TWENTY-EIGHTH EDITION

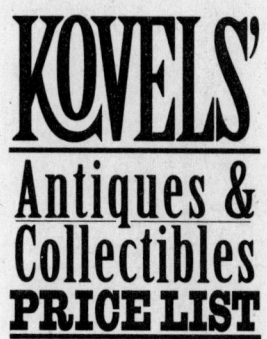

KOVELS'
Antiques &
Collectibles
PRICE LIST

BOOKS BY RALPH AND TERRY KOVEL

American Country Furniture 1780–1875

A Directory of American Silver, Pewter, and Silver Plate

Kovels' Advertising Collectibles Price List

Kovels' American Art Pottery: The Collector's Guide to Makers,
Marks, and Factory Histories

Kovels' American Silver Marks: 1650 to the Present

Kovels' Antiques & Collectibles Fix-It Source Book

Kovels' Antiques & Collectibles Price List

Kovels' Book of Antique Labels

Kovels' Bottles Price List

Kovels' Collector's Guide to American Art Pottery

Kovels' Collector's Source Book

Kovels' Depression Glass & American Dinnerware Price List

Kovels' Dictionary of Marks—Pottery & Porcelain

Kovels' Guide to Selling, Buying, and Fixing Your Antiques and Collectibles

Kovels' Illustrated Price Guide to Royal Doulton

Kovels' Know Your Antiques

Kovels' Know Your Collectibles

Kovels' New Dictionary of Marks—Pottery & Porcelain

Kovels' Organizer for Collectors

Kovels' Price Guide for Collector Plates, Figurines,
Paperweights, and Other Limited Editions

Kovels' Quick Tips—799 Helpful Hints on How to Care for Your Collectibles

TWENTY-EIGHTH EDITION

KOVELS'

Antiques &
Collectibles
PRICE LIST

For the 1996 Market
ILLUSTRATED

CROWN TRADE PAPERBACKS   NEW YORK

Published by Crown Publishers, Inc., 201 East 50th Street, New York,
New York 10022. Member of the Crown Publishing Group.
Random House, Inc. New York, Toronto, London, Sydney, Auckland
CROWN TRADE PAPERBACKS and colophon are trademarks of Crown Publishers,
Inc.
Manufactured in the United States of America
Library of Congress Catalog Card Number: 83-643618

ISBN: 0-517-88462-3 (pbk.)
10 9 8 7 6 5 4 3 2 1
First Edition

This is a book for the average collector. We check prices all year, visit shops and shows, read our mail, check on-line computer services and the Internet, and decide what antiques and collectibles are of most interest. We do not list the top of the market but concentrate on the average pieces in any category. We will often add one or two high-priced pieces in a category so you will realize that some of the rarities are quite valuable. For example, Ohr pottery can sell for $300 to $22,000. Most pieces we list are less than $10,000. Although pieces of furniture, silver, Tiffany, or art pottery may sell for more than $50,000, we list few of those examples here. The highest price in this book is $57,500 for a coin-operated gum machine. The lowest price is 5¢ for a bottle cap. We even list the weird and wonderful, and this year you can find prices for a Jayne Mansfield hot water bottle, Hitler's toilet paper, leg irons, a bee smoker, a pair of alligator platform shoes, a plastic mesh dress, and a whale bone birdcage. The smallest object is a button; the largest, a sixteen-foot backbar.

The book is changed slightly each year. Categories are added or omitted to make it easier for you to find your antiques. The book is kept about 800 pages long because it is written to go with you to sales. We try to have a balanced format—not too much glass, pottery, or collectibles, not too many items that sell for over $5,000. The prices are *from* the American market *for* the American market. Few European sales are reported. We take the editorial privilege of not including any prices that seem to result from "auction fever."

The computer-generated index is so complete it amazes us. Use it often. An internal alphabetical index is also included. For example, there is a category for "Celluloid." Most items made of celluloid will be found there, but if there is a toy made of celluloid, it will be listed under "Toy" and also indexed under "Celluloid." All pictures and prices are new every year, except pictures that are pattern examples shown in "Depression Glass" and "Pressed Glass." Pictured antiques are not museum pieces but items offered for sale. The hints are set in easy-to-notice special type. Leaf through the book and learn how to wash porcelains, store textiles, guard against theft, and much more. Old Kovels' price books should be saved for future reference, tax, and appraisal information.

RECORD PRICES

Auctions of well-known collections at prestigious auction houses are often reported by the media. The high prices encourage the average person to think that not just the one special table is worth a million dollars but that many other treasures like this might be in the attic. Sometimes sales of unusual collections also are reported. This year sales of Kewpies, advertising trade cards, Royal Bayreuth matchholders, and oyster memorabilia generated high prices and collector interest that will probably raise prices in coming years. Major auctions of Tiffany lamps, arcade machines, and the famous Eddy Nicholson collection of furniture and Dedham pottery brought media coverage and record-setting prices.

Prices of toys continue to soar. A G.I. Joe Action Fighter Pilot figure made in 1994, one of a kind, fought to $5,750. A "Lost in Space" Roto-Jet Gun blasted to a price of $14,880. A boy cyclist toy made by Ferdinand Martin wheeled in at $8,100 and a No. 2, brunette ponytail Barbie, with stand and box, busted out at $5,100. Toy cars raced to high values: a Dinky Toy Bentalls Van sold for $20,240, and a set of eight Dinky toy cars in the No. 24 series box for $22,700. Someone is now hugging a "Teddy Girl" cinnamon Steiff bear, c. 1904, which sold for $176,000. So many marbles rolled to records it is hard to see what is winning. The top price for a single marble this year was $7,700 for a 2½-inch Indian swirl, but also high was a set of Christensen Agate Company marbles, 25 in a box, for $10,925.

Other records were set in unexpected places. A Pabst Indian calendar for the year 1906, a "yard long," brought $1,430. The costume worn by a munchkin in the "Wizard of Oz" movie went for $23,000, and *the* Maltese Falcon, the original prop from the 1941 movie, sold for an astounding $398,500. A super price of $22,000 was paid for a 1939–1940 Action Comics Superman ring.

Furniture records this year included pieces in many styles. The famous Nicholson carved mahogany Chippendale tea table (Philadelphia, 1760–1780) sold for $2,422,500. Another Nicholson table, a carved mahogany Queen Anne tea table (Boston, 1740-1760), sold for $552,500. A record for a Shaker rocking chair was set at $37,400 for a birch chair with original red stain and rush seat. A 6-piece parlor set by John Henry Belter, made of carved and laminated rosewood in Rococo Revival style about 1850, was auctioned off at $134,750. A museum traveling exhibition of Herter furniture excited many, and when a rare, carved oak console made by Herter Brothers of New York about 1881 was sold in San Francisco, it set a record at $288,500. Arts and Crafts furniture sold well also. A Plail Brothers 3-piece set of barrel-shaped furniture with narrow vertical slats and drop-in spring seats set a record for the maker at $13,200. A Roycroft magazine pedestal sold for $9,900, and a Roycroft Morris chair (# 044) for $7,700.

Two glass paperweights set records: an American weight with a parrot on a latticinio ground at $34,100 and a French pear on a red ground at $22,500. A free-blown early American olive-amber colored glass pitcher, with a gadrooned design, brought $23,100. This year's record-setting Tiffany lamp was the Virginia Creeper, made of Favrile glass around 1900, with amethyst glass beads and a bronze base. The $18\frac{1}{4}$-inch lamp sold for $1,102,500.

Pottery of many types set records. A student character stein made in Sarrequemines, France, was auctioned off for $5,390. Four different Mettlach steins set records when they sold for $2,200–$3,520 each. English wares included a creamware teapot made in 1743, decorated with birds and oriental foliage for $63,000 and a Clarice Cliff Etna pattern charger, made in the 1930s, that sold for $20,200. Record-setting American ceramics included a $10\frac{1}{2}$-inch-high Grand Feu vase made in Los Angeles in 1910 at $8,250 and a Newcomb four-color vase by Lenore Nicholson for $29,700.

The prices in this book are reports of the general antiques market, not the record-setting examples. Each year, every price in the book is new. We do not estimate or "update" prices. Prices are actual asking prices, although a buyer may have negotiated a price to a lower figure. No price is an estimate. We do not ask dealers and writers to estimate prices. Experience has shown that a collector of one type of antique is prejudiced in favor of that item, and prices are usually high or low, but rarely a true report. If a price range is given, it is because at least two identical items were offered for sale at different times. The computer records prices and prints the high and low figures. Price ranges are found only in categories like "Pressed Glass," where identical items can be identified. Some prices in *Kovels' Antiques & Collectibles Price List* may seem high and some may seem low because of regional variations. But each price is one you could have paid for the object.

If you are selling your collection, do not expect to get retail value unless you are a dealer. Wholesale prices for antiques are from 20 to 50 percent less than retail. Remember, the antiques dealer must make a profit or go out of business.

ACKNOWLEDGMENTS

Special thanks should go to those who helped us with pictures and deeds: Noel Barrett Antiques & Auctions, Ltd., Frank H. Boos Gallery Auctioneers & Appraisers, Christie's East, Garth's Auctions, Lynn Geyer Advertising Auctions, Glass-Works Auctions, Morton M. Goldberg Auction Galleries, Inc., Willis Henry Auctions Inc., Joy Luke Fine Arts Brokers, Auctioneers & Appraisers, Mapes Auctioneers & Appraisers, McMasters Doll Auctions, Neal Auction Company, Phillips, David Rago Arts & Crafts, Lloyd Ralston Gallery, Red Baron's Antiques, Skinner, Inc., Sotheby's, Theriault's the Dollmasters, Winter Associates Auctioneers & Appraisers, and Woody Auction. Special help was given by Robert E. Davis, Dave Lewis, Lee Markley, Paula and Steve Ockner, and Darryl Rehr.

To the others in the antiques trade who knowingly or unknowingly contributed prices to this book, we say "thank you!" We could not do it without you. Some of you are: A Look Back, Accent East Gallery, The Ackerman's, Jack Adamson, Richard Alan Antiques, Alan's Antiques, Albury-Eagles Gallery, Inc., All That Jazz, Paula Allegretti, America's Pride, The Anderson Gallery, Antique Cupboard, ARK Antiques, Around the World, Arts & Crafts Emporium, Asiantiques Inc., Larry Atkinson, Autumn Pond, Richard S. Axtell, Aram H. Azadian, Sr., Lee Backulich, Al & Judy Bagon, Robert & Cynthia Baker, Barbara A. Bako, Mannie Banner, Donald P. Bean, John E. Bilane, Carolyn Blake, Blanche's Collectibles, R.C. Blankenhorn, Richard Blue, Blue and Gray Antiques, Boar's Head Antiques, Leota Bohnert, Philip Bongiorno, Boomerang Antiques, Rennette Boucher, Irvin & Dolores Boyd, Briskin Antiques, Florence Brodwith, Scott Brown Antiques, Thomas Brown Antiques, Bud's Barn, Alfred Bullard, Inc., Jo Calame, Alfred Cali, Cambrae Antiques, Campbell House, Candelstick Antiques, Candlewick & Cathay, C. M. Carey, Carousel Antiques, Tom Casey, Cat's Paw Antiques, Tony Charlton, Charon's Antiques, Mick & Lorna Chase, Chew & Formicola, Peter W. Chillingworth, Circa Antiques, Cobweb Corner, Marilyn Colby, Country Cousin Antiques, Gary Crossen, John Crouse, Sandra W. Crowther, Currier Antiques, Dale's Decoy Den, Michael D. Danton, Dave's Electric Avenue, John M. Davis, Inc., Rachel Davis Fine Arts, Lila de Lellis, Scott & Elizabeth De Wolfe, Dekor Antiques, Dee's Antiques, Del's Antiques, Maralyn DelGross, Doug Dezso, Richard Diehl, Pat Doyle, Don Dutcher, E & J Antiques, Don Eager, East Bay Gallery, Eastland Galleries, David Eich, Larry Eisenstein, Cliff Ekdahl, Elegant Reflections, Kenneth D. Erwin, Excelsior Coin & Collectible,

Michael Fallon, Bill Feiner, John Finch, Millie Fishman, Flo-Blue Shoppe, Eva Flynn, Forever Heisey, Lee Foster, Fred & Alma Fowler, Gerald Frank Gallery, Frank's Antiques, Gary Franzen, Tucker Frey Antiques, G & M Antiques, G. S., Inc., Gaab's Antiquarian Prints, Laura Galbraith, Helen Garneau, Jim Gartner, David R. Geiger, Georgian House, Leigh Giarde, Lynda Givens, Glass 'n' Glass, The Gold Man, Charles Golden Jr., Lawrence C. Goodhue, Inc., Harry Gordon, Grandma's Attic, R. Greenan, Greene Acres Antiques, John Grogan, Gwynby Antiques, Hall & Winter, Hammer Antiques, Hanes & Ruskin, Harmonite Stohr Antiques, Susan & Jim Harran, Hastings House, Dianne Hermes, Hesson Collectables, Hi-De-Ho Collectibles, The Hickory Tree, Robert Hinde, Hodge Podge Antiques, Joyce Hornback, Billie Hoskins Antiques, Cheryl & Cleve Hostetter, Paul & Carol Hrics, Treesa Hudson, Lori Hughes, David Hunkins, Frances Hursey, Bill Hyde, Jean-Paul Iannantvoni, In Love with Nippon, Jo Irwin, Isaacs Gallery, B. Issod Antiques, Michael Ivankovich, Jackie's Antiques, James Gallery, Jay-Q Antiques, Jerry's Antiques, JP Antiques, Carol Kahn, Kaleidoscope, George Kamm, Bob Kay, Bob & Linda Keimig, Michael Kellogg, Kelly's Antiques, Ken's Collectibles, James Kennedy Antiques Ltd., Kent Farm Antiques, Joan King, King of Prussia Antiques, Robert P. Kipp, Kirtland Antiques, Janet Klumpp, Gus Knapp, Ron & Maureen Kovacs, Virginia Kreutzer, Ted Kromer, Bob & Gay Krug, La Verrerie D'Art, Lady Rose Antique Glass, Darcy Lange, Langford Antiques, Robert Dean Leath, Darrell Lehman, Craig Leverenz, Mimi & Steve Levine, Inc., Howard Lewis Antiques, Lindberg-Townsend, Lion's Den Antique Holiday Decorations, Lombard Antiquarian Maps & Prints, Gary & Martha Ludlow, Debbie Lund, Lynn's Unique & Antique, Clarence & Betty Maier, Magnificent Obsession, Chris Mahloch, The Maine Idea, Janet Mansholt, Marsha's Antiques, Ruth & Dave Martens, Tim & Barb Martien, Matrix Quality Antique Dolls, McAfee & Lynch, Craig McIver, McLean Ribbehege, Melton's Antique Dolls, John Merher III, Merry Walk Antiques, Mike's General Store, Militia Hill Antiques, Milmac Antiques, Aileen Minor, John F. Moe, Joan Mogensen, Mongenas Antiques, S. Moore, Carolyn Moore, Moore's Antiques, Wm. Morford, Robert Morin, Ron Mossing, The Mouse Man Ink, Muddy River Trading Co., Nancy Antiques, R.R. Nery, New-Strom Antiques, Nikel Enterprises, Inc., Noll & McGee, Nostalgia Antiques, Nutting House Antiques, E. L. Oakes, Old Telephones, Olde Gold Estate Jewelry, Danny Owens, P & M Antiques, P. V. Antiques, Anita Pagani Antiques, Jean & Don Parrett, Pascoe & Co., Inc., Crystal Payton, The Pearl Antiques, Ltd., Jackie Peay,

Alan Pedel, Jennifer Petersen, Gary N. Peterson, Marsha Petrella Antiques, Plantation Galleries, Ted Polhman, Bonita Pontillo, J. E. Porcelli, Porte Galleries, Pots-n-Such Antiques, Prairie Home Antiques, Greg Price, Howard Price Fine Art, James Proctor, John R. Prunier, Cathy Pudlo, Tom Quinn, Rabideau & McKerrow, Ragman Antiques, Don Raitzer, Dennis Raleigh, Carl Rauch, Richard & Barbara Reddock, Red's Antiques, Diane Reh Antiques, Susan Reid, Jack & Berta Reynolds, DeDe Ritner Antiques, Estee Roll, Rosemarie Antiques, Roseville Pottery Mart, Helen & Phil Rosso, Route 66 Antiques, Steven J. Rowe, Running Rabbit Video Auctions, Ryan's Fine Arts, G. W. Samaha Antiques, H. J. Saunders, Debbie Schaffer, Schiller Antiques, Ken Schneringer, Donald R. Schoonover, Scientific Medical & Mechanical Antiques, Norb Seeley, Shaker Square Antiques, Inc., Shawnee Auction Center, Miriam Sherrer, Showcase Antique Center, Inc., Jim Sinsley, Bill Smith, Elizabeth Lisy Smith, Herb Smith, Snow Hill Antiques, So Rare! Galleries, Sandra Solomon, The Spare Room, Nancy Splitstoser, Spruce Antiques, Constance St. Clair Antiques, Jack Stecher, Stein's Antiques, Steve Stephens, Al Sternagle, Eve Stone Antiques, Ltd., Dodie Strandberg, Studio Moderne, Frank Swala, John Sweetman, Sweetwater Trading Co., J. Simon Taylor, Joyce Taylor, Judy Taylor, Teacher's Room Antiques, Team Antiques, Temple's Antiques, Rick & Ricki Thompson, Three's Company, Phil & Nyla Thurston, Times Square Records, Tomlinson Antiques, Tonquish Creek Fire Company, Joe Torre Antiques, Toy Scouts, Inc., Tulip Manor, Mary Tupta, Turn of the Century Antiques II, Uncle Sam's Antiques, Ralph Van Brocklin, Van Why's Antiques, Lenny Veneziano, Victorian House Antiques, Victorian Images, Christine Vining Antiques, Ltd., Vixseboxse Art Galleries, Inc., Rick Waggoner, Walker & Ewing, Walrick Antiques, Larrin Wanechek, Weiss Gallery, Lynn Weler, Lynn E. Wesch, Jean Whelan, Wicker's Antiques, Dee Wilhelm, James Wilhoit Antiques, Linda Willauer Antiques, Taylor B. Williams, Willow House Antiques, Mark Wiskow, The Wizards of Odd, Jane Woodring, John Woytowicz, John A. Wright, Yankee Tools & Collectables, Yesterday's Treasures, John L. Young, Young's Oldies.

Special Thanks

Special thanks to Gay Hunter who was responsible for proofing, coordinating, and solving all the problems created by both humans and computers. And more thanks to the rest of the Kovel crew: Carmie Amata, Grace DeFrancisco, Amy Garvey, Marcia Goldberg, Harriet Goldner, Evelyn Hayes, Mary Anne Klasen, Eleanore Melzak, Gloria Pearlman, Nancy Saada, Vijay Shah, Cherrie Smrekar, Edie Smrekar, Hillary Stone, and Virginia Warner. And to those who helped at Crown: Sharon Squibb, our editor who sees all of the materials first, Michelle Sidrane, Steve Magnuson, Pam Stinson, Ken Sansone, Laurie Stark, Teresa Nicholas, Jessica Allan, Lenny Henderson, and Merri Ann Morrell.

MORE ANTIQUE PRICE NEWS

Have you kept up with prices? They change! Last year a "Lost in Space" Roto-Jet gun sold for $14,880, a No. 2 Brunette ponytail Barbie with stand and box was $5,100, a Dinky toy van was $20,240. A rare and famous Chippendale tea table from 18th-century Philadelphia set a record price at over two million dollars and a piece of Victorian furniture made by Herter Brothers sold for $288,500. How did the owners know these collectibles had such a special value? Prices change with discoveries, auction records, even historic events. Every entry and every picture in this book is new and current thanks to modern computer technology, making this book a handy overall price guide. But you also need current news about collecting. Books on your shelf get older each month, and prices do change. Important sales produce new record prices. Rarities are discovered. Fakes appear. You will want to keep up with developments from month to month rather than from year to year. *Kovels on Antiques and Collectibles,* a nationally distributed, illustrated newsletter, includes up-to-date information on the world of collectors. This monthly newsletter reports current prices, collecting trends, landmark auction results for all types of antiques and collectibles, and tax, estate, security, and other pertinent news for collectors. Additional information and a free sample newsletter are available from the authors at P.O. Box 420420, Palm Coast, FL 32142.

If sports are your interest, write the same P.O. box for a sample of our other newsletter, *Kovels Sports Collectibles.* It has news about old and new sports items including baseball cards, hockey shirts, golf clubs, and stadium seats. A special monthly feature is a "Freebies" list of the collectibles being offered with products found at the grocery store.

HOW TO USE THIS BOOK

There are a few rules for using this book. Each listing is arranged in the following manner: CATEGORY (such as Pressed Glass or Furniture), OBJECT (such as vase), DESCRIPTION (as much information as possible about size, age, color, and pattern). Some types of glass are exceptions to this rule. These are listed CATEGORY, PATTERN, OBJECT, DESCRIPTION. All items are presumed to be in good condition and undamaged, unless otherwise noted.

Several special categories were formed to make the most sensible listing possible. For instance, "Tool" includes special equipment because the casual collector might not know the proper name for an "adze." A few years ago we reorganized the glass entries into these categories: "Glass-Art," "Glass-Contemporary," "Glass-Midcentury," and "Glass-Venetian." Major glass factories are still listed under the factory names, and well-known types of glass such as cut, pressed, Carnival, etc., can be found in their own categories. This year, heeding the suggestions of readers, we eliminated all guns except toy types. It is not legal to sell weapons without a special liscense, and so guns are not part of the general antiques market. Airguns, B-B guns, rocket guns, and others are listed in the "Toy" category. New categories include "Bow," "Caughley," "Holt Howard," and "Movie." Actual costumes used in movies are in the new movie category and are no longer found in "Clothing." The index can help you locate items.

Several idiosyncrasies of style appear because the book is printed by computer. Everything is listed according to the computer alphabetizing system. This means words such as "Mt." are alphabetized as "M-T," not as "M-O-U-N-T." All numerals are before all letters; thus "2" comes before "A." A quick glance will make this clear, as it is consistent throughout the book.

We made several editorial decisions. A bowl is a "bowl" and not a "dish" unless it is a special dish, such as a pickle dish. A butter dish is a "butter." A salt dish is called a "salt" to differentiate it from a saltshaker. It is always "sugar and creamer," never "creamer and sugar." Political collectors often refer to "pinbacks," the round celluloid or tin pins that are decorated with candidates names and faces. The word "button" is sometimes used in this book instead of the word "pinback." Of course, the word "button" is also used when referring to the fasteners used on clothing. Where one dimension is given, it is the height; or if the object is round, the dimension is the diameter. The height of a picture is listed before width. Glass is clear unless a color is indicated.

Every entry is listed alphabetically, but the problem of language remains. Some antiques terms, such as "Sheffield" or "Pratt," have two meanings. Be sure to read the paragraph headings to know the meaning used. All category headings are based on the language of the average person at an average show, and we use terms like "mud figures" even if not technically correct.

This book does not include price listings of fine art paintings, stamps, coins, most types of books, although *Big Little Books* are included, comic books, although original comic art is listed, and a few other special categories.

All pictures in *Kovels' Antiques & Collectibles Price List* are listed with the prices asked by the seller. "Illus" (illustrated nearby) is part of the description if a picture is shown.

There have been misinformed comments about how this book is written. We *do* use the computer. It alphabetizes, ranges prices, sets type, and does other time-consuming jobs. Because of the computer, the book can be produced quickly. The last entries are added in June; the book is available in October. This is six months faster than would be possible any other way. But it is human help that finds prices and checks accuracy. We read everything at least twice, sometimes more. We edit from 100,000 entries to the 50,000 entries found here. We correct spelling, remove incorrect data, write category headings, and decide on new categories. We sometimes make errors. Information in the paragraphs is reviewed and updated each year. This year more than forty corrections and additions were made in the category headings.

Prices are reports from all parts of the United States and Canada (translated to U.S. dollars at the rate of $1.42 U.S. to $1 Canadian) between June 1994 and June 1995. Prices are from auctions, shops, and shows. Every price is checked for accuracy, but we are not responsible for errors.

It is unprofessional for an appraiser to set a value for an unseen item. Because of this, we cannot answer your letters asking for specific price information. But please write if you have any requests for categories to be included in future editions or any corrections to information in the paragraphs.

When you see us at the shows, stop and say hello. Since our television show has been aired in all parts of the country, we find we can no longer be anonymous buyers. It may mean the dealers know us before we ask a price, but it has been wonderful to meet all of you. Don't be surprised if we ask for your suggestions for the next edition of *Kovels'*

Antiques & Collectibles Price List. Or you can write us at P.O. Box 22200-K, Beachwood, Ohio 44122.

Ralph & Terry Kovel
Accredited Senior Appraisers
American Society of Appraisers
July 1995

TWENTY-EIGHTH EDITION

KOVELS'
Antiques &
Collectibles
PRICE LIST

A. WALTER made pate-de-verre glass under contract at the Daum glassworks from 1908 to 1914. He started his own firm in Nancy, France, in 1919. Pieces made before 1914 are signed *Daum, Nancy* with a cross. After 1919 the signature is *A. Walter Nancy*.

Bowl, Beetle In Corners, Pinecone & Needle Panels, Signed, c.1925, 6 In.	3737.00
Bowl, Lizard Perched On Rock At Rim, Signed, c.1925, 4 3/8 In.	5462.00
Bowl, Pate-De-Verre, Mold Blown	4840.00
Figurine, Buddha, Lotus Position, Amber, Signed, 6 3/4 In.	1725.00
Light, Boudoir, Oval Shade, Raised Green Berries, Iron Base, Signed, 5 3/4 In.	4888.00
Paperweight, Pate-De-Verre Stag Beetle, Red, Brown & Black	1495.00
Pendant, Green & Black Insect, Turquoise Ground, Signed, 2 1/8 In.	402.00
Vase, Trumpet, Amber, Yellow Streaks, Pinecones, Needles, c.1920, 4 In.	1880.00

ABC plates, or children's alphabet plates, were most popular from 1780 to 1860, but are still being made. The letters on the plate were meant as teaching aids for children learning to read. The plates were made of pottery, porcelain, metal, or glass. Mugs and other items were also made with alphabet decorations.

Bowl, Dutch Children	88.00
Bowl, Little Bopeep	90.00
Bowl, Little Bopeep, c.1900, 7 1/2 In.	23.00
Bowl, Old Lady In Balloon Sweeping Sky	88.00
Bowl, Old Woman, In Basket, 4 Children	85.00
Cup, Plate & Bowl, Green Enameled	115.00
Plate, Baby Bunting, Cat, Dog, Gold Letters, 6 In.	75.00
Plate, Ben Franklin, Maxim	75.00
Plate, Birds & Animals, Silver Plate, 20th Century, 8 In.	15.00
Plate, Blind Girl, Colored Transfer, Creamware	145.00
Plate, Blue Train Transfer	120.00
Plate, Boy, Bee On Cheek, Flint Glass, c.1900, 6 1/4 In.	15.00
Plate, Braille, Guide Dog Center, 6 1/4 In.	75.00
Plate, Button Pattern, Clear Glass, c.1900, 6 In.	45.00
Plate, Centennial, 1776-1876, Glass, c.1876, 6 3/4 In.	45.00
Plate, Child Swinging, Tin, Red, Yellow, 3 1/2 In.	65.00
Plate, Children With Hoops, Cast Iron, 2 7/8 In.	148.50
Plate, Clock Center	45.00
Plate, Cock Robin, Tin	60.00
Plate, Geese, Amber, 6 In.	25.00
Plate, Grinding Old Into Young, Miniature	145.00
Plate, Hey Diddle Diddle, Tin	85.00
Plate, Hunter, Hounds, Fox, Horse, 8 1/2 In.	150.00
Plate, Lady On Mule, Side Saddle, Tin, c.1880, 2 1/2 In.	350.00
Plate, Lion, Tin, c.1880	500.00
Plate, London Dog Seller, 8 1/4 In.	150.00
Plate, Marine Railway Station, Manhattan Beach Hotel, 8 1/4 In.	135.00
Plate, Morning Walk, Black & White Transfer, Pearlware	130.00
Plate, Old Into Young, c.1880, 2 1/8 In.	470.00
Plate, Punch	168.00
Plate, Sign Language, Tea Party, Staffordshire	295.00
Plate, Sir Colon Camprell, Tin, c.1880, 4 1/4 In.	1500.00
Plate, Stork With Baby, Orange Carnival Glass, 20th Century, 7 1/2 In.	10.00
Plate, Wooden Dolls, Green Transfer, Red Rim Stripe, 6 1/4 In.	182.00

ABINGDON POTTERY was established in 1934 by Raymond E. Bidwell as the Abingdon Sanitary Manufacturing Company. The company made art pottery and other wares. Sixteen varieties of cookie jars are known. The factory ceased production of art pottery in 1950.

Bookends, Horse Head, Label	45.00
Compote, No. 568	25.00
Console, Gray-Green, 14 x 9 In.	18.00

Console, Rose, Scalloped, Scroll Handles, Interior Relief, 17 x 6 x 3/4 In.	22.00
Cookie Jar, Bopeep	425.00
Cookie Jar, Buick, White	600.00
Cookie Jar, Choo Choo	250.00
Cookie Jar, Fat Boy	550.00
Cookie Jar, Hippo	525.00
Cookie Jar, Hobby Horse	450.00
Cookie Jar, Jack-In-The-Box	325.00
Cookie Jar, Jack-O'-Lantern	300.00 to 435.00
Cookie Jar, Little Miss Muffet	225.00 to 425.00
Cookie Jar, Little Old Lady	185.00 to 255.00
Cookie Jar, Money Bag	60.00 to 75.00
Cookie Jar, Mother Goose	600.00
Cookie Jar, Tepee	895.00
Cookie Jar, Train	195.00
Cookie Jar, Wigwam	750.00 to 875.00
Cookie Jar, Witch	1600.00
Figurine, Goose, Pink	35.00
Figurine, Nude, Kneeling, Holding Bouquet Flowers, Pink, Gold Trim, 10 In.	175.00
Planter, Deer	12.00
String Holder, Mouse	195.00 to 230.00
Tile, Coolie	50.00
Vase, Flower Holder, Fan, White, Ribbed Base, Fan & Scroll, 5 x 5 x 7 In.	22.00
Vase, Iris, Paper Labels, 8 In.	40.00
Vase, Sea Gull, No. 3468	35.00
Wall Pocket, Blue	25.00
Wall Pocket, Butterfly	95.00

ADAMS china was made by William Adams and Sons of Staffordshire, England. The firm was founded in 1769 and is still working. All types of tablewares and useful wares have been made through the years. Other pieces of Adams will be found listed under Flow Blue.

Bowl, English Scenes, 10 x 4 3/4 In.	58.00
Bowl, Vegetable, Carolyn, Calyxware, 9 1/4 In.	45.00
Cup & Saucer, Carolyn, Calyxware	12.00
Cup & Saucer, New York, From Weehawk	225.00
Hair Receiver, Horse & Hunt Design, Dogs, Dark Blue, Jasperware	50.00
Plate, American Express Train, Currier & Ives, 10 1/2 In.	45.00
Plate, Blenheim, Blue, Oxfordshire, 10 In.	165.00
Plate, Fairy Villas, Flow Blue, 10 In.	95.00
Plate, Kyber, Flow Blue, 8 In.	75.00
Plate, Kyber, Flow Blue, 9 In.	78.00
Plate, Mitchell & Freeman China & Glass Warehouse, 8 7/8 In.	725.00
Plate, Monte Video, Pink, 7 In.	85.00
Plate, Woodcock Shooting, Currier & Ives, 10 1/2 In.	45.00 to 50.00
Platter, Carolyn, Calyxware, 11 1/2 In.	60.00
Platter, Falls Of Niagara, Black, 19 5/8 In.	1200.00
Platter, Windsor Castle, Berkshire, 19 1/4 In.	1225.00
Soup, Dish, Fairy Villas, Flow Blue, 9 In.	75.00
Spill Holder, Neo-Classical Muses, Making Offerings, Jasperware, Tunstall, 1900, 7 In.	82.00
Tureen, Sauce, Lily, Underplate	150.00

ADVERTISING containers and products sold in the old country store are now all collectibles. These stores, with the crackers in a barrel and a potbellied stove, are a symbol of an earlier, less hectic time. Listed here are many of the advertising items. Other similar pieces may be found under the product name, such as Planters Peanuts. We have tried to list items in the logical places, so large store fixtures will be found under the Architectural category, enameled tin dishes under Graniteware, paper items in the Paper category, etc. Store fixtures, cases, and other items that have no advertising as part of the decoration are listed in the Store category.

Apron, Alka-Seltzer, Red Flames, Says To The Rescue, Cloth, Unused	40.00
Apron, Change, Chicago Daily Times	18.00

Ashtray, American Export Airlines 55.00
Ashtray, Anheuser-Busch, Raised Logo, Owner's Name, Brass, 1930s, 6 1/2 In. 25.00
Ashtray, Ballantine's Scotch, Blue, Glass, Ceramic, Square, 1/2 x 6 1/2 x 2 In. 12.00
Ashtray, Beaumet, Green, White, Porcelain, Rectangular, 5 x 4 1/2 x 1 In. 6.00
Ashtray, Blue Diamond Coal Co., Brass 35.00
Ashtray, Boeing 247, 1935 .... 145.00
Ashtray, Brezner Shoe Co., Figural, Mr. Cobbleright, Sirocco Wood, 1930s 100.00
Ashtray, Bridgestone, Box, 5 In. 15.00
Ashtray, Bryers Ice Cream, China, 1950s 15.00
Ashtray, Camel Cigarettes, Camel Bronze, 6 x 3 1/2 In. 8.00
Ashtray, Campari Cordial, Blue, White, Gold, Ceramic, Round, 8 1/4 x 2 1/4 In. 22.00
Ashtray, Carling Black Label Beer, Black, White, Gold, Ceramic, Round, 8 x 1 1/2 In.. · 15.00
Ashtray, Champion Spark Plugs, Plug Mounted On Rim 100.00
Ashtray, Chilean RR, Brown, Beige, Ceramic, Square, 5 1/2 x 1 In. 10.00
Ashtray, Ciga Hotel, White, Black, Ceramic, Square, 3 3/4 x 1 In. 6.00
Ashtray, Crodo Water, White Green, Black, Porcelain, Triangular, 4 1/2 x 1 1/2 In. 9.00
Ashtray, Cusenier Brandy, Brown, Beige, Ceramic, Round, 5 3/4 x 1 3/4 In. 9.00
Ashtray, Cutty Sark, Green, Yellow, Ceramic, Round, 9 x 2 In. 16.00
Ashtray, Dom Perignon Champagne, Red, Gold, Ceramic, Triangular, 1/2 x 1 In. 8.00
Ashtray, Dr. Scholl's Foot Powder, Nickel Plated, 4 In. 45.00
Ashtray, Dubonnet Cordial, Blue, White, Glass, Round, 5 1/4 x 2 In. 7.00
Ashtray, Gilbey's Gin, White, Red, Ceramic, Square, 6 1/2 x 2 In. 12.00
Ashtray, Glen Grant's Scotch, Brown, Gold, Ceramic, Rectangular, 4 1/4 x 1 1/4 In. 5.00
Ashtray, Goodrich Silvertown, Tire 17.00
Ashtray, Goodrich, 100th Anniversary 15.00
Ashtray, Goodyear Super Cushion, 4-Ply Tire 25.00
Ashtray, Goodyear Tire, Ted's Tire Service 20.00
Ashtray, Gordon's Gin, Yellow, Ceramic, Rectangular, 8 x 8 x 2 1/4 In. 25.00
Ashtray, Green River Whiskey, With Matchbox Holder, Ornate 55.00
Ashtray, Guinness Beer, Black, Gold, Glass, Round, 7 x 2 In. 10.00
Ashtray, Haig, White, Black, Gold, Porcelain, Rectangular, 5 1/2 x 4 x 1 In. .... 7.00 to 9.00
Ashtray, Hood Tires 135.00
Ashtray, Howard Johnson's Motor Lodge, Blue Logo 20.00
Ashtray, J & B Scotch, Black, Ceramic, Rectangular, 3 1/2 x 6 x 1 In. 6.00
Ashtray, John Smith's Beer, Clear, Red, Glass, Square, 3 3/4 x 1 In. 3.00
Ashtray, Kelly Springfield, Rubber Tire Rim, Green Glass Center 45.00
Ashtray, L & M, Black, Red, White, Ceramic, Round, 4 x 1 3/4 In. 7.00
Ashtray, La Pinede, St. Tropez, Beige, Ceramic, Rectangular, 3 3/4 x 3/4 In. 4.00
Ashtray, Loburg Beer, Brown, Gold, Glass, Round, 5 3/4 x 1 1/2 In. 7.00
Ashtray, Lucky Strike, White, Red, Black, Yellow, Glass, Round, 4 1/4 x 1 3/8 In. 7.00
Ashtray, Mack Truck, Bulldog 22.00
Ashtray, Madrid Palace, White, Red, Porcelain, Rectangular, 5 x 3 x 1/2 In. 8.00
Ashtray, McKinley's Scotch, Glass, 9 x 7 x 1 1/4 In. 8.00
Ashtray, Michelin, Hard Plastic, 3-Dimensional Figure, 1930s, Base 5 1/2 In 150.00
Ashtray, Michelin, Mr. Bib, 1940 .... 65.00
Ashtray, Moet Et Chandon, Green, White, Ceramic, 5 1/2 x 4 1/2 x 1 In. 8.00
Ashtray, Mohawk Tires, Rubber 10.00
Ashtray, Moxie Maid, Wooden .... *Illus* 250.00

Advertising, Ashtray,
Moxie Maid, Wooden

Advertising, Ashtray,
Red Heart Rum, c.1900

◆◆◆◆◆◆◆◆◆◆◆◆◆◆◆◆◆◆◆◆◆◆◆

Moving your own belongings?
Be careful about insurance.
Rental trucks or your car may
have coverage for antiques
that is too low. Your home-
owner's policy probably does
not cover damage from poor
packing. Check with your
agent before you move!

◆◆◆◆◆◆◆◆◆◆◆◆◆◆◆◆◆◆◆◆◆◆◆

Ashtray, Moxie, White Ceramic	30.00
Ashtray, Muehlebach Hotel	30.00
Ashtray, Normandy Ferries, Blue, White, Ceramic, Rectangular, 7 x 1 In.	7.00
Ashtray, Otard Brandy, Green, White, Ceramic, Square, 8 x 8 x 2 1/2 In.	20.00
Ashtray, Pa. Stove Co., Agate	38.00
Ashtray, Palm Beer, White, Gold, Glass, Square, 4 3/4 x 4 3/4 x 1 In.	7.00
Ashtray, Playboy, Orange	18.00
Ashtray, Post Cereal, Various Post Cereals	45.00
Ashtray, Red Heart Rum, c.1900 ....*Illus*	210.00
Ashtray, Reddy Kilowatt, Glass ....15.00 to	20.00
Ashtray, Royal Crown Cola, Glass, 1940	18.00
Ashtray, Ruffino Wine, Green, Gold, Glass, Round, 4 x 1 1/2 In.	7.00
Ashtray, Sabena Airline, White, Blue, Glass, Round, 4 1/4 x 1 1/4 In.	8.00
Ashtray, Schweppes, White, Blue, Ceramic, Round, 5 x 1 In.	5.00
Ashtray, Seagrams VO, Blue, Gold, Ceramic, Round, 5 1/2 x 1 1/2 In.	8.00
Ashtray, St. Louis Car Co., Horsehead & Crop, Copper	125.00
Ashtray, Stardust Hotel, Las Vegas, Black Glass	1.00
Ashtray, The Queens, White, Blue, Porcelain, Square, 3 3/4 x 3/4 In.	9.00
Ashtray, Trenton Security National Bank Of New Jersey, 1927	15.00
Ashtray, Vat 69, White, Ceramic, Square, 4 1/4 x 1/2 In.	4.00
Ashtray, Vought Kimmich Republic Staghound, Tire	85.00
Ashtray, Zenith Tire, Tire Shape	12.00
Automaton, Animal Orchestra, Baranger	4400.00
Automaton, Diamond Cleaners, 4 Workers, Polishing Diamond Ring, Baranger	3850.00
Automaton, Lighthouse, Rolling Waves, Sailboat, Baranger	3850.00
Badge, Tab Bread, Cisco Kid	20.00
Bag, Butter-Kist, Glassine, Pictures Holcome & Hole Kids, 1914	4.00
Banner, Chippewa Salt, Feathered Indian Brave, Cloth, 24 1/2 x 60 1/2 In.	203.00
Banner, Hercules Powder, Grand Prize Winner, Cloth, 19 In.	220.00
Banner, Kellogg's Castor Oil, Baby, Teething Ring, Cloth, c.1921, 30 1/2 In.	220.00
Bill Hook, Austex Chile Products, Metal, Celluloid, Colorful	32.00
Bill Hook, Walker's Mexene Chili	25.00
Bin, Calypso Baking Powder, Wooden, Blue Paint	205.00
Bin, German Coffee, Slant Top, Green Metal, Toledo Spice Co.	450.00
Bin, Honest Breakfast Java Coffee, 3 Sides Stenciled, Tin, 22 1/2 In.	231.00
Bin, Honest Scrap Tobacco, Store Size	1250.00
Bin, Polar Bear Tobacco, Counter, Lift Lid, Tin	225.00
Bin, Pure Spices, 6 Doors, Ovoid Portraits, Tin, 21 x 24 1/4 In.	850.00
Bin, Seed, 18 Glass Front Drawers, W.B. & Co., Oak, 37 x 76 In.	2350.00
Bin, Sweet Cuba, Slant Top, Tin, Counter	50.00
Bin, Tea, Montgomery Ward & Co., Oriental Girl Pictured	110.00
Bin, Tea, Young Hyson, Stenciled, Toleware, Cylinder Roll	165.00
Blotter, Brown's Iron Bitters, Woman's, Desk, Children, Frame, 3 1/2 x 6 1/2 In.	58.00
Blotter, Calendar, Ward's Tip-Top Cakes, 1949	8.50
Blotter, Dodge Bros., Pictures Cars	9.00
Blotter, Emerson Fan, Fan Picture	12.00
Blotter, Kellogg's Rice Krispies, 1940s ....20.00 to	22.00

Blotter, Kellogg's Whole Wheat Krumbles 6.00
Blotter, Mentholatum For Croup & Sore Throats 4.00
Blotter, Neverfals Products, All American Girl, 1915, 6 x 3 1/2 In. 12.00
Blotter, Shadow Blue Coal, 1930s 45.00
Blotter, Ward's Clothing, Archie Gunn 18.00
Books may be included in the Paper category
Booklet, Faultless Starch, Children's Type, 1905-1910 .... 6.00
Booklet, Franco-American Soup, 1908 .... 22.00
Booklet, McDonald's, Let's Eat Out, 28 Pages, 1965 .... 25.00
Booklet, Sapolio Cleaning Product, Story 1 Side, 1880s, 3 x 4 In. 20.00
Bookmark, Old Nick Candy Bar, Mechanical Glad-Sad Face 8.00
Bottles are listed in their own category
Bottle Openers are listed in their own category
Bottle Topper, Royal Crown Cola, Figural, Santa Claus 15.00
Bowl, Baby's, Ralston Purina, 1925 .... 85.00
Bowl, Cereal, Cap'n Crunch, Embossed, 1960s 30.00
Bowl, Cereal, Grape-Nuts Flakes, Mickey Mouse, Yellow, Beetleware, 1930s 50.00
Bowl, Howard Johnson, 5 1/2 In. 35.00
Box, see also Box category
Box, 1 Kote Roof Barn Bridge Paint, Wooden, Empty 22.50
Box, 3 Little Kittens Castile Soap, Molded, Display 60.00
Box, Barbie, Display, Cardboard, 1963 .... 250.00
Box, Bazooka Bubble Gum, 3 Baseball Cards On Back 38.00
Box, Beechnut Gum, Display, 14 In. 65.00
Box, Black Jack Candy, Man Dancing Across Front, Top Hat, 100 Count.................. 198.00
Box, British Beechnut Gum, Display, 100 Pack, 1940s.. 65.00
Box, Capwell Horse Nails, Dovetailed, Stenciled 32.00
Box, Cheerios, Unopened, Contents, 1975 .... 25.00
Box, Cigar, Henry George 105.00
Box, Cigar, Virginia Cheroots, Wooden 155.00
Box, Cigarette, Benson & Hedges, 20 .... 20.00
Box, Colman's Mustard, Wooden 150.00
Box, D.M. Ferry Co., Oak, Mitered Corners, 7 x 12 x 4 In. 75.00
Box, Dauntless Cheese 3.00
Box, Donkey Kong Cereal, With Baseball Cards, 1984 .... 25.00
Box, Eli Cutter, Cigarettes... 6.00
Box, Epsom Salts, Wooden 75.00
Box, Gold Dust Twins Washing Soap, Unopened 95.00
Box, Gold Tip Gum, Cardboard, Holds 10 Sticks Of Gum, Sterling Mint Co. 35.00
Box, Happy Meal, Kansas City Royal Players, Burger Chef 18.00
Box, Happy Meal, Star Trek, McDonald's, 1979, 4 Piece 35.00
Box, Hat, John Cavanaugh, Black, Gold Letters, With Velvet & Straw Hat 25.00
Box, Hershey's Milk Chocolate Candy, 1960 .... 23.00
Box, Hiawatha Long Cut Tobacco, Scotten & Co., Indians, 4 Oz, 2 x 3 x 15 In. 95.00
Box, Jack Sprat Codfish, Wooden 35.00
Box, Krispy Kernel Popcorn, Never Folded, 1930s 8.00
Box, Log Cabin Tobacco, Black Man Smoking, 1880s, 8 x 16 In. 250.00
Box, Mother Hubbard Energy Wheat, Cereal, 1940s 130.00
Box, National Biscuit Shredded Wheat, 1930 .... 50.00
Box, News Boy Rough & Ready Pocket Plug Tobacco, Wooden............................... 65.00
Box, Pikes Scythestone, Wooden 50.00
Box, Post Grape-Nuts Flakes, Baseball Cards, c.1961 .... 175.00
Box, Post's Sugar Crisp Order Form, 1955 .... 15.00
Box, Pulver Hi-Lo Gum 285.00
Box, Ralston, Space Patrol Phones, 1950 .... 145.00
Box, Shipping, Maypo Hot Cereal, 1950s 75.00
Box, Soap, Swift Co. Heliotrope Soap, Art Nouveau Graphics................................ 25.00
Box, T.N.T. Popcorn, Firecracker Each Side, Cardboard, 1920-1930 .... 25.00
Box, TWA Winston Cigarette, Jet, Sample, Contents ....25.00 to 35.00
Box, Wilbur's Horse & Cattle Food, Yellow, Black Stenciling.................................. 1395.00
Bracelet, Heinz Products, Silvered Brass, 5 Charms, 1940s 47.00
Brush, Baldwin Park Poultry Farms, Celluloid, Round.. 12.00
Bucket, Paint, Dutch Boy, Bail Handle... 18.00

◆◆◆◆◆◆◆◆◆◆◆◆◆◆◆◆◆◆◆◆◆◆◆◆

Be very careful when handling old bottles or medical equipment. The remains of old drugs, even toxic materials, may still cling to the surface. A broken bit of glass or a sliver could let these toxic materials reach your bloodstream.

◆◆◆◆◆◆◆◆◆◆◆◆◆◆◆◆◆◆◆◆◆◆◆◆

Advertising, Cabinet, Humphrey's Veterinary Remedies, 21 x 33 x 60 In.

Cabinet, Boye Needles, Wooden	125.00
Cabinet, Diamond Dyes, Baby In Frame, 16 x 20 In.	825.00
Cabinet, Diamond Dyes, Governess, Cherry, Lithographed Panel, 30 x 23 In.	495.00
Cabinet, Diamond Dyes, Washer Woman, Tin Front, 29 3/4 In.	1015.00
Cabinet, Dr. Daniels Veterinary Medicine Products, Tin Front, 21 x 27 In.	1045.00
Cabinet, Feen-A-Mint Laxative, Mirror On Marquee, Tin, 16 In.	410.00
Cabinet, Gargoyle Mobiloil, Globe, Padlow, 99 In.	3575.00
Cabinet, Humphrey's Veterinary Remedies, 21 x 33 x 60 In. ....*Illus*	3685.00
Cabinet, Munyon's Homeopathic Home Remedies, Drawer, Metal	150.00
Cabinet, Peerless Dyes, Roll Top, Tin Front, Gypsy Girl, 18 1/2 In.	495.00
Cabinet, Perfection Dyes, Tin Insert, 24 1/4 x 17 1/4 In.	990.00
Cabinet, Putnam Dyes, General Putnam On Horseback, Contents	140.00
Cabinet, Ribbon, Floor Model, Oak, 32 x 48 In.	990.00
Cabinet, Spool, Lily Sewing Threads, Slant Top, Glass Front, Tin Sides	65.00
Cabinet, Spool, Belding Bros. & Co., 10 Glass Front Drawers, Cherry	300.00
Cabinet, Spool, Belding Bros. & Co., 8 Glass Front Drawers, Cherry	550.00
Cabinet, Spool, Belding Bros. & Co., Drawers, Oak, 22 x 18 In.	385.00
Cabinet, Spool, Belding Brothers, Brass & Glass Drawers, Wooden, 39 In.	660.00
Cabinet, Spool, Brainerd & Armstrong Co.	1750.00
Cabinet, Spool, Clark's O.N.T. Cotton, 4 Drawers, Hinged Top, Oak, 34 x 30 In.	5175.00
Cabinet, Spool, Clark's O.N.T. Cotton, Wooden, Brass, Red Glass Panels	355.00
Cabinet, Spool, Clark's Thread, 2 Black-Fronted Drawers	265.00
Cabinet, Spool, Corticelli, 3 Drawers, Gold Stenciled Sides, Wooden, 22 In.	245.00
Cabinet, Spool, J. & P. Coats' Spool Cotton, 4 Drawers, Walnut, 22 x 26 In.	452.00
Cabinet, Spool, J. & P. Coats, Tambour Door, 20 In.	715.00
Cabinet, Spool, Lily Sewing Threads, Slant Glass Front, 30 Compartments	100.00
Cabinet, Spool, Richardson's, 9 Drawers, Glass Front, 18 1/4 x 22 In.	632.00
Cabinet, Spool, Royal Society, Oak, 12 Drawers, 36 x 19 x 19 In.	550.00
Cabinet, Spool, Willimantic Thread For Sewing Machines, 6 Drawers, Label	2300.00
Cake Plate, Nelson Furniture Store, Homer Laughlin, 11 In.	30.00
Cake Plate, Nelson Furniture Store, Homer Laughlin, 9 In.	25.00
Cake Plate, Star Furniture Store, Homer Laughlin, 9 In.	25.00
Calendars are listed in their own category	
Can, Duplex Motor Oil, Pierce Arrow Car Picture, 5 Gal.	990.00
Can, Gold Dust Cleanser	50.00
Can, Old Dutch Cleanser, Contents, 1945	27.00
Can, Sunoco Household Oil, Gas Pump Picture	35.00
Can, Underhay Oil, Wooden Shipping Crate, 5 Gal.	150.00 to 195.00
Can Opener, Blatz Beer	6.00
Can Opener, Budweiser Beer	8.00

Advertising, Carrier, Bottle, Moxie Carousel,
Carnival Of Fun

Watch out for exploding antiques! Guns, shells, powder cans, nitrate movie film, and some chemicals left in old bottles or cans are dangerous. If you don't know about these items, contact your local police or fire department for help.

Can Opener, Coors Beer	10.00
Can Opener, Hershey's Chocolate Can, Dazy, 1976	15.00
Can Opener, Jax Beer, Bar Mounted	45.00
Can Punch, Pet Milk, Wooden	15.00
Candy Jar, Necco Sweets, Paneled, Ground Stopper Cover, Tall	85.00
Canisters, see introductory paragraph to Tins in this category	
Canoe, Old Town, Green Paint, Red Letters, Salesman's Sample, 50 x 4 x 9 1/2 In.	9350.00
Cards are listed in their own category	
Carrier, Bottle, Moxie Carousel, Carnival Of Fun .... *Illus*	425.00
Carton, Chesterfield Cigarettes, Arthur Godfrey, Bing Crosby, Perry Como	75.00
Carton, Milk, Elsie The Cow, Borden, 1950s, 1 Qt.	8.00
Case, Arrow Collar, Various Styles & Sizes, 33 1/2 x 21 In.	880.00
Case, Deuce Cigars, Playing Cards On Sides, 4 x 9 x 7 In.	83.00
Case, Diamond Dyes, Glass Lift Top, Back Drawer, Stenciled Only 10 Cents	165.00
Case, Dr. Raibert's Pine Tar Tablets, Glass, Metal, Schmitt & Co., 9 In.	523.00
Case, Eveready Flashlight & Batteries, Counter, Glass, Metal, 17 In.	50.00
Case, Karbar Knives, Stag Handle, Folding, Hunter In Wood	285.00
Case, Philip Morris, Oak Framed, 18 x 12 In.	95.00
Case, Ray-O-Vac Batteries, Color, Tin	215.00
Chair, Folding, Schenley Whiskey, Decal On Seat, Folded Becomes Cane, 36 In.	105.00
Chair, Page's Ice Cream, Blue & White, Back To Back Signs, Tin, 32 1/2 In.	330.00
Chair, Smoke Piedmont Cigarettes, Folding, Porcelain Back, Pair	200.00
Chair, Smoke Piedmont, Folding, Wooden, Tin Back, Pair	385.00
Chalkboard, 5 Roses, Cardboard, 20 x 15 In.	375.00
Charm, Nipper, Celluloid, Cream, Loop On Side, Pink Cork, 1 In.	27.00
Cigar Cutter, Brown's Mule, Countertop, 1920s	125.00
Cigar Cutter, Swift's Bacon, Iron, Pocket	65.00
Clicker, Chevrolet, Tin Lithograph, 1950s, 1 3/4 In.	19.00
Clicker, Real Kill Bug Killer, Tin	15.00
Clip, Pencil, Celluloid, Hires' Household Extract, Genuine Root Beer, 1 5/8 In.	35.00
Clip, Pencil, Red Goose Shoes For Boys & Girls, Metal, Celluloid, 1940s	30.00
Clocks are listed in their own category	
Coaster, Otis Elevator, U.S. & Canadian Symbols, Lenox, 1970s, 4 In., 15 Piece	85.00
Coaster, Pabst Blue Ribbon Beer, 4 In.	2.00
Coaster, Sprite Boy, Coke Hat, 1950s	8.00
Coaster Set, Beverwyck Beer, Horse & Rider, Embossed, All Different, 4 Piece	25.00
Cooler, Budweiser Beer, Red	165.00
Cooler, Dr Pepper, Green	25.00
Cooler, Maxwell House Iced Tea, Barrel Shape, Watt Pottery, 1940s	235.00
Cover, Pillow, Lithographed Cotton, Jack Bachelor Celibate's Club, 1905	187.00
Creamer & Sugar, Kennel Ration Dog & Cat Food, F & F	90.00
Crock, Fountain, Syrup, Orange Crush, Tin, 1 Gal.	50.00
Crock, Heinz Tomato Preserves, Stoneware, 1883, 5 1/2 In.	165.00
Crock Set, Heinz 57 Baked Beans, With 10 Bean Pots, 1950	125.00

Cuff Links, Kraft Jelly, 1957 .... 20.00
Cuff Links, Reddy Kilowatt 75.00
Cuff Links, Western Airlines, The Only Way To Fly 30.00
Cup, California Raisins, In Conga Line, Plastic, White, CALRAB, 1987, 4 1/8 In. 1.00
Cup, Measuring, Kodak, Glass 27.00
Cup, Shoney's Big Boy, Waxed Paper, Dixie, 1960s, 5 In. 37.00
Cup, Tony The Tiger, Glass 10.00
Cup, Winchell's Donuts, Ceramic 3.00
Curtain, General Tire, Fringed, On Wooden Rod, Finials, 45 x 45 In. 95.00
Decanter, Stoughton Bitters, Cut Glass 75.00
Dish, Corn, Miracle Maid 30.00
Dish, Sundae, Borden's, Elsie, Box, 4 Piece 125.00
Dispenser, Boraxo Soap, Moisten Hands Before Using, Porcelain 35.00
Dispenser, Buckeye Root Beer, Name On Front, Black, 11 1/2 x 8 In. 275.00
Dispenser, Chocolate Cone, 5 Cent 2900.00
Dispenser, Fowler's Cherry Smash Syrup, Bellied, Gold Trim, 14 In. 1540.00
Dispenser, Heinz Vinegar, Barrel Shape, Countertop, 10 In. 225.00
Dispenser, Hires Munimaker, Marble Base, Polished Plating 8250.00
Dispenser, Hires, Stainless, Medallions, c.1940 .... 450.00
Dispenser, Howell's Orange Julep, 5 Cent, 14 x 9 In. 770.00
Dispenser, Lash's California Orangeade 495.00
Dispenser, Massey's Root Beer 1350.00
Dispenser, Middeby Root Beer, Mug Shape 245.00
Dispenser, Mission Orange Soda, Black Amethyst Base, Pink Globe, 1920s 295.00
Dispenser, Nesbitt, Counter Clamp On, Glass 125.00
Dispenser, Soda, Arctic, Marble, T.W. Tufts, Boston 3500.00
Dispenser, Soda, Charles Lippincott, Philadelphia, Marble 3100.00
Dispenser, Ward's Lemon Crush, Figural, Flowered Base, 13 x 12 In. 825.00
Dispenser, Ward's Lime, Figural 1210.00
Display, Aurora Models Catalog, 1960 .... 45.00
Display, Blatz Beer Man, For Bar, 1950s 60.00
Display, Box, Sunshine Custard Creams, Bakery, Wiles Biscuit Co., 1900s 75.00
Display, Boye Needle Selector, Orange & Cream Tin, 1909 .... 150.00
Display, Bud Light, Spuds MacKenzie, Light-Up, Plastic, 1987 ....*Illus* 100.00
Display, Burry's Cookies, Green Hornet Bike Badge, Plastic, 1966, 34 x 48 In. 1705.00
Display, Champion Spark Plugs, Tin, Yellow, Black Letters, 12 x 18 x 5 1/2 In. 220.00
Display, Courvoisier Cognac, Napoleon Bust, Counter, Bronze 65.00
Display, Crayola, Cardboard, Stand-Up, c.1940 .... 35.00
Display, Dutchman, Bois Liqueurs, Holds Bottle, Plaster, 17 In. ....*Illus* 85.00
Display, Goebel Beer Bottle, Chicken, Plaster, 8 x 10 In. ....*Illus* 105.00
Display, Gold Dust, Letter Over Each Box, Cardboard, Hanging, 60 In. 8800.00
Display, Green River Whiskey, Man, Horse, Bred In Kentucky, 1899, 14 x 11 In. 175.00
Display, Hickory Garters, Die Cut, Wooden, 19 1/2 x 13 In. 550.00
Display, Johnnie Walker, Figural, Born 1820, Still Going Strong 175.00
Display, Keen Kutter, Draw Knife, Board, Simmons Hardware, 1904 .... 2900.00
Display, Kellogg's, Snap, Crackle & Pop, Cardboard, Die Cut, 36 In., Set Of 3 .... 200.00
Display, Ko-Pak-Ta, Hot Nuts, Dancing Natives 350.00
Display, L.Z. Forster Brewing Co., Figure, Clock, Train & Ship, Iron, 12 In. 560.00
Display, Lucky Lager Bottle, Elf, Plaster, 11 x 7 x 4 In. ....*Illus* 171.00
Display, Lucky Strike, Store Display, Figural, Stand-Up, 1940s 69.00
Display, Marine, Camel Cigarette Pack, World War II, Easel Back, Cardboard 195.00
Display, McDonald's Cinderella Premiums, Translucent Sign, 1987 .... 70.00
Display, Meerschaum Pipes, Corncob, 36 In. 275.00
Display, Nestle Chocolate, Girl, Die Cut Cardboard, 1940s, 36 In. 550.00
Display, Norvell-Shapleigh Razors, Etched Logo, Oak Frame, c.1910 .... 725.00
Display, PEZ, Revolving, Countertop 175.00
Display, Philip Morris, Cardboard, 43 1/2 In. ....*Illus* 375.00
Display, Polly Soda Pop Bottle, Mounted In Cardboard, Parrot 180.00
Display, Raid, Inflatable Figure 35.00
Display, Red Goose Shoes, Figural, Papier-Mache, Mechanical, Lays Golden Egg 600.00
Display, Red Goose Shoes, Revolving Rack, Cardboard, 36 x 32 In. 330.00
Display, Shredded Wheat, Glass Dome, Wooden Base, Holds 12 Biscuits 425.00
Display, Slinky Toy, Electric, Store 225.00

Display, Toy, Warriors Of The World Figures, Marx, 1950s 275.00
Display, Vernor's Ginger Ale, Automated, Eyes Roll, Mouth Moves, 45 In. 6500.00
Display, Wonder Bread, Loaf, c.1950 .... 15.00
Display Case, Curved Front, Mirrored Sliding Glass Doors, Nickel, 27 1/2 In. 247.00
Display Case, Hunt's Pens, Oak 450.00
Display Case, Keen Kutter Knives, Pocket 700.00
Display Case, Keen Kutter Roller Skates, Steel 350.00
Display Case, Remington, Holds 22 Shells, Wooden 85.00
Display Case, Sanford Ink, Reverse On Glass, Oak, 18 In. 550.00
Display Case, Victorian, Revolving Shelves, Oak 1325.00
Display Rack, Chandler's Laxative, Cardboard, 18 Sample Boxes 25.00
Display Rack, Topps Gum, Metal & Plastic, Countertop, 1940s, 8 x 6 In. 55.00
Display Rack, Winchester, Roller Skates, Countertop 350.00
Dolls are listed in their own category
Dominoes, Lord Calvert Whiskey, 1939 .... 65.00
Door, Paneled Wood, Salesman's Sample 247.00
Door Push, 7-Up, Porcelain, 3 x 32 In. ....55.00 to 70.00
Door Push, Ex-Lax 25.00
Door Push, Salada Tea, Porcelain ....45.00 to 85.00
Door Push, Schweppes, Porcelain 100.00
Door Push, Sky Chief Gasoline, Porcelain, 12 x 22 In. ̇... 85.00
Door Push, Vicks, Porcelain, Graphic, 4 x 6 In. 350.00
Door Push, We Recommend & Sell Winchester Cartridges & Guns 125.00
Fans are listed in their own category
Figure, Air India, Indian Man, Turban, Mustache, 16 In. 125.00
Figure, Beefeater, Gin Man, Figural, Ceramic, Wade Pourer, Box 28.00
Figure, Big Boy, 1972, 8 In. 16.00
Figure, Boy, Modeling Carter's Underwear, Papier-Mache, 33 In. 725.00
Figure, Burgermeister Beer, Gold Plaster, 16 x 14 x 6 1/2 In. .... *Illus* 127.00
Figure, California Raisin, 1st Edition, 2 1/2 To 3 In., Set Of 4 .... 10.00

Advertising, Display, Bud Light,
Spuds MacKenzie, Light-Up,
Plastic, 1987

Advertising, Display, Dutch-
man, Bois Liqueurs, Holds
Bottle, Plaster, 17 In.

Advertising, Display, Lucky Lager Bottle, Elf, Plaster,
11 x 7 x 4 In.; Advertising, Goebel Beer Bottle,
Chicken, Plaster, 8 x 10 In.

Advertising, Display,
Philip Morris, Cardboard,
43 1/2 In.

Advertising, Figure, Burgermeister
Beer, Gold Plaster, 16 x 14 x 6 1/2 In.

Advertising, Figure, Pabst Blue
Ribbon, Girl With Bonnet

Advertising, Figure, Dachshund, Doggone Good Beer
& Ale, Frankenmuth, 7 In.;

Advertising, Figure, Man,
Carter's Knit Underwear,
Papier-Mache, 33 1/2 In.

Advertising, Figure, Heidelberg
Beer, Student Prince, Plaster

Figure, Chicken Of The Sea, Mermaid, Mattel, 1974, 15 In. 45.00
Figure, Cliquot Club Soda, Papier-Mache, Full Bodied, Original Clothes, 33 In. 375.00
Figure, Count Chocula, Vinyl, 1975, 8 In. 55.00
Figure, Crosley Pup 65.00
Figure, Dachshund, Doggone Good Beer & Ale, Frankenmuth, 7 In. ....*Illus* 20.00
Figure, Dog, Bryant Pup, Papier-Mache 400.00
Figure, Elsie The Cow, 2 Calves, Borden's, Rubber Face, Dated 1957, Pair 85.00
Figure, Elsie, Borden's, Bendee Type 25.00
Figure, Frankenmuth Beer, Dog 40.00
Figure, Hamm's Bear, Bartender Bear, 1973 .... 65.00
Figure, Heidelberg Beer, Student Prince, Plaster ....*Illus* 100.00
Figure, Jack Daniels Whiskey, Black Tie, 36 In. 125.00
Figure, Kraft, Cameraman 85.00
Figure, Laughing Lena, Arms Raised, Missing Front Tooth, c.1920, 79 In. 6900.00
Figure, Magic Chef Ovens, Vinyl 30.00
Figure, Man, Carter's Knit Underwear, Papier-Mache, 33 1/2 In. ....*Illus* 777.00
Figure, Michelin Man, Hard Plastic, Standing, 12 In. ....55.00 to 95.00
Figure, Nathan's, Hot Dog Man 10.00
Figure, Nauga, Naugahyde, 1960s 60.00
Figure, Nipper, Papier-Mache, 36 In. 875.00
Figure, Nipper, Victor, His Master's Voice, Papier-Mache, King Cole Co., Oh. 850.00
Figure, Nipper, Victor, Papier-Mache, Repaired Legs, 12 In. 325.00

Figure, Nipper, Victor, Polyethylene, 13 In.	450.00
Figure, Pabst Blue Ribbon, Girl With Bonnet .... *Illus*	116.00
Figure, Raid, Bug, Plastic, Battery Operated, Remote Control	195.00
Figure, Red Goose Shoes, Goose, Plaster, Inscribed, 12 In.	165.00
Figure, Reddy Kilowatt, Glow-In-The-Dark Hands, Plastic, 1961, 5 1/2 In.	220.00
Figure, Schlitz Beer, Golden Girl Holding World Globe, 45 In.	78.00
Figure, Shoe, Children, Weatherbird Shoes, All Leather Always, Bisque, 4 1/2 In.	60.00
Figure, Sinclair Oil, Dinosaur, c.1950, On Card, 4 Piece	15.00
Figure, Smilin' Sprite, Vinyl, Talking	20.00
Figure, Spalding, Li'l Ballboy, Terra-Cotta, c.1912, 43 1/2 In.	9200.00
Figure, Tagament Antacid, Stomach, Bendable Arms, Smiling Face, Pedestal, 5 In.	12.00
Figure, Travelodge, Sleepy Bear, Vinyl	35.00
Figure, Wieland, Bartender, On Bottle	80.00
Figure, Windmill, Heineken's Beer, Brewed In Holland, Lights, Turns	265.00
Flashlight, Energizer Bunny	20.00
Flower Holder, Stork Club	135.00
Folder, Remingrton Arms, Ducks & Hunter In Rain, 3-Fold, 39 1/2 In.	1760.00
Game, Carling Black Label, Cribbage, Cards & Board	25.00
Game, Checkers, Poll-Parrot, 2 1/2 x 5 In. Box	30.00
Game, Elsie And Her Family, 1941, Box	155.00
Game, Hawaiian Punch, Mattel, 1977	50.00
Game, Quaker Oats, Marathon Race	50.00
Game, Shell Stop & Go, 1936	55.00
Game, Tootsie Roll Train Game, Hasbro, 1969	29.00
Glass, 7-Up, Green	22.00
Glass, Arby's, Casper, Midnight Ride, 5 In.	15.00
Glass, Beer, Cliff House Picture, San Francisco	75.00
Glass, Beer, Yosemite Lager	85.00
Glass, Big Top Peanut Butter, Pop Goes The Weasel, Blue	5.00
Glass, Big Top Peanut Butter, Yankee Doodle, Red	5.00
Glass, Bob's Big Boy, 50th Anniversary	10.00
Glass, Borden's, Elsie, Elmer & Family, 12 Oz.	8.00
Glass, Charlie Tuna, Original Box, Late 1960s, Set Of 6	30.00
Glass, Dr Pepper, Star Trek, Set Of 3	140.00
Glass, Jack Daniels, Square	5.00
Glass, Kool Glass, Wall Match Hanger	22.50
Glass, McDonald's, Camp Snoopy, The Struggle For Security Is No Picnic, 1965	8.00
Glass, McDonald's, Camp Snoopy, There's No Excuse, 1968	8.00
Glass, Moerlein's Beer	59.00
Glass, Passport Scotch Whiskey, Etched	12.50
Glass, Phospo Bottle, Soda, 3 9/16 In.	6.00
Glass, Popeye's Fried Chicken, 10th Anniversary	11.00
Glass, Speedy Gonzales, Speedy Snaps Up The Cheese, Porky In Bottom, 1974	4.00
Glass, Star Wars, Burger King, 1980, 4 Piece	25.00
Glass, Taco Villa, 1979, Beauregard	8.00
Glass, Taco Villa, 1979, Frawley	9.00
Glass, Taco Villa, 1979, Harley	10.00
Glass, Taco Villa, 1979, Irving	20.00
Glass, Taco Villa, 1979, Julius	7.00
Glass, Taco Villa, 1979, Lazlo	8.00
Glass, Taco Villa, 1979, Mortimer	9.00
Glass, Taco Villa, 1979, Sigmund	7.00
Glass, Welch, Archie, Betty & Veronica Give A Party, Hot Dog In Bottom, 1973	4.00
Glass, Welch, Archie, Reggie Makes The Scene, Veronica, 1971	8.00
Glass, Welch, Archie, The Archies Having A Jam Session, Sabrina In Bottom, 1971	4.00
Glass, Welch, Bugs Bunny, Bugs Leads A Merry Chase, Yosemite On Bottom, 1974	4.00
Glass, Welch, Elmer Fudd, Porky In Bottom, Warner Bros., 1976	6.00
Glass, Wendy's, Where's The Beef, 1984	18.00
Glass, Wonder Woman, Brockway Style	25.00
Goblet, Lone Star, Red Pyro Stars, Footed, Round	10.00
Grill Plate, Howard Johnson	35.00
Hand Puppet, Sealtest, Mr. Cool, 1962	60.00
Hat, Delivery Man's, Holsum Bread	65.00

*Advertising, Hat Cleaner, Bailey's,
Cleveland, O.,
Leather, 1930s, 4 In.*

◆◆◆◆◆◆◆◆◆◆◆◆◆◆◆◆◆◆◆◆◆◆

Some of the moisturizing creams that are sold at the cosmetics counter are equally useful to keep leather soft. Best are moisturizers that have shea butter as an ingredient. Dried leather purses can be rejuvenated with a treatment from a moisturizer with an oil in it. Try a small spot first or it may darken the leather.

◆◆◆◆◆◆◆◆◆◆◆◆◆◆◆◆◆◆◆◆◆◆

Hat, Hauze, Motor Oil, R.P.M., 1930s	38.00
Hat, Texaco Fire Chief	45.00
Hat Cleaner, Bailey's Cleveland, O., Leather, 1930s, 4 In. ....*Illus*	15.00
Hatpin, Economy Stoves & Ranges, 10-In. Shank	55.00
Headdress, Indian, Sunbeam Bread, Child's, 1958	10.00
Holder, Old Dutch Cleanser	12.50
Ice Bucket, Booth's London Gin, Double-Decker Bus	25.00
Ice Bucket, Joe Camel, With 4 Glasses, 5 Piece	22.00
Ice Chest, Royal Crown Cola, Double Door Lift Top, Steel, 30 x 31 In.	275.00
Jar, Adams Gum, Etched	175.00
Jar, Barbasol, 8 Sides	125.00
Jar, Blue Boy Peanut Butter, Blue Boy Picture, Square, 8 Oz.	75.00
Jar, Jumbo Peanut Butter, White Screw Lid, 1930, 7 Oz.	100.00
Jar, Kis-Me Chewing Gum, 2 Kissing Children, Glass, 11 x 4 1/2 In.	385.00
Jar, Paul Jones, Embossed, Brown, 1/2 Pt.	10.00
Jar, Snack, Alpo Dog Snacks	44.00
Jar, Tom's Peanuts, Glass, Black Pyroglazed Paint, Red Finial Lid, Countertop	55.00
Jar, Wesson Oil, Stoneware	85.00
Jug, Kodak, Stenciled Text, Cobalt Blue, Early Logo, 5 Gal.	230.00
Keg, Alpine Bitters, Pewter	60.00
Keg, Hires Root Beer, Brass Claw Feet	2975.00
Key Fob, Esso, Put A Tiger In Your Tank, White Metal, Tiger Logo, 1960s	8.00
Kite, California Raisin, Windsock, Color, 1987, 44 x 27 In.	10.00
Knife, Dixson's Cameras, Pearl Handle, Bottle Shape, 2 In.	15.00
Knife, Swift's Premium Dry Sausage	30.00
Label, Abraham Lincoln, Orange Crate	12.00
Label, Amstr-Dam Beer, Los Angeles, California	10.00
Label, Ascot, Wm. Cameron & Bros., Dark Aromatic Tobacco, 1891	100.00
Label, Atlas Malt Tonic, Atlas Brewing Co., Chicago	23.00
Label, Blue Moon Coffee	9.00
Label, California Mission Lemon, 1930s, 9 x 12 In.	6.00
Label, Cerveza Hidalgo Beer, Lynwood, California	32.00
Label, Chickie Brand, California Asparagus, A. Levy & J. Zenter	5.00
Label, Chummy Brand California Grapes, 4 x 13 In.	3.00
Label, Cigar Box, Ethel Barrymore	980.00
Label, Cigar Box, Grant & Lee, Fellow Citizens	240.00
Label, Cigar Box, Uncle Sam, Honest Yankee	135.00
Label, Cincinnati Cream Ale, Jackson Brewery Co., Cincinnati, Ohio	22.00
Label, Coors Bock Beer, Golden, Colorado	42.00
Label, Diamond Bell & Full Jewel 5 Cent Cigars, Black, White & Red, 1890s	175.00
Label, Fresno Bohemian Beer, Fresno, California	15.00
Label, Gilt Edge Lager, Sacramento, California	15.00
Label, Glacier Beer, Kalispell Malt & Brewing, Kalispell, Montana	80.00
Label, Hahn & Livingston, Spitz Brand, Emperor Grapes, 4 x 13 In.	5.00
Label, Japan Tea, Garden Flowers, Multicolor, 1870-1880, Frame, 13 x 15 In.	80.00

Label, Kimbriel & Co., Top Stock Citrus Fruits From Texas...................................... 5.00
Label, Kitsap Hair Tonic, Cottel Drug Co., Indian Chief's Head, 7 In...................... 16.00
Label, Klausman Brewing Co. 42.00
Label, Koppitz Victory Beer, Koppitz-Melcher's, Detroit, Michigan 25.00
Label, La Rose De Mix, Vernon, California 20.00
Label, Largay's Pale Lager, Waterbury, Connecticut... 18.00
Label, London Bobby Beer, Miami Valley Brewing Co., Dayton, Ohio 50.00
Label, Lucky Lager, San Francisco, California.. 20.00
Label, Matz Bock Beer, Matz Brewing Co., Bellaire, Ohio...................................... 42.00
Label, Mefisto, Art Deco 72.00
Label, Meister-Brau Beer, Cleveland Home Brewing Co., Cleveland, Ohio 18.00
Label, Midnight Sun Beer, Fairbanks, Alaska.. 25.00
Label, Munchner Beer, Frankenmuth, Michigan.. 20.00
Label, Old Bohemian Beer, Chicago, Illinois.. 13.00
Label, Old Heidelbrau, Pacific Brewing, Sacramento, California ...:......................... 15.00
Label, Osceola Brand Tobacco 60.00
Label, Paradise Lager, Honolulu, Hawaii 102.00
Label, Pony Boy, Honeydew Melons Vine Ripened, Boys, Ponies, 7 1/2 x 5 In............ 6.00
Label, Regal Amber Bock, San Francisco, California.. 17.00
Label, Santa Lemon, Crate, 1928, 9 x 12 In. 10.00
Label, Select Lager, Honolulu, Hawaii 113.00
Label, Snow Owl Brand Apples, Image Of Snowy Owl, 8 1/2 x 10 1/2 In. 5.00
Label, Southern Tier Beer, Jos. Laurer, Binghamton, New Jersey 65.00
Label, Student Prince Beer, Heidelberg Brewing Co., Covington, Kentucky................. 13.00
Label, The Queen, Royal Delight, 1882.. 100.00
Label, Trading Post Lager, Chicago, Illinois.. 12.00
Label, White Top Beer, Capital Brewing & Ice Co., Montgomery, Alabama 55.00
Label, White Top Beer, Montgomery, Alabama 71.00
Label, Wise Bird Brand, Citrus Growers Assoc., 9 x 9 In.. 5.00
Label, Yako Chief Beer, Yakima Brewery & Bottling Co., Yakima, Washington 35.00
Lamp, Beer, Old Schiltz Globe 65.00
Lamp, Charlie Tuna, 1970 .... 70.00
Lamp, G & W Whiskey, Composition, Electric, 1930s, 15 In. 395.00
Letter Opener, Fuller Brush 5.00
Lid Top, Crispo Cereal, Cast Iron, 1 3/4 In. 50.00
Lunch Boxes are listed in their own category
Menu Board, Dr Pepper, Embossed Tin, 33 1/2 x 20 1/2 In. 170.00
Menu Board, Miss Rheingold, 1959.. 40.00
Menu Board, Squirt, Raised Green Bottle & Little Boy 75.00

Advertising pocket mirrors range in size from 1 1/2 to 5 inches in diameter.
Most of these mirrors were given away as advertising promotions.

Mirror, Anderson Jewelry, Silverware, 68 Nassau St., New York, 2 1/4 In. 40.00
Mirror, Angelus Marshmallow, Pocket...60.00 to 75.00
Mirror, Beauty Skin Products, Woman's Face, Pocket 75.00
Mirror, Bedford Peanut Butter, Pocket.. 75.00
Mirror, Big Jo Flour, Oval, Pocket.. 20.00
Mirror, Black & White, Scotch, Wall.. 50.00
Mirror, Brunswick Records, Pocket 45.00
Mirror, Buckeye Grain Drill, Pocket.. 85.00
Mirror, Case Threshing Machine Co., Celluloid, Pocket.. 65.00
Mirror, Ceresota Flour, Logo, White On Brown Rim, Pocket, 2 In............................ 45.00
Mirror, Clarehose Hosiery, Pocket.. 50.00
Mirror, Dr. Daniels Veterinary Medicines, Celluloid, Pocket, 2 1/4 In......................... 100.00
Mirror, Drink Plezio, The New Drink, Pocket 65.00
Mirror, Eiden Bonnet & Hat Frames, Hand Type, Pocket.. 35.00
Mirror, Garrett's Rye, Celluloid, Pocket, 2 3/4 In... 205.00
Mirror, Hires Root Beer, Boy Pointing Finger, Round, Pocket 95.00
Mirror, His Pleasure, Nude, Taking California Fig Bitters, Find Yours, 2 In.............. 75.00
Mirror, Horlick's, Pocket 50.00
Mirror, Joe Grein's Sauerkraut Juice, Chicago, Pocket.. 35.00
Mirror, John Deere, New Way Air Cooled Engine, Pocket...................................... 110.00
Mirror, Kelly-Springfield Tires, Celluloid, Pocket 132.00

Mirror, Kelly-Springfield Tires, Devil, Pocket 660.00
Mirror, Kleinert's Dress Shields, Celluloid, Pocket 35.00
Mirror, Laurel Stoves, Pocket 65.00
Mirror, Life Savers, Pocket 9.00
Mirror, Lightolier, 10 x 12 In. 21.00
Mirror, Miss Lang, Celluloid, Pocket 120.00
Mirror, Nature's Remedy, Tablets On Extended Tongue, Pocket, 2 1/8 In. .... 36.00 to 55.00
Mirror, New King Snuff, Celluloid, Pocket, 2 3/4 In. 38.50
Mirror, Nude, Full Frontal Female, Pocket, 2 1/4 In. 70.00
Mirror, Old Reliable Coffee, Pocket 65.00
Mirror, Old Spice, Hand Painted, Pocket 23.00
Mirror, Oxford Chocolates, Celluloid, Pocket 85.00
Mirror, Pond's Extract, Lettered Promotion, Oak Frame, Beveled, 11 1/2 In. 143.00
Mirror, Queen Shoes, Pocket 65.00
Mirror, Red Goose Shoes, Floor Stand 135.00
Mirror, Robin Hood Flour, None So Good As Robin Hood, Germany, Pocket, c.1930s . 18.00
Mirror, Rose Distillery, Jacksonville, Florida, Handle, Pocket 95.00
Mirror, Sherman Music Co., Harp, Pocket 25.00
Mirror, Star Soap, Round, Pocket 7.00
Mirror, Victor, His Master's Voice, Nipper Figure, Celluloid, c.1910, Pocket 173.00
Mirror, Western Employment Counselors, Kansas City, Pocket 30.00
Mirror, With Thermometer, Diekorns Bread, Color Loaf Of Bread 295.00
Money Clip, Anheuser-Busch 10.00
Money Clip, Philip Morris, Celluloid 20.00
Moxie Fountain Piece, Held Jug Of Moxie Syrup 425.00
Mug, A & W Root Beer 5.00
Mug, Auto Ignition Co., Pittsburgh, Pa., 1926 .... 45.00
Mug, Beer, Anheuser-Busch, Glass, Embossed Emblem, 1890-1905 .... 425.00
Mug, Beer, Bartholomay, N.Y., 1911, Miniature 80.00
Mug, Beer, Budweiser, Anheuser & Eagle 50.00
Mug, Beer, Budweiser, Christmas, 1981 .... 200.00
Mug, Beer, Cardinal, Scranton, Pa., Milk Glass 88.00
Mug, Beer, For Health Drink Trommer's Bottled Beer 237.00
Mug, Beer, G. Brehm & Son, Miniature 160.00
Mug, Beer, Miller High Life, Miniature 15.00
Mug, Beer, Pabst, Gnomes 78.00
Mug, Buick, 1924 .... 60.00
Mug, Champion Clydesdales, Clear Glass, Applied Metal Label, 3 In. 3.00
Mug, Dad's Root Beer, Barrel Shape 6.00
Mug, Dr. Swett's Root Beer, c.1916 .... 60.00
Mug, Drink Hires Root Beer, Child Picture 385.00
Mug, Joe Camel, Glass 4.00
Mug, Kool-Aid, Purple, 1960s 15.00
Mug, Maxwell House, 1984 Olympics 10.00
Mug, Nestle's Chocolate, Farfel The Dog Picture, Signed Jimmy Nelson, 1954 .... 40.00
Mug, Nestle's Quick, Rabbit 20.00
Mug, Pabst Beer, Wisconsin, Miniature 120.00
Mug, Quaker Oats, Plastic 8.00
Mug, Raid Bug, Ceramic 25.00
Mug, Round Oak Stoves, Doe Wah Jack Indian 395.00
Mug, Schmidt's Beer, Miniature 15.00
Mug, Sprudel Water & Salt, West Baden, Indiana, Buildings & Gnome 125.00
Necktie, RCA Nipper 35.00
Oil Can, Singer Sewing Machine 6.00
Oil Kit, Glass Vial, Dan L. Muffen, Leather Case, 9 3/8 x 4 3/8 In. 185.00
Opener, Beer, Box, Dixie 45.00
Oven Mitt, Reddy Kilowatt, Package 65.00
Pack, Cigarette, Chesterfield, 1947, Full 15.00
Pack, Cigarette, L & M, Man & Woman By Lake, 1970s 10.00
Paddle, Wrigley's Gum, Wooden, For Opening Cartons, Oak, 2 x 14 In. 85.00
Padlock, Shapleigh Hardware 225.00
Pan, Cake, Hetty Harper Mixes, Square, 7 In. 6.50
Paperweight, Brownie Baking Co. 125.00

Paperweight, Buffalo Insurance Co. 38.00
Paperweight, Griswold, No. 30, Puppy 220.00
Party Kit, Circus, Pillsbury Flour, Premium, Original Mailer 20.00
Peeler, Morton Salt, Nickel 5.00
Pen Holder, Calgary Stampede, Marble 45.00
Pencil Case, A & W Root Beer Bear 20.00
Pillow, Hershey's Mr. Goodbar, Candy Bar Shape, 4 x 6 In. 8.00
Pillow, Little Sprout, Cloth, 13 In. 10.00
Pin, Alka-Seltzer, Try It You'll Like It, 1980s... 5.00
Pin, Campbell's Girl, Enamel On Brass, New Jersey Jaycee-Ettes, 1 3/4 In. 50.00
Pin, Chessie C & O, Sleeping Cat, 1940s, 1 1/2 In. 41.00
Pin, Elsie The Cow, Borden's 5.00
Pin, Firestone Non Skid Tires, Celluloid, Figure Holding Tire, 1910, 1 1/2 In. 29.00
Pin, Gold Dust Washing Powder, Inscription Side Of Washtub, 1898, 7/8 In. 50.00
Pin, Manager's, Burger King, 14K Gold... 35.00
Pin, Reddy Kilowatt, Brass, 1950s... 45.00
Pin, Yellow Kid, High Admiral Cigarettes, Kid With Poster 13.00
Pitcher, Cutty Sark Scotch 25.00
Pitcher, Farmers Union, Co-Op Creamery, Brown & Green, 5 In. 225.00
Pitcher, Finley Acker & Co., Acker's High Grade Groceries, Philadelphia, 1 Qt. 60.00
Pitcher, Home Oil & Gas, Waukomis, Okla., Spongeware 90.00
Pitcher, Imported Black Velvet, Blended Canadian Whiskey.................................... 8.50
Pitcher, West Texas Gin, Paducah, Texas, Spongeware, 1942 .... 120.00
Place Setting, RCA Victor, Silver Plate, 1935, 5 Piece 45.00
Plaque, Falstaff Beer, Family Gathered Around Table, Round, 24 In. 95.00
Plate, Anheuser-Busch Malt, Blue, Gold Rim 110.00
Plate, Budweiser, Anheuser & Eagle, White, 10 In. 50.00
Plate, Crosley, Dishwasher Safe, Homer Laughlin 25.00
Plate, Dinner, Moxie, White Ceramic, Bird Border 1700.00
Plate, Pimm's Tea, Tin, Suit Border, Lithograph, 1930, 10 In. 121.00
Plate, Standard Brewing Co., New Orleans, Shonk Royal Art................................... 100.00
Plate, Standard Oil Co., Commemorative, 1870-1970, Black Glass 50.00
Platter, Howard Johnson, Round, 13 In. 70.00
Poster, Kickapoo Indian Remedies, Liebler & Mass Lith., 38 x 27 In. 172.00
Poster, Peabody-Martini Rifle, 1878, 2 Pages, 9 1/2 x 12 1/2 In.............................. 49.00
Rack, Bottle, 7-Up, 1940s... 175.00
Rack, Display, Griswold, For Skillets..350.00 to 375.00
Rack, Saddle Display, A & W Horseshoes, 43 In. 750.00
Rack, Spice, Slade's Pure Spices, Store, Tin 115.00
Radio, California Raisin... 100.00
Radio, NBC, Plastic, Microphone Shaped, 1950s, 12 In. 95.00
Ring, Apple Jacks, H.R. Puff N' Stuff, Premium, 1969 .... 60.00
Ring, Chex, Agent Decoder, Cellophane Wrapper, 1960s... 25.00
Ring, Elsie The Cow, Plastic, Green, c.1950... 50.00
Ring, Little King Post Toasties, Package 20.00
Ring, Post Toasties, Smilin' Jack.. 12.00
Ring, Red Goose Shoes, Jet Pilot.. 45.00
Ruler, Baptist Book Store, Dallas, Wooden, 6 In. 6.00
Ruler, Dr Pepper, Frosty Man, Wooden... 10.00
Ruler, Joseph D. Spiegel, 1 Ft., Oversized, 36 In. 150.00
Ruler, Wonder Bread ....5.00 to 10.00
Sack, Morton Salt 20.00
Salt & Pepper Shakers are listed in their own category
Scales are listed in their own category
Shaving Mug, Elkhardt & LeDuc, Grooming Products... 20.00
Shot Glass, Jim Beam, Embossed.. 25.00
Shot Glass, Wells Pharmacy, Danvers, Mass., Etched 150.00
Sign, A. Lewis's Inn, 1812, Masonic Design, 2 Sides, Tree Other Side, Carved 9075.00
Sign, A.L. Owl Co., Grinding, Sharpening, 181 Bleeker St., Oval, 36 x 20 In. 350.00
Sign, Alpenbrau Neon Light 375.00
Sign, American Family Soap, Porcelain, 26 x 19 In.. 800.00
Sign, American Lady Corsets, Printed On Paper, 36 x 11 In...................................... 350.00
Sign, American President Steamship Lines, Painted Wood 3630.00

Sign, Amoco Motor Oil, Cat Trying To Catch Goldfish, Logo, 28 x 40 In...................... 150.00
Sign, Anheuser-Busch, Doctor & Stork, Tin On Cardboard, 7 3/4 x 12 3/4 In. 95.00
Sign, Antiques, Pocket Watch Shape, Metal, Hollow Body... 440.00
Sign, Apollo Chocolates, Silhouette Of Gentleman, Porcelain, 12 x 32 In. 148.00
Sign, Apothecary, Mortar & Pestle, 26 In.. 495.00
Sign, Approved DeSoto Service, Round, 30 In... 235.00
Sign, Armour Star, Black Man Slicing Ham, Tin, Self-Framed, 15 x 22 In. 550.00
Sign, Artie Cigars, The Vest, Tin, 14 x 10 In. 725.00
Sign, Authorized Studebaker Service, Round, 42 In... 750.00
Sign, Barbershop, Ask For Wildroot, 39 x 14 In. 172.00
Sign, Barq's Root Beer, 2 Sides, Art Deco, Privilege Panel, 20 x 28 In. 475.00
Sign, Barq's Root Beer, Bottle Picture, Tin, 12 x 30 In. 125.00
Sign, Belar Cigar, Self-Framed, 8 x 10 In.. 175.00
Sign, Bixby's Royal Polish, Old Woman Sees Reflection, Paper, 20 x 12 1/2 In. 275.00
Sign, Black Label T.V. Time, Light 35.00
Sign, Blackstone Cigars, Frame, 1933, 26 x 32 In. 275.00
Sign, Blatz Pilsner Beer, Tin Over Cardboard, Bottle Dated 1941, 9 x 13 In. 138.00
Sign, Boot Maker's, Boot Form, 2 Sides, Mauve Ground, c.1870, 22 In. 750.00
Sign, Boot, 3-Dimensional, Carved Pine, c.1900, 28 In. 275.00
Sign, Borden's, Cardboard, Die Cut, Blue, Red, White, 20 In. ....*Illus* 209.00
Sign, British Railways, Porcelain, 5 1/4 x 26 3/4 In. 65.00
Sign, Brown, Forman Distillers, Salesman At Bar, Tin, 27 x 19 In. 2420.00
Sign, Buckeye Beer, Light.. 35.00
Sign, Budweiser, Neon, Bow Tie Logo.. 225.00
Sign, Burma Shave, Bearded Lady Tried A Jar, Now A Movie Star, 22 x 12 In. 65.00
Sign, Burma Shave, Poorest Guy, Million Dollar Face, Red, White, Set, 1949 .... 995.00
Sign, Burma Shave, Red & White, Wooden 80.00
Sign, Butternut Bread, 1924, 22 x 12 In.. 45.00
Sign, Butternut Bread, Colorful Baker Boy, Cardboard, 1930s, 10 x 14 In. 23.00
Sign, Butternut Bread, Girl With Loaf Of Bread, Cardboard, 1930s, 7 x 9 In................ 10.00
Sign, C.H. Case Drugs & Stationery, Pestle Shape.. 575.00
Sign, Campbell's Soup, Soup Can Shape, Porcelain, 22 1/2 x 14 In............... 1800.00 to 2420.00
Sign, Canadian Home Insurance, Tin, 13 x 19 In. 50.00
Sign, Card, Free Standing, Wardonia Razor Blades, Holds 6 Boxes............................. 40.00
Sign, Case Farm Machinery, Painted, 30 x 72 In. 750.00
Sign, Castoria, 35 Doses, 35 Cents, Girl On Front, Cardboard, 13 x 6 In. 85.00
Sign, Cataract Cream Ale, Tin Over Cardboard, 8 x 13 In... 155.00
Sign, Centlivre Tonic, Cardboard, 22 x 12 In.. 27.50
Sign, Cerveza Coors, Neon... 95.00
Sign, Clear Club Soda, Bear, 2 1/2 Ft. 800.00
Sign, Coles Peruvian & Wild Cherry Bitters, Porcelain, 6 x 16 In. 395.00
Sign, Common Sense Truss, Reverse Painted, Patriotic Symbols, 30 In. 440.00
Sign, Congress Playing Cards, Pictorial Backs, c.1903, 12 x 18 In. 550.00
Sign, Cook's Beer & Ale, Hand Holding 2 Bottles, 12 x 18 In. 175.00
Sign, Coors Beer, Neon, Oval 95.00
Sign, Cork Distillers Whiskey, Tin, Color, 12 x 8 In. 125.00
Sign, Cresent Beverage, Embossed Moon & Star, Metal.. 55.00
Sign, De Laval Cream Separators, Bonneted Baby, Frame, Tin, 40 1/2 In. 495.00
Sign, De Laval Cream Separators, Girl Leaning On Cow, Tin, 1907, 31 x 41 In. 1250.00
Sign, De Laval Cream Separators, Self-Framed, Red, Tin, Round, 26 In. 1200.00
Sign, Diamond Bell & Full Jewel 5 Cent Cigars, Smoke 'Em, 14 x 8 In. 175.00
Sign, Dr Pepper, Embossed, Metal 85.00
Sign, Dr Pepper, Horse Soldiers, Harry Payne, 12 x 18 In. 350.00
Sign, Dr Pepper, Porcelain, Red, White, Black, Green, 10 1/2 x 26 1/2 In. 175.00
Sign, Dr. Bell's Pine Tar Honey, Cures Coughs, Cardboard, 13 x 14 In......................... 75.00
Sign, Dr. Le Gear Medicine, Veterinary Cure, Giant Horse, 14 x 17 1/2 In. 135.00
Sign, Dr. Pierce's Family Remedies, Cardboard, 1920s, 14 x 18 In. 495.00
Sign, Drink Orange Kist, Hanging, c.1940, 2 1/2 x 8 In. 35.00
Sign, Duffee's Cough Syrup, Tin, 9 x 14 In. 100.00
Sign, Eat Little General Bread, Lithographed Metal, Yellow, 1912, 9 3/4 In. 2310.00
Sign, Eigenbrot Brewery, Baltimore, Gold On Red On Black, 9 x 13 In. 100.00
Sign, Ever-Ready Safety Razor, Cardboard, Countertop, 1920s, 11 x 27 In. 45.00
Sign, Eveready, Porcelain, India, 12 x 18 In. 225.00

Sign, Excelsior Trunk Locks, Tin, 6 x 8 In. 35.00
Sign, Falstaff Beer, Castle Scene, Tin, Round, 24 In. 450.00
Sign, Falstaff, Fiberoptic Light 150.00
Sign, Farmers Insurance Co., Iowa, Self-Framed, Tin, 1900s, 13 x 37 In. 195.00
Sign, Fern Glen Rye, Black Man, Chicken Under Arm, Tin, Frame, 33 x 23 In. 1980.00
Sign, Fine Paints & Varnishes, F.O. Pierce Co., Barrel Shape, Metal, 36 In. 95.00
Sign, Fisk Tires, Reclining Baby In Tire, Oilcloth, 8 Ft. 150.00
Sign, Fleckenstein Brewing, Beer Sampled By Workers, Tin, 13 3/4 x 19 In. 495.00
Sign, Florsheim Shoes, Pink & Orange Neon, 15 x 21 1/2 In. 950.00
Sign, Ford Genuine Parts, 2 Sides, Porcelain, Oval 595.00
Sign, Foss's Extracts, Curved, Porcelain, 14 x 10 In. 245.00
Sign, Four Roses Whiskey, Wild Game, Tin, 1930s, 36 x 25 In. 125.00
Sign, Fry's Cocoa, Black Boy, I'se Raised On It, Tin, 17 1/2 x 11 1/2 In. 660.00
Sign, G.W. Cramer, Druggist, Urbana, Ohio, Covered Bridge, Tin, 17 x 26 In. 385.00
Sign, General Electric, Mr. Magoo, Cardboard, 18 x 7 In. 95.00
Sign, Gold Flake Cut Plug & Cigarettes, Tin, 20 x 14 In. 275.00
Sign, Gold Medal Flour, Green, White, Porcelain, 10 x 60 In. 175.00
Sign, Golden Garage, 2 Sides, Black & Gold, Wooden, 11 1/2 x 69 1/2 In. 38.00
Sign, Goldfield's Modern Hotel, Goldfield, Nevada, Dated 1907, 8 1/2 x 11 In. 45.00
Sign, Goodrich Automobile Tires Sold Here, 2 Sides, Porcelain, 16 In. 275.00
Sign, Grape Smash, Better Than Juice, Tin, 13 1/2 x 9 1/2 In. 675.00
Sign, Grape-Nuts, Girl With St. Bernard Dog, Self-Framed, Tin, 20 x 30 In. .....965.00 to 2000.00
Sign, Green River Whiskey, Tin, Frame, 27 x 21 In. 275.00
Sign, Grennan Cake, Embossed Tin, 3 Colors, 1930s, 13 1/2 x 35 1/2 In. 62.00
Sign, Greyhound Bus Depot, Red, White & Blue, 2 Sides, Porcelain 1650.00
Sign, Gulf Solar Heat, Porcelain, Single Face, 58 x 46 In. 275.00
Sign, H.M.V. & Columbia Records, Porcelain, England, Round, 24 In. 325.00
Sign, Haberdashery Shop, Top Hat & Glove, Cast Bars, Sheet Metal, 46 In. 4600.00
Sign, Hambone Tobacco, Cardboard, Round, 9 In. 60.00
Sign, Harley-Davidson Motor Cycles, Sales & Service, Tin, 23 x 30 In. 275.00
Sign, Hartford Insurance, Soldier, Tin, 19 x 11 In. 55.00
Sign, Headquarters For Keen Kutter Pocketknives, Logo, 22 x 15 1/2 In. 35.00
Sign, Hercules Spring, Woman On Bed, Tin, Frame, 8 3/4 x 19 In. 190.00
Sign, Hess, 18 Wheeler & Racer, White Border, 29 x 43 1/2 In. 150.00
Sign, Hills Bros., Tea & Coffee, Curved, Porcelain, 19 x 11 In. 895.00
Sign, Hohner, Light-Up, Tin & Glass, 12 x 10 In. 85.00
Sign, Hollanbru, 2 x 4 Ft. 450.00
Sign, Home Insurance Co., New York, Tin, 14 x 23 In. ....65.00 to 75.00
Sign, Hood's Ice Cream, Embossed, Tin, 36 x 28 In. 350.00
Sign, Hood's Ice Cream, Tin, Embossed Cow & Cone, 20 x 26 In. 500.00
Sign, Hoosier Beer, Man In Boat, Tin Over Cardboard, 1930s, 12 x 15 In. 555.00
Sign, Hot Chili Cold Bud, Neon 200.00
Sign, Indian Rubber Girl, Hand Brushed, Carnival, 8 x 10 Ft. 450.00
Sign, Izaak Walton League Of America, Indian In Canoe, Tin, 18 x 12 In. 260.00
Sign, Jacob Ruppert Knickerbocker Beer, Cardboard, Frame, 1918, 14 x 30 In. 65.00
Sign, Jenny Aero Solvenized Pump, Airplane Graphics, Round, 12 In. 2640.00
Sign, Jersey-Creme, Girl, Shawled Bonnet, 12 In. 55.00
Sign, Jos. A. Enzler, Trunk Factory, 2 Sides, Iron-Bound Trunk, Metal 1760.00
Sign, Kamm & Schellinger, Lithograph, Frame, 40 x 29 In. 730.00
Sign, Kato Beer, Embossed Tin, White Letters, Black Ground, 11 x 17 In. 55.00
Sign, Kay Flange, Round, 1957 .... 300.00
Sign, Kayo Chocolate Drink, Tin Lithograph, Chalkboard, 13 x 27 In. 125.00
Sign, Keds, Girl Holding Doll, Man Making Call, 4 Different Style Shoes 143.00
Sign, Kool Cigarette, Penguin, Tin, 1950s 65.00
Sign, Labelle Chocolatiere, Walter Baker, Tin, Self-Framed, 22 1/4 x 28 In. 715.00
Sign, Leaping Deer, Plow, Cast Iron, Hanging, 1847 .... 600.00
Sign, Lee Shirts & Pants, Embossed Tin, 11 x 23 In. 265.00
Sign, Lily Starch, Roll Down, Babies, Paper, 28 x 12 In. 1540.00
Sign, London Life Cigarettes, Tin Lithograph, People, 1900s, 27 x 39 .... 1500.00
Sign, Lost In The 50s, Neon 260.00
Sign, Lucky Strike Cigarettes, Tobacco Leaf, Cardboard, c.1934, 13 x 18 In. 100.00
Sign, Luxeberry Varnish, Product Can, Embossed Tin, 12 3/4 x 25 1/2 In. 192.00
Sign, Marlboro Man, Metal, 34 x 23 In. 25.00

Advertising, Sign, Oakite Cleaner,
Die Cut, 26 In.

Advertising, Sign, None Such Mince Meat,
Tin, 20 x 28 In.

Advertising, Sign, Schrafft's,
Chromolithograph, 1912, 32 x 23 In.

Advertising, Sign, Borden's, Cardboard,
Die Cut, Blue, Red, White, 20 In.

Sign, Masury's Paint, Lithograph, 20 x 12 In.	215.00
Sign, McAlpin Tobacco, Plantation Family, Paper, 22 x 17 In.	2640.00
Sign, Mercedes-Benz, 42 In.	950.00
Sign, Mil-Kay, Waiter With Tray, 1941, 40 x 23 In.	250.00
Sign, Miller Guitar, Neon	200.00
Sign, Miller High Life, Tin Over Cardboard, 9 x 13 In.	248.00
Sign, Missing Miss Cigar, Image Of Viola, Tin, Square, 14 1/2 In.	357.00
Sign, Mission Orange Soda, Metal, Orange & Silver, 1950s, 3 x 24 In.	55.00
Sign, Missouri Pacific, Train, River, With Removable Calendar Cards	345.00
Sign, Mobil Gasoline, Flying Horse, 2 Sides, Motor	4500.00
Sign, Mobil Oil, Gargoyle, Porcelain, 19 1/2 x 24 In.	495.00
Sign, Mobil Oil, Sidewalk, 2 Sides, Oval, 24 x 32 In.	650.00
Sign, Model Tobacco, Pictures Wooden Indian, Tin, 16 x 6 In.	150.00
Sign, Model Tobacco, Porcelain, 36 x 12 In.	275.00

Sign, Moxie Nerve Food, Cardboard, Frame, 13 x 10 In. 330.00
Sign, Moxie, Die Cut Cardboard, Uncle Sam, With Arms, 30 In. 750.00
Sign, Moxie, Embossed Tin, Slogan, Sidewalk, 36 x 20 1/4 In. 467.00
Sign, Mr. Magoo, General Electric, Cardboard, Easel, 18 x 7 In. 60.00
Sign, Mutual Life Assurance, Curved, Porcelain, 20 x 14 In. 990.00
Sign, Nabisco, Slicker Boy, Cornucopia, Cardboard, 1948, 24 x 20 In. 55.00
Sign, National City Bank Of New York, Curved, Bronze, 24 In. 385.00
Sign, Nature's Remedy, 3 Sides, 2 Ft. 290.00
Sign, Nehi Soda, Cardboard, 12 x 8 In. 20.00
Sign, New Home Sewing Machine, Woman Stitching Pants, 40 x 25 1/2 In. 1320.00
Sign, Nichol Kola, Tin Embossed, 1930s, 18 1/2 x 11 In. 70.00
Sign, None Such Mince Meat, Tin, 20 x 28 In. .... *Illus* 8250.00
Sign, North Pole Cut Plug, Polar Bears Killing Walrus, Iceberg, Tin, 5 x 6 In. 578.00
Sign, Oakite Cleaner, Die Cut, 26 In. .... *Illus* 286.00
Sign, Oilzum, Man Inside "O" In Oilzum, Tin, 60 x 12 In. 660.00
Sign, Old Dutch, Neon 180.00
Sign, Old Nelson Club Whiskey, Curly Beveled Edge, 8 1/2 x 14 In. 250.00
Sign, Old Stock Cigar, Cardboard, Silver Letters, 1910, 5 x 12 In. 12.00
Sign, Omar Cigarettes, Men In Tuxedos, Cardboard, Lithograph, 18 1/2 x 25 In. 265.00
Sign, Optician, Eye Glass Form, 2 Cobalt Blue Glass Inserts, 29 In. 2310.00
Sign, Orange Crush, Paper, 14 x 22 In. 30.00
Sign, Orangeine Powders, Medicinal Cures, Cardboard, 25 x 17 In. 38.50
Sign, Oxygenated Bitters, Reverse On Glass, Frame, Wooden Back, 6 x 12 In. 265.00
Sign, Pabst Malt Extract, Best Tonic, Brass, 7 x 10 In. 150.00
Sign, Pastum Hair Tonic, Barber Poles, Chains, 1910, 7 x 18 In. 85.00
Sign, Paul Jones Four Roses Whiskey, 36 x 24 In. 250.00
Sign, Pennzoil, Tin, 60 x 12 In. 150.00
Sign, Petoskey Chief Cigars, Feathered Indian Chief, Paper, 27 1/2 x 20 In. 2750.00
Sign, PEZ Space Gun, 6 Guns & Registration Certificates, Display Card, 1950s 800.00
Sign, PEZ, Drugstore Ad, Color, 1950s 350.00
Sign, Phillies Cigars, Only 5 Cents, Tin Bound, Chipboard, 14 x 42 In. 75.00
Sign, Plainville Post Office, Wooden, Oval, 18 1/4 x 11 In. 247.00
Sign, Polar Bear Chew, Porcelain, 29 x 50 In. 275.00
Sign, Polarine Oil, Shape Of Hot Air Balloon, Hanging 900.00
Sign, Poll-Parrot Shoes, Pencil, Large 48.00
Sign, Poll-Parrot, Neon, Porcelain 1045.00
Sign, Pontiac Silver Anniversary, 10 Different Models Pictured, 1951 .... 85.00
Sign, Postal Telegraph Here, Steel, Enameled, 2 Sides, 30 1/4 x 16 In. 750.00
Sign, Potosi Beer, Indian Drinking From Spring, Aluminum, Round, 10 In. 165.00
Sign, Public Bar, Glass, White Letters, Metal Mounted, Electrified, 23 In. 165.00
Sign, Pump, Sinclair Oil Co., Porcelain, 13 3/4 x 12 In. 45.00
Sign, Red Goose, Porcelain, 2 Sides, Neon, Art Deco, Late 1940s, 108 x 48 In. 2500.00
Sign, Red Man Chewing Tobacco, 4 Men, 19 x 14 In. 363.00
Sign, Ritchey's, Burlington, Wooden, Worn Paint, 74 x 49 1/2 In. 385.00
Sign, Rockford Watch, Girl Holds Pocket Watch, 17 x 23 In. 605.00
Sign, Roll Down, Happy Thought Tobacco, Paper, c.1884 .... 1210.00
Sign, Royal Amber, Neon 190.00
Sign, Royal Crown Cola, Embossed Tin, 1940s, 21 x 4 In. 35.00
Sign, Royal Crown Cola, Tin, 12 x 31 In. 180.00
Sign, Ruppert Ale, Glass Shield, 10 In. 90.00
Sign, S & H Green Stamps, Light-Up 145.00
Sign, San-Cura Ointment, 1920s, 8 x 11 In. 22.00
Sign, Savard, Georgeon Cognac, Turkish Beauty, Embossed Tin, 19 x 13 In. 190.00
Sign, Savory Beer, Comic Fellow, Hooked Fish, Tin, Frame, 15 1/2 x 19 In. 1300.00
Sign, Schenley Whiskey, Buckskin & Beaver Hatted, Tin, 27 1/2 x 19 1/2 In. 415.00
Sign, Schiltz Famous Malt Syrup, Tin, Embossed, 1929, 23 1/2 x 11 3/4 In. 115.00
Sign, Schrafft's, Chromolithograph, 1912, 32 x 23 In. .... *Illus* 467.00
Sign, Schwinn-Built Bicycles, Reverse On Glass, Frame, 9 x 19 In. 105.00
Sign, Shapleigh Warehouse, Reverse Painted On Glass, 5 1/2 x 2 1/2 Ft. 1750.00
Sign, Sinclair Credit Cards, Porcelain, Hanging, 2 Sides, 23 x 14 In. 75.00
Sign, Sinclair Products Approved Dealer, Porcelain, 8 1/4 x 4 In. 1870.00
Sign, Singer Sewing Machine, Woman Sitting At Machine, Porcelain, 25 x 32 In. 1100.00
Sign, Smoke El Baton, Follow The Leader, Easel Back, Cardboard, 6 1/2 x 7 In. 85.00

Advertising, Sign, Watch, Iron, Tin,
19th Century, 20 In.

◆◆◆◆◆◆◆◆◆◆◆◆◆◆◆◆◆◆◆◆◆◆◆

Good tips for care of Fiesta and any other heavy, color-glazed dishes of the 1930s. Bauer is oven safe for baking—up to 350 degrees. Do not use in a microwave. Do not use on a direct flame. Do not wash in an automatic dishwasher. The detergent may discolor the glaze. Do not scour. Store with felt between stacked plates to avoid scratching. Early 1930 to 1942 dishes used a lead in the glazing, so do not use scratched dishes with acidic foods. Lead poisoning is possible with prolonged use.

◆◆◆◆◆◆◆◆◆◆◆◆◆◆◆◆◆◆◆◆◆◆◆

Sign, Sonny 5 Cent Cones, Cardboard, Child & Ice Cream Cone, 1920s, 8 x 19 In.	17.00
Sign, Spitting On Sidewalk Prohibited, Tin, 7 x 10 In.	90.00
Sign, Spring Soda, Green & Cream, Metal, 1940s, 30 x 12 In.	65.00
Sign, Squirt Boy, Tin, 1950s, 4 x 10 Ft.	950.00
Sign, Stadhouder, Celluloid, Round, 1942, 18 x 12 In.	95.00
Sign, Standard Feeds, Barn Shape, Tin	45.00
Sign, Stanley Tools, Small Town Scene, Die Cut Cardboard, 33 In.	495.00
Sign, Stoneware Crock, Boy Pulling Roll From Crock, Self-Framed, Tin, 19 In.	1045.00
Sign, Store Display, P.F. Flyers, 32 x 19 In.	125.00
Sign, STP, Double Face, Metal, 11 x 15 In.	15.00
Sign, Sunbeam Bread, Metal, Oval, 32 x 52 In.	95.00
Sign, Texaco Aviation Products, Red, Green, Black, White, Porcelain, 24 In.	5225.00
Sign, Texaco Fire Chief, Porcelain, 12 x 18 In.	85.00
Sign, Texaco Marine Lubricants, Porcelain, 15 x 30 In.	4400.00
Sign, Uncle John's Syrup, Stone Lithograph, Cardboard, 1915, 12 x 18 In.	26.00
Sign, United States Fur Co., Paper Lithograph, 2 Black Boys, 15 x 31 In.	385.00
Sign, United States Fur Co., St. Louis, Mo., Paper Lithograph, 15 x 21 In.	325.00
Sign, Use Maclin Zimmer's Tobacco, Paper, Multicolor Lithograph, 7 x 13 1/2 In.	275.00
Sign, Van Merritt, Burlington Brewing Co., Reverse On Glass, 5 x 10 In.	30.00
Sign, Vreeland & Siemer Divers For Hire, Demilune Form, Wooden, 38 1/2 In.	385.00
Sign, Warn's Jewelers, Pocket Watch Form, Cast Iron & Tin, 20 In.	247.00
Sign, Warner's Bra & Girdle, 3 Models In Bras, England, 1920s, 23 x 36 In.	300.00
Sign, Watch, Iron, Tin, 19th Century, 20 In. ....*Illus*	225.00
Sign, Watchmakers Trade, Eagle, Spread Wings, Post-Civil War Style, 1870	2400.00
Sign, Waterman's Ideal Fountain Pen, Tin, 6 x 27 In.	250.00
Sign, Watermelons For Sale, Comical Black Man, Tin, 26 x 47 In.	1100.00
Sign, Watson-Plummer Shoe Co., Children In School Yard, Tin, Oval, 17 x 14 In.	575.00
Sign, Weatherbird Shoes, Red Chicken, Black Accents, Neon, 25 x 17 In.	1870.00
Sign, Weatherbird Shoes, Super Circus, Paper, 1950s, 10 x 17 In.	45.00
Sign, Welle-Boettler Bakery, Baby In High Chair, Porcelain, 15 x 36 In.	195.00
Sign, Whippet & Willys-Knight, 2 Sides, Porcelain, 24 x 35 1/2 In.	305.00
Sign, Whistle Soda Pop, Child & Bottle, Cardboard, 11 x 14 In.	10.00
Sign, White Star Line, Largest In World, Red Flags, White Stars, Brass, 6 x 15 In.	143.00
Sign, Whitman's Chocolates, Teden's Drug Store, Bronze, 5 1/2 x 21 3/4 In.	175.00
Sign, Wiedemann Beer, 1968, 14 x 17 1/2 In.	35.00
Sign, Wildroot Hair Tonic, Barber Pole Picture, Tin, 4 x 1 Ft.	390.00
Sign, Winchester, 3 Panels, Trap Range, 1930s, 18 x 40 In.	795.00
Sign, Wrigley's Chewing Gum, Trademark Arrow, 10 1/2 x 20 1/2 In.	192.00
Sign, Wrigley's Gum, Streamlined Locomotive, 11 x 21 In.	120.00

Sign, Wrigley's Juicy Fruit Chewing Gum, Die Cut Cardboard, 1930s, 14 In.	75.00
Sign, Your Independent Hardware Store, Tin, Bracket Frame, 27 x 21 In.	260.00
Silk, University Of California, Tobacco, Color, 5 In.	28.00
Silk, Zira Cigarette, Rockaway Girl	20.00
Skillet, Byran Smokey Hollow, Cast Iron, 10 In.	12.00
Skillet, White's Auto Store, Rosenberg, Tex., 4 In.	18.00
Soap, Sinclair Dino, With Box, 1960s	28.00
Spatula, Antiphlogisstine, Metal, 7 In.	7.00
Spoon, Slotted, Brooklyn Edison, Electrical Home Appliances, Wire Handle	4.00
Squeeze Bottle, California Raisins, Plastic, Straw, CALRAB, 1987	3.00
Stickpin, Banner Buggies	50.00
Stickpin, Dr. Bell's Pine Tar Honey	25.00
Stickpin, Gorton's Fish Food	35.00
Stickpin, Peters Cartridge, .22-Caliber Cartridge Soldered To Pin, Early 1900s	40.00
String Holder, Beymer-Bauman, Dutch Boy, Tin, 28 In.	3100.00
String Holder, Chase & Sanborn, Red, Green & White, c.1905, 10 x 14 In.	295.00
String Holder, Heinz Pickle, Figural, Tin, 17 x 15 In.	3575.00
String Holder, Lawney's Cocoa, Tin, 24 x 16 In.	385.00
String Holder, Post Toasties, Swiveling Sign, c.1916, 12 In.	185.00
String Holder, Postum, Rotating Tin Sign, Health First, 11 1/2 In.	300.00
String Holder, Red Goose Shoes, Die Cut Tin, 18 x 26 In.	1650.00
Sugar & Creamer, Cover, Elsie & Elmer, Borden's, Plastic, F & F	70.00 to 100.00
Sugar Shaker, Poppin' Fresh	8.00
Swizzle Stick, Jack Daniels, 12 Piece	29.00
Swizzle Stick, Jack Daniels, Figural, Plastic	5.00
Swizzle Stick, Wurlitzer Phonograph, Music Figural	7.00
Swizzle Stick, Zulu, On Card, 1950s, 5 Piece	16.00
Syrup, Gold Medal Products, Pottery, Mauve	165.00
Tap Knob, Ballantine Beer, Ball Shape	32.00
Tap Knob, Baseball, Iron City Beer, Beat Em Bucs	40.00
Thermometers are listed in their own category	
Thermos, Tim Horton Donuts, 13 In.	35.00
Tie Clasp, Chain Saw, Remington, Kinney Co., Provs., R.I., 1950s	25.00
Tie Clasp, Muffler, Sears Logo, Silver Tone, 1950s	20.00
Tie Tack, Big Boy, 3-Dimensional Figure, Holding Burger, 7/8 In.	20.00
Tin, Huntley & Palmer, Roman Column, Female Figures, Biscuit, 8 In.	225.00

Advertising tin cans or canisters were first used commercially in the United States in 1819 and were called *tins*. The English language is sometimes confusing. Today the word *tin* is used by most collectors to describe many types of containers, including food tins, biscuit boxes, roly poly tobacco containers, gunpowder cans, talcum powder sprinkle-top cans, cigarette flat-fifty tins, and more. Beer cans are listed in their own category. Things made of undecorated tin are listed under Tinware.

Tin, 3 Knights Condom	80.00
Tin, 3MW Perfectos, Condom	25.00
Tin, Abbey Tobacco, Pocket, 4 x 3 x 1 In.	125.00
Tin, Albert L. Richa Ginger	250.00
Tin, American Home Coffee, House, Paper Label, c.1920, 1 Lb., 6 x 4 1/2 In.	55.00
Tin, Anne Page Allspice	8.00
Tin, Anne Page, Pepper	8.00
Tin, Annette's Cleaner, Dated 1930, Salesman Sample	15.00
Tin, Apache Trail Cigars, Tin, 6 x 6 x 4 In.	1275.00
Tin, Astor White, Pepper	10.00
Tin, Atwood Private Blend Coffee, 1 Lb.	40.00
Tin, Barrington Ball Coffee, Key Wind, 1 Lb.	35.00
Tin, Benton Mixture Tobacco, Pictures Thomas Hart Benton, 3 1/4 x 4 1/4 In.	95.00
Tin, Beringaria Passenger Liner, Biscuit	850.00
Tin, Betsy Ross Brand Coffee, 6 x 4 In.	95.00
Tin, Between The Acts, Cigar, Pocket, 4 x 2 In.	20.00
Tin, Big Ben, Canada, Pocket	650.00
Tin, Black Beauty Stove Polish, Horse In Horseshoe Frame Picture	45.00
Tin, Blackstones Tasty-Lax	20.00

Tin, Blue Boar Tobacco, Canister 40.00
Tin, Blue Boy Toffee 40.00
Tin, Bokar Coffee, A & P, Red, Brown, 1 Lb. 35.00
Tin, Bond Street, Pocket, 6 x 4 In. 20.00
Tin, Boot Jack Tobacco, Chewing, 6 x 3 In. 185.00
Tin, Boy-Ur-Ready Marshmallow Ice Cream Topping 35.00
Tin, Breakfast Call Coffee, 1 Lb., 6 x 3 In. 50.00
Tin, Briggs Pipe Mixture, Light Brown, Pocket, 4 1/2 x 3 1/4 In. 8.00
Tin, Brilliantone Phonograph Needles, Cloth Bottom, Round 28.00
Tin, Buckingham Cut Plug, American Tobacco Co., 1917 Stamp, Pocket 115.00
Tin, Buckingham Tobacco, Pocket 35.00
Tin, Bugler Cigarettes, Pocket 18.00
Tin, Bulldog Tobacco, Pocket, 4 x 2 In. 295.00
Tin, Calumet Baking Powder, Paper Label 3.00
Tin, Camel Cigarettes, Flat, 50 .... 40.00
Tin, Campbell's Shag Tobacco, Pocket, 4 x 2 In. 350.00
Tin, Candy, Land Of Disney, Lithographed, 1930s 325.00
Tin, Capstan Navy Cut, American Tobacco Co., Paper Label, Round, 50s 40.00
Tin, Caravan Condom, Contents, Rectangular 46.00
Tin, Caravan, Condom 95.00
Tin, Cardinal Cut Plug, Pocket, 4 1/2 x 3 In. 275.00
Tin, Cardinal Tobacco, Pocket, 4 x 2 In. 1500.00
Tin, Cashmere Bouquet Talc, Sample 40.00
Tin, Central Union Cut Plug, Pocket, 4 1/2 x 3 1/2 x 1 In. 65.00
Tin, Chariots, Condom 125.00
Tin, City Club Crushed Cubes Tobacco, Pocket, 4 1/2 x 3 In. 220.00
Tin, Clabber Girl, Baking Powder 10.00
Tin, Clark's Teaberry Gum, Counter Display 125.00
Tin, Commodore Coffee, 8 x 5 In. 65.00
Tin, Continental Cubes Tobacco, Concave Front, Pocket .... 225.00 to 450.00
Tin, Crane's Private Mixture, 4 1/2 x 3 1/4 x 1 In. 200.00
Tin, Culture Smoking Tobacco, 4 1/2 x 3 1/2 x 3 In. 120.00
Tin, Daily Mail Tobacco, Airmail Plane 50.00
Tin, Dan Patch Coffee 880.00
Tin, Davis Baking Powder, Sample 60.00
Tin, De Reszke Tobacco, Pocket, 3 x 3 In. 45.00
Tin, Dead Shot Dupont Gunpowder, 1 Lb. 300.00
Tin, Delicious Coffee, McTighe Grocery Co., Binghamton, N.Y., 1 Lb. 35.00
Tin, Dill's Best Cut Plug, Flat, Pocket, 4 x 3 x 1 In. 20.00
Tin, Dill's Best Cut Plug, Square Corner 25.00

Advertising, Tin, Double 00 cigar

Tin, Dill's Best Sliced Plug, Flat, 3 1/2 x 3 In.. 5.00
Tin, Dill's Best Smoking Tobacco, Girl In Reserve 30.00
Tin, Double 00 Cigar... *Illus* 325.00
Tin, Dr. Baxter's Mandrake Bitters Tablet, Hinged Cover, 2 x 3 In. 110.00
Tin, Dr. Nebbs, Talcum, Baby & Blocks 90.00
Tin, Dr. Pierce, Suppositories.. 25.00
Tin, Dr. Robinson, Condom 65.00
Tin, Dream Girl, Talcum, Deco Woman 65.00
Tin, Dupont Gunpowder, Indian Label 70.00
Tin, Edgeworth Extra High Grade Sliced Pipe Tobacco, 2 x 3 In. 35.00
Tin, Edward G. Robinson Pipe Mixture, Full Pack 25.00
Tin, Egyptian Henna.. 125.00
Tin, Eight Brothers Cut Plug, Dark Yellow, 6 x 3 In. 70.00
Tin, English Breakfast Tea, Red Paint, 19th Century, 20 x 14 x 15 In. 225.00
Tin, Epicure Tobacco, Pointed End, Pocket 240.00
Tin, Eskimo Anti Freeze, Eskimo Picture 18.00
Tin, Flame Room Coffee, McGarvey's, Black, Red 35.00
Tin, Foltz Maid Coffee, Girl Drinking Coffee, Cinci., 1 Lb. 1000.00
Tin, Forest & Stream Tobacco, Fisherman, Pocket 80.00
Tin, Forest & Stream Tobacco, Gold Duck, Pocket.. 65.00
Tin, Four Roses Tobacco, Green 75.00
Tin, French's Chili Powder, Colorful, Round 20.00
Tin, Frontenac Peanut Butter, 1927 ....35.00 to 50.00
Tin, Full Dress, Patterson Tobacco Co., 1902 Stamp, Contents, Pocket....................... 40.00
Tin, Gannon Grocery Co., Michigan, Peanut Butter, 1920s....................................... 45.00
Tin, Gold Bond Coffee, 1 Lb. 68.00
Tin, Golden Circle, Condom, Round Case, Set Of 3 .... 10.00
Tin, Golden Lustre Long Cut Virginia Tobacco, 5 x 4 x 3 1/4 In............................... 375.00
Tin, Golden Pheasant, Bird, Condom 60.00
Tin, Golden Rule Blend Tea 75.00
Tin, Goodrich Tires, Tire Holder, Folds Flat, Blue, White, Red & Green, 1950s.......... 125.00
Tin, Granulated 54 Tobacco, Sample 80.00
Tin, Half & Half Burly & Bright, Cargo, Pocket 20.00
Tin, Harvard Peanuts, 10 Lb. 190.00
Tin, Hazard Shotgun Powder, Geese, Ducks, Hunter, 1893 .... 130.00
Tin, Hi-Plane Tobacco, 1 Engine, 4 1/2 x 3 3/4 In. 45.00
Tin, Hiawatha Straight Cut Tobacco, Green, 4 x 3 x 1 In.. 65.00
Tin, Hills Brothers Coffee, 20 Lb... 70.00
Tin, Huntley & Palmer, Roman Column, Female Figures, Biscuit, 8 In...................... 225.00
Tin, Imperial Mocha & Java, Wm. S. Scull Co. 75.00
Tin, Indian Sewan Scott, Oyster, 1 Pt.. 195.00
Tin, Japp's Hair Rejuvenator, Man & Woman, 1920 .... 100.00
Tin, Jim Dandies Peanuts, Children Playing Baseball, 10 Lb. 440.00
Tin, Johnson & Johnson Adhesive Tape, Miniature 8.00
Tin, Johnson & Johnson Floss, On Card.. 12.00
Tin, Just Suits Cut Plug, 5 x 4 In... 65.00
Tin, Justrite Cigars, Canister 35.00
Tin, Kentucky Club Tobacco, Pocket, 4 x 3 In. 18.00
Tin, Kingsbury Mixture, 4 x 2 In... 700.00
Tin, Kleeko Brand Coffee.. 80.00
Tin, Knights, Condom 80.00
Tin, Kool Cigarettes, Penguin, Flat, 1950s 45.00
Tin, Kraft Sweetened Chocolate Flavored Malted Milk, Square, 5 Lb. 15.00
Tin, Lady Helen Coffee, 1 Lb.. 50.00
Tin, Little San, Canister.. 40.00
Tin, Log Cabin Syrup, Towle, 1 1/2 Oz.. *Illus* 375.00
Tin, Loose-Wiles, World War II Ships, Biscuit.. 30.00
Tin, Lucky Strike, Flat, 1950s 25.00
Tin, Lucky Strike, It's Toasted, Pocket 55.00
Tin, Luer Bros., Sweet Home Lard, 1 Lb. 100.00
Tin, Luzianne Coffee, Silver Lid, White, c.1940, 3 Lb... 175.00
Tin, Luzianne Mammy Coffee & Chicory, 5 Cents Off, White Label, 1 Lb. 35.00
Tin, Mammy's Favorite Brand Coffee, Lithograph, 4 Lb. ....400.00 to 650.00

Tin, Mariners Reier Cocoa, Knob Top 110.00
Tin, McGill Tobacco, Rugby Game Picture 50.00
Tin, Mellor & Rittenhouse Cough Drops, Green 75.00
Tin, Mennen's Borated Talc, Free Sample 48.00
Tin, Merry Widows Perfectos, Condom 25.00
Tin, Mickey Mouse, Chased By Lion, Biscuit 550.00
Tin, Monarch Union, Typewriter Ribbon 15.00
Tin, Moon Kist, Talcum 100.00
Tin, Morton House Coffee 75.00
Tin, Mother's Mustard Plaster, Old Woman On Cover, Flat, Contents 45.00
Tin, Muhammad Ali Shoe Polish, Unused 32.00
Tin, Neatsfoot, Oil, 10 1/2 In. 75.00
Tin, Negro Head Oysters, Black Servant Picture, Unopened 200.00
Tin, Never Dull Aircraft Polish, Planes Picture 44.00
Tin, Niggerhair Tobacco, Man With Afro, 6 1/2 In. 93.00
Tin, Nugget Boot Polish 12.00
Tin, Nyte Brand, Condom 20.00
Tin, O'Neill's Vegetable Remedy, 1919 .... 12.00
Tin, Oh-Boy Peanut Butter, Kids Playing Around Tin, 1 Lb. 165.00
Tin, Old Abe Tobacco, Abe Lincoln Pictured, Round, 8 1/4 In. 440.00
Tin, Old Southern Coffee, Larkin, Woman In Chair 85.00
Tin, Old West Coffee, Key Wind, 1 Lb. 25.00
Tin, Orchard Park Coffee, Key Wind, Buffalo, N. Y. 32.00
Tin, Owl Brand Shoe Polish 35.00
Tin, Palmolive After Shave Talc, Sample 38.00
Tin, Palmy Days Tobacco, Upright, Red Letters, Pocket, 4 1/2 x 3 3/4 In. 125.00
Tin, Peachey Tobacco, Pocket, 3 x 2 In. 95.00
Tin, Peacock Coffee, Bird On Label, 1 Lb. 65.00
Tin, Plow Boy Tobacco, 1918, 7 x 3 In. 125.00
Tin, Powow Brand Peanuts, Indian In Headdress, 1 Lb. 275.00
Tin, Prince Albert Crimp Cut Tobacco, 4 1/4 x 3 3/4 In. 10.00
Tin, Profex Prophylactic 8.50
Tin, Punch Polish Mop, Full Figure Punch, Nose Is Handle 165.00
Tin, Ramses Condom 65.00
Tin, Rawleigh's Talc & Baby Powder, Baby In Locket 34.00
Tin, Rawleigh's Talcum, Nursery Rhyme Characters 95.00
Tin, Red Raven Tobacco, Ask The Man, Pocket 425.00
Tin, Red Wolf Coffee, Wolf Picture, 1 Lb. 120.00
Tin, Revelation, Philip Morris, Short, Pocket 20.00
Tin, Rex Tobacco, Pocket, 4 x 2 In. 125.00
Tin, Rices Lard, Pig, 4 Lb. 21.00
Tin, Richard Hudnut, Marvelous, Dusting Powder, Male Nude 55.00
Tin, Richelieu Tarter, Gold Metallic Lithograph 15.00
Tin, Riley's Toffee 55.00
Tin, Robinson's Patent Barley, Red & Black On Blue Lithograph, Contents 40.00
Tin, Rod & Reel Cut Plug, 5 x 3 x 4 In. 220.00
Tin, Roly Poly, Mammy, Mayo's Cut Plug Tobacco, Tin, 7 1/2 x 7 In. .... 247.00 to 400.00
Tin, Roly Poly, Satisfied Customer, Mayo's 240.00
Tin, Roly Poly, Singing Waiter 145.00
Tin, Royal Baking Powder Absolutely Pure, 1 Lb., 5 1/8 In. 22.00
Tin, Runkel's Chocolate 220.00
Tin, Sano-Flush, For Cleaning Closet Bowl, 1913 .... 35.00
Tin, Sarony Cigarettes, Roulette Wheel & Layout, 1920, 6 x 13 In. 94.00
Tin, Schepp's Cake, Hinged Lid, Advertising Inside, Rectangular, 9 x 12 In. 38.00
Tin, Sheik Condom, Contents .... 20.00 to 35.00
Tin, Silver Brand Typewriter 10.00
Tin, Silver Gem Gum 225.00
Tin, Sinclair Opaline, 5 Gal. 125.00
Tin, Sir Walter Raleigh Tobacco, Pocket 5.00
Tin, Smyth Hamburger, 10 Lb. 40.00
Tin, Sparrer Brand Shucked Oysters, 1 Gal. 65.00
Tin, Star Tobacco, Contents, Box, 1898, 2 x 1 In. 15.00
Tin, Sterling Plaid, Store, Canister 125.00

Tin, Suchard Cocoa 125.00
Tin, Sugar Barrel Tobacco... 6.00
Tin, Sure Shot Tobacco, 4 x 10 In. 478.00
Tin, Sweet Georgia Brown Hair Pomade 50.00
Tin, Sweetheart Talc, Box 95.00
Tin, Tao Tea, Black & Gold Dragon On Front, Rectangular 95.00
Tin, Texide Water Cured Prophylactic, Blacks Harvesting Rubber, 1931 ....175.00 to 325.00
Tin, Three Knights, Condom 35.00
Tin, Times Square Tobacco, Pocket, 4 1/2 x 3 In.................... 275.00
Tin, Towle's Log Cabin Syrup, 12 Oz..................................... 350.00
Tin, Trilby, Condom 25.00
Tin, Trout-Line Tobacco, Fisherman On Front, Pocket, 3 1/2 x 4 In. 165.00
Tin, True Cigarettes, Round 35.00
Tin, Turkish Mixture, Allen & Ginter 180.00
Tin, Tuxedo Tobacco, 6 x 3 In. 325.00
Tin, Twin Oaks Tobacco, Flat Top, Pocket 25.00
Tin, Uncle Ben's Rice, 1983.. 40.00
Tin, Uncle Remus Syrup, 4 1/2 In... 150.00
Tin, Uncle Remus Syrup, 7 1/2 In... 225.00
Tin, Uneeda Baker's Graham Wafers 55.00
Tin, Uneeda Biscuit, Lithograph, Handle, Closure, 5 3/4 x 4 1/2 x 5 In. 22.00
Tin, Union Leader Chewing Tobacco, Tin, Wire Handle 55.00
Tin, Union Leader Cut Plug... 300.00
Tin, Union Leader, Eagle, Pipe Or Cigarette, Pocket 25.00
Tin, Venizelos Coffee, Man's Face On Label, 1 Lb. 450.00
Tin, Viceroy Cigarettes, Aluminum, Flat, 50s 55.00
Tin, Violet Chips Gum, Dated 1910 .... 35.00
Tin, Wagon Wheel Tobacco, Pocket, 4 x 2 In. 170.00
Tin, Warnick & Brown, Utica, N.Y., Tobacco, Black On Mustard Lithograph 50.00
Tin, White Bear Coffee, Cardboard & Tin, Polar Bear, 6 x 4 1/2 In. 100.00
Tin, White House Coffee, Building, 4 x 5 In. 75.00
Tin, White Witch Talc.. 58.00
Tin, Whitman's Treasure Island Candy, Rectangular, 1920 ...... 24.00
Tin, William's Baby Talc 500.00
Tin, William's La Tosca Rose Talc, Sample 85.00
Tin, Win Ola Salted Peanuts, Yellow, Red Lettering 425.00
Tin, Winston, Crush Proof Cigarettes...................................... 15.00
Tin, Zanot Babymine Talc 95.00
Tin, Zeppelin Motor Oil, Zeppelin Picture, 2 Gal.................... 650.00
Tin, Huntley & Palmer, Roman Column, Female Figures, Biscuit, 8 In. 225.00

Advertising tip trays are decorated metal trays less than 5 inches in diameter.
They were placed on the table or counter to hold either the bill or the coins
that were left as a tip. Change receivers could be made of glass, plastic, or
metal. They were kept on the counter near the cash register and held the
money passed back and forth by the cashier. Related items may be listed in
the Advertising category under Change Receivers.

Tip Tray, Bartels Brewing Co., Syracuse, N.Y., 1893-1972 .... 70.00
Tip Tray, Beaverhead Brewery, Dillon, Mont., 1908-1918 .... 748.00
Tip Tray, Borden's, Woman In Maid's Uniform, Serving, 4 1/2 In.............................. 95.00
Tip Tray, Century Beer, Man & Woman With Beer, Pre-Prohibition ....85.00 to 135.00
Tip Tray, Cottolene, Black Woman & Child, Picking Cotton...............................140.00 to 175.00
Tip Tray, Dogs Playing Poker With Monkey, Glass, 1900, 3 1/2 x 7 In..................... 110.00
Tip Tray, Evinrude Boat Motor Co.. 275.00
Tip Tray, Fairy Soap, Have You A Little Fairy In Your Home, 4 1/4 In...................... 75.00
Tip Tray, Fank Ruhstall, City Brewery, Sacramento, Calif., 1881-1920 .... 226.00
Tip Tray, Frank Jones Ale 45.00
Tip Tray, Germania Brewing Co., Buffalo, N.Y., 1894-1912 .... 165.00
Tip Tray, Goebel Brewing Co., Detroit, Mich., 1874-1964 .... 35.00
Tip Tray, Havana Ribbon Cigars, Roulette Wheel, 1910, 8 In. 330.00
Tip Tray, Junket, Blond Girl Eating Cup Of Dessert, 4 1/2 In.................................... 325.00
Tip Tray, Junket, Souvenir, St. Louis World's Fair, 4 1/4 In.. 165.00
Tip Tray, La Creole Hair Dressing, Victorian Ladies, Copper, Glass, 4 1/2 In. 65.00

Advertising, Tip Tray,
Skat Players Dream

Advertising, Tray,
Old Saratoga Whiskey

Tip Tray, Luden's Cough Drops	175.00
Tip Tray, Man & Woman, Erotic, White Metal, 3 1/2 x 5 In.	78.00
Tip Tray, Minneapolis Brewing Co., Minneapolis, Minn., 1893-1975	55.00
Tip Tray, Moxie, Woman's Face	150.00
Tip Tray, National Brewing Co., Cowboy Riding Horse, Holding Beer Bottle	350.00
Tip Tray, Old Angus Whiskey	19.00
Tip Tray, Old Reliable Coffee, Beautiful Woman, 1906	125.00
Tip Tray, Perrier, Girl On Bar Stool, Limoges	135.00
Tip Tray, Philip Kling Brewing Co., Detroit, Mich., 1856-1919	40.00
Tip Tray, Prudential Insurance, 1930s	40.00
Tip Tray, Royal Crown Cola, Pyramid Bottle, 2 Girls	85.00
Tip Tray, Skat Players Dream	*Illus* 200.00
Tip Tray, Smith Brothers, New Bedford, Me.	12.00
Tip Tray, Stegmaier Beer, Factory View, Oval, Pre-1920, 6 x 4 3/8 In.	85.00
Tip Tray, Tivoli Brewing Co., Detroit, Mich., 1897-1948	75.00
Tip Tray, Versa Cigars, Glass	20.00
Tip Tray, Western Brewing Co., Belleville, Ill., 1875-1920	25.00
Tip Tray, Yuengling Brewing Co., Pottsville, Pa., 1829-Present	120.00
Tire Holder, Goodrich Tires, Tin, Blue, Red, White & Green	85.00
Tobacco Cutter, Enterprise, Champion Knife Improved, Counter	65.00
Tobacco Cutter, Griswold, Erie, 1883	95.00
Tobacco Cutter, Jockey On Horseback, Iron	450.00
Tobacco Cutter, May Brothers Groceries, Counter Type, 1914	75.00
Tobacco Cutter, R.J. Reynolds Tobacco Co., Counter	75.00
Tobacco Cutter, S.C.W.W. & Co., Triumph, Counter	45.00
Tobacco Pouch, Dixie Kid Tobacco, Black Boy Picture	40.00
Towel, Beach, Keebler	40.00
Toy, Beech-Nut Peppermint Gum, Squeak, Rubber, Gum-Pack Shape, 7 In.	74.00
Toy, Bi-Plane, Wrigley's Juicy Fruit Gum, Package On Wing	36.00
Toy, Borden's Milk Wagon, Horse, Carrier Has 2 Bottles	495.00 to 795.00
Toy, Bunny, Beats Drum, Duracell, Box	200.00
Toy, Bus, Archway Cookies	40.00
Toy, Canteen, Kool Aid, Clear Strap	75.00
Toy, Dinosaur, Stegosaurus, Copper Color, Sinclair, Plastic, 1960s	45.00
Toy, Dinosaur, Tyrannosaurus Rex, Pink, Sinclair, Plastic, 1960s	45.00
Toy, Dog, Bob Evans Restaurant, Plush	10.00
Toy, Frisbee, Speedy Alka-Seltzer	8.00
Toy, Game, Tiddley Winks, Trix Premium, 1960s	10.00
Toy, Glow Sticker, Count Chocula, Yellow, 1975	17.00
Toy, Grimace, In United Plane, McDonald's, Box	2.00 to 7.00
Toy, Hand Puppet, Snap, Rice Krispies, 1950s	45.00

Toy, Jolly Green Giant Squeeze, 1970s 50.00
Toy, Jolly Green Giant, Squeeze 50.00
Toy, Kellogg's, Crackle, Rice Krispies, Premium ....15.00 to 30.00
Toy, Kellogg's, Pop, Vinyl 12.00
Toy, Kite, Borden's, Elsie 20.00
Toy, Magic Color Cards, Snap, Crackle & Pop, 1933 .... 100.00
Toy, Raid Robot, Remote Controlled 375.00
Toy, Restaurant Set, Kentucky Fried Chicken, HO Scale, Box 35.00
Toy, Ring, Red Goose Shoes, Plastic 20.00
Toy, Sugar Bear Yo-Yo, Sugar Crisp, Premium 8.00
Toy, Train, Coco Puffs, Linemar 65.00
Toy, Truck, Rice Krispies, Box 5.00
Toy, Whistle, Hush Puppies, Plastic, Figural 5.00
Tray, Ambrosia Beer, 3 Monks Drinking, Red 45.00
Tray, Arctic Ice Cream, Polar Bear On Iceberg, 13 1/2 In. 88.00
Tray, Baby Ruth Gum, Glass 95.00
Tray, Beadleston & Woerz Brewing, Woman Setting Table, Square, 13 1/4 In. 220.00
Tray, Black Horse Beer, Dawes, Round, 13 In. 60.00
Tray, Budweiser Beer, Blacks Loading Cases, c.1914, 17 1/2 x 12 3/4 In. 50.00
Tray, Burger Beer Brewing Co., Zinzinnati, Oval, 1910, 12 x 15 In. 121.00
Tray, Canandaigua, N.Y., Oval, 16 In. 50.00
Tray, City Dairies Co., Ice Cream, Boy & Girl, Tin Lithograph, 13 1/2 In. 265.00
Tray, Cold Spring Brewing Co., Girl Leaning On Tiger's Head, 13 1/2 In. 245.00
Tray, Concumers Brewing Co., Feathered Chief, Porcelain, 16 x 13 In. 440.00
Tray, Cornelius Rohles Brewery, Phila., 4 Card Players, Tin, Oval, 1910, 14 x 16 In. ... 121.00
Tray, Dawes Brewery Black Horse Ale & Porter, Horse & Bottle, Porcelain 350.00
Tray, Dawson's Ale & Lager, Man & Woman Scene, Round, 1920, 12 In. 44.00
Tray, Eastside Beer, Los Angeles Brewing Co., 13 In. 82.00
Tray, Falstaff, Tavern Scene, 24 In. 175.00
Tray, Fan Tan Chewing Gum, Oriental Scene, 13 1/4 x 10 1/2 In. 275.00
Tray, Frank X. Schwab Ale, Fuggalo, N.Y., Tin, 13 1/4 x 10 1/2 In. 165.00
Tray, Frostie Root Beer, c.1950 .... 50.00
Tray, Furnas Ice Cream, Rolled Edge, 13 In. 220.00
Tray, Guggenheim Bros., Cleveland Distiller, Girl, Oval, 13 3/4 x 16 1/2 In. 220.00
Tray, Hutchinson's Purity Ice Cream, Woman In Yellow Dress, 13 In. 250.00
Tray, James Pepper Whiskey, Large Bottle, Revolutionary Soldiers, 14 x 17 In. 165.00
Tray, Liberty Beer & Tam-O-Shanter Ale, American Brewing Co., 14 In. 25.00
Tray, Miller High Life Beer, Girl Sitting On Moon ....35.00 to 75.00
Tray, Moxie, Pretty Woman, Tin, 6 In. 425.00
Tray, Nip Cigar, Wire Display Stand, 12 In. 385.00
Tray, Old Barbee Whiskey, College Girl In Coat, Feathered Hat, 12 3/4 x 16 In. 165.00
Tray, Old Pepper Whiskey, Patriotic Border 260.00
Tray, Old Saratoga Whiskey .... *Illus* 1100.00
Tray, Pabst Blue Ribbon Beer, Older Man Pouring 45.00
Tray, Patton's Ice Cream, Dish Of Ice Cream, Square, 13 3/4 In. 105.00
Tray, Port Townsend Brewing Co., Stag, Washington 325.00
Tray, Prince Albert Tobacco, Round, 24 In. 115.00
Tray, Rainier Beer, Mountain Scene, Porcelain On Metal, 9 In. 50.00
Tray, Robinson's Sons Pilsner Beer, Couples In Rowboat, 12 In. 275.00
Tray, Rolling Rock Beer, Horsehead, 14 In. 85.00
Tray, Ruppert's Beer, Cartoon People, Post-Prohibition 11.00
Tray, Standard Brewing Co., Mankato, Minn., Execution Of Sioux Indians 435.00
Tray, Tip, see Tip Trays in this category
Tray, Virginia Dare Wine, c.1915 .... 395.00
Tray, West End Brewing Co., Liberty Lady With Eagle, Flags, 13 In. 302.00
Tray, White Cap Ale, Frontenac Special Lager Bottle, Beer, Porcelain 235.00
Tray, Wieland's Beer, Pretty Girl, Bowl Of Roses, 10 1/2 x 13 1/4 In. 105.00
Tray, Wright & Taylor Distillers, 13 In. 75.00
Water Set, Esso, Tiger, Glass 35.00
Whiskey Glass, J. F. Cutter, Star In Shield 30.00
Whiskey Glass, Nipper, Glad Hand, Figural, Hand, Porcelain 95.00
Whiskey Glass, Standard Diamond Liquor Co. 20.00

Whistle, Peters Shoes, Weatherbird, Tin 20.00
Whistle, Russell's Velvet Ice Cream, Tin 25.00

AGATA glass was made by Joseph Locke of the New England Glass Company of Cambridge, Massachusetts, after 1885. A metallic stain was applied to New England Peachblow and the mottled design characteristic of agata appeared.

Toothpick, Cactus, Red 175.00
Toothpick, Flared, Green, Gold Trim, 2 1/2 In. 750.00

AKRO AGATE glass was made in Clarksburg, West Virginia, from 1932 to 1951. Before that time, the firm made children's glass marbles. Most of the glass is marked with a crow flying through the letter *A*.

Ashtray, Leaf, Blue 8.00
Cup, Child's, Concentric Ring, Pumpkin 45.00
Cup, Child's, Octagonal, Pumpkin .... 25.00 to 45.00
Dish Set, Play-Time, Cobalt Blue, Box, 1930, 9 Piece 185.00
Flowerpot, Marbleized, Flared Rim 28.00
Flowerpot, Stacked Disc, Blue Marble, 3 In. 12.00
Lamp, TV, Shop, 1950s 38.00
Plate, Child's, White 20.00
Plate, Octagonal, Lime Green, Small 6.00
Powder Jar, Colonial Woman, Blue .... 65.00 to 80.00
Powder Jar, Scotty, Light Blue 75.00
Powder Jar, Victorian Woman 140.00
Saucer, Child's, Lime Green 22.00
Tea Set, Child's, Little American Maid, 17 Piece, Box 325.00
Tea Set, Child's, Octagonal, Multicolored, 17 Piece 110.00
Teapot, Child's, Light Blue 24.00
Teapot, Lid, Stacked Disc & Panel, White, 2 5/8 In. 25.00
Tumbler, Octagonal, Lime Green, Small 18.00
Water Set, Pan, Disc Pitcher, Green, 7 Piece 75.00

ALABASTER is a very soft form of gypsum, a stone that resembles marble. It was often carved into vases or statues in Victorian times. There are alabaster carvings being made even today. Because the alabaster is very porous, it will dissolve if kept in water, so do not use alabaster vases for flowers.

Bust, Young Girl, Cap, 14 3/4 In. 160.00
Compote, Brown, Scalloped, 7 3/4 x 4 1/2 In. 18.00
Figurine, Arctic Explorer With Dog Sled, White Metal, 14 1/4 In. 138.00
Figurine, Diana & Hound, L. Morelli, 21 In. 1265.00
Figurine, Horsehead, Marble Base, Inscribed Studio Proof G. Bessi, 15 In. 500.00
Figurine, Loon, Bud Hurst, 11 x 9 1/2 In. 45.00
Figurine, Seated Nude Woman, On Rock, Signed, 16 In. 520.00
Group, La Lutte Pour Le Coeur, Falconet 2300.00
Lamp, Columnar Form, 30 In. 99.00
Lamp, Urn Shape, Dancing Nymphs, White, 16 In. 358.00
Lamp, Vines & Grapes, Square Pedestal Base, Pair 440.00
Lamp, Young Woman, White, 24 In. 413.00
Powder Holder, Enamel, 8 x 3 1/2 In. 80.00
Urn, Neoclassical Style, Pierced Cover, Ovoid, Handles, Italy, 17 1/4 In., Pair 3450.00

ALEXANDRITE is a name with many meanings. It is a form of the mineral chrysoberyl that changes from green to red under artificial light. A man-made version of this mineral is sold in Mexico today. It changes from deep purple to aquamarine blue under artificial light. The Alexandrite listed here is glass made in the late nineteenth and twentieth centuries. Thomas Webb & Sons sold their transparent glass shaded from yellow to rose to blue under the name Alexandrite. Stevens and Williams had a cased Alexandrite of yellow, rose, and blue. A. Douglas Nash Corporation made an amethyst-colored Alexandrite. Several American glass companies of the 1920s made a glass that changed color under electric lights and this was also called Alexandrite.

Figurine, Hippopotamus, 7 In. 45.00
Goblet, Lancaster, 8 Piece.. 450.00
Sugar & Creamer, Footed 175.00
Vase, Yellow To Purple, Gold Filigree Design, 24 1/2 x 7 In. 950.00

ALUMINUM was more expensive than gold or silver until the 1850s. Chemists learned how to refine bauxite to get aluminum. Jewelry and other small objects were made of the valuable metal until 1914, when an inexpensive smelting process was invented. The aluminum collected today dates from the 1930s through the 1950s. Hand-hammered pieces are the most popular.

Ashtray, Chrysanthemums, Continental, 7 In. 3.00
Basket, Intaglio Wheat, Double Bar Handle, Center Twist, Milcraft, 14 In. 23.00
Basket, Leaves, Blossoms, Keystone Paisley, 13 x 2 In. 10.00
Basket, Scalloped, Acorn Design, Continental, 12 x 6 In. 12.00
Basket, Wastepaper, World Map Pattern, Hammered 250.00
Bowl, Bronze Base, Kensington, 12 In. 40.00
Bowl, Circle Of Holly, Monogram MGC, Arthur Armour.................................... 15.00
Bowl, Cover, Kensington, 9 In. 40.00
Bowl, Cover, Ring Finial, Incised Flowers, Buenilum, 5 1/4 In. 15.00
Bowl, Cover, Steamer Ring, Rosette & Leaves, Continental, 10 In. 25.00
Bowl, Fish, 3-Footed, Royal Hickman Design, Bruce Fox 65.00
Bowl, Grapes, Hammerkraft, 11 1/2 In. 6.00
Bowl, Intaglio Design, Forged, 12 In. 28.00
Bowl, Intaglio Wheat, Bar & Coil Handles, Milcraft, 15 1/4 In. 23.00
Bowl, Leaf Shape, Coiled Stem Handle, Triangular, Buenilum, 10 x 11 x 2 In. 6.00
Bowl, Nut, Grape Pattern, Hammered 23.00
Bowl, Orange Knob Surrounded By Leaves, Cover, Shup Laird, 7 1/4 In. 35.00
Bowl, Pine & Mounts, Gold Anodized, Arthur Armour 35.00
Bowl, Serving, Cover, Glass Insert, Buenilum 25.00
Bread Tray, Corduroy, Continental.. 15.00
Bread Tray, Everlast.. 8.00
Bread Tray, Grape Cluster & Leaf, 13 1/2 In. 6.00
Bread Tray, Tulip, Rodney Kent.. 7.00
Cake Basket, Rodney Kent, Flat 15.00
Candy Dish, Rosette Center Knob, Mums, 3 Sections, Continental, 7 In. 7.00
Casserole, Bamboo, Everlast, 12 1/2 In. 15.00
Casserole, Cover, Glass Dish, Paper Label, Everlast 35.00
Cheese & Cracker Set, Tulip, Rodney Kent, 12 In. 15.00
Coaster Set, Leaves, Basket Handled Holder, Rodney Kent, Set Of 6 .... 8.00
Cocktail Set, Pitcher, Stirrer, Bronze Band At Base, 5 Glasses, Leumas....................... 70.00
Coffeepot, Drip, Club 40.00
Coin Changer, Gargoyles On Sides, c.1921... 220.00
Cooler, 7-Up 50.00

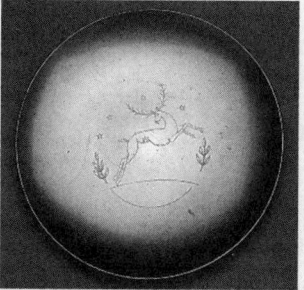

Fifties aluminum chairs and other brushed aluminum can be cleaned with a paste silver polish or a metal cleaner like Nevr-Dull.

Aluminum, Plate, Jumping Deer, Kensington, 10 In.

Cup & Plate, Snack, Rainbow Design On Handles, Chase, 8 Sets 185.00
Dish, Chafing, Wood Handle, Buenilum.. 30.00
Dish, Dogwood & Butterfly, Scalloped, Arthur Armour, 6 1/2 In. 6.00
Dish, Grapes, Ruffled, Handle, Hammerkraft, 7 1/2 In.. 4.00
Dish, Oak Leaf, Bruce Fox 45.00
Dish, Serving, Cover, Hyde Park, Kensington, 13 In.. 55.00
Ice Bucket, Cover, Ring Finial, Curved Band Tab Handles, Buenilum.......................... 35.00
Ice Bucket, Insulated, Hammerkraft 9.00
Lazy Susan, 8-Petal Flower, Scalloped, Buenilum, 17 1/2 In.. 12.00
Lazy Susan, Tulip, 4-Part Insert, Rodney Kent, 18 In. 14.00
Mold, Cake, Santa In Chimney, 2 Piece.. 25.00
Pan, Royal Super Ware, Waterless Cooking, Salesman Sample, 1 1/2 x 3 In. 110.00
Pitcher, Syrup, Wood Handle, Buenilum 18.00
Plate, 4 Stems Wild Rose, Fluted, Handwrought, Continental 30.00
Plate, Jumping Deer, Kensington, 10 In..*Illus* 8.00
Rack, Magazine, World Map Pattern, Hammered 350.00
Server, 2 Tiers, Acorns, Continental, 12 1/2 In. 12.00
Server, 2 Tiers, Bamboo, Round, Everlast, 7 3/4 x 6 In. 8.00
Server, 2 Tiers, Dogwood, Rose, Everlast, Rectangular, 11 x 7 1/2 x 9 1/4 x 5 In. 10.00
Silent Butler, Pine Cones, Needles, Everlast... 6.00
Silent Butler, Wheat, Kraftware... 20.00
Syrup, Karo Syrup 15.00
Tidbit, 2 Tiers, Everlast 15.00
Tray, Acorn, Leaf Design, Handles, Round, Continental, 15 In...................................... 30.00
Tray, Arthur Armour, 9 x 12 In... 70.00
Tray, Berries, Round, Farberware 7.00
Tray, Cattails, Flying Geese, Gold Anodized, Square, Arthur Armour, 11 1/2 In........... 45.00
Tray, Chrysanthemum, Handles, Continental Silver, 8 1/2 x 16 In. 10.00
Tray, Dahlias, Loop Handles, Openwork Panels, Farberware, 15 1/2 In........................ 10.00
Tray, Daisies, Interlocking Petals, Scalloped Flower Look, Continental, 14 In.............. 25.00
Tray, Dip, Hammered Lid, Divided Glass Dish, Cromwell 23.00
Tray, Floral Band, Open Handles, Everlast, 14 1/2 In.. 10.00
Tray, Fruit Flowers, Hand Finished, 11 3/4 x 7 In.. 6.00
Tray, Fruit, Flowers, Cromwell, 15 In. 7.00
Tray, Fruit, Flowers, Keystone Paisley, 16 1/2 In... 8.00
Tray, Fruit, Flowers, Ruffled Edge, 13 1/4 x 9 3/4 In... 6.00
Tray, Grape Cluster & Leaves, Hammerkraft, Hand Hammered, Square, 11 In. 6.00
Tray, Grape Cluster & Leaves, Loop Handle, Hammercraft, 16 3/4 x 11 3/4 In............... 10.00
Tray, Loop Handles, Grape Cluster, Buenilum, 14 1/2 In. 8.00
Tray, Plain, Leaf Bud Handles, Continental, 15 1/2 In. 12.00
Tray, Poinsettia, Loop Handle, Farber & Shlevin, 15 In.. 8.00
Tray, Ribbon & Flower Handles, Rodney Kent, 11 1/2 x 16 1/2 In. 27.00
Tray, Sailboat, 11 In.. 75.00
Tray, Serving, Brass Handles, Bruce Fox, 24 In. 65.00
Tray, Serving, Clipper Ship, Kensington 30.00
Tray, Tile Inset, Cellini Craft... 100.00
Tray, Tulip, Basket Handles, Rodney Kent, 12 x 7 In.. 9.00
Tray, Vegetables, Keystone, 13 x 10 In... 7.00
Tray, Wild Rose Pattern, Rose Handles, Continental, 10 1/2 x 14 1/2 In........................ 21.00
Tumbler, Anodized Color, 6 Piece 18.00
Undertray, Zigzag Design Edge, Shup Laird, 6 1/4 In. 15.00
Vanity Set, Airplane Shape, Compartments, D.R.G.M., Germany, 10 In. 1150.00
Vase, Cobalt Blue Glass, Kensington 195.00

AMBER, see Jewelry category

AMBER GLASS is the name of any glassware with the proper yellow-brown
shading. It was a popular color just after the Civil War and many pressed
glass pieces were made of amber glass. Depression glass of the 1930s–1950s
was also made in shades of amber glass. All types are being reproduced.

Basket, Blue Ruffled Edge, Applied Twisted Rope Handle, Blue, 6 3/4 x 6 1/2 In......... 145.00
Creamer, Cross Bar Daisy & Button, Pedestal, 6 In... 30.00

Powder Jar, Bambi 18.00

AMBERINA is a two-toned glassware made from 1883 to about 1900. It was patented by Joseph Locke of the New England Glass Company, but was also made by other companies. The glass shades from red to amber. Similar pieces of glass may be found in the Baccarat category. Glass shaded from blue to amber is called *Blue Amberina* or *Bluerina*.

Bottle, Liquor, Allover Ripple Design, 9 1/2 In.	125.00
Bowl, 6-Crimp Top, Thumbprint, Scroll Feet, 5 3/4 In.	325.00
Bowl, Cranberry Shading To Amber, 5 1/4 In.	135.00
Bowl, Finger, Hobnail, Rose Amber, Square, Mt. Washington	225.00
Bowl, Swirl, Applied Handles, Base Forming Feet, Amber Glass Rim, Oval, 12 x 7 In.	325.00
Butter, Inverted Thumbprint, Hobbs, 5 In.	220.00
Canoe, Button & Daisy, Tufts Holder, 8 In.	475.00
Castor, Pickle, Rib Pattern On Insert, Tongs	395.00
Celery Vase, Diamond-Quilted, New England, 6 1/2 In.	325.00
Celery Vase, Melon Sections, Inverted Thumbprint	150.00
Celery Vase, New England	375.00
Celery Vase, Thumbprint & Swirl	170.00
Creamer, Swirl, Cranberry Shaded To Golden Amber, Bulbous, Handle, 4 1/2 x 3 In.	135.00
Creamer, Thumbprint, 2 1/2 In.	165.00
Cruet, Baby Thumbprint, Blue To Amber, Amber Stopper, 6 3/4 In.	315.00
Cruet, Bulbous To 1 Inch Of Base, Flares To Form Pedestal, Amber Handle	265.00
Cruet, Inverted Thumbprint	325.00
Daisy & Button, Canoe, 8 x 4 In.	200.00
Finger Bowl, Fuchsia, Ruffled	185.00
Finger Bowl, Melon Sectioned, Inverted Thumbprint	110.00
Pitcher, Bulbous, Applied Amber Handle	225.00
Pitcher, Claw Handle, Inverted Thumbprint, New England, 8 x 7 In.	425.00
Pitcher, Diamond-Quilted, Applied Handle, 2 3/4 x 5 1/2 In.	110.00
Pitcher, Inverted Thumbprint, Square Rim, Reeded Handle, 7 1/2 In.	375.00
Pitcher, Milk, Melon Sections, Herringbone, Blue	325.00
Pitcher, Milk, Wood Bark Design, Amber Handle, Ruffled Top, 5 3/4 In.	250.00
Pitcher, New England Glass Co., 5 In.	350.00
Pitcher, Red To Amber, Swirled, Applied Handle, Bulbous Bottom, 6 5/8 x 5 3/8 In.	195.00
Pitcher, Ribbed Amber Handle, Honeycomb Pattern, 4 7/8 In.	121.00
Punch Cup, Amber Handle, 2 1/2 In.	85.00
Punch Cup, Amber Reeded Handle, 2 1/2 In.	75.00
Punch Cup, Diamond-Quilted, Amber Ribbed Handle, 2 3/4 In.	115.00
Punch Cup, Diamond-Quilted, Purple	120.00
Punch Set, Diamond-Quilted, 9 Piece	1750.00
Shade, Swirl Pattern, Gas, 4 In. Fitter	75.00
Spooner, Honeycomb Pattern, Amber Ruffled Rim	125.00
Syrup, Thumbprint, Silver Top	875.00
Toothpick, Daisy & Button	250.00 to 350.00
Toothpick, Fuchsia, Square Top, 2 1/2 In.	165.00
Toothpick, Ground Pontil	25.00
Toothpick, Inverted Thumbprint, 2 1/4 In.	27.00
Toothpick, Inverted Thumbprint, Bulging Base	150.00
Toothpick, Moon & Star	20.00
Toothpick, Tri-Corner, New England, 2 In.	195.00 to 300.00
Toothpick, Tri-Corner, Rose Amber, No. 39	395.00
Toothpick, Tri-Corner, Venetian Diamond, 2 1/4 In.	275.00
Toothpick, Tri-Corner, Venetian Diamond, Fuchsia, 2 1/4 In.	450.00
Toothpick, Urn, Diamond-Quilted, Fuchsia	465.00
Tumbler, Diamond Design, New England, 3 3/4 In.	200.00
Tumbler, Diamond-Quilted, 3 3/4 In.	71.00
Tumbler, Inverted Thumbprint, Footed, 3 7/8 In.	75.00
Tumbler, Thumbprint	100.00
Vase, Basket Handle, Pink Enamel Floral Spray, Leaf Pattern Feet, 9 1/4 In.	475.00
Vase, Crystal Spiral Trim, Red To Amber, 8 x 2 1/2 In.	195.00
Vase, Diamond-Quilted, Scalloped Rim, 6 1/2 In.	110.00

Vase, Diamond-Quilted, Square Mouth, Scalloped, 6 1/2 In.	38.00
Vase, Flared Top, Ruffled Rim, 10 In.	235.00
Vase, Swirl Pattern, Enameled Floral, 12 In.	535.00

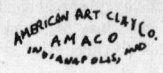

AMERICAN ART CLAY Company of Indianapolis, Indiana, made a variety of art pottery wares, especially vases, from about 1930 to after World War II. The company used the mark AMACO, as well as the company name. Do not confuse this company with an earlier art pottery firm from Edgerton, Wisconsin, called the American Art Clay Works.

Figurine, Deco Woman Holding Tray, Aqua, 8 In.	125.00
Tile, Stylized Flowers, Brown, 8 In.	50.00

AMERICAN DINNERWARE is the name used by collectors for ceramic dinnerware made in the United States from the 1930s through the 1950s. Most was made in potteries in southern Ohio, West Virginia, and California. Dishes were sold in gift shops and department stores, or were given away as premiums. Many of these patterns are listed in this book in their own categories, such as Autumn Leaf, Coors, Fiesta, Franciscan, Hall, Harker, Harlequin, Red Wing, Riviera, Russel Wright, Vernon Kilns, and Watt. For more information, see *Kovels' Depression Glass & American Dinnerware Price List.*

Ashtray, Poppy Trail, Metlox	10.00
Banana Boat, Gulfstream, Glidden, 10 In.	110.00
Berry Bowl, Lu-Ray, Blue, Taylor, Smith & Taylor	6.00
Bonbon, Shell, French Peasant, Blue Ridge	145.00
Bowl, Afrikans, Glidden, 7 1/2 In.	80.00
Bowl, California Ivy, Metlox, 6 3/4 In.	8.00
Bowl, Cereal, Red Rooster, Poppy Trail, Metlox	6.00
Bowl, Circus, Universal, 6 In.	10.00
Bowl, Cover, Santa Anita, Gray, 5 In. ....*Illus*	5.00
Bowl, Crab Apple, Blue Ridge, Oval, 9 1/4 In.	25.00
Bowl, Fruit, Poinsettia, Blue Ridge, 5 In.	9.00
Bowl, Lu-Ray, Vegetable, Blue, Oval	15.00
Bowl, Mar-Crest, Western Stoneware, 5 1/2 In.	7.00
Bowl, Orange Tree, Turquoise, Homer Laughlin, 10 In.	40.00
Bowl, Poppy Trail, Beige, Metlox Stamp, 9 In. ....*Illus*	18.00
Bowl, Taverne, Taylor Smith & Taylor, 5 1/4 In.	8.00
Bowl, Vegetable, Aztec, Loop Handle, Metlox	45.00
Bowl, Vegetable, California Ivy, Metlox, Round, 9 In.	19.00
Bowl, Vegetable, Normandy Plaid, Purinton	20.00
Bowl, Vegetable, Poppy Trail, Blue Provincial, Basket Weave, Metlox	20.00
Bowl, Vegetable, Taverne, Taylor, Smith & Taylor, 8 3/4 In.	22.00
Bowl Set, Orange Tree, Turquoise, Homer Laughlin, 5, 6, 7 & 8 In., 4 Piece	150.00
Bread Plate, Cheers, Blue Ridge	90.00
Butter, Lu-Ray, Blue	35.00
Cake Plate, Dutch Tulip, With Server, Blue Ridge	58.00
Cake Plate, Lu-Ray, Blue	40.00
Candleholder, Apple, Purinton	145.00
Candy Box, French Peasant, Blue Ridge	235.00
Casserole, Cover, California Ivy, Metlox	40.00
Casserole, Cover, Platter, Epicure, Charcoal, Homer Laughlin	65.00
Casserole, Glidden, Large	145.00
Casserole, Jubilee, Gray, Homer Laughlin	30.00
Casserole, Warming Stand, Mar-Crest, Western Stoneware	25.00
Celery Dish, French Peasant, Leaf Shape, Blue Ridge	60.00
Celery Dish, Leaf, Summertime, Blue Ridge	45.00
Chocolate Pot, French Peasant, Blue Ridge	285.00
Chocolate Set, Elegance, Blue Ridge, 4 Piece	600.00
Chocolate Set, Palace, Blue Ridge, 4 Piece	650.00
Chocolate Set, Summertime, Blue Ridge, 3 Piece	275.00
Chop Plate, Apple, Purinton, 12 In.	60.00
Chop Plate, California Ivy, Metlox, 13 In.	25.00

American Dinnerware, Bowl, Cover,
Santa Anita, Gray, 5 In.

American
Dinnerware, Dish,
Shell Shape,
Southern
Potteries,
9 1/4 In.

American Dinnerware, Bowl,
Poppy Trail, Beige,
Metlox Stamp, 9 In.

Chop Plate, Intaglio, Purinton	50.00
Coaster, Homestead, Metlox	15.00
Coffee Set, Evetide, Blue Ridge, 3 Piece	325.00
Coffeepot, California Provincial, Metlox	55.00
Coffeepot, Daisy, Metlox	55.00
Coffeepot, Fruit, Purinton	65.00
Coffeepot, Jubilee, Celadon, Homer Laughlin	45.00
Coffeepot, Lid, Village, Pfaltzgraff	30.00
Cookie Jar, Squirrel On Pine Cone, Metlox	85.00
Creamer, Apple, Purinton	30.00
Creamer, Century, Mexicana, Homer Laughlin	25.00
Creamer, Circus, Universal	12.00
Creamer, George Washington, Metlox	95.00
Creamer, Poinsettia, Blue Ridge	4.00
Creamer, Poppy Trail, Blue Provincial, Metlox	8.00
Cruet, Oil & Vinegar, Daisy, Purinton	65.00
Cruet, Oil & Vinegar, Dog Design, Regal	150.00
Cruet Set, Rooster, Green, Holder, Metlox, 5 Piece	230.00
Cup, Christmas Tree, Blue Ridge	33.00
Cup, Dutch, Purinton	75.00
Cup & Saucer, Aztec, Metlox	25.00
Cup & Saucer, Brittany, Majestic, Homer Laughlin	5.00
Cup & Saucer, California Ivy, Metlox	8.00
Cup & Saucer, Christmas Tree, Mistletoe, Blue Ridge	45.00
Cup & Saucer, Christmas, Classic Style, Blue Ridge	50.00
Cup & Saucer, Fantasia, Blue Ridge	14.00
Cup & Saucer, Lu-Ray, Blue, Taylor, Smith & Taylor	9.00
Cup & Saucer, Lu-Ray, Chocolate, Yellow, Blue	110.00
Cup & Saucer, Peach Blossom, Metlox	14.00 to 15.00
Cup & Saucer, Red Rooster, Poppy Trail, Metlox	8.00
Cup & Saucer, Rhythm, Homer Laughlin	5.00
Cup & Saucer, Silhouette, Crooksville	25.00
Cup & Saucer, Trellis, Pink Roses, Homer Laughlin	7.00
Dish, Chip 'n' Dip, Cowboy Hat, Metlox, 14 In.	35.00
Dish, Shell Shape, Southern Potteries, 9 1/4 In. *Illus*	12.00

Eggcup, Mexicana, Homer Laughlin.. 35.00
Fork & Spoon, Red Rooster, Metlox... 35.00
Fruit Dish, Apple Form, Turquoise, Hoenig Of California, 6 Piece 40.00
Gravy Boat, Countess, Georgian, Eggshell, Homer Laughlin..................................... 15.00
Gravy Boat, Epicure, Turquoise, Homer Laughlin 22.00
Gravy Boat, Rustic Plaid, Blue Ridge 9.00
Jam Jar, Cover, Apple, Purinton 60.00
Jug, Ball, Cobalt, Pfaltzgraff, 7 1/2 In... 45.00
Jug, Cover, Calico Fruit, Universal 40.00
Jug, Rebecca, Mountain Rose, Purinton 40.00
Jug, With 4 Mugs, Dutch, Purinton, 5 Piece.. 140.00
Lazy Susan, Red Rooster, Metlox.. 165.00
Mug, Cockeyed Charlie, Pfaltzgraff 30.00
Mug, Jerry The Jerk, Pfaltzgraff.. 30.00
Mug-Jug, Apple, Purinton 65.00
Pitcher, Antique Pattern, Blue Ridge 70.00
Pitcher, Apple, Purinton, 5 Pt. 145.00
Pitcher, Aztec, Metlox 90.00
Pitcher, Bird, Pearlized Blue, Gold Trim, Purinton 160.00
Pitcher, Dutch Girl, Blue Ridge.. 75.00
Pitcher, Green, Taylor, Smith & Taylor 95.00
Pitcher, Jane, Blue Ridge.. 125.00
Pitcher, Lu-Ray, Footed, Blue 77.00
Pitcher, Pansy Trio, Spiral, Blue Ridge 90.00
Pitcher, Rooster, Metlox... 700.00
Pitcher, Water, Lu-Ray, Yellow, Taylor, Smith & Taylor 60.00
Pitcher, Wild Irish Rose, Spiral, Blue Ridge, 7 In. 85.00
Place Setting, California Ivy, Metlox, 4 Piece 175.00
Planter, Train, Black, Gold Trim, Metlox... 95.00
Plate, Apple Pattern, Purinton, 10 In. 30.00
Plate, Aztec, Metlox, 8 In. 15.00
Plate, Aztec, Metlox, 10 In. 30.00
Plate, Bolero, W.S. George, 9 1/4 In. 6.00
Plate, California Ivy, Metlox, 6 1/4 In. 4.00
Plate, California Ivy, Metlox, 10 1/4 In. 10.00
Plate, Cheers, Blue Ridge, 8 In. 40.00
Plate, Christmas Tree, Blue Ridge, 10 1/2 In. 50.00
Plate, Countess, Georgian, Eggshell, Homer Laughlin, 6 In. 5.00
Plate, Crab Apple, Blue Ridge, 10 In. 8.00
Plate, Crab Orchard, Green Rim, Blue Ridge, 6 In. 2.00
Plate, Fantasia, Blue Ridge, 9 1/2 In. 9.00
Plate, Flower Cabin, Blue Ridge.. 650.00
Plate, Flowers In Vase, Blue Ridge, 8 1/2 In. 25.00
Plate, Freeform, Metlox, 10 In.. 25.00
Plate, French Peasant, Blue Ridge, 10 In. 50.00
Plate, Greenbriar, Blue Ridge, 9 1/2 In. 8.00
Plate, Language Of Flowers, Blue Ridge 90.00
Plate, Lu-Ray, Pink, 8 In. 12.00
Plate, Luncheon, Lu-Ray, Pink, Taylor, Smith & Taylor... 6.00
Plate, Pastel Tulip, Nautilus, Eggshell, Homer Laughlin, 10 In...................................... 6.00
Plate, Peach Blossom, Metlox, 6 In. 7.00
Plate, Peach Blossom, Metlox, 10 1/4 In. .... 14.00 to 15.00
Plate, Quaker Apple, Blue Ridge, 9 1/2 In... 9.00
Plate, Red Rooster, Poppy Trail, Metlox, 7 1/2 In. 6.00
Plate, Red Rooster, Poppy Trail, Metlox, 10 In. 10.00
Plate, Rustic Plaid, Blue Ridge, 9 1/2 In.. 4.00
Plate, Stanhome Ivy, Skyline Shape, Blue Ridge, 9 1/2 In. 6.00
Plate, Taverne, Taylor, Smith & Taylor, 7 1/4 In. 10.00
Plate, Tic Tack, Blue Ridge, 10 In.. 13.00
Plate, Weathervane, Blue Ridge, 6 In. 10.00
Platter, Brittany Hemlock, Red, Homer Laughlin, 11 In. 13.00
Platter, California Provincial, Metlox, 11 In. 20.00

Platter, California Provincial, Metlox, 13 In. 25.00
Platter, Conchita, Homer Laughlin, Rectangular 18.00
Platter, Countess, Homer Laughlin, 13 In. 15.00
Platter, Crab Apple, Blue Ridge, Oval, 13 In. 29.00
Platter, Jubilee, Celadon, Homer Laughlin, Small 12.00
Platter, Jubilee, Pink, Homer Laughlin, Large 15.00
Platter, Lu-Ray, Green, Taylor, Smith & Taylor, Small 13.00
Platter, Mexicana, Square Well, Homer Laughlin, 11 1/2 In. 28.00
Platter, Poinsettia, Blue Ridge, 13 1/2 In. 35.00
Platter, Red Rooster, Metlox, 16 In. 95.00
Platter, Red Rooster, Poppy Trail, Metlox, 13 In. 15.00
Platter, Rustic Plaid, Blue Ridge, 11 1/2 In. 7.00
Relish, 3 Sections, Apple, Purinton 55.00
Relish, 3 Sections, Fruit, Purinton ....35.00 to 50.00
Relish, Chintz, Leaf, Blue Ridge, Large 75.00
Relish, Easter Parade, Blue Ridge, Round 75.00
Relish, Normandy Plaid, 3 Sections, Purinton 44.00
Relish, Shell, Rose, Blue Ridge 45.00
Salt & Pepper, Chicken, Black & White, Blue Ridge 85.00
Salt & Pepper, Epicure, Turquoise, Homer Laughlin 22.00
Salt & Pepper, Palm Tree, Shake & Pour, Purinton 450.00
Salt & Pepper, Rhythm, Homer Laughlin 7.00
Salt & Pepper, Sir Francis Drake, Metlox ....55.00 to 65.00
Sauce Boat, Mexicana, Homer Laughlin 55.00
Saucer, Peach Blossom, Metlox 3.00
Soup, Dish, Countess, Homer Laughlin 7.00
Soup, Dish, Red Rooster, Poppy Trail, Metlox 8.00
Sugar, Cover, Fruits, Purinton 28.00
Sugar, Cover, Majestic, Brittany 12.00
Sugar, Lu-Ray, Blue, Taylor, Smith & Taylor 6.00
Sugar, Virginia Rose, Patrician 12.00
Sugar & Creamer, Apple, Purinton ....45.00 to 60.00
Sugar & Creamer, Apple, Purinton, Miniature 50.00
Sugar & Creamer, Cover, California Ivy, Metlox 15.00
Sugar & Creamer, Cover, Nautilus, Homer Laughlin 28.00
Sugar & Creamer, Crab Apple, Blue Ridge 25.00
Sugar & Creamer, Easter Parade, Pedestal, Blue Ridge 85.00
Sugar & Creamer, Fruit, Purinton 40.00
Sugar & Creamer, Red Ivy, Purinton 30.00
Sugar & Creamer, Silhouette, Crooksville 55.00
Teapot, Apple, Purinton, 2 Cup 20.00
Teapot, Apple, Purinton, 6 Cup ....55.00 to 85.00
Teapot, Colonial, Blue Ridge ....65.00 to 100.00
Teapot, Fruit, Purinton 40.00
Teapot, Ivy, Red, Purinton, 2 Cup 35.00
Teapot, Jubilee, Celadon, Homer Laughlin 40.00
Teapot, Lu-Ray, Straight Spout, Pink, Taylor, Smith & Taylor 45.00
Teapot, Lu-Ray, Yellow 65.00
Teapot, Nautilus, Eggshell, Iridescent, Gold, Homer Laughlin 95.00
Teapot, Niagara Falls, Stadler 70.00
Teapot, Pyramidal, 3 Stars, White Rim, Green Base, Purinton 85.00
Teapot, Red Rooster, Metlox 75.00
Teapot, Rose, Purinton, 2 Cup 25.00
Teapot, Silhouette, Crooksville 55.00
Teapot, Tic Tack, Blue Ridge 150.00
Teapot, Yellow Ivy, Purinton, 2 Cup 35.00
Tidbit, Lu-Ray, Yellow, 2 Tiers 75.00
Tile, Tea, Nocturne, Yellow, Blue Ridge 50.00
Toilet Set, Duchess, Gold Greek Key, Homer Laughlin, 6 Piece 595.00
Tumbler, Poppy Trail, Cobalt Blue, Metlox 12.00
Tureen, Cover, Ladle, Village, Pfaltzgraff 65.00
Vase, Cornucopia, Purinton 25.00

AMERICAN ENCAUSTIC TILING COMPANY was founded in Zanesville, Ohio, in 1875. The company planned to make a variety of tiles to compete with the English tiles that were selling in the United States for use in fireplaces and other architectural designs. The first glazed tiles were made in 1880, embossed tiles in 1881, faience tiles in the 1920s. The firm closed in 1935 and reopened in 1937 as the Shawnee Pottery.

Tile, 4 Butterflies In Relief, Olive Majolica, 4 1/4 In.	72.00
Tile, Classical Woman Profile, Amber Majolica Glaze, Frame, 8 In.	137.00
Tile, Embossed Stag, Black Ground, Art Deco, Frame, 6 In.	248.00
Tile, Lotus Flower In Relief, Amber Majolica, 4 1/4 In.	94.00
Tile, Old Man, Beard, Hat, Olive Majolica Glaze, Frame, 6 In.	325.00
Tile, Plant Opening, Zanesville, Ohio, 1892, 4 In.	195.00
Tile, Raised Cockatoo, Branch, Leaves, 6 x 12 In.	187.00
Tile, William Jennings Bryan, 1896, 3 In.	145.00
Tile, William McKinley Profile, Blue Majolica, 1896, 3 In.	215.00
Tile, Woman, Sticks On Back, Gold Majolica, Frame, 6 In.	303.00

AMETHYST GLASS is any of the many glasswares made in the dark purple color of the gemstone called amethyst. Included in this category are many pieces made in the nineteenth and twentieth centuries. Very dark pieces are called *black amethyst* and are listed under that heading.

Box, Enamel Flowers, Hinged, Brass Feet & Rings, 4 x 3 5/8 In.	225.00
Lamp, Hand, Little Buttercup, 19th Century, 2 3/4 In.	144.00
Vase, Bud, Clear Stem & Base, 8 In.	5.00
Vase, Enameled Design, 19th Century, 7 1/2 In., Pair	132.00
Vase, Trumpet, Freeblown, Mid 19th Century, 7 1/8 In.	747.00

ANIMAL TROPHIES, such as stuffed animals or fish, rugs made of animal skins, and other similar collectibles, are listed in this category. Collectors should be aware of the endangered species laws that make it illegal to buy and sell some of these items. Any eagle feathers, many types of cats (such as leopards), and many forms of tortoiseshell can be confiscated if discovered by the government.

Alaskan Moose, Head, Antlers, 62-In. Spread	1870.00
Alaskan Moose, Head, Antlers, 63-In. Spread	1650.00
Argali Sheep, Full Mounted	550.00
Ashtray, Buffalo Hoof	45.00
Bear, Wall Hanging	495.00
Buffalo, Head	1600.00 to 2000.00
Caribou, Head, Newfoundland	220.00
Coyote, Full Mounted	400.00
Dall Ram Sheep, Head, Near Full Curl	500.00
Deer Antlers, Large	50.00
Giraffe, Shoulder Mount, 6 Ft.	220.00
Glacial Bear, Alaska, Full Mounted	5830.00
Grizzly Bear, On Rock, Half Mounted	990.00
Horns, Water Buffalo, Mounted	100.00
Jack-Alope, Head	165.00
Kodiak Bear, Rearing, 10 Ft.	7260.00
Moose Head, Antlers, Maine, 50-In. Spread	357.00
Mountain Goat, Full Mounted	2750.00
Mountain Goat, Head	275.00
Mountain Goat, Head, British Columbia	357.00
Rug, African Lion Skin	1650.00
Rug, Bear Skin, Stuffed Head	575.00
Rug, Black Bear	500.00
Rug, Cinnamon Bear, Felt Lined, 5 Ft. 3 In.	600.00
Rug, Mountain Lion, 8 1/2 Ft.	1295.00
Rug, Polar Bear, 101 x 98 In.	1600.00
Russian Wild Boar, Full Mounted	605.00
Skin, Zebra, 1950s	1800.00

Skull, Alligator, 80 Teeth	285.00
Skull, Black Bear	27.00
Skull, Black Wolf, Alaska	94.00
Skull, Grizzly Bear	165.00
Walrus, Head Mounted	1430.00
Water Buffalo, Horns, Mounted	100.00 to 595.00

ANIMATION ART collectibles include cels that are painted drawings on cellu-loid needed to make animated cartoons shown in movie theaters or on TV. Hundreds of cels were made, then photographed in sequence to make a car-toon showing moving figures. Early examples made by the Walt Disney Stu-dios are popular with collectors today. Original sketches used by the artists are also listed here. Modern animated cartoons are made using computer-gen-erated pictures. Some of these are being produced as cels to be sold to collec-tors. Other cartoon art is listed in Comic Art and Disneyana.

Cel, Alice In Wonderland, Mad Hatter, Walt Disney, 1951, 7 In.	1955.00
Cel, Archie, Reggie, Jughead, Betty, Dilton Doily, 1960s, 9 x 29 In.	288.00
Cel, Beatles, Paul McCartney & G. Harrison, Yellow Submarine, 1968, 2 Piece	863.00
Cel, Beatles, Paul McCartney & Ringo Starr, Yellow Submarine, 1968, 2 Piece	920.00
Cel, Beatles, Yellow Submarine, George, John, King Features, 1968, 8 Piece	2587.00
Cel, Bugs Bunny, Playing Baseball, Warner Bros., Frame, 17 x 21 In.	99.00
Cel, Bugs In Storyland, Warner Bros., 1949, 9 1/2 x 11 1/2 In.	1610.00
Cel, Casper, 1 Cat	200.00
Cel, Casper, 2 Cats & Sack	250.00
Cel, Casper, Down By The Old Mill Stream, 1953	75.00
Cel, Casper, Full Figure	150.00
Cel, Cinderella, Pumpkin Changes To Coach, Walt Disney, 1950, 8 x 10 In.	805.00
Cel, Daisy Mae, Al Capp, 1975	900.00
Cel, Donald Duck & Daisy, Clasping Hands, Al Stetter, 1945, 5 x 6 In.	440.00
Cel, Donald Duck & Pluto, Marching, Al Stetter, 1945, 5 x 7 In.	465.00
Cel, Donald Duck, Eyes Open, Double Matte, Shoulders Up Image, 4 In.	400.00
Cel, Donald Duck, Funny, You Don't Look 2000, Double Matted	400.00
Cel, Donald Holds Mickey, Alpine Climbers, Walt Disney, 1936, 7 In.	6325.00
Cel, Fantasia, 3 Dancing Mushrooms, Walt Disney, 4 x 5 In.	2860.00
Cel, Flintstones, Fred & Barney, Driving, Hanna-Barbera, 1963, 7 x 9 In.	920.00
Cel, Flintstones, Fred & Barney, Hanna-Barbera Studios, 1965, 7 x 9 In.	690.00
Cel, Flintstones, Wilma & Fred, Hanna-Barbera, 11 x 9 In.	345.00
Cel, Fred Flintstone's Head, Cowboy Hat, Frame	50.00
Cel, Fred Flintstone, Full Figure, Cowboy Hat	110.00
Cel, Goofy, Art Of Skiing, Walt Disney, 1941, 3 x 7 In.	4025.00
Cel, How The Grinch Stole Christmas, MGM, 1966, 11 x 7 3/4 In.	2588.00
Cel, Jiminy Cricket, Eyes Open, Frame, 6 x 6 1/2 In.	300.00
Cel, Journey Back To Oz, Frame	700.00
Cel, Jungle Book, Mowgli, King Louie, Walt Disney, 9 1/2 x 11 1/2 In.	1150.00
Cel, Ludwig Von Drake, Disney TV Show, Matted, 1960s, 6 In.	400.00
Cel, Mickey Mouse, Dangles Fish By Tail, Walt Disney, 1948, 6 1/2 In.	2070.00
Cel, Mountain Lion, Fish, Hook, Lion & Sinker, Walt Disney, 1950, 5 In.	115.00
Cel, Pink Panther, Depatie-Freleng Ent., 8 x 9 1/2 In.	460.00
Cel, Pinocchio Listens To Jiminy Cricket, Walt Disney, 1940, 10 x 10 In.	8625.00
Cel, Pluto, Surrounded By 6 Puppies, Al Stetter, 1945, 6 1/2 x 8 1/2 In.	440.00
Cel, Snow White & Seven Dwarfs, Dopey, Walking, 1937, 7 1/2 In.	5750.00
Cel, Snow White & Seven Dwarfs, Dopey, Standing, 7 1/2 In.	6200.00
Cel, Snow White & Seven Dwarfs, No Grumpy, Courvoisier	7500.00
Cel, Star Wars, Ewoks, Frame	550.00
Cel, Superman, Matted, Frame	195.00
Cel, Teenage Mutant Ninja Turtles, Matted	20.00
Cel, Tiger, TV Cartoon, Disney, 6 In.	225.00
Cel, Winnie The Pooh, Tigger, Forest Scene, 6 In.	225.00
Cel, Yogi Bear & Quick Draw McGraw, Laser Ground, Frame, 8 1/2 x 9 1/2 In.	220.00
Drawing, Donald Duck, Action Pose For 50th Birthday, Red, Black Pencil	95.00
Drawing, Mickey Mouse, Alpine Climbers, Red, Blue & Gray Pencil, 4 In.	900.00
Drawing, Scrooge McDuck, Rescue Rangers, Mister Money Bags, 3 In.	65.00

Architectural, Balusters, Staircase, Lion,

32 In., Pair

✦✦✦✦✦✦✦✦✦✦✦✦✦✦✦✦✦✦✦✦✦✦

You and your antiques may have different ideas about ideal temperature and humidity. Bronzes and photographs like 40% humidity, stone carvings and oil paintings like 50%, wooden pieces and paper prefer 55%. The level, whatever you choose, should be constant. It can be measured by a hygrometer you will be able to find at a hardware store.

✦✦✦✦✦✦✦✦✦✦✦✦✦✦✦✦✦✦✦✦✦✦

Drawing, Sleeping Beauty, Goons Huddled Together, Gray Pencil 95.00
Drawing, Wicked Witch, Snow White, Red & Gray Pencil, 5 In. 925.00

ARC-EN-CIEL is the French word for rainbow. A pottery factory named Arc-en-ciel was founded in Zanesville, Ohio, in 1903. The company made art pottery for a short time, then became the Brighton Pottery in 1905.

Vase, Bud, Honey Mustard High Glaze, Brown Flecks, No. 549, 6 In. 121.00
Vase, Gold Luster, 12 In. 220.00
Vase, Leaves, Stems, Blue-Green, 1904, 6 1/2 In. 275.00

ARCHITECTURAL antiques include a variety of collectibles, usually very large, that have been removed from buildings. Hardware, backbars, doors, paneling, and even old bathtubs are now wanted by collectors. Pieces of the Victorian, Art Nouveau, and Art Deco styles are in greatest demand.

Backbar, Barber Shop, Marble Counter, Sink, Oak, 7 x 14 Ft. 2800.00
Backbar, Mirrors Across Back, Oak, 92 x 120 In. 7500.00
Backbar, Mirrors, Chrome Hardware, Birch & Mahogany, 1940, 16 Ft. 8750.00
Backbar, Stained & Leaded Glass, Cherry, 9 Ft. 2 In. x 8 Ft. 3000.00
Backbar, Stained Glass Side, 4 Doors, Cherry, 2 Piece 800.00
Balusters, Staircase, Lion, 32 In., Pair................................*Illus*   900.00
Bar, Walnut Inlay, Oak, 12 Ft. 2400.00
Bathtub, Copper Lined, Hardwood Rim, Cast Iron Footed, 19th Century...... 330.00
Bathtub, Iron, Oak Trim, Victorian... 850.00
Bracket, Roof Snow Fence, Cast Iron, 18th Century, 11 1/2 x 6 1/2 In., 4 Piece 250.00
Brick, Culver Block, From Indianapolis Motor Speedway, Paved In 1909.................... 50.00
Chimney Pot 145.00
Column, Corinthian, Iron, Zinc, Glass Globe, Pair............................... 2595.00
Cover, Gutter, Open Triangular Form, Frank Lloyd Wright, 1940, 66 In. 1265.00
Cupola, Pagoda Style, Open Pole Work, England, 1800s, 10 Ft.................... 3500.00
Door Surround, Painted, Garnered, Late 19th Century 4887.00
Doorknob, Glass Faceted, With Connector, 2 In. 8.00
Doorknob, Green Glass 32.00
Fence, Double Gates, French Castle, 7 Ft. 7000.00
Fountain, Willimantic, Conn., Main Street, Cast Iron, c.1909 .... 5500.00
Frame, Window, Lozenge Design, Frank Lloyd Wright, 47 x 49 1/4 In. 1495.00
Gate, Georgian, Iron, Mahogany, 1780, 100 x 82 In. 2750.00
Grille, Elevator, Grid & Scrolling, Cast Iron, Jenney & Mundie, 1889, 78 1/2 In. 1840.00
Heater, Bath Water, Humphrey Co., Copper, 2 Spigots, 30 In. 70.00
Mantel, Carved Oak, Country Scene, With Log Cabin.............................. 1400.00
Mantel, Detailed Molding, Brown Grained Repaint, Walnut, 32 x 44 In. 330.00

Mantel, Fireplace, Quarter Sawn Oak, Victorian, 6 Ft. 2 In. x 5 Ft. 1 In. 1100.00
Mantel, Fireplace, Victorian, Cupid & Thistle Tiles 750.00
Mantel, Fireplace, White Marble, Rococo, France 8800.00
Mantel, Frieze With Shell Carvings, Carved Columns, Oak & Iron, 43 x 48 In. 425.00
Mantel, Fruit & Grapes Panels, Figure With Urn, Gessoed Pine, c.1811, 61 In. 3162.00
Mantel, Louis VI Style, Black Marble, Shaped Shelf, 37 1/2 x 48 1/2 In. 412.00
Mantel, Mirror Top With Shelves, Walnut 500.00
Mantel, Pine, Poplar, Black & Brown Graining, Black Trim, 53 x 50 1/4 In. 385.00
Newel Post, Carved Griffins, Pair 418.00
Newel Post, Elliptical Pattern, Foliage, Cast Iron, Adler & Sullivan, 1893, 65 In. 3450.00
Ornament, Roof, Sunflower, Zinc, c.1860, 54 In. 575.00
Panel, Frieze, Low Relief Pattern, Adler & Sullivan, Cast Iron, 1893, 42 3/4 In. 690.00
Panel, Hearse, Carved As Drawn-Back Drape, Blue & Red Paint, Pair 950.00
Panel, Saints, Carved Wood, Gilt Design, 20 1/2 In. 1320.00
Spire, Church, Iron, c.1870 .... 2500.00
Stair Riser, L.H. Sullivan, Chicago Stock Exchange, Iron, 42 1/2 x 7 1/2 In. 660.00
Staircase, Iron, 3 Stories, Circular, Victorian 3000.00
Surround, Wooden, Painted, Weathered 440.00
Swag Carved Panel, Carved & Painted Pine, c.1803, 32 x 37 1/2 In. 6900.00
Tile, Roof, Warrior Riding A Leaping Horse, 19th Century, 14 In. 287.00
Window Guard, Balcony, Iron, Ornate, Victorian, Single 400.00

AREQUIPA POTTERY was produced from 1911 to 1918 by the patients of the
Arequipa Sanitarium in Marin County Hills, California.

Bowl, Carved Flower Design, Matte Blue, Impressed Oval Mark, 2 1/4 x 6 1/2 In. 220.00
Bowl, Flowers, Leaves, Black, White, 9 In. 165.00
Bowl, Matte Brown Glaze, Flat, Impressed Oval Mark, 1 3/4 x 6 In. 358.00
Jar, 2 Handles, Incised Geometrics, Light Blue Matte, 5 In. 330.00
Pot, Modeled Flowers, Matte Gray & Pink Glaze, Bulbous, 3 1/4 x 4 In. 275.00
Vase, Blue Drip Over Tan 595.00
Vase, Carved Design, Allover Hanging Wisteria, Green Glaze, 12 In. 4950.00
Vase, Matte Brown, No. 1524, 3 1/2 In. 187.00
Vase, Painted Flowers, Gunmetal To Dark Blue Ground, 4 In. 550.00
Vase, Stylized Flowers, Under Black High-Gloss, Bulbous, Stamped, 3 1/4 In. 220.00
Vase, Stylized Grass Blades, Creamy White Glaze, Bulbous, Oval Mark, 7 1/4 In. 825.00
Vase, Tan, Blue, Flambe, 4 In. 525.00

ARGY-ROUSSEAU, see G. Argy-Rousseau category

ART DECO, or Art Moderne, a style started at the Paris Exposition of 1925, is
characterized by linear, geometric designs. All types of furniture and decorative arts, jewelry, book bindings, and even games were designed in this style.
Additional items may be found in the Furniture category or in various glass
and pottery categories, etc.

Ashtray, Bulldog 25.00
Cocktail Set, Gold & Green Bands 75.00
Coffee Urn, Sugar & Creamer, Globe, 3 Piece 100.00
Dispenser, Cigarette, Pottery & Chromium, Bulbous, Sports Figures, 7 In. 225.00
Figurine, Musician, Rosewood, 9 In., Pair 33.00
Fish Bowl, Green Glass, Iron Base, 1930 .... 350.00
Sculpture, Torso, Chrome, Berrocal, 1970s, 5 In. 950.00
Vase, Metal, Silver Stylized Diana, With Boy, Greyhounds, France, 12 In. 550.00

ART GLASS, see Glass-Art

ART NOUVEAU is a style of design that was at its most popular from 1895 to
1905. Famous designers, including Rene Lalique and Emile Galle, produced
furniture, glass, silver, metalwork, and buildings in the new style. Ladies with
long flowing hair and elongated bodies were among the more easily recognized design elements. Copies of this style are being made today. Many modern pieces of jewelry can be found. Additional Art Nouveau pieces may be
found in Furniture or in various glass categories.

Lamp, Hand Painted, Landscape Design Shade, Frosted, Metal Frame, 22 In................. 418.00
Vase, Cobalt Blue, Hand Painted Design, 10 In.. 195.00
Vase, Sterling, Crimped & Flared, Floral Top & Foot, 1900.. 1725.00

ART POTTERY was first made in America in Cincinnati, Ohio, during the 1870s. The pieces were hand thrown and hand decorated. The art pottery tradition continued until the 1920s when studio potters began making the more artistic wares. American and English art pottery by less well-known makers is listed here. Other makers, such as Arequipa, Ohr, Rookwood, Roseville, and Weller, are listed in their own categories. More recent pottery is listed under the name of the maker or in the Pottery category.

Bookends, Eagle, Blue Matte, California Faience... 650.00
Bowl, Burgundy Glaze, Closed, California Faience, 2 3/4 x 4 3/4 In. 55.00
Bowl, Crackled Matte Blue & Green Glaze, Double Gourd, Wm. P. Jervis, 3 3/4 In....... 1210.00
Bowl, Currant Pattern, Orange, 2 Handles, 9 3/8 x 4 In. 120.00
Bowl, Green & Blue Matte Flambe Glaze, Footed, Flared, Byrdcliffe, 3 1/2 x 8 In........ 358.00
Bowl, Mottled Leathery Blue-Green Matte Glaze, Squatty, Zark, 4 x 7 1/4 In. 605.00
Bowl, Red & Brown Mottled Glaze, Bulbous, A. Delaherche, 3 1/4 x 4 In..................... 770.00
Box, University City, Lines & Beads, Swirled Cover, White High Glaze, 1914, 2 In...... 308.00
Candlestick, Enameled Geometric Design, Rhead, Signed, 6 x 4 1/2 In., Pair 1430.00
Candlestick, Mottled Green & Brown, Glazed, Zanesville, 8 In. 85.00
Dish, Aubergine Matte, Crackled Persian Blue Interior, Durant Kilns, 2 3/4 x 6 In. 275.00
Figurine, Veiled Woman, Holding Fan, All Cream, 1920, 9 1/2 In. 50.00
Jardiniere, Art Nouveau, 3 Snails At Rim, Daubac, c.1900, 7 3/4 In. 1380.00
Jardiniere, Burgundy, Blue & Green, Stylized Flowers, A. Delaherche, 22 In. 2300.00
Lamp, Table, Green, Blue, Black, Wicker Shade, c.1900, Wannopee, 18 In. 786.00
Loving Cup, Clover, Green To Brown Ground, La Moro, Zanesville, 6 In...................... 165.00
Mug, Cooperage Design, Blue Glaze, C.A.P., 7 In. 100.00
Pitcher, Green & Yellow Streaks, Flowers, Stockton, 7 In. 165.00
Pitcher, William Shakespeare's Birthday, 1892, Chesapeake Pottery, 6 3/4 In.............. 220.00
Plate, Art Deco Design, P. & M. St. Gaudens, 9 1/2 In., 4 Piece 385.00
Trivet, Matte Green, Pardee, Mahogany Frame, Square, 5 1/2 In.... 100.00
Umbrella Stand, Water Lilies, Floral, Amber, Green, Majolica, Isaac Broome, 19 In.... 605.00
Vase, 2 Handles, White Curdled Glaze, Gold Iridescent, Swastika Keramos, 8 In......... 165.00
Vase, 4-Sided Teardrop, Mottled Matte Glaze, Byrdcliffe, 6 3/4 In. 325.00
Vase, 6 Vertical Leaves, Olive Green Over Brown, Chicago Crucible, 6 1/4 In. 467.00
Vase, Band Of Pachyderms & Palm Trees, Charles Catteau, c.1925, 16 In. 5750.00
Vase, Bands Of Calligraphy, Turquoise Ground, Theodore Deck, c.1890, 14 In. 3162.00
Vase, Bird, Flowering Tree, Shaded Apricot To Green Glaze, Bretby, 9 x 4 1/4 In. 165.00
Vase, Black Stylized Trees, Orange Black & Green, Bottle Shape, Avon, 6 x 4 In. 605.00
Vase, Blue High Glaze, Flowers, Bag Outlines, Avon, No. 126, F. Rhead, 5 In.............. 1320.00
Vase, Brown, A. Delaherche, 5 1/2 In. 950.00
Vase, Cabinet, Crystalline, Robineau 4400.00
Vase, Carved, 2-Tone Green Matte Glaze, Chicago Crucible, 4 1/2 In.......................... 825.00
Vase, Chicago Crucible, 5 In. 245.00
Vase, Cobalt Glaze, Spherical Base, Neck, Bottle Shape, Pauline Pottery, 5 1/2 In. 220.00
Vase, Etched Organic Designs, Cream, Rust, Yellow, No. 6316, Markham, 7 In........... 605.00
Vase, Floral Design, Mottled Yellow Ground, California Faience, 8 x 4 In. 1650.00
Vase, Gourd Shape, Gold Luster, Arc-En-Ciel, J. Lessell, 7 1/2 In. 400.00
Vase, Gray-Brown Glaze, Green Hint, Handles, Chauncey R. Thomas, 1907, 8 x 7 In... 770.00
Vase, Iridescent Landscape, Viennese Style, Swastika Keramos, 8 In. 465.00
Vase, Landscape Design, High Glaze, Avon, 6 In. 440.00
Vase, Leathery Matte Slate Gray Glaze, Bulbous, Rhead, 3 1/2 x 3 3/4 In..................... 275.00
Vase, Magenta Flowers, Iridescent Copper Ground, Swastika Keramos, 8 In. 330.00
Vase, Matte Blue, Tapered, California Faience, Impressed, 7 1/4 x 4 1/4 In. 665.00
Vase, Matte Green, Stippled, No. 605, Strobl, 3 1/4 In. 319.00
Vase, Medicine Man, Rydings, 13 1/2 In. 715.00
Vase, Metallic Dark Blue & Apple Green Flambe, Spherical, Cabat, 4 1/4 x 4 In.......... 247.00
Vase, Mottled Purple Glaze, Flared Rim, Byrdcliffe, 8 1/4 In. 325.00
Vase, On Stand, Purple & Red Mottled Glaze, c.1920, Ruskin, 16 3/4 In. 5430.00
Vase, Pottery, Dark Green Glazed, 2 Handles, Wannopee 150.00
Vase, Sculpted Flowers, Matte Green Glaze, Valentine, 5 In. 1870.00

Vase, Stylized Floral, Matte Green Microcrystalline Glaze, Valentine, 5 In................. 1870.00
Vase, Swollen Shape, Blue Crystals On Cream Ground, Norweta, 8 In. 220.00
Vase, Thera, Pink & Lavender Flowers, Matte Green Ground, Radford, 12 1/2 In........ 385.00
Vase, Turquoise Jewels, Ring Handles, Matte, Bretby, 9 1/2 In., Pair 250.00
Vase, Viking Ship, Cylindrical Neck, c.1906, Bernard Moore, 7 1/2 In. 500.00
Vase, Viking Ship, On Waves, Opalescent Glaze, Bernard Moore 4800.00

ARTS & CRAFTS was a design style popular in American decorative arts from 1894 to 1923. In the 1970s collectors began to rediscover Mission furniture, art pottery, metalwork, linens, and light fixtures from this period. The interest has continued. Today everything from this era is collectible, including jewelry, graphics, and silverware. Additional items may be found in the Furniture category, various glass categories, etc.

Basket, Waste, Post & Panel, Cut-Out Handles, Signed, 17 1/2 In.............................. 425.00
Box, Hammered Copper, Sterling Rivets & Clasp, 5 x 1 1/2 In. 412.00
Candlestick, Water Lily Design 165.00
Frame, Hammered Art Nouveau Design, Cameo, 2 Green Stones 165.00
Lantern, Stained Red & Caramel Glass, Hanging, 13 1/2 x 9 1/2 x 9 1/2 In.................. 302.00
Pillow, 3 Embroidered Vertical Patterns, 12 x 18 In. 245.00
Pitcher, Hammered Copper & Brass, H.H.D., 10 3/4 In. 145.00
Rug, Donegal, Wool, Gavin Morton & G.K. Robertson, c.1900, 7 Ft. x 6 Ft. 11 In. 3220.00
Runner, Embroidered Linen, Pink Flowers, Natural Ground, 10 x 16 1/2 In. 225.00
Table Cover, Reversible, Brown, Green & Ivory, 8 Ft. 4 In. x 5 Ft. 350.00
Teaspoon Set, Hammered Handle, Chased Design, Elverhoj Craft, 6 In., 6 Piece 495.00
Tile, Incised Leaf Pattern, Speckled Glaze, Ochre Ground, Octagonal, 6 3/4 In. 82.00
Tile, Lion & Lioness, Medallion, Matte Blue, Green Frame, 6 1/2 In. 385.00
Tile, White & Blue Iris, Blue-Gray Ground, Rectangular, 1915, 9 x 5 In...................... 193.00
Umbrella Stand, Brass, Hammered, Bulbous Foot, Wide Shoulder, 25 In. 660.00
Vase, 4 Buttresses Rising To Rim, Teco Form, Tan Glaze, No. 3664, 9 In.................... 330.00
Vase, Blue-Green Glaze, A. Courant 175.00
Vase, Copper Buttressed Legs, Teardrop & Dot Design, 10 x 13 In. 1430.00
Vase, Turned Wood, Pair 48.00
Wastebasket, Wooden, Square, 15 x 11 1/2 x 11 1/2 In. 385.00
Wood Block, Gnarled Trees, Snow On Ground, Helen Hyde, 6 1/2 x 8 In. 385.00

AURENE glass was made by Frederick Carder of New York about 1904. It is an iridescent gold or blue glass, usually marked *Aurene* or *Steuben*.

AURENE

Basket, Gold, Crimped Rim, Applied Berry Prunts, Steuben, 12 1/2 In. 1150.00
Bowl, ABC, Gold Daisies Over Alabaster, Steuben, 7 In. 2300.00
Bowl, Blue, Steuben, 10 In. 695.00
Bowl, Calcite Exterior, Gold Iridescent Interior, Steuben, 10 In. 300.00
Bowl, Calcite, No. 3200, Gold, Steuben, 10 In. 375.00
Bowl, Chinese Pattern, Gold Overlay On Alabaster, Steuben, 7 In. 2415.00
Bowl, Gold Iridescent, White Calcite Interior & Exterior, Steuben, 9 7/8 In.................. 1150.00
Bowl, Gold, No. 2887, Steuben, 6 x 4 In. 242.00
Compote, Sterling Silver Holder, Steuben 265.00
Cordial, Twisted Stem, Gold Iridescent, Signed, 3 1/2 In. 225.00
Darner, Blue, Steuben 375.00
Goblet, Twisted Stem, Gold Iridescent, Steuben, 6 1/4 In. ....165.00 to 240.00
Lamp Shade, Gold, Fleur-De-Lis Mark, Steuben, 5 In. 126.00
Salt, Ruffled Edge 265.00
Shade, Iridescent, Steuben, c.1920, 4 1/2 In.. 172.00
Shade, Ruby, Steuben, 9 In. 150.00
Vase, Blue Chain, Flared Body, Steuben, 5 1/4 In. 3100.00
Vase, Blue Flowers, Red, Steuben, 9 In. 4000.00
Vase, Blue Iridescent, Steuben, 8 1/2 In. 154.00
Vase, Blue, Elongate Stick Body, Dish Foot, Steuben, 8 /18 In. 430.00
Vase, Blue, Flower Form, Steuben, 12 1/2 In. 2200.00
Vase, Blue, No. 2812, Steuben, Paper Label, 4 x 4 In. 450.00
Vase, Floriform, Gold, On Calcite, Steuben 495.00
Vase, Gold Iridescent Trailings & Leaves, Red, Steuben, c.1910, 8 7/8 In................... 8625.00
Vase, Oviform, Everted Rim, Gold Iridescent, No. 2685, 11 In................................ 1035.00

Vase, Red, Flared Cylinder, Gold Iridescent, No. 723, Steuben, 5 In. 5750.00

AUTO parts and accessories are collectors' items today. Gas pump globes and license plates are part of this specialty. Prices are determined by age, rarity, and condition. Signs and packaging related to automobiles may also be found in the Advertising category. Lalique hood ornaments will be listed in the Lalique category.

Air Pump, Eco, Stand	300.00
Antifreeze Tester, Amoco, Sealed In Original Box	75.00
Can, Travelene Motor Oil, 5 Gal.	38.00
Certificate, Stock, Reo Motor Car Co., January, 1916, 10 Shares................................	500.00
Dashboard, Ornament, Car, Hula Girl	55.00
Extinguisher, Shur-Ex Motor Guardian	30.00
Fan, Dashboard, Advertising Auburn & Saxon Autos, Cardboard, 1916, 13 1/2 In.	35.00
Gas Pump, Red, White Trim, 1929, 10 Gal., 13 Ft.	1400.00
Gas Pump, Wayne, Visible, 10 Gal.	850.00
Gas Pump Globe, Aerio, Green Gill Ripple, Plane In Flight..	9350.00
Gas Pump Globe, Diamond D, Milk Glass	395.00
Gas Pump Globe, Magnolia Ethyl, Metal Body, 16 1/2 In.	850.00
Gas Pump Globe, Metro, 3 Piece	300.00
Gas Pump Globe, Musgo, Indian Chief, Multicolored, 1928	5225.00
Gas Pump Globe, Phillips 66, Mae West	1200.00
Gas Pump Globe, Pittman Streamlined, Blue Gill Ripple, Plane	7700.00
Gas Pump Globe, Shell, Shell Shape, 1 Piece	450.00
Gas Pump Globe, Sinclair Aircraft, Airplane Graphics	4950.00
Gas Pump Globe, Sinclair HC...	600.00
Gas Pump Globe, Sinclair Power X Gas	350.00
Gas Pump Globe, Sky Chief, Glass, 3 Piece	500.00
Gas Pump Globe, Texaco, Glass, 1 Piece	950.00
Gas Pump Globe, Tydol, 16 1/2 In.	600.00
Gas Pump Globe, White Eagle, Milk Glass, Walnut Base, 20 1/2 In.	1150.00
Gas Pump Globe, White Star Gasoline	375.00
Gas Pump Plate, Mobilgas, Shield Shape..	125.00
Grill, Dodge Bros., Shell Emblem, Porcelain..	60.00
Handbook, Chevrolet Owner's, Complete, 1929-1950..	10.00
Handbook, Volkswagen Service Repair, 1962-1973	15.00
Holder, Flag, Radiator, 1940s..	18.00
Hood Ornament, Airplane, Wooden, 9 In.	20.00
Hood Ornament, Cowboy On Horse	25.00
Hood Ornament, Duesenberg Pegasus, Plexiglas Pedestal, 5 1/2 In.	515.00
Hood Ornament, Oldsmobile, Streamlined Airplane	11.00
Hood Ornament, Packard, Winged Woman	50.00
Hood Ornament, Pontiac, Chief, Lighted, 1950..	75.00
Hood Ornament, Pontiac, Goose...	22.00
Hood Ornament, Pontiac, Super Chief, 1953	75.00
Hood Ornament, Winged Flight Goddess, Red Plastic Wing, Unused, Box	75.00
Knob, Gear Shift, Orange-Red, Marble	40.00
Knob, Gear Shift, Triumph	10.00
License Plate, Alabama, 1954	15.00
License Plate, Alaska, 1960	22.00
License Plate, Alberta, Canada, 1960...	9.00
License Plate, Arizona, 1963...	8.00
License Plate, Arizona, Cactus, 1982	3.00
License Plate, Arizona, Copper, 1933	150.00
License Plate, Arkansas, 1926...	70.00
License Plate, California, 1924	10.00
License Plate, California, 1929 ....8.00 to 15.00
License Plate, California, 1938	8.00
License Plate, California, 1958	12.00
License Plate, California, 1963, Black	7.00
License Plate, Connecticut, 1956	12.00
License Plate, Dominican Republic, 1981..	15.00
License Plate, Maine, Brass, 1948..	100.00

License Plate, Massachusetts, Porcelain, 1914	25.00
License Plate, New Hampshire, 1914	70.00
License Plate, Ohio, 1923	14.00
License Plate, Ohio, 1950	7.00
License Plate, Ontario, Canada, 1916	125.00
License Plate, Ontario, Canada, 1946	40.00
License Plate, Pennsylvania, 1938	10.00
License Plate, South Carolina, 1926	18.00
License Plate, Texas, 1917	275.00
License Plate, Texas, 1918	275.00
License Plate, Texas, 1919	200.00
License Plate, Washington, D.C., Bicentennial, 1976	40.00
License Plate, Washington, D.C., Inaugural, 1953	90.00
License Plate, Wisconsin, 1928	10.00
License Plate, Yukon, Canada, 1958	190.00
Motometer, Buick, 1928, Box	85.00
Motor Oil, Cuplex, Pierce Arrow Motor Car, 5 Gal.	990.00
Pail, Duplex Auto, Kansas	30.00
Sign, Conoco Gasoline, Green Porcelain	75.00
Sign, Direction Of Highway Commission, Porcelain, 25 x 25 In.	395.00
Sign, Gas Pump, Atlantic Refining Company, Porcelain, Fried Egg Type	550.00
Sign, Gas Pump, Gulf No-Nox Motor Fuel, Porcelain, Gulf Refining Co., Flange Type	425.00
Sign, Gas Pump, Marine Regular & Ethyl, Seahorse, Pair	300.00
Sign, Gas Pump, Supreme Auto Oil, Gulf Refining Co., Porcelain, Flange Type	675.00
Sign, Iron Fireman Automatic Coal Burner, Robot, Porcelain, Round, 12 In.	425.00
Sign, Marathon Ethyl, Porcelain, Round, 30 In.	1250.00
Sign, Sinclair Opaline Motor Oil, Porcelain, 19 x 46 In.	495.00
Step, Running Board, Model A Ford, Aluminum, Ford Logo	80.00
Traffic Signal, Electric, Rewired	85.00
Wrench, Model T	4.00

AUTUMN LEAF pattern china was made for the Jewel Tea Company beginning in 1933. Hall China Company of East Liverpool, Ohio, Crooksville China Company of Crooksville, Ohio, Harker Potteries of Chester, West Virginia, and Paden City Pottery, Paden City, West Virginia, made dishes with this design. Autumn Leaf has remained popular and was made by Hall China Company until 1978. Some other pieces in the Autumn Leaf pattern are still being made. For more information, see *Kovels' Depression Glass & American Dinnerware Price List*.

Baker, French, 4 3/4 In.	40.00
Baker, Oval, 7 1/2 In.	95.00
Bean Pot	90.00
Bowl, Oval, Hall	15.00
Bowl, Salad, 9 In.	32.00
Bowl, Vegetable, Divided	70.00
Cake Stand	175.00
Candy Dish	525.00
Casserole, Cover	48.00
Casserole, Flat	20.00
Clock, Electric, 1956	500.00 to 550.00
Clock, Teapot Shape, Hall	495.00
Coaster, Jewel Tea, 6 Piece	25.00
Coffeepot, 9 Cup	80.00
Coffeepot, Drip, Jewel Tea	37.00 to 57.00
Cookie Jar, Big Ear	175.00
Cookie Jar, Ear Handles, Hall	325.00
Cookie Jar, Radiance	225.00
Cookie Jar, Rayed	235.00
Cookie Jar, Tootsie	200.00
Cookie Jar, Tootsie, Floral, Hall	98.00
Cup, Oyster	225.00
Cup & Saucer	10.00 to 17.00
Cup & Saucer, St. Dennis, Hall	18.00

Gravy, Underplate, Hall 40.00
Jug, Ball, Hall 45.00
Mixing Bowl Set, Jewel Tea, 3 Piece 55.00
Percolator, Electric 250.00
Pitcher, Hall, 2 1/2 Pt. 15.00
Pitcher, Tilt 100.00
Plate, 7 In. 8.00
Plate, 8 In. 8.00
Plate, 9 In. 10.00
Platter, Hall, 11 1/2 In. 15.00
Platter, Hall, 13 1/2 In. 18.00
Saucer, Hall 2.00
Sifter 140.00
Stack Set, Cover, 3 Piece 110.00
Sugar & Creamer 15.00
Sugar Packet Holder 100.00
Tablecloth, 54 x 54 In. 75.00
Teapot, Aladdin 35.00
Teapot, Donut, Jewel Tea 250.00
Teapot, Newport, 1930s 175.00
Tidbit, 3 Tiers .... 90.00 to 110.00
Tumbler, Brockway, 9 Oz. 45.00
Tumbler, Iced Tea, Frosted, Jewel Tea, 5 1/2 In. 20.00
Vase, Bud 100.00

BACCARAT glass was made in France by La Compagnie des Cristalleries de Baccarat, located 150 miles from Paris. The factory was started in 1765. The firm went bankrupt and began operating again about 1822. Cane and millefiori paperweights were made during the 1860 to 1880 period. The firm is still working near Paris making paperweights and glasswares.

Bottle, Dresser, Figural, Cupid Holding Cornucopia, 6 3/4 In., Pair 110.00
Bowl, Floral & Geometric Design, Gilt, Snowflake Texture, 9 In. 405.00
Box, Rose Teinte, Sunburst Pattern, Amberina, Covered, 3 x 3 1/4 In. 110.00
Candlestick, Rose Teinte, Swirl, Amberina, 7 x 4 In., Pair 295.00
Champagne Flute, Prestige, 24K Gold Trim, Pair 600.00
Compote, Rose Teinte Swirl, 4 3/4 In. 70.00
Cruet, Wine, Rose Teinte, Swirl, Applied Handle, Stopper, 10 1/4 In. 225.00
Decanter, Missouri 170.00
Decanter, Remy Martin, Signed, Wooden Box 267.00
Decanter, Saint-Remy, Satin-Lined Wooden Box 155.00
Dresser Set, Amberina, Swirled Ribs, Cut Panels In Necks, 4 Piece 275.00
Epergne, Bowl & Vase Over Dolphin, Signed, 1900s, 21 1/2 In. 715.00
Figurine, Duck 95.00
Figurine, Giraffe 175.00
Figurine, Panther, Crouching 5050.00
Figurine, Panther, Crouching, Display Case, Wooden Crate 7979.00
Figurine, Rabbit 75.00
Ice Bucket, Cut Glass 145.00
Ice Bucket, Rose Teinte Swirl, Bronze Foot & Rim, Bail Handle, Signed, 5 1/2 In. 345.00
Lamp, Crystal & Bronze Floor Lamp, 19th Century, 75 In. ....*Illus* 4400.00
Lamp, Fairy, Pinwheel Swirl, Signed, 4 1/8 x 5 3/4 In., Pair 235.00
Mustard, Glass Spoon, 5 In. 45.00
Paperweight, Aires 43.00
Paperweight, Center Star, Leafy Stem, 2 1/2 In. 435.00
Paperweight, Sulphide, Lafayette 85.00
Perfume Bottle, Invitation, Signed, 4 1/4 In. 325.00
Perfume Bottle, Joy, Diamond Cut, Silk Lined Box 205.00
Perfume Bottle, Malmaison 174.00
Perfume Bottle, Rose Teinte, Diamond Point Swirl, 5 1/2 In. 100.00
Perfume Bottle, Rose Teinte, Swirl, Amberina, Stopper, 7 x 2 5/8 In. 75.00
Perfume Bottle, Round, Spiked Diamonds, Silver-Plated Stand, 4 In., Pair 258.00
Perfume Bottle, Sun Ray Stopper, Black Birds, Gilt Metal Box, c.1945, 6 5/8 In. 8625.00
Toothpick, Brilliant Diamond Point, Clear 52.00

Baccarat, Lamp, Crystal & Bronze
Floor Lamp, 19th Century, 75 In.

◆◆◆◆◆◆◆◆◆◆◆◆◆◆◆◆◆◆◆◆◆◆◆

Always use a metal polish on
the metal it was made for.
Don't clean silver with pewter
or chrome polish. The wrong
formulation may scratch the
metal.

◆◆◆◆◆◆◆◆◆◆◆◆◆◆◆◆◆◆◆◆◆◆◆

Tray, Absinthe Green, Signed, 9 1/2 x 3 1/2 In.	35.00
Tumbler, Harcourt, 5 1/2 In.	50.00
Tumbler, Rose Teinte, Signed.	35.00
Tureen, Cover, Canary, 1850, 7 In.	1000.00
Vase, Lobster, 7 /12 In.	275.00
Vase, Overall Floral & Vine Etching, Signed, 6 1/4 In.	85.00
Vase, Paneled & Scalloped, Leaf Tips Top Of Standard, Signed, 16 In., Pair	4600.00
Vase, Poppy Blossoms, Raspberries, Gilt Metal Foot, c.1900, 10 5/8 In., Pair	4025.00
Vase, Red & Clear, Orsay, 9 1/2 In.	395.00
Wine, Colbert, 5 1/8 In.	65.00

BADGES have been used since before the Civil War. Collectors search for examples of all types, including law enforcement and company identification badges. Well-known prison or law enforcement badges are most desirable. Most are made of nickel or brass. Many recent reproductions have been made.

American Express	90.00
Broadmoor Fire Department, Senior Captain	100.00
Canadian Mounted Police	24.00
Chauffeur, Colorado, 1951	25.00
Chauffeur, Illinois, 1936.	30.00
Chauffeur, Kentucky, 1929	25.00
Chauffeur, Minnesota, 1931	25.00
Chauffeur, New York State, 1926	38.00
Chauffeur, New York, 1916	25.00
Chauffeur, New York, 1928	25.00
Chauffeur, Ohio, 1938	25.00
Chief, Charlestown, New Hampshire	45.00
Dallas Railway, Cap	35.00
Employee's, Bulldog Clip Back, St. Louis Button Co., 2 1/4 In.	3.00
Exposition, Brass, Portland, 1905	32.00
Fire, Chestertown, N.Y.	45.00
Fire, Super Surgeon	85.00
Fire Department, Hanover, New Hampshire	45.00
Fireman's, Reading, Penn., Nickel Plated Brass, 1870s	225.00
Forest Ranger, New York	85.00
Forest Warden, Conn.	90.00
Greyhound, Cap.	95.00
Harley-Davidson, Brass	5.00

Highway Patrol Auxiliary, Ohio	60.00
Junior G-Man, Special Investigator, Tab Type, Painted Tin	35.00
Lockheed Overseas Corps Chief Of Police	185.00
Municipal Court Probation Officer, Roxbury, Mass.	40.00
National Rifle Association, Member	25.00
Park Department, Watchman, City Of St. Louis	95.00
Park Superintendent, State Of North Carolina, Enameled, Leather Case	125.00
Police, Park Department, Worcester, Maine	80.00
Police, Sheridan, Wyoming, No. 1, Eagle Over Shield, Brass	575.00
Post Office Dept., Boston	15.00
Probation Officer, Waltham, Mass.	40.00
Radio City Music Hall, Cap	150.00
Radio City Music Hall, Collar	65.00
Ribbon, Box, Joseph K. Davison's Inc.	60.00
Royal Typewriter, Plant	25.00
Seaboard Freight, Cap	25.00
Sheriff, Flying Posse, Shasta, Ca., 1930s	65.00
Ship Building, War Service, 1940s	35.00
Special Police, Alford, Ma.	55.00
Special Police, Kansas City, 1922	75.00
Texaco Oil Co., Employee, Nickel Plated, 1930s	8.00
United Aircraft, Plant, Blue	35.00
Wells Fargo, Service Shield Type	70.00

BANKS of metal have been made since 1868. There are still banks, mechanical banks, and registering banks (those that show the total money deposited on the face of the bank). Many old iron or tin banks have been reproduced since the 1950s in iron or plastic. Pottery, glass, and plastic banks are also listed here. Mechanical banks are grouped alphabetically under "m" in this section. Mickey Mouse and other Disneyana banks are listed in Disneyana.

3 Little Pigs, Tin, 3 In.	121.00
1876 Bank, Cast Iron, 3 3/8 In.	165.00 to 286.00
Admiral Appliances, Vinyl, Package	15.00
Air Mail, Cast Iron, 6 3/8 In.	660.00
Airplane, Texaco, Box	95.00
American Can Co., Century Of Progress, Tin Can	25.00
Andy Gump, Cast Iron, 1980, 4 1/2 In.	30.00
Apple, Tin, Plastic, Windup, Yone, Japan, Box, 1960	50.00
Artillery, Officer & Mortar, J. & E. Stevens, Cast Iron, 8 1/4 In.	990.00
Aunt Jemima, Cast Iron, 6 In.	135.00
Baby Sleeping, Cradle That Rocks, Bluebird On Cradle, 4 x 2 3/4 x 3 In.	195.00
Bailey's Centennial, Cast Iron, 4 1/2 In.	121.00
Bank Building, Cast Iron, 5 3/4 In.	319.00
Bank Building, Red, Yellow & Black, Cast Iron, 6 In.	302.00
Baseball, Flying Red Horse	65.00
Baseball Player, Gold Uniform, Red Hat, A.C. Williams, Cast Iron, 1909, 5 3/4 In.	145.00
Baseball Player, Penny, Cast Iron, Moore No. 20, Gold Paint, 5 3/4 In.	247.00
Basket, Bushel, 1902	100.00
Be Wise Owl, Cast Iron, 5 In.	135.00 to 145.00
Bean Pot, Cast Iron, 3 In.	209.00
Bear, Beating Drum, Lead & Tin, 3 3/4 In.	715.00
Bear, Hubley	245.00
Bear, Square, Jointed, Dakin, 1970s	65.00
Bear, Standing, With Staff, Ceramic, 5 1/4 In.	66.00
Beauty, Cast Iron, 4 1/8 In.	82.00
Bell With Indian Head Shield, Tin, 4 3/8 In.	88.00
Ben Franklin, Wire Glasses, 11 In.	25.00
Billiken, A.C. Williams, 1909, 4 1/4 In.	69.00
Billiken, White Metal, 3 3/4 In.	165.00
Black Boy, 2 Faces, A.C. Williams, 4 In.	259.00
Black Boy, 2 Faces, Cast Iron	145.00
Black Woman On Commode, Billy Brand Laxative, Cast Iron, 8 In.	495.00
Bob's Big Boy, Vinyl, 1973	15.00 to 25.00

Bank, Magic, *Bank, Trader's Bank,* *Bank, Panorama, Off-White,*
Green, Iron *Yonge St., Iron* *Lithograph*

Bank, Boston
State House,
Iron, 1800s

♦♦♦♦♦♦♦♦♦♦♦♦♦♦♦♦♦♦♦♦♦♦♦
To clean small pieces of iron,
try soaking them in white vinegar for 24 to 48 hours.
♦♦♦♦♦♦♦♦♦♦♦♦♦♦♦♦♦♦♦♦♦♦♦

Bokar Coffee, Tin	12.00
Bonzo, Chalkware	72.00
Book, My Book Bank, Cast Iron, 4 3/8 In	605.00
Boston Bull, Seated, Cast Iron, 4 3/8 In	247.00
Boston State House, Iron, 1800s *Illus*	6612.00
Bozo The Clown, Chalkware, 1950s	48.00
Bubble Bank, Save For The Day He Returns, World War II, Glass, Wood, 6 1/2 In	99.00
Buffalo, Cast Iron, 4 In	25.00 to 45.00
Bugs Bunny, 1960s	35.00
Building, Candy Container, Glass & Tin, 3 In	50.00
Building, Flat Iron, Cast Iron, 5 1/2 In	154.00 to 302.00
Building, Flat Iron, Original Trap	425.00
Building, Raised Slot, Tin, 3 1/8 In	132.00
Building, Tin, 3 1/8 In	27.00
Building, Widow's Walk, Dormer Windows, Arcade, 4 1/4 In	225.00
Bulldog, Cast Iron	70.00
Bulldog, Seated, Cast Iron, 3 7/8 In	308.00
Bullet Head, 4 1/2 In	77.00
Bungalow, Green & White, Grey Iron Casting Co., Green & White, 3 3/4 In	175.00
Bust, Girl In Cap, Ceramic, 3 5/8 In	220.00
Bust, John F. Kennedy, Metal, 1917-1963	35.00
Bust, Man, Hat, Ceramic, 3 1/2 In	247.00 to 253.00
Cabin, J. & E. Stevens, Cast Iron, 4 1/4 In	805.00
Cadet, Cast Iron	425.00
California Raisins, 1987	15.00 to 25.00
Calumet Baking Powder, Paper Label, 6 In	225.00
Camel, Cast Iron, 4 3/4 In	121.00 to 180.00
Camel, Cast Iron, 7 1/4 In	413.00 to 440.00

Camel, Kneeling, Cast Iron, 2 1/2 In.	687.00
Camel, Oriental, Cast Iron, 3 3/4 In.	605.00
Campbell Kids, Cast Iron, 3 5 /16 In.	330.00
Can Shape, Pabst Beer	15.00
Captain Kidd	290.00
Car, 1917 Model T, Coors Malted Milk	13.00
Car, 1939 Model Mercury Sedan	60.00
Car, 1940 Model Ford Sedan Delivery, Sturgis No.2, Hood Opens To Engine	60.00
Car, Buick, Arcade, Cast Iron, 8 In.	1100.00
Car, Chevrolet, White Metal, 2 7/8 In.	71.00
Car, Ford Touring Car, Removable Chauffeur, Cast Iron, Arcade, c.1923, 6 1/2 In.	690.00
Car, Limousine, Green	3500.00
Car, Nash, Banthrico	125.00
Cash Register, Crescent, J. & E. Stevens Co., 6 In.	460.00
Casper, Coin In One Hand, Money Bag, Ceramic, Marked USA, 1960s, 3 x 5 x 8 In.	200.00
Casper The Friendly Ghost, American Bisque	395.00 to 450.00
Castle, Cast Iron, 3 In.	577.00
Cat, Cast Iron	55.00 to 100.00
Cat, Grapette	50.00
Cat, In Egg, Ceramic, 2 3/8 In.	93.00
Cat, With Ball, Cast Iron	290.00
Cat, With Bow, Seated, Cast Iron, 4 3/8 In.	302.00
Cathedral, Tin, Chein	75.00 to 85.00
Charlie Tuna, Ceramic	35.00 to 65.00
Chest, White Clay, Amber Glaze, 6 3/4 In.	770.00
Chewbacca, Ceramic	120.00
Chinaman, Mammy, Ceramic, 3 1/4 In.	330.00
Chippendale's Strip Joint Man, Sitting, Vinyl, 16 1/2 In.	95.00
Chocolate Cow, Tin, Cow Picture	40.00
Chuck E. Cheese, Plastic	16.00
Church Towers, Cast Iron, 6 3/4 In	715.00
Circus Elephant, Cast Iron, 3 7/8 In.	275.00
City Bank With Chimney, Cast Iron, 6 3/4 In.	3080.00
City Bank With Teller, Cast Iron, 5 1/4 In.	550.00
Clown, Cast Iron, 6 3/16 In.	66.00 to 165.00
Clown, Del Monte Foods	40.00
Clown, Grapette, Glass	38.00 to 60.00
Clown Bust, Ceramic, 3 1/2 In.	247.00
Colonial House, Cast Iron, 4 In.	99.00
Coronation Crown, White Metal, 3 1/2 In.	25.00
Cow, Celluloid	85.00
Crowing Rooster, Tin	1870.00
Cupola Bank, Cast Iron, 4 1/8 In.	175.00
Cupola Building, Cast Iron, 3 1/4 In.	225.00
Daffy Duck At Tree Trunk, White Metal, 4 1/4 In.	121.00
Darth Vader	100.00
Destroyer, Chalkware, 4 1/2 In.	44.00
Dime Register, Cannon, Save For Victory, Tin, Wood	200.00
Dime Register, Dopey	100.00
Dime Register, Kiddie Clock	20.00
Dime Register, New York Life Insurance Co., Calendar	125.00
Dime Register, Prudential Dual Registering, Cast Iron, 7 3/8 In.	302.00 to 440.00
Dime Register, Snow White, 1938	115.00
Dime Register, Trunk, Cast Iron, 3 3/4 In.	99.00
Dime Register, Uncle Sam	35.00
Dog, Fido On Pillow, Cast Iron, 5 3/4 In.	264.00
Dog, Fido, Hubley, 5 In.	65.00
Dog In Doghouse, Lead, 2 7/8 In.	412.00
Donkey, Cast Iron, 4 1/2 In.	66.00
Double Door, Cast Iron	165.00
Doughboy, Cast Iron, 7 In.	962.00
Dr. Zaius, Plastic, 1967	25.00
Duck, Cast Iron, 4 3/4 In.	286.00

Duck, White Metal, 5 1/8 In.	121.00
Duck On Tub, Cast Iron, 5 3/8 In.	143.00
Dutch Boy, Cast Iron, 8 1/2 In.	190.00
Dutch Boy On Barrel, Cast Iron, 5 5/8 In.	71.00
Dutch Boy On Barrel, Cast Iron, 9 1/2 In.	75.00
Dutch Girl, Cast Iron	110.00
Dutch Girl, Standing, Cast Iron, 6 1/2 In.	825.00
Dutch Girl With Flowers, White Metal, 5 1/2 In.	60.00
Eagle, Immigrant, Ceramic, Box	45.00
Eagle On Rock, Ceramic, 5 In.	170.00
Electrolux Vacuum Cleaner	50.00
Elephant, Grapette	18.00
Elephant, Seated, White Metal, 5 In.	55.00
Elephant, Tin, c.1920, 5 In.	65.00
Elf With Tree Trunk, Lead, 2 5/8 In.	165.00
Elmer Fudd At Tree Trunk, White Metal, 5 1/2 In.	85.00 to 137.00
Elsie The Cow, Borden's, Wall, Gardner Corbin, Inc., 1940-1950	495.00
Enarco Oil Co., Gear Compound, Gun Grease, Small Version Of Can, 3 x 3 In.	55.00
Esso, Tiger's Head, Plastic	50.00
Faith, Hope & Charity	4025.00
Felix The Cat, Ceramic	13.00 to 55.00
Ferdinand The Bull, Composition	125.00
Fidelity Safe, Cast Iron, 3 In.	143.00
Fidelity Trust, 6 Point Star On Side, Cast Iron, 1930s	48.00
Filter Queen Canister Vacuum Cleaner, Plastic, Gold & Brown, 1950s, 4 x 4 In.	70.00
Fortune Ship, Cast Iron, Brighton Moore, No.1457	900.00 to 1800.00
Fortune Teller, Savings, Baumgarten & Co., 5 1/2 In.	575.00
Foxy Grandpa, Cast Iron	295.00
Fred & Wilma Flintstone, American Bisque	290.00
G.E. Refrigerator, Cast Iron, 3 3/4 In.	143.00
G.E. Refrigerator, Cast Iron, 4 1/4 In.	187.00
G.E. Refrigerator, Green, Small	65.00
Gas Pump, Sinclair Gasoline, 1960s	90.00
General MacArthur Bust, White Metal, 5 7/8 In.	25.00
General Pershing, Original Paint	450.00
General Pershing Bust, Cast Iron, 7 3/4 In.	55.00
General Sheridan	705.00
Globe, Cast Iron, 5 3/8 In.	165.00
Globe, Coin Sorter, Tin, Chein, c.1920, 4 In.	50.00
Globe, Tin	10.00
Golliwog, Standing, Red & Blue, Cast Iron, 6 1/2 In.	245.00
Gothic, Tin 4 1/8 In.	44.00
Gothic Bank, Time Is Money, Tin, 4 1/4 In.	55.00
Hall Clock, Cast Iron, 5 5/8 In.	412.00
Hansel & Gretel, Tin Lithograph, Box, Germany	20.00 to 30.00
Home Savings, Cast Iron, 3 1/2 In.	220.00
Home Savings, Cast Iron, 5 3/4 In.	357.00
Home Savings, Cast Iron, 10 1/2 In.	1200.00
Home Savings, Cast Iron, J. & E. Stevens	295.00
Honey Bear, Cast Iron, 2 1/2 In.	935.00
Horse, Prancing, Cast Iron	85.00 to 135.00
Horse, Rearing, Cast Iron	25.00
Horse On Tub, Cast Iron, 4 5/16 In.	220.00
Horse On Tub, Decorated, Cast Iron, 5 5/16 In.	192.00
Horseshoe, Good Luck, Buster Brown & Tige, Cast Iron.	250.00
House, Tin, Smoke Decorated, 19th Century, 7 1/2 x 7 1/2 In.	431.00
House, With Basement, Black, Red Bricks, Ohio Foundry Co., c.1893, 5 x 4 In.	1610.00
House With Bay Window, Cast Iron, 4 7/8 In.	2200.00
Howard Johnson's, Restaurant Shape	28.00
Humpty-Dumpty, Tin 5 1/4 In.	220.00
Humpty-Dumpty, White Metal	15.00
I Hear A Call, Cast Iron, 5 3/8 In.	275.00
Ice Cream Freezer, 1902	65.00

Icebox, Souvenir, Alaska, Cast Iron 225.00
Indian, Cast Iron .... 60.00 to 120.00
Indian, With Tomahawk, Cast Iron .... 175.00 to 325.00
Institution For Savings, Tin, 4 In. 275.00
Jean Lafoote, Cap'n Crunch, Vinyl, 7 1/2 In. 150.00
Jukebox, Windup, Plastic, Ideola 125.00
Kangaroo, Kirby Vacuum Cleaner, Vinyl 45.00
Liberty Bell, 1926 Sesquicentennial, Cast Iron, 3 3/4 In. 55.00
Liberty Bell, With Yoke, Cast Iron & Steel, 3 3/8 In. .... 11.00 to 16.00
Lilliput, Red, White, Blue, Halls 1850.00
Lindbergh, Bust, Aviator Dress, Cast Iron, 9 In. 295.00
Lindbergh, Painted Gold, Cast Metal, Grannis & Tolton, U.S., c.1929 .... 250.00
Lion, Cast Iron, 2 1/2 In. 165.00
Lion, Open Mouth, Cast Iron, 5 In. .... 65.00 to 85.00
Lion, Tail, Cast Iron, 4 In. 44.00
Lion Of Lucerne, Ceramic, 4 1/2 In. 247.00
Little Lulu, 7 1/2 In. 45.00
Little Lulu, With Carriage 65.00
Little Sprout, Ceramic 55.00
Loaf Of Bread, Wonder 20.00
Log Cabin, Ceramic 25.00
Lucky Joe, Nash's Mustard, Glass .... 22.00 to 26.00
Lucky Savings Bank, Tin, 5 In. 176.00
Magic, Green, Iron .... Illus 1150.00
Magic Chef, Vinyl, 7 1/2 In. 18.00
Magic Safe, White Metal, 4 1/2 In. 55.00
Mailbox, Cast Iron, 3 3/4 In. 36.00
Mammy, Cast Iron 65.00
Mammy, Hands On Hips, Cast Iron, 5 1/4 In. 231.00
Mammy, With Spoon, Cast Iron, 5 7/8 In. 302.00
Man Astride Sack, Ceramic, 3 1/2 In. 308.00
Marky Maypo, Vinyl 55.00
Master's House, Iron 1870.00
McColl's Peanut Butter, Ceramic, 6 In. 20.00

Mechanical banks were first made about 1870. Any bank with moving parts
is considered mechanical. The metal banks made before World War I are the
most desirable. Copies and new designs of mechanical banks have been made
in metal or plastic since the 1920s.

Mechanical, 2 Kids, Cast Iron, 4 1/2 In. 1402.00
Mechanical, 2-Car Garage, Cast Iron, 2 1/2 In. 175.00
Mechanical, 3 Stars, Cast Iron 660.00
Mechanical, Always Did 'Spise A Mule, J. & E. Stevens, Worn Paint, 10 In. 650.00
Mechanical, Always Did 'Spise A Mule, J. & E. Stevens, 10 In. 8800.00
Mechanical, Bad Accident 3600.00
Mechanical, Bad Accident, Cast Iron, Worn Paint, 11 In. 715.00
Mechanical, Balky Mule, Lehmann 495.00
Mechanical, Bank Of Industry, Cast Iron, 5 3/8 In. .... 150.00 to 209.00
Mechanical, Battleship Ohio 900.00
Mechanical, Bear & Tree Stump, Cast Iron 550.00
Mechanical, Bear On Hind Legs, Cast Iron, 6 1/8 In. 110.00
Mechanical, Bear With Honey Pot, Cast Iron, 6 1/2 In. 132.00
Mechanical, Bear, Seated With ABC Ball, White Metal, 4 7/8 In. 110.00
Mechanical, Billy Bounce, Cast Iron 4 11/16 In. 907.00
Mechanical, Billy Goat, J. & E. Stevens, 5 1/2 In. .... 550.00 to 1725.00
Mechanical, Bird On Roof, J. & E. Stevens, 4 3/16 In. 1725.00
Mechanical, Bird On Stump, Chalkware, 11 In. 357.00
Mechanical, Birdhouse, Tin, 5 1/4 In. 143.00
Mechanical, Birdie Putt, Cast Iron, 7 In. 231.00
Mechanical, Boy On Trapeze, J. Barton Smith, Cast Iron, c.1891, 5 In. .... 1725.00 to 3450.00
Mechanical, Boy Scout Camp, J. & E. Stevens Co., 9 7/8 In. 1850.00
Mechanical, Boy Scout, Cast Iron, 5 7/8 In. 99.00

Bank, Mechanical, Mammy & Child,
Kyser & Rex Co., Excellent Paint,
7 1/2 In.

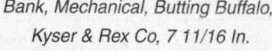

Bank, Mechanical, Butting Buffalo,
Kyser & Rex Co, 7 11/16 In.

Mechanical, Bull Dog Savings Bank, Windup, Ives, Blakeslee, 8 1/2 In.......... 960.00 to 1850.00
Mechanical, Bulldog, Seated, Chalkware, 11 3/4 In. 357.00
Mechanical, Bulldog, Standing, Cast Iron 742.00
Mechanical, Butting Buffalo, Kyser & Rex Co, 7 11/16 In. ....*Illus* 5175.00
Mechanical, Butting Goat, Judd Mfg., 4 3/4 In. 460.00
Mechanical, Butting Goat, White, Cast Iron 2970.00
Mechanical, Cabin, J. & E. Stevens, Cast Iron, 1885, 4 3/16 In. ....1045.00 to 1610.00
Mechanical, Cabin, Serrated Roof, Green Cabin, J. & E. Stevens, 3 1/2 In................... 660.00
Mechanical, Calamity, Football Action, Pre-1940... 250.00
Mechanical, Cat & Mouse, Cat Balancing, J. & E. Stevens, 5 3/8 In. ....1035.00 to 2530.00
Mechanical, Cat With Long Tail, Cast Iron, 4 3/8 In... 1210.00
Mechanical, Chief Big Moon, J. & E. Stevens, Cast Iron, 1899, 10 In. ....1265.00 to 2450.00
Mechanical, Chinaman, Moves Arm, Reveals Cards, J. & E. Stevens, 8 1/2 In. 1430.00
Mechanical, Church, Tin, Chein, 4 7/8 In... 55.00
Mechanical, Circus Elephant, Cast Iron, 3 7/8 In. 253.00
Mechanical, Clown On Globe, J. & E. Stevens, Cast Iron, c.1890 ....3500.00 to 5175.00
Mechanical, Clown, Chein, Tin.. 58.00 to 115.00
Mechanical, Clown, Square Kit, Tin, Chein, 5 In.. 121.00
Mechanical, Columbian Magic Savings Bank, Cast Iron, Introduction Co......... 207.00 to 357.00
Mechanical, Creedmoor, Man Firing Into Tree, 9 3/4 x 6 In. .... 355.00 to 825.00
Mechanical, Darktown Battery, J. & E. Stevens, c.1888 .... 990.00 to 3500.00
Mechanical, Darktown Battery, Pitcher Tossing Coin, Book Of Knowledge, Iron......... 165.00
Mechanical, Darky In Cabin.. 675.00
Mechanical, Dentist, Hammacher Schlemmer, 1990s 35.00
Mechanical, Dentist, J. & E. Stevens Co., 9 1/2 In.. 4830.00
Mechanical, Dinah, Cast Iron, 5 1/2 x 6 1/2 In... 385.00
Mechanical, Dog In Doghouse Door, Tin, 2 In.. 165.00
Mechanical, Dog On Box With Stand, Tin & Lead, 3 3/4 In. 330.00
Mechanical, Dog On Turntable .... 300.00 to 523.00
Mechanical, Dracula, Hand Ready To Snatch Coin, Battery Operated, 1960s. 115.00
Mechanical, Eagle & Eaglets, Iron, J. & E. Stevens, 1883, 6 11/16 In. .... 635.00 to 1300.00
Mechanical, Economy Is Wealth, Gothic, Tin 4 1/4 In.....:.. 33.00
Mechanical, Elephant & 3 Clowns ....3250.00 to 5500.00
Mechanical, Elephant On Bench On Tub, Cast Iron, 3 7/8 In.. 110.00
Mechanical, Elephant On Tub, Decorated, Cast Iron, 5 3/8 In. 121.00
Mechanical, Elephant With Blanket, Cast Iron, 3 1/8 In. 715.00
Mechanical, Elephant With Blanket, Ceramic, 3 In.. 55.00
Mechanical, Elephant With Raised Trunk, Ceramic With Metal Trap, 5 1/2 In. 22.00
Mechanical, Elephant With Tucked Trunk, Cast Iron, 2 3/4 In. 198.00

Mechanical, Elephant, 3 Stars.. 625.00
Mechanical, Elephant, Aluminum, 4 1/2 In. 104.00
Mechanical, Elephant, Gold Trim, Aluminum Tail, Hubley, 1930s, 7 1/2 In. 517.00
Mechanical, Elephant, Howdah, Cast Iron, 2 1/2 In. 110.00
Mechanical, Elephant, Howdah, Man Pops Out, Cast Iron 522.00
Mechanical, Elephant, Howdah, Pull Tail, Aluminum, 4 3/4 In. 115.00
Mechanical, Elephant, Howdah, Pull Tail, Cast Iron 1127.00
Mechanical, Elephant, Howdah, Pull Tail, Wright, Box 85.00
Mechanical, Elephant, Lifts Trunk, Chein, Tin Lithograph 110.00
Mechanical, Ferris Wheel, Hubley 6900.00
Mechanical, Football Kicker, Wooden Ball Attached To String, Cast Iron, 8 In. 385.00
Mechanical, Football Player, Cast Iron 435.00
Mechanical, Football Player, Cast Iron, 5 7/8 In. 467.00
Mechanical, Frog On Rock, Cast Iron.. 1100.00
Mechanical, Frog On Round Base, J. & E. Stevens, Cast Iron 605.00
Mechanical, Frog, Round Base, J. & E. Stevens.. 460.00
Mechanical, Frogs, J. & E. Stevens Co., 8 1/2 In.. 460.00
Mechanical, Girl Skipping Rope, Key, 17 Revolutions, J. & E. Stevens, 8 In. 11500.00
Mechanical, Hall's Excelsior, Teller, Cast Iron, J. & E. Stevens, 5 In............... 410.00 to 605.00
Mechanical, Hen On Nest, Cast Iron, 3 In. 1210.00
Mechanical, Hen On Nest, Ceramic, 3 1/2 In. 220.00
Mechanical, Home Bank, Brass & Cast Iron, 4 In. 308.00
Mechanical, Home Bank, Cast Iron, 5 1/2 In.. 4675.00
Mechanical, Hoop-La, Cast Iron 6710.00
Mechanical, Horse Race, J. & E. Stevens, 4 3/8 In. 1150.00
Mechanical, House With Dormers 6050.00
Mechanical, House, Two Story, Cast Iron, 3 1/16 In. 110.00
Mechanical, Humpty-Dumpty, Cast Iron, Excellent Original Paint 8800.00
Mechanical, Humpty-Dumpty, Coin In Clown's Mouth, Shepard Hardware, 1884 .... 575.00
Mechanical, Humpty-Dumpty, Shepard Hardware, Pat. 1883 .... 200.00 to 978.00
Mechanical, Independence Hall Tower, Bell Rings, Cast Iron, 1876, 9 1/2 In.... 440.00 to 632.00
Mechanical, Independence Hall, Cast Iron, 10 In. 577.00
Mechanical, Independence Hall, Enterprise Mfg., 1875 .... 575.00 to 3450.00
Mechanical, John Deere, Blacksmith With Sledgehammer, 1950s 170.00
Mechanical, Jolly Clown With Hat, Aluminum 203.00
Mechanical, Jolly Nigger, Aluminum.. 165.00
Mechanical, Jolly Nigger, Cast Iron, 6 In. 260.00
Mechanical, Jolly Nigger, Cast Iron, Steel.. 557.00
Mechanical, Jolly Nigger, Good Paint, Cast Iron... 1100.00
Mechanical, Jolly Nigger, Polychrome Paint, Cast Iron, 6 3/4 In. 445.00
Mechanical, Jolly Nigger, Red Jacket, Green Tie, 5 1/4 In..................................... 435.00
Mechanical, Jolly Nigger, Top Hat, 1880s.. 600.00
Mechanical, Jonah & The Whale, Shepard Hardware............................... 920.00 to 55000.00
Mechanical, Leap Frog, Shepard Hardware .... 2310.00 to 2420.00
Mechanical, Lilliput.. 650.00
Mechanical, Lion & Monkeys, Kyser & Rex, Cast Iron, 1883, 9 1/16 In. .... 800.00 to 2200.00
Mechanical, Lion Hunter, J. & E. Stevens, Cast Iron, 1911, 10 3/4 In. .... 4510.00 to 4600.00
Mechanical, Lion On Wheels, Cast Iron, 4 1/2 In. 187.00
Mechanical, Lion, Tail Left, Cast Iron, 3 3/4 In. 121.00
Mechanical, Little Joe, Cast Iron, 4 1/2 x 5 In. 110.00
Mechanical, Lost Dog, Cast Iron, 5 3/8 In. 385.00
Mechanical, Magic Bank, Cast Iron.. 1485.00
Mechanical, Magician, J. & E. Stevens, 4 In. 4025.00
Mechanical, Magician, Pink Flocking, J. & E. Stevens, Cast Iron, 1901, 6 3/16 In........ 3220.00
Mechanical, Mammy & Child.. 3500.00
Mechanical, Mammy & Child, Feeds Child, Cast Iron, 8 In. 1485.00
Mechanical, Mammy & Child, Kyser & Rex Co., Excellent Paint, 7 1/2 In. .... *Illus* 10350.00
Mechanical, Mammy & Child, Kyser & Rex, Cast Iron, 1884.................................... 6600.00
Mechanical, Mammy With Basket, White Metal, 5 1/4 In. 192.00
Mechanical, Milking Cow, J. & E. Stevens, 10 In. 4600.00
Mechanical, Monkey 990.00
Mechanical, Monkey & Cocoanut, J. & E. Stevens, 5 In. 1150.00
Mechanical, Monkey & Cocoanut, J. & E. Stevens, Cast Iron, 8 1/4 In.......................... 1760.00

Mechanical, Monkey & Cocoanut, James Bowen, Pat.1886 .... 3190.00
Mechanical, Monkey & Organ, Bell, Kyser & Rex, Cast Iron, 1881, 6 In. ....185.00 to 220.00
Mechanical, Monkey Tips Hat, Chein, Tin ....110.00 to 187.00
Mechanical, Monkey, Coin In Stomach, S.S. & S.D. Tallman 3220.00
Mechanical, Monkey, Hubley, Cast Iron, 1920s, 8 13/16 In. 632.00
Mechanical, Monkey, Square Kit, Tin, Chein, 5 1/2 In. 187.00
Mechanical, Mule Entering Barn, J. & E. Stevens, 8 1/2 In. ....575.00 to 1100.00
Mechanical, Novelty Bank, Cast Iron...2050.00 to 2750.00
Mechanical, Organ Bank, Cat & Dog, Cast Iron 5665.00
Mechanical, Organ Boy & Tambourine Girl, Cast Iron, Original Paint, 7 x 5 In. 990.00
Mechanical, Organ Grinder & Performing Bear, Kyser & Rex, 7 In............................ 5520.00
Mechanical, Owl, Slot In Book, Cast Iron.. 1210.00
Mechanical, Owl, Slot In Head, Cast Iron, Worn Paint 605.00
Mechanical, Owl, Turns Head, Cast Iron 632.00
Mechanical, Owl, Turns Head, Cast Iron, 1880 .... 4400.00
Mechanical, Owl, Turns Head, Cast Iron, 1950s 275.00
Mechanical, Owl, Turns Head, J. & E. Stevens, Cast Iron, 7 1/2 In. ....259.00 to 545.00
Mechanical, Paddy & The Pig, Original Paint, 8 In. ....2500.00 to 2550.00
Mechanical, Palace... 900.00
Mechanical, Panorama, J. & E. Stevens, 4 3/16 In.. 3220.00
Mechanical, Panorama, James Butler, Cast Iron, 1875... 2990.00
Mechanical, Pay Phone, Cast Iron & Steel 990.00
Mechanical, Pay Station Telephone, Plastic, 5 1/2 In.. 88.00
Mechanical, Pelican, Baseball Player, Thumbs Nose, Trenton Lock & Hardware, 8 In. 1800.00
Mechanical, Pig In High Chair, Cast Iron 1045.00
Mechanical, Postal Scale, U.S. Mail, Tin, Japan, Miniature 35.00
Mechanical, Professor Pug Frogs Great Bicycle Feat, Cast Iron, 10 1/2 In. ......230.00 to 2970.00
Mechanical, Punch & Judy, Fine Paint, Iron, 1884 .... 2750.00
Mechanical, Punch & Judy, Shepard Hardware, 1884, 6 1/8 In. ....2760.00 to 3450.00
Mechanical, Punch & Judy, Shepard Hardware, 1884, 7 1/2 x 6 In. 1150.00
Mechanical, Punch & Judy, Small Letter Variant 5720.00
Mechanical, Punch & Judy, Tin, 3 In.. 220.00
Mechanical, Rabbit In Cabbage, Cast Iron 1072.00
Mechanical, Rabbit On Mound, Ears Extend When Coin Drops, Cast Iron, 4 In. 220.00
Mechanical, Rabbit, Seated, White Metal, 4 1/2 In. 165.00
Mechanical, Rabbit, Standing, Bronze Plated, Lockwood, 5 3/4 In. ....435.00 to 880.00
Mechanical, Radio, Green, Cast Iron & Tin, 3 In. 286.00
Mechanical, Radio, Red, Cast Iron & Tin, 3 In. 231.00
Mechanical, Risque Pig, Cast Iron 165.00
Mechanical, Rocket, White Metal, 1 7/8 In...44.00 to 110.00
Mechanical, Rocket, White Metal, Vinyl, 13 In. 44.00
Mechanical, Rooster, Iron, Gold Paint 100.00
Mechanical, Rooster, Kyser & Rex, 6 1/2 In.. 1095.00
Mechanical, Santa Claus, 3 3/4 In. 467.00
Mechanical, Santa Claus, Iron, 6 In. 50.00
Mechanical, Santa In Chimney, White Metal, 5 In.. 280.00
Mechanical, Shot A B'ar, White Metal, 7 1/2 In. 220.00
Mechanical, Smyth X-Ray Bank, Cast Iron... 4125.00
Mechanical, Speaking Dog, J. & E. Stevens, Cast Iron ....450.00 to 2550.00
Mechanical, Tabby, White Metal, 4 1/4 In. ....148.00 to 165.00
Mechanical, Tammany, Cast Iron, 6 In. ....300.00 to 660.00
Mechanical, Teddy & The Bear, J. & E. Stevens, 10 1/2 In. 1840.00
Mechanical, Treasure Chest, Music Box, White Metal 6500.00
Mechanical, Trick Dog Bank, Cast Iron, 1888 .... 1815.00
Mechanical, Trick Dog, c.1920 .... 650.00
Mechanical, Trick Dog, Green Base, Cast Iron 1540.00
Mechanical, Trick Dog, Hubley, 1930s, 8 11/16 In... 517.00
Mechanical, Trick Dog, Penny, Cast Iron 125.00
Mechanical, Trick Pony, Cast Iron, Pat. 1885, 8 In... 575.00
Mechanical, Tricky Pig, Bronze, 5 In. 357.00
Mechanical, U.S. Mail, Large Trap, Cast Iron, 4 3/4 In. 110.00
Mechanical, U.S. Tank Bank, 1918, Cast Iron, 2 3/8 In. 137.00

Mechanical, U.S. Treasury Bank, Cast Iron & Steel, 3 1/4 In. 495.00
Mechanical, Uncle Sam's Hat, Glass, Tin, 2 1/2 In. 55.00
Mechanical, Uncle Sam's Hat, Tin 3 1/8 In. 38.00
Mechanical, Uncle Sam, Cast Iron, Pat. June 8, 1886, 11 1/4 In. 517.00
Mechanical, Uncle Sam, Shepard Hardware, 5 In. 3220.00
Mechanical, Uncle Sam, Tin, 3 1/4 In. 50.00
Mechanical, Uncle Tom, No Stars, Lapels, Cast Iron, 1882, 5 1/4 In. 550.00
Mechanical, Uncle Tom, Polkadot Tie, Lapels 875.00
Mechanical, Whale, Red, White Metal 605.00
Mechanical, Whale, White Metal 687.00
Mechanical, Wild West, Key 250.00
Mechanical, William Tell, J. & E. Stevens .... 490.00 to 1090.00
Mechanical, World Time Bank, Cast Iron & Paper, 4 1/8 In. 302.00
Merry-Go-Round, Cast Iron, 4 5/8 In. .... 115.00 to 660.00
Mighty Mouse, Vault, Box 40.00
Miss Piggy, Ceramic 65.00
Monkey, Tin, Chein, 3 x 5 1/2 In. 65.00
Mosque, Domed, Cast Iron 115.00
Musical Bank, Wood 99.00
Mutt & Jeff, Cast Iron, 4 1/4 In. .... 145.00 to 165.00
National Safe, Cast Iron, 4 3/8 In. 330.00
National Safe Deposit, Cast Iron & Tin, 5 7/8 In. 198.00
North Pole 650.00
Old Doc Yak, Cast Iron 875.00
Old South Church, Lead, 9 In. 770.00
Orange, Ceramic, 3 In. 44.00
Ornate Carved Coconut Shell, 2 1/2 In. 11.00
Panorama, Off-White, Lithograph ....*Illus* 5750.00
Penny Pineapple, Cast Iron, 8 5/8 In. 302.00
Pennzoil Motor Oil, Oil Can Shape, Red & Black Letters 80.00
Pig, Gattuso Olives, Glass 30.00
Pig, Iowana, Cast Iron, Decker, 2 1/4 x 4 1/4 In. 95.00
Pig, Seated, Cast Iron, 3 In. 49.00
Pig In Poke, Ceramic, 2 1/8 In. 132.00
Pillsbury Doughboy 30.00
Pillsbury Goose, Maddux 95.00
Platypus Duck, Fitz & Floyd, 1960 .... 50.00
Policeman, Arcade, 5 In. 305.00
Policeman, Cast Iron, 5 1/2 In. 660.00
Porky Pig, Metal 75.00
Post Office Box 35.00
Prancing Horse, Cast Iron, 7 3/16 In. 121.00
Preferred Life Building, Lead, 2 7/8 In. 209.00
Puppy, Black & White, Red Collar, Cast Iron, 5 In. 42.00
Raggedy Ann, Vinyl, Box, 15 In. 55.00
Red Goose Shoes, Cast Iron, 4 1/4 In. .... 135.00 to 185.00
Register, 3 Coins, Universal, 1905 .... 125.00
Register, Uncle Sam, 3 Coins, Durable Toy 35.00
Retriever, Pack On Back, Cast Iron 90.00
Rival Dog Food, Blue, Red, Yellow Lithograph, 1950s 33.00
Rocket, Astro, Plated, 12 In. 75.00
Rocket, Cast Iron, 1957 .... 43.00
Rocket & Planet, Plated, Strato, Salesman Sample, 8 In. 65.00
Rocky, Ceramic, Jay Ward Comic Character, Copyright 1960, 5 1/4 In. 174.00
Roof Bank, Cast Iron, 5 1/4 In. 302.00
Rooster, Chalkware, 10 In., Pair 165.00
Rumpelstiltskin .... 375.00 to 650.00
Saddle Horse, Cast Iron, 2 3/4 In. 187.00
Safe, Burglar Proof House, Ornate, J. & E. Stevens, 1870 .... 195.00
Safe, Cast Iron, 3 1/8 In. 55.00
Safe, Horse Design, Kenton, c.1911, 6 x 4 In. 165.00

Safe Deposit, Plated Cast Iron, Ideal 95.00
Santa Claus, Cloth, Tin, Rings Bell, Eyes Flash, Arms Move, Battery Operated, Japan   165.00
Santa Claus, Removable Tree, Cast Iron, 7 1/4 In. 935.00
Santa Claus, With Tree, Iron, 5 7/8 In. ....400.00 to 935.00
Saturn Guided Missile, Rocket Style, Rubber Cone, Tin, Box, 11 In. 220.00
Save Your Money, Cast Iron 190.00
Savings For Baby, Book, Iron 28.00
Scotty, Seated, Cast Iron, 4 7/8 In. 203.00
Scotty, Seated, White Metal, 4 3/4 In. 82.00
Scotty, Seated, White Metal, 6 In. 88.00
Scotty, Standing, Iron, 3 5/16 In. 110.00
Scrubbing Bubbles, Ceramic 10.00
Sea Lion, Arcade, Black Paint, 4 1/4 In. 488.00
Seamen's Saving Bank, Figural, Ceramic 55.00
Second National Duck Bank, Tin, 3 1/2 In. 137.00
Security Bank, 5 Coin, Tin, 7 In. 132.00
Security Safe, Cast Iron, 6 In. 297.00
Sharecropper, Painted, Cast Iron, 5 1/2 In. .... 150.00 to 225.00
Shopkeeper, Tin, 6 5/8 In. 302.00
Skyscraper, Cast Iron 3 9/16 In. 93.00
Skyscraper, Cast Iron, 5 1/2 In. 60.00
Skyscraper, Cast Iron, 6 1/2 In. 126.00
Smokey Bear, Seated, Ceramic 65.00
Snoopy, Basketball, Ceramic, 1966 .... 25.00
Snoopy, Glass 12.00
Snuffy Smith Hootin' Holler, Decal, Ceramic 65.00
Space Capsule, Alan Shepard Information On Base, 1961 .... 35.00
Speedy Alka-Seltzer, Rubber, Squeeze, 5 3/4 In. .... 235.00 to 350.00
Spiderman, Vinyl, Green Web, 1977 .... 43.00
Spinaround Planet, Box 225.00
Sport Safe, Cast Iron 90.00
St. Bernard, Pack, A.C. Williams, 7 1/2 In. 115.00
State, Cast Iron, 5 1/2 In. ....50.00 to 187.00
Statue Of Liberty, Cast Iron, c.1920, 6 1/2 x 10 In. ....50.00 to 187.00
Steamboat, 2 Slots, 2 Stacks, Gold, Cast Iron, A.C. Williams, 7 5/8 In. 95.00
Stork, Saving For Baby, Metal 30.00
Suitcase, Fold-Down Handle Top, Metal Tag, Bank Of Morley, Michigan 150.00
Suitcase, Tin 8.00
SunMaid, California Raisins 25.00
Tank, Cast Iron, 1919, 9 1/2 In. 632.00
Tank, Save For Victory, Chalkware, 5 3/4 In. 88.00
Teddy Bear, Cast Iron, 2 1/2 In. 209.00
Telephone Booth, Bell, Tin Lithograph, Japan, 1950s, 9 In. 175.00
Texaco, No. 3 .... 100.00
Thrifty Pig, Hubley 185.00
Tom & Jerry, Tom Holding Jerry, Plastic, Transogram, 1960s 45.00
Toonerville Trolley, Tin Lithograph, Turning Wheels, Penny Toy, 1 1/2 In. 355.00
Town Hall Bank, Cast Iron, 4 5/8 In. 1272.00
Trader's Bank, Yonge St., Iron .... *Illus* 1495.00
Treasure Chest, Battery Operated ....55.00 to 100.00
Treasure Chest, Bowery Savings, New York City 20.00
Treasure Safe, J. & E. Stevens, 1897 .... 85.00
Troll, Pirate, 1960s, 8 In. 48.00
Trolley, Hershey's, 100th Anniversary 21.00
Truck, 1905 Ford, Anheuser Busch, No. 10, Ertl 19.00
Truck, 1905 Ford, Kodak, No. 2, Red Spokes, Ertl 75.00
Truck, Pick-Up, Ford, Indian Motorcycle, Red, Black, Chrome, Hood Opens, 1940 ...... 38.00
True Value, No. 5, Box 25.00
Trunk, Tin, 2 In. 38.00
Turkey, Cast Iron, 3 3/8 In. 137.00
Turkey, Cast Iron, Small 125.00
Tweety Bird, Composition, Milton Bradley 100.00

U.S. Mail, Cast Iron, 3 5/8 In.	38.00
U.S. Mail With Eagle, Cast Iron, 4 1/8 In.	121.00
U.S. Tank Bank, 1918, Cast Iron, 2 3/8 In.	55.00
Uncle Remus, Cast Iron, 5 In.	100.00
Uncle Sam, Purinton	150.00
Uncle Sam, With Umbrella	1200.00
Uncle Sam Bust, Ceramic, 4 3/8 In.	71.00
USN Spain, Rudder, Cast Iron, 9 1/4 In.	38.00
Vending Machine, Hershey Bar, 1960s	130.00
Victory V Bank, Ceramic, 5 1/2 In.	88.00
Villa, 1892, Cast Iron, 5 7/8 In.	550.00
Washington Bell	325.00
Washington Redskins, Helmet, Plastic, 3 x 4 In.	7.00
Watch Me Grow Tall, Tin, Apex	45.00
Wienermobile, Oscar Mayer, 9 1/2 In.	40.00
Wimpy, Cast Iron, 1940s	90.00
Windmill, Japan, Box, 3 1/2 In.	70.00
Wise Pig, Cast Iron, 6 5/8 In.	110.00
Woody Woodpecker, Ceramic	12.00 to 40.00
World's Fair Administration Building, Cast Iron, 6 In.	1595.00

BANKO, Korean ware, and Sumida are terms that are often confusing. We use the names in the way most often used by antiques dealers and collectors. Korean ware is now called *Sumida Gawa* or *Sumida* and is listed in this book in the Sumida category. Banko is a group of rustic Japanese wares made in the nineteenth and twentieth centuries. Some pieces are made of mosaics of colored clay, some are fanciful teapots. Redware and other materials were also used.

Butter, Cover, Enamel Flowers & Birds, Signed	195.00
Wall Pocket, Geisha, Mirror Image, 9 In., Pair	125.00

BARBED WIRE was first patented in 1867. Collectors want eighteen-inch samples.

2 Point, Orlando M. Pond, January, 1883, 18 In.	200.00
Block & Spike, A.G. Hulbert, April, 1884, 18 In.	200.00
Diamond, George Dewalt, February, 1885, 18 In.	150.00
Horn Barb, Dobbs-Booth, December, 1875, 18 In.	250.00
Loop Lock, A.W. Stevens, June, 1884, 18 In.	250.00
Spread With Center Barb, Ellwood, January, 1882, 18 In.	200.00
Stretcher	13.00

BARBER collectibles range from the popular red and white striped pole that used to be found in front of every shop to the small scissors and tools of the trade. Barber chairs are wanted, especially the older models with elaborate iron trim.

Back Bar, Porcelain Sterilizer, Marked DeWitt-Steri-Tool, 9 Sections	95.00
Cabinet, Eastlake, Cherry, Burl Veneer, 2 Doors, Marble, Mirror, 39 x 15 x 104 In.	1815.00
Cabinet, Razor, 3 Glass Shelves, 1 Door, Pine, 13 x 11 x 7 In.	75.00
Cabinet, Shop, Oak, 2 Glass Doors, 2 Small Drawers Over Doors, Tall	375.00
Chair, Carved Gargoyle Heads, Walnut, 1890	1000.00
Chair, Carved Lion's Heads, Walnut, 1880s	1100.00
Chair, Child's, Car, Packard, Restored, 1928	4510.00
Chair, Child's, Pedal Car, Packard Roadster, American National	5500.00
Chair, Child's, Porcelain Horsehead	2500.00 to 2850.00
Chair, Hercules, Tufted Velour, Cast Swan Supports, Metal Base, 46 x 48 In., Pair	3520.00
Chair, Hydraulic, Brass Plated Hardware, Mahogany, 49 x 47 In.	935.00
Chair, Koch, Iron & Oak, 48 x 36 In.	605.00
Chair, Koken, Nickel Plated, Padded Seat, Footrest & Headrest, 1930s	950.00
Chair, Koken, Porcelain	600.00
Pole, Koken, Leaded Glass	1250.00
Pole, Koken, Porcelain & Stained Glass, 48 In.	1200.00
Pole, Painted, Decorated, 19th Century, 59 In.	287.00
Pole, Red & White, Turned Wood, 66 In.	330.00

Pole, Red, White & Blue Stripes, Turned Wood, 73 In. 385.00
Pole, Wall Mount, Cast Iron, 44 In. 650.00
Pole, Wall Mount, Porcelain, Electrified, 48 x 12 In. 330.00
Pole, Wall Mount, Turned Ball At Ends, White & Red, Wooden, 72 In. 935.00
Pole, Wall Mount, Wooden, 36 x 14 1/4 In. 170.00
Shaving Brush, Bakelite Handle, Peerless 8.00

BAROMETERS are used to forecast the weather. Antique barometers with
elaborate wooden cases and brass trim are the most desirable. Mercury column barometers are also popular with collectors. It is difficult to find someone to repair a broken one, so be sure your barometer is in working condition.

A. Tarelli, Newcastle, England, 39 In. 550.00
Aneroid, LaEsmeralda, Philippines, Fitted Case, 1905 .... 92.00
Aneroid, Nautical, Oak Case, 32 In. 99.00
Banjo, Federal, Mahogany, 36 In. 430.00
Banjo, Mahogany, G.Introvini, Manchester, England, 19th Century, 37 3/4 In. 345.00
Banjo, Mahogany, Inlaid, 38 1/2 In. 332.00
Banjo, String, Shell & Floral Inlays, Mahogany, Lambardini, 39 In. 345.00
Brass Finial, Celti & Co., London, 38 1/2 In. 805.00
Charles Wilder, New Hampshire, 37 1/2 In. 1995.00
Charpentier, Louis XVI Style, Giltwood, Painted Dial, Paris, 36 1/2 In. 1265.00
Eastlake Style, Thermometer, Porcelain Faces, Carved, Turned, Victorian, 17 1/2 In. ... 180.00
Edwardian, Marquetry, Mahogany, c.1900, 41 In. 230.00
Eglomise, Diamond Shape, France 770.00
Louis XVI, Giltwood, Carved Scrolls & Drapery, Lovebirds, France, c.1780 .... 1200.00
Louis XVI Style, Giltwood, Painted Dial, Calsen, Paris, 37 1/2 In. 2185.00
Oak, Gothic, Carved, c.1870, 42 In. 373.00
Porcelain Dial, Carved Frame, c.1880 .... 300.00
Rodaris & Co., Walnut Veneer, 37 In. 632.00
Stick, Mahogany Case, 36 In. 550.00
Stick, Mercury, Brass, Blackened Metal, 38 In. 110.00
Victorian, Shaped Neck Over Numeral Dial, Walnut, 44 In. 515.00

BASKETS of all types are popular with collectors. Indian, Japanese, African,
Shaker, and many other kinds of baskets can be found. Of course, baskets are
still being made, so the collector must learn to tell the age and style of the
basket to determine the value.

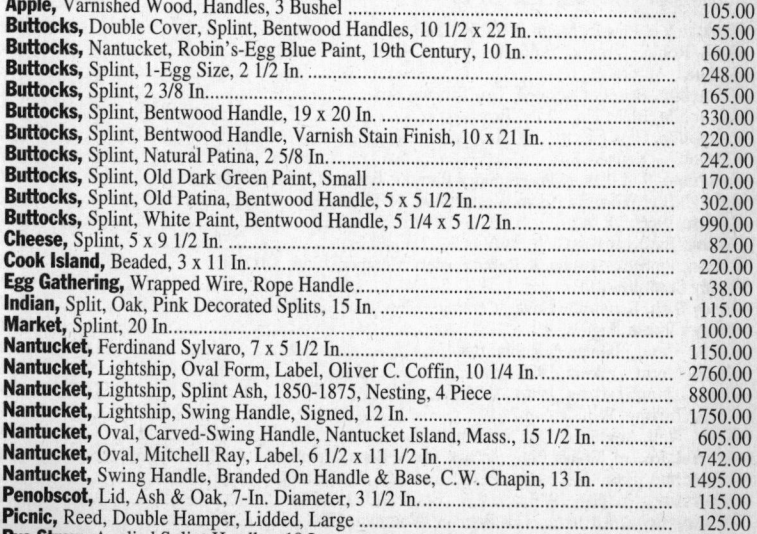

Apple, Varnished Wood, Handles, 3 Bushel 105.00
Buttocks, Double Cover, Splint, Bentwood Handles, 10 1/2 x 22 In. 55.00
Buttocks, Nantucket, Robin's-Egg Blue Paint, 19th Century, 10 In. 160.00
Buttocks, Splint, 1-Egg Size, 2 1/2 In. 248.00
Buttocks, Splint, 2 3/8 In. 165.00
Buttocks, Splint, Bentwood Handle, 19 x 20 In. 330.00
Buttocks, Splint, Bentwood Handle, Varnish Stain Finish, 10 x 21 In. 220.00
Buttocks, Splint, Natural Patina, 2 5/8 In. 242.00
Buttocks, Splint, Old Dark Green Paint, Small 170.00
Buttocks, Splint, Old Patina, Bentwood Handle, 5 x 5 1/2 In. 302.00
Buttocks, Splint, White Paint, Bentwood Handle, 5 1/4 x 5 1/2 In. 990.00
Cheese, Splint, 5 x 9 1/2 In. 82.00
Cook Island, Beaded, 3 x 11 In. 220.00
Egg Gathering, Wrapped Wire, Rope Handle 38.00
Indian, Split, Oak, Pink Decorated Splits, 15 In. 115.00
Market, Splint, 20 In. 100.00
Nantucket, Ferdinand Sylvaro, 7 x 5 1/2 In. 1150.00
Nantucket, Lightship, Oval Form, Label, Oliver C. Coffin, 10 1/4 In. 2760.00
Nantucket, Lightship, Splint Ash, 1850-1875, Nesting, 4 Piece 8800.00
Nantucket, Lightship, Swing Handle, Signed, 12 In. 1750.00
Nantucket, Oval, Carved-Swing Handle, Nantucket Island, Mass., 15 1/2 In. 605.00
Nantucket, Oval, Mitchell Ray, Label, 6 1/2 x 11 1/2 In. 742.00
Nantucket, Swing Handle, Branded On Handle & Base, C.W. Chapin, 13 In. 1495.00
Penobscot, Lid, Ash & Oak, 7-In. Diameter, 3 1/2 In. 115.00
Picnic, Reed, Double Hamper, Lidded, Large 125.00
Rye Straw, Applied Splint Handles, 19 In. 2185.00

Splint, Bentwood Handle, Round, 15 x 9 1/2 In. 225.00
Splint, Bentwood Rim Handles, Round, 7 x 20 In. 247.00
Splint, Cheese, Weathered Gray Finish, 26 1/2 In. 247.00
Splint, Goose Feather, Bentwood Rim Handles, 21 1/2 In. 225.00
Splint, Half, 2 1/8 In. 121.00
Splint, Herb Drying, Openworked Bottom, Bentwood Handle, 23 x 25 1/2 In. 220.00
Splint, Market, Round, Bentwood Handle, 3 1/4 In. 522.00
Splint, Melon Rib, Bentwood Handle, Orange Painted Trim, 19 In. 330.00
Splint, Melon Rib, Round, Bentwood Handle, 15 x 16 In. 22.00
Splint, Picnic, Hinged Lid, Swivel Handle, Green Paint, 14 In. 176.00
Splint, Rectangular, Bentwood Handle, 14 x 21 In. 82.00
Splint, Reed, Oblong, Old Patina, Bentwood Handle, 3 3/8 x 6 1/4 In. 220.00
Splint, Round, 15 1/2 x 19 In. 70.00
Splint, Wooden Bottom, Bentwood Rim Handles, Oblong, 11 x 21 1/2 In. 220.00

BATCHELDER products are made from California clay. Ernest Batchelder established a tile studio in Pasadena, California, in 1909 and expanded until in 1916 he built a larger factory with a new partner. The Batchelder-Wilson Company made all types of architectural tiles, garden pots, and bookends. The plant closed in 1932. In 1936 Batchelder opened Batchelder Ceramics, also in Pasadena, and made bowls, vases, and earthenware pots. He retired in 1951 and died in 1957. Pieces are marked *Batchelder Pasadena* or *Batchelder Los Angeles*.

**BATCHELDER
LOS ANGELES**

Ashtray, Hexagonal, Blue Matte, c.1925, 4 1/2 In. 175.00
Bookends, Tan & Blue 150.00
Bowl, Advertising, 2 x 4 In. 425.00
Tile, 2 Doves, White Clay, Blue & Brown Slip, Marked, 3 3/4 In. 94.00
Tile, 5 Animals & Birds, Dealer Tile, Die Stamped, 3 3/4 In., 6 Piece 385.00
Tile, Buff Clay Lion, Matte Blue Ground, Marked, 3 3/4 In. 248.00
Tile, Cartoon-Type Hunter, Dog, Red Clay, Matte Yellow Ground, Stamped, 4 In. 88.00
Vase, Closed Rim, Mottled Glossy Blue Glaze, Marked, 5 1/2 In. 357.00
Vase, Mottled Chinese Blue Glaze, Signed, 6 1/4 In. 665.00
Vase, Pale Green High Gloss, Drip Glaze, 3 1/2 In. 275.00

BATMAN and Robin are characters from a comic strip by Bob Kane that started in 1939. In 1966, the characters became part of a popular television series. There have been radio and movie serials that featured the pair. The first full-length movie was made in 1989.

Bank, Joker, Plastic, Mego, 1974, 8 1/2 In. 40.00
Bank, Robin, Ceramic, 1966, Box 65.00
Batboat, Aurora 275.00
Batmobile, Battery Operated, Tin, Taiwan, Box 175.00
Batmobile, Blue, Tin, 12 In., Box 265.00
Batmobile, Husky Extra, 1960s 145.00
Batmobile, Kenner, Box 180.00
Batphone, Red Plastic, Programmed Phrases, Battery Operated, Marx, 1966, 8 In. 900.00
Belt, Utility, Worn By Adam West, 1960s, 41 1/4 In., Box 865.00
Button, 1966, 7/8 In. 1.00
Button, Bat Kids Fan Club, 2 1/2 In. 2.00
Button, Pinback, Batman & Robin Society Member, 1966, 3 1/2 In. 25.00
Candy Container, PEZ 10.00
Candy Dish, Batmobile Cover, Ceramic, 1966 .... 135.00
Change Purse, Figural, 1966 .... 65.00
Clock, Alarm, Batman & Robin, Box .... 125.00 to 145.00
Clock, Alarm, Talking, 1974 .... 65.00
Clock, Alarm, Talking, Janex, 1975 .... 75.00 to 110.00
Clock, Talking, With Robin 130.00
Clock, Wall, Animated, On Card, England 35.00
Club Set, Record, Flasher Ring, Pinback, Comic Book, Membership Card, 1966, Box ..195.00 to 225.00
Colorforms, 1966 .... 14.00
Colorforms, No. 401, 1976 .... 60.00
Coloring Book, Adventures Of Batman, Whitman, 1966 .... 6.00
Coloring Book, Batman Meets Blockbuster, Whitman, 1966 .... 6.00

Comic Book, No. 9 .... 895.00
Costume, c.1950 .... 95.00
Doll, Penguin, Top Hat & Cloak, 9 In. 14.00
Game, 50th Anniversary 15.00
Game, Electronic Pinball, England, 1989 .... 98.00
Game, Gyro-Powered Stunt Cycle, On Car, 1974 .... 55.00
Game, Japan, 1966 .... 275.00
Glass, Black & Yellow Images, 1989, 8 Oz., 4 1/4 In., Set Of 6 .... 25.00
Gun, Escape, Red, Plastic, Dual-Action Launcher, Lincoln International, 1966 ......45.00 to 95.00
Jigsaw Puzzle, Game, No. 4693, Milton Bradley, 1966 .... 85.00
Lamp, Desk, Figural, Batman, Standing, Bat Cave 95.00
License Plate, Batmobile, Tin Lithograph, 1966 .... 35.00
Lunch Box, 1985 .... 85.00
Lunch Box, Action Scenes On All 4 Panels, Aladdin, 1966 .... 70.00
Model Kit, Batplane, Sealed, Aurora, 1967 .... 279.00
Mug, Milk Glass, Westfield, 1966 .... 18.00
Mug Set, Batman & Robin, Milk Glass, Fire-King, 1966 .... 28.00
Night-Light, Full Figure, 3 In., 1966 .... 30.00
Pedal Car, Power Wheels Batmobile, Box 200.00
Photograph, Batman & Robin, A. West & Burt Ward Autograph, Frame, 7 x 9 In. 20.00
Photograph, Batman, A. West Autographed, Frame, 8 x 10 In. 15.00
Poncho, Hooded, Mask, Batman Emblem, 1976 .... 32.00
Poster, Batwoman, 1966 .... 110.00
Puppet, Hand, Ideal, 1965 .... 85.00
Puppet, Marionette 25.00
Puzzle, Sliding, American Publishing, 1978 .... 12.00
Record, Album, TV Theme, 1960s 25.00
Record, Comic Book, Late 1970s, 45 RPM, Plastic Wrap 10.00
Reel, Viewmaster, Batman & Robin, Original 25.00
Ring, Bat, 1966 .... 25.00
Ring, Cartoon Flicker, 1960s 15.00
Roller Skates, Over The Shoe, Batman Face, 1966 .... 25.00
Siren, Figural 45.00
Sleeping Bag, Bat Girl, 1960s 225.00
Soaky, Batman & Robin, 1966, Pair ....65.00 to 85.00
Soccer Ball, Animated, Spain 30.00
Squirt Gun, Figural 45.00
Telephone, Batmobile, Box 36.00
Toy, Batboat, Coupling, Corgi, Box 250.00
TV Magazine, Full-Color Cover With Bat Signal, Boston, 1966 .... 40.00
TV Photo Flicker, 1960s 35.00
Wallet, Robin, Vinyl, 1966 .... 95.00
Wristwatch, Bat Shape, Gilbert 175.00
Wristwatch, Right Hand Holding Rope, Dabs Co., 1977 .... 125.00
Wristwatch, Robin, 1976 .... 85.00

BATTERSEA enamels, which are enamels painted on copper, were made in
the Battersea district of London from about 1750 to 1756. Many similar
enamels are mistakenly called *Battersea.*

Box, Man Wearing Wig 365.00
Box, Mirrored & Scene Cover, Dots, Esteem The Giver, 1 1/2 In. 275.00
Box, Patch, Blue Swag & Floral Vignettes, Pink Ground, 19th Century, 3 1/4 In. 195.00
Box, Patch, Cover, Figural Designs, Putti Painting, c.1800, 2 In. 1325.00
Box, Patch, Legend, Blue & White, Red Dots, 19th Century, 1 3/4 In. 150.00
Box, Patch, Legend, Pink & Black, Cover, 19th Century, 1 5/8 In. 210.00
Box, Pink Polychrome Cover, Hobby Horse, 1 3/4 In. 305.00
Box, Virtue Is The Greatest Ornament, Pink, White, 1 3/4 In. 575.00

BAUER pottery is a California-made ware. J.A. Bauer moved his Kentucky
pottery to Los Angeles, California, in 1909. The company made art pottery
after 1912 and dinnerwares marked *Bauer* after 1929. The factory went out of
business in 1962.

Bowl, Beater, Ring, Yellow, 5 In. 35.00

Bowl, Mixing, Ring, Bluish Green	40.00
Bowl, Mixing, Ring, Yellow	25.00
Bowl, Organic Form, Gunmetal Glaze, Russel Wright, 5 x 13 In.	1320.00
Butter, Cover, Ivory	65.00
Butter, Cover, Ring, Blue	175.00
Butter, Cover, Ring, Orange	135.00
Butter, Cover, Ring, Red	150.00
Candlestick, 2-Light, Cal-Art, White, Pair	45.00
Canister, Coffee, Wooden Cover, Hand Painted, Oval	58.00
Carafe, Orange Ring, Copper Fittings	80.00
Carafe, Red, Copper Fittings	85.00
Carafe, Ring, Orange, Copper Fittings	80.00
Casserole, Cover, Warmer, Metal Stand	55.00
Casserole, Ring, Red, Rack	145.00
Charger, Ring, Red, 17 In.	225.00
Chop Plate, Ring, Cobalt Blue, 12 1/2 In.	75.00
Chop Plate, Ring, Green, 12 1/2 In.	65.00
Chop Plate, Ring, Yellow, 12 1/2 In.	65.00
Coffee Set, Carafe, Ring, Red, Yellow & Red Tumblers, 7 Piece	275.00
Cup & Saucer, Ring, Yellow, Demitasse	175.00
Custard, 2 Handles	10.00
Jar, Oil, Medium Green, No. 100	750.00
Mixing Bowl, No. 12	35.00
Pitcher, Ring, Black	240.00
Pitcher, Ring, Red	75.00
Planter, Vertical Ribs, Black, Round, 5 3/4 In.	35.00
Plate, Cobalt Blue, 10 3/4 In.	85.00
Plate, Orange Red, 9 In.	20.00
Plate, Ring, Black & White, 10 In.	75.00
Plate, Ring, Green, 10 3/4 In.	75.00
Plate, Ring, Yellow, 5 In.	40.00
Relish, 5 Sections, Ring, Orange	75.00
Sherbet, Ring, Yellow	65.00
Sherbet, Ring, Yellow, Low	35.00
Stack Set, Leftover, Ring, Yellow	75.00
Sugar Shaker, Orange Red	225.00
Sugar Shaker, Ring, Red	225.00
Teapot, Hi Fire, Rust	125.00
Teapot, Monterey	70.00
Teapot, Orange Red	150.00
Teapot, Ring, Cobalt Blue	135.00
Teapot, Ring, Red	175.00
Vase, Atlanta	125.00
Vase, Corsage, No. 3	39.00
Vase, Mission, Tan, Green, 9 In.	225.00
Vase, Russel Wright, Organic Ovoid Shape, Gray & White Speckled, 5 In.	214.00

BAVARIA is a region in Europe where many types of porcelain were made. In the nineteenth century, the mark often included the word *Bavaria*. After 1871, the words *Bavaria, Germany,* were used. Listed here are pieces that include the name *Bavaria* in some form, but major porcelain makers, such as Rosenthal, are listed in their own categories.

Ashtray, Rose Medallion, Gold, Maroon Border, Flowers & Lattice, 4 1/4 x 3 1/4 In.	9.00
Bowl, Rose Buds, Leaves, Scalloped, 10 x 2 1/4 In.	35.00
Bowl, Roses, Daises, Scalloped, 11x 3 In.	75.00
Cake Stand, Floral Spray, Scrolled Blank, 10 1/2 x 4 1/2 In.	18.00
Chocolate Set, Roses, Woman Oval Scenes, Gilt, 5 Piece	60.00
Dessert Set, Strawberries, Hand Painted, 7 Piece	130.00
Dish, Hand Painted, Handles, Signed	85.00
Dish, Oak Leaf, White & Pink Blossoms, Gold Stem, 4 1/2 x 11 In.	20.00
Figurine, Bathing Beauty, Pastel Enameled, Marked, 7 In.	148.00
Pitcher, Gold Leaf Dragonflies & Butterflies, White Art Co.	185.00
Plate, Arbutus, Pink & Green Flower Border, Gold Trim, 7 3/4 In.	12.00

Plate, Reticulated, Roses Transfer, Schumann, 10 In. 10.00
Powder Box, Red, Lover's Transfer, Square, Schwarzhammer, 1948 .... 33.00
Powder Jar, Porcelain, Multicolored, A.Koch, Round, 1940, 3 x 6 In. 45.00
Tray, Lotus Blossoms, Double Handles, Pale Blues & Greens, Gold Edge, Artist, 8 In.. 17.00
Vase, Pink Top, Colorful Flowers On White, Gold Trim, 9 1/4 x 5 1/4 In. 12.00

BEATLES collectors search for any items picturing the four members of the
famous music group or any of their recordings. Because these items are so
new, the condition is very important and top prices are paid only for items in
mint condition. The Beatles first appeared on American network television in
1964. The group disbanded in 1971. Ringo Starr, George Harrison, and Paul
McCartney are still performing. John Lennon died in 1980.

Award, Brass, Apple Form, 1st Apple Single, Hey Jude, 4th September, 1968, 4 In. 3105.00
Bank, Head, Package, 1964 .... 25.00
Banner, 4 Beatles In Black, Printed Nylon, 1966, 44 x 58 In. 1150.00
Binder, 3-Ring, Red, Vinyl, Standard Plastic Products 145.00
Brush, Autographed Picture Card, 1960s, Sealed 45.00
Brush, Photograph Of 4, Display Package 9.00
Bust, John Lennon, Bronze, Glasses, Wooden Base, 12 1/2 In. 2588.00
Cake Decorating Set, Plastic Figures, Holding Instruments, Blue 12.00
Card Set, 220 Piece 20.00
Change Purse, Blue Plastic, Spring Opening, Pictures 4 Beatles 10.00
Change Purse, Pictures, NEMS, 1964 .... 6.00
Coin Wallet, Red, Snap, 4 Enclosed Signed Pictures 55.00
Color Flickers, Green, Red, Blue, Black, 1960s, 4 Piece 45.00
Coloring Book, Saalfield, Partly Colored 22.00
Disk-Go-Case, 1966 .... 115.00
Doll, Bobbin' Head, Hand Painted, Car Mascots Inc., 1964, 8 In., Set Of 4 ....425.00 to 920.00
Doll, Hamilton Gilts, 10 In., Set Of 4 .... 65.00
Doll, Ringo, Blow-Up, 1964 .... 55.00
Eraser, 4 Pictures, 2 1/2 In. 1.00
Figurine, John Lennon, George Harrison & Ringo Starr, Goebel, 1968, 3 Piece 5750.00
Figurine, Plaster, 14 In., 4 Piece 290.00
Figurine, With Instruments, 1964, Set Of 4 .... 300.00
Glass Set, Joseph Lang & Co. Ltd., London, Box, 4 Piece 1035.00
Jacket, 1964 Tour, Great Britain 950.00
Key Ring, Official Fan Club Issue, Photograph 1 Side, Logo On Back, 1964 .... 4.00
Knife, John Lennon Picture, October 9, 1940, To December 8, 1980, 2 Blades 5.00
Lobby Card, Hard Day's Night 85.00
Lunch Bag, Vinyl, 4 Faces 325.00
Lunch Box, Metal, 1966 .... 250.00
Lunch Box, Yellow Submarine, Thermos, 1968 ....195.00 to 375.00
Pencil Case, Red, White & Blue, Pictures, NEMS, 1964 .... 9.00
Pennant, Red & White, Pictures All 4, Wool, 1964, 30 In. 20.00
Pillow, 1964 .... 75.00
Pillow, Character, Blue Suits On White Ground, Red Ties, Guitars, 1964, NEMS 200.00
Pin, Fan Club, Photograph, Color, 2 1/4 In. 2.00
Pin, Figural, George, Package, 4 In. 20.00
Pin, Get Your Beatles Buttons Here, Color 2.00
Pin, Guitar, Pictures 4 Beatles, On Card, NEMS, 1964 .... 20.00
Pin, Sgt. Pepper, Set Of 4 .... 25.00
Pin, Yellow Submarine 50.00
Pin, Yellow Submarine, King Features, England, 1968, 3/1/2 In., Set Of 4 .... 19.00
Pin, Yellow Submarine, Pictures, 1 1/4 In., Set Of 4 .... 6.00
Postcard, London Concert Promotion, Photograph, 1963 .... 2.00
Postcard, Peppermint Lounge, Color, Paul McCartney, Ringo Starr, John Lennon 402.00
Poster, Beatles Picture, Dell, 1965 .... 55.00
Poster, Beatles Playing Instruments, Hand Painted, 1960s, 6 In. 50.00
Poster, Original Concert, 1965 .... 250.00
Puzzle, Yellow Submarine, Put Together, 1968, Box ....60.00 to 120.00
Record, Help, Photo Sleeve, 45 RPM 20.00
Record, Let It Be, Apple, 33 RPM 10.00
Record, Sgt. Pepper, Apple, 33 RPM 12.00

Record, Starting Over, John Lennon, 45 RPM 10.00
Ring Set, Flicker, Picture Of Different Beatle On Each Ring, 1960s, Set Of 4 .... 25.00 to 35.00
Ruler, Photograph, Gold, Birthdays, NEMS, 12 In. 5.00
Scarf, 4 Heads, Instruments & Records, White Ground, Box 25.00
Sheet Music, Day Tripper, 1964 .... 20.00
Soaky, Bubble Bath, Paul McCartney, 1965 .... 200.00
Song Book, Help, Japan 30.00
Thermometer, Fan Club, Photographs, Autographs, 7 1/2 In. 5.00
Towel, Beach 35.00
Tray, Photograph Of 4, 13 x 13 In. 25.00
Wig, On Card 125.00
Wig, Package 55.00
Wrapper, Gum, Group Silhouette, Official Beatles Fan Club, NEMS, 1964 .... 1.00

BEEHIVE, Austria, or Beehive, Vienna, are terms used in English-speaking
countries to refer to the many types of decorated porcelain bearing a mark
that looks like a beehive. The mark is actually a shield, viewed upside down.
It was first used in 1744 by the Royal Porcelain Manufactory of Vienna. The
firm made porcelains, called *Royal Vienna* by collectors, until it closed in
1864. Many other German, Austrian, and Japanese factories have reproduced
Royal Vienna wares, complete with the original shield or *beehive* mark. This
listing includes the expensive, original Royal Vienna porcelains and many
other types of beehive porcelain. The Royal Vienna pieces include that name
in the description.

Plate, Girl Holding Mirror, Gold Rim, Hearts, Trees, Bird, Marked, 9 1/2 In. 795.00
Plate, Portrait, Ruth, Gold Trim On Rim, 9 3/4 In. 1195.00
Plate, Seated Girl, Raised Gold Border, Signed Wagner, 9 1/2 In. 805.00
Powder Box, Cobalt Blue Border, Marked 70.00
Tea Set, Tavern Scene, Signed Fisher, 4 Piece 250.00
Urn, Cover, Neo-Classical, Gilt Tracery, Mythological Scene, Handles, 18 1/2 In., Pair 4840.00
Vase, Woman's Portrait, Long Black Hair, Turquoise Beading, Marked, 9 3/4 In. 1050.00

BEER CANS are a twentieth-century idea. Beer was sold in kegs or returnable
bottles until 1934. The first patent for a can was issued to the American Can
Company in September of that year; and Gotfried Kruger Brewing Company,
Newark, New Jersey, was the first to use the can. The cone-top can was first
made in 1935, the aluminum pop-top in 1962. Collectors should look for cans
in good condition, with no dents or rust. Serious collectors prefer cans that
have been opened from the bottom.

Ace Hi, Extra Strong Stamped On Lid, Flat Top, 1960s 22.00
Ace Lager, Australia, Pull Tab 3.00
Acme, Acme Bottling Co., San Francisco 32.00
Alt Seidel Brau, Student Prince Castle, Germany, 12 Oz. 4.00
Ambassador, Flat Top, 1950s 15.00
Arnold Pilsener, Germany, 5 Liter 4.00
Ballantine Ale, Copper Lid, 1950s 8.00
Banner, Flat Top, 12 Oz. 7.00
Blackhawk, Davenport, Iowa, Cone Top 33.00
Brown Derby, Flat Top, 12 Oz. 20.00
Bruenig's, Cone Top 6.00
Bull Dog, Acme Bottling, Flat Top 55.00
Bull Dog Ale, Grace Bros. Brewing 17.00
Burgermeister, Flat Top, 1950s 20.00
Burgermeister, Silver Ground 27.00
Canadian Ace, Chicago, Cone Top 21.00
Coburger, Old Dutch Brewing Co., Flat Top, 12 Oz. 11.00
Croft, Flat Top 4.00
Crystal Rock White Label, 1950s 15.00
Dommelsch Pilsener, Germany, 5 Liter 4.00
Eastside Old Tap, Flat Top, 11 Oz. 9.00
El Rancho, 1960s 8.00
Famous Beverwyck Ale, Cone Top, Albany, N.Y. 52.00
Fitzgerald's, Troy, N.Y., Crowntainer 40.00

Fort Pitt, Fort Pitt Brewing Co., Instructional 400.00
Fox Head Sparkling Malt Liquor, 12 Oz. 7.00
Fursten Pils, Germany, 5 Liter 6.00
Gilde Pilsener, Wood Grain, Germany, 5 Liter 4.00
Gold Brau, Flat Top 5.00
Gold Fassel Pils, Germany, 5 Liter 6.00
Grain Belt, Cone Top 12.00
Guarana, Primeiro, Brazil, Pull Tab 4.00
Heidel-Brau, Cone Top 11.00
Highlander, Missoula Bottling Co., Flat Top 10.00
Hyde Park 75 .... 31.00
Iron City, Pitt Helmet, Football Schedule, 1974, Tab 77.00
Isenbeck, Germany, 1970s, 3.8 Liter 11.00
Krueger Cream Ale, Newark, N.J. 200.00
Kulmbacher Eku Pils, Germany, 5 Liter 6.00
Kutscher Alt, Wood Grain, Germany, 5 Liter 6.00
Lindener Spezial, Wood Grain, Germany, 5 Liter 4.00
Lowenbrau Munchen, Germany, 1960s 5.00
Monchshop Pilsener, Germany, 5 Liter 4.00
Old Topper, Rochester Bottling, Crowntainer 40.00
Old Vienna, Chicago, Ill. 24.00
Old Vienna, Maier Brewing Co. 18.00
Pabst Old Tankard Ale 10.00
Patrizier Pils, Wood Grain, Germany, 5 Liter 4.00
Pearl, San Antonio, Tex. 4.00
Peter Doelger, Harrison, N.J. 297.00
Piels 8.00
Reidenbach, Flat Top, 12 Oz. 24.00
Rheingold Scotch Ale, Flat Top, 1940s 21.00
Royal Pilsener, Cone Top 18.00
Schlitz, Dated 1954 .... 5.00
Schmidt Draft, Pull Tab, 16 Oz. 8.00
Shandy, White Bread, London, Pull Tab 1.00
Shenandoah, Crown Cork, Winchester, Va., 41st Annual 2.00
Sierra, Reno Bros., Cone Top. 82.00
Stag's Head Ale, Cone Top, 1950s 67.00
Storz-Ette, Orchid On Lid, 1950s 22.00
Tennent's Girl, Ann At Pool, 15 1/2 Oz. 10.00
Tennent's Girl, Ann On Bonnie Banks Of Loch Lomond, 15 1/2 Oz. 9.00
Tijuana, Multicolor, 1950s, 12 Oz. 16.00
Tube City, Cone Top, McKeesport, Pa., 12 Oz 50.00
Tucher Pilsener, Germany, 5 Liter. 4.00
Unset Burgerbrau, Wood Grain, Germany, 5 Liter 6.00
Walter's Bock, Pull Tab, 1960s 11.00
Welde, Wood Grain, Germany, 5 Liter 6.00
West End, S. Australia, Pull Tab 12.00
Westover, Pull Tab, 1960s 87.00
Wieninger, Germany, 5 Liter 5.00
Zunft Kolsch, Germany, 5 Liter 6.00

BELL collectors collect all types of bells. Favorites include glass bells, figural bells, school bells, and cowbells. Bells have been made of porcelain, china, or metal through the centuries.

Alice In Daliland, Salvador Dali, c.1970, Signed, 7 x 2 1/2 In. 495.00
Bronze, Lappet Border Below Shoulder Flange, Bowl Of Grapes, Buddhist, 20 In. 230.00
Chimes, Dinner, Resonator Box, Signed Quaint, Stickley Brothers, 10 x 11 1/2 In. 700.00
Cow, Strap, Brass Buckles, No. 1 & No. 3 Size, 2 Pieces 135.00
Dinner, With Yoke 125.00
Fire Engine, Base 275.00
Gong, Trolley, Brass & Iron, 12 x 9 x 4 In. 135.00
Hairpin Pattern, Glass, Clear, Iron & Wire Clapper, 5 3/4 x 3 1/4 In. 39.00
Railroad Size, Yoke & Harp, Brass 375.00
School, Cast Iron, National Bell Foundry, Saddle & Wheel, 26 In. 950.00

Shop, Brass, Steel Spring, c.1830, 2 1/2 x 3 In.	140.00
Sleigh, Brass, 15 Bells, Strap, Pat. 1878	120.00
Sleigh, Strap, 24 Bells	250.00
Sleigh, Strap, 29 Bells, 1870s, 90 In.	345.00
Sleigh, Strap, 34 Graduated Bells, 1 To 2 1/2 In.	350.00
Sleigh, Strap, Brass, 10 Bells, 3 Ft.	20.00
Sleigh, Strap, Brass, 20 Bells, 5 Ft.	26.00
Sleigh, Strap, Brass, 30 Bells, 6 1/2 Ft.	30.00
Sleigh, Strap, Nickel, 10 Bells, 3 Ft.	18.00
Sleigh, Strap, Nickel, 20 Bells, 5 Ft.	23.00
Tea, Woman's Head, Flowing Hair, Sterling Silver	125.00
Temple, Dragon Figural Top, Incised Design, Bronze, Chinese, 26 In.	2530.00
Wooden, Set, 1940s	50.00

BELLEEK china was made in Ireland, other European countries, and the United States. The glaze is creamy yellow and appears wet. The first Belleek was made in 1857. All pieces listed here are Irish Belleek. The mark changed through the years. The first mark, black, dates from 1863 to 1890. The second mark, black, dates from 1891 to 1926 and includes the words *Co. Fermanagh, Ireland.* The third mark, black, dates from 1926 to 1946 and has the words *Deanta in Eirinn.* The fourth mark, same as the third mark but green, dates from 1946 to 1955. The fifth mark, green, dates from 1955 to 1965 and has an R in a circle added in the upper right. The sixth mark, green, dates after 1965 and the words *Co. Fermanagh* have been omitted. The seventh mark, gold, was used from 1980 to 1993 and omits the words *Deanta in Eirinn.* The eighth mark, introduced in 1993, is similar to the second mark but is printed in blue. The word *Belleek* is now used only on the pieces made in Ireland even though earlier pieces from other countries were sometimes marked *Belleek.* These early pieces are listed by manufacturer, such as Haviland, Lenox, and Ott & Brewer.

Basket, 2nd Mark, Black	450.00
Basket, 3 Strand, Sprigged Flowers, 1st Mark, Black	795.00
Basket, Shamrock Shape, Spring Flowers, 1st Mark, Black	425.00
Bowl, Shell Plateau, Pink Trim, 2nd Mark, Black, 6 1/2 x 6 1/2 In.	295.00
Cake Plate, 4-Strand Thorn Handle, 3rd Mark, Black	600.00
Coffeepot, Harp, 6th Mark, Green	160.00
Coffeepot, Shamrock, 6th Mark, Green	185.00
Creamer, Neptune, Pink, 5th Mark, Black	80.00
Creamer, Undine, Girl, 2nd Mark, Green	95.00
Cup & Saucer, Artichoke, 1st Mark, Black	195.00
Cup & Saucer, Harp, Shamrock, 3rd Mark, Black	120.00
Cup & Saucer, Mask, Tea, 3rd Mark, Black	155.00
Cup & Saucer, Shamrock, 2nd Mark, Black	220.00
Cup & Saucer, Shamrock, Tea, 3rd Mark, Black	110.00
Cup & Saucer, Thistle, 1st Mark, Black	200.00
Dinner Set, Limpet Pattern, 59 Piece	1400.00
Dish, Heart, 3rd Mark, Green, 4 In.	50.00
Dish, Heart-Shaped Shell, 4th Mark, Green, 6 In.	25.00
Dish, Jelly, Nautilus On Coral, Oblong, 1st Mark, Black	200.00
Figurine, Erin Awakening From Her Slumber, Rocky Base, c.1870, 16 3/4 In.	690.00
Figurine, Leprechaun, Yellow Luster Trim, 2nd Mark, Black, 5 In.	445.00
Figurine, Pig, 2nd Mark, Black, 3 In.	375.00
Jar, Cover, Pineapple Shape, Gilt, 7 1/4 In., Pair.	155.00
Mug, Shamrock, 3rd Mark, Black	100.00
Pitcher, Harp Handle, 1st Mark, Black, 6 x 4 In.	325.00
Pitcher, Pink Roses & Shamrocks, 5th Mark, Green	85.00
Plate, 3rd Mark, Black, 7 In.	125.00
Plate, Butter, Shamrock, 3rd Mark, Black	67.00
Plate, Christmas, 1970	29.00
Plate, New Shell, 4th Mark, Green, 7 In.	305.00
Plate, Shamrock, 3rd Mark, Black, 6 1/4 In.	67.00
Salt, Green & Tan Leaves, Gold Trim, 3 Footed, Master, 2 1/8 In.	64.00
Sugar & Creamer, Neptune, 6th Mark, Green	90.00

Sugar & Creamer, Shamrock, 3rd Mark, Black... 120.00
Tea Set, 3rd Mark, Black, 3 Piece 585.00
Tea Set, Neptune, 2nd Mark, Black, 3 Piece 545.00
Tea Set, Shamrock, 3rd Mark, Black, 15 Piece.. 595.00
Teakettle, Shamrock, 5th Mark, Green 225.00
Vase, Cornucopia, 2nd Mark, Black, 5 1/2 In. 2100.00
Vase, Cornucopia, Ruffled Top, 2nd Mark, Black, 5 1/2 In., Pair.............................. 755.00
Vase, Cornucopia, Seahorse, White Base, 1st Mark, Black, 3 3/4 In. 325.00
Vase, Horn Shape, 9 In. 249.00
Vase, Horn, 2nd Mark, Black, 9 In.. 225.00
Vase, Shamrock, Tree Trunk, 2nd Mark, Black, 6 1/4 In.. 150.00
Vase, Tree Trunk, 2nd Mark, Green, 6 1/2 In. 95.00

BENNINGTON ware was the product of two factories working in Bennington, Vermont. Both the Norton Company and the Lyman Fenton Company were out of business by 1896. The wares include brown and yellow mottled pottery, Parian, scroddled ware, stoneware, graniteware, yellowware, and Staffordshire-type vases. The name is also a generic term for mottled brownware of the type made in Bennington.

Bottle, Book, Scroddled Ware, Applied Star, Label, 5 5/8 In. 2585.00
Bottle, Coachman, Marked Lyman Fenton, 1849, 11 In. 546.00
Creamer, Cow, Rockingham Glaze, 5 5/8 In. 247.00
Cuspidor, Scroddled Ware, Scalloped Rib, 9 1/4 In. 440.00
Figurine, Lion, Green & Red, Flint Enamel, Cole-Slaw Mane 3850.00
Figurine, Poodle, Mottled Brown & White, 8 /12 x 8 In. 6000.00
Flask, Book, Departed Spirits, Rockingham Glaze, 5 1/2 In. 292.00
Flask, Departed Spirits, Greens, Yellow-Browns, Flint Glaze, 1 Pt., 6 In. 580.00
Jar, Reclining Deer, 2 Fences, Tree & Stump, 2 Gal. 5720.00
Jug, Peacock On Stump, 3 Gal. 2640.00
Pitcher, Molded Grapes, Rockingham Glaze, Fenton, c.1845, 7 In. 165.00
Pitcher, Molded Hunt Scenes, Rockingham Glaze, 9 3/4 In. 88.00
Pitcher, Oak Trees, 5 In.. 135.00
Pitcher, Water, Parian, Wild Rose, 10 In... 195.00
Pot, Drip Glaze, Dimples, David Gil, 4 In. 60.00
Teapot, Molded Chinamen, Rockingham Glaze, 9 3/4 In. 93.00
Toby Bottle, Mustache & Tassel, L. Fenton & Co. Enamel, 1849, 10 In. 1450.00
Vase, Cottage, Classical Picture, 8 1/2 In., Pair 2500.00
Vase, Tapering Bulbous Form, 7 1/4 In., Pair 68.00

BERLIN, a German porcelain factory, was started in 1751 by Wilhelm Kaspar Wegely. In 1763, the factory was taken over by Frederick the Great and became the Royal Berlin Porcelain Manufactory. It is still in operation today. Pieces have been marked in a variety of ways.

Box, Cover, Rococo Cartouche, Gilt Edge, Silver-Gilt Collar, c.1765, 6 In. 1265.00
Plaque, Cupid With Reclining Sea Nymph, Signed, 7 In.. 5175.00
Plate, Antikzierat, 3 Birds Perched On Branch Center, Insects, c.1772, 9 3/4 In. 5462.00
Platter, Konisch, Gentleman Conversing With Lady, Octagonal, c.1790, 13 In. 690.00
Snuffbox, Cover, European & Turkish Encampment Scenes, c.1765, 3 1/8 In. 3162.00
Soup, Dish, Reliefziert, Center Floral Spray, Sprays On Rim, c.1773, 9 3/4 In. 4025.00
Tea Caddy, Palette Of Figures, Conversing By Tent, c.1775, 4 1/4 In. 575.00
Urinal, Swan Shape 1035.00
Vase, Cover, Sprays & Sprigs Of Tulips & Roses, c.1785, 11 5/16 In......................... 3450.00
Vase, Mask Sides, S Scrolling Dolphin Handles, Bronze Mounted, 10 1/2 In. 376.00

BESWICK started making earthenware in Staffordshire, England, in 1936. The company is now part of Royal Doulton Tableware, Ltd. Figurines of animals, especially dogs and horses, Beatrix Potter animals, and other wares are still being made.

Bust, Shakespeare, On Pedestal, No. 2243, 5 In. 60.00
Cornucopia, Palm Tree... 70.00
Figurine, American Blue Jay, No. 925 .... 60.00
Figurine, Appley Dappley.. 45.00

Figurine, Aunt Pettitoes	45.00 to 55.00
Figurine, Basset Hound, Ski Country	40.00
Figurine, Bay Foal	25.00
Figurine, Bay Horse	65.00
Figurine, Benjamin Bunny, With Peter Rabbit	95.00
Figurine, Blue Jays	90.00
Figurine, Border Collie, 3 3/4 In.	38.00
Figurine, Chippy Hackee	35.00 to 50.00
Figurine, Christopher Robin	95.00
Figurine, Cocker Spaniel	85.00
Figurine, Colt	25.00
Figurine, Fisher Digging	155.00
Figurine, Flopsy, Mopsy & Cottontail	50.00
Figurine, Foxy, Whiskered Gentleman	50.00 to 65.00
Figurine, Goody & Timmy Tiptoes	220.00
Figurine, Goody Tiptoes	55.00
Figurine, Horse, 4 In.	35.00
Figurine, Hunca Munca	55.00
Figurine, Irish Setter, On Plateau	195.00
Figurine, Jack Russell Dog	20.00
Figurine, Jeremy Fisher Digging	185.00
Figurine, John Townmouse	50.00
Figurine, Koala Bear, No. 1038, 3 1/2 In.	60.00
Figurine, Mr. Jackson	55.00
Figurine, Mr. Pricklepin	100.00 to 125.00
Figurine, Mrs. Tiggy Winkle	100.00
Figurine, Mrs. Tiggy Winkle Takes Tea	100.00
Figurine, Old Bardstown Bulldog	135.00
Figurine, Old Mr. Brown	55.00 to 60.00
Figurine, Orioles	90.00
Figurine, Parakeet	85.00
Figurine, Parsley	95.00
Figurine, Penguin, With Walking Stick	35.00
Figurine, Persian Cat, Standing, Gray, 5 In.	65.00
Figurine, Pheasant, In Flight	125.00
Figurine, Piggly Bland	60.00
Figurine, Potter's, Dog Sled	240.00
Figurine, Puppy Dog	65.00
Figurine, Raylene's Bulldog	50.00
Figurine, Siamese Cat, No. 1559	55.00
Figurine, Siamese Cat, Sitting, No. 1887, 4 In.	35.00
Figurine, Simpkin	450.00
Figurine, Sir Isaac Newton	300.00
Figurine, Tabby, Cat	25.00
Figurine, Tabitha Twichit	120.00
Figurine, Tailor Of Gloucester, Beatrix Potter	47.00
Figurine, Tanager	90.00
Figurine, Thomasina Tittlemouse	80.00
Figurine, Timmy Tiptoes	47.00 to 220.00
Figurine, Tiswell Pony & Rider	75.00
Figurine, Tom Kitten & Butterfly	220.00
Figurine, Woodpecker, Green, No. 1218, 9 In.	180.00
Figurine, Yorkie	80.00
Plate, America, 1978	55.00
Plate, Bulgaria, 1974	55.00
Plate, England, 1972	55.00
Plate, Mexico, 1973	55.00
Tankard, Christmas Carolers At Scrooge's Door, Dickens Ware, 1972, 5 1/8 In.	115.00
Tankard, Ghost Of Christmas Past, Dickens Ware, 1975, 5 1/8 In.	95.00
Teapot, Character	75.00
Teapot, Dolly Varden	110.00
Teapot, Peggotty	110.00
Vase, Palm Trees, Blown Out, Textured, Semimatte, 7 1/4 In.	65.00

BETTY BOOP, the cartoon figure, first appeared on the screen in 1931. Her face was modeled after the famous singer Helen Kane and her body after Mae West. In 1935, a comic strip was started. Her dog was named Bimbo. Although the Betty Boop cartoons ended by 1938, there was a revival of interest in the Betty Boop image in the 1980s and new pieces are being made.

Ashtray, With Bimbo	225.00
Bank, Figural, Ceramic	45.00
Bank, Vandor	95.00
Bookends, Vandor	113.00 to 225.00
Candleholder, Figural, Standing, Vandor	100.00
Cookie Jar, Head, Top Hat	175.00
Cookie Jar, Standing, Vandor	550.00 to 650.00
Doll, Box, 1984, 19 In.	195.00
Doll, Celluloid, Gold Hair, Movable Arms, Nude, 3 In.	10.00
Doll, Composition & Wood Jointed, Cotton Outfit, Cameo, Joseph Kallus, 11 In.	402.00
Doll, Composition Head & Body, Jointed Wood Arms & Legs, c.1930	450.00
Doll, Composition, Molded & Painted Hair & Dress, Fleischer Studios, 12 In.	900.00
Figurine, Full Figure, Vandor	995.00
Figurine, Theda, Chalkware, 9 In.	155.00
Mask, Face	45.00
Nodder, Windup, Celluloid	900.00
Parasol, Fleischer	250.00
Vase, Piano	65.00

BICYCLES were invented in 1839. The first manufactured bicycle was made in 1861. Special ladies' bicycles were made after 1874. The modern safety bicycle was not produced until 1885. Collectors search for all types of bicycles and tricycles. Bicycle-related items are also listed here.

5-Seater, Tigerquint Model, Steel Frame, Bells, Horns, Dutch, 14 Ft.	2875.00
Blue Star, Generator For Front & Back Light, England, 26 In.	75.00
Boneshaker, Forged Iron & Wood, Pin Striping, 36- & 32-In. Wheels, 75 In.	3250.00
Boneshaker, France, 1862	5600.00
Boneshaker, Iron & Wood, Green Pin Striping, Pad, c.1850	3200.00
Bowden, Spacelander, 1959	7500.00
Columbia, Boy's, 3 Star	475.00
Columbia, Girl's, 3 Star	1265.00
Dayton Streamliner, 26 In.	5720.00
Elgin Bluebird, Blue, Red Strip, Sears & Roebuck, Mid-1930s	9350.00
Elgin Robin, Red & White, Zeppelin-Shaped Tank On Top Tube, 26 In.	3680.00
Geo. L. Brownell, Red & Black, Leather Covered Seat, Wood & Iron, 46 x 65 In.	2310.00
High-Wheeler, Child's, 35 x 38 In.	440.00
High-Wheeler, Original Paint, 50-In. Front Wheel, 1880	2310.00
High-Wheeler, Spoked Front Wheel, Rubber Tires, c.1880, 68-In.Wheel	2875.00
High-Wheeler, Steel Frame & Handlebars, Leather Saddle, Rubber Tires, 51-In.Wheel	1495.00
Iver Johnson, Decals, Early 1900s	1200.00
J.C. Higgens, Girl's, Built-In Head Lamp & Taillight	55.00
License Plate, Detroit	22.00
Mercury Quad, 1890s	3190.00
Motor-Bike, Whizzer Sportsman, 21 In.	5500.00
Pink Panther, Japan	100.00
Roadmaster, Boy's, Streamlined Tank & Horn, 1941	525.00
Rollfast, Hopalong Cassidy, Western Style Saddle Bags, 24 In.	1870.00
Schwinn, Boy's, Stingray	250.00
Schwinn, Boy's, Western Flyer Buzz	250.00
Schwinn, Boys, Black Phantom, Restored	3500.00
Schwinn, Man's, Black Phantom, 26 In.	600.00
Schwinn, Woman's, 1941	450.00
Shelby, Airflow, 26 In.	2200.00
Shelby, Boy's, Neon Blue Trim, Blue Banana Seat, 1940s	300.00
Tricycle, Black Leather Seat, Black, 28 In.	132.00
Tricycle, Child's, Lever-Powered, Mixed Woods, 34 x 22 In.	198.00
Tricycle, Garton, 1931	450.00

Bicycle, Tricycle, Murray, Airflow Jr.
Style, Red, 17 1/2 In.

It is said creativity comes from a messy, cluttered environment. It inspires ideas. Remember that the next time you rearrange your collectibles. Looking back at our son's room we realize there may be a reason why he is in a creative business.

Tricycle, J.G. Rideout Type, 1930s	250.00
Tricycle, Murray, Airflow Jr. Style, Red, 17 1/2 In. ....*Illus*	220.00
Tricycle, Red & Black, Metal, c.1900, 29 In.	165.00
Tricycle, Wooden & Metal, 19th Century, 29 In.	165.00
Tricycle, Wooden Handlebars, Spoke Wheels, Orange	1600.00
Tricycle, Wooden, Blue & White Paint, Upholstered Seat, Iron Wheels, 35 x 51 In.	1650.00
Velocipede, Wire Spoked Wheels, Rubber Tread, 19th Century	275.00
Waverly, 1890s	310.00
Wolf-American, Side-By-Side, 2 Seats, Restored, 1930s	5170.00

BING & GRONDAHL is a famous Danish factory making fine porcelains from 1853 to the present. Underglaze blue decoration was started in 1886. The annual Christmas plate series was introduced in 1895. Dinnerwares, stoneware, and figurines are still being made today. The firm has used the initials B & G and a stylized castle as part of the mark since 1898.

B&G
TJOBENHAVN
MADE IN
DENMARK

Compote, Low, Flowers, Blue	55.00
Figurine, 2 Boys, No. 1648	115.00
Figurine, 2 Children With Coat, No. 2312	95.00
Figurine, Ballerina, Seated On Floor, 6 1/4 In.	250.00
Figurine, Bird, No. 1852	75.00
Figurine, Bird, No. 2310	75.00
Figurine, Blacksmith, At Anvil, No. 2225, 12 In.	500.00
Figurine, Boy Skier, No. 2358, 9 In.	295.00
Figurine, Boy, Kissing Girl, No. 2162, 8 In. .... 100.00 to	110.00
Figurine, Boy, With Bear, No. 2231	60.00
Figurine, Boy, With Cup, No. 1713	85.00
Figurine, Foundry Worker, 11 3/4 In.	250.00
Figurine, Girl, Feeding Cat, No. 1745	120.00
Figurine, Girl, With Cat In Apron, No. 1779	90.00
Figurine, Girl, With Doll, No. 1721	150.00
Figurine, Girl, With Purse, No. 1574, 6 1/2 In.	145.00
Figurine, Kitten, White	65.00
Figurine, Seal, No. 1733, 8 In.	150.00
Ornament, Christmas In America, 1986	50.00
Plaque, Figures Of Day & Night, White Parian, 11 3/8 In., Pair	295.00
Plate, 1949, Danish Soldier, Fredericia, Hyldahl	70.00
Plate, Christmas, 1895, Behind Frozen Windows	4425.00
Plate, Christmas, 1896, New Moon Over Snow-Covered Spruce Trees	1975.00
Plate, Christmas, 1898, Roses And Star	638.00
Plate, Christmas, 1900, Bells Chiming	750.00
Plate, Christmas, 1901, 3 Wise Men From East	356.00
Plate, Christmas, 1903, Children's Expectation, Hyldahl	150.00
Plate, Christmas, 1905, Anxiety Of Coming Night	150.00
Plate, Christmas, 1907, Little Match Girl, Plockross	125.00
Plate, Christmas, 1910, The Old Organist	90.00

Plate, Christmas, 1915, Chained Dog, Double Meal... 135.00
Plate, Christmas, 1920, Hare In Snow 75.00
Plate, Christmas, 1924, Lighthouse 74.00
Plate, Christmas, 1927, Skating Couple, Friis 125.00
Plate, Christmas, 1929, Fox Outside Farm 71.00
Plate, Christmas, 1931, Arrival Of The Christmas Train, Friis................................ 75.00
Plate, Christmas, 1963, Christmas Elf, Thelander ....63.00 to 120.00
Plate, Christmas, 1964, Spruce Tree, Thelander 26.00
Plate, Christmas, 1968, Church On Christmas Eve, Thelander......................12.00 to 17.00
Plate, Christmas, 1969, Christmas At Parsonage, Thelander 15.00
Plate, Mother's Day, 1971... 25.00
Sign, Dealer 60.00
Vase, Windjammer Eagle, Ovoid, 10 In... 400.00

BINOCULARS of all types are wanted by collectors. Those made in the eighteenth and nineteenth centuries are favored by serious collectors. The small, attractive binoculars called *opera glasses* are listed in their own category.

Celestron, Right-Angle Tripod Adapter, Case, 11 In.. 160.00
Lemaire, Case ....45.00 to 65.00

BIRDCAGES are collected for use as homes for pet birds and as decorative objects of folk art. Elaborate wooden cages of the past centuries can still be found. The brass or wicker cages of the 1930s are popular with bird owners.

4 Tiers, Late 19th Century 1800.00
Arched Dome, Brass, Brass Stand, 16 1/4 In. 85.00
Brass, Germany 150.00
Hanging, Bronze, 26 1/2 In... 4070.00
Hendryx, Cast Iron Stand ....65.00 to 95.00
Indonesian, White & Blue Trim 155.00
Mahogany, 5 Domed Cupolas, 32 Ornate Carved Columns, 60 x 60 x 96 In. 12500.00
Pagoda Shape, Oriental Design 100.00
Parcel Gilt Wire, Circular Turrets, 7 False Doors, Stand, Green, Victorian 9775.00
Parrot, Balloon Shape, Wrought Iron, French Style, 5 x 4 Ft. 330.00
Pavilion Form, Inlaid Floral Marquetry At Base, Walnut & Wire, 21 1/2 In. 550.00
Pierced Gallery, 2 Sliding Doors, Polychromed, Metal, Oriental, 33 1/2 In. 495.00
Tole, Birds, Geometric, Green Ground, 27 In. 192.00
Victorian-Style Stand, Parcel Gilt Mahogany, 73 In. 460.00
Whalebone, Arched Top, Door, Tapering Finials, 17 3/4 x 18 In................................ 8050.00
White, Wrought Iron, 2 Ft... 85.00
Wicker, Domed Top, White Paint 85.00

BISQUE is an unglazed baked porcelain. Finished bisque has a slightly sandy texture with a dull finish. Some of it may be decorated with various colors. Bisque gained favor during the late Victorian era when thousands of bisque figurines were made. It is still being made. Additional bisque items may be listed under the factory name.

Box, Egg Shape, Windmill, Footed 50.00
Figurine, Baby, Standing, Blowing Kiss 175.00
Figurine, Boy On Potty, Bottle, Germany, 3 1/2 In... 35.00
Figurine, German Boy, Accordion, Nubby Sweater 20.00
Figurine, Girl, With Basket, Barefoot, Continental, 12 1/2 In................................. 88.00
Figurine, Little Red Riding Hood & Wolf, Hand Painted, 8 1/2 In............................ 16.50
Figurine, Pastoral Pair, Binoculars, Gold Beading, Pastel Colors, 9 In........................... 50.00
Flowerpot, Figural Carriage, Blue, Pink, Gold Dots 140.00
Planter, Girl, Basket, Pastel Colors, Gold Trim, Hat & Dress, Germany, 7 x 7 x 3 In. ... 75.00
Plaque, Napoleon Profile, Green Ground, Bronze Dore Frame, 19th Century, 10 1/2 In. 550.00
Relish Jar, French Chef, Cardinal China.. 45.00
Salt, Figural, Man, Sitting By Basket, Germany 25.00
Tobacco Jar, Indian Head, Figural 165.00
Toothbruch Holder, Clown, Germany, 5 In.. 155.00
Toothbrush Holder, Boy, Playing Violin, Little Dog, Japan, 5 In. 65.00
Toothbrush Holder, Boy, With Flowers, With Picnic Basket, Japan, 4 1/2 In.............. 50.00
Toothbrush Holder, Cat, Seated, Art Deco, 4 In. 205.00

Toothbrush Holder, Dog, Seated, Germany, 4 3/4 In. 145.00
Toothbrush Holder, Duck & Bucket, Germany, 3 1/4 In. 135.00
Toothbrush Holder, Little Girl & Dog, Japan, 6 In. 88.00
Toothbrush Holder, Penguin, Painted & Glazed, Japan, 5 1/2 In. 143.00
Toothbrush Holder, Two Children, Wearing Goggles, Japan, 5 In. 155.00
Toothpick, Bearded Man, Elf Costume, Kneeling, Blue, Gold Dots, 4 In. 45.00

BLACK memorabilia has become an important area of collecting since the
1970s. The best material dates from past centuries, but many recent items are
also of interest. F & F is the mark used on plastic made by Fiedler & Fiedler
Mold & Die Works, Inc. in the 1930s and 1940s. Objects that picture a black
person may also be listed in this book under Advertising, Tins; Banks; Bottle
Openers; Cookie Jars; Salt & Pepper; Sheet Music; etc.

Ashtray, Coon Chicken Inn, Glass, 1950s .... 22.00 to 75.00
Book, Little Black Sambo 48.00
Book, Little Black Sambo, Linenette 48.00
Book, Little Black Sambo, Pop-Up, C. Carey Cloud, Blue Ribbon Press, 1934 .... 225.00
Book, Pickings, From The Picayune, New Orleans 165.00
Booklet, How To Get Up A Cake Walk, Illustrations, 31 Pages, 5 x 7 In. 22.00
Brush, Whisk, Americana Mandy, Box 45.00
Candleholder, Aunt Jemima, F & F, Pair 35.00
Cookie Jar, Black Chef, Star, Not Painted 150.00
Cookie Jar, Mammy, Southwest Colors, Hattie 150.00
Document, Inventory, Estate, Aaron Tilghman, Boy, Woman, Children, 1834, 7 3/4 In. ... 85.00
Doll, Boy, Cloth, Norah Wellings, England, 8 In. 160.00
Doll, Bye-Lo, Sleep Eyes, Celluloid Hands, Dress & Hat, 11 1/4 In. 1500.00
Doll, Cloth, 1940s, 9 1/2 In. 85.00
Doll, Diana & Wade, Aunt Jemima, Cloth, Uncut, 1924, Pair 335.00
Doll, Effanbee, Grumpykins, Composition Head & Hands, Cloth Body, 12 In. 275.00
Doll, Hannibal The Cannibal, Black Sock 37.00
Doll, Heubach Koppelsdorf, Baby, Bisque, Painted, Earring, 9 In. 225.00
Doll, Honeysuckle Mammy, Sachet, Box 195.00
Doll, Kammer & Reinhardt, Bisque Head, Brown Glass Eyes, c.1909, 11 In. .... *Illus* 3162.00
Doll, Mammy, Cloth, Tennessee, 1920s 50.00
Doll, Minstrel 275.00
Doll, Rag, Woman, Embroidered Face, Handmade Costume, 23 In. 165.00
Doll, Redd Foxx, Cloth, Double Sided, Redd Foxx Enterprises, 1976 .... 25.00

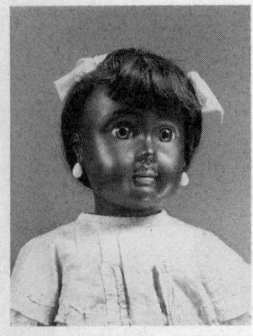

Black, Doll, Steiner, A Series, Bisque, c.1890, 27 1/2 In.

Black, Doll, Kammer & Reinhardt, Bisque Head, Brown Glass Eyes, c.1909, 11 In.

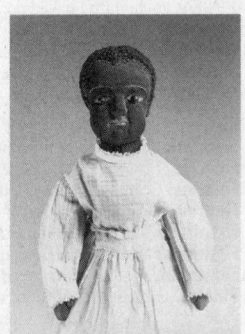

Black, Doll, Stockinet, Embroidered, Looped Wool Hair, 20th Century, 20 In.

Doll, Steiner, A Series, Bisque, c.1890, 27 1/2 In... *Illus* 6325.00
Doll, Stockinet, Embroidered, Looped Wool Hair, 20th Century, 20 In. .... *Illus* 4312.00
Doll, Wool Twill Body, Oilcloth Limbs, Embroidered Features, 18 In. 1380.00
Doll Set, Aunt Jemima Family, 4 Piece.. 795.00
Egg Timer, Black Chef, Germany 85.00
Figure, Ball Tossing Game, Black Minstrel Man, Open Mouth, Papier-Mache 3500.00
Figure, Dancing Sambo, Cardboard, Jointed, 1940s, 12 In. ....24.00 to 30.00
Figure, Pickaninnies Ride Alligator, Heads Jiggle When Shaken, Celluloid, 8 In. 100.00
Figurine, Blue Dress, Pink Drape, Turban, Bird, Cornucopia, Bisque, 1860, 11 x 3 In. . 550.00
Figurine, Boy Eating Watermelon, Bisque, 5 In. 65.00
Figurine, Boy On Potty, Holding Watermelon, Bisque, Japan, 4 In............................... 65.00
Figurine, Darky On Fence, Eats Watermelon, Lead, Painted, Manoil, 3 In. 75.00
Game, Little Black Sambo, Board 135.00
Game, Puzzle, Changeable Charlie 25.00
Handbill, Hire Of Negroes, Fayette County, Ga., 1831, 5 1/2 x 7 1/2 In........................ 45.00
Marriage License, Slave, Nathan Smith & Josey Johnson, Ga., Frame, 1870, 7 x 8 In.. 50.00
Menu, Coon Chicken Inn 45.00
Menu, Coon Chicken Inn, Small 65.00
Notepad, Mammy, Wooden, Painted, Folk Art 85.00
Pancake Shaker, Aunt Jemima, 1960s... 15.00
Pancake Shaker, Aunt Jemima, Pair.. 110.00
Paper, Estate Sale, Negro Woman, Anaka, Infant Child Called Arch, 1831 .... 700.00
Paperweight, Lawn Jockey, Cast Iron 25.00
Paperweight, Singing Butler 75.00
Picture, Coon Chicken Inn, 8 x 10 In. 22.00
Pie Bird, Black Chef, 1950s.. 75.00
Pin, Golliwog 20.00
Pin, Topsy Club 18.00
Pincushion Doll, Man, Carved Wood 55.00
Pincushion Doll, Tropicana 22.00
Plaque, Mammy, Chef, Green 95.00
Plate, 2 People, Talking On Phone, Cupid On Line, Saying On Bottom 145.00
Postcard, Hanging Of Black Man, Monroe, La., Photograph, 1910 .... 500.00
Postcard, Skinning A Coon, White Man Picking Pocket Of Black Woman, 1909 .... 27.00
Postcard, Who's A Nigger, Black Boy In Fight, c.1900 .... 30.00
Poster, Booker T. Washington, 1936, 20 x 16 In.. 125.00
Poster, Crosman Bros' Seed, Black Boys Carrying Watermelon, 23 1/2 x 16 3/4 In...... 1980.00
Poster, Dark Town Brotherhood Vs. Blackville Little League, Thatcher, 39 1/2 x 29 In. 4950.00
Poster, Hiram Sibley Seed, Black Boy Eating Watermelon, Frame, 24 1/2 x 16 In. 1705.00
Poster, Hy-Beavie Hair Dressing, 1940s, 10 x 14 In. 18.00
Poster, Minstrel Show, Dark Town Brotherhood, 39 x 29 In. .... *Illus* 4950.00
Poster, Poor Little Mose & Hatchet, Color, Outcault, Frame 80.00
Print, 10 Kids Peer Over Board Fence, Child Eating Watermelon, Oak Frame 135.00
Sheet Music, 3 Little Words, Amos 'n' Andy... 25.00

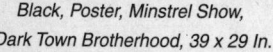

Black, Poster, Minstrel Show,
Dark Town Brotherhood, 39 x 29 In.

Black, Sign, Aunt Jemima Pancake Flour,
Jemima On Swing, Hanging, Die Cut, 17 1/2

Black, Sign, Aunt Jemima, Die Cut, Red, White, Yellow, Black, 21 In.

Sheet Music, Babylon Is Fallen, Black Civil War Infantry, 1862	125.00
Sheet Music, Carolina Mammy	25.00
Sheet Music, I Am Going There Or The Death Of Little Eva, Uncle Tom's Cabin	35.00
Sheet Music, Little Eva, Uncle Tom's Cabin, Uncle Tom's Guardian Angel, 1852	58.00
Sheet Music, Little Sam, Black Child Marches With Broom, 1869	85.00
Sheet Music, Old Folks At Home, Christy's Minstrels, Late 1800s	30.00
Sheet Music, Pickaninny Blues, Kickmann, 1919	7.00
Sheet Music, Plantation Melodies, Young Black Musicians, 1867	85.00
Sheet Music, Rastus On Parade, 1896	45.00
Sheet Music, Shew Fly, Minstrel Dancer, In Action, 1869	65.00
Sign, Aunt Jemima Breakfast Club, Hanging, Round, 6 In.	10.00
Sign, Aunt Jemima Flour, Cardboard, Hanger, 9 1/2 x 17 1/2 In. ....*Illus*	5940.00
Sign, Aunt Jemima Pancake Flour, Jemima On Swing, Hanging, Die Cut, 17 1/2 In.	6000.00
Sign, Aunt Jemima, Die Cut, Red, White, Yellow, Black, 21 In. ....*Illus*	5170.00
Soap Dish, Mammy, Painted, 1920	360.00
Spice Set, Aunt Jemima, F & F, 6 Piece	300.00
Spoon Rest, Mammy, Rockingham	175.00
Stand, Butler, Wooden, Painted, Folk Art, 36 In.	295.00
String Holder, Porter, Fredricksburg	200.00
Sugar & Creamer, Aunt Jemima, F & F	150.00
Sugar & Creamer, Clown	55.00
Sugar & Creamer, Mammy & Butler, F & F	125.00
Syrup, Aunt Jemima, F & F	75.00
Syrup, Mammy, F & F	65.00
Tablecloth, Mammy, Paper Label	98.00
Tea Towel, Chef	35.00
Teapot, Mammy	30.00
Teapot, Salt & Pepper, Clown	145.00
Thermos, Sambo	35.00
Toaster Cover, Mammy, Pressed Cardboard Top	20.00
Toothbrush Holder, Baker, Tray	400.00
Towel, Black Waiter Picture, Tray In Hand, Red, Black & Gray, 1940s, 15 1/2 x 29 In.	100.00
Tumbler, Coon Chicken Inn	45.00
Wall Pocket, Chef	225.00
Wall Pocket, Mammy	225.00

BLACK AMETHYST glass appears black until it is held to the light, then a dark purple can be seen. It has been made in many factories from 1860 to the present.

Ashtray, Round, 3 Cigarette Rests, 5 In.	8.00
Bowl, Cone Shape, Diamond Faceted Base	8.00
Bowl, Rolled Edge, Gold Encrusted Rim, 9 x 3 1/4 In.	30.00
Candy Dish, Cover, Cloverleaf Shape, 7 In.	22.00
Coaster, 5 In.	8.00
Decanter, Hunt Scene, Sterling Silver Overlay, Marked Scotch & Rye, Pair	135.00
Plate, Decagon, 8 In.	15.00
Plate, Round, 8 In.	4.50
Plate, Square, Open Work, 6 1/2 In.	20.00

Tumbler, Diamond Point, 10 Oz., 5 3/8 x 2 3/4 In. 8.00
Vase, Bud, Bulbous Bottom, Multicolor Floral Decal, 8 In. 15.00
Vase, Decagon, Ruffled, 4 In. 15.00
Vase, Enamel Scenes, White Herons Amid Swamp, Triangular, 7 1/2 In. 175.00

BLOWN GLASS was formed by forcing air through a rod into molten glass.
Early glass and some forms of art glass were hand blown. Other types of
glass were molded or pressed.

Bottle, Vinegar, Sapphire, 3 Mold, Flint 375.00
Candlestick, Pewter Insert, Clear, 11 1/4 In. 1980.00
Canister, Tin Lid, Clear, 13 In. 192.50
Cordial Set, Gilt, Stopper, Tray, Mahogany Case, 1780, 8 In., 4 Piece 725.00
Decanter, Cut Design, Panels, Engraved Fish, Flowers, Crane, Stopper, 7 7/8 In. 82.00
Decanter, Wine, Diamond, Etched Grape Band, Stopper, 14 In. 185.00
Decanter, Wine, Vintage, Stopper, Bohemia, 9 In. 75.00
Decanter Set, White Nude Women Stands, Bemini Werkstatte, 7 Piece 985.00
Ewer, Raspberry Pink, White Lining, Amber Applied Handle 125.00
Figurine, Bluebird, Ball Base, 13 1/2 In., Pair 247.00
Pitcher, Chain Design, Thomas Caine, Boston, c.1820, 6 1/4 In. 920.00
Pitcher, Clear, Hollow Handle, 8 3/8 In. 825.00
Pitcher, Milk, 3 Mold 1600.00
Pitcher, Olive-Amber, Lily Pad, Stoddard, 7 1/2 In. 6600.00
Pitcher, Water, Aquamarine, 1820-1830, 7 1/4 In. 2310.00
Steigel-Type, Rummer, Blown, Man, Hat & Long Frock, Scene 175.00
Tumbler, 3 Mold, Clear, 5 1/2 In. 137.50
Vase, Tulip, Wafer Stem, c.1830, 11 In. 175.00
Whimsy, Powder Horn, Clear, White Looping, Applied Rigaree, 10 In. 104.00
Witch's Ball, Double Cased, White, Blue & Violet Spotted, Germany, 6 x 6 In. 400.00
Witch's Ball, Teal Green, Closed Pontil, 5 1/2 In. 120.00
Witch's Ball, Tortoiseshell, Brown Splotches, Footed Metal Stand, 11 In. 200.00

BLUE GLASS, see Cobalt Blue category

BLUE ONION, see Onion category

BLUE WILLOW pattern has been made in England since 1780. The pattern
has been copied by factories in many countries, including Germany, Japan,
and the United States. It is still being made. Willow was named for a pattern
that pictures a bridge, birds, willow trees, and a Chinese landscape.

Bowl, 5 3/4 x 2 1/2 In. 22.00
Bowl, 6 1/4 x 1 1/4 In. 22.00
Bowl, Cereal, Flair, Japan, 6 1/2 In. 5.00
Bowl, Dipping, 12 Piece 275.00
Bowl, Homer Laughlin, 5 1/4 In. 3.50
Bowl, Sauce, Royal, Sebring, Ohio, 5 1/2 In. 3.50
Bowl, Soup, Ridgway 22.00
Bowl, Vegetable, Allerton 85.00
Bowl, Vegetable, Cover, Square, Stevenson & Sons, Pair 350.00
Bowl, Vegetable, Royal, 9 In. 12.00
Butter Chip, Allerton 22.50
Cake Plate, Maruyama 90.00
Cake Server, Maruyama 150.00
Casserole, 5 In. 25.00
Casserole, 7 1/4 In. 35.00
Cup & Saucer, Farmer 23.00
Cup & Saucer, Japan 12.00
Cup & Saucer, Meakin 12.00
Cup & Saucer, Occupied Japan 15.00
Cup & Saucer, Stacking 3.50
Fork & Spoon, Salad, Japan 20.00
Gravy Boat 25.00
Grill Plate, Japan, 9 3/4 In. 12.00
Lamp, Oil, 8 In. 60.00

Mug, Design On Handles & Inside, Japan 15.00
Pitcher, Milk, Abbey Pattern 110.00
Plate, Child's, Japan, 3 1/2 In. 5.00
Plate, Dinner, Meakin 18.00
Plate, Johnson Bros., 6 1/2 In. 3.00
Plate, Luncheon, Carter & Hall, 8 Piece 200.00
Plate, Meakin, 6 In. 8.00
Plate, Royal, 6 3/8 In. 3.00
Plate, Royal, Sebring, Ohio, 9 In. 5.00
Plate, Royal, Sebring, Ohio, 12 1/4 In. 15.00
Plate, Salad, Meakin 15.00
Plate, Senango, 7 In. 4.00
Platter, England, 7 x 14 In. 225.00
Platter, England, 14 x 17 In. 300.00
Platter, Homer Laughlin, 11 1/2 In. 16.00
Platter, Pre-1890, 16 In. 120.00
Platter, Ridgway, 15 1/2 In. 120.00
Saucer, Royal 1.00
Soup, Dish, Johnson Bros., 8 In. 9.00
Soup, Dish, Royal, Sebring, Ohio, 8 1/2 In. 8.00
Sugar & Creamer, Allerton 115.00
Sugar & Creamer, Cover, Child's, Japan 15.00
Sugar & Creamer, Cover, Meakin 40.00
Teapot, Meakin 65.00
Teapot, Sadler, England 150.00
Tumbler, Flat, 5 In. 12.00

BOCH FRERES factory was founded in 1841 in La Louviere in eastern Belgium. The wares resemble the work of Villeroy & Boch. The factory is still in business.

Bowl, Flowers, Green Leaves, 4 1/2 In. 75.00
Plate, Farm Scenes, 6 In. 22.00
Vase, Band Of Stylized Cranes, Crackled White, c.1925, 35 1/2 In. 9200.00
Vase, Fluted Panels, Black Outlining, White Crackle Ground, c.1922, 23 In. 862.00
Vase, Glazed Black Rings, Charles Catteau, c.1920, 5 1/4 In. 345.00
Vase, Polychrome Enamel Design, Black Outlining, c.1905, 9 In. 173.00
Vase, Stylized Birds, Charles Catteau, 1925, Pair 3700.00

BOEHM is the collector's name for the porcelains of Edward Marshall Boehm. In 1953 the Osso China Company was reorganized as Edward Marshall Boehm, Inc. The company is still working in England and New Jersey. In the early days of the factory, dishes were made, but the elaborate and lifelike bird figurines are the best-known ware. Edward Marshall Boehm, the founder, died in 1961, but the firm has continued to design and produce porcelain. Today, the firm makes both limited and unlimited editions of figurines and plates.

Bust, Madonna, 6 1/2 In. 150.00
Coffeepot, Rose, c.1956 .... 175.00
Figurine, American Bald Eagle, Young & Spirited, No. 400-49, c.1976, 9 1/4 In. ... 546.00
Figurine, Baby Bird Set, Goldfinch, Bluebird & Wood Thrush, 3 Piece 330.00
Figurine, Barn Owl, No. 1005, 20 x 25 1/2 In. 575.00
Figurine, Bird On 3 Rocks, White Flowers, 6 In. 110.00
Figurine, Black Grouse, 15 In. 575.00
Figurine, Black-Eared Wheatear, No. BJF-8, 13 x 8 In. 980.00
Figurine, Blue Jays, 29 x 9 In. 4600.00
Figurine, Bluebird, 13 x 9 In. 5400.00
Figurine, Crested Flycatcher, 19 In. 1430.00
Figurine, Cygnet, Pair 385.00
Figurine, Flowers, Daisies, No. 3002 .... 750.00
Figurine, Foxhound, Reclining 2500.00
Figurine, Golden Oriental Pheasant, No. 414, 8 x 19 In. 325.00
Figurine, Hooded Merganser, 14 In., Male, 13 In., Female, Pair 1320.00
Figurine, Hummingbird, No. 440 .... 900.00

Boehm, Figurine, Peregrine Falcon
With Young, 14 1/2 x 11 In.

Boehm, Figurine, Red-Shouldered
Hawk, 26 1/2 x 19 In.

Figurine, Jaguar, No. 500-20, 9 1/2 x 18 In. 515.00
Figurine, Jenny Wren, 6 In. ....220.00 to 230.00
Figurine, Junco, No. 400-12, 11 1/2 In. 285.00
Figurine, Lesser Prairie Chicken, 10 In., Pair 259.00
Figurine, Madonna, 9 1/4 In. 145.00
Figurine, Mallard, Male & Female, 10 1/2 x 12 In., Pair 550.00
Figurine, Meadowlark, 8 In. 316.00
Figurine, Mockingbirds, No. 459, 12 In. 750.00
Figurine, Mountain Bluebirds, No. 470, 12 1/2 x 16 In. 1725.00
Figurine, Mute Swan, Water Foliage, No. 400-14, 17 3/4 In. 1380.00
Figurine, Northern Oriole, No. 401.94, 12 1/2 x 9 In. 515.00
Figurine, Northern Water Thrush, No. 490J, 10 3/4 In. 405.00
Figurine, Nyala, 18 x 15 In. 880.00
Figurine, Orchard Oriole, No. 400, 11 x 11 In. 632.00
Figurine, Owl, c.1980, 18 3/8 In. 862.00
Figurine, Partridges, 11 In. 1090.00
Figurine, Peregrine Falcon With Young, 14 1/2 x 11 In. ....*Illus* 863.00
Figurine, Peregrine Falcon, 22 x 30 1/2 In. 2100.00
Figurine, Poodle 25.00
Figurine, Prothonotary Warbler, No. 445 .... 1100.00
Figurine, Queen Elizabeth Rose, No. 161, 6 1/2 In. 430.00
Figurine, Raccoons, No. 4002, 12 x 12 In. 480.00
Figurine, Racquet-Tail Hummingbird, No. 40105, 9 1/2 x 8 In. 980.00
Figurine, Red Fox, No. 4003, 12 1/2 x 13 In. 285.00
Figurine, Red-Shouldered Hawk, 26 1/2 x 19 In. ....*Illus* 4600.00
Figurine, Royal Terns, No. 10047, 1983, 31 3/4 In. 488.00
Figurine, Snow Buntings, No. 400-21, 7 x 13 In. 485.00
Figurine, Squirrel, No. 400-94 .... 180.00
Figurine, St. Francis With Brother Wolf, 13 1/2 In. 172.00
Figurine, Stonechats, No. 1003, 11 1/2 In. 430.00
Figurine, Treecreepers, No. 1007, 17 x 9 In. 860.00
Figurine, Trumpeter Swan, No. 40266, c.1985, 14 1/4 In. 460.00
Figurine, Varied Thrush & Parrot Tulip, 18 x 10 In. 920.00
Figurine, Yellow-Breasted Warbler, No. 431 .... 400.00
Figurine, Yellow-Shafted Flicker, No. 400-16, 13 1/4 In. 805.00
Group, Fledgling Canadian Warbler, No. 491, 8 1/2 In. 517.00
Group, Goldfinches, No. 457, 11 1/2 In. 460.00
Group, Rhododendron, Butterflies, No. 243, 8 1/4 In. 747.00
Group, Tufted Titmice, No. 482, 12 3/4 In. 575.00
Plaque, Nature's Bounty, Frame 4300.00
Plate, Bird Of Peace, Case, 1972, 12 In. 200.00
Plate, Owl Series, No. 7, Box 385.00

Tile, 2 Mockingbirds, 1 Sparrow, 11 x 8 In., 3 Piece 1610.00

BOHEMIAN GLASS is an ornate overlay or flashed glass made during the Victorian era. It has been reproduced in Bohemia, which is now a part of the Czech Republic. Glass made from 1875 to 1900 is preferred by collectors.

Basket, Malachite, 5 1/2 In. 98.00
Decanter, Clear Cut, Flashed Ruby Red, 9 1/4 In. 72.00
Decanter, Cranberry, Clear Design, 18 1/2 In. 44.00
Decanter, Ruby To Clear Glass, Etched Dog & Stag, 14 1/2 In. 88.00
Goblet, Cover, Gilt Leaves, Enameled Floral Medallion, 11 1/4 In. 345.00
Mug, Engraved Castle & Trees, Applied Handle, Red, 6 In. 80.00
Salt, Fluted Oval Form, Enameled Portraits In Bottom, c.1823, 9 Piece 4140.00
Sugar Shaker, Bird, Castle, Red 70.00
Vase, Floral, Frosted Ground, 11 In. 60.00

BONE DISHES were considered a necessary part of a table setting for the Victorian table. The crescent-shaped dish was kept at the edge of the dinner plate so the bones removed from the fish could be stored away from the uneaten food. Some bone dishes were made in more fanciful shapes and many resemble fish.

Floral, Blue & White, Meakin 8.00

BOOKENDS have probably been used since books became inexpensive. Early libraries kept books in cupboards, not on open shelves. By the 1870s bookends appeared, especially homemade fret-carved wooden examples. Most bookends listed in this book date from the twentieth century.

Abraham Lincoln, Hollow Cast White Metal, Brass Finish, 7 1/2 In. 38.00
Abraham Lincoln, Sitting, Bronzed Metal, D.C. French, 7 In. 133.00
Airedales, Full-Bodied, Polychrome, 4 1/2 In. 210.00
Airedales, Polychrome, Hubley, 5 1/4 In. 120.00
Anchor, Brass 75.00
Aventurine, Metallic Glaze, Kenton Hills, 6 1/2 x 3 1/2 x 6 In. 250.00
Boston Terrier Heads, Protrude From Bronze Finish 90.00
Boston Terriers, Copper Over Iron 145.00
Bouquet, Silvered Bronze Figures, Sibylle May, c.1930, 8 3/4 In. 4025.00
Boy, Lying Next To Cornstalk, Copper.. 30.00
Brass, Ceramic Deer, c.1930, 8 x 4 1/2 In. ....*Illus* 45.00
Brass & Copper Concentric Bands, Ball Feet 275.00
Bulldog, Heads, Bronze, Cast, 4 5/8 In. 83.00
Camels, Polychrome, Cast Iron, 5 1/4 In. 93.00
Captain & Ship's Wheel, Jennings Brothers 60.00
Cats, Cubist, White Crackle Glaze, Adnet, France, c.1930, 4 1/2 x 10 In. 308.00
Child, Reading A Book, Matte Pink, Fred H. Robertson, 4 1/2 x 5 x 3 1/2 In. 715.00
Cobra, Wrought Iron, Edgar Brandt, c.1925, 7 5/8 In. 7475.00
Cocks, Fighting, Cast Iron, c.1880, 7 x 9 x 10 In. 295.00
Cowboy, Cast Iron 75.00

Bookends, Brass, Ceramic Deer, c.1930, 8 x 4 1/2 In.

Cutout Poppies, Hammered Copper, Dirk Van Erp, 1912, 5 x 6 In. 775.00
Elephant Motif, Bronze, Austria, c.1890, 5 x 5 1/2 In. 575.00
Elephants, Red, Marked 112, Cast Iron, 4 In. 82.00
Fencing Figures, Patinated Cast Metal, Marble Base, Bruno Zack, Austria, 5 In. 715.00
Figural, Nude On Top Of Book, Bronze, Austria, 11 1/2 In. 2990.00
German Shepherds, Seated, Bronze Finish 45.00
Hartford Fire Insurance, Bronze, 1935 .... 75.00
Horse, Art Deco, Bronzed White Metal 85.00
Horse, Painted, Cast Iron, 1914 .... 40.00
Indian Bust, Cast Iron 195.00
Jumping Trout, Aluminum 145.00
Lions, Cast Brass, England, 5 1/2 In. 138.00
Medieval Knight, Galloping Steed, Bronze, c.1890 .... 215.00
Mother Mary & Baby Jesus, Cast Iron 31.00
Mountain Boys, Paul Webb 25.00
Nude, Bronze, Art Deco 95.00
Nude Child, Kneeling, Parsons, Bronze, Gorham Foundry, 1913, 6 1/4 In. 1035.00
Owl, Chalkware 45.00
Pointers, Full-Bodied, Polychrome, 4 1/2 In. 110.00
Prancing Horse, Hollow Glass 85.00
Punch & Judy, Cast Bronze, 7 1/4 In. 104.00
Quail, Cast Iron, 5 1/2 In. 137.00
Rooster, Wrought Iron, Edgar Brandt, c.1925, 8 In. 7200.00
Saddled Horses, Marked 110, Cast Iron, 4 5/8 In. 60.00
Sailing Ship, Hubley 45.00
Scotty Dog, At Fence, Cast Bronze, 6 1/2 In. 115.00
Seal, Iridescent Blues & Greens, Rambervilliers, 8 x 6 1/2 In. 475.00
Seal, White Onyx Base, Bronze, Marcel Bouraine, c.1925, 13 1/2 In. 2300.00
Setter At Point, Bronze, Atmor 150.00
Shepherdess, Bronze 125.00
Ships, Galleon, M-M Co., No. 700, Cast Iron, 5 3/8 In. 27.00
Skull, Bronze Wrapped Plaster Of Paris, Armor Bronze Corp. 40.00
Square Cutouts, Hammered Copper, Forest Craft Guild, 4 1/2 x 6 x 3 In. 99.00
Stitched Border, Hammered Copper, Dirk Van Erp, 3 1/2 x 4 1/2 In. 330.00
Swordfish, Brass 95.00
Tree Shape, Painted Golfers, Cast Iron, 8 In. 220.00
Trojan Horsehead, Glass 95.00
Wirehaired Fox Terriers, Brass Plated, c.1929 .... 85.00
Women In Pink Dresses, Seated, 1 Holds Book, 1 Holds Fan, Pottery, 6 In. 145.00

BOOKMARKS were originally made of parchment, cloth, or leather. Soon woven silk ribbon, thin cardboard, celluloid, wood, silver, tortoiseshell, and metals were used. Examples made before 1850 are scarce, but there are many to be found dating before 1920.

Punch Work, To My Dear Mama 24.00
Sterling Silver, Repousse, S. Kirk & Son 50.00
TV Guide, Tin 22.00

BOSSONS character wall masks, plaques, figurines, and other decorative pieces are made by W.H. Bossons, Limited of Congleton, England. The company was founded in 1946 and is still working.

BOSSONS

Figurine, Lords Of The Desert ....95.00 to 125.00
Head, Corsican 50.00
Head, Mexican .... 300.00 to 500.00
Head, Persian 75.00
Plaque, Market Days, Round, 14 In. 85.00
Plaque, Sioux Warrior Panel 100.00

BOTTLE collecting has become a major American hobby. There are several general categories of bottles, such as historic flasks, bitters, household, and figural. Pyro is the shortened form of the word pyroglaze, an enameled lettering used on bottles after the mid-1930s. For more bottle prices, see the book *Kovels' Bottles Price List* by Ralph and Terry Kovel.

Apothecary, Green, Stars, Marked I, 40 Oz. 20.00

Avon started in 1886 as the California Perfume Company. It was not until
1929 that the name *Avon* was used. In 1939, it became Avon Products, Inc.
Avon has made many figural bottles filled with cosmetic products. Ceramic,
plastic, and glass bottles were made in limited editions.

Avon, Decanter, Cape Cod	20.00
Avon, Decanter, Cape Cod, Red..	14.00
Avon, Fly-A-Balloon, 1975-1977..	20.00
Avon, Tiffany Lamp, 1972-1974..	12.00
Bar, Pillar Mold, Conical, Flint, 1850s, 11 In.	175.00
Barber, Cobalt Blue, Enameled Dot & Flower Design	160.00
Barber, Cobalt Blue, White & Orange Flowers, Gold Trim, 11 In.	250.00
Barber, Cranberry Opalescent Swirl, Rolled Lip, Square....................	210.00
Barber, Cut Glass, Enameled Design, Amethyst, 9 1/4 In.	120.00
Barber, Enameled Gold Leaf Design, Opalescent, Pontil	75.00
Barber, Flowers & Leaves, White Enameled, Frosted Brown, Stopper, 9 In....	125.00
Barber, Milk Glass, Basket Weave Gold Trim....................................	25.00
Barber, Polka Dot, White Opalescent..	100.00
Barber, Ribs Swirled Right, Yellow, Tool Sheared Lip, 6 1/2 In.	55.00
Barber, Venetian Type, Blue, White & Gold Stripes, Pontil	119.00

Beam bottles were made to hold Kentucky Straight Bourbon, made by the
James B. Beam Distilling Company. The Beam series of ceramic bottles
began in 1953.

Beam, Grant Locomotive Train, 5 Cars, Track, 1983, 7 Pieces.............	600.00
Beam, Liberty Eagle, 6 Coins, Blue & White, 1970, 9 1/2 In...............	48.00
Beer, Acme Brewing, San Francisco, Calif., Miniature	30.00
Beer, Adam's Ale House, Concord, N.H., Red Amber, 1 Pt.	125.00
Beer, August Stoer Milwaukee Lager, Manchester, N.H., Yellow, Orange Tint, 1 Pt.....	30.00
Beer, Black Label, Ohio, Miniature..	5.00
Beer, Blackwood's Ginger, Winnipeg, Canada, 1 Qt.	100.00
Beer, Blatz Old Heidelberg, Label, Case, May, 1935	195.00
Beer, Blatz Old Heidelberg, Wis., Miniature....................................	7.00
Beer, Budweiser, Missouri, Miniature	10.00
Beer, Bunker Hill Lager, Charlestown, Mass., 1 Pt.	20.00
Beer, C. Berry, Boston, Watermelon Slugplate Shoulder, Porcelain Stopper, 1 Pt.	35.00
Beer, C. Schmidt & Sons, Hoboken, N.J., 1 Pt................................	20.00
Beer, Charles E. Lehnert Brewery, Catasauqua, Pa., Aqua, Crown Top, Contents, 1900s	25.00
Beer, Charles Joly, Philadelphia, Emerald Green, 1 Pt.	45.00
Beer, Chicago Lager, San Francisco, Script, Applied Top, 1 Qt.	70.00
Beer, Clark & Roberts, Boston, Monogram, Whittled, Honey Amber, 1 Pt.	35.00
Beer, Columbia Weiss Beer Brewery, St. Louis, Emerald Green, Teepee, 1 Pt.............	65.00
Beer, Columbia Weiss Beer Brewery, St. Louis, Mo., Teepee, Red Amber, Stopper, 1 Pt.	65.00
Beer, Coors Export Lager, Ceramic, 1940, Miniature	35.00
Beer, Coors Golden, Ceramic, Miniature	25.00
Beer, Coors Pilsner, Gold Waterfall	7.00
Beer, Creedmore, New York, Aqua, Squatty, Lightning Stopper, 1 Qt.	75.00
Beer, Cripple Creek Bottling Works, Amethyst, Blob Top, 8 1/4 In.	60.00
Beer, Eastside Pabst, California, Miniature......................................	10.00
Beer, Edward Wagner, Aqua, 1 Pt...	35.00
Beer, Eldelweiss, Illinois, Miniature	5.00
Beer, Excelsior Lager, Aqua, Applied Blob	15.00
Beer, Excelsior Lager, Aqua, Unusual Cork & Lead Stopper, 1 Pt.	35.00
Beer, Florida Brewing Co., Tampa, Fla..	25.00
Beer, Frank Jones Ale, In Shield, Smoky Clear, Early Crown..............	25.00
Beer, George Frank, Orange, N.J., Citron Green, Blob Top, 1 Pt.	75.00
Beer, Hamm's, Minnesota, Miniature..	5.00
Beer, Haverhill, Massachusetts, Whittled, Aqua, Lightning Stopper, 1 Pt.	100.00
Beer, Hinkel Brewing Co., Smoky Yellow Amber, 1 Pt........................	20.00
Beer, Hohmann & Bartlett Schlitz, Manchester, N.H., 1903, 1 Pt........	17.00
Beer, I. Joseph, Pittsburgh, Pa., Amber, Blob Top, Large	25.00
Beer, J. Gahn, Boston, Mass., Yellow Gold, Applied Blob Top	25.00

  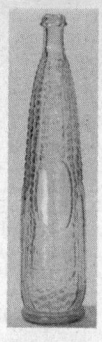 

Bottle, Bitters, Drake's, Plantation, 6 Log, Amber, 1870, 10 In.

Bottle, Bitters, Brown's Celebrated Indian Herb, Queen, Yellow Green, 1870, 12 In.

Bottle, Bitters, National, Ear Of Corn, Aqua, 1867, 12 In.

Bottle, Decanter, Mt. Vernon, Olive, 1820, 6 7/8 In.

Beer, J. Lebkuchner, N.Y., Eagle, 2 Flags, Aqua, Whittled, Lightning Stopper, 1 Pt.	30.00
Beer, J. Nash, Pittston, Pa., Greenish Aqua, 1 Pt.	8.00
Beer, John McGinty's Brewery, Tamaqua, Pa., Light Yellow	20.00
Beer, Keep Cool & Keep Coolidge With Near Beer, White Pottery, 1/2 Pt.	35.00
Beer, Meister Brau, Illinois, Miniature	5.00
Beer, National Bottling Works, San Francisco, Eagle, Chocolate Amber, 1 Pt.	150.00
Beer, Old Crown Ale, Presentation, With Letter Dated Dec. 12, 1939	50.00
Beer, Old Dutch Ale, Pennsylvania, Miniature	75.00
Beer, Old Export, Maryland, Miniature	20.00
Beer, Otis Neale, Boston, Slug Plate, Aqua, Lightning Stopper, 1 Pt.	16.00
Beer, P. Herringbone Bottler Of Milwaukee Lagers, Porcelain Stopper, 1 Pt.	125.00
Beer, Pabst Ale, Wisconsin, Miniature	8.00
Beer, Pabst Blue Ribbon, Metal	7.00
Beer, Phoenix Bottling Co., N.Y., Blob Top	10.00
Beer, Rainier, Seattle, Light Amber, Miniature	55.00
Beer, Roshirt Bros., Rens Co., Amber, 1 Pt.	15.00
Beer, S.B. Doty Bottler, Morrisville, Vt., Aqua, Embossed, Lightning Stopper, 1 Pt.	65.00
Beer, San Jose Bottling Co., Golden Honey Amber, Whittled, Lightning Stopper, 1 Qt.	100.00
Beer, Stoddard, 1 Pt.	30.00
Beer, Sunset Bottling Co., San Francisco, Reddish Amber, 1 Qt.	55.00
Beer, U.S. Bottling, John Fauser & Co., Red Amber, Whittled, Applied Top, 1 Qt.	65.00
Binniger, Cannon, Light Amber.	400.00
Binniger, Regulator, Clock Face, Light Amber...	185.00
Bitters, Beggs Dandelion, Strap Flask	100.00
Bitters, Bourbon Whiskey, Deep Claret, 9 In.	325.00
Bitters, Brillanteen, Ruby Red Paneled Design, Stopper, 3 7/8 In.	350.00
Bitters, Brown's Celebrated Indian Herb, Queen, Yellow Green, 1870, 12 In. .... *Illus*	3300.00
Bitters, Brown's Celebrated Indian Herb, Golden Amber, 12 1/2 In.	550.00
Bitters, Buhrer's Gentian, Dug, Light Stain, 8 1/2 In.	210.00
Bitters, California Fig, Golden Amber, Panels, Cover, Square, 9 1/2 In.	45.00
Bitters, Clarke's Compound Mandrake, Aqua, Oval, Label, 7 1/2 In.	65.00
Bitters, DeMuth's Stomach, Square, Light Golden Amber, 9 1/4 In.	165.00
Bitters, Dr. Ball's Vegetable Stomachic, Aqua, Open Pontil, 7 In.	160.00
Bitters, Dr. Blake's Aromatic Bitters, New York, Aqua, Open Pontil	225.00
Bitters, Dr. Fisch's, Cover, Light Amber, 11 1/2 In.	180.00
Bitters, Dr. Geo. Pierce's Indian Restorative, Lowell, Mass., Aqua, 7 1/2 In. .... 45.00 to 85.00
Bitters, Dr. Gilmore's Laxative, Kidney & Liver, Medium Amber, 10 1/2 In.	150.00
Bitters, Dr. Hopkins Union Stomach, Panels, Cover, Yellow Amber, Square, 9 1/2 In..	285.00
Bitters, Dr. J. Sweet's Strengthening, Aqua, Square, 8 1/2 In.	70.00
Bitters, Dr. Langley's Root & Herb, Light Green, 7 In.	25.00

Bitters, Dr. Mampe's Herb Stomach, Aqua, 7 In. 75.00
Bitters, Dr. Russell Pepsin Calisaya, Lime Green 75.00
Bitters, Dr. S.O. Richardson, Sherry Wine, South Reading, Mass., Aqua, 6 1/2 In. 25.00
Bitters, Dr. Solomon's Indian Wine, Aqua 40.00
Bitters, Dr. Von Hopf's Curacoa, Amber Flask, 7 7/8 In. .... 70.00 to 80.00
Bitters, Dr. Wilcox' Compound Extract Of Sarsaparilla, Blue-Green 350.00
Bitters, Drake's Plantation, 4 Log, Amber, 1860 .... 135.00
Bitters, Drake's Plantation, 4 Log, Yellow, Amber Tones, Open Bubble On Corner 95.00
Bitters, Drake's Plantation, 5 Log, Honey Amber 175.00
Bitters, Drake's Plantation, 5 Log, Red Amber 175.00
Bitters, Drake's Plantation, 6 Log, 4 Label Panels 225.00
Bitters, Drake's Plantation, 6 Log, Amber, 1870, 10 In. ....*Illus* 105.00
Bitters, Drake's Plantation, 6 Log, Deep Strawberry 225.00
Bitters, Drake's Plantation, 6 Log, Medium Apricot Puce, Embossed 175.00
Bitters, Drake's Plantation, 6 Log, Topaz Orange 95.00
Bitters, Greeley's Bourbon Whiskey, Pinkish Copper 225.00
Bitters, Greeley's Bourbon, Dark Red Puce, 9 1/8 In. 250.00
Bitters, Green Mountain Cider, Cylinder, 10 1/4 In. 125.00
Bitters, Greer's Eclipse, Amber, Sunken Panels, Square, 8 3/4 In. 100.00
Bitters, Hartwig Kantorowicz, 3 Labeled Sides, Milk Glass, Contents 80.00
Bitters, Kidney & Liver, Cover, Light Amber Square, 8 5/8 In. 175.00
Bitters, Lohengrin, Milk Glass, 9 In. 135.00
Bitters, National, Ear Of Corn, Aqua, 1867, 12 In. ....*Illus* 3135.00
Bitters, Old Homestead, Wild Cherry, Cabin, Orange Amber, Squatty Neck, 9 1/2 In. ... 250.00
Bitters, Pepsin Calisaya, Bright Lime Green, 8 In. 80.00
Bitters, Phoenix, John Moffat, Aqua, 6 In. 45.00
Bitters, Prickly Ash, Yellow Amber, Panel, Cover, Square, 9 1/4 In. 125.00
Bitters, Red Jacket, Monheimer & Co., Amber, Square 100.00
Bitters, Roback's Stomach, Amber, Barrel, Large 225.00
Bitters, Turner Bros., Olive Amber, Barrel, 9 In. 350.00
Bitters, Warner's Safe, Amber, Applied Mouth, 7 3/8 In. 275.00
Bitters, Warner's Safe, Medium Amber, 1 Pt. 525.00
Blown In Mold, Geometric, Amber 550.00
Coca-Cola bottles are listed in the Coca-Cola category
Cosmetic, Loxor Cold Cream, Milk Glass, Barrel Shape, 3 1/8 In. 3.00
Cosmetic, Mascara Tonique For The Hair, Rochester, N.Y., Embossed 60.00
Cosmetic, Parker's Hair Balsam, New York 25.00
Cosmetic, Rachael Talcum, Art Deco 65.00
Creamer, Borden's, Red, 1/2 Oz. 15.00
Creamer, Dairy Products, Brand, Red Pyro 20.00
Creamer, Gerbers Central, Red, 1/2 Oz. 20.00
Creamer, Golden Royal, Red, 1/2 Oz. 20.00
Creamer, Missouri Pacific Lines, Service Institution 22.00
Creamer, Quality Dairy, None Better, Red, 1/2 Oz. 12.00
Creamer, Rosebud Creamery, Sideways, Maroon, 1 Oz. 20.00
Creamer, Sanitary Farm Dairies, Red, 1/2 Oz. 20.00
Creamer, Tastemark Cream, Red, 1/2 Oz. 20.00
Creamer, Valley Farm Dairy Products, Orange, 1/2 Oz. 20.00
Cure, Dr. Daniels' Veterinary Colic Cure, Amber 75.00
Cure, Langenbach's Dysentery Bottle, Seal, Contents 37.00
Cure, Total Eclipse Spavin Bottle, Dr. J.G. Leisure & Co., Keene, N.H., Aqua 35.00
Decanter, Mt. Vernon, Olive, 1820, 6 7/8 In. ....*Illus* 3080.00
Decanter, Pinch, Half Post, Sea Green, Pewter Cap, Germany, 18th Century, 11 In. 500.00
Decanter, Whiskey, Bulbous Base, Cover, Fluted, White, Orange Enamel, 3 1/4 In. 275.00
Demijohn, Kidney Shape, Orange Amber, Whittle Marks, 1 Qt. 29.00
Demijohn, Stoddard, Seed Bubbles, Pontil, 1 Gal. 85.00
Dresser, Clear, Ornate, 1940s, Pair 95.00
Drug, B.Ward Druggist, Mobile, Ala., Amber, Rectangular 17.00
Drug, Bromo Seltzer, Cobalt, Measuring Cap, 5 In. 8.00
Drug, Bromo Seltzer, Emerson Drug Co., Baltimore, Cobalt Blue, Tin Lid, 8 In. 20.00
Drug, Doherty Apothecary, Atlantic City, N.J., Cobalt Blue, 4 7/8 In. 75.00
Drug, Keystone Drug Co., Deer Lodge, Mont., 2 7/8 In. 7.00
Drug, Palmer Druggists, Santa Cruz, Amber, 4 1/4 In. 45.00

Drug, Reed & Garnick Pharmacists, Honey Amber, Whittle Marks, Maltine Shape 25.00
Drug, T.H. VanHorn Druggist, Lockport, N.Y., Aqua, 10 x 4 In. 30.00
Drug, Vauhn's Vegetable Lithantriptic Mixture, Buffalo, Aqua, 8 1/4 In. 125.00
Drug, Vick's Drops, Embossed, Cobalt, 1 7/8 In. 8.00
Ezra Brooks, Decanter, VFW, Cobalt Blue, Red, White & Gold, No. 185, 1973 .... 75.00
Ezra Brooks, Muscleman, 1974 .... 25.00
Figural, Banjo, Yellow Olive-Green, Monogram MFJ, 8 In. 30.00
Figural, Bat Masterson 24.00
Figural, Bell, Melvale Pure Rye, Clear, Cut Glass, Bar, 1 Qt. 59.00
Figural, Dachshund, Whiskey, Opalescent Glass, Italy, 18 In. 90.00
Figural, Pig, Paperweight, Theodor Netter, Philadelphia 89.00
Figural, Pig, Standing On Hind Legs, 9 In. 50.00
Figural, Pig, White, Black Spots, Stoneware, Limaville, Ohio, 1880 .... 1400.00
Figural, Pineapple, Bitters, Medium Amber 72.00
Figural, Woman, On Head, On Ball, 16 1/2 In. 35.00
Flask, 24 Ribs, Swirled At Neck, Amber, Blown, Folded Lip, 7 5/8 In. 1430.00
Flask, 24 Ribs, Swirled, Zanesville, Aqua, Pontil, 7 1/2 In. 302.00
Flask, 24 Ribs, Swirled, Zanesville, Citron, Pontil, 8 1/4 In. 2200.00
Flask, 24 Ribs, Swirled, Zanesville, Olive Amber, Pontil, 9 1/2 In. 1045.00
Flask, Baltimore Glassworks & Resurgam, Variant, Aqua 85.00
Flask, Blown, Globular, Folded Lip, Dark Amber, 11 1/2 In. 385.00
Flask, Blown, Molded, Cobalt, 19th Century, 5 In. 115.00
Flask, Chestnut, 10 Diamonds, Zanesville, Amber, Sheared Pontil, 5 In. 1210.00
Flask, Chestnut, 10 Diamonds, Zanesville, Aqua, Pontil, 1/2 Pt., 5 1/4 In. 605.00
Flask, Chestnut, 10 Diamonds, Zanesville, Dark Amber, Pontil, 4 5/8 In. 495.00
Flask, Chestnut, 10 Diamonds, Zanesville, Olive Yellow, 1/2 Pt., 5 3/8 In. 2420.00
Flask, Chestnut, 20 Ribs, Broken Swirl, Golden Amber, 6 /34 In. 935.00
Flask, Chestnut, 24 Ribs, Broken Swirl Ribs, Zanesville, Dark Amber, Pontil, 6 5/8 In. 2090.00
Flask, Chestnut, 24 Ribs, Swirled, Zanesville, Aqua, 7 1/2 In. 522.00
Flask, Chestnut, 24 Ribs, Swirled, Zanesville, Dark Amber, Pontil, 4 3/4 In. 412.00
Flask, Chestnut, 24 Ribs, Swirled, Zanesville, Golden Amber, 1/2 Pt., 5 In. 275.00
Flask, Chestnut, 24 Ribs, Vertical, Zanesville, Olive Yellow, Pontil, 4 3/4 In. 445.00
Flask, Chestnut, Flattened, Amber, Handle, Open Pontil 55.00
Flask, Chestnut, Painted Floral Design, Olive Green, 5 In. 120.00
Flask, Chestnut, Sapphire Blue, Handle, Pontil, Applied Lip, 1820-1840 .... 950.00
Flask, Clasped Hands, Eagle In Flight, Banner, Adams & Co., 7 1/2 In. 225.00
Flask, Coffin, Robert J. Crispin, Wellington Hotel, Salt Lake City, Aqua, 9 1/4 In. 70.00
Flask, Cornucopia & Urn, Yellow-Olive, 1 Pt. 85.00
Flask, Cornucopia Side, Flower Basket On Reverse, Olive Green, 1/2 Pt. 45.00
Flask, Double Broken Swirl, Pitkin, Olive Amber, New England 4125.00
Flask, Double Eagle, Aqua, 1/2 Pt. 110.00
Flask, Double Eagle, Granite Glass Co., Deep Yellow Amber, Burst Bubble Base 95.00
Flask, Double Eagle, Olive, 5 5/8 In. 143.00
Flask, Eagle & Anchor, New London, Medium Orange, 1/2 Pt. 425.00
Flask, Eagle & Cornucopia, Aqua, 1/2 Pt. 258.00
Flask, Eagle & Pike's Peak, Aqua, 9 In. 77.00
Flask, Eagle, Green, 1 Pt. 240.00
Flask, Ear Of Corn, Washington Monument, Aqua, 6 3/4 In. 300.00
Flask, Flag, New Granite Glass Works, Stoddard, N.H., c.1850 .... 8525.00
Flask, Gunpowder, Silver Tulip & Birds Front, Wriggled Tulip Back, Brass, 6 1/2 In. ... 375.00
Flask, Hayner Whiskey, Fluted Shoulder & Base, Label 20.00
Flask, Henry Chapman & Co., Montreal, Amber, Screw Threads Cap, Pocket 179.00
Flask, It's A Long Time Between Drinks, Playing Card Clock, 1890, 4 1/2 In. 770.00
Flask, Kossuth & Tree, Calabash, Yellow Green 220.00
Flask, Liberty & Union, Calabash, Aqua, 1 Qt. 175.00
Flask, Liberty 1 Side, Company Name On Other, Olive Green, 1/2 Pt. 135.00
Flask, Morning Glory & Eagle, Brilliant Aqua 235.00
Flask, Neller & Shirmer, San Francisco, Slug Plate, Tooled Screw Top, 1 Pt. 45.00
Flask, Old Homestead Fine Bourbon Whiskey, Floral Design, Ground Tip 235.00
Flask, Olive Green, Ovoid, 1860s, Pocket 29.00
Flask, Pictorial, Adams & Jefferson, Olive Green, 1/2 Pt. 132.00
Flask, Pretzel, Pottery ....65.00 to 95.00
Flask, Pumpkinseed, Merry Christmas 18.00

Flask, Scroll, Light Green	95.00
Flask, Success To The Railroad, Both Sides, Fired Polished Lip	220.00
Flask, Success To The Railroad, Eagle, Olive Amber, 1 Pt., 7 In.	170.00
Flask, Success To The Railroad, Eagle, Olive Green, 1 Pt.	110.00
Flask, Summer & Winter, Aqua	85.00
Flask, Swirl, Midwestern, Chartreuse, 8 In.	2200.00
Flask, Urn & Cornucopia, Deep Olive Green, 1 Pt.	105.00
Flask, Urn & Cornucopia, Olive Amber, 1/2 Pt.	93.00
Flask, Washington & Taylor, Yellow Olive, Open Pontil, 1 Pt.	495.00
Food, Aqua, 12 Sides, Open Pontil, 4 1/2 In.	19.00
Food, Capers, Dark Emerald Green, 9 In.	22.00
Food, Giessen's Union Mustard, 4 5/8 In.	88.00
Food, Nemo Korn Syrup, Boston, Round, 1pt.	12.00
Food, Pickle, Cathedral, Gothic Pattern, 13 In.	250.00
Food, Vinegar, White House, 1 Pt.	12.00
Food, Vinegar, White House, 1 Qt.	18.00
Food, Vinegar, White House, Dark Green	16.00
Fruit Jar, Atlas, Good Luck, 1 Pt.	27.50
Fruit Jar, Atlas, Good Luck, 1 Qt.	24.00
Fruit Jar, Ball Ideal, Aqua, Glass Top, Pat. July 14, 1908, 1 Qt.	5.00
Fruit Jar, Excelsior, Aqua, 1 Qt.	575.00
Fruit Jar, Gem, Aqua, CFJ Co., Nov. 30, 1858	80.00
Fruit Jar, Globe, Blue, Glass Lid, 1 Qt.	25.00
Fruit Jar, Globe, Brands, 1/2 Gal.	104.00
Fruit Jar, Lafayette, 3 Piece Glass & Metal Stopper, 1885-1900, 1/2 Gal.	154.00
Fruit Jar, Lafayette, Profile, Aqua, 1 Qt.	655.00
Fruit Jar, Mason's, Keystone In Circle, Yellow-Green, 1880-1910, 1 Qt.	522.00
Fruit Jar, Mason, Medium Yellow-Green, Pat. Nov. 30th, 1858, 1qt.	200.00
Fruit Jar, Mason-Improved, Aqua, Screw Band	40.00
Fruit Jar, Newman's, Patent Dec. 20th, 1859, Aqua, 1 Qt.	605.00
Fruit Jar, Safety, Yellow Amber, 1870-1890, 1 Qt.	143.00
Fruit Jar, Trademark, Lightning, Amber, 1 1/2 Pt.	75.00
Fruit Jar, Whitmore's, Patent, Rochester, N.Y., Wire Bail, 1 Qt.	385.00
Household, Black Cat Stove Enamel, 6 In.	5.00
Household, Crystal Cleaner, Embossed Winchester, Paper Label, Box, 5 In.	110.00
Household, Glue, Te-Nex-Ine, Pyramid, Aqua, Cone, 2 7/8 In.	20.00
Ink, 3 Mold, Medium Olive Green, Seed Bubbles, Spout, Master	60.00
Ink, Arnolds Ink, Bakelite, Round, 2 1/4 In.	35.00
Ink, Blackstone's, Bimal, 3 Oz.	10.00
Ink, Carter's, Amber, Embossed, Master, 5 In.	35.00
Ink, Carter's, Ma Carter, Bisque, Germany, 3 5/8 In.	75.00
Ink, Carter's, Pa Carter, Bisque, Germany, 3 5/8 In.	145.00
Ink, Cone, Olive Green	32.00
Ink, Cut Glass, Diamond Pattern, Fluted Neck, Twisted Pontil	16.00
Ink, Free Blown, Green, Folded Lip, 2 1/2 In.	55.00
Ink, Kirkland's Writing Fluid, Aqua, Cone, Applied Square Cover, 2 5/8 In.	40.00
Ink, Kwikstick, Cone, Applicator Cap, Mint, 2 1/2 In.	30.00
Ink, Milk Glass, Cylindrical, 5 1/2 Oz.	10.00
Ink, P & J Arnold, England, Cylinder, 4 1/2 In.	40.00
Ink, Pomeroy's Fountain Pen Ink, Round Shoulder, 2 3/4 In.	40.00
Ink, S.B. Dunbar's Black, Aqua, 6 3/4 In.	55.00
Ink, Stafford's Ink, Teal Green, Pouring Lip, Master	85.00
Ink, Teakettle, Cobalt Blue, 8 Sided Facets	390.00
Ink, Teakettle, Cobalt Blue, Curved Spout	300.00
Ink, Teakettle, Deep Puce-Amethyst, 8 Sided Facets	550.00
Ink, Umbrella, Blue-Green, Open Pontil	55.00
Ink, Underwood's Ink, Cover, Aqua 8 Sides, 2 1/4 In.	30.00
Ink, Worden's, Threaded Metal Cap, Aqua, Round Shoulder, 2 5/8 In.	30.00
Jar, Cheese, Northampton Sanitary Dairy, 1/2 Pt.	15.00
Jar, Cigar, William Tegge & Co., 50 Cigars, Slug Plate, No Cover, Round, 5 In.	45.00
Jar, Cosmetic, Richard Hudnut Flower Sachet, Floral Tin Cover, Floral Shaped Soap ...	25.00
Jar, Eat Tom's Toasted Peanuts	30.00
Jar, Elephant Peanuts, Round	290.00

Jar, Globe, Orange Amber, Original Closure & Lid, 1 Qt.	85.00
Jar, Mayonnaise, Paper Label, Lithographed Lid	8.00
Jar, McMechen's, Always The Best Old Virginia, Wheeling, Square, Glass Cover, 5 In.	75.00
Jar, Mustard, Nash, Bank, Paper Lips	45.00
Jar, Pickle, Mason, Original Tin Lid & Handle, 24 In.	40.00
Jar, Preserve, Cover, Green Glaze, Brown Splotches, Gonic, N.H.	950.00
Jar, Reliance Coffee, Paper Label, Lithographed Cover	25.00
Jar, Tobacco, Wm. S. Kimball & Co., Yellow Amber, 8 Sides, Ground Top, 6 In.	50.00
Jug, Casey's Malt Whiskey, Tan, Ovoid, Miniature	89.00
Jug, Charles H. Gring, Sinking Springs, Pa., Merry Christmas, Brown, Cream, Miniature	300.00
Jug, Glen Garry Scotch, 1 Handle, Pottery, Transfer	20.00
Jug, Golden Hills, Toledo, Ohio, Blue Stenciled, 1905-1914, 1/2 Pt.	80.00
Jug, Grey Beard Heather Dew Whiskey, 2 Scotsmen Toasting, Transfer	65.00
Jug, H.J. Kuhr, 906 South St., Dark Black Lettering, Miniature	60.00
Jug, I.W. Harper, Nelso Co., Kentucky, Miniature	45.00
Jug, Jos. Leopold Whiskey, 1 Gal.	90.00
Jug, Key & Co.'s Pure Hand Made Corn Whiskey, Brown Over Cream, 1 Gal.	200.00
Jug, Meredith's Diamond Club Pure Rye Whisky, For Medicinal Use, Green Letters	65.00
Jug, Mulland's Dairy, Watertown, Wis., 1 Gal.	30.00
Jug, O'Keefe's Malt Whiskey, Oswego, N.Y., Tan, Brown Top, Design	65.00
Jug, Oertel's Ale, Little Brown Jug	22.00
Jug, Old Cold Spring Sour Mash Whiskey, Stoneware, Brown, Tan, 1 Qt.	129.00
Jug, Old Rose Distilleries, Chicago, 1/2 Gal.	10.00
Jug, Wanzer's On Milk Is Like Sterling On Silver, 1 Gal.	22.00
Medicine, Burks Medicine Co., New York, Maple Balsam, Label, Contents, 6 1/4 In.	17.00
Medicine, Congreves Elixir For Coughs, Whooping Cough & Asthma	15.00
Medicine, Dr. J.W. Bull's Cough Syrup, Aqua	20.00
Medicine, Dr. J.W. Bull's Vegetable Pills, 8 Sides, Ground Top, 2 1/2 In.	20.00
Medicine, Dr. Jones' Liniment, Embossed Beaver, Green, Partial Contents, Tooled Top	18.00
Medicine, Dr. Kilmer's Autumn Leaf Uterine Injection, 4 1/2 In.	20.00
Medicine, Dr. Kilmer's Swamp Root Kidney Remedy, 3 In.	22.00
Medicine, Dr. White's Dandelion Compound, Blood Purifying Tonic, Label, Blue	25.00
Medicine, Dr. Wynkoop's Katharismic Honduras Sarsaparilla, N.Y., 1850s, 10 In.	8525.00
Medicine, Harper Headache Co., Washington, D.C., 6 In.	18.00
Medicine, Hough's Vegetable Life Preserver, Keene, N.H., Glassworks, c.1840	7700.00
Medicine, Humphrey's Homopathic, Veterinary	265.00
Medicine, J.R. Nicholson & Co., Boston, Green, Cylindrical, Flared Top, Whittled	145.00
Medicine, John J. Smith, Louisville, Ky., Ice Blue, Cylinder, 6 In.	10.00
Medicine, Julius Hospital, Wurzburg, Pius Emblem, Claret, Kidney Shape	95.00
Medicine, Mexican Mustang Liniment, 5 1/2 In.	45.00
Medicine, Paregoric, Advertising & Doses For Infants, Violet, Swirls	200.00
Medicine, Pawnee Indian Too-Re, Dark Aqua, 7 1/2 In.	35.00
Medicine, Sanitarium, Yellow Green, Triangular, Replaced Collar	40.00
Medicine, South Carolina Dispensary, Palm Tree, Aqua, 6 In.	75.00
Medicine, U.S. Army, Medical Department, U.S. Army, 4 3/4 x 3 1/2 In.	15.00
Medicine, Winslow's Improved, Olive Amber, 5 In.	330.00
Medicine, Wm. E. Zoellers, Pittsburgh, Pa., Hostetter Shape	50.00
Milk, Alex Campbell Milk Co., 1 Qt.	25.00
Milk, Alpenrose, The Very Best, Portland, Ore., Red, Square, 1 Pt.	12.00
Milk, Anderson Erickson Dairy Co., Des Moines, Iowa, Orange, Square, 1 Qt.	50.00
Milk, Associated Bottle Supply Co., 2 Neck Rings, Embossed, 1 Pt.	12.00
Milk, Athens Co-Op Creamery, War Bonds For Victory, Uncle Sam, Green Pyro, 1 Qt.	60.00
Milk, Babyface, Brookfield, 1/2 Pt.	50.00
Milk, Babyface, Cream Top	75.00
Milk, Babyface, Red & Yellow Printing, White's Farm Dairy, 9 1/2 In.	75.00
Milk, Bailey's Dairy, Riverside, Calif., Slug Plate, Embossed, 1 Qt.	25.00
Milk, Bellview Dairy, Himrod, N.Y., Amber, White, Square, 1 Qt.	10.00
Milk, Broquiere's, Montebello, Calif., Baby In High Chair, Square, 1 Qt.	12.00
Milk, Cambridge Dairy, Black & Orange Pyro, 1 Qt.	35.00
Milk, Capital Dairy, Chicago, Cream, 1/2 Pt.	32.00
Milk, Carnation Dairy, Milk Glass, Red Carnation Spray, 1 Qt.	48.00
Milk, Carnation, Fresh Milk Over Circle, Red Pyro, Square, 1/2 Pt.	30.00
Milk, Carnation, Script, 1/2 Pt.	20.00

Milk, Castle Rock Barbecue, Smart To Drink Bottle, Milk, Green Pyro, 1/3 Qt.	25.00
Milk, Cedar Grove Dairy, Memphis, Tenn., Slug Plate, Embossed, 1 Qt.	12.00
Milk, Chicago Sterilized Milk Co., Blob Top, Aqua, No Closure, 1 Qt.	65.00
Milk, Clare, King & Queen Picture, Red Pyro, 1 Qt.	280.00
Milk, Cloverleaf Farms, Stockton, Orange Pyro, 1 Pt.	12.00
Milk, College Dairy For High Quality Dairy Products, Green Pyro, Square, 1 Qt.	22.00
Milk, Cosgrove, Tin Top, Registered, 1 Pt.	45.00
Milk, Crown Dairy, Pickaninny Picture, Red & Black Pyro, 1 Qt.	438.00
Milk, Dairylea, Owl & Figures, 1/2 Pt.	12.00
Milk, Damascus Fresh Dairy Products, Amber, Square, 1 Pt.	80.00
Milk, Double Babyface, Bargeware, 1892..	300.00
Milk, Dublin Co-Op, Red Pyro, Buy War Bonds, 5 Cents Deposit, 1 Qt.	35.00
Milk, Elmog Dairy, Coatesville, Pa., It Whips On Cream Top, 1 Qt.	35.00
Milk, Eurkeka Dairy, Amethyst, Embossed, Slug Plate, 1 Pt.	20.00
Milk, Farmer's Dairy Co., Inc., Baby's Picture, Black Pyro, 1 Pt.	17.00
Milk, Farmer's Dairy, Howell & Demarest, Tin Stopper, 1/2 Pt.	95.00
Milk, Farmers Creamery, Livingston, Mont., Embossed, 1/2 Pt.	38.00
Milk, Federal Dairy, Dish Of Ice Cream, Amber, Square, 1 Qt.	18.00
Milk, Frasure-Brown, Logan, Ohio, Embossed, 1/2 Pt.	24.00
Milk, Fredericktown Ice & Dairy Co., Slug Plate, Embossed, 1 Qt.	15.00
Milk, Gagnon's, Huron, S.D., Invest In Victory, Planes, War Bonds, Red, Blue Pyro, 1 Qt.	75.00
Milk, Gold Medal, Award Ribbon, Crown City Dairy Co., 1/3 Qt.	20.00
Milk, Gold Spot Homogenized & Pasteurized Milk, Orange Pyro, 1 Pt.	10.00
Milk, Grandy, Guardian Of Health, Tanks Picture, Red Pyro, 1/2 Pt.	180.00
Milk, Haleakala Dairy, Makawao, 1 Embossed Ring, 1 Qt.	12.00
Milk, Haleakala Dairy, Orange & Gray Pyro, Orange, 1963, 1/2 Pt.	8.00
Milk, Happy, 1 Qt.	60.00
Milk, Highclere, Churchill & Roosevelt Picture, Brown Pyro, 1 Qt.	1087.00
Milk, Highland B-B Dairy, California, Slug Plate, Embossed, 1 Pt.	20.00
Milk, Hover, Pelican Picture, Red Pyro, 1 Qt.	100.00
Milk, J.H. Rich Dairy, Banner Over Neck, Embossed, 1 Pt.	13.00
Milk, Jersey Farms, Yuma, Ariz., Amber, Square, 1 Qt.	25.00
Milk, Leafy Lane Dairy, Princeton, Ill., Amber, 1 Qt.	18.00
Milk, Live Oak Riviera Farms, Santa Barbara, Eagle, Red Pyro, 1/2 Pt.	30.00
Milk, Long Acres, 1 Qt.	25.00
Milk, Lucerne Homogenized, Square, Red Plastic Handle, 1 Gal.	30.00
Milk, Mayflower, Farm Scene, Red, Squatty, 1 Qt.	60.00
Milk, Mayflower, Pilgrim, Red Pyro, Square, 1 Pt.	12.00
Milk, McCarthy Dairy, Fillmore, N.Y., Buy Locally-Profit Locally, Deposit, Black, 1 Qt.	22.00
Milk, McClain Dairy Farm, Gadsden, Ala., Embossed, 1 Qt.	20.00
Milk, Meadow Gold, Cream Top, 1 Qt.	25.00
Milk, Meadow Gold, Himes Bros. Dairy Co., Dayton, Amber, Square, 1 Qt.	18.00
Milk, Meadow Gold, Square, 1/2 Gal.	12.00
Milk, Medo-Land, Maroon Pyro, 1/2 Pt.	15.00
Milk, Metzger's, Baby's Head, Embossed, 1 Pt.	60.00
Milk, Mid Valley Farm, Boy & Girl, Milk Bottle, Green, Square, 1/2 Pt.	6.00
Milk, Mission Creameries, Inc., Red Pyro, 1 Qt.	10.00
Milk, Mission Milk Creameries, Inc., Tower & Building, Pyro, 1/2 Pt.	18.00
Milk, Model Dairy, Galveston, Tex., Keep His America, Soldier, Orange Pyro, Dacro, 1 Qt.	25.00
Milk, Morningside Farm, Stockton, Calif., Dairy Farm Scene, Orange Pyro, 1 Qt.	28.00
Milk, Newport Dairy, Newport, Ky., Neck Hobnails, Embossed, 1 Qt.	15.00
Milk, Niday's Dairy, Molalla, Ore., Cow's Head, Blue, Square, Plastic Handle, 1 Gal. ..	30.00
Milk, North Yarmouth Dairy Inc., Pyro, 1/3 Pt.	24.00
Milk, Northside Dairy, Aurora, Ind., 1 Qt.	20.00
Milk, Oatman's Dairy, Cream, Dark Brown, Cardboard Cover, 1 Pt.	28.00
Milk, Paterson Dairy, Clifton, Ariz, Orange, Pyro, 1 Qt.	75.00
Milk, Port Colbourne, Tank, Boy & Go-Cart Picture, Both Need Fuel, Red Pyro, 1 Pt. ..	240.00
Milk, Price's Farm Dairy, Hazelton, Pa., 1 Qt.	24.00
Milk, Quality Dairy Co., Connellsville, Pa, Orange Pyro, 1/2 Pt.	6.00
Milk, Renovo Milk Co., Renovo, Pa., 1/2 Pt.	25.00
Milk, Reuger's Premium Milk Dairy, Evergreen Park, Ill., 1 Qt.	18.00
Milk, San Bernardino Creamery, Crown Top, Embossed, Slug Plate, 1 Pt.	10.00
Milk, Scott Powell Dairies, Philadelphia, 1/2 Pt.	7.00

Milk, Seneca Guernsey Farms, Geneva, N. Y., Blue Pyro, 5 Cent Deposit, 1 Qt. 25.00
Milk, Smith Bros. Dairy, Yellow Pyro, Amber, Square, 1 Qt. 15.00
Milk, Snider Dairy & Produce Co., Slug Plate, 1/2 Pt. 25.00
Milk, Somerset Farms Dairy, Middlebush, N.J., Amber, Square, 1 Qt. 12.00
Milk, Spokane Bottle Exchange Inc., Blue Pyro, Round, 1 Qt. 15.00
Milk, St. Mary's Dairy, George M. Erich, St. Mary's, Pa., Maroon Pyro, 1 Qt. 18.00
Milk, Stokely's Dairy, Newport, Tenn., Red Shield, Pyro, 1 Qt. 48.00
Milk, Sunland Dairy, Yuma, Ariz., Amber, White, Square, 1 Qt. 25.00
Milk, Sunrise Dairy, Red, Squatty, 1 Qt. 30.00
Milk, Sunrise Farm Dairy, Baltic, Conn., Orange Sunrise, Square, 1/2 Pt. 7.00
Milk, Sunshine Dairy, Florida, Cream Top, 1 Qt. 32.00
Milk, Superior Bottle, Milk, Pueblo, Colo., Green Pyro, 1 Qt. 30.00
Milk, Supreme Dairy, Peru, Ill., Baby In Crib With Bottle, Baby's Choice, Blue, 1 Qt... 24.00
Milk, Terrace Farm Dairy Co., Slug Plate, Embossed, 1 Qt. 18.00
Milk, Terry Dairy Co., Little Rock, Ark., Pasteurized Milk & Cream, 1 Qt. 35.00
Milk, Thatcher's Dairy, Embossed Man Milking Cow, 1884, 1 Qt. 250.00
Milk, Tin Top & Handle, Pat. 1898, 1 Pt. 150.00
Milk, Tri-State Milk Bottle Supply Co., Ashland, Ky., Embossed, 1 Qt. 30.00
Milk, Union Milk Co., Ltd., Calgary, Round, 1 Qt. 15.00
Milk, Universal Store Bottle, Embossed, 1/2 Pt. 9.00
Milk, Valley Gold, Albuquerque, N.M., Orange In Blue Shield, Square, 1 Qt. 12.00
Milk, Victoria Guernsey, San Bernardino, Orange, Squatty, 1 Qt. 45.00
Milk, Wayne County Hospital Diet Kitchen, Black Pyro, Round, 1/2 Pt. 50.00
Milk, West End Dairy, C.C. Rebert, Hanover, Pa., Embossed, 1 Pt. 20.00
Milk, Willow Farm Products, La Grange, Ill., 1 Qt. 28.00
Milk, Wm. E. Hemming, Whiteboro, N.Y., Tin Top, 1 Pt. 45.00
Milk, Wm. Weckerle & Sons, Emblem, Amber, 1 Qt. 60.00
Milk, Wood County Dairymen, Parkersburg, W.V., Safety Ring, 1 Pt. 24.00
Milk, York Dairy Co., Inc., Brooklyn, N.Y., Deposit, Round, 1 Pt. 12.00
Mineral Water, Bailey's Island Spring Water, Red Amber, Gloppy Applied Top, 9 In. ... 400.00
Mineral Water, Deep Rock Artesian Fresh, Los Angeles, Calif., Red Pyro, Green, 1/2 Gal. 65.00
Mineral Water, Highland Spring Water, St. Paul, Minn., Square, 1/2 Gal. 10.00
Mineral Water, Kissingen, Hanbury Smith, Deep Yellow Olive, 1 Pt. 90.00
Mineral Water, Milton Aerated Water Works Queens Co., Nova Scotia, Codd 90.00
Mineral Water, New Almaden, W & W, 1870 .... 95.00
Mineral Water, Owl, 2 Wing, Teal Blue, 9 1/2 In. 65.00
Mineral Water, Twitchell Superior, Philadelphia, Pale Green, Iron Pontil 35.00
Nurser, Sonny Boy 18.00
Nurser, Universal Feeder, 8 Oz. 25.00
Nurser, Welfare, Double Ended, England 35.00
Oil, Mobil, Gargoyle, Flat Sides, Arctic Grade, 1 Qt. 95.00
Oil, Shell, Raised Logo, Ribbed Design, 1 Qt. 85.00
Perfume bottles are listed in their own category
Poison, Black Flag Powder, Contents, Label, Box 8.00
Poison, C.L.G. Co., Pat. Applied For, Cobalt Blue, 4 1/4 In. 45.00
Poison, J.G. Godding & Co., Apothecaries, Boston, Cobalt Blue, Ribbed, 6 1/4 In. 425.00
Poison, Jeye's Fluid, Amber, Oval, 6 In. 35.00
Poison, KO-1, Skull & Crossbones, Yellow Amber, 4 3/4 In. 595.00
Poison, Krieger's Pharmacy, Poughkeepsie, Embossed, Label, 1900 .... 28.00
Poison, Mercury Bichloride, Poison Antiseptics, Label, Amber, 3 Sides, 8 In. 60.00
Poison, Not To Be Taken, Emerald Green, Bimal, Rectangular, 4 1/4 In. 13.00
Poison, Owl Drug, 3 3/8 In. 55.00
Poison, Owl Drug, Dark Cobalt Blue, 1 7/8 In. 65.00
Poison, Poison Tincture Iodine, Skull & Crossbones, Amber, Rubber Stopper 30.00
Poison, Quilted Design, Cobalt Blue 85.00
Poison, Radams Microbe Killer, Medium Amber, Man Beating Skeleton, 10 1/4 In. 55.00
Poison, Styrnia, 2 5/8 In. 55.00
Poison, Tincture Of Iodine, Skull & Crossbones, Glass Rod, Rubber Stopper 55.00
Poison, Undertakers Supply Co., Embalming Fluid, Chicago, 7 1/2 In. 60.00
Poison, Wyeth, Cobalt Blue, Embossed Dots Base, 2 3/4 In. 29.00
Sarsaparilla, Enameled White & Gold, Pewter Top, 11 1/2 In. 139.00
Seal, Initials PHO, England, c.1765, 10 1/2 In. 295.00
Seal, P.F. Heering, Amber, Bubbles, Whittled, Long Ribbon Seal 215.00

Seltzer, 7-Up, New Orleans, Pinkish Rose, 3/4-In. Lip 30.00
Seltzer, C. Frieds, Brooklyn, N.Y., Dark Green 12.00
Seltzer, Fountain Mineral Water, Bronx, N.Y., Czechoslovakia 15.00
Seltzer, Green, 1930 .... 160.00
Seltzer, Jas. Doughan, Parlor City Bottling Works, New York, Pewter Fittings, 1 Qt. ... 35.00
Seltzer, Jay-EFF, Sparkling Beverage, Brooklyn, N.Y., Bright Blue 22.00
Seltzer, Puroxia, 1930 .... 50.00
Seltzer, Ray Bottling Works, Brooklyn, N.Y., Aqua, Czechoslovakia 15.00
Snuff, Characters Subduing Horse, Wooden Spoon, 3 1/4 In. 190.00
Snuff, Comical Figures Of English & Dutch Men, Chinese Export, 2 3/4 In. 220.00
Snuff, Internal Scene, Bonsai Tree In Planter, China, 3 In. 210.00
Snuff, Jade, Rose Quartz Stopper 550.00
Snuff, Mottled Pink & Gray, Green Stone Top, Wooden Spoon, Stone, 2 3/4 In. 210.00
Snuff, Painted Warrior, Orange & Black Enamel, Silver & Glass Stopper, 3 3/4 In. 65.00
Snuff, Red Relief Design, Birds Sitting In Bush, Snowstorm Ground, Peking, 3 In. 225.00
Snuff, Relief Carved Dragon, Green Jade, 2 3/4 In. 95.00
Soaky, Alvin Chipmunk 15.00
Soaky, Bozo.. 15.00
Soaky, Broom Hilda, Black Outfit, Green Face, 1977, 9 In...........................*Illus* 32.00
Soaky, Bugs Bunny, Pale Blue & White, Hard Plastic, c.1960s, 10 1/2 In. 30.00
Soaky, Bullwinkle, Blue & Yellow Swim Suit, Yellow Antlers 60.00
Soaky, Bullwinkle, Brown 40.00
Soaky, Bullwinkle, Inserted Antlers, Plastic, 1960s, 10 1/2 In. 35.00
Soaky, Bullwinkle, No Clothes... 40.00
Soaky, Casper The Friendly Ghost 25.00
Soaky, Casper, Harvey Cartoon Character, 1960s, 10 In. ....*Illus* 37.00
Soaky, Chipmunks, Alvin, Simon, Theodore, 3 Piece 65.00
Soaky, Creature From The Black Lagoon 85.00
Soaky, Deputy Dawg.. 20.00
Soaky, Deputy Dawg, Screw-Off Hat Style, 1966 .... 36.00
Soaky, Elmer Fudd, Elmer Goes Hunting, Red & Black, 1960s 18.00
Soaky, Felix The Cat 35.00
Soaky, Frankenstein, 1960s ....70.00 to 75.00
Soaky, Lippy The Lion.. 45.00
Soaky, Mighty Mouse.. 33.00
Soaky, Mighty Mouse, Removable Head, Yellow Body, Vinyl, 10 In. 35.00
Soaky, Monster.. 60.00
Soaky, Mr. Magoo, 1960s.. 54.00
Soaky, Porky Pig 15.00
Soaky, Pumpkin Puss, Purex, 1960s 45.00
Soaky, Quick Draw McGraw, Blue, Black Hat, 1960s, 10 In. ....*Illus* 37.00

Bottle, Soaky, Broom Hilda, Black Outfit, Green Face, 1977, 9 In.

Bottle, Soaky, Casper, Harvey Cartoon Character, 1960s, 10 In.

Bottle, Soaky, Quick Draw McGraw, Blue, Black Hat, 1960s, 10 In.

Soaky, Rocky The Squirrel	30.00
Soaky, Rocky, 1960s	40.00
Soaky, Smokey The Bear	13.00
Soaky, Spouty Whale, Unused	8.00
Soaky, Tweety	25.00
Soaky, Tweety, 1960s	30.00
Soaky, Wendy, Red Outfit, Yellow Accents, Yellow Hair, Vinyl, c.1960s, 10 1/4 In.	18.00
Soaky, Wolfman, Blue Pants, 1963	85.00 to 90.00
Soaky, Woody Woodpecker	18.00
Soaky, Yoda, Star Wars	10.00
Soda, 9th Cola Clan Convention, Washington D.C., 1983	40.00
Soda, Burke Mt., Mountain & Trees, 7 Oz.	70.00
Soda, C. Brandt, Carlisle, Dyottville Glass Works, Emerald Green, Iron Pontil	170.00
Soda, Chico Club, Indian's Head, 7 Oz.	6.00
Soda, Crump & Fox, Bernardston, Mass., Superior Mineral Water, Green, Iron Pontil..	750.00
Soda, Dr Pepper, Good For Life, 6 1/2 Oz.	35.00
Soda, Dr Pepper, Thieves	100.00
Soda, Dr Pepper, Waco, Texas, 1885-1985	20.00
Soda, Dr. Nut, Punxsutawney, Complimentary, 1949	25.00
Soda, E. Duffy, No. 44 Filbert St., Dyottville Glass Works, Green, Iron Pontil	225.00
Soda, Grand Pop Hits The Spot, 6 1/2 Oz.	7.00
Soda, Hippo Size, San Antonio, Tex., Embossed Hippo, Pate. 1926, Large	20.00
Soda, Hires Root Beer Extract, Aqua	10.00
Soda, Hoxie, Albany, Ice Blue, Square Shoulders	35.00
Soda, Hygia Soda Works, Kahului, Hawaii, Aqua, Hutchinson	95.00
Soda, J. Pabst & Sons, Hamilton, Ontario, Hutchinson	15.00
Soda, Meyer & Rottman, New York, Pale Green, Iron Pontil	65.00
Soda, Moxie, Blob Top, 6 1/2 In.	10.00
Soda, Phosphorize, Cobalt, Embossed Across Shoulder	190.00
Soda, Southern Bottling Works, Atlanta, Aqua, Hutchinson, 7 1/4 In.	10.00
Soda, Taylor's Sarsaparilla Root Beer, Trenton, N.J., Aqua, Miniature	15.00
Soda, Tifton, Ga., Aqua, Hutchinson	12.00
Soda, Wm. Pond, XX Philadelphia Ale & Porter, N.Y., Emerald Green, Small	100.00
Soda, Wm. Russell, Baltimore, Deep Blue Green, Iron Pontil	150.00
Tonic, Dr. Stewart's Tonic, Bitters, Columbus, Ohio, Amber, Label	100.00
Wheaton, George Washington, Amethyst	10.00
Whiskey, 4 Aces American Rye, Ace Design, 8 In.	94.00
Whiskey, 4 Aces American Rye, British Columbia Dis., Fancy, 1920s, 1 Pt.	15.00
Whiskey, Castle, Amber, Inside Threads	25.00
Whiskey, Cherry Cordial, Victorian Blond Woman Label, Foil Over Top, Contents	35.00
Whiskey, Dark Green, Dutch, Squatty, 1720, 8 In.	145.00
Whiskey, Fine Bourbon Whiskey, Milk Glass, Floral Design	235.00
Whiskey, Golden Wedding, Carnival Glass, Label, 1 Pt.	50.00
Whiskey, Green, Barrel Shape Dispenser, Stopper, Metal Spout, 1 Qt.	115.00
Whiskey, Harvard Rye, Rectangular, 6 1/8 In.	15.00
Whiskey, Hermitage, 1 Qt., 11. In. .... *Illus*	6.00
Whiskey, Hettermann, Amber, In Wicker Basket, 9 1/4 In.	20.00

Bottle, Whiskey,
Hermitage,
1 Qt., 11. In.

◆◆◆◆◆◆◆◆◆◆◆◆◆◆◆◆◆◆◆◆◆◆

To remove a dried cork that
has fallen inside a bottle, try
this: Pour some household
ammonia in the bottle. Let it
sit for a few days. Most of the
cork should dissolve and can
easily be removed.

◆◆◆◆◆◆◆◆◆◆◆◆◆◆◆◆◆◆◆◆◆◆

Whiskey, I. Goldbery, New York City, Golden Amber, 9 Vertical Panels, 1 Qt. 40.00
Whiskey, James Woodburn Co., Sacramento, Calif., Deep Amethyst, Tooled Top 20.00
Whiskey, Joseph Fetz, Importer, Amethyst, Cylinder, 1 Fifth 125.00
Whiskey, Mammoth Cave, Oval, Cover, White Enamel Dots, Bar 3800.00
Whiskey, Nip, Woman's, Boot Shape.. 18.00
Whiskey, Pottery, Embossed Eagle, Multicolored, 3 1/2 In.. 35.00
Whiskey, Roehling & Shultz, Semi-Cabin, Chicago, Red Amber, 9 1/2 In. 75.00
Whiskey, S. Rosenthal & Co., Golden Amber, Paneled, Cylinder, 2 Qt. 50.00
Whiskey, Squatty, Cylindrical, c.1750, 7 3/4 In. 235.00
Whiskey, Udolpho Wolfe's Aromatic Schnapps, Light Yellow Amber, 9 1/4 In. 30.00
Whiskey, Udolpho Wolfe's Aromatic Schnapps, Olive Green, Iron Pontil 75.00
Whiskey, Udolpho Wolfe's Scheidam Aromatic Schnapps, Light Green, Open Pontil ... 135.00
Wine, Cobalt Blue, Bimal, 12 In.. 125.00
Wine, Wicker Top, Huge... 50.00

BOTTLE CAP collectors search for the printed cardboard caps used during the
past 80 years.

Booth's Dairy, Dunkirk, N.Y., Skimmed Milk, Paper... .05
Coopers New Jersey Pasteurized Milk, Aluminum .... .05
Darigold Whatcom Co., Dairymens Assoc., 2 1/4 In... 1.00
Golden State, Los Angeles, Pasteurized Milk, Red Aluminum.................................. .50
Littleton's Milk, San Bernardino .... .25
Pasteurized Homogenized Milk, Plug Type .... .10
Quality Dairy, Redlands Buttermilk, 1 1/2 In... .10
Quality Dairy, Redlands Low Fat, Paper... .05
Quality Dairy, Redlands Orange Juice, 1 1/2 In... .10
Quality Dairy, Redlands Punch Drink, Paper, 2 1/4 In... .05
Shady Grove Ice Cream, Plug Type .... .10
Teakwood Farms, Bakersfield, Calif. Milk, Paper.. .10

BOTTLE OPENERS are needed to open many bottles. As soon as the commercial bottle was invented, the opener to be used with the new types of closures
became a necessity. Many types of bottle openers can be found, most dating
from the twentieth century. Collectors prize advertising and comic openers.

Anchor, Metal... 2.00
Baseball Cap, Cast Iron 20.00
Black Man, Cast Iron 145.00
Budweiser Starr, Wall Mount... 5.00
Cowboy, With Guitar, Cactus, Cast Pot Metal, 4 7/8 In. 395.00
Dog, Cast Iron.. 40.00
Drink Dick Bros. Beer, Quincy, Ill. 5.00
Drink Moxie, 100% The Home Of Moxie 6.00
Drunk, On Sign Post.. 40.00
French Maid 35.00
Golden Pheasant, Cast Iron... 265.00
Helmet, Fireman's, Base Plate... 45.00
Indian, Iroquois Beer... 25.00
Irish Setter, Cast Iron 38.00
Isaac Leisy Brewing Co., Figure Of Baseball Pitcher, Pat. 1914 .... 32.00
Jimmy Carter, 1976... 40.00
Lovable Bar Bum, Box... 150.00
Man At Palm Tree, Iron 50.00
Monkey, Cast Iron 265.00
Ortlieb's Beer, Green Wooden Handle, Pat. 1933.. 3.00
Palm Tree, Cast Iron 130.00
Parrot, Cast Iron.. 45.00
Parrot On Perch, Iron, 5 1/2 In... 45.00
Pelican 65.00
Rheingold Extra Dry 2.00
Rooster, Painted, Iron, 3 3/4 In. 60.00
Seahorse, Cast Iron... 130.00
Silver Inlaid, Colonial Style, Mexico 550.00
Tavern Pale Atlantic Beer, Metal... 35.00

Toucan, Cast Iron 145.00
Zepp Malt Tonic, Gross Akron's Best Beer, Ice Pick, 1912 .... 25.00

BOW is an English porcelain works started in the eighteenth century. Most
items sold as Bow today were made after 1750.

Bowl, Quail, Shell Form, Interior Design, Trefoil Base, c.1755, 5 1/2 In........ 1840.00
Box, Partridge, Cover, c.1760, 4 7/16 In. 4600.00
Dish, Sweetmeat, 3 Scalloped Shells, Trefoil Base, 8 1/4 In. 460.00
Figurine, Abbess, Robe, Seated, Reading Bible, White, c.1755, 5 3/4 In. 575.00
Figurine, Allegorical, Autumn & Winter, c.1755, 5 3/16 & 4 7/8 In., Pair 805.00
Figurine, Goldfinch, Perched On Tree Stump, c.1760, 5 3/16 In. 2587.00
Figurine, Henry Woodward, Tricorner Hat, Frock Coat, c.1750, 10 1/8 In....... 2300.00
Figurine, James Quin As Falstaff, c.1750, 9 1/4 In. 2875.00
Figurine, Thames Waterman, Tree Stump, c.1753, 7 13/16 In. 9200.00
Salt Cellar, 3 Prunus Sprigs, Cherub's Mask & Paw Feet, 3 1/16 In. 3162.00
Sauceboat, Scroll Rim, Blossoms & Leaves At Back, Handle, 7 3/4 In. 4025.00
Teapot, Mushroom Knop, Spray & Sprigs Of Roses, 1760, 5 5/16 In. 2070.00
Vase, Kakiemon, Phoenix In Flight, Flowering Plant, c.1753, 3 9/16 In., Pair 1035.00

BOXES of all kinds are collected. They were made of thin strips of inlaid
wood, metal, tortoiseshell, embroidery, or other material. Additional boxes
may be listed in other sections, such as Advertising, Battersea, Ivory, Shaker,
Tinware, and various Porcelain categories. Tea Caddies are listed in their
own category.

Agate, Bird On Hinged Cover, Silver Mounted, Oval, 1930, 5 1/8 In.............. 1725.00
Band, Wallpaper Covered, Blue & Brown, Oval, Large 235.00
Band, Wallpaper Covered, Blue, Orange, Yellow Leaves & Flowers, 6 x 11 In. 4025.00
Band, Wallpaper Covered, Figural Design, 1859 Newspaper Lined, 12 x 21 In. 135.00
Band, Wallpaper Covered, Floral & Feather, Marked Anna L. Bowman, 2 7/8 x 4 1/2 In. 19.00
Band, Wallpaper Covered, Geometric & Floral Designs, Bentwood, 15 In. 220.00
Band, Wallpaper Covered, Geometric Print, Cardboard, Oval, 13 In. 225.00
Band, Wallpaper Covered, Scenes Of Capitol, Bentwood, 17 1/2 In. 990.00
Bentwood, Black & Red Trim, Stenciled Flower On Lid, Wire Handle, 9 3/4 In. 357.00
Bentwood, Domed Cover, Laced Seams, Engraved Geometric Design, 1821, 5 1/2 In. .. 165.00
Bentwood, Single Finger Construction, Wrought Iron Tacks, Oval, 10 In. ....110.00 to 165.00
Bible, Cleated Hinged Lid, Painted Stylized Circles & Birds, Walnut, 1740s, 23 1/2 In. .. 2012.00
Bible, Molding On Lid, Turned Feet & Base, Tabletop, 10 x 21 x 14 In. 522.00
Bible, Shoe Feet, Iron Lock 285.00
Bride's, Pennsylvania German, Painted Bride & Groom, Oval 3000.00
Bride's, Polychrome Floral, Gray Ground, Bentwood, Oval, 18 In. 250.00
Bride's, Woman On Lid, Polychrome Flowers, Black Ground, Pine, 18 In. 995.00
Burl, Ivory Inlay, Anchor, Stars & Moon, 19th Century, 4 1/4 In. 430.00
Camphorwood, Carved, China, 8 In. 29.00
Candle, Beveled Edge Lid, Lollipop Hanger, Oak, 19 In. 300.00
Candle, George III, Mahogany, Brass Bound, 2 Sloped Lids, 1780, 19 x 14 In. 825.00
Candle, Green Paint, 13 In. 410.00
Candle, Hanging, 1 Drawer, Lift Top, Iron Pull, Walnut, 15 1/4 In. 660.00
Candle, Hinged Cover, 1 Dovetailed Drawer, Butternut, 16 In. 385.00
Candle, Hinged Cover, Fluted Quarter Columns, Drawer, Oak, Scotland, 1790, 17 In. . 750.00
Candle, Hinged Cover, Hanging, Dovetailed Case, Walnut & Poplar, 14 In. 495.00
Candle, Sliding Cover, Dovetailed, Beaded Edge, 19 In. 105.00
Candle, Sliding Cover, Mahogany, Dovetailed, Hand Cut Screws, Nails, 1820, 9 1/2 In. . 275.00
Candle, Sliding Cover, Pine & Poplar, Yellow Repaint, Dovetailed, Initials CF, 12 In.. 220.00
Candle, Walnut, Carved Starbursts, No Cover, 1800, 11 x 5 x 18 1/4 In. 420.00
Candy, Little Girl, 1939s, 3 x 5 In. 12.00
Chalice, Wooden, Large 105.00
Cherry, Cutout Heart Hanging Hole, Dovetailed, 14 1/2 In. 385.00
Coal, Brass, Ornate, Tavern Drinking Scenes, Castors 120.00
Collar, Celluloid, Cupids, Flowers, Red Satin Lined 80.00
Deed, Copper, 12 1/2 x 5 1/2 x 2 1/2 In. 45.00
Desk, Tabletop, Pine, Painted, Applied Base Molding, Slant Lift Top, 21 In. 385.00
Ditty, Hollowed From Log, Iron Bound, Studs, Leather Strap & Hinges, 1800s, 9 x 5 In. 175.00
Document, Alligatored Black Paint, Gold Trim, Flowers, 11 1/2 x 3 x 4 In. 125.00

Document, Allover Birds, Flowers & Leaves, Wooden, Pennsylvania German, 1840 .... 670.00
Document, Allover Gold Embossed Black Leather, Brass Lock, 1785, 4 x 8 In. 295.00
Document, Georgian, Mahogany, Rosewood, Brass Bound, 13 In. 110.00
Document, Leather Hinges, Newspaper Lining, 1828, 9 x 4 1/4 x 4 1/2 In. 65.00
Document, Lift Top, Painted Black & Red, Iron Handles, 7 1/2 x 18 In. 255.00
Document, Painted Flower & Basket On Hinged Lid, Compartmented, Pine, 13 1/4 In. 8350.00
Dome Top, Dovetailed, Pine, Blue Paint, Polychrome Floral Design, 17 In. 1450.00
Dome Top, Dovetailed, Pine, Floral Design, Yellow Striping, Painted, 11 1/2 In. 385.00
Dome Top, Dovetailed, Poplar, Green Paint, Hinged, 20 In. 110.00
Dome Top, Dovetailed, Poplar, Iron Lock, Brass Keyhole Cover, 24 In. 138.00
Dome Top, Dovetailed, Red Paint, Black Sponging, Lined, 30 1/4 In. 230.00
Dome Top, Hinged Lid, Wooden, Red & Black Paint, 19th Century, 12 x 25 1/2 x 12 In. 460.00
Dome Top, Poplar, Red Brown Grained Paint, 8 In. 355.00
Dome Top, Poplar, Wallpaper Covering, Tin Hinges & Hasp, 5 1/4 In. 195.00
Dome Top, Theorem Baskets Of Flowers On Sides, Florals On Top, 7 1/2 x 18 In. 605.00
Dome Top, Tooled & Gilded Leather, John Clements Label, London, 7 In. 160.00
Dome Top, Vining Flowers, Birds, Wire Staple Hinges, Handle, Lock, 14 1/2 In. 990.00
Double Sliding Covers, Walnut, Europe, 13 3/4 In. 93.00
Dough, Cover, Poplar, Refinished, Dovetailed, 15 1/2 x 26 In. 135.00
Dough, Poplar, Dovetailed Splay Case, Lid, 32 1/2 In. 135.00
Dovetailed, Marbleized Paint, Wallpaper Interior, Copper Hasp, 18 1/2 In. 248.00
Dovetailed, Pine, Carved, Fan Shaped Ornaments, 26 In. 138.00
Dovetailed, Pine, Early 1800s 125.00
Dovetailed, Wood & Ivory Inlaid, Yellow Velvet Upholstered Top, 11 1/2 In. 115.00
Dresser, Bronze, Cupids Scenic Plaque, Original Lining, 6 x 8 x 3 In. 215.00
Dresser, Man In Doghouse, Head Peeks Out, Whimsy Type, Villona Starr, Small 95.00
Dresser, Relief Nude Woman, Wrapped In Cloth, Malachite Glass 235.00
Enameled Scrollwork, Faceted, Gilt & Ruby Starburst Medallions, 3 x 4 In. 440.00
Firkin, Butter, Polychrome Flowerhead On Lid, Catharine V.P., 5 In. 4600.00
Fruitwood, Circular, Carved Lid, Bagard De Nancy, c.1700, 5 1/2 In. 2185.00
Fruitwood, Satinwood Inlay, Music Motif, Holland, 19th Century, 9 1/2 x 6 In. 805.00
Game, Rosewood, Brass Bound, Chess, Checkers, Backgammon, Cribbage, Tiffany 860.00
Gaming, Rosewood, Mother-Of-Pearl Inlays, c.1870 .... 1400.00
Geometric Marquetry Design On Top & Sides, Tufted Silk Lining, 11 In. 82.00
Glove, Inlaid Walnut, 11 In. 60.00
Glove, Rosewood, Mother-Of-Pearl & Brass Inlay, Hinged Cover, 9 5/8 In. 80.00
Hardwood, Hanging, Cutout Bird Crest, 2-Tone Brown, Wire Nail, 7 1/2 x 8 1/4 In. 440.00
Hat, Clear Plastic & Fabric, 1940s 35.00
Honor, Dispensing Tobacco, Coin Opens Compartment, Brass, 9 1/4 In. 1100.00
Horse Hoof, Silver Plated Hinged Cover, 19th Century, Pair 396.00
Instrument, Inlaid, Mahogany, 8 In. 155.00
Iron, Hammered, Arts & Crafts, Black Finish, Snake Finial, Maple Liner, 9 In. 467.00
Jewelry, Brass, Inlaid, Marble Top, 6-Drawer Fitted Interior, 11 1/4 x 7 1/4 In. 198.00
Jewelry, Embossed Design, Assorted Stones, Brass, 2 1/2 x 8 In. 295.00
Jewelry, Gilt-Metal, Italian Baroque, Cabinet Shape, Hinged Cover, 7 1/4 x 4 1/4 In. 1380.00
Jewelry, Inlaid Geometric Marquetry On Lid, Velvet Lined, 10 1/4 In. 192.00
Jewelry, Mirror Top, England 495.00
Jewelry, Silver, Art Deco, Ahrendt & Taylor, Newark, N.J., c.1925, 4 1/2 x 3 1/2 In. 80.00
Jewelry, Trick, Carved Stags, Austria, 9 1/2 In. 330.00
Jewelry, Tunbridgeware 77.00
Knife, 1 Drawer, Scalloped Ends, Wire Nail, 14 1/2 In. 302.00
Knife, Dovetailed, Dark Finish, Oak, 13 3/4 In. 93.00
Knife, Dovetailed, Walnut, Cutout Handle, 10 x 13 1/2 In. 193.00
Knife, Georgian, Mahogany, Inlaid, Sloping Lid 523.00
Knife, Hepplewhite Style, Bracket Feet, String Inlays, Berkey & Gay, 27 x 11 In., Pair. 2415.00
Knife, Hepplewhite, Serpentine, Star Inlay, Ivory Handled Cutlery, England 880.00
Knife, Tiger Pale, Pencil Inscription, Kennebunk, Me, 10 1/2 In. 402.00
Knife, Walnut, Inlaid Star, Williamsburg, Va., c.1780, 9 x 15 1/2 In. 350.00
Lace Maker's, Sliding Lids, Inner Compartments, Drawers, Cherry, 22 In. 825.00
Lap, Wooden, Blue Paint, Oval, 19th Century 380.00
Leather, Tooled, Red, France, 10 In. 94.00
Letter, Burl Walnut, Perpetual Calendar, Fitted Interior, Leather Top, Victorian 770.00
Lift Cover, Yellow Grain Paint, Bootjack Sides, Small 155.00

Made From Violin, Tiger Stripe Maple, 14 1/2 In. 104.00
Mahogany Marquetry, Geometric Foliage Bands, Worn, 9 In. 82.00
Maple, Bentwood, 1-Finger, 19th Century, Oval, 2 1/8 x 5 1/4 In. 345.00
Maple & Pine, 3-Finger, Oval, 6 1/2 In. 220.00
Maple & Pine, 4-Finger, Copper Nails, 4 1/4 x 10 1/4 In. 550.00
Medallion Of Ruins On Cover, Micro-Mosaic, Gilt Metal, Enameled, 2 3/4 In. 287.00
Pantry, Mustard Yellow 525.00
Pantry, Rosewood Grain Painting, 19th Century, 7 x 5 1/2 In. 225.00
Pen, Persian Lacquer, Allover Birds & Trees, Inner Inkwell, 8 7/8 In. 115.00
Pencil, Felix The Cat, Playing Fiddle, American Pencil Co., 1939 .... 100.00
Pine, 2 Drawers, Brown Vinegar Grained, Black Trim, Green Knobs, 5 x 8 x 9 In. 621.00
Pine, Red Flame Graining, Brass Ring Handle, 18 In. 220.00
Pinwheels, Black, Small 2300.00
Pipe, Hanging, 1 Drawer 3450.00
Pipe, Red Flame Graining, 1 Drawer, Scrolled Open Top, Pine & Maple, 23 In. 3355.00
Pipe, Wooden, Carved, Lead Lined, Early 19th Century, 18 In. 460.00
Pressed Floral Cover, Mirrored Base 18.00
Putty & Vinegar, Grained, 19th Century, 6 x 12 In. 5750.00
Salt, Wall, Folk Art, Red 195.00
School, Space Shuttle Illustration, Cardboard 10.00
Secret Drawer In Base Molding, Walnut, 20 1/2 In. 192.00
Sewing, Woman's, Faux Tortoise With Inset Lacquered Panels, Oriental, 14 In. 396.00
Shirtwaist, Copper Hardware, Cedar Lining, Gustav Stickley, No. 95, 16 x 32 In. 6750.00
Silver Overlay On Copper, Over Wood, Inlaid Ivory, King Tut's Copy, 1930s, 7 In. 220.00
Sliding Cover, Blue Paint, Yellow & Ochre Grained Panel 8625.00
Sliding Cover, Forged Nails, Pine, 11 x 22 In. 48.00
Sliding Cover, Red & Green Tulip, Initials M.M. 3220.00
Speckled Gold, Black & Mica Flakes Bound, Edo Japanese, Lacquer, 12 In. 1400.00
Spice, Sliding Cover, 4-Part Interior, Dovetailed, Walnut, 8 1/2 In. 220.00
Spice, Sliding Cover, Divided Interior, Poplar, Painted, 11 1/4 In. 297.00
Stamp, White Porcelain, Gold Enameled Butterfly 12.00
Strong, Hinged Cover, Straps, Painted, Germany, c.1600, 4 5/8 x 6 3/4 x 4 3/4 In. 1380.00
Tin, Painted, Amish, Mary Lapp 295.00
Traveling, Walnut Veneered, Brass Hardware, Velvet Lining, 19th Century, 9 x 8 In. 210.00
Trinket, Rosewood, Key, 12 In. 60.00
Wall, Cutout Of Heart & Reverse Heart, White Over Green Over Red, Square Nails 1100.00
Watch, Curly Maple, Cathedral Style 625.00
Wooden, Abstract & Figural Painted, Orange, Black, Green, Blue, 2 x 8 x 4 In. 110.00
Wooden, Painted Deer Scene, 15 1/2 In. 2800.00
Wooden, Painted Farm Scene, Wolf, 16 In. 3500.00
Writing, Engraved Abalone Shell Inlay On Cover, Bird's-Eye Veneer, 14 3/4 In. 105.00
Writing, Fitted Interior, Bands Of Inlay, Walnut, 10 1/2 In. 93.50
Writing, Fitted Interior, End Drawer, Brass Bound, Mahogany, c.1800 .... 650.00
Writing, Papier-Mache, Lacquered, Mother-Of-Pearl Inlay Of Windsor Castle 495.00
Writing, Rosewood Grained, Brass Tack Design, Escutcheons, 13 In. 180.00
Writing, Walnut Veneer, Brown Finish, Gilding, Fitted, 11 1/2 In. 60.00

BOY SCOUT collectibles include any material related to scouting, including patches, manuals, and uniforms. The Boy Scout movement in the United States started in 1910. The first Jamboree was held in 1937. Girl Scout items are listed under their own heading.

Baseball Cover, Hickory Ridge Boy Scouts, Fast Nine, 1913 .... 26.00
Bookmark, Original Card 20.00
Calendar, Scout Standing By Liberty Bell, Goodyear, 1947, Large 10.00
Camera, Seneca, Box 65.00
Compass, Bakelite 12.00
Cover, Silver Jubilee Boy Scouts 18.00
Flashlight, Metal 20.00
Handbook, 1940 .... 13.00
Handbook, Leaper's, 1st Edition, 1918 .... 75.00
Hat, Scout Master, 1900s, Box 95.00
Hatchet, Bridgeport 35.00
Knife Set, Remington, Lithographed Inside Cover, 9 1/4 x 3 1/2 In. 615.00

Neckerchief Holder, Bronze, Eagle Emblem, Domed, 1 1/2 x 1 1/4 In. 8.00
Planetarium, 2 Planet Cards, Inside Packet, 1948 .... 6.00
Ring, Sterling... 10.00
Shirt, Patches, East Pittsburgh, Pa., 1930s-1940s... 95.00
Tie Pull, Leather, Dated 1958 .... 15.00
Uniform, 1920s 50.00
Utensil, Spoon-Knife, 1930s 8.00

BRADLEY & HUBBARD is a name found on many metal objects. Walter Hubbard and his brother-in-law, Nathaniel Lyman Bradley, started making cast iron clocks, tables, frames, andirons, lamps, chandeliers, sconces, and sewing birds in 1854 in Meriden, Connecticut. The company became Bradley & Hubbard Manufacturing Company in 1875. Charles Parker Company bought the firm in 1940. Their lamps are especially prized by collectors.

Andirons, Scrolled Fiddle Head, Half-Round, Cast Iron, 12 In. 575.00
Bookends, Boston Terriers.. 295.00
Bookends, Classical Greek Arches 75.00
Bookends, Longfellow ....65.00 to 95.00
Calendar, Perpetual, 13 Celluloid Inserts, Brass 65.00
Chandelier, 5-Light, Baluster Form Column, Electrified, Signed, 18 In. 145.00
Doorstop, Warrior 170.00
Fireplace Set, Andirons & 4-Piece Tool Set, Fenter, 24 x 12 In. 1200.00
Fish Plate Set, Fish & Crabs, 19th Century, 12 Piece... 805.00
Lamp, 2-Light, 8 Amber Slag Panels, Floral Frame, Signed, 22 In. 575.00
Lamp, 2-Light, Brass, Conical Slag Shade, 18 1/2 In. 385.00
Lamp, 2-Light, Octagonal Conical Shade, 18 1/2 In... 385.00
Lamp, 6-Paneled Slag Glass Shade, Signed, 1910 .... 875.00
Lamp, 8 Slag Glass Inserts, Metal Frame, 2 Socket Base, 21 In. 862.00
Lamp, Banquet, Coiled Wire Design, Oil Canister, Shell Shade, 29 In. 690.00
Lamp, Colorless Bent Paneled Shade, 4 Lions Base, Signed, 18 In. 345.00
Lamp, Floor, Attached Ashtray & Match Holder 475.00
Lamp, Floor, Green Slag, Leaded, Gold Key Border, Circular Foot, 56 In...................... 375.00
Lamp, Gone With The Wind, Yellow Floral 110.00
Lamp, Green Shade, Signed, 1917-1920 .... 925.00
Lamp, Hammered Shade, Bronze Base, 16 1/2 In. 635.00
Lamp, Library, Apricot Diamond-Quilted Shade 1250.00
Lamp, Octagonal Shade, Gridwork, Floral, Red Slag Glass Inserts, 18 In. 747.00
Lamp, Octagonal, 8 Slag Panels, 22 In. ....*Illus* 978.00
Lamp, Oil, Emeralite Shade, Nickel Plate Over Brass 245.00
Lamp, Oil, Pierced Floral & Scroll Design, Electrified, Signed, 29 In. 175.00
Lamp, Palm Tree Overlay, Slag Glass Shade, 1900-1920 .... 2900.00
Lamp, Table, Green Cased Melon Ribbed Shade, 2 Handles...................................... 250.00
Lamp, White Slag Glass, No. 6822.. 300.00
Letter Holder, Cherubs, Brass, Art Nouveau, Signed.. 155.00

*Bradley & Hubbard, Lamp, Octagonal,
8 Slag Panels, 22 In.*

◆◆◆◆◆◆◆◆◆◆◆◆◆◆◆◆◆◆◆◆◆◆

Tired of scrubbing and scrubbing glass to remove marks from masking tape and labels? Get some commercial hand cleaner, pat some on the stain, let it stay for 30 minutes. Then rub it off with a cloth and wash the glass.

◆◆◆◆◆◆◆◆◆◆◆◆◆◆◆◆◆◆◆◆◆◆

Sconce, Beveled Mirror, Wall, 19 1/2 x 13 In. 450.00

BRASS has been used for decorative pieces and useful tablewares since ancient times. It is an alloy of copper, zinc, and other metals. Additional brass items may be found under Bell, Candlestick, Tool, or Trivet.

Ashtray, 3 Cigarette Rests, Scrolled Rim, Korea, 4 1/2 In. 4.00
Ashtray, Enameled, Slipper, Magenta Dragon On Blue, White Interior, 3 3/4 x 2 In. 18.00
Ashtray, Floral, Scroll, Scalloped, 3-Footed, Near Eastern Style, 4 3/8 In. 3.00
Ashtray, Flowers, Nest Of 4, Scalloped, China, 2 3/4 In. 12.00
Ashtray, Hammered, Signed Jack Clausen, 4 1/2 In. 220.00
Ashtray, Oriental Monster God, 3-Footed, 6 1/2 In. 4.00
Ashtray, Owl, Deep Feathered, England, 5 1/2 x 3 1/2 In. 24.00
Ashtray, Panel, 12 Animals In Relief Around Rim, 4 1/4 In. 8.00
Ashtray, Scallop Shell, Anodized Blue On Top, Brass Rim, Black Bottom, Israel, 3 3/4 In. 3.00
Ashtray, Tooled, Enameled, India Behares Brass, 3 5/8 x 1 7/8 In. 5.00
Bar Holder, Horses, Wagon, Driver, 2 Pressed Glass Decanters, 6 Shot Glasses, 1940s 95.00
Beaker, Repousse Gadrooning, Punch Work, Dutch, Late 18th Century 195.00
Bed Warmer, Copper, Engraved Peacocks, Turned Wooden Handle, 42 In. 165.00
Bed Warmer, Engraved Design Cover, Cut Down Handle, America, 33 In. 84.00
Bed Warmer, Engraved, Pierced, Wooden Handle, 19th Century, 44 In. 172.00
Bed Warmer, Incised Floral Design, 42 In. 250.00
Bed Warmer, Pierced & Chased Lid, Woman's Head Outline, Iron Shaft, 46 In. 467.00
Bed Warmer, Tooled Lid, 40 In. 126.00
Bed Warmer, Tooled Lid, Turned Handle, 43 In. 275.00
Bed Warmer, Tooled Lid, Wooden Handle, 40 In. 203.00
Bookrack, Bronze Owl, Expandable 62.00
Bowl, Mission Symbols, Hammered, Mission Inn, 2 x 5 In. 82.00
Box, Cover, Foreign Script & Woman In Landscape, Oval, 5 In. 84.00
Bucket, Kerosene, Fireplace Starter, Hammered, Old Mission Kopper Kraft, 9 x 8 In. . 165.00
Bucket, Swing Handle, Mid-19th Century, 11 In. 50.00
Cachepot, Ring Handles, India, 15 In. 172.00
Caddy, Desk, Tripartite Form, Bracket Feet, Bell, England, 18th Century, 7 x 6 In. 825.00
Candle Snuffer, Stagecoach 25.00
Candy, Compote, Scalloped Foot, Engraved Flowers, China, 6 x 3 3/8 In. 23.00
Canterbury, Rectangular, Casters, 17 x 12 x 17 In. 104.00
Chalice, Turned Pedestal, England, c.1760, 6 1/2 In. 260.00
Chamberstick, Gimbal Socket, 6 1/4 In. 72.00
Chamberstick, Repousse, Punch, Wriggled Design, Dutch, Late 18th Century, 13 In. ... 175.00
Chamberstick, Scalloped Edged Saucer, England, Pair, 5 x 1 5/8 In. 30.00
Chest, Allover Relief Scenes, Mid-1800s, 17 x 12 1/2 x 19 3/4 In. 210.00
Chocolate Pot, Continental, 18th Century, 10 1/2 In. 690.00
Cups, Engraved Flowers, China, 2 1/4 x 1 4 1/2 In. 4.00
Cuspidor, Enamel Insert 48.00
Cuspidor, England 50.00
Cuspidor, Havana Cigars, 5 Cents, Large 45.00
Cuspidor, Rochester Stamping Co. 48.00
Decanter, Cast, Heavy, 1 3/4 In. 6.00
Door Knocker, Flower Basket 75.00
Door Knocker, Kissing Couple, Roses Ground, 5 1/2 In. 74.00
Door Knocker, Regency, Dolphin Shape 231.00
Door Knocker, Woodpecker 25.00
Dredger, England, c.1730, 4 1/2 In. 195.00
Dresser Set, Velvet Box, 5 Piece 235.00
Easel, Frames, Pierced Leaf Scrolls, Ovals, 10 x 9 In. 90.00
Figurine, Drunk, Holding Signpost, Canterbury Coat Of Arms, England, 4 1/2 In. 15.00
Figurine, Rhino, Filigree, Turquoise, Studded With Carnelians, 3 1/2 x 2 In. 25.00
Figurine, Seated Hoi Toi, Carved Native Wood, Throne, 10 x 12 In. 175.00
Figurine, Squirrel, Solid, England, 1/2 x 2 In. 20.00
Flask, Figural, Flapper, Pocket, Japan, 4 In. 50.00
Humidor, Roycroft, Cylindrical, Twisted Design, 8 In. 605.00
Incense Burner, Hinged Turtle, Hinged Back, 4 1/4 In. 18.00
Incense Burner, Incised Dragon, 3-Footed, Handles, Chinese Characters, China 12.00
Incense Burner, Open-Mouthed Chick, 2 1/4 x 2 1/2 In. 12.00

Jardiniere, Floral Basket Frieze Around Rim, Ring Handles, 3-Footed, 10 1/2 x 9 In. 28.00
Jardiniere, Leaf Forms, Engraved Dragons, Geometrics, China, 9 1/2 x 6 1/2 In. 45.00
Jardiniere, Sculptured Roses In Heavy Relief Around Rim, 9 3/4 x 11 1/2 In. 42.00
Kettle, Spun, Wire Bail Handle, Hayden Pat. Label, 14 1/2 In. 82.00
Lamp, Floor, Adjustable, Kerosene Burner, Electrified, Milk Glass Globe, 58 In. 192.00
Lipstick Case, Forever Amber 10.00
Magnifier, Composition Head Of Retriever Dog 125.00
Mortar & Pestle, Square Handles, 9 In. 65.00
Mortar & Pestle, Zigzag, Square Handles, 3 7/8 x 4 3/8 In. 64.00
Notary Seal, Recorder's Office Of Forest County Penna., 1 7/8 In. 28.00
Pail, Rattail Handle, Signed 55.00
Pan, Marmalade, Georgian, 1800, 22 In. 110.00
Plaque, Fruit, Leaves, Beetle, Ring Handle, England, 14 1/2 In. 8.00
Plaque, Picture, English Garden, Tudor House, Brass Rim, England, 10 In. 15.00
Plaque, Picture, Fox Hunt Scenes, Scrolled, Feathered Rim, England, 14 1/4 In. 10.00
Plaque, Ship, 3-Masted, Fancy Relief Rim, England, 11 3/4 In. 8.00
Plaque, Wall, Fruits & Fancy Scrolled Rim, 11 3/4 In. 5.00
Plate, Pierced Bands, Griffin Heads, Toothed Rim, 10 1/4 In. 45.00
Powder Flask, Embossed Clasped Hands, Eagle & Flags, Stamped Ames Spout, 1844 . 220.00
Salver, Arabesque, Turned & Carved Folding Base, Middle East, 29 x 24 In. 220.00
Samovar, Hammered & Pierced, Chimney, Ivan Katineva, Pre-1917, 28 1/2 In. 450.00
Sander, Barrel, Banded Sides, Pierced Top, 2 1/4 In. 287.00
Shoehorn, Traces Of Wriggle Design, 18th Century, 9 In. 165.00
Spoon, Tea Caddy, Shakespearean 12.00
Stamp Holder, Double, Sunflowers 55.00
Stand, Parrot, Copper 135.00
Stand, Umbrella, Dish Bottom, Ovoid, 17 1/4 x 5 1/2 x 19 3/4 In. 58.00
Stand, Umbrella, Relief Scene 35.00
Sundial, Folding Gnomon, Late 17th Century, Brass 750.00
Tea Caddy, Spoon, Shakespearean 12.00
Tea Set, Floral Enameled, Middle East, Miniature, 4 Piece 22.00
Teapot, Gooseneck Spout, Tin Lined, Bail Handle, 8 1/4 In. 28.00
Tie Back, Victorian, Curved Design, Foliate Ends, Oval Pastoral Prints, 6 Piece 258.00
Tray, Engraved Flowers, Basket Lattice Ground, Scalloped Rim, Oval, 16 x 11 3/4 In. . 12.00
Tray, Engraved Flowers, Double Bamboo Bail Handle, China, 10 1/2 In. 40.00
Tray, Geometrics, Tooled Moorish, 19 3/4 In. 38.00
Trivet, Embossed, Polished, Expandable, Manning Bowman, 13 1/2 x 17 In. 65.00
Umbrella Stand, Aesthetic Style, Twisted Columns, Florals, Shells, 27 1/2 In. 440.00
Vase, Baluster Shape, 2 1/4 x 7/8 In. 6.00
Vase, Bud, Engraved Florals, Scalloped, China, 5 In. 7.00
Vase, Classic Shape, Footed, 2 1/4 x 7/8 In. 5.00
Vase, Fluted Hammered Bowl, Scrolling Handles, c.1924, J. Hoffman, 7 In. 9400.00
Vase, Incised Allover Design, China, 7 1/2 x 3 1/4 In. 32.00
Vase, Overall Raised Chrysanthemums, Bulbous, China, 16 3/4 In. 315.00
Vase, Urn Shape, 1 3/8 In. 5.00
Wall Sconce, Round Back, Punched, Candleholder, England, 17th Century, 16 1/2 In. . 316.00
Warming Pan, Chased Cover, 19th Century 165.00

BRASTOFF, see Sascha Brastoff category

BREAD PLATE, see various silver categories, porcelain factories, and pressed
glass patterns

BRIDE'S BASKETS OR BRIDE'S BOWLS were usually one-of-a-kind novelties made in American and European glass factories. They were especially
popular about 1880 when the decorated basket was often given as a wedding
gift. Cut glass baskets were popular after 1890. All bride's baskets lost favor
about 1905.

BRIDE'S BASKET, Beaded Loops, Melon Ribbed Bowl, Tufts, 13 1/4 x 11 In. 395.00
    Cased Glass, Figural Scene, Enameled, Gilt 165.00
    Cranberry To Pink Glass, Silver Overlay, Pleated Scallops, Enameled 275.00
    Daisy & Button Insert, Honey Amber, Ornate Footed Frame, 12 x 12 1/2 In. 100.00
    Dark To Light Red, Cased, Ruffled, Silver Plated Holder, 11 1/2 In. 220.00

Enameled Bird & Floral, Pleated Rim, Silver Plated Frame, 10 3/4 In. 325.00
Glass, Peach To Apricot, Pleated Rim, Ribbon Edge, Braided Handle, 10 In. 225.00
Opalescent Spanish Lace, Ruffled Rim, Cranberry, 10 In. 295.00
Peachblow, Ruffled Rim, Enameled & Gilt Flowers, Silver Plated Frame, 9 1/2 In. 99.00
Ruffled Bowl, Enamel, White Scrolls, Blue Forget-Me-Nots, Satin, Victorian 450.00
Ruffled Edge, Enameled Flowers & Leaves, Cobalt Blue, Silver Plated Frame 440.00
Ruffled Rim, Pink Flowers, Gold Leaves 295.00
Silver Plate, Scrollwork, Arched Handle, Pierced Hearts, 17 In. 523.00
Silver Plated Frame, Crystal Insert, Tufts 225.00
Star Shape Insert, Golden Amber, Daisy & Button, 10 In. 195.00
Victorian, Birds, Ruffled Bowl, Apricot, Stevens & Williams, 1880s 850.00
BRIDE'S BOWL, Beaded Drape, Opalescent Green, Silver On Basket 215.00
Burmese, Enameled, Floral Clusters, Double Cherub Silver Base 1250.00
Burmese, Yellow Enameled Daisies & Blue Berries, Ornate Silver Base 2200.00
Cranberry Opalescent, Crimped, Vertical Stripe, 10 5/8 x 3 3/4 In. 150.00
Enameled, Gold Floral, Scalloped 165.00
Enameled, Ruffled, Silver Frame 195.00
Enameled, Yellow Daises, Rust Centers, Pink Overlay, 11 1/4 In. 195.00
Floral On White Satin Glass, Green Scalloped Rim, 12 In. 225.00
Grape, Vaseline, Silver On Stand 225.00
Hickman, Emerald Green 75.00
Hobnail, Cranberry 395.00
Opalescent Seaweed, Raspberry, Crimped Rim, 10 In. 175.00
Ruffled, Aqua, Cased White, Mica Flakes, 8 In. 60.00
Ruffled, Robin's-Egg Blue, Blue Flowers, Gold Coralene Buds, 4 3/4 x 8 In. 295.00

BRISTOL glass was made in Bristol, England, after the 1700s. The Bristol glass most often seen today is a Victorian, lightweight opaque glass that is often blue. Some of the glass was decorated with enamels.

Chandelier, 4-Light, Bells, Prisms, 1880 .... 2200.00
Dish, Lozenge Shape, Central Floral Spray, Gilt, Bands, 1775, 10 1/8 In., Pair 690.00
Jug, Success To Papermaking, 1814, 15 In. 2800.00
Lamp, Enameled Flowers, Flying Birds, Shell Feet, Square Shade, 10 In. 650.00
Shade, Melon Ribbed, Brass Font 1100.00
Sweetmeat Dish, Shell Shape, Fluted, c.1770, 5 1/4 In. 690.00
Vase, Coach & Horses, 14 In. 125.00
Vase, Egg Shape, Bird On Limb, Pin, Blue White Flowers, Leaves, Pedestal, 10 In. 95.00
Vase, Enameled Bird & Floral Scene, Crimped Pink Top, Blue Ground 145.00
Vase, Green & Gilt Leaf, 9 1/2 In., Pair 50.00
Vase, Hydrangeas, Hand Painted & Gilt, 18 In. 150.00
Vase, Pink Ruffled Rim, Pussy Willows On Clambroth Ground, 6 1/4 In. 55.00
Vase, Red & Purple Poppies, Shaded Yellow Ground, 13 In. 125.00

BRITANNIA, see Pewter category

BRONZE is an alloy of copper, tin, and other metals. It is used to make figurines, lamps, and other decorative objects.

Ashtray, Bull's Head 42.00
Ashtray, Bulldog, Flint Holder In Head 65.00
Ashtray, Deer Standing Over Fallen Hunter, England 42.00
Ashtray, Spaniel, Duck In Mouth 65.00
Bookrack, Owl, Brass, Expandable 63.00
Bowl, Swan Form, Oriental, 10 1/2 In. 115.00
Box, Hinged Cover, Ormolu Band, Blue Opaline Mounted, 2 1/4 x 5 1/2 x 3 1/2 In. 440.00
Buddha, Hollow Cast, Symbol On Back, 3 1/8 x 4 x 5 1/2 In. 255.00
Burner, Incense, Exotic Bird Shape, Design On Wings, c.1860, 17 1/2 In. 1500.00
Burner, Incense, Globular Form, Twig Handle, Pierced Trivet Base, c.1850, 8 1/2 In. ... 750.00
Bust, Albert Laessle, Maurice Molarsky, 1923, 25 In. 742.00
Bust, Bissell, Abraham Lincoln, 1899, 25 1/2 In. 2530.00
Bust, Byron, Marble Pedestal, 7 3/4 In. 176.00
Bust, Cain, A., Lion, 18 In. 2070.00
Bust, Dumaige, H., Young Woman, Daphnis, Signed, France, 1830-1888, 17 1/4 In. 577.00
Bust, Henry-Bonnard Bronze Co., New York, George Washington, Stamped, 1899, 9 In. 402.00

Bust, Madrassi, Woman, Marble Base, 23 1/2 In. 1445.00
Bust, Muller, H., Maiden, Flower Garland, 5 In. 230.00
Bust, Muller, H., Richard Wagner, Red Marble Pedestal, Brown Patina, 7 x 11 In. 450.00
Bust, Muller, Maiden, In Garland Of Flowers, 5 In. 230.00
Bust, Napoleon, 2 Cannon Balls On Square Base, Pedestal, 19th Century, 15 In. 990.00
Bust, Quinn, Gentleman, Walnut Base, 1907, 19 In. 468.00
Bust, Shakespeare, Marble Pedestal, 20 In. 176.00
Bust, Van Der Straeten, Woman, Art Nouveau, 12 In. 1350.00
Bust, Villanis, E., Diane, 24 In. 690.00
Candelabrum, 3 Foliate Cups, Curved Stem, George De Feire, c.1900, 13 1/4 In., Pair. 4025.00
Card Tray, Chiparus, School Girl, No. 5414, Ivory, Gilt & Polychrome, 7 In. 975.00
Casket Handle, Tiger Face, Ring, China, 4 1/2 In., Pair 2500.00
Centerpiece, Water Sprite, Marble Base, 10 In. 1815.00
Cigar Cutter, Austria, Figural Man At End, Match Holder, Sliding Drawer, 4 1/2 In. 425.00
Coffeepot, Silver Banding & Spout, Turkish 2000.00
Cup, Wine, Traveling, Stem Unscrews Through Inside, Scotland, 1830s, 4 In. 115.00
Dish, Round, Zodiac Signs, Signed Nuss '46, 10 1/2 In. 132.00
Ewer, Jozon, Thistles & Leaves, c.1900, 9 In. 1610.00
Figurine, Aichele, Diane, Marble Vase, c.1900, 32 1/2 In. 690.00
Figurine, Allgayer & Co., Indian Scout, Onyx Base, 10 1/2 In. 1045.00
Figurine, Arab, Raised Arms, On Prayer Rug, Marble Base, Geschutz, 7 1/2 In. 900.00
Figurine, Aristotle, Seated, 10 1/2 In. 303.00
Figurine, Assyrian-Babylonian, Anthropomorphic Bull, Winged, Plinth, 8 In. 385.00
Figurine, August Moreau, Le Travail 525.00
Figurine, Austria, Arab Man In Tent, 20th Century, 11 1/2 In. 3450.00
Figurine, Austria, Crouching Fox, Cold Painted, 3 3/4 In. 225.00
Figurine, Austria, Dancing Mice, Cold Painted, 2 In. 325.00
Figurine, Austria, Kitten, In Doctor's Bag, Cold Painted, 2 In. 200.00
Figurine, Austria, Pheasant, Original Paint, 12 In. 565.00
Figurine, Barrias, Nature Revealing Herself Before Science, c.1900, 22 7/8 In. 9775.00
Figurine, Barrias, Woman, Marble Base, 24 In. 4800.00
Figurine, Barye, Crouching Vulture, Granite Base, 7 1/2 In. 715.00
Figurine, Barye, Dog, Hound, 5 x 10 In. 750.00
Figurine, Barye, Lion, 3 x 8 In. 715.00
Figurine, Barye, Lion, Attacking Horse, 8 In. 770.00
Figurine, Barye, Rabbit, Crouching, 3 1/2 In. 550.00
Figurine, Bianchi, Boy, With Parrots, 37 1/2 In. 5225.00
Figurine, Bizard, Seated Shepherdess, Gold Patina, Marble Base, 9 In. 230.00
Figurine, Bonheur, Isidore, Bull Stampeding 5500.00
Figurine, Bonheur, R., Bull, Lying Down, Signed, 20th Century 1950.00
Figurine, Boulle, Father Time, Scales In Hand, Velvet Covered Stand, 17 3/4 In. 1725.00
Figurine, Brault, 3 Terns, Onyx & Marble Base, c.1925, 27 In. 1840.00
Figurine, Breton, Greyhound Chasing Hare, 24 In. 1375.00
Figurine, Chariot, 4 Rearing Horses, Driver, Gilded, Onyx Base, 17 x 24 1/2 x 16 In. ... 1375.00
Figurine, Chaudet, Seal, With Napoleon Bust & Eagle, Gilded, Paris, 3 In. 275.00
Figurine, Chiparus, Boy With Accordion, Cold Painted, Ivory, 9 1/2 In. 1095.00
Figurine, Chiparus, Russian Dancer, Ivory Arms & Face, c.1925, 23 In. 9200.00
Figurine, Chretien, Roman Swordsmith, 29 In. 2090.00
Figurine, Clara, Child, Seated On Pillow, Black Marble Base, 6 3/4 In. 715.00
Figurine, Clara, Young Girl, With Dog, 8 In. 715.00
Figurine, Clesinger, Bull, 17 1/4 In. 1870.00
Figurine, Clodion, Mercury, Marble Base, 34 In. 6495.00
Figurine, Clodion, Winged Victory, 28 In. 1705.00
Figurine, Cormier, Female, Nude, Kneeling, France, Barbedienne, 16 1/4 In. 1265.00
Figurine, Cormier, Kneeling Female Nude, 16 1/4 In. 1265.00
Figurine, Dana, Boy, By Street Lamp, 11 5/8 In. 270.00
Figurine, Delabrier, Game Bird, 10 x 16 In. 345.00
Figurine, Dog, Setter, Stalking, Patinated, c.1900, 2 1/4 In. 154.00
Figurine, Drivier, Archer, Paris, 19 3/4 In. 6325.00
Figurine, Drouot, Female Sprinter, Brown & Black Marble Base, France, 21 3/4 In. 1380.00
Figurine, Dumaige, Victory, 2 Rearing Stallions, 1830-1888, 20 1/2 In. ....*Illus* 1430.00
Figurine, Eagle, Dore, On Fluted Column, France, 6 In. 248.00
Figurine, Elephant, 12 1/2 In. 137.00

Bronze, Figurine, Dumaige,
Victory, 2 Rearing Stallions,
1830-1888, 20 1/2 In.

Bronze, Figurine, Enrique Alfirez,
Woman Washing Hair

Bronze, Figurine, Preiss, Archer, Ivory,
Art Deco, 1930, 18 In.

Figurine, Elephant, Standing On Ball, Marble Base, 23 In. 385.00
Figurine, Elephant, Standing, Wooden Base, Signed, Oriental, 8 x 14 In. 690.00
Figurine, Emily Clayton Bishop, Woman In Flowing Robe, 1909, 9 1/2 In. 1045.00
Figurine, Enrique Alfirez, Woman Washing Hair .... *Illus* 6050.00
Figurine, Enzo Plazzotta, Male Dancer, 22 1/2 In. 1265.00
Figurine, Fayral, Kneeling Partially Nude Maiden, Marble Base, 16 3/4 In. 630.00
Figurine, Ferrari, Arab, On Camel, 21 In. 3300.00
Figurine, Flapper, Seated, 1920s, 30 In. 8500.00
Figurine, Focht, Spirit Of Flight, Marble Base, c.1925, 30 1/4 In. 6325.00
Figurine, Fraser, End Of A Trail, Green Marble Base, 1894, 13 x 10 1/2 In. 675.00
Figurine, Fraser, L., Dog, Seated, 1930, 5 1/4 In. 715.00
Figurine, Fredericks, Mother & Child 7700.00
Figurine, Gautherin, Man Sharpening Scythe, Marble Base, 14 3/4 In. 750.00
Figurine, Gerdago, Dancer, Ivory Face, Polychrome Costume, c.1925, 13 1/4 In. 6900.00
Figurine, Giraud, Dog, Hound, Reclining, Barbedienne, 9 1/2 In. 935.00
Figurine, Gueyton, Jester & Zany, Red Marble & Bronze Stand, 1880, 31 In. 1300.00
Figurine, Guillemin, Harlequin, 39 3/4 In. 6325.00
Figurine, Hagenaur, African Woman, Brass Earrings, Black Finish, 7 1/2 In. 605.00
Figurine, Hagenaur, Girl, Flowing Hair, Black Finish 1100.00
Figurine, Hagenaur, Maiden, Carved Wooden Skirt, 12 In. 1150.00

Figurine, Hagenaur, Native Girl, Black, Gold, 5 1/2 In. 385.00
Figurine, Hatvany, Doe, France, 15 In. 1840.00
Figurine, Humphriss, Appeal To Great Spirit, 1906 .... 4600.00
Figurine, Injalbert, Winged Boy & Love Birds, 20 1/2 In. 2587.00
Figurine, Kalish, Female Nude, Andro Fondeur, 7 x 15 1/4 In. 1035.00
Figurine, Kelety, Hunter With Gazelles, Silver Patina, 44 In. 2875.00
Figurine, Laporte, E., Boy In Knickers 465.00
Figurine, Larche, Nymph, 25 In. 2587.00
Figurine, Lavergne, Young Fisherman, c.1900 .... 1100.00
Figurine, Levasseur, Diana, 30 In. 4600.00
Figurine, Lorengi, Girl, Ivory Face & Hands, Marble Base, 9 1/2 In. 1200.00
Figurine, Magnus, Spirit Of America, Eagle's Head 280.00
Figurine, Male & Female Nude, Signed PM, 1920s, 10 In., Pair 650.00
Figurine, Mene, Dog, Retriever, With Bird, 11 In. 595.00
Figurine, Mene, Horse, Jockey, Vainqueur Du Derby 3200.00
Figurine, Mene, Mountain Goat, 9 1/2 In. 852.00
Figurine, Moigniez, Bird & Butterfly, Late 19th Century, 4 3/4 x 4 1/2 In. 345.00
Figurine, Monkey, Seated, Wearing Coat, Root-Carved Base, Japan, 3 3/4 In. 632.00
Figurine, Moreau, M., Kneeling Maiden With Cupid, 12 1/2 x 13 In. 1610.00
Figurine, Moreau, M., Woman, 45 In. 6900.00
Figurine, Neptune, Right Foot On Dolphin, Italy, 13 1/8 In. 6612.00
Figurine, Nitken, Nude With Cymbals 1155.00
Figurine, Parsons, Running Terrier, 7 3/4 In. 575.00
Figurine, Picault, Archangel, Les Grande Hommes, Phares De Humanite, 29 In. 1045.00
Figurine, Picault, Archer 4400.00
Figurine, Picault, Roman Soldier, 69 1/2 In. 1540.00
Figurine, Picault, Winged Man, Holding Scroll, Pax, Labor, Progressus, 20 In. 900.00
Figurine, Pierre Blanc, Cockatoo, Black Patina, 16 3/4 In. 2760.00
Figurine, Potter, E.C., Sleeping Child With Rabbit, 13 In. .... *Illus* 935.00
Figurine, Preiss, F., Archer, Ivory, Art Deco, 1930, 18 In. .... *Illus* 23000.00
Figurine, Preiss, F., Ballerina, Ivory Trim, 7 3/4 In. 1375.00
Figurine, Preiss, F., Nude, With Scarf, Onyx & Marble Base, 5 3/4 In. 2100.00
Figurine, Preiss, F., Seated Girl, Marble & Green Onyx Base, 6 In. 4000.00
Figurine, Preiss, J., Autumn Dancer, Ivory Limbs & Face, 14 1/2 In. 7360.00
Figurine, Prost, M., Panther, Sloping Marble Base, 14 3/4 x 7 3/4 In. .... 2570.00 to 2585.00
Figurine, Rosse, Boy, Carrying Water, 15 In. .... 805.00 to 1150.00
Figurine, Sherbell, Mother & Child, 20 In. 632.00
Figurine, St. Gaudens, Dog, Bulldog, 6 In. 715.00
Figurine, Steiner, Winged Woman, Brown Patina, 34 1/2 In. 3335.00
Figurine, Sylvestre, Leda & Swan, 29 3/4 In. 2875.00
Figurine, Tiger, Standing, Wooden Base, 4 1/4 In. 70.00
Figurine, Varenne, Dancer, Gilded Baton, c.1900, 36 In. 9775.00
Figurine, Vedam, Woman, With Tambourine, 15 In. 330.00
Figurine, Venus, Crouching, Knee On Scallop Shell, France, 19th Century, 15 1/2 In. .. 2875.00
Figurine, Vincenzo Alfano, Woman, 1904, 19 In. 2013.00
Figurine, Woman, Dancing, Art Deco, Ivory Head, Arms & Feet, France, 16 In. 1610.00
Figurine, Woman, Diving From Rock, Marble Base, 17 1/2 x 13 1/2 In. 605.00
Figurine, Woman, Nude, Reclining, 12 In. 302.00
Figurine, Zach, Female Nude, 34 1/4 In. 4025.00
Figurine, Zach, Hugger, Flapper Hugging Penis 595.00
Figurine, Zach, Midnight Lovers, 2 Women 225.00
Figurine, Zach, Woman, c.1925, 17 In. 1725.00
Figurine, Zach, Woman, With Fox Stole, Onyx Base, 17 1/4 In. 3220.00
Figurine, Zach, Woman, With Fur Coat, Marble Base, 17 In. 2760.00
Garniture Set, Clock, Sevres, Courting Scenes, A.G. Mougin, c.1900, 3 Piece 2185.00
Group, 2 Women Picking Flowers, Germany, 1850s, 19 In. 2500.00
Group, Austria, Salve Girl, With Arab, Polychrome, Marble Base, 16 In. 3680.00
Group, Bergman, Arab Maiden, Reclining, Polychrome, Lamp Wired, 16 In. 2990.00
Group, Bergman, NamGreb, Reclining Arab Maiden, Polychrome, Austria, 16 In. 2990.00
Group, Bitter, 2 Children, 2 Fauns, Green Marble Base, France, 11 x 23 In. 345.00
Group, China, Man, On Elephant, 16 x 14 In. 1200.00
Group, Coulin, 4 Seasons Of A Woman, Art Nouveau, 1915 .... 2395.00
Group, Descomps, Cormier, Kissing Couple, 1929, 31 In. 3450.00

Group, Drivier, Archer, 19 3/4 In... 6325.00
Group, Gratcheff, Cossack, Kissing Woman, Saddled Horse, Russia, 13 1/2 In. 2185.00
Group, Lanceray, Mounted Herdsman, Child, 3 Horses, Russia, 22 In. 5750.00
Group, Lefagauys, Bacchanalian Group, c.1925, 26 In... 4600.00
Group, Mene, Jockey, On Prancing Steed, Plinth, 24 x 18 1/2 In. 495.00
Group, Picault, Pegasus & Perseus, 19 1/4 In. 630.00
Group, Rozet, Lady, Embraces Clown, c.1910, 18 1/2 In. 4025.00
Group, Vital-Cornu, 2 Allegorical Figures, 48 In. 4887.00
Hand, Volk, Lincoln's, Signed A. Lincoln, 1860, 6 1/2 In. 2300.00
Head, Buddha, Oriental, Late 17th-Early 18th Century 2530.00
Incense Burner, Foo Dog Finial Cover, 2 Dragon Panels, Elephant Head Base, 17 In. . . 350.00
Jar, Cover, Stand, Elephants & Birds, Stand, China, 19 In. 200.00
Letter Holder, 3 Tier, Bouquet Of Flowers Form, 1870, 9 In.. 155.00
Letter Holder, Medallion, Man, Lion Face & Paws.. 225.00
Mascot, Rolls Royce, Spirit Of Ecstasy, Silvered, Marble Socle, 27 1/2 In. 3450.00
Medallion, Young Boy, St. Gaudens, 4 In. 440.00
Obelisk, Grand Tour, Thermometer, Marble Base, Continental, 19th Century, 11 In. 385.00
Planter, Hanging, Demilune Basket, Pierced, Copper Liner, 25 1/2 In., Pair 660.00
Plaque, Baskin, L., Prometheus Bound, Low Relief, 1970, 23 x 13 1/2 In. 990.00
Plaque, Bust, Bismarck, Military Uniform, Signed, 1898, 8 1/2 In. 300.00
Plaque, Carved Wooden Frame, Japan, Signed, 11 1/8 x 15 In....................................... 750.00
Plaque, Goddess Of Harvest, Offering Wheat To Draped Citizens, Round, 8 1/2 In...... 110.00
Plaque, Konig Grau, Frederick The Great, On Horseback, 9 1/2 x 7 1/2 In. 660.00
Plaque, Terzinka, L., Lorilie, Repousse, 9 3/4 x 7 In., Pair 275.00
Plaque, Theodore Roosevelt's Bust, 12 1/2 x 9 1/2 In. 220.00
Plaque, Thorwaldsen, Apollo & Muses, 1920s, 4 1/2 x 9 5/8 In. 120.00
Plate, Christmas, 8 Figures In Design, Gorham, 1925, 7 In... 120.00
Rack, Coat, Wall, Tiger's Head, Victorian, 13 x 9 In.. 412.00
Rice Table, Tooled, Oriental, 7 1/4 x 8 In... 82.00
Sculpture, 3 Devils, Holding Crystal Sphere, Japan, 8 3/4 x 3 5/8 In............................ 4400.00
Tazza, Renaissance Style, Flat Handles, Center Relief Of Jason, 21 In. 287.00
Teakettle, Dragon Design Handle & Spout, Lizard Finial, Oriental, 8 x 7 In.................. 300.00
Teapot, Dragon Form, China, 8 In. 66.00
Teapot, Swing Handles, Formed Spout, 2 Side Panels, Japan, 9 1/2 In. 58.00
Tray, Art Nouveau, Nude Woman, Owl, 10 1/2 x 7 In... 225.00
Tray, Dragons, China, 19th Century, 11 In.. 117.00
Tray, Moigniez, Hunting Scene, Fox Finial, Vulture Form Stem, French, 9 1/2 In......... 345.00
Tray, Villanis, Women's Heads, Cutout Handles, Green Highlights, 11 x 20 In............. 330.00
Umbrella Stand, Allover Raised Foliate, Floral & Bird Design, Oriental, 23 3/4 In. 315.00
Urn, Moreau, Girl Sitting On Urn, 12 In. ....995.00 to 1200.00
Urn, Philippe, L., Couple, Campana Shape, Patinated, Sienna Marble, 9 1/4 In., Pair.... 2875.00
Urn, Regency Style, Black Patinated, Leaf-Shaped Handles, Fluted Finial, 16 In., Pair . 3450.00
Vase, Bulbous Bottom, Flared Top, 3 x 4 1/2 In. 26.00
Vase, Dragon Wound Around Neck, Lobed Body, Japan, c.1900, 18 1/2 In.................... 275.00
Vase, Fish Shape, 16 1/2 In... 302.00
Vase, Fluted Narrow Neck, Overall Standing Cranes, Japan, 23 1/2 In. 1090.00
Vase, Inlaid Gold, Silver, Mother-Of-Pearl Patina, Orchid Design, Japan, 9 1/2 In. 2587.00
Vase, Kunst, Figural, Egyptian Revival, 11 1/2 In. 715.00
Vase, Label, Art Nouveau, Irises, Foliage, Flower Handles, c.1900, 19 3/4 In. 2500.00
Vase, Narrow Neck, Inlaid & Raised Silver & Gold Duck, Japan, 7 1/2 In. 515.00
Vase, Raised Florals & Birds, Gold, Silver, Japan, 7 In.. 1495.00

BROWNIES were first drawn in 1883 by Palmer Cox. They are characterized
by large round eyes, downturned mouths, and skinny legs. Toys, books, dinnerware, and other objects were made with the Brownies as part of the
design.

Blocks, Paper Lithographed Scenes, McLoughlin Bros., Box, 14 x 11 In....................... 850.00
Book, Brownies & Other Stories, Palmer Cox, 225 Pages 90.00
Bowl, Golf Scenes, Palmer Cox 495.00
Cup & Plate, Palmer Cox, 6 In. 165.00
Cup & Saucer, Tug Of War, Palmer Cox 95.00
Game, Nine-Pins, Palmer Cox, Pasteboard Figures, Box, 1883 .... 1495.00
Label, Crate, Palmer Cox, 1930s, 10 x 12 In... 14.00

Mug, Silver Plate	185.00
Napkin Ring, Figural, Palmer Cox, Meriden	325.00
Plate, Palmer Cox, 8 In.	165.00
Stickpin, Palmer Cox	35.00
Wrapper, Ice Cream Bar	5.00

BRUSH Pottery was started in 1925. George Brush first worked in 1901 in Zanesville, Ohio. He started his own pottery in 1907, but it burned to the ground and he joined McCoy in 1909. After a series of name changes, the company became The Brush Pottery. It closed in 1982. Collectors favor the figural cookie jars made by this company.

Bank, Pig, Formal, Green	295.00
Cookie Jar, Bunny Chef	225.00
Cookie Jar, Cinderella Pumpkin	425.00 to 495.00
Cookie Jar, Circus Horse, Brown	700.00 to 950.00
Cookie Jar, Clown	500.00
Cookie Jar, Clown Bust	350.00
Cookie Jar, Clown, Yellow Pants	475.00
Cookie Jar, Covered Wagon	475.00 to 760.00
Cookie Jar, Cow, Brown	95.00 to 130.00
Cookie Jar, Cow, Purple	1100.00
Cookie Jar, Davy Crockett	425.00
Cookie Jar, Elephant With Ice Cream Cone	485.00 to 525.00
Cookie Jar, Granny, Green	375.00
Cookie Jar, Hillbilly Frog	4395.00 to 5000.00
Cookie Jar, Hippo Sitting	325.00
Cookie Jar, Humpty Dumpty, With Peaked Hat	296.00
Cookie Jar, Little Angel	675.00
Cookie Jar, Little Boy Blue	125.00 to 595.00
Cookie Jar, Owl, Yellow	225.00
Cookie Jar, Panda	120.00
Cookie Jar, Panda, Black & White	395.00
Cookie Jar, Peter Pan, Large	875.00
Cookie Jar, Peter Pumpkin Eater	425.00
Cookie Jar, Pumpkin With Lock On Door	550.00
Cookie Jar, Rabbit, White	265.00
Cookie Jar, Squirrel On Green Log	55.00
Cookie Jar, Squirrel With Top Hat, Brown, With Green Coat	495.00
Doll, Box	55.00
Figurine, Hillbilly Frog	5000.00
Flower Frog, Kingfisher	60.00
Jardiniere, Birds, Green, 8 In.	130.00
Jardiniere, Pedestal, Blue & Gold Glazes, 1920s, 16 In.	150.00
Mug, Peter Pan	150.00
Pitcher, Kissing Dutch Children, Green, 7 In.	55.00
Planter, Figural, Southern Belle, With Basket, Ivory Gloss, 7 1/2 x 6 x 4 In.	25.00
Planter, Green, Flared, Scalloped, 4-Footed, 11 x 5 x 5 In.	12.00
Planter, Rabbit On Log	25.00
Planter, Squirrel On Log, Gold	35.00
Wall Pocket, Boxer Dog	150.00
Wall Pocket, Duck	80.00
Wall Pocket, Grazing Horse	125.00

BRUSH MCCOY, see McCoy category

BUCK ROGERS was the first American science fiction comic strip. It started in 1929 and continued until 1965. Buck has also appeared in comic books, movies, and, in the 1980s, a television series. Any memorabilia connected with the character Buck Rogers is collectible.

Atomic Pistol, Holster	425.00
Battle Cruiser, Tootsie Toy, 1937	135.00
Book, Big Little Book, City Of Floating Globe, Cocomalt	50.00
Book, Big Little Book, Doom Comet	125.00

Book, Coloring, 1979	8.00
Car, Police Patrol, Tin Windup, Box	1495.00
Doll, Killer Kane, Mego, 12 In., Box	50.00
Doll, Twiki, Walking, Mego, Box	40.00
Figure, Lead, Cocomalt, 1933	150.00
Flying Saucer, 1940s, 6 In.	95.00
Pinback	45.00
Pistol, Atomic, Daisy, 1930s	220.00
Pistol, Lazer Light, Battery Operated, 1979	20.00
Record, Original Radio Broadcast, 1979, 33 1/3 RPM	30.00
Rocket Ship, Marx	295.00
Shaker Maker, Pour Mix In Mold, Ideal, 1980, Box	25.00
Space Gun, 4 Fins In Middle, 3 Fins On End	325.00
Space Gun, Daisy, Metal, 7 In.	2745.00
Space Pistol, Steel, 1930s	145.00
Space Ship, Tin Windup, Marx	895.00
Squirt Gun, Liquid Helium	210.00
Strato-Kite, 1946	65.00
Walkie Talkie, Plastic Phones, Moving Decoder Disc, 8 1/2 x 13 In.	150.00
Water Pistol, Liquid Helium, Red, Yellow, 1930s	700.00

BUFFALO POTTERY was made in Buffalo, New York, after 1902. The company was established by the Larkin Company, famous manufacturers of soap. The wares are marked with a picture of a buffalo and the date of manufacture. Deldare ware is the most famous pottery made at the factory. It has khaki-colored or green background with hand painted transfer designs.

BUFFALO POTTERY, Bone Dish, Geometric Design	25.00
Bowl, Blue Willow, 1911, 8 1/2 In.	30.00
Chop Plate, Buffalo, 13 1/2 In.	500.00
Cup & Saucer, Bluebird	18.00
Mug, Beer, Celebration	40.00
Mug, Cardinal Bust, Reverse Advertising, Bing & Nathan, Buffalo, N.Y.	110.00
Pitcher, Gaudy Willow, 7 In.	335.00
Pitcher, George Washington, With Gold, 7 1/2 In.	400.00 to 550.00
Plate, Child's, Lamb, Ducklings, Chicken, 8 Kate Greenaway Children	55.00
Plate, Christmas, 1950	55.00
Plate, Christmas, 1951	40.00
Plate, Christmas, 1956	50.00
Plate, Christmas, 1958	45.00
Plate, Christmas, 1959	40.00
Plate, Christmas, 1960	40.00
Plate, Christmas, 1962	245.00
Plate, Elias Big Boy, 9 In.	40.00
Plate, Great Falls, Mont., Smelter	150.00
Plate, New Bedford, Me., 10 1/2 In.	135.00
Plate, Vienna, 8 1/4 In.	20.00
Plate, Wild Rose, 6 In.	715.00
Soup, Dish, New England Steamship Company, 8 7/8 In.	60.50
Sugar & Creamer, Bluebird, 1919	18.00
Tankard, Abino, Sail Boats, 10 1/2 In.	990.00
Teapot, Tea Ball, Argyle	220.00
BUFFALO POTTERY DELDARE, Bowl, Ye Village Tavern, 1908, 9 In.	350.00 to 385.00
Candlestick, Village Life, 9 In., Pair	570.00
Chop Plate, Ye Lion Inn, 14 In.	325.00 to 525.00
Coffee Set, Scenes Of Village Life, In Ye Olden Days, 3 Piece	850.00
Creamer, Standing Rabbit Front, Back Side Rabbit In Profile	3410.00
Humidor, There Was An Old Sailor, 8 In.	750.00 to 900.00
Jardiniere, Ye Village Street, 8 In.	280.00
Mug, Emerald, Dr. Syntax Returned Home, 3 1/2 In.	295.00
Mug, Fallowfield Hunt, Breaking Cover	350.00
Mug, Ye Lion Inn, 4 1/4 In.	225.00 to 300.00
Pitcher, Emerald, Dr. Syntax Sketching Lake, 9 In.	650.00
Pitcher, Fallowfield Hunt, At Three Pigeons, Octagonal, 6 In.	775.00

Pitcher, Fox Hunt, Whirl Of The Town, 7 In. 495.00
Pitcher, The Great Controversy, 12 1/2 In. 1250.00
Plate, Emerald, Misfortune At Tulip Hall, 8 1/2 In. 550.00
Plate, Fallowfield Hunt, The Dash, 1909, 6 1/2 In. 125.00
Plate, Fallowfield Hunt, The Dash, 9 1/2 In. 140.00
Plate, Lion Tapestry, 8 1/2 In. 880.00
Plate, Ye Olden Times, 9 1/4 In. 150.00
Plate, Ye Village Gossips, 10 In. 170.00
Saucer, Village Life, 6 In. 50.00
Sugar, Cover, Village Life, 4 1/2 In. .... 175.00 to 250.00
Sugar, Cover, Village Life, Signed W.F., 1924 .... 300.00
Sugar & Creamer, Village Life 295.00
Tankard, Fallowfield Hunt, The Death, Signed, 12 In. 850.00
Teapot, Village Life, 1909, 3 1/4 In. .... 245.00 to 275.00
Tile, Traveling In Ye Olden Days, Trivet, Round, 1908, 6 1/4 In. 385.00
Vase, Emerald, Kingfisher, Green, White, J. Gerhardt, 1911, 7 3/4 In. 2645.00

BURMESE GLASS was developed by Frederick Shirley at the Mt. Washington Glass Works in New Bedford, Massachusetts, in 1885. It is a two-toned glass, shading from peach to yellow. Some pieces have a pattern mold design. A few Burmese pieces were decorated with pictures or applied glass flowers of colored Burmese glass. Other factories made similar glass also called *Burmese*. Related items may be listed in the Fenton category, the Gunderson category, and under Webb Burmese.

Bowl, 6 Lobes, 5 1/2 In. 77.00
Bowl, Applied Feather, Folded Over Scalloped Rim, Pale Yellow To Pink, 2 1/2 In. 220.00
Bowl, Crimped, Polished Pontil, Pedestal Foot, 3 1/2 In. 330.00
Castor, Ribbed, Cylinder, 4 In., Pair 220.00
Celery Vase, Mt. Washington, 6 1/2 In. 550.00
Creamer, Pale Yellow To Pale Pink, Applied Yellow Handle, 3 5/8 In. 82.00
Cruet, Floral, 1880s 1200.00
Cruet, Flowers All Around, Striped Stopper & Handle, c.1885 .... 1450.00
Dish, Ice Cream, Salmon To Yellow, 4 In., 6 Piece 440.00
Ewer, Ruffled Rim, Ear Handle, 7 1/2 In. 350.00
Fairy Lamp, 2 Dome Shades, Metal Holder, Cut Glass Base, 3-Part, 17 In. 500.00
Fairy Lamp, Double, Dome Shades, Clarke Inserts, Dolphin Stem 1100.00
Fairy Lamp, Pale Yellow To Deep Pink, Enameled Leaves & Berries, 5 3/4 In. 330.00
Fairy Lamp, Woodbine Leaves & Berries, Fall Colors, 3-Part, 10 1/2 In. 4500.00
Finger Bowl, Salmon Pink To Yellow, Crimp Top, Mt. Washington, 2 x 4 3/8 In. 225.00
Pitcher, Enameled Floral, Ring White Dots, Tiny Spout, Mt. Washington, 11 1/2 In. 2950.00
Pitcher, Tankard Shape, Country Scene, Flowers, Longfellow Poem, 9 In. 3250.00
Salt & Pepper, Painted, Enamel Flowers, Silver Plated Holder, Mt. Washington 850.00
Shade, Electric, 2 In. Fitter 125.00
Sugar & Creamer, Footed, Mt. Washington 550.00
Toothpick, Acid Finish Polished Pontil, 6-Sided Top, 3 In. 275.00
Toothpick, Diamond-Quilted, Square Top, Bulbous, Mt. Washington, 2 1/2 In. 615.00
Toothpick, Mt. Washington, Acid Finish, Diamond-Quilted, Tricornered 395.00
Tumbler, Mt. Washington, 4 In. 110.00
Tumbler, Mt. Washington, Acid Finish, 4 In. 200.00
Tumbler, Pale Yellow To Pink, Yellow Rim, 3 5/8 In. 38.00
Tumbler, Peaches, Cream, Shiny Finish, Mt. Washington 375.00
Tumbler, Yellow Roses, Mt. Washington, 3 3/4 In. 565.00
Vase, Ball Shape, Star-Shaped Top, Salmon Pink To Yellow, Mt. Washington, 3 In. 180.00
Vase, Custard To Deep Pink, Glossy Finish, 3 1/2 In. 275.00
Vase, Custard To Pink, Enameled Flowers, Flared Ruffled Lip, 4 3/8 In. 160.00
Vase, Custard To Pink, Enameled Flowers, Hexagonal Mouth, 3 1/4 In. 148.00
Vase, Gourd, 2 Handles, Mt. Washington, 5 3/4 In. 165.00
Vase, Grapes, Vines, Leaves, 4 3/4 In. 750.00
Vase, King Tut, Yellow To Pink, Queen's Design, Scrolled Handles, Satin, 11 In. 797.00
Vase, Lily, Salmon To Yellow, Mt. Washington, 7 1/4 In. 195.00
Vase, Mt. Washington, 5 x 4 1/2 In. 450.00
Vase, Pale Yellow To Pale Pink, Hexagonal Mouth, 2 5/8 In. 104.00
Vase, Pale Yellow To Pink, Enameled Flowers, Mt. Washington, 11 5/8 In. 588.00

Vase, Ribbed, Bulbous, Scalloped Rim, Matte Finish, Mt. Washington, 4 1/2 In. 550.00
Vase, Rolled Pentastar, Salmon To Custard, Mt. Washington, 3 3/4 x 2 1/2 In. 210.00
Vase, Ruffled, Pale Yellow To Pink, 2 1/2 In. 88.00
Vase, Scalloped Lip, Yellow To Pink, Glossy Finish, 6 3/4 In. 522.00
Vase, Trumpet, Lily Top, Mt. Washington, 23 1/2 In. 1250.00
Vase, Trumpet, Trefoil Mouth, Pale Yellow To Pink, 7 1/8 In. 104.00
Vase, Trumpet, Yellow To Pink, Satin Finish, 8 1/4 In. 220.00

BUSTER BROWN, the comic strip, first appeared in color in 1902. Buster and his dog, Tige, remained a popular comic and soon became even more famous as the emblem for a shoe company, a textile firm, and others. The strip was discontinued in 1920, but some of the advertising is still in use.

Bandanna, Club, Smiling Ed, Froggy, Buster & Tige, 1940s, 22 x 24 In. 150.00
Bandanna, Features All The Gang 90.00
Bank, Ceramic, 1950s 295.00
Bill Holder 30.00
Book, Coloring, Unused, 1940s 45.00
Cards, Playing, Buster With Tige Picture, 1906 .... 242.00
Clock, Buster Brown Shoes 200.00
Cookie Jar, Tige, California Originals 165.00
Cup, ABC 95.00
Cup, Child's, Tin 40.00
Cup & Saucer, Boy Pouring Tea For Bulldog 120.00
Game, Pin The Tie On Buster 125.00
Handkerchief 60.00
Kite, Buster Brown Shoes, 1940s 38.00
Kite, Paper, 1950s 28.00
Mannequin, Movable Arms, Clothes, Buster & Tige On Base, 1920s, 34 In. 1400.00
Mirror, Pocket 45.00
Nodder, Tige, Germany, 2 1/2 In. 65.00
Periscope, Secret Agent 25.00
Platter, Buster Serving Tea To Tige, 9 1/2 In. 58.00
Puppet, Hand, Yakety-Yak, 1950s 3.00
Sign, Buster Brown Bread, Embossed Tin, Buster Brown & Tige, 28 In. 330.00
Sign, Hosiery Box, 1920 .... 50.00
Sign, Tin Whistle, 1930 .... 45.00
Stickpin, Figure, Brass, Enameled, 1900s, 2 1/2 In. 150.00
Whistle, Tin, 1930s 45.00

BUTTER CHIPS, or butter pats, were small individual dishes for butter. They were the height of fashion from 1880 to 1910. Earlier as well as later examples are known.

Blue And White Scene, Horses, English 17.00
Church, House In Winter Scene, Royal Copenhagen 13.00
Hus Odense, H.C. Andersen, Royal Copenhagen 13.00
Ironstone, White, Brown Band 15.00
Pink Flowers, Germany 15.00
Viking Skibe, Royal Copenhagen 13.00

BUTTER MOLDS are listed in the Kitchen category under Mold, Butter.

BUTTONS have been known throughout the centuries, and there are millions of styles. Gold, silver, or precious stones were used for the best buttons, but most were made of natural materials, like bone or shell, or from inexpensive metals. Only a few types are listed for comparison.

AF Of L, Truck Driver, Early 1940s, 8 Piece 40.00
Carnival Glass, Set, 6 Piece 18.00
Carved Jade, Oval Shape, On Purple Silk, 10 Piece 135.00
Gutta Percha, Set, 1860s 45.00
Man's Shirt, Pearl, Harvey Chalmers & Sons, Picture Of Man 4.00
Metal, Floral, 10 Piece 22.00
Pearl, Baby, On Card, Baby With Pacifier, 2 1/4 x 3 1/8 In. 5.00

Uniform, New Hampshire Volunteers 9.00

BUTTONHOOKS have been a popular collectible in England for many years but only recently have gained the attention of American collectors. The buttonhooks were made to help fasten the many buttons of the old-fashioned high-button shoes and other items of apparel.

Silver Plate, Filigree Work Handle 30.00
Sterling Silver, Pat. 1891 .... 30.00
Sterling Silver, Raised Flowers & Scrolls, Pat. 1891 .... 35.00
Tortoiseshell, Celluloid, Beaded Scroll Handle, 7 In. 9.00

CALENDARS made to hang on the wall or to be displayed on a desk top have been popular since the last quarter of the nineteenth century. Many were printed with advertising as part of the artwork and were given away as premiums. Calendars with guns, gunpowder, or Coca-Cola advertising are most prized.

1883, Dr. Morse's Indian Root Pills 45.00
1896, Metropolitan Insurance Co., Child In Straw Hat, Frame 70.00
1897, Reyman Brewing Company, Mug Of Frothing Beer, 14 x 22 In. 1155.00
1898, Continental Fire Ins. Co., Betsy Ross Sewing American Flag 25.00
1900, Keystone Union Made Overalls 40.00
1901, Prudential Ins., Women Center 40.00
1903, Continental Fire Ins. Co., Gen. Stark, Battle Of Bennington, Vt. 25.00
1904, Bromo-Quinine, Colorful, Envelope 24.00
1904, Hood's Sarsaparilla, Woman, Die Cut Cardboard .... 225.00 to 300.00
1905, Armour, Lithographed Women 160.00
1905, Weisbrod & Hess Beer 75.00
1906, Pabst Extract, Indian, Yard Long Print, 7 x 36 In. ....*Illus* 1430.00
1907, Winchester, Hunting Dogs, 14 1/2 x 13 1/2 In. 660.00
1908, Dr. Miles 45.00
1910, Kimmel Seeds, Girl, Dog, 26 1/2 x 12 In. 420.00
1910, Peters Cartridge Co., Bull Moose, 25 1/2 x 15 1/2 In. 1375.00
1912, Esso 12.00
1912, Penn Beer, Stylishly Clothed Woman, 30 x 15 1/2 In. 330.00
1913, Berkshire Brewery, Cowgirl & Horse, 20 x 15 1/2 In. 1210.00
1913, Marble City Garage, Man & Woman In Touring Car, 20 x 15 In. 105.00
1914, Osborne 30.00
1915, Hood's Sarsaparilla, School Days 60.00
1917, De Laval Cream Separators, Farm Girl, Collie In Lap, 24 x 12 In. 770.00
1917, Jahne's Medizinisher ....6.00 to 8.00
1919, Clay Robinson & Co., Livestock Commission, 12 x 36 In. 145.00
1920, Chevrolet Motor Cars, Open Touring Car, 27 1/2 x 14 1/2 In. 220.00
1920, Chevrolet, Green, White Letters, 30 1/2 x 16 In. 150.00

*Calendar, 1906, Pabst
Extract, Indian, Yard Long
Print, 7 x 36 In.*

◆ ◆ ◆ ◆ ◆ ◆ ◆ ◆ ◆ ◆ ◆ ◆ ◆ ◆ ◆ ◆ ◆

Never store old paper collectibles in ordinary cardboard boxes or plastic bags. Buy the acid-free boxes and Mylar wrapping film that are approved for long-term storage. Many picture-framing and supply stores will have these items.

◆ ◆ ◆ ◆ ◆ ◆ ◆ ◆ ◆ ◆ ◆ ◆ ◆ ◆ ◆ ◆ ◆

1923, Blue Star Line 150.00
1924, Wrigley's Gum.. 25.00
1925, Drink Ward's Orange Crush, Woman With Orange-Red Hair 250.00
1926, Child By Flour Sack, Full Pad, 14 x 22 In.. 18.00
1926, Smith's Confectionery, Lawrenceburg, Ind... 22.00
1927, Harrington & Richardson Arms Co., Setter Dog, 16 x 9 In................................ 495.00
1927, Seneca Cameras, Seneca Princess, 22 1/2 x 10 1/2 In. 385.00
1929, Pompeian Perfume, Card.. 17.00
1930, Schultz Produce, Parrot Design, Spencer, Neb., 10 1/2 In. 65.00
1930, Shapleigh 100.00
1931, Indian Neck Land Co., Branford, Conn., Country Picture, 11 1/2 x 12 In. 8.00
1936, Keen Kutter, Hand Saws On Sides 180.00
1937, Hi-Plane Tobacco, Indians, Inset Of Tobacco Can, 30 x 17 1/2 In..................... 110.00
1938, Albany Creamery Assoc., Oregon, Only God Can Make A Tree 175.00
1938, De Laval, Pictures Cows & Equipment 60.00
1938, Standard Oil, 36 x 18 In. 25.00
1939, Batchelder Bros., Centennial, Baseball Players, 28 x 21 In. 175.00
1939, St. John Motors, Ford Dealer, 45 x 22 In. 605.00
1940, TWA Airlines... 125.00
1941, Union Oil, 6 Color Photographs, Unused, 7 1/2 x 9 In....................................... 55.00
1942, Morrell's Walt Disney, 12 Different Pictures, Incomplete, 8 x 10 1/2 In. 115.00
1943, Esquire, Vargas 65.00
1945, Chesapeake & Ohio Railroad 35.00
1945, Keen Kutter, Box 400.00
1946, Washington's Prayer, Historical Art 25.00
1947, Petty... 85.00
1948, Esquire, Envelope 60.00
1948, Mobilgas, Western Scenes 65.00
1948, Rolf Armstrong, Let's Go, Pinup, 22 x 45 In. 165.00
1949, Grapette.. 65.00
1950, Royal Crown Cola, Wanda Hendrix 35.00
1950, Royal Crown Soda, Girl With Bottle Of Royal Crown Soda............................. 65.00
1951, Dr Pepper 55.00
1953, Ford Motor Co., 50th Anniversary, 1903-1953 .... 25.00
1953, Marilyn Monroe 225.00
1955, Keen Kutter 145.00
1955, Marilyn Monroe, 1955 .... 25.00
1955, Pennsylvania Railroad, Army & Navy Game.. 90.00
1955, Royal Crown Cola 55.00
1960, Playboy, Envelope 75.00
1961, Hummel 33.00
1961, Playboy, Envelope 45.00
1967, Playboy, Desk Type, Envelope 50.00
1968, Hummel 15.00
1970, Hummel 20.00
1974, Playboy 15.00
1976, Hummel 7.00

CALENDAR PLATES were very popular in the United States from 1906 to 1929. Since then, plates have been made every year. A calendar and the name of a store, a picture of flowers, a girl, or a scene were featured on the plate.

1908, Dog, Pittston, Pa. 35.00
1909, Andover, Me. 25.00
1909, Friars, Fruit & Goose, Harry Bragg Hardware, Kansas, 9 1/4 In....................... 45.00
1910, J.H. Hillsbury, Ely, Nev., Months In Horseshoe 175.00
1910, Poppies, New York 36.00
1910, Sailboats On Water 35.00
1911, Deer In Meadow.. 35.00
1912, Airplanes.. 35.00
1912, Milton, N.H... 25.00
1913, Airplane 40.00
1914, Mt. Vernon 25.00
1955, Fiesta, Green 75.00

1974, Currier & Ives 15.00
1991, Compliments EA Conover, Maple Plain, Minn. 50.00

CAMARK POTTERY started in 1924 in Camden, Arkansas. Jack Carnes founded the firm and made many types of glazes and wares. The company was bought by Mary Daniel. Production was halted in 1983.

Basket, Bird Handle 65.00
Bowl, Birds Of Paradise Flower Frog, Black, 10 In. 45.00
Bowl, Green, Melon Rib, Scalloped Edge, Paper Label, 9 1/2 x 4 In. 10.00
Bowl, Iris, Handles, 7 3/4 x 6 x 15 In. 80.00
Candleholder, Aladdin 220.00
Pitcher, Bead & Scroll Relief, White, 3 1/4 In. 4.00
Pitcher, Cat Handle, Pink 85.00
Pitcher, Green, 4 In. 16.00
Pitcher, Swirl 25.00
Pitcher, Undertray, Embossed Flowers, Ivory 25.00
Planter, Rooster, Chartreuse, 9 In. 30.00
Sugar & Creamer 25.00
Teapot, Swirl 40.00
Tray, Floral Design, Matte Blue & White, Marked, 13 1/2 In. 75.00
Vase, Bud, Orange, Green Drip, 6 In. 50.00
Vase, High Mirror Black Glaze, Double Handles, 5 In. 125.00
Vase, Leaf Form, Footed, Split Top, Flared, Black, 5 In. 6.00
Vase, Maroon, Label, Marked, Handles, 5 1/4 In. 20.00
Vase, Mottled Glaze, Foil Label, 4 1/2 x 4 3/4 In. 60.00
Vase, Mottled Green & Blue, Paper Label, 6 In. 80.00
Vase, Orange & Green Drip, 6 In. 50.00
Vase, Stylized Trees & Mountain, 8 3/4 In., Pair 550.00

CAMBRIDGE GLASS Company was founded in 1901 in Cambridge, Ohio. The company closed in 1954, reopened briefly, and closed again in 1958. The firm made all types of glass. Their early wares included heavy pressed glass with the mark *Near Cut*. Later wares included Crown Tuscan, etched stemware, and clear and colored glass. The firm used a C in a triangle mark after 1920. Some Cambridge patterns may be included in the Depression Glass category.

Apple Blossom, Ashtray, Filigree Holder, Yellow 85.00
Apple Blossom, Bonbon, Handle, Yellow, 5 1/2 In. 22.00
Apple Blossom, Bowl, Yellow, 6 In. 45.00
Apple Blossom, Bowl, Yellow, 12 In. 65.00
Apple Blossom, Candlestick, Yellow, 4 In., Pair 75.00
Apple Blossom, Candy Dish, Cover, Footed, Yellow, 7 In. 145.00
Apple Blossom, Cocktail, Yellow, 3 Oz. 35.00
Apple Blossom, Compote, Yellow, 4 In. 35.00
Apple Blossom, Cup & Saucer, Yellow 39.00
Apple Blossom, Goblet, Yellow, 8 Oz. 45.00
Apple Blossom, Grill Plate, Yellow, 10 In. 55.00
Apple Blossom, Ice Bucket, Yellow 85.00
Apple Blossom, Pickle, Yellow, 9 In. 45.00
Apple Blossom, Pitcher, 6 In. 8.00
Apple Blossom, Pitcher, Blue, 11 1/2 In. 65.00
Apple Blossom, Plate, Yellow, 9 1/2 In. 95.00
Apple Blossom, Relish, 2 Handles, Yellow, 8 In. 45.00
Apple Blossom, Relish, 4 Sections 65.00
Apple Blossom, Sandwich Plate, Yellow, 12 In. 65.00
Apple Blossom, Sherbet, Yellow, 6 Oz. 25.00
Apple Blossom, Sugar & Creamer, Yellow .... 47.00 to 55.00
Apple Blossom, Sugar, Cover 37.00
Apple Blossom, Tumbler, Footed, Yellow, 5 Oz. 35.00
Apple Blossom, Wine, Yellow 50.00
Bashful Charlotte, Flower Frog, Blue, Frosted, 11 In. 550.00
Bashful Charlotte, Flower Frog, Mocha, 11 In. 225.00
Blossom Time, Candy Dish, Cover, Martha 95.00

Calla Lily, Candlestick, Green, Pair 35.00
Candlelight, Candy Dish, Cover, 3 Sections 150.00
Candlelight, Shrimp Cocktail 79.00
Candlelight, Tumbler, Footed, 5 Oz. 45.00
Candlelight, Tumbler, Footed, 10 Oz. 39.00
Candlewick, Bowl, Heart Shape, 9 In. 75.00
Cape Cod, Punch Cup 5.00
Caprice, Ashtray, Cardholder Indentation, 2 3/4 In. 8.00
Caprice, Ashtray, Mandarin Gold, 2 1/4 x 3 1/2 In. 12.00
Caprice, Ashtray, Shell, 3-Footed, 2 3/4 In. 5.00
Caprice, Ashtray, Triangular, Moonlight Blue, 3 In. 15.00
Caprice, Bonbon, Blue, Footed, 6 In. 50.00
Caprice, Bonbon, Upright Handles, Square, 5 In. 12.00
Caprice, Bowl, 2 Handles, Blue, 4 1/2 In. 20.00
Caprice, Bowl, Blue, 11 In. 100.00
Caprice, Bowl, Blue, Handles, Footed, 11 In. 110.00
Caprice, Bowl, Crimped, Footed, 10 1/2 In. 35.00
Caprice, Bowl, Crimped, Footed, 13 In. 30.00
Caprice, Cabaret Plate, 3-Footed, Blue, 14 In. 80.00
Caprice, Candlestick, 2-Light, Blue, Pair ....50.00 to 100.00
Caprice, Candlestick, 2-Light, Flame, Pair 225.00
Caprice, Candlestick, 5 In., Pair 99.00
Caprice, Candy Dish, Alpine 145.00
Caprice, Candy Dish, Cover 52.00
Caprice, Candy Dish, Cover, Alpine 79.00
Caprice, Candy Dish, Footed, Cover, Alpine 100.00
Caprice, Compote, Pink, 7 In. 159.00
Caprice, Cordial, 1oz. ....38.00 to 42.00
Caprice, Cup & Saucer, Pink 52.00
Caprice, Holder, Place Card 7.00
Caprice, Ice Bucket 50.00
Caprice, Oyster Cocktail, Alpine 39.00
Caprice, Plate, Blue, 8 1/2 In. ....9.00 to 29.00
Caprice, Plate, Blue, 13 3/4 In. 85.00
Caprice, Plate, Blue, Alpine, 8 1/2 In. 29.00
Caprice, Plate, Lemon, Handles, 5 In. 8.00
Caprice, Plate, Lemon, Handles, 6 1/2 In. 10.00
Caprice, Relish, 3 Sections, Blue, 8 1/2 In. ....40.00 to 50.00
Caprice, Salad Set, Black 75.00
Caprice, Salt & Pepper, Individual 69.00
Caprice, Sherbet 29.00
Caprice, Sugar & Creamer 25.00
Caprice, Sugar, 2 1/2 In. 9.00
Caprice, Tumbler, Iced Tea, Footed 49.00
Caprice, Wine, Blue, 2 1/2 In. 45.00
Chantilly, Cake Plate 129.00
Chantilly, Sherbet, Tall, 7 Piece 14.00
Cleo, Bowl, Blue, 12 In. 69.00
Cleo, Bowl, Green, 5 In. 17.50
Cleo, Cup & Saucer, Amber 25.00
Cleo, Cup & Saucer, Blue 40.00
Cleo, Cup & Saucer, Green 22.00
Cleo, Cup & Saucer, Pink 45.00
Cleo, Cup, Blue 25.00
Cleo, Goblet, Water 30.00
Cleo, Ice Bucket, Pink 159.00
Cleo, Platter, Amber, Oval, 10 1/2 In. 59.00
Cleo, Sandwich Server, Blue, Center Handle 150.00
Cleo, Sherbet, Tall 22.00
Cleo, Soup, Cream, Liner, Amber 39.00
Cleo, Tumbler, Pink, 4 1/2 In. 59.00
Cleo, Tumbler, Pink, Gold Rim, 12 Oz., 5 1/2 In. 45.00
Colonial, Toothpick, Cobalt Blue 30.00

Coronet, Sugar & Creamer	12.00
Crown Tuscan, Box, Cover, Dolphin Feet, 5 x 4 In.	50.00
Crown Tuscan, Candy Dish, Cover, 3 Sections	22.00
Crown Tuscan, Compote, Sea Shell, Footed, 4 x 6 3/4 In.	43.00
Crown Tuscan, Nut Dish, 3-Footed, Gold Rim, 3 In.	12.00
Crown Tuscan, Shell Dish, Oval, 4-Footed, 8 1/4 x 4 3/4 x 3 1/4 In.	42.00
Crown Tuscan, Swan, 3 In.	30.00 to 38.00
Crown Tuscan, Vase, Shell Base, 9 In.	56.00
Decagon, Bowl, Vintage Etch, Cupped, Pink, 12 1/2 x 5 In.	65.00
Decagon, Goblet, Blue, 9 Oz., 7 1/4 In.	25.00
Decagon, Ice Pail, Metal Bail Handle & Tongs, Amethyst	30.00
Decagon, Plate, 2 Handles, Polished Bottom, Blue	10.00
Decagon, Plate, Amber, 8 In.	4.00
Decagon, Saucer, Green	1.00
Decagon, Sherbet, Blue, 8 Oz.	15.00
Decagon, Sugar, Blue	12.00
Diane, Bell, Dinner	95.00
Diane, Bowl, Flared, Footed, 12 In.	40.00 to 42.00
Diane, Candleholder, 3 1/2 In.	15.00
Diane, Candlestick, 2-Light, 5 In.	25.00
Diane, Cordial, 1 Oz.	40.00
Diane, Cruet, 6 Oz.	10.00
Diane, Ice Bucket, Bail Handle	65.00
Diane, Ice Bucket, Tongs	85.00
Diane, Sugar & Creamer, Scrolled Handles	24.00 to 30.00
Dolphin, Candlestick, Amber, 9 3/4 In., Pair	140.00
Draped Lady, Flower Frog, 8 1/2 In.	80.00
Draped Lady, Flower Frog, Champagne, 8 1/2 In.	150.00
Draped Lady, Flower Frog, Dark Amber, 8 1/2 In.	160.00
Draped Lady, Flower Frog, Green, 8 1/2 In.	95.00 to 115.00
Draped Lady, Flower Frog, Pink, 8 1/2 In.	80.00
Draped Lady, Flower Frog, Pink, 13 1/2 In.	215.00
Draped Lady, Flower Frog, Yellow, 8 1/2 In.	240.00
Eagle, Bookend	65.00
Elaine, Bowl, 3 Sections, 11 In.	38.00
Elaine, Creamer, Footed	14.00
Elaine, Cup & Saucer	24.00
Elaine, Goblet, 9 Oz.	20.00
Elaine, Goblet, 10 Oz.	20.00
Elaine, Oyster Cocktail	15.00
Elaine, Plate, 6 1/2 In.	15.00
Elaine, Relish, 2 Sections, 7 In.	24.00
Elaine, Sherbet	15.00
Elaine, Sherbet, Tall	16.00
Gadroon, Bowl, 2 Handles, Footed, 7 1/2 In.	15.00
Gadroon, Dish, 2 Handles, 8 In.	10.00
Gadroon, Relish, 3 Sections, Footed, 10 In.	25.00
Gadroon, Soup Cream, Liner	10.00
Georgian, Tumbler, Ruby, 9 Oz.	5.00
Georgian, Tumbler, Sapphire, 3 1/4 In.	6.00
Heron, Flower Frog, 9 In.	85.00
Keyhole, Candlestick, 2-Light, Pair	129.00 to 169.00
Keyhole, Vase, Emerald, Footed, 11 1/2 In.	45.00
Lamp, Dealer's, Crown Tuscan, Gold Logo	150.00
Mandolin Lady, Flower Frog, Green, 9 In.	390.00
Marjorie, Compote, Blown, 7 In.	99.00
Marjorie, Plate, 6 In.	10.00
Marjorie, Wine, Footed	39.00
Martha Washington, Candlestick, 2-Light, 4 In., Pair	159.00
Martha Washington, Finger Bowl, Cobalt Blue	15.00
Martha Washington, Grape Bowl, Old Fashion, 4 3/4 In.	12.00
Mt. Vernon, Cocktail, 3 1/4 Oz.	9.00
Mt. Vernon, Compote, Twist Stem, 6 In.	25.00

Mt. Vernon, Cup & Saucer, Forest Green	20.00
Mt. Vernon, Decanter Set, Stopper, 11 Oz., 6 Cordials, 7 Piece	125.00
Mt. Vernon, Plate, 8 1/2 In.	7.00
Mt. Vernon, Plate, 10 1/2 In.	28.00
Mt. Vernon, Sherbet, Stemmed, 6 1/2 Oz.	9.00
Mt. Vernon, Tumbler, 10 Oz.	15.00
Mt. Vernon, Tumbler, Footed, 5 Oz.	12.00
Nude, Ashtray, Cobalt Blue	399.00
Nude, Ashtray, Yellow	395.00
Nude, Cigarette Box, Red	550.00
Nude Stem, Brandy, Amber	80.00
Nude Stem, Brandy, Gold Crystol, 1 Oz.	95.00
Nude Stem, Candy Dish, Cover, Red	2500.00
Nude Stem, Claret, Red, 4 1/2 Oz., 5 In.	145.00
Nude Stem, Cocktail, Amethyst	75.00
Nude Stem, Cocktail, Pistachio	115.00
Nude Stem, Compote, Flared, Amber	140.00
Nude Stem, Cordial, Green	250.00
Nude Stem, Goblet, Cobalt Blue	450.00
Nude Stem, Goblet, Red	265.00
Nude Stem, Ivy Ball, Amber, 10 In.	195.00
Nude Stem, Wine	150.00
Oakwood, Vase, 6 In.	65.00
Plate, Green, 5 3/4 In.	12.00
Primrose, Bowl, Opaque Yellow, 12 x 1 3/4 In.	50.00
Primrose, Compote, 6 In.	40.00
Pristine, Bowl, Divided Bowl Liner, 5 3/8 x 3 In.	18.00
Pristine, Celery, 5 Sections, 10 In.	20.00
Pristine, Cocktail, Shaker Decanter, Wheat Cut, 32 Oz.	30.00
Pristine, Relish, 3 Sections, Handles, 12 In.	24.00
Punch Bowl, Base, No. 3200	195.00
Raleigh, Creamer, 4 In.	7.00
Raleigh, Cup & Saucer	6.00
Ram's Head, Candlestick, Pair	225.00
Regency, Sherbet, Low, 7 Oz.	10.00
Rosalie, Bowl, Down-Turned Rim, Blue, 11 1/2 In.	42.00
Rosalie, Syrup	95.00
Rose Lady, Flower Frog, Amber	195.00
Rose Lady, Flower Frog, Green, Frosted	210.00
Rose Lady, Flower Frog, Mocha	175.00
Rose Point, Basket, Handle	295.00
Rose Point, Bonbon, Footed, Handle, 7 In.	38.00
Rose Point, Butter, Cover, Round	175.00
Rose Point, Champagne, Footed	32.00
Rose Point, Cheese & Cracker	135.00
Rose Point, Cocktail, 3 Oz.	30.00
Rose Point, Jam Jar, Sterling Cover	120.00
Rose Point, Mayonnaise	55.00
Rose Point, Oyster Cocktail	35.00
Rose Point, Plate, 7 1/2 In.	14.00
Rose Point, Plate, 10 1/4 In.	159.00
Rose Point, Relish, 5 Sections	60.00
Rose Point, Sherbet, Gold Trim	28.00
Rose Point, Sherbet, Tall, 6 Piece	165.00
Rose Point, Sugar & Creamer, Piecrust Edge, Individual	40.00
Rose Point, Tray, Square, 6 In.	150.00
Rose Point, Tumbler, 12 Oz.	42.50
Rose Point, Tumbler, Footed, 10 Oz.	25.00
Seagull, Flower Frog, 8 1/2 In.	28.00
Swan, Amber, With Frog, Signed, 10 In.	550.00
Swan, Carmen, 3 In.	55.00
Swan, Cobalt, Signed, 3 In.	325.00
Swan, Ebony, Signed, 10 1/2 In.	285.00

Swan, Emerald, Label, 3 In.	25.00
Swan, Punch Cup, Set Of 12	395.00
Tally-Ho, Bowl, Flared, Chrome Rim, Polished Bottom, Amber, 6 3/4 x 2 1/8 In.	8.00
Tally-Ho, Bowl, Ruby, 13 x 3 5/8 In.	62.00
Tally-Ho, Cup & Saucer, Ruby	22.00
Tally-Ho, Plate, 8 In.	13.00
Tally-Ho, Platter, Punch	150.00
Vintage, Candy Dish, 3 Sections, Footed, 7 x 2 1/2 In.	20.00
Wildflower, Bonbon, Footed, Gold Trim, 7 In.	33.00
Wildflower, Bowl, Handle, 2 Sections	22.00
Wildflower, Cake Plate, Handle, 11 In.	45.00
Wildflower, Cake Plate, Handle, 13 1/2 In.	30.00
Wildflower, Cocktail, Tall, 3 Oz.	20.00
Wildflower, Compote, Gold Etched	35.00
Wildflower, Salt, Footed	9.00
Wildflower, Sherbet, Tall	18.00
Wildflower, Sugar & Creamer, Individual	30.00
Wildflower, Torte Plate, Gold Trim, 14 In.	55.00

CAMBRIDGE POTTERY was made in Cambridge, Ohio, from about 1895 until World War I. The factory made brown glazed decorated art wares with a variety of marks, including an acorn, the name *Cambridge*, the name *Oakwood*, or the name *Terrhea*.

Ewer, Oakwood, Marbleized Green, Brown, Yellow, 5 In.	85.00
Ewer, Yellow & Orange Blossoms, Brown Ground, No. 240, 7 1/2 In.	132.00
Tile, Dog's Head Profile, Green Majolica Glaze, Marked, 6 In.	193.00
Tile, Girl Profile, Long Hair In Relief, Amber Majolica Glaze, Frame, 4 1/2 In.	121.00
Vase, Floral Glaze, Double Handles, Bulbous, 4 In.	95.00
Vase, Portrait Of Young Girl, No. 211, A. Williams, 24 In.	4125.00
Vase, Yellow & Caramel Blossoms, No. 211, A. Williams, 24 In.	1540.00

CAMEO GLASS was made in much the same manner as a cameo in jewelry. Parts of the top layer of glass were cut away to reveal a different colored glass beneath. The most famous cameo glass was made during the nineteenth century. Signed cameo glass pieces are listed under the glasswork's name, such as Daum or Galle.

Box, Jewelry, Cover, 3 1/4 x 8 /12 In.	1500.00
Lamp, Oil, Overall Floral Design, English, 5 3/4 In.	430.00
Perfume Bottle, Yellow-Green, White Overlay, Blossoms, 2 1/4 In.	525.00
Vase, Amethyst, Arsall, 12 In.	1950.00
Vase, Blossoms, Buds, Leafage, D. Christian Meisenthal, c.1900, 11 1/2 In.	8050.00
Vase, Chrysanthemums, Leafage, Silver Mounted, Bergun & Schverer, 8 In.	8912.00
Vase, Enameled Oriental Brocade Design, Auguste Jean, c.1880, 7 5/8 In.	2875.00
Vase, Morning Glory, Vines Above & Below Borders, England, 5 1/2 In.	632.00
Vase, Pink, Turquoise, Geese, Landscape, Rectangular, E. Rousseau, 1885, 8 In.	8360.00
Vase, Purple Cut To Clear, Landscape, Cylindrical, 12 1/2 In.	220.00
Vase, Red, Amber, Squirrel-Like Animal, Branch, Bird, Leveille, c.1895, 4 1/2 In.	3340.00
Vase, Rose Colored, 6 In.	740.00
Vase, Stick, Azalea Blossoms, Blue, Bulbous, Prussian, 9 In.	2299.00
Vase, White Morning Glories, Leaf Band At Rim, England, 5 x 3 1/4 In.	1220.00

CAMPBELL KIDS were first used as part of an advertisement for the Campbell Soup Company in 1906. The kids were created by Grace Drayton, a popular illustrator of the day. The kids were used in magazine and newspaper ads until about 1951. They were presented again in 1966; and in 1983, they were redesigned with a slimmer, more contemporary appearance.

Dish, Feeding	110.00
Display, Cardboard Cutout, Boy, Backpack, School Book, 1980s, 16 In.	10.00
Doll, Bicentennial, Pair	125.00
Doll, Boy, Bicentennial, 1976	75.00
Doll, Girl, Bicentennial, 1976	65.00
Doll, Hat, Kerchief, Knickerbocker, 11 In., Pair	35.00
Doll, Ideal	16.00

Doll, Knickerbocker	65.00
Doll, Velvetine, Pair	195.00
Lunch Box, Metal	110.00
Mug, Boy & Girl Rag Doll, Pair	28.00
Mug, Plastic	20.00
Salt & Pepper, Eyelashes, 4 1/4 In.	40.00

CAMPHOR GLASS is a cloudy white glass that has been blown or pressed. It was made by many factories in the Midwest during the mid-nineteenth century.

Creamer, 3 3/4 In.	25.00
Lamp, Vanity, Pair	35.00
Vase, Fan Shape, Leaf Design, 8 In.	85.00

CANDELABRUM refers to a candleholder with more than one arm to hold many candles; a candlestick is designed to hold one candle. The eccentricity of the English language makes the plural of candelabrum into candelabra.

2-Light, Circular Domed Base, Swans, Fountains, 2-Part, 18 1/4 In., Pair	3162.00
2-Light, Figural, Cherub, Square Base, Bronze, Dore, 4 In.	550.00
2-Light, Giltwood & Painted Tole, Square Base, Electrified, 29 In.	2990.00
2-Light, Louis XVI, Ormolu, Fluted Baluster, Eagles' Heads, 16 In., Pair	2875.00
2-Light, Louis XVI, Putto Holding Torches, Bronze, 17 1/2 In., Pair	3737.00
2-Light, Louis XVI, Satyr Youth Supporting Branches, 16 In., Pair	3450.00
2-Light, Sterling Silver, Georg Jensen, 9 1/4 x 10 In.	6050.00
2-Light, Stylized Seahorses, Aged Patina, Mark, E.T. Hurley, 12 1/2 In., Pair	880.00
3-Light, Directoire, Patinated Bronze, Central Urn, Anthemion, 16 In., Pair	4600.00
3-Light, Figural, Marble, Gilt Bronze, 12 In., Pair	1870.00
3-Light, Georgian, 2 Scrolled Candle Arms, Sheffield Plated, 19 In.	1955.00
3-Light, Girandole, Jenny Lind, White Marble Base, 17 In.	143.00
3-Light, Louis XVI, Scrolled Arms With Bells, Electrified, 28 In.	4830.00
3-Light, Ram's Head Jointed By Wreaths, Gilt Bronze, 16 In.	1092.00
3-Light, Silver Plated, Adam Style, 13 In., Pair	302.00
3-Light, Wave Surface, Removable Branches, Shreve, 19 1/2 In., Pair	2300.00
4-Light, Charles X Style, Ormolu, Patinated Bronze, Paw Feet, 21 In., Pair	2300.00
4-Light, Faceted Drops & Squares, Miter Diamond Basket, 17 3/4 In.	2250.00
4-Light, Fluted Marble Base, Tripod Feet, France, 20 1/2 In.	150.00
4-Light, Regency, Central Flame Finial, Matthew Boulton, c.1815, 30 In.	2990.00
4-Light, Regency, Chased Stiff Leaves, Matthew Boulton, c.1815, 29 In.	2760.00
5-Light, 4 Brackets, Bobeches & Sockets, Laurel Wreath, Bronze, 24 In.	440.00
5-Light, Charles X, Patinated Bronze, Winged Male & Female, 31 In., Pair	5462.00
5-Light, Gilt Bronze, French Empire Style, Cornucopia Arms, Cherub, 42 In.	525.00
5-Light, Marble Stems & Bases, 30 In.; Pair	3740.00
6-Light, Brass, Prisms, 17 In., Pair	282.00
6-Light, Charles X Style, Ormolu, Patinated Bronze, Paw Feet, 27 In., Pair	5175.00
6-Light, Charles X, Leaf Tips & Flower Heads On Standard, 29 1/4 In., Pair	6325.00
6-Light, Marble Standard, Foliate Arms, Marble & Bronze Standard, Lamp, 41 In.	1430.00
6-Light, Removable Flame Finials, Bronze, France, 1830-1888, 22 In., Pair	1800.00
6-Light, Rococo Style, Painted Tole & Porcelain, 24 In.	2760.00
7-Light, Empire, Bronze Dore, Acanthus, Black Marble, 19th Century, 37 In.	3080.00
7-Light, Gilt, Patinated Bronze, Floral Bouquet Arms, 26 1/2 In., Pair	915.00
9-Light, Shaped Arms, Beaded Pendants, 36 In., Pair	1150.00
Garden Topiary Form, Prisms On Branches, Tripod Metal Base, 29 In.	138.00

CANDLESTICKS were made of brass, pewter, Sandwich glass, sterling silver, plated silver, and all types of pottery and porcelain. The earliest candlesticks, dating from the sixteenth century, held the candle on a pricket (sharp pointed spike). These lost favor because in times of strife the large church candlesticks with prickets became formidable weapons, so the socket was mandated. Candlesticks changed in style through the centuries, and designs range from classic to rococo to Art Nouveau to Art Deco.

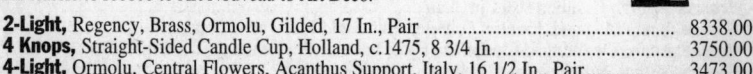

2-Light, Regency, Brass, Ormolu, Gilded, 17 In., Pair	8338.00
4 Knops, Straight-Sided Candle Cup, Holland, c.1475, 8 3/4 In.	3750.00
4-Light, Ormolu, Central Flowers, Acanthus Support, Italy, 16 1/2 In., Pair	3473.00

7-Light, Brass, Adjustable Arms, 18 In., Pair 250.00
Altar, Baroque, Tripod Base, Paw Feet, Electrified, 28 In. 1380.00
Base Metal, Trumpet, Mid-Drip, Turned Stem, England, c.1650, 6 7/8 In. 3100.00
Bell Metal, Engraved, France, 1740, 9 3/4 In. Pair. 1250.00
Brass, Altar, Pricket, Repousse, Italy, Late 18th Century, 18 1/2 In., Pair 805.00
Brass, Art Nouveau Lady, Trailing Vines, Benedict Mfg. Co., 8 In. 165.00
Brass, Arts & Crafts, Cupped Bobeches, Jarvie Style, 14 1/4 x 5 In., Pair 385.00
Brass, Ball & Claw Footed, 9 In., Pair 121.00
Brass, Baluster Turned Nozzle, Stepped Domed Foot, 13 In., Pair 58.00
Brass, Beaded Design, England, c.1780, 9 1/4 In. 95.00
Brass, Beehive, Diamond Design, 10 In. 78.00
Brass, Beehive, England, Pair, 9 In. 140.00
Brass, Bell Base, Nuremberg, Signed, 5 1/4 In., Pair 3950.00
Brass, Beta Form, Robert Jarvie, 12 In., Pair 2090.00
Brass, Bulbous Candle Cup, Bobeche, Robert Jarvie, 14 In., Pair 1380.00
Brass, Bulbous, Bobeche, Thin Stem, Circular Foot, Robert Jarvie, 14 In., Pair 1380.00
Brass, Butterfly Base, Turned Stem, China, 5 In. 12.00
Brass, Capstan, Dark Patina, Spain, c.1550 .... 385.00
Brass, Capstan, Spain, 1530s, 3 1/2 In. 425.00
Brass, Continental, Triangular Base, Baluster Stem, 17th Century, 18 In., Pair 2875.00
Brass, Cylindrical, Stepped Domed Base, Russia, c.1880, Pair 2185.00
Brass, Delta Model, Bobeche, Robert Jarvie, Script Signed, 14 In. 770.00
Brass, Diamond & Beehive, Push-Ups, Victorian, 11 3/4 In., Pair 88.00
Brass, Dolphin Shape, 9 In., Pair 88.00
Brass, Domed Hexagonal Base, 10 1/8 In. 575.00
Brass, Enameled Engraving, India, 8 3/4 In. 8.00
Brass, Flared Bobeche, Square Base, Scandinavian, 1780, 9 1/2 In., Pair 288.00
Brass, French Empire Style, Screw-On Base, 9 3/4 In., Pair 220.00
Brass, Georgian, 9 In., Pair 99.00
Brass, Georgian, Petal Base, Side Ejector, England, c.1745, Pair 770.00
Brass, Green Globes, France, Dated June 1931, 17 In., Pair 250.00
Brass, Hagenauer, 10 1/2 In. & 8 1/2 In., Pair 165.00
Brass, Heart Shape, Pennsylvania Dutch, Signed, Dated 1703 .... 395.00
Brass, Jack Of Diamonds, England, 12 In. 187.00
Brass, King Of Diamonds, 12 1/4 In., Pair 595.00
Brass, Mini, Classical Shape, Hexagonal Base, 2 5/8 In., Pair 12.00
Brass, Octagonal Balusters, 5-In. Base, 10 In. 118.00
Brass, Octagonal Base, 5 5/8 In. 248.00
Brass, Openwork Flat Stem Forms, Oriental Emblem, 4 Footed, 6 In. 11.00
Brass, Pricket, Mid-Drip Pan, 8 In., Pair 11.00
Brass, Prince Of Diamonds, 12 1/4 In., Pair 550.00
Brass, Push Ejectors, Swirl Base, England, c.1740, 8 In., Pair 2650.00
Brass, Push-Up, Petal Base, 19th Century, 9 3/4 In., Pair 977.00
Brass, Push-Up, Square Base, Victorian, 6 In. 72.00
Brass, Queen Anne, 7 3/8 In. 275.00
Brass, Queen Anne, Polished, 6 7/8 In. 220.00
Brass, Queen Anne, Scalloped Base, 7 3/4 In. 330.00
Brass, Queen Anne, Scalloped Base, Geo. Grove, 7 1/4 In. 900.00
Brass, Shaped Bobeche, Conical Domed Square Base, 19th Century, 6 In., Pair 115.00
Brass, Shaped Column, 7 1/2 In., Pair 66.00
Brass, Square Base, Polished, England, 11 1/4 In., Pair 1500.00
Brass, Stylized Shade Shaped Design, 13 1/2 In., Pair 1650.00
Brass, Swelling Standard, Bobeches, Robert Jarvie, c.1910, 13 1/2 In., Pair 3450.00
Brass, Tapering Standard, Circular Stepped Cavetto Base, Beading, c.1790 .... 330.00
Brass, Twist Stem, Saucer Base, China, Pair, 6 1/2 In. 48.00
Brass, Wide Base, Arts & Crafts, 6 In., Pair 55.00
Bronze, Baroque Style, Patinated, Baluster Standard, Electrified, 31 1/2 In. 550.00
Bronze, Charles X, Patinated, Gilt, Spiral Turned Standard, Paw Feet, 21 In., Pair 1870.00
Bronze, Empire Style, Acanthus Clad Support, Eagle Knop, 24 In., Pair 955.00
Bronze, Figural, Cavalier, 9 3/4 In., Pair 515.00
Bronze, Lamp Mounted, Empire, Ormolu, Adjustable Tole Peinte Shade, 14 In. 5750.00
Bronze, Louis XV, Winged Cherub On Foot On Orb, 19th Century, 10 3/4 In. 352.00
Bronze, Seated Putto Holding Candle Arm, Griffins, c.1820, 12 In., Pair 4830.00

Glass, Blue Opalescent, Moon & Stars, Pair 35.00
Glass, Flint, Ring & Baluster Knopped Support, Stepped Base, 10 5/8 In., Pair 495.00
Glass, Frosted, Hexagonal Pedestal & Base, 3 In., Pair 58.00
Glass, Vaseline, Art Nouveau Design, 11 In. 75.00
Iron, Hog Scraper, Shaw, England, Early 19th Century, 7 In. 110.00
Ivory, Open, Double Twist Stem, Acanthus Leaf Relief On Cup, 7 1/2 In., Pair 60.00
Marble, Rouge, Rococo, Leafy Nozzle, Lamp Mounted, 34 In. 605.00
Ormolu, Beaded Drip Pan, Cabochon Molding, Caryatid Pedestal, 11 In., Pair 1390.00
Ormolu, Charles X, Waisted Nozzle, Reeded Stem, Floral Wreath, 14 1/2 In., Pair 5462.00
Ormolu, Empire, Entwined Dolphins, Putto, Chariots, 11 3/4 In., Pair 3820.00
Ormolu, Leaf-Cast Nozzle, Flame Finial, Lion's Mask, Caryatids, 14 1/2 In., Pair 4340.00
Ormolu, Neoclassical, Spiral Twisted Stem, Domed Base, Baltic, 10 1/2 In. 2300.00
Ormolu, Urn-Shaped Nozzle, Berries, Flowers, Satyr Stem, 13 1/2 In., Pair 6950.00
Pewter, Jack-O'-Diamonds, England, 7 1/2 In., Pair 95.00
Plaster, Man & Woman Nude Both Sides, A. St. Gaudens, 34 In. 1100.00
Porcelain, Putti Riding Dolphins, France, Pair 99.00
Silver Over Copper, England, 18th Century, 7 In., Pair 175.00
Steel, Hog Scraper, Tin Plate, Brass Knob On Push-Up, 6 1/2 In. 93.50
Steel & Brass, Adjustable, Tripod Base, 73 1/2 In. 450.00
Sterling Silver, Dominick & Haff, c.1899, 9 1/2 In., Pair 230.00
Tin, Hog Scraper, Push-Up, Lip Hanger, Shaw, 7 1/4 In. .... 126.00 to 143.00
Tin, Hog Scraper, Push-Up, Lip Hanger, 5 1/2 In. 143.00
Tin, Weighted Capstan Base, Push-Ups, Brass Knobs, 9 1/4 In., Pair 605.00

CANDY CONTAINERS have been popular since the late Victorian era. Collectors have long favored the glass containers, but now all types, including tin and papier-mache, are collected. Probably the earliest glass container sold commercially was the Liberty Bell made in 1876 for sale at the Centennial Exposition. Thousands of designs were made until the cost became too high in the 1960s. By the late 1970s, reproductions were being made and sold without the candy. Containers listed here are glass unless otherwise described.

Ambulance, Military, Tin, France, 1930s, 6 1/2 In. 450.00
Amos 'n' Andy 600.00
Auto, 1940s Chevrolet 15.00
Barney Google, By Barrel 750.00
Battleship, Contents 25.00
Battleship, Maine, Milk Glass 95.00
Belsnickle, White Coat, Mica Accents, Germany, 1910s, 11 1/8 In. 632.00
Box, Paper, Cannon On Caisson, Sand Covered, Diamond Shape, 4 1/2 In. 195.00
Bunny, Standing, Life-Size, Glass Eyes, Early 20th Century, 21 x 12 In. 460.00
Bus, Jitney, On Wheels 450.00
Camel, Rider, Bisque Head, Germany, 12 In. 1275.00
Camera, On Tripod 400.00
Cannon 400.00
Car, Jeep Scout 25.00
Car, Racing, Driver 75.00
Car, Sedan, 4 Door, Tin Wheels, No. II 245.00
Car, Volkswagen 20.00
Cash Register 250.00
Cat, Papier-Mache, Yellow & Black, 1950s, 7 1/2 In. 45.00
Chauffeur, Dapper, Molded Hat, 16 In. 3550.00
Chicken, Composition, Painted Orange, Yellow, White, 3 In. 60.00
Child, Naked 60.00
Clown, Standing, Ruffled Costume 900.00
Dog, Bulldog, Sitting, 3 In. 15.00
Dog, Next To Barrel 325.00
Dog, Paper & Metal Hat 30.00
Dog, Terrier, Glass, Frosted, 15 In. 15.00
Drum Mug, Gold, No Closure 50.00
Duck, Large Bill 150.00
Duck, Nodder, West Germany 50.00
Duck, Round Base 395.00

Duckling, Mohair, Egg-Shaped Body Opens, Glass Eyes, Germany, 5 In.	140.00
Elephant	225.00
Elephant, Tail Suit	300.00
Fat Boy, On Drum	250.00
Father Christmas, Basket On Back, Fur Beard, Feather Tree, 10 In.	865.00
Father Christmas, Cotton Batting, 5 In.	200.00
Father Christmas, Feather Tree, Polychrome Face, Papier-Mache, 9 1/2 In.	495.00
Father Christmas, Feather Tree, Yellow Coat, Papier-Mache, 6 7/8 In.	305.00
Father Christmas, Nodder, c.1940s, 13 In.	295.00
Fire Engine, Large Boiler	110.00
Football, Tin, Germany	22.00
George Washington, Composition, Germany, 3 In.	95.00
Girl, Victorian, Egg Shape, Papier-Mache, Germany	65.00
Girl Holding Child, Santa Claus, Feather Tree, Pull Slide, Germany, 6 1/2 In.	395.00
Guitar, Cardboard, Strings	68.00
Gun, 6-Sided Barrel	30.00
Gun, Revolver, V-Shaped Trigger	40.00
Gun, Toy	228.00
Happifats, Glass, Tin Base, Coin Slot, 4 1/2 In.	110.00
Happifats, On Drum	200.00
Hen On Nest, Label, Papier-Mache, 6 1/2 In.	49.00
Horn, Yellow, Candy	25.00
Horse, Pulling Cart	2.00
Horse & Cart, 2 Wheels, 4 1/2 In.	12.00
Kiddie Clock	20.00
Lady, Bisque Head & Arms, Glued-On Fabric Costume, c.1890, 5 In.	300.00
Lamp, Ribbed Base	180.00
Lamp, Shade	250.00 to 275.00
Lantern, Barn, Green Glass	85.00
Lantern, Barn, Wire Bail	50.00
Lantern, Little Ball	30.00
Lantern, Victory Glass Co.	10.00 to 20.00
Liberty Bell, No. 3, Amber	55.00
Liberty Bell, No. 3, Wire Bail Type, Clear	45.00
Locomotive, Double Window	50.00
Locomotive, Friction Cap	225.00
Locomotive, Pink	40.00
Mail Box, Clear	300.00
Megaphone	10.00
Mule, Pulling 2-Wheeled Barrel, Driver	110.00
Mule, Pulling Cart, Glass	40.00
No Parking Sign, 4 1/2 In.	60.00
Nursing Bottle, Rubber Nipple	20.00
Opera Glasses, Brass Frame	125.00
Peanut, Papier-Mache	25.00
Pencil	60.00
Peter Rabbit, Box, Tin, Art Deco	70.00
PEZ, Barney Bear	15.00
PEZ, Batgirl, Rubber Head	45.00
PEZ, Blob, Green Stem, Black Head, 1970s	80.00
PEZ, Bugs Bunny, On Feet, Card	1.50
PEZ, Bullwinkle	125.00
PEZ, Cabbage-Head Man	1265.00
PEZ, Captain America	20.00
PEZ, Captain America, Candy, Bag	39.00
PEZ, Casper, Die Cut	85.00 to 95.00
PEZ, Cat In Hat, Black, 1970s	40.00
PEZ, Charlie Brown, Cap	40.00
PEZ, Charlie Brown, Frowning, On Card	6.00
PEZ, Clown, With Chin	35.00
PEZ, Cocoa-Marsh Spaceman	135.00
PEZ, Creature From The Black Lagoon, 1963	150.00 to 185.00

PEZ, Dalmatian	20.00
PEZ, Donald Duck, 1950s	140.00
PEZ, Donkey, Merry Melody Makers, Card	6.00
PEZ, Dumbo, Blue Head	15.00
PEZ, Easter Bunny, Die Cut	285.00
PEZ, Frankenstein, 1963	135.00 to 150.00
PEZ, Frog	15.00
PEZ, Garfield, With Teeth, On Card	6.00
PEZ, Goofy	8.00
PEZ, Gorilla	35.00
PEZ, Green Hornet, 1966	198.00
PEZ, Huey, Card	6.00
PEZ, Hulk	10.00
PEZ, Hulk, Painted Face	225.00
PEZ, Indian Chief, Multicolored Headdress, 1970s	65.00
PEZ, Kermit, On Feet, Card	1.50
PEZ, King Louie	15.00
PEZ, Koala	20.00
PEZ, Koala, Whistle Head	45.00
PEZ, Lamb, Whistle Head	15.00
PEZ, Lion, With Crown	30.00
PEZ, Little Bad Wolf	15.00
PEZ, Merlin The Mouse	6.00
PEZ, Merry Melody Panda	6.00
PEZ, Mickey Mouse	8.00
PEZ, Mimic The Monkey	40.00
PEZ, Miss Piggy, On Feet, Card	1.00
PEZ, Monkey Sailor	35.00
PEZ, Mr. Ugly	18.00 to 35.00
PEZ, Nurse, Blond Hair	48.00
PEZ, Nurse, Brown Hair	70.00
PEZ, Peace Pipe, Brown, Germany, 1970s	45.00
PEZ, Pear-Head Man	795.00 to 1100.00
PEZ, Penguin, Merry Melody Makers, Card	6.00
PEZ, Peter PEZ	55.00
PEZ, Petunia Pig	15.00 to 30.00
PEZ, Pirate	45.00
PEZ, Policeman	25.00
PEZ, Pooh	20.00
PEZ, Road Runner, 1970s	30.00
PEZ, Road Runner, Card	6.00
PEZ, Rooster	35.00
PEZ, Santa Claus, Full Body, Instruction Sheet	115.00
PEZ, Santa Claus, On Feet, Card	1.00
PEZ, Santa Claus, Unpainted Beard	75.00
PEZ, Santa Claus, Unpainted Eyes	10.00
PEZ, Scrooge McDuck	10.00
PEZ, Smurfette	6.00 to 8.00
PEZ, Snow White	75.00
PEZ, Space Gun, 1980s	75.00
PEZ, Space Trooper, Full-Bodied, Red	550.00
PEZ, Spaceman	80.00
PEZ, Spiderman, Candy, Bag	7.00
PEZ, Spiderman, Package	8.00
PEZ, Thor	150.00
PEZ, Thumper	20.00
PEZ, Wile E. Coyote	15.00
PEZ, Wolfman	225.00
PEZ, Woodstock, Painted Feathers, Package	10.00
PEZ, Zorro	45.00 to 75.00
Piano, Brown Paint	350.00
Pigeon On 3 Wheels, Windup, Composition, 6 1/2 In.	330.00

Policeman, Pumpkin Head	975.00
Potato, Germany	70.00
Pumpkin, Papier-Mache, Orange & Green, Germany, 7 In.	45.00
Pumpkin Head, Children, 3 Piece	330.00
Pumpkin Head, Policeman	400.00
Pumpkin Head, Woman	385.00
Rabbit, Composition Head & Body, Movable Arms, 9 /12 In.	1815.00
Rabbit, Easter, Papier-Mache, White Paint, Glass Eyes, Cotton Coat, 6 1/4 In.	77.00
Rabbit, Eating Carrot	175.00
Rabbit, Emerging From Egg, Composition, Applied Sparkles, 8 In.	220.00
Rabbit, Fur & Fabric Covering, Paper Egg, Papier-Mache, 10 In.	905.00
Rabbit, Lady, Pull-Off Head, Apron, Blouse Holds Egg, Germany, 8 In.	375.00
Rabbit, Nibbling Carrot	35.00
Rabbit, On Log	250.00
Rabbit, Paper, Germany	125.00
Rabbit, Papier-Mache	50.00
Rabbit, Pushing Buggy	350.00
Rabbit, Running On Log	350.00
Rabbit, Wearing Glasses, Banjo, Composition, 14 In.	365.00
Rabbit, White & Green Paint, Papier-Mache, 7 1/4 In.	27.00
Rabbit, With Basket, Ears Set On Springs, Papier-Mache	125.00
Rocketeer, Plastic, Topps, Small	40.00
Rocking Horse	275.00
Rocking Horse, Clown Rider	225.00
Rooster, Crowing	145.00 to 225.00
Saltshaker, Benjamin Franklin, Original Cover	325.00
Santa Claus, Banded Coat, Contents	250.00
Santa Claus, Bells On Hat, 7 In.	95.00
Santa Claus, Fur Beard, Squeaks When Pushed Down, 7 1/2 In.	55.00
Santa Claus, Fur Beard, With Tree, 9 1/2 In.	48.00
Santa Claus, Head, Papier-Mache	65.00
Santa Claus, Leaving Chimney	125.00
Santa Claus, Painted, Plastic Head, Contents, 6 In.	125.00
Santa Claus, Standing, Germany	75.00
Santa Claus, Tree, Fur Beard, Toy Sack, Papier-Mache, 7 1/2 In.	22.00
Santa Claus, Wooden Platform, Fur Beard, Cloth Pants, Germany, 11 In.	785.00
Scotty, 5 1/4 In.	13.00
Scrub Board, Midget Washer	25.00
Skookum	255.00 to 350.00
Snowman, Composition, Pull-Off Head, Top Hat, Germany, 4 In.	235.00
Snowman, Mica Cardboard, 1930s	55.00
Snowman, Musical Instrument, Papier-Mache, Box	195.00
Snowman, Plastic, Red & White, 4 In.	12.00
Snowman, Top Hat, Papier-Mache, 6 1/2 In.	28.00
Snowman, With Umbrella, Papier-Mache, 6 1/2 In.	36.00
Soda Fountain, Yellow, Box Of Candy	125.00
Soldier, Bisque Head, Cardboard Torso, Wooden Legs, 1900, 8 In.	950.00
Soldier, Doughboy, Tin Hat	650.00
Soldier, On Monument	900.00
Spark Plug	65.00 to 125.00
Spirit Of Goodwill	165.00
Spirit Of St. Louis, Tin & Glass, 1920s, 4 3/4 x 6 3/16 In.	345.00
Suitcase, Milk Glass, Painted Sailboats	150.00
Tank, World War I, Blue Glass	110.00
Tank, World War I, Clear Glass	100.00
Taxi, Boyd Glass	15.00
Telephone, Dial	40.00
Telephone, Red Flashed, Label, Victory Glass	50.00
Truck, Ladder	150.00
Trumpet, Milk Glass	150.00
Trunk, Milk Glass, Gold Trim	150.00
Uncle Sam	495.00

Veggie Boy, Pull-Off Head, 4 In.	375.00
Village, Glass Liner	150.00
Watermelon, Green, Dark Serrations, Germany, 4 In.	245.00
Willys Jeep	65.00
Windmill	20.00 to 110.00
Windmill, Blades	130.00
Windmill, Pewter Top	800.00
World Globe, On Stand	500.00

CANES and walking sticks were used by every well-dressed man in the nineteenth century, but by World War I the style had changed. Today canes are used by few but the infirm. Collectors prize old canes made with special features, like hidden swords, whiskey flasks, or risqué pictures seen through peepholes. Examples with solid gold heads or made from exotic materials, such as walrus vertebrae, are among the higher priced canes.

Automaton, Parrot, Movable Lower Beak, Rolling Eyes	1500.00
Bird-Shaped Whistle Handle, Simmons	770.00
Cap Bomb, Forged Iron, Wooden Shaft, Carved Snake & Fourth Of July, 1809	250.00
Cherry, Mermaid Handle, Flowing Hair, Carved Shaft, 1870s, 35 1/4 In.	3737.00
Ebony, Ivory Handle, Brass Collar, 33 In.	250.00
Glass, Red & White Swirled Stripes, Blue, Crook Handle, 34 In.	195.00
Glass, Spiral Twisted Shaft & Handle, Victorian, 45 In.	58.00
Glass Cylinder, Oak, Case, 36 In.	800.00
Harmonica, Walnut With Ebony Cap & Separator, England, 1900-1925, 36 In.	1100.00
Head Of Indian Squaw Handle, Bed Set, C.L. Morris, 1986, 35 In.	60.00
Hickory, Pouting Man Handle, White Metal Ferrule, Folk Art, c.1880	127.00
Ivory, Brass Spyglass Handle, Rosewood Shaft	687.00
Ivory, Breast Of Disraeli, Rosewood, Brass Ferrule, Sterling Silver Collar, 36 1/2 In.	1870.00

Cane, Ivory Handle, Shakespeare, Rosewood, c.1870

Cane, Pewter Handle, Columbus, Chicago Fair, 34 In.

Cane, Sterling Silver Handle, Acorns, Leaves, Ebony, c.1880

Cane, Sterling Silver Handle, Eagle With Apple, c.1880

Cane, Walking Stick, Ivory Cat Head, Knob, Silver, Rosewood, c.1890

Ivory, Carved Tassels, Brass Ring & Tip, 1800s, 35 1/2 In... 215.00
Ivory, Carved, Legend Of St. Hubertus, Malacca Shaft 3025.00
Ivory, Fist Clutching Head Of Snake, Rope Twist Shaft, Whalebone Tip, 34 In. 2990.00
Ivory, Head, Malacca Shaft, Brass Ferrule, Dated 1700.. 495.00
Ivory, Leda & Swan, 3 Nude Maidens & Swan, c.1860, 36 In....................................... 3850.00
Ivory, Spy Glass, Brass, Rosewood, Band, Brass Ferrule, c.1920, 36 1/2 In.................. 688.00
Ivory, Sterling Silver Mounted, Rosewood Shaft.. 852.00
Ivory, Tiger, Glass Eyes, Snakewood, Horn Ferrule, Gold, France, 1900-1925.............. 880.00
Ivory Handle, Shakespeare, Rosewood, c.1870 ....*Illus* 1320.00
John The Baptist, Metal Ferrule, Snakewood Shaft, America, c.1900, 35 1/2 In. 3080.00
Macrame Covered, Lacquered, 36 In.. 285.00
Malacca, Silver Dragonfly Handle, Art Nouveau, 3 Opals, France, c.1900 .... 2300.00
Narwhal, Coin Silver End Cap, Polished Tusk, America, c.1850, 38 3/4 In.................... 4180.00
Oak, Carved, No Tip, 34 3/4 In... 125.00
Owls, Glass Eyes, Bone 195.00
Panther Head Handle, Silver Monogram, Mahogany, c.1912, 23 1/2 In...................... 402.00
Pekinese Handle, Charles L. Morris, 33 In.. 40.00
Pewter Handle, Columbus, Chicago Fair, 34 In..*Illus* 248.00
Shooting Stick, Pull-Ring Released Handle & Turned Into Seat, Chestnut 220.00
Silver, Hippopotamus Head, Stone-Set Eyes, Gilded Borders, Birch Stick, Russia 8625.00
Silver Handle, Bamboo, England 132.00
Silver Top & Ring, Ash, Brass Blade, 19th Century, 38 1/4 In. 115.00
Snuffbox Top, Opened To Painting Of Victorian Couple, 1914 .... 3850.00
Spectroscope, Concealed, Silver Sterling Cap, Brigg, London, 1929............................ 467.00
Sterling Silver Handle, Acorns, Leaves, Ebony, c.1880 ....*Illus* 330.00
Sterling Silver Handle, Eagle With Apple, c.1880 ....*Illus* 743.00
Sword, Indian Head Handle, Florals On Shaft, Mahogany, c.1850, 37 1/2 In. 345.00
Sword, Rapier Style Blade, With Fuller, Brass Tip, 1775-1825, 34 1/4 In. 575.00
Sword, Wooden Carved Head, 35 In. 990.00
Walking Stick, Blown Glass, Spirals Of Yellow, Blue & Green, 47 In. 165.00
Walking Stick, Blown, Aqua With Amber Center, Twisted, 34 1/2 In. 71.00
Walking Stick, Bone Male Head Handle, Ebony, 35 1/2 In. 402.00
Walking Stick, Carved Cone Hold Of Dog, 19th Century 445.00
Walking Stick, Donkey Head, Folk Art, 35 In. 357.00
Walking Stick, Engraved Gold Handle, Horn Tip 235.00
Walking Stick, Gilded Barrels, Foliate Carved, c.1917, 37 In..................................... 920.00
Walking Stick, Gold-Filled Top, Ebonized Shaft, Dieaton, Child's, 1882, 24 1/4 In. 210.00
Walking Stick, Ivory Cat Head, Knob, Silver, Rosewood, c.1890 ....*Illus* 1980.00
Walking Stick, Ivory Handle, 35 1/2 In. 55.00
Walking Stick, Ivory Handle, Knight In Armor On Shaft, Ebony, 37 In........................ 1035.00
Walking Stick, Ivory Hold Of Man's Head, Hallmarked Silver Band............................ 445.00
Walking Stick, Ivory, 37 In. 330.00
Walking Stick, Ivory, Dog Handle, Bone, 34 1/8 In... 1150.00
Walking Stick, Japanese Shibayama Finial, Vine & Insect Design, 32 In...................... 260.00
Walking Stick, Multicolored Geometric & Striped Beading, 33 1/2 In. 690.00
Walking Stick, Silver Elephant Hold, Bone Tusks 445.00
Walking Stick, Whale Tooth Hand Grip, Malacca Shaft, c.1825 .... 445.00
Walking Stick, Whalebone Shaft, Baleen Inserts, Whale Tooth Knob, 32 3/4 In............ 950.00
Walking Stick, Whalebone Shaft, Ivory Hold, Marked H. Perkins Winsted, 1844 .... 900.00
Walking Stick, Whalebone, Handle With Ebony Spacers, 36 1/2 In. 375.00
Walking Stick, Whalebone, Incised Knob, 38 1/2 In... 375.00
Walking Stick, Woman's, Dog-Form Gold Head, Ebony, 38 In. 370.00
Whalebone, Whale Tooth Handle 750.00
Whalebone & Ivory, Fist Handle, Mother-Of-Pearl Inlay, 36 In. 2090.00
White Metal, Eagle Handle, Flag, Branch Insignia, Striped Wooden Shaft, GAR 100.00
Wood, Carved Eagle & Snake, Bullfights, Tex-Mex, 38 In. 625.00
Wood, Carved, Snake, Rhinestone Eyes, 37 In... 220.00

CANTON CHINA is blue-and-white ware made near Canton, China, from
about 1785 to 1895. It is hand decorated with Chinese scenes.

Basket, Fruit, Undertray, 19th Century, 9 3/4 In.. 750.00
Bowl, Fruit, Underplate, 19th Century, 9 3/4 In. 635.00
Bowl, Salad, 19th Century, 10 In. 690.00

Box, Brush, Divided Interior, 19th Century, 7 5/16 x 3 5/8 In. 635.00
Butter Plate, Cover, Strainer, 19th Century, 13 1/4 x 15 7/8 In. 550.00
Chamber Pot, Domed Cover, 19th Century, 8 1/2 In. 290.00
Curry Dish, Blue & White, 9 1/2 In., 3 Piece 550.00
Dish, Hot Water, c.1840, 11 In. 500.00
Dish, Oval, 7 In. 77.00
Dish, Serving, Cover, Shaped Corners, Rectangular, 19th Century, 9 1/4 In. 230.00
Dish, Shrimp, 19th Century, 9 1/4 In. 635.00
Fruit Basket, Underplate, 19th Century, 10 3/4 In. 1035.00
Ginger Jar, Cover, Blue & White, 7 In. 145.00
Jug, Cider, Cover, 1820s, Miniature... 2200.00
Mug, Strap Handle, Large 445.00
Planter, Riverscapes, Everted Rim, Oval, 10 7/8 In., Pair.. 920.00
Plate, Hot Water, 10 1/2 In. 120.00
Platter, Blue & White, Octagonal, 13 1/2 In. 357.00
Platter, Blue & White, Octagonal, 16 In. 357.00
Platter, Cut Corner, Rectangular, 19th Century, 17 1/4 x 14 In. 400.00
Platter, Footed, Shaped Edge, Oval, 19th Century, 14 7/8 In. 1150.00
Platter, Insert, Octagonal, 14 x 17 In. 1155.00
Platter, Octagonal, 14 1/2 In. 420.00
Platter, Octagonal, 19th Century, 17 In. 374.00
Teapot, 5 1/2 In. 605.00
Tray, Ice Cream, 19th Century, 13 3/4 In. 1150.00
Tureen, Cover, Hill & Stream, 19th Century, 13 In. 1495.00
Tureen, Sauce, Cover, Undertray, Blue & White, 6 In. 330.00
Tureen, Soup, Cover, 19th Century, 11 5/8 x 9 1/4 x 7 1/2 In. 748.00
Tureen, Soup, Platter, 19th Century 546.00
Urinal, Blue Floral Design 405.00
Vase, Cylinder, 9 3/4 In. 484.00
Vase, Diaper Trellis, 15 1/4 In. 2300.00

CAPO-DI-MONTE porcelain was first made in Naples, Italy, from 1743 to 1759. The factory moved near Madrid, Spain, reopened in 1771, and worked to 1834. Since that time, the Doccia factory of Italy acquired the molds and is using the N and crown mark. Societe Richard Ceramica is a modern-day firm often referred to as Ginori or Capo-di-Monte. This company uses the crown and N mark.

Ashtray, Square, 6 In. 45.00
Basket, Openwork Basket Weave, Applied Flowers, 4 x 4 In. 13.00
Bowl, 5 Panels, Semi-Nude Classical Figures, 5 Footed 65.00
Box, 10 In... 220.00
Box, Bacchanalian Scenes, Hinged Cover, Blue Crown Mark, 5 x 3 1/4 In. 340.00
Box, Classical Figures, Panels, Hinged Cover, Blue Crown Mark, 8 x 5 1/2 In. 535.00
Box, Hinged Cover, Trees, People Scenic, Oval, 3 1/2 x 1/2 In. 75.00
Box, Jewelry, Piano Shape, Man, Woman & Cupids, Garden, 5 1/2 x 13 1/2 In. 150.00
Bust, Napoleon I, N & Crown, Porcelain, 19th Century, 5 1/8 In. 210.00
Cache Pot, Oriental Scenes, Ivory Ground, 9 In.. 110.00
Casque, Jewel, Hinged Cover, Cherubs, Large.. 450.00
Chamberstick, Floral, 4 1/2 In. 75.00
Cup & Saucer, Nymphs In Ocean, Flowers, Putti, 24 Piece 2450.00
Dish, Figural Finial Cover, Young Children & Flowers, Oval, 8 In. 100.00
Ewer, Pedestal, Relief, Gentleman, Woman, Cupids & Floral, Mask Handle, 46 In. 225.00
Figurine, 5 Musicians 900.00
Figurine, Female Exotic Dancer, Marked, c.1920, 8 1/2 In. 193.00
Figurine, Girl, Ponytail, Short Dress, Wooden Stand, Signed, 7 3/4 In. 80.00
Figurine, Putti With Grapes, 6 In. 358.00
Figurine, Ragamuffin Band, 8 In., 8 Piece 880.00
Plaque, Semi-Nude Lovers In Garden, Gold Trim, 5 1/2 In. 10.00
Plate, Raised Cherub Faces & Wing Border, 9 1/2 In. 100.00
Plate, Wall, Bacchus Scene, Gold Trim, 6 1/2 In. 55.00
Urn, Campana Shape, Mask Handles, Molded Satyrs & Putti, 7 3/4 In., Pair 1100.00
Urn, Cover, Cherubs & Satyrs, Nymph Handles, Ginori, 14 In. 715.00
Urn, Cover, Classical Scene Of Romans At Bath, Handles, 12 3/4 In., Pair.................. 880.00
Vase, White, Applied Bow, Richard Ginori, 6 In. 45.00

CAPTAIN MARVEL was introduced in February 1940 in Whiz comic books. An orphan named Billy Batson met the wizard, Shazam, and whenever he said the magic word he was transformed into a superhero. A movie serial was released in 1940. The comic was discontinued in 1954. A second Captain Marvel appeared in 1966, a third in 1967. Only the original was transformed by shouting *Shazam*.

Button, 1 3/4 In.	2.00
Comic Book, Whiz Comics, No. 65, England, Oversized, 1950	20.00
Lobby Card	25.00
Membership Button, Club, Red, White & Blue	65.00
Paper Doll, 3 Famous Flying Marvels, Fawcett, 1945, Uncut	20.00
Photograph, Premium, 1942	70.00
Puzzle, Captain Marvel Rides The Engine Of Doom, Fawcett, 1941, Box	85.00
Puzzle, Jigsaw, No. 1, Box, 1940s	75.00
Puzzle, One Against Many, Original Envelope	45.00

CAPTAIN MIDNIGHT began as a radio show in September 1940. The first comic book appeared in July 1941. Captain Midnight was really the aviator Captain Albright, who was to defeat the Nazis. A movie serial was made in 1942 and a comic strip was published for a short time. The comic book Captain Midnight ended his career in 1948. The radio premiums are the prized collector memorabilia today.

Better Little Book, Sheik Jomak	20.00
Book, Trick & Riddle, 1939	40.00
Decoder, Key-O-Matic, 1949	115.00
Handbook, Flight Commander's, Ovaltine Premium Booklet, 1957	265.00
Handkerchief, Secret Squadron Emblem	225.00
Medal, Flight Patrol, Membership, Skelly Oil Co.	17.00
Member Kit, Secret Squadron, Mailing Envelope, 1955	760.00
Membership Card, Secret Squadron, Signed, 1957	50.00
Mug, Character	30.00
Mug, Shake-Up, Orange With Blue Top, Embossed	140.00
Patch, Cloth, Secret Squadron, Cellophane Wrapper, 1955-1956	50.00
Ring, Secret Compartment	125.00
Toy, Magni-Matic Code-O-Graph, 1945	95.00
Toy, Mirro-Flash Code-O-Graph, 1946	65.00

CARAMEL SLAG, see Chocolate Glass category

CARDS listed here include advertising cards, greeting cards, baseball cards, playing cards, valentines, and others. Color pictures were rare in the nineteenth century, so companies gave away colorful cards with pictures of children, flowers, products, or related scenes that promoted the company name. These were often collected and stored in albums. Greeting cards are also a nineteenth-century idea that has remained popular. Baseball cards also date from the nineteenth century when they were used by tobacco companies as giveaways. The gum cards were started in 1933, but it was not until after World War II that the bubble gum cards favored today were produced. Today over 1, 000 cards are issued each year by the gum companies. Related items may be found in the Postcard and Movie categories.

Advertising, Alexander Bros. Leather Belting	25.00
Advertising, American Eagle Bank, S.O. Barnum & Son	1017.00
Advertising, Babbitts Soap, Mechanical, Girl Washing Clothes In Bucket, 1907	20.00 to 25.00
Advertising, Babcock Fire Extinguisher	250.00
Advertising, Bad Accident Bank, H. Partridge & Co.	2310.00
Advertising, Barney Thompson Wagons & Wagon Wheels	20.00
Advertising, Bear Hunt Bank, J. & E. Stevens Co.	27.00
Advertising, Becker Croton Flour Mills, 1860s	30.00
Advertising, Blood Will Tell, Currier & Ives, 1879	45.00
Advertising, Brown Iron Bitters, Sailboat, Flowers	6.00
Advertising, Buffalo German Insurance Company Building	40.00
Advertising, Buffalo Robes, Woodcut Of Buffalo	110.00

Advertising, Buy Raser's Root Beer Extract, Children 10.00
Advertising, Carter's Little Liver Pills, Cats, Palette Shape...................................... 7.00
Advertising, Child Shopping Card, 1950 .... 250.00
Advertising, Christ Bros., House Furnishings 30.00
Advertising, Church & Co.'s Soda, Arm & Hammer Logo, Caricature, 5 x 6 In. 110.00
Advertising, Clark's O.N.T. Spool Cotton, Image Of Pike's Peak, 5 x 7 In.................. 9.00
Advertising, Columbus Buggy Co... 20.00
Advertising, Congress Bitters, View Of Capitol 30.00
Advertising, Empire Strikes Back, Burger Chef, 36 Piece 1800.00
Advertising, Estey Organs Works, Orchestra Club 20.00
Advertising, Gall's Corsets 35.00
Advertising, Geneva Hand Fluter, Girl Making Victorian Ruffles............................. 20.00
Advertising, Geo. J. Raymond, Men's Hats, Darktown Trial By Jury, 3 x 4 In. 20.00
Advertising, Grayvita, Anti-Gray Hair Treatment, Female Heads, 1942, 8 1/2 x 5 In. ... 8.00
Advertising, Green Hornet, 1966, 44 Piece.. 475.00
Advertising, Hawley & Hoops Breakfast Powdered Extract Of Cocoa, 5 x 6 In. 19.00
Advertising, Heinz, Pickle Shape, Salesman's Business, 1890s.................................. 24.00
Advertising, Hennepin Shoes, Kate Claxton Pictured, c.1880 .... 20.00
Advertising, Hercules Steam Tug Corp., Liverpool 35.00
Advertising, Humpty-Dumpty, Bank, Mechanical, Selchow & Righter......................... 357.00
Advertising, Humpty-Dumpty, Bank, Mechanical, Kennedy, Spaulding & Co. 550.00
Advertising, Indian Queen Perfume, Maiden 40.00
Advertising, J. & P. Coats, Animals As Soldiers, 3 Piece.. 15.00
Advertising, J. & P. Coats, Women Sewing, 1879 Calendar Back, 3 1/2 In.................. 22.00
Advertising, James Bond, Glidrose, 1965, 66 Piece.. 195.00
Advertising, Jazz Greats, Armstrong, Teagarden, Morton, Goodman, Box, 36 Cards 10.00
Advertising, John Deere, Rawlings Implement Co. 25.00
Advertising, Jolly Nigger, Campbell, Porter & Smith... 357.00
Advertising, Kansas City Chiefs Football, Hardee's, 1979, 10 Piece.......................... 12.00
Advertising, Le Page's Glue, Man Glued To Bench, Police Pulling Him, 3 1/4 x 5 1/2 In. 10.00
Advertising, Lindbergh, Flyer And Airplane Spirit, 1927.. 35.00
Advertising, Lion Coffee, Easter Bunny & Boy, 1893, 5 x 7 In.................................. 12.00
Advertising, Lion Coffee, Humpty-Dumpty, Children's Dolls, Stories 6.00
Advertising, Lost In Space, 1966, 55 Piece.. 350.00
Advertising, Lyons Tea, Australia, 1 3/8 x 2 5/8 In., 20 Piece.................................. 5.00
Advertising, Marquette Club Ginger Ale, Die Cut Pretty Girl, 5 1/2 x 9 In. 17.00
Advertising, Mason Bank, S.G. Dickinson.. 1320.00
Advertising, McLaughlin's XXXX Coffee, Congo Negro, 3 3/4 x 5 In.......................... 10.00
Advertising, McLaughlin's XXXX Coffee, Fiji Islands, c.1889, 3 3/4 x 5 In. 12.00
Advertising, Merrick Thread Co., Centennial Medals... 20.00
Advertising, Messageries Royales Paris, Coach Rental, Bilingual............................. 25.00
Advertising, Morell's French Lotion, Fairy With Blue Wings, c.1880, 4 x 3 In. 25.00
Advertising, New England Boat & Shoe House, Girl, Oval Frame, 1900s, 8 x 12 In. 7.00
Advertising, New York Fire Insurance, 1835 Wall Street Fire 75.00
Advertising, Nixon's Stove Polish, Black Lady Cleaning Child 20.00
Advertising, Parker Brothers Toys, Boston.. 40.00
Advertising, Pep Cereal, Premium 20.00
Advertising, Piper & Sons Railway Equipment, List Of Products 25.00
Advertising, Punch & Judy, Bank, Mechanical, Shepard Hardware 357.00
Advertising, Punch & Judy, Bank, Mechanical, Selchow & Righter 440.00
Advertising, Quaker Bitters, Girl In Barrel.. 8.00
Advertising, Red Spruce Gum 30.00
Advertising, Rising Sun Stove Polish 25.00
Advertising, Sapolio, Black Boy, Watermelon, Die Cut 10.00
Advertising, Snow White, Panini, 360 Piece 450.00
Advertising, Speaking Dog, Bank, Mechanical, Selchow & Righter ....330.00 to 550.00
Advertising, Stump Speaker, Bank, Mechanical, Weaver & Goss Hardware Co. 412.00
Advertising, Stump Speaker, Bank, Mechanical, J.G. Lauer..................................... 275.00
Advertising, Sweetser & Co., Fine Boots & Shoes 45.00
Advertising, Thurber's Preserves & Jellies 10.00
Advertising, Traveler's Insurance Co., Bird's-Eye View.. 25.00
Advertising, Uncle Sam, Bank, Mechanical, E.I. Horsman...................................... 440.00

Advertising, Uncle Sam, Bank, Mechanical, Shepard Hardware 550.00
Advertising, Universal Fire Extinguisher Co. 350.00
Advertising, Valentine, Figural, Edwardian Gentleman, Tipsy, String Operated, 14 In. . 20.00
Advertising, White House Coffee 25.00
Advertising, Wichita Wings Soccer Team, Burger King, 1984-1985, 20 Piece 15.00
Advertising, Zebra Navy Plug Tobacco, Black Man Taking Nap, 3 3/8 x 6 In. 5.00
Baseball, Bobby Bonilla, Autographed, 1988 .... 45.00
Baseball, Bohemian Hearth Bread, San Diego Padres, Tim Flannery .... .25
Baseball, Carlos May .... .25
Baseball, Cracker Jack, Tris Speaker No. 65, 1915 .... 1840.00
Baseball, St. Louis Stars Ladies' Baseball Club, 1910 .... 88.00
Baseball, Topps Set, 1964, Includes Mantle & Rose 1725.00
Baseball, Ty Cobb, T206 .... 20123.00
Basketball, Wilt Chamberlain, Rookie, 1961-62 Fleer No. 8 .... 1045.00
Basketball, Wilt Chamberlain, Topps No. 1, 1969-70 .... 195.00
Boxing, Famous Prizefighters, Burstein Isaacs & Co., 1923, Set Of 50 .... 789.00
Boxing, Gene Tunney, Fro-Joy Ice Cream, 1927 .... 150.00
Boxing, Ringside, Jack LaMotta, Max Baer, Rocky Marciano, 96 Piece 1232.00
Cigarette, Gallaher LTD, Great War Series, 1 3/8 x 2 5/8 In., 10 Piece 5.00
Cigarette, Life On Board A Man Of War, Player Cigarettes, 1 3/8 x 2 5/8 In., 48 Piece   16.00
Cigarette, Player & Sons & Gallaher, Military, 1 3/8 x 2 5/8 In., 8 Piece 4.00
Cigarette, Players, Aircraft Of Royal Air Force, 1 3/8 x 23 5/8 In., 48 Piece 31.00
Cigarette, Players, Army Life, 12 3/8 x 2 5/8 In., 23 Piece 13.00
Cigarette, Players, Drum Banners & Cap Badges, 1 3/8 x 2 5/8 In., 21 Piece 7.00
Cigarette, Players, International Air Lines, 1 3/8 x 2 5/8 In., 34 Piece 21.00
Cigarette, Players, Uniforms Of British Empire Overseas, 1 3/8 In., 50 Piece 38.00
Cigarette, W.D. & H.O. Wills, Aviation, 1 3/8 x 2 5/8 In., 50 Piece 39.00
Cigarette, W.D. & H.O. Wills, Military Motors, 1 3/8 x 2 5/8 In., 16 Piece 7.00
Flags Of World, Gum, 30 Piece 40.00
Football, Bowman, 1955, Set Of 160 .... 300.00
Football, Card, O.J. Simpson, Rookie 180.00
Football, Fran Tarkenton, Topps No. 90, 1962 .... 150.00
Golf, Donruss, 1981, 166 Cards 65.00
Golf, Goudey Sport King, Bobby Jones, 1933 .... 1375.00
Greeting, Valentine, Pinocchio, Die Cut, Mechanical, 1939 .... 40.00
Greeting, Valentine, Snow White, Die Cut, Mechanical, 1938 .... 40.00
Hockey, Alex Peter Delvecchio, Parkhurst, No. 63, 1951-52 .... 85.00
M*A*S*H, 1982, Gum, Set 27.00
McHale's Navy, 1966, Gum, Set 70.00
Mork And Mindy, Gum, 1978, 99 Piece 27.00
Playing, Bicycle, Rider Back, Russell & Morgan Co., 1890 .... 468.00
Playing, Burlington Vista Dome Zephyr 25.00
Playing, Chicago, Milwaukee & St.Paul RR, 1910 .... 72.00
Playing, Columbia River, Ore., 1909 .... 187.00
Playing, Delta Airline, In United Box 3.00
Playing, Frisco Railroad, Double Deck 12.00
Playing, Golden Lights Cigarettes, Sealed 7.00
Playing, Harlequin, Tiffany Transformation, 1879 .... 2530.00
Playing, Johnson Outboard Motors, Logo On Cards & Box, 1950s, Double Deck 38.00
Playing, League, Red, 1920 .... 72.00
Playing, Milwaukee Railroad 25.00
Playing, Norman Rockwell, Double Deck 15.00
Playing, Pall Mall 6.00
Playing, Panama Inaugural, 1915 .... 72.00
Playing, Pullman RR, 1915 .... 94.00
Playing, Reddington Electric Service Co., Boston, Double Deck, Box 25.00
Playing, Southern Pacific RR, 1910 .... 33.00
Playing, TWA Airline, Opened 5.00
Playing, TWA, Box, Sealed 5.00
Playing, Union Oyster House, Boston, Double Deck, Box 40.00
Playing, Union Pacific RR, 1910 .... 60.00
Playing, Union Pacific RR, 1950s 15.00
Playing, Washington & Pacific Northwest, 1900 .... 110.00

Playing, Washington, D.C. Views, 1910 .... 72.00
Playing, Winchester, 1929 .... 325.00
Wings, Cigarette, Set 1, 1940s, 50 Piece 100.00
Wings, Cigarettes, World War II Allied Planes, 12 Piece 25.00

CARLSBAD, Germany, is a mark found on china made by several factories in
Germany. Most of the pieces available today were made after 1891.

Chocolate Pot, Portrait, Blue, 10 In. 110.00
Chocolate Set, Demitasse, 13 Piece 187.00
Ewer, Enamel Poppies, Enamel Ground, Figural Handle, 9 1/2 In. 245.00
Plate, Austrian Blue & White Windmill 25.00
Platter, Trout, Polychrome, 1907, 10 x 24 1/2 In. 195.00
Powder Box, Multicolored Flowers Cover, Gold, Black & Red, Footed 65.00

CARLTON WARE was made at the Carlton Works of Stoke-on-Trent,
England, about 1890. The firm traded as Wiltshaw & Robinson until 1957. It
was renamed Carlton Ware Ltd. in 1958.

Bowl & Pitcher Set, Soap Bowl, Chinese Kang Hsi Pattern, 15 1/4 In., 3 Piece 358.00
Cup & Saucer, Yellow Poppy 75.00
Dish, Australian, Iris, Cream Ground 25.00
Pitcher, Yellow & Green, Potter, 4 1/2 In. .... *Illus* 35.00
Sugar Shaker 175.00
Vase, Birds & Flowers, Gold Tracery, 10 In. 245.00
Vase, Gold & Enamel Birds & Flowers, Pearl Interior, Maroon Ground, 7 In. 240.00

CARNIVAL GLASS was an inexpensive, iridescent, pressed glass made from
about 1907 to about 1925. More than 1, 000 different patterns are known.
Carnival glass is currently being reproduced. Additional pieces may be found
in the Northwood category.

Acanthus, Bowl, Green, 8 In. 85.00
Acanthus, Chop Plate, Marigold 140.00
Acorn, Bowl, Blue, 7 1/2 In. 50.00
Acorn Burrs, Pitcher, Amethyst 525.00
Acorn Burrs, Pitcher, Green 800.00
Acorn Burrs, Pitcher, Purple 900.00
Acorn Burrs, Tumbler, Amethyst 60.00
Acorn Burrs, Tumbler, Green .... 85.00 to 100.00
Acorn Burrs & Bark pattern is listed here as Acorn Burrs
Amaryllis pattern is listed here as Tiger Lily
American Beauty Roses pattern is listed here as Wreath of Roses
Apple Blossom Twigs, Banana Boat, Peach 175.00
Apple Tree, Water Set, Marigold, 7 Piece 500.00
Apple Tree, Water Set, White, 5 Piece 1250.00
April Showers, Vase, Blue, 12 In. 65.00
Arcs, Bowl, Ruffled Edge, Marigold, 8 1/2 In. 30.00
Banded Vintage, Mug, Marigold 26.00
Banded Vintage, Water Set, Marigold, 7 Piece 500.00

Carlton Ware, Pitcher, Yellow & Green,
Potter, 4 1/2 In.

Battenburg Lace No. 1 pattern is listed here as Hearts & Flowers
Battenburg Lace No. 3 pattern is listed here as Fanciful
Beaded Cable, Rose Bowl, Aqua 350.00
Beaded Shell, Mug, Amethyst 65.00
Beaded Shell, Sugar, Purple 90.00
Birds & Cherries, Bonbon, Amethyst 85.00
Birds On Bough pattern is listed here as Birds & Cherries
Blackberry & Checkerboard pattern is listed here as Blackberry Block
Blackberry B. pattern is listed here as Blackberry Spray
Blackberry Block, Tumbler, Amethyst 95.00
Blackberry Block, Tumbler, Green 195.00
Blackberry Bramble, Compote, Ruffled Edge, Marigold, 6 1/2 In. 38.00
Blackberry Spray, Bowl, Flared, Ruffled Edge, Marigold, 5 1/2 x 3 1/2 In. 45.00
Blackberry Spray, Marigold, 5 1/2 In. 45.00
Blackberry Wreath, Bowl, Marigold, 7 1/2 In. .... 50.00 to 65.00
Blackberry Wreath, Bowl, Marigold, 8 In. 45.00
Blackberry Wreath, Bowl, Purple, 7 In. .... 65.00 to 125.00
Blackberry Wreath, Bowl, Scalloped, Green, 8 In. 90.00
Blossom Time, Compote, Ruffled Edge, Amethyst 200.00
Blossom Time, Compote, Ruffled Edge, Marigold 425.00
Blueberry, Tumbler, White 175.00
Bouquet, Water Set, Blue, 7 Piece 950.00
Broken Arches, Punch Bowl, Stand, Marigold 300.00
Butterfly, Bonbon, Threaded Back, Purple 275.00
Butterfly & Berry, Bowl, Footed, Blue, 9 1/4 In. 75.00
Butterfly & Berry, Bowl, Marigold, 9 1/4 In. 80.00
Butterfly & Berry, Water Set, Blue, 4 Piece 1100.00
Butterfly & Berry, Water Set, Marigold, 6 Piece 600.00
Butterfly & Fern, Water Set, Amethyst, 5 Piece 825.00
Butterfly & Fern, Water Set, Marigold, 7 Piece .... 700.00 to 750.00
Butterfly & Grape pattern is listed here as Butterfly & Berry
Butterfly & Plume pattern is listed here as Butterfly & Fern
Butterfly & Stippled Rays pattern is listed here as Butterfly
Cabbage Rose & Grape pattern is listed here as Wine & Roses
Cactus Leaf Rays pattern is listed here as Leaf Rays
Cattails & Fish pattern is listed here as Fisherman's Mug
Cattails & Water Lily pattern is listed here as Water Lily & Cattails
Cherries & Mums pattern is listed here as Mikado
Cherry Chain, Plate, Marigold, 6 In. 40.00
Cherry Wreathed pattern is listed here as Wreathed Cherry
Christmas Cactus pattern is listed here as Thistle
Christmas Plate pattern is listed here as Poinsettia
Christmas Rose & Poppy pattern is listed here as Six-Petals
Chrysanthemum, Bowl, Footed, Marigold, 10 In. 120.00
Chrysanthemum Wreath pattern is listed here as Ten Mums
Coin Dot, Bowl, Amethyst, 8 3/4 In. 40.00
Coin Dot, Bowl, Amethyst, Ruffled Edge, 9 1/2 In. 62.00
Coin Dot, Bowl, Ruffled Edge, Blue, 9 1/2 In. 55.00
Coin Spot, Compote, Peach 95.00
Concave Diamonds, Tumbler, Vaseline 165.00
Concord, Bowl, Ruffled Edge, Green, 9 In. 575.00
Constitution pattern is listed here as God & Home
Corinth, Banana Boat, Marigold 35.00
Cosmos & Cane, Butter, Cover, Honey Amber 190.00
Cosmos & Cane, Tumbler, Honey Amber 55.00
Crab Claw, Tumbler, Marigold 70.00
Crab Claw, Water Set, Marigold, 7 Piece .... 950.00 to 1350.00
Crackle, Rose Bowl 30.00
Dahlia, Pitcher, White 1250.00
Dahlia, Tumbler, Marigold 145.00
Daisy & Drape, Vase, Aqua, 6 In. 800.00
Daisy & Plume, Candy Dish, Green 75.00
Daisy & Plume, Compote, Ruffled Edge, Amethyst 40.00

Daisy & Plume, Rose Bowl, Aqua 850.00
Daisy & Plume, Rose Bowl, Marigold 50.00
Daisy Wreath, Bowl, Marigold, 9 In. 110.00
Dandelion, Mug, Aqua 550.00
Dandelion, Mug, Marigold 425.00
Dandelion, Tumbler, Green 175.00
Dandelion Variant pattern is listed here as Panelled Dandelion
Diamond, Pitcher, Water, Marigold 135.00
Diamond & Cable pattern is listed here as Fentonia
Diamond & Daisy, Water Set, Marigold, 7 Piece 750.00
Diamond Lace, Bowl, Purple, 9 In. 95.00
Diamond Point & Daisy pattern is listed here as Cosmos & Cane
Diamond Points, Vase, Amethyst, 10 In. 85.00
Dogwood & Marsh Lily pattern is listed here as Two Flowers
Double Star, Pitcher, Green 350.00
Double Star, Water Set, Green, 7 Piece ....800.00 to 925.00
Dragon & Lotus, Bowl, Flat, Marigold, 9 In. 135.00
Dragon & Lotus, Bowl, Ice Cream Shape, Red 1150.00
Dragon & Lotus, Bowl, Ruffled Edge, Marigold, 8 1/2 In. 65.00
Drape & Tie pattern is listed here as Rosalind
Enameled Crocus, Tumbler, Amethyst 30.00
Estate, Mug, Marigold 70.00
Fan & Arch pattern is listed here as Persian Garden
Fanciful, Plate, Blue, 9 In. 375.00
Fashion, Creamer, Smoke 70.00
Fashion, Punch Cup, Marigold 15.00
Feather & Heart, Tumbler, Green 25.00
Feathered Scroll pattern is listed here as Feathered Serpent
Feathered Serpent, Sauce, Green 20.00
Feathers, Vase, Marigold, 6 1/4 In. 55.00
Featherstitch, Bowl, Ruffled Edge, Marigold 70.00
Fenton's Butterfly pattern is listed here as Butterfly
Fentonia, Water Set, Blue, 3 Piece 675.00
Fentonia, Water Set, Marigold, 3 Piece 550.00
Field Flower, Tumbler, Amethyst 55.00
Field Rose pattern is listed here as Rambler Rose
Field Thistle, Water Set, Marigold, 7 Piece ....525.00 to 990.00
Fine Cut & Roses, Rose Bowl, Amethyst 115.00
Fine Cut & Roses, Rose Bowl, Green 160.00
Fine Rib, Vase, Green, 10 In. 55.00
Fine Rib, Vase, Marigold, 16 In. 45.00
Finecut & Star pattern is listed here as Star & File
Fish Net, Epergne, Amethyst 345.00
Fisherman's Mug, Mug, Souvenir, Amethyst, 1910 .... 145.00
Fisherman's Net pattern is listed here as Tree Bark
Floral & Diamond Point pattern is listed here as Fine Cut & Roses
Floral & Grape, Pitcher, Water, White 425.00
Floral & Grape, Tumbler, White 65.00
Floral & Grape, Water Set, Marigold, 7 Piece 350.00
Floral & Grape Variant, Water Set, Blue, 7 Piece 550.00
Floral & Grapevine pattern is listed here as Floral & Grape
Flowering Almonds pattern is listed here as Peacock Tail
Fluffy Bird pattern is listed here as Peacock
Fluffy Peacock, Water Set, Amethyst, 6 Piece 825.00
Fluffy Peacock, Water Set, Amethyst, 7 Piece 995.00
Flute, Punch Bowl, Base, Marigold 450.00
Four Flowers, Bowl, Ruffled Edge, Amethyst 135.00
Four Flowers, Bowl, Ruffled Edge, Green 85.00
Four-70-Four, Goblet, Marigold 55.00
Four-70-Four, Pitcher, Milk, Marigold 145.00
Fruits & Flowers, Bonbon, Aqua 535.00
Fruits & Flowers, Bonbon, Blue ....150.00 to 250.00
Fruits & Flowers, Bonbon, Marigold 35.00

Fruits & Flowers, Bowl, Purple, 10 In. .... 150.00 to 160.00
Garland, Rose Bowl, Marigold.. 25.00
God & Home, Tumbler, Blue.. 250.00
Good Luck, Bowl, Basketweave Exterior, Marigold, 8 3/4 In. 280.00
Good Luck, Bowl, Ruffled, Electric Blue 350.00
Good Luck, Bowl, Scalloped Edge, Marigold, 9 1/2 In. 145.00
Good Luck, Plate, Green, 9 In. 500.00
Grape & Cable, Banana Boat, Amethyst .... 350.00 to 425.00
Grape & Cable, Banana Boat, Marigold... 175.00
Grape & Cable, Berry Bowl, Amethyst, 6 Piece... 125.00
Grape & Cable, Bonbon, Green.. 50.00
Grape & Cable, Bowl, 3 Spade Feet, Marigold, 7 3/4 In. 50.00
Grape & Cable, Bowl, Ball Foot, Green, 8 In... 75.00
Grape & Cable, Bowl, Green, 9 In. 95.00
Grape & Cable, Bowl, Ruffled Edge, Stippled, Blue, 9 In. 285.00
Grape & Cable, Bowl, Ruffled Edge, Stippled, Ribbed Back, Green, 8 1/2 In. 495.00
Grape & Cable, Butter, Cover, Amethyst.. 375.00
Grape & Cable, Dish, Sweetmeat, Amethyst.. 250.00
Grape & Cable, Humidor, Marigold.. 325.00 to 425.00
Grape & Cable, Humidor, Purple 800.00
Grape & Cable, Plate, Amethyst, 9 In. 195.00
Grape & Cable, Powder Jar, Amethyst 325.00
Grape & Cable, Powder Jar, Marigold 200.00
Grape & Cable, Powder Jar, Purple.. 125.00
Grape & Cable, Punch Bowl, Purple, 10 1/2 In. 110.00
Grape & Cable, Punch Set, Purple, 6 Piece... 1500.00
Grape & Cable, Spooner, Marigold.. 65.00
Grape & Cable, Sweetmeat, Amethyst 265.00
Grape & Cable, Table Set, Amethyst, 4 Piece.. 595.00
Grape & Cable, Tobacco Jar, Green... 250.00
Grape & Cable, Tumbler, Amethyst, 4 In. 42.00
Grape & Cable, Tumbler, Marigold 46.00
Grape & Cable, Water Set, Amethyst, 5 Piece... 350.00 to 425.00
Grape & Cable, Water Set, Amethyst, 7 Piece 495.00
Grape & Gothic Arches, Tumbler, Blue... 45.00 to 50.00
Grape & Gothic Arches, Water Set, Marigold, 7 Piece 525.00
Grape Arbor, Water Set, Blue, 5 Piece 3500.00
Grape Arbor, Water Set, Marigold, 7 Piece.. 600.00
Grape Arbor, Water Set, White, 4 Piece... 750.00
Grape Delight pattern is listed here as Vintage
Greek Key, Water Set, Marigold, 7 Piece 1050.00
Hearts & Flowers, Compote, Aqua .... 550.00 to 575.00
Hearts & Flowers, Compote, Marigold .... 130.00 to 200.00
Heavy Iris, Tumbler, Marigold.. 80.00
Heavy Iris, Water Set, Marigold, 7 Piece.. 800.00
Heron & Rushes pattern is listed here as Stork & Rushes
Hobnail pattern is listed in this book as its own category
Hobstar & Arches, Bowl, Ruffled, Marigold, 9 x 3 In.. 45.00
Hobstar & Feather, Punch Cup, Marigold... 20.00
Hobstar & Torch pattern is listed here as Double Star
Hobstar Flower, Compote, Marigold 55.00
Holly, Bowl, Marigold, 8 In. 55.00
Holly, Bowl, Marigold, 9 In. 75.00
Holly, Compote, Amethyst.. 150.00
Holly, Compote, Vaseline 125.00
Holly, Goblet, Marigold 50.00
Holly, Plate, Blue 350.00
Holly Spray pattern is listed here as Holly Sprig
Holly Sprig, Bonbon, Marigold.. 60.00
Holly Sprig, Bowl, Marigold, 8 In. 75.00
Honeycomb & Clover, Bonbon, Amethyst 40.00
Horse Medallions pattern is listed here as Horses' Heads
Horses' Heads, Bowl, Footed, Blue... 150.00

Horses' Heads, Plate, Marigold, 9 1/2 In. 195.00
Horses' Heads, Rose Bowl, Marigold 150.00
Imperial Grape, Decanter, Stopper, Marigold 60.00
Imperial Grape, Pitcher, Water, Marigold 40.00
Imperial Grape, Plate, Amethyst, 6 1/2 In. 200.00
Imperial Grape, Tumbler, Amethyst 45.00
Imperial Grape, Tumbler, Marigold 15.00
Imperial Grape, Wine, Purple 38.00
Intaglio pattern is listed here as Hobstar & Feather
Interior Of Cherries & Mums pattern is listed here as Mikado
Inverted Strawberry, Bowl, Amethyst, 10 In. 245.00
Inverted Strawberry, Tumbler, Amethyst 225.00
Irish Lace pattern is listed here as Louisa
Kimberly pattern is listed here as Concave Diamonds
Kittens, Toothpick, Marigold ....170.00 to 175.00
Lattice & Grape, Tankard, Marigold, 11 3/4 In. 260.00
Lattice & Grape, Tumbler, Blue 35.00
Lattice & Grape, Tumbler, White 200.00
Lattice & Grape, Water Pitcher, Blue 300.00
Lattice & Grape, Water Set, Blue, 7 Piece 750.00
Lattice & Grape, Water Set, Marigold, 7 Piece 600.00
Lattice & Grapevine pattern is listed here as Lattice & Grape
Leaf & Beads, Candy Dish, Footed, Marigold, 8 1/4 In. 72.00
Leaf & Beads, Candy Dish, Marigold 75.00
Leaf & Beads, Rose Bowl, Amethyst 125.00
Leaf & Beads, Rose Bowl, Marigold 125.00
Leaf Chain, Plate, White, 9 /14 In. 145.00
Leaf Medallion pattern is listed here as Leaf Chain
Leaf Pinwheel & Star Flower pattern is listed here as Whirling Leaves
Leaf Rays, Nappy, Marigold ....20.00 to 72.00
Lion, Bowl, Ruffled, Marigold, 7 In. 90.00
Little Barrel, Tumbler, Green 200.00
Little Flowers, Bowl, 9 1/4 In. 135.00
Loop & Column pattern is listed here as Pulled Loop
Looped Petals pattern is listed here as Scales
Lotus & Grape, Bonbon, 2 Handles, Green 50.00
Lotus & Grape, Bonbon, Marigold 40.00
Louisa, Rose Bowl, Footed, Amethyst 50.00
Lustre Rose, Bowl, Marigold, 5 1/2 In. 40.00
Lustre Rose, Bowl, Marigold, 11 In. 35.00
Magnolia & Poinsettia pattern is listed here as Water Lily
Maple Leaf, Water Set, Amethyst, 7 Piece ....500.00 to 750.00
Maryland pattern is listed here as Rustic
Melinda pattern is listed here as Wishbone
Mikado, Compote, Clear Foot, Marigold, 9 5/8 In. 450.00
Morning Glory, Vase, Funeral, Marigold 160.00
Morning Glory, Vase, Funeral, Purple 275.00
Morning Glory, Vase, Marigold, 7 In. 30.00
Oak Leaf & Acorn pattern is listed here as Acorn
Octagon, Decanter, Stopper, Marigold 60.00
Octagon, Goblet, Marigold 55.00
Open Edge, Basket, Red 395.00
Open Rose, Berry Set, Purple, 7 Piece 325.00
Orange Tree, Bowl, Footed, White, 10 In. 200.00
Orange Tree, Bowl, Ruffled Edge, Blue 90.00
Orange Tree, Jelly Compote, Marigold, 4 1/2 x 3 In. 40.00
Orange Tree, Loving Cup, Blue 300.00
Orange Tree, Mug, Blue 60.00
Orange Tree, Plate, Marigold, 10 In 175.00
Orange Tree, Powder Jar, Blue 145.00
Orange Tree, Powder Jar, Marigold ....75.00 to 95.00
Orange Tree, Shaving Mug, Marigold 60.00
Orange Tree Varient, Water Set, Marigold, 6 Piece 1200.00

Orange Tree Varient, Water Set, Marigold, 7 Piece .... 800.00 to 1200.00
Oriental Poppy, Tankard, Marigold 595.00
Oriental Poppy, Tumbler, Amethyst 70.00
Oriental Poppy, Tumbler, Green 275.00
Oriental Poppy, Tumbler, White 160.00
Oriental Poppy, Water Set, Amethyst, 7 Piece 1500.00
Oriental Poppy, Water Set, Marigold, 7 Piece .... 850.00 to 975.00
Palm Beach, Tumbler, Silver Rim, White 250.00
Panelled Dandelion, Pitcher, Marigold 395.00
Panelled Dandelion, Water Set, Blue, 7 Piece 1200.00
Panelled Dandelion, Water Set, Green, 7 Piece 975.00
Pansy, Relish, Green 50.00
Parlor Panels, Vase, Marigold, 12 In. 100.00
Peacock, Bowl, Ruffled Edge, Aqua, 8 1/2 In. 450.00
Peacock, Bowl, Ruffled Edge, Marigold, 8 1/2 In. 225.00
Peacock, Plate, Ice Green, 9 In. 450.00
Peacock & Urn, Bowl, Marigold 45.00
Peacock & Urn, Compote, Marigold 45.00
Peacock & Urn, Sauce, Purple 125.00
Peacock At The Fountain, Butter, Cover, Purple 250.00
Peacock At The Fountain, Orange Bowl, Purple 450.00
Peacock At The Fountain, Pitcher, Marigold 250.00
Peacock At The Fountain, Tumbler, Amethyst 35.00
Peacock At The Fountain, Tumbler, Green 325.00
Peacock At The Fountain, Water Set, Blue, 7 Piece 1400.00
Peacock At The Fountain, Water Set, Marigold, 7 Piece 675.00
Peacock At The Fountain, Water Set, White, 7 Piece 2400.00
Peacock Eye & Grape pattern is listed here as Vineyard
Peacock On Fence pattern is listed here as Peacocks
Peacock Tail, Bowl, Ruffled Edge, Marigold, 6 In. 30.00
Peacock Tail, Compote, Amethyst 20.00
Peacocks, Bowl, Marigold, Ruffled, 8 1/2 In. 225.00
Peacocks, Marigold, 9 In. 375.00
Persian Garden, Dish, Ice Cream, White, 6 In. 60.00
Persian Garden, Dish, Ice Cream, White, 11 In. 145.00
Persian Garden, Dish, Ice Cream, White, 12 In. 250.00
Persian Garden, Plate, Marigold, 6 In. .... 65.00 to 100.00
Persian Garden, Plate, Pool Of Pearls Back, White 150.00
Persian Medallion, Berry Set, Purple, 7 Piece 400.00
Persian Medallion, Bowl, Blue, 5 In. 55.00
Persian Medallion, Bowl, Marigold, 5 In. 35.00
Persian Medallion, Bowl, Ruffled Edge, Blue, 10 In. 225.00
Pine Cone, Plate, Marigold, 6 1/2 In. 100.00
Pine Cone Wreath pattern is listed here as Pine Cone
Plume Panels, Vase, Marigold, 10 1/4 In. 40.00
Poinsettia, Pitcher, Milk, Marigold .... 85.00 to 185.00
Poinsettia & Lattice pattern is listed here as Poinsettia
Poppy, Dish, Pickle, Oval, Marigold 90.00
Poppy Scroll pattern is listed here as Poppy
Princess Lace pattern is listed here as Octagon
Pulled Loop, Vase, Amethyst, 10 In. 5.00
Pulled Loop, Vase, Marigold, 10 1/2 In. 30.00
Quill, Tumbler, Marigold 350.00
Raindrops, Bowl, Footed, Peach, 9 In. 100.00
Rambler Rose, Water Set, Marigold, 7 Piece 450.00
Raspberry, Pitcher, Green 450.00
Raspberry, Tumbler, Aqua 295.00
Raspberry, Water Set, Amethyst, 7 Piece .... 525.00 to 700.00
Raspberry, Water Set, Green, 6 Piece 650.00
Raspberry, Water Set, Green, 7 Piece 750.00
Ripple, Vase, Green, 8 1/4 In. 75.00
Ripple, Vase, Marigold, 8 In. 22.00
Ripple, Vase, Purple, 12 1/2 In. 95.00

Robin, Water Set, Marigold, 7 Piece ....600.00 to 650.00
Robin Red Breast pattern is listed here as Robin
Rosalind, Bowl, Green, 10 In.. 275.00
Rose & Ruffles pattern is listed here as Open Rose
Rose Show, Bowl, White 415.00
Rustic, Vase, Amethyst, 11 In. 40.00
Rustic, Vase, Ruffled Edge, Marigold, 15 In... 55.00
Rustic, Vase, White, 10 In. 90.00
Rustic, Vase, White, 11 In. 80.00
S-Repeat, Punch Cup, Amethyst...85.00 to 110.00
Sailboat & Windmill pattern is listed here as Sailboats
Sailboats, Goblet, Marigold 95.00
Sailboats, Sauce, Ruffled Edge, Marigold.. 45.00
Sailboats, Wine, Marigold... 35.00
Scales, Bowl, Marigold, 6 In. 20.00
Scales, Plate, Amethyst, 6 In. 25.00
Scroll-Cable pattern is listed here as Estate
Shell & Wild Rose pattern is listed here as Wild Rose
Singing Birds, Mug, Cobalt Blue...160.00 to 275.00
Singing Birds, Mug, Marigold.. 150.00
Singing Birds, Pitcher, Green 450.00
Singing Birds, Pitcher, Purple 850.00
Singing Birds, Tumbler, Green.. 70.00
Six-Petals, Bowl, Amethyst, 7 In... 60.00
Six-Petals, Bowl, Tricornered, Peach Opalescent 85.00
Spring Flowers pattern is listed here as Bouquet
Stag & Holly, Bowl, Amethyst, 10 In. 350.00
Stag & Holly, Bowl, Marigold, 8 In. 125.00
Stag & Holly, Bowl, Marigold, 10 3/4 In. 150.00
Stag & Holly, Bowl, Marigold, 12 In. 95.00
Stag & Holly, Bowl, Spade-Footed, Marigold, 7 3/4 In. 125.00
Star & File, Compote, Marigold, 6 3/4 x 6 3/8 In. 45.00
Star Medallion, Chop Plate, Marigold.. 40.00
Star Medallion, Pitcher, Milk, Marigold 25.00
Star Medallion, Punch Cup, Marigold.. 20.00
Star Of David & Bows, Bowl, Footed, Purple, 8 In....................................... 95.00
Star Of David Medallion pattern is listed here as Star of David & Bows
Starflower, Pitcher, Water, Blue 1300.00
Stippled Diamond & Flower pattern is listed here as Little Flowers
Stippled Leaf & Beads pattern is listed here as Leaf & Beads
Stippled Petals, Bowl, Dome-Footed, Amethyst, 9 In. 65.00
Stippled Posy & Pods pattern is listed here as Four Flowers
Stippled Rays, Bowl, Amethyst, 10 In.. 45.00
Stippled Rays, Bowl, Marigold, 5 5/8 In... 40.00
Stippled Rays, Compote, Blue... 325.00
Stippled Rays, Dish, Ice Cream, Red, 6 In. 425.00
Stippled Rays, Plate, Marigold, 7 In. 40.00
Stork & Rushes, Water Set, Blue, 7 Piece 425.00
Stork & Rushes, Water Set, Marigold, 7 Piece.. 425.00
Strawberry pattern is listed here as Wild Strawberry
Strawberry Scroll, Tumbler, Blue 185.00
Stream Of Hearts, Bowl, Green, 9 In... 70.00
Strutting Peacock, Sugar & Creamer, Amethyst 110.00
Sunflower pattern is listed here as Dandelion
Sunflower & Wheat pattern is listed here as Field Flower
Swirl Hobnail, Cuspidor, Marigold 375.00
Teardrops pattern is listed here as Raindrops
Ten Mums, Bowl, Marigold, 10 1/4 In.. 120.00
Thin Rib, Vase, Blue, 15 1/2 In. 20.00
Thistle, Banana Boat, Blue.. 550.00
Thistle, Bowl, Ruffled Edge, Amethyst, 9 In... 125.00
Thistle, Bowl, Three-In-One Edge, Amethyst, 8 In.. 85.00
Thistle, Candy Dish, Green 80.00

Three Fruits, Bowl, Dome-Footed, White, 8 3/4 In. 225.00
Three Fruits, Bowl, Footed, Amethyst 275.00
Three Fruits, Bowl, Green, 9 In. 100.00
Three Fruits, Bowl, Ruffled, Stippled, Green 595.00
Three Fruits, Plate, Amethyst 240.00
Three Fruits, Plate, Basketweave Exterior, Purple 500.00
Three Fruits Medallion, Bowl, Amethyst 175.00
Three Fruits Medallion, Bowl, Footed, Purple 275.00
Tiger Lily, Water Set, Green, 3 Piece 400.00
Tree Bark, Pitcher, Marigold, 8 1/2 In. 45.00
Tree Of Life, Rose Bowl, Marigold 30.00
Tree Trunk, Vase, Purple, 6 1/4 In. 70.00
Twins, Bowl, Pedestal, Marigold 55.00
Two Flowers, Bowl, Blue, 10 In. 140.00
Two Flowers, Bowl, Footed, Marigold, 8 In. 45.00
Two Flowers, Bowl, Marigold, 10 In. 65.00
Vineyard, Pitcher, Water, Marigold 135.00
Vineyard, Water Set, Marigold, 5 Piece 275.00
Vintage, Bowl, Blue, 5 1/2 In. 50.00
Vintage, Bowl, Ruffled Edge, Marigold, 8 In. 50.00
Vintage, Rose Bowl, Amethyst, 6 Footed, 5 In. 75.00
Vintage, Rose Bowl, Blue .... 75.00 to 140.00
Waffle Block, Pitcher, Marigold 80.00
Water Lily, Sauce, Footed, Green, 6 In. 110.00
Water Lily & Cattails, Table Set, Marigold, 4 Piece 395.00
Whirling Leaves, Bowl, Marigold, 10 In. .... 75.00 to 80.00
Wild Rose, Syrup, Marigold 695.00
Wild Strawberry, Bonbon, Handles, Marigold 32.00
Wild Strawberry, Bowl, Cobalt Blue 150.00
Windflower, Bowl, Marigold, 8 1/2 In. 80.00
Windmill, Pitcher, Milk, Marigold 70.00
Windmill Medallion pattern is listed here as Windmill
Wine & Roses, Pitcher, Cider, Marigold 665.00
Wishbone, Bowl, Amethyst, 7 1/2 In. 125.00
Wishbone, Bowl, Ruffled Edge, Footed, Amethyst, 7 1/2 In. 125.00
Wreath Of Roses, Bonbon, Green, 3 3/4 x 5 In. 50.00
Wreath Of Roses, Compote, Footed, Amethyst, 5 1/2 In. 50.00
Wreath Of Roses, Rose Bowl, Marigold 30.00
Wreathed Cherry, Berry Bowl, Purple, Large 150.00
Wreathed Cherry, Bowl, Oval, Purple, 9 x 12 In. 130.00

CAROUSEL or merry-go-round figures were first carved in the United States
in 1867 by Gustav Dentzel. Collectors discovered the charm of the hand-
carved figures in the 1970s, and they were soon classed as folk art. Most
desirable are the figures other than horses, such as pigs, camels, lions, or
dogs. A jumper is a figure that was made to move up and down on a pole; a
stander was placed in a stationary position.

Burro, Wooden 1150.00
Chariot, Wooden, Painted, c.1905, 32 x 41 In. 3737.00
Cow, Child's, Green Blanket, Tan Saddle, Iron Horns, Bayol, c.1905, 4 Ft. 3162.00
Dragon Car, 5 Seats, Head Of Sea Monster, Interior Light, S.G. Spooner 6325.00
Dragon Head, Orton & Spooner, c.1890 .... 7500.00
Horse, 1 Front Hoof Up, Carved Cherub On Side, Indiana, 1950 .... 300.00
Horse, Armored, Parker, Large 9500.00
Horse, Bucking Bronco, Herschell-Spillman, c.1910, 49 1/2 In. 4312.00
Horse, Charles Carmel 4125.00
Horse, Jumper, Green, Black, Red, Glass Eyes, Charles Dare, 40 x 47 In. 2750.00
Horse, Jumper, Herschell-Spillman, Pole, 1906-1910 .... 5995.00
Horse, Jumper, Illions, c.1910, 52 In. 6050.00
Horse, Jumper, White, Black Mane, Charles Carmel, c.1910, 58 x 54 In. 4125.00
Horse, Laminated Carved Wood, Glass Eyes, Dentzel, 50 In. 6050.00
Horse, Out-Side Stander, Hand Carved, Carmel, Early 1900s 7500.00
Horse, Parker, Armored 9500.00

Horse, Prancer, Herschell-Spillman 8500.00
Lion, Wooden, Spiral Base Handle, 1900 .... 2500.00
Ostrich, Carved Plumage, Wooden Base, c.1900, 66 In. 4887.00
Ox, Laminated Carved Wood, Finials On Base & Pole, 37 1/4 In. 467.00
Panel, Swan, Philadelphia Toboggan Co., Painted Pine, c.1900, 30 In. 1725.00
Woman, Tulip Headdress, Standing, No Arm, Philadelphia Toboggan Co., 42 In. 4600.00

CARRIAGE means several things, so this category lists baby carriages, buggies for adults, horse-drawn sleighs, and even strollers. Doll-sized carriages
are listed in the Toy category.

Baby Buggy, American Gothic, Leather, Iron & Wood, Fringed Canopy, 50 In. 357.00
Baby Buggy, Attached Parasol, Wicker 325.00
Baby Buggy, Bathtub Style, Silk Hood, Built-In Diaper Bag, Marklin, 9 In. 4000.00
Baby Buggy, Brown Wicker, Lace Parasol, Metal Springs & Wheels, 36 In. 1075.00
Baby Buggy, Double Facing Seats, Woven Reed, Silk On Seats, 56 In. 850.00
Baby Buggy, Hand Woven Reed 1550.00
Baby Buggy, The Tourist, Model T Top 5000.00
Baby Buggy, Victorian, Movable Cover, Fringe, Four Wheels, 28 x 28 In. 345.00
Baby Buggy, Wicker, Movable Hood, 1910 .... 330.00
Baby Buggy, Wooden, Leather Folding Top, Four Wheels, 24 x 24 In. 115.00
Buggy, 1-Horse, Black Painted Wooden Body, Red Trim, c.1890 .... 575.00
Buggy, Bamboo 675.00
Buggy, Pony, Wicker Seat 1000.00
Buggy Seat, Child's, Iron, Folding, 1895 .... 45.00
Cart, Victorian, Running Hide-Covered Horse, c.1880 .... 3695.00
Push Cart, Wooden Horse Rocks When Pushed, Wicker Seat, 65 In. 2850.00
Sleigh, Albany Cutter, Swan, Red & Black Trim, Velvet Upholstery, c.1901 .... 3950.00
Sleigh, Child's, Dutch Countryside Scenes, Fretwork-Type Trim, Late 18th Century 5500.00
Sleigh, Child's, Push Type, Ivory, Gold Striping, Velvet Seat, Paris Mfg. Co., 1900 ..... 1200.00
Sleigh, Child's, Wooden Runners, Primitive 165.00
Sleigh, Doll's Wooden Runners, Curved Handles, Red Upholstery, Wooden, 36 In. 1045.00
Sleigh, Doll's, Gilt Painted Medallions, Leather Seat, Metal Frame, Wooden, 23 In. 2100.00
Sleigh, Doll's, Green, Gold & Red Design, Stencil, Long Tongue Handle 605.00
Sleigh, Merritt, Painted, 1850 .... 1300.00
Sleigh, Open, 1-Horse Type, Brass Trim, 1880s 2300.00
Sleigh, Push, Victorian, 52 In. 450.00
Stroller, Wicker, Wooden, Metal Back Wheels, Upholstered Seat, 27 In. 200.00
Stroller, Wicker, Wooden, Ornate, Velvet Upholstery, 29 In. 440.00
Sulky, Pedal, Pulled By 2 Black Horses, Painted Wood & Metal, 46 In. 495.00
Wagon, Cretor's Popcorn, Red, White Wheels, 1906 .... 6500.00
Wagon, Model, Aurora Wagon Co., 1892 Chicago Expo., 23 In. 6600.00
Wagon Seat, Splint, Old Red, Colonial 1000.00

CASH REGISTERS were invented in 1884 because an eye on the cash was a
necessity in stores of the nineteenth century, too. John and James Ritty
invented a large model that resembled a clock and kept a record of the dollars
and cents exchanged in the store. John Patterson improved the cash register
with a paper roll to record the money. By the early 1900s, elaborate brass registers were made. About World War I, the fancy case was exchanged for the
more modern types.

Imperial, Chrome Plated, 18 1/2 x 18 1/2 In. 110.00
National, 1 Drawer, 27 Keys, c.1914 .... 750.00
National, 1 Drawer, Tape Dispenser, Brass & Wood, 30 x 28 In. 440.00
National, 1 Drawer, Tape Reel, Name Plate, Brass, c.1915 .... 7500.00
National, Model 7, Original Top Sign 550.00
National, Model 35, Nickel Plated, c.1891 .... 1600.00
National, Model 47, Amount Purchased Sign, Marble & Glass, c.1896 .... 800.00
National, Model 211 .... 800.00
National, Model 226, Bilingual Top Sign 700.00
National, Model 250 .... 600.00
National, Model 311 .... 650.00
National, Model 313 .... 425.00
National, Model 316, 15 Key, Marble Shelf 500.00

National, Model 317, Candy Store, Tape Dispenser, 21 x 17 1/4 In.	605.00
National, Model 347	225.00
National, Model 442XX, Brass	600.00
National, Model IVIVI, Nickel Plated Brass, Tape Dispenser, 20 1/2 In.	165.00
Peck, No. 5, Syracuse, Wooden	300.00
Sun Mfg., Oak, Nickel Plated Fittings, Brass Plate Top, 17 x 10 1/2 x 19 In.	308.00
Union, 4 Rows Of Levers, Up To $99.99, Money Drawer, Oak Case, 17 In.	460.00
Verdic-Corbin, Barber Shop, Embossed Cast Iron, Sales To 1 Dollar, 21 In.	825.00

CASTOR JARS for pickles are glass jars about six inches in height, held in special metal holders. They became a popular dinner table accessory about 1890. Each jar had a top that was usually silver or silver plate. The frame, also of a silver metal, had a handle that arched above the jar and a hook that held a pair of tongs. By 1900, the pickle castor was out of fashion. Many examples found today have reproduced glass jars in old holders. Additional pickle castors may be found in the various Glass categories.

Pickle, Blue Opalescent Swirled Windows, Silver Frame & Tongs	345.00
Pickle, Cow, Ferns, Flowers, Beaded Edge	58.00
Pickle, Cranberry, Bubbled, Florence Plate Co.	375.00
Pickle, Cupid & Venus	195.00 to 245.00
Pickle, Cut Glass, Amber, Small	310.00
Pickle, Cut Glass, Small	110.00
Pickle, Daisy & Button, Vaseline Insert	125.00
Pickle, Daisy & Fern, Blue Opalescent	460.00
Pickle, Diamond Point Insert, Forbes Silver Plated Frame, Tongs	210.00
Pickle, Inverted Thumbprint, Enamel Florals, Cranberry	345.00
Pickle, Inverted Thumbprint, Gold Enamel, Barbour Frame, Cranberry	495.00
Pickle, Inverted Thumbprint, Gold Silver Plate, Loop Frame	305.00
Pickle, Inverted Thumbprint, Silver Plated Cover, Cranberry, 4 1/2 In.	155.00
Pickle, Mechanical, Meriden Frame, Hand Painted Cranberry Bottle	535.00
Pickle, Pink Opalescent Stripes, Enamel Florals, Tongs, Silver Frame, Small	345.00
Pickle, Reverse Thumbprint, Plated Cover & Handle, Sterling Fork	360.00
Pickle, Rubina Verde, Hobnail Insert, Frame & Tongs, Breakfast Size	265.00
Pickle, Sapphire Blue Inverted Thumbprint Jar, Silver Frame, 11 3/4 In.	475.00
Pickle, Sapphire Blue, Inverted Thumbprint, Enameled Floral, Tongs	335.00
Pickle, Silver-Sterling, Samuel Wood, 1735, 8 In.	1350.00
Pickle, Standing & Lying Deer, Frosted Bottom, Clear Top	75.00
Pickle, Thumbprint, Cranberry	195.00

CASTOR SETS holding just salt and pepper castors were used in the seventeenth century. The sugar castor, mustard pot, spice dredger, bottles for vinegar and oil, and other spice holders became popular by the eighteenth century. These sets were usually made of sterling silver. The American Victorian castor set, the type most collected today, was made of silver plated Britannia metal. Colored glass bottles were introduced after the Civil War. The sets were out of fashion by World War I. Be careful when buying sets with colored bottles; many are reproductions. Other castor sets may be listed in various porcelain and glass categories in this book.

3 Bottle, Pewter Frame, Doll's	110.00
3-Bottle, Daisy & Button, Blue, Amber & Clear Bottles, Clear Crystal Frame	120.00
3-Bottle, Daisy & Button, Pressed Glass	125.00
3-Bottle, Silver Plated, Etched Bohemian Glass, Victorian, 19 In.	920.00
6-Bottle, Cut Glass, Diamond Point, Silver Frame, Gorham, c.1880, 11 1/2 In.	2420.00
6-Bottle, Ornate, Silver Frame, With Lily Toothpick In Handle	250.00

CAUGHLEY porcelain was made in England from 1772 to 1814. See the Salopian category for related items.

Eyebath, Lozenge Shape Bowl, Baluster Form Stem, 1785, 2 1/8 In.	1725.00
Jug, Cabbage Leaf, Pagoda On Reverse, Triple C-Scroll Handle, 1783, 8 5/8 In.	2760.00

CELADON is the name of a velvet-textured green-gray glaze used by Chinese, Japanese, Korean, and other factories.

Bowl, 2 Rows Of Incised Petals, Song Style, 7 In. 57.00
Bowl, Floral, China, 10 1/2 In. 138.00
Bowl, Horizontal Potting Ridges, Crackled Glaze, Song Dynasty, 7 In. 632.00
Jardiniere, Green, Flowers, Deer, Owls, Birds, 12 In., Pair.................................... 550.00
Teapot, Pink Blossoms, 4 In. 45.00
Vase, Polychrome Flowers, Birds & Butterflies, 12 In., Pair 660.00

CELLULOID is a trademark for a plastic developed in 1868 by John W. Hyatt. Celluloid Manufacturing Company, the Celluloid Novelty Company, Celluloid Fancy Goods Company, and American Xylonite Company all used Celluloid to make jewelry, games, sewing equipment, false teeth, and piano keys. Eventually, the Hyatt Company became the American Celluloid and Chemical Manufacturing Company, the Celanese Corporation. The name *Celluloid* was often used to identify any similar plastic. Celluloid toys are listed under Toys.

Box, Collar & Cuff, Bicycle Scene Top, 9 x 5 In. 495.00
Box, Cows On Lid, 6 x 4 1/2 In. 295.00
Brush, Baby's, 3 Cat's Faces 32.00
Comb, Leaf Design, Dated 1916 .... 40.00
Figure, Skippy, Jointed, 5 1/2 In. 165.00
Key Chain, Cowboy, Original Tag, 1930s... 48.00
Lion, Roly Poly, 3 1/2 In. 45.00
Pin, Scotty, Wearing Beret, Czechoslovakia 35.00
Reindeer, White, Pink Lips & Ears, 6 x 5 In. 16.00
Strainer, Child's 35.00

CERAMIC ARTS STUDIO was founded in Madison, Wisconsin, by Lawrence Rabbett and Ruben Sand. Their most popular products were expensive molded figurines. The pottery closed in 1955. Do not confuse these products with those of the Ceramic Art Co. of Trenton, New Jersey.

Candleholder, Speak No Evil 58.00
Figurine, Accordion Boy 60.00
Figurine, Archibald The Dragon ....45.00 to 145.00
Figurine, Boy, With Pig 35.00
Figurine, Cat, Bright Eyes 20.00
Figurine, Cat, Green Bowl, 3 In. 15.00
Figurine, Cat, Siamese 35.00
Figurine, Cat, Standing 38.00
Figurine, Chinese Girl, White Jacket, Black Pants, Pigtails 45.00
Figurine, Dog, Scotty 35.00
Figurine, Drum Girl 60.00
Figurine, Dutch Girl...32.00 to 33.00
Figurine, Katrinka, Dutch Dancing Girl, 7 In. 45.00
Figurine, Lamb ....10.00 to 18.00
Figurine, Little Bo Peep... 35.00
Figurine, Manchu & Lotus, Pair 110.00
Figurine, Mexican Children 60.00
Figurine, Mo-Pi & Smi-Li, 6 In., Pair.. 35.00
Figurine, Mo-Pi, 6 In. 18.00
Figurine, Mouse & Cheese... 25.00
Figurine, Mr. Skunk... 25.00
Figurine, Petruska 30.00
Figurine, Rhumba Dancer, Woman, Blue, 7 In. 70.00
Figurine, Saxophone Boy 60.00
Figurine, Skunk, Daddy 20.00
Figurine, Summer Belle 20.00
Figurine, Ting-A-Ling & Sung-Tu, Chartreuse, Green, Black, Red, 6 In., Pair 25.00
Figurine, Turtle, With Cane 32.00
Figurine, Winter Belle 40.00
Head Vase, Lotus & Fu Manchu, Pair 145.00
Humidor, Acorns, Brown Ground, Belleek 285.00
Mug, Gooseberries, Signed M.B.L., Purple Palette Mark, 5 3/4 In. 125.00

Planter, Oriental Girl 18.00
Plaque, Harlequin & Jester, 8 In., Pair.. 150.00
Plaque, Wall, Zor & Zorinda, Pair 90.00
Salt & Pepper, Bear & Cub.. 45.00
Salt & Pepper, Bears, White... 47.00
Salt & Pepper, Black Boy On Elephant 145.00
Salt & Pepper, Cat, Siamese, Sitting 62.00
Salt & Pepper, Cats, Siamese, Mother & Baby 55.00
Salt & Pepper, Cow & Calf, Nesting 95.00
Salt & Pepper, Elephant ....45.00 to 49.00
Salt & Pepper, Elephant & Native... 85.00
Salt & Pepper, Farmer Boy & Girl, Bench, Pole 95.00
Salt & Pepper, Frisky Lamb 20.00
Salt & Pepper, Hillbillies, Lying Down, Knee Up, 5 In. 25.00
Salt & Pepper, Kangaroo, Gray, Nesters 75.00
Salt & Pepper, Leopard 75.00
Salt & Pepper, Lucinda & Colonel Jackson.. 90.00
Salt & Pepper, Mama Bear, Baby Bear, Brown 45.00
Salt & Pepper, Monkeys.. 25.00
Salt & Pepper, Monkeys, Nesting... 60.00
Salt & Pepper, Mouse & Cheese 25.00
Salt & Pepper, Mr. Skunk.. 30.00
Salt & Pepper, Parakeets, Pudgie & Budgie, Metal Birdcage 95.00
Salt & Pepper, Penguin... 30.00
Salt & Pepper, Skunks, Inky & Dinky.. 25.00
Salt & Pepper, Snuffle, White.. 50.00
Salt & Pepper, Thai & Thai Thai.. 95.00
Saltshaker, Dog, Scotty, Black 29.00
Saltshaker, Elephant 50.00
Shelf Sitter, Baby Camel... 89.00
Shelf Sitter, Ballerina.. 35.00
Shelf Sitter, Cat 35.00
Shelf Sitter, Cat, Pair 96.00
Shelf Sitter, Cat, Persian 35.00
Shelf Sitter, Cat, White 30.00
Shelf Sitter, Dog, Collie.. 50.00
Shelf Sitter, Lady Bell 40.00
Shelf Sitter, Maurice & Michele, Pair...90.00 to 125.00
Stein, 3 Boy Scene, Playing Football, Artist, 5 1/2 In. 325.00
Vase, Red & Yellow Roses, Handle, Green Palette Mark, 17 In. 450.00

CHALKWARE is really plaster of Paris decorated with watercolors. One type
was molded from Staffordshire and other porcelain models and painted and
sold as inexpensive decorations in the nineteenth century. Figures of plaster,
made from about 1910 to 1940 for use as prizes at carnivals, are also known
as chalkware. Kewpie dolls made of chalkware will be found in their own
category.

Bank, Dog, Collie, 10 1/2 In... 40.00
Bust, Abraham Lincoln 65.00
Figurine, Bluebird 48.00
Figurine, Boy, Dog Under Each Arm, c.1890.. 300.00
Figurine, Camel, Carrying Paul Jones Whiskey, Back Bar 100.00
Figurine, Cat, 19th Century, 6 1/4 In. 198.00
Figurine, Cat, Painted Yellow, 19th Century, 10 In.............................*Illus* 1265.00
Figurine, Cat, Seated, Paint Decorated, 19th Century, 9 3/4 In. 431.00
Figurine, Cat, Seated, Painted & Smoke Design, 15 In. 4312.00
Figurine, Cat, Sitting, Gray & Beige, Black Eyes, 7 1/2 In. 45.00
Figurine, Cat, White, Seated, Black, Red & Yellow Paint, 6 5/8 In. 1155.00
Figurine, Dog, Pekinese, 6 x 10 In. 45.00
Figurine, Dog, Spaniel, King Charles, 7 3/4 In.. 245.00
Figurine, Dog, Spaniel, Painted, Pennsylvania, 19th Century, 10 3/8 In. ....*Illus* 115.00
Figurine, Dog, Spaniel, Staffordshire Type, 10 In... 150.00
Figurine, Drum Majorette, 13 In. 60.00

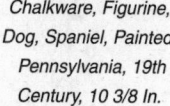

Chalkware, Figurine,
Dog, Spaniel, Painted,
Pennsylvania, 19th
Century, 10 3/8 In.

Chalkware, Figurine,
Cat, Painted Yellow,
19th Century, 10 In.

◆ ◆ ◆ ◆ ◆ ◆ ◆ ◆ ◆ ◆ ◆ ◆ ◆ ◆ ◆ ◆ ◆ ◆

Look in your hardware store
for the new glues that can
fix almost anything. Buy the
proper one to fix transparent
glass, porous pottery, or non-
porous metals. There will be
one that will work.

◆ ◆ ◆ ◆ ◆ ◆ ◆ ◆ ◆ ◆ ◆ ◆ ◆ ◆ ◆ ◆ ◆ ◆

Figurine, Girl, Puppy Tucked In Muff, c.1890	300.00
Figurine, Girl, With Wolfhound, 10 1/2 In.	45.00
Figurine, Kissing Doves	585.00
Figurine, Nude Girl, 8 In.	30.00
Figurine, Ox, Wooden Horns & Ears, Red & White, 19 In.	50.00
Figurine, Parrot, Pair	4200.00
Figurine, Seal	48.00
Figurine, Squirrel, White With Yellow, Black & Red, 5 1/4 In.	55.00
Garniture, Fruit, 19th Century, 14 In., Pair	1745.00
Salt & Pepper, Skull	12.00
Statue, Red Goose Shoes, 11 In.	125.00
String Holder, Cat Holding Ball Of Red Yarn	45.00
Urn, Fruit Filled, Polychromed, Pennsylvania	800.00

CHARLIE CHAPLIN, the famous comic and actor, lived from 1889 to 1977. He
made his first movie in 1913. He did the movie *The Tramp* in 1915. The character of the Tramp has remained famous, and in the 1980s appeared in a series of
television commercials for computers. Dolls, candy containers, and all sorts of
memorabilia picture Charlie Chaplin. Pieces are being made even today.

Ashtray	50.00
Book, Little Tramp Cover, S. Gabriel, 1916, 6 1/2 x 11 In.	80.00
Candy Container	188.00
Chocolate Mold, Tin, 7 1/2 In.	105.00
Cigarette Box, Tramps Regular, 1972	15.00
Doll, Bisque, 18 In.	65.00
Doll, Carved Head, Hands & Feet, Stuffed Cloth Body, 11 In.	287.00
Doll, Composition, Painted Eyes, Mustache & Hair, Original Clothing, 15 In.	400.00
Figurine, Chalk, 2 In.	48.00
Figurine, Papier-Mache, Metal Cane, Germany, 4 1/2 In.	145.00
Photograph, Autograph, Matte, Frame, 11 x 9 In.	978.00
Sheet Music, Charlie Chaplin Walk, 1915	70.00
Slate Dancer, Crank Mechanism, Germany, 1920s	1600.00
Snow Globe, 5 In., Box	9.00
Stickpin, Gold Finish, Die Cut Figure Of Charlie, 1930s	60.00
Wristwatch, Bradley, Box	65.00

CHARLIE MCCARTHY was the ventriloquist's dummy used by Edgar Bergen
from the 1930s. He was famous for his work in radio, movies, and television.
The act was retired in the 1970s.

Car, Buggy, Charlie & Edgar Bergen On Back, 8 In.	275.00
Doll, Composition, All Original, Pin, Effanbee, 16 1/2 In.	650.00

Doll, Composition, String-Pull Mouth 325.00
Doll, Ventriloquist, Composition, Box, 31 In... 400.00
Game, Radio, Chase & Sanborn Mailer, 1938 .... 55.00
Pencil, Sharpener, Bakelite 45.00
Puppet, Cardboard, 1950s 65.00
Puppet, Hand, Cloth Body, Composition Head, 1940s.. 125.00
Puppet, Hand, Composition 135.00
Radio, Majestic, 1930s 1250.00
Radio Party, Mailing Package, c.1938 .... 150.00
Salt & Pepper, Porcelain... 85.00
Soap, 5 In... 48.00
Spoon, Detective Hat.. 24.00
Toy, Charlie McCarthy, Windup, Marx... 350.00
Toy, Crazy Car, Marx, c.1939 .... 700.00

CHELSEA GRAPE pattern was made before 1840. A small bunch of grapes in a raised design, colored with purple or blue luster, is on the border of the white plate. Most of the pieces are unmarked. The pattern is sometimes called *Aynsley* or *Grandmother*. Chelsea Sprig is similar but has a sprig of flowers instead of the bunch of grapes. Chelsea Thistle has a raised thistle pattern. Do not confuse these Chelsea patterns with Chelsea Keramic Art Works, which can be found in the Dedham category, or with Chelsea porcelain, the next category.

Teapot, Paneled, Floral Design, Copper Luster Grape Finial, 8 3/4 In. 825.00
Tureen, Soup, Octagonal, Ladle, Ironstone, Marked 200.00
CHELSEA SPRIG, Cup & Saucer, Purple Luster Flowers, White .... *Illus* 18.00
Tea & Coffee Set, Sprigware, Incomplete, 54 Piece 110.00

CHELSEA PORCELAIN was made in the Chelsea area of London from about 1745 to 1784. Some pieces made from 1770 to 1784 may include the letter *D* for *Derby* in the mark. Ceramic designs were borrowed from the Meissen models of the day. Pieces were made of soft paste. The gold anchor was used as the mark but it has been copied by many other factories. Recent copies of Chelsea have been made from the original molds. Do not confuse Chelsea porcelain with Chelsea Grape, the preceding category.

Beaker, Famille Rose, Raised Anchor Mark, c.1750, 2 3/4 In., Pair 4600.00
Beaker, Kakiemon, Ho Ho Bird On Rock, c.1747, 2 3/4 In. 1265.00
Beaker, Molded Scolopendrium, Floral Sprigs, Insects, c.1752, 2 7/8 In....................... 1600.00
Beaker, Tea Plant, Lobed Body, Spiraling Branches, c.1745, 2 7/8 In. 1725.00
Bonbonniere, Enamel Cover, White Ruffled Cap, c.1755, 2 5/8 In. 3738.00
Bottle, Bouquet Of Summer Flowers On Front, 5 Sides, c.1755, 7 1/4 In....................... 6325.00
Bust, William Augustus, Duke Of Cumberland, Pedestal, c.1750, 5 3/8 In..................... 6900.00
Cream Boat, Acanthus Leaf, White, c.1745, 3 13/16 In... 1725.00
Cup & Saucer, Multicolored Birds, c.1765 .... 825.00
Dish, 2 Overlapping Leaves, Double Leaf, Signed, 1750, 8 3/16 In. 460.00
Dish, Decagon, Imari, Insects, Bird In Flight, c.1755, 6 5/8 In....................................... 2415.00
Dish, Sunflower, Red Anchor Mark, c.1755, 9 In... 6400.00

Chelsea Sprig, Cup & Saucer,
Purple Luster Flowers, White

◆ ◆

Do not use gold- or silver-decorated glasses if the trim has turned chalky gray. This is a source of lead poisoning.

◆ ◆

Etui, Bust Of Lady Cover, c.1760, 5 5/16 In. 2875.00
Figurine, Cupid, In Disguise, c.1758, 4 3/16 In. 345.00
Figurine, Lady, White Greyhound, 19th-Century Hunting Costume, 7 1/2 In. 475.00
Figurine, Man & Woman, Marked, 22 1/2 In.Pair 2450.00
Figurine, Musician, Blackamoor, Red & Turquoise Hat, c.1760, 5 1/2 In. 925.00
Figurine, Woman, 18th Century, 10 1/2 In. 1300.00
Jug, Goat & Bee, Pear Shape, Signed, 4 1/4 In. 2012.00
Jug, Goat & Bee, White, c.1747, 4 3/8 In. 5500.00
Plate, Botanical, Garlic, Brown Anchor Mark, c.1760, 8 1/2 In. 575.00
Plate, Bouquet & Sprigs Center, Exotic Birds, 1757, 8 5/8 In., 11 Piece 2070.00
Plate, Floral Bouquet Center, Diaperwork, Red Anchor Mark, 13 In., Pair 2013.00
Plate, Floral Bouquet Center, Scattered Sprigs On Rim, c.1755, 9 7/16 In. 2070.00
Plate, Imari Brocade Pattern, c.1756, 9 13/16 In. 690.00
Plate, Kakiemon, Flying Fox Over Squirrel, Cinquefoil, c.1754, 8 7/8 In. 1265.00
Sauceboat, Strawberry Leaf, Berries & Leaves, c.1754, 6 5/16 In. 690.00
Saucer, Butterfly, 2 Moths, Ladybird, Signed, c.1755, 6 7/16 In. 690.00
Saucer, Dog & Fox, c.1752, 5 5/8 In. 6037.00
Teabowl & Saucer, Kakiemon, Seated Oriental Woman, c.1750 .... 1265.00
Teabowl & Saucer, Recumbent Putti, Red Anchor Mark, c.1755. .... 1840.00
Tureen, Cover, Asparagus, c.1755, 7 1/8 In. 6900.00
Tureen, Cover, Cauliflower, c.1755, 4 1/2 In. 4600.00

CHINESE EXPORT porcelain comprises all the many kinds of porcelain made in China for export to America and Europe in the eighteenth, nineteenth, and twentieth centuries. Other pieces may be listed in this book under Canton, Celadon, Nanking, and Rose Medallion.

Basin, Scalloped Shell Shape, Gilt, Imari-Style Colors, 4 1/2 x 15 x 12 In. 3300.00
Basket & Tray, Reticulated, Varied Colors, 11-In. Tray 850.00
Bowl, Barber, Shield, Gelderlant 2820.00
Bowl, Court Scenes, Floral Panel, Famille Rose, 1900, 11 1/2 In. 1100.00
Bowl, Fruit, Green Fitzhugh, 19th Century, 8 7/8 In. 800.00
Bowl, Fruited Branches Around Bamboo, Famille Rose, 4 1/8 In. 575.00
Bowl, Green & Gilt, Central Floral Cartouche, 11 1/2 In. 715.00
Bowl, Hunt, Scene Of Hunters, 18th Century, 5 1/2 In. 1150.00
Bowl, Painted Fruiting Vine & Butterflies, Famille Rose, 4 1/8 In. 316.00
Bowl, Rose Sprays & Butterflies, Rose & Gilt Puce Border Interior, 7 3/4 In. 635.00
Bowl, Salad, Blue Fitzhugh, 19th Century, 10 1/4 In. 575.00
Bowl, Waste, Dragon Pattern, c.1775, 6 1/8 In. 700.00
Bowl, Water Landscapes, Square, 19th Century, 9 1/2 In. 1035.00
Charger, Dragon In Flowers, Famille Rose, 15 In. 185.00
Charger, Floral Design, Gilt & Grisaille, 18th Century, 13 In. 315.00
Cider Jug, Coat Of Arms, Success To Bombay, Ship, 18th Century, 11 1/4 In. 2530.00
Cider Jug, Masonic Symbols, Gilt, Polychrome Enameled, 11 In. 925.00
Coffeepot, Rose Mandarin, 19th Century, 10 1/4 In. 1850.00
Coffeepot, Sampan Beyond Island Pavilions, 1780, 9 5/8 In. 1265.00
Creamer, Armorial, 5 In. 715.00
Creamer, Floral Design, Grisaille Helmet Shape, 5 1/2 In. 95.00
Cuspidor, Famille Rose, 7 x 7 1/2 In. 245.00
Demitasse Set, Blue Fitzhugh, 12 Piece 990.00
Dish, Famille Rose, 19th Century, 9 In., Pair 800.00
Dish, Garden, Basketry Rim, Famille Rose, Oval, 8 1/2 In. 770.00
Dish, Hot Water, Rose Mandarin, 19th Century, 9 3/4 In. 750.00
Dish, Noblemen & Ladies, Garden Pavilion, Famille Rose, Oval, 10 1/2 In. 805.00
Dish, Serving, Oval, Armorial, Porcelain, Gilt & Enamel, 12 In. 345.00
Dish, Shaped, Fitzhugh, Blue, 19th Century, 8 In. 750.00
Dish, Shrimp, Rose Mandarin, 19th Century, 10 5/8 In., Pair 1380.00
Dish, Warming, Sacred Bird & Butterfly, c.1870, 13 In. 1650.00
Figurine, Attendant, High-Necked Robe, Famille Rose, 8 1/4 In. 485.00
Figurine, Buddhist Lion, Famille Verte, 19th Century, 18 1/4 In., Pair 8000.00
Figurine, Crane, On Blue Rockwork Base, Famille Rose, 14 5/8 In., Pair 8350.00
Fish Bowl, Ovoid, Exotic Birds & Flowers, Blue & White, 25 In. 2875.00
Fruit Set, Square Bowl, Monogrammed Plates, 9 Piece 4400.00
Inkwell, Sprigs On Sides, 4 Quill Holes, c.1795, 3 In. 6350.00

Jar, Cover, Birds Perched On Rockwork, Famille Noire, 17 1/4 In., Pair	6325.00
Jug, Cider, Armorial, Porcelain, 19th Century, 8 1/2 In.	345.00
Jug, Hill & Stream, Arched Bamboo Handle, Pear Shape, 13 1/4 In.	2070.00
Jug & Basin, Hill & Stream, Plain Arched Handle, 13 1/8 & 15 1/2 In.	3220.00
Mug, Flower Garlands & Beading, Double Twist Handles, Pair	1800.00
Mug, Reserve Of Personages, Exotic Bird On Back, Famille Rose	185.00
Pitcher, Cream, Blue, White, Gold, 19th Century, 5 3/4 In.	290.00
Pitcher, Mandarin Pattern, Famille Rose, 8 /34 In.	110.00
Plate, Allover Roses, Heraldic Center, Gilt & Blue Borders, 9 1/2 In.	125.00
Plate, American Eagle, Fitzhugh, Early 19th Century, 9 3/4 In., Pair	95.00
Plate, Bird, Peonies, Famille Rose, 9 In.	150.00
Plate, Birds & Butterflies, Orange, White, 10 In., 12 Piece	330.00
Plate, Enameled Coastal Landscape, Late 18th Century, 9 In., Pair	370.00
Plate, Frolicking Red Kylins Center, Ribbon Border, 9 3/4 In., 13 Piece	3450.00
Plate, Green Fitzhugh, Brown Center, Fitzhugh, 9 3/4 In.	1265.00
Plate, Hot Water, Armorial, Rose Mandarin, 19th Century, 9 3/8 In.	1725.00
Plate, Octagonal, Bull, Stream, Lion's Head, Blue & White, 8 1/4 In., Pair	575.00
Plate, Rose Medallion, 10 1/2 In.	715.00
Plate, Underglaze, Blue Fitzhugh, 9 1/2 In., 12 Piece	2750.00
Platter, Armorial, Arms Of Cooke, 18th Century, 17 3/4 In.	1600.00
Platter, Blue Fitzhugh, 19th Century, 17 1/8 In.	635.00
Platter, Dragons Chasing Pearls, Gold Rim, 18 1/4 x 15 3/4 In.	500.00
Platter, Floral Design, Landscape, Orange Peel Glaze, 12 3/8 In.	195.00
Platter, Footed, Rose Mandarin, 19th Century, 14 1/4 In.	750.00
Platter, Japan Pattern, Famille Rose, 13 In., Pair	1100.00
Platter, Japan Pattern, Famille Rose, 14 1/2 In., 4 Piece	1450.00
Platter, Lake Scene, Blue & White, 12 In.	385.00
Platter, Landscape Scene, Octagonal, 17 In.	1265.00
Platter, Orange Fitzhugh, 18th Century, 18 1/2 x 15 1/2 In.	1150.00
Platter, Oval, Blue Fitzhugh, 19th Century, 19 1/8 In.	920.00
Platter, Oval, Cranberry & Cobalt Blue Enameled Berries, 12 In.	300.00
Punch Bowl, Blue & White, Cut Corners, Basketweave Border, 10 In.	670.00
Punch Bowl, Hunting Scenes, 18th Century, 11 1/4 In.	1955.00
Punch Bowl, Spearhead Medallion Each Side, Fitzhugh, 16 In.	1380.00
Soup, Dish, Armorial, Arms Of Boyd, 18th Century, 8 1/2 In.	805.00
Sweetmeat Set, Red Shou Character, Turquoise Ground, 11 In., 8 Piece	518.00
Tazza, Rose Mandarin, 19th Century, 4 x 10 In.	1265.00
Tea Caddy, Blue & White, Gold Trim, Silver Cap, 5 In.	245.00
Teapot, Couple & Child, Polychrome Scene, 5 1/4 In.	500.00
Teapot, Cover, Gilt, Scrolled Floral, Iron Red, Black, c.1770, 2 3/4 In.	175.00
Teapot, Cylindrical, Entwined Handle, Blue Design, 9 7/8 In.	230.00
Teapot, Famille Rose, Drum Shape, Wicker Carrying Box	140.00

Chinese Export, Tureen, Soup, Famille Rose,
c.1760, 15 x 11 x 9 In.

Teapot, Polychrome Floral, Gilt Trim, 5 1/4 In.	220.00
Teapot, Twisted Handle, Leaf & Berry Design	275.00
Teapoy, Cover, Geometric, Peacocks, Black, 18th Century, 4 1/2 In.	230.00
Tureen, Cover, Landscape Scene, Boar's Head Handles, 10 1/4 In.	1035.00
Tureen, Cover, Landscape, Blue & White, Octagonal, 12 In.	2200.00
Tureen, Sauce, Underplate, Flowers, American Eagles, 7 x 9 In., Pair	230.00
Tureen, Soup, Cover, Finial, Boar Head Handles, 7 5/8 x 12 1/2 In.	862.00
Tureen, Soup, Famille Rose, c.1760, 15 x 11 x 9 In.	*Illus* 10000.00
Tureen, Underplate, Cover, Boar's Head Handles, 14 x 10 In.	1800.00
Tureen, Underplate, Flowers, American Eagles, Marked, 7 3/4 x 7 1/2 In.	290.00
Urinal, Coat Of Arms	925.00
Urn, Baluster, Stylized Dog Handles, Blue & White, 41 1/2 In., Pair	7500.00
Vase, Beaker, Fitzhugh, 13 1/8 In.	1380.00
Vase, Foliate Panels, Famille Rose, Gilt Bronze Mounts, 27 In.	1150.00
Vase, Panels, Famille Verte, 17 In., Pair	470.00
Vase, Rouleau, Pheasant On Rockwork, Famille Noire, 17 In.	3350.00
Vase, Sepia & Gilt Design, 18th Century, 21 1/2 In.	2300.00
Vase, Stylized Peonies, Famille Verte, Lamp Mounted, 13 3/4 In.	3735.00
Vase, Temple, Allover Floral, Hawthorn, 22 In.	770.00
Vase, Temple, Rose Mandarin, 19th Century, 23 1/2 In.	865.00
Wig Stand, Reserve Or Birds, Foliate Ground, Famille Rose, 11 In., Pair	160.00

CHOCOLATE GLASS, sometimes mistakenly called caramel slag, was made by the Indiana Tumbler and Goblet Company of Greentown, Indiana, from 1900 to 1903. Fenton Art Glass Co. also made chocolate glass from about 1907 to 1915. More recent pieces have been made by Imperial, Heisey, and others.

Animal, Colt, Standing, Imperial	22.00
Animal, Donkey, Imperial, 6 1/2 In.	22.00
Animal, Owl, Imperial	25.00
Berry Set, Cactus, 7 Piece	420.00
Bowl, 5 Lobes, Scalloped, 9 In.	295.00
Bowl, Geneva, 8 1/2 x 15 In.	160.00
Butter, Cover, Cactus	165.00 to 180.00
Butter, Cover, Geneva	450.00
Butter, Cover, Leaf Bracket	170.00
Compote, Cactus, Footed, Greentown, 5 In.	155.00
Compote, Jelly, Geneva	140.00
Creamer, Cactus, Greentown	70.00
Creamer, Leaf Bracket	80.00
Creamer, Shuttle, Tankard Shape, 6 In.	85.00
Cruet, Cactus	175.00
Cruet, Herringbone & Buttress	325.00
Cruet, Imperial, Sticker	65.00
Cruet, Leaf Bracket	175.00
Dish, Bird With Berry Cover	1000.00
Dish, Cat On Hamper Cover	725.00
Dish, Dolphin Cover, Beaded	950.00
Dish, Fighting Cocks Cover	1700.00
Figurine, Dolphin, Beaded Edge	195.00
Hatpin Holder, Orange Tree	325.00
Mug, Drinking Scene, 5 1/2 In.	150.00
Mug, Herringbone	45.00
Nappy, Leaf Bracket, Greentown	50.00 to 60.00
Pitcher, Feather	950.00
Pitcher, Heron	550.00
Pitcher, Racing Deer & Doe	500.00 to 650.00
Pitcher, Ruffled Eye, Greentown	800.00
Pitcher, Serenade	1000.00
Pitcher, Shuttle, 6 In.	160.00
Pitcher, Squirrel	590.00
Plate, Cactus, 7 1/2 In.	95.00
Plate, Serenade, 6 1/4 In.	325.00

Punch Cup, Herringbone Buttress 80.00
Salt & Pepper, Cactus, Greentown 150.00
Sauce, Cactus, 4 In. 225.00
Sauce, Leaf Bracket, Greentown 45.00
Sauce, Teardrop & Tassel, 4 1/2 In. 245.00
Spooner, Leaf Bracket .... 50.00 to 65.00
Sugar, Cover, Geneva 250.00
Sugar, Cover, Wild Rose & Bowknot 425.00
Syrup, Cord Drapery .... 205.00 to 325.00
Toothpick, Cactus, Greentown 40.00
Tumbler, Cactus, 5 In. 58.00
Tumbler, Shuttle 70.00
Water Set, Cactus, 7 Piece 850.00

CHRISTMAS collectibles include not only Christmas trees and ornaments listed below, but also Santa Claus figures, special dishes, and even games and wrapping paper. A Belsnickle is a nineteenth-century figure of Father Christmas. A kugel is an early, heavy ornament made of thick blown glass, lined with zinc or lead, and often covered with colored wax. Christmas trees are listed in the section below.

Bell, Garfield The Cat, Ceramic, Cat Handle, Enesco, 1984 .... 50.00
Bell, Looney Tunes, 1977 .... 15.00
Box, Cookie, Santa Claus, Children, Radio Receiver, Toy Model T Under Tree, 2 x 4 In. 69.00
Creche, Figure Carved & Painted Face, Twine Body, Dressed, 11 3/4 In. 110.00
Figurine, Child, Cotton, Bisque Face, On Wooden Sled, Germany 260.00
Figurine, Father Frost, Blue Sash & Bag, White Mittens, Red Hat, 13 In. 425.00
Figurine, Santa Claus, Celluloid, Holding Doll, 7 In. 110.00
Figurine, Santa Claus, On Rotating & Lighted Globe, Rings Bell, Box 485.00
Figurine, Santa Claus, On Skis, Bisque, Red, Silver, Brown, 2 In. 85.00
Figurine, Santa Claus, On Skis, Sack On Back, Red Coat, Blue Pants, Fur Beard, 6 In. . 275.00
Figurine, Santa Claus, On Sled, Hand Painted, Germany, 5 x 4 1/2 In. 185.00
Figurine, Santa Claus, Papier-Mache, 16 In. 125.00
Figurine, Santa Claus, Papier-Mache, Cloth Coat, Blue Pants, Gold Feather Tree, 8 In.. 125.00
Figurine, Santa Claus, Riding Polar Bear, Bisque, 6 In. 300.00
Figurine, Santa Claus, Rolled Cotton, Crepe Coat, Holding Staff, 13 In. 385.00
Figurine, Santa Claus, Waving, Celluloid, Holding Lantern, 5 1/2 In. 65.00
Figurine, Santa Claus, With Dog Sled, Bisque, 5 In. 160.00
Figurine, Santa Claus, With Sack, Bisque, 2 1/2 In. 45.00
Figurine, Snow Princess, Rolled Cotton & Crepe, Composition Face, Russian, 6 In. 350.00
House, Composition, Stone House Style, Red Cellophane Windows, 2 1/4 x 4 In. 62.00
Mask, Father Christmas, Papier-Mache, Germany 175.00
Nativity Scene, Stable, Papier-Mache, Italy, Box 400.00
Nativity Set, Cardboard Manger, Simulated Straw Roof, Italy, 9 Figures 50.00
Nativity Set, Cardboard Manger, Straw Roof, Italy, Figures, 1955, 15 Piece 55.00
Nativity Set, Heavy Cardboard, 1933 .... 85.00
Nativity Set, Velvet Clothing, Wax Faces 295.00
Pin, Christmas, Swarovski 32.00
Pin, Merry Christmas, Tracy Bros., Wreath Type, 1940s, 1 1/2 In. 8.00
Planter, Santa Claus, Skiing, Snowy Tree 14.00
Plaque, Santa Claus, Plaster, 1930s, 17 In. 125.00
Plates are listed in the Collector Plate category
Scene, Nativity, Fold Out, Die Cut, Blue & Red Tissue Ground 125.00
Snow Dome, Santa Claus, In Sleigh, Reindeer 10.00
Snow Dome, Santa Claus, Sled, Reindeer, Toy, Red Cabin, Large 20.00
Spotlight, Revolving, 4 Colors 20.00
Suit, Santa Claus, 1920s 95.00
Toy, Handcar, Mr. & Mrs. Santa Claus, Electric, Lionel 75.00
Toy, Happy Santa Claus, Playing Drum, Eyes Light, Battery Operated, Japan 195.00
Toy, Pull, St. Nicholas On Nodder Donkey, Papier-Mache, c.1885, 9 In. 1400.00
Toy, Santa Claus, Riding Mohair Covered Deer, Windup, Tin & Rubber, 6 1/4 In. 160.00
Toy, Santa Claus, Rings Bell & Sways, Battery Operated, Japan, Box, 18 In. 475.00
Toy, Santa Claus, Rings Bell, Ho-Ho, Battery Operated, 18 In. 395.00
Toy, Santa Claus, Windup, Tin, Box, 1950s 155.00

CHRISTMAS TREES made of feathers and Christmas tree decorations of all types are popular with collectors. The first decorated Christmas tree in America is claimed by many states, including Pennsylvania (1747), Massachusetts (1832), Illinois (1833), Ohio (1838), and Iowa (1845). The first glass ornaments were imported from Germany about 1860. Dresden ornaments were made about 100 years ago of paper and tinsel. Manufacturers in the United States were making ornaments in the early 1870s. Electric lights were first used on a Christmas tree in 1882. Character light bulbs became popular in the 1920s, bubble lights in the 1940s, twinkle bulbs in the 1950s, plastic bulbs by 1955. In this book a Christmas light is a holder for a candle used on the tree. Other forms of lighting include light bulbs. Other Christmas memorabilia is listed in the section above.

Aluminum, Box, 1950s, 4 Ft.	75.00
Aluminum, Box, 1950s, 6 Ft.	65.00
Aluminum, Pompon Ends, Unused, 1950s, Box, 8 Ft.	85.00
Candleholder, Tin, 23 Piece	35.00
Carpet, Chromolithographed Scene, Square, c.1920, 44 In.	390.00
Ceramic, 15 In.	88.00
Feather, 2 Ft.	200.00
Feather, With Ornaments, 20 In.	350.00
Fence, Wicker, Green, 12 Wooden Posts, Hazelton, Pa., 6 1/2 In. Posts	245.00
Fence, Wooden, 4 x 82 In.	95.00
Fence, Wooden, Red Frame, Green Pickets, Square, 4 x 18 In.	115.00
Garland, Beaded, Gold Beads, 8 Ft.	26.00
Light, Diamond Design, Brocks Illumination Lamp Mfg., France, 1880, 4 In.	60.00
Light, Diamond Design, Deep Cobalt Blue, Folded Rim, c.1900, 2 7/8 In.	75.00
Light, Diamond Design, Milk Glass, Flared Rim, England, c.1880, 3 3/8 In., Pair	140.00
Light, Diamond Design, Pinkish Amethyst, Pains Patent 1882, 3 1/2 In.	40.00
Light, Diamond Design, Purple Streaks, c.1870, 3 In.	65.00
Light, Diamond Design, Red Amber, Rolled Rim, England, 2 3/8 In.	150.00
Light, Diamond Design, Ruby Red, Brocks Illumination Lamp, Bohemia, 4 In.	275.00
Light, Diamond Design, Swirl Of Black, England, c.1870, 2 7/8 In.	55.00
Light, Harlequin Diamond, Cobalt Blue, Tooled Lip, England, c.1880, 3 1/2 In.	190.00
Light, Harlequin Diamond, Emerald Green, Smooth Base, England, 3 1/2 In.	210.00
Light, Harlequin Pattern, Purple, 3 3/8 In. *Illus*	110.00
Light, King Edward Bust, Regd No. 298588, England, c.1900, 4 1/8 In.	550.00
Light, King Edward, Amethyst, 4 1/8 In. *Illus*	715.00
Light, Queen Mary Bust, Eclipse Lamp, Medium Green, c.1870, 4 1/8 In.	675.00
Light, Queen Victoria Bust, Hearn Wright, 1900, 3 7/8 In. *Illus*	198.00
Light, Queen Victoria Bust, Hearn, Wright & Co., Cobalt Blue, c.1910, 4 In.	350.00
Light, Ribbed Design, Amethyst, Allover Swirling, England, c.1880, 2 5/8 In.	85.00
Light, Ribbed Design, Flared-Out Rim, Deep Amethyst, c.1900, 2 3/4 In.	65.00
Light, Ribbed Design, Gray Amethyst, Folded Rim, English, c.1880, 2 5/8 In.	65.00
Light, Ribbed Design, Sapphire Blue, American, c.1870, 2 1/2 In.	70.00
Light, Tulip Form, Hearn, Wright & Co., Medium Green, c.1880, 3 1/2 In.	325.00
Light, Turquoise, Embossed Crown, Rose & Thistle, c.1902, 4 3/4 In.	425.00
Light Bulb, Betty Boop	68.00 to 78.00

◆ ◆

Glass becomes cloudy if not kept completely dry when not in use. That is why decanters and vases often discolor. Drain them upside down.

◆ ◆

Christmas Tree, Light, Queen Victoria Bust, Hearn Wright, 1900, 3 7/8 In.

Christmas Tree, Light, Harlequin Pattern, Purple, 3 3/8 In.

Christmas Tree, Light, King Edward, Amethyst, 4 1/8 In.

Christmas Tree, Ornament, Kugel, European, c.1880, 2 3/4 In.

Christmas Tree, Ornament, Kugel, Ribbed, Green, 1880, 5 In.

Light Bulb, Ear Of Corn	35.00
Light Bulb, Lion, With Mandolin	25.00
Light Bulb, Little Girl, In Rose	30.00
Light Bulb, Moon Mullins	70.00
Light Bulb, Old King Cole, Egg Shape	40.00
Light Bulb, Peach	25.00
Light Bulb, Popeye, Set	90.00
Light Bulb, Rose	15.00
Light Bulb, Santa Claus, Belsnickle Form, Bakelite Base, 9 In.	355.00
Light Bulb, Snow White & Seven Dwarfs, Noma, Box	325.00
Light Bulb, Strawberry	10.00
Light Bulb, Tulip	15.00
Light Bulb, Yellow Bird	15.00
Light Bulb, Zeppelin	40.00
Light Bulb Set, 21 Figurals, Comic Characters, Santa Claus, Birds, Fruit	115.00
Ornament, Airplane, Blown Glass, Crinkled Wire, Cotton Santa, 1920s, 6 In.	144.00
Ornament, Airplane, Long White Opaque Beaded Wings, 3 In.	68.00
Ornament, Angel, Treetop, 1950s	20.00
Ornament, Barbie, Hallmark, 1st	90.00
Ornament, Bird, Red, 2 3/4 In.	25.00
Ornament, Blue & White Glass, Blown, Germany, Box, 15 1/2 In.	375.00
Ornament, Boy Holding Catsup Over Bag Of Fries, McDonald's	10.00
Ornament, Cherub, Wax Covered Composition, Blue Costume, 4 In.	11.00
Ornament, Cross, Sterling Silver, Reed & Barton, Box, 1972	40.00
Ornament, Father Christmas, Tinsel Scrap	27.00
Ornament, Floral, Sterling Silver, Towle, 1983	32.00
Ornament, Gold & Silver Glass, Man In The Moon Inside	40.00
Ornament, Grapes, Blown Blue Glass, Kugel, 3 In.	45.00
Ornament, Grumpy	20.00
Ornament, Here Comes Santa, Hallmark, 1979	395.00
Ornament, Iridescent, Pinecone Shape, Mt. St. Helens Ash	20.00
Ornament, Kayo	50.00
Ornament, Kugel, Blue Grape, Molded, 7 1/2 In.	565.00
Ornament, Kugel, European, c.1880, 2 3/4 In. .... *Illus*	138.00
Ornament, Kugel, Grapes, Amethyst, 6 1/2 In.	27.00
Ornament, Kugel, Grapes, Blue, Silvered, 4 In.	225.00
Ornament, Kugel, Grapes, Green, Silvered, 3 3/4 In.	49.00
Ornament, Kugel, Ribbed, Green, 1880, 5 In. .... *Illus*	193.00
Ornament, Kugel, Silver, Ribbed, Oval, Large	175.00
Ornament, Peacock, Glass	15.00
Ornament, Reindeer, Celluloid	18.00
Ornament, Santa Claus, Head, Blue & Red	35.00
Ornament, Santa Claus, Pipe Cleaner Trim, Black Boots, Cotton, 8 1/2 In.	710.00
Ornament, Santa Claus, With Cane, 3 In.	55.00
Ornament, Santa's Helpers, Round, & Flat, 2 1/2 In.	20.00
Ornament, Silver Mandolin, Dresden, 3 3/8 In.	200.00

Ornament, Snoopy, As Davy Crockett 22.00
Ornament, Snoopy, As Gondolier 15.00
Ornament, Snow White & Seven Dwarfs, Glass, 1938 .... 825.00
Ornament, Snow White's Surprise, Round & Flat, 2 1/2 In. 20.00
Ornament, Swan, Red Glass, Wire Wrapped, Spun Glass Tail, 4 1/2 In. 65.00
Ornament, Treetop, Angel, Doll, Satin Dress, Gold Wings, Victorian 95.00
Ornament, Treetop, Angel, Spun Glass, Gold Wings, 8 In. 78.00
Ornament, Treetop, Star, Says Merry Christmas, Lights, Tin 25.00
Reflector, Light Bulb, Paper, Sparkle, 7 Piece 15.00
Stand, Cast Iron, Brass Trim, Fancy, Germany 70.00
Stand, Green, 4 Legged, Gold Star On Legs, Cast Iron, 3-In. Opening .... 52.00 to 55.00
Stand, Poinsettia, Iron 135.00
Stand, Revolving, Musical, 1950s 30.00

CHROME items in the Art Deco style became popular in the 1930s. Collectors are most interested in high-style pieces made by the Connecticut firms of Chase Brass and Copper Company and Manning Bowman.

Ashtray, Art Deco, Sailfish, Gustav Bohland 25.00
Ashtray, Jeep, CJ-5 Mounted On Top, c.1950 .... 125.00
Ashtray, Spinning Bucket Center, Bird Cigarette Grips, Hamilton, 5 3/4 In. 9.00
Bowl, Lotus, Chase 40.00
Bucket, Champagne, Bacchus, Rockwell Kent, Chase, 9 1/4 In. .... 475.00 to 770.00
Butter Pitcher, Chase 95.00
Candy Dish, 2 Sections, Handles, Glass Insert, Chase 45.00
Candy Dish, Cover, Sferrazza 30.00
Candy Dish, Upside Down Whale In Middle, Circular Handle, Chase 32.00
Cocktail Ball, Box 48.00
Cocktail Set, Hammered, Black Plastic Handle, Goblet, Farberware, 6 1/4 In. 28.00
Cocktail Set, Handled Shaker, Goblet, Flared, 7 In. 28.00
Cocktail Shaker, Art Deco, Manning Bowman 25.00
Cocktail Shaker, Art Deco, Red Bakelite Lid, Knob & Handle 48.00
Cocktail Shaker, Black Trim, Chase Brass, 11 In. 40.00
Cocktail Shaker, Grapes With Leaves Etch, Handle, Spout, 11 3/4 In. 12.00
Cocktail Shaker, Handles, 11 1/2 In. 9.00
Cocktail Shaker, Penguin, On Tray, 6 Goblets, 7 Piece 395.00
Cocktail Shaker, Zeppelin, Gold Washed Interior, Flask, Cups, c.1928, 9 In. 357.00
Coffee Set, Coronet, Chase, 3 Piece 225.00
Coffee Set, Percolator, Forman, 3 Piece 45.00
Coffee Set, Yellow & Green Catalin Handles, Tray Base, Manning Bowman, 4 Piece .. 605.00
Compote, Nude Stem, Scalloped, Grape & Leaf Pierced Bowl, Sferrazza, 7 3/4 x 8 In. 24.00
Dish, Sundae, Footed, Flared, Set Of 6, 3 3/8 In. 15.00
Tray, Deco Tooling, Rounded Rectangle, 14 x 9 1/4 In. 7.00
Tray, Leaf & Scroll Center, Pierced Double Scallop Rim, Kromekraft, 13 1/2 In. 11.00
Tray, Machine Age, Reverse-Painted Art Deco Graphic, c.1935, 12 x 18 In. 550.00
Tray, Scroll & Lattice, Chased Flowers, 12 3/4 In. 5.00
Tray, Scroll & Lattice, Pierced Floral, Scroll Medallions, 16 3/4 x 12 In. 8.00

CIGAR STORE FIGURES of carved wood or cast iron were used as advertisements in front of the Victorian cigar store. The carved figures are now collected as folk art. They range in size from counter type, about three feet, to over eight feet high.

Bearded Man, Turban, Carved, Wooden, Paint, 41 In. 220.00
Black Man, Holding Package Of Cigars, 63 In. 825.00
Indian, 19th Century, 83 In. 8350.00
Indian, Cigars & Tobacco, Wheeled Base, Wooden, 65 1/2 In. 5750.00
Indian, Headdress, Holding Box Of Cigars, 1920s, 74 In. 10350.00
Young Man, Scotsman's Outfit, 1880s, Countertop 625.00

CINNABAR is a vermilion or red lacquer. Pieces are made with tens to hundreds of thicknesses of the lacquer that is later carved.

Box, Lid, Carved Flowering Lotus, Black Interior, Red, 7 x 6 In. 460.00
Cigarette Case, Court Scene, Key-Fret Border, 6 In. 350.00
Dish, Floral Form, Figure In Landscape, 8 In. 460.00

Urn, 18 1/2 In.	295.00
Vase, Magnolias & Cardinals, China	90.00

CIVIL WAR mementos are important collector's items. Most of the pieces are military items used from 1861 to 1865.

Ammunition Pouch	295.00
Binoculars, Case	65.00
Boots, Cowhide, Wooden Pegs, 20 x 11 In.	165.00
Box, Ballot, Black & White Marbles, Mahogany	110.00
Brass, Oil Can	45.00
Bullet Pouch, Belt, Eagle Buckle, 1864	885.00
Canteen, Blue Cover	175.00
Canteen, Bull's Eye	75.00
Canteen, Copper, Confederate, Belt Loop, Carrying Strap, 4 1/2 In.	275.00
Canteen, Copper, Sling Guides, Chain, Cork Stopper, 7 1/2 In.	390.00
Canteen, Union, Concentric Ring, 1864, 7 1/2 In.	302.00
Cap, Kepi	135.00
Cartridge Pouch, Oval Lead-Backed Buckle	302.00
Case, Courier, Tin, 11 1/2 x 8 x 3 3/8 In.	120.00
Comb, Folding, Ivory, Case	45.00
Crutch, Rosewood, Brass Plated Hardware, 55 In., Pair	71.00
Desk, Lap, Walnut, 8 x 12 x 3 3/4 In.	150.00
Drum, Brass Body	250.00
Flag, 35 Hand-Sewn Stars, 120 x 71 In.	522.00
Headdress, Shako, Leather, Mass. Troops At Bull Run, No Pompon	450.00
Mirror, Folding, Mahogany, A.H. Dyson	85.00
Pouch, Bullet, Model 1855, Brass U.S. Plate, Broken Shoulder Strap	235.00
Pouch, Bullet, Model 1864, Tins	185.00
Pouch, Pistol Ammunition	50.00
Print, Andersonville Prison, Ariel & Small Views, Siebert, Frame, 49 x 69 In.	286.00
Saber, Confederate Officer's Cavalry, Nashville Plow Works, 35 1/2-In. Blade	9200.00
Saber Sash, Officer's, Maroon & Red, 10 1/2-In. Tassel Ends, 173 x 4 In.	302.00
Sheet Music, O Search Ye Well The Lists, Mother, 1865	30.00
Shot Pouch, Mattress Ticking, Thread Spool Throat, 6 1/2 In.	65.00
Surgeon's Kit, H.M. Merrell, Instruments, Brass Bound Mahogany, 15 1/2 In.	1870.00
Telescope, Red, 3 Sections, Pocket	55.00
Watering Bridle, Leather	50.00

CKAW, see Dedham category

CLAMBROTH glass, popular in the Victorian era, is a grayish color and is somewhat opaque, like clam broth.

Bowl, Luster Rose	49.00
Candlestick, Crucifix, 9 3/4 In., Pair	55.00
Candlestick, Petal & Loop, Blue Top, Flint	300.00
Eggcup, 1880s	225.00
Holder, Spill, Diamond & Thumbprint, 4 3/4 In.	45.00
Mug, Lacy Medallion	35.00

CLARICE CLIFF was a designer who worked in several English factories after the 1920s. She died in 1972.

Bowl, Vegetable, Tonquin	35.00
Dish, Tea, Bizarre, Silver Plated Handle, 9 In.	92.00
Flower Frog, Autumn Crocus	374.00
Jam Jar, Bizarre, Crocus	225.00
Mask, Face Of Woman, Flowers In Hair, 14 1/2 x 14 In.	1150.00
Pitcher, Dragon, Bizarre, House Design	375.00
Pitcher, Tonquin, Pink, 6 1/4 In.	30.00
Plate, Bizarre, Scenic Design, Signed, 9 In., Pair	288.00
Plate, Copper Luster, 1940s, 9 In. ....*Illus*	35.00
Plate, Leaf Design, 8 In.	150.00
Platter, Tonquin, Blue & White	89.00
Sauce, Tonquin, Liner	36.00
Teapot, Teepee, Marked, 6 5/8 In.	690.00

Clarice Cliff, Plate, Copper Luster, 1940s, 9 In.

Toby Jug, Seated Man, Drinking Beer, 8 1/2 In.	1800.00
Vase, Fantasque, Black & Orange Bands, Center Landscape, 11 3/4 In.	1265.00
Vase, No. 205, Geometric Design, Signed, Late 1920s, 8 In.	390.00

CLEWELL ware was made in limited quantities by Charles Walter Clewell of
Canton, Ohio, from 1902 to 1955. Pottery was covered with a thin coating of
bronze, then treated to make the bronze turn different colors. Pieces covered
with copper, brass, or silver were also made. Mr. Clewell's secret formula for
blue patinated bronze was burned when he died in 1965.

Bowl, Copper Over Pottery, Riveted Panels, Fowler Simpson Advertising, 4 In.	165.00
Candlestick, Dark Brown & Green, 10 In., Pair	600.00
Ewer, Raised Arts & Crafts Style Design, Ribbed Body, Signed, 4 1/2 In.	605.00
Pitcher, Copper Clad, 5 3/4 In.	165.00
Vase, Bud, Orange To Green Patina, Corseted, Signed, 6 1/2 In.	275.00
Vase, Copper Clad, Allover Verdigris & Orange Patina, Signed, 5 1/2 In.	600.00
Vase, Copper Clad, Bulbous, Narrow Neck, 4 1/2 In.	275.00
Vase, Copper Clad, No. 187, 4 In.	522.00
Vase, Copper Clad, No. 321-2, 6 In.	468.00
Vase, Copper Clad, No. 433-25, 4 1/2 In.	522.00
Vase, Copper Electroplating, Mottled Green	975.00
Vase, Copper, Squatty Base, Long Neck, Flared, Incised, 12 3/4 x 6 3/4 In.	413.00
Vase, Cylinder, Brown To Green Patina, No. 328-2-6, 9 1/2 In.	880.00
Vase, Incised Floral Design, Molded At Base, 6 1/2 x 6 In.	660.00
Vase, Voluted Handles Rise From Sides, Copper Plated, 9 1/2 In.	450.00

CLEWS pottery was made by George Clews & Co. of Brownhill Pottery,
Tunstall, England, from 1806 to 1861. Additional pieces may be listed in the
Flow Blue category.

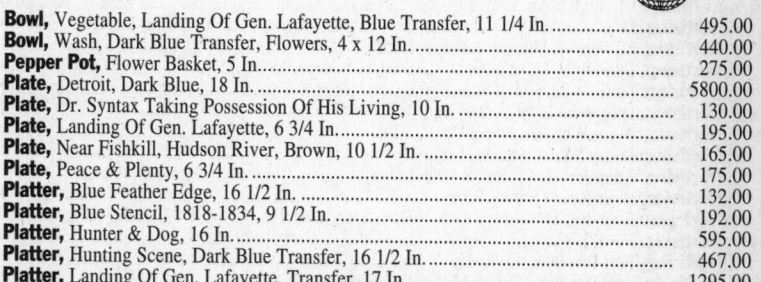

Bowl, Vegetable, Landing Of Gen. Lafayette, Blue Transfer, 11 1/4 In.	495.00
Bowl, Wash, Dark Blue Transfer, Flowers, 4 x 12 In.	440.00
Pepper Pot, Flower Basket, 5 In.	275.00
Plate, Detroit, Dark Blue, 18 In.	5800.00
Plate, Dr. Syntax Taking Possession Of His Living, 10 In.	130.00
Plate, Landing Of Gen. Lafayette, 6 3/4 In.	195.00
Plate, Near Fishkill, Hudson River, Brown, 10 1/2 In.	165.00
Plate, Peace & Plenty, 6 3/4 In.	175.00
Platter, Blue Feather Edge, 16 1/2 In.	132.00
Platter, Blue Stencil, 1818-1834, 9 1/2 In.	192.00
Platter, Hunter & Dog, 16 In.	595.00
Platter, Hunting Scene, Dark Blue Transfer, 16 1/2 In.	467.00
Platter, Landing Of Gen. Lafayette, Transfer, 17 In.	1295.00

CLIFTON POTTERY was founded by William Long in Clifton, New Jersey, in
1905. He worked there until 1908 making a line called *Crystal Patina*. Clifton Pottery made art pottery. Another firm, Chesapeake Pottery, sold majolica marked *Clifton ware*.

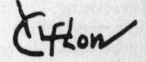

Bowl, Indian Ware, Bulbous, Brown Bands, 8 In.	165.00

Candlestick, Conical Standard, Matte Green Glaze, Paper Label, 5 In. 250.00
Humidor, Cover, Indian Ware, Terra-Cotta, Geometric Relief, Painted Design 95.00
Humidor, Incision & Excision Indian Design, Place For Sponge In Top, 5 3/4 In. 375.00
Teapot, Cover, Indian Ware, Impressed Design, Mottled, Gold Trim, 7 1/2 In. 50.00
Teapot, Modernistic Form, Green Semigloss, 4 x 5 In. 295.00
Teapot, White, c.1910 .... 75.00
Vase, Bulbous, Green & Cream Over Brown & Tan, 5 In. 440.00
Vase, Celadon & Cream Crystalline Glaze, Pinched Organic Handles, 1906, 10 1/2 In.. 330.00
Vase, Celadon Crystalline Glaze, 2 Flaring Handles, 1905, 5 x 6 In. 195.00
Vase, Crystal Patina, 1905, 6 1/2 In. 250.00
Vase, Indian Ware, Bulbous, Flared Rim, 2 3/4 x 3 In. 138.00
Vase, Indian Ware, Stepped Shoulder, 2 1/4 x 4 x 4 In. 140.00
Vase, Lamp Base, Celadon Crystalline Over Clear Amber Base, 1906, 5 x 7 3/4 In. 360.00
Vase, Matte Green To Olive Green Crystalline Glaze, Bottle Shape, 1905, 10 1/2 In. 385.00
Vase, Olive & Brown Crystalline Glaze, Double Gourd, 2 Handles, 1906, 4 x 3 3/4 In.. 220.00
Vase, Olive, Light Gold Crystalline, Bulbous, 4-Sided Flared Neck, 7 1/4 x 4 1/2 In. 220.00
Vase, Squatty, 2 Handles, Green Crystalline Over Light Green, 1906, 3 1/2 .... 195.00
Vase, Tirrube, Yellow Jonquils, Brick Red Ground, E.B., 8 x 4 1/4 In. 335.00

CLOCKS of all types have always been popular with collectors. The eighteenth-century tall case, or grandfather's clock, was designed to house a
works with a long pendulum. In 1816, Eli Terry patented a new, smaller
works for a clock, and the case became smaller. The clock could be kept on a
shelf instead of on the floor. By 1840, coiled springs were used and even
smaller clocks were made. Battery-powered electric clocks were made in the
1870s.

Advertising, Another 48 Hours, Movie, Box 40.00
Advertising, Ansonia, Cream Mustard, Regulator, Brass Bezel, 25 In. 440.00
Advertising, Atlas Tires, Wall, c.1950 .... 175.00
Advertising, Aunt Jemima Face, Cooking Oil, Gong Type Alarm, Metal & Glass, 1907 325.00
Advertising, Barq's Soda Pop, Light-Up .... 150.00 to 250.00
Advertising, Blatz Beer, Made Of 1/2 Beer Barrel 475.00
Advertising, Budweiser Beer, Clydesdale Horses 595.00
Advertising, Budweiser Bud Man, Man Holding Bottle, Light-Up 180.00
Advertising, Budweiser, Rotating Grandfather Sign, c.1970 .... 95.00
Advertising, Bulova, Light-Up, 15 x 15 In. 95.00
Advertising, Bulova, Light-Up, Square 85.00
Advertising, Cain's Potato Chips, Light-Up 175.00
Advertising, Calumet Baking Powder, Oak, Calendar, Sessions, Forestville, Ct., 1900 .. 750.00
Advertising, Calumet Baking Powder, Wall, Time To Buy, Scrolled Molding, 40 In. 215.00
Advertising, Case XX Cutlery 165.00
Advertising, Champion Spark Plugs, Light-Up 25.00
Advertising, Chapples Milk, Double Bubble 265.00
Advertising, Clicquot Club 300.00
Advertising, D. Ghirardelli's Chocolates, & Breakfast Cocoa, Figure 8 Form, Label 2970.00
Advertising, Dr Pepper, Diamond Shape, c.1950 .... 225.00
Advertising, Dr Pepper, Double Glass, Light-Up, Square, 15 In. .... 140.00 to 175.00
Advertising, Duffy's Pure Malt Whiskey 950.00
Advertising, Duquesne Pilsner, Bar Sign, 1953-1958 .... 145.00
Advertising, Elgin Watches, Light-Up 150.00
Advertising, Enjoy Squirt, Square, Light-Up 200.00
Advertising, Enna Jetticks, Neon, 8 Sides 425.00
Advertising, Ever-Ready Safety Razor 1100.00
Advertising, Ever-Ready Safety Razor, 8-Day, Embossed Tin, 12 1/2 x 17 3/4 In. 1650.00
Advertising, Ford, Light-Up 175.00
Advertising, Fort Pitt Beer, Light-Up 150.00
Advertising, Fort Pitt Beer, White Milk Glass Face, 1940s 130.00
Advertising, Fram Filters, Light-Up, 1950s 90.00
Advertising, Frostie Root Beer, Frostie Swings On Pendulum 125.00
Advertising, Frostie Root Beer, The Smooth One 75.00
Advertising, General Electric Lamps, Light-Up, Metal, Wall 135.00
Advertising, General Electric, Blue Mirror 150.00
Advertising, General Electric, Monitor-Top Refrigerator, Figural, c.1930 .... 175.00 to 180.00

Clock, Advertising, Moxie, Compound
For Nervous System

Clock, Advertising, Moxie, Old Fashion,
Round Face, Square

Advertising, General Electric, Refrigerator, Metal	325.00
Advertising, Gibbons Beer & Ale, Bakelite, 14 In.	35.00
Advertising, Grapette, Neon, Octagonal, 1940s	1200.00
Advertising, Greyhound Bus, Glass & Metal, Electric, Round, 15 In.	1120.00
Advertising, Gruen Watches, Metal, Glass, Octagonal, 1940s	85.00
Advertising, Gulf Gasoline, Gas Pump Face, Porcelain	650.00
Advertising, Hamburger Helper, Helping Hand, Box	45.00 to 50.00
Advertising, Hires Root Beer, 1950s	50.00
Advertising, Holland Dairy	90.00
Advertising, Keebler, Wag	48.00
Advertising, Keen Kutter, Electric, 18 In.	650.00
Advertising, Keen Kutter, Wrought Iron Stand	2100.00
Advertising, Kendall Motor Oil, Light-Up	175.00
Advertising, Kodak	200.00
Advertising, Kool-Aid, Alarm	24.00
Advertising, Lowenbrau Beer, Electric, Lucite Box	30.00
Advertising, Lowenbrau Beer, Lions Holding Clock	55.00
Advertising, McCreary Tires, Light-Up, Round	265.00
Advertising, Michelin Man, Figural, Leaded Crystal	300.00
Advertising, Moxie, Baird, Logo On Face, Wooden, 31 x 18 In.	7700.00
Advertising, Moxie, Compound For Nervous System	*Illus* 7700.00
Advertising, Moxie, Old Fashion, Round Face, Square	*Illus* 9000.00
Advertising, Nu-Grape, Light-Up	225.00
Advertising, Old Crow Whiskey	225.00
Advertising, Orange Crush, Light-Up, 15 In.	585.00
Advertising, Oshkosh B'Gosh Work Clothes	750.00
Advertising, Pam, Light-Up, 1950	200.00 to 400.00
Advertising, Pard Dog Food, Head Moves Up & Down, Eating From Bowl, Electric	200.00
Advertising, Pearl Beer, Light-Up, Neon Tube Around Edge	400.00
Advertising, Peter Pan Peanut Butter, Attached Neon Sign	850.00
Advertising, Philadelphia Times Newspaper, Logo, Baird	2200.00
Advertising, Polly Trading Stamps	450.00
Advertising, Procter & Gamble, Square	125.00
Advertising, Quaker State Oil, Spinner, Neon, Round, 22 In.	650.00
Advertising, Red Goose Shoes, Alarm, Gilbert	275.00
Advertising, Red Goose, Alarm, New Haven, Pat. 23	135.00
Advertising, Reed's Tonic, Wall, Logo On Bottom Glass, 36 x 4 In.	185.00
Advertising, Revco, Light-Up, Round	155.00
Advertising, Rexall, Pharmacist	100.00
Advertising, Roxana Shell Petroleum Co., 8-Day, Hour Chime	2530.00
Advertising, Royal Crown Cola, Light-Up	105.00
Advertising, Sauers Flavoring Extracts, Pendulum, Oak, Wall	625.00

Advertising, Schaefer Beer, Art Deco, Ship Shape, 1940s 60.00
Advertising, Schlitz, Lowenbrau, Electric, Light-Up, 11 x 4 x 5 In. 40.00
Advertising, Shapleigh, R-U-Up, Alarm 350.00
Advertising, Sprite Soda, Alarm, Sprite Boy On Face, 1978 .... 75.00
Advertising, Squirt, Light-Up 125.00
Advertising, Squirt, Windup, Alarm, 1978 .... 55.00
Advertising, St. Joseph Aspirin, 15 In. Diam. 65.00
Advertising, Standard Brand Shoes, Gilbert 75.00
Advertising, Star Wars, Box 65.00
Advertising, Suncrest Orange Soda, Light-Up 250.00
Advertising, Sundial Shoes, Lux, 3 1/4 In. 75.00
Advertising, Valvoline Motor Oil, Light-Up 125.00
Advertising, Victory V Lozenge, Egyptian Stylized Paintings, Mantel, Key Wind 66.00
Advertising, Western Union Station, Marked National Observatory Time 95.00
Advertising, Westinghouse, Revolving, Light-Up, Wooden Case 95.00
Advertising, Winchester, Horse & Rider, More Than A Gun, American Legend 300.00
Advertising, Wolf's Head, Light-Up, Round 225.00
Alabaster, Ormolu & Pink Onyx Trim, Face Marked Chapman, 13 1/2 In. 220.00
Alarm, Flintstones, Key Wind 15.00
Alarm, Golf Ball, Open Reveals Clock, Welby, Germany, 7 Jewels 175.00
Alarm, Snoopy, Tennis Player, Windup, Metal Case, Equity, Hong Kong, 1970s, 4 In. .. 40.00
Animated, Alarm, Woody Woodpecker 145.00
Animated, Covered Wagon, 4-Horse Team, Driver's Arm Moves, Electric 125.00
Animated, Haddon, Ship Ahoy, Celluloid Ship, Rocking In Waves, Electric ... 350.00
Animated, Hula Girl 275.00
Animated, Owl, Wall, Wooden, Eyes Move, Replaced Pendulum 175.00
Animated, Panda Bear, Eyes Move 35.00
Animated, Queen Of Hearts Playing, Hand Painted, Ivory, c.1900 .... 1100.00
Animated, Seesaw, Lighted, Electric 175.00
Ansonia, Mantel, Blue & Pink Floral, Dated 1892 .... 850.00
Ansonia, Mantel, Blue Floral, Pink, Royal Bonn 650.00
Ansonia, Mantel, Grecian Woman, Seated, Black Base 600.00
Ansonia, Mantel, Metal, Bird & Figural Applied Design 330.00
Ansonia, Mantel, Spelter, Allegorical Woman On Bench, c.1870, 15 x 19 1/2 In. 575.00
Ansonia, Mantel, Wild Rose Pattern, Red, Royal Bonn 650.00
Ansonia, Siren, Figural, Open Escapement, c.1900 .... 675.00
Art Nouveau, Silver Patinated Bronze, Dancing Maidens, M. Dufrene & Voulot, 21 In. 7300.00
Atkins Clock Co., Shelf, Rosewood, Fuse Movement, c.1840 .... 2300.00
Attleboro, Mantel, 8-Day 185.00
Bagues & Fils, Wall, Gilt Bronze, Wreath Decoration, Ribbon Support, Paris, 18 In. 300.00
Baird, Regulator, Figure 8, Open Pendulum Window, 27 In. 935.00

Clock, Banjo, Curtis & Dunning, Mahogany, 1820, 41 In.

Clock, Banjo, Curtis, Mahogany, 1830, 36 x 11 1/2 In.

Clock, Banjo, David Williams, Giltwood, Eglomise, 1815, 41 x 10 In.

Banjo, Chelsea, Wall, Time & Strike, Eglomise Column... 500.00
Banjo, Cummens, William, Federal, Mahogany, Ball & Eagle, c.1825, 33 x 10 In. 2300.00
Banjo, Curtis & Dunning, Mahogany, 1820, 41 In..*Illus* 2587.00
Banjo, Curtis, Mahogany, 1830, 36 x 11 1/2 In...*Illus* 8050.00
Banjo, David Williams, Giltwood, Eglomise, 1815, 41 x 10 In. ....*Illus* 5175.00
Banjo, Eagle Finial, Acorn Drop Shelf 1700.00
Banjo, Federal, Gilt Gesso & Mahogany, c.1820, 30 In...860.00 to 920.00
Banjo, Federal, Gilt Gesso & Mahogany, 19th Century, 35 In................................ 920.00
Banjo, Federal, Mahogany, c.1826, 36 x 10 In. 4315.00
Banjo, Federal, Mahogany, Eglomise, Giltwood, c.1820, 41 x 10 In. 6325.00
Banjo, Federal, Stenciled Mahogany, Eglomise, c.1825, 33 x 10 In. 5175.00
Banjo, Mahogany Veneer, Pine, Gilded Facade, 40 In.. 440.00
Banjo, Mahogany, Eglomise Panels, Gilt Flowers, Fighting Ships, c.1820, 53 In. 415.00
Banjo, Mahogany, Reverse-Painted Horse & Chariot, Gilt Acorn Finial, 33 In............. 1200.00
Banjo, Mahogany, Washington & Mt. Vernon, Eagle Finial, 43 In. 770.00
Banjo, Willard, Aaron, Eagle Finial, Naval Battle Lower Glass 3300.00
Banjo, Willard, Glazed Hinged Door, Painted Dial, American Eagle, 37 In.................. 4600.00
Banjo, Willard, Simon, Father Time Panel, Eglomise Panel Restoration...................... 2600.00
Banjo, Willard, Simon, Federal, Inlaid Mahogany, Brass, c.1815, 34 1/2 x 9 7/8 In. 4315.00
Banjo, Willard, Simon, Federal, Mahogany, Eglomise, c.1810, 32 1/2 x 9 1/2 In. 23000.00
Birge, Mallory & Co., Mahogany, 8-Day, Ball Feet, Thistle Carving, Conn., c.1830 ..... 600.00
Birge & Fuller, Double Gothic Steeple, Wagon Spring 2200.00
Blinking Eye, Barefoot Black Man, Clock Face On Back, Cast Iron, 11 1/2 In.............. 8500.00
Blinking Eye, Man In Red Coat, Napoleonic Hat, Cast Iron, 16 1/2 In. ....1760.00 to 3400.00
Blinking Eye, Organ Grinder, Monkey & Hurdy-Gurdy, Cast Iron, 17 1/4 In.............. 2650.00
Blinking Eye, Owl, Clock In Beak, Cast Iron, 8 1/2 In.. 5200.00
Blinking Eye, Sambo, Black Man Playing Banjo, Cast Iron, 16 In............................... 6600.00
Blinking Eye, St. Nicholas, Holding Toys, Bronze Finish Cast Iron, 14 In. 10450.00
Blinking Eye, Toby, Man In Top Hat, Striped Trousers, Cast Iron, 16 1/2 In................ 2650.00
Bracket, Chiming, Brass Face, Carved Acanthus Leaves, Grapevines, Oak, 24 In......... 635.00
Bracket, Regency, Brass Dial, Fusee Movement, Inlaid Mahogany, 20 x 27 In. 3100.00
Brass, Spherical Form, 2 Lions Support, Candelabra, 9-Light, 3 Piece 715.00
Bronze, Figural, Man & Woman, Holding Branch, France, 1900s, 35 In. 1195.00
Bronze Dore, Marble, Mounted Cupids, Le Roy, Paris, c.1850 .... 3750.00
Caldwell, E.F., Desk, Gilt Dolphins, Marble Base, Swiss Movement, 1910, 7 In. 445.00
Calendar, 8-Day, Time & Strike, Rosewood Veneer, Paper Label, B.B. Lewis, 32 In. .. 1210.00
Carriage, Brass, Beveled Glass, Porcelain Face, Mercury Pendulum, France, 10 In. 165.00
Carriage, Duverdry & Bloquel, Brass, Beveled Glass, Key, 2 1/2 x 3 x 4 In. 290.00
Carriage, Repeater, Porcelain Dial, France, Brass, 7 In.. 1925.00
Chadwick, Clock Top, New Hampshire, 30 In.. 4600.00
Desk, H. Bohm, Silver, Enamel, Oval, Pelican Wing Supports, c.1885, 7 3/4 In. 2645.00
Desk, Kem Weber, Digital, Copper, Brass Bands, Lawson, c.1933, 3 1/2 In. 385.00
Elaner, Elijah, Wall, Mahogany, Tiger Maple, Paper Label, c.1855, 34 1/4 In.............. 3025.00
Empire, Bronze, Gilt, Ebony, France, 20 In.. 2250.00
F. Ripponden, Tall Case, Federal, Mahogany, Pierced Fretwork, 91 1/2 In. 6900.00
Federal, Tall Case, Pine, Gothic Arch, Above Glazed Door, Waisted Case, 88 In. 805.00
Figural, Archer, Gilt Bronze & Marble, Louis Philippe, 26 1/2 In.............................. 4025.00
Figural, Smokey The Bear, Plastic, Wall 225.00
Figural, Statue Of Liberty, Bronze... 85.00
Figural, Statue Of Liberty, Waving Flag, Tin Lithograph.. 95.00
G. Raub, Alarm, Reverse Painted Glass... 45.00
George Nelson, Wall, Asterisk, Battery Operated, Howard Miller, 1950s, 10 In. 495.00
George Nelson, Wall, Spun Brass, Conical Markers, Howard Miller, 1950s, 14 In. 385.00
Gilbert, Cottage, Small Reverse Painting... 375.00
Gilbert, Mantel, Ebonized Wooden Case, 1870s, 11 x 16 In... 70.00
Gilbert, Mantel, Faux Marble, Brass Feet & Face, c.1900 .... 130.00
Gilbert, School, Oak 100.00
Gilbert, Steeple, Walnut... 210.00
Gilbert Rohde, Table, Round, Chrome, Cylindrical Feet, H. Miller, 1930s, 6 In........... 467.00
Gilbert Rohde, Table, Z-Shaped Chrome Bar, H. Miller, 1933, 12 1/2 In. 7150.00
Girandole Shape, Ornate, Wall, France, 40 In. 880.00
Girl, Teaching Time To Doll, Germany, 10 In. 30.00
Gruby, Edward, Round Framed Gallery, Gilt Frame, Drop Strike, Round 3300.00

◆◆◆◆◆◆◆◆◆◆◆◆◆◆◆◆◆◆◆◆

Put about 15 inches of plastic "popcorn" in the bottom of your tall case clock cabinet. The weights sometimes fall, damaging the bottom boards, and this will solve the problem before it happens.

◆◆◆◆◆◆◆◆◆◆◆◆◆◆◆◆◆◆◆◆

Clock, Louis XV Style, Boulle, Dore, France, 19th Century

Gustav Becker, Tall Case, Open Well, c.1900	1700.00
Hoadley, Mantel, Painted Dial, Reverse Painted Tablet, Upside Down Works, 26 In.	2200.00
Howard, Arabic Numerals On Round Face, Dark Wood, 7 Ft.	3100.00
Howard, Wall, Keyhole	3200.00
Howard, Wall, Model 58, c.1880, 62 1/2 In.	3950.00
Howard & Davis, Banjo, Rosewood, 30 In.	1815.00
Indian, Green & Red, Neon	1895.00
Ingraham, Calendar, Ionic, Gold Paint At Rims, 8-Day, Walnut Veneer, 30 In.	825.00
Ingraham, Capitol Dome, Gingerbread, Oak	300.00
Ingraham, Paper Face, Hour & Half-Hour Strike, 8-Day, 15 1/2 In.	200.00
Ingraham, Wall, Arched Case, String & Diamond Inlay, 8-Day, 16 In.	60.00
International, Time, Oak Case	395.00
Ithaca, Calendar, Shelf, Silver Trim, Label, Mahogany Case, 20 1/4 In.	198.00
Ithaca, Wall, Scroll Cut Case, Round Calendar Face, 26 In.	175.00
J. Barnish, Tall, Mahogany, Musical, Rochdale, England, 1820	3400.00
J.B. Benoits, Louis XV Style, Cartel, Round Enamel Dial, 34 1/2 In.	4885.00
J.C. Brown, Shelf, 8-Day, Eglomise Panel, Rosewood, Mahogany, c.1855	2300.00
J.H. Potter, Bracket, Carved Oak	2500.00
Jacob Geiger, Scroll Top, Fluted Quarter Columns, 30-Hour	7000.00
James McCabe, Regency, Bracket, c.1805	1750.00
Japy Freres, Elephant, Bronze & Ormolu, 23 In.	3300.00
Jerome, Calendar, Perpetual, Walnut, 32 In.	2045.00
Kennard, C., Handle, Can Shape, Leather Case, c.1882	2200.00
Kirke,Charles, Pillar & Scroll, Reverse Painted Federal Farm House, 29 In.	2200.00
Liberty, Tudric, Pewter, Cast Trees, Bowed Triangular Face, A. Knox, c.1905, 9 In.	2090.00
Louis XV Style, Boulle, Dore, France, 19th Century............*Illus*	6000.00
Lux, Black Alligator	175.00
Lux, Black Man Polishes Lady's Shoes	150.00
Lux, Black Man, Alarm	115.00
Lux, Cuckoo, Keebler	45.00
Lux, Doghouse, Scotty Dog's Head Moves	300.00
Lux, Figural, Black	275.00
M. & S. Wherly, Skeleton, Brass, White Marble Base, Sunderland, England, 15 1/2 In..	977.00
Mantel, Biedermeier, Fruitwood, Ebonized, Parcel Gilt, Eagle, Figural Supports	1840.00
Mantel, Boulle, Louis Philippe, De La Garde A Paris	522.00
Mantel, Bronze, Brass Cylinder, Striking, Late 19th Century, France, 28 1/2 In.	880.00
Mantel, Charles X, Ormolu, Woman, Seated Top, c.1825, 16 1/2 x 12 3/8 In.	1155.00
Mantel, Double Figure, Moreau, Bronze & Gilt, France, 22 x 9 x 19 In.	2450.00
Mantel, Empire, Ormolu, Bookshelf, Children Reading, Moinet Eline A Paris, 15 In.	3737.00
Mantel, Empire, Ormolu, Hero, Hound, Seated Couple, c.1810, 25 1/4 x 9 1/2 In.	9550.00
Mantel, Empire, Ormolu, Patinated Bronze, Cupid, Dog, Enameled Dial, 18 1/2 In.	7475.00
Mantel, French Empire Style, Alabaster & Bronze, Samuel Marti, 1900, 19 1/4 In.	405.00

Mantel, Gilt Metal, Bronze, Florals, G. Beal, France, c.1920, 13 In. 300.00
Mantel, Gilt, Patinated Bronze, Charles X, 14 In. 517.00
Mantel, Louis Philippe, Ormolu, Patinated Bronze, Winged Putti, Thomire A Paris 3450.00
Mantel, Louis XV Style, Porcelain, Gilt, France, 19th Century, 17 1/2 In. 460.00
Mantel, Louis XV, Ormolu Mounted, Black & Gilt Japanned, Cartouche Shape 2085.00
Mantel, Louis XVI, Allegorical Group, Ormolu, Marble, Enameled Dial, 13 1/4 In. 5750.00
Mantel, Louis XVI, Cupid, Woman, Dove, Ormolu, Marble Base, 16 In. 5175.00
Mantel, Napoleon III, Rosewood, Fruitwood, C.F. Cronier, Paris, 16 1/2 In. 1850.00
Mantel, Neoclassical, Fossilized Marble, Ormolu, Block Feet, Russia, 19 1/2 In. 3737.00
Mantel, Ormolu, Sevres Pattern Porcelain, Berthoud, Paris, 17 x 15 1/2 In. 7825.00
Mantel, Ornate Gilt Iron Frame, Black Enameled, 19th Century, 9 1/4 In. 175.00
Mantel, P.H. Mourey, Louis XVI Style, Gilt Metal, Painted Porcelain, 19 In. 345.00
Mantel, Pierre-Philippe Thomire, Empire, Ormolu Mounted, 15 1/2 x 20 In. 9000.00
Mantel, Psyche With Eros, Bronze, Dore, White Marble, 31 x 22 x 10 In. 7700.00
Mantel, Sitzendorf, 4 Seasons 2200.00
Mantel, Tilden Thurber, Black & Red Marble, Enameled Face, Eastlake, France, 12 In. 198.00
Mueller, Cherub Figural, Gold Paint 450.00
National Clock Co., Wall, Mission, Hour Strike 200.00
New Haven, Art Nouveau Woman On Base, Small 55.00
New Haven, Banjo, Federal Style, Time & Strike, 41 1/2 In. 230.00
New Haven, Gingerbread 160.00
New Haven, Mantel, Onyx, Portico Form, Paper Face, Arabic, Second Hand, 7 3/4 In. . 175.00
New Haven, Octagon Gem, Rosewood, 8-Day, 17 1/4 In. 115.00
New Haven, Regulator, 8-Day, No Strike 425.00
New Haven, Rosewood Veneered Case, 14 x 11 In. 145.00
New Haven, School, Calendar, Strike, Long Drop 495.00
New Haven, Shelf, Rosewood Veneer, Eglomise Glass, Paper Label, 12 In. 72.00
New Haven, Shelf, Rosewood Veneered Case, 14 In. 143.00
Owen, Tall Case, Domed Top, Brass Finials, Painted Dial, Mahogany Case, 86 In. 1550.00
Paul Frankl, Mantel, Telechron, Brushed Silver, Chrome, Enamel, 1929, 5 x 3 x 8 In. . 775.00
Paul Frankl, Mantel, Warren Telechron Co., Silver, Brass, Bakelite, c.1930 .... 1850.00
Petel & Co., Empire Style, Ebonized Portico, 18 In. 230.00
Pirisma, Rectangular Chrome Case, Electric Works, 7 1/2 In. 315.00
Portico, Charles X, Black & White Marble, Ormolu, Paris, 18 x 10 1/2 In. 1210.00
Portico, Louis Philippe, Ebonized, Ormolu, Architectural Case, 19 1/4 In. 630.00
Regulator, Empire, Mahogany, Ormolu Griffins, Paris, c.1810, 21 1/2 x 11 1/2 In. 8050.00
Regulator, Mahogany, Carved, Ebonized Trim, Pendulum & Key, 39 In. 220.00
Regulator, Walnut, Neoclassical Mask Design, Weight Driven, N.Z. Kirch, 42 1/2 In. . 385.00
S. Guiguichon, Urn Shape, Gilt Bronze, Square Foot, c.1925, 12 In. 4025.00
Samuel Terry, Pillar & Scroll, Federal, Mahogany, c.1825, 30 x 17 1/2 In. 2990.00
Sawin & Dyer, Banjo, Mahogany, Scroll Front Lyre, Eagle Top 1540.00
Sessions, Horse, 12 In. 60.00
Sessions, Kitchen, Teapot Shape, Red, 1950s 20.00
Sessions, Little Red Riding Hood, Bluebird 275.00
Sessions, Mantel, Reclining Classical Woman, Arabic Numbers, 16 x 6 x 16 1/4 In. 58.00
Sessions, Swimming Fish, Light-Up 395.00
Seth Thomas, Art Deco, Red, Gold, Electric 30.00
Seth Thomas, Banjo, Federal Style, 28 In. 225.00
Seth Thomas, Bell-Over Model 1540.00
Seth Thomas, Bell-Under Model 880.00
Seth Thomas, Calendar, Double Dial, Weight Driven, Rosewood 1250.00
Seth Thomas, Empire, Crystal Regulator 275.00
Seth Thomas, Mantel, Aesthetic, Ebonized, Carved Friezes, Inlaid, 15 In. 600.00
Seth Thomas, Mantel, Black Wood, Red Marble 145.00
Seth Thomas, Mantel, Mahogany, 8 1/2 x 15 1/4 In. 35.00
Seth Thomas, Mantel, Mahogany, Eglomise Panel, Striking, Rectangular, 10 x 14 In. . 77.00
Seth Thomas, Pillar & Scroll, Reverse Painted Lakeside House, Boat, 32 In. 1815.00
Seth Thomas, Railroad Engineer's 295.00
Seth Thomas, Shelf, Split Turned Columns, Reverse Painted, Mahogany, 25 In. 145.00
Seth Thomas, Ships Bell, 8-Day, Silvered Face, Bronze Base, 23 In. 632.00
Seth Thomas, Wall, Gilded Glass Door, Hour Strike, 20 In. 60.00
Seth Thomas, Wall, Oak, 30-Day, 24 In. 660.00
Shelf, Cherubs, Porcelain Face, French Style, Cast Metal, New Haven U.S.A., 10 In. 115.00

Clock, Tall Case, Walnut,
Arched Hood, Flower
Spandrels, 1775, 92 In.

Clock, Wall, Federal,
Mahogany, Giltwood,
Eglomise, 1835, 43 In.

Shelf, Louis XV Style, Boulle, Dore, Paris, France, 39 1/2 x 18 In. 7900.00
Shelf, T.M. Roberts, Classical, Mahogany, Gilt, Paint, Connecticut, 33 In. 316.00
Singing Bird, On Wirework Tree, Painted Landscape, Gilt & Enamel 9600.00
Skeleton, Bronze Face, Black Belgian Marble, Columns, c.1815, 20 In. 1322.00
Skeleton, Gothic Cathedral, Double Fusee, Chain Drive, England, c.1880 .... 1490.00
Southern Calendar Clock Co., Shelf Or Hanging, Double Dials, Pat. 1875, 32 In. 345.00
Tall Case, Allen, Bonnet, Free Standing, Columns, Curly Birch, Steel Face, 84 In. 770.00
Tall Case, Benjamin Swan, Mahogany, 19th Century, 92 In. 4400.00
Tall Case, Bradford, Georgian, Mahogany, 30-Hour, Painted Face, 95 In. 1155.00
Tall Case, Broken Arch Pediment, Hand-Painted Face, Eagle Finial, Scotland 935.00
Tall Case, Broken Arch Top, 8-Day, Painted Metal Dial, Moon Phase, Penna. 6100.00
Tall Case, D & W Morice, Brass Works, London, 82 In. 1870.00
Tall Case, Edward Smith, Georgian, Lacquered, Date Aperture, 90 x 16 In. 5775.00
Tall Case, Federal, Grain Painted, Waisted Case, Glazed Door, 81 3/4 x 22 1/2 In. 690.00
Tall Case, Federal, Mahogany Inlay, John Baily, c.1795, 94 1/2 In. 9200.00
Tall Case, Federal, Painted Metal Dial, Paneled Door, Mahogany, 89 In. 1495.00
Tall Case, Georgian Provincial, Painted Dial, 30-Hour, c.1780, Otelli, Buckingham 880.00
Tall Case, Gilbert, No.18, Regulator, Mercury Pendulum 6800.00
Tall Case, Griffin Reyment, Brass Face & Dial, Oak Case, 81 In. 880.00
Tall Case, Herschede, Moon Phase, Pewter Face, Mahogany, 85 1/2 In. 1840.00
Tall Case, Herschede, Walnut, 5 Tubes 1000.00
Tall Case, J. Brunner, Regency, Oak, 1830, 86 In. 1650.00
Tall Case, James Black, Mahogany, 8-Day, Peterhead, England, c.1830, 82 In. 2420.00
Tall Case, James Peterson, George III, Chinoiserie, Banff, 90 In. 2185.00
Tall Case, Mahogany, Chippendale Style, Brass & Silver Face, Moon Dial, 97 In. 1760.00
Tall Case, Mahogany, Domed Door, Reeded Quarter Columns, French Feet, 87 In. 1100.00
Tall Case, Mahogany, Fan & Line Inlaid Design, Moon Phase Dial 3190.00
Tall Case, Mahogany, Veneer, 8-Day, Scrolled Bonnet, Pillars, c.1860, England 1700.00
Tall Case, Maple, Wooden Movement, c.1820, 84 In. 1092.00
Tall Case, Mission Oak, Quartersawn Oak, Side Shelves, Leaded Glass Door, 76 In. 770.00
Tall Case, Oak, Arched Pediment, Moon Phase, Germany, 20th Century, 22 In. 1210.00
Tall Case, Oak, Glass Door, Beveled Edge, Brass Face & Works, 86 1/2 In. 440.00
Tall Case, Pennsylvania Dutch, Finials, Hand Painted Face 3500.00
Tall Case, Ransbottom, George II, Hall, Green, Lacquered, Silver Chapter Ring 4950.00
Tall Case, Ridgway, Acorn Finials, Gilt Moon Face Dial, Oak, 86 In. 460.00
Tall Case, Riley Whiting, Grain Painted, Bonnet 1485.00
Tall Case, Samuel Mauss, Seconds, Calendar, Painted Dial, c.1810, 89 In. 6900.00
Tall Case, Seth Thomas, Wooden Works, 1840s, 92 In. 3850.00
Tall Case, Smith Paterson, Mahogany, Victorian, Chiming, 94 In. 2875.00
Tall Case, Songbird & Foliate Spandrels, 30-Hour Wooden Movement, 16 x 12 In. 690.00
Tall Case, T.S. Gainsboro, Oak, Broken Pediment, Roman & Arabic, Striking, 84 In. ... 863.00

Tall Case, Thomas West, Calendar Window, 8 Bells, Bracket Feet, 1830s, 103 1/2 In. . 5750.00
Tall Case, Walnut, Arched Hood, Flower Spandrels, 1775, 92 In........................... *Illus* 12650.00
Tall Case, Waltham, Mahogany, Arched Bonnet, Moon Phases, 7 Ft. 10 In.................. 8580.00
Tall Case, Whiting, Wooden Works, Decorated Face, c.1840 .... 1800.00
Tall Case, Wooden Works, Grain Painted, New England, c.1825, 82 In. 1150.00
Terry, Eli, Pillar & Scroll, Shelf, Eglomise On Lower Panel, Brass Finials................... 750.00
Terry, Eli, Pillar & Scroll, Shelf, Quarter Columns, Pineapple Finial 750.00
Terry, Eli & Samuel, Painted Dial, Reverse Painted Mt. Vernon, 30 In. x 30 In............ 517.00
Terry & Andrews, Mantel, Beehive, Metal, Mother-Of-Pearl Design, 16 In.................. 387.00
Terry & Andrews, Mantel, Ogee, 30-Hour, Time & Strike, Mahogany, 26 In. 130.00
Thomas, Regency, Bracket, Brass Inlaid, London, c.1825, 16 In.................................. 1210.00
Tiffany clocks are listed in the Tiffany category
Wall, Federal, Mahogany, Giltwood, Eglomise, 1835, 43 In............................... *Illus* 4025.00
Wall, Mahogany, Turned Half Columns, Porcelain Face 440.00
Wall, Mission Oak, Lyre Shape, 31 In. 99.00
Wall, Regulator, Walnut, Viennese, 19th Century... 825.00
Waterbury, Kitchen, Gilt Designed Glass Door... 170.00
Waterbury, Shelf, Porcelain, Floral Garlands, Gold, Chimes 225.00
Welch, Alexis, 30-Day.. 1100.00
Welch, Calendar, Brass Rimmed Glasses, 8-Day, Time & Strike, Walnut, 20 In. 605.00
Welch, Spring & Co., Shelf, Beehive... 585.00
Willard, Shelf, Mahogany, Satinwood Veneer 31000.00
Woman Bowler, Trophy, Bakelite 65.00
Wood & Hudson, Tall Case, Rosettes Around Brass Face, 8-Day, c.1790, 93 In. 4250.00

CLOISONNE enamel was developed during the tenth century. A glass enamel
was applied between small ribbons of metal on a metal base. Most cloisonne
is Chinese or Japanese. Pieces marked *China* are twentieth-century examples.

Ashtray, Red Floral, White Cloud Ground, 2 Rests, China, 4 1/2 In............................ 26.00
Bowl, 4 Running Foo Lions, 4 Horses Interior, Blue Ground, 7 3/4 In. 2415.00
Bowl, Black Clouds With Pink Flowers, Green Leaves, Turquoise, China, 3 1/2 In. 20.00
Bowl, White Flowers, Leaf Border, Red Scrolls, Teak Stand, 4 3/8 x 2 In. 28.00
Box, Fields Of Grain, Mt. Fuji, Ando Jubei, Rectangular, 6 1/8 In. 1760.00
Box, Gold Wire Bird, Flying Moonlit Sky, Japan, Round, 2 5/8 In............................. 1100.00
Box, Hinged Cover, Floral Spray, 4 Ball Footed, 3 1/2 x 3 x 1 1/2 In....................... 35.00
Box, Pink, Brown, 6 1/2 x 3 1/2 In.. 325.00
Charger, Polychrome, Phoenix, Floral Lappets, China, 14 1/2 In............................... 550.00
Clock, Porcelain Face & Side Panels, Painted, People's Republic Of China, 11 In. 110.00
Goose, Cover, Black, Blue, Pink, White, Rust, 15 x 7 In., Pair.................................... 465.00
Hat Stand, 19th Century, 12 In.. 585.00
Jar, Potpourri, Green & Gold, Wooden Stand.. 175.00
Lamp, Multicolored Floral Design, Green, Blue, Black Ground, Japan, 12 x 24 In. 148.00
Napkin Ring, Berries, Flowers With Leaves On Geometric Background, Pair 45.00
Plate, Birds & Flowers, Multicolored, Turquoise Ground, Japan, 12 In. 350.00
Tray, Multicolored Floral & Dragon Design, Round, 11 3/4 In. 80.00
Urn, Yellow & Red Birds, Landscape, Black Ground, Japan, 12 In. 4600.00
Vase, Allover Flowers, Multicolored, 9 1/4 In... 100.00
Vase, Chrysanthmum Design, Pale Green Ground, Seed Form, 19th Century, 5 In. 125.00
Vase, Flowers, China, 10 1/2 In.. 150.00
Vase, Flowers, Red, Yellow, Blue With Green Foliage, China, 3 In............................. 15.00
Vase, Goldfish & Water Lilies, Red Ground, Japan, 7 In.. 71.00
Vase, Pigeon Blood Ground, Yellow Daisies, c.1930, 7 1/2 In. 1035.00
Vase, Pinch Neck, Yellow Ground, 8 In... 145.00
Vase, Trumpet, Blue & Green Morning Glory, Red, Kichisaburo, 2 1/2 In. 935.00
Vase, White & Lavender Mums, Small Flowers, Green Interior, 8 3/4 In., Pair 595.00

CLOTHING of all types is listed in this category. Dresses, hats, shoes, underwear, and more are found here. Other textiles are to be found in the Coverlet,
Movie, Quilt, Textile, and World War I and II categories.

Apron, Hostess, Ecru, Lacy Openwork, Pink 6.00
Apron, Hostess, White Lace Corners, Blue Stitched Edge, Pocket................................ 6.00
Apron, Work, Check Gingham, Blue & White... 50.00
Bandanna, Red Cotton, White Factory Picture, Lee Work Clothes, 1950s, 21 x 23 In... 85.00

Belt, Leather, Metal Eyelets, 40-46 In. 10.00
Belt, Silver Link Chain, Whiting & Davis 16.00
Bloomers, Gym, Blue Wool, 1900s 40.00
Blouse, Aqua, Rayon, Button Down Back Short Sleeves, Embroidered Neck, 1940s 3.00
Blouse, Beaded, Gold Satin, Sleeveless, Scoop Neck, 2-In. Border 32.00
Blouse, Crocheted, Off-White, Short Sleeves, Scalloped, Size 36 .... 6.00
Blouse, Embroidered, Pin Tucks, Lace Trim, High Neck 68.00
Blouse, Ivory Rayon, Sleeveless, Collarless, Lace Edge, Sorority Girl, Size 34 .... 5.00
Blouse, Lace, Long Sleeves, Black, c.1920 .... 25.00
Blouse, Sheer Print, Stylized Flowers, Black & White Stripes, Size 15-16 .... 5.00
Blouse, Silk, Charles Jourdan 12.00
Blouse, Velvet, Black, Bows, Embroidered, Early 1900s 5.00
Blouse, White Rayon, Short Sleeves, Delicate White Paisley Loops, 1940s 3.00
Boots, Cowboy, Polychrome & Appliqued, Azure Ground, 1950s, Size 7 .... 180.00
Boots, Cowboy, Polychrome & Appliqued, Black Ground, 1950s, Size 6D 180.00
Boots, Cowboy, Polychrome & Appliqued, Brown & Rust, 1940s, Size 10 .... 180.00
Camisole, Crocheted Yoke, 1900s 50.00
Camisole, Crocheted Yoke, Drawstring, 1890s 60.00
Cap, Miner's, Attached Lantern, Coal King, Canvas, Leather, Brass, c.1927 .... 220.00
Cape, Beaded, Organdy Trim, Lace, c.1860 .... 880.00
Cape, Burgundy Wool, 1900s 10.00
Christening Gown, Lace & Tulle Over Cotton, c.1870 .... 172.00
Christening Outfit, C.1885 .... 75.00
Cloak, Sister's, Violet Wool, Silk Brocade Lining, Labeled The Dorothy 715.00
Coat, Baby's, c.1902, 25 In. 75.00
Coat, Evening, Black Velvet, 1930s 100.00
Coat, Lambskin, New Zealand, 3/4 Length 55.00
Coat, Man's, Charcoal Wool, Hart, Schaeffner & Marx 35.00
Coat, Persian Lamb, With Muff & Pillbox Hat, 3 Piece 175.00
Coat, Square Collar, Soutache Embroidery On Sleeves & Hem, Purple 340.00
Collar, Bib Or Yoke, Crocheted, Bone, Squared Bottom, Flowers, Leaves, 13 1/2 In. 18.00
Collar, Crocheted, Full Circle For Yoke, Wide Scoop Neck, 1-In. Scalloped Lace Edge ... 2.00
Collar, Crocheted, Off-White, Threaded, Floral Open Sections, 14 x 3 3/4 In. 9.00
Collar, Crocheted, Off-White, With Cuffs, 4 In. 2.00
Collar, Crocheted, Rosy Rust, Threaded, Fancy Lace Stitch, 3 1/2 x 12 In. 5.00
Collar, Dotted Cotton, White, Wide Square Yoke 2.00
Collar, Eyelet, Pink, Floral, Ruffled Eyelet Edge 2.00
Collar, Jeweled, Graduated Pearls, Silver Lining, Silver Metallic Thread, 2 In. 5.00
Collar, Pearls, Divided Front, Adjustable Hook Closure, 13 In. 8.00
Collar, Pearls, Satin Backing, Heavy, Hook/Eye Front, 1 1/4 In. 9.00
Collar, White Cotton, 2 Sections, 8 1/2 x 3 In. 2.00
Collar, White Cotton, 3-D Petals In Front, Lace Edge, 3 In. 4.00
Collar, White, Ecru, Lace Rose At Points, Round Lapels, 1/2-In. Border 2.00
Dickey, Lace, White, Collar & Front 3.00
Dickey, Nylon Organza, White Eyelet Floral Embroidery, Bib Front, 13 1/2 x 12 1/2 In. ... 3.00
Dickey, Nylon Organza, White, Lace Edge Ruffle, Front & Back 2.00
Dickey, Organza, Black, Looped Lace, Low V-Neck 5.00
Dickey, Sheer Black Rayon, Gold Sequins, Ruffled, V-Neck 5.00
Dress, Ball, Pale Butter Yellow, Silk Chiffon, Crinoline, Maggy Rouff, 1957 .... 6958.00
Dress, Beaded, Brown Silk, 1920s 65.00
Dress, Black Rayon Crepe, Scoop Neck Front, Sleeveless, 1940s, 31 In. 10.00
Dress, Black Rayon Crepe, Squared Scoop Neck, Full Satin Lining, 1940s, 28 In. 10.00
Dress, Black Silk, Lace, Bustle 60.00
Dress, Black, Heavy Satin Black Poppies, Sleeveless, Floor Length, Size 14 .... 12.00
Dress, Brown, Long Chiffon Sleeves, Rounded V-Neck, Floor Length 10.00
Dress, Child's, Pin Tucked, 1860 .... 58.00
Dress, Cream Silk, Trailing Lace Point In Back 85.00
Dress, Evening, Beads, Sequins, 1920s 350.00
Dress, Evening, Silk, Velvet, Embroidered, Rhinestones, Beaded, Schiaparelli 6958.00
Dress, Flapper, Beaded, Red, 1930s .... 155.00 to 175.00
Dress, Flapper, Black Lace, Tassels, 1926 .... 160.00
Dress, Flapper, Black, Purple Beading, Floor Length 35.00
Dress, Flapper, Metallic Lace, Green Velvet Trim 98.00

Dress, Floral Print, High Ruffled Neck, Long Sleeves, Floor Length, 26 In................... 8.00
Dress, Garden, Chiffon, Tiered Skirt, 1920 .... 90.00
Dress, Gold, Chanel, 1960s 495.00
Dress, Plastic Mesh, Paco Rabanne, 1967 .... 725.00
Dress, Prairie, Expandable Under-Bodice For Use When Pregnant, 1880 .... 195.00
Dress, Purple Velvet, Luster Beads In Intricate Design 258.00
Dress, Satin, Battenburg Lace Collar, c.1860 .... 650.00
Dress, Sheath, Pink Linen, Sleeveless, Cutwork, Flowers Down Front, Size 18 .... 6.00
Dress, Wedding, Duchesse Lace, Organdy Puff Sleeves, 19th Century 2700.00
Dress, Wedding, Ivory, 1950, Size 5-6 .... 500.00
Duster, Man's, Horsehide & Horsehair 110.00
Gloves, Crocheted, 1940s 65.00
Gloves, Fingerless, Green Mesh, 1930s 25.00
Handkerchief, Crocheted, White Lace Edge .... .75
Handkerchief, Framed, Columbian Exposition, Chicago, 1892, 25 3/4 x 26 1/2 In........ 165.00
Handkerchief, White & Yellow Embroidered Flowers, Fruit Of Loom 3.00
Handkerchief, White Lace, Gray Pink Orchid, Leaves, Fruit Of Loom, 6 In. 3.00
Handkerchief, White, Applique Flowers, Dainty Embroidered Lace 8.00
Handkerchief, White, Colored Crocheted Border.. .50
Handkerchief, White, Threaded, Embroidered Lace .... .75
Hat, Black, Large Brim, 1910 .... 90.00
Hat, Child's, Beaver, Bent & Bush, Paper & Silk Lining, Iron Buckle 130.00
Hat, Child's, Velvet, Midnight Blue 65.00
Hat, Confederate States Of America, Felt & Leather, Pettibone Bros. 165.00
Hat, Good Humor Man, 1930s 50.00
Hat, Indiana Jones Type, Felt, Stetson, Size 7 1/2 .... 18.00
Hat, Man's, Seal, Black 15.00
Hat, Mink, Light Brown, Sewed On Combs... 9.00
Hat, Pillbox, Mink, Beige, Allover Swirled Stripes, Sewed On Combs 8.00
Hat, Pillbox, Rust Satin, Brown Velvet, Veil 3.00
Hat, Robinson Crusoe, Black, Pelts On Stiff Mesh 10.00
Hat, Salvation Army, 1900s... 45.00
Hat, School Safety Patrol, AAA, Blair County Motor Club 30.00
Hat, Sheared Beaver, Black.. 10.00
Hat, Sheared Beaver, Tall Beret Type, Beige, Brown Satin Band 12.00
Hat, Stovepipe, Dunlap & Co.. 48.00
Hat, Straw, Ostrich Feathers, 1880s 68.00
Hat, Top, Beaver Skin, Case 70.00
Hat, Tricornered, Black Curly Fur 10.00
Hat, Woman's, Edwardian, Beaver Plush, Feather Trim 65.00
Hat, Woman's, Picture, Straw, Flower, 1930s 35.00
Hat & Collar, Leopard, Bun Warmer Type, 2 Piece... 40.00
Jacket, Combing, White Linen, Lace Inserts 75.00
Jacket, Encrusted With Jet Beading, Black, Short 400.00
Jacket, Flight, Leather, Patches, American 175.00
Jacket, Flight, Soyuz 23 Mission, Suit & Union Suit, Russia, Oct. 1976, 3 Piece.......... 5463.00
Jacket, Motorcycle, Brown, Harley-Davidson, Medium 95.00
Jacket, Vanson Motorcycle, Harley Patch On Back, Size 42..................................... 195.00
Jacket & Muff, Mole Fur, Gray & Brown, 2 Piece 65.00
Kimono, Gilt Dragon Design, Magenta Silk, Embroidered, China, 56 In. 198.00
Muff, Child's, Black Seal 5.00
Muff, Mink 37.00
Pantaloons, Embroidered Edges, Cotton, 1900s 125.00
Pantaloons, Split Crotch, Lace... 20.00
Petticoat, Amish 330.00
Playsuit, Child's, Drop Seat, 1930s 12.00
Poncho, Hooded, Red Plaid, Fringed.. 12.00
Robe, Dragon, Chinese Silk, 19th Century... 405.00
Robe, Embroidered Silk, Floral, Bird, Dragon & Bat, China, 56 In. 400.00
Robe, Sleigh, Foxes, Glass Eyes 250.00
Robe, Sleigh, With Stag, Victorian 200.00
Robe, Woven Bands, Silk Velvet, Overall Palmettes, Mid-19th Century...................... 4312.00
Romper, Gym, 1920s.. 40.00

Clothing, Suit, Penguin, Russian Space,
Blue, 12/10/82, Salyut 7

◆◆◆◆◆◆◆◆◆◆◆◆◆◆◆◆◆◆◆◆◆

Don't hang valuable old clothing on hangers. This puts a strain on the shoulders. Store clothing flat or folded on a shelf.

◆◆◆◆◆◆◆◆◆◆◆◆◆◆◆◆◆◆◆◆◆

◆◆◆◆◆◆◆◆◆◆◆◆◆◆◆◆◆◆◆◆◆

Stuff hats with acid-free tissue for storage. Try to make the stuffing deep enough so the hat brim does not touch the shelf.

◆◆◆◆◆◆◆◆◆◆◆◆◆◆◆◆◆◆◆◆◆

Sailor Suit, Child's, Black Wool, Size 1	45.00
Sailor Suit, Child's, Gabardine, With Hat, Size 3, 1940	65.00
Shawl, Silk, Black, Embroidered, Fringe	75.00
Shawl, Silk, Cream, Crocheted, Fringe	65.00
Shirt, Homespun, Brown & White, 35 In.	137.00
Shoes, 2 Buckles, Civil War	300.00
Shoes, Baby's, White, 3 Buttons	35.00
Shoes, Boy's, High Top, Black, Unused	75.00
Shoes, Child's, High Button, Dark	85.00
Shoes, Child's, High Button, Red Leather, 5 In.	68.00
Shoes, Platform, Alligator, Adrian, 1940s	80.00
Shoes, Toddler's, Leather, Cutout, Button Strap	40.00
Shoes, Woman's, High Top, Brown	57.00
Skirt, Gibson Girl, Sport, White Linen	70.00
Skirt, Hula, Girl's, Woven Grass, Vegetable Dyed, 1940s, 17-In. Waist	125.00
Skirt, Poodle Type, Felt, Chess Game Design	75.00
Spats, Gray Felt, Bond Street Box	20.00
Spats, Taupe	25.00
Stole, Mink, Autumn Haze	60.00
Suit, Child's, Brown Linen, 2 Piece	58.00
Suit, Leisure, Man's, Rust, Polyester, 1970s	50.00
Suit, Man's, Brown Tweed, Jaymar	20.00
Suit, Penguin, Russian Space, Blue, 12/10/82, Salyut 7 ....*Illus*	4600.00
Suit, Walking, Black Brocade Skirt, Crepe Bodice, Leg-A-Mutton Sleeves	190.00
Suit, Woman's, Norell, 1959	450.00
Suit, Woman's, Rayon, Black & White, 1935	60.00
Sweater, Ivory Wool, Beaded, Lined, Flowers At Neck, Cuffs & Front	28.00
Sweater, Mother-Of-Pearl Sequined Scrolls Bugle Beads, Light Blue Pearls, Size 42	24.00
Swimsuit, Woman's Red & White Striped, 1920s	45.00
Swimsuit, Woman's, Wool, 1920s	50.00
Uniform, Campfire Girl, Book, c.1922	50.00
Vest, Crocheted, Orange, Yellow & White Ombre, V-Neck, 28 In.	5.00

CLUTHRA glass is a two-layered glass with small air pockets that form white spots. The Steuben Glass Works of Corning, New York, made it after 1903. Kimball Glass Company of Vineland, New Jersey, made Cluthra from about 1925. Victor Durand signed some pieces with his name. Related items are listed in the Steuben category.

Lamp, Original Finial, Green, 21 In.	375.00
Vase, Amethyst, Steuben, 10 1/2 In.	1100.00
Vase, Blue, Steuben, 8 In.	1300.00

Vase, Classical Form, Dark Blue, Steuben, 8 In.	1300.00
Vase, Kimball, 8 x 7 In.	175.00
Vase, Monart, Orange-Red, 10 x 7 In.	250.00
Vase, Mottled Lavender, Trapped Bubbles, Steuben, 6 3/4 In.	430.00
Vase, Red & Yellow, Silver Mark, 7 In.	395.00
Vase, White, Signed, 4 In.	300.00

COALPORT ware has been made by the Coalport Porcelain Works of England from 1795 to the present time. Early pieces were unmarked. About 1810–1825 the pieces were marked with the name *Coalport* in various forms. Later pieces also had the name *John Rose* in the mark. The crown mark has been used with variations since 1881. The date 1750 is printed in some marks but it is not the date the factory started.

BONE   CHINA
COALPORT
MADE IN ENGLAND
EST. 1750

Bowl, Bird Of Paradise, White Ground, 19th Century, 11 1/2 In.	345.00
Bowl, Soup, Apple Green Border, Raised & Fired Gold Edge, 9 1/2 In., 12 Piece	805.00
Bulb Pot, Cover, D-Shaped, Purple Winged Cupid, c.1810, 8 5/8 In.	1035.00
Candelabrum, 4-Light, Figural, Bacchanalian Figures, Applied Floral Design, 17 1/2 In.	115.00
Cup & Saucer, Bluebird	49.00
Cup & Saucer, Cardinal, Demitasse, 16 Piece	110.00
Cup & Saucer, Flowerpot, After Dinner	40.00
Cup & Saucer, Japan Pattern, c.1800	185.00
Cup & Saucer, Jewels On Gold Ground, Miniature	135.00
Desert Set, Botanical, Green Border, 2 Compotes, 9 In., 16 Piece	3000.00
Figurine, Christine, Green Flowing Dress, Signed, 7 3/8 In.	85.00
Fruit Cooler, Cover, Gilt Handles, Floral Springs, c.1805, Pair	1725.00
Holder, Place Card, Flowered, 16 Piece	80.00
Jardiniere, Stand, Tapering Cylinder, Shepherds & Sheep, c.1810, 5 5/8 In.	460.00
Plate, Dragon In Compartments Pattern, Green Ground, 1805, 4 Piece	1265.00
Plate, Japan, Iron Red Ground, Leafy Branches, c.1815, 12 Piece	2300.00
Plate, Mythological, Life Of Cupid, c.1805, 9 1/2 In., 6 Piece	2013.00
Plate Set, Desert, Blue, Yellow, Red Green & Pink Floral, With Platter, 1840, 11 Piece	985.00
Rose Bowl, Ming Rose	25.00
Soup, Dish, Gilt Floral & Geometric Design, 10 In., 10 Piece	575.00
Sucrier, 2 Scrolled Handles, Blue Banding, Gold Trim, 7 1/2 In.	165.00
Tea Set, Blue, Red, Gold Flowers, Leaves, White Ground, 3 Piece	225.00
Tea Set, Dark Blue, Red, Gold Flowers, Green Leaves, White Ground, 1 1/2 In.	225.00
Teapot, Landscape, Sepia, 6 1/2 In.	440.00
Tureen, Soup, Cover, Circular, Gilt Bands, Flowers, c.1810, Pair	2875.00

COBALT BLUE glass was made using oxide of cobalt. The characteristic bright dark blue identifies it for the collector. Most cobalt glass found today was made after the Civil War.

Decanter, Stopper, Cut To Clear, Everted Rim, Starburst, Thumbprint, 15 3/4 In.	242.00
Decanter Set, Enameled Flowers, Gold Trim, Bohemian, 7 Piece	50.00
Jar, Grape & Leaf Design, 9 1/2 In.	24.00
Platter, Cut To Clear, Thumbprint, Diamonds, Fans, Starburst, Round, 14 In.	220.00
Snack Set, Capri, Seashell Swirl, 8 Piece	32.00
Sugar, 12 Diamonds, Applied Petals On Foot, Blown, 4 1/2 x 4 In.	110.00
Vase, Cover, Man & Woman Scene Panel, Metal Mount, 16 In.	225.00
Vase, Ruffled, Ribbed Interior, 6 In., Pair	65.00

COCA-COLA was first served in 1886 in Atlanta, Georgia. It was advertised through signs, newspaper ads, coupons, bottles, trays, calendars, and even lamps and clocks. Collectors want anything with the word *Coca-Cola*, including a few rare products, like gum wrappers and cigar bands. The famous trademark was patented in 1893, the *Coke* mark in 1945. Many modern items and reproductions are being made.

Ashtray, Metal, Red, 1960s, 4 1/2 In.	8.00
Ashtray, Wood Grain, 1960s, 4 1/2 In.	10.00
Bank, Cardboard, c.1960, 4 In.	5.00
Bank, Santa Claus, Mechanical, Trains Moves As Santa Lifts Bottle To Drink	30.00
Bank, Vending Machine, Linemar	700.00
Banner, Winter Scene, Paper, 18 x 56 In.	195.00

Blotter, Man & Woman, 1929 .... 75.00
Bottle, 75th Anniversary, Amber .... 8.00 to 12.00
Bottle, Altoona, Pa., Christmas, 6 Oz. 15.00
Bottle, Commemorative, Rockies, 1993 .... 4.00
Bottle, Jackson, Tenn., 75th Anniversary, Brown, Contents 15.00
Bottle, Macon, Ga., 1918 .... 25.00
Bottle Cap, Magnetic, Red, White, Package, 3-In. Diam. 8.00
Bottle Opener, Flat Handheld Design, Logo, 1960s 7.00
Bottle Opener, Wall Mount, Cast Iron 5.00
Calendar, 1923, Woman With Bottle 450.00
Calendar, 1924, Smiling Girl, Holding Glass, Frame 750.00
Calendar, 1927, Woman, Holding Glass 1500.00
Calendar, 1947, Wholesome Woman, Skiing, Sunglasses, Complete 275.00
Calendar, 1954, Pause, Refresh, 2 Months On Sheet, Athelete 75.00
Calendar, 1959, Teenaged Girl, 2 Months On Sheet 165.00
Calendar, 1971, Page A Day Type 12.00
Can, Washington Redskins Super Bowl XXVI Champs, Contents 5.00
Cap, Baseball, Adult Size, 1950s 18.00
Card, Playing, Airplane Silhouettes, World War II, 1943, 4 Decks 855.00
Card, Playing, Woman Drinking Coca-Cola, USPC Co., Ohio, 1915 .... 3100.00
Card, Playing, WWII Airplane Spotter 98.00
Carrier, 6-Bottle, Aluminum, Bottles, 1950s 62.00
Carrier, 6-Bottle, Yellow, With Wings, 1940s 95.00
Carrier, Wooden, Yellow & Red 60.00
Clock, 1910, Gilbert Regulator, Oak 1700.00
Clock, 1950s, Round 185.00
Clock, 1950s, Silver & Red, Round 150.00
Clock, 1959, Golden Girl, Bottle, Light-Up, Metal, Glass 200.00
Clock, 1960, Counter, Light-Up 525.00
Clock, Ingraham, Regulator, Pressed Oak, Red Lettering 1300.00
Coaster, World's Fair, Cardboard, 3-D, 1939, 5 In. 35.00
Coin-Operated Machine, Jacobs 26 Coke 2000.00
Coin-Operated Machine, Vendo, 1939 .... 1750.00
Comb Set, Drink Coca-Cola 5 Cents, Red Comb, Metal Nail File 3.00
Cookbook, Coca-Cola, Pause For Living, Summer, 1955 .... 5.00
Cookie Jar, Coke Can, McCoy, Box 150.00
Cookie Jar, Polar Bear 125.00
Cooler, 2 Doors, Westinghouse, 1939 .... 275.00 to 495.00
Cooler, Canvas 12.00
Cooler, Vendorator, Model UMC44, 5 Cent, 57 x 15 1/2 In. 4500.00
Dart Board, Frame, 1943, Square, 15 In. 70.00
Dispenser, Cornellis, Light-Up Fishtail Sign 250.00
Dispenser, Syrup, Delicious & Exhilarating, Urn Shape, 11 x 20 In. 2200.00
Display, Snowman, Cardboard, 1942 .... 850.00
Door Push, Steel, Red Letters, White Ground, 24 In. 90.00
Flashlight, Bottle Shape 125.00
Fly Swatter, Wooden Handle, Wire Mesh, 1942 .... 6.00
Game, Bingo, 1940s, Contents, Box .... 50.00 to 55.00
Game, Bingo, Drink 60.00
Glass, Christmas, Holly Hobbie, Holding Sprig Of Holly 3.50
Glass Set, Snow White, Pinocchio, Fantasia & Peter Pan, Canada, 1980s, 4 Piece 50.00
Handkerchief, Kit Carson, 1953, 20 x 22 In. .... 50.00 to 60.00
Hat, Baseball, Felt, 1950 .... 18.00
Hat, Soda Jerk, Things Go Better With Coke, Logo, 1950s 10.00
Kayak, Blow-Up, Manager's Incentive, Box, 1970s 125.00
Lighter, Bottle Shape 17.50
Lunch Box, 2 Handles, Metal 25.00
Marble, Giveaway, Mesh Bag, 1960s 16.00
Menu Board, Wooden, 3 x 2 Ft. 500.00
Napkin, Bottle Picture, Paper 1.00
Paper Cup, Unused, c.1960 .... 20.00
Pencil, Bullet 8.00
Pencil Sharpener, Bottle Shape, 2 In. 30.00

Pillow, 3 x 11 x 13 In. 25.00
Pitcher, Water, Dallas Cowboys, Green 25.00
Plane, 1929 Model, Lockheed Vega Air Express, Yellow, Red, Box 24.00
Postcard, International Truck, 1940s, 7 1/2 x 4 In. 10.00
Poster, 1960, 20 x 36 In. 90.00
Poster, Coca-Cola Float, 1962, 9 x 20 In. 5.00
Poster, Man, Popping Cap, Sandwich On Plate, Paper, 20 x 12 In. 330.00
Punch Board, 1940, 7 x 8 In. 10.00
Radio, Bottle Shape, AM, 1976, Box 37.00
Radio, Cooler Shape, 1949, 7 x 12 x 9 1/2 In. 650.00
Rain Coat, Size 7 .... 20.00
Ruler, Wooden, 12 In. 4.00
Sailboat, Coke Is It, Fiberglass, 12 Ft. 275.00
Sign, Canadian, Paper, Star Wars Characters 65.00
Sign, Cap, Bottle, White, Porcelain, 24 In. 375.00
Sign, Christmas Bottle, 1930s, 36 In. 1000.00
Sign, Coca-Cola For Passover, Fishtail Logo, 18 x 18 In. 20.00
Sign, Coke Float, Neon 285.00
Sign, Coke Headquarters, People At Refrigerator, Cardboard, 16 x 21 In. 600.00
Sign, Coke, 72 In. 450.00
Sign, Coke, Take Home A Carton, 1938, 10 x 15 In. 21.00
Sign, Delicious & Refreshing, 1932, 3 x 5 In. 750.00
Sign, Drink Coca-Cola In Bottles, Celluloid, Multicolored, Button Shape, 9 In. 9.00
Sign, Drink Coca-Cola, Bottle, Embossed Tin, 6 x 13 In. 350.00
Sign, Drink They All Expect, Boy & Girl, Paper, 13 x 22 In. 575.00
Sign, Enjoy Coke, Red, White & Silver, Metal, 1965, 24 x 24 In. 40.00
Sign, Fountain Service, Porcelain, 12 x 42 In. 300.00
Sign, Hot Dog, 3-D, Cardboard Cutout, 1932 .... 600.00
Sign, In Bottles, 5 Cents, Embossed Tin, 1922 .... 650.00
Sign, Mom Knows Her Groceries, Girl At Refrigerator, Cardboard, 29 x 50 In. 900.00
Sign, Old Dispenser Picture, Porcelain, 27 x 28 In. 585.00
Sign, Pause That Refreshes, Girl Leaning On Table, Cardboard, 20 x 36 In. 650.00
Sign, Please Pay When Served, Thank You, Reverse Glass, Round, 11 In. 550.00
Sign, Refresh Yourself, Cardboard, 12 x 20 In. 450.00
Sign, Santa Claus, Lionel Train, Countertop, 1960, 24 In. 248.00
Sign, Santa Claus, Sleeping Boy, Toy Trains, Cardboard, 23 1/2 In. 138.00
Sign, Santa Claus, With Elves, Christmas, 22 x 12 In. 100.00
Sign, So Refreshing, Drink Coca-Cola, Girl, Cardboard, 27 x 56 In. 475.00
Sign, Thirst Knows No Season, Man, Woman, Snowman, Cardboard, 29 x 50 In. 750.00
Sign, World War II Scene, Cardboard, 1943, 13 x 14 In. 35.00

Coca-Cola, Tray, 1908, Topless Girl,
Highball & Gin-Rickies, 12 In.

◆ ◆ ◆ ◆ ◆ ◆ ◆ ◆ ◆ ◆ ◆ ◆ ◆ ◆ ◆ ◆ ◆ ◆ ◆ ◆

Moving is a collector's nightmare. Rolls of paper that schools use to cover lunch tables are best. Cut the paper to different sizes before starting to pack. Put paper plates between plates. Wrap saucers 10 to 15 together at one time. Put paper napkins between the cover of a teapot and the upside down lid. Toilet paper tubes are good holders for mustard spoons or ladles. Disposable diapers are best for large items.

◆ ◆ ◆ ◆ ◆ ◆ ◆ ◆ ◆ ◆ ◆ ◆ ◆ ◆ ◆ ◆ ◆ ◆ ◆ ◆

Table, Card, 1930 .... 125.00
Thermometer, Bottle Shape, Tin Lithograph, 1950s, 17 In. ....25.00 to 80.00
Thermometer, Drink Coca-Cola, 5 Cents, Wooden, 1915, 21 x 5 In. 275.00
Thermometer, Drink, 6 1/2 In. 20.00
Thermometer, Silhouette Girl, Porcelain, 1940s, 6 1/2 x 16 In. 450.00
Tip Tray, 1903, Hilda Clark, 6 In. ....825.00 to 995.00
Tip Tray, 1907, Drink Coca-Cola, 5 Cents 150.00
Tip Tray, 1907, Girl, With Glass, Cocoa Beans On Rim, 6 x 4 1/4 In. 330.00
Tip Tray, 1909, Girl, With Large Hat, Oval, 4 3/8 x 6 1/8 In. ....550.00 to 700.00
Tip Tray, 1913, Girl, With Glass 550.00
Tip Tray, 1914, Betty, Oval, 4 3/8 x 6 1/8 In. 440.00
Tip Tray, 1917, World War I Girl, 4 3/8 x 6 1/8 In. 400.00
Tongs, Ice, All Metal, 1940s 325.00
Toy, Car, Volkswagen Van, Red & White, 1/43 Scale, Box 25.00
Toy, Truck, Bottling, Steel, Rubber Wheels, 2 Bottles, Metalcraft, 1932, 11 In. 230.00
Toy, Truck, Boy, Heavy Tin, Marx, 1940s, 21 In. 250.00
Toy, Truck, Corgi, No. 95, 1978, 3 In. 15.00
Toy, Truck, Delivery, Buddy L, 1979, 5 In. 20.00
Tray, 1903, Hilda Clark, Round, 9 1/4 In. 4500.00
Tray, 1905, Lillian Nordica, 10 1/2 x 13 In. 1500.00
Tray, 1908, Topless Girl, Highball & Gin-Rickies, 12 In. ....*Illus* 13200.00
Tray, 1914, Betty, 10 1/2 x 13 1/4 In. 330.00
Tray, 1931, Barefoot Boy, With Dog, 10 1/2 x 13 1/4 In. ....350.00 to 425.00
Tray, 1938, Girl In Afternoon ....125.00 to 225.00
Tray, 1939, Springboard Girl, 10 1/2 x 13 1/4 In. 195.00
Tray, 1941, Girl Ice Skater, 10 1/2 x 13 1/4 In. ....200.00 to 345.00
Tray, 1942, Girl Standing Next To Auto, 10 1/2 x 13 1/4 In. 70.00
Tray, 1955, Girl With Menu, 10 1/2 x 13 1/4 In 40.00
Tray, 1961, Pansy Garden, 10 1/2 x 13 1/4 In. 12.00
Truck, Pressed Steel, Metal Wheels, Marx, 20 In. 465.00
Umbrella 25.00
Watch Fob, Strap Type 130.00
Yo-Yo 8.00

COFFEE GRINDERS of home size were first made about 1894. They lost favor by the 1930s. Large floor-standing or counter-model coffee grinders were used in the nineteenth-century country store. The renewed interest in fresh-ground coffee has produced many modern electric and hand grinders, and reproductions of the old styles are being made.

Adams, Cast Iron 225.00
Arcade, Lap Model 105.00
Arcade, No. 4, Glass Hopper, Wall Mount 85.00
Ceramic, Glass, Wooden Base, Germany, 15 1/2 In. 72.00
Clark, Cast Iron, Salesman Sample, Brass Trim, Painted, February 17, 1842 .... 475.00
Dutch Windmill Scene, Blue, White Ground, Wall Mount ....45.00 to 65.00
Elgin, Double Wheel, 18 In. 230.00
Elgin National, Edwards Co., Cast Iron, 28 In. 525.00
Elgin National, Original Paint 500.00
Elgin National, Twin Wheel, Store, Floor Mount 350.00
Enterprise, Cast Iron Wheels, Wooden Base, Small Drawer, 15 1/2 In. 375.00
Enterprise, Drawer In Front, Wooden Handle, 12 1/2 x 8 In. 185.00
Enterprise, Eagle, Pat. 1873, 72 In. 3850.00
Enterprise, No. 2, 2 Wheels 650.00
Fairbanks & Morse, Pat. 1889 .... 600.00
Grand Union, No. 1, Factory Scene, Tin, Wall Mount 165.00
Griswold, Original Paint 995.00
Hobart, Porcelain Case, Lighted Glass Front, Electric, Commercial 325.00
Holwick, Green, Electric 60.00
Kitchen Air, Model A-O, Glass Top, Electrical, 1937 .... 140.00
Landers, Frary & Clark, 2 Wheels, Counter Type, 1880 .... 1200.00
Landers, Frary & Clark, New Britain, Conn., 2 Wheels 325.00
Landers, Frary & Clark, No. 20, 8-In. Wheel 950.00
Leinbrock Ideal 40.00

National Specialty, Cast Iron, Philadelphia, Wall Mount 85.00
Parker, Wall Mount, Tin & Cast Iron 45.00
Red & Black Tin, Lithograph, Red Tin Cup, Wall Mount 70.00
Simmons Hardware, Koffee Krusher, 2 Wheels 1800.00
Swift Mill, Lane Brothers, Red & Black Paint, c.1870, 20 In. 1250.00
Wooden, Cast Iron Fittings, 7 1/2 In. 198.00

COIN SPOT is a glass pattern that was named by the collectors for the spots resembling coins, which are part of the glass. Colored, clear, and opalescent glass was made with the spots. Many companies used the design in the 1870–1890 period. It is so popular that reproductions are still being made.

Castor, Pickle, Cranberry Opalescent, Grapes & Vines Frame 650.00
Compote, Amber, 8 1/2 In. 30.00
Cruet, Ring Neck, Blue 125.00
Pitcher, Blue, 9 In. 98.00
Sugar Shaker, Ring Neck Mold 250.00
Sugar Shaker, Tapered, Blue 145.00
Syrup, Silver Plated Top, Clear Handle 245.00
Tumbler, Ruby, 3 5/8 In. 40.00

COIN-OPERATED MACHINES of all types are collected. The vending machine is an ancient invention dating back to 200 B.C. when holy water was dispensed in a coin-operated vase. Smokers in seventeenth-century England could buy tobacco from a coin-operated box. It was not until after the Civil War that the technology made modern coin-operated games and vending machines plentiful. Slot machines, arcade games, and dispensers are all collected. An important collection of rare coin-operated machines was sold this year for record prices and some of these are listed.

Band Box, Miniature Figures With Instruments, 1950, 28 In. 8625.00
Baseball, Marble Rolls Down Chute, Batter Swings, 10 Cent 100.00
Baseball, Williams 2200.00
Bubble Gum, Space, Spacegun Shape, 6 For 1 Cent 175.00
Bull's-Eye Baseball, Chicago's Coins 225.00
Candy, Mills, Windmill, Floor Model, Oak Case, 1 Cent, 1920, 20 In. 2587.00

Coin-Operated Machine, Doctor Vibrator,
1 Cent, Iron, Watling, 96 x 45 In.

Coin-Operated Machine, Fortune Teller,
Enchantress, Oak, 1925, 80 In.

Card Vendor, Western Theme, John Wayne, 1950s 22.00
Chocolate, Wilbur's Sweet Clover, Ryede, Oak Case, 1912, 35 In. 1840.00
Cigar, Zinc Bust, Black Man, Whistles, Moves Eyes, 1895, 69 In. 7475.00
Cigarette, U-Need-A-Pack, 8 Rotating Columns, 54 In. 345.00
Coin Changer, Wall Mount, Have A Coke, 5 & 10 Cent, 1950, 15 In. 805.00
Collar Button, 6 Columns, 10 Cent Coin Slot, 1905, 10 1/2 In. 1035.00
Condom Dispenser, Harmon, 25 Cent 125.00
Condom Dispenser, Masters 1475.00
Condom Dispenser, Prophy Decal, 6 Doz. Condoms, 25 Cent 100.00
Derby Roll, Horse Race, Wooden Case 600.00
Digger Claw, Crane, Stutz, Yankee, Iron Base, 1 Cent, 1920, 41 In. 8035.00
Digger Claw, Exhibit, Floor Stand, 1 Cent, 1920s, 70 In. 1955.00
Digger Crane, 1930s .... 1250.00 to 2600.00
Doctor Vibrator, 1 Cent, Iron, Watling, 96 x 45 In. .... *Illus* 26450.00
Drink, Golden Orangeade, Countertop, Hungerford Smith, 5 Cent 920.00
Electric Shock, Advance, Brass Grip Handles, 1 Cent, 1925, 13 In. 800.00
Fortune Teller, Enchantress, Oak, 1925, 80 In. .... *Illus* 12650.00
Fortune Teller, Genco, Gypsy Grandma, 10 Cent, 76 In. 2185.00
Fortune Teller, Mills, Wizard, Aluminum Front, c.1919, 1 Cent, 1919 .... 1265.00
Fortune Teller, Mills, Wizard, Moving Pointer, c.1910, 16 1/2 In. 575.00
Fortune Teller, Mills, Wizard, Wooden, 1904 .... 475.00
Game, Bean 'Em, Ristaucrat Mfg., Wooden, 5 Cent 975.00
Grip Tester, Uncle Sam, 1 Cent, Iron, 1904, 66 In. .... *Illus* 17250.00
Gum, Adams, Du Greiner 150.00
Gum, California Fruit & Pepsin 700.00
Gum, Chicklets, Dentyne, Mills, 4 Columns, Wall Mount, 1915, 30 In. 57500.00
Gum, Columbus, Model L, Cast Iron, Figural Door, 16 1/2 In. 7150.00
Gum, Happy Jap, Gum From Mouth, 1 Cent, 1902, 13 In. 3162.00
Gum, Masters, White Porcelain, 1 Cent 195.00
Gum, National Auto Vending Machine Co., Model G, 1 Cent, 17 x 17 In. 325.00
Gum, Northwestern, Quarters 36.00
Gum, Pulver Kola Pepsin 3300.00
Gum, Pulver, HotChu, 1900s 175.00
Gum, Pulver, Porcelain Sided, 1 Cent For 2 Chews, 24 In. 715.00
Gum, Scoopy 1675.00
Gum, Taffy Tolu, Colgan, Red Face Plate, Metal 3100.00
Gum, Tutti-Frutti, Adams, 1 Cent, Mirror At Top 1600.00
Gum, Wilbur-Suchard 400.00
Gum, Yellow Kid, Pulver, Animated, Kid Pushes Gum, 1925, 20 In. 575.00
Gum, Zeno, Clockwork, Oak Case, 1 Cent, 17 x 10 In. 440.00
Gum, Zeno, Yellow Porcelain, 1 Cent 320.00
Gumball, 5 Star Baby Grand, Oak Case 75.00
Gumball, Acorn, Oak 50.00
Gumball, Atlas Master, 1954, 16 In. 90.00
Gumball, Baby Grand, Oak Case, Restored, 1940s 100.00
Gumball, Bluebird, 1920s, 14 x 7 In. 120.00
Gumball, Ford's, 1950, 14 In. .... 75.00 to 140.00
Gumball, Hart 65.00
Gumball, Marvel, 11 In. 160.00
Gumball, Watling, 1 Cent .... 2195.00 to 2695.00
Handkerchiefs, Men's, 10 Cent, 1920-1930 .... 77.00
Honor Box, Pipe Tobacco Or Snuff, England, Brass 402.00
Horse Race, Dice, Kentucky Derby, 5 Cent, Metal Case, 1930, 11 In. 230.00
Ice Water, Cup Dispenser, Cast Iron, 1 Cent, 1910, 63 In. 2185.00
Kotex, Thin Model, 10 Cents 125.00
Lighter Fluid, Gas Pump Shape, Kautz Van-Lite, 1 Cent, 1930, 19 In. 575.00
Lung Tester, Hats Off, 1 Cent, Oak, 1905, 96 In. .... *Illus* 43125.00
Lung Tester, How Many Lamps Can You Light, Gasser, 1 Cent, 1898 .... 6325.00
Match, Advance, Glass Dome, Cast Iron, 1 Cent, 18 In. 550.00
Match, Glass Dome, Oak Case, Cigar Cutter Attachment, 1 Cent 165.00
Match, Wooden Ware Co., Cat Iron, 1910 .... 375.00
Music Box, Caille, New Century, 5 Cent, 64 In. 10450.00
Mutoscope, Child's, Metal Drum Case, Floor Stand, 42 In. 1150.00

Coin-Operated Machine,
Grip Tester, Uncle Sam,
1 Cent, Iron, 1904, 66 In.

Coin-Operated Machine,
Lung Tester, Hats Off, 1 Cent,
Oak, 1905, 96 In.

Coin-Operated Machine,
Perfume Lady, Papier-Mache,
Full Size, 98 In.

Mutoscope, Shoot-O-Matic, Chromed Target, 5 Cent, 1930s..................................... 4025.00
Mutoscope, Tin Viewer, 5 Cent, Marque, Early 1900s ....1150.00 to 1955.00
Nut, Hot Nuts, Challenger... 400.00
Nut, Smilin' Sam From Alabam', Aluminum, 1 Cent, 1931, 11 In. 1265.00
Peanut, Columbus, Porcelain, 5 Cent 170.00
Peanut, Dean, 1 Cent... 80.00
Peanut, Northwestern, No. 60 .... 50.00
Peanut, Spanish, Vendex.. 175.00
Peanut, Tall Glass Globe, Acorn, 1950s.. 75.00
Peanut & Candy, Sunburst, Caille, Cherub Legs, c.1908, 21 In. 8050.00
Pencil, With Your Embossed Name, C. Weeks, 5 Cent, 1920, 22 In. 402.00
Penny Flip, Rainbow, Jennings, 5 Payout Jackpots, 1930, 20 In. 1150.00
Perfume, Bull's Head, Pull Horns To Dispense, 1904, 16 In. 3162.00
Perfume, Perfumatic, 4 Coin Slots, 10 Cent, Wall Mount, 1930, 16 In. 460.00
Perfume Lady, Papier-Mache, Full Size, 98 In.............................. *Illus* 18400.00
Perfume Your Handkerchief, Mills, 1 Cent, c.1916, 17 In. 3450.00
Pinball, Aerial Photograph, Chicago Fair, 10 Balls, 5 Cent 1035.00
Pinball, Bally, Delta Queen 475.00
Pinball, Bally, Fireball... 1870.00
Pinball, Bally, Triumph, 1939.. 950.00
Pinball, Gottlieb, Spin Out.. 475.00
Pinball, Jennings, Sportsman, Payout, 42 x 43 In. 355.00
Pinball, Rock-Ola, World's Fair, Floor Model, 1933... 2300.00
Pinball, Star Fair, Electric.. 125.00
Pinball, Whiffle, Countertop, 10 Balls, 5 Cent, 1930s, 36 In. 575.00
Polyphon, Disc, Burled Walnut, 79 In. 7975.00
Postcard, Exhibit Ideal, Wooden Case, 1 Cent, 12 In. 345.00
Ride, Elephant, Child's... 2475.00
Scopitone, Video, 36 Color & Sound Film Sections, 25 Cent, 79 In. 575.00
Shooting Gallery, Spaceship Targets, W.A. Tratch 2000.00
Slot, American Indy Driving.. 400.00
Slot, Baker's Pacer, Horse Racing, 7 Slots, 5 Cent, 1930s, 40 In...................... 1610.00
Slot, Bally, Double Bell, 5 Cent.. 3295.00
Slot, Bower, Master Mechanic, 6 Slots, Floor Model, 1902, 65 In. 6325.00
Slot, Buckley, 50 Cent.. 1350.00
Slot, Bull Durham, Triple Jackpot, Gold Coin Award... 6000.00
Slot, Callie, Baseball, Cast Iron, 1 Cent 9700.00
Slot, Callie, Dough Boy, 5 Cent... 695.00

Slot, Columbus, Tri-More, Stand.. 1075.00
Slot, Jennings, Big Chief, 50 Cent, 29 In... 1150.00
Slot, Jennings, Chief, 1 Dollar.. 1950.00
Slot, Jennings, Club Special, 5 Cent.. 1750.00
Slot, Jennings, Comet, 1 Cent, England, 25 1/4 In.. 172.00
Slot, Jennings, Dutch Boy & Girl, 5 Cent... 1400.00
Slot, Jennings, Electro-Vendor... 2295.00
Slot, Jennings, Extraordinary, Aluminum Front, 10 Cent, 32 In............................. 1380.00
Slot, Jennings, Four Star, Victoria Chief, 5 Cent... 1075.00
Slot, Jennings, Golf Ball, Floor Model, 25 Cent... 4995.00
Slot, Jennings, Little Duke, 3 Reel, 1 Cent, 21 In... 1150.00
Slot, Jennings, Peacock, 5 Cent... 1995.00
Slot, Jennings, Prospector, Stand, 1 Dollar.. 4495.00
Slot, Jennings, Rol-A-Top, Castle Front, 5 Cent... 3900.00
Slot, Mills Dewey, Upright... 10000.00
Slot, Mills, 1920s... 1450.00
Slot, Mills, Blue Bell, 50 Cent.. 1800.00
Slot, Mills, Castle Front, 10 Cent.. 1950.00
Slot, Mills, Diamond Front.. 1200.00
Slot, Mills, Futurity, 5 Cent... 3500.00
Slot, Mills, Goldenfalls, 5 Cent.. 1495.00
Slot, Mills, High Top, 10 Cent.. 18.00
Slot, Mills, High Top, 3 Reel, 23 In.. 690.00
Slot, Mills, High Top, 5 Cent.. 1800.00
Slot, Mills, Horsehead Bonus, 10 Cent... 1750.00
Slot, Mills, Lion Front, 5 Cent.. 1795.00
Slot, Mills, Little Kuke, Oak Cabinet, Decals, 5 Cent... 1800.00
Slot, Mills, No. 12, Gold Design, 24K Gold Plated.. 5995.00
Slot, Mills, Roman Head, 3 Reel, 5 Cent, 1932, 26 In... 1955.00
Slot, Mills, Silver Dollar, Stand-Up Console.. 3995.00
Slot, Mills, Skyscraper, 5 Cent.. 1495.00
Slot, Pace, Kitty, 10 Cent... 3995.00
Slot, Rol-Let... 400.00
Slot, Standard Chief, 10 Cent, Jennings... 1100.00
Slot, Watling, Baby Lincoln, 5 Cent.. 1795.00
Slot, Watling, Rol-A-Top, 1930s... 4800.00
Slot, Watling, Rol-A-Top, Cherry, Diamond Bell Model, 5 Cent............................ 4900.00
Slot, Watling, Treasury, 1 Cent.. 4495.00
Slot, Watling, Treasury, Twin Jackpot, 3 Reel, 5 Cent, 1936, 24 In.................... 3162.00
Stamp, American Banner, Aluminum Front, 5 Cent, 1915, 18 1/2 In................... 2185.00
Stamp, U.S. Mailbox, With Scale, Tin Lithograph 25.00
Stamp, Uncle Sam, 1 Cent, 17 In.. 220.00
Stamp, Uncle Sam, Tin Marquis, Iron Base, 5 Cent, 21 x 11 1/2 In..................... 412.00
Strength Tester, Practical Joke, Water, Powder & Cap, 19 In............................... 805.00
Strength Tester, Tiger Tail Pull, Roars, 5 Cent, 1925, 64 In................................. 6900.00
Trade Stimulator, Fairest Wheel, Penny Drop, 1895, 22 In.................................. 1610.00
Trade Stimulator, Fairest Wheel, Roulette, Cigars, 17 1/2 In............................... 460.00
Trade Stimulator, Liberty, 5 Cent.. 475.00
Trade Stimulator, Mills, Perfection, Upright, 1901... 1750.00
Trade Stimulator, Waddel Bicycle Wheel 900.00
Viewer, Mills, Girlie Drop Cards, Counter Model, 1904... 1100.00
Weight & Fortune, Watling, Mirror Front, Oak Case, 1 Cent, 77 In...................... 1600.00

COLLECTOR PLATES are modern plates produced in limited editions. Some
may be found listed under the factory name, such as Bing & Grondahl, Royal
Copenhagen, Royal Doulton, and Wedgwood.

Anri, Anniversary, 1981.. 79.00
Anri, Christmas, 1978 ....67.00 to 115.00
Artaffects, Pocahontas, Perillo, 1981... 50.00
Avon, Christmas, 1973.. 35.00
Avon, Christmas, 1974.. 15.00
Avon, Christmas, 1975, Box... 10.00
Cast Art Ind., Steve Garvey, Hackett, 1982 .... 150.00

Gorham, Letter To Santa, Rockwell, 1980 .... 40.00
Gorham, No Swimming, Rockwell, 1974 .... 65.00
Gorham, Santa Plans His Visit, Rockwell, 1981 .... 40.00
Hadley, Coming Home, Redlin 59.00
Hadley, Evening Retreat, Redlin 39.00
Hummel, Golden Tranquillity, Schmid, 1978 .... 34.00
Rorstrand, Sailing Home, Fisherman, Christmas, G. Nyland, 1969 .... 17.00
Royal Devon, Doctor & Doll, Rockwell, 1975 .... 75.00
Schmid, Caroling, 1975 .... 15.00
Schmid, Santa's Surprise, 1979 .... 15.00
Schmid, Sneak Preview, Christmas, 1983 .... 15.00
Schmid, Valentine's Day, Charles Schulz, Box, 1980 .... 15.00
Viletta, Algonquin, Zolan, 1983 .... 50.00
Viletta, Christie's Kitty, Zolan, Box 23.00
Viletta, Touching The Sky, Zolan 19.00

COMIC ART, or cartoon art, is a relatively new field of collecting. Original comic strips, magazine covers, and even printed strips are collected. The first daily comic strip was printed in 1907. The paintings on celluloid used for movie cartoons are listed in this book under Animation Art.

Book, High Chaparral No. 1, Gold Key, 1968 .... 8.00
Book, Jetsons No. 6, Gold Key, 1963 .... 10.00
Book, Linus The Lionhearted No. 1, Gold Key, 1965 .... 25.00
Book, Orange Rider No. 8, Dell, 1955 .... 10.00
Book, Peter Potamus No. 1, Gold Key, 1964 .... 12.00
Book, Supercar No. 2, Gold Key, 1962 .... 65.00
Book, Wagon Train No. 5, Dell, 1960 .... 2.00
Book, Yakky Doodle & Chopper No. 1, Gold Key, 1962 .... 12.00
Book, Zorro, Dell, 1955 .... 15.00
Drawing, Bugs Bunny, Tasmanian Devil, Warner Bros., 1960, 9 x 10 In., 2 Piece 690.00
Drawing, Dumbo, Peering Out From Fallen Tent, Walt Disney, 1942, 8 3/4 In. 748.00
Drawing, Flash Gordon, Pen & Ink, Alex Raymond, Sept. 5, 1937 .... 8625.00
Drawing, Li'l Abner, Pencil, Al Capp, 15 x 17 In. 4950.00
Drawing, Prince Valiant, Pen & Ink, H. Foster, Dated Jan. 28, 1940, 34 x 26 In. 10925.00
Drawing, Snow White & Seven Dwarfs, Grumpy 750.00
Drawing, Snow White & Seven Dwarfs, Happy, 1937, 10 x 12 In. 345.00
Lithograph, An Orchestra Of Stars, Hanna & Barbera, 18 x 31 3/4 In. 220.00
Storyboard, Woody Woodpecker Polka, Walter Lantz, 1951, 4 x 5 In., 8 Piece 1092.00

COMMEMORATIVE items have been made to honor members of royalty and those of great national fame. World's fairs and important historical events are also remembered with commemorative pieces. Related collectibles are listed in the Coronation and World's Fair categories.

Ashtray, Pennsbury Pottery State Education, 1957 .... 40.00
Beaker, King Edward VII & Alexandria, Royal Doulton, c.1902 .... 145.00
Cuff Links & Tie Bar, Queen Elizabeth, 1930 .... 95.00
Cup & Saucer, Edward VII 30.00
Cup & Saucer, George & Elizabeth, 1937 .... 22.00
Goblet, Abraham Lincoln, Gilt & Enamel Design, 19th Century, 5 1/2 In. 345.00
Jug, In Honor Of 1840 Wedding Of Prince Albert 695.00
Plate, British Royalty Visit Canada & USA, Royal Winton, 1939 .... 20.00
Plate, Charles & Diana Marriage, July 29, 1981, Crest & Portrait, 9 3/4 In. 42.00
Plate, Edward & Alexandra, 6 In. 60.00
Spoon, Queen Elizabeth II Visits Canada, 1959 .... 50.00
Tin, Queen Elizabeth & Prince Phillip, Edward Sharp & Sons Ltd., 7 x 10 In. 15.00

COMPACTS hold face powder. A woman did not powder her face in public until after World War I. By 1920, the beauty parlor, permanent waves, and cosmetics had become acceptable. A few companies sold cake face powder in a box with a mirror and a pad or puff. Soon the compact was designed by jewelers and made of gold, silver, and precious materials. Cosmetic companies began to sell powder in attractive compacts of less valuable metal or plastic. Collectors today search for Art Deco designs, commemorative com-

pacts from world's fairs or political events, and unusual examples. Many were made with companion lipsticks and other fittings.

Art Deco, Triangular Shape, Striped, Ring Chain, Sapphire Clasp	150.00
Bluebird, Petit Point	32.00
Butterfly Wing, Iridescent Blue Wings	75.00
Central Savings Bank Of New York, Art Deco	35.00
Cigarette Case, Mother-Of-Pearl, Gold Mesh Handle, Large	38.00
Coro, Horseshoe Shaped, Black Enamel, Compartments, c.1920	150.00
Coty, Flying Colors	100.00
Djer Kiss, Nymphs Lid	65.00 to 85.00
Dorothy Gray, Hat Picture, Goldtone	65.00 to 75.00
Dresser, Military Hat Shape, Flashed Amber Glass, Mirror Lid, 5 x 4 1/2 In.	40.00
Dunhill, Clearview	95.00
Eagle, War Logo Border, Chain, c.1916	50.00
Elgin, Engraved Floral	95.00
Elgin, Gold Bands, Sterling Silver	95.00
Elgin, Gold Flower Basket, Floral Sprays, Sterling Silver	42.00
Elgin, Musical, Anniversary Song, Goldtone, Fleur-De-Lis Border, Rectangular	65.00
Elgin, Rebekah, Box	25.00
Elgin, Scrolls, Glass Beadwork, Box	52.00
Elgin American, Coin	40.00
Elgin American, Mirror, 3 x 3 In.	25.00
Enamel, Blue Guilloche, 3 Pug Dogs, Sterling Silver, 2 1/2 In.	1320.00
Enamel, God Bless America	40.00
Enamel, Red Roses, Green Leaves, Fluted Edge, Marked Stratton, England	22.00
Enamel, Silver-Gilt, 3 Compartments, Diamond-Set, Russia, c.1910, 3 7/8 In.	4600.00
Enamel On Sterling Silver, Floral Design, Chain, 12 In.	695.00
Enameled Silhouette Buildings, Art Deco, Chrome, Chain Handle, 2 1/2 In.	75.00
Evans, Cigarette Case, Metal, Bronze Color, White Cloisonne Lid, c.1930	75.00
Evans, Clock On Top	75.00
Evans, Floral, Pouch, Enamel, Dark Blue, c.1948, 3 In.	95.00
Evans, Sterling Silver, Basket Weave, Pink, Yellow, 4 In.	150.00
Evans, Wrist, Carryall, Gold Metal, 6 Compartments	150.00
Finebery Pendant, Etched Bimetal, Finger Ring	72.00
Golden Gate Exposition, C.1939	45.00
Goldtone, Art Deco, Striped Lid, Metal Tassel, Chain Has Ring, June 15, 1920	45.00
Goldtone, Deer	48.00
Henrette, Enamel Basket	70.00
Illinois, Inset Watch	110.00
Jules Richard, Tan To Brown Enamel, Red Cabochon Stone, Rhinestone Circle	25.00
Lucite, Etched Floral Design, 1940s	45.00
Majestic Roulette, Brass, Wheel	110.00
Map Of Hawaiian Islands, 1950s	48.00

Compact, Silver Plated, Cane Handle, c.1925

◆ ◆ ◆ ◆ ◆ ◆ ◆ ◆ ◆ ◆ ◆ ◆ ◆ ◆ ◆ ◆ ◆ ◆

To remove old protective lacquer from a piece of silver, immerse the piece in very hot water for a few hours. This should loosen the lacquer. The process may have to be repeated to get all of the lacquer off. Several commercial lacquer removers are available.

◆ ◆ ◆ ◆ ◆ ◆ ◆ ◆ ◆ ◆ ◆ ◆ ◆ ◆ ◆ ◆ ◆ ◆

Military Hat, Red, White & Blue 95.00
Mondaine, Enamel, Painted Woman Cameo, Filigree 75.00
Pendant, Floral Design, Sterling Silver, c.1905 .... 85.00
Peruvian, Aztec Design, Square, 2 In. 48.00
Revlon, Blue Stone Surrounded By Diamonds, Gold Finish, Box 40.00
Rex, Red Snakeskin, Loop Holds Lipstick, Square 36.00
Rex, Woman On Bridge Oriental Scene, Red & Blue, Gold Trim, Black Ground 45.00
Richard Hudnut, Cloth, White, Gold, Tree With Green Stones, c.1940 .... 100.00
Richard Hudnut, Double, Floral Design, Silver 55.00
Richard Hudnut, Gold, Rectangular 30.00
Royale Volupte, Hearts, Flowers, Diamonds, Felt Case 40.00
Sesquicentennial, Colored Stones In Lid, c.1926 .... 60.00
Silver Finish, Art Deco, With Chain, 3 Sections 50.00
Silver Plated, Cane Handle, c.1925 .... *Illus* 578.00
Sterling Silver, Pine Cone & Leaf, Automatic Mirror Cleaner, Georg Jensen, 2 3/4 In.. 350.00
Sterling Silver, Pink & Green Floral, Enamel On 12-In. Chain 695.00
Sterling Silver & 14K Gold, Lighter 145.00
Stork Club, 1940s ....95.00 to 110.00
T. Muto Silversmiths, Allover Birds, Flowers & Foliage 125.00
Tango, Art Deco, Green & Black 165.00
Volupte, 2 Sections, Comb, Lipstick, Original Case, 3 x 4 In. 45.00
Volupte, Black Matte Goldtone, Musical, Stardust, Slide Out Lipstick 85.00
Volupte, Jeweled 19.00
Volupte, Mirror, Sterling Silver, 4 In. 45.00
Volupte, Mother-Of-Pearl 32.00
Volupte, Musical, Lipstick Holder 150.00
Volupte, Oriental Scene, Enamel 38.00
Volupte, Woman Tennis Player, Double Sifter, Silver 55.00
Yardley, Blue Enamel Arc Designs, White, Red Clasp 25.00

CONSOLIDATED LAMP AND GLASS COMPANY of Coraopolis, Pennsylvania, was founded in 1894. The company made lamps, tablewares, and art glass. Collectors are particularly interested in the wares made after 1925, including black satin glass, Cosmos (listed in its own category in this book), Martele (which resembled Lalique), Ruba Rombic (1928–1932 Art Deco line), and colored glasswares. Some Consolidated pieces are very similar to those made by the Phoenix Glass Company. The colors are sometimes different. Consolidated made Martele glass in blue, crystal, green, pink, white, or custard glass with added fired-on color or a satin finish. The company closed for the final time in 1967.

Biscuit Jar, Diamond-Quilted, Phlox, Pink Satin 175.00
Biscuit Jar, Victorian, Silver-Plated Lid & Bail, Cranberry 300.00
Bowl, Compote, Orchids, Honey Yellow, 10 In. Diam. 130.00
Bowl, Console, Gold Traces, Line 700, 13 In. 95.00
Bowl, Mayonnaise, Iris, Honey Yellow, 6 In. Diam. 35.00
Box, Cigarette, Ruba Rombic, Lilac 80.00
Cake Plate, Iris & Bird Of Paradise, Green, 12 In. 70.00
Candleholder, Iris, Honey Yellow, 10 1/2 In., Pair 145.00
Castor, Pickle, Florals In Open Heart Arches, Frame, Tongs 335.00
Compote, Fish, Green 90.00
Condiment Set, Guttate, Cased, Pink 225.00
Cup, Dancing Nymph, Frosted 85.00
Jug, Iris, Transparent Green Over White Casing, 1/2 Gal. 850.00
Lamp, Chrysanthemum, 11 In. 175.00
Lamp, Foxglove, Blue On Satin Custard 135.00
Lamp, Lovebirds 459.00
Lamp, Parrot, Blue 549.00
Lamp, Pinecone, Cockatoo 150.00
Night-Light, Elk, 12 In. 1210.00
Night-Light, Lovebirds, 10 In. 770.00
Night-Light, Owl, 8 In. 355.00
Night-Light, Santa Claus, 9 In. 1210.00
Plate, Bird Of Paradise, Amber Wash, 8 1/4 In. 45.00

Plate, Five Fruits, Green, 8 In. 25.00
Snack Set, Five Fruits, Sundae & Tray, Pink... 45.00
Sugar Shaker, Cone.. 1235.00
Tray, Fish, Amber Stain 300.00
Tumbler, Dancing Nymph 85.00
Tumbler, Dancing Nymph, Frosted 110.00
Vase, Chrysanthemum, Sculptured Coral Flowers, Green Vines, White Ground, 12 In. . 235.00
Vase, Con-Cora, Hand Painted Violets, Gold Trim, Oval, 7 In. 50.00
Vase, Crimped, Dancing Nymph, Ruby Wash.. 200.00
Vase, Dancing Nymph, Art Nouveau, Brass Ormolu Mounted, 8 In. 325.00
Vase, Dancing Nymph, Frosted Ground, Clear Nude, Pan Center, 11 3/4 In................ 425.00
Vase, Dogwood, Green, Brown, 11 In. 125.00
Vase, Dogwood, White, 11 In... 150.00
Vase, Lovebirds, Blue On Satin Custard.. 230.00
Vase, Pinecone, Brown On Satin 80.00
Water Set, Pink Shiny Guttate, 7 Piece... 425.00
Whiskey, Ruba Rombic, Green, 2 3/4 In. 250.00

CONTEMPORARY GLASS, see Glass-Contemporary

COOKBOOKS are collected for various reasons. Some are wanted for the recipes, some for investment, and some as examples of advertising. Cookbooks
and recipe pamphlets are included in this category.

All About Cookery, Mrs. Isabella Beeton, London, 476 Pages, 1906 .... 45.00
American Woman's, Berolzheimer, 1943 .... 20.00
American's Cookbook, New York Herald, Hard Cover, 1, 032 Pages, 1944 .... 19.00
Arm & Hammer Baking Powder, Good Things To Eat, 1938.. 12.00
Barbie Easy-As-Pie, Random House, 1964 .... 45.00 to 80.00
Better Homes & Gardens, Junior Cookbook, 1963 .... 12.00
Betty Crocker, Cookbook For Boys & Girls, 1978 .... 12.00
Betty Crocker, General Mills, Illustrated, Hard Cover, 463 Pages, 1950...................... 23.00
Betty Crocker, Holidays On Parade, 1965 .... 6.00
Betty Crocker, Hostess Cookbook, Hard Cover, 1st Edition, 1967 .... 10.00
Borden, An Epicure's Book Of Cheese Recipes, 68 Pages, 1931 .... 15.00
Borden, Elsie, Envelope, 1930s... 18.00
Borden's Eagle Brand 70 Magic Recipes, 1952 .... 8.00
Brer Rabbit Molasses Recipes, 24 Pages 4.00
Buckeye Cookery, 1880 .... 75.00
Calumet Baking Powder, Baking Secrets, 1942 .... 8.00
Campbell's Cooking With Soup, 1969 .... 5.00
Campfire Marshmallows 5.00
Carnation, 1942 .... 15.00
Chiquita Banana Recipe Book, 1950 .... 6.00
Colburn's Condiment Recipes, Philadelphia, 25 Pages, 1920...................................... 3.00
Cookin' With Dr Pepper, 1965 .... 5.00
Cooking For 2, Janet M. Hill, Boston, 407 Pages, 1929 .... 25.00
Crisco Shortening, A Few Cooking Suggestions, 1928 .... 12.00
Detroit Times Cookbook, 1933... 20.00
Fashions In Foods, Beverly Hills, Will Rogers Introduction, 1930 .... 45.00
Fleischmann's Recipes, Woman With Bread Picture, 1917 .... 15.00
Freezer Cookbook, Hazel Meyer, 1970 .... 7.00
Galloping Gourmet, Graham Kerr, 286 Pages, 1969... 12.00
General Foods, Illustrated, Hard Cover, 144 Pages, 1933... 20.00
Glenwood Range Co., 72 Pages, 1933 .... 4.00
Gold Medal Flour, 1910 .... 13.00
Good Housekeeping, Illustrated, Hard Cover, Dorothy B. Marsh, 803 Pages, 1963....... 17.00
Home Comfort, Wrought Iron Range Co., St. Louis, 212 Pages, 1910 .... 20.00
How To Keep Him-After You've Caught Him-Cookbook, 1968 .... 12.00
Jell-O, New Jell-O Book Of Surprises, 1930... 14.00
Jell-O Girl Entertains, Rose O'Neill, 1914.. 50.00
Jewel Tea Company, Mary Dunbar's Favorite Recipes, 1939 .... 10.00
Joys Of Jewish Cooking, 1974... 14.00
Kerr, Modern Homemaker, Victory Canning Edition, 1943 .... 10.00

Kerr, Your Guide To Home Canning, 1938 .... 5.00
King's Daughter, Advertising, 1908 .... 35.00
Kraft, Kitchen Fresh Ideas, Marye Dahnke, Phoenix Cheese, 1931 .... 12.00
Maytag Dutch Oven Gas Range Cookbook, 1949 .... 8.00
Mennonite Community, Mary Showwalter, Illustrated, 494 Pages, 1951, 6 x 9 In. 22.00
Metropolitan Life Insurance Co., Soft Cover, 1922, 5 x 7 In. 6.00
Mrs. Curtis, 1205 Pages, 1914 .... 45.00
Mrs. Knox's Top 20 Delicious Salads & Desserts, 1942 .... 10.00
New England Cookbook, Chas. E. Brown, Boston, 286 Pages, 1905 .... 35.00
New Receipts For Cooking, T.B. Peterson, Philadelphia, 520 Pages, 1854 .... 125.00
Ocean Spray, Cape Cod's Famous Cranberry Recipes, 1941 .... 4.00
Pillsbury, 12 New Cake Recipes, Sno-Sheen, 1945 .... 8.00
Pillsbury, Best Of The Bake-Off Collection, Hard Cover, 1959 .... 30.00
Planters Oil, 1948 .... 22.00
Prudential Insurance Co., 30 Pages, 1900 .... 12.00
Rice: 200 Delightful Ways To Serve It, Southern Rice Indust., 95 Pages, 1935 .... 6.00
Roquefort, 1978 .... .75
Royal Cookbook, 1932 .... 12.00
Rumford, 1940 .... 8.00
Rumford, Pretty Girl On Cover, 1911 .... 20.00
Someone's In The Kitchen With Dinah, 1971 .... 15.00
Sperry Flour Co. Cookbook, Pre-General Mills, 1920s 15.00
Spry Shortening, What Shall I Cook Today?, 1930s 5.00
Sunkist Recipes For Every Day, 1934 .... 14.00
Teen Cuisine, Peter Max, 1969 .... 45.00
The Salad Bowl, Nucoa Shortening, 1927 .... 13.00
Treasury Of Great Recipes, Mary & Vincent Price, 1974 .... 48.00
Uneeda Bakers 6th Book Of Menu Magic, 1934 .... 6.00
Union Pacific 5.00
Velvet Cake Flour, Good Things To Eat, 1954 .... 4.00
Watkins, 1938 .... 25.00
White House, 1900 .... 65.00
White House, 1917 .... 10.00
White House, 600 Pages, 1887 .... 125.00
You Can Be A Better Cook Than Mama Was, Hard Cover, 322 Pages, 1968 .... 23.00

COOKIE JARS with brightly painted designs or amusing figural shapes became popular in the mid-1930s. Many companies made them and collectors search for cookie jars either by design or by maker's name. Listed here are examples by the less common makers. Major factories are listed under their own names in other categories of the book, such as Abingdon, Brush, Hull, McCoy, Red Wing, and Shawnee. See also the Black and Disneyana categories.

Acorn, Oakleaf Relief, Acorn Finial, Rush Basket Handle, Japan, 7 In. 16.00
Airplane With Pilot, California Originals 475.00
Ali Cat, Metlox 495.00
Alice In Wonderland, Looking Glass Cover 675.00
Alice In Wonderland, Regal .... 2650.00 to 3600.00
Apple, California Originals 75.00
Aramis Bear 130.00
Aunt Jemima, Fitz & Floyd 400.00
Avon Bear, Red Sweater, California Originals 146.00
Avon House 250.00
Baby Bluebird, On Pinecone, Metlox 185.00
Barrel Of Apples, Metlox 50.00
Baseball Boy, California Originals 35.00
Basket Handle Mammy, Maruhan Ware 750.00
Basset Dog, Metlox .... 825.00 to 975.00
Bear, American Bisque 55.00
Bear, Flasher, American Bisque 535.00
Bear, Girl, American Bisque 45.00
Bear, On Roller Skates, Metlox 125.00
Bear, With Hat, American Bisque 65.00

Cookie Jar, Casper, American Bisque

Never put your name on the mailbox. Do put the street number in reflecting numerals more than 3 inches high, in clear view. Make it easy for the police & fire departments to find your house.

Beau Bear, Metlox	65.00 to 75.00
Betsy Ross, Enesco	225.00
Billy & Dolly, Starnes	1200.00
Black Chef, Artistic Potteries	300.00
Blackboard, American Bisque	190.00
Blue Bonnet Sue	49.00
Blue Rex, Metlox	150.00
Bluebird On Stump, Metlox	250.00
Boots, American Bisque	115.00
Brown Bagger, Doranne	20.00
Brown Owl, Metlox	45.00
Buick Convertible, Gray, Appleman	800.00
Calico Cat, Metlox	200.00
Campbell Soup, Red & White	125.00
Candy Baby, American Bisque, Ungemach	325.00
Carousel, Napco, Japan	150.00
Casper, American Bisque ....*Illus*	1610.00
Cat, Gold, Regal	400.00
Cat, Kliban	275.00
Cat, On Stool, With Guitar, Kliban	225.00
Cat's Head, Metlox	125.00
Century 21, House	1500.00
Cheerleaders, Flasher, American Bisque	425.00 to 495.00
Chef, Pearl China	525.00 to 600.00
Chef, Regal	390.00
Chef Entenmann's	125.00
Chevrolet, North American Ceramics, 1957	80.00
Chick, Yellow, American Bisque	70.00
Churn, American Bisque	20.00
Churn Boy, Regal	90.00
Cinderella, Napco	135.00 to 300.00
Circus Tent, Brayton Laguna	120.00
Clown, DeForest	85.00
Clown, On Elephant, California Originals	65.00
Clown, On Stage, Flasher, American Bisque	355.00
Cookie Boy, Metlox	650.00
Cookie Bus, Cardinal	560.00 to 650.00
Cookie Jarrin's Little Angel, Regal China	360.00
Cookie Monster, California Originals	25.00
Cookie Shack, Green, Twin Winton	95.00
Cow, On Moon, Green, Doranne	250.00
Cow, Over Moon, American Bisque	1100.00
Cow, Purple, Metlox	400.00 to 765.00
Cow, Twin Winton	175.00
Cow, Yellow, Metlox	275.00 to 375.00
Cream Of Wheat Chef	800.00
Cub Scout, Metlox	1050.00
Darth Vader, Hexagonal, Sigma	98.00

Diaper Pin Pig, Regal China.. 400.00
Dino With Golf Clubs 825.00
Dog, Schnauzer, California Originals 150.00
Dog House, Howling Cat On Roof, Starnes 425.00
Dolly, Starnes 750.00
Donald Duck, Flour On Pocket 90.00
Dutch Boy, American Bisque 20.00
Dutch Girl, Regal China 970.00
Eddie Bauer Bear 89.00
Eggplant, Metlox ....:..... 245.00
Elf Schoolhouse, Gilner 275.00
Elsie, Pottery Guild, 1950s, 11 1/2 In. ....225.00 to 495.00
Emmett Kelly Jr., On Barrel, Flambro 650.00
Family Circus, Billy, Starnes 725.00
Farmer Pig, Treasure Craft 50.00
Ferdinand Calf, Metlox 125.00
Fi Fi Poodle, Regal 775.00
Fire Truck, Red, California Originals 395.00
Flower Lady, Brayton Laguna 750.00
Fred Flintstone, American Bisque 675.00
Fred Flintstone, Golfing, American Bisque 850.00
Fred Flintstone, Golfing, Dino Finial, American Bisque, Paper Label........ 1000.00
Fred Flintstone, Standing, Vandor 175.00
Fred Flintstone's Head 150.00
Garfield, Enesco, 1981 ....75.00 to 95.00
Gingerbread House 25.00
Girl, With Freckles, Cardinal.. 100.00
Girl, With Ponytail, DeForest 1200.00
Goldilocks, Regal..125.00 to 300.00
Graduate Owl, Dorrane of California..125.00 to 300.00
Grandma Gold, American Bisque 150.00
Green Cow, On Moon, Doranne... 250.00
Green Giant Sprout 110.00
Halo Boy, DeForest...750.00 to 925.00
Harpo Marx 1500.00
Hippo, Fishing, Japan.. 30.00
Hobo Clown, With Chalkboard, American Bisque 300.00
Hubert The Lion, Regal China.. 750.00
Humpty Dumpty, Metlox 375.00
Humpty Dumpty, Red Bottom 300.00
Humpty Dumpty, Regal 230.00
Humpty Dumpty, Underglaze, Maddux 295.00
Jazz, Singer, Billie Holiday, Clay Art 69.00
Jazz'e Junque Cookie Shop, Decals.. 350.00
Jolly Chef, Head, Metlox.. 850.00
Jukebox, Treasure Craft.. 50.00
Jukebox, Vandor... 175.00
Katrina, Treasure Craft... 395.00
Ken-L-Ration Dog, Fitz & Floyd 200.00
Kitten & Beehive, American Bisque 95.00
Koala Bear, California Originals ....250.00 to 345.00
Koala Bear, Metlox ....85.00 to 265.00
Koala Bear, On Limb, California Originals.. 450.00
Leprechaun, Doranne 150.00
Little Red Riding Hood, Regal 300.00
Ludwig Von Drake 1200.00
Lunch Box, Blue, Dorrane Of California ....58.00 to 60.00
Magic Bunny, American Bisque 35.00
Majorette, Regal...375.00 to 725.00
Mammy, Blue, Metlox ....475.00 to 600.00
Mammy, Gold Tooth, Erwin Pottery, Negatha.. 260.00
Mammy, Googly Eyed, Basket Handle 1500.00
Mammy, Luzianne 650.00

Mammy, Mosaic Tile Co. 675.00
Mammy, Pearl China .... 495.00 to 650.00
Mammy, Polka Dot, Gold Tooth, Erwin Pottery 200.00
Mammy, Rockingham .... 596.00 to 795.00
Mammy, Yellow Bandanna, Gilner 1950.00
Man With Chicken, Animals & Company 850.00
Matilda, Brayton 675.00
Merlin The Magician, Gold Trim, Alfano 495.00
Milk Bone Dog Biscuits 125.00
Mohawk Indian, American Bisque 3500.00
Mona Lisa, Vandor 35.00
Monkey, DeForest 195.00
Mrs. Fields Cookie Sack 25.00
Mrs. Tiggy Winkle, Sigma 650.00
Nerd, On Skateboard, Blue & Yellow 110.00
Nestle's Toll House 45.00
Noah's Ark, Brown 55.00
Noah's Ark, Starnes 295.00
Noah's Ark, Treasure Craft 55.00
Noah's Ark, Twin Winton 375.00
Nun, DeForest .... 325.00 to 345.00
Old Woman In A Shoe, Fitz & Floyd 135.00
Orange, Metlox 75.00
Oriental Lady, Regal 795.00
Paddington Bear 675.00
Panda Bear With Lollipop, Metlox 600.00
Parrot, Metlox .... 345.00 to 375.00
Peasant Girl, American Bisque 900.00
Peek-A-Boo, Regal China .... 1500.00 to 1650.00
Penguin, Metlox .... 75.00 to 95.00
Pepperidge Farm 60.00
Peter Peter Pumpkin Eater, Vallona Starr 410.00
Pig In Poke, Regal 30.00
Pillsbury Doughboy, 1988 .... 45.00
Pinky Lee, American Bisque 325.00
Pinocchio, California Originals 1500.00
Pinocchio, Metlox .... 290.00 to 390.00
Polka Dot Witch, Fitz & Floyd 420.00
Poodle, Gold Trim, American Bisque 210.00
Poodle, Sierra Vista 325.00
Porky Pig, Sitting In Chair, Dugan, Warner Bros. Inc., 1975 .... 85.00
Professor Snail, Treasure Craft 650.00
Puddles The Duck, Metlox 45.00
Purple Cow, Metlox .... 485.00 to 600.00
Quaker Oats, Regal China .... 75.00 to 155.00
Rabbit, California Originals 20.00
Rabbit, In Hat, DeForest 150.00
Rabbit, On Cabbage, Metlox 225.00
Rabbit, On Stump, California Originals 42.00
Rabbit, White, Gold Trim, Pink Glass Eyes, California Originals 325.00
Raccoon, Bisque Finish, Metlox, Sticker 235.00
Radio, California Originals 70.00
Rag Doll, Starnes 165.00
Raggedy Andy, Maddux .... 85.00 to 150.00
Raggedy Ann, California Originals 78.00
Raggedy Ann, Metlox 250.00
Ranger Bear, Twin Winton 140.00
Red Corvette, Appleman 1400.00
Red Riding Hood, Pottery Guild 125.00
Rio Rita, Fitz & Floyd .... 90.00 to 195.00
Rocking Horse, Lane 160.00
Romper Room 495.00
Rooster, Twin Winton 50.00

Cookie Jar, Yogi Bear, Hanna-Barbera,
American Bisque

✦ ✦ ✦ ✦ ✦ ✦ ✦ ✦ ✦ ✦ ✦ ✦ ✦ ✦ ✦ ✦

Safety tips: If garage windows are painted, burglars won't be able to tell if cars are home or not. Use translucent paint to get light in the closed garage, if it has an entrance to your house. Mailboxes large enough to conceal several days' mail make daily pickup unnecessary. Don't put your name on signs outside your house. Install large windows; burglars avoid shattering them because of noise.

✦ ✦ ✦ ✦ ✦ ✦ ✦ ✦ ✦ ✦ ✦ ✦ ✦ ✦ ✦ ✦

Rubbles House, American Bisque	995.00
Sailor Elephant, American Bisque	45.00 to 95.00
Sailor Monkey, Yellow Hat, Deforest	225.00
Santa, In A Christmas Car, Fitz & Floyd	600.00
Santa, Winking, American Bisque	505.00
Santa Claus, On Motorcycle, Fitz & Floyd	420.00 to 600.00
Santa Claus, Standing, White, Metlox	895.00
Santa Claus, White Face, Metlox	595.00
Scarecrow, California Originals	170.00
Seabag, American Bisque	140.00
Seal, On Igloo	385.00
Sheriff, Fitz & Floyd	280.00
Sheriff, Gondor	1500.00
Sheriff, Lane	650.00
Sid's Taxi, Appleman	900.00
Sir Francis Drake, Metlox	55.00
Smokey Mountain Boy, Paul Webb	495.00
Snowman, Doranne	160.00
Snowman, Fitz & Floyd	200.00
Southwestern Santa, Fitz & Floyd	550.00
Space Cadet, California Originals	78.00
Space Ship, American Bisque	295.00 to 350.00
Squirrel, On Stump, Gilner	55.00
Stagecoach, Sierra Vista	210.00 to 250.00
Stan Laurel, Cumberland	595.00
Stove, Cleminson	160.00
Strawberry, Metlox	110.00
Swee' Pea, American Bisque	3800.00
Tasmanian Devil, Certified International	45.00
Tat-L-Tale, Helen Hutula	550.00 to 1200.00
Teddy Bear, Blue Sweater, Metlox	40.00
Tony The Tiger, Head	130.00
Toothache Dog, American Bisque	700.00
Topsy, Blue Apron, Metlox	595.00
Toy Soldier, American Bisque	110.00
Train, California Originals	40.00
Transformer, Hasbro	165.00
Umbrella Kids, American Bisque	325.00
Uncle Sam, Bear, Metlox	1450.00
W.C. Fields, Cumberland Ware	700.00

Walrus, Blue Scarf, Metlox 275.00
Watermelon Sammy, Gifford 500.00
Wilma, On Telephone, American Bisque .... 800.00 to 1000.00
Wonder Woman, Silver, California Originals 800.00
Woody Woodpecker, Head, Walter Lantz .... 800.00 to 1125.00
Yarn Doll, Green, American Bisque 135.00
Yogi Bear, Hanna-Barbera, American Bisque .... *Illus* 288.00

COORS ware was made by a pottery in Golden, Colorado, owned by the
Coors Beverage Company. Dishes and decorative wares were produced from
the turn of the century until the pottery was destroyed by fire in the 1930s.
The name *Coors* is marked on the back. For more information, see *Kovels'
Depression Glass & American Dinnerware Price List.*

COORS
U.S.A.

Apple Baker, Cover, Rosebud, Red.. 38.00
Apple Baker, Rosebud, Maroon 50.00
Bean Pot, Rosebud, Rose, 10 In. 65.00
Bowl, Batter, Maroon, 3 1/2 Pt... 85.00
Bowl, Mixing, Rosebud, Green, 7 In. 55.00
Bowl, Rosebud, Green Tab Handle 15.00
Bowl, Vegetable, Rosebud, Maroon, Deep 40.00
Cake Plate, Rosebud, Orange 65.00
Creamer, Rock-Mount, Orange 38.00
Honey Pot, Green 150.00
Jug, Rosebud, Blue 95.00
Jug, Rosebud, Maroon, Stopper.. 110.00
Muffin Set, Rosebud, Maroon 200.00
Pie Plate, Coorado, Ivory... 45.00
Pie Plate, Rosebud, Green, 11 1/2 In. 35.00
Pitcher, Rosebud, Green 175.00
Plate, Rosebud, Maroon, 10 1/4 In. 15.00
Soup, Dish, Rosebud, Maroon 35.00
Sugar, Cover, Rosebud, Maroon 45.00
Teapot, Rosebud, Orange 95.00
Vase, Bulbous, Tan, Turquoise Interior, Rope Handle, 8 In. 50.00
Vase, Coorado, Satin Ivory, Turquoise, Bulbous, 6 In.. 55.00
Vase, Handles, 5 In... 40.00
Vase, Matte Yellow, 12 In. 125.00
Vase, Semicircular Handle, Matte Green Glaze, 7 1/2 x 8 1/2 In. 135.00
Vase, Signed, 6 In... 50.00
Vase, Trinidad, Ivory & Turquoise, 8 In.. 55.00
Vase, Urn, Orange, 8 In. 75.00

COPELAND pieces listed here are those that have a mark used between 1847
and 1976. See also Copeland Spode and Royal Worcester.

Bowl, Blue & White, Marked.. 38.00
Bust, Woman, John Hancock, Impressed Mark, Parian, c.1863, 11 In. 373.00
Creamer, Horse & Rider Scenes, 4 In. 55.00
Figurine, Girl, Standing, Holding Dog, Parian, c.1876, 14 In. 550.00
Figurine, Nude Woman, Shackled Wrists, Chain, Impressed Mark, Parian, 18 1/2 In. ... 747.00
Mug, Green Band, White Classical Figures, 3 Handles, Yellowware, 5 1/4 In. 137.00
Pitcher, Water, Going To Halloa, 7 1/2 In. 88.00
Plate, Country Sporting Series, Copeland & Garrett, c.1833, 9 5/16 In., 6 Piece 1840.00

COPELAND SPODE appears on some pieces of nineteenth-century English
porcelain. Josiah Spode established a pottery at Stoke-on-Trent, England, in
1770. In 1833, the firm was purchased by William Copeland and Thomas
Garrett and the mark was changed. In 1847, Copeland became the sole owner
and the mark changed again. W. T. Copeland & Sons continued until a 1976
merger when it became Royal Worcester Spode. Pieces are listed in this book
under the name that appears in the mark. Copeland Spode, Copeland, and
Royal Worcester have separate listings.

Basin, Italian, 12 In. 195.00
Bowl, Embossed Flowers, White, c.1920, 10 1/2 In.. 125.00

Butter, Cover, Tower, Pink, Square.. 75.00
Cake Stand, Tower, Pink, Footed, 9 1/2 In. 100.00
Chocolate Pot, Trade Winds 110.00
Creamer, Trade Winds 45.00
Cup & Saucer, Tower, Blue.. 32.00
Cup & Saucer, Tower, Blue, Demitasse 27.00
Game Set, Game Birds, Cobalt Blue Underglaze, 41 Piece 6600.00
Gravy Boat, Blue.. 110.00
Plate, Constitution Hall, Blue Transfer, c.1920, 10 1/2 In. 50.00
Plate, Memorial Continental Hall, Blue Transfer, c.1920, 10 1/2 In............ 50.00
Plate, Tower, Pink, 7 1/2 In.. 18.00
Plate, Tower, Pink, 10 1/2 In.. 30.00
Platter, Oval, Birds, Tree Trunk, Oriental Flowers, 9 1/2 In. 100.00
Platter, Tower, Pink, 14 1/2 x 11 1/2 In. 110.00
Sugar & Creamer, Cover, Tower, Pink 50.00
Tea Set, Pink & Blue Landscape, Flowers, White Ground, 53 Piece.............. 605.00

COPPER has been used to make utilitarian items, such as teakettles and cooking pans, since the days of the early American colonists. Copper became a popular metal with the Arts & Crafts makers of the early 1900s, and decorative pieces, like bookends and desk sets, were made. Other pieces of copper may be found in the Arts & Crafts, Bradley & Hubbard, Kitchen, and Roycroft categories.

Ashtray, Hammered, Crimped Top, No. 182, Benedict Studios, 6 In............ 165.00
Ashtray, Stand, Hammered, Removable Liner, Kopper Kraft, 29 x 8 In........ 165.00
Basket, Canoe Shape, Riveted Handle, Dirk Van Erp, 5 1/4 x 12 In. 600.00
Bed Warmer, Brass Lid, Wooden Handle, Basket Of Flowers, 43 1/2 In. 330.00
Bed Warmer, Pierced & Engraved Lid, Wooden Handle, Brass Trim, 43 In.............. 104.00
Boiler, Laundry, Cover, Spigot, Large 140.00
Bowl, Fluted, Enameled Yellow Interior With Green Border, Handicraft Shop, 7 In. 675.00
Bowl, Fluted, Hammered, Self-Footed, Karl F. Leinonen, 3 x 9 In. 495.00
Bowl, Footed, Hammered, Cupped & Scalloped, Georgian, 8 1/2 x 3 In....... 15.00
Bowl, Fruit, Hammered, Scalloped Rim, Red & Brown Patina, Dirk Van Erp, 3 1/2 In.. 1210.00
Bowl, Fruit, Reticulated, Pedestal, Manning Bowman, 4 x 7 1/2 In. 22.00
Bowl, Fruit, Straight, Angled Rim, Dirk Van Erp, San Fran. Mark, 4 1/4 x 10 3/4 In..... 880.00
Bowl, Hammered, Jarvie, 4 1/2 x 8 1/2 In. 330.00
Bowl, Hammered, Scalloped Rim, Flared, Pratt, 2 3/4 x 6 1/2 In. 165.00
Box, Cover, Hammered, Curved Handle, Curly Legs, Benedict, 7 x 10 x 6 In. 165.00
Box, Enameled Cover, Art Deco Floral, Black Ground, 2 1/4 x 4 1/4 x 6 In.................. 600.00
Box, Handled Cover, Hammered, Footed, Benedict Studio, 6 1/2 x 10 x 6 1/2 In. 275.00
Box, Intricate Cutout, Hammered Silver Design On Cover, Dirk Van Erp, 6 1/2 x 4 In. 1430.00
Box, Stamp, Hammered Copper, Gustav Stickley, 2 x 4 1/4 x 2 1/4 In. 412.00
Bucket, Brass Handle, 3 Gal.. 90.00
Candlestick, 2-Arm, Hammered, Square Base, Karl Kipp, 6 1/2 In., Pair...... 715.00
Candlestick, Beveled Base, 4 Stems, Rohlfs, 13 1/2 In. 715.00
Candlestick, Hammered, 2 Handles, Benedict Studios, 9 3/4 x 4 1/2 In. 99.00
Candlestick, Hammered, Apollo Studios, 8 3/4 x 3 3/4 In. 138.00
Candlestick, Hammered, Applied Handles, Onondaga Metal Shops, 3 x 4 In., Pair 165.00
Candlestick, Hammered, Karl Kipp, 7 1/2 In., Pair...................................... 1430.00
Candlestick, Princess, Hammered, Square Base, Karl Kipp, 7 1/2 x 3 1/4 In., ... 220.00
Candlestick, Princess, Woodgrain Pattern, 4-Sided Stems, Karl Kipp, 8 In., Pair.......... 605.00
Candlestick, Stylized Leaves Above Base, Sloping Handles, Benedict Studios, 9 In..... 355.00
Centerpiece, Hand Hammered, Elephant Floral Camel Medallions, 16 x 4 In. 40.00
Chamberstick, Looped Riveted Handle, G. Stickley, Signed, 9 In., Pair 825.00
Chamberstick, Riveted Handle, Cylinder Base, G. Stickley, Bobeche, 9 In. ... 467.00
Charger, Rolled Rim, Embossed Hearts, Center Medallion, Arts & Crafts, 12 In. 475.00
Coffee Server, Brass Fittings & Finial, Wood Stick Handle 22.00
Coffee Set, Raised Triangles, Hammered, Wertembergische, 4 Piece 400.00
Coffeepot, Dovetailed, Brass Acorn Finial, England, c.1750, 12 1/2 In. 450.00
Colander, Iron Handles, Middle Eastern, 15 In. 38.00
Cuspidor, Turtle, Golden & Jackson's, Chicago Pat. 1891, 14 1/2 In.......... 259.00
Desk Set, Ivory Trim, Pen Tray, 2 Pens, Impressed Mark, Albert Berry, 1 Piece........... 600.00
Desk Set, Silvercrest, Silver Edged, Circle Mark, 5 Piece............................... 137.00

Copper, Vase, Red Wash, Dirk Van Erp, 7 In.

Fern Holder, 4 Curled Iron Feet, Gustav Stickley, No. 299, 6 x 9 In. 1760.00
Finial, Eagle, Gilt Verdigris Surface, 12 1/2 In. 546.00
Frame, Hammered Design Of Stems, Blossoms, Arts & Crafts, 9 1/2 x 11 1/2 In. 550.00
Frame, Hammered, Arts & Crafts, 9 x 6 In. 75.00
Frying Pan, Dovetailed, Cast Iron Handles, S.B. Traub, 17 x 17 In. 137.00
Gong, Dinner, Triangular Wall Plate, Flower, Hammered, Mission Studios, 9 1/2 In. 110.00
Jardiniere, Flared, 2 Braided Handles, Dirk Van Erp, 8 x 9 1/4 In. 880.00
Jardiniere, Hammered, 3 Handles, Stickley, 7 1/2 x 11 3/4 In. 330.00
Jardiniere, Scalloped Border, Applied Top, Stickley Bros., No. 156, 8 x 7 In. 300.00
Kettle, Bail Handle, Dovetail Seams, Riveted Handle Loops, Lacquered, 5 1/2 x 4 In. .. 60.00
Kettle, Canning, Iron Handle, Large. 170.00
Kettle, Cover, Cast Iron Handles, J. Van Range Co., 15 x 13 In. 95.00
Kettle, Handle Stamped W. Shilling, Early 19th Century 9775.00
Kettle, Spigot, Brass Trim, Swivel Handle, Dovetailed, 17 In. 95.00
Letter Holder, Hammered, Enamel Viking Ship Plaque, G. Twitchell, 4 1/2 x 5 1/2 In. 625.00
Molds are listed in the Kitchen category
Night-Light, Hammered, Candle Shape, Craftsman Studios, 10 1/2 x 8 In. 220.00
Pan, Embossed Apple & Pear, Deep, 14 x 2 3/4 In. 110.00
Pan, Tin Lining, Iron Handle, Rivets, 16 1/2 x 2 1/4 In. 140.00
Panel, Birth Of Venus, 27 1/2 In. 770.00
Panel, Woman, Scepter, Science, Chemistry & Art, Relief, Signed, c.1888, 21 x 11 In. 275.00
Planter, 4 Riveted Legs, 4 Panels, Mushrooms, Karl Kipp, 4 x 7 In. 6500.00
Plaque, Gentleman, Oval, 23 In. 110.00
Plaque, Profile Bust Of Woman, Floral, Gustav Stickley, Round 350.00
Tea Urn, Engraved Pierced Base, Adams, 21 In. 495.00
Teapot, Brass Stand, Burner, Polished, Dated 1904 .... 145.00
Tray, Card, Notched & Fluted Rim, Purple Enamel Interior, Panis Gallery, 4 1/4 In. 75.00
Tray, Embossed Daisies, Rebaje, Round, 16 In. 225.00
Tray, Etched, Benares, 29-In. Diam. 100.00
Tray, Hammered, 2 Handles, Gustav Stickley, 23 x 11 1/4 In. 660.00
Tray, Hammered, Concave Raised Handles, Round, Dirk Van Erp, 12 In. 660.00
Tray, Hammered, Concave Scallops, Round, Dirk Van Erp, 17 1/2 In. 1200.00
Tray, Hammered, Joseph Heinrichs, Round, 17 1/2 In. 138.00
Tray, Hammered, Overlapping Rectangles, Peacock Corners, Laguna, 15 x 11 In. 275.00
Tray, Undulating Rim, Cutout Handles, Jarvie, 18 1/2 In. 1850.00
Umbrella Stand, Stickley Bros., Hexagonal, Riveted Rim, No. 180, 26 In. 715.00
Vase, Applied Silver Tree, Silvercrest, 4 1/2 In. 220.00
Vase, Baluster, Rolled Rim, Dark Patina, Dirk Van Erp, Signed, 11 1/2 In. 1900.00
Vase, Baluster-Form, Hammered, Open-Box Mark, Dirk Van Erp, 9 In. 1050.00
Vase, Bulbous, Rolled Rim, Red Patina, Dirk Van Erp, c.1912, 8 In. 4370.00
Vase, Hammered Copper, Rolled Rim, Green & Black Patina, Dirk Van Erp, 11 In. 4950.00
Vase, Hammered Diamond Design Body, Harry Dixon, 17 In. 2970.00
Vase, Hammered, Rolled Rim, Closed-Box Mark, Dirk Van Erp, 11 3/4 In. 1320.00
Vase, Hammered, Spherical, San Francisco Mark, Dirk Van Erp, 3 x 4 In. 770.00
Vase, Hammered, Squatty, Flared Rim, Dirk Van Erp, 3 1/2 x 4 1/2 In. 192.00

Vase, Hammered, Windmill Mark, Dirk Van Erp, 5 In.	880.00
Vase, Hand Hammered, Red Patina, Dirk Van Erp, 7 In.	4125.00
Vase, Hand Hammered, Rolled Rim, Dirk Van Erp, 4 1/2 In.	1320.00
Vase, Hand Hammered, Swollen Shoulder, Dirk Van Erp, 8 1/2 In.	770.00
Vase, Low Form, Rolled Rim, Hand Hammered, Dirk Van Erp, 5 1/2 x 11 In.	2640.00
Vase, Red Wash, Dirk Van Erp, 7 In. *Illus*	4125.00
Vase, Rolled Rim, Red Patina, Dirk Van Erp, c.1912, 8 In.	4370.00
Wall Sconce, Hammered, Impressed Circular Mark, Albert Berry, 11 x 5 In., Pair	522.00
Warming Pan, Cover, Fruitwood Handle, 12 In.	77.00
Warming Pan, Engraved Cover, 12 1/2 In.	121.00
Warming Pan, Reticulated Cover, 11 In.	99.00

CORALENE glass was made by firing many small colored beads on the outside of glassware. It was made in many patterns in the United States and Europe in the 1880s. Reproductions are made today. Coralene-decorated Japanese pottery is listed in the Japanese Coralene category.

Pitcher, Fruit & Leaves, Orange, Applied Amber Handle, Enameled, 3 x 2 5/8 In.	245.00
Pitcher, Pink To Deep Pink, White Casing, Clear Handle, Yellow Seaweed, 5 7/8 In.	291.00
Pitcher, Seaweed, Yellow, White, 6 1/4 In.	350.00
Tumbler, Yellow Seaweed, Orange Fish, Light To Medium Blue, 3 7/8 In.	143.00
Vase, Allover Designs, Dusty Rose At Top, 11 1/4 In.	890.00
Vase, Green Floral, Pale Yellow, Crystal Rim, Waisted, Crimped, 5 In., Pair	325.00

CORDEY China Company was founded by Boleslaw Cybis in 1942 in Trenton, New Jersey. The firm produced gift shop items. In 1969 it was acquired by the Lightron Corp. and operated as the Schiller Cordey Co., manufacturers of lamps. About 1950 Boleslaw Cybis began making Cybis porcelains, which are listed in their own category in this book.

Bust, Josephine, No. 5039	50.00
Bust, Raleigh, No. 5034	50.00
Figurine, Gentlemen, No. 5091	150.00
Figurine, Lady With Fan, Peach & Fuchsia, 16 In.	105.00
Figurine, Man, Ruffled Shirt, 14 In.	115.00
Lamp, Figural, Woman, Victorian, Outstretched Hands, 20 In.	175.00
Sugar & Creamer, No. 622 & 623, 4 In.	85.00
Wall Pocket, Face, 10 In.	250.00

CORKSCREWS have been needed since the first bottle was sealed with a cork, probably in the seventeenth century. Today collectors search for the early, unusual patented examples or the figural corkscrews of recent years.

Bottle, Imperial Pale Beer	50.00
Bottle, Lion Brewery	50.00
Brass, Brush, Embossed Lion & Unicorn Label, Bone Trim, 5 1/2 In.	203.00
Dog's Profile Shape, Silver Plate	55.00
Elephant, Brass, England, c.1930	30.00
Ensign Southwest Corner, San Francisco, Wooden Handle	25.00
Lady's Legs, Celluloid	250.00
Listerine	12.00
McAvoy Brewery, Wooden Handle	25.00
Old Snifter, With Bottle Opener, Metal, Demley	150.00
Slepp Brewery, Wooden Handle	21.00
Snake Type, Larson P & R, 9 Oz.	55.00
Stroh's Beer, Bottle	75.00
Woman, Celluloid, White, Germany	525.00

CORONATION souvenirs have been made since the 1800s. Pottery, glass, tin, silver, and paper objects with a picture of the monarchs and date have been sold at many coronations. The pieces that mention King Edward VIII, the king who was never crowned, are not rare; collectors should be sure to check values before buying. Related pieces are found in the Commemorative category.

Beaker, George V, 1911, 3 3/4 In.	70.00
Bowl, Elizabeth II, Pressed Glass, 1953, 4 /34 In.	60.00

Dish, Green, Animals, Wade, 1952... 95.00
Loving Cup, George VI, 1937, 3 1/4 In. 140.00
Mug, George V 35.00
Mug, Queen Elizabeth, 3 1/2 In. 24.00
Pin Tray, Elizabeth II 15.00
Plate, Edward VII, Blue, White, Royal Copenhagen, 1902, 7 In. 210.00
Plate, George VI & Queen Elizabeth, 1937.. 50.00
Scarf, Queen Elizabeth, II, Hand Painted, Dated 1953, 30 x 32 In. 35.00
Tumbler, King George VI & Queen Elizabeth, 1937... 50.00

COSMOS is a pressed milk glass pattern with colored flowers made from 1894 to 1915 by the Consolidated Lamp and Glass Company. Tablewares and lamps were made in this pattern. A few pieces were also made of clear glass with painted decorations. Other glass patterns are listed under Consolidated Lamp and also in various glass categories.

Lamp, Oil, Clear, Painted Flowers... 195.00
Lamp, Painted Base, Clear Pattern Shade, 8 In.. 225.00
Salt & Pepper, Pink Band 110.00

COVERLETS were made of linen or wool during the nineteenth century. Most of the coverlets date from 1800 to 1850. Four types were made: the double weave, jacquard, summer and winter, and overshot. Later coverlets were made of a variety of materials. Quilts are listed in this book in their own category.

Double Weave, Snowflake & Pine Tree, 84 x 96 In. 280.00
Double Weave, Yo-Yo, Doll's, 28 x 17 In. 28.00
Jacquard, 4 Rose Medallions With Stars, Bird Border, 78 x 87 In.................. 305.00
Jacquard, 4 Rose Medallions, Andrew Hoover, c.1843, 82 x 92 In. 385.00
Jacquard, 4 Rose Medallions, Emanuel Ettinger, Aronsburg, 70 x 84 In. 55.00
Jacquard, Bird & Flower Pattern, c.1840, 85 x 80 In. 275.00
Jacquard, Bird & Tree Border, Dated 1843, 82 x 80 In. 450.00
Jacquard, Central Floral Medallion, Swag & Tassel Borders, 71 x 81 In. 71.00
Jacquard, Central Star, Flowers, Eagle Spandrels, Scrolled Border, 77 x 88 In. 225.00
Jacquard, Floral Medallions With Stars, Bird Border, Fringe, 84 x 96 In. 467.00
Jacquard, Floral Medallions, Birds & Trees, Pennsylvania, Label, c.1838, 79 x 88 In. .. 550.00
Jacquard, Floral Medallions, Pine Tree Borders, Mary Cook, c.1837, 83 x 90 In.......... 248.00
Jacquard, Floral Medallions, Stag & Floral Border, Label, 2-Piece, 80 x 92 In. 880.00
Jacquard, Floral Medallions, William Fleck, Findlay, Ohio, c.1861, 67 x 76 In. 192.00
Jacquard, Floral Stripes & Stars, Long Necked Birds Border, 72 x 96 In. 137.00
Jacquard, Floral, Willows, Eagles, Turkeys, Orleans County, N.Y., c.1839, 75 x 85 In. 215.00
Jacquard, Foliate Medallions, Rose Border, Red, Blue, Green, Fringe, 98 x 48 In. 230.00
Jacquard, Geometric Floral Design, Star Corners, Lydia Thomas, 82 x 90 In. 495.00
Jacquard, Geometric Floral, Tomato Red & White, 72 x 84 In. 357.00
Jacquard, Geometric Square Pattern, c.1850, 86 x 144 In. 192.00
Jacquard, Masonic, American Independence, Mary Crouch, c.1843, 86 x 74 In. 345.00
Jacquard, Masonic, Inscribed, Blue & White, 85 x 73 In. 172.00
Jacquard, Navy & White, Floral, 19th Century, 88 x 84 In. 287.00
Jacquard, Nine Floral Medallions, Birds, 75 x 84 In. 325.00
Jacquard, Red, White & Blue, Peacocks, Compotes Of Fruit, Flowers, 78 x 72 In. 632.00
Jacquard, Single Weave, Floral Medallions, Navy & White Border, 71 x 90 In. 220.00
Jacquard, Single Weave, Medallion, Angels, Floral Border, Label, 72 x 81 In. 165.00
Jacquard, Star Medallion, Vining Flowers, Bird Border, L.S., c.1862, 82 x 90 In. 385.00
Jacquard, Stars & 4 Rose Medallions, James Spence, c.1850, 80 x 96 In...... 1155.00
Jacquard, Tulip Clusters, Floral, Blue & White, D.D. Haring, c.1835, 94 x 76 In. 575.00
Jacquard, Urns Of Flowers, Christian & Heathen Border, 76 x 88 In. 192.00
Jacquard, Washington On Horseback, 92 x 78 In. 1092.00
Overshot, Embroidered, 1792 MCS, 89 x 68 In. 373.00
Overshot, Navy & White Optical Design, 2-Piece, 66 x 84 In. 143.00
Overshot, Optical Pattern, Rust, Red, Green, Natural, Fringe, 2-Piece, 85 x 101 In. 302.00
Overshot, Plaid Pattern, Red, Navy Blue & White, Fringe, 66 x 84 In. 55.00
Pieced & Appliqued, John Hewson, Textile Printer, 18th Century, 98 x 88 In. 6325.00
Star, Flowers & Seaweed Design, Navy & Natural, 70 x 72 In. 110.00
Summer & Winter, Blue & White Optical Design, 81 x 96 In. 82.00
Summer & Winter, Stripes, Red, Gray-Blue, Olive Brown, 2-Piece, 74 x 75 In. 302.00

COWAN POTTERY made art pottery and wares for florists. Guy Cowan made pottery in Rocky River, Ohio, a suburb of Cleveland, from 1913 to 1931. A stylized mark with the word *Cowan* was used on most pieces. A commercial, mass-produced line was marked *Lakeware*. Collectors today search for the Art Deco pieces by Guy Cowan, Viktor Schreckengost, Waylande Gregory, or Thelma Frazier Winter.

Ashtray, Duck, Turquoise	95.00
Ashtray, Shell Shape, Black	60.00
Bookends, Boy & Girl, Cream Gloss, No. 519, Frank N. Wilcox, 6 1/2 In.	220.00
Bookends, Nude Children	375.00
Bookends, Sunbonnet, Green & Brown Crystalline Glaze, No. 521, 7 1/2 In.	440.00
Bowl, Cream Exterior, Green Interior, Scalloped, Footed, 9 1/2 In.	24.00
Bowl, Crystalline Glaze, 13 1/2 In.	275.00
Bowl, Dawn, 8 x 11 In.	115.00
Bowl, Footed, Tan, Green Wash, Molded Leaves, c.1929, 16 x 6 In.	121.00
Bowl, Sea Horse, 15 In.	65.00 to 75.00
Box, Cover, Flame-Shaped Finial, Flowers, Ivory Crackled Glaze, Stamped, 4 1/2 x 6 In.	247.00
Candelabrum, Figural Nude Woman Between 2 Lights, Ivory, No. 745, 9 1/2 In.	605.00
Candleholder, Leaves, Powder Blue Glaze, Floriform, Stem Handle, 8 x 3 In., Pair	193.00
Candleholder, Turquoise, Pair	50.00
Candlestick, Double Handle, Orange Luster, 3 1/2 In., Pair	35.00
Candlestick, Marigold, 8 In.	60.00
Candlestick, Sea Horse, April Green, 4 In., Pair	50.00
Candlestick, Sea Horse, Pink, No. 716, Pair	50.00
Candlestick, White, Triangular Shape, Scroll Base, 3 In., Pair	35.00
Charger, Art Deco Design, Dancing Nude, Greyhound, Signed, 15 In.	660.00
Charger, Thunderbird, Melon Green Crackle Glaze, Blazys, 15 1/2 In.	650.00
Compote, Tulip Shape, Caramel	40.00
Console Set, Apple Blossom Pterodactyl Bowl, Ivory Lotus Candleholder, 3 Piece	275.00
Dish, Embossed Antelope, Blue	78.00
Figurine, Bird & Wave, Blue High Glaze, No. 749B, 14 In.	247.00
Figurine, Nude, Kneeling, Ivory, Walter Sinz	2000.00
Figurine, Owl, Introspection, Art Deco Design, No. D-1, A. Drexel Jacobson, 8 In.	1210.00
Figurine, Primrose Spanish Dancers, Pair	1350.00
Figurine, Spanish Dancer, Female No. 793, Male No. 794, E. Anderson, 9 In., Pair	1045.00
Figurine, Spanish Dancers, Primrose, Pair	1500.00
Figurine, Woman Nude, Peach Tint, Waylande Gregory, Tall	1800.00
Flower Frog, 2 Nude Women, No. 685, R. Guy Cowan, 7 1/2 In.	297.00
Flower Frog, Figure Standing In Pool Of Water, Signed, c.1931, 12 In.	522.00
Flower Frog, Figure Wrapped In Swirling Cloth, White High Glaze, Signed, 8 In.	265.00
Flower Frog, Nude Woman, 7 In.	165.00
Flower Frog, Nude Woman, 9 In.	135.00
Flower Frog, Nude Woman, No. 680, 1925, 8 1/2 In.	467.00
Flower Frog, Swirl Dancer, Nude, White High Glaze, No. 720, 10 In.	495.00
Jar, Cigarette, Urn, Pink, Yellow Glaze, Molded Medallions, People, Animals, 3 1/2 In.	209.00
Lamp, Foliage, 8 1/2 In.	175.00
Lamp, October Rocket	950.00
Lamp, Orange & Beige Crystalline Glaze, 10-In. Base	275.00
Match Holder, Ivory	35.00
Match Holder, Sea Horses, Ivory	45.00 to 50.00
Paperweight, Elephant, Oriental Red Glaze, No. D-3, Margaret Postgate, 4 1/2 In.	209.00
Pitcher, Blue Luster, 5 In.	60.00
Pitcher, Delphinium, 5 In.	150.00
Plate, Fish, Soft Sea Green & Blue, Thelma Frazier Winter	650.00
Radio Figure, Art Deco Woman, Bowed Head, White Crackle, No. 853, 9 In.	2640.00
Sculpture, Heart In Cage, Orange Heart, Thelma Frazier Winter	3900.00
Strawberry Pot, Attached Saucer, Pink & Green Glaze, 6 1/2 In.	160.00
Tile, Yellow Blossoms, Foliage, Teal Ground, Self-Framed, Hexagonal, 5 3/4 In.	302.00
Vase, Antique Green, 5 3/4 In.	200.00
Vase, Apricot & Peach, Beehive Shape, 9 In.	275.00
Vase, Blue, Green, Iron Stand, 30 In.	770.00
Vase, Egyptian Blue, Chinese Bird	750.00

Vase, Fan, Light Orange Crystalline, R.G. Cowan, No. V-801, 5 In.	99.00
Vase, Flemish Blue, Lakeware, 4 3/5 In.	95.00
Vase, Flemish Blue, Lakeware, 9 1/4 In.	150.00
Vase, Geometric Design Of Women, Leaves, Thelma Frazier Winter, 1930, 9 1/2 In. ...	2400.00
Vase, Green Crackle Glaze, Metal Glazed Stand, Marked, 8 In.	172.00
Vase, Green Staircase Line, Mottled Brick Brown Ground, Bulbous, Stamped, 6 1/2 In.	247.00
Vase, Larkspur Luster, 7 1/2 In.	110.00
Vase, Light Blue High Glaze, Lavender Highlights, No. 847, Impressed J, 12 In.	165.00
Vase, Marigold Lustre, No. 562, 12 In.	220.00
Vase, Pillow, 7 In.	125.00
Vase, Swirled, Blue & Turquoise, 12 In.	325.00
Vase, Swirling Aqua & Blue High-Glaze, Signed, c.1930, 12 In.	230.00

CRACKER JACK, the molasses-flavored popcorn mixture, was first made in 1896 in Chicago, Illinois. A prize was added to each box in 1912. Collectors search for the old boxes, toys, and advertising materials. Many of the toys are unmarked.

Angelus Marshmallows Wagon, Horse, 2 In.	95.00
Booklet, Uncle Sam's Famous National Songs, 16 Pages, 1918	60.00
Card, Birthday, Horoscope, Victorian Boy	25.00
Game, 1 Prize Missing, 1978	40.00
Horse-Drawn Wagon, Tom	52.00
Lunch Box, Metal, Aladdin, 1969	30.00
Riddle Card	15.00
Street Car, Metal	25.00
Toonerville Trolley	500.00
Truck, Angelus Marshmallows, 1 1/2 In.	85.00
Watch, Tin Lithograph, 1940s	85.00

CRACKLE GLASS was originally made by the Venetians, but most of the ware found today dates from the 1800s. The glass was heated, cooled, and refired so that many small lines appeared inside the glass. It was made in many factories in the United States and Europe.

Vase, Cover, Blue & White, 11 In.	66.00

CRANBERRY GLASS is an almost transparent yellow-red glass. It resembles the color of cranberry juice. The glass has been made in Europe and America since the Civil War. It is still being made, and reproductions can fool the unwary. Related glass items may be listed in other categories, such as Northwood, Rubena Verde, etc.

Basket, Cut Glass, Large	95.00
Bottle, Gold Bands, Dotted & Daisylike Flower, Facet Stopper, 9 x 3 In.	100.00
Candlestick, Optic Diamond, Bobeche Top, c.1910, 3 In., Pair	295.00
Casket, Jewel, Gilt Metal Mounts, Key, Enameled, 5 3/4 x 3 3/16 In.	200.00
Cologne Bottle, Gold Scrolls & Flowers, Squared Bubble Stopper, 8 5/8 In.	165.00
Cruet, Encased In Teal Base, Handle & Band On Neck, Facet Stopper, 8 In.	165.00
Cup, Raised Flowers, Hand Blown, 10 Piece	575.00
Decanter, Crystal Handle, Bubble Stopper, Basket Of Flowers, 12 1/4 In.	195.00
Decanter, Victorian, 12 In.	140.00
Decanter, White Vertical Stripe, Bulbous Base, Cork & Metal Stopper	150.00
Dish, Jam, Clear Rim, Silver Plated Holder, 4 1/2 In.	100.00
Epergne, 6 Trumpets, Central Flower, Applied Design, c.1870, 23 In.	575.00
Jar, Ginger, Silver Overlay, Bulbous, 7 1/4 In.	60.00
Lamp, Beaded Swirl, Chimney Shade, Brass Burner, 8 1/2 x 4 1/2 In.	395.00
Lamp, Oil, Blown Molded, Milk Glass Base, Electrified, 12 In.	132.00
Lamp, Peg, Pair	459.00
Lemonade Set, Enameled Roses, 7 Piece	600.00
Pitcher, Bladder, Twisted Braided Rope Handle, 9 3/4 In.	295.00
Pitcher, Bulbous Base, 19th Century, 9 In.	137.00
Pitcher, Coin Spot, Applied Clear Handle, 6 3/4 In.	90.00
Pitcher, Daisy & Fern, Opalescent, 8 In.	350.00
Pitcher, Inverted Thumbprint, Clear Handle, 3-Way Top, 6 1/4 In.	101.00
Pitcher, Optic Pattern, Tankard Shape, Clear Handle, 8 3/8 In.	110.00

Pitcher, Rippled Pattern, Clear Handle, Bulbous Mouth, 6 1/2 In. 95.00
Pitcher, Water, Overshot, Tankard Shape, 9 3/8 x 4 1/2 In. 165.00
Powder Box, Enameled.. 295.00
Shade, Lamp, Swirl, 10-In. Diam. 35.00
Shaker, Nutmeg, Pair 149.00
Sugar Shaker, Coin Spot... 275.00
Sugar Shaker, Inverted Thumbprint, Tapered..85.00 to 110.00
Sugar Shaker, Leaf Umbrella, 5 In. 350.00
Sugar Shaker, Reverse Swirl 65.00
Sugar Shaker, Vertically Paneled, Sterling Silver Cover, 5 3/4 In.............................. 95.00
Sugar Shaker, White Spots 295.00
Swan, Blown, 2 x 2 In.. 45.00
Toothpick, Baby Thumbprint... 45.00
Urinal, Gilded Rim.. 315.00
Vase, Enamel Flowers, Fan & Leaf Design, Crystal Handles, 9 1/2 x 6 In. 475.00
Vase, Jack-In-The-Pulpit, Clear Base, 11 5/8 x 5 7/8 In. 145.00
Vase, Relief Ribbing, 7 7/8 x 3 1/2 In.. 148.00
Water Set, Enameled Lilies, Gold Trim, 11 3/4-In. Pitcher, 7 Piece 275.00

CREAMWARE, or queensware, was developed by Josiah Wedgwood about
1765. It is a cream-colored earthenware that has been copied by many factories. Similar wares may be listed under Pearlware and Wedgwood.

Candlestick, Spherical Knop, Feather Edge, Staffordshire, c.1775, 3 In. 230.00
Jug, Wine Measure, Lady's Mask Spout, Feather Headdress, c.1783, 6 3/4 In. 2645.00
Match Holder, Scratcher, Gold Luster.. 225.00
Mug, Floral Border, Verse, Enamel, 3 1/8 In. 316.00
Pitcher, Band Of Hearts, Swags, Enamel, 19th Century, 7 3/4 In............................... 172.00
Pitcher, Cider, Masonic, Early 19th Century 750.00
Pitcher, Classical Transfer, Zodiac Border, 19th Century, England, 10 1/2 In. 862.00
Pitcher, Strawberry Pattern, Quilted... 475.00
Pitcher, Tavern Scene & Vignette Transfer, 19th Century, 7 In................................... 575.00
Pitcher, Tavern Scene, Verses, Flutist On Back, 7 In. 373.00
Planter, Square, 5 In.. 85.00
Pot, Pepper, Black Transfer 110.00
Teapot, Floral Finial Slide Back Cover, Salt Glaze, 9 1/4 x 5 5/8 In. 460.00
Tray, Basket Weave, Reticulated Rim, Oval, 10 In. 88.00
Tureen, Cover, Seed Pattern Panels, Floral Finial, 18th Century, 9 1/2 In.................... 575.00
Urinal, Allover Blue Stenciled Design, Wicker Carrying Case 230.00

CREDIT CARDS, credit tokens, metal charge plates, and other similar collectibles are now part of the numismatic collecting hobby.

Gimbel Bros., Cover 15.00
Gulf Gasoline, 1977 .... 22.00
Mobil Gas, 1940... 28.00
Sinclair Gasoline 75.00
Skelly Gasoline, Tin Flange.. 135.00
Standard Oil Of Indiana, Paper, Bifold, Expires Jan., 1952....................................... 15.00
Standard Oil Of Indiana, Paper, Bifold, Expires May, 1954 .... 15.00

CROWN DERBY is the name given to porcelain made in Derby, England,
from the 1770s to 1935. Pieces are marked with a crown and the letter *D* or
the word *Derby*. The earliest pieces were made by the original Derby factory,
while later pieces were made by the King Street Partnerships (1848–1935) or
the Derby Crown Porcelain Co. (1876–1890). Derby Crown Porcelain Co.
became Royal Crown Derby Co. Ltd. in 1890. It is now part of Royal Doulton Tableware Ltd.

Dish, Serving, Japan Pattern, Imari Palette, Oval, Painted Red Mark, 10 In. 201.00
Plate, Imari, 1940, 10 3/4 In., 12 Piece... 690.00

CROWN DUCAL is the name used on some pieces of porcelain made by A. G. CROWN
Richardson and Co., Ltd., England. The name has been used since 1916. DUCAL
WARE

Bowl, 6 1/4 In... 15.00
Charger, Blue & Violet Flowers, White Ground, C. Rhead, 13 In................................. 440.00

CROWN MILANO glass was made by Frederick Shirley at the Mt. Washington Glass Works about 1890. It had a plain biscuit color with a satin finish. It was decorated with flowers and often had large gold scrolls.

Biscuit Jar, Pink Flowers On Shaded Yellow Ground, Silver Deposit	865.00
Biscuit Jar, Pond Lilies, Melon Ribbed, Signed, 6 1/4 x 7 In.	770.00
Bowl, Tricorner, Gold Rim, Roses & Forget-Me-Not Panels, Signed, 9 1/2 In.	460.00
Bride's Basket, White, Pleated Rim, Enameled Bird & Floral, Frame, 10 x 10 In.	245.00
Dish, Pansy, Triangular, Rolled Edge, Multicolored Flowers	475.00
Dish, Sweetmeat, Melon Ribbed, Multicolored Flowers, Lid, Handle, 4 x 5 1/2 In.	830.00
Pitcher, Gold & Silver Azaleas & Branches, Rope Handle, Signed, 8 In.	1980.00
Pitcher, Jeweled Holly Design, Bulbous, 9 In.	3025.00
Salt, Melon Ribs, 2 In.	85.00
Syrup Pitcher, Bee, Flowers, Embossed Cover, 6 1/2 In.	1375.00
Toothpick, Powder Blue & Purple Floral, 2 1/2 In.	385.00
Vase, Blue Scrolling, Gold Outlined Buds & Blossoms, Signed, 7 In.	978.00
Vase, Distant Desert City, Palm Trees, Dotted Gold Border Rim, 8 In.	748.00
Vase, Gold Rococo Scrolls, White Ground, Ball Shape, 6 1/2 x 7 In.	985.00
Vase, Green Maiden Hair Allover Design, 3 Gold Medallions, 9 In.	460.00
Vase, Milky Sides, Enameled Flamingos In Water, c.1890, 9 3/4 In.	1380.00
Vase, Pansies Outlined In Gold, Triangular, 3 Leaf Handles, 8 In.	1875.00
Vase, Raised Gold Flowers & Leaves, Beige Ground, Label, 7 3/4 In.	895.00

CRUETS of glass or porcelain were made to hold vinegar, oil, and other condiments. They were especially popular during Victorian times and have been made in a variety of styles since the eighteenth century. Additional cruets may be found in the Castor Set category and also in various glass categories.

Cranberry Glass, Swirl	125.00
Daisy Design, Blue, Clear Pointed Stopper	190.00
Glass, Silver Plated Stand, Ring Handle, Set Of 6 Bottles	72.00
Pink Satin Glass, Quilted	795.00
Pressed Glass, Broken Column	65.00
Satin Glass, Cranberry, Frosted Handle	330.00
White Finish, Applied Clear Handle With Swan Head, Stopper, Swansbill, 5 1/2 In.	575.00
Yellow Satin Glass, White Birds & Foliage, Trefoil Lip	345.00

CUP PLATES are small glass or china plates that held the cup while a diner of the mid-nineteenth century drank coffee or tea from the saucer. The most famous cup plates were made of glass at the Boston and Sandwich factory located in Sandwich, Massachusetts. There have been many new glass cup plates made in recent years for sale to gift shops or limited edition collectors. These are similar to the old plates but can be recognized as new.

Battery, New York, Dark Blue Transfer, Staffordshire, 3 3/4 In.	110.00 to 350.00
Blue, Luster Rim, Staffordshire	140.00
Blue Opalescent, Scallop Spalls	325.00
Cadmus, Trefoil Border, Staffordshire	350.00
Flow Blue, In Wire Basket	180.00
Gaudy Rose Design, Staffordshire, 3 3/4 In.	165.00
General Andrew Jackson, Staffordshire	1250.00
Glass, 1 Scallop & 4 Points	42.00
Landing Of General Lafayette At Castle, N.Y., August 1824, Staffordshire, 4 In.	288.00
Light Blue Glass, Lacy Design, 16 Large Scallops, Europe, 4 1/8 In.	45.00
Red Peafowl Spatterware, P.W. & Co. Stoneware, 4 1/8 In.	632.00
Roman Rosette, Blue-Green	300.00
South Carolina, Mayer, 4 In.	650.00
Staffordshire, South Carolina, 4 In.	650.00

CURRIER & IVES made the famous American lithographs marked with their name from 1857 to 1907. The mark used on the print included the street address in New York City, and it is possible to date the year of the original issue from this information. Earlier prints were made by N. Currier and use that name from 1835 to 1847. Many reprints of the Currier or Currier & Ives prints have been made. Some collectors buy the insurance

calendars that were based on the old prints. The words *large*, *small*, or *medium folio* refer to size. The original print sizes were very small (up to about 7 x 9 in.), small (8.8 x 12.8 in.), medium (9 x 14 in. to 14 x 20 in.), and large (larger than 14 x 20 in.). Other sizes are probably later copies. Other prints by Currier & Ives may be listed in the Card category under Advertising and in the Sheet Music category.

American Fruit Piece, Walnut Shadowbox Frame, 13 3/4 x 16 3/4 In.	220.00
American Homestead, Autumn, 1869, Frame, Small Folio	525.00
American Homestead, Winter, Frame, 13 1/2 x 16 1/2 In.	525.00
Autumn Fruits, 1861, Medium Folio	425.00
Battle Of Chickamauga, Frame, 12 x 16 In.	175.00
Blue Fishing, Small Folio	995.00
Catherine, Beveled Frame, 9 1/2 x 15 1/2 In.	192.00
Central Park, N.Y., The Bridge, Frame, 9 x 13 In.	60.00
Clipper Ship, Queen Of Clippers, Small Folio	595.00
Death Of President Lincoln At Washington, April 5, 1865	110.00
First Smoke-All Right, 1870, Small Folio	165.00
Frolicsome Pets, Hand Colored, Frame, 13 3/4 x 17 3/4 In.	192.00
George Washington, Black & White, Medium Folio	95.00
Good Morning, Little Favorite, Black & White, Small Folio	75.00
Grand Racer Kingston By Spendthrift, 1891, Large Folio	1575.00
Grandpa's Cane, Medium Folio	120.00
Harvesting, Frame, 13 x 16 1/2 In.	165.00
Home Of The Deer, 13 x 18 In.	50.00
Hunting On The Plains, 1871	2185.00
Lafayette At The Tomb Of Washington, 1845, Frame, 10 1/2 x 14 1/2 In.	235.00
Life Of A Fireman, The Race, 22 3/4 x 30 1/4 In.	2100.00
Lincoln Family, Hand Watercolored, Frame, 1964	150.00
New England Home, Small Folio	250.00
New York Crystal Palace, Large Folio	2650.00
Pair Of Nutcrackers, Small Folio	175.00
Philadelphia From The Navy Yard, Black & White, 11 x 13 3/4 In.	85.00
Rabbit Catching, Trap Sprung, Small Folio	725.00
Return From The Woods, Maple Frame, Medium Folio	295.00
Snowy Morning, F.F. Palmer, 12 x 16 1/2 In.	3100.00
Southern River Scenery, 1870, Small Folio	195.00
Steamboats Passing At Midnight, Long Island Sound, Small Folio	330.00
The American Patriot's Dream, Medium Folio	33.00
The Levee, New Orleans, Frame, 20 x 30 In.	3410.00
The Sale Of The Pet Lamb, Frame, 10 x 14 In.	175.00
Through Express, 1850	2100.00
Trotting Mare Belle Hamlin, Small Folio	55.00
Trotting Queen Alix, 1894, Large Folio	1100.00
Trotting Stallion Mambrino Gift, Small Folio	365.00
Two Little Fraid Cats, Frame, 12 3/8 x 16 1/4 In.	258.00
View On Long Island, Frame, 22 1/4 x 26 In.	600.00
William Penn's Treaty With Indians, 10 x 14 1/4 In.	185.00
William Penn's Treaty With The Indians, Black & White, 1875, Large Folio	995.00
Winter Morning In The Country, 1873, Small Folio	1380.00 to 1450.00
Winter Sports, Pickerel Fishing, 1872	2300.00
Yosemite Falls, Black Frame, Gilded Liner, 14 x 18 In.	140.00
Young Blood In An Old Body, Frame, 13 3/4 x 16 3/4 In.	250.00

CUSTARD GLASS is a slightly yellow opaque glass. It was first made in the United States after 1886 at the La Belle Glass Works, Bridgeport, Ohio. It is being reproduced. Additional pieces may be found in the Cambridge, Fenton, Heisey, and Northwood categories.

Argonaut Shell, Berry Set, 7 Piece	550.00
Argonaut Shell, Pitcher	375.00
Argonaut Shell, Pitcher, Gold Trim	350.00
Argonaut Shell, Pitcher, Water	475.00
Argonaut Shell, Spooner	110.00 to 125.00

Beaded Cable, Rose Bowl, Nutmeg 50.00
Chrysanthemum Sprig, Berry Bowl, Master... 200.00
Chrysanthemum Sprig, Celery 795.00
Chrysanthemum Sprig, Compote 100.00
Chrysanthemum Sprig, Compote, Jelly.. 125.00
Chrysanthemum Sprig, Creamer 105.00
Chrysanthemum Sprig, Cruet, Original Stopper....................................... 325.00
Chrysanthemum Sprig, Pitcher 495.00
Chrysanthemum Sprig, Salt & Pepper.......................... 140.00 to 195.00
Chrysanthemum Sprig, Spooner... 140.00
Chrysanthemum Sprig, Spooner, Green, Pink, Gold, Signed..................... 110.00
Chrysanthemum Sprig, Sugar 43.00
Chrysanthemum Sprig, Sugar, Cover 90.00
Chrysanthemum Sprig, Tumbler .... 38.00 to 70.00
Diamond With Peg, Butter, Cover ....200.00 to 215.00
Fine Cut & Roses, Rose Bowl, Nutmeg 55.00
Geneva, Banana Boat, Green Stain 150.00
Geneva, Cruet, Blue... 225.00
Geneva, Salt & Pepper, Green, Red Design.. 225.00
Geneva, Sauce, Green & Red Design, Oval... 35.00
Geneva, Toothpick, Plain 70.00
Georgia Gem, Powder Jar, Cover, Souvenir... 35.00
Grape & Cable, Banana Boat, Nutmeg 275.00
Grape & Cable, Cologne Bottle, Nutmeg 525.00
Grape & Gothic, Goblet, Northwood... 50.00
Grape & Gothic Arches, Goblet 65.00
Grape & Gothic Arches, Goblet, Nutmeg......................... 45.00 to 60.00
Grape Arbor, Vase, Whimsy, Nutmeg Stain.. 25.00
Intaglio, Berry Set, 7 Piece.. 395.00
Intaglio, Butter, Cover, Green, Gold Trim.. 225.00
Intaglio, Compote, Jelly, Green, Gold Trim 120.00
Intaglio, Pitcher, Water, Green Design 395.00
Intaglio, Saltshaker, Green Design... 125.00
Intaglio, Spooner, Design.. 110.00
Inverted Fan & Feather, Butter, Cover.. 345.00
Inverted Fan & Feather, Compote, Jelly 450.00
Inverted Fan & Feather, Toothpick... 695.00
Ivorina Verde pattern is in this category under Winged Scroll
Jackson, Tumbler, 4 In... 25.00
Jefferson Optic, Toothpick 55.00
Little Gem, see Georgia Gem pattern in this category
Lotus & Grape, Bonbon, Green Stain... 60.00
Lotus & Grape, Bonbon, Rose Stained Rim, 2 Handles 32.00
Louis XV, Berry Bowl, Gold Trim.. 40.00
Louis XV, Berry Bowl, Master... 200.00
Louis XV, Butter, Cover..40.00 to 190.00
Louis XV, Spooner, Gold Trim .... 75.00 to 78.00
Louis XV, Tumbler.. 50.00
Maize is its own category in this book
Maple Leaf, Spooner.. 110.00
Maple Leaf, Sugar, Cover 200.00
Peacock At Urn, Bowl, Ice Cream, 5 In. 45.00
Poppy, Relish, Nutmeg Stain......................................25.00 to 35.00
Prayer Rug, Bonbon.. 35.00
Ribbed Drape, Cruet 975.00
Ribbed Thumbprint, Toothpick, Rose Buds.. 90.00
Ring Band, Butter, Cover, Rose Design 245.00
Ring Band, Toothpick, Flower Bud... 165.00
Ring Band, Toothpick, Rosebuds... 125.00
Vermont, Toothpick.. 145.00
Vermont, Toothpick, Green Trim.. 95.00
Victoria, Celery, Gold Trim.. 195.00
Winged Scroll, Berry Set, 6 Piece 350.00

Winged Scroll, Berry Set, Gold Trim, 6 Piece 445.00
Winged Scroll, Box, Trinket, Cover, 3 In. 125.00
Winged Scroll, Butter, Cover, Round, 7 1/2 In. 195.00
Winged Scroll, Creamer, Gold Trim, 4 In. 110.00
Winged Scroll, Spooner, 3 3/4 In. 75.00
Winged Scroll, Spooner, Gold Trim 65.00
Winged Scroll, Water Set, 6 Piece 375.00

CUT GLASS has been made since ancient times, but the large majority of the
pieces now for sale date from the brilliant period of glass design, 1880 to 1905.
These pieces have elaborate geometric designs with a deep miter cut. Modern
cut glass with a similar appearance is being made in England, Ireland, and the
Czech and Slovak Republics. Chips and scratches are often difficult to notice
but lower the value dramatically. A signature on the glass adds significantly to
the value. Other cut glass pieces are listed under factory names.

Banana Boat, Hobstars, Miters, Strawberry Diamonds, Maple City, 10 In. 300.00
Basket, Hobstar & Cane Design, Twist Handle, 7 x 10 x 7 In. 675.00
Berry Set, Strawberry Diamond, 11 Piece 595.00
Biscuit Barrel, Brilliant, Hobstar Base, 8 In. 700.00
Bonbon, X-Cut Diamond 120.00
Bottle, Cologne, Hobstars, Step Cutting On Neck, 7 1/2 In. 325.00
Bottle, Cologne, Princess, Dorflinger, 7 In. 425.00
Bowl, 5 Geometric Floral Engraved, Sterling Silver Base, Hawkes, 8 x 4 In. 110.00
Bowl, 5 Point Flower Center, Brilliant, 12 x 3 In. 302.00
Bowl, Belmont, Hobstars & Buzz Stars, 8 In. 110.00
Bowl, Caroline, Teardrop From Underside Of Bowl To Base, 8 x 10 In. 825.00
Bowl, Comet, 8 x 3 1/2 In. 235.00
Bowl, Florals & Panels, 19th Century, England, 8 1/4 In. 402.00
Bowl, Flower, Turned-In Rim, Cobwebs, Garlands, Foliage, Curled Handles, 10 In. 265.00
Bowl, Green To Clear, Engraved, Footed, 10 3/4 In. 850.00
Bowl, Hobstar Center, Crosshatching On Other Areas, 3 Handles, 7 1/4 In. 375.00
Bowl, Hobstars, Fans, Crosshatching & Hobnails, Blackmer, 9 1/2 In. 275.00
Bowl, Hobstars, Fans, Miters, 8 In. 48.00
Bowl, Marlboro, Green To Clear, Dorflinger, 9 In. 2795.00
Bowl, Marquise, Egginton, 9 In. 200.00
Bowl, Orange, Hobstar, Clear Buttons, 11 1/4 x 5 1/2 In. 375.00
Bowl, Pinwheels, Hobstars Center, Crosshatching, Unger, 8 In. 100.00
Bowl, Russian, 13 1/2 In. 1210.00
Bowl, Sawtooth Rim, Hobstars, Crosshatching, Hobnails & Miters, Straus, 9 In. 300.00
Bowl, Serving, Swirl Design, 9 1/4 In. 360.00
Bowl, Starflowers & Strawberry Cut Bars, Scalloped, Brilliant, 9 1/4 x 4 In. 82.00
Bowl, Stars, Dentil Edge, Frosted Banners, Hawkes, 6 In. 66.00
Bowl, Strawberry Diamonds With Fans, Starflower Bottom, 9 x 3 3/4 In. 132.00
Bowl, Trellis, Egginton, 1 3/4 x 7 1/4 In. 1450.00
Bowl, Triple Miter Hobstars, Encircled By Ring Of Cane, 4 1/2 x 10 In. 575.00
Bowl, Triumph, Laurel & Co., 4 x 8 In. 350.00
Bowl, Waste, Miter Pattern, Cobalt Blue To Clear, Dorflinger 110.00
Box, Candy, Cover, Square Finial, Allover Hobstars & Lace, 7 x 8 In. 85.00
Box, Cracker, Allover Hobstars, Fans & Crosshatching, 9 x 2 1/2 In. 195.00
Box, Glove, Flowers & Harvard Pattern, Hinged, J.D. Bergen 2300.00
Bread Tray, Cane, Hobstars & Fans, Engraved Leaf Design, Clark, 12 1/2 In. 275.00
Bread Tray, Royal, Hunt, 5 1/2 x 11 1/2 In. 275.00
Cake Plate, Butterfly & Daisy, 10 In. 225.00
Candlestick, Crosscut Diamonds & Fans, 5 1/2 x 3 In. 1250.00
Candlestick, Hobstar, Cane, Crosscut Diamond, Teardrop Stem, 6 In., Pair 550.00
Candlestick, Strawberry Diamond Band, Pewter Insert, 10 3/4 In. 975.00
Candlestick, Teardrop, Diamonds Of Crosshatching, Hoare, 8 In., Pair 1050.00
Canoe, Harvard, 11 1/2 In. 200.00
Carafe, Drape, Hobstar Base, Straus, 7 1/4 x 7 In. 180.00
Carafe, Geometric Patterns, 1850s, 6 In. 195.00
Carafe, Hobstar, Fan & Strawberry Diamond Cut, Ringed Neck, 10 In. 225.00
Carafe, Water, Peerless, Empire Glass Co., 7 3/4 In. 110.00
Casserole, Cover, Wild Rose, Intaglio, 6 x 8 In. 1100.00

Celery, 2 Rows Of Offset Flutes, Bucket Shape, c.1845, 9 1/2 x 5 1/2 In. 375.00
Celery, Strawberry-Diamond & Fan, Bladed Knot Stem, 7 1/2 x 5 51/2 In. 275.00
Celery, Triple Square, Clark, 12 1/2 In. 425.00
Celery Dish, Harvard, 10 1/2 In. 95.00
Celery Dish, Plaza, Canoe Shape, Pitkin & Brooks, 12 x 4 3/4 In. 335.00
Champagne, Flute, Star Foot, Strawberry-Diamond & Fans Panels, 7 In. 295.00
Champagne, Hobstars, Fan & Cane, Rayed Base, 3 1/2 In., 10 Piece 190.00
Champagne, Panels Under Row Of Miter Cut Diamonds, 7 In., 8 Piece 1200.00
Cheese Dish, 18 Scalloped Panels, Faceted Knop, Gold Band Trim 68.00
Clock, Mantel, Harvard, New Haven, 10 x 6 In. 1250.00
Cocktail Shaker, Diamond Pattern, Hawkes Cover, 9 In. 245.00
Compote, Crosshatched Vesicas, Alternating Strawberry Diamonds, 7 /12 In. 750.00
Compote, English Hob, Dorflinger, 5 1/2 x 8 In. 1200.00
Compote, Hobstar Base, Notched Prisms On 6-Sided Stem, 9 In. 325.00
Compote, Memphis, Handles, Short Standard, 10 In. 160.00
Compote, Monarch, Scalloped Base, Teardrop Stem, Hoare, 7 x 8 In. 375.00
Compote, Strawberry-Diamonds & Fan, Baluster Stem, 7 x 7 In., ... 1125.00
Compote, Teardrop, Notched Prism Stem, Hobstars, Fan, 7 1/2 x 6 In. 225.00
Compote, Teardrop, Notched Stem, Star Cut Base, Hobstar Center, Signed, 8 x 5 In. 375.00
Cordial, Diamond, Square Base, Hawkes, 1 Oz., 8 Piece 375.00
Cordial, Hobstars & Strawberry-Diamond, 3 1/2 In., 6 Piece 270.00
Cracker Jar, Russian, Rayed Buttons, Full Cut Lid, 7 In. 950.00
Cream & Sugar, Square Dentillated Rim, Crosshatched Stars 99.00
Cruet, Cosmos, 9 In. 250.00
Cruet, Marlboro, Steeple Stopper, Dorflinger, 10 1/4 In. 290.00
Decanter, George III, Stylized Drapery Folds, Circular Stopper, 10 3/4 In., Pair 4025.00
Decanter, Green To Clear Diamond, Cathedral Shape, 12 1/2 In. 88.00
Decanter, Harvard, Bowling Pin Form, 13 1/2 In. 1250.00
Decanter, Hobstar Panels, Scalloped Foot, Cut-In Pattern Stopper, 16 In. 785.00
Decanter, Lapidary Cut Stopper, Bowling Pin Form, 13 In. 5000.00
Decanter, Offset Flutes Below Silver Diamonds, Dorflinger, 1870s, 12 In. 450.00
Decanter, Pillar Cut, 10 1/2 In. 325.00
Decanter, Strawberry-Diamond & Fan, Teardrop & Bubble Stopper, 14 1/2 In. 475.00
Decanter, Strawberry-Diamond Under Roundels, Bakewell, 9 In. 650.00
Decanter, Strawberry-Diamond, Faceted Neck Rings, 1830s, 8 3/4 In. 435.00
Decanter, Wheat & Thistle, Swirls, Sterling Silver Stopper, Hoare, 9 In. 1150.00
Dish, Heart Shape, Hobstars, Snowflakes, Fans, Sawtooth Edge, 5 1/4 In. 110.00
Dish, Ice Cream, Stars & Fans, Hunt, 5 In., 5 Piece 200.00
Dish, Rosemere, Alternating Hobstars, Oval, 7 1/4 x 4 1/4 In. 250.00
Dish, Sweetmeat, Cover, Footed, Diamonds & Hatching, Anglo-Irish, 12 In., Pair. 1430.00
Ewer, Thumbprint Handle, 4 Variations Of Designs, 32 Rayed Base, 11 1/2 In. 225.00
Finger Bowl, Kalana Poppy, Dorflinger 125.00
Flask, Diamond & Hobstars, Brass Shot Glass Cap, 6 1/2 In. 88.00
Flower Center, Step Cutting On Neck, Hobstar Base, 9 x 11 In. 1050.00
Frame, Satin Tulips, Cut Leaves, Notched, 9 x 7 In. 275.00
Frame, Tulips & Deeply Cut Leaves, Notched Edge, 9 x 7 In. 295.00
Goblet, Croesus, 6 In. 285.00
Goblet, Strawberry-Diamond & Fan, Bucket Shape, 5 1/4 In. 150.00
Humidor, Allover Hobstars, Cut-In Prism Lid, 7 In. 515.00
Humidor, Glenwood, Bulbous Lid, Bergen, 8 In. 850.00
Humidor, Hindoo, Hoare, 6 1/4 In. 285.00
Humidor, Marlboro Pattern, Dorflinger, 7 1/2 x 6 1/4 In. 1075.00
Ice Bucket, Floral Design, Silver Trim & Handle, Kirby Beard & Co., 8 1/2 In. 632.00
Ice Bucket, Harvard & Intaglio 210.00
Ice Bucket, Undertray, Hobstar On Field Of Prism Cutting, 6 1/4 x 9 In. 1850.00
Ice Cream Plate, Hobstars, Fans & File, Serrated Rim, 11 1/4 In. 115.00
Jar, Caviar, 16 Point Hobstar, Stopper, 6 x 3 3/4 In. 415.00
Jug, Whiskey, Monarch, Hoare, 11 In. 1240.00
Knife Rest, Allover Crosscut Diamond Cutting, 4 1/4 In. 65.00
Knife Rest, Strawberry-Diamond & Single Star Cutting, 4 1/8 In. 50.00
Lamp, Mushroom Shade, Hobstar & Diamond, Prisms, Signed, 29 In. 5300.00
Lemonade Set, Feathered Hobstar & Diamond, 7 Piece 172.00
Lemonade Set, Starburst, 8 Piece 220.00

Mustard, Charles II, Strawberry-Diamond & Crosshatching, Sterling Ladle	250.00
Mustard, Concave Hexagons, Cincinnati, Sterling Silver Spoon, 4 In.	250.00
Nappy, Miter & Silver Diamond, Dorflinger	185.00
Nappy, Prima Donna, Clark, 5 In.	125.00
Orange Bowl, Lotus, Egginton, 7 1/2 In.	275.00
Paperweight, Hobstars, Buttons, Crosshatching, Heart Shape, 3 1/2 In.	195.00
Perfume Bottle, Buzz Stars, Fans, & Diamond Cut, Bowling Pin Shape, 4 In.	165.00
Perfume Bottle, Miters, Oval Thumbprints, Stars, Atomizer, 4 1/4 x 4 3/4 In.	48.00
Perfume Bottle, Parisian, Dorflinger, 7 1/2 In., Pair	600.00
Pitcher, Buttermilk, Geometric, Notched Handle, 7 In.	175.00
Pitcher, Cider, Hobstar Base, 6 x 8 1/2 In.	450.00
Pitcher, Cider, Hobstars, Cane, Fan, Diamond Point, 8 In.	375.00
Pitcher, Cider, Large Expanding Star, Notched Handle, 6 1/4 In.	220.00
Pitcher, Cosmos, Flowers & Leaves, 10 1/2 In.	225.00
Pitcher, Diamonds & Fans, Brilliant, Applied Handle, 11 1/2 In.	77.00
Pitcher, Diamonds, Panels & Prismatic Miter Cuts, Richardson, 6 3/4 In.	850.00
Pitcher, Dorflinger, 8 1/4 In.	400.00
Pitcher, Fans, Swag Miters, Diamond Miters, Seed Cut, Piecrust Rim, 7 1/4 In.	98.00
Pitcher, Harvard, 9 1/2 In.	275.00
Pitcher, Harvard, Double Notched Handle, 13 In.	525.00
Pitcher, Lemonade, Engraved Wild Rose, 9 3/4 In.	55.00
Pitcher, Star Pattern, Notched Handle, Silver Rim & Spout, 9 7/8 In.	405.00
Pitcher, Starflower Design, 8 1/2 In.	66.00
Pitcher, Starflowers, Circles & Fans, Brilliant, Applied Handle, 11 1/4 In.	115.00
Pitcher, Starflowers, Fans & Panels, Brilliant, Applied Handle, 8 1/2 In.	126.00
Pitcher, Strawberry Diamonds Below Roundels & Rays, Bakewell, 7 1/2 x 8 In.	1125.00
Pitcher, Thumbprint Band, Zipper Swags, Crosshatched, 6 1/2 x 5 In.	80.00
Pitcher, Thumbprint Neck, Zigzag & Crisscross Miters, Bulbous Belly, 6 1/2 x 5 In.	92.00
Pitcher, Water, Etched Vintage Design, 19th Century, 11 In.	201.00
Pitcher, Water, Russian, Square, Silver Trim, Hinged Cover, c.1900, 12 1/4 In., Pair	3162.00
Plate, Allover Chrysanthemums & Scrolling, 8 1/2 In.	48.00
Plate, Butterflies Around Central Flower, Niland, 7 In., 4 Piece	300.00
Plate, Diamond & Fan, 6 1/4 In.	125.00
Plate, Sandwich, Festoon & Urn, Straus, 10 In.	210.00
Punch Bowl, Hobstar & Prism, Straight Sides, 12 x 12 In.	1375.00
Punch Bowl, Pedestal, Deep Hobstars, 12 In.	1695.00
Punch Bowl, Royal, Hunt, 2 Piece	1500.00
Punch Bowl Set, Overall Canes, Notched Shafts, Hobstar Base, 13 Piece	1092.00
Relish, Allover Cut, Nailhead Maltese Cross Center, Hobstars, Oval, 8 1/2 x 5 In.	110.00
Relish, Expanding Star, 4 Sections, Notched Handles, Elite Glass Co., 8 In.	385.00
Relish, Star Flower & Fans, Boat Shape, Brilliant, 11 3/4 In.	104.00
Rose Bowl, Royal, Hunt, 7 x 7 /12 In.	560.00
Salad Set, Parisian, Matched Bowl & Undertray, Dorflinger, 10 In.	1875.00
Salad Set, Russian, Bowl & Underplate, 4 1/4 x 11 In.	985.00
Salt, Hobstars & Strawberry-Diamond, 2 1/8 In.	40.00
Salt, Master, Feathered Design, Teardrop Stem, 3 3/8 x 3 In., Pair	390.00
Salt & Pepper, Miters & File, Chrome Tops, Footed, Square Shoulders, 5 In.	25.00
Server, Sandwich, Engraved Fruit, Signed Hunt, c.1904	295.00
Sherbet, Intaglio Cut Blossom, Buds & Stems, Amethyst, 3 7/8 In., 10 Piece	375.00
Sherry, Block Cutting, Hobstar Base	55.00
Sherry, Monarch, Hoare	65.00
Spooner, Cup Shape, Hobstars, 5 x 5 /12 In.	140.00
Spooner, Stars, Hobnails & Miters, Egginton, 8 In.	80.00
Sugar & Creamer, Buzz Stars, Thumbprints On Handle	125.00
Sugar & Creamer, Colonial, Notched Prism Handles, Dorflinger	250.00
Sugar & Creamer, Comet-Type Design, Swirled Hobstars & Fans, Hoare	135.00
Sugar & Creamer, Cut Thistle, Clark, 3 1/2 In.	125.00
Sugar & Creamer, Geometric, 4 1/2 In.	100.00
Sugar & Creamer, Handleless Sugar, Pluto, Hoare, 3 1/2 x 4 In.	395.00
Sugar & Creamer, Heart & Hobstar	85.00
Sugar & Creamer, Hobstar & Fan	350.00
Sugar & Creamer, Pedestal, Carolyn, Hoare, 5 1/2 In.	895.00
Sugar & Creamer, Royal, Hunt	350.00

Sugar & Creamer, Ruby Pattern, Blackmer, 4 In.. 130.00
Sugar & Creamer, Star Flowers, Brilliant, 3 In. 71.00
Sugar Shaker, 3 Hobstars, Separated By Zipper Cutting, Silver Collar........................ 125.00
Sugar Shaker, Allover Diamonds, 3 x 5 3/4 In. 72.00
Sugar Shaker, Brilliant, Hobstar, Silver Plated Cover, 4 In.................................... 95.00
Syrup, Stars Alternating With Hobstars All Around, Plated Top & Handle 115.00
Tankard, Hobart, Unger, 11 In. 250.00
Tray, Chrysanthemum, Square, Brilliant, 11 In.. 475.00
Tray, Ice Cream, Allover Hobstar & Lace, Panel Of Cane, 14 In. 1210.00
Tray, Ice Cream, Allover Hobstar Cutting, Hoare, 17 1/2 In. 2530.00
Tray, Ice Cream, J. Hoare 2530.00
Tray, Ice Cream, Miter Cuts, Hobstars, Crosshatching, Sawtooth Rim........................ 595.00
Tray, Ice Cream, Palm & Fan, Ovoid, Ohio Glass Co., 14 In. 140.00
Tray, Ice Cream, Sultana, Dorflinger... 1200.00
Tray, Stafford, Hunt, 14 1/2 In.. 590.00
Tray, Star, Meriden, 12 1/2 In... 3250.00
Tumble-Up, Hobstars & Flowers, Handle, Rayed Bottom 135.00
Tumbler, Allover Hobstar Cutting, Hobstar Base, 5 1/4 In. 185.00
Tumbler, Croesus, Hoare, 3 3/4 In... 165.00
Tumbler, Crosshatched Triangles Under Diamonds & Fans, 3 1/2 In. 175.00
Tumbler, Hobstars, Swirls, Fans, 8 Piece 185.00
Tumbler, Juice, Royal, Hobstar Base, Dorflinger... 50.00
Tumbler, Strawberry-Diamond & Fan, Star Cut Base, Pair 450.00
Tumbler, Strawberry-Diamond, Roundels & Rays, Bakewell, 3 1/2 In., Pair................ 750.00
Vase, Butterflies, Daisy Blossoms, Herringbone Stepped Stem, 14 1/2 In. 690.00
Vase, Diamond Facets, Baluster Shape, Dentil Rim, 11 3/4 In. 110.00
Vase, Harvard, Hobstar & Cane, Footed, Scalloped 24-Point Hobstar Foot, 10 In......... 650.00
Vase, Hobstars & Diamond Cut Fields, 11 3/4 In. 172.00
Vase, Mistletoe, Clark, 10 1/4 x 8 1/2 In... 1260.00
Vase, Monarch, 2 Handles, Hoare, 12 In. 1445.00
Vase, Notched Prism, Hobstars, Diamond Point, Columns Of Russian, 18 In................ 1250.00
Vase, Star Flower & Fans, Scalloped, Brilliant, 12 In. 137.00
Vase, Star Flower & Fans, Vertical Bars, Brilliant, 11 7/8 In. 104.00
Vase, Star, Strawberry-Diamond & Zipper Cutting, 16 In....................................... 302.00
Vase, Stars With Hobnail, Button Centers, Allover Engraved Flowers, 10 1/2 In. 125.00
Vase, Victoria, Cylindrical, Egginton, 12 In... 190.00
Water Set, Floral Cutting, Signed, 7 Piece.. 375.00
Water Set, Harvard, Rayed Bases, Tankard, 10 In., 7 Piece 625.00
Water Set, Hobnails & Mitered Stars, 10 1/2-In. Pitcher, 5 Piece 325.00
Whiskey, Old Colony, Dorflinger... 42.00

CUT VELVET is a special type of art glass, made with two layers of blown
glass, which shows a raised pattern. It usually had an acid finish or a texture
like velvet. It was made by many glass factories during the late Victorian
years.

Ewer, Diamond Quilted, Blue, Applied Handle, 4 3/4 In... 165.00
Vase, Yellow, Small 275.00

CYBIS porcelain is a twentieth-century product. Boleslaw Cybis came to the
United States from Poland in 1939. He started making porcelains in Long
Island, New York, in 1940. He moved to Trenton, New Jersey, in 1942 as one
of the founders of Cordey China Co. and started his own Cybis Porcelains
about 1950. The firm is still working. (See also Cordey.)

CYBIS

Bell, Christmas, 1983...75.00 to 95.00
Box, Heart, Thinking Of You, No. 817R ....95.00 to 150.00
Candlestick, Iris, White 75.00
Carafe, Bacchus 250.00
Compote, Iris, White 95.00
Cup, Bacchus, 4 Piece.. 195.00
Figurine, Baby Owl, No. 334, 4 1/2 In. 85.00
Figurine, Bathsheba, No. 452, 14 In. 1300.00
Figurine, Beatrice, No. 445, 12 In. 287.00
Figurine, Calla Lily, No. 515, 16 1/2 In. 800.00

Figurine, Cinderella, No. 429, 7 1/2 In. 350.00
Figurine, Deer Mouse, In Clover, No. 660, 3 1/2 In. 95.00
Figurine, Elizabeth Ann, No. 490, 5 In. 125.00
Figurine, Eskimo Child Head, Snow Bunting, No. 466, 10 1/2 In. 225.00
Figurine, George Washington Bust, No. 482, 12 In. 1100.00
Figurine, Guinevere, No. 448, 12 In. 1650.00
Figurine, Hamlet, No. 446, 12 In. 460.00
Figurine, Hermit Thrush, No. 380, 15 1/2 x 9 In. 1000.00
Figurine, Holiday Child, Panda, 5 1/2 In. 195.00
Figurine, Jeanie, No. 4012, 9 1/2 In. 185.00
Figurine, Kitten Topaz, No. 684R, 3 x 5 1/2 In. 110.00
Figurine, Little Boy Blue, No. 4000, 9 In. 400.00
Figurine, Little Miss Muffet, No. 4008, 7 1/4 In. 275.00
Figurine, Moses, Great Lawgiver, No. 411, 20 In. 1092.00
Figurine, Mr. Snowball, No. 611, 4 In. 55.00
Figurine, Penguin, No. 365, 5 1/2 In. 200.00
Figurine, Peter Pan, No. 430, 7 1/2 In. 475.00
Figurine, Pinto Colt, No. 670, 5 1/2 x 9 In. 250.00
Figurine, Queen Esther, No. 98, 13 In. 950.00
Figurine, Queen Esther, No. 496, 13 1/2 In. 460.00
Figurine, Turtle Doves Of Peace, No. 331, 12 In. ....175.00 to 345.00
Figurine, Walrus Wellington 110.00
Figurine, Wendy, No. 433, 6 1/2 In. 85.00
Figurine, Wood Wren With Dogwood, No. 336, 5 1/2in. 350.00
Vase, Daisy 195.00

CZECHOSLOVAKIA is a popular term with collectors. The name, first used as
a mark after the country was formed in 1918, appears on glass and porcelain
and other decorative items. Although Czechoslovakia split into Slovakia and
the Czech Republics on January 1, 1993, the name continues to be used in
some trademarks.

Ashtray, Alligator, In Relief 15.00
Basket, Glass.. 76.00
Basket, Hand Painted, Ceramic, Barta & Rose, 5 In.. 48.00
Basket, Purple & Green Flowers, Yellow Ground, Pottery, 9 x 7 3/4 In. 225.00
Candlestick, Varicolored, Cased Glass, Signed, 8 1/2 In. 79.00
Canister Set, Blue & Yellow, Wood Shelving, Bauhaus, Pottery, 10 Piece 800.00
Canister Set, Colored Design, Cream Ground, Yvonne, Pottery, 5 x 5 In. 350.00
Demitasse Set, Teahouse, Red, 13 Piece 100.00
Figurine, Bull, Mottled, 10 In. 65.00
Lamp, Flowers, Orange Ground, Peasant Art Industries, Pottery, 10 In. 300.00
Perfume Bottle, Cut Glass Rose Top, Glass Dabber 65.00
Perfume Bottle, Dresser Set, Malachite Glass, Intertwined Nudes, 7 In. 2420.00
Perfume Bottle, Filigree, Inset Stones, Purse Size 90.00
Perfume Bottle, Woman, Full Skirt, Flowers & Bird, Long Stopper, 10 In. 650.00
Pitcher, Air Brushed Bubbles, Checked Ground, Erphila, Pottery, 6 3/4 In. 300.00
Pitcher, Brown Crosshatching, Amber Ground, Signed Celebrate, Pottery 125.00
Pitcher, Coin Dots, Blue, 3 3/4 In. 55.00
Pitcher, Cut Glass, Squatty, Signed.. 33.00
Pitcher, Spots, On Red Ground, Green Handle, Lustro, Pottery, 8 1/2 In. 150.00
Pitcher, Vase, Green Cased, Clear Handle, Ruffled Top, Signed, 9 In. 75.00
Pitcher, White, Cat Handle, Black Dots, 4 In. 32.00
Pitcher, Yellow, Green, Purple Design, Black Ground, Pottery, 9 In. 175.00
Planter, Art Deco, Floral Design, Yellow Ground, Ditmar Urbach, Pottery 250.00
Planter, Basket Of Flowers, On Black Medallion, Erphila, Pottery, 7 In.............. 200.00
Plaque, Engraved Giraffe Design, Cased Glass, Artist, Square, 6 In. 150.00
Plate, Colonial Couple, Orchid, Gold, Pirkenhammer, 10 1/2 In. 35.00
Teapot, Art Deco, Peasant Art Industries, Stepped Lid, Pottery, 7 x 9 1/4 In. 300.00
Teapot, Yellow Lusterware, Black Handle & Trim, 4 3/4 In. 30.00
Vase, Alternate Vertical Panels, Ditmar Urbach, Pottery, 10 In. 400.00
Vase, Art Deco, Geometric Diamond Pattern, Signed, Pottery, 7 x 5 In. 175.00
Vase, Black & Tan Design, Cream Ground, Signed, Pottery, 10 In. 225.00
Vase, Blue Oil Spot Design, Yellow, Signed, 8 In... 1375.00

Vase, Embossed Woman Profile, White, Handle, Stepped Top, Art Deco, 9 In. 125.00
Vase, Floral, Red Ground, Signed, Pottery, 12 In. 225.00
Vase, Fluted, 16 Faceted Sides, Signed HP, Pottery, 8 In. 175.00
Vase, Glass, Floriform, Applied Lily Leaves, Footed, 8 In. 460.00
Vase, Hand Painted Floral, Tulips, Black Ground, Signed, Pottery, 8 In. 250.00
Vase, Multicolored Eyes, Signed, Pottery, 10 In. 3375.00
Vase, Orange & Cobalt Trim, 7 1/2 In., Pair 185.00
Vase, Orange, Beige, Pottery, Signed, 8 1/4 In. 89.00
Vase, Panels Of Abstract Flowers, Ditmar Urbach, Pottery, 10 In. 300.00
Vase, Red & Green Design, Cream Ground, Ditmar Urbach, Pottery, 7 In. 175.00
Vase, Red, Applied Cobalt Blue, 4 3/4 In. 95.00
Vase, Tic-Tac-Toe, Red & Black, Cream Ground, Signed, Pottery, 8 In. 250.00
Vase, Varicolored, Blue-Orange, Cased Glass, Signed, 8 In. 79.00
Window Box, Red & Cream Desgin, Black Top Band, Pottery, 5 x 9 In. 175.00

D'ARGENTAL is a mark used in France by the Compagnie des Cristalleries de
St. Louis. The firm made multilayered, acid-cut cameo glass in the late nine-
teenth and twentieth centuries. D'Argental is the French name for the city of
Munzthal, home of the glassworks. Later they made enameled etched glass.

Chandelier, Orchid Blossoms, 3 Iron Chain Links, Signed, c.1920, 26 In. 4025.00
Vase, Large Pinecones, Pine Needles, 3 Color, c.1920, 9 In. 2500.00
Vase, Riverbank Landscape, House, Castle, Bridge, Brown, Yellow, Cameo, 14 In. 990.00

DANIEL BOONE, a pre-Revolutionary War folk hero, was a surveyor, trapper,
and frontiersman. A television series, which ran from 1964 to 1970, was
based on his life and starred Fess Parker. All types of Daniel Boone memorabilia are collected.

Coloring Book, 1965 .... 10.00
Doll, Marx, 11 In. 200.00
Slate, 1965 .... 45.00
Thermos, For Lunch Box, 1965 .... 85.00 to 90.00
Viewer, Movie, With Film, Original Package, 1964 .... 34.00

DAUM, a glassworks in Nancy, France, was started by Jean Daum in 1875.
The company, now called *Cristalleries de Nancy*, is still working. The *Daum
Nancy* mark has been used in many variations. The name of the city and the
artist are usually both included.

Bowl, Chestnut Leaves & Branches, Gray Overlay, c.1910, 11 1/8 In. 3163.00
Bowl, Dragonflies & Flowers, Cameo, Signed, 10 In. 9775.00
Bowl, Etched & Enameled, Trefoil Rim, Dandelions, 5 2/3 In. 3680.00
Bowl, Gold Foil Design, Orange & Yellow Mottling, Signed, 8 7/8 x 4 1/2 In. 924.00
Bowl, Riverside Landscape, Frosted Quatraform, Signed, 6 In. 1955.00
Bowl, Trefoil Rim, Enameled Dandelions Going To Seed, Signed, 5 2/3 In. 3680.00
Box, Art Deco Design, Smoky Amber, 5 x 3 In. 412.50
Box, Cover, Enameled Carnations & Clover, Signed, c.1910, 5 1/2 In. 3737.00
Box, Cover, Etched, Enameled, Yellow, Pink, Sailing Vessels, Seagulls, c.1900, 4 In. .. 2090.00
Box, Cover, Molded Overall Floral, Oval, 2 1/2 x 5 1/2 In. 1955.00
Box, Landscape, Defoliated Trees On Cover, Signed, Round, c.1910, 7 In. 3450.00
Box, Silver Cover, Etched, Enameled, Flowering Poppies, Circular, 3 1/2 x 6 In. 1495.00
Chandelier, Etched Furrows, Raised Dots, Leaf & Tendril Finial, c.1925, 38 In. 7475.00
Chandelier, Vertical Stringing, Clear & Frosted, c.1925, 15 3/4 x 13 7/8 In. 5750.00
Figurine, Cat, Signed, 10 1/2 In. 695.00
Figurine, Owl, 3 1/2 In. 65.00
Flask, Pansy Blossoms Enameled On White, Screw Top Cup, c.1900, 5 7/8 In. 3162.00
Lamp, Boudoir, River Landscape, 3-Arm Foliate Metal Mount, Signed, 11 In. 6900.00
Lamp, Gray, Mottled Lemon & Salmon, Signed, 18 1/2 In., Pair 5750.00
Lamp, Winter Landscape, 3-Arm Iron Mount, Signed, 19 1/4 In. 6900.00
Perfume Bottle, Coppella, Pate-De-Verre, 6 In. 325.00
Pitcher, Yellow Enameled Under Lip, Clear, Ribbed, Signed 300.00
Plate, Four Seasons, Various Colors, 10 1/2 In., 4 Piece 545.00
Powder Box, Vase, Silver Cover, Foliate Design, 2 Red Blossoms, Signed, 2 1/4 In. 920.00
Souvenir Cup, Opalescent Frosted, Clear, Cut Raspberries, Leaves, 1900, 4 In. 1200.00

Toothpick, Cameo, Gold Leaves, Green Base.. 395.00
Toothpick, Gold Cut Back To Chipped Ice, Frosted Peach Ground................................ 495.00
Vase, Acid-Sculptured, Geometric Design, Smoky-Amber, 1930s, 9 1/2 In.................. 2100.00
Vase, Apple Blossom, Brown Speckled Ground, Ovoid 1980.00
Vase, Bottle Form, Morning Glories, Molded, 9 1/4 In... 7260.00
Vase, Bud, Sunflowers, Daisies, Green Cut To Ochre, Signed, 5 1/2 In..................... 2118.00
Vase, Bulbous, Blue Base, Cut Leaves, Signed, c.1900, 5 1/4 In........................... 2070.00
Vase, Concentric Bands, Signed, c.1925, 10 7/8 In.. 3680.00
Vase, Cornflower, Gray Walls, Mottled, Overlaid Enamels, Signed, 15 1/4 In. 7187.00
Vase, Cornflowers, Leafage, Signed, c.1900, 3 3/4 In.. 4312.00
Vase, Cut Iris Flower, Dragonfly, Gilt Bronze Foliage, Signed, c.1900, 16 In. 6900.00
Vase, Cylindrical, Footed, Frosted Clear Shading To Dark Violet, Gilded, 9 In............ 4600.00
Vase, Double Overlay, Etched, Trumpet Shape, Wheel-Carved Daisies, 9 1/2 In.......... 3220.00
Vase, Enameled Landscape Scene, Birch Trees, Lake, Mottled, 12 In....................... 4200.00
Vase, Enameled Spring Violets & Leaves, Signed, 5 In.. 3025.00
Vase, Etched & Enamel Painted Waterfront Riverscape, Mountains, Signed, 9 5/8 In. ... 7475.00
Vase, Etched & Enameled Flowering Fuchsia Blossoms, Signed, 9 In. 4600.00
Vase, Etched & Enameled, Sphere, Spring Landscape, Pink Ground, 3 In. 1265.00
Vase, Etched Geometrics, Amber, Foil Inclusions, 10 In...................................... 4025.00
Vase, Etched, Wheel-Carved, Footed, Oviform, Inverted Rim, Leaves, Beetle, 5 1/2 In. 4025.00
Vase, Flattened Shape, Mottled Yellow & Blue, 7 x 5 In...................................... 231.00
Vase, Forest Scene, Shades Of Green & Charcoal, Signed, c.1900, 6 3/4 In. 2300.00
Vase, Frosted Orange, Oak Leaves, Foil-Backed Acorns, Beetle, Signed, 5 1/2 In........ 4025.00
Vase, Geometric Band, Raised Dots, Signed, c.1926, 13 3/4 In............................. 9200.00
Vase, Gold Foil Inclusions, Geometric Pattern, Signed, 10 In. 4025.00
Vase, Green Holly Berries, White Ground, 15 1/2 In... 1200.00
Vase, Green Mottled Glass, Foil Inlay, Signed, 5 In... 275.00
Vase, Internal Stripes, Poppy Blossoms & Leafage, Signed, c.1910, 6 In................. 4900.00
Vase, Irises & Leaves, Green, Satin Finish, Overlay, Gilt Signature, 7 In. 995.00
Vase, Lake Scene, Signed, 4 In. 400.00
Vase, Lemon Yellow Streaks, Primroses & Leafage, c.1910, 14 7/8 In..................... 7200.00
Vase, Martele, Cameo Rose Sprays, Squat Shape, c.1900, 5 3/4 In. 4180.00
Vase, Mottled Surface, Earth Tones, Signed, 4 x 4 In... 385.00
Vase, Mottled, Layered Orange & Green, Etched Fruits, Signed, 14 In..................... 7475.00
Vase, Mustard To Burnt Orange Leaf Design, Cross Of Lorraine Mark, 7 In. 1980.00
Vase, Orchid Blossoms, Buds & Leafage, Signed, 1910, 12 7/8 In.......................... 4025.00
Vase, Overlaid Ferns, Enameled, Signed, c.1900, 3 1/4 In.................................. 2100.00
Vase, Oviform, Tripod Base, Scalloped Rim, Woods & Lake, Sailboats, 5 3/4 In. 2990.00
Vase, Peacock, Cut Feathers, Inlaid Eyes, Signed, 7 3/8 In. 5750.00
Vase, Purple Passion Flower, Green Leaves & Vines, Signed, 4 3/4 In..................... 1045.00
Vase, Red & Green Foliate, 14 In... 2860.00
Vase, River Landscape, Leafy Trees, Signed, c.1900, 8 In. 2590.00
Vase, Scenic, Yellow Center, Amethyst Below, Autumnal Trees, Signed, 27 In. 9775.00
Vase, Sprays Of Wildflowers & Leaves, Green, Charcoal, Signed, 1910, 13 1/2 In. 4900.00
Vase, Spring Landscape Scene, Pale Green, Spherical Form, Signed, 3 In. 1265.00
Vase, Spring Landscape, Rolling Hills, Signed, c.1900, 19 3/4 In........................... 6900.00
Vase, Square, Etched, Enameled, Gray, Cornflowers, c.1920, 4 3/4 In. 2500.00
Vase, Stems Of Bleeding Hearts, Mottled Foot, Signed, c.1910, 8 1/2 In. 4800.00
Vase, Streaked, Woodland Bells, Spiky Leafage, Signed, c.1910, 18 3/8 In. 6615.00
Vase, Summer Landscape, Signed, c.1910, 5 1/2 In. 2185.00
Vase, Textured Fluting, Ring Foot, Signed, 13 1/2 x 14 In.................................... 465.00
Vase, Thistle, Baluster Form, Overall Scrolling Thorny Branches, Signed, 7 1/8 In. 2400.00
Vase, Trees Bending In Rainstorm, Signed, c.1910, 1 5/8 In................................ 2585.00
Vase, Violets, 4-Sided, Enameled, Cameo, Signed, 4 1/2 x 2 In. 1800.00
Vase, Winter Forest Landscape, Signed, c.1915, 6 1/2 In. 2875.00
Vase, Winter Landscape, Black & Frosty White, Signed, 6 1/4 In.......................... 2530.00

DAVENPORT pottery and porcelain were made at the Davenport factory in Longport, Staffordshire, England, from 1793 to 1887. Earthenwares, creamwares, porcelains, ironstone, and other ceramics were made. Most of the pieces are marked with a form of the word *Davenport*.

DAVENPORT
LONGPORT
STAFFORDSHIRE

Bowl, With Plate, Black Transfer, Landscape Scene, Cover, c.1825, 8 3/4 In................ 290.00

Cup Plate, Teaberry, Pink Luster 30.00
Pitcher, Water, View In Geneva, White Ground, Loop & Scoop Handles, 11 1/4 In. 575.00
Soup, Dish, Pearlware, Green Edge, Multicolored House, 8 In. 400.00
Toby Jug, 1820, 9 1/2 In. 900.00

DAVY CROCKETT, the American frontiersman, was born in 1786 and died in 1836. The historical character gained new fame in 1954 when the Walt Disney television show ran a series of episodes featuring Fess Parker as Davy Crocket. Coonskin caps and buckskins became popular and hundreds of different Davy Crockett items were made.

Badge 25.00
Bandanna, Yellow With Red & Black Lettering 45.00
Bank, Pony Express, Randy Inc., Package 15.00
Bank, Pot Metal, Figural 45.00
Bathrobe, Reversible 443.00
Belt, Powder Horn & Compass, Original Card 65.00
Billfold, Box 85.00
Bookends 150.00
Bracelet, Charm 45.00
Cap, Raccoon 38.00
Cap Gun, Flintlock, Hubley, 1950s 148.00
Cards, Gum, Topps, 1950, 23 Piece 54.00
Clothes Rack, Saddle 35.00
Comic Book, Davy Crockett & River Pirates, Fess Parker, 1955 .... 14.00
Cookie Jar, American Bisque .... 485.00 to 500.00
Cufflinks, Metal, 1950s 9.00
Doll, Plush, 1940s, 19 In. 135.00
Flashlight 75.00
Game, Horseshoes, Rubber, Box .... 75.00 to 95.00
Hat, Straw, Child's 60.00
Horseshoe Set, Box 95.00
Jackknife 35.00
Knife, Pocket, Disney, Small 40.00
Lamp, Electric, Motion 295.00
Lamp, With Shade, Premco .... 150.00 to 195.00
Lunch Box, Frontier, Green, Plastic, Dome, Red Handle, Paper Label, 1950s .... 185.00 to 300.00
Mug, Blue & White 15.00
Mug, Red .... 8.00 to 16.00
Mug, White Glass, 3 Pictures, W.D. Productions, 1950s 45.00
Nodder 150.00
Pajamas, Child's, 2 Piece 200.00
Pinback, Kresge 15.00
Pistol, Model Kit, Box 95.00
Poster, Davy Crockett & River Pirates, Cardboard, England, 1956, 22 x 28 In. 110.00
Poster, Movie, Davy Crockett & River Pirates, 27 x 41 In. 125.00
Powder Horn, Box 60.00
Puzzle, Jigsaw, Fess Parker Photo, No. 4423, Whitman, 1955 .... 43.00
Record, Ballad Of Davy Crockett, Little Golden Record, No. D197, 78 Rpm, 1950s 32.00
Record, Comic Book, Late 1970s, 45 RPM, Plastic Wrap 10.00
Rifle, Buffalo, Hubley 175.00
Ring, 1950s 25.00
Sheet Music, Ballad Of Davy Crockett, 1954 .... 10.00
Spurs, Engraved Steel, Wide Straps 325.00
Stamp Book, King Of The Wild Frontier, Complete, 1955 .... 30.00
Suspenders, Fess Parker .... 55.00 to 67.00
Thermos, Crockett Fighting Indians, Steel, Holtemp, 1950s .... 37.00 to 63.00
Tie, Leather, Hand Painted Picture Of Davy And Powder Horn 20.00
Tie, String, Clip-On 23.00
Tomahawk, Pocket Knife, Fess Parker, Imperial, 1950s 50.00
Tumbler, Orange, White, Old Grumpy Bear Made His Mistake, 15 In. 10.00
Wall Pocket 48.00
Watch, Complete With Horn, Windup 495.00
Watch, Toy, On Card 50.00

DE VEZ was a signature used on cameo glass after 1910. E. S. Monot founded the glass company near Paris in 1851. The company changed names many times. Mt. Joye, another glass by this factory, is listed in its own category.

Vase, Cameo Glass, Bird, Landscape, Tree, Ships, Purple To Gray, 4 1/2 In.	907.00
Vase, Exotic Flowers & Leaves, Chartreuse Ground, Signed, 7 1/2 In.	940.00
Vase, Flared Petticoat Vasiform, Pond Lily Blossoms, Signed, 6 In.	632.00
Vase, Sailboats, Village, Signed, 6 1/4 In.	850.00
Vase, Stick, Exotic Flowers & Leaves, Chartreuse Ground, Signed, 7 /12 In.	940.00

DECOYS are carved or turned wooden copies of birds, fish, or animals. The decoy was placed in the water or propped on the shore to lure flying birds to the pond for hunters. Some decoys are handmade, some are commercial products. Today there is a group of artists making modern decoys for display, not for use in a pond.

Black Duck, 4-Part Body, Glass Eyes, Decoys Unlimited, 20 1/2 In.	62.00
Black Duck, G.C. Hendrickson	525.00
Black Duck, Inset Glass Eyes, Lead Weight	3450.00
Black Duck, Ned Burgess	6600.00
Black Duck, Original Paint, Primitive, 15 In.	70.00
Black Duck, Shot Scars, Glass Eyes, Dr. Miles Pirnie, Michigan, 17 3/4 In.	193.00
Black Duck, Tack Eyes, Hollow Body, Branded C.R.W., 16 1/2 In.	300.00
Blackbellied Plover, Glass Eyes, Relief Carved Wings & Split Tail, Tom Wilson	1380.00
Blackbellied Plover, Obediah Verity	7150.00
Blue-Winged Teal, Mason	7700.00
Bluebill, Chesapeake Bay	110.00
Bluebill Drake, Carved Detail, Glass Eyes, Ben Schmidt, 14 3/4 In.	220.00
Bluebill Drake, Glass Eyes, Paul Arness, 13 In.	55.00
Bluebill Drake, Turned Head, Glass Eyes, Old Paint, Dark Varnish, 15 3/4 In.	110.00
Bluebill Drake, Working, Repaint, Glass Eyes, Shot Scars, 13 In.	95.00
Bluebill Drake, Worn Old Paint, Shot Scars, Primitive, 11 5/8 In.	60.00
Bluebill Hen, Eli Doughty	8800.00
Brant, Hollow Block, Glass Eyes, William Goenne, 19 1/2 In.	105.00
Bufflehead, Nick Purdo	635.00
Canada Goose, Balsa, Wooden Head, Glass Eyes, Wild Fowler Decoys, 19 In.	95.00
Canada Goose, Black & White Paint, 2-Piece Head, 22 In.	195.00
Canada Goose, Carved, Painted, Joe Lincoln, Massachusetts, 5 3/4 x 14 In.	3100.00
Canada Goose, Carved, Signed J. Lapham, 6 1/2 In.	210.00
Canada Goose, Cork & Wood, Glass Eyes, 21 1/4 In.	170.00
Canada Goose, Molded Papier-Mache, Glass Eyes, General Fibre Co., 26 In.	27.50
Canada Goose, Original Paint, Glass Eyes, Clare Londrigan, 1978, 10 1/2 In.	27.50
Canada Goose, Painted, Wood & Canvas, A.C., 32 In.	100.00
Canada Goose, Primitive, Original Paint, 17 In.	66.00
Canada Goose, Stick-Up, Glass Eyes, Driftwood Base, 16 1/2 x 29 In.	440.00
Canada Goose, Stick-Up, Tin, 21 In.	160.00
Canvasback Drake, August George Heinfield, Rock Hall, Md., 12 In.	165.00
Canvasback Drake, Hollow Body, High Head, Glass Eyes, 16 3/4 In.	525.50
Canvasback Drake, John Daddy Holly, Havre De Grace, Md., 13 In.	275.00
Canvasback Drake, Oversized Head, Glass Eyes, Mike Bonnet, 15 1/2 In.	105.00
Canvasback Hen, Bobtail, Glass Eyes, Down River, Mich., 14 1/ 4 In.	60.00
Canvasback Hen, Glass Eyes, Shot Scars, Dobson, 16 1/2 In.	160.00
Canvasback Hen, Rankin	750.00
Crow, Papier-Mache, Glass Eyes, Original Paint, 16 In.	33.00
Dowitcher, Walter Brady	7700.00
Eider Drake, Hollow Carved, Glass Eyes, Wood Mussel In Bill, 20th Century	575.00
Fish, Pike, Hand Carved, Early 1900s, Large	60.00
Fish, Tin Fins, Brown & Yellow Paint, Spots, Wooden, 14 In.	150.00
Fish, Tin Fins, Polychrome Paint, Weighted, Wooden, 12 1/2 In.	165.00
Goldeneye, Hen, Adam Brown, St. Lawrence River, c.1920s, 10 3/4 In.	357.00
Goldeneye, Stamped Mark On Base, A. Elmer Crowell, 2 3/4 In.	800.00
Goose, Cork & Wood, Glass Eyes, 19 1/2 In.	50.00
Green-Winged Teal Drake, 1949	65.00
Green-Winged Teal Drake, Original Paint, Branded Walker, 12 1/2 In.	165.00

Green-Winged Teal Drake, Wood & Canvas Over Wire Hoops, Initialed W.M., 10 In.   49.50
Herring Gull, Carving, Antiqued Painting, 15 In.. 50.00
Long-Billed Curlew, Hollow Carved, Glass Eyes, Original Paint, Cedar........................ 345.00
Mallard Drake, Carved, A. Elmer Crowell, East Harwich, Mass., 13 1/2 In. 1850.00
Mallard Drake, Charlie Perdew, 1930s.. 775.00
Mallard Drake, Hollow Block, Glass Eyes, Initialed P.A., 19 1/2 In............................... 95.00
Mallard Drake, Sleeper, Inletted Ballast Weight, Maumee Bay, Ohio, 14 In. 192.00
Mallard Hen, Folk Art Repaint, Glass Eyes, 16 In. 115.00
Mallard Hen, Original Paint, Combed Feather, Green Lake, Wis., 18 In. 70.00
Mallard Hen, Original Paint, Glass Eyes, J. M. Hayes Co., 15 1/2 In............................. 115.00
Mallard Hen, Original Paint, Glass Eyes, Shot Scars, 16 In. 126.00
Merganser Drake, Glass Eyes, Original Paint, Tom Wilson 6600.00
Pigeon, Carved, Painted, Glass Eyes, 19th Century, 9 1/4 In.. 285.00
Pintail, Orton Griebler, Worn Repaint, Bead Eyes, 14 3/4 In. 105.00
Pintail Drake, Jack Sweet, Erie, Pa., Original Paint, Glass Eyes, 11 3/4 In..................... 70.00
Pintail Hen, Glass Eyes, Wing Tip Carving, Richard Jansen, 16 3/4 In.......................... 275.00
Red-Breasted Merganser, A. Elmer Crowell, 3 1/8 In. 865.00
Red-Breasted Merganser, H.Conklin, New Jersey, Pair... 1325.00
Red-Breasted Merganser, Horsehair Tufts, 13 1/2 In. 440.00
Redhead Drake, Glass Eyes, 13 1/2 In.. 150.00
Redhead Drake, Glass Eyes, J.H. Oser, '79, 5 3/4 In. 40.00
Redhead Drake, Hollow, Thomas Chambers, 1920... 1825.00
Redhead Drake, Oversized Humped Back, Carved Wing Tips, 16 3/4 In. 66.00
Ringed Plover, A. Elmer Crowell, Massachusetts, Full Size 5500.00
Seagull, Glass Eyes, Tom Martindale, 15 1/4 In.. 80.00
Shorebird, Folding, Tin, Label Pat. Oct. 27, 1874, 11 1/2 In. 165.00
Sturgeon, Attached Measuring Device, Leather Fins, Manitowoc, Wis., 37 1/2 In. 650.00
Sturgeon, Metal Fins & Hanger, Full Size, 40 1/2 In... 335.00
Swan, Charles Hart 6325.00
Swan, Painted, John T. Lewark, North Carolina, 24 x 22 In. 1845.00
Swan, Solid, 3-Piece Construction, Tack Eyes, Horseshoe Weight, Charles Hart........... 3740.00
Turkey, Wild, Hardy's, Roanoke Rapids, N.C., Stand, 26 In. 550.00
Whistling Swan, Painted Eyes, Weight, Branded CWJ, Maryland 6325.00
Widgeon Drake, Glass Inset Eyes, Tom Wilson 1600.00
Widgeon Drake, Wildfowler Decoy Co., Connecticut.. 165.00
Willet, Charles Thomas, Oversized... 5000.00
Willet, Inset Glass Eyes, Original Bill, Over Sized, Charles Thomas............................... 4887.00
Yellowlegs, Inset Glass Eyes, Relief Carved Wings & Split Tail, Tom Wilson 1380.00

DEDHAM Pottery was started in 1895. Chelsea Keramic Art Works was
established in 1872 in Chelsea, Massachusetts, by members of the Robertson
family. The firm used the mark *CKAW*. The factory closed in 1889 and was
reorganized as the Chelsea Pottery U.S. in 1891. It became the Dedham Pottery of Dedham, Massachusetts. The factory closed in 1943. It was famous
for its crackleware dishes, which picture blue outlines of animals, flowers,
and other natural motifs.

Bowl, Blue Swans Band, Cattails, Crackleware, White Ground, Ink Stamp, 2 x 5 In. 330.00
Bowl, Rabbit, Double Blue Stamp, 6 x 12 In... 460.00
Bowl, Rice, Chick, Marked, 3 1/8 In.. 1265.00
Creamer, Night & Day, Owl & Moon One Side, Hen & Sunrise On Other, 5 In........... 440.00
Dish, Bacon, Rabbits, Crackleware, White Ground, Signed, 9 1/4 x 6 In....................... 325.00
Dish, Ducks & Pond Lilies, 9 1/4 In... 350.00
Eggcup, Rabbit 350.00
Humidor, Elephants, 7 In. 2000.00
Plate, 5 Blossom Pods Perimeter, Outlined Lily.. 572.00
Plate, Butterfly, Blue Stamp, 8 5/8 In.. 400.00
Plate, Horsechestnut, Double Stamp, 8 1/4 In.. 50.00
Plate, Mushroom Pattern, 8 1/2 In.. 4840.00
Plate, Polar Bear, 8 1/2 In.. 302.00
Plate, Pond Lily Border, 9 3/4 In.. 220.00
Plate, Pond Lily Border, Maude Davenport, 6 In. 1100.00
Plate, Reverse Rabbit, Clover Mark, 9 13/16 In. 1840.00

Plate, Snowtree, Blue Stamp, 6 In.	70.00
Plate, Turtle, Blue Stamp, 10 In.	800.00
Platter, Rabbits Around Edge, 10 1/2 x 17 1/2 In.	4400.00
Tile, Elephant, Blue Ground, Crackleware, Square, 5 3/4 In.	525.00
Tile, Iris, Square, 5 1/2 In.	185.00
Tile, Rabbit, 5 1/2 In.	250.00
Tray, Cheese, Rabbit Border, Square	1540.00
Vase, 4-Sided, Scrolled Base, Metal Shape, Chelsea Keramic, 12 1/2 x 5 In.	550.00
Vase, Blue Branches, Blossoms, Crackleware, Artist, Rabbit Mark, 7 1/4 In.	1500.00
Vase, Bud, High Gloss Green & Brown Glaze, Signed, 5 In.	225.00
Vase, Covered In Thick Green & Blue-Gray Flambe, Hugh Robertson, 7 1/4 In.	700.00
Vase, Sang De Boeuf Flambe Allover, Orange Peel Texture, Signed, 6 1/4 In.	1300.00
Vase, Sang De Boeuf, Orange Peel Texture, Signed, 4 1/2 In.	650.00
Vase, Sang De Bouef, Red Metallic, Gray, Hugh Robertson, 5 In.	605.00
Vessel, Double Gourd Shape, Orange Peel Texture, Signed, 7 1/2 In.	2300.00
Wash Basin, Band Of Rabbits Nibbling, 12 1/8 In.	4730.00

DEGENHART is the name used by collectors for the products of the Crystal Art Glass Company of Cambridge, Ohio. John and Elizabeth Degenhart started the glassworks in 1947. Quality paperweights and other glass objects were made. John died in 1964 and his wife took over management and production ideas. Over 145 colors of glass were made. In 1978, after the death of Mrs. Degenhart, the molds were sold. The D in a heart trademark was removed, so collectors can easily recognize the true Degenhart piece.

Cup Plate, Heart & Lyre, Cobalt	15.00
Dish, Hen, Blue, 3 In.	20.00
Dish, Turkey, Covered, Cream Colored, Opaque	75.00
Figurine, Owl, Green	42.00
Salt, Bird With Cherry, Yellow	20.00
Toothpick, Colonial Drape, Purple	18.00
Toothpick, Forget-Me-Not	30.00

DEGUE is a signature acid-etched on pieces of French glass made in the early 1900s. Cameo, mold blown, and smooth glass with contrasting colored rims are the types most often found.

Lamp, Deco Stripes & Geometric Devices, Cone Shade, Signed, 16 1/2 In.	2415.00
Lamp, Forest Scene, Mottled Blue To Amethyst, 3 Arms, Iron, c.1925, 19 In.	7475.00

DELATTE glass is a French cameo glass made by Andre Delatte. It was first made in Nancy, France, in 1921. Lighting fixtures and opaque glassware in imitation of Bohemian opaline were made. There were many French cameo glass makers, so be sure to look in other appropriate categories.

Lamp, Birds In Flight, Sailing Ships On Standard, Signed, c.1925, 17 1/2 In.	2875.00
Vase, Bands Of Chevrons, Middle Band Of Flowers, Signed, c.1925, 15 1/2 In.	3450.00

DELDARE, see Buffalo Pottery Deldare

DELFT is a tin-glazed pottery that has been made since the seventeenth century. It is decorated with blue on white or with colored decorations. Most of the pieces sold today were made after 1891, and the name *Holland* appears with the Delft factory marks. The word *delft* also appears on pottery from other countries.

Ashtray, 3 Cigarette Rests, Florals, 6 1/2 x 2 In.	12.00
Ashtray, Shoe, Windmill Scene, 2 5/8 In.	8.00
Bottle, Floral Design, Blue & White, Liverpool, England, c.1760, 10 1/4 In.	450.00
Bowl, Playing Cards On Exterior, 5 Cards On Interior, Dutch, c.1750, 9 In.	3450.00
Bowl, Stylized Leaf & Scroll Design, Melon Rib, Footed, Tab Handles, 6 1/4 x 3 In.	40.00
Brick, Floral, English, 18th Century, 5 1/2 In.	325.00
Brick, Flowers & Leaves, Beribboned Oriental Objects, Dublin, c.1760, 5 7/8 In.	1265.00
Butter, Lid, Windmill Scene, 1/4 Lb.	16.50
Charger, Blue & White, Landscape, Cattle, 16 1/4 In.	132.00
Charger, Chinese Fisherman, Landscape, Blue & White, England, c.1740, 13 In.	375.00

Charger, Floral Landscape, Blue & White, 13 1/2 In. 400.00
Charger, Girl By River, Boat, Windmills, 20th Century, 14 1/2 In. 60.00
Clock, Tall Case, Paper Label, Miniature 715.00
Coffeepot, Lid, Blue Parsley, Floral, Foliage Border, Parsley Sprays, 8 In. 110.00
Cup, Fuddling, 3 Vessel Form, Rope Twist Handles, Southwark, 1700s, 3 1/4 In. 5175.00
Dish, Allover Berry & Floral Design, Blue & White, c.1770, 12 1/4 In. 500.00
Dish, Floral Design, Scalloped Leafy Border, Blue & White, c.1750, 11 3/4 In. 375.00
Dish, Floral Landscape, Floral & Berry Border, Blue & White, Ireland, c.1760, 11 In. .. 259.00
Dish, Oriental Figural Landscape, Lobed, 18th Century, 14 In. 925.00
Dish, Polychrome Compote Of Flowers, 18th Century, 5 1/4 In. 247.50
Dish, Royalist, William Of Orange, Fruit & Floral Border, 1680s, 12 In. 1265.00
Figurine, House, Signed Henkes Holland, 6 In. 15.00
Figurine, Woman, Feather Hat, 5 In. 15.00
Inkstand, Oriental Designs, Bristol, 18th Century, 6 In. 560.00
Inkwell, Wagon, Blue House 55.00
Jar, Drug, Bergemot, Lamp Base, 9 In. 400.00
Muffineer, Woman At Seashore, Flowers On Neck & Foot, c.1800, 5 1/2 In. ... 145.00
Pill Slab, Crest Of Worshipful Society Of Apothecaries, London, 1750s, 12 1/2 In. 3737.00
Pitcher, Blue Scenes Both Sides, Off-White, Soft Paste, 1820-1840, 5 3/4 x 7 1/4 In. ... 130.00
Pitcher, Polychorme Floral, Armorial Crest, 7 In. 190.00
Pitcher, Underplate, Stylized Flowers, 3 x 2 1/2 In. 22.00
Plaque, Birdcage, Canary, Blue & Yellow Cage, Drapery, Dutch, 1700, 16 5/8 In. 5175.00
Plate, Birds & Flowers, 14 1/2 In. 137.00
Plate, Blue & White, Floral, Bristol, c.1760, 9 1/4 In. 325.00
Plate, Center Balloon In Flight, Feathered Edge, Lambeth, c.1785, 9 1/8 In. ... 1150.00
Plate, Center Floral, Blue Band Rim 25.00
Plate, House & Landscape, Blue & White, Bristol, c.1760, 9 1/4 In. 325.00
Plate, Polychrome House, 8 3/4 In. 165.00
Plate, Village Scene, Blue & White 195.00
Platter, Blue Parsley, 11 1/2 In. 30.00
Punch Bowl, Blue & White, Oriental Man Fishing, London, c.1766, 10 1/2 In. 2000.00
Puzzle Jug, Blue & White, Spherical, Peonies, Liverpool, c.1745, 7 In. 2000.00
Salt & Pepper, Windmill, Box 25.00
Sugar & Creamer, Blue Parsley 45.00
Tankard, Polychrome Decoration, Pewter Mounts, Hinged Lid, Germany, 9 3/4 In. ... 1265.00
Teapot, Gentleman, Woman On Reverse, Leaping Stag, Dutch, 1700s, 4 5/8 In. 3175.00
Tile, Arts & Crafts, Galleon, 9 x 5 In. 225.00
Tile, Dragonfly 75.00
Tile, Landscape, Church, Sponged Purple, 5 1/4 In. 50.00
Tile, River, Boat, Horse, Holland, 17 x 12 In. 440.00
Tile, Water Scenes, Floral Corners 50.00
Toby Jug, Modeled As Napoleon, Allover Scrolled Leaf Design, 13 In. 287.50
Tureen, Sauce, Cover, Nesting Plover Form, 1850s, 6 In. 2550.00
Vase, Blue & White Oriental Design, 7 1/4 In. 55.00
Vase, Flared Cylinder, Red & Green High Glaze, 9 1/2 In. 66.00

DENTAL cabinets, chairs, equipment, and other related items are listed here.
Other objects may be found in the Medical category.

Barber's Bowl, Blue & White Floral, Delft, 10 In. 715.00
Barber's Bowl, Blue & White, Blossom & Leaves, Delft, c.1750, 11 1/2 In. 1035.00
Barber's Bowl, Flowers, Garden Fence, Blossom Rim, Dutch, Delft, c.1780, 9 In. 700.00
Cabinet, Hutch, Mirror, Marble 2150.00
Cabinet, Revolving, Clark 9500.00
Case, Traveling, Black Leather, Oak Drawers 200.00
Chest, Lift Top, Name On Brass Plaque, 6 Drawers, Civil War Period 600.00
Drill, Foot Pedal, Cast Iron, 1850-1860 .... 650.00
Drill, Foot Pedal, Cast Iron, 1870s 350.00
Drill, SS White, Foot Pedal, Cast Iron Base 320.00
Machine, Saliva Suction, Air Blowing, Chromed Flywheel, Gauges, Early 1900s 950.00
Mold, Denture, Marked B.D.M. Co., No. 22 A, Buffalo, N.Y., Brass 80.00
Mold Guide, Trubyte, Encased Teeth, 1952 .... 35.00
Picture, Dentist, Pulling Old Woman's Tooth, Photo-Engraved, 1880s, 5 x 9 In. 6.50
Teeth, Model For Filling, Bone 45.00

Tooth Extractor, Iron, Albany, N.Y. 39.00

DEPRESSION GLASS was an inexpensive glass manufactured in large quantities during the 1920s and early 1930s. It was made in many colors and patterns by dozens of factories in the United States. The name *Depression glass* is a modern one. For more descriptions, history, pictures, and prices of Depression glass, see the book *Kovels' Depression Glass & American Dinnerware Price List.*

Adam, Bowl, Pink, 4 3/4 In. 12.00
Adam, Bowl, Square, Green, 8 In. 25.00
Adam, Cake Plate, Footed 24.00
Adam, Candy, Cover 92.00
Adam, Pitcher, 8 In. 42.00
Adam, Plate, Pink, 6 In. 10.00
Adam, Plate, Pink, 9 In. 25.00
Adam, Sugar & Creamer 19.00
Adam, Sugar, Cover 43.00
Alice, Cup & Saucer, Blue 9.50
Alice, Cup & Saucer, Jadite .... 4.50 to 6.00
Alice, Cup & Saucer, White 9.50
Alice, Plate, Blue, 9 In. .... 9.50 to 17.00
Alice, Saucer, Jadite 1.50
Alice, Saucer, White 2.50
Alpine Caprice, Candleholder, 3-Arm, Pink, Frosted 50.00
American Pioneer, Bowl, Green, 9 1/2 In. 20.00
American Pioneer, Cup & Saucer, Pink 14.00
American Pioneer, Platter, Green, 12 1/2 In. 15.00
American Sweetheart, Bowl, Monax, 6 In. ....6.50 to 12.00
American Sweetheart, Console, Red, 18 In. 985.00
American Sweetheart, Creamer, Monax 7.00
American Sweetheart, Cup, Pink 15.00
American Sweetheart, Plate, Monax, 8 In. 11.00
American Sweetheart, Plate, Monax, 9 In. 5.50
American Sweetheart, Plate, Monax, 15 1/2 In. 170.00
American Sweetheart, Salver, Monax, 12 In. 45.00
American Sweetheart, Saucer, Monax 4.00
American Sweetheart, Saucer, Pink 4.00
American Sweetheart, Tray, Monax, 12 In. 45.00
Apple Blossom pattern is listed here as Dogwood
Aunt Polly, Berry Bowl, Blue, 7 In. 20.00
Aunt Polly, Plate, Blue, 6 In. 10.00
Aunt Polly, Sherbet, Blue 10.00
Aunt Polly, Tumbler, Blue 20.00
Aurora, Bowl, Deep, Cobalt Blue, 4 1/2 In. 27.00
Aurora, Cup & Saucer, Cobalt Blue 20.00
Aurora, Cup, Cobalt Blue 10.00
Aurora, Plate, 6 1/2 In. 15.00

Depression glass, Adam   Depression glass,   Depression glass, Bubble
Block Optic

Depression glass, Cherry Blossom

Depression glass, Cloverleaf

Avocado, Creamer, Footed	10.00
Ballerina pattern is listed here as Cameo	
Banded Rib pattern is listed here as Coronation	
Banded Rings pattern is listed here as Ring	
Baroque, Rose Bowl, Topaz	85.00
Basket pattern is listed here as No. 615	
Beaded Block, Bowl, Green, 7 1/2 In.	27.00
Beaded Block, Pitcher, White, 1 Pt.	160.00
Beaded Block, Plate, Round, Pink, 8 3/4 In.	10.00
Beaded Block, Plate, Square, Green, 7 1/4 In.	16.00
Block pattern is listed here as Block Optic	
Block Optic, Bowl, Green, 4 1/4 In.	8.00
Block Optic, Candleholder, Green, 1 3/4 In., Pair	45.00
Block Optic, Candy Dish, Cover, Green	45.00
Block Optic, Cup, Green	7.00
Block Optic, Plate, 8 In.	5.00
Block Optic, Plate, Green, 6 In.	4.00
Block Optic, Plate, Green, 9 In.	18.00
Block Optic, Saltshaker	20.00
Block Optic, Saucer, Green, Ring, 5 1/2 In.	8.50
Block Optic, Sherbet, Green, 3 1/4 In.	6.00
Block Optic, Sherbet, Green, 4 3/4 In.	15.00
Block Optic, Sugar & Creamer, Footed	23.00
Block Optic, Tumbler, Footed, 9 Oz.	20.00
Bouquet & Lattice pattern is listed here as Normandie	
Bubble, Berry Bowl, Blue, 5 1/4 In.	6.50
Bubble, Berry Bowl, Blue, 8 3/8 In.	12.00 to 15.00
Bubble, Cup & Saucer, Blue	6.00 to 7.50
Bubble, Cup, Blue	5.00
Bubble, Goblet, Forest Green, 5 5/8 In.	10.00
Bubble, Plate, 9 3/8 In.	4.00
Bubble, Plate, Blue, 6 3/4 In.	3.00
Bubble, Platter, Blue	17.50
Bubble, Sherbet, Forest Green, 3 3/4 In.	8.00
Bubble, Sugar & Creamer, Green	17.50
Bullseye pattern is listed here as Bubble	
Butterflies & Roses pattern is listed here as Flower Garden With Butterflies	
Buttons & Bows pattern is listed here as Holiday	
Cabbage Rose pattern is listed here as Sharon	
Cameo, Candlestick, Green, 4 In., Pair	135.00
Cameo, Cup, Green	10.00 to 11.00
Cameo, Grill Plate, Green	9.50
Cameo, Pitcher, Green, 6 In.	80.00
Cameo, Plate, Green, 6 In.	2.50 to 4.00
Cameo, Plate, Green, 8 In.	7.00
Cameo, Plate, Green, 9 1/2 In.	15.00 to 16.00

Cameo, Plate, Yellow, 6 In. 4.50
Cameo, Plate, Yellow, 9 1/2 In. 8.50
Cameo, Saltshaker, Green 32.50
Cameo, Sherbet, 6 In. 25.00
Cameo, Sherbet, Green, 4 7/8 In. 30.00
Cameo, Tumbler, 9 Oz. 17.00
Cameo, Vase, Green, 8 In. 20.00
Candlewick pattern is listed in the Imperial Glass category
Cape Cod, Goblet, 6 3/8 In. 9.00
Cape Cod, Sherbet, 5 In. 8.00
Caprice pattern is included in the Cambridge Glass category
Caribbean, Relish, 5 Sections, Blue, 12 1/2 In. 95.00
Century, Sugar & Creamer 29.00
Chantilly, Plate, 10 In. 88.00
Cherokee Rose, Plate, 8 In. 15.00
Cherry Blossom, Bowl, Pink, 5 3/4 In. 30.00
Cherry Blossom, Bowl, Vegetable, Oval, Pink, 9 In. 35.00
Cherry Blossom, Butter, Cover, Pink 70.00
Cherry Blossom, Cake Plate, Footed 27.00
Cherry Blossom, Creamer & Sugar, Pink, Child's 80.00
Cherry Blossom, Cup & Saucer, Delphite 30.00
Cherry Blossom, Dinner Set, Pink, Child's, 14 Piece 275.00
Cherry Blossom, Grill Plate, Pink, 9 In. 24.00
Cherry Blossom, Pink, Cup 16.00
Cherry Blossom, Pitcher, Pink, 42 Oz., 8 In. 50.00
Cherry Blossom, Plate, Delphite, 10 1/4 In. 125.00
Cherry Blossom, Plate, Pink, 7 In. 17.00
Cherry Blossom, Plate, Pink, 9 In. 20.00
Cherry Blossom, Platter, Pink, 13 In. 60.00
Cherry Blossom, Sugar, Cover, Pink ....25.00 to 27.00
Cherry Blossom, Tumbler, Pink, 4 1/2 In. 28.00
Christmas Candy, Cup & Saucer, Teal Blue 40.00
Christmas Candy, Sugar & Creamer, Teal Blue 75.00
Circle, Cup & Saucer, Green 6.00
Circle, Goblet, Green, 8 Oz. 9.00
Circle, Goblet, Wine, Green, 4 1/2 In. 12.00
Circle, Pitcher, Green, 8 In. 22.50
Circle, Sherbet, Green, 4 3/4 In. 5.00
Cloverleaf, Creamer, Green .... 7.50 to 9.50
Colonial, Cup & Saucer, Pink 16.00
Colonial, Sherbet 5.50
Colonial, Sugar & Creamer 25.00
Colonial Block, Bowl, Green, 7 In. 15.00
Colonial Block, Sugar, Cover, Green 9.00
Columbia, Bowl, 5 In. 12.50
Columbia, Bowl, 8 1/2 In. 14.50
Columbia, Bowl, 10 1/2 In. 13.50

Depression glass, Colonial

Depression glass, Cubist

Columbia, Butter, Cover...17.00 to 25.00
Columbia, Chop Plate, 11 In.. 7.50
Columbia, Cup & Saucer.. 8.50
Columbia, Plate, 9 1/2 In... 7.50
Coronation, Tumbler, Pink.. 15.00
Cube pattern is listed here as Cubist
Cubist, Berry Bowl, 4 1/2 In... 8.00
Cubist, Candy Jar, Cover.. 27.00
Cubist, Coaster... 11.00
Cubist, Pitcher, Green 225.00
Cubist, Plate, 8 In.. 9.00
Cubist, Saucer... 10.00
Cubist, Sugar & Creamer, Cover, Green 25.00
Dancing Girl pattern is listed here as Cameo
Diamond Pattern is listed here as Miss America
Diamond Quilted, Candlestick, Flat, Pair.. 22.00
Diamond Quilted, Plate, 6 In... 5.50
Diamond Quilted, Sugar & Creamer 23.00
Diana, Bowl, 5 In.. 3.50
Diana, Cup & Saucer...4.00 to 9.50
Diana, Plate, Amber, 9 1/2 In. 7.50
Diana, Saucer... 1.50
Diana, Saucer, Amber.. 2.00
Dogwood, Bowl, Green, 10 1/2 In. 245.00
Dogwood, Cup & Saucer, Green... 40.00
Dogwood, Plate, 8 In. 6.00
Dogwood, Plate, Green, 8 In.. 12.00
Dogwood, Plate, Pink, 8 In. 26.00
Doric, Bowl, Oval, Green, 9 In.. 39.00
Doric, Cake Plate, Footed, Green, 10 In. 27.00
Doric, Candy Dish, Cover, Pink.. 40.00
Doric, Coaster, Green 25.00
Doric, Relish, Green, 4 x 4 In... 14.00
Doric, Relish, Green, 4 x 8 In... 21.00
Doric, Sherbet, Green, Footed 17.50
Doric, Sugar, Cover, Green... 38.00
Doric, Tumbler, Pink, 4 In.. 65.00
Double Shield pattern is listed here as Mt. Pleasant
Dutch Rose pattern is listed here as Rosemary
Early American Rock Crystal pattern is listed here as Rock Crystal
English Hobnail, Tumbler, Iced Tea, 10 Oz. 8.00
Fire-King, Hot Plate, Ivory 6.50
Fire-King, Plate, 9 In. 6.00
Flat Diamond pattern is listed here as Diamond Quilted
Floragold, Ashtray.. 8.50
Floragold, Bowl, Deep, 9 1/2 In. 40.00

Depression glass, Dogwood

Depression glass, Doric

Depression glass, Florentine No.1

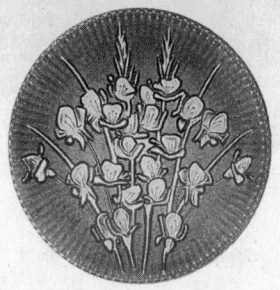

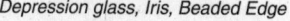

Depression glass, Iris, Beaded Edge

Depression glass, Mayfair Federal

Floragold, Bowl, Ruffled, 5 1/2 In.	9.50
Floragold, Bowl, Square, 4 1/2 In.	8.50
Floragold, Cup	8.50
Floragold, Pitcher	3.50
Floragold, Sherbet, 2 1/2 In.	11.00
Floragold, Tumbler, Footed, 10 Oz.	15.00
Floral, Butter, Cover, Pink	75.00
Floral, Butter, Pink	20.00
Floral, Platter, Oval, Green, 10 3/4 In.	17.50
Floral, Platter, Pink, 10 3/4 In.	11.50
Floral & Diamond Band, Bowl, Green, 4 1/2 In.	9.50
Florentine No. 1, Sherbet, Green	8.50
Florentine No. 1, Sugar, Ruffled Edge, Pink	30.00
Florentine No. 2, Coaster, Green	10.00
Florentine No. 2, Cup & Saucer, Yellow	12.00
Florentine No. 2, Plate, Yellow, 8 1/2 In.	7.00 to 7.50
Florentine No. 2, Saltshaker, Yellow	22.50
Florentine No. 2, Sherbet, Green	8.00
Florentine No. 2, Sherbet, Yellow	7.50
Florentine No. 2, Sugar, Yellow	8.00
Flower Garden With Butterflies, Candy Jar, Cover, Amber, 7 1/2 In.	75.00
Flower Garden With Butterflies, Plate, Green, 8 In.	17.50 to 25.00
Forest Green, Vase, 6 1/2 In.	4.00
Forest Green, Vase, 9 In.	8.00
Fortune, Candy Dish, Cover, Pink	22.50
Fruits, Cup & Saucer, Green	8.50
Georgian, Bowl, Green, 4 1/2 In.	7.50
Georgian, Bowl, Green, 6 1/2 In.	19.50
Georgian, Butter, Cover, Green	75.00
Georgian, Creamer, Green	7.50
Georgian, Plate, Green, 6 In.	4.50
Georgian, Plate, Green, 8 1/2 In.	8.50
Georgian, Plate, Green, 9 1/4 In.	30.00
Georgian, Sugar & Creamer, Green	45.00
Hairpin pattern is listed here as Newport	
Harp, Cake Stand, Ruffled Edge, Blue	20.00
Harp, Coaster	3.50
Harp, Tray, Handle, 12 3/4 In.	25.00
Heritage, Bowl, 10 1/2 In.	10.00
Heritage, Cup & Saucer	8.00
Hobnail pattern is listed in the Hobnail category	
Holiday, Berry Bowl, Pink, 5 1/8 In.	9.50
Holiday, Creamer, Pink	7.50
Holiday, Sherbet, Pink	5.50
Horizontal Ribbed pattern is listed here as Manhattan	
Horseshoe pattern is listed here as No. 612	
Iris, Bowl, Beaded Edge, 4 1/2 In.	6.00

Depression glass, Miss America

Depression glass, Moderntone

Iris, Bowl, Ruffled Edge, Iridescent, 11 1/2 In. .... 10.00 to 15.00
Iris, Butter, Cover 45.00
Iris, Goblet, 4 1/4 In. 25.00
Iris, Lamp Shade, White 40.00
Iris, Sherbet, Footed, 4 In. 20.00
Iris, Tray 25.00
Iris, Tumbler, Footed, 6 1/2 In. .... 19.50 to 29.50
Iris, Vase, 9 In. 29.50
Iris, Vase, Iridescent, 9 In. .... 20.00 to 22.50
Iris & Herringbone pattern is listed here as Iris
Jamestown pattern is listed here as Tradition
Jane Ray, Cup & Saucer, Jadite .... 3.00 to 4.50
Jane Ray, Plate, Dinner, Jadite 5.00
Jane Ray, Soup, Dish, Jadite 14.00
Jane Ray, Sugar & Creamer, Cover, Jadite 10.00
Jane Ray, Sugar, Cover, Jadite 8.00
Jubilee, Cake Plate, 2 Handles, Topaz 28.00
Jubilee, Creamer, Footed, Yellow 22.00
Jubilee, Cup & Saucer, Yellow 15.00
Jubilee, Plate, Yellow, 7 In. 14.00
Jubilee, Plate, Yellow, 8 3/4 In. 16.00
Jubilee, Sugar, Yellow 35.00
Jubilee, Tumbler, Footed, Yellow, 6 In. 42.00
Katy Blue pattern is listed here as Laced Edge
Knife & Fork pattern is listed here as Colonial
Lace Edge, Bowl, Pink, 7 3/4 In. 25.00
Lace Edge, Cup & Saucer, Pink 20.00
Lace Edge, Grill Plate, Pink 20.00
Lace Edge, Plate, Pink, 8 1/2 In. 20.00
Lace Edge, Sugar, Pink 20.00
Laced Edge, Bowl, 7 3/4 In. 26.00
Laced Edge, Bowl, Ribbed, 9 1/2 In. 24.00
Laced Edge, Plate, 8 In. 8.00
Laced Edge, Tumbler, Footed, 5 In. 80.00
Lake Como, Sugar 28.00
Laurel, Bowl, Ivory, 6 In. 9.50
Lorain pattern is listed here as No. 615
Lorna pattern is included in the Cambridge Glass category
Louisa pattern is listed here as Floragold
Lovebirds pattern is listed here as Georgian
Madrid, Bowl, Amber, 5 In. .... 4.50 to 6.50
Madrid, Bowl, Oval, 10 In. 21.00
Madrid, Butter, Amber 24.00
Madrid, Cup & Saucer, Amber 9.50
Madrid, Cup, Green 7.00
Madrid, Pitcher, Pink, 5 1/2 In. 50.00
Madrid, Plate, Green, 8 7/8 In. 8.00
Madrid, Platter, Oval, 11 1/2 In. 20.00
Madrid, Sherbet, Green 9.00

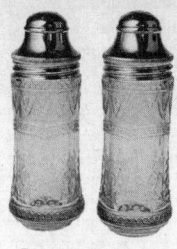

Depression glass, No. 615

Depression glass, Patrician

Depression glass, Petalweare

Madrid, Soup, Dish, 7 In...15.00 to 19.00
Madrid, Sugar, Amber 8.00
Madrid, Tumbler, Footed, Green, 4 In. 37.50
Madrid, Tumbler, Footed, Green, 5 1/2 In. 37.50
Madrid, Tumbler, Green, 5 1/2 In. 38.00
Manhattan, Berry Bowl, Underplate 30.00
Manhattan, Plate, 10 1/4 In. 15.00
Manhattan, Sugar & Creamer, Pink 16.00
Manhattan, Tumbler, 10 Oz. 14.00
Martha Washington pattern is included in the Cambridge Glass category
Mayfair Federal, Grill Plate, Amber.. 12.50
Mayfair Open Rose, Bowl, Blue, 5 1/2 In. 40.00
Mayfair Open Rose, Bowl, Blue, 7 In. 45.00
Mayfair Open Rose, Cake Plate, Pink.. 25.00
Mayfair Open Rose, Console, Green, 3-Footed, 9 In. 6950.00
Mayfair Open Rose, Cookie Jar, Blue 275.00
Mayfair Open Rose, Pitcher, Blue, 6 In. 135.00
Mayfair Open Rose, Plate, Blue, 10 /14 In. 75.00
Mayfair Open Rose, Plate, Yellow, 9 1/2 In. 135.00
Mayfair Open Rose, Platter, Oval, Closed Handles, Yellow, 12 1/2 In. 225.00
Mayfair Open Rose, Relish, 4 Sections, Blue 40.00
Mayfair Open Rose, Sandwich, Server, Green, Center Handle.................................... 37.50
Mayfair Open Rose, Soup, Cream, Blue 50.00
Mayfair Open Rose, Vase, Sweet Pea, Blue 100.00
Miss America, Bowl, 6 1/4 In. 7.50
Miss America, Bowl, Green, 6 1/4 In. 12.00
Miss America, Bowl, Pink, 9 In. 45.00
Miss America, Cake Plate.. 15.00
Miss America, Celery Dish, Green 27.50
Miss America, Celery Dish, Pink 27.50
Miss America, Cup & Saucer, Pink 30.00
Miss America, Cup, Green 7.00
Miss America, Grill Plate 9.50
Miss America, Plate, Green, 6 3/4 In. 10.50
Miss America, Saucer.. 5.00
Miss America, Sugar & Creamer, Pink.. 50.00
Miss America, Tumbler, Green, 4 1/2 In. 15.00
Moderntone, Cup, Pink 3.00
Moderntone, Little Hostess, Tea Set, Turquoise, 15 Piece 195.00
Moderntone, Mustard, Cobalt Blue 22.00
Moderntone, Pitcher, Cobalt Blue 35.00
Moderntone, Plate, 6 3/4 In. 5.00
Moderntone, Plate, Cobalt Blue, 5 7/8 In. 6.50
Moderntone, Plate, Cobalt Blue, 6 3/4 In. ....9.00 to 11.00
Moderntone, Plate, Cobalt Blue, 7 3/4 In. 10.00
Moderntone, Plate, Cobalt Blue, 8 7/8 In. 15.00
Moderntone, Plate, Sherbet, Pink.. 5.00

Moderntone, Platter, Cobalt Blue, Oval, 12 In. 40.00
Moderntone, Punch Bowl, Stand, Cobalt Blue 100.00
Moderntone, Sherbet, Yellow Platonite 21.00
Moderntone, Soup, Cream, Cobalt Blue 18.00
Moderntone, Soup, Cream, Yellow Platonite 6.00
Moderntone, Sugar, Cover, Cobalt Blue 5.00
Moonstone, Bowl, Ruffled Edge, 9 1/2 In. 9.00
Moonstone, Candlestick, Pair 20.00
Moonstone, Creamer 20.00
Moonstone, Cup & Saucer 15.00
Moonstone, Goblet 20.00
Moonstone, Plate, 8 1/2 In. 12.50
Moonstone, Plate, Ruffled, 10 In. 15.00
Moonstone, Relish, 2 Sections 18.00
Moonstone, Sherbet 9.00
Moonstone, Sugar 8.00
Moroccan Amethyst, Bowl, 6 In. 10.00
Moroccan Amethyst, Tumbler, 3 1/4 In. 12.00
Mt. Pleasant, Sherbet, Cobalt Blue 10.00
Mt. Vernon pattern is included in the Cambridge Glass category
Navarre, Goblet, 7 5/8 In. 30.00
Navarre, Relish, 2 Sections, 6 In. 27.50
Navarre, Sherbet, 5 1/2 In. 25.00
Navarre, Sugar & Creamer, Tray 55.00
New Century, Sugar, Cover 16.00
New Century, Tumbler, 4 1/4 In. 16.50
Newport, Saucer, Amethyst 4.50
Newport, Soup, Cream, Amethyst 15.00
No. 601 pattern is listed here as Avocado
No. 610, Ice Tub, Cover, Yellow 1295.00
No. 610, Pitcher, Yellow 795.00
No. 612, Bowl, Green, 7 1/2 In. 22.50
No. 612, Plate, Green, 8 3/8 In. 9.50
No. 612, Plate, Green, 9 3/8 In. 13.50
No. 612, Plate, Sandwich, Green, 11 1/2 In. 20.00
No. 612, Relish, 3 Sections, Round, Green 25.00
No. 615, Bowl, Green, 7 1/2 In. 45.00
No. 615, Bowl, Vegetable, Oval .... 20.00 to 40.00
No. 615, Cup 8.50
No. 615, Cup & Saucer, Yellow 17.50
No. 615, Plate, Green, 5 1/2 In. 4.00
No. 615, Plate, Green, 8 3/8 In. 14.00
No. 615, Plate, Yellow, 5 1/2 In. 15.00
No. 615, Plate, Yellow, 7 3/4 In. 25.00
No. 615, Sherbet, Green 20.00
No. 615, Sherbet, Yellow 25.00
No. 615, Tumbler, Green, 4 3/4 In. 20.00

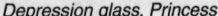

Depression glass, Princess

Depression glass, Rosemary

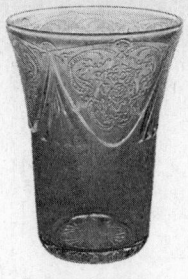

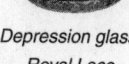

Depression glass,
Royal Lace

Depression glass, Sierra

Depression glass,
Waterford

No. 615, Tumbler, Yellow, 4 3/4 In. 25.00
Normandie, Cup & Saucer, Pink.. 12.50
Normandie, Sherbet, Pink... 8.50
Old Cafe, Pitcher, Pink, 80 Oz. 60.00
Old Colony pattern is listed here as Lace Edge
Old English, Pitcher 55.00
Old Florentine pattern is listed here as Florentine No. 1
Open Lace pattern is listed here as Lace Edge
Open Rose pattern is listed here as Mayfair Open Rose
Optic Design pattern is listed here as Raindrops
Oyster & Pearl, Bowl, Heart, Pink Shape, 5 1/4 In... 14.00
Oyster & Pearl, Plate, 13 1/2 In... 29.00
Oyster & Pearl, Relish, Divided, Pink, 10 In. 15.00
Patrician, Bowl, Vegetable, Oval, Amber, 10 In. 35.00
Patrician, Grill Plate, Amber.. 13.50
Patrician, Plate, Amber, 9 In. 13.50
Patrician, Plate, Amber, 10 1/2 In. 8.50
Patrician, Sherbet, Amber 9.00
Patrician, Soup, Cream, Amber... 12.00
Petalware, Salver, Monax, 11 In. 5.00
Philbe, Casserole, Cover, Individual, 4 Piece 45.00
Pinwheel pattern is listed here as Sierra
Poinsettia, pattern is listed here as Floral
Poppy No. 1 pattern is listed here as Florentine No. 1
Poppy No. 2 pattern is listed here as Florentine No. 2
Pretty Polly Party Dishes, Ultramarine, 14 Piece 325.00
Princess, Cake Plate, Footed 29.00
Princess, Candy Dish, Cover, Green 45.00
Princess, Coaster, Green 30.00
Princess, Cookie Jar, Cover, Green.. 85.00
Princess, Cup & Saucer, Green 20.00
Princess, Grill Plate, Amber.. 9.00
Princess, Platter, Oval, 12 In... 28.00
Princess, Platter, Topaz, 12 In. 35.00
Princess, Sherbet, Green 20.00
Prismatic Line pattern is listed here as Queen Mary
Provincial pattern is listed here as Bubble
Pyramid pattern is listed here as No. 610
Queen Mary, Bowl, 5 1/2 In. 18.00
Queen Mary, Butter, Cover.. 22.50
Queen Mary, Dish, Cloverleaf Shape, Metal Cover 60.00
Queen Mary, Relish, Square, Inserts... 65.00
Queen Mary, Tumbler, Pink, 4 In. 8.00
Radiance, Sugar, Creamer & Tray, Etched.. 55.00
Raindrops, Cup & Saucer, Green 6.50

Ribbon, Sugar, Green 9.00
Ring, Water Set, Green, 5 Piece... 125.00
Rock Crystal, Bowl, 7 In.. 15.00
Rock Crystal, Compote, Amber, 7 In. 40.00
Rock Crystal, Tray, 11 1/2 x 8 1/4 In. 30.00
Rosemary, Bowl, Amber, 5 In. ....5.00 to 7.00
Rosemary, Cup & Saucer, Amber 13.00
Rosemary, Cup, Amber 3.00
Rosemary, Grill Plate, Amber 11.50
Rosemary, Plate, Amber, 6 3/4 In. ....2.50 to 6.50
Rosemary, Platter, Amber, Oval, 12 In. 12.50
Rosemary, Soup, Cream, Amber 12.50
Round Robin, Cup, Green 4.50
Round Robin, Sherbet, Green.. 6.00
Royal Lace, Berry Bowl, 10 In. 37.00
Royal Lace, Butter, Cover, Cobalt Blue................................ 510.00
Royal Lace, Candy Dish, Cover, Ribbed Bottom, Pink 67.50
Royal Lace, Cookie Jar, Cover, Cobalt Blue.......................... 200.00
Royal Lace, Cookie Jar, Cover, Crystal 35.00
Royal Lace, Creamer, Cobalt Blue, Footed........................... 50.00
Royal Lace, Cup & Saucer, Cobalt Blue................................ 40.00
Royal Lace, Plate, Amber, 9 7/8 In...................................... 14.00
Royal Lace, Plate, Cobalt Blue, 9 7/8 In. 38.00
Royal Lace, Platter, Oval, Cobalt Blue, 13 In. 52.00
Royal Lace, Salt & Pepper, Cobalt Blue................................ 230.00
Royal Lace, Salt & Pepper, Green.. 120.00
Royal Lace, Soup, Cream, Cobalt Blue 35.00
Royal Lace, Sugar & Creamer, Cobalt Blue 85.00
Royal Lace, Sugar, Cover, Cobalt Blue................................. 130.00
Royal Lace, Sugar, Footed 18.00
Royal Lace, Tumbler, 4 1/8 In. 23.00
Royal Lace, Tumbler, Cobalt Blue, 3 1/2 In. 105.00
Royal Ruby, Cup & Saucer 8.00
Royal Ruby, Sherbet, Footed 8.00
Sail Boat pattern is listed here as Sportsman Series
Sandwich Anchor Hocking, Bowl, Oval, 9 In. 4.00
Sandwich Anchor Hocking, Butter, Cover............................. 35.00
Sandwich Anchor Hocking, Creamer.................................... 4.00
Sandwich Anchor Hocking, Cup & Saucer............................ 3.00
Sandwich Anchor Hocking, Cup & Saucer, Green 20.00
Sandwich Anchor Hocking, Plate, 8 In. 3.00
Sandwich Anchor Hocking, Punch Set, 7 Piece..................... 30.00
Sandwich Anchor Hocking, Sugar, Cover 15.00
Saxon pattern is listed here as Coronation
Sharon, Bowl, 6 In. 25.00
Sharon, Bowl, Amber, 8 1/2 In. 8.50
Sharon, Bowl, Green, 5 In.. 11.50
Sharon, Bowl, Pink, 5 In. ....13.00 to 18.00
Sharon, Candy Dish, Amber 35.00
Sharon, Cup & Saucer, Pink 23.00
Sharon, Plate, Amber, 9 1/2 In. 12.50
Sharon, Plate, Green, 7 1/2 In. 17.00
Sharon, Plate, Pink, 9 1/2 In. 18.50
Sharon, Platter, Oval, Amber, 12 1/2 In. 18.50
Sharon, Tumbler, 5 1/4 In. 44.00
Sierra, Bowl, Cereal, 5 1/2 In. 14.00
Sierra, Creamer 22.00
Sierra, Cup & Saucer, Pink 15.00
Sierra, Salt & Pepper, Pink 40.00
Spoke pattern is listed here as Patrician
Sportsman Series, Salt & Pepper, Cobalt Blue 58.00
Sunflower, Cake Plate, Green.....................................12.00 to 19.50
Sunflower, Cake Plate, Pink... 4.00

Sunflower, Creamer, Pink .... 9.00 to 14.00
Sunflower, Cup & Saucer 18.00
Tea Room, Candlestick, Pink, Pair 55.00
Tea Room, Vase, 11 In. 55.00
Threading pattern is listed here as Old English
Tradition, Goblet, Water, Pink 25.00
Tradition, Tumbler, Pink, 4 1/4 In. 20.00
Turquoise Blue, Bowl Set, 3 Piece 27.50
Turquoise Blue, Cup 3.00
Turquoise Blue, Mug 8.00
Turquoise Blue, Plate, Indentation, 9 In. 6.00
Twisted Optic, Plate, Green, 8 In. 3.50
Vertical Ribbed pattern is listed here as Queen Mary
Waffle pattern is listed here as Waterford
Waterford, Butter, Cover 25.00
Waterford, Coaster 4.00
Waterford, Creamer 4.00
Waterford, Pitcher, Water 35.00
Waterford, Plate, 7 1/8 In. 4.50
Waterford, Plate, 9 5/8 In. 8.50
Waterford, Salt & Pepper 5.00
Waterford, Sherbet 5.00
White Ship pattern is listed here as Sportsman Series
Wild Rose pattern is listed here as Dogwood
Windsor, Bowl, Boat Shape, Pink, 7 x 11 3/4 In. 30.00
Windsor, Chop Plate, Green .... 35.00 to 40.00
Windsor, Salt & Pepper, Pink .... 25.00 to 27.50
Windsor, Sugar & Creamer, Green 20.00
Windsor Diamond pattern is listed here as Windsor
Woolworth, Creamer, Pink 8.00

DERBY has been marked on porcelain made in the city of Derby, England, since about 1748. The original Derby factory closed in 1848, but others opened there and continued to produce quality porcelain. The Crown Derby mark began appearing on Derby wares in the 1770s.

Cup, Stirrup, Hound Head, Tally Ho, Stevenson & Hancock, c.1875, 5 7/16 In. 1495.00
Dish, Oval, Molded Vines, Scrolled Ends, c.1765, 10 7/8 In. 1610.00
Figurine, Chinese Boy, Belted Jacket, Holding Bottle, 1752, 5 1/2 In. 1495.00
Figurine, Kitty Clive As Mrs. Riot, c.1755, 9 5/16 In. 7475.00
Figurine, Pug Dog, Seated, Black Muzzle & Toes, Red Mouth, 1765, 3 1/4 In. 920.00
Figurine, Shepherds & Companion, Dog At Feet, c.1770, 8 9/16 In. 1380.00
Group, Ewe & Lamb, Green Mound Base, c.1765, 4 In. 805.00
Plate, Gilt Rim, Summer Flowers, Foliate Vine, Yellow Ground, 1790, 9 7/16 In. 460.00
Toothpick, Victorian Woman 80.00
Urn, Potpourri, Flowerhead Knop, 3 Panels, Landscape & River, 1825, 11 1/2 In., Pair 4312.00
Vase, Shield Shape, Painted Fruit-Filled Basket, Molded Gilt Handles, c.1820, 9 In. 635.00

DICK TRACY, the comic strip, started in 1931. Tracy was also the hero of movies from 1937 to 1947 and again in 1990, and starred in a radio series in the 1940s and a television series in the 1950s. Memorabilia from all these activities is collected.

Badge, Crimestopper, Silver, 1940s 65.00
Badge, Member Secret Service Patrol, Tin Lithograph, Dick & Junior 40.00
Badge, Membership, Brass, 1939 .... 65.00
Badge, Secret Service Patrol, Lieutenant, Silver Plate, Black Etched Face, 1938 .... 120.00
Badge, Sergeant, Secret Service Patrol, 1938 .... 95.00
Book, Big Little Book, The Phantom Ship 45.00
Book, Big Little Book, Yoggee Yamma 30.00
Book, Comic, Ltd. Edition, 1975, 10 x 13 In. 4.00
Book, Comic, Motorola TV Giveaway, 1953 .... 20.00
Book, Little Golden, No.497, 1962 .... 13.00
Book, Pop-Up, 1935 .... 250.00
Box, Submachine Water Gun 55.00

Camera, Candid, Black, Plastic, Seymour Sales, c.1950 .... 120.00
Car, Green, Windup, Marx, 1940s 195.00
Car, Tin, Windup, Marx USA, 1950s, 11 In. 195.00
Cartoon Kit, 1961, Colorforms 39.00
Charm Bracelet 145.00
Crimestoppers Kit, TV Premium, Sealed Mailer, 1960s 95.00
Detective Game, Whitman, 1937 .... 139.00
Flashlight, Bullet Shape, Tracy's Bust, Red, Pocket, 1939 .... 70.00
Flashlight, Tin, Black, 1940s, 3 In. 60.00
Game, Board, 1962 .... 20.00
Game, Crime Stopper, Ideal, 1963 .... 45.00
Game, Master Detective 75.00
Gun, Cap/Water, Riot Rifle, Mattel, 1961 .... 45.00
Knife, Magnifier, Whistle, Glow In Dark, Dick & Junior 48.00
Knife, Pocket, ... 40.00
Lunch Box, Metal, Aladdin, 1967 .... 75.00 to 135.00
Lunch Pail, Aladdin, Vinyl, 1960s, 8 1/2 In. 45.00
Mug, Coffee, Ceramic, Color Portraits, 1940s 125.00
Postcard, World War II, Unused 20.00
Puppet, Molded Vinyl Head, Printed Cloth Body, Ideal, 1961 .... 45.00 to 65.00
Puzzle, Manhunt For Mumbles, Jaymar, 1960s, 10 x 14 In. 75.00
Ring, Secret Compartment 400.00
Salt & Pepper, Dick Tracy, Junior, Chalkware 45.00
Soaky, 1960s .... 35.00 to 80.00
Suspenders, On Card 75.00
Target Board, Gould Illustration, c.1940 .... 95.00
View-Master, Gift Set, Madonna On Box 22.00
Wrist Radio, 2-Way Electronic, Remco, Box 175.00
Wrist Radio Set, 1950s 95.00
Wristwatch, 2-Way Integrated Circuit, 1960s 55.00

DINNERWARE, see American Dinnerware

DIONNE QUINTUPLETS were born in Canada on May 28, 1934. The publicity about their birth and their special status as wards of the Canadian government made them famous throughout the world. Visitors could watch the girls
play; reporters interviewed the girls and the staff. Thousands of special dolls
and souvenirs were made picturing the quints at different ages. Emilie died in
1954, Marie in 1970. Yvonne, Annette, and Cecile still live in Canada.

Book, Dionne Quintuplets, History Of Birth, Whitman, 40 Pages, 1935 .... 18.00
Calendar, 1937 .... 28.00
Calendar, 1940, Original Envelope .... 15.00 to 18.00
Dish, Chrome 20.00
Doll, Composition, Brunette, Madame Alexander, 1935, 8 In., 5 Piece 1150.00
Doll, Original Clothes, Diapers, Effanbee, 7 In., 5 Piece 895.00
Doll Set, Jointed Arms, Printed Dress, Japan, 5 Piece 95.00
Doll Set, Nurse, Each Has Button Photo Of Real Quint, Alexander, 6 Piece 1795.00
Handkerchief 48.00
Magazine, Carnation Milk, 1935 .... 20.00
Magazine, Life, c.1937 .... 75.00
Spoon, Figural, Silver, In Rack, Set Of 5 .... 135.00

DISNEYANA is a collector's term. Walt Disney and his company introduced
many comic characters to the world. Collectors search for examples of the
work of the Disney Studios and the many commercial products modeled after
his characters, including Mickey Mouse, Donald Duck, and recent films, like
Beauty and the Beast and *The Little Mermaid*.

Bank, Baby Dinosaur, Figural, Epcot Center, Vinyl, 1982 .... 13.00
Bank, Cinderella, Ceramic, 1950 .... 80.00
Bank, Dime Register, Snow White, Walt Disney Ent., 1938 .... 95.00
Bank, Donald Duck, Astronaut, Nabisco Puppets, 1966 .... 40.00
Bank, Donald Duck, Ceramic, 6 1/2 In. 143.00
Bank, Donald Duck, Composition, 6 1/4 In. 60.00

Bank, Donald Duck, Long Bill, Cast Metal, Painted, 1930s, 6 In. 575.00
Bank, Dumbo, Dakin, 1960s 45.00
Bank, Ferdinand The Bull, Chalkware 58.00
Bank, Ferdinand The Bull, Composition, Crown Toy Co., 1938, 5 In. 185.00
Bank, Jam Jar, Mickey On Tin Lithograph Cover, 4 Molded Figures, 1930s ......175.00 to 200.00
Bank, Mickey Mouse Book, Vinyl & Metal 4 1/4 In. 110.00
Bank, Mickey Mouse Suitcase, Metal, 3 In. 396.00
Bank, Mickey Mouse, Ceramic, 6 1/4 In. 143.00
Bank, Mickey Mouse, Figural, Mouse Club, Brown Glass, 1970s 15.00
Bank, Mickey Mouse, Mechanical, Plastic 50.00
Bank, Mickey Mouse, Plastic, 7 In. 6.50
Bank, Mickey Mouse, World's Fair, Leather, Brass Trim, 1933 .... 395.00
Bank, Mickey Mouse, Wright 175.00
Bank, Pinocchio's Head, 1971 .... 20.00
Bank, Pinocchio, On Stack Of Books, Walt Disney Prod., 12 In. 15.00
Bank, Uncle Scrooge, Composition, Early 1960s, 10 In. 75.00
Birthday Card, Mickey Mouse, Cowboy, Inside Writing, Hallmark, 1936 .... 65.00
Blotter, Donald Duck, Typing At Typewriter 1942, Etc., Sunoco 22.00
Blotter, Sunoco Oil, Mickey Mouse, Defend Your Car's Life, 1942, 3 1/2 x 6 In. 40.00
Blouse & Shorts, Mickey Mouse, Red, White, 1930s, 2 Piece 65.00
Book, Alphabet, Mickey Mouse, 1936 .... 95.00
Book, Babes In Toyland, Golden Press, 1961, Large Size 30.00
Book, Coloring, Mickey Mouse Club, 1955 .... 12.00
Book, Comic, Donald Duck, Dell No. 50, Dec. 1956 .... 25.00
Book, Comic, Mickey Mouse, 1946 .... 65.00
Book, Guide, Disneyland, 1962, 28 Pages 45.00
Book, Mickey Mouse & Dude Ranch Bandit, Big Little Book, Whitman, 1943 .... 46.00
Book, Mickey Mouse & Missing Mouseketeers, Big Little Book, 1956 .... 12.00
Book, Mickey Mouse & Pluto The Racer, Big Little Book, 1936 .... 65.00
Book, Mickey Mouse & Stolen Jewels, Big Little Book, 1949 .... 75.00
Book, Mickey Mouse Fire Brigade, Whitman, 1936 .... 17.00
Book, Mickey Mouse On Sky Island, Better Little Book, Whitman, 1941 .... 15.00
Book, Mickey Mouse Sails For Treasure Island, Big Little Book, 1933 .... 65.00
Book, Mickey Mouse The Detective, Big Little Book, 1935 .... 25.00
Book, Mickey Mouse, Mail Pilot, Amoco, Big Little Book, 1933 .... 125.00
Book, Paint, Cinderella, 1956, Unused 48.00
Book, Paint, No. 1150, Mickey Mouse, Whitman, Unused, 1946 .... 75.00
Book, Paint, Snow White & Seven Dwarfs, Whitman, Unused, 1938 .... 65.00
Book, Punch-Out, Babes In Toyland, Whitman, 1981, 22 1/2 x 11 In. 48.00
Book, Seven Dwarfs Find A House, Simon & Schuster, 1952 .... 15.00
Book, Sleeping Beauty, Little Golden Book, 1957 .... 22.00
Book, Snow White & Seven Dwarfs Jingle, Olson's Bakery, 20 Pages, 1938, 4 x 5 In. .. 50.00
Book, Souvenir, Disney On Parade, 1973, 28 Pages 20.00
Book, Uncle Scrooge, The Lemonade King, Tip Top Tales, Whitman, 1960 .... 12.00
Book, Walt Disney's Famous 7 Dwarfs, Whitman, 1938 .... 82.00
Book, Walt Disney's Toby Tyler, Little Golden Book, 1960 .... 12.00
Book Bag, Snow White & The Seven Dwarfs, 1950s 165.00
Bookends, Mickey & Minnie Mouse, Seated, Composition, 1930s Type, 1960s 165.00
Bookends, Mickey Mouse, Minnie Mouse, Ceramic, 7 In. 95.00
Bottle, Mickey Mouse Pale Dry Ginger Ale, Green, 1930s 700.00
Bowl, Dewey, Donald Duck's Nephew, Sango, 1957, 4 5/8 In. 35.00
Bowl, Mickey Mouse, Alphabet & Numbers On Rim, 1930s 65.00
Bowl, Mickey Mouse, Green Plastic, Abex, England, 1930s, 5 1/2 In. 125.00
Bowl, Pink Luster Band, Seven Disney Characters, 6 In. 50.00
Box, Brush, Mickey Mouse, Orange, 1930s, 5 x 2 x 2 In. 100.00
Box, Cookies, Mickey Mouse, c.1940 .... 125.00
Box, Paint, Donald Duck, Nephews & Mickey, Tin Lithograph, Transogram, 1940s 45.00
Box, Pencil, Mickey Mouse, Pie-Eyed, Long-Billed Donald Duck, Dixon 55.00
Bracelet, Charm, Snow White & Seven Dwarfs, Gold, Enameled, 1930s 95.00
Brush, Donald Duck, Box 110.00
Brush, Mickey Mouse, Metal 60.00
Brush, Mickey Mouse, Walking, Aluminum, Henry L. Hughs Co., 1936, 2 Piece 275.00
Button, Star Tours Disneyland, 1980s, 3 In. 5.00

Cake Candles, Tinkerbell, Disneyland Box, 1960s	10.00
Camera, Donald Duck, Black Plastic, Herbert-George Co., 1946	85.00
Camera, Figural, Mickey Mouse, Nose Is Lens, Walt Disney	35.00
Camera, No. 1, Mickey Mouse, 2 Rolls Of Mickey Film, Ettelson, 1950s	125.00
Candy Box, Snow White & Forest Friends, Tin Lithograph, Belgium, 1930s	285.00
Cane, Mickey Mouse Figural Head, 1930s	125.00
Card, Euro Disney Meal, Euro Castle & Moat, 1990s, 2 x 3 1/4 In.	25.00
Card, Playing, Disneyland, 4 Each Of 11 Characters, 1964	15.00
Card, Playing, Mickey Mouse Old Maid, 1937, 5 Piece	138.00
Cards, Playing, Cinderella	5.00
Case, Jungle Book, Vinyl, 1966	75.00
Cel, see Animation Art category	
Cereal Box, Pinocchio, Post Toasties, 1939	300.00
Chair, Beach, Mickey Mouse, Canvas	475.00
Christmas Card, Epcot Center, Mickey, Donald, Goofy, Pluto, With Tree, 1982	12.00
Christmas Lights, Mickey Mouse, Plastic Light Cover, Noma, Box, 1930s	300.00
Christmas Tree Ornament, Bambi, Baby, 1st Christmas	9.50
Christmas Tree Ornament, Santa's Helpers, Round, 1985, 2 1/2 In.	25.00
Clock, Alarm, Big Bad Wolf, Ingersoll	300.00
Clock, Alarm, Mickey Mouse & Goofy On Face, Bradley	35.00
Clock, Alarm, Mickey Mouse, 2 Bells On Top, Red & Yellow	75.00
Clock, Alarm, Mickey Mouse, Figural	125.00
Clock, Alarm, Mickey Mouse, Ingersoll, 1940s	145.00
Clock, Alarm, Mickey Mouse, Ingersoll, 1955	125.00
Clock, Alarm, Pluto, Bayard	255.00
Clock, Mickey Mouse, School House, 1960s	60.00
Clock Radio, Mickey Mouse, Mickey On Dial, General Electric, 1960s	110.00
Cookie Jar, Dumbo	100.00
Cookie Jar, Mickey Mouse, Black, Colorful Mickey Holds Pie, 1930s	225.00
Cookie Jar, Mickey Mouse, Hand Painted, 12 In.	55.00
Cookie Jar, Mickey Mouse, On Birthday Cake	700.00
Cookie Jar, Mickey Mouse, Turnabout	100.00
Cookie Jar, Mickey Mouse, Walt Disney, Hoan Ltd., 11 In.	125.00
Cookie Jar, Mrs. Potts, Treasure Craft	48.00
Cookie Jar, Santa Mickey Mouse	75.00
Cookie Jar, Tigger, Walt Disney	185.00
Cookie Jar, Winnie-The-Pooh	100.00
Creamer, Gus, From Cinderella, Figural, Weetman	95.00
Creamer, Mickey Mouse, Figural, China, Cold Painted, 1930s	100.00
Cup, Practical Pig, Lusterware, Gold Rim, Japan, 1930s	15.00
Dinner Set, Snow White & Seven Dwarfs, Louis Marx, 14 Piece	95.00
Dish, Child's, Mickey & Minnie Mouse, 3 Compartments, Porcelain, 1930s	175.00
Display, Donald Duck Cola, Donald Standing, On Bottle, 1950s, 9 x 19 1/2 In.	200.00
Doll, Goofy, Talking, Battery Operated, 1960s, 19 1/2 In.	250.00
Doll, Grumpy, Cloth, Soft Plastic Hands, Japan, 7 In.	9.00
Doll, Mary Poppins, Handbag, Umbrella, Box, Horsman	125.00
Doll, Mickey Mouse, Bisque, Japan, 9 In.	3000.00
Doll, Mickey Mouse, Celluloid, Spring Arms & Legs, France	295.00
Doll, Mickey Mouse, Cloth, Paper Label, Knickerbocker, 1940s, 11 In.	518.00
Doll, Mickey Mouse, Knickerbocker, c.1936, 11 In.	350.00
Doll, Mickey Mouse, Orange Shoes, Knickerbocker, c.1935, 10 In.	220.00
Doll, Mickey Mouse, Steiff, 16 In.	2500.00
Doll, Mickey Mouse, Stuffed Velvet, Floppy Arms & Legs, c.1940, 16 In.	250.00
Doll, Minnie Mouse, Plush, Knickerbocker	125.00
Doll, Roger Rabbit, Talking, Box	50.00
Doll, Snow White, Ideal, 1940s, 22 In.	275.00
Dollhouse, Mickey Mouse, Tin, Plastic Furniture, Marx	125.00
Doorstop, Donald Duck, Cast Iron, 1970	145.00
Drum, Mickey Mouse Club, Tin Lithograph, Sticks, Noble & Cooley, 1970s, 11 In.	48.00
Drum, Mickey, Minnie, Clarabelle, Horace, Donald & Pluto, Tin, 1930s, 11 x 5 In.	275.00
Fan, Silly Symphony, 1930	95.00
Figure, Mickey Mouse, Baseball, Painted, 1930s	175.00
Figurine, Bambi, With Thumper, Goebel, 3 Line Mark, 1950, 3 1/4 In.	175.00

Figurine, Donald Duck, 13 1/2 In. 65.00
Figurine, Donald Duck, Riding Rocking Horse, Bisque, 1930s, 3 1/4 In. ....225.00 to 250.00
Figurine, Donald Duck, Sailor Suit, Green Scooter, Bisque, 3 In. 55.00
Figurine, Dopey, Bisque, Impressed, Japan, 2 In. 18.00
Figurine, Dwarf, Happy, Goebel, 1950, 3 In. 80.00
Figurine, Elmer Elephant, Standing Bisque, Movable Trunk, 4 In. 250.00
Figurine, Elmer Elephant, Standing, Bisque, Painted, 1930s, 4 In. 300.00
Figurine, Geppetto, Green, Porcelain, National, 1940s, 2 3/4 In. 50.00
Figurine, Goofy, Bisque, Painted, 1930s, 1 7/8 In. 100.00
Figurine, Hippopotamus, Fantasia, American Pottery 350.00
Figurine, Jiminy Cricket, White Glazed Ceramic, National Porcelain Co., 3 In. 55.00
Figurine, Mary Poppins, Umbrella, Original Tag, Disneyland 1964, 6 In. 55.00
Figurine, Mickey & Minnie Mouse, Bisque, 3 In., Set 250.00
Figurine, Mickey & Minnie Mouse, Pie-Eyed, Germany, Bisque, Set 650.00
Figurine, Mickey Mouse, Holding A Sword, 3 1/4 In. 100.00
Figurine, Mickey Mouse, Playing Saxophone, Bisque, 6 In. 275.00
Figurine, Mickey Mouse, Riding Pluto, Bisque, 4 In. 100.00
Figurine, Mickey Mouse, Standing Hands On Hips 75.00
Figurine, Mickey Mouse, With Baseball Bat, Painted, 1930s, 3 1/4 In. 200.00
Figurine, Mickey Mouse, Wood, 5 1/2 In., 1930s 375.00
Figurine, Mickey Mouse, Wooden, Hand Carved, Red & Black, Label, 1940s, 7 In. 207.00
Figurine, Minnie Mouse, Nurse's Kit, Bisque, 1930s, 3 1/4 In. 150.00
Figurine, Minnie Mouse, Red Night Shirt, Bisque, 1930s, 4 In. 150.00
Figurine, Pinocchio, Carved Wood, Jointed, Composition Head, Ideal, 1940s, 10 In. 81.00
Figurine, Pinocchio, Chalkware, 14 1/2 In. 95.00
Figurine, Pinocchio, Glazed Bisque, Japan, 1940s, 2 3/4 In. 215.00
Figurine, Pluto, Sitting, Howling, Brayton Laguna, 1930s, 6 In. 150.00
Figurine, Scamp, Lady & The Tramp, Hagen-Renaker, 1950s, 1 In. 50.00
Figurine, Sgt. Tibbs, Wade 110.00
Figurine, Sneezy, Snow White & Seven Dwarfs, Goebel, 1950s, 3 In. 75.00
Figurine, Snow White & Seven Dwarfs, Bisque, 1930s 450.00
Figurine, Snow White & Seven Dwarfs, Bisque, Japan, Late 1930s, 3 & 4 In., 8 Piece . 350.00
Figurine, Snow White & Seven Dwarfs, Bisque, Borgfeldt, 1938, 4-In. Dwarfs, Box 850.00
Figurine, Snow White & Seven Dwarfs, Disneykins, 1960s, Complete 60.00
Figurine, Snow White & Seven Dwarfs, Painted, 1930s, 4 & 3 1/2 In., 8 Piece 275.00
Figurine, Snow White, Hagen-Renaker, 5 3/4 In. 288.00
Figurine, Thumper's Girlfriend, Label, 4 In. 85.00
Figurine, Thumper, Label, 3 x 3 In. 85.00
Figurine, Thumper, Sitting, Goebel, 1950s, 3 In. 165.00
Figurine, Thumper, Standing On Hind Legs, Laughing, Goebel, Full Bee, 1950s, 3 In.. 125.00
Figurine Set, 101 Dalmations, Plastic, Unpainted, 1960s 35.00
Flashlight, Pluto, Red Plastic, Push Tail To Turn On 35.00
Game, Create Your Own Disneyland, Playboy Products, 1968, 9 x 17 In. Folder 110.00
Game, Donald Duck Bean Bag, 14 x 16 In. Board 25.00
Game, Mickey & Minnie Mouse, Snakes & Ladders, Chad Valley, England, 1930s 133.00
Game, Mickey Mouse Going Home, 1930s 175.00
Game, Mickey Mouse Spin, Box 50.00
Game, Mickey Mouse, Target, Baseball On Reverse, Marks Bros. 250.00
Game, Pinocchio The Merry Puppet, Board, Milton Bradley, 1939 .... 75.00
Game, Riverboat, Parker Bros., 1960 .... 75.00
Game, Snow White, Board, 1930s 125.00
Geppetto, Wooden, Multi-Products, 1940 .... 85.00
Glass, 101 Dalmations, Wonderful World Of Disney 14.00
Glass, Donald Duck, Bricking A Wall, Mickey Mouse Club 5.00
Glass, Ferdinand The Bull, All Star Parade, 1939, 4 3/4 In. 45.00
Glass, J.W. Foulfellow, Brown, 1940s, 4 3/4 In. 18.00
Glass, Juice, Mickey Mouse Club, Logo, 1970s, 3 5/8 In. 5.00
Glass, Mickey Mouse, Black, 1930s, 3 1/2 In. 30.00
Glass, Mickey Mouse, Name Is Vertical 30.00
Glass, Minnie Mouse, Pie-Eyed, Umbrella, Black, 1930s, 4 1/4 In. 40.00
Glass, Pinocchio, Red, 1940s, 4 5/8 In. 15.00
Glass, Robin The Boy Wonder, 5 In. 18.00
Glass, Sleeping Beauty, Good Fairies, 1958, 5 In. ....18.00 to 25.00

Glass, Snow White, All Star Parade, 1939	40.00
Glass, Snow White, Pinocchio, Fantasia, Peter Pan, McDonald's, Coca-Cola, 4 Piece	50.00
Globe, World, Disney Characters, Tin	225.00
Handkerchief, Mickey Mouse, Kiddie Hankies, c.1940, 2 Piece	125.00
Holder, Pencil, Happy, Porcelain, Painted, Figural, Disneyland, 1960, 4 In.	35.00
Holder, Pencil, Mickey Mouse, Composition	200.00
Iron-On, Donald Duck, Original Store Card, 1946	15.00
Iron-On, For T-Shirt, Mickey Mouse, 1940s	6.00
Jack-In-The-Box, Mickey Mouse & Friends, Pie Eyed, Musical, Carnival	85.00
Knife, Pocket, Mickey Mouse Handle, Remake 1933 World's Fair, 1980s	10.00
Knife, Pocket, Mickey Mouse, Welcome To Disneyland, 7/17/1955	5.00
Lamp, Baby's, Mickey & Minnie Mouse, 1984	25.00
Lamp, Donald Duck The Sailor, Figural, Illustrated Shade, 1960s	49.00
Lamp, Snow White, Figural, Making Pie, Animals, Lamode Studios, 1938	475.00
Lunch Box, Bedknobs & Broomsticks, Metal, Aladdin, 1972	45.00
Lunch Box, Disney Express, Metal, Aladdin, 1979	12.00
Lunch Box, Disneyland Castle, 1957	155.00
Lunch Box, Magic Kingdom	45.00
Lunch Box, Mickey Mouse, Metal, 1980s	12.00
Lunch Box, Snow White, Plastic, Thermos	12.00
Lunch Box, Tinker Bell, Vinyl, 1969	200.00
Lunch Pail, Mickey Mouse's Head	35.00
Magic Slate, Donald Duck, T.X. Products Co., England, 1950s, 6 1/4 x 9 In.	55.00
Marionette, Donald Duck	125.00
Marionette, Mickey Mouse	225.00
Marionette, Minnie Mouse, Pelham, England, Box	350.00
Marionette, Minnie Mouse, Wood, Papier-Mache, Cloth Costume, 13 1/2 In.	160.00
Marionette, Pinocchio, 1850s	15.00
Marionette, Snow White, Madame Alexander	85.00
Mask, Jiminy Cricket, Gillette Blue Blade, Paper, 1939	15.00
Mask, Pinocchio, Gillette Blue Blade, Paper, 1939	15.00
Mask, Snow White, Paper, Par-T-Mask, Eison-Freeman Co., Inc., 1937	50.00
Mickey Mouse, Circus, Mickey Lithograph, Box	900.00
Mirror, Snow White & Seven Dwarfs, Raised Figures Around Frame, Oval	225.00
Model Kit, Satellite Launcher, Strombecker, 1950s	200.00
Mug, Ludwig Von Drake, Ceramic, Raised Graphics, Late 1950s	45.00
Mug, Ludwig Von Drake, Face, W.D. Productions, 1961	17.00
Mug, Mickey Mouse	150.00
Mug, Smokey The Bear, Glass, Milk	14.00
Mug, Snow White, Plastic, Decal	10.00
Mug, Sonic Silver, 1959-1984	11.00
Mug, Sonic, 1983	11.00
Mug, Three Little Pigs, Patriot China	65.00
Music Box, Cinderella	45.00
Music Box, Donald Duck & Nephews On Seesaw, Wooden	175.00
Napkin Ring, Mickey Mouse, Bakelite, Decal, 1930s, 2 3/4 In.	90.00
Newspaper, Disney Land News, Vol. 1, No. 1, July 1955	1500.00
Nodder, Donald Duck, Celluloid	950.00
Nodder, Dumbo's Mother	225.00
Nodder, Ferdinand	225.00
Nodder, Mickey Mouse, Celluloid	1300.00
Nodder, Winnie The Pooh	150.00
Pail, Donald Duck, Tin Lithograph, Ohio Art, 1939	100.00
Pencil, Mickey & Friends, 3 Characters, Walt Disney, 1960s	2.00
Pencil Sharpener, Bambi, Figural, Red, 1940s	65.00
Pencil Sharpener, Donald Duck	25.00
Pencil Sharpener, Donald Duck, Desk Or Wall Mount, 1960	35.00
Pencil Sharpener, Pinocchio, 4 1/2 In.	75.00
Photograph, Walt Disney, Black & White, Autographed, 8 x 10 In.	825.00
Picture, 3-D, Color, Walnut Frames, 1966, 2 Piece	35.00
Pin, Convention, Flasher, Sorcerer Mickey Mouse, Logo	10.00
Pin, Donald Duck's 55th Birthday, June 9, 1989, 2 1/4 In.	10.00
Pin, Dumbo, Kay Kaymen Paper, 1940s	45.00

Pin, Epcot Center, Flag, Mickey Mouse Center, Enameled, 1980s 6.00
Pin, Goofy, Figural, Brass, Enameled 30.00
Pin, Huey, Dewey, Louis, 1950s 85.00
Pin, Mickey Mouse Sitting In Director's Chair, Cloisonne 10.00
Pin, Mickey Mouse Store, Pinback, 1940, 1 In. 28.00
Pin, Mickey Mouse's 60th, Old & New, Shaking Hands, 1988, 3 In. 8.00
Pin, Mickey Mouse's Face, Boston Sunday Advertiser, 1930s 95.00
Pin, Mickey Mouse, Walt Disney, 1937 .... 20.00
Pin, Mouse Club East, 1st Logo, Enameled, 1980s 5.00
Planter, Alice In Wonderland, Figural, Leeds, 1950s .... 95.00 to 150.00
Planter, Cowboy, Mickey Mouse 185.00
Planter, Donald Duck Holding Flower, Leeds, 1940s 28.00
Planter, Pluto, Gold Trim, Leeds 70.00
Planter, Snow White, At Wishing Well, 1960s 96.00
Planter, Snow White, Leeds China Co., 1949 .... 54.00
Plate, Christmas, 1972, Snoopy Guides The Sleigh, C. Schulz, Schmid, Japan 90.00
Plate, Christmas, 1973, Sleigh Ride, Schmid, Japan 400.00
Plate, Christmas, 1977, Down The Chimney, Schmid, Japan 25.00
Plate, Mickey Mouse, Minute Man Clothes, Bicentennial, Schmid, 1776-1976 .... 20.00
Plate, Mother's Day, 1976, Minnie Mouse & Friends, Schmid, Japan 20.00
Postcard, Donald Duck, Spanish, 1956 .... 45.00
Postcard, Seven Dwarfs, 1938 .... 35.00
Program, Fantasia 65.00
Projector, Mickey Mouse, Model E-18, Green, Keystone, c.1930, 9 x 9 In., Box 110.00
Puppet, Hand, Dopey, Composition Head, Yellow Hat, W.D.E. ....65.00 to 125.00
Puppet, Hand, Pinocchio, Walt Disney Prod., Japan, 1960s 27.00
Puppet, Pinocchio, Walt Disney Enterprises, 1937 .... 95.00
Puppet, Push, Dumbo, Wooden, Plastic, Kohner, 2 1/2 In. 150.00
Puzzle, Disneyland Christmas, Whitman, 1955, 7 1/2 x 15 In. 25.00
Puzzle, Dopey, Frame Tray, Judy Toys, 1950s 30.00
Puzzle, Snow White 30.00
Puzzle, Ugly Duckling, Jigsaw, 1940s, Box, 7 x 10 1/2 x 2 In. 16.50
Radio, Mickey Mouse's Head 20.00
Record, Cinderella, Mickey Mouse Club, No. D281, 78 Rpm, 1950s 28.00
Record, Little Toot, 1948 .... 12.00
Record, Walt Disney's Song Parade, 1955, 8 Piece, Box 75.00
Record Set, Three Caballeros, Movie End Papers, 1944 .... 20.00
Ring, Mickey Mouse Club, Flasher, Plastic, c.1950, Vari-Vue 15.00
Ring Toss, Donald Duck 45.00
Rug, Snow White & Seven Dwarfs, 22 x 39 In. 115.00
Rug, Snow White, Seven Dwarfs Carrying Tools Over Bridge, 22 x 45 In. 200.00
Salt & Pepper, Ferdinand The Bull, Japan, 1930s, 2 1/2 In. 40.00
Salt & Pepper, Flower, Skunk From Bambi, Goebel, 1950s 175.00
Salt & Pepper, Hop & Low, Fantasia, Ceramic, Vernon Kilns 195.00
Salt & Pepper, Mickey & Minnie Mouse, Leeds, 1940s 20.00
Salt & Pepper, Pinocchio & Jiminy Cricket 300.00
Scarf, Cinderella 38.00
Sheet Music, A Dream Is A Wish Your Heart Makes, Cinderella, 1954 .... 12.00
Sheet Music, Bibbidi-Bobbidi-Boo, 1949 .... 10.00
Sheet Music, Mickey Mouse's Birthday Party, Characters Around Cake, 1936 .... 30.00
Sheet Music, Snow White & Seven Dwarfs, Book, 1938 .... 45.00
Sheet Music, Whistle While You Work, Walt Disney Enterprise, Copyright 1937 .... 100.00
Sheet Music, You Belong To My Heart, Three Caballeros, 1944 .... 5.00
Sheet Music, Zip-A-Dee-Doo-Dah, Song Of The South, 1946 .... 10.00
Soaky, Bambi, 1960s 23.00
Soaky, Cinderella 20.00
Soaky, Donald Duck 18.00
Soaky, Dopey, 1960s 22.00
Soaky, Pinocchio 35.00
Soaky, Snow White, Movable Arms 20.00
Soap, Snow White & Seven Dwarfs, Figural, Box, c.1938 .... 175.00
Spoon, Mickey Mouse, William Rogers & Son, 1930s 15.00
Spoon, Sculpted Castle, Sterling Silver, 1950s-1960s, 4 In. 12.00

Spoon Holder, Mickey Mouse, Hoan	30.00
Spoon Set, Mickey & Minnie Mouse, Goofy, Disney, 4 In., 3 Piece	30.00
Tambourine, Mickey Mouse Club	12.00
Tea Set, Helpmates, Tin, Ohio Art, c.1936	245.00
Tea Set, Mickey & Minnie Mouse, Lusterware, 1930s, 21 Piece	250.00
Tea Set, Mickey & Minnie, Lusterware, Japan, 1930s, 6 Piece	85.00
Tea Set, Mickey Mouse, Magic Kingdom, Box	30.00
Telephone, Mickey Mouse, Figural, 1960s	85.00
Telephone, Mickey Mouse, Yellow Handset	275.00
Tin, Land Of Disney, 1940s, 12 1/2 x 7 3/4 x 2 1/2 In.	335.00
Tin, Snow White Biscuit, Belgium	165.00
Toothbrush Holder, Bashful, Figural, China, England, Late 1930s, 4 In.	100.00
Toothbrush Holder, Dumbo, Bisque, Painted, 1940s	425.00
Toothbrush Holder, Mickey & Minnie Mouse, Standing, Bisque, 1930s, 4 1/2 In.	275.00
Toothbrush Holder, Mickey Mouse, Movable Arm, 5 In.	385.00
Toothbrush Holder, Mickey Mouse, Yellow Pants, String Tail, Bisque	250.00
Toothbrush Holder, Sleepy & Dopey, Double, Bisque	1007.00
Toothbrush Holder, Three Little Pigs	135.00
Toothbrush Holder, Three Little Pigs, Bisque	120.00
Toy, Acrobat, Mickey Mouse, Box	895.00
Toy, Airplane, Mickey Mouse, Sun Rubber	85.00
Toy, Baloo, Jungle Book, 2nd Series, Disneykin, 1960s	45.00
Toy, Bambi, Steiff, 1940s, 6 In.	95.00
Toy, Car, Ludwig Van Drake, Friction	425.00
Toy, Car, Mickey Mouse, Anniversary, Lionel, Box	385.00
Toy, Casey Jr., Train, Mickey Mouse, Windup, Marx	75.00
Toy, Cinderella & Prince Charming, Windup, Irwin, Box	175.00
Toy, Cinderella & Prince, Dancing, Battery Operated, Box	175.00
Toy, Danny, Song Of The South, Stuffed Animal, 1945	150.00
Toy, Disney Express, Marx	125.00
Toy, Donald Duck & Goofy Duet, Tin, Windup, 1941	875.00
Toy, Donald Duck Choo Choo, Fisher-Price, 1942	200.00
Toy, Donald Duck In Police Car	28.00
Toy, Donald Duck, Acrobat, Celluloid, Gym Toys, Box	750.00
Toy, Donald Duck, Celluloid, Nodder, 5 3/4 In., 1930s	1750.00
Toy, Donald Duck, Celluloid, Windup, Tin Base, Label, 1930s, 6 In.	690.00
Toy, Donald Duck, Climbing Fireman, Windup, Tin Lithograph, Line-Mar, 1950s	225.00
Toy, Donald Duck, Dipsy Car, Windup, Marx	550.00
Toy, Donald Duck, Rides Tricycle, Tin, Celluloid, Linemar, Box	650.00
Toy, Donald Duck, Squirt Gun, Figural	35.00
Toy, Donald Duck, Standing, Rubber, Sun Rubber Co., Box, 1950s, 10 In.	75.00
Toy, Donald Duck, Toss-Up Balloon, Package	95.00
Toy, Donald Duck, Train, Lithograph, No. 450, Fisher-Price, 1942	225.00
Toy, Donald Duck, Tricycle, Celluloid, Tin Lithograph, Linemar, 3 1/2 In.	632.00
Toy, Donald Duck, Windup, Celluloid, Borgfeldt, 5 In.	800.00
Toy, Donald Duck, Windup, Spinning Tail, Plastic, 1960s	125.00
Toy, Donald Duck, Windup, Tail Spins, 1960s	125.00
Toy, Drum, Mickey Mouse, Playing Various Instruments, Happynak, 4 In.	195.00
Toy, Ferdinand The Bull, Jointed, Composition, Ideal Toy & Novelty, 1930s	165.00
Toy, Ferdinand The Bull, Seiberling Rubber, 1930s	95.00 to 185.00
Toy, Fire Truck, Mickey Mouse, Sun Rubber	60.00
Toy, Goofy The Gardner, Windup, Tin, Marx, England, 8 x 10 In.	1195.00
Toy, Handcar, Donald Duck & Pluto, Clockwork	450.00
Toy, Handcar, Mickey Mouse & Minnie Mouse, Painted Steel, Lionel, 7 1/2 In.	525.00
Toy, Hurdy-Gurdy, Mickey Mouse, Minnie Mouse & Donald, Salco, 3 1/2 In.	95.00
Toy, Jiminy Cricket, Ramp Walker, Marx	30.00
Toy, Jiminy Cricket, Windup, Tin, Linemar	300.00
Toy, Krazy Kar, Mickey Mouse, Battery Operated, Marx, c.1970	150.00
Toy, Ludwig Von Drake, Car, Marline Friction, Tin, Plastic, 1961	425.00
Toy, Mickey & Minnie Acrobats, Windup Trapeze, Celluloid, Borgfeldt, 1930s	1750.00
Toy, Mickey Mouse & Friends, Spinning Top, Lackawanna Mfg., Co., c.1930, 10 In.	287.00
Toy, Mickey Mouse Bus Line, Bus, Walt Disney Stars, 19 In.	195.00
Toy, Mickey Mouse Krazy Kar, Battery Operated, Marx, Box	150.00

Toy, Mickey Mouse On Pluto, 3 Wheel, Key Wind, Celluloid, 1940s, 5 1/2 In. Box 6325.00
Toy, Mickey Mouse On Trapeze, Wooden, 1930s 75.00
Toy, Mickey Mouse Service Truck, Friction, Plastic, Linemar, 1950s, 4 1/2 In. ......55.00 to 75.00
Toy, Mickey Mouse Tow Truck, Battery Operated, Andygard, Box 225.00
Toy, Mickey Mouse Trapeze, Push Buttons, Kohner, 5 1/2 In. 25.00
Toy, Mickey Mouse, Acrobat, Wooden, Handheld 45.00
Toy, Mickey Mouse, Bendable, Marx 75.00
Toy, Mickey Mouse, Celluloid, Spring Arms & Tail, 1930s 250.00
Toy, Mickey Mouse, Celluloid, Spring Arms & Legs, France 325.00
Toy, Mickey Mouse, Corn Popper, Musical 25.00
Toy, Mickey Mouse, Crazy Car 600.00
Toy, Mickey Mouse, Ferris Wheel, Tin, Chein 490.00
Toy, Mickey Mouse, Jointed, Cardboard, String Action, 1930s, 9 In. 550.00
Toy, Mickey Mouse, Magician, Battery Operated, Box 2400.00
Toy, Mickey Mouse, On Trapeze, Windup, Celluloid, 1930s 950.00
Toy, Mickey Mouse, On Unicycle, Marx 525.00
Toy, Mickey Mouse, Pie-Eyed, Chaps & Neckerchief, Knickerbocker, 11 2/ In. 155.00
Toy, Mickey Mouse, Plastic, Rubber, Dakin, 7 In. 19.00
Toy, Mickey Mouse, Playing Xylophone, Linemar 1000.00
Toy, Mickey Mouse, Plush Cloth, Black, Battery Operated, Mechanical, 14 In. 35.00
Toy, Mickey Mouse, Pull Toy, Xylophone Player, Fisher-Price, 1939, 9 x 11 In. 330.00
Toy, Mickey Mouse, Ramp Walker 20.00
Toy, Mickey Mouse, Rattle, Roly-Poly, Mirror, 7 1/2 x 5 1/4 In. 25.00
Toy, Mickey Mouse, Roller Skater, Tin, Linemar, 7 In., Box 660.00
Toy, Mickey Mouse, Steiff, 16 In. 2500.00
Toy, Mickey Mouse, The Engineer, Pull, Wooden, Fisher-Price 175.00
Toy, Mickey Mouse, Train Set, Engine & 4 Cars, Track, Tin Lithograph, Windup, Box 525.00
Toy, Mickey Mouse, Train, 1936, Lionel, Box ....*Illus* 14000.00
Toy, Mickey Mouse, Windup, Wheelbarrow, Marx 85.00
Toy, Mickey Mouse, Wooden, Articulated Hands, 4 Fingers, 7 In. 250.00
Toy, Mickey Mouse, Xylophone 265.00
Toy, Mickey, Goofy, Donald & Pluto, Xylophone, Tin Lithograph, Tudor, 1960s 75.00
Toy, Minnie Mouse Knitting Rocking Chair, Windup, Linemar, Box 1150.00
Toy, Minnie Mouse, Jointed, Celluloid, 5 In. 250.00
Toy, Minnie Mouse, Plastic, Rubber, Dakin, 7 In. 19.00
Toy, Minnie Mouse, Windup, Linemar, 1950s, 7 In. 460.00
Toy, Mouse, Gus, Cinderella, Plush, Original Package, 5 In. 65.00
Toy, Nautilus, Sub, 20,000 Leagues Under The Sea, Windup, Tin, Box ....245.00 to 295.00
Toy, Pail, Donald Duck & Nephews, Atlantic City 450.00
Toy, Pail, Mickey Mouse, Chein, 5 1/2 In. 165.00
Toy, Pail, Mickey Mouse, Chein, Shovel, 7 1/2 In. 250.00
Toy, Paint Box, Snow White & 7 Dwarfs, Tin, Belgium 75.00
Toy, Phonograph, 78 RPM, Chein 285.00
Toy, Phonograph, Character Decals, 1950s 110.00
Toy, Pinocchio's Christmas Party, Spear Store Giveaway, 1939, 8 x 10 3/4 In. 38.00

◆◆◆◆◆◆◆◆◆◆◆◆◆◆◆◆◆

Printed game boards
from the 1940s to
the 1960s fade very
quickly. Older print-
ing seems to be less
damaged by ultravi-
olet exposure.

◆◆◆◆◆◆◆◆◆◆◆◆◆◆◆◆◆

Disneyana, Toy, Mickey Mouse, Train, 1936, Lionel, Box

Toy, Pinocchio, Acrobat, 1930s 90.00
Toy, Pinocchio, Shovel, Holding Candle 65.00
Toy, Pinocchio, Squeeze, Hard Rubber, 1930s 85.00
Toy, Play Set, Rocket Ship, Control Board, Box 115.00
Toy, Pluto Pup, Wooden & Fiber, Geo. Borgfeldt Co., 5 3/4 In. 115.00
Toy, Pluto, On Wheels, Plastic, Marx, 1960s, 3 In. 15.00
Toy, Pluto, Paddle Toy, Fisher-Price, 1930s 80.00
Toy, Pluto, Pop-Up, Critter, Blue Paddle, Fisher-Price 45.00
Toy, Pluto, Windup, Plastic, Marx 165.00
Toy, Pluto, Wooden, Pop-Up, Fisher-Price, 1930s... 80.00
Toy, Professor Ludwig Von Drake, Tin, Friction, Marline, 1961 .... 425.00
Toy, Snow White & Seven Dwarfs, Hard Rubber, 3 1/2 To 5 1/2 In., 8 Piece 350.00
Toy, Tea Set, Disneyland, Chein, Service For 2, Box, 1940s 175.00
Toy, Tea Set, Mickey Mouse, Happynak, Tin, Box, 8 Piece 325.00
Toy, Tea Set, Mickey Mouse, Tan Luster, Box, 23 Piece....................................... 425.00
Toy, Top, Mickey Mouse, Tin Lithograph, Chein, 1975, 5 In. 20.00
Toy, Top, Mickey, Pluto, Donald, Goofy, Tin Lithograph, LBZ, 1970s, 9 In. 30.00
Toy, Tractor, Mickey Mouse, Sun Rubber 165.00
Toy, Tramp The Dog, Vinyl, Mohair, Felt, Chimes, Gund, 1955, 8 1/2 In. 65.00
Toy, View-Master, Mickey Mouse Face 5.00
Toy, Xylophone, Donald Duck, Pull Toy, Paper Lithograph On Wood, Fisher-Price 240.00
Toy, Xylophone, Mickey Mouse, Windup, Linemar 750.00
Train, Casey Jr. Express, Tin, Windup 125.00
Tray, Donald Duck, Tea Set, Tin Lithograph, 1930s, Ohio Art, 8 x 10 In. 95.00
Tray, Seven Dwarfs, Wooden Veneer, Hasko, 1955, 7 1/2 x 16 In. 30.00
Umbrella, Mickey Mouse, Full Figural Mickey Handle, 1950s............................. 90.00
Umbrella, Snow White, 1950 .... 55.00
Viewer, Mickey Mouse, Film Strips, Display Box 175.00
Watch, Bradley Cinderella, Walt Disney... 12.50
Watch, Mickey Mouse, Pocket, Fob, 1933.. 650.00
Whistle, Donald Duck, Celluloid... 45.00
Wristwatch, Beauty & The Beast, Employee-Only Premium.................................. 175.00
Wristwatch, Donald Duck, 20th Birthday, US Time, 1948 .... 400.00
Wristwatch, Fantasia.. 200.00
Wristwatch, Mickey Mouse, Box, 1939 .... 400.00
Wristwatch, Mickey Mouse, Ingersoll... 450.00
Wristwatch, Mickey Mouse, Ingersoll, c.1936.. 287.00
Wristwatch, Mickey Mouse, Pie-Eyed Mickey On Face, 50th Birthday 150.00
Wristwatch, Pluto, Wagging Head, Bradley, Box 575.00
Wristwatch, Snow White, U.S. Time, 1958 .... 25.00
Wristwatch, Steamboat Willie 250.00
Wristwatch, Zorro On Black Hat In Box, Zorro On Face.. 450.00

DOCTOR, see Dental; Medical

DOLL entries are listed by marks printed or incised on the doll, if possible. If
there are no marks, the doll is listed by the name of the subject or country.

A.B.G., 639, Fashion Lady, Closed Mouth, Kid Body, Antique Dress & Shoes, 16 In. 1150.00
A.M., 1894, Original Wig, Pink Silk Dress, Hat & Shoes, 16 In.................................... 550.00
A.M., 243, Toddler, Closed Mouth, 5-Piece Composition Body, Sleep Eyes, 10 In......... 1800.00
A.M., 252, Googly, Molded Painted Topknot, Dress & Socks, 10 In. 1550.00
A.M., 253, Googly, Bisque Head, Toddler Body, Eyes To Side, 7 1/2 In. 775.00
A.M., 323, Googly, Bisque Socket Head, Mohair Wig, 5-Piece Composition Body, 7 In. 625.00
A.M., 323, Googly, Toddler Body, Dressed, 10 In. 1650.00
A.M., 341, Dream Baby, Blue Sleep Eyes, Composition Baby Body, 8 1/4 In. 275.00
A.M., 370, Bisque Head, Hands, Sleep Eyes, Kid Body, Cloth Legs, c.1900, 20 In......... 975.00
A.M., 370, Bisque, Brown Eyes & Hair, Open Mouth, 19 In. 150.00
A.M., 390, Bisque Head, Ball-Jointed Composition Body, Redressed, 33 In. 330.00
A.M., 390, Bisque Head, Sleep Eyes, Jointed Stick Leg, 18 In. 105.00
A.M., 390, Bisque Head, Sleep Eyes, Lace Trimmed Dress, 20 In. 200.00
A.M., 390, Bisque, Dutch Boy Outfit, Open Mouth, Sleep Eyes, 18 In........................... 220.00
A.M., 390, Sleep Eyes, Chunky Ball-Jointed, Composition, Brown Hair, 34 In............... 1050.00
A.M., 990, Baby, Bisque Head, Bent Leg, Composition Body, Dressed, 18 In. 220.00

A.M., 990, Baby, Bisque Head, Sleep Eyes, Composition, Bent Limb, Dressed, 14 In. .. 325.00
A.M., 990, Blond Human Hair Wig, White Dress, Pink Silk Trim, 28 In. 875.00
A.M., 995, Bisque, Brown Eyes & Hair, Open Mouth, 28 In.. 258.00
A.M., Bisque, Blond, Sleep Eyes, Open Mouth, 14 In... 68.00
A.M., Bisque, Brown Wig, Braids, Blue Eyes, Open Mouth, 22 In. 247.00
A.M., Bisque, Composition Body, Blond Wig, Open Mouth, 23 In. 143.00
A.M., Bisque, Wig, Blue Sleep Eyes, Open Mouth, White Lacy Dress, 23 In. 220.00
A.M., Boy, Bisque, Kid Body, Closed Mouth, 13 In... 375.00
A.M., Composition, Brown Sleep Eyes, Open Mouth, Wig, 24 In.................................. 220.00
A.M., Florodora, Bisque Head, Composition Body, 24 In. 250.00
A.M., Florodora, Bisque Head, Sleep Eyes, 18 1/2 In. 315.00
A.M., Florodora, Bisque Shoulder Head, Sleep Eyes, Blond, Kid Body, Dressed, 21 In. 165.00
A.M., Florodora, Fur Eyebrows, Green Print Dress, Lace Trim, 21 In. 400.00
A.M., Head, 990, Bisque... 187.00
A.M., Queen Louise, Bisque, Sleep Eyes, French Style Dress, 28 In. 895.00
Advertising, Art Fabric Mills, Cloth Original Dress, 1900, 17 In. 135.00
Advertising, Arthur Murray Dance Studios, Man & Woman, Let's Twist, Pair.............. 229.00
Advertising, Bell Telephone Co., Telephone Co. Clothes, Box, 15 In. 48.00
Advertising, Big Boy's Dolly, Pillow Doll, 1978, 4 In. 35.00
Advertising, Blue Bonnet Sue, Dakin, 1986... 25.00
Advertising, Blue Ribbon Malt Extract, Cloth, Uncut... 135.00
Advertising, Buddy Lee, Composition, Denim Jacket, 1930s, 12 1/2 In. 325.00
Advertising, Burger King, Stuffed, Bag, 13 In.. 19.50
Advertising, Burger King, With Necklace, 1973, 15 In. 20.00
Advertising, C & H Sugar, Boy, Box :... 15.00
Advertising, California Raisin, 25 In... 12.00
Advertising, California Raisin, Cloth, Stuffed, 33 In., 1988 .... 50.00
Advertising, California Raisin, Plush, 18 In.. 15.00
Advertising, California Raisin, Plush, 1988, 10 In.. 15.00
Advertising, California Raisin, Plush, Plastic Face, 15 In. 25.00
Advertising, Ceresota Boy, Lithographed Cloth, Uncut.. 200.00
Advertising, Chicken Of The Sea, Mermaid, Stuffed, Acme Premium 75.00
Advertising, Chiquita Banana, Oilcloth, Kellogg's Premium, 1950s, 10 1/2 In. 65.00
Advertising, Domino's Noid, Plush, 26 In... 25.00
Advertising, Eskimo Pie, Cloth, Box, 1976.. 45.00
Advertising, Fig Newton, Box 12.00
Advertising, Fisk Tire Boy, Box 65.00
Advertising, Hawaiian Punch, Punchy 20.00
Advertising, Huggie, Speedy Alka-Seltzer, Cloth, 1988 .... 4.00
Advertising, Jack Frost, Cloth, 1950s 9500.00
Advertising, Kellogg's, Chiquita Banana, Cloth, Uncut, Mailer, 1944 .... 95.00
Advertising, Kellogg's, Goldilocks & 3 Bears, Cloth, 13-In. Doll, 4 Piece 170.00
Advertising, Kellogg's, Pop, Rice Krispies, Vinyl, 8 In..30.00 to 40.00
Advertising, Kellogg's, Pop, Rice Krispies, Vinyl, Squeeze, 7 1/2 In. 45.00
Advertising, Kimberly-Clark, Patient Pat, 6 1/2 In. 20.00
Advertising, Levi, Denim, Box, 1973 .... 38.00
Advertising, Levi, Denim, Rag, Red Hair, Knickerbocker, 1970s, 10 In. 30.00
Advertising, Little Debbie, Barbie Type, Box 35.00
Advertising, Little Sprout, Vinyl 10.00
Advertising, Miss Revlon, 15 In. 195.00
Advertising, Miss Revlon, Fur Stole, 18 In... 225.00
Advertising, Miss Tastee Freez, American Sweetheart, Movable Eyes, 1950s 25.00
Advertising, Morton Salt Girl, Cloth, Mattel, 1974, 14 In. 45.00
Advertising, Mountain Dew, Hillbilly, Stand 800.00
Advertising, Nabisco, Mr. Salty, Rag, Box, 10 In... 20.00
Advertising, National Blue Ribbon Freezer Food Service, Bonnie, 18 In., 1960s, Box .. 125.00
Advertising, Natural Gas, Genie, Stuffed, Flame-Shaped Vinyl Face, Late 1960s 50.00
Advertising, Nauga, Orange Naugahyde, 1967... 75.00
Advertising, Naughty Naugahyde, Light Brown, 10 In.. 65.00
Advertising, Pillsbury Doughboy, 1971... 8.00
Advertising, Pillsbury, Poppin' Fresh, Terry Cloth... 30.00
Advertising, Playboy Rabbit, Cheerleader 45.00
Advertising, Playboy Rabbit, Tuxedo, 35 In.. 50.00

Advertising, Reddy Kilowatt, Glow-In-The-Dark, 1961, 5 In. ....215.00 to 225.00
Advertising, Ronald McDonald, Stuffed, 1971, 17 In. 30.00
Advertising, Ronald McDonald, Stuffed, 1977.. 14.00
Advertising, Senor Taco, Rag, Multicolor, Box, 14 In. 20.00
Advertising, Smokey The Bear, Cloth, Dakin, Box, 6 In. 10.00
Advertising, Speedy Alka-Seltzer, Vinyl, 8 In. 850.00
Advertising, Sprite, Talking, Vinyl, Box 15.00
Advertising, Stay-Puft Marshmallow Man 10.00
Advertising, Trix, Rabbit, Squeeze, 1970s, 8 1/2 In. 45.00
Advertising, Twinkle The Kid, Inflatable, 28 In.. 28.00
Alexander dolls are listed in this category under Madame Alexander
Alice, Blonde Hair, Molded Black Band, Cloth Body, Leather Arms, Blue Dress, 15 In. 115.00
Alma, Character Boy, Fat Molded Face, Riding Outfit & Crop, 19 In. 1250.00
Alt, Beck & Gottschalk, 698, Bisque, Sleep Eyes, Kid Body, Antique Dress, 19 In. 450.00
Alt, Beck & Gottschalk, Bisque, Open Mouth, Wig, Pierced Ears, Pink Dress, 24 In...... 220.00
Amberg, Baby Peggy, Brown Sleep Eyes, Kid Body, Bisque Hands, 20 In. 2495.00
American Character, Toni, Bride, All Original, 13 In. 175.00
Amish, Family, Cloth, Oilcloth Face, No Features, 1950, 9 To 13 In., 3 Piece................ 345.00
Amusco, Baby, Sleep Eyes, Shift & Booties, Signed, Box, 14 In. 495.00
Annalee, Colonial Rabbit, 34 In. 295.00
Annalee, Frosty The Snowman, 34 In. 350.00
Annalee, Mouse, Pregnant, 1971, 7 In.. 85.00
Annalee, Mr. & Mrs. Bunnies, 37 In., Pair.. 450.00
Armand Marseille dolls are listed in this category under A.M.
Arranbee, Nancy, Composition, 16 In. 250.00
Automaton, Alice In Wonderland, 22 1/2 x 15 In. 1815.00
Automaton, Amazing Feats, Acrobat & Clown, Metal, Hinged Limbs, 31 1/2 In. 1955.00
Automaton, Animal Orchestra, 16 x 13 In. 4400.00
Automaton, Ballerina, Clockwork, Bisque Head, Mohair Wig, 16 1/2 In. 1000.00
Automaton, Boy On Bicycle, Wooden Body, Curly Wig, Key-Wind Wheel, Germany .. 2200.00
Automaton, Cowboy, 15 x 18 In. 2750.00
Automaton, Elopement, 25 1/2 x 23 In. 1595.00
Automaton, Juggler, Bisque Head, Balancing Ball On Head, Germany, 17 In. 1610.00
Automaton, Lady, Chicken In Basket, Flower, Clockwork, Lambert, France, 1890 ...15000.00
Automaton, Lambert, Clown, Playing Mandolin, Bisque Hands, Clown Suit, 21 In. 4600.00
Automaton, Lute Player, Music, Open Mouth, Blue Set Eyes, Mohair Wig, 14 In. 1850.00
Automaton, Monkey, Key Wind, Phalbois.. 5750.00
Automaton, Seated On Chair, Turn Knob, Plays Music, Arms Up & Down, 12 In........ 1695.00
Averill, American Indian Girl, Cloth, 1930 .... 65.00
Averill, Bonnie Babe, Dressed, 16 In. 1695.00
Averill, Bonnie Babe, Toddler, Bisque, Swivel Head, Glass Sleep Eyes, Tag, 6 In. 1250.00
Baby, Cloth, Oil-Painted Hair & Feathers, Stockinet Body, Cotton Shift, 8 In................ 315.00
Baby, Mechanical, Wax Over Papier-Mache, Original Clothes, 11 1/2 In. 1750.00
Bahr & Proschild, 201, Bisque Head, Sleep Eyes, Jointed Composition Body, 15 In..... 675.00
Bahr & Proschild, 204, Closed Mouth, 24 In.. 2500.00
Bahr & Proschild, 224, Bisque, Blue Paperweight Eyes, Dressed, 12 In. 1400.00
Bahr & Proschild, 323 3/0, Googly Eyes, Composition Body, Dressed, 1915, 10 In...... 1955.00
Bahr & Proschild, Baby, Bisque, Composition Body, Sleep Eyes, Teeth, 18 In. 375.00
Barbie dolls are listed in this category under Mattel
Barrois, Bisque, Kid Body, Plum Gown, Cap, Leather Shoes, 1870s, 17 In.................... 2900.00
Barrois, Bisque, Kid Body, Stitched Fingers, Diamond Ring, 22 In. 3700.00
Barrois, Fashion, Bisque Head, Kid Body, Brown Wig, Marked E.B., 17 1/2 In. 3000.00
Barrois, Parisienne, Blue Eyes, Original Pate & Wig, Victorian Clothes, 17 In............. 2900.00
Belton Type, Closed Mouth, Straight Wrists, Composition Body, 18 In. 2400.00
Belton Type, Sonnenberg Body, Closed Mouth, Mohair Wig, 2 Holes, 24 1/2 In. 2800.00
Bergmann dolls are also in this category under S & H and Simon & Halbig
Bergmann, Bisque Head, Sleep Eyes, Jointed Composition Body, 22 In. 287.00
Bergmann, Bisque, Sleep Eyes, Open Mouth, Composition Body, 23 In. 330.00
Bierschenk, Bisque Head, Sculpted Tongue, Flocked Hair, Bent Limb, 12 In................ 1000.00
Bierschenk, Character, Lady, Bisque, Straight Limb, Satin Dress, 1910, 13 In. 2875.00
Bisque, Bebe, Blue Eyes, Dressed, 22 In.. 7200.00
Bisque, Bebe, Paperweight Eyes, Mohair Wig, Silk & Lace Costume, 29 In. 3500.00
Bisque, Bebe, Swivel Head, Pierced Ears, Kid Body, c.1882, 16 In.............................. 5400.00

Bisque, Mr. & Mrs. Happifats, Googly Eyes, Jointed, Germany, 4 In., Pair 650.00
Bisque, Princess No. 1, Christening Dress, Germany, 22 In. 320.00
Bisque, Shoulder Head, Molded Blue Scarf On Head, Cloth Body, 21 In. 1050.00
Bisque, Walking, Blue Sleep Eyes, Open Mouth, Mohair Wig, Brevete, Box, 6 In. 350.00
Black dolls are included in the Black category
Borgfeldt, Girl, Holding Rocking Horse, Complete Outfit, 24 In. 550.00
Borgfeldt, My Girlie III, Bisque, Composition, Open Mouth, Wig, Lacy Gown, 25 In. .. 220.00
Boudoir, Cloth Face, Swedish, 28 In. 225.00
Boudoir, Marlene Dietrich, Smoker, 30 In. 795.00
Boudoir, Silk Hair, France, 18 In. 275.00
Bozo The Clown, Vinyl, Cloth, 30 In. 32.00
Bru Jne, Baby, Nursing, Composition Body, Old Costume, 24 1/2 In. 6800.00
Bru Jne, Bebe, Mechanical Walker, Gray Sleep Eyes, Open Mouth, 5 Teeth, 21 In. 1380.00
Bru Jne, Bisque, Blue Eyes, Blond Mohair Wig, Old Costume, 22 In. 9800.00
Bru Jne, Bisque, Closed Mouth, Paperweight Eyes, Original Dress, Box, 26 In. 11800.00
Bru Jne, Fashion, Bisque, Mohair Wig, Cork Pate, Kid Body, Wool Dress, 1875, 14 In. 4025.00
Bru Teteur, Bisque Swivel Head & Arms, Nursing Mechanism, Lace Gown, 14 In. 6500.00
Bruno Schmidt, Wendy, Wood & Composition Body, Floral Dress, Hat, 1912, 11 In... 3450.00
Bubbles, Heart Tag Neckline, Life-Size, 24 In. 895.00
Buffy & Mrs. Beasley, Box, 1967 .... 170.00
Bugs Bunny, Rubber Face & Hands, Stuffed 100.00
Bye-Lo, Baby, Bisque, Brown Eyes, Celluloid Hands, Original Dress & Slip, 10 In. 525.00
Bye-Lo, Baby, Closed Mouth, Cloth Body, Celluloid Hands, Label On Torso, 18 1/2 In. 265.00
Bye-Lo, Baby, Glass Eyes, Closed Mouth, Cloth Body, Celluloid Hands, 11 1/2 In. 300.00
Bye-Lo, Baby, Stamped Body, Celluloid Hands 367.00
Bye-Lo, Bisque Socket Head, Brown Baby Hair, Bent-Limb Body, c.1923, 13 In. 1300.00
Bye-Lo, Bisque Swivel Head, Bisque Torso & Limbs, c.1923, 5 In. 600.00
Bye-Lo, Wax, Celluloid Hands, Baby Clothes, 14 1/2-In. Head 5500.00
Carl Bergner, Faces, Crying, Laughing, Sleeping, Glass Eyes, Clothes 1895.00
Catterfelder Puppenfabrik, 201, Toddler, Bisque, Socket Head, 10 In. 900.00
Catterfelder Puppenfabrik, 263, Antique Gown, Bonnet, 26 In. 900.00
Catterfelder Puppenfabrik, Bisque Head, Smiling Expression, Bent Limb, 12 In. 1000.00
Celluloid, Baby Boy, Jointed Shoulders & Hips, 12 In. 95.00
Celluloid, Baby, Crawling, Tin Body, Celluloid Head, Arms & Legs, Windup 65.00
Celluloid, Character Baby, Slanted Eyes, Chinese Costume, 11 In., Pair 1250.00
Celluloid, Child, Glass Eyes, Germany, 17 In. 159.00
Celluloid, Nun, Adult Face, Habit, 17 In. 250.00
Chad Valley, Bambina, Glass Eyes, 18 In. 795.00
Chad Valley, Girl, Tagged Feet, 15 In. 350.00
Chad Valley, Long John Silver, 15 In. 225.00
Chase, Baby, Oil-Painted Stockinet Head, Cloth Body, Pale Blue Dress, 17 In. 275.00
Chase, Baby, Separate Thumbs, Stitched Fingers & Toes, Hospital Gown, 21 In. 500.00
Chase, Bobbed Hair, Period Clothes, 16 In. 1200.00
Chase, Child, Applied Ears, Cloth Body, Jointed Limbs, Clothes, 24 In. 1295.00
Chase, Painted Hair & Features, Cloth, 19 In. 165.00
Chase, Stockinet Head, Oil Painted Facial Features & Hair, Dressed, 19 In. 1600.00
Chase, Stockinet Head, Painted Facial Features & Hair, Sateen Body, Dress, 20 In. 900.00
China, Spit Curl, Molded & Painted Black Hair, Cloth Body, 25 In. 700.00
China Head, Blond, Marianne On Chest 60.00
China Head, Cloth Body, Kid Arms, Stitched Fingers, Underclothes, c.1870s, 26 In. ... 748.00
China Shoulder Head, Navy Silk Dress, Leather Boots, Pique Coat, 1860s, 19 In. 395.00
China Shoulder Head, Painted Blue Eyes, Jointed Cloth Body, Leather Arms, 29 In. ... 400.00
China Shoulder Head, Painted Eyes, Cloth Body, Jewels, 20 In. 200.00
Chinese, Silk Kimono, Carrying Stool & Ladder On Head, 7 In. 20.00
Cloth, Little Orphan Annie, Sandy In Pocket, 16 In. 20.00
Cloth, Monkey, Sock 30.00
Cloth, Raggedy Andy, Brown Checked Shirt, Tan Corduroy Pants, 20 In. 130.00
Cochran, Solemn Expression, Cotton Frock, c.1965, 11 In. 1100.00
Coleco, Cat In The Hat, Plush 35.00
Coleco, Grinch, How The Grinch Stole Christmas, Plush, Santa Suit, 1983, 24 In. 150.00
Composition, Nun, Tin Sleep Eyes, 5-Piece Body, White Habit, Box, 13 In. 95.00
Composition, Nursing Baby, Jointed Body, 16 In. 9500.00
Cruckner, Topsy-Turvy 575.00

Cuno & Otto Dressel, 1349, Bisque, Sleep Eyes, Jointed Composition, Wig, 18 In.	375.00
Cuno & Otto Dressel, 1469, Flapper, Bisque, Wooden Ball-Jointed Body, 14 In.	2800.00
Cuno & Otto Dressel, Admiral Dewey, Bisque, 5-Piece Papier-Mache Body, 1900, 8 In.	400.00
Cuno & Otto Dressel, Bisque, 5 Upper Teeth, Jointed, White Antique Dress, 23 In.	195.00
Cuno & Otto Dressel, Uncle Sam, 13 In.	1700.00
Cuno & Otto Dressel, Uncle Sam, Bisque Head, Incised Wrinkles, Ball Jointed, 12 In..	900.00
Dennis The Menace, Original Clothes, 1950s	200.00
Dennis The Menace, Soft Rubber Face & Hands, 1950s	120.00
Dennis The Menace, Vinyl, Movable Head, 1959	45.00
DEP, 109, Blue Eyes, Open Mouth, Composition Jointed Body, Dressed, 26 In.	795.00
DEP, Bisque, Sleep Eyes, Jointed French Body, Pale Green Satin Dress, 34 In.	2500.00
DEP, Bisque, Snow Figures, Captain Cook, Admiral Perry At North Pole, 5 1/2 In.	750.00
DEP, Brown Sleep Eyes, Ball-Jointed Composition Body, 31 In.	2400.00
DEP, Chunky Body, Antique Pearl Silk Dress, Socks & Shoes, 31 In.	2895.00
Dollhouse, Family, Bisque & Cloth, Unused, Germany, 1890, 4 Piece	395.00
Dorothy, Wizard Of Oz, Judy Garland, Black Dog, 15 1/2 In.	995.00
Dream Baby, Bisque, Composition Body, Brown Sleep Eyes, Christening, 24 In.	850.00
Dream Baby, Cloth Body, Celluloid, Clothes & Hat, 10 1/2-In. Head	325.00
Dressmaker, Powderweight Eyes, Original Clothes, Germany, 16 1/4 In.	1495.00
Dutch Girl, Cloth, Box, 1930s, 18 In.	135.00
Ed Wynn, Fire Chief, Wooden, Jointed, 4 In.	125.00
Eden Bebe, Blue Paperweight Eyes, Ball-Jointed Body, 30 In.	2950.00
Effanbee, Anne Shirley	275.00
Effanbee, Baby Grumpy, Composition & Cloth, 12 In.	200.00
Effanbee, Bubbles, Cloth Body, Composition Arms & Legs, 24 In.	595.00
Effanbee, Dy-Dee, Clothes, Layette, Trunk, Wardrobe, 12 In.	157.00
Effanbee, Dy-Dee, Jointed Rubber Body, Plastic Head, 24 In.	350.00
Effanbee, Girl Scout, 2 Uniforms	50.00
Effanbee, Groucho Marx, Box	35.00
Effanbee, Liberace, Box	175.00
Effanbee, Little Lady Majorette	300.00
Effanbee, Little Lady, Yarn Hair, Cape, 18 In.	350.00
Effanbee, Louie Armstrong, Poseable, Diamond Ring, Handkerchief, Trumpet, 15 In...	135.00
Effanbee, Nancy Lee, Composition, Extra Clothes, Trunk, 18 In.	236.00
Effanbee, Patsy Ann, Composition Body, Sleep Eyes, Original Clothes, 19 In.	1025.00
Effanbee, Patsy Ann, Composition, Painted Lashes, 5-Piece Body, Wrist Tag, 19 In.	205.00
Effanbee, Patsy Ann, Sleep Eyes	225.00
Effanbee, Patsy Jr.	235.00
Effanbee, Patsy, Porcelain, 14 In.	70.00
Effanbee, Patsy, Sleep Eyes, c.1920, 14 In.	125.00
Effanbee, Patsyette, Original Clothes, Trunk, 10 In.	262.00
Effanbee, Rosemary, Composition, 25 In.	150.00
Effanbee, Skippy, Forelock Curl, Jointed 1 Piece Arms & Legs, Dec. 1935, 15 In.	375.00
Effanbee, Suzanne, Composition, Long Brown Hair	95.00
Effanbee, Sweetie Pie, Hard Plastic, Nonworking Voice Box, Pink Taffeta Dress, 27 In.	115.00
Effanbee, Teddy Roosevelt, Rubber Head, 16 In.	145.00
Effanbee, Wizard Of Oz, Dorothy, Witch, Tin Man, Scarecrow, Lion	150.00
Emma Clear, 1947, Shy Lady, Dressed, 22 In.	495.00
Emma Clear, Jenny Lind, Corsets, Dressed, 20 In.	495.00
Eskimo, Painted Features, Fur Clothes, 10 1/2 In.	375.00
Fam-Lee, Composition, Head Screws Into Body, 6, Blue Eyes, April 12, 1921, 6 In.	450.00
Fashion, Wooden Body, Swivel Head, Original Wig & Boots, 14 1/2 In.	4800.00
Flip Wilson-Geraldine, Not Talking, Box	20.00
Foxy Grandpa, Cloth, 16 1/2 In.	250.00
France, Pierre, Organ Grinder, Music Box, Stocking Face, Painted Features, 13 1/2 In.	385.00
Franz Schmidt, Bisque, Composition Body, Wobbly Tongue, 24 In.	875.00
French, Bisque, Closed Mouth, Paperweight Eyes, Dressed, 20 In.	5750.00
French, Character, Blue Paperweight Jeweled Eyes, 2 Rows Teeth, Clothes, 15 In.	950.00
French, Fashion, Bisque, Blue Eyes, Gusseted Leather Body, 1860s, 25 In.	3900.00
French, Fashion, Bisque, Cobalt Blue Eyes, Trunk, 3 Dresses, 16 1/2 In.	6500.00
French, Fashion, Kid Body, Painted Eyes, Antique Clothes, Cape, 13 In.	1207.00
French, Fashion, Papier-Mache, Original Clothes & Wig, 13 In.	1495.00
French, Mystery, Bulging Paperweight Eyes, Long Curls, Closed Mouth, 29 In.	3750.00

Freundlich, General MacArthur, 18 In. 450.00
Frozen Charlie, China, Painted Black Hair, Painted Eyes, No Clothes, 12 In. 165.00
Frozen Charlie, Painted Face & Hair, Ridged Arms, Stiff Legs, 15 In. 437.00
Frozen Charlie, Pink Luster Face, Square Cheeked, 15 In. 650.00
Fulper, Bisque Head, Celluloid & Metal Eyes, Mohair Wig, Composition, c.1920, 15 In. .. 287.00
Fulper, Composition Body, Blond Wig, Blue Eyes, Open Mouth, Lacy Clothes, 23 In. . . 330.00
G.I. Joe figures are listed in the Toy category
Gaultier, Bebe, Paperweight Eyes, Tooth, Dressed, Bonnet, Boots, 20 In. 2400.00
Gaultier, Bisque Head, Kid Body, Paperweight Eyes, Boots, Undies, 17 In. 3500.00
Gaultier, Bisque, Kid Fashion Body, Costume, c.1875, 19 In. 3000.00
Gaultier, Fashion, Bisque, Swivel Head, Fabric Body, Kid Arms, c.1875, 16 In. 1265.00
Gaultier, Fashion, Black Satin Gown, Bustle Bow, Leather Boots, 17 In. 1995.00
Gaultier, French Fashion, Paperweight Eyes, Swivel Head, Dressed, 13 In. 1850.00
Gaultier, Man, French Fashion, Cape, Turban, Mechanical, Musical, 18 In. 3800.00
Gebruder Heubach dolls are also in this category under Heubach
Gebruder Heubach, 5689, Child, Blue Sleep Eyes, Ball-Jointed, Straw Hat, 21 In. 3400.00
Gebruder Heubach, 7623, Bisque, Forelock Curl, Provincial Costume, c.1910, 20 In. ... 1200.00
Gebruder Heubach, 7822, Boy, Molded Curls, Intaglio Eyes, Wood Body, 14 In. 1950.00
Gebruder Heubach, 8192, Character, Girl, Ball-Jointed, Human Hair Wig, 17 In. 850.00
Gebruder Heubach, 8192, Large Sleep Eyes, Round Cheeks, 2-Piece Suit, 15 In. 695.00
Gebruder Heubach, Bisque, Baby Stuart, Baby Gown, 1912, 9 In. 805.00
Gebruder Heubach, Character, Intaglio Eyes, Cotton Dress, 1925, 9 In. 2070.00
Gebruder Heubach, Character, Smiler, Kid Body, Mohair Wig, 27 In. 2995.00
Gebruder Heubach, Child, Bisque, Wooden Jointed Body, Cinderella Tag, 1904, 22 In. 1050.00
Gebruder Heubach, Coquette, Smiling, Leather Body, Celluloid Arms, 11 3/4 In. 895.00
Gebruder Heubach, Dolly Dimple, Bisque, Sleep Eyes, Original Costume, 13 1/2 In... 2800.00
Gebruder Heubach, Pouty, Bisque, Intaglio Blue Eyes, Flocked Hair, 17 In. 695.00
Gebruder Kuhnlenz, Bisque, Paperweight Eyes, Kid Body, Satin Dress, 18 In. 1000.00
Geisha, Holding Wig, Silk, 1930, 14 1/2 In. 25.00
General Douglas MacArthur, Composition, All Original, 17 In 325.00
Georgene, Little Lulu 475.00
Georgene, Raggedy Andy, Box, 1951, 14 In. 250.00
Georgene, Raggedy Ann & Andy, New York, c.1930s, 20 In., Pair 725.00
Georgene, Raggedy Ann & Raggedy Andy, New York, c.1930s, 20 In., Pair 725.00
Georgene, Raggedy Ann, 22 In. 198.00
Georgene, Raggedy Ann, Box, 1951, 14 In. 250.00
Georgene, Raggedy Ann, Original Clothes, 15 In. 75.00
Georgene, Raggedy Ann, Outlined Nose, 20 In. 650.00
Georgene, Sailor, Wrist Tag, 14 In. 225.00
German, Child, Bisque Head, Set Blue Eyes, 5 Teeth, Jointed, Antique Dress, 18 In. ... 90.00
German, Closed Mouth, Bulbous Paperweight Eyes, Ball-Jointed, 17 In. 1800.00
German, Fashion, Paperweight Eyes, Swivel Head, Cloth Body, Clothes, 16 In. 1495.00
German, Fashion, Swivel Neck, Paperweight Eyes, Silk Ensemble, 14 In. 1795.00
German, Flirty Eye, Plastic, 1940s, 12 In. 80.00
German, Florodora, Bisque Socket Head, Composition Body, Sailor Dress, 15 In. 1000.00
German, Pansy II, Sleep Eyes, Teeth, Human Hair, Jointed, Lavender Dress, 23 In. 330.00
German, Queen Louise, Bisque Socket Head, Mohair Wig, Jointed Child's Body, 25 In. 375.00
German, Queen Louise, Bisque, Sleep Eyes, 4 Upper Teeth, Human Hair, Jointed, 28 In. 325.00
Gilbert, Napoleon Solo, Box, 1965 .... 250.00
Googly, Blue Eyes To Side, Watermelon Mouth, Toddler Body, 11 In. 2800.00
Gund, Jiminy Cricket, 1940 .... 400.00
Gund, Little Lulu, Cloth, 1972, 19 In. 85.00
Gund, Little Lulu, Felt, 22 In., Pair 50.00
Halbig, Baby Blanche, Bisque, Mohair Wig, Dotted Swiss Dress, Shoes, 24 In. 750.00
Half Dolls are listed in the Pincushion category
Halle Blakely, Abraham Lincoln, Mary Todd Lincoln, Muslin, 1950, Pair 1100.00
Handwerck, 69, Juliet Wig, Ball-Jointed Body, Old Dress, Extra Outfit, 24 In. 850.00
Handwerck, 99, Ball-Jointed, Swing Leg, All Original, 28 In. 1200.00
Handwerck, 99, Bisque, Sleep Eyes, Old Dress & Shoes, Marked, 21 In. 995.00
Handwerck, 99, Black, Mohair Wig, Stationary Eyes, Ball-Jointed, 21 In. 1350.00
Handwerck, 99, Brown Sleep Eyes, Human Hair Wig, Original Dress & Shoes, 22 In. . . 800.00
Handwerck, 109, Bisque Socket Head, Brown Sleep Eyes, Teeth, Antique Dress, 26 In. 450.00
Handwerck, 109, Bisque, Blue Sleep Eyes, Pastel Silk Dress, Human Wig, 25 In. 1250.00

Handwerck, 109, Human Hair Wig, Salmon Brown Eyes, 25 In. 1275.00
Handwerck, 119, Bisque Head, Sleep Eyes, Mohair Wig, Wood, Composition, 19 In.... 350.00
Handwerck, 119, Bisque, Sleep Eyes, Human Hair Wig, Dress, Boots, 28 In. 1395.00
Handwerck, 119, Bisque, Sleep Eyes, Human Hair Wig, Pink Underdress, 28 In. 900.00
Handwerck, Bisque, Antique Clothes, Leather Shoes, 30 In. 1200.00
Handwerck, Child, Bisque, Mohair Wig, Jointed Body, Floral Dress, 31 In. 550.00
Handwerck, Lady In Red, Ball-Jointed, Painted Lashes, High Boots, 22 In. 575.00
Heebee-Shebee, Painted Eyes, Composition, Molded Chemise, Pink Booties, 10 In. 170.00
Hertel Schwab, 136, Bisque, Outlined Lips, Dressed, Feathered Hat, 29 In. 1100.00
Hertel Schwab, 136, Sleep Eyes, Brown Mohair Wig, Dressed, 29 In. 925.00
Hertel Schwab, 151, Character Baby, Bisque, Solid Dome, 22 In. 470.00
Hertel Schwab, 152, Open Closed Mouth, Original Gown, 12 In. 495.00
Hertel Schwab, 157, Sleep Eyes, Fat Cheeks, Ball Jointed, Old Clothes, 15 In. 2800.00
Hertel Schwab, 172, Googly, Bisque, Composition, Shirt & Diaper, 12 In. 3400.00
Hertel Schwab, 222/28, Our Fairy, Googly Eyes, Gauze Short Dress, c.1915, 11 In. 2587.00
Hertel Schwab, Bisque, Composition Body, Sleep Eyes, Open Mouth, 14 In. 220.00
Heubach dolls are also in this category under Gebruder Heubach
Heubach, 312, Bisque Face, Composition Body, 18 In. 350.00
Heubach, 321, Baby, Sleep Eyes, Bent Limb Composition, Dress, 15 In. 250.00
Heubach, 7602, Bisque, Intaglio Eyes, Dressed, 23 In. 1950.00
Heubach, 9167, Tousled Hair, Crooked Smile, Fancy Gown, 18 In. 750.00
Heubach, 10332, Baby Face, Gown, Blanket, 9 In. 695.00
Heubach, Baby Stuart, 14 In. 1695.00
Heubach, Baby, Bisque, Painted Lashes, 4 Upper Teeth, Bent Limb, Mohair Wig, 19 In.   325.00
Heubach, Boy, Sailor Suit, 12 In. 2000.00
Heubach, Flapper, Fancy Wig, 10 In. 350.00
Heubach, Googly, Bisque, Wire Lever Moves Eyes, Calico Costume, 11 In. 3200.00
Heubach, Googly, Intaglio Eyes, Pursed Mouth, Lederhosen, 7 In. 875.00
Heubach, Googly, Molded Topknot, Triangular Mouth, Crepe-Paper Dress, 10 In. 1550.00
Heubach, Pouty, Intaglio Eyes, Marked, 8 In. 495.00
Heubach Koppelsdorf, 339, Bisque Head, Sleep Eyes, Painted Hair, 15 In. 595.00
Highland Mary, Bisque, Painted Blue Eyes, Blond Hair, Pinafore, 24 In. 220.00
Hilda, Baby, Bisque, Christening Gown, 27 In. 5500.00
Hilda, Solid Dome, Blue Sleep Eyes, Clothes, 18 In. 4700.00
Horsman, Baby, Composition Head, 15 In. 25.00
Horsman, Dimples, Tin Sleep Eyes, Composition & Cloth, Pink Dress, 23 In. 450.00
Horsman, HEbee-SHEbee, 6 In. 600.00
Horsman, Jennie, Composition, Box.1937 .... 95.00
Horsman, Mary Poppins, Picture Window Box, 12 In. 135.00
Horsman, Tynie Baby, Bisque, Painted Hair, Pouty Lips, Muslin Body, 8 1/2 In. 550.00
Horsman, Wendy Ann, Bride, 11 In. 75.00
Huret-Type, French Fashion, China Face, Glass Eyes, Original Clothes, 14 In. 3000.00
Ideal, Baby, Plastic Head, Magic Skin, Wrist Tag, 16 In. 225.00
Ideal, Bam-Bam, Hanna-Barbera Prod., 16 In. 160.00
Ideal, Bonny Braids, 1951, Box 295.00
Ideal, Bull Fighter, Cloth, From Ferdinand The Bull, Hat, Cape, Yellow Coat, 20 In. 460.00
Ideal, Captain Action, Box 225.00
Ideal, Deanna Durbin, Composition, Original Clothes, 24 In. 288.00
Ideal, Deanna Durbin, Pin, 20 In. 550.00
Ideal, Harriet Hubbard Ayer, Dressing Table, Make-Up, Box, 14 In. 300.00
Ideal, Miss Revlon, Vinyl, 5-Piece Body, Yellow Taffeta Dress, Box, 19 In. 250.00
Ideal, Mitzi, Teen Doll, 1965, 12 In. 35.00
Ideal, Posie, 17 In. 20.00
Ideal, Samantha, Bewitched, Red Dress 85.00
Ideal, Sleepy, Dwarf, Cloth, Coat, Pants & Hat, Sleepy Printed On Brim, 12 In. 58.00
Ideal, Snow White & Seven Dwarfs, 1937 .... 950.00
Ideal, Snow White, Composition, White & Yellow Dress, Yellow Shoes, 16 In. 81.00
Ideal, Toni, Brunette, Permanent Set, Paper Tag, Box, 14 In. 395.00
Ideal, Toni, Hard Plastic, Original Clothes, Marked, 14 In. 165.00
Ideal, Walker, Closed Mouth, Original Clothes, 14 In. 55.00
Indian dolls are listed in the Indian category
J.D.K. dolls are also listed in this category under Kestner
J.D.K., 211, Sammee, Blue Sleep Eyes, Original Wig, Old Clothes, 14 In. 695.00

J.D.K., 211, Sammy, Original Skin Wig, Blue Sleep Eyes, 2 Lower Teeth, 24 In. 1950.00
J.D.K., 226, Original Pate & Wig, Antique Gown, 11 In. 695.00
J.D.K., Character, Boy, Brown Sleep Eyes, 5-Piece Toddler Body, Pajamas, 13 In. 550.00
J.D.K., Ivory Bisque, Brown Eyes, 2 Lower Teeth, Chubby Body, 26 In. 1695.00
Japanese, Papier-Mache, Wooden Case, Accessories, c.1910, 5 In. 750.00
Japanese, Water Bearer, c.1830, 15 1/2 In. 675.00
Jester, On Stick, Bells, Blue & White. 495.00
Jumeau, American School Boy, Kid Body, 17 In. 500.00
Jumeau, Bebe, Bisque Socket Head, Paperweight Eyes, Composition Body, 28 In. 4300.00
Jumeau, Bisque Head, Blue Glass Eyes, Closed Mouth, Cork Plate, Jointed, 19 In. 2530.00
Jumeau, Bisque Head, Glass Eyes, Human Hair Wig, Composition Body, 24 In. 2875.00
Jumeau, Bisque Head, Paperweight Eyes, Mohair Wig, Jointed Body, 1907, 22 In. 2700.00
Jumeau, Bisque, Bulging Blue Eyes, Straight Wrists, Costume, 19 In. 8500.00
Jumeau, Bisque, Hair On Cork Pate, Jointed Body, Lace Frock, Bonnet, 27 In. 3700.00
Jumeau, Bisque, Paperweight Eyes, Closed Mouth, Antique Outfit, 25 In. 6600.00
Jumeau, Bisque, Paperweight Eyes, Walker, Head Moves, Label, 20 In. 2300.00
Jumeau, Blue Paperweight Eyes, Antique Clothes & Shoes, 22 1/4 In. 1850.00
Jumeau, Blue Sleep Eyes, Composition, Jointed, Long Curls, 32 1/2 In. 2200.00
Jumeau, Brown Paperweight Eyes, Sailor Suit, Straight Wrists, 20 In. 5200.00
Jumeau, Open Mouth, Brown Paperweight Eyes, 1907, 15 In. 2200.00
Jumeau, Pale Bisque, Blue Paperweight Eyes, 29 In. 9800.00
Jumeau, Portrait, Wrap-Around Oval Eyes, 14 1/2 In. 6500.00
Juro, Dick Clark, All Original, 27 In. 450.00
Juro, Pinkie Lee, All Original, 23 1/2 In. 395.00
Just Me, Bisque, Blue Sleep Eyes, Rosebud Mouth, 9 1/2 In. 1750.00
Jutta, 1348, Bisque Head, Sleep Eyes, Human Hair Wig, Jointed Flapper Body, 23 In. .. 400.00
Jutta, 1349, Child, Vintage Clothes, 27 In. 950.00
K * R, 22, Baby, Blue Sleep Eyes, 17 In. 595.00
K * R, 46, Girl, Blue Flirty Eyes, Composition, Jointed, White Cotton Dress, 18 In. 700.00
K * R, 100, Baby, Molded Hair, Bent Limb, Composition Body, 14 In. 489.00
K * R, 101, Bisque, Sleep Eyes, Human Hair, Provincial Costume, c.1910, 18 In. 8000.00
K * R, 101, Marie, Jointed Body, Chemise, 12 In. 1750.00
K * R, 101, Marie, Mohair Wig, Vintage Clothes, 19 1/2 In. 735.00
K * R, 101, Marie, Pouty, Wig & Clothes, All Original, 14 In. 5900.00
K * R, 109, Ball-Jointed, Original Wig & Clothes, 9 1/2 In. 4000.00
K * R, 114, Painted Eyes, Blond Braids In Buns, Crocheted Dress, 11 In. 2950.00
K * R, 114, Wooden Ball-Jointed Body, Wool Frock, Straw Bonnet, c.1910, 17 In. 6500.00
K * R, 115, Pouty, Chubby Toddler Body, 16 In. 5975.00
K * R, 115A, Toddler, Bisque, Sleep Eyes, Jointed Body, Dress & Shoes, 18 In. 5500.00
K * R, 117, Mein Leibling, Brown Sleep Eyes, Lashes, Clothes, Box, 23 In. 9500.00
K * R, 117N, Bisque Head, 4 Teeth, Composition & Wooden Body, 21 In. 1600.00
K * R, 117N, Flirty, Working Eyes, Tin Lids, Crepe Dress, 16 In. 2400.00
K * R, 121, Baby, Bisque Head, Open Mouth, Bent Limb, Composition, 13 In. 800.00
K * R, 122, Blue Eyes, Dimples, Wobble Tongue, Blond, Yellow Organdy Dress, 15 In. .. 895.00
K * R, 122, Toddler, Bisque, Sleep Eyes, Jointed Body, Wobble Tongue, 16 In. 2150.00
K * R, 126, Baby, Bisque, Sleep Eyes, Antique Gown Bonnet, 20 In. 850.00
K * R, 126, Baby, Brown Sleep Eyes, Bent Limb, Composition, Baby Dress, 12 In. 300.00
K * R, 126, Baby, Flirty Eyes, Composition, Double Chin, 23 In. 1050.00
K * R, 126, Toddler Body, Jointed, Original Dress & Wig, 23 In. 1800.00
K * R, 126, Toddler Body, Jointed, Strawberry Blond Wig, Dress & Bonnet, 23 In. 1500.00
K * R, 126, Toddler, Brown Sleep Eyes, Lashes, Bent-Limb Body, 18 In. 695.00
K * R, 127, Bisque Socket Head, Painted Hair, 2 Teeth, c.1912, 15 In. 1150.00
K * R, 177, Flirty, Tin Eye Lids, Jointed, Panties, Slip, Leather Shoes, 26 In. 2400.00
K * R, 192, Child, Bisque, Glass Eyes, Composition, Ball-Jointed, Mohair Wig, 23 In. .. 1300.00
K * R, 406, Molded Celluloid Head, Sleep Eyes, Ball-Jointed, Clothes, 18 In. 500.00
K * R, Bisque, Rose Dress, Rose Leather-Heeled Shoes, 24 1/2 In. 1150.00
K * R, Bisque, Sleep Eyes, Mohair Wig, Pink Silk Dress, Shoes & Socks, 26 In. 1100.00
K * R, Boy, Scottish, Painted Black Boots & Stockings, 5-Piece Body, 7 In. 495.00
K * R, Brown Sleep Eyes, 4 Teeth, Human Hair Wig, Jointed, Walker, 20 In. 450.00
K * R, Child, Brown Sleep Eyes, Auburn Mohair Wig, 25 In. 750.00
K * R, Flirty Eyes, Mohair Long Thick Wig, Matching Shoes, 21 In. 1550.00
K * R, Wobble Tongue, Baby Body, 26 In. 1800.00
Kallus, Bisque Head, Baby Bo-Kaye, Muslin Body, Celluloid Hands, 1923 .... 1400.00

Kamkins, Dress, Wool Coat & Hat, 18 In. 1250.00
Kamkins, Jackie Coogan, Cloth, Blond Mohair Wig, Original Outfit, 1925, 18 3/4 In. .. 977.00
Kathe Kruse, Cloth, Painted Face, Human Hair Braids, 1930s, 19 1/2 In. 1150.00
Kathe Kruse, Du Mein, Life-Size, Stockinet Body, 19 In. 2400.00
Kathe Kruse, Du Mein, Original Costume, 14 1/2 In. 2850.00
Kathe Kruse, Mannequin, Smiling, Fabric Covered Wire Frame, 56 In. 2600.00
Kathe Kruse, Stitch Shaped Head, Oil Painted Hair, All Muslin, c.1930, 18 In. 2300.00
Kathe Kruse, Vinyl Head, Celluloid Body, Dress, Tag, 16 In. 450.00
Kathy Kruse, Baby, Plastic, Cloth 5 Piece Body, Blue Floral Dress, 19 In. 150.00
Kenner, Baby Alive, Black, 1972, Box.. 70.00
Kestner dolls are also in this category under J.D.K.
Kestner, 129, Bisque Head, Sleep Eyes, Human Hair Wig, Jointed Body, 21 In. 430.00
Kestner, 142, Bisque, Chunky Body, Sleep Eyes, Human Hair Wig, 36 In. 2695.00
Kestner, 143, Chin Dimple, Bowed Upper Lip, Composition, Jointed Body, 24 In. 2450.00
Kestner, 143, Square Teeth, Human Hair Wig, Ball-Jointed Legs, 9 In. 850.00
Kestner, 147, Shoulder Head, Brown Sleep Eyes, 21 1/2 In. 595.00
Kestner, 152, Bisque, Original Wig, Leather Shoes, Lace & Silk Costume, 20 In. 895.00
Kestner, 152, Riding Hood, Mohair Wig, Ball-Jointed Body, Pink Dress, 23 In. 1095.00
Kestner, 154, Baby Blanche, 23 In.. 525.00
Kestner, 154, Bisque, Brown Eyes, Original Dress, Crown Label, 24 In. 825.00
Kestner, 154, Blue Sleep Eyes, 16 In... 450.00
Kestner, 154, Blue Sleep Eyes, Leather Jointed Body, Mohair Wig, 26 In. 895.00
Kestner, 154, Child, Bisque Shoulder Head, Sleep Eyes, Kid Body, Roller Skates, 20 In. 245.00
Kestner, 164, Brown Sleep Eyes, Mohair Wig, Composition Body, 16 In. 575.00
Kestner, 166, Boy, Blue Sleep Eyes, Kid Body, Bisque Hands, 22 In. 350.00
Kestner, 167, Bisque, Sleep Eyes, 4 Teeth, Mohair Wig, Ball-Jointed, 23 In. 1000.00
Kestner, 168, Bisque, Molded Hair, Uncut Wig, Lace Clothes, Bonnet, 22 In................ 750.00
Kestner, 171, Daisy, Bisque, Original Wig, 18 1/2 In. 1500.00
Kestner, 171, Daisy, Bisque, Pantalets, Shoes, Socks, 20 In. 750.00
Kestner, 171, Daisy, Bisque, Plaster Pate, Mohair Wig, Sleep Eyes, 20 In. 995.00
Kestner, 171, Daisy, Blue Sleep Eyes, Bisque, White Dress, 27 In................................ 985.00
Kestner, 171, Nun, Sleep Eyes, Bisque, Angelic Look, Vintage Clothes, 28 In. 1495.00
Kestner, 172, Gibson Girl, Cloth Body, Bisque Limbs, Underwear, 11 In. 1025.00
Kestner, 195, Kid Body, Human Hair Curls, Old Clothes, 21 In. 550.00
Kestner, 241, Composition Body, Open Mouth, Sleep Eyes, Original Costume, 19 In. .. 1150.00
Kestner, 243, Oriental Baby, Bisque Head, Bent-Limb Body, 13 In. 2600.00
Kestner, 243, Oriental Baby, Bisque, Sleep Eyes, Costume With Beads, 14 In. 6200.00
Kestner, 247, Bisque Head, Flirty Eyes, Incised Eyeliner, Dressed, 1912, 16 In. 1700.00
Kestner, 257, Bisque, Victorian Christening Gown & Coat, 23 In................................. 1700.00
Kestner, 260, Bisque, Threaded Blue Eyes, Lace & Silk Dress, 36 In. 2995.00
Kestner, 260, Oily Bisque Head, Wooden Ball-Jointed Toddler Body, c.1915, 19 In. 950.00
Kestner, Baby, Fat Cheeks, Sleep Eyes, Open Mouth, 2 Teeth, Double Chin, 14 In. 695.00
Kestner, Bisque Head, Flanged Neck, Half-Moon Eyes, Bent Limb, Dressed, 13 In. 900.00
Kestner, Bisque, Open-Close Mouth, Wood & Composition Body, Dressed, 15 In. 3450.00
Kestner, Bisque, Sleep Eyes, Jointed Body, Human Hair Wig, Dressed, 22 In. 1600.00
Kestner, Bisque, Sleep Eyes, Jointed, 8 In. 225.00
Kestner, Bisque, Toddler, Molded Hair, Sleep Eyes, Antique Clothes, 19 In. 1850.00
Kestner, Bisque, Wig, Brown Eyes, Open Mouth, White Lacy Blouse, Blue Skirt, 21 In. 176.00
Kestner, Blue Sleep Eyes, Turned Head, Bisque Hands, Kid Body, Clothes, 27 In. 850.00
Kestner, Composition, Brown Eyes, Open Mouth, Brown Lacy Dress, 23 In. 412.00
Kestner, Crying Baby, Bisque Head, Squinting Eyes, Baby, c.1920, 10 In. 1800.00
Kestner, Gibson Girl, Fabric Body, Painted Boots, Satin & Lace Gown, 1900, 10 In..... 805.00
Kestner, Gibson Girl, Kid Body, Bisque Hands, Dressed, 20 In. 3900.00
Kestner, Hilda, Bisque Head, 23 In.. 6250.00
Kestner, Hilda, Bisque Head, Upper Teeth, Bent-Limb Body, Undergarments, 14 In. ... 2400.00
Kestner, Hilda, Bisque, 2 Upper Teeth, Dressed, 15 In. 3600.00
Kestner, Hilda, Bisque, Christening Outfit, 26 1/2 In. 6800.00
Kestner, Lady, Bisque Shoulder, Cobalt Powderweight Eyes, Clothes, 24 In. 2800.00
Kestner, Lady, Bisque, Full Lips, French Ensemble, Leather Boots, 21 In. 1250.00
Kestner, Lady, Pouty, Large Paperweight Eyes, Kid Body, Green Gown, 21 In............. 1250.00
Kestner, Little Emma, Long Tresses, Traveling Cloak, Dress, 16 1/2 In. 950.00
Kestner, Long Face, Dressed, Marked, 29 In.. 1495.00
Kestner, Pouty, Bisque, Sleep Eyes, Straight Wrist, 24 In. 3500.00

Kestner, Pouty, Closed Mouth, Sonneburg Body, Dimple In Chin, 15 1/2 In. 895.00
Kestner, Sleep Eyes, Open-Close C Mouth, Molded Hair, 14 In. 895.00
Kestner, Swivel Head, Bisque Head & Arms, Kid Body, All Original, 15 1/2 In. 650.00
Kestner, XI, Pouty, Sleep Eyes, Bisque, Straight Wrists, Schmitt Body, 16 In. 3875.00
Kewpie dolls are listed in the Kewpie category
Kiddiejoy, Baby, Bisque Flange Head, Cloth Body, Dressing Gown, 20 In. 550.00
Kley & Hahn, 161, Baby, Crier, Sleep Eyes, Baby Doll Clothes, 14 In. 950.00
Kley & Hahn, 525, Character, 15 In. 1500.00
Kley & Hahn, Walkure, Bisque, Brown Eyes, Antique Clothes, 31 In. 900.00
Kley & Hahn, Walkure, Bisque, Set Eyes, Dress, Matching Shoes, 18 In. 675.00
Kley & Hahn, Walkure, Bisque, Sleep Eyes, 4 Teeth, Jointed Body, 33 In. 1000.00
Kley & Hahn, Walkure, Brown Sleep Eyes, Ball-Jointed, Clothes, 34 In. 1295.00
Kley & Kahn, Bisque Head, Bent-Limb Body, Cotton Sailor Suit, c.1912, 10 In. 375.00
Kling, 189, Blond, Leather Arms & Stitched Boots, 20 In. 550.00
Kling, Bisque Feet, Paperweight Eyes, Blond Wig, Scandinavian Attire, 15 In. 775.00
Knickerbocker, Bozo, Bend 'Em, 9 In. 28.00
Knickerbocker, Flintstones, Pebbles & Bam-Bam, 1960s, Pair 65.00
Knickerbocker, Incredible Hulk, 17 In. 9.00
Knickerbocker, Laurel & Hardy, Rubber, Clothes, 1940s, 10 In., Pair 145.00
Knickerbocker, Puppet, Alvin, From The Chipmunks, 1963, 11 In. 88.00
Knickerbocker, Raggedy Andy, 39 In. 120.00
Knickerbocker, Raggedy Andy, 40 In. 135.00
Knickerbocker, Raggedy Andy, Tag, Box, c.1973, 38 1/2 In. 200.00
Knickerbocker, Raggedy Ann & Andy, 38 In., Pair 195.00
Knickerbocker, Raggedy Ann & Andy, Box, 18 In., Pair 170.00
Knickerbocker, Raggedy Ann & Andy, Tag, 20 In., Pair 75.00
Knickerbocker, Raggedy Ann, 15 In. 12.00
Knickerbocker, Raggedy Ann, 1964, Box 225.00
Knickerbocker, Raggedy Ann, 24 In. 50.00
Knickerbocker, Raggedy Ann, 30 In. 85.00
Konig & Wernicke, Baby, Bisque, Bent Limb, 22 In. 1050.00
Konig & Wernicke, Bisque, Side Glancing Eyes, Painted Shoes, Socks, c.1915, 8 In. 575.00
Koppelsdorf, Baby, Gown, All Original, 10 In. 375.00
Kuhnlenz, Black Girl, Mohair Wig, Red Sailor Type Clothes, SFBJ Label, 16 1/2 In. 3750.00
Laurel & Hardy, Dakin, Original Tag, Bag, Pair. 60.00
Lawton, Drummer Boy 400.00
Lawton, Katie & Kewpie 400.00
Lawton, Patsy. 400.00
Lenci, 300, Girl, Russian, Felt Swivel Head, Braids, Muslin Body, c.1930, 17 In. 1500.00
Lenci, Baseball Player, Short Pants, Leather Shoes, Felt, 1920, 17 1/2 In. 3450.00
Lenci, Boy & Girl, 36 In. 5400.00
Lenci, Boy, Blond Mohair Wig, Eyes To Side, 17 In. 395.00
Lenci, Boy, Vested Suit, Leggings, Spats, 14 In. 775.00
Lenci, Fascist Boy, 13 In. 1100.00
Lenci, Felt & Cloth, High Spanish Comb In Hair, Tagged Costume, 15 In. 550.00
Lenci, Googly, Italian Cloth, Swivel Head, Glass Eyes, c.1930, 19 In. 4200.00
Lenci, Italian Soldier, 16 In. 2200.00
Lenci, Marlene Dietrich, Box, 12 In. 1400.00
Lenci, Opium Smoker, Felt Head, Cloth, Closed Eyes, Yarn Hair, Yellow Jacket, 12 In. 270.00
Lenci, Pouty Girl, 18 In. 995.00
Lenci, Russian Boy & Girl, 36 In. 5400.00
Lenci, Woman, Cloth, Organdy Dress, Wooden Shoes, 37 1/2 In. 3800.00
Lenci, Woman, Yellow Braids, Organdy Dress, Picture Hat, Wooden Shoes, 37 1/2 In. 2200.00
LHB, 2 1/2, Brown Sleep Eyes & Hair, Open Mouth, 21 In. 258.00
Louis Wolfe, 152, Baby, Gray Sleep Eyes, Dressed As Boy, 13 In. 350.00
Madame Alexander, 1520, Goldilocks, Classic Series, 1978, Box 45.00
Madame Alexander, 1610, Elise, Ballerina, Box, 17 In. 70.00
Madame Alexander, Amy, Little Women, Box, 1959-1966, 12 In. 175.00
Madame Alexander, Beth, Little Women, Box, 1959-1966, 12 In. 175.00
Madame Alexander, Brenda Starr, 1964, Box 165.00
Madame Alexander, Cinderella. 60.00
Madame Alexander, Cissette, Queen, Plastic, Wig, Jointed Knees, Yellow Dress, 10 In. 150.00
Madame Alexander, Cissette, Southern Belle 400.00

Madame Alexander, Cissy, Black Taffeta Dress, 21 In. 295.00
Madame Alexander, Cissy, Plastic, Sleep Eyes, Ivory Satin Dress, Box 825.00
Madame Alexander, Dionne Quintuplets, With Nurse Louise, Button 1795.00
Madame Alexander, Ginny.. 160.00
Madame Alexander, Jane Withers, Composition, 13 In.. 750.00
Madame Alexander, Jo, Little Women, Box, 1959-1966, 12 In...................................... 175.00
Madame Alexander, Jo, Little Women, Walker, Straight Leg, 1950s.............................. 195.00
Madame Alexander, Little Colonel, Composition, Yellow Organdy Dress, 18 In. 1100.00
Madame Alexander, Little Women, 14 In., 5 Piece 1100.00
Madame Alexander, Mary, Mary, Box, 8 In. 65.00
Madame Alexander, Marybel, Case With Accessories, 1959, 15 In. 295.00
Madame Alexander, Meg, Little Women, Box, 1959-1966, 12 In................................... 175.00
Madame Alexander, Princess, 12 In. 70.00
Madame Alexander, Scarlett O'Hara, Bride, 21 In... 450.00
Madame Alexander, Scarlett O'Hara, Composition, Original Hat, 1939-1946, 17 In..... 795.00
Madame Alexander, Scarlett O'Hara, Composition, White Floral Dress, 17 In. 1600.00
Madame Alexander, Scarlett O'Hara, Green Satin Gown, 21 In. 850.00
Madame Alexander, Scarlett O'Hara, Yellow Dress, Pink Hat & Trim, 15 In. 895.00
Madame Alexander, Sleeping Beauty, Elise Face, All Original, Tag, 16 1/2 In. 450.00
Madame Alexander, Sonja Henie, All Original, 18 In. 550.00
Madame Alexander, Sonja Henie, Composition, Sleep Eyes, Human Hair, 17 In. 350.00
Madame Alexander, Sonja Henie, Replaced Clothes, Ice Skates, 18 In. 625.00
Madame Alexander, Winnie Walker, Box, 18 In... 290.00
Majestic, 18, Bisque Socket Head, Open Mouth, Human Hair, Jointed, 36 In. 1200.00
Mannequin, On Carved Wooden Pedestal, E.G. Buste Girard, Paris, 1920, 24 In.......... 575.00
Marilyn Houchen, Leslie Caron, Gigi, Lace & Feathers Dress, 27 In. 2200.00
Marilyn Houchen, Susan Hayworth, Suede Suit, 27 In. 1695.00
Marilyn Monroe, Gentlemen Prefer Blondes, Box, 12 In. 65.00
Marionette, Black Man, Wood & Papier-Mache, 24 In.. 220.00
Marionette, Effanbee, Clippo Clown, Wrist Tag, 1936.. 75.00
Marionette, Effanbee, Emily Ann, Box 95.00
Marionette, Felix, Suspended From Spring Wire, 5 In 110.00
Marionette, Punch & Judy, c.1840, Set Of 4 .... 395.00
Marionette, Santa Claus, Composition Face 125.00
Marionette, Wonder Woman, Box 95.00
Mascotte, Clown, Original Clothes, 10 In... 1300.00
Mason, Taylor, Wooden, 12 In.. 250.00
Mattel, Baby Burp 150.00
Mattel, Baby First Step, Skates, 1964 .... 80.00
Mattel, Barbie, 35th Anniversary, Box.. 50.00
Mattel, Barbie, American Girl, Pale Blond, Beige Lips, Swimsuit, 1966 .... 400.00
Mattel, Barbie, Bendable, 1976 .... 55.00
Mattel, Barbie, Benefit Performance ....;................ 450.00
Mattel, Barbie, Black, Box, 1979 .... 60.00
Mattel, Barbie, Blond Bubble Cut, Pink Gown, White Stole 110.00
Mattel, Barbie, Blond Ponytail, Red Jersey Swimsuit, High Heels, Pearl Earrings, 1962 295.00
Mattel, Barbie, Blue Rhapsody, Porcelain.. 695.00
Mattel, Barbie, Brunet Ponytail, Box.. 2200.00
Mattel, Barbie, Brunet, 35th Anniversary... 85.00
Mattel, Barbie, Brunet, No. 2, Stand 5100.00
Mattel, Barbie, Bubble Cut... 80.00
Mattel, Barbie, Cinderella, Shoulder-Length Dark Blond, Gown, Box 52.00
Mattel, Barbie, Egyptian 50.00
Mattel, Barbie, Empress Bride ....431.00 to 450.00
Mattel, Barbie, Enchanted Evening, Blond, Pink Satin Gown....................................... 1380.00
Mattel, Barbie, Evergreen Princess 75.00
Mattel, Barbie, Fashion Queen, Painted Brown Hair, 1964... 95.00
Mattel, Barbie, Going To Prom, Box, Pair 40.00
Mattel, Barbie, Gold Jubilee... 2000.00
Mattel, Barbie, Growing Pretty Hair, Blond, 1970, Box... 105.00
Mattel, Barbie, Happy Holidays, 1988 ....450.00 to 500.00
Mattel, Barbie, Happy Holidays, 1992 .... 75.00
Mattel, Barbie, Happy Holidays, Black, Box, 1990.. 65.00

Mattel, Barbie, Happy Holidays, Special Edition, 1988	546.00
Mattel, Barbie, Ken & Midge, On Parade Gift Set, 1963	2070.00
Mattel, Barbie, Long Velvet Dress	110.00
Mattel, Barbie, Mardi Gras, 1988	75.00
Mattel, Barbie, Masquerade	350.00
Mattel, Barbie, Miss Barbie, Sleep Eye, Red Swimsuit, 1964	375.00
Mattel, Barbie, Neptune Fantasy, 4th Edition	345.00
Mattel, Barbie, No. 2, Brunette, Original Stand & Box	5100.00
Mattel, Barbie, No. 3, Curved Eyebrows	300.00
Mattel, Barbie, No. 4, Tan Skin, Vinyl, Mint In Box	275.00
Mattel, Barbie, No. 5, Mint In Box	275.00
Mattel, Barbie, No. 6, Brunet, Ponytail, 1963	375.00
Mattel, Barbie, Platinum	405.00
Mattel, Barbie, Ponytail Mint, Box	5100.00
Mattel, Barbie, Ponytail, Blond, Red Lips, Black & White Striped Swimsuit	100.00
Mattel, Barbie, Ponytail, Dark Blond, 1964	155.00
Mattel, Barbie, Ponytails	375.00
Mattel, Barbie, Queen Of Hearts	190.00
Mattel, Barbie, Round The Clock, Box	4300.00
Mattel, Barbie, Scarlet Flame, Exclusive To Sears	690.00
Mattel, Barbie, Swan Lake, Musical, Box, 1991	160.00
Mattel, Barbie, White Magic, Satin Coat & Hat, 1964	170.00
Mattel, Barbie, Winter Princess	150.00
Mattel, Captain Lazer	250.00
Mattel, Doctor Doolittle, Talking, 1967, 23 In.	65.00
Mattel, Francie, Brunet, Short Flip Style, Tagged Dress, 1966	85.00
Mattel, Francie, Growin' Pretty Hair, Blond, 1970	40.00
Mattel, Francie, Twist 'n Turn Waist, Short Brunet, Nude, 1969	55.00
Mattel, Jamie, Barbie's Friend, Walking, Original Clothes	65.00
Mattel, Jamie, New & Wonderful Walking, 1969	747.00
Mattel, Julia, Nurse Outfit, Box	158.00
Mattel, Ken, Flocked Hair, Original Clothes, 1961	50.00
Mattel, Midge, Bendable Legs, Brunet, 1965	85.00
Mattel, Midge, Blond, Pink Lips, Blue Swimsuit, 1964, Box	55.00
Mattel, Midge, Wedding Party, 1990, Box, 6 Piece	90.00
Mattel, Ricky, Lights Out, Yellow Pajamas, Box, 1964	30.00
Mattel, Skipper, Blond, Pink Lips, Red & White Swimsuit, Box, 1963	55.00
Mattel, Skipper, Fun At McDonald's, No. 4276, 1982	17.50
Mattel, Skipper, Pale Blond, Pink Lips, Box, 1963	135.00
Mattel, Skipper, Red Hair, Ballet Class	75.00
Mattel, Skooter, Blond, Bent Knee, Denim Swimsuit	70.00
Mattel, Skooter, Silk N Fancy, Brunet	85.00
Mattel, Skooter, Titian, Pink Lips, Box, 1964	95.00
Mattel, Twiggy, 1967	230.00
Mattel, Wayne Gretzky, Vinyl, Oiler Home Jersey, Box, 12 In.	150.00
Maxine Doll Co., Mitzi, Knockoff On Patsy, Composition, 13 1/2 In.	250.00
Morimura, Twins, Composition, Jointed, Pink Dress & Hat, 9 In., Pair	262.00
Mrs. Beasley, Cloth, 11 In.	65.00
Nancy Ann, Storybook, Miss Lullaby, No. 212, 12 In.	495.00
Nancy Ann, Storybook, Muffie, Mexican Outfit, Brown Eyes, 8 In.	125.00
Nancy Ann, Storybook, Muffie, Pink Ballerina Outfit, 8 In.	135.00
Nancy Ann, Storybook, Plastic, Box, 5 1/2 In.	40.00
Norah Wellings, Boy & Girl, Felt, Swivel Head, Mohair Wig, Jointed, 15 In., Pair	950.00
Norah Wellings, Costume Woman, Felt, Swivel Head, Floss Hair, 1930, 26 In.	1500.00
Norah Wellings, Felt Face, Velvet Body, Glass Eyes, Original Clothes, 15 In.	495.00
Norah Wellings, Guardsman, Tag, 9 In.	15.00
Norah Wellings, Sailor, 10 In.	35.00
Paper Dolls are listed in their own category	
Papier-Mache, Boy & Girl, Alsatian Costume, Glass Eyes, 12 & 14 In.	850.00
Papier-Mache, Child, Boyish Hair, 4 Teeth, Muslin Body, Costume, c.1885, 11 In.	375.00
Papier-Mache, Cloth Body, Redressed, 12 In.	70.00
Papier-Mache, Gibson Girl, Jointed Hips & Shoulders, Dressed, 13 1/2 In.	295.00
Papier-Mache, Glass Eyes, Hair, 28 In.	345.00

Papier-Mache, Mammy, Dressed, 19th Century, 10 In.	395.00
Papier-Mache, Milliner's Model, Head, Wooden Limbs, Leather Body, 9 1/2 In.	750.00
Papier-Mache, Painted Black Hair, Homemade Cloth Body, Cotton Dress, 24 In.	400.00
Papier-Mache, Shoulder Head, Cloth Body, Leather Arms, Germany, 23 In.	200.00
Parian, Alice, Bisque, Painted Blond Hair, Cloth Body, Silk Taffeta Dress, 13 In.	325.00
Parian, China Head Body, Blond, Curly Hair, 12 In.	100.00
Parian, Cloth Body, Molded Bodice, Dressed, 12 1/2 In.	27.50
Parian, Molded Bodice, Blond Hair, 13 In.	135.00
Parian, Swivel Head, Painted Hair, Glass Eyes, Cloth Body, Red Satin Dress, 24 In.	825.00
Parian, Woman, Fancy Hairdo, Snood, Pierced Ears, 22 In.	1395.00
Pee Wee Herman, 40 In., 1989	700.00
Peter Pan, Sun Rubber, 1950s, 11 In.	45.00
Phoenix, Brown Paperweight Eyes, Lashes, Ball-Jointed, Clothes, 19 1/2 In	1250.00
Phoenix Star, 90, Bisque, Blond Curls, 16 1/2 In.	2350.00
Phonograph, Mae Starr, Blond Curly Hair, 1 Cylinder, Battery-Operated	450.00
Pincushion dolls are listed in their own category	
PM, 194, Baby, 1 Blue & 1 Brown Sleep Eyes, Gown, Mohair Wig, Basket, Petite, Pair	393.00
Puf 'n' Stuf, Vinyl, Plush, My Toy Co., Box, 23 In.	1100.00
Puppet, Curly, Three Stooges, Vinyl Head, Cloth Body, 1950	145.00
Puppet, Danny O'Day, Moving Eyes, Eyelids, Hair, 33 In.	600.00
Puppet, Donald Duck, Kohner	175.00
Puppet, Dorothy, Wizard Of Oz, Eyes & Mouth Move, 1960s, 20 In.	275.00
Puppet, Finger, Monkees, 1970, 3 Piece	65.00
Puppet, Finger, Three Stooges, 4 1/2 In., 3 Piece	10.00
Puppet, Fred Flintstone, Hand, 1960s	69.00
Puppet, Hand, Cat In The Hat, Talking, Mattel	68.00
Puppet, Hand, Gomez, Addams Family	95.00
Puppet, Hand, King Friday The 13th, Mr. Rogers, 1950s	25.00
Puppet, Hand, Magilla Gorilla, Printed Cloth, Ideal, 1960s	42.00
Puppet, Hand, Mr. Ed, Talking, 1962	165.00
Puppet, Hand, Mr. Magoo, Ideal, 1962	48.00
Puppet, Hand, Steiff, Boxer Dog	80.00
Puppet, Hand, Stingray, Aquaphibian, Lakeside Toys, 1966	125.00
Puppet, Hand, Three Stooges, Larry & Moe, 1950s, Pair	100.00
Puppet, Hand, Tiger, Steiff	195.00
Puppet, Hand, Yogi Bear, Cloth Body, Vinyl Head, Knickerbocker, 1960s, 9 In.	30.00
Puppet, Howdy Doody, Kohner	125.00
Puppet, Lamb Chop, 1960	20.00
Puppet, Mr. Turnip, Metal, Luntoy, 6 3/4 In. *Illus*	264.00
Putnam, Bye-Lo, Baby, Bisque Flange Head, Sleep Eyes, Cloth Body, 11 In.	250.00
Putnam, Bye-Lo, Baby, Bisque Flange Head, Sleep Eyes, Cloth Body, 14 In.	325.00

Doll, Puppet, Mr. Turnip, Metal, Luntoy, 6 3/4 In.

◆◆◆◆◆◆◆◆◆◆◆◆◆◆◆◆◆◆◆◆◆◆

When storing dolls (old or new), be sure to remove any sticky tape that might have been used to hold bows, etc., in place. The glue from the tape will eventually discolor the fabric. If dolls are to be stored a long time, put tissue between clothing and doll to keep bright colors from 'bleeding' onto the doll. Remove metal that might rust. Save the box and all tags.

◆◆◆◆◆◆◆◆◆◆◆◆◆◆◆◆◆◆◆◆◆◆◆

Rabery & Delphieu, Bisque, Almond Paperweight Eyes, Dimple In Chin, 24 In. 6200.00
Rabery & Delphieu, Bisque, Cork Pate, Silk Frock, Silk Bonnet, 26 In. 4400.00
Rabery & Delphieu, Paperweight Eyes, Mohair Wig, Old Clothes, 28 In. 5500.00
Rag, Baby, Cloth Over Wax, Pressed Facial Features, Muslin Body, Leather Arms, 11 In. 110.00
Rag, Baby, Maude Tousey Fangel, 14 In. 725.00
Rag, Girl, Embroidered Face, Sundress & Bonnet, 29 In. 55.00
Raynal, Flirty, Glass Eyes, Celluloid, Original Clothes, 20 In. 575.00
Remco, Phantom Of The Opera, Box 350.00
Revalo, Girl, Antique Pink Striped Silk Costume, Fur Muff, 22 In. 393.00
Roche, 150, Florence, Bisque, Wooden Articulated Body, Winter Outfit, c.1985, 17 In. 1500.00
Rollinson, Original Paint, Embroidered Gown, 20 In. 895.00
Ron Kron, Marilyn Monroe, Feather Boa, 18 In. 950.00
Rubber, Black, 1950s, 10 In. 38.00
S & H dolls are also listed here as Bergmann and Simon & Halbig
S & H, 1019, Blue Sleep Eyes, Ball-Jointed Body, Human Hair, Clothes, 30 1/4 In. 1800.00
S & H, 1039, Child, Luminous Bisque, Mohair Wig, 23 In. 1375.00
S & H, 1079, Bisque, Blue Eyes, Clothes, 26 1/2 In. 1400.00
S & H, 1079, Bisque, Sapphire Blue Eyes, Ecru Silk & Lace Dress, 30 In. 1650.00
S & H, 1249, Composition, Sleep Eyes, Lacy Pink & White Dress, Bonnet, 26 In. 2195.00
S & H, 1249, Santa, Original Wig, Original Clothes, 23 In. 2350.00
S & H, 1249, Santa, Walker, Mohair Curls, Old Clothes, Shoes, 23 In. 950.00
S & H, 1294, Character Baby, Mechanical, Flirty Rolling Eyes, 21 1/2 In. 2200.00
S & H, 1299, Baby, Dimples, Pursed Lips, Pinwheel Eyes, Dressed, 14 In. 1195.00
S & H, 1428, Bisque Head, Slanted Brows, Mohair Wig, Baby Clothes, 12 In. 1200.00
S.F.B.J., 26, Boy, Oily Bisque, 5-Piece Body, Waffle-Weave Suit, 15 1/2 In. 1100.00
S.F.B.J., 226, Character Boy, Sailor Suit, 20 In. 2875.00
S.F.B.J., 230, Character, Bisque, Paperweight Eyes, Dressed, 24 In. 2775.00
S.F.B.J., 236, Laughing Jumeau, Bisque, Toddler Body, 14 In. 1595.00
S.F.B.J., 236, Laughing Jumeau, Toddler Body, Open-Close Mouth, 15 In. 1250.00
S.F.B.J., 238, Bisque, Jewel Eyes, Teeth, Dressed, c.1912, 19 In. 3800.00
S.F.B.J., 248, Bisque Head, Jointed Composition Body, Dressed, 10 In. 4700.00
S.F.B.J., 301, Blue Sleep Eyes, Lashes, Human Wig, Dress & Undies, 22 In. 1395.00
S.F.B.J., 301, Walker, Bisque Socket Head, Voice Box, Antique Lace Dress, 22 In. 900.00
S.F.B.J., 301, Walker, Sleep Eyes, Head Turns When Walking, Dress, 22 In. 1100.00
S.F.B.J., Bisque Head, Composition Body, Walking, Kissing, Flirty Eyes, 23 In. 875.00
S.F.B.J., Bisque, Blue Eyes, Human Wig, Chunky Body, Antique Dress, 35 In. 2995.00
Santa Claus, Velvet Suit, 1930s, 8 In. 45.00
Schmidt, Bisque Socket Head, Brush Stroke Hair, Bent-Limb Body, 12 In. 1000.00
Schoenau & Hoffmeister, 4711, Bisque, Wooden Body, Costume, c.1900, 38 In. 1500.00
Schoenau & Hoffmeister, Japanese Soldier, Bisque, Papier-Mache, 1912, 9 In. 325.00
Schoenau & Hoffmeister, Princess Elizabeth, Lush Curls, Silk Dress, 17 In. 2200.00
Schoenhut, 19/314, Child, Full Lips, Quiet Eyes, Wool Suit & Cap, c.1912, 19 In. 1250.00
Schoenhut, 101, Girl, Carved Hair, 14 In. 1000.00
Schoenhut, 102, Carved Hair, Vintage Clothes & Shoes, 17 In. 1900.00
Schoenhut, 105, Girl, Carved Hair, 14 In. 95.00
Schoenhut, 311, Heart-Shaped Face, Dimple On Cheek, Intaglio Eyes, 16 In. 2200.00
Schoenhut, Bareback Rider, Composition Head, Hair To Bun On Top, 7 In. 180.00
Schoenhut, Boy, Heavy Lids, Intaglio Eyes, Full Lips, 16 In. 1500.00
Schoenhut, Boy, Sober Face, Fully Jointed, c.1913, 17 In. 316.00
Schoenhut, Carved Hair, Pulled To Back, Blue Ribbon, 15 In. 1500.00
Schoenhut, Child, Carved Wavy Hair, Intaglio Eyes, Pantalets, Shoes, 17 In. 1950.00
Schoenhut, Felix The Cat, 8 In. 395.00
Schoenhut, Felix The Cat, Jointed, Wooden, 4 In. 195.00
Schoenhut, Girl, Carved Bonnet, 16 In. 4500.00
Schoenhut, Girl, Sleep Eyes, Wooden Spring-Jointed Body, Dressed, 15 In. 1000.00
Schoenhut, Intaglio Eyes, Teddy Under Striped Drop-Waist Dress, Bonnet, 16 In. 1550.00
Schoenhut, Open Mouth, Wooden, Spring-Jointed, 15 In. 110.00
Schoenhut, Period Clothes, 1913, 14 In. 425.00
Schoenhut, Policeman, Roly Poly 450.00
Schoenhut, Pouty, Undergarment, Shoes, Tag, 17 In. 1200.00
Schoenhut, Toddler, Wooden Socket Head, Painted Eyes, Mohair Wig, 11 In. 625.00
Schoenhut, Wooden, Bobbed Wig, Spring-Jointed, Gauze Dress, 18 1/2 In. 575.00
School Boy, Bisque Shoulder Head, Cloth Body, Squeaker, Cotton Suit, 12 1/2 In. 250.00

Schuetzmeister & Quendt, 201, Baby, Red Hair, Blue Eyes, Bonnet, Clothes, 27 In..... 995.00
Schuetzmeister & Quendt, Toddler, Jointed, Frilled & Lace Dress, 15 In. 1100.00
Shirley Temple dolls are included in the Shirley Temple category
Simon & Halbig dolls are also listed here under Bergmann and S & H
Simon & Halbig, 129, Baby, Toddler Body, Christening Dress & Bonnet, 25 In. 1250.00
Simon & Halbig, 155, Baby, Brown Flirty Eyes, Blond Mohair, Cabinet Size 393.00
Simon & Halbig, 550, Bisque, Ball-Jointed Body, Dress, 23 In............................... 595.00
Simon & Halbig, 939, Belton Head, Paperweight Eyes, Mohair Wig, 25 In.................... 5500.00
Simon & Halbig, 939, Bisque, Blue Paperweight Eyes, Rosy Cheeks, 29 In. 3600.00
Simon & Halbig, 939, Sleep Eyes, Ball-Jointed Body, Open Mouth, Marked, 24 In....... 2250.00
Simon & Halbig, 949, Oily Bisque, Blond Curls, Walking Dress, 18 In................. 1795.00
Simon & Halbig, 1009, Bisque, Straight Wrist, Composition 1470.00
Simon & Halbig, 1009, Brown Sleep Eyes, Bisque, Jointed Wrists, 16 In. 656.00
Simon & Halbig, 1039, Black, 28 In... 4500.00
Simon & Halbig, 1078, Brown Bisque Head, Teeth, Mohair Wig, Jointed Body, 22 In. . 1300.00
Simon & Halbig, 1078, Sleep Eyes, Human Hair Wig, Ball-Jointed Body, 40 In. 3500.00
Simon & Halbig, 1079, Bisque, Glass Sleep Eyes, Human Hair, Fully Jointed, 26 In. 546.00
Simon & Halbig, 1079, Bisque, Sleep Eyes, Mohair Wig, Old Dress, Bonnet, 23 In. 995.00
Simon & Halbig, 1079, Bisque, Sleep Eyes, Painted Shoes & Socks, Dress, 7 In. 750.00
Simon & Halbig, 1079, Blue Eyes, Blond Human Hair Wig, Dressed, 27 In.................. 1450.00
Simon & Halbig, 1080, Bisque, Sleep Eyes, Mohair Wig, Kid Body, 17 In. 650.00
Simon & Halbig, 1159, Fashion Lady, Wooden Ball-Jointed Body, Lace Dress, 20 In. .. 1200.00
Simon & Halbig, 1159, Lady, Bisque, Glass Eyes, Composition, Ball-Jointed, 19 In. 1700.00
Simon & Halbig, 1199, Oriental, Bisque, Jointed Body, Silk Kimono, 15 In. 3750.00
Simon & Halbig, 1249, Character, Sleep Eyes, Mohair Wig, Ball-Jointed Body, 34 In. . 5500.00
Simon & Halbig, 1249, Santa, Bisque, Sleep Eyes, Human Hair Wig, Silk Dress, 26 In. 2575.00
Simon & Halbig, 1329, Olive Tone Ball-Jointed Body, Oriental Clothes, 13 In.............. 1595.00
Simon & Halbig, 1428, Freddy, Jointed Baby Body, 13 In...................................... 1900.00
Simon & Halbig, Adult, Blue Paperweight Eyes, Ball-Jointed, 16 In. 1800.00
Simon & Halbig, Bisque Arms, Twill Body, Swivel Head, Mohair Wig, 10 In. 4800.00
Simon & Halbig, Bisque, Black, Wood & Composition Body, Pinafore, 1888, 13 In...... 1610.00
Simon & Halbig, Bisque, Brown Eyes, Open Mouth, Wig, Black Dress, 21 In. 110.00
Simon & Halbig, Bisque, Brown Sleep Eyes, Open Mouth, Pierced Ears, 21 In. 288.00
Simon & Halbig, Bisque, Composition Body, Sleep Eyes, Open Mouth, 25 In. 357.50
Simon & Halbig, Bisque, Pierced Ears, Open Mouth, Beaded Cape, 29 In..................... 495.00
Simon & Halbig, Bisque, Sleep Eyes, Blond Wig, Open Mouth, White Gown, 21 In. 495.00
Simon & Halbig, Bisque, Sleep Eyes, Brown Wig, Pierced Ears, Open Mouth, 18 In..... 286.00
Simon & Halbig, Bisque, Sleep Eyes, Human Hair Wig, Dress, Boots, 32 In. 2100.00
Simon & Halbig, Child, Bisque Socket Head, Sleep Eyes, Organdy Dress, 22 In. 400.00
Simon & Halbig, Composition, Pierced Ears, Open Mouth, Lace Dress, 17 In. 220.00
Simon & Halbig, Jointed Wrists & Knees, Original Silk Costume, 10 In.................. 472.00
Simon & Halbig, Slanted Brown Sleep Eyes, Composition, Ball-Jointed, 21 In............ 595.00
Skookum, Brave, 11 1/2 In.. 165.00
Skookum, Chief, Headdress, 14 In. 185.00
Skookum, Indian, 22 In.. 595.00
Skookum, Squaw & Brave, Papier-Mache Face, Straw-Filled Body, 35 In., Pair 3300.00
Skookum, Squaw With Papoose, 10 1/2 In. 165.00
Skookum, Squaw, 10 1/2 In.. 125.00
Soldier, Beetle Bailey, On Stand, Original Tags 20.00
Soldier, Japanese, Cloth, Handmade, World War II 100.00
Sonneberg Taufling, Child, Kicking-Screaming, Cloth Over Composition, 12 In. 2450.00
Spanky & Our Gang, Jointed, 1975, 6 1/2 In., 5 Piece 90.00
Steiff, Character Boy, All Felt, 8 Buttons, 13 In... 367.00
Steiff, Gabi, Box, 1987... 700.00
Steiff, Navy Goat... 325.00
Steiner, Baby, Black, Closed Mouth, Sleep Eyes, 17 In. 695.00
Steiner, Baby, Large Lips, Bakelite, 13 In. 260.00
Steiner, Bisque Head, 24 In. 6500.00
Steiner, Bisque Head, Trunk & Wardrobe, 9 1/2 In. 4000.00
Steiner, Bisque Shoulders, Hips & Lower Limbs, Tiered Gown, c.1870, 14 In. 6500.00
Steiner, Bisque, Paperweight Eyes, Silk & Lace Dress, 27 In................................. 8200.00
Steiner, Le Parisien, Walking, Human Wig, Jointed Composition, Voice Box, 24 In...... 2000.00
Steiner, Mechanical, Key Wind, 2 Rows Of Teeth, Label, 17 1/2 In. 2400.00

Doll, Volland, Raggedy Ann, 16 In.

◆◆◆◆◆◆◆◆◆◆◆◆◆◆◆◆◆◆◆◆◆◆◆◆

If you have a vinyl doll with dirt or pencil marks on the head or body, try this: Wrap the doll so that only the marked part shows. Rub the mark with solid vegetable shortening and put the doll in the sun for the day. Try this for several days, and the mark should disappear.

◆◆◆◆◆◆◆◆◆◆◆◆◆◆◆◆◆◆◆◆◆◆◆◆

Steiner, Mohair Wig, Dressed, French Hat, 19 In.	6950.00
Terri Lee, Hard Plastic Body, Brown Painted Eyes, Synthetic Wig, 16 In., Box	340.00
Terri Lee, Original Outfit, Western, Denim, Plaid Shirt, White Boots, 16 In.	295.00
Terri Lee, Tagged Dress, 16 In.	225.00
Tete Jumeau, Bebe, Painted, Paperweight Eyes, Closed Mouth, Dressed, 22 In.	3900.00
Tete Jumeau, Bisque, Blue Eyes, Clothes, Shoes, 20 In.	3600.00
Tete Jumeau, Bisque, Mohair Wig, Mama & Papa Pull Strings, 20 In.	5900.00
Tete Jumeau, Bisque, Sleep Eyes, Mama & Papa Pull Strings, Dressed, 22 In.	2900.00
Tete Jumeau, Blue Powderweight Eyes, Closed Mouth, Box, 29 In.	9500.00
Tete Jumeau, Paperweight Eyes, Open Mouth, Human Hair Wig, 14 In.	1975.00
Tete Jumeau, Sleep Paperweight Eyes, Human Hair Wig, Clothes, 22 1/2 In.	5200.00
Toddler, Ball-Jointed Composition Body, Fixed Eyes, Smiling Mouth, 15 In.	250.00
Topsy-Turvy, Hand-Painted Faces, 1900	225.00
Troll, Dam, Purple Hair, Green Eyes, Nude, 1964, 12 In.	175.00
Tubby Tom, Georgene	1200.00
Ventriloquist Dummy, Black Male, Papier-Mache, Wood & Straw, Dressed, 3 Ft.	1000.00
Ventriloquist Dummy, Jerry Mahoney, 1940s, Box	375.00
Ventriloquist Dummy, Jerry Mahoney, Original Box	85.00
Ventriloquist Dummy, Moe, Three Stooges, Box	100.00
Vogue, Cathy, Hard Plastic, Sleep Eyes, Synthetic Wig, Dress, Straw Hat, Box	1320.00
Vogue, Ginny, Cinderella, Plastic, Costume, Tag, 8 In.	288.00
Vogue, Ginny, Fairy Godmother, Costume, Tag, 8 In.	315.00
Vogue, Ginny, Walker, Straight Leg, 1956	150.00
Vogue, Toddles, Eyes To Side, Mohair Wig In Braids, Pinafore, Shoes, 7 1/2 In.	270.00
Volland, Beloved Belindy, Cotton, Stuffed, Stitched Jointed, Red Bandanna, 15 In.	1250.00
Volland, Raggedy Ann & Andy, Muslin, Stuffed, Painted Face, 16 & 17 In., Pair	1100.00
Volland, Raggedy Ann, 16 In. .... *Illus*	850.00
Volland, Raggedy Ann, Cloth Head, Yarn Hair, Cardboard Heart, 15 In.	1050.00
Walkure, Bisque Head, Sleep Eyes, Ball-Jointed, Composition Body, Dressed, 20 In.	330.00
Walkure, Brown Sleep Eyes, Synthetic Wig, Jointed Body, Coat Dress, 26 In.	425.00
Wax, Blue Glass Eyes, Original Wig, Clothes, England, 15 In.	795.00
Wax, Child, Inset Hair, Print Dress, Leather Shoes, F.E. Drew, London, 24 In.	2500.00
Wax, Child, Layers Of Elegant Clothes, 18 In.	1650.00
Wax, Fashion, Green Eyes, Dropped Bustle Dress, Silk Bows, 19 In.	375.00
Wax, Kid Body, Blond Ringlet Wig, Taffeta Dress, 18 In.	450.00
Wax, Long Blond Hair, Glass Eyes, Swivel Wrists & Ankles, 18 1/2 In.	395.00
Wax, Open-Close Eyes, Fitted Dress, Cape, Crocheted Slippers, 20 In.	1350.00
Wax, Over Composition, Stationary Eyes, Human Hair Wig, Cloth Body, 14 In.	85.00
Wax, Over Composition, Walker, Wooden Limbs, Glass Eyes, 12 In.	250.00
Wax, Over Papier-Mache, Hair Wig, Motschmann-Style Body, Ermine Cape, 22 In.	1200.00
Wax, Rooted Hair, Glass Eyes, Clothes, England, 18 In.	1595.00
Wax, Ver Papier-Mache, Glass Eyes, Clockwork, Key Wind, Germany, 10 In.	1900.00
Webber, Dolly Madison, Singing Mechanism, China Head, Cloth Body, 22 In.	305.00
Wooden, Nesting, Salyut 7 Mission, Russia, 1982, Pair .... *Illus*	3163.00
Wooden, Woman, Painted Face, Muslin Arms, Skirt With Apron, Switzerland, 17 In.	300.00

Doll, Wooden, Nesting, Salyut 7 Mission,
Russia, 1982, Pair

◆ ◆ ◆ ◆ ◆ ◆ ◆ ◆ ◆ ◆ ◆ ◆ ◆ ◆ ◆ ◆ ◆ ◆ ◆ ◆

Green ears are a problem for Barbie dolls. The green is a reaction between the vinyl head and the metal posts that hold the earrings. Remove Barbie's head. Put Clearasil maximum strength vanishing lotion or Tarnex silver polish on a piece of cotton. Put the cotton on each ear. Put the Barbie's head in a covered dish and ignore it for 4 days. The stain should be bleached out.

◆ ◆ ◆ ◆ ◆ ◆ ◆ ◆ ◆ ◆ ◆ ◆ ◆ ◆ ◆ ◆ ◆ ◆ ◆ ◆

WPA, Child, Oil Painted Face, 23 In.	925.00
WPA, Greek Scholar Outfit, 18 In.	595.00
WPA, Man, Costume, 18 In.	595.00
WPA, Revolutionary Soldier, 16 In.	595.00

DOORSTOPS have been made in all types of designs. The vast majority of the doorstops sold today are cast iron and were made from about 1890 to 1930. Most of them are shaped like people, animals, flowers, or ships. Reproductions and newly designed examples are sold in gift shops.

Aunt Jemima, Full Figure, Cast Iron, 9 In.	275.00
Aunt Jemima, Full Figure, Iron, Worn Paint, 9 x 4 1/2 In.	250.00
Aunt Jemima, Green Dress, White Apron, Red Scarf, Cast Iron, 1900s, 8 1/2 In.	395.00
Baby, Crying, Cast Iron, 4 1/2 x 8 3/4 In.	82.00
Baby, Yawning, Marked M.L. Corp., 1931, Cast Iron, 4 1/2 x 8 3/4 In.	55.00
Baker's Chocolate Lady, Gold Gilt, Cast Iron	180.00
Bellhop, Black, Cast Iron	950.00
Bird In Cage, Cast Iron, 7 x 8 In.	60.00
Bird On Stump, Cast Iron, 6 1/2 In.	38.50
Calla Lilies, Hubley	375.00
Cat, American Bisque	178.00
Cat, Cast Iron, 5 1/2 x 8 1/2 In.	60.00
Cat, Hubley	139.00
Cat, Yellow Glass Eyes, Early 20th Century, Cast Iron, 12 In.	316.00
Charleston Dancers, Cast Iron	1400.00
Chef Piggy, Painted Iron	66.00
Cockatiel, Cast Iron, 5 1/4 x 8 1/2 In.	115.00
Cornucopia, Cast Iron, 6 7/8 x 6 1/4 In.	180.00
Dog, 3 Puppies In Basket, Cast Iron, 7 x 7 3/8 In.	440.00
Dog, Boston Bull, 7 In.	80.00
Dog, Boston Terrier, Cast Iron, 10 x 10 In.	85.00 to 165.00
Dog, Boston Terrier, Cast Iron, Painted, 19th Century, 9 3/4 x 10 1/4 In.	92.00
Dog, Boston Terrier, Iron, 10 In.	55.00 to 150.00
Dog, English Bulldog, Haley's Ale, Cast Iron	425.00 to 575.00
Dog, Fox Terrier, Large	200.00
Dog, German Shepherd	70.00
Dog, Greyhound, Cast Iron, 12 1/2 In.	150.00
Dog, Pekinese, Chalkware	35.00
Dog, Pekinese, Full-Bodied, Cast Iron, 14 In.	1320.00
Dog, Puppy, Sitting, Cast Iron	20.00

Dog, Retriever, Standing In Grass, Laddie Boy Inscribed, 1920 .... 250.00
Dog, Scotty, Cast Iron, Relief, 7 In. 88.00
Dog, Setter, Black & White, 8 3/4 x 15 7/8 In. 235.00
Dog, Spaniel, Stoneware, Salt Glaze, Blue Slip Design 1250.00
Dog, Wolfhound, Cast Iron, 8 x 12 In. 88.00
Duck, Full Figure, Pants & Top Hat, Cast Iron, 8 1/4 In. 565.00
Dutch Boy Kissing Dutch Girl, Cast Iron, 8 1/2 In. 192.50
Elephant, Cast Iron, Large 195.00
Fantail Fish, Hubley, 5 1/2 x 9 3/4 In. 45.00
Flamenco Dancer, Female, Cast Iron, 10 In. 215.00
Flower Basket, Greenblat Studios, Boston, 1927, Cast Iron, 9 In. 99.00
Flower Basket, Hubley 125.00
Frog, Cast Iron 18.00
Fruit Bowl, Hubley 95.00
Geisha On Pillow, Hubley, 7 In. 220.00
Gnome In Jacket, Cast Iron .... 195.00 to 225.00
Gnome With Barrel, Cast Iron 475.00
Golfer, Putting, Cast Iron, 8 In. .... 250.00 to 495.00
Hedgehog, Cast Iron 225.00
Horse, Black, Cast Iron 98.00
Horse, Cast Iron, 12 x 10 1/2 In. 105.00
Horse, Hubley, 10 x 12 In. 135.00
Horse, With Saddle, Cast Iron 60.00
Jungle Boy, Cast Iron, 12 3/4 In. .... 715.00 to 915.00
Lighthouse, Cast Iron 150.00
Little Red Riding Hood, With Wolf, Iron 155.00
Little Southern Belle, Cast Iron, 6 3/4 In. 100.00
London Mail Coach, Cast Iron 150.00
Maid, Cast Iron, 9 In. 220.00
Major Domo, Cast Iron, 8 x 8 1/2 In. 185.00
Mammy, Painted, Cast Iron 130.00
Man, With Dog, Cast Iron 85.00
Narcissus, Hubley 325.00
Old Salt, Yellow, Cast Iron, 14 In. 288.00
Owl, Cast Iron, 4 1/2 x 7 In. 65.00
Owl, Cast Iron, 5 7/8 x 4 1/4 In. 165.00
Owl On Stump, Cast Iron, J. Co., 10 1/2 In. 495.00
Parrot, In Ring, 9 In. 325.00
Penguin, Cast Iron 250.00
Persian Cat, Sitting, Gray, Hubley, 9 1/2 In. .... 145.00 to 250.00
Poppies, Hubley 165.00
Poppies & Snapdragons, Cast Iron 75.00
Rabbit, Red Jacket, In Front Of White Picket Fence 95.00
Race Horse, King's Genius, Rife Loth Corp, Virginia, 12 1/4 In. 72.00
Ram, Cast Iron, 7 1/8 x 9 1/2 In. 160.00
Ram, On Base, Cast Iron, 10 1/2 x 7 3/4 In. 105.00
Raven, Cast Iron, 5 7/8 In. 125.00
Rooster, French, Cast Iron 495.00
Santa Claus, No. 2, E. Conley EMC 3520.00
Senorita, Cast Iron, 9 3/4 In. 247.00
Ship, 3-Masted Schooner, Cast Iron, 1920 .... 150.00
Ship, 3-Masted, 11 1/4 In. 20.00
Ship, Cast Iron 75.00
Ship, Sailing On Waves, Cast Iron 165.00
Soldier, Civil War, Cast Iron, 7 1/2 In. 99.00
Southern Belle, National Foundry 295.00
Spanish Girl, Cast Iron, 9 1/2 In. 330.00
Squirrel, Cast Iron, 11 x 9 1/2 In. 165.00
Squirrel, Gold, Black Details, Cast Iron, 6 1/4 In. 170.00
Sunbonnet Girl 210.00
Tiger Lilies, Hubley 290.00
Tropical Woman, Cast Iron, 12 In. 245.00
Warrior, Bradley & Hubbard 495.00

Whistling Jim, Cast Iron	4510.00
Windmill, Multicolored, 6 3/4 In.	95.00
Woman, Chalkware	80.00
Young Black Boy On Back Of Frog, Iron, 6 1/2 In.	165.00
Zebras, Cast Iron, 6 x 5 In.	135.00

DOULTON pottery and porcelain were made by Doulton and Co. of Burslem, England, after 1882. The name *Royal Doulton* appeared on their wares after 1902. Other pottery by Doulton is listed under Royal Doulton.

Barrel, Biscuit, Motto, Brown & Tan Panels, Lambeth, 1897-1902, 4 3/4 In.	375.00
Bibelot, With Bird, Polychrome Glazes, Lambeth, c.1925, 5 3/4 In.	230.00
Bibelot, With Polar Bear, Polychrome Glazes, Lambeth, c.1925, 4 1/4 In.	258.00
Biscuit Jar, Frieze Of Goats, H. Barlow, Silver Plated Base, Lambeth, 1877, 6 3/4 In.	805.00
Biscuit Jar, Incised Sheep, H. Barlow, Lambeth, c.1873, 8 1/2 In.	345.00
Biscuit Jar, Pate-Sur-Pate Design, H. Barlow, Lambeth, 7 In.	862.00
Bowl, Melrose, Cover, Flow Blue, 10 3/4 In.	65.00
Bowl, Melrose, Cover, Flow Blue, 11 In.	225.00
Bowl, Possett, Briar Rose	1200.00
Bowl, Vegetable, Watteau, Flow Blue, 10 In.	150.00
Butter, Watteau, Cover, Flow Blue	425.00
Candlestick, Leaf & Floral Design, Emily Partington, c.1910, 11 3/4 In., Pair	485.00
Candlestick, Raised & Incised Foliate, E. Simmance, Lambeth, 7 3/8 In., Pair	375.00
Cup, Hounds, Silver Ring, 3 Handles, Lambeth, H. Barlow, c.1876, 6 1/2 In.	490.00
Dessert Set, Persian Spray, Flow Blue, Service For 6	1250.00
Flask, Figural, Old Crow Bourbon, Bone China, c.1954, 13 In.	86.00
Flower Holder, Persian Spray, Flow Blue, 3 x 7 In.	165.00
Foot Warmer, Lambeth, Stoneware	295.00
Ginger Jar, Cover, Red Glaze, Dripped Crackle Glaze, Chang Ware, c.1925, 11 1/2 In.	6900.00
Humidor, Tobacco Leaf	195.00
Jar, Cover, Silicon Ware, Blue, White On Brown, 5 3/4 In.	140.00
Jug, Fish Pattern, Slip Design, Burslem, 1902, 13 1/2 In.	375.00
Jug, Maidens Dancing & Playing Instruments, Flow Blue, Burslem, 1913, 5 In.	375.00
Jug, Queen Victoria 1897 Jubilee, Barrel Shape, Portraits, 7 /34 In.	295.00
Jug, Wine, Raised Figural Design, Silver Plated Stopper, 9 1/2 In.	135.00
Lamp, Kerosene, Floral Medallions, Leafy Border, Brass Mounts, c.1900, 15 In.	230.00
Lamp, Kerosene, Leaf & Floral Design, Brass Finish, 19th Century, 17 3/8 In.	575.00
Lamp, Kerosene, Owl, Silicon Ware, Brass Fittings, Bronze Base, 1883, 19 In.	1380.00
Letter Holder, Leaf & Scrolled Design, Lambeth, Frank A. Butler, 5 1/2 In.	1150.00
Mug, Beadwork Framed Panels, Silver Plated Ring, H. Barlow, Lambeth, 1884, 7 In.	1095.00
Mustard Pot, Cover, Rhaddlan Castle, Brown Transfer, 1895, 2 5/8 In.	140.00
Pitcher, Figaro, No. 26970, Burslem, 7 7/8 In.	75.00
Pitcher, Galleon, Ship Design, Burslem	300.00
Pitcher, Horse, Acanthus Leaf Borders, Lambeth, H. Barlow, c.1880, 10 3/4 In.	430.00
Pitcher, Leaf Design, Silver Rim, A. Barlow, Lambeth, c.1873, 11 In.	315.00
Pitcher, Leaves Around Medallions Of Flowers, Lambeth, c.1882, 9 3/4 In.	345.00
Pitcher, Panels Of Golfers, Floral Border, Signed Lambeth, c.1900, 7 1/2 In.	520.00
Pitcher, Poppy, Flow Blue	225.00
Pitcher, Raised Florets, George Tinworth, c.1882, 9 1/2 In.	400.00
Pitcher, Watteau, Flow Blue, 7 1/2 In.	300.00
Pitcher & Bowl, Watteau, Flow Blue	1250.00
Planter, Floral, Blue Transfer, Burslem, Ovoid, 1902, 7 1/4 x 9 1/2 In.	450.00
Plaque, Hound Design, H. Barlow, Lambeth, Wooden Stand, c.1874, 8 In.	518.00
Plate, Leafy Gilt Decorations, Burslem, c.1900, 10 In., 12 Piece	979.00
Plate, Watteau, Flow Blue, 6 1/2 In.	30.00
Platter, Watteau, Flow Blue	300.00
Platter, Watteau, Flow Blue, 9 1/2 x 12 In.	125.00
Punch Bowl, Ivoryware, Burslem, 16 x 9 1/4 In.	212.00
Stand, Pocket Watch, Dragon Supporting Frame On Back, Lambeth, 5 1/8 In.	315.00
Tankard, Cover, Rabbit Design, Pewter Rim & Lid, H. Barlow, Lambeth, 1878, 5 In.	980.00
Tobacco Jar, Frieze Of Sheep, H. Barlow, c.1900, 6 In.	200.00
Tureen, Sauce, Watteau, Underplate	600.00
Tureen, Soup, Watteau, Underplate	900.00 to 1000.00
Vase, Birds In Tall Grass, F. Barlow, Signed, c.1900, 11 In.	575.00

Vase, Bud, Art Union Of London, Leaf Design, E.E. Stormer, c.1895, 8 1/2 In. 115.00
Vase, Burslem, Multicolored Floral, Curved Handles, Baroque Style, 1877, 10 In. 1800.00
Vase, Carrara Ware, Children Either Side Of Floral, c.1890, 10 1/2 In. 115.00
Vase, Cows & Goats Grazing, H. Barlow, Lambeth, c.1895, 8 1/4 In. 430.00
Vase, Doune Castle, Blue Transfer, Burslem, Ovoid, 1911, 7 1/2 In. 495.00
Vase, Dragon Surrounding Leaf Design, Eliza Simmance, c.1879, 15 1/4 In. 2530.00
Vase, Figural, Waning Of The Honeymoon, Lambeth, c.1895, 6 1/2 In. 1495.00
Vase, Floret & Incised Foliage, George Tinworth, c.1900, 11 In. 285.00
Vase, Flowers, Cheesecloth Texture, Squeezebag Enamel, 16 1/2 In. 176.00
Vase, Frieze Of Cows Grazing, H. Barlow, Lambeth, c.1882, 11 1/4 In. 200.00
Vase, Goats Grazing, Leaf Border, H. Barlow, Lambeth, c.1874, 9 In. 405.00
Vase, Hand-Tooled Spiraling Design, 3 Handles, Gold Leaf Finish, 1904, 9 In. 800.00
Vase, Painted Flower Pattern, Gilt, Bulbous, 1886, 10 7/8 In. 275.00
Vase, Pink Rose Pattern, Carrara Ware, Lambeth, Pre-1891, 8 7/8 In. 225.00
Vase, Presentation, Railway, Panels Of Runners, c.1900, 25 In. 2645.00
Vase, Sheep Grazing, Stylized Floral Border, Hannah Barlow, c.1905, 10 3/4 In. 747.00
Vase, Silicon, Brown, Tan, Light Blue Medallions, No. 2424, 4 1/2 In. 65.00
Vase, Sphinx Form, Classical Figures, E. Eggleton, c.1876, 9 1/4 In. 575.00
Vase, Twin Boys Incised On Front, Words The Twins On Back, 5 1/2 In. 175.00
Vase, Woman In Garden Landscape, Gilt Trim, Luscian Ware, Signed, c.1895, 9 In. 920.00

DRAGONWARE is a form of moriage pottery. Moriage is a type of decoration on Japanese pottery. Raised white designs are applied to the ware. White dragons are the major raised decorations on the moriage called *dragonware*. The background color is gray and white, orange and lavender, or orange and brown. It is a twentieth-century ware.

Condiment Set, Pair Of Cruets, Salt & Pepper, Mustard & Lid, Tray 58.00
Cup & Saucer, Brown Rim, Orange Luster Inside, Japan 10.00
Cup & Saucer, Pearlized Interior, Blue Highlights, Demitasse 9.00
Plate, Brown Edge, Twin T Diamond, 7 1/2 In. 12.00
Plate, Brown Raised Dragon, Beige Ground, Blue & Pink, Japan, 7 In. 12.00
Saki Set, Orange 35.00
Sugar, Lid, Blue Highlights, Gold Trim, Japan 15.00
Tea Caddy, Nippon 185.00
Tray, Loop Handle 35.00
Vase, Luster, Double Handles, 2 1/2 In. 12.00
Vase, Orange Luster Interior, Shoulder Handles, Pink & Blue, 6 x 3 x 9 In. 80.00

DRESDEN china is any china made in the town of Dresden, Germany. The most famous factory in Dresden is the Meissen factory. Figurines of eighteenth-century ladies and gentlemen, animal groups, or cherubs and other mythological subjects were popular. One special type of figurine was made with skirts of porcelain-dipped lace. Do not make the mistake of thinking that all pieces marked *Dresden* are from the Meissen factory. The Meissen pieces usually have crossed sword marks, and are listed under Meissen. Some recent porcelain from Ireland, called *Irish Dresden*, is not included in this book.

Basket, Nut, Applied Flowers, Woven Porcelain, 8 Piece 345.00
Bowl, Center, Multicolored Floral Design, Gilt, Ivory Ground, 9 1/4 In. 230.00
Bowl, Hand Painted Flowers, Reticulated, c.1910, 7 1/2 In. 165.00
Bowl, Multicolored Flowers Inside, Gold Trim, Openwork Edge, Schumann, 7 x 9 In... 75.00
Bowl, Portrait Panels, Flowers, Yellow & White, c.1900, 5 3/4 In. 50.00
Cake Stand, Floral, Openwork, Multicolored, Gold Trim, Marked, 4 3/4 x 12 In. 395.00
Candelabrum, Standing Putto Holding Flower, 18 3/4 In., Pair 860.00
Candleholder, Gold Trim, Embossed Handle, Crossed Swords, 6 x 4 3/4 In. 70.00
Candy Container, Cross, Gold & Silver With Pearl, 3 1/2 x 2 1/2 In. 165.00
Candy Container, Drum, Red, White, Blue & Gold, Pulls Apart 110.00
Candy Container, Guitar, Wire & Tinsel, Gold, Pull Apart, 7 1/2 In. 110.00
Candy Container, Mandolin, 5 1/2 In. 110.00
Carriage, Girl & Gentleman In Back, 4 Horses, Dog Chasing 700.00
Casket, Gilt & Floral Painted Country Scenes, Crossed Swords 1210.00
Centerpiece, Gold, White, 10 1/2 In. 85.00
Centerpiece, Reticulated Basket, Cupids Base, 11 3/4 x 12 In. 539.00
Clock, Boudoir, Applied Flowers & Leaves 165.00

Compote, Openwork Edge & Foot, Multicolored Flowers, Schumann, 5 5/8 x 6 In. 195.00
Cup & Saucer, Lovers, Pale Blue Ground, 2 Handles 165.00
Cup & Saucer, Multicolored Flowers, Scalloped, Gold Trim, After Dinner, c.1886...... 125.00
Dish, Flowers, Blue & Yellow, Handle, 5 x 3 1/2 In. 15.00
Figurine, Ballerina, Lacy Skirt, Gold Bands, c.1930, 12 In. 207.00
Figurine, Ballerina, Pink, White, Flowers, 7 In. 225.00
Figurine, Boar, Running, Grayish, 6 In. 395.00
Figurine, Child Ballerina, Pink Dress, 7 In. 60.00
Figurine, Gentleman, Riding Horse, Holding Parrot, 7 In. 225.00
Figurine, Girl Dancing, Gold Gown, Blue Shoes, 7 In. 180.00
Figurine, Man & Woman Dancing, 2 Playing Piano & Guitar, 19 In. 850.00
Figurine, Napoleonic General Murat, Equestrian, 10 1/2 In. 325.00
Figurine, Turkey, 5 1/2 In., Pair 175.00
Figurine, Woman Playing Piano, Man Playing Cello, c.1950, 8 x 6 In. 275.00
Figurine, Woman, Dancing, 11 In. 350.00
Figurine, Woman, Seated, Buffing Nails, Mark, 5 1/2 In. 143.00
Group, Europa & Bull, 8 3/4 x 9 1/4 In. 345.00
Group, German Man Holding Woman's Hand, Little Black Boy 475.00
Group, Little Tea Party, 3 Victorian Ladies, Butler 300.00
Group, Maroon Overland Coach, 4 Horses, Meadow, Ausfahr Der Prinzessin................ 1600.00
Group, Ring Around The Rosie, 3 Little Girls, 8 In. .... 145.00 to 250.00
Lamp, Oil, Blue & White, Applied Young Girl & Flowers, Chimney, 19 In. 220.00
Pitcher, Hand Painted Flowers, White Ground, c.1910, 4 1/2 In. 75.00
Plate, Floral, Reticulated Border, Center Floral Monogram, c.1930s, 8 1/2 In. 95.00
Plate, Hand Painted Flowers, c.1910, 10 In. 200.00
Plate, Portrait, Konigin Louise, Gold Rim, 10 1/2 In. 1295.00
Plate Portrait, Women, Artist, 6 Piece 3900.00
Potpourri Jar, Young Woman & Old Woman, Blue With Ivory Trim, 7 1/8 In. 165.00
Reamer, Hand Painted, Franziska Hirsch, c.1890 .... 350.00
Tea Set, Figures In Garden, Wine & Gold, 3 Piece.. 605.00
Urn, Cover, Stand, Painted Panel Under Heraldic Shield, 2 Putti, 46 In. 5175.00
Vase, Cover, Flowers, Figures, Marked, 14 1/2 In. 1210.00
Vase, Cover, Stand, Figural, Painted Bacchanalian Scene, 34 In. 1265.00
Vase, Green, Gilt, Frieze Of Musical Putti, 9 In. 410.00
Vase, Urn Shape, Portrait Of Woman In Robe, Flowing Hair, Signed Wagner, 9 In. 385.00

DUNCAN & MILLER is a term used by collectors when referring to glass
made by the George A. Duncan and Sons Company or the Duncan and Miller
Glass Company. These companies worked from 1893 to 1955, when the use
of the name *Duncan* was discontinued and the firm became part of the United
States Glass Company. Early patterns may be listed under Pressed Glass.

Adoration, Sherbet, 6 Piece.. 75.00
American Way, Candlestick, Pair.. 30.00
Astaire, Bowl, Finger, Red 35.00
Astaire, Plate, Red, 7 1/2 In. 12.50
Butter, Teardrop, Silver Plate Cover, 1/4 Lb.. 35.00
Canterbury, Ashtray, Rectangular, 3 1/2 x 2 3/4 In.. 6.00
Canterbury, Bonbon, Handles, Square, 6 In. 10.00
Canterbury, Bowl, Crimped, Oval, Ruby, 11 1/2 In. 65.00
Canterbury, Bowl, Flared, Oval, 13 In.. 32.00
Canterbury, Bowl, Rolled-In Rim, 9 1/4 In... 24.00
Canterbury, Bowl, Ruffled, Blue Opalescent, 10 In. 52.00
Canterbury, Candy Dish, Chartreuse.. 32.00
Canterbury, Celery, 11 In.. 15.00
Canterbury, Compote, Chartreuse, 7 1/8 x 5 1/2 In... 28.50
Canterbury, Mayonnaise, 2 Piece 20.00
Canterbury, Nappy, Fruit, 5 In. 12.00
Canterbury, Pickle, Clear, 8 1/2 In. 12.00
Canterbury, Plate, 8 1/2 In.. 8.00
Canterbury, Relish, 5 Sections, 12 In. 28.00
Canterbury, Sugar & Creamer.. 15.00
Canterbury, Sugar & Creamer, Individual .... 15.00 to 18.00
Canterbury, Vase, Cloverleaf, 4 In.. 15.00

Canterbury, Vase, Cream, 5 1/2 In. 22.00
Caribbean, Bowl, Blue, Round, 5 In. 30.00
Caribbean, Candy Dish, Blue, 7 In. 95.00
Caribbean, Celery, 11 In. 45.00
Caribbean, Cocktail, Blue, 3 3/4 Oz., 4 1/8 In. 45.00
Caribbean, Console Set, Candelabrum, 2 Light, 3 Piece 395.00
Caribbean, Pitcher, Milk, Blue 350.00
Caribbean, Pitcher, Water, Blue 950.00
Caribbean, Plate, Handle, Blue, 6 In. 18.00
Caribbean, Punch Cup 25.00
Caribbean, Punch Set, Underplate, Cobalt Handles, 12 Cups 360.00
Caribbean, Relish, 2 Sections, Round, Blue, 6 In. 30.00
Caribbean, Relish, 5 Sections 95.00
Caribbean, Water Set, Blue, 7 Piece 1000.00
Compote, Tree Of Life, Hand Stem 60.00
First Love, Bowl, Flared, 10 In. 45.00
First Love, Candy Dish, Crown Finial Cover, 3 Sections 48.00
First Love, Champagne, Saucer 14.00
First Love, Cordial 75.00
First Love, Creamer 14.00
First Love, Decanter, Stopper, 32 Oz. ....110.00 to 295.00
First Love, Saucer 8.00
Georgian, Mug, Amber Handle, 5 In. 20.00
Goose, Doorstop 195.00
Hobnail, Basket, Pink Opalescent, 10 1/2 In. 150.00
Hobnail, Bowl, Crimped, 9 In. 22.00
Hobnail, Goblet, Water 15.00
Hobnail, Plate, 6 1/4 In. 9.00
Hobnail, Punch Set, 12 Piece ....150.00 to 200.00
Hobnail, Punch Set, Pink Opalescent, 15 Piece 750.00
Hobnail, Vase, Ovoid, Plum, 4 1/2 In. 35.00
Indian Tree, Plate, 8 1/2 In. 16.00
Indian Tree, Relish, 2 Sections, 6 In. 20.00
King Arthur, Punch Cup 8.00
Mardi Gras, Carafe 110.00
Mardi Gras, Champagne, Straight Stem 20.00
Mardi Gras, Cruet 65.00
Mardi Gras, Punch Set, 10 Piece 175.00
Mardi Gras, Punch Set, 15 Piece 425.00
Mardi Gras, Toothpick 35.00
Pall Mall, Ashtray, Duck, 4 3/4 In. 18.00
Pall Mall, Candleholder, Swan, Dark Green, 6 In. 20.00
Pall Mall, Duck, 4 In. ....35.00 to 40.00
Pall Mall, Swan, 3 In. 15.00
Pall Mall, Swan, 5 In. 20.00
Pall Mall, Swan, Ruby, 7 1/2 In. 45.00
Plaza, Bowl, Deep, Pink, 8 In. 145.00
Puritan, Cup & Saucer, Pink, Demitasse 20.00
Puritan, Plate, Floral Cut, 10 1/2 In. 22.00
Puritan, Plate, Green, 8 1/2 In. 8.00
Radiance, Cup & Saucer, Light Blue 25.00
Radiance, Plate, 8 In. 13.00
Radiance, Plate, Light Blue, 8 5/8 In. 20.00
Radiance, Sugar, Light Blue 20.00
Sandwich, Bowl, Mayonnaise 10.00
Sandwich, Cake Plate, Pedestal, 13 In. 110.00
Sandwich, Candelabrum, 10 In., Pair. 150.00
Sandwich, Candelabrum, 3-Light, 16 In. 250.00
Sandwich, Candelabrum, Prism, Pair. 195.00
Sandwich, Candy Dish, Cover, Footed 70.00
Sandwich, Coaster, 4 1/2 In. 7.00
Sandwich, Condiment Set, 5 Piece 65.00
Sandwich, Creamer, 3 In. 8.00

Sandwich, Cruet, Oil & Vinegar, Tray	45.00
Sandwich, Cruet, Oil, Stopper	25.00
Sandwich, Cup & Saucer	8.00
Sandwich, Cup, Amber	20.00
Sandwich, Egg Plate	55.00
Sandwich, Goblet, 9 Oz.	15.00 to 17.00
Sandwich, Ice Cream, 5 Oz., 4 1/2 x 3 1/2 In.	10.00
Sandwich, Juice, Footed, 3 3/4 In.	11.00
Sandwich, Nappy, Handle, 4 1/2 In.	8.00
Sandwich, Oil, Wrong Stopper	5.00
Sandwich, Plate, 8 1/4 In.	14.00
Sandwich, Plate, Amber, 7 In.	20.00
Sandwich, Plate, Amber, 8 In.	24.00
Sandwich, Plate, Deviled Egg	90.00
Sandwich, Plate, Hostess, Amber, 16 In.	105.00
Sandwich, Saucer	3.00
Sandwich, Sherbet	10.00 to 11.00
Sandwich, Sugar & Creamer, Tray	82.00
Sandwich, Sugar & Creamer, Tray, Individual	30.00
Sandwich, Tumbler, Footed, 5 Oz.	7.00
Sandwich, Tumbler, Footed, 9 Oz.	8.00 to 14.00
Sandwich, Tumbler, Footed, Amber, 8 Oz.	20.00
Sandwich, Tumbler, Iced Tea, 13 Oz.	12.00
Sandwich, Tumbler, Old-Fashioned, 7 Oz.	8.00
Sanibel, Tray, Mint, Yellow, 7 In.	21.00
Spiral Flutes, Bowl, Green, 6 3/4 In.	17.00
Spiral Flutes, Candlestick, Green, 9 1/4 In., Pair	90.00
Spiral Flutes, Console, Amber, 12 In.	30.00
Spiral Flutes, Cup & Saucer, Green	10.00
Spiral Flutes, Dish, Pickle, Green, 8 1/2 In.	15.00
Spiral Flutes, Goblet, Amber, 6 1/4 In.	14.00
Spiral Flutes, Goblet, Green, 6 1/4 In.	17.10
Spiral Flutes, Pickle, Green, 8 1/2 In.	15.00
Spiral Flutes, Plate, Green, 6 In.	5.00
Spiral Flutes, Plate, Green, 7 1/2 In.	4.00 to 7.00
Spiral Flutes, Tumbler, Green, Footed, 3 1/4 In.	9.00
Spiral Flutes, Vase, Footed, Green, 8 1/2 In.	20.00 to 40.00
Swan, White, Green Neck, 7 In.	290.00
Sylvan, Candy Dish, 7 1/2 In.	24.00
Sylvan, Dish, Green Handle, 7 1/2 In.	16.00
Teardrop, Ashtray, Individual, 3 In.	6.00
Teardrop, Basket, Candy	68.00
Teardrop, Candy Basket, Excluding Handles, 10 x 8 x 3 1/4 In.	80.00
Teardrop, Champagne, 3 Bead Stem, 5 1/8 In.	10.00
Teardrop, Champagne, Footed, 5 In.	5.00
Teardrop, Compote, Cheese	18.00
Teardrop, Goblet, Footed, 9 Oz., 7 In.	8.50
Teardrop, Plate, 11 In.	30.00
Teardrop, Plate, Butter Silver Plate Cover	20.00
Teardrop, Relish, 5 Sections, 12 In.	15.00
Teardrop, Relish, 6 Sections, Round, 12 In.	28.00
Teardrop, Sugar & Creamer	20.00
Teardrop, Tumbler, Footed, 9 Oz.	8.00
Teardrop, Wine, Footed, 3 Oz.	13.00
Terrace, Ashtray, Red, Square	35.00
Terrace, Bowl, Crystal, 5 In.	12.00
Terrace, Creamer, Red	42.00
Terrace, Plate, 2 Handles, Cobalt Blue, 5 In.	30.00
Terrace, Plate, Crystal, 7 1/2 In.	9.00
Terrace, Plate, Red, 8 1/2 In.	25.00
Terrace, Plate, Red, Square, 7 1/3 In.	25.00
Terrace, Plate, Red, Square, 9 In.	85.00
Three Feathers, Vase, 4 In.	20.00

Three Feathers, Vase, Cornucopia, Blue Opalescent 165.00

DURAND glass was made by Victor Durand from 1879 to 1935 at several factories. Most of the iridescent Durand glass was made by Victor Durand, Jr., from 1912 to 1924 at the Durand Art Glass Works in Vineland, New Jersey.

Bowl, Riffled Rim, Cased Body, Allover Iridescent Gold, Signed, 6 In. 430.00
Centerpiece, Egyptian, Red, 11 In. 350.00
Centerpiece, Red Crackle, Stretched & Ruffled, 11 In. 385.00
Compote, Gold Iridescence, Footed, 7 1/2 In., Pair 660.00
Lamp, Art Glass, Victorian, Signed, 10 In. 1080.00
Lamp, Pulled Leaf Design, Overlay Threading, 24 In. 295.00
Lamp, Vine & Leaf Pattern, Iridescent Green-Gold Pulled Glass, Metal, 27 3/4 In. 330.00
Vase, 3-Layer, Orange, Textured, Raised Amethyst Netting, White Center, 6 x 2 1/2 In. 300.00
Vase, 5 Pulled Feathers, Blue Outlines, Gold Iridescent, Signed, 10 In. 575.00
Vase, Ambergris, White Pulls, Signed, 7 In. 450.00
Vase, Bulb, Gold Iridescent, 7 1/4 In. 330.00
Vase, Gold Inverted Handles, Blue Aurene, 12 In. 2500.00
Vase, Purple Feather & String Design, Mounted As Lamp, 20 In. 315.00
Vase, Taupe Threading, Stepped Neck, Ginger Jar Shape, Green, Signed, 5 1/2 In. 645.00

ELFINWARE is a mark found on Dresden-like porcelain that was sold in dime stores and gift shops. Many pieces were decorated with raised flowers. The mark was registered by Breslauer-Underberg, Inc. of New York City in 1947. *Elfinware* Pieces marked *Elfinware Made in Germany* had been sold since 1945 by this importer.

Basket, Flowers, 5 In. 120.00
Box, Stamp, Hand Painted Floral Cover, 1 1/2 x 3 1/2 In. 45.00
Figurine, Cradle 25.00
Figurine, Piano 15.00
Lighter .... 35.00 to 295.00
Salt, Swan, 3 1/2 In. .... 45.00 to 75.00
Salt & Pepper, 3 1/2 In. 100.00
Shoe, Applied Flowers, 3 x 1 In. 35.00
Shoe, Baby's, Pale Blue, Applied Rose, 4 In. 45.00
Slippers, Double 135.00
Tea Set 135.00

ELVIS PRESLEY, the well-known singer, lived from 1935 to 1977. He became famous by 1956. Elvis appeared on television, starred in twenty-seven movies, and performed in Las Vegas. Memorabilia from any of the Presley shows, his records, and even memorials made after his death are collected.

Belt, White Leather, Brass Eagle Buckles, Silver Chains, Mike McGregor, 1972 .... 4312.00
Book, Elvis Presley Greatest Hits Songbook, 120 Songs, 30 Pages 8.00
Bracelet, Anklet, Dog Tag, Elvis Presley Ent., On Card, 1955 .... 14.00
Bracelet, Charm, Guitar, Heart Break, Hound Dog & Elvis Picture, RCA, 1957 .... 30.00
Bracelet, Charm, Loving You, 4 Charms, Picture, 1956, On Card 75.00
Bracelet, Photograph, 1956, On Card 180.00
Briefcase, Elvis Tour Labels, Black Leather 5462.00
Calendar, Pocket, RCA, 1969 .... 85.00
Card, Gum, Color Photographs, Donruss, 1978, 66 Piece 45.00
Card Set, 40 Piece 395.00
Cards, Playing, Elvis Playing Cars, Color 5.00
Cards, Playing, Elvis, Karate Suit, Color, Sealed 6.00
Clock, Figural, Elvis, Swinging Legs, Box, 14 In. 20.00
Clock, In Guitar, Elvis, Composition, Red, Wall Display 120.00
Credit Card, Exxon Gasoline, 1976 .... 3162.00
Dog Tags, Gold Metal, On Chain, Picture, Elvis Presley Ent., 1956 .... 8.00
Earrings, 14K Gold Plated, Picture In Frame, Elvis Presley Ent., 1955 .... 35.00
Earrings, Loving You, Hanging Picture Of Elvis, 1956 .... 130.00
Guitar, Emenee, Box, 1956 .... 1300.00
Hat, With Tag, 1956 .... 55.00
Knife, Photograph, 2 Blades, Pocket, 5 1/2 In. 4.00

Marble, Picture, Red Hearts, Glass, Love Me Tender, 1 In. 2.00
Mirror, Photograph, Color, Century Fox Film Corp, 1956, Pocket 2.00
Newspaper, Memphis Press, August 17, 1977 .... 14.00
Paper Doll Book, With Priscilla, Uncut 45.00
Pin, Don't Be Cruel, Pinback, 1950s, 1/2 In. 22.00
Postcard, Portrait, Young, Laser Printed, E.P. Ent., Inc., 1986, 5 x 5 In. 1.00
Poster, Las Vegas, 1976, 22 x 28 In. 16.00
Poster, Movie, Double Trouble, 1967, 1 Sheet, 27 x 41 In. 275.00
Record, Album, Christmas Treasure From Avon, RCA, LP 10.00
Record, Album, Madison Square Garden 12.00
Record, Album, Pure Gold, RCA, LP 15.00
Record, How Great Thou Art, So High, Picture Sleeve, RCA 200.00
Record, Jail House Rock, Picture Sleeve, 45 RPM 30.00
Record, Just For You, RCA, 45 RPM 75.00
Record, Love Me Tender, 78 RPM 55.00
Record, The Real Elvis, RCA, 45 RPM 75.00
Record, The Wonder Of You, Photo Sleeve, 45 RPM 20.00
Sheet Music, All Shook Up, 1957 .... 25.00
Sheet Music, Love Me Tender .... 15.00 to 40.00
Sheet Music, My Way, French Edition, 1967 .... 25.00
Sheet Music, Suspicion, Photo On Cover, 1962 .... 48.00
Sheet Music, Wooden Heart, 1960 .... 10.00
Sunglasses, Aviator Style, Brown Lenses, Gold Plated, Neostyle, Germany 4025.00
Swizzle Stick, 12 Piece 19.00
Thimble, Commemorative, Blue, King Of Rock & Roll, 1977 .... 1.00
Wallet, 1950s 300.00
Wristwatch, Woman's 35.00
Yearbook, Hume High School, 1953 .... 8625.00

ENAMELS listed here are made of glass particles and other materials heated and fused to metal. In the eighteenth and nineteenth centuries, workmen from Russia, France, England, and other countries made small boxes and table pieces of enamel on metal. One form of English enamel is called *Battersea* and is listed under that name. There was a revival of interest in enameling in the thirties and a new style evolved. There is now renewed interest in the artistic enameled plaques, vases, ashtrays, and jewelry. Enamels made since the 1930s are usually on copper or steel, although silver was often used for jewelry. Graniteware is a separate category and enameled metal kitchen pieces may be included in the Kitchen category.

Ashtray, Red Fish, Neckrasoff, 7 1/2 In. 35.00
Bowl, Oval, Courting Couples Interior & Exterior, Vienna, c.1880, 7 1/2 In., Pair 1725.00
Bowl, Red, White Crackle, Winter, 8 In. 55.00
Cigarette Case, Blue, Red, Green, Silver Trim, Pavel Mishukova, 4 In. 1380.00
Cigarette Case, Silver-Gilt, Stylized Foliage, Stippled, Russia, c.1910, 4 3/8 In. 632.00
Cup, Flaring Rim, 4 Portrait Medallions, Gold, Persia, c.1830, 2 3/4 In. 4887.00
Cup, Silver-Gilt, 3 Handles, Floating Swans, Flowers, Russia, c.1900, 5 In. 8050.00
Dresser Set, Gilt & Polychrome, 3 Piece 143.00
Figurine, Crucifix, Copper Gilt, Blue Glass Eyes, France, 13th Century, 9 3/8 In. 3737.00
Plaque, Blue, Green, Abstract, Silver, Puskas, 4 x 6 In. 800.00
Vase, Blue, Green, White, Spelter, H.G., 8 In. 40.00
Vase, Fish Scale, Scarlet & Violet Irises, Green Foliage, Japan, 8 3/4 In. 176.00

ERPHILA is a mysterious mark found on 1930s Czechoslovakian pottery and porcelain. It is thought that the mark was used on items imported by Eberling & Reuss, Philadelphia, a giftware firm that is still operating in Pennsylvania. The mark is a combination of the letters *E* and *R* (Eberling & Reuss) and the first letters of the city, Phila(delphia). Many whimsical figural pitchers and creamers, figurines, platters, and other giftwares carry this mark.

Pitcher, Stylized Ram 200.00
Plate, Grapes, Leaves, 7 3/4 In. 45.00
Salt & Pepper, Mexican Couple 24.00
Salt & Pepper, Mrs. Gamp & Pickwick 30.00
Teapot, Dog, Begging, 8 In. 65.00

Teapot, Stylized Rabbit 225.00

ES GERMANY porcelain was made at the factory of Erdmann Schlegelmilch from 1861 to 1925 in Suhl, Germany. The porcelain, marked *ES Germany* or *ES Suhl*, was sold decorated or undecorated. Other pieces were made at a factory in Saxony, Prussia, and are marked *ES Prussia*. Reinhold Schlegelmilch made the famous wares marked *RS Germany*.

Inkwell, Blue Daisies, Purple Floral, Wing Mark, 2 1/2 In. 50.00
Plate, Fox Hunters On Horses, Hounds, 10 In. 75.00
Plate, Sitting Bull, White Ground, 5 1/4 In. 70.00
Server, Robin Scene, Center Handle, 6 1/2 In. 60.00

ESKIMO artifacts of all types are collected. Carvings of whale or walrus teeth are listed under Scrimshaw. Baskets are in the Basket category. All other types of Eskimo art are listed here.

Cribbage Board, Ivory, Black Pigment, Map Of Coastal Alaska, Seals, 16 1/4 In. 1035.00
Doll, Carved Bone, Fur Parka, Ketchikan, Alaska, 1930, 7 In. 850.00
Doll, Man, Carved Wood, Sealskin Suit, Hood, Boots, Greenland, 1930-1940 .... 450.00
Doll, Woman, Baby, Carved Wood, Sealskin Suit, Hood, Greenland, 1930s 850.00
Figurine, Ivory, Reindeer Pulling Sleigh, 10 In. 82.00
Kayak, Newfoundland 295.00
Moccasins, Beaded 200.00
Needle Case, Inlaid Ivory, 3 Parts, Stylized Seal, Engraved 316.25

FABERGE was a firm of jewelers and goldsmiths founded in St. Petersburg, Russia, in 1842, by Gustav Faberge. Peter Carl Faberge, his son, was jeweler to the Russian Imperial Court from about 1870 to 1914. The rare Imperial Easter eggs, jewelry, and decorative items are very expensive today.

ФАБЕРЖЕ
КФ

Ashtray, Imperial Eagle Center, War, Brass, c.1914, 4 1/4 In. 805.00
Bookmark & Letter Opener Combined, Moonstone Finial, Case, 3 3/4 In. 3680.00
Box, Oyster Over Guilloche Ground, Gold Thumbpiece, c.1910, 1 1/2 In. 2990.00
Buttonhook, Translucent Blue, Gold, c.1900, 1 7/8 In. 1495.00
Case, Cigarette, Gray Wolf, Red Hardstone Thumbpiece, Silver, 4 3/8 In. 2530.00
Cuff Links, Tied Knot Form, Sapphire & Rubies, c.1910, 3/4 In. 8050.00
Ewer, Hinged Cover, Ribbon Bows At Neck, Silver Mounted, c.1900, 11 In. 2760.00
Frame, Ribbon Over Enamel Band, Band Of Seed Pearls, Silver & Enamel, 3 In. 2750.00
Holder, Collar, Applied Silver Arrows, Enameled Border, c.1910, 5 1/2 In. 6038.00
Holder, Matchbox, Nephite Panel, Gold Borders, Gold Leaf Tips, c.1890, 1 3/4 In. 5060.00
Holder, Pencil, Enameled Oyster Over Guilloche Ground, Gold, 3 1/8 In. 1725.00
Inkwell, Flowering Foliage On Silver, Red Marble Base, c.1900, 7 3/8 In. 2530.00
Knife, Paper, Carved Nephrite, Handle Set With Moonstone, c.1900, 4 3/4 In. 4887.00
Kovsh, Gilded Silver, Enameled Siren, Scrolling Foliage, c.1900, 14 5/8 In. 7475.00
Locket, Pendant, Diamonds & Sapphires, Fitted With Mirror, c.1900, 3 In. 4600.00
Pendant, Easter Egg, Gold-Mounted Smoky Quartz, c.1900, 3/4 In. 2760.00
Pendant, Icon, Risen Christ, Silver & Enamel, Red Stone, c.1910, 2 7/8 In. 3450.00
Tea Set, Medusa Masks, Dolphins, J. Rappoport, Silver, Enamel, c.1895, 3 Piece 6050.00
Tray, Mirrored, Loop Handles, Wirework Gallery, c.1890, 22 In. 8625.00

FAIENCE refers to tin-glazed earthenware, especially the wares made in France, Germany, and Scandinavia. It is also correct to say that faience is the same as majolica or Delft, although usually the term refers only to the tin-glazed pottery of the three regions mentioned.

Bottle, Pilgrim, Reticulated, France, Pair 210.00
Bowl, 2 Handles, France, 4 1/2 In. 55.00
Bowl, Barber's, France, 12 1/2 In. 198.00
Bowl, Blue, Yellow, Green, 15 1/4 In. 145.00
Bowl & Pitcher, Blue & Gold Design, Neiderviller, 1920, 12-In. Bowl, 9 In. 230.00
Bulb Pot, Cover, Half-Round, Footed, Sceaux, 1780s, 8 3/4 In. 1450.00
Candlestick, 10 In., Pair 165.00
Canister, Tea, Stopper, Painted Flowers, Stripes, Blue & White, Octagonal, 6 In. 635.00
Dish, Serving, 2 Sections 145.00
Figurine, Horse, Gold With Green & Brown, 10 1/2 In. 195.00
Humidor, Pipe Smoking Frog Cover, 7 1/4 In. 350.00

Inkwell, Multicolored Scrolls & Flowers, Coat Of Arms, Scrolled Lid, 4 x 3 In. 25.00
Jar, Drug, Painted Manganese & Blue, Floral Garland, Savona, c.1711, 4 5/8 In. 635.00
Jug, Cover, Cream, Marked Gien, 4 In., Pair 165.00
Lamp, Gold & Figural Designs, Brass Fittings, 30 1/2 In., Pair 100.00
Lavabo, Blue & White, Wooden Backboard, Italy, 30 In. 140.00
Mug, Blue, Yellow & Green, Cream Ground, Stencil, France, 18th Century, 5 In. 300.00
Planter, Ear Of Corn Shape, 6 In. 125.00
Plate, Blue, Yellows & Pink, Ivory Ground, Octagonal 165.00
Plate, Figural Landscape, Armorial, Lille 1767 Mark, France, Square, 8 In., 4 Piece..... 345.00
Plate, Figural Landscape, Leaf Mark, France, Square, 8 In., 5 Piece 550.00
Plate, Oriental Figure Center, Ivory Ground, Scalloped... 110.00
Plate, Shell Shape, 5 In. 35.00
Platter, St. Clement, Oriental Scene, Gilt, Red, Square, c.1870, 12 3/4 In. 750.00
Snuffbox, Scene, Marked VP 350.00
Soup, Dish, Building Center, Mustard, Tin Glazed 200.00
Tea Caddy, Dutch Type, 5 In., Pair 375.00
Tray, Desk, Heraldic Lion, Shield, Blue, Red, Cream, Gilt, St. Clement, c.1870, 14 In. . 835.00
Tureen, Cover, Underplate, Blue Painted Design, Off-White, Itay, 21 x 18 x 13 In........ 60.00
Tureen, Soup, Domed Cover, Handles, Footed 198.00

FAIRINGS are small souvenir china boxes and figurines that were sold at
country fairs during the nineteenth century. Most were made in Germany.
Reproductions of fairings are being made, especially of the famous *twelve
months of marriage* series.

Figurine, Napoleon & Horse 100.00
Match Striker, Puppy Kissing Girl, Table Model 110.00
Pin Box, Shall We Sleep First 160.00
Pin Box, Welsh Tea Party... 135.00
Trinket, Box, Boy Looking In Mirror, Staffordshire 195.00

FAMILLE ROSE, see Chinese Export category

FANS have been used for cooling since the days of the ancients. By the eighteenth century, the fan was an accessory for the lady of fashion and very elaborate and expensive fans were made. Sticks were made of ivory or wood, set
with jewels or carved. The fans were made of painted silk or paper. Inexpensive paper fans printed with advertising were giveaways in the late nineteenth
and early twentieth centuries. Electric fans were introduced in 1882.

Abalone Shell, Paper, French Garden Scene, Gilt Frame, 21 1/2 x 14 In. 247.00
Advertising, Dr. Morse's, Indian Root Pills, Lithograph, Wooden Handle, 8 In. 55.00
Advertising, Hand Holding Bottle, 1940 .... 50.00
Advertising, Infallible Coffee, Leftlore Coffee Co., Paper, 1920s.................................... 25.00
Advertising, Marcy Funeral Home, Cardboard, Last Supper On Reverse, 1940s 7.00
Advertising, Mrs. Winslow's Soothing Syrup, Mother & Baby, Handheld, 8 In. 28.00
Advertising, Optometrist, Illustrated, Cardboard, Wooden Handle, 2 Sides................... 16.00
Advertising, Putnam Dye, Handheld 12.00
Advertising, Putnam Fadeless Dyes, Paper, 1920s 20.00
Advertising, Savory Hotel, Wooden, Paper, Celluloid Design, England 25.00
Advertising, Savoy Hotel, Wooden, Paper 15.00
Beadwork, Floral, Gilt Handles, Circular, Pair.. 138.00
Electric, 2 Rotate As Ceiling Unit, Adams Bagnall Gyrofan 2500.00
Electric, C & C Electric Motor Co., Bipolar, c.1887 ....13200.00
Electric, Century, Ceiling, Cast Iron Head, Wooden Paddles.. 5.00
Electric, Emerson, Desk Type, Oscillating, 13 In. 25.00
Electric, Emerson, Oscillating, 12 In. 130.00
Electric, General Electric, Coin-Operated, Brass Blades, 19 x 14 In............................... 330.00
Electric, Leather Blades, Soviet Union, Tabletop, 1940s 65.00
Electric, Luminaire, Bronze Base, Louvers, Lights, 1920 .... 750.00
Electric, Robbins & Myers, Chrome 225.00
Electric, Victor, Breeze Spreader, 14 1/2 In... 225.00
Electric, Victron, Chrome Blades, 10 In.. 70.00
Electric, Western Electric, Brass, Fancy Metal, 16 In 85.00
Embroidered Roses, Hand-Painted Musical Instruments, Silk, Case................................ 68.00

Feather, Ghost Dance	60.00
Hand Painted, Mother-Of-Pearl Mounts, France, 26 In.	363.00
Ivory, Pierced Geometric Sticks, Conforming Shaped Case, China, 20 x 49 1/2 In.	92.00
Kerosene, Jost Sterling, Hot Air Type, 1910	5225.00
Lace, Silver Sequins, Ivory, Gilt Frame, 11 1/2 x 19 1/2 In.	27.00
Peacock Feathers, Figural Vignette, Ivory Fansticks, China	160.00
Satin, Hand-Painted Pink Flower Blossoms, Lily-Of-The-Valley, Feather Edge	150.00
Slk, Continental, Demilune Shape, Sequined, Rhinestones, Tortoiseshell, 17 In.	132.00
Whalebone, Folding, Green Cloth	45.00

FEDERZEICHNUNG is the very strange German name for a pattern of mother-of-pearl satin glass. The pattern had irregularly shaped sections of brown glass covered with a pattern of gold squiggle lines. It was first made in the late nineteenth century.

Vase, Mother-Of-Pearl, Brown, Maze Of Pearl Air Traps, Pink Lining, 6 In.	2125.00
Vase, Octopus, Allover Gold Scrolled Design, White Lining, 8 3/4 In.	1925.00

FENTON Art Glass Company, founded in Martins Ferry, Ohio, by Frank L. Fenton, is now located in Williamstown, West Virginia. It is noted for early carnival glass produced between 1907 and 1920. Some of these pieces are listed in the Carnival Glass category. Many other types of glass were also made.

Aqua Crest, Relish, Heart Shape, Handle	58.00
Aqua Crest, Vase, 4 In.	20.00
Aqua Crest, Vase, 8 In.	35.00
Captive Rose, Bowl, 8 In.	135.00
Coin Dot, Pitcher, Small	35.00
Coin Dot, Vase, 5 In.	60.00
Coin Dot, Vase, Cranberry Opalescent, 5 In.	58.00
Coin Dot, Water Set, Blue, 7 Piece	200.00
Coin Dot, Water Set, Lime Opalescent, 5 Piece	245.00
Daisy & Button, Hat, 4 In.	20.00
Daisy & Fern, Pitcher, Vaseline	160.00
Diamond Lace, Epergne, Milk Glass, 3 Lily, 1948	50.00
Diamond Optic, Bonbon, Dolphin Handles, Ruffled, 6 In.	65.00
Diamond Optic, Salt & Pepper, Ruby	250.00
Emerald Crest, Compote, Footed, 7 x 3 5/8 In.	35.00
Emerald Crest, Flowerpot, Saucer	65.00
Emerald Crest, Plate, 12 In.	50.00
Figurine, Alley Cat, Green Carnival, 10 1/2 In.	75.00
Figurine, Alley Cat, Pink Carnival, 10 1/2 In.	66.00
Figurine, Elephant, Rosalene, Small	48.00
Figurine, Happiness Bird, Rosalene, Long Tail	24.00
Figurine, Shoe, Milk Glass, Hand Painted	40.00
Georgian, Goblet, Pink, 10 Oz., 5 1/2 In.	13.00
Gold Crest, Vase, Crimped, 4 In.	30.00
Hobnail, Basket, Blue, 4 1/2 In.	35.00
Hobnail, Basket, Blue, Crystal Handle, Cone Shape, 5 1/2 In.	60.00
Hobnail, Basket, Cranberry Opalescent, 4 1/2 In.	46.00 to 55.00
Hobnail, Bonbon, Blue Opalescent	20.00
Hobnail, Bonbon, Cranberry Opalescent, Square, 6 In.	30.00
Hobnail, Bonbon, Cranberry, 6 1/2 In.	35.00
Hobnail, Bonbon, Handle, French Opalescent, 5 In.	17.00
Hobnail, Bowl, Blue, 10 In.	55.00
Hobnail, Bowl, Cranberry, 6 In.	38.00
Hobnail, Bowl, Cranberry, 10 In.	55.00
Hobnail, Bowl, Crimped, Fluted, 7 1/2 In.	25.00
Hobnail, Bowl, Ruffled, Opalescent, 8 1/2 In.	45.00
Hobnail, Cake Stand, Blue, Smooth Edge	100.00
Hobnail, Cake Tray, Yellow, 13 In.	125.00
Hobnail, Compote, Amber, Footed, 6 x 6 1/4 In.	12.00
Hobnail, Cornucopia, Blue Opalescent	18.00
Hobnail, Cranberry, Crimped, 5 In.	65.00

Hobnail, Creamer, Blue Opalescent, Handle, 4 1/2 In.	65.00
Hobnail, Creamer, Topaz Opalescent	24.00
Hobnail, Cruet, Cranberry Opalescent, Pair	90.00
Hobnail, Cruet, Green	350.00
Hobnail, Epergne, 3-Lily	275.00
Hobnail, Epergne, 3-Lily, Vaseline, Medium	265.00
Hobnail, Hat, Blue Opalescent, 3 1/2 In.	37.00
Hobnail, Hat, Pink Opalescent	25.00
Hobnail, Jug, Blue Opalescent, 4 1/2 In.	65.00
Hobnail, Lamp, Cranberry	135.00
Hobnail, Lamp, Cranberry Opalescent, White Painted, Half Shade & Font	259.00
Hobnail, Lavabo, Milk Glass, 3 Piece	65.00
Hobnail, Mustard, Cover, Blue	19.00
Hobnail, Pitcher, Squatty, Cranberry, 4 1/2 In.	55.00
Hobnail, Punch Set, Octagonal, White, 14 Piece	690.00
Hobnail, Sugar & Creamer, Blue Opalescent, 3 1/2 In.	35.00
Hobnail, Sugar & Creamer, Blue, Individual	20.00
Hobnail, Sugar & Creamer, French Opalescent, Individual	25.00
Hobnail, Syrup, Amethyst	50.00
Hobnail, Toothpick	5.00
Hobnail, Tray, Fan, Cranberry, 10 In.	47.00
Hobnail, Vase, Blue, Conical, 8 In.	36.00 to 55.00
Hobnail, Vase, Cranberry, 4 In.	25.00
Hobnail, Vase, Fan, Opalescent, 8 3/4 In.	40.00
Hobnail, Vase, Fan, Yellow Opalescent	50.00
Hobnail, Vase, Fluted, 11 In.	75.00
Hobnail, Vase, Green Opalescent, 4 1/2 In.	30.00
Hobnail, Vase, Woman's Boot, Cranberry, 4 1/2 In.	36.00
Hobnail, Vase, Woman's Boot, Cream, Frosted, 4 1/2 In.	34.00
Hobnail, Water Set, Aqua, 7 Piece	200.00
Hobnail, Wine	22.50
Hobnail, Wine Set, 7 Piece	225.00
Jadite, Basket, 7 In.	35.00
Lamp, Sea Mist Green, Hand Painted Floral	165.00
Lily-Of-The-Valley, Candy Box, Opalescent	30.00
Lily-Of-The-Valley, Rose Bowl, Blue	25.00
Lions, Bowl, Green, Carnival Glass, 3-Footed	25.00
Lotus, Ashtray, No. 848, Jade, 3-Footed	5.00
Lotus, Ashtray, No. 848, Ruby, 3-Footed	8.00
Moonstone, Bowl, Cupped, Footed, 11 In.	60.00
Orange Tree, Bowl, Ruffled, Blue, 9 In.	1850.00
Peach Crest, Basket, Handle	75.00
Peach Crest, Bowl, 7 1/2 In.	40.00
Peach Crest, Bowl, Ruffled, Large	125.00
Peach Crest, Vase, Pink Roses, Gold, 8 In.	125.00
Perfume Bottle, Hand Painted Orchid, Black	45.00
Perfume Bottle, Stopper, French Opalescent	10.00
Plate, Christmas, Blue Satin, 1970	25.00
Plate, Christmas, Blue Satin, 1974	20.00
Plate, Christmas, Carnival Glass, 1970	9.00
Plate, Christmas, Carnival Glass, 1972	25.00
Plate, Christmas, Carnival Glass, 1977	22.00
Plate, Christmas, White, 1974	20.00
Plate, Christmas, White, 1975	20.00
Plate, Christmas, White, 1977	17.00
Plate, Craftsman, Carnival Glass, 1970	7.00
Plate, Mother's Day, Red Carnival Glass, 1979	29.00
Powder Jar, Military Hat Shape, Amber	25.00
Rose Crest, Vase, 8 In.	45.00
Silver Crest, Banana Boat, Low Footed	40.00
Silver Crest, Basket, Cranberry	60.00
Silver Crest, Cake Plate, Low Footed, 13 In.	55.00
Silver Crest, Candlestick, Cornucopia, Pair	50.00

Silver Crest,	Candlestick, Pair	12.00
Silver Crest,	Candy Box, Stem	110.00
Silver Crest,	Epergne, 3-Horn, 12 In.	110.00
Silver Crest,	Plate, 8 In.	19.00
Silver Crest,	Plate, 8 1/2 In.	27.00
Silver Crest,	Plate, 11 In.	20.00
Silver Crest,	Relish, 2 Sections, Round	3.00
Silver Crest,	Sherbet	20.00
Silver Crest,	Tidbit, 2 Tiers, Ruffled	75.00
Silver Crest,	Tidbit, 3 Tiers	50.00
Silver Crest,	Vase, Fan, 12 In.	80.00
Snow Crest,	Lamp, Emerald Green	95.00
Snow Crest,	Lamp, Hurricane, Emerald, 11 In.	100.00
Snow Crest,	Lamp, Hurricane, Emerald, Milk Glass Base, 11 In.	110.00
Snow Crest,	Vase, Corset Shape, Cranberry, 8 1/2 In.	150.00
Spiral Optic,	Vase, Hat Shape, 3 In.	95.00
Spiral Optic,	Vase, Opalescent, Cranberry, 8 In.	85.00
Stippled Rays,	Compote, Amethyst	40.00
Strawberry,	Bonbon, Amber	120.00
Swirl,	Lamp, Matching Shade, Cranberry, Milk Glass Base, 17 In.	335.00
Thumbprint,	Candlestick, Amber, Pair	37.00
Vase,	Black Amethyst, Footed, Paper Label, 8 In.	50.00
Vase,	Black, Etched Flowers & Leaves, 1930s, 5 3/4 In.	35.00
Vase,	Jack-In-The-Pulpit, Black, Roses	120.00
Vase,	Jack-In-The-Pulpit, Cranberry Opalescent	85.00

FIESTA, the colorful dinnerware, was introduced in 1936 by the Homer Laughlin China Co., redesigned in 1969, and withdrawn in 1973. It was reissued again in 1986 in different colors and is still being made. The simple design was characterized by a band of concentric circles, beginning at the rim. Cups had full-circle handles until 1969, when partial-circle handles were made. Harlequin and Riviera were related wares. For more information and prices of American dinnerware, see the book *Kovels' Depression Glass & American Dinnerware Price List.*

Ashtray,	Chartreuse	68.00
Ashtray,	Green	35.00
Ashtray,	Ivory	45.00
Ashtray,	Light Green	35.00
Ashtray,	Medium Green	225.00
Ashtray,	Red	45.00
Ashtray,	Rose	68.00
Ashtray,	Turquoise	35.00
Ashtray,	Yellow	25.00
Bowl,	Cereal, Light Green, 5 1/2 In.	20.00
Bowl,	Cereal, Medium Green, 5 1/2 In.	60.00
Bowl,	Cereal, Yellow, 5 1/2 In.	20.00
Bowl,	Chartreuse, 8 1/2 In.	18.00
Bowl,	Dessert, Chartreuse, 6 In.	50.00
Bowl,	Dessert, Cobalt Blue, 6 In.	50.00
Bowl,	Dessert, Ivory, 6 In.	40.00
Bowl,	Dessert, Red, 6 In.	50.00
Bowl,	Fruit, Cobalt Blue, 11 3/4 In.	195.00
Bowl,	Fruit, Gray, 4 3/4 In.	30.00
Bowl,	Fruit, Light Green, 4 3/4 In.	18.00
Bowl,	Fruit, Medium Green, 5 1/2 In.	75.00
Bowl,	Fruit, Red, 5 1/2 In.	30.00
Bowl,	Fruit, Turquoise, 4 3/4 In.	25.00
Bowl,	Fruit, Yellow, 11 3/4 In.	125.00
Bowl,	Green, 4 3/4 In.	18.00
Bowl,	Ivory, 4 3/4 In.	18.00
Bowl,	Kitchen Kraft, 14 In.	30.00
Bowl,	Medium Green, 5 1/2 In.	55.00
Bowl,	Mixing, No. 1, Cobalt Blue	110.00
Bowl,	Mixing, No. 2, Cobalt Blue	80.00

Bowl, Mixing, No. 3, Cobalt Blue, Cover, 7 In. 600.00
Bowl, Mixing, No. 4, Ivory, Cover, 8 In. 550.00
Bowl, Mixing, No. 6, Red, 10 In. 75.00
Bowl, Salad, Medium Green, Individual, 7 1/2 In. 175.00
Bowl, Salad, Yellow, Individual, 7 1/2 In. 75.00
Bowl, Turquoise, 5 1/2 In. 24.00
Bowl, Vegetable, Medium Green, 8 In. 100.00
Bowl, Vegetable, Red, 8 In. 40.00
Bowl, Yellow, 4 3/4 In. 18.00
Bread Plate, Medium Green 20.00
Cake Plate, Light Green 30.00
Cake Plate, Red, Kitchen Kraft .... 40.00 to 130.00
Candleholder, Bulb, Cobalt Blue 115.00
Candleholder, Bulb, Ivory 95.00
Candleholder, Bulb, Red, Pair 80.00
Canister, Yellow, Kitchen Kraft 295.00
Carafe, Cobalt Blue 225.00
Carafe, Red 200.00
Carafe, Turquoise 265.00
Carafe, Yellow 180.00
Casserole, Cover, Ivory 175.00
Casserole, Cover, Kitchen Kraft, Decal, 8 In. 36.00
Casserole, Cover, Medium Green 650.00
Casserole, Cover, Red 225.00
Casserole, Red 125.00
Casserole, Turquoise 85.00
Casserole, Yellow 210.00
Chop Plate, Gray, 13 In. .... 65.00 to 75.00
Chop Plate, Gray, 15 In. 90.00
Chop Plate, Green, 13 In. 25.00
Chop Plate, Green, 15 In. 22.00
Chop Plate, Ivory, 13 In. 42.00
Chop Plate, Ivory, 15 In. 50.00
Chop Plate, Red, 13 In. 38.00
Chop Plate, Red, 15 In. 38.00
Chop Plate, Yellow, 13 In. .... 20.00 to 25.00
Coffeepot, Ivory, After Dinner 325.00
Coffeepot, Light Green, After Dinner 195.00
Coffeepot, Red 175.00
Coffeepot, Rose 220.00
Coffeepot, Turquoise .... 110.00 to 145.00
Coffeepot, Yellow 155.00
Compote, Ivory, 12 In. 95.00
Compote, Sweets, Yellow, 10 1/4 In. 65.00
Compote, Turquoise, 12 In. 125.00
Creamer, Chartreuse 12.00
Creamer, Medium Green .... 50.00 to 75.00
Creamer, Rose 25.00
Cup, Ivory, After Dinner 4.00
Cup, Medium Green .... 35.00 to 45.00
Cup & Saucer, Chartreuse .... 19.00 to 45.00
Cup & Saucer, Cobalt Blue 25.00
Cup & Saucer, Gray 30.00
Cup & Saucer, Green 25.00
Cup & Saucer, Ivory 60.00
Cup & Saucer, Light Green 20.00
Cup & Saucer, Light Green, After Dinner 65.00
Cup & Saucer, Medium Green 65.00
Cup & Saucer, Red .... 28.00 to 35.00
Cup & Saucer, Rose 30.00
Cup & Saucer, Turquoise 25.00
Cup & Saucer, Turquoise, After Dinner .... 35.00 to 75.00
Cup & Saucer, Yellow .... 20.00 to 25.00

Cup & Saucer, Yellow, After Dinner 75.00
Eggcup, Cobalt Blue ....35.00 to 45.00
Eggcup, Red.. 60.00
Gravy Boat, Cobalt Blue 50.00
Gravy Boat, Ivory 55.00
Gravy Boat, Turquoise 38.00
Gravy Boat, Yellow 30.00
Grill Plate, Gray.. 52.00
Grill Plate, Green, 10 1/2 In... 20.00
Grill Plate, Medium Green, 10 1/2 In. 85.00
Jam Jar, Cover, Turquoise 225.00
Juice Set, Yellow, 7 Piece 175.00
Mug, Forest Green 85.00
Mug, Gray ....45.00 to 88.00
Mug, Light Green.. 100.00
Mug, Medium Green ....85.00 to 125.00
Mug, Rose ....85.00 to 88.00
Mug, Tom & Jerry, Child's, Animal Characters, Ink Mark 175.00
Mug, Tom & Jerry, Light Blue, 2 Piece 50.00
Mug, Tom & Jerry, Light Green 42.00
Mug, Tom & Jerry, Rose.. 58.00
Mug, Tom & Jerry, Yellow 40.00
Mug, Yellow 35.00
Mustard, Red.. 145.00
Nappy, Ivory, 8 1/2 In.. 45.00
Nappy, Red, 8 1/2 In... 65.00
Nappy, Turquoise, 8 1/2 In... 75.00
Pitcher, Disk, Chartreuse.. 225.00
Pitcher, Disk, Cobalt Blue 160.00
Pitcher, Disk, Gray 250.00
Pitcher, Disk, Green 75.00
Pitcher, Disk, Ivory 115.00
Pitcher, Disk, Red.. 155.00
Pitcher, Disk, Rose..200.00 to 250.00
Pitcher, Disk, Turquoise.. 80.00
Pitcher, Disk, Yellow... 50.00
Pitcher, Ice Lip, Cobalt Blue 120.00
Pitcher, Ice Lip, Turquoise.. 145.00
Pitcher, Ivory 25.00
Pitcher, Juice, Red... 340.00
Pitcher, Juice, Yellow ....42.00 to 50.00
Pitcher, Light Green 135.00
Plate, Calendar, Green, 1955, 10 In... 75.00
Plate, Calendar, Ivory, 1954, 10 In.. 45.00
Plate, Chartreuse, 6 In. 8.00
Plate, Chartreuse, 7 In. 11.00
Plate, Chartreuse, 9 In. 16.00
Plate, Gray, 7 In. ....9.00 to 11.00
Plate, Green, 6 In.. 2.00
Plate, Green, 7 In.. 8.00
Plate, Green, 9 In.. 11.00
Plate, Ivory, 6 In... 7.00
Plate, Ivory, 7 In... 7.00
Plate, Light Green, 10 In. 22.00
Plate, Medium Green, 9 In. ....35.00 to 38.00
Plate, Red, 6 In... 8.00
Plate, Red, 7 In... 8.00
Plate, Red, 9 In... 22.00
Plate, Rose, 9 In.. 17.00
Plate, Salad, Medium Green, Individual, 7 1/2 In... 95.00
Plate, Turquoise, 6 In. 5.00
Plate, Turquoise, 9 In. 11.00
Plate, Turquoise, 10 In. ....14.00 to 25.00

Plate, Yellow, 6 In. .... 3.00 to 6.00
Plate, Yellow, 7 In. 6.00
Plate, Yellow, 10 In. .... 10.00 to 22.00
Platter, Medium Green, 12 1/2 In. 75.00
Platter, Rose, 12 1/2 In. 45.00
Platter, Turquoise, 12 1/2 In. 25.00
Platter, Yellow .... 20.00 to 30.00
Platter, Yellow, 12 1/2 In. 30.00
Relish, Cobalt Blue, Green, Yellow, Red 285.00
Relish, Red 235.00
Salad Fork, Green 95.00
Salt & Pepper, Red, Kitchen Kraft 40.00
Salt & Pepper, Yellow 25.00
Sauceboat, Chartreuse 55.00
Sauceboat, Gray 65.00
Sauceboat, Ivory 65.00
Sauceboat, Turquoise 35.00
Saucer, Chartreuse 5.00
Saucer, Medium Green 55.00
Saucer, Yellow, After Dinner 10.00
Soup, Cream, Cobalt Blue .... 30.00 to 60.00
Soup, Cream, Red .... 50.00 to 55.00
Soup, Cream, Turquoise 37.00
Soup, Cream, Yellow .... 25.00 to 30.00
Soup, Onion, Green 395.00
Soup, Onion, Ivory .... 200.00 to 500.00
Spoon, Red, Kitchen Kraft 115.00
Sugar & Creamer, Cover, Red .... 65.00 to 80.00
Syrup, Cobalt Blue 195.00
Syrup, Green 285.00
Syrup, Ivory .... 100.00 to 200.00
Tray, Utility, Red 40.00
Tumbler, Juice, Cobalt Blue .... 30.00 to 35.00
Tumbler, Juice, Red 35.00
Tumbler, Juice, Turquoise 35.00
Tumbler, Juice, Yellow .... 25.00 to 35.00
Tumbler, Water, Light Green 50.00
Tumbler, Water, Red 60.00
Tumbler, Water, Turquoise 50.00
Vase, Bud, Green, 6 1/2 In. 35.00
Vase, Cobalt Blue, 8 In. 495.00
Vase, Gray, 10 In. 225.00
Vase, Ivory, 8 In. 595.00
Vase, Ivory, 10 In. 450.00
Vase, Light Green, 10 In. 795.00
Vase, Turquoise, 10 In. .... 250.00 to 675.00
Vase, Yellow, 8 In. .... 450.00 to 495.00

FINCH, see Kay Finch category

FINDLAY ONYX AND FLORADINE are two similar types of glass made by
Dalzell, Gilmore and Leighton Co. of Findlay, Ohio, about 1889. Each piece
was made using three layers of glass. Onyx is a patented yellowish white
opaque glass with raised silver daisy decorations. A few rare pieces were
made of rose, amber, orange, or purple glass. Floradine is made of raspberry
or tan-colored opaque glass with opalescent white raised floral pattern. The
same molds were used for both types of glass.

Butter, Cover 600.00
Celery, 6 1/2 In. 900.00
Muffineer, Cased Raspberry 3700.00
Mustard, Raspberry 1400.00
Spooner, Raspberry 950.00
Sugar Shaker, Floradine 2100.00

Sugar Shaker, Silver Luster, 5 3/4 In..400.00 to 465.00
Syrup, Applied Handle, Lift Lid 450.00
Syrup, Opalescent Handle, Tin Lid, 7 3/4 In.. 715.00
Syrup, Silver Blossom & Foliage, Handle 985.00
Tumbler, Apricot 2200.00
Vase, Allover Floral Design, Shaped Neck, Bulbous, 4 1/2 x 5 1/4 In. 200.00

FIREFIGHTING equipment of all types is wanted, from fire marks to uniforms to toy fire trucks. It is said that every little boy wanted to be a fireman or a train engineer 75 years ago and the collectors today reflect this interest.

Alarm, Autocall, Industrial, Time & Date Stamp, Brass, Glass Case, 15 In. 1550.00
Alarm, Center Wound, Screw-In Key, Brass, 10 In... 206.00
Alarm, Faraday, Direct Acting Tapper, Chrome Bell, Gray Case, 11 In................................ 90.00
Alarm, Gamewell Fire Alarm & Telegraph Co., Brass Gong, Oak Case, 33 In. 2750.00
Alarm, Gamewell, Brass Register 225.00
Alarm, Gamewell, Fire Station, Oak Case, 27 In. 1155.00
Alarm, Gamewell, Pull Chain, Chrome, 10 In... 190.00
Alarm, Gamewell, Punch Cup & Key, Brass.. 1400.00
Ax, Crash, World War II... 25.00
Backpack, Water Tank, Brass, D.B. Smith.. 125.00
Badge, Fireman, Alliance, Ohio 40.00
Badge, Reading, Pa., No. 12, Hose & Hat, Nickel Plated, 2-Part, Chair Links, 1870s ... 485.00
Badge, Steamer, Hat, Hose, Nickel Plated Brass, Reading, Penn., 1870s 175.00
Bucket, Banner, Clasped Hands, Salem, Mass., Leather, T. Ropes, 1807...................... 4440.00
Bucket, Brass Riveted Rim, Seam & Base, Tulip Shape, Leather.............................. 350.00
Bucket, Canvas, Painted, Scene, Alon Somers, 2, Bergen Hose, 12 1/2 In. 525.00
Bucket, Green & Black, Grafton Norton, 1836.. 660.00
Bucket, Jefferson Fire Society, 1807, Pair.. *Illus* 9900.00
Bucket, Jefferson Fire Society, Charlestown, Mass., 1830 .... 9300.00
Bucket, Leather, Cartouche Of Burning Building, 19th Century, 8 1/2 In. 750.00
Bucket, Leather, No. 1 Calyin Haven, Gold On Green Ground, 1821, 20 In. 1045.00
Bucket, Leather, Spread-Winged Eagle, S.S. Raymond, Charlestown, Bag, Pair 9900.00
Bucket, Leather, Stenciled, D. Van Alstyne, Waterford 300.00
Bucket, Leather, Wrapped Leather Handle, 1850, 15 In....................................... 275.00
Bucket, Masonic Symbols, Eagle With Banner In Beak, Leather 4800.00
Bucket, Matthew Cobb, Died In Barnstable, May 18th, 1863.................................. 358.00
Call Box, Fire Alarm Telegraph, Gamewell, Cast Aluminum, 1928 .... 125.00
Cap, Parade, Red & Blue Oilcloth, Maltese Cross Badge, 1850s 195.00
Certificate, N.Y.C. Fireman Appointment, July 2, 1787, Copied From Original............ 65.00
Certificate, Presentation, Brookline Hook & Ladder Co., Frame, 17 x 18 In. 220.00
Extinguisher, Arrow, Copper... 110.00
Gong, Edwards, Loper Rotary Hammer, Oak Case, 16 In. 870.00

Firefighting, Bucket,
Jefferson Fire Society, 1807, Pair

When you buy antiques, you should beware of stickers, Magic Marker numbers, or other dealer-added labels that may damage the antique. Any type of sticky tape or label will leave marks on paper or paint finishes. Metal with an oxidized finish is damaged when ink marks are removed. Pencil or pen notations often leave indentations.

Grenade, B. & O. R. R., Star, Yellowish Green, Contents, May 27, '84, 1885, 8 In. 425.00
Grenade, Firex, Cobalt Blue, Contents, Box, c.1900, 3 3/4 In. 45.00
Grenade, Firex, Metal Hanger, Contents, Red Sealing Wax, c.1900, 4 In. 65.00
Grenade, Harden Star, Sapphire Blue, Contents 90.00
Grenade, Harden, Star, Clear Tube, c.1880, 16 7/8 In. 230.00
Grenade, Harden, Star, Cobalt Blue, Neck Label, France, c.1885, 6 3/4 In. 210.00
Grenade, Harden, Star, Original Plug, c.1880, 6 1/2 In. 90.00
Grenade, Harden, Star, Yellow Green, Contents, c.1880, 8 In. 300.00
Grenade, Harden, Turquoise Blue, Contents, Patent May 27, '84, 6 5/8 In. 210.00
Grenade, Hayward's, Aqua, Applied Mouth, c.1871, 6 1/4 In. 275.00
Grenade, Hayward's, Clear, Tooled Lip, Patent 1871, 6 In. 230.00
Grenade, Hayward's, Yellow Olive, c.1871, 6 In. 110.00
Grenade, Hayward's, Yellow Olive, Contents, Neck Seal, c.1871, 6 In. 125.00
Grenade, Haywards, New York, Amber, Patent 1871 .... 395.00
Grenade, Haywards, New York, Cobalt Blue, Patent 1871 .... 365.00
Grenade, Pyro, Tube Type 38.00
Grenade, Red Comet 20.00
Grenade, Unembossed, Raised Vertical Ribs, Turquoise Blue, 5 1/2 In. 550.00
Grenade, Wire Carrying Rack, 2 Glass Grenades, Contents, Sealed 440.00
Hat, Parade, Attached Beacon Lamp, 1875 .... 1750.00
Hat, Parade, Stovepipe, Weccacoe On Front, Gold Lettering 2900.00
Helmet, Aide, New York City Fire Commissioner, 1930 .... 205.00
Helmet, Aluminum, Cairns 95.00
Helmet, Brass Crossed Axes, Cork & Fabric, Belgium 120.00
Helmet, Leather Shield, Metal 100.00
Helmet, Leather, Front 325.00
Helmet, Leather, Inscribed Rescue, Crossed Hook & Ladder, 1850 .... 3162.00
Helmet, Leather, Metal Eagle, Boston Veteran Fire Assoc., 15 1/2 x 11 x 9 In. 260.00
Helmet, London Fire Brigade Decal, Cork & Fabric 150.00
Helmet, Presentation, Chief, J.F.M., Hand-Painted Front, Reverse Badge 2178.00
Helmet, Top Guard, Leather Front, VIFS, St. Croix, Red, MSA 60.00
Helmet, Union On Back Brim, Brass Shield, Gold Chin Strap, Leather 1075.00
Helmet, White Leather Front, Gold Lettering, Washington No. 2, 1840 .... 2600.00
Horn, Chain, Nickel Plated, 16 In. 275.00
Hose Reel, Wooden, Iron Wheels, Tool Box 248.00
Kit, Red Comet, Salesman's Sample 120.00
Lamp, Engine, Red, Blue & Clear Beveled Glass, Bracket 1320.00
Lantern, Chief's, Adams & Westlake, Model 39, Patent 1864 .... 795.00
Lantern, Chief's, Peter Gray, Boston, Nickel Plated, No. 3, Brass 475.00
Lantern, Dietz, American LaFrance & Foamite Corp, Steel 330.00
Mark, Banner & Torch, Iron, 10 1/2 In. 100.00
Mark, Fire Hydrant & Serpentine Hose, Cast Iron, 11 1/2 In. 120.00
Mark, Hydrant, Hose, Cast Iron, Marked FA, 11 x 7 1/4 In. 120.00
Mark, Lion's Face, Gold Paint, Cast Iron, 19th Century, 8 In. 575.00
Nozzle, Brass, Large 45.00
Nozzle, Elkart 60.00
Nozzle, Fire Hose, Brass, 1900s 95.00
Nozzle, Morse & Son, Red Cord, Brass, 30 In., Pair... 300.00
Torch, Parade, Tin, 1880s 125.00
Torch, Turned & Ebonized Wooden Handle, Brass, 28 In. 220.00
Trumpet, Collapsing, 13 Brass Telescoping Segments, Extended 14 In......................... 2130.00
Trumpet, Fireman Rescuing Baby Scene, Delaware Fire Co., No. 4, 23 1/2 In.............. 7140.00
Trumpet, Fireman's... 575.00
Trumpet, Presentation, Silver Plaque, Columbia Fire Dept., Brass & Pewter 2100.00
Trumpet, Speaking, Embossed, Applied Washington Medallions..................................... 1430.00
Tumbler, Negaunee Fire Dept., Milk Glass, Bead Swag 135.00
Wagon, Fire Patrol, Wooden, 4 Large Wooden Wheels, 1890 .... 4800.00

FIREPLACES were used to cook and to heat the American home in past centuries. Many types of tools and equipment were used. Andirons held the logs in place, firebacks reflected the heat into the room, and tongs were used to move either fuel or food. Many types of spits and roasting jacks were made and may be listed in the Kitchen category.

Andirons, Brass, Acorn Above Urn, Square Molded Base, Penny Feet, 26 3/8 In. 1495.00
Andirons, Brass, Acorn Finial, Ring Turned Urn, Garlands, American, 1800, 19 In. 2530.00
Andirons, Brass, Ball & Spur Feet, Bell Top, 1810, 20 In. 200.00
Andirons, Brass, Ball Capital, Ring-Turned Columnar Shaft, 1830s, 18 In. 920.00
Andirons, Brass, Ball Finial, Log Stops, 19th Century 200.00
Andirons, Brass, Ball Finial, Slipper Footed, 1795, 11 In. 495.00
Andirons, Brass, Cannonball Finial, Log Stops, Hoofed Feet With Spurs, 14 1/2 In. 350.00
Andirons, Brass, Cannonball, 1800, 21 In. 1500.00
Andirons, Brass, Chippendale, Painted Ball Finials, 20 In. 3450.00
Andirons, Brass, Federal, Floral & Urn Design, Ball Feet, 19 3/4 In. 4715.00
Andirons, Brass, Federal, Steeple Finials, 1800, 21 In. 1150.00
Andirons, Brass, Federal, Urn Finials, Gadrooned Skirt, 1790-1815, 29 In. 4025.00
Andirons, Brass, Figural, Leaping Trout 660.00
Andirons, Brass, Finials, Dogs Pass Through Shaft & Spit Hooks, 1775, 39 1/2 In. 385.00
Andirons, Brass, Flame & Reeded Ball, Ball & Claw Footed, 18th Century, 21 In. 5175.00
Andirons, Brass, French Style, Pinecone Finials, Pierced Bases 110.00
Andirons, Brass, Georgian Style, Knopped Standard, 25 In. 460.00
Andirons, Brass, Iron, Aesthetic, Pierced Foliate Disc, 19th Century, 27 In. 990.00
Andirons, Brass, Lemon Finial, Ball Feet, 24 In. 825.00
Andirons, Brass, Louis XVI Style, Ribbon Tied Tapering Stem, 24 In. 545.00
Andirons, Brass, Right & Left, Massive 880.00
Andirons, Brass, Rococo Style, Knopped Standard, Scrolling Base, 22 In. 575.00
Andirons, Brass, Spiral, Rampant Lion Finials, McKinney, 16 1/2 In. 110.00
Andirons, Brass, Spire & Ring Turned Ball, Spurred Arch Legs, Bailey, 26 1/4 In. 4025.00
Andirons, Brass, Square Cap Over Column, Arts & Crafts, 19 x 7 In. 1045.00
Andirons, Brass, Steel, Draped Urn & Flame Finials, Leaf & Scroll, 38 1/2 In., Pair..... 605.00
Andirons, Brass, Turned Shafts, Spurred Arched Legs, 1830, 22 In. 230.00
Andirons, Brass, Turned, 19th Century, 23 1/2 In., Pair 259.00
Andirons, Brass, Urn Above Turned Shaft, Shovel & 2 Jamb Hooks, 19 In. 865.00
Andirons, Bronze, French Empire, Dolphin Feet, Grecian Athlete Finials, 1840s, 17 In. 1350.00
Andirons, Bronze, Louis XV Style, Lion Resting On Shield, 21 In. 7415.00
Andirons, Bronze, Louis XV, Bonheur Freres 1000.00
Andirons, Bronze, Louis XVI Style, Recumbent Lion, 9 1/2 In., Pair 1265.00
Andirons, Bronze, Rococo Style, Knopped Standard, 24 In. 632.00
Andirons, Cast Metal, Cartoon Figure Popeye, Half-Round, 14 1/4 In. 1380.00
Andirons, Gilt & Patinated Bronze, Reclining Lions, Short Legs, 16 In. 5750.00
Andirons, Gilt Bronze, Louis XV Style, Figures Of Putti Eating Grapes, 14 In. 1600.00
Andirons, Iron, Cutout Design, Howes, Oval Raised Mark, 18 x 9 1/2 In. 165.00
Andirons, Iron, Duck, 20th Century.. 220.00
Andirons, Iron, Gargoyle, Bat Wings, Bradley & Hubbard.. 3500.00
Andirons, Iron, Greek Goddesses, Flowing Dresses, Torch, 1850, Pair......................... 325.00
Andirons, Iron, Hanging Horseshoe-Shaped Loops, Arts & Crafts, 15 In...................... 300.00
Andirons, Iron, Heart Shape, 14 1/2 In. 345.00
Andirons, Iron, Hessian Soldiers, 17 In. 140.00
Andirons, Iron, Penny Feet, Pigtail Tops, New England, 1750, 9 3/4 In. 325.00
Andirons, Iron, Sawtooth Stems, Spit Rod, Finials Hold Hot Toddy, 26 In. 495.00
Andirons, Iron, Textured, Black, Rectangular Base, George Maher, 16 x 26 In. 715.00
Andirons, Iron, Tweedledee & Tweedledum 425.00
Andirons, Wrought Iron & Brass, Arched Base, Italy, 16th Century, 34 x 20 In. 2600.00
Andirons, Wrought Iron, Black, Arts & Crafts, Rectangular Column, Flower................ 1200.00
Andirons, Wrought Iron, Brass, Arched Base, Scrolling Band, 17th Century, 26 In. 1495.00
Andirons, Wrought Iron, Renaissance Revival, Fold-Over Pot Holders, 44 In. 175.00
Andirons, Wrought Iron, Renaissance Revival, Knights, 44 In..................................... 170.00
Andirons, Wrought Iron, Swivel Crane & Shelf, Brass Ball Finial, 47 In. 200.00
Bellows, Brass, Wood, Hand-Painted Cherries, 16 1/2 In. 132.00
Bellows, Jenny Lind, Woman At Spinning Wheel 45.00
Bellows, Stenciled & Freehand Floral, Yellow, Brass Nozzle, 18 3/4 In. 110.00
Bellows, Stenciled & Freehand Fruit & Foliage, Brass Nozzle, 17 1/2 In...................... 120.00
Bellows, Stenciled Floral, Smoked White Painted Leather, Brass Nozzle, 17 In. 71.00
Bellows, Turtle Back, Mourning Scene, Woman At Tomb, Brass Nozzle, 18 1/2 In. 2100.00
Bellows, Turtle Back, Stenciled Gilded Fruit, Brass Nozzle, 17 In. 245.00
Bellows, Turtle Back, Yellow Paint, Smoked Graining, Brass Nozzle, 16 1/4 In........... 82.00
Broiler, Grease Trap In Handle, Wrought Iron, 24 In. 300.00

Fireplace, Mantel, Pine, Flower Garlands, R. Welford, 1800, 6 Ft. 6 In.

Chenet, Bronze, Brass, Cherub Holding Torch, Rocaille Base, 17 1/2 x 15 1/2 In., Pair 1320.00
Coal Box, Hand Hammered Brass, Arts & Crafts, 14 x 17 In. 172.00
Coal Box, Tiled Castle Ruin Slant Lid, Lion Head Handles & Feet, 1900, 22 In. 248.00
Coal Box, Victorian, Repousse, Rectangular, 1850 .... 60.00
Coal Hod, Oak, Brass Mounted, 15 In. 115.00
Coal Scuttle, Carved Gallery, Lion Carved Fall Front, 26 x 18 1/2 In. 250.00
Coal Scuttle, Copper, Helmet Shape, 19th Century 66.00
Coal Scuttle, Cover, Campana Shape, Brass, 16 In. 143.00
Coal Scuttle, Helmet Shape, Copper, Dovetailed, Wooden Handles, 10 In. 99.00
Coal Scuttle, Liner, Painted Floral, Female Mask Handles & Feet, Tin, 23 1/2 In. 575.00
Fan, Front Stenciled Grapes, Turned Wooden Handle, Maple, 14 1/2 In. 1035.00
Fender, Bell Metal, Pierced Front, Engraved Paterae & Guilloches, 41 In. 2185.00
Fender, Brass & Wire, 19th Century, 36 1/2 x 12 In. 172.00
Fender, Brass, Art Nouveau, Central Bar With 3 Urns, Scroll Sides, 1910, 11 In. 518.00
Fender, Brass, D-Shaped Form, 2 Pierced Leaf Bands, Paw Feet, 41 1/4 x 11 In. 575.00
Fender, Brass, Georgian Style, 41 x 11 1/2 x 9 1/2 In. 190.00
Fender, Brass, Iron Wire Screen, Swag Top, Serpentine Base, 12 x 46 x 14 In. 1955.00
Fender, Brass, Pierced, 19th Century, 43 In. 287.00
Fender, Brass, Pierced, Footed, 13 x 54 In. 195.00
Fender, Bronze, Link Chain, Neoclassical, Ormolu, Patinated, Sea Serpents, Pair 1150.00
Fender, Bronze, Louis XV Style, Reclining Cupid Amid Foliage, 18 1/2 In. 635.00
Fire Board, Delft-Type Tile Frame, Trompe L'Oeil, Oil On Pine, 30 1/2 x 44 In. 9200.00
Fireback, Iron, Arched Top, Royal Arms, England, 17th Century, 24 x 22 In. 977.00
Fireback, Iron, Caricatured Figure, 18th Century, 24 In. 575.00
Fireback, Iron, Heraldic Lion Design, 18th Century, 33 In. 575.00
Fireback, Iron, Horse & Rider, 18th Century, 24 In. 805.00
Fireback, Iron, Man On Horse, Louis XV, Roy De France Et De Navarre, 22 x 17 In. .. 143.00
Fireback, Iron, Mask Design, 1763, 15 1/2 In. 201.00
Fireback, Iron, Tombstone Shape, 18th Century, 24 In. 230.00
Frying Pan, Wrought Iron, Handle Stamped Foster, 53 In. 467.00
Grate, Cast Iron, Prairie School, 16 x 29 x 14 1/2 In. 467.00
Guard, Iron, Winter, Diana Goddess Of Hunt, 1900 .... 225.00
Mantel, Pine, Flower Garlands, R. Welford, 1800, 6 Ft. 6 In. ....*Illus* 8050.00
Pot Hanger, Double Hook, Wrought Iron, 18th Century, 11 1/2 In. 45.00
Pot Hanger, Large Hook & Link, Wrought Iron, 18th Century, 9 1/2 In. 45.00
Pot Holder, For Crane, Loop Top, 12 x 9 In. 35.00
Rail, Brass, 20th Century, 8 1/2 x 48 x 14 In. 85.00
Screen, 4 Panels, Stylized Tree, Greene & Greene, Wrought Iron, 1905, 36 In. 6900.00
Screen, Aesthetic Movement, Leaded Glass, Walnut Frame.. 2310.00
Screen, Art Nouveau, Brass & Glass Bead, Floral Design, Brass Frame, 28 In. 650.00
Screen, Bamboo, Butterflies Under Glass, 42 x 30 In. 1800.00

Screen, Beveled Leaded Glass Insert, ... 350.00
Screen, Burgundy Silk Panels, Sliding, Mahogany, England, 11 1/4 x 35 1/2 In. 60.00
Screen, Egg & Dart Border, Trophy On Claw Feet, Brass, Gilt Metal, 28 3/4 In. 745.00
Screen, Empire, Needlepoint, Carved, Mahogany, 51 x 30 In. 475.00
Screen, Folk Art, Hounds & Stags, Large Crest, 52 In. 440.00
Screen, Gilt Bronze, Louis XV Style, Cartouche, 4 Scrolled Legs, 30 x 32 In. 1265.00
Screen, Horse & Rider, Fall Wooded Scene.. 80.00
Screen, Inlaid Rosewood, England.. 4675.00
Screen, Iron, Brass Rim, 24 x 56 In.. 1100.00
Screen, Leaded Glass Panels, Mahogany Frame, Abel Landry, 1900, 39 In. 3737.00
Screen, Louis XV, Arched, Adjustable Brocaded Silk Panel, 33 1/2 x 16 In. 800.00
Screen, Mahogany, Marquetry, Urn-Shaped Finials, Floral Needlework 880.00
Screen, Painted Wrought Iron, Wire Mesh, Rearing Gazelles, 1925, 29 In. 4600.00
Screen, Pole, Attached 1810 Sampler, Abigail Graham 1870.00
Screen, Pole, Needlework Scene On Frame, Canvas, Mahogany Veneer, 53 In. 357.00
Screen, Wire, Brass Rails & Finials 440.00
Screen, Woven & Hand Painted Design, Renaissance Revival 2050.00
Screen, Wrought Iron, Flat Pad Feet, Italy, 16th Century, 50 x 48 In. 2185.00
Spit, Iron, American, 18th Century 535.00
Striker, Flint, Wooden Handle, 5 1/2 In. 65.00
Surround, Cast Iron, 1860, 60 In.. 248.00
Surround, Louis XVI Style, Marble, D Shape, Frieze Carved Corners.......................... 5750.00
Surround, Pierced Stylized Scrolling, Cast Iron, 1900, 36 In. 3737.00
Tongs, Ember, Wrought Steel, 17 3/4 In. 176.00
Tool Set, Brass & Steel, Engraved Brass Crown Finial, 18th Century, 3 Piece.............. 776.00
Tool Set, Brass, Stand, 4 Piece 44.00
Tool Set, Child's, Jester Handles, Brass, Late 19th Century, 12 In. 275.00
Tool Set, Iron, Stand, 3 Piece... 24.00
Tool Set, Modernist Design, Metal, Rattan Handle... 110.00
Trammel, Catch In Form Of Bird's Head, Dutch, 1750, 18 In. 325.00
Trammel, Chain, Twisted, 66 In. 95.00
Trammel, Iron Chain, Pot Hook, Early 18th Century, 82 In. 250.00
Trammel, Ratchet Teeth, 37 In. 125.00

FISCHER porcelain was made in Herend, Hungary, by Moritz Fischer. The factory was founded in 1839 and continued working into the twentieth century. The wares are sometimes referred to as *Herend* porcelain.

MF

Cachepot, Oriental Design, 4 Feet On Square Base, 3 3/4 In., Pair 185.00
Cachepot, Oriental Figural Design, Flared, Square Base, 3 3/4 In., Pair 184.00
Cup & Saucer, 1870 .... 180.00
Dinner Set, Chinese Bouquet, Rust, 38 Piece 978.00
Figurine, Boy On Goose, Herend, 3 In.. 80.00
Figurine, Boy Who Slipped, Herend, 3 In. 100.00
Figurine, Hadik Hussar, 15 In. 925.00
Figurine, Schoolchildren Playing, 8 x 10 In... 525.00
Figurine, Woody Woodpecker 900.00
Inkwell, Double, Bird... 350.00
Inkwell, Porcelain, Hand Painted, Hungary, 2 1/2 In. 135.00
Pitcher, Queen Victoria Pattern, 4 1/2 In. 55.00
Powder Box, Butterflies, Flowers, Vines, Rose Finial, Artist, 1949, Round................... 55.00
Salt, Double, Bird 250.00
Sauceboat, Underplate, Butterflies, Ladle... 250.00

FISHING reels of brass or nickel were made in the United States by 1810. Bamboo fly rods were sold by 1860, often marked with the maker's name. Metal lures, then wooden and metal lures were made in the nineteenth century. Plastic lures were made by the 1930s. All fishing material is collected today and even equipment of the past thirty years is of interest if in good condition with original box. Other fishing equipment may be listed in the Sports category.

Bait Casting, Vom Hofe, Commander Ross Model 14/0 .... 1925.00
Box, Tackle, Presentation, A.& F... 770.00
Box, Tackle, Tole 1320.00

Bucket, Minnow, Fall City Brand, Oval, Fish Illustration	75.00
Bucket, Minnow, Floating	45.00
Bucket, Minnow, Green Finish, Handle, 13 In.	45.00
Bucket, Minnow, Green River Brand	30.00
Bucket, Minnow, Sturdibilt Brand, Oval	35.00
Creel, Birch Bark, Design Of Bears & Loons, Indian, 6 x 8 In.	495.00
Creel, Hardy Perfect	880.00
Creel, Trout, Wicker	65.00
Creel, Willow, Center Holder, Slant Front, Hinged, c.1850	200.00
Cuff Links, 14K Gold, Encased Fly, Glass	95.00
Dinghy, Arlie Bowen, Oars	4950.00
Fly Reel, Pflueger Progress	12.00
Fly Rod, Fred Devine, Bag, Tag, c.1920s, 9 In.	450.00
Fly Rod, South Bend, Bamboo, 9 Ft.	125.00
Harpoon, Shoulder Held, Double Shank, Toggle Head, 27 1/2 In.	355.00
License, California, 1943	15.00 to 25.00
License, New York, 1940	20.00
Line, Shapleigh, Keen Kutter, Roll	95.00
Lure, Al Foss Skidder, Colorado Spinner, 1916	93.00
Lure, Arbogast Weedless Kicker	65.00
Lure, Baby Lucky, 13s, Mounted, 3 Piece	45.00
Lure, Bass Bait, Decker	390.00
Lure, Dipsy Doodle, Wooden, 1947, 1 1/2 In.	12.00
Lure, Flying Helgramite, Comstock, Type II	6600.00
Lure, Frog, Cork, C.R. Harris, c.1897	550.00
Lure, Frog, Stud Eyes, Wooden	40.00
Lure, Frog, Tempter, Weedless, Rubber-Jointed Legs, c.1928, 4 In.	150.00
Lure, Green, Al Foss, Tin	28.00
Lure, Heddon Lucky, 13s, Mounted, 3 Piece	40.00
Lure, Helga Devil, Box, c.1946	25.00
Lure, Helin, Swimmer Spoon, Pair	23.00
Lure, K & K	412.00
Lure, Mac Fox, Rubber Band & Propeller Powered	1000.00
Lure, Manitou Minnow, Box, c.1905	1210.00
Lure, Miller's Reversible	3025.00
Lure, Minnow, Glass Eyes, Wooden	40.00
Lure, Minnow, Haskell, c.1859	7480.00
Lure, Minnow, Heddon No. 150, Tan With Gold Scales, 3 1/2 In.	510.00
Lure, Minnow, Metal-Plated	385.00
Lure, Mouse, Hairy, Mounted, 1900s, 3 Piece	550.00
Lure, Revolution, Cork, Shakespeare	1201.00
Lure, Shakespeare Pups, Mounted, 3 Piece	25.00
Lure, Spinner, No. 9624	55.00
Lure, Underwater Minnow, No. 33	358.00
Lure, Wiggler, Wilcox	2475.00
Net, Metal, Canada	95.00
Net, Wooden	85.00
Pole, Cane	25.00
Reel, Atlas	20.00
Reel, Bass Caster	35.00
Reel, Bourne & Bond, Open Multiplying	115.00
Reel, Cascade	35.00
Reel, Casting, Bait, German Silver, Ivory Handle, c.1903	550.00
Reel, Edward Vom Hofe, Leather Case	600.00
Reel, Edward Vom Hofe, No. 1	4400.00
Reel, Edward Vom Hofe, Perfection, Model 360, 2 3/4 In.	6270.00
Reel, Fly, Heddon, No. 37, Box	65.00
Reel, Follett, c.1885	800.00
Reel, Hawg, Telescoping Rod	15.00
Reel, Hurron, Black Plastic Finish	32.00
Reel, J.A. Coxe, No. 25-2	50.00
Reel, Jr. Ace, Tin Case	35.00
Reel, Leader, Small	40.00

Reel, Pflueger Supreme, Steel Rod, 1930s	50.00
Reel, Quadruple, Multiplying Casting	20.00
Reel, Salmon, Edward Vom Hofe Model 423, Pat. 1902, 4 In.	770.00
Reel, Salmon, Edward Vom Hofe, c.1926	1210.00
Reel, Shakespeare, Model 1960	15.00
Reel, St. George Jr.	525.00
Reel, Trout, Conroy, Bissett & Malleson, c.1878	415.00
Rod, C.W. Jenkins, 8 1/2 Ft.	495.00
Rod, Casting, South Bend, 2 Piece Split Bamboo, 9 Ft.	100.00
Rod, Dirigo, Thomas, 9 Ft.	440.00
Rod, Heddon Deluxe Pal, Steel, Casting, Gold, Model 3151-L, 1930	90.00
Rod, Heddon, Pal Steel, Original Case, 1950s	38.00
Rod, Impregnated Bamboo Bait, Orvis	175.00
Rod, Leonard, Model 46-4	2475.00
Rod, Leonard, Model 50DF	1100.00
Rod, Leonard, Model 66, 8 Ft.	770.00
Rod, Orvis, 6 1/2 Ft.	415.00
Rod, P.H. Young, Princess, 7 Ft.	1760.00
Rod, Payer, Trout, 7 Ft. 9 In.	1650.00
Rod, Payne, 7 1/2 Ft.	1700.00
Rod, Poacher's, Telescopic, Concealed In Bamboo Walking Stick	550.00
Rod, Salmon, Forrest Kelso	750.00
Rod, South Bend, No. 59, Bamboo	85.00
Rod, South Bend, No. 359, Bamboo	125.00
Rod, W.G. Soeffker, 8 Ft.	1375.00
Rod, Walt Carpenter, Model 199 Special, 7 Ft.	2100.00
Spinning Spool, Simplistic, Plastic, 1940	10.00
Tackle Box, Metal, Multilevel, Green, Leather Handle, 46 Modern Lures, 1920s	70.00
Trap, Minnow, 3 Hole, Marked Camp Minnow, Checotah, Okla., 1 Gal.	125.00

FLASH GORDON appeared in the Sunday comics in 1934. The daily strip started in 1940. The hero was also in comic books from 1930 to 1970, in books from 1936, in movies from 1938, on the radio in the 1930s and 1940s, and on television from 1953 to 1954. All sorts of memorabilia are collected, but the ray guns and rocket ships are the most popular.

Book, Big Little Book, Fiery Desert Of Mongo, 1948	40.00
Book, Big Little Book, The Perils Of Mongo, 1940s	50.00
Card, Christmas, Unused, 1951	20.00
Colorforms, Adventure Set, 1980	21.00
Coloring Book, McWilliams Cover, Whitman, 1952	35.00
Gun, Air Ray, 1948	195.00
Gun, Arresting Ray, 1932	225.00 to 232.00
Gun, Ray, Holster, On Card	40.00
Gun, Stun, Telescopic Sight, Box	150.00
Jigsaw Puzzle, Flash & Dale, Spaceship Cockpit, No. 4216, Milton Bradley, 1951	65.00
Model Kit, Revell, 1965	189.00
Pistol, Holster, 1970s, On Card	40.00
Play Set, Tootsietoy, Sealed, 1978	50.00
Puzzle, Built-Rite Frame, 1949	65.00
Puzzle, Tray Frame, Sleeve, 1951	75.00
Spaceship, Die Cast, Tootsietoy, 1978	26.00
Stamp Pad Set, Card, 1970s	30.00
Thermos, 1979	10.00
Uniform Patch, Multicolored, Name Embroidered On Top, Copyright, 1930s	175.00

FLORENCE CERAMICS were made in Pasadena, California, from World War II to 1977. Florence Ward created many colorful figurines, boxes, candle-holders, and other items for the gift shop trade. Each piece was marked with an ink stamp that included the name *Florence Ceramics Co.* The company was sold in 1964 and although the name remained the same the products were very different. Mugs, cups, and trays were made.

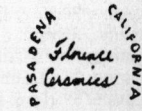

Bird, California Quail, Matte, White	329.00
Bird, Cardinal	329.00

Bird, Mockingbird 199.00
Bust, Oriental Man, Cream Uniform, Gold, Black Trim, 8 x 6 In. 60.00
Bust, Oriental Woman & Man, 7 In., Pair 150.00
Figurine, Abigail, Green, Blue, Tan, 8 1/2 In. .... 85.00 to 139.00
Figurine, Adeline 100.00
Figurine, Amelia, Brown, 9 1/4 In. 159.00
Figurine, Ann 65.00
Figurine, Annette 189.00
Figurine, Belle 125.00
Figurine, Blue Boy & Pinky, 11 In., Pair .... 650.00 to 660.00
Figurine, Blue Boy, 12 In. .... 150.00 to 295.00
Figurine, Camille, Blue, 9 In. .... 180.00 to 225.00
Figurine, Catherine, On Bench, Teal 525.00
Figurine, Charmaine 150.00
Figurine, Choir Boy .... 35.00 to 40.00
Figurine, Clarissa, Green & Pink, 8 In. .... 75.00 to 110.00
Figurine, Delilia, Rose, 8 1/2 In. 225.00
Figurine, Della, Rosy Purple, 8 In. 85.00
Figurine, Diane, White, Gold Trim Coat, Turquoise Dress, 8 1/2 In. 95.00
Figurine, Douglas, White 229.00
Figurine, Edward, Gray Suit, Blue Chair 430.00
Figurine, Elizabeth, Blue Dress, Gray Sofa 429.00
Figurine, Elizabeth, On Settee, Open Fingers, Green 275.00
Figurine, Eugenia 225.00
Figurine, Eve & Charles, Pair 350.00
Figurine, Gary, Green 230.00
Figurine, Gary, Pink 260.00
Figurine, Georgette, Cranberry 105.00
Figurine, Grace, Blue .... 195.00 to 229.00
Figurine, Her Majesty .... 85.00 to 150.00
Figurine, Jeannette 159.00
Figurine, Jennifer, Pink, 8 1/2 In. 279.00
Figurine, Jim .... 65.00 to 90.00
Figurine, Josephine .... 100.00 to 135.00
Figurine, Joyce, Pink 279.00
Figurine, Karla, Ballerina, Matte Pink 349.00
Figurine, Lilian, Gray .... 85.00 to 110.00
Figurine, Linda Lou 95.00
Figurine, Louis 149.00
Figurine, Louis XIV 295.00
Figurine, Louise, Label, 8 In. 60.00
Figurine, Madonna 189.00
Figurine, Madonna With Child 400.00
Figurine, Marie Antoinette 430.00
Figurine, Marie, Rose 289.00
Figurine, Marilyn, Carrying Hat Box 150.00
Figurine, Mary, Gray Dress, Mauve Chair 429.00
Figurine, Matilda, Tan, Blue 125.00
Figurine, Melanie 125.00
Figurine, Memories .... 275.00 to 550.00
Figurine, Mermaid 135.00
Figurine, Oriental Girl, White-Gold Trim, Applied Chrysanthemums, 8 In. 45.00
Figurine, Oriental, Haru & Misha, Red, 11 In., Pair 459.00
Figurine, Oriental, She-Ti & Kiu, White, 11 In., Pair 429.00
Figurine, Pat & Mike, Pair 125.00
Figurine, Pinkie & Blue Boy, Pair 300.00
Figurine, Rebecca .... 125.00 to 140.00
Figurine, Rose Marie, Rose 289.00
Figurine, Sarah, Gray, 8 In. .... 75.00 to 100.00
Figurine, Scarlet & Rhett, Green, Red, Pair 450.00
Figurine, Scarlett, Purple 150.00
Figurine, Southern Belle, White 240.00
Figurine, Sue Ellen 140.00

Figurine, Swan, 12 In.	195.00
Figurine, Victoria, Burgundy Dress, Gray Sofa	429.00
Figurine, Victoria, Sofa, Gold Trim	200.00
Figurine, Wickum, Boy & Girl, Pair	239.00
Figurine, Woman, Dancing, Basket On Head	149.00
Flower Holder, Oriental Boy	39.00
Flower Holder, Violet, Head Vase	95.00
Head Vase, Violet	95.00
Lamp, Dear Ruth, Green	295.00
Lamp, Figural, David & Betsy, Pair	459.00
Planter, Lantern Boy	50.00
Planter, Man, Pushing Cart	170.00
Plaque, 2 Girls, Brunette & Blond, Gold Muff, 6 1/2 x 9 In., Pair	195.00
Wall Pocket, Florane	55.00

FLOW BLUE, or flo blue, was made in England about 1830 to 1900. The plates were printed with designs using a cobalt blue coloring. The color flowed from the design to the white plate so that the finished plate has a smeared blue design. The plates were usually made of ironstone china.

Berry Bowl, Argyle, Gold Trim, Grindley	40.00
Berry Bowl, Lois, 9 In.	85.00
Berry Bowl, Roseville, Maddock, 5 In.	35.00
Berry Set, Oregon, Johnson Bros., 6 Piece	175.00
Bone Dish, Duchess, Grindley	30.00
Bone Dish, Touraine, Alcock, 8 Piece	325.00
Bone Dish, Touraine, Stanley	85.00
Bone Dish, Touraine, Stanley, 12 Piece	650.00
Bowl, Conway, 9 In.	120.00
Bowl, Florida, 8 In.	40.00
Bowl, Keswick, Wood & Sons, 12 In.	41.00
Bowl, Messina, Leaf & Acorn Handles, Alfred Meakin, Large	145.00
Bowl, Moreau, 9 In.	285.00
Bowl, Nonpareil, Cover, Square	320.00
Bowl, Paris, New Wharf Pottery, 8 In.	50.00
Bowl, Possitt, Briar Rose	1100.00
Bowl, Serving, Watteau, New Wharf Pottery, 8 3/4 In.	80.00
Bowl, Vegetable, Baltic, Cover, Burgess & Leigh	275.00
Bowl, Vegetable, Blue Danube, Cover, Johnson Bros.	195.00
Bowl, Vegetable, Delamere, Cover, Alcock	275.00
Bowl, Vegetable, Grace, Cover, Grindley	275.00
Bowl, Vegetable, Jeddo, Cover	260.00
Bowl, Vegetable, Marechal Niel, Cover, Grindley	235.00
Bowl, Vegetable, Touraine, Cover	375.00
Bowl, Waldorf, 9 In.	90.00
Butter, Nonpareil, Cover, Burgess & Leigh	275.00 to 300.00
Butter Chip, Argyle, Grindley	35.00
Butter Chip, Blue Danube	35.00
Butter Chip, Florentine	35.00
Butter Chip, Georgia, Alfred Meakin	35.00
Butter Chip, Hofburg	35.00
Butter Chip, Romeo	35.00
Butter Chip, Vermont, Burgess & Leigh	30.00
Casserole, Nonpareil, Cover, 8 In.	365.00
Casserole, Watteau, Cover, 7 x 12 In.	225.00
Chamber Pot, Hong Kong, Cover	600.00
Chamber Set, Syrian, 7 Piece	2250.00
Charger, Nonpareil, Burgess & Leigh, 12 In.	143.00
Chocolate Pot, Orchid, Maddock & Sons, 12 1/2 In.	235.00
Chop Plate, La Belle, 11 In.	175.00
Cigarette Box, 3 Ashtrays, Grimwades	75.00
Creamer, Abbey	90.00
Creamer, Amoy, Davenport	225.00
Creamer, Athol	120.00

Creamer, Bamboo, Large 350.00
Creamer, Claremont, Johnson Bros. 125.00
Creamer, Indian 395.00
Creamer, Kyber 90.00
Creamer, Lancaster 185.00
Creamer, Manilla 500.00
Creamer, Morning Glory 175.00
Creamer, Temple, Podmore, Walker & Co. 250.00
Creamer, Touraine, Stanley 235.00
Cup & Saucer, Argyle, Grindley 95.00
Cup & Saucer, Bentick 120.00
Cup & Saucer, Chain Of States 75.00
Cup & Saucer, Child's, Basket Pattern 65.00
Cup & Saucer, Claremont, After Dinner 95.00
Cup & Saucer, Clarence, Grindley .... 70.00 to 85.00
Cup & Saucer, Kermlin, Alcock 160.00
Cup & Saucer, Oregon, Johnson Bros. 95.00
Cup & Saucer, Temple 150.00
Cup & Saucer, Touraine, Alcock 85.00
Cup & Saucer, Trent, New Wharf Pottery 65.00
Cup Plate, Amoy 110.00
Dish, Cheese, Ivy, Utzschneider 250.00
Dish, Elaine, Brown-Westhead Moore, 8 In. 30.00
Dish, Hong Kong, Cover 500.00
Dish, Sundae, Warwick 75.00
Dish, Vegetable, Kyber, Cover, 2 Handles, 11 In. 192.50
Dish, Vegetable, Lorne, 7 x 10 In. 140.00
Gravy Boat, Dresden, Underplate, Grindley 75.00
Gravy Boat, Manilla 345.00
Gravy Boat, Nonpareil, Double Spout 325.00
Gravy Boat, Touraine, Alcock 175.00
Gravy Boat, Warwick, Figural Handle, Underplate 95.00
Mug, Wheel 75.00
Pitcher, Clayton, Johnson Bros. 200.00
Pitcher, Haddon, Gridley, 5 In. 395.00
Pitcher, Haddon, Gridley, 8 In. 298.00
Pitcher, Hong Kong, 11 1/2 In. 440.00
Pitcher, Melton, 7 In. 135.00
Pitcher, Milan, 5 1/2 In. 145.00
Pitcher, Milk, Kyber, 8 1/2 In. 275.00
Pitcher, Oregon, 12 1/2 In. 880.00
Pitcher, Ormonde, Alfred Meakin 200.00
Pitcher, Touraine, 7 1/2 In. 350.00
Pitcher, Watteau, New Wharf Pottery 250.00
Pitcher & Bowl, Seine 225.00
Plate, Alaska, Grindley, 10 In. 95.00
Plate, Arcadia, 10 In. 70.00
Plate, Argyle, Grindley, 7 In. 35.00
Plate, Ashton, Pountney, c.1901, 7 1/2 In. 40.00
Plate, Bamboo, Dimmock, 10 1/4 In. 135.00
Plate, Belmont, 8 In. 65.00
Plate, Bentick, 6 In. 45.00
Plate, Colonial, Hanley 68.00
Plate, Conway, 10 In. .... 90.00 to 95.00
Plate, Denver, Souvenir, 1890 .... 35.00
Plate, Duchess, 10 In. 40.00
Plate, Eclipse, Johnson Bros., 10 In. .... 80.00 to 85.00
Plate, Formosa, Mayer, 9 1/4 In. 85.00
Plate, Grace, 10 In. 30.00
Plate, Holland, Alfred Meakin, 10 In. 75.00
Plate, John Alden & Priscilla 110.00
Plate, Lancaster, 9 In. 37.00
Plate, Leicester, 9 In. 100.00

Plate, Lorne, 9 In. 75.00
Plate, Louise, Johnson Bros., 7 In. 35.00
Plate, Madras, 7 1/2 In. 55.00
Plate, Messina, 10 In. 65.00
Plate, Montana, 10 In. 55.00
Plate, Neapolitan, Johnson Bros., 10 In. 50.00
Plate, Nonpareil, 10 In. 50.00
Plate, Nonpareil, Burgess & Leigh, 9 3/4 In. 90.00
Plate, Normandy, Johnson Bros., c.1901, 10 In. 85.00
Plate, Oriental, Alcock, 9 1/2 In. 125.00
Plate, Oriental, New Wharf Pottery, 9 In. 78.00
Plate, Pelew, 8 In. 59.00
Plate, Plate, Duchess, 8 In. 35.00
Plate, Savoy, Johnson Bros., 9 7/8 In. 72.00
Plate, Scinde, Alcock, 10 1/2 In. 185.00
Plate, Scinde, Walker, 9 1/4 In. 110.00
Plate, Shanghai, 9 In. 95.00
Plate, Shanghai, Grindley, 10 In. 80.00
Plate, Temple, 7 In. 85.00
Plate, Temple, 8 3/4 In. 115.00
Plate, Touraine, 8 1/2 In. 65.00
Plate, Touraine, 9 1/2 In. 65.00
Plate, Touraine, 10 In. 100.00
Plate, Trent, Wood, 6 1/8 In. 35.00
Plate, Waldorf, 9 1/2 In. 100.00
Plate, Waldorf, 10 In. 78.00
Plate, Waldorf, New Wharf Pottery, c.1894, 10 In. 90.00
Plate, Waverly, 8 In. 52.00
Plate, Wentworth, 8 In. 50.00
Platter, Argyle, 15 In. 225.00
Platter, Argyle, Ford & Sons, 12 In. 100.00
Platter, Argyle, Ford & Sons, 13 In. 150.00
Platter, Argyle, Grindley, 17 x 12 In. 250.00
Platter, Argyle, Grindley, 19 In. ....250.00 to 495.00
Platter, Argyle, Grindley, 19 x 13 1/4 In. 550.00
Platter, Ayr, 10 1/2 In. 120.00
Platter, Bacon, Marie, Grindley, 8 x 11 In. 135.00
Platter, Baltic, Grindley, 9 x 12 In. 140.00
Platter, Cashmere, 17 1/2 In. 1625.00
Platter, Castle, 15 In. 175.00
Platter, Cauldon, 15 3/4 In. 137.00
Platter, Colonial, Alfred Meakin 185.00
Platter, Conway, 10 1/2 In. ....95.00 to 115.00
Platter, Daisy, 16 In. 198.00
Platter, Duchess, 12 In. 135.00
Platter, Duchess, 15 In. 165.00
Platter, Dundee, Ridgways, 12 3/4 x 8 1/2 In. 65.00
Platter, Eclipse, 10 1/2 x 14 In. ....135.00 to 185.00
Platter, Egg, Waldorf, 10 1/2 x 8 In. 65.00
Platter, Excelsior, 11 In. 250.00
Platter, Georgia, Alfred Meakin, 12 1/4 x 9 1/4 In. 145.00
Platter, Harvard, Maddock, c.1886, 15 In. 125.00
Platter, Hindustan, 18 In. 398.00
Platter, Imperial, 12 In. 115.00
Platter, Indian Jar, J. & T. Furnival, 12 In. 215.00
Platter, Kelmscott, Oval, 18 In. 225.00
Platter, Kin Shan, Challinor, 15 1/4 x 12 In. 325.00
Platter, Kyber, 12 x 16 In. 445.00
Platter, Kyber, 18 In. 275.00
Platter, LaFrancais, French China, 13 In. 70.00
Platter, Lawrence, 13 In. 195.00
Platter, Lawrence, Scalloped Rim, 16 In. 250.00
Platter, Lorne, 10 1/2 x 14 In. 155.00

Platter, Lorne, 14 In. 235.00
Platter, Lorne, 16 1/2 In. 110.00
Platter, Lotus, 14 In. 235.00
Platter, Lotus, 16 In. 225.00
Platter, Marechal Niel, 12 1/2 In. 225.00
Platter, Marguerite, Grindley, 18 x 13 In. 200.00
Platter, Mayfair, 15 In. 115.00
Platter, Mayfair, 17 In. 168.00
Platter, Messina, 13 In. 145.00
Platter, Minwood, Alcock, c.1891, 19 1/2 In. 150.00
Platter, Nonpareil, Burgess & Leigh, 13 In. 275.00
Platter, Normandy. 185.00
Platter, Oriental Scene, Oval, 18 1/2 In. 80.00
Platter, Ormonde, Keeling, c.1912, 10 1/2 In. 50.00
Platter, Osborne, Rathbone, Oval, 13 1/2 In. 170.00
Platter, Persian, 1902, 12 x 16 In. 295.00 to 450.00
Platter, Rock, 12 1/2 In. 365.00
Platter, Rolland, Johnson Bros., c.1900, 14 In. 125.00
Platter, Scinde, 13 In. 95.00
Platter, Scinde, 15 1/2 In. 475.00
Platter, Scinde, Scalloped, Alcock, 18 1/4 x 14 1/2 In. 665.00
Platter, Scroll, Morely, 15 1/2 In. 350.00
Platter, Touraine, 12 1/2 In. 170.00
Platter, Touraine, Alcock, 15 1/2 In. 230.00
Platter, Watford, 13 In. 140.00
Platter, Waverly, 17 In. 340.00
Relish, Abbey, 11 1/4 x 5 3/4 In. 95.00
Shaving Mug, Wagon Wheel. 140.00
Soup, Dish, Carlton, 10 1/4 In. 150.00
Soup, Dish, Chusan, Morley, 10 3/8 In. 75.00
Soup, Dish, Conway, 9 In. 70.00
Soup, Dish, Duchess. 35.00
Soup, Dish, Florida, 7 3/4 In. 32.00
Soup, Dish, Florida, 9 1/2 In. 40.00
Soup, Dish, Louise, New Wharf Pottery 35.00
Soup, Dish, Monarch, Myott, 9 In. 40.00
Soup, Dish, Nonpareil, Burgess & Leigh, 8 1/4 In. 80.00
Soup, Dish, Pekin, Johnson Bros. 67.50
Soup, Dish, Waldorf, New Wharf Pottery 501.00
Soup, Dish, Waverly, 8 In. 55.00
Soup Tureen, Chusan, Podmore, Walker & Co. 200.00
Soup Tureen, Clarence, Grindley. 500.00
Soup Tureen, Excelsior, Underplate, Cover, Ladle, Thomas Fell 770.00
Spooner, Nonpareil. 220.00
Sugar, Albany, Grindley 175.00
Sugar, La Francais, Windmills 57.00
Sugar, Mandarin. 250.00
Sugar, Scinde. 450.00
Sugar, Scinde, Cover, Pumpkin Shape 495.00
Sugar, Temple, Cover, Podmore, Walker & Co. 250.00
Sugar, Windmill, French China Co. 70.00
Tea Set, Scinde, 3 Piece 1750.00
Teapot, Amoy. 900.00
Teapot, Chinese, Dimmock 695.00
Teapot, Cypress, Davenport 995.00
Tureen, Alleghany, Octagonal, Goodfellow 465.00
Tureen, Sauce, Argyle, Cover, Underplate, Johnson Bros. 275.00
Tureen, Sauce, Shrewsbury, Underplate, Ladle 225.00
Tureen, Soup, Bamboo, Alcock. 1550.00
Tureen, Soup, Grace, Grindley, 6 1/2 x 12 1/2 In. 395.00
Tureen, Trent, Wood & Sons, 6 x 11 1/2 In. 225.00
Vase, Rhine, Stoke On Trent, Dimmock, c.1844, Pair. 1350.00
Waste Bowl, Cashmere, Morley. 850.00

Waste Bowl, Timor	75.00
Waste Bowl, Touraine	125.00
Waste Bowl, Touraine, Stanley	250.00

FLYING PHOENIX, see Phoenix Bird category

FOLK ART is also listed in many categories of this book under the actual name of the object. See categories such as Box, Cigar Store Figure, Weather Vane, Wooden, etc.

Bank, Wooden, Carved & Painted, 19 1/2 In.	1035.00
Baseball Toss Target, Happy Hooligan, Hit Makes Eyes Move, 1910, 56 In.	4025.00
Basket, Twig, Twisted Handle, Picket Fence Edge, Round	60.00
Birdcage, Full-Rigged Ship Shape, Wire & Wooden, Signed G. Bret, 1900	3400.00
Birdhouse, Built As Maryland Shore Fishing Shack	2500.00
Birdhouse, Castle, 2 Story, Red, White & Blue, Large	125.00
Birdhouse, Church, Christmas, Snow Covered, Evergreens, Sparkle Bell Tower & Bell	95.00
Birdhouse, Log Cabin	225.00
Birdhouse, Log Cabin Shape, Twig & Branches, 4 Unit	200.00
Birdhouse, Log Cabin, 1930s	365.00
Birdhouse, Log Cabin, Slant Roof	225.00
Birdhouse, Red, Green & White Painted	225.00
Birdhouse, Wooden, Sections, Removable Roof	80.00
Box, Carved, Cutouts With Inset Mirrors, Brasses, 14 x 6 x 7 1/2 In.	350.00
Box, Document, Applied Trees & Stars, Original Painted & Shellacked, 1860	3800.00
Box, Jewelry, Chip Carved, Red Velvet Lining, C. B., 8 In.	110.00
Carving, Eagle, Spread Wings, Pine, 13 In.	300.00
Carving, Gray Cat, Grasping Mouse In Mouth, Wooden, Relief, Nova Scotia	325.00
Carving, Ivory On Board, Dog Sled, Driver, Grenfell, 1930	3800.00
Checkerboard, Reverse Painted, Molded Frame, 14 3/4 x 13 1/4 In.	50.00
Comb Box, Comb Slot, Shelf, 2 Tiny Pockets, Blue Paint, Yellow Trim	210.00
Figure, Eaglet, Folded Wings, Carved Claws, Schimmel, 1865, 7 In.	6325.00
Figure, Elephant, Pine, Papier-Mache, Felt, 19th Century, 4 x 5 Ft.	660.00
Figure, Parrot, Colored Beads, 1890s, 11 3/4 In.	1995.00
Figure, Poodle, Carved & Painted, Pine, Aaron Mountz	3220.00
Figure, Uncle Sam, Cut-Out Board	225.00
Frame, Easel, Bent Twig, Silver Accents, Fancy	75.00
Lamp, Wishing Well, Man, Red Shirt, String, 14 In. *Illus*	245.00
Model, Church, Country, Wooden, Red, Black & White Paint	375.00
Pillow, Penny, 17 x 17 In.	40.00
Retablo, E. Santo Nino De Praga, Jose Rafeal Aragon, 1820-1862	8625.00
Rolling Pin, Hand Carved, 17 In.	35.00

Folk Art, Lamp, Wishing Well, Man, Red Shirt, String, 14 In.

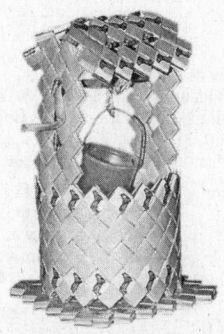

Folk Art, Wishing Well, Cigarette Packs, Made By Prisoner, 6 1/2 In.

Folk Art, Wishing Well, Red, White, Bird, Directional, 51 In.

Rug, Penny, Unhemmed, 33 x 17 In. 40.00
Sailor's Valentine, Double-Type, Shells, Ever Thine, 8 1/4 In. 1760.00
Scarecrow, Old Jacket & Hat, Pair 700.00
Sideshow Banner, Fifi, Indian Rubber Girl, Oil On Canvas, 1910s, 12 x 9 Ft.............. 2185.00
Sideshow Banner, Jolly Joe, Seated Fat Man, Weighing 585 Pounds 1725.00
Sideshow Banner, King Of Swords, Painted Canvas 2597.00
Sideshow Banner, Two-Headed Cow, O. Henry Tent & Awning Co., 7 Ft. 7 In. 805.00
Snow Goose, Wooden, Sheet Metal, Original Paint, On Stand, Herman Glick, 23 In. 94.00
Squirrel Cage, Tin, Mansion, Revolving Exercise Side Drums, Painted, 1900.............. 1200.00
Stone Fruit, Peach, Orange & Pear, Original Paint, 3 Piece.. 148.00
Stone Fruit, Pear, Apple & Plum, Original Paint, 3 Piece.. 82.00
Stone Fruit, Potato, Peach & Pomegranate, Original Paint, 3 Piece........................ 181.00
Table, Parcheesi Top, Legs Made Of Thread Spools, Rectangular............................ 1650.00
Toy, Airplane Ride, 4 Planes, Suspended From Cross Arms, Haag 330.00
Toy, Ferris Wheel, Carts Made Of Tobacco Tins 1275.00
Toy, Mule Cart, 2 Wheels, Man 400.00
Uniform, Cap, Red & Green Postage Stamps, Eastern Carnival, Milo, Maine.......... 2700.00
Whimsy, Chain With Ring & Hook, Dated 1891, 20 In.. 193.00
Whirligig, Airplane, 20th Century, 18 x 18 In. 55.00
Whirligig, Animated Horse Cart, Old Man, Masonite, Wire & Sheet Metal, 12 In......... 550.00
Whirligig, Farmer & Wife, Sharpening Wheel, 1930s 925.00
Whirligig, Gentleman, Double-Sided, Black Bowler, Striped Trousers, Pine, 15 3/4 In. . 2588.00
Whirligig, Indian, In Canoe, Paddles, Wooden, Painted, 19th Century, 16 In............... 3000.00
Whirligig, Keystone Cop, Metal Cap & Hands, Brass Buttons, 17 1/2 In. 2875.00
Whirligig, Man On Bone Shaker Bicycle, Pine & Metal, American, 1910s, 40 In........... 5175.00
Whirligig, Man On Unicycle, Blue & Yellow Clothes, Large Wheel.......................... 575.00
Whirligig, Sailor Boy, Painted, 12 1/2 In... 715.00
Whirligig, Uncle Sam In Airplane, 19 x 11 In. 715.00
Whirligig, Weight Lifter, c.1900... 1795.00
Wishing Well, Cigarette Packs, Made By Prisoner, 6 1/2 In......................*Illus*   85.00
Wishing Well, Red, White, Bird, Directional, 51 In. ....*Illus*   285.00

FOOTBALL collectibles may be found in the Card and the Sports categories.

FOOT WARMERS solved the problem of cold feet in past generations. Some
warmers held charcoal, others held hot water. Pottery, tin, and soapstone
were the favored materials to conduct the heat. The warmer was kept under
the feet, then the legs and feet were tucked into a blanket, providing welcome
warmth in a cold carriage or church.

Coach, Double Size... 295.00
Drilled Hole Designs, Red Paint, Tin Pan, Cherry, 7 x 10 In. 192.00
Hinged Round Door, Wire Bail Handle, Cherry, 9 1/2 x 11 1/2 In............................ 358.00
Hot Water, Copper 75.00
Iron Handle, Soapstone 15.00
Pierced Tin, Wooden 88.00
Punched, Brass, Dutch, c.1720, 5 1/4 In. 525.00
Punched Circles & Hearts, Wooden Frame, 9 In. 94.00
Punched Tin, Drum Shape, Wooden Frame, 9 3/4 In... 275.00
Stagecoach, Tin & Wooden Pillars, Heart Design, Side Coal Container...................... 250.00
Stoneware, Brown Glaze, c.1860, 11 1/4 x 6 1/4 In... 135.00
Tin & Glass, Kerosene Burner, Carpet Covered, D.L. Jaques Patent, 9 1/2 In. 193.00

FOSTORIA glass was made in Fostoria, Ohio, from 1887 to 1891. The factory
was moved to Moundsville, West Virginia, and most of the glass seen in
shops today is a twentieth-century product. The company was sold in 1983;
new items will be easily identifiable, according to the new owner, Lancaster
Colony Corporation. Additional Fostoria items may be listed in the Milk
Glass category.

American, Ashtray, Oval, 3 7/8 In. 9.00
American, Ashtray, Square, 2 3/4 In. 6.00
American, Basket, Reed Handle ....75.00 to 87.00
American, Boat, 2 Handles, 12 In.. 14.00
American, Boat, 2 Sections, 2 Handles, 12 In. 17.00

American, Bonbon, Amber, Footed 135.00
American, Bonbon, Red.. 35.00
American, Bottle, Stopper, 9 Oz.. 75.00
American, Bowl, 16 x 20 In. 140.00
American, Bowl, 2 Sections, Oval 35.00
American, Bowl, 3 1/2 In.. 15.00
American, Bowl, 3-Footed, 10 1/2 In. 25.00
American, Bowl, Cover, 2 Sections, Rose, 5 1/4 In. 22.00
American, Bowl, Fruit, Footed, 16 In. 225.00
American, Bowl, Hat Shape.. 150.00
American, Bowl, Lily Pond, 12 In. ....55.00 to 60.00
American, Bowl, Salad, Liner, 10 In. 50.00
American, Bowl, Shrimp, 12 1/4 In. 375.00
American, Bowl, Wedding, Cover, Footed 80.00
American, Butter, Cover, Dome.. 95.00
American, Cake Plate, 7 1/2 In. 10.00
American, Cake Salver, Pedestal, Square, 10 In. 110.00
American, Candlestick, 3 In., Pair 28.00
American, Candy Dish, Cover, Hexagonal, Footed 35.00
American, Celery Dish, 10 In. 15.00
American, Cheese & Cracker... 40.00
American, Cigarette Box, Cover 35.00
American, Creamer, 9 1/2 Oz. 11.00
American, Cup & Saucer, Flared, Footed, 7 Oz.. 12.00
American, Cup & Saucer, Footed 11.00
American, Decanter, Scotch, Stopper 125.00
American, Decanter, Sterling Silver Labels On Chains, Stopper, 7 3/8 In., 7 Piece 346.00
American, Decanter, Stopper, 24 Oz. 80.00
American, Dish, Lemon, Cover, 5 1/4 In. 42.00
American, Fernery, 3-Footed... 8.00
American, Goblet, Hexagonal, Footed, 10 Oz. 12.00
American, Goblet, Round Foot, 9 Oz. 11.00
American, Hat, 2 1/2 In. 10.00
American, Hat, 3 In. 20.00
American, Ice Bucket, 6 1/2 In. 45.00
American, Mayonnaise Set, 3 Piece.. 35.00
American, Mayonnaise, Liner... 25.00
American, Napkin Ring 18.00
American, Nappy, 1 Handle, 4 1/2 In. 7.00
American, Nappy, Handle, Shallow, Round, 5 In. 12.00
American, Nappy, Loop Handle, Triangular.. 11.00
American, Perfume Lamp.. 50.00
American, Pitcher, 10 In. 105.00
American, Pitcher, 44 Oz., 7 3/8 In. 55.00
American, Pitcher, Water, 8 In. 95.00
American, Plate, 7 In. 11.00
American, Plate, 8 1/2 In. ....10.00 to 13.00
American, Plate, 12 1/2 In. 16.00
American, Plate, 13 In. 28.00
American, Plate, Torte, 14 In...30.00 to 55.00
American, Plate, Vaseline, 7 1/2 In. 85.00
American, Puff Box, Cover, Square, 3 In. 125.00
American, Punch Bowl, High Foot, 14 In. 165.00
American, Punch Set, Stand, 3 3/4-Gal. Bowl, 14 Piece 325.00
American, Relish, 2 Sections, Oblong, 11 In. 20.00
American, Relish, 3 Sections, Oval, 9 1/2 In. 35.00
American, Relish, 3 Sections, Oval, 10 1/2 x 7 In. 28.00
American, Relish, 4 Sections, Square, 11 In. 175.00
American, Salt & Pepper 20.00
American, Sauceboat & Underplate... 35.00
American, Server, Center Handle 35.00
American, Sherbet, Low Footed, Flared 9.00
American, Sherbet, Octagonal Bead Stem, 3 1/2 x 3 1/4 In. 10.00

American, Soup, Cream, Handle 42.00
American, Sugar & Creamer, 3 In. 15.00
American, Sugar & Creamer, Individual, 2 1/2 In. 17.00
American, Sugar & Creamer, Tray 22.00
American, Sugar, 3 In. 8.00
American, Syrup, Bakelite Handle 75.00
American, Toothpick 16.00
American, Tray, Round, 12 In. 175.00
American, Tub, Ice, No Liner, 5 1/2 In. 30.00
American, Tumbler, 8 Oz., 3 7/8 In. 12.00
American, Tumbler, Flared, 4 In. 14.00
American, Tumbler, Footed, 6 In. 20.00
American, Tumbler, Footed, 7 In. 8.00
American, Tumbler, Old-Fashioned, 6 Oz. .... 12.00 to 14.00
American, Vase, Bud, Footed, 6 In. 11.00
American, Vase, Bud, Red, 6 In. 38.00
American, Vase, Cupped, 10 In. 195.00
American, Vase, Flared, 6 In. 15.00
American, Vase, Flared, 9 1/2 In. 150.00
American, Vase, Flared, 10 In. 75.00
American, Vase, Footed, 10 In. 40.00
American, Vase, Square Foot, 9 In. 32.00
American, Vase, Swung, 14 In. 200.00
American Lady, Goblet, 10 Oz. 17.00
American Lady, Wine, 3 1/2 Oz. 6.00
Arcady, Wine, 3 Oz. 26.00
Argus, Candy Dish, Cover, Red, 8 In. 65.00
Argus, Sugar & Creamer, Cover, 6 In. 65.00
Baroque, Bowl, Handle, Footed, 10 1/2 In. 30.00
Baroque, Cake Plate, 10 In. 15.00
Baroque, Candlestick, 2-Light, Blue, Pair 80.00
Baroque, Candy Dish, Cover, Blue, 9 1/2 In. 70.00
Baroque, Celery, Topaz 30.00
Baroque, Compote, Blue, 5 In. 30.00
Baroque, Ice Bucket, Topaz 55.00
Baroque, Mayonnaise, 2 Sections, Blue, 8-In. Tray 135.00
Baroque, Plate, Topaz, 6 In. 10.00
Baroque, Plate, Torte, 14 In. 20.00
Baroque, Relish, Topaz, 3 Sections 22.00
Baroque, Sauceboat, Oval, Blue, 6 1/2 In. 65.00
Baroque, Sweetmeat, Cover, Blue, 9 1/2 In. 395.00
Baroque, Tray, Oblong, Blue, 8 In. 65.00
Baroque, Tumbler, Footed, Blue, 14 Oz. 75.00
Beverly, Butter, Blue 275.00
Beverly, Pitcher, Amber 295.00
Bookends, Colt, Rearing, 5 1/4 In. 35.00
Bouquet, Vase, Bud, 6 In. 45.00
Brocade, Bonbon, Acorns 50.00
Brocade, Bonbon, Daffodil, Green 75.00
Brocade, Bonbon, Daffodil, Pink 75.00
Brocade, Compote, Daffodil, White 75.00
Buddha, Bookends, Black 495.00
Buttercup, Creamer 18.00
Buttercup, Goblet, 10 Oz. 30.00
Buttercup, Pitcher, 53 Oz. 295.00
Buttercup, Salt & Pepper 35.00
Buttercup, Sugar 20.00
Buttercup, Wine, 3 1/2 Oz. .... 18.00 to 30.00
Camellia, Cruet, Pair 95.00
Camellia, Cruet, Stopper 65.00
Camellia, Tray, 7 In. 15.00
Camellia, Wine, 3 1/4 Oz. 30.00
Century, Bonbon, Round, 3-Footed, 7 In. 18.00

Century, Bowl, Flared, 12 In.. 35.00
Century, Bowl, Handle, 4 1/2 In... 10.00
Century, Bowl, Rolled, Footed, 10 In. 45.00
Century, Bowl, Triangular, 3-Footed, 7 1/8 In. 14.00
Century, Candlestick, 3-Light, 7 3/4 In. 30.00
Century, Candlestick, 4 1/4 In., Pair 20.00
Century, Compote, 4 3/8 In... 22.00
Century, Cup & Saucer..15.00 to 18.50
Century, Cup & Saucer, Ring 30.00
Century, Goblet, 10 1/2 Oz... 15.00
Century, Ice Bucket, 4 7/8 In... 50.00
Century, Mayonnaise, Liner 24.00
Century, Mustard, Cover, Footed, Spoon 55.00
Century, Pickle, 8 3/8 In... 15.00
Century, Pitcher, 48 Oz.. 85.00
Century, Plate, 7 1/2 In. 13.00
Century, Platter, 12 In.. 55.00
Century, Relish, 2 Sections, 7 3/8 In. 12.00
Century, Relish, 3 Sections, 11 1/8 In. 25.00
Century, Salt & Pepper 18.00
Century, Sugar & Creamer... 21.00
Century, Sugar & Creamer, Tray, Individual 28.00
Century, Tumbler, Footed, 12 Oz. 28.00
Century, Vase, 2 Handles, 7 1/2 In. 40.00
Chintz, Bonbon, Footed, 7 3/8 In. 25.00
Chintz, Cake Plate, Handle, 10 In. 45.00
Chintz, Candlestick, 2-Light, 4 1/2 In. 29.00
Chintz, Candlestick, 2-Light, 4 1/2 In., Pair...55.00 to 75.00
Chintz, Candlestick, 3-Light, 6 In., Pair 43.00
Chintz, Celery, 11 In. 45.00
Chintz, Champagne, 6 Oz. 20.00
Chintz, Cocktail, 4 Oz. 25.00
Chintz, Compote, Cheese, 3 1/4 In. 50.00
Chintz, Compote, Crystal, 5 1/2 In. 40.00
Chintz, Cordial, 1 Oz. ....48.00 to 59.00
Chintz, Creamer 20.00
Chintz, Creamer, Baroque, Individual 16.00
Chintz, Cruet, Oil... 90.00
Chintz, Goblet, Juice, Footed, 5 Oz. 20.00
Chintz, Goblet, Water, 9 Oz. 33.00
Chintz, Plate, 7 1/2 In. ....8.00 to 14.00
Chintz, Plate, Tidbit, 3-Footed 23.00
Chintz, Relish, 3 Sections 40.00
Chintz, Sherbet, 6 Oz. ....12.00 to 20.00
Chintz, Sugar & Creamer, Footed 35.00
Chintz, Sugar, Baroque, 3 1/2 In. 10.00
Chintz, Tumbler, Footed, 5 Oz. 18.00
Chintz, Wine, 4 1/2 Oz. 15.00
Coin, Ashtray, Emerald Green 39.00
Coin, Ashtray, Olive, 7 1/2 In. 20.00
Coin, Ashtray, Round, 7 1/2 In.. 30.00
Coin, Bowl, Amber, Frosted, 8 In. 35.00
Coin, Bowl, Oval, Ruby, Frosted, 9 In. 48.00
Coin, Candleholder, 4 1/2 In., Pair 27.00
Coin, Candy Jar, Cover 35.00
Coin, Jelly, Olive, 3 3/4 x 4 3/8 In. 15.00
Coin, Lamp, Courting, Shade, Amber 150.00
Coin, Nappy, Handle 35.00
Coin, Nappy, Red, Handle.. 85.00
Coin, Punch Set, Ladle, 20 Cups 750.00
Coin, Salt & Pepper, Amber... 40.00
Coin, Salt & Pepper, Red 40.00
Colonial, Toothpick 35.00

Colonial Dame, Goblet, Green, 11 Oz.. 17.00
Colonial Dame, Sherbet, Green, 6 1/2 Oz. 14.00
Colonial Dame, Tumbler, Green, 12 Oz. 15.00
Colony, Bonbon, 3-Footed, 7 In. 25.00
Colony, Bowl, Celery, 11 1/2 In... 25.00
Colony, Bowl, Flared, 11 In... 33.00
Colony, Bowl, Mayonnaise, Ladle 28.00
Colony, Bread Plate 3.00
Colony, Cake Stand, 10 In. 50.00
Colony, Candlestick, 9 In. 25.00
Colony, Cocktail, 3 1/2 Oz. 7.00
Colony, Dish, Pickle, Double Swirl 35.00
Colony, Goblet, 9 Oz. ....12.00 to 13.00
Colony, Lamp, Large 175.00
Colony, Pitcher, Ice Lip, 48 Oz... 100.00
Colony, Plate, 9 In. 20.00
Colony, Plate, Luncheon 8.00
Colony, Plate, Upturned Handles, 9 In... 23.00
Colony, Relish, 2 Sections, Handles, 7 In. 14.00
Colony, Sherbet, 5 Oz. ....6.00 to 8.00
Colony, Sugar & Creamer, Footed, 3 3/4 In... 11.00
Colony, Sugar, 3 /12 In... 5.00
Colony, Sugar, Individual 4.00
Colony, Tray, Handle, 11 In... 20.00
Colony, Vase, 13 In. ....50.00 to 95.00
Colony, Vase, Bud, Footed, 6 In.. 14.00
Colony, Vase, Cupped, 7 In. 40.00
Colony, Vase, Flared, Footed, 7 1/2 In. 30.00
Corsage, Celery.. 35.00
Corsage, Cup & Saucer 24.00
Corsage, Goblet, 9 Oz.. 18.00
Corsage, Oyster Cocktail, 4 Oz. 22.00
Corsage, Tumbler, Footed, 12 Oz. 24.00
Dolly Madison, Goblet, 9 Oz... 12.00
Dolly Madison, Sherbet, Low, 6 Oz.. 10.00
Fairfax, Bonbon, Handle, Blue 23.00
Fairfax, Bouillon, Handle, Footed, Blue 12.00
Fairfax, Candy Dish, Cover, 3 Sections, Orchid... 95.00
Fairfax, Compote, Green, 6 In... 33.00
Fairfax, Cup & Saucer, Footed, Green 9.00
Fairfax, Cup & Saucer, Green 12.00
Fairfax, Cup & Saucer, Orchid 12.00
Fairfax, Cup & Saucer, Topaz, After Dinner 18.00
Fairfax, Pail, Whipped Cream, Blue 75.00
Fairfax, Parfait, Blue 30.00
Fairfax, Plate, Amber, 6 In. 2.00
Fairfax, Plate, Blue, 8 /12 In.. 14.00
Fairfax, Plate, Green, 9 In. 5.00
Fairfax, Platter, Green, 12 In... 20.00
Fairfax, Platter, Pink, 12 In. ....50.00 to 60.00
Fairfax, Relish, 3 Sections, Green, 8 1/2 In... 9.00
Fairfax, Relish, Oval, Pink, 8 1/2 In. 20.00
Fairfax, Sandwich Tray, Center Handle, Amber... 35.00
Fairfax, Sauce Boat, Liner, Amber.. 40.00
Fairfax, Soup, Cream, Amber, Footed 7.00
Fairfax, Soup, Cream, Topaz... 9.00
Fairfax, Sugar & Creamer, Blue, Individual 40.00
Fairfax, Sugar & Creamer, Footed, Green 15.00
Fairfax, Sugar & Creamer, Green 25.00
Fairfax, Sugar & Creamer, Green, Individual... 25.00
Fairfax, Tumbler, Topaz, 5 Oz. 11.00
Fairfax, Whiskey, Orchid 30.00
Fern, Cocktail, Oyster, 8 Piece 90.00

Figurine, Madonna, 10 In. 15.00
Figurine, Madonna, Silver Mist, Frosted, 10 In. 60.00
Heather, Cake Plate, Handle.. 28.00
Heather, Cup & Saucer.. 20.00
Heather, Plate, 6 In.. 7.00
Heather, Plate, 7 In.. 9.00
Heather, Plate, 8 In.. 17.00
Heather, Plate, 9 In.. 25.00
Heather, Relish, 3 Sections, 11 In. 38.00
Heather, Salt & Pepper... 25.00
Heather, Sherbet, 7 Oz. 14.00
Heather, Sugar & Creamer ....30.00 to 35.00
Heather, Tumbler, 12 Oz.. 22.00
Heather, Vase, Bud, Footed, 8 In. 48.00
Heirloom, Bonbon, Orange, 7 In. 26.00
Heirloom, Bowl, Blue Opalescent, 7 In. 30.00
Heirloom, Bowl, Oval, Pink, 13 In. 60.00
Heirloom, Candleholder, Opalescent, 3 1/2 In. 18.00
Heirloom, Epergne, Blue Opalescent, 9 1/2 In. 95.00
Hermitage, Ashtray Set, 4 Yellow Ashtrays, 5 Piece 38.00
Hermitage, Cocktail, Footed, Wisteria, 4 Oz. 12.00
Hermitage, Compote, Wisteria, 6 In. 30.00
Hermitage, Finger Bowl, Wisteria 12.00
Hermitage, Plate, Wisteria, 8 In. 14.00
Hermitage, Sherbet, Wisteria, 5 1/2 Oz. 12.00
Hermitage, Tumbler, Wisteria, 2 Oz.. 12.00
Hermitage, Vase, Yellow, 6 In. 38.00
Holly, Cocktail, Footed, 3 1/2 Oz. 18.00
Holly, Goblet, 10 Oz..18.00 to 20.00
Holly, Relish, 2 Sections, 8 1/4 In. 15.00
Holly, Sherbet, 6 Oz. 11.00
Holly, Tray, Center Handle... 28.00
Holly, Tumbler, Footed, 5 Oz. 12.00
Holly, Tumbler, Footed, 12 Oz. ....18.00 to 22.00
Horizon, Sugar & Creamer... 35.00
Iris, Candy Dish, Cover.. 145.00
Jamestown, Goblet, 9 1/2 Oz. 4.00
Jamestown, Goblet, Blue, 6 Piece 20.00
Jamestown, Goblet, Pink, 10 Oz... 25.00
Jamestown, Goblet, Red, 10 Oz.. 18.00
Jamestown, Plate, 14 In 43.00
Jamestown, Sherbet, Green, 6 1/2 Oz. 17.00
Jamestown, Tumbler, Amber, Footed, 11 Oz. 17.00
Jamestown, Tumbler, Blue, Footed, 11 Oz... 17.00
Jamestown, Tumbler, Green, Footed, 11 Oz. ....14.00 to 17.00
Jenny Lind, Pitcher, Milk Glass, 8 In.. 110.00
June, Ashtray, Blue, Small.. 75.00
June, Champagne, Pink.. 48.00
June, Console, Footed, Pink, 8 In. 85.00
June, Cup & Saucer.. 28.00
June, Cup & Saucer, Yellow... 28.00
June, Cup, Blue.. 20.00
June, Parfait, Pink, 5 1/4 In. 18.00
June, Plate, Fairfax, Topaz, 7 1/2 In. 7.00
June, Plate, Yellow, 7 1/2 In. 9.00
June, Plate, Yellow, 9 In... 25.00
June, Salt & Pepper, Blue 250.00
June, Salt & Pepper, Yellow... 165.00
June, Sherbet, Yellow, Low, 6 Oz. 25.00
June, Sugar, Cover, Yellow 225.00
June, Tumbler, Footed, 12 Oz.. 30.00
Lafayette, Cordial, Wisteria 150.00
Lafayette, Cup & Saucer, Wisteria 24.00

Lafayette, Plate, Wisteria, 6 In.......	13.00
Lafayette, Sugar & Creamer, Pink	38.00
Lido, Candy Dish, Cover, 3 Sections	50.00
Manor, Champagne, Topaz, 4 1/2 Oz.	20.00
Mayflower, Bowl, Handle, 8 1/2 In.......	35.00
Mayflower, Mayonnaise, Ladle, 2 Piece	45.00
Meadow Rose, Bowl, 12 1/2 In.	65.00
Meadow Rose, Cup, Footed	18.00
Meadow Rose, Goblet, 10 Oz.	28.00
Meadow Rose, Plate, 9 In.	45.00
Meadow Rose, Saucer	7.00
Meadow Rose, Sugar & Creamer, Footed, 3 1/2 In.	24.00
Meadow Rose, Tidbit, Round, 3 Footed, 8 In.......	32.00
Meadow Rose, Wine, 3 1/4 Oz....	38.00
Meadow Rose Sherbet, Low, 6 Oz.	23.00
Midnight Rose, Cake Plate, Handle, 10 1/2 In.	40.00
Midnight Rose, Relish, 3 Sections, Round, 7 1/2 In.	35.00
Midnight Rose, Sugar & Creamer	35.00
Midnight Rose, Vase, Footed, 10 In.	55.00
Minuet, Bowl, Handle, Green, 6 In.......	15.00
Minuet, Cup & Saucer, Green	15.00
Minuet, Vase, Topaz, 8 In.	75.00
Morning Glory, Mayonnaise, Liner	35.00
Navarre, Bell, Dinner	43.00
Navarre, Bonbon, Footed, 7 In.	25.00
Navarre, Bowl, 12 In.	50.00
Navarre, Bowl, Handle, 10 1/2 In.......	60.00
Navarre, Cake Plate, Handles, 10 In.......	35.00 to 45.00
Navarre, Candlestick, 2-Light, Pair	60.00
Navarre, Champagne, 6 Oz.	25.00
Navarre, Claret, 4 1/2 Oz.	45.00
Navarre, Claret, Blue, 4 1/2 Oz.	50.00
Navarre, Cocktail, 4 Oz.	16.00
Navarre, Compote, 5 1/2 In.	25.00
Navarre, Compote, Cheese, 3 1/4 In.	23.00
Navarre, Cordial, 3/4 Oz.	35.00 to 50.00
Navarre, Cup & Saucer	25.00 to 28.00
Navarre, Goblet, Water, Blue, 10 Oz.......	40.00
Navarre, Pitcher, 3 Pt.	365.00 to 400.00
Navarre, Plate, 8 In.	15.00
Navarre, Plate, 9 1/2 In.	45.00 to 65.00
Navarre, Relish, 3 Sections	65.00
Navarre, Relish, 5 Sections	95.00
Navarre, Sherbet, 6 Oz.	14.00
Navarre, Sugar & Creamer, Footed, 3 5/8 In.......	40.00 to 55.00
Navarre, Sugar & Creamer, Individual	30.00
Navarre, Tumbler, 13oz.	20.00 to 35.00
Navarre, Tumbler, Footed, 5 Oz.......	15.00
Navarre, Tumbler, Footed, Blue, 10 Oz.	40.00
Navarre, Vase, Flip, 5 In.	70.00
Navarre, Wine, 3 1/4 Oz.	45.00
Navarre Crown, Bowl, Ruby, 9 In.	60.00
New Garland, Cup & Saucer, After Dinner	18.00
Pine, Mayonnaise, 3 Piece, 3 1/4 In.	40.00
Pine, Relish, 3 Sections, 10 3/4 In.	30.00
Pioneer, Plate, 8 In.......	8.00
Pioneer, Plate, Amber, 7 In.	6.00
Pioneer, Plate, Amber, 9 In.	10.00
Pioneer, Platter, Amber, Oval, 12 In.	25.00
Priscilla, Butter, Cover, Green, Gold Trim.......	129.00
Priscilla, Mug, Green, 4 Piece.......	50.00
Priscilla, Pitcher, Water, Green, Gold Trim	195.00
Priscilla, Tumbler, Footed, Handle, Amber.......	14.00

Rambler, Candleholder, 2-Light, Pair 45.00
Rogene, Goblet 15.00
Romance, Bowl, 10 In. 35.00
Romance, Bowl, Lily Pond, 12 In. 40.00
Romance, Champagne, 6 Oz. 24.00
Romance, Cocktail, 3 1/2 Oz. 23.00
Romance, Cordial, 3/4 Oz. 60.00
Romance, Cup & Saucer 20.00
Romance, Oyster Cocktail, 4 Oz. 22.00
Romance, Plate, 7 In. 8.00
Romance, Plate, 8 In. 17.00
Romance, Plate, 9 In. 35.00
Romance, Sherbet, Champagne, 6 Oz. ....15.00 to 18.00
Romance, Sugar & Creamer ....30.00 to 35.00
Romance, Tumbler, 5 Oz. 18.00
Romance, Tumbler, 9 Oz. 15.00
Rose, Wine, 3 Oz. 75.00
Royal, Console, Amber, 11 In. 22.00
Royal, Cordial, 3/4 Oz. 35.00
Royal, Goblet, Green, 9 Oz. 25.00
Royal, Plate, Blue, 6 In. 6.00
Seascape, Bowl, Footed, Blue, 10 In. 45.00
Seascape, Relish, 2 Sections 28.00
Serenity, Goblet, 13 Oz. 25.00
Seville, Cup & Saucer, Amber 15.00
Seville, Goblet, Footed, Amber, 9 Oz. ....8.00 to 15.00
Seville, Plate, Amber, 7 1/2 In. 5.00
Seville, Plate, Amber, 8 1/2 In. 3.00
Silver Flutes, Goblet, 9 Oz. ....18.00 to 28.00
Silver Flutes, Sherbet, 7 Oz. ....12.00 to 25.00
Sunray, Bonbon, Handle 18.00
Sunray, Cup & Saucer 10.00
Sunray, Nappy, Handle, Red, 5 1/2 In. 25.00
Trojan, Berry Bowl, Yellow 28.00
Trojan, Candlestick, 3-Footed, Topaz 17.00
Trojan, Goblet, Yellow, 10 Oz. 30.00
Trojan, Plate, Yellow, 7 1/2 In. 8.00
Trojan, Salt & Pepper, Yellow 125.00
Vernon, Berry Bowl, Blue, 5 In. 30.00
Vernon, Bouillon, Liner, Footed, Blue 50.00
Vernon, Grapefruit, Insert, Green 110.00
Versailles, Bowl, Blue, 5 In. 30.00
Versailles, Bowl, Flared, Footed, Yellow, 12 In. 45.00
Versailles, Bowl, Yellow, 5 In. 20.00
Versailles, Bowl, Yellow, Footed, 12 In. 45.00
Versailles, Celery, Yellow, 12 In. 35.00
Versailles, Console Set, Footed, Green, 3 Piece 110.00
Versailles, Cup & Saucer, Blue ....35.00 to 39.00
Versailles, Lemon Dish, Fairfax, Green 16.00
Versailles, Parfait, Pink 28.00
Versailles, Plate, Blue, 7 1/2 In. ....13.00 to 17.00
Versailles, Plate, Pink, 9 1/2 In. 40.00
Versailles, Plate, Topaz, 9 1/2 In. 23.00
Versailles, Plate, Yellow, 7 1/2 In. ....8.00 to 13.00
Versailles, Platter, Blue, 12 In. 125.00
Versailles, Sugar & Creamer, Blue 70.00
Versailles, Sugar, Cover, Pink 175.00
Versailles, Tumbler, Blue, 5 Oz. 48.00
Versailles, Tumbler, Blue, Footed, 12 Oz. 45.00
Vesper, Cordial, Amber, 3/4 Oz. 80.00
Vesper, Cup & Saucer, Footed, Amber 20.00
Vesper, Plate, Amber, 7 1/2 In. 7.00
Vesper, Plate, Amber, 8 1/2 In. ....7.00 to 8.00

Vesper, Sherbet, Amber, 5 In.	18.00
Vesper, Tumbler, Amber, 9 Oz.	28.00
Victoria, Celery, Frosted	125.00
Victoria, Cruet, Frosted	265.00
Victoria, Nappy, Handle, 9 In.	120.00
Victoria, Plate, 4 1/2 In.	85.00
Victoria, Spooner, Frosted	129.00
Victoria, Toothpick	225.00
Victoria, Tumbler, Frosted, 9 Oz.	89.00
Willowmere, Cordial, Paper Label, 1 Oz.	18.00
Willowmere, Cup & Saucer	23.00
Willowmere, Oyster Cocktail, Paper Label, 4 Oz.	18.00
Willowmere, Plate, 7 In.	14.00

FOVAL, see Fry category

FRANCISCAN is a trademark that appears on pottery. Gladding, McBean and Company started in 1875. The company grew and acquired other potteries. They made sewer pipes, floor tiles, dinnerwares, and art pottery with a variety of trademarks. In 1934, dinnerware and art pottery were sold under the name Franciscan Ware. They made china and cream-colored, decorated earthenware. Desert Rose, Apple, El Patio, and Coronado were best sellers. The company became Interpace Corporation and in 1979 was purchased by Josiah Wedgwood & Sons. The plant was closed in 1984 but a few of the patterns are still being made. For more information, see *Kovels' Depression Glass & American Dinnerware Price List*.

Ashtray, Apple	12.00
Ashtray, Apple, Individual	23.00
Ashtray, Apple, Oval	62.00 to 65.00
Ashtray, Coronado	8.00
Ashtray, Desert Rose, Individual	10.00
Ashtray, Desert Rose, Oval	75.00
Ashtray, Desert Rose, Square	75.00
Ashtray, Ivy	32.00
Ashtray, Ivy, Individual	30.00
Ashtray, Starburst, Large	70.00
Baking Dish, Desert Rose, 1 1/2 Qt.	250.00
Baking Dish, Desert Rose, 1 Qt.	200.00
Baking Dish, Forget-Me-Not, 1 1/2 Qt.	125.00
Bell, Dinner, Desert Rose	150.00
Berry Bowl, Starburst	9.00
Bowl, Apple, 5 1/4 In.	8.00
Bowl, Apple, 5 3/4 In.	15.00
Bowl, Apple, 6 In.	12.00
Bowl, Apple, 7 In.	35.00
Bowl, Apple, 8 In.	39.00
Bowl, Cereal, Desert Rose	8.00
Bowl, Cereal, Starburst	6.00
Bowl, Desert Rose, 2 Sections, Oval	35.00
Bowl, Desert Rose, 5 1/4 In.	8.00
Bowl, Desert Rose, 8 In.	25.00
Bowl, Fruit, Desert Rose, 5 In.	6.00 to 10.00
Bowl, Fruit, Desert Rose, 6 In.	4.00
Bowl, Fruit, Ivy	10.00
Bowl, Fruit, Starburst	4.00
Bowl, Ivy, 2 Sections	40.00
Bowl, Ivy, 5 3/4 In.	20.00
Bowl, Salad, Apple, 10 In.	95.00
Bowl, Salad, Desert Rose, 10 In.	95.00
Bowl, Salad, Ivy, 11 In.	150.00
Bowl, Salad, Ivy, Individual	40.00
Bowl, Salad, Starburst	75.00
Bowl, Soup, Dish, Apple	18.00

Bowl, Starburst, Oval, 8 In. 15.00
Bowl, Vegetable, 2 Sections, Ivy 75.00
Bowl, Vegetable, Apple, 2 Sections ....43.00 to 50.00
Bowl, Vegetable, Apple, 7 1/2 In. 25.00
Bowl, Vegetable, Apple, Round, 8 In. 25.00
Bowl, Vegetable, California Poppy, 8 1/2 In. 125.00
Bowl, Vegetable, Desert Rose, 2 Sections, Oval 50.00
Bowl, Vegetable, Desert Rose, 8 In. ....20.00 to 40.00
Bowl, Vegetable, Ivy, 8 In. 35.00
Bowl, Vegetable, Ivy, Cover 150.00
Bowl, Vegetable, October, Round, Small 25.00
Bowl, Vegetable, Starburst, 2 Sections 45.00
Bowl Set, Mixing, Apple 365.00
Bowl Set, Mixing, Desert Rose 350.00
Box, Cigarette, Apple ....135.00 to 175.00
Bread Plate, Fruit 15.00
Bread Plate, Ivy 12.00
Bread Plate, Poppy 20.00
Bread Plate, Tiempo, Gray 6.00
Butter, Apple, 1/4 Lb. 50.00
Butter, Desert Rose, Cover ....35.00 to 40.00
Butter, Iris, Cover 65.00
Butter, Ivy, 1/4 Lb. 45.00
Butter, Ivy, Cover 65.00
Butter, Starburst ....26.00 to 32.00
Butter, Tiempo, Cover, Chartreuse 40.00
Butter, Wheat 20.00
Candleholder, Apple, Pair 40.00
Candleholder, Desert Rose 65.00
Candleholder, Desert Rose, Pair 125.00
Candy Dish, Desert Rose 125.00
Casserole, Apple, Cover, 10 In. ....50.00 to 69.00
Casserole, Apple, Square 35.00
Casserole, Desert Rose, Cover 85.00
Chop Plate, Apple, 14 In. ....28.00 to 35.00
Chop Plate, Desert Rose, 14 In. 85.00
Chop Plate, Ivy, 14 In. 150.00
Chop Plate, Meadow Rose, 14 In. 48.00
Chop Plate, October, 14 In. 65.00
Clock, Apple, Electric 125.00
Coffeepot, Apple ....85.00 to 125.00
Coffeepot, Coronado, White, After Dinner 45.00
Coffeepot, Denmark 58.00
Coffeepot, Desert Rose ....75.00 to 95.00
Coffeepot, Desert Rose, After Dinner ....195.00 to 350.00
Coffeepot, Ivy ....145.00 to 225.00
Coffeepot, Starburst, 8 Cup 110.00
Compote, Apple ....50.00 to 70.00
Cookie Jar, Apple ....165.00 to 250.00
Cookie Jar, Desert Rose ....150.00 to 265.00
Creamer, Apple ....15.00 to 25.00
Creamer, Fresh Fruit 19.00
Creamer, Oasis 8.00
Creamer, Strawberry 32.00
Cup, Desert Rose 7.00
Cup & Saucer, Apple ....7.00 to 15.00
Cup & Saucer, Apple, After Dinner 43.00
Cup & Saucer, Apple, Jumbo 65.00
Cup & Saucer, Bountiful 35.00
Cup & Saucer, California Poppy 25.00
Cup & Saucer, Desert Rose ....6.00 to 15.00
Cup & Saucer, Desert Rose, After Dinner ....30.00 to 45.00
Cup & Saucer, Ivy ....10.00 to 20.00

Cup & Saucer, Ivy, Jumbo	55.00
Cup & Saucer, October	15.00
Cup & Saucer, Poppy	35.00 to 40.00
Cup & Saucer, Starburst	6.00 to 10.00
Cup & Saucer, Strawberry Time	35.00
Cup & Saucer, Tiempo, Chartreuse	13.00
Cup & Saucer, Tiempo, Dark Brown	13.00
Cup & Saucer, Tiempo, Salmon	13.00
Cup & Saucer, Twilight Rose	35.00
Dinner Set, Woodside, 78 Piece	950.00
Dish, Child's, Starburst, 3 Sections	42.00
Dish, Desert Rose, Heart Shape	85.00
Eggcup, Desert Rose	35.00
Ginger Jar, Desert Rose	250.00
Gravy Boat, Apple, Underplate	30.00
Gravy Boat, Denmark, Underplate	48.00
Gravy Boat, Desert Rose, Underplate	35.00
Gravy Boat, Ivy, Underplate	40.00 to 46.00
Gravy Ladle, Starburst	110.00
Grill Plate, Apple, 10 1/4 In.	85.00
Grill Plate, Desert Rose, 11 In.	75.00 to 85.00
Jam Jar, Apple, Cover	85.00 to 90.00
Lamp, Hurricane, Desert Rose	225.00
Mug, Apple, 12 Oz.	35.00 to 40.00
Mug, Cocoa, My First Piece Of Franciscan On Bottom	150.00
Mug, Coffee, Apple	12.00
Mug, Desert Rose, 7 Oz.	12.00 to 20.00
Mug, October, 7 Oz.	18.00
Mug, Saucer, Apple, 10 Oz.	40.00
Mug, Starburst	12.00
Napkin Ring, Apple	50.00
Napkin Ring, Desert Rose	38.00
Napkin Ring, October, 4 Piece	110.00
Pitcher, Apple, Ice Lip	110.00
Pitcher, Desert Rose	110.00
Pitcher, Ivy	115.00
Pitcher, Milk, Desert Rose, 6 1/2 In.	75.00
Pitcher, Milk, Twilight Rose	135.00
Pitcher, October	125.00 to 225.00
Pitcher, Starburst	125.00
Plate, Apple, 6 1/2 In.	5.00 to 6.00
Plate, Apple, 9 1/2 In.	11.00 to 13.00
Plate, Apple, 10 1/2 In.	10.00 to 14.00
Plate, Buffet, Ivy, 11 In.	95.00
Plate, California Poppy, 9 1/2 In.	35.00
Plate, Coronado, 9 1/4 In.	6.00
Plate, Coronado, Green, 8 In.	10.00
Plate, Coronado, Rose, 6 1/2 In.	6.00
Plate, Desert Rose, 6 In.	5.00
Plate, Desert Rose, 8 In.	12.00
Plate, Desert Rose, 9 1/2 In.	10.00 to 14.00
Plate, Desert Rose, 10 1/2 In.	15.00
Plate, Forget-Me-Not, 9 1/2 In.	13.00 to 20.00
Plate, Fresh Fruit, 10 1/4 In.	20.00
Plate, Ivy, 6 1/2 In.	7.00
Plate, Ivy, 8 1/2 In.	10.00
Plate, Ivy, 9 1/2 In.	22.00 to 30.00
Plate, Ivy, 10 1/2 In.	15.00
Plate, Oasis, 10 In.	6.00
Plate, October, 9 1/2 In.	20.00
Plate, Poppy, 9 1/2 In.	35.00 to 40.00
Plate, Starburst, 6 In.	3.00
Plate, Starburst, 9 1/2 In.	9.00 to 10.00

Plate, Strawberry, 10 In.	30.00
Plate, Tiempo, Dark Green, 9 1/2 In.	12.00
Plate, Tiempo, Salmon, 9 1/2 In.	12.00
Plate, Twilight Rose, 10 In.	30.00
Platter, Apple, 12 1/2 In.	25.00 to 35.00
Platter, Apple, 19 In.	250.00
Platter, Apple, Turkey, 19 1/2 In.	250.00
Platter, Desert Rose, 12 1/2 In.	30.00
Platter, Desert Rose, 19 In.	195.00 to 265.00
Platter, Forget-Me-Not	65.00
Platter, Fresh Fruit, 14 In.	48.00
Platter, Ivy, 12 1/2 In.	35.00
Platter, Ivy, 19 1/2 In.	275.00
Platter, October, 14 In.	65.00
Platter, Starburst, 12 1/2 In.	27.00
Relish, Apple	30.00
Relish, Apple, 10 In.	35.00
Relish, Apple, 3 Sections	62.00 to 85.00
Relish, Desert Rose, 2 Sections	40.00
Relish, Desert Rose, 3 Sections	65.00
Relish, El Patio, 2 Sections	18.00
Relish, Ivy, Divided	95.00
Salt & Pepper, Apple	25.00
Salt & Pepper, Apple, Bulbous	225.00
Salt & Pepper, Apple, Small	20.00 to 39.00
Salt & Pepper, Apple, Tall	55.00
Salt & Pepper, California Poppy	55.00
Salt & Pepper, Desert Rose, Bulbous	195.00 to 225.00
Salt & Pepper, Desert Rose, Rosebud	20.00
Salt & Pepper, Desert Rose, Small	23.00
Salt & Pepper, El Patio	12.00
Salt & Pepper, Forget-Me-Not	48.00 to 55.00
Salt & Pepper, Fresh Fruit	48.00
Salt & Pepper, Strawberry	38.00
Salt & Pepper, Tiempo, Chartreuse	22.00
Salt & Pepper Mill, Apple	20.00
Salt & Pepper Mill, Meadow Rose	255.00
Saltshaker, October	15.00
Saucer, Green	3.00
Saucer, White Satin	3.00
Sherbet, Apple	30.00
Sherbet, Ivy	37.00
Snack Tray, Echo	40.00
Snack Tray, Starburst	115.00
Soup, Dish, Apple	22.00
Soup, Dish, Apple, Cover, Lug Handle	85.00
Soup, Dish, Desert Rose	15.00
Soup, Dish, Ivy	25.00

*Franciscan, Sugar, Cover, Salmon, Handles, Square,
3 x 3 In.*

Sugar, Apple	40.00
Sugar, Apple, Cover	20.00
Sugar, Coronado, Cover	9.00
Sugar, Cover, Salmon, Handles, Square, 3 x 3 In. *Illus*	12.00
Sugar, Forget-Me-Not	29.00
Sugar, Ivy, Cover	35.00
Sugar, Oasis	10.00
Sugar, Strawberry	38.00
Sugar, Wildflower, Cover	125.00
Sugar & Creamer, Apple	15.00
Sugar & Creamer, California Poppy, Cover	95.00
Sugar & Creamer, Fresh Fruit	50.00
Sugar & Creamer, Starburst	15.00
Sugar & Creamer, Tiempo, Gray, Cover	13.00
Syrup, Apple	95.00
Tea Caddy, Cafe Royal, Cover	65.00
Tea Set, Coronado, After Dinner, 13 Piece	195.00
Teapot, Apple	80.00 to 95.00
Teapot, Coronado, Aqua	40.00
Teapot, Desert Rose	85.00 to 125.00
Teapot, October	75.00
Teapot, Poppy	375.00
Teapot, Shasta	99.00
Teapot, Starburst	95.00
Teapot, Wildflower	850.00
Thimble, Desert Rose	75.00
Tray, TV, Starburst	85.00
Trivet, Desert Rose, Fluted	125.00
Trivet, Fresh Fruit, Square	32.00
Tumbler, Apple, 10 Oz.	35.00
Tumbler, Desert Rose, 10 Oz.	25.00
Tumbler, Iced Tea, Apple, Hand Painted	15.00
Tumbler, Ivy, 10 Oz.	25.00 to 40.00
Tureen, Desert Rose, Flat Base	650.00
Tureen, Desert Rose, Footed	700.00
Tureen, Soup, Apple	395.00 to 475.00

FRANKART, Inc., New York, New York, mass-produced nude *dancing lady* lamps, ashtrays, and other decorative Art Deco items in the 1920s and 1930s. They were made of white lead composition and spray-painted. *Frankart Inc.* and the patent number and year were stamped on the base.

Ashtray, Bear	65.00
Ashtray, Dog, Scotty	50.00
Ashtray, Nude, Kneeling, 6 In.	210.00
Ashtray, Nude, Pearlized, Art Deco	259.00
Bookends, Dog, Scotty	135.00
Bookends, Dutch Girl & Boy	135.00
Bookends, Eagle, Outstretched Wings	140.00
Bookends, Horsehead, 5 In.	45.00
Bookends, Peek-A-Boo, Green	190.00
Bookends, Sailor Boy & Dog, Marked	95.00
Bookends, Team Of Horses	150.00
Lamp, Nude, Holding Globe, No. L210	500.00
Lamp, Woman, Sitting On Pillar, Holding Globe	450.00
Night-Light, 2 Nudes, Opaque Glass Panel	1100.00
Night-Light, Woman, Standing, Outstretched Arms, Signed, Dated	375.00

FRANKOMA POTTERY was originally known as The Frank Potteries when John F. Frank opened shop in 1933. The factory is now working in Sapulpa, Oklahoma. Early wares were made from a light cream-colored clay, but in 1956 the company switched to a red burning clay. The firm makes dinnerwares, utilitarian and decorative kitchenwares, figurines, flowerpots, and limited edition and commemorative pieces.

Ashtray, Cocker Spaniel 60.00
Ashtray, Road Runner.. 5.00
Bookends, Dog, Green 140.00
Bowl & Pitcher, Blue, Brown, Oval Bowl, 4 1/2 & 6 In. 10.00
Candlestick, Christ The Light Of The World, Oral Roberts, Pair.................. 18.00
Cookie Jar, Barrel, Yellow.. 28.00
Cup & Saucer, Mayan Aztec, Woodland Moss 5.00
Cup & Saucer, Wagon Wheel, Green, Brown 6.00
Dish, Leaf, Prairie Green, 12 1/2 In. 12.00
Dish, Plainsman, 4-Leaf Clover, Bronze, 6 1/2 In. 6.00
Figurine, Amazon Woman, 6 1/4 In.. 225.00
Figurine, Cowboy Boot, 3 1/2 In. 12.00
Figurine, English Setter, Miniature... 59.00
Figurine, Trojan Horse... 59.00
Flower Frog, Duck, Ada Clay 150.00
Mug, Elephant, 1968 Through 1987, 20 Piece 495.00
Mug, Elephant, White, 1968 ....80.00 to 100.00
Mug, Uncle Sam, Red, White & Blue, 1976.. 17.00
Pitcher, Prairie Green, Ice Lip, 8 In. 140.00
Pitcher, Wagon Wheel 42.00
Plate, Bicentennial, 1976 ....17.00 to 20.00
Plate, Christmas, 1965 .... 300.00
Plate, Christmas, 1968 ....32.00 to 45.00
Plate, Christmas, 1969 .... 35.00
Plate, Christmas, 1971 .... 25.00
Plate, Christmas, 1972 .... 20.00
Plate, Christmas, 1975 .... 20.00
Plate, Christmas, 1977 .... 10.00
Plate, Christmas, 1978 .... 17.00
Plate, Plainsman, Woodland Moss, 6 1/2 In. 2.00
Plate, Teenagers Of The Bible, 1972-1973 .... 25.00
Salt & Pepper, Black Cat 45.00
Salt & Pepper, Bull 65.00
Salt & Pepper, Oil Well, Black 45.00
Salt & Pepper, Puma 95.00
Tile, Will Rogers, Portrait, Crystalline Green Self-Frame, Incised, 6 x 5 1/4 In. 148.00
Vase, Wagon Wheel, Green, 4 In. 22.00
Wall Pocket, Acorn, Green, Ada Clay.. 35.00

FRATERNAL objects that are related to the many different fraternal organizations in the United States are listed in this category. The Elks, Masons, Odd Fellows, and others are included. Furniture is listed in the Furniture category. Shaving mugs decorated with fraternal crests are included in the Shaving Mug category.

Elks, Badge, Chicago, 56th Reunion, 1920 .... 15.00
Elks, Badge, Reunion, 2 Chains, Medal Of 5 Center, Purple Ribbon, 1905, 2 x 5 In. 25.00
Elks, Plate, Luncheon, Huntington Lodge.. 12.00
Elks, Plate, Tin Lithograph, 9 In. 50.00
Elks, Tie Tack, Red Star, 10K Gold.. 32.00
Knights Of Pythias, Paperweight, Black, Milk Glass Bottom, Milwaukee, Wis., 1890.. 75.00
Masonic, Apron, Lamb Skin 25.00
Masonic, Apron, Silk, Schoolgirl's Needlework, 1815, 12 x 14 In. 2400.00
Masonic, Ashtray, Brass, G Center, Eye At Top, Hammer Trowel, 5 1/2 In. 68.00
Masonic, Chocolate Pot, Hermann Lodge, Porcelain, 1914, 9 In................ 85.00
Masonic, Clock, Waltham, Masonic Insignia, Wooden Case, Round 40.00
Masonic, Creamer, Masonic Temple, Ruby Thumbprint, 1893 .... 25.00
Masonic, Cross, Jeweled, Enameled, Glass Outlined Symbols, 5 In............ 3450.00
Masonic, Cup & Saucer, Eastern Star, Demitasse 15.00
Masonic, Diploma, Royal Arch, Peter Schultz To Mark Master, Fold-Out, 1854 .... 75.00
Masonic, Hat, Feathered 40.00
Masonic, Loving Cup, Syria Shrine, Niagara Falls...................................... 120.00
Masonic, Medal, Washington's Death, 1799 .... 80.00
Masonic, Mirror, Knights Templar, Pocket 25.00

Masonic, Money Clip	30.00
Masonic, Watch Fob, Eagles	45.00
Masonic, Watch Fob, Masonic Emblem, Gold-Filled Chain	75.00
Odd Fellows, Badge, 3 Crosses, Ribbon, Black, White, Leather Case, Early 1920s	20.00
Odd Fellows, Medallion, Rope Necklace, 1934	100.00
Odd Fellows, Watch Fob, Chain	20.00
Shriner, Bowl, Ascalon Commandery, No. 59, K.T. Pittsburgh, Footed, Gold Trim, 1898	75.00
Shriner, Champagne, Alligators, Advertising	75.00
Shriner, Champagne, Rochester, Camel, Photographer	95.00
Shriner, Champagne, Syria, Pittsburgh, New Orleans, Alligator Handles, 1910	85.00
Shriner, Cup, Gold Sword Handle, Blown Out Indian, Saratoga, Pittsburgh, 1903	85.00
Shriner, Mug, 1911	12.00
Shriner, Plate, Los Angeles, 1906	35.00
Shriner, Tumbler, Gold, 1963, 6 Piece	36.00
Shriner, Tumbler, Lady Crying, I Want To Be A Shriner, Detroit, 1897	95.00

FRY GLASS was made by the H. C. Fry Glass Company of Rochester, Pennsylvania. The company, founded in 1901, first made cut glass and other types of fine glasswares. In 1922, they patented a heat-resistant glass called *Pearl Oven glass.* For two years, 1926–27, the company made Fry Foval, an opal ware decorated with colored trim. Reproductions of this glass have been made. Depression glass patterns made by Fry may be listed in the Depression Glass category. Some pieces of cut glass may also be included in the Cut Glass category.

FRY, Cake Plate, Floral, Royal Blue Handle, Cut Engraving	450.00
Creamer, Flower Engraving	75.00
Ivy Bowl, Fuchsia, Swirl Ball Connector	100.00
Pitcher, Green Handle, 64 Oz., 6 x 6 1/2 In.	55.00
Reamer	25.00
Vase, Oriole & Flower Design, Signed, 14 In.	320.00
FRY FOVAL, Candlestick, Cobalt Blue, 9 In., Pair	250.00
Casserole, Cover, 2 Qt.	28.00
Cup & Saucer, Cobalt Blue	60.00
Cup & Saucer, Opalescent	35.00
Grill Plate	25.00
Lemonade Set, Delft Blue, 9 Piece	1000.00
Teapot, White Opalescent Handle & Finial	195.00
Tumbler, Blue Applied Rim, 2 1/2 In.	65.00

FULPER is the mark used by the American Pottery Company of Flemington, New Jersey. The art pottery was made from 1910 to 1929. The firm had been making bottles, jugs, and housewares from 1805. Doll heads were made about 1928. The firm became Stangl Pottery in 1929. Fulper art pottery is admired for its attractive glazes and simple shapes.

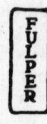

Ashtray, Frog, Seated On Edge	95.00
Bookends, Figural Face, Blue Drip Glaze	350.00
Bookends, Polar Bear, Feet In Air, Paws In Lap, White Matte Glaze, Signed, 7 1/2 In..	2100.00
Bookends, Rameses, Cucumber Green	800.00
Bottle, Dark Blue, Metallic Highlights, 3 Sides, Pinched Top, Ink Mark, 8 x 4 1/4 In....	137.00
Bowl, Flower Frog, Matte Purple, Ink Stamp, 1 3/4 x 6 In.	55.00
Bowl, Incised Collar Rim, Cafe-Au-Lait Matte Glaze, Signed, 6 x 8 1/2 In.	425.00
Bowl, Ivory To Mahogany Flambe Interior, Elephant's Breath Feet, 11 3/4 In.	660.00
Bowl, Scalloped Sides, Blue Matte, Glaze, Signed, 3 x 15 In.	440.00
Bowl, Stylized Square Leaves, Green, Yellow & Brown, Ink Stamp Mark, 3 1/2 x 8 In.	302.00
Candlestick, Blue Flambe, Crystalline Glaze Over Brown Glaze, 4 1/4 In., Pair	400.00
Doorstop, Chinese Cat, Sleeping, Mahogany Flambe, Label, 5 x 9 1/2 In.	705.00
Flask, Pilgrims, Mirror Green & Black, White Dripped Glaze, Ink Stamp, 10 In.	522.00
Flower Frog, Bird On Log	70.00
Jar, Matte Green, No. 564, 6 1/4 In.	260.00
Jug, Copper Dust Crystalline Glaze, Music Box In Base, Handle, 8 x 5 In.	165.00
Jug, Musical, Hexagonal, Flemington Green, 8 In.	195.00
Jug, Musical, How Dry I Am, 9 In.	250.00
Jug, Musical, How Dry I Am, Electroplated Sterling Sports Figures	175.00

Lamp, Apple Green Glaze, Silver Crystals, Claw-Footed Bronze Base, 19 In. 275.00
Lamp, Cutout Floral Design, Mica Shade, c.1925, 26 In. 3737.00
Lamp, Perfume, Ballerina, Pink 325.00
Lamp, Perfume, Cockatoo, Blue & Yellow Feathers, 13 x 5 1/2 In. 385.00
Lamp, Perfume, Girl In Pink Dress, Matching Hat, Hand Painted 225.00
Lamp, Perfume, Lady, Pink 185.00
Lamp, Perfume, Robin, Crimson Chest, Brown Feathers, 8 x 5 In. 550.00
Lamp Base, Bulbous, Tapered Body, Green & Gunmetal, 8 x 16 In. 165.00
Pitcher, Cider 175.00
Pitcher, Ice Lip, Cat's-Eye Glaze 250.00
Pot, Green, Crystalline, Drip Glaze, 6 1/2 x 12 In. 295.00
Powder Box, Art Deco Woman 150.00
Powder Box, Woman, Yellow & Orange Skirts, Hat, Holding Fan, Bisque 140.00
Tile, Ostrich Silhouette, Reeds, Matte Dark Green, Light Green Ground, Round, 6 In. .. 688.00
Urn, Green Over Cobalt Crystalline Glaze, Footed, Corseted Neck, Ink Mark, 9 1/2 In. 605.00
Vase, 2 Buttressed Handles, Copper Dust Crystalline Glaze, Signed, 9 1/2 In. 475.00
Vase, 7 Sides, Blue & Brown Drip Over Cream, 9 3/4 In. 440.00
Vase, 7 Sides, Blue To Mahogany To Ivory Flambe, Signed, 10 In. 440.00
Vase, 7 Sides, Chinese Blue To Mahogany To Ivory Flambe, Ink Mark, 10 x 5 1/2 In. . 523.00
Vase, Anniversary Sticker, 8 In. 150.00
Vase, Baluster Shape, 2 Handles, Royal Blue Ground, Green Glazes, 10 1/2 In. 483.00
Vase, Baluster Shape, Pale Green Glazes, Handles, Signed, 10 1/2 In. 483.00
Vase, Barrel Shape, Cobalt Blue To Ivory Flambe, Signed, 8 3/4 In. 412.00
Vase, Barrel Shape, Flowing Turquoise Flambe Glaze, Signed, 10 1/2 In. 350.00
Vase, Beehive, Brown To Mahogany Flambe, 2 Curved Handles, Stamped, 10 x 9 In. .. 357.00
Vase, Blue & Ivory Matte, Wisteria, No. 584, Signed 125.00
Vase, Blue Green, Over Pink, 7 1/2 In. 500.00
Vase, Brown Flambe, 6 In. 77.00
Vase, Bud, Green Matte Ground, Brown Drip, 6 In. 50.00
Vase, Cafe-Au-Lait Glaze, Ring Handles, Signed, 12 1/2 In. 475.00
Vase, Caramel Brown Glaze, 2 Handles, Ink Stamp, 6 x 5 3/4 In. 137.00
Vase, Carved Stems & Leaves, Geometric Hearts, Marked, 9 1/2 In. 286.00
Vase, Chinese Baluster Shape, Blue Flambe, Marked, 11 In. 395.00
Vase, Closed Rim & Base, Flowing Turquoise Flambe Glaze, Signed, 10 1/2 In. 350.00
Vase, Cobalt Blue Drip, Over Light Matte Blue Glaze, Acorn Shaped Base, 16 In. 1045.00
Vase, Cobalt Drip Glaze, Over White, Cylindrical, Paper Label, 8 1/2 x 4 3/4 In. 247.00
Vase, Copper Dust Over Green Glaze, Tapered Neck, 2 Handles From Top, 9 In. 495.00
Vase, Cucumber Glaze, 8 In. 175.00
Vase, Cylinder, Green Crystalline, Blue & Cream, 8 x 10 1/4 In. 465.00
Vase, Dark Blue & Yellow Flambe Glaze, Handles, Bulbous, Incised Oval Mark, 12 In. 495.00
Vase, Dark Green Flambe Dripping Glaze, Sandy Ground, Incised Mark, 5 x 6 In. 275.00
Vase, Flaring Rim, Wisteria Matte Finish, Signed, 11 3/4 In. 400.00
Vase, Flemington Green Luster Glaze, Rolled Rim, 6 x 3 1/2 In. 137.00
Vase, Flemington Green Over Cucumber Green, 17 In. 2000.00
Vase, Flemington Green, Gunmetal Drop, 8 In. 300.00
Vase, Flemington Green, Mirror Black Overglaze, Signed, 5 1/2 In. 125.00
Vase, Frothy Flambe Over Mustard Ground, Squatty, Signed, 7 3/4 x 10 In. 990.00
Vase, Green & Pink Matte Glaze, 3 Handles, Bullet, 6 3/4 x 5 In. 385.00
Vase, Green Over Rose Glaze, Signed, 13 1/2 In. 550.00
Vase, Ivory To Gun Metal To Blue Textured Flambe, Signed, 10 1/4 In. 522.00
Vase, Leopard Skin Crystalline Glaze, Drilled For Lamp, 17 In. 510.00
Vase, Leopard-Skin Glaze, 2 Handles, 12 In. 440.00
Vase, Mirror Black Overglaze, 9 1/4 In. 225.00
Vase, Mirror Black, Over Blue & Mauve Flambe, Bulbous, Oval Mark, 7 1/2 In. 385.00
Vase, Mirrored Black Gloss, Silver Crystals, Signed, 7 In. 495.00
Vase, Mission Matte Brown, No. 23, 5 x 7 In. 325.00
Vase, Olive To Blue Crystalline Flambe, Looping Handles, Signed, 11 1/2 In. 825.00
Vase, Rafco, Blue Crystalline Glaze, 4 1/2 In. 95.00
Vase, Raised Beads On Handles, Periwinkle Blue Glaze, Signed, 12 In. 990.00
Vase, Ribbed, Copper Dust, 13 In. 1050.00
Vase, Ribbed, Gunmetal Glaze, Tan Matte To Rim, 13 1/2 In. 425.00
Vase, Rouge Flambe Glaze, Bulbous Base, Cylindrical Neck, Racetrack Mark, 8 x 5 In. 247.00
Vase, Sage-Green Dripping Glaze, Sandy Ground, Squatty, Incised Mark, 5 x 6 In. 247.00

Vase, Semi-Matte Green Glaze, Small Opening, Ink Stamp, 3 x 5 In............................... 165.00
Vase, Tan, Green Overglaze, 8 In.. 175.00

FURNITURE of all types is listed in this category. Examples dating from the
seventeenth century to the 1950s are included. Prices for furniture vary in different parts of the country. Oak furniture is most expensive in the West; large
pieces over eight feet high are sold for the most money in the South, where
high ceilings are found in the old homes. Condition is very important when
determining prices. These are NOT average prices but rather reports of
unique sales. If the description includes the word *style*, the piece resembles
the old furniture style but was made at a later time. It is not a period piece.

Armchairs may also be listed under Chair in this category.
Armchair, A. Lorenzebent Beechwood, Leather.. 2300.00
Armchair, A. Waterhouse, Oak, Vertical Supports, Brown Hide, 1874.......................... 835.00
Armchair, Arched Floral Carved Crest, Silk, Pair 3450.00
Armchair, Arrowback, Foliage & Cornucopias With Fruit, Painted White, Pair 1650.00
Armchair, Art Deco, Sleigh Shape, Square Legs, American, 33 1/2 In., Pair.................. 1035.00
Armchair, Art Deco, Striped Silk Fabric, c.1925, Pair.. 2875.00
Armchair, Art Nouveau, Mahogany, Paw Footed, Crest, Vinyl Seat, Scrolled Arms 127.00
Armchair, Ash, Black Stained, Trapezoidal Plank Seat, H Stretcher, England, 49 In. 690.00
Armchair, Bamboo, Painted Black, 18-In. Seat, 34 In.. 495.00
Armchair, Banister Back, Maple, Carved, 1780-1800, 48 1/2 In. 2760.00
Armchair, Banister Back, Maple, Rush Seat, Painted, 1750 .... 1725.00
Armchair, Banister Back, Rush Seat, Painted & Turned Maple, c.1780........................ 4313.00
Armchair, Baroque Style, Walnut, Parcel Gilt, Leather, Pair 1840.00
Armchair, Baroque, Needlepoint, Arched Back, H Stretcher...................................... 4025.00
Armchair, Barrel Back, Mahogany, Upholstered, Open Arms, New York, 1830, Pair 10925.00
Armchair, Barrel Back, Rush Seat, Fruitwood, Open Arms, 1930s 70.00
Armchair, Belter, Rococo, Rosewood & Laminated, Serpentine Seat, Cabriole Legs 4180.00
Armchair, Belter, Rosalie Pattern 7500.00
Armchair, Belter, Scroll, Laminated Rosewood 1650.00
Armchair, Bembe & Kimbel, Carved Oak, Leather, Congress, 1857, 39 In. 6325.00
Armchair, Bentwood, Upholstered Back & Seat 258.00
Armchair, Biscuit Tufted Yoke Back, Trapezoidal Upholstered Seat, Casters 220.00
Armchair, Bow Back, Rush Seat, Stenciled Lion, Child's...................................... 330.00
Armchair, Bruno Methesson, Birch 1210.00
Armchair, Campeachy, Carved Walnut, Scrolled Arms, Louisiana, c.1850 .... 1650.00
Armchair, Carved Back & Arms, Cloud Design Splat, 19th Century, 37 In., Pair........... 460.00
Armchair, Carved Frame & Arms, Cabriole Legs, Upholstered, Continental, 38 In........ 357.00
Armchair, Carved Paw & Cornucopia Feet, Lyre Arms, Eaglehead Crest...................... 1555.00
Armchair, Carved Walnut, Claw Feet, Flowers, Needlepoint, France 1100.00
Armchair, Classical, Mahogany, Carved, Upholstered, c.1825, 33 1/2 In., Pair............. 3450.00
Armchair, Concave Back, Bowed Arms, Pierced Side Panels, c.1900, 39 3/4 In. 800.00
Armchair, Corner, Elmwood, 2 Pierced Splats, Reeded Columns, Drop-In Seat 1725.00
Armchair, Desk, Charles X, Mahogany, Tub Back, 1840... 935.00
Armchair, Donald Deskey, Rounded, Wooden Block Feet, Schmieg & Kotzian, 30 In. .. 1045.00
Armchair, Dutch Style, Carved Hardwood, Upholstered Seat, 53 In., Pair 979.00
Armchair, Eastlake, Walnut, Turned, Carved, Upholstered, Victorian, 33 1/2 In............ 55.00
Armchair, Edwardian, Paint Decorated, Pierced Back, Cane Seat, Spade Feet, 37 In. 460.00
Armchair, Edwardian, Satinwood, Cane, Paint Decorated 920.00
Armchair, Elizabethan Style, Carved Walnut, Caned Back & Seat 690.00
Armchair, Empire, Mahogany, Parcel Gilt, Upholstered Back, Dolphins' Heads, Pair ... 8625.00
Armchair, F.L. Wright, Price Tower, Cast Aluminum, Hexagonal Back, Red Trim........ 7700.00
Armchair, Finger Carved, Cabriole Legs, Button-Tufted Back, Open Arms, Victorian .. 110.00
Armchair, Finn Juhl, Chieftain, Teak Frame, Leather, 36 3/4 x 41 In. 1380.00
Armchair, Flemish Baroque Style, Walnut, 45 In. 345.00
Armchair, Franco-Flemish Style, Walnut, Floral Gros Point Cover 3220.00
Armchair, French Provincial, Cherrywood, Rush Seat, 1800 .... 385.00
Armchair, French Style, Brass Inlay In Crest, Fruitwood Veneer, Pair 165.00
Armchair, French Style, Button Tufted, Cabriole Legs 110.00
Armchair, George III Style, Mahogany, Late 19th Century, 39 In. 1380.00
Armchair, George III Style, Walnut, Late 19th Century, 38 1/2 In., Pair 745.00
Armchair, Georgian Style, Upholstered Back & Seat, Shell-Carved Knees, Pair 978.00

◆◆◆◆◆◆◆◆◆◆◆◆◆◆◆◆◆◆◆◆◆◆◆◆

To see if a worm hole is real or a fake made by a drill, use this test. Put a needle in the hole. If it goes in for more than 1/8 inch, the hole was made by a drill.

◆◆◆◆◆◆◆◆◆◆◆◆◆◆◆◆◆◆◆◆◆◆◆◆

Furniture, Armchair, Gilbert Rohde, Walnut,
Upholstered, 1930

Armchair, Gilbert Rohde, Streamline, Block Feet, Herman Miller, 31 x 45 In.	3850.00
Armchair, Gilbert Rohde, Walnut, Upholstered, 1930 .... *Illus*	3575.00
Armchair, Gilded Low Back, Tapestry Seat, Velvet Back, 27 In.	400.00
Armchair, Gio Ponti, Chrome, Red Vinyl, 1938	2500.00
Armchair, Gothic Revival, Carved Mahogany, Upholstered Seat, Arms, N.Y., 1850	4025.00
Armchair, Gothic Revival, Walnut, Carved Heads Of Dogs, Animal Claw Feet	345.00
Armchair, Gothic Revival, Walnut, Pointed Back, Foliate Finial	745.00
Armchair, Gustav Stickley, 3 Vertical Back Slats, Added Color, Leather Seat	1045.00
Armchair, Gustav Stickley, Morris, Curved Slate Back, No. 332, 1904	3680.00
Armchair, Heart And Crown, 5 Banisters, Rush Seat, Sausage-Turned Stretcher	550.00
Armchair, Hepplewhite, Mahogany, Prince Of Wales Shield Back, 39 In.	1200.00
Armchair, Hitchcock, Painted Black, Rush Seat, Stenciled Back, 20th Century	45.00
Armchair, Hitchcock, Rush Seat, Stenciled Over Grain Painting	135.00
Armchair, Islamic, Fruitwood, Mother-Of-Pearl Inlay, Damask, Pair	2090.00
Armchair, Italian Neoclassical Style, Walnut, Ribbon-Carved Crest, Pair	546.00
Armchair, J. & W. Meeks, Laminated Rosewood, Henry Ford Pattern, Pair	8800.00
Armchair, J. Hoffman, Bentwood, Padded Curved Back, c.1905, 30 1/2 In., Pair	435.00
Armchair, J. Hoffman, Bentwood, Upholstered Seat, Horseshoe Base, 29 In.	230.00
Armchair, Jacobean Style, Mahogany, Bobbin-Turned Frame, Upholstered, Pair	358.00
Armchair, Jacobean Style, Walnut, Acanthus-Carved Open Arms	100.00
Armchair, Jacobean, Oak, Turkey Work Cushion, 43 3/4 In.	1035.00
Armchair, L. & J.G. Stickley, Morris, Upholstered, Slat To Floor	6500.00
Armchair, L. & J.G. Stickley, No. 348, 3/4 Size Arms, Slat Back, Leather Seat, 38 In.	770.00
Armchair, Ladder Back, 3 Arched Slats, Paper Rush Seat, 58 In.	110.00
Armchair, Ladder Back, 4 Horizontal Slats, Rush Seat, Painted, 46 1/4 In., Pair	1725.00
Armchair, Ladder Back, 4 Slats, Sausage Turning, Rush Seat, 18th Century	1300.00
Armchair, Ladder Back, Hardwood, 5 Graduated Arched Slats, 45 In.	770.00
Armchair, Ladder Back, Mahogany, Pretzel-Carved Slats, Slip Seat, c.1780	5750.00
Armchair, Ladder Back, Maple & Hardwoods, 4 Slats, Turned Finials, 46 In.	275.00
Armchair, Ladder Back, Maple, 4 Graduated Slats, Rush Seat, 43 In.	1555.00
Armchair, Ladder Back, Painted Black, Rush Seat, Lemon Finials, Sausage Turnings	330.00
Armchair, Ladder Back, Painted Red, Scrolled Arms, Splint Seat	165.00
Armchair, Ladder Back, Painted Red, Woven Seat, New England, 42 x 17 In.	2185.00
Armchair, Ladder Back, Turned Finials & Stiles, Splint Seat	165.00
Armchair, Leaf-Carved Oval Back, Loose Cushion, Brocade, Pair	8625.00
Armchair, Library, Regency, Mahogany, Upholstered, 1820	303.00
Armchair, Lifetime, Horizontal Slat Over Upholstered Back, 27 In., Pair	1100.00
Armchair, Louis XIV, Carved Walnut, Tall Back, Tapestry, 1700	1100.00
Armchair, Louis XV Style, Carved Gesso & Giltwood, Foliate Crest, Pair	1035.00
Armchair, Louis XV Style, Giltwood, Upholstered, Serpentine Rails, Paris, Pair	8050.00
Armchair, Louis XV, Beechwood, Serpentine Top, Upholstered, Cabriole Legs	2300.00
Armchair, Louis XV, Giltwood, Upholstered Backrest, Carved Flower Heads, Pair	9200.00
Armchair, Louis XVI Style, Carved Frame, Needlepoint, 35 In.	302.00
Armchair, Louis XVI Style, Gilt, Medallion Back Crest, Silk, Pair	1430.00
Armchair, Louis XVI, Painted, Bowfront Seat, Upholstered, Late 18th Century	3795.00

Armchair, Mahogany, Leather Seat, Tooled Leather Back, c.1900 .... 160.00
Armchair, Mahogany, Pierced Backrest, Ring-Turned Spindles, Casters, Victorian 2587.00
Armchair, Mahogany, Upholstered Seat, St. John, Canada 950.00
Armchair, Maple & Ash, Norwich, Lebanon, 1680-1720, 45 1/2 In. 3735.00
Armchair, Marquetry, Barrel-Shaped Down Cushion, Holland, 19th Century 2300.00
Armchair, Martha Washington, Claw & Ball Feet, Brocade 715.00
Armchair, Modern, Bent & Laminated Wood & Steel Wire, Upholstered Seat, Pair 220.00
Armchair, Neoclassical, Mahogany, Birch, Pierced Backrest, Paw Feet, Italy 2300.00
Armchair, Neoclassical, Mahogany, Brass Mounted, Bowfront Seat, Russia, Pair............ 4600.00
Armchair, Neoclassical, Mahogany, Ebonized, Concave Back, Demilune, Pair.............. 7475.00
Armchair, Neoclassical, Mahogany, Painted, Parcel Gilt, Arched Back, Russia 6325.00
Armchair, Neoclassical, Mahogany, Parcel Gilt, Foliate-Scroll Top Rail, Russia, Pair .. 9200.00
Armchair, Norman Cherner, Bentwood, Walnut, Plycraft, 24 x 24 x 29 In. 185.00
Armchair, Oak, Painted Red, Spindle Back, Child's, Pair.. 110.00
Armchair, Oak, Pierced Splat & Crest, Block & Spool Sides.. 860.00
Armchair, Oak, Pierced Splat, Block & Spool Sides, Trapezoidal Seat, England 965.00
Armchair, Open Arms, Original Upholstery, Ball & Claw Feet, Victorian 950.00
Armchair, Oriental Style, Yoke Back, Square Legs, Brass Toe Caps 230.00
Armchair, Oriental, Native Wood, Mother-Of-Pearl Inlay Overall, Pair........................ 460.00
Armchair, Ottoman, Y. Ekstrom, Laminated Plywood, Sweden, c.1945, 39 3/4 In........ 1260.00
Armchair, P. Paulin, Brown Wool, 4-Legged Aluminum Pedestal, Artifort, 28 In.......... 305.00
Armchair, Paul Frankl, Bentwood, Black Finish, c.1928, 26 3/4 In. 690.00
Armchair, Plail Brothers, Curved Vertical Slats, Spring Seat, 40 1/2 In. 2300.00
Armchair, Porcelain Plaques, Laminated & Rosewood 770.00
Armchair, Queen Anne Style, Walnut, Upholstered Back & Seat, Pad Feet 172.00
Armchair, Queen Anne, Maple, Inversely Arched Crest, Splint Seat, 1760s................. 1725.00
Armchair, Queen Anne, Maple, Oxbow Crest, Spanish Feet, Bulbous Stretcher............ 4125.00
Armchair, Raj Style, Rosewood, Rattan Seat 895.00
Armchair, Red Lacquer, Polychrome Decoration, China, 36 In. 865.00
Armchair, Red Leather, Chromed Tubular Steel, Jazz U.S.A. 100.00
Armchair, Regency, Beechwood, Silk Cushion Back & Seat, c.1730............................ 8050.00
Armchair, Restauration, Mahogany, Swan Arms, Silk, 1840, Pair............................... 4180.00
Armchair, Rococo Continental, Cartouche Backrest, Upholstered, 18th Century........... 4025.00
Armchair, Rococo Revival, Mahogany, Upholstered, Victorian, 42 In. 165.00
Armchair, Rococo Revival, Walnut, Rose Crest, Velvet, Victorian 140.00
Armchair, Rococo, Parcel Gilt, Cartouche-Shaped Back, Serpentine Front, Italy 5175.00
Armchair, Shaker, Maple, Straw-Filled Seat, Mt. Lebanon, c.1880, 38 In. 110.00
Armchair, Shaker, Maple, Taped Seat, Mt. Lebanon, N.Y., c.1880, 39 In., Pair 2420.00
Armchair, Shaker, Mt. Lebanon, No. 1, Taped Seat, Child's, 28 In. 1925.00
Armchair, Shaker, Red & Black Taped Seat, No. 5, Mt. Lebanon, Pair 2420.00
Armchair, Sheraton, Figural Carved Star Burst Panel, c.1800, 40 In............................ 2000.00
Armchair, Slat Back, Mule Ear, Taped Seat 110.00
Armchair, T. Molesworth, Leather, Chimayo Cushion, 1948 .... 9500.00
Armchair, Walnut, Burl Veneer Trim, Velvet, Tufted Back, Victorian, 36 In. 165.00
Armchair, Walnut, Ebony, Triangular Top, Carved & Turned Finials, c.1870 .... 5850.00
Armchair, Walnut, Floral & Shell Crest Rail, Cabriole Legs, Open Arms, Victorian 190.00
Armchair, Walnut, Foliate & Fruit Carved Crest Rail 258.00
Armchair, Walnut, Parcel Gilt, Ebonized, Padded Back, Victorian, 40 1/2 In............... 1610.00
Armchair, Walter, Curule Base, Spindle Stretcher, Crushed Velvet, Victorian 248.00
Armchair, Warren McArthur, Spun Aluminum, Upholstered Seat, c.1920, 21 In. 1650.00
Armchair, Warren McArthur, Tubular Aluminum, Leather, 1913, Pair 7800.00
Armchair, Warren Platner, Upholstered 700.00
Armchair, Weathered Gray, Carved, Face Crest, Upholstered, 20th Century 360.00
Armchair, Wicker, Magazine Racks On Each Side 120.00
Armchair, William & Mary Style, Walnut, Center Caned Back Panel, Miniature 800.00
Armchair, Windsor Style, Hoop Back, Maple, 4 .... 287.00
Armchair, Windsor, 7 Spindle Back, Oval Seat, Scrolled Arm Ends 825.00
Armchair, Windsor, Bow Back, Bamboo, 9 Spindle Back, Black Painted, 37 In............ 880.00
Armchair, Windsor, Bow Back, Continuous Arm, Black Finish, 19th Century, 37 In. 325.00
Armchair, Windsor, Bow Back, Knuckle Arms, Spindle Back, 38 1/2 In....................... 1100.00
Armchair, Windsor, Bow Back, Oak, Pierced Splat, Miniature.................................... 2070.00
Armchair, Windsor, Bow Back, Painted Black, H Stretcher, Knuckle Arms, 38 In......... 2200.00
Armchair, Windsor, Bow Back, Painted Red, 37 1/2 In. 1430.00

Furniture, Armchair, Windsor,
Sack Back, Grain Painted,
1750, 43 In.

♦ ♦ ♦ ♦ ♦ ♦ ♦ ♦ ♦ ♦ ♦ ♦ ♦ ♦ ♦ ♦ ♦ ♦ ♦

Serious collecting of antique furniture began in the 1920s. Fakers began to make great pieces from average pieces. Butterfly tables were made from tavern tables, block-front bureaus from plain bureaus; inlaid eagles and other designs were added to furniture and clocks. Plain highboys were 'improved' with scroll tops. Plain legs of tea tables were carved. Birdcage supports and piecrust edges were added to plain tables.

♦ ♦

Armchair, Windsor, Bow Back, Saddle Seat, Spindle Back, Grain, Repainted	220.00
Armchair, Windsor, Brace Back, Painted Green, c.1780, 37 In.	2185.00
Armchair, Windsor, Comb Back, D-Shaped Plank Seat, Pa., 18th Century	5750.00
Armchair, Windsor, Continuous Arm, Dark Brown Varnish	1980.00
Armchair, Windsor, Continuous Arm, Painted Black, c.1780, 36 1/2 In.	1600.00
Armchair, Windsor, Fan Back, Painted Black, New England, c.1780, 40 1/2 In.	1380.00
Armchair, Windsor, Oak & Yew, Paint Traces, England, 18th Century, Pair	1650.00
Armchair, Windsor, Painted Black, Continuous Arm, Saddle Seat, 39 In.	395.00
Armchair, Windsor, Sack Back, Grain Painted, 1750, 43 In. .... *Illus*	2760.00
Armchair, Windsor, Sack Back, Painted Black, New England, c.1780, 37 In.	1725.00
Armchair, Windsor, Sack Back, Painted, Carved Knuckle Arms, c.1780	2300.00
Armchair, Windsor, Saddle Seat, Bulbous Turned Stretcher, 7-Spindle Back	440.00
Armchair, Windsor, Spindle Bow Back, Saddle Seat, 37 In.	670.00
Armchair, Windsor, Wallace Nutting, Comb Back, No. 415	415.00
Armchair, Wing, George II, Walnut, Bowed Seat, Acanthus Carved Legs	9200.00
Armchair, Wing, Mahogany, Serpentine Crest, Ogival Wings, Loose Cushion	4315.00
Armchair Set, Boardroom Type, Mahogany, Leather, Nail Trim, 1930, 6	4500.00
Armoire, American Gothic, Mahogany, Cornice, 1840, 89 x 78 In. .... *Illus*	2475.00
Armoire, Baltic Neoclassical, Mahogany, Frieze Drawer, Paw Feet, 34 x 24 In.	1840.00
Armoire, Burl Walnut, Carved, Birch Lined, France, 98 In.	3800.00
Armoire, C.A. Baudouine, Rococo, Rosewood, Mirrored Door, 101 x 42 x 21 In.	4180.00
Armoire, Continental, Pine, Painted Blue, Flowers, 2 Drawers, 1 Door, 37 x 70 In.	525.00
Armoire, Diamond Pattern Veneer, Gilt Bronze Mounted, Maple, c.1940, 64 In.	4025.00
Armoire, Empire, Gothic Paneled Doors, Ogee Bracket Feet, Louisiana, 1835	1760.00
Armoire, Fall Front, Oak, Paneled Doors, Fitted, Continental, 75 x 79 In.	2090.00
Armoire, French Provincial, Arch Top, 1 Base Drawer, 1780, 84 x 46 x 17 In.	1550.00
Armoire, French Provincial, Cherry, 2 Paneled Doors, 90 In.	4600.00
Armoire, French Provincial, Oak, Scroll Feet, 1800, 98 x 54 x 20 In.	3300.00
Armoire, George III Style, Bowfront, 3 Doors, Ball & Claw, Oval, 72 x 63 x 24 In.	550.00
Armoire, Hand-Cut Dovetailing, Beveled Mirrors, Victorian, 7 Ft.	2900.00
Armoire, Louis XV, Provincial, Fruitwood, Marquetry, 2 Wirework Doors	2750.00
Armoire, Louis XV, Provincial, Paneled Doors, 84 x 51 x 24 In. .... *Illus*	3520.00
Armoire, Mahogany, 2 Doors, Egg & Dart Frieze, New Orleans, Victorian, 98 In.	2420.00
Armoire, Mahogany, Mirror, 1 Door, Base Drawer	3500.00
Armoire, Mahogany, Molded & Paneled Doors, Lower Drawer, Mid-19th Century	1045.00
Armoire, Mirrored Door, String-Banded Shelves, c.1840	2090.00
Armoire, Napoleon III, Marquetry, Bombe Form, 1860, 78 x 60 x 19 In.	880.00
Armoire, Oak, 2 Doors, Molded Cornice, 1880	895.00

Furniture, Armoire, American Gothic,
Mahogany, Cornice, 1840, 89 x 78 In

Furniture, Armoire, Louis XV, Provincial, Paneled Doors, 84 x 51 x 24 In.

Furniture, Armoire, Rococo,
Rosewood, Bonnet Top, 1900s,
123 x 65 x 24 In.

Furniture, Armoire,
Walnut, 2 Doors,
Germany, 18th
Century,
89 x 60 In.

Armoire, Olive Wood Veneer, Mahogany, Marquetry, Mirrored Doors, 98 In.	2750.00
Armoire, Provincial, Carved Walnut, Pine, Canted Cornice, Paneled Doors, 81 In.	1870.00
Armoire, Rococo, Rosewood, Bonnet Top, 1900s, 123 x 65 x 24 In. ....*Illus*	10450.00
Armoire, Rosewood, Dome-Curved Top, Victorian, 1830, 89 x 44 x 18 In.	1430.00
Armoire, Rosewood, Mirror Front, Arched Cornice, 5 Shelves, Victorian, 87 In.	2310.00
Armoire, Rosewood, Oval Mirrored Door, Crest, Paneled Maple Interior, 1 Drawer	4950.00
Armoire, Victorian, Walnut, Burl Walnut Veneers, Double Door, 111 In.	2200.00
Armoire, Walnut, 2 Doors Over Drawer Base, 1880, 7 1/2 Ft.	1250.00
Armoire, Walnut, 2 Doors, Germany, 18th Century, 89 x 60 In. ....*Illus*	2760.00
Armoire, Walnut, Dome Top, Carved, Mirror, 1860, 50 x 50 x 20 In.	715.00
Armoire, Walnut, Double Door, Ogee Molded Cornice, 90 1/2 x 60 1/2 In.	1650.00
Baker's Rack, Brass, Iron, 3 Shelves, Sheaf Of Wheat Cornice, 88 x 28 In.	575.00
Banquettes, Regency Style, Beech, Marble, Serpentine Frieze, 42 x 17 In., Pair	3000.00
Bar, Art Deco, Oak, 4 Doors, 1930	695.00
Bed, 21 Spindles Between Posts, Arts & Crafts, 3/4 Size, 42 x 75 In.	605.00

Furniture, Bed, Four-Poster,
Mahogany, Cornucopia,
90 x 50 x 90 In.

Furniture, Bed, Brass, French Style, Foliate
Scrollwork, 39 x 78 x 53 In.

Bed, Bentwood, Open Scrolls, Cane Sides, Arched Head & Footboard, Art Nouveau.... 2420.00
Bed, Brass, French Style, Foliate Scrollwork, 39 x 78 x 53 In. .... *Illus* 550.00
Bed, Cannonball, Maple, c.1840, 50 x 51 In. 225.00
Bed, Canopy, Chamfered & Fluted Posts, Crewel Hangings, Mahogany, Double Size... 360.00
Bed, Canopy, Cherry, Reeded Posts, c.1820 .... 3200.00
Bed, Canopy, Federal, Birch, Stained Red, New England, c.1815, 77 x 54 x 70 In. ... 4025.00
Bed, Canopy, Federal, Maple, Tall Post, c.1820, 72 x 48 x 72 In. 1610.00
Bed, Canopy, Rosewood, India Raj Era, Double Size 4800.00
Bed, Canopy, Twig, Painted White, No Bark, Country, Ohio 4250.00
Bed, Chippendale, Tall Post, Curly Maple, Scrolling, 72 x 80 x 60 In. 3000.00
Bed, Double, Maple, Carved Pineapples & Flowers, Turned Head & Foot Rails 525.00
Bed, Eastlake Style, Ivy Spoon Carving, Twin Size 700.00
Bed, Empire, Mahogany, Ormolu, Boat-Shaped Rail, Masks, 85 x 43 In. 6900.00
Bed, Eric Bagge, Pollarded Elm & Bird's-Eye Maple, c.1927, 6 Ft. 8 In. 5175.00
Bed, Federal, Maple, Shaped Headboard, Ring & Baluster Turned Legs, 61 In. 1380.00
Bed, Field, Peaked Headboard, Pine & Poplar, 28 1/2 x 71 1/2 In. 55.00
Bed, Four-Poster, Carved Wheat Ears, Fluted, Mahogany, 7 Ft. x 5 Ft. 8 In. 4887.00
Bed, Four-Poster, Davis Cabinet Co., Spool 925.00
Bed, Four-Poster, Federal Style, Carved Mahogany, Double Size 700.00
Bed, Four-Poster, Federal, Tester, Mahogany, Fluted Columns, 87 x 68 x 84 In. 805.00
Bed, Four-Poster, Mahogany, Carved Posts, 1840, 84 In. 1750.00
Bed, Four-Poster, Mahogany, Cornucopia, 90 x 50 x 90 In. .... *Illus* 7425.00
Bed, Four-Poster, Mahogany, Reeded Posts, Leaf, 85 x 59 x 76 In. .... *Illus* 5060.00
Bed, Four-Poster, Mahogany, Scroll Crest, New Orleans, 1850s, 92 x 71 x 62 In. 6600.00
Bed, Four-Poster, Mahogany, Wm. McCracken, 1850 .... *Illus* 11000.00
Bed, Four-Poster, Maple, Acorn Finials, Turned & Baluster Supports, 44 x 55 In. 1155.00
Bed, Four-Poster, Sheraton, Carved Mahogany, Crotch Veneer, c.1810 .... 4675.00
Bed, Four-Poster, Sheraton, Mahogany, Scalloped Headboard, American, c.1810 .... 4675.00
Bed, Frank Lloyd Wright, Oak, Equal Ends, 78 In., Pair 2070.00
Bed, Gustav Stickley, Vertical Posts, 5 Wide Slats, c.1907, Double Size 725.00
Bed, Half-Tester, Mahogany, Sunburst Medallion, 103 x 52 In. .... *Illus* 4950.00
Bed, Half-Tester, Rococo, Carved Mahogany, New Orleans, 100 x 60 x 81 In. 7700.00
Bed, Half-Tester, Walnut .... *Illus* 14300.00
Bed, Iron, Brass Trim, White Paint, Rails, Single, 59 1/2 In. 137.00
Bed, Lincoln, Walnut, High Back, c.1840, 9 Ft. 4500.00
Bed, Low Post, Mahogany, Acanthus-Carved Arched Head & Footboard, Pair 2530.00
Bed, Mahogany, Acorn & Leaf Urn Finial, Claw Feet, Victorian, 75 x 38 In., Pair 1045.00
Bed, Murphy, Beveled Mirror On Front Of Case 1100.00
Bed, Murphy, Oak, Side-By-Side Chest, Mirror, 79 x 55 x 30 In. .... *Illus* 2530.00
Bed, Neo Grec, Ebonized, Victorian, 76 x 58 x 86 In. .... *Illus* 2750.00
Bed, Oak, Carved Scrolls, Foliate Foot & Headboard, Victorian, Youth, 34 In. 230.00
Bed, Opium, Mother-Of-Pearl & Marble Inlay, Native Wood, 77 x 50 1/2 In. 1725.00

Furniture, Bed, Four-Poster, Mahogany,
Reeded Posts, Leaf,
85 x 59 x 76 In.

Furniture, Bed, Four-Poster,
Mahogany, Wm. McCracken,
1850

Bed, Painted Red, New England, 1810, Twin Size 2200.00
Bed, Plantation, Full-Tester, Mahogany, Square Posts, Damask, 102 x 80 In. 4950.00
Bed, R. Thompson, Adzed Paneled Oak, Horsehair Mattress, 40 3/4 In., Pair 1775.00
Bed, Red Wash, Square Nails, Child's, 1840.. 150.00
Bed, Renaissance Revival, 1860s, Double Size, 89 x 57 In. 1495.00
Bed, Renaissance Revival, Walnut, Burl Walnut, 57 x 89 In... 1500.00
Bed, Rope, Cannonball, Painted Red, Scrolled Headboard, Rails, 52 x 50 In. 495.00
Bed, Rope, Cannonball, Tiger Maple, Scrolled Headboard, Single Size 265.00
Bed, Rope, Cherry, Scrolled Broken Arch Headboard, Ball Finials, 3/4 Size................. 450.00
Bed, Rope, Cherry, Turned Posts & Rails, 28 1/2 x 75 1/2 In. 495.00
Bed, Rope, Curly Maple, Square Posts, Paneled Headboard, Blanket Rail Foot............. 3575.00
Bed, Rope, Curly Maple, Turned Posts, Shaped Headboard, Rails, 52 x 72 x 32 In. 715.00
Bed, Rope, Maple, Turned Posts, Attached Canopy Frame, 65 In. 1650.00
Bed, Rope, Poplar, Mushroom-Type Turned Posts... 525.00
Bed, Rope, Tall Post, Maple, Acorn Finials, Blanket Rail, 80 x 93 x 70 In. 1485.00
Bed, Rope, Tiger Maple, Turned Finials, Square Posts, 1840s, 7 Ft................................ 4500.00
Bed, Shaker, Maple & Pine, Painted Green-Blue, Wooden Rollers, 6 Ft. 1 In. x 3 Ft. 770.00
Bed, Sheraton, Red & Black, Design On Rails, Double Size.. 1100.00
Bed, Sleigh, Classical, Mahogany, Serpentine Head & Foot, 44 x 49 x 78 In. 4600.00
Bed, Sleigh, Empire, Mahogany, Flame Veneer, S-Curve Head & Foot, 64 x 44 In. 605.00
Bed, Sleigh, Mahogany, Scroll Form, Scalloped Side Rails, 40 x 53 3/4 In. 1210.00
Bed, Sleigh, Mahogany, Twin Size 70.00
Bed, Sleigh, Pine, Grape Design... 1320.00
Bed, Sleigh, Tiger Maple, Double Size 3750.00
Bed, Tall Post, Cherry & Maple, Late 18th Century, 47 1/2 In.. 4025.00
Bed, Tall Post, Federal, Mahogany, Carved, Inlaid, c.1800, 87 x 54 x 7 1/2 In.............. 2645.00
Bed, Tall Post, Sheraton, Walnut, Flat Canopy Frame, 72 In. 1450.00
Bed, Tester, Arched Headboard, Serpentine Footboard, Vasiform Capitals, c.1835........ 2550.00
Bed, Tester, Federal, Butternut, Arched Headboard, 67 In., Pair...................................... 690.00
Bed, Tester, George III, Mahogany, 19th Century, 88 x 75 x 54 In..........................*Illus* 1760.00
Bed, Tester, Mahogany, Acanthus Urn-Turned Posts, 70 1/2 In. 2240.00
Bed, Tester, Mahogany, Carved, Salem, McIntyre School, Double Size 8800.00
Bed, Tester, Mahogany, Everted Crest Head & Footboard, American, 100 In. 5225.00
Bed, Tester, Rosewood, Silk Hangings..11500.00
Bed, Tester, Sheraton, Mahogany, Scalloped Headboard, Drapery, c.1810.................... 675.00
Bed, Tester, Walnut, Victorian, 92 x 73 x 54 In. ....*Illus* 2420.00
Bed, Turned Post, Hinged Frame, Single Size.. 165.00
Bed & Dresser, Louis XV Style, Brass Inlay, Copper & Mother-Of-Pearl 7500.00

*Furniture, Bed, Half-Tester,
Mahogany, Sunburst
Medallion, 103 x 52 In.*

Furniture, Bed, Half-Tester, Walnut

*Furniture, Bed, Murphy, Oak,
Side-By-Side Chest, Mirror,
79 x 55 x 30 In.*

Bed Steps, Ceramic Chamber Pot, Carpet Covered, 1850s, 16 1/4 x 17 In.	220.00
Bed Steps, Federal, Mahogany, 19th Century, 26 In.	460.00
Bed Steps, Wallace Nutting, Mahogany	470.00
Bedroom Set, Burl Walnut, Acorns, Floral, Marble, 3 Piece	2750.00
Bedroom Set, Chippendale Style, Mahogany, Mahogany Veneer, c.1930, 5 Piece	825.00
Bedroom Set, Cottage, Landscapes Medallion, Gray-Green, Single Bed, 8 Piece	1250.00
Bedroom Set, John Widdicomb, Carved Walnut, Hand-Painted Reserves, 6 Piece	6050.00
Bedroom Set, Mahogany, Sleigh Bed, Dolphins, 3 Piece	2000.00
Bedroom Set, Oak, Carved, Brass Handles, 3 Piece	1650.00
Bedroom Set, Oak, Carved, Oval Mirror Dresser, Commode, 3 Piece	1815.00
Bedroom Set, Pine, Design, Commode, Bureau, Night Stand, Chairs, 6 Piece	1100.00
Bedroom Set, Rococo Revival, Burl Walnut, Carved, Marble Top, 3 Piece	4400.00
Bedroom Set, Rococo Revival, Rosewood, Marble Top, Victorian, 2 Piece	3080.00
Bedroom Set, Rococo, Serpentine, Dresser & Armoire, Victorian, 1890, 3 Piece	2750.00
Bedroom Set, Spoon-Carved Oak, 4 Piece	500.00
Bedroom Set, Thomas Brooks, Rosewood, White Marble Top, Crest, 3 Piece	9900.00
Bedroom Set, Walnut, Bed, 97 1/2-In. Dresser, Victorian	9400.00
Bedroom Set, Walnut, Shell, Scroll & Foliate Carving, Gilt, Victorian, 2 Piece	5775.00
Bench, Arts & Crafts, Limbert, Oak, 4 Square Cutouts, Leather Cushion, 24 In.	4500.00
Bench, Bucket, Pine, 48 x 48 In.	330.00
Bench, Carnival, Arm Rests In Shape Of Animal, Seascape Painted On Back	4400.00
Bench, Carved Swan, Small	275.00
Bench, Country French Style, Walnut, Upholstered Seat, Carved Apron, 31 In.	345.00
Bench, Country French, Pine, Needlepoint, Cabriole Legs, 30 In.	110.00
Bench, Crock, Dovetailed Top Board, Mortised Shelves, Painted Red	180.00
Bench, Curule, Neo-Classical, Fruitwood, Silk, Greek Key Rail, 20 In.	495.00
Bench, Deacon's, Arrow-Back, Stenciled, Short	1760.00
Bench, Deacon's, Grain Painted, 9 Ft. 6 In.	275.00
Bench, Deacon's, Painted Black, Gold Stenciled, Pa., Scroll Arms	700.00
Bench, Deacon's, Rocking	600.00

Furniture, Bed, Tester, George III, Mahogany, 19th Century, 88 x 75 x 54 In.

Furniture, Bed, Tester, Walnut, Victorian, 92 x 73 x 54 In.

Bench, Ebonized Wooden Top & Legs, Slat, Leather Cushion, 72 In. 935.00
Bench, F.L. Wright, Angled Ends, 4 Short Legs, Plank Stretcher, Cypress, 73 In. 2990.00
Bench, Fiberglass, Figural, Couple Embracing Form Back, Lap Is Seat 185.00
Bench, Fireside, Brass, Olive Leather Padded Seat, England, 60 x 22 In. 1380.00
Bench, Fireside, Rococo Style, Carved Mahogany, Upholstered, 43 In. 770.00
Bench, Fireside, Wrought Iron, Velvet Seat 120.00
Bench, George II, Walnut, Needlepoint, 15 1/2 x 18 1/2 In. 1265.00
Bench, George Nelson, Slat, 6 Legs 2500.00
Bench, Georgian Style, Mahogany, Upholstered Slip Seat, Carved Rails, 21 In. 200.00
Bench, Greene & Greene, Inglenook, Fir & Oak, Paneled Back, 79 x 25 x 54 In. 2530.00
Bench, Gustav Stickley, Horizontal Slat Back, Tenon, Leather Seat, 40 In. 8800.00
Bench, Kneeling, Pine, 67 1/2 In. 55.00
Bench, Louis XV Style, 16 x 17 x 13 In. 85.00
Bench, Louis XV Style, Gros Point, Oak, 19 x 38 In. 920.00
Bench, Louis XVI Style, A.A. Rateau, Painted, Parcel Gilt, Upholstered, 70 1/2 In. 4312.00
Bench, Mahogany, Needlepoint Seat, 23 In. 185.00
Bench, Mahogany, Shell & Foliage Carved Back, X Shaped Legs, 50 In. 575.00
Bench, Piano, French Provincial, Fruitwood, Floral Upholstered Seat, 34 In. 405.00
Bench, Piano, Needlepoint, Petit Point Birds 330.00
Bench, Piano, Roycroft, Keyed-Through-Tenons, No. 71, 42 In. 4125.00
Bench, Plank Seat, Painted Red-Brown, Child's 85.00
Bench, Railroad Station, Folding, 19th Century 950.00
Bench, Regency Style, Walnut, Needlework, Tasseled Fringe, 34 In. 1840.00
Bench, Regency, Parcel Gilt, Ebonized, Cane Seat, 38 x 22 In., Pair 9200.00
Bench, Renaissance Style, Walnut, Armless, Needlepoint, c.1920 .... 690.00
Bench, Roycroft, Ash, No. 046, Ali Baba, Bark Exterior, 42 In. 6900.00
Bench, Shaker, Oak, Blue-Green Painted Top, Salmon Base, 19 x 37 x 11 1/2 In. 220.00
Bench, Shaker, Visitor's, Pierced Laminated Seat, Our Sabbath Home, 77 In. 880.00
Bench, Shoe Shine, Oak, 3 Seat, Brass Foot Rests, Marble On Pedestal, 85 In. 2090.00
Bench, Trolley, Reversible Back, 96 In. 190.00
Bench, U-Shaped Seat, Spindle Legs, Stained, Victorian 170.00
Bench, Water, Ash & Pine, Cutout Feet, Shelf In Base, Recessed Top, 44 1/2 In. 770.00
Bench, Water, Painted Green, 42 In. 175.00
Bench, Water, Painted Pine, Step-Back Top Shelf, 46 In. 2145.00
Bench, Water, Pine, 2 Doors In Base, Shelves Mortised Through Ends, 64 In. 1705.00
Bench, Water, Pine, 4 Shelves, 58 1/2 In. 1650.00
Bench, Water, Pine, Dovetailed Corners, Cutout Feet, 30 x 39 1/2 In. 385.00
Bench, Willow, Folk Art Design, Arms, S.C. 2650.00
Bench, Window, Edwardian, Boxwood, Hinged Cushion Seat, c.1900 .... 220.00
Bench, Window, William IV, Rosewood, Padded Sides, Cushion Seat, 47 In. 920.00
Bench, Windsor, D-Shaped Seat, Low Rail Back, 8 Bamboo-Turned Legs 9800.00

◆◆◆◆◆◆◆◆◆◆◆◆◆◆◆◆◆◆◆◆◆

To remove wet glass rings from furniture, first try rubbing in a little cigar ash to open the finish lightly. If this doesn't work, thoroughly rub in a nondrying oil such as lemon or almond oil. Follow with a regular paste wax. The same procedure can be used to remove white marks caused by heat.

◆◆◆◆◆◆◆◆◆◆◆◆◆◆◆◆◆◆◆◆◆

Furniture, Bed, Neo Grec, Ebonized, Victorian,
76 x 58 x 86 In.

Bergere, Art Nouveau, Carved Giltwood, Upholstered, Scroll Feet	1200.00
Bergere, Regency, Beechwood, Arched Padded Back, Senelepere, c.1709	7815.00
Bergere, Regency, Ebonized, Curved Inset Backrest, Drop-In Seat, Saber Legs	3165.00
Bibliotheque, Charles X, Fruitwood, Flared Rectangular Cornice, 76 x 80 3/4 In.	9775.00
Bonheur Du Jour, Napoleon III, Writing Drawer, Gallery, Sevres Mount, 1860	3575.00
Book Rack, Mahogany, Divided Center Compartment, 1 Drawer, 36 x 25 In.	375.00
Book Stand, Stickley Bros., 3 Tiers, 2 Small Over Long Rack, Metal Tag, 42 In.	1650.00
Book Stand, Two Hinged Sections, Carved Rocaille, Paw Feet, Italy, 13 x 17 In.	1035.00
Book Trough, Gustav Stickley, 2 Lower Shelves, Tenon & Key, 32 x 10 In.	1210.00
Book Trough, Gustav Stickley, Half Circle Cutouts At Sides, Black Finish, 31 In.	3025.00
Book Trough, Stickley, Half-Circle Cutout Sides, Black Finish, 30 x 10 x 31 In.	3025.00
Bookcase, 2 Doors, 5 Adjustable Shelves, Quartersawn Oak, 99 1/2 In.	935.00
Bookcase, Biedermeier Style, Birch, Part Ebonized, Open Shelves, 57 In.	1380.00
Bookcase, Cherrywood, String Inlay, 2 Doors, Gothic Panels, 73 x 53 In.	2640.00
Bookcase, Eastlake, Ebonized Finish, 3 Drawer Base, 42 1/2 x 50 In.	357.00
Bookcase, Eastlake, Walnut, 2 Glass Doors, 2 Base Drawers, c.1880, 66 x 50 In.	1035.00
Bookcase, Eastlake, Walnut, Burl Veneer, 3 Adjustable Shelves, 31 x 11 x 63 In.	250.00
Bookcase, Empire Revival, Mahogany, 1 Door, Fluted Flanking Columns	600.00
Bookcase, Federal, Mahogany, 2 Doors, 1810, 67 x 48 In.	3500.00
Bookcase, Frank Lloyd Wright, Mahogany, 3 Gilt Edged Shelves, 1923, 48 In.	2760.00
Bookcase, French Provincial, Oak, Carved Doors, Beveled Glass Panels, 71 In.	1725.00
Bookcase, George Nakashima, Headboard, 2 Sliding Doors, 54 In.	635.00
Bookcase, Gustav Stickley, 1 Door, 16 Panes, Decal, 56 In.	4025.00
Bookcase, Gustav Stickley, 2 Doors, 8 Panes, Decal & Label, No. 716, 56 In.	8250.00
Bookcase, Gustav Stickley, 2 Doors, 8 Panes Each Door, Oak, c.1902, 56 In.	6325.00
Bookcase, Gustav Stickley, 2 Doors, 8 Panes Each, No. 717, 56 In.	4125.00
Bookcase, Gustav Stickley, 2 Doors, Slab Sides, No. 542, 56 x 36 x 12 1/4 In.	6325.00
Bookcase, Gustav Stickley, Oak, 2 Doors, No. 716, c.1909, 56 x 43 12 In.	4025.00
Bookcase, Kingwood, Ebonized Fret, Lion Marquetry, 37 x 13 x 68 In.	2070.00
Bookcase, L. & J.G. Stickley, 1 Door, 16 Panes, Keyed-Tenon, No. 641, 55 In.	6050.00
Bookcase, L. & J.G. Stickley, 2 Doors, No. 645, Oak, 55 1/4 In.	5465.00
Bookcase, L. & J.G. Stickley, 8 Panes, Double Doors, No. 643, 40 x 12 x 55 In.	4125.00
Bookcase, L. & J.G. Stickley, Open, 4 Shelves, Keyed Tenons, No. 646, 55 In.	2425.00
Bookcase, Lifetime, 1 Door Overlaid With 10 Small Sections, No. 7218, 55 In.	1980.00
Bookcase, Lifetime, 4 Shelves, 1 Door, Copper Pull, No. 7360, 31 x 58 In.	1200.00
Bookcase, Lifetime, Oak, Medium Finish, No. 727, c.1910, 56 x 48 1/8 In.	1495.00
Bookcase, Limbert, 8 Pane Doors, Copper Hardware, 8 Shelves, 1907, 60 In.	2185.00
Bookcase, Limbert, Oak, 4 Shelves	525.00
Bookcase, Limbert, Oak, Backsplash, Wicker Panels, No. 801-22, 60 In.	3400.00
Bookcase, Limbert, Single Door, 6 Panes, 4 Shelves, Copper Pulls, No. 377	1500.00

Furniture, Bookcase, Queen Anne, Walnut,
Mirror Doors, 82 In.

◆◆◆◆◆◆◆◆◆◆◆◆◆◆◆◆◆◆◆◆◆◆

The eighteenth-century bookcase had shelves that were
placed symmetrically. If the
bottom shelf is 8 inches from
the bottom, the top shelf
should be 8 inches from the
top. If the permanent grooves
for the shelves are not
spaced this way, look carefully to be sure you have an
antique piece.

◆◆◆◆◆◆◆◆◆◆◆◆◆◆◆◆◆◆◆◆◆◆

Bookcase,	Louis Philippe Style, Walnut, 4 Grillwork Doors, 94 x 84 In.	1265.00
Bookcase,	Mahogany, Peaked Pediment, Glazed Doors, Germany, 73 In.	6900.00
Bookcase,	Mission, Oak, c.1910, 54 x 39 x 13 In.	400.00
Bookcase,	Neoclassical, Mahogany, Canted Corners, Brass Mounts, Russia, 22 In.	2875.00
Bookcase,	Oak, 2 Glazed Doors, Lower Paneled Cupboard Doors, 92 In.	2300.00
Bookcase,	Oak, 2 Stained Leaded Glass Doors	800.00
Bookcase,	Oak, Lift & Roll Doors, 3 Stack	500.00
Bookcase,	Oak, Lift & Roll Doors, 4 Stack	600.00
Bookcase,	Oak, Lift & Roll Doors, 5 Stack	625.00
Bookcase,	Quartersawn Oak, 3 Doors, Carved Columns, Victorian	1200.00
Bookcase,	Queen Anne, Walnut, Mirror Doors, 82 In. ....*Illus*	10350.00
Bookcase,	Roycroft, 1 Door, 16 Panes, 33rd Degree, No. 086, 40 x 15 x 55 In.	5225.00
Bookcase,	Roycroft, Architectural Form, Applied Columns	7500.00
Bookcase,	Satinwood, Open, Inlaid, Spade Feet, 36 x 66 In.	550.00
Bookcase,	Wallace Nutting, Oak, Leaded Glass Top, 4 Shelves, 5 Ft. 2 In.	625.00
Bookcase,	Walnut, Glass Doors, Molded Base Doors, Phila., 1865, 107 x 54 In.	3575.00
Bookcase,	Walnut, Step-Up, Triple, Mirrored Back, 7 x 6 Ft.	2860.00
Bookcase,	Wanamaker's, Walnut, Revolving, Square, 19th Century, 57 x 24 x 24 In.	900.00
Bookcase,	William IV, Mahogany, 2 Glazed Arched Doors, Plinth Base, 1835, 76 In.	770.00
Box,	Blanket, 6 Board, Snipe Hinges, Bootjack Ends, 19th Century	330.00
Box,	Blanket, Painted Black, Amber Faux Marble, Varnished, N.J., 21 x 32 In.	635.00
Box,	Blanket, Painted Blue, Bootjack End, Initials J.E.L. Front, N.Y., 1800	2500.00
Box,	Blanket, Poplar, Lift Top, Ditty Box, Grain Paint, 23 x 43 In.	138.00
Box,	Blanket, Shaker, Pine, Poplar, Orange Wash, Lid, New Lebanon, 1850, 33 In.	605.00
Box,	On Stand, Georgian, Mahogany, Fan Inlay, 16 In.	275.00
Bracket,	Corner, Tulipwood, 4 Shelves, Brass Borders, 34 1/4 In., Pair	8050.00
Bracket,	George III, Giltwood, Above Spread-Winged Eagle, 13 1/4 In., Pair	6900.00
Breakfront,	Fruitwood, Glass Door, 2 Drawers, Bun Feet, 97 In.	1100.00
Breakfront,	George III Style, Mahogany, 4 Glass Paneled Doors, 81 1/2 In.	1600.00
Breakfront,	Georgian Style, Mahogany, 4 Mullioned Doors, 4 Drawers, 78 In.	1980.00
Breakfront,	Mahogany, China Cabinet Top, Inlaid Base, 87 In.	2200.00
Breakfront Bookcase,	Chippendale, Mahogany, Broken Arch Pediment, 4 Doors	5500.00
Breakfront Bookcase,	Mahogany, Glazed Doors, Lower Drawers, 92 In.	5175.00
Buffet,	Adirondack, George LeClerk, Marquetry, Mirror, 1925, 55 1/2 x 66 In.	6200.00
Buffet,	Baroque Revival, Oak, 2 Glazed Doors, 2-Door Carved Base, 19th Century	770.00
Buffet,	E. Galusha, Burl Walnut, Pink Marble, 2 Drawers Over 2 Doors, 1845	1800.00
Buffet,	French Provincial, Cherry, 2 Drawers Over Cupboard Doors, 42 In.	2760.00
Buffet,	French Provincial, Oak, 2 Drawers Over 2 Doors, 1700	1870.00
Buffet,	French Provincial, Walnut, Scalloped Rim, Carved Doors, 80 3/4 In.	1980.00
Buffet,	G. Rohde, Walnut, Burl Veneer, Chromed U-Shaped Legs, 1930s, 66 In.	4675.00

Buffet, Neo-Grecian, Hand Painted & Carved, 34 x 60 In. 700.00
Buffet, Oak, Claw Feet, Glass Door, Mirror, c.1915.. 265.00
Buffet, Walnut, Carved, Glazed Doors, Lower Panel Door, c.1800, 88 x 48 In. 2415.00
Bureau, 4 Drawers, Marble Top, Drop Pulls, Victorian, 36 x 41 x 18 In...................... 330.00
Bureau, Bird's-Eye Maple, 3 Drawers, Oval Brasses, 36 1/2 x 42 x 17 In. 495.00
Bureau, Bowfront, Sheraton, Mahogany, 6 Drawers, M. Mellen, Boston, 49 In............. 1875.00
Bureau, Chippendale, Bowfront, Maple, Painted, c.1790, 36 x 37 x 18 In. 2990.00
Bureau, Eastlake, Walnut, 3 Drawers, Carved, Mirror, 89 x 50 x 23 In. 880.00
Bureau, Empire, Mahogany, Bird's-Eye Maple Veneers, 5 Drawers, Split Columns 215.00
Bureau, Empire, Mahogany, Mirror, Child's, 37 x 31 In.. 255.00
Bureau, Federal, Bird's-Eye Maple, c.1820, 43 x 43 1/2 In.. 1495.00
Bureau, Federal, Bowfront, Mahogany, 4 Drawers, c.1815-1825, 37 x 43 x 20 In........ 1495.00
Bureau, Federal, Bowfront, Mahogany, Birch, Veneers, c.1800, 37 x 40 In.................. 1150.00
Bureau, Federal, Bowfront, Mahogany, Veneer, Original Pulls, c.1820, 39 x 41 In...... 980.00
Bureau, Federal, Bowfront, Maple, c.1800, 38 x 39 x 22 In.. 1850.00
Bureau, Federal, Bowfront, Maple, Oval Brass Pulls, c.1790, 32 x 38 x 21 In............. 2990.00
Bureau, Federal, Cherry, Veneer, Serpentine, 4 Drawers, c.1800, 40 x 40 x 26 In....... 2875.00
Bureau, Federal, Inlaid Mahogany, 4 Drawers, Original Brasses, c.1815, 38 x 40 In..... 2875.00
Bureau, Federal, Mahogany & Veneer, 4 Drawers, c.1800, 37 1/2 x 41 x 17 1/2 In. 1035.00
Bureau, Federal, Mahogany & Veneer, c.1815, 41 x 43 x 19 1/2 In............................ 690.00
Bureau, Federal, Walnut, 32 1/2 x 33 x 18 In... 1495.00
Bureau, Hepplewhite, Cherry, Inlaid Edge, Bird's-Eye Maple Veneer, 43 In. 2420.00
Bureau, Mahogany, 5 Drawers, Chamfered Ends, Applied Carvings, Victorian, 39 In. . 495.00
Bureau, Mahogany, Serpentine Front, 4 Drawers, c.1780, 36 In. 6820.00
Bureau, Napoleon III, Marquetry, Ormolu, Leather, 3 Drawers........................... *Illus* 11000.00
Bureau, Queen Anne, Carved Walnut, Faux Frieze Drawer, Bracket Feet, 37 x 40 In. .. 2640.00
Bureau, Sheraton, Mahogany Veneer, 5 Drawers, 49 x 43 x 20 In. 215.00
Bureau, Sheraton, Mahogany, 4 Drawers, Rope-Turned Legs, 44 x 27 x 20 In............. 2200.00
Bureau, Tiger Maple, 7 Drawers, Scrolled Apron, 40 x 40 x 20 In. 1540.00
Bureau, Walnut, Slant Front Desk, Fitted Interior, 6 Drawers, Walnut, 39 In. 1150.00
Bureau Bookcase, George III, Slant Front, Mahogany, Dentil Frieze, Glazed Door 3850.00
Bureau Plat, Louis XV Style, Tulipwood, Serpentine, Leather Inset, 67 x 35 In. 9200.00
Bureau Plat, Regency, Ebonized, Ormolu, Leather Top, 2 Short Drawers, 29 1/2 In. ... 5750.00
Butler's Tray, Stand, Walnut, X-Form, 19th Century, American, 28 x 16 In. 1955.00
Cabinet, Aesthetic Movement, Rosewood, Marquetry, Galleried Top, 54 x 109 In........ 2400.00
Cabinet, American Renaissance, Carved Walnut, Herter Bros. Style, 1870 .... 995.00
Cabinet, Arts & Crafts, 3 Bottom Graduated Drawers, Castors, England, 1905-1910 .... 850.00
Cabinet, Arts & Crafts, Oak, 3 Full-Length Glass Doors, Mirrored, 72 x 56 In. 550.00
Cabinet, Black Lacquer, Gilt Painted Scenes, Fitted Interior, China, 19 x 14 In. 600.00
Cabinet, China, Alvar Aalto, Birch Veneer, 2 Doors, Artek, 1940s, 47 1/2 x 49 In........ 525.00
Cabinet, China, Gilbert Rohde, Burl Walnut, Chrome Legs, Herman Miller, 36 In........ 4950.00
Cabinet, China, Gustav Stickley, 2 Doors, Mirror, Glass Shelves, 42 x 15 x 64 In. 2530.00

Furniture, Bureau, Napoleon III, Marquetry, Ormolu, Leather, 3 Drawers

Cabinet, China, Gustav Stickley, 2 Doors, 16 Panes, Shelves, No. 815, 63 1/2 In. 7250.00
Cabinet, China, Gustav Stickley, 8 Panes Each Door, Glass Sides, Signed, 63 In. 9350.00
Cabinet, China, Gustav Stickley, Oak, 12-Paned Door, No. 820, 1905, 62 In. 3450.00
Cabinet, China, L. & J.G. Stickley, 2 Doors, No. 746 .... 5500.00
Cabinet, China, Lifetime, Backsplash, Signed, 61 In. 1800.00
Cabinet, China, Mahogany, 2 Sections, Drawers At Mid Area, Mirrored Panels 4400.00
Cabinet, China, Mahogany, Curved Glass, Beveled Mirrors 2900.00
Cabinet, China, Oak, 2 Glass Doors, 2 Glass Sides, Shelves, 37 x 64 x 18 In. 600.00
Cabinet, China, Oak, 4 Stained Glass Doors, 5 Drawers Each Section, 10 Ft. 5465.00
Cabinet, China, Oak, Carved Crest, Glazed Door, Curved Glass Door, 45 1/4 In. 1035.00
Cabinet, China, Oak, Carved Lions Front, Claw Feet, 1900, 66 x 44 x 18 In. 770.00
Cabinet, China, Oak, Curved Glass, Lions' Heads & Claw Feet 2395.00
Cabinet, China, Onondaga, No. 729 .... 9350.00
Cabinet, China, Queen Anne Style, Walnut, 2 Glazed Doors, 47 x 15 x 68 In. 175.00
Cabinet, China, Roycroft, Leaded Glass Doors & Sides, Copper Pulls, 55 In. 9900.00
Cabinet, China, Walnut, Step-Back Drawers, 6-Pane Glass Doors, Biscuit Knobs 750.00
Cabinet, Cigar, Inlaid Mahogany, Linen Press Form, Victorian, Miniature 7360.00
Cabinet, Corner, American Federal, Cherry 5500.00
Cabinet, Corner, Bowfront, Mahogany, 2 Glazed Doors, 2 Drawers & Base Doors 385.00
Cabinet, Corner, Cherry, 12 Pane 1350.00
Cabinet, Corner, Curio, Georgian Style, Fruitwood, 70 1/2 In. 195.00
Cabinet, Corner, Dentil Molding, 2 Bowfront Glazed Doors, 1 Drawer 690.00
Cabinet, Corner, Display, Bowfront, Trapezoidal Form, 49 1/2 In. 175.00
Cabinet, Corner, Edwardian, Mahogany, Glazed Door, Velvet Interior, 70 x 22 In. 550.00
Cabinet, Corner, Elm & Maple, Mullioned Glass Door, 19th Century, 43 x 83 In. 1450.00
Cabinet, Corner, Federal, Cherry, 2 Doors Over Cupboard Doors, 9 Ft. 1600.00
Cabinet, Corner, Federal, Cherry, 4 Doors, 55 x 108 x 24 In. 1400.00
Cabinet, Corner, Grained, Pa., 96 In. 6000.00
Cabinet, Corner, Hanging, Georgian, Walnut, 1800 .... 725.00
Cabinet, Corner, Hanging, Mahogany, Mullioned Doors, 50 x 30 In. 1015.00
Cabinet, Corner, Maple, Mullioned Doors, 3 Short Drawers, 2 Doors, 50 x 85 In. 1955.00
Cabinet, Corner, Maple, Pine, Pa., Red Finish 9500.00
Cabinet, Corner, Oak, 5 Shelves, Convex Glass Door 1300.00
Cabinet, Corner, Poplar, Mullioned Glass Doors Over 2 Drawers, 77 1/2 In. 3600.00
Cabinet, Corner, Round Front, 3 Drawers, Original Hardware, England 2950.00
Cabinet, Corner, W. Gropius, Mahogany, Fluted Curved Doors, c.1913, 35 3/4 In. 4200.00
Cabinet, Corner, Walnut, 2 Paneled Doors, 3 Silver Drawers, c.1840 .... 4995.00
Cabinet, Corner, Walnut, 6-Paned Door, Rattail Hinges, Pa., 1790 .... 7800.00
Cabinet, Corner, Yellow Pine, 1 Mullioned Glass Door Over Door 4750.00
Cabinet, Curio, Carved Fret Work, Doors In Base & Top, China, 77 In. 1450.00
Cabinet, Curio, Cloverleaf Shape, Gold-Leaf Finish, Beveled Glass, 4 Ft. 2500.00
Cabinet, Curio, Hanging, Burl Walnut, Mullioned Door & Sides, 23 1/2 In. 750.00
Cabinet, Curio, Louis XV Style, Serpentine, Painted Armorial Panel, 26 x 57 In. 1260.00
Cabinet, Curio, Mahogany, Art Nouveau Panels, Reticulated, Glass Shelves 3950.00
Cabinet, Curio, Reeded Corner Columns, Bronze Mounted, France 3300.00
Cabinet, Curio, Teak, Black Lacquer, Landscape Scene Doors, China, 69 In. 525.00
Cabinet, Document, 12 Shallow Drawers, Pullout Work Surface 400.00
Cabinet, Drexel, Bleached Maple, 2 Sliding Doors, 44 x 19 x 35 In. 60.00
Cabinet, Edwardian, Mahogany, Mirrored Back, Glazed Doors, 72 In., Pair 1100.00
Cabinet, Federal Style, Cherry, Glass Panes, 12 Drawers, Bracket Feet, 36 x 82 In. 1300.00
Cabinet, File, Globe, Oak, 4 Stack, 35 Drawers 2595.00
Cabinet, File, Oak, 33 Drawers 650.00
Cabinet, French Provincial, Walnut, 1 Door, Carved Panels, 86 In. 1955.00
Cabinet, G. Nelson, Walnut, 8 Drawers, Brushed-Chrome Pulls, Herman Miller, 57 In. 385.00
Cabinet, George III Style, Satinwood, Rosewood Inlay, 95 1/2 In., Pair 9775.00
Cabinet, Georgian Style, Bowfront, Mahogany, Geometric Mullioned Doors, 69 In. 980.00
Cabinet, Gothic Style, Oak, Carved Dragon Center Of Number 1900, 67 In. 690.00
Cabinet, Gothic, Oak, Dentil Frieze, Leaded Latticework Doors, 67 x 22 x 18 In. 690.00
Cabinet, Gun, Rom-Weber, Oak, Painted Hunt Scenes On Doors, 79 In. 495.00
Cabinet, Hanging, 9-Light Center Door, 3-Light Sides, 37 In. 495.00
Cabinet, Hanging, Mahogany, Beveled Glass Door, 23 x 11 3/4 In. 200.00
Cabinet, Hanging, Paneled Door, 2 Shelves, Painted Green, 29 x 19 3/4 In. 7475.00
Cabinet, Heywood-Wakefield, Sliding Doors, Interior Drawers, 34 x 44 In. 1100.00

Cabinet, Kitchen, Porcelain Top, c.1910, Small 1295.00
Cabinet, Lacquer, Gilt Figures & Pagodas, 3 Lower Panels, China, 77 x 54 In. 2587.50
Cabinet, Library, 2 Open Shelves Over 2 Doors, Black & Gilt Lacquer, 61 In. 865.00
Cabinet, Liquor, Edwardian, Mahogany, Satinwood Inlay, Fitted Interior 440.00
Cabinet, Liquor, Lift Top, Suede Lined, Compartments, Arts & Crafts, 30 x 18 In. 1265.00
Cabinet, Liquor, Marble Top, Mounted Ormolu, France, 62 In. 450.00
Cabinet, Liquor, Stickley Bros., Top Doors, Pullout Shelf, No. 77, 51 In. 880.00
Cabinet, Louis XVI Style, Kingwood, Marble Top, Parquetry, 30 In., Pair 1035.00
Cabinet, Magazine, Gustav Stickley, No. 72, c.1907, 42 In. 2070.00
Cabinet, Mahogany, Ormolu Mounts, Fretted Tier, Marble Top, France, 19th Century . 1995.00
Cabinet, Mahogany, Pitched Top, Mirrored Door, Bronze Figures, 7 Ft. 5 In. 6900.00
Cabinet, Majorelle, Closed Cabinet & Open Bay, Scenic Marquetry, 66 x 31 In. 3680.00
Cabinet, Music, Bowfront, Walnut, 1 Cupboard Door, 39 1/2 In. 80.00
Cabinet, Music, Galle, Walnut, Marquetry, Iris 2310.00
Cabinet, Music, Gustav Stickley, 1door, Iron Hardware, No. 70, 46 In.......................... 5500.00
Cabinet, Music, Gustav Stickley, 4 Ft. 7000.00
Cabinet, Music, Kimbel & Cabus, Door Over Drawer, Incised, Ebonized, 47 In. 1265.00
Cabinet, Music, Mahogany, Gadrooned Edge, 1 Short Drawer, 35 1/2 In. 225.00
Cabinet, Music, Mahogany, Inlaid Urn & Floral, 1 Drawer Over 1 Door..................... 110.00
Cabinet, Music, Rosewood, Marble, Opens To 1 Drawer, 5 Compartments, 31 x 21 In. 3740.00
Cabinet, Neoclassical, Karelian Birch, Ebony, Fruitwood, 3 Drawers, 2 Doors, Russia. 5750.00
Cabinet, Oak, 2 Part, Upper Doors, Shelves, Lower Doors, 7 Ft. 1 In............................. 4900.00
Cabinet, Oak, Acanthus Scroll, Berries & Jester, 17th Century, 80 In.......................... 4025.00
Cabinet, Oriental, 8 Drawers, Dark Red Lacquer, Black Hardware, 41 1/4 In. 135.00
Cabinet, Paul Frankl, Skyscraper, Juxtaposed Sections, 2 Drawers, 1928, 4 Ft............. 4600.00
Cabinet, Renaissance Revival, Walnut, Marquetry, 65 x 43 x 19 1/2 In......................... 1725.00
Cabinet, Rosewood Veneer, Porcelain Panels, Painted Cherubs, 46 3/4 In. 2090.00
Cabinet, Rosewood, Marble Top, Shelved Interior, Nickel Trim, 1930, 4 Ft. 7 In. 4025.00
Cabinet, Sacristy, Mary & Holy Child, Oak, Germany, 15th Century 5400.00
Cabinet, Side, Boullework, Gilt Bronze, Rouge Marble Top, Bombe-Shaped Door........ 1870.00
Cabinet, Side, Renaissance Style, Walnut, Iron Mounted, 62 x 28 1/2 x 14 In. 2590.00
Cabinet, Smoker's, Gustav Stickley, 1 Door, Arched Apron, No. 89, 20 x 19 x 29 In. .. 4125.00
Cabinet, Smoker's, Gustav Stickley, No. 522:.. 5000.00
Cabinet, Stand, Black Lacquer & Parcel Gilt, Chinese Export, 1830s, 5 Ft. 5 In. 5463.00
Cabinet, T. Molesworth, 2 Drawers, Open Shelf, Pole Dividers, Leather Covered 825.00
Cabinet, Wall, Charles Rohlfs, Open Carving, Copper Hardware, 1898, 63 In. 3850.00
Cabinet, Wall, Folk Art, Chip Carved, Geometric Design, 1 Side Door......................... 750.00
Cabinet, Wall, Pine, 2 Paneled Doors, 8-Sectioned Interior, 31 x 37 1/2 In. 1495.00
Cabinet-On-Stand, Baroque Style, Bone Inlay, Engraved, 20 x 40 x 12 In. 3450.00
Cabinet-On-Stand, C. Spooner, Mahogany, Satinwood, Ogee Latticework, 5 Ft. 6270.00
Cabinet-On-Stand, Georgian Style, Carved Mahogany, Molded Cornice, 75 3/4 In. 1210.00
Cabinet-On-Stand, Louis XVI, Mahogany, Parquetry, Ormolu Mounted, 1890, 63 In. . 1650.00
Canape, Louis XVI Style, Carved & Painted, Upholstered Back & Seat, 54 In.............. 1210.00
Candlestand, Cherry, Birch, Round Top, Turned Shaft, Snake Leg, 1880, 24 In. 2750.00
Candlestand, Cherry, Scalloped Top... 1400.00
Candlestand, Cherry, Tripod Base, Snake Feet, Turned Column, 16 x 16 x 25 1/2 In. ... 660.00
Candlestand, Cherry, Tripod Base, Turned Shaft, 18th Century, 25 x 11 x 16 1/4 In. ... 690.00
Candlestand, Cherry, Turned Post, Spider Leg 250.00
Candlestand, Chippendale, Cherry Stellate Device Inlaid, c.1790, 27 In. 3450.00
Candlestand, Chippendale, Cherry, Claw Feet, Turned Column, Drawer, 18 x 20 In. ... 220.00
Candlestand, Chippendale, Cherry, New England, c.1780, 27 x 18 x 19 In. 5175.00
Candlestand, Chippendale, Cherry, Tripod, Snake Feet, 2 Board Top, 14 x 15 In. 935.00
Candlestand, Chippendale, Mahogany, Dish Top, Tilt Top, c.1780, 28 x 19 1/2 In. 2415.00
Candlestand, Chippendale, Mahogany, Octagonal Top, 28 1/2 In. 860.00
Candlestand, Chippendale, Tilt Top, Cherry, c.1780, 27 1/4 x 18 x 17 3/4 In. 1955.00
Candlestand, Chippendale, Tilt Top, Mahogany, Snake Feet, 27 In. 220.00
Candlestand, Chippendale, Tilt Top, Walnut, Snake Feet, 28 1/2 In. 5290.00
Candlestand, Classical, Tilt Top, Birch, Carved, Carved Post, c.1820, 27 x 18 In........ 405.00
Candlestand, Country Chippendale, Cherry, Snake Feet, 28 In. 2035.00
Candlestand, Dish Top, Tiger Maple, Spade Feet, c.1800 .... 1540.00
Candlestand, Empire, Tiger Maple, Oval Top, American, 1825-1830 .... 4950.00
Candlestand, Empire, Tilt Top, Cherry, 1-Board Top, 30 3/4 In................................. 330.00
Candlestand, Federal, Cherry, Cut Corners, Turned Column, c.1795, 18 In. 1000.00

Furniture, Candlestand, Tripod, Mahogany,

c.1790, 28 x 21 In.

◆◆◆◆◆◆◆◆◆◆◆◆◆◆◆◆◆◆◆◆◆◆◆◆◆

We had a friend whose pet cougar liked to chew on the legs of her 18th-century American chairs. Not good for the chairs. Don't even let your dogs or cats near valuable old furniture.

◆◆◆◆◆◆◆◆◆◆◆◆◆◆◆◆◆◆◆◆◆◆◆◆◆

Candlestand, Federal, Cherry, New England, c.1790, 28 x 20 x 17 In.	750.00
Candlestand, Federal, Mahogany, Carved, Massachusetts, c.1790, 28 x 22 x 15 In.	1150.00
Candlestand, Federal, Mahogany, Cloverleaf Tilt Top, Tripod, 28 x 27 x 18 In.	640.00
Candlestand, Federal, Mahogany, Serpentine Square Top, Pedestal, 1790, 25 In.	2070.00
Candlestand, Federal, Square Top, Urn-Turned Pedestal, Maple, 26 1/2 In.	1035.00
Candlestand, Federal, Tilt Top, Mahogany	575.00
Candlestand, Federal, Tilt Top, Mahogany, Oval Top, Tripod Legs, 28 x 25 x 16 In.	1035.00
Candlestand, Grained Red & Black, Cut-Corner Top	2150.00
Candlestand, Hardwoods, Adjustable Candle Arm, 2 Sockets, 35 1/2 In.	1045.00
Candlestand, Hepplewhite, Mahogany, Oval, Turned Pedestal, Splayed Legs	1045.00
Candlestand, Hepplewhite, Mahogany, Spade Feet, 28 In.	550.00
Candlestand, Inlaid Ash & Maple, Victorian	300.00
Candlestand, J. Hoffman, Bentwood, Round, c.1905, 21 1/4 In.	400.00
Candlestand, Mahogany, Carved Standard, Urn Pendant, c.1830, 26 1/2 In.	360.00
Candlestand, Mahogany, Ornately Carved Legs, Victorian, 26 1/2 In.	245.00
Candlestand, Mahogany, Serpentine Top, Federal, c.1790, 28 x 20 x 20 In.	7475.00
Candlestand, Maple & Birch, Adjustable, Swiveling Top, 1770, 28 1/2 In.	690.00
Candlestand, Maple & Birch, Screw Standard, Double Candle Arm, 37 In.	1725.00
Candlestand, Maple & Cherry, Turned Pediment, 27 1/2 x 17 1/2 x 18 1/2 In.	300.00
Candlestand, Maple, Turned Standard, 4 Scroll Legs, Round, 19th Century, 18 In.	69.00
Candlestand, Pine, Burl Wood Inlay, Octagonal Top, 28 1/2 In.	550.00
Candlestand, Queen Anne, Cherrywood, Round, Pedestal, Pad Feet, 1750, 15 In.	460.00
Candlestand, Queen Anne, Maple, Tripod, Snake Leg, Square Top, 1 Black, Pair	1700.00
Candlestand, Queen Anne, Painted Black, Portsmouth, N.H.	2600.00
Candlestand, Queen Anne, Tiger Maple, Urn-Form Standard, c.1790, 27 In.	2300.00
Candlestand, Queen Anne, Walnut, Tripartite Cabriole Legs, 25 1/2 In.	345.00
Candlestand, Ratchet, Tray Top, Painted Green	1500.00
Candlestand, Shaker, Cherry & Birch	2750.00
Candlestand, Shaker, Cherry, Round Top, Spider Legs, New Lebanon	990.00
Candlestand, Sheraton Style, Vase-Turned Pedestal, Sawn Snake Feet, 17 1/2 In.	495.00
Candlestand, Square Top, Applied Edge, 26 In.	385.00
Candlestand, Tilt Top, Birch, Vase Of Flowers Inlay	9900.00
Candlestand, Tilt Top, Dish Top, Mahogany, Baluster Turned, Tripod Base, c.1800	330.00
Candlestand, Tilt Top, Hexagon Top, Reverse Scrolls Legs, c.1810, 26 1/2 In.	790.00
Candlestand, Tilt Top, Mahogany, Oval, Baluster Standard, Tripod Base, Slipper Feet	880.00
Candlestand, Tilt Top, Walnut Top, Scrolled Feet, Tripod Base, 28 1/2 In.	195.00
Candlestand, Tripod, Mahogany, c.1790, 28 x 21 In. ....*Illus*	1150.00
Candlestand, Walnut, Carved Bellflowers & Leaves On Standard, 33 In.	2300.00
Candlestand, Walnut, Dish Top, Configured Legs	205.00
Candlestand, Walnut, Pa., 1740-1760, 28 3/4 x 17 In. ....*Illus*	4025.00
Canterbury, George III Style, Mahogany, Lower Shelf, Casters, 41 In.	1090.00
Canterbury, Mahogany, 3 Spindled Gallery Sections, Drawer, Victorian, 22 In.	935.00
Canterbury, Walnut, Pierced, Handle, Fitted, 1 Drawer, Castors, 19th Century, 22 In.	920.00
Card Press, Mahogany, Floral Petit Point, Carving, 1860-1880	463.00
Card Press, Mahogany, Inlaid Mother-Of-Pearl Flowers, 1860-1880	705.00
Card Press, Rosewood, Ivory Finial, Brass Bound, 1860-1880	467.00

Cart, Flower, 2 Tiers, Iron, 31 1/2 In. 315.00
Case, Gun, Brass Bound Mahogany, Hinged Lid, Stand, 20 1/2 x 36 In. 460.00
Cellarette, Federal, Sectioned Interior, Fixed Frame, c.1810, 23 1/4 In. 2250.00
Cellarette, George III, Inlaid Mahogany, Fitted Interior, 1760s, 23 In. 1840.00
Cellarette, George III, Inlaid Mahogany, Hinged Top, Fitted Interior, 27 1/2 In. 575.00
Cellarette, Georgian Style, Mahogany, Satinwood Inlay, Lead Liner, 29 In. 1650.00
Cellarette, Lift Top, Fitted Interior, 2 Base Drawers, c.1910 .... 660.00
Cellarette, Limbert, Slide-Out Shelf Over Drawer, Shelf, No. 751, 36 In. 5250.00
Cellarette, Mahogany, Beveled Glass, Hinged Panels, Box, c.1860, 32 x 19 In. 1610.00
Cellarette, Mahogany, Brass, 6-Sided, Original Key, England 2255.00
Cellarette, Mahogany, Hinged Cover, 1800, 28 x 35 x 20 In. .... *Illus* 5500.00
Cellarette, Rosewood, Tapering Case, Lion's-Head Brasses, 8 1/4 x 13 1/4 In. 690.00
Cellarette, Stand, Georgian Style, Mahogany, 5 Sections, Lead Liner, 24 1/4 In. 1100.00
Chair, Aesthetic, Herter Brothers, Trapezoidal Seat, 1880-1885, Pair 575.00
Chair, Alfred Waterhouse, Leather Back & Arms, Vertical Supports, 1874, Pair 1725.00
Chair, Arched Dragon & Floral Crest, Caned Back & Seat, Folding, Pair 290.00
Chair, Arne Jacobsen, Swan, Leather, 4-Footed Swivel Post 425.00
Chair, Arrow-Back, Maple, Plank Seat 35.00
Chair, Art Deco, Over-Scrolling Padded Back & Seat, American, 30 1/2 In., Pair 1095.00
Chair, Arts & Crafts, Willow, Drink, Magazine Holders On Arms, 32 x 25 x 36 In. 770.00
Chair, Balloon Back, Carved Sides & Crest, Tufted Arms, Casters, 19th Century 205.00
Chair, Balloon Seat, Mahogany, New England, c.1750, 40 1/2 In. 2185.00
Chair, Balloon, Upholstered Seat, Cabriole Legs, 19th Century, Pair 202.00
Chair, Banister Back, Grain Painted, 18th Century, 43 In. 2550.00
Chair, Banister Back, Maple, Arched Crest, 4 Split Spindles, Rush Seat, New England 460.00
Chair, Banister Back, Painted Brown, 1780-1800, 40 1/2 In. 450.00
Chair, Banister, Black Over Red, Painted Design, Rhode Island, 1740 .... 2000.00
Chair, Baroque Style, Ebonized, Upholstered Back & Seat, Padded Arms, 46 In. 175.00
Chair, Baroque Style, High Carved Back, Scrolling Carved Arms, Pair 440.00
Chair, Bernard Maybeck, Honduras Mahogany, Rush Seat, c.1910 .... 4400.00
Chair, Biedermeier, String Inlay, Ribbons & Leaves, A. Bembe, c.1860 .... 2550.00
Chair, Black Wood, Curved Splat, Marble Inset, Open Apron, China, Pair 1500.00
Chair, Boardwalk, Wicker 50.00
Chair, Boudoir, Maple, Dark Walnut Stain, Taped Seat, Mt. Lebanon, 28 In. 550.00
Chair, Boudoir, Walnut, Incised Carved Feet, Brass Casters, Tufted Back 355.00
Chair, Bugatti, Mahogany, Ivory Inlay, Copper, Suede Leather Seat, Rawhide 1760.00
Chair, Bugatti, Painted Parchment, Inlaid Ebony, Square Seat, Fringe, 41 In. 5520.00
Chair, Bugatti, Walnut, Pewter & Brass Inlay, 1902, Pair 9775.00
Chair, Cane Back & Seat, 17th Century, Flemish 1150.00
Chair, Captain's, Elm, Spindle Back, England, Pair 345.00
Chair, Carved & Figured Mahogany, Saber Leg, Loose Cushion, c.1820 .... 2875.00
Chair, Carved Bear Set Into Back, Concealed Music Box, Child's 4000.00
Chair, Charles & Ray Eames, Molded Plywood, Child's, c.1945 .... 3737.00
Chair, Charles Eames, Dowel Leg, Fiberglass Shell, Herman Miller, 24 x 22 In. 825.00
Chair, Charles Eames, Rosewood Plywood Seat, Black Metal Frame 145.00
Chair, Charles Stickley, 9-Spindle Back, Drop-In Cushion, 18 x 17 x 36 In. 495.00

Furniture,
Candlestand,
Walnut, Pa.,
1740-1760,
28 3/4 x 17 In.

Furniture, Cellarette, Mahogany,
Hinged Cover, 1800, 28 x 35 x 20 In.

Chair, Cherry, Office, Cane Seat & Back, Arms	575.00
Chair, Chippendale Style, Mahogany, Ribbon Back, Cabriole Legs, Ball & Claw	288.00
Chair, Chippendale, Birch, Shaped Carved Shell Crest Rail, Rush Seat	1610.00
Chair, Chippendale, Carved Ears, Pierced Splats, Rush Seat, Country, Pair	495.00
Chair, Chippendale, Carved Mahogany, Ball & Claw Feet, c.1780, Pair	3300.00
Chair, Chippendale, Cherry, Rush Seat, Conn., 1790-1810	625.00
Chair, Chippendale, Corner, Walnut, Upholstered Slip Seat, 30 In.	450.00
Chair, Chippendale, Curly Maple, Serpentine Crest, c.1780, Pair	3450.00
Chair, Chippendale, Mahogany, Ball & Claw Feet, Cabriole Legs, c.1780, Pair	3000.00
Chair, Chippendale, Mahogany, Carved, c.1770, 38 In.	5462.00
Chair, Chippendale, Mahogany, Serpentine Crest Rail, Trapezoid Seat	1290.00
Chair, Chippendale, Mahogany, Square Legs, Crest, Needlework Seat, 38 In.	495.00
Chair, Chippendale, Mahogany, Strapwork Splat, Slip Seat, N.Y., 1735-1795, Pair	3680.00
Chair, Chippendale, Maple & Cherry, Vasiform Splat, 1760-1790, 40 x 17 In.	770.00
Chair, Chippendale, Walnut, Crest, Strapwork Splat, Balloon Seat, 1750, Pair	4600.00
Chair, Chippendale, Walnut, Owl's-Eye Splat	650.00
Chair, Club, Art Deco, Mahogany, Parquetry, American, 29 In.	1840.00
Chair, Club, F.L. Wright, Taliesan Design Legs, Heritage Henredon, 33 x 35 x 26 In.	705.00
Chair, Coconut, George Nelson, Triangular, White Metal, Herman Miller, 40 In.	3100.00
Chair, Commode, Chippendale, Walnut, Pierced Splat, Skirt, 1760, 33 1/2 In.	1435.00
Chair, Commode, Shaker, Watervliet, F.W., 1861, Arms	5600.00
Chair, Corner, Arched Splats, Rush Seat, Turned Stiles, c.1800	415.00
Chair, Corner, Bentwood Back Rail Forms Arms, Paper Rush Seat, 27 In.	325.00
Chair, Corner, Bugatti, Ebony, Brass Inlay, Horseshoe-Shaped Arms, 28 1/2 In.	1610.00
Chair, Corner, Bugatti, Inlaid Ebony, Block Feet, Suede, 31 1/2 In.	3680.00
Chair, Corner, Cherry, Scalloped Slats, Rush Seat, Country, 30 3/4 In.	1375.00
Chair, Corner, Chippendale Style, Walnut, Rush Seat Insert	330.00
Chair, Corner, Chippendale, Maple, Rush Seat, 1785 ....*Illus*	2300.00
Chair, Corner, Chippendale, Scrolled Arms, Vasiform Splats, Slip Seat	440.00
Chair, Corner, George II, Slip Upholstered, Cabriole Legs, 18th Century	690.00
Chair, Corner, Georgian, Mahogany, Cabriole Legs, 1750	605.00
Chair, Corner, Mahogany, Foliate-Carved Cresting, Needlework Seat	205.00
Chair, Corner, Mahogany, Heraldic Lion's-Mask Back, Rope Columns, 30 1/2 In.	440.00
Chair, Corner, Original Black Paint, Leather Over Splint Seat, 1740s	7475.00
Chair, Corner, Painted, Splint Seat, 18th Century, 31 In.	1610.00
Chair, Corner, Queen Anne Style, Fruitwood, Heart-Shaped Splats	210.00
Chair, Corner, Queen Anne, Birch, Removable Rush Seat, c.1770	4025.00
Chair, Corner, Queen Anne, Maple, Rush Seat, Double Box Stretchers, 1760	865.00
Chair, Corner, Queen Anne, Walnut, 2 Vasiform Splats, Shaped Skirt, 1750	2587.00
Chair, Corner, Regency, Elm, Time-Out Type, Child's, 1835, Pair	770.00
Chair, Corner, Rosewood, Ox-Horn-Shaped Armrests, Marble Inlay, China	360.00
Chair, Corner, Rush Seat, Conn., 1740	3900.00
Chair, Corner, Turned Legs, Posts & Stretchers, Square Seat, 31 1/2 In.	770.00
Chair, Corner, William & Mary, Leather Seat, Painted, 18th Century, 30 In.	7475.00
Chair, Corner, William & Mary, Turned, Painted Black, Leather Seat, 30 In.	545.00

Furniture, Chair, Corner, Chippendale,
Maple, Rush Seat, 1785

❖ ❖ ❖ ❖ ❖ ❖ ❖ ❖ ❖ ❖ ❖ ❖ ❖ ❖ ❖ ❖ ❖

Remove dripped candle wax
on a tabletop with a credit
card. Scrape with the grain of
the wood. When finished use
furniture polish or wax to
restore the top's luster.

❖ ❖ ❖ ❖ ❖ ❖ ❖ ❖ ❖ ❖ ❖ ❖ ❖ ❖ ❖ ❖ ❖

Chair, Corner, With Table, Bamboo, 3 Piece 445.00
Chair, Crown, Painted, Rush Seat, 1750-1770, 43 1/2 x 16 1/2 In. 1035.00
Chair, Curly Maple, Cane Seat, Saber Legs, Pair 400.00
Chair, Desk, Knoll, Star Pedestal Base, Upholstered 140.00
Chair, Desk, Mahogany, Swivel Type, Victorian 115.00
Chair, Desk, Michigan Chair Co., Oak, 5 Spindles, Saddle Seat, 38 In. 495.00
Chair, Desk, Rush Seat, c.1710, 36 In. 750.00
Chair, Desk, Tilt Back, Bentwood Arms 395.00
Chair, Dutch Baroque Style, Walnut, Arched Crest, Shell Over Vase Splat, Pair 1380.00
Chair, Dutch Marquetry, 1800 .... 495.00
Chair, Easy, Chippendale, Mahogany, Rolled Arms, Bowed Seat, England, 45 In. 1955.00
Chair, Easy, Federal, Mahogany, Trapezoidal Upholstered Seat 1380.00
Chair, Easy, Queen Anne, Maple, Shaped Wings, Upholstered, Cabriole Legs, 46 In. 1955.00
Chair, Easy, Walnut, Shaped Wings, Scrolling Arms, Cabriole Legs, 47 1/4 In. 405.00
Chair, Edwardian, Rosewood, Marquetry, Leather, c.1900, Pair 1760.00
Chair, Federal Style, Mahogany, Shield Back, Trapezoidal Seat, Pair 165.00
Chair, Federal, Cherry, Carved, Vasiform Back, c.1790, 39 In. 632.00
Chair, Federal, Mahogany, Carved, c.1810, 35 In. 865.00
Chair, Finn Juhl, Teak, Leather, Pair 1750.00
Chair, Flemish, Beech, Carved, Spanish Foot, England, 18th Century, 48 In. 546.00
Chair, Folding, Bentwood, Upholstered Back & Seat 517.00
Chair, Folding, Hans J. Wegner, Oak, Rush, Johannes Hansen, Denmark, 30 In. 2530.00
Chair, Folding, Walnut, Tapestry Seat, Boston Furniture Co., Victorian, 1890 .... 100.00
Chair, Frank Lloyd Wright, Hexagonal Back & Seat, Oil Cloth, 1922, 37 3/4 In. 4600.00
Chair, Frank Lloyd Wright, Oak, Hexagonal Back & Seat, c.1916, 38 In. 5520.00
Chair, Frank Lloyd Wright, Oak, Slab Back, Handhold Joined To 2 Stiles, 1902 .... 5175.00
Chair, Frank Lloyd Wright, Stiles Fitted With Block To Top & Bottom, Birch 4600.00
Chair, French Style, Floral Crest, Velvet, Cabriole Legs 165.00
Chair, Fruitwood, Tablet Crest Rail, Gilt Painted Roman Figures, Rush Seat, Pair 1925.00
Chair, G. Rohde, Leatherette, Chromium Plated, Troy Sunshade, c.1934, 30 x 17 In. 115.00
Chair, George II, Leather, Serpentine Seat & Padded Backrest 7475.00
Chair, George II, Mahogany, Vasiform Splat, Trifid Feet, Ireland, 40 In. 460.00
Chair, George III, Mahogany, Wheel Back, Open Arms, Pierced Spoke, c.1780 .... 4600.00
Chair, George Nakashima, Curved Back 1000.00
Chair, Georgian Style, Carved Oak, Cane Back, Upholstered Seat, Pair 115.00
Chair, Gilbert Rohde, Sling, Chromed Steel Bands, Vinyl, Troy Sunshade, 1930s 1210.00
Chair, Gio Ponti, Chrome, Red Vinyl, 1938 .... 1200.00
Chair, Gothic Revival, Mahogany, Arched Crest Rail, Barley Twist Columns 315.00
Chair, Gothic Style, Upholstered Dolphin Support Arms, 55 In. 715.00
Chair, Gothic, Church, Burl Walnut, c.1860, Pair 1895.00
Chair, Gothic, Mahogany, Shaped Back, Fleur-De-Lis Crest, Floral Silk, Pair 715.00
Chair, Great, William & Mary, Heart Crest, Painted Red, Rush Seat, Arms, 1735 .... 2760.00
Chair, Gustav Stickley, 3 Vertical Slats, Leather Seat, No. 350, 17 x 39 In. 550.00
Chair, Gustav Stickley, Cube, 6 Vertical Slats Under Side, Leather, 29 In. 2200.00
Chair, Gustav Stickley, Curly Maple, H-Back, 1 Back Slat, Pewter Flower Inlay 2100.00
Chair, Gustav Stickley, Leather, No. 342, Child's, 14 x 13 x 26 In. 495.00
Chair, Hall, Walnut, Stylized Foliage On Back, Lion On Crest, c.1865, Pair 3737.00
Chair, Hans J. Wegner, Jakkens Hvile, 3 Legs, Storage Seat, Denmark, 37 In. 1150.00
Chair, Hardwood, Scooped Back Seat On Back Of Standing Elephant 2300.00
Chair, Hepplewhite, Feather Splat, Bellflowers Inlay, 1800, Salem, Mass., Pair 2850.00
Chair, Hepplewhite, Mahogany, Urn Splat, 36 In. 450.00
Chair, Heywood Bros., Wicker, 40 In. 575.00
Chair, Hitchcock, Gilt Design Of Mount Vernon, Caned Seat 90.00
Chair, Hitchcock, Painted Yellow, Stenciled, Painted Rush Seat, 1830, Pair 350.00
Chair, Horn, Child's, 1915 .... 1250.00
Chair, Italian Neoclassical, Walnut, Caned, Carved Splat Back, Spade Feet, Pair 1035.00
Chair, J. & J. Kohn, Bentwood, Open Arms, Upholstered Seat, c.1930, Pair 750.00
Chair, Jacobean Style, Oak, Bearded Man Finial, Upholstered Seat, England, Pair 198.00
Chair, Jacobean Style, Oak, Foliate, Berry & Rope Turned Back, Pair 125.00
Chair, Jacobean, Caned Back, Carved Crest, Child's 2200.00
Chair, Jacobsen, Upholstered Fiberglass Shell, Aluminum Swivel Base, 1960s 2450.00
Chair, James Perry, Painted Canvas Cover, Abstract Figures, 33 3/4 In. 85.00
Chair, John Henry Belter, Laminated Rosewood, Pierce Carved 2150.00

Chair, John Henry Belter, Laminated Rosewood, Rosalie, Carved Rose On Seat Rail 1750.00
Chair, Josef Hoffmann, Bentwood & Aluminum, Painted, Leather, 1901 .... 3300.00
Chair, Kangaroo, George Nelson, Upholstered, Steel Frame, 1956, 39 In. 2530.00
Chair, Kitchen, Oak, Pressed Back, Separated By Twist Carved Stretchers 70.00
Chair, L. & J.G. Stickley, Mission, Oak, Horizontal Splat Back 145.00
Chair, L. & J.G. Stickley, Oak, 4 Splat Back, Plank Seat, Label, 37 In., Pair 121.00
Chair, L. & J.G. Stickley, Prairie School, Dropped Arm, No. 428, 28 x 30 In. 4950.00
Chair, Ladder Back, 3 Slats, Bulbous Finials, Painted Red, 39 1/2 In. 412.00
Chair, Ladder Back, 4 Shaped Splats, Turned Knob Finials, Rush Seat, c.1800 .... 110.00
Chair, Ladder Back, Birch & Ash, Rush Seat, 1830 .... 1955.00
Chair, Ladder Back, Chippendale, Carved, Mahogany, c.1775, 37 In., Pair 1960.00
Chair, Ladder Back, Chippendale, Mahogany, Pierced Crest Rail & Splats, Pair 865.00
Chair, Ladder Back, Maple, Rush Seat, New England, 18th Century 632.50
Chair, Ladder Back, Painted Black, Sausage Turned, Rush Seat, Stencil Honor Old Age 302.00
Chair, Ladder Back, Rabbit Ear, Splint Seat, 33 In. 55.00
Chair, Ladder Back, Rush Seat, Turned Finials, Child's 330.00
Chair, Ladder Back, Sir Gordon Russell, Oak, Shaped Arms & Sides 1552.00
Chair, Ladder Back, Wallace Nutting, Maple, c.1924, Pair 895.00
Chair, Limbert, Bicycle, Saddle Seat, Loose Leather Back, Signed, 42 In. 750.00
Chair, Lolling, Chippendale, Mahogany, Leather, c.1780, 36 In. 2760.00
Chair, Lolling, Federal, Mahogany, Canted Upholstered Back & Seat, Mass., 1790 .... 5175.00
Chair, Lolling, Federal, Mahogany, Inlaid, Serpentine Crest, H Stretcher, 44 In. 1380.00
Chair, Lolling, Federal, Mahogany, Serpentine Crest, Upholstered, 40 In. 345.00
Chair, Lolling, Federal, Mahogany, Serpentine Crest, Shaped Arms, c.1800 .... 3737.00
Chair, Lolling, Hepplewhite Style, Mahogany, Silk, 41 In. 330.00
Chair, Lolling, Inlaid Mahogany, Upholstered Back & Crest, c.1800 .... 5750.00
Chair, Lolling, Mahogany, c.1790, 44 In. 977.00
Chair, Lolling, Mahogany, Serpentine Crest, Damask, Open Arm, 1780 .... 990.00
Chair, Lolling, Mahogany, Serpentine Crest, Down Curving Arms, c.1800 .... 4025.00
Chair, Lolling, Mahogany, Upholstered Crest & Seat, Shaped Arms, c.1800 .... 6325.00
Chair, Lolling, Regency, Mahogany, Leather, c.1800 .... 2800.00
Chair, Loose Cushion, Silk Brocade, Painted Green, 1770s 4830.00
Chair, Louis XV Style, Walnut, Carved, Cabriole Legs, Pair 220.00
Chair, Louis XV Style, Walnut, Curved Back, Shell-Carved Crest, Silk 880.00
Chair, Louis XV Style, Walnut, Rocaille Crest, Down-Curved Arms, Silk 825.00
Chair, Louis XV, Caned, Loose Cushion, Leather 2070.00
Chair, Louis XVI Painted, Gray, Beaded Back, Padded Seat, Fluted Legs, 35 1/2 In. 3300.00
Chair, Louis XVI Style, Beechwood, Arched Upholstered Back & Seat 138.00
Chair, Louis XVI Style, Carved Giltwood, Oval Back, Fluted Leg, c.1900, Pair 1035.00
Chair, Louis XVI Style, Lyre Back, Carved & Gilded Frame, Tapestry Seat, 36 In. 550.00
Chair, Louis XVI Style, Wedgwood Medallions, White Classical Relief, White, Pair 373.75
Chair, Lounge, B. Mathsson, Plywood, Webbed Jute, Sweden, c.1945 .... 575.00
Chair, Lounge, Charles Eames, Laminated & Molded Plywood, Black Dye 660.00

Furniture, Chair, Molesworth, Black & Red
Leather, Chemayo Cushions

If the screw holding a hinge is loose, try this old-fashioned remedy. Break the heads off several large wooden kitchen matches. Put the wooden strips in the hole with some glue, then screw the old screw back into place.

Chair, Lounge, Plywood Joined With Metal Rivets, 2 Positions, H.V. Thaden, 1947 .... 4125.00
Chair, Mahogany, Child's Head Surrounded By Foliate Scrolling, Pair 460.00
Chair, Mahogany, Turned Stretcher, Upholstered Seat, Boston, Pair.......................... 8250.00
Chair, Mahogany, Upholstered, c.1770, 39 In... 747.00
Chair, Maple, Molded Corners, Vase Splat & Yoke Crest, Carved Ears....................... 418.00
Chair, Maple, Painted, Turned Side, Leaf Design, Heart-Pierced Crest, 1735, 42 In. 1495.00
Chair, Miles Van Der Rohe, Bent Tubular Steel, Painted Red, Caned Seat & Back 7500.00
Chair, Molesworth, Black & Red Leather, Chemayo Cushions .... *Illus* 11000.00
Chair, Moravian, Pine & Hardwood, 38 1/2 In. 82.50
Chair, Morris, Arts & Crafts, 4 Slats Under Arms, Adjustable Back, Cushion 2420.00
Chair, Morris, Gustav Stickley, 18 Side Spindles, No. 367, 40 1/2 x 30 x 36 In. 8250.00
Chair, Morris, Gustav Stickley, 5 Slats, Leather, No. 332, 31 x 38 In. 6050.00
Chair, Morris, Gustav Stickley, Bow Arm, Rope Foundation 5000.00
Chair, Morris, Gustav Stickley, Flat Arm, Drop-In Spring Seat, No. 346, 40 In............. 1300.00
Chair, Morris, Gustav Stickley, Open Arms, Spring Seat, No. 336, Decal, 36 In. 9350.00
Chair, Morris, J.M. Young, 4 Slats Under Each Arm, Paper Label, 38 1/2 In. 2420.00
Chair, Morris, L. & J.G. Stickley, Adjustable Back, 40 In.. 1430.00
Chair, Morris, L. & J.G. Stickley, 5 Slats Under Arms, No. 497, 32 x 36 x 41 In. 4400.00
Chair, Morris, L. & J.G. Stickley, Open Arm, 38 1/2 In. 990.00
Chair, Morris, Limbert, Front & Back Corbels, Extended Arms, No. 530, 32 x 44 In. ... 4950.00
Chair, Morris, Limbert, No. 818, Marked, c.1910, 32 1/2 In. 2070.00
Chair, Morris, Mission, Upholstered Back & Seat, Arms 150.00
Chair, Morris, Oak, 5 Vertical Slats Under Arms, Webbed Drop-In Seat, American 3680.00
Chair, Neoclassical, Mahogany, Hourglass-Shaped Back, Rosette Carving, Russia 6037.00
Chair, Neoclassical, Painted Land & Seascapes, Baltimore, c.1830, Pair 4850.00
Chair, Oak, Carved Old Man Winter, Natural, Leather Seat, Cabriole Legs, 1880s........ 250.00
Chair, Oak, Office, Cane Seat & Back, Arms 575.00
Chair, Oak, Upholstered Back & Seat, 19th Century, England 150.00
Chair, Office, Roycroft, Swiveling, 1 Vertical Back Slat, Leather Seat, 42 In................ 1800.00
Chair, Openwork Splat, Paint Design, Arms... 88.00
Chair, Ottoman, Bertoia, Elliptical, High Back, Knoll International, 1952, 38 1/2 In..... 518.00
Chair, Owl's-Eye Splat 5462.50
Chair, P. Fornasetti, Guitar, Bentwood, Metal Legs, 16 x 19 x 37 In. 770.00
Chair, Painted Basket Of Flowers, Compote Of Fruit Splat, c.1820, Pair 2990.00
Chair, Painted Green, Split Oak Base, Child's.. 68.00
Chair, Painted Hudson Valley Scenes On Slats, Rush Seat.. 1400.00
Chair, Parlor, Inlaid Rosewood, Marquetry, Pair .... *Illus* 550.00
Chair, Pilgrim, Cherry, Finials Over Ball Stiles, 5 Upright Rails, Rush Seat, 1680........ 5750.00
Chair, Porter's, George III, Mahogany, Upholstered Sides, 1780s 2415.00
Chair, Potty, Pressed Back, High-Chair-Type Tray 145.00
Chair, Potty, Stenciling, Yellowware Potty, 19th Century 150.00

Furniture, Chair, Parlor, Inlaid Rosewood, Marquetry, Pair

Chair, Pressed Back, Crest, Spindle Back, Trapezoidal Seat, American 24.00
Chair, Pressed Back, Oak, Face 65.00
Chair, Pressed Back, Plank Seat 25.00
Chair, Pressed Back, Rectangular Crest, Grapes, Spindles, Pair 150.00
Chair, Queen Anne Style, Rectangular Carved Back, Shaped Seat, H Stretcher, Pair 550.00
Chair, Queen Anne Style, Walnut, Open Arms, Upholstered, 41 In. 145.00
Chair, Queen Anne Style, Walnut, Upholstered, Back & Seat, 39 1/2 In., Pair 230.00
Chair, Queen Anne, Back Splat, Rush Seat, Delaware River Valley, 18th Century 900.00
Chair, Queen Anne, Centennial, Mahogany, Pair 4800.00
Chair, Queen Anne, Cherry, Vasiform Splat, Balloon Seat, 1740 .... 805.00
Chair, Queen Anne, Cherrywood, Black, Rush Seat 395.00
Chair, Queen Anne, Cherrywood, Rush Seat 295.00
Chair, Queen Anne, Mahogany, Massachusetts, c.1760, 39 1/2 In. 1955.00
Chair, Queen Anne, Maple, Carved Crest, Rush Seat, Spanish Feet, 40 1/2 In. 488.00
Chair, Queen Anne, Maple, Vase Splat, Trapezoidal Rush Seat, Spanish Feet, 42 In. 690.00
Chair, Queen Anne, Rush Seat, Spanish Feet, Carved Crest Rail, Portsmouth, N.H. 2900.00
Chair, Queen Anne, Stained Maple, Vasiform Splat, Scrolled Arms, Rush Seat 6325.00
Chair, Queen Anne, Vasiform Splat, Turned Base, Spanish Feet, Country 330.00
Chair, Queen Anne, Walnut, Cabriole Legs, Slip Seat, Vasiform Splat, 43 In. 770.00
Chair, Queen Anne, Walnut, Chamber Pot, Chair Cover, Arms, Mid-1700s 9775.00
Chair, Queen Anne, Walnut, Serpentine Rail, Vasiform Splat, Slip Seat, 1750 .... 4600.00
Chair, Queen Anne, Walnut, Vasiform Splat, Slip Seat, William Savery, 40 In. 3000.00
Chair, Queen Anne, Walnut, Vasiform Splat, Slip Seat, Maryland, 1740, Pair 6325.00
Chair, Queen Anne, Walnut, Yoke Crest Rail, Shaped Apron, c.1760, Pair 4312.00
Chair, Queen Anne, Yoke Crest, Voluted Stiles, Slip Seat, Pair 4600.00
Chair, Reclining, Leather, Pullout Foot Rest 325.00
Chair, Regency, Ebonized, Cane Seat, Ormolu Mounted, 33 In. 55.00
Chair, Renaissance Revival, Spiral Turned Arm Rests & Base 385.00
Chair, Ribbon Back, Rush Seat, 33 In., Pair 1200.00
Chair, Rocker, look under Rocker in this category.
Chair, Rococo, Walnut, Carved, Needlepoint Seat, Cabriole Legs, Victorian 415.00
Chair, Rosewood, Carved & Molded Back, Seat Rail, Cabriole Legs, Pair 550.00
Chair, Rosewood, Tall Back, Needlepoint Seat, Victorian, Pair 170.00
Chair, Sausage Turned, Child's, c.1750 .... 1200.00
Chair, Serge Chermayeff, Brown Enameled Metal, Canvas Seat, PEL, 1934, 22 In. 600.00
Chair, Settle Type, Green Over Red, Child's 750.00
Chair, Shaker, 2-Rod Slat Back, Cloth Tape Woven Seat, Mt. Lebanon, 27 1/2 In. 1610.00
Chair, Shaker, 4 Slat, Original Finish, Mt. Lebanon Transfer, 1900 .... 3800.00
Chair, Shaker, Curly Maple, Tilters, Rush Seat, Mt. Lebanon 6325.00
Chair, Shaker, Maple, Cane Seat, Tilters, No. 19, Canterbury, N.H., c.1830, 41 In. 4620.00
Chair, Shaker, Maple, Mt. Lebanon, Plush Seat, Child's, 27 1/2 In. 990.00
Chair, Shaker, Maple, No. 3 .... 2600.00
Chair, Shaker, Maple, Rush Seat, Mt. Lebanon, No. 4, 34 In. 415.00
Chair, Shield Back, Mahogany, Upholstered Seat, Pair 2600.00
Chair, Slip Seat, Leather, Holland, 39 In., Pair 1100.00
Chair, Slipper, Belter, Fountain Elm Pattern, Pair 8625.00
Chair, Slipper, Belter, Laminated Rosewood 5500.00
Chair, Slipper, Belter, Rosalie, Rosewood, Velvet, Pair 2475.00
Chair, Slipper, Button Tufted, Pair 330.00
Chair, Slipper, Cherry & White Pine, Blocked Serpentine Front Seat Rail 7500.00
Chair, Slipper, Gustav Stickley, Rails Side Of Seat, No. 2578, Decal, 29 In. 440.00
Chair, Slipper, Mahogany, Pierced Carved Scrollwork Back, c.1850 .... 425.00
Chair, Slipper, Painted Maple, Vasiform Splat, Removable Rush Seat, ... 690.00
Chair, Slipper, Walnut, Upholstered Back & Seat, Casters, Victorian 175.00
Chair, Spectator's, Pool 650.00
Chair, Spinning Wheel Frame, Bobbin Spindle, 30 1/2 In. 192.50
Chair, Stickley & Brandt, 2 Slats Under Each Arm, Decal, 34 3/4 In. 2200.00
Chair, Swirled Comb Paint, Brown Over Mustard, Plank Seat, Child's 145.00
Chair, Swiss Revival, Walnut, Carved Crest, Down-Curved Arms, Barrel Seat 515.00
Chair, Tall Back, Carved & Upholstered Back, Saddle Seat, Black, 54 In. 400.00
Chair, Tete-A-Tete, Wicker, Padded Seats 1650.00
Chair, Thonet, Bentwood, Scrolled Back & Arms, Cane Seat, c.1900 .... 300.00
Chair, Thonet, Pine, Cafe, Curved Backrest, Down-Curving Legs, Pair 255.00

Chair, Tiger Maple, 5-Slat Ladder Back, Rush Seat, Delaware Valley 3000.00
Chair, Wainscot, Elizabethan Gothic, Carved Arms, Trapezoidal Seat 1150.00
Chair, Wakefield Rattan Co., Wicker, Paint Decorated, No. 3612, 40 In., Pair 1150.00
Chair, Wallace Nutting, Ladder Back, Rope Seat, Turned Legs & Arms 255.00
Chair, Wallace Nutting, Windsor, No. 349 .... 688.00
Chair, Wallace Nutting, Writing Arm, Fanback, Paper Labels 1650.00
Chair, Walnut, Balloon Back, Pierced Crest, Needlepoint Seat 90.00
Chair, Walnut, Brocade, Finger Carved, Victorian, 38 In. 275.00
Chair, Walnut, Carved, Newport, Rhode Island, c.1750, 39 In. 8000.00
Chair, Walnut, Dolphin Crest, Dark Finish, Needlepoint, Victorian 195.00
Chair, Walnut, Finger-Roll Back, Needlepoint Seat, Victorian 175.00
Chair, Walnut, Heart Cutout Back, Balloon Seat, Norwich, Conn., Pair 7975.00
Chair, Walnut, High Back, Lion Carved Ears, Shaped Seat, Paw Feet, Pair 270.00
Chair, Walnut, Molded Arm Supports, Gros & Petit Point, c.1930 .... 400.00
Chair, Walnut, Open Arms, Carved Crests, Velvet, Victorian, Pair 575.00
Chair, Walnut, Pierced Rectangular Back, Needlepoint Seat, Casters, 19th Century 175.00
Chair, Walnut, Yoked Crest, Pierced Splat 2200.00
Chair, Wassily, Black Leather & Tubular Chromed Steel, 1925 .... 220.00
Chair, Weaver's, Taped Seat, 19th Century 295.00
Chair, Wicker, Painted Cream, Late 19th Century, American 220.00
Chair, William & Mary, Banister Back, Painted, 18th Century, 44 1/2 In. 745.00
Chair, William & Mary, Padded Back & Overupholstered Seat, Black, 37 In. 405.00
Chair, William IV, Mahogany, Panel, 1833 .... 165.00
Chair, Windsor, 8 Spindles, Bulbous Turnings, Saddle Seat, 35 3/4 In. 100.00
Chair, Windsor, Arrow-Back Splats, Bamboo Turnings, Shaped Seat, 35 In. 72.00
Chair, Windsor, Arrow-Back, Yellow Striping, Floral Swags, Plank Seat, 36 In. 275.00
Chair, Windsor, Bamboo Turned, 7 Spindles, Bow Back, 19th Century, 36 In. 80.00
Chair, Windsor, Bamboo Turnings, Spindle Back, Painted, Crest, Child's, 25 In. 1155.00
Chair, Windsor, Bamboo, 34 In. 250.00
Chair, Windsor, Bamboo, 7 Spindles, Splayed Legs, Shaped Seat, 34 In. 88.00
Chair, Windsor, Bamboo, Painted, Floral Design, Spindle Back, Branded, 35 In. 715.00
Chair, Windsor, Bamboo, Splayed Legs & Seat, Step-Down Crest, 34 1/4 In. 195.00
Chair, Windsor, Bow Back, Added Rockers, Saddle Seat, 9 Spindles, 31 In. 220.00
Chair, Windsor, Bow Back, Bamboo Turnings, Saddle Seat, 39 In. 550.00
Chair, Winsor, Bow Back, Bamboo Turnings, 7 Spindles, Shaped Seat, 35 In. 300.00
Chair, Windsor, Bow Back, Bowed Crest Rail, 7 Spindles, Bamboo Turned Legs 345.00
Chair, Windsor, Bow Back, Brace Back, Painted Black, c.1780, 40 In. 1150.00
Chair, Windsor, Bow Back, Grain Painted, New Hampshire, Pair 7425.00
Chair, Windsor, Bow Back, H Stretcher, Bamboo Turnings, 36 In., Pair 660.00
Chair, Windsor, Bow Back, T.C. Hayward, Bamboo, Painted Brown, 37 3/4 In., Pair ... 865.00
Chair, Windsor, Bow Back, Turned Arm Supports, Spindle Back, 35 2/3 In. 360.00

Furniture, Chair, Windsor, Fanback,
Floral, Painted, 1765, 35 In.

◆◆◆◆◆◆◆◆◆◆◆◆◆◆◆◆◆◆◆◆◆◆

Slightly scratched or damaged wooden furniture will
look better if it is waxed with a
high-quality paste wax. Do not
use spray or liquid wax
because it has other added
chemicals that may cause
problems. Apply the wax with
a tightly woven soft cotton
cloth, not cheesecloth because it may snag. Wax only
once a year. Buff monthly.

◆◆◆◆◆◆◆◆◆◆◆◆◆◆◆◆◆◆◆◆◆◆

Chair, Windsor, Brace Back, Arched Crest Rail, 9 Spindles, 37 1/4 In., Pair 1725.00
Chair, Windsor, Comb Back, 9 Tapered Spindles, Flared Handholds, Green 3175.00
Chair, Windsor, Fanback, Ash & Pine, Late, 18th Century, 35 1/2 In. 435.00
Chair, Windsor, Fanback, Bamboo, 8-Spindle Back, 35 1/2 In. 415.00
Chair, Windsor, Fanback, Brace Back, Painted Red 2310.00
Chair, Windsor, Fanback, Floral, Painted, 1765, 35 In. ....*Illus* 5175.00
Chair, Windsor, Fanback, Painted Black, New England, c.1780, 31 In. 259.00
Chair, Windsor, Fanback, Painted Black, c.1780, 38 In. 2070.00
Chair, Windsor, Fanback, Saddle Seat, Spindle Back, 35 1/2 In. 275.00
Chair, Windsor, Fanback, Splayed Base, Saddle Seat 330.00
Chair, Windsor, Fanback, Whale's-Tail-Shaped Brace, Painted Brown Over Red 6500.00
Chair, Windsor, George Nakashima, Solid Walnut, 38 In. 2530.00
Chair, Windsor, J. Lambert, Bow Back, Upholstered, c.1810, 37 In., Pair 1380.00
Chair, Windsor, Plank Seat, Straight Crest Rail, Bamboo Turnings 100.00
Chair, Windsor, S.J. Tucke, Bow Back, Painted, c.1790-1796, 38 In. 920.00
Chair, Windsor, Sack Back, Painted, 18th Century, 37 1/2 In. 1840.00
Chair, Windsor, Saddle Seat, Bamboo Turned Legs 300.00
Chair, Windsor, Saddle Seat, Continuous Arm, Spindle Back, Green 1320.00
Chair, Windsor, Samuel Moon, 9 Spindles 995.00
Chair, Windsor, Step, Black & Red, Green Leaves, Pair 825.00
Chair, Windsor, Wallace Nutting, Brace Back, No. 301 .... 635.00
Chair, Wing, Chippendale Style, Floral Brocade, 45 In. 245.00
Chair, Wing, Chippendale, Mahogany, Scrolled Arms, Upholstered Seat 1380.00
Chair, Wing, Chippendale, Square Molded Legs, Damask, 48 In. 2860.00
Chair, Wing, George III, Mahogany, Barrel Back, c.1800 .... 1265.00
Chair, Wing, Louis XV Style, Carved, Painted Wood, Pair 1755.00
Chair, Wing, Mahogany, Upholstered, Molded Straight Legs, Philadelphia 8800.00
Chair, Wing, Pink Damask, Ball & Claw Feet 175.00
Chair, Wing, Queen Anne Style, Walnut, Upholstered, 19th Century 375.00
Chair, Wing, Queen Anne, Colonial Revival, Mahogany, Youth-Size, c.1900, 35 In. 660.00
Chair, Wing, Rolled Arms, Tufted Back, Upholstered 75.00
Chair, Woman's, Mahogany, Cabriole Legs, Upholstered, Victorian, American, 1850 .. 220.00
Chair, Womb, Knoll 687.00
Chair, Yellow Striping, Brushed Foliage On Posts, Floral, Plank Seat, Pair 155.00
Chair & Ottoman, Bruno Mathsson, Laminated Birch, Organic Shape, Web, 1940s 880.00
Chair & Ottoman, Charles Eames, Molded Rosewood, Leather, Herman Miller 1650.00
Chair & Ottoman, Eero Saarinen, Grasshopper, Molded Birch, Knoll 1870.00
Chair & Ottoman, Eero Saarinen, Womb, Molded Fiberglass, Chrome Legs, Knoll 1200.00
Chair Set, Alvar Aalto, Plywood Back, Birch Frame, Upholstered Seat, c.1935, 3........ 355.00
Chair Set, American Renaissance, Walnut, Fruit & Berries Frieze, Fluted Legs, 11....... 6050.00
Chair Set, Arrow-Back, Apple Green, 6... 1925.00
Chair Set, Art Deco, Mahogany, Upholstered, 4.. 9240.00
Chair Set, Arts & Crafts, Inlaid High Back, Leather Seat, England, 8 .... 8250.00
Chair Set, Balloon Back, Molded Frame, Velvet Tapestry, 8....................................... 1430.00
Chair Set, Balloon Back, Painted Design On Brown Paint, 6.. 1500.00
Chair Set, Balloon Back, Walnut, Foliate Carved Frame, 4 .... 250.00
Chair Set, Banister Back, Rush Seat, Turned Front Stretcher, 1 Armchair, 2................. 145.00
Chair Set, Baroque Style, Walnut, Parcel Gilt, Tapestry, Italy, 6................................. 9775.00
Chair Set, Biedermeier, Fruitwood, 37 1/2 In., 4 .... 1725.00
Chair Set, Biedermeier, Fruitwood, Pierced Scrolled Back, Drop Seat, Saber Legs, 4 ... 6325.00
Chair Set, Birch, Rosewood Simulated Paint, Upholstered Seat, 19th Century, 5.......... 450.00
Chair Set, Brown, Yellow & Red Pineapple Design, Balloon Back, 4 .... 895.00
Chair Set, Cast Iron, Painted Brown, Lyre Back, Arms, 3 .... 3200.00
Chair Set, Chinese Export, Bamboo, Parcel Gilt, Caned, Arched Crest, Red, 4 .... 7475.00
Chair Set, Chippendale Style, Arched Scrolling Crest Rail, Slip Seat, 4....................... 1840.00
Chair Set, Chippendale Style, Pierced Splat, Square Legs, 2 Armchairs, 10.................. 6900.00
Chair Set, Chippendale, Cherry Serpentine Crest, Pierced Vasiform Splat, 6 .... 2990.00
Chair Set, Chippendale, Cherry, Arched Crest Over Vasiform Splat, Slip Seat, 8 .... 1840.00
Chair Set, Chippendale, Ladder Back, Mahogany, Slip Seat, 37 1/2 In., 4 .... 220.00
Chair Set, Chippendale, Ladder Back, Mahogany, Shipley, c.1780, 37 In., 6................. 5750.00
Chair Set, Chippendale, Molded Front Legs, Pierced Splat Back, 37 In., 6 .... 2100.00
Chair Set, Chippendale, Rib Band Back, Upholstered Seat, 2 Armchairs, 12 .... 4400.00
Chair Set, Chippendale, Walnut, Pierced Splat, Upholstered, 2 Armchairs, 9 .... 5520.00

Chair Set, Crest Rail Above Urn-Shaped Splat Back, Upholstered Seat, 10.................. 7500.00
Chair Set, Curly & Tiger-Stripe Maple, Cane Seat, 1850s, 4 .... 650.00
Chair Set, Curly Maple, Rolled Crest, Cane Seat, Saber Legs, 4................................ 900.00
Chair Set, Dutch Neoclassical, Mahogany, Marquetry, 8 .... 5175.00
Chair Set, E. Gimson, Shaped Slats, Rush Seat, 2 Armchairs, 6 .... 1840.00
Chair Set, Empire, Mahogany, Flame Veneer Splat, Crest, Slip Seat, Saber Leg, 6....... 825.00
Chair Set, Empire, Saber Leg, 7 .... 2530.00
Chair Set, F. Brooks, Thumb Back, Grain Painted, Stenciled, 1946, 6 .... 715.00
Chair Set, F.L. Wright, Mahogany, Greek Key Trim, Armchairs, Henredon, 6 .... 1000.00
Chair Set, Federal, Curly Maple, Pierced Back Rail, Rush Seat, 1820, 12 .... 5750.00
Chair Set, Federal, Mahogany, 3 Urn-Shaped Uprights, Trapezoidal Seat, 5 .... 2530.00
Chair Set, Federal, Mahogany, Carved, c.1800, 38 1/2 In., 8 .... 4887.00
Chair Set, Federal, Mahogany, Ladder Back, Leaf-Carved Ears, 3 Slats, 4.................. 8625.00
Chair Set, Frank Gehry, Laminated Cardboard, 3 .... 1840.00
Chair Set, Frank Lloyd Wright, Upholstered Back & Seat, 6 .... 1150.00
Chair Set, French Provincial, Baker, 2 Armchairs, 8.. 135.00
Chair Set, French Provincial, Fruitwood, Lyre Splats, 4 .... 1210.00
Chair Set, French Provincial, Fruitwood, Rush Seat, 8 .... 5740.00
Chair Set, French Provincial, Oak, Rush Seat, 19th Century, 2 Armchairs, 8 .... 1870.00
Chair Set, French Provincial, Rush Seat, Stretcher, 6... 1430.00
Chair Set, G. Stickley, 5-Slatted Back, Leather Seat, No. 312, 18 x 17 In., 6 .... 7150.00
Chair Set, George III Style, 1 Armchair, 38 In., 8.. 5175.00
Chair Set, George III, Mahogany, c.1770, 8... 8050.00
Chair Set, George III, Mahogany, Lattice Type Back, Upholstered Seat, 8.................. 5175.00
Chair Set, George III, Mahogany, Leather, 2 Armchairs, 10 .... 8050.00
Chair Set, Georgian, Chinese Chippendale Style, Mahogany, 4 .... 1275.00
Chair Set, Gio Ponti, Chromed Steel Frame, Woven Vinyl Rope Seat, 4 .... 258.00
Chair Set, Golden Oak, Quartersawn Wood, Slip Vinyl Seat, 8 In., 4 .... 264.00
Chair Set, Gustav Stickley, 2 Armchairs, Rush Seat, Decal, No. 354A & 354, 6 .... 8800.00
Chair Set, Gustav Stickley, H-Back, Cutout Back Slat, Drop-In Seat, 4....................... 1760.00
Chair Set, Half Spindle, Red & Black Grained, Stenciled Florals, Plank Seat, 6 .... 925.00
Chair Set, Half Spindle, Yellow & Gold Striping, Dished Plank Seat, 32 In., 5............ 577.50
Chair Set, Half-Arrow Back, Green & White Striping, Black Label, 6 .... 3300.00
Chair Set, Half-Spindle Back, Black Striping, Stenciled Design, 32 3/4 In., 6.............. 630.00
Chair Set, Half-Spindle Back, Plank Seat, Stenciled Design, 32 3/4 In., 6................... 990.00
Chair Set, Henri IV Style, Walnut, Bowed Arms, Tapestry, c.1700, 4 .... 9200.00
Chair Set, Hepplewhite, Mahogany, String Inlay, Pierced Shield, c.1810, 8 .... 4950.00
Chair Set, Hitchcock, Rush Seat, Stenciled, 2 Armchairs, 6.................................... 795.00
Chair Set, Horizontal Crest & Splats, Cane Seat, Turned Legs, 19th Century, 8 .... 970.00
Chair Set, Jacobean Revival, Oak, 6.. 345.00
Chair Set, Jacobean, Wainscot Back, Leather Cushion, 2 Armchairs, 4 .... 220.00
Chair Set, Jens Risom, Birch Frame, Canvas Webbing, Knoll, c.1940, 4 .... 440.00
Chair Set, Keyhole, Floral Stenciled, Pennsylvania, 6 .... 2000.00
Chair Set, Knoll, Curved Seat, Wire Mesh Back, Trapezoidal Wire Legs, 32 In., 4....... 115.00
Chair Set, L. & J.G. Stickley, Drop Seat, Decal, No. 804, c.1910, 6............................. 1495.00
Chair Set, Ladder Back, 3 Horizontal Slats, No. 306, 17 x 17 x 36 In., 4..................... 357.50
Chair Set, Ladder Back, Foliate Carved Crests, Rush Seat, 4................................... 345.00
Chair Set, Ladder Back, Mahogany, 4 Cross Splats, Square Legs, 12 .... 1980.00
Chair Set, Ladder Back, Rush Seat, 20th Century, 4 .... 65.00
Chair Set, Larkin, Oak, Pressed Back, No. 1, 4 .... 975.00
Chair Set, Le Corbusier, Stainless, Pony-Hide, Strap Arms, c.1975, 4....................... 2070.00
Chair Set, Louis XV Style, Beechwood, Swivel Seat, Leather, 4 .... 1235.00
Chair Set, Louis XV Style, Carved Giltwood, 10 .... 2875.00
Chair Set, Mahogany, Foliate Crest Rail, Wicker, 2 Armchairs, Victorian 1840.00
Chair Set, Mahogany, Gondola Vase Back, 7.. 1870.00
Chair Set, Mahogany, Ladder Back, Incised Shipley On Seat Rails, 6 .... 5750.00
Chair Set, Mahogany, Wheel Back, Carved, Upholstered Seat, 12 .... 385.00
Chair Set, Metal, White Painted, France, 1920, 6.. 2900.00
Chair Set, Neoclassical, Birch, Parcel Gilt, Foliate Scrolled Frieze, Russia, 6 .... 6900.00
Chair Set, Neoclassical, Mahogany, Gilt, Arched Back, Foliate Frieze, Russia, 7 .... 4890.00
Chair Set, Neoclassical, Mahogany, Parcel Gilt, Outscrolled Back, Russia, 4 .... 6900.00
Chair Set, Neoclassical, Mahogany, Parcel Gilt, Foliate Carving, Russia, 4 .... 6325.00
Chair Set, Neoclassical, Mahogany, Parcel Gilt, Drop Seat, Russia, 6 .... 7700.00

Chair Set, Oak, Captain's, Caned Seat, 4 .... 425.00
Chair Set, Oak, Leather Back & Seat, Applied Angel's Head, Victorian, 6 .... 1150.00
Chair Set, Oak, Lion & Scroll Crest Rail, Pressed Leather Back & Seat, 6 .... 1150.00
Chair Set, Plank Seat, Painted Design, 6... 450.00
Chair Set, Queen Anne Style, Mahogany, Vasiform Splats, Raised Legs, 4 .... 465.00
Chair Set, Queen Anne Style, Walnut, 2 Armchairs, 8 .... 3960.00
Chair Set, Queen Anne Style, Walnut, Old Finish, Slip Seats, 20th Century, 8 .... 2335.00
Chair Set, Queen Anne Style, Walnut, Pierced, Slip Seat, 2 Armchairs, 8...................... 2530.00
Chair Set, Queen Anne Style, Walnut, Upholstered Back & Seat, Drake Feet, 6 .... 1035.00
Chair Set, Queen Anne, Walnut, Yoked Crest Rail, Vasiform Splat, 8 .... 4025.00
Chair Set, Quervelle, New York, 1825, 6.. 7800.00
Chair Set, Quervelle, Saber Leg, Philadelphia, 6 .... 7800.00
Chair Set, Reeded Back Frame, Carved Swags, Upholstered Seat, 33 In., 4 .... 242.00
Chair Set, Regency, Ebonized, Parcel Gilt, Cane, 2 Armchairs, c.1800, 8.................... 12650.00
Chair Set, Regency, Mahogany, Reeded Diamond Medallions Back, Leather Seat, 4 .... 572.00
Chair Set, Renaissance Revival, Walnut, Needlepoint Seat, 19th Century, 4.................. 385.00
Chair Set, Renaissance Style, Oak, Leather, 8 .... 3105.00
Chair Set, Ribbonback, Custom Made, 8 .... 3520.00
Chair Set, Rosewood, Painted Grain, Saber Leg, c.1840, 6 .... 850.00
Chair Set, Russel & Sons, Ladder Back, Hide Straps, 2 Armchairs, 8 .... 3130.00
Chair Set, Saber Legs, Spindle Back, Woven Cane Seats, Victorian, 33 In., 6 .... 297.00
Chair Set, Sheraton, Bird's-Eye Maple, Paper Rush Seat, 6 .... 825.00
Chair Set, Sheraton, Mahogany, 8... 3080.00
Chair Set, Sir Gordon Russell, Oak, Woven Leather Seat, c.1924, 6 .... 1380.00
Chair Set, Spindle Back, Plank Seat, Rabbit Ear Finials, 33 In., 4 .... 374.00
Chair Set, Stickley, Mahogany, 3 Vertical Slats, Heart-Shaped Cutout, 38 In., 6 .... 2090.00
Chair Set, Tablet Crest Rail, Foliate Splat, Caned Seat, 6... 2070.00
Chair Set, Tall Back, Swivel Seat, Polished Steel, 1930s, 6... 3400.00
Chair Set, Thonet, Barrel Back, 5 .... 440.00
Chair Set, Thonet, Bentwood, Arched Back Rail, D-Shaped Seat, 39 In., 4 .... 2185.00
Chair Set, Thonet, Bentwood, Fledermaus Style, J. Hoffman, 29 In., 3 .... 865.00
Chair Set, Tiger Maple & Cherry, Cane Seat, 6 .... 300.00
Chair Set, Wallace Nutting, Banister Back, No. 380, 4... 935.00
Chair Set, Walnut, Open Arms, Caned Crest Rail, Leather Slip Seat, 8.......................... 9200.00
Chair Set, Walnut, Tooled Leather Back & Seat, Trapezoidal Seat, 4 .... 375.00
Chair Set, William IV, 2 Armchairs, 34 1/4 In., 8.. 1955.00
Chair Set, Windsor, Arrow-Back, Painted, Gold Stencil, 1810-1840, 34 x 18 In., 6 ...... 1380.00
Chair Set, Windsor, Bamboo-Turned Legs, Rod Back, c.1800, 8 .... 6750.00
Chair Set, Windsor, Chicken-Coop, Painted Black, 4 .... 4800.00
Chair Set, Windsor, Hoop Back, Bamboo, 7 Spindles, 6... 2145.00
Chair Set, Windsor, Painted Yellow, Swans, 6 .... 5200.00
Chair Set, Windsor, Rabbit Ear, Striping On Floral Crest, Initialed MA, Utica, 6 .... 528.00
Chair Set, Windsor, Rod Back, Bamboo Turnings, Philadelphia, 8 .... 7425.00
Chair Set, Windsor, Thumb Back, Black, Gilt Fruit Stencil, c.1830, 33 In., 6 .... 747.00
Chair Set, Windsor, W. Evans, Bamboo, Splayed Legs, Spindle Back, 35 3/4 In., 5 ...... 2310.00
Chair Set, Windsor, Wing Back, Painted Black, Pa., 6 .... 1200.00
Chair Set, Wing, Mahogany, H Stretcher, Shaped Crest Rail, 8...................................... 5175.00
Chair Table, Round Top, Painted Red, 29 x 48 In.. 3575.00
Chaise Longue, Bentwood, Ash, Maple, Leather, Snowshoe Style 935.00
Chaise Longue, Duncan Phyfe Style, Mahogany Frame, c.1820 .... 3400.00
Chaise Longue, Empire Style, Mahogany, Outscrolled Backrest, 38 1/2 In................... 3165.00
Chaise Longue, G. Nelson, Black Wool, Steel Frame, Herman Miller, 70 x 30 In. 5500.00
Chaise Longue, Louis XV, Beechwood, Serpentine Sides & Front, Scrolled Legs......... 4600.00
Chaise Longue, Mahogany Frame, Horsehair Mattress, Damask, c.1830 .... 3893.00
Chaise Longue, Sheraton Style, Writing Arm, Old Red Paint... 385.00
Chaise Longue, Silk Back & Seat, Painted Gray, Pair 2300.00
Chaise Longue, Wicker, Natural, 1905 .... 1250.00
Chaise Longue, Windsor Style, Bamboo, Painted Decoration, Cane Seat......................... 550.00
Chest, 2 Short, 2 Long Drawers, Brass Lock Plates, Inlaid Back Stop, 34 1/2 In. 920.00
Chest, 3 Short & 6 Graduated Drawers, Mahogany, 41 x 20 x 62 In.............................. 3165.00
Chest, 3 Short Over 4 Long Drawers, Shell Carved 385.00
Chest, 4 Dovetailed Drawers, Cherry, 43 In. 275.00
Chest, 4 Drawers, Bird's-Eye Maple, Spiral Turned Front Columns, 36 In. 220.00

Chest, 4 Drawers, Cherry & Curly Maple, Cock-Beaded Edges, 53 In. 935.00
Chest, 4 Drawers, Cherry, Barber Pole Inlay, Naval Insignia, 38 In. 2000.00
Chest, 4 Drawers, Cherry, Scrolled Bracket Base, 38 x 40 x 19 In. 1320.00
Chest, 4 Drawers, Grain Painted, Maine, 1830 .... 1200.00
Chest, 4 Drawers, Grain Painted, Scroll Front, 1845, 11 3/4 x 11 1/8 x 7 In. 445.00
Chest, 4 Drawers, Mahogany, Fluted Quarter Columns, Molded Top, Ogee Bracket 1550.00
Chest, 4 Drawers, Oak, Ebonized Moldings, Inscribed R.P.-A.P., 17th Century 1150.00
Chest, 4 Drawers, Straight Bracket Feet, England, 36 x 30 In. 220.00
Chest, 4 Graduated Drawers, Cherry, Flat Front, Turned Foot, Painted Mustard 375.00
Chest, 4 Graduated Drawers, Mahogany & Cherry, Eliphalet Briggs, 1810, 33 In. 7187.00
Chest, 6 Drawers, Hidden Locking Device, Enamel Pulls, Brass Inlay, 1879 .... 5500.00
Chest, 6 Drawers, Walnut, Side Lock, Gallery, 1875, Victorian 2250.00
Chest, 9 Overlapping Drawers, Walnut, Dovetailed Case, 62 3/4 x 43 In. 1740.00
Chest, Aaron Deihl, Painted Red, Signed, Dated 1784 .... 2800.00
Chest, American Empire, 2 Short Over 2 Long Drawers, Mahogany, 52 x 45 In. 862.00
Chest, Apothecary, 10 Drawers, Glass Pulls, Drawer Labels 300.00
Chest, Apothecary, 14 Dovetailed Drawers, Poplar, 37 x 54 In. 1430.00
Chest, Apothecary, 8 Drawers, Painted, 33 x 20 In. 330.00
Chest, Apothecary, 9 Drawers, Painted Mustard 895.00
Chest, Bachelor, Georgian Style, 4 Graduated Drawers, Burl Walnut 770.00
Chest, Bachelor, Georgian, 3 Long Drawers, Oak, Frieze, 30 1/2 x 19 x 30 In. 230.00
Chest, Baker Co., Mahogany, Bowed Top, Slide Over 4 Drawers, 34 1/2 In. 900.00
Chest, Biedermeier, 4 Drawers, Fruitwood Veneer, Ebonized Columns 7500.00
Chest, Blanket, 1 Drawer, Signed, Rhode Island 895.00
Chest, Blanket, 2 Drawers, Brass Inlay, Carved Front, Turned Feet 800.00
Chest, Blanket, 2 Drawers, Hepplewhite, Grain Painted 1450.00
Chest, Blanket, 2 Drawers, Pine, Lift Top, Oval Brasses, 36 1/2 x 40 x 19 In. 385.00
Chest, Blanket, 2 Drawers, Pine, Sponge Painted, Yellow & Brown 3025.00
Chest, Blanket, 2 False Over 2 Drawers, Grain Painted, 1780, 44 In. 6900.00
Chest, Blanket, 3 Drawers, 3 False, Lift Top, New England, 47 x 42 In. 650.00
Chest, Blanket, 3 Drawers, Pine, Lift Top, Molded Feet, 43 1/2 x 38 1/2 x 21 In. 990.00
Chest, Blanket, Blue-Green, Bracket Feet, Scalloped Molding, 46 x 27 1/2 In. 250.00
Chest, Blanket, Carved Oak, Paneled Sides, England, 25 x 48 3/4 x 23 In. 1840.00
Chest, Blanket, Cherry, Ash Panels, Till With Lid, 24 x 38 In. 220.00
Chest, Blanket, Chippendale, 2 Overlapping Drawers, Walnut Inlay, 49 In. 3080.00
Chest, Blanket, Chippendale, Pine, Painted, 1780, 44 x 42 x 20 In. 2070.00
Chest, Blanket, Chippendale, Pine, Painted Black, Scalloped Apron, 24 x 12 In. 5750.00
Chest, Blanket, Chippendale, Red Flowers, 1782, 24 x 51 In. .... *Illus* 4025.00
Chest, Blanket, Connecticut River Valley, Painted Red, 42 1/2 In. 8500.00
Chest, Blanket, Dovetailed Case, Pine, Till, Iron Strap Hinge & Handles, 50 In. 260.00
Chest, Blanket, Dovetailed Case, Poplar, Till, Wrought Iron Strap Hinge, 37 In. 165.00
Chest, Blanket, Dovetailed Case, Red Grain Painted, Till, 41 In. 275.00
Chest, Blanket, Federal, Till, Thumb-Molded Drawer, 45 1/2 x 32 In. 945.00
Chest, Blanket, Floral, Lebanon County, Pa., 1795 .... 5500.00
Chest, Blanket, Gray, Cotter Pin Hinges, 6 Board, Bootjack Ends 675.00
Chest, Blanket, Mustard Grained, Hinged Top, 3 Astral Panels, 1806, 52 In. 9200.00
Chest, Blanket, Oak, Opens To Well With Till, John Thurston, c.1685, 49 In. 3165.00

Furniture, Chest, Blanket, Chippendale,
Red Flowers, 1782, 24 x 51 In.

Furniture, Chest, Bridal,
Gustav Stickley

Chest, Blanket, Painted Mustard, Hand-Wrought Strap Hinges, Miniature 795.00
Chest, Blanket, Pine, 2 Drawers, Sponge Painted, Yellow & Brown, Child's 1430.00
Chest, Blanket, Pine, Iron Handles, Bracket Feet, 19th Century, 39 x 20 x 21 In. 260.00
Chest, Blanket, Pine, Lift Top, False Drawers Over 3 Working Drawers, c.1800 .... 770.00
Chest, Blanket, Pine, Lift Top, Snipe Hinges, 40 x 41 In. 715.00
Chest, Blanket, Pine, Painted Red, Ditty Box Interior, 25 x 48 x 18 In. 275.00
Chest, Blanket, Pine, Red Flame Grained, Till With Lid, 24 1/2 x 38 In. 190.00
Chest, Blanket, Pine, Rose Mulled Design, Till, Painted, European, 51 In. 605.00
Chest, Blanket, Pine, Worn Red Paint, Black Trim, 37 1/2 x 19 1/2 x 25 In. 550.00
Chest, Blanket, Pine, Yellow & Red Grained, Painted Black, Miniature 850.00
Chest, Blanket, Poplar, Blue Vinegar Grained, 17 1/2 In. 195.00
Chest, Blanket, Poplar, Compass Stars On Lid, Flame Graining, Ohio, 40 1/2 In. 1980.00
Chest, Blanket, Poplar, Red Comb Graining Over Yellow, 28 x 47 1/2 In. 275.00
Chest, Blanket, Queen Anne, 4 Drawers, Maple, Scalloped Apron, 36 x 18 In. 6900.00
Chest, Blanket, Queen Anne, Original Blue, Provenance Under Cover, Dated 1764 ..... 2500.00
Chest, Blanket, Red Over Yellow Grained, Turnip Feet, 1853 .... 895.00
Chest, Blanket, Shaker, Pine, Drawer, Bootjack Feet, Painted & Grained, c.1835 .... 4025.00
Chest, Blanket, Shaker, Pine, Yellow Stained, Mt. Lebanon, 18 x 37 1/2 In. 1830.00
Chest, Blanket, Shaker, Watervliet, 22 x 46 x 17 In. 3500.00
Chest, Blanket, Sheraton, 2 Drawers, Painted Red 700.00
Chest, Blanket, Sheraton, 2 Hidden Vertical Drawers, Painted Design 2900.00
Chest, Blanket, Snipe Hinges, Ditty Box Interior, Bootjack Base, 25 x 46 In. 330.00
Chest, Blanket, Traces Of Old Red, Pine, 6 Board, 27 In. 250.00
Chest, Blanket, Zoar, Poplar, Cherry, Brown Paint, Green Panels, 43 x 20 In. 660.00
Chest, Bowfront, 4 Drawers, Mahogany, French Feet, 36 1/2 In. 1430.00
Chest, Bowfront, 4 Drawers, Mahogany, Inlaid, Mayflower Furn. Co., 30 x 24 In., Pr. . 525.00
Chest, Bridal, Gustav Stickley .... *Illus* 13200.00
Chest, Campaign Style, 2 Doors, 4 Drawers, Beacon Hill Collection 165.00
Chest, Campaign, Mahogany, Brassbound, England, 2 Sections 3000.00
Chest, Camphor Wood, Brassbound, Brass Handles, 12 x 28 In. 395.00
Chest, Chippendale, 3 Drawers Over 5 Graduated Drawers, 63 1/2 In. 925.00
Chest, Chippendale, 4 Drawers, Cherry, Connecticut, c.1780, 36 In. 3410.00
Chest, Chippendale, 4 Drawers, Cherry, Ogee Feet, Fluted Columns, 39 x 22 x 41 In. .. 4070.00
Chest, Chippendale, 4 Drawers, Cherry, Serpentine, Top Drawer For Writing, 38 In..... 8050.00
Chest, Chippendale, 4 Drawers, Dovetailed, Bracket Feet, 31 1/2 x 35 1/2 In. 880.00
Chest, Chippendale, 4 Drawers, Folding Top, 19th Century 2090.00
Chest, Chippendale, 4 Drawers, Mahogany, Reverse Serpentine, 1760, 31 In. 7475.00
Chest, Chippendale, 4 Drawers, Mahogany, Ogee Bracket Feet, 34 x 39 In. 7475.00
Chest, Chippendale, 4 Drawers, Maple, Brass Pulls, c.1790, 35 x 36 x 18 In. 4600.00
Chest, Chippendale, 4 Drawers, New England, Maple, c.1790, 29 1/2 x 36 1/2 In. 2645.00
Chest, Chippendale, 4 Drawers, Tiger Maple, New England, 1760, 35 x 40 x 21 In....... 3680.00
Chest, Chippendale, 4 Graduated Drawers, Tiger Maple, Ogee Feet 6875.00
Chest, Chippendale, 4 Graduated Drawers, Mahogany, 1760, 35 x 37 x 19 In. 2990.00
Chest, Chippendale, 4 Graduated Drawers, Cherry, Overhung Molded Top, 32 1/2 In... 4675.00
Chest, Chippendale, 4 Graduated Drawers, Cherry, 1780, 36 x 39 In. 4310.00
Chest, Chippendale, 4 Graduated Thumb-Molded Drawers, Maple, 1770, 36 x 19 In. ... 2990.00
Chest, Chippendale, 5 Drawers, Cherry, Dovetailed, Bracket Feet, 39 x 20 x 41 In. 3630.00
Chest, Chippendale, 5 Drawers, Maple & Birch, Brass Pulls, c.1780, 44 x 36 In........... 1495.00
Chest, Chippendale, 6 Drawers, Maple, Molded Cornice, Scrolled Apron, 62 In. 3520.00
Chest, Chippendale, 6 Graduated Drawers, Maple, Tiger Maple, New England, 51 In... 5750.00
Chest, Chippendale, 6 Graduated Drawers, Maple, c.1780, 51 1/2 x 35 1/2 In. 4312.00
Chest, Chippendale, 7 Drawers, Maple, Bracket Base, 55 In. 2860.00
Chest, Chippendale, 7 Drawers, Walnut, Dovetailed Case, 60 x 41 In. 5500.00
Chest, Chippendale, Poplar, Dust Shelves Between 5 Drawers, 42 1/2 In. 3355.00
Chest, Chippendale, Walnut, 1770-1790, 41 x 38 x 22 In. .... *Illus* 3680.00
Chest, Chippendale, Walnut, On Frame, 77 In. 2750.00
Chest, Classical, 2 Over 3 Bowfront Drawers, Mahogany, 46 x 22 In. 2970.00
Chest, Classical, 4 Graduated Drawers, Tiger Maple, Mirror, Baltimore, 1830-1840 .... 6500.00
Chest, Classical, 5 Drawers, Mahogany, Brass Inlay, Gallery, 56 In. 1870.00
Chest, Concave Front, Mirrored Top Drawer, European, 1790, 34 x 41 In. 7500.00
Chest, Continental, 6 Drawers, Floral Marquetry, Claw Feet, 56 x 40 In. 1650.00
Chest, Country Chippendale, 4 Drawers, Maple, Brass Bails, 32 3/4 In. 825.00
Chest, Dower, 2 Drawers, 2 Panels, Stylized Pinwheels & Tulips 3500.00

*Furniture, Chest, Chippendale, Walnut,
1770-1790, 41 x 38 x 22 In.*

*Furniture, Chest, Federal,
Curly Maple, Cherry, 1820, 38 x 41 In.*

Chest, Dower, 3 Drawers, Black & White Stylized Flowers, Johanes Hort, 1808 .... 3800.00
Chest, Dower, Grain Painted, Gold & Brown, Early 19th Century, 29 x 48 x 24 In. 1840.00
Chest, Dower, Walnut, Inlaid, Initialed, LR 1776, Pennsylvania, 23 x 52 x 22 In. 5462.00
Chest, Dower, Walnut, Inlaid, Pennsylvania, c.1780, 29 x 47 x 21 1/2 In. 5175.00
Chest, Dressing, 4 Drawers, Rosewood, Marble Top, Oval Mirror, 68 1/2 x 42 In. 880.00
Chest, Drexel, 1 Narrow Above 3 Long Drawers, Bleached Maple, 38 x 15 x 33 In...... 230.00
Chest, Dunlap Style, 6 Graduated Drawers, Birch, Crown Molding, N.H. 6500.00
Chest, Eastlake, Walnut, Burl Veneer, 6 Drawers, Hinged Locking Strip, 55 In. 990.00
Chest, Egyptian Revival, 4 Drawers, Red, Black & Yellow Grain Painted 825.00
Chest, Empire Style, 5 Drawers, Mahogany, Ormolu Mounted, 45 3/4 x 48 1/2 In........ 2300.00
Chest, Empire Style, Brown & Yellow Grain Painted, Miniature.................................... 700.00
Chest, Empire, 3 Short, 4 Long Drawers, Mahogany, Recessed Galleried Top, 50 In. ... 900.00
Chest, Empire, 4 Drawers, Painted Yellow, Smoke Design Columns............................ 5060.00
Chest, Empire, 4 Drawers, Zebra Red & Black Grained, Spiral-Turned Columns.......... 1659.00
Chest, Empire, Poplar & Pine, c.1820-1840 .... 450.00
Chest, English Provincial, 6 Drawers, Oyster Pattern, Burl Walnut, 44 In. 4950.00
Chest, F.L. Wright, 6 Drawers, No. 2000, Taliesan, Heritage Henredon, 27 x 52 In...... 1650.00
Chest, Federal, 2 Over 3 Long Drawers, Mahogany, Paterie Inlay, 40 x 39 x 21 In. 978.00
Chest, Federal, 4 Drawers, Cherry Inlay, Bracket Feet 550.00
Chest, Federal, 4 Drawers, Cherrywood, New England, 1790, 42 x 44 x 19 In. 1600.00
Chest, Federal, 4 Drawers, Mahogany, French Feet, Brass Pulls, 44 1/2 x 46 1/4 In...... 2100.00
Chest, Federal, 4 Drawers, Mahogany, Scrolled, Turned Columns, c.1830................... 467.50
Chest, Federal, 4 Graduated Drawers, Mahogany, Inlaid, Mass., 1800, 36 In. 9775.00
Chest, Federal, 4 Mahogany Veneer Drawer Fronts, Cherry & Maple, 52 In. 1150.00
Chest, Federal, 9 Drawers, Walnut, Quarter Pillars, Bracket Feet ....; 5500.00
Chest, Federal, Bowfront, Mahogany, Inlay, 4 Graduated Drawers, 47 x 41 x 26 In...... 3220.00
Chest, Federal, Curly Maple, Cherry, 1820, 38 x 41 In.   *Illus* 7475.00
Chest, Federal, Walnut, Inlaid, c.1800, 20 1/2 x 39 x 19 In.. 6325.00
Chest, French Empire, 3 Drawers, Marble Top, Eagle Brasses...................................... 3300.00
Chest, George III, 3 Drawers, Bowfront, Inlaid Mahogany, c.1800, 37 1/4 In. 1150.00
Chest, George III, Bowfront, Mahogany, Fruitwood String Inlay, c.1800 .... 935.00
Chest, Georgian Style, 2 Short, 2 Long Drawers, Mahogany, D-Shaped Top, 38 x 19 In. 360.00
Chest, Georgian Style, 2 Small Over 3 Long Drawers, Mahogany, 40 x 42 In. 1100.00
Chest, Georgian Style, Serpentine, Brush Slide, Cross-Banded Top, 1900, 28 x 17 In... 415.00
Chest, Georgian, 2 Over 3 Drawers, Bowfront, Mahogany, 1800, 44 x 43 x 22 In......... 825.00
Chest, Georgian, 5 Drawers, Bowfront, Mahogany, 41 x 41 x 20 In. 1545.00
Chest, Georgian, 5 Drawers, Fruitwood, Bracket Feet, Provincial, 1750, 37 In. 715.00
Chest, Georgian, 5 Drawers, Mahogany, Splayed Feet, 1800, 42 x 43 x 21 In. 1100.00
Chest, Gustav Stickley, 2 Over 4 Drawers, No. 627, 39 x 22 x 59 In. 6600.00
Chest, Gustav Stickley, 2 Short Over 2 Wide Drawers, Mirrored, No. 911, 66 In. 2500.00
Chest, Gustav Stickley, 2 Small Over 4 Long Drawers, No. 626.................................... 2400.00

Chest, Hepplewhite, 4 Drawers, Cherry, French Feet, Dovetailed, 19 x 39 x 39 In. 440.00
Chest, Hepplewhite, 4 Graduated Drawers, Glass Knobs, 40 In. 1650.00
Chest, Hepplewhite, Bowfront, French Feet, Pennsylvania.. 1650.00
Chest, Hepplewhite, Cherry & Pine, Diamond Escutcheons, 71 1/4 In. 8250.00
Chest, Immigrant's, Pine, Dome Top, Painted Black Label, 34 In. 195.00
Chest, Immigrant's, Pine, Dovetailed, Dome Top, Painted, Floral Panel, 1864, 35 In. 385.00
Chest, Immigrant's, Pine, Stenciled Flowers & 1746, Bear Trap Lock, 17 x 42 In. 165.00
Chest, Lingerie, Georgian Style, Burl Yew Wood 1705.00
Chest, Liquor, Mahogany, Brass Handles, Blown Glass Bottles, c.1812, 10 3/8 In........ 2000.00
Chest, Maple, Carved, New England, c.1770, 85 x 39 x 19 In.. 9775.00
Chest, Military Campaign, On Reverse Mrs. Rae, 11 x 39 x 35 In................................... 1485.00
Chest, Mule, 2 Drawers, 2 False Drawers, Pine, Straight Apron, 41 1/4 In................... 430.00
Chest, Mule, Chippendale, 3 Drawers, 2 Fake Drawers, Pine, Hinged Lid, 50 1/4 In. ... 1265.00
Chest, Mule, Hepplewhite, 2 Dovetailed & 2 False Drawers, Red, Country, 42 In. 1980.00
Chest, Neoclassical, 3 Drawers, Karelian Birch, Canted Corners, Russia, 36 x 47 In. 8050.00
Chest, Pine, 5 Drawers, East Indian Co., Cargo To All Ports, Painted, 1851 .... 385.00
Chest, Pine, 5 Graduated Drawers, Bracket Feet, Spurs, New England, 44 x 36 In. 225.00
Chest, Queen Anne, 5 Graduated Drawers, Maple, Painted, c.1760, 49 x 36 In............. 4025.00
Chest, Queen Anne, Cherry, Bonnet Top, Carved, c.1770, 82 x 38 In. 9775.00
Chest, Queen Anne, Mahogany, Bonnet Top, Cock-Beaded, Mass., 1750-1760, 84 In... 9300.00
Chest, Queen Anne, Maple, Graduated Drawers, Cabriole Legs, 69 x 40 x 20 In.... 1725.00
Chest, Regency, 5 Drawers, 1810, 40 x 40 x 20 In.. 1045.00
Chest, Regency, 5 Drawers, Bowfront, Mahogany, Ivory Escutcheon Inlay, 1830 .... 910.00
Chest, Regency, 5 Drawers, Mahogany, Inlaid, Lion's-Head Handles, 57 x 52 x 21 In.. 715.00
Chest, Regency, Mahogany, 5 Drawers, Lion's-Head Handles, 37 x 47 In. 715.00
Chest, Scratch-Carved Pine, Incised Pinwheel & Geometric Design, c.1710, 39 In. 2875.00
Chest, Shaker, 5 Graduated Drawers, Pine, Harvard Community, c.1840, 5 Ft.............. 2300.00
Chest, Sheraton, 2 Over 3 Drawers, Cherry & Maple, Shaped Backboard, Finials 1320.00
Chest, Sheraton, 4 Drawers, 2 Small Top Drawers, Cherry, Mahogany, New England .. 1950.00
Chest, Sheraton, 4 Drawers, Cherry, 40 x 37 In. 1100.00
Chest, Sheraton, 4 Drawers, Figured Wood, Inlaid, Country 1150.00
Chest, Sheraton, 4 Graduated Beaded Drawers, Walnut, c.1830, 40 x 39 In. 575.00
Chest, Sheraton, 4 Graduated Drawers, Tiger Maple, Cherry Top, 19th Century........... 1760.00
Chest, Sheraton, 5 Drawers, Mahogany, 1790, 39 x 35 x 20 In. 1430.00
Chest, Sheraton, 5 Drawers, Mahogany, Beaded Edges, Turned Legs, 42 x 40 In. 855.00
Chest, Sheraton, Bowfront, Painted Design, Turned Legs, Brasses, Maine, 1820.......... 3200.00
Chest, Sheraton, Cherry, Mahogany Veneer, Brasses, Hartford, Conn., 1820-1830....... 4500.00
Chest, Sheraton, Painted Design, Pinwheel Wooden Knobs, Maine, 1825.................... 3600.00
Chest, Sheraton, Step Back, Bowfront, Backsplash, Rope-Turned Supports 705.00
Chest, Smoke Grained, 6 Board, Yellow & Black Trim, New England, 1825................. 2750.00
Chest, Storage, 1 Drawer, Lift Top, Bracket Base 305.00
Chest, Storage, Dome Top, Painted, Polly Draper's Property, c.1830, 22 x 44 In. 546.00
Chest, Storage, Shaker, Pine, Cherry, Painted, Black Handles, Dovetailed, 22 x 37 In... 1325.00
Chest, Sugar, Cherry, c.1820.. 3600.00
Chest, Sugar, Poplar, Bracket Feet, Arched Apron 250.00
Chest, Sugar, Shaker, 2 Drawers, Maple, Pine, Oak, Hinged Lid, Door, 47 x 25 In. 4025.00
Chest, Tall, Federal, Walnut, 5 Short Over 4 Thumb-Molded Long Drawers 4025.00
Chest, Tall, Louis XV Style, Kingwood, 6 Drawers, Marble Top, Ormolu, 1880 .... 1320.00
Chest, Tall, Mahogany, Serpentine, 1 Long Over 4 Graduated Drawers, 1870, 59 In. ... 1840.00
Chest, Thomas A. Braman, 3 Graduated Drawers, Gallery Drawers, Butternut 450.00
Chest, Victorian, 5 Drawers, Mahogany, Plinth Base, 38 x 39 x 22 In. 412.00
Chest, Victorian, 6 Drawers, Walnut, Carved Backsplash, Plinth Base, 60 x 41 In. 2035.00
Chest, Victorian, Marble Top, Carved Lions' Heads & Paw Feet................................... 1800.00
Chest, Walnut, Bracket Feet, Handmade, 1775 .... 4200.00
Chest, Walnut, Eastlake, Entleman's, Side Lock 1430.00
Chest, William & Mary, 5 Drawers, Walnut Veneer, Inlaid, England, 36 x 34 In. 3080.00
Chest, William & Mary, Birch, Maple, c.1730, 67 x 36 x 18 1/2 In............................... 5462.00
Chest, William & Mary, Maple, Cup-Turned Legs, Secret Door, 1720 .... 7300.00
Chest, William & Mary, Walnut Veneer, Pine, Drawers, 60 x 35 1/2 In......................... 5175.00
Chest, William & Mary, Walnut, 36 x 36 1/2 x 24 1/4 In. 2185.00
Chest-On-Chest, 2 Short Over 3 Graduated Drawers, Walnut, Oak, England, c.1780 .... 1650.00
Chest-On-Chest, 3 Over 3 Drawers, Oak, Columns, Dental Molding, 1780, 74 In. 7800.00
Chest-On-Chest, Chippendale, Birch, Massachusetts, c.1780, 78 x 39 x 19 1/2 In. 4312.00

Chest-On-Chest, Chippendale, Mahogany, Pullout Shelf In Base, 74 1/4 In. 4290.00
Chest-On-Chest, England, Mahogany, Serpentine Front, 65 In. 2750.00
Chest-On-Chest, Fret-Carved Corners, Slide Over 3 Drawers, 1870s, 6 Ft. 2 In. 4887.00
Chest-On-Chest, George III, Mahogany, 78 3/4 In. 4025.00
Chest-On-Chest, George III, Mahogany, c.1785, 72 3/4 x 42 x 21 3/4 In. 2300.00
Chest-On-Chest, George III, Mahogany, Molded Cornice, 1780, 75 x 40 x 23 In. 2530.00
Chest-On-Chest, Georgian, Mahogany, Bracket Feet, Swan Handles, c.1780 .... 1850.00
Chest-On-Chest, Georgian, Mahogany, Ogee Bracket Feet, 1780, 70 x 42 x 22 In. 2310.00
Chest-On-Chest, Regency, Bowfront, Carved Mahogany, Brass Hairy Paw Feet 6050.00
Chest-On-Frame, 6 Graduated Drawers, Maple, Bandy Legs, 36 In. 6820.00
Chest-On-Frame, 8 Overlapping Drawers, Walnut, Trifid Feet, 65 1/2 In. 6050.00
Chest-On-Frame, Queen Anne, 2 Graduated Long Drawers, Maple, 54 x 37 x 19 In. 1150.00
Chest-On-Frame, Queen Anne, 5 Graduated Drawers, Poplar, 18th Century 6875.00
Chiffonier, Boudin, Tulipwood, Marble Top, 6 Drawers, Tambour Slide, 45 1/2 In. 9200.00
Chiffonier, Empire, Mahogany, Ormolu, Concave Marble Top, 63 x 33 1/4 In. 6035.00
Chiffonier, Limbert, 5 Drawers, Wooden Knobs, Arched Bottom, No. 487, 50 In. 3300.00
Chiffonier, Louis XV Style, Kingwood, Tulipwood, Marble Top, 32 3/4 x 23 3/4 In. 690.00
Chiffonier, Louis XV, Fruitwood, Marquetry, Serpentine, 3 Drawers, 19 x 14 In. 9200.00
Chiffonier, Louis XV-XVI, Tulipwood, Fruitwood, Marquetry, 1 Drawer, 29 In. 4600.00
Chiffonier, Louis XV-XVI, Tulipwood, Purplewood, Parquetry, 7 Drawers, 58 In. 6900.00
Claret, Beidermeir, Walnut, Down Curving Hinged Top, Parquetry, 25 In. 1850.00
Coal Holder, Victorian, Oak, Beveled Mirror, 1840 .... 730.00
Coat Rack, Adirondack, Hickory Style, 4 Slanted Legs, 8 Racks, 65 3/4 In. 195.00
Coat Rack, Bentwood, Clustered Central Shaft, 4 Down-Scrolled Legs, 96 In. 660.00
Coat Rack, Lifetime, Angled Feet, 4 Brass Hooks, Dark Finish, 67 x 20 x 20 In. 250.00
Coat Rack, Stickley Brothers, Brass Hooks, Label, 72 x 23 1/2 In. 715.00
Coat Tree & Umbrella Stand, Oak & Brass, c.1880 .... 285.00
Coffer-On-Stand, George III, Mahogany, Domed Lid, Interior Tray, Drawer, 30 In. 1955.00
Commode, 1 Drawer & 1 Door, Marble Top, France 330.00
Commode, 1 Drawer Over 2 Paneled Doors, Pine, Shaped Back 83.00
Commode, 1 Drawer, 2 Doors Over 1 Drawer, Mahogany Veneer, 20 1/2 x 31 In. 225.00
Commode, 2 Doors, Drawer, Legs, Mahogany Veneer, 19th Century, 20 x 30 In. 275.00
Commode, 3 Drawers, Fruitwood, Brass Gallery, Marble Top, 29 In. 430.00
Commode, 3 Drawers, Walnut, Carved Wooden Pulls 280.00
Commode, 3 Drawers, Walnut, Serpentine, Marble Top 6050.00
Commode, 3 Long Drawers, Fruitwood, Thumb Molded Apron, Shaped Top, 39 In. 865.00
Commode, 4 Drawers, Ormolu Mounted, Sun King Bronze Design, France, Pair 7700.00
Commode, Baroque, Walnut, Marquetry, Molded Top, Germany, c.1750, 34 x 49 In. 2875.00
Commode, Baroque, Walnut, Marquetry, Serpentine Top, Germany, 35 1/4 x 51 In. 5465.00
Commode, Bombe, 2 Drawers, Parquetry, Marble Top, 33 x 44 3/4 In. 1760.00
Commode, Bombe, Rococo Style, Fruitwood, Italy, 31 x 29 1/2 In., Pair 3025.00
Commode, Charles X, Burl Birch, Ormolu, Marble Top, Bracket Feet, 49 1/4 In. 8050.00

Furniture, Commode, Louis XV, Bombe, Walnut, French, 34 x 49 x 24 In.

Commode, Empire, 4 Graduated Drawers, Mahogany, Ormolu, 36 x 50 x 26 In. 9200.00
Commode, Empire, Mahogany, Ormolu, Gray Marble Top, Female Capitals, 51 In. 8625.00
Commode, Flemish Style, 2 Drawers, Shaped Marble Top, 22 x 14 x 26 In., Pair 635.00
Commode, French Style, Fruitwood Veneer, Marble Top, Cabriole Legs 440.00
Commode, French Style, Fruitwood Veneer, Marble Top, Brass Mounts 330.00
Commode, Georgian, Burl Elm, Tray Top, 3/4 Gallery, 1760, 30 x 21 x 18 In. 1100.00
Commode, Gio Ponti, 4 Drawers, Burl Walnut, Bowed, Tapered Legs, 1930, 35 In. 4600.00
Commode, Italian Rococo, Walnut, Serpentine, 36 1/4 x 46 1/2 In. 5750.00
Commode, Italian Rococo, Walnut, 31 x 20 1/2 In., Pair 4025.00
Commode, Louis XV Style, Bombe, 3 Drawers, Faux Painted, Splayed Feet, 68 1/4 In. 860.00
Commode, Louis XV Style, Fruitwood, Metal Mounts, 27 x 15 x 29 In. 375.00
Commode, Louis XV Style, Rosewood, Marble Top, Marquetry, c.1900, 54 In. 4400.00
Commode, Louis XV, 3 Drawers, Pine 6500.00
Commode, Louis XV, Bombe, 3 Drawers, Kingwood, Ormolu, Marquetry, 23 In. 1540.00
Commode, Louis XV, Bombe, 3 Drawers, Walnut, Ormolu, France, 49 x 24 In. 7475.00
Commode, Louis XV, Bombe, French, 18th Century 6500.00
Commode, Louis XV, Bombe, Walnut, French, 34 x 49 x 24 In. ....*Illus* 7475.00
Commode, Louis XVI Style, Kingwood & Tulipwood Parquetry, 32 3/4 In. 1265.00
Commode, Louis XVI, 3 Graduated Drawers, Mahogany, Marble, 37 x 17 In. 4600.00
Commode, Louis XVI, Mahogany, Brass Mounted, Chavignau, 35 x 50 x 22 In. 6325.00
Commode, Mahogany, Pullout Bottom, English, 30 x 20 In. 355.00
Commode, Marquetry On Drawer Fronts, Side Panels & Top, 33 x 45 In. 4400.00
Commode, Neoclassical Style, 2 Short Over 2 Long Drawers, Parcel Gilt, Italy 8050.00
Commode, Pine, Lift Top, Dovetail Construction, 18 x 19 In. 110.00
Commode, Pine, Painted Scene Of General Washington & Troops, 31 x 29 In. 2750.00
Commode, Queen Anne, 3 Drawers, Walnut, Serpentine, 19 In. 192.00
Commode, Regency, 2 Doors, 1 Drawer, Mahogany, Bowed Top, French Feet, 23 In. .. 858.00
Commode, Regency, Kingwood, Ormolu, Serpentine Front, Marble Top, 51 1/2 In..... 9775.00
Commode, Swedish Rococo, Kingwood, Ormolu Mounted, Bombe Case, 41 In. 6325.00
Console, Empire, Mahogany, Serpentine, 3 Tiers, Marble Top, 1825 .... 1045.00
Console, Neoclassical Style, Marble Top, Winged Female Terns, Parcel Gilt, 34 In. 4312.00
Console, Neoclassical, Ebonized, Parcel Gilt, Marble Top, Leaf-Tip Carving, Sweden . 6900.00
Console, Neoclassical, Mahogany, Parcel Gilt, Marble Top, Paw Feet, Sweden 5175.00
Console, Neoclassical, Mahogany, Parcel Gilt, Leaf-Tip Border, Fretwork, 26 1/2 In. ... 4025.00
Console, Regency, Oak, 3 Drawers, Mask Scroll Handles, Marble, 38 In. 6325.00
Console, Rococo, Carved Giltwood, Pierced Serpentine Skirt, Animal Paw Feet 2200.00
Cradle, Bentwood Ends, Late 1800s, 36 x 27 In. 395.00
Cradle, Biedermeier, Mahogany, Columnar Supports, Swan's Head, 41 In., Pair 2300.00
Cradle, Birch, Red Stained, Arched Head & Footboard, Iron Handles, 20 x 37 In. 605.00
Cradle, Bird's-Eye Maple, Turned Posts, Spindles, Laced Canvas Bottom, 30 In. 1100.00
Cradle, Curly Maple, Canted Sides, Scalloped Step-Down Edges, 41 In. 495.00
Cradle, Federal, Mahogany, Heart Cutouts, Rectangular Frame, 1800, 30 In. 425.00
Cradle, Field, On Rockers, Patent October 17, 1876, Gold Lettering............................... 850.00
Cradle, Jacobean, Hooded, England 2300.00
Cradle, Mahogany, Hooded, 40 In. 145.00
Cradle, On Frame, c.1850 .... 1795.00
Cradle, Painted Red-Brown, New England, c.1830, 22 x 16 x 50 1/2 In. 285.00
Cradle, Painted Wood, Red, Yellow & Black Geometrics, 33 In. 330.00
Cradle, Pine, Scalloped Sides, Painted Red.. 200.00
Cradle, Poplar, Dark Worn Finish, Posts, Spindles, 20 x 40 In. 140.00
Cradle, Swinging, 2 Wheels In Front, Handle In Back, Slats, Ford Johnson Co. 1150.00
Cradle, Walnut, Cutout Rockers, 37 In. 225.00
Cradle, Walnut, Painted, Dark Greenish Black, 36 1/2 In. 245.00
Cradle, Walnut, Pierced-Cut Scrollwork On Ends & Splat Sides 975.00
Cradle, Walnut, Scrolled Ends & Crest, 42 1/4 In. 205.00
Cradle, Windsor, Painted, New England, c.1810, 24 x 17 1/2 x 38 In............................ 2300.00
Credenza, Baroque Style, Walnut, Canted Corners, Italy, 33 x 28 x 13 In. 1265.00
Credenza, Continental, Burl Walnut, Rosewood, Satinwood, 3 Doors, 64 In. 3300.00
Credenza, Dutch Baroque Style, Oak, Carved Panel Of Dutch Farmers, 67 In. 1925.00
Credenza, Late Renaissance Style, Overhanging Frieze, Italy, 46 x 92 x 22 In. 7475.00
Credenza, Regency, Mahogany, 1 Drawer Over 2 Paneled Doors, 37 x 39 x 14 In. 825.00
Credenza, Rosewood, Serpentine Top, Glazed Cabinet Doors, 37 x 48 In..................... 690.00
Credenza, Walnut, Marble Top, Oval Mirrors On 4 Cabinet Doors, 1860, 73 In. 1760.00

Crib, Arts & Crafts, Cutout Spade Design, Mattress, 40 x 48 1/2 x 25 In. 990.00
Crib, Gothic Revival, Walnut, Pointed Pillar Posts, N.Y., 1840, 45 x 29 x 43 In. 1495.00
Crib, White Wicker, Large 600.00
Cube, Storage, Hans Wegner, Teak, Brushed Steel Legs, Denmark, 19 x 20 x 20 In. 990.00
Cupboard, 12 Pane Doors, 3 Drawers, Half Columns, Spoon Notches, Pa. 2600.00
Cupboard, 12 Panes Over Pie Shelf, 3 Drawers, 2 Doors, Mixed Wood 2600.00
Cupboard, 8 Paned Doors, Painted Red, Indiana 380.00
Cupboard, Amish, Pine, Hinged Work Top, Dough Box, Flour Bin, Pa. 2195.00
Cupboard, Baker's, Pullout Table 2700.00
Cupboard, Baroque Revival, White Oak, Brown Finish, 3 Glass Doors, 63 x 99 In. 2310.00
Cupboard, Bird's-Eye Maple, Paneled, 1 Door 625.00
Cupboard, Cherry, Raised Panel Construction, 2 Pairs Of Doors, 86 In. 1980.00
Cupboard, Cherry, Upper Doors, 3 Center Drawers, 19th Century, 87 In. 3300.00
Cupboard, Chimney, 1 Door, Shelves, Painted Red, 42 In. 200.00
Cupboard, Chimney, 3 Lower Drawers, Painted Blue 410.00
Cupboard, Chimney, 4-Panel Door, Painted Red, 7 Ft. 975.00
Cupboard, Chimney, Shaker, Pine, Dark Brown, Painted Cream Interior, 1 Door, 7 Ft. 4950.00
Cupboard, Chippendale, 12-Pane Top Door, 2-Door Base, 1820, 2 Piece 4850.00
Cupboard, Chippendale, Paneled Doors, Chester County, 81 x 55 In. 3680.00
Cupboard, Corner, Alternate Cherry & Curly Maple Blind Doors, 88 In. 2860.00
Cupboard, Corner, Cherry, 3 Drawers, 1 Top Door, 12 Panes, 84 In. 2530.00
Cupboard, Corner, Cherry, Double Door Base, 2 Upper Doors, c.1800, 84 In. 8250.00
Cupboard, Corner, Cherry, Glazed, 2 Doors, New England, 19th Century 1800.00
Cupboard, Corner, Cherry, Glazed, c.1830, 89 1/2 x 46 1/2 x 32 1/4 In. 3450.00
Cupboard, Corner, Cherry, Paneled Base Doors, 8 Panes Each Door, 85 3/4 In. 1980.00
Cupboard, Corner, Cherry, Paneled Doors, 2 Drawers, 8 Glass Panes, 88 In. 6325.00
Cupboard, Corner, Cherry, Paneled Doors, 80 In. 1550.00
Cupboard, Corner, Cherry, Paneled Doors, Cove Molded Cornice, 84 3/4 In. 2100.00
Cupboard, Corner, Cherry, Pie Shelf, 1 Drawer, 1-Pane Doors, 89 1/4 In. 2145.00
Cupboard, Corner, Chippendale, Painted, 1 Drawer & Door, Pa., 1760-1780 .... 5250.00
Cupboard, Corner, Curly Maple, 4 Doors & 2 Middle Drawers, Butternut Cutouts 3300.00
Cupboard, Corner, Federal, Cherry, Hinged Paneled Door, 74 3/4 In. 2415.00
Cupboard, Corner, Federal, Pine Glazed, Pa., c.1810, 85 x 50 x 26 In. 2415.00
Cupboard, Corner, Mahogany & Veneer, Glazed, c.1800, 94 x 48 x 22 1/2 In. 2990.00
Cupboard, Corner, Mahogany, Holland, 94 In. 6875.00
Cupboard, Corner, Pine, Painted, 4 Doors, Arts & Crafts Hardware, 74 x 46 In. 2425.00
Cupboard, Corner, Pine, Raised Panel Doors, Bracket Base, 75 x 41 In. 1100.00
Cupboard, Corner, Pine, Refinished, 4 Raised Panel Doors, Cornice, 50 x 94 In. 880.00
Cupboard, Corner, Poplar, Pie Shelf, Feather Grain Painted, 4 Doors 1200.00
Cupboard, Corner, Walnut, Blind Door, c.1850 .... 2200.00

Furniture, Cupboard, Dutch, Baroque, Oak,
88 x 59 x 23 In.

♦♦♦♦♦♦♦♦♦♦♦♦♦♦♦♦♦♦♦♦♦♦♦

To remove a smell from a
drawer, sprinkle the inside of
the drawer with baking soda
and leave it there for a week.
Vacuum. Repeat if necessary.
If the smell is from an animal,
try washing the wood with a
solution of neutroleum alpha,
found in pet stores.

♦♦♦♦♦♦♦♦♦♦♦♦♦♦♦♦♦♦♦♦♦♦♦

Cupboard, Corner, Walnut, Glazed Doors, Shelves, c.1800, 7 Ft. 11 In. 8625.00
Cupboard, Corner, Walnut, Paneled Doors, 1 Drawer, 87 1/4 In. 1870.00
Cupboard, Corner, Walnut, Paneled Doors, Zigzag Trim, 79 In. 825.00
Cupboard, Corner, Walnut, Raised Panel Door, Scalloped Apron, 84 3/4 In. 1870.00
Cupboard, Corner, Walnut, Shelved Interior, Lower Doors, c.1780, 8 Ft. 1 In. 3450.00
Cupboard, Country, 2 Shelves Over Single Drawer, Painted Backboard 225.00
Cupboard, Court, George III, Ebony Escutcheons, 74 1/4 x 54 1/4 In. 3335.00
Cupboard, Crock, Open, Painted Blue-Green.. 1300.00
Cupboard, Curly Maple, 16-Pane Doors, Flat Front, Paneled Lower Doors 1175.00
Cupboard, Dutch, Baroque, Oak, 88 x 59 x 23 In. ....*Illus* 5750.00
Cupboard, Federal, 2 Doors, Shelves, Grain Painted, 55 1/2 In. 4150.00
Cupboard, Flame Grained, 9-Pane Glass Door, Pa. 2200.00
Cupboard, Flat Front, Curly Maple Panels On Lower Doors 1175.00
Cupboard, Fluting Down Sides, Raised Panels, Base Doors, Brown.............................. 4500.00
Cupboard, French Provincial, Carved Fruitwood, 2 Parts, 2 Frieze Drawers, 86 In........ 1200.00
Cupboard, Glazed Mullioned Doors, Shelves, Grain Painted, 78 1/2 In. 2580.00
Cupboard, Hanging, Continental, Carved Brass, Mounted Walnut, Female Bust........... 145.00
Cupboard, Hanging, Painted Black, Yellow Striping, Doors, Locks, 21 1/2 In.............. 1650.00
Cupboard, Hanging, Pine, Painted Gray Interior, Paneled Door, England, 39 In. 525.00
Cupboard, Hanging, Red Interior, Yellow & Blue Tulips On Door 385.00
Cupboard, Hanging, Walnut, 1 Door, Glazed Side Lights, Scalloped Shelves, 32 In. 660.00
Cupboard, Hanging, Walnut, Dentil Mold At Cornice, 32 In. 440.00
Cupboard, Hanging, Walnut, Glass Door, 1 Shelf, 2 Short Drawers, Penna. 8625.00
Cupboard, Hanging, Walnut, Paneled Door, Shelf, Beaded Frame, 26 1/2 In. 2100.00
Cupboard, Jelly, 2-Section Paneled Door, 5 Shelves, 19th Century 660.00
Cupboard, Jelly, Grain Painted, 2 Curly Maple Drawers, Dovetailed Gallery 1700.00
Cupboard, Jelly, Hardwood, Board & Batten Door, 44 1/2 In. 230.00
Cupboard, Jelly, Painted Design, 3 Drawers Over 2 Doors, 1830.................................. 1850.00
Cupboard, Jelly, Painted Red, 1-Panel Door, 4 Shelves, Shaped Cornice Molding 2100.00
Cupboard, Jelly, Pine & Poplar, Paneled Doors, Drawer, Scalloped Gallery, 54 In........ 825.00
Cupboard, Jelly, Pine, Raised Beaded Framed Panel Doors, 64 In. 2530.00
Cupboard, Jelly, Pine, Red, Paneled Door, 1 Drawer, Country, 36 x 18 x 55 In. 880.00
Cupboard, Jelly, Poplar, Dovetailed Case, Brass Thumb Latches, 59 3/4 In.................. 1100.00
Cupboard, Jelly, Poplar, Old Red Paint, Paneled Doors, 5 Shelves, Country, 68 In. 605.00
Cupboard, Jelly, Poplar, Paneled Doors, Red Grained, 71 1/2 In.................................. 1870.00
Cupboard, Kitchen, Pine, England, 1875 .... 3400.00
Cupboard, Kitchen, With Dry Sink, Oak, 5 Legs.. 2300.00
Cupboard, Molded Top, 4 Inside Shelves, 2 Panel Doors, 45 1/2 x 47 x 19 1/2 In. 385.00
Cupboard, Oak, 8 Stained Glass Doors Over 5 Drawers 5465.00
Cupboard, On Stand, Georgian, 1 Paneled Door, Provincial, 1750, 68 x 31 x 17 In. 1155.00
Cupboard, Pantry, Cutout Finials, Old Red Paint... 600.00
Cupboard, Parlor, Carved, 3 Doors, Figural Supports, Metal Hardware, 51 In. 550.00
Cupboard, Pewter, H-Hinged Panel Door, Painted Mustard, 6 Ft. 2800.00
Cupboard, Pewter, Pine, Paneled Doors, Open Top, Spoon Rack, 80 In. 1750.00
Cupboard, Pewter, Pine, Step Back, Open Shelves, 78 In... 2100.00
Cupboard, Pewter, Poplar, Open Top, 3 Shelves, Plate Bars, 75 3/4 In. 7375.00
Cupboard, Pewter, Poplar, Paneled Doors In Base, 3 Shelves, 73 1/2 In. 2860.00
Cupboard, Pewter, Poplar, Paneled Pine Doors, Open Top, 79 In. 385.00
Cupboard, Pewter, Step Back, 1 Door Base 350.00
Cupboard, Pine, Cleaned Natural Patina, 1 Door, 2 Drawers, Denmark, 31 x 63 In. 330.00
Cupboard, Pine, Hanging, Painted Blue & Red, 1 Door & Drawer, 1861, 25 x 27 In. 1155.00
Cupboard, Pine, Mullioned Upper Doors, Bracket Feet, 76 In...................................... 2000.00
Cupboard, Pine, Paneled Door, Back Splash, 16 1/2 x 20 1/2 x 9 In............................. 145.00
Cupboard, Pine, Upper Glazed Doors, Lower Paneled Doors, 88 In............................. 1325.00
Cupboard, Press, James II, Oak, 2 Upper Drawers, 2 Doors, Interior Drawers.............. 4400.00
Cupboard, Shaker, 2 Drawers Base, Painted Brownish Ochre, 1840, 71 In. 2200.00
Cupboard, Shaker, Chimney, Dark Brown, Cream Interior, 7 Ft.................................... 4950.00
Cupboard, Shaker, Gray Paint Traces, 2 Doors, Painted Blue Interior, Enfield, 38 In. ... 3300.00
Cupboard, Shaker, Pine, 1 Door, Small 1475.00
Cupboard, Shaker, Walnut & Poplar, 2 Drawers, Brass Thumb Latch, 89 In.................. 3750.00
Cupboard, Step Back, Cherry, 12 Pane Top, 2 Drawers Over 2 Door 700.00
Cupboard, Step Back, Cherry, 16 Pane Doors, Paneled Doors Base 2350.00
Cupboard, Step Back, Cherry, 2 Board Doors, Wooden Knobs, 72 3/4 In. 1100.00

Cupboard, Step Back, Cherry, Maple & Figured Maple, 1830s, 80 x 60 In................. 5900.00
Cupboard, Step Back, Country Chippendale Feet, Narrow, Painted Blue...................... 2400.00
Cupboard, Step Back, Painted Blue, Glass Top Doors, N.Y.. 10000.00
Cupboard, Step Back, Pine, Paneled Base Door, Brass Hinges, 83 1/2 In. 935.00
Cupboard, Step Back, Victorian, Child's... 650.00
Cupboard, Step Back, Walnut, 2 Doors Above Pie Shelf, 2 Narrow Drawers 1350.00
Cupboard, Step Tack, Walnut, Pie Shelf, Crown Molding, 19th Century...................... 2990.00
Cupboard, Wall, Oak, Flat, 2 Glass Doors, Over 2 Doors, Dark Varnish 250.00
Cupboard, Walnut, 2 Glass Pane Doors, 5 Drawers, Pennsylvania, 1860, 2 Piece 5500.00
Cupboard, Walnut, Curly Maple, 4 Doors & 3 Middle Drawers, 2 Piece 3900.00
Cupboard, Walnut, Pierced Tin Sides, Double Door 1075.00
Cupboard, Welsh, George III, Elm, 76 In.. 2990.00
Cupboard, Welsh, Oak, Panel Inset Doors, 5 Lower Drawers, 6 Ft. 8 In....................... 5175.00
Cupboard, White & Red Paint, Scrolled Top, 2 Doors, Lower Base Drawer.................. 475.00
Cupboard, Zinc Top, Tilt-Out Bin, Wainscot Front.. 195.00
Daybed, Adjustable Head Rest, Curved Posts, Flame Stitch Pillows, 80 In. 440.00
Daybed, Directoire, Painted, Anthemion Reserves, Toupie Feet, 78 1/2 In., Pair 6900.00
Daybed, Empire Style, Outscrolled Headboard, Rounded Footrest, 74 In., Pair 3750.00
Daybed, Empire, Carved Mahogany, 1835.. 660.00
Daybed, Folding, Wooden, Spindle Sides, 1900 .... 30.00
Daybed, Frank Lloyd Wright, Oak, Equal Ends, Horizontal Moldings, c.1902, Pair 8050.00
Daybed, George Nelson, Hairpin Legs, Upholstered, 27 x 75 In....................................... 1325.00
Daybed, Gustav Stickley, Oak, Knock-Down, Slats, No. 220, 34 x 84 x 36 In. 4600.00
Daybed, L. & J.G. Stickley, 4 Slats Each End, Tapering Posts, No. 292, 80 In. 2700.00
Daybed, Limbert, Angled Sides, Lower Corbels, No. 870, 33 x 82 In. 1875.00
Daybed, Louis XV Style, Carved & Painted Wood, 76 In. 800.00
Daybed, Neoclassical, Painted, Outscrolled Sides, Upholstered Seat, Italy, 89 In. 5750.00
Desk, 10 Spindles Each Side, 2 Drawers, Square Brass Pulls, 36 x 20 x 29 In. 2860.00
Desk, 3 Graduated Drawers Each Side, Marquetry, Folk Type 1550.00
Desk, Architectural Design, Wood, Bakelite, Celluloid & Chrome, 1920s 4400.00
Desk, Art Deco, Rosewood & Mahogany, Inlaid, Ebonized, France, 1925, 36 In.......... 1870.00
Desk, Arts & Crafts, Roll Top, Oak, 6 Drawers, 50 x 37 x 36 In. 800.00
Desk, Butler's, Bird's-Eye Mahogany, Acanthus Leaf, Hairy Paw Feet 550.00
Desk, Butler's, Federal, 3 Drawers, Top Drawer Pulls Out, Fitted Interior, 49 In. 275.00
Desk, Butler's, Federal, Mahogany, Hinged Drawer Over Drawer, 1810, 46 x 43 In. ... 4600.00
Desk, Butler's, Sheraton, Mahogany, Server Type, 2 Bowed Doors, 47 x 40 In............. 1210.00
Desk, Butler's, Walnut, Acanthus Leaves, Cubby Holes, 1840s 3300.00
Desk, C Roll Top, Quartersawn Oak, Card Files.. 2500.00
Desk, Captain's, Painting Of Sea Schooner Top, 1859, 5 Ft. 1200.00
Desk, Captain's, Sheraton, Mahogany, Fold-Out Front, Rope-Turned Legs, 28 x 18 In. 2200.00
Desk, Carlo Bugatti, Fall Front, 2 Sections, Inlaid, c.1900, 15 1/2 In............................ 8625.00
Desk, Cartonnier, Biedermeier, Black Walnut, Burl Birch, Tambour Slide, 43 In. 6900.00
Desk, Chippendale Style, Block Front, Mahogany, Kneehole, 29 x 36 In....................... 750.00
Desk, Chippendale Style, Slant Front, Mahogany, Serpentine, Rockford Furn. Co. 285.00
Desk, Chippendale Style, Slant Front, Curly Maple, 1930s 3100.00
Desk, Chippendale, Drop Front, Cherry, 4 Graduated Drawers, 1790, 40 In. 5000.00
Desk, Chippendale, Slant Front, Birch, Fitted Interior, 4 Drawers, 43 In....................... 1200.00
Desk, Chippendale, Slant Front, Birch, Double-Stepped Fan, Oxbow 4510.00
Desk, Chippendale, Slant Front, Birch, c.1780, 43 x 42 x 21 In...................................... 2760.00
Desk, Chippendale, Slant Front, Figured Maple, 4 Molded Drawers, 1770, 40 In. 5750.00
Desk, Chippendale, Slant Front, Mahogany, Serpentine Interior, 39 x 51 3/4 In. 3850.00
Desk, Chippendale, Slant Front, Mahogany, Reverse Serpentine, 4 Drawers, 42 In. 9200.00
Desk, Chippendale, Slant Front, Mahogany, Reverse Serpentine, 1760, 41 x 44 In........ 4025.00
Desk, Chippendale, Slant Front, Mahogany, Oxbow, 4 Graduated Drawers, 44 In......... 7590.00
Desk, Chippendale, Slant Front, Mahogany, 3 Drawers, 42 x 21 x 43 In........................ 3520.00
Desk, Chippendale, Slant Front, Maple, Rhode Island, c.1780, 41 x 34 x 18 In. 4025.00
Desk, Chippendale, Slant Front, Maple, New England, c.1780, 42 x 36 x 18 In. 3450.00
Desk, Chippendale, Slant Front, Maple, c.1790, 42 x 39 x 18 1/2 In. 2875.00
Desk, Chippendale, Slant Front, Maple, c.1780, 40 x 39 x 19 1/2 In. 2415.00
Desk, Chippendale, Slant Front, Maple, 4 Graduated Drawers, 1760, 42 x 37 In. 4600.00
Desk, Chippendale, Slant Front, Oak, 4 Drawers, Fitted, England, 50 x 20 x 44 In........ 600.00
Desk, Chippendale, Slant Front, Walnut, Inlaid, Bracket Feet, 41 x 35 x 19 In. 4600.00
Desk, Clerk's, Slant Front, Hepplewhite, Cherry, Lift Top, 1 Drawer, Country, 36 In. ... 690.00

Desk, Counting House, Pine, 50 1/2 x 38 In... 330.00
Desk, Cylinder, Eastlake, Walnut, Pull-Out Writing Surface, Large 2895.00
Desk, Double Roll Top, Indianapolis Cabinet Co., Walnut, Cupboard Base, 59 In. 5225.00
Desk, Drop Front, Birch, Serpentine, 41 1/2 In. 4510.00
Desk, Drop Front, Cherry, 4 Graduated Drawers, Shaped Bracket Base......................... 1860.00
Desk, Drop Front, Oak, Carved, 1880s... 990.00
Desk, Dutch Marquetry, Bombe, Mahogany, Cabriole Leg, 36 x 32 x 20 In. 1760.00
Desk, Dutch Rococo Style, Slant Front, Mahogany, Marquetry 4880.00
Desk, Edwardian, Mahogany, Kidney Shape, Satinwood Inlay, c.1890, 49 x 27 In. 2200.00
Desk, Edwardian, Satinwood, Square Tapering Legs, Paint Decorated, 53 x 28 In. 2645.00
Desk, Elm, 3 Drawers, Middle Drawer, Square Legs, Hoof Feet, 32 x 46 In. 635.00
Desk, Empire Style, Drop Front, Mahogany & Veneer, Carved Paw Feet....................... 385.00
Desk, F.L. Wright, Cypress, Triangular Top, Angled Legs, 1951, 57 1/2 x 49 In. 5750.00
Desk, Fall Front, Cherry, Document Drawers, Pigeonholes, c.1790, 45 In..................... 8500.00
Desk, Fall Front, Victorian Style, Walnut, 38 1/2 x 20 x 34 1/2 In. 115.00
Desk, Federal, Lift Top, Mahogany, Fitted Interior, Eagle & Masonic Inlay 4400.00
Desk, Federal, Mahogany, Tambour, Mullioned Doors, 1810s, 70 In. 8625.00
Desk, Frank Lloyd Wright, Triangular, Corner Drawers, Cypress, 1951, 25 3/4 In......... 5750.00
Desk, French Empire, Fall Front, Mahogany, Bronze Trim, Side Columns, 55 In........... 2587.50
Desk, G. Nelson, Drop Leaf, 3 Drawers, Brushed Tubular Steel, Herman Miller........... 715.00
Desk, George I Style, Yew, Kneehole, Central Recessed Cupboard, Bracket Feet......... 975.00
Desk, George III Style, Tooled Leather Over 2 Pedestals, Drawers, 55 3/4 In. 3335.00
Desk, George III, Mahogany, Hinged Writing Surface, 37 x 63 x 22 In....................... 935.00
Desk, George III, Satinwood, Painted, Ormolu, Leather Top, 30 x 57 x 29 In. 5775.00
Desk, George Nakashima, Walnut, Free Edge, Butterfly Fissure, Y Support, 54 In........ 4675.00
Desk, George Nelson, Forest Green Lacquer, Leather Top, Aluminum Legs 7000.00
Desk, Gilbert Rohde, Biomorphic Paldao Top, Herman Miller, 1940s, 52 x 26 In. 1980.00
Desk, Governor Winthrop, Mahogany, 1830, 68 x 34 x 17 In. 715.00
Desk, Gustav Stickley, 2 Drawers, Gallery, Paneled Sides, 35 x 40 In........................ 1450.00
Desk, Gustav Stickley, Copper Pulls, Letter Files, Decal, No. 708, Label, 36 x 40 In. ... 1760.00
Desk, Gustav Stickley, Drop Front, 1 Drawer, Branded Mark, 43 x 30 x 13 In. 825.00
Desk, Gustav Stickley, Drop Front, Copper Strap Hinges, No. 518, 51 1/4 In. 4675.00
Desk, Gustav Stickley, Fall Front, Copper Strap Hardware, No. 518, 52 In. 7150.00
Desk, Gustav Stickley, Flat, 2 Drawers Back & Front, V-Pulls, No. 720, 37 In. 3850.00
Desk, Gustav Stickley, Oak, Wooden Pulls, No. 430, c.1901, Youth's, 29 1/4 In. 575.00
Desk, Hepplewhite, Mahogany, 3 Drawers, Fold-Down Surface, 50 1/2 In. 1595.00
Desk, High School, Oak, Inkwell, Seat Slides On Metal Runners 375.00
Desk, Kidney Shape, Mahogany, 7 Drawers, Glass Top, Chair.................................... 325.00
Desk, Kneehole, 4 Drawers Either Side, Circular Legs, China Trade, 30 x 45 In. 575.00
Desk, Kneehole, Heywood Wakefield, Birch, 1950s, 49 x 24 In. 605.00
Desk, Lap, Boulle, Fully Fitted Interior, France, 19th Century, 8 1/2 x 12 1/2 In. 1975.00
Desk, Lap, Brassbound, Mother-Of-Pearl Inlay, Center Medallion, 10 1/2 x 15 In. 140.00
Desk, Lap, Burl Walnut, Brassbound, 6 x 16 In.. 300.00
Desk, Lap, Federal, Hinged Lid, Brass Corners, Fitted Interior, 5 x 13 1/2 In................ 258.00
Desk, Lap, Federal, Mahogany, Baize-Lined Compartments, Inlaid, 7 1/4 x 21 In. 1210.00
Desk, Lap, Papier-Mache, Scenes Of Battle Of Monitor & Merrimac On Lid............... 230.00
Desk, Lap, Rosewood, Mother-Of-Pearl, Lock, Hinges, 1850, 14 x 9 1/2 x 3 3/8 In....... 230.00
Desk, Lap, Simulated Rosewood, 13 In.. 38.00
Desk, Lap, Tiger Maple, 19th Century, 6 1/2 x 16 In. 747.00
Desk, Lap, Traveling, Boulle Work, Ebonized, Hinged Hood Cover, Paris, 14 x 11 In... 770.00
Desk, Lap, Walnut, Mother-Of-Pearl & Ebony Inlay 150.00
Desk, Lap, Walnut, Tambour Section, Opens When Drawer Pulled, 16 1/2 In................ 860.00
Desk, Larkin, Oak, Beveled Mirror 385.00
Desk, Lift Top, 1 Drawer, Square Tapered Legs, 19th Century 300.00
Desk, Louis XVI Style, Tambour Top, Ormolu Punts, 1 Drawer, c.1840...................... 450.00
Desk, Mahogany, 5 Drawers, Swag Design, France, 60 x 36 x 31 In. 1452.00
Desk, Mahogany, Center Drawer, Flanked By Banks Of 3 Drawers............................ 2640.00
Desk, Mahogany, Kneehole, Parchment Top, 2 Storage Wells, 1935, 5 Ft. 10 In. 4313.00
Desk, Mahogany, Veneer, Wavy Glass Doors, 4 Drawers, 76 In., 2 Piece 5610.00
Desk, Majorelle, Poppy Design, 1 Drawer, Bronze Pull, 29 1/2 In. 2500.00
Desk, Maple & Veneer, Kneehole, Ring Turned Legs, c.1830, 31 x 42 1/2 In. 2300.00
Desk, Marshall Field Co., Roll Top, Oak, 3/4 Size.. 425.00
Desk, Marshall Field, Walnut, 2 Slide Out Shelves, 8 Drawers, 33 x 54 x 30 In............. 350.00

Desk, Napoleon III Style, Slant Front, Mahogany, 5 Drawers, 33 x 20 In. 290.00
Desk, Neoclassical Provincial, Slant Front, Walnut, Marquetry, Italy, 42 x 49 In. 3165.00
Desk, On Frame, Hepplewhite, Slant Front, Pine, Wood Pegged, Country 550.00
Desk, On Frame, Queen Anne, Slant Front, Shell-Carved Interior, 1900s 3400.00
Desk, On Stand, Rosewood, Mother-Of-Pearl, Inlay, Victorian 210.00
Desk, Partner's, 2 Pedestals, Green Leather Inset Drawers, 1850, 44 x 73 In. 4400.00
Desk, Partner's, Chippendale, Mahogany, 10 Drawers, Cabriole Legs, 61 In. 1430.00
Desk, Partner's, Mahogany, Black Leather Inset, 9 Drawers, Plinth Base, 4 x 6 Ft. 3300.00
Desk, Partner's, Renaissance Style, Oak, Paneled Door, 30 x 59 In. 865.00
Desk, Pedestal, Walnut, Victorian, 43 x 54 x 27 In. 3750.00
Desk, Plantation, Drop Front, Glass Doors, Mixed Woods, 8 Ft. 2650.00
Desk, Plantation, Fall Front, Mahogany, Pigeonhole, Long Drawer, Ring-Turned Legs 360.00
Desk, Plantation, Lift Top, Walnut, 2-Piece Base, Double Door, 85 In. 1430.00
Desk, Queen Anne Style, Maple, 54 x 25 x 30 In. 288.00
Desk, Queen Anne, Slant Front, Cherry, Bandy Legs, 44 1/2 In. 5500.00
Desk, Queen Anne, Slant Front, Maple, 4 Graduated Drawers, 36 In. 5800.00
Desk, Railroad, Potter's Place, New Hampshire, Red 185.00
Desk, Regency, Mahogany, Double Pedestal, England 2875.00
Desk, Renaissance Revival, H. Closterman, Walnut & Burl, Cincinnati, Pat. 1878 .... 575.00
Desk, Roll Top, Mahogany, Gilt Metal Handles, Keyhole Escutcheons, 48 x 44 In. 2300.00
Desk, Roll Top, Oak, Child's 220.00
Desk, Roll Top, Oak, Raised Panel, 4 Side Drawers, Derby Co. 1995.00
Desk, Roll Top, Oak, Raised Panels, Fitted Drawer Interior, Grand Rapids Plate, 72 In. .. 9100.00
Desk, Roll Top, Secretary, Oak, 2 Glass Top Doors, Victorian 1800.00
Desk, Rosewood, Floral Abalone Inlay, 3 Drawers, Double Pedestal, 30 x 79 In. 975.00
Desk, S Roll Top, Indianapolis Cabinet Co., Walnut, Kneehole, 60 x 53 In. 2100.00
Desk, S Roll Top, Mahogany, c.1915, 66 In. 2500.00
Desk, S Roll Top, Oak, Fully Paneled, 55 x 45 In. 1800.00
Desk, School, Wooden, Iron Base 500.00
Desk, Schoolmaster's, Drawer, Slant Front, Pine, Fitted Interior, 36 3/4 In. 600.00
Desk, Schoolmaster's, Slant Front, Lift Top, Cherry, Turned Legs, 20 x 18 x 31 In. 165.00
Desk, Secretary, Burl & Bird's-Eye Maple, Crest, Fitted, 44 x 38 x 74 In. 7425.00
Desk, Secretary, Fall Front, Oak, Veneer, 2 Drawers, Cabriole Lets, 2 Part 1430.00
Desk, Secretary, Governor Winthrop, Mahogany, Serpentine, Ball & Claw Feet 520.00
Desk, Sewing, Shaker, Alfred, Maine 19000.00
Desk, Sewing, Shaker, Birch, Pine 14000.00
Desk, Sewing, Shaker, Pine, Canterbury 1725.00
Desk, Sewing, Shaker, Pink, 19th Century, 30 1/2 x 22 x 17 In. 1725.00
Desk, Shaker, Painted Red Over Salmon, Enfield, 53 In. 3850.00
Desk, Sheraton Style, Woman's, Mahogany, Leather, Satinwood Inlay 880.00
Desk, Slant Front, Bombay, Dutch Marquetry, England, 1730 .... 12500.00
Desk, Slant Front, Burl Walnut, Sweden, 41 x 38 x 22 1/4 In. 3750.00
Desk, Slant Front, Cherry, 3 Tiger Maple Drawer Fronts, 41 1/2 x 43 1/2 x 19 In. 935.00
Desk, Slant Front, Cherry, 4 Overlapping Drawers, Fitted Interior, 1893, 42 1/4 In. 3190.00
Desk, Slant Front, Cherry, Compartmented Interior, 36 1/2 In. 990.00
Desk, Slant Front, Cherry, Original Finish, 1900s, 42 x 26 In. 750.00
Desk, Slant Front, Federal, Cherry, Stepped Valance, 44 x 40 x 18 In. 2185.00
Desk, Slant Front, Mahogany, Brass Gallery, Inlaid Front, Victorian, 31 In. 1100.00
Desk, Slant Front, Mahogany, Gilt Tooled Leather, Fitted Interior, c.1825 .... 1210.00
Desk, Slant Front, Mahogany, Interior Pigeonholes, Shaped Bracket Feet, c.1800 .... 935.00
Desk, Slant Front, Oak, Claw Feet, Carved Lid, 1900 .... 1500.00
Desk, Slant Front, Oak, Fold-Out Surface, Cubby Holes, 19th Century, 39 1/4 In. 1490.00
Desk, Slant Front, Oak, Secret Compartment, 4 Drawers, England, 37 x 19 x 39 In. 1495.00
Desk, Slant Front, On Frame, Fitted Interior, Cherry, c.1760, 36 1/2 In. 8625.00
Desk, Slant Front, Pigeonholes Over Drawers, Applewood, c.1760, 43 1/4 In. 9775.00
Desk, Slant Front, Queen Anne, Walnut, c.1750, 39 x 34 1/2 In. 5465.00
Desk, Slant Front, Square Tapering Legs, Painted, 19th Century, 36 x 32 In. 550.00
Desk, Slant Front, Swell Front, Stepped Interior, Marquetry, France, 38 1/2 In. 1155.00
Desk, Slant Front, Tiger Maple, 4 Graduated Drawers, Conn. River Valley, 1765 .... 8900.00
Desk, Slant Front, Walnut, Beaded Tapered Block Legs, 40 x 48 In. 1550.00
Desk, Slant Front, Walnut, Fitted Interior, Document Drawers, 42 In. 2585.00
Desk, Slant Front, Walnut, Interior Cubbyholes & Drawers, Pull-Out Bench 230.00
Desk, Slant Front, Walnut, Joseph Kindig III, 3 Graduated Drawers 14950.00

Desk, Slant Front, Walnut, Virginia 2600.00
Desk, Slant Top, Mahogany & Marquetry, 1890s, 42 1/2 x 50 In. 4900.00
Desk, Spinet, Fitted Interior, Turned Legs, American, 19th Century, 46 x 31 In. 195.00
Desk, Spinet, Rosewood, 2 Drawers Over Scroll-Cut Apron, Casters, 56 1/2 In. 520.00
Desk, Spinet, Rosewood, American, 2 Drawers Over Cup Apron, Bulbous Legs, 56 In. 520.00
Desk, Spinet, Rosewood, Foldover Top, Cubbyholes, Drawers, 31 1/4 In. 1090.00
Desk, Table Top, Lift Top, Curly Maple, Interior Shelf, 3 Drawers, 18 x 28 1/2 In. 990.00
Desk, Teakwood, Carved Dragons, Curio Niches, Cabinets, 3 Drawers, China 2875.00
Desk, Tobey Furniture Co., Leather Top, Cutout Sides, No. 3688, 29 In. 880.00
Desk, Traveling, Shaker, Walnut, Lift Top, Brass Hinges, 1880, 3 x 14 3/4 x 7 1/2 In. .. 440.00
Desk, Walnut, 6 Drawers, Side Door, 1880-1890, 56 x 30 x 30 In. 1175.00
Desk, William & Mary, Walnut, 1 Long & 2 Short Drawers, 54 x 28 x 30 In. 210.00
Desk, William & Mary, Walnut, Upper Long Drawer, 2 Short On Side, 30 In. 145.00
Desk, Writing, French Provincial, Walnut, 2-Drawer Gallery, Scalloped Sides 1045.00
Desk, Writing, Woman's, American Aesthetic, Ebonized Cherry, c.1885, 30 In. 1150.00
Desk Bookcase, Art Deco, Slant Front 650.00
Desk Bookcase, Hinged Writing Space, Fitted, 2 Parts, 79 x 34 x 20 In. 2530.00
Desk Bookcase, Sticher & Clemmens, Mahogany, Inlaid, c.1804, 7 Ft. 5 In. 8625.00
Desk Bookcase, Walnut, Burl Trim, Fitted, Victorian, 1870 .... 6450.00
Dining Set, Edward Doff, Oak, Woven Splint Seats, 4 Leaves, 13 Piece 690.00
Dining Set, Eero Saarinen, Pedestal Table, Eggshell Chairs, Knoll, 7 Piece 1540.00
Dining Set, F.L. Wright, Mahogany, Copper, Heritage-Henredon, c.1955, 5 Piece 1150.00
Dining Set, Federal Style, Mahogany, Baker, Double Pedestal Table, 8 Piece 6050.00
Dining Set, L. Jallot, Mahogany & Rosewood, Draw Leaf, 8 Chairs, c.1930, 9 Piece 5500.00
Dining Set, Mahogany & Birch, Draw Leaf, 6 Upholstered Chairs, 1935, 8 Ft. 4 In..... 6325.00
Dining Set, Mahogany, Banded Inlay, China Cabinet, 1900s, 9 Piece 6200.00
Dining Set, Nichols & Stone, Painted Green, Black Windsor Chairs, 8 Piece 1495.00
Dining Set, Oak, Northwind Carved, Round Table, 6 Chairs, Victorian, 1890, 9 Piece .. 3850.00
Dining Set, Queen Anne, Table Opens To 8 1/2 Ft., 1910, Belgium, 7 Piece 2295.00
Dining Set, Roycroft, 1909, 4 Piece 23000.00
Dining Set, Rustic, Rev. Ben Davis, 1887-1968, 5 Piece 6900.00
Dining Set, Waterfall, Leather Seat, Table & 4 Chairs 850.00
Dining Set, White Wicker, Round Table, Chintz Cushions, 5 Piece 2450.00
Dining Set, White Wrought Iron, Glass Top Table, 2 Armchairs, 1930s, 5 Piece 1400.00
Dining Set, William & Mary Style, Oak, Host & Hostess Chair, 11 Piece 460.00
Divan, Victorian, Meridienne, Wicker, Curvilinear Design, Beads, 38 In. 1045.00
Dresser, Classical, Mahogany, Gilt Stencil, 5 Drawers, 67 x 29 In. 1980.00
Dresser, Eastlake, Marble Top, Mirror, 3 Drawers, 2 Glove Drawers 220.00
Dresser, Eastlake, Walnut, 3 Drawers, Marble Top, Mirror, Lamp Shelves, 43 x 88 In. . 275.00
Dresser, Golden Oak, 2 Over 4 Drawer, Curved Front, Locking Drawers 270.00
Dresser, Heywood-Wakefield, 4 Drawers, Splayed Legs, 32 x 20 x 43 In...................... 495.00
Dresser, L. & J.G. Stickley, Oak, 4 Drawers, Copper Hardware, Mirror, 36 x 42 In. 2530.00
Dresser, Mahogany, Short Over 5 Long Drawers, Fan-Carved Skirt 410.00
Dresser, Maple, 5 Drawers, Serpentine 270.00
Dresser, Mirror, White Marble Insert, Candle Shelves, 2 Hankie Drawers 400.00
Dresser, Oak, Serpentine Front, 3 Drawers, Towel Bar, Claw Feet 100.00
Dresser, Oak, Tilt Beveled Mirror, Slide Hatbox, 2 Long Drawers 450.00
Dresser, Queen Anne Style, Oak, Rack, 19th Century, Welsh, 74 x 76 x 20 In. 2750.00
Dresser, Renaissance Revival, Walnut, Marble Top, 3 Graduated Drawers, Child's 1100.00
Dresser, Rococo Revival, Marble Top, Carved Walnut Mirror, Plated Pulls, 1850s........ 1650.00
Dresser, Rococo, Rosewood, Serpentine, Marble, 4 Graduated Drawers, 1850, 83 In.... 1980.00
Dresser, Rosewood, Marble, 3 Drawers, Arched Mirror, Victorian, 95 x 49 In. 1650.00
Dresser, Walnut & Burl, Drop Well, 93 1/2 x 50 1/8 In. 1035.00
Dresser, Walnut, 2 Handkerchief & 3 Drawers, Mirror, Marble, Victorian, 74 In. 385.00
Dresser, Walnut, 3 Drawers, Marble Top, Mirror, Shelves, Victorian, 44 x 80 In. 385.00
Dresser, Walnut, 4 Drawers, Fruit Pulls, Lyre Form, Mirror, Victorian, 40 x 69 In. 385.00
Dresser, Walnut, Bombe Front, 3 Banks Of Drawers, Cabriole Legs............................. 330.00
Dresser, Walnut, Full-Length Mirror, Marble Top, Pedestal Sides, Victorian 800.00
Dresser, Walnut, Glove Boxes, 4 Drawers, Wishbone Mirror.. 325.00
Dresser, Walnut, Marble Top, Candle Shelves, Carved Frame 1300.00
Dresser, Walnut, Marble Top, Victorian, Glove Boxes, Mirror 800.00
Dresser, Walnut, Pine, 2 Over 3 Drawers, 1860, 40 x 18 x 40 In.................................. 375.00
Dry Sink, 2 Blind Doors Above Sink, 2 Blind Doors Below... 850.00

Dry Sink, Green Paint, 2 Doors, 1 Small Side Drawer, Original Zinc Lining 1600.00
Dry Sink, High Back, Lancaster County, 1840, Small 1200.00
Dry Sink, Pine, 2 Paneled Doors, Drawer, 40 x 60 x 18 In. 825.00
Dry Sink, Pine, Paneled Doors, Brown Graining, Iron Latches, 36 x 48 In. 1045.00
Dry Sink, Pine, Paneled Doors, Country, 30 1/2 x 49 In. 990.00
Dry Sink, Poplar, Porcelain Pulls, Large 275.00
Dry Sink, Scrolled Apron & Backsplash, Paneled Door, 1850s 2350.00
Dry Sink, Walnut, American, Late 19th Century, 35 1/2 In. 315.00
Dry Sink Cupboard, 2 Top Doors, Zinc Sink Over Doors 3575.00
Drying Rack, Wooden Frame, Splint, 4 3/4 x 18 x 10 1/2 In. 130.00
Dumbwaiter, Chippendale, Mahogany, 3 Graduated Dished Tiers, 1760, 43 In. 3220.00
Dumbwaiter, George III, Mahogany, 2 Tiers, Marble Tops, Brass Gallery, 40 In. 2588.00
Dumbwaiter, Georgian Style, 2 Tiers, Cabriole Legs, 36 3/4 In. 60.00
Dumbwaiter, Mahogany, 4 Graduated Tiers, Tripartite Base, 51 1/2 In. 1465.00
Dumbwaiter, Mahogany, Graduated Tiers, Baluster Stem, 41 In. 290.00
Dumbwaiter, Rosewood, 3 Graduated Dished Tiers, Victorian, Miniature 1035.00
Easel, Bamboo 55.00
Easel, Peacock On Cornice, Flower Heads & Snakes On Stand, 7 Ft. 2070.00
Etagere, Aesthetic Movement, Mirrors, Carved Crane-Type Supports, American 1100.00
Etagere, Carved Mahogany, Gallery Top, Drawer, Scrolled, Victorian, 67 In. 990.00
Etagere, Empire Style, Mahogany, Ormolu, White Marble Top, 59 1/4 In. 6900.00
Etagere, Federal, Mahogany, 4 Shelves, 1 Base Drawer, N.Y., 1790, 53 x 27 1/2 In. 6670.00
Etagere, Fruitwood, D Shape, Foliate Carved Supports, 49 In., Pair 500.00
Etagere, Mahogany, 3 Lower Shelves, Upper Drawer, Writing Surface 415.00
Etagere, Mahogany, 4 Tiers, Bamboo Turnings, 1840s, 48 x 17 5/8 In. 1950.00
Etagere, Mahogany, Acorn Finials, 3 Shelves, X-Form Dividers, c.1820, 55 In. 4315.00
Etagere, Mahogany, Ball Finials, 3 Scalloped Shelves, Drawer, c.1820, 5 Ft. 4900.00
Etagere, Neoclassical Style, Mahogany, Brass Mounted, 3 Tiers, 34 1/4 x 36 In. 1725.00
Etagere, Oak, Quartersawn Shelves, Old Finish, 20th Century, 22 x 42 x 36 In., Pair ... 495.00
Etagere, Rococo Revival, Mahogany, Hanging, Openwork, American, 1850, 48 In. 415.00
Etagere, Rosewood, Marble Top, Pierced Carved Crest, Arched Mirror, 97 In. 8880.00
Etagere, Rosewood, Marble Top, Victorian, 87 x 50 In. 3025.00
Fauteuil En Cabriolet, Louis XV, Painted Gray, Foliate Top, Serpentine Front, Pair 2600.00
Fauteuil En Cabriolet, Louis XVI, Painted, Oval Upholstered Back, Fluted Legs, Pair. 5750.00
Footstool, Aesthetic Movement, Velvet Covered Rolling Pin Rest 200.00
Footstool, Beadwork, Victorian, 1850, 17 In. 138.00
Footstool, Cabriole Legs, Needlepoint Top 75.00
Footstool, Carved Rosewood, Needlepoint, Cabriole Legs, 14 x 17 In. 415.00
Footstool, Empire, Mahogany, Ogee Molded Frame, 10 x 17 In. 55.00
Footstool, Georgian Style, Upholstered, Pad Feet, 18 1/2 x 30 x 23 In. 110.00
Footstool, Gothic-Arch Feet, Scalloped Apron, Oval Top, 7 3/4 x 14 In. 82.00
Footstool, Gustav Stickley, 7-Spindled Sides, No. 395, 20 x 16 x 15 In. 1910.00
Footstool, Gustav Stickley, Square Stretcher, No. 300, 15 x 20 x 16 In. 200.00
Footstool, Gustav Stickley, Upholstered Seat, No. 300, 20 x 16 x 15 In. 715.00
Footstool, L. & J.G. Stickley, Oak, Leather Top, 4 Square Legs, No. 311, 16 In. 345.00
Footstool, L. & J.G. Stickley, Oak, Tacked Aprons, Leather Top, No. 311, 16 In. 345.00
Footstool, Lakeside Crafters, Flared Legs, 8 x 17 x 10 In. 220.00
Footstool, Mahogany, Adjustable, 1800s, 15 1/2 x 21 In. 200.00
Footstool, Mahogany, Serpentine Sides, Damask, 19th Century, 14 x 22 In. 385.00
Footstool, Maple, Dark Walnut Varnish, Taped, Mt. Lebanon, 1870, 9 x 12 x 10 In. 495.00
Footstool, Needlepoint Top, Round Tapered Legs, 19 1/2 In. 44.00
Footstool, Needlework Panel, Canister Form 210.00
Footstool, Peter Hunt, 8 1/2 In. 110.00
Footstool, Pine, Painted Red, Tulips, Stars & Bird, Primitive, 19th Century, 15 In. 22.00
Footstool, Raised Corduroy Pile, Spotted Dog, Tree, 19th Century, 14 1/2 In. 1380.00
Footstool, Red & Black Graining, White Striping, 5 3/4 x 16 In. 89.00
Footstool, Regency, Saber Leg, 1825, 20 In. 83.00
Footstool, Roycroft, Drop-In Leather Cushion, 17 x 12 x 14 In. 660.00
Footstool, Roycroft, Upholstered Cushion, No. 048, 10 x 15 x 9 In. 605.00
Footstool, Rush Top, Ring & Baluster Turned Legs, Painted Flowers, 11 1/4 In. 170.00
Footstool, Shaker, Pine, Bootjack End, Stained Red, c.1840, 7 x 13 x 8 In. 165.00
Footstool, Shaker, Slanted Top, Mt. Lebanon, Label, 11 1/2 x 11 1/2 In. 523.00
Footstool, Solid Bird's-Eye Maple, Cabriole Legs, 9 x 13 1/2 In. 600.00

Footstool, Wallace Nutting, Maple, Rush, No. 166, 16 In. 440.00
Footstool, Walnut, Floral Needlepoint, Victorian 176.00
Footstool, Walnut, Pierced, Floral Petit Point, Victorian, 14 1/2 x 23 x 18 In. 385.00
Footstool, Windsor, Curly Maple, Turned & Splayed Legs, 8 x 12 In. 165.00
Footstool, Windsor, Oval Top, Splayed Base, Turned Legs, Muslin, 16 In. 110.00
Footstool, Windsor, Painted Brown, Turned Legs, Country, 7 x 13 In............................. 137.00
Frame, Egg & Dart Edges, Leaf Carving, 41 x 35 In. 60.00
Frame, Floral & Leaf Molding, Gilt, 38 x 34 In. 160.00
Frame, Shadowbox, Walnut, Ebonized Bands, Gilt Liner 415.00
Glider, Porch, Old Hickory, Martinsville, Indiana 360.00
Globe, Celestial, George III, Mahogany, Turned Tripod Support, W.S. Jones, c.1800.... 550.00
Globe, Tin, Astrological Signs On Base, c.1930, 10 In... 95.00
Gueridon, Empire Style, Mahogany, Ormolu, 3 Columnar Support, Round, 20 In. 1840.00
Gun Case, Regency, Walnut, 54 In. 88.00
Hall Seat, Golden Oak, Hand Carved, c.1900, 82 In.. 1495.00
Hall Seat, Oak, Griffins & North Wind Carvings. 1320.00
Hall Seat, Oak, North Wind Cartouche, Mirror, Victorian, 87 x 48 In. 1820.00
Hall Stand, Black Forest, Carved Walnut, Figural Bear Holding Tree, 80 In. 4600.00
Hall Stand, Carved Oak, Lion's Head Drawer 1025.00
Hall Stand, Cast Iron, Faux Bamboo, Central Mirror, Victorian, 72 In. 490.00
Hall Stand, Cast Iron, Painted White, 1867 .... 1950.00
Hall Stand, Eastlake, Oak, Mirror, Umbrella Rack, Hooks, Victorian, 27 x 85 In. 440.00
Hall Stand, Hanging, Golden Oak, Quartersawn Oak, Mirror, 6 Hooks, 37 x 26 In........ 170.00
Hall Stand, Mirror, 7 Pegs Over Inset Marble, Victorian, 94 x 47 In............................... 865.00
Hall Stand, Mirror, Walnut & Burl Walnut, Coat Hooks, 2 Umbrella Stands 550.00
Hall Stand, Oak, Beveled Glass Mirror, 5 Ft. 350.00
Hall Stand, Oak, Beveled Mirror, Carved Lift Top, Paw Feet, Oak 1100.00
Hall Stand, Walnut, 6 Coat Hooks, Umbrella Rack Each Side, Mirror, Victorian 1000.00
Hall Stand, Walnut, Mirror, Brown Marble Shelf, Iron Drip Pans 2750.00
Hall Tree, Eastlake Style, Oak, Boar's Head, Carved, 96 In. 850.00
Hall Tree, Stickley Brothers, Cruciform Base, 4 Hooks, Label, No. 187, 68 In............... 660.00
Hat Rack, Hanging, Oak Frame, Turned Spindle, Center Mirror, 5 Hooks 165.00
Hat Rack, Poplar, Accordion Folding, 120 Porcelain Button Pegs, Victorian, 79 In........ 115.00
Hat Rack, Walnut, 10 Extensions, c.1760, 75 In. 3900.00
Head & Footboard, Spool-Turned Walnut, Twin Size, 48 x 42 1/4 In. 1100.00
Headboard, F.L. Wright, No. 2001, Heritage Henredon, King, 79 x 40 In. 1210.00
High Chair, 3 Spindle Back, Stenciled Design On Crest, Plank Seat, 36 In..................... 195.00
High Chair, Blue Paint, 19th Century 65.00
High Chair, Gustav Stickley, 3 Back Slats, Rush Seat, No. 388, 37 1/2 In. 850.00
High Chair, H. Goshon, Black Striping, Floral On Crest, Bentwood Arms, 35 In. 247.00
High Chair, Hardwood, Paper Rush Seat, Country, 19 3/4 In. 155.00
High Chair, Hardwood, Woven Splint Seat, Foot Bar, 36 In. 138.00
High Chair, Jumping Chair, Spindle Back, Piano Stool Base, 1858 .... 475.00
High Chair, Limbert, No. 875, 2-Slat Back, Tray, Leather Seat, Mark, 38 x 19 In.......... 1210.00
High Chair, Maple & Ash, Delaware River Valley, Late 18th Century, 40 3/4 In. 920.00
High Chair, Painted Green, Mid-19th Century, 32 In. 450.00
High Chair, Red Paint Traces, Early 19th Century 1125.00
High Chair, Welsh, c.1820 .... 395.00
High Chair, Windsor, Bamboo Turned, Painted Red 1265.00
High Chair, Windsor, Bamboo, Thumb Back, c.1830, 34 In. 230.00
High Chair, Windsor, Painted Red, 1840-1860 .... 115.00
High Chair, Windsor, Yellow Striping, Foot Shelf, Country, 34 In. 165.00
High Chair-Stroller, Folding, Pressed Design On Back, Iron Wheels 225.00
Highboy, Cherry, Bonnet Top, Fan-Carved Apron, Conn., 81 x 39 x 22 In., 2 Part......... 9350.00
Highboy, Cherry, Bonnet Top, Finger-Fluted Quarter Columns, 7 Ft. 6 In. 11250.00
Highboy, Chippendale Style, 9 Graduated Drawers, Cabriole Legs, 36 x 19 x 76 In. 990.00
Highboy, Queen Anne Style, 4 Graduated Drawers, 3 Aligned Drawers, Mahogany 1940.00
Highboy, Queen Anne Style, Maple, Banded Inlay On Drawers, 70 1/2 In. 1430.00
Highboy, Queen Anne, 5 Top & 3 Base Drawers, Oak, Legs Cut, England, 44 In. 1020.00
Highboy, Queen Anne, Cherry & Pine, 4 Over 9 Drawers, 76 3/4 In. 3410.00
Highboy, Queen Anne, Flat Top, Spliced Cabriole Legs 6600.00
Highboy, Queen Anne, Oak, Ireland.. 2750.00
Highboy Base, Goddard-Townsend, Undercut Talons, 39 1/2 x 36 In. 4950.00

Holder, Magazine, Painted, France, 19th Century 240.00
Holder, Towel & Comb, Eastlake, Walnut, Mirrored, 32 In. 105.00
Hoosier Cabinet, 4 Doors, Pull-Down Cover 895.00
Hoosier Cabinet, 40 x 20 x 73 1/2 In. 288.00
Hoosier Cabinet, Birch, Painted White 115.00
Hoosier Cabinet, Saves Steps 620.00
Hoosier Cabinet, Tambour Doors, Frosted Glass, Zinc Surface, Auglaize Co. 985.00
Hoosier Cabinet, With Flour Bin, Oak, Apartment Size 1195.00
Huntboard, Hepplewhite, Yellow Pine, 4 Overlapping Drawers, 53 1/4 In. 3300.00
Huntboard, Yellow Pine, 1 Drawer In Apron, 43 x 47 1/2 In. 1320.00
Hutch, Peter Hunt, Decoration, Provincetown, 1943 .... 4950.00
Hutch, Peter Hunt, Floral Urn Design, Dated 1928, 68 x 42 In. 1980.00
Hutch, Peter Hunt, Painted Hearts, Angels, Flowers, 3 Shelves Over 5 Drawers 4950.00
Hutch, Pine, 3 Open Shelves Over Case Of 2 Drawers & 2 Doors, 84 3/4 In. 460.00
Hutch, Pine, Storage Under Seat, 29 x 45 x 66 In. 825.00
Ice Cream Set, Bent Wire, Table & 4 Chairs 450.00
Kas, Architectural Carved Doors, Europe, Late 17th Century, 87 x 72 In. 6010.00
Kas, Chippendale, Cherry, 2 Doors, Shelves, Fluted Pilasters, 1770s, 75 In. 6035.00
Kas, George Duppel, Original Red, 1860 .... 5200.00
Kas, Hinged Long Door, Ball Feet, Painted Brown, 78 In. 1210.00
Kas, Mennonite, Walnut, Paint Decorated, 2 Interior Drawers 3600.00
Kas, Oak, Allover Carved Grape Leaves & Cherubs, 19th Century 3080.00
Lacquer, Tray, Floral Roundels, Ebonized Stand, Japan, 48 x 61 In. 175.00
Library Steps, Black Lacquer, Leather Treads, Cabinet Door, 1780s, 39 In. 4025.00
Library Steps, Lamp, Mahogany, 4 Spiral Steps 230.00
Library Steps, Mahogany, 3 Treads, Oriental Carpet Covered, 1840s 920.00
Library Steps, Mahogany, Leather On 2 Steps 1350.00
Library Steps, Maple & Bird's-Eye Maple, Laminated Bentwood, c.1972 .... 345.00
Library Steps, Walnut, Carpet Treads, Victorian 645.00
Linen Press, Colonial, Hardwood, Carved Cornice, Doors, Lower, Drawers, 7 Ft. 8060.00
Linen Press, Crotch Mahogany, England 2400.00
Linen Press, Georgian, Mahogany, 2 Doors Over 2 Drawers, 1760, 85 x 57 x 21 In. 1980.00
Linen Press, Grain Painted, 2 Doors Top, 3 Long Drawers, 85 x 41 x 20 In., 2 Part 1725.00
Linen Press, Mahogany, Satinwood String Inlay, Adjustable Shelves, 90 In. 1760.00
Linen Press, Pine, England, 1890, 88 In. 2150.00
Linen Press, Sheraton, Mahogany, Inlaid, Splayed Feet, 1790, 82 x 48 x 21 In. 2420.00
Liqueur Set, Napoleon III, Lift-Out Tray, 4 Decanters, 16 Liqueurs, 11 x 14 In. 1437.00
Lounger, Barca, Tubular Aluminum, Stretch Canvas, 2 Positions, 1950s 99.00
Love Seat, 4 Toss Pillows, Upholstered, 62 In., Pair 115.00
Love Seat, American Empire, Flame Mahogany, Serpentine Crest, c.1820, 78 In. 805.00
Love Seat, Carved Base, Upholstered, Victorian 295.00
Love Seat, Empire, Mahogany, Upholstered, Carved Swan Neck Arm, 19th Century 825.00
Love Seat, Johnson-Kurtz, Twisted Wicker 450.00
Love Seat, Scrolled Carved Floral Frame, Upholstered, Victorian 220.00
Love Seat, Shaped & Carved Crest Rail, Ball & Claw Feet, Upholstered 440.00
Love Seat, Walnut, Yoke Shape Chair Back, Upholstered, Cabriole Legs, 60 In. 320.00
Love Seat, Windsor, Bamboo Back, Arms, 1810 .... 850.00
Love Seat & Chair, Mahogany, Carved Lion's Heads, Velvet, 2 Piece 750.00
Love Seat & Chair Set, Flowing Medallion Backs, Spoon Carving, 5 Piece 3200.00
Lowboy, Carved Mahogany, Frieze Drawer, 2 Small Drawers, 28 1/2 In. 1725.00
Lowboy, Chippendale Style, Carved, Scalloped, 33 x 34 x 19 In., Pair 2750.00
Lowboy, Fruitwood, 3 Frieze Drawers, Ball & Claw Feet, 29 x 33 In. 1265.00
Lowboy, Queen Anne, Walnut, 1 Long Over 2 Short Drawers, 29 x 34 1/2 In. 3737.00
Lowboy, Queen Anne, Walnut, 1 Long, 2 Short Drawers, c.1745, 32 1/4 In. 9200.00
Lowboy, Queen Anne, Walnut, 3 Drawers, Cabriole Legs, Early 18th Century, 42 In. ... 605.00
Lowboy, Queen Anne, Walnut, Notched Corners, 1 Long, 3 Short Drawers, 1730 .... 8625.00
Lowboy, William & Mary Style, Oak, 29 x 23 In. 1980.00
Mirror, 3-Way, Tooled Folding Oak Frame, Winged Cupids, Chain 145.00
Mirror, Adam Style, Urn, Giltwood, Bellflower Swags, Oval, 40 x 20 In. 2990.00
Mirror, Aesthetic Period, Daniel Pabst, c.1880, 92 In. 3525.00
Mirror, American Classical, Giltwood, Rectangular, 24 x 50 In. 770.00
Mirror, Bull's-Eye, Regency, Giltwood, Ebonized, Carved Acanthus, c.1815, 26 In. 935.00
Mirror, Carved Wood, Gilded, Gesso, 19th Century, 26 In., Pair 545.00

Mirror, Charles II, Stumpwork, Queen Anne Style Giltwood Frame, 23 1/4 In. 2070.00
Mirror, Cheval, Biedermeier, Maple, 72 x 30 In. 770.00
Mirror, Cheval, George III, Mahogany, Tubular Molded Frame, Brass Feet, 68 In. 1045.00
Mirror, Chippendale Style, Mahogany Veneer & Gilt, 50 1/2 x 25 In. 440.00
Mirror, Chippendale, Giltwood, Rococo, Pagoda Design Edges, 1770 .... 2100.00
Mirror, Chippendale, Hardwood, Flowers In Crest, Bird's Heads, 19 1/4 In. 690.50
Mirror, Chippendale, Mahogany Veneer On Pine, Scroll, 28 3/4 x 17 1/2 In. 2805.00
Mirror, Chippendale, Mahogany, Giltwood, Phoenix Pediment, 1760, 38 x 20 In. 3450.00
Mirror, Chippendale, Mahogany, Line Inlay, 37 1/2 x 20 In. 575.00
Mirror, Chippendale, Mahogany, Parcel Gilt, Spread-Wing Eagle, 41 1/2 x 22 In. 690.00
Mirror, Chippendale, Scrolled Crest, Inset Gilt, Phoenix, Mahogany, 1760, 46 In. 4370.00
Mirror, Classical, Gilt Gesso, New England, c.1825, 57 x 33 In. 949.00
Mirror, Classical, Gilt Gesso, Overmantel, c.1830, 28 x 60 In. 460.00
Mirror, Classical, Giltwood, Eagle, Chain, Eglomise Panels, 50 x 19 In. 3450.00
Mirror, Classical, Overmantel, Gilt, Gesso, 19th Century, 24 x 60 1/2 In. 316.00
Mirror, Convex, 19th Century, 45 x 23 In. 4600.00
Mirror, Convex, Giltwood, Spread-Eagle Finial, Ball & Chain From Beak, 42 In. 7475.00
Mirror, Courting, Mahogany Veneer, Reverse-Painted Floral, Crest, 15 x 10 In. 385.00
Mirror, Courting, Reverse-Painted, Compote Of Flowers, 15 3/4 In. 325.00
Mirror, Courting, Walnut, Eglomise Floral Panel, 9 1/2 x 6 1/4 In. 805.00
Mirror, Dressing, Gibbons Style, Walnut, Scrolled Arms, 4 Paw Feet, 28 x 20 In. 825.00
Mirror, Dressing, Queen Anne, Japanned, 7 Drawers 2970.00
Mirror, Eastlake, Pier, Walnut, White Marble Shelf In Base, 95 1/2 x 30 In. 880.00
Mirror, Elaborately Carved Crest, Gilt, Gesso, Victorian, c.1850 .... 1320.00
Mirror, Empire, Convex, Gilt Frame, Minerva Heads, Eagle, 46 In. 90.00
Mirror, Empire, Mahogany, Gilt Slip & Angled Frame, c.1850, 16 3/4 x 23 In. 138.00
Mirror, Empire, Mahogany, Ormolo Mounted, Flanking Columns, 6 Ft. 1650.00
Mirror, Empire, Ogee, Gold-Leaf Edge, 3 Sections 525.00
Mirror, Empire, Walnut, Eglomise Reverse Glass, Ship, Shield & Eagle, 39 3/4 In. 385.00
Mirror, Federal Style, Gilt Finial, Shell Inlay 745.00
Mirror, Federal, Eglomise Tablet With Swan, Label, 32 x 16 In. 1725.00
Mirror, Federal, Gilt Gesso, Standing Figure Of America, c.1815, 33 x 16 In. 9775.00
Mirror, Federal, Gilt, Eglomise Panel, Gilt Frieze, American, 1790-1810, 36 x 24 In. ... 1150.00
Mirror, Federal, Giltwood Frame, Eglomise Panel With Sailboat, 27 1/2 x 14 In. 430.00
Mirror, Federal, Giltwood, Broken Cornice, Pendants, Colonettes, 39 x 24 In. 690.00
Mirror, Federal, Giltwood, Eagle Crest, Drapery Swag, N.Y., 1790, 47 x 22 In. 8050.00
Mirror, Federal, Giltwood, Eglomise, Floral Wreath, Half Columns, 32 x 16 In. 460.00
Mirror, Federal, Giltwood, Label, 30 x 13 1/2 In. 980.00
Mirror, Federal, Giltwood, Tabernacle, Flowers, c.1810, 42 3/4 In. 1320.00
Mirror, Federal, Girandole, Eagle & Dolphin, Gilt, Black Bezel, 2 Candle Arms 3410.00
Mirror, Federal, Mahogany Frame, Molded Cornice Pediment, Carved Pilasters 192.00
Mirror, Federal, Mahogany, Inlaid Conch Shell Crest, Satinwood Inlay, 33 In. 1380.00
Mirror, Federal, Mahogany, Scrolled Frame, String Inlay, 36 x 19 In. 550.00
Mirror, Federal, Pier, Giltwood, Eglomise Panel, 3 Figures, Seaside, c.1800, 55 In. 8050.00
Mirror, Federal, Reverse-Painted Panel, Grain Painted, 22 x 13 1/2 In. 175.00
Mirror, Federal, Split Columns, Dentil Top, Canada 975.00
Mirror, Federal, Wood & Gilt Gesso, c.1825, 36 x 18 1/2 In. 1265.00
Mirror, Frame, Bull's-Eye, Gold, Eagle, 3 Candleholders, 48-In. High 1700.00
Mirror, French Rococo, 4 Porcelain Medallions, Birds & Flowers, 56 x 32 In. 3410.00
Mirror, French Style, Gold-Leaf Frame, Floral Wreaths, 68 x 52 In. 1650.00
Mirror, Fruitwood, Giltwood Eagle Crest, Laurel Leaves, 50 x 28 In. 620.00
Mirror, George II, Shell & Foliate Carved Crest, Ribbon Borders, 56 x 36 In. 5175.00
Mirror, George III, Giltwood, 50 1/4 x 25 In. 3100.00
Mirror, George III, Pier, Cartouche Shape, Honeysuckle Surround, 4 Ft. 5 In. 2875.00
Mirror, George III, Surround Of Scrolls & Flower Heads, Oval, 40 x 25 In. 5750.00
Mirror, Gilt Gesso, Carved Girandole, Early 19th Century, 38 x 22 In. 3450.00
Mirror, Gilt, Eagle, Flowers, Convex, 44 In. 635.00
Mirror, Gilt, Pierced Urn & Leaf Crest, Foliate Design On Sides 495.00
Mirror, Gilt, Scroll Carved, 4 Ft. x 2 Ft. 9 In. 110.00
Mirror, Giltwood, Broken Pediment, Acorn Shaped Drops, 44 1/2 x 26 In. 345.00
Mirror, Girandole, Eagle Crest, Convex, Gilt 3575.00
Mirror, Girandole, Eagle On Rocky Plinth, Rosettes, Round, 1780s, 43 1/2 In. 2530.00
Mirror, Girandole, Eagle Pediment, Gilt, 42 x 26 In. 1100.00

Mirror, Gothic, Giltwood, Architectural, Crest, American, 1830, 106 x 52 In. 2640.00
Mirror, Gustav Stickley, Arched Oak Frame, Decal, No. 904, 32 x 54 In. 4600.00
Mirror, Gustav Stickley, Inverted V Crest Rail, Copper Mounted, 23 x 28 1/2 In. 1400.00
Mirror, Gustav Stickley, Oak Frame, 4 Iron Coat Hooks, No. 66, c.1904 .... 2100.00
Mirror, Gustav Stickley, Oak, Arched Top, No. 904, c.1904, 32 x 54 In. 4600.00
Mirror, Gustav Stickley, Tenon, Chamfered Board Back, Red Decal, 29 x 42 In. 2860.00
Mirror, Hall, Walnut, Parcel Gilt, 72 x 31 1/2 In. 345.00
Mirror, Hall, Walnut, Turned Spindle Columns, Curved Legs, Victorian, 8 Ft. 2 In. 1495.00
Mirror, Italian Rococo, Giltwood, Late 18th Century, 28 x 21 1/2 In. 975.00
Mirror, Italian Rococo, Pierced Rocaille & Floral Cresting, 37 x 29 In., Pair 6900.00
Mirror, John Elliot, Mahogany, Philadelphia, c.1753-1762, 42 1/2 x 19 In. 4312.00
Mirror, Louis Phillippe, Gold Leaf, Rounded Corners, 1850, 55 x 38 In. 990.00
Mirror, Louis XIV, Giltwood, Rectangular, Beaded, Shell Carving, 29 1/2 x 18 In. 4312.00
Mirror, Louis XVI Style, Carved Frame, Drooping Flowers, 57 x 40 In. 460.00
Mirror, Louis XVI, Giltwood, Rectangular, Kissing Lovebirds, Arrows, 74 1/2 In. 4887.00
Mirror, Mahogany, Mahogany Veneer, Ogee, Eglomise Panel, c.1840 .... 215.00
Mirror, Mahogany, Scrolled, Crest Center, Late 18th Century, 37 x 19 In. 2420.00
Mirror, Mantel, Rococo Carved Giltwood, Triple Arched, 1850s, 71 1/2 x 73 In. 2310.00
Mirror, Mask Figural Crest, Gilt Scrolling, 19th Century, 56 1/2 x 26 In. 515.00
Mirror, Mourning, Abraham Lincoln, Eagle Pediment, Iron, 19 x 11 1/2 In. 258.00
Mirror, Neoclassical, Arched Pediment, Baltic, 52 In. 750.00
Mirror, Neoclassical, Fruitwood, Parcel Gilt, Fluted Columns, 83 x 53 In. 8625.00
Mirror, Neoclassical, Painted, Parcel Gilt, Fluted Pilasters, Sweden, 70 x 58 In. 3165.00
Mirror, Neoclassical, Parcel Gilt, Painted, Lion's Head & Paws, 68 1/2 In. 6325.00
Mirror, Neoclassical, Parcel Gilt, Painted, Double-Arched Frame, 61 x 38 1/4 In. 5175.00
Mirror, Neoclassical, Pier, Parcel Gilt, Painted, Griffins, Sweden, 73 In. 1725.00
Mirror, Neoclassical, Thuya, Ormolu, Stepped Rectangular Cornice, 67 1/2 In. 4025.00
Mirror, Parcel Gilt, Broken Pediment, Eagle, Pierced, 19th Century, 46 x 24 In. 1500.00
Mirror, Paul Frankl, Geometric Chrome Frame, Round, c.1932, 30 In. 1980.00
Mirror, Pier, Corinthian Columns, Oriental, 79 1/2 In. 1725.00
Mirror, Pier, Gilt, Stand, Pediment Top, 8 Ft. 1200.00
Mirror, Pier, Half Round Columns, Gilt Bronze Mounted, 87 In. 1495.00
Mirror, Pier, Mahogany, Flower Basket Finial, Shell Inlay, c.1790, 60 In. 8625.00
Mirror, Pier, Vase Top, Holland, 67 In., Pair 7150.00
Mirror, Plate Within Double Giltwood Frame, Birds, Female Bust, 9 Ft. 4025.00
Mirror, Plateau, Double Beveled Glass, Chains & Beads, 16 In. 130.00
Mirror, Queen Anne Style, Curly Maple, Prince Of Wales Plume, 38 x 21 In. 415.00
Mirror, Queen Anne, Black & Chinoiserie Lacquer, 3-Part Glass, 47 x 16 1/2 In. 3850.00
Mirror, Queen Anne, Parcel Gilt Walnut, Shaped Cresting, 53 x 22 In. 3165.00
Mirror, Queen Anne, Walnut & Gilt Gesso, 18th Century, 48 1/2 x 24 In. 4025.00
Mirror, Queen Anne, Walnut, Beveled Plate, Parcel Gilt, 2 Part, c.1740, 40 In. 3740.00
Mirror, Queen Anne, Walnut, Parcel Gilt, Shaped Crest, Veneered, 1740, 31 x 15 In. 2185.00
Mirror, Queen Anne, Walnut, Parcel Gilt, Crest, C-Scroll, Mid-18th Century, 35 In. 1035.00
Mirror, Queen Anne, Walnut, Shell-Scrolled Crest Rail, 1740, 15 x 18 In. 2300.00
Mirror, Regency, Convex, Early 19th Century, 40 In. 1380.00
Mirror, Regency, Convex, Giltwood, Eagle, Early 19th Century 440.00
Mirror, Regency, Convex, Giltwood, Ebony Design, 28 In. 770.00
Mirror, Regency, Rosewood, Landscape, 1830 .... 110.00
Mirror, Revival, Gesso On Wood, 26 1/2 x 14 1/4 In. 220.00
Mirror, Rococo, Fruits, Flowers & Vegetables Frame, Oval, With Straight Base 3500.00
Mirror, Rococo, Gilt Gesso, 18th Century, 14 x 8 In. 375.00
Mirror, Shaving, 1 Drawer, Oval Mirror, 1900 .... 165.00
Mirror, Shaving, Bowfront, Mahogany Veneer, 21 Drawer, 20 In. 300.00
Mirror, Shaving, Georgian, 6 Lower Drawers, 38 In. 302.00
Mirror, Shaving, Georgian, Mahogany, Cheval Mirror, 3 Drawers, 23 x 23 In. 290.00
Mirror, Shaving, Gold Paint Over Silver, Convex Lens In Top Arch, 16 1/4 In. 165.00
Mirror, Shaving, Hepplewhite, Figured Mahogany Veneer On Pine, 16 In. 72.00
Mirror, Shaving, Hepplewhite, Mahogany Inlay, Scalloped Apron, 2 Drawers, 23 In. 165.00
Mirror, Shaving, Hepplewhite, Walnut & Mahogany, Oval, Beaded Frame, 22 In. 305.00
Mirror, Shaving, Mahogany Veneer On Pine, Drawer, Adjustable Mirror, 18 In. 110.00
Mirror, Shaving, Mahogany, 2 Short Drawers, Victorian, 22 3/4 x 18 In. 65.00
Mirror, Shaving, Mahogany, Line Inlay, Ball Feet, 26 In. 330.00
Mirror, Shaving, Tilting, Mahogany, Drawer In Base, Oval, c.1890, 12 In. 195.00

Mirror, Shelf & Letter Tray, Painted Wood.. 45.00
Mirror, Sheraton, Acanthus Capped Barley Twist Columns, c.1820, 32 1/4 x 18 In. 800.00
Mirror, Shoe, Wrought Iron, Double Sided, Scrolls On Frame, c.1925, 28 3/8 In. 4600.00
Mirror, Tabernacle, Sheraton, Fruit-Carved Upper Panel, 38 x 25 In. 385.00
Mirror, Tortoiseshell Frame, Metallic Embroidered Stumpwork, 25 x 23 In. 5750.00
Mirror, Venetian, Parcel Gilt, Painted, Late 19th Century, 29 In., Pair 575.00
Mirror, Walnut Architectural Frame, 38 1/4 x 26 1/4 In. 140.00
Mirror, Walnut Veneer, Gilt, Gesso, 18th Century, 39 x 15 1/2 In. 517.00
Mirror, Walnut, 3 1/2-In. Gold Liner, Victorian, 17 x 19 In. 95.00
Mirror, Walnut, Beehive Shape, Gilt Trim, Victorian 132.00
Mirror, Walnut, Carved Flowers, Carved Animal's Head Top, 1850, 9 Ft. x 52 In. 2750.00
Mirror, Wiener Werkstatte, Giltwood, Carved Overlapping Leaves, 19 x 18 In. 7100.00
Mirror, Wrought Iron, Hammered, Openwork Scrolls & Foliage, France, 46 x 39 In. 800.00
Music Stand, Bowfront, Walnut, Cupboard Door, Carved Paw Feet, 38 In. 150.00
Music Stand, Drawer, Carved Marble Top, Victorian, 32 x 19 1/2 x 32 In. 1595.00
Noga-Hibachi, Copper Lined, 3 Drawers, Lift Top Panel Base, Japan, 19th Century..... 950.00
Ottoman, American Classical, Mahogany, Ogee Frame, Scrolled Feet, c.1840 .... 300.00
Ottoman, Needlepoint, Scroll Feet, 1820, Pair.. 2400.00
Ottoman, Paul Frankl, Rattan, Square, Rounded Corners, 24 x 24 x 14 In..................... 150.00
Ottoman, Suede Velvet, 3-Layer Tasseled Fringe, Victorian, 19 x 21 In. 468.00
Parlor Set, Aesthetic Movement, Gilded Rosewood, 5 Piece 3025.00
Parlor Set, Belter, Carved, Laminated Rosewood, Scroll Pattern Recamier, 6 Piece...... 8910.00
Parlor Set, Belter, Rosalie Pattern, Upholstered, 5 Piece...16500.00
Parlor Set, Ice Cream, Bent Metal, Round Table, 5 Piece 350.00
Parlor Set, Jeliff, Renaissance Revival, Walnut, Triple-Back Sofa, 1870, 5 Piece 3300.00
Parlor Set, Renaissance Revival, Burled Walnut, Upholstered, 1870, 3 Piece............... 1045.00
Parlor Set, Rococo Revival, Mahogany, Upholstered, 5 Piece 3300.00
Parlor Set, Walnut, Woman's-Head Arm Support, c.1870, 3 Piece 3250.00
Pedestal, Art Deco, Walnut Veneer, Inlaid Bands, 49 1/2 In. 2100.00
Pedestal, Art Nouveau, Mahogany, Carved Animal Corners, 48 x 9-In. Square Top 1100.00
Pedestal, Directoire Style, Glass Inset, Ram's-Head Standards, Hoof Feet, 10 In.......... 400.00
Pedestal, Gilt Ormolu, Peacock Feather, Paw Feet, 42 In. 1375.00
Pedestal, John Elliot, Walnut, Carved Fruit, 35 In. 1840.00
Pedestal, Mahogany, Barley Twist, Victorian, 5 In. 210.00
Pedestal, Mahogany, Brass Gallery, Fluted, 42 x 13 In. 66.00
Pedestal, Mahogany, Victorian-Style, Fluted Columns, 1930s, Pair 660.00
Pedestal, Marble, Columnar Base, 16 In.. 65.00
Pedestal, Marble, Mythical Demon Carved Support.. 3565.00
Pedestal, Neoclassical Style, Mahogany, Ormolu, Marble Top, Sweden, 36 In. 6325.00
Pedestal, Onyx, Cylindrical Standard, Square Base, 44 In. 2185.00
Pedestal, Rococo Style, Parcel Gilt, Scrolled, Dragon Mask, Italy, 36 In., Pair........... 2587.00
Pedestal, Rococo Style, Wooden, Gilt & Painted, 45 In. 285.00
Pedestal, Rouge Granite, Rectangular Column, Cavetto Base, 33 1/2 In. 495.00
Pedestal, Roycroft, Magazine, 5 Shelves, Carved Leaves On 2 Panels, 64 In. 8000.00
Pedestal, Tripod, Stylized Bird Supports, Claw Feet, Iron Pedestal, 48 In. 1045.00
Pedestal, Verde Antico Marble, Oval Top, Twisted Fluted Column............................ 1725.00
Pedestal, Verde Marble, Contemporary, Paneled Rectangular Form, 30 x 10 x 36 In. ... 316.00
Pedestal, Walnut, Blackamoor, Carved, 1825, 24 In. 1650.00
Pie Safe, 10 Circular Punched Tins, Lower Drawer.. 395.00
Pie Safe, 6 Panel Heart & Flower, Penna... 1600.00
Pie Safe, 6 Panel Punched Star, Green Over Mustard 1250.00
Pie Safe, 6 Punched Tins, Painted Green, 1 Bottom Drawer.................................... 3350.00
Pie Safe, Cherry & Walnut, 3 Tin Panels, 2 Doors, Painted Blue, 52 1/2 In. 525.00
Pie Safe, Leaf & Floral Punch Panels 1450.00
Pie Safe, Pine, 2 Doors, Screened Mesh, Shelves, Bracket Feet, 54 In. 285.00
Pie Safe, Pine, 2 Drawers, 2 Doors, Inside Shelves, Painted Red, Pierced Tin Sides...... 495.00
Pie Safe, Pine, 2 Screened Doors, 1 Drawer, 57 x 42 In. 400.00
Pie Safe, Poplar, Scalloped Apron, Drawer, Star & Circle In Doors, 41 1/2 In. 505.00
Pie Safe, Punched Tin Front & Sides, Painted Green.. 1650.00
Pie Safe, Tin Covered Wood, Punched Compass & Flower, Painted Blue, 27 In.......... 220.00
Pie Safe, Walnut, Single Door, 5 Punched Tin Panels, 76 1/2 In. 2860.00
Pie Safe, Walnut, Tapered Legs, Double Door, 3 Punched Tin Panels, 39 x 41 In. 990.00
Planter, Walnut, Acanthus Leaf & Geometric Carving, Metal Liner, 26 x 36 In. 550.00

Rack, Blanket, Brass, 27 x 35 1/4 In. 72.00
Rack, Boot, Mahogany, Brass Handle, Over Square Supports, 26 In. 400.00
Rack, Drying, 4-Sections, 30 1/2 x 60 In., Folded 83.00
Rack, Drying, Shoe Feet, 3 Dowel Rod Bars, 49 x 39 /12 In. 55.00
Rack, Drying, Shoe Foot, Wooden 190.00
Rack, Drying, Trestle Feet, Grained All Over In Ochre, New England, 19th Century.... 545.00
Rack, Hat, Mirror, Victorian, Oval 50.00
Rack, Magazine, Art Deco, Tubular Chrome, Wooden Handle, Ball Feet, 18 x 16 In. ... 440.00
Rack, Magazine, Cast Iron, Twisted Handle 120.00
Rack, Magazine, Chippendale Style, 2 Slots, Cutout Sides.............................. 55.00
Rack, Magazine, Rattan, Natural, Chair Side, ... 40.00
Rack, Magazine, Rosewood, 3 Sections, Shell & Scroll Dividers, 1840, 18 1/4 In....... 990.00
Rack, Plate, Carved Wood, Dogs & Horse Upper Panel, Polychrome, 44 x 58 In. 850.00
Rack, Robe, Softwood, Scrolled Galleried Rack, Scrolled Trestle Base, 68 In. 345.00
Recamier, Belter, Laminated Rosewood, Scroll, Pair.................................... 5280.00
Recamier, Carved Mahogany Frame, Tufted Upholstered, 72 In. 920.00
Recamier, Classical, Mahogany, Acanthus Crest, Upholstered, 1825, 82 In. 8050.00
Recamier, Classical, Rosewood, Carved, Gilded, Hairy Paw Feet, N.Y., c.1820 .... 6875.00
Recamier, Empire, Mahogany, Paw Feet, Floral Brocade 550.00
Recamier, Mahogany, Brass Feet, 6 Ft. 1800.00
Recamier, Neoclassical, Mahogany, Parcel Gilt, Undulating Back, Germany, 75 In...... 6900.00
Recamier, Scalloped Back, Serpentine Seat, Carved Arms, Victorian, 80 In. 2200.00
Rocker, 5 Spindles, Bamboo Turned, Stenciled Crest, Grain Painted, Child's, c.1829... 1150.00
Rocker, Amish, Hickory & Oak, 35 In. 385.00
Rocker, Arms, Shaker, Maple, No. 7, Taped Back & Seat, Mt. Lebanon, c.1880, 42 In. 825.00
Rocker, Arms, Wicker, c.1890, Child's, 27 3/4 In. 375.00
Rocker, Arrow-Back, Grain Painted, 19th Century..................................... 690.00
Rocker, Balloon Back, Black Graining, Yellow Striping, Floral, 40 In. 110.00
Rocker, Banister Back, Painted Black, Crest, Woven Splint Seat, Arms 660.00
Rocker, Baroque, Grotto, Arms, Italy, 19th Century...................................... 3220.00
Rocker, Bedroom, Roycroft, Oak, Incised, 34 In. 1050.00
Rocker, Bent Willow, Painted Green, Arms, 43 1/2 In. 360.00
Rocker, Bentwood Back & Seat, Scrolled Branch-Form Stiles & Arms 1380.00
Rocker, Boston, Grain Painted, Stencil, c.1840 .... 295.00
Rocker, Boston, Yellow Striping, Stenciled Fruit & Foliage Crest, 39 In..... .... 165.00
Rocker, Caned, Mahogany, Lion's Paw Feet, Scrolled Arms, West Indian, c.1920....... 825.00
Rocker, Carved Clasped Hands Top Rail, Upholstered Seat, Arms 675.00
Rocker, Carved Shells On Back & Seat & Arm Supports, Italy.......................... 3220.00
Rocker, Charles Eames, Black Wire Struts On Birch Runners, Fiberglass Shell 770.00
Rocker, Charles Eames, Black Wire, Birch Runners, Fiberglass, Herman Miller.......... 525.00
Rocker, Curly Maple, 4 Slats, 1830 .... 6900.00
Rocker, Eagle Crest, Arms, 19th Century 4600.00
Rocker, Eastlake, Platform, Victorian 33.00
Rocker, Empire, Red & Black Flame Grained, White Striping, 41 In...................... 160.00
Rocker, George Nakashima, Walnut, Exaggerated Spindle Back, 19 x 32 In. 660.00
Rocker, Gooseneck, Cane Seat & Back 120.00
Rocker, Grotto, Painted, Shell-Carved Seat & Back, Dolphin Rockers 3220.00
Rocker, Gustav Stickley, 4-Slat Back, Drop-In Leather Cushion, Arms, 25 x 23 In....... 935.00
Rocker, Gustav Stickley, High Back, 3 Slats Back & Sides, No. 387, 20 x 18 x 43 In. ... 715.00
Rocker, Gustav Stickley, Ladder Back, Arms, Child's 750.00
Rocker, Gustav Stickley, Oak, 3 Horizontal Slats, c.1905 .... 525.00
Rocker, Gustav Stickley, Oak, 5-Slat Sides, 4-Slat Back, Cushion, 35 1/2 In. 2530.00
Rocker, Gustav Stickley, Oak, No. 343, Decal, Child's, c.1909 .... 1035.00
Rocker, Gustav Stickley, Spindled Back, Broad Arms, Leather Seat, No. 375, 45 In.... 5520.00
Rocker, Harden Co., Oak, 5 Pierced Back Slats, Paper Label, 37 3/4 In. 200.00
Rocker, Hardwood, Curved Back, Scrolled Arms, Chinese 345.00
Rocker, High Back, Black & Gold Striping, Stenciled Fruit, Green 550.00
Rocker, Hitchcock, Green, Stenciled Design, Arms, 20th Century....................... 90.00
Rocker, Hoopskirt, Southern, 1840 .... 275.00
Rocker, Italian Baroque, Shell Carved Seat & Back, Dolphin Arm Supports 3220.00
Rocker, J.M. Young, Deep, 4 Slats Under Arm, Leather Cushion, 31 In..................... 2300.00
Rocker, J.M. Young, Slatted Back & Sides, Arched Crest Rail, 34 x 29 x 33 In. 400.00
Rocker, J.M. Young, Under Arm Slats, Leather Cushion, 37 In. 2300.00

Furniture, Rocker, Shaker,
Elder's, Tiger Maple, Varnish,
Blue Seat, 1820

Furniture, Rocker,
Platform, Lollipop, Oak,
Hunzinger, 1822, 40 In.

Furniture, Rocker, Shaker,
Birch, Red Stain Rush Seat,
Enfield, 1830

Rocker, L. & J.G. Stickley, Spindled Arms, 10-Spindle Back, Marked, 34 In. 825.00
Rocker, Ladder Back, 4 Slats, Rope Seat 231.00
Rocker, Ladder Back, 5 Arched Slats, Turned Finials, Shaped Arms, 47 In. 545.00
Rocker, Ladder Back, Curly Maple, Rush Seat, 34 3/4 In. 165.00
Rocker, Ladder Back, Hardwood, 4 Slats, Finials, Arms, Paper Rush Seat, 44 In. 110.00
Rocker, Ladder Back, Rush Seat, American, 19th Century 65.00
Rocker, Ladder Back, Shaped Arms, 4 Arched Slats, Tape Seat, 42 In. 225.00
Rocker, Limbert, No. 1894 .... 650.00
Rocker, Lincoln, Cane, Arms, Child's 150.00
Rocker, Lyre Back, Stenciled Design On Back & Crest, Green 250.00
Rocker, Mahogany, Carved Crest, Upholstered Seat & Back, Scrolled Arms 99.00
Rocker, Mahogany, Lion's-Heads Sides Of Headrest, Gargoyle In Center, 1840 .... 525.00
Rocker, Maple, Wicker Seat, 9-Spindle Back 120.00
Rocker, Mission Oak, Leather Seat 225.00
Rocker, Mission Style, Oakcraft Shops, Oak, Impressed Mark, Pair 375.00
Rocker, Mission, Oak, Child's 58.00
Rocker, Nursing, Gustav Stickley, Oak, Leather Seat, Red Stamp, 31 In. 695.00
Rocker, Oak, Leather Seat, American, 19th Century, Child's 80.00
Rocker, Oak, Platform, Rush Back & Seat, Child's 150.00
Rocker, Oak, Pressed Back, Cane Seat, Arms, Child's, 28 In. 105.00
Rocker, Oak, Pressed Lion's-Head Back, 7 Spindles, Pressed Seat 130.00
Rocker, Oak, Slat Back, Arms 85.00
Rocker, Old Hickory, Woven Back & Seat, Arms, 32 In. 265.00
Rocker, Painted Green, Rush Seat, Child's, 33 In. 25.00
Rocker, Platform, Eastlake, Victorian 38.50
Rocker, Platform, Lollipop, Oak, Hunzinger, 1822, 40 In.......................................*Illus* 2760.00
Rocker, Platform, Oak, Pressed Back, Star Design In Wooden Seat 185.00
Rocker, Platform, Pressed Crest, Composition Seat, 17 Dowel-Type Spindles.............. 425.00
Rocker, Platform, Upholstered Back, Seat & Arms... 190.00
Rocker, Platform, Wicker, Arms 55.00
Rocker, Rococo, Laminated Mahogany, Reticulated, Acanthus Armrests, Velvet 880.00
Rocker, Salem, Scribbles & Melons Painted Design, Child's 1050.00
Rocker, Sea Grass, Child's.. 245.00
Rocker, Sewing, Gustav Stickley, Leather, No. 305, c.1910 .... 230.00
Rocker, Sewing, High Half-Spindle Back, Plank Seat, 42 In. 80.00
Rocker, Sewing, Pierced Back, Finial Posts 110.00
Rocker, Shaker, Arms, Taped Seat, No. 6, c.1920.. 1350.00
Rocker, Shaker, Birch, Red Stain Rush Seat, Enfield, 1830.................................*Illus* 37400.00
Rocker, Shaker, Bulb Finials, Rush Seat, Harvard Community, c.1840 .... 2590.00

Rocker, Shaker, Checkerboard Taped Seat, Mt. Lebanon, Child's 1210.00
Rocker, Shaker, Elder's, Bird's-Eye Maple, Splint Seat, Arms, New Lebanon, 1830 .... 6600.00
Rocker, Shaker, Elder's, Tiger Maple, Brown Taped Seat, New Lebanon, 1830, 45 In. 4400.00
Rocker, Shaker, Elder's, Tiger Maple, Varnish, Blue Seat, 1820 .... *Illus* 4400.00
Rocker, Shaker, Figured Maple, Acorn Finial, Trapezoidal Splint Seat, 19th Century ... 1150.00
Rocker, Shaker, Ladder Back, 3 Slats, Taped Seat 600.00
Rocker, Shaker, Man's, Taped Seat 650.00
Rocker, Shaker, Maple, 4-Slat Back, Red & Gray Taped Seat, Mt. Lebanon, 38 1/2 In. 715.00
Rocker, Shaker, Maple, Bird's-Eye Maple, Rush Seat, c.1830, 36 In..... 440.00
Rocker, Shaker, Maple, Dark Stain, Mt. Lebanon, 1870, 41 In. .... *Illus* 880.00
Rocker, Shaker, Maple, Painted, Woven Splint Seat & Back, Mt. Lebanon, 1880, 43 In. 550.00
Rocker, Shaker, Maple, Splint Seat, Child's, 31 x 11 In.. 1380.00
Rocker, Shaker, Maple, Stained Dark Walnut, Taped Seat, No. 7, Mt. Lebanon, Arms . 440.00
Rocker, Shaker, Maple, Taped Back & Seat, No. 2, Mt. Lebanon, c.1880, 34 1/2 In. 385.00
Rocker, Shaker, Maple, Tiger Maple, Light Finish, Taped Seat, Mt. Lebanon, 1860 ..... 495.00
Rocker, Shaker, Mt. Lebanon, Impressed 6, Woven Tape Seat, 41 1/2 In. 880.00
Rocker, Shaker, Mushroom Caps, No. 0 .... 1450.00
Rocker, Shaker, No. 1, Child's 825.00
Rocker, Shaker, Oak, Stenciled Back, Child's, c.1899 .... 375.00
Rocker, Shaker, Painted Black, Black & Red Taped Seat, No. 6, 19th Century............. 690.00
Rocker, Shaker, Painted, Red & Black Taped Seat, No. 6, Mt. Lebanon, 41 3/4 In....... 415.00
Rocker, Shaker, Rush Seat, Mt. Lebanon, 1875.. 5000.00
Rocker, Shaker, Rush Seat, No. 7 .... 1200.00
Rocker, Splint Seat, Painted White, Child's 65.00
Rocker, Stained Wood, Rush Back & Seat, Victorian 55.00
Rocker, Tall Back, Polychrome, Painted, Sailboat, Arms, c.1830, 43 In. 2530.00
Rocker, Thonet, Bentwood, Double-Cane Back, 1880-1890s 95.00
Rocker, Turned & Cutout, Arms, 45 In... 192.50
Rocker, Twig, c.1870.. 375.00
Rocker, Walnut Frame, Upholstered, Victorian... 110.00
Rocker, Walnut, Foliate Carved Crest, Arms, Victorian 115.50
Rocker, Weil & Co., Store With A Million Friends, Child's 145.00
Rocker, Wicker, Floral Cushion, Child's... 85.00
Rocker, Wicker, Ram's-Horn-Shaped Top Rail, Reeded, Basketweave Back 550.00
Rocker, Wicker, White, Cushioned Seat & Back 70.00
Rocker, Wicker, Yoke Back, Painted Brown, c.1920.. 125.00
Rocker, Windsor, Arrow-Back, Pine & Maple, Painted Designs, 1830s...................... 2200.00
Rocker, Windsor, Bamboo, Black Striping, Shaped Seat, Arms 275.00
Rocker, Wing Back, Potty, Hardwood, Cut Out Heart In Crest, 27 3/4 In. 525.00
Rocker, Wrought Iron, Arms, Child's... 35.00
Rocker & Folding High Chair, Caned Seat, Quartersawn Oak, Child's......................... 410.00
Screen, 2-Panel, Carved Bird & Foliate, Inset Ivory Birds, 69 x 26 3/4 In. 400.00
Screen, 2-Panel, Ink & Color On Gold Leaf Paper, 18th Century 9250.00
Screen, 2-Panel, Ivory Mounted, Red Lacquer, Lotus Blossoms, 71 3/4 In................. 935.00
Screen, 3 Panel, Diagonally Painted, Arts & Crafts, Gordon Saint Clair, 66 In. 1090.00
Screen, 3 Panel, Thonet, Bentwood, Spanish Wand, Cut Geometrics, Glass, c.1904 ..... 3000.00
Screen, 3-Panel, 1 Mirrored, Molded Floral & Beaded Walnut Frame, 68 In. 920.00

Furniture, Rocker,
Shaker, Maple, Dark
Stain, Mt. Lebanon,
1870, 41 In.

Screen, 3-Panel, Arts & Crafts, Oak, Neoclassical Children, 68 x 72 In........................ 550.00
Screen, 3-Panel, Canvas, Gilt Frame, Birds One Side, Design Other, 24 In. 1095.00
Screen, 3-Panel, Carved Camphor Wood, 67 In.. 140.00
Screen, 3-Panel, Different Pictures, Ball & Stick Design 275.00
Screen, 3-Panel, Directoire Style, Mahogany, 70 1/2 x 72 1/2 In. 1725.00
Screen, 3-Panel, Gilt Acanthus Leaves, Shells & Flowers, Mahogany, 71 In. 640.00
Screen, 3-Panel, Louis XV Style, Bronze & Mesh, 30 In. 520.00
Screen, 3-Panel, Needlepoint Inset, 1860 .... 715.00
Screen, 3-Panel, Neoclassical Vase & Flowers, Painted Canvas, 68 x 19 3/4 In. 745.00
Screen, 3-Panel, Pierced Foliate Design, Oriental, Sandalwood, 63 In. 145.00
Screen, 4 Panel, Gothic Revival, Walnut, 1900, 74 In..................................... 3250.00
Screen, 4 Panels, Painted Canvas, Figural Landscape, France, 61 x 94 In. 1320.00
Screen, 4-Panel, Arched Top, Abalone Shell Inserts, Rosewood, 42 3/4 In. 575.00
Screen, 4-Panel, Black Lacquer, Abalone Shell, Flowers, China, 10 x 35 In. 105.00
Screen, 4-Panel, Carved Birds & Florals, Chinese, Black Lacquer, 72 x 16 In. 148.00
Screen, 4-Panel, Carved Indian Teak, 65 x 19 3/4 In..................................... 85.00
Screen, 4-Panel, Embroidered Panels, Landscape, Birds, Oriental, 72 3/4 In. 60.00
Screen, 4-Panel, Figures In Landscape, Oriental, Lacquer, 72 1/2 In. 800.00
Screen, 4-Panel, Figures In Landscape, Gold Ground, Japan, 36 x 18 In.................... 60.00
Screen, 4-Panel, Figures In Summer House, Birds, Red Lacquer, 73 x 83 In. 5400.00
Screen, 4-Panel, Gothic Revival, Carved Walnut, c.1900, 74 In x 76 In.................... 3740.00
Screen, 4-Panel, Hunting Scene, Double-Sided, Chinese............................... 400.00
Screen, 4-Panel, Inset Hard Stones, Oriental, 36 1/2 x 11 1/2 In. 100.00
Screen, 4-Panel, Lacquer, Embroidered, Landscape, 66 3/4 In. 345.00
Screen, 4-Panel, Leather, 2 Portraits Each Panel, 19th Century, 7 Ft. 1 1/4 In. 5465.00
Screen, 4-Panel, Mahogany, Decoupage One Side, Lacquered Paper Other Side 1430.00
Screen, 4-Panel, Needlepoint Figures & Animals, Mahogany, 75 In. 1610.00
Screen, 4-Panel, Neoclassical, Paper, 102 In. 600.00
Screen, 4-Panel, Padded Brocade.. 25.00
Screen, 4-Panel, Patchwork Quilt Inset, Spiral Supports, Rosewood, 61 1/2 In............ 715.00
Screen, 4-Panel, Upper Glazed Panels, Lower Petit Point Panels, 69 In.................... 4312.00
Screen, 6-Panel, Allover Gold Landscape, Black Ground, Oriental, 16 x 68 In............. 230.00
Screen, 6-Panel, Charles Eames, Folding, Birch, Canvas Hinges, 61 x 68 In. 3300.00
Screen, 6-Panel, Chinese Figures, Wood Block Feet, Wood & Silk, 84 x 18 In. 115.00
Screen, 6-Panel, Gold Landscape, Figural Hard Stones, Oriental, 68 x 16 In............. 230.00
Screen, 6-Panel, Max Kuehne, Lacquered Jungle Scene, 1930, 8 Ft. 3 In. 6900.00
Screen, 8-Panel, Charles Eames, Birch Plywood, Canvas Hinges, 34 x 78 In.............. 3575.00
Screen, 8-Panel, Coromandel, Black & Gold Lacquer, Garden Scene, 96 x 140 In. 4950.00
Screen, 12-Panel, Brown & Black Lacquer, Parcel Gilt, Landscape, China, 90 In......... 5750.00
Screen, Dressing, Coromandel & Ivory, Teakwood, 79 x 79 In............................ 1650.00
Screen, Pole, Classical, Mahogany, Needlework Panel, Isaac Vose, 58 In., Pair 2900.00
Screen, Pole, English Rococo, Mahogany, Needlepoint, Beadwork, 62 1/2 In. 880.00
Screen, Table, 6-Panel, Moon Hanging Low, Grass Field, 14 x 36 In. 115.00
Screen, Table, Famille Rose Style Porcelain Panel, Hardwood Frame, 23 3/4 In. 345.00
Screen, Table, Jade Panels, Rosewood, 13 In. 165.00
Seating System, R. Sebastian, Polyurethane Foam, Orange Upholstery, 64 In............. 1955.00
Secretaire, Kingwood, Parquetry, Ormolu Mounted, Canted Rectangle, 19 1/2 In. 2600.00
Secretaire, Marquetry, Faux Leather Bindings, France 9500.00
Secretaire, Neoclassical, Brass Mounted, Painted Chinoiserie, Italy, 100 In.............. 9200.00
Secretaire, Spanish Revival, Walnut, 2 Figural Painted Doors, Rope Legs, 70 In........... 3636.00
Secretaire A Abattant, Denis Genty, Tulipwood, Amaranth, Ormolu Mounted 5200.00
Secretaire A Abattant, Louis Phillippe, Drop Front, Mahogany, 62 x 38 x 21 In. 1430.00
Secretaire A Abattant, Louis XV, Kingwood, Ormolu, Fall Front, Serpentine Front 6900.00
Secretary, Biedermeier, Birch & Part Ebonized, 52 In. 3750.50
Secretary, Biedermeier, Drop Front 7700.00
Secretary, Biedermier, Drop Front, Fitted Interior, 3 Drawers, 51 x 57 In. 4750.00
Secretary, Birch, Secret Drawers, Candia, N.H., 1805.................................... 7500.00
Secretary, Burl Walnut, Cylinder Roll, 1870s 3450.00
Secretary, Cherry, Double Glazed Doors, c.1820, 80 x 40 In. 5900.00
Secretary, Chippendale, Fall Front, Walnut, 2 Panel Doors, c.1780, 78 In. 5500.00
Secretary, Cylinder Roll, Burl Panels, Bird's-Eye Interior 6710.00
Secretary, Empire, Curly Maple, Double Doors, Figured Veneer, Country, 65 1/2 In.... 2200.00
Secretary, Empire, Pine, Dovetailed Case, 3 Drawers, Paneled Doors, 76 1/4 In. 3575.00

Furniture, Secretary-Bookcase, George III,

Inlaid Mahogany, 1780, 96 In.

✦✦✦✦✦✦✦✦✦✦✦✦✦✦✦✦✦✦✦✦✦✦✦✦✦

It is safe to use spray or paste wax on your furniture but be careful about changing brands. It is okay to put paste wax over spray wax. It is not safe to put spray wax over paste wax because it may soften the paste wax and spoil the finish.

✦✦✦✦✦✦✦✦✦✦✦✦✦✦✦✦✦✦✦✦✦✦✦✦✦

Secretary, Fall Front, Marble Top, Interior Drawers, Parquetry, 49 In.	690.00
Secretary, Federal, Cherry, Mahogany, 1790-1820, 52 In.	5250.00
Secretary, Federal, Mahogany, Dovetailed, Drawer Veneer, 1800.	3800.00
Secretary, George III, Slant Front, Walnut, Mirrored Panels, 18th Century, 65 In.	2750.00
Secretary, Georgian, Slant Front, Mahogany, Inlaid, Glazed Doors, 84 x 23 In.	1900.00
Secretary, Judkins & Senter, Birch, Portsmouth, N.H., 1810, 78 x 41 1/2 In.	8580.00
Secretary, Mahogany, Fold-Out Writing Surface, c.1850, 69 x 40 In.	575.00
Secretary, Mahogany, Marquetry, Ormolu, Spain, 79 3/4 In.	880.00
Secretary, S.R. Howland, Mahogany Veneers, N.Y., 67 3/4 x 35 In.	3750.00
Secretary, Shaker, Slant Front, 2 Top Doors	4500.00
Secretary, Slant Front, Walnut, Fitted Interior, 3-Pane Doors, 83 In.	1650.00
Secretary, Walnut, Glass Above Drawers, Bracket Base, c.1850	2900.00
Secretary, William & Mary Style, Hinged Slant Front, Oak, 41 1/2 In.	460.00
Secretary-Bookcase, 3 Burled Drawers, Glass Doors, 5 Ft.	2600.00
Secretary-Bookcase, Classical, Slant Front, Mahogany, 3 Drawers, N.Y., 86 x 55 In.	5775.00
Secretary-Bookcase, Drop Front, Mahogany, Cavetto Cornice, Glazed Doors, 89 In.	1760.00
Secretary-Bookcase, Eastlake, Pullout Writing Surface, 73 x 33 1/2 x 20 In.	600.00
Secretary-Bookcase, Fall Front, Mahogany, Veneer, Broken Arch Pediment, 2 Doors	415.00
Secretary-Bookcase, Fall Front, Walnut, Bird's-Eye Maple	6450.00
Secretary-Bookcase, Fall Front, Walnut, Mirrored Doors, 86 In.	6670.00
Secretary-Bookcase, George III, Inlaid Mahogany, 1780, 96 In. .... *Illus*	7475.00
Secretary-Bookcase, George III, Satinwood, Mahogany, 81 x 36 1/2 In.	6035.00
Secretary-Bookcase, Georgian Style, Mahogany, Inlaid Slant Front, 78 1/2 In.	880.00
Secretary-Bookcase, Georgian, Mahogany, Glazed Doors, 92 x 84 In.	3960.00
Secretary-Bookcase, Georgian, Slant Front, Mahogany, Geometric Glazed Doors	2640.00
Secretary-Bookcase, Gothic Revival, Drop Front	1485.00
Secretary-Bookcase, Mahogany, 2 Glazed Doors, Above 2 Drawers, 41 x 22 x 87 In.	575.00
Secretary-Bookcase, Mahogany, 2 Piece, Ogee Cornice, Carved, c.1840, 94 1/2 In.	3520.00
Secretary-Bookcase, Mahogany, Glazed Doors, 3 Drawers, Fitted Interior, 87 In.	9775.00
Secretary-Bookcase, Mahogany, Multipaned Doors, Drawers, 93 In.	660.00
Secretary-Bookcase, Mahogany, Upper Glazed Doors, Lower Drawer, 103 In.	6900.00
Secretary-Bookcase, Satinwood Banded, Eagle & Brass Ball Finials, 82 In.	1320.00
Server, 2 Leaded Glass Doors, 5 Drawers, Mirror, Victorian, 1890, 61 x 48 In.	440.00
Server, Art Deco, Walnut, France, 1920	2250.00
Server, Blind Drawer, Back Splash, L.& J.G. Stickley, 32 In.	600.00
Server, E. Wormley, 3 Drawers Over 3 Woven Splint Doors, 61 In.	520.00
Server, Eastlake, Marble Top, 2 Drawers Over 1 Door, 37 x 40 x 18 In.	250.00
Server, Empire, Marble Top, Boston, 31 x 30 In.	3900.00
Server, George II Style, Serpentine, 3 Drawers, Square Tapering Legs, 52 In.	825.00
Server, George III Style, Mahogany & Yew Wood, 1880s, 31 x 42 1/2 In.	1380.00
Server, Jacobean Style, Mahogany, 2 Cupboard Doors, 35 x 40 In.	68.00

Furniture, Settee, Classical, Scroll Arm, Tubular Crest, Velvet, 37 x 90 In.

Server, Mahogany, Foliate Carving, Cabriole Legs, Lower Shelf, 32 x 59 In. 460.00
Server, Mahogany, Frieze With Foliate Carving, 1 Shelf, Victorian, 32 x 59 In. 460.00
Server, Mahogany, Reverse-Curved Skirt, Molded Edge, 3 Drawers............................ 880.00
Server, Oak, 2 Drawers, Scroll-Cut Apron, Shelf, England, 31 1/2 x 57 1/2 In. 1100.00
Server, Oak, Mirror, 4 Drawers Over 2 Doors, Carved 1250.00
Server, Oak, Mirror, 4 Drawers, 2 Side Doors, Victorian 600.00
Server, Pine, 2 Drawers, Embossed Escutcheons, Shaped Apron, 1860...................... 485.00
Server, Walnut, Marble Top, Victorian 2530.00
Settee, 1 Arm, Ball & Spindle Back... 250.00
Settee, Arched Ladder Back, Open Arms, Upholstered Seat, 53 In. 200.00
Settee, Art Deco, Velvet, c.1925, 5 Ft. 11 In.. 4320.00
Settee, Biedermeier Style, Arched Back Ending In Scrolls, 61 In............................. 690.00
Settee, Brocade Gilded, France, c.1860 .... 2200.00
Settee, Camelback, Serpentine Back Rest, Damask, 76 In.. 745.00
Settee, Camelback, Walnut, Upholstered, 40 x 57 In.. 385.00
Settee, Carved Rosewood Frame, Upholstered Back & Seat, Victorian 575.00
Settee, Charles X, Mahogany, Ormolu Mounted, Upholstered Back, 58 In. 4600.00
Settee, Cherry, Curved Arms, Upholstered Back, 1825, 84 In. 2000.00
Settee, Classical, Mahogany, Serpentine Crest Rail, Upholstered, 1825, 36 x 68 In....... 5175.00
Settee, Classical, Scroll Arm, Tubular Crest, Velvet, 37 x 90 In. ....*Illus* 3080.00
Settee, Continental Baroque Style, Studded Leatherette, 59 In. 1840.00
Settee, Empire Revival, High Back, Down-Curved Arms, Ball & Claw Feet, 51 In. 715.00
Settee, Empire, Mahogany, Floral & Foliate Carved Crest, 19th Century, 77 In. 413.00
Settee, Franco-Flemish, Gros Point Needlework, 51 1/2 In....................................... 6325.00
Settee, French Style, Fruitwood, 49 In... 665.00
Settee, George III Style, Roll Arm, Fretwork, 19th Century, 81 In. 1320.00
Settee, George III Style, Walnut, Carved Crest, Marlboro Legs, 34 x 40 In., Pair......... 2530.00
Settee, George III, Mahogany, Square Back, 1880s, 65 In. 345.00
Settee, George III, Painted, Parcel Gilt, Padded Backrest, Loose Cushion, 5 Ft. 9 In..... 4600.00
Settee, Gothic Revival, Leaf-Carved Frame, Velvet, c.1845, 7 Ft. 10 In....................... 5750.00
Settee, Grape-Carved Crest, Horsehair, Victorian 220.00
Settee, Green, Black, Gilt, Melon Leaves, Pa., 1840 .... 4250.00
Settee, Gustav Stickley, No. 221, c.1905... 3850.00
Settee, Louis XV Style, Beechwood, Arched Crest, Floral Spray Center, 47 In. 8005.00
Settee, Louis XV Style, Carved Giltwood, 66 In. 690.00
Settee, Louis XV Style, Giltwood, Pierced Foliate Back & Sides, 44 In. 18540.00
Settee, Louis XV, Walnut, Carved Crest, Serpentine Top Rail, Velvet, 80 In. 825.00
Settee, Louis XVI Style, Carved Giltwood, Oval Back, Tapestry, 55 In....................... 1100.00
Settee, Mahogany, 10 Legs, Cloven Hoofs, Upholstered Seat & Wing Back 3000.00
Settee, Mahogany, Satinwood Inlay, Caned Back, Medallions, 56 In............................ 1200.00
Settee, Neoclassical, Walnut, Guilloche-Carved Backrest, Italy, 37 In., Pair 8050.00
Settee, Provincial, Pegged Construction, 57 In.. 440.00

*Furniture, Settee, Tiger &
Bird's-Eye Maple, Refinished,
Cane Back, 55 In.*

*Furniture, Settee, Windsor,
Chicken Coop, Green
Paint, 77 In.*

Settee, Regency Style, Giltwood Upholstered Back, Leaf-Tip Apron	3450.00
Settee, Renaissance Revival, Ormolu, Rosewood, Marquetry, Applied Medallions	3450.00
Settee, Rococo Revival, Cast Iron, Stamped Hinderer, Arms	1325.00
Settee, Rosewood, Fully Carved, Victorian, 1860	8500.00
Settee, Rosewood, Triple Back, Scalloped Crest, Carved Lilies & Roses	1760.00
Settee, Scroll Arm, Tubular Crest Rail, Velvet, 90 In.	3080.00
Settee, Scroll Crest Rail, High Arms, Scroll Cut Apron, Canada, 87 1/4 In.	2000.00
Settee, Shaped Seat, Bronze Medallion Set In Crest, 70 In.	550.00
Settee, Shells In Geometric Pattern On Backrest, Monopodie Legs, 5 Ft. 3 In.	5465.00
Settee, Tiger & Bird's-Eye Maple, Refinished, Cane Back, 55 In. *Illus*	3450.00
Settee, Tiger Maple Arms, Half-Spindle Back, Painted, Stenciled, 6 Ft. 5 In.	6250.00
Settee, Triple Back, Arrow-Back Stiles, Balloon Seat, Painted Yellow, 68 1/2 In.	1380.00
Settee, Triple Chair Back, Upholstered Back & Seat, Tufted Arms, 1870s, 71 In.	430.00
Settee, Tufted Back, Adjustable Sides, Plush Mohair, 5 Ft. 9 In.	8050.00
Settee, Windsor, Bamboo Turned, 51 Spindles, H Stretcher, Green, 77 x 23 In.	1500.00
Settee, Windsor, Bamboo-Turned Spindles, Arms, 19th Century, 109 In.	6900.00
Settee, Windsor, Bowen & Hayes, Low Back, Knuckle Arms, 78 In.	5500.00
Settee, Windsor, Cage Back, 7 Bamboo-Turned Supports, 71 1/2 In.	2415.00
Settee, Windsor, Chicken Coop, Green Paint, 77 In. *Illus*	3520.00
Settee, Windsor, Low Back, Scroll Arms, Bamboo Turnings, 61 1/2 In.	1700.00
Settee, Windsor, Painted Green, Gold Striping, Arms, Pennsylvania	750.00
Settle, Arrow-Back, Turned Legs, Plank Seat, Scrolled Arms, 75 In.	135.00
Settle, Barrel Back, Arms, 18th Century	2995.00
Settle, Black Striping, Stenciled & Freehand Floral, Plank Seat, 82 In.	685.00
Settle, Brown Graining, Striping, Gilt Foliage, Plank Seat, Pennsylvania, 76 In.	1870.00
Settle, George III, Provincial, Oak, Cupboard Over Arms, Hinged Seat, 59 1/2 In.	865.00
Settle, Georgian, Mahogany, Double Back, Interlaced Splat, Restored, 1780, 43 In.	1100.00
Settle, Gustav Stickley, 2-Slats, Cutback Slab Side, No. 215, 38 x 13 x 30 In.	1045.00
Settle, Gustav Stickley, Back And Arm Slats	9900.00
Settle, Gustav Stickley, Even Arm, 8-Slat Back, Tenons, No. 208H, 39 x 76 In.	4950.00
Settle, Gustav Stickley, Even Arm, No. 221	3520.00
Settle, Half-Spindle Back, Yellow Striping, 74 In.	440.00
Settle, L. & J.G. Stickley, Bent Arm, 7 Slats Back, No.263, 77 x 29 In.	6050.00
Settle, L. & J.G. Stickley, Box, No. 232, 5-Slat Back, Brown Leather, 28 x 72 In.	2750.00

Settle, L. & J.G. Stickley, Even Arm, 5 Slats Under Arms, 16 On Back, 1906, 76 In. ... 6325.00
Settle, Oak, 17th-Century Style, Child's, 30 x 24 In. 275.00
Settle, Pine, 2 Drawers, Beaded Edge Back, Painted Black Paint, Pine, 60 x 61 In. 1870.00
Settle, Pine, Base Folds Out To Bed, 65 1/2 In. 305.00
Settle, Pine, Seat Folds Out To Bed, Brown Finish, 69 In. 275.00
Settle, Polychrome Floral, Rush Seat, 2-Slat Back, 78 In. 1265.00
Settle, Softwood, Drawers Above & Below, Varnished, Arms, 79 x 69 In. 2145.00
Settle, Stickley Brothers, 3 Side Slats, 11 Back Slats, Paper Label, 84 In. 5225.00
Settle, Stickley Brothers, 5 Slats, Even Arm, Leather Cushions, No. 226 .... 7000.00
Settle, Stickley Brothers, Canted Sides, Vertical Splats, Oak, 62 In. 5175.00
Settle, Stickley Brothers, Oak, Crib Style, Drop-In Seat, No. 3863, 36 x 62 x 30 In. 5175.00
Settle & Armchair, Jacobean Style, Oak, Chip-Carved Back, 1870s, Miniature 1380.00
Shelf, Hanging, Mahogany, 3 Graduated Shelves, 2 Drawers, Inlaid, 23 In. 1455.00
Shelf, Hanging, Poplar, Painted Brown, Tapered Ends, 3 Shelves, 20 x 27 In. 550.00
Shelf, Hanging, Sponged Edge, Cut-Out Sides, 3 Shelves, Painted, 11 x 22 In. 550.00
Shelf, Hanging, Walnut, 3 Shelves, Shaped Sides, England, 28 1/2 x 32 x 5 1/2 In. 345.00
Shelf, Kettle, England, 10 x 15 1/2 x 10 1/2 In. 165.00
Shelf, Kettle, Wooden Handle, Brass Top, Wrought Iron, 16 1/2 In. 300.00
Shelf, Music, Mahogany, Stick & Ball, 40 In. 220.00
Shelf, Standing, 3 Tiers, 3 Shelves, Painted Robin's-Egg Blue, 25 1/2 In. 2645.00
Sideboard, Aesthetic-Colonial Revival, Mahogany, Carved 850.00
Sideboard, Art Deco, Burl Walnut, Veneered, Silver Drawers, Germany 6500.00
Sideboard, Arts & Crafts, Oak, Blue Wash Carving, 4 Doors & Drawers, 90 x 50 In. ... 880.00
Sideboard, Bowfront, 3 Drawers, Center Cupboard Doors, 78 1/4 In. 2530.00
Sideboard, Carved Oak, Rouge Marble Top, Beveled Mirror Back, 1840s 4400.00
Sideboard, Carved Walnut, Burl Panels, Marble, Fox Pulling Grapes, Mirror 3775.00
Sideboard, Cherry, 2 Doors, 2 Faux Drawers, Marble Top, Dolphin Supports 1500.00
Sideboard, Classical, Inlaid, Mirror, 1890 .... 6500.00
Sideboard, Classical, Mahogany, 3/4 Gallery, Punched Columns, 53 x 70 x 23 In. 1495.00
Sideboard, Classical, Mahogany, Brass Inlay, Acanthus Gilt Legs, 49 x 47 In. 1955.00
Sideboard, Classical, Mahogany, Splashback, 2 Paneled Doors, 1820, 56 x 37 In. 2300.00
Sideboard, Empire Style, Mahogany, Bowfront Doors, Reeded Legs, 66 In. 440.00
Sideboard, Empire, Mahogany Veneers, 2 Over 3 Drawers & 2 Doors, 45 x 58 In. 275.00
Sideboard, Empire, Mahogany, Ormolu Capped Columns, Paw Feet, 72 In. 2530.00
Sideboard, F.L. Wright, Mahogany, 8 Drawers, 2 Doors, Greek Key Design, 1955 .... 1495.00
Sideboard, Federal Style, Cherry, Tambour Doors, Serpentine Front 7900.00
Sideboard, Federal Style, Irwin, Mahogany, 2 Doors Base, 50 x 18 x 36 1/2 In. 385.00
Sideboard, Federal, Mahogany Inlaid, 3 Drawers, Doors, c.1790, 43 x 59 In. 8625.00
Sideboard, Federal, Mahogany, 1 Long Drawer Over 2 Doors, 40 1/2 x 63 x 23 In. 1955.00
Sideboard, Federal, Mahogany, Inlaid, Drawers, Compartments, c.1800, 43 x 67 In. 7475.00
Sideboard, Federal, Medial Shelf, Mirror, Boston, Small 1650.00
Sideboard, Federal, Tiger Maple, Cherry, Vermont 1700.00
Sideboard, French Provincial, Walnut, Breakfront Type, 4 Doors, Marble Top 880.00
Sideboard, George III Style, Mahogany Inlaid, Late 19th Century, 43 x 72 In. 3737.00
Sideboard, George III Style, Satinwood, Mahogany, Bowed Top, 36 1/2 In. 1610.00
Sideboard, George III, Mahogany, Tambour Slides, Cellaret Drawers, 6 Ft. 5 In. 3450.00
Sideboard, Georgian Style, 3 Drawers Over Doors, Burl Walnut, 48 1/4 In. 860.00
Sideboard, Georgian Style, Mahogany, Bowfront, Beaded Carved Borders, 66 In. 1540.00
Sideboard, Gilbert Rohde, Walnut, 4 Drawers, 2 Doors, H. Miller, 66 In. 440.00
Sideboard, Gio Ponti, Parchment & Birch, Center Glass Panel, 1950, 92 In. 6325.00
Sideboard, Gustav Stickley, 2 Drawers Over Long, Iron Pulls, Strap Hinges, 45 In. 9200.00
Sideboard, Gustav Stickley, 3 Drawers Over Long Drawer 3250.00
Sideboard, Gustav Stickley, 8 Pegged Legs, Copper Straps, No. 1301, 70 x 50 In. 8800.00
Sideboard, Gustav Stickley, No. 1 .... 3250.00
Sideboard, Gustav Stickley, Square Wooden Knobs & Copper Pulls, 1903 .... 8800.00
Sideboard, Hepplewhite Style, Mahogany, c.1880, 40 3/4 x 65 1/2 In. 2950.00
Sideboard, Incised, Black Lacquer, 2 Doors, J. Adnet, c.1940, 6 Ft.6 1/2 In. 8050.00
Sideboard, Knoll & Assoc, Pine Shelves, 75 1/2 In. 825.00
Sideboard, L. & J.G. Stickley, Oak, No. 738, c.1910 .... 2090.00
Sideboard, Lifetime, Overhang On Mirror, 2 Doors, 3 Drawers, Brass Pulls, 55 In. 900.00
Sideboard, Limbert, 2 Drawers, Hammered Copper Hardware, Arched Back, 66 In. 2860.00
Sideboard, Mahogany, 4 Drawers Over 4 Doors, Columns At Corners, Marble Top 715.00
Sideboard, Mahogany, Art Deco, 2 Lower Drawers, Brass, c.1935, 7 Ft. 7 In. 7475.00

Furniture, Sideboard, Regency, Ebony Inlaid,
Convex Mirror, c.1810

Sideboard, Mahogany, Carved Scrolled Gallery, Paw Feet, c.1840, 51 1/2 In. 825.00
Sideboard, Mahogany, Paper Label, Gloucester, Mass., 1804, 40 x 60 In. 8800.00
Sideboard, Mission Oak Style, Beveled Mirror, 2 Drawers, 2 Doors Over 1 Drawer 500.00
Sideboard, Queen Anne Style, Mahogany, Cupboard, Drawers, 1896, 60 In. 275.00
Sideboard, Regency, Ebony Inlaid, Convex Mirror, c.1810 .... *Illus* 9000.00
Sideboard, Robsjohn-Gibbings, 6-Side-By-Side Drawers, Widdicomb 875.00
Sideboard, Rococo, Rosewood, Serpentine Marble, Etagere Top, 84 x 81 x 24 In. 8800.00
Sideboard, Rosewood, 2 Glass Doors, Side Shelves, Marquetry, c.1900, 85 In. 2760.00
Sideboard, Sheraton Style, Mahogany, Rosewood, Serpentine, 19th Century, 66 In. 1870.00
Sideboard, Sheraton, Curly Maple, 5 Dovetailed Drawers, Paneled Ends 4620.00
Sideboard, Sheraton, Mahogany, Concave Center, Fitted Drawers, 67 1/2 In. 1870.00
Sideboard, Stickley Bros., 2 Side Doors, 4 Drawers, Gallery 950.00
Sideboard, Walnut, 2 Glass Doors, Side Shelves, Eastlake, 3 Drawers........................ 1400.00
Sideboard, Walnut, 2 Upper & 4 Base Cabinets, 3 Drawers, Vienna, 92 x 64 In. 2875.00
Sideboard, Walnut, Carved Fowl & Horn, Pheasants, Nuts & Grapes, 89 In. 6050.00
Sideboard, Walnut, Fruit Carved, Marble, Victorian, 1860 .... 5495.00
Sideboard, Walnut, Marble Top, 2 Open Shelves, Over 2 Drawers, 2 Doors, 81 In....... 775.00
Sideboard, Walnut, Shell & Floral Inlay, Tapered Legs, c.1810, 34 x 63 x 22 In. 2200.00
Sideboard, Wylie & Lockhead, Inlaid, Curved Side Panels, 73 3/4 x 36 1/4 In. 6250.00
Sofa, American Empire, Mahogany, Loral Carved Back, 80 In. 230.00
Sofa, Arched Back, Serpentine Seat, Silk Brocade, 73 1/2 In., Pair............................. 4600.00
Sofa, Carved Top Rail, Upholstered 550.00
Sofa, Carved Wooden Frame, Brocade, 1930, 85 In. 275.00
Sofa, Carved, Mahogany, New York, 1820, 33 x 77 x 23 In...................................... *Illus* 6670.00
Sofa, Cast Aluminum Frame, Alexander Girard, Winged Arms 4125.00
Sofa, Chippendale Style, Mahogany, Camelback, Outward Scrolling Arms, 83 In......... 550.00
Sofa, Chippendale, Mahogany, c.1780, 37 x 74 x 24 In... 2415.00
Sofa, Classical, Carved Mahogany, Serpentine Sides, Philadelphia, c.1830, 79 In. 1430.00
Sofa, Classical, Flame Mahogany, Scrolled Arms, Upholstered, 87 In. 2750.00
Sofa, Classical, Mahogany, Carved, c.1825, 35 x 86 x 24 1/2 In. 8652.00
Sofa, Classical, Mahogany, Carved, Paw Feet, American, 1820s, 34 x 92 In. 10925.00
Sofa, Classical, Mahogany, Carved, Veneer, c.1825, 35 1/4 x 84 x 21 In....................... 2300.00
Sofa, Classical, Mahogany, Padded Seat, Scrolled Arms, 19th Century, 87 In. 1380.00
Sofa, Classical, Mahogany, Quadripartite Caned Back, Removable Seat, 78 In. 4370.00
Sofa, Classical, Mahogany, Scrolled Arms, Upholstered, Hairy Paw Feet, 85 In. 2530.00
Sofa, Cornucopia, Upholstered Squabs, Acanthus Crest Rail, c.1810, 61 1/2 In............ 2500.00
Sofa, Country, Upholstered, c.1810, 16 x 71 x 20 In. 2415.00
Sofa, Eastlake, Burl Walnut Carved, Upholstered, Victorian, 53 In. 467.00
Sofa, Eastlake, Walnut, Carved, Upholstered, Brass Tacks 415.00
Sofa, Edwardian, Hand-Carved Frame, Upholstered, 88 In. 855.00
Sofa, Egyptian Revival, Walnut, Upholstered, Sectional, 1870s.................................. 7425.00

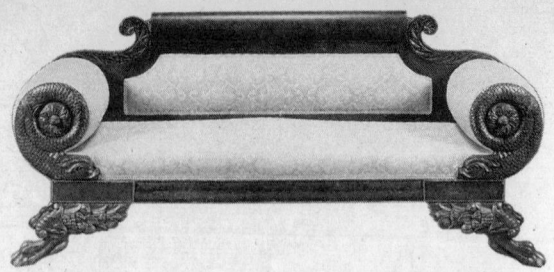

Furniture, Sofa, Carved, Mahogany, New York, 1820, 33 x 77 x 23 In.

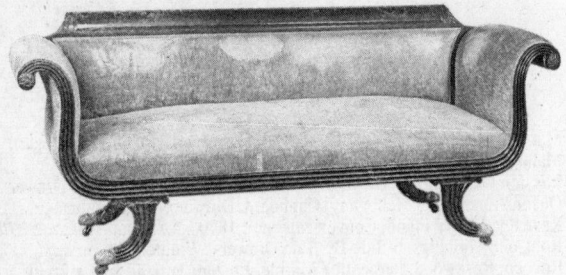

Furniture, Sofa, Mahogany, Acanthus, John Needles, 1825, 7 Ft. 9 In.

Sofa, Empire Regency, Carved Arms, Velvet.. 705.00
Sofa, Empire, Claw Feet, Carved Back, Rolled Arms, c.1840, 87 x 35 x 23 In. 1800.00
Sofa, Empire, Floral & Scroll Crest, Upholstered Back & Seat, American, 85 In. 275.00
Sofa, Empire, Mahogany, Rectangular Floral-Carved Back, 19th Century, 80 In. 230.00
Sofa, Empire, Mahogany, Scrolled Arm, Claw, Ball Feet, Upholstered, 19th Century.... 2200.00
Sofa, Empire, Scrolled Arms, Carved Feet, Mahogany, 95 In. 550.00
Sofa, Federal, Inlaid Mahogany, c.1815, 38 x 77 1/2 x 22 In. 5465.00
Sofa, Federal, Mahogany, c.1815, 38 x 78 x 26 In. 1150.00
Sofa, Federal, Mahogany, Carved Thunderbolts Tied To Bow & Knot Crest, 6 Ft. 4025.00
Sofa, Federal, Mahogany, Open Arms, Brocade, 78 In. 2530.00
Sofa, Frank Lloyd Wright, Sectional, 3-Piece, Linen, 104 In. 2090.00
Sofa, Frank Lloyd Wright, Taliesin Design, Heritage Henredon, 101 x 33 x 30 In. 1045.00
Sofa, Georgian Style, Mahogany, Camelback, Rolled Arms, Ball & Claw Feet, 77 In.... 805.00
Sofa, Jacobean Style, Walnut, Rope Turned & Block Legs, 78 In................................... 185.00
Sofa, Louis XV, Fruitwood Gilt, 51 In.. 865.00
Sofa, Louis XVI Style, Fruitwood, 54 In... 575.00
Sofa, Mahogany, Acanthus Crest Rail, Padded Back & Seat, c.1830, 89 1/2 In. 6035.00
Sofa, Mahogany, Acanthus, John Needles, 1825, 7 Ft. 9 In. ....*Illus* 8625.00
Sofa, Mahogany, Boston, 19th Century..*Illus* 1100.00
Sofa, Mahogany, Curved Back, Loose Cushion, Embroidered Silk Cover, 75 In. 4025.00
Sofa, Mahogany, Inlaid, c.1815, 77 1/2 In... 5650.00
Sofa, Mahogany, Molded Crest, Upholstered Back, Loose Cushion, c.1805, 6 Ft.......... 8625.00
Sofa, Mahogany, Scrolled Crest Rail, Upholstered Back & Sides, 73 1/2 In.................. 1380.00
Sofa, Marshmallow, Black & White, Herman Miller, c.1956................................*Illus* 16500.00
Sofa, Modernist, Upholstered Cushions, Arms, 64 In.. 415.00
Sofa, Paul Franke, 6 Rattan Bands, Muslin, c.1930, 78 In... 1210.00
Sofa, Provincial, Painted, 82 In... 1100.00
Sofa, Regency, Alexander Lawrence, Upholstered, 1820s 2600.00
Sofa, Renaissance Revival, Rosewood, Gilt, Damask, American.................................... 1100.00
Sofa, Rococo Revival, Rosewood, Laminated, Serpentine Seat, 1850-1870, 75 In. 5750.00
Sofa, Rococo Revival, Rosewood, Upholstered, Victorian, 76 In. 495.00

Furniture, Sofa, Mahogany, Boston, 19th Century

Sofa, Rococo Revival, Walnut, Finger Carved, Velvet, 69 In. 415.00
Sofa, Rococo Revival, Walnut, Finger Carved, Velvet, 60 In. 360.00
Sofa, Sofa, Federal, Rolled Arms, Brass Inlaid 1760.00
Sofa, T. Molesworth, Leather Upholstered, Chimayo Woven Pillows, 83 In. 9900.00
Sofa, Walnut, Carved Scroll & Rose Back, Upholstered, Victorian, 40 x 81 In. 440.00
Sofa, Walnut, Floral Carved Frame, Button-Tufted, Victorian 660.00
Sofa & Armchair, Eastlake, Walnut, Burl Veneer, Minerva Heads, Velvet, 2 Piece 415.00
Sofa & Chair, Downcarved Arms & Back, Brocade 1500.00
Sofa & Chair, Mies Van Der Rohe, Chromed Block Legs, 260 Series, Knoll................ 2300.00
Sofa Set, White Wicker, Floral Chintz Cushions, Table, Ottoman, 5 Piece.................... 3950.00
Stand, 4 Drawers, Carved, Cabriole Legs 467.50
Stand, Breadboard Top, Red, 1 Drawer, Thin Taper Leg, New Hampshire 575.00
Stand, Bucket, Pine & Maple, 2 Shelves, 1 Drawer, Cabinet Door, 47 In. 385.00
Stand, Butler's, Biedermeier, 2 Tier, 50 In. 440.00
Stand, Butler's, Georgian Style, Mahogany, 28 x 19 In. 247.00
Stand, Carved Teak, Pierced Apron, Straight Legs, Claw Feet, China, 22 x 22 In. 330.00
Stand, Carved, Marble Top, Lower Shelf, Ball & Claw Feet, China, 32 x 21 In. 515.00
Stand, Chamber, Classical, Painted, New England, c.1820, 33 x 20 x 17 In. 230.00
Stand, Cherry & Curly Maple, 2 Drawers, Glass Pulls, 28 1/4 In. 70.00
Stand, Cherry, Turned Legs, Dovetail Drawer, 2-Board Top, Country, 20 x 22 In........ 415.00
Stand, Coat & Umbrella, Leaf Design, Mirror, Cast Iron 850.00
Stand, Corner, Pine, 4 Graduated Shelves, Primitive, 34 In. 110.00
Stand, Corner, Walnut, 5 Tiers, 19th Century, 57 1/4 In. 155.00
Stand, Curly Maple, Dovetailed Drawer, 2-Board Top, 28 In. 660.00
Stand, Dictionary, Oak, Folding Top, Cast-Iron Base 240.00
Stand, Drink, L. & J. G. Stickley, Leather Top, Arched Cross Stretcher, No. 22, 29 In. 3575.00
Stand, Drink, Lower Shelf, Tapered Legs, Square, 31 1/2 x 13 1/2 In. 385.00
Stand, Drop Leaf, Butternut, Turned Legs, 2 Dovetailed Drawers, 16 x 18 x 29 In. 440.00
Stand, Drop Leaf, Cherry & Maple, Bird's-Eye Veneer Posts, 19 In. 415.00
Stand, Empire, Tilt Top, Mahogany, Turned Pedestal, 29 1/2 x 23 In........................... 250.00
Stand, Federal, Birch & Mahogany, Cherry Inlay, Turned Reeded Legs, 28 x 16 In..... 2300.00
Stand, Federal, Cherry, 1 Drawer, Inlaid Edge, Conn., 1790, 19 In. 690.00
Stand, Federal, Mahogany & Birch Veneer, Drawer, 2 Doors, c.1800, 25 x 24 In. 1840.00
Stand, Federal, Tilt Top, Mahogany, Tripod Base, c.1760, 29 1/2 In. 5750.00
Stand, Federal, Walnut, 1 Drawer, Square Tapering Legs, 29 x 19 1/4 x 19 In. 230.00
Stand, Galle, Mahogany, Magnolia Blossoms Inlay, Lower Shelf, c.1900, 43 In. 4600.00
Stand, Hepplewhite, Bird's-Eye Maple Top, Hardwood, Drawer, 30 1/2 In. 220.00
Stand, Hepplewhite, Cherry, 2-Board Top, 28 1/2 In. 247.50
Stand, Hepplewhite, Cherry, Drawer, Tapered Legs 415.00
Stand, Hepplewhite, Cherry, Molded-Edge Drawer, 28 1/2 In. 550.00
Stand, Hepplewhite, Cherry, Poplar Top, Square Tapered Legs, Drawer, 28 3/4 In....... 250.00
Stand, Hepplewhite, Drop Leaf, Mahogany, Line Inlay, 1 Drawer, 27 In. 545.00
Stand, Hepplewhite, Mahogany, Drawer, 18 x 15 1/2 x 26 1/2 In. 485.00
Stand, Hepplewhite, Pine, Cherry, Tapered Legs, Drawer, 18 x 24 x 28 In. 300.00
Stand, Light, Federal, Birch, Bird's-Eye Maple, New Hampshire, c.1825, 27 x 20 In. .. 3220.00

Stand, Light, Federal, Cherry, Drawer, New England, c.1810, 27 x 18 x 17 In. 1495.00
Stand, Magazine, Gustav Stickley, 3 Shelves, Single Side Slat, 30 x 27 In. 1320.00
Stand, Magazine, Gustav Stickley, Cutout Handles, 4 Shelves, No. 79, 40 In. 1540.00
Stand, Magazine, L. & J.G. Stickley, 4 Shelves, 3 Slats Each Side, 42 x 19 In. 1760.00
Stand, Magazine, L. & J.G. Stickley, Shelves, Arched Supports, No. 45, 21 x 45 In. 2000.00
Stand, Magazine, Limbert, 3 Shelves, Tapered, Cutouts, No. 352, 16 x 10 x 28 In. 825.00
Stand, Magazine, Stickley Bros., 5 Shelves, No. 4753, 14 x 11 x 42 In. 1210.00
Stand, Mahogany, Drawer, Turned Legs, Brass Pulls, 28 1/2 x 21 1/2 x 16 In. 440.00
Stand, Mahogany, Inlaid Cuff On Legs, String Inlay Allover Body, 1780, 28 In. 2700.00
Stand, Mahogany, Ring & Block-Turned Legs, 2 Drawers 225.00
Stand, Muffin, Mahogany, 3 Round Shelves 200.00
Stand, Music, Adjustable, Tapered Legs, Mid-19th Century 450.00
Stand, Music, American Renaissance, Walnut, 3 Tiers, 19th Century, 35 x 23 x 15 In. .. 1870.00
Stand, Music, Lyre, Mahogany 176.00
Stand, Music, Marquetry, Walnut, 35 x 23 In., Pair.....................................*Illus* 1870.00
Stand, Music, Oak, Lyre In Top Gallery, Ball & Stick 195.00
Stand, Music, William IV, Rosewood, 2 Candlesticks, Nettlefold & Son, 1820, 42 In... 2300.00
Stand, Night, Gustav Stickley, 2 Drawers, Backsplash, 31 In. 2090.00
Stand, Oak, 1 Drawer, Turned Legs, 26 In... 55.00
Stand, Oak, 2 Shelves, Square, 16 In. 30.00
Stand, Onyx & Brass, Raised On Scroll Feet, 2 Tiers, Victorian, 32 x 14 In. 250.00
Stand, Pine, Harlequin Chamfer Legs, Drawer, Painted, 18 1/2 x 29 In. 385.00
Stand, Pine, Old Red, Turned Legs, 1-Board Top, 19 x 20 x 29 In. 360.00
Stand, Plant, Charles Rohlfs, Wood & Hammered Metal 8800.00
Stand, Plant, L. & J.G. Stickley, Handcraft Decal, No. 587, 16 x 27 In. 715.00
Stand, Plant, Limbert, 4 Splayed Legs, Arched Apron, 10 x 10 x 28 In......................... 605.00
Stand, Plant, Limbert, Flush Top, Arched Rails, Signed, 27 In...................................... 700.00
Stand, Plant, Limbert, Square Top, Splayed Legs, Lower Stretcher, 12 x 12 x 16 In. 490.00
Stand, Plant, Oak, Pineapple-Skin Pedestal 175.00
Stand, Plant, Painted Mahogany, 3 Tiers, 1920... 450.00
Stand, Plant, Rope-Twist Brass, 2 Oak Shelves 500.00
Stand, Plant, Wicker 38.00
Stand, Portfolio, Mirrors, Minton Plaques, Marquetry... 3850.00
Stand, Portfolio, Walnut, Folding, Victorian 2050.00
Stand, Roycroft, Little Journeys, Tenon & Key Construction, Tag, 26 x 26 x 14 In. 880.00
Stand, Sewing, Astragal, Frederick County, Md., 1815 .... 2200.00
Stand, Sewing, Drop Leaf, 2 Drawers, 28 x 16 x 16 In.. 550.00
Stand, Sewing, Drop Leaf, Mahogany, 2 Drawers, c.1830, 28 1/4 In. 465.00
Stand, Sewing, Federal, Mahogany, Reeded Legs, Cookie Corner Top, 31 x 16 In. 3630.00
Stand, Sewing, Heywood-Wakefield, Shelf, 27 1/2 x 14 1/2 In. 125.00
Stand, Sewing, Louis Philippe, Rosewood, Marquetry, Sarcophagus, Lift Top, 23 In.... 440.00
Stand, Sewing, Mahogany, Leather Top, Tole 126.00
Stand, Sewing, Mahogany, Shaped Gallery, 2 Drawers, Cabriole Legs 140.00
Stand, Sewing, Regency, Rosewood, Drop Leaf, Brass, Lyre Legs, 2 Drawers, 28 In.... 1870.00
Stand, Sewing, Satinwood, Hinged Octagonal Top, 19th Century, 28 In. 375.00
Stand, Sewing, Shaker, Tiger Maple, Pine, 2 Drawers, New Lebanon, 1840, 24 In........ 2860.00
Stand, Sewing, Sheraton, Martha Washington, Mahogany 330.00

♦ ♦ ♦ ♦ ♦ ♦ ♦ ♦ ♦ ♦ ♦ ♦ ♦ ♦ ♦ ♦

Watch out for a married
piece of furniture: a top
and bottom section that
did not start out together.

♦ ♦ ♦ ♦ ♦ ♦ ♦ ♦ ♦ ♦ ♦ ♦ ♦ ♦ ♦ ♦

Furniture, Sofa, Marshmallow, Black &
White, Herman Miller, c.1956

Stand, Sewing, Walnut, Lift Top, Fitted Interior, Walnut, 1840s, 30 1/4 In. 250.00
Stand, Sewing, Wicker 90.00
Stand, Shaker, Birch Top, Red, 1 Drawer, Pencil-Post Leg, 27 x 16 x 17 In. 17600.00
Stand, Shaker, Cherry, Butternut, Pine & Poplar, 2 Drawer, New Lebanon 6050.00
Stand, Shaving, Faux Bamboo, Chinoiserie Panels, 3 Legs, Circular Shelf, 56 In. 825.00
Stand, Shaving, Hepplewhite, Bowfront, Mahogany, Mirror, 2 Drawers, 16 x 17 In. 220.00
Stand, Shaving, Mahogany Veneer, 1 Drawer 100.00
Stand, Shaving, Mahogany, Drawers, 3 Leaf-Carved Feet, Victorian, 56 In. 345.00
Stand, Shaving, Mahogany, Oblong Swivel Mirror, 1 Drawer, Stringing 140.00
Stand, Shaving, Metal, Beveled Swivel Mirror, Milk Glass, Ornate Brush, 12 In. 250.00
Stand, Sheraton, 1 Drawer, New England 1200.00
Stand, Sheraton, Cherry, Bird's-Eye Maple Veneer Front, Drawer, 28 1/2 In. 415.00
Stand, Sheraton, Cherry, Inlaid, Beaded-Edge Drawer, 28 1/4 In. 1375.00
Stand, Sheraton, Cherry, Splayed Leg, Penna. 1750.00
Stand, Sheraton, Drop Leaf, Mahogany, Rope-Turned Legs, 2 Drawers, 28 x 16 In. 660.00
Stand, Sheraton, Mahogany, 2 Drawers, Rope-Turned Legs, 26 In. 330.00
Stand, Sheraton, Maple, Turned Legs, Drawer, 29 x 19 x 21 In. 470.00
Stand, Sheraton, Walnut, Removable Marble Top, c.1840, 21 x 37 1/2 In. 500.00
Stand, Smoking, Figural, Standing Black Man, 35 1/2 In. 200.00
Stand, Table, Mahogany, Inset Marble Top, Eagle Trestle Base, 27 x 18 x 20 In. 525.00
Stand, Teakwood, Carved, Marble Top, Cross-Stretcher Base, Oriental 300.00
Stand, Telephone Chair, Upholstered Seat, Faux Victorian, 1940s 65.00
Stand, Tiger Maple, Snake Foot, Serpentine Top 1350.00
Stand, Tilt Top, Cherry, Mahogany Finish, Spider Leg, Urn-Shaped Pedestal, 28 In. ... 110.00
Stand, Tilt Top, Mahogany, Dish Edge, Vasiform Standard, Tripod Slipper Feet 357.50
Stand, Umbrella, Black Forest, Cub Standing Upright, Mouth Open, 32 In. 2200.00
Stand, Umbrella, Brass & Iron, 24 1/4 In. 150.00
Stand, Umbrella, Cylindrical, Painted Green, 19 1/2 In. 55.00
Stand, Umbrella, Dutch Style, Brass, Figural Lion's Mask Ring Handle, 10 x 6 x 22 In. 35.00
Stand, Umbrella, Figural, Iron, Dog Holding Riding Crop In Mouth, England 1750.00
Stand, Umbrella, Gustav Stickley, Copper Handles, Leaves At Sides, No. 382, 25 In. ... 2970.00
Stand, Umbrella, Gustav Stickley, Copper Drip Pan, No. 54, 33 In. .... 425.00 to 850.00
Stand, Umbrella, Gustav Stickley, Plank Sides, Wrought Iron Bands, No. 100, 24 In. .. 2300.00
Stand, Umbrella, Hammered Copper 470.00
Stand, Umbrella, Mahogany, Brass Carrying Handles, Metal Tray, 40 In. 690.00
Stand, Urn, Giltwood, Scroll-Carved Frieze, Veined Green Marble Top, 40 1/2 In. 230.00
Stand, Walnut, Folding, Portfolio, Victorian 2050.00
Stand, Walnut, Spool Legs, Octagonal, 26 In. 55.00
Stand, Walnut, Turtle Top, Eastlake, 29 In. 275.00
Stand, Wig, Papier-Mache, Bust Of Elegantly Dressed Man, 17 1/2 In. 3105.00
Stand, Work, Shaker, Maple, Tiger, 2 Drawers, 1830, 23 x 21 In. .... *Illus* 16500.00

Furniture, Stand, Music, Marquetry, Walnut, 35 x 23 In., Pair

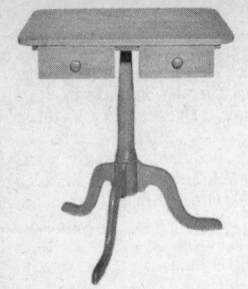

Furniture, Stand, Work, Shaker, Maple, Tiger, 2 Drawers, 1830, 23 x 21 In.

If you reupholster an antique piece of furniture, save some of the original fabric. Put it in an envelope and tape it to the bottom of the seat so future owners can know more about the original appearance. When selling a piece, this sort of history will add to the value.

Steps, Library, 5 Rungs, Hold-On Pole, England, 6 Ft.	440.00
Stool, Art Deco, Ebonized & Gilt, Brocade, Fluted Legs, c.1920	1150.00
Stool, Arts & Crafts, Rectangular Seat, Oak, 16 x 20 In.	515.00
Stool, Bar, White, Wicker	15.00
Stool, Biedermeier, Fruitwood, Penwork, Circular, Square Tapering Legs, Pair	2875.00
Stool, Charles II, Oak, Scratch-Carved Frieze, 1670s	3680.00
Stool, Cherry & Poplar, Hooked Rug Cushion, Felt Skirt, 15 1/2 In.	690.00
Stool, Concave Seat, Bamboo-Turned Splayed Legs, Painted Green, c.1795	1380.00
Stool, Continental Baroque, Walnut, Pierced Heart Top Center, 22 1/2 In., Pair	5750.00
Stool, D-Shaped Top, 5 Baluster Turned Supports, Oak, 1660s, 21 In.	4025.00
Stool, Empire, Mahogany, French Feet, 23 In.	275.00
Stool, Florence Knoll, Black Wrought-Iron Triangular Legs, Formica Top, 13 In.	110.00
Stool, George I, Walnut, Drop-In Needlepoint Seat, 23 In.	2300.00
Stool, George II Style, Mahogany, Drop-In Seat, Paw Feet, 18 x 20 In.	1840.00
Stool, Gout, Mahogany, Adjustable, Brass-Studded Vinyl, 16 x 21 x 16 In.	495.00
Stool, Joint, William & Mary, Ring & Baluster Turned Legs, Painted Black, 21 In.	3335.00
Stool, L. & J.G. Stickley, No. 1292, 7 Side Spindles, Leather, 16 1/4 In.	2200.00
Stool, Louis XVI, Walnut, Cut-Velvet, Fluted Legs, 15 x 19 In.	460.00
Stool, Neoclassical, Mahogany, Rectangular, Papyrus-Carved Arms, 22 3/4 In., Pair	4025.00
Stool, Neoclassical, Painted, Parcel Gilt, Floral Needlepoint, Pair	4025.00
Stool, Oak, Fluted Frieze On Legs, Block Feet, England, 18 x 24 In., Pair	2760.00
Stool, Piano, Adjustable Height, By Lever, Needlepoint	160.00
Stool, Piano, Classical, Mahogany, Revolving Seat, Boston, 1830, 21 x 14 1/2 In.	920.00
Stool, Piano, Mahogany, Chair Back	170.00
Stool, Piano, Mahogany, Regency, Screw Standard, Needlework, 19 In.	690.00
Stool, Piano, Rosewood, Needlework, Canted Frame, 19 1/2 In.	400.00
Stool, Piano, Swivel, Round, Glass Ball & Claw Feet	90.00
Stool, Piano, Venetian Style, Carved & Painted Wood, Swivel Seat	460.00
Stool, Piano, Walnut, Needlepoint, Cabriole Legs, Late 19th Century	385.00
Stool, Pine, Hooked Rug Cover, Painted Yellow	460.00
Stool, Pine, Primitive, Box Stretcher, 1690-1710	595.00
Stool, Raymond Subes, Wrought Iron, Leather, c.1925, 18 In., Pair	6325.00
Stool, Rocking, Isamu Noguchi, Walnut Seat, Chromed Steel Struts, c.1955	6050.00
Stool, Rococo Style, Mahogany, Cotton, 21 In.	60.00
Stool, Shaker, 2 Steps, Pine, Painted, Half-Moon Cutouts, 22 1/2 x 16 In.	3190.00
Stool, Shaker, Figured Walnut, 2 Steps, Varnish, N.Y., 1860, 24 x 16 x 18 In.	1430.00
Stool, Shaker, Pine, 3 Steps, Putty Brown Over Gray, Mortise & Tenon, 27 In.	990.00
Stool, Shaker, Pine, Double C Arch Ends, Labeled Andrews, 2 Steps, 9 x 12 x 8 In.	385.00
Stool, Shaker, Walnut, 2 Steps, New York, 24 1/2 In.	1430.00
Stool, Shoe Salesman's, Attached Footrest, 5 Twisted Iron Legs	65.00
Stool, Vanity, Gilbert Rohde, White Holly Ring, No. 3323, Herman Miller, c.1934	330.00
Stool, Walnut, Gouge Carved, England	525.00
Stool, Wharton Esherick, Ash, Irregularly Shaped Seat, 1964, 19 3/4 In.	2300.00
Stool, Windsor, Bamboo Legs, Painted Green, Philadelphia, c.1780, 27 /12 In.	4500.00
Storage Unit, Charles Eames, Birch, 4 Tiers, Iron, E.S.U.400, c.1952, 47 x 58 In.	4675.00

Sugar Chest, Tabletop, Grain Painted, Dovetailed.. 350.00
Table, 2 Splayed Legs, Breadboard Top 1700.00
Table, A.J. & J. Kohn, Bentwood, Circular Top & Base, 4 Pairs Of Ovoid Legs, 28 In. 2090.00
Table, Aesthetic, Walnut, Inset Rectangular Onyx Top, 29 1/4 x 24 x 16 In. 460.00
Table, Altar, Native Wood, Overall Foliate & Dragon Design, Oriental, 82 In. 315.00
Table, Altar, Red Lacquer, Scrolled Ends, Polychrome Design, 50 1/2 In.................... 435.00
Table, Alter, Ming Style, Burled Wood Top, Scrolling Frieze, 35 x 65 In................... 460.00
Table, American Aesthetic, Giltwood, Onyx, Painted & Gilt Frieze, 55 x 35 In. 2415.00
Table, Art Nouveau, Fruitwood, Marquetry Butterflies, Foliage On Top, 29 In. 1035.00
Table, Bagatelle, Telescopic Base, Turned Legs, Extra Balls & Rules, 1850s 800.00
Table, Banquet, Drop Leaf, Mahogany, Oval, 82 In. Opened 1540.00
Table, Banquet, Federal, Triple Pedestal, Bronze Paw Feet, Acanthus Legs 3850.00
Table, Banquet, Hepplewhite, Wallace Nutting, Mahogany, No. 670, Round, 3 Part 4540.00
Table, Banquet, Jacobean Style, Walnut, Pullout Leaves, Bun Feet, 54 1/2 In. 800.00
Table, Banquet, Mahogany, 4 Leaves, Carved Base, Paw Feet, Oval, 19th Century 2860.00
Table, Banquet, Wallace Nutting, Mahogany, 3 Part, Marked 4125.00
Table, Beau Brummell, Mahogany, Flip Top, Fitted Interior, 2 Drawers, 36 In.............. 1610.00
Table, Bedside, Louis XV Style, Fruitwood, 3 Drawers, 28 1/2 In. 635.00
Table, Bedside, Louis XVI Style, 1 Drawer, 2 Shelves, Gilt, France, Pair.................... 415.00
Table, Biedermeier, Fruitwood, Ebonized, 1860s, 31 1/2 x 40 In. 1610.00
Table, Biedermeier, Fruitwood, Round Top, 3 S-Scroll Supports, 29 3/4 In.................. 225.00
Table, Black Lacquer, Gilt Villages, Mountainous Landscape, 24 In., Pair 8625.00
Table, Black Lacquer, Mother-Of-Pearl, Cartouche Shape, Korea, 27 x 22 1/4 In.......... 5750.00
Table, Book, L. & J.G. Stickley, 4 Sides, 7 Slats, No. 516, 27 x 27 x 29 In. 7150.00
Table, Book-Shaped, Faux Leather Finish, Lift Top, Compartments, 1920, 33 1/2 In. 1980.00
Table, Boulle, 1 Drawer, Masks Of Mythical Figures On Sides, 19th Century 2415.00
Table, Breakfast, Chippendale, Mahogany, Drawer, New England, 18th Century, 28 In. 550.00
Table, Breakfast, Federal, Mahogany, Clover Drop Leaf, 1810, 28 x 40 x 48 In. 5175.00
Table, Breakfast, Grain Painted, Conn., 1840 .... 695.00
Table, Breakfast, Late Classical, Tilt Top, Mahogany, 3-Part Pedestal, 1840 .... 1650.00
Table, Breakfast, Loop Top, Column Base, Victorian, 1860, 52 x 29 In........................ 1045.00
Table, Breakfast, Mahogany, Hipped Downswept Legs, 5 Ft. 6 In. 4600.00
Table, Breakfast, Mahogany, Painted Black Banding, 53 3/4 In. 1035.00
Table, Breakfast, Mahogany, Rounded Tilt Top, Brass Claw Casters, 56 In. 2200.00
Table, Breakfast, Queen Anne, Maple, Drop Leaf, c.1750, 24 3/4 In. Extended............. 8050.00
Table, Breakfast, Queen Anne, New England, 1760, 40 In. 12500.00
Table, Breakfast, Regency Style, Rosewood, Oval, Quadruped Base, 78 x 54 In. 1320.00
Table, Breakfast, Regency, Rosewood, Round Top, 1810, 52-In. Diam. 2530.00
Table, Breakfast, Regency, Tilt Top, Mahogany, England, 35 x 54 x 28 In.................... 1760.00
Table, Breakfast, Rosewood, Veneered, Pedestal, 3 Carved Feet, Round, England 3300.00
Table, Breakfast, William IV, Mahogany, Scrolled Feet, England, c.1880 .... 3500.00
Table, Butler's, Kittinger, Center Oval Satinwood Panel, 22 x 26 3/4 In....................... 150.00
Table, Butterfly, Splayed Baluster-Turned Legs 8675.00
Table, Cabinet, Fruitwood, Architectural Shrine Shape, Ivory, Bronze, Brass, 24 In. 4025.00
Table, Cabinet, Walnut, Box Stretcher, Turned Legs, Drawer, 27 x 41 x 23 In. 300.00
Table, Card, Carved Rosewood, Swing Leg, Molded Edge, S-Scroll Legs, N.Y., c.1850 1870.00
Table, Card, Chippendale, Mahogany, 1 Cock-Beaded Drawer, Phila., 36 x 17 In. 3475.00
Table, Card, Classical, Mahogany, c.1820, 34 3/4 x 17 1/2 In. 1265.00
Table, Card, Classical, Mahogany, Veneered Top, Pedestal, N.Y., 1815, 36 x 18 In....... 1840.00
Table, Card, Edwardian, Mahogany, Handkerchief Foldover, Black Felt, 29 x 21 In. 440.00
Table, Card, Empire, Mahogany, Lyre Form Base, Lift Top, 36 x 38 In.......................... 330.00
Table, Card, Federal, Fold Top, Inlaid Banded Edge, Square Legs, 27 x 32 x 15 In....... 635.00
Table, Card, Federal, Mahogany & Birch, Veneer, Inlaid, c.1790, 30 x 37 In. 2415.00
Table, Card, Federal, Mahogany, 5 Legs, Line Inlay, c.1800, 28 1/4 In. 1495.00
Table, Card, Federal, Mahogany, c.1810, 29 3/4 x 40 In... 1895.00
Table, Card, Federal, Mahogany, Carved Pedestal, Brass-Footed Casters, 36 In. 1650.00
Table, Card, Federal, Mahogany, Clover-Shaped Top, 5 Legs, N.Y., 1800, 36 In. 2530.00
Table, Card, Federal, Mahogany, D-Shaped Top, Inlaid, R.I., 1790, 36 x 18 In............. 2300.00
Table, Card, Federal, Mahogany, Demilune, Inlaid Edge, Concealed Drawer, c.1800.... 2645.00
Table, Card, Federal, Mahogany, Demilune, Decorative Stringing, c.1810 .... 1100.00
Table, Card, Federal, Mahogany, Demilune, Bellflower Inlay, 1790, 36 x 18 In. 5520.00
Table, Card, Federal, Mahogany, Demilune, Inlaid, 1780-1810, 36 x 18 In. 2990.00
Table, Card, Federal, Mahogany, Flame Birch Veneer, Massachusetts, 30 x 37 In......... 2587.00

Fakers sometimes make a round table with leaves from a square table with leaves because round tables have more value. This can be spotted if you carefully examine the overall proportion of the table and the edges of the top.

Furniture, Table, Card, Mahogany,
Swivel Top, Brass Feet, 1830, 29 x 35 In.

Table, Card, Federal, Mahogany, Haines-Connelly, Philadelphia, 1810 .... 4400.00
Table, Card, Federal, Mahogany, Inlaid, c.1790, 30 x 35 x 16 1/2 In. 2300.00
Table, Card, Federal, Mahogany, Inlaid, c.1790, 29 x 35 x 17 1/2 In. 2760.00
Table, Card, Federal, Mahogany, Inlaid, D-Shaped, Square Legs, 29 x 36 x 17 In. 1495.00
Table, Card, Federal, Mahogany, Inlaid, Serpentine, Hinged Top, c.1800, 36 x 17 In. 1725.00
Table, Card, Federal, Mahogany, Lyre Base, Boston 3800.00
Table, Card, Federal, Mahogany, Swivel Top, 1820, 37 1/4 x 42 In. Open 3500.00
Table, Card, Federal, Mahogany, Wavy Birch Inlay, c.1825, 29 x 36 x 18 In. 1610.00
Table, Card, Flame, Turned Legs, New Hampshire 3800.00
Table, Card, French Provincial, Walnut, Cabriole Legs, Swivel Top 440.00
Table, Card, Mahogany, Demilune Banded, 29 x 36 In. 2200.00
Table, Card, Mahogany, Line Inlay, Bellflower & Leaf Inlay, c.1805, 35 In. 7475.00
Table, Card, Mahogany, Lyre Base, Brass Paw Feet, 30 x 36 In. 2200.00
Table, Card, Mahogany, Swivel Top, Brass Feet, 1830, 29 x 35 In. ....*Illus* 1725.00
Table, Card, Mahogany, Swivel Top, Leaf, Dolphin-Shaped Feet, c.1825, 37 In. 4600.00
Table, Card, Oak, 4 Hinged Triangular Sections, Baize Lined, H. Vollmer, 25 In. 1095.00
Table, Card, Sheraton, Mahogany, Turned Legs, c.1820, 29 x 36 In. 1100.00
Table, Card, Sheraton, Shaped Apron, Mahogany, 29 In. 825.00
Table, Card, Sheraton, Thomas Seymour, 36 In. 4400.00
Table, Center, American Classical, Mahogany, Marble Top, Veneered Skirt, 43 In. 2200.00
Table, Center, Biedermeier, Fruitwood, Painted, Parcel Gilt, Round, Bun Feet, 56 In. ... 3737.00
Table, Center, Charles X, Rosewood, Fruitwood, Marble Top, Hexagonal Baluster 5750.00
Table, Center, Classical, Mahogany, Stenciled, Marble Top, N.Y., 1810, 37 In. 4830.00
Table, Center, Edwardian, Crossbanded Top, Double U-Stretchers, Oval, 31 x 20 In. ... 275.00
Table, Center, French Empire, Faux Malachite Painted, Brass, 27 x 24 In. Diam. 1210.00
Table, Center, French Empire, Mahogany, Marble Top, Egyptian Designs, 46 In. 5060.00
Table, Center, Louis Philippe, Boullework, Serpentine Top, Female Masks 1650.00
Table, Center, Louis Philippe, Walnut, Fleur-De-Lis & Scroll, 51 x 35 In. 1210.00
Table, Center, Louis XV Provincial Style, Dish Rim, 19th Century, 30 x 17 In. 522.00
Table, Center, Neoclassical, Mahogany, Gilt, Oval, 4-Part Base, Sweden 8050.00
Table, Center, Onyx Top, Gilt Carved, France 1925.00
Table, Center, Rococo, Marble Top, Serpentine Shape, Cabriole Legs, 41 x 21 1/2 In. .. 1320.00
Table, Center, Tilt Top, Regency Style, Mahogany, 4 Splayed Legs, 39 1/2 In. 355.00
Table, Center, Walnut, Marble Inset, Round Base Shelf, 1870 .... 1025.00
Table, Cherry, Empire, Country, Drop Leaf, 6 Rope-Carved Legs, 46 In. 385.00
Table, Child's, Gustav Stickley, No. 639, Tenon & Key Construction, 22 x 36 In. 1760.00
Table, Coffee, F.L. Wright, Mitered Drop Side, Heritage Henredon, 61 x 20 x 14 In. 3190.00
Table, Coffee, Frank Lloyd Wright, Mahogany, Greek Key Trim, 17 x 42 In. 865.00
Table, Coffee, G. Poillerat, Gilt, Wrought Iron, Black Marble Top, 17 x 38 x 17 In. 3450.00
Table, Coffee, Georgian Style, Yew Wood, Tray Type, Oval 330.00
Table, Coffee, Glass, Chrome Base, Square, 40 In. 800.00

Furniture, Table, Dining, Mahogany, Circular, 4 Scrolled Supports, 47 In.

Table, Coffee, Mahogany, Square, Carved Cabriole Legs, Inset Leather Top 99.00
Table, Coffee, Marble Top, Iron Corners & Legs, 18 1/2 x 43 In. 80.00
Table, Coffee, Noguchi, Adjustable Base, Triangular Glass Top, c.1947, 50 x 36 In. 1320.00
Table, Coffee, Paul Frankl, Biomorphic Cork Top, c.1940, 36 x 47 In. 2420.00
Table, Coffee, Paul Frankl, Round, 3 Rattan Legs, 42 x 16 In. 550.00
Table, Coffee, Wolfgang Hoffman, Chromed Steel, Glass Top, Howell, c.1930, 36 In. . 2200.00
Table, Conference, Herman Miller, Marble Top, Stainless Steel Trestle, 76 1/2 In. 500.00
Table, Conference, Regency, Inlaid Segmented Top, Round, 1820, 7-Ft. Diam. 1925.00
Table, Conference, Walnut, Stretcher Base, 1940, 96 x 42 x 30 In. 1200.00
Table, Console, Adam Style, Polychrome, Demilune, Painted Center, 44 In. 770.00
Table, Console, Baroque Style, Walnut, Serpentine Top, Tapered Legs, 33 x 63 In. 978.00
Table, Console, Ebonized Rosewood, Marble Top, Egyptian Figures, 32 1/2 In. 9775.00
Table, Console, Empire, Mahogany, Ormolu Mounted, Gray Marble Top, 52 In. 4860.00
Table, Console, Federal Style, Mahogany, Demilune, Decorative Banding, Pair............ 467.50
Table, Console, Georgian Style, Marble Top, Pierced Apron, Cabriole Legs, 36 x 18 In. 302.00
Table, Console, Italian Neoclassical, Walnut, Ebonized, Demilune, 16 x 31 x 32 In...... 1840.00
Table, Console, Lifetime, Octagonal, 1 Drawer, Triangular Platforms, 20 x 60 In. 3680.00
Table, Console, Louis XVI, Giltwood, Semielliptical Marble Top, 47 x 37 1/4 In. 7815.00
Table, Console, Ormolu Mounted, Mahogany, Brass Inlay, Marble Top, 38 1/2 In. 5900.00
Table, Console, Regency, Walnut, Marble Top, Pierced Frieze, 39 x 21 x 34 In. 6950.00
Table, Console, Rosewood, Carved Human & Animal Figures, 48 In. 5000.00
Table, Console, Sheraton, Birch, Faux Drawer, Oak-Turned Legs, 17 x 36 In. 715.00
Table, Cricket, Oak, Round Top, Triangular Stretcher, Miniature, 8 1/2 x 8 In. 2645.00
Table, Demilune, Painted, Floral Design, Tapering Legs, 30 x 32 x 17 1/2 In 2530.00
Table, Dessert, 2 Tiers, China, 32 In. 575.00
Table, Dice Throwing, Pink Velvet Top, Curved Backboard 150.00
Table, Dinette, Noguchi, White Formica, Crisscross Wire Struts, Knoll, 36 In. 1540.00
Table, Dining, Ash, Grand Rapids Folding Table & Chair Co., Folding, 2 Leaves......... 1295.00
Table, Dining, Charles Eames, Grained Plywood Top, Metal Folding Legs, 34 In. 935.00
Table, Dining, Cherry, Barley-Twist Legs, Wooden Ball & Bronze Claws, 2 Leaves 1600.00
Table, Dining, Cherry, Drop Leaf, Chamfered Swing Legs 220.00
Table, Dining, Classical, Mahogany, Veneer, Carved Pedestal, c.1825, 48 x 48 In. 1725.00
Table, Dining, Claw Feet, Victorian, 48 In. 1900.00
Table, Dining, Danish Provincial, Oak, 2 Leaves, 29 /12 x 69 In. 345.00
Table, Dining, Derby Furniture Co., Pedestal, 3 Leaves, Signed, 30 x 54 In. 1100.00
Table, Dining, Drop Leaf, Empire, Mahogany, Acanthus Carved Pedestal, Claw Feet... 990.00
Table, Dining, Drop Leaf, Federal, Mahogany Inlaid, c.1800, 28 1/2 x 56 x 44 In. 575.00
Table, Dining, Drop Leaf, Mahogany, 2 Consoles Form Ends, 105 In. Extended.......... 2750.00
Table, Dining, Drop Leaf, Pine, Hinged Leaves, Square Legs, 29 x 91 In. 2990.00
Table, Dining, Drop Leaf, Sheraton, Mahogany, Turned & Ribbed Legs, 28 x 48 In. 797.50
Table, Dining, Empire, Mahogany, Molded Frieze, 3 Leaves, Casters, 88 x 35 In. 2760.00
Table, Dining, Federal, Cherry, Drop Leaf, c.1800, 28 1/2 x 41 x 54 In. 520.00

Table, Dining, Federal, Mahogany, 3 Pedestal, 2 Large Leaves, 19 1/2 Ft..................... 7700.00
Table, Dining, Frank Lloyd Wright, Cypress, Rectangular, Slab Legs, 2 Parts, 1940 ..... 2100.00
Table, Dining, George III Style, Mahogany, Double Pedestal, Casters, 82 1/2 In. 825.00
Table, Dining, George III Style, Mahogany, Blind Fret Carved Legs, 72 In. 1840.00
Table, Dining, George III, Mahogany, 3 Shaped Ends, Square Legs, 48 x 140 In........... 2300.00
Table, Dining, George Nelson, Lazy Susan, Gray Laminate, Plywood, Pedestal, c.1950 415.00
Table, Dining, Georgian Style, Mahogany, Triple Pedestal, 2 Leaves, 140 In. 6050.00
Table, Dining, Gustav Stickley, 5 Legs, Signed, 1904, 48 In. 2500.00
Table, Dining, L. & J.G. Stickley, Oak, Open Rectangular Standard, 2 Leaves, 48 In. ... 3680.00
Table, Dining, Lifetime, Round, Cross Stretchers, Corbels On Legs, 48 x 29 In............ 880.00
Table, Dining, Louis XV Style, Mahogany Veneered, 31 x 32 In. 555.00
Table, Dining, M. Breuer, Bent & Laminated Plywood, Tapering Legs, 26 3/4 In......... 7310.00
Table, Dining, Mahogany, Circular Top, Rectangular Base, 31 1/2 x 54 1/2 In. 345.00
Table, Dining, Mahogany, Circular, 4 Scrolled Supports, 47 In.............................*Illus* 2310.00
Table, Dining, Mahogany, D-Shaped Ends, Hinged Leaves, c.1810, 8 Ft. 6 In. 3450.00
Table, Dining, Mahogany, Grained Top, Leaf & Dart Skirt, 9 Leaves, 30 1/4 In. 3520.00
Table, Dining, Mahogany, Rectangular, Rounded Corners, France, 30 x 85 x 39 In. 3450.00
Table, Dining, Mahogany, Triple Pedestal, Reeded Edge, Brass Caps, 2 Leaves 1210.00
Table, Dining, Marquetry, 2 Pedestals, 2 Leaves, Holland, 19th Century 2860.00
Table, Dining, Oak, Canted Square Legs, L. & J.G. Stickley, No. 548, c.1910, 7 Ft....... 7475.00
Table, Dining, Oak, Claw Feet, 6 Leaves, Victorian, 54 In. 3500.00
Table, Dining, Oak, Cylindrical Standard, 2 Leaves, Round, American, 42 x 28 In....... 137.00
Table, Dining, Oak, Square, Rope-Turned Legs, 3 Leaves... 525.00
Table, Dining, Queen Anne, Walnut & Cherry, c.1760, 27 x 41 x 44 In. 920.00
Table, Dining, Regency Style, Mahogany, Inlaid Banding, Brass Casters, 91 In........... 575.00
Table, Dining, Regency, Mahogany, 1815, 7 Ft. 4 In. 5000.00
Table, Dining, Regency, Mahogany, Double Pedestal, Brass Casters, 1800, 84 In......... 7475.00
Table, Dining, Russel Workshop, Oak, Octagonal Section Legs, 77 x 35 1/2 In. 5850.00
Table, Dining, Sheraton, Drop Leaf, Cherry, 28 1/2 In.. 495.00
Table, Dining, Solid Maple, Self-Contained Extension Leaves 4450.00
Table, Dining, Stickley Bros., Corbeled Feet, 4 12-Ft. Leaves, 48 x 29 In. 2420.00
Table, Directoire Style, Fruitwood, Gilt, Marble, 1 Drawer, 22 x 27 x 23 In., Pair........ 115.00
Table, Dish Top, Chippendale, Mahogany, J. Goddard, 1760 ....*Illus* 7475.00
Table, Dish, Charles Eames, Birch Plywood Top, Wooden Legs, c.1946, 34 In. 935.00
Table, Dressing, Bamboo, Lacquer, Embossed Wallpaper, Victorian, 21 x 14 In. 865.00
Table, Dressing, Black, Gilt Stencil, Original Brasses, New Hampshire 1600.00
Table, Dressing, Chippendale Style, Drawers, Oriental Export, 21 x 34 In. 385.00
Table, Dressing, Federal, Walnut, Hinged Top, Fitted, 29 x 25 x 18 In. 405.00
Table, Dressing, George III, Mahogany, Satinwood Inlay.. 750.00
Table, Dressing, Georgian Style, Mahogany, 4 Drawers, 34 x 18 x 30 In. 920.00
Table, Dressing, Goddard & Engs, Federal, Mirrored Lid, Marble Insert, 1780............. 4600.00
Table, Dressing, Gustav Stickley, 3 Top Drawers, Iron Pulls, Mirror, No. 632, 1992 ..... 5520.00
Table, Dressing, Herman Miller, Oak Bowed Doors, Fitted Interior, 58 In. 345.00
Table, Dressing, Louis XV Style, Fruitwood, 1 Drawer, Banks Of 2 Drawers, 30 In...... 460.00
Table, Dressing, Mahogany, Hinged Lid, Fitted Interior, Adjustable Mirror, 32 In. 9200.00
Table, Dressing, Mahogany, Marble Top, Arched Mirror, 1 Veneered Drawer, Trestle.. 770.00

Furniture, Table, Dish Top, Chippendale, Mahogany, J. Goddard, 1760

Table, Dressing, Mahogany, Shaped Top, Serpentine Drawer, Early 20th Century 155.00
Table, Dressing, Mahogany, X-Stand, Reeded Legs, Lion's-Head Brasses, 36 In. 3850.00
Table, Dressing, Oval Swivel Mirror, Carved Legs, Oriental, 66 1/2 In. 575.00
Table, Dressing, Painted Leaves On Drawer, Bird On Back Panel, 1810 .... 2900.00
Table, Dressing, Pine, 1 Drawer, Scrolled Crest, Red & Black Grained, 31 In. 550.00
Table, Dressing, Poplar & Pine, 2 Drawers, Scalloped Crest, 37 1/4 In. 485.00
Table, Dressing, Queen Anne, Walnut, 1 Drawer, Cabriole Legs, 28 x 31 x 18 In. 1035.00
Table, Dressing, Queen Anne, Walnut, 1 Over 3 Drawers 1350.00
Table, Dressing, Red & Black, Gold Stencil, 1 Drawer 2200.00
Table, Dressing, Sheraton, 2 Tiers, Painted Yellow, Stencils, 32 In. 250.00
Table, Dressing, Stool, R. Thompson, Adzed Paneled Oak, 53 3/4 x 19 3/4 In. 3340.00
Table, Dressing, White Marbleized Top, Blue & Black Striped, Gray Ground 890.00
Table, Drop Leaf, American Classical, Mahogany, 1 Drawer, Pedestal Base, 47 In. 1650.00
Table, Drop Leaf, American Empire, Cherry, Leaf-Carved Spiral Legs, 41 In. 690.00
Table, Drop Leaf, Birch, Shaped Skirt, Square Molded Legs 470.00
Table, Drop Leaf, Cherry, 1 Drawer, Cross Stretcher Base 440.00
Table, Drop Leaf, Cherry, Victorian, 29 x 39 In. 460.00
Table, Drop Leaf, Chippendale Style, Mahogany, 28 x 47 1/2 In. 300.00
Table, Drop Leaf, Chippendale, Mahogany, Square Molded Legs, 14 x 47 In. 275.00
Table, Drop Leaf, Chippendale, Mahogany, Philadelphia, 1700s 1500.00
Table, Drop Leaf, Chippendale, Mahogany, Massachusetts, c.1780, 29 x 44 In. 690.00
Table, Drop Leaf, Chippendale, Maple, Cutout Corners, 27 x 46 In. 1045.00
Table, Drop Leaf, Chippendale, Maple, Square Legs, Swing-Leg Support, 14 x 42 In... 990.00
Table, Drop Leaf, Classical, Mahogany, Carved, c.1825, 29 x 39 x 50 3/4 In. 545.00
Table, Drop Leaf, Classical, Mahogany, Drawer, c.1815, 28 x 38 x 51 1/2 In. 865.00
Table, Drop Leaf, Classical, Mahogany, Faux Drawer Front, N.Y., 51 x 37 In. 2200.00
Table, Drop Leaf, Classical, Mahogany, Pedestal, Trefoil Feet, 1840, 56 x 42 In. 825.00
Table, Drop Leaf, Curly Maple, 6 Legs, 2 Swing Legs, 29 1/4 x 45 1/4 In. 770.00
Table, Drop Leaf, Federal Style, Mahogany, Swing Legs, Decorative Banding 495.00
Table, Drop Leaf, Federal, Cherry Inlay, c.1790, 28 x 36 x 18 In. 2185.00
Table, Drop Leaf, Federal, Mahogany, 1 Frieze Drawer, Ivory Pull, R.I., 41 x 36 In. 5175.00
Table, Drop Leaf, Federal, Mahogany, D-Shaped Leaves, Apron, 28 x 48 x 42 In. 115.00
Table, Drop Leaf, Federal, Mahogany, Turned Legs, Apron, c.1815, 29 x 31 In. 805.00
Table, Drop Leaf, Federal, Pembroke, Mahogany, Inlaid, 1 Drawer, 1790, 37 x 32 In. ... 2760.00
Table, Drop Leaf, Federal, Tiger Maple, New England, c.1820, 29 x 39 x 19 1/2 In. 2645.00
Table, Drop Leaf, Georgian, Mahogany, 1780, 29 x 42 x 61 In. 75.00
Table, Drop Leaf, Hepplewhite, Birch, Scrubbed Top, Country, 36 x 29 In. 300.00
Table, Drop Leaf, Hepplewhite, Mahogany, Square Tapered Legs, 27 1/2 x 26 In. 1045.00
Table, Drop Leaf, Hepplewhite, Mahogany, Square Tapered Legs, 36 x 16 1/2 In. 165.00
Table, Drop Leaf, Hepplewhite, Walnut, Line Inlay, 36 x 39 In. 700.00
Table, Drop Leaf, Jacobean, Walnut, 28 x 36 In. 1495.00
Table, Drop Leaf, Mahogany, Cherry, Carved Legs 405.00
Table, Drop Leaf, Mahogany, Drawer, 4 Column Pedestal, Claw Feet, 38 In. 990.00
Table, Drop Leaf, Oak, 3 Leaves, Twist Legs, 19th Century, American, 40 x 24 In. 160.00
Table, Drop Leaf, Oak, Block & Spool Gate Legs, England, 27 x 34 3/4 In. 115.00
Table, Drop Leaf, Pine, Hardwood, Painted Red, Country, 18 3/4 x 42 In. 190.00
Table, Drop Leaf, Queen Anne, Mahogany, England, 18th Century, Small 1575.00
Table, Drop Leaf, Queen Anne, Maple, Shaped Skirt, 26 x 44 x 48 In. 6325.00
Table, Drop Leaf, Queen Anne, Maple, Wing Leg, Duck Feet, Oval, 27 1/4 In. 2300.00
Table, Drop Leaf, Queen Anne, Scalloped Apron, Oval, 46 1/2 x 47 1/3 In. 1840.00
Table, Drop Leaf, Queen Anne, Walnut, Drake Feet, 28 1/2 In. 2930.00
Table, Drop Leaf, Queen Anne, Walnut, Duck Feet, Pa., 17 x 43 In. 2750.00
Table, Drop Leaf, Regency, Mahogany, 1 Drawer, Brass Casters, England, 19 x 42 In. . 325.00
Table, Drop Leaf, Sheraton Style, Mahogany, 1 Frieze Drawer, 19th Century 1200.00
Table, Drop Leaf, Sheraton, Cherry, Drawer, Turned Legs, 28 x 35 1/2 x 16 In. 195.00
Table, Drop Leaf, Sheraton, Mahogany, 28 x 36 x 36 In. 385.00
Table, Drop Leaf, Tiger Maple, 1 Drawer, D-Shaped Leaves, 26 x 27 x 18 In. 978.00
Table, Drop Leaf, Tiger Maple, Oval Top, Trestle Base, 25 1/4 In. 345.00
Table, Drop Leaf, Walnut, c.1820, 51 x 56 In. Extended 2000.00
Table, Drop Leaf, Walnut, Mahogany, 1 Drawer, Turned Legs, 1820 .... 375.00
Table, Drum, Italian Neoclassical, Walnut, Parquetry, 29 1/2 x 14 3/4 In. 800.00
Table, Drum, Regency, Mahogany, Crossbanded Inlay, Drawers, 40 1/4 In. 3165.00
Table, Dutch Rococo, Walnut, Marquetry, Faux Hinged Top, Fitted, 31 x 23 In. 2645.00

Furniture, Table, Ebonized, Marquetry Inlay, c.1875

Furniture, Table, Mahogany, Octagonal, 8 Drawers, 27 x 28 In.

Table, Eames, Surfboard, Black Laminated Plywood, Wire Cage Bases, c.1952		4400.00
Table, Ebonized, Marquetry Inlay, c.1875	*Illus*	1100.00
Table, Eero Saarinen, Walnut, Pedestal, Knoll, Round		3000.00
Table, Eero Saarinen, White Marble, Cast Aluminum Base, Knoll, 20 In.		495.00
Table, End, Frank Lloyd Wright, Angled Legs, Lower Tier, 1951, 23 1/2 In.		3680.00
Table, End, Mission Oak, 2 Open Shelves, 31 x 15 3/4 In.		630.00
Table, English Style, Drop Leaf, Oak, Spool-Turned Gate Legs, 15 x 35 x 27 In.		1115.00
Table, Entry, Louis XV, Pink Marble Insert		4600.00
Table, Farm, Pine, 3 Drawers In Base, 2-Board Top, c.1860, 33 x 72 In.		1250.00
Table, Farm, Poplar, Pine, Turned Legs, Country, 1835, 26 x 42 In.		510.00
Table, Farm, Walnut, Wide 2-Board Top		300.00
Table, Fornasetti, Colorful Round Top, Cards, Brass Tripod Feet, 13 In.		415.00
Table, Frank Lloyd Wright, Cypress, Rectangular Top, Angled Legs, 1951, 10 1/8 In.		2760.00
Table, Frank Lloyd Wright, Greek Key Frieze Above 6 Legs, Oak, 1916, 25 In.		6325.00
Table, Frank Lloyd Wright, Low, Auldbrass Plantation, Hexagon, 59 In.		1955.00
Table, Frankl, Silver Trim, Black Lacquer, Stepped Shelf, Under Tier, 17 x 30 In.		2300.00
Table, French Bistro, Cast Iron, Brown Paint, 3 Legs		995.00
Table, French Style, Mahogany, Fruitwood, Marquetry, Turtle, Tripod, Masks, 25 In.		600.00
Table, French Style, Mahogany, Marquetry, 1 Drawer, 1920s, 31 x 40 In.		1100.00
Table, Fruitwood, Gilt Metal Mounts, Marquetry Overall, 22 1/2 x 28 In.		1495.00
Table, G. Rohde, Chromed Steel, Black Lacquer, Troy Sunshade, 25 In.		1045.00
Table, Galle, Carved Mahogany, Marquetry, Under Tier, 30 1/2 In.		4600.00
Table, Galle, Daffodil Blossoms Inlay, Wild Grass Inlay Under Tier, 32 In.		4600.00
Table, Galle, Fruitwood, 2 Tiers, Moonlight Landscape On Tray, 1900, 29 /12 In.		2300.00
Table, Galle, Inlaid Fern Leaves, 2 Butterflies, Inlaid Lower Gallery, Signed, 30 In.		4600.00
Table, Galle, Mahogany, Doves Amid Grapes, 44 In.		6050.00
Table, Galle, Marquetry, 2 Tiers, Flying Swallows, Signed, 30 In.		2000.00
Table, Galle, Nesting, Marquetry, Seascape, Cats, Jonquils, c.1900, 28 In.		2760.00
Table, Game, American Classical, Carved Mahogany, Foldover Top, 34 3/4 In.		1100.00
Table, Game, Bagatelle, Collapsible, Folds Into Regency Side Table		3410.00
Table, Game, Black Lacquer & Parcel Gilt, Chinese Export, 30 x 29 In.		3165.00
Table, Game, Burl Walnut, Tooled Leather Surface, Shell-Carved Knees		1430.00
Table, Game, Chippendale, Mahogany, Needlepoint Playing Field, 28 x 31 In.		6500.00
Table, Game, Classical, Mahogany, Lift Top, Canted Corners, N.Y., 36 x 18 In.		5500.00
Table, Game, Dominique, Inlaid Board, Ivory Banding, Drawer Each End, c.1925		8625.00
Table, Game, Edwardian, Mahogany, Swivel Top		220.00
Table, Game, Empire, Mahogany, Lift Top, 19th Century, 34 x 17 x 30 In.		385.00
Table, Game, Empire, Mahogany, Lyre Base, c.1820, 28 x 34 In.		1250.00
Table, Game, Empire, Mahogany, Swivel Rectangular Top, American, 1895, 36 In.		470.00
Table, Game, Gateleg, Regency, Rosewood, Drawer, Tapering Legs, 33 In.		300.00
Table, Game, George II, Mahogany, Needlepoint Playing Surface, 28 x 33 In.		2590.00

Table, Game, George III, Mahogany, Folding, Concertina Action, England, 17 x 35 In. 660.00
Table, Game, George III, Mahogany, Open Fretwork Corner, Veneered Frieze, 34 In... 880.00
Table, Game, George III, Mahogany, Shell Above Inlaid Frieze, 1780s, Pair 7475.00
Table, Game, Georgian, Mahogany, Folding, 1780, 37 In. 495.00
Table, Game, Gustav Stickley, Lift Top, Inner Compartments, No. 643, 1904, 42 In..... 3220.00
Table, Game, Hepplewhite Style, Potthast, 3-Ft. Diam. 1200.00
Table, Game, Kingwood, Hinged Square Top, Leather Inlay, 30 x 35 1/2 In. 3220.00
Table, Game, Louis XVI, Mahogany, Brass Mounted, Leather Surface, 35 1/2 In. 6900.00
Table, Game, Mahogany, 4 Square Tapering Legs, 28 x 35 In. 1265.00
Table, Game, Mahogany, Double Swing Leg, Late 19th Century, England, 41 In.......... 1495.00
Table, Game, Mahogany, Foldover, Stylized Plinth, American, 28 x 36 x 17 In. 385.00
Table, Game, Mahogany, Pierced-Heart Column, Tapered Legs, Scalloped Apron 165.00
Table, Game, Maple, Swivel Top, Bun Feet, Victorian, c.1840, 29 1/2 x 36 In. 1725.00
Table, Game, Napoleon II, Ebonized, 1870s, 28 1/2 x 31 1/2 In. 260.00
Table, Game, Neoclassical, Mahogany, Inset Board, Frieze Drawer, Russia 9775.00
Table, Game, Oak, Drink Pockets, Cast-Iron Base, 34 In. 650.00
Table, Game, Outset Corners, Ball & Claw Feet, Mahogany, 1850s, 28 3/4 In. 4315.00
Table, Game, Paul Frankl, Cork Top, Johnson Furniture Co., c.1938, 36 In. 1430.00
Table, Game, Regency, Mahogany, Ebonized Inlay, Rounded Corners, 36 x 18 In. 500.00
Table, Game, Regency, Mahogany, Sliding Top, Leather Checkerboard, Drawer, 37 In. 825.00
Table, Game, Regency, Rosewood, Brass Inlay, Felt Surface, 28 1/2 In. 2300.00
Table, Game, Rococo Revival, 1860 .... 800.00
Table, Game, Snooker, Brunswick, 1893 .... 5500.00
Table, Game, Walnut & Yew Wood, Inset Chess & Checkerboard, 26 x 36 In. 575.00
Table, Game, Walnut, Burl Walnut, Shaped-Supports, Victorian, 28 3/4 In. 460.00
Table, Game, Walnut, Storage Drawer, Swivel Top 985.00
Table, Gateleg, George III, Mahogany, Rectangular Flaps, Miniature 1840.00
Table, Gateleg, Oak, 1 Drawer, England, 26 x 47 In. 880.00
Table, Gateleg, Pine, Oval, Bobbin-Turned Legs, 2 12-In. Leaves, 27 x 27 In. 99.00
Table, George II, Mahogany, Dish Rim, Tripod, Birdcage, 27 In. 1265.00
Table, George II, Mahogany, Piecrust, Tilt Top, Birdcage Support, 1760s, 28 In. 2185.00
Table, George III, Satinwood, Inlaid Conch Shells, Painted Foliage, 34 In. 5750.00
Table, Georgian Style, Mahogany, Bowfront, 1 Drawer, Tapering Legs, 46 In. 275.00
Table, Georgian Style, Oak, Feather Inlay, 3 Drawers, 27 x 50 x 26 In. 288.00
Table, Georgian, Dish Top, Tripod, Rectangular, 1780 .... 385.00
Table, Georgian, Mahogany, Bowfront, 2 Tiers, 1780 .... 220.00
Table, Georgian, Mahogany, Tripod With Snake Feet, Round, 32 1/2 x 29 In. 115.00
Table, Georgian, Mahogany, Tripod, Birdcage Support, 32 In. 935.00
Table, Gilbert Rohde, Cloud, Biomorphic Top, Black Legs, Herman Miller 1045.00
Table, Gio Ponti, Parchment, Wood & Brass, X-Form Pedestal, 1945, 30 1/2 In. 6900.00
Table, Glass Top, Kneeling Blackamoor Supports, Painted, Italy, 29 1/2 In. 575.00
Table, Gustav Stickley, Cut Corners, Lower Shelf, No. 611, 24 x 24 x 29 In. 2860.00
Table, Gustav Stickley, Leather Top, Lower Shelf, No. 609, Paper Label...................... 4250.00
Table, Hall, Wolfgang Hoffman, Tubular Chrome, Black Lacquer, Howell, 30 x 70 In. 1540.00
Table, Hans Bellman, Blond Wood, Tripod Base, Knoll, 24 In.................................... 770.00
Table, Harvest, 2-Board Top, 6 Rock Maple Legs, c.1880, 9 x 3 Ft. 1450.00
Table, Harvest, Drop Leaf, Birch Base, Pine Top, 1-Board Top, 18 3/4 x 96 In. 3740.00
Table, Harvest, Poplar, Painted Dark Green, 3-Board Top, 27 x 84 x 39 In. 660.00
Table, Hepplewhite, Demilune, Conn., 1790, Pair.. 2250.00
Table, Hunt, Drop Leaf, Chippendale, Mahogany, 8 Legs, Ireland, 15 x 83 In. 2090.00
Table, Hutch, 2-Board Top, Full Mortise & Wedged Construction, Painted Green 600.00
Table, Hutch, Pine Top, Painted Red, 18th Century, 28 x 53 x 37 In............................ 4025.00
Table, Hutch, Pine, Painted Red, Square Post Legs, Drawer, 53 x 28 1/2 In. 2000.00
Table, Hutch, Pine, Shoe Foot, 27 x 40 In. 1320.00
Table, Hutch, Poplar, Drawer, Round 4-Board Top, 28 x 56 In. 836.00
Table, Ice Cream Parlor, Bent Wire, Oak Top, Chair & Stool, 3 Piece 137.00
Table, Ice Cream, Marble Top, Wooden Base, 36 x 20 In. 110.00
Table, Inlaid Fruitwood, 2 Tiers, Carved, Circular, Pad Feet, c.1905, 31 x 45 1/2 In. 2560.00
Table, Isamu Noguchi, Interlaced Tubular Pedestal, Round, Knoll, 48 In. 1540.00
Table, Italian Baroque, Walnut, 2 Drawers, Rectangular Molded Top, 33 In. 9775.00
Table, J & J.W. Meeks, Rosewood, Serpentine Marble Top, 37 x 21 In......................... 880.00
Table, J. & J.D. Howe, Oak, Extension, 19th Century 1500.00
Table, J. Gruber, Fruitwood Marquetry Flowers, 2 Tiers, Leaves, 1900, 30 1/2 In......... 9775.00

Table, James I, Oak, 1 Drawer, Grooved Sides, Turned Legs, 37 x 38 x 19 In. 1035.00
Table, Kitchen, Pine, 1 Drawer, Drop Leaf, 29 x 42 In. 120.00
Table, Kitchen, Pine, Drawers Each Side, 1850, 34 x 55 In. 715.00
Table, L. & J.G. Stickley, Trestle Base, Key & Tenon Construction, No. 594, 72 In. 9350.00
Table, L. & J.G. Stickley, Oak, 6-Sided Top, 6 Legs, Wagon Wheel Stretcher, 48 In..... 9775.00
Table, Lacquer Top, Painted Landscapes, Chinese Export, 18 x 32 In. 1495.00
Table, Lamp, Limbert, Cutout, Flat Splayed Legs, Octagonal, 29 x 30 x 30 In. 1760.00
Table, Lamp, Oak, Ball & Stick Design, Circular Shelves 675.00
Table, Library, A. Waterhouse, Carved Legs, Twin-Arched Aprons, c.1880, 66 In. 1840.00
Table, Library, Arts & Crafts, Book Compartments, Inlaid Panels, 32 1/2 In. 1725.00
Table, Library, Arts & Crafts, Quartersawn Oak, 2 Drawers, 34 1/4 x 48 In. 495.00
Table, Library, Carved Oak, Faux Marble Top, Egg & Dart Border, Victorian, 53 In..... 2200.00
Table, Library, Chippendale Style, Mahogany, 4 Drawers, Ball & Claw Feet, 72 In. 990.00
Table, Library, Empire, Mahogany, Round, Ormolu Pedestal, 3 Feet, 65 In. 2100.00
Table, Library, Empire, Oak, 1 Drawer 295.00
Table, Library, George III, Late 18th Century, 31 x 54 In. 6100.00
Table, Library, Gothic, Frieze, Turned Legs, England, 113 x 27 x 29 In. 1265.00
Table, Library, Gustav Stickley, 1 Drawer, Lower Shelf, No. 653, 42 x 27 x 29 In. 1870.00
Table, Library, Gustav Stickley, Leather Top, No. 407, c.1902, 48 x 30 In. 3100.00
Table, Library, Gustav Stickley, Trestle, Double-Keyed Tenons, No. 3403, 36 x 24 In.. 2750.00
Table, Library, Horner, Oak, Each Leg Carved With Different Face, Paper Label......... 5750.00
Table, Library, Jacobean Style, Oak, 3 Drawers, Carved Supports, 32 x 47 In. 975.00
Table, Library, L. & J.G. Stickley, 1 Drawer, Hammered Copper Pulls, 42 x 28 In. 1760.00
Table, Library, L. & J.G. Stickley, 2 Drawers, Arched Corbels, No. 520, 29 x 42 In...... 700.00
Table, Library, L. & J.G. Stickley, Trestle, Leather Top 900.00
Table, Library, Lifetime, 1 Drawer, Original Hardware, Label, 48 In. 1650.00
Table, Library, Lifetime, Oak, Six Sides, 2 Drawers, Iron Hardware, 52 x 26 In. 1575.00
Table, Library, Limbert, Geometric Ebony Inlay On Drawer, 41 1/4 In. 2750.00
Table, Library, Mahogany, Bronze Dragon With Snake In Mouth Mounts 1500.00
Table, Library, Mission Oak, 1 Drawer, 29 3/8 x 36 In. 290.00
Table, Library, Mission Oak, 2 Drawers, 2 Lower Shelves 250.00
Table, Library, Oak, 1 Drawer, Stretched Shelf, Paw Feet 220.00
Table, Library, Oak, Bookshelf Cutout Sides, Center Drawer 300.00
Table, Library, Oak, Carved Dragons On Apron, North Wind Faces, 30 x 58 In. 3300.00
Table, Library, Oak, Carved Drawer, Square Tapered Legs 520.00
Table, Library, Oak, University Of Michigan Symbol, Long Drawer, 40 x 39 In. 920.00
Table, Library, Provincial, Shaped Top, Turned Legs, 51 In. 358.00
Table, Library, Regency, Mahogany, Leather Top, Round 1840.00
Table, Library, Stickley Bros., Blind Drawer, No. 2818, Signed, 30 x 42 x 27 1/2 In. 600.00
Table, Library, Walnut, 1 Drawer, Original Finish, Victorian 4495.00
Table, Library, Walnut, Double-Urn Pedestal, Quadruped Feet, 24 x 72 x 30 In. 520.00
Table, Library, Walnut, Double-Urn Pedestal, Quadruped Feet, 30 x 72 In. 515.00
Table, Limbert, Round, Square Cutout Base, No. 148, 30 x 29 In. 2750.00
Table, Limbert, Square Cutouts On Stretcher, Round Top, No. 148, 30 x 30 In............ 2200.00
Table, Louis XV Style, Giltwood, Inset Onyx Top, 30 In. 345.00
Table, Louis XV, Purplewood, Fruitwood, Marquetry, Writing Slide, 33 x 20 In. 1450.00
Table, Louis XV, Rosewood & Mahogany, Drawer, Floral Marquetry, 33 1/2 In. 895.00
Table, Louis XVI Style, Fruitwood, Marble Top, Gallery Top, 24 In., Pair 205.00
Table, Louis XVI Style, Mahogany, Marble Top, Brass Gallery, Reniform, 21 In......... 4370.00
Table, Low, Hard Stone, Down-Curved Sides, Oriental Inlay, China, 13 In. 660.00
Table, Lunch, Gustav Stickley, No. 647, Tenon & Key, 29 1/2 x 40 In. 2200.00
Table, Mahogany, Carved Apron, Short Cabriole Legs, Ball & Claw Feet.................... 35.00
Table, Mahogany, Crossbanded Top, Center Lifts On Ratchet Support, 4 Ft. 3450.00
Table, Mahogany, Octagonal, 8 Drawers, 27 x 28 In. ....*Illus* 715.00
Table, Mahogany, Swan Pedestal, Round Glass Top.. 415.00
Table, Mahogany, Tripartite, Pierced Gallery, Brass Handle & Stretcher, 34 x 17 In. 290.00
Table, Mahogany, Veined Marble Top, Pierced Gallery, Human Feet, 29 In. 1150.00
Table, Majorelle, Fruitwood, 2 Tiers, Trefoil Top, Marquetry Flowers, 29 1/2 In. 3000.00
Table, Majorelle, Mahogany, Buttress Supports, Lower Shelf, 1900, 45 In. 5175.00
Table, Micro Mosaic, Round, Ebonized Stand, Center Medallion, c.1850, 15 In. 2850.00
Table, Mixing, Federal Style, Mahogany, Frieze, 1 Short Drawer, 38 x 17 x 32 In......... 800.00
Table, Molded Scrubbed Top, Dark Green Base, 2 Drawers 650.00
Table, Mother-Of-Pearl, Ebonized, Octagonal, Dished Top, Near East, 14 x 14 In. 1150.00

Furniture, Table, Pembroke,
Inlaid Mahogany, Ovolo
Corners, 28 1/2 In.

Furniture, Table, Pembroke, Bird's-Eye
Maple Veneer, c.1810, 29 In.

Furniture, Table, Pembroke, Chippendale,
Mahogany, Pierced Leg Brackets, c.1785

Table, Musician's, For Stringed Instrument, Hardwoods, Qinzhuo, 36 1/2 In.	1000.00
Table, Neoclassical Style, Rose Des Pyrenees Marble, Round, 39 1/2 In.	8050.00
Table, Neoclassical, Fruitwood, Bone Marquetry, Hunting Scene, Italy, 25 x 18 In.	6900.00
Table, Nesting, Bent Beechwood, Spherical Handles, Glass & Fabric Tops, 1904	4600.00
Table, Nesting, Round, Pierced Apron, Burl Inset Tops, Oriental, 4	465.00
Table, Oak & Wicker, Lower Tier, 30 x 72 1/3 x 36 1/2 In.	385.00
Table, Oak, Celtic Design, Frieze, 2 Short Drawers, England, 74 x 28 x 33 In.	3200.00
Table, Oak, Claw Feet, 4 Lions' Heads On Pedestal	350.00
Table, Oak, Frieze, 2 Short Drawers, Celtic Design, Bun Feet, 33 x 74 1/2 In.	3155.00
Table, Omega Workshops, Ebony & Fruitwood, Marquetry, Holly, 29 1/2 In.	8775.00
Table, P.G. Durand, Walnut, 1850s	3950.00
Table, Parlor, Eastlake, Walnut, Oval Marble Top, Carved & Turned, 18 x 24 In.	250.00
Table, Parlor, Oak, Spool-Turned Legs, Lower Shelf, Square	250.00
Table, Parlor, Rosewood, Turtle Shape, 2 Side Drawers, H Stretcher, 50 x 33 In.	1215.00
Table, Parlor, Walnut, Dark Finish, Marble Turtle Top, Victorian, 17 x 29 x 27 In.	360.00
Table, Parlor, Walnut, Gray Marble Top	250.00
Table, Parlor, Walnut, Marble Top, Drawer, 21 x 28 x 30 In.	360.00
Table, Paul Frankl, Square Top, Black Stepped Shelf, Silver Trim, 17 1/2 In.	2300.00
Table, Pembroke, Bird's-Eye Maple Veneer, c.1810, 29 In. *Illus*	4111.00
Table, Pembroke, Cherry, Shaped Leaves, Scalloped Stretcher, c.1780, 27 In.	3165.00
Table, Pembroke, Chippendale, Mahogany, Pierced Leg Brackets, c.1785 *Illus*	7590.00
Table, Pembroke, Chippendale, Walnut, Drawer, 28 1/2 In.	495.00
Table, Pembroke, Federal, Cherry, Scalloped Top, c.1795, 29 In.	920.00
Table, Pembroke, Federal, Mahogany, 1800, 27 1/2 x 21 In.	1035.00
Table, Pembroke, Federal, Mahogany, Hinged Leaves, 1 Drawer, Oval, 41 x 35 In.	1955.00
Table, Pembroke, Federal, Mahogany, Inlaid, New York, c.1800, 29 x 22 x 32 In.	3850.00
Table, Pembroke, Federal, Walnut, Cock-Beaded Apron, 1770s, 29 1/2 In.	2530.00
Table, Pembroke, George II, Mahogany, 1 Drawer, 29 x 52 x 34 In.	1540.00
Table, Pembroke, George III Style, A. Lewis & Sons, Satinwood, Mahogany	2300.00
Table, Pembroke, George III, Mahogany, Ireland, 1870s, 28 x 30 1/2 In.	1495.00

Table, Pembroke, George III, Satinwood, Rosewood Banding, 30 1/4 x 27 3/4 In. 1150.00
Table, Pembroke, Georgian, Mahogany, Tapering Legs, c.1780 .... 325.00
Table, Pembroke, Georgian, Simulated Door One End, Butterfly Supports 600.00
Table, Pembroke, Hepplewhite, Mahogany, 1 Drawer, Icicle Inlay, 28 In. 4950.00
Table, Pembroke, Hepplewhite, Pinned Apron, 28 1/2 In... 495.00
Table, Pembroke, Inlaid Mahogany, Ovolo Corners, 28 1/4 In. ....*Illus* 2760.00
Table, Pembroke, Mahogany, Bowed Ends, Serpentine Shaped Leaves, c.1770 .... 5175.00
Table, Pembroke, Mahogany, Bowed Skirt, String & Geometric Inlay, 41 x 37 In. 3525.00
Table, Pembroke, Mahogany, Molded Oval Top, Bellflower Inlay 2425.00
Table, Pembroke, Mahogany, Tapered Legs, England, c.1800 .... 745.00
Table, Pembroke, Sheraton Style, Walnut, Ring-Turned Legs, 29 In. 550.00
Table, Pembroke, Sheraton, Mahogany, Brass Pull, c.1810, 28 In. 1760.00
Table, Pier, American Classical, Gilt Stenciled, Rosewood Marble Top, N.Y. 7975.00
Table, Pier, American Classical, Mahogany, Marble Top, 19th Century, 38 x 18 In. 1435.00
Table, Pier, Charles X, Rosewood, Inlaid, c.1850, 33 x 38 x 17 In. 1840.00
Table, Pier, Charles X, Rosewood, Long Skirt Drawer, 19th Century, 37 x 17 In. 1980.00
Table, Pier, Classical, Mahogany, Marble Top, Gilt Stencil, Columns, 46 x 24 In. 2640.00
Table, Pier, Classical, Mahogany, S-Scroll Supports, Marble Top, c.1840 .... 2860.00
Table, Pier, Mahogany, Marble Top, Mirror, Pillars, 1825-1835, 38 x 40 x 20 In. 2990.00
Table, Pier, Oak, Elm, Inlaid, Fluted Stiles & Base, England, 31 1/2 x 46 x 17 In. 3740.00
Table, Pier, Rosewood, Marble Top & Support Columns, Bronze Mounts, 41 1/2 In. 7975.00
Table, Pierro Fornasetti, Ancient Coins & Medals Within Bands, 21 In. 4830.00
Table, Pine & Hardwood, Square Tapered Legs, Mortised & Nailed Apron, 29 In. 55.00
Table, Pine, Square Tapered Legs, T-Apron, Semi-Circular Top, Country, 18 x 36 In. .. 525.00
Table, Provincial, Walnut, Square, Cabriole Legs, Continental, 39 x 40 In.................... 550.00
Table, Pub, Cast Iron Base, England, 1890.. 375.00
Table, Queen Anne, Maple, 1 Drawer, Overlapping 2 Boards, 44 x 26 In...................... 715.00
Table, Reading, William IV, Mahogany, 29 x 29 1/4 In... 2300.00
Table, Refectory, Carved Oak, Turned Legs, 30 1/2 x 82 In.. 920.00
Table, Refectory, French Provincial, Cherrywood & Poplar, 1 Drawer, 35 x 75 In.......... 1430.00
Table, Refectory, French Provincial, Walnut, 2 Drawers, Trestle, 30 x 84 x 26 In. 1540.00
Table, Refectory, Georgian, Elm, Square Legs, 1800, 29 x 87 x 36 In. 1870.00
Table, Refectory, Jacobean Style, Oak, 31 x 70 1/2 In.. 520.00
Table, Refectory, Jacobean, Oak, Raised Trestle Base, 87 1/4 x 31 1/4 In. 1265.00
Table, Refectory, Oak, Carved Legs Depicting Roman Men, 19th Century 5060.00
Table, Refectory, Renaissance Style, Walnut, Lyre Supports, 36 x 120 x 27 In. 8625.00
Table, Refectory, Spanish Baroque Style, Walnut, Bun Feet, 33 x 90 x 29 In. 6325.00
Table, Refectory, Teak & Ash, 11 Ft. 2800.00
Table, Refectory, Walnut & Cedar, 2 Frieze Drawers, Bun Feet, 1670s, 85 In............... 7475.00
Table, Refractory, Walnut, Urn Shaped Ends, Claw Feet, Carved Stretcher, 58 In. 3520.00
Table, Regency, Chinoiserie, Black Lacquer, Oriental Figures, 17 x 35 In. 1155.00

Furniture, Table, Rosewood, Serpentine Shaped,
Marble Top, 30 x 37 x 37 In.

Furniture, Table, Tea, Tilt Top,
Chippendale, Mahogany, 34 In. Diam.

Table, Renaissance Style, Walnut, Fruit Carved Trestle Supports, c.1920 .... 1840.00
Table, Robert Lorimer, Oak, Center Square, 4 Panels, Fluted Legs, 29 1/4 In. 3225.00
Table, Rococo Revival, Cast Iron, Small 135.00
Table, Rococo, Rosewood, Drawer Each End, 34 x 49 In. 2800.00
Table, Rosewood, Blackamoor Supports, Ivory Marquetry 4500.00
Table, Rosewood, Serpentine Shaped, Marble Top, 30 x 37 x 37 In. .... *Illus* 880.00
Table, Roussel, Tulipwood, Quarter Veneered Top, Fitted Drawer, 28 In. 9200.00
Table, Roycroft, Little Journeys, 2 Tiers, Trestle Base, Oak, Metal Tag, 26 1/4 In. 633.00
Table, Roycroft, Mahogany, 4-Leg Pedestal, 2 Leaves, Carved Mark, 28 1/2 x 48 In. ... 3850.00
Table, Sawbuck, Pine & Poplar, 2-Board Top, 30 x 71 1/2 In. 385.00
Table, Sawbuck, Pine, 1840s, 36 x 28 In. 575.00
Table, Sawbuck, Pine, Dark Patina Base, Scrubbed 2-Board Top, 28 x 45 x 27 In. 550.00
Table, Sawbuck, Walnut, Breaks Down Into Scroll Cut Legs, 3-Board Top, 74 In. 2145.00
Table, Serving, Federal, Mahogany, 2 Drawers, Ring-Turned Tapering Legs, 43 x 20 In. 865.00
Table, Serving, Sheraton, Edwards & Roberts, Mahogany, D Shape, 1 Drawer, 80 In. .. 4950.00
Table, Sewing, Burl Maple, c.1820, 29 1/2 In. 6750.00
Table, Sewing, Cherry, Tripod, Snake Feet, Drawer, Hinged Top, 16 x 27 In. 440.00
Table, Sewing, Chippendale, Chestnut & Pine, Drawer, Breadboard Top, 26 1/2 In. 550.00
Table, Sewing, Dimensions Incised On Top, 19th Century, 22 x 36 In. 750.00
Table, Sewing, Empire, Drop Leaf Mahogany Veneer, 2 Drawers, 1850s 260.00
Table, Sewing, Federal, Bird's-Eye Maple & Mahogany, c.1810, 29 1/2 In. 3165.00
Table, Sewing, Federal, Drop Leaf, Mahogany, 3 Drawers, Spiral Legs, 30 x 18 In. 460.00
Table, Sewing, Federal, Figured Mahogany, 2 Divided Drawers, c.1825, 29 3/4 In. 2070.00
Table, Sewing, Federal, Mahogany, 2 Drawers, 1810-1830, 28 x 35 x 17 1/2 In. 1035.00
Table, Sewing, Federal, Mahogany, Astragal End, 2 Bowed Drawers, 1800, 29 In. 1610.00
Table, Sewing, Federal, Mahogany, Hinged Top, 2 Drawers, Fluted Sides, 20 x 17 In. .. 1840.00
Table, Sewing, Federal, Mahogany, Maple Inlaid, c.1810, 29 1/8 In. 2875.00
Table, Sewing, Federal, Mahogany Veneer, Spiral Carved Legs, c.1820, 31 x 16 In. 460.00
Table, Sewing, Federal, Tiger Maple, 1 Drawer, Splayed Square Legs, 17 1/2 x 17 In. .. 1380.00
Table, Sewing, Mahogany & Maple, Checker Inlaid Edge, c.1800, 28 3/4 In. 9200.00
Table, Sewing, Mahogany, 2 Drawers, Line Inlay, 31 In. 275.00
Table, Sewing, Mahogany, Adjustable Baize-Lined Writing Flap, Inkwell, c.1810 .... 4900.00
Table, Sewing, Mahogany, Canted Corners, Inset Carved Disks, 1780, 27 1/2 In. 5175.00
Table, Sewing, Mahogany, Hinged Cover, Cavetto Edge, 1 Drawer, 31 x 21 x 16 In. 660.00
Table, Sewing, Mahogany, Hinged Top, Writing Compartment, Phila., 1815, 39 In. 6325.00
Table, Sewing, Mahogany, Lift Top Writing Desk, 2 Drawers, 29 x 21 In. 1550.00
Table, Sewing, Mahogany, Veneer, 2 Drawers, Spiral Carved Legs, 25 x 16 x 18 In. 920.00
Table, Sewing, Maple, 2 Drawers, 3-Board Removable Top, 28 x 73 In. 800.00
Table, Sewing, Mother-Of-Pearl Inlay, Painted Landscape, England, Victorian 665.00
Table, Sewing, Papier-Mache, Mother-Of-Pearl Inlay 1400.00
Table, Sewing, Queen Anne, Maple, Splayed Base, Breadboard Top, 32 x 44 x 25 In. .. 1595.00
Table, Sewing, Rosewood, Maple Interior, Incurved Legs, N.Y., 32 x 21 x 16 In. 1320.00
Table, Sewing, Shaker, Birch, Rounded Drop Leaves, 27 x 30 1/2 x 15 In. 880.00
Table, Sewing, Shaker, Cherry & Butternut, Tapered Legs, Drawers, 22 1/2 x 31 In. 490.00
Table, Sewing, Shaker, Cherry, Pine, Varnish, Painted Red, 2 Drawers, 27 x 20 x 24 In. 660.00
Table, Sewing, Shaker, Drop Leaf, Mahogany, 2 Drawers, 29 x 36 In. 1100.00
Table, Sewing, Shaker, Maple Base, 2-Board Pine Top, Tapered Legs, 27 x 50 x 29 In. 1650.00
Table, Sewing, Shaker, Pine & Maple, 2-Board Top, Turned Legs, c.1840 .... 495.00
Table, Sewing, Shaker, Pine, Red Paint, Drawer, 29 x 18 x 18 In. 2530.00
Table, Sewing, Shaker, Pine, Shelf Top, Breadboard Ends, Anderson, 35 x 30 In. 1725.00
Table, Sewing, Sheraton, Mahogany, 2 Drawers, Turned Ribbed Legs, 28 x 20 x 20 In. 880.00
Table, Sewing, Sheraton, Mahogany, 2 Drawers, Tapering Legs, 28 x 18 1/2 In. 285.00
Table, Sewing, Sheraton, Mahogany, 3 Drawers, 19th Century, 30 x 24 x 17 In. 1045.00
Table, Sewing, Sheraton, Maple, 2 Drawers, Turned Legs, 29 x 17 x 18 In. 385.00
Table, Sewing, Sheraton, Maple, 2 Drawers, Turned Legs, 21x 17 1/2 x 28 In. 220.00
Table, Sewing, Sheraton, Maple, Collapsible Leg, Yardstick Top, 19 x 36 x 25 In. 110.00
Table, Sewing, Stretcher Base, Drawer, Iron Pulls, Turned Feet, 20 x 33 In. 450.00
Table, Sewing, Walnut, 2 Dovetailed Drawers, Removable 3-Board Top, 35 3/4 In. 1650.00
Table, Sewing, Walnut, Foldover, Turned Legs, Long Drawers, 32 1/2 x 56 x 38 In. 935.00
Table, Shaker, Trestle, Birch & Pine, Shirley Shaker Settlement, 26 x 102 In. 6900.00
Table, Sheraton, Cherry, Tiger Maple Drawer, Reeded Leg, Cloverleaf, New York 985.00
Table, Side, Baroque Style, Walnut, Rectangular Top, Frieze Drawer, 28 x 39 In. 3165.00
Table, Side, Biedermeier, Burl Birch & Walnut, Ebonized, Giltwood Paw Feet 5750.00

Table, Side, Biedermeier, Mahogany, Parcel Gilt, Circular, Scrolled Base, Pair 5175.00
Table, Side, Biedermeier, Walnut, Parcel Gilt, Marble Top, Tripartite Base, Pair 9775.00
Table, Side, Cherry, Maple, Inlay, Stepped Front, Square Tapered Legs, 28 x 33 In. 1700.00
Table, Side, Cherry, Tiger Maple Front, Drawer, Turned Legs, 29 1/2 x 21 x 21 In. 440.00
Table, Side, F.L. Wright, Lower Shelf, Drawer, Heritage Henredon, 27 x 21 x 22 In. 800.00
Table, Side, G. Rohde, Black Lacquer, Tubular Chrome Frame, Troy Sunshade, c.1930 825.00
Table, Side, George II, Mahogany, Gray Marble Top, Shell Carvings, 89 x 21 In. 6325.00
Table, Side, Neoclassical, Fruitwood, Oval, Inlaid Urn, Frieze Drawer, Russia, 28 In. .. 5175.00
Table, Side, Neoclassical, Karelian Birch, Oval, Conforming Apron, Russia, 38 1/2 In. 5465.00
Table, Side, Rosewood, Rope-Twist Carved, Portugal, 17th Century, 18 x 28 x 18 In.... 5500.00
Table, Sofa, Drop Leaf, Duncan Phyfe Style, Mahogany, 2 Drawers, Brass Feet 2750.00
Table, Sofa, Neoclassical, Birch, Parcel Gilt, Beaded Border, Paw Feet, Sweden........... 6325.00
Table, Sofa, Neoclassical, Bleached Mahogany, Parcel Gilt, Canted Corners, 45 In. 4025.00
Table, Sofa, Neoclassical, Bleached Mahogany, Lyre-Shaped Pedestal, Russia, 46 In. .. 4315.00
Table, Sofa, Neoclassical, Fruitwood, Mahogany, Inlaid, Hinged Top, 59 x 25 1/4 In. .. 6900.00
Table, Sofa, Neoclassical, Karelian Birch, Elm, Walnut, Serpentine Sides, Russia........ 8050.00
Table, Sofa, Neoclassical, Mahogany, Canted Corners, Paw Feet, Russia, 42 1/2 In. 9200.00
Table, Sofa, Sir Ambrose Heal, Oak, Twin Flap Top, 2 Drawers, c.1915, 72 1/2 In. 1495.00
Table, Stickley Brothers, 4 Splayed Legs, Keyed Tenons, 72 In. 1325.00
Table, Store, Oak, Turned Legs, 30 1/4 x 29 /12 In.. 275.00
Table, Sutherland, Mahogany, Overall Floral Inlay, 22 1/2 In..................................... 750.00
Table, T.H. Robsjohn-Gibbings, Tripod Base, Round Top, 28 In., Pair 770.00
Table, Tavern, Birch Wood & Pine, Oval Top, Splayed Legs, 1880s, 27 1/2 In.............. 1400.00
Table, Tavern, Cherry, Breadboard Ends, Ring & Baluster Legs, 1740, 27 In. 6900.00
Table, Tavern, George III, Oak, Spiral Turned Legs, Flattened Ball Feet, 28 In. 520.00
Table, Tavern, Hardwood & Pine, Butterfly Arms Support Top, 24 In. 1320.00
Table, Tavern, Maple, Pine, Turned Legs, Cross Stretcher, 23 1/2 x 24 In. 400.00
Table, Tavern, Molded Edge, Painted Brown, 18th Century, 24 x 27 x 21 In................. 4315.00
Table, Tavern, Oblong Top, 1 Drawer, Ring And Baluster Turned Legs...................... 935.00
Table, Tavern, Pine & Maple, Drawer, Painted Base, 18th Century, 27 x 37 1/2 In. 2100.00
Table, Tavern, Pine & Poplar, Scalloped Apron, 1 Drawer, 26 1/2 In. 935.00
Table, Tavern, Pine, Box Stretcher, 27 x 42 In.. 740.00
Table, Tavern, Queen Anne, Maple, Breadboard Top, Duck Feet, 27 x 44 x 28 In. 3960.00
Table, Tavern, Queen Anne, Walnut, Square Apron, Short Over Long Drawer, 43 In.... 2800.00
Table, Tavern, Scrubbed Top, Base Mustard Painted, Drawer, c.1800, 28 x 47 In.......... 2070.00
Table, Tavern, Scrubbed Top, Breadboard End, Red Turned Leg Base.......................... 585.00
Table, Tavern, Shaped Top, Button Feet, 26 x 35 1/2 In.. 990.00
Table, Tavern, Square Molded Legs, Painted Red, c.1780, 26 x 31 x 23 1/2 In. 1400.00
Table, Tavern, Walnut, Poplar, Pine, 2 Drawers, Box Stretcher, 30 x 60 In. 1200.00
Table, Tavern, Walnut, Stretcher Base, 1 Drawer, 1780.. 3200.00
Table, Tavern, William & Mary, Cusped Corners, 1730s, 25 In.................................. 3105.00
Table, Tavern, William & Mary, Maple, Pine Drawer, 18th Century, 29 x 36 In............. 1380.00
Table, Tea, Birdcage, Cherry, Dish Top, 44 In. 8800.00
Table, Tea, Birdcage, Walnut, Dish Molded Top, 18th Century, 32 x 28 In................... 1400.00
Table, Tea, Gustav Stickley, Arched Cross Stretchers, No. 604, 26 x 20 In. 935.00
Table, Tea, Mahogany, New England, c.1780, 28 1/2 x 34 In..................................... 1035.00
Table, Tea, Painted Black, Triangular Base, Round Top, 23 In. 24000.00
Table, Tea, Painted, New England, 18th Century, 26 x 32 x 22 In. 9200.00
Table, Tea, Queen Anne, Cherrywood, Scalloped Apron, 27 x 30 x 22 In. 2100.00
Table, Tea, Queen Anne, Maple & Pine, Oval Top, Scalloped Skirt, 36 3/4 In. 3450.00
Table, Tea, Queen Anne, Maple, Scrolled Apron, Tray Top, 24 3/4 In. 7800.00
Table, Tea, Samuel Newman, Mahogany, Ring & Vase Standard, 1880, 11 1/2 In......... 1265.00
Table, Tea, Satinwood & Mahogany, Fold Top, Line Inlay, 30 In. 1100.00
Table, Tea, Splayed Legs, Painted Red, 26 In. 9200.00
Table, Tea, Tilt Top, Chippendale, John Goddard, Mahogany, Dish Top, Tripod, 28 In. 1955.00
Table, Tea, Tilt Top, Chippendale, Mahogany, 34 In. Diam. ....*Illus* 1955.00
Table, Tea, Tilt Top, Chippendale, Mahogany, Carved, c.1780, 28 1/2 x 33 In. 7475.00
Table, Tea, Tilt Top, Chippendale, Mahogany, Birdcage, 1770, 36 1/4-In. Diam. Top.... 4900.00
Table, Tea, Tilt Top, Chippendale, Maple, Birdcage, 27 x 35 In. Diam. 460.00
Table, Tea, Tilt Top, Chippendale, Walnut, Dished, Birdcage, 1770, 28 x 32 In. 2550.00
Table, Tea, Tilt Top, Federal, Mahogany, Inlaid, Urn Form, 29 1/2 x 20 x 19 In........... 865.00
Table, Tea, Tilt Top, Mahogany, Round Top, Vasiform Standard, Tripod Base 350.00
Table, Tea, Tilt Top, Mahogany, Round, Turned Vasiform Pedestal, Claw & Ball Feet. 835.00

Furniture, Table Set, Frank Lloyd Wright, 2 Stools, 1956, 3 Piece

Table, Tea, Tilt Top, Mahogany, Snake Feet, 27 In.	385.00
Table, Tea, Tilt Top, Mahogany, Vasiform Standard, Tripod Base, c.1800	385.00
Table, Tea, Tilt Top, Queen Anne, Mahogany, Snake Foot Tripod Base	1150.00
Table, Tea, Tilt Top, Queen Anne, Maple, Tripod Cabriole Legs, 28 1/4 x 30 In.	290.00
Table, Tea, Walnut, Pennsylvania, c.1780, 29 1/2 x 34 In.	2415.00
Table, Teak, Red Marble Top, Medial Shelf, Carved, Round, China, Large	1000.00
Table, Telephone, A. Girard, Plastic Coated, Walnut, Aluminum, 19 1/2 x 16 In.	1100.00
Table, Tiger Maple, 1 Drawer, 1 Board Top	750.00
Table, Tiger Maple, Spider Leg, Spade Feet, New England, 1780	3600.00
Table, Tilt Top, Cast Bronze, Painted Roundel, Tripod Base, Victorian, 30 1/4 In.	2300.00
Table, Tilt Top, Cherry, Tiger Maple Shaft, 5 Boards, Square, 42 In.	660.00
Table, Tilt Top, Classical, Carved Mahogany, Scalloped Edges, N.Y., 30 x 21 In.	990.00
Table, Tilt Top, Federal, Mahogany, 28 1/2 x 23 1/2 x 23 In.	2300.00
Table, Tilt Top, Federal, Mahogany, Ball Feet, 29 In.	405.00
Table, Tilt Top, Mahogany, Round, Diamond Veneered Top, Hairy Paw Feet	1430.00
Table, Tilt Top, Octagonal Brass Bordered Marble Top, 27 In.	1725.00
Table, Tilt Top, Papier-Mache, Floral Painted, Abalone, Oval Top, 26 x 21 In.	665.00
Table, Tilt Top, Papier-Mache, Mother-Of-Pearl Inlay, Victorian	770.00
Table, Tilt Top, Papier-Mache, Mother-Of-Pearl Inlay, 29 x 31 1/2 In.	440.00
Table, Tilt Top, Papier-Mache, Mother-Of-Pearl Inlay, 1850, 23 x 22 In.	415.00
Table, Tilt Top, Papier-Mache, Painted, Mother-Of-Pearl Inlay, 40 In.	995.00
Table, Tilt Top, Queen Anne, Maple, Pine, Urn Standard, 3 Cabriole Legs, 1760	1725.00
Table, Tilt Top, Regency, Mahogany, Tapered Pilaster, 1840, 40-In. Diam.	1210.00
Table, Tilt Top, Rosewood, Satinwood, Trifid Padded Feet, 28 x 15 1/2 x 22 In.	275.00
Table, Tilt Top, Stenciled, Painted Lake Scene, 3 Legs, Victorian, 38-In. Diam.	995.00
Table, Toilet, Louis XV, Mechanical, Kingwood, Marquetry, 28 x 25 x 16 In.	2200.00
Table, Trestle, Gustav Stickley, Lower Tier, No. 403, Decal, c.1901	5175.00
Table, Trestle, Shaker, Cut Down & Modified	800.00
Table, Walnut & Cypress, Scalloped Frieze, Deep Drawer, 1760s, 25 1/2 In.	9350.00
Table, Walnut Top, Pine Brackets, Bracket Feet, Block Supports, 23 x 75 x 22 In.	1150.00
Table, Walnut, Cypress, Cabriole Legs, Drawer, Scalloped Frieze, Louisiana, 25 In.	9350.00
Table, Walnut, Marble Top, Flaring Pedestal, Openwork Floral Feet, 27 In.	1265.00
Table, Walnut, Marble Top, Shell-Carved Legs, 1750s, 31 In.	6900.00
Table, Walnut, Marble Top, Turned & Block Base, 1 Shelf, Casters, 30 In.	402.00
Table, Walnut, Mission Style, Median Shelf, 29 1/2 x 36 In.	115.00
Table, Walnut, Split Pedestal Base, Center Leg, 5 Leaves, Victorian, c.1860	4350.00
Table, Walnut, Sugar Bin, Half Hinged Top, 1 Section Interior, 31 1/2 In.	1430.00
Table, Wicker, Oak, Oval Top, c.1890, 30 x 31 1/2 x 25 In.	2415.00
Table, Wicker, Oak, Rectangular, Scrolled Sides, Lower Shelf, c.1910, 28 x 23 In.	1380.00
Table, Wicker, Round Oak Top, 4 Scrolling Side Supports, Lower Shelf, 28 In., Pair	2415.00
Table, William & Mary Style, Drop Leaf, Gateleg, Box Stretchers, Ring Turnings	660.00
Table, William & Mary, Oak, Frieze Drawer, 17th Century, 26 x 29 x 19 In.	1320.00

Table, Work, Classical, Mahogany, Veneer, New England, c.1825, 28 x 19 x 20 In....... 345.00
Table, Writing, Architect's, Adjustable Top, Fitted Drawer, Leather Surface, 37 In....... 5175.00
Table, Writing, Biedermeier, Fruitwood, Geometric Exotic Wood Inlay, 30 In. 2100.00
Table, Writing, Georgian, Mahogany, Leather Insert, 6 Drawers, 1820, 51 x 36 In. 1540.00
Table, Writing, Hepplewhite Style, Demilune, Floral & Urn Inlay, 36 In...................... 357.50
Table, Writing, Neoclassical, Mahogany, Rectangular, Canted Corners, 2 Drawers 6900.00
Table, Writing, Red & Black Grain Painted, Floral Stencil, Yellow Banded Legs 605.00
Table, Writing, Regency, Ebonized, Parcel Gilt, c.1820, 27 3/4 x 34 3/4 In. 4312.00
Table, Writing, Tooled Leather, Candle Slides, Fire Screen, 18th Century, Small 1675.00
Table, Writing, Tulipwood, Leather Surface, 4 Side & Center Drawer, Parquetry 7475.00
Table De Nuit, Empire, Mahogany, Ormolu, Circular Marble Top, 31 1/2 In., Pair........ 5750.00
Table Set, Frank Lloyd Wright, 2 Stools, 1956, 3 Piece ....*Illus* 10400.00
Table Set, Ice Cream, Wood, Dark Red Paint, Copper Gilded Metal, Child's, 3 Piece.... 255.00
Tabouret, Brooks, Octagonal, Canted Slab Sides, Square Cutouts, 18 x 28 In................ 825.00
Tabouret, Gustav Stickley, Oak, Arched Stretcher, No. 602, c.1907, 18 In. 575.00
Tabouret, L. & J.G. Stickley, Octagonal, Cross Stretchers, No. 558, 19 x 15 In............. 1100.00
Tabouret, Stickley, Bros., Hexagonal, 3 Splayed Legs, Cutouts, No. 111, 19 In. 550.00
Tabouret, Woodcraft Guild, Cut Corner, Slab Sides, Cutouts, 17 x 23 In...................... 715.00
Tansu, Rosewood, 8 Drawers, 2 Sliding Doors, Japan, 68 x 47 In., 4 Part.................... 2860.00
Tea Cart, Maple, Folding Sides, 1 Shelf, Casters, 32 3/4 x 29 In.................................. 100.00
Tea Cart, Wooden Wheels, Green Wicker 420.00
Tete-A-Tete, Horn, Tufted Leather, 53 In. 8500.00
Tray, Thuyawood, Pierced Handle Holds, Silver Mounted, Oval, 23 1/2 In. 3750.00
Tray-On-Stand, Dutch Marquetry, Brass Handles, Tapered Leg, Round, 21 In.............. 700.00
Tray-On-Stand, George II, Walnut, Spiral Twist & Block Legs, 1750s 6325.00
Trumeau, Louis XVI, Painted, Parcel Gilt, Gray Highlights, 6 Ft. 5 In. x 47 In. 6900.00
Umbrella Stand, Iron, Branches Hold Umbrella, Black, 19th Century, 58 In. 440.00
Vanity, Danish Modern, Walnut, Drop Front Top Drawer, 34 1/8 x 39 1/2 In................. 435.00
Vanity, Empire, Mahogany, Hinged Top, Marble Lined, Mirror, 3 Drawers, 40 In. 405.00
Vanity, Federal, Mahogany Veneer, Marquetry, Kidney Shape, Mirror, 52 x 30 In. 385.00
Vanity, Gilbert Rohde, Walnut, 3 Rounded Drawers, Glass Shelf, 57 x 25 In. 770.00
Vanity, Gilbert Rohde, White Holly, Red Ash, Chrome Base, Herman Miller, c.1934.... 2750.00
Vanity, Gustav Stickley, Mirror, 5 Drawers, Copper Hardware, 48 x 22 In.................... 3850.00
Vanity, Mahogany, Oval Beveled Mirror, 34 x 61 In... 325.00
Vanity, Metal, Demilune Top, Glass Top, Frameless Mirror, 1930, 42 In. 600.00
Vanity, Rosewood, Serpentine Marble Top, Rosette Roundels, 59 x 40 x 19 In. 825.00
Vanity, Stool, Gilbert Rohde, Light, Dark Mahogany, Streamlined, Cavalier, c.1930..... 990.00
Vanity & Chair, Gustav Stickley, Mirror, 2 Drawers, Butterfly Joints, 53 3/4 In. 3000.00
Vitrine, French Provincial, Floral Carved Design Domed Top, 86 x 40 In..................... 275.00
Vitrine, French Style, Marble Top, Central Drawer Over 2 Paneled Glass Doors 880.00
Vitrine, Hanging, Chinoiserie Shagreen, Painted, Scrolled Pediment, c.1930 .... 8375.00
Vitrine, Louis XV Style, Fruitwood, Demilune Glazed Case, Floral Inlay, 63 In. 925.00
Vitrine, Louis XV Style, Kingwood, Gilt Bronze, Silk Damask Interior, 62 1/2 In. 1325.00
Vitrine, Louis XV Style, Ormolu, Painted Scene Of Eros, Landscapes 2650.00
Wagon Bench, Maple, Splint Seat, Arms, 19th Century 495.00
Wagon Seat, Ladder Back, Rush Seat, Painted Red, Arms 600.00
Waiter, Wicker, Rolling, Painted Yellow, 36 x 31 In. 45.00
Wardrobe, Biedermeier, Serpentine Paneled Doors, 76 x 40 In. 6210.00
Wardrobe, Bonnet, Painted Blue-Gray, Sweden, Early 19th Century 1295.00
Wardrobe, Edwardian Style, Mahogany, Small 950.00
Wardrobe, Hanging Space, 4 Doors, 4 Drawers, Copper Pulls, 69 x 56 x 25 In. 4400.00
Wardrobe, L. & J.G. Stickley, One Door, Arched Bottom, 26 x 21 x 74 In. 2425.00
Wardrobe, Long-Grained Pine, 2 Doors, Sweden 5000.00
Wardrobe, Mahogany, Inset Parchment Squares In Door, France, 5 Ft. 3 In. 3450.00
Wardrobe, Oak, 6 Drawers, 2 Doors, 1870, 7 Ft... 2475.00
Wardrobe, R. Thompson, Adzed Paneled Oak, Wrought Iron Door, 71 3/4 In. 6300.00
Wardrobe, T. Justice, Twin Paneled Doors, Latch Device, Exposed Hinges, c.1900....... 5850.00
Wardrobe, Walnut, 2 Doors, 2 Drawers, Victorian, 54 x 85 1/2 In. 715.00
Washstand, Bird's-Eye Maple, Shaped Gallery, 1 Drawer, Open Shelf 1050.00
Washstand, Cherry & Walnut, Double Turkey Breast, Brass Thumb Latch, 1830s........ 875.00
Washstand, Connersville Furniture Co., Oak, Towel Bar, Brass Plated Pulls 225.00
Washstand, Corner, Mahogany, Three-Quarter Gallery, Line Inlay Legs, 19 In. 1290.00
Washstand, Corner, Sheraton, Hard & Soft Wood, Shelf, 2 Drawers, 30 In.................... 255.00

Furniture, Window Bench, William IV, Paw Feet, 30 x 47 x 17 1/2 In.

Washstand, Corner, Walnut, Drawer, 2 False Drawers, 19th Century, 18 x 43 In.	325.00
Washstand, Empire, Bird's-Eye Maple Frieze Drawer, Painted Brown, 35 In.	690.00
Washstand, Federal, Copper Basin, Drawer At Lower Shelf, 33 1/2 In.	825.00
Washstand, Federal, Tapered Saber Legs, Cutout Galley, Grained, 1800, 31 1/2 In.	700.00
Washstand, Figured Maple, Shelf, Drawers, Turned Legs, Hole, 36 In.	300.00
Washstand, Hepplewhite, Mahogany, Bowfront, 3 Bowl Cutouts, 43 1/2 In.	357.50
Washstand, J.H. Read, Walnut, Veneered Front, Marble Top, N.J.	475.00
Washstand, Jacobean Style, Oak, Marble Backsplash	230.00
Washstand, Napoleon III, Marble Top, 1860, 35 In.	360.00
Washstand, Painted Pine, Splashboard, 1 Drawer, 1820s, 37 1/4 x 35 3/4 In.	9775.00
Washstand, Pine, Base Shelf, Dovetailed Gallery, 39 In.	415.00
Washstand, Pine, Cutout Cabriole Legs, Fall Front Door, Painted Brown, 38 In.	220.00
Washstand, Pine, Cutout For Bowl, Gallery, Painted Yellow, 29 1/2 In.	225.00
Washstand, Pine, Marble Top, Gallery Over Frieze, 1 Drawer, Shelf, 38 In.	150.00
Washstand, Pine, Yellow Striping, Bottom Shelf, 1 Drawer, 29 3/4 In.	140.00
Washstand, Regency, Naval Officer's, Pembroke, Fitted, 1830, 29 x 38 x 10 In.	415.00
Washstand, Rosewood, 3 Drawers, Serpentine, Marble Top	1750.00
Washstand, Sheraton, Mahogany, Splashboard, Base Shelf With Drawer, 1820, 36 In.	250.00
Washstand, Sheraton, Pine, Painted Foliage & Red Berries, 36 In.	715.00
Washstand, Stepped, 2 Drawers, Back Splash, 40 1/2 x 35 In.	230.00
Washstand, Walnut, Scroll Cut Backsplash, 3 Drawers, 35 x 30 1/2 In.	140.00
Window Bench, William IV, Paw Feet, 30 x 47 x 17 1/2 In. ... *Illus*	9200.00
Window Seat, Empire, Mahogany, Saber Leg	1650.00
Window Seat, French Empire, Carved, Swan, 1800	1430.00
Window Seat, Gustav Stickley, Leather, No. 178, c.1902, 36 x 19 x 26 In.	385.00
Window Seat, Michigan Chair Co., 11-Spindle Sides, 24 x 17 x 30 In.	660.00
Window Seat, Neoclassical, Guilloche, Painted, Silk, 30 x 47 In.	1760.00
Window Seat, Rosewood, Serpentine Seat, Velvet, 40 In., Pair	2090.00
Wine Cooler, Regency, Domed Cover, Lead Lined, Brass Mounted, 31 In.	1600.00

GUNS that may be classed as toys, such as BB guns, air rifles, and cap guns, are listed in the Toy category.

G. ARGY-ROUSSEAU is the impressed mark used on a variety of objects in the Art Deco style. Gabriel Argy-Rousseau, born in 1885, was a French glass artist.

G-ARGY-
ROUSSEAU

Bowl, Pate-De-Verre, Coupe Sur Pied Aux Anses, c.1927, 8 1/2 In.	2990.00
Bowl, Red Grape Clusters, Trailing Leaves, Gray Ground, Signed, 3 1/2 In.	5000.00
Box, Cover, Round, Pate-De-Verre, Hortensias, c.1926, 4 In.	5750.00
Cup, Central Blossoms, Wing-Form Handles, c.1927, 4 1/8 In.	3450.00
Lamp Base, Roses, Stems Of Roses, Signed, c.1919, 7 1/2 In.	9200.00
Pendant, Pate-De-Verre, Flower Cluster, Blue, Green, Lilac, c.1920, 2 In.	1380.00
Plate, Floral On Mottled Ground, Pate-De-Verre, 7 In.	1265.00

Vase, Allover Stylized Hydrangea Blossoms, Signed, c.1926, 4 In. 5750.00
Vase, Bands Of Lozenges, Geometric Design, Signed, 3 3/8 In. 4370.00
Vase, Furling Spotted Leaves, Signed, c.1925, 6 1/2 In. 4025.00
Vase, Pate-De-Verre, Chardons Rouges, c.1920, 6 In. 5175.00
Vase, Pate-De-Verre, Vase A Palmettes, c.1930, 3 3/8 In. 4370.00
Vase, Petite Roses, Band Of Roses, Signed, c.1921, 2 3/4 In. 2875.00
Vase, Stylized Thistle Blossoms & Foliage, Signed, 6 In. 5175.00
Vase, Swirling Foliate Repeating Design, Signed, 5 In. 3105.00
Vase, Thistle Blossoms, Leaves, Signed, c.1915, 3 7/8 In. 3450.00

GALLE was a designer who made glass, pottery, furniture, and other Art Nouveau items. Emile Galle founded his factory in France in 1874. After Galle's
death in 1904, the firm continued to make glass and furniture until 1931. The
name *Galle* was used as a mark, but it was often hidden in the design of the
object. Galle Pottery is listed below and his furniture is listed in the Furniture
category.

Beaker, Enameled, Rampant Lions, Floral Sprays, Red, White, Black, c.1884, 5 1/2 In.   2925.00
Bottle, Enameled Festoons With Ribbons, Flowers & Bees, Signed, 4 In., Pair............. 450.00
Bottle, Enameled, Bulbous, Ribbon Festoons, Flowers, Bees, Stopper, 4 In., Pair......... 1150.00
Bowl, Cover, Internal Green Streaks, Flowering Tulips, Dutch Seascape, 6 In. 3450.00
Bowl, Inverted Trefoil Rim, Yellow, Red, Blue, Cameo Rose Sprays, c.1900, 6 1/4 In.... 2300.00
Coupe, Internal Red, Green & Ocher Swirls, Silver Foil Inclusions, c.1902, 4 1/2 In..... 3760.00
Coupe, Inverted Bowl, Blue, Green, Pink Overlay, Cameo Flowers, c.1900, 7 In.......... 9400.00
Decanter, Paneled, Apple Blossoms Sprays, Dragonfly, Signed, c.1890, 11 1/4 In. 1380.00
Dish, Trefoil, Circular Foot, Amber, Red, Cameo Flowers, Grasses, c.1893, 6 3/4 In..... 2300.00
Ewer, Wild Flowers, Olive Green, Signed, c.1900, 11 1/4 In. 3450.00
Inkwell, Berries & Branches, Layered Amber Glass, Squatty, Signed, 5 3/4 In.:............. 1725.00
Lamp, Domed Shade, 27 Butterflies, Candlestick Base, Parlor ....*Illus* 11000.00
Perfume Bottle, Riverside Landscape, Fall Trees In Front, Gilt Metal Fittings, 7 In. 748.00
Vase, 2 Jewel Flower Centers, Etched Leaves, Signed, 11 1/2 In.................................... 2185.00
Vase, 3 Large Nasturtium, Buds, Leaves, Signed, 6 In... 825.00
Vase, Acid Cut Leaf & Berry Design, Purple, Frosted Ground, Signed, 5 In. 885.00
Vase, Applied Crystal Rigaree, Enameled Design, Signed, 7 3/4 In............................... 1325.00
Vase, Autumnal Colors, Tapered, 18 In... 2850.00
Vase, Beetle, Oak Leaves, Autumnal Colors, Signed, 14 In.. 6700.00
Vase, Bell Form Pods, Tapered Shoulder, Signed, 20 1/2 In. 2000.00
Vase, Brown To Frost, Leaves & Berries, Flattened Ovoid, Signed, 8 1/4 In. 1265.00
Vase, Brown To Purple Flowers, Frosted Yellow Ground, 6 In....................................... 1100.00
Vase, Brown To Yellow, Flowers & Leaves, Signed, 4 In.. 865.00
Vase, Bud, Trailing Leaves & Buds, Burnt Orange Over Frosted, 7 In. 400.00
Vase, Bud, Trees, Mountains, Lake, Red On Pale Ocher, Cameo, 6 3/4 x 2 1/2 In. 1150.00

Galle, Lamp, Domed Shade,
27 Butterflies, Candlestick Base, Parlor

Vase, Caramel Over Yellow, Trees & River, Cylindrical, Peaked Rim, 8 In. 1725.00
Vase, Cherries & Leaves, Frosted, Slender Neck, Cameo, Signed, 7 In. 850.00
Vase, Chestnuts & Leafage, Signed, c.1900, 16 3/4 In. 4890.00
Vase, Clematis Blossoms, Buds & Leaves, Signed, c.1900, 9 3/8 In. 9775.00
Vase, Delphinium Blossoms, Leaves, Signed, c.1900, 18 1/2 In. 6050.00
Vase, Enameled, Sphere, Swirled Interior, White Asters, Red Flowers, 7 1/4 In. 2300.00
Vase, Etched Oak Leaves & Acorns, Wheel Cut Caps, Signed, 10 1/4 In. 1495.00
Vase, Etched, Enameled, Smoky, Flowers, Honeycomb Ground, c.1898, 11 In. 5430.00
Vase, Falling Maple Leaves, Signed, c.1900, 19 1/2 In. 3165.00
Vase, Fiddle Head Fern Design, c.1890, 13 3/4 In. 5500.00
Vase, Flared Cylinder, Inverted Rim, Internal Design, Flowers, 5 In. 3450.00
Vase, Flared Rim, Mauve To Yellow Frost, Flowers & Leaves, Signed, 5 1/4 In. 2530.00
Vase, Flared, Gray, Pale Pink Lining, Green Overlay, Maple Leaves, 5 In. 1840.00
Vase, Floral Design, Amber Ground, Flagon Shape, Inverted Neck, Acid Cut, 7 In. 995.00
Vase, Gold & Blue Bamboo Shoots Pattern, Ivory Ground, Signed, 9 3/4 In. 1100.00
Vase, Gothic Designs, Bands Of Acanthus Scrolls, Blossoms, Signed, 6 1/4 In. 2530.00
Vase, Grape Pods, Cylindrical, 23 1/2 In. 3000.00
Vase, Joan Of Arc, Etched, Enameled, Flared Foot, Pink, c.1890, 7 In. 6270.00
Vase, Leafy Branches Pendent With Berries, Signed, c.1900, 14 In. 4600.00
Vase, Morning Glories, Footed, Oviform, 10 In. 4780.00
Vase, Mottled Caramel & Green Ground, Silver Foil Inclusions, Signed, 5 In. 3450.00
Vase, Peaked Rim, Etched Trees Along River, Signed, 8 In. 1725.00
Vase, Pendant Squash Blossoms, Trailing Leaves, Signed, c.1900, 7 1/4 In. 6037.00
Vase, Purple Clematis, Cut To Clear, Signed, 7 In. 775.00
Vase, Purple Floral Design, Frosted, Bulbous, Long Neck, Cameo, 6 1/2 In. 600.00
Vase, Purple Floral, Frosted Clear Ground, Flared Foot, Cylindrical, Cameo, 8 3/4 In. .. 588.00
Vase, Red Cherries, Leaves, Vines, Flared, Cameo, Signed, 6 3/4 In. 850.00
Vase, Red Orchids, Yellow Ground, Cameo, 8 In. 600.00
Vase, River Landscape, Leafy Trees, Signed, c.1900, 12 5/8 In. 4600.00
Vase, Rondels Of Animals, Gilt Coral Ground, Signed, c.1890, 7 3/4 In. 4600.00
Vase, Saddle-Shaped Mouth, Suspended Flowers, Cameo, 4 x 2 1/2 In. 1200.00
Vase, Sprays Of Blossoms, Grasshopper Amid Fern Fronds, Signed, c.1900, 4 In. 4025.00
Vase, Sprays Of Thistles, Leaves, Gilding, Signed, c.1890, 7 In. 5175.00
Vase, Streaky Yellow, White, Purple, Intarsia Leaves, c.1900, 6 1/2 In. 1670.00
Vase, Stylized Flowers & Leafage, Applied Cabochons, Signed, c.1890, 8 3/4 In. 8625.00
Vase, Trees & Stream, Oviform, Signed, 11 In. 2700.00
Vase, Triple Overlay, Cameo, 1st Period, 12 In. 4800.00
Vase, White Asters, Red Flowers, Vines, Dragonfly, Enameled, c.1890 .... 2300.00
Vase, Wisteria, Amethyst Blossoms, Frosted, Pink Interior, Signed, 4 1/2 In. 805.00
Vase, Wisteria, Gray Walls Shading To Lavender At Base, Signed, c.1900, 17 In. 1840.00
Vase, Yellow, Blue & Aubergine Overlay, Cut Violets, Ovoid, Footed, Signed, 4 In. ... 690.00

GALLE POTTERY was made by Emile Galle, the famous French designer, after 1874. The pieces were marked with the initials *E. G.* impressed, *Em. Galle Faiencerie de Nancy*, or a version of his signature. Galle is best known for his glass, listed above.

Ewer, Red Poppies, Dark Brown 1500.00
Vase, Blue Flowers, 14 In. 975.00

GAME collectors like all types of games. Of special interest are any board games or card games. Transogram and other company names are included in the description when known. Other games may be found listed under Card, Toy, or the name of the character or celebrity featured in the game.

77 Sunset Strip, Lowell, 1960 .... 80.00
Addams Family, Card, Milton Bradley, 1965 .... 45.00 to 50.00
Addams Family, Milton Bradley, 1973 .... 55.00
All In The Family, Card, Archie Bunker, 1972, Milton Bradley 18.00
Aquaman, Hasbro, 1965 .... 75.00
Authors, Card, McLoughlin, 1889 .... 60.00
Authors, Card, Milton Bradley 20.00
Authors, Fairchild, Box, 1945 .... 12.00
Automobile Tour Game, En-Ar-Co, 1919 .... 115.00
Babe Ruth Baseball, Official, Toy Town 300.00

Balcony Bound, Tin, Shoot Marble To Score 80.00
Ball Toss, Yogi Bear, 1960.. 60.00
Bambi, Card, Russell Mfg., 1965 .... 10.00
Barber Pole, Parker Brothers 100.00
Barbie's Keys To Fame Game, Mattel, 1963.. 40.00
Baseball, Countertop, Tin, Akins Company, Patent 1915, 18 1/2 x 24 In. 165.00
Bat Masterson, 3-Dimensional Cardboard Buildings, 1959 .... 100.00
Battleboard, Ideal, 1972 .... 10.00
Bean Toss, Black Man In Barrel, Carnival, 45 x 22 In. 990.00
Beany & Cecil, Jumpin' DJ, 3-Dimensional Figures, Mattel, 1950 .... 45.00 to 60.00
Ben Casey M.D., Transogram, 1961.. 20.00 to 40.00
Beverly Hillbillies, Card 13.00
Beverly Hillbillies, Card, 1963... 25.00
Beverly Hillbillies, Jumbo Cards, Milton Bradley, Jumbo Co. Of Holland, 1965 .... 145.00
Bewitched, Game Gems, 1965 .... 58.00
Bewitched Stymie, Card, No. 4534, Milton Bradley, 1964 .... 40.00
Billie Bumps Visit To Boston, Geo. S. Parker & Co., 1888 .... 75.00
Bingo, Lithograph Box, 1936 .... 150.00
Bingo, Marble, Tin Lithograph, Wolverine, Box .... 55.00 to 65.00
Bionic Woman, Parker Brothers, Box, 1976... 38.00
Black Beauty, Transogram, 1957 .... 25.00
Blondie Goes To Leisureland, Spinner & Envelope, 1940 .... 85.00
Board, 2-Sided, Parcheesi & Checkers, Pine, 18 x 18 In. 550.00
Board, 2-Sided, Parcheesi & Checkers, Tin 145.00
Board, Black Surface, Faux Marble Border, Painted Slate, Square, 22 In. 285.00
Board, Good Ol' Charlie Brown, Milton Bradley, 1971 .... 22.00
Board, Mahogany, Clay Marbles, 19th Century, 6 7/8 x 8 3/8 In. 115.00
Board, Parcheesi, Painted.. 1800.00
Board, Red & Black Paint, Yellow & Blue Striping, Flowers, 15 x 23 1/2 In. 403.00
Board, Round The World With Nellie Bly, McLoughlin, 1890.. 195.00
Board, Slate Top, Oak Bottom, 1940s.. 450.00
Bob Feller's Big League Baseball, Saalfield, c.1950... 80.00
Bop The Beetle, Ideal, 1962... 65.00
Bowling Alley, Wooden, 32 x 6 1/2 In... 27.00
Box, Folding Board, Fitted, Card, Cribbage, Chess, Checkers, Whist, 1884, 6 3/4 x 12 In. 815.00
Box, Poker Chips, Burnt Wood, Aces, 2 Men Playing Cards, 1900, 6 1/2 x 9 1/2 In. 242.00
Box, Poker Chips, Cutout Playing Card Suit Signs, Primitive, 1900, 9 x 18 In. 60.00
Box, Poker Chips, Leather, Compartments, 200 Chips & 2 Decks, 1900, 9 x 12 In......... 83.00
Box, Tiger Oak, Scrimshaw Horsehead Design, 300 Ivory Chips, 1890......................... 6270.00
Bozo, Pin The Button Party Game 7.00
Bozo The Clown, Ball Toss, Box 35.00
Bull In The China Shop, Milton Bradley, 1937.. 55.00
Camp Granada, Milton Bradley, 1965 .... 35.00
Captain Kangaroo, Kangadoodles, Hasbro, 1956.. 45.00
Carpet Bowling, Bandor, Box, England 40.00
Casper, Box Of Games, No. 4932, 1958 .... 42.00
Casper, EduCards... 8.00
Casper The Friendly Ghost, 1969.. 9.00
Cat & Mouse, Board, McLoughlin Bros... 500.00
Charlie Brown's All-Stars Baseball, Parker Brothers 35.00
Checkerboard, Black Squares, Yellow Trim, Pine, 14 x 27 1/4 In. 440.00
Checkerboard, Dark Red & Black Paint, Yellow Striping, 17 1/2 x 24 In. 220.00
Checkerboard, Green & Black Paint, Poplar, 14 1/4 x 23 1/4 In. 330.00
Checkerboard, Inlaid Cherry & Walnut, 12 3/4 x 12 3/4 In. 71.00
Checkerboard, Inlaid Wood, Yellow & Olive Paint, 19 x 19 In. 120.00
Checkerboard, Pine, Plywood, Red & Black Painted, 18 1/2 x 18 1/2 In. 50.00
Checkerboard, Recessed Frame, Pine, 21 1/4 x 21 1/4 In... 412.00
Checkerboard, Red & Black Paint, Alp Monogram, Poplar, 19 x 25 In. 220.00
Checkerboard, Red & Black, Green Border, Masonite, 17 x 17 In. 55.00
Checkers, Solitary, Akro Agate, 1939, Box 25.00
Checkers, Wood, Stenciled Flowers, Board, Checkers, Victorian, 20 1/2 x 17 In. 259.00
Chess Set, Ivory & Dark Red, Mahogany Case 138.00
Chess Set, Ivory, Carved, Oriental, Papier-Mache Box, 1880s.. 905.00

Chess Set, Ivory, Chinese Figure Standing On Floating Sphere, China 1150.00
Chess Set, Ivory, On Carved Ball, 5 To 7 Floating Nested Spheres, China, 8 In. 1150.00
Chessboard, Ivory Inlaid, White & Brown.. 192.00
Chessboard, Reverse-Painted Glass, Frame, 29 x 29 In. 250.00
Cheyenne, Milton Bradley, 1958 .... 59.00
Chinese Checkers, Wood & Cardboard, Hop Ching 20.00
Chiromagica, 3 Answer Sheets, Question Disk, McLoughlin, 1901 .... 115.00
Clubhouse Bingo, Little Rascals, Box, 1958 .... 55.00
Clue, 1972 .... 9.00
Columbo Detective, Board, Milton Bradley, 1973 .... 20.00
Combat, Board, Ideal, 1963, 10 x 20 In. ....55.00 to 72.00
Concentration, Milton Bradley, 1959.. 55.00
Cowboy Roundup, Parker Brothers, 1952 .... 15.00
Cribbage Board, Carved, Crayoned Surface Design, 1917, 10 3/4 x 20 3/4 In.............. 187.00
Croquet Set, 1940s, Small 65.00
Croquet Set, 8 Mallets, 8 Balls, Wire Hoops, Wooden Box, 33 1/2 In.......................... 27.00
Croquet Set, Box, Instructions, Victorian 225.00
Croquet Set, Floor, Milton Bradley, 1932, 20 x 5 In. 10.00
Croquet Set, Parlor, Bliss, c.1895, Box 220.00
Croquet Set, Wooden Stenciled Box, Victorian, 1900 .... 145.00
Cross Up, Lucille Ball Cover, Cards, 1974 .... 15.00
Dallas, Card, Mego, 1980 .... 8.00
Dart Board, Little Black Sambo, Wyandotte 85.00
Dart Board, Matador, Unused, 1974.. 50.00
Dennis The Menace, Baseball 95.00
Devil's Dice Brain Buster, Parachute Golf Balls.. 45.00
District Messenger Boy, McLoughlin, 9 x 17 In... 495.00
Dominoes, Catalin, Box 45.00
Dominoes, Handmade Bone-Ivory, Late 18th Century, 28 Piece 225.00
Dominoes, Ivory & Ebony, Tin Box 75.00
Dr. Busby, Card, McLoughlin Bros., 1890... 125.00
Dr. Doolittle, Post Cereal Premium, Cards, 1967... 32.00
Dr. Quack, Card 20.00
Dragnet, Transogram, 1957 .... 60.00
Duck Pins, 8 Wood Pins, 2 Wood Balls, Box, No. 604, Concord Toy Co. 8.00
Easy Money, Milton Bradley, 1936.. 50.00
Electric Football, Tudor, Model 500, Metal, 1960s.. 25.00
Elsie & Her Family, Box, 1941 ....130.00 to 165.00
Felix The Cat, Milton Bradley, 1960 .... 65.00
Fighting Knights, Builtrite, 1950s 23.00
Flintstones, Board, Milton Bradley, 1971 .... 35.00
Flintstones, Giant Checkers 150.00
Flintstones, Target Gun & Dart, Transogram 48.00
Flipper, Japan, 1966.. 165.00
Fortune Telling, Card, U.S. Playing Card Co., 52 Cards, 1900s 25.00
Game Of Flowers, Card, Cincinnati Game Co. 35.00
Game Of Yertle, Dr. Seuss, Balancing Game, Revell 175.00
Going To Jerusalem, Board, Parker Brothers, 1955... 65.00
Gomer Pyle, Transogram, 1964 .... 30.00
Gong Show, American Publishing, 1977 .... 10.00
Green Ghost 50.00
Hank Aaron, Baseball, Box... 50.00
Happy Days, Fonzie Real Cool, Board, Parker Brothers, 1976 .... 12.00
Harlem Globetrotters, Board, Milton Bradley, 1971.. 40.00
Have Gun, Will Travel, Parker Brothers, 1959...55.00 to 90.00
Hogan's Heroes, Transogram, 1966 .... 40.00
Home Team Baseball, 1930s... 75.00
Honeymooners, Board, 1986 .... 14.00
Horseshoes, Little Jim Toys, Tin 45.00
Hot Potato, Remco 15.00
I Dream Of Jeannie, Milton Bradley, 1965... 40.00
I Spy, Ideal, 1965 .... 85.00
Jetsons, Milton Bradley, Box, 1986... 18.00

Jeu Du Cirque, Traveling, 10 Piece, Box	308.00
Johnny Get Your Gun, Colorful Lithograph, 1920s...	85.00
Johnny Quest, Card, Milton Bradley, 1964	50.00
Johnny Quest, Card, Score Pad, Vacuform Playing Tray, Box...........................	60.00
Junior Motor Race, 11 1/2 x 11 1/2 In.	110.00
Kentucky Derby Racing, Whitman, 1938	20.00
Kiddie Kamper, Wolverine	375.00
Kimba The Lion, Japan, 1966..	199.00
Kojak, Milton Bradley, 1975	18.00
Land Of The Lost, Milton Bradley, 1975	30.00
Laurel & Hardy, Transogram, 1962...	12.00
Lee Vs. Mead, Battle Of Gettysburg, Box, Gamut Of Games	40.00
Lindy, The New Flying Game, Card, Parker Brothers, 1927...................55.00 to 65.00
Little Black Sambo, Board, Cadaco-Ellis .... 110.00 to 175.00
Little House On The Prairie, Box	25.00
Lloyd Thaxton Dawk, Transogram	125.00
Lost In Space, Board	75.00
Lotto, Milton Bradley, 1932..	12.00
Lucy's Tea Party, Milton Bradley, Box, 1971..	30.00
Mad Magazine, Parker Brothers, 1979	40.00
Magic Robot, England, 1950s	50.00
Mah-Jongg, Ivory & Bamboo, Rosewood Cabinet, Signed, 9 x 6 1/4 x 6 1/4 In.	935.00
Mah-Jongg, Ivory, Bamboo, Rosewood Box	165.00
Major Matt Mason Space Exploration, 1967	265.00
Man From U.N.C.L.E., Card, Ilya Kuryakin, Milton Bradley, 1966	45.00
Marble, Kick Back	35.00
Maze, Marble, 1960...	20.00
McHale's Navy, Transogram, 1962	40.00
Melvin The Moon Man, Remco..	80.00
Monday Night Football, Staubach On Cover	35.00
Monopoly, First Edition, Parker Brothers, 1935	160.00
Mother Hen, Target, Knickerbocker	15.00
Motorcycle Tag, Roulette, Flashing Bulbs, 1925-1930, Box..................................	1350.00
Movie Land Keeno, 1929	75.00
Mrs. Potatohead, 1950s, Box	110.00
Nancy Drew, Metal Cars..	27.00
Nancy Drew Mystery, Parker Brothers, 1950s..	130.00
National Defense, Shooting, Marx, 22 x 11 In..	60.00
National Velvet, Transogram, 1961	38.00
Outlaw The Outlaw, Target, Mattel, 1959	150.00
Parachute Golf Balls	45.00
Partridge Family, Milton Bradley, 1971	23.00
Peg Solitaire	45.00
Perry Mason Case Of The Missing Suspect, Transogram, 1959 .... 30.00 to 103.00
Peter Pan, Board, Selchow & Righter, 1927...	110.00
Pick-Up Sticks, Spears, Shovels, Knives, Hammers, 35 Sticks, Mahogany Case	120.00
Pinball, 6 Marbles, 2-Star Design, Tin	65.00
Pinball, Lindstrom	65.00
Pinball, Poosh-M-Up, 1933..	95.00
Ping-Pong, Box, Parker Brothers, c.1902..	45.00
Pinocchio, Marble, 1939..	150.00
Pitch, Oak & Cast-Iron Stand, 35 In...	275.00
Planet Of The Apes, Milton Bradley, 1974	49.00
Poker Chips, 200 Fan Ivory Piece, Tiger Oak Box, 1890	5060.00
Poker Chips, Composition Chips, Oak Case, Interior Insert	118.00
Poker Chips, Mahogany Veneered Case, 20th Century, 12 x 7 x 5 In.	48.00
Politics, Parker Brothers, 1952...	65.00
Poosh-M-Up Jr., 4-In-1 Pinball, Glass & Wood, 1940s, 17 x 11 In.	100.00
Post Office, Parker Brothers, c.1910...	125.00
Prince Valiant, Yellow Box, Transogram, 1955	45.00
Punch & Judy, Parker Brothers, 13 x 11 In.	192.00
Puppet Pinball, Marx, 1950s, Box...	45.00
Puss In Boots, Box Bottom Is Field, 2 Figures, McLoughlin, 1897............................	747.00

Pussy Cat Ten Pins, Lithographed Paper On Cardboard, Box, McLoughlin Bros. 805.00
Puzzle, Banana Splits, Whitman, 1968 .... 35.00
Puzzle, Beverly Hillbillies, Car Scene, Jaymar, 1963 .... 30.00
Puzzle, Bewitched, Along For The Ride, Color Portrait Of Samantha, 1964 .... 65.00
Puzzle, Cap'n Crunch, No. 4569, Whitman, 1968 .... 35.00
Puzzle, Columbia Space Shuttle, Box 20.00
Puzzle, Donkey, Lithograph, Late 1800s, 3 x 4 1/2 In. 20.00
Puzzle, Folgers Coffee, 57 Pieces, In Folgers Can .... 30.00 to 35.00
Puzzle, G.I. Joe, 2 Men Charging, 150 Pieces, Whitman, No. 4647, 14 x 18 In. 32.00
Puzzle, Holiday Inn Map 25.00
Puzzle, Hoppity Hopper, Whitman, 1965 .... 50.00
Puzzle, Huckleberry Hound, Whitman Jr., 1959 .... 30.00
Puzzle, James Bond, Thunderball, No. 1, 1965 .... 30.00
Puzzle, Jigsaw, Atom Ant, Whitman, 1967 .... 35.00
Puzzle, Jigsaw, Banana Splits, Whitman, 1968 .... 35.00
Puzzle, Jigsaw, Bozo The Clown, No. 4516, Whitman, 1965 .... 30.00
Puzzle, Jigsaw, Felix The Cat, No. 18, Built-Rite, 1949, 9 x 12 In. 90.00
Puzzle, Jigsaw, James Bond, Goldfinger Fort Knox Finale, Whitman, 1965 .... 55.00
Puzzle, Jigsaw, Man From U.N.C.L.E., No. 4, Whitman, 196 .... 55.00
Puzzle, Jigsaw, Tales Of Wells Fargo, Dale Robertson, No. 4427, Whitman, 1958 .... 32.00
Puzzle, Jigsaw, Underdog, No. 4610, 1975 .... 35.00
Puzzle, Jigsaw, Wild Bill Hickok, Famous TV Stars, Built-Rite, 1956 .... 45.00
Puzzle, Keen Cutter, I.G. Simmons, Box 1500.00
Puzzle, Little Black Sambo, 1930s 50.00
Puzzle, Major Matt Mason, 1968, Whitman 48.00
Puzzle, Map, United States, Paper Lithograph, McLoughlin, 9 1/2 In. 120.00
Puzzle, Mary Poppins, With Comic 20.00
Puzzle, Model Ship, Paper Lithograph On Cardboard, Hinged Lid, Milton Bradley 175.00
Puzzle, Mummy, Jaymar, 1963 .... 95.00
Puzzle, Outer Limits 250.00
Puzzle, Ovaltine ROA, 1933 .... 60.00
Puzzle, Planet Of The Apes, On Patrol, 96 Pieces, H-G Toys, 1967, 10 x 14 In. 12.00
Puzzle, Playboy, 1968 .... 10.00
Puzzle, Rin Tin Tin, 1952 .... 16.00
Puzzle, Rin Tin Tin, Whitman, 1956 .... 30.00
Puzzle, Roger Rabbit, Waddington, 1989 .... 45.00
Puzzle, Starsky & Hutch, Street Fight, Box 12.00
Puzzle, Steam Fire Engine, Horse Drawn, Milton Bradley, Board, 1904 .... 165.00
Puzzle, Stingray, Whitman, 1965 .... 45.00
Puzzle, Sword In The Stone, 1968 .... 15.00
Puzzle, The Prince, Maxfield Parrish, 1926 .... 125.00
Puzzle, Tip Top Bread, Dated 1952, Original Envelope 85.00

Game, Quarterback,
Littlefield Mfg. Co., c.1914

◆◆◆◆◆◆◆◆◆◆◆◆◆◆◆◆◆◆◆◆◆◆◆◆

If you are moving or if you are storing paper collectibles and pictures for a long period of time, remember that extreme changes of temperature are damaging. Air trapped inside a picture frame may condense and cause moisture damage.

◆◆◆◆◆◆◆◆◆◆◆◆◆◆◆◆◆◆◆◆◆◆◆◆

Puzzle, Tray, Tom Corbett Space Cadet, 1950 .... 35.00
Puzzle, US Map, Wooden, Sifo 55.00
Puzzle, Wolfman, Jaymar, 1963 .... 9500.00
Puzzle, Wyatt Earp, Hugh O'Brien Photo, Whitman, 1958 .... 40.00
Quarterback, Littlefield Mfg. Co., c.1914 ....*Illus*   385.00
Quick Draw McGraw, Milton Bradley, 1960 .... 40.00
Quiz Kids Radio Question Bee, Card, Whitman, Box 20.00
Raggedy Ann & Raggedy Andy, 1974 .... 28.00
Red Riding Hood, Parker Brothers 110.00
Reward Of Virtue, Ives, 1850, 13 5/8 In. 1380.00
Rich Uncle, Milton Bradley, 1946 .... 35.00
Rifleman, Board, 1959 .... 55.00
Rifleman, Milton Bradley, 1959 .... 40.00 to 75.00
Ring Toss, Beany & Cecil, Tin Lithograph, 1961 .... 95.00
Ring Toss, Clown 25.00
Ring Toss, Parker Brothers, 1925 .... 8.00
Ring Toss, Sappy, Box, 1930s 50.00
Road Runner, Whitman, 1969 .... 60.00
Robinson Crusoe, Lowell Toys 23.00
Rockets To The Moon 75.00
Rocky & Bullwinkle Electronic Quiz, On Card, 1971 .... 18.00
Roulette Wheel, Brass & Cast Iron Hardware, Black & White, 20 In. 203.00
Sambo, Board, Wyandotte.. 165.00
Shooting Gallery, Circus Carnival, Windup, Ohio Art, Box, 11 x 17 In. 145.00
Shooting Gallery, Posse, Marx 70.00
Six Million Dollar Man, Parker Brothers, 1975 .... 15.00
Skeet-Shoot, Irwin 38.00
Skill Ball, Marble, Tin Lithograph, Marx, Box 50.00
Skittles, Paper Lithograph On Cardboard, La Grande Semaine D'Aviation 3850.00
Skunk, Illustrated Inlay Tray, Dice, Chips, Score Sheets, Box, 1950s, 8 x 10 In. 20.00
Smokey Bear 55.00
Snoopy, Board 377.00
Snoopy & The Red Baron, 1971, Milton Bradley 25.00
Snoopy Bowling Ball, Romper Room 20.00
Snoopy Come Home, Milton Bradley, 1970s 14.00
Soccer, Tabletop, Tudor Rose, England, Box 65.00
Space Race, Card, Box, 1969 .... 35.00
Spin-It, Elenee 59.00
Sports Illustrated Pro Football, Box 16.00
Star Reporter, 1960 .... 79.00
Sub Attack, Card, Firefighters, Milton Bradley, Box 65.00
Surfside 6, Lowell, 1962 .... 65.00
Target, Crows In The Corn, Wilder, Box, c.1930 .... 180.00
Telephone, J.H. Singer, 1898 .... 50.00
Terry & The Pirates, Board, Wooden Pegs & Tabs, 1937 .... 25.00
The Lid's Off, Board, With Wyandotte Pop Gun, 1930s, 24 In. Square 125.00
Three Men On A Horse, Board, Milton Bradley, 1936 .... 75.00
Ticker, 17 x 22 In. Green Felt Playing Mat, Glow Products Co., 1929 .... 90.00
Tiddlywinks, 1932 .... 18.00
Time Tunnel, Ideal, 1966 .... 125.00 to 145.00
Tom & Jerry, 1968 .... 30.00
Tom & Jerry Merry-Go-Round Game, Watkins, 1959 .... 40.00
Tom Hamilton's, Football 295.00
Uncle Wiggily, 1967 .... 26.00
Uncle Wiggily, Box, Milton Bradley, 6 1/2 x 5 1/4 In. 11.00
Untouchables, Transogram, 1961 .... 125.00
Wacky Races, Milton Bradley, 1970 .... 90.00
Watergate Scandal, Card 10.00
What Shall I Be? Various Careers, Selchow & Righter, 1968 .... 38.00
Wheel Of Fortune, Hand-Painted Horses & 4 Clowns, Large 1595.00
White House, Card, President's Pictures, U.S. Playing Card Co., 1895 .... 35.00
White Shadow, Basketball, Cadaco 95.00

Who's On First, Abbott & Costello, 1978	30.00
Why, Alfred Hitchcock, 1961	48.00
Woody Woodpecker, 1958	45.00
World's Game Of Baseball, McLoughlin, 1889	3100.00
Yacht Race, Parker Brothers, 1961	105.00

GAME PLATES are plates of any make decorated with pictures of birds, animals, or fish. The game plates usually came in sets consisting of twelve dishes and a serving platter. These sets were most popular during the 1880s.

Ducks, Gold Rococo Border, Limoges	125.00
Fish, Limoges, 9 In., 6 Piece	275.00
GAME SET, Bird, 2 Quail On Gold Platter, Various Birds On Plates, Platter, Limoges, 20 In.	1375.00
Fish, Hand Painted Center Fish, Gold Border, Platter, Limoges, 12 Plates, c.1895	2200.00

GARDEN FURNISHINGS have been popular for centuries. The stone or metal statues, wire, iron, or rustic furniture, urns and fountains, sundials, and small figurines are included in this category. Many of the metal pieces have been made continuously for years.

Armchair, Schinkel, Iron, Berlin, 1925	440.00
Bench, 3-Pierced Back, Leaf Turned Legs, Marble, India, 5 Ft. 8 In.	6900.00
Bench, 3-Panel Back, Scrolls Above Tracery, Pierced Seat, Iron	865.00
Bench, Armorial & Trefoil Back, Iron Rod Seat, Wood & Perot, 59 In.	3100.00
Bench, Bentwood, Slanted Back, Weathered Black Painted, Arms, 72 In.	300.00
Bench, Carved, 4-Panel Slat Back, Scroll Armrests, Anglo Indian, 76 In.	440.00
Bench, Egg & Dart Border, Scroll Paw Feet, Stone, 5 Ft. 3 In.	1050.00
Bench, French Revival, Bronze	3750.00
Bench, Gothic, Green Paint, Carved Armrests, Iron, 35 x 39 In.	1200.00
Bench, Green Paint, Kramer Bros., Dayton, Ohio, Cast Iron, c.1880	1100.00
Bench, Griffon Arms, Foliage & Berry Back, Cast Iron, 44 In.	90.00
Bench, Regency, Painted Wirework, Tub Shape, Scrolled Supports, 74 In.	1495.00
Bench, Scrolled Legs, Paw Feet, Marble, 44 In., Pair	8050.00
Bench, Twig Pattern, Cast Iron, c.1865	1500.00
Bench, White Paint, 19th Century	880.00
Birdbath, Baluster Turned Base, Masonry, 27 3/4 In.	50.00
Birdbath, Ceramic, Masque Of The Hours, June 20, 1905, 31 In.	1485.00
Birdbath, Frogs, Pair	400.00
Chair, Iron, Shield Back, White Paint, Trapezoidal Slip Seat, 37 In., Pair	460.00
Chair, Oval Back, Center Cartouche, Harvester Figure, Pair	575.00
Chair, Rococo, Swivel, Cast Iron, Scrolled Legs, Victorian, 32 In.	1100.00
Chair, Windsor, Metal, Ohio, 1890-1920	375.00
Dog, Whippet, Recumbent, Concrete, Black Painted, 14 1/2 In., Pair	55.00
Figure, Cherub, Allegory Of Spring, Stone, France, 28 In.	1500.00
Figure, Cherub, Allegory Of Winter, Stone, France, 36 In.	1750.00 to 2010.00
Figure, Dog, Cast Iron, Painted, 40 x 28 1/2 In.	3000.00
Figure, Sculpture, Cherub, Allegory Of Spring, Stone, France, 28 In.	1725.00
Font, Bowl, Carved Leaf Tips, Baluster Pedestal, Marble, 4 Ft.	9775.00
Font, Pedestal Supporting Well, Gadrooned Lion Masks, Limestone, 4 Ft.	6900.00
Fountain, Cherub, With Reed Pipes, Lead, c.1920, 36 In.	1380.00
Fountain, Figural, Seminude Supporting Basin, Cast Iron, 56 1/2 In.	3450.00
Fountain, Mask At Font, Lion Headed Monopodia, Marble, 5 Ft. 2 In.	9775.00
Fountain, Putto Blowing On Conch Shell Horn, White Marble, 49 In.	3950.00
Fountain, Shell Basin, Frogs & Standing Girl, Lead, 27 x 21 In.	200.00
Fountain, Youth, Holding Fish, Incorporating Nozzle, Lead, 23 1/2 In.	3450.00
Gate, Scrolls & Panels, Wrought Iron, 4 Sections, 10 Ft., Pair	1725.00
Hitching Post, Jockey, Cast Iron	700.00
Jardiniere, Flanked By Mask & Snake Handles, Terra-Cotta, 18 In., Pair	3150.00
Lantern, Carved Zodiac Designs, Granite, China, 7 Ft. 8 In.	6025.00
Lavabo, Art Nouveau, Child Holding Conch Shell, Cast Stone, 22 In.	865.00
Love Seat, Adirondack Type, Slanted Roof, Percy Kelly, 1913	1850.00
Love Seat, Wrought Iron, 2 Women Bust Form Back, 1950s	875.00
Planter, Carved Masks Hung With Swags, Marble, Pair	4600.00
Planter, Leaf-Tip Form, Marble, 13 In., Pair	4025.00

Planter, Lion Masks All Sides, Stone, 28 In. 460.00
Sarcophagus, 3 Sides, Carved, Sea Horses, Cherubs, Masks, Marble, 6 In. 8625.00
Seat, Arms Formed As Griffins, Wing Backrests, Terra-Cotta, 29 In., Pair 9220.00
Seat, Barrel Form, Foo Lions At Play, Studded Borders, 19 1/2 In., Pair 9485.00
Seat, Egg & Spinach Glaze, Majolica, Late 19th Century, 21 In. 575.00
Seat, Famille Rose, Writhing Dragons, Barrel Form, 22 In. 115.00
Seat, Multicolored Glaze, Hexagonal Bulbous Form, 19 1/4 In., Pair 745.00
Seat, Mushroom Form, Marked WS & S 6332, Earthenware, 18 In., Pair 3450.00
Seat, Pottery, Multicolored, Hexagonal, Oriental, 1900s, 14 x 19 In., Pair 748.00
Seat, Rose Medallion, 18 1/2 In. 1980.00
Seat, Tang Style Colors, China, 18 In. 90.00
Settee & Armchair, Cast Iron, Schinkel, Berlin, 1925, 2 Piece 2650.00
Sprinkler, Figural, Winged Victory, Part Arm Missing, Lead, 20 In. ʹ495.00
Sprinkler, Lawn Tractor, Brass Tube, Cast Iron 95.00
Sprinkler, Lawn, Tractor Style, Model 101 .... 350.00
Sprinkler, Lawn, Western Cartridge Co., Brass. 75.00
Statue, Child With Bird's Nest, Marble, 1880s, 30 1/2 In. 2070.00
Statue, Crane, Bronze, 7 Ft., Pair 6325.00
Statue, Foo Lion, On Plinth, 1 With Pup, Bronze, 53 In., Pair. 2875.00
Statue, Goose, Bronze, 29 In., Pair 4025.00
Statue, Lion, Seated Upright, Stone, 42 In., Pair 6325.00
Statue, Lion, Seated, Paw Resting On Crown Shield, Stone, 28 In., Pair 7475.00
Statue, Mushroom, Concrete. 2100.00
Statue, Nude Boy, Holding Shell Shape Basin, Cast Iron 880.00
Statue, Sphinx, Stone, 33 1/2 In., Pair 8050.00
Statue, Spirited Neapolitan Peasant Boy, 42 In. 2000.00
Statue, Whippet, Lead, 4 Ft., Pair 4887.00
Sundial, Classic Woman, Standing, Pottery, L. & A. St. Gaudens, 41 In. 2750.00
Sundial, Griswold Mfg Co., No. 357, Iron 510.00
Sundial, Inset Top With Bronze Dial, Marble, 48 In. 1495.00
Table, Foliage Scroll Leg, Center Hole For Umbrella, Cast Iron, 39 In. 105.00
Urn, All Around Birds & Foliage, Earthenware, 24 In., Pair 5175.00
Urn, Bluebird Design Base, Cast Iron, 34 In., Pair 880.00
Urn, Cherub Holding Oval Basket Weave Bowl, Cast Iron, 45 In., Pair 5950.00
Urn, Classical Style, Handles, Cast Iron, 10 1/2 In., Pair. 385.00
Urn, Foliage Scrolls, Buffalo Heads, Scrolled Ears, Cast Iron, 42 1/2 In. 2050.00
Urn, Lead, Classical Panels, Scrolled Handles, 18th Century, 23 In., Pair 745.00
Urn, Loop Handles, Cast Iron, 24 In., Pair. 2600.00
Urn, Lotus Leaf Design, Cast Iron, 18 In. 210.00
Urn, Spigot Near Bottom, Cast Iron, Pair 600.00

GAUDY DUTCH pottery was made in England for America from about 1810 to 1820. It is a white earthenware with Imari-style decorations of red, blue, green, yellow, and black. Only sixteen patterns of Gaudy Dutch were made: Butterfly, Carnation, Dahlia, Double Rose, Dove, Grape, Leaf, Oyster, Primrose, Single Rose, Strawflower, Sunflower, Urn, War Bonnet, Zinnia, and No Name. Other similar wares are called *Gaudy Ironstone* and *Gaudy Welsh*.

Creamer, Dahlia 850.00
Creamer, Oyster 185.00
Cup, No Handle, Double Rose 330.00
Plate, Butterly, 9 In. 110.00
Platter, War Bonnet, 10 1/2 In. 2500.00

GAUDY IRONSTONE is the collector's name for the ironstone wares with the bright patterns similar to Gaudy Dutch. It was made in England for the American market. There may be other examples found in the listing for Ironstone or under the name of the ceramic factory.

Pitcher, Imari Design, Snake Handle, 5 1/2 In. 115.00
Plate, Allover Oriental Scenes, Mason 32.00
Plate, Floral Design, Mason, 9 In. 132.00
Plate, Morning Glory, 8 1/2 In. 98.00
Plate, Strawberry, 8 In. 200.00
Sugar, Cover, Urn Of Flowers, Lion's-Head Handles 85.00

GAUDY WELSH is an Imari-decorated earthenware with red, blue, green, and gold decorations. Most Gaudy Welsh was made in England for the American market. It was made after 1820.

Chamber Pot, 9 In.	880.00
Creamer, Daisy & Chain	88.00
Cup & Saucer, Red, Blue	110.00
Cup & Saucer, Wagon Wheel	72.00
Jug, Buddha, 4 1/2 In.	95.00
Jug, Tulip	395.00
Server, Hot Water, Cobalt, Terra-Cotta, Gold Florals, Pivoting Lid	125.00
Sugar, Tulip, Polychrome, 7 1/8 In.	385.00

GEISHA GIRL porcelain was made for export in the late nineteenth century in Japan. It was an inexpensive porcelain often sold in dime stores or used as free premiums. Pieces are sometimes marked with the name of a store. Japanese ladies in kimonos are pictured on the dishes. There are over 125 recorded patterns. Borders of red, blue, green, gold, brown, or several of these colors were used. Modern reproductions are being made.

Biscuit Jar, Orange Trim	85.00
Bowl, Nut	25.00
Chocolate Pot, Cobalt Blue	75.00
Cup, Parasol	18.00
Plate, 6 In.	10.00

GENE AUTRY was born in 1907. He began his career as the *Singing Cowboy* in 1928. His first movie appearance was in 1934, his last in 1958.

Book, Big Little Book	40.00
Book, Gene Autry & Bad Men Of Broken Bow, Cover, Whitman, 1951	16.00
Book, Gene Autry Land Grab Mystery, Better Little Book, 1948	20.00
Book, Law Of The Range, Big Little Book, 1939	35.00
Book, Rearing Champion, Little Golden Book, 1955	28.00
Book, Song, 1938	35.00
Cap Gun, Gold	140.00
Cap Gun, Kenton	55.00
Cap Gun, Leslie Henry, 10 In., Pair	240.00
Cap Gun, Pearl Handle	125.00
Guitar, Roundup Scene, Pick, 1938	140.00
Lamp, Covered Prairie Wagon, Gene, Champion & Melody Ranch, 12 In.	475.00
Lunch Box, Melody Ranch, Metal, Universal, 1954-1955	800.00
Pennant, Back In The Saddle Again, Purple, Cloth	45.00
Pistol, Golden, No. 103, Die Cast, Leslie-Henry, 1950, 7 1/2 In., Box	285.00
Pistol, Kenton, Cast Iron, 1940	125.00
Postcard, Gene Autry Shirts, Sturdiboy, 5 x 3 1/4 In.	5.00
Poster, Movie, Gene Autry & The Mounties, P. Buttram, 1950, 27 x 41 In.	150.00
Puzzle, 1950, 20 Piece	30.00
Puzzle, Color Photo With Champion, No. 2628, Whitman, 1954	42.00
Record Set, Gene Autry Melody Ranch, 33 RPM, 1954, 4 Piece	50.00
Sheet Music, That Silver Haired Daddy Of Mine, Gene Autry Picture, 1932	10.00
Ukulele	90.00
Viewmaster Reel, No. 950	15.00
Wristwatch, Moving 6 Gun, 1948	185.00
Wristwatch, Six Shooter, Animated Gun, Box, 1951	475.00

GIBSON GIRL black-and-blue decorated plates were made in the early 1900s. Twenty-four different 10 1/2-inch plates were made by the Royal Doulton pottery at Lambeth, England. These pictured scenes from the book *A Widow and Her Friends* by Charles Dana Gibson. Another set of twelve 9-inch plates featuring pictures of the heads of Gibson Girls had all-blue decoration. Many other items also pictured the famous Gibson Girl.

Drawing, Bust Portrait, Oval, Signed C.D. Gibson, 13 x 9 1/4 In.	715.00
Engraving, Lady Driving Car, Sickels, Frame, 11 1/2 x 15 In.	47.00
Plate, Miss Babbles Brings A Copy, 10 1/2 In.	100.00 to 125.00

Print, Somewhere In France, Fisher, Frame, 1918 .... 40.00

GIRL SCOUT collectors search for anything pertaining to the Girl Scouts, including uniforms, publications, and old cookie boxes. The Girl Scout movement started in 1912, two years after the Boy Scouts. It began under Juliette Gordon Low of Savannah, Georgia. The first Girl Scout cookies were sold in 1928.

Clip, Sweater.. 20.00
Compass, Nickel, Box, 1943 .... 25.00
Manual, Scouting For Girls, 557 Pages, 1920 .... 22.00

GLASS-ART. Art glass means any of the many forms of glassware made during the late nineteenth or early twentieth century. These wares were expensive and production was limited. Art glass is not the typical commercial glass that was made in large quantities, and most of the art glass was produced by hand methods. Later twentieth-century glass is listed under Glass-Contemporary, Glass-Midcentury, or Glass-Venetian. Even more art glass may be found in categories such as Burmese, Cameo Glass, Tiffany, Venini, and other factory names.

Basket, Amber With Cream & Brown Spatter, Pulled Up Corner Edges, Handle, 6 In... 355.00
Bottle, Irregular Rim, Internal Fissured Glass, Maurice Marinot, 1925, 7 1/2 In. 6900.00
Bowl, Floral & Foliate Gilt Design, Open Handles, Loetz Type, Round, 8 x 4 1/2 In. 99.00
Candlestick, Stylized Florals, Karl Massanetz, c.1914, 5 3/4 In., Pair............................ 7475.00
Charger, Carp, Ruby Cut To Clear, Shallow Lip, Concave, France, 19 1/2 In. 330.00
Cologne, Pink & White Spatter, White Blown Ball Stopper... 75.00
Compote, Stylized Florals, Karl Massanetz, c.1914, 7 In., Pair 2875.00
Enameled, Cylindrical, Everted Rim, 3 Panels, Hunter, Deer, M. Goupy, 6 1/4 In. 2990.00
Pitcher, Georges De Feure, c.1910 .... 495.00
Powder Jar, Cover, Rosaline, Alabaster Knob, c.1900, 7 In. 275.00
Punch Set, Amethyst Blown Glass, Carved Lines, 8 Tumblers, France, c.1930 .... 330.00
Tumbler, Pink Ear Of Corn, Cased... 29.00
Vase, Aventurine, Footed 75.00
Vase, Band Of Floral Arabesques, August Jean, c.1880, 7 1/4 In............................... 1725.00
Vase, Emerald Cut To Clear, Fired-On Gold, Hohners, Austria, c.1910, 13 In. 110.00
Vase, Neoclassical, Blue, Eagle, Chains, Marble, 19th Century, 8 1/2 In., Pair 4025.00
Vase, Stylized Nude Male Hunter, Deer On Reverse, Marcel Goupy, 6 1/4 In. 2940.00

GLASS-CONTEMPORARY includes pieces by glass artists working after 1975. Many of these pieces are free-form, one-of-a-kind sculptures. Paperweights by contemporary artists are listed in the Paperweight category. Earlier studio glass may be found listed under Glass-Midcentury or Glass-Venetian.

Bowl, Irregularly Cut, Painted Segments, Jay Musler, 1987, 10 1/2 In............................ 3700.00
Bowl, Wavy Rim, Multicolored, Toots Zynsky, 1987, 11 1/4 In. 3450.00
Sculpture, Cube, Fused & Laminated, J. Kuhn, 1987, 7 1/4 In..................................... 1050.00
Sculpture, Homage To Escher, Diamond Mark, M. Peiser, 1986, 10 In. 9775.00
Sculpture, IS068, Triangular, Colored Layers, M. Peiser, 1983, 7 In. 2185.00
Sculpture, Magnum Scarlet Kiss, J. Kuhn, 1982, 8 1/4 x 6 1/2 In. 3000.00
Sculpture, Messa III, 3 Obelisk Forms, Jose Chardiet, 1988, 28 In. 4000.00
Shade, Gold Iridescent, Flaring To 5-In. Fluted Lip, Lundberg, 7 In............................. 100.00
Vase, Flora, Lotton, 10 1/4 In.. 630.00
Vase, Internal Cane & Ribbon Design, Richard Ritter, 1980, 9 In. 750.00
Vase, Iridized Blue, Silver Heart & Vine, Lundberg Studios, 1979 .... 250.00
Vase, Iridized Opalescent, Charles Lotton, 5 1/2 In. 595.00
Vase, Jack-In-The-Pulpit, Rainbow Iridescent, Deep Ruby, 10 1/4 In........................... 100.00
Vase, Paperweight, Country Road, M. Peiser, 1981, 7 3/8 In....................................... 9775.00
Vase, Silver King Tut Design, Red, Lotton, 1978 .... 550.00
Vessel, Round, Geometric Surface Design, William LeQuier, 1984, 5 In. 1265.00
Vessel, Twisted Shoulder, Iridized Shards, W. Morris, 1981, 9 In.................................. 1725.00

GLASS-MIDCENTURY refers to art glass made from the 1950s to the 1980s. Some glass factories, such as Baccarat or Orrefors, are listed under their own categories. Earlier glass may be listed in the Glass-Art and Glass-Contemporary categories. Italian glass may be found under Venini and Glass-Venetian.

Bowl, Multicolored, Lobed, Glass & Silver, 1950s, Italy, 10 1/2 In. 375.00
Bowl, Rounded Triangle, Translucent Blue, P. Holmegaard Lutken, 12 In. 60.00
Sculpture, Jonah & Whale, Kosta 195.00
Vase, Bulbous, Narrow Neck, Charles Lotton, 1971, 4 In. 350.00
Vase, Deep Red, Gold Iridescent Highlights, Dominick Labino, 5 5/8 In. 495.00
Vase, Flared, Angled Top, Translucent Blue, P. Holmegaard Lutken, 10 In. 60.00
Vase, Mold-Blown, Clear Tapio Wirkkala, Iittala, No. 3429, 9 1/2 In. 88.00
Vase, Unica, Bottle Shape, Opaque White, Leerdam, Meydam, 15 1/2 In. 225.00

GLASS-VENETIAN. Venetian glass has been made near Venice, Italy, since
the thirteenth century. Thin, colored glass with applied decoration is favored,
although many other types have been made. Collectors have recently become
interested in the Art Deco and fifties designs. Glass was made on the Venetian island of Murano from 1291. The output dwindled in the late seventeenth
century, but began to flourish again in the 1850s. Some of the old techniques
of glassmaking were revived, and firms today make traditional designs and
original modern glass. Since 1981, the name *Murano* may only be used on
glass made on Murano Island. Other pieces of Italian glass may be found in
the Glass-Contemporary, Glass-Midcentury, and Venini categories of this
book.

Basket, Green, Red Label, Murano 22.00
Berry Bowl, Mica Flecked Connector, Ruby 45.00
Bottle, Clown, Large, Murano 85.00
Bowl, Dense Bubbles, Internal Colors, Aureliano Toso, Dino Martens, 6 In. 300.00
Bowl, Entwined Blue & White Helix Design, 9 1/4 In. 150.00
Bowl, Intarsia, Red, Clear, Triangular Patchwork, E. Barovier, 10 In. 690.00
Bowl, Mezza-Filigrana Bianca/Nera, Aureliano Toso, D. Martens, 8 In. 250.00
Bowl, Multicolored Applied Designed Handles, Footed, 6 x 11 1/2 In. 10.00
Bowl, Owl Shape, Murrina Eyes, Cenedese, 1960, 9 In. 120.00
Candlestick, Amethyst, Applied Feet, Cappellin, V. Zecchin, 1920, 13 In., Pair 700.00
Candlestick, Cylindrical, Cupped Holders, Iridescent, Murano, 6 In., Pair 220.00
Candy Dish, Swan Shape, Pink With Apple Green Head, 6 In. Diam 85.00
Centerpiece, Cornucopia Type, Green, Murano, 17 In. 40.00
Compote, Red Ribbing, Green, Paper Label, Salviati & Co., 6 1/4 In. 295.00
Cordial, Green, Floral & Gilt Design, 3 3/4 In., 6 Piece 66.00
Decanter, Smiling Clown Form, White & Amber Eyes & Stopper, 11 1/2 In. 38.00
Figurine, 2 Birds, On Stand, Red & Blue, 8 In. 90.00
Figurine, Angel Fish, Morretti, 15 1/2 x 13 In. 600.00
Figurine, Bear, 6 In. 35.00
Figurine, Bird, Internal White Latticino, Black Legs, Salviati, 17 1/2 In. 385.00
Figurine, Bird, Yellow, White Gold Aventurine, 10 In. 110.00
Figurine, Clown, Spangle Glass, Murano, 8 1/2 In. 85.00
Figurine, Clown, With Accordion, Murano, 12 In. 45.00
Figurine, Colonial Woman, Latticino Skirt, Gold Leaf, Murano, 11 In. 120.00
Figurine, Creche Scene, Salviati & Co., 11 1/4 In., 7 Piece. 1200.00
Figurine, Duck, 6 In. 35.00
Figurine, Fish, 7 In. 65.00
Figurine, Man & Woman, A. Canne, Barovier & Toso, 1960, 11 1/2 In., Pair 1430.00
Figurine, Peasant Man & Woman, Holding Basket Of Apples, 12 In., Pair 575.00
Figurine, Pelican, Red, 8 In. 85.00
Figurine, Pheasant, Cranberry, Gold Deposits, Murano, Savatini & Co., 15 In. 185.00
Figurine, Red Bird, Pedestal, Amber Tail, Signed 35.00
Figurine, Rooster, Multicolor, 10 In. 65.00
Figurine, Swan, White & Gold Filigrana, Aureliano Toso, D. Martens, 5 1/2 In. 250.00
Figurine, Woman, Blue Gown, Large Hat, 12 In. 250.00
Figurine, Woman, Swirled Skirt & Shawl, Murano, 9 1/2 In. 66.00
Paperweight, Frosted, Cobalt To Clear, Thin Neck, Wavy Lip, Murano, 12 In. 195.00
Paperweight, Pear, Murano 110.00
Paperweight, Swan, Murano 56.00
Perfume Bottle, Gold Dust Stopper, Segusso, 5 In. 295.00
Perfume Bottle, Latticino, Conic Base, Gold Crown Stopper, Seguso, 5 In. 295.00
Perfume Bottle, Seguso, Goll Dsu Crown, 5 In. 295.00
Pezato, Symmetrical Patchwork, Pale Colors, Barovier & Toso, 17 In. 2990.00

Vase, Allover Design Of Cut Canes, 1950, 12 In. 95.00
Vase, Allover Multicolored Floral Design, Cream Ground, 5 3/4 In. 160.00
Vase, Applied Pink Roses, Footed, 8 1/2 In. 145.00
Vase, Basilissa, Bell Shape, Short Neck, Vistosi, E. Sottsass Jr., 1977, 10 In. 2420.00
Vase, Bell Shape, Yellow, Black, Vistosi, E. Sottsass Jr., 1977, 8 In. 1870.00
Vase, Blue, Rigaree Ruffled, Murano, 10 In. 325.00
Vase, Bulbous Bottom, Flared, Spout, Applied Canes, Fratelli Toso, 1960, 8 In. 175.00
Vase, Controlled Bubbles, Donut Handles, Barovier & Toso, 1940, 6 In. 500.00
Vase, Controlled Bubbles, Iridized, Applied Handles, Murano, 5 In. 330.00
Vase, Enameled Flower, Green, Murano, Tall 45.00
Vase, Grillwork, Baluster, Flared Rim, Gold Leaf, Archimede Seguso, 16 In. 470.00
Vase, Handkerchief, Mezza Filigrana 70.00
Vase, Intarsia, Multicolored Triangles, Barovier & Toso, 1961, 14 In. 7150.00
Vase, Patchwork, Internal Gold Foil Inclusions, 1970s, 20 3/4 In. 5175.00
Vase, Pezatto, Fulvio Bianconi, 7 In. 7425.00
Vase, Pezatto, Fulvio Bianconi, 11 In. 5225.00
Vase, Pezatto, Pale Patchwork, Barovier & Toso, 17 In. 3000.00
Vase, Plum Canes, Spiral Bands, Alberto Toso, 1950, 15 In. 525.00
Vase, Pulegoso-Type, Zecchin-Martinuzzi, N. Martinuzzi, 1933, 6 In. 2530.00
Vase, Sommerso, Cased, Blue, Green, Murano, 1950, 20 In. 360.00
Vase, Sommerso, Curved Teardrop, 4 Internal Layers, Seguso, F. Polo, 7 In. 255.00
Vase, Sommerso, Green Interior, Cased, Seguso Vetri D'art, 10 In. 66.00
Vase, Squared Shape, Controlled Bubbles, Barovier & Toso, 1940, 8 In. 60.00
Vase, Swirled Body, Internal Bubbles, Blue & White, 8 1/4 In. 40.00
Vase, Swirling White & Green Canes, Multifold Rim, Alberto Toso, 11 In. 300.00
Wine, Gilt Floral Design, 8 1/4 In., 6 Piece 99.00

GLASSES for the eyes, or spectacles, were mentioned in a manuscript in 1289 and have been used ever since. The first eyeglasses with rigid side pieces were made in London in 1727. Bifocals were invented by Benjamin Franklin in 1785. Lorgnettes were popular in late Victorian times. Opera glasses are listed in their own category.

Brass, Flat X-Shaped Nasal Bridge, Loop Temporal Piece, Oval Green Lenses, 1840 ... 145.00
Brass, O. Parker, Pat.1872, Canada, Cigar Shaped Tin Case 45.00
Brass, Turnpin Type Temporal Pieces, Ends In Loops, Oval Lenses, Running Deer Mark 88.00
Coin Silver, Extendible Temporal Ending In Loops, Cigar Shaped Leather Case 90.00
Coin Silver, Long Temporal Piece, Loops, Oval Lenses, Marked Pure Coin & No. 6 ..... 48.00
Coin Silver, Oval Lenses, Oval Loops, McAllister, Philadelphia 185.00
Coin Silver, Turnpin Type Temporal Pieces, Loops, Green Lenses, Fisher, Philadelphia 195.00
Lorgnette, Mother-Of-Pearl, Silver Frame, Fixed Round Lenses, Mid-19th Century 110.00
Lorgnette, Sterling Silver, Round Bifocal Lenses, Decorated Handle, Releasing Knob . 85.00
Lorgnette, Textres Scrolling Handle, Flora Link Chain 315.00
Lorgnette, Unplated Steel, Large Round Lenses, Releasing Knob On Shaft 42.00
Magnifying, Round In Gold Mount, Figure Of Child, Ruby Accent, Tiffany 460.00
Plated Brass, Extendible Temporal Piece, Oval Loop, Papier-Mache Case 65.00
Sharpshooter, Amber, Clear Centers, Civil War, Case 130.00
Silver, Extendible Temporal Pieces Ends In Shields, Oval Lenses, London, 1809 .... 125.00
Silver, Wide Extendible Temporal Pieces, Ending Small Shields, London, 1825 .... 115.00
Silver Frame, Folding, Into Mother-Of-Pearl Cover, Scissor Type, Early 1800s 950.00
Spectacles, Brass Nose Rest, Plain Glass, Salesman's Sample, 15 1/4 In. 255.00
Steel, Flat x Shaped Nasal Bridge, Large Circular Lenses, Early 19th Century 95.00
Steel, Wide Extendible Temporal Pieces, Circular Loops, Oval Steel Case 95.00
Tortoiseshell, Folding, Short Handle, Circular Loop 48.00
White Metal, Extendible Temporal Pieces, Ending In Loops, Oval Lenses 26.00

GOEBEL is the mark used by W. Goebel Porzellanfabrik of Oeslau, Germany, now Rodental, Germany. Many types of figurines and dishes have been made. The firm is still working. The pieces marked *Goebel Hummel* are listed under Hummel in this book.

Ashtray, Cardinal Tuck, Red 425.00
Ashtray, Friar Tuck 30.00
Bank, Money Sack 15.00

Bookends, Bulldog, Blue, Gray, & White 125.00
Condiment Set, Friar Tuck, Stylized Mark 75.00
Cookie Jar, Monk 495.00
Creamer, Cardinal Tuck 125.00
Figurine, After Tea, No. 1874 .... 50.00
Figurine, Bambi, Full Bee 18.00
Figurine, Boy, Carrying Ladder, Full Bee 55.00
Figurine, Boy, Seated, Playing Accordion 55.00
Figurine, It's Cold, No. 421 .... 160.00
Figurine, Ride Into Christmas, No. 396 .... 225.00
Figurine, Schnauzer, 7 3/4 x 8 1/2 In. 45.00
Figurine, Viscountess Diana, No. 1769 .... 50.00
Holder, Cigarette, Cardinal Tuck, Red 450.00
Mug, Nude Handle, Marked, 4 1/2 In. 88.00
Pitcher, Cardinal, No. 541/0, Stylized Mark 275.00
Pitcher, Elephant, Orange, Crown Mark, 5 In. 80.00
Pitcher, Friar Tuck, No. 141/0, Stylized Mark 225.00
Plate, Midnight Clear 15.00
Plate, Santa's Helpers, Poole, Box, 1978 .... 50.00
Salt & Pepper, Bride & Groom, Full Bee 65.00
Salt & Pepper, Cats 30.00
Salt & Pepper, Chicken 20.00
Salt & Pepper, Chimney Sweep 50.00
Salt & Pepper, Flower, Skunks, Full Bee, 3 In. 155.00
Salt & Pepper, Friar Tuck, Full Bee .... 25.00 to 65.00
Salt & Pepper, Monk, Full Bee Mark 30.00
Salt & Pepper, Rabbit & Chick, 1960 .... 30.00
Salt & Pepper, Skunks, Full Bee 55.00
Salt & Pepper, Squirrel & Acorn, Bull Bee 48.00
Sugar & Creamer, Friar Tuck 60.00
Sugar & Creamer, Tray, Friar Tuck, Stylized Mark, 3 Piece 60.00

GOLDSCHEIDER has made porcelains in three places. The family left Vienna in 1938 and started factories in England and in Trenton, New Jersey. The New Jersey factory started in 1940 as Goldscheider-U.S.A. In 1941 it became Goldscheider-Everlast Corporation. From 1947 to 1953 it was Goldcrest Ceramics Corporation. In 1950 the Vienna plant was returned to Mr. Goldscheider and the company continues in business. The Trenton, New Jersey, business, now called *Goldscheider of Vienna*, imports all of the pieces.

Bust, Foo Girl 50.00
Bust, Madonna, 9 In. 65.00
Dish, Powder, Woman Emerging From Disk Lid, Ball Feet, 7 1/2 In. 258.00
Figurine, Afghan Hound, 12 In. 125.00
Figurine, Austrian Terrier, 7 In. 225.00
Figurine, Butterfly Girl, c.1930, 11 1/2 In. 1550.00
Figurine, Cotillion, 5 3/4 In. 85.00
Figurine, Courtesy, 10 In. 160.00
Figurine, Dancing Nude Indian Maiden, Terra-Cotta, 14 In. 110.00
Figurine, Girl, Holding Skirt, 5 In. 250.00
Figurine, Goldcrest Pheasant, 14 In. 100.00
Figurine, Juliet With Doves, Rose, Gray, Cobalt Blue, 12 1/4 In. .... 200.00 to 225.00
Figurine, Lady, With Parasol, 11 In. 150.00
Figurine, Nude Female, Seated, Terra-Cotta, 25 In. 460.00
Figurine, Old Virginia, Signed, 8 1/2 In. 125.00
Figurine, Penguin 245.00
Figurine, Red Headed Bird 35.00
Figurine, Royal Blackamoor, Barbara Loveday, 15 In., Pair 1500.00
Figurine, Seated Nude, Matte Rust, No. 8726-15, 25 In. 460.00
Figurine, Sing Lo, Oriental, Holding Bird, Pagoda & Bird House, 7 1/4 In. 32.00
Figurine, Summer, Woman 65.00
Figurine, Viennese Woods 135.00
Figurine, White Christmas 135.00

Figurine, Woman With Parasol, Skirt, Muff, Ermine Trim, 11 In.	175.00
Figurine, Woman, Long Dress, White, Blue & Yellow, Hat & Muffler, 8 1/2 In.	95.00
Group, 3 Dancing Girls, Ruffled Skirts, c.1925, 14 In.	3795.00
Plate, Mermaid	150.00

GOLF, see Sports category

GONDER Ceramic Arts, Inc., was opened by Lawton Gonder in 1941 in Zanesville, Ohio. Gonder made high-grade pottery decorated with flambe, drip, gold crackle, and Chinese crackle glazes. The factory closed in 1957. From 1946 to 1954, Gonder also operated the Elgee Pottery, which made ceramic lamp bases.

Bank, Sheriff, Green	450.00
Bank, Sheriff, Yellow	600.00
Ewer, Shell & Star, Green, 13 In.	50.00
Figurine, Black Panther, 18 1/2 In.	75.00
Figurine, Modern Cat, No. 521, Yellow & Brown Drip Glaze, 12 In.	475.00
Figurine, Swan, Gray	20.00
Lazy Susan, Signed, Miniature	250.00
Planter, Swan, Yellow, Pink Mottling, 5 In.	16.00
Vase, Aqua, 6 1/2 In.	30.00
Vase, Handles, Aqua, 6 1/2 In.	30.00
Vase, Turquoise, Pink, Gray, Mottled, Twisted High Side Handles, 8 3/4 x 5 3/4 In.	15.00

GOOFUS GLASS was made from about 1900 to 1920 by many American factories. It was originally painted gold, red, green, bronze, pink, purple, or other bright colors. Many pieces are found today with flaking paint and this lowers the value.

Bowl, Roses, 10 1/2 In.	35.00
Plate, Red & Silver	28.00
Vase, Bird, Vines & Berries, 9 In.	65.00
Vase, Cockatoo, 9 In.	55.00
Vase, Cockatoo, 12 1/2 In.	85.00
Vase, Statue Of Liberty, 13 In.	175.00

GOUDA, Holland, has been a pottery center since the seventeenth century. Two firms, the Zenith pottery, established in the eighteenth century, and the Zuid-Hollandsche pottery, made the brightly colored wares marked *Gouda* from 1880 to about 1940. Many pieces featured Art Nouveau or Art Deco designs.

Chamberstick, Atrium, 6 1/2 In.	100.00
Creamer, Enamel Highlights, Black, 2 1/2 In.	45.00
Decanter, Applied Bead Design, Shades Of Green, 1928, 9 1/2 In.	230.00
Decanter, Nadra, 10 1/2 In.	150.00
Dish, Cover, Flowers, Leaves, Anjer House Mark, Gouda, Holland, 1888	73.00
Ewer, White Paisley Type Design, Blue, Angular Handle, Royal Plazuid, 1950s, 11 In.	70.00
Figurine, Skier & Dancer, Pair	75.00
Inkwell, Pen Tray, Cover, Ivora, Signed, 10 1/2 In.	325.00
Inkwell, Triangle Shape, Black Ground, Marked, Regina WB, House	150.00
Lamp, Oil, Roba, 7 1/2 In.	185.00
Lantern, Candle, 7 In.	250.00
Pitcher, Embossed Bali Dancers, Blue & White	195.00
Pitcher, Zwaro Mark, 4 In.	30.00
Tobacco Jar, Verona, 5 In.	85.00
Vase, Art Nouveau Design, High Glaze, Zuid, c.1896, 11 In.	650.00
Vase, Baluster Shape, 2 Handles, Floral Design, B.O. Ivora, Holland, 16 1/2 In.	460.00
Vase, Curra, Bulbous, 7 In.	125.00
Vase, Damascus Lotus, Matte Glaze, Signed, 11 In.	230.00
Vase, Green, Black & Red, 5 In.	80.00
Vase, Holland Palma, Florals, 6 x 5 In.	125.00
Vase, Matte Glaze, Green & Cobalt Blue Design, Cream Ground, Signed, 10 1/4 In.	375.00
Vase, Multicolored Flowers, High Glaze, 11 1/2 In., Pair	440.00
Vase, Roosters, Blue & Mustard, Emerald Ground, 19 In.	500.00

Vase, Stick, Colorless Glaze Over Green, Gold & Orange Design, 8 1/2 In. 210.00
Vase, Stylized Blue & Mustard Roosters, Emerald Ground, 19 In. 500.00
Vase, Woman's Portrait, Handles, 12 In. 350.00

GRANITEWARE is an enameled tinware that has been used in the kitchen
from the late nineteenth century to the present. Earlier graniteware was green
or turquoise blue, with white spatters. The later ware was gray with white
spatters. Reproductions are being made in all colors.

Ashtray, Polar Wear 115.00
Bidet, Cover, Portable, French, Porcelain Over Tin 225.00
Bowl, Blue Mottled, 12 In. 75.00
Bucket, Black & White Speckled, Majestic, 10 In. 35.00
Bucket, Brown & White Mottled, 11 In. 70.00
Can, Milk, Blue & White 165.00
Canister, Tea, Blue 70.00
Canister Set, Cobalt Blue, White Plaid, 6 Piece 195.00
Canister Set, Robin's-Egg Blue, 4 Piece 130.00
Churn, Butter, Blue, 1873 .... 2100.00
Churn, No. 30, Flower Molded On Base 235.00
Coffee Boiler, Cover, Blue & White Mottled 175.00
Coffee Boiler, Cover, Emerald With Cream Swirl, Large 335.00
Coffee Boiler, Green & White Swirl 195.00
Coffeepot, Chrysolite 250.00
Coffeepot, Gooseneck, Yellow, Guard Top 60.00
Coffeepot, Gray, Medium 30.00
Coffeepot, Green & White Swirl 240.00
Coffeepot, Light Blue Sponged, Large 140.00
Coffeepot, Swan Neck Handle, Blue & White 45.00
Coffeepot, Tin Hinged Spout, Wooden Handle, Speckled Green 90.00
Coffeepot, Tin Lid, Brown 100.00
Coffeepot, Tin Lid, Gray, 6 Cup 42.00
Coffeepot, Tin Lid, Wooden Knob, Lilac & White, Garnet Label, 8 Cup 115.00
Colander, Blue & White Swirl 85.00
Colander, Octagonal, Footed 90.00
Cooking Set, Child's, White, Black Trim, 5 Piece 195.00
Cup & Saucer, Cobalt & White Swirl 120.00
Cuspidor, Hand-Held 170.00
Cutter, Biscuit, Gray 350.00
Double Boiler, Blue & White 100.00
Funnel, Black Handle, Blue, Medium Size 15.00
Funnel, Blue Swirl, White Interior 260.00
Kettle, Preserving, Green & White, Austria 150.00
Ladle, Blue, Black Handle, Small 8.00
Lunch Bucket, White 100.00
Milk Can, Lid, Blue & White, Mottled, 11 In. 120.00
Mold, Melon, Tin Bottom & Band, Gray 145.00
Muffin Tin, Dark Cobalt Blue, Marbleized 300.00
Pail, Berry, Blue 110.00
Pail, Berry, Robin's-Egg Blue Swirl 65.00
Pail, Blue & White Marbleized, Small 95.00
Pan, Angel Food Cake, Gray 40.00
Pan, Blue & White Marbleized, 9 x 12 In. 100.00
Pan, Muffin, Mottled Gray, 8 Cup 40.00
Pan, Muffin, Turk's Head, Gray, 6 Cup 125.00
Pie Plate, Purple, White Mottled, 9 1/2 In. 15.00
Pitcher, Blue & White Swirl, 7 1/2 In. 110.00
Pitcher, Child's, Blue Mottled 66.00
Pitcher, Measuring, Gray, 1 Qt. 35.00
Pitcher, Snow On The Mountain, 8 In. 55.00
Platter, Meat, Aqua & White Swirl, White Inside, Black Trim 95.00
Roaster, Cover, Dark Blue Spatter, Savory 13.00
Roaster, Light Blue Speckled, Savory 20.00
Roaster, Robin's-Egg Blue, Dated 1911, 4 Piece 95.00

Roaster, Robin's-Egg Blue, Mottled, Oval, 3 Piece 60.00
Roaster, With Tray, Blue & White... 95.00
Rolling Pin, White, Gray Handles 695.00
Salt Box, Hanging, Blue 75.00
Skillet, Dark Blue Spatter, 6 In... 12.00
Skillet, Wagner, Red & Black, Cast Iron, No. 0 .... 26.00
Skimmer, Gray.. 8.00
Skimmer, Hand, Crysolite 200.00
Spoon, Mixing, White 10.00
Table, Alphabet, Numbers 1 To 10 In Center, Storybook Characters 225.00
Tea Set, Blue, Teapot, Creamer, Sugar, 4 Cups & Saucers, Germany, Box 575.00
Teapot, Black Handle, Blue, 3 Cup ......) 22.00
Teapot, Blue Swirl, 4 Cup .... 100.00 to 120.00
Teapot, Gooseneck, Cream & Green 65.00
Teapot, Green, 2 Cup 40.00
Teapot, Green, Tangerine Interior, 6 In. 75.00
Teapot, With Stand, Blue 795.00
Trivet, Green.. 79.00
Wash Pan, Blue & White Marbleized 65.00

GREENTOWN glass was made by the Indiana Tumbler and Goblet Company of Greentown, Indiana, from 1894 to 1903. In 1899, the factory name was changed to National Glass Company. A variety of pressed, milk, and chocolate glass was made. Additional pieces may be found in other categories, such as Chocolate Glass, Custard Glass, Holly Amber, Milk Glass, and Pressed Glass.

Berry Set, Cord Drapery, 6 Piece 125.00
Bowl, Cord Drapery, 7 1/2 In. 22.00
Butter, Cover, Herringbone Buttress, Green 200.00
Cake Stand, Emerald Green... 525.00
Cracker Jar, Emerald Green... 375.00
Creamer, Dewey, Amber, 5 In. 25.00
Creamer, Lattice, Blue 38.00
Cruet, Dewey, Amber, Original Stopper 105.00
Dish, Cat On Hamper Cover, Red Agate Ears, Brown 525.00
Dish, Fighting Cocks Cover, Canary.. 2700.00
Dish, Fighting Cocks Cover, Emerald Green 1600.00
Dish, Hen On Nest Cover, Golden Agate 1500.00
Dish, Hen On Nest Cover, Milk Glass 125.00
Dish, Mitted Hand, Crystal, 7 In. 25.00
Goblet, Austrian, Blue 60.00
Mustard, Cover, Daisy, White 75.00
Pitcher, Cactus 350.00
Pitcher, Diamond, Amber 900.00
Pitcher, Ruffled Eye, Amber... 125.00
Pitcher, Ruffled Eye, Canary 500.00
Pitcher, Squirrel.. 150.00 to 500.00
Punch Cup, Herringbone Buttress.. 80.00
Sugar, Cover, Austrian.. 52.00
Sugar, Cover, Dewey 115.00
Sugar, Cover, Leaf Bracket 85.00
Sugar, Dolphin, Blue... 150.00
Toothpick, Sheaf Of Wheat, Nile Green... 475.00
Tray, Dewey, Serpentine, Amber, 8 1/4 In. 40.00
Tumbler, Cactus 65.00
Tumbler, Goblet 60.00
Tumbler, Pleat Band, Etched 55.00
Tumbler, Tassel, Blue 75.00
Tumbler, Teardrop & Tassel, Blue 75.00
Tumbler, Teardrop, Blue 75.00

GRUEBY Faience Company of Boston, Massachusetts, was incorporated in 1897 by William H. Grueby. Garden statuary, art pottery, and architectural tiles were made until 1920. The company developed a matte green glaze that was so popular it was copied by many other factories making a less expensive type of pottery. This eventually led to the financial problems of the pottery.

Bowl, Circular High Glaze, Ribbed Matte Exterior, 9 x 2 In.	250.00
Bowl, Doughnut, Textured Blue-Green, 4 In.	240.00
Bowl, Finger Rings On Bottom, Green Glaze, Signed, 9 1/2 In.	606.00
Bowl, Thick Green Glaze, Signed, 1 1/2 x 4 1/2 In.	385.00
Lamp Base, Quatrefoils & Leaves, Acorn Pattern Shade, Signed, 20 x 16 In.	1875.00
Tile, 2 Winged Angels, Family Crest, White, Pale Brown Glaze, 6 x 6 In.	325.00 to 360.00
Tile, Brown & Ivory Galleon, Blue Sky, Trivet, Copper Mounted, 6 1/4 In.	1085.00
Tile, Brown Clay Geometric Design, Blue Matte Ground, Die Stamp, 3 In., 12 Piece	220.00
Tile, Brown Ship, White Sails, Dark Green Ground, Oak Frame, 8-In. Square	1800.00
Tile, Frieze, Water Lilies, Green Pads, Matte Green Pond, Framed, 6-In. Tiles, 3 Piece	6600.00
Tile, Galleon Ship, On Unglazed Bisque, Red Ground, 6 x 6 In.	495.00
Tile, Geometrics, 2 Colors, Signed, 3 x 3 In.	75.00
Tile, Heraldic Flower, Ocher Ground, Stylized, Painted KC, 6 In.	640.00
Tile, Knight On Horseback, Polychrome, Square, 6 In.	275.00
Tile, Landscape, Mountain & Sky, Oak Frame, 4 1/2 In.	1045.00
Tile, Mermaid Rising From Waves, Holding Mirror, Stylized Design, Square, 6 In.	825.00
Tile, Monk Playing Cello, Matte Blue & Brown Glaze, 6 x 6 In.	495.00
Tile, Pine Trees, Green Shades, Blue & Brown Glaze, 6 x 6 In.	1325.00
Tile, Sailing Ship, Signed, c.1909, 4 x 4 In.	345.00
Tile, Spanish Ship, Oak Frame, M.D., Square, 4 In.	550.00
Tile, St. Matthew, Stylized Angel, Matte Pumpkin & Dark Blue, 7 3/4 In.	1075.00
Tile, Textured & Crackled White Glaze, Red Ground, Signed, Square, 7 3/4 In.	350.00
Tile, Turtle, Green Leaves, Brown Ground, Signed, Square, 6 In.	525.00
Tile, Water Lily Design, 3 Piece	6600.00
Tile, White Bird, Black Beak, On Branch, Blue Ground, Green Frame, 6 In.	640.00
Tile, Yellow Rabbit, Cabbage Patch, Dark Green Ground, Trivet, Painted CA, 6 In.	1265.00
Vase, 5 Vertical Leaves, Marie Seaman, 5 x 3 3/4 In.	825.00
Vase, Allover Textured Matte Green Glaze, Signed, 4 1/4 In.	425.00
Vase, Allover Thick Yellow Glaze, Signed, 2 x 4 In.	358.00
Vase, Alternating Low Relief Buds On Long Stem, Signed, c.1905, 7 In.	1600.00
Vase, Alternating Low Relief Laces, Buds, Green Glaze, Signed, 12 In.	2105.00
Vase, Alternating Low Relief Leaves & Buds, Signed, 5 1/2 In.	800.00
Vase, Applied & Tooled Leaves, Yellow Matte Suspended Glaze, 14 1/2 In.	3850.00
Vase, Baluster Form, Stylized Leaves, Green Glaze, Marked, 22 1/2 In.	8975.00
Vase, Bulbous Bottom, Rising To Flaring Neck, Green Glaze, Signed, 8 In.	990.00
Vase, Bulbous, Applied Leaves, Vertical Ribs, Blue Matte Glaze, 8 1/2 In.	2200.00
Vase, Bulbous, Tooled Leaves, Oatmeal Matte Glaze, 3 1/2 In.	1045.00
Vase, Carved Leaves, Oatmeal Matte Glaze, 5 In.	385.00
Vase, Carved Vertical Leaf Design, Dark Green Glaze, Signed, 10 1/2 In.	3190.00
Vase, Incised Lines Between 6 Vertical Panels, Signed, 9 In.	1600.00
Vase, Leaves Below Vertical Ribs, Thick Blue Glaze, Signed, 11 1/2 In.	2200.00
Vase, Light Blue Matte Glaze, Broad Shoulders, 4 1/2 x 3 In.	660.00
Vase, Lotus Bud Design, Matte Yellow Glaze, 6 3/4 In.	6325.00
Vase, Rolled Rim, Curdled Mustard Matte Glaze, Signed, 7 In.	550.00
Vase, Squatty, 6 Leaves Encircling Body, Matte Green, 5 1/2 x 6 In.	1980.00
Vase, Stovepipe Neck, Applied Leaves, Organic Matte Green Glaze, Signed, 5 In.	950.00
Vase, Thin Leaves, Matte Green, Ruth Erickson, 3 1/2 In.	495.00
Vase, Tooled Leaves, Yellow Blossoms, Squatty, Wilhemina Post, 4 3/4 In.	2970.00
Vase, Vertical Leaf Design, Signed, 4 1/2 x 6 In.	1325.00
Vase, Vertical Leaves Covered In Green Glaze, Signed, 6 x 9 1/2 In.	5225.00
Vase, White Matte Glaze, Flower Impressed Mark, 3 x 2 1/4 In.	330.00

GUNDERSON glass was made at the Gunderson-Pairpoint Glass Works of New Bedford, Massachusetts, from 1952 to 1957. Gunderson Peachblow is especially famous.

Bowl, Peachblow, Footed, 10 1/2 In.	275.00
Champagne, Peachblow, Stemmed, 5 1/2 In.	350.00
Epergne, Peachblow, 10 1/2 x 9 In.	278.00
Pitcher, Peachblow, 4 3/4 In.	154.00

A glass vase or bowl can be cleaned with a damp cloth. Try not to put the glass in a sink filled with water. Hitting the glass on a faucet or the sink is a common cause of breakage.

Gustavsberg, Vase, Silver Crowns, Blue, S. Jonson, 5 1/8 In.

Vase, Peachblow, 3 3/4 In., Pair	82.00
Vase, Peachblow, Matted, 6 1/2 In.	95.00

GUNS that may be classed as toys, such as BB guns, air rifles, and cap guns, are listed in the Toy category.

GUSTAVSBERG ceramics factory was founded in 1827 near Stockholm, Sweden. It is best known to collectors for its twentieth-century art wares, especially a green stoneware with silver inlay called *Argenta*. **Gustafsberg**

Ashtray, West Highland, Green Sponging, Signed	65.00
Bowl, Fish Blowing Bubbles, Argenta, 6 1/2 In.	315.00
Figurine, Cat, Carved & Patinated, Hollow, 12 x 4 In.	358.00
Jar, Cover, Silver Inlay, 3 3/4 In.	385.00
Pitcher, Leaf Design, White, Stig Lindberg, 5 x 6 In.	40.00
Smoke Set, Holder & 4 Ashtrays, Argenta, Green	125.00
Urn, Cover, Flattened, 2 Handles, Mottled Green, Silver Maidens, 1930, 9 1/2 In.	1360.00
Urn, Cover, Silver Diaphanously Draped Maidens, Signed, 1930, 9 /12 In.	1380.00
Vase, Incised & Painted Organic Design, Blue Ground, 1920, 13 In.	468.00
Vase, Ship, Silver Crowns, S. Jonson, 5 In.	145.00
Vase, Silver Crowns, Blue, S. Jonson, 5 1/8 In. ....*Illus*	125.00
Vase, Silver Florals & Butterflies, White Ground, Grazia, Marked, 6 In.	175.00
Vase, Silver Inlay, 8 In.	550.00

GUTTA-PERCHA was one of the first plastic materials. It was made from a mixture of resins from Malaysian trees. It was molded and used for daguerreotype cases, toilet articles, and picture frames in the nineteenth century.

Case, Beehive Design, Ambrotype Bearded Man, Dated 1857, 1/6 Plate	70.00
Case, Cartouche Design, Tintype, Baby Girl & Boy, 1/6 Plate	95.00
Case, Green Velvet, Tintype, Man, Business Suit, 1/4 Plate	75.00
Pedestal, Classical Maiden Form Support, White Marble Top, Victorian, 43 In.	825.00
Pipe, Bowl, Pipe In Form Of Gun	50.00
Ward's Collar Box, Brown, Picture Of Playing Cards	120.00

HAEGER Potteries, Inc., Dundee, Illinois, started making commercial art wares in 1914. Early pieces were marked with the name *Haeger* written over an *H*. About 1938, the mark *Royal Haeger* was used. The firm is still making florist wares and lamp bases.

Bookends, Ram, Pink	37.00
Bowl, Freeform Oval, Cream, 11 x 6 In.	12.00
Candlestick, Double, Trumpet Flowers On Leaf Form, Black, 8 x 5 1/2 In.	22.00
Centerpiece, Leaf, Applied Fruit Cluster, Black Exterior, 20 x 6 In.	32.00
Cookie Jar, Keebler Tree House	95.00

Figurine, Egyptian Cat, No. 658, Green... 35.00
Figurine, Mountain Lion.. 55.00
Planter, Figural, Mermaid, Flesh Tones, Gold Highlights, 22 In............................... 85.00
Planter, Girl Holding Basin In Lap, Green Dress, Long Braid, 11 x 9 x 10 In. 25.00
Vase, Brown, Orange & Yellow Snakeskin, Square, 10 In. 45.00
Vase, Figural, Gazelle, Brown, Green Streaks, 13 In. 65.00
Vase, Figural, Swan, Dark Green, Mottled, Gunmetal, 13 In..................................... 35.00
Vase, Gold Fluted, Art Deco, 9 In... 35.00
Vase, Leaf & Berry, Mottled Brown 20.00
Vase, Mermaid & Shell, Gray & Blue, 15 In. 90.00
Vase, Snake Skin, Brown Base, Square, 10 In. ....60.00 to 90.00

HALF-DOLL, see Pincushion Doll category

HALL CHINA Company started in East Liverpool, Ohio, in 1903. The firm made many types of wares. Collectors search for the Hall teapots made from the 1920s to the 1950s. The dinnerwares of the same period, especially Autumn Leaf pattern, are also popular. The Hall China Company is still working. For more information, see *Kovels' Depression Glass & American Dinnerware Price List*. Autumn Leaf pattern dishes are listed in their own category in this book.

Blue Blossom, Batter Bowl... 130.00
Blue Blossom, Batter Jug, Banded.. 175.00
Blue Blossom, Cookie Jar, 5 Bands.. 250.00
Blue Blossom, Jug, 1 1/2 Pt. 45.00
Blue Blossom, Jug, 2 Pt... 55.00
Blue Blossom, Jug, Ball, No. 1.. 175.00
Blue Blossom, Jug, Ball, No. 2.. 175.00
Blue Blossom, Jug, Ball, No. 3.. 150.00
Blue Blossom, Jug, Banded, 1 1/2 Pt... 95.00
Blue Blossom, Salt & Pepper, Handles 75.00
Blue Garden, Casserole, Cover, Cobalt Blue 55.00
Bouquet, Plate, Dinner, 9 In... 13.00
Casual Living, Bowl, Salad.. 80.00
Casual Living, Sugar & Creamer 45.00
Cattail, Casserole, Cover, 8 1/2 In. 45.00
Cattail, Casserole, Cover, 9 1/4 In. 45.00
Cattail, Platter, 15 In.. 40.00
Cattail, Soup, Dish.. 20.00
Christmas Tree, Plate, 10 In... 20.00
Christmas Tree, Plate, 7 1/4 In... 16.00
Crocus, Bean Pot.. 150.00
Crocus, Cup & Saucer 15.00
Flareware, Casserole, 3 Pt. 15.00
Flareware, Coffee Server... 30.00
Flareware, Cookie Jar... 45.00
Flareware, Cookie Jar, White, Gold Lace, 2 Handles ....75.00 to 100.00
Flareware, Trivet, Gold Lace... 15.00
Floral Lattice, Syrup 40.00
French Russet, Coffeepot, Drip 30.00
Heather Rose, Mug, Irish Coffee 12.00
Holly, Sugar & Creamer 35.00
Hotpoint, Leftover, Daffodil, No. 4, Square, 6 3/4 In. 22.00
Marine, Cereal Set.. 550.00
Morning Glory, Bean Pot, Pastel.. 110.00
Mt. Vernon, Creamer, Sears.. 5.00
Old Crow, Punch Set, 11 Piece..130.00 to 165.00
Pheasant, Coffeepot, Percolator.. 95.00
Poppy, Bean Pot, Orange 75.00
Poppy, Bowl, 6 In. 8.00
Poppy, Casserole, Oval, 8 In..55.00 to 75.00
Poppy, Coffeepot 30.00
Poppy, Cookie Jar... 110.00

Poppy, Jug Ball, Red 28.00
Poppy, Mixing Bowl, 10 In. 85.00
Poppy, Salt & Pepper, Handles 35.00
Poppy, Sifter, Tin 45.00
Poppy, Sugar, Cover 20.00
Poppy & Wheat, Casserole, 5 Band, 8 In. 90.00
Poppy & Wheat, Pitcher, Cover, Small 100.00
Radiance, Jug, Sunshine, No. 1 .... 125.00
Radiance, Jug, Sunshine, No. 2 .... 125.00
Red Poppy, Bread Box 23.00
Red Poppy, Bread Plate 6.00
Red Poppy, Coffeepot, Daniel .... 30.00 to 45.00
Red Poppy, Coffeepot, Drip 35.00
Red Poppy, Cup & Saucer 8.00
Red Poppy, Plate, 10 In. 9.00
Red Poppy, Plate, 9 In. 6.00
Red Poppy, Salt & Pepper, Handles 40.00
Red Poppy, Salt & Pepper, Range 30.00
Red Poppy, Sugar & Creamer 40.00
Red Poppy, Tumbler, Frosted, 6 Piece 90.00
Refigerator Ware, Jug, Loop, Yellow 125.00
Rose Parade, Baker, French 15.00
Rose Parade, Bean Pot, Cadet Blue, Tab Handles 45.00
Rose Parade, Bowl, Salad, 9 In. 22.00
Rose Parade, Casserole, Blue, Tab Handle 50.00
Rose Parade, Casserole, Cover, Tab Handles, Blue 28.00
Rose Parade, Creamer 15.00
Rose White, Casserole, Round, Tab Handle 35.00
Shaggy Tulip, Coffee Set, Drip, Kadota, 8 Piece 120.00
Shaggy Tulip, Coffeepot, Metal Drip 70.00
Shaggy Tulip, Sugar, Handle 30.00
Silhouette, Baker, French 12.00
Silhouette, Casserole 42.00
Silhouette, Coffeepot 90.00
Silhouette, Leftover, Rectangular 27.00
Silhouette, Pretzel Jar 115.00
Silhouette, Tray, Rectangular 35.00
Springtime, Plate, 8 1/4 In. 5.00
Stonewall, Sugar Shaker, Handle 45.00
Sundial, Coffeepot, Red 260.00
Sundial, Cookie Jar, Saf-Handle 225.00
Teapot, Airflow, Cobalt Blue, Gold Trim .... 60.00 to 95.00
Teapot, Airflow, Maroon 120.00
Teapot, Airflow, Red .... 100.00 to 140.00
Teapot, Aladdin, Cadet Blue, Gold Trim .... 50.00 to 125.00
Teapot, Aladdin, Infuser, Pink 55.00
Teapot, Aladdin, Oval Infuser, Pink 85.00
Teapot, Aladdin, Wildfire 175.00
Teapot, Aladdin, Yellow 32.00
Teapot, Alton, Delphinium Blue 185.00
Teapot, Autumn Leaf 45.00
Teapot, Baltimore, Yellow 50.00
Teapot, Basket, Canary 75.00
Teapot, Boston, Canary, 2 Cup 50.00
Teapot, Boston, Dresden, Gold, 6 Cup 38.00
Teapot, Boston, Emerald, Gold Trim 50.00
Teapot, Bouquet, Zeisel 60.00
Teapot, Cameo Rose 50.00
Teapot, Car, Blue, Silver Spout From Grill 350.00
Teapot, Cleveland, Yellow 55.00
Teapot, Cube, Green 50.00
Teapot, Delphinium, Gold Trim 275.00
Teapot, Donut, Chinese, Red .... 150.00 to 415.00

Teapot, Donut, Red...295.00 to 550.00
Teapot, Flareware, Gold Lace.. 45.00
Teapot, Football, Red 950.00
Teapot, French Lipton 55.00
Teapot, French, Brown, Gold Trim, 1 Cup 65.00
Teapot, Globe, Delphinium 90.00
Teapot, Gold Band, Yellow 95.00
Teapot, Gold Dot, Windshield... 55.00
Teapot, Grape, Cobalt Blue 225.00
Teapot, Hook Cover, Canary 30.00
Teapot, Hook Cover, Chinese Red.. 95.00
Teapot, Illinois, Maroon 155.00
Teapot, Indiana, Warm Yellow... 150.00
Teapot, Kansas, Emerald 385.00
Teapot, Los Angeles, Yellow, Gold Trim.............................. 22.00
Teapot, Margaret Thatcher 250.00
Teapot, Marine, Car.. 750.00
Teapot, McCormack, Maroon.. 20.00
Teapot, McCormack, Old Rose.. 20.00
Teapot, McCormick, Burgundy 25.00
Teapot, Melody, Poppy 290.00
Teapot, Nautilus, Maroon 225.00
Teapot, New York, Cobalt Blue, 2 Cup 65.00
Teapot, New York, Green, 4 Cup 25.00
Teapot, New York, Red Poppy 72.50
Teapot, Parade, Yellow 55.00
Teapot, Philadelphia..22.00 to 35.00
Teapot, Poppy, Boston 55.00
Teapot, Poppy, Donut 375.00
Teapot, Poppy, Streamline... 275.00
Teapot, Radiance 275.00
Teapot, Red Poppy 40.00
Teapot, Ronald Reagan..25.00 to 65.00
Teapot, Rose Parade 25.00
Teapot, Rose Parade, Boston 110.00
Teapot, Royal Rose, French... 65.00
Teapot, Rutherford, Orange Dot 275.00
Teapot, Saf-Handle, Yellow 60.00
Teapot, Silhouette, Colonial 50.00
Teapot, Star, Orange... 180.00
Teapot, Streamline, Poppy 250.00
Teapot, Streamline, Silhouette.. 325.00
Teapot, Surfside, Emerald 95.00
Teapot, Surfside, Emerald & Gold 80.00
Teapot, Tea For 2, Blue.. 165.00
Teapot, Town & Country, Zeisel 345.00
Teapot, Twin Spout, Chinese Red 125.00
Teapot, Twin Spout, Forest Green 70.00
Teapot, Wildfire, With Sugar & Creamer, 3 Piece................. 110.00
Teapot, Windshield, Golden Clover 190.00
Tom & Jerry, Cup... 5.00
Tritone, Pitcher, Large.. 175.00
Tulip, Bean Pot... 90.00
Tulip, Coffee Set, Dripolator, 4 Piece 125.00
Westinghouse, Jug, Tilt, Delphinium Blue, No. 3................... 28.00
Westinghouse, Leftover, Cover, Yellow, Oval 30.00
Wildfire, Bowl, Vegetable, 9 In. 25.00
Wildfire, Tidbit, 3 Tiers 50.00
Zeisel, Butter, Cover, Painted 50.00
Zeisel, Coffeepot, Classic White ....250.00 to 320.00
Zeisel, Cookie Jar, Golden Clover 150.00
Zeisel, Creamer, Classic White, After Dinner 25.00
Zeisel, Gravy Boat, Classic White 35.00

Zeisel, Plate, Salad	35.00
Zephyr, Bottle, Water, 7 Oz.	275.00
Zephyr, Butter, Cover	425.00

HALLOWEEN is an ancient holiday that has been changed in the last 200 years. The jack-o'-lantern, witches on broomsticks, and orange decorations seem to be twentieth-century creations. Collectors started to become serious about collecting Halloween-related items in the late 1970s. The papier-mache decorations, now replaced by plastic, and old costumes are in demand.

Candy Container, Cat, Black, Molded Cardboard, Spring Neck, Germany, 6 In.	35.00
Candy Container, Cat, Papier-Mache, Germany, 1950s, 7 1/2 In.	32.00
Candy Container, Jack-O'-Lantern, Slanted Eyes	65.00
Candy Container, Pumpkin Head, Bulging Eyes, Pulls Apart, 5 In.	185.00
Candy Container, Pumpkin Head, Witch	750.00
Candy Container, Pumpkin, Orange, Painted Face, Pull Slide, Germany, 3 x 2 In.	175.00
Candy Container, Pumpkin, Papier-Mache, Germany, 1950s, 4 In.	32.00
Candy Container, Witch On Pumpkin	110.00
Candy Container, Witch, Composition, Germany	185.00
Candy Container, Witch, Composition, Straw Hair, Broom, Pull-Off Head, 7 In.	595.00
Candy Container, Witch, Papier-Mache, Germany, 1950s, 7 1/2 In.	32.00
Candy Container, Witch, Papier-Mache, Red & Black, Germany, 1950s, 7 1/2 In.	45.00
Cat, Orange, Pulp, 7 In.	245.00
Costume, Addams Family, Morticia, Box	198.00
Costume, Annie Oakley, c.1950	65.00
Costume, Annie Oakley, Playmaster, Box	105.00
Costume, Bewitched, Samantha	38.00
Costume, Bigfoot, Sid & Marty Krofft, Box, 1977	95.00
Costume, Bret Maverick, Boxed, 1950s	155.00
Costume, Casper, Box, 1950s	100.00
Costume, Cowboy, Child's, Neiman Marcus	150.00
Costume, Darth Vader, Box, 1977	35.00
Costume, Dr. Jekyll & Mr. Hyde, 2-Face Mask, 1964	98.00
Costume, Empire Strikes Back, Ben Cooper	75.00
Costume, Fred Flintstone, Ben Cooper, Box, 1961	55.00
Costume, Jetson, Masquerade, 1972	55.00
Costume, Mary Hartline, 1950s	95.00
Costume, Mighty Mouse, Child's, Flannel, 1958	35.00
Costume, Quick Draw McGraw, Ben Cooper, Box, 1959	55.00
Costume, Shazzan, Ben Cooper, Box, 1967	75.00
Costume, Skeleton, Sears, 3 Pieces, Box, Large Size	40.00
Costume, Snoopy, Collegeville, Box	20.00
Costume, Snow White, Box, 1940s	60.00
Costume, Tonto, Hatchet, String Of Beads, 1950s	85.00
Costume, Witch, Collegeville, Box	15.00
Costume, Wyatt Earp, 1930s	95.00
Costume, Zorro, Ben Cooper, 1950s	25.00
Doorstop, Black Cat Silhouette, Cast Iron, 9 1/4 In.	65.00
Flashlight, Pumpkin Head, Celluloid, 2 1/2 In.	85.00
Game, Cat And Witch, Box	45.00
Game, Spook Cat, Glow-In-The-Dark Tail, Envelope	45.00
Hat, Pirate Shape, Crepe Tassel, Honeycomb Insert, 1920	22.00
Jack-O'-Lantern, Orange, Black Molded Hair Bows, 5 In.	75.00
Jack-O'-Lantern, Spring Arms & Legs, Battery Operated, Box	115.00
Jack-O'-Lantern, Tin, Painted Face, Kazoo Nose, U.S. Metal Toy Mfg. Co., 1940s	95.00
Jack-O'-Lantern, Torch Light, Tin, c.1930	85.00
Jack-O'-Lantern, Trick Or Treat, Tin Litho, U.S. Metal Toy Mfg. Co., 6 In.	165.00
Lantern, Black Cat	140.00
Lantern, Cat Head Shape, Orange Paint	85.00
Lantern, Devil Head, Germany, 2 1/4 x 2 1/2 In.	245.00
Lantern, Owl, Pumpkin Face, Witch & Cat, Cardboard, Black, 6 In.	62.00
Lantern, Skull, 2 x 3 In.	150.00
Lantern, Skull, Orange Paper Inserts, 1940s	45.00
Lantern, White Skull, Black, Cardboard, 5 x 10 In.	75.00

Mask, Alien, Plastic	7.00
Mask, Colonel Sanders	25.00
Mask, Devil, Tip-Top Bread Give-A-Way, 1948	25.00
Mask, Fred Munster, Rubber, 1990s	35.00
Napkins, Vegetable People, Sealed Package, 1940s	38.00
Noisemaker, 2 Jack-O'-Lanterns, Tin, Wooden Stick, 1940s, 10 x 5 In.	38.00
Noisemaker, Black Cat, Tin	15.00 to 35.00
Noisemaker, Elsie Head, Tin	150.00
Noisemaker, Pumpkin, Witch, Cat, Metal, Wooden Handle, 4 In.	32.00
Noisemaker, Safety Cracker, Red, White & Blue, Patent 1918	25.00
Noisemaker, Witch & Devil Ball	195.00
Paper Doll, Dolly Dingle Celebrates Halloween, 1927	15.00
Pattern, Devil's Costume, Butterick, 1921	20.00
Pumpkin Face, Cardboard Hat, 8 In.	45.00
Scarecrow, Orange & Black, Honeycomb Tissue, Pull Up Arms, Cardboard, 7 3/4 In.	43.00
Skeleton, Die Cut, Germany, 37 In.	175.00
Squeaker, Smiling Face, German, 5 In.	295.00
Tambourine, Black Cat Head, Witch & Cat Head Rings, Painted	45.00
Tambourine, Metal, 6 In.	35.00
Whirligig, Witch, On Broomstick, Wooden, Painted	2750.00

HAMPSHIRE pottery was made in Keene, New Hampshire, between 1871 and 1923. Hampshire developed a line of colored glazed wares as early as 1883, including a Royal Worcester–type pink, olive green, blue, and mahogany. Pieces are marked with the printed mark or the impressed name *Hampshire Pottery* or *J.S.T. & Co., Keene, N.H.* Many pieces were marked with city names and sold as souvenirs.

Bowl, Carved Geometrics, Green Matte Glaze, 5 1/2 In.	385.00
Bowl, Closed Rim, Alternating Leaves & Buds, Green Glaze, Signed, 10 In.	325.00
Bowl, Embossed Flowers, Green Matte Glaze, Squatty, Impressed, 2 x 5 1/2 In.	250.00
Bowl, Embossed Leaves & Buds, Green Matte Glaze, Low, Incised, 3 x 9 3/4 In.	330.00
Bowl, Green Matte Glaze, Closed, Impressed Mark, 3 1/4 x 6 1/2 In.	440.00
Bowl, Interior Drip Green Glaze, 9 In.	145.00
Bowl, Stylized Buds At Rim, Green Matte Glaze, 2 x 9 In.	300.00
Chamberstick, Rolled Rim, Thick Pink-Brown Matte Ground, Signed, 5 3/4 In.	175.00
Compote, 2 Handles, Ivy, Footed, 13 1/4 In.	150.00
Ewer, High Glazed Brown, Signed, 10 x 9 1/2 In.	90.00
Lamp, Veined Green Matte Glaze, Electrified, Bulbous, No Shade, Label, 15 In.	1100.00
Mug, High Glazed Brown, Signed, 5 In.	40.00
Pitcher, Green Matte Glaze, 6 In.	145.00
Pitcher, Palm Trees, Textured & Veined Matte Glaze, Signed, 11 1/4 In.	325.00
Pitcher, Salem Witch, 6 1/2 In.	175.00
Vase, Blue Green Glaze, Signed, 6 In.	325.00
Vase, Blue Matte Glaze, Cylinder, Incised Mark, 5 1/4 x 3 In.	165.00
Vase, Bulbous, Textured Blue Matte Glaze, 6 1/4 x 5 1/4 In.	385.00
Vase, Dark Blue Matte Drip Over Blue & White Mottled Body, 5 1/2 In.	360.00
Vase, Deep Green Matte Glaze, Finish, 5 In.	225.00
Vase, Dripping Dark To Medium Green Matte Flambe Glaze, Marked, 6 x 3 3/4 In.	275.00
Vase, Embossed Petals, Green, 6 In.	90.00
Vase, Embossed Spade-Shaped Leaves, Green Matte Finish, 7 1/4 In.	550.00
Vase, Full-Length Leaves & Buds, Flowing Blue Matte Glaze, Signed, 6 1/2 In.	450.00
Vase, Grained Green Matte Glaze, Bulbous, Closed Rim, Impressed Mark, 4 x 5 In.	195.00
Vase, Greek Key Design, Mottled Brown, Blue, Green & Gray, Incised, 5 x 5 3/4 In.	315.00
Vase, Green Matte & Red Veinlike Glaze, Impressed Mark, 4 1/4 x 3 1/4 In.	220.00
Vase, Green Matte Glaze, Double Handles, 5 In.	250.00
Vase, Green Matte Glaze, Signed, 8 1/4 In.	450.00
Vase, Green Matte, 2 Handles, Flared, J.S.T. & Co., 14 3/4 x 4 3/4 In.	1650.00
Vase, Leaves Alternating With Buds, Green Matte Glaze, Marked, 7 x 4 1/2 In.	470.00
Vase, Molded Leaves & Buds On Stems, Blue & Black Matte Glaze, 7 In.	415.00
Vase, Overlapping Leaves, Cadmon Robertson, 8 3/8 In.	490.00
Vase, Speckled Gray Matte Glaze, Melon Ribbed, Impressed Mark, 5 1/2 x 6 In.	415.00
Vase, Stylized Leaves, Green Matte Finish, Signed, 7 3/4 In.	550.00
Vase, Twisted Vertical Stems, Folded Rim, Green Matte Glaze, Signed, 8 1/2 In.	660.00

Handel, Lamp, Chipped Ice,
Daffodils, 26 In.

Handel, Lamp, Reverse
Painted Shade, Floral,
22 1/2 In.

Handel, Lamp, Reverse
Painted Shade,
Hollyhocks, Flowers

Handel, Lamp, Table,
Reverse Painted Shade,
Scenic, The Chestnut, 18 In.

Handel, Lamp, Reverse
Painted Shade,
Floral, 25 In.

HANDEL glass was made by Philip Handel working in Meriden, Connecticut, from 1885 and in New York City from 1893 to 1933. The firm made art glass and other types of lamps. Handel shades were made not only of leaded glass in a style reminiscent of Tiffany but also of reverse painted glass. Handel also made vases and other glass objects.

Chandelier, Amber Globe, Painted Forest Scene, Signed, c.1923, 41 In.	4888.00
Humidor, 3 Puppies In Grass, Signed, 6 1/4 x 7 In.	1650.00
Humidor, Green Etched Glass, Copper Fittings, 5 In.	467.50
Humidor, Horse & Dog, Pewter Pipe On Lid	600.00
Humidor, Pipe On Lid	475.00
Lamp, 3 Abalone Shell Shades, Curved Bronze Arms, 14 x 11 In.	770.00
Lamp, 3-Light, Glass Segments Arranged As Flowers, Within Latticework, 18 1/2 In.	3450.00
Lamp, Boudoir, Bronzed Metal & Slag, Signed, 13 1/2 In.	630.00
Lamp, Boudoir, Hexagonal Shade, Interior Landscape	1980.00
Lamp, Boudoir, Reverse Painted Shade, Nocturnal Landscape, No. 6451, 14 In.	1870.00
Lamp, Boudoir, Reverse Painted Shade, Landscape, Bronze Base, No. 6150, 14 In.	2200.00
Lamp, Boudoir, Reverse Painted Shade, Metal Base, Signed, 15 1/2 In.	2310.00
Lamp, Boudoir, Reverse Painted, Chipped Ice Shade, Landscape, Signed, 13 In.	2640.00
Lamp, Boudoir, Slag Glass Shade, Bronzed Metal, Signed, 13 1/2 In.	590.00

Lamp, Bridge, Half-Harp Shade Supports, Bronze, 55 In. 748.00
Lamp, Chipped Ice, Daffodils, 26 In. .... *Illus* 7500.00
Lamp, Cone-Shaped Shade, Caramel Slag, Floral Frame, 16 x 8 In. 660.00
Lamp, Desk, Brown Glass Shade, Bronze Adjustable Base 925.00
Lamp, Egyptian, 18 In. 3500.00
Lamp, Globe, Parrot On Branches Front & Back, Tassel, 10 In. 460.00
Lamp, Mottled Yellow Domed Shade, Orange Wave Pattern, Bronze, 14 In. 1092.00
Lamp, Pendant, Birds, Teroma Surface, 8 In. 4312.00
Lamp, Pine Needle, Red Glass Shade, c.1920, 22 1/2 In. 2875.00
Lamp, Reverse Painted Dome Shade, Landscape, Shaded Sky, Signed, 23 In. 3220.00
Lamp, Reverse Painted Shade, Chrysanthemum, Signed, c.1911, 24 In. 4888.00
Lamp, Reverse Painted Shade, Evergreens, Hampshire Base, Signed, 19 x 14 In. 3100.00
Lamp, Reverse Painted Shade, Floral, 22 1/2 In. .... *Illus* 15000.00
Lamp, Reverse Painted Shade, Floral, 25 In. .... *Illus* 7150.00
Lamp, Reverse Painted Shade, Hollyhocks, Flowers .... *Illus* 30800.00
Lamp, Reverse Painted Shade, Landscape, Bird, No. 7024, John Baily, 18 x 22 In. 4400.00
Lamp, Reverse Painted Shade, Landscape, Green, Tan Trees, Orange Water, 15 In. 2970.00
Lamp, Reverse Painted Shade, Mountain & River, Tree Trunk Metal Base, 18 In. 7700.00
Lamp, Reverse Painted Shade, Treasure Island, Metal Base, Signed, 24 1/2 In. 8050.00
Lamp, Reverse Painted Shade, Treasure Island, Cruciform Foot, Signed, 27 In. 7425.00
Lamp, Reverse Painted Shade, Winter Scene, Metal Base, Signed, 21 In. 3025.00
Lamp, Student, Frosted Tam-Shaped Shade, Green & Pink Floral 1300.00
Lamp, Table, Dutch Harbor Scene, Shade, 17 3/4 In. 5195.00
Lamp, Table, Reverse Painted Shade, Scenic, The Chestnut, 18 In. .... *Illus* 13200.00
Torchere, Cylinder Shade, Molded Bronzed Metal Base, 57 In. 1100.00
Torchere, Cylinder Shade, Yellow Daisies, Bronzed Metal Base, 13 In., Pair............... 2035.00
Vase, Cut Back Floral, Frosted Colorless, Signed, 10 In. 1495.00

HARDWARE, see Architectural category.

HARKER Pottery Company of East Liverpool, Ohio, was founded by Benjamin Harker in 1840. The company made many types of pottery but by the Civil War was making quantities of yellowware from native clays. They also made Rockingham-type brown-glazed pottery and whiteware. The plant was moved to Chester, West Virginia, in 1931. Dinnerwares were made and sold nationally. In 1971 the company was sold to Jeannette Glass Company and all operations ceased in 1972. For more information, see *Kovels' Depression Glass & American Dinnerware Price List.*

Berry Bowl, Everglades, Coral, 5 2/3 In. 5.00
Bowl, Mallow, 6 1/4 In. 14.00
Bowl, Pate-Sur-Pate, Green & White, 5 1/2 In. 1.50
Bowl, Utility, Red Apple, Set Of 3 .... 65.00
Cake Plate, Corinthian, Handled, Teal & Cream Gadroon Border, 10 1/2 In. 8.00
Cake Server, Petit Point 15.00
Casserole, Cover, Everglades, Coral 35.00
Cup & Saucer, Cameo Rose, Demitasse, Light Blue & White 12.00
Cup & Saucer, Mallow 14.00
Custard, Cameoware, Blue, Rack, 6 Piece 40.00
Pie Lifter, Pastel Tulip 30.00
Pie Plate, Petit Point, 9 In. 15.00
Pie Server, Lovelace 30.00
Pitcher, Oriental Poppy 45.00
Plate, Everglades, Coral, 10 In. 12.00
Plate, Laurelton, 8 In. 44.50
Plate, Mallow, 6 In. 4.00
Plate, Mallow, 9 In. 14.00
Plate, Petit Point, 10 In. 10.00
Rolling Pin, Amy 135.00
Rolling Pin, Modern Tulip 95.00
Rolling Pin, Petit Point Rose... 65.00 to 135.00
Rolling Pin, Red Apple II... 135.00
Soup, Dish, Everglades, Coral, 7 1/2 In. 8.00
Sugar & Creamer, Cameoware, Blue 22.00
Teapot, Cameoware, Blue... 35.00

HARLEQUIN dinnerware was produced by the Homer Laughlin Company from 1938 to 1964, and sold without trademark by the F. W. Woolworth Co. It has a concentric ring design like Fiesta, but the rings are separated from the rim by a plain margin. Cup handles are triangular in shape. For more information, see *Kovels' Depression Glass & American Dinnerware Price List.*

Ashtray, Saucer Type, Red	75.00
Bowl, Salad, Gray, Individual	20.00
Candleholder, Yellow, Pair	225.00
Casserole, Turquoise	95.00
Creamer, Maroon	20.00
Creamer, Rose, Individual	30.00
Cup, Turquoise, Demitasse	28.00
Cup, Yellow, Demitasse	28.00
Cup & Saucer, Medium Green	18.00
Eggcup, Chartreuse	30.00
Eggcup, Double, Gray	25.00
Eggcup, Double, Yellow	25.00
Eggcup, Spruce Green	38.00
Figurine, Cat, Maroon	165.00
Figurine, Cat, Yellow	145.00
Figurine, Donkey, Spruce	90.00
Figurine, Duck, Maroon	115.00
Figurine, Duck, Yellow	125.00
Figurine, Fish, Mauve	125.00
Figurine, Lamb, Mauve	110.00
Figurine, Penguin, Maroon	120.00 to 170.00
Gravy Boat, Red	22.00
Jug, Yellow, 22 Oz.	55.00
Nappy, Chartreuse, 9 In.	45.00
Pitcher, Ball, Red	50.00 to 65.00
Pitcher, Ball, Spruce	60.00
Pitcher, Chartreuse, 22 Oz.	85.00
Pitcher, Orange	50.00
Pitcher, Red	40.00
Pitcher, Rose, Medium Green, 10 In.	30.00
Pitcher, Spruce	85.00
Pitcher, Water, Rose	75.00
Plate, Chartreuse, 7 In.	8.00
Plate, Chartreuse, 9 In.	15.00
Plate, Maroon, 9 1/2 In.	12.00
Plate, Red, 10 In.	28.00
Plate, Salad, Mauve, Individual	45.00
Platter, Chartreuse, 13 In.	30.00
Platter, Turquoise, 10 1/2 In.	6.00
Soup, Cream, Maroon	20.00
Soup, Cream, Spruce Green	20.00
Soup, Dish, Mauve	30.00 to 35.00
Sugar, Cover, Chartreuse	20.00
Sugar, Cover, Maroon	40.00
Sugar, Turquoise Handle	20.00
Teapot, Mauve	95.00
Teapot, Red	105.00
Teapot, Rose	85.00
Teapot, Turquoise	55.00
Teapot, Yellow	70.00

HATPIN collectors search for pins popular from 1860 to 1920. The long pin, often more than four inches, was used to hold the hat in place on the hair. The tops of the pins were made of all materials, from solid gold and real gemstones to ceramics and glass. Be careful to buy original hatpins and not recent pieces made by altering old buttons.

Art Deco, White, Black & White Rhinestones, Pair 24.00
Art Nouveau, Green Stones 125.00
Art Nouveau, Webb-Like Design, Turquoise Pearls & Diamonds Both Sides, France ... 2300.00
Black Opaque Glass 5.00
Cameo, Lady At Well & Lady By House 165.00
Crystal, Rhinestone & Pearl 10.00
Garden Path, Carnival Glass 145.00
Greyhound Route, 10 In. 65.00
Lady's Head, Art Nouveau, Brass 48.00
Marcasite, Sterling Silver 15.00
Openwork, Garnet, Gold Filled, 9 1/2 In. 75.00
Owl, Blue, Robert Hanson 160.00
Rhinestone, Square, 1 1/2 In. 85.00
Rhinestones, Bakelite, Black 35.00
Rooster, Carnival Glass, Blue 60.00
Sword Shape, 60 Seed Pears, 1 Sapphire, 14K Yellow Gold 275.00
Tennis Racket, Silver Plated 25.00
Turban, Carnival Glass 150.00

HATPIN HOLDERS were needed when hatpins were fashionable from 1860 to
1920. The large, heavy hat required special long-shanked pins to hold it in
place. The hatpin holder resembles a large saltshaker, but it often has no
opening at the bottom as a shaker does. Hatpin holders were made of all types
of ceramics and metal. Look for other pieces under the names of specific
manufacturers.

Blue & White, Germany 39.00
Figural, Bear & Tree Stump, Heart Shape Base, 3 1/4 In. 85.00
Figural, Poodle 110.00
Hand-Painted Violets, Beaded, 4 In. 75.00
Hanging, Cornucopia Shape, Apple Blossoms, Nippon 275.00
Jasperware, Cherubs 65.00
Pastel Roses, Germany 120.00

HAVILAND china has been made in Limoges, France, since 1842. The factory
was started by the Haviland Brothers of New York City. Pieces are marked *H
& Co.*, *Haviland & Co.*, or *Theodore Haviland*. It is possible to match exist-   HAVILAND & CO.
ing sets of dishes through dealers who specialize in Haviland china. Other
factories worked in the town of Limoges making a similar chinaware. These
porcelains are listed in this book under Limoges.

Berry Bowl, Blue Garland, 5 In. 8.00
Berry Bowl, Trailing Vines, Violet Flowers 12.00
Chocolate Set, Baltimore Rose, 13 Piece 1650.00
Chocolate Set, Dainty Flower Sprays, Pink Shades, Gold Trim, Ruffled, 5 Piece 185.00
Coffeepot, Apple Blossom, Gold Trim, Red Mark, No. 146 .... 295.00
Compote, Roses, Hand Painted, Porcelain, 4 3/4 In. 93.50
Compote, White Ground, Hand Painted, Silver & Gilt Decoration 77.00
Cracker Jar, Bluebells, Cobalt Blue, Gold 125.00
Cup & Saucer, Apple Blossom, Gold Trim 25.00
Ice Cream Set, Blown Roses, Foliage, Gold Edge, Hand Painted, 1890s, 7 Piece 875.00
Mustard, Cover, Rabbit, White, Gold Trim, G.M. Sandoz, 2 x 3 In. 275.00
Oyster Plate, Pink & Blue Flowers, 9 In. 80.00
Oyster Plate, Yellow Roses, Brown Leaves, 4 Wells 80.00
Plate, Apple Blossom, Gold Trim, 8 In. 20.00
Plate, Clover, 6 In. 12.00
Plate, Cobalt & Gilt Border, 9 1/2 In., Pair 115.00
Plate, Dessert, 7 1/4 In., 10 Piece 247.00
Plate, Swirls, Hand Painted, Blackberries & White Flowers, c.1887, 8 1/2 In. 40.00
Plate, Thistles, Butterfly & Bird, Open Handles, 9 1/2 In. 48.00
Plate, Trailing Vines, Violet Flowers, 9 In. 15.00
Platter, Apple Blossom, Gold Trim, Oval, 12 In. 55.00
Platter, Athena, 14 In. 190.00
Platter, Springtime, 16 In. 95.00

Sauce Boat, Apple Blossom, Flow Blue 12.00
Server, Vegetable, Cover, Trailing Vines, Violet Flowers, 1930s 125.00
Sugar, Cover, Flowers, Gold Lines & Trim 12.00
Sugar & Creamer, Apple Blossom, Gold Trim, Tall 135.00
Tray, Hand Painted, Scalloped Edges, Gold Gilt & Roses, 14 x 7 In................. 125.00
Tureen, Cover, Delicate Floral, Ivory Ground, 12 In. 88.00
Urn, Alpine Landscape Scene, Geometric Border, Ernest Chaplet, 16 In. 5750.00
Vase, Sang De Boeuf, Chaplet, 3 1/2 In.. 450.00

HAWKES cut glass was made by T. G. Hawkes & Company of Corning, New York, founded in 1880. The firm cut glass blanks made at other glassworks until 1962. Many pieces are marked with the trademark, a trefoil ring enclosing a fleur-de-lis and two hawks. Cut glass by other manufacturers is listed under either the factory name or in the general Cut Glass category.

Bowl, Allover Geometric Design, Signed, 8 In.. 75.00
Bowl, Blown-Out, 8 Panel, Marked, 3 x 10 In. 1425.00
Bowl, Chrysanthemum, Oval, 9 3/4 In. 580.00
Bowl, Hamilton, Signed, 8 In... 350.00
Bowl, Hobstar & Fan, Notched 6-Petal Center, 19th Century, 8 In.................... 290.00
Bowl, Iris, Sterling Silver Base, 6 x 8 In. 350.00
Casserole, Cover, Pedestal Base, Notched Rim, 6 x 8 In. 1950.00
Champagne, Morning Glories, Signed, 6 In... 55.00
Cocktail Mixer, Sterling Silver Top, Signed, 7 1/4 In. 85.00
Cocktail Shaker, Sterling Silver Cover, 13 In. 475.00
Compote, Hobstars, Diamond Point, Teardrop Stem, 12 x 7 In......................... 425.00
Cordial, Louis XIV, 10 Piece 525.00
Cordial Set, Key Pattern, Tray, Decanter, 4 Cordials, Signed 685.00
Dish, Cheese & Cracker, Rose Type Cutting, 4 x 9 In. 55.00
Flower Holder, Cosmos, Signed, 4 x 8 In. 325.00
Lamp, Newport Starred Mushroom Shade, Horizontal Stepped Shaft, 23 In.... 2415.00
Pitcher, Cocktail, Engraved Fighting Cocks, Stirrer, Signed, 16 1/4 In. 230.00
Pitcher, Step-Cut Top, Diamond Point, Hobstar, Fan, 7 In................................ 475.00
Plate, Brilliant Cut, Signed, 10 In. 525.00
Plate, Imperial, Signed, 6 1/2 In. 595.00
Plate, Strawberry & Fan, Signed, 8 In. 60.00
Rose Bowl, Norwood Pattern, 6 1/2 In. 245.00
Sugar & Creamer, Diamond & Geometric Cut Design, Signed, 3 1/2 In........... 40.00
Sugar & Creamer, Hobstars, Cane, Fans, Zipper Handles, 4 1/2 In. 750.00
Tray, Ice Cream, Empress, Signed, 13 In.. 1100.00
Tumbler, Hobstar Design, Triple Notched Handles, 4 1/2 In. 270.00
Tumbler, Russian Cut, 3 3/4 In... 60.00
Tumbler, Russian Cut, Square, 4 1/2 In. 175.00
Vase, Cone Shape, Signed, c.1930, 13 In. 460.00
Vase, Fan, Allover Florals, Notched Ends, Signed, 11 1/4 In............................. 360.00
Vase, Fan, Florals & Ribbons, Applied Green Base, 11 In. 225.00
Vase, Queen's, Trumpet Shape, Lapidary Cut Knop In Stem, Signed, 16 In..... 1320.00
Vase, Stick, Engraved Tiger Lilies, Leaves & Stems, Signed, 16 1/2 In. 220.00
Vase, Trumpet, Teutonic, 10 In. 225.00
Vase, Wild Turkey, Layered Red & Crystal Body, Signed, 12 1/2 In................. 920.00
Water Set, Iris, 7 Piece 600.00

HEAD VASES, generally showing a woman from the shoulders up, were used by florists primarily in the 1950s and 1960s. Made in a variety of sizes and often decorated with imitation jewelry and other lifelike accessories, the vases were manufactured in Japan and the U.S.A. Less elaborate examples were made as early as the 1930s. Religious themes, babies, and animals are also common subjects.

African Woman 65.00
Art Deco, Woman, Brimmed Hat, Yellow Pearl Necklace 55.00
Baby 30.00
Beethoven 85.00
Boy, Winter Hat.. 62.00

Clown, 7 1/4 In.	35.00
Clown, Blue Coat, Yellow Tie, Black Hat, Cole Plate 173, 5 1/4 In.	25.00
Clown, Finger Up To Lips, Red Hat, Yellow Band, Green Tie, Cole Plate 170, 5 1/4 In.	30.00
Double, Boy & Girl	95.00
Girl, Earrings, Pearls	55.00
Girl, Wearing Santa Claus Outfit	25.00
Grandmother, Eyeglasses & Hat	35.00
Halloween, Girl	35.00
Kennedy Set, Jackie, John, Caroline, 1964, Set Of 3	500.00
Kewpie Doll	65.00
Lucille Ball, Tall Hat, Large, Box	400.00
Lucy	42.00
Madonna, Rubens Original	3.00
Margo, 6 In.	55.00
Nun	25.00
Poodle	12.50
Posegay, Green, 8 In.	150.00
Posegay, No. 158	60.00
Praying Boy	55.00
Teenager, Gold Trim	42.00
Woman, Bare Shoulders, Hands Under Chin, Roses, Earrings, 7 In.	50.00
Woman, Blond, Closed Eyes, Earrings, Black Glove, Enesco Label, 6 In.	55.00
Woman, Blond, Pearl Necklace	26.00
Woman, Christmas, Blond, Green Coat, Fur Collar, Eyes Shut, Hat, 1961, 6 1/2 In.	40.00
Woman, Hair Eyelashes, Napco, 159	35.00
Woman, Holding Fan, Black Glove, Closed Eyes, Earrings, Inarco, 6 In.	85.00

HEDI SCHOOP Art Creations, North Hollywood, California, started about 1945 and was working until 1954. Schoop made ceramic figurines and lamps.   *Hedi Schoop S*

Candlestick, Oriental Children, White, Pair	90.00
Cookie Jar, Darner Doll	165.00
Cookie Jar, Queen	1100.00
Dish, Apple, 13 1/2 In.	37.00
Figurine, Bowl, Attached Figural Young Girl, Large	50.00
Figurine, Chinese Child Crying, With Mother	35.00
Figurine, Girl, Oriental	50.00
Figurine, Lady Basket, 7 1/2 In.	30.00
Figurine, Man, Carrying Buckets	45.00
Figurine, Oriental With Buckets, Pair	125.00
Figurine, Oriental Woman, 12 In.	38.00
Figurine, Oriental Women, Holding Parasols, Gold Trim, Facing, 12 In., Pair	125.00
Figurine, Peasant Lady, Ruffled Dress, Bonnet, Drawstring Purse, 10 In.	65.00
Flower Frog, Oriental Boy & Girl, Signed	150.00
Lamp, Oriental Woman, Parasol, Gold Trim, Pair	175.00
Lamp, TV, Comedy & Tragedy	350.00
Planter, French Peasants, Figural, Man & Woman, Pair	135.00
Planter, Horse	45.00
Planter, South American Woman, Long Gown, Basket Over Head, 12 In.	60.00
Vase, Figural, Maria, 12 1/2 In.	55.00
Vase, Stylized Rooster, Iridescent Copper, 14 In.	85.00

HEINTZ ART Metal Shop made jewelry, copper, silver, and brass in Buffalo, New York, from 1906 to 1935, when a new company name was taken and the mark became *Silvercrest*. The most popular items with collectors today are the copper desk sets and vases made with applied silver designs.

Ashtray, Standing, Match Stand, Stylized Floral, Signed, 31 1/2 In.	475.00
Box, Cigarette, Sterling On Bronze	150.00
Box, Sterling On Bronze, 3 1/2 x 4 In.	95.00
Box, Sterling On Bronze, Floral Silver Overlay, Green Patina, Mark, 5 x 10 1/4 In.	275.00
Candlestick, 5 1/2 In., Pair	145.00
Candlestick, Floral Silver Overlay Design, Sterling On Bronze, 5 1/2 In., Pair	275.00
Candlestick, Pointed Drop Design, Silver On Bronze, 5 1/2 In., Pair	357.00

Desk Set, Sterling Silver Flowers, No. 1203, 6 Piece 550.00
Humidor, Cover, Rectilinear Silvered Design, Bronze Ground, Signed, 7 1/2 In. 350.00
Lamp, Bronze Patina, Silver Floral Overlay, Label, 9 1/2 In. 805.00
Lamp, Bulbous Base, Silver Florals, Cutout Shade, 10 In. 1320.00
Lamp, Dark Copper, Silver Stylized Design, Helmet Shade, Flared Base, 10 1/4 In. 660.00
Lamp, Helmet Shade, Art Nouveau Floral, 14 x 13 1/4 In. 1000.00
Smoking Set, Silver On Bronze, Humidor, 8 /14 In., 6 Piece 330.00
Tobacco Jar, Sterling Silver On Bronze, Round, 8 In. 260.00
Vase, Flared Rim, Geometric Design, Silver On Bronze, Monogram, 8 In. 247.00
Vase, Flared Rim, Overlaid Freesia Blossoms, Bronze Ground, Signed, 11 In. 400.00
Vase, Mistletoe, Overlay, Sterling, 9 In. 135.00
Vase, No. 3654X, Sterling Silver & Bronze, 3 3/4 In. 165.00
Vase, Orchid, Corseted Green, Mark, Sterling On Bronze, 12 x 4 1/2 In. 495.00
Vase, Silver Birds & Cattails, Bronze Ground, Signed, 12 In. 400.00
Vase, Silver Flowers, Dark Bronze Ground, Signed, 9 In. 300.00
Vase, Silver Iris Blossoms, Bronze Patina, Signed, 12 In. 2700.00
Vase, Silver Wild Rose, Dark Brown Ground, Signed, 5 x 5 In. 300.00

HEISEY glass was made from 1896 to 1957 in Newark, Ohio, by A. H. Heisey and Co., Inc. The Imperial Glass Company of Bellaire, Ohio, bought some of the molds and the rights to the trademark. Some Heisey patterns have been made by Imperial since 1960. After 1968, they stopped using the *H* trademark. Heisey used romantic names for colors, such as *Sahara*. Do not confuse color and pattern names. The Custard Glass and Ruby Glass categories may also include some Heisey pieces.

Alexandrite, Plate, Square, 7 In. 60.00
Animal, Goose, Wings Down 400.00
Animal, Goose, Wings Up 125.00
Animal, Kicking Colt, 4 In. 175.00
Animal, Kicking Mule, 4 In. 175.00
Animal, Mallard, Wings Up 175.00
Animal, Pony, Standing, 5 In. 50.00
Aristocrat, Candlestick, 1-Light, 7 1/2 In., Pair 110.00
Athena, Sugar & Creamer 45.00
Banded Flute, Cocktail, 3 Oz. 14.00
Banded Flute, Cordial, 1 Oz. 75.00
Banded Flute, Pickle Jar 85.00
Banded Flute, Pitcher, 3 Pt. 195.00
Banded Flute, Sugar & Creamer, Cover 85.00
Banded Flute, Toothpick .... 65.00 to 75.00
Basket, Cruet, Cut 130.00
Beaded Panel, Cruet 60.00
Beaded Swag, Berry Bowl, Emerald 25.00
Beaded Swag, Berry Set, 5 Piece 90.00
Beaded Swag, Berry Set, Opaque White Opalescent, Rose Design, Signed, 7 Piece 410.00
Beaded Swag, Cocktail Shaker, Under Cutting 75.00
Beaded Swag, Goblet, Custard, 8 Oz. 54.00
Beaded Swag, Salt & Pepper 60.00
Beaded Swag, Table Set, Opalescent, 4 Piece 285.00
Beaded Swag, Tankard, Cornflower 150.00
Belle-le-Rose Etch, Goblet, Queen Ann 25.00
Carcassonne, Lafayette Etch, Goblet, Sahara 25.00
Carcassonne, Soda, Classic Etch, Sahara, 12 Oz. 22.50
Carcassonne, Tumbler, Cobalt, 12 Oz. 85.00
Carcassonne, Tumbler, Footed 20.00
Charter Oak, Compote, Pink, 7 In. 75.00
Chintz, Cup & Saucer 27.50
Chintz, Goblet, Water 25.00
Circle Pair, Goblet, Moongleam, 9 Oz. 60.00
Coarse Rib, Sugar & Creamer, Cover, Hotel 48.00
Colonial, Basket, Floral Cut, Mark, 13 1/8 In. 209.00
Colonial, Champagne, 4 1/2 Oz. 5.00
Colonial, Compote 28.50

Colonial, Cordial	6.00
Colonial, Covered Candy With Cut, 1 Lb.	155.00
Colonial, Jug, 3 Qt.	150.00
Colonial, Mustard, Cover, Crystal	32.00
Colonial, Plate, 7 In.	10.00
Colonial, Punch Bowl, Crystal, 14 In.	50.00
Colonial, Punch Cup	8.00
Colonial, Punch Cup, 12 Piece	85.00
Colonial, Sherbet, Low Footed, Deep, 5 Oz.	5.00
Colonial, Spooner, Crystal	25.00
Colonial, Syrup, Sanitary, 5 Oz.	50.00
Colonial, Tumbler, 4 3/4 In.	10.00
Colonial, Tumbler, 5 Oz.	25.00
Columbia, Candleholder, Pair	80.00
Concord Etch, Spanish, Goblet	45.00
Continental, Bottle, Water	50.00
Continental, Creamer	65.00
Continental, Toothpick	145.00
Crystolite, Ashtray, Zircon, Round, 3 1/4 In.	70.00
Crystolite, Bonbon, Heart Shape, Handles, 7 In.	15.00
Crystolite, Bottle, Bitters	175.00
Crystolite, Bowl, Gardenia, Square, 10 In.	95.00
Crystolite, Candle, Black, Round	15.00
Crystolite, Candy, Cover, Footed, Round	80.00
Crystolite, Coaster	6.00
Crystolite, Cruet, Stopper, 3 Oz.	40.00 to 45.00
Crystolite, Cup	16.00
Crystolite, Jug, Ice	100.00
Crystolite, Lamp, Hurricane, Cut	265.00
Crystolite, Mayonnaise, Tray, 2 Handles, Oval, 8 In.	15.00
Crystolite, Nut Cup, Handles, Individual	9.00
Crystolite, Pitcher, Ice, 1/2 Gal.	115.00
Crystolite, Plate, 13 In.	28.00
Crystolite, Plate, 7 In.	9.00
Crystolite, Plate, 8 1/2 In.	10.00
Crystolite, Powder Box, Cover, 4 3/4 In.	50.00
Crystolite, Punch Cup	4.00
Crystolite, Relish, 3 Sections, 8 In.	35.00
Crystolite, Relish, 3 Sections, 9 1/2 In.	22.50
Crystolite, Relish, 3 Sections, Oval, 13 In.	40.00
Crystolite, Relish, 5 Sections, 10 In.	40.00
Crystolite, Sherbet	10.00
Crystolite, Syrup	100.00
Crystolite, Tumbler, 10 Oz.	32.00 to 65.00
Danish Princess, Sherbet, 10 In.	20.00
Dawn, Jam Jar	50.00 to 52.00
Eileen, Sugar & Creamer	45.00
Empress, Ashtray	295.00
Empress, Ashtray, Cobalt	350.00
Empress, Candlestick, Dolphin, Sahara, 6 In.	335.00
Empress, Candlestick, Yellow, Pair	210.00
Empress, Candy Dish, Blank Etched, Dolphin-Footed, Crystal, 6 In.	50.00
Empress, Compote, Yellow, 6 In.	50.00
Empress, Cup & Saucer, Sahara	65.00
Empress, Cup & Saucer, Yellow, Round	42.00
Empress, Cup, Etched, Yellow	32.00
Empress, Dish, Oval	40.00
Empress, Goblet, Water, Pink	70.00
Empress, Liner, Sahara, 6 7/8 In.	12.00
Empress, Mayonnaise, Sahara, Footed, 5 1/2 In.	45.00
Empress, Mustard, Cover, Flamingo	65.00
Empress, Mustard, Sahara	100.00
Empress, Pitcher, Sahara, 3 Pt.	295.00

Empress, Plate, 8 In.	12.00
Empress, Plate, Green, 7 In.	23.00
Empress, Plate, Moonbeam, 7 In., 8 Piece	155.00
Empress, Plate, Red Rosebuds, Green Leaves, Gold Hobnails, Round, 8 In.	75.00
Empress, Plate, Sahara, 6 In.	14.00
Empress, Plate, Sahara, 8 In.	20.00
Empress, Plate, Square, Sahara, 8 In.	20.00
Empress, Plate, Tangerine, Plate, 8 In, 4 Ea.	105.00
Empress, Relish, Buffet, 4 Sections, 16 In.	50.00
Empress, Sahara, Salt & Pepper	130.00
Empress, Sugar & Creamer, Flamingo, Individual	65.00
Empress, Sugar & Creamer, Individual	35.00
Empress, Sugar & Creamer, Sahara	70.00
Empress, Tumbler, Iced Tea, Pink, Footed	55.00
Fancy Loop, Bowl, 8 In.	20.00
Fancy Loop, Goblet, 8 Oz.	50.00
Fancy Loop, Toothpick	85.00
Fancy Loop, Toothpick, Green With Gold	165.00
Fancy Loop, Wine, Green, Gold Trim	65.00
Fandango, Cruet	145.00
Fandango, Footed, 4 1/2 In.	84.00
Fandango, Punch Cup	25.00
Fandango, Salt & Pepper	95.00
Fandango, Sugar & Creamer Set, Individual	62.00
Fandango, Toothpick	35.00
Fern, Candlestick, 2-Light With Etch	45.00
Fern, Dish, Jelly, Handles, 6 In.	15.00
Fish, Angelfish	105.00
Fisherman Etching, Greek Key, Cocktail Shaker	135.00
Flamingo, Sugar, Hotel, Ribbed, Octagon	25.00
Flamingo, Syrup	45.00
Flamingo Empress, Nut Dish	24.00
Grape Cluster, Candlestick, Pair	285.00
Greek Key, Almond Dish, Individual	45.00
Greek Key, Bowl, 9 1/2 In.	60.00
Greek Key, Celery Dish, 9 In.	100.00
Greek Key, Goblet, 9 Oz.	135.00
Greek Key, Ice Tub, Individual	85.00
Greek Key, Jelly, Footed, 5 In.	45.00
Greek Key, Punch Cup, 6 Piece	115.00
Greek Key, Punch Cup, Flamingo	30.00
Greek Key, Sherbet, Low Footed, 4 Oz.	20.00
Greek Key, Spooner, Small	85.00
Greek Key, Straw Holder, 12 In.	440.00
Greek Key, Tankard, 3 Sections	350.00
Greek Key, Wine	160.00
Horse Head, Bookends, Single	135.00
Horseshoe, Pitcher	175.00
Icicle, Cruet	119.00
Idyll, Toothpick	45.00
Ipswich, Candlestick, Evergreen, Pair	40.00
Ipswich, Candlestick, Ruby, Pair	55.00
Ipswich, Candy, Cover	95.00
Ipswich, Cocktail, Oyster	16.00
Ipswich, Cruet, Stopper, Marked, 2 Oz.	85.00
Ipswich, Glass, Soda, Footed, 5 Oz.	28.00
Ipswich, Jar, Cover, Amethyst, Signed	150.00
Ivy Etch, Champagne, Plantation	20.00
Jack-Be-Nimble, Candlestick, Toy, Marked, Pair	70.00
Jamestown, Goblet, Narcissus Cut	23.00
Kimberly Classic, Dolly Madison, Wine, Rose, 2 Oz.	65.00
Kohinoor, Soda, Zircon, 12 Oz.	80.00
Lady Leg, Goblet, Champagnes	150.00

Lariat, Basket, Handle, Blown, 9 In. 160.00
Lariat, Bowl, Crimped Edges, 11 In. 30.00
Lariat, Bowl, Punch, Ladle 130.00
Lariat, Candlestick, 2-Light, Pair 50.00
Lariat, Candy Dish, Cover, 5 In. 50.00
Lariat, Candy Dish, Cover, Hand Painted Roses, 4 In. 14.00
Lariat, Cologne Oil Bottle, No. 117, Stopper, 4 Oz. 90.00
Lariat, Goblet, 10 Oz. 14.00
Lariat, Mayonnaise, Footed 65.00
Lariat, Plate, 6 In. 4.50
Lariat, Platter, Round, 14 In. 25.00
Lariat, Relish, 3 Sections, 6 1/2 x 10 In. 28.00
Lariat, Tray, Round, 21 In. 125.00
Liberty, Candlestick, 3 In. 50.00
Locket On Chain, Cake Salver, 9 In. 120.00
Locket On Chain, Compote 115.00
Locket On Chain, Goblet 160.00
Locket On Chain, Wine 110.00
Lodestar, Bowl, Floral, Crimped, Dawn, 11 In. 165.00
Lodestar, Glass, Soda, Dawn, 13 Oz. 55.00
Mercury, Candlestick, Hawthorne 115.00
Mercury, Candlestick, Sahara, 3 In. 62.00
Minuet, Champagne 24.00
Minuet, Cocktail, 3 1/2 Oz., 5 7/8 In. 30.00
Minuet, Plate, Salad, 7 In. 11.00
Minuet, Saucer, Champagne, 6 Oz. 18.50
Minuet, Sherbet, 6 Oz. 13.50
Minuet, Tumbler, Water .... 29.00 to 30.00
Moonglo Cut, Glass, Old Fashion, National, 8 Oz. 15.00
Narrow Flute, Nappy, 8 In. 38.00
Narrow Flute, Pitcher, Flamingo 195.00
Narrow Flute, Salted Nut, With Rim, Star Base, Flamingo 20.00
Narrow Flute, Sugar & Creamer, Marked 30.00
Narrow Flute, Sugar, Footed, Domingo 59.00
Narrow Flute, Tray, Sugar, Flamingo 95.00
New Era, Cordial, 1 Oz. 32.00
Octagon, Sugar & Creamer Set 65.00
Octagon, Sugar, Yellow 20.00
Old Colony, Plate, Sahara, Round, 8 In. 42.00
Old Dominion, Goblet, Alex, 10 Oz. 210.00
Old Dominion, Goblet, Tall Stem, Alexandrite, 10 Oz. 195.00
Old Dominion, Tumbler, Footed, Sahara, 2 Oz. 40.00
Old Dominion, Tumbler, Footed, With Rim 65.00
Old Dominion, Tumbler, Soda, Sahara, Footed, 12 Oz. 110.00
Old Fitz, Whiskey, Hot, Amber, 4 1/2 Oz. 70.00
Old Sandwich, Candlestick, Yellow, 6 In., Pair 195.00
Old Sandwich, Champagne, Yellow 35.00
Old Sandwich, Compote, Footed, Moongleam, Marked, 6 In. 165.00
Old Sandwich, Cruet, No Stopper 45.00
Old Sandwich, Cruet, Salt & Pepper, Silver Holder 250.00
Old Sandwich, Finger Bowl 15.00
Old Sandwich, Mug, Beer, 12 Oz. 45.00
Old Sandwich, Mug, Beer, Sahara, 12 Oz. 150.00
Old Sandwich, Mug, Beer, With Silver Rim, 18 Oz. 65.00
Old Sandwich, Mug, Cobalt, 18 Oz. 350.00
Old Sandwich, Mug, Moongleam, 18 Oz. 350.00
Old Sandwich, Parfait, 4 1/2 Oz. 28.00
Old Sandwich, Plate, Yellow, 6 In. 20.00
Old Williamsburg, Candelabrum, 3-Light, Pair 425.00
Old Williamsburg, Candlestick, 1 Light, 8 3/4 In., Pair 115.00
Old Williamsburg, Candlestick, 9 In., 1 Pair 160.00
Old Williamsburg, Goblet, 9 Oz., 6 1/2 In. 18.00
Old Williamsburg, Juice, Footed, 5 Oz. 10.00

Omega, Goblet, Silver Leaf Cut	17.50
Orchid Etch, Bowl, Lily, Queen Ann, 7 In.	130.00
Orchid Etch, Butter	190.00
Orchid Etch, Butter, Cover	175.00
Orchid Etch, Butter, Cover, Waverly	165.00
Orchid Etch, Butter, Horse Head, Waverly	135.00
Orchid Etch, Candlestick, 2-Light, Waverly, Pair	75.00
Orchid Etch, Candlestick, 3-Light, Cascade	165.00
Orchid Etch, Candy Dish	190.00
Orchid Etch, Compote	50.00
Orchid Etch, Compote, Footed, 6 In.	45.00
Orchid Etch, Compote, Low Footed, 6 In.	45.00
Orchid Etch, Compote, Oval, 7 In.	110.00
Orchid Etch, Compote, Oval, Waverly	175.00
Orchid Etch, Goblet, 10 Oz.	35.00 to 45.00
Orchid Etch, Goblet, 8 1/12 In.	35.00
Orchid Etch, Pitcher	475.00
Orchid Etch, Plate, 15 In.	72.00
Orchid Etch, Plate, 6 In.	22.50
Orchid Etch, Relish, 3 Sections	70.00
Orchid Etch, Relish, 3 Sections, Waverly, 11 In.	75.00
Orchid Etch, Salt & Pepper	85.00
Orchid Etch, Sherbet	35.00
Orchid Etch, Sugar & Creamer	65.00
Orchid Etch, Sugar & Creamer, Waverly, Individual	69.00
Orchid Etch, Torte Plate, 14 In.	45.00
Orchid Etch, Tray, Center Dolphin Handle, Waverly, 14 1/2 In.	165.00
Orchid Etch, Tumbler	50.00
Orchid Etch, Tumbler, Iced Tea, 12 Oz.	65.00
Oxford, Goblet	15.00
Park Lane, Goblet, 10 Oz., 3 Ea.	32.00
Park Lane, Wine, 2 1/2 Oz.	30.00
Patrician, Candlestick, 1-Light, 7 1/2 In., Pair	115.00
Peerless, Pitcher, 3 Pt.	175.00
Peerless, Sherbet, Low Footed, Shallow, 4 1/2 In.	12.00
Peerless, Toothpick	50.00
Petal, Sugar & Creamer, Flamingo	45.00
Petticoat Dolphin, Compote, Flamingo	225.00
Pied Piper, Wine, 10 Oz.	25.00
Pineapple & Fan, Biscuit Jar, Cover	175.00
Pineapple & Fan, Bowl, Rose, Emerald, 4 In.	95.00
Pineapple & Fan, Pitcher, Souvenir, Marked	85.00
Pineapple & Fan, Spooner	35.00
Pineapple & Fan, Toothpick, Green, Gold Trim	225.00
Pineapple & Fan, Tumbler, Emerald	36.00
Pineapple & Fan, Vase, Emerald, 6 In.	55.00
Pinwheel & Fan, Basket, Diamond H Mark, 11 5/8 In.	192.00
Plain Band, Toothpick, Clear	28.00
Plantation, Bowl, Flared, 12 In.	55.00
Plantation, Butter, Cover, 1/4 Lb.	85.00
Plantation, Cake Stand, Marked	160.00
Plantation, Candlestick	50.00
Plantation, Candlestick, 2-Light, Pair	130.00
Plantation, Candlestick, 3-Light	80.00
Plantation, Candlestick, Ivy, Pair	195.00
Plantation, Candy Dish, Cover, 5 In.	375.00
Plantation, Champagne	15.00
Plantation, Claret, 4 Oz., 2 Ea.	31.00
Plantation, Claret, Footed, 4 1/2 Oz.	50.00
Plantation, Cruet, 3 Oz.	95.00
Plantation, Cruet, With 125 Stopper	100.00
Plantation, Footed Sugar & Creamer	55.00
Plantation, Goblet, 8 Oz.	30.00

Plantation, Goblet, Footed, 10 Oz. 40.00
Plantation, Iced Tea, Footed, 12 Oz. 40.00
Plantation, Plate, Round, 8 In. 17.00
Plantation, Plate, Sandwich, 14 In. 85.00
Plantation, Punch Cup. 5.00
Plantation, Punch Set, 10 Piece. 750.00
Plantation, Punch Set, Bowl, Underplate, 32 Cups 1200.00
Plantation, Relish, 3 Sections. 55.00
Plantation, Salt & Pepper. 69.50
Plantation, Sherbet, 4 1/2 In. 22.00
Plantation, Sugar. 20.00
Plantation, Syrup. 135.00
Plantation, Tumbler, Iced Tea, 12 Oz. 50.00
Plantation, Vase, Flared, Footed, 5 1/2 In. 75.00
Pleat & Panel, Candy Dish, Cover, Flamingo 85.00
Pleat & Panel, Candy Dish, Pedestal, Flamingo, 8 1/2 In. 95.00
Pleat & Panel, Compote, Cover, Low, Flamingo 135.00
Pleat & Panel, Compote, Cover, Pink, 6 In. 95.00
Pleat & Panel, Compote, Low, Footed, Moongleam, 6 In. 78.00
Pleat & Panel, Compote, Moongleam, 6 In. 78.00
Pleat & Panel, Cruet, 3 Oz. 65.00
Pleat & Panel, Cup & Saucer, Flamingo 32.50
Pleat & Panel, Tray, Spice 45.00
Pleat & Panel, Tumbler, Pink, 8 Oz. 30.00
Press Cut, Pitcher, Clear, Applied Handle, 6 1/2 In. 176.00
Prince Of Wales, Toothpick, Ruby 250.00
Priscilla, Compote, 12 In. 265.00
Priscilla, Toothpick, Cut Flowers 75.00
Priscilla, Toothpick, Marked 40.00
Priscilla, Vase, Sweet Pea, 3 1/2 In. 35.00
Prison Stripe, Jam Jar, Footed, 5 In. 48.00
Prison Stripe, Toothpick 425.00
Provincial, Candy Dish, Cover 65.00
Provincial, Mayonnaise, 3-Handled, Limelight 125.00
Provincial, Sugar & Creamer, 1 1/2 In. 40.00
Punty & Diamond Point, Toothpick 260.00
Punty & Diamond Point, Vase, 6 In. 38.00
Punty Band, Syrup 195.00
Puritan, Cup, Plate, 4 1/2 In. 25.00
Puritan, Jug, Three Pint 95.00
Puritan, Pitcher, Applied Handle, 7 1/2 In. 137.00
Puritan, Water Set, 8 Piece 150.00
Queen Ann, Candelabrum, 1 Light, 7 1/2 In. 112.00
Queen Ann, Nut Dish. 15.00
Queen Ann, Saucer 4.25
Queen Ann, Toothpick 365.00
Recessed Panel, Candy Jar, Cover. 50.00
Revere, Candy Dish, Cover, 1/2 Lb. 135.00
Revere, Mayonnaise, Underplate, Dawn, Marked. 85.00
Rib & Panel, Compote, Cover, Moongleam. 125.00
Ribbed Octagon, Cup & Saucer, Green 45.00
Ridgeleigh, Ashtray, Diamond. 10.00
Ridgeleigh, Ashtray, Square 4.00
Ridgeleigh, Bowl, 10 In. 30.00
Ridgeleigh, Bowl, Fruit, Crystal, 12 In. 40.00
Ridgeleigh, Candleblock, 3 In. 60.00
Ridgeleigh, Candlestick, 2-Light, Pair. 185.00
Ridgeleigh, Candlestick, Bobeche, 7 In., Pair. 265.00
Ridgeleigh, Candlevase, Zircon, 6 In. 210.00
Ridgeleigh, Celery Dish, 2 Sections, Oval, 12 In. ....35.00 to 37.50
Ridgeleigh, Coaster. 6.50
Ridgeleigh, Coaster, 3 1/2 In. 42.00
Ridgeleigh, Compote, 6 In. 20.00

Ridgeleigh, Cruet, 3 Oz. 40.00
Ridgeleigh, Goblet, Mariemont, 10 Oz. 100.00
Ridgeleigh, Ice Tub 65.00
Ridgeleigh, Lemon Dish, Cover, Crystal 35.00
Ridgeleigh, Mustard, Cover 40.00
Ridgeleigh, Nut Dish, 2 Handles, Individual 10.00
Ridgeleigh, Pitcher, 1/2 Gal. 275.00
Ridgeleigh, Plate, 13 In. 32.00
Ridgeleigh, Plate, Cheese, 2 Handles, 6 In. 19.00
Ridgeleigh, Plate, Crystal, 11 In. 35.00
Ridgeleigh, Puff Box 175.00
Ridgeleigh, Punch Cup .... 9.00 to 10.00
Ridgeleigh, Punch Set, 11 Piece 165.00
Ridgeleigh, Relish, 5-Point Star 35.00
Ridgeleigh, Relish, 5 Sections 65.00
Ridgeleigh, Sugar & Creamer, Individual 35.00
Ridgeleigh, Sugar, Oval 18.00
Ridgeleigh, Tray, Oblong, 10 1/2 In. 47.50
Ridgeleigh, Vase, Individual 35.00
Ring Band, Toothpick, Gold Trim 48.00
Rococo, Celery, 13 In. 75.00
Rococo, Compote, 6 In. 80.00
Rooster, Cocktail 45.00
Rooster, Cocktail Shaker 100.00
Rooster, Cocktail Shaker, Wheat Etching 140.00
Rose Etch, Butter, Cover, Waverly, 6 In. 185.00
Rose Etch, Cake Plate, Footed, 13 1/2 In. 295.00
Rose Etch, Candlestick, 3-Light, Pair 195.00
Rose Etch, Claret 145.00
Rose Etch, Creamer 20.00
Rose Etch, Cruet, Footed 225.00
Rose Etch, Cup 65.00
Rose Etch, Cup & Saucer 85.00
Rose Etch, Mayonnaise, Liner 85.00
Rose Etch, Plate, 8 In. 25.00
Rose Etch, Plate, Center Design, Waverly, 11 In. 95.00
Rose Etch, Relish, 4 Sections 110.00
Rose Etch, Relish, 4 Sections, Round, 9 In. 95.00
Rose Etch, Sugar & Creamer, Waverly 85.00
Rose Etch, Torte Dish, Demitasse 87.00
Rose Etch, Tumbler, Iced Tea 35.00
Rose Etch, Tumbler, Juice, Footed 47.50
Rose Etch, Vase, Footed, Waverly, 7 In. 375.00
Sandwich Star, Goblet, Purple, 10 Oz. 20.00
Satellite, Creamer 25.00
Saturn, Goblet, 10 Oz. .... 12.00 to 30.00
Saturn, Mayonnaise, Footed, 4 3/4 x 3 In. 8.00
Saturn, Mustard, Cover 40.00
Saturn, Plate, Limelight, Round, 7 In 40.00
Saturn, Shaker, Sterling Top 80.00
Sawtooth Band, Cake Stand, 9 3/4 x 5 3/8 In. 75.00
Sawtooth Band, Salver, Signed, 11 In. 85.00
Saxony, Sherbet, Sahara 25.00
Spanish, Cordial, Pairpoint, 1 Oz. 75.00
Spanish, Goblet, Etched 25.00
Spanish, Goblet, Riviere, 10 Oz. 70.00
Spanish, Tumbler, Cobalt, Footed, 12 Oz. 50.00
Stanhope, Wine 10.00
Sunburst, Cruet .... 60.00 to 90.00
Sunburst, Goblet, 7 Oz. 215.00
Sunburst, Pitcher, 2 Pt. 250.00
Sunburst, Pitcher, 64 Oz. 195.00
Sunburst, Plate, Herringbone, 7 In. 50.00

Sunburst, Punch Cup	15.00
Sunflower, Plate, 7 In.	17.50
Thumbprint & Panel, Candlestick, 2-Light, Pair	80.00
Trident, Candlestick, 2-Light, Pair	65.00
Trojan, Pitcher, Yellow	365.00
Trojan, Whipped Cream Pail, Yellow	165.00
Twist, Bottle, French Dressing, Moongleam	85.00
Twist, Bowl, Floral, Alexandrite	595.00
Twist, Cruet, 4 Oz.	65.00
Twist, Cruet, Flamingo	100.00
Twist, Ice Tub, Tongs	595.00
Twist, Mayonnaise, Handle, Square Pedestal, Marigold	55.00
Twist, Mustard, Cover, Green	75.00
Twist, Mustard, Cover, Moongleam	70.00
Twist, Nut Dish, Handle, Flamingo, Individual	20.00
Twist, Toothpick, Green	40.00
Versailles, Cordial, Yellow, 4 In.	85.00
Victorian, Glass, Old Fashion, 8 Oz.	26.00
Victorian, Jar, Oil	35.00
Victorian, Sherbet, 5 Oz.	15.00
Victorian, Wine, Flamingo, 2 1/2 Oz.	24.00
Wabash, Pitcher, Green Footed & Applied Handle, 13 In.	165.00
Wampum, Cigarette Set, 5 Piece	85.00
Warwick, Vase, Horn Of Plenty Form, Cobalt Blue, 5 In., Pair	450.00
Warwick, Vase, Horn Of Plenty, Crystal, 9 In.	55.00
Waverly, Bowl, Ruffled & Flared, 12 In.	13.00
Waverly, Candlestick, Epergne, Fits In Epergnette	5.00
Waverly, Celery Tray, 12 In.	15.00
Waverly, Chocolate Box, Cover, Marked	75.00
Waverly, Relish, 2 Sections, Footed	20.00
Waverly, Sugar & Creamer, Individual	70.00
Whirlpool, Butter, Cover, 1 Lb.	90.00
Wigwam Etch, Tumbler, Yeoman, 10 Oz.	80.00
Willowmere, Goblet, Water	25.00
Yeoman, Bowl, Pink, Oval, 6 In.	13.00
Yeoman, Cake Salver, Footed, 12 In.	135.00
Yeoman, Cruet, Flamingo, 4 Oz.	54.00
Yeoman, Cruet, Pink, 3 Oz.	85.00
Yeoman, Cruet, Sahara, Crystal Stopper, 20 Oz.	65.00
Yeoman, Cup & Saucer	10.00
Yeoman, Gravy Boat, Green	45.00
Yeoman, Plate, Hawthorne, 8 In.	25.00
Yeoman, Saucer, After Dinner, Pink	4.50
Yeoman, Sugar & Creamer, Flamingo	65.00
Yeoman, Sugar & Creamer, Hawthorne	95.00
Yeoman, Tumbler, Flared, Sahara, 2 1/2 Oz.	15.00
Yeoman, Tumbler, Footed, Sahara, 8 Oz.	18.00
Yeoman, Vase, Moongleam, Oval, 7 In.	95.00
Zodiac, Juice, Marked, 5 Oz.	24.00

HEREND, see Fischer category

HEUBACH is the collector's name for Gebruder Heubach, a firm working in Lichten, Germany, from 1840 to 1925. It is best known for bisque dolls and doll heads, their principal products. They also manufactured bisque figurines, including piano babies, beginning in the 1880s, and glazed figurines in the 1900s. Piano babies are listed in their own category. Dolls are included in the Doll category under *Gebruder Heubach* and *Heubach*. Another factory, Ernst Heubach, working in Koppelsdorf, Germany, also made porcelain and dolls. These will also be found in the doll category under Heubach Koppelsdorf.

Figurine, Child, On Skis, Bisque Face, Rolled Cotton Clothes	275.00
Figurine, Child, On Wooden Sled, 3 1/2 x 3 1/4 In.	335.00
Figurine, Girl Holding Bouquet Of Flowers, 7 1/2 In.	175.00

Figurine, Man With Ax, Woman With Baby, 12 1/2 In., Pair	725.00 to 825.00
Figurine, Pup With A Muzzle, Impressed Mark, 5 In.	125.00
Vase, Art Nouveau Women, 4 1/2 In.	125.00

HIGBEE glass was made by the J. B. Higbee Company of Bridgeville, Pennsylvania, about 1900. Tablewares were made and it is possible to assemble a full set of dishes and goblets in some Higbee patterns. Most of the glass was clear, not colored. Additional pieces may be found in the Pressed Glass category by pattern name.

Bowl, Flared Panel, Marked, 10 1/4 In.	25.00
Cup, Teardrop Row	25.00
Pitcher, Gem Pattern, 9 In.	55.00
Spooner, Pineapple	45.00
Sugar, Cover, Pineapple	65.00

HISTORIC BLUE, see factory names, such as Adams, Clews, Ridgway, and Staffordshire

HOBNAIL glass is a style of glass with bumps all over. Dozens of hobnail patterns and variants have been made. Clear, colored, and opalescent hobnail have been made and are being reproduced. Other pieces of hobnail may also be listed in the Duncan & Miller, Fenton, and Francisware categories.

Basket, Amber, Pleated Top, Applied Handle, 7 In.	35.00
Bone Dish, Blue Opalescent	15.00
Bottle, Barber, Cranberry Opalescent	349.00 to 350.00
Celery Vase, Square, Footed	20.00
Cuspidor, Amethyst, Millersburg	500.00
Mug, 3 x 2 1/2 In.	8.00
Perfume Bottle, Stopper, 8 In.	15.00
Pitcher, Cranberry To Clear, Hobbs, Brockunier	495.00
Pitcher, Water, Rubena Opalescent, Hobbs	325.00
Rose Bowl, White Opalescent	75.00
Rose Bowl, White Opalescent, Collar Foot, Small	25.00
Shade, Hanging, Pink, 14 In.	1350.00
Sugar Shaker, Amber, Pointed	45.00
Toothpick, White Opalescent	25.00
Tumbler, Amethyst To Blue	195.00
Tumbler, Vaseline	20.00
Tumbler, Vaseline Opalescent	95.00
Vase, Cranberry, Ruffled, Clear Applied Feet, 7 5/8 x 2 1/2 In.	85.00

HOCHST, or Hoechst, porcelain was made in Germany from 1746 to 1796. It was marked with a six-spoke wheel. Be careful when buying Hochst; many other firms have used a very similar wheel-shaped mark.

Cup & Saucer, Swan & Duck On Cup Front, Cranes On Saucer, c.1770	690.00
Figurine, Little Girl With Muff, Rocky Mound Base, c.1785, 6 1/8 In.	920.00
Plate, 2 Men In Center, Astride Mounts, Reticulated, c.1770, 10 In.	4025.00

HOLLY AMBER, or golden agate, glass was made by the Indiana Tumbler and Goblet Company of Greentown, Indiana, from January 1, 1903, to June 13, 1903. It is a pressed glass pattern featuring holly leaves in the amber-shaded glass. The glass was made with shadings that range from creamy opalescent to brown-amber.

Bowl, Rectangular, 4 x 10 In.	950.00
Butter, Cover	575.00 to 1350.00
Cake Stand, Cover, Pedestal, 8 1/4 In.	2300.00
Compote, Beaded, Stem, 5 x 4 1/2 In.	475.00
Compote, Cover, 7 1/4 In.	2100.00
Compote, Cover, 8 1/4 In.	2300.00
Compote, Fruit	3000.00
Compote, Jelly, Cover, 4 1/4 In.	800.00
Compote, Jelly, Low Pedestal	1475.00

Creamer	700.00
Dish, Pickle, 2 Handles	500.00
Parfait	575.00
Pitcher	1900.00
Plate, Square, 7 1/2 In.	800.00
Salt & Pepper	750.00 to 1500.00
Spooner	425.00 to 600.00
Sugar, Cover	3000.00
Syrup, Metal Lid	2600.00
Toothpick, Pedestal	2100.00
Tray, Round, 9 1/4 In.	1200.00
Tumbler	425.00

HOLT HOWARD was an importer who started working in 1949 in Stamford, Connecticut. He sold many types of table accessories, such as condiment jars, decanters, spoon holders, and salt shakers. The figures shown on some of his pieces had a cartoon-like quality. The company was bought out by General Housewares Corporation in 1969. Holt Howard pieces are often marked with the name and the year or HH and the year stamped in black. There was also a black and silver label.

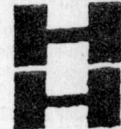

Ashtray, Snow Baby	45.00
Bowl, Condiment, Stinky Cheese	35.00
Butter, Dish Cover	35.00
Cocktail Shaker, Bartender, 4 Tumblers, Stirrer, 6 Piece	65.00
Cookie Jar, Apple	24.00
Eggcup	9.00
Jam Jar, Rooster	35.00
Jar, Condiment, Cherries, Spoofy Spoon, 1958	50.00
Jar, Condiment, Ketchup, Spoofy Spoon, 1958	45.00
Jar, Condiment, Mayonnaise, Spoofy Spoon, 1958	50.00
Jar, Condiment, Olives, Spoofy Spoon, 1958	50.00
Jar, Condiment, Onions, Spoofy Spoon, 1958	50.00
Pixie, Hors D'Oeuvres, 7 In.	50.00
Pixie, Mayonnaise	45.00
Pixie, Olive	45.00
String Holder, Kitty	45.00
Sugar & Creamer, Reindeer	45.00

HOPALONG CASSIDY was a character in a series of twenty-eight books written by Clarence E. Milford, first published in 1907. Movies and television shows were made based on the character. The best-known actor playing Hopalong Cassidy was William Lawrence Boyd. His first movie appearance was in 1919, but the first Hopalong Cassidy film was not until 1934. Sixty-six films were made. In 1948, William Boyd purchased the television rights to the movies, then later made fifty-two new programs. In the 1950s, Hopalong Cassidy and his horse, named *Topper*, were seen in comics, records, toys, and other products. Boyd died in 1972.

Bank, Yellow Plastic	90.00
Barrette, Girl's, Metal	45.00
Barrette, Hair, Silver Color	25.00
Bedspread, Chenille	250.00
Bicycle, Rolfast, Western Style Saddle Bags	1870.00
Binoculars	85.00 to 100.00
Book, Pop-Up, 1950	55.00
Book, Pop-Up, Lends A Helping Hand	50.00
Bottle, Hair Trainer, Contents	50.00
Bracelet, Sterling Silver, Box	60.00
Card, Birthday, Savings Club, Tan, Brown, Signed & Dated 1950	2.50
Card, Trading, Ways Of The West, Bond Bread, 1950s, 3 Piece	75.00
Chaps, Hoppy On Topper Each Side	195.00
Charm, Gold Metal, Loop Top Of Hat, 1950s, 1 1/4 In.	15.00

Chow Set, 3 Piece, Original Box	70.00
Coaster, Hopalong Cassidy Favors Spun Honey, Multicolor, 4 In.	2.00
Cookie Jar	850.00
Cookie Jar, Short	400.00
Display, Langendorf Loaf Of Bread, 1951	38.00 to 50.00
Figure Set, Hoppy & Topper, With Hat, Ideal	145.00
Film, Doomed Wagon Train, 8 mm Castle Film	45.00
Flashlight	125.00
Floor Mat, Chenille, Large	175.00
Game, Chinese Checkers, Box	230.00 to 275.00
Game, Dominoes, Box	225.00
Game, Milton Bradley, 1950	100.00 to 250.00
Game, Target, 2-Sided, Tin, Darts & Instructions, Box	275.00
Guitar, Black Edges, Tan Face, Pictures Hoppy & Topper, Jefferson	275.00
Guitar, Picture Of Hoppy	275.00
Gun, Zommerange	125.00
Hat, Black, Leather Chin Strap & Buckle	145.00
Holster, Double, 2-Tone Brown	100.00
Ice Cream Container, Wm. Boyd, 1950s, 1 Qt.	65.00
Jacket & Pants, Lined	225.00
Knife, Black Bakelite, 3 Blades, Imperial	90.00
Knife, Hoppy & Topper Picture	90.00
Knife, Pocket, Metal Lanyard Chain	115.00
Linoleum, Hoppy & Topper Center, Frame, 24 x 32 In.	295.00
Lobby Card, Fighting Texan, 14 x 11 In.	25.00
Lobby Card, Man From Butte, 14 x 11 In.	25.00
Lobby Card, Strange Gamble, Movie, 1947, 14 x 11 In.	30.00
Lunch Box, Blue, Square Decal, Thermos, 1954	175.00 to 250.00
Milk Carton, 1 Pt.	10.00
Movie, 8 mm, Square Illustrated Box, 3 1/2 In.	29.00
Mug, Coffee, Milk Glass, Man On Horse Roping Cow, 1950s	34.00 to 40.00
Neckerchief, Child's, Hopalong, Riding Topper, Gold, Signed, 1950	8.00
Night-Light, Gun & Holster, Figural, Milk Glass, Hoppy Decal	250.00 to 350.00
Night-Light, Spun Honey Spread, 1950	25.00 to 45.00
Notebook, Loose Leaf, Hoppy On Topper, Western Guide Inside	120.00
Pencil Case, Tan, Complete	145.00
Pennant, Felt, Hoppy With Cole Bros. Circus, Rope Letters, 12 x 28 1/2 In.	75.00
Pin, Green & Black, 1 1/4 In.	1.00
Pin, Hopalong & Topper, Red & Black, 1 3/4 In.	2.00
Pin, Hoppy & Topper, Color, Pinback, 1 1/4 In.	2.00
Pin, Tin Lithograph, Chicago Tribune Comic Strip, 1 1/2 In.	40.00
Plate, Luncheon, Milk Glass, Black Design	70.00
Pop-Up Book, 1950	55.00
Postcard, Happy Birthday Savings Club, 1950	35.00
Postcard, Hopalong Cassidy Club, 1950s	5.00
Postcard, Hopalong Cassidy, 1942 Chrysler Station Wagon, Photograph	4.25
Poster, Sunny Spread	17.00
Puzzle, Frame Tray, Original Sleeve	75.00
Puzzle Set, Western Scene, Box, 3 Puzzles	125.00
Saddle, Child's	2600.00
Shooting Gallery, Box	295.00
Sun Glasses	100.00
Sweater, Embroidered Hoppy On Front, Topper On Back	125.00 to 225.00
Television Set, No. 352, Box	400.00
Thermos, Yellow	30.00
Toy, Hoppy On Horse, Windup, Marx	575.00
Toy, Range Rider, Tin Lithographed, Hoppy Both Sides, Windup	695.00
Tumbler, Black & White	45.00
Tumbler, Milk Glass	45.00
Wallet, Ornate Gold	310.00
Waste Pail, Hoppy, On Topper, Leather	275.00
Wood Burning Set, Wm. Boyd Prod., American Toy & Furniture Co., 1950	175.00 to 295.00
Wristwatch, Papers, Box, 1950s	355.00

Wristwatch, Saddle Style Box 295.00

HOWARD PIERCE has been working in southern California since 1936. In 1945, he opened a pottery in Claremont. His contemporary-looking figurines are popular with collectors. Pieces are marked with his name. He stopped making pottery in 1991.

Howard Pierce

Figurine, 2 Birds On Branch	75.00
Figurine, 3 Ducks	95.00
Figurine, Deer	20.00 to 48.00
Figurine, Flower Girl	85.00
Figurine, Geese, Pair, 8 1/4 In.	125.00
Figurine, Madonna	75.00
Figurine, Native Woman	85.00
Figurine, Owl, Brown, 8 In.	50.00
Figurine, Owl, Pair	70.00
Figurine, Quail, 3 Piece	75.00
Figurine, Water Bird, Black Matte, 14 In.	60.00

HOWDY DOODY and Buffalo Bob were the main characters in a children's series televised from 1947 to 1960. Howdy was a redheaded puppet. The series became popular with college students in the late 1970s when Buffalo Bob began to lecture on campuses.

Album, Air-O-Doodle, RCA, 2 Records	45.00
Album, American History, Wonder Bread Premium, 1950s	125.00
Bandanna, Club, Square, 1950s, 20 In.	65.00 to 75.00
Bank, Howdy On TV	95.00
Bank, Purinton	995.00 to 1250.00
Book, Clarabelle Clown, 1955	25.00
Book, Coloring, 1951	40.00
Book, Howdy Doody's Circus, Little Golden Book, 1952	15.00
Book, Howdy Doody's Lucky Trip, Little Golden Book, 1952	15.00
Bottle, Welch Juice, Cover	70.00
Cap, Poll-Parrot Shoes, 1952	25.00
Card Game, Russell Mfg., Early 1950s	60.00
Clock, Alarm, Talking, Box	170.00
Clown, Clarabelle, Tin, Lithograph, Mechanical, Linemar, Box	995.00
Cookie Jar, Head .... *Illus*	650.00
Cookie Jar, Purinton	650.00
Cookie Jar, Vandor	495.00
Cup, Decal, Howdy Figure, Blue Plastic	40.00
Doll, Movable Eyes & Mouth, Bandanna, Ideal, 1950s	165.00
Doll, Open-Close Eyes, 1950s, Ideal, 21 In.	95.00
Doll, Ventriloquist, Box, Small	105.00
Doll, Ventriloquist, Dummy	150.00
Drum, Indian, Stick	80.00
Figure, Howdy, Jointed, Wooden, With NBC Mike, Kohner	95.00
Figure, Push-Up, Flub-A-Dub, Kohner	250.00
Figure, Standing, NBC Mike, Jointed, Push-Up	195.00
Funbook, 1951	25.00
Funbook, No. 2187, Whitman, 1953	42.00
Game, Bean Bag, Box	175.00
Game, Bowling, Parker Bros., 1050s	85.00
Game, Circus, 3 Ring	95.00
Game, Howdy Doody's T.V. Game, Milton Bradley	75.00
Game, TV Studio, Board, Box	120.00
Glass, Painted Fishing Scene, Welch's	25.00
Glass Set, Welch's, All Different, 1953, 6 Piece	69.00
Handkerchief, Signed By Bob Smith	40.00
Key Chain, Puzzle	40.00
Lamp, Wall, Howdy & Santa Claus, Raised Figures, 14 x 10 In.	145.00
Lunch Box, Dome, Hard Plastic, 1977	39.00
Mug, Drink Chocolate Flavored Ovaltine, Red Celluloid	50.00
Mug, Red, Celluloid, Howdy, Be Keen, Be Keen, Drink Chocolate Ovaltine	40.00 to 50.00

Howdy Doody, Phonodoodle, Paper,
Sheratons, 78 RPM, 12 In.

Howdy Doody,
Cookie Jar, Head

Night Light, Glass, Leco, 1950s		150.00
Phonodoodle, Paper, Sheratons, 78 RPM, 12 In.	*Illus*	121.00
Pin, Figural, I'm For Howdy Doody		45.00
Puppet, Howdy Doody, Terry Cloth		22.00
Puppet, Mr. Bluster, Terry Cloth		22.00
Puppet Show Set, Tee Vee, 1950s		210.00
Purse, Child's, Howdy's Face Front, Red Clasp		95.00
Put On Your Own Puppet Show, 5 Plastic Figures, Mouths Move, On Card		195.00
Puzzle, Figural, Key Chain, Instructions, Cellophane Package		60.00
Puzzle, Is That You Clarabelle?, Tray Type, 1952		33.00
Puzzle, Jigsaw, At Campsite, 1953		35.00
Puzzle, Tray, 1953		38.00
Ring, Flashlight, Original Battery		150.00
Rocker, Bell On Base		250.00
Salt & Pepper, Howdy In Pink Cadillac, Vandor		75.00
Salt & Pepper, Huggers, Purinton		500.00
Sign, Die-Cut Cardboard, Colgate Dental Cream, c.1950, 22 x 14 In.		295.00
Slippers, Plastic Puppet Head, Plaid Shirt, Blue Scarf, Child's Size		55.00
Spoon, Figural, Silver Plate, 1950s, 7 In.		47.00
Spoon, Ice Tea, Figural, Crown Silverplate, 1950s		90.00
Tin, Cookie, Cookie-Go-Round, Lithograph		135.00
Tin, Cookie-Go-Round		200.00
Toy, Acrobat, Tin Lithograph Trapeze, Composition Head, Arnold Toys, 1950s		100.00
Toy, Band, Bob Smith, Tin Lithograph, Windup, Unique Art, 8 x 6 1/2 In.		862.00
Toy, Pump-Mobile		350.00
Toy, Time Teacher, Howdy Doody & Clock Face, 1970s		25.00
Toy, Ukulele, Emenet		120.00
Tube Patch, Swim, Child's		45.00
Tumbler, Doodyville Elephant Squirts Clarabelle, Yellow		13.00
Tumbler, Hey Kids What A Shot, Clarabelle In Bottom, Yellow, 1953		10.00
Tumbler, Wherever We Eat - Favorite Treat, Howdy In Bottom, 1953		12.00
TV Tray, Yankee Doodle Wood Products, 11 x 16 In.		125.00
Wall Lamp, Santa Claus, Howdy On Chimney		175.00
Wallet, Child's, 1950s		45.00
Wallet, Howdy Doody, 1950s		125.00
Wristwatch, Eyes Rotate, 1950s		235.00

HULL pottery was made in Crooksville, Ohio, from 1905. Addis E. Hull bought the Acme Pottery Company and started making ceramic wares. In 1917, A. E. Hull Pottery began making art pottery as well as the commercial wares. For a short time, 1921 to 1929, the firm also sold pottery imported from Europe. The dinnerwares of the 1940s, including the Little Red Riding Hood line, the high gloss artwares of the 1950s, and the matte wares of the 1940s, are all popular with collectors. The firm officially closed in March 1986.

Hull
U.S.A.

Ashtray, Butterfly, 7 In.	50.00
Ashtray, Ebb Tide, Mermaid, Green & Pink	95.00

Hull, Cookie Jar,
Little Red Riding Hood,
Open Basket

◆◆◆◆◆◆◆◆◆◆◆◆◆◆◆◆◆◆◆◆◆◆◆◆◆

To ship small pieces of glass, try this trick: Put the glass in a Styrofoam cup, then wrap in bubble wrap or several layers of paper. Stuff sides and bottom of a large box with Styrofoam trays. Then put the antiques on the trays. Pack more Styrofoam around them. Maybe you can get extra trays at your grocery store.

◆◆◆◆◆◆◆◆◆◆◆◆◆◆◆◆◆◆◆◆◆◆◆◆◆

Bank, Corky Pig, Brown	25.00 to 28.00
Bank, Corky Pig, Pink	50.00 to 85.00
Bank, Little Red Riding Hood, 7 In.	500.00 to 650.00
Bank, Wall Hanging, Little Red Riding Hood	2800.00
Basket, Blossom Flite, Cobalt Trim, 4 1/2 x 6 In.	32.00 to 35.00
Basket, Bow Knot, 10 1/2 In.	625.00
Basket, Bow Knot, Yellow Flower, 10 1/2 In.	495.00
Basket, Butterfly, Matte, 8 In.	85.00
Basket, Ebb Tide, Shrimp	140.00
Basket, Green & Rose Accents, High Gloss, Dark Handle, 10 In.	65.00
Basket, Hanging, Woodland, Glossy, Heavy Gold Trim, Pre-1950	400.00
Basket, Magnolia, 10 1/2 In.	225.00
Basket, Magnolia, Matte, 10 1/2 In.	225.00
Basket, Mardi Gras, 8 In.	85.00
Basket, Moon, Tuscany	38.00
Basket, Morning Glory	300.00
Basket, Parchment & Pine, 16 In.	50.00 to 150.00
Basket, Royal, 8 3/4 In.	50.00
Basket, Tokay, Green & White, 11 In.	75.00
Basket, Tokay, White, 12 In.	160.00
Basket, Water Lily, 10 1/2 In.	320.00
Basket, Woodland, Chartreuse, 8 3/4 In.	110.00
Basket, Woodland, Chartreuse, 10 1/2 In.	230.00
Basket, Woodland, Green, Pink	85.00
Bowl, Batter, Little Red Riding Hood	385.00
Bowl, Bow Knot, 5 3/4 In.	165.00
Bowl, Flower, Blossom Flite	50.00
Bowl, Magnolia, Brown, Yellow, 12 In.	33.00
Bowl, Orchid, 13 In.	350.00
Bowl, Wild Flower, Matte, 12 In.	150.00
Butter, Cover, House 'n' Garden	10.00
Butter, Cover, Little Red Riding Hood	295.00 to 315.00
Butter Dish, Westinghouse, Green	30.00
Candleholder, Bow Knot, Pair	125.00
Candleholder, Dogwood, Peach & Turquoise, 5 1/2 x 3 7/8 In.	125.00
Candleholder, Woodland, Chartreuse, Pair	85.00
Candy Dish, Tokay, Pink	80.00
Canister, Salt, Little Red Riding Hood	750.00
Canister, Sugar, Little Red Riding Hood	475.00
Clock, Bluebird, Sessions	135.00 to 425.00
Clock, Fruit Basket	90.00
Coffeepot, Crestone	30.00

Coffeepot, House 'n' Garden 25.00
Console, Dogwood, Cream & Aqua, 11 1/2 In. 125.00
Console, Parchment & Pine, Green & Brown, 15 3/4 In. 55.00
Console Set, Parchment & Pine, 3 Piece 100.00
Console Set, Woodland, Green Over Pink, 3 Piece 110.00
Cookie Jar, Barefoot Boy .... 450.00 to 495.00
Cookie Jar, Gingerbread Boy, Brown 150.00
Cookie Jar, Gingerbread Man 400.00
Cookie Jar, Little Red Riding Hood, Open Basket .... *Illus* 345.00
Cookie Jar, Little Red Riding Hood, Stars On Apron .... 275.00 to 475.00
Cookie Jar, Red Riding Hood, Poinsettia 550.00
Cookie Jar, Train Canister Set 2200.00
Cornucopia, Athena, Chartreuse, Green, 9 In. 25.00
Cornucopia, Blossom Flite .... 37.50 to 65.00
Cornucopia, Bow Knot, Blue & Green, 7 1/2 In. .... 95.00 to 120.00
Cornucopia, Calla Lily, Turquoise & Cream 110.00
Cornucopia, Double, Water Lily, Aqua, Pink 195.00
Cornucopia, Ebb Tide, Mermaid, 7 1/2 In. 65.00
Cornucopia, Magnolia, Yellow & Maroon, Gloss, Gold Trim, Hand Decorated, 9 In. ... 52.00
Cornucopia, Parchment & Pine, 8 In. 25.00
Cornucopia, Sunglow, 8 1/2 In. 40.00
Cornucopia, Wild Flower, 8 1/2 In. 100.00
Cornucopia, Wild Flower, Cream, Rose, 7 1/2 In. 55.00
Cornucopia, Wild Flower, Pink, Blue, 7 1/2 In. 50.00
Cornucopia, Woodland, High Gloss, 11 In. 55.00
Cornucopia, Woodland, Pink & Cream, Pre-1950 .... 100.00
Creamer, Little Red Riding Hood, Head Pour 350.00
Creamer, Little Red Riding Hood, Side Pour 150.00
Dish, Tuscany, Leaf Shape 26.00
Ewer, Bow Knot, 5 1/2 In. 165.00
Ewer, Bow Knot, 13 1/2 In. 1100.00
Ewer, Butterfly, 14 In. 100.00
Ewer, Magnolia, 7 In. 85.00
Ewer, Open Rose, 4 1/2 In. 85.00
Ewer, Orchid, Pink & Blue, 13 In. 650.00
Ewer, Poppy, 4 1/2 In. 115.00
Ewer, Royal, Woodland, 13 1/2 In. 95.00
Ewer, Sueno, 7 In. 90.00
Ewer, Wild Flower, 5 1/2 In. 30.00
Ewer, Wild Flower, 8 1/2 In. .... 150.00 to 175.00
Ewer, Woodland, Glazed, 13 1/2 In. 175.00
Figurine, Accordion Boy 70.00
Figurine, Girl, Dancing, Pink, White, Matte Glaze, 7 In. 22.00
Figurine, Goose, No. 69 .... 25.00
Flowerpot, Tulip, 4 3/4 In. 80.00
Flowerpot, Tulip, 6 In. 145.00
Garlic Cellar, Brown 20.00
Honey Jug, Blossom Flite 35.00
Jar, Dresser, Little Red Riding Hood 550.00
Jar, Grease, Little Red Riding Hood, Yellow 1150.00
Jar, Grease, Wolf 950.00
Jar, Nutmeg Spice, Little Red Riding Hood 675.00
Jardiniere, Bow Knot .... 195.00 to 225.00
Jardiniere, Iris 155.00
Jardiniere, Tulip, 7 In. 250.00
Jardiniere, Woodland, Open Handle, Pink, 5 1/2 In. 45.00
Lamp, Little Red Riding Hood, Gold Trim 2225.00
Lavabo Set, Butterfly, 2 Piece .... 95.00 to 125.00
Magnolia, Ewer, 7 In. .... 45.00 to 85.00
Match Holder, Little Red Riding Hood 625.00
Pitcher, Bow Knot, Pink & Blue, 5 In. 145.00
Pitcher, Butterfly, 8 1/4 In. 90.00

Pitcher, Capri, 12 In. 75.00
Pitcher, Cow, Blue & White 200.00
Pitcher, Dogwood 95.00
Pitcher, Ebb Tide ....60.00 to 125.00
Pitcher, House & Garden, Brown, 9 1/2 In. 25.00
Pitcher, Little Red Riding Hood, Side Pour 150.00
Pitcher, Magnolia, Pink To Blue, Matte, 4 3/4 In. 40.00
Pitcher, Milk, Little Red Riding Hood, 8 In. ....235.00 to 265.00
Pitcher, Open Rose, 7 In. 145.00
Pitcher, Open Rose, White, No.128, 4 3/4 In. 22.00
Pitcher, Orchid, Pink, 13 In. 695.00
Pitcher, Sun Glow, Pink & Yellow Flower 28.00
Planter, Baby & Pillow 20.00
Planter, Bandanna Duck 45.00
Planter, Double Ducks, 10 In. 25.00
Planter, Duck, No. 75 .... 45.00
Planter, Elephant 20.00
Planter, Goose, Chartreuse & Green, 4 1/2 In. 15.00
Planter, Goose, Small & Large 40.00
Planter, Hanging, Iris 165.00
Planter, Hanging, Little Red Riding Hood 345.00
Planter, Little Boy 20.00
Planter, Parchment & Pine, Pink & Gray 20.00
Planter, Pheasant 30.00
Planter, St. Francis 20.00
Planter, Standing Poodle, Pink 45.00
Planter, Swan, 9 x 11 In. 40.00
Planter, Swan, Gold Trim, 6 In. 26.00
Planter, Twin Geese 25.00
Planter, Wishing Well, 6 1/2 In. 40.00
Planter, Woodland, Yellow & Green, 10 1/2 In. 65.00
Salt & Pepper, Little Red Riding Hood, 3 1/2 In. 42.00
Salt & Pepper, Little Red Riding Hood, 4 1/2 In. 725.00
Salt & Pepper, Little Red Riding Hood, 5 1/2 In. ....110.00 to 160.00
Salt & Pepper, Poppygold Trim 35.00
Salt & Pepper, Sunglow 15.00
Sconce, Sunglow, Cast Iron 85.00
Soap Dish, Blue & White, Round 170.00
Sugar, Cover, Basket Weave, Blue & White 140.00
Sugar, Cover, Blossom Flite, Pink, Black 35.00
Sugar, Cover, Cinderella Blossom 22.00
Sugar, Royal, Woodland, Blue, Speckled, Open 12.00
Sugar & Creamer, Cover, Butterfly, Blue 80.00
Sugar & Creamer, Little Red Riding Hood, Side Pour 300.00
Tea Set, Ebb Tide, 3 Piece 225.00
Tea Set, Wild Flower, 4 Piece 1500.00
Teapot, Car, Chinese Red 650.00
Teapot, Dogwood 250.00
Teapot, Ebb Tide, Chartreuse, Wine 150.00
Teapot, Little Red Riding Hood ....255.00 to 350.00
Teapot, Magnolia, Blue Base, Pink Top 170.00
Teapot, Magnolia, Glossy 35.00
Teapot, Nautilus, Delphinium Blue, Gold Trim 285.00
Vase, Blossom Flite, Black, 9 1/2 In. 65.00
Vase, Bow Knot, 8 1/2 In. ....135.00 to 200.00
Vase, Bow Knot, Blue Turquoise, 10 1/2 In. 250.00
Vase, Bow Knot, Pink, Blue, 6 1/2 In. ....95.00 to 110.00
Vase, Bud, Ebb Tide 95.00
Vase, Bud, Iris 90.00
Vase, Calla Lily, No. 4 .... 120.00
Vase, Dogwood, Turquoise, Cream, 4 3/4 In. 55.00
Vase, Ebb Tide, Fish, 11 In. 100.00

Hull, Vase, Forest Green, Black, White Marble, 1930, 6 In.

If you are having your antiques moved in a van to a new home, watch out for damage. Check the antiques as they are unloaded. Sweep the inside of the moving van and save any small pieces of veneer or wood that might have chipped off your furniture.

Vase, Fan, Magnolia, Gold Side Handle, Blue Flowers, 8 1/2 In.	55.00
Vase, Fan, Wild Flower, 10 1/2 In.	110.00
Vase, Forest Green, Black, White Marble, 1930, 6 In. *Illus*	18.00
Vase, Imperial, Bell, White, 10 In.	12.00
Vase, Iris, Beige, Pink, Yellow, 8 1/2 In.	95.00
Vase, Little Red Riding Hood	275.00
Vase, Magnolia, 12 1/2 In.	85.00 to 175.00
Vase, Magnolia, Matte, Peach, 6 1/4 In.	32.00
Vase, Magnolia, Matte, Pink, Blue, 8 1/2 In.	50.00
Vase, Magnolia, Pink Flowers, 12 1/2 In.	125.00
Vase, Magnolia, Rose & Cream, Handle, 8 1/2 In.	65.00
Vase, Magnolia, Swan Handles	280.00
Vase, Mardi Gras, Pink, 6 In.	20.00
Vase, Open Rose	120.00
Vase, Open Rose, Swan	165.00
Vase, Orchid, 8 1/2 In.	130.00
Vase, Pine Cone, Pink, 6 1/2 In.	95.00
Vase, Poppy, 4 3/4 In.	135.00
Vase, Sueno, Matte Blue, Paper Label, 6 In.	95.00
Vase, Tulip, 10 In.	180.00
Vase, Unicorn, 9 1/2 In.	60.00
Vase, Water Lily, 6 1/2 In.	45.00
Vase, Water Lily, 8 1/2 In.	125.00
Vase, Water Lily, Glossy White, Gold Trim, 5 1/2 In.	38.00
Vase, White & Pink Blossoms, Foliage, Yellow Ground, Bennett, 9 In.	2200.00
Vase, Wild Flower, 8 1/2 In.	200.00
Vase, Wild Flower, Matte, 8 1/2 In.	105.00
Vase, Wild Flower, Pink Over Blue, 4 1/2 In.	50.00
Vase, Wild Flower, Pink Over Blue, 6 1/2 In.	65.00
Vase, Wildflower, Cornucopia, Peach, 10 x 8 1/2 In.	60.00
Vase, Woodland, 6 1/2 In.	50.00
Vase, Woodland, Matte, 7 1/2 In.	85.00
Wall Pocket, Bow Knot	225.00
Wall Pocket, Bow Knot, Whiskbroom, Original Sticker	195.00
Wall Pocket, Mandolin	45.00
Wall Pocket, Match Holder	750.00
Wall Pocket, Pitcher, Label	715.00
Wall Pocket, Poppy, 9 In.	350.00
Wall Pocket, Rosella, Pair	65.00
Wall Pocket, Royal, Woodland	25.00
Wall Pocket, Shell, 7 1/2 In.	35.00
Wall Pocket, Woodland	40.00
Window Box, Fantasy, Pink & Pale Green, 12 1/2 In.	20.00
Window Box, Woodland, Green Over Pink, 10 In.	40.00

Window Box, Woodland, Pink Base, Green Top 65.00

HUMMEL figurines, based on the drawings of the nun Berta Hummel, are made by the W. Goebel Porzellanfabrik of Oeslau, Germany, now Rodenthal, Germany. They were first made in 1934. The mark has changed through the years. The following are the approximate dates for each of the marks: *Crown* mark, 1935 to 1949; *U.S. Zone, Germany*, 1946 to 1948; *West Germany*, after 1949; *full bee* with variations, 1950 to 1959; *stylized bee*, 1960 to 1972; *three line mark*, 1968 to 1979; *vee over gee*, 1972 to 1979; *new mark, West Germany* 1979 to 1990; *G Mark, Goebel* 1979 to 1991; and the *Goebel, Germany*, mark introduced in 1991. Other decorative items and plates that feature Hummel drawings have been made by Schmid Brothers, Inc., since 1971.

Ashtray, No. 34, Singing Lesson, Full Bee	106.00
Ashtray, No. 114, Let's Sing, Full Bee	225.00
Bell, Annual, 1978, Let's Sing	29.00
Bookends, No. 14/A & B, Bookworms, Stylized Bee	300.00
Bookends, No. 251/A & B, Good Friends & She Loves Me, Stylized Bee	275.00
Bookends, No. 252/A & B, Apple Tree Boy & Apple Tree Girl, Full Bee	350.00
Box, No. III/110, Let's Sing, Full Bee	150.00
Candleholder, No. 38, Angel, With Mandolin, Full Bee	200.00
Candleholder, No. 39, Angel, With Accordion, Full Bee	200.00
Candleholder, No. 40, Angel, With Trumpet, Full Bee	200.00
Figurine, No. 1, Puppy Love, Stylized Bee	240.00
Figurine, No. 2/0, Little Fiddler, Stylized Bee	130.00
Figurine, No. 2/0, Little Fiddler, Vee Over Gee	50.00
Figurine, No. 2/II, Little Fiddler, Vee Over Gee	650.00
Figurine, No. 3/I, Bookworm, Full Bee	325.00
Figurine, No. 4, Little Fiddler, Full Bee	195.00 to 225.00
Figurine, No. 5, Strolling Along, Full Bee	375.00
Figurine, No. 5, Strolling Along, Vee Over Gee	135.00
Figurine, No. 6/0, Sensitive Hunter, Full Bee	210.00
Figurine, No. 6/0, Sensitive Hunter, Stylized Bee	120.00 to 144.00
Figurine, No. 8, Bookworm, Full Bee	210.00
Figurine, No. 8, Bookworm, Stylized Bee	138.00 to 250.00
Figurine, No. 9, Begging His Share Without Can, Vee Over Gee	126.00
Figurine, No. 9, Begging His Share, Stylized Bee	115.00
Figurine, No. 10/I, Flower Madonna, Stylized Bee	185.00
Figurine, No. 10/III, Flower Madonna, Full Bee	385.00
Figurine, No. 12/1, Chimney Sweep, Full Bee	236.00
Figurine, No. 12/2/0, Chimney Sweep, Full Bee	100.00
Figurine, No. 13/0, Meditation, Full Bee	247.00
Figurine, No. 13/0, Meditation, Stylized Bee	126.50
Figurine, No. 13/II, Meditation, Vee Over Gee	216.00
Figurine, No. 15/0, Hear Ye, Hear Ye, Three Line Mark	97.75
Figurine, No. 16/1, Little Hiker, Full Bee	236.00
Figurine, No. 16/I, Little Hiker, Stylized Bee	65.00
Figurine, No. 17/0, Congratulations, Vee Over Gee	102.00
Figurine, No. 18, Christ Child, Full Bee	165.00
Figurine, No. 20, Prayer Before Breakfast, Crown Mark	450.00
Figurine, No. 21/0, Heavenly Angel, Stylized Bee	110.00
Figurine, No. 21/0, Heavenly Angel, Stylized Mark	100.00
Figurine, No. 23/I, Adoration, New Mark	180.00
Figurine, No. 23/I, Adoration, Stylized Bee	295.00
Figurine, No. 32, Little Gabriel, Stylized Bee	105.00
Figurine, No. 42/0, Good Shepherd, Full Bee	230.00
Figurine, No. 42/I, Good Shepherd, Large, Full Bee	5200.00
Figurine, No. 47/0, Goose Girl, Full Bee	370.00
Figurine, No. 47/0, Goose Girl, Stylized Bee	150.00
Figurine, No. 47/3/0, Goose Girl, Full Bee	115.00 to 187.00
Figurine, No. 47/3/0, Goose Girl, Stylized Bee	92.00
Figurine, No. 49/0, To Market, Stylized Bee	204.00

Figurine, No. 49/3/0, To Market, Full Bee 195.00
Figurine, No. 51, Village Boy, Full Bee 115.00
Figurine, No. 51/0, Village Boy, Full Bee 262.00
Figurine, No. 52, Going To Grandma's, Crown Mark 1000.00
Figurine, No. 52/0, Going To Grandma's, Full Bee .... 175.00 to 300.00
Figurine, No. 52/0, Going To Grandma's, Stylized Bee 225.00
Figurine, No. 52/1, Going To Grandma's, Vee Over Gee 250.00
Figurine, No. 56/A, Culprits, Stylized Bee Mark 225.00
Figurine, No. 56B, Out Of Danger, Stylized Bee 235.00
Figurine, No. 57, Chick Girl, Stylized Bee 100.00
Figurine, No. 57/0, Chick Girl, Full Bee .... 150.00 to 187.00
Figurine, No. 57/0, Chick Girl, New Mark 80.00
Figurine, No. 57/I, Chick Girl, Stylized Bee 220.00
Figurine, No. 58/1, Playmates, Stylized Bee .... 150.00 to 220.00
Figurine, No. 59, Skier, Full Bee 195.00
Figurine, No. 63, Singing Lesson, Full Bee 125.00
Figurine, No. 63, Singing Lesson, Vee Over Gee 60.00
Figurine, No. 66, Farm Boy, Stylized Bee 135.00
Figurine, No. 66, Farm Boy, Vee Over Gee 120.00
Figurine, No. 68, Lost Sheep, Full Bee, 6 1/4 In. 250.00
Figurine, No. 68/0, Lost Sheep, Vee Over Gee 50.00
Figurine, No. 69, Happy Pastime, Full Bee 165.00
Figurine, No. 69, Happy Pastime, Stylized Bee 84.00
Figurine, No. 70, Holy Child, Full Bee 105.00
Figurine, No. 71, Stormy Weather, Stylized Bee .... 270.00 to 325.00
Figurine, No. 71, Stormy Weather, Vee Over Gee 99.00
Figurine, No. 74, Little Gardener, Stylized Bee 85.00
Figurine, No. 79, Globe Trotter, Three Line Mark 103.50
Figurine, No. 80, Little Scholar, Full-Bee 243.00
Figurine, No. 80, Little Scholar, Stylized Bee 180.00
Figurine, No. 81/0, School Girl, Stylized Bee 230.00
Figurine, No. 82/0, School Boy, Full Bee 210.00
Figurine, No. 82/0, School Boy, Stylized Bee 150.00
Figurine, No. 83, Angel Serenade, Lamb, Full Bee 270.00
Figurine, No. 84/0, Worship, Full Bee 172.50
Figurine, No. 84/0, Worship, Vee Over Gee 84.00
Figurine, No. 85/0, Serenade, Stylized Bee 120.00
Figurine, No. 87, For Father, Full Bee 243.00
Figurine, No. 87, For Father, Stylized Bee .... 126.50 to 165.00
Figurine, No. 88/II, Heavenly Protection, Stylized Bee 635.00
Figurine, No. 89/I, Little Cellist, Stylized Bee 165.00
Figurine, No. 89/I, Little Cellist, Vee Over Gee 125.00
Figurine, No. 94/3/0, Surprise, Full Bee 187.00
Figurine, No. 95, Brother, Stylized Bee 150.00
Figurine, No. 98, Sister, Crown Mark 360.00
Figurine, No. 98, Sister, Full Bee 225.00
Figurine, No. 98, Sister, Stylized Bee .... 165.00 to 220.00
Figurine, No. 111/I, Wayside Harmony, Full Bee .... 250.00 to 300.00
Figurine, No. 112, Just Resting, Crown Mark 500.00
Figurine, No. 112/3/0, Just Resting, Full Bee .... 100.00 to 187.00
Figurine, No. 112/3/0, Just Resting, Three Line Mark .... 100.00 to 120.00
Figurine, No. 112/I, Just Resting, Full Bee 250.00
Figurine, No. 112/L, Just Resting, Stylized Mark 195.00
Figurine, No. 123, Max & Moritz, Three Line Mark .... 103.50 to 145.00
Figurine, No. 124/0, Hello, Full Bee .... 220.00 to 225.00
Figurine, No. 127, Doctor, Full Bee 175.00
Figurine, No. 127, Doctor, Stylized Bee .... 92.00 to 105.00
Figurine, No. 128, Baker, Full Bee .... 180.00 to 225.00
Figurine, No. 128, Baker, Stylized Bee 85.00
Figurine, No. 129, Band Leader, Full Bee 143.00
Figurine, No. 129, Band Leader, Stylized Bee .... 112.00 to 185.00
Figurine, No. 130, Duet, Full Bee 337.00

Figurine, No. 131, Street Singer, Full Bee 225.00
Figurine, No. 131, Street Singer, Stylized Bee.. 170.00
Figurine, No. 132, Star Gazer, Full Bee 210.00
Figurine, No. 135, Soloist, Full Bee ....50.00 to 168.00
Figurine, No. 135, Soloist, Stylized Bee 102.00
Figurine, No. 136, Friends, 10 1/2 In., Crown Mark 345.00
Figurine, No. 136/I, Friends, Vee Over Gee 114.00
Figurine, No. 136/V, Friends, Full Bee 936.00
Figurine, No. 141/1, Apple Tree Girl, Vee Over Gee 100.00
Figurine, No. 141/3/0, Apple Tree Girl, Full Bee 187.00
Figurine, No. 141/I, Apple Tree Girl, Full Bee 220.00
Figurine, No. 142/3/0, Apple Tree Boy, Stylized Bee ....80.50 to 120.00
Figurine, No. 142/I, Apple Tree Boy, Tree Base, Crown Mark 600.00
Figurine, No. 142/I, Apple Tree Boy, Vee Over Gee 95.00
Figurine, No. 142/V & 141/V, Apple Tree Boy & Girl, Pair, Vee Over Gee 1050.00
Figurine, No. 142/V, Apple Tree Boy, Vee Over Gee 675.00
Figurine, No. 143/0, Boots, Stylized Bee 144.00
Figurine, No. 143/1, Boots, Vee Over Gee 150.00
Figurine, No. 144, Angelic Song, Full Bee 175.00
Figurine, No. 150/0, Happy Days, Full Bee 375.00
Figurine, No. 150/2/0, Happy Days, Full Bee ....27.00 to 225.00
Figurine, No. 152/B/0, Umbrella Girl, Three Line Mark 450.00
Figurine, No. 152/B/0, Umbrella Girl, Vee Over Gee. 325.00
Figurine, No. 152A, Umbrella Boy, Full Bee 1250.00
Figurine, No. 153/0, Auf Wiedersehen, With Hat, Full Bee 2200.00
Figurine, No. 157, Doctor, Full Bee 165.00
Figurine, No. 169, Bird Duet, Stylized Bee 120.00
Figurine, No. 170/3, School Boys, Vee Over Gee. 1300.00
Figurine, No. 171, Little Sweeper, Stylized Bee 105.00
Figurine, No. 174, She Loves Me, She Loves Me Not, Full Bee 175.00
Figurine, No. 175, Mother's Darling, Full Bee 240.00
Figurine, No. 175, Mother's Darling, Stylized Bee... 126.50
Figurine, No. 175, Mother's Darling, Vee Over Gee 82.00
Figurine, No. 178, Photographer, Full Bee 225.00
Figurine, No. 178, Photographer, Three Line Mark 220.00
Figurine, No. 182, Good Friends, Stylized Bee 195.00
Figurine, No. 184, Latest News, Full Bee 60.00
Figurine, No. 185, Accordion Boy, Full Bee 160.00
Figurine, No. 185, Accordion Boy, Stylized Bee ....109.25 to 172.50
Figurine, No. 188/0, Celestial Musician, New Mark 108.00
Figurine, No. 195/2/0, Barnyard Hero, Full Bee ....150.00 to 168.00
Figurine, No. 195/2/0, Barnyard Hero, Three Line Mark 90.00
Figurine, No. 197, Be Patient, Full Bee 143.75
Figurine, No. 197/2/0, Be Patient, Full Bee 243.00
Figurine, No. 198/2/0, Home From Market, Three Line Mark 95.00
Figurine, No. 198/I, Home From Market, Vee Over Gee 114.00
Figurine, No. 199/0, Feeding Time, Full Bee 240.00
Figurine, No. 199/0, Feeding Time, Three Line Mark 120.00
Figurine, No. 200/0, Little Goat Herder, Stylized Bee 120.00
Figurine, No. 200/I, Little Goat Herder, Three Line Mark 115.00
Figurine, No. 200/I, Little Goat Herder, Vee Over Gee 120.00
Figurine, No. 201/2/0, Retreat To Safety, Full Bee 275.00
Figurine, No. 204, Weary Wanderer, Full Bee ....175.00 to 300.00
Figurine, No. 214/A, Virgin Mary, Three Line Mark 111.00
Figurine, No. 217, Boy With Toothache, Three Line Mark 175.00
Figurine, No. 218/0, Birthday Serenade, Full Bee 300.00
Figurine, No. 220/0, Little Goat Herder, Vee Over Gee 50.00
Figurine, No. 226, Mail Is Here, Vee Over Gee. 285.00
Figurine, No. 239/B, Girl With Doll, Three Line Mark 30.00
Figurine, No. 255, Stitch In Time, Vee Over Gee... 120.00
Figurine, No. 260/F, We Congratulate, Vee Over Gee 200.00
Figurine, No. 260P, King, Kneeling, Large, Three Line Mark 299.00

Figurine, No. 261, Angel Duet 105.00
Figurine, No. 304, The Artist, Three Line Mark 172.50
Figurine, No. 305, Builder, Three Line Mark 175.00
Figurine, No. 309, With Loving Greetings, New Mark 105.00
Figurine, No. 311, Kiss Me, Socks On Doll, Stylized Bee 490.00
Figurine, No. 317, Not For You, Three Line Mark 150.00
Figurine, No. 319, Doll Bath, Three Line Mark .... 130.00 to 180.00
Figurine, No. 322, Little Pharmacist, Three Line Mark 115.00
Figurine, No. 328, Carnival, Gee Mark 60.00
Figurine, No. 328, Carnival, Three Line Mark 109.25
Figurine, No. 331, Cross Roads, Vee Over Gee 250.00
Figurine, No. 334, Homeward Bound, Three Line Mark 479.00
Figurine, No. 336, Close Harmony, Three Line Mark 225.00
Figurine, No. 340, Letter To Santa Claus, Vee Over Gee 210.00
Figurine, No. 344, Feathered Friends, Vee Over Gee 100.00
Figurine, No. 347, Adventure Bound, Vee Over Gee 2200.00
Figurine, No. 348, Ring Around The Rosie, Vee Over Gee .... 1350.00 to 1550.00
Figurine, No. 353/1, Spring Dance, Vee Over Gee 375.00
Figurine, No. 355, Autumn Harvest, Vee Over Gee 105.00
Figurine, No. 361, Favorite Pet, Three Line Mark 210.00
Figurine, No. 367, Busy Student, Three Line Mark .... 80.50 to 130.00
Figurine, No. 385, Chicken Licken, Three Line Mark 100.00
Figurine, No. 394, Timid Little Sister, New Mark 225.00
Figurine, No. 399, Valentine Joy, Gee Mark 82.00
Font, No. 36/I, Child With Flowers, Stylized Bee 100.00
Font, No. 91/A, Angel Facing Left, Vee Over Gee 25.00
Lamp, Boy In Tree Form 190.00
Plaque, Auf Wiedersehen, 5 x 5 In. 75.00
Plaque, Collectors Club, 1976 .... 5.00
Plaque, Little Fiddler, Crown Mark 350.00
Plaque, No. 187A, Dealer, Moon Top, Three Line Mark 359.00
Plaque, No. 690, Smiling Through 125.00
Plate, Anniversary, 1980 .... 39.00
Plate, Annual, Heavenly Angel, 1971 .... 595.00
Plate, Christmas, Angel, Schmid, 1971 .... 12.00
Plate, Christmas, Schmid, 1973 .... 34.00
Plate, Collector Club, 1978 .... 30.00
Plate, No. 735, Celebration Series, Valentine Gift, 1986 .... 45.00
Plate, No. 736, Celebration Series, Daisies Don't Tell, 1988 .... 59.00
Plate, No. 737, Celebration Series, Valentine Joy 45.00

HUTSCHENREUTHER Porcelain Company of Selb, Germany, was established in 1814 and is still working. The company makes fine quality porcelain dinnerwares and figurines. The mark has changed through the years, but the name and the lion insignia appear in most versions.

Dinner Set, Meriden, Floral Design, Gold Trim, 36 Piece 140.00
Figurine, 3 Children, Hands Clasped, 6 1/2 x 7 In. 300.00
Figurine, Bison Fighting Mountain Lion, Painted, Germany, 9 x 14 In. 495.00
Figurine, Blue Jay 85.00
Figurine, Cocker Spaniel 185.00
Figurine, Dachshund, Standing, Paper Label, 5 1/2 In. 195.00
Figurine, Dancing Couple 75.00
Figurine, Great Blue Heron, 19 1/2 x 22 In. 3220.00
Figurine, Gull In Flight, 7 1/2 In. 90.00
Figurine, Kissing Budgie Birds, Yellow & Green, 8 1/2 x 13 In. 295.00
Figurine, Musicians Of Bremen, 7 1/2 In. 275.00
Figurine, Nude Girl, On Knee, Feeding Doe, 13 x 10 In. 595.00
Figurine, Owl 45.00
Figurine, Running Nude Woman, On Gold Pedestal Ball 225.00
Figurine, Siamese Cat, Cream, Brown & Blue Eyes, 7 1/2 In. 295.00
Group, Nymph Riding Stag, Signed C. Werner, 9 1/4 In. 150.00
Plate, Center Fruit, Baskets Surround, Gilt Border, 11 In., 12 Piece 750.00
Plate, Mozart, Gilt Edge, Cobalt Blue Rim, 10 1/2 In. 65.00

ICONS, special, revered pictures of Jesus, Mary, or a saint, are usually Russian or Byzantine. The small icons collected today are made of wood and tin or precious metals. Many modern copies have been made in the old style and are being sold to tourists in Russia and Europe.

Annunciation, Brass Border, Russia, 17th Century, 11 1/4 x 9 1/4 In.	1200.00
Bishop Saint, Dalmatian, 17th Century, 10 x 8 In.	4150.00
Burning Bush, Russia, 19th Century, 12 1/4 x 10 5/8 In.	925.00
Christ Pantocrator, 19th Century, 12 x 10 1/2 In.	865.00
Christ Pantocrator, Silver, Enamel, Russia, c.1900, 10 5/8 x 8 7/8 In.	1600.00
Crucifix, Oil On Wood, 14 x 12 In.	440.00
Holy Trinity, Russia, 14 x 12 In.	1150.00
Iverskaya Mother Of God, Silver, Red Stones, Russia, c.1910, 12 1/4 x 10 1/2 In.	6900.00
Kazan Mother Of God, Russia, 19th Century, 12 1/4 x 10 1/4 In.	800.00
Madonna & Child, 2 Saints, Olive Tree Trunk Carved, Tin Hinges, 1800s, 7 1/2 x 8 In.	420.00
Madonna & Child, Wood Panel, Russia, 10 x 7 1/2 In.	385.00
Pokrov, 19th Century, 13 3/4 x 12 1/4 In.	1035.00
Resurrection With Feasts, Surrounded By 12 Festivals Of Church, 12 x 11 3/8 In.	1380.00
Saint, 2 Women Saints, Papier-Mache Box, Mirror, Europe, Early 1800s, 2 x 3 In.	480.00
St. Elijah, Museum Of Kiev, Paint & Gilt On Wood, Russia, c.1750, 12 1/4 x 10 1/2 In.	635.00
St. George, Silver Plated, Riza, 7 x 5 3/4 In.	220.00
St. John The Forerunner, Baptist Holds Chalice, 18th Century, 28 x 21 In.	1850.00
St. Nicholas, Patron Saint Of Russia, Painted Face, Silver Front, c.1807	3200.00
St. Nicholas, Russia, 19th Century, 16 3/4 x 13 3/4 In.	980.00
St. Yerimin, Russia, c.1700, 20 x 14 3/4 In.	1725.00
Transfiguration Of Christ, Russia, 19th Century, 12 1/4 x 10 1/4 In.	920.00

IMARI patterns are named for the Japanese ware decorated with orange and blue stylized flowers. The design on the Japanese ware became so characteristic that the name *Imari* has come to mean any pattern of this type. It was copied by the European factories of the eighteenth and early nineteenth centuries.

Bowl, Blue & Orange Panels, 6 Character Mark, c.1900, 9 1/2 In.	200.00
Bowl, Cover, Polychrome, Marked Lid, 19th Century, 4 1/4 In., 6 Piece	475.00
Bowl, Fish, Blue & Iron Red Floral & Figural Design, 14 In.	405.00
Bowl, Flower Shape, Cartouches Of Carp & Flowers, 11 In.	220.00
Bowl, Flower Shape, Scrolling Floral Panels, Late 19th Century, 15 In.	920.00
Bowl, Flowers & Vines, Peony Center, Landscape Cartouches Interior, 13 1/2 In.	1100.00
Bowl, Foliage & Birds, Scrolled Handles, Bronze Mounted, 12 1/2 In.	2185.00
Bowl, Polychrome Herons, Brown Rim, 6 In.	325.00
Bowl, Round, Figures On Exterior, Interior Landscape, 7 1/4 In.	750.00
Brush Pot, 6 In.	165.00
Charger, 6 Panels, Alternating Scenes, Stylized Florals, Gold, 16 In.	150.00
Charger, Blossoming Peony In Vase, Phoenix Amid Branches, 12 1/2 In.	978.00
Charger, Blue & White, 15 3/4 In.	230.00
Charger, Flower Shape, Peony Center, 12 1/2 In.	155.00
Charger, Round Center Design, 18 1/2 In.	495.00
Dish, Boat, 19th Century, 13 1/4 In.	900.00
Dish, Dragon, Blue & White, 18th Century	300.00
Dish, Fish Shape, 10 In.	286.00
Dish, Fluted, Scalloped, 12 1/2 In.	195.00
Pitcher, Floral Spray, Iron Red & Cobalt Blue, White Ground	135.00
Plate, 4 Character Mark, 9 In.	80.00
Plate, Octagonal, 11 1/2 In.	470.00
Plate, Scalloped, 8 1/2 In.	90.00
Platter, Fish Form, 23 In.	460.00
Platter, Fish, Underwater Scene, Water Lilies, Oval, Large	95.00
Punch Bowl, Bird & Floral Design, Scalloped Rim, 19th Century, 10 1/4 In.	290.00
Punch Bowl, Blue & White, 19th Century, 15 In.	1695.00
Sugar, Blue, Gold, Red On White, Silver Bail Handle & Cover, England	90.00
Teapot, Ribbed Melon, 18th Century	850.00
Tureen, Domed Lid, Handles, Mason, 1840	590.00
Vase, Bottle, 3 1/2 In.	45.00

Vase, Faceted, 4 In. 90.00
Vase, Multiform Panels Over Floral Ground, 19th Century, 30 In. 1840.00

IMPERIAL GLASS Corporation was founded in Bellaire, Ohio, in 1901. It
became a subsidiary of Lenox, Inc., in 1973 and was sold to Arthur R. Lorch
in 1981. It was sold again in 1982, went bankrupt that same year, and some of
the molds and assets were sold to other companies. The Imperial glass preferred by the collector is art glass, carnival glass, slag glass, stretch glass, and
other top-quality tablewares. Tablewares and animals are listed here. The others may be found in the appropriate sections.

Animal, Asiatic Pheasant, Amber 110.00
Animal, Clydesdale, Amber, 5 1/4 In. 330.00
Animal, Colt Set, Amber, 3 Piece 270.00
Animal, Cygnet, Light Blue, 4 In. 25.00
Animal, Donkey, Wild Jack, Ultra Blue, 6 In. 70.00
Animal, Elephant, Green Carnival Glass, 1 In. 90.00
Animal, Elephant, Light Blue, 4 In. 190.00
Animal, Gazelle, Ultra Blue, 11 In. 110.00
Animal, Giraffe, Etched, 10 1/4 In. 190.00
Animal, Hen, Font, Sun Yellow, 4 1/2 In. 110.00
Animal, Mallard Set, Amber, 3 Piece 440.00
Animal, Pig, Amber, 3 1/8 In. 440.00
Animal, Piglet, Pink, 1 In. 40.00
Animal, Rabbit, Ultra Blue, 4 3/8 In. 165.00
Animal, Swan, Green Iridescent, 4 1/2 x 3 3/4 In. 28.00
Animal, Woodchuck, Amber, 4 1/2 In. 55.00
Beaded Block, Bowl, Green, 7 1/2 In. 38.00
Beaded Block, Sugar, Vaseline Opalescent 38.00
Bookends, Scotty Dog, Carmel Slag 375.00
Candlewick, Ashtray, Eagle 57.00
Candlewick, Ashtray, Rectangular, 4 1/4 x 3 In. 3.00
Candlewick, Basket, Beaded, Handle, 5 In. 185.00
Candlewick, Bowl, 2 Sections, Handles, 6 In. 18.00
Candlewick, Bowl, Blue, 10 x 7 In. 125.00
Candlewick, Bowl, Flared, Graduated Beads, 11 In. 75.00
Candlewick, Bowl, Fruit, Fluted, Footed, 10 In. 200.00
Candlewick, Bowl, Handle, 6 In. 18.00
Candlewick, Bowl, Heart, Handle, 5 In. 18.00
Candlewick, Bowl, Star Cut, 4 3/4 In. 18.00
Candlewick, Bowl, Star Cut, 7 In. 30.00
Candlewick, Butter, Beaded Cover, 1/4 Lb. .... 25.00 to 27.00
Candlewick, Candlestick, Flower 150.00
Candlewick, Compote, 5 1/2 In. .... 25.00 to 36.00
Candlewick, Cruet, Oil, Bulbous, 6 Oz. 50.00
Candlewick, Cup Plate, With Cup, Oval 11.00
Candlewick, Egg Tray 115.00
Candlewick, Goblet, 9 Oz. 18.00
Candlewick, Goblet, 10 Oz. 21.00
Candlewick, Ice Bucket 45.00
Candlewick, Nut Cup 10.00
Candlewick, Plate, 8 In. 12.00
Candlewick, Plate, 10 In. 42.00
Candlewick, Punch Bowl .... 89.00 to 110.00
Candlewick, Punch Cup 8.00
Candlewick, Punch Set, Box, 9 Piece 275.00
Candlewick, Punch Set, Mallard Etched, 13 Piece 395.00
Candlewick, Relish, 3 Section, 3-Footed, 10 In. 95.00
Candlewick, Relish, 4 Sections, 12 In. 100.00
Candlewick, Relish, 4 Sections, Gold Trim, 8 1/2 In. 65.00
Candlewick, Relish, 5 Sections, 13 In. .... 45.00 to 60.00
Candlewick, Relish, 6 Sections 45.00
Candlewick, Salt & Pepper 15.00
Candlewick, Salt, 2 1/2 In. 8.00

Candlewick, Server, Center Handle, Heart Handle, 8 1/2 In. 25.00
Candlewick, Server, Sandwich, Center Handle, Red 650.00
Candlewick, Sherbet, Footed, 5 Oz. 20.00
Candlewick, Spoon & Fork. 25.00
Candlewick, Sugar & Creamer 22.00
Candlewick, Sugar & Creamer, Individual 14.00
Candlewick, Tray, 3 Sections, Green, Round, 7 In. 25.00
Candlewick, Tray, Lemon, Handle 45.00
Candlewick, Tray, Oval, 9 In. 30.00
Candlewick, Tumbler, Footed, 12 Oz. 22.00
Candlewick, Vase, Bud, 4 In. 48.00
Candlewick, Vase, Fan, Beaded Handles, 8 In. 20.00
Candlewick, Wine, 4 Oz. ....22.00 to 25.00
Cape Cod, Bowl, 5 In. 6.00
Cape Cod, Bowl, 11 In. 35.00
Cape Cod, Bowl, Baked Apple, 6 In. 5.00
Cape Cod, Bowl, Footed, 9 1/2 In. 37.00
Cape Cod, Cake Plate, 72 Candle Holes 300.00
Cape Cod, Champagne, Azalea. 20.00
Cape Cod, Compote, 6 In. 12.00
Cape Cod, Cruet, 4 Oz. 20.00
Cape Cod, Cup & Saucer 5.00
Cape Cod, Decanter, Square, 24 Oz. 60.00
Cape Cod, Goblet, 9 Oz. 5.00
Cape Cod, Goblet, Azalea, 9 Oz. 22.00
Cape Cod, Goblet, Red 15.00
Cape Cod, Jam Jar 30.00
Cape Cod, Marmalade 30.00
Cape Cod, Parfait, 6 Oz. 7.50
Cape Cod, Plate, 7 1/4 In. 6.00
Cape Cod, Plate, 8 In. ....5.00 to 6.00
Cape Cod, Plate, 10 In. 35.00
Cape Cod, Plate, Azalea, 8 1/4 In. 20.00
Cape Cod, Relish, 3 Sections, 9 1/2 In. 28.00
Cape Cod, Sherbet, Amberina 20.00
Cape Cod, Sherbet, Footed 7.00
Cape Cod, Stein, Milk Glass, Handle 85.00
Cape Cod, Sugar, Footed, 3 1/2 In. 7.00
Cape Cod, Wine, 3 Oz. 5.00
Cape Cod, Wine, 4 1/2 In. 7.00
Cathay, Ashtray, Pillow, Jade. 45.00
Cathay, Ashtray, Wuling, Verde Green 55.00
Cathay, Ashtray, Yang & Yin, Red. 150.00
Cathay, Bookends, Empress. 150.00
Cathay, Pagoda, Frosted 850.00
Dish, Lion Cover, Gold Satin, 7 x 7 1/2 In. 55.00
Dish, Rooster Cover, Carnival Glass, 8 1/2 x 8 In. 75.00
Dresser Set, 2 Bottles, Puff Box, Hand Painted Red Flowers, 3 Piece 75.00
Duck, Ashtray 25.00
Mayonnaise, Liner, Ladle, Blue Opalescent 165.00
Old Williamsburg, Goblet, Water 7.00
Old Williamsburg, Tumbler, Iced Tea, Footed 7.00
Pillar Flute, Bowl, Blue, Flower, 5 In. 25.00
Pillar Flute, Celery, Blue 27.00
Pillar Flute, Creamer, Blue 22.00
Pillar Flute, Pickle, Blue, Handle 25.00
Pillar Flute, Plate, Blue, 8 In. 18.00
Pillar Flute, Vase, Blue, 6 In. 65.00
Plate, Christmas, 1970. .... 7.00
Reeded, Cocktail, Footed, Cobalt Blue, 3 1/2 Oz. 16.00
Reeded, Pitcher, Teal, 80 Oz. 95.00
Reeded, Rose Bowl, Red 45.00
Reeded, Tumbler, Teal, 14 Oz. 15.00

Reeded, Vase, Ivy Ball, Crystal, Red, 4 In. 65.00
Snake Dance, Urn, Cranberry, 8 /12 In. 77.00

INDIAN art from North America has attracted the collector for many years.
Each tribe has its own distinctive designs and techniques. Baskets, jewelry,
pottery, and leatherwork are of greatest collector interest. Eskimo art is listed
in another category in this book.

Bag, Doctor's, Sioux, Beaded Leather, Steel Faceted Beads, 1880s 4320.00
Bag, Nez Perce, Corn Husk, Brown, Green, Blue & Orange 795.00
Bag, Nez Perce, Corn Husk, Polychrome Geometric Design, 20 x 15 In. 200.00
Bag, Pipe, Cree, Floral Design, Fringe 1495.00
Bag, Pipe, Sioux, Geometric Shapes 2400.00
Basket, Algonquin, Splint, Lid, Natural, Red & Green, 1835 Newspaper Lining, 12 In.   248.00
Basket, Apache, Burden, Cloth Attached, Tin Cones, 9 x 9 In. 495.00
Basket, Cheese, Micmac 195.00
Basket, Coiled, Red & Natural, Inverted Lip, c.1900, 5 1/2 In. 103.50
Basket, Navajo, Woven Geometric Design, 18 1/2 In. 195.00
Basket, Nootka, Cover, Polychrome Whale Boats, Whalers, 2 1/2 x 3 7/8 In. 165.00
Basket, Northeastern Woodlands, Splint, Painted Design, Cover, 10 1/2 In. 690.00
Basket, Papago, 5 3/4 x 7 1/4 In. 235.00
Basket, Papago, Arrowhead Pattern, 3 x 6 In. 190.00
Basket, Penobscot, Cover, Sweet Grass, c.1930, 8 1/2 In. 55.00
Basket, Pima, Bowl, Grass Design, 14 1/4 x 3 3/4 In. 575.00
Basket, Pima, Urn Shape, Step Design, 8 1/2 x 8 In. 225.00
Basket, Pomo, Coiled, Dark Stepped Zigzag, Seed Beads Top, Quail Feathers 3410.00
Basket, Pomo, Geometric Design, 3 x 5 1/4 In. 175.00
Basket, Pomo, Stepped Zigzag Design, Quail Feathers On Body, 7 1/2 In. 310.00
Basket, Taconic, Swing Handle, Concave Base 400.00
Basket, Woodland, Splint, Loom, Woven, Green, Red & Natural, 9 1/2 In. 330.00
Basket, Woodlands, Ash Splint, Lined With 1861 Newspaper, 10 1/2 In. 440.00
Belt, Crow, Leg Drop, Religious Design 895.00
Belt, Southwest, Silver, Alternating Thunderbird Rondels, Cabochon Turquoise, 1900 .   288.00
Birdstone, Ohio, Glacial Kame Banded-Slate, 4 3/4 In. 230.00
Blanket, Chimayo, Black & White Stripes & Patterns, Red Field, 76 x 38 1/2 In. 150.00
Blanket, Chimayo, Red, Black & Blue, Mexico 150.00
Blanket, Cree, Saddle, Wool, Floral Beadwork, Fringe, c.1880, 32 x 55 In. 1331.00
Blanket, Navajo, 45 Brown Diamonds, Gray & White Field, 42 x 70 In. 50.00
Blanket, Navajo, Checkerboard Pattern, 1930s, 30 x 50 In. 425.00
Blanket, Navajo, Chief's Pattern, Stripes With Diamonds, 52 x 60 In. 4600.00
Blanket, Navajo, Child's, Wool, Interlocking Diamonds & Cross, c.1880, 32 x 46 In. 5000.00
Blanket, Navajo, Geometric Design, Gray Ground, 58 x 81 In. 690.00
Blanket, Navajo, Geometric Design, Red Ground, 31 x 49 In. 1610.00
Blanket, Navajo, Red & Brown Saw-Tooth Border, Brown, Gray & White, 47 x 65 In..   65.00
Blanket, Navajo, Red, Brown, Gray, White Geometric Diamond Design, 69 x 52 In. 1100.00
Bowl, Black On Black Pottery, Globular Shape, Dragon Design, M. Martinez, 6 In. 660.00
Bowl, Burl, Turned Lip, Large 1265.00
Bowl, Hopi, 4 x 5 In. 195.00
Bowl, Hopi, Painted, 2 5/8 x 5 1/4 In. 60.00
Bowl, Hopi, Polychrome, Pottery, Black & Red Over Orange, 10 1/4 In. 316.00
Bowl, Nootka, Basketry, Trinket, Polychrome Twine, Pacific Northwest, 6 1/2 In. 575.00
Bowl, Northeastern Woodlands, Burl, Traces Of Paint, 19th Century, 9 5/8 In. 745.00
Bowl, Papago, Stepped Cross Design, Martynia & Willow, 4 1/2 x 8 1/4 In. 110.00
Bowl, Papago, Straight Sided Basketry, Stepped Design, Yarn Handle, 4 3/4 In. 73.00
Bowl, Pima, Martynia & Willow, Basketry, 2 3/8 x 4 7/8 In. 330.00
Bowl, San Ildefonso, Black Pottery, Ovoid, Wave Design, 5 1/4 In. 195.00
Bowl, San Ildefonso, Blackware, Shallow, Gun Metal Finish, Rose Gonzales, 7 3/8 In. .   175.00
Bowl, Sioux, American Horse, 13 In. 135.00
Bowl, Tubatulabal, Polychrome, Basketry, Coiled, Bundle Foundation, 6 1/2 In. 2645.00
Bowl, Washoe, 1 Rod Coil, Triangular Design Around Body, 3 1/4 x 5 1/2 In. 330.00
Bowl, Zia, Dough, Red & Black On White, Feather Design Interior, 5 x 12 In. 1650.00
Box, Navajo, Stone-Set Cover, Turquoise & Silver, Footed, 1 1/2 x 4 1/2 x 3 In. 1150.00
Bracelet, Navajo, Silver, Wide Tooled Band 165.00
Breechcloth, Ojibwa, Floral Design, Civil War 695.00

◆◆◆◆◆◆◆◆◆◆◆◆◆◆◆◆◆◆◆◆◆◆◆◆

Microcrystalline waxes, like Quake Wax or Quake Hold or the wax used by dentists to keep braces from hurting, are good to stick ceramics and glass on shelves, but don't use them on soft unglazed ceramics like Indian pots. They may leave an oil stain.

◆◆◆◆◆◆◆◆◆◆◆◆◆◆◆◆◆◆◆◆◆◆◆◆

Indian, Jar, Acoma, Red & Black
On White, c.1900, 10 1/2 x 12 In.

Canoe, Birch Bark, 48 In.	525.00
Canoe, Great Lakes, Birch Bark	2530.00
Canteen, Marked U.S., Cover	85.00
Carrying Case, Drum, Mimac, Geometric Design, c.1930	750.00
Cradle, Micmac, Hood	370.00
Doll, Cherokee, Red Cotton Clothes, Wooden, c.1920	450.00
Doll, Hopi, Kachinas, 2 Heads, Ceremonial, Fur Trim	75.00
Doll, Kachina, Signed, 1930s, 18 In.	395.00
Doll, Navajo, Metal Belt, Beads, Cloth, 11 In.	195.00
Doll, Plateau, Wool Dress, Beaded Leather Belt, Moccasins, Late 19th Century, 9 In.	285.00
Doll, Sioux, Beaded, 1890-1900	375.00
Doll, Skookum, Standing Man & Woman, Each With Child, c.1940, 16 & 17 In., Pair	287.00
Doll, Zuni, Kachina, Yamuhakto, c.1980, 8 1/4 In.	172.00
Dress, Navajo, Woman's, Hand Spun, Raveled Wool	6900.00
Dress, Sioux, Fringed Hide, Flag Design Yoke	7475.00
Fan, Feather, Ghost Dance	60.00
Gloves, Northern Plains, Beaded Moose Hide, 1890	400.00
Gorget, Trade, Eagle, Peace, J. Monroe Medallion, Gilt Traces, Silver, 19th Century	1400.00
Hatchet, Seminole, Iron & Wooden, 19th Century, 23 In.	630.00
Holder, Pocket Watch, Blackfoot, Beaded, c.1890	750.00
Jar, Acoma, Red & Black On White, c.1900, 10 1/2 x 12 In. *Illus*	4887.00
Jar, Cochiti, Polychrome, Indented Base, Gray-White Slip, Pink Ground, 10 1/2 In.	1437.00
Jar, Hopi, Hano Polychrome, Avian Figures, Cream Slip, c.1910, 14 In.	632.00
Jar, Kawaiisu, Deer Grass, Willow Coil, 6 1/4 x 8 3/4 In.	1705.00
Jar, San Ildefonso, Blackware, Serpent, c.1950, 6 In.	1600.00
Jar, San Ildefonso, Blackware, Southwestern, Rose Gonzales, 7 In.	690.00
Jar, San Ildefonso, Polychrome, Pottery, Indented Base, Flared Lip, Red, Black, 11 In.	8050.00
Jar, Santa Clara, Black Pottery, Globular Shape, Feather Design, G. Suazo, 3 3/4 In.	192.00
Jar, Santo Domingo, Blackware, Gun Metal Finish, R. Aguilar, 13 In.	575.00
Jar, Zuni, Polychrome, Southwestern, Dark Brown & Red Paint, White Slip, 6 In.	260.00
Jewelry, Bracelet, Navajo, Twisted Silver, 6 Bezel Set Turquoise, c.1914, 2 3/4 In.	1380.00
Knife, Northern Plains, Trade, Double Edge, Bone Handle, Jukes Couls	13800.00
Knife, Posey County, Paleo, Ind., 4 In.	17.00
Knife Case, Plains, Beaded, Sinew, Hide Front, Parfleche Back, 10 In.	460.00
Leggings, Arapaho, Quilled Hide Sinew Sewn, Maidenhair Fern	9200.00
Mask, Zuni, Ceremonial Dance, Cotton Batting Over Cloth Covered Wire Frame, 1925	1500.00
Medallion, Navajo, Silver, 7 Buttons & 1 Brooch, 2 In., 8 Piece	165.00
Moccasins, Beaded, Soft Soles, Turquoise Ground, Concentric Design, 10 1/4 In.	1725.00
Moccasins, Great Lakes, Ribbon, Appliqued Hide, Silk & Sinew Thread, 10 1/8 In.	4025.00
Moccasins, Plains, Beaded	225.00
Moccasins, Plains, Beaded Cloth & Hide, Geometric, c.1900, 8 1/4 In.	165.00
Moccasins, Plains, Child's, Beaded Hide, Cross Pattern, c.1900, 5 In.	165.00

Indian, Rug, Navajo, c.1910, 6 Ft. 11 In. x 4 Ft. 3 In.

Moccasins, Plains, Child's, Beaded Hide, Terraced Diamond, c.1900, 6 In. 300.00
Moccasins, Sioux, Beaded, 9 In. 145.00
Model, Totem Pole, Northwest Coast, Sisiootl, Serpentine Body, Wooden, 38 In. 8050.00
Olla, Acoma, c.1900 .... 9775.00
Olla, Acoma, Geometric & Curvilinear Design, 5 1/4 x 6 3/4 In. 412.00
Olla, Santa Clara, Blackware, Indented Base, Flared Sides, Southwestern, 11 In. 2185.00
Olla, Santo Domingo, Black Avian & Geometric Design, 12 1/2 In. 1380.00
Olla, Zuni, Polychrome Pottery.. 7475.00
Parfleche, Crow, Painted Buffalo Hide 5750.00
Pincushion, Navajo, Painted Face, Beaded Dress, Pink Skirt, 6 In. 30.00
Pipe, Southeastern Woodlands Style, Figural, Stylized Frog, 4 1/2 In. 35.00
Pipe, Wood Puzzle Stem, 8 Carved & Pierced Panels, Brass Tacks, 25 1/2 In. 1265.00
Pipe Bag, Cheyenne 9775.00
Pipe Bag, Cree 1955.00
Pipe Bag, Sioux.. 5750.00
Pitch Fork, Cherokee, 1 Piece Of Wood 95.00
Plate, San Ildefonso, Black On Black, Feather Design, Maria Popovi, 10 1/4 In. 330.00
Pot, Acoma, Gourd Shape, 14 1/2 In. 5775.00
Pouch, Cheyenne, Quills, Beads & Tin Cones 2500.00
Pouch, Hide, Beaded, Flaring Square Shape, Glass & Brass Suspensions, 4 In. 1265.00
Pouch, Woodlands, Beadwork, Multicolored Oak Leaf Design, 10 x 7 1/2 In. 605.00
Purse, Woodlands, Beaded, Small 35.00
Robe, Plains, Painted Bison Hide, Standing Bear In Field Of Red Dots 7475.00
Rug, Navajo Native American, c.1910, 79 x 59 In. 4950.00
Rug, Navajo, 1910, 45 x 54 In. 1250.00
Rug, Navajo, 44 x 78 In. 1850.00
Rug, Navajo, Banded Design, Alternating Stripes, Diamonds, 2 Ft. 7 In. x 3 Ft. 126.00
Rug, Navajo, Bright Colors, 1920s, 26 x 45 In. 275.00
Rug, Navajo, c.1910, 6 Ft. 11 In. x 4 Ft. 3 In. ....*Illus* 3300.00
Rug, Navajo, Central Block, Diamonds, Red, Gray, Tan, Natural Ground, 44 x 66 In. 522.00
Rug, Navajo, Chief's Blanket Design, Red, Black & White, 68 x 79 In. 1650.00
Rug, Navajo, Double Dye Red, Diamond Design, Border, Fylfots, 3 x 5 Ft. 715.00
Rug, Navajo, Homespun Wool, Banded Sawtooth, Red Ground, 63 x 42 In. 805.00
Rug, Navajo, Homespun Wool, Multicolored, Ivory Ground, Vellero Star, 57 x 35 In. .. 316.00
Rug, Navajo, Homespun Wool, Natural & Aniline Dye, Red, Black, Gray, 92 x 37 In. .. 287.50

Rug, Navajo, Homespun Wool, Pictorial, Stylized Indian Dancers, 89 x 66 In. 1610.00
Rug, Navajo, Homespun, Banded Geometrics, Brown Ground, 70 x 38 In. 316.00
Rug, Navajo, Interlocking Diamonds, Wool, c.1910-1920, 54 x 84 In. 275.00
Rug, Navajo, Latch Hook Design, 59 x 39 In. 385.00
Rug, Navajo, Serrated Diamonds, Red, Black, Natural, 48 x 66 In. 220.00
Rug, Navajo, Shades Of Brown, Tan Wool, 4 Ft. x 6 Ft. 3 In. 220.00
Rug, Navajo, Step Design, X Pattern, Black Border, 82 1/2 x 62 1/4 In. 880.00
Rug, Navajo, Traditional, c.1920, 48 x 72 In. 775.00
Rug, Navajo, Two Gray Hills Design, 44 x 73 In. 797.00
Rug, Navajo, Two Gray Hills, 54 x 73 In. 550.00
Rug, Navajo, Yei Design, 6 Standing Figures, 31 x 61 In. 770.00
Rug, Navajo, Yei Figures, Dance Rattles, Feather Motifs, c.1915, 45 x 72 In. 2200.00
Saddlebag, Sioux, Buffalo Hide, Canvas, Geometric Beadwork, 14 x 70 In. 3575.00
Scraper, Turkey Tail, Flint, Scioto County, Ohio 17.00
Serape, Navajo, Wool, Figures In Boxes At Edges 6900.00
Sheath, Knife, Sioux, Beaded 595.00
Shirt, Northern Plains, Muslin, Strips Of Striped Beadwork, Stroud Cloth Bib 6900.00
Sioux, Legging Strips, Red Beads On White Bead Ground, c.1910, 30 In., Pair 522.00
Spoon, Northwest Coast, Soapberry, Totemic Design 8337.00
Spoon, Woodlands, Wood, Shallow Bowl, Back-Curved Handle, Perched Bird, 5 In. ... 1150.00
Totem Model, Haida, Northwest Coast, Argillite, Flat Back, Incised, Pierced, 8 In. 747.00
Totem Pole, Northwest Coast, Eagle Atop Bear, 1880s, 11 1/2 In. 880.00
Totem Pole, Northwest Coast, Wing Span-24 In. 385.00
Totem Pole, Sisiootl, Northwest Coast, Model, Sisiootl, Mask Like Head, Carved 4025.00
Totem Pole, Sisiootl, Northwest Coast, Red Cedar, Polychrome, 38 In. 8050.00
Tray, Apache, Corn Meal, Braided Rim, 16 1/2 In. 165.00
Tray, Cherokee, Pine Needle, Rafia, Seashells Under Glass 55.00
Vase, Acoma, Pottery, White, Black, Brown, Checkered, 6 In. 126.00
Vase, Santa Clara, Wedding, Blackware, Southwestern, Carved Water Serpent, 11 In. ... 230.00
Walking Stick, Makah, Grass Dyed Cover, Brass Rifle Shell Tip, 34 1/2 In. 550.00
Weaving, Navajo, 2nd Phase Chief's Pattern, Wool, Raveled, Hand Spun, 56 x 68 In. ... 6325.00
Weaving, Navajo, Chief's Blanket Pattern, Natural, Aniline Dyed Homespun Wool 6900.00
Weaving, Pictorial, Geometrics & Arrows, Homespun Wool, 77 x 44 In. 747.00

INDIAN TREE is a china pattern that was popular during the last half of the nineteenth century. It was copied from earlier Indian textile patterns that were very similar. The pattern includes the crooked branch of a tree and a partial landscape with exotic flowers and leaves. Green, blue, pink, and orange were the favored colors used in the design.

Butter Dish, Cover, Johnson Bros. 45.00
Dish, Pierced Handle, Coalport, 7 1/2 In. 27.00
Tureen, Soup, Cover, Ladle, Maddock & Sons, 10 In. 150.00

INKSTANDS were made to be placed on a desk. They held some type of container for ink, and possibly a sander, a pen tray, a pen, a holder for pounce, and even a candle to melt the sealing wax. Inkstands date to the eighteenth century and have been made of silver, copper, ceramics, and glass. Additional inkstands may be found in these and other related categories.

Brass, 2 Cut Glass Lidded Bottles, Lidded Box, Foliate Handles, 16 In. 805.00
Brass, Pierced Foliate & Scroll Allover, Beaded Border, 16 In. 80.00
Bronze, 2 Wells, Wingless Griffin Figures, Back Panel Scenes, 6 3/4 x 12 In. 230.00
Bronze, Enameled, Baluster, Scrolling Acanthus Struts & Footed, France, 4 1/2 In. 69.00
Bronze & Marble, 2 Ink Pots, Center Aspiring Eagle Of Waterloo, 16 1/2 In. 690.00
Bull, Standing, Bronze, Lift-Top Reveals Sander, 4 x 4 In. 437.00
Eagle Perched On Rocky Ledge, Bronze, A. Marionnet, 16 In. 460.00
Enameled, Center Handle, Rectangular, England 4500.00
Enameled, Painted Flowers, Reserves Of Country Views, 3 Wells, 7 1/4 In. 690.00
English Mastiff, Seated, Jacob Petit, 9 1/2 In. 1980.00
Faience, Chantilly, Ormolu Wells, Octagonal, France 742.00
Fruitwood, Neoclassical, Brass Accents, Green Glass Bottle, 11 3/8 In. 460.00
Gondola, Porcelain, Flanked By Pair Of Covered Jars, 7 In. 245.00
Heintz, Copper, Silver Overlay, Arts & Crafts 195.00
Malachite, Ormolu, 2 Cut Glass Ink Pots, Leaf-Molded Bell, 9 1/2 In. 1035.00

Papier-Mache, Sterling Silver Cap, 1850s 250.00
Porcelain, Louis XV Style, Foliate Scroll Cresting, Center Eagle, Sander, 15 In. 1495.00
Silver, Applied Scrolling Rim, 4-Footed, Victorian, London, c.1870, 9 1/4 In............... 630.00
Sterling Silver, Rectangular, Engraved, G. Jensen, c.1934, 12 3/16 In. 2875.00
Woman's Head, Candleholder At Top, Chased Owl, Gorham, c.1900, 12 In. 5175.00

INKWELLS, of course, held ink. Ready-made ink was first made about 1836 and was sold in bottles. The desk inkwell had a narrow hole so the pen would not slip inside. Inkwells were made of many materials, such as pottery, glass, pewter, and silver. Look in these categories for more listings of inkwells.

Arabian, Seated, Bronze, Head & Shoulder Hinged Cover, Vienna, 5 1/2 In. 120.00
Blown Glass, 3-Mold, Waffle, Dark Olive Green, 2 x 2 1/2 In... 99.00
Blown Glass, Conical, Octagonal Base, 2 1/2 In. 36.00
Brass, Art Deco, 2 Wells, Pen Tray, B & H 145.00
Bronze, 2 Horse Heads Lift For Glass Insert, Austria, 9 /12 In. 490.00
Bronze, Foliated Baluster Form Shaft, Floral Wreath, French Empire, 7 1/4 In.............. 440.00
Cameo Glass, Amethyst To Clear, Metal Mounted, 5 In.. 715.00
Carved Boar's Head, Black Forest... 400.00
Cat, Woman In Gold Dress, Male In Trousers, Porcelain, 5 x 2 1/4 In., Pair 295.00
Copper, Hammered, Rivets At Base, Gustav Stickley, 2 x 5 3/4 In................................ 302.00
Cut Glass, Octagonal... 45.00
Daisy & Button High Backed Chair, Cat On Cover... 175.00
Dog, Reclining, Staffordshire 135.00
Dragons, Enameled, Diamond Border, Onyx Plinth, 18K Gold 1495.00
Glass, Controlled Bubbles, Periwinkle Blue, Hinged Cover, 4 1/2 x 5 1/4 In. 295.00
Glass, Silver Overlay, Square, Monogram, Black, Starr & Frost, 3 In. 450.00
Golf Ball, Bronze, Insert, Marble Stand 265.00
Grand Tour, Brass, Floral Frame, 2 Crystal Wells, Shell Dish, 19th Century, 2 1/2 x 6 In. 138.00
Iver Johnson Revolver, Milk Glass Insert, Eclipse Light Co., Dated 1906 .... 325.00
Jar, Candlestick, Crystal, Sterling, Jos. & Albert Sovary, 1853........................*Illus* 2645.00
Milk Glass Wells, Brass Stand & Cover, Pat. 1897 .... 40.00
Mother-Of-Pearl, 2 Wells, Hinged Tortoise Lids, 19th Century, 9 1/2 In. 1000.00
Napoleon III, 2 Wells, Paneled Marble Reserves, Rosettes On Feet, 9 1/2 In. 2300.00
Nude Male In Sea, Bronze, H. Muller, 8 1/2 x 15 In... 920.00
Pagoda, Bronze, Inner Candle Holder & Well, Stepped Oval Base, 5 1/4 In. 475.00
Pewter, Shield-Shaped Cover, Round Body, No. 0140, Liberty & Co., 5 1/2 x 3 In. 275.00
Phrenologist, Blue & White, Bennington, F. Bridge, 5 1/2 In... 825.00
Rabbit, With Mandolin, Rustic Bench, Cast Metal, Nodding Head, Glass Well, 4 In. 195.00
Railroad Flatcar, Walnut 175.00
Sang De Boeuf, Silver-Gilt Mounts, Stone Finial, 19th Century, 3 1/4 In. 575.00
Silver, Crystal, Shell & Scroll Design, J. & A. Savory, London, c.1854, 4 Piece........... 2645.00
Silver, Traveling, Chased, Gorham, 2 1/2 In... 165.00
Silvered Brass, Wooden Pluto Figure, Stepped, Slide Compartment, 15 3/8 In............. 5460.00
Skull, With Ivory Snake, Wooden, Hand Carved, Frog Lid, Glass Insert, 2 1/2 x 3 In. ... 180.00

Inkwell, Jar, Candlestick, Crystal, Sterling, Jos. & Albert Sovary, 1853

Snail, Louis Philippe, Porcelain, Pink, Gold, c.1850, 5 1/4 In. 250.00
Stag's Head, Bronze, Cut Glass, 2 x 2 In. 450.00
Suffrage Movement, Woman With Crossed Arms, Doulton, 3 1/4 In. 430.00
Vaseline Glass, Daisy & Button, 2 In. 175.00
Venetian Gondolier, Gilt Bronze, Candleholder, Oval Base, 7 In. 210.00
Whippet, Cobalt Blue Base, Staffordshire 295.00
Woman, Holding Basket, Bronze, Round Marble Base, 5 In. 302.00

INSULATORS of glass or pottery have been made for use on telegraph or telephone poles since 1844. Thousands of different styles of insulators have been made. Most common are those of clear or aqua glass; most desirable are the threadless types made from 1850 to 1870.

AA, Mossy Blue-Green 125.00
Agee, Purple 125.00
American Telephone, Dark Green, Amber Swirls 400.00
Armstrong, DP1, Light Green 5.00
Armstrong, Root Beer, Amber 25.00
B.G.M. Co., Purple ....50.00 to 200.00
Brookfield, Aqua ....8.00 to 10.00
Brookfield, Emerald Green, New York 5.00
Brookfield, Small Spiral, Aqua 135.00
C.E.W., Aqua 130.00
C.G.I., Sage Green 15.00
California, Aqua 10.00
California, Purple 35.00
California, Santa Ana, Purple 100.00
California, Santa Ana, Yellow-Green 60.00
Canadian Pacific Railway, Ice Blue 4.00
Chicago, Embossed, Blue 50.00
Chicago, Embossed, Blush 50.00
Chicago Insulating Co., Embossed Base, Aqua 60.00
Columbia, Light Blue 400.00
Confederate Egg, Dark Green 450.00
Diamond, Gray 300.00
Diamond, Ice Green 6.00
Diamond, Medium Purple 250.00
Diamond, No. 13, Dark 20.00
Dominion, No. 42, Cornflower Blue 650.00
Duquesne, Teal Blue 25.00
F.M. Locke, Victor, N.Y., Aqua 20.00
G.T.P., Dark Green, Amber In Base 9.00
Green Aqua, Bits Of Slag, Patented June 17, 1890 .... 65.00
H.G. Co., Aqua, Milk Glass 12.00
H.G. Co., Beehive, Milky Swirling 40.00
H.G. Co., Cornflower Blue 350.00
H.G. Co., Patd May 2nd 1893, Blue Aqua, Inner Outer Drips 10.00
H.G. Co., Petticoat, Blue 500.00
H.G. Co., Petticoat, Light Apple Green 15.00
H.G. Co., Petticoat, SB, Aqua 3.00
Hawley, Aqua 95.00
Hemingray, No. 1, High Voltage Triple Petticoat, Patent May 2, 1893 .... 15.00
Hemingray, No. 3, Cable, Drips, Aqua 35.00
Hemingray, No. 9, Jade Milk Glass 30.00
Hemingray, No. 38, Aqua 7.00
Hemingray, No. 40, Aqua, Amber Swirls 8.00
Hemingray, No. 42, Green 125.00
Hemingray, No. 79, Aqua 25.00
Hemingray, No. D-990, Aqua 4.00
Hemingray, Patented, Backward 2nd E, Oct 8th, 1907, Aqua 5.00
Hemingray No. 3 Cable, Drips, Aqua 35.00
Human Services Telephone Pioneers, Lilac 15.00
Human Services Telephone Pioneers, Milk Glass 12.00
Lynchburg, No. 44, Clear 5.00

Lynchburg, No. 44, Light Aqua	5.00
Lynchburg, No. 44, Light Blue, With Snow	8.00
Lynchburg, No. 44, Olive Green	18.00
Manhattan, Bluish Aqua	50.00
McLaughlin, Blue	25.00
McLaughlin, No. 14, Green	4.00
McLaughlin, No. 14, Olive Green, Black Glass	15.00
McLaughlin, No. 19, Emerald Green	18.00
McLaughlin, No. 42, Apple Green	25.00
N.E.G.M., Green	150.00
N.E.G.M., Sapphire Blue	75.00
N.E.G.M., Straight Side, Aqua	65.00
Nacionales Telegrafos, Dark Red Amber	18.00
National, Embossed New England Telephone, Aqua	235.00
O Provo, Aqua	150.00
Orlando Commemorative, Blue Carnival & Lilac	35.00
Peacock, Blue Mickey Mouse	900.00
Portland Commemorative, Cobalt Blue, Milk Glass Swirls	25.00
Pyrex, Sombrero, Carnival	12.00
Pyrex, Yellow Tinge, 38 Lbs.	250.00
Star, Dark Olive	8.00
Star, Olive Green	4.00
T.H.E. Co., Light Blue	5.00
T.T.C., Royal Purple, Canada	15.00
W. Brookfield, 45 Cliff St., Aqua, Amber Swirls	20.00
W. Brookfield, Deep Purple	300.00
W. Brookfield, Green	12.00
W. Brookfield, New York, Celery Green, Milk Glass Swirls	20.00
W.F.G., Pale Silver	15.00
W.G.M., Dark Amethyst	18.00
W.U.T. Co., Carnival, Copper Insert	15.00
Westinghouse, No. 6, Aqua	250.00
Westinghouse, No. 6, Light Green	285.00
Whitall Tatum Co., No. 1, Pink	3.00
Whitall Tatum Co., No. 1, Purple	10.00

IRISH BELLEEK, see Belleek category

IRON is a metal that has been used by man since prehistoric times. It is a popular metal for tools and decorative items like doorstops that need as much weight as possible. Items are listed here or under other appropriate headings, such as Bookends, Doorstop, Kitchen, Match Holder, or Tool. The tool that is used for ironing clothes, an iron, is listed in the Kitchen category under Iron and Sadiron.

Ashtray, Griswold, No.570A	30.00
Ashtray, Skillet, Griswold, No. 00, White Enamel	60.00
Ashtray, Skillet, Griswold, No. 770, Square Form	35.00
Barrel Lifter, Cooper's, Hand Forged, 17 5/8 In.	90.00
Bell, Farm, Dinner, A.F. Shapleigh, Cast	400.00
Bill Spike	45.00
Bill Weight, NCR	55.00
Birdhouse, Cast, c.1880	2500.00
Birdhouse, Miller Iron Works, Providence, Rhode Island, c.1869	3900.00
Boot Scraper, Dachshund, 13 In.	95.00
Boot Scraper, Dachshund, Green, Cast, 21 In.	280.00
Boot Scraper, Dachshund, Open Mouth, Curled Tail, Old Black Paint, 21 In.	95.00
Boot Scraper, Dachshund, Original Paint Traces, 22 x 7 5/8 In.	240.00
Boot Scraper, Regency, Double Sphinx Form	137.00
Boot Scraper, Scrollwork Finial, Stone Base, 19th Century, 14 1/2 In.	220.00
Bootjack, Black	65.00
Bootjack, Floral, Hand Forged	165.00
Bowl, Patty, Iron, Griswold, No. 871	125.00
Cage, Bank, Beveled Etched Glass Windows, c.1899, 17 x 10 In.	1200.00

Candleholder, Pricket Socket, Primitive, Wrought Iron, Adjustable, 17 In. 275.00
Candlestick, Spiral, Oak Base, England, c.1750, 8 In. 265.00
Carriage Step, Tip-Proof Legs, Cast, 60 x 4 1/4 In. 185.00
Cigar Cutter, J.G. Hutchinson & Co., Embossed Lettering, 8 1/2 x 15 In. 165.00
Cuspidor, Graniteware Insert, Cast 550.00
Door Knocker, Forged, Lucifer & Horse Hinge, Old Black Paint 230.00
Eagle, Outspread Wings, 30 1/2-In. Wingspan 845.00
Eagle, Standing, Polychrome Paint, 35 In. 3600.00
Figure, Rooster, Shooting Gallery 88.00
Figure, Whippet, Painted, 19th Century, 66 In., Pair 10350.00
Figurine, Classical Maiden, Paris, Life Size, Corneau Freres, Pair 11550.00
Figurine, Dancer & Musician, 50's Style, 4 1/2 In. 13.00
Figurine, Dog, Scottie, Black, 3 7/8 x 4/12 In. 9.00
Figurine, Owl, Painted Black, 2 3/8 In. 10.00
Figurine, Rooster, Cast Iron, 7 x 9 3/4 In., Pair 600.00
Figurine, Turtle, Primitive, Old Paint, 6 In. 137.00
Finial, Horse Head, Hitching Post, Ring 75.00
Footman, Pierced Top & Apron, c.1860, 13 x 11 x 12 3/4 In. 285.00
Hitching Post, Black Boy, Polychromed, 19th Century, Pair 5225.00
Hitching Post, Horsehead 300.00
Hitching Post, Steer Head, Pair 2500.00
Kettle, Rendering, Built-In Wood Stove, Embossed Cattle Heads, Corn Stalks 400.00
Key, Fancy Shape, England, 11 In. 34.00
Leg Irons, Mattatuck Mfg. Co., Waterbury Conn., USA, 14-In. Chain. 185.00
Magazine Rack, Lyre Shape, Black, 9 x 12 3/4 In. 120.00
Mailbox, Griswold, No. 3PN106 .... 50.00
Mirror, Dressing, Mother-Of-Pearl, Painted, Oval, 19th Century, 22 In. 825.00
Planter, Bulb, Bronze Plated, 11 3/4 x 7 3/4 x 2 1/8 In. 25.00
Porringer, Flowered Handle, c.1800, 5 1/8 In. 125.00
Rack, Wine, 17 Shelves, Green Paint, Holds 6 Bottles, 19th Century, 71 x 23 In., Pair . 550.00
Rushlight & Candleholder, Forged, Octagonal Wooden Base, c.1740 .... 260.00
Stove Plate, Tulips & Hearts, Inscription, 18th Century, 22 x 23 In. 425.00
Tea Kettle, 5 In. 12.00
Tongs, Pipe, 19th Century, 21 1/2 In. 575.00
Tray, Erotic, Woman's Derriere Showing On Back, 6 In. 19.00
Windmill Weight, Ball, For Hummer 350.00
Windmill Weight, Bobtailed Horse, White Paint, 17 x 18 In. 185.00
Windmill Weight, Bobtailed Horse, 17 x 17 In. 350.00
Windmill Weight, Crescent, Fairbanks, Morse & Co., Chicago, 10 1/2 In. 93.50
Windmill Weight, Fairbury Bull, Standing 700.00
Windmill Weight, Fairbury Bull, White 585.00
Windmill Weight, Horse 412.00
Windmill Weight, Horse, Short Tail 250.00
Windmill Weight, Hummer, Rooster, On Weight Ball 1250.00
Windmill Weight, Letter W, Weight Box On Left Side 400.00
Windmill Weight, Long-Tailed Horse 495.00
Windmill Weight, Rainbow Tail Rooster 2500.00
Windmill Weight, Rooster, Elgin Wind Power & Pump Co., Paint Traces, 20 In. 1265.00
Windmill Weight, Rooster, Elgin, White Repaint, 16 In. 528.00
Windmill Weight, Rooster, Hollow, 1880s 3200.00
Windmill Weight, Rooster, No. 2, Box 700.00
Windmill Weight, Rooster, Rainbow, Tall 1600.00
Windmill Weight, Woodmanse Rooster 800.00

IRONSTONE china was first made in 1813. It gained its greatest popularity
during the mid-nineteenth century. The heavy, durable, off-white pottery was
made in white or was decorated with any of hundreds of patterns. Much flow
blue pottery was made of ironstone. Some of the decorations were raised.
Many pieces of ironstone are unmarked, but some English and American factories included the word *Ironstone* in their marks. Additional pieces may be
listed in other categories, such as Chelsea Grape, Chelsea Sprig, Flow Blue,
Gaudy Ironstone, Moss Rose, Staffordshire, and Tea Leaf Ironstone.

Box, Salt, Hinged Wooden Lid, Blue & White, 6 1/2 In. 71.00

Chamber Set, 3 Little Maids, T.P.C. Co., 8 Piece 200.00
Chamber Set, Cobalt Blue & Gilt, Warwick, 6 Piece 275.00
Chamber Set, Richelieu Pattern, Brown, 4 Piece 350.00
Churn, 6 Gal. 650.00
Coffeepot, Teaberry 65.00
Compote, Gilt, Avian Design, Booth, 9 x 5 3/8 In, Pair 184.00
Ewer, Snake Handle, Polychrome, Mason's, 12 1/4 In. 625.00
Feeder, Invalid, Gilt Highlights, 19th Century, 7 In. 6.00
Luncheon Set, Apple Blossoms, Branches, Allover Brown, White, England, 37 Piece .. 225.00
Plate, Mason's, 10 In., Pair 99.00
Platter, Blue & White Transfer, England, 19th Century, 17 3/4 x 14 In. 150.00
Platter, Blue Transfer, European Harbor, 14 1/2 In. 165.00
Platter, Blue Transfer, Wild Turkey, Marked, 19 In. 302.00
Platter, Light Blue Transfer, Gothic Cottage, 15 3/4 In. 105.00
Platter, Oriental Scene, Brown, Oval, Large 37.00
Platter, Tree & Well, Imari Pattern, Marked, 21 In. 330.00
Soup, Dish, Flower Basket Center, Mason's 75.00
Soup Set, Corey Hill, Polychrome, 8 Piece 297.00
Teapot, Paneled, Black Transfer, Oriental Design, 6 In. 235.00
Teapot, Vista, Mason's 70.00
Tureen, Ladle, White, Lion & Unicorn Mark, Wm. Adams, 15 In. 55.00
Tureen, Soup, Cover, Underplate, Maroon, Square, Handles, 19th Century, 10 In. 275.00
Tureen, Vegetable, Dainty, Cover, John Maddock & Sons 175.00
Vase, Floral Cluster Knop, Japan Pattern, Mason's, c.1830, 21 In. 575.00
Wash Set, Red, Blue Flowers, Mason's, 5 Piece 975.00

ISPANKY figurines were designed by Laszlo Ispanky, who began his American career as a designer for Cybis Porcelains. In 1966, he established his own studio in Pennington, New Jersey; since 1976, he has worked for Goebel of North America. He works in stone, wood, or metal, as well as porcelain. The first limited edition figurines were issued in 1966.

Figurine, Shakespearean Lovers, 11 1/2 x 13 1/2 In. 185.00
Figurine, Swan Lake, No. 97/300, 10 1/2 x 14 In. 70.00

IVORY from the tusk of an elephant is thought by many to be the only true ivory. To most collectors, the term *ivory* also includes such natural materials as walrus, hippopotamus, or whale teeth or tusks, and some of the vegetable materials that are of similar texture and density. Other ivory items may be found in the Scrimshaw and Netsuke categories. Collectors should be aware of the recent laws limiting the buying and selling of elephant ivory and scrimshaw.

Bird, Brass Claws, Mother-Of-Pearl Eyes, Mounted As Lamp, c.1900, 14 1/2 In. 2090.00
Bone, Oriental Scenes, Elephant Tusk Shape, 7 1/4 In., Pair 4500.00
Box, Carved Figural Scenes, Continental, c.1900, 1 3/4 In. 550.00
Box, Carved Panels With Genre Scenes, Hinged Cover, 5 In. 85.00
Box, Shell Shape, Carved Lid, Continental, c.1780, 3 In. 747.00
Cup, Cover, Leaves, Figureheads, Fruits, Mother-Of-Pearl Figural Finial, 13 3/4 In. 2760.00
Figurine, Cabbage, China, 9 In. 135.00
Figurine, Camel, Middle East, 5 x 5 1/2 In., Pair 340.00
Figurine, Empress, Case, 13 In. 275.00
Figurine, Fisherman, Putting Fish Into Basket, Fish On Hook, 4 3/4 In. 350.00
Figurine, Flying Cherubs, Holding Floral Wreaths, 6 1/4 In. 400.00
Figurine, Maiden, Holding Flowering Sprig, 15 In. 1495.00
Figurine, Man, With Pipe, Mask, Monkey, Carved, Polychromed, 10 In. 495.00
Figurine, Nude, Doctor's Model, Hardwood Stand, 6 In. 125.00
Figurine, Nude, Doctor's Model, Wooden Base, China, 18 1/2 In. 550.00
Figurine, Old Man, Holding Umbrella, 7 In. 50.00
Figurine, Pagoda, Hand Carved, Inset Turquoise & Carnelian, Polychromed, 23 In. 1325.00
Figurine, Quan Yin, Fruit Bowl, 5 1/2 In. 80.00
Figurine, Reclining Nude, Rosewood Stand, Japan, 2 1/2 x 9 3/4 In. 300.00
Figurine, Renaissance Style Woman, Holding Book, 19 1/2 In. 5750.00
Figurine, Warrior, Holding Blade, Hand Carved, Polychromed, 20 In. 990.00
Figurine, Warrior, Holding Spear, Carved, Polychromed, 8 In. 440.00

Figurine, Woman, 18th Century Dress, Hinged Skirt Reveals Courting Scene, 8 In....... 1210.00
Figurine, Woman, Holding Fan, Carved, 5 In... 275.00
Flagon, Silver Fittings, Carved Battle Scene, Knights, Horses, 15 3/4 In. 4300.00
Frame, Miniature Of Woman, 4 1/4 x 4 1/2 In. 154.00
Group, 7 Oriental Figures, Wooden Stand, 31 In. 800.00
Group, Man & Woman, Classical Pose, Oval Base, Marble Plinth, 11 1/2 In., Pair........ 3300.00
Group, Samurai In Tree, Fighting Off Two Oni, Oriental, 6 In.. 115.00
Inro, Curled Rabbit, Inlaid Eyes, Early 19th Century 275.00
Inro, Dancer, Seated Man, Kyonin, Signed, 19th Century 330.00
Inro, Hawk & Dragon, 19th Century.. 300.00
Inro, Puppies, Masayoshi, Signed, 19th Century.. 350.00
Letter Opener, Silver Mounted, Art Nouveau, Russia, 11 1/2 In. 745.00
Miniature, Engraved Portrait Bust, Bearded Man, Frame, 5 x 4 1/2 In. 290.00
Necklace, Carved Wafers, Balls & Beads, Bone, c.1850, 25 In. 195.00
Okimono, Chinese Sage, Staff & Gourd, Attendant, Wooden Stand, 12 x 6 In. 1980.00
Okimono, Kaikoku, Upraised Hammer, 2 Rice Bales, Wooden Stand, 4 1/2 In. 325.00
Okimono, Kintaro, Standing On Wild Board, Goddess, Basket, Late 19th Century, 5 In. 1650.00
Phoenix Birds, On Stump, Teakwood Base, c.1900, 12 In. 2475.00
Plaque, Frolicking Putti, After F. Duquesnov, Flemish, Oval, 4 /12 x 5 3/4 In. 3000.00
Plaque, George Washington Portrait, Wooden Frame, 2 1/4 In. 690.00
Ruler, Folding, No. 99, Stephens & Co... 245.00
Scene, Woman, Feeding Chickens, In Yard 1195.00
Shadow Box, Baroque, Garden Scene, Arches, Urns, Giltwood Case, 22 x 16 1/2 In..... 5175.00
Tusk, African Man's Head, 28 In... 400.00
Tusk, Carved To Form 8 Graduated Elephants, Wooden Base, Pair 250.50
Tusk, Uncarved, Africa, 72 In... 1600.00

JACK ARMSTRONG, the all-American boy, was the hero of a radio serial from 1933 to 1951. Premiums were offered to the listeners until the mid-1940s. Jack Armstrong's best-known endorsement was for Wheaties.

Book, Big Little Book, 1939 .... 19.00
Book, Big Little Book, Jack Armstrong & The Ivory Treasure, 1937 .... 25.00
Explorer Telescope, 1938 ....30.00 to 50.00
Hike-O-Meter, 1934 .... 30.00
Pedometer, Silver Aluminum, 1939... 35.00
Training Kit, Preflight, How To Fly Manual, Star Transfers, 1943................................... 95.00

JACK-IN-THE-PULPIT vases, oddly shaped like trumpets, resemble the wild plant called jack-in-the-pulpit. The design originated in the late Victorian years. Vases in the jack-in-the-pulpit shape were made of ceramic or glass and the complete list of page references can be found in the index.

Vase, Cased Glass, Floral & Gilt Painting, 13 In. 220.00
Vase, Glass, Enameled Gold Roses, Swirled, 11 1/2 In. 50.00
Vase, Green Overlay, Flower Petal Top, Off-White, Applied Feet, 7 x 5 In. 79.00
Vase, Iridescent Amethyst, Gold Luster, Feathered 200.00
Vase, Ruffled Rim, White To Peachblow, 7 1/4 In. 440.00
Vase, Ruffled Top, Pink, Opaque Off-White, 6 1/2 x 6 1/2 In. 89.00
Vase, Satin Glass, Pale Yellow To White, Enameled Flowers, 15 5/8 In........................ 203.00

JACKFIELD ware was originally a black glazed pottery made in Jackfield, England, from 1750 to 1775. A yellow glazed ware has also been called Jackfield ware. Most of the pieces referred to as *Jackfield* today are black-glazed, red-clay wares made at the Jackfield Pottery in Shropshire, England, in Victorian times.

Coffeepot, Black, Camel-Form Spout, Bird Finial, Chain, 18th Century, 12 1/2 In........ 374.00
Teapot, 18th Century 185.00

JADE is the name for two different minerals, nephrite and jadeite. Nephrite is the mineral used for most early Oriental carvings. Jade is a very tough stone that is found in many colors from dark green to pale lavender. Jade carvings are still being made in the old styles, so collectors must be careful not to be fooled by recent pieces. Jade jewelry is found in this book under Jewelry.

Bowl, Carved Dragons, Key Fret Border, Dragon Form Handle, 4 1/2 In. 920.00

Box, Floral Form, Lotus Flowers On Stems, Ruby Encrusted In Cover, 4 In. 172.00
Cup, Boat Shape, Dragon Handles, White, China, 4 1/2 In. 350.00
Figurine, Foo Lion, Lying Crouched, Raised Head, Black, 3 1/2 In. 805.00
Figurine, Quan Yin, Holding Vase, Crane, 16 1/2 In. 690.00
Frame, Peering Mirror, Gilt Metal Back, Precious Stones, China, 3 In. Diam. 132.00
Inkstand, Carved, China.. 150.00
Pitcher, Spiral Bands, Rope Borders, Strap Handle, 5 1/2 In. 525.00
Screen, Carved Leaping Fish, Parrot On Flowering Branches, Wooden Base, 12 In. 460.00
Seal, Square Form, Pierced Center, Seal On Base, Brown, 4 x 4 In. 460.00
Vase, Flattened Baluster, Birds & Rookery, White, 19th Century, 4 7/8 In. 2990.00

JAPANESE CORALENE is a ceramic decorated with small raised beads and
dots. It was first made in the nineteenth century. Later wares made to imitate
coralene had dots of enamel. There is also another type of coralene that is
made with small glass beads on glass containers.

Pitcher, Red, Brown, Yellow Daffodils, 1909, 4 1/2 In. 950.00
Vase, Hollyhocks, Lavender Ground, Gold On Rim, 12 3/4 In. 665.00

JASPERWARE can be made in different ways. Some pieces are made from a
solid colored clay with applied raised designs of a contrasting colored clay.
Other pieces are made entirely of one color clay with raised decorations that
are glazed with a contrasting color. Additional pieces of jasperware may also
be listed in the Wedgwood category or under various art potteries.

Ashtray, Classical Maidens, Scalloped, Square, Marked, 2 3/4 In.................................. 6.00
Box, Green Ground, White Cherubs & Lovebirds, 6 In. 175.00
Plaque, Blue Ground, White Classical Figures, E. Wood, 3 1/2 x 4 1/2 In., 3 Piece 385.00
Plate, Indian, White Chief, Raised, Full Headdress, Green, 5 1/2 In. 39.00
Vase, Ewer, Little Girl In White, 2 5/8 In.. 9.00
Vase, Scrolls & Leaves, Applied Pink Flower, Square Handles, 2 3/4 In. 9.00
Vase, Victorian Child, Green, 5 In. 125.00

JEWELRY, whether made from gold and precious gems or plastic and colored
glass, is popular with collectors. Values are determined by the intrinsic value
of the stones and metal and by the skill of the craftsmen and designers. Victorian and older jewelry have been collected since the 1950s. More recent interests are Art Deco and Edwardian styles, Mexican and Danish silver jewelry,
and beads of all kinds. Copies of almost all styles are being made. Indian jewelry is listed in the Indian category.

Amulet, 14K Gold Chain, c.1840.. 195.00
Barrette, Gold, Tortoiseshell, Grapevines, Fruit Cluster, Art Nouveau, O. Heintz, 4 In. 1200.00
Bead Set Corals, Barrel Shape Links, Gold Twist Links 1150.00
Belt Buckle, Rhinestone, Square, 2 Triangular Sections, 4 In. 65.00
Bib, Citrine Stones & Pearls 175.00
Bolo Tie, Silver, Turquoise, Buffalo Head, Signed J. Nezzie 325.00
Bracelet, 5 Rows Of Arched Rhinestones, Weiss 125.00
Bracelet, 6 Lozenge-Shaped Links, H. Koppel For G. Jensen, c.1950........................... 1880.00
Bracelet, 8 Enameled Aces & Kings Sections, Sterling Silver, 1920.............................. 523.00
Bracelet, 15 Hemispherical Plaques, R. Lalique, France, c.1920.................................. 2185.00
Bracelet, 17 Gold Coins, Claw Mounted, Dated 1911 .... 975.00
Bracelet, Amethyst Stones, Pearls, Gold Tone, Schiaparelli 135.00
Bracelet, Aurora Borealis Rhinestones, Weiss... 35.00
Bracelet, Bakelite, Geometric Expandable Plastic Discs, Butterscotch Color................ 265.00
Bracelet, Bangle, 12 Love Tokens, Sterling Silver, c.1850... 375.00
Bracelet, Bangle, 7 Round Diamonds, Reticulated Band, 14K Yellow Gold 518.00
Bracelet, Bangle, Bakelite, Black Double Flower, Hinged 340.00
Bracelet, Bangle, Bakelite, Dark Caramel, Carved Stylized Leaf Flowers, 1/2 In. Wide 27.00
Bracelet, Bangle, Bakelite, Green, Carved Stylized Leaf Flowers, 1/2 In. 27.00
Bracelet, Bangle, Bakelite, Orange, Carved Stylized Flowers & Crossed Lines, 1/2 In.. 25.00
Bracelet, Bangle, Enameled Ladies, Gold Inset Seed Pearls, Victorian 2645.00
Bracelet, Bangle, Etruscan Design, Green Center Stone, 2 Rhinestones, Brass 60.00
Bracelet, Bangle, Flat Beads, Black, Orange, Caramel, Double Cone............................ 27.00
Bracelet, Bangle, Green & Pink Leaves, Beaded Edge, Sterling Silver 258.00
Bracelet, Bangle, Hand Painted, Enameled Horses & Stable Boys, Hermes, Paris 375.00

Bracelet, Bangle, Opals, Filigree, 14K Yellow Gold.. 650.00
Bracelet, Bangle, Pearls, Blue Enamel Borders, Gold, c.1890.................................... 978.00
Bracelet, Bangle, Whiting Davis, Wide.. 25.00
Bracelet, Bangle, Wide Hinge Clasp, Engraved, Safety Chain.................................... 425.00
Bracelet, Brushed Gold, Hinged Intertwining, Trifari, 1 3/4 In.................................. 25.00
Bracelet, Central Floral Medallion, Hammered Band, Roycroft, Sterling Silver........... 375.00
Bracelet, Charm, 7 Animal Charms, Brilliant-Cut Diamonds, Sapphires, Rubies......... 2415.00
Bracelet, Charm, Around The World Charms, 12K To 18K Gold, 7 In.......................... 421.00
Bracelet, Charm, Related To Cowboys, Sterling Silver.. 95.00
Bracelet, Child's, Poodle, Werther, 1950s.. 15.00
Bracelet, Collet Set Pearls, Sterling Silver, 7 Circular Links, Edward E. Oakes, 7 In.... 4900.00
Bracelet, Coral, 18K Gold, 1940s, 7 In.. 200.00
Bracelet, Diamonds, Open & Crossed Square Plaques, Platinum, c.1930.................... 6325.00
Bracelet, Double Strands, Faceted Crystal Beads, Discs.. 10.00
Bracelet, Flexible Mesh, Adjustable, Buckle Clasp With Fringe, Wide......................... 850.00
Bracelet, Flexible, Black Onyx, Sterling Silver, Taxco, 1-In. Wide............................... 45.00
Bracelet, Flexible, Wide Baton Links, 2-Color Gold, Star Pattern, c.1950.................... 1035.00
Bracelet, Freeform Links, Sterling Silver, Spratling, Mexico, c.1940, 8 In.................. 825.00
Bracelet, Green Stones, Masks, Sterling Silver, Taxco... 85.00
Bracelet, Hammered Sterling Silver, Onyx, Arts & Crafts, Bjarne, 12 1/4 In............... 165.00
Bracelet, Leaf Beads, Amber & Green, Iridescent, Regency, 7/8-In. Wide.................. 78.00
Bracelet, Leaf Shape, Lopez, Sterling Silver, Taxco, Mexico.. 88.00
Bracelet, Link, Enameled Florals, Black & White.. 12.00
Bracelet, Link, Floral, Red Stones, 1 1/8 In... 8.00
Bracelet, Link, Gold, Red Stones, Kramer.. 38.00
Bracelet, Oval & Round Jade Links, Coiled Rope Frame.. 860.00
Bracelet, Rhinestone, 3 Stones, 1/2 In.. 6.00
Bracelet, Rock Crystal Links, Rose Diamonds, Platinum, Art Deco............................. 2070.00
Bracelet, Row Of Brilliants, Center Appears As Diamonds, Sterling Silver, 1915........ 295.00
Bracelet, Seed Pearls, Victorian, 14K Yellow Gold, Pair... 1705.00
Bracelet, Silver & Abalone Shell Cameo, Neoclassical Figures..................................... 345.00
Bracelet, Snake, Coralcraft... 115.00
Bracelet, Spiral, Sterling Silver, Anni & Bert Knudsen, Denmark................................ 93.00
Bracelet, St. Jude Charm & Tassel, 14K Gold Rope Type Link..................................... 300.00
Bracelet, Sterling Wire, Henry Steig, 3 In... 880.00
Bracelet, Tennis, 43 Bezel-Set Brilliant-Cut Diamonds, 14K Yellow Gold Mount....... 1150.00
Bracelet, Thief Of Bagdad, David Andersen, 1940s.. 95.00
Bracelet, Thief Of Bagdad, Korda, 1940s.. 95.00
Bracelet, Turquoise & Blue Enamel, 18K Yellow Gold, Tiffany & Co........................... 1725.00
Bracelet, Twisted, Linked Chain, Heavy, Monet.. 14.00
Bracelet, Yellow Gilt-Metal Chevron Links, Seed Pearl Slider Clasp, c.1930, Pair....... 431.00
Bracelet & Earrings, Black Enameled Fans & Dancers, Sterling Silver, Siam............. 90.00
Bracelet & Earrings, Cameo, Oval Link Bracelet Set With Cameos............................. 385.00
Bracelet & Earrings, Flexible Micromosaic, Italy.. 38.00
Bracelet & Earrings, Micromosaic, Multicolored, c.1910, Italy, 3 Piece..................... 172.00
Bracelet & Necklace, Repeated Cylinder Center, Staggered Links, 14K Yellow Gold. 687.00
Buckle, Belt, Whiplash Floral Design, Copper, Art Nouveau, 2 3/8 x 3 7/8 In.............. 395.00
Buckle, Black, Metal Beads, Rectangular, 2 1/4 x 1 1/2 In, Pair.................................. 6.00
Buckle, Bronze, Gold & Silver Inlaid, Tang, 7 1/2 In.. 1250.00
Buckle, Cut Metal, Oval, 1 1/4 x 3/4 In, Pair... 4.00
Buckle, Gold, Rectangular, Calif., c.1860.. 1495.00
Buckle, Gott Mit Uns, Brass, Germany.. 30.00
Buckle, Grosgrain, Black Bows, 3 x 1 1/4 In., Pair... 6.00
Buckle, Marcasite, 2 1/2 In... 25.00
Buckle, Sash, Rhinestone, Art Deco... 18.00
Buckle, Shoe, Faceted Colorless Glass, Copper & Silvered Metal, Lined Case............ 345.00
Chain, Braided, Overlapping Links, Sterling Silver, 19 In... 22.00
Chain, Textured Curb Links, Swivel Clasp, 15K Gold, England, Victorian, 64 In......... 1840.00
Chain, Watch, Agate, Bar Lines, 14K Yellow Gold, 16 In.. 632.00
Chain, Watch, Gold Filled Heart, Seed Pearls.. 125.00
Chain, Watch, Human Hair... 57.00
Chatelaine, 4 Sewing Accessories, Sterling Silver.. 385.00
Chatelaine, Armor Mesh, Corn Drops, Finger Ring, Sterling Silver, 4 1/2 x 6 In.......... 175.00

Chatelaine, Finger Ring, 7 Implements, Engraved, Sterling Silver, c.1890 .... 1500.00
Chatelaine, Sterling Silver, 5 Chains 800.00
Chatelaine, Sterling Silver, 6 Chains 950.00
Clip, Diamond, Emeralds, Colored Stone, Pierced Foliate Mount, Art Deco 2300.00
Clip, Dress, Art Deco, Stones 90.00
Clip, Dress, Leaf & Blossom, Silver Sterling, Pearl, Peer Smed, 1 3/4 x 1 In., Pair 235.00
Clip, Figural, Toastmaster, Movable Limbs, Top Hat, White Tie & Tails, Bakelite 694.00
Clip, Fur, Faux Rubies, Diamonds & Turquoise, Sterling Silver, Trifari, 2 1/2 In. 150.00
Clip, Ivy Leaf, 14K Yellow Gold 287.00
Clip, Owl, Aqua Rhinestone Eyes, Aqua Enamel Body, Coro, Pair 185.00
Comb, Horn, Cluster Of Flower Heads, Center Pearls, E. Gaillard, c.1900, 6 1/8 In. 3550.00
Cross, 12 Brilliant-Cut Diamonds, 18K Yellow Gold, Chain 1840.00
Cross, Cat's-Eye Center, 26 In. Chain, Bethlehem 275.00
Cross, Oval Rubies, Blue Enameled Leaves, Diamonds, 15K Yellow Gold, Birks 2070.00
Cuff Links, 14K Gold, White Enamel, Rubies, Diamonds, Faberge, c.1900, Pair 4312.00
Cuff Links, 4 Brilliant-Cut Sapphires, Platinum Mount, Tiffany, Fitted Case 690.00
Cuff Links, Amber, White & Green Enamel, Center Diamond, 18K Gold Mount 575.00
Cuff Links, Butterfly, Enamel Wings, Diamond Body, 18K Yellow Gold Mount 690.00
Cuff Links, Cameo, Button Closure 50.00
Cuff Links, Coiled Serpent, Gilt Mounts, Signed, Lalique, c.1912 .... 3335.00
Cuff Links, Kum-A-Art, 1923 .... 10.00
Cuff Links, Pointer Dog, Intaglio, Beveled Links, Hickok 65.00
Cuff Links, Raised Open Diamond Design, Black Oxidized Ground, Kalo Shop, 3/4 In. 300.00
Cuff Links, Reverse Crystal, Pair Of Polo Ponies, 14K Yellow Gold 432.00
Cuff Links, Rock Crystal, Lapis Lazuli, Diamonds Form X, 18K Yellow Gold 1150.00
Cuff Links, Seahorse, Old Type Closure 35.00
Cuff Links, Silver Scalloped Ovals, Flowers & Lines, 1 3/4 In. 5.00
Cuff Links, Stirrup Shape, 4 Cabochon Sapphires, Yellow Gold, Cartier 862.00
Cuff Links, White Black Design Embossed Square, Snap Set 5.00
Cuff Links & Tie Clip, Anson 35.00
Cuff Links & Tie Clip, Fishing Fly, Gold Filled, Crystal, Van Guard 32.00
Dress Clip, Crown On Shield, Sterling Silver, Peruzzi, 1930s, Pair 350.00
Dress Clip, Marcasite, Sterling Silver, France, Pair 50.00
Dress Clip, Wooden Red Sunflower, Bakelite, 3 In. 190.00
Ear Pendants, Pear-Shaped Emerald, Diamond Set Mount, c.1920 .... 3450.00
Earrings, Black Enamel, Flowers, 14k Gold, Victorian 275.00
Earrings, Bow, 2 Pearls, Screw Back, 14K Yellow Gold 77.00
Earrings, Buttercup, .56 Ct. Diamond, Threaded Posts, White Gold 550.00
Earrings, Cluster Of Citrines, Small Diamonds Accent, 14K Yellow Gold 690.00
Earrings, Comma Shape, 18K Yellow Gold, Elsa Peretti, Tiffany, Box, Suede Bag 525.00
Earrings, Concentric Circle Flowers, Clip-On, Aurora Borealis, 4 Pair 18.00
Earrings, Contemporary Design, Sterling Silver, Georg Jensen, c.1945 .... 150.00
Earrings, Dove, Sterling Silver, Georg Jensen 190.00
Earrings, Drop, 14 Graduated Round Diamonds, 14K Yellow Gold 750.00
Earrings, Freeform Fans, Marcasite On Sterling Silver, Clip-On 48.00
Earrings, Gold Leaf, Clip-On, Trifari 8.00
Earrings, Jade Plaque, Enamel Frame, Diamond Tassels, Platinum & 18K Gold 8050.00
Earrings, Kidney Bean Shape, Clip-On, Aurora Borealis, 1 1/4 x 5/8 In. 18.00
Earrings, Pear-Shaped Diamond, 7.98 Total Cts., Platinum 8050.00
Earrings, Pearls, Ringed With Black Onyx, 14K Yellow Gold, 1 In. 290.00
Earrings, Pearls, Spray Design, Screw Back, 14K Gold, Gilbert Oakes, 1 In. 1150.00
Earrings, Rhinestone Bow, Camel Drops, Ora 20.00
Earrings, Rhinestone, Faceted Yellow Glass 6.00
Earrings, Spray, Each Set With 16 Pearls, 14K Yellow Gold 115.00
Earrings, Stylized Leaf Shape, Red Stone, Weiss, 1 1/2 In. 22.00
Earrings, Sunburst, Plain & Textured Stylized Rays, 18K Gold, Tiffany & Co. 750.00
Earrings, Tassel, Seed Pearls, Blue & White Enameled, 14K Yellow Gold 289.00
Earrings & Pendant, Enamel, Bright Pastels, Eisenberg, 1940s 200.00
Hatpins are listed in this book in the Hatpin category
Locket, 4 Aces, Opens For 2 Photos, Loop, c.1920 .... 187.00
Locket, Dome Center, Shell Design, 19 Link & Circle Chain, 14 In. 135.00
Locket, Enamel Flower Basket Center, Wire Work Border, Mesh Chain, 1 1/2 In. 135.00
Locket, Enamel, Diamond & Polychrome Enamel, 18K Yellow Gold, French, c.1823 .. 4025.00

Locket, Engraved Castle, Flowers, Gold Filled, Victorian... 30.00
Locket, Gold, Half Pearl, Cross Design, Stylized Floral Pendant Loop, Oval, c.1880.... 690.00
Locket, Memorial, Hair, Hand Painted, Oval, c.1850, 3 x 2 3/8 In............................ 192.00
Locket, Profile Of Woman, Diamonds & Rubies, Link Chain, Austria 575.00
Lorgnette, Fluted Stem, 2-Color Gold, Shell & Acanthus Leaves, 18K Gold, France.... 575.00
Maltese Cross, 53 Mine-Cut Diamonds, Continental, Silver, 19th Century, 1 1/2 In..... 3450.00
Medallion, 18K Yellow Gold, Becker, 19th Century 400.00
Necklace, 1 Row Of Red Heart Dangles, Red Celluloid Chain, Bakelite 330.00
Necklace, 2 Of Each Heart, Spade, Club & Diamond, Chain, c.1920, 14 In. 265.00
Necklace, 20 Amoeboid Links, 18K, H. Koppel For G. Jensen, c.1966 .... 7300.00
Necklace, 3-Shell Cameo, Chariot Scenes, 14K Yellow Gold, 14 1/2 In. 1265.00
Necklace, 6 Strands Of Amber Glass Beads, Spacers, Miriam Haskell 175.00
Necklace, Abalone Insets, Cut-Outs, Sterling Silver, Kalo, 13 In. 2000.00
Necklace, Abstract Design, Blue Enamel, Margot De Taxco 185.00
Necklace, Amber, Large Cubes, 31 In. 125.00
Necklace, Amethyst, Nuggets, Silver Links, 38 In. 24.00
Necklace, Aurora Borealis, 14 1/2 In. 12.00
Necklace, Aurora, Double Strands, 14 In. 13.00
Necklace, Aurora, Triple Strands, 16 In. 23.00
Necklace, Beads, Black & White, Textured, 13 1/2 In. 15.00
Necklace, Beads, Blue, Double Oval, 22 1/2 In. 15.00
Necklace, Beads, Faceted, Double Strands, 14 1/2 In. 13.00
Necklace, Beads, Faceted, Green Strung On White, 16 In. 18.00
Necklace, Beads, Faceted, Gunmetal, Iridescent, 36 In. 42.00
Necklace, Beads, Faceted, Jet, 34 In. 28.00
Necklace, Beads, Light Blue & White, Glass, Rhinestone, 17 In. 22.00
Necklace, Beads, Marbleized Green & White With Brass, White Tooth 6.00
Necklace, Beads, Turquoise And Black Oval, Round, 16 In. 15.00
Necklace, Bib, Oval Pearls, Glass Stones, 2 Rows Of Tortoise Glass, Pearl Dangles 130.00
Necklace, Brick Pattern, Diamonds, 14K Yellow Gold 1850.00
Necklace, Choker, 1 Strand, Haskell 65.00
Necklace, Choker, Aurora Borealis, Triple Strands 18.00
Necklace, Choker, Beads, Brass, 4 Strands 5.00
Necklace, Choker, Blue Glass & Beads, Filigree, DeMario 65.00
Necklace, Choker, Clear Round Rhinestones, Eisenberg... 25.00
Necklace, Choker, Double Ribbed, Coro, 17 In. 8.00
Necklace, Choker, Gold & Silver 10.00
Necklace, Choker, Gold, Flat, 5 Strands, 16 In. 4.00
Necklace, Choker, Gold, Polished Wire Into Central Knot, Georg Jensen 1095.00
Necklace, Choker, Pearl, Cultured, 3 Rosettes, 12K Gold...................................... 6.00
Necklace, Choker, Pearls & Butterfly, Miriam Haskell 75.00
Necklace, Choker, Rhinestones, Pave & Prong Set, Large Drop Rhinestone, Jomaz 25.00
Necklace, Colored Glass Beads, Metal Fittings, Woven Bands, Mandarin, 26 In........... 460.00
Necklace, Coral, 15 In. 18.00
Necklace, Crystals, Faceted, Round Beads, 18 In. 20.00
Necklace, Cut Glass, 35 In. 46.00
Necklace, Daisy, Green Leaves, Gold Frame, 19 In. 16.00
Necklace, Faceted, Butterfly, Double Heart, 15 In. 13.00
Necklace, Floral Design, Clasps Of Etruscan Design Pendant, Chain Drops 120.00
Necklace, Gold Double Leaf Links, Trifari, 14 In. 80.00
Necklace, Green Stones, Bogoff 55.00
Necklace, Heart, Marble, 16 In.. 3.00
Necklace, Jade, Oriental Character, Oval, 1 3/8 In. 7.00
Necklace, Links, Brass, 3/8 In... 8.00
Necklace, Openwork Panels, Baroque Pearls, A. Knox, Liberty & Co., c.1900 .... 5430.00
Necklace, Pearl, Cultured, 81 Graduated, Sapphire & Amethyst Clasp, 23 In.............. 805.00
Necklace, Pearl, Natural, White Gold Clasp, 1920s, 17 In. 6000.00
Necklace, Pearls, 1 Strand, 17 In. 15.00
Necklace, Pearls, 2 Strands, Pink, 16 In. 5.00
Necklace, Pearls, 2 Strands, Rhinestone Clasp, Ciner, 25 In. 35.00
Necklace, Pearls, Cultured, 1 Strand, 14K White Gold Clasp 195.00
Necklace, Pearls, Cultured, 4 Strands, Graduated, Gold Pearl & Sapphire Clasp........... 920.00
Necklace, Pearls, Cultured, 4 Strands, Multi-Gem Set Clasp 747.00

Necklace, Pearls, Cultured, 4 Strands, White Gold Clasp 575.00
Necklace, Pearls, Cultured, 46 In. 690.00
Necklace, Pearls, Cultured, 8 mm, 14K Gold Clasp, 22 In. 745.00
Necklace, Pearls, Cultured, Creamy Lustre, 8 mm Evenly Matched, Clasp, 20 In. 575.00
Necklace, Pearls, Cultured, Graduated, 14K White Gold Filigree Clasp, 20 1/2 In. 247.00
Necklace, Pearls, Cultured, Graduated, 5 mm, 18 In. 245.00
Necklace, Pearls, Cultured, Graduated, Silver Clasp, 15 In. 345.00
Necklace, Pearls, Graduated, 14K White Gold Clasp 154.00
Necklace, Pearls, Graduated, White Gold Filigree Clasp, 16 In. 250.00
Necklace, Pendant, 2 Large Grape Clusters, Snake Chain, Napier, 14 In. 135.00
Necklace, Raised Flower Links, Yellow & Rose Gold, Victorian, 18 In. 75.00
Necklace, Rhinestones, Faceted, 15 In. 6.00
Necklace, Swag Design, Amethyst & Freshwater Pearl, Double Chain, Edwardian 40.00
Necklace, Teardrop Pendant, Faceted Garnet, Foliate Chain, c.1900 .... 5175.00
Necklace, Textured White Beads, Rhinestone Cluster Center, Miriam Haskell 150.00
Necklace, Women's Head Links, Egyptian Dress, Enamel & Gilt 430.00
Necklace, Yellow Gold, Citrine, Arts & Crafts, Hale, c.1910 .... 6325.00
Necklace, Zigzag, Blue & Clear, Silk Cord, Signed, Lalique, c.1927 .... 3795.00
Necklace & Bracelet, Amethyst Cabochon, Sterling Silver Leaves, Mexico 225.00
Necklace & Bracelet, Choker, Hinged, Inset Amethyst, Silver, Sigi, Taxco 412.00
Necklace & Earrings, Copper, Matisse 45.00
Necklace & Earrings, Drops, Rhinestone, Screw Back, Coro, Lined Box 125.00
Necklace & Earrings, Hinged Amethyst Drops, Silver, Antonio 1100.00
Pendant, 1 Oval Cut Amethyst, 14K Yellow Gold Bezel 375.00
Pendant, 50 Pts. Diamonds Heart, 18K Gold, Cartier 1600.00
Pendant, Arrowhead Shape, Gold, Pearls, Art Nouveau, James H. Winn, 1 1/4 In. 3200.00
Pendant, Briolette-Cut Green Tourmaline, Diamonds, Platinum Mount, Art Deco 2645.00
Pendant, Cameo, Woman Playing Zither, 10K Yellow Gold Frame, Gold Chain 135.00
Pendant, Carved Carnelian, 14K Gold Frame, c.1920 .... 155.00
Pendant, Cat, Chain, Marked HBS, 14K Yellow Gold, 2 In. 440.00
Pendant, Cross, 19 Full Cut Brilliant Diamonds, Chain, Platinum, Edwardian 635.00
Pendant, Cross, Multicolored Glass Stones, Bale On Link Chain, Metal 105.00
Pendant, Floral Form, Synthetic Sapphires, Simulated Diamonds, c.1910 .... 2300.00
Pendant, Heart Shape, Asymmetrical, Pear-Shaped Amethyst, Pave-Set Diamonds 1380.00
Pendant, Maltese Cross, Green Enamel, Diamonds, Amethysts, Maggie Hayes, c.1930 ..... 635.00
Pendant, Mother-Of-Pearl, Hand Painted Birds, Etched Frame, Victorian 40.00
Pendant, Mourning, Amber, Yellow Gold 145.00
Pendant, Nugget, Applied Ring, Gold Filled Chain, 14K Yellow Gold 440.00
Pendant, Oval Plaque Set With Mine Cut Diamond, Rock Crystal, Chain, 15 1/2 In. 430.00
Pendant, Oval, Frolicking Mermaids, Turquoise Silk Cord, R. Lalique 1725.00
Pendant, Parrot, Rose-Cut Diamonds, Onyx Frame, Diamond Loop, 14K Chain 285.00
Pendant, Pear Shaped Emerald Cabochon, Collet Diamonds, White Gold, Platinum 800.00
Pendant, Perfume Bottle, Molded Frosted Glass, Stylized Acorn, Cord, Lalique 400.00
Pendant, Silver Gilt, Micromosaic, 2 Oval Drops, White Birds, Red Ground, Italy 175.00
Pendant, Sterling Cage Enclosing Stone, Rebajes, 2 1/2 In. 210.00
Pendant, Wings, Green & Yellow Frosted Plique-A-Jour Enamel, Silver 805.00
Pendant & Earrings, Enamel Pastels, Eisenberg, 1940s 200.00
Pin, 12-Pointed Star, Graduated Diamonds & European-Cut Diamonds, c.1880 ...... 1035.00
Pin, 2 Dolphins, Georg Jensen 440.00
Pin, 3 Round Brilliant Cut Diamonds, White Gold 115.00
Pin, 4 Perched Birds Form, Turquoise, 14K Yellow Gold 80.00
Pin, 4-Leaf Clover, Rhinestones, Weiss 50.00
Pin, 5 Amethysts, Stippled Gold Plate, Coro, 2 In. 95.00
Pin, 5-Sided Shield Shape, Dark Green Cabochon, Z Design, Brass, Forest Craft, 2 In. .. 300.00
Pin, Abstract Fish, Georg Jensen, 2 1/2 In. 308.00
Pin, Abstract, Silver, Ed Weiner, c.1950, 2 1/2 In. 220.00
Pin, Abstract, Tourmalines, Aquamarines, Amethysts 518.00
Pin, Agate, Gold-Plated Back, Victorian, 1 1/2 In. 23.00
Pin, Agate, Scotland, Victorian 145.00
Pin, Amethyst, Citrines, Center Cherub, Citrine Briolette, Yellow Gold, 19th Century .. 150.00
Pin, Angelfish, Gold, Jelly-Belly, Trifari 150.00
Pin, Apple, Carved Lucite Leaves, Red Bakelite 65.00
Pin, Bar, 14K White Gold Filigree, 2 1/2 Point Diamond Center, Victorian, 2 x 3/4 In. .. 250.00

Pin, Bar, 14K Yellow Gold, Foxtail Link Chain, Etruscan Revival, Victorian 175.00
Pin, Bar, 18K Gold, Platinum & Diamond Set Bow, Black Enameled, Pearls, Edwardian 450.00
Pin, Bar, Amethyst, 10K White Gold 75.00
Pin, Bar, Center Baroque Pearl, Sea Plants, Sterling, Rokesley Shop, 2 3/4 In. 1200.00
Pin, Bar, Center Row Of Sapphires, Diamond Set Platinum Mount............................ 1380.00
Pin, Bar, Diamond, Filigree, 14K White Gold 155.00
Pin, Bar, Floral Design, Oval Sapphire, 2 Brilliant Cut Diamonds, Platinum Mount...... 865.00
Pin, Bar, Geometric Pierced, Quartz Cabochon Center, Oval, Sterling, 2 1/2 In........... 130.00
Pin, Bar, Green Plastic, Rhinestones, Kenneth Lane 50.00
Pin, Bar, Horseshoe Center, Set With Seed Pearls, Victorian 105.00
Pin, Bar, Openwork Floral, Mine & Rose-Cut Diamonds, Platinum Mount.................... 920.00
Pin, Bar, Rhinestones, Green Plastic, Kenneth Lane 50.00
Pin, Bar, Rolled Gold Plate, Space For Photograph On Back 80.00
Pin, Bar, Trefoil, Diamonds, 18K Gold, Victorian.. 628.00
Pin, Biomorphic Shape, Silver, Georg Jensen, No. 325, 2 1/4 In. 176.00
Pin, Bird Of Paradise, Coro.. 125.00
Pin, Bird, Sapphire Wings, Brilliant-Cut Diamond Body, Cabochon Ruby Eye 489.00
Pin, Blue Baroque Pearls, Miriam Haskell... 85.00
Pin, Bow, 14K Yellow Gold, Laykin & Cie.. 690.00
Pin, Bow, Green & Red Stones, Bogue.. 80.00
Pin, Bow, Green & Blue Rhinestones, Clear Round Rhinestone Knot, Trifari, 1 1/2 In. 135.00
Pin, Bow, Pave Diamonds, Emeralds & Onyx, 14K Gold, Art Deco 2300.00
Pin, Bow, Pave-Set Clear Round Rhinestones, Jomaz, 2 In. 25.00
Pin, Branch With Flowers & Leaves, Sterling Silver, Beau 12.00
Pin, Brass Disk, Abstract Design In Copper, Ed Weiner, 2 1/2 In. 520.00
Pin, Brass, Clear Glass Stone, Scales Of Justice, Round, Forest Craft Guild, 2 3/8 In.... 300.00
Pin, Brass, Cut Cornered Oval, Embossed Salamander, Hammered, 2 x 2 1/2 In. 185.00
Pin, Brushed Gold, Citrine Applied Design, Sorrento, 2 1/2 In.................................... 25.00
Pin, Bug On Ladder, 18K Yellow Gold, 2 In. 50.00
Pin, Butterfly, Diamonds, Emeralds, Pave-Set Diamond Body, 14K Gold 2875.00
Pin, Butterfly, Enamel, Andersen, 3 In. 45.00
Pin, Butterfly, Garnet, Victorian, 2 In. 230.00
Pin, Butterfly, Hollycraft 45.00
Pin, Butterfly, Mother-Of-Pearl, Sterling Silver, Art Nouveau 85.00
Pin, Butterfly, Multicolor Foil Backed Stones, Wax Pearls, Emmons, 2 1/4 In. 18.00
Pin, Butterfly, Pink Stones, Regency 30.00
Pin, Cameo, Buxom Woman, Flower In Hair, 14K White Gold Frame......................... 350.00
Pin, Cameo, Coral, 10K Gold Mounting.. 115.00
Pin, Cameo, Gold, Creme Parfum On Chain, Box... 58.00
Pin, Cameo, Oval, 16K Yellow Gold 575.00
Pin, Cameo, Oval, Gold, 2 In. 127.00
Pin, Cameo, Portrait, Seed Pearls On 10K Yellow Gold Frame, 1 5/8 In....................... 137.00
Pin, Cameo, Rebecca At The Well, 1 3/4 In.. 75.00
Pin, Cameo, Shell, Cupid & Psyche, Gold Mount, 1 5/8 In. 180.00
Pin, Carved Ivory Hand, Holding Rose, Victorian.. 130.00
Pin, Cat, Gold Tone, Trifari 20.00
Pin, Catalin Horse, Glass Eye, Metal Bridle, Bakelite, c.1937 .... 295.00
Pin, Center Pearl, Brass, Art Nouveau, 1 1/2 In. 80.00
Pin, Chevron Design, Sterling Silver, Hans Hansen, No. 113, 3 In............................. 66.00
Pin, Christmas Tree, Red, Green, Blue & Clear Rhinestones, Joseph Warner, 2 In. 65.00
Pin, Circle, Art Deco, Diamonds, Sapphires, Platinum Mount, J.E. Caldwell 6100.00
Pin, Circle, European-Cut Diamonds Set Into Number 21, c.1880 .... 805.00
Pin, Citrine, Pierced Greek Key Design, Pearls, 14K Yellow Gold, Art Nouveau 250.00
Pin, Clip, Allover Different Cut Diamonds, Foliate Engraved Reverse, c.1930............. 4025.00
Pin, Cluster, Brilliant, Pear & Marquise-Cut Diamonds, Platinum 3105.00
Pin, Crescent, Sterling Silver, Rhinestones 75.00
Pin, Crown, Cabochon Stones, Red & Green, Trifari, Large....................................... 200.00
Pin, Crown, Pave-Set Clear Rhinestones, Baguettes, Trifari, 1940s............................ 35.00
Pin, Daisy, Enameled, Monet, 2 1/2 In. 8.00
Pin, Dangling Red Bakelite Cherries, Green Leaves, Celluloid Chain 92.00
Pin, Deux Aigles, 2 Eagles, Gilt Metal & Glass, Signed, Lalique, c.1911, 3 3/4 In. 1150.00
Pin, Doves, Wheat Shaft, Art Deco, Georg Jensen, 1 1/2 In. 200.00
Pin, Dragonfly, Garnets, Ruby Eyes, Diamond Wings, Platinum, 18K Yellow Gold 4885.00

Pin, Dragonfly, Rubies, Sapphire, Emerald, Pave-Diamond Wings & Tail 1035.00
Pin, Dutch Shoe, Tulips & Windmill, Plastic, On Card, 3 Piece 18.00
Pin, Eagle, Carved Opal, Diamond-Set Eye, Yellow Gold Branch, Enamel Leaves 3450.00
Pin, Edelweiss, Gold Plated, 3 1/4 In. 357.00
Pin, Elephant, Openwork Design, Pave-Set Clear Rhinestones, Kenneth Lane 105.00
Pin, Enamel & Jeweled, Feodor Lorie, c.1910, 2 1/2 In. 8050.00
Pin, Five-Point Crown, European-Cut And Rose-Cut Diamonds, c.1870 .... 805.00
Pin, Flag, Rubies, Sapphires, Diamonds, 18K White Gold Mount 1380.00
Pin, Flower Basket, Blue & Yellow Sapphires, Rubies, Diamonds, 2 Tone Gold 1380.00
Pin, Flower Blossom, Carnelian, Sterling Silver, Kalo Shop, 2 3/4 x 3 In. 795.00
Pin, Flower, Clear Rhinestones, Marcel Boucher 395.00
Pin, Flower, Diamond Stem, Multishaped Tanzanites & Brilliant-Cut Diamonds 1150.00
Pin, Flower, Enameled, Coro, 4 In. 15.00
Pin, Flower, Gold Plated Pave Rhinestones, Weiss 150.00
Pin, Flower, Sterling Silver, Nettie Rosenstein 175.00
Pin, Fox, Reds, Browns & Black, Marble Effect, Plastic, Leah Stein 145.00
Pin, Free Form Design, 3 Moonstones, Sterling Silver, 2 1/4 In. 95.00
Pin, Frog, Green Enamel, Diamond Eyes, 14K Gold... 285.00
Pin, Gargoyle, Ruby Eyes, Unger Brothers 385.00
Pin, Garnet, Openwork Star Design, Victorian 130.00
Pin, Gold & Enameled Florets, Cabochon Garnet, Yellow Gold, c.1880 .... 518.00
Pin, Green Stone, Mask, Sterling, Diaz Santoya, Taxco, 2 1/4 In............................ 55.00
Pin, Green Tourmaline Bead, Enameled, Art Nouveau, Yellow Gold, M & Co. 920.00
Pin, Heart, Sterling Silver, Castlecliff 65.00
Pin, Horse, Painted Trim, Clear, Carved Lucite.. 80.00
Pin, Horsehead, Clear Baguette Rhinestones On Rein, Red Cabochon Eye, Trifari 25.00
Pin, Horseshoe, Graduating Mine-Cut Diamonds, Platinum & Gold Mount 920.00
Pin, Horseshoe, Yellow Gold, Graduated Amethysts Row, Cartier 920.00
Pin, Irish Wolfhound, Sterling Silver, Monet, 1960s, 3 In...................................... 75.00
Pin, Ivory Rose, Gold, Accessocraft, 1 1/2 In.. 25.00
Pin, Jade, 14K Yellow Gold, Art Nouveau, Mildred G. Watkins, 7/8 x 1 3/4 In. 5500.00
Pin, Lapel, Avon Lady Door Knocker 15.00
Pin, Leaf & Bead Work, Pearls, Round, Gold, Sterling, Gilbert Oakes, 1 3/4 In........... 2850.00
Pin, Leaf Shape, Sapphires, Brilliant-Cut Diamonds, Diamond Stem, Yellow Gold 431.00
Pin, Leaf, Blue Enamel, David Andersen ....55.00 to 65.00
Pin, Leaf, Pastel Stones, Lucite 60.00
Pin, Lizard, Marcasite.. 25.00
Pin, Lizard, Pave Pearls, Garnets, 15K Yellow Gold, Edwardian................................ 1725.00
Pin, Mine-Cut Diamond Center, Pave-Set Leaves, Platinum Mount................................ 3220.00
Pin, Moon Walk, Enameled, 14K Gold, Tiffany 325.00
Pin, Mourning, Floral, Jet, France 55.00
Pin, Mourning, Hair, Rectangular Black Onyx, Yellow Gold................................. 115.00
Pin, Mushroom, 3-D, Copper Wash, Silver 22.00
Pin, Oval Outline, Row Of Tapering Collet Set Diamonds, Platinum Mount 7475.00
Pin, Oval, Chased Pear Design, Sterling, Kalo Shop, 1 1/2 x 2 In. 450.00
Pin, Oval, Pink Topaz, Diamonds, Seed Pearls, Marcus & Co., c.1910...................... 1610.00
Pin, Owl, Kenneth J. Lane.. 55.00
Pin, Pansy, Enameled 17.00
Pin, Parrot, Rhinestone Eyes, Bakelite 50.00
Pin, Peacock, Seed Pearls On Body, Ruby Eye, Enameled Flower, Victorian................ 287.00
Pin, Pearls, Filigree, Miriam Haskell... 60.00
Pin, Pendant, Cross, Lamb Center, Mosaic, Floral, Sacred Letters, Gold, Italy, c.1850 .. 3000.00
Pin, Penguin, Goldtone, Red Enamel Beak, Jelly Belly, 2 1/2 In. 135.00
Pin, Pierced Floral Design, Center Sapphire & Diamond Cluster, France 978.00
Pin, Porcelain, Portrait Of Woman, Gold-Plated Back, Victorian, 1 3/4 In. 40.00
Pin, Portrait Of Beauty, Rose-Cut Diamonds, Pearl Set Border, 19th Century 1207.00
Pin, Portrait, Brass Filigree Frame, Hinged Swivel 45.00
Pin, Red Stones, Barclay 150.00
Pin, Rhinestones, Large Topaz, Sarah Coventry, 5 In. 25.00
Pin, Rhinestones, Red & White, Eisenberg, 1940s 100.00
Pin, Ribbon, Center Blue Cabochon Sapphire, Diamond Scrolls, 14K Gold 259.00
Pin, Rooster, Enamel, Jelly Belly, 3 In. 145.00
Pin, Round Diamonds Center, Pearl Surround, 14K Yellow Gold............................ 345.00

Pin, Round Foliate Design, Base Cityscape, 41 Diamonds, Art Deco 2415.00
Pin, S Shape, Rose-Cut Diamonds, Russian Gold, c.1900 .... 575.00
Pin, Salamander, Clear Stomach, Trifari.. 650.00
Pin, Scarecrow, Sterling Silver, Trifari.. 80.00
Pin, Scarf, Benzel-Set, Gray Pearl, 18K Yellow Gold, c.1900.................................... 445.00
Pin, Scarf, Rhodolite Garnets, Gold, Victorian 165.00
Pin, Seahorse, Oval Jade Within Mount, Rubies, Pave-Set Diamond Head 405.00
Pin, Seed Pearls, Surrounded By Round Garnets 105.00
Pin, Sgt. Preston, With King, Figural, Wood Composition, Cutout, 1950s 120.00
Pin, Shield Shape, Tassel Drops, Scrolling Vine, Yellow Gold 690.00
Pin, Shield, Stylized Design, Brass, Verdigris Ground, Forest Craft, 2 3/4 In. 300.00
Pin, Silver Sheet & Wire Construction, Ed Weiner, c.1948, 3 1/2 x 2 In. 1200.00
Pin, Silver, Rock Crystal & Onyx, Wiwen Nilsson, 1940s, 1 1/2 In. 2300.00
Pin, Silver, Woman, Flowing Hair, Flowers, Sterling, Art Nouveau, No. 1307, 1 1/2 In. 110.00
Pin, Sleeping Cat, Shades Of Rust & Black, Plastic, Leah Stein, 3 1/2 In. 145.00
Pin, Snail, Diamond-Set Yellow-Gold Body, Ribbed Shell, Pearl 259.00
Pin, Snakes Around Amber Stone, Sterling, Arts & Crafts, 2 1/2 In. 286.00
Pin, Sombrero, With 2 Cherries, Green Plastic Leaf, Bakelite 565.00
Pin, Sphinx, Sterling Silver, Coro, 3 In. 175.00
Pin, Sports Car, Yellow & Blue Enameled, Sapphires, 18K Gold, Hase, c.1950 .... 1380.00
Pin, Spray, Turquoise & Rose-Cut Diamonds, Silver, Gold, Victorian 628.00
Pin, St. Angelo's Cathedral, Micromosaic Inlay, Black Onyx, 14K Gold Frame 770.00
Pin, Star Comet, Blue & Clear Rhinestones, Lisner 65.00
Pin, Stylized Blossom, Bat Shape, Acid-Etched Copper, Carence Crafters, 1 1/2 x 2 In. 375.00
Pin, Stylized Floral, Rounded Shield Shape, Nickel Silver, Carence Crafters, 1 3/4 In. . 275.00
Pin, Stylized Insect, Etched Butterfly, Brass, Hammered, Marshall Field, 3 In. 300.00
Pin, Stylized Palm, Sapphires, Diamonds, Coral, 18K Yellow Gold 402.00
Pin, Stylized Violin, Silver, Paul Lobel, 1950s, 3 In.. 415.00
Pin, Sword, Moonstones & Garnets, Sterling Silver, Georg Jensen, Large.................... 145.00
Pin, Trois Marguerites, 3 Daisies, Gray Patina, Signed, Lalique, c.1912, 1 1/4 In......... 1035.00
Pin, Turtle, Opal, Mine-Cut Diamonds, Garnet, With Chain 1850.00
Pin, Turtle, Textured Gold Head, Ruby Eyes, 15K Gold 175.00
Pin, Winged Scarab, Enameled, Sterling Silver, Charles Horner 275.00
Pin, Yellow Glass Cabochon, Hammered Leaf & Stem, Sterling, 1 1/4 x 2 In. 225.00
Pin & Earrings, Leaf, Light & Dark Blue Stones, Coro, 3 In....................................... 28.00
Pin & Earrings, Leaf, Marcasite, Weiss.. 185.00
Pin & Earrings, Pink Ice, Eisenberg, 2 1/4 In.. 125.00
Pin-Pendant, Mourning, Oval, Garnet, Gold Filled, Victorian, 2 3/4 In. 460.00
Ring, 1891 Indian Head Penny, 18K Yellow Gold... 71.00
Ring, Amethyst, 2 Side Beads, Sterling, Art Deco, Kalo Shop, Size 6 3/4 In. 650.00
Ring, Bean, 18K Gold, Elsa Peretti, T & Co. 2650.00
Ring, Black Star Sapphire, 18K Gold, Spain, 1800s 1695.00
Ring, Blue Wedgwood Portrait, Classical Woman, 14K Yellow Gold 85.00
Ring, Butterfly, Enameled Wings, Diamond Eyes, 18K Yellow Gold Mount 230.00
Ring, Cameo Lapis, Profile Of Woman, 14K Gold Frame 920.00
Ring, Cameo, Hardstone, Female Head, 14K Yellow Gold Mount 460.00
Ring, Cameo, Red Jasper, Female Satyr, 18K Gold Mount c.1860 .... 1150.00
Ring, Carved Half-Hood, Pearls, Diamond Points, 18K Gold, Victorian 632.00
Ring, Cat's Eye Chrysoberyl, 8 Cts., 14K Yellow Gold Mount 9775.00
Ring, Chrysoprase In Bezel, 14K Gold, Edward E. Oakes, Size 7 1/4 In. 3600.00
Ring, Circular Diamonds For Initials G E, White Gold Mount 115.00
Ring, Citrine Surrounded By Seed Pearls, Miriam Haskell 125.00
Ring, Citrine, Surrounded With 4 mm. Pearls, 14K Yellow Gold, Size 10 .... 295.00
Ring, Cocktail, 21 Brilliant-Cut Diamonds, 14K Yellow Gold 805.00
Ring, Cognac-Colored Brilliant-Cut Diamond, 2.8 Cts, Platinum Mount, c.1930 .... 1150.00
Ring, Coral, Carved, Emerald & Diamond Shell Pattern Supports, Yellow Gold 805.00
Ring, Diamond, 4 Rows Channel Set Sapphires, Pierced Platinum, European, 1900 ...... 725.00
Ring, Dinner, Natural Coral & 6 Square-Cut Emeralds, 14K Yellow Gold.................... 170.00
Ring, Domed Setting, 1 Full Carat Small Diamonds 310.00
Ring, Emerald Step-Cut Diamond, Small Diamonds Around, Platinum, c.1920 .... 4025.00
Ring, Eternity, Multicut Diamonds, 3 Cts. Total Weight 1725.00
Ring, Filigree, European Cut Diamond, Platinum, Art Deco.. 2650.00
Ring, Half-Loop Design, Round Sapphires, Diamonds, 18K Yellow Gold 173.00

Ring, Mabe Pearl Center, Hammered 18K Gold Mount 1035.00
Ring, Mabe Pearl, Diamond Surround, White Gold 402.00
Ring, Malachite, Cat's-Eye, Diamond, 14K Gold 121.00
Ring, Man's, 1/2 Carat Diamonds, Handmade 400.00
Ring, Man's, Oval Cabochon Jade Plaque, Yellow Gold Mount 1093.00
Ring, Man's, Star Ruby, 9 Cts., Oval, Platinum Mount 8625.00
Ring, Marquis Diamonds, Oval Sapphire Surrounds, c.1960 .... 2000.00
Ring, Memorial, Bowknot Frame, Pearls, Weeping Willows, Ivory & Gold 690.00
Ring, Mine-Cut Diamond, .80 Carat, 18K White Gold Filigree 625.00
Ring, Mourning, Enamel & Gold, England, c.1752 .... 750.00
Ring, Mourning, Hair, 2 Braid, Gold Joinings 60.00
Ring, Oblong Fire Agate, 14K Gold 120.00
Ring, Opal, Art Nouveau, 14K Yellow Gold 250.00
Ring, Opal, Rose Gold Basket Filigree Mount, Victorian 495.00
Ring, Oval 5.9-Cts. Sapphire, Triangular-Cut Diamonds, 18K White Gold Mount 2300.00
Ring, Oval Green Agate Cabochon, Pierced Sides, 14K Gold, Kalo Shop, Size 4 .... 2900.00
Ring, Pearl, Cultured, Rose-Cut Diamonds, Rubies, 14K Gold, Art Nouveau 275.00
Ring, Pink Panther, Carol Kee 175.00
Ring, Polychrome Enamel, 1920s 115.00
Ring, Rose Gold, Garnet, Pearls, Victorian 85.00
Ring, Rose-Cut Diamond Cluster, 5 Rubies, Georgian, c.1770 .... 920.00
Ring, Ruby, Abstract Snake Design, Rose-Cut Diamonds, 18K Yellow Gold 375.00
Ring, Ruby, Diamond, Emeralds & Rubies, 18K Yellow Gold Stylized Buckle, 1940s .. 200.00
Ring, Small Round Diamonds & Emeralds, 14K White Gold 138.00
Ring, Solitaire, Diamond, Yellow & White Gold 1150.00
Ring, Step-Cut Emerald, Cluster Of 22 Brilliant Diamonds, 14K Gold Mount 546.00
Ring, Tourmaline, Gilbert Oakes 1150.00
Ring, Turquoise, Elongated Oval Cabochon, Yellow-Gold Band, c.1820 .... 80.00
Ring, Yellow Gold, Cabochon Cut Opal, Surrounded By Rose-Cut Diamonds 345.00
Rosary, Blue Crystal 25.00
Rosary, Monk's, Carved Wooden Beads, Early 1900s, France, 7 Ft. 95.00
Rosary, Sterling Silver 30.00
Stickpin, Case, Eagle On Globe 25.00
Stickpin, George Washington's Hatchet, Feb. 22, Gilt Finish, Red Highlights 65.00
Stickpin, Man's, Fleur-De-Lis, Seed Pearl, Yellow Gold, c.1890 .... 110.00
Stickpin, Mutt & Jeff, 1920s 130.00
Stickpin, Pear, Emerald, Art Deco, Monet 45.00
Stickpin, Rhinestone, Florenza 75.00
Tie Bar, Twisted Rope Design, Sterling Silver, Kalo Shop, 1/4 x 2 3/4 In. 265.00
Watches are listed in their own category
Watch Chain, Box Links, 14K Yellow Gold, 13 1/2 In. 127.00
Watch Ring, Gubelin, Sapphire, Roman Numerals, Hinged Cover, 14K Gold, c.1960 ... 2185.00
Wristwatches are listed in their own category

JOHN ROGERS statues were made from 1859 to 1892. The originals were
bronze, but the thousands of copies made by the Rogers factory were of
painted plaster. Eighty different figures were created. Similar painted plaster
figures were produced by some other factories. Rights to the figures were
sold in 1893 and they were manufactured for several more years by the Rogers Statuette Co. Never repaint a Rogers figure because this lowers the value
to collectors.

Group, Coming To The Parson .... 175.00 to 330.00
Group, It Is So Nominated In The Bond 385.00
Group, One More Shot 430.00
Group, Private Theatricals 600.00

JUDAICA is any memorabilia that refers to the Jews or the Jewish religion.
Interests range from newspaper clippings that mention eighteenth- and nineteenth-century Jewish Americans to religious objects, such as menorahs or
spice boxes. Age, condition, and the intrinsic value of the material, as well as
the historic and artistic importance, determine the value.

Box, Charity, 833 Silver, 8 In. 2000.00
Bust, Semitic Youth With Pais & Yarmulke, Bronze, Painted, Israel, 4 7/8 In. 18.00

Candlestick, Sabbath, A. Katz, London, c.1894, 16 1/4 In., Pair 1100.00
Carving, Dome Of The Rock, Hebrew Script, Wood, 1800s, 4 3/4 In............................ 250.00
Etrog Box, Succah Dinner Engraved On Cover, Silver, I. Schor, c.1950, 5 1/8 In.......... 8337.00
Ketubah, Peacock, Lions, Foliate, Persian, Frame, 1865 .... 625.00
Kiddish Cup, Engraved Menorah, Silver, German Mark 145.00
Kiddush Cup, Applied Star Of David, Sterling Silver, 4 1/2 In. 85.00
Kiddush Cup, Footed, Applied Hebrew Letters, c.1950, Israel.................................. 80.00
Kiddush Cup, Silver Gilt, Poland, c.1770, 5 1/4 In.. 950.00
Kiddush Cup, Swags Above Stiff Leaves, Carl Friederich, c.1804, 5 In. 6037.00
Spice Box, Bird On Top, Sterling Silver, 1800s, 8 In. 2950.00
Spice Box, Silver, Brass, 19th Century.. 475.00
Torah Finials, 2 Rows Of Gilt Bells, Crown Finials, Parcel Gilt Silver, 15 1/2 In., Pair 4887.00
Torah Finials, Tribes Of Israel, Tree Of Life, Silver, c.1960, 3 Piece 3450.00
Window, Central Cartouche Of Torah, Leaded Glass, 19 x 42 In............................... 990.00

JUGTOWN Pottery refers to pottery made in North Carolina as far back as the 1750s. In 1915, Juliana and Jacques Busbee set up a training and sales organization for what they named *Jugtown Pottery*. In 1921, they built a shop at Jugtown, North Carolina, and hired Ben Owen as a potter in 1923. The Busbees moved the village store where the pottery was sold to New York City. Juliana Busbee sold the New York store in 1926 and moved into a log cabin near the Jugtown Pottery. The pottery closed in 1958. It reopened and is still working near Seagrove, North Carolina.

Bowl, Blue, 8 In... 160.00
Creamer, Cover, Yellow, 4 3/4 In... 50.00
Eggcup, Blue.. 15.00
Jar, Cover, Frogskin Glaze... 75.00
Jardiniere, Quartz Inclusions, Black Tenmoku Glaze 95.00
Pitcher, Frogskin, Pinched Spout, 3 1/2 In. 35.00
Pot, Red & Turquoise, 6 1/2 In. 425.00
Vase, Chinese Blue Drip, Red-Brown Body, 5 1/2 In. 550.00
Vase, Chinese Blue Glaze Drip, Over Red Clay, Impressed Circle, 7 x 4 3/4 In............. 495.00
Vase, Chinese Blue Glaze, 4 1/2 In. 660.00
Vase, Chinese Blue Glaze, Banded, Oviform, Impressed Mark, 6 3/4 x 4 In. 468.00
Vase, Chinese Blue Glaze, Sloped Shoulder, Flared Rim, Signed, 6 x 8 In. 605.00
Vase, Dark Brown High Glaze, 8 In... 225.00
Vase, Frogskin, 10 In. 195.00
Vase, Frogskin, Signed, 5 In. ....65.00 to 75.00
Vase, New Chinese Blue, Vernon Owen, 1985, 8 1/2 In. 225.00
Vase, Thick Mottled Dark Blue Matte Glaze, Ovoid, Marked, 5 x 3 1/2 In. 523.00
Vase, Tobacco Spit Brown Glaze... 75.00

JUKEBOXES play records. The first coin-operated phonograph was demonstrated in 1889. In 1906 the *Automatic Entertainer* appeared, the first coin-operated phonograph to offer several different selections of music. The first electrically powered jukebox was introduced in 1927. Collectors search for jukeboxes of all ages, especially those with flashing lights and unusual design and graphics.

Rock-Ola, Model 1422, 1946 .... 1870.00
Rock-Ola, Model 1426, Bakelite Front Panels, 20 Records, 1946, 56 In..........5300.00 to 5750.00
Rock-Ola, Model ST-20, Standard, 20 Selections, Deco Shape, 55 1/2 In. 2300.00
Seeburg, Mayfair.. 1050.00
Seeburg, Model 100, Happy Days, 54 x 36 In... 1210.00
Seeburg, Model W, Hideaway, 1953 .... 350.00
Wurlitzer, Model 61, Counter, 1937-1939 .... 3500.00
Wurlitzer, Model 600, 24 Selections, 1938-1939.. 6200.00
Wurlitzer, Model 780, 24 Selections, Colonial, 1941 ....3500.00 to 7500.00
Wurlitzer, Model 800, 24 Selections, Glazed Front, 3 Bubble Tubes, 37 In. 5175.00
Wurlitzer, Model 1100, 24 Selections, 25 Cents, 59 In. ....2400.00 to 4600.00
Wurlitzer, Model 1800, 104 Selections, Chrome Frame, 55 In. 3450.00
Wurlitzer, Model 3510, Zodiac 500.00
Wurlitzer, Model P-12, 12 Selections, Walnut, Simplex, 1934.................................... 900.00

KATE GREENAWAY, who was a famous illustrator of children's books, drew pictures of children in high-waisted Empire dresses. She lived from 1846 to 1901. Her designs appear on china, glass, and other pieces. Figural napkin rings depicting the Greenaway children may also be found in the Napkin Ring category under Figural.

Doll, Muff, DN 25, Stand, Case, 1982, 12 In.	350.00
Napkin Ring, Figural, Girl, Beating Drum, Drum Is Ring, Silver Plate	325.00
Plate, Aries, The Ram, Almanack, 1978, 8 1/4 In.	65.00
Salt & Pepper, Boy & Girl, Wearing Hats, Long Coats, Silver Plated, 4 1/4 In.	195.00
Tea Set, Child's, Scenic, Multicolored, 15 Piece	450.00

KAY FINCH Ceramics were made in Corona Del Mar, California, from 1935 to 1963. The hand-decorated pieces often depicted whimsical animals and people. Pastel colors were used.

Kay Finch
CALIFORNIA

Figurine, Angel, Boy, No. 212	55.00
Figurine, Angel, No. 4909 & No. 4910, Pair	100.00
Figurine, Bear, Standing, No. 5004	125.00
Figurine, Boy & Girl, 8 In.	55.00
Figurine, Cat, Ambrosia	450.00
Figurine, Cat, Jezebel	125.00 to 150.00
Figurine, Cat, Mehitable, No. 181	225.00
Figurine, Cat, Persian, 11 In.	450.00
Figurine, Cat, Puff, No. 183	48.00
Figurine, Choir Boy, No. 210 & No. 211, Pair	125.00
Figurine, Donkey	75.00
Figurine, Draft Horses, 3 Piece	195.00
Figurine, Duck, Fat, 3 In.	35.00
Figurine, Duck, Peep & Jeep, No. 178, Pair	80.00
Figurine, Elephant, Baby, 5 In.	50.00
Figurine, Elephant, Peanuts, No. 191	225.00
Figurine, Godey Couple	150.00
Figurine, Kitten	50.00
Figurine, Lamb, Kneeling, No. 136	40.00
Figurine, Lamb, Seated	45.00
Figurine, Missouri Mule	60.00
Figurine, Owl, 5 3/4 In.	40.00
Figurine, Owl, 8 1/2 In.	60.00
Figurine, Owl, 9 In.	125.00
Figurine, Pig, Sassy, No. 166, 4 1/4 x 3 1/2 In.	38.00
Figurine, Pig, Winkie, No. 185	65.00
Figurine, Rooster & Hen, Pair	45.00
Figurine, Yorkie Pup, No. 171, 5 1/2 In.	185.00
Figurine, Yorkie Pup, Standing, Foot Up, 6 1/2 In.	125.00
Figurine, Yorkshire Puppy, No.170	150.00
Planter, Book Shape, Lamb, 6 In.	40.00
Planter, Our Baby Book, Bunny	65.00

KAYSERZINN, see Pewter category

KELVA glassware was made by the C. F. Monroe Company of Meriden, Connecticut, about 1904. It is a pale, pastel-painted glass decorated with flowers, designs, or scenes. Kelva resembles Nakara and Wave Crest, two other glasswares made by the same company.

KELVA

Box, Floral, Gray, Blue, 3 1/2 In.	500.00
Box, White Flowers, Beads, Roses	500.00
Humidor, Cigar, Flowers	625.00

KENTON HILLS Pottery in Erlanger, Kentucky, made art wares, including vases and figurines that resembled Rookwood, probably because so many of the original artists and workmen had worked at the Rookwood plant. Kenton Hills opened in 1939 and closed during World War II.

Dish, Red Aventurine Glaze, Bulbous, Squatty, Impressed KH, 3 1/4 x 4 In.	275.00

KEW BLAS is the name used by the Union Glass Company of Somerville, Massachusetts. The name refers to an iridescent golden glass made from the 1890s to 1924. The iridescent glass was reminiscent of the Tiffany glass of the period.

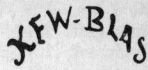

Pitcher, Pulled Feathers, Green, 4 1/2 In.	880.00
Vase, Diagonal Stripes, Gold & Green, 7 In.	600.00

KEWPIES, designed by Rose O'Neill, were first pictured in the *Ladies' Home Journal*. The figures, which are similar to pixies, were a success, and Kewpie dolls started appearing in 1911. Kewpie pictures and other items soon followed. Collectors search for all items that picture the little winged people.

Bank, Doll, Chalkware, 13 In.	45.00
Bank, Painted Kewpie, Next To Jar, Glass, Geo. Borgfeldt, 3 In.	70.00
Beaming Smile, Wings, Rose O'Neill, c.1912, 3 In.	400.00
Bell, Brass	65.00
Bisque, 6 1/2 In.	385.00
Bisque, Baseball Uniform, Blue Wingers Team, Plastic Mitt & Ball, 1956, 4 1/2 In.	125.00
Bisque, Bride & Groom, Jointed Arms, Dressed, Rose O'Neill, 5 In., Pair	400.00
Bisque, Bride, Jointed Arms, Eyes Left, Ivory Crepe Paper Gown, Veil, 4 1/2 In.	50.00
Bisque, Eyes Left, Aviator Helmet, Goggles, Signed, 8 1/2 In.	775.00
Bisque, Groom, Jointed Arms, Rose O'Neill, 5 In.	150.00
Bisque, Holding Pen	495.00
Bisque, Kicker On Basket, Blue Basket Weave Design, Black Mark, 2 x 2 1/2 In.	800.00
Bisque, Lying On Stomach, Arms Outstretched, Eyes Right, Rose O'Neill, 4 In.	275.00
Bisque, Molded Head, Jointed Body, Eyes Left, Rose O'Neill, 5 3/4 In.	100.00
Bisque, Reading Book, Standing, Pair	805.00
Bisque, Santa Claus, Counter Stand Up, Signed, Rose O'Neill, 1913	145.00
Bisque, Scootles, Composition, Jointed, Bib Overalls, Effanbee, 1949, 12 In.	700.00
Bisque, Scootles, Jointed Arms, Toddler Body, Rose O'Neill, 8 In.	2700.00
Bisque, Sitting Sucking Thumb, 4 1/2 In.	15.00
Bottle, Nurser, Figural, Glass, Rose O'Neill, 1919, 8 Oz., 7 In.	1000.00
Boutonniere, Bisque, Figural, Lapel Stud Back, Ribbon On Chest, 2 In.	150.00
Bowl & Pitcher, Lusterware, 3 Colors, O'Neill, Germany, 6 1/2 In.	575.00
Button, Bisque, Figural, Raised Arms, Square Button Hole Back, O'Neill Label, 2 In.	250.00
Candy Container, Barrel	150.00
Candy Container, Borgfeldt & Co.	85.00
Candy Container, With Barrel, Glass	150.00
Card Holder, Bisque, Figural, Hanging, 2 1/2 In.	250.00
Celluloid, Bride & Groom, 3 In.	45.00
Celluloid, Occupied Japan	25.00
Chalkware, Full Figure, 12 In.	65.00
Charm, Figural, Silver, Arms At Sides, 1 1/4 In.	50.00
Clock, Mantle, Blue Jasperware, 3 White Kewpies, 6 x 5 3/4 In.	425.00
Cloth, Arabella, 16 In.	600.00
Composition, Black, Hottentot, Jointed Arms, Red Wings, 1946, 11 In.	525.00
Composition, Cloth, Jointed, Floral Dress, Flange Neck, 1915-1916, 11 In.	800.00
Composition, Jointed, Floral Romper, Cameo, Box, 1946, 13 In.	700.00
Composition, Jointed, Original Tag & Box, Rose O'Neill, 12 1/2 In.	495.00
Composition, Rose O'Neill, Red Label, 11 1/2 In.	235.00
Creamer, Green Jasperware, 7 White Kewpies, Butterflies, Glazed Interior, 2 1/2 x 4 In.	110.00
Doll, All Bisque, Side Wings, Rose O'Neill, c.1910, 12 In.	950.00
Doll, Bisque, Doodles, 4 1/2 In.	275.00
Doll, Cameo, Scootles, Composition, Original Dress, 16 1/4 In.	495.00
Doll, Hard Plastic, Bonnet & Shoes, Cameo, 26 In.	350.00
Doll, Hinged Joints, Cameo, 16 In.	125.00
Doll, Scootles, Bisque, Molded & Painted Blond Hair, Shirt & Shorts, 7 In.	355.00
Doll, Scootles, Composition Head, Sleep Eyes, Forehead Curls, Cameo, 12 In.	1000.00
Handkerchief, Dotty Darling With Kewpies, & Baby, 1914, Box, Pair	260.00
Hatpin Holder	595.00
Hugger, Glitter, Germany, 1930s	125.00
Light Bulb, Christmas Tree	45.00

Mold, Candy, Figural, Standing, Metal, 2 Part, 5 In. 80.00
Mold, Chocolate, Figural, Pewter, Hinged, Mar. 4, '13, 6 In. 150.00
Ornament, Christmas Tree, Bisque, Figural, Hands To Side, 1 Piece, Loop, 2 1/2 In. 275.00
Ornament, Christmas Tree, Bisque, Kewpie, Swing, Mandolin, Black Stamp, 2 1/2 In. .. 4000.00
Paperweight, Cast Iron 75.00
Pitcher, Blue Jasperware, 4 White Kewpies, Floral, Glazed Interior, 4 In. 525.00
Plate, Being Loved, 1973 .... 12.00
Plate, Child's, ABC, Porcelain, Gold Edge, 7 1/2 In. 250.00
Plate, Rose O'Neill, Germany, 7 In. 95.00
Postcard, Christmas 35.00
Seated, Reading Book, Eyes Right, Bisque, Black C Stamp, 2 In. 200.00
Shaker, Talcum Powder, Figural, Composition, 1913 Label, Box, 7 In. 110.00
Sheet Music, My Kewpie Doll, Nat Goldstein, San Francisco 90.00
Soap, Figural, Box, O'Neill, Harry Leon Wilson, 1917, 4 In. 100.00
Soldier, With Rifle & Helmet 705.00
Spoon, Dixie Cup, Sharpless Ice Cream, Wrapper 10.00
Stickpin, Figural, Sterling Silver, 1/2 In. 40.00
Sugar, Cover, 3 Kewpies, Porcelain, Embossed Border, O'Neill, Wilson, 3 In. 80.00
Sugar, Cover, Green Jasperware, 6 Pink Kewpie Figures, Glazed Interior, 3 x 4 In. 140.00
Sweeper, Head Turned Down, O'Neill, 3 1/2 In. 525.00
Tea Set, Child's, Pink Daisy, C.A. Lehmann, Rose O'Neill, 10 Piece 450.00
Tea Set, Child's, Pink Lusterware, C.A. Lehmann, Rose O'Neill, 22 Piece 1050.00
Thinker, Seated, Bisque, Eyes Right, O'Neill, 5 In. 200.00
Thinker, With Pen, Rose O'Neill, 2 In. 385.00
Traveler, Large 405.00
Tray, Desk, Kewpie, Seated, With Pen, Bisque, Rose O'Neill, 4 x 4 1/2 In. 675.00
Vase, Bud & Card Holder, Seated, With Rose, Bisque, 2 1/2 In. 300.00
Vase, Farmer, Bisque, Art Nouveau Design, Black Stamp, 6 1/2 In. 825.00
With Banjo, 2 In. 325.00

KIMBALL, see Cluthra category

KING'S ROSE, see Soft Paste category

KITCHEN utensils of all types, from eggbeaters to bowls, are collected today.
Handmade wooden and metal items, like ladles and apple peelers, were made
in the early nineteenth century. Mass-produced pieces, like iron apple peelers
and graniteware, were made in the nineteenth century. Other kitchen wares
are listed under manufacturers' names or under Advertising, Iron, Tool, or
Wooden.

Baking Cabinet, Unfolded In Flour Bin & Doughbox... 2195.00
Baster, Tite-Top, Griswold, No. 10.. 175.00
Beater, Rug, Bentwood, Goodenough's Improved Carpet & Rug Beater, 41 In............. 95.00
Beater Jar, Green Glass, Green Handle 32.50
Blender, Oesterizer, Art Deco, Chrome, Large .... 105.00 to 155.00
Board, Smoothing, Carved Tulip, Heart & Compass Star, Poplar, 1798, 29 1/2 In. 578.00
Board, Smoothing, D-Shaped Handle, Corrugated Surface, Wooden, c.1810, 29 In. 150.00
Board, Springerle, 1 Side 12 Designs, Reverse 9 Designs, Scrubbed, 8 x 6 1/2 In.......... 495.00
Bowl, Butter, Wooden, Green Paint, Miniature.. 420.00
Bowl, Griswold, No. 4, Scotch... 45.00
Bowl, Mixing, Kitchen Kraft, Nested, Homer Laughlin, 3 Piece 95.00
Bowl, Wooden, Green Paint, 20 In.. 380.00
Bread Maker, Universal, Bucket Type, Tin 27.00
Broiler, Game, Fireside, Drip Pan, Wrought Iron, Penny Feet, 16 In. 550.00
Bucket, Sugar, Wooden Stave, Dark Brown Patina, Bentwood Handle, 14 x 14 In. 82.00
Butter Mold, look under Mold, Butter in this category
Butter Paddle, Curly Maple, 9 In. 159.00
Butter Stamp, Acorn & Oak Leaf, 3 3/4 In... 220.00
Butter Stamp, Cow, 3 7/8 In. 125.00
Butter Stamp, Crosshatched Heart, Foliage, Semi-Circular, Inserted Handle, 6 In. 363.00
Butter Stamp, Floral Design, Stylized, Scrubbed, Round, 3 7/8 In. 60.00
Butter Stamp, Heart Design, Primitive, Marked April 22, 1829 On Back, 4 In.............. 302.00
Butter Stamp, Indian Shawl, Knob Handle 130.00
Butter Stamp, Leaf 1 Side, Spray Of Roses On Other, Brass Tacks, 4 7/8 In................. 330.00

Butter Stamp, Lollipop, Eagle 1 Side, Star Flower On Other, Pine, 9 In. 990.00
Butter Stamp, Pineapple & Foliage, Hand Grip, 3 3/8 x 4 1/2 In. 143.00
Butter Stamp, Pineapple Pattern, Basswood, Hand Carved, c.1830, 3 3/4 In. 65.00
Butter Stamp, Pineapple, Stylized, Scrubbed, Round, 3 7/8 In. 82.00
Butter Stamp, Pinwheel, Inserted Handle, 5 1/4 In. 412.50
Butter Stamp, Tulip, Carved, Primitive, Rectangular, 3 1/4 x 4 7/8 In. 82.00
Butter Stamp, Tulip, Stylized, Round, Turned Handle, 3 1/2 In. 357.00
Cake Mold, Lamb, Griswold, No. 866 ....95.00 to 150.00
Cake Pan, Fred Flintstone, Aluminum, Wilton Ent., 1979, 8 1/2 x 17 In. 30.00
Cake Pan, Harvest, Iron, Black, Griswold 175.00
Cake Pan, Hetty Harper Mixes 6.00
Can Opener, Corkscrew, Steel 3.00
Can Opener, Figural, Bull, Wooden Handle, Hand Type 45.00
Can Opener, Pet Milk, 2 Harpoon Points, Metal 9.00
Can Opener, Red Chrome, Wall Mount, Rival 25.00
Carving Set, Steel, Staghorn Handles, Silver Trim, England, 2 Piece 16.50
Casserole, Griswold, Red & Cream, Rectangular 85.00
Cheese Saw, Wire Saw, Forged Iron, 21 1/2 x 22 1/4 In. 145.00
Cheese Shaker, Organ Grinder, Victoria Ceramics 12.50
Cherry Pitter, Enterprise, Pat. 1895 .... 35.00
Cherry Pitter, Goodell Co., c.1895 .... 55.00
Cherry Pitter, Goodell, Double 55.00
Cherry Pitter, New Standard, Mt. Joy, Pennsylvania, Iron 40.00
Chopper, Food, Puritan, Griswold, No. 10 .... 37.00
Chopper, Food, Wrought Steel, Heart Cutout, Turned Handle, 5 x 6 3/4 In. 357.00
Churn, Advertising, White, Blue Letters, Brass Spigot 85.00
Churn, Barrel, Hawthorne, No. 0, Montgomery Ward 495.00
Churn, Bentwood, Wapakoneta, Ohio, Black Stenciling 220.00
Churn, Crown, Solid Lid, Red Bail Handles 200.00
Churn, Davis Swing Churn No. 2, Bellows Falls, Vt., 40 x 48 x 20 In. 121.00
Churn, Dazey, 1 Qt. 1300.00
Churn, Dazey, 3 Qt. 200.00
Churn, Dazey, 6 Qt. 160.00
Churn, Dazey, Floor Standing, Tin 150.00
Churn, Gray-Green Painted, Huge 357.00
Churn, Sears, Electric, Glass 25.00
Churn, Standard Churn Co., Wapakoneta, Ohio, Oak 280.00
Churn, Stave Construction, Metal Bands, Turned Lid, 22 In. 165.00
Churn, Stave, Wire, Galvanized Metal Bands, 22 In. 55.00
Churn, Superior Sanitary, Crock, Wooden Lid, Stand On Wheels, 1910, 8 Gal. 550.00
Churn, Tabletop, Glass, Wooden Paddles 150.00
Clothespin, Willow, Tin Binding Ring, 1 Piece, c.1830, 6 In. 19.00
Coffee Grinders are listed in their own category
Coffee Urn, Electric, Proctor, Boston, Mass. 125.00
Coffeepot, Cast Iron, Erie 40.00
Colander, Heart Shape, Tin, 3 Punched Hex Designs, 14 In. 478.00
Cooker, Egg, Electric, Instructions 30.00
Cooker, Egg, Hankscraft, Metal Top, Self-Cord, 1930s 45.00
Cooker, Egg, Premier Egg Cup Co., Patent 1893, Small 18.00
Cooker, Hot Dog, Coney, Porcelain, 1940s 175.00
Cookie Board, 14 Carved Animals, Chestnut, 4 3/4 x 22 1/2 In. 275.00
Cookie Board, 15 Designs, Including Masonic, Pewter, Wood Back, 6 1/8 x 10 In. 165.00
Cookie Board, Boy On Rocker 1 Side, Angel & Swan On Other, 10 x 12 1/2 In. 1760.00
Cookie Board, Full Length Hunter In Lederhosen, 7 1/4 x 18 3/8 In. 275.00
Cookie Board, Grapes, 19 1/4 x 3 1/2 In. 425.00
Cookie Board, Round, Handle, 15 1/2 In. 55.00
Cookie Board, Scene Of George Washington, Justice & Columbia, 12 x 11 3/4 In. 3630.00
Cookie Board, Slate, Handle, 18 In. 209.00
Cookie Board, Springerle, 6 Designs, c.1830, 7 x 3 1/2 In. 325.00
Cookie Board, Walnut, Running Dog, Indian, Happy New Year On Back, 5 x 6 In. 137.00
Cookie Cutter, Bird, Tin, 5 In. 40.00
Cookie Cutter, Chick, Tin 20.00
Cookie Cutter, Dog, Tin 20.00

Cookie Cutter, Fish, Tin 13.00
Cookie Cutter, Frosty The Snowman, Corncob Pipe, Stovepipe Hat, Tin, 8 In............... 70.00
Cookie Cutter, Heart & Hand, Tin, 3 1/2 In... 660.00
Cookie Cutter, Heart In Hand 895.00
Cookie Cutter, Horse, Tin, 1930s 13.00
Cookie Cutter, Horse, Tin, c.1890, 7 1/4 In. 248.00
Cookie Cutter, Lamb, Aluminum, 4 In. 3.00
Cookie Cutter, Large Stag, Tin, 7 1/2 In. 330.00
Cookie Cutter, Lion, Tin 20.00
Cookie Cutter, Rooster, Tin, 7 In. 77.00
Cookie Cutter, Rosette, Aluminum, 2 1/2 In. 1.00
Cookie Cutter, Woman, With Full Skirt, Tin, 11 In. 115.00
Corn Holder, Owl, F & F, Plastic, 4 Piece 18.00
Corn Popper, Embossed Instructions & Brand Names, Mazola & Karo, Tin................... 35.00
Cover, Toaster, Black Girl 40.00
Cover, Toaster, Mammy Doll 55.00
Cup, Measuring, Aluminum, 1930s 6.00
Cup, Measuring, Hocking, Green 15.00
Cup, Measuring, Purple Cow's Head, Ceramic.. 18.00
Cup, Measuring, Shaker Top, Aluminum, 1 Cup 4.00
Cup, Measuring, Swan's Down Flour 10.00
Cupboard, Opossum-Bellied Bottom Drawers, Pullout Work Shelf..................................... 795.00
Curler, Hair, Electric, 1900 .... 13.00
Cutter, Biscuit, Rumford 28.00
Cutter, Cabbage, 3 Blade, Indianapolis Sanitary Kraut Cutter, Patent, April 18, 1905 ... 38.00
Cutter, Cabbage, Cutout Hanging Hole, Poplar, A. J. Kuhn, 8 1/4 x 25 1/2 In. 99.00
Cutter, Cabbage, Heart Cutout, 46 In. 82.00
Cutter, Cabbage, Heart Cutout, Poplar, Old Patina, 9 3/4 In. 385.00
Cutter, Doughnut, Rolling 26.00
Cutter, French Fry, Sled Style, Wood Handle 4.00
Cutter, Herb, Go Devil, Cast Iron, 10 x 16 In. 440.00
Cutter, Tobacco, Griswold, No. 1, Erie 80.00
Dipper, Bird's Head Handle Hook, Treen Ware, Carved From 1 Piece, 16 In. 192.00
Dipper, Ice Cream, Clipper, No. 5 .... 295.00
Dipper, Maple, Bird Head Handle, 5 5/8 In. 360.00
Dipper, Maple, Burl Bowl & Hook Handle, Treen Ware, Carved From 1 Piece, 18 In. .. 579.00
Dispenser, Dixie Cup 95.00
Dough Box, Poplar, Red Repaint, Cutout Heart Handles, Dovetailed, 14 x 30 In. 220.00
Dough Scraper, Heart Cut Out, Wrought Iron, 5 In. 412.00
Dutch Oven, Chuck Wagon, Griswold, No. 10... 150.00 to 225.00
Dutch Oven, Flat Top, Griswold.. 95.00
Dutch Oven, Griswold, No. 8, Marked Glass Cover 45.00
Dutch Oven, Griswold, Tile-Top, No. 9, Lid & Handle 40.00
Dutch Oven, Griswold, Tile-Top, No. 10 .... 105.00 to 200.00
Egg Carrier, 4 Tiers, Black & Yellow Design, Red Ground... 385.00
Egg Cooker, Sunbeam, Automatic, Box 18.00
Egg Separator, Rumford 48.00
Egg Timer, Chef .... 65.00 to 95.00
Egg Timer, Chef, Seated... 95.00
Egg Timer, Girl, Arms Out.. 110.00
Egg Timer, Mammy, Tin Lithograph 145.00
Egg Warmer, Rooster, Steiff, 1913 .... 60.00
Egg Whipper, Slotted, Tin... 15.00
Eggbeater, Angel Wing Shape, Wire 55.00
Eggbeater, Betty Taplin, 1930s... 16.00
Eggbeater, Dover... 35.00
Eggbeater, Green Wooden Handle 13.00
Eggbeater, High Speed Super Center Drive Beater, Wooden Handle 6.00
Eggbeater, Ladd, Blue T Handle, Ball Bearings, 1926-1929 .... 10.00
Eggbeater, Patent Sept. 12, 1886 .... 1300.00
Eggbeater, Taplin 45.00
Eggbeater, Worldbeater, 1940s... 45.00
Firken, Gray, Painted, Covered, 19th Century, 14 In... 115.00

Irresistible Buys from Shops and Shows
(And Why the Kovels Bought Them)

Ten years after we started collecting, we went to a show with 50 dealers. We walked two feet into the room and both of us said, "Quick, check on the booth at the end of this aisle." On a shelf filled with dishes, we both spotted a piece of 18th-century English marbleized ware, our passion at the time. How we saw that teapot in a room with thousands of items is a mystery that only another collector could understand. Your antique will call out from anywhere in the room, asking to be taken home. This almost mystical experience is not just luck. After many years of study and examination of a special collectible, we can quickly recognize the subtle signs of quality. It is said that collectors are like squirrels hunting for nuts. The skillful squirrel learns to read the signals in fallen oak leaves and changes in the weather, and finds the best nuts. The skillful collector spots the best booths, the rarest forms, and the most desirable "look" before the less knowledgeable collector does.

You may wonder what we, the people who write the price book each year, collect. We buy like you do at the shops and shows. In some places we negotiate, in some shops we know we should expect to pay the ticketed price. But we buy almost everything that calls out to us and says, "I am special, I am unique, I want to be loved, but no one has noticed me yet."

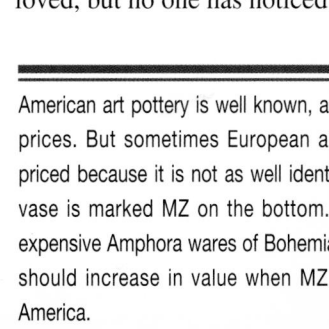

American art pottery is well known, and dealers know the prices. But sometimes European art pottery is underpriced because it is not as well identified. This 11$\frac{1}{2}$-inch vase is marked MZ on the bottom. It is related to the expensive Amphora wares of Bohemia. It sold for $95 and should increase in value when MZ is better known in America.

These are some of our finds from the past year. They were purchased in a show or shop after others had seen and ignored them. You may think our choices odd, but each one is special to us, and to us a bargain. To prove it we have listed our purchase price and the probable price if we had bought our treasure in a good antiques store in the Midwest. Some we bought for the current price, knowing we would be happy to own the piece in later years.

Brass and copper in the Mission style has become popular in the last few years. These 4$^{1}/_{2}$-inch-high bookends are brass with ceramic deer and enameled leaves. Although unsigned, they are probably 1930s pieces by the Potter Studio of Cleveland, still a relatively unknown maker. Cost, $45. Value today, $100.

Tramp art was rediscovered by collectors in the 1970s. Today a small group of collectors are searching for "recycled art" and post-1940s folk art. This Popsicle-stick flowerpot holder was probably made in the 1950s by a housewife or student. It is 8$^{1}/_{2}$ inches high. Cost, $25. Value today, $25—but wait a few years.

This wooden grapes box has a lithographed black–and–white scene on the cover. It is marked "Lettington Paper Box Maker, 25 Exchange Place, Rochester, New York." We happily paid $45 for this rare 19th-century container.

Work by fifties designers and artists are becoming more collectible. Waylande Gregory did statues and pottery in Ohio and Michigan. He started as a designer with Cowan Pottery. This 10¹/₂-inch plate with gold pear decorations would cost $100 at a major fifties show. We found it for $35 at a flea market.

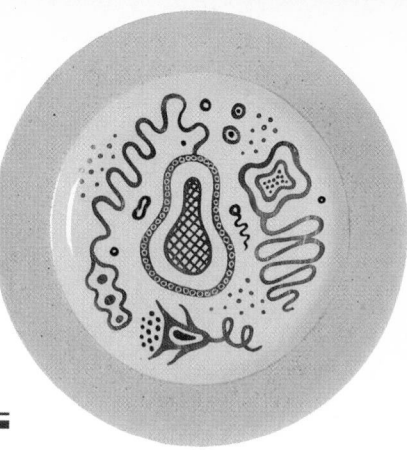

European and American furniture, silver, and porcelains inspired by Japanese designs were popular in the last part of the 19th century. Museums stress this influence in exhibits and books. But we just like the look, so we got this brown transferware Staffordshire creamer to use. It was only $9. We checked the diamond-shaped registry mark and learned it was made in 1881. Current value is $15-$20.

"We never saw anything like it." We are often told by collectors that an item must be valuable because it is so unfamiliar. But we really never have seen another plate like this. The photograph is surrounded by signatures, creating a "friendship" memento. We have always been interested in photographs that are reproduced on tiles, metal, celluloid, or porcelain, so we paid $65 for this 8¹/₂-inch plate. The date 1892 is included with the signatures, which gives the plate added value.

We once stopped at a motel in Louisville, and the next morning a flea market was set up in the parking lot. This 3¹/₂-inch–long lithographed tin toy that advertises coffee was only 75 cents. It must be worth at least $2.

We spotted this 7-inch-high rubber toy at a large flea market late in the day. It was marked "Fred G. Reiner, Akron, O," and was priced $35. We bought it quickly because we recognized it as the Brooklyn Bum, a choice collectible for baseball fans. Retail price, $150.

Small toy metal trucks and cars are being saved by the savvy collector. We found some of our son's toys that were inexplicably saved in a box of tools in the basement. This 4¹/₄-inch Dinky Toy lift truck and Corgi toy Bentley were among the finds. Value of the Bentley is $35; value of the Dinky is $60. There were also several model sets, a tin tobacco box filled with old marbles, and some campaign buttons, all dating from the 1960s—a treasure trove for today's collector.

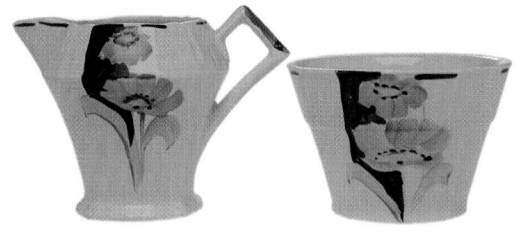

English porcelains with Art Deco and modern designs are rising in price in England. The American market is bound to follow. We found this sugar and creamer by Myott, Son & Company of England for $12. The set is sure to go up in price.

White figurines are always wanted by decorators. This "Chinese Modern" design by Roselane Pottery of Pasadena, California, was probably made in 1945. The firm worked from 1938 to1973. The 11-inch figure is marked with the incised word Roselane and the number 401. It also has a foil label, "Roselane, Pasadena." Cost $15, value over $35.

We needed some decorations for a rental unit in a ski resort, so we decided to scour the flea markets for inexpensive but large pieces of green pottery. The 1940s 13-inch West Coast Pottery (Burbank, California) vase was $15. This 8-inch, two-tone vase made in 1935 by Nelson McCoy Pottery Company cost $35, and the 6-inch unmarked streaked turquoise vase that resembles Fulper was $23.

Advertising signs and boxes now overflow the shelves in our basement replica of a country store. These egg cartons were only $2 each, too good to pass by. They were in a booth of expensive antiques in a Chicago show, but the dealer had hundreds of them.

Another advertising item is this pen wiper with the name Bailey's, a long-defunct Cleveland, Ohio, department store. The 4$^1/_2$-inch felt wiper cost $4—a high price—but like other collectors, we often pay more for local artifacts.

This cloth banner ad for Butterick patterns just shouts "1960s." The $12 price seemed low for a 69$^1/_2$-inch-long, 21-inch-wide picture. And we collect datable printed fabrics.

19 KENTUCKY 67
341·412
FRANKLIN

Save your old license plates. This one came from a garage sale for 50 cents. It is worth more to a collector.

Handkerchiefs are bought both for use and for display. This machine-embroidered handkerchief has the hand-embroidered words "To my dearest wife, 1917." It was in a box with other war scarves and badges. It was probably embellished by a soldier and then sent home as a gift from France. Five dollars seemed like a low price for a dated war souvenir.

We bought this 3-inch-long toy bronze cannon because it looked like a quality bronze. It was only $1. We often buy on a hunch and later learn what we have.

Everyone knows about baseball cards. We like these Salada tea and Junket desserts baseball coins. Each is made of plastic with a printed paper picture pasted to the $1^3/_8$-inch disk. The ad is on the back. We found them in a box of stored stuff that belonged to our son. Cost: free. Today's value, $1 to $4, depending on the player.

Every perfume bottle has a value today. We found this one at a house sale for $2. It is Madame Rochas, a 3-inch bottle made in the 1960s by Marcel Rochas of Paris. Value today, $35-$50.

Twenty years ago we found Roseville and Weller pottery at low prices. Today we buy pieces from the fifties and after. This Royal Haegar cigarette box and ashtray is $10^1/_2$ inches long. It was $13 at a shop. Its value should rise.

The enamels made in the 1950s are starting to interest collectors, but prices are still low. Signed pieces are the most valuable. These lighters should interest both cigarette lighter collectors and enamel lovers. We recognized the enamels as the work of Edward Winter, a well-known maker. The large walnut lighter is 5½ inches high. Cost for the two at an antiques shop that was going out of business, $20.

If you like computer bulletin boards for collectors, you have noticed great interest in new commemorative tins, the kind that come out each Christmas filled with candy or raisins or rice. Collectors have always liked commemorative and fancy gift-box tins. This Whitman's chocolates box, 3¼ by 6½ inches, cost only $12 at a flea market. Current value, $30.

Yes, there are collectors of razor blades and razor blade packages. There are also collectors of typewriter ribbon tins, phonograph needle tins, and cigarette packs. Almost any type of packaging that displays different designs and brands is collected. Razor blade aficionados often also want razors and other hair-cutting equipment. This box with about 35 packaged Enders safety blades was $5 at a show. A good Gillette package is worth $3.

We bought this solid brass whistle so we could use it. It is a regulation U.S. Army whistle, 2 inches long. Cost, $2. Value, probably $2—but it is useful!

Letter openers make good gifts. New ones are very expensive. We buy any attractive old brass openers we can find that sell for under $25. This eagle-decorated opener was only $12 at a flea market. It is about 50 years old. Most bronze letter openers retail at $50.

The studious-monk bookends will find a place in our library, holding some of the thousands of books we also collect. A thin sheet of decorated metal was applied to a plaster-like form. This type of bookend was made in the 1930s. When we started to buy them about 15 years ago, a good pair of bookends cost under $15. Today they are a bargain at $25, and often sell for $50 in excellent condition. These were a bargain.

This 15-inch-long musical instrument is labeled "Jink-E-Jink, Tamberina." We have no idea how old it is or what it is worth, but it is amusing. We paid $26.

This electric lamp has a paper shade picturing Niagara Falls. Inside is a revolving wheel that casts shadows on the shade, making it appear that the falls are running. It was a bargain at a thrift shop, just $15. Most motion lamps are over $50. We wanted it because we have many items that picture Niagara Falls, but not quite enough to call it a collection.

This patinated bronze candy dish is signed with the cipher CS. We have seen many similar pieces marked this way but have not yet learned the history of Sorrenson, the maker. Not too bad for $60. Worth much more, we hope!

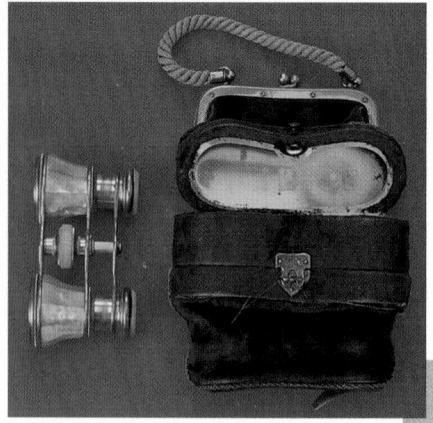

Looks like opera glasses and a case, but it is more. The top of the case is a purse, the center a compact with a powder puff. Because of the great interest in purses and compacts and the rarity of this set, it is worth over $250. We received it as a gift.

This 3¼-inch–long sterling silver pin is unmarked, but by the shape of the leaves and the flowers we recognized it as a piece by Hobé, the American costume jewelry firm. We paid $20. A piece of Hobé is worth twice as much.

Beaded fruit is popular in New York City but almost ignored in other parts of the country. The fruit is made by pinning colored beads to a lightweight plastic form. This fruit came in a bag for $3 at a house sale. Each apple or orange sells for $25 in New York City.

We have assembled a set of goblets to use on the table from hundreds of patterns of pressed glass made in the 19th and early 20th centuries. This Columbian Frosted Coin glass cost $60—a high price, but the pattern is rare. We use the goblets regularly.

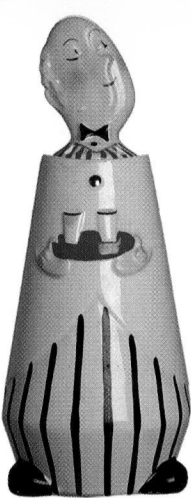

Collecting Holt Howard pieces has become one of our family projects. Everyone buys them for us. The pieces were made in the 1960s and are marked with the name and often a date. This 9-inch condiment jar came from a Florida flea market for $50. We just missed the very expensive decanter that later sold at a Modernisme show for $400.

Souvenir buildings have been discovered by a group of collectors who have even formed a club. This 3$\frac{1}{4}$–inch Eiffel Tower made of bronze-colored white metal cost 25 cents at a yard sale. Value, $10.

This lithographed tin tea set was made as a child's toy in the 1940s. We bought all 19 pieces for $30 at a country antiques show. The set is incomplete, but it is an interesting decoration in our grandchild's room. Value today, about $100.

This 6-inch-high pitcher is marked "Manchester, Germany." It is typical of a design popular in Germany and other parts of Europe in the 1930s. We own an almost identical pitcher with orange glaze that is marked "Holland," so we decided to buy this mate. Price, $8. We think anything with orange glaze (notice the dots) will go up in value.

This 4¹/₂-inch 1930s teapot is a late piece of Banko, a Koreanware that we have collected for years. It was a bargain at $9. We have seen them for $25.

Poole Pottery of England is rising in price. The modern designs appeal to the fifties collector. We paid $65 for this 7³/₄-inch-high bud vase.

Czechoslovakian pottery has just started to interest collectors. This 5¹/₂-inch-high creamer is marked "Peasant Art Industry, made in Czechoslovakia." Peasant Art was a major pottery producer. Its current $45 value should rise.

Few people know about pieces marked "Raymor, Italy." Fifties collectors know that many of the ceramics marked "Raymor" were made by important designers and firms. Raymor was an importing firm that ordered high-style wares from many companies, including Glidden. We bought the 10-inch–high vase for a bargain $65. It will go up in value.

Years ago in college in a class on abnormal psychology, we learned about Louis Wain, an English illustrator who drew cats with special appeal. He was institutionalized as insane but continued to draw. The series of cat pictures reflected his deteriorating mental state, and the cuddly cats of early years became ferocious beasts at the end. Some of his cat pictures inspired figurines by Max Emmanuel and Co., "Futuristic Cats in China," in 1914. We have tried to buy these figurines, but they sell for over $500 each. We were delighted to spot this 2-inch-high "Made in Japan" copy at a flea market for $30.

Our kitchen is ringed with pitchers shaped like birds. So how could we resist this 7-inch-wide "Made in Japan" nut dish for only $30? It holds flowers on the shelf.

Black memorabilia is going up in price as the country looks at its history. This charming photograph of a well-dressed black woman and child is printed on a flowered celluloid circle that is $7^{1}/_{2}$ inches in diameter. There is a stand in the back so the picture could be displayed on a tabletop. Obviously a clever product by a photographer working about 1900. Price: $65 at a Chicago antiques show. We bought it because of its historic interest and because it is an unusual type of photograph.

The flea market booth in the field was filled with furniture. A shell-shaped teapot that resembled a Royal Bayreuth piece was on a dresser. Probably a Japanese copy, it had a bamboo handle. "How much?" we asked. It was $9. We bought it even though by then we had noticed the word "Florida" impressed on the cover, proving it was a 1930s tourist piece. The dealer started to put it in a box, then added the sugar and creamer and salt and pepper. "Can't do better on the price, but $9 seems like a fair price for the set," he said. We know it's a bargain, and it was a good gift for our Florida relatives.

We know many pieces marked "Georges Briard" are found at yard sales and flea markets and do not sell for much. We know that Mr. Briard is alive and well, so we couldn't resist this 5½-inch-square dish for $6. If you want a more valuable example of a Briard, look for one decorated in silver, not the more common gold. Notice the square shape. Originally, the textured glass was made to be a cover for a ceiling light fixture. Mr. Briard bought the shades from the factory and created decorative bowls and trays.

Giveaways from fast-food restaurants are another new collecting area. This windup Volkswagen, 1¾ inches long, cost 50 cents in a box at a large Florida mall show. It should go up in value.

Firkin Set, White Paint, Graduated, 5 Piece 300.00
Flue Cover, Griswold, 5 In... 7.00
Flue Cover, Moorish Dressed Woman, 1910 .... 75.00
Fork, Roasting, Wrought Iron, Brass Inlaid, Pennsylvania 4025.00
Fork, Wrought Iron, Heart Tines, Pennsylvania, 17 1/4 In. 1155.00
Fork-Turner, Twist, Wrought Iron, 18th Century, 13 7/8 In. 185.00
Fryer, Chicken, Griswold, No. 8, Cover.. 20.00
Fryer, Chicken, Griswold, No. 8, Cover, Iron Mountain 75.00
Gas Burner, 2, Griswold, No. 1002, Tabletop 55.00
Grater, Cheese, 1 Drawer... 100.00
Grater, Cheese, Green Handle, Tin 22.00
Grater, Cheese, Iron, Tin, Wooden Top, 3 Legs, Germany.. 25.00
Grater, Revolving, Regina, Clamp On, Wooden Handle, Cast Iron, 12 1/2 In. 26.00
Griddle, Favorite, No. 9 .... 40.00
Griddle, Griswold, Diamond Logo.. 80.00
Griddle, Griswold, No. 9, Round 15.00
Griddle, Griswold, No. 14, Round, Bailed, Block Logo 45.00
Griddle, Griswold, No. 109 .... 65.00
Griddle, Vapor, Griswold, 12 In.. 350.00
Griddle, Wagner, Bail Handle 125.00
Griddle, Wagner, Fat-Free Fryer 40.00
Grinder, Cavanagh, Cast Iron, Legs With Claw Feet, Glass Container Base, 1885 .... 625.00
Grinder, Food, Griswold, No. 1 .... 15.00
Grinder, Food, Griswold, No. 2 .... 60.00
Grinder, Food, Keen Kutter 20.00
Grinder, Meat, Griswold, No. 2 .... 25.00
Grinder, Meat, Griswold, No. 4 .... 23.00
Grinder, Meat, Griswold, No. 12, Erie... 18.00
Grinder, Meat, Winchester.. 75.00
Grinder, Universal No. 1, Meat, Wooden Handle, Table Clamp, 9 In............................. 10.00
Hanger, Laundry Clothes, Wooden, Collapsible Arms 45.00
Hatchet, Butcher's... 25.00
Heater, Gas, Griswold, No. 200... 250.00
Holder, Broom, Advertising Garland Stoves & Ranges, 4 1/4 x 4 In. 45.00
Holder, Dixie Cup 60.00
Holder, Napkin, Figural, Flat Iron Shape, Pottery... 40.00
Holder, Scouring Pad, Black Chef 165.00
Hook, Meat, 3 Prongs, Wrought Iron 45.00
Hot Plate, Gas, Griswold, No. 713, 3 Burners 125.00
Ice Cream Freezer, Dazey 995.00
Ice Cream Freezer, North Pole, 1910... 32.00
Ice Cream Freezer, White Mountain, Hand Crank, 1 Qt. 75.00
Ice Crusher, Jiffy Ice Crax, Deluxe Model, Spring Action, Bottle Opener Top, Box 10.00
Ice Pick, Wooden Handle, Varnished, 9 1/2 In.. 5.00
Ice Shave, Griswold 140.00
Icebox, 4 Doors, Porcelain Interior, Wire Shelves, Galvanized Ice Section 1000.00
Icebox, Alaska Star, 2 Doors, Oak 650.00
Icebox, Eddy & Sons, Locking Lid, 2 Inner Doors, 1905, 48 x 32 In. 1295.00
Icebox, Macy & Co., 2 Doors, 48 x 20 In.. 565.00
Icebox, Oak, Original Hardware 425.00
Icebox, Zinc Lining, Brass Hardware, 1891.. 495.00
Iron, Flat, Wapak, No. 7 .... 15.00
Iron, Flat, Wapak, No. 12 .... 85.00
Iron, Fluting, Geneva ....28.00 to 29.00
Iron, Fluting, Hand Rock, The Best 55.00
Iron, Fluting, Knox, 1877 .... 150.00
Iron, Goffering 280.00
Iron, Griswold, Waffle, Indian Head... 155.00
Iron, Hinged Back Opening, Hand Sewn Leather Handle 125.00
Iron, Removable Lid, Slide Vent Each Side, Pat. Aug. 18, 1914 .... 95.00
Iron, Silver Streak, Cast Glass, Chrome Plate, Red.. 605.00
Iron, Sunbeam, Steel, Box, 1925.. 65.00
Jar, Grease, Old McDonald, Regal.. 225.00

Juicer, Dazey, Aluminum Crank In Base, 2 Piece	8.00
Juicer, Sunkist, Chrome, Green Glass, Drugstore Soda Fountain	25.00
Juicer, Sunkist, White, Orange Logo, Electric, Squatty	85.00
Juicer, Tin, Crank Handle	13.00
Keg, Oak, Iron Bound, Marked W.H., 1730-1825, 8 x 5 In.	210.00
Kettle, Candy, Copper, Dovetailed	100.00
Kettle, Tea, Griswold, Cast Iron	125.00
Kettle, Tea, Shinnick, Patent 1863	65.00
Kettle, Waterbury Brass Co., Spun Brass, Cast Feet, Lion Head Ring Handles, 11 In.	83.00
Ladle, Roasting, Wrought Iron, Rattail Handle, 32 1/4 x 8 1/2 In.	135.00
Lard Press, Griswold, No. 2, 2 Qt.	125.00
Lemon Squeezer, Griswold, No. 9	250.00
Lemon Squeezer, Little Giant, Cast Iron, Dated May 3, 1818	100.00
Lid, Skillet, Drip Drop, Wagner, No. 8, Raised Letter	45.00
Lid Lifter, Erie, Stove	65.00
Lid Lifter, Ideal, Face On End, Coiled Handle	18.00
Lifter, Pie, Harker	14.00
Match Holders can be found in their own category	
Match Safes can be found in their own category	
Mayonnaise, Metal Beater Top, Glass	25.00
Measure, Jennyware, Ultramarine, 1 Cup	50.00
Melon Baller, Wing Action, Wood Handle, Makes 1 1/4-In. Balls	4.00
Melon Baller, Wire Handle	3.00
Milk Shake Machine, Hamilton Beach, 3 Heads, Green Enamel	265.00
Milk Shake Machine, Hamilton Beach, Single Head, 2 Speed, Cream Porcelain	150.00
Milk Shake Machine, Hamilton Beach, Stainless Mixing Cup, 1950s	155.00
Milk Shake Machine, Hires Root Beer	1750.00
Milk Shake Machine, Horlick, Blue Design Square, White, Marked	75.00
Milk Shake Machine, Machine Craft, California, Green Granite	295.00
Mixer, Double Coiled Wire, Wooden Handle, 1920	29.00
Mixer, Mixmaster, Box, Dated May 7, 1927	110.00
Mixer, Mixmaster, Sunbeam, Red, Green Bowls, Juicer Top	75.00
Mixer, Mixmaster, Sunbeam, Turquoise	50.00
Molds may also be found in the Pewter and Tinware categories	
Mold, Butter, 4 Designs, Rose, Wheat, Grapes, Letter B, Wooden, 4 3/8 x 5 In.	65.00
Mold, Butter, Deer, Wooden	325.00
Mold, Butter, Round, 1/2 Lb.	65.00
Mold, Butter, Wooden, 1 Lb.	40.00
Mold, Cake, Gingerbread Boy, Aluminum, 9 x 10 1/2 In.	11.00
Mold, Cake, Lamb, Griswold, Cast Iron, 2 Piece	150.00
Mold, Cake, Lamb, Griswold, No. 866, Box	90.00 to 120.00
Mold, Cake, Rabbit, Griswold, Cast Iron, 2 Piece	220.00 to 240.00
Mold, Cake, Santa Claus, Griswold	595.00 to 750.00
Mold, Candle, see Tinware category	
Mold, Candle, 24 Tubes, Redware, Frame, 22 1/4 In.	1320.00
Mold, Candy Clark Bars, 6 Bars, 7 x 16 In.	15.00
Mold, Candy, 5 Geometric Carved Designs, Wooden, 30 In.	127.00
Mold, Candy, Swan, 2 Sections, 2 7/8 x 3 1/2 In.	44.00
Mold, Cheese, c.1880	375.00
Mold, Chocolate, Daniel Boone	45.00
Mold, Chocolate, Heart, 2 Sections, 6 In.	65.00
Mold, Chocolate, Lion, Standing, Copper	145.00
Mold, Chocolate, Pipe, Tin	50.00
Mold, Chocolate, Rabbit, Standing, Basket On Back, Hinges, Spring Clips, 5 x 16 In.	110.00
Mold, Chocolate, Rabbit, With Cart	65.00
Mold, Chocolate, Rabbits, With Easter Egg Cart, 4 In 1 Group, Hinges, 11 x 6 x 3 In.	80.00
Mold, Chocolate, Santa Claus	75.00
Mold, Cookie, Cornucopia, Cast Iron, 4 x 5 1/4 In.	165.00
Mold, Fish Shape, Clear Glaze, Redware, Brown Flecks & Splotches, 11 5/8 In.	440.00
Mold, Fish, Leaping Fish, Copper, 9 x 8 1/2 In.	120.00
Mold, Fish, Ring For Hanging, Germany, 8 In.	10.00
Mold, Food, Ear Of Corn, Tin, Copper, 4 x 6 In.	110.00
Mold, Food, Feathered Bird, Metal Rim, 13 x 19 In.	35.00

Mold, Ice Cream, see Pewter category
Mold, Jell-O, Fluted, Aluminum, Impressed In Bottom, 3 In., Set Of 13 .... 9.00
Mold, Jell-O, Rabbit, Tin, 8 In. 30.00
Mold, Patty, Griswold, No.1 ....25.00 to 32.00
Mold, Turk's Head, Dark Brown Sponging, Redware, Scalloped, 7 1/4 In. 71.00
Mold, Turk's Head, Yellow Slip Rim, Green & Brown Daubs, Redware, 8 3/4 In. 84.00
Muffin Pan, Erie, No. 3 .... 125.00
Muffin Pan, Griswold, No. 18, Tin 45.00
Napkin Holder, Prayer Lady 16.00
Nipper, Sugar, Brass Mount, On Wooden Board 225.00
Nipper, Sugar, Wrought Steel, 9 3/4 In. 105.00
Nut Chopper, Red Metal, Glass Bottom, Flower Decal 10.00
Oven, Roasting, For Game Birds, Tin 800.00
Pan, Breadstick, 7 Hole, Griswold, No. 21-961 .... 100.00
Pan, Breadstick, 11 Hole, Griswold, No. 954 .... 50.00
Pan, Breadstick, Griswold, No. 22, Erie 60.00
Pan, Brownie, Griswold, No. 9, Pattern No. 947 .... 185.00
Pan, Bundt, Griswold, Handle, Iron 1000.00
Pan, Cake, Angel Food, Swan's Down, Metal 18.00
Pan, Corn Stick & Wheat, Griswold, No. 1270, Sears Roebuck & Co. 105.00
Pan, Corn Stick, Griswold, Miniature 80.00
Pan, Corn Stick, Griswold, No. 273 .... 25.00
Pan, Frying, Griswold, Square 35.00
Pan, Ham Boiler, Griswold, No. 2364, Slant Mark, Large 750.00
Pan, Krispy Korn Kobs, Wagner, Cast Iron, 1906 .... 85.00
Pan, Muffin, Griswold, No. 17-6140 .... 100.00
Pan, Muffin, Russell-Ervin, Cast Iron 35.00
Pan, Popover, 6 Cup, Griswold, No. 18-6141 .... 100.00
Pan, Popover, Griswold, No. 10 .... 35.00
Pan, Popover, Griswold, No. 11 .... 45.00
Pan, Popover, Wagner, 8 Cups 35.00
Pan, Roll, Vienna, Griswold, No. 26 .... 95.00
Pan, Sauce, Copper & Iron, England, 1700-1720, 10 In. 145.00
Pan, Turk's Head, 12, Griswold, No. 140 .... 250.00
Pan, Vienna Roll, Griswold, No. 6 .... 160.00
Pan, Wagner, Tin Cover, Cast-Iron Base 40.00
Pan, Wheat Stick, Griswold, No. 27 .... 240.00
Pastry Cutter, Lady Finger 85.00
Peel, Double Hearts Handle, Hand Wrought Iron, 20 1/2 In. 546.00
Peel, Ram's Horn Handle, Wrought Iron, 41 1/2 In. ....82.00 to 105.00
Peeler, Apple Corer, Sinclair, Apple & Pear, Cast Iron 95.00
Peeler, Apple, Bay State, Oak Base 110.00
Peeler, Apple, Cast Iron, Counter Top, Pat. 1880 .... 68.00
Peeler, Apple, Centennial, 1873 .... 120.00
Peeler, Apple, Hand Held, Hand Hewn, Forged Blade, 1800, 4 1/2 In. 85.00
Peeler, Apple, Keen Kutter ....65.00 to 85.00
Peeler, Apple, Primitive, 1700s 375.00
Peeler, Apple, Reading, Penn. 45.00
Peeler, Apple, Sinclair, Scott & Co., Baltimore, Table Clamp, Cast Iron 82.00
Peeler, Apple, Sinclair-Scott 85.00
Peeler, Apple, Wooden, 22 In. 100.00
Peeler, Apple, Wooden, 31 In. 83.00
Peeler, Potato, Morton's Salt 35.00
Pie Bird, Black Chef Holding Pie, England, 4 1/2 In. 60.00
Pie Bird, Black, Royal Worcester 35.00
Pie Bird, Chick, Josef 28.00
Pie Bird, Duck, Yellow 43.00
Pie Bird, Flour Fred 55.00
Pie Bird, Little Red Riding Hood 25.00
Pie Bird, Pig, Pink, Bride's Clothes, England, 4 In. 50.00
Pie Bird, Pink & Blue Trim, White 35.00
Pie Bird, Pirate, England, 4 In. 50.00
Pie Bird, Yelling Bear 90.00

Kitchen, Pie Funnel, Pottery, c.1890, 3 In.

Oil your butcher-block table to keep it from splitting at the seams. Use cooking oil if you plan to cut food on the block, mineral oil if it will be used only as a table. You must oil it at least once a month.

Pie Bird, Yellow, Small	49.00
Pie Funnel, Pottery, c.1890, 3 In. *Illus*	35.00
Pitcher, Measuring, For Household Use Only, Tin, 1 Qt.	22.00
Platter, Steak, Wagner, No. 40 & 45, Al Carder, Cast Aluminum, Pair	80.00
Popcorn Popper, Hand Forged Iron Trivet	145.00
Pot Scraper, 4 x 5 In.	25.00
Pot Scraper, Gottlieb Patent, 5 x 8 1/2 In.	45.00
Pot Scraper, Large Double Rings, 8 x 13 In.	65.00
Pot Scraper, Snow King Baking Powder, Metal, Lithographed	900.00 to 1000.00
Pot Scraper, Urias Cramer, Cast Iron, September, 1874, 4 In.	90.00
Potato Masher, Natural Finished Turned Handle	3.00
Potato Masher, S & S, Rake Style, Metal	8.00
Potato Masher, Wooden, 1930s	8.00
Potato Masher, Wooden, Turned Handle, Button Knob Finial, 11 In.	7.00
Rack, Baked Potato, 6, Tin	45.00
Rack, Drying, Pine, Folding, 4 Bars Each Section, 49 x 39 In.	40.00
Rack, Hanging, Iron, 12 Hooks, 9 1/2 x 11 In.	125.00
Reamers are listed in their own category	
Refrigerator, General Electric, Model CG 1A16, Electric, Makes Ice In 2 Hours	250.00
Refrigerator, General Electric, Top Motor, 1930s, 64 In.	425.00
Roaster, Chestnut, 24 In.	210.00
Roaster, Chestnut, Brass, England, 1890	425.00
Roaster, Griswold, No. 5, Aluminum, Oval	75.00
Roaster, Griswold, No. 5, Cover, Aluminum	145.00
Roaster, Griswold, No. 7, Oval, Cover, Aluminum	190.00 to 495.00
Roaster, Wagner, No. 9, Oval	275.00 to 350.00
Roasting Stand, Iron, Urn Finial Above Shaft, Rotating Plate, Tripod Legs, 30 In.	288.00
Roll Pan, French, Griswold, No. 15	225.00
Rolling Pin, Baker's, Wooden, 4 Ft.	110.00
Rolling Pin, Curly Maple, 16 1/4 In.	110.00
Rolling Pin, Glass, Metal Cap	20.00
Rolling Pin, Milk Glass, Victorian, 5 1/2 In.	80.00
Rolling Pin, Red Apple, Harker	135.00
Rolling Pin, Red Bands, Stoneware	350.00
Rolling Pin, Rollrite	60.00
Rolling Pin, S.E. Roth, Ipava, Illinois, Pumpkin, White Ground	550.00
Rolling Pin, Springerle, 12 Designs, 13 In.	203.00
Rolling Pin, Stoneware, Red Banded	350.00
Rolling Pin, Tiger Maple, Depression Era	15.00
Sadiron, Cover Dolly Iron, Wooden Detachable Handle	50.00
Sadiron, Sensible, 1887, 4 Piece	65.00
Sadiron, Wapak, Griswold	45.00
Salt & Pepper Shakers are listed in their own category	
Salt Box, Handing, Cherry	750.00
Scoop, Banana Split, Gilchrist, No. 34, Enamel Handle, 1930, 11 In.	165.00
Scoop, Cranberry	85.00
Scoop, Ice Cream, Arnold No. 50	25.00

Scoop, Ice Cream, Banana 690.00
Scoop, Ice Cream, Cold Dog 650.00
Scoop, Ice Cream, College.. 1800.00
Scoop, Ice Cream, Cone Shape 80.00
Scoop, Ice Cream, Gilchrist, No. 10, Wooden Handle ....45.00 to 75.00
Scoop, Ice Cream, Gilchrist, No. 31 ....45.00 to 55.00
Scoop, Ice Cream, Hamilton Beach 20.00
Scoop, Ice Cream, Red Wooden Handle 15.00
Scoop, Ice Cream, Sky High.. 850.00
Scoop, Icypi, Square Bowl, Wooden Handle, 10 Cents A Scoop 220.00
Scoop, Slicer, Dober, Enamel Handle, 1924, 11 In.. 165.00
Scoop, Sugar, Harker.. 20.00
Scoop, Wagner Ware, Aluminum 15.00
Scraper, Pot, Commander Flour Mill Co. 60.00
Seeder, Cherry, Double, 2 Tracks & 2 4-Pointed Seeders, Box 110.00
Seeder, Cherry, Goodells Family Cherry Stoner 40.00
Shaker, Pancake, Aunt Jemima 65.00
Sharpener, Knife, Cream & Green Handle.. 4.00
Sharpener, Knife, Eversharp, Disc Type, Wood Handle 3.00
Sharpener, Knife, Steel Disc, Maple Holder, Ace Ladle, Aluminum, 12 In.................. 3.00
Shears, Poultry, Lily Pattern, Sterling Silver Handle, 10 1/2 In. 115.00
Sieve, Cheese, Woven Splint, 25 In. 550.00
Sifter, Flour, Androck 12.00
Sifter, Flour, Cream City 395.00
Sifter, Flour, Watkins 20.00
Sifter, Flour, Wooden, Bloods Patented, Dated Sept. 17, 1861, 9 x 10 1/2 x 13 In......... 350.00
Sifter, Screen Bottom, Dowel Style Handle, Push-Pull Action, Wooden 295.00
Skewer, Meat, Iron, Pair 35.00
Skewer Holder, Bird's Head Finial, Wrought Iron, 20 x 12 In. 400.00
Skewer Set, Holder, Iron, With 12 Skewers 715.00
Skillet, Bacon & Egg Breakfast, Wagner Ware 20.00
Skillet, Bacon & Egg Breakfast, Wagner, 3 In 1, Polished 25.00
Skillet, Breakfast, Griswold, Colonial, Iron 40.00
Skillet, Breakfast, Griswold, No. 665, 5-In-1, Block Logo... 180.00
Skillet, Breakfast, Griswold, No. 666, Square, White Enamel Interior 100.00
Skillet, Double, Griswold, No. 80 .... 60.00
Skillet, Eagle Stove Works, No. 12.. 400.00
Skillet, Erie, No. 1 .... 140.00
Skillet, Forged Handle, Iron.. 60.00
Skillet, Griswold No. 4 .... 30.00
Skillet, Griswold No. 8, Deep, Hinged Lid, Small Logo... 37.50
Skillet, Griswold, 1 Egg, Square 40.00
Skillet, Griswold, Egg, Square 35.00
Skillet, Griswold, Hammered Cover 80.00
Skillet, Griswold, No. 4 .... 30.00
Skillet, Griswold, No. 6, Aluminum, Small Trademark 8.00
Skillet, Griswold, No. 9, Smooth, Offset Logo Lid... 80.00
Skillet, Griswold, No. 11, Block ....140.00 to 225.00
Skillet, Griswold, No. 12, Cover ....120.00 to 150.00
Skillet, Griswold, No. 13, Emblem In Slant Letters, Heat Ring.................................... 1200.00
Skillet, Griswold, No. 14 .... 150.00
Skillet, Griswold, No. 20, Block Letters, Heat Ring 625.00
Skillet, Griswold, No. 20, Cast Iron, Hotel Type 500.00
Skillet, Griswold, No. 2106, Square... 80.00
Skillet, Rotating, Wrought Iron, 19th Century, 24 In. 230.00
Skillet, Sperry, Deep, Patent 1887, Size 8.. 40.00
Skillet, Wagner, No. 2..150.00 to 200.00
Skillet, Wagner, No. 11.. 200.00
Skillet, Wagner, No. 12.. 95.00
Skillet, Wapak, No. 8... 95.00
Skillet Griddle, Excelsior Stove Co., No. 7 .... 40.00
Skimmer, Maple Syrup, Tin, Pierced Holes, 8-In. Pan, 4 1/2-In. Handle 25.00
Slicer, Meat, Bird's-Eye Maple 125.00

Slicer, String Bean, Cast Iron, Germany.. 60.00
Spatula, Forged Iron, Keyhole, Late 18th Century... 65.00
Spatula, Tulip Cut In Blade, Wrought Steel, 17 1/2 In.. 236.00
Spatula, Wrought Iron, Brass Inlays With Heart & 1823, 15 1/4 In.............................. 357.00
Spice Box, 6 Small Over 1 Large Drawer, Wooden, Germany, 9 1/2 x 9 1/4 In. 395.00
Spice Box, Divided Interior, Red Over Yellow Paint, Wooden................................... 250.00
Spice Box, Hanging, Lift Lid, 1 Drawer, 4-Part Divided Interior, 12 1/2 In. 275.00
Spice Set, Old McDonald, Regal, 3 Piece... 125.00
Spoon, Measuring, Aluminum, Set.. 3.00
Spoon, Tasting, Maple, Burls, 2 Hearts Carved In Handle, 18th Century, 5 1/4 In. 195.00
Spoon Rest, Mammy, Rockingham... 140.00
Sprinkler Bottle, Chinaman, Green & Yellow 20.00
Sprinkler Bottle, Clothes, Peasant Girl 35.00
Sprinkler Bottle, Clothespin 95.00
Sprinkler Bottle, Elephant ....40.00 to 55.00
Sprinkler Bottle, Mammy 235.00
Sprinkler Bottle, Rooster 75.00
Sprinkler Bottle, Siamese Cat 85.00
Sprinkler Bottle, Tin Tubular Handle, c.1840, 5 1/2 x 2 In. 59.00
Stirrer, Laundry, Double Prong At End, Wooden 220.00
Strainer, Cheese, Heart Shape... 395.00
Strainer, Chittlin, Wooden Handle, 1896 .... 45.00
Strainer, Fine Mesh, Wire Handles, Tin, 4-Footed Self Stand 6.00
Strainer, Flat, To Fit On Cup, Aluminum 2.00
String Holder, Bulldog, China.. 45.00
String Holder, Butler, Full Figure 450.00
String Holder, Cleminson, Heart Shape 80.00
String Holder, Mammy, Large 295.00
String Holder, Mammy, Plaid 165.00
String Holder, Mammy, Pottery, Japan 170.00
String Holder, Mammy, Pudgy, 7 In. 275.00
String Holder, Witch, Celluloid Head & Arms, Oilcloth Outfit 60.00
Sugar Nippers, Brass Mount On Wooden Board, c.1750 .... 225.00
Sweeper, Bissell, American Queen, Cyco Ball Bearing, Walnut & Cast Iron 195.00
Sweeper, Karpet King, Wooden.. 185.00
Tea Cozy, Doll, Large... 55.00
Teakettle, Copper, Square, 19th Century 535.00
Teakettle, Erie, Aluminum, 4 Qt.. 35.00
Teakettle, Wagner Ware, J.C. Rideout, Sydney, Ohio, Black Handle 85.00
Toaster, Foldover, Double Handle, Wire, 9 x 10 In. 65.00
Toaster, GE, Spider Web Design, 1940 .... 15.00
Toaster, Handy Hot Side Loader, Chrome, 1930s 475.00
Toaster, Hotpoint, Crumb Tray & Timer, Original Cord, 1930s 475.00
Toaster, Porcelier Ceramic, 2 Slice, Floral Design, Electric 675.00
Toaster, Reed & Cameron, Early 1920s 45.00
Toaster, Sunbeam, No. 1... 100.00
Toaster, Swivel, Iron, New England, 8 In. 335.00
Toaster, Torrid, 1920s.. 45.00
Toaster, Wrought Iron, Twisted Trim, Shaped Handle, 14 x 19 In. 247.00
Toaster Cover, Art Deco Doll, Dressed, 16 In. 20.00
Toaster Cover, Cat, Kliban 25.00
Vacuum Cleaner, Oreck, Upright... 97.00
Wafer Iron, Japan, 1915, 10 x 10 In. 125.00
Wafer Iron, Makes Waffle-Like Pastries, Rectangular, 4 3/8 x 7 1/4 In.................... 220.00
Wafer Iron, Makes Waffle-Like Pastries, Round, 1800, 26 In. Handle, 4 5/8 In.......... 190.00
Wafer Iron, Masonic Pyramid, Waffle & Sun Rays Design, Handles, 29 In. 95.00
Waffle Iron, Andersen Heart 135.00
Waffle Iron, Folding, Wrought Iron, 22 x 6 x 4 In. 65.00
Waffle Iron, Griswold, Heart & Star 175.00
Waffle Iron, Griswold, No. 3... 50.00
Waffle Iron, Griswold, No. 8, Low Frame, 1910 .... 125.00
Waffle Iron, Griswold, No. 9, Low Base 75.00
Waffle Iron, Griswold, No. 11, Wooden Handles, Square...........................120.00 to 150.00

Waffle Iron, Griswold, No. 21, American-French Pattern	1500.00
Waffle Iron, Griswold, No. 919, Heart & Stars	200.00
Waffle Iron, Hearts & Diamonds, No. 7, Cast Iron, 6 3/4 In.	145.00
Waffle Iron, Keen Kutter, Child's	85.00
Waffle Iron, Krumkake, Nordic Ware	45.00
Waffle Iron, Sidney, No. 7, Wooden Handles, Low Base, Patent 1892	75.00
Waffle Iron, Smith Francis Wells, Hearts, Diamonds, Scroll Design Cover, 8 In.	185.00
Waffle Iron, Wagner, National, No. 8, Patent 1911	60.00
Waffle Iron, Wagner, No. 8, High Frame, 1910	135.00
Waffle Iron, Wapak, Indian Mark	160.00
Waffle Iron, Wearever, No. 8	65.00
Waffle Iron, Winchester	175.00
Wash Boiler, Cover, Copper, Insert	115.00
Washboard, Dubl Handi Columbus Washboard Co., Metal Scrubber, Bicentennial	9.00
Washboard, Glass, 8 1/2 x 18 In.	50.00
Washboard, Maple, 18th Century, 21 x 10 In.	395.00
Washboard, National, No. 197, Cobalt Blue Enamel	75.00
Washboard, Rockingham Insert In Frame, 12 x 22 In.	16.00
Washboard, Stoneware Insert, Albany Slip, 25 x 13 1/4 In.	182.00
Washboard, Wooden, Wide Slant Bar, 1 Piece	120.00
Washing Machine, Maytag, Wooden, Missing Agitator	110.00
Washing Machine, Solid Copper	180.00
Washing Machine, Wringer, Green Speckled Porcelain, 1933	225.00
Water Dispenser, Refrigerator, Porcelain, Spring Action, Folding Spigot, c.1930	87.00
Whisk, Spoon Shape Coiled Wire	6.00

KNIFE collectors usually specialize in a single type. In the 1960s, the United States government passed a law that required knife manufacturers to mark their knives with the country of origin. This seemed to encourage the collectors, and knife collecting became an interest of a large group of people. All types of knives are collected, from top quality twentieth-century examples to old bone- or pearl-handled knives in excellent condition.

American United Life, Embossed, Pocket	28.00
Army, Survival, Sheath, Camillus, 12 In.	40.00
Benedictine, Pearlized, With Corkscrew, Pocket	19.00
Bowie, Black Composition Haft, Brass Screws, 7 In.	185.00
Bowie, Elliot & Son, Stag Haft, Silver Mountssilver Blade, c.1860, 7 3/4 In.	395.00
Bowie, Joseph Rodgers & Sons, Clip-Point Blade, Stag Grip, 8 1/2 In.	1500.00
Bowie, Mother-Of-Pearl Hilt, Coffin Shape, 9 7/8 In.	900.00
Bowie, Painted Wooden Haft, Brass Rivets, 6 In.	140.00
Bowie, Rosewood Handle, Brass Guard, 9 1/4 In.	137.50
Bowie, Stag Haft, 19th Century, 5 3/8 In.	120.00
Butcher, Shapeleigh	30.00
Case XX, Lock Blade, 4 Blades	125.00
Case XX, Sunfish, 1964	100.00
Cheese, Geo. Lautz, Boston, Country Store, 22 1/2 In.	110.00
Commando, Brass Knuckle Grip, Scabbard, 6 3/4 In.	185.00
Congress Beer & Derby Cream Ale, Bottle Opener, 3 In.	85.00
Dagger, 2-Piece Curved Bone Grip, Indo-Persian, c.1700	175.00
Dagger, Iron Blade, Wooden Grip With Floral Design, 16th Century, 13 3/4 In.	225.00
Dagger, Scottish Highland, Fullered Blade, Antler Grip, c.1820, 12 1/2 In.	375.00
Dagger, Tapered Handle, Double Ring Handle, Bronze, China, 16 3/4 In.	3105.00
Dagger, Wave Blade, Java, 14 1/4 In.	290.00
Electrician's, Remington, Wooden Handle	45.00
Elephant, Armor Piercing Section, 5-Bar Grip, India, 7 1/2-In. Blade	225.00
Halberd, Crude Forged Iron, Gold Paint Traces, 18th Century, 61-In. Blade	320.00
Hunting, Leather Handle & Sheath, Finish, Miniature	25.00
Hunting, Randall, 6-In. Blade, 4 3/4-In. Composition Handle, Leather Scabbard	275.00
Pen, Geo. Wostenholm, Embossed, Corkscrew, Key, Pipe & Cards, 2 Blades, 1900, 3 In.	99.00
Pipe, Kershaw	15.00
Pocket, Boubon DeLuxe, Pearlized, Bottle Opener	18.00
Pocket, Bridge Cutlery, Official League Ball, Bat Shape, 4 In.	85.00
Pocket, Case, 2 Blades, Leather Case	95.00

Pocket, Case, 3 1/2-In. Bone Handle, 4-In. Blade	55.00
Pocket, Diamond Edge	35.00
Pocket, Jubilee Rye, Bone	34.00
Pocket, Lung Tonic	95.00
Pocket, Monkees, Guitar Logo, Picture Of 4, Opens To 6 In.	3.00
Pocket, Movado, Henckels, 1930s	175.00
Pocket, Purina	10.00
Remington, Bone Handle	150.00
Remington, Drink Nehi, Bottle Opener, Lady's Leg	195.00
Switch Blade, Schrade Cutlery Co., Patent 1916	200.00
Switch Blade, Shapleigh Hardware	175.00

KOREAN WARE, see Sumida

KOSTA, the oldest Swedish glass factory, was founded in 1742. During the 1920s through the 1950s, many pieces of original design were made at the factory. The firm is still working.

KOSTA

Bowl, Freeform, Internal Red Bands, Vicke Lindstrand, c.1955, 6 In.	358.00
Bowl, Frosted Blue Swirls, 6 In.	225.00
Bowl, Kayak Shape, White & Clear, Signed, 7 In.	125.00
Candy Dish, Swan, 6 In.	45.00
Decanter, Black Stripe Up Sides, Clear, Signed, 10 In.	180.00
Vase, Bud, Mushroom Shape, Signed, 4 In.	30.00
Vase, Cover, Faceted Base, Engraved Greek Youth, Lyre, c.1927, E. Dahlskog, 29 In.	5850.00
Vase, Frosted Color Stripes, Bartil Vallien, 3 x 3 In.	150.00
Vase, Frosted, Wheel-Cut, Intaglio Prehistoric Figures, Vicke Lindstrand, c.1955, 8 In.	3135.00
Vase, Nude Woman Looking Into Mirror, Signed, c.1955, 8 1/2 In.	385.00
Vase, Pinched-In Shape, Cut Tree Branches, Vicke Lindstrand, No. 42104, 11 1/2 In.	220.00
Vase, Rainbow, 7 In.	175.00
Vase, Seaweed, Ovoid, Internal Green Forms & Bubbles, Vicke Lindstrand, c.1962, 6 In.	66.00
Vase, Seaweed, Teardrop Shape, Bubbles, Vicke Lindstrand, c.1962, 8 In.	195.00
Vase, Surface Wrap Of Multicolored Confetti-Like Design, Bartil Vallien, 6 3/8 In.	258.00
Vase, Threads Of Red, Black & White, c.1950, 4 x 7 In.	305.00
Vase, Tiered, Clear, Internal Yellow Bubbles, No. 48760, 7 1/2 In.	99.00

KPM refers to Berlin porcelain, but the same initials were used alone and in combination with other symbols by several German porcelain makers. They include the Konigliche Porzellan Manufaktur of Berlin, initials used in mark, 1823–1847; Meissen, 1723–1724 only; Krister Porzellan Manufaktur in Waldenburg, after 1831; Kranichfelder Porzellan Manufaktur in Kranichfeld, after 1903; and the Kister Porzellan Manufaktur in Scheibe, after 1838.

KPM

K.P.M

Basket, Reticulated, Octagonal, Slot Handles, Blue Scepter Mark, 10 x 7 1/2 In.	395.00
Candleholder, Wide Scalloped Edge, Pink & Yellow Flowers, Receptacle, Round, 6 In.	40.00
Charger, Allegorical Scene, Cupid, 2 Women With Quivers, Flowers, c.1900, 12 In.	805.00
Coffee Set, Gold Floral & Vine, 3 Piece	120.00
Dinner Set, Floral Sprays & Insects, Hand Painted	8500.00
Figurine, Boy, Holding Flute To Mouth, Carrying Birdcage, 12 In.	245.00
Figurine, Monkey, White Porcelain, 17 In.	385.00
Jar, Cover, Portraits Of Young Couple, White Ground, 7 In.	395.00
Lithophane, see also Lithophane category	
Lithophane, Girl & Child, 4 1/2 x 5 In.	250.00
Miniature, Woman, Portrait, Frame, 2 1/2 x 3 In.	99.00
Miniature, Woman, Profile, Oval Gilt Frame, 4 x 5 In.	165.00
Mirror, Miniature, Woman Portrait, Sterling Silver, 7 1/2 In.	154.00
Plaque, Angel, Woman In Black, 9 x 11 In.	3105.00
Plaque, Child, With 2 Cats, Marked, 9 1/2 x 6 1/2 In.	3737.00
Plaque, Girl, Holding Chamberstick, Gute Nacht, Signed, L. Gross, Frame, 7 1/2 x 5 In.	1500.00
Plaque, Madonna, Matter Dolorosa, Oval, 1850s, 7 In.	950.00
Plaque, Peasant Girl, Carrying Water Jug, 19th Century, 10 x 7 1/2 In.	2300.00
Plaque, Pensive Angel, Marked, 4 1/4 x 5 1/2 In.	750.00
Plaque, Portrait, Angelique, Giltwood Frame, Scepter Mark, 12 3/8 x 10 1/8 In.	5750.00
Plaque, Portrait, Woman, M.H. Green	950.00 to 995.00
Plaque, Woman, In Garden, Carved Frame, 6 x 9 In.	3500.00

Plaque, Woman, Long Flowing Hair, Sommer, Wagner, Scepter Mark, 9 1/2 x 6 1/2 In. 2875.00
Plate, Alpine Scene, Hand Painted, F. Tamrath, 7 1/8 In... 220.00
Portrait, Young Girl, Rococo Frame, Signed, 6 1/2 In. 715.00
Teapot, Figures, Gilt, 6 In. 70.00
Urinal, Blue & Gold Bands 145.00
Vase, Lily Leaves & Blossoms, Brown, Green & Pink Glaze 8925.00
Vase, Portrait, Woman Sitting On Garden Bench, Cupids, Signed, c.1920, 6 1/4 In........ 750.00

KTK are the initials of the Knowles, Taylor & Knowles Company of East Liverpool, Ohio, founded by Isaac W. Knowles in 1853. The company made many types of utilitarian wares, hotel china, and dinnerwares. They made the fine bone china known as Lotus Ware from 1891 to 1896. The company merged with American Ceramic Corporation in 1928. It closed in 1934. Lotus Ware is listed in its own category in this book.

K.T.&K.
CHINA

Chamber Pot, White Porcelain, Handle 115.00
Coaster, Yorktown, Russet.. 18.00
Jug, Whiskey, Maryland Club, 1881 .... 125.00
Pitcher, Large Red Raspberries, Leaves, Scrolled Handle, Sponged Rim, 8 In. 95.00
Plate, Tiajuana, 6 In... 3.00
Shaving Mug, Enameled Skull & Crossbones, J.D. Blevins 19.00

KU KLUX KLAN items are now collected because of their historic importance. Literature, robes, and memorabilia are available. The Klan is still in existence, so new material is found.

Flag, 1920s, 45 x 81 In. 430.00
Pin, Ribbon & Bell... 138.00
Robe, With Hood, Patch 160.00
Sign, Ku Klux Klothes, Klansman Picture, Die Cut On Board, Frame, 5 x 3 In. 85.00
Stamp, Women Of Bucyrus, Ohio 225.00

KUTANI ware is a Japanese porcelain made after the mid-seventeenth century. Most of the pieces found today are nineteenth-century. Collectors often use the term *kutani* to refer to just the later, colorful pieces decorated with red, gold, and black pictures of warriors, animals, and birds.

Bottle, Allover Red & Gold Geometric, Long Rimmed Neck, 19th Century, 8 3/4 In.... 35.00
Bowl, Figures All Sides, Floral & Medallion Border, Interior Dragons, 4 3/4 In. 259.00
Chocolate Pot, Bird & Flower Design, Late 19th Century, 11 In.................................. 36.00
Figurine, Buddha, Marked, 8 In. 115.00
Figurine, Foo Dog, Rust & Cream Ground, Gold Trim, Artist, 1920, 8 1/2 In., Pair 350.00
Jar, Cover, Warriors, Molded Tasseled Handles, Multicolored Brocade, 20 1/2 In., Pair 1300.00
Salt & Pepper, White Elephants, Red, Green, Gold Time, 1940s 20.00
Tea Caddy, c.1900, 5 1/2 In.. 275.00
Teapot, One Thousand Faces.. 225.00
Vase, Cover, Allover Figural & Floral Design, Paneled, 1890s, 31 In. 430.00

LACQUER is a type of varnish. Collectors are most interested in the Chinese and Japanese lacquer wares made from the Japanese varnish tree. Lacquer wares are made from wood with many coats of lacquer. Sometimes the piece is carved or decorated with ivory or metal inlay.

Box, Book-Shaped, Gilt Trim, Chinoiserie Decoration, 13 1/4 x 14 x 3 1/4 In. 175.00
Box, Rectangle, Cinnamon Color, Flowers, Dragons, Brass Lock, 16 x 8 In. 920.00
Box, Sewing, Lift Top, China, 6 x 10 1/2 x 8 In.. 187.00
Box, Temple, Cover, China, 6 x 11 In. 24.00
Box, Tortoiseshell Cover, Japan, 11 In. 88.00
Box, Writing, Fitted Interior, Japan, 9 In. 880.00
Egg, 1909 Bank Notes, Catherine The Great Portrait, Over Wood, Russia, 4 In. 132.25
Tray, On Stand, Black, 1850, Japan, 28 x 16 In. 605.00

LADY HEAD VASE, see Head Vase

LALIQUE glass was made by Rene Lalique in Paris, France, between the 1890s and his death in 1945. The glass was molded, pressed, and engraved in Art Nouveau and Art Deco styles. Pieces were marked with the signature *R. Lalique*. Lalique glass is still being made. Pieces made

Lalique

after 1945 bear the mark *Lalique*. Jewelry made by Rene Lalique is listed
in the Jewelry category.

Ashtray, Deux Zephyrs, Gray, Signed, c.1913, 3 1/4 In.	402.00
Ashtray, Jamaique, Amber, Signed, c.1928, 5 1/2 In.	947.00
Ashtray, Moineau, Sparrow, Green, Signed, c.1925	925.00
Bell, Finch Finial	175.00
Bookends, Gazelle, Leaping, Circular Ground, Acid Stamp, 4 x 4 In., Pair	395.00
Bookends, Hirondelles, Swallows, 6 1/4 In.	545.00
Bottle, Myosotis, Forget-Me-Nots, Nude Woman Stopper, No. 613, 9 In.	605.00
Bowl, Calypso, Circular, Nude Maidens In Sea, 14 1/4 In.	1610.00
Bowl, Sparrow Motif, 9 In.	431.25
Bowl, Spiral Pattern, Signed, 8 In.	470.00
Box, 3 Dahlias, Opalescent, Blue Cast, Signed, 1932, Round, 8 1/2 In. Diam.	1000.00
Box, 4 Swimming Fish On Underside Of Lid, Satin On Bottom, Signed, 1921, 10 In.	2760.00
Box, Chantilly, Deer, Sepia Patina, Signed, c.1924, 3 3/4 In.	575.00
Box, Cover Molded As Dahlia, Black Enamel, Signed, 1931, 5 1/2 In.	1380.00
Box, Vallauris, Cover, Signed, c.1928, 5 1/2 In.	690.00
Candelabrum, 4-Light, Brown Pheasants	2100.00
Candlestick, Mesanges, Birds In Floral Arbor, Signed, 6 1/8 In., Pair	235.00
Chalice, Leafy Branches, Melon-Shaped Bowl, Signed, 9 1/2 In.	287.50
Champagne, L'Ange, Frosted Angel, Signed, 8 In.	155.00
Champagne, L'Ange, Signed, 1970s, 6 Piece	977.00
Chandelier, Champs Elysees, Leaf Form, Chrome Standard, Signed, 45 1/2 In.	4600.00
Chandelier, Charmes, Amber, Molded Branches, Domed Shade, 13 1/2 In.	4370.00
Chandelier, Noisettier, Star-Shaped Shade, Leaves & Branches, Signed, 26 In.	920.00
Clock, Birds, Frosted, Signed, 5 x 11 In.	1800.00
Clock, Deux Colombes, 2 Doves, Battery Movement, Signed, c.1926, 8 3/4 In.	5750.00
Clock, Moineaux, Sparrows, Electric Movement, Signed, c.1924, 6 1/4 In.	1725.00
Clock, Naiades, Water Nymphs, Signed, c.1926, 4 7/8 In.	2300.00
Comb, 3 Pearls In Foliate Mount, Signed, c.1900, 4 1/2 In.	2645.00
Crucifix, Figure In Relief, Frosted, Bronze Lighted Base, 19 In.	1750.00
Dish, Cover, Round, Opalescent Raised Flowers, Blue Tint, 6 1/4 In.	1100.00
Figurine, Buffalo	1700.00
Figurine, Cat, Crouching, Frosted, Signed, 4 1/4 x 9 In.	605.00 to 825.00
Figurine, Cat, Sitting, 8 1/4 In.	795.00 to 935.00
Figurine, Chrysis, Mythical Female Nude, Signed, c.1965, 5 3/4 In.	310.00
Figurine, Cockatoo, 11 3/4 In.	2200.00
Figurine, Crouching Cat, Signed, 4 1/4 x 9 In.	585.00
Figurine, Danseuse, Dancer, Arms Raised, Nude, R. Lalique, 9 1/4 In.	330.00
Figurine, Deux Danseuses, 2 Dancers, Signed, c.1965, 9 3/4 In.	1265.00
Figurine, Diane, 4 3/4 In.	215.00
Figurine, Fish, Frosted, Script Marked, 6 In.	220.00
Figurine, Floral, Frosted Nude, Hair Of Flowers, Signed, 3 3/8 In.	258.75
Figurine, Leda, Nude With Swan, 4 3/4 In.	215.00
Figurine, Nude Woman, Signed, 13 1/2 In.	395.00
Figurine, Owl, On Stump, 3 In.	88.00
Figurine, Owl, Signed, 8 1/2 In.	800.00
Figurine, Sainte Therese De L'enfant Jesus, Crystal Block, Signed, 15 In.	805.00
Figurine, Sparrow, 4 In.	110.00
Figurine, Swan, Etched Glass, 14 1/2 In., Pair	2310.00
Figurine, Water Buffalo, Box, 12 1/2 In.	1649.00 to 2930.00
Flower Frog, Towel Draped Nude Woman, Clear, 7 In.	150.00
Handle, Parasol, Enameled, Carved Ivory, Maidens' Heads, c.1903, 8 In.	8625.00
Hood Ornament, Chrysis, Kneeling Nude, Flowing Hair, Signed, 5 1/4 In.	1955.00
Hood Ornament, Grande Libellule, Dragonfly, 8 1/4 In.	4400.00
Hood Ornament, Hirondelles, Swallows, Signed, c.1928, 5 7/8 In.	2300.00
Hood Ornament, Levrier, Greyhound, Chromium Mount, Signed, c.1928, 7 3/4 In.	1380.00
Hood Ornament, Tete D'aigle, Eagle's Head, Signed, c.1928, 4 5/8 In.	1495.00
Hood Ornament, Victoire, Woman's Head, Streaming Hair, 1928, 10 In.	9487.00
Hood Ornament, Vitesse, Nude Maiden, 1929, 7 In.	4312.00
Lamp, 5 Panels Of Peonies, Leafage, Marble Base, Signed, c.1925	3162.00
Liquor Set, Pouilly, Blue Wash, Signed, 9 Piece	2350.00

Lalique, Perfume Bottle, Blue Glass,
Ridged Design, Camille, 5 1/2 In.

◆◆◆◆◆◆◆◆◆◆◆◆◆◆◆◆◆◆◆◆◆◆◆◆◆

To dust small, fragile items
like flower-decorated figurines, try blowing the dust
away with a hand-held hair
dryer set on low. For large,
sturdy items, cover the end of
the vacuum cleaner nozzle
with an old nylon stocking,
then vacuum.

◆◆◆◆◆◆◆◆◆◆◆◆◆◆◆◆◆◆◆◆◆◆◆◆◆

Medallion, International Exposition Of Art & Industry, 1937, 3 1/2 In. 1610.00
Night-Light, Nude Dancer, Outstretched Fabric-Draped Arms, 1925, 12 3/4 In. 5750.00
Paperweight, Bison, Frosted, No. 1196 ....325.00 to 400.00
Paperweight, Chouette, Barn Owl, No. 1193, 3 1/2 In. 325.00
Paperweight, Coq Nain, Frosted Rooster, No. 1135 .... 475.00
Paperweight, Thistle Intaglio Design, Frosted & Clear, Rectangular, Signed 45.00
Pendant, Panier De Fruits, Charcoal Gray, Silk Cord, c.1922, 1 7/8 In. 575.00
Perfume Bottle, Blue Glass, Ridged Design, Camille, 5 1/2 In. .... *Illus* 2970.00
Perfume Bottle, Butterflies, Signed, c.1922, 4 In. 402.00
Perfume Bottle, Coeur Joie, Heart Shape, Signed ....375.00 to 475.00
Perfume Bottle, Dahlia 150.00
Perfume Bottle, Deux Fleurs, 2 Flowers Form, 3 5/8 In. ....132.00 to 345.00
Perfume Bottle, Duncan, 3 Female Nudes, Signed, c.1950, 7 1/2 In. 1380.00
Perfume Bottle, Epines, Signed, 4 In. 385.00
Perfume Bottle, Glycines, Wisteria, Blue Patina, Signed, 1920, 4 3/4 In. 920.00
Perfume Bottle, Houbigant, La Belle Saison, 1925, 3 3/4 In. 1725.00
Perfume Bottle, Molinard De Molinard, Frosted Nudes 55.00
Perfume Bottle, Molinard, La Provencal, 5 1/4 In. 250.00
Perfume Bottle, Narcisse Et Elegance, Square, 2 Women, Flowers, D'orsay, 3 3/4 In. .. 275.00
Perfume Bottle, Nina Ricci, Air Du Temps, Double Dove, Frosted Bottom 125.00
Perfume Bottle, Worth, Dans La Nuit, 4 1/4 In. 700.00
Perfume Bottle, Worth, Je Reviens, Unopened, 3 In. 450.00
Perfume Bottle, Worth, Vers Le Jour, Amber, c.1926, 4 In. 977.00
Plate, 1965, Deux Oiseaux, 2 Birds, Marie-Claude Lalique, 8 1/2 In. 800.00
Plate, 6 Nude Maidens On Reverse, Bubbling Water, 1921, 10 7/8 In. 2070.00
Plate, Campanules, Stylized Tulips, Signed, c.1932, 12 1/4 In. 747.00
Plate, Chardon, Thistle, Crescent Form, 6 Frosted Pods, Signed, 8 In. 345.00
Plate, Christmas, 1965, Box 895.00
Plate, Crescent, Dandelion Leaves 295.00
Powder Box, 2 Entwined & Draped Females On Cover, Signed, 3 1/2 x 2 1/4 In. 350.00
Sconce, Stylized Leaf Form, Signed, 10 In. Pair 1495.00
Tray, Pin, Eagle, Black Box, Labels, 1976 .... 112.00
Tray, Pin, Eagle, Box 85.00
Tray, Pissenlit, Dandelion Leaves, Signed, c.1921, 11 5/8 In. 747.00
Tumbler, Bunches Of Grapes At Base, Signed, 4 1/4 In., 6 Piece 350.00
Vase, Albert, Flanking Eagle Heads, Signed, 6 3/4 In. 975.00
Vase, Archers, Amber, Signed, c.1921, 10 1/4 In. 6900.00
Vase, Archers, Topaz, 10 1/2 In. 4675.00
Vase, Bacchantes, Carved Field Of Female Nudes, 9 1/2 In. 1950.00
Vase, Bagatelle, Numerous Birds In Floral Arbors, Signed, 6 3/4 In. 160.00
Vase, Beauvais, Faceted, Cylindrical, Graduated Coiled Fern Leaves, c.1940, 8 In. 2500.00
Vase, Birches, Clear & Frosted, Late 1940s Mark, 6 1/2 In. 350.00
Vase, Birds In Various Poses, Perched On Branches, Signed, 1923, 9 1/4 In. 9775.00
Vase, Birds, Raised, 6 In. 225.00
Vase, Ceylan, Perching Lovebirds, Opalescent, Signed, 9 1/2 In. 3450.00

Vase, Ceylan, Perching Lovebirds, Signed, 1914, 9 3/8 In. 3737.00
Vase, Courges, Molded Gourds Overall, Signed, 7 1/2 In. 690.00
Vase, Cover, 2 Birds Eating Fruit On Handles, 1929, 8 3/4 In. 6900.00
Vase, Danaides, Frieze Of Neoclassical Figurines, Signed, c.1926, 7 1/4 In. 4140.00
Vase, Davos, Simulates Sharkskin, Signed, c.1932 .... 1495.00
Vase, Domremy, Signed, c.1926, 8 5/8 In. 3220.00
Vase, Druides, Berries & Leaves, Signed, c.1924, 7 1/2 In. 1150.00
Vase, Eglantines, Frosted Bottle Form, Wild Rose Blooms, Signed, 4 1/2 In. 345.00
Vase, Eucalyptus, Leaves, Blue, Signed, c.1925, 8 3/4 In. 1265.00
Vase, Formose, Swimming Fish, Smoky, Signed, 6 1/2 x 7 In. 1540.00
Vase, Frosted Birds, Signed, 5 In. 250.00
Vase, Grenade, Allover Geometric Flower Petals, Signed, Black, 4 3/4 In. 3220.00
Vase, Gros Scarabees, Large Beetles, Frosted & Clear, Signed, 1923, 11 1/2 In. 5175.00
Vase, Gui, Allover Stylized Mistletoe, Amber, Signed, 6 1/2 In. 2070.00
Vase, Gui, Amber, Stylized Mistletoe, 6 1/2 In. 2070.00
Vase, Gui, Blown-Out Flowers, Etched Vines, Frosted, R. Lalique, 7 In. 1100.00
Vase, Guirlande De Roses, Footed, Oviform, Oval Shaped Rose Garlands, 5 1/2 In. 460.00
Vase, Leaf & Vine Handles, Signed, 9 1/2 In. 750.00
Vase, Lievres, Hares, Sepia Patina, Signed, c.1923, 6 In. 977.00
Vase, Lotus Blossoms, Frosted Ground, Block Letters, 5 3/4 x 5 In. 700.00
Vase, Moses, Amber, 8 In. 3000.00
Vase, Nude Maidens, Brown Patina, Signed, 1927, 9 5/8 In. 8337.00
Vase, Oran, Opalescent, Peony Blossoms, 10 1/4 In. 8625.00
Vase, Ormeaux, Overlapping Leaves, Frosted, Narrow Neck, 1932, 6 1/2 In. 850.00
Vase, Overlapping Thorny Brambles, Signed, 1921, 9 1/4 In. 412.00
Vase, Pairs Of Lovebirds, Amid Rushes, Amber, Signed, 10 In. 5750.00
Vase, Pairs Of Lovebirds, On Flowering Branches, Signed, 1919, 10 In. 3450.00
Vase, Palissy, Sphere, Everted Rim, Snail Shells, 6 3/4 In. 1380.00
Vase, Perruches, Amber, Lovebirds, 10 In. 5750.00
Vase, Perruches, Parakeets, Blossoms, Frosted Blue, Branches, 10 1/4 In. 2530.00
Vase, Pinsons, Raised Band Of Finches, Cherry Tree, Signed, 7 1/4 In. 920.00
Vase, Piriac, Circling Fish, Frosted, No. 1043 .... 450.00
Vase, Poissons, Large Finned Fish, Amber, Signed, 9 1/2 In. 7475.00
Vase, Poissons, Overlapping Spiky Fish, Signed, 1921, 9 In. 3450.00
Vase, Rampillon, Raised Diamonds & Flowers, 5 1/4 In. 920.00
Vase, Ricquewihr, Bands Of Grapevines, 5 In. 402.00
Vase, St. Marc, c.1950, 6 1/2 In. 475.00
Vase, Violettes, Stylized Leaves, Signed, c.1920, 6 1/4 In. 690.00
Wine Cooler, Constance, Black Enamel, Anemones Handles, c.1970, 7 In. 805.00

LAMPS of every type, from the early oil-burning Betty and Phoebe lamps to the recent electric lamps with glass or beaded shades, interest collectors. Fuels used in lamps changed through the years; whale oil (1800–1840), camphene (1828), Argand (1830), lard (1833–1863), turpentine and alcohol (1840s), gas (1850–1879), kerosene (1860), and electricity (1879) are the most common. Other lamps are listed by manufacturer or type of material.

Aladdin, 550, Original Shade 500.00
Aladdin, 7005, Bridge, Refinished 75.00
Aladdin, B-27, Simplicity, Alacite, Gold Luster 250.00
Aladdin, B-41, Lincoln Drape, Short Style, Amber 2500.00
Aladdin, B-49, Washington Drape, Amber 300.00
Aladdin, B-75, Scalloped Foot 295.00
Aladdin, B-76, Lincoln Drape, Blue, Burner, 10 In. 1600.00
Aladdin, B-77, Tall Lincoln Drape, Ruby, Burner 625.00
Aladdin, B-85, White Moonstone, Burner 310.00
Aladdin, B-86, Green Moonstone, Whip-O-Lite, Shade 250.00
Aladdin, B-88, Vertique, Yellow Moonstone 475.00
Aladdin, B-88, Yellow Moonstone, Burner 575.00
Aladdin, B-93, Vertique, White Moonstone 75.00
Aladdin, B-98, Queen, Rose Moonstone, Vertical Ribbed Bowl 100.00
Aladdin, B-100, Corinthian, Clear 85.00
Aladdin, B-110, Cathedral, White Moonstone 275.00
Aladdin, B-111, Cathedral 275.00

Aladdin, B-112, Cathedral Pattern, Rose Moonstone, Nickel Burner 295.00
Aladdin, B-116, Rose Moonstone 235.00
Aladdin, B-120, Majestic, White Moonstone 285.00
Aladdin, B-122, Majestic, Green Moonstone 175.00
Aladdin, B-124, Corinthian, White Moonstone Font, Black Font 225.00
Aladdin, B-131, Oriental, Green 65.00
Aladdin, C-130, Amber Bowl, Shade & Finial, 1934 .... 200.00
Aladdin, Cathedral, Rose Moonstone, Nickel Burner 250.00
Aladdin, G-16, Figurine, Alacite 550.00
Aladdin, G-16, Opalique, Alacite, Original Shade 475.00
Aladdin, G-18, Black Chromium, Finial 75.00
Aladdin, G-23, Alacite, Pair 75.00
Aladdin, G-27, Clear, Miss Ophelia Finial 800.00
Aladdin, G-40, Boudoir, No. 1541 Shade, Pair 175.00
Aladdin, G-49, No. 866 Square Shade 285.00
Aladdin, G-67, Velvex 750.00
Aladdin, G-141, Frosted, Wreath Finial 280.00
Aladdin, G-214, Alacite, Oriental, Tan Design, Metal 40.00
Aladdin, G-228, Alacite, Fluted Urn, Flowers, Table 55.00
Aladdin, G-232a, Alacite, Urn, Pair 270.00
Aladdin, G-267a, Alacite 45.00
Aladdin, G-274, Pink Trim, Wheat Finial, Shade 60.00
Aladdin, G-301, Green, Fluted Shade, Pair 275.00
Aladdin, G-303, Alacite, Gray & Ivory, Glass Finial 60.00
Aladdin, G-321, Fluted Shade, Finial, Pair 70.00
Aladdin, G-326, Red, Lighted Base 45.00
Aladdin, G-333, Bride & Groom, Green 75.00
Aladdin, G-376, Urn, Sticker, Pair 305.00
Aladdin, Internal White Leaf Design, Wreath Form Finial, 22 3/4 In. 50.00
Aladdin, Lomax Star, Peg Front 50.00
Aladdin, Model C-164, Burner, Brazil, Shelf 80.00
Aladdin, No. 21C, Caboose, Rock Island & Pacific Railroad, Case 105.00
Aladdin, No. 23C, Caboose 55.00
Aladdin, No. 105, Colonial, Green Beta 95.00
Aladdin, No. 301, Green, Fluted Shade, Pair 275.00
Aladdin, No. 501, Model 11 Shade, Electric, c.1950 .... 140.00
Aladdin, No. 516, White Paint, Hanging, Shade 125.00
Aladdin, No. 783, Black Vase 425.00
Aladdin, No. 1240, Variegated Verde, Burner 130.00
Aladdin, No. 1243, Green Vase 350.00
Aladdin, No. 1244, Vase, No. 301 Chip, Shade 475.00
Aladdin, No. 3982, Alacite Ring, Floor 75.00
Aladdin, Piano, Painted Swiveling Shade, Brass Wash, 15 x 6 1/2 In. 300.00
Aladdin, Ribbed Milk Glass Shade, Electrified, Brass, 17 1/2 In. 100.00
Aladdin, W-161, Walnut 100.00
Argand, 1-Arm, Neoclassical, Etched & Frosted Shade, Electrified, 1830s, 17 In., Pair 1210.00
Argand, 1-Arm, Urn Form Reservoir, Globe, Bronze, Electrified, 14 1/4 In., Pair 1210.00
Argand, Brass, Clear Blown Shade, Floral Engraved, Modified Burner, 16 7/8 In. 250.00
Argand, Bronze, Glass, Lion's Mask & Ring Legs, Paw Feet, Wood Base, 31 1/4 In., Pair 4887.00
Argand, Empire, 2-Light, Bronze, Electrified, 1830-1845, 15 In., Pair 1955.00
Argand, Frosted Shades, Name Plate, J.B. Wilbor, Electrified, 14 1/2 In., Pair 1100.00
Argand, Garniture Set, J. Cox, New York, 3 Piece 1650.00
Argand Diamond, Opaque White Base, Brass, 23 1/2 In. 125.00
Astral, Argand Burner, Parker's Sinambra Font, Frosted To Clear 770.00
Astral, Classical Bronze, Tri-Column Standard, Neoclassical Masks, 22 In. 825.00
Astral, Double, Gilt Brass, Frosted Glass Globe, Cut Glass Prisms, 17 In. 520.00
Astral, Frosted Snowflake Shade, Marble Base, Cut Prisms, Electrified 235.00
Astral, Gilt Brass, Wheel Cut & Etched Glass Shade, 25 1/2 In. 460.00
Astral, Gilt Bronze, Cut Glass, Faceted Prisms, Thumbprints, Flowers, 29 In. 1100.00
Betty, Primitive, Hinged Lid, Wrought Iron, 6 In. 100.00
Betty, Twisted Top, Wooden Trammel, Cast Iron, 39 In. 1035.00
Betty, Wrought Iron, Bird Silhouette Cover, Hanger, 3 1/2 In. 300.00
Betty, Wrought Iron, Replaced Hanger, 4 In. 195.00

Bicycle, Solar, Hall Lampco.. 70.00
Bradley & Hubbard lamps are included in the Bradley & Hubbard category
Bradley & Hubbard, Cranberry Bull's-Eye Shade, Stick & Ball Frame........................ 1000.00
Bradley & Hubbard, Student, Double, Painted Milk Glass Shades, 20 In..................... 935.00
Bradley & Hubbard, Table, Slag Glass Shade, Filigree, Brass Base, 18 In................... 522.50
Candelabrum, 2-Light, Ormolu Mounted Cut Glass, 17 In.. 520.00
Candle, Adjustable, Brass Double Candle Arm, Green Shades, 20 1/2 In....................... 385.00
Candle, Garden, Brass & Glass, Spring-Loaded, 15 1/2 In.. 195.00
Candle, Tole, Brown Japanning, Gold Painted, Snuffer, 19 1/4 In................................ 880.00
Chandelier, 2 Pierced Graduated Tiers, Crosses & Balls On Chains, 5 Ft...................... 2300.00
Chandelier, 3-Light, Roycroft, Copper, Torch-Shaped Lights, Electrified, 47 x 39 In.... 5225.00
Chandelier, 3-Light, Wrought Iron, Twisted Detail, 12 3/4 In..................................... 357.00
Chandelier, 4 Hanging Lanterns, Slag Glass, 4 Faces, Iron, Arts & Crafts, 15 x 19 In... 1300.00
Chandelier, 4 Hanging Shades, Hammered Brass, New Mica Insert, Chain, 17 x 22 In. 660.00
Chandelier, 4-Light, Arts & Crafts Style, Brass.. 55.00
Chandelier, 4-Light, Brass, Ring & Baluster Standard, 19th Century, England, 13 In.... 575.00
Chandelier, 4-Light, Candle, Forged Iron... 180.00
Chandelier, 5-Light, Empire Style, Laurel Wreath Mounts, Electrified, Bronze, 32 In... 2550.00
Chandelier, 5-Light, Scrolling Tendrils, Daum Shade, Wrought Iron, E. Brandt, 42 In.. 9200.00
Chandelier, 6-Light, Baroque, Removable Candle Arms, Brass, Electrified, 20 In......... 3450.00
Chandelier, 6-Light, Bowknot Ceiling Plate, Dresden Flowers, Bronze, 32 x 34 In....... 6325.00
Chandelier, 6-Light, Crystal, Scrolling Arms, Swags & Drops, 24 x 31 In..................... 635.00
Chandelier, 6-Light, Louis XV Style, Cage Shape, Ormolu, Cut Glass, 40 x 23 In....... 3740.00
Chandelier, 6-Light, Louis XVI Style, Foliate Branches, Ram Busts, Bronze, 30 In...... 4315.00
Chandelier, 6-Light, Louis XVI, Trumpet Corona, Faceted Orb Center, 45 x 36 In...... 2640.00
Chandelier, 6-Light, Queen Anne, Turnip Form Pendant, 15 In................................... 2875.00
Chandelier, 6-Light, Victorian, Tinted Glass, Baluster Columns, Swags, 40 In.............. 2875.00
Chandelier, 8-Light, Art Deco, Silvered Metal, Alabaster Shades, c.1930, 36 In.......... 3450.00
Chandelier, 10-Light, Prisms, Bronze... 990.00
Chandelier, 12-Light, Empire Style, Foliate Arms, Pendants, Gilt Bronze, 30 In.......... 1495.00
Chandelier, 15-Light, Regency Style, Rams Heads, Shells On Standard, 36 In............. 6900.00
Chandelier, 15-Light, Tin, Prickets Instead Of Sockets.. 17250.00
Chandelier, 16-Light, Cut Crystal, Tiered, Concave Scalloped Corona, 65 x 46 In....... 4400.00
Chandelier, 57-Light, Louis XV Style, Gilt Metal, Cut Glass, Flower Heads, 40 x 53 In. 8700.00
Chandelier, Bell Form, Heart & Vine Shade, 3 Chain Drops, 5 1/2 In........................... 460.00
Chandelier, Black Paint, 17th Century Style, 22 In.. 55.00
Chandelier, Charles X Style, 10-Light, Ormolu, Patinated Bronze, Flower Baskets....... 5750.00
Chandelier, Copper, Relief Sea Horses, Chiton Shells, E.E. Burton, c.1910, 25 3/4 In... 5750.00
Chandelier, Edgar Brandt, Iron, Scrolling Tendrils, Daum Glass, 21 x 42 In................. 9200.00
Chandelier, Elk Antlers, Wall, 1920s... 1250.00
Chandelier, French Style, Foliate Bronze Rings, Crystal Strands, Bronze, 40 In........... 450.00
Chandelier, Frosted Shades, Chrome Frame, Arrow Drop Finial, 1930, 19 1/2 In......... 330.00
Chandelier, Glass, Acorn-Shaped, Multicolored, 3 Arms, France, c.1910, 22 x 20 In.... 1380.00
Chandelier, Globe, Richmond Ship, Etched Ship's Name... 495.00
Chandelier, Hammered & Pierced Shade, Copper & Chiton, E.E. Burton, 1910, 25 In.. 5750.00
Chandelier, Louis XV Style, 9-Light, Cage, Ormolu, Rock Crystal, Glass, 24 1/2 In..... 5462.00
Chandelier, Louis XV Style, Basket Form, Quiver, Torches, Gilt Bronze, 33 In............. 2760.00
Chandelier, Neoclassical, 9-Light, Gilt-Metal, Cut & Cobalt Glass, 42 x 33 In............. 4887.00
Chandelier, Wrought Iron, Conical Shade, Openwork Flower Panels, France, 37 1/2 In. 920.00
Cigar, Genie Head, Metal... 170.00
Cigar, Gnome Head, Metal... 65.00
Cigar Lighter, Brass Barrel On Stand, Cranberry Shade, 2 Lighters, 10 3/4 In............. 220.00
Crusie, Double, Scottish, 1740s... 185.00
Electric, 3 Nude Women, Art Deco.. 250.00
Electric, 3 Nude Women, Holding Light Bulb, Art Nouveau.. 160.00
Electric, 3 Women, Art Deco, Multicolor Glass Globe Shade...................................... 150.00
Electric, 3-Light, Conical Shade, Dirk Van Erp, 22 1/2 In... 4370.00
Electric, 4 Putti Climbing Grapevine On Standard, Alabaster, 76 In............................ 6875.00
Electric, Airplane, Art Deco, Chrome, Light In Cabin & Base, 1930............................ 145.00
Electric, Anywhere, G. Von Nessen, Enameled Shade, Cantilevered Base, 1952, 14 In. 660.00
Electric, Arrow Collars & Shirts.. 150.00
Electric, Art Deco, Apple Green Glass, Satin Shade, 1930s, 10 In.............................. 145.00
Electric, Bellova, Desk, Double Knuckle, Acorn Base, Reverse Painted Shade.............. 585.00

Lamp, Electric, Dirk Van Erp, Copper, Mica, 1912

Electric, Billiard, Slag Glass 4500.00
Electric, Black Cat, Royal Hickman, 13 In. 150.00
Electric, Blackamoor, Composition, Painted, 1925, Pair 660.00
Electric, Blackamoor, Red Pantaloons, Turban, Red Pleated Paper Shade, Plaster 75.00
Electric, Brass Tripod, Milk Glass Reflector & Fringed Shade, Floor 75.00
Electric, Brass, Green Glass, Hanging, Cabriole Form Arm, Wall Mount, 13 In., Pair .. 1035.00
Electric, Brass, Iridized Green Shade, Threading, Brass Base, 6 In. 325.00
Electric, Bronze, Electrolier, Art Nouveau, c.1900 .... 1500.00
Electric, Bubble, George Nelson, Spherical Shade, Wall Mount, Howard Miller, 15 In. 220.00
Electric, Budweiser, Motion, Box 45.00
Electric, Candelabrum, 2-Light, Scrolling Branch Arms, Prisms, 1915, 8 1/2 In. 105.00
Electric, Cat, Bronze 150.00
Electric, Charlie Tuna, Figural, Composition, 1960s 95.00
Electric, Chinoiserie, Quatrefoil Stand, Floor 357.00
Electric, Classique, Reverse-Painted, Snow Scene, Arts & Crafts, 16 x 22 In. 1430.00
Electric, Cobalt Blue, Mica Flecks, Clear Shade, 14 1/2 In. 110.00
Electric, Cranberry Opalescent, Clear Pedestal Base 3750.00
Electric, Cut Glass, Cut Flowers & Leaves, Prisms 250.00
Electric, Dancer, Pink, Gold Painted Ground, Original Shade, Pair 65.00
Electric, Desk, Acorn Base, Reverse Painted Shade, Ellova 585.00
Electric, Desk, Arteluce, Square, Black Enameled, Magnetized Socket, 3 x 9 In. 525.00
Electric, Desk, Brass, Rectangular Green Overlay Shade, Adjustable, Emeralite 137.00
Electric, Desk, Leaded Green Slag, Adjustable Weighted Bronze Base, 16 In. 750.50
Electric, Desk, Polaroid, Bakelite, Aluminum, Hood Shade, W.D. Teague, c.1939, 12 In. 400.00
Electric, Desk, Woman Golfer, Swing 350.00
Electric, Dirk Van Erp, Copper, Mica, 1912 .... *Illus* 23000.00
Electric, Dirk Van Erp, Copper, Mica, Conical Shade, 22 1/2 x 19 In. 9200.00
Electric, Dirk Van Erp, Copper, Onion Shape Base, Mica, 1911, 20 In. 12650.00
Electric, Double, Partner's Desk, Elongated Green Shades 800.00
Electric, Econolite, Fountain Of Youth 55.00
Electric, Econolite, Ships 65.00
Electric, Econolite, Trains, Motion, Multiple Animation 175.00
Electric, Econolite, White Christmas Tree, Motion 55.00
Electric, Edgar Brandt, La Tentation, Bronze Cobra, Basket Base, Daum Shade, 64 In. 18150.00
Electric, Egyptian Man, Holding Ball Shade, Etched With Grapes, Silver Plate, 23 In. .. 750.00
Electric, Figural, Betsy, Gold, No Shade, Blue Ridge Pottery, Pair 875.00
Electric, Figural, Bloodhounds, Ice Bag On Head, Enesco, 10 In. 35.00
Electric, Figural, Bowl Of Flowers, Venetian Glass Petals, Leaves, Socket Center, 21 In. 44.00
Electric, Figural, Pixie, Ivory Face, Millefiori Round Shade, Marble Base, Art Nouveau 720.00
Electric, Figural, Scotty Dog, Metal, Glass Shade, 1930s 150.00
Electric, Figural, Victorian Lady, 6 Radiating Flower Lights 1980.00
Electric, Figural, Woman & Man, Sitting, With Violin, Polychrome 165.00
Electric, Fixture, Ceiling, Inverted Dome, Colored Geometric Shape, 6 1/2 x 12 1/4 In. 15.00

♦ ♦

When starting a dirty job like cleaning metal or refinishing pewter, try this trick. Rub your nails into a bar of soap. At cleanup time the dirt will easily come out from under the nail tips.

♦ ♦

Lamp, Electric, Jefferson, Reverse
Painted Shade, Landscape, 16 In.

Electric, Fixture, Hanging, Crystal Twist Drops, Brass	288.00
Electric, Floor, 3 Adjustable Arms Pivot In Sockets, Circular Metal Base, 1950s, 83 In.	880.00
Electric, Floor, Kurt Versen, Iron, Enameled Aluminum Swivel Shade, 1950s, 50 In. ...	550.00
Electric, Gustav Stickley, Hammered Copper, Original Wicker Shade, 1910	4785.00
Electric, Heat Motion, Econolite, Snow Scene, Houses, Church In Background, 1957...	95.00
Electric, Heinz, Bronze Tapered Base, Harp Support, Helmet Shade, No. 5501, 7 x 11 In.	330.00
Electric, Hula Girl, Metal	495.00
Electric, Jefferson, Cottage Scene On Shade, Pebble Finish To Glass, 16 3/4 In.	880.00
Electric, Jefferson, Reverse Painted Shade, Winter Scene, Lighted Base	750.00
Electric, Jefferson, Reverse Painted Shade, Landscape, Metal Base, Signed, 21 1/2 In..	1035.00
Electric, Jefferson, Reverse Painted, Landscape, 16 In. ....*Illus*	1750.00
Electric, Jesus Christ, Plastic, 1940s	25.00
Electric, Laconlite, Niagara Falls, Motion	50.00
Electric, Lighthouse, Art Deco, Green Globe, 1920s, 15 1/4 In.	135.00
Electric, Lightolier, Frosted Shades, 3-Tube Standard, 65 1/2 In., Pair	220.00
Electric, Limbert, Hammered Copper, Octagonal Shade, Overlaid Dutch Scene, 24 In..	6050.00
Electric, Limed & Stained Oak, Geometric Contour, Pierre Legrain, c.1925	4315.00
Electric, Little Sprout, Touch, Box	95.00
Electric, Loetz Type, Bronze & Art Glass, Pulled Leather Design, Green Patina, 16 In.	2100.00
Electric, Luminaire, Carved Glass, Peacock Feather, Onyx Base, c.1920, 17 x 12 In.	2860.00
Electric, Miller, Spelter Floral & Acanthus, Slag Glass, Hexagonal Paneled Shade, 21 In.	195.00
Electric, Mission & Prairie, Oak, Slag Glass Shade, 20 1/4 x 13 1/2 x 13 1/2 In.	660.00
Electric, Modernaire, Black, Gold Trim, Original Shade, Pair	65.00
Electric, Moe Bridges, 2-Armed Base, Reverse Painted Ducks, No. 104, 23 In.	4950.00
Electric, Moe Bridges, 2-Light, Urn Form, 4 Paw Beet, Signed, 28 In.	175.00
Electric, Moe Bridges, Mushroom, Green Landscape Shade	300.00
Electric, Moe Bridges, Reverse Painted Scene, Bronzed Base, No. 251, 16 x 21 In.	1430.00
Electric, Moe Bridges, Reverse Painted Shade, Small	650.00
Electric, Moe Bridges, Reverse Painted Shade	300.00
Electric, Moore, Cupids Base, Orchid Cactus Design Shade, 19th Century, 16 1/2 In. ...	1545.00
Electric, Motion, Blazing Fire, Deer In Foreground, Drinking Water	150.00
Electric, Motion, Budweiser, Box, 1993	40.00
Electric, Motion, Burning Fireplace, Mastercrafters	125.00
Electric, Motion, Butterflies	50.00
Electric, Motion, Campfire, Waterfall	80.00
Electric, Motion, Christmas Tree	65.00
Electric, Motion, Colonial Fountain, Montgomery	140.00
Electric, Motion, Dance At Dawn, Revolite, 1930s	125.00
Electric, Motion, Ducks Flying, Pedestal Base	175.00
Electric, Motion, Ducks Red, Trees	120.00
Electric, Motion, Forest Fire & Waterfall, 1955	58.00
Electric, Motion, Forest Fire, Roto-Vue	75.00
Electric, Motion, Fountain Of Youth	95.00
Electric, Motion, Garden Scene, Dancer, Revolite	145.00
Electric, Motion, Geese Flying, Goodman	190.00

◆◆◆◆◆◆◆◆◆◆◆◆◆◆◆◆◆◆◆◆◆◆◆◆

If you are moving, be sure to get special insurance coverage for damage to your antiques. You may want valuable pieces covered by your insurance, not by the mover's policy.

◆◆◆◆◆◆◆◆◆◆◆◆◆◆◆◆◆◆◆◆◆◆◆◆

Lamp, Electric, Paneled Slag Glass, M. Gale Bros., 23 In.

Electric, Motion, Genesee Beer, 1950s	40.00
Electric, Motion, Japanese Women At A Volcano	165.00
Electric, Motion, Lacolite Waterfall, c.1971	30.00
Electric, Motion, Merry-Go-Round, Econolite, Blue	175.00
Electric, Motion, Merry-Go-Round, Red Rotovue	140.00
Electric, Motion, Mill Scene, Econolite	75.00
Electric, Motion, Mill, Water Flowing Over Wheel	150.00
Electric, Motion, Niagara Falls, 1950s	125.00 to 250.00
Electric, Motion, Niagara Falls, Dietz, Lantern, Flash Buckeye	50.00
Electric, Motion, Niagara Style, Picture Frame, Econolite	135.00
Electric, Motion, Peace Symbols, Animated, 1960s	65.00
Electric, Motion, Santa Claus, Econolite, Box, 12 In.	75.00
Electric, Motion, Snow Falling On Country Church, Horse-Drawn Sled	225.00
Electric, Motion, Train, Econolite, 1953	175.00
Electric, Motion, Train, Econolite, 1956	100.00
Electric, Motion, Tropical Fish	88.00
Electric, Motion, Twilight, Metal, Mt. Fuji Scene	185.00
Electric, Motion, Vintage Cars	90.00
Electric, Motion, Waterfall, Men At Campfire, Goodman	75.00
Electric, Motion, Winter Snow Scene, Econolite	45.00
Electric, Motion, Yosemite Falls	85.00 to 175.00
Electric, Multicolored Slag, Turtleback Slag Panels, Griffin Base	495.00
Electric, Night-Light, Fred Flintstone, Plug In, Leviton, 1974, 4 In.	17.00
Electric, Night-Light, Figural, Dragon, Winged, Metal, 11 1/2 x 4 In.	325.00
Electric, Onondaga Period, L. & J.G. Stickley, Table Model	2400.00
Electric, Oriental Style Shade, Wicker, 70 In.	485.00
Electric, Paneled Slag Glass, M. Gale Bros., 23 In. .... *Illus*	575.00
Electric, Panther, Black, Large	36.00
Electric, Peter, Peter, Pumpkin Eater, Shade	225.00
Electric, Pharmacy, Rick Boxie, Brass, Frosted Lucite Trim, Travertine Base, 40 In.	250.00
Electric, Piano, Bakelite	25.00
Electric, Piano, Floral Design On Globe, Brass, 5 Ft.	800.00
Electric, Porch, Forged Iron, Hanging, Cutout Design, Arts & Crafts, 12 x 5 1/2 In.	358.00
Electric, Radio & Lamp Combination, Art Deco, Radio Lamp Company Of America	650.00
Electric, Salt Glazed, Geometric, 19th Century, 30 In.	110.00
Electric, Sewing, Miller, Embossed, Green Ribbed Shade, Brass	220.00
Electric, Square Shade, 4 Trapezoidal Slag Glass Panels, Mission Oak, 22 1/2 In.	575.00
Electric, Student, 2 Shades, Green Slag Glass, Wooden, Arts & Crafts, 18 In.	825.00
Electric, Student, Double, Brass, Green Shade, 24 1/2 In.	880.00
Electric, Student, Double, Manhattan, Yellow Cased Ribbed Shades	950.00
Electric, Student, Glass Shades, Maroon Case	215.00
Electric, Student, Ornate Brass, Gilt, Green Shade, White Chased, 26 In.	850.00

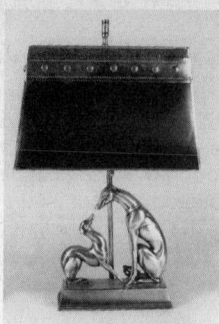

*Lamp, Electric, Table, Art Deco,
Silvered Metal, 23 1/2 In.*

*Lamp, Fairy, Thistle, Pressed
Glass, Ruby Font, England,
1880, 5 3/8 In.*

*Lamp, Electric, Wilkinson,
Leaded Glass Shade, Bronze
Foliate Base, 27 In.*

*Lamp, Electric,
Umbrella Shade,
Stag, 23 In.*

Electric, Suess, 3-Light, Tulip, Domed Shade, Bronze Base, 25 1/2 In.	3795.00
Electric, Suess, 3-Light, Wreath & Torch, Rippled & Smooth, Bronze Base, 24 1/2 In.	925.00
Electric, Table, Art Deco, Silvered Metal, 23 1/2 In. ....*Illus*	748.00
Electric, Table, Bronze, Gilt, Segar Studios, 1925, 25 In.	402.00
Electric, Table, Cut Crystal, Cranberry Flashing, Silk Shade, 22 x 41 In.	90.00
Electric, Table, Duffner & Kimberley, Square Shade, Striated Panels, Egyptians, 30 In.	6200.00
Electric, Tiffany Style, Bronze, Stained Glass Apple Blossom Shade, 18 1/2 In.	495.00
Electric, Tole Shade, Painted Bronze, 62 In.	2990.00
Electric, TV, White Panther	200.00
Electric, Umbrella Shade, Stag, 23 In. ....*Illus*	770.00
Electric, Wilkinson, Leaded Glass Shade, Bronze Foliate Base, 27 In. ....*Illus*	2875.00
Electric, Woven Wicker Base, Wide-Weave Wicker Shade, Arts & Crafts, 24 In.	302.00
Empire Style, 3 Black Caryatids, Standing, Pedestal, Bronze, Gilt, 15 1/4 In.	1100.00
Erin Brew Beer	25.00
Fairy, Blue Nailsea Shade, White Loops, Clark Base, 4 3/4 x 4 In.	180.00
Fairy, Blue Satin Finish Glass, Embossed Mold In Shade, 6 1/2 In.	480.00
Fairy, Cranberry Glass, White Nailsea Loops, 5 In.	205.00
Fairy, Figural, Bisque Cat, Pink Collar, 3 5/8 In.	60.00
Fairy, Melon Font, Clambroth Chimney, Patent 1895	160.00
Fairy, Metal Pyramid, Ironstone Insert, Glass Holder, Marked	85.00

Fairy, Owl's Head, Clarke Base, Face On Both Sides, Enamel Eyes, 4 1/2 In. 295.00
Fairy, Peacock Blue Shade, Matching Ruffled Saucer, Clarke Base 605.00
Fairy, Pink Ribbon, Satin Shade, Matching Base 300.00
Fairy, Satin Glass, Yellow, Clarke, 2 7/8 In. 125.00
Fairy, Swirl Pattern, Crystal Dripping From Rim Forming Feet, 4 1/4 In. 420.00
Fairy, Thistle, Pressed Glass, Ruby Font, England, 1880, 5 3/8 In. .... *Illus* 138.00
Fat, Tinware, Hinged Lid & Wick Support, 2 3/4 In. Pair 805.00
Fat, Trammel, Rectangular Pan, Extended, 31 In. 675.00
Fluid, Brass, Ruffled Glass Shade, Etched, Marble, 1880s 118.00
Fluid, Cut Crystal & Bronze, Hinks & Sons, Mushroom Shaped Shade, 27 In., Pair 1955.00
Fluid, Tulip Form, 2-Tier Base, 11 1/2 In, Pair 330.00
Gas, Carriage, Tin, Worn Paint, Copper, Brass, Beveled Glass, Converted, 27 In., Pair. 300.00
Gas, Cranberry Glass, Hanging 450.00
Gas, Gasolier, 4-Light, Rows Of Thumbprints, Scalloped Bobeche, 46 1/2 In. 2090.00
Gas, Table, Marble Base, Brass Columnar Stem, Green Cased Shade, 20 1/2 In. 110.00
Gasolier, 5-Light, Fluted & Frosted Globes, Electrified, Brass, 53 1/2 In. 2310.00
Girandole, Louis XIV Style, 4-Light, Gilt Metal, Rock Crystal, Bun Feet, 36 In., Pair.. 8050.00
Gone With The Wind, Etched Grape Design, Chimney, Frosted & Clear, 9 x 4 1/2 In... 45.00
Gone With The Wind, Green, Vintage, Electrified, 20th Century, 24 In......................... 110.00
Gone With The Wind, Miller 345.00
Gone With The Wind, Vaseline Glass, Fern, Gold Base, Electrified 215.00
Handel lamps are included in the Handel category
Hanging, Ansonia, Gold Herringbone Mother-Of-Pearl Shade, Brass Holder, 14 In. 1550.00
Hanging, Brass, Center Duck Painted Shade, 4 Hanging Shades, Victorian, 24 x 16 In. 225.00
Hanging, Domed Painted Shade, Prisms, Can Be Pulled Down When Needed............... 400.00
Hanging, Hall, Opalescent, Pale Coin Spots, Brass Frame, Electrified, 12 In. 110.00
Hanging, Hall, Pink With Opalescent Diamond Quilted Net, Brass Frame, Chain, 10 In. 192.00
Hanging, Harem, Brass Star Shape, Colored Glass Jewels 99.00
Hanging, Leaded Glass, Green, 15 In. 230.00
Hanging, Shade, Silvered Metal, Leaded Glass, C.R. Mackintosh, c.1900, 14 1/4 In. 5850.00
Jefferson, Rose Blossom, Hexagonal, Reverse Paint, Gilt Metal, 22 In. .... *Illus* 1380.00
Kerosene, 3-Light, Louis XVI, 3 French Horn Branches, Tole Shade, 26 3/4 In........... 6325.00
Kerosene, Adams & Westlake Co., Cast Bronze & Sheet Bronze, 20 1/2 In. 225.00
Kerosene, Aladdin, Washington Drape, Chimney, Model B 100.00
Kerosene, Angle, Clear Elbow & Petal Top Globe, Copper, Bottom Screw, Single....... 225.00
Kerosene, Avalon, Faience, Eagle's Heads, Faces For Feet, Double Burner, 2 Piece 375.00
Kerosene, Banquet, 2-Light, Silver Plate, Hanks & Birmingham, England, 7 12 In....... 1320.00
Kerosene, Banquet, 3 Tiers, Multicolored Floral, Victor Burner, 17 In......................... 100.00
Kerosene, Banquet, Octagonal Base, Gilded Stem, Amber Font, Brass Collar, 15 1/2 In. 50.00
Kerosene, Bopeep With Lamb, Marble Base 275.00
Kerosene, Bronze, Devil Face, Flanked By 2 Winged Figures 1495.00
Kerosene, Bronze, Figural, Sphinx, Gilt, Marble Base 195.00
Kerosene, Bronze, Striated Panels, Majorelle, c.1900, 21 1/2 In................................. 3450.00
Kerosene, Carriage, Iron, Clear Front, Red Lens In Back, C.T. Ham, 1905, 9 x 3 1/2 In. 35.00
Kerosene, Carriage, Tin, Black Paint, Brass Trim, Nickel Plate, 15 In., Pair 100.00
Kerosene, Coin Pattern 150.00
Kerosene, Double Arch, Flint... 60.00
Kerosene, Finger Hold, Frosted Heart Pattern, Clear Font, Green, 7 In. 950.00
Kerosene, Finger, Blue Opalescent, Windows Pattern 770.00
Kerosene, Finger, Nickel Plated Saucer, Metal 105.00
Kerosene, Gilt Bronze, Raoul Larche, Siot-Decauville Foundry, 13 1/2 In. 2990.00
Kerosene, Girandole, 3-Light, Brass, Marble Base, Prisms, 22 1/2 In., Pair 605.00
Kerosene, Green Opaque, 10 1/4 In.. *Illus* 495.00
Kerosene, Hanging, Brass, Clear Font, Milk Glass Shade, Chrysanthemums, 14 In. 193.00
Kerosene, Mercury Glass Stem, White Opaque Cut To Clear, Cast-Iron Base, 10 3/8 In. 220.00
Kerosene, Monks, Keg Of Spirits, Ball Shade, Electrified, 29 In............................ *Illus* 3410.00
Kerosene, Nailsea Type Shade, Base & Chimney, Crystal Feet, 11 3/8 In. 2970.00
Kerosene, Nellie Bly, Horner Burner, Pink Floral On Base & Shade, 9 In..................... 175.00
Kerosene, Painted Violets & Pansies, Milk Glass, 7 In.. 40.00
Kerosene, Peanut Pattern, Clear Glass, Brass, Beaded Chimney, 10 In......................... 65.00
Kerosene, Piano, Silver Plated, Etched Glass Shade, Late 19th Century, 18 In. 205.00
Kerosene, Prince Edward, Yellow, Clear Base, 9 3/4 In.. *Illus* 605.00
Kerosene, Rib Band & Loop, Milk Glass Base.. 80.00

Lamp, Kerosene, Prince Edward,
Yellow, Clear Base, 9 3/4 In.

Lamp, Kerosene, Green
Opaque, 10 1/4 In.

Lamp, Jefferson, Rose Blossom, Hexagonal,
Reverse Paint, Gilt Metal, 22 In.

Lamp, Kerosene, Monks, Keg Of Spirits,
Ball Shade, Electrified, 29 In.

Kerosene, Sheaf Cut Font, Goat Head Tripod, Marble Foot, Electrified, 10 1/2 In.	1500.00
Kerosene, Sheldon Swirl, Green Opalescent	550.00
Kerosene, Store, Hanging, Nickel Plated Brass Font, The Rochester	137.50
Kerosene, Student, Brass, Crystal Chimney, Green Porcelain Shade, 21 In.	425.00
Kerosene, Student, Brass, Green Glass Shade, Cased	175.00
Kerosene, Table, Marble Base, Glass Font, Floral Decorated Porcelain Column, Pair	95.00
Kerosene, Table, Rochester, Green Ribbed Shade, Nickel	170.00
Kerosene, Victorian, Mushroom Beaded Shade, Marked Success, P.L.B. & Co., 21 In.	345.00
Kerosene, White Baroque Base, Flint 3-Mold Font, Sandwich Glass	180.00
Lace Maker's, Freeblown, 2 Part, 10 1/2 In.	440.00
Metal & Slag Glass Top, Geometric Shade, Square, Arts & Crafts, 23 x 12 In.	800.00
Miner's, Autolite, Clip-On	25.00
Miner's, Carbide, With Cap, Guys Dropper, Box	25.00
Miner's, Cast Steel, Brass Chicken Finial, Hanger, 8 In.	250.00
Miner's, Husson, No. 6.	125.00
Miner's, Sticking Tommy	35.00
Miner's, Winchester	55.00
Newel Post, Bronze Griffin, Victorian, 35 In.	4250.00
Nude, Sitting, Next To Globe, Art Deco, 1920s	250.00
Oil, Agate, Spotted, New England Glass Company	4895.00
Oil, Banquet, Ball Shade, Hunting Dogs & Duck, 21 In.	1400.00
Oil, Banquet, Bristol Glass, Enamel, White Stem & Font, Electrified, 28 1/2 In.	165.00
Oil, Banquet, Opalescent Striped, Ruffled Shade, Brass Base & Stem, 21 1/4 In.	750.00

Lamp, Parlor, Ball Shade, Stag & Wolf, 27 In.

Oil, Banquet, Windmills & Sailboats On White Shade, Parker, 29 In. 990.00
Oil, Blown Font, 4-Step Base, Brass Burner, 7 1/4 In. 220.00
Oil, Brass Plated, Opalescent Globe, Electrified 75.00
Oil, Brass, Belted Ball Font, Turned Standard, c.1840, 10 1/2 In., Pair 489.00
Oil, Brass, Cranberry Glass Font, Victorian, 25 In. 247.00
Oil, Brass, Red Painted, Etched Glass Globular Shade, 19 1/2 In. 165.00
Oil, Bronze, Figural, Bacchus Holding, Coiled Serpent, Rampant Lions, 34 In. 2200.00
Oil, Candy Stripe, Crystal Feet, 8 In. 4125.00
Oil, Cherub Heads Metal Base, Floral Shade, Prisms Round Edge, Victorian 360.00
Oil, Cranberry Opalescent, Clear Pedestal Base, 7 1/2 In. 3740.00
Oil, Fern & Palm Font, Upper Section Frosted, Cast-Iron Base, 10 In. 240.00
Oil, Grecian Key, Miniature 125.00
Oil, Hand, Flat, Coin Dot, Cranberry Opalescent, No Chimney, 3 In. 1050.00
Oil, Ice Skater, Dated 1864-1867 .... 625.00
Oil, Krinkel & Beaded Drape 120.00
Oil, Maroon Ball Shade, Roses, Lily-Of-The-Valley, Gargoyle Legs, Electrified, 21 In. 1000.00
Oil, Metal, Painted Floral Design, Milk Glass, Electrified, 21 In. 99.00
Oil, Molded Font, Ruby Cut To Clear Overlay Standard, Impressed, 13 1/2 In. 402.00
Oil, Monot Stumpf, Pantin, Swirl Base, Square Shade, 10 In. 850.00
Oil, Nutmeg Burner, Owl Form Globes, White Milk Glass, 19th Century, 8 In. 1575.00
Oil, Oval Miter, Brass Stem, Marble Base, Flint 200.00
Oil, P & G Duplex, Brass, Pink & White Slag Glass Panels, Matching Shade, 27 1/2 In. 1634.00
Oil, Parlor, Ball Shade, 4 Monks Painted Scene, 29 1/2 In. 3100.00
Oil, Parlor, Ball Shade, Stag & Wolf, 27 In. 1375.00
Oil, Parlor, Umbrella Shade, Stags & Flying Ducks, Yellow Ground, Electrified, 23 In. 700.00
Oil, Pink Opalescent, Applied Green Glass Leaves 2475.00
Oil, Ribbed Forget-Me-Not, Flint 125.00
Oil, Santa Claus, White Milk Glass, 9 1/2 In. 1650.00
Oil, Shade, Cranberry Diamond-Quilted 130.00
Oil, Shade, Cranberry Hobnail, 10 In. 270.00
Oil, Shade, Etched Crown, Windmills & Castles 140.00
Oil, Skeleton, White Bisque, Green Glass Eyes, 6 3/4 In. 550.00
Oil, Solar, Classical, Urn Shaped Reservoir, Marble, Ring With Spear Prisms, 12 1/4 In. 715.00
Oil, Spelter, Cold Painted Men Discussing Carpets, European, 9 1/2 In. 230.00
Oil, Student, Double, Plume & Atwood, Green Shades 1195.00
Oil, Student, Lincoln Log Style, Milk Glass Shade 275.00
Oil, Student, Pink Swirl Shade & Font, 1850-1860 .... 1450.00
Oil, Student, Wall Mount, White Slant Shade, Brass, Shade-6 In. 260.00
Oil, Student, White Milk Glass Shade, New Vestal, E.M. & Co., Brass, 20 1/4 In. 440.00
Oil, Verse, Little Biddy O'Toole & Pig, Porcelain, c.1880 .... 300.00
Organ, Rope Twist Post, Etched Ball Shade With Dolphins, Cast Brass 1050.00
Pairpoint lamps are in the Pairpoint category
Parlor, Ball Shade, Stag & Wolf, 27 In. .... *Illus* 1513.00
Peg, Blue Satin Shades & Fonts, Brass Base, Ribbed, 15 In., Pair 1480.00

Peg, Pink Shading Top To Bottom, Swirled Rib Pattern, Pleated Shade, 11 1/4 In. 495.00
Perfume, Floral & Gilt Design, Porcelain, H. Berger, 6 3/4 In. 75.00
Perfume, Glass Eyes, Germany 145.00
Perfume, Richard Hudnut, Reverse Glass Panels 2500.00
Pincushion Doll, Boudoir, Parasol, Dress, Hands Away 75.00
Rush, Wrought Iron, Twisted, Turned Oak Base, 15 1/2 In., Pair 385.00
Rushlight, Holder, Iron, Turned Wooden Base, 6 In. 385.00
Sconce, 1-Light, Cartouche Shaped Plate, Leaf Cast Branch, Brass, 8 In., Pair 8050.00
Sconce, 1-Light, Louis XV, Pierced Foliate, Flowerhead On Arm, 14 1/2 In., Pair 4600.00
Sconce, 2-Arm, Ribbon Back Plate, Tassel Tips, Porcelain Flowers, 18 x 10 In. 5225.00
Sconce, 2-Light, Brass, Mirror Back, Urn & Dolphin Cartouche, 22 In. 99.00
Sconce, 2-Light, Brass, Scrolled Arm, 1 Socket, 9 In., Pair 357.00
Sconce, 2-Light, Gilt Metal & Cut Glass, Pierced Back Plate, 24 1/2 In., Pair 2706.00
Sconce, 2-Light, Louis XVI Style, Dore Bronze, 12 1/2 In., Pair 375.00
Sconce, 2-Light, Porcelain Floral Portrait Plate, Gilt Metal, 7 x 10 In., Pair 315.00
Sconce, 3-Light, Brass, Lyre Back, 10 In. 137.00
Sconce, 3-Light, Directoire Style, Gilt Metal, Petal Nozzles, 25 x 9 1/4 In., Pair 770.00
Sconce, 3-Light, Louis XVI, Foliate Back Plate, Scrolled Branches, 29 1/2 In., 4 Piece 8625.00
Sconce, 3-Light, Mask Backplate, Foliate Branches, 1880s, 15 In., Pair 5750.00
Sconce, 3-Light, Napoleon III, Fluted & Swag Standard, Love Birds, Bronze, Pair 4312.00
Sconce, Baroque, Shells & Scrolls, 18th Century, Flemish, Pair 1870.00
Sconce, Bride's, Hand Cut & Hammered Brass, 2 Tin Holders, c.1820, 13 3/4 In. 330.00
Sconce, Candle, 3-Light, Bronze, Rococo, Floral Wax Pan, 9 x 13 In., Pair 605.00
Sconce, Candle, Mirror Fragments In Frame, Tin, Brass Medallion, 11 In., Pair 307.00
Sconce, Crimped Circular Crests, Tooled Designs, Tin, 13 1/2 In., Pair 440.00
Sconce, Gilt Carved Cupid, Pair 825.00
Sconce, Louis XVI Style, 3-Light, Female Head Over Swags, Bronze, 20 In. 1035.00
Sconce, Louis XVI Style, Lyre & Urn Shape Design, Italy, 39 x 14 1/2 In. 100.00
Sconce, Owl Center, Copper, John Pearson, c.1895, 15 1/2 x 11 In. 632.00
Sconce, Silver Plate, Scrolled Arms, Teardrop Prisms, Pair 495.00
Sconce, Wall, 2-Arm, Wrought Iron & Alabaster, Edgar Brandt, c.1925, 16 In. 3450.00
Skater's, Brass, Clear Globe, 7 In. 154.00
Skater's, Tin, Clear Globe, 7 In. 100.00
Tiffany lamps are listed in the Tiffany category
Torchere, 6 Candle Nozzles, Wrought Iron, Electrified, 60 In. 85.00
Torchere, Art Deco, Alabaster Shade, Wrought Iron Base, 74 In. 805.00
Torchere, Empire Style, Brass & Patinated Metal, 71 In. 975.00
Torchere, Griffin & Foliate Design, Art Glass Shades, Bronze Stand, 71 In., Pair 860.00
Torchere, Molded Mask & Entwined Scrolling Standard, Gilt Metal, 32 In. 110.00
Torchere, Scrolling, Alabaster Shade, R. Subes, Wrought Iron, 1925, 5 Ft. 9 3/4 In. 7762.00
Torchere, Stylized Palm Tree, Gilt Plaster, Emile Terry, c.1935, 6 Ft., Pair 5750.00
Vapo Cresolene, Box With Contents, 1910 .... 125.00
Wax Or Oil, Ceiling Fixture, Continental, Etched & Hand Blown, 16 In. 650.00
Whale Oil, Almond Thumbprint, Flint Baroque Base, Sandwich Glass 400.00
Whale Oil, Blown Font, Hollow Stem, Wafered To Waterfall Base, 12 In. 400.00
Whale Oil, Blown Font, Waterfall Base, Flint 250.00
Whale Oil, Brass Collar, 4-Lobed Base, 12 In. 200.00
Whale Oil, Brass, Acorn Font, U.S., c.1800, Pair 247.50
Whale Oil, Brass, Acorn Font, U.S., c.1825, Pair 165.00
Whale Oil, Brass, Owls, Ducks, Swans & Snails, 3 Chains, 19th Century, 23 1/2 In. 138.00
Whale Oil, Brass, Saucer Base, U.S., c.1800, Pair 412.50
Whale Oil, Brass, Wm. H. Webb, Warren, Maine, c.1805, Pair 1155.00
Whale Oil, Bull's Eye & Fleur-De-Lis, Brass Stem, Black Base, Flint 180.00
Whale Oil, Double Marble Base 525.00
Whale Oil, Flint & Sandwich Glass, Shade, Electrified 200.00
Whale Oil, Flint, Acanthus, 13 In. 300.00
Whale Oil, Freeblown, 8 In. 1350.00
Whale Oil, Glass, Paneled Font, Knopped Standard, Square Base, 1850, 10 1/2 In. 110.00
Whale Oil, Hexagonal Base, Ellipse Font, Pewter Collar, 7 7/8 In. 110.00
Whale Oil, Pewter, Yale & Curtis, c.1858 .... 650.00
Whale Oil, Sandwich Star, Burner, Flint 275.00
Whale Oil, Sickroom, Nurse's 140.00
Whale Oil, Thumbprint, Amethyst 850.00

Whale Oil, Tulip, Flint 200.00
Whale Oil, Waterfall Base, Pewter Burner, Blown Font 250.00

LANTERNS are a special type of lighting device. They have a light source, usually a candle, totally hidden inside the walls of the lantern. Light is seen through holes or glass sections.

Boat, Adirondack, Reflector, Ham Co., No. 20, Clip-On, 1900, 15 In. 100.00
Brass, Electrified, Beveled Glass Shade 55.00
Buggy, Rayo, Red Glass 20.00
Candle, Horn Lights, Ring Handle, Tin, 16 In. 300.00
Candle, Lace Maker's, 19th Century, 14 1/2 In. 175.00
Candle, New England, Wooden, 18th Century 995.00
Candle, Tin, Ring Handle, 18 In. 75.00
Carriage, Brass, 1 With 2 Green Lenses, 1 With 2 Red Lenses, 19th Century, 12 In., Pair 55.00
Coach, Kerosene, Brass, Rectangular, 12 In. 105.00
Dietz, Copper Font, Steel, 19 In. 220.00
Dietz, King Fire, Swing-Up Cage, Brass, 19 In. 355.00
Dietz, King, Tin & Copper 165.00
Dietz, Police 185.00
Dietz, Queen, Brass 645.00
Dietz, Ruby Red Glove, Nickel Plating, Brass, 19 In. 355.00
Dietz, Seagrave, Brass, 19 In. 240.00
Dietz, Tin, Buggy, Shale Oil Burner 95.00
Dietz, Tubular, Square Tubes, Slide Cage, Patent Jan. 2, 1889, 19 In. 425.00
Hall, Blown Glass, Etched Stylized Fruit, Smoke Bell, Brass Frame & Chains, 16 In. ... 825.00
Hall, Classical, Floral Etched Glass Globe, Gilt Brass Fittings, c.1840, 14 1/2 In. 865.00
Horn, Sheet Iron, English, c.1760, 12 1/2 In. 335.00
Iron, Pierced Sides, Rectangular, Oriental, 12 In. 180.00
Kerosene, C.T. Ham Mfg.Co., No. 8 Tubular Square Lamp, Pat.1886, 24 1/2 In. 150.00
Kerosene, Red Globe, Warsaw, New York 65.00
Newel Post, Copper & Glass, Gustav Stickley, No. 702, 21 1/2 In. 3680.00
Onion, Squatty Shade, Tin Whale Oil Burner, Crystal Font, 8 1/2 In. 320.00
Painted Panels, Nobles, Hexagonal Base, Chinese, Porcelain, 12 1/2 In. 285.00
Punched Tin, Revere Type, Ring Handle, 13 In. 195.00
Punched Tin, Revere, Ring Handle, 14 In. 150.00
Punched Tin, Ring Handle, 13 1/2 In. 160.00
Tin, Bull's-Eye Lens, Peter Gray & Sons, Removable Font, Kerosene, 8 1/2 In. 115.00
Tin, Clear-Blown Globe, Partial Stamped With Sangs, Ring Handle, 11 In. 385.00

LE VERRE FRANCAIS is one of the many types of cameo glass made in France. The glass was made by the C. Schneider factory in Epinay-sur-Seine from 1920 to 1933. It is a mottled glass, usually decorated with floral designs, and bears the incised signature *Le Verre Francais.*

Lamp, Cameo, Elephants, Palm Trees, Wrought Iron, 12-In. Shade, 21 In. 9350.00
Vase, Gourd Shape, Red With Green Mottling, Applied Dripping, 8 1/2 In. 1300.00
Vase, Stylized Architectural Design, Band Of Cats, c.1925, 18 1/2 In. 4312.00

LEATHER is tanned animal hide and it has been used to make decorative and useful objects for centuries. Leather objects must be carefully preserved with proper humidity and oiling or the leather will deteriorate and crack. This damage cannot be repaired.

Animal, Rhinoceros, Molded, Brown, 9 In. 55.00
Animal, Tiger, Molded, Brown, 10 In. 55.00
Belt, Black, 10 In., Size 6 & 6 1/2 .... 4.00
Belt, Tan, Cut, Size 6 1/2 In. 8.00
Bull Whip, Rawhide 95.00
Case, Make Up, Brass Snap Closures, Mae West On Front, 10 x 14 1/2 In. 1840.00
Case, Travel, Cosmetic Jars, Perfumes, Compacts, Cara Nome 125.00
Gauntlets, Small Butterfly On Cuff, Multicolored Flowers 500.00
Gloves, Buffalo Bill Cody's, Beaded Design Of Bumble Bee, c.1920 .... 6000.00
Holster, Gaskills Nonpullout, Patent 1914 .... 150.00
Luggage Set, Arthur Gilmore, N.Y., 4 Piece 192.50
Purse, Floral Design, Spanish Steerhide, Fitted, Arts & Crafts, 5 1/2 x 10 In. 38.00

◆◆◆◆◆◆◆◆◆◆◆◆◆◆◆◆◆◆◆◆◆◆◆◆

Check the metal strips holding any heavy wall-hung
shelves. After a few years,
the shelf holder may develop
'creep' and gradually bend
away from the wall.

◆◆◆◆◆◆◆◆◆◆◆◆◆◆◆◆◆◆◆◆◆◆◆◆

Leeds, Pitcher, Silver Luster, Lion Pattern,
England, c.1813

Purse, Tooled Design, Sailing Ship, Spanish Steerhide, Arts & Crafts, 4 1/2 x 6 In.	77.00
Saddle, Cavalry, McCullen	275.00
Saddle, Fork, Cheyenne Cantle, 15 1/2-In. Seat, Original Lapaderos, 1890	1100.00
Saddle, Hamley & Co., c.1915	750.00
Saddle, Pony, J.C. Higgins	95.00
Saddle Bag, Cowboy's, Angora Hair Cover	450.00

LEEDS pottery was made at Leeds, Yorkshire, England, from 1774 to 1878. Most Leeds ware was not marked. Early Leeds pieces had distinctive twisted handles with a greenish glaze on part of the creamy ware. Later ware often had blue borders on the creamy pottery.   **LEEDS POTTERY,**

Bowl, Oval, 8 Pierced Side Panels, Floral Garland, c.1800, 8 In.	357.00
Chamberstick, 8 Pierced Octagonal Panels, c.1800, 2 1/4 In., Pair	330.00
Creamer, Gaudy Floral, Pearlware, 3 5/8 In.	192.00
Dish, Creamware, Reticulated Border, Shell Corners, Oval, 3 Spiral Feet, 8 1/2 x 7 In.	302.00
Figurine, Psyche & Cupid, Dolphin, Pearlware, Impressed, 7 In.	50.00
Jug, Puzzle, Polychrome, 19th Century, 6 3/4 In.	517.00
Mug, Pearlware, Flowers	160.00
Pitcher, Silver Luster, Lion Pattern, England, c.1813 ....*Illus*	3105.00
Plate, Eagle Center, Green Feather Edge, Pearlware, 8 In.	495.00
Plate, John The Baptist, Creamware, Shaped Feather Edge, 10 In.	330.00
Plate, Multicolored House, Sponged Trees, 6 1/2 In.	325.00
Plate, Oriental Transfer, Pearlware, 8 1/4 In.	50.00
Platter, Blue & White, 17 In.	65.00
Platter, Eagle With Blue Feather, Polychrome, 19th Century, 16 1/4 In.	1495.00
Sauce Boat, Raised Bust Of George Washington & Eagle, Blue Ground, 4 x 6 In.	412.50
Sauce Tureen, Underplate, 19th Century	242.00
Tea Caddy, Creamware, Floral Crested Cover, Tree, Vines, 18th Century, 8 x 5 In.	1100.00
Tea Caddy, Creamware, Lion Top Cover, Cherub Corners, Inscription, 1796, 6 In.	1045.00

LEFTON is a mark found on many pieces. The Geo. Zoltan Lefton Company has imported porcelains to be sold in America since 1940. The firm is still in business. The company mark has changed through the years; but because marks have been used for long periods of time, they are of little help in dating an object.

Bank, Hubert Lion	45.00
Bank, Leprechaun	30.00
Bank, Owl	25.00
Bank, Snail	25.00
Cake Topper, Bride & Groom	22.50
Cookie Jar, Bluebird	300.00
Cookie Jar, Cat's Head, Blue	90.00 to 145.00
Cookie Jar, Winking Santa Claus	235.00

Creamer, 2 Cats, Black Tips, 4 x 5 1/2 In. 40.00
Figurine, Dog, St. Bernard 35.00
Figurine, Frog 10.00
Figurine, William & Mary, Pastel Hand Painted, Bisque, 11 In., Pair 95.00
Head Vase, Woman, Black Hat, Paper Label, 5 1/4 In. 65.00
Salt & Pepper, Bluebird 40.00
Salt & Pepper, Christmas Tree 10.00
Salt & Pepper, Owl ....8.00 to 20.00
Sugar & Creamer, Bluebird 75.00
Teapot, Cat 35.00
Toby Mug, George Washington 30.00
Vase, Roses, Vines, Hand Painted, 6 In. 26.00

LEGRAS was founded in 1864 by Auguste Legras at St. Denis, France. It is best known for cameo glass and enamel-decorated glass with Art Nouveau designs. Legras merged with Pantin in 1920 and became the Verreries et Cristalleries de St. Denis et de Pantin Reunies.

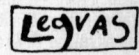

Bowl, Cameo Cut Leaf Clusters, Amber, Green, Enameled, 7 In. 786.50
Compote, Tricon, Cameo Leaf Design, Signed, 5 1/4 x 7 1/2 In. 575.00
Vase, Cameo, Bowling Pin Shape, Amethyst Fountain, Stippled Lavender, 14 x 5 In. ... 950.00
Vase, Cameo, Bulbous, Frosted Mauve, Cherry Blossoms & Branches, 8 1/2 In. 495.00
Vase, Cameo, Woodland Scene, Gray, Flaring Round Base, 22 In. 1155.00
Vase, Etched Apple Blossoms, Maroon Enameling, Signed, 8 In. 287.50
Vase, Etched Mistletoe & Vines, Amber, 7 In. 550.00
Vase, Etched Surface, Enameled Waterfront Scene, Signed, 3 1/2 x 5 In. 315.00
Vase, Landscape, 10 In. 600.00
Vase, Lavender Flowers, Crystal Ground, 13 1/4 In. 1650.00
Vase, Maple Leaves, Purple Shades, Frosted Ground, Signed, 15 1/4 In. 522.00
Vase, Sea Grasses & Shells, Overlaid Beige Carnelian, Signed, 6 1/4 In. 402.50
Vase, Stick, Forest Scene, Green Foliaged Trees, Signed, 10 1/2 In. 800.00
Vase, Wisteria, Tricorn Stick Form, Signed, 13 In. 747.50
Vase, Woodland, 8 In. 550.00

LENOX is the name of a porcelain maker. Walter Scott Lenox and Jonathan Cox founded the Ceramic Art Company in Trenton, New Jersey, in 1889. In 1906, Lenox left and started his own company called *Lenox*. The company makes a porcelain that is similar to Irish Belleek. The marks used by the firm have changed through the years and collectors prefer the earlier examples. Related pieces may also be listed in the Ceramic Art Co. category.

Basket, Handle, 24K Gold Trim, Signed, 2 1/2 x 6 In. 50.00
Bouillon Cup, Pierced Sterling Holder, Loop Handles, 12 Piece 330.00
Bowl, Vegetable, Wheat, Oval 38.00
Breakfast Set, Mt. Vernon, Made For Tiffany, 11 Piece 195.00
Candlestick, Art Modern, Green Mark 35.00
Candlestick, Scalloped Cuff, Gold Trim, 4 1/2 In., Pair 60.00
Chocolate Set, Golden Wreath, 13 Piece 275.00
Cup & Saucer, Bellevue, Green 35.00
Cup & Saucer, Golden Wreath 20.00
Cup & Saucer, Harvest ....10.00 to 125.00
Cup & Saucer, Laurent 95.00
Cup & Saucer, Wheat 18.00
Dinner Service, Golden Wreath, 58 Piece 550.00
Dinner Set, Moonspun, 53 Piece 920.00
Dinner Set, Pine, 85 Piece 1200.00
Dinner Set, Rose, 80 Piece 1500.00
Dinner Set, Springdale, 20 Piece 280.00
Dinner Set, Westbury, 56 Piece 330.00
Dinner Set, Westchester, Service For 8, 43 Piece 1095.50
Figurine, Swan, Peach & Gold, Green Wreath, 4 1/2 x 3 1/4 In. 30.00
Goblet, Wine, Impromptu, Amber 4.00
Loving Cup, Silver Overlay, 3 Handles, Signed, 7 3/8 In. 1650.00
Plate, Boehm Bird, 1970, Wood Thrush, 10 1/2 In. 175.00
Plate, Boehm Bird, 1972, Mountain Bluebird, 10 1/2 In. 65.00

Plate, Cobalt Blue & Gilt Border, Ivory Ground, 10 1/2 In., 8 Piece	160.00
Plate, Dinner, Green, Cream, Eggshell, Elaborate Gold Trim, 10 1/2 In., 18 Piece	1150.00
Plate, Dinner, Wheat	25.00
Plate, Oak Leaf, 10 1/2 In., 12 Piece	230.00
Plate, Salad, Carolina	75.00
Platter, Noblesse, 13 1/2 In.	175.00
Platter, Noblesse, 16 In.	220.00
Platter, Peachtree, 13 In.	65.00
Platter, Rose, 13 1/2 In.	148.00
Salt & Pepper, Lennie	45.00
Service For 12, Ivory, Encrusted Gold Rims, 38 Piece	550.00
Soup, Cream, Bellaire, Underplate	20.00
Soup, Dish, Belvedere	55.00
Soup, Dish, Washington, Wakefield	30.00
Stein, 3 Boys Playing Football, Signed, 5 1/2 In.	325.00
Tea Strainer & Drain, Rose, Lavender Mark, c.1910, 6 In.	137.50
Teapot, White Silver Overlay, Finial, 3 1/2 x 7 In.	135.00
Tile, Tea, Silver Overlay, White, Round, 4 1/2 In.	190.00
Urn, Coral Glazed Body, Ovoid, Curled Handles, 14 In.	115.00
Vase, Cobalt Blue, Sterling Overlay, 4 In.	135.00
Vase, Ivory, Flared, Fluted, Scalloped Neck, Bulbous, Green Wreath, 8 In., Pair	52.00
Vase, Roses, W. Morley, 6 In.	165.00
Vase, Silver Overlay, Green, 5 3/4 In.	770.00
Vase, Swan Handles, Green Mark, 10 3/4 In., Pair	185.00

LETTER OPENERS have been used since the eighteenth century. Ivory and silver were favored by the well-to-do. In the late nineteenth century, the letter opener was popular as an advertising giveaway and many were made of metal or celluloid. Brass openers with figural handles were also popular.

Brass, Abstract, Green & Red Enamel, Arts & Crafts, 12 In.	110.00
Brass, Knights Insurance Co.	10.00
Brass, Sword Shape, Hammered, E.T.C. Fish, 9 In.	88.00
Bulldog Head, Wooden, Carved, 19th Century	138.00
Cartier, Engraved, Silk Padded Box, 5 1/2 In.	535.00
Celluloid, Diamond Disc Record, Edigon	45.00
Celluloid, Doll Figure On End	75.00
Copper, Etched Pinecone Design, Arts & Crafts, 9 1/2 In.	55.00
Knitting Co., With Pocket Knife	15.00
MacKenzie Candy, Solinger, With Cigar Cutter	85.00
Neptune Seafood, Fish Logo, Imitation Ivory, 6 In.	29.50
Owl, Bronzed Handle	38.00
Peruvian Sun God Handle, Sterling Silver	95.00
Phillips Milk Of Magnesia, Metal, With Magnifier	17.00
Plastic, Fuller Brush, Salesman Figure	65.00
San Francisco Golden Gate International Exposition	25.00
Silver Plate, Stieff	30.00
Squirrel, Carved Wood, Japan	14.00
Uneeda Crackers, Kid In Raincoat	895.00

LIBBEY Glass Company has made many types of glass since 1888, including the cut glass and tablewares that are collected today. The stemwares of the 1930s and 1940s are once again in style. The Toledo, Ohio, firm was purchased by Owens-Illinois in 1935 and is still working under the name *Libbey* as a division of that company. Additional pieces may be listed under Amberina, Cut Glass, and Maize.

Bowl, Circular Design, Star Flowers & Fans, 9 x 4 1/4 In.	357.50
Bowl, Cut Glass, Fan & Hobstar, Brilliant Period, 8 In.	172.50
Bowl, Diana, Signed, 8 1/2 x 3 1/2 In.	395.00
Bowl, Fruit, Strawberries & Leaves, Signed, 2 1/2 x 9 In.	350.00
Bowl, Nut, Lovebirds, Cherry Blossoms & Ferns, Cut Allover, Signed, 5 1/4 In.	145.00
Bowl, Regis, 8 In.	230.00
Champagne, Squirrel, 6 In.	200.00
Claret, Bear	165.00

Compote, Cut Glass, Star & Diamond, Notched Edge, 11 In., Pair 488.75
Compote, Rolled Rim, Crystal, Signed, 7 In. 225.00
Compote, Star & Diamond, 11 In. 488.00
Cordial, Green Knob, 6 Piece 300.00
Cordial, Greyhound 175.00
Cruet, Harvard, Triple Notch Handle, Triform Spout 125.00
Decanter, Kimberly, Double Gooseneck, Cut Stopper, 12 1/2 In. 895.00
Decanter, Nailhead Diamond In Band Of Circles, Steeple Stopper, 13 In. 245.00
Decanter, Whiskey, Glass Stopper, Signed, 11 1/2 In. 135.00
Dish, Hobstar, 9 In. 285.00
Dish, Hobstar, Notched Panels, Shallow, 9 In. 287.50
Goblet, Cat 200.00
Jar, Empress, Signed, 8 3/4 In. 1295.00
Nappy, Cut Glass, Handle, Signed 145.00
Nappy, Shooting Star, Sawtooth Rim, Signed, 7 In. 75.00
Pitcher, Brilliant Period, Signed, 8 3/4 In. 275.00
Pitcher, Cut Glass, Bulbous, Signed, 9 In. 260.00
Pitcher, Wine, Kimberly, Cut Glass, 10 In. 725.00
Platter, Ice Cream, Star Center, 12 In. 405.00
Platter, Ice Cream, Star Center, Cut Glass, Brilliant Period, 12 In. 402.50
Punch Bowl, Stand, Repeating Star & Zipper, Repeated On Base, 11 x 12 In. 632.00
Relish, Cut Glass, Brilliant Cut, Starburst & Hobstar, Scalloped 200.00
Salt & Pepper, Cut Glass, Hobstars & Sunburst, Sterling Tops 250.00
Sherbet, Rabbit, Low 75.00
Sherbet, Silhouette Pattern, Black Rabbit Stem, Signed .... 110.00 to 138.00
Sherbet, Squirrel, Footed, 4 In. 125.00
Sherry, Monkey 145.00
Tray, Anita, Oval, 12 x 8 In. 385.00
Tray, Ellsmere, Signed, 12 In. 2650.00
Tray, Ice Cream, Band Of Hobstar, Rayed Hobstar Bottom, Signed, 13 1/2 In. 1210.00
Tumbler, Cane Wheat, Sunbursts, 11 Piece 269.50
Vase, Amberina, 10 In. 200.00
Vase, Cherry Blossoms, Cut Glass, Flared, 4 In. 50.00
Vase, Cut, Flowers, Flutes, c.1910, 12 In. 295.00
Vase, Floral & Ovals Of Lily-Of-The-Valley, Scalloped Rim, Label, 13 1/4 In. 220.00
Vase, Fuschia Flared Rim, Amberina Base, Signed, 11 1/2 In. 1250.00
Vase, Intaglio Cut Peacock, Signed, 12 In. 150.00
Vase, Paperweight Base, Floral Cutting, Signed, 4 In. 85.00
Vase, Turquoise Zipper Pattern, On Clear, Signed, 10 In. 425.00
Wine, Black Kangaroo Stem 110.00
Wine, Black Monkey Stem 110.00
Wine, Frosted Kangaroo Stem 110.00

LIGHTERS for cigarettes and cigars are collectible. Cigarettes became popular in the late nineteenth century, and with the cigarette came matches and cigarette lighters. All types of lighters are collected, from solid gold to the first of the recent disposable lighters. Most examples found were made after 1940.

Airplane, Art Deco, Chrome .... 40.00 to 60.00
Airplane, Occupied Japan, Chrome 200.00
Aladdin Lamp, Occupied Japan, Metal 25.00
Ashtray & Cigarette Holder, Orange Glass, Gold Dust, 3 Piece Set 35.00
Aurora, Built-In Flashlight, Alligator Finish, Box 38.00
Baseball, 2 Criss-Crossed Bats Attached, 1940s 65.00
Beer Bottle Shape, Ballantine Beer, N.J. 20.00
Beer Bottle Shape, Canadian Ace 25.00
Bottle Shape, Everves 70.00
Bottle Shape, J & B Scotch, Japan, 7 1/2 In. 35.00
Bottle Shape, Patrick Henry Beer, Mich. 75.00
Bottle Shape, Royal Crown Cola, 1940s .... 45.00 to 55.00
Bottle Shape, Stag Beer, St. Louis 35.00
Bowling Pin 10.00
Buffalo Bill, Lookout Mountain, Omega 12.00

Cable Car, San Francisco	35.00
Camel, Joe Cool, Christmas, 5 Piece Set, Box	35.00
Camel, Syria Masonic Lodge	35.00
Camera Shape, 3 Metal Legs	55.00
Can Shape, Buckeye Draft Beer	15.00
Can Shape, Michelob Beer	15.00
Can Shape, Schlitz Beer	10.00
Cartier, 14K Gold	465.00
Chesterfield	20.00
Cigar, Wall, Figural, Sea Captain, Pipe In Mouth, Germany, Copper	140.00
Cigar, Wired To Transformer, Oak Base	450.00
Cowboy, Occupied Japan	85.00
Derringer, Table	45.00
Dog, Brass	100.00
Dunhill, Inset Watch, Sterling Silver	1000.00
Dunhill, Ribbed, Rectangular, 14K Yellow Gold	290.00
Dunhill, Silent Flame, Sally Rand	100.00
Dunhill, Sylph	75.00
Dunhill, Tinder Pistol	75.00 to 125.00
Dunhill, Yellow Gold, Ribbed Decoration, No. 750	287.50
Evans, Case & Lighter, Chrome	15.00
Flaminaire Gentry	400.00
Flashlight, Chrome, Box	25.00
Frank Lloyd Wright, Replica Of Johnson Wax Research Tower, Chrome, 6 In.	412.00
Golf Bag, Box, c.1940	65.00
Gun, Enameled Card Suits On Side, Silver, 1890	50.00
Gun, Flashlight, Large	55.00
Gun, Mother-Of-Pearl Handle, Occupied Japan	22.50
Horsehead, Japan, Table	20.00
Joe Camel, Unused	3.50
Knight's Head, Table	25.00
Letter Opener, Masonic	32.00
Limoges, Gold	25.00
Musical, Advertising, Dubonnet	40.00
Musical, Smoke Gets In Your Eyes	35.00
Parker, Flaminaire, Box	45.00
Parker, Silent Flame, Nude On Box, England, Square, 2 3/4 In.	45.00
Parrot, Flashlight	25.00
Pen Shaped, Japan, Box	25.00
Piano, Occupied Japan	100.00
Pistol Shape	10.00 to 25.00
Playboy, Bunny Logo	16.50 to 35.00
Queen Of Hearts Card Shape, Enameled, 1940	16.00
Reliable Pocket Lamp, 1890s	350.00
Rivo, With Watch	40.00
Rocket, Occupied Japan	100.00
Ronson, Angels	14.50
Ronson, Art Deco, Silver Plate, Table	55.00
Ronson, Banjo	350.00
Ronson, Bartender, Touch Tip, 1936, Table	1200.00 to 1500.00
Ronson, Crown, No. 19023	15.00
Ronson, Leona, Brass, Table, 4 In.	75.00
Ronson, Monkey, Pickacig, Table	550.00
Ronson, Pal, Art Deco, Chrome, Box	35.00
Ronson, Pencil Bottle Opener, With Corkscrew, Parrot, Art Deco, Chrome	30.00
Ronson, Pencil, Box	55.00
Ronson, Penciliter	35.00 to 65.00
Ronson, Touch Tip Octet	75.00
Ronson, Varaflame Comet, Box	22.00
Ronson, Viking, Black, Red Stripe	20.00
Ronson, Whirlwind, Alligator Cover	35.00
Ronson, Woman On Black Metal Base, Table	550.00
Ronson Mastercase, Chrome, Flannel & Box	40.00

Roulette Wheel, Pocket	45.00
Royal Doulton, Long John Silver, 1958	125.00
Royal Doulton, Rip Van Winkle, 1958	480.00
Sedan, Chrome, 1940s	90.00
Sgt. Lee, Poker Chips, Enameled Aces On Side, 1945	28.00
Sheffield, Watch On Side, Gold Color	45.00
Ship, Chrome, Occupied Japan	200.00
Ship's Wheel, Chrome	16.00 to 40.00
T-Bird, Metal	45.00
Tinder Pistol, 18th Century	500.00
Tobacco Store, Gas, Black Dandy Form, Polychromed Zinc, 31 In.	3300.00
Tom Mix, Figural, Metal	45.00
Triplex, Austria	15.00
Vulcan, 1st Field Artillery General's	45.00
Whiskey, American Rye, 4 Aces, Pearlized Celluloid, 1920, 1 1/2 x 2 In.	55.00
Wolverine Boots & Shoes	20.00
Zippo, 1957 Model Ford Truck, Box	45.00
Zippo, American Embassy, Rome, Italy	25.00
Zippo, Aztec Design, Sterling Silver	65.00
Zippo, Beachcraft	24.00
Zippo, Clark Candy Bar	55.00
Zippo, Cover Slots, 1936	235.00
Zippo, Cowboy & Bucking Bronco	52.50
Zippo, Embossed Iron City Beer	65.00
Zippo, Heineken Beer Logo	25.00
Zippo, Koch Office Supply	40.00
Zippo, Lord Selkirk	55.00
Zippo, Military Logo	35.00
Zippo, Outside Hinge, Sterling Silver Etched Case, Enamel Work, Italian	52.00
Zippo, Reddy Kilowatt	35.00
Zippo, Santa Claus	25.00
Zippo, State Of New Jersey Emblem	17.00
Zippo, World War II Battleship USS Robinson	15.00

LIMOGES porcelain has been made in Limoges, France, since the mid-nineteenth century. Fine porcelains were made by many factories, including Haviland, Ahrenfeldt, Guerin, Pouyat, Elite, and others. Modern porcelains are being made at Limoges and the word *Limoges* as part of the mark is not an indication of age. Haviland, one of the Limoges factories, is listed as a separate category in this book.

Bone Dish, Fish, Hand Painted	25.00
Bowl, Fruit & Grapes, Gold Border, Signed, 10 In.	235.00
Bowl, Hand Painted Flowers, Fluted, Gold Scrolls, 9 x 2 In.	35.00
Bowl, Portrait Of Cherub, Metal Feet, Dolphin Handles	190.00
Box, Cherubs, Signed, c.1900	225.00
Box, Cover, Scalloped, Purple Flowers, Large Center Flower, Hand Painted, 6 In.	130.00
Box, Dresser, Cover, Hunt Scene	35.00
Box, Pate-Sur-Pate Lid, Flowers In Relief, c.1890, 5 1/2 In.	175.00
Cake Plate, Gold Medallion, Ivory Ground, Gold Rim, 11 1/2 In.	70.00
Cake Plate, Open Handles, Boisbertrand, Floral Design, c.1890	75.00
Cake Plate, Speckled Orchids, Open Handles, Green, Brown, Gold, 1898	95.00
Cake Set, White Ground, Gold, Bands Of Daisies, 5 Piece	495.00
Candlestick, Hand Painted Floral & Gilt, 6 1/2 In., Pair	60.00
Chocolate Pot, Lid, Green & Gold Trim, White Ground, Marked	125.00
Chocolate Pot, Morning Glories, Gold Trim, Bamboo-Shaped Handle & Finial	140.00
Chocolate Pot, Violets, Cream Ground, Gold Handle, 13 In.	325.00
Chop Plate, Grape Cluster, 13 1/2 In.	275.00
Chop Plate, Grape Cluster, Hersey, 1909, 13 In.	175.00
Coffee Set, Moss Rose, Molded Rope Design, c.1876, 34 Piece	750.00
Cup & Saucer, Geometric & Floral Design	15.00
Cup & Saucer, Roses, Leaf Garlands, Gold, Demitasse	24.00
Dessert Plate Set, Game Birds, Hand Decorated, c.1910-1920, 8 5/8 In., Set Of 4	400.00
Dessert Set, Floral, Fluted Rim, 15 Piece	500.00

Dresser Set, Lilacs, Oval Tray, Pin, Tray, Ring Tree, Box, Candlestick 160.00

Dresser Set, White, Gold Trim, Covered Jar, Hair Receiver, Tray 175.00

Dresser Tray, Hand Painted, Yellow Flowers, Aqua, Signed, c.1915, 10 x 8 1/2 In. 95.00

Dresser Tray, White & Yellow, Pink Flowers, 8 x 12 In. 125.00

Ewer, Pink & Gold Flowers, Gold Ribbing & Handle, 1892, 6 In. 150.00

Fish Service, Gilt Decorated Scalloped Rims, Realistic Painted Fish, 15 Piece 525.00

Fruit Plate, Dubois, 10 1/4 In. 295.00

Humidor, Melon Ribbed, Leaves, White Pipes 130.00

Ice Cream Set, Scalloped Border, Forget-Me-Nots, Rosebuds, Tray, 10 Dishes 425.00

Jar, Biscuit, Hand Painted Flowers, White Ground, Ribbed, c.1890 .... 65.00

Mug, Cider, Gilt Design, Grapes & Vines, 5 3/4 In. 130.00

Mug, Green Grapes, Vines, Leaves, Pastel Green To Tan, 6 x 4 In. 95.00

Mustache Cup, White, Gold Design 33.00

Pitcher, Hand Painted Grapes, Artist Signed, 11 In. 395.00

Plaque, Blond Woman, Red Bonnet, Enameled, Catalina, Gilt Frame, 3 1/2 In. 247.00

Plaque, Bust Length View Of Madonna, Head Shawl, Framed, 11 3/8 In. 230.00

Plaque, Dutch Scene, Gold Rococo Border, 12 In. 245.00

Plaque, Dutch Scene, Gold Rococo Border, Signed, 12 In. 225.00

Plaque, Figure On Horse, House, Square, c.1890, 10 1/2 In. 350.00

Plaque, Hand Painted Flowers, Gold Rococo Border, Signed, 11 In. 190.00

Plaque, Hunting Dog Chasing Mallard Beside Lake, 13 1/2 In. 250.00

Plaque, Lovers In Sailboat, Carved Wood & Gilt Frame, c.1900, 10 x 7 In. 975.00

Plaque, Man & Woman, Gold Rococo Border, 10 In. 225.00

Plaque, Rabbits, 10 1/2 In. 200.00

Plaque, Scene, 2 Stags Facing 2 Does, Gold Rococo Border, Signed, 13 1/4 In., Pair.... 845.00

Plaque, Wall, Holly Berries, Scrolls, A. Lanternier Mark, Round, 11 1/2 In. 150.00

Plaque, Wild Boars, 10 1/2 In. 250.00

Plaque, Woman, Full Length, Gold Rococo Border, 10 In. 225.00

Plaque, Woman, Full Length, Man & Woman On Other, Signed, 10 In., Pair 450.00

Plaque, Woman, Semi-Nude, Hand Painted, Signed Baumy, 12 In 300.00

Plate, Cat Looking At Dragonfly, Signed L. Coudert, 9 3/4 In. 175.00

Plate, Coronet, Game Bird, Signed, 10 In. 80.00

Plate, Fish, Pair 85.00

Plate, Flowers, Pastel Colors, Art Nouveau Style, 9 In. 30.00

Plate, Fruit, Dubois, 10 1/4 In. 285.00

Plate, Fruit, Signed, 10 1/4 In. 300.00

Plate, Game Bird, Hand Painted, Scalloped Edge, Leaves & Berries, 9 1/2 In., Pair 225.00

Plate, Gilt Rim, Gilt Traced Borders, Center Flowers, 10 1/4 In., 12 Piece 370.00

Plate, Hand Painted, Flowers & Hummingbird, Scalloped Border, 9 In. 25.00

Plate, Hand Painted, Moss Rose, Gold Rim, 8 In. 15.00

Plate, Hanging, Flying Ducks, Gold Rococo Border, 11 1/4 In. 225.00

Plate, Hunter & Dog, Scalloped Edge, Marked, 13 1/2 In., Pair 650.00

Plate, Quails On 1, Pheasants On 1, Facing, Gold Rim, Marked, 9 1/2 In., Pair 265.00

Plate, Raised Gilt Tracery Design, Cobalt Blue Ground, 10 3/4 In., 12 Piece 990.00

Plate, Woman, Seated On Tree Branch, Flowers & Bird, 12 In. 700.00

Platter, Blue Flowers, Gold Handles, C. Ahrenfeldt, 16 x 11 In. 30.00

Platter, Flying Bird, Scalloped Rim, Rococo Border, 18 3/4 x 12 In. 175.00

Platter, Pink Forget-Me-Nots, Leaves, Scroll Rim, 17 In. 125.00

Powder Box, Cover, Roses 25.00

Powder Jar, Lid, Stylized Leaf Fronds & Lines, Eggshell Ground 30.00

Punch Bowl, Hand Painted Reserve, 19th Century, 20 In. 385.00

Punch Bowl, Pink & Yellow Currants, Gold Band, Signed, 5 1/4 x 12 In. 220.00

Punch Set, Grapes Inside & Out, Gold Trim, 9 Piece 1295.00

Ramekin Set, Cranberry & Gilt Rim, Underplates, 10 Piece 66.00

Rose Bowl, Hand Painted Roses, Gold Trim, 7 1/4 In. 110.00

Salad Set, Shrimp, Pastel Seashells, Gold Scalloped, Bowl, 10 In., 7 Piece 375.00

Shaving Mug, Occupational, Cabinetmaker Working With Circular Saw, Gold 325.00

Tankard, Cider, Dragon Handle, Bunches Of Grapes, 14 1/2 In. 275.00

Tankard, Floral & Grapes, Gold Dragon Handle, Late 19th Century, 14 1/2 In. 475.00

Tankard, Large Yellow & Red Roses, Defaye, Coronet, France 450.00

Tea & Dinner Set, Floral, Wine Decanter, Tumblers, Flatware, Box, 1914 .... 1575.00

Tobacco Set, Tray, Humidor, Card & Match Holder, Signed 240.00

Toothpick, Basket, With Gold 40.00

Tray, Gold Roses, Flowers, White Ground, Gold Rim, 16 1/2 x 11 In. 85.00
Trivet, Yellow Roses, Hand Painted, 3-Button Feet, Pastel Ground, Signed, 6 In. 48.00
Tureen, Cover, Pink Forget-Me-Nots, Leaves, Scrolled Handles & Rim...................... 150.00
Urn, French Fishing Scene, Pink, 13 1/2 In. 350.00
Vase, Pastel Floral, Ivory Ground, Pale Blue Trim, Gilt, J.P.L. France, 14 In. 247.00
Vase, Water Lilies, Gold Trim, Low, Round, T & V, 11 In. Base.................................. 160.00

LINDBERGH was a national hero. In 1927, Charles Lindbergh, the aviator,
became the first man to make a nonstop solo flight across the Atlantic Ocean.
In 1932, his son was kidnapped and murdered, and Lindbergh was again the
center of public interest. He died in 1974. All types of Lindbergh memorabilia are collected.

Book, Lindbergh's Lone Eagle, 1928... 35.00
Bottle, Spirit Of St. Louis, New York To Paris 25.00
Film, Motion Picture, Lindbergh's Paris Flight, Pathex 60.00
Sheet Music, Oh, Charlie Is My Darling, Lindbergh Photo 25.00
Watch Fob, Compass, New York To Paris 75.00

LITHOPHANES are porcelain pictures made by casting clay in layers of various thicknesses. When a piece is held to the light, a picture of light and
shadow is seen through it. Most lithophanes date from the 1825–1875 period.
A few are still being made. Many lithophanes sold today were originally panels for lampshades.

Lamp, 5 Panels, Children, PPM, 8 x 8 In. 445.00
Panel, Woman With Admiring Man, Mountain Scenery, 5 x 4 1/4 In. 185.00
Stein, Floral & Soldier, 1/2 Liter 150.00

LIVERPOOL, England, was the site of several pottery and porcelain factories
from 1716 to 1785. Some earthenware was made with transfer decorations.
Sadler and Green made print-decorated wares from 1756. Many of the pieces
were made for the American market and feature patriotic emblems, such as
eagles, flags, and other special-interest motifs.

Charger, Oriental Coastal Landscape Scene, Blue & White, 13 1/2 In. 258.00
Coffeepot, Hunt Scene & Dogs, Black, Small 295.00
Dish, Soup, Black Transfer, Yellow Flag Ship, Firing Cannon, 10 In. 250.00
Dish, Soup, Ship, Charles Lauwereins, Black Transfer, 9 1/2 In. 275.00
Figurine, Winter, Allegorical, Putto, Wearing Mantle Over Naked Body, 5 In. 2600.00
Mug, Transfer, Creamware, 19th Century, 5 In. 430.00
Pitcher, American Ship Design, Water Around Entire Body, 10 In.......................... 4850.00
Pitcher, Arms Of United States & Free Trade & Sailors Rights, Polychrome 2650.00
Pitcher, Boston Fusiliers, Reverse United We Stand-Divided We Fall, 9 1/4 In. 2180.00
Pitcher, Creamware, Baluster Form, Figure Of Hope & Sailing Ship, 10 In. 1035.00
Pitcher, Creamware, Independence, Washington, Justice, Liberty, c.1800 .... 1650.00
Pitcher, Creamware, Poor Jack The Sailor, c.1870, 10 1/4 In. 140.00
Pitcher, Decatur & Bainbridge, Luster, 1812, 4 1/2 In. 1400.00
Pitcher, Faith, Hope & Charity Transfer, Monogram, Creamware, 1792, 11 1/2 In. 546.00
Pitcher, Forester's Arms, Reddish Brown Transfer, 5 5/8 In. 126.50
Pitcher, George Washington Transfer, 13 Original Colonies, Plus 2, 8 In. 1320.00
Pitcher, Glory Of Washington, 15 In. 880.00
Pitcher, Hunting Scene Transfer, Creamware, Inscribed, 19th Century, 8 In. 920.00
Pitcher, Lafayette & Benjamin Franklin, Richard Hall & Son, 5 3/4 In. 450.00
Pitcher, Masonic Symbols, Verse, Inscribed, 10 3/4 In. 1150.00
Pitcher, Portrait Of Washington, Verse, Funeral Urn, 8 1/4 In. 1495.00
Pitcher, Puzzle, Verse, Woman Holding Bird, 3 Nozzles, Delft, c.1760, 8 In. 2875.00
Pitcher, Ship, American Flag, Large 1980.00
Pitcher, Shipwright's Arms & View Of Vessel In Dry-Dock, 10 In. 1760.00
Pitcher, Washington In Glory, Virtue & Valor, 8 3/4 In. 1600.00
Pitcher, Washington Map Transfer, Creamware, 19th Century, 9 In. 1725.00
Plate, 3-Masted Ship Transfer, 10 In. 86.00
Plate, East Indian Man Sailing From The Downs, Black, 9 3/4 In. 1750.00
Plate, Map Of East Coast & Washington Transfer, 10 3/8 In. 2600.00
Plate, O Liberty Thou Goddess, Poem & U.S. Ship, 7 7/8 In. 1650.00
Tankard, U.S. Ship, 6 In. 1200.00

Teapot, Oriental Figures, c.1775, 8 1/2 In... 835.00
Teapot, Polychrome Floral, Gilt Trim, 5 1/2 In.. 175.00

LLADRO is a Spanish porcelain. Juan, Jose, and Vicente Lladro opened a ceramics workshop in Almacera in 1951. They soon began making figurines in a distinctive, elongated style. In 1958 the factory moved to Tabernes Blanques, Spain. The company makes stoneware and porcelain vases and figurines in limited and unlimited editions. Dates given are first and last years of production.

LLADRÓ°

Bell, 1987, Christmas.. 35.00
Figurine, A Lady Of Taste, No. 1495, 1986, 14 1/2 In... 625.00
Figurine, At The Circus, Clown & Girl 1150.00
Figurine, Autumn Glow, No. 2250, 1993, 10 3/4 In.. 750.00
Figurine, Billy Football Player, 1983 .... 600.00
Figurine, Boy With Drum, No. 4616, 1969-1979, 4 1/4 In.. 500.00
Figurine, Bunny Girl, No. 5162, 1982-1985.. 345.00
Figurine, Cadet Captain, No. 5404, 1987-1990, 12 1/2 In.. 325.00
Figurine, Can I Play?, No. 7610, 1990, 8 1/4 In..............................250.00 to 350.00
Figurine, Cat Girl, Girl Standing, With Tail, 9 In.. 500.00
Figurine, Chinese Farmer, With Staff, Matte Finish, 22 In. 1500.00
Figurine, Cinderella, No. 4828, 9 3/4 In... 1150.00
Figurine, Clown With 2 Puppies, 8 1/2 In. ....2750.00 to 2825.00
Figurine, Clown, Holding Bag Behind Back, 8 1/2 In.. 935.00
Figurine, Columbus, No. 1432, 1982, 16 1/2 In.. 1500.00
Figurine, Cougar, No. 5435, 1987-1990, 2 In.. 450.00
Figurine, Crawling Baby, With Pacifier 140.00
Figurine, Deep In Thought, No. 5389, 1986-1990, 4 1/2 In. 350.00
Figurine, Dentist, No. 4762, 1971-1985, 15 3/4 In.. 150.00
Figurine, Dog, Playing The Tymbal, No. 1156, 1971-1978, 7 1/2 In. 250.00
Figurine, Don Quixote, No.1030, 1969, 14 1/2 In... 1200.00
Figurine, Donkey In Love, No. 4524, 1969-1985, 5 In.. 225.00
Figurine, Drummer Boy, No. 5403, 1987-1990, 12 1/4 In... 500.00
Figurine, El Greco, No. 5359, 1986-1990, 12 1/2 In.. 650.00
Figurine, Fairy Queen, No. 5068, 1980-1983, 12 3/4 In.. 1000.00
Figurine, Flag Bearer, No. 5405, 1987-1990, 12 1/2 In... 450.00
Figurine, Flock Of Birds, No. 1462, 1985, 11 1/2 In... 1750.00
Figurine, Flower Peddler, Cart Full Of Flowers 1000.00
Figurine, Flower Song..400.00 to 450.00
Figurine, Garden Of Dreams ....900.00 to 1250.00
Figurine, Girl With Love, No. 4910, 8 1/2 In.. 300.00
Figurine, Girl, Manicuring, No. 1082, 1969-1985, 7 1/2 In... 195.00
Figurine, Girl, Shampooing, No. 1148, 1971-1985, 8 1/2 In.. 250.00
Figurine, Girl, Singer, Slit Skirt, With Microphone, 7 1/2 In...................................... 600.00
Figurine, Girl, Soccer Player, No. 5134, 1982-1983, 9 In... 600.00
Figurine, Girl, With Cockerel, No. 4591, 1969, 9 3/8 In. ....90.00 to 100.00
Figurine, Girl, With Dog, No. 4806, 1972-1982, 12 1/2 In.. 250.00
Figurine, Girl, With Doll, No. 1083, 1969-1985, 7 In.. 295.00
Figurine, Girl, With Domino, No. 1175, 1971-1981, 7 1/2 In....................................... 275.00
Figurine, Girl, With Lamb, No. 4584, 1969, 10 1/2 In.............................115.00 to 130.00
Figurine, Girl, With Lamb, No. 4835, 1972, 10 5/8 In... 115.00
Figurine, Girl, With Mother's Shoe, No. 1084, 1969-1985, 7 1/2 In. 380.00
Figurine, Girl, With Pigeons, No. 4915, 1974-1990, 8 3/4 In...................................... 300.00
Figurine, Girl, With Ukulele 75.00
Figurine, Groom Carrying Bride, No. C-27N, 1985 .... 120.75
Figurine, Hand Of Justice, No. 6035 .... 1250.00
Figurine, Heavenly Swing, No. 1739, 1991, 8 3/4 In.. 2050.00
Figurine, Hebrew Student, No. 4684, 1970-1985, 11 1/2 In. 350.00
Figurine, Holiday Glow.. 750.00
Figurine, I Love You Truly, No. 1528, 1987, 14 1/2 In... 316.25
Figurine, Indian Brave.. 1250.00
Figurine, Jester's Serenade, No. 5932, 1993, 14 1/2 In... 1200.00
Figurine, Jockey, 1341, 1977-1979, 12 1/4 In... 315.00
Figurine, Kitty Bunny Girl, No. 5164, 1982-1985, 9 In. 450.00
Figurine, Little Couple Kissing, No. 1188, 1972-1989, 8 1/2 In.................................. 375.00

Figurine, Little Pals, No. 7600, 1985, 8 3/4 In. 1800.00
Figurine, Little Traveler, No. 7602, 1986, Limited Edition, 8 1/2 In. ....1000.00 to 1500.00
Figurine, Love Boat 1350.00
Figurine, My Buddy, No. 7609, 1969-1985, 8 In. 300.00
Figurine, Napoleon Bonaparte, No. 5338, 1985, 13 1/4 In. 495.00
Figurine, New World Medallion, No. 5808, 1991, 6 1/4 In. 200.00
Figurine, Obstetrician, No. 4763, 1971-1975, 16 1/2 In. 275.00
Figurine, Pegasus 1950.00
Figurine, Peter Pan, No. 7529, Limited Edition, 1993 .... 1295.00
Figurine, Picture Perfect ....350.00 to 700.00
Figurine, Playful Piglets, No. 5228, 1984, 3 In. 80.00
Figurine, Poodle, No. 1259, 1974-1985, 5 1/2 In. 285.00
Figurine, Praying Angel, 4538, 1969, 5 In. 45.00
Figurine, Rescue, No. 3504, 1978, 17 In. 3800.00
Figurine, Rey De Bastos, No. 5369, 1986, 11 In. 550.00
Figurine, Sad Parting, No. 5583, 1989, 13 In. 525.00
Figurine, School Days, No. 7604, 1988, 8 1/4 In. 430.00
Figurine, See Saw, No. 1255, 1974, 9 1/4 In. 575.00
Figurine, Skye Terrier, No. 4643, 1969-1985, 6 In. 375.00
Figurine, Small Dog, No. 4749, 1971-1985, 3 In. 95.00
Figurine, Snow White 800.00
Figurine, Soccer Players, No. 1266, Limited Edition, 1974, 27 1/2 In. 1490.00
Figurine, Sorrowful Mother, No. 5849, 1992, 12 1/2 In. ....1400.00 to 1850.00
Figurine, Spring Bouquet, No. 7603, 1987, 8 1/4 In. 650.00
Figurine, Summer Stroll 225.00
Figurine, Tennis Young Lady, No. 4798, 1972-1981, 12 1/2 In. 195.00
Figurine, Tinker Bell, No. 7529, Limited Edition, 1992 ....2000.00 to 2095.00
Figurine, Torero Seated, No. 1162, 1971-1973, 11 3/4 In. 485.00
Figurine, Veterinarian, Matte Finish, 13 1/4 In. 500.00
Figurine, Voyage Of Columbus 14500.00
Figurine, Way Of The Cross 1050.00
Figurine, Wedding, No. 4808, 1972, 7 3/4 In. 105.00
Mug, Columbus Discovery, No. 5967 .... 100.00
Plate, Christmas, 1971, Caroling, 8 In. 30.00
Plate, Christmas, 1979, Snow Dance, 8 In. 80.00
Plate, Mother's Day, 1977, Mother & Daughter 60.00
Sign, Dealer's 11.00

LOCKE ART is a trademark found on glass of the early twentieth century. Joseph Locke worked at many English and American firms. He designed and etched his own glass in Pittsburgh, Pennsylvania, starting in the 1880s. Some pieces were marked *Joe Locke*, but most were marked with the words *Locke Art*. The mark is hidden in the pattern on the glass.

Cordial, Poppy, Optic Ribbed 80.00
Pitcher, Grapes & Lines, Hour Glass Shape, 8 1/2 x 7 1/2 In. 670.00
Sherbet, Grapes & Lines, Saucer Base, Signed 145.00
Sherbet, Poppy Pattern, Attached Underplate, Signed 185.00
Wine, Poppy, Ribbed 75.00

LOETZ glass was made in many varieties. Johann Loetz bought a glassworks in Austria in 1840. He died in 1848 and his widow ran the company; then in 1879, his grandson took over. Most collectors recognize the iridescent gold glass similar to Tiffany, but many other types were made. The firm closed during World War II.

Basket, Flower Prunts, Purple & Green Oil Spots, Handle, 9 In. 185.00
Biscuit Jar, Blown-Out Corners, Pink Iridescent, Square 485.00
Bowl, Flared, Marked, 5 1/2 In. 190.00
Bowl, Green, Iridescent, Cuspidor Shape, Crimped, 6 1/2 x 3 1/2 In. 220.00
Centerpiece, Cylindrical, Iridescent Green-Gold To Purple, Signed, 10 In. 195.00
Cookie Jar, Lavender Floral, Green 495.00
Inkwell, Fern Design, Green 250.00
Rose Bowl, Globe Shape, Pinched Rim, Blue & Gold Iridescent, 1900s, 4 1/2 In. 110.00
Rose Bowl, Amethyst, Mottled Blue, Purple, Gold Iridescent, 5 1/4 x 4 1/2 In. 115.00

Shade, Cameo Cut, Iridescent, 4 1/2 In. 275.00
Shade, Green & Gold Mottled Feathering, Gold Interior, 6 3/4 In., Pair 495.00
Vase, 4 Applied Spiraling Columnar Handles, c.1902, 11 5/8 In. 3450.00
Vase, Applied Loops, Rainbow Iridescent Gold Ground, 11 1/2 In. 1320.00
Vase, Aubergine, Melon Trailings, Signed, c.1901, 3 1/4 In. 8050.00
Vase, Austrian Design, Iridescent White, 6 1/2 In. 530.00
Vase, Baluster, Everted Rim, Pink, Silver & Blue Iridescent Oil Spots, 7 3/4 In. 1380.00
Vase, Blue Oil Spot, 5 In. 450.00
Vase, Blue-Green Swirl, Enameled Blue & Gold Flowers, 4 In. 178.00
Vase, Bud, Art Glass, Stick Neck, Fluted Body, Banding, Iridescent Green To Blue, 7 In. 110.00
Vase, Butterscotch Oil Spot Over White, Silver Overlay, 6 In. 575.00
Vase, Cased With Vertical Lines, 6 In. 535.00
Vase, Cobalt Blue, 6 In. 875.00
Vase, Cobalt Reverse Feather, Gold Raindrop Ground, 4 In. 135.00
Vase, Contorted Body, Dimpled, Metal Collar, Eagles On Laurel Swags, 10 In. 450.00
Vase, Corset Shape, Flared Rim, Iridescent, Green, Rippled, 7 x 3 1/2 In. 140.00
Vase, Dark Green, Gold Overlay, 12 1/4 In. 225.00
Vase, Dimpled, Twisted Shape, Blue, Green, Gold Iridescent, 11 x 4 In. 450.00
Vase, Double Gourd Shape, Yellow, Silver-Green Iridescent, Wavy Lines, 4 In. 920.00
Vase, Free Form Ripples, 4 Convex Sides, Purple On Amber, 10 1/4 In. 750.00
Vase, Golden Combed Iridescent, Recessed Pontil, Signed, 12 1/2 In. 3000.00
Vase, Green & Silver Loops & Swirls, Ruffled Collar, c.1900, 10 In. 1795.00
Vase, Green Oil Spot, Iridescent Handles, 6 1/4 In. 375.00
Vase, Inverted Baluster Shape, Papillon Finish, c.1900, 11 3/4 In. 330.00
Vase, Iridescent Amber, 9 In. 150.00
Vase, Iridescent Spots, Hooked Feathering, Dots, Pinched Sides, 4 1/4 In. 1100.00
Vase, Iridescent Waves, Silver Lily Pad Pulls, Pinched Sides, 7 1/4 In. 2185.00
Vase, Iridized Silver Zippered Design, Green, 12 In. 200.00
Vase, Oil Spot, Rolled Rim, Green, 7 1/2 In. 175.00
Vase, Oil Spots, 3 Pinched Sides, Blue-Purple, 3 In. 150.00
Vase, Oviform, Pinched Sides, Gold Iridescent Waves, Lily Pad Pulls, 7 1/4 In. 2185.00
Vase, Pinched Sides, Gold Oil Spot, 4 In. 300.00
Vase, Pinched Sides, Metal Rim, Footed, Marigold, c.1900, 7 In., Pair 405.00
Vase, Pinched Sides, Oviform, Salmon Iridescent, Blue Waves, Silver Spots, 9 In. 4370.00
Vase, Pinched Teardrop Shape, Random Trailings, Signed, c.1900, 5 In. 5175.00
Vase, Pinched, Iridescent Green, Silver Sterling Rims, c.1924, 7 1/2 In., Pair.............. 600.00
Vase, Platinum & Blue Pulls, Navy Ground, White, 4 In. 880.00
Vase, Rain Drops, Green Iridescent, Bulbous, 8 In. 150.00
Vase, Random Threads, Green, Platinum & Blue Oil Spots, 9 In. 2310.00
Vase, Red Oil Spot, Platinum Design, 10 In. 525.00
Vase, Red, Light Green Threading Rim, 9 1/2 x 8 1/2 In. 300.00
Vase, Rib & Horizontal Wavy Line Design, Gold Iridescent, Blue Highlights, 7 7/8 In. 192.00
Vase, Silver Blue Drapery, 4 Sides, 7 In. 1000.00
Vase, Silver Scroll, Floral Wrap Marked Sterling Silver Deposit, 6 3/8 In. 2185.00
Vase, Silvery Blue Swirls, Amber, c.1900, 8 3/4 In. 4312.00
Vase, Snake Coiled, Around, Green, 7 In. 66.00
Vase, Snakeskin, Green, Flared Rim, 5 In. 285.00
Vase, Spotted, Ruby Red Ground, Flared Rim, Signed, 3 3/4 In. 2300.00
Vase, Squatty, Dimpled, Pink Iridescent, Intermittent Patches, c.1900, 6 1/4 In. 3760.00
Vase, Stylized Roses, Mother-Of-Pearl Ground, 7 In. 3000.00
Vase, Swirling Purple-Blue Iridescent, Flared, Squatty Bulbous, 9 x 6 In. 550.00
Vase, Tapered, Reeded, Angular Shoulder, Green, Purple Iridescent Cast, 4 In. 85.00
Vase, Textured Glass Cased In Clear, c.1900, 11 1/8 In. 5750.00
Vase, Threaded, Iridescent Green, 16 In. 450.00
Vase, Twisted Filigree, Green, 6 In. 275.00
Vase, Twisted Shape, Purple Iridescent Swirl, Green Ground, 8 In. 495.00
Vase, Waves, Trailings, Blue Swirl Base, Signed, c.1900, 8 In. 8050.00
Vase, White & Purple Pulled Swirl, Pinched, Twisted, 13 In. 650.00

LONE RANGER, a fictional character, was introduced on the radio in 1932.
Over three thousand shows were produced before the series ended in 1954. In
1938, the first Lone Ranger movie was made. Television shows were started
in 1949 and are still seen on some stations. The Lone Ranger appears on
many products and was even the name of a restaurant chain for several years.

Badge, Bond Bread Safety Club, 6 Points, Lone Ranger Figure, T.L.R. Inc., 1938 .... 12.00
Badge, Deputy, Secret Compartment, 1949 ....35.00 to 50.00
Badge, Silvercup Bread, Safety Scout, Metal, Premium, 1930s, 1 In. 12.00
Bank, Strong Box, Leather Covered, Sun Life Insurance, 1938, 3 x 4 In. ....225.00 to 250.00
Book, Big Little Book 60.00
Book, Coloring, 64 Pages, 1980 ....11.00 to 12.00
Book Bag, Leather, Raised Image Of The Lone Ranger, Late 1940s 200.00
Brush, Wooden, 1938, 5 In. 95.00
Button, Long Ranger, Hi-Yo Silver, Color, Pinback, 7/8 In. 2.00
Card, Peace Control Member, Clayton Moore, Signed, 1950s, 2 1/2 x 4 In. 3.00
Comic Book, No.2, 1952 .... 15.00
Costume, Tonto, Complete, Hatchet, String Of Beads, 1950s 85.00
Doll, Composition, Muslin Jointed Body, 1940-1950, Box, 20 In. 1400.00
Figure, Horse, Silver, Castile Soap, Box 75.00
Figure, Horse, Silver, Plastic, Jointed Legs 35.00
Figure, Lone Ranger & Tonto, With Silver & Scout, Gabriel, Box 154.00
Figure, Tonto, Castile Soap, Box 75.00
Flasher, Varivue, c.1970, 1 1/2 x 2 1/2 In. 5.00
Flashlight, Ranger Signal Siren, Silver Bullet Secret Code, Usalite, Box, 1950s 200.00
Game, Board, Metal Playing Pieces, Milton Bradley, 1938 .... 110.00
Game, Board, Parker Bros., Box, 1938 .... 85.00
Game, Hi-Yo Silver, 1940s, Box 95.00
Game, Skill Ball 30.00
Guitar, Box 145.00
Gun, Click, Metal 65.00
Hat, Hi-Yo Silver, Cloth 150.00
Knife, Bullet, Red, Pocket ....40.00 to 65.00
Lunch Box, Red, Metal, 1954 .... 275.00
Model Kit, Aurora, 1967, Box 200.00
Pedometer, Mailing Box, 1943 .... 110.00
Pen, Silver Bullet, Lone Ranger Picture, Key Ring, 4 1/2 In. 6.00
Postcard, Bond Bread, Membership, Safety Club, 1939, 3 1/2 x 5 1/2 In. ....10.00 to 24.00
Puppet, Hand, Molded Rubber Head, Cloth Body, Felt Hands, 1950 .... 95.00
Puppet, Tonto, Molded Rubber Head, Cloth Body, Hand, 1940s 125.00
Puzzle, Story, 1950s 95.00
Puzzle, Tray, 1950 .... 38.00
Radio, Airline 1050.00
Record, 1950s 25.00
Record, Radio Shows, 33 RPM, 1977 .... 20.00
Record Player, Decca, Wooden, 1940s 225.00
Ring, Atom Bomb 125.00
Ring, Flashlight, Premium, 1948 .... 120.00
Snow Dome 95.00
Soap, Figural, Tonto, Castile, Box 65.00
Spoon, Figural, Sterling Silver, 1938 .... 35.00
Tent, Box 225.00
Tonto Soap, Figural, Castile, Original Display Box 50.00
Toothbrush Holder, Lone Ranger On Silver, Wooden, Syrocco Co., 1938, 4 In. 80.00
Toy, Lone Ranger, Silver, Rotating Lasso, Tin, Windup, Marx, 1938.................350.00 to 400.00
View-Master Set, 1956 .... 28.00
Wristwatch, New Haven, 1939 .... 295.00

LONGWY Workshop of Longwy, France, first made ceramic wares in 1798.
The workshop is still in business. Most of the ceramic pieces found today are
glazed with many colors to resemble cloisonne or other enameled metal. The
factory used a variety of marks.

Box, Cover, Multicolored Flowers, Gold, Square, 5 In. 125.00
Charger, Stylized Jungle Scene, 15 In. 2070.00
Plate, Mosaic Design, 8 In. 195.00
Tile, Deco Woman & Flowers, Square, Marked 250.00
Vase, Geometric Vertical Chain Links, Enamel Outlining, Crackle Glaze, 11 In. 695.00

LONHUDA Pottery Company of Steubenville, Ohio, was organized in 1892 by William Long, W. H. Hunter, and Alfred Day. Brown underglaze slip-decorated pottery was made. The firm closed in 1896. The company used many marks; the earliest included the letters *LPCO*.

LONHUDA

Bowl, Orange Geraniums, Green Foliage, Flared Rim, Signed, 6 1/2 x 7 In.	575.00
Vase, Flowers, Brown Glaze, Jessie Spaulding, 7 1/2 In.	450.00

LOTUS WARE was made by the Knowles, Taylor & Knowles Company of East Liverpool, Ohio, from 1890 to 1900. Lotus Ware, a thin porcelain which resembles Belleek, was sometimes decorated outside the factory. Other types of ceramics that were made by the Knowles, Taylor & Knowles Company are listed under KTK.

Bowl, Flowers, Twig Handles, 9 In.	1430.00
Bowl, Shell Shape, 5 1/2 In.	135.00
Creamer, Fish Net Allover	500.00
Vase, Orange Flowers, Fishnet, Ball Feet, 8 In.	500.00

LOW art tiles were made by the J. and J. G. Low Art Tile Works of Chelsea, Massachusetts, from 1877 to 1902. A variety of art and other tiles were made. Some of the tiles were made by a process called *natural*, some were hand modeled, and some were made mechanically.

J.&J.G.LOW

Tile, Boy Reading Book, c.1861, Square, 6 In.	250.00
Tile, Bust Of Old Woman, Arthur Osborne, Signed	100.00
Tile, Grazing Sheep, Herders, c.1880, 7 3/4 x 11 In.	1955.00
Tile, Group Of Sheep, Herded Down Village Street, 10 x 18 In.	750.00
Tile, Stylized Vegetation, Art Nouveau, 1890s	95.00
Tile, Zigzag Pattern, Blue & Buff, Square, 4 1/2 In.	85.00

LOY-NEL-ART, see McCoy category

LUNCH BOXES and lunch pails have been used to carry lunches to school or work since the nineteenth century. Today, most collectors want either early tobacco advertising boxes or children's lunch boxes made since the 1930s. Boxes listed here include the original Thermos bottle inside the box unless otherwise indicated. Movie, television, and cartoon characters may be found in their own categories.

LUNCH BOX, A-Team, Metal, King Seeley Thermos, 1985	25.00
Adam-12, Metal, Aladdin, 1972	45.00
Addams Family, Metal, Aladdin, 1974	75.00
Alice In Wonderland, Vinyl, Walt Disney Productions, Aladdin, 1974	175.00
Annie Oakley, Metal, Adaddin, 1956	200.00
Archies, Metal, Aladdin, 1969	28.00
Astronauts Moon Landing, 1970	50.00
Barbie, Campus Queen	65.00
Barbie, Hologram	15.00
Barbie, Vinyl, 1962	69.00 to 75.00
Barbie & Midge, Metal, Canada, 1962	295.00
Beatles, Aladdin	275.00
Bee Gees, Barry, Metal, King Seeley Thermos, 1978	28.00
Beverly Hillbillies, Metal, Aladdin, 1963	65.00 to 95.00
Bionic Woman, Metal, Aladdin, 1976	39.00
Boston Bruins, Metal, Okay Industries, 1973	300.00
Boston Red Sox, Vinyl	35.00 to 55.00
Bozo The Clown, Metal, Aladdin, 1963	180.00
Brady Bunch, King Seeley Thermos, 1970	250.00
Buck Rogers, Metal, Aladdin, 1979	16.00
Bullwinkle, Yellow, Vinyl	275.00
Charlie's Angels, Metal, Aladdin, 1978	35.00 to 50.00
Chuck Wagon, Metal, Aladdin, 1958-1960	200.00
Circus Wagon, Dome Top, Metal, American Thermos, 1958	175.00
Color Me Happy, Metal, Ohio Art, 1984	25.00
Doctor Doolittle, Metal, Aladdin, 1968	40.00 to 95.00

Dome, Red Barn, Metal, American Thermos, 1957 .... 39.00 to 90.00
Dr. Seuss, Metal, Aladdin, 1970.. 89.00
Dutch Cottage, Dome, Metal, American Thermos, 1958 .... 195.00
Evel Knievel, Metal, Aladdin, 1974 .... 45.00
Fireball XL5, Metal, King Seeley Thermos, 1964.. 125.00
Flipper, Metal, King Seeley Thermos, 1966 .... 100.00
Fox & Hound, Metal, Aladdin, 1981 .... 30.00
G.I. Joe, Metal, King Seeley Thermos, 1967 .... 65.00 to 125.00
Get Smart, Metal, King Seeley Thermos, 1966 .... 150.00 to 225.00
Gomer Pyle, U.S.M.C., Metal, Aladdin, 1966 .... 95.00
Green Hornet, Metal, King Seeley Thermos, 1967.. 120.00
Gremlins, Metal, Aladdin, 1984.. 20.00
Guns Of Will Sonnett, Metal, King Seeley Thermos, 1968 .... 175.00
Hansel & Gretel, Metal, Ohio Art, 1982.. 75.00
Hee-Haw, Metal, King Seeley Thermos, 1970 .... 85.00 to 90.00
Hogan's Heroes, Dome Top, Metal, Aladdin, 1966 .... 50.00
Hometown Airport, Dome Top, Metal, King Seeley Thermos, 1960s 135.00
Huckleberry Hound, Metal, Aladdin, 1961 .... 40.00 to 114.00
It's About Time, Dome Top, Metal, Aladdin, 1967 .... 315.00
James Bond 007, Metal, Aladdin, 1966.. 100.00
Jetsons, Dome Top, Metal, Aladdin, 1963 .... 642.00
Joe Palooka, Metal, Continental Can, 1949.. 180.00
Junior Miss, Basset Hound, Metal Aladdin, 1978.. 15.00
Just Suits Tobacco, Tin 30.00
Kung Fu, Metal, King Seeley Thermos, 1974 .... 145.00
Lance Link, Metal, Aladdin, 1971 .... 100.00
Land Of The Giants, Metal, Aladdin, 1968.. 95.00
Land Of The Lost, Metal, Aladdin, 1975 .... 60.00
Landers, Frary, Clark, Tin 65.00
Lawman, Metal, King Seeley Thermos, 1961 .... 95.00 to 150.00
Little Ballerina, Red, Vinyl, Bayville, 1975 .... 35.00
Lost In Space, Dome Top, Metal, King Seeley Thermos, 1967 .... 375.00 to 445.00
Man From U.N.C.L.E., Metal, King Seeley Thermos, 1966 .... 89.00 to 330.00
Mighty Mouse, Hard Plastic, 1979 .... 20.00
Muppets, Metal, King Seeley Thermos, 1979 .... 15.00
Osmonds, Metal, Aladdin, 1973 .... 30.00 to 35.00
Partridge Family, Metal, King Seeley Thermos, 1971 .... 39.00 to 45.00
Pebbles & Bamm Bamm, Metal, Aladdin, 1971 .... 80.00
Peter Pan Sandwich, Metal, 1974 .... 265.00
Police Patrol, No. 9, Metal, Aladdin, 1978.. 85.00
Psychedelic Dome Top, Metal, Aladdin, 1969.. 140.00 to 149.00
Raggedy Ann & Andy, Metal, Aladdin, 1973.. 20.00
Rat Patrol, Metal, Aladdin, 1967.. 75.00 to 95.00
Road Runner, Metal, King Seeley Thermos, 1970 .... 65.00
Robin Hood, Metal, 1956.. 150.00
Rocketeer, Plastic, Aladdin, 1990 .... 25.00
Secret Agent, Metal, King Seeley Thermos, 1968 .... 65.00 to 78.00
Sesame Street, Yellow, Vinyl, 1985.. 15.00
Six Million Dollar Man, Metal, Aladdin, 1974 .... 15.00 to 20.00
Sleeping Beauty, White Vinyl, 1970.. 175.00
Smokey Bear, Timberwolves, Plastic, Premium Giveaway................................ 55.00
Snoopy, Lunch With Snoopy, Dome Top, Metal, King Seeley Thermos, 1968 .... 81.00 to 85.00
Soupy Sales, Vinyl, King Seeley Thermos, 1966.. 395.00
Speed Buggy, Metal, King Seeley Thermos, 1974 .... 15.00
Star Wars, Stars On Band, Metal, King Seeley Thermos, 1977 .... 28.00
Star Wars, X-Wing Fighter, Black, Metal, King Seeley Thermos, 1978 .... 25.00
Stars & Stripes, Dome Top, Metal, Aladdin, 1976 .... 65.00
Strawberry Shortcake, Metal, Aladdin, 1980 .... 12.00
Strawberry Shortcake, Vinyl, Aladdin, 1981 .... 22.00
The Astronauts, Metal, Aladdin, 1969 .... 95.00
Thermos Only, Gunsmoke, Steel, Glass, 1958 .... 50.00
Thermos Only, Monkees, 1967 .... 20.00
Thermos Only, Tarzan, 1966.. 60.00

Thermos Only, The Flintstones, Metal, 1964	50.00
Thermos Only, Twiggy, 1967	35.00
Thermos Only, Wild, Wild West, 1969	30.00
Thermos Only, Wonder Woman, 1977	9.00
Thermos Only, Woody Woodpecker, Plastic, Glass, 1971	40.00
Thermos Only, World Of Barbie, 1971	35.00
Tom Corbet, Space Cadet, Metal, Aladdin, 1950s	330.00
Tom Corbett, Red, Decal	100.00
Tropicana Premium, 1989	65.00
U.S. Mail, Dome Top, Metal, Aladdin, 1969	85.00
Universal Movie Monsters, Metal, Aladdin, 1979	45.00 to 125.00
Voyage To The Bottom Of The Sea, Metal, Aladdin, 1967	100.00
Wagon Train, Metal, King Seeley Thermos, 1964	190.00
Welcome Back Kotter, Metal, Aladdin, 1977	35.00
Wild Frontier, Metal, Ohio Art, 1977	40.00 to 80.00
Winner Tobacco	225.00
Winnie The Pooh, Vinyl, 1964	300.00
Woody Woodpecker, Metal, Aladdin, 1972	65.00
LUNCH PAIL, Bengal Brand Peanut Butter, 1 Lb.	4500.00
French Market Coffee, 3 Lb.	70.00
Frontenac Peanut Butter, 12 Oz.	40.00
Jackie Coogan Peanut Butter, Tin, 3 x 3 In.	350.00
Kung Fu, 1974	45.00
Magic Of Lassie, 1978	45.00
Monarch Peanut Butter	14.50
Niggerhair Tobacco, Tin, 6 1/2 In.	192.00
Noble Popcorn, Lid, 4 Lb.	16.00
O'Boy Peanut Butter, 1 Lb.	925.00
Ox-Heart Peanut Butter, Cover	165.00
Pinocchio, 1940	250.00
Pride Of Ontario Honey	125.00
Schepp's Coconut, Green	155.00
Shedds Peanut Butter, 5 Lb.	25.00
Squirrel Brand Peanut Butter, 2 Lb.	125.00 to 175.00
Staple Brand Peanut Butter, Tin Litho, Blue, White & Yellow, 25 Lb.	55.00
Sultana Peanut Butter, 1 Lb.	45.00
Sunny Boy Peanut Butter, Boy Holding Sandwich, 1 Lb.	75.00
Tiger Tobacco, Red, 5 Lb.	125.00
Union Leader Cut Plug, Spread Winged Eagle, Tin, 9 x 5 In.	110.00
Uzar Peanut Butter, 2 Lb.	350.00
Wilson's Peanut Butter, Mother & Child Scene, Bail, Cover, 11 Oz.	105.00
Winner Cut Plug Tobacco, Racing Scene, Square, Handle, 1910	200.00

LUNEVILLE, a French faience factory, was established about 1730 by Jacques Chambrette. It is best known for its fine biscuit figures and groups and for large faience dogs and lions. The early pieces were unmarked. The firm was acquired by Keller and Guerin and is still working.

Candlestick, Faience, Rococo Baluster, Pink, Green & Blue Painted Design, 10 In.	230.00
Urn, Floral, Gold Handles, 4-Footed	420.00
Vase, Art Nouveau Form & Design, 14 1/4 In.	175.00
Vase, Pillow, Pierced Handles, Purple & Gray Majolica Glaze, 10 1/2 In.	895.00

LUSTER glaze was meant to resemble copper, silver, or gold. It has been used since the sixteenth century. Most of the luster found today was made during the nineteenth century. The metallic glazes are applied on pottery. The finished color depends on the combination of the clay color and the glaze. Tea Leaf pieces have their own category.

Copper, Goblet, Polychrome Design, 9 In.	125.00
Copper, Jug, C Handle, 5 Beaded Bands Top, 5 In.	45.00
Copper, Jug, Transfer Print, Tolls Taken At The Menai Bridge, 19th Century, 4 1/2 In.	230.00
Copper, Mug, Wide Pink House Band, 5 1/2 In.	175.00
Copper, Pitcher, Cherubs, Tending Goat, 8 In.	93.00
Copper, Pitcher, Cobalt Band, 6 In.	20.00

Luster, Pink, Creamer, Cow, England, 6 1/2 In.,
Luster, Pink, Watch Holder, Pocket, Lion Finial, England, 1825, 7 1/2 In.

Luster, Pink, Pitcher, Officer, Horseback, 18th Century, England, 5 In.;
Luster, Pink, Pitcher, Classical Figures, Purple, Sewell, 1825, 9 In., Pair;
Luster, Pink, Pitcher, Queen Caroline, Verse, England, 1820, 5 1/4 In.

Luster, Silver Deposit, Jug, Sporting, Blue Transfer, England, 1815, 5 In.;
Luster, Silver, Pitcher, Floral, Enameled, England, 1815, 8 3/8 In.;
Luster, Silver, Jug, Sporting, Blue Transfer, England, 1815, 6 1/4 In.

Copper, Pitcher, Father Mathew, Advocate Of Temperance, Administrating Pledge	90.00
Copper, Pitcher, Floral Decoration, 8 1/4 In.	132.00
Copper, Pitcher, Harrison & Reform, 1840	2090.00
Copper, Pitcher, Scene On Blue Band, c.1809, 6 In.	135.00
Copper, Pitcher, Yellow & Black Transfer, Lafayette & Cornwallis, 5 1/2 In.	715.00
Cranberry To Clear, Prisms, Bohemian, 12 In., Pair	165.00
Fairyland luster is included in the Wedgwood category	
Orange, Creamer	20.00
Pink, Condiment Set, Footed Holder, China Shovel Spoons	45.00
Pink, Creamer, Cow, England, 6 1/2 In., 2 Piece ....*Illus*	259.00
Pink, Cup & Saucer, House	27.00
Pink, Cup & Saucer, House Pattern, 12 Piece	535.00
Pink, Figurine Set, Figure For Each Season, Enamel Decorated, c.1825, 9 In., Set Of 4	1380.00
Pink, Figurine, Strawberry, Embossed	259.00

Pink, Jug, Black Transfer, MacDonough's Victory On Lake Champlain, 8 1/2 In. 5170.00
Pink, Jug, Black Transfer, War Heroes, Eagle & Shield, Encircled Frigate, 7 In. 1870.00
Pink, Mustache Cup & Saucer, Cobalt Blue, Gold Fruit, Emblem, Victorian.................. 110.00
Pink, Pitcher, Classical Figures, Purple, Sewell, 1825, 9 In., Pair............................*Illus* 489.00
Pink, Pitcher, House Design, 6 In. 99.00
Pink, Pitcher, Officer, Horseback, 18th Century, England, 5 In. ....*Illus* 519.00
Pink, Pitcher, Officers On Horseback, Titles Wellington & Blucher, 5 1/8 In. 518.00
Pink, Pitcher, Queen Caroline, Verse, England, 1820, 5 1/4 In. ....*Illus* 633.00
Pink, Sugar & Creamer... 66.00
Pink, Tea Set, Children's Pictures, Crown Mark 275.00
Pink, Tea Set, Grape Vines, Red Enameled, England, 19th Century, 16 Piece.............. 288.00
Pink, Tea Set, Slop & Milk, 3 Piece 329.00
Pink, Tea Set, Three Pigs, Service For Two 325.00
Pink, Teapot, Chrysanthemum, Paste .... 249.00 to 250.00
Pink, Watch Holder, Pocket, Lion Finial, England, 1825, 7 1/2 In.........................*Illus* 805.00
Pitcher, Marquis Wellington & The Farmer's Arms, 19th Century, 8 1/4 In. 6325.00
Silver, Creamer... 150.00
Silver, Jug, Sporting, Blue Transfer, England, 1815, 6 1/4 In...........................*Illus* 460.00
Silver, Mug, Mother & Child Scene, Canary 420.00
Silver, Pitcher, Fallow Deer, Wedgwood, 4 In. 95.00
Silver, Pitcher, Floral, Enameled, England, 1815, 8 3/8 In.....................................*Illus* 1380.00
Silver, Pitcher, Floral, Polychrome Enameling, c.1815, 8 3/8 In. 1380.00
Silver Deposit, Jug, Sporting, Blue Transfer, England, 1815, 5 In.......................*Illus* 633.00
Sunderland luster pieces are in the Sunderland category
Tea Leaf luster pieces are listed in the Tea Leaf Ironstone category

LUSTRE ART GLASS Company was founded in Long Island, New York, in 1920 by Conrad Vahlsing and Paul Frank. The company made lampshades and globes that are almost indistinguishable from those made by Quezal. Most of the shades made by the company were unmarked.

    Shade, Gold & Blue Hearts, Threading, Calcite.. 150.00

LUSTRES are mantel decorations or pedestal vases with many hanging glass prisms. The name really refers to the prisms, and it is proper to refer to a single glass prism as a lustre. Either spelling, luster or lustre, is correct.

    Continental, Each With Pendants, 12 In., Pair... 1840.00
    Deer, Castle, Ruby Glass, Bohemian, 10 In... 245.00
    Mantel, Deer & Castle Scenes, Bohemian, Long Prisms, Late 1800s, Pair 545.00
    Prisms, Vaseline, 11 In., Pair.. 900.00
    Ruby Cut To Clear, Prisms, 12 In., Pair 350.00
    White Cut To Cranberry, 13 In.. 575.00
    Wide Vesicas & Diamonds Below Edge, Prism Hung, 13 x 6 In., Pair 225.00

MAASTRICHT, Holland, was the city where Petrus Regout established the De Sphinx pottery in 1836. The firm was noted for its transfer-printed earthenware. Many factories in Maastricht are still making ceramics.

    Bowl, Pack Horse, 6 In. 40.00
    Bowl, Pink Transfers, Pack Horse, Windmill, Draped Ribbon Interior, 6 In.................... 75.00
    Pitcher & Bowl, Sprays Of Hydrangeas Inside & Out, 12-In. Pitcher 650.00

MAIZE glass was made by W. L. Libbey & Son Company of Toledo, Ohio, after 1889. The glass resembled an ear of corn. The leaves were usually green, but some pieces were made with blue or red leaves. The kernels of corn were light yellow, white, or light green.

    Celery Vase, Green Husks, Opaque, Libbey.. 145.00
    Vase, Blue Leaves, Crystal, Libbey 158.00

MAJOLICA is a general term for any pottery glazed with an opaque tin enamel that conceals the color of the clay body. It has been made since the fourteenth century. Today's collector is most likely to find Victorian majolica. The heavy, colorful ware is rarely marked. Some famous makers include Wedgwood; Minton; Griffen, Smith and Hill (marked *Etruscan*); and Chesapeake Pottery (marked *Avalon* or *Clifton*).

Majolica, Bowl, Lily, Dolphin Footed,
Holdcroft, 9 1/2 x 9 1/2 In.

Majolica, Cheese Keeper, Underplate,
Rope & Fern, 11 1/2 In.

Ashtray & Match Holder, Black Boy On Stone Wall, Eating Ear Of Corn	175.00
Bowl, Dolphin & Lily, Twist Pedestal, Holdcroft, 9 1/2 x 9 1/2 In.	1265.00
Bowl, Green Lily Pad, White Water Lily, 11 1/2 In.	475.00
Bowl, Lily, Dolphin Footed, Holdcroft, 9 1/2 x 9 1/2 In.	*Illus* 1265.00
Bowl, Paneled Sides, Alternating Lobsters & Vegetables, c.1882, 11 In.	805.00
Bowl, Shell, Seaweed, Etruscan	170.00
Bowl, Underplate, Wheat & Daisy, Turquoise, Lavender Interior, Jones, 6 1/2 In.	1750.00
Bowl, Water Lily, Oval, Samuel Lear, 9 1/2 In.	358.00
Box, Sardine, Cover, Mottled, Pink Interior, Underplate	350.00
Box, Sardine, Fish Draped On Cover, George Jones, c.1875, 7 1/2 x 8 1/2 In.	1035.00
Box, Sardine, Underplate, George Jones	1320.00
Butter Chip, Fan & Floral	110.00
Butter Chip, Leaf, Veined, Teal Green, 3 In.	18.00
Cake Plate, Maple Leaf Design, Footed, Etruscan, Signed, 9 In.	415.00
Cake Plate, Morning Glories, Signed	625.00
Cake Plate, Shell, Raised On 3 Dolphins, 8 3/4 In.	425.00
Cake Stand, Bird & Holly, Yellow, Brown	265.00
Cake Stand, Lily Pad, Footed	330.00
Candleholder, Cherub, Riding Dolphin, Large	195.00
Candleholder, Elephant, On Rear Legs, Dressed In Coat, Top Hat, 8 In.	310.00
Candlestick, Venezia Pattern, Austria, 12 1/2 In.	90.00
Centerpiece, 4 Winged Cherubs Seated At Each Foot, Minton, c.1875, 23 In.	3165.00
Centerpiece, Shell Shaped Oval Top, Mermaid Standard, Shell Feet, 16 1/2 In.	250.00
Charger, Crab, Mussels & Seaweed, Red, 13 In.	295.00
Charger, Portrait Of Beatrice D'Este, c.1880, 16 In.	60.00
Charger, Portrait Of Ludovico Sforza, c.1880, 16 In.	60.00
Charger, Procession Of Magi, Cobalt Border With Serpents, c.1870, 17 1/2 In.	190.00
Cheese Keeper, Rope & Fern, 11 1/2 In.	3000.00
Cheese Keeper, Swan & Lily White Ground, Etruscan	825.00
Cheese Keeper, Underplate, Rope & Fern, 11 1/2 In.	*Illus* 2970.00
Compote, Stork Pedestal, Green & Brown, 5 3/4 In.	395.00
Compote, Water Lily, Sea Nymph On Dolphin's Back Support, c.1880, 12 1/4 In.	1495.00
Creamer, Bird & Iris	110.00
Creamer, Corn	38.00
Creamer, Goat	130.00
Cup & Saucer, Fish & Seaweed, Cobalt Blue, Pink Interior	220.00
Dish, 2 Salamanders, Palissy, 12 1/2 In.	990.00
Dish, Blackberries, Vines & Leaves, Clifton, 9 1/2 In.	120.00
Dish, Figures In Boat, Florentine, 15 1/2 In.	440.00
Dish, Floral Strawberry, White Ground, George Jones, 10 In.	1000.00

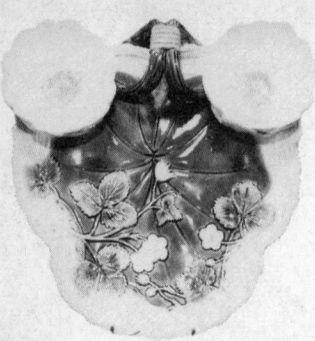

Majolica, Dish, Serving, Floral
Strawberry, White, George Jones

Majolica, Pitcher, Stork In Marsh,
Eel Handle, 11 In.

Dish, Game, Molded Game, Signed, c.1886, 9 1/2 In.	430.00
Dish, Leaf Shape, Applied Bucket Spilling Out Dice, Aqua, Green & Pink, 5 3/4 In.	125.00
Dish, Sardine, Cover, 8 1/2-In. Underplate	1100.00
Dish, Serving, Floral Strawberry, White, George Jones ....*Illus*	990.00
Ewer, Cover, On Stand, Salamander Handle, Palissy, 14 In.	1650.00
Figurine, Black Boy Eating Watermelon	125.00
Figurine, Boy & Girl Fishing, With Boats, 9 1/2 In., Pair	358.00
Figurine, Magpies, Marked, Minton, 21 1/2 In., Pair	518.00
Humidor, Black Boy Reclining On Coconut, c.1890	795.00
Humidor, Scotsman	90.00
Jardiniere, Classical Figure, Blue & White, 12 In.	265.00
Jardiniere, Raised Fruit, Brown, Blue, 19th Century, 8 1/2 In.	115.00
Jardiniere, Underplate, Spiral Fluted Body, Fruit & Floral Swags	2415.00
Letter Holder, Art Nouveau, Continental	1035.00
Match Holder, Town Crier	55.00
Mug, Black Berry, 3 1/4 In.	90.00
Mug, Corn, 5 1/2 In.	38.00
Mug, Pineapple, Etruscan	165.00
Oyster Server, 3 Tiers, Minton	4180.00
Oyster Server, 4 Tiers, Minton	4180.00
Pitcher, Allover Scrolled Leaf Design, 11 In.	460.00
Pitcher, Bird & Nest, Blue Eggs, 6 In.	90.00
Pitcher, Bird Design, Strawberry & Green, 7 In.	150.00
Pitcher, Bird With Nest, Leaves, White Ground, 9 3/4 In.	357.00
Pitcher, Birds Feeding Young, 6 In.	300.00
Pitcher, Castle Body, Medieval Figures, Jester Finial, Hinged Cover, c.1874, 13 In.	632.00
Pitcher, Corn, 8 In.	290.00
Pitcher, Duck, Beak Spout, 10 In.	135.00
Pitcher, Figural, Owl, 8 1/4 In.	300.00
Pitcher, Fish, 10 In.	295.00
Pitcher, Fish, Glug-Glug, 10 In.	330.00
Pitcher, Floral, 9 In.	775.00
Pitcher, Floral, Fruit & Armorial, Yellow, Blue, Orange & Green, 9 In.	115.00
Pitcher, Fruit & Leaf Design, 7 In.	220.00
Pitcher, Fruiting Grapevines, Stippled Ground, Twig Handle, c.1880, 11 5/8 In.	172.00
Pitcher, Large Leaf, Fern Sprigs, Brown Tree Bark Ground, 8 1/2 In.	100.00
Pitcher, Lily-Of-The-Valley, Ferns, Ropes, 11 1/2 In.	1005.00
Pitcher, Milk, Baseball & Soccer Players, Wedgwood, 7 1/2 In.	1325.00
Pitcher, Milk, Leaves On Basket Weave, English Registry Mark, 6 1/2 In.	165.00
Pitcher, Morning Glory, Yellow Ground, Pink Flowers, 7 In.	65.00
Pitcher, Owl, 8 In.	425.00

Pitcher, Pineapple, Lavender Interior, 7 In... 195.00
Pitcher, Pink 5-Petal Open Rose, Bud, Leaves, Basket Weave, Greek Key Top, 7 In. ... 225.00
Pitcher, Raised Circle Design, Hinged Pewter Cover, 12 1/2 In.............................. 245.00
Pitcher, Rooster, 8 In.. 200.00
Pitcher, Stork In Marsh, Eel Handle, 11 In... *Illus* 440.00
Pitcher, Stork With Fish, Bamboo Bottom, 7 1/4 In.. 265.00
Pitcher, Water Lily, 9 In.. 210.00
Place Card Holder, Floral Basket, Porcelain Tag For Name, 2 Piece........................... 35.00
Planter, Fish On Outside, Rustic Forms All Around, 11 x 16 In. 1375.00
Plaque, Landscape Hunt Scene, Green Glaze, Marked, 7 1/2 In............................. 193.00
Plaque, Mythological Scenes, Wedgwood, 10 1/2 In., Pair 825.00
Plaque, Naughty Girl, Pantaloons On Back, 7 In... 200.00
Plate, Basket Weave & Blackberry, Brown Ground, 10 In. 135.00
Plate, Begonia Leaf, Green, Yellow & Deep Rose Shades, 10 In. 110.00
Plate, Begonia, Brown Ground, 9 In. 95.00
Plate, Bird, Trenton Type 160.00
Plate, Cabbage Leaf Form, Wedgwood, 7 3/4 In., 6 Piece 515.00
Plate, Cauliflower, Etruscan, 9 1/4 In. 220.00
Plate, Fern Pattern, White Flowers, Pink Ground, c.1870 .... 165.00
Plate, Floral & Cherry Design, 11 1/2 In.. 95.00
Plate, Floral, 3 Leaves, White Basket Weave, Yellow Rim, 9 In........................... 72.00
Plate, Girl, Netting Sea Creatures, Seaweed & Shell Rim, 8 1/2 In. 192.00
Plate, Leaf, 7 3/4 In., 8 Piece.. 187.00
Plate, Leaf, Fern, 6 1/4 In. 40.00
Plate, Leaf, Scalloped Rim, Etruscan, 12 x 9 In. 165.00
Plate, Mermaid Riding Dolphins, Shells & Lobsters On Rim, 8 1/2 In. 225.00
Plate, Overlapping Begonia Leaves, Dark Greens, Rose & Yellow......................... 80.00
Plate, Oyster, Insect & Fan, Fielding 688.00
Plate, Peach Flowers, Shaded Green Ground, 9 1/2 In.. 45.00
Plate, Peacock, Spreading Tail, 6 In. 55.00
Plate, Pond Lily, 8 1/4 In. 55.00
Plate, Raised Berries & Leaves, 7 1/2 In. 110.00
Plate, Snake & Toad, Palissy, Jose Alves Cunha, 9 1/2 In. .... 440.00 to 550.00
Plate, Star Center, Leaf Border, Etruscan, 9 1/8 In. 220.00
Plate, Strawberry, 7 1/4 In... 45.00
Platter, Bird & Fan, Eureka, Lavender, Turquoise & Yellow, 15 1/2 x 10 1/2 In. 605.00
Platter, Fish, Beige, Brown & Pink, Royal Doulton, 12 In. 325.00
Platter, Fruits, Avalon, 16 1/2 x 9 1/2 In.. 110.00
Platter, Ribbon & Bowl, 8 Matching Dishes, Wedgwood, 13 x 11 In. 1540.00
Platter, Water Lily, Samuel Lear, 12 1/2 x 10 In.. 385.00
Platter, Worble Fern, Basket Weave, 14 In. 150.00
Pot, Frog, 3 Footed, Green Glaze, Minton, England, c.1858, 6 3/4 In., Pair.................. 1092.00
Salt, Figural, Sailor, Minton 660.00
Spooner, Bamboo, Etruscan 138.00
Sugar, Cover, Brown To Gold Basket Weave, Green Leaves, Red Roses 145.00
Syrup, Sunflower, Etruscan, 8 In. 550.00
Tea Set, Wild Rose, England, 3 Piece 555.00
Teapot, Bird & Iris, 19th Century.. 160.00
Teapot, Bird's Nest Shape, Bird Cover 400.00
Tile, Wall, Repeating Floral Trellis, c.1875, 8 x 8 In. 860.00
Tobacco Jar, Alpine Man 150.00
Tobacco Jar, Figural, Bear, Blue Jacket, Pipe In Hand, 6 1/2 In. 160.00
Tobacco Jar, Figural, Elephant, Gray, Pink Jacket, Pipe In Mouth, 7 In. 175.00
Tray, Bird & Flower Design, Marked, 12 1/2 In. 150.00
Umbrella Stand, Molded Scroll & Floral Design, Pierced Collar, 22 In. 60.00
Umbrella Stand, Panels Of Flying Cranes, c.1875, 24 In. 1380.00
Umbrella Stand, Side Handles, Foliate Scrolls Within Borders, 24 1/8 In. 863.00
Vase, 4 Pink Water Lilies, Buds Around Rim, Gold Trim, Footed 165.00
Vase, Applied Red Cherries, Cream Ground, Austria, 10 1/2 In. 60.00
Vase, Full Figure Dragon Surrounds Vase, Field Of Clouds, Cobalt, 1880s, 28 In......... 690.00
Vase, Opposing Noblemen, Lion Heads, Rings In Mouth, Animals, 18 1/2 In. 675.00
Wall Pocket, Dog, With Collar, Glazed, c.1900, France, 7 1/2 In. 320.00
Wall Pocket, Shoe, Pair.. 710.00

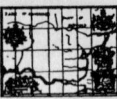

MAPS of all types have been collected for centuries. The earliest known printed maps were made in 1478. The first printed street map showed London in 1559. The first road maps for use by drivers of automobiles were made in 1901. Collectors buy maps that were pages of old books, as well as the multifolded road maps popular in this century.

Albany, N.Y., 1830	45.00
Auto Trails, Pennsylvania & New Jersey, 1923	12.00
Auto Trails In New York, 1918	10.00
Devonshire, John Speed, London, 1611	375.00
Dioecesis Berginsis Tabula, Colored, Frame, 18 x 22 In.	110.00
Florida, N. & S. Carolina, Florida Forts & Swamps, 1866, 3 Sections, 12 x 15 In.	35.00
Globe, Celestial, Floor Stand, Weber Costello Co.	875.00
Globe, Celestial, Iron Stand, Claw Feet Holding Glass Balls	925.00
Globe, Celestial, Mahogany Tripod Support, W.S. Jones, 24 x 17 In.	2760.00
Globe, G. & J. Carey, Terrestrial, On Stand, Dated 1816, 25 In., Pair	14950.00
Globe, Puzzle, Terrestrial, Geographic Educator, c.1928, 6 In.	2850.00
Globe, Terrestrial, Copper Stand, Animal Head Feet, W. & A. D. Johnson, 45 x 24 In.	2640.00
Globe, Terrestrial, Table, Iron Base, Joslin's, Boston, 19th Century, 19 x 17 In.	1610.00
Globe, Terrestrial, W. & T.M. Bardin, Mahogany Stand, 1807, 18 1/2 In.	3738.00
Maine, From Carey's American Atlas, Colored, Frame, 1814, 14 3/4 x 12 3/4 In.	138.00
Mississippi River, Ribbon, Lithographed On Linen, Wooden Roller Case	3630.00
Monterey Peninsula, California, History In Cartoon Form, 1920s	55.00
New York City, Manhattan & Brooklyn Sections, Hand Colored, 1866, 12 x 15 In.	35.00
North America, Robert De Vaugondy, France, Frame, 18th Century, 13 3/4 x 12 In.	195.00
Northern Europe, 5 Germanial Interiors, Frame, 19 3/8 x 22 3/4 In.	200.00
Railroad, United States, Depots, Stations, Ensign, Bridgman & Fannings, Frame	175.00
Railway, Ohio, Linen, 1902	60.00
Southern California, Southern Pacific Railroad, 1927	15.00
Street, Portland, Oregon, Fold-Out, 1910	18.00
Territorial Growth Of The U.S., Between 1776 & 1887, Color, 1892	10.00
Texas, Powers Colony, Plat Holders, 1886	55.00
Train Routes, Textile, England, 19th Century	185.00
Universal Atlas, Rand McNally, 1898	165.00
Walt Disney's Guide To Disneyland, Paper, Color, 1968, 20 x 44 In.	125.00
West India Isles, London, J. Cary, 1883, 18 1/2 x 20 1/2 In.	90.00
Westchester County, New York, 1910, 22 x 33 In.	30.00
White Plains, New York, 1910, 22 x 33 In.	60.00

MARBLE collectors pay highest prices for glass and sulphide marbles. The game of marbles has been popular since the days of the ancient Romans. American children were able to buy marbles by the mid-eighteenth century. Dutch glazed clay marbles were least expensive. Glazed pottery marbles, attributed to the Bennington potteries in Vermont, were of a better quality. Marbles made of pink marble were also available by the 1830s. Glass marbles seem to have been made later. By 1880, Samuel C. Dyke of South Akron, Ohio, was making clay marbles and The National Onyx Marble Company was making marbles of onyx. The Navarre Glass Marble Company of Navarre, Ohio, and M. B. Mishler of Ravenna, Ohio, made the glass marbles. Ohio remained the center of the marble industry, and the Akron-made Akro Agate brand became nationally known. Sulphides are glass marbles with frosted white figures in the center.

Akro Agate, Orange & Blue, Corkscrew, 1 1/4 In.	525.00
Banded Swirl, 5/8 In.	45.00
Clambroth, Black, 9/16 In.	175.00
Cobalt Blue, Mica, 1 7/16 In.	295.00
Corkscrew, Popeye, Akro Agate Co., Shooter Size Hybrid, 23/32 In.	120.00
End Of Day, Onionskin, 1 3/8 In. ....*Illus*	205.00
End Of Day, Onionskin, 2 1/32 In.	210.00
End Of Day, Ribbon Core, 13/16 In.	310.00
Lutz, End Of Day, Onionskin, 3/4 In. ....460.00 to 483.00
Lutz, Joseph's Coat, 1 9/16 In.	1300.00
Lutz, Lavender Ribbon, 7/8 In.	600.00

Marble, End Of Day, Onionskin, 1 3/8 In.

Marble, Ribbon Swirl

Marble, Swirl Flame, Christensen Agate Co., 19/32 In.

Lutz, Opaque White, Blue Lines	650.00
Lutz, Solid Core, 2 1/32 In.	225.00
Lutz, Swirl, Blue Opaque	140.00
Mica, End Of Day, Onionskin, 2 In.	300.00 to 315.00
Onionskin, 1 3/4 In.	400.00
Onionskin, 2 5/8 In.	3050.00
Onionskin, 4 Panels, 2 1/4 In.	135.00
Onionskin, Blue & Orange, 1 15/16 In.	172.00
Orphan Annie	80.00
Pee Wee, Divided Core, 1 1/2 In.	20.00
Peppermint, Swirl, 11/16 In.	90.00 to 120.00
Ribbon Swirl	*Illus* 1150.00
Sulphide, Bird	105.00
Sulphide, Donkey	90.00
Sulphide, Frog, 1 1/4 In.	150.00
Sulphide, Frog, 1 13/16 In.	260.00 to 273.00
Sulphide, Girl, 1 9/16 In.	175.00
Sulphide, Head, Oriental Gentleman, 1 5/8 In.	1725.00
Sulphide, Horse, 1 3/16 In.	125.00
Sulphide, Indian, 15/16 In.	135.00
Sulphide, Jenny Lind, Double Overlay	135.00
Sulphide, Lady & Basket, 1 3/8 In.	750.00
Sulphide, Lion	80.00 to 90.00
Sulphide, Pit, 2 In.	75.00
Sulphide, Rabbit, 1 5/16 In.	180.00
Sulphide, Rooster	250.00
Sulphide, Santa Claus, Amber	2550.00
Sulphide, Sheep	150.00
Swirl, Bright Blue, Yellow Core, 1 9/16 In.	840.00
Swirl, Joseph's Coat, 7/8 In.	55.00
Swirl, Pastel Core, 1 5/16 In.	260.00
Swirl, Solid Core, 2 1/32 In.	27.00
Swirl, White, Red, Green, Blue, Outer Bands, Latticinio Co., 2 1/8 In.	200.00
Swirl Flame, Christensen Agate Co., 19/32 In.	*Illus* 150.00

MARBLE CARVINGS, such as large or small figurines, groups of people or animals, and architectural decorations, have been a special art form since the time of the ancient Greeks. Reproductions, especially of large Victorian groups, are being made of a mixture using marble dust. These are very difficult to detect and collectors should be careful. Other carvings are listed under Alabaster.

2 Winged Cherubs, Riding, With Bird's Nest, 38 In.	4600.00
Ariadne, Seated On Panther, White, c.1880, 48-In. Pedestal	8625.00
Ariadne, White, 18 x 15 1/2 In.	1092.00
Bust, Augustus Caesar, Cuirass, Italy, 19th Century, 31 1/4 In.	7475.00
Bust, Bearded Man, Tie, Vest & Jacket, c.1890, 28 x 20 In.	748.00
Bust, Caesar, Wooden Frame, Late 17th Century, 11 3/8 x 6 7/8 In.	3220.00

Bust, Little Girl, C. Zalli, 10 In. 330.00
Bust, Napoleon, Campaign Hat, Socle Base, 19th Century, 18 In. 1760.00
Bust, Roman Emperor, Full Armor, Cloak On Shoulder, c.1800, 17 1/2 In. 3450.00
Bust, Sir Percival, 21 1/2 In. 1375.00
Bust, Young Lady, White, Gray Marble Base, Houdon, 18 In. 2200.00
Candleholder, Boar's Head Shape, 5 1/2 In. 154.00
Capital, Entwined Beasts & Birds, France, 12th Century, 11 In. 1035.00
Fountain, 2 Putti, Standing & Drinking, Dolphin, Italy, c.1900 .... 20000.00
Group, Dancers, P. Wolfers, Green Base, 18 3/4 In. 5750.00
Head, Michelangelo, Italy, 16th Century, 10 3/4 In. 5175.00
Inuit, Monukana, 22 In. 302.00
Lamp, Black, Ormolu Mounted, Divided Cylindrical Stem, 32 In., Pair 4025.00
Marsyas, Roped To Tree, Wooden Base, France, 35 In. 4600.00
Memorial, Book With Rose & Banner, Forget-Me-Not, F.C.M., 6 In. 75.00
Model, Roman Temple, Italy, 19th Century, Pair 4140.00
Pedestal, Cylinder Form, 1850 .... 825.00
Pedestal, Fluted Column, Removable Square Top, 32 In. 200.00
Pedestal, Fluted Spiral Standard, Green, 42 In. 515.00
Pedestal, Square, Medallions Above Leaf Base, 7 1/2 In. 2300.00
Plaque, Old Gentleman, Beaded, M.F. Foley, c.1865, 29 In. 880.00
Putto, White, Steiner, 35 In. 4025.00
Relief, Goddess Hebe, Long Flowing Hair, Eagle, Italy, 18th Century, 19 In. 1725.00
Relief, Horse, Henry Schonbauer, 1943 .... 137.50
Tazza, Neoclassical Style, Everted Rim, Square Base, Italy, 16 x 21 In., Pair 6325.00
Urn, Ram Heads Sides, Putto Base, Bronze Mounted, 27 In. 6900.00
Urn, Stepped Cover, George III, Ball Finial, Ribbed, 12 3/4 In. 7475.00
Woman, Adorned With Flowers, Continental, 24 1/2 In. 575.00
Woman, Affortunato Gory, Marble Base, Signed, 26 In. 6325.00
Woman, Seated, Outstretched Arm, G.B. Lombardi, Italy, 45 In. 2530.00

MARBLEHEAD Pottery was founded in 1905 by Dr. J. Hall as a rehabilitative
program for the patients of a Marblehead, Massachusetts, sanitarium. Two
years later it was separated from the sanitarium and it continued operations
until 1936. Many of the pieces were decorated with marine motifs.

Basket, Blue Matte Glaze, 3 Loop Handles, Pointed Base, 4 x 4 1/2 In. 220.00
Basket, Hanging, Gray Glaze, Projectile Shape, 3 x 3 3/4 In. 285.00
Bowl, 2-Tone Blue Leaves & Vines, Gray Ground, Hanna Tut, 6 1/2 x 2 In. 1210.00
Bowl, 2-Tone Green, Textured, 7 1/2 x 4 1/2 In. 220.00
Bowl, Closed, Matte Lavender Glaze, Impressed Mark, 3 x 5 1/2 In. 360.00
Bowl, Green, Blue Matte Interior, Arthur E. Baggs, 4 x 12 In. 415.00
Bowl, Inverted Rim, Olive Green, 6 In. 380.00
Bowl, Matte Blue Glaze, Impressed Mark, 4 1/2 x 6 1/2 In. 470.00
Bowl, Matte Gray Glaze, Impressed Mark, 1 1/2 x 6 1/4 In. 195.00
Bowl, Rolled Rim, Gray Matte Glaze, Signed, 6 In. 230.00
Bowl, Semimatte Glaze, Blue Interior, Blue, 6 1/4 In. 395.00
Bowl, Wide Rolled Rim, Gray Glaze, Impressed Mark, 6 In. 230.00
Chamberstick, Ring Handle, Green Glaze, Marked, 4 1/2 In. 750.00
Perfume Bottle, Sarcophagus Shape, Mottled Violet, Label, 5 x 1 1/2 In. 415.00
Pitcher, Green Top & Base, Sandy Matte Center, Signed, 8 1/2 In. 350.00
Pitcher, Tan, Brown, Sailing Ship, Yellow & Red, Billowing Flag, 2 Sides, 5 In. 1200.00
Teapot, Cover, Arts & Crafts Geometric Design, Woven Fiber Handle, 7 1/2 In. 2530.00
Tile, 4 Stylized Galleons, Speckled Green, Signed, Square, 6 1/4 In. 1100.00
Vase, Allover Blue Matte Glaze, Signed, 6 In. 275.00
Vase, Allover Dark Blue Matte Glaze, Signed, 4 1/2 In. 175.00
Vase, Blue Matte Glaze, Signed, 5 1/4 In. 195.00
Vase, Bud, Matte Mauve Glaze, Squatty Base, Cylindrical Neck, 6 x 2 3/4 In. 195.00
Vase, Bulbous, Blue High Glaze, 5 In. 140.00
Vase, Bulbous, Tapered, Stylized Trees, Oatmeal Ground, Hanna Tutt, 4 1/2 In. 715.00
Vase, Carved Floral, Blossoms, Berries, Lavender Ground, Signed, 5 In. 770.00
Vase, Classic Shape, Blue Glaze, Signed, 8 1/2 In. 1045.00
Vase, Dark Blue, Ball Feet, 3 In. 165.00
Vase, Deep Blue, Cylindrical, Impressed Mark, 6 In. 275.00
Vase, Finger Marks, Medium Blue Glaze, Wide Rim, Signed, 4 1/2 x 6 In. 235.00

Martin Brothers, Vase, Creatures, 10 In.

◆ ◆ ◆ ◆ ◆ ◆ ◆ ◆ ◆ ◆ ◆ ◆ ◆ ◆ ◆ ◆ ◆ ◆ ◆

Don't load your dishwasher with fine crystal, gold decorated glass or china, dishes with crazed glaze, lacquered metal, bone- or ivory- or wood-handled serving pieces, or wooden wares. They should never be cleaned in a dishwasher. The hot water and strong detergent will damage them.

◆ ◆ ◆ ◆ ◆ ◆ ◆ ◆ ◆ ◆ ◆ ◆ ◆ ◆ ◆ ◆ ◆ ◆ ◆

Vase, Flared Shape, Lavender Matte Glaze, 4 x 7 In.	250.00
Vase, Gray & Blue Flowers, Sea Gull Mark, 4 In.	1100.00
Vase, Gray Glaze, Blue Flecks, Finger Marks Interior, Label, 9 In.	825.00
Vase, Matte Speckled Gray Glaze, Impressed Slip Mark, 3 1/2 x 2 1/4 In.	140.00
Vase, Ovoid, Matte Yellow Glaze, 5 1/4 x 3 1/4 In.	225.00
Vase, Repeating Floral Design, Speckled Gray Base, Hanna Tutt, 4 1/2 In.	1550.00
Vase, Silver Trees, Blue Matte Ground, Signed H.T., 7 1/4 In.	2500.00
Vase, Stylized Arts & Crafts Design, Speckled Ground, Signed, 3 x 5 1/2 In.	1100.00
Vase, Stylized Tree, Green, Black Outling, Marked, 7 In.	1725.00

MARTIN BROTHERS of Middlesex, England, made martinware, a salt-glazed stoneware, between 1873 and 1915. Many figural jugs and vases were made by the three brothers. Of special interest are the fanciful birds, usually made with removable heads.

Martin Bro / *London*

Pitcher, Handle, Raised & Etched Flowers, Blues, 10 In.	825.00
Vase, 5 Incised Grotesque Dragons, 10 In.	5225.00
Vase, Creatures, 10 In.	*Illus* 5225.00
Vase, Grotesque Fish, Ribbed, Raised Bubbles, Gunmetal, 2 Handles, 5 In.	2000.00
Vase, Gun-Metal Glaze, Turned Body, Footed, 1902, 8 In.	110.00
Vase, Incised & Painted Long-Beaked Birds, Orchids, June 1897, 7 In.	1710.00
Vase, Incised Lilies, Cream, Brown, Flared Neck & Rim, 9 In.	1000.00

MARY GREGORY is the name used for a type of glass that is easily identified. White figures were painted on clear or colored glass as the decoration. The figures chosen were usually children at play. The first glass known as Mary Gregory was made about 1870. Similar glass is made even today. The traditional story has been that the glass was made at the Sandwich Glass works in Boston by a woman named Mary Gregory. Recent research suggests that it is possible that none was made at Sandwich. In general, all-white figures were used in the United States, tinted faces were probably used in Bohemia, France, Italy, Germany, Switzerland, and England. Children standing, not playing, were pictured after the 1950s.

Bottle, Sapphire Blue, Girl Enameled In White, Bubble Stopper, 9 1/2 x 3 1/2 In.	195.00
Bottle, White Boy, Golden Amber, Stopper, 9 1/4 In.	195.00
Bowl, Girl Fishing, 5 In.	75.00
Bowl, Sugar, Cover, Boy, White Enamel, Amber, 5 x 3 1/2 In.	195.00
Box, Boy With Sprig Of Flowers On Hinged Cover, Amber, 3 1/2 x 4 In.	435.00
Candy Dish, Cover, 2 Children, Amber, 3 Footed, Signed, 7 1/2 In.	228.00
Cruet, Green, Crystal Stopper	100.00
Cruet, Vinegar, Amber, Young Girl, White Enamel, Matching Stopper, 8 3/4 In.	245.00
Cruet, Wine, Boy Sitting On Chair, Green, 10 1/4 x 5 1/2 In.	235.00
Cruet, Young Boy, Bubble Stopper, Amber, 9 1/2 In.	245.00
Decanter, Diamond Optic, Crimped Rim, Silver Stand, c.1890, 11 In.	185.00
Dish, Cheese, High Dome, Scene Of 2 Girls & Boy, Cranberry, 9 In.	365.00

Ewer, White Elk, Lime Green, 7 In.	135.00
Goblet, White Elk, Emerald Green	135.00
Muffineer, Boy In Reeds, Peach Ground, Silver Plated Cover, 5 1/2 In.	100.00
Mug, Barrel Shape, Boy & Girl Facing Each Other, Golden Amber, 4 In., Pair	145.00
Perfume Bottle, Atomizer, Boy & Girl Facing Each Other, Cranberry, 5 In.	360.00
Pitcher, Boy With Flowers Amid Lilies-Of-The-Valley, Green, Gold Trim, 5 In.	170.00
Pitcher, Little Girl, Trees, Flowers, Applied Handle, 9 In.	125.00
Rose Bowl, Boy Holds Bird, Gold Scrolls & Lattice, Green, 6 1/2 In.	210.00
Stein, Girl With Parasol, Birds, Fence, Trees, Amber Cover, Metal Trim, 6 In.	250.00
Syrup, Ruby	495.00
Tray, Boy With Cane, Deer, Girl, Green, 11 In.	450.00
Tumbler, Boy, Flowers & Trees	25.00
Vase, Boy & Girl, White Enamel, Sapphire Blue, 6 1/4 x 2 3/4 In., Pair	145.00
Vase, Boy Chasing Butterflies With Net, Black Base, 15 In.	475.00
Vase, Boy In Knickers, Sword & Bugle, Girl, Flowers, Trees, 8 x 3 3/8 In., Pair	475.00
Vase, Boy In Suit, White Enamel, Lime Green, Round Top, 11 In.	85.00
Vase, Boy On His Knee, Holding Heart Out To Girl, Sapphire Blue, 11 3/4 In.	460.00
Vase, Bud, Hand-Enameled Putto, Green, 19th Century, 6 3/4 In.	46.00
Vase, Cobalt Blue, 12 In.	130.00
Vase, Girl In Hat, Black Amethyst, 9 3/4 In.	195.00
Vase, Green Enamel Woman & Man, White Tree Ground, 12 In., Pair	475.00
Vase, White Boy & Girl, Cranberry, 10 In., Pair	345.00
Vase, Woman Sitting On Bench, Light Green, 14 In.	195.00

MASONIC, see Fraternal

MASSIER, a French art pottery, was made by brothers Jerome, Delphin, and Clement Massier in Vallauris and Golfe-Juan, France, in the late nineteenth and early twentieth centuries. It has an iridescent metallic luster glaze that resembles the Weller Sicard pottery glaze. Most pieces are marked *J. Massier.*

Bird Bath, Basket Weave Design, Turquoise Interior, Doves On Rim, 25 In.	2500.00
Bowl, Squares Of Mosaic, 4 1/2 In.	295.00
Charger, French Scene, Juniper Tree, Shoreline, Signed, c.1901, 12 1/2 In.	1100.00
Figurine, Grasshopper, Handmade, Glazed, c.1870	3250.00
Jardiniere, Art Nouveau Maidens, Poppies At Base, c.1900, 4 Ft. 8 1/2 In.	6612.00
Vase, 3-Leaf Clovers, Gold & Green, Paper Label, 2 1/4 In.	288.00
Vase, Applied Birds, Majolica Glaze, Blue & Purple Luster Glaze, 9 1/2 In., Pair	3500.00
Vase, Daisies, Mustard Ground, Baluster, 2 Handles, Golfe-Juan, 18 3/4 In.	345.00
Vase, Enamel Over Unglazed Buff Body, Incised Lines, Signed	350.00

MATCH HOLDERS were made to hold the large wooden matches that were used in the nineteenth and twentieth centuries for a variety of purposes. The kitchen stove and the fireplace or furnace had to be lit regularly. One type of match holder was made to hang on the wall, another was designed to be kept on a tabletop. Of special interest today are match holders that have advertisements as part of the design.

Ace Of Clubs, Sterling Silver, Enameled, 1900	33.00
Aladdin	35.00
Black Boy Emerging From Egg	145.00
Black Boys, Cotton Bale	139.00
Blackamoor, Porcelain, Germany	30.00
Boots, Cast Iron, Black & Gold, 3 1/8 x 3 7/8 In.	80.00
Brass, Marbles Brand, 1900	20.00
Bulldog Head, Cast Iron, 2 1/2 x 2 3/4 In.	45.00
Bust Of Columbus, Cast Iron	80.00
Ceresota	80.00
Child, Heubach-Type, Says Strike My Back, Bisque	95.00
Christopher Columbus, Cast Iron	37.00
Clover, 4-Leaf, Sterling Silver, Black, Starr & Frost Co., 1900	77.00
Coon Kitchen	225.00
De Laval, Figural	180.00 to 285.00
Dutch Boy Paints, Figural, Tin, 6 1/2 x 3 In.	247.00
Giesecke Brand Shoe, St. Louis, Tin Lithograph	85.00

Match Safe, Hand Holding Cards, Four Aces, Silver, c.1890;
Match Safe, Hand Holding Cards, I'll Try Solo, Silver, c.1890;
Match Safe, Roulette, Enamel On Silver, c.1900

Goebel Beer	150.00
Gold, 18K Yellow, With Cigar Cutter, Engraved Crown, England	432.00
Kaiers Beer, Pa.	150.00
Keen Kutter, Cast Iron, Wall	100.00
Kool Cigarettes	30.00
Little Red Riding Hood, Wall	300.00
Mammy, Figural, Hammered Tin, Copper, Painted, Striker, Double, 4 1/2 x 5 In.	245.00
Michigan Stove Co., The Best, Rabbit Shape	150.00
Modoc, Indiana, Tin, Wall	22.00
Mother & Father Cat, Holding Kitten, Porcelain, 4 1/2 In., Pair	90.00
National Cash Register Logo	30.00
Old Judson, Tin Lithograph, Wall	135.00
Phil Mayer's New Orleans Cuban Cigars, Gray & Cobalt Blue	150.00
Salem Cigarettes, Tin	20.00
Smith, Lawless Shoe Co., Metal	47.00
Universal Stove & Ranges	175.00

MATCH SAFES were designed to be carried in the pocket. Early matches were made with phosphorus and could ignite unexpectedly. The matches were safely stored in the tightly closed container. Match safes were made in sterling silver, plated silver, or other metals. The English call these *vesta boxes*.

Alcorn Hotel, Celluloid	50.00
Anheuser-Busch	125.00
Daisies, Hand Painted, Horseshoe Shape	68.00
Dancing Couple, Race Horses, Horseshoe, Sterling Silver, 1890	275.00
Flag & Eagle, Brass	40.00
Floral Design, Silver	20.00
Floral Engraving, Silver	65.00
Game Design, Iron	70.00
Good Luck, 4-Leaf Clover, Dice, Wishbone, Silver, 1890	385.00
Hand Holding Cards, Four Aces, Silver, c.1890 .... *Illus*	357.00
Hand Holding Cards, I'll Try Solo, Silver, c.1890 .... *Illus*	275.00
Havana American Cigars, 1904	55.00
Monmouth Gravel Co., Nude On Reverse, Celluloid, Pocket, 2 3/4 In.	357.00
Nude Woman, Full Figure, Silver	90.00
Pig, Figural, Head Flips Open, Brass	95.00
Roulette, Enamel On Silver, c.1900 .... *Illus*	550.00
Scotty, Figural	45.00
Silver, Aces, Poker Chips, 1890	360.00
Silver, Enameled Cards, 1880	415.00
Smoking Woman, Various Animals Playing Cards, Sterling Silver	385.00
Spades Royal Flush Hand, Enameled, Silver, 1890	900.00
Summertime, Kate Greenaway	80.00
Sunny Clime Havana Cigars, 10 In.	50.00

Unger Bros., Cupid Kissing Woman 185.00
Violin Shape, 1930s.. 195.00
Whistle & Compass, Combination, Plastic, Red, Kumbak, West Germany 10.00

MATSU-NO-KE was a type of applied decoration for glass patented by Frederick Carder in 1922. There is clear evidence that pieces were made before that date at the Steuben glassworks. Stevens & Williams of England also made an applied decoration by the same name.

Vase, Green Shaded To White, Design, 9 In. 626.00

MATT MORGAN, an English artist, was making pottery in Cincinnati, Ohio, by 1883. His pieces were decorated to resemble Moorish wares. Incised designs and colors were applied to raised panels on the pottery. Shiny or matte glazes were used. The company lasted less than two years.

Dish, White Cherry Blossoms, Japanese Style, 2 Handles, Artist, 3 3/4 In. 165.00
Tile, Allover Morning Glory Blossoms, Bisque, Marked, 4 In. 121.00
Tile, Stylized Poppies & Leaves, Bisque, Marked, 6 In. 193.00
Vase, Limoges-Style Oriental Scene, Brown Ground, 1883, 5 3/4 x 6 In. 230.00

MCCOY pottery was made in Roseville, Ohio. The J. W. McCoy Pottery was founded in 1899. It became the Brush McCoy Pottery Company in 1911. The name changed to the Brush Pottery in 1925. The word *Brush* was usually included in the mark on their pieces. The Nelson McCoy Sanitary and Stoneware Company, a different firm, was founded in Roseville, Ohio, in 1910. The firm made art pottery after 1926. In 1933 it became the Nelson McCoy Pottery. Pieces marked *McCoy* were made by the Nelson McCoy Company. Cookie jars were made from the 1930s until December 1990 when the McCoy factory closed. In 1990 the McCoy mark was put back on pottery by a firm unrelated to the original company.

Ashtray, Smokey The Bear... 50.00
Banana Boat, Calypso, 1959... 75.00
Bank, Immigrant Savings 15.00
Bank, Lion.. 95.00
Bank, Rabbit... 95.00
Bank, Seaman's, White Sailor 30.00
Bank, Woodsey Owl... 100.00
Basket, Hanging, Basket Weave, Turquoise, Molded Loop Handles, 7 x 4 1/2 In. 35.00
Basket, Hanging, Pale Yellow Green 20.00
Bean Pot, Heinz, Brown, Small 5.00
Bookends, Elephant 180.00
Bowl, Antique Rose Flower, 6 x 2 In. 30.00
Bowl, Dark Teal, Incised Scrolls, Rays, Scalloped, Marked, 6 x 2 1/4 In. 12.00
Bowl, Leaf, Green, Oval, Marked, 10 3/8 x 6 1/2 x 2 1/2 In. 12.00
Bowl, Mixing, Green, Large 20.00
Bowl, Turtle, Light Brown, 5 3/4 x 4 1/2 In. 25.00
Clock, Chef.. 65.00
Coffeepot, El Rancho 125.00
Console Set, Rockraft, Stone Finish, 3 Piece 150.00
Cookie Jar, American Eagle 35.00
Cookie Jar, Apollo With Stickers .... 810.00 to 1200.00
Cookie Jar, Astronauts 1000.00
Cookie Jar, Bananas .... 115.00 to 145.00
Cookie Jar, Barn... 235.00
Cookie Jar, Barnum's Animal Crackers .... 210.00 to 425.00
Cookie Jar, Bear With Cookies In Vest 45.00
Cookie Jar, Bobby The Baker .... 40.00 to 85.00
Cookie Jar, Boy On Baseball .... 225.00 to 400.00
Cookie Jar, Boy On Football .... 155.00 to 225.00
Cookie Jar, Caboose.. 175.00
Cookie Jar, Chairman Of The Board, Brown .... 695.00 to 900.00
Cookie Jar, Chef's Head .... 95.00 to 125.00
Cookie Jar, Chipmunk.. 110.00

Cookie Jar, Christmas Tree..750.00 to 1000.00
Cookie Jar, Clown, Bust ....75.00 to 90.00
Cookie Jar, Clown, In Barrel, Green.....................................120.00 to 125.00
Cookie Jar, Coalby Cat ....275.00 to 350.00
Cookie Jar, Coffee Grinder 15.00
Cookie Jar, Coke Can 275.00
Cookie Jar, Cook Stove, Black ....30.00 to 40.00
Cookie Jar, Cookie Boy, White..160.00
Cookie Jar, Cookie House 110.00
Cookie Jar, Corn 135.00
Cookie Jar, Covered Wagon ....65.00 to 90.00
Cookie Jar, Dalmatian, 1961..*Illus*   403.00
Cookie Jar, Dog In House, Blue Bird...250.00
Cookie Jar, Dutch Boy, Full Paint ....40.00 to 45.00
Cookie Jar, Engine, Black...125.00
Cookie Jar, Engine, Silver 225.00
Cookie Jar, Engine, Yellow 200.00
Cookie Jar, Fireplace 85.00
Cookie Jar, Freddie The Gleep, Yellow..280.00
Cookie Jar, Frog On Stump 55.00
Cookie Jar, Globe 190.00
Cookie Jar, Goodie Goose 20.00
Cookie Jar, Grandma ....65.00 to 150.00
Cookie Jar, Hamm's Bear 150.00
Cookie Jar, Happy Face, Yellow 25.00
Cookie Jar, Heart, Hobnail, Blue 195.00
Cookie Jar, Hen On Nest 55.00
Cookie Jar, Hobby Horse...125.00 to 145.00
Cookie Jar, Honey Bear..50.00 to 110.00
Cookie Jar, Honey Bear, Dark Glaze 75.00
Cookie Jar, Honey Bear, Yellow..135.00
Cookie Jar, Indian Head ....270.00 to 350.00
Cookie Jar, Kangaroo, Tan 350.00
Cookie Jar, Keebler ....40.00 to 75.00
Cookie Jar, Kettle, Bronze 45.00
Cookie Jar, Kittens In Basket..400.00
Cookie Jar, Kookie Kettle...20.00
Cookie Jar, Lamb, On Basket Weave 49.00
Cookie Jar, Leprechaun, Green...1250.00
Cookie Jar, Log Cabin 100.00
Cookie Jar, Mac Dog 75.00
Cookie Jar, Mammy, Aqua 315.00
Cookie Jar, Mammy, With Cauliflowers...........................600.00 to 1500.00
Cookie Jar, Owl, Beige 30.00
Cookie Jar, Owl, Mr. And Mrs. 125.00
Cookie Jar, Panda Bear, Upside Down ....30.00 to 45.00
Cookie Jar, Penguin, All White 75.00

McCoy, Cookie Jar, Dalmatian, 1961

McCoy, Cookie Jar,
Purple Cow, 1950

Cookie Jar, Pineapple 40.00
Cookie Jar, Popeye, Cylinder 150.00
Cookie Jar, Purple Cow, 1950 .... *Illus* 1035.00
Cookie Jar, Quaker Oats 500.00
Cookie Jar, Red Apple 20.00
Cookie Jar, Rocking Chair, Dalmatians .... 295.00 to 425.00
Cookie Jar, Snoopy On Doghouse 210.00
Cookie Jar, Stagecoach .... 125.00 to 895.00
Cookie Jar, Teepee .... 175.00 to 325.00
Cookie Jar, Tulip 170.00
Cookie Jar, W.C. Fields .... 175.00 to 250.00
Cookie Jar, Winking Pig 200.00
Cookie Jar, Woodsey Owl .... 190.00 to 295.00
Cookie Jar, Wren House, 1960 .... 85.00 to 110.00
Creamer, Pine Cone 8.50
Cuspidor, Standard Glaze, Cigar Design, 5 In. 88.00
Decanter, Phantom, 1932 .... 40.00
Dish, Dog, Loy-Nel-Art 100.00
Dispenser, Tea, Chuck Wagon 235.00
Flower Frog, Rockraft, Stone Finish 20.00
Flowerpot, Double Beetle Band, Orange, Dark Green, 5 In. 8.00
Flowerpot, White 37.00
Holder, Toothbrush, Peter Rabbit 80.00
Jar, Grease, Cabbage 75.00
Jardiniere, Butterfly, Lavender, 3 x 3 3/8 In. 14.00
Jardiniere, Flying Birds, Green 40.00
Jardiniere, Loy-Nel-Art, Pansies, No. 205, 6 In. 66.00
Jug, Dutch, Musical, Ivotint 80.00
Lamp, Black Panther & Tree 35.00
Mug, Buccaneer 22.00
Pitcher, Acorn & Oak Leaf 25.00
Pitcher, Angel Fish, Brown 35.00
Pitcher, Buttermilk, Green 30.00
Pitcher, Fish Handle 40.00
Pitcher, Hobnail, Purple, Tall 85.00
Pitcher, Red 15.00
Planter, Bird Dog 50.00
Planter, Bird On The Rim 25.00
Planter, Blossomtime, Square, 5 3/4 x 5 1/4 x 5 In. 22.00
Planter, Brocade Artisan Pedestal, Pink 15.00
Planter, Butterfly 30.00
Planter, Deer & Fawn 6.00
Planter, Dog & Cart 20.00
Planter, Dopey, Figural 85.00
Planter, Double Shell, Green 6.00
Planter, Down By The Old Mill Stream 10.00
Planter, Duck, With Egg 35.00
Planter, Frog, Green, 8 In. 20.00
Planter, Goose & Cart, White 16.00
Planter, Hillbilly, Aqua 25.00
Planter, Liberty Bell, July 8 .... 100.00
Planter, Pine Cone Window Box, Rose, Gloss, 7 1/2 x 4 In. 16.00
Planter, Pineapple, Gold Trim 140.00
Planter, Pussy At Well 80.00
Planter, Quail .... 30.00 to 75.00
Planter, Spinning Wheel, Dog & Cat 25.00
Planter, Spinning Wheel, Scotty Dog 20.00
Planter, Sylvan, Small 12.00
Planter, Wishing Well 16.00
Planter, Zebra 225.00
Rose Bowl, Ruffled Top, Orange & Yellow Fruit, 4 In. 44.00
Scoop, Flour, Mammy 165.00
Stand, Umbrella, Green, 21 In. 45.00

McCoy, Vase, Green Glaze Floral, 1930s,
8 1/2 In.

McCoy, Vase, Urn, Salmon Top With
Green Base, 1935, 7 1/2 In.

String Holder, Chef	65.00
String Holder, Mammy	150.00
Tankard, Set, Rust	70.00
Tea Set, Ivy	80.00
Tea Set, Pine Cone, 3 Piece	45.00
Tureen, Soup, El Rancho, Sombrero Cover	195.00 to 295.00
Vase, Aegean, Matte Green, 9 In.	175.00
Vase, Amaryllis, Kolorkraft, Green, 11 In.	65.00
Vase, Bird, Green, Bulbous, Berries & Leaves, Rim Handles, 6 x 7 1/4 In.	35.00
Vase, Birdbath	45.00
Vase, Brocade Pillow, Green	20.00
Vase, Brocade Pillow, Red	20.00
Vase, Cornucopia, Cream, 7 In.	9.00
Vase, Crown Top, Leaves, Loy-Nel-Art, 14 In.	175.00
Vase, Double Bud, Aqua	20.00
Vase, Double Bud Dish, Matte Green	45.00
Vase, Fan, Grapes & Leaves, Brown Over Green, 8 In.	28.00
Vase, Green Glaze Floral, 1930s, 8 1/2 In. *Illus*	55.00
Vase, Hand, White	20.00
Vase, Lizard Handle, White	70.00
Vase, Lizard Skin, Dark Green, 9 3/8 In.	14.00
Vase, Painted Floral Spray, Baluster, Cylindrical, Loy-Nel-Art, 1906	99.00
Vase, Tulip Design, Green Glaze, 10 In.	24.00
Vase, Tulips, Buds, Footed, Green, 8 In.	18.00
Vase, Urn, Salmon Top With Green Base, 1935, 7 1/2 In. *Illus*	35.00
Vase, Vesta, Green, 13 In.	15.00 to 30.00
Wall Pocket, Banana	30.00
Wall Pocket, Dutch Shoe, Blue	20.00
Wall Pocket, Mailbox	40.00
Wall Pocket, Mexican, Aqua	35.00
Wall Pocket, Owl	125.00
Wall Pocket, Pear	40.00
Wall Pocket, Violin, Brown	55.00
Wall Pocket, Woman In Bonnet, 8 In.	14.00
Window Box, Apple Blossom, Blue	100.00

MCKEE is a name associated with various glass enterprises in the United States since 1836, including J. & F. McKee (1850), Bryce, McKee & Co. (1850 to 1854), McKee and Brothers (1865), and National Glass Co. (1899). In 1903, the McKee Glass Company was formed in Jeannette, Pennsylvania. It became McKee Division of the Thatcher Glass Co. in 1951 and was bought out by the Jeannette Corporation in 1961. Pressed glass, kitchenwares, and tablewares were produced. Jeannette Corporation closed in the early 1980s. Additional pieces may be included in the Custard Glass category.

PRESCUT

Bowl, Rock Crystal, Cream	27.00
Butter, Chalaine Blue	325.00

Candleholder, Rock Crystal, Satin Glass, Pair 30.00
Candlestick, Boston, 10 In. 95.00
Canister, Yellow, Round 40.00
Compote, Champion, Scalloped Edge, 8 In. 25.00
Cordial, Ruby, Rock Crystal, 3 In. 40.00
Creamer, Berry 20.00
Cup, Measure, Chalaine Blue, 4 Cup 185.00
Custard Cup, Jadite 5.00
Dish, 2-Head Chick Cover, Basket Base, Marked, 5 1/2 In. 1100.00
Dish, 4-Chicks Cover, Woven Basket Base, 2 3/4 x 4 1/4 In. 525.00
Dish, Dove Cover, Split Rib Base, Marked 550.00
Dish, Frog Cover 950.00
Eggcup, Jadite, Footed 12.00
Goblet, Rock Crystal, Red, Low-Footed 37.00
Measure, Seville, Yellow, 32 Oz. 60.00
Pickle, Aztec 15.00
Reamer, Grapefruit, Chalaine Blue 1000.00
Relish, Rock Crystal, 6 Sections 25.00
Toothpick, Colonial, Green 30.00
Toothpick, Colonial, No. 75 .... 25.00
Toothpick, Wisconsin, Purple 25.00

MEDICAL office furniture, operating tools, microscopes, thermometers, and other paraphernalia used by doctors are included in this category. Medicine bottles are listed in the Bottle category. There are related collectibles listed under Dental.

Amputation Set, Knives, Capital, Saws, Rosewood Case, Tiemann, c.1860 .... 1900.00
Back Brace, Woman's, Orthopedic, 1900, 18 In. 395.00
Bag, Doctor's, Alligator Skin 260.00
Bleeder, Brass, 3 Blades, Late-1700s 50.00
Bleeder, Brass, Germany, Case 125.00
Box, First Aid, Chemical Warfare, Metal, Empty 6.00
Box, Molded Glass Bottles, Rectangular Case, Mahogany, 9 x 9 1/2 In. 630.00
Breast Pump, 9 Glass Cups, Syringe, Card Cased, c.1910, France 150.00
Cabinet, Mirror, Base Drawer, Green, Red Horse's Head Top, Folk Art 795.00
Cabinet, Sterilizer, Hinged Glass Door & Sides, Shelves, 1920s, 17 1/2 In. 250.00
Chest, Medicine, St. John Ambulance Assn. CPR Center, Metal, Wall, 19 3/8 x 14 In. .. 120.00
Coagulator, Cameron, Art Deco 400.00
Crutches, Rosewood, Leather Arm Rests, Plated Brass Bands, 51 In., Pair 50.00
Dose Indicator, Dr. Wilson's, Tin Spoon Holder, Lithographed Box 110.00
Ear Trumpet, London Hearing Horn 275.00
Ear Trumpet, Lorgnette, Tortoiseshell, Curved Japanned Metal Ear Piece, 11 In. 2850.00
Eyecup, Cobalt Blue, Pedestal, Marked British Made 25.00
Eyecup, Cobalt, Wyeth 15.00
Eyecup, John Bull, Green, Pedestal, 1917 .... 70.00
Eyecup, Milk Glass 16.00
Eyecup, White Ceramic, Pinched Sides 14.00
Fleam, 2 Blades, Brass Case, Morris 115.00
Fleam, 3 Blades, Horn & Brass Case, GNJ. B 130.00
Forceps, Obstetrics, c.1800 .... 265.00
Glass Eye, Human, Blue 35.00
Glass Eyes, Artificial, Fitted Box, 25 Piece 150.00
Glass Eyes, Replacement, Oak Case, 50 Piece 1000.00
Healing Chair, Electro-Mechanical, Wappler 27500.00
Hot Water Bottle, Baby's, Red Rubber, 3 Little Kittens 30.00
Instrument, Bone Handle, 5 Piece 100.00
Invalid Feeder, Blue & White, Canton 40.00
Kit, 20 Bottles, Leather Case, Handle, F.S. & Asprey, London, 1860, 4 3/4 x 7 3/4 In. .. 300.00
Kit, Handle, Lock, 1900, 11 In. 995.00
Kit, Optician's, 19th Century, Fitted, Case 600.00
Knife, Bistoury, 1 Curved Blunt End, 1 Curved Pointed Blade, Otto & Sons 65.00
Lamp, Medication, Cresoline, Milk Glass Hurricane Globe 40.00
Lancet, Veterinary, Spring, Will & Fink, Case 250.00

Lens & Glasses, Optometrist's, F.A. Hardy & Co., Recovered Black Case 185.00
Machine, Electric Shock, Western Coil Co. 75.00
Machine, Electro-Magnetic, Williams Perfection, Oak Case 175.00
Microscope, Physician's, Single Pillar, Bausch & Lomb, Slide Carrier & Case............. 1250.00
Mortar, 4 Portraits Of Charles II, Bronze, England, c.1660, 4 1/4 In. 685.00
Mortar, Bronze, 12 In., Pair... 1650.00
Mortar, Sawtooth Border Base, Dated 1675, Brown Patina, Bronze, 5 1/2 In. 950.00
Mortar & Pestle, Griswold Mfg. Co., 1 Pt. 500.00
Mortar & Pestle, Lignum Vitae, Hand Turned, c.1820, 6 3/4 In., 10 3/4-In., Pestle 185.00
Nasal Douche, Box... 18.00
Optometer, Count The Dots, Nickel-Silver, Wooden Handle... 135.00
Optometrist, Lens Kit, Glass Top, 2 Drawers, Frames & Lenses, Welch Allyn Co. 330.00
Otophone, E.B. Meyrowitz, New York, Otophone 1C, Serial No. 3555 .... 120.00
Saw, Bone, Ciercker, 16 In... 125.00
Scalpel, Folding, Simulated Ebony Handle, B.M. & Co., Germany, 3 In. 30.00
Scalpel, Wester Bros., Germany, Bone Handle... 18.00
Stethoscope, Dr. Kehler's, Brass Chest Piece, Pilling & Son, Patent 1897................. 70.00
Stethoscope, Metal Ear Holder, Double Rubber Hoses, 1920s 75.00
Surgical Instrument Set, Bone Handle, 5 Piece 100.00
Table, Examination, Hamilton, Wood & Steel, Stool & Cabinet 4300.00
Tenaculum, Ivory Handle, Unsigned.. 15.00
Wheel Chair, Oak, Caned Back & Foot Rest 75.00

MEERSCHAUM pipes and other pieces of carved meerschaum, a soft mineral, date from the nineteenth century to the present.

Holder, Cigarette, Case 45.00
Pipe, Bearded Male In Turban, Fitted Case, 20th Century, 22 1/4 In......................... 460.00
Pipe, Cavalier In Plumed Hat.. 50.00
Pipe, Display, 36 Corncob Pipes, Missouri... 275.00
Pipe, Figure Of Young Boy & Horse, Amber Stem, Case, 7 In. 165.00
Pipe, Moorish Potentate, Ornamented Turban, Amber Stem, 5 3/4 In. 58.00
Pipe, Nautical, Carved Mermaid, c.1850s... 165.00
Pipe, Nude Woman, Amber Stem, Case, 9 1/2 In. 385.00
Pipe, Nude, Case.. 575.00
Pipe, Roman's-Head Bowl, Amber Stem... 55.00
Pipe, Victorian Lady's Head, Silver Plate & Amber Stem, Case, 4 1/2 In. 135.00

MEISSEN is a town in Germany where porcelain has been made since 1710. Any china made in the town can be called Meissen, although the famous Meissen factory made the finest porcelains of the area. The crossed swords mark of the great Meissen factory has been copied by many other firms in Germany and other parts of the world. Pieces of Meissen dinnerware in the Onion pattern are listed in their own category in this book.

Beaker & Saucer, Chinaman Strolling, Chinaman Leaning On Chair, c.1723, 5 3/8 In. 4600.00
Bottle, Gelber Lowe Pattern, Tiger Curling Around Bamboo, c.1740, 2 3/8 In. 635.00
Bowl, Blanc De Chine, Grape Vines, Oval, Marked, 10 x 14 In................................... 450.00
Bowl, Imari Pattern, Lobed, Oval, c.1735, 14 3/8 In.. 2185.00
Bowl, Reticulated, 4-Cherubs Base, Gilt, Oval, 12 1/2 In. 275.00
Bowl, Waste, Chinaman Approaching Others, Gilt Border, Hausmaler, c.1725, 7 In..... 4315.00
Bowl, Waste, Kakiemon, Phoenix In Flight, c.1735, 6 3/4 In.. 800.00
Candelabrum, Applied Flowers, Gilt, Basket Of Flowers Base, 20 In., Pair 495.00
Candlestick, Armorial, Border Of Acanthus Leaves At Top, c.1739, 8 1/8 In. 5750.00
Candlestick, Cherubs & Flowers, Gilt, 20 1/4 In., Pair 495.00
Candlestick, Gilt, Leaf-Molded Trim, Yellow, Late 19th Century, 11 1/2 In., Pair 230.00
Candlestick, Ormolu Mounted, Central Swan, Flower Heads, 6 1/2 In., Pair................ 3475.00
Centerpiece, Bacchanalian Figures, Wheat Gatherers, Signed, 17 In............................ 3350.00
Centerpiece, Center Bouquet, Gold Embossed Flowers, 12 In...................................... 950.00
Clock, Cherub Design, Double Bird Finial, Marked, c.1910, 12 In................................. 1210.00
Coffeepot, Parrots Perched On Rose Stem, c.1740, 7 1/8 In... 6900.00
Compote, Flowers, Gold Reticulated Rim 95.00
Cup & Saucer, Flaring Rim, Rose Sprigs, Double Scrolled Handle, 3 1/2 In................. 518.00
Cup & Saucer, Greek Key Handle, Late 1700s 175.00
Cup & Saucer, Kakiemon-Style, Birds, Flowers 275.00

Cup & Saucer, Pink Flowers.. 77.00
Cup & Saucer, Scroll Handle, Husk & Dot Design, c.1740, 2 5/8 In............................. 3450.00
Dessert Set, Floral Sprays, 6-In. Teapot, 3 Piece 690.00
Dish, Center Floral Spray, Intertwining Vines Surround, Signed, 10 1/2 In. 115.00
Dish, Leaf Shape, Gilt, Cobalt, 19th Century, 8 1/2 In., 5 Piece..................................... 660.00
Dish, Sauce, Figural, Reclining Courtier Holding Bowl, 11 In., Pair............................. 1725.00
Dish, Schmetterling Pattern, Scalloped Rim, Signed, c.1740, 13 1/4 In. 920.00
Dish, Tiger, Puce Tree Trunk, Floral Sprigs, Gelber Lowe, 13 7/8 In., Pair 7475.00
Eggcup, Hand Painted Roses, Fired-Gold Trim, c.1910, 2 1/4 In.................................... 80.00
Figurine, After The Ball, 10 In.. 1950.00
Figurine, Amorous Couple, Marked, 9 3/4 In. 920.00
Figurine, Baby, Reclining, Quilts & Pillows, With Dog... 3850.00
Figurine, Bagpipe Player, 18th Century Costume, Marked, 13 1/2 In. 990.00
Figurine, Bolognese Terriers, Seated, Curly White Coat, Signed, 5 3/8 & 6 1/8 In. 2585.00
Figurine, Boy, Fishing Basket & Fish, 7 In. 975.00
Figurine, Cat, 6 1/2 In. 165.00
Figurine, Chocolate Maker, Enameled, Crossed Swords, 4 1/4 In.................................... 860.00
Figurine, Cupid, 4 In. 750.50
Figurine, Cupid, Signed, 5 1/2 In. 920.00
Figurine, Dove, Black & Red Eyes, Signed, 3 3/4 In. 805.00
Figurine, Farmer, Pulling Cows, 11 x 17 In. 1150.00
Figurine, Gardener, Enameled, Crossed Swords, 7 1/2 In. 690.00
Figurine, Gardener, Ribbon In Hair, Bustled Skirt, c.1770, 9 In. 1035.00
Figurine, Juno & Peacock, Marked, 6 1/4 In. 975.00
Figurine, Laundress, Black Cap, Turquoise Skirt, Apron, c.1755, 4 3/8 In. 1035.00
Figurine, Mongolian, Man & Woman, Freeform Scrolled Base, 13 In., Pair.................... 1150.00
Figurine, Putto, Marked, 7 In. 825.00
Figurine, Seminude Woman, Blue Crossed Swords Mark, 18 In.................................*Illus* 2760.00
Figurine, Shoe, With 2 Angels, 5 1/2 In. ....353.00 to 405.00
Figurine, Spaniel, Begging, On Hind Legs, Shaggy Coat, Signed, 10 1/8 In. 975.00
Figurine, Wheat Gatherers At Rest, Marked, 6 1/8 In. 490.00
Figurine, Woman, Carrying Basket, Crossed Swords, 5 1/2 In... 660.00
Figurine, Woman, Holding Basket Of Flowers, Lace Work, c.1850, 6 1/2 In. 1050.00
Figurine, Young Girl, Basket Of Vegetables, 5 1/2 In... 352.00
Figurine, Young Man, Reading Book, 18th Century Costume, Marked, 8 In. 650.00
Group, 2 Putti, Holding Human Mask, Cat Emerging From Mouth, 6 In. 775.00
Group, Man & Woman, Seated, Reading Letter, Man Looking Over Shoulder, 6 In....... 875.00
Group, Man, Kissing Woman's Hand, Satyr, Crossed Swords, 5 3/4 In. 1090.00
Group, Partially Draped Females, Putti, Signed, 13 In. 2185.00
Group, Putti, Holding Flowers, c.1890, 3 1/2 x 4 In... 795.00
Group, St. Matthew & Cherub, Holding Book, Cherub At Feet, c.1740, 9 1/8 In. 5750.00

◆ ◆ ◆ ◆ ◆ ◆ ◆ ◆ ◆ ◆ ◆ ◆ ◆ ◆ ◆ ◆ ◆ ◆ ◆

The material used to make repairs is warmer to the touch than the porcelain. Feel the surface of a figurine to determine if there are unseen repairs.

◆ ◆ ◆ ◆ ◆ ◆ ◆ ◆ ◆ ◆ ◆ ◆ ◆ ◆ ◆ ◆ ◆ ◆ ◆

Meissen, Figurine, Seminude Woman,
Blue Crossed Swords Mark, 18 In.

Inkwell, Louis XV, Pot, Animal Masks, Ormolu Cover, 18th Century, 4 1/2 In. 1840.00
Jug, Milk, Floral Sprig Knop, Birds On Tree, Grassy Plateau, c.1745, 5 3/16 In. 1380.00
Lamp, Painted Shasta Daisies, Portraits & Flowers, 18 In. 850.00
Plate, Animal, Pots, White Ground, Kakiemon Style, 10 1/2 In. 198.00
Plate, Birds, Scalloped Ring, Pierced Border, c.1880, 9 1/4 In., 11 Piece 3450.00
Plate, Bouquet Center, Butterflies & Floral, Crossed Swords, 10 In. 175.00
Plate, Fruit Design, Gilt Ring, Late 19th Century, 9 3/4 In., 12 Piece 2300.00
Plate, Imari Pattern, Blossoms & Dotted Circlets, c.1740, 9 1/2 In. 1265.00
Plate, Swirled, Gold & White, c.1927, 8 3/4 In. 200.00
Plate, Tiger, Tree Trunk, Floral Sprigs, Gelber Lowe, Signed, c.1735, 13 3/16 In. 2012.00
Powder Box, Pink Roses, White Ground, Rosebud Handle Cover, Marked 175.00
Shelf, Bracket, Cherub, 8 1/2 In. 247.00
Soup, Dish, Central Figures Conversing Near Barrels, c.1765, 9 3/8 In. 1265.00
Sugar Castor, Armorial, Flowering Plants Under Butterfly, c.1745, 6 3/4 In. 9200.00
Tazza, Scrolling Leafy Vines, Yellow & Cream, Marked, 11 In. 175.00
Tea Caddy, 6 Recessed Panels, Bird Perched On Plant, Hexagonal, c.1730, 5 In. 6325.00
Tea Caddy, Spiraling Swags, Gilt Scrollwork Edge, c.1760, 5 In. 1955.00
Tea Set, White & Gold, Crossed Swords, 14 Piece 495.00
Teabowl & Saucer, Ornithological, Cafe-Au-Lait Ground, c.1755, 5 1/8 In. 1495.00
Teabowl & Saucer, Rural Landscape, Interior Spray, c.1725, 5 In. 2587.00
Teapot, Hen & Chicks, Beak Spout, 1 Chick On Back, c.1735, 7 In. 8625.00
Teapot, Serpent Headed Spout, Wishbone Handle, c.1765, 4 5/16 In. 3162.00
Tray, Floral, Gilt, Crossed Swords, 16 1/4 x 16 1/2 In. 467.00
Tray, Shell Corners, Acanthus Leaf Handles, Tiny Flowers, Signed, 16 In. 795.00
Tray, Spoon, Tischenmuster, Lobed, Oval, c.1740, 6 1/4 In. 1265.00
Tureen, Cover, Bienenmuster, Boar's Head Handles, 1740, 12 1/8 In. 8625.00
Tureen, Cover, Dolphin Shape, Scale-Molded Body, c.1765, 9 7/16 In. 4887.00
Tureen, Cover, Topographical Panels, Arms, Saxony & Poland, 10 1/2 In. 7475.00
Urinal, Blue Floral Design 748.00
Urn, Cobalt Blue & White, Double Coiled Snake Handles, Gold Leaf, 15 In., Pair 2310.00
Urn, Cobalt Blue & White, Double Coiled Snake Handles, Gold Leaf, 19 In., Pair 2860.00
Vase, Yellow, Twining Snake Handle, Baluster, 10 3/4 In., Pair 1380.00

MERCURY GLASS, or silvered glass, was first made in the 1850s. It lost
favor for a while but became popular again about 1910. It looks like a piece
of silver.

Candlestick, Gold, White Enameled Trim, 11 In., Pair 78.00
Candlestick, Raised Design Base, 13 1/2 In., Pair 130.00
Candlestick, Silver, 9 In. 40.00
Compote, 5 In. 20.00
Mug, Child's, 3 In. 20.00
Stand, Wig, 10 1/2 In. 210.00
Vase, Allover Pattern, 10 In. 18.00
Vase, Blue & White Flowers, Bulbous, 14 1/4 In. 250.00
Vase, Etched Floral, Spreading Mouth, Spread Foot, 10 1/2 In., Pair 125.00
Vase, White & Purple Flowers, Red Berries, Butterfly, 9 1/2 In. 90.00

MERRIMAC POTTERY Company was founded by Thomas Nickerson in
Newburyport, Massachusetts, in 1902. The company made art pottery, garden
pottery, and reproductions of Roman pottery. The pottery burned to the
ground in 1908.

Vase, Bottle Shape, Volcanic Orange & Green Matte, Signed, 7 1/2 In. 900.00
Vase, Bulbous, Feathered, Blue-Green Matte, 12 In. 550.00
Vase, Cylindrical, 5 Trees, Carved, Raised, 6 x 4 1/4 In. 1100.00
Vase, Stylized Flowers, Green & Gunmetal, 6 In. 990.00
Vase, Textured & Feathered, Orange & Yellow Matte Glaze, 4 1/2 In. 650.00
Vase, Thick Matte Eggplant Glaze, Paper Labels, 6 1/2 x 3 1/2 In. 165.00

METTLACH, Germany, is a city where the Villeroy and Boch factories
worked. Steins from the firm are known as Mettlach steins. They date from
about 1842. *PUG* means painted under glaze. The steins can be dated from
the marks on the bottom, which include a date-number code. Other pieces
may be listed in the Villeroy & Boch category.

Beaker, No. 2327, Hamburg, 1/4 Liter 85.00
Flagon, No. 2690, Men Drinking, Jeweled Base, 1/4 Liter 747.50
Loving Cup, No. 2169, 3-Paneled Drinking Scene, 1894 .... 400.00
Pitcher, No. 171, Pewter Cover, White & Cream, Black Enameled, 1/4 Liter 357.00
Pitcher, No. 1028, Brown, White, 2 Cream Shades, 11 3/4 In. 275.00
Pitcher, No. 2076, White, Cream & Rust Red, Pewter Fittings, 3.2 Liter 220.00
Pitcher, No. 2947, Trees, Art Nouveau Style, 1/4 Liter 195.00
Plaque, Cameo, Bust Of Woman, Green Ground, Oval, 7 1/2 x 8 3/4 In. 450.00
Plaque, Mutterdag, 1978 .... 45.00
Plaque, No. 307, Dutch Scene, 12 1/2 In. 110.00
Plaque, No. 1108, Castle On Rhine, Gold Edge, 17 In. 1150.00
Plaque, No. 1385, Knight, Shield & Club, 1910, 14 1/4 In. 995.00
Plaque, No. 2322, Knight, With Maiden, 1909, 15 In. 995.00
Plaque, No. 2442, Trojan Warrior, In Boat, Green Ground, 19 In. 1150.00
Plaque, No. 2443, Trojan Lady, Dancing, Servants, Green Ground, 19 In. 1150.00
Plaque, No. 2622, Cavalier, Holding Glass, 7 1/2 In. 275.00
Plaque, No. 2624, Cavalier, Smoking Pipe, 7 1/2 In. 275.00
Plaque, No. 7032, Woman's Profile, Oval, 9 In. 395.00
Plate, Christmas, 1977 .... 44.00
Plate, Christmas, 1979 .... 64.00
Stein, No. 228, 1/2 Liter, German Verse Each Panel, Silver Grapes 365.00
Stein, No. 775, 1 Liter, Garde-Kurassier-Regiment, Albert Oppermann, 1906-1907 ...... 547.00
Stein, No. 941, 1/2 Liter, Tavern Beer Barometer, Pewter Cover 288.00
Stein, No. 1028, 1/2 Liter, Grotesque Face On Cover, Tree Trunk 195.00
Stein, No. 1300, 1/2 Liter, Medallions, Pewter Fittings 330.00
Stein, No. 1395, 1/2 Liter, French Card, Inlaid Pewter Cover 403.00
Stein, No. 1467, 1/2 Liter, 4 Panels, People Picking Fruit 295.00
Stein, No. 1508, 1/2 Liter, Tavern Scene 550.00
Stein, No. 1526, Ges. Gesch, Brown, Marked, 3 3/4 x 4 3/8 In. 145.00
Stein, No. 1526/1108, 1 Liter, Quilmes Brewery 350.00
Stein, No. 1527, 1/2 Liter, 4 Men Drinking, Inlaid Pewter Cover 258.00
Stein, No. 1536, 1/2 Liter, Man With Pipe, PUG, Pewter Cover 302.00
Stein, No. 1733, 1/2 Liter, Horse & Jockey, Signed Warth 1265.00
Stein, No. 1745, 1/2 Liter, Leaves & Scroll, Inlaid Pewter Cover 144.00
Stein, No. 1786, 1/2 Liter, St. Florian, Putting Out Fire, Dragon Handle 633.00
Stein, No. 1909, 1/2 Liter, Pilsner Export Beer 400.00
Stein, No. 1932, 1/2 Liter, Cavaliers Drinking, Inlaid Pewter Cover 547.00
Stein, No. 1998, 1/2 Liter, Trumpeter From Sakingen, Inlaid Pewter Cover 258.00
Stein, No. 2008, 1/2 Liter, Trumpeter On Black Horse, Stuck 156.00
Stein, No. 2024, 1/2 Liter, Shield Of Berlin, Inlaid Pewter Cover .... 385.00 to 490.00
Stein, No. 2035, 1/2 Liter, Bacchus, Frolicking, Inlaid Pewter Cover 547.00
Stein, No. 2057, 3/10 Liter, Peasants Dancing, Inlaid Pewter Cover 345.00
Stein, No. 2065, 1.5 Liter, Cavalier & Barmaid, Garden, Jeweled Base, Schlitt 1350.00
Stein, No. 2066, Maiden & Cavalier Scene, H. Schlitt, 14 In. 1150.00
Stein, No. 2090, 3/10 Liter, Club, Inlaid Pewter Cover 345.00
Stein, No. 2097, 1 Liter, Musical Notes 550.00
Stein, No. 2134, 1/2 Liter, Gnome In Tree, Schlitt 2970.00
Stein, No. 2204, 1 Liter, Blue Max, Prussian Eagle 880.00
Stein, No. 2230, 1/2 Liter, Man & Barmaid, Inlaid Pewter Cover 376.00
Stein, No. 2324, 1/2 Liter, Football Game 2200.00
Stein, No. 2391, 1/2 Liter, Wedding March, Swan Knight, Pewter Cover 770.00
Stein, No. 2394, 1/2 Liter, Siegfried's Youth, Pewter Cover .... 748.00 to 850.00
Stein, No. 2557, 1/2 Liter, Drinking Scenes, Pewter Fittings 192.00
Stein, No. 2728, 1/2 Liter, Brewer 3300.00
Stein, No. 2776, 1/2 Liter, Keeper Of Wine Cellar, Inlaid Pewter Cover 690.00
Stein, No. 2780, 1/2 Liter, Man Playing Guitar For Lady, Inlaid Pewter Cover 518.00
Stein, No. 2823, 1/2 Liter, Woman, Rifle, Pewter Figural Cover 375.00
Stein, No. 2951, 1 Liter, Prussian Eagle, White On Sage, Pewter Cover 795.00
Stein, No. 2957, 1/2 Liter, Bowling Scene, Inlaid Pewter Cover 258.00
Stein, No. 3351, 1/2 Liter, Rugby Players, Inlaid Pewter Cover 805.00
Tray, No. 2960, Carved Art Nouveau Trees, Blue, White, Tan, Round, 15 In. 248.00
Vase, Classical Maidens, Tulip-Form Mouth, Scroll Handles, 13 1/2 In., Pair 800.00

MILK GLASS was named for its milky white color. It was first made in England during the 1700s. The height of its popularity in the United States was from 1870 to 1880. It is now correct to refer to some colored glass as blue milk glass, black milk glass, etc. Reproductions of milk glass are being made and sold in many stores. Related pieces may be listed in the Cosmos, Vallerysthal, and Westmoreland categories.

Basket, Waffle Block	52.00
Bottle, Jenny Lind, Pink, 8 In.	120.00
Box, Patch, Enameled, 2 In.	175.00
Butter, Cover, Child's	60.00
Butter, Cover, Wild Iris	40.00
Cake Stand, Shell, Pink	25.00
Candlestick, 2-Light, Shell, Pink	22.00
Candlestick, Portieux, Signed, 9 1/2 In.	45.00
Compote, Blue, Lattice Top	20.00
Creamer, Chrysanthemum Sprig Pattern, Northwood, 4 3/4 In.	192.00
Creamer, Roman Cross	40.00
Creamer, Swan	38.00
Dish, Battleship Maine Cover, 7 3/4 x 3 3/4 In.	44.00 to 46.00
Dish, Boar's Head Cover, 1888	1800.00
Dish, Double Head Chick Cover	1100.00
Dish, Eagle, On Nest Of Eggs Cover, Puerto Rico, Cuba	125.00
Dish, Hen Cover, Dominecker	400.00
Dish, Hen Cover, Ribbed Base, Blue Head, 5 1/2 In.	65.00
Dish, Lacy Base, Blue, Atterbury	600.00
Dish, Pekinese Cover, Diamond & Stippled Base	300.00 to 800.00
Dish, Pope Leo Cover	145.00
Egg, Easter, Hand Painted, Large	22.00
Eggcup, Birch Leaf, Fling	28.00
Eggcup, Blackberry	25.00
Goblet, Romeo	35.00
Lamp, Ball Shade, Pink Floral, Green Leaves; 7 1/4 x 3 In.	275.00
Lamp, Elephant, Hurricane Globe, Metal Connector, Miniature	500.00
Lamp, Owl, Painted, 7 1/2 In.	1100.00
Lamp, Shield Design, Pair	88.00
Match Holder, Cylindrical	65.00
Match Holder, Witch's Kettle	35.00
Mug, Deer & Cow, 2 In.	48.00
Mug, Deer & Cow, 2 x 1 3/4 In.	48.00
Mug, Liberty Bell, Miniature	110.00
Pitcher, Paneled Grape, Westmoreland, 1 Qt.	25.00
Pitcher, Paneled Grape, Westmoreland, 2 Qt.	20.00
Pitcher, Water, Guttate, Pink Glaze	250.00
Plate, Ancient Castle, 7 In.	57.00
Plate, Angel & Harp, 8 In.	35.00
Plate, Columbus, 9 1/2 In.	65.00
Plate, Fish, Embossed, Pat. June 4, 1872, 10 In.	135.00
Plate, Imperial Grape	110.00
Plate, Roosevelt Bears, Souvenir, Allison, Iowa	110.00
Punch Bowl, Pineapple, Westmoreland	50.00
Punch Set, Child's, Nursery Rhyme, 7 Piece	300.00
Punch Set, Child's, White Rose, 7 Piece	200.00
Relish, Blackberry, 5 1/4 x 9 1/4 In.	20.00
Relish, Ivy In Snow, 4 1/2 x 8 In.	22.00
Rose Bowl, Double Stem	90.00
Salt & Pepper, Tray, Fleur-De-Lis Design, Miniature	24.00
Sauce, Footed, Crossed Fern, 4 In.	12.00
Shade, Ceiling Fixture, Brass Plated Rims, 8 x 12 In., 8 Piece	300.00
Shaker, Salt, Pepper, Sugar & Flour, Glenwood Gas Ranges, 4 Piece	75.00
Spooner, Melon With Leaf & Net	85.00
Sugar & Creamer, Enamel Flowers, Pink Cased, Pleated Top, Amber Handle, 7 In.	200.00
Sugar & Creamer, Teardrop & Tassel	175.00

Sugar Shaker, Forget-Me-Not, Blue	95.00
Syrup, Blue	230.00
Syrup, Iris, Gold Trim	135.00
Syrup, Painted Flower, Pewter, Cover, Pat. 1884	125.00
Syrup, Tree Of Life, Challinor	60.00
Toothpick, Button Arches, Pink, Christmas 1903	25.00
Toothpick, Cobalt Blue, Westmoreland	75.00
Toothpick, Gnome's Head, Wall Mount	55.00
Toothpick, Paneled Sprig, Blue	25.00
Toothpick, Pleat & Bow	35.00
Toothpick, Vermont, Blue Design	75.00
Toothpick, Witch's Head, Blue	6.00

MILLEFIORI means, literally, a thousand flowers. Many small pieces of glass resembling flowers are grouped together to form a design. It is a type of glasswork popular in paperweights and some are listed in that category.

Bottle, Paperweight, Base & Stopper, 6 In.	330.00
Bottle, Red, White, Blue, Ground Stopper, 6 In.	125.00
Dish, Green, Blue, Red, 8 In.	120.00
Figurine, Bird, 6 In.	90.00

MINTON china has been made in the Staffordshire region of England from 1793 to the present. The firm became part of the Royal Doulton Tableware Group in 1968, but the wares continued to be marked *Minton*. Many marks have been used. The one shown dates from about 1873 to 1891, when the word *England* was added.

Bread Plate, Molded Stylized Foliage & Wheat, Waste Not, Want Not, c.1849, 12 In.	1775.00
Cup, Saucer & Dessert Plate, Swirled, Gold Flowers, 1950s	250.00
Cup & Saucer, Aesthetic, Demitasse, c.1870	25.00
Cup & Saucer, Ashbourne	20.00
Dinner Service, Ancestral, 98 Piece	863.00
Dinner Set, Marlow, Stenciled Pastel Florals, Fired-On Gold Rim, 65 Piece	605.00
Dish, Flower Encrusted, Basket Work Rim, 4 Gilt Scroll Feet, c.1830, 10 7/8 In.	4025.00
Dish, Walnut Encrusted, Circles & Triangles Rim, c.1830, 7 1/2 In.	2530.00
Figure, Ariadne, Seated On Panther, Parian	1045.00
Figurine, Hearing, Allegorical, Woman, Lace Bonnet, Petticoat, c.1840, 5 3/8 In.	345.00
Garden Seat, Majolica, Passion Flower	3450.00
Garden Seat, Stylized Prince Of Wales Feathers, Majolica, 1872, 18 In.	3750.00
Mug, Rural Landscape On Front, Gilt Branches, c.1800, 3 1/8 In.	230.00
Plate, Debutante, Pink, Set Of 8	125.00
Plate, Dinner, Vermont	25.00
Sconce, Wall, Angels, Pair	5650.00
Server, Oyster, Majolica, 4 Tiers, 10 In. ....*Illus*	4180.00
Soup, Dish, Gilded Anthemion Design, White Ground, 9 1/2 In., 8 Piece	305.00
Tea Set, Cockatrice, 3 Piece	350.00
Tea Set, Pink & Blue Flowers, White Ground, c.1890, 3 Piece	395.00

Minton, Server, Oyster, Majolica,
4 Tiers, 10 In.

✦✦✦✦✦✦✦✦✦✦✦✦✦✦✦✦✦✦✦✦✦

An old Staffordshire or majolica pitcher has a small hole inside where the handle meets the body. A new pitcher will not have this hole but will often have a large hole in the base.

✦✦✦✦✦✦✦✦✦✦✦✦✦✦✦✦✦✦✦✦✦

Tile Set, Shakespeare Scenes, Polychrome, Signed, 6 x 6 In., 16 Piece 575.00
Tile Set, Stylized Design, c.1890, 6 Piece 250.00
Tray, Torte, Floral Enamel Design, Blue Border, c.1912, 12 x 11 3/4 In. 105.00
Vase, Gilt, Polychrome Enamel, Turquoise Ground, C. Dresser, c.1871, 11 In., Pair 7300.00
Vase, Imari Type Flowers & Vines, Gold Handles & Trim, 24 1/2 In., Pair 495.00
Wine Cooler, Bacchus Figures, c.1850 .... 3250.00

MOCHA pottery is an English-made product that was sold in America during the early 1800s. It is a heavy pottery with pale coffee-and-cream coloring. Designs of blue, brown, green, orange, black, or white were added to the pottery and given fanciful names, such as *Tree, Snail Trail,* or *Moss.*

Bowl, Black & White Geometric Rim, Marbleized Band, 7 1/2 In. 149.00
Bowl, Brown & White Stripes, Yellowware, 6 1/2 In. 82.00
Bowl, Earthworm, Blue Band, Teal Stripes, 6 In. 192.00
Bowl, Earthworm, Blue Stripe, 6 1/2 In. 400.00
Bowl, Earthworm, Pale Blue Band, Black Stripes, Blue & White, 6 1/2 In. 165.00
Bowl, Marbleized White, Black & Brown, Yellow Rim, Strap Handle, 4 1/4 In. 632.00
Bowl, Waste, Blue & White Earthworm, Gray Band, Brown Stripes, 5 In. 385.00
Cider Pot, Cover 1595.00
Creamer, Green Band, Dark Brown Stripes, Seaweed, Leaf Handle & Spout 1375.00
Creamer, Leaf Handle & Spout, Black Seaweed, Beige Rim, 4 1/4 In. 853.00
Eggcup, Black Stripes, Seaweed, Blue Bands, Brown, 2 7/8 In. 330.00
Jug, Allover Design, Wavy Lines, Circles, 2 Gal. 6500.00
Jug, Milk, Brown Seaweed, Pumpkin Ground, Blue Enamel, 5 1/2 In. 977.00
Mug, Applied Swag Design, Marbleized Brown & Pumpkin Body, 6 1/4 In. 747.00
Mug, Bands, Seaweed Designs, Blue & Browns, 5 3/4 In. 230.00
Mug, Black & White Geometric, Barrel, Applied Leaf Handle, 2 3/4 In. 50.00
Mug, Brown Stripes, White Band, Ribbed Handle, Yellowware, 3 7/8 In. 60.00
Mug, Child's, Banded, A Trifle For George, 19th Century, 2 3/4 In. 460.00
Mug, Fern, Light Brown Ground, 5 In. 400.00
Mug, Fern, Mustard Ground, Unusual Shape 850.00
Mug, Gray Stripes, Feather Type Designs, Leaf Handle, Green Rim, 4 3/4 In. 1100.00
Mug, Light Blue Band, Black Stripes, White Ground, Leaf Handle, 2 7/8 In. 99.00
Mug, Molded Swag, Marbleized, 3 5/8 In., Pair 3220.00
Mug, Pearlware, Looped Cable, 1830, 5 5/8 In. .... *Illus* 460.00
Mug, Pearlware, Oval & Dots, 1840 .... *Illus* 690.00
Mug, Pearlware, Twig, Dot, 1840, 5 7/8 In. .... *Illus* 2587.00
Mug, Seaweed, 1 Qt. 235.00
Mustard, Cover, Yellow, Blue Banding 242.00
Pepper Pot, 2 Band Top, 3 3/4 In. 450.00
Pepper Pot, Beige & Brown Earthworm, Stripes, White, 3 3/4 In. 1100.00
Pepper Pot, Black Seaweed, Brown Stripes, Tan Band, 3 3/4 In. 550.00
Pepper Pot, Domed Top 550.00
Pepper Pot, Seaweed, Blue Bands, 4 In. 75.00
Pitcher, Black & White Earthworm, Blue & Gray Bands, Stripes, 6 In. 165.00
Pitcher, Blue Bands, White & Brown Stripes, Earthworm Design, 6 7/8 In. 550.00
Pitcher, Earthworm, 6 1/2 In. 950.00
Pitcher, Looping Earthworm, Blue & Brown Banding, c.1840, 6 In. 525.00
Pitcher, Tooled Design, Olive Green, Orange Stripes, Blue & White Band, 6 5/8 In. 247.00

Mocha, Mug, Pearlware, Looped Cable, 1830, 5 5/8 In.; Mocha, Mug, Pearlware, Twig, Dot, 1840, 5 7/8 In.; Mocha, Mug, Pearlware, Oval & Dots, 1840.

Pitcher, White & Black Stripes, Leaf Handle, 4 7/8 In.	220.00
Shaker, Blue, White & Black Stripes, 4 1/2 In.	137.00
Sugar, Marbleized Tan, Brown & White, 4 1/2 In.	55.00
Tankard, Green Coggle Wheel	1895.00
Tea Set, Sea Design, Pumpkin Ground, Miniature, 19th Century, 12 Piece	4887.00

MONMOUTH Pottery Company started working in Monmouth, Illinois, in 1892. The pottery made a variety of utilitarian wares. It became part of Western Stoneware Company in 1906. The maple leaf mark was used until 1930. If *Co.* appears as part of the mark, the piece was made before 1906.

Jardiniere, Woven Branch Design	175.00
Pitcher, Tan, Horizontal Ribs, 5 1/2 In.	8.00
Vase, Blue, Cream Design, Signed, 13 In.	175.00

MONT JOYE, see Mt. Joye

MOORCROFT pottery was first made in Burslem, England, in 1913. William Moorcroft had managed the art pottery department for James MacIntyre & Company of England from 1898 to 1913. The Moorcroft pottery continues today, although William Moorcroft died in 1945. The earlier wares are similar to the modern ones, but color and marking will help indicate the age.

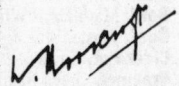

Bowl, Claremont, 2 Handles, Footed, Blue Ground, Mushrooms, 6 1/2 In.	440.00
Bowl, Hibiscus Design, Red, Yellow & Blue, White Ground, 10 x 2 1/2 In.	310.00
Bowl, Pansy Design, Glossy Green Ground, c.1913, 4 5/8 In.	632.00
Bowl, Red Hibiscus, Light Green Ground, Paper Label, 6 In.	95.00
Box, Cover, Polychrome Floral, Blue Ground, Labels, c.1930, 4 3/4 x 3 1/2 In.	225.00
Box, Cover, Poppy Design, Paper Label, c.1945, 4 1/2 In.	200.00
Candlestick, Sterling Mounted Rim, 1930, 6 1/2 In., Pair	1250.00
Chalice, Multicolored Flowers, Beige Ground, 7 1/2 In.	1215.00
Compote, Luster Ware, 2 Handles, Rose-Colored Berries, For Liberty & Co., 7 In.	1650.00
Jug, Floral Designs, MacIntyre	3250.00
Lamp, Flambe, Orchid, 12 1/2 In.	195.00
Lamp, Fruit & Leaves, Cobalt Blue Ground, Table Type	275.00
Mug, Commemorative, Dark Blue Letters, Peace June 28th, 1919, 3 1/2 In.	770.00
Plate, Floral Design, Off-White Ground, Signed, 10 1/4 In.	110.00
Plate, Floral, 4 1/2 In.	40.00
Plate, Grape Leaf, 4 1/2 In.	35.00
Plate, Moonlit Blue Landscape, Green Initials WM, 8 1/2 In.	770.00
Teapot, Blue Luster, Individual, 6 1/4 In.	95.00
Vase, Anemone, Burgundy, Pink, Blue, Red, Green Ground, Blue Interior, 12 1/2 In.	220.00
Vase, Anemone, Flambe, 6 In.	350.00
Vase, Anemone, Green, 2 In.	135.00
Vase, Anemone, Pink & Purple, Green Ground, 5 1/2 x 12 1/2 In.	275.00
Vase, Baluster, Everted Rim, Flambe Orchids, Burgundy Ground, 10 1/2 In.	690.00
Vase, Bud, Baluster, Red Flowers, Blue Ground, 6 In.	115.00
Vase, Clematis, 5 In.	175.00
Vase, Double Pansy, White Ground, c.1920, 9 1/4 In.	600.00
Vase, Floral, Cobalt Blue, 5 1/4 In.	210.00 to 220.00
Vase, Florian Ware, Blue Slip Irises, MacIntyre, 8 3/4 In.	800.00
Vase, Grapes, Leaves & Pomegranate, 3 1/2 In.	250.00
Vase, Hibiscus, Bulbous, 3 In.	95.00
Vase, Hibiscus, Green Ground, 7 In.	225.00
Vase, Hibiscus, Multicolored, Cobalt Ground, Bulbous, 4 x 5 1/2 In.	195.00
Vase, Incised Poppy Design, Blue & Green Glaze, c.1898, 8 1/8 In.	700.00
Vase, Landscape Scene, 6 In.	400.00
Vase, Moonlit Blue Design, Royal Blue Ground, Signed, 9 1/2 In.	1150.00
Vase, Multicolored Floral Design, MacIntyre, c.1904, 11 1/4 In.	1000.00
Vase, Orange Hibiscus, Green Ground, Bulbous, 4 x 5 1/2 In.	185.00
Vase, Orchid, Signed, 8 1/2 In.	305.00
Vase, Pansy Design, Green Ground, Signed, c.1920, 9 In.	575.00
Vase, Pansy, Blue Ground, Impressed Mark, England, c.1945, 6 1/4 In.	172.00
Vase, Pansy, c.1920, 3 1/2 x 4 In.	295.00
Vase, Pomegranate, 4 1/2 In.	175.00

Vase, Pomegranate, Grapes, Bulbous, Signed, 10 1/2 In.	985.00
Vase, Pomegranate, Hammered Silver Footed Base, Tudric No. 01518, 6 1/2 In.	880.00
Vase, Pomegranate, Handles, Signed, c.1925, 10 1/4 In.	978.00
Vase, Pompeian Style, Swags Of Roses, Ribbons, Signed, c.1907, 6 3/4 In.	1895.00
Vase, Powder Blue Cornflower, 5 Flowers, Blue Ground, No. 101, 14 1/2 In.	2090.00
Vase, Tudor Rose, Squeezebag, Lime Ground, For Liberty & Co., c.1905, 8 In.	2090.00
Vase, Wisteria, Purple, Red, Yellow, No. 55, 5 x 7 In.	247.00

MORIAGE is a special type of raised decoration used on some Japanese pottery. Sometimes pieces of clay were shaped by hand and applied to the item; sometimes the clay was squeezed from a tube in the way we apply cake frosting. One type of moriage is called *Dragonware* and is listed under that name.

Ewer, Forest Scene, Gold, 14 In.	150.00
Jam Jar, Underplate, Gold & Magenta Roses, Green Ground	435.00
Vase, Pastel Colors, Handles, 15 In.	550.00

MOSAIC TILE COMPANY of Zanesville, Ohio, was started by Karl Langerbeck and Herman Mueller in 1894. Many types of plain and ornamental tiles were made until 1959. The company closed in 1967. The company also made some ashtrays, bookends, and related giftwares. Most pieces are marked with the entwined *MTC* monogram.

American Patriotic Scene, Panel, David Fink, Frame, 6 In., 4 Piece	605.00
Ashtray, Figural, Hunting Dog, Glazed	115.00
Asian Child Profile, Pink Halo, Cobalt Blue Ground, 5 3/4 In.	248.00
Black Sea Horses, Orange Ground, 4 In.	247.00
Cookie Jar, Mammy, White & Peach Striped Apron	1385.00 to 1800.00
Cookie Jar, Mammy, Yellow Dress	645.00 to 650.00
Delft-Type Transfer, House, Dutch Landscape, Impressed M, 4 1/4 In.	88.00
Figurine, German Shepherd, Lying Down, Tan, 10 1/2 x 6 In.	95.00
Hispanol-Moresque, Yellow, Brown, Green & Blue, 6 In.	77.00
Lincoln	75.00
Man That Pleased None, Moral, Walter Crane, 6 In.	192.00
Tile, African Boy Profile, Halo, Cobalt Blue Ground, Frame, Stamped, 6 In.	302.00

MOSER glass is made by Ludwig Moser und Sohne, a Bohemian glasshouse founded in 1857. Art Nouveau-type glassware and iridescent glassware were made. The most famous Moser glass is decorated with heavy enameling in gold and bright colors. The firm is still working in Czechoslovakia. Few pieces of Moser glass are marked.

Basket, Molded Malachite, Cherubs, Green, 5 1/2 In., Pair	800.00
Box, Raised Enamel, Amethyst, Mark, 3 x 3 1/2 In.	245.00
Candlestick, Gold Band Of Warriors, Amethyst, Signed, 10 1/2 In.	325.00
Centerpiece, Intaglio Cut, Amethyst To Clear, 7 x 8 In.	1500.00
Cologne Bottle, Garlands, Scrolls, Bands, Bubble Stopper, Amethyst To Clear, 6 In.	225.00
Compote, Broad Gold Etched Band, Amazon Women, 8 3/4 In.	575.00
Cordial Set, Allover Tiny Florals, Cranberry Panels Cut To Clear, 5 Piece	295.00
Cordial Set, White Branches, Dotted Flowers, Blue Dotting, 4 Piece	165.00
Ewer, Allover Multicolor Enameled Ferns, Green Ground, 6 In.	525.00
Figurine, Colonial Lady, 6 In.	150.00
Figurine, Polar Bear, Crystal, Pair	150.00
Liqueur Set, Fired Gold Design, Cranberry, 8 Piece	517.00
Pitcher, Crackle Glass, Enamel Fish & Seaweed, 7 x 6 In.	295.00
Tumbler, Gilded Floral Band, Cut Diamond Nail Heads, Band Of Ovals, 5 1/4 In.	145.00
Tumbler, Juice, Grape Leaves & Foliage, Gold Enameled, Green, 3 3/4 x 2 3/8 In.	225.00
Vase, Acorn, Insects, 5-Footed, Cranberry	1200.00
Vase, Allover Enameling, Gold Paneled Sides, 9 In.	450.00
Vase, Applied Metal Bees, Raised Scrolls, Enamel, Signed, 12 3/8 In.	500.00
Vase, Bud, Gold Vine & Flowers, Green Shaded To Clear, 6 1/2 In.	70.00
Vase, Classical Women Engaged In Combat, Amethyst To Clear, Signed, 5 In.	312.00
Vase, Domed Ring Foot, Woman Warrior, Gold Band, 8 5/8 In.	575.00
Vase, Enamel Fish, Seaweed, Crackle Glass, 5 In.	225.00
Vase, Enamel Flowers & Birds, Aqua Blue, 5 3/4 In.	310.00
Vase, Enamel Flowers, Butterflies & Bees, Blue, 12 1/2 In.	250.00

Vase, Engraved Wildlife Scene, Translucent Yellow, 10 Sides, 6 In. 350.00
Vase, Flower Shape, Gold Trim, Vaseline To Cranberry, 15 In. 895.00
Vase, Gold Band Of Warriors, Amethyst, Signed, 11 1/2 In. 695.00
Vase, Multicolor Floral Design, Gold Trim, Signed, 12 In. 300.00
Vase, Nude Woman Under Grapevine, Green Malachite, 4 7/8 In. 230.00
Vase, Pedestal, Portrait Transfer, Cranberry Ground, Clear Base, 8 1/2 In. 250.00
Vase, Pink & Blue Floral Enamel, Green Ground, 16 In. 1275.00
Vase, Ruffled Flared Top, Spattered Gold Edge, Clear, 10 In. 145.00
Vase, Stick, Green, Pink & Blue Floral, Gold Trim, 16 In. 495.00
Vase, Trumpet, Enamel Flowers, Gold Trim, White To Cobalt Blue, Signed, 13 In. 275.00

MOSS ROSE china was made by many firms from 1808 to 1900. It has a typical moss rose pictured as the design. The plant is not as popular now as it
was in Victorian gardens, so the fuzz-covered bud is unfamiliar to most collectors. The dishes were usually decorated with pink and green flowers.

Bowl, Pedestal, Hand Painted, Gold Rim, 10 x 5 In. 20.00
Cup & Saucer, Fancy Handles & Feet, Demitasse 8.00
Plate, 7 In. 42.00
Platter, Oval, c.1850 .... 595.00

MOTHER-OF-PEARL GLASS, or pearl satin glass, was first made in the 1850s
in England and in Massachusetts. It was a special type of mold-blown satin
glass with air bubbles in the glass, giving it a pearlized color. It has been
reproduced. Mother-of-pearl shell objects are listed under Pearl.

Cruet, Frosted Handle & Stopper, Blue 475.00
Ewer, Herringbone, Salmon, Camphor Handle, 7 1/2 In. 115.00
Perfume Bottle, Peacock Eye, Bridal White, Stopper, 3 3/4 In. 635.00
Rose Bowl, Concentric Circles, 6-Crimp Top, 4 3/8 In. 850.00
Tumbler, Enamel Flowers 200.00
Vase, Blue Raindrop, Ruffled Top, White Lining, 7 1/2 In. 175.00
Vase, Coin Spot, Enamel Design, 3 1/2 x 2 1/4 In. 325.00
Vase, Coraline Seaweed, Cylindrical Neck, Pink, 4 1/2 In. 350.00
Vase, Diamond Quilted, Coraline Fleur-De-Lis, Yellow, 6 3/4 In. 660.00
Vase, Diamond Quilted, Frosted Serpent Entwined At Middle, 7 In. 135.00
Vase, Diamond Quilted, White Lining, Blue, 12 In. 225.00

MOTORCYCLES of all types are being collected today. Examples can be
found that date back to the early years of the twentieth century.

BMW R60, 600cc, 1967 .... 1945.00
Harley-Davidson, 45 Cubic In. Motor, Blue, Restored, 1946 .... 7150.00
Harley-Davidson, Sprint, Black, Original, 1967 .... 1650.00
Honda, Dream, 305cc, 1965 .... 2750.00
Indian, Chief, 1947 Motor, Dark Blue, Overhauled Engine, 1948 .... 12100.00

*Motorcycle, Indian, Road Warrior, Vertical
Twin Motor, 500cc, c.1951*

*Motorcycle, Indian, Sport Scout Racer,
Red & Black, 45 Cubic In. Motor, 1937*

Indian, Military Model 741, 1942... 6050.00
Indian, Road Warrior, Vertical Twin Motor, 500cc.1951 .... *Illus* 7150.00
Indian, Sport Scout Racer, Red & Black, 45 Cubic In. Motor, 1937............................. 8800.00
Norton, 850 Commando, 1975... 4125.00

MOUNT WASHINGTON, see Mt. Washington

MOVIE memorabilia of all types is collected. Animation cels, games, sheet music, toys, and some celebrity items are listed in their own sections. Listed here are costumes and paper collectibles. A lobby card is 11 by 14 inches. A set of lobby cards includes seven scene cards and one title card. A one sheet, the standard movie poster, is 27 by 41 inches. A half sheet is 22 by 28 inches. A window card, made of cardboard, is 14 by 22 inches. An insert is 14 by 36 inches. A herald is a promotional item handed out to patrons. A press book was sent to newspapers and magazines to promote a picture.

Bank, Mechanical, Marilyn Monroe, Dress Blows Up, 7 In. 55.00
Clock, Figural, Marilyn Monroe, Legs Swing, Black & White, Box, 5 In...................... 17.00
Costume, Dress, Star Trek, TV, Paramount, 1966-1969... 9200.00
Costume, Fez, Sons Of The Desert, Laurel & Hardy, 1933 .... 5750.00
Costume, Jacket, Patton, George C. Scott 9775.00
Costume, Kit Carson, Bill Williams, 1950s.. 125.00
Costume, Romeo & Juliet, Leslie Howard 9200.00
Costume, Shirt & Vest, Dances With Wolves, Kevin Costner................................. 5750.00
Costume, Suit, Sound Of Music, Julie Andrews, Wool, 3 Piece............................... 7475.00
Costume, Tunic, Star Trek, TV, Paramount, 1966-1969 .... 18400.00
Game, Deputy, Henry Fonda, No. 4044, Milton Bradley, 1960 .... 100.00
Herald, All The President's Men, R. Redford, D. Hoffman, 1976, 8 x 11 In. 5.00
Herald, Secrets, N. Talmadge, Head Shape, 1924, 10 In. 45.00
Hot Water Bottle, Jayne Mansfield, Bathing Suit Model, 1957 ....79.00 to 145.00
Lobby Card, A Streetcar Named Desire, Marlon Brando, 1951 .... 45.00
Lobby Card, From Here To Eternity, Burt Lancaster, 1953 .... 25.00
Lobby Card, Funny Face, Audrey Hepburn, 1957 .... 15.00
Lobby Card, Goldfinger, Sean Connery, 1964 .... 45.00
Lobby Card, Jack And The Beanstalk, Abbott & Costello, 1952 .... 25.00
Lobby Card, Let's Make Love, Marilyn Monroe, 1960 .... 45.00
Lobby Card, Man Of A Thousand Faces, James Cagney, 1957 .... 15.00
Lobby Card, Mickey Mouse Anniversary Show 25.00
Lobby Card, Moon Spinners, Hayley Mills 15.00
Lobby Card, Queen Christina, Garbo, 1933 .... 750.00
Lobby Card, Silent Movie, Mel Brooks, 1976 .... 8.00
Lobby Card, Tramp, Tramp, Tramp, Jackie Gleason, 1942 .... 75.00
Lobby Card, Twelve O'Clock High, Gregory Peck, 1949...................................... 15.00
Lobby Card, Veracruz, Gary Cooper, 1954.. 15.00
Lobby Card, Whatever Happened To Baby Jane, Davis, Crawford, 1962.................. 25.00
Lobby Card Set, Patton, G.C. Scott, 1970, 8 Piece... 60.00
Photograph, Boris Karloff, Signed, 1939, 10 x 8 In.. 575.00
Photograph, Cary Grant, Evening Dress, Signed Birth Name, Archie Leach................ 1265.00
Photograph, Dorothy Gish, Signed, c.1930.. 85.00
Photograph, James Dean, Signed, 3 1/2 x 2 1/2 In.. 2300.00
Photograph, Johnny Weissmuller, Tarzan Character, Signed, 10 x 8 In. 230.00
Photograph, Marx Brothers, Sepia Tone, Denver, Colorado, 10 x 35 In..................... 1495.00
Photograph, Mary Pickford & Douglas Fairbanks, Signed, 1924 .... 288.00
Poster, Abbott & Costello, London Palladium, 31 x 21 In. 805.00
Poster, Air Meet, 1913, One Sheet... 2800.00
Poster, Apple Dumpling Gang, Folded, 1975, One Sheet 10.00
Poster, Breakfast At Tiffany's, Audrey Hepburn, 1961, One Sheet 1840.00
Poster, Canary Murder Case, Wm. Powell, Louise Brooks, 1929, One Sheet 10350.00
Poster, Casablanca, H. Bogart, I. Bergman, Insert, 1942 .... 1200.00
Poster, Chinatown, Nicholson, Dunaway, 1974, Insert.....................200.00 to 300.00
Poster, Coquette, Mary Pickford's First Talking Picture, 1929, Half Sheet 488.00
Poster, Day Mars Invaded Earth, Half Sheet.. 40.00
Poster, Day The Earth Stood Still, M. Rennie, P. Neal, 1951, Three Sheet................ 8200.00
Poster, Dracula, Prince Of Darkness, Christopher Lee, 1966, Half Sheet 30.00

Poster, Fear Strikes Out, T. Perkins, 1956, Three Sheet 75.00
Poster, Girl Of The Golden West, Jeanette MacDonald, Nelson Eddy, 1938, One Sheet 373.00
Poster, It's A Wonderful Life, J. Stewart, D. Reed, 1946, One Sheet 5000.00
Poster, James Dean Story, Documentary, 1 Sheet, 1957 .... 250.00
Poster, Mickey Mouse 50th Anniversary, Germany, 1978, 23 1/2 x 33 In. 80.00
Poster, New Adventures Of Winnie The Pooh, Disney Press, 1980s, 18 x 23 In. 12.00
Poster, Pearl Of Death, B. Rathbone, N. Bruce, 1944, Three Sheet 1050.00
Poster, Phantom Of The Opera, Universal, 1925, 11 x 14 In. 1420.00
Poster, Roman Holiday, A. Hepburn, G. Peck, 1953, Insert 500.00
Poster, Royal Scandal, Tallulah Bankhead, Charles Coburn, 1945, One Sheet 200.00
Poster, Second Chorus, F. Astaire, P. Goddard, 1940, One Sheet 900.00
Poster, Singin' In The Rain, G. Kelly, D. Reynolds, 1952, Insert 850.00
Poster, Sleeping Beauty, Maleficent, Re-Release, 1979, 27 x 40 In. 25.00
Press Kit, Blade Runner, H. Ford, 1982, 21 Stills 20.00
Pressbook, African Queen, H. Bogart, K. Hepburn, 20 Pages, Uncut, 1951 .... 200.00
Pressbook, Gold Diggers Of 1933, R. Keeler, G. Rogers, 8 Pages, Uncut, 1933 .... 150.00
Pressbook, L. Ball, 14 Pages, Uncut, 1974 .... 20.00
Pressbook, Lion In Winter, K. Hepburn, P. O'Toole, 12 Pages, Uncut, 1968 .... 15.00
Pressbook, Taras Bulba, T. Curtis, Y. Brynner, 20 Pages, Uncut, 1962 .... 12.00
Program, Gone With The Wind, Metro-Goldwyn-Mayer, Color Scenes, 1939, 9 x 12 In. 45.00
Program, Souvenir, Funny Girl, B. Streisand, 1968 .... 10.00
Program, Souvenir, Julius Caesar, M. Brando, J. Mason, 1953 .... 35.00
Prop, Chariot, Ben Hur, Charlton Heston 48500.00
Prop, Mirror, Star Trek, Nichelle Nichols, 2 Piece 4000.00
Prop, Robe, Coronation, Lined In Fur, Desiree, Marlon Brando 2875.00
Puzzle, Marilyn Monroe, Nude 25.00
Spoon, Medical, Musical, Mary Poppins 100.00
Tunic, Star Trek, TV, Leonard Nimoy, 1966-1969, 2 Piece 7000.00
Window Card, Actress Norma Shearer, 1928 .... 230.00

MT. JOYE is an enameled cameo glass made in the late nineteenth and twentieth centuries by Saint-Hilaire Touvier de Varraux and Co. of Pantin, France.
This same company made De Vez glass. Pieces were usually decorated with
enameling. Most pieces are not marked.

Vase, Cameo, Light Puce, Green Gold Enameled Floral Design, Cylindrical, 7 3/4 In. .. 220.00
Vase, Dragonfly In Flight, Maroon & Gold Enameled, 9 1/4 In. 275.00
Vase, Enameled Violets, Textured & Frosted, Scrolling Border, Signed, 13 3/4 In. 862.00
Vase, Gold Tree, Green Leaves, Amber Hammered Ground, Signed, 6 1/2 In. 550.00
Vase, Purple & White Violets, Gold Trim, Frosted Ground, 11 1/2 In. 385.00

MT. WASHINGTON Glass Works started in 1837 in South Boston, Massachusetts. In 1870 the company moved to New Bedford, Massachusetts. Many
types of art glass were made there until 1894, when the company merged
with Pairpoint Manufacturing Co. Amberina, Burmese, Crown Milano, Cut
Glass, Peachblow, and Royal Flemish are each listed in their own category.

Bowl, Bulged Out Optic Ribbed Sides, Triangular, 5 x 5 In. 325.00
Bride's Basket, White, Rose Lining, Original Frame, 12 1/4 x 12 In. 400.00
Bride's Bowl, Jack-In-The-Pulpit Style, Bird On Gingko Branch, 12 In. 330.00
Condiment Set, Wilcox Frame, Swan Footed, Center Handle 135.00
Creamer, White & Yellow Spider Mums, Square Mouth 600.00
Cruet, Melon Ribbed, Mushroom Stopper, Blush, Satin Finish, 6 1/2 In. 1085.00
Cruet, Mother-Of-Pearl Satin Glass, Loop Handle, Frosted Stopper, 5 3/4 In. 440.00
Dresser Tray, Orchids, Enameled, Gold Trim 85.00
Ewer, Mother-Of-Pearl Herringbone Pattern, Frosted Handle, 6 1/2 In. 55.00
Pickle Castor, Flowers, 4 Point Star Ground, Pairpoint Frame, 8 1/2 In. 1120.00
Pin Jar, Floral Design, Gilt 77.00
Pitcher, Inverted Thumbprint, Rainbow, Reed Handle, 8 1/2 In. 675.00
Powder Box, Black Base, Green Figurine Top, New Martinsville 335.00
Punch Bowl, Triple Miter, 14 1/2 x 13 1/2 In. 5500.00
Ring Holder, Lusterless, Saucer, Beaded Ring Stick, Forget-Me-Nots 85.00
Rose Bowl, Apricot, Yellow, Purple Pansies, Gold Trim, 5 In. 220.00
Salt & Pepper, Loop & Daisy 70.00
Saltshaker, Lusterless, Floral Design, White, Egg Shape .... 60.00 to 75.00

Sugar Shaker, Mother-Of-Pearl, Light To Dark Pink 195.00
Toothpick, Little Lobe, Enamel Floral, Melon Shape 110.00
Tumbler, Diamond Thumbprint, Rose Amber, 3 3/4 In. 135.00
Vase, Art Glass, Verona, 16 In. 800.00
Vase, Berries, Leaves, Crimson Shading To Blue, Amber Handles, 11 In. 850.00
Vase, Bulbous, Black, Reeded Handles, Colored Glass Inserts, 5 3/4 In. 2250.00
Vase, Chestnut Tree Branch, Verona, 15 1/2 In. 450.00
Vase, Cut Velvet, Frosted Leaf & Acorn, White Lining, 7 1/2 In. 105.00
Vase, Lily, 4 Medallions Of Warrior, Meriden Holder, 8 In. 265.00
Vase, Lily, Amberina, 6 In. 195.00

MUD FIGURES are small Chinese pottery figures made in the twentieth century. The figures usually represent workers, scholars, farmers, or merchants. Other pieces are trees, houses, and similar parts of the landscape. The figures have unglazed faces and hands but glazed clothing. They were originally made for fish tanks or planters. Mud figures were of little interest and brought low prices until the 1980s. When the prices rose, reproductions appeared.

Seated, Man, Wooden Stand, 4 In. 22.00
Woman, Standing, 7 In. 44.00

MULBERRY ware was made in the Staffordshire district of England from about 1850 to 1860. The dishes were decorated with a reddish brown transfer design, now called *mulberry*. Many of the patterns are similar to those used for flow blue and other Staffordshire transfer wares.

Cup & Saucer, Handleless 65.00
Plate, Corean, 9 In. 48.00
Plate, Moss Rose, 10 In. 65.00
Plate, Oriental, Polychromed, 1881, 8 In. 40.00
Plate, Oriental, Scalloped, 10 3/8 In. 55.00
Plate, Vincennes, 8 In. 65.00
Platter, Corean, 16 In. .... 200.00 to 250.00
Platter, Cyprus, 12 1/2 In. 125.00
Platter, Cyprus, 18 In. 275.00
Platter, Indian Encampment, St. Lawrence, Morley, 12 In. 250.00
Platter, Oriental, 1881, 16 1/4 In. 150.00
Platter, Pelew, 18 In. 275.00
Punch Cup, Corean, 6 Piece 425.00
Soup, Dish, Madras 30.00
Soup, Dish, Oriental, 1881, 9 In. 55.00
Sugar & Creamer, Corean 200.00
Teapot, Pelew 295.00
Teapot, Tivoli 325.00

MULLER FRERES, French for Muller Brothers, made cameo and other glass from the early 1900s to the late 1930s. Their factory was first located in Luneville, then in nearby Croismaire, France. Pieces were usually marked with the company name.

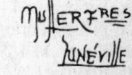

Lamp, Etched Thorny Branches, Berries, Dome Shade, Signed, 19 1/2 In. 8625.00
Lamp, Flowering Branches, Wrought Iron Mounts, c.1920, 22 In. 6325.00
Lamp, Pheasant, Silver Foil, Marble Base, Wrought Iron, c.1920, 16 1/4 In. 4600.00
Lamp, Red Poppy, 11 In. 4500.00
Lamp, Snail, Glass & Chapelle, Wrought Iron, c.1925, 14 In. 4025.00
Vase, Blooming Irises, Green Over White, 6 3/4 In. 925.00
Vase, Field Mouse Munching Seed, Amber, Signed, c.1920, 5 3/8 In. 4313.00
Vase, Internal Layered Gold Flecks, Cluthra-Type Inclusions, 9 1/2 In. 545.00
Vase, Lily Blossoms & Leaves, Signed, c.1920, 11 In. 2550.00
Vase, Overlaid, Etched, Wheel Carved, Lake, Water Lilies, Bugs, 12 2/3 In. 2550.00
Vase, Rhododendron Flowers & Leaves, Signed, c.1920, 9 3/4 In. 3750.00

MUNCIE Clay Products Company was established by Charles Benham in Muncie, Indiana, in 1922. The company made pottery for the florist and gift-shop trade. The company closed by 1939. Pieces are marked with the name *Muncie* or just with a system of numbers and letters, like *1A*.

Figurine, Canoe, Green To Lavender, 11 1/2 In. 90.00
Figurine, Canoe, Insert 165.00
Juice Set, Yellow, 5 Piece 175.00
Lamp, Horsemen & Deer, Aqua High Glaze 170.00
Pitcher, Green Flambe On Pink, 6 In. ....60.00 to 85.00
Pitcher, Matte Pink & Green, 7 In. 165.00
Vase, Art Deco Star, Lavender, Green, 4 In. 85.00
Vase, Gunmetal Black, 12 In. 245.00
Vase, Slate Gray, Green High Glaze Over Lemon, Brown Mottling, 7 1/2 In. 50.00
Wall Pocket 70.00

MURANO, see Glass-Venetian

MUSIC boxes and musical instruments are listed here. Phonograph records, jukeboxes, phonographs, and sheet music are listed in other categories in this book.

Accordion, Hohner, Mother-Of-Pearl Inlay, Case 350.00
Accordion, Majestic, Mother-Of-Pearl Trim 195.00
Accordion, Scandell, Red Swirl Plastic 200.00
Banjo, Bacon, Professional, Pearl Inlay, 4 Strings, Case 275.00
Banjo, H.G. Shultz Inc., Detroit, Cleveland, Maple 100.00
Bow, Violoncello, Silver Mounted, James Tubbs 5175.00
Box, Automaton, French Cylinder, Square, 1843 .... 4700.00
Box, Criterion, Double Comb, Storage Cabinet, 15 1/2-In. Disc .... 5500.00 to 6500.00
Box, Cylinder, 6 Tunes, Single Comb, Inlaid, 20th Century, Switzerland, 11 In. 490.00
Box, Cylinder, Windup, 8 Tunes, 16 In. 357.00
Box, D'Allard & Sandoz, Cylinder, Inlaid Burled Case 7000.00
Box, Jerome Thibouville-Lamy, Bells-In-Sight, 12 Tunes, Boxwood Stringing, 28 In. 5175.00
Box, Longue Marche Sublime Harmone, 1881, 45 In. 7700.00
Box, Marquetry Inlay, Crank Wind, 10 Tunes, Rosewood Case, 9 x 28 In. 2300.00
Box, Mermod Freres, 12 Tunes 1150.00
Box, Mermod Freres, Forte Piccolo, Interchangeable Cylinder 4180.00
Box, Mermod Freres, Stella, Carved Front, Drawer, 17 1/4-In. Disc 5200.00
Box, Mermod Freres, Stella, Mahogany, Floor Model, 42 x 29 In. 6050.00
Box, Mermod Freres, Stella, No. 24189, 15 Discs, 9 1/2-In. Disc, 17 x 14 In. 2310.00
Box, Mermod, 11-In. Cylinder, 10 Tunes For Nickel, 1895 .... 5500.00
Box, Olympia, 12 In. 2200.00
Box, On-Coming Tide, Bronze, Swiss Chalet, Clock, 1880, 24 In. 4800.00
Box, Operatic Tune Cylinder, Mahogany, Switzerland, 8 x 24 In. 1870.00
Box, Orchestral, 12 Tunes, Tune Sheet, Butterfly Striker Bells, Switzerland, 32 In. 5175.00
Box, Orchestrion, Mythological Figures, Tin Lithograph, 1900, 7 x 4 In. 500.00
Box, Ornithological, Blown Glass Dome, Brass Base, 18 In. 1320.00
Box, Orphenion, 16 1/8-In. Disc 2900.00
Box, Perfection, 14-In. Disc 1350.00
Box, Piccola Forte, Peerless 3100.00
Box, Porter, 15 1/2-In. Discs 6750.00
Box, Regina, 12 1/4-In. Disc 2500.00
Box, Regina, Bowfront Glass Door, Automatic Changer, 12 Discs, 15-In. Discs 23000.00
Box, Regina, Casket, 27 In 8500.00
Box, Regina, Double Comb, Oak, 15 1/2-In. Disc, Table Model 4600.00
Box, Regina, Double Comb, Records, Mahogany Cabinet 4700.00
Box, Regina, Mahogany, 21 15 1/2-In. Discs, c.1894, 18 x 8 1/2 In. 3575.00
Box, Regina, No. 61, Walnut, Carved, 11-In. Disc, 1903 .... 5500.00
Box, Regina, Tiger & Quartersawn Oak, 12 Discs 6500.00
Box, Reginaphone, Style 171, 16-In. Disc, Double Comb, 1907, 10 x 21 x 19 In. 4600.00
Box, Reuge, Interchangeable Cylinders, 72-Tooth Comb, Box 1500.00
Box, Rosenfield, Columbia AZ Mechanism, Floor Model, 1 Cent, 1920s, 72 In. 5750.00
Box, Singing Bird, Automaton, Sevres Plaques At Bottom, Gilt Bronze, 17 In. 4887.00
Box, Singing Bird, Birdcage, Reuge, Brass, 1950 .... 2600.00
Box, Singing Bird, Gilt Filigree, Enameled Mountain Scene, 19th Century 7700.00
Box, Singing Bird, On Branch, Cage, Germany 900.00
Box, Sublime Harmonie, 6 Tunes On Each Cylinder, Walnut, Switzerland, 29 x 53 In. .. 6900.00
Box, Symphonion, 1 Tune A Disc, England, 1895 .... 2900.00

Box, Symphonion, 28 Discs, Cabinet 4250.00
Box, Symphonion, Single Comb, 10 In. 1200.00
Box, Thorens, Ornate Brass Case, 25 Discs, 4 1/2-In. Disc 550.00
Box, Thorens, Silvered & Gilt Metal Case, Bust Of Beethoven, 4 Tunes, 10 1/2 In. 230.00
Box, Universal, Cylinder, 6 Cylinders 3500.00
Box, Victorian Boy & Girl, Chrome, Windup, Round, 1890, 3 In. 100.00
Box, Walnut, 27 1/2-Perforated Metal Tune Sheets, 12 Sheets, Floor Console, 1902 ..... 11500.00
Calliope, Railer, Generator & Rolls, 1980s 7800.00
Clavichord, John Challis, Fruitwood Case, Signed, 4 Ft. 9 In. 2185.00
Drum, Base, Marching Band 145.00
Dulcimer, Walnut, Case 195.00
Fife, Civil War 250.00
Grafonola, Columbia, Oak, Floor Model 260.00
Gramophone, Swiss Flingsor, Vibrating Wire System, Wooden Case, 3 Ft. 1300.00
Guitar, Bigby, Custom-Made, Arch Top, 1961 .... 6500.00
Guitar, Chet Atkins, Case 880.00
Guitar, D'Angelico, Arch Top, Acoustic, Sunburst Finish, Maple, Hardshell Case, 1938 9775.00
Guitar, Fender Stratocaster, Electric, Chuck Berry & Bo Diddley 1150.00
Guitar, Fender Stratocaster, Electric, White Finish, 1966 .... 4600.00
Guitar, Gibson L-5, Arch Top, Electric, Sunburst Finish, Black Hardshell Case, 1968 .. 5750.00
Guitar, Gibson, Les Paul, 1956 .... 8000.00
Guitar, Gibson, Les Paul, Gold Top, 1982 .... 1195.00
Guitar, Gibson, Les Paul, Standard, White, Gold Hardware, 1988 .... 895.00
Guitar, Gibson, SG Custom, White, 1964 .... 3000.00
Guitar, Gretsch, Arch Top, Electric, Maple, Black Hardshell Case, 1955 .... 3220.00
Guitar, Paramount 55.00
Guitar, Steel, Dickerson, Tortoiseshell Finish, Case, Matching Amplifier, 1940s 300.00
Guitar, Steel, Dickerson, Tortoiseshell Finish, Case, Amplifier, 1940s 265.00
Guitar, Stratocaster, Fender, Solid Body, Cream, Rosewood Neck, 1962 .... 750.00
Guitar, Stratocaster, Series 10, Electric, Beach Boys Autographed 978.00
Guitar, Vivitone No. 577, Acoustic, Sunburst Finish, Hardshell Case 3450.00
Harmonica, Borah Minivich, 5 1/2 In. 70.00
Harmonica, Chromatic, Finger-Push Lever, Germany, Box 35.00
Harmonica, Hohner, Box, 1915 .... 65.00
Harmonica, Hohner, Herb Shriner's Hoosier Boy, Box 85.00
Harmonica, Hoosier Boy, Herb Shriner, Red & Blue Graphics, Box 50.00
Harmonica, Rolmonica, 12 Paper Rolls, Bakelite. 125.00
Harmonica, Rolmonica, 4 Rolls 85.00
Harp, Coliate Finial, Oak Leaf & Acorn Wreathed Column, Pleyed Wolff, No. 542 ..... 1650.00
Harp, Gerard Mengers, Neoclassical Ram's Heads, Giltwood, 19th Century, 66 In. 1100.00
Harp, L.V.R. Lewis, Gothic Tracery Panels, Saints & Angels, 67 3/4 In. 4180.00
Harp, Painted, Gilt Design, 19th Century, Cardiff, Wales 3850.00
Harp, Rosewood, Gilded 4180.00
Harpsichord, John Challis, Fruitwood Case, 8 x 4 Ft. 3270.00
Harpsichord, Sabattil & Sons, 20th Century 3500.00
Horn, Brass, Original Mouthpiece, 3 1/4 x 15 In. 115.00
Hurdy-Gurdy, Molinari, 20 Keys, Tune Sheet, 14 x 15 Ft. 4995.00
Hurdy-Gurdy, Victorian, Inlaid Walnut, 22 1/4 x 21 3/4 In. 4400.00
Hurdy-Gurdy, With Cart, c.1910, Miniature 1800.00
Mandolin, Label, Roger H. Hildreth, Dartmouth, Hanover, N.H., 1930 .... 180.00
Metronome, Paquet, 19th Century, 9 In. 80.00
Nickelodeon, Coinola, Cupid, Stained Glass Panels, Piano & Mandolin, 1920, 55 In. 8050.00
Nickelodeon, Cremona, Style A 5300.00
Nickelodeon, Peerless, Elite 8900.00
Nickelodeon, Peerless, Elite, 10 Rolls 9995.00
Nickelodeon, Seeburg, Style A 9000.00
Nickelodeon, Seeburg, Style A, Mandolin & Orchestration Bells 4500.00
Orchestrelle, Style V 6500.00
Organ, Barrel, Fruitwood Inlay, Front Handle, 43 Notes, Germany, 1900, 30 In. 4025.00
Organ, Barrel, James Davis 6900.00
Organ, Barrel, Lamy 4200.00
Organ, Barrel, Wilhelm Bruder 9500.00
Organ, Gem, Concert Roller, 17 Wooden Cob Rolls, 1880 .... 750.00

Organ, Kimball, Eastlake, Stool, Stick & Ball, Oak Cabinet 2250.00
Organ, Monkey, Gavioli, 25 Keys 7500.00
Organ, Monkey, Haufbauer, 39 Keys 6000.00
Organ, Monkey, Molinari, 20 Keys 4500.00
Organ, Monkey, Molinari, 26 Keys 8000.00
Organ, Monkey, O.G.M., 41 Keys 7500.00
Organ, Monkey, Reed, Thibouville, France, 1865, 6 Tunes 11000.00
Organ, Monkey, Remote Controlled 550.00
Organ, Pipe, Built-In Roll Player, Simplex Roll Frame 850.00
Organ, Pipe, Milwaukee Organ Co., Player & Manual, 7 Rows Of Pipes, 38 Rolls 5000.00
Organ, Player & Manual, 7 Rows Of Pipes, 36 Rolls, 1932 .... 5000.00
Organ, Player, Angelus 175.00
Organ, Player, Kimball 400.00
Organ, Player, Kimball, Rolls 1800.00
Organ, Player, Reed, Aeolian Orchestrelle, Mahogany Case, 50 Rolls, 1903 .... 3900.00
Organ, Player, Theater, Manual, 4 Banks, 38 Rolls 5000.00
Organ, Pump, Cutout Trim, Applied Carving 210.00
Organ, Pump, Taylord Farley, Ornate, Swivel Stool, 6 Ft. 600.00
Organ, Reed, Aeolian Orchestrelle, Mahogany Case, 40 Rolls 3900.00
Organ, Reed, Pump, Farrand 7500.00
Organ, Roller, Chautaugua, 6 Cobs 850.00
Organ, Roller, Little Gem, 10 Cobs 825.00
Organ, Seeburg, Style K, Xylophone 9500.00
Organ, Wurlitzer, No. 1100, Carved Wood 3500.00
Orguinette, 5 Paper Rolls, Table Model 600.00
Piano, Adam Schaff, Tiger Mahogany Case, Grand 1900.00
Piano, Aeolian, Player, 65 To 88 Notes, Electrified, 40 Rolls 2000.00
Piano, Baldwin Welte, Bench, Grand, 6 Ft. 3800.00
Piano, Baldwin, Baby Grand, Ebonized, Bench, 38 1/2 x 56 1/2 In. 5940.00
Piano, Baldwin, No. B1715, Mahogany Case, Grand, Bench 2760.00
Piano, Barnes Bros., Cottage Grand, Removable Carved Legs, 1853, 36 In. x 6 Ft. 5000.00
Piano, Barrel, Coin Operated 4500.00
Piano, Bechstein, Mahogany, Grand 3450.00
Piano, Chickering & Sons, Console, Mahogany, No. 177029, Bench, 60 x 23 x 39 In. .. 330.00
Piano, Chickering, Square, Carved Legs, Grand, 1893 .... 2500 to 3000.00
Piano, Franklin, Ampico, Baby Grand 1200.00
Piano, Franz Wirth, Brass Inlaid Mahogany, Baby Grand, 5 Ft. 8 In. 345.00
Piano, G.A. Miller, Boston, Square, Grand 725.00
Piano, Grovesteen & Fuller, Square, Grand, 1880 .... 7000.00
Piano, Haddorff, Vertichord, Grand, Bench 375.00
Piano, John Broadwood, Rosewood, Grand, Late 19th Century 3960.00
Piano, Knabe, Louis XV Style, Grand, 1926 .... 7500.00
Piano, Knabe, Upright, Oak, 1892 .... 1000.00
Piano, Ludwig, Player, 38 Rolls, 1920s 2500.00
Piano, Marshall & Wendell, Ampico, 4 Ft. 10 In. 8800.00
Piano, Marshall & Wendell, Ampico, Grand, 5 Ft. 1200.00
Piano, Marshall & Wendell, Upright, Ampico 3500.00
Piano, Mason & Hamlin, Ebony Finish, Grand, 5 Ft. 8 In. 6900.00
Piano, Nelson-Wiggen, Player, A-Roll, Coin Operated 1500.00
Piano, Player, Honky Tonk Attachment, Electric & Manual, Upright, 88 Notes 2500.00
Piano, Reproducing, Knabe, Ampico, 55 Rolls 4750.00
Piano, Reproducing, Knabe, Grand, Ampico A, Rolls 4750.00
Piano, Reproducing, Steck, Duo-Art, Grand, 1930s 8000.00
Piano, Schaeffer, Player, Matching Bench, Roll Cabinet, 70 Rolls 950.00
Piano, Schomacher & Co., Square, Carved Legs, Grand, 1800s 7000.00
Piano, Spinet, Marantz, Pianocorder System, 40 Cassettes 3000.00
Piano, Steck, Duo-Art, Grand, 5 Ft. 4 In. 9500.00
Piano, Steinway, Grand, 1911, 5 Ft. 8 In. 5900.00
Piano, Steinway, Hepplewhite Style, Black Lacquer, Grand, 1925, 65 x 56 In. 9200.00
Piano, Steinway, Mahogany, Baby Grand 8337.00
Piano, Stroud, Player, Grand, Duo-Art, Rolls, 5 Ft. 6500.00
Piano, Symphonique, Ampico, Grand 3950.00
Piano, W.P. Emerson, Bulbous Legs, Rosewood 1000.00

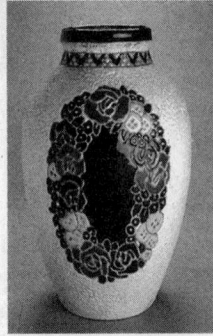

MZ Austria, Vase, 11 1/2 In.

◆◆◆◆◆◆◆◆◆◆◆◆◆◆◆◆◆◆◆◆◆◆◆
Don't scrub gilding and gold
edges on porcelains.
◆◆◆◆◆◆◆◆◆◆◆◆◆◆◆◆◆◆◆◆◆◆◆

◆◆◆◆◆◆◆◆◆◆◆◆◆◆◆◆◆◆◆◆◆◆◆
Stains on porcelains can be
removed by soaking in a mixture of 2 tablespoons Poli-
dent denture cleaner in 1
quart tepid water.
◆◆◆◆◆◆◆◆◆◆◆◆◆◆◆◆◆◆◆◆◆◆◆

Piano, Weber, Duo-Art, Baby Grand, 1927-1930	16000.00
Piano, Weber, Duo-Art, Mahogany, Grand, Matching Bench, 100 Rolls	6000.00
Piano, Weber, Grand, Duo-Art, 100 Rolls, Bench, Mahogany	6000.00
Piano, Wing & Sons, Mandolin, 5 Pedals, Bench	2295.00
Pianoforte, F. Stevens, Mahogany & Tiger Maple	990.00
Pianoforte, Loud Brothers, Philadelphia, Rosewood Veneer, Stencil, 1820s, 70 In.	2070.00
Pianola, Aeolian Metro Style, Mahogany Case	1750.00
Pitcher, John Peel, England Crown Devon Fieldings, 8 In.	165.00
Rolmonica, 21 Rolls	175.00
Rolmonica, Bakelite, 4 Rolls, Box, 1925	110.00
Singing Bird, Beak Opens, Tail Moves, Birdcage, Germany, 20th Century, 11 1/2 In.	488.00
Violano, Mills Novelty Co., Converter, Mahogany	9500.00
Violin, Label Copie De Ludovicus Ricozali, 2 Bows, Case, 1891, Full Size	70.00
Whistle, Sweet Potato	150.00
Zither, Gullar, Panama Model, 1915	100.00

MUSTACHE CUPS were popular from 1850 to 1900 when the large, flowing mustache was in style. A ledge of china or silver held the hair out of the liquid in the cup. This kept the mustache tidy and also kept the mustache wax from melting. Left-handed mustache cups are rare but are being reproduced.

Clydesdale Mare, Colt, Left-Handed	125.00

MZ AUSTRIA is the wording on a mark used by Moritz Zdekauer on porcelains made at his works in Altrolau, Austria, from 1884 to 1909. The mark was changed to MZ Altrolau in 1909 when the firm was purchased by C.M. Hutschenreuther. The firm operated under the name Altrolau Porcelain Factories from 1909 to 1945. It was nationalized after World War II. The pieces were decorated with lavish floral patterns and overglaze gold decoration. Full sets of dishes were made as well as vases, toilet sets, and other wares.

MZ Austria

Biscuit Jar, Water Lilies, Hand Painted, Green, White & Gold	225.00
Vase, 11 1/2 In. .... *Illus*	195.00

NAILSEA glass was made in the Bristol district in England from 1788 to 1873. It was made by many different factories, not just the Nailsea Glass House. Many pieces were made with loopings of either white or colored glass as decoration.

Demijohn, 1800, 12 In.	1200.00
Lamp, Fairy, Cranberry	185.00
Lamp, Fairy, Ruffled Base, Blue & White, 6 x 6 1/2 In.	485.00
Pitcher, Rust, Yellow, White & Blue Flecks, Green Ground, 1800, 11 In.	2200.00
Rolling Pin, Blue & White Swirl, 1850	305.00
Shade, Fairy Lamp, Ruffled Under Base, Citron	450.00
Vase, White Loopings, Rolled Edge, Blue, 4 1/2 In.	135.00

NAKARA is a trade name for a white glassware made about 1900 by the C. F. Monroe Company of Meriden, Connecticut. It was decorated in pastel colors. The glass was very similar to another glass made by the company called *Wave Crest*. The company closed in 1916. Boxes for use on a dressing table are the most commonly found Nakara pieces. The mark is not found on every piece.

NAKARA

Bonbon, Enameled Daisy, Marked, 7 1/2 x 6 In.	275.00
Box, Collars & Cuffs, Roses	850.00
Box, Girls Tea Party On Hinged Lid, 6 x 3 1/2 In.	950.00
Box, Portrait, Green Satin Finish, 4 1/2 In.	525.00
Box, Portrait, Lady With Rose In Hair, Green, 4 1/2 In.	525.00 to 595.00

NANKING is a type of blue-and-white porcelain made in Canton, China, since the late eighteenth century. It is very similar to Canton, which is listed under its own name in this book. Both Nanking and Canton are part of a larger group now called *Chinese Export* porcelain. Nanking has a spear-and-post border and may have gold decoration.

Bowl, 7 x 9 In.	225.00
Bowl, Salad, 19th Century, 9 1/2 In., Pair	690.00
Cider Jug, Cover, Gold Trim, 19th Century, 9 1/4 In.	977.00
Coffeepot, Lighthouse, Gold Trim, 19th Century, 9 3/4 In.	862.00
Dish, Pudding, Blue & White, c.1790, 5 In.	240.00
Platter, Blue & White, 17 3/4 In.	320.00
Platter, Cover, Oval, 19th Century, 15 In.	805.00
Platter, Pierced Insert, 19th Century, 15 1/2 In.	345.00
Sauce Boat, Underplate, 19th Century, 6 1/2 In.	316.00
Teapot, 19th Century, 9 In.	345.00
Teapot, Twist Handle, Gold Trim, 5 In.	330.00
Tureen, Soup, Cover, 19th Century, 9 x 13 In.	488.00

NAPKIN RINGS were in fashion from 1869 to about 1900. They were made of silver, porcelain, wood, and other materials. They are still being made today. The most popular rings with collectors are the silver plated figural examples. Small, realistic figures were made to hold the ring. Good and poor reproductions of the more expensive rings are now being made and collectors must be very careful.

Bakelite, Jade Green, 8 Piece	90.00
D Shape, Repousse Dolphin, Enameled, Sterling Silver, England, 1905, 2 1/8 In.	250.00
Figural, Bear, Silver Plate	60.00
Figural, Bird & Floral, Basketweave, Silver Plate, 2 3/4 x 8 1/2 In.	60.00
Figural, Birds, 3 Parrots Holding Cobalt Blue Vase	90.00
Figural, Boy, Holding Book, Kate Greenaway	160.00
Figural, Boy, In Harness, Pulling Cart With Ring, Silver Plate	375.00
Figural, Boy, Pulling Ring On Sled, Silver Plate	325.00
Figural, Boy, Riding Dolphin, Silver Plate, Meriden	250.00
Figural, Cherub & Bird On Wishbone, Silver Plate	95.00
Figural, Cherubs, Footed Base, Silver Plate	335.00
Figural, Chick, Ring Rests On Wishbone, Best Wishes, Silver Plate	75.00
Figural, Deer, Ring On Back, Silver Plate	175.00
Figural, Dog, Chained, Silver Plate	175.00
Figural, Dog, Menacing Cat, On Top Of Ring, Silver Plate	225.00
Figural, Dog, Wilcox	115.00
Figural, Eagles, Silver Plate, Meriden	65.00
Figural, Egyptian Busts At Sides, Hoofed Legs, Bud Vase Top, Silver Plate, 6 In.	125.00
Figural, Foxes, After Bird On Nest, Silver Plate	148.00
Figural, Giraffe, Eating Leaves, Silver Plate	150.00
Figural, Goat, Rectangular Ring, Silver Plate	50.00
Figural, Grouse, Silver Plate	150.00
Figural, Heron, Long Beak, Silver Plate, Reed & Barton	300.00
Figural, Ostrich, Standing, Silver Plate, Australia	90.00
Figural, Putti On Chariot, Silver Plate, Pair	77.00
Figural, Rabbits, Ring On Ornate Base, Silver Plate, Pairpoint	400.00

Figural, Suffragette, Holding Megaphone 250.00
Figural, Tennis Player, Woman, Racquet, Silver Plate 350.00
Figural, Turtle, Propped On Back, 3-Tiered Base, Derby 235.00
Figural, Winged Cherubs, In Canoe, Oars Are Arrows, 4 1/2 In. 115.00
Hammered Silver, Applied Block E, Rectangular, Lebolt & Co., 7/8 x 3 x 5/8 In. 75.00
Hammered Silver, Applied Block J, Rectangular, Lebolt & Co., 3/4 x 2 1/4 x 5/8 In. ... 65.00
Pewter, Relief Scene, Scrolled Border 15.00

NASH glass was made in Corona, New York, from about 1928 to 1931. A.
Douglas Nash bought the Corona glassworks from Louis C. Tiffany in 1928
and founded the A. Douglas Nash Corporation with support from his father,   **NASH**
Arthur J. Nash. Arthur had worked at the Webb factory in England and for
the Tiffany Glassworks in Corona.

Bowl, Chintz, Crystal Foot, Signed, 4 In. 120.00
Bowl, Green Iridescent, Petal Edge, Signed, 10 In. 430.00
Bowl, Opalescent Stripes, Pedestal 150.00
Dish, Chintz, Raised Scalloped Rim, Orange & Yellow, Signed, 7 In. 165.00
Vase, Gold Iridescent, Disk Foot, Signed, 4 1/4 In., Pair 747.50
Vase, Pulled Feather Design, White Luster Cased, Signed, 11 In. 1850.00

NAUTICAL antiques are listed in this category. Any of the many objects that
were made or used by the seafaring trade, including ship parts, models, and
tools, are included. Other pieces may be found listed under Scrimshaw.

Aneroid Barometer, Brass, Open Face Dial, Beveled Glass, 5 In. 77.00
Asparagus Fork, Cunard White Star, Silver Plate 75.00
Barometer, Marine, Gimbal, Rope Carving, Ivory Scales, Vernier Adjustment 2750.00
Barometer-Thermometer, Schatz & Sohne, Wall Mount, 7 In. 115.00
Bell, Ship's, Great Lakes Grain Carrier, Charles C. West, Dated 1925, 14 In. 930.00
Binnacle, Ship's, White, Lionel Compass 880.00
Binnacle, Yacht, Brass, Oil Burner, 10 In. 900.00
Binoculars, Ship's, Krauss, Paris, Brass, Chrome Mounts, 68 In. 445.00
Binoculars, Submarine, Mounted On Conning Tower 350.00
Blubber Spade, Original Wooden Pole Mounted, P. Butts & Son, New Bedford 600.00
Box, Blanket, Fisherman's, Deep Green, Nova Scotia, 1840-1860 .... 1800.00
Brush, Shaving, Prisoner Of War, Bone Handle, Pierced Carving, 6 1/2 In. 90.00
Cannon, Bronze, Wooden Carriage, D. Kahnellers & Sons, 1831, 27 In. 3300.00
Cannon, Starting Signal For Yacht Races, Chrome Plated 16-In. Barrel, Lock Sets 1700.00
Cannon, Starting Signal, Brass, Strong & Co., 16-In. Mahogany Base, 11 In. 1760.00
Canoe, Old Town, Green, Letters, Salesman's Sample, 50 x 9 In. .... *Illus*   9350.00
Canoe, R.J. Robertson, 17 Ft. 6 In. 660.00
Canoe, William English, c.1910 .... 3025.00
Case, Needle, Sail Maker's, With Needles, Oak, 7 1/2 In. 115.00
Case, Needle, Sail Maker's, With Needles, Oak, 5 1/2 In. 95.00
Chair, Deck, Mahogany, Green Leather, Brass Studs, From Queen Elizabeth I, Pair 4400.00
Chest, Crackled Blue Paint, British Bark In Full Sail On Inside Lid, 42 x 16 x 19 In. 3575.00
Chest, Dovetail Construction, Blue Paint, 17 3/4 x 39 1/2 In. 770.00
Chest, Hinged Paneled Top, Stepped Base, Oak, American 110.00
Chest, Medicine, Painted New Zealand Flags, Ship's Name, Pine, 27 x 48 In. 1760.00
Chest, Till, Rope Becket Handles, Pine & Poplar, 27 3/4 In. 140.00
Chronometer, Brass Clock, Mounted On Gimbals, Mahogany 3575.00

Nautical, Canoe, Old Town, Green, Letters, Salesman's Sample, 50 x 9 In.

Clock, Bell, Chelsea Mariner, Wheel Design..	2200.00
Clock, Chelsea, Engine Room, Brass, 10 In..	395.00
Clock, Perkinson & Frodsham, Peary's Arctic Expedition, Wooden Stand, 6 1/4 In........	1320.00
Clock, Seth Thomas, Outside Bell, Brass, 10 1/2 In.......................................	600.00
Clock, Seth Thomas, Outside Bell, Nickel Plate, 10 1/2 In..............................	550.00
Clock, Seth Thomas, Ship's Bell, 11 In..	465.00
Clock, Ship's, Brass, Smith, Astral, 8-Day, 8 In...	220.00
Clock, Ship's, Chelsea, Brass, Spokes, Wooden Base, Bells, 14 1/2 x 17 1/2 In.	2200.00
Clock, Ship's, Seth Thomas, Outside Bell	880.00
Clock, Ship's, Trophy, Awarded In Pinehurst, N.C., Brass, Spokes, 1939	660.00
Clock, Strikes Every 4 Hours, Exposed Bell...	500.00
Compass, Boat, Baker Of Boston, Box, 5 In.	88.00
Compass, Cased, Charles Laughlin Co., 5 In.	100.00
Compass, Mariner's, Wooden Dovetailed Box	95.00
Compass, Tell-Tale, Captain's, Nickel, Brass, Mounting Bracket, Potter, Toronto, 6 In.	990.00
Compass, Tell-Tale, Nickel, 6 In...	550.00
Desk, Captain's, c.1920	2200.00
Ditty Bag, Sailor's, Knife, Fid, Palm, From Maine Ship, 15 Piece......................	45.00
Dividers, Chart, H. Hughes & Co., Brass Folding Tripod, Wooden Case, 25 1/2 In........	330.00
Figurehead, Flying Dutchman, English-Type Sailor, 58 1/2 In.	9350.00
Foghorn, Foot Powered, Siebe, Gorman, Wood & Leather Bellows, 28 x 23 In.	357.50
Fork, Lee Line Steamers, Reed & Barton, Silver Plate, c.1900	50.00
Gangway Board, Ship's, Carved Mahogany, Brass, 19th Century, 44 x 12 In., Pair........	2750.00
Goblet, Presented To Capt. Bristow, By Dan Bennett & Son, 1846, S. Hennel Marks	1100.00
Grappling Hook, Wooden Handle, 65 In..	82.00
Harpoon, Iron, 38 In...	825.00
Harpoon, Temple, Toggle Barb, Iron, 1848, 41 In.	990.00
Harpoon, Toggle, 29 In..	330.00
Harpoon, Whaling, Hand Forged Steel, 32 In.	247.00
Harpoon, Whaling, Hand Forged Steel, 35 3/4 In.	121.00
Harpoon, Whaling, Hand Forged Steel, Flat Blade, Wooden Handle, 73 In.................	93.00
Harpoon, Whaling, Hand Forged Steel, Rope, Ferrule End, Incised W.D.B., 32 In.	275.00
Harpoon Whaling Gun, Shoulder, Percussion, Open Stock, CC Brand, 1850, 36 In.	1540.00
Lamp, Kerosene, Lighthouse, Chimney, 4th Order, Fresnel Lens, 26 In.	2310.00
Lamp, Marquetry Lighthouse Base, Boat Helm Top, Natural Wood, 17 x 28 In.	400.00
Lamp, Port & Starboard, Copper, China, 1920s, 18 In., Pair............................	195.00
Lamp, Starboard, Brass, 11 In...	66.00
Lance, Whaling, 50 In...	412.00
Lance, Whaling, Iron, 53 In...	165.00
Lantern, Mounted To Sway With Ship's Motion, Nickel Over Brass	35.00
Lantern, Ship's, Marine Lighting, Ward Henickson, Akin & Co.	135.00
Lantern, Starboard, Blue-Green Lens, Copper, 23 In.....................................	90.00
Ledger, Listing Cargo On Sonoma, 1884	360.00
Light, Anchor, Brass, Electrified, 18 In..	165.00
Light, Anchor, Copper, 20 1/2 In..	195.00
Light, Starboard, Hugh Douglas, Liverpool, Copper, 24 In.	110.00
Lights, Running, Full Round, Brass, Electric, Pair	75.00
Lights, Running, Port & Starboard, From Maritime Electric, Sank 1983, 18 In., Pair.....	187.00
Measure, Cordage, Scales 1 Side, Manufacturer Other, Maple, Brass, 1850, 6 1/2 In. ...	575.00
Model, 2-Masted Schooner, Female Figurehead, Wooden, 19 x 24 In.	865.00
Model, 3-Masted Schooner, Lucia A. Simpson, H.W. Potter, 1943, 36 x 23 In..............	2415.00
Model, 3-Masted Ship, Inez, Bath, Carved Figurehead, Working Pulleys, 34 In.	1250.00
Model, 3-Masted Ship, Plank-On-Frame, Cloth Sails, Case, 36 1/2 x 43 In.	1045.00
Model, 3-Masted Square Rigger, Formosa, Case, 27 1/2 x 39 1/2 In......................	1430.00
Model, 4-Masted Ship, Yellow, Blue & Black, 60 In.	350.00
Model, Adirondack Skiff, Pond Boat, Home-Built, Red, 1950, 24 3/4 In.	42.00
Model, America's Cup Yacht, Valkyrie III, Mahogany Case, 26 x 24 In.	1540.00
Model, American Sailing Ship, Evangeline, Mahogany Case, 28 x 16 In..................	880.00
Model, Amphibian Plane, Blackburn Perth, Wm. Doylend, 1934-1935	2300.00
Model, Amphibian Plane, Short Singapore I, Wm. Doylend	1155.00
Model, Azorian Whaleboat, Pink & Blue Interior, White & Yellow, Case, 24 In.	1100.00
Model, Battleship Courbet, France, 51 In..	7700.00
Model, Boat, Fuller Bros., Buzzard's Bay, Cape Cod, 6 1/2 In...........................	64.00

Model, British Brig, Case, 14 x 22 In. 495.00
Model, British Gunboat, H.M.S. Victory, 43 In. 2200.00
Model, Clipper Ship, Sovereign Of The Seas, Case, 26 x 14 In. 1595.00
Model, Clipper Ship, W.T. Babcock, N.Y., American Flag, Case, 31 x 21 In. 1325.00
Model, Clipper Ship, Wooden, 38 1/2 In. 7700.00
Model, Clipper, Great Republic, H.W. Potter, Birmingham, Mich., 1943, 53 x 30 In. 3200.00
Model, Eastport Pinky, Full Suit Of Sails, Black Rail, Pine Cradle, 23 x 23 In. 405.00
Model, English Steamer Hobart, 70 In. 4125.00
Model, Four Winds, London, 48 In. 595.00
Model, French Warship, Le Superbe, 38 In. 1100.00
Model, Frigate, Essex, Copper Clad Hull, 26 In. 1320.00
Model, Fully-Rigged, Hand Sewn Linen Sails, Hand Painted, 1800s, 31 x 32 In. 1150.00
Model, Half Moon, Henry Hudson's, Running Rigging, 22 x 28 In. 220.00
Model, Half, Clipper Ship, Cutty Sark, Carved, Fully Rigged, Frame, 11 x 20 In. 460.00
Model, Half, Mayflower, Carved, Full Sail, Shadowbox Frame, 24 x 34 In. 865.00
Model, Half, Sloop, William Quincy, Painted Red & White, 6 x 21 In. 120.00
Model, Hudson River Day Liner, New York, 1860, 42 In. 3850.00
Model, New England Whaleboat, Tubs, Buckets, Oars, 21 x 22 In. 505.00
Model, New York, Shadowbox, Carved, Painted, 9 1/2 x 19 In. 115.00
Model, Ocean Liner, Ile De France, Waterline, 54 In. 2750.00
Model, Paddle Wheel, John F. Tobin, Vicksburg & New Orleans Packet, Tin 9625.00
Model, Plane, HP42 Hannibal, Imperial Airways, Wm. Doylend 1155.00
Model, Planked Sailboat, Cloth Sails, Mahogany, Stand, 1950s, 33 x 25 In. 240.00
Model, Prisoner Of War, Victory, Bone, Wooden Case, 11 1/2 x 13 In. 1650.00
Model, Privateer Rattlesnake, Wooden, 28 In. 495.00
Model, Side Wheel Steamship, Robert E. Lee, 20 3/4 In. 435.00
Model, Sloop, Friendship, Mahogany, Brass Pedestal, 40 x 45 In. 1545.00
Model, Steam Trawler, Storm King, Glass Display Case, 15 x 28 In. 1100.00
Model, USS Frigate, Constitution, Wooden, 58 In. 4400.00
Model, Whale Ship, Alice Mandell, Fully Fitted, Hardwood Base, 26 x 32 In. 2200.00
Octant, John Holdsworth, Ebony & Ivory, 1791, 16 1/2 In. 350.00
Octant, Spence, Barrett & Co., Cased 1045.00
Oil Can, Machinist's, With Tray, For Steam Engine, Brass, 4 Cans, 2 Spouts, 18 x 15 In. ... 907.00
Passenger List, Queen Mary, 1957 .... 10.00
Plaque, Cunard Lines, SS Franconia, Cardboard, Wood Frame, 18 x 23 In. 200.00
Pond Boat, Silver Spray, Brass Deck Fittings, White, Blue & Varnish 1320.00
Quadrant, Cased, J. Smith, London, Box 440.00
Quadrant, J. Soulby & Co., Ebony Frame, Ivory Scale, 12 In. 385.00
Quadrant, Spencer, Browning & Rust, Case 440.00
Sextant, Box, England, c.1880 .... 950.00
Sextant, Brass, Silver Scales, Cary, London, Unusual Frame, 1 Eyepiece, Case 1210.00
Sextant, Brass, Spencer, Browning & Rust, London, Case, Label, David Baker 1035.00
Sextant, Ebony & Brass, Ivory, Wooden Case, 16 In. 357.00
Sextant, Flat, Sheet Brass, Cory, London 1210.00
Sextant, U.S. Navy, Mark 1, Mahogany Case 192.00
Ship Model, see Nautical, Model
Sighting Vane, Boxwood Scales, Fruitwood, American 3850.00
Sign, American President Steamship Lines, Carved Dolphins, Painted, 36 x 48 In. 3630.00
Sign, Harbormaster's, Rates For Dockage, Newburyport, 60 x 35 In. 1430.00
Sink, Ship's, Unusual Chestnut Grain Painted, With Tap 250.00
Spear, Eel, 6 Prongs, 15 1/2 In. 25.00
Spyglass, Brass & Rosewood, Extends To 37 In. 187.00
Stand, Dressing, Ship's Officer, Mechanical, Mirror Top, Tall 220.00
Swordfish Bill, Painted Ship & Mermaids, Fish Other Side, 23 1/2 In. 155.00
Telescope, Brass, Leather & Vellum Covered Barrel, Flags Of World, 34 1/2 In. 445.00
Telescope, Captain's, Single Draw, Wooden, 18th Century, Ramsden, London, 46 In. .. 1320.00
Telescope, Single Draw, Bate, London, Objective Lens, Owner F. Cresser, 31 In. 415.00
Telescope, US Navy, Bronze, 1920, 22 12 In. 365.00
Telescope, Wooden Barrel, Single Draw, 30 In. 440.00
Wheel, Bronze Fittings, Mahogany, 29 In. 126.00
Wheel, Pilot, Double Circle, C.C. Slider, Wooden, 120 In. 605.00
Wheel, Ship's, Brass & Mahogany, 36 In. 247.00
Wheel, Ship's, Brass Hardware, 30 In. 250.00

Wheel, Ship's, Brass Hub, 10 Walnut & Oak Spokes	1500.00
Wheel, Ship's, Brass Hub, Turned Handles, 37 In.	66.00
Whistle, Hand-Pumped, Brass, 21 In.	100.00
Whistle, Steam, Triple Chime, Lunkenheimer, Brass, Copper & Cast Iron, 48 In.	1210.00

NETSUKES are small ivory, wood, metal, or porcelain pieces used as toggles on the end of the cord that held a Japanese money pouch. The earliest date from the sixteenth century. Many are miniature, carved works of art.

Ivory, Monkey, Fighting 2 Sparrows, Signed Seigyoku, Late 19th Century	3750.00
Ivory, Mouse Resting On Basket, Movable Cat, 1 3/4 In.	175.00
Ivory, Puppy, Licking Flank, Inlaid Eyes, Kyoto School, 1800	7150.00
Wood, Coiled Rat, Black Inlaid Eyes, Masamitsu	1980.00
Wood, Monkey, Eating Fruit, Young On Back, Signed Masanao	2530.00
Wood, Owl, Perched On Branch, Ivory Beak & Horn, Amber Eyes, Bishu, Box	1320.00
Wood, Puppy, Seated, Black Stone Eyes, 19th Century, Masayoshi	2425.00
Wood, Shoki Clutching His Beard, Halberd, Gold & Silver Lacquered, 18th Century	4400.00

NEW HALL Porcelain Manufactory was started at Newhall, Shelton, Staffordshire, England, in 1782. Simple decorated wares were made. Between 1810 and 1825, the factory made a glassy bone porcelain sometimes marked with the factory name. Do not confuse New Hall porcelain with the pieces made by the New Hall Pottery Company, Ltd., a twentieth-century firm.

Coffee Can, Oriental Flowers	150.00
Cup & Saucer, Chinese Figures	125.00

NEW MARTINSVILLE Glass Manufacturing Company was established in 1901 in New Martinsville, West Virginia. It was bought and renamed the Viking Glass Company in 1944 and is still producing fine glasswares.

Batter Set, Tray	500.00
Bookends, Cornucopia	45.00
Bookends, Nautilus Shell	60.00 to 120.00
Bride's Bowl, Raspberry To Cream, Ruffled Edge, 12 1/2 x 11 1/4 In.	295.00
Candlestick, Single Wing, Moondrops, Pair	42.00
Figurine, Baby Bear, 3 In.	35.00
Figurine, Bear, 4 1/2 In.	35.00
Figurine, Hen, 5 In.	50.00
Figurine, Janice Swan, Clear, Ruby, 7 1/2 In.	25.00
Figurine, Pelican, 8 In.	50.00
Figurine, Seal, With Ball, 7 In.	45.00
Pitcher, Florene, Ruby Stained	135.00
Sugar & Creamer, Moondrops, Red	20.00
Tumbler, Janice, Red	30.00
Vase, Melon Shape, Ribbed Neck, 26 Ruffled Top, Orange Cased	145.00

NEWCOMB Pottery was founded by Ellsworth and William Woodward at Sophie Newcomb College, New Orleans, Louisiana, in 1895. The work continued through the 1940s. Pieces of this art pottery are marked with the printed letters *NC* and often have the incised initials of the artist as well. Most pieces have a matte glaze and incised decoration.

Bowl, Band Of White Blossoms, Green Leaves, Anna Frances Simpson, 7 In.	715.00
Bowl, Carved & Painted, Green, Rose, Blue Ground, Sadie Irvine, 4 x 8 In.	475.00
Bowl, Carved Pink & Lavender Poppies, Sadie Irvine, 1918, 11 In.	1600.00
Bowl, Rose Blossoms, Leaves, Purple Ground, Henrietta Bailey, 1910, 7 In.	1600.00
Humidor, Tobacco Leaves & Blossoms, Sadie Irvine, 1925, 5 1/2 In.	2100.00
Pitcher, Stems Around Shoulder, Square Handle, Anna Frances Simpson, 7 In.	1870.00
Pitcher, White Ducks, Blue River, Sadie Irvine, 1917, 4 In.	2530.00
Plaque, Arts & Crafts Landscape, Cypress Trees, Amelie Roman, 1906, 7 3/4 In.	3500.00
Plaque, Moon Reflecting On Pot Behind Trees, 3 1/2 x 5 12 In.	3950.00
Plate, Moonlit Bayou Landscape, Aurelia Arbo, 4 3/4 In.	1550.00
Pot, Floral, Sadie Irvine, 8 3/4 In.	2530.00
Trivet, Espanol, 1929	1450.00
Vase, 3 Handles, Carved & Painted Flowers, Leona Nicholson, No. BK79, 5 In.	4400.00
Vase, 3 Handles, Incised & Painted Moss-Laden Trees, Sadie Irvine, 5 In.	2200.00

◆◆◆◆◆◆◆◆◆◆◆◆◆◆◆◆◆◆◆◆◆◆◆◆◆

A vase that has been drilled
for a lamp, even if the hole for
the wiring is original, is worth
30% to 50% of the value of
the same vase without a hole.

◆◆◆◆◆◆◆◆◆◆◆◆◆◆◆◆◆◆◆◆◆◆◆◆◆

Newcomb, Vase, Woodland Scene,
Marie De Hoa Le Blanc, 1909, 12 In.

Vase, Blue, Pink Dribbling Band, Baluster, Joseph Meyer, 1925, 6 3/4 In.	665.00
Vase, Bottle Shape, Stylized Leaves, Green Ground, Sabina Wells, 1903, 6 In.	2300.00
Vase, Bulbous Flowers, Blue & Green Ground, Maude Robinson, 1908, 8 3/4 In.	3000.00
Vase, Espanol, Anna Frances Simpson, 1929	3750.00
Vase, Flared Cylinder, Blue To Pink Daffodil, Green Leaves, 10 1/2 In.	2425.00
Vase, Floral Band At Shoulder, Anna Frances Simpson, 3 1/2 In.	550.00
Vase, Floral Design, 12 In.	1450.00
Vase, Floral Design, Green Leaves, Blue Ground, No. 223, 9 In.	2200.00
Vase, Floral, Corset, 1910, 12 In.	3850.00
Vase, Floral, Stems Surrounding Shoulder, Henrietta Bailey, 11 1/2 In.	4125.00
Vase, Grapes, 5 1/2 x 3 1/2 In.	1200.00
Vase, Jonquil, 10 In.	1650.00
Vase, Landscape, Closed-In Rim, Anna Frances Simpson, 1918, 5 x 5 In.	2550.00
Vase, Matte Green, Brown Drip, Joseph Meyer, 5 In.	335.00
Vase, Mistletoe, High Glaze, Squatty, 6 In.	1100.00
Vase, Oak Tree Scene, Landscape, Yellow Moon, Sadie Irvine, J.H., 5 In.	1650.00
Vase, Oak Trees, Spanish Moss, Moon, Bulbous, Henrietta Bailey, 1933, 5 x 6 In.	1200.00
Vase, Painted Wisteria Clusters, Maude Robinson, 1904, 8 1/4 In.	3850.00
Vase, Pine Cones & Needles, Cream Interior, Henrietta Bailey, 1915, 6 7/8 In.	1495.00
Vase, Scenic, Carved, Stylized Green & Blue Trees, Mark, Henrietta Bailey, 7 In.	4125.00
Vase, Sculpted Landscape, Oak Trees, Harvest Moon, Sadie Irvine, 6 In.	3575.00
Vase, Stylized Daffodils & Foliage, Cream Ground, Marked, 11 1/2 In.	4600.00
Vase, Stylized Landscape, Cynthia Littlejohn, 1915, 4 In.	1450.00
Vase, Swamp Scene, Trees, Moss, Blue Tone Glazes, Sadie Irvine, 5 x 4 In.	2300.00
Vase, Tall Trees, Blue Matte Glaze, Sadie Irvine, 1915, 7 1/4 In.	2000.00
Vase, Trumpet Form, Stylized Blue Flowers, Band Of Foliage, Marked, 9 In.	3450.00
Vase, White Narcissus, Foliage, Blue Ground, Anna Frances Simpson, 1922, 4 In.	700.00
Vase, Woodland Scene, Marie De Hoa Le Blanc, 1909, 12 In. .... *Illus*	25300.00

NILOAK Pottery (Kaolin spelled backward) was made at the Hyten Brothers
Pottery in Benton, Arkansas, between 1909 and 1946. Although the factory
did make cast and molded wares, collectors are most interested in the marbleized art pottery line made of colored swirls of clay. It was called *Mission
Ware.*

Bowl, Marbleized Clay, Tones Of Brown, Signed, 5 3/4 x 8 In.	400.00
Bowl, Marbleized, 3 In.	50.00
Candlestick, Marbleized, 9 In.	20.00
Clock Case, Mission Ware	800.00
Jar, Finial Cover, Marbleized, Blue, Brown, Gray & Ivory, Impressed, 4 1/4 In.	330.00
Pitcher, Ball, Black, Ice Lip, Cast	35.00
Pitcher, Grease Pencil Markings, Cast, 5 1/2 In.	40.00
Pitcher, Ozark Dawn, Pink, Blue	35.00
Pitcher, Rose & Misty Green, Round, 5 In.	60.00
Planter, Deer, Blue, 7 In.	22.00
Planter, Kangaroo, Boxing Gloves, Cast	15.00

Planter, Squirrel, Brown, Matte, Cast 30.00
Planter, Swan, Black, Cast, 7 1/2 In. 35.00
Planter, Swan, Pink, Cast, 7 In. 24.00
Vase, Bud, Marbleized, Blue, Pink, Gray & Cream, Speckled Blue Interior, 6 In. 88.00
Vase, Bud, Marbleized, Narrow Cylinder, Flared Bottom, Blue, Tan, Brown, 8 1/2 In. ... 275.00
Vase, Cylinder, Flared Base, Brown, Blue, Cream & Orange Swirls, 8 1/2 In. 330.00
Vase, Fan, Marbleized, Gray, Ivory, Blue & Terra-Cotta, Stamped, 6 1/4 x 5 3/4 In. 193.00
Vase, Marbelized, Blue-Gray & Brown Matte, Flared, 7 1/2 x 4 1/2 In. 193.00
Vase, Marbleized, 4 5/8 In. 65.00
Vase, Marbleized, 8 1/4 In. 225.00
Vase, Marbleized, 9 1/4 In. 250.00
Vase, Marbleized, Broad Base, Wide Flared Top, Blue, Brown, Tan, Cream, 11 1/2 In.. 385.00
Vase, Marbleized, Broad Shoulder, Raised Rim, Tan, Blue, Red-Brown, Brown, 10 In.. 440.00
Vase, Marbleized, Brown, Light Brown, Rust, Closed In Rim, Stamped, 10 In. 385.00
Vase, Marbleized, Browns, Orange, Blue, Cream, 8 1/2 In. 110.00
Vase, Marbleized, Bulbous, Thin Neck, Flared Rim 138.00
Vase, Marbleized, Dark Blue, Brown & Beige, Impressed Mark, 9 x 3 1/2 In. 220.00
Vase, Marbleized, Gray, Blue, Cream, 11 In. 495.00
Vase, Marbleized, Notched Shoulder, Flared Rim, Impressed Mark, 9 1/2 x 4 1/4 In. .. 248.00
Vase, Marbleized, Rust, Brown, Blue, Cream, 13 In. 495.00
Vase, Marbleized, Signed, 4 1/2 x 3 1/2 In. 85.00
Vase, Marbleized, Signed, 4 x 4 In. 125.00
Vase, Marbleized, Signed, 5 1/2 In. 125.00
Vase, Marbleized, Swirls Of Brown, Tan & Blue, Signed, 10 In. 187.00
Vase, Ozark Dawn, Rose & Misty Green, 14 In. 250.00
Vase, Wing Shoulder Handles, Flared, Rose, 6 x 3 1/2 In. 10.00

NIPPON porcelain was made in Japan from 1891 to 1921. *Nippon* is the Japanese word for *Japan*. A few firms continued to use the word *Nippon* on ceramics after 1921 as a part of the company name more than as an identification of the country of origin. More pieces marked Nippon will be found in the Dragonware, Moriage, and Noritake categories.

Ashtray, Beaded, Scenic, 6 In. 200.00
Ashtray, Match Holder, Trees, Shoreline, Yellow, Mark No. 47 .... 75.00
Ashtray, Sailboat, Round, 5 In. 35.00
Basket, Hand Painted Roses, Pastel Ground, Green Maple Leaf 85.00
Bowl, 9 1/2 In. 100.00
Bowl, Allover Violet Floral, Gold Border, 10 In. 90.00
Box, Trinket, Hand Painted Roses, Squatty & Bulbous, Green M Wreath 42.00
Celery, Hand Painted Violets & Leaves, Geometric Gold Design, 12 x 5 In. 48.00
Celery Dish, Flowers, Open Handles, 12 In. 40.00
Cheese & Cracker, Hand Painted Swags, Roses, Scrolled Band, 9 In. 65.00
Coffeepot, Gold, White Ground, 9 1/2 In. 125.00
Compote, Beaded, Cobalt Blue & Gold 450.00
Compote, Scenic, Cobalt & Gold Borders, Double Handle, Blue Mark, 7 In. 200.00
Cup & Saucer, Chocolate, Alpine Scene, Beaded Rim, Gold Trim 9.00
Cup & Saucer, Gold Trim, Footed, Green M Wreath 80.00
Ewer, Lavender Poppies, Gold Enamel Outlining, Cobalt Trim 135.00
Fernery, Paisley Design, Turquoise 135.00
Figurine, Musical Couple, 8 In. 100.00
Hair Receiver, Cover, Coral Flowers, White & Black 25.00
Hatpin Holder, Roses, Gold Trim, Ewer Shape, 5 In. 135.00
Hatpin Holder, Roses, Gold, Hanging 610.00
Humidor, Cherries, Cobalt Blue, Gold & Brown Ground 495.00
Humidor, Cover, Portrait, Painted, Cylindrical 2500.00
Humidor, Indian Head 1 Side, Pipe Other, Hexagonal 375.00
Humidor, Playing Cards, Shaded Brown, 3 Handles, 6 In. 125.00
Jug, Whiskey, Moriage, Scenic, 8 In. 550.00
Lemonade Set, Geometric Leaf Design, Branched Fruit, 5 Piece 180.00
Match Holder, Trees With Shoreline, Yellow, Green, Mark No. 47, 3 In. 125.00
Mayonnaise Set, Garland Of Roses On Border, 3 Piece 45.00
Mug, Deer, In Forest, Moriage Trim Handles & Neck, Green M Mark, 4 1/2 In. 175.00
Mug, Grapes, Gold Trim 15.00

Mug, Steer, On Sand Scene, Green Mark, 3 3/4 In. 195.00
Mustard, Lid, Attached Saucer, Lakeside Sunset Scene, Cherry Blossom Mark 75.00
Mustard, Yellow Luster.. 25.00
Nut Set, Hand Painted Flowers, Gold Trim, 7 Piece... 125.00
Plaque, 3 White Swans, Draped Moriage Border, 10 In. 275.00
Plaque, Bison, Blown Out, Green Mark, 10 1/2 In. 595.00
Plaque, Indian, Bird & Bow, Blown 600.00
Plaque, Man, On Camel, Cobalt Blue, 10 In. 375.00
Plaque, Meadow, Pond & Trees, 10 In. 75.00
Plaque, Wall, Scene, Trees, Meadow, Path, Green Wreath Mark, 10 In. 165.00
Plaque, Windmill Scene, Earth Colors, 8 3/4 In. 190.00
Plate, Doll's Face, 6 In. 35.00
Plate, Game, 2 Deer On Hill, Sunset, Blue Trim, Beaded Overlay, 8 1/2 In. 150.00
Plate, Hanging, Landscape Scene, Satin Finish, Green Mark, 10 1/4 In. 195.00
Plate, Lake, Trees, Mountains, Bird & Flower Border, Blue Maple Leaf Mark, 10 In. .. 95.00
Plate, Painted Farm Scene, Wicker Handle, 8 In. 22.00
Plate, Windmill, 6 1/2 In. 10.00
Relish, White, Handles, Square.. 15.00
Spooner, Azalea, 7 In. 75.00
Tea Set, Child's, Silhouettes, White, Pink Trim, 16 Piece... 210.00
Tea Set, Doll's, Birds & Flowers.. 48.00
Tea Set, Doll's, Yellow Birds, Bouquets Of Roses, Rising Sun Mark, 9 Piece 135.00
Tea Set, Scenic, Swans, Gold Beaded Trim, 19 Piece 115.00
Tea Set, White Crane, 18 Piece 275.00
Tobacco Jar, Playing Cards, Chips & Pipe, Hand Painted, 4 In. 132.00
Tray, Round, Multicolored Scene... 20.00
Vase, 3 Peasants, Lake On Reverse, Interior Scene, 13 1/2 In. .... 1100.00 to 1210.00
Vase, Boat Scene.. 225.00
Vase, Cameo, Scene, Handle, Cobalt Blue... 575.00
Vase, Dogwood Blossoms, 8 In. 60.00
Vase, Fisherman & Cart, Tall.. 1295.00
Vase, Floral Center, Gilded Designs & Handles, Blue Maple Leaf Mark, 10 x 8 In. 300.00
Vase, Floral Enamel Design, Gold Handles, Green Mark, 5 In. 225.00
Vase, Floral, Handles, 11 In., Pair 475.00
Vase, Gold Beading, Handles, Blue, Tan, Brown, 8 In. 150.00
Vase, Iris, Hand Painted, 14 In. 297.00
Vase, Lake Scene, Flowers, Jeweled, Green M Wreath, 4 3/4 In. 58.00
Vase, Landscape Scene, 2 Handles, 14 In. 295.00
Vase, Lavender, Pink & Gold, Blue Mark, Small 10.00
Vase, Man, On Camel, Handles, 10 1/2 In. 395.00
Vase, Poppies, Leaves Extend From Top Handle, 12 In. 695.00
Vase, Raised Branches & Flowers, 7 1/2 In. 95.00
Vase, Roses, Tan & Green, 9 In. 75.00
Vase, Roses, Tan, Green Mark, 8 In. 125.00
Vase, Scene, Hand Painted, Jeweled Neck, 9 1/2 In. 195.00
Vase, Scenic Panels, All Different, Gold Trim, Signed, 12 In. 325.00
Vase, Scenic Panels, Gold Tracery, 1900, 8 In. 490.00
Vase, Sunflowers, 14 In. 400.00
Vase, Violets, 2 Angled Handles, Pair 265.00
Vase, Yellow Rose, Leaves, Light Green Ground, Brown Handles, Beaded, 7 In. 80.00

NODDERS, also called nodding figures or pagods, are porcelain figures with
heads and hands that are attached to wires. Any slight movement causes the
parts to move up and down. They were made in many countries during the
eighteenth, nineteenth, and twentieth centuries. A few Art Deco designs are
also known. Copies are being made. A more recent type of nodder is made of
papier-mache or plastic. These often represent sports figures or comic characters.

Bank, Black Boy, Mission Donation, Drop Coin, Head Nods, Plaster, 10 1/4 In. 165.00
Bank, Black Man, Hand Carved, 3 x 4 7/8 In... 350.00
Baseball, Washington Senators, Miniature 155.00
Beetle Bailey 45.00
Ben Casey, Box 85.00

Nodder, Brewmaster, Figural,
Plaster, Sicks' Ranier, 15 1/2 In.

◆◆◆◆◆◆◆◆◆◆◆◆◆◆◆◆◆◆◆◆◆◆◆◆◆

A photoelectric cell can be put into an existing exterior light to turn the light on at dusk, off at dawn. Another kind of adapter will turn a light on when there is motion in your yard.

◆◆◆◆◆◆◆◆◆◆◆◆◆◆◆◆◆◆◆◆◆◆◆◆

Big Tex, Composition, 1960s	175.00
Black Boy, Sitting On 2 Bananas, Florida	65.00
Bowler, Ceramic, Best Power Award	65.00
Brewmaster, Figural, Plaster, Sicks' Ranier, 15 1/2 In. ....*Illus*	138.00
Cart, With Alphonse, Cast Iron, Kenton, 1910	1075.00
Cat, Halloween, Germany	175.00
Charlie Brown, Composition, Painted Clothes, Lego, Japan, 1960s, 5 1/2 In.	60.00
Charlie Weaver	175.00
Chicago Cub, Plaster, 8 In.	25.50
Cincinnati Red Player, Baseball Shape	195.00
Clown, Polychrome Design, France, 5 1/2 In.	115.00
Colonel Sanders, Plastic, 1960 ....65.00 to 100.00	
Cow, Hide Covered	400.00
Cowboy, Pumpkin Head, Papier-Mache, 8 1/2 In.	299.00
Dallas Cowboy	150.00
Danny Kaye, Celluloid, Lead Weight Mechanism, 1930s, 7 In.	650.00
Dog, Spring Driven, Celluloid, 1910s, 3 1/2 x 5 1/2 In.	92.00
Donald Duck, Tag	850.00
Donkey, Celluloid, Red & Black, 6 1/2 x 5 1/2 In.	22.00
Dr. Kildare, 6 1/2 In.	40.00
Famous Cartoon Characters From The Funnies, Bisque, Box, 12 Piece	2500.00
Golfer, Comic	55.00
Golfer, Golf Ball Head, 1900, 6 In.	195.00
Goose, Celluloid, Germany	20.00
Green Bay Packer, Gold Base	75.00
Kangaroo	60.00
Kissing Couple, Plastic	35.00
Mammy	295.00
Max, Bisque, Germany, 1930s	500.00
Mickey Mouse	95.00
New York Yankees, 1960s	275.00
NFL Cheerleader	30.00
Old Timer, Bisque, Germany, 1930s	250.00
Oriental Kissing Couple, Japan, 5 In., Pair	30.00
Oriental Man, Seated, Bisque, 6 3/4 In.	195.00
Oriental Woman, Holds Fan Behind Head, Bisque, Pastels, Gold Trim, Nodder	500.00
Rattlesnake, Vandor	18.00
Salt & Pepper, Abe Lincoln & Black Children, Regal	325.00
Santa Claus, Candy Container, Pressed Cardboard, West Germany	65.00
Smitty, Bisque, Germany, 4 1/2 In.	72.00
Snake Charmer ....350.00 to 500.00	
Snoopy, Aviator, Composition, Painted, Spring-Mounted Head, 5 1/2 In. ....30.00 to 60.00	
Snoopy, Composition	50.00
Snoopy, Joe Cool, Spring-Mounted Head, Painted, Composition, 3 3/4 In.	12.00
Space Man, 5 In. ....35.00 to 75.00	

Tiger, Esso Gasoline, 12 In. 125.00
Topo Gigio, Ceramic 100.00
Uncle Walt, Bisque, Germany, 4 1/2 In. 100.00
Veggie Man, Pumpkin Head, 4 1/2 In. 385.00

NORITAKE porcelain was made in Japan after 1904 by Nippon Toki Kaisha. The best-known Noritake pieces are marked with the M in a wreath for the Morimura Brothers, a New York City distributing company. This mark was used until 1941. Another famous Noritake china was made for the Larkin Soap Company from 1916 through the 1930s. This dinnerware, decorated with azaleas, was sold or given away as a premium. There may be some helpful price information in the Nippon category, since prices are comparable.

Bouillon, Plate, Celon 12.00
Bowl, Dessert, Azalea, 5 1/2 In. 11.00
Bowl, Figural Squirrel On Edge 70.00
Bowl, Footed, 7 In. 100.00
Bowl, Soup, Granada 12.50
Bowl, Vegetable, Cover, Azalea 45.00
Bowl, Vegetable, Cover, Corinth 40.00
Butter, Cover, Savona 35.00
Candy Dish, Cover, Stylized Floral 85.00
Candy Jar, Azalea 750.00
Casserole, Azalea, Gold Finial 435.00
Celery Dish, Goat Head Handles 35.00
Celery Set, Painted Vegetable, 12-In. Dish, 7 Piece 165.00
Chamberstick, Orange & Black Luster 75.00
Cheese Dish, Blue & Brown Flowers, 8 In. 33.00
Coffeepot, Azalea, After Dinner 395.00
Coffeepot, Sutherland 65.00
Condiment Set, Azalea, 5 Piece 45.00
Creamer, Savona 20.00
Cruet, Azalea 190.00
Cup, Granada 10.00
Cup & Saucer, Athlone, Demitasse 10.00
Cup & Saucer, Azalea 12.00
Cup & Saucer, Maywood 15.00
Cup & Saucer, Tree In Meadow 12.00
Dish, 2 Part, Bird In Center, 7 x 8 In. 80.00
Dish, Mayonnaise, Azalea, 3-Footed 25.00
Dish, Pink Daisies, Gold Rim, 3 Open Handles, 7 In. 22.00
Doll, Dresser, Blue Floral Skirt, 4 1/2 In. 350.00
Eggcup, Azalea 40.00
Figurine, Oriental Woman, 9 In. 75.00
Gravy Boat, Avalon 35.00
Gravy Boat, Azalea 40.00
Humidor, Figural, Owl 38.00
Mustard Jar, Roseara 18.00
Napkin Ring, Man & Woman, Pair 75.00
Nut Set, Bowl & 6 Serving Cups, Painted Walnuts, 7 Piece .... 160.00 to 165.00
Plate, Arab At Campfire, Cobalt Blue, 8 1/2 In. 125.00
Plate, Azalea, 8 1/2 In. 20.00
Plate, Dinner, Avalon 15.00
Plate, Dinner, Azalea 18.00
Plate, Dinner, Granada 15.00
Plate, Dinner, Maywood 15.00
Plate, Luncheon, Azalea 14.00
Plate, Salad, Maywood 8.00
Plate, Tree In Meadow, Red M Wreath, 8 5/8 In. 7.00
Platter, Avalon, Large 45.00
Platter, Azalea, 14 In. 90.00
Platter, Granada, Small 20.00
Powder Box, Painted Floral 200.00

Salt, Swan, Master	70.00
Salt & Pepper, Azalea	20.00
Sugar, Cover, Azalea, No. 7	18.00
Sugar, Cover, Savona	35.00
Sugar & Creamer, Japanese Lanterns & Flowers, Orange Pearlized	30.00
Sugar Shaker, Azalea	90.00
Tea Set, Child's, White, Gold, Silverware, Box, 15 Piece	85.00
Tea Set, Figural, Birds, Luster	175.00
Tea Set, Rainbow Luster, Cobalt Blue Butterfly, Pink Roses, 21 Piece	650.00
Toothpick, Azalea	125.00
Vase, Dragon, Moriage, 4 3/4 In.	39.00
Wall Pocket, Poppies	95.00

NORSE Pottery Company started in Edgerton, Wisconsin, in 1903. In 1904 the company moved to Rockford, Illinois. The company made a black pottery, which resembled early bronze relics of the Scandinavian countries. The firm went out of business in 1913.

Pitcher, Abstract Green Designs, Black Ground, Stopper, Stamped, 7 In.	385.00
Vase, Dragon, Black Matte Glaze, Footed, Flared, Impressed, 12 x 6 1/2 In.	935.00
Vase, Green Owls, Black Matte Ground, Bulbous, Squatty, 4 x 5 1/2 In.	467.00

NORTH DAKOTA SCHOOL OF MINES was established in 1892 at the University of North Dakota. A ceramic course was included and pieces were made from the clays found in the region. Students at the university made pieces from 1909 to 1949. Although very early pieces were marked *U.N.D.*, most pieces were stamped with the full name of the university.

Bowl, Geometric Indian, Red-Orange Ground, 1931, 5 x 7 In.	357.00
Bowl, Mixing, Glossy Cream & Brown, 6 3/4 In.	85.00
Bowl, Multicolored Abstract Spokes, Rose Ground, 9 In.	165.00
Bowl, Yellow Flowers, Pink Ground, F. Huckfield, 1933, 5 In.	358.00
Figurine, Fish, Carved, 13 In.	125.00
Tile, Green Grasshopper, Grass, White Ground, 4 1/2 In.	456.00
Tile, Medallion, Round, Emma Lou Mariman, 4 1/4 In.	100.00
Tile, Ship, Blue Sky, Hazel Rohde, 1933, 4 1/2 x 4 In.	525.00
Tray, Leaf Shape, Shaded Green, 14 In., Pair	675.00
Trivet, Blue Flowers, White, Caramel, F. Huckfield, 5 In.	250.00
Vase, Blossoms, Stems & Leaves, Prairie Rose, 3 In.	285.00
Vase, Carved & Painted Birds, Signed Mary E., 8 1/4 In.	4400.00
Vase, Carved & Painted Flowers, Signed Huck, 6 1/2 In.	1400.00
Vase, Carved & Painted Roses, Signed Huck, 4 In.	605.00
Vase, Carved Daffodils & Leaves, Yellow To White, J.T., 5 1/2 In.	467.00
Vase, Carved Zigzag & Dot Design, Signed, 2 x 4 In.	4680.00
Vase, Cowboys, Brown, F.J. Anderson, 1947, 3 1/2 x 5 1/4 In.	660.00
Vase, Crosses, Stars, Moons, Tulips, J. Mattson, 9 1/2 x 5 In.	385.00
Vase, Geometric, Dark Blue, Bulbous, M.T., 3 3/4 x 5 1/2 In.	330.00
Vase, Poppy Blossoms, Twisted Stems, Signed, 10 In.	2420.00
Vase, Prairie Rose, 2-Tone Green, Signed Huck	390.00
Vase, Prairie Rose, Flowers, Ribbed, Brown, 2 3/4 x 5 In.	275.00
Vase, Stylized Plants, Olive Green Ground, 5 1/4 In.	440.00

NORTHWOOD Glass Company was founded by Harry Northwood, a glassmaker who worked for Hobbs, Brockunier and Company, La Belle Glass Company, and Buckeye Glass Company before founding his own firm. He opened one factory in Indiana, Pennsylvania, in 1896, and another in Wheeling, West Virginia, in 1902. Northwood closed when Mr. Northwood died in 1923. Many types of glass were made, including carnival, custard, goofus, and pressed. The underlined N mark was used on some pieces.

Banana Boat, Opalescent, Light Green, 8 1/2 x 3 In.	250.00
Berry Bowl, Opalescent Blue, Master	45.00
Berry Bowl, Regent, Master	35.00
Berry Bowl, Strawberry & Cable, Ruby & Gold	30.00
Berry Set, Paneled Holly, Green, Gold, 13 Piece	325.00
Bowl, Blue Opalescent, Footed, 9 In.	65.00

Bowl, Drapery, White Opalescent, 9 In. 60.00
Bowl, Grape & Cable, Blue, Carnival Glass 459.00
Bowl, Lattice Medallion, Blue Opalescent, Ruffled.. 35.00
Bowl, Leaf Umbrella, Turquoise, 8 In. 225.00
Butter, Cherry Thumbprint, Ruby & Gold... 125.00
Butter, Cover, Blue Opalescent Drapery.. 185.00
Butter, Cover, Sunburst On Shield, Blue... 295.00
Butter, Cover, Wild Bouquet, Custard 550.00
Butter, Creamer & Spooner, Bloom & Blossom, 3 Piece.............................. 275.00
Butter, Pod & Posies, Green, Gold Trim 175.00
Butter, Rose, Green, Gold Trim 125.00
Compote, Grape & Cable, Vaseline, 6 x 8 In.. 95.00
Creamer, Beaded Circle, Custard, Floral, Gilt 180.00
Creamer, Cherry Thumbprint, Ruby & Gold 45.00
Creamer, Fan, Green, Gold Trim 35.00
Creamer, Memphis, Green, Gold Trim 65.00
Creamer, Wild Bouquet, Custard 300.00
Cruet, Green.. 195.00
Cruet, Swirl Daisy & Fern, Blue 75.00
Daisy & Plume, Bowl, White Opalescent, Candy Ribbon Rim, Goofus Design............. 58.00
Goblet, Water, Gothic Arches, Custard, 3 Piece.. 75.00
Jam Jar, Opalescent Intaglio Blue 35.00
Pitcher, Coin Spot, Cranberry Opalescent, Star Crimp 150.00
Pitcher, Leaf Umbrella, Blue, Cased Satin 425.00
Pitcher, Leaf Umbrella, Rose Agate 475.00
Pitcher, Oriental Poppy 95.00
Rose Bowl, Pull-Up, Satin Glass, White Ground, Thorny Feet, 3 1/4 In............ 295.00
Spooner, Grape & Gothic Arch, Green, Gold 35.00
Spooner, Holly & Berry, Ruby & Gold 75.00
Spooner, Wild Bouquet, Custard 300.00
Sugar, Cover, Blue Opalescent Intaglio 75.00
Sugar, Cover, Wild Bouquet, Custard 500.00
Sugar & Creamer, Wild Bouquet 350.00
Tumbler, Cherry & Lattice, Ruby & Gold 35.00
Tumbler, Chrysanthemum Sprig, Blue... 150.00
Tumbler, Inverted Feather, Green, Gold Trim 35.00
Tumbler, Inverted Feather, White, Gold Trim 60.00
Tumbler, Strawberry, Ruby & Gold, 6 Piece 300.00
Vase, Funeral, Fluted, 19 x 5 In. 150.00
Vase, Palisades, White Opalescent, 5 In... 45.00
Water Set, Circled Scroll, Blue, 6 Piece 725.00
Water Set, Grape & Cable, Ruby & Gold, 5 Piece 200.00
Water Set, Grape & Gothic Arch, Green, Gold, 6 Piece................................. 200.00
Water Set, Grape, Custard, 7 Piece 750.00

NU-ART, see Imperial Glass

NUTCRACKERS of many types have been used through the centuries. At first
the nutcracker was probably strong teeth or a hammer. But by the nineteenth
century, many elaborate and ingenious types were made. Levers, screws, and
hammer adaptations were the most popular. Because nutcrackers are still useful, they are still being made, some in the old styles.

Dog, Aluminum.. 39.00
Dog, Brass, 19th Century, 8 In.. 75.00
Dog, Cast Iron... 200.00
Monk's Face, Hand Carved, Germany 18.00
Nude Woman, Wooden.. 20.00
Rooster, Brass.. 28.00 to 30.00
Squirrel, Cast Iron... 35.00
Squirrel, Mahogany, 7 5/8 In. 115.00
Superman, Standing, Wooden 25.00
Wolf's Head, Chrome On Wooden Base, June, 1920 .... 75.00

NYMPHENBURG, see Royal Nymphenburg

OCCUPIED JAPAN was printed on pottery, porcelain, toys, and other goods made during the American occupation of Japan after World War II, from 1945 to 1952. Collectors now search for these pieces. The items were made for export.

Ashtray, Indian Head, Pair	17.00
Ashtray, Willow Pattern, Multicolored, Lavish Gold, 4 x 3 In.	4.00
Bowl, Chrysanthemums, Turquoise Centers, Gold Oriental Mark, 3 1/4 In.	4.00
Bowl, Salad, Wooden, Black Lacquered, Hand Turned, 11 1/2 x 4 In.	18.00
Cup & Saucer, Blue & White	7.00
Dancer, Oriental Man, Holding 2 Paddles, 7 1/4 In.	25.00
Figurine, Ballerina, Toe Dancing, Blue Fabric Tutu, 4 1/4 In.	12.00
Figurine, Black Boy & Girl, Blue & White Striped Clothes, 4 1/4 In., Pair	40.00
Figurine, Boy & Girl At Fence, Bisque, Andrea Mark, 9 1/4 In., Pair	95.00
Figurine, Boy Violinist, Sitting On Wall, Green Hat, Brown Shorts, 4 In.	10.00
Figurine, Canadian Mountie, 4 1/2 In.	15.00
Figurine, Colonial Man & Woman, 7 1/2 In., Pair	50.00
Figurine, Gentleman Dancing, Green Coat, Striped Pants, 4 3/4 In.	12.00
Figurine, Girl, With Basket, Turquoise Bandanna, 4 In.	10.00
Figurine, Girl, With Umbrella, Dog, 8 In.	65.00
Figurine, Goose, Black Neck & Head, Green Tail & Back, Yellow Breast, 3 3/4 In.	6.00
Figurine, Hula Dancer, 4 1/4 In.	15.00
Figurine, Man Pushing Lady In Sleigh, Dog, Mirrored Pair	125.00
Figurine, Man, Playing Piano, 2 Piece	18.00
Figurine, Oriental Man & Woman, Blue Jackets, Yellow Pants, 7 In., Pair	15.00
Figurine, Oriental Woman, On Stair Step Base, 10 In.	25.00
Figurine, Siamese Dancers, 7 1/2 In., Pair	75.00
Figurine, Uncle Sam, 4 3/8 In.	20.00
Lamp, 2 Dancers, Brass Base	135.00
Lamp, Bedroom, Colonial Couple, Pair	145.00
Mug, Barrel, Figural Handle, Man, Ranger Hat, Holster & Gun, Horseshoe	20.00
Mug, Hunting & Archery Scene, Figural Handle, Cobalt & Tan, 5 1/4 In.	25.00
Planter, Boat With Driver, Porcelain	25.00
Planter, Woman Bowler	10.00
Planter, Zebra, 5 In.	20.00
Plaque, Colonial Couple, Pastels, 6 7/8 x 4 1/2 In., Pair	80.00
Plate, Sailing Ship, Blue & White, 8 In.	20.00
Shelf Sitter, Black Boy & Girl, Porcelain	35.00
Sugar, Cover, Cottage	7.00
Sugar & Creamer, Turquoise, 2 1/4 In.	15.00
Tea Set, Pink Flowers On White, Covered Teapot	45.00
Toby Jug, Devil	35.00
Toby Jug, General MacArthur	50.00
Tray, Souvenir, Niagara Falls, 3 1/2 In.	4.00
Wall Pocket, Woman, Bisque	35.00

OHR pottery was made in Biloxi, Mississippi, from 1883 to 1918 by George E. Ohr, a true eccentric. The pottery was made of very thin clay that was twisted, folded, and dented into odd, graceful shapes. Some pieces were life-like models of hats, animal heads, or even a potato. Others were decorated with folded clay *snakes*. Reproductions and reworked pieces are appearing on the market. These have been reglazed, or snakes and other embellishments have been added.

Bowl, Brown & Chartreuse Crystalline Glaze, Body Twist, Low, 1 1/2 x 5 In.	385.00
Bowl, Closed, Flat Rim, Folded & Twisted, Bisque, Signed, 3 x 6 In.	880.00
Bowl, Crushed & Tortured, Speckled Green & Brown, Impressed Mark, 2 x 5 In.	990.00
Bowl, Folded Rim, Speckled Black Glaze, Raspberry Interior, Signed, 4 1/2 In.	2100.00
Bowl, Torn Rim, Pinched, Gunmetal Exterior, Mahogany Interior, Signed, 4 1/2 In.	900.00
Candlestick, Multiple Knop, Green & Silver Luster Glaze, Marked	850.00
Jardiniere, Grotesquely Folded, Reddish Glaze, Pig Latin Saying On Base, Large	1995.00
Match Holder, Incised Flowers, Bisque, Poem, A Biloxi Welcome, 1895, 5 3/4 x 3 In.	330.00
Mug, 1 Curved & 1 Angular Handle, Brown Glaze, Green Interior, Signed, 6 In.	1495.00

Mug, Joe Jefferson, In-Body Twist & Dimples, Pink Glaze, Blue Interior, 3 3/4 In.	1600.00
Mug, Puzzle, Gunmetal & Olive Green, Rope Handle, Holes, Script, 3 1/2 x 5 In.	440.00
Mug, Puzzle, Misshapen, Mottled Gunmetal & Green Glaze, Signed, 4 x 4 3/4 In.	600.00
Mug, Puzzle, Rabbit Head Handle, Brown & Black High Gloss, Signed, 6 In.	715.00
Pitcher, Cutout Handle, Sponged Onto Spinach Green Base, 4 x 4 In.	1210.00
Pitcher, Mottled & Spattered Brown Glaze, Strap Handle, Marked, 6 1/2 In.	600.00
Pitcher, Red Glaze, Green Spatter, Strap Handle, Footed, 7 In.	2900.00
Pitcher, Ruffled Rim, Orange Interior, Gunmetal Glaze, Signed, 3 x 5 In.	1000.00
Vase, Cranberry Glaze, Mottled Brown Interior, Thumbprint, 6 In.	1600.00
Vase, Cupped Rim, Mottled Green, Red & Gunmetal Flambe, Signed, 7 3/4 In.	130.00
Vase, Dimpled Body, Ruffled Rim, Iron Oxide Wash, Signed, 5 1/2 In.	1200.00
Vase, Double Gourd, Gunmetal Gray, Dark Brown Glaze, Script Mark, 5 x 4 In.	425.00
Vase, Green & Burgundy Flambe Glaze, Signed, 5 1/2 In.	495.00
Vase, Green, Pinch Rim, 6 1/2 In.	775.00
Vase, Gunmetal & Brown Glaze, Spherical, Footed, Script Mark, 3 3/4 x 4 In.	350.00
Vase, In-Body Twist, Pinched & Folded Rim, Bisque, Signed, 4 1/2 x 4 3/4 In.	1100.00
Vase, In-Body Twist, Rolled Rim, Dark Pink Finish, Signed, 4 In.	3500.00
Vase, Metallic Black & Brown Pebbled Finish, Signed, 5 1/2 In.	1000.00
Vase, Metallic Mottled Gunmetal Black, Green Glaze, Corseted Neck, 7 x 3 In.	885.00
Vase, Pinched Body, Undulating Rim, Silvery Textured Glaze, Signed, 3 3/4 In.	450.00
Vase, Stovepipe Neck, Lustered Green & Black Gunmetal Glaze, Signed, 8 1/4 In.	2100.00
Vase, Terra-Cotta Bisque, Overlapping Pinched Sides, 6 3/4 x 3 1/2 In.	385.00
Vase, Twist & Cupped Neck, Peacock Feather Blue Glaze, Signed, 5 In.	1450.00
Vessel, Allover Mottled Glossy Finish, Bottle Shape, Signed, 9 1/4 In.	1700.00
Vessel, Bulbous Middle, Crimped Rim, Cobalt Blue High Glaze, Signed, 7 In.	1600.00

OLD IVORY china was made by Hermann Ohme in Silesia, Germany, at the end of the nineteenth century. The ivory-colored dishes have flowers, fruit, or acorns as decoration and are often marked with a crown and the word *Silesia.* Some pieces are also marked with the words *Old Ivory.* The pattern numbers appear on the base of each piece.

Berry Bowl, No. 82, 5 1/2 In.	25.00
Berry Set, No. 16, 5 Piece	225.00
Bowl, Waste, No. 75, Signed..	110.00
Cake Plate, No. 15, Open Handle, 10 In.	110.00
Chocolate Pot, No. 16	350.00
Cracker Jar, No. 15, Barrel Shape...	25.00
Creamer, No. 16	80.00
Cup & Saucer, Chocolate, No. 7	50.00
Plate, Holly, 6 In.	65.00
Plate, No. 15, 7 1/2 In..	20.00
Plate, No. 16, 6 1/4 In..	25.00
Plate, Orange Flowers & Buds, Green, Silesia, 7 1/2 In., Pair...................................	75.00
Platter, No. 16, Handles, 11 1/2 In...120.00 to 140.00
Salt & Pepper, No. 16	115.00
Saucer, No. 16, Beige & Pink Roses, 5 1/2 In..	38.00
Sugar & Creamer, Cover, No 84 ....170.00 to 225.00
Sugar & Creamer, Flowers, Gold Design, Pedestal	60.00
Teapot, No. 84	350.00

OLD PARIS, see Paris

OLD SLEEPY EYE, see Sleepy Eye

ONION PATTERN, originally named *bulb pattern,* is a white ware decorated with cobalt blue or pink. Although it is commonly associated with Meissen, other companies made the pattern in the late nineteenth and the twentieth centuries. A rare type is called *red bud* because there are added red accents on the blue-and-white dishes.

Clock, Kitchen, Wall, Key, Meissen	125.00
Coffeepot, Meissen, c.1900	655.00
Cup & Saucer, Scalloped Rim, Dresden...	25.00
Dish, Leaf Shape, Meissen, 9 In...	125.00

Eggcup, Meissen	85.00
Funnel, Loop Handle, Germany	125.00
Matchbox & Striker, Wall Mount	125.00
Meat Tenderizer, Hanging	95.00
Plate, Floral, Reticulated, Meissen, 8 In.	95.00
Platter, Blue & White, Meissen, 13 1/4 x 18 In.	235.00
Salt, Double, Meissen	125.00
Soup, Dish, Flow Blue, Meissen	125.00
Tureen, Cover, Meissen, 12 1/4 In.	405.00
Tureen, Handle, Liner, Round, 9 In.	30.00

OPALESCENT GLASS is translucent glass that has the tones of the opal gemstone. It originated in England in the 1870s and is often found in pressed glassware made in Victorian times. Opalescent glass was first made in America in 1897 at the Northwood glassworks in Indiana, Pennsylvania. Some dealers use the terms *opaline* and *opalescent* for any of these translucent wares. More opalescent pieces may be listed in Hobnail, Northwood, Pressed Glass, Spanish Lace, and other glass categories.

Basket, Raindrop, Flares At Sides, Piecrust Edge, Bamboo Handle	275.00
Berry Set, Tokyo, Green, 7 Piece	110.00
Bowl, Barbells, Aqua, 8 In.	30.00
Bowl, S-Repeat, Blue, Master	75.00
Butter, Cover, Colorado, Green, Gold Trim	90.00
Butter, Cover, Flora, Blue, Gold Trim	250.00
Butter, Cover, Iris With Meander, White	150.00
Butter, Cover, Jewel & Flower, Blue	275.00
Butter, Cover, Palm Beach	250.00
Butter, Cover, Sunburst On Shield, Blue	250.00 to 295.00
Butter, Cover, Swag With Brackets, Blue	190.00 to 210.00
Butter, Cover, Wreath & Shell, Blue	200.00
Butter, Cover, Wreath & Shell, Vaseline	100.00
Butter, Swag With Bracket, Vaseline	125.00
Celery, Beatty Rib, Blue	55.00 to 65.00
Celery, Bubble Lattice, Blue	150.00
Celery, Chrysanthemum Base Swirl, Cranberry	200.00
Celery, Sunburst On Shield, Blue	115.00
Celery, Swirl, Blue, 5 1/2 In.	85.00
Compote, Hobnail, Cranberry, 5 1/2 x 9 In.	250.00
Compote, Jelly, Coin Spot, Green	30.00
Compote, Jelly, Everglades, Yellow	135.00
Compote, Jelly, Maple Leaf, Blue	40.00
Compote, Jelly, Tokyo, Blue	35.00
Compote, Popsicle Sticks, Green, 8 In.	40.00
Compote, Swag With Brackets, Jelly, Green	32.00
Creamer, Argonaut Shell, Blue	75.00
Creamer, Colorado, Green	35.00
Creamer, Diamond Spearhead, Blue	180.00
Creamer, Flora, White	40.00
Creamer, Ivy Scroll, Blue, Gold Trim	95.00
Creamer, Scroll With Acanthus, Blue	50.00
Cruet, Daisy & Fern, Blue	165.00
Cruet, Intaglio, White	100.00
Cruet, Iris With Meander, White	225.00
Cruet, Seaweed, Blue	225.00
Cruet, Seaweed, Cranberry	850.00
Cruet, Swag With Brackets, Vaseline	350.00
Dish, Jelly, Everglades, Blue	75.00
Dish, Many Loops, Trefoil, Green	30.00
Epergne, 3-Lily, Vaseline, 18 In.	700.00
Gravy Boat, Fan, Peach	110.00
Lamp, Oil, Hearts & Flowers, Miniature	195.00
Match Holder, Beatty Rib, White	20.00
Pitcher, Alaska, Blue	335.00 to 495.00

Pitcher, Argonaut Shell, Blue 575.00
Pitcher, Buttons & Braids, Green 150.00
Pitcher, Daisy & Crisscross, White, 1885 .... 525.00
Pitcher, Daisy & Fern, Cranberry 300.00
Pitcher, Everglades, White 95.00
Pitcher, Herringbone, White 395.00
Pitcher, Jewel & Flower, Blue, Gold Trim 345.00
Pitcher, Jewel & Flower, White 345.00
Pitcher, Lattice Medallions, White 280.00
Pitcher, Milk, Wide Stripe, Cranberry 500.00
Pitcher, Palm Beach, Blue 395.00
Pitcher, Pump & Trough, Blue 110.00
Pitcher, Swirl, Crimped Top, Blue 155.00
Pitcher, Swirl, Square Top, Blue 200.00
Pitcher, Tokyo, Green 200.00
Pitcher, Windows, Cranberry 600.00
Sauce, Plumes, Acorn Base, Flint 125.00
Saucer, Beatty Rib, Blue 28.00
Spooner, Argonaut Shell, Blue 75.00
Spooner, Daisy & Fern, White 48.00
Spooner, Drapery, Blue 95.00
Spooner, Flora, Green 30.00
Spooner, Inverted Fan & Feather, White ....85.00 to 95.00
Spooner, Swag With Brackets, Blue 120.00
Spooner, Swag With Brackets, Green 65.00
Spooner, Wild Bouquet, Blue 140.00
Spooner, Wreath & Wheel, Vaseline, 4 1/2 In. ....70.00 to 95.00
Sugar, Cover, Alaska, Blue 130.00
Sugar, Cover, Daisy & Button, Blue 45.00
Sugar, Cover, Diamond Spearhead, Vaseline ....75.00 to 185.00
Sugar, Cover, Wild Bouquet, White 125.00
Sugar & Creamer, Wreath & Shell, Blue 195.00
Sugar Shaker, Leaf Umbrella, Blue 300.00
Sugar Shaker, Polka Dot 95.00
Sugar Shaker, Ribbed Lattice, Blue 235.00
Swan, Blue, England, 1880s, 4 3/4 x 3 x 6 In. 125.00
Syrup, Coin Spot, Blue 200.00
Syrup, Honeycomb, White, Metal Top 225.00
Syrup, Reverse Swirl, Blue 195.00
Table Set, Drapery, Blue, 4 Piece 425.00
Table Set, Intaglio, Green, Gold Trim, 4 Piece 495.00
Table Set, Tokyo, Blue, 4 Piece 600.00
Toothpicks are listed in the Toothpick category
Tumbler, Chrysanthemum Base Swirl, Blue 140.00
Tumbler, Fluted Scrolls, Vaseline 65.00
Tumbler, Jackson, Blue 50.00
Tumbler, Jewel & Flower, Blue 85.00
Tumbler, Jewel & Heart, Blue 85.00
Tumbler, Regal, Blue 50.00
Tumbler, Reverse Swirl, Cranberry 100.00
Tumbler, Seaweed, Blue 125.00
Tumbler, Swag With Brackets, Green 75.00
Tumbler, Swirl, Cranberry 95.00
Tumbler, Swirling Maize, Green 65.00
Tumbler, Water Lily & Cattails, Marigold, 6 Piece 250.00
Tumbler, Wild Bouquet 48.00
Tumbler, Windows, Cranberry 150.00
Tumbler, Windows, White 43.00
Vase, Polka Dot, Cranberry, 6 In. 48.00
Water Set, Beatty Rib, White, 6 Piece 175.00
Water Set, Daisy & Fern, Cranberry, 5 Piece 495.00
Water Set, Jewel & Flower, Blue, 7 Piece 765.00
Water Set, Tokyo, Blue, 7 Piece 750.00

OPALINE, or opal glass, was made in white, green, and other colors. The glass had a matte surface and a lack of transparency. It was often gilded or painted. It was a popular mid-nineteenth-century European glassware.

Box, Dresser, Hand Painted Winter Scene, 4 1/4 x 4 In.	105.00
Vase, Trumpet, Blue, Birds, Allover Foliate & Leaf, 50 1/4 x 14 3/4 In., Pair	288.00

OPERA GLASSES are needed because the stage is a long way from some of the seats at a play or an opera. Mother-of-pearl was a popular decoration.

Enameled, Floral Medallions, Gold & Silver Design, French	200.00
Faux Tortoiseshell	66.00
Gilt Brass & Mother-Of-Pearl, France, 2 1/2 In.	110.00
Mother-Of-Pearl, Leather Case, Colmont, Paris	135.00
Mother-Of-Pearl, Leather Case, France	98.00
Napoleonic, Blue Enamel, Hand Painted Vignettes	175.00
Scroll Pattern, White Metal, Mother-Of-Pearl Eye Pieces, Tiffany & Co.	748.00
Smoky Mother-Of-Pearl & Brass, Audeaiare, Paris	42.00
Sportiere, Brass & Nickel Plate, Paris	15.00
Victorian, Hinged, Gold Plated Holder, Floral Design, Case, 1800s	150.00

ORPHAN ANNIE first appeared in the comics in 1924. The redheaded girl and her friends have been on the radio and are still on the comic pages. A Broadway musical show and a movie in the 1980s made Annie popular again and many toys, dishes, and other memorabilia are being made.

Badge, Decoder, Brass, Radio, 1936	45.00
Book, Big Little Book, Little Orphan Annie & Ghost Gang, 1935	80.00
Book, Drawing & Tracing, McLoughlin, 1932	85.00
Clothespin Set, 12 x 6 1/4 In.	82.00
Crayons, Milton Bradley, 1930	45.00
Decoder Badge, Ovaltine, Secret Compartment, 1936	35.00
Doll, Cloth, 1930s	98.00
Doll, Cloth, Sandy In Pocket, 16 In.	20.00
Doll, Composition, Molded Hair, Painted Eyes, Original Dress	125.00
Manual, Secret Society, 1937	65.00
Mug, Ovaltine, Annie On Front, Sandy On Back	55.00 to 65.00
Pin, Secret Society, 1934	25.00
Plate, 4 In.	25.00
Puzzle, Ovaltine, Box, 1933	65.00
Ring, Silver Star Secret Message	200.00
Salt & Pepper, Orphan Annie & Sandy, Chalkware	30.00
Skipping Rope, Windup, Tin, 5 In.	165.00
Toy, Stove, Metal, 5 x 4 In.	65.00
Toy, Tea Set, Tan Luster, 17 Piece	300.00
Wristwatch	200.00

ORREFORS Glassworks, located in the Swedish province of Smaaland, was established in 1898. The company is still making glass for use on the table or as decorations. There is renewed interest in the glass made in the modern styles of the 1940s and 1950s. Most vases and decorative pieces are signed with the etched name.

Orrefors

Bowl, Etched Woman & Child, 5 In.	195.00
Bowl, Garden Of Paradise, Engraved Naked Figures, Simon Gate, c.1928, 11 In.	940.00
Bowl, Internal Geometric Rectangles, Signed, c.1960, 10 1/2 In.	3300.00
Bowl, Thousand Windows, 7 1/8 In.	227.00 to 300.00
Decanter, Art Nouveau Woman, Crystal	295.00
Decanter, Melon Ribbed Stopper, 11 In.	88.00
Figurine, Elephant, Crystal	195.00
Fish Bowl, 4 Fish, With Aquatic Plants Interior, Signed, 6 x 8 3/4 In.	862.00
Goblet, Tulpenglaser Exposition, Nils Landberg, c.1957, 16 3/4 In.	934.00
Lamp, Crystal, Signed, Numbered, 36 x 10 In.	1200.00
Vase, 3 Sides, Deep Green To Clear, Marked, 8 In.	225.00
Vase, Angular Shape, Clear Over Smoke, Somerso, 7 In.	85.00

Vase, Angular, Art Deco, Crystal, 6 x 7 1/2 In. 165.00
Vase, Beaker Shape, Applied Green Base, Engraved Fish, Bubbles, No. HE199, 10 In.   195.00
Vase, Black Disc Footed, 3 Nude Male Divers, Vicke Lindstrand, c.1934, 13 3/4 In. 3680.00
Vase, Clear & Blue Wavy Lines, 7 In. 75.00
Vase, Clear, Internal Gray, Engraved, c.1960, 6 1/2 In. 100.00
Vase, Clown, Sven Palmquist, 7 In. 250.00
Vase, Dykaren Diver, Nude Male Diver, Ocean Ripples Ground, Signed, 9 In. 975.00
Vase, Full Length Male Nude Diver, Signed, 7 1/8 In. 635.00
Vase, Global, Edward Hald... 750.00
Vase, Graal Fish, Internal Design, Edward Hald, No. NR2467G, c.1955, 4 1/2 In. 525.00
Vase, Ocean Scene, Internal Fish & Seaweed, Signed, 4 3/4 In. 545.00
Vase, Olive Green Faces, Signed, c.1969, 7 1/2 In. 1955.00
Vase, Oval Paperweight, Internal Fish & Marine Shapes, Signed, 5 1/4 In. 345.00
Vase, Portrait Of Maiden, Headdress, Sea Shapes, Signed, c.1949, 6 3/4 In. 3450.00
Vase, Singing Gondolier, Guitar, Maiden On Reverse, Signed, 1950, 8 1/4 In. 2576.00
Vase, Triangular Shape, Clear Over Smoke, Somerso, 7 In. 95.00
Vase, Young Girl With Flowers, Sven Palmquist, 12 In. 425.00

OTT & BREWER Company operated the Etruria Pottery at Trenton, New Jersey, from 1863 to 1893. They started making belleek in 1882. The firm used a variety of marks that incorporated the initials *O & B*.

Bowl, Flowers, Leaves, Gold, Scalloped, 2 1/2 x 4 1/2 In. 195.00
Creamer, Flowers, Gold Handle, 4 1/2 In. 70.00
Cup, Shell, Belleek.. 45.00

OVERBECK pottery was made by four sisters named Overbeck at a pottery in Cambridge City, Indiana. They started in 1911. They made all types of vases, each one-of-a-kind. Small, hand-modeled figurines are the most popular pieces with today's collectors. The factory continued until 1955, when the last of the four sisters died.

Figurine, Squirrel, Brown, 3 In. 165.00
Tile, 2 Horses At Play, Lavender, Black & Aqua, Signed, 6 1/2 In. 1045.00
Vase, Geometric Design, Random Triangles, Signed, 6 In. 1100.00
Vase, Geometric Florals, 3 Panels, Brown Matte, Incised E.F., 6 3/4 In. 2300.00
Vase, Geometric, Gray & Brown Matte Glaze, Cylindrical, 2 3/4 x 2 1/2 In. 100.00
Vase, Stylized Deer Design, Amid Branches, Red Flecks, Signed, 5 x 6 In. 4400.00

OWENS Pottery was made in Zanesville, Ohio, from 1891 to 1928. The first art pottery was made after 1896. Utopian Ware, Cyrano, Navarre, Feroza, and Henri Deux were made. Pieces were usually marked with a form of the name *Owens*. About 1907, the firm began to make tile and discontinued the art pottery wares.

Bowl, Cyrano, White Design, Dark Ground, c.1890... 250.00
Bowl, Venetian, Undulating Surface, Gold Nacreous Glaze, 7 In. 150.00
Candleholder, White Matte Glaze, Circle Mark, 9 x 4 In., Pair. 220.00
Cider Set, Stylized Fruit Tree Design, Matte Green, Impressed Mark, 8 Piece 468.00
Jardiniere, Lotus, Slip Painted, Butterflies Around Rim, 10 1/2 x 7 1/2 In. 200.00
Jardiniere, Raised Child & Shells. 450.00
Lamp Base, Utopian, Black, Orange & Cream Flowers, Green Ground, 13 In. 100.00
Mug, Utopian, Green Berries, Light Brown, 5 1/4 In. 145.00
Pot, Aborigine, Pseudo Indian, c.1903... 495.00
Tile, Egyptian Style, Art Deco, Leather Raspberry Pink Glaze, Green Ground, 6 In. 137.00
Tile, Green Oak Leaves, Acorns, Mustard Ground, Stamped, 5 3/4 In. 165.00
Tile, Scenic, c.1910, 6 1/8 x 6 1/8 In. 750.00
Vase, Aborigine, 8 In. 150.00
Vase, Floral Design, 2 Handles, 4 In. 135.00
Vase, Gold Flower Design, Black Ground, 10 x 5 In. 302.00
Vase, Gunmetal, Green Glaze, Thrown, 5 In. 48.00
Vase, Incised Leaves & Berries, Green Matte Glaze, 2 Handles, No. 235, 5 In. 192.00
Vase, Indianware, Handle, Incised G.B., 5 1/4 x 6 1/2 x 3 1/2 In. 55.00
Vase, Lotus, Italian Blue To Cream, 10 1/2 In. 700.00
Vase, Matte Green, Tapering, Buttressed Top, 9 1/2 x 4 In., Pair.................................. 523.00
Vase, Orange Clover, No. 1047, 4 1/2 In. 121.00

Vase, Painted Santa Barbara Mission, Towers, Fountain, Signed, 12 In.......................... 605.00
Vase, Trumpet Top, Opalescent, 13 In. 595.00
Vase, Utopian, 3 Sides, Orange & Green Leaves, No. 116, 3 1/2 In............................... 66.00
Vase, Utopian, Coralene, 11 1/4 In. 850.00
Vase, Utopian, Orange, Yellow & Green Pansies, 2 Handles, No. 879, 6 In. 132.00
Vase, Utopian, Painted Daisies, Shaded Ground, 4 In. 275.00
Vase, Utopian, Slip Painted Broad Leaves, Matte Brown Ground, 13 x 7 In. 275.00
Vase, Utopian, Yellow Floral, Twisted Body, 4 1/2 In. 95.00
Vase, White & Gray Kitten Portrait, Standard Glaze, 8 In. 3080.00

OYSTER PLATES were popular from the 1880s. Each course at dinner was
served in a special dish. The oyster plate had indentations shaped like oysters.
Usually six oysters were held on a plate. There is no greater value to a plate
with more oysters, although that myth continues to haunt antiques dealers.
There are other plates for shellfish, including cockle plates and whelk plates.
The appropriately shaped indentations are part of the design of these dishes.

Floral Design, Haviland, 8 In. 70.00
Gray Shells, Aqua Ground, Orchies, 9 1/2 In., 9 Piece 235.00
Green & Beige Florals, Gold Trim, Limoges, 6 Piece 375.00
Lavender, Gold Lustre Trim.. 98.00
Limoges, Signed CDA/CDM, 7 1/2 In., 6 Piece 695.00
Pink, Pottery, 6 Piece 125.00
Polychrome & Gilt, Haviland, 8 3/4 In. 1017.00
Purple & Gold, White Ground, Limoges, 9 In. 75.00
Turkey Design, White Glaze, Signed 175.00
White Ground, Gold Starburst Center, Gold Trim, 9 In., 6 Piece 425.00

PADEN CITY Glass Manufacturing Company was established in 1916 at
Paden City, West Virginia. It is best known for glasswares but also produced
a pottery line. The firm closed in 1951.

Bookends, Pouter Pigeon 170.00
Bowl, Gothic Garden, Pink, Footed, Square, 9 In. 98.00
Bowl, Peacock Reverse, Crow's Foot Blank, Pink, 12 In.. 105.00
Cake Plate, Crow's Foot, Red, Footed, Square... 80.00
Candy Dish, Cover, Gothic Garden, Yellow, Footed.. 145.00
Compote, Crow's Foot, 6 5/8 In. 60.00
Compote, Peacock & Wild Rose, Green, 7 In. 75.00
Creamer, Penny, Ruby 8.00
Figurine, Chanticleer, 7 1/4 x 9 1/2 In. 88.00
Figurine, Pheasant, Blue, 14 In. ....95.00 to 125.00
Figurine, Pony, Standing, 11 1/2 In. 90.00
Ice Tub, Cupid Etching, Pink 150.00
Jug, Cream, Off-White Drip Glaze, 1940s, 2 3/4 x 3 1/2 In. 20.00
Plate, Peacock & Wild Rose, Pink, Indentation, 10 1/2 In. 60.00
Plate, Penny, Ruby, 6 In. 4.00
Plate, Penny, Ruby, 8 In... 6.00
Sandwich Server, Crow's Foot, Center Handle, Red, Square 40.00
Sandwich Server, Lela Bird, Center Handle, 9 1/2 In. 98.00
Sugar, Penny, Ruby... 8.00
Tumbler, Penny, Footed, Ruby, 8 Oz. 9.00
Tumbler, Penny, Ruby, 10 Oz. 10.00
Vase, Gazebo Etching, Topaz, 10 In. 85.00
Vase, Gleaners, Harvesting Grapes, Amber, 10 In. 75.00
Vase, Peacock & Wild Rose, Pink, 10 1/2 In. 145.00
Vase, Peacock Reverse, Green, Black Forest Blank, 6 In. 155.00
Wine, Penny, Ruby, 2 Oz... 14.00

PAINTINGS listed in this book are not works by major artists but rather decorative paintings on ivory, board, or glass that would be of interest to the average collector. To learn the value of an oil painting by a listed artist you must
contact an expert in that area.

Oil On Board, 2 Children Kissing, Brotherly Love, Frame, 14 3/8 x 11 7/8 In. 71.00
Oil On Board, Barnyard Animals, Gilt Frame, Signed Hunt, 12 1/2 x 14 1/2 In. 137.00

Oil On Board, Floral Bouquet, McCary, 11 1/2 x 15 1/2 In.. 35.00
Oil On Board, Landscape, Harbor, Steam Ship, Sail Boats, Primitive, Frame, 19 x 21 In. 330.00
Oil On Board, Portrait, Woman In Lace Bonnet, Frame, 16 1/4 x 12 In................................ 1092.00
Oil On Board, River Fort, Frame, 1840, 2 5/8 x 4 1/2 In.. 240.00
Oil On Board, Ship, 5 Masted Schooner 385.00
Oil On Board, Snow Covered Mountains, F. Chade, Frame, 15 x 18 1/4 In. 75.00
Oil On Board, Snowscape, Notations, 13 1/2 x 22 1/2 In.. 220.00
Oil On Board, Vase Of Tulips, Gilt Frame, 26 3/4 x 21 In... 104.00
Oil On Brass, Gentleman, Red Coat, Embroidered Frame, 1740 .... 115.00
Oil On Canvas, Arabs Selling White Female Slaves, Frame, 1903, 4 x 5 Ft. 1100.00
Oil On Canvas, Child, Lacy Coat, Holding Book, Frame, England, 37 x 29 In. 1430.00
Oil On Canvas, Church Scene, Autumn Trees, Signed LL, Frame, 19 x 15 1/2 In. 88.00
Oil On Canvas, Figures In Town, Mexican, 20th Century, 24 x 20 In. 143.00
Oil On Canvas, Flower Market, M. Lichtenberg, 19 x 28 In. 270.00
Oil On Canvas, French Girl In Garden, Gilt Frame, 20th Century, 24 3/4 x 28 3/4 In. 110.00
Oil On Canvas, Genre Scene, Women, Men, Cottage, Gilt Frame, Victorian, 12 x 13 In. 300.00
Oil On Canvas, Idyllic European Landscape, Frame, Gilded Liner, 25 x 32 In. 176.00
Oil On Canvas, Just Punishment, School Room Scene, 19th Century, 30 x 34 In. 1725.00
Oil On Canvas, Landscape Scene, Middleville, New York, Frame, 14 1/4 x 20 In. 431.00
Oil On Canvas, Landscape With Cabin, Frame, 10 x 14 In. 192.00
Oil On Canvas, Landscape, Cows, Primitive, Shadowbox Frame, 29 x 24 3/4 In. 55.00
Oil On Canvas, Landscape, Farmhouse, Barn Yard, Primitive, Frame, 28 x 40 In. 1100.00
Oil On Canvas, Landscape, Mount Vernon, Primitive, Frame, 29 x 40 1/2 In. 3300.00
Oil On Canvas, Landscape, Mountains & Clouds, Signed, J.H. Mosler 700.00
Oil On Canvas, Man & Woman Victorian Portrait, Frame, 24 x 20 In., Pair 880.00
Oil On Canvas, Pastoral Scene With Milkmaids, Russia, 24 x 20 1/2 In........................ 258.00
Oil On Canvas, Pastoral Scene, Cows, C.D. Spangler, 9 1/2 x 13 1/2 In. 245.00
Oil On Canvas, Plowing The Fields, Figures & Oxen, Frame, 14 x 22 In. 316.00
Oil On Canvas, Portrait Of A Blond, Campagnola, 24 x 19 1/2 In. 92.00
Oil On Canvas, Portrait, Gentleman, Period Frame, Inscribed Label, 26 x 20 In. 805.00
Oil On Canvas, Portrait, Gentleman, Restored, Frame, 29 1/2 x 22 In. 247.00
Oil On Canvas, Portrait, Sea Captain, Frame, 38 x 31 In. 1017.00
Oil On Canvas, Portrait, Woman, 24 3/4 x 19 3/4 In.. 253.00
Oil On Canvas, Portrait, Woman, Black Dress, White Lace, Primitive, 28 x 25 1/2 In... 1540.00
Oil On Canvas, Portrait, Young Girl, Gilded Frame, 19th Century, 14 1/2 x 12 1/2 In... 300.00
Oil On Canvas, Portrait, Young Girl, Red Dress, Full Length 3465.00
Oil On Canvas, Schooner In High Seas, 19th Century, Frame, 14 x 18 In. 575.00
Oil On Canvas, Still Life, Fruit In Bowl, C. Haberman, Gilt Frame, 19 x 23 In. 60.00
Oil On Canvas, Summer Landscape With Bridge, Saul Schary, 20 x 24 In. 100.00
Oil On Canvas, Sunnyside Ltd., Brooklyn Heights, Lewandowski, 16 x 20 In. 230.00
Oil On Canvas, Woman Seated At A Window, Book In Lap, Frame, 36 x 29 In. 920.00
Oil On Canvas, Yellow Roses, E. Spencer, 18 x 14 In... 250.00
Oil On Canvas Board, Farmyard, People, Animals, Frame, 26 x 32 In........................... 55.00
Oil On Copper, Landscape, Black Man, Lake, Brass Frame, 1840, 2 7/8 x 3 5/8 In........ 220.00
Oil On Ivory, French Judge, Oval, 2 x 1 3/4 In. 192.00
Oil On Ivory, Young Woman, Gold Cross On Chain, Gilt Metal Frame, Oval, 4 1/4 In. . 165.00
Oil On Masonite, East Rock, New Haven, Conn., Scene, Frame, 9 1/4 x 13 In. 275.00
Oil On Masonite, Nude Woman, Standing In Stream, 22 x 11 In. 145.00
Oil On Masonite, Tug Boat In Harbor, Melvin Miller, 1963, 9 1/2 x 15 In. 245.00
Oil On Panel, Young Woman & Cherub, Frame, 5 3/4 x 4 In. 33.00
Oil On Paper, Glued On Board, Lamb, Primitive, Frame, 14 3/4 x 17 3/4 In. 275.00
Oil On Tin, Lion Of Cunne Shote, Feathered Headdress, 1835, 5 x 3 3/4 In. 3450.00
Oil On Wood, Cat On Pillow, Primitive, Gold Painted Frame, 3 5/8 x 5 In.................... 300.00
Oil On Wood, Nursery Rhyme, 7 x 9 1/2 In. 40.00
Oil On Wood, Village Road, Stagecoach, Cornelius, 4 x 6 In. 300.00
On Ivory, American Gentleman, Frame, 1840, 2 5/8 In.. 625.00
On Ivory, Bearded Gentleman, Brass Easel Frame, 3 x 4 In. 195.00
On Ivory, Blond Little Girl, Pink Ribbons, Silver Frame, 1920s, 3 5/8 x 2 3/4 In. 287.00
On Ivory, Bust Of 18th-Century Woman, Frame, 2 x 2 1/4 In. 172.00
On Ivory, Clementine D'Orleans, 3 1/2 x 2 3/4 In. 317.00
On Ivory, Elegant Woman, 19th Century, Signed NK, 2 1/4 x 2 In.............................. 155.00
On Ivory, English Lady, Frame, 1790, 2 5/8 In. 800.00
On Ivory, Gentleman, Tousled Hair, Black Coat, 2 1/2 x 2 1/8 In. 1495.00

On Ivory, Gentleman, Wearing Glasses, Early 19th Century, 2 5/8 x 2 In. 248.00
On Ivory, George Washington, Portrait, Latour, 3 1/8 x 2 1/2 In. 660.00
On Ivory, Lady, In Pink, Gilt Frame, 2 1/4 x 2 3/4 In. 260.00
On Ivory, Lady, Pink Roses In Hat, Signed Getta, 3 1/2 x 2 1/2 In. 345.00
On Ivory, Lady, With Turban, Brass Frame, 2 1/4 x 3 1/8 In. 265.00
On Ivory, Madam Clarion, Ivory Frame, 6 x 3 1/2 In. 330.00
On Ivory, Mourning, Trees & Tomb, 18th Century, Frame, Oval, 2 3/8 x 2 7/8 In. 670.00
On Ivory, Napoleon & Josephine, Ivory Frame, 3 1/4 x 2 1/2 In. 375.00
On Ivory, Napoleon, Gilt Metal Frame, Dupre, 8 1/2 x 7 1/8 In. 925.00
On Ivory, Portrait, Woman, Pastel Colors, Inscription, Watercolor, Case, 3 1/4 In. 247.00
On Ivory, Prince Bernhard Von Bulow, Tortoiseshell & Ivory Frame, 6 In. 230.00
On Ivory, Queen Louise, Ivory & Wooden Frame, 1 3/8 x 1 7/8 In. 280.00
On Ivory, Watercolor, Portrait, Gentleman, Signed, Pendant Frame, 1 1/2 In. 920.00
On Ivory, Watercolor, Young Woman, Blue Dress, Black Frame, 5 1/4 x 4 1/2 In. 225.00
On Ivory, Woman, 3 Children, Reynolds, Rosewood & Ivory Frame, c.1825, 3 1/4 In. ... 495.00
On Ivory, Woman, Basket Of Kittens, Blue & Green Enamel Frame, 3 3/4 In. 357.00
On Ivory, Young Woman, Off The Shoulder Lace Dress, Ivory Frame, 5 x 5 In. 165.00
On Ivory, Young Woman, Wearing Flowers, 19th Century, 2 5/8 x 2 1/4 In. 150.00
On Paper, Basket Of Fruit & Flowers, Watercolor, Gilt Frame, 8 3/8 x 11 1/2 In. 412.00
On Paper, Mother & Child, Charles Deklyn, Watercolor, 1892, 8 x 5 1/2 In. 17.00
On Paper, New Dog Old Trick, Watercolor, Frame, 10 5/8 x 13 3/8 In. 575.00
On Paper, Seascape, Geo. Howell Gay, Watercolor, Gilt Frame, 18 x 28 In. 742.00
On Paper, Shorebird, Pencil Label, Watercolor, Matted, Frame, 21 3/4 x 17 3/4 In., Pair 319.00
On Paper, Tanker, Clyde Singer, Watercolor, 1942, 11 1/2 x 8 5/8 In. 295.00
On Porcelain, Empress Josephine, Bronze Frame, 2 1/2 x 3 1/2 In. 495.00
On Porcelain, Gibson Girl, Large Hat, Frame, 10 x 6 1/2 In. 295.00
On Porcelain, Marie Antoinette, Florentine Frame, 5 5/8 In. 110.00
On Porcelain, Young Woman, Brown Hair, Ivory Frame, 4 1/4 In. 205.00
On Porcelain, Young Woman, Classical Dress, Brass Frame, M. Arnold, 5 1/2 In. 137.00
On Porcelain, Young Woman, Red Cape, Brass Frame, 1 3/4 x 2 1/4 In. 385.00
On Silk, Roses With Butterfly, Gilt Frame, Oriental, 15 3/4 x 18 In. 16.00
On Silk, Scroll, Swallows In Weeping Cherry Tree, Frame, Japan, Signed, 34 x 14 In. ... 302.00
On Silk, Watercolor, Girl In Blue, Blond, Hat & Bouquet, Frame, 1880, 3 3/4 x 4 1/2 In. 160.00
On Velvet, Large Basket Of Fruit, 15 x 18 In. 440.00
Reverse On Glass, Portraits, Frame, 15 1/4 x 13 1/2 In., Pair 154.00

PAIRPOINT Manufacturing Company started in 1880 in New Bedford, Massachusetts. It soon joined with the glassworks nearby and made glass, silver-plated pieces, and lamps. Reverse-painted glass shades and molded shades known as *puffies* were part of the production until the 1930s. The company reorganized and changed its name several times but is still working today. Items listed here are glass or glass and metal. Silver-plated pieces are listed under Silver Plate.

Biscuit Barrel, Inverted Thumbprint, Teal Blue, 7 1/2 x 5 In. 445.00
Bottle, Whiskey, Cut & Engraved, Cut Stopper 625.00
Bowl, Crystal, Diamond Cut, Silver Plated Frame, Claw Feet, No. 553c, 9 In. 600.00
Bowl, Turned-In Rim, Blue Handles, 10 In. 135.00
Box, Collar Button, Collar Shaped Base, Lined, Round, 1894, 2 1/2 In. 68.00
Box, Dresser, Hinged Cover, Enameled Blossoms, Lined, Silver Plate, 4 1/2 In. 230.00
Candlestick, Crystal, Silver Plate, Onyx Base, 15 1/2 In., Pair 550.00
Candlestick, Engraved Vine, Trapped Air Bubbles In Sphere, 10 In., Pair 400.00
Candlestick, Intaglio & Geometric Cutting, 16 In., Pair 585.00
Candlestick, Viscaria, Teardrop Stem, Rayed Base, 9 1/4 In., Pair 255.00
Centerpiece, Cherub, Floral Garland, Marble Base, Removable Silver Plate Holder 850.00
Centerpiece, Cherub, Holding Art Glass Peach Bowl, Ruffled, Marble Base, 17 In. 1000.00
Compote, Amethyst, Engraved Grape Design, 7 1/2 x 4 In. 110.00
Compote, Bubble Connestor, Vaseline, 12 In. 550.00
Compote, Cobalt Blue, Ruffled Rim, 5 In., Pair 165.00
Ewer, Ruffled Poppies, 1890, 15 1/2 In. 795.00
Globe, Hurricane, White Birch Trees, Yellow Ground, 8 3/4 In. 225.00
Lamp, Bombay Shade, Continuous New Bedford Harbor Scene, Signed, 18 In. 5250.00
Lamp, Boudoir, Papillon Shade, Roses & Butterflies ....*Illus* 5500.00
Lamp, Boudoir, Puffy, Black Field, Signed, 8 3/4 In. 4995.00

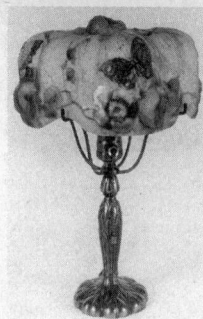

Pairpoint, Lamp, Boudoir,
Papillon Shade, Roses
& Butterflies

Pairpoint, Lamp, Puffy,
Apple Blossom Shade,
Tree Trunk Base, 27 In.

Pairpoint, Lamp, Puffy,
Floral, 20 In.

Pairpoint, Lamp, Reverse
Painted, Autumn Scene
Shade, 24 In.

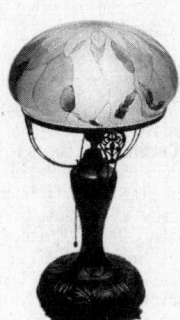

Pairpoint, Lamp,
Sunflower Shade,
20 In.

Lamp, Boudoir, Puffy, Floral, Blue Ground, Signed, 9 In.	3450.00
Lamp, Boudoir, Puffy, Reverse Painted, Rose & Butterfly Shade, Tree Trunk, 14 In.	4715.00
Lamp, Boudoir, Reverse Painted Shades, 2 Candle Arms, Bronze, 16 In.	1320.00
Lamp, Hanging, Puffy, Reverse Painted, Butterflies, Blue Ground, 1907, 13 3/4 In.	10000.00
Lamp, Metal, No. B3050, Patinated & Lacquered, Signed, 15 In.	115.00
Lamp, Persian Design, Exeter Shade	2300.00
Lamp, Puffy Lotus Shade, Yellow, Art Nouveau Molded Base, Signed	8800.00
Lamp, Puffy, Apple Blossom Shade, Tree Trunk Base, 27 In. .... *Illus*	26400.00
Lamp, Puffy, Butterflies & Roses, Patinated Metal, 1915, 12 In.	4600.00
Lamp, Puffy, Butterflies, Burgundy Rose, Brass Base, 15 In.	5500.00
Lamp, Puffy, Floral, 20 In. .... *Illus*	16500.00
Lamp, Puffy, Reverse Painted, Hummingbird, No. 3066, 21 1/2 In.	5980.00
Lamp, Puffy, Rose & Butterfly, Interior Butterflies, 22 In.	8800.00
Lamp, Reverse Painted, 5 Clipper Ships	4500.00
Lamp, Reverse Painted, Autumn Scene Shade, 24 In. .... *Illus*	2750.00
Lamp, Reverse Painted, Band Of Roses, Hummingbirds On Shade, 21 1/2 In.	6000.00
Lamp, Reverse Painted, Chestnut Tree, Signed, Numbered, 17 3/8 In.	3750.00
Lamp, Reverse Painted, Chipped-Ice Shade, Colored Border	3500.00
Lamp, Reverse Painted, Copley Shade, Urn Form Base, Logo, 22 In.	1610.00
Lamp, Reverse Painted, Flowers & Branches, Black Enameling, Signed, 15 In.	1925.00
Lamp, Reverse Painted, Inverted Shade, Enameled, 13 In.	1200.00

Lamp, Reverse Painted, Landscape Scene, 2 Candle Arms, Marble, 26 1/2 In. 1840.00
Lamp, Reverse Painted, Mountain & Meadow Scene, N. Gifford, 24 x 18 In. 3575.00
Lamp, Reverse Painted, Sunflower, Flower Form Feet, 1904, 20 In. 3850.00
Lamp, Reverse Painted, Venice Shade, Signed, 1915, 22 In. 5750.00
Lamp, Sunflower Shade, 20 In. ....*Illus* 3500.00
Lamp, Table, English Castle Scene, Signed.. 2500.00
Lamp, Table, Flowers & Birds On Shade, 17 In. 4400.00
Perfume Bottle, Swirl Mold, Enamel Lily-Of-The-Valley, Allover Scrolling, 6 In........ 285.00
Salt, Master, Old Colony, Teardrop Stem, Pedestal, 3 1/2 x 3 In., Pair 450.00
Shade, Puffy, Floral Design, 6 In... 1850.00
Shade, Reverse Painted, Horizontal Danver Glass Beehive, Cottage, 15 In. 1265.00
Spooner, Daisy & Button, Amberina, 4 3/4 In. 49.00
Tray, Molded Grapes Trim, 15 1/2 In. 85.00
Vase, Cornucopia, Clear Controlled Bubble Base, 8 3/4 In., Pair 450.00
Vase, Cut & Etched Florals, Amethyst, 12 In.. 400.00
Vase, Trumpet, Cobalt Blue... 190.00
Vase, Vintage Pattern, Double Handles, 12 In.. 295.00

PALMER COX, BROWNIES, see Brownies

PAPER collectibles, including almanacs, catalogs, children's books, stock certificates, and other paper ephemera, are listed here. Paper calendars are listed separately in the Calendar category.

Almanac, Kodol, 1905... 8.00
Almanac, Miles Nervine, 1937... 5.00
Almanac, Peruna Almanac Lucky Day, 1909 .... 10.00
Almanack, Published By Nathaniel Ames, Boston, 1765 .... 165.00
Birth & Baptismal Certificate, Johann Ritter, Hand Colored, Pennsylvania, 1831 .... 160.00
Blotter, Sophie Feldman, Stenographed Transcribing, 1923 Calendar 12.00
Book, Atlas, Colorado, U.S. Dept. Of Interior, 1877 .... 300.00
Book, Atlas, Minnesota, A.T. Andrea, Chicago, 1874 .... 325.00
Book, Atlas, W. Roxbury, Mass., Bromley 210.00
Book, Big Little Book, Bonanza, 1967 .... 7.00
Book, Big Little Book, Brad Turner In Transatlantic Flight 15.00
Book, Big Little Book, G-Man & Red X, 1936... 22.00
Book, Big Little Book, G-Man, On The Trail, 1938 .... 35.00
Book, Big Little Book, Houdini's Magic 35.00
Book, Big Little Book, Pat Nelson Ace Of Jet Pilots, 1937 .... 7.00
Book, Big Little Book, Peggy Brown & Runaway Auto Trailer 35.00
Book, Big Little Book, Peter Pan & The Indians, 1952 .... 15.00
Book, Big Little Book, Prairie Bill, 1934.. 15.00
Book, Big Little Book, Return Of Phantom, Flip Pictures 65.00
Book, Big Little Book, Tailspin Tommy Last Transport, 1939...................................... 22.00
Book, Big Little Book, Uncle Wiggly.. 65.00
Book, Coloring, Archie, Whitman, 1970 .... 12.00
Book, Coloring, Barbie, Superstar Barbie, 1977, Whitman 8.00
Book, Coloring, Ben Casey, No. 9532, Saalfield Artcraft, 1968.................................... 28.00
Book, Coloring, Ben-Hur, Movie, Lowe, 1959... 45.00
Book, Coloring, Betty Hutton & Her Girls, Whitman, 1951 .... 29.00
Book, Coloring, Brady Bunch, No. 1035, Whitman, 1972 .... 35.00
Book, Coloring, Bullwinkle & Dudley Doright, 1971 .... 13.00
Book, Coloring, Captain Kangaroo, Dot-To-Dot, 150 Pages, Whitman, 1959................. 10.00
Book, Coloring, Dennis The Menace, Cartoon, Golden, 1964 .... 25.00
Book, Coloring, Doris Day, Doris In Locket, Uncolored, Whitman, 1958 .... 25.00
Book, Coloring, Dudley Doright, Artcraft, 1962 .... 20.00
Book, Coloring, Johnny Quest, Whitman, 1965 .... 49.00
Book, Coloring, Lad, A Dog, Saalfield, 1962.. 18.00
Book, Coloring, Lassie, Whitman, 1969, 8 x 11 In. 8.00
Book, Coloring, Terry & The Pirates, Uncolored, 1946 .... 45.00
Book, Coloring, Tom Corbett, Saalfield, 1950 .... 70.00
Book, Coloring, Treasure Island, Abbott, Unused, 1950s.. 20.00
Book, Coloring, Wagon Train, Whitman, 1959 .... 20.00
Book, Diet, Calories Don't Count, 1961 .... 5.00

Book, Flip, Dance Lesson, 1941 .... 20.00
Book, Little Big Book, Lassie Adventures In Alaska, 1967 .... 5.00
Book, Little Golden, Hokey Wolf, 1964 .... 20.00
Book, Little Golden, Huckleberry Hound, 1960 .... 12.00
Book, Pop-Up, Astronauts On Moon 15.00
Book, Pop-Up, Billy Boy, Jack In The Book, 1953 .... 25.00
Book, Pop-Up, Christmas Time In Action, 1949 ....30.00 to 48.00
Book, Pop-Up, Dr. Doolittle 28.00
Book, Pop-Up, Huckleberry Hound 25.00
Book, Pop-Up, Jolly Jump Up, 1939 .... 75.00
Book, Pop-Up, Jolly Jump-Up's ABC Book, McLaughlin, 1946 .... 30.00
Book, Pop-Up, Pirate Treasure, 1969 .... 10.00
Book, Pop-Up, Red Barn Farm, Hallmark 25.00
Book, Pop-Up, Santa In Toyland, 1951 .... 25.00
Book, Pop-Up, Santa's Fun Book, 1954 .... 15.00
Book, Pop-Up, Santa's Workshop, 1951 .... 25.00
Book, Pop-Up, Yogi Bear 25.00
Book, Souvenir, Ewing High School, Photograph Insert, 3 x 5 In. 12.00
Booklet, New York Life Insurance Co., The America's Cup, Embossed Cover, 1899 ... 55.00
Booklet, Palmolive, Doctrine Of Soap & Water, Color Prints, Early 1900s 10.00
Booklet, Warner's Safe Bottle, Cure, 32 Pages 12.00
Catalog, A.G. Spalding & Bros., 1903, Athletic Library, 84 Pages 15.00
Catalog, Alton Bicycle, 1901, Pocket Size 15.00
Catalog, Aultman-Taylor Machinery, 1917, 64 Pages 35.00
Catalog, Avery, 1920, Threshing & Road Building, 96 Pages 45.00
Catalog, Avon, 1936, 1900 Pages 30.00
Catalog, Avon, Gifts, 1956, Christmas 75.00
Catalog, Bakery Equipment, 1937, 254 Pages 32.00
Catalog, Buescher Musical Instruments, 1934 .... 16.00
Catalog, Buffalo Threshers, 32 Pages 20.00
Catalog, Carson, Pirie, Scott & Co., 1929 .... 40.00
Catalog, Case, 1913, Machinery & Automobiles, 83 Pages 45.00
Catalog, Chainless Bucket Elevators, Bloomington, Ill. 10.00
Catalog, Cleveland Model Co., 1937, Planes & Trains Supplies 75.00
Catalog, Colt Firearms, 1978, Pistols 15.00
Catalog, Craftsman Power Tools, 1934, 40 Pages 18.00
Catalog, David Cook, 1933, Sunday School, Supplies & Holiday Specialties 125.00
Catalog, Denver Dry Goods, 1946, Spurs, Saddles 25.00
Catalog, Dixson Pencils, 1910 .... 35.00
Catalog, Eastman Kodak, 1919, 64 Pages 19.00
Catalog, Evenrude Outboard Motor, 1954 .... 20.00
Catalog, F.A.O. Schwarz, 1964, Christmas 35.00
Catalog, General Electric Co., 1929, Refrigerators, 24 Pages 18.00
Catalog, Goodyear Tire & Rubber Co., 1919, Akron, Ohio, 36 Pages 29.00
Catalog, Goodyear Tire, 1932 .... 9.00
Catalog, Hall Fishing Line, 1938 .... 10.00
Catalog, Harley Davidson, 1922 .... 45.00
Catalog, Herman Miller Collection, 1948, 11 x 9 In. 357.00
Catalog, Hot Wheels, 1969 .... 40.00
Catalog, Ideal Model Airplanes, 1928 .... 35.00
Catalog, Illinois Prison Board, 1908, Wood Furniture Made By Prisoners 75.00
Catalog, Indian Motorcycle, 1911, 24 Pages 150.00
Catalog, Jenny Semple Hill Furniture, 1925, 300 Pages ....35.00 to 40.00
Catalog, Johnson Smith Co., 1944, Novelties, Toys 75.00
Catalog, Keen Kutter, 1909, 4200 Pages 850.00
Catalog, Kodak Cameras & Kodak Supplies, 1924, 64 Pages 45.00
Catalog, L.L. Bean, 1927, Fall, 24 Pages 32.00
Catalog, Liggett & Myers Tobacco, 1910, Premiums 45.00
Catalog, Lionel, 1940, 64 Pages 120.00
Catalog, Lorillard Tobacco, 1922, Price List, 28 Pages 15.00
Catalog, Lyman Wood Mfg., 1900s, Buggy Wagon, Saddlery Specialties 100.00
Catalog, Maher & Grosh, 1899, Barber Supply, Toledo, Ohio 85.00
Catalog, Marklin, 1965, Toy Trains, Cars 40.00

Catalog, Marshall Fields, 1955, Fashions & Gifts, Christmas 25.00
Catalog, McArthur, Wirth & Co., 1900, Country Store Fixtures, 84 Pages, 8 x 10 In. 24.00
Catalog, Mead Cycle Co., 1918, Ranger Bicycles & Supplies 80.00
Catalog, Milton Bradley, 1930 .... 20.00
Catalog, Montgomery Ward, 1893, Vehicles Of All Kinds, 144 Pages 125.00
Catalog, Montgomery Ward, 1916, Sept. & Oct., Pure Food Groceries 40.00
Catalog, Montgomery Ward, 1917, Building Materials 65.00
Catalog, Montgomery Ward, 1919, No. 91, Wrapper 95.00
Catalog, Montgomery Ward, 1933 .... 60.00
Catalog, Montgomery Ward, 1937, Power Tools 25.00
Catalog, Montgomery Ward, 1950, Winter 25.00
Catalog, Montgomery Ward, 1964, Christmas 35.00
Catalog, Montgomery Ward, 1966, Christmas 35.00
Catalog, Montgomery Ward, 1968, Christmas 50.00
Catalog, Mueller Saddles & Ranchware, 1965 .... 10.00
Catalog, National Cloak & Suit, 1914, Fall & Winter Fashions 100.00
Catalog, Olson Rug Co., 1937, Household Carpeting 30.00
Catalog, Otto Young, 1913, Chicago, Jewelry, 800 Pages 500.00
Catalog, Popsicle, 1959-1960, Gift List, 8 Pages 15.00
Catalog, Ranger Bicycles, 1920, Mead Cycle Co., 57 Pages .... 75.00 to 90.00
Catalog, Remington Bicycle, 1893 .... 195.00
Catalog, Sears Roebuck, 1920, Your Grocery Store, September & October 40.00
Catalog, Sears Roebuck, 1942, Christmas 60.00
Catalog, Sears Roebuck, 1948, Christmas 34.00
Catalog, Sears Roebuck, 1954, Christmas 40.00
Catalog, Sears Roebuck, 1967, Christmas 25.00
Catalog, Sears Roebuck, 1978, Christmas 15.00
Catalog, Shapleights Auto Equipment & Supplies, 1920 .... 100.00
Catalog, Sharp & Smith, 1935, Surgical Instruments, Equipment 100.00
Catalog, Simplicity Pattern Book Fashions, August, 1954 .... 60.00
Catalog, Singer Sewing Machine, 1929, How To Make Drapes, 64 Pages 5.00
Catalog, Snap-On Tools & Shop Equipment, 1962 .... 30.00
Catalog, Spiegel, 1937 .... 25.00
Catalog, Spiegel, 1951, Christmas 65.00
Catalog, Stanley Tools, 1939, 240 Pages 20.00
Catalog, Stanley, 1900, August, 80 Pages, 5 x 7 1/4 In. 185.00
Catalog, Stanley, 1938, April, Parts Index, Supplement, 204 Pages, 5 x 7 In. 100.00
Catalog, Star Windmills & Towers, 1908 .... 20.00
Catalog, Wollensak Co., 1914, Cameras & Lens Supplies 40.00
Deed, Lehigh County, Pa., 1856 .... 5.00
Fraktur, Birds & Flowers, Birth Of Christian Erb, 1758, Frame, 16 x 20 In. 2750.00
Fraktur, Birth Record, Elizabeth Jung, Dauphin County, Born In 1801, 18 1/4 x 21 In. . 385.00
Fraktur, Certificate Of Birth & Baptism, 1829, Frame, 19 1/4 x 15 1/4 In. 825.00
Fraktur, Floral Wreath, Tauf Zedel, 1809, 8 x 7 In. 300.00
Fraktur, Flying Angel, German, Birth, 1807, Frame, 16 3/4 x 19 3/4 In. 2695.00
Fraktur, Geburts Und Taufschein, 1923 Birth Record, Montgomery Co., Penn. 110.00
Fraktur, Geburts Und Taufschein, Wullimann Family Births, 1840-1877, 15 1/2 In. 445.00
Fraktur, Mermaids & Hearts, 2 Women, Friederich Speyer, 1800 .... 5300.00
Fraktur, Mother, Midwife, Musical Lyrics In Latin, Flowers, Baby 850.00
Greeting Card, Valentine, Mechanical, Felix The Cat, Germany, 1930 .... 95.00
Greeting Card, Valentine, Musical Instruments, Birds, Message, 1895, 8 x 6 In. 50.00
Greeting Card, Valentine, Pretty Girl, Heart Shaped, Gold Edges, Envelope, c.1912, 6 In. 15.00
Greeting Card, Valentine, Snow White, Mechanical 30.00
Invitation, Barnum & Bailey, Opening Day Performance, 1911 .... 45.00
Letter, Commission, Abraham Lincoln, Frame 4750.00
Magazine, Life, Jayne Mansfield Cover, 1956 .... 48.00
Magazine, The Gentleman's, December 1752, London, On How To Build A Kite 60.00
Magazine, TV Guide, Garrison's Gorillas Cover, November 25, 1967 .... 16.00
Magazine, TV Guide, Ironsides Cover, February 15, 1969 .... 17.00
Manual, Harley Davidson, Owner's, 1941 .... 85.00
Menu, Cafe Rouge, Hotel Pennsylvania, August, 1943, Autographs 25.00
Menu, Franklin & Eleanor Roosevelt, 1932, Autographed By Both 1450.00
Newspaper, London Daily Post, 1738-1740 .... 17.00

Notepad, Lost In Space, June Lockhart, 1960s	42.00
Playbill, Sound Of Music, Mary Martin & Troupe On Cover, 1961	10.00
Program, Annie Get Your Gun, San Francisco Civic Light Opera, 1975	35.00
Program, Closing Literary Exercise, Mt. Union Women's College, March 6, 1856	45.00
Program, Commencement Exercise, Mt. Union College, 1864, 6 1/2 x 6 In.	50.00
Program, Conjoint Of Republic & Linnean Literary Society, Mt. Union College, 1856	50.00
Program, Dance, Decatur Athletic Club, Brooklyn, 1913	18.00
Program, Miss America, 1941	16.00
Program, Olympics, Los Angeles, With Ticket Stub, 1932	200.00
Reward, Merit, Gibson & Co., Gilt Card Stock, 1880, 11 x 3/4 In.	40.00
Stock Certificate, American Linen Co., Fall River, Mass., 2 Women Shield, 1924	15.00
Stock Certificate, Colorado Mining Co., 1909	31.00
Stock Certificate, Dodge Gold Mining Co., S.D., Miners, Stream, 1908	15.00
Stock Certificate, National Consolidated Oil Corp, Liberty, With Flag, Delaware, 1922	8.00
Stock Certificate, National Consolidated Oil Corp, Liberty Design, 1922	6.00
Stock Certificate, Old Colony Railroad Co., Boston, Mass., 1881	15.00
Stock Certificate, Utica Sunday Tribune Co., N.Y., 9 Stamps, 1899	18.00
Tickets, Brooklyn Bridge Trolley, Strip Of 5	45.00

PAPER DOLLS were probably inspired by the pantins, or jumping jacks, made in eighteenth-century Europe. By the 1880s, sheets of printed paper dolls and clothes were being made. The first paper doll books were made in the 1920s. Collectors prefer uncut sheets or books or boxed sets of paper dolls. Prices are about half as much if the pages have been cut.

Amy Carter, Toy Factory, 14 In., Uncut	25.00
Ann Sothern, 1943, Uncut	75.00
Archie, 5 Dolls & Outfits, Whitman, 1970, Uncut	19.00
Barbie, Boutique, Whitman, 1973	20.00
Barbie, Pretty Changes, Whitman	10.00
Barbie & Ken, Sun Valley Wardrobe, 31 Pieces, Whitman, 1974, Uncut	15.00
Blondie, Dagwood, Daisy & Baby Dumpling, 1940, Cut	72.00
Buffy, Family Affair, Whitman, 1968, Uncut	25.00
Buster Brown & Tige, Outfits, J. Ottmann, Envelope, Cut	115.00
Carmen Miranda, 1940s	5.00
Charlie's Angels, Farrah Fawcett, 14-In. Doll, Toy Factory, 1977	25.00
Charlie's Angels, Jill, Magic Touch Clothes, 14-In. Doll, Toy Factory, 1977	45.00
Charlie's Angels, Kelly, Magic Touch Clothes, 14-In. Doll, Toy Factory, 1977	40.00
Chrissy, 1971, Uncut	12.00
Chuck & Di Have A Baby, Uncut	15.00
Claudette Colbert, 1940s	5.00
Colonial, Saalfield, Missing Stands	18.00
Cynthia Pepper As Margie, 1963, Uncut	25.00
Dinah Shore, 1 Missing Doll, 1963	15.00
Elizabeth Taylor, As Cleopatra, Blaise Publishing, 1963, Uncut	25.00
Family Affair, Buffy & Mrs. Beasley	30.00
Francie, Malibu, Whitman, 1973	20.00
Gilda Radner, Uncut	12.00
Gone With The Wind, 1940, Uncut	275.00
Hayley Mills, Moon Spinners Movie, Whitman, 1964, 6 Uncut Sheets	100.00
Hedy Lamarr, Saalfield, Uncut	150.00
It's A Small World, 10 Dolls Of Many Lands, Walt Disney, Whitman, 1966	22.00
Jack & Jill, New Frocks & Frills, Regensteiner, Uncut, 1925	35.00
Jane Withers, Ruhman, 10 Pages, 3 Cut, 7 Uncut	30.00
Judy Garland, Queen, Holden, Uncut	22.00
Kopy Kate, 1971, Uncut	12.00
Lion Coffee, 4 Piece, Cut	60.00
Little Lulu, Valentine, 1951	11.00
Little Lulu & Tubby, Whitman, Uncut, 1974	45.00
Little Lulu Majorette, Kleenex Advertising, Cardboard, 1956, 10 1/2 In.	12.00
Lucy & Desi	50.00
Mary Poppins, Whitman, 1964, Uncut	50.00
Miss America, 1974	12.00
Miss Piggy, Colorforms, Uncut	15.00

Munsters, Whitman, 1966... 55.00
Nanny & The Professor, Saalfield, 1971, Uncut... 31.00
Osmonds, Donny & Marie, Whitman, 1977, Uncut 20.00
Partridge Family, Artcraft, 1972... 50.00
Patience & Prudence, Abbott, 1959, Uncut... 35.00
Playmates, Box, Whitman, Uncut... 28.00
Rapsy & Ritzy, Complete.. 200.00
Reagan, 1st Family, Uncut... 10.00
Rhonda Fleming, Saalfield, 1954, Uncut 45.00
Richard Burton, As Mark Antony, Blaise Publishing, 1963 .... 25.00
Ricky Nelson, 1959, Uncut... 125.00
Ronald & Nancy Reagan, First Family, Patti & Ron, Dell, Jr., 1981 ....10.00 to 12.00
Ronald Reagan, 32 Outfits, 1984, Uncut.. 10.00
Sandra Dee, Saalfield, 1969, Uncut 40.00
Slumber Party, Merrill, Uncut 25.00
That Girl, Artcraft, No. 4471, 1969, Uncut.. 67.00
Tom Corbett Space Cadet, Push-Out Book, Saalfield, 1952... 35.00
Tricia, Julie & Pat Nixon, White House, Saalfield, 1969, Uncut 35.00
Twiggy, Whitman, 1967... 30.00
Waltons, 1974 .... 25.00
Waltons, Whitman, 1975, Uncut ....30.00 to 40.00

PAPERWEIGHTS must have first appeared along with paper in ancient Egypt. Today's collectors search for every type, from the very expensive French weights of the nineteenth century to the modern artist weights or advertising pieces. The glass tops of the paperweights sometimes have been nicked or scratched, and this type of damage can be removed by polishing. Some serious collectors think this type of repair is an alteration and will not buy a repolished weight; others think it is an acceptable technique of restoration that does not change the value. Baccarat paperweights are listed separately under Baccarat.

Advertising, Airship Scene, Enameled Pewter 95.00
Advertising, Alshuler Co., Racine, Wis. 40.00
Advertising, American President Lines, Steamship, Brass, Box 85.00
Advertising, American School Of Osteopathy, Glass, 1895 .... 48.00
Advertising, Boehringer & Soehue, Makers Of Quinine & Cocaine, 2 x 4 In. 70.00
Advertising, Brownie Baking Co., Spokane, Washington, Figural, 1920s....................... 125.00
Advertising, Buick.. 16.00
Advertising, Chicago Tailor, Glass... 22.00
Advertising, D.R. Woerffel, Russia, Tiger, Chinese Chop Form, Bronze, 4 In................. 275.00
Advertising, Dog, Standing, Figural, Funeral... 85.00
Advertising, Dutch Boy Paint, National Lead Co. 75.00
Advertising, Hallden Machine Co., Figural, Printing Press, Metal, 1930s, 7 x 4 In. 49.00
Advertising, Hayes Equipment Co. 75.00
Advertising, Intervale Manufacturing Co., 1882 .... 180.00
Advertising, J.C. Shaffer & Co., Grain Merchants, Celluloid Mirror, c.1890................. 35.00
Advertising, John Frick Jewelry Co., N.Y., Rock Of Gibraltar, Lead, Embossed 28.00
Advertising, Kaiser Co., Pig Leaning Against Iron Ingot, Iron, 1943 .... 90.00
Advertising, Keen Kutter, Pen Rest, Glass 375.00
Advertising, Lion Oil, Figural 70.00
Advertising, MGM Lion, Standing, Script On Base, 2 x 5 In. 85.00
Advertising, National Lead Company, Dutch Boy Logo 35.00
Advertising, Parched Rolled Oats, Quail Brand, Nebraska City Cereal Mills................... 130.00
Advertising, Parry-Ford Automobiles, ... 50.00
Advertising, Stoughton Wagon, Reverse Painted Glass, 3 In. 135.00
Advertising, Tri-State Pottery Festival, Door-Knob Shape.. 6.00
Advertising, Ward's Vitovim Bread 65.00
Advertising, Workingmen's Clothes.. 40.00
Ayotte, Summer, Carnations, Daisies, Freesia & Mums 950.00
Bird, Garden Of Paper 10.00
Blown Glass, Clear, Green & Pink Millville Rose, 3 1/8 In. 330.00
Book Shape, Cut Glass, Sandwich, Miniature... 150.00

Canoe, Glass, Flowers, Souvenir, Youngstown, Ohio	20.00
Cenedese, Internal Fish & Seaweed, Lion Hand Inscribed, Blue Ground, 4 x 5 In.	95.00
Clichy, Cane, Pink, Green, 2 In.	750.00
Clichy, Cane, White, Pink, Rose, 1 7/8 In.	540.00
Clichy, Millefiori, Green, Pink, White Canes, 3 1/8 In.	800.00
Clichy, Millefiori, Red, White, Blue Canes, 2 5/8 In.	800.00
Clichy, Miniature Spaced Millefiori, 9 Canes, 2 In.	450.00
Clichy, Nosegay, 1 3/4 In. Diam.	550.00
Ebelhare, Pink & White Swirl, Blue Complex Center Cane, 2 1/2 In.	175.00
Egg, Crystal, Bubbles, 1 Large Black Bubble, Mt. St. Helen Ash	20.00
Frog, Silver, Signed S. Kirk & Sons, No. 1 In Circle	250.00
Gentile, Star Medallion, Signed	395.00
Jon Lewis, Moon	250.00
Kaziun, 7 Canes Within Heart Canes In Center, 1 7/8 In.	525.00
Kaziun, Floral Trellis	900.00
Lookout Mountain, Tenn.	20.00
Lundberg, Daffodil, 6 Leaves, Cobalt Blue Ground, 3 1/2 In.	125.00
Lundberg, Daniel Salazar's Golden Clematis, Butterfly	320.00
Lundberg, Pine Moon, Pine Branches & Needles, Outlined By Moon	280.00
Lundberg, Purple, Yellow Butterfly, Striping, Tiffany Type, 1974	50.00
Millefiori, 4 Wedges, Multicolor Canes, Spiral Cones, Gold Dust, 3 In.	50.00
Millefiori, 6 Turquoise Canes, Pink Center, Gold Dust, 3 In.	50.00
Millefiori, Canes, Red & White Center, White & Pink Middle, Oyster-Shell Rolls	125.00
Millefiori, Rosette, Multicolor Canes, Straw & White, 3 In.	95.00
New England Glass, Symmetrical Design, Fruits On Swirling Basket	550.00
Perthshire, Thistles Within Stardust Canes, 6 Millefiori Canes, 3 1/4 In.	385.00
Rooster, Signed, 7 7/8 In.	165.00
Sandwich Glass, White Rose, Cobalt Blue Petals & Leaves, 2 x 3 1/8 In.	488.00
Sanglier, Wild Boar, Signed, 2 1/2 In.	288.00
Scotty Dog, Cast Iron	28.00
Simpson, Planet, 4 In.	350.00
Snow Dome, Creature Of Black Lagoon, 5 In.	15.00
Snow Dome, Flintstones, Days Inn	30.00
Snow Dome, Polar Bear, Ceramic	58.00
Snow Dome, Rudolph	22.00
Spanish Armada, Central Ship Silhouette, 400th Anniversary	190.00
Spatter Glass, 3 Flowers, Multicolored, Bubble Centers	40.00
St. Clair, 8 Flowers, Blue Puff, Bubbles, Dome, 3 In.	45.00
St. Clair, Frog Inside	110.00
St. Clair, Maude & Joe, White Flowers, 1974	85.00
St. Clair, Owl Inside	100.00
St. Louis, Clemantis, Red, 2 3/8 In.	1175.00
St. Louis, Crown, Red, Green Ribbons, 3 In.	2500.00
St. Louis, Pear, Green Leaves, White Latticinio Ground, 2 1/8 In.	1095.00
Stickley, Glass, Marked, 1918, 1 x 3 In	300.00
Sulphide, Eisenhower, c.1954	190.00
Sulphide, Kennedy	75.00
Sulphide, Kossuth Inscription, People Of U.S. Of America, 1851, 2 3/4 In.	225.00
Sulphide, Lincoln, Abraham, Ruby Base	310.00
WAC Saluting	60.00
Whitefriars, 30th Anniversary, State Of Israel, 1978	400.00
Whitefriars, Bicentennial, 1975	350.00
Whitefriars, Christmas, 1975	450.00
Ysart, Butterfly, Multicolored, Green Ground, Garland, 2 15/16 In.	1200.00

PAPIER-MACHE is made from paper mixed with glue, chalk, and other ingredients, then molded and baked. It becomes very hard and can be painted. Boxes, trays, and furniture were made of papier-mache. Some of the nineteenth-century pieces were decorated with mother-of-pearl. Furniture made of papier-mache is listed in the Furniture category.

Bowl, Black Lacquer, Gold, Roses, Butterflies, Tiered, Bamboo Frame, England	85.00
Box, Correspondence, Mother-Of-Pearl Design Cover, Victorian	225.00
Box, Writing, Slant Front, Gilt Decorations, Ivory Pulls, 8 1/4 x 10 1/2 In.	275.00

Figure, Rabbit, Standing, Green, White & Red, 9 1/2 In. 85.00
Figurine, Turtle, On Back Of Another, Triangular Scales, China, 5 In. 230.00
Race Horse, Leather Covered, 25 In. 935.00
Tray, Interval Painting Of Gilt Foliate, Ribbon Garlands, 12 1/2 In. 375.00
Tray, Oval, Gilded Geometric Painting, Black Ground, Victorian, 29 In. 405.00

PARASOL, see Umbrella

PARIAN is a fine-grained, hard-paste porcelain named for the marble it
resembles. It was first made in England in 1846 and gained in favor in the
United States about 1860. Figures, tea sets, vases, and other items were made
of Parian at many English and American factories.

Box, Trinket, Dove, 6 In. 65.00
Bust, Henry Wadsworth Longfellow, 13 1/2 In. 115.00
Figurine, Girl, Victorian, Dress, Basket, Hat, 16 In. 250.00
Figurine, Mercury, England, c.1850, 23 1/4 In. 1495.00
Figurine, Napoleon, On Rearing Horse, Rockwork Base, 10 1/2 In. 264.00
Figurine, Toymaker, Santa Claus, Elves & Tops, White, 6 In. 95.00
Lamp, Hanging, 3 Chains, Greek Key Acanthus Design, 8 1/2 x 16 In. 450.00
Pitcher, Dolphin Form, 8 1/2 In. 150.00
Vase, Baluster, Flared Neck, Flowers, Elongated Leaves, 11 x 4 In., Pair 150.00

PARIS, Vieux Paris, or Old Paris, is porcelain ware that is known to have
been made in Paris in the eighteenth or early nineteenth century. These porcelains have no identifying mark but can be recognized by the whiteness of the
porcelain and the lines and decorations. Gold decoration is often used.

Bowl, Paris Building, Shell Form, Gilt Border, Schoelcher Mark, 9 x 8 In., Pair 3960.00
Cachepot, Frolicking Cherubs, Pair 2475.00
Compote, Gilt & Cobalt Blue Trim, Crown Monogram, 7 1/2 x 8 /12 In., Pair.............. 880.00
Cup & Saucer, Classical Robed Figures Interior, Leaf Borders, Dagoty, c.1810, 3 In. 935.00
Cup & Saucer, From Franklin Pierce White House Service, 1853 .... 375.00
Cup & Saucer, Molded Swan Feathers & Head Forms Handle, 4 1/2 In. 1650.00
Group, Europa & Bull, c.1870, 11 In. 495.00
Inkwell, Boat Shape, Gilt Sea Sprite, Painted Stripes, Square Well, 8 In. 990.00
Jar, Tobacco, Black & Gilt Striped Barrel Body, Seraph Cover, 8 3/4 In. 990.00
Jardiniere, Scenic Medallion, Gilded, 1850s 7150.00
Jardiniere, Tapering Circular Body, Gilt Trim, Chinese Nobles, 8 3/4 In., Pr................ 5775.00
Lamp, Carcel, Gray-Blue Ground, Floral Panels, c.1850, 19 In., Pair 1320.00
Perfume Bottle, Capstand Shape, Stopper, Gilt Tracery, 8 1/4 In................................ 440.00
Perfume Bottle, Porcelain, Birds, 6 1/2 In., Pair... 247.00
Pitcher, Foliated Lip & Handle, Gilt Trim, 8 3/4 In.. 98.00
Plate, Brown Transfer Of Marseilles, Gilt Border, c.1810, 10 1/2 In. 880.00
Punch Bowl, Painted Fruit Reserves, Gilt Scrolling, c.1850, 14 1/4 In. 522.00
Teapot, On Warmer, Castle Form, All White, 10 In.. 247.00
Teapot, On Warmer, Gothic Church Form, Reticulated Balcony, 9 3/4 In. 440.00

Paris, Tureen, Cover, Shell Shape, Jacob Petit

Tureen, Cover, Shell Shape, Jacob Petit .... *Illus* 2588.00
Urn, Allegorical, Rural Landscapes, Mythological Handles, 8 3/4 In., Pair 880.00
Urn, Cover, White, Gold, c.1860, 19 1/2 In. 1995.00
Urn, Flared Rim, Foliate Scrolled Handles, Plinth Base, c.1860, 13 3/4 In., Pair 1437.00
Urn, Gilt Tracery, Continuous Estate Scenes, Mythological Handles, 7 1/2 In., Pair 715.00
Urn, Gothic-Style Design, Tied Loop Handles, 4 Paw Feet, c.1835, Pair 1650.00
Urn, Parian Wisdom & Learning Figures, Pair... 1100.00
Vase, Bird & Flower Design, 8 In., Pair... 209.00
Vase, Enamel, Gilt, Seated Figure Supports Leaf-Shaped Vase, 12 In. 370.00
Vase, Figural, Musician, Sitting By Horse, Gilt & Green, 19th Century, 6 1/2 In., Pair . 87.00
Vase, Garden Flower Reserves, Gilt Trimmed Handles, Gilded Plinth, 11 1/2 In., Pair . 240.00
Vase, Garniture, Stag's Head, Arrows & Quivers, 14 3/4 In., Pair 1210.00
Vase, Gilt Tracery, Raised Floral Handle, c.1830, 14 In.. 275.00
Vase, Hand-Painted Floral, Floral Handles, 12 x 10 In... 325.00
Vase, Painted Courtly Love Scenes, Voluted Handles, 10 1/4 In., Pair......................... 550.00
Vase, Portrait & Floral Reserves, Waisted Neck, Late 19th Century, 16 1/2 In. 230.00
Vase, Portrait, Gilded, Painted, 1850s, Pair 4180.00
Vase, Posy, Flowers, 5 In., Pair 209.00
Vase, Woman, Shoulder Handles, 16 1/2 In.. 600.00

PATE-DE-VERRE is an ancient technique in which glass is made by blending and refining powdered glass of different colors into molds. The process was revived by French glassmakers, especially Galle, around the end of the nineteenth century.

Bowl, Center Swirling Star, Francois Decorchement, c.1925, 11 3/4 In......................... 3162.00
Perfume Bottle, Atomizer, Rose Body, Leaves, Red Berries, Signed, 4 x 1 1/2 In. 2500.00
Plaque, Bust Of Caesar Augustus, Carder, 4 x 2 3/4 In. 3450.00
Plaque, St. Theresa Of Lisieux, Rectangular, 10 x 12 In. 1650.00
Vase, Gray, Purple, Molded Seaweed & Sea Horses, Despret, c.1905, 8 1/3 In. 2925.00

PATE-SUR-PATE means paste on paste. The design was made by painting layers of slip on the ceramic piece until a relief decoration was formed. The method was developed at the Sevres factory in France about 1850. It became even more famous at the English Minton factory about 1870. It has since been used by many potters to make both pottery and porcelain wares.

Charger, White Nymphs, Landscape, Green Ground, George Jones, c.1875, 12 In........ 575.00
Plaque, Cherub Leaning On Pedestal, Oval, Green & White, 5 3/4 In. 1760.00
Plaque, Nude Woman, Near Birdcage, Oak Frame, 7 x 4 1/2 In. 1540.00
Urn, Allegorical Figures, Pink Ground, Converted Into Lamp, 20 In. 1955.00
Vase, Art Nouveau Baluster Form, Teal Ground, 9 1/2 In. 230.00
Vase, Female Nymph At Sunset, Landscape, Schenck, c.1875, 8 In.............................. 632.00
Vase, Flowers, Gold Serpent Skin Twisted Handle, 7 1/4 In., Pair 995.00
Vase, Pilgrim, White Relief, Brown Ground, Gilt Feet & Border, c.1870, 7 In. 258.00

PAUL REVERE POTTERY was made at several locations in and around Boston, Massachusetts, between 1906 and 1942. The pottery was operated as a settlement house program for teenage girls. Many pieces were signed *S.E.G.* for Saturday Evening Girls. The artists concentrated on children's dishes and tiles. Decorations were outlined in black and filled with color.

Bookends, Owls 1500.00
Bowl, Incised Daffodils, SEG, 1914, 8 1/4 In. 1320.00
Bowl, Stylized Blossoms, Slate Blue Ground, SEG, Dated May 1917, 9 In. 1430.00
Bowl, Tulip Band, SEG, 3 x 8 1/2 In.. 850.00
Box, Cover, Painted Sailing Ship, E. Bown, 1923, 2 x 4 In.. 605.00
Box, Cover, White Flowers, Blue Band, SEG, 3 x 1 1/2 In. 385.00
Candlestick, Crystalline Glaze, SEG, 3 1/2 In., Pair 550.00
Demitasse Set, White & Black Lilies, Yellow & White, 6 Piece 660.00
Flower Frog, Green, SEG, 1 1/4 x 2 1/2 In. 55.00
Inkwell, Brown Glaze, SEG 355.00
Jar, 6 Sides, Incised & Painted Landscape, House, Hill, Water, Trees, SEG, 4 1/2 In. ... 357.00
Paperweight, Stylized Trees, Blue Ground, SEG, Octagonal, 2 1/2 In........................ 250.00
Pitcher, Ducks Against Blue Water, SEG, 3 1/8 In. 287.00

Pitcher, Flowing Mottled Blue Glaze, SEG, 7 In.	525.00
Plate, Incised Running Pig, SEG, 8 1/2 In.	1495.00
Plate, Smiling Pigs Border, SEG, 8 1/2 In.	1400.00
Tile, Irregular Geometric Design, Black Outlining, 3 In.	275.00
Tile, Landscape Ring, Mustard & Yellow, Signed, 5 1/2 In.	460.00
Trivet, Trees, Blue Ground, SEG, 1/2 x 5 1/2 In.	350.00
Vase, 4 Sides, Flared Shape, Incised & Painted Flowers, SEG, 19 In.	605.00
Vase, Black Textured Glaze, 4 1/2 In.	220.00
Vase, Blue High Glaze, SEG, 10 In.	400.00
Vase, Blue-Gray Flecked Glaze, SEG, 7 In.	188.00
Vase, Cream Matte Over Brown Clay, Signed, 6 In.	120.00
Vase, Dark Green High Glaze, 4 In.	66.00
Vase, Raised Rim, Cream Glaze, Brown Clay, Impressed Mark, 6 In.	121.00
Vase, Yellow Blossoms, Curdled Green Ground, Signed, 9 In.	2310.00

PEACHBLOW glass originated about 1883 at Hobbs, Brockunier and Company of Wheeling, West Virginia. It shades from yellow to peach and is lined with white glass. New England peachblow is a one-layer glass shading from red to white. Mt. Washington peachblow shades from pink to blue. Reproductions of all types of peachblow have been made. Some are poor and easy to identify as copies, others are very accurate reproductions and could fool the unwary. Related pieces may be listed under Gunderson and Webb Peachblow.

Bride's Bowl, Enamel Spider & Flies, Etched Web In Bottom, Brass	495.00
Creamer, K. Haught, 5 In.	88.00
Creamer, Pale Blue To Pink, Applied Handle, Mt. Washington, 3 5/8 In.	715.00
Cruet, Wheeling, Thin Walls	1250.00
Fairy Lamp, Wheeling, 5 In.	985.00
Finger Bowl, Asters, Mt. Washington	3015.00
Mustard, Wheeling, Silver Plated Fittings, 2 7/8 In.	192.00
Pitcher, Kanawha Glass, 5 1/2 In.	55.00
Pitcher, Wheeling, Claret, Amber Reeded Handle, Neck Rigaree, 9 3/4 In.	1840.00
Pitcher, Wheeling, Fuschia To Amber, Cream Lining, 10 1/2 In.	1500.00 to 2750.00
Rose Bowl, Acid-Finish, Raspberry To Off-White, 7-Crimp Top, 2 1/2 x 2 3/4 In.	295.00
Salt & Pepper, Wheeling	350.00
Salt & Pepper, Wheeling, Bulbous	775.00
Saltshaker, Matte, New England, 4 In.	950.00
Stand, Wig, Victorian, Opalescent Base, 6 In.	175.00 to 200.00
Sugar, New England, World's Fair, 1893, 2 1/2 In.	450.00
Sugar, Wheeling, Glossy, 3 x 4 In.	795.00
Toothpick, New England, White To Raspberry	595.00
Toothpick, Pink To Soft White, Glossy Finish	425.00
Tumbler, Mt. Washington, Wheeling, 3 3/4 In.	187.00
Tumbler, New England, Glossy Finish, 3 3/4 In.	600.00
Tumbler, New England, Matte Finish, 3 3/4 In.	600.00
Tumbler, Wheeling, Glossy, 3 3/4 In.	400.00
Vase, Stick, Wheeling, 11 In.	895.00
Vase, Stick, Wheeling, Matte, Bulbous Base, 8 1/2 x 4 In.	1065.00
Vase, Wheeling, Bulbous, 3 3/4 In.	250.00
Vase, Wheeling, Elongated Pear Form, Red To Amber, 9 1/4 In.	220.00
Vase, Wheeling, Morgan, Amber Base, 10 In.	1705.00
Vase, Wheeling, Oriental Shape, Bulbous Base, Brockunier, 8 1/8 In.	715.00
Wig Stand, Opal Base, Victorian, 6 In.	140.00

PEARL items listed here are made of the natural mother-of-pearl from shells. Such natural pearl has been used to decorate furniture and small utilitarian objects for centuries. The glassware known as mother-of-pearl is listed by that name. Opera glasses made with natural pearl shell are listed under Opera Glasses.

Card Case, 3 3/4 In.	88.00
Card Case, Inlaid Bird & Flowers, 3 5/8 In.	55.00
Card Case, Side Opening, 4 1/2 In.	66.00
Figure, Jesus On Cross, Wooden, 12 In.	65.00
Fish Set, Knives & Fork	78.00

Flatware, Pearl Handles, Wooden Case, 33 Piece.. 450.00

PEARLWARE is an earthenware made by Josiah Wedgwood in 1779. It was copied by other potters in England. Pearlware is only slightly different in color from creamware and for many years collectors have confused the terms.

Pearl

Bowl, Floral Design, 19th Century, 9 In.	230.00
Bowl, Fruit, Floral Design, 19th Century, 12 1/2 In.	488.00
Bowl, Leaf Design, Late 18th Century, 7 In.	260.00
Bowl, Oriental Transfer, Polychrome Enamel, Floral Ground, England, 9 1/2 In.	460.00
Bowl, Waste, Oriental Design, Signed, 5 5/8 In.	77.00
Dish, Blue Transfer, Arms Of City Of London, Lozenge Shape, 10 3/4 In.	125.00
Mug, Chinoiserie, Blue & White, 19th Century, 3 3/8 In.	86.00
Mug, Floral Design, 4 3/4 In.	316.00
Pitcher, Enamel Design, Bees & Skep, 19th Century, 7 3/4 In.	575.00
Pitcher, Flower & Swag Design, Inscribed Gamelia Bingly 1800, 7 In.	850.00
Pitcher, Landscape Of Masonic Symbols, 19th Century, 8 1/2 In.	747.00
Puzzle Jug, Ovoid, Dimpled Ground, Acanthus Leaves, England, c.1790, 8 7/8 In.	575.00
Teapot, Green & Black Stripes, Miniature, 3 3/4 In.	27.00

PEKING GLASS is a Chinese cameo glass first made popular in the eighteenth century. The Chinese have continued to make this layered glass in the old manner, and many new pieces are now available that could confuse the average buyer.

Bowl, Foliate Shape, Ribbed Body, 11 In.	345.00
Snuff Bottle, Painted Peony In Vase, Sailing Ship, Green Over White, 3 In.	345.00
Vase, Carved Pink Floral Design, Milk Glass, 3 1/2 In.	150.00
Vase, Cover, Blue Design, White Ground, 19th Century	920.00
Vase, Dragonfly, Water Lilies, Teal To White, 8 In.	225.00
Vase, Opaque Apple Green, High Shoulders, 8 1/4 In.	172.00
Vase, Taotie Masks, Upright Leaf Design, 9 In., Pair	4312.00

PELOTON glass is a European glass with small threads of colored glass rolled onto the surface of clear or colored glass. It is sometimes called spaghetti, or shredded coconut, glass. Most pieces found today were made in the nineteenth century.

Biscuit Jar, Pink Ribbed, White Interior, Multicolored Strands, 7 3/4 In.	1170.00
Bowl, 4 Pulled-Up Points, Coconut Strings, 6 Shell Feet, 3 3/4 x 3 1/2 In.	330.00
Jar, Sweetmeat, Coconut Strings, Silver Plated Fittings, 6 1/2 In.	660.00
Pitcher, Butterfly In Shades Of Blues & Greens, Enameled, 8 In.	995.00
Plate, Pink, 9 1/4 x 6 1/2 In.	125.00
Vase, Multicolored Threading, Ruffled Rim, Clear Glass Pulled Up & Down, Pair	370.00
Vase, Pink, Bulbous, 5 3/4 In.	155.00

PENS replaced hand-cut quills as writing instruments in 1780 when the first steel pen point was made in England. But it was 100 years before the commercial pen was a common item. The fountain pen was invented in the 1830s but was not made in quantity until the 1880s. All types of old pens are collected.

PEN, Ball-Point, Martin Luther King, King Picture Clip	35.00
Ball-Point, Monkees, Group Photograph, 1967	3.00
Banker, Pearl & Black, Lever, 14K Gold Nib	22.00
Carved Clear Rock Crystal, 18K Gold, Lapis Lazuli, Bic Pen Cartridge	490.00
Chilton, Fountain, c.1935	165.00
Chilton, Woman's, Fountain, Pat. 1926	125.00
Conklin, Blue Speckled	40.00
Cowhide Design, Fountain, Black & White	10.00
Dip, American Pencil Co., Wooden Handle, Red, White & Blue, 13 1/2 In.	60.00
Esterbrook, Bell Telephone	45.00
Eversharp, Skyline, 14K Gold Point, Blue & Gold	85.00
Eversharp, Skyline, Fountain, Black	40.00
Eversharp, Skyline, Fountain, Dark Green, 14K Gold Filled Cap & Nib	39.00
Grieshaber, Gold Banded, Orange	70.00
Grieshaber, No. 8, Black & Gold Pattern, 1930s	403.00
Kraker, Filigree Design, Gold Filled	630.00

Majestic, Red Pearl, Lever, 14K Gold Nib	18.00
Moore, Fountain, Black Bakelite, Gold Clip, 5 1/4 In.	15.00
Morrison, Gold Filled Overlay	65.00
Papermate, Tootsie Roll	435.00
Parker, Big Red	125.00
Parker, Duofold, Woman's	50.00
Parker, Fountain, 1930s	20.00
Parker, Lady Duofold, Fountain, c.1930	85.00
Parker, Lucky Curve, Sept. 5, 1916	125.00
Parker, V-S, Lustraloy Cap, Gray, 14K Gold Nib	128.00
Parker, Vacumatic Jr., Gray Marbleized	50.00
Parker, Vacumatic, Fountain, Brown	50.00
Parker 25, Aqua, Gold Filled Cap, 14K Gold Nib, England	33.00
Parker 45, 2-Tone Lustraloy Cap & Barrel	40.00
Parker 45, Lustraloy Cap, Black	35.00
Parker 51, Aero Metric, Case	50.00 to 60.00
Parker 51, Fountain, Maroon, Gold Filled Cap	49.00
Parker 51, Lustraloy Cap, Maroon	40.00
Parker Duofold, Lucky Curve, Woman's, Orange	60.00
Parker Duofold, Silver & Black Stripes	75.00
Parker Duofold Sr., Red	95.00
Peter Pan, 3 In.	25.00
Salz Brothers, Gray Pearl Orange, Lever, 14K Gold Nib	26.00
Secretary, Green Pearl, Gold Trim, 14K Gold Nib	22.00
Sheaffer, Lifetime, Fountain, 14K Gold Trim, c.1925	375.00
Sheaffer, Admiral Snorkel, Green, Gold Filled Trim, 14K Gold Nib	39.00
Sheaffer, Dual Pen, Folding Case, 1930s	15.00
Sheaffer, Lifetime, Balance, Red, Lever, 1935	3795.00
Sheaffer, Lifetime, Flat Top, Black Ends & Nib, 1930s	4830.00
Sheaffer, Lifetime, No. 876, 14K Gold Tip	25.00
Sheaffer, Lifetime, Triumph 2000, 14K Gold Trim, 1940s	65.00
Sheaffer, Pre-Lifetime, No. 8, Line Design, 14K Yellow Gold	6555.00
Sheaffer, Valiant White Dot, Brown, Gold Filled Trim, Triumph 14K Gold Nib	60.00
Sheaffer, Valiant White Dot, Fountain, Royal Blue, Gold Fill Trim, 14K Gold Nib	65.00
Swan, Burgundy	75.00
Wahl, Woman's, Gold Filled, Allover Design, Box, 4 1/4 In.	48.00
Waterman, Fountain, Sterling Overlay, c.1915	725.00
Waterman, Ideal	75.00
Waterman, Inkvue Silver Ray	100.00
Waterman, Woman's, Engraved Vine, Sterling Silver	90.00
Waterman 52, Gold Filled Overlay, 5 In.	220.00
Webster, Green Pearl Black, Gold Trim, 14K Gold Nib	20.00
PEN & PENCIL, Planters Peanuts, Envelope, Woman's, Sterling Silver, Box, 1920s	1035.00
S. Mordan, Inscribed & Cased, 18K Yellow Gold	978.00
Shaeffer, Lifetime, White Dot	150.00
Sheaffer, Penvelope, Woman's, Feather Touch, Double Ended, Black, 1920s	1035.00
Sheaffer, White Dot, Green Chrome, Gold Trim, Case	125.00
Wahl, No. 3, Yellow Gold	633.00

PENCILS were invented, so it is said, in 1565. The eraser was not added to
the pencil until 1858. The automatic pencil was invented in 1863. Collectors
today want advertising pencils or automatic pencils of unusual design. Boxes
and sharpeners for pencils are also collected.

PENCIL, 3 Little Pigs & Big Bad Wolf, Colored, Cardboard Box	35.00
Carpenter's, Cover, Shapleigh	20.00
Duro Lite, Spinner For Dial Telephone	35.00
Gold, 14K, BWU Monogram, 1915, 4 1/2 In.	60.00
Mechanical, AC Spark Plugs	12.00
Mechanical, Floating Mobil Oil Can	36.00
Reddi Kilowatt, 4 Piece	10.00
Sheaffer Lifetime, Gold Filled, Green Marbleized	20.00
St. Clair Lumber Co., Kansas City	18.00
Sterling Silver, Embossed Race Horse, Woman & Playing Cards, 1900, 3 In.	66.00

PENCIL SHARPENER, Airplane, Bakelite 35.00
  Baker's Chocolate Girl 36.00
  Boxer, Occupied Japan 85.00
  Bozo The Clown, Wall Mount.. 99.00
  Climax, No. 3, Pat. 1921 .... 88.00
  Clock, Germany 20.00
  Cowboy 45.00
  Dexter, Bronze, Mail Receiver, Pat. 1907.. 65.00
  Dick, In Row Boat, Figural, Hard Plastic 65.00
  Figural, Dinosaur, Metal.. 22.00
  French Phone 22.00
  G Man Gun, Bakelite... 45.00
  Gun 42.00
  Satellite, 1958.. 25.00
  Snoopy, Box, 1974 .... 30.00
  Traffic Signal, Germany 75.00
  Uncle Sam 38.00

PENNSBURY Pottery worked in Morrisville, Pennsylvania, from 1950 to 1971. Full sets of dinnerware as well as many decorative items were made. Pieces are marked with the name of the factory.

Pennsbury Pottery

  Ashtray, Outen The Light 20.00
  Ashtray, Such Schmootzers 22.00
  Bird, Nuthatch, No. 110 .... 140.00
  Bowl, Pretzel, Eagle, 12 In. 55.00
  Butter, Cover, Rooster 32.00
  Canister Set, Red Rooster, 4 Piece 365.00
  Cruet, Oil & Vinegar, Rooster Stopper, Pair.................................... 125.00
  Feeder, Rabbit, Label 125.00
  Mug, Coffee, Black Rooster 20.00
  Mug, Hex Store Label 20.00
  Pie Plate, Boy & Girl, 9 In. 80.00
  Pitcher, Black Rooster, 4 In.. 22.00
  Pitcher, Hexagonal, 6 In. 50.00
  Pitcher, Red Rooster, 4 In. 30.00
  Pitcher, Rooster, Black, 2 1/2 In... 28.00
  Pitcher, Tulip, Advertising, 4 In.. 22.00
  Plaque, Clipper Lighting, 9 1/2 In. 45.00
  Plaque, Western Atlantic Steam Engine, 1855 .... 40.00
  Plate, Christmas, 1970 .... 20.00
  Plate, Glenview, 1971 .... 26.00
  Plate, Mother's Day, 1974 .... 32.00
  Plate, Treetops, 1966.. 32.00
  Plate, U.S. Steel, 8 In. 22.00
  Snack Set, Rooster 22.00
  Stein, Barbershop... 35.00
  Sugar & Creamer, Rooster ....35.00 to 45.00
  Tile, Farm Scene, Wheeling, Sterling Silver Rim.............................. 45.00
  Vase, Straight Sides, 5 In. 35.00
  Wall Pocket, Woman's Head.. 150.00

PEPSI-COLA, the drink and the name, was invented in 1898 but was not trademarked until 1903. The logo was changed from an elaborate script to the modern block letters on the 1970 Pepsi label. All types of advertising memorabilia are collected, and reproductions are being made.

  Bank, Trolley, Red, White & Blue, Logo On Sides 35.00
  Bottle, Glass, Mini, 6 Pack 75.00
  Bottle, Raleigh, North Carolina 98.00
  Bottle, Warrenton, Va., Red, White & Blue, Pyro Label 20.00
  Bottle Cap, Cork Lined, 1950s 2.00
  Bottle Opener, Brass 55.00
  Bottle Opener, Figural, Bottle, Sheet Iron, Lithographed, 4 In. 49.00
  Calendar, 1950 .... 235.00

Cannister, Glass 5.00
Carrier, 6 Bottles, 1940 .... 295.00
Carrier, Metal, Double Dot 45.00
Carrier, Picnic, Metal 55.00
Chair, Folding, Pepsi Light Refreshment 350.00
Clock, Light Up, Square 65.00
Clock, Light-Up, Double Dot, 1940s 300.00
Dispenser Radio, Countertop, Leather Carrying Handles, 1960, 7 In. ... 350.00
Figure, Santa Claus, Stand Up, Die Cut, Holding Pepsi In Hand, With Pack, 20 In. 120.00
Glass, Bagheera, Jungle Book 49.00
Glass, Bianca, Rescuers, 1977 .... 7.00
Glass, Big Baby Huey, Circus Design, c.1970s, 5 1/4 In. 7.00
Glass, Detroit Grand Prix IV ....2.00 to 3.00
Glass, Diet, 1 Calorie 2.00
Glass, Diet, Everything Yoghurt 22.00
Glass, Elmer Fudd, 1973, 6 1/4 In. 3.00
Glass, Free, Round Base, 6 In. 14.00
Glass, Goblet, Blue 6.00
Glass, Irving Gasoline 45.00
Glass, Kentucky Fried Chicken 20th Anniversary, Red, White 33.00
Glass, Louisville, No. 1 Choice, Football Shape 36.00
Glass, Michigan Sesquicentennial, 1987 .... 10.00
Glass, Mighty Mouse, Brockway, 16 Oz. 539.00
Glass, Mowgli, Jungle Book 38.00
Glass, Pepsi & Krogers 100th Anniversary 3.00
Glass, Pitcher, White Tole Work Design, Chase Kelly 18.00
Glass, Porky Pig, Hardee, 1973, 16 Oz. 4.00
Glass, Posters, Antique, Lace Panel 5.00
Glass, Road Runner, 1973, 6 1/4 In. 3.00
Glass, Sea World, Dinosaur 15.00
Glass, Shere Kahn, Jungle Book 43.00
Glass, Stained, Tulsa & Pepsi 75th Anniversary 5.00
Glass, Support The Home Team, Milwaukee Brewers 13.00
Glass, Taco Time, Cactus, Orange 5.00
Glass, Tweety Bird, 1973, 6 1/4 In. 3.00
Glass, United Oil, Lou Gehrig 10.00
Glass, United Oil, Roberto Clemente 14.00
Glass, United Oil, Ty Cobb 15.00
Glass, Vertical Design, 32 Oz. 3.00
Glass, Wisconsin Badgers, Baseball, 16 Oz. 10.00
Glass, Wisconsin Badgers, Hockey, 16 Oz. 10.00
Glass, Yosemite Sam, 1973, 6 1/4 In. 3.00
Headdress, Indian 18.00
Mug, 1940 Sorcerer Mickey Mouse, White Glass, 1980s, 4 In. 7.00
Mug, Memphis Bottling Co., White Ceramic, Blue Lettering 7.00
Penny, Rescuers, 1977 .... 7.00
Pin, Drink Up Pepsi, 3 In. 7.00
Place Mat, Daffy Duck & Peppy La Pew, Plastic, 1976 .... 18.00
Rack, Bottle, 1950s 125.00
Radio, Cooler, 1955 .... 1000.00
Salt & Pepper, Bottle Shape, Miniature 10.00
Sign, 5 Cents, 1940 .... 600.00
Sign, Bottle Cap, Porcelain, 42 In. 500.00
Sign, Bottle Form, Tin, 30 In. 145.00
Sign, Button, Tin, 1960, 38 In. 775.00
Sign, Button, Tin, 1963, 28 In. 475.00
Sign, Counterspy Radio Show 50.00
Sign, Indian Gasoline, Porcelain 275.00
Sign, Trolley, Pepsi & Pete, Double 1200.00
Straw Jar 22.00
Tap Knob, 1930s 75.00
Thermometer, 27 In. 18.00
Thermometer, Green & White, Glass, 11 x 4 In. 195.00

Thermometer, Light Refreshment, Tin, 1957 .... 185.00
Thermometer, Metal, Bottle Cap Picture, Say Pepsi Please, 28 1/2 In. 75.00
Tip Tray, Girl In Green Hat & Dress, 4 1/4 x 6 In. 715.00
Toy, Semitruck, Mack, Pepsi Bottling Co., 1960 .... 62.00
Tray, Hits The Spot, Musical Notes, 1940s 55.00
Wristwatch, Round 38.00

PERFUME BOTTLES are made of cut glass, pressed glass, art glass, silver, metal, enamel, and even plastic or porcelain. Although the small bottle to hold perfume was first made before the time of ancient Egypt, it is the nineteenth- and twentieth-century examples that interest today's collector. DeVilbiss Company has made atomizers of all types since 1888 but no longer makes the perfume bottle tops so popular with collectors. These were made from 1920 to 1968. The glass bottle may be by any of many manufacturers even if the atomizer is marked *DeVilbiss*. Glass or porcelain examples may be found under the appropriate name such as Lalique, Czechoslovakia, etc.

Amber, Floral Etching, Gold Trim 40.00
Atomic Cloud, Steuben, 9 3/4 In. 4400.00
Birds, Czechoslovakia, Bright Red & Green, Ingrid .... *Illus* 3300.00
Blown Glass, Overlay, Light Blue Cut To Dark Blue, Gilt Trim, 11 In. 440.00
C'Est La Vie, Factice, Store Display 400.00
Chanel No. 5, Cordon Stopper, Contents, Double Box, 2 1/2 In. 29.00
Chevalier Du Garde, Frosted Double Eagle Stopper 215.00
Chloe, Factice, Store Display, Large 450.00
Chloe, Factice, Store Display, Small 275.00
Cologne, Brilliant Amethyst, 12 Sides, 4 1/2 In. 185.00
Cologne, Brilliant Amethyst, Corset Waisted, 4 1/2 In. 688.00
Coty, Ambre Antique, Grecian Maidens, Frosted, 6 In. .... *Illus* 2420.00

Perfume Bottle, Birds, Czechoslovakia, Bright Red & Green, Ingrid

Perfume Bottle, D'Orsay, Divine, Blue Box, 7 In.

Perfume Bottle, DeVilbiss, Peach Shading To Blue, Signed, 7 In.

Perfume Bottle, Coty, Ambre Antique, Grecian Maidens, Frosted, 6 In.

Perfume Bottle, Dancer, Czechoslovakia, Flowers, Turquoise, 5 1/2 In.

Countess Maritza Toilet Water	49.00
Cranberry Glass, Enameled, Laydown	165.00
Cut Glass, Cranberry, Silver Cap Both Ends, 4 1/2 In.	250.00
Cut Glass, Diamond Pattern, Gold Leaf Top, 5 1/2 In.	135.00
Cut Glass, Swirl Pattern, Silver Top, Glass Stopper	160.00
Cut Glass, Whirling Stars & Fans, Bulbous Base, Stopper, 6 In.	110.00
D'Orsay, Divine, Blue Box, 7 In. *Illus*	385.00
Dancer, Czechoslovakia, Flowers, Turquoise, 5 1/2 In. *Illus*	770.00
Dauber, Pink, Cambridge	55.00
DeVilbiss, Atomizer, Opalescent Swirled Glass, Original Green Pump, 4 In.	74.75
DeVilbiss, Hawkes, Gold Encrusted, 10 In.	450.00
DeVilbiss, Peach Shading To Blue, Signed, 7 In. *Illus*	3575.00
Emerald Green, Cylinder, Original Stopper, 1840-1850, 9 1/2 In.	189.00
Emerald Green, Towle Sterling Filigree Stopper & Overlay, 5 In.	185.00
Evening In Paris, Vial Shape, Contents	29.00
Flask, Margaine, Maiden Shape, Paris, 1840	302.00
Fortune Tellers, Gypsy Couple, Porcelain, Jacob Petit, 8 1/2 In., Pair	445.00
Gold Floral, Cranberry Glass, Bubble Stopper, 6 1/2 In.	145.00
Hattie Carnegie, Bust Shape, Gold, 4 In.	575.00
Iridescent Gold, Flame Stopper, Steuben, 8 In.	350.00
Japanesque Silver, Gorham, Pair	2090.00
Kazium, Faceted, Offset Stopper, Spider Lilies, Gold Ground, 2 In.	978.00
L'Air Du Temps, Double Dove, Sealed, 8 Oz.	950.00
Louis D'Or, Famous 6, Box	100.00
Maggie Noir, Factice, Store Display	350.00
Malachite Glass, Intaglio Cut Leaf Design, Floral Stopper	395.00
Malachite Glass, Relief Rose Design	430.00
Milot, Crepe De Chine, 3 Oz.	24.00
Monument, Clear, Amethyst Tint, Applied Collar Mouth, Mid-1880s, 11 3/4 In.	110.00
Monument, Green, Boston & Sandwich Glassworks, c.1860, 8 In.	2970.00
Nailsea Type, Opaque Yellow, Rose & Blue Swirls, 2 3/4 In.	90.00
Obsession, Men's, Factice, Store Display	95.00
Orrefors, Art Deco, 5 1/2 In.	185.00
Orrefors, Art Deco, Cut Glass, 4 1/2 In.	125.00
Oscar, Factice, Store Display, Small	250.00
Oscar, Red, Factice, Store Display	350.00
Passion, Factice, Store Display	500.00
Porcelain, Leather Case, England	325.00
Prince Matchabelli, Gypsy Pattern, Box	135.00
Rafael Replique, Cordon Stopper, Sealed, Box, 1/4 Oz.	35.00
Rocket, Peacock Blue, Steuben, 10 1/4 In.	1485.00
Satin Glass, Pansies, Hinged Cover	85.00
Scent Vial, Blue Frosted Glass, Enameled, Nickle Cap	45.00
Silver Deposit, 3 In.	44.00
Sterling Overlay, Globe Shape Stopper, c.1900, 5 In.	220.00
Sterling Silver, Enameled, 2 In.	100.00
T.J. Holmes, Etched, Footed, Atomizer, Paper Label, Boston, 1923	295.00
Vigny, Golliwog, Black Face & Furry Hair Stopper, Box	175.00

PETERS & REED Pottery Company of Zanesville, Ohio, was founded by John D. Peters and Adam Reed in 1897. Chromal, Landsun, Montene, Pereco, and Persian are some of the art lines that were made. The company, which became Zane Pottery in 1920 and Gonder Pottery in 1941, closed in 1957. Peters & Reed pottery was unmarked.

Cuspidor, Moss Aztec, Dark Red, Raised Rose, Sprayed Green Ground, 4 3/4 In.	44.00
Jardiniere, Stylized Mushroom Design, Red Bisque, 6 3/4 x 7 1/2 In.	605.00
Jug, Sprigged Ware, Monk On Either Side, Globular	150.00
Mug, Grape Pattern	50.00
Tile, Moss Aztec, Classical Figures, Picking From Trees, 8 1/4 x 5 1/4 In.	523.00
Umbrella Stand, Ribbed, Black Ground, Blue, Yellow, Caramel, 23 In.	525.00
Vase, Bud, Brown Landsun Glaze, 5 1/2 In.	60.00
Vase, Bud, Brown, 11 1/2 In.	125.00
Vase, Chromal, Landscape, With Cabin, 7 In.	242.00

Vase, Chromal, Scenic, 13 1/2 In.	500.00
Vase, Flower Medallions, 6 Sides, Pinched, Brown, 4 x 6 In.	46.00
Vase, Flower Swags, Molded, Brown, Shoulder Handles, Bulbous, 5 x 5 1/2 In.	30.00
Vase, Landsun Glaze, 6 In.	55.00
Vase, Moss Aztec, 14 1/2 In.	165.00
Vase, Persian Ware, Striped, 1920s, 5 1/2 In.	95.00
Vase, Shadow Ware, Black Mirror Glaze, Green Drip, 13 1/2 In.	357.00
Vase, Shadow Ware, Dark Glaze Drip Over Light Ground	125.00
Vase, Zane Ware, Blue, Yellow & Brown Landsun Glaze, 9 In.	66.00
Wall Pocket, Matte Green, Fern Design	185.00

PETRUS REGOUT, see Maastricht

PEWABIC POTTERY was founded by Mary Chase Perry Stratton in 1903 in Detroit, Michigan. The company made many types of art pottery, including pieces with matte green glaze and an iridescent crystalline glaze. The company continued working until the death of Mary Stratton in 1961. It was reactivated by Michigan State University in 1968.

Bowl, Chinese Green & Red Interior, Purple & Gray Exterior, 4 1/2 In.	300.00
Bowl, Luster Turquoise Glaze, Black Ground, Signed, 6 1/2 In.	905.00
Box, Cover, Cut Corners, Peacock, Blue-Green, 5 x 3 3/4 x 1 3/4 In.	250.00
Candlestick, Flower Petal Shape, Iridescent Pink To Blue, 1 1/2 In., Pair	110.00
Plate, Red & Yellow Apples Rim, Ivory Crackled Ground, Signed, 9 In.	410.00
Tile, Fish, Burgundy Glaze, Flowing Matte Khaki Crystalline, 2 3/4 In.	165.00
Tile, Stations Of Cross, Blue Sky, Self-Framed, 8 1/4 x 5 3/4 In.	195.00
Vase, Blue, Copper, 4 In.	575.00
Vase, Burgundy Glaze Dripping Over Purple Ground, Signed, 4 1/2 In.	465.00
Vase, Flared Rim, Feathered Persian Blue, Glossy Glaze, 5 1/2 In.	330.00
Vase, Flower Frog, Purple & Red Iridescent Glaze, Squatty, Stamped, 2 x 3 In.	110.00
Vase, Iridescent Blue, Turquoise Flambe, Bulbous, Flared, Circular Mark, 5 x 4 In.	660.00
Vase, Iridescent Gold & Blue Flambe, Signed, 3 3/4 In.	450.00
Vase, Maroon & Gunmetal, Bulbous Base, Tapered Shoulder, 4 In.	415.00
Vase, Matte Blue, Angled Shoulder, Impressed Rectangular Mark, 9 In.	715.00
Vase, Matte Yellow & Brown, 7 In.	465.00
Vase, Metallic Glaze Around Flared Rim, Signed, 5 In.	600.00
Vase, Multicolored Drip Glazes, Mary Chase Perry, 4 In.	225.00
Vase, Slanted Shoulder, Gray-Green Glaze, Pink Luster Overglaze, 9 3/4 In.	1870.00
Vase, Swirling Lines, Celadon, Gold & Burgundy Glaze, Incised Mark, 2 1/4 In.	415.00
Vase, Turquoise Over Metallic Copper, 4 In.	575.00

PEWTER is a metal alloy of tin and lead. Some of the pewter made after 1840 has a slightly different composition and is called *Britannia metal*. This later type of pewter was worked by machine; the earlier pieces were made by hand. In the 1920s pewter came back into fashion and pieces were often marked *Genuine Pewter*. Eighteenth-, nineteenth-, and twentieth-century examples are listed here.

Basin, English Export Sheaf Of Wheat Touch, c.1750, 6 1/2 In.	250.00
Basin, Peter Young, Deep, 10 7/8 In.	2300.00
Basin, Robert Bush & Co., England, 7 5/8 In.	150.00
Basin, Thomas Boardman, Early 1800s, 8 In.	125.00
Beaker, Munden & Grove, Hallmarks Of John Carpenter, 1760-1763, 4 1/4 In.	315.00
Beaker, Scotch, Robert Whyte, c.1805, 3 1/2 In.	290.00
Beaker, Timothy Boardman & Co., 1822-1825, 5 1/4 In.	920.00
Beaker, U.S., Handle, c.1825, 2 3/4 In.	60.00
Bottle, Nursing, 18th Century, 6 1/2 In.	430.00
Bottle, Ring Cup, Engraved H.L., Square, 7 3/4 In.	83.00
Bowl, Kayserzinn, Oval, Flowers, Leaves, Handles, 13 In.	165.00
Bowl, Liberty & Co., Rolled Rim, Molded Feet, Conical, 1905, 4 In.	350.00
Bowl, Potter Studio, Low Ring Footed, Applied Wire Rim, 2 1/4 x 4 3/4 In.	55.00
Bowl, S. Ellis, London, 8 In.	95.00
Box, Rebecca Cauman, Hinged Cover, Blue Enameled Plaque, 1 3/4 x 4 5/8 In.	1200.00
Bread Tray, Kayserzinn, No. 322	300.00
Bread Tray, Scroll Handles, 4 Scrolled Feet, 14 1/2 x 5 1//2 x 2 In.	15.00

Bread Tray, Scrolled Rim, Etched, Lattice, Marked... 18.00
Candle Mold, 12 Tubes, Pine Frame, 16 1/2 x 16 In. 660.00
Candlestick, Ball Knobbed Trumpet Base, c.1660.. 3750.00
Candlestick, Fleur-De-Lis & H. E. Mark, Domed Base, 6 1/2 In., Pair 440.00
Candlestick, Rope Trim, Base, Classic Shape, 8 1/2 In. 125.00
Charger, B & Co., R. Bush, Bristol, 14 3/4 In. 335.00
Charger, George Rooke, London, Broad Rim, c.1673, 16 3/8 In. 550.00
Charger, Helmet & Shield, Dragon Crest, Relief Molded, c.1763, 11 x 1 In. 395.00
Charger, John Duncomb, England, 1724-1750, 18 In. 575.00
Charger, John Townsend, London, Plain Rim, c.1748, 15 In. 295.00
Charger, Samuel Danforth, Eagle Touch, 11 In. 660.00
Charger, Samuel Duncomb, England, Engraved Rim, 1740-1780, 16 1/2 In. 230.00
Charger, Samuel Ellis, London, 13 1/2 In.. 110.00
Charger, Samuel Hamlin, 15 In. 920.00
Charger, T. Cloudsly, England, 16 3/4 In.. 220.00
Charger, Thomas D. Boardman, Eagle Touch, 13 In.. 605.00
Charger, Thomas Swanson, London, 1753-1789, 15 In. 316.00
Coffee Set, Joh Prip, Tray, Black Cane Wrap Handle, 4 Piece..................................... 475.00
Coffeepot, Boardman & Co., New York, Double Bellied, Marked Thomas, 12 1/2 In.... 632.00
Coffeepot, Boardman & Hart, 11 In. 305.00
Coffeepot, Dixon & Son, Wooden Finial, Melon Rib Design, 11 1/2 In. 140.00
Coffeepot, H. Homan, Cincinnati, Ohio, Floral Finial, 11 In. 220.00
Coffeepot, Oliver Trask, Lighthouse, c.1825 .... 460.00 to 475.00
Coffeepot, Rufus Dunham, Domed Cover, Scrolled Handle, c.1860 .... 200.00
Coffeepot, Sellew & Co., Hinged Cover, 10 1/2 In. 250.00
Coffeepot, W.S., Open Winged Bird On Grape Leaves Finial, 11 1/2 In. 295.00
Coffeepot, William Calder, Lighthouse... 275.00
Creamer, Edward Quick, London, 3-Footed, 1735-1760, 3 1/2 In. 1840.00
Cup, Birch & Villers, England, Double Handle, c.1800 .... 110.00
Cup, C. Bently, London, Footed, c.1840.. 40.00
Cup, Traveling, Collapsible, Leather Case, 2 1/2 x 3 In. 49.00
Dish, Freeform Leaf Shell, 3 Ball Feet, 8 1/2 x 5 In. 10.00
Dish, Reeded Wavy Rim, Dated 1774, 16 1/2 In. 185.00
Dish, Scrolled Rim, 4-Lobed, Center Ball Knob, Square, 9 1/2 In................................. 12.00
Ewer, Art Nouveau, Snakes & Women's Heads, 10 1/2 In. 206.00
Figurine, Emile Loiseau, Horse, Standing, Hound, Holding Horse's Reins, 9 1/2 In. 690.00
Flagon, Boardman & Hart 3500.00
Flagon, Communion, 12 3/8 In.. 935.00
Flagon, France, 18th Century Touch, 9 1/2 In. 143.00
Flagon, Oliver Trask.. 950.00
Flask, Rectangular, Triangular Applied Gold Monogram, 128 Oz., 2 1/2 In. 35.00
Foot Warmer, Brass Spout & Plug, Unusual Shape, 8 x 4 1/4 x 2 1/8 In. 180.00
Funnel, England, Egg Shape, Hinging Ring, 6 In.. 195.00
Hat, Wales, Birch & Villers Touch On Rim, 1800, 8 x 12 3/4 In. 413.00
Inkwell, England, Raised Flowers, Glass Insert, 5 x 1 1/2 In....................................... 275.00
Jardiniere, China, Ruffled, Flared, Applied Foliage, 4 1/4 x 6 In. 48.00
Knife Rest, Kayserzinn, Figural, Dog.. 55.00
Lamp, Hand, Bell-Shaped Font, Cast Ear Handle, Single Spout Burner, 3 1/4 In........... 110.00
Lamp, M. Hyde, Hand, Cast Ear Handle, Brass & Pewter Burner, 3 3/8 In.................... 264.00
Lavabo, Walnut Stand, 71 In. 3705.00
Measure, C.M. Mark, England, Hinged Cover, 5 1/4 In. 275.00
Measure, Dry, W.& J. Burrow, Brass Rim, England, 1870s 75.00
Measure, Gaskell & Chambers, 1 Pt. 11.00
Measure, James Yates, Bellied, 5 In. 33.00
Measure, Munster Iron Works, Haystack, Ireland, 1 Qt... 300.00
Measure, Wine, Double Volute, England, c.1760, 5 In... 310.00
Mold, Candle, 12 Tubes, Pine Frame, 18 x 12 3/4 In. 715.00
Mold, Candle, 18 Tubes, Pine Cast, Hand Cut Nails, 1800... 1650.00
Mold, Candle, 24 Tubes, Pine Frame, Worn Finish, 7 x 18 3/4 x 14 In. 825.00
Mold, Ice Cream, Heart, Cupid, 4 In. 55.00
Mold, Ice Cream, Log, Hinged, 10 In. 40.00
Mold, Ice Cream, Rabbit, Pair 44.00
Mold, Ice Cream, Turkey.. 70.00

◆◆◆◆◆◆◆◆◆◆◆◆◆◆◆◆◆◆◆◆◆◆◆◆◆

Rub cabbage leaves on pewter to clean it.

◆◆◆◆◆◆◆◆◆◆◆◆◆◆◆◆◆◆◆◆◆◆◆◆◆

◆◆◆◆◆◆◆◆◆◆◆◆◆◆◆◆◆◆◆◆◆◆◆◆◆

Cheesecloth is a good polishing cloth.

◆◆◆◆◆◆◆◆◆◆◆◆◆◆◆◆◆◆◆◆◆◆◆◆◆

Pewter, Tankard, Double Scroll Handle, 7 3/4 In.

Mug, Danforth, Connecticut, Late 18th Century, 1 Qt.	750.00
Mug, Scroll Handle, Bud Terminal, Philadelphia, 1760-1790, 4 3/8 In.	515.00
Pitcher, Derby Sp. Co., Scrolled Rim, 8 1/2 In.	28.00
Pitcher, Epca Co., Floral Scrolled, Ice Cover, Gadroon Border, 9 In.	32.00
Pitcher, James Yates, Handle, c.1840, 1 Qt.	92.00
Pitcher, Kayserzinn, Laughing Man, Beard Under Spout, 1902	195.00
Pitcher, Kayserzinn, Satyr & Iris, No. 4061, 1900	450.00
Pitcher, R. Dunham, 7 In.	330.00
Plate, Blakslee Barnes, c.1812, 7 7/8 In.	250.00
Plate, Jonas Durand, 1 Side, c.1720, 9 In.	330.00
Plate, Joseph Danforth, 18th Century, 8 In.	200.00
Plate, Marie Antoinette, c.1850, 9 In.	160.00
Plate, Thomas Danforth Boardman, Lion Touch, 9 In.	385.00
Plate, Thomas Danforth II, 1775-1782	575.00
Plate, Thomas Danforth III, 8 5/8 In.	475.00
Plate, William Greenbanck, Reeded, 17th Century, Pair	925.00
Porringer, Boardman, Old English Handle, J.C.T. Mark, 3 1/4 In.	690.00
Porringer, Gero, Cover, Ball Finial, Fan Handle, 6 In.	45.00
Porringer, Gershom Jones, Lion On Flowered Handle, Marked, 1774-1809, 5 1/2 In....	1092.00
Porringer, Rhode Island, Floral Handle, c.1800, 5 1/2 In.	395.00
Porringer, S.C., Crown Handle, c.1820, 5 In.	530.00
Porringer, S.G., Boston, Cast Crown Handle, 4 1/4 In.	275.00
Porringer, William Billings, Providence, R. I., 1791-1806, 3 1/4 In.	275.00
Pot, Tall, R. Gleason, Eagle Touch, 11 In.	248.00
Pot, Tavern, Thomas & Townsend, Compton, London, c.1801, 1 Qt.	425.00
Salt, William Will, Pyriform Bowl, Gadrooned Molding Foot, 2 3/8 In.	2185.00
Sauce Boat, Henry Joseph, London, 1736-1780, 18th Century, 4 x 7 In.	920.00
Silent Butler, Hank & Debler, Lucite Handle, 5 5/8 In.	35.00
Sugar, Cover, Boardman, 2 Handles	900.00
Sugar, Cover, James Dixon & Sons, 6 1/2 In.	65.00
Sugar & Creamer, Cover, Dixon & Son, Sheffield, c.1823	275.00
Sugar Castor, England, 1780, 7 3/4 In.	285.00
Sundial, Windowsill, Heavy Patina, c.1750, 4 1/2 In.	395.00
Tankard, Domed Cover, Double C Handle, Open-Chair Thumbpiece	750.00
Tankard, Domed Cover, Robert Bush, Sr., Bristol, c.1770	495.00
Tankard, Domed Cover, William Eddon, England, c.1720, 1 Qt.	1495.00
Tankard, Double Scroll Handle, 7 3/4 In. *Illus*	1380.00
Tankard, England, Double Scroll Handle, 18th Century, 7 3/4 In.	1800.00
Tankard, Glass Bottom, 1750-1825, 1 Pt.	90.00
Tankard, Hinged Cover, England, Old Country Rose Pewter	48.00
Tankard, John Donne, London, 2 Banded, 1 Pt.	8000.00
Tankard, Peter Yates, Ear Handle, 1/2 Pt.	120.00
Tankard, Peter Yates, Handle, 1 Pt.	140.00
Tankard, Reed & Barton, Britannia, 1st Prize, c.1911	110.00
Tea Set, Child's, Service For 4	150.00
Teapot, A. Griswold, No. 154, Eagle Touch, 7 In.	275.00
Teapot, Ashbil Griswold, 6 5/8 In.	55.00

Teapot, Boardman & Hart, New York & Hartford, c.1827, 1 Cup, 5 In. 1840.00
Teapot, Cincinnati, Ohio, Fruit Finial, 8 1/2 In. 82.00
Teapot, Domed Hinged Cover, W. Will, Wooden Handle, Late 1700s, 6 1/2 In. 21850.00
Teapot, Gleason, 8 1/2 In. 375.00
Teapot, Hinged Cover, Reed & Barton, Handle, 8 Oz. 15.00
Teapot, Hinged Cover, Rogers Bros., Colonial Flute, Handle 35.00
Teapot, J. Townsend, Pear Shape, Wooden Handle, London, England, 1748-1801, 7 In. 2875.00
Teapot, James Allan, Sheffield... 125.00
Teapot, Leonard Reed & Barton, 9 1/2 In. 82.00
Teapot, M. Simon, Pear Shape, Beehive Finial, Pat. March 17, 1868 .... 58.00
Teapot, R. Dunham, Lighthouse, 11 In. 355.00
Teapot, Robert Bush Jr., Egg Shape, Bristol, England, 18th Century, 7 1/4 In. 489.00
Teapot, Samuel Ellis, Pear Shape, 3-Footed, Wooden Handle, c.1750, 6 3/4 In. 4600.00
Teapot, Smith & Feltman, c.1848 .... 100.00
Teapot, W.W. Allis, 6 3/8 In. 10.00
Tray, Silberzinn, Flowers, Butterfly, Oval, 11 3/4 x 8 1/4 In................................... 68.00
Tureen, Soup, Cover, Underplate, 14 In. 248.00
Tureen, Soup, Dautzenburg, Lobster Finial, Ladle, 10 In. 120.00
Urn, Chestnut, Lion's Head Pull Handles, 12 1/2 In., Pair....................................... 275.00
Vase, Kayserzinn, Art Nouveau, 3 Slender Base Handles, 4 3/4 In. 80.00
Vase, Liberty Tudric, 8 In. 110.00

PHOENIX BIRD, or Flying Phoenix, is the name given to a blue-and-white
kitchenware popular between 1900 and World War II. A variant is known as
Flying Turkey. Most of this dinnerware was made in Japan for sale in the
dime stores in America. It is still being made.

Bowl, Japan, 4 3/4 In. 7.00
Bowl, Oval, Blue M Wreath, Japan, 7 3/4 x 6 In.. 20.00
Console 75.00
Creamer, Japan 12.00
Cup & Saucer 12.00
Cup & Saucer, Demitasse ....16.00 to 20.00
Cup & Saucer, Japan 9.00
Eggcup 13.00
Plate, Blue M Wreath, Japan, 6 In... 5.00
Plate, Blue M Wreath, Japan, 8 1/2 In... 22.00
Salt & Pepper 18.00
Salt & Pepper, Self Tops, 3 In. 17.00
Sugar & Creamer 25.00
Teapot, Demitasse... 55.00
Trivet, China... 75.00

PHOENIX GLASS Company was founded in 1880 in Pennsylvania. The firm
made commercial products, such as lampshades, bottles, and glassware. Col-
lectors today are interested in the "Sculptured Artware" made by the company from the 1930s until the mid-1950s. Some pieces of Phoenix glass are
very similar to those made by the Consolidated Lamp and Glass Company.
Phoenix made Reuben Blue, lavender, and yellow pieces. These colors were
not used by Consolidated. In 1970 Phoenix became a division of Anchor
Hocking, then was sold to the Newell Group in 1987. The company is still
working.

Banana Boat, Lovebirds 125.00
Bowl, Console, Hummingbird, Yellow Frost 150.00
Bowl, Tiger Lily, Yellow, 11 1/2 In. 125.00
Candlestick, Tropical Fish, Yellow Wash, Pair 575.00
Candy Box, Cover, Phlox, Blue & White, Gold On Handle....................................... 150.00
Candy Dish, Cover, Phlox, Blue Flowers, Leaves, White Ground, 6 3/4 In.................... 155.00
Cigarette Box, Lid, Phlox, Light Periwinkle Blue Cameo, 4 1/2 In. 135.00
Lamp, Chrysanthemums, Brown & Custard, 9 In. 100.00
Lamp, Foxglove, Yellow, Green & White, 10 1/2 In. 85.00
Lamp, Lovebirds, Pearl White, 10 1/2 In.. 100.00
Lamp, Pinecone, White Frosted, 6 1/2 In. 110.00

Lamp, Red, Brown, Green & Custard	125.00
Lamp, Reverse Painted, Country Cottage By Pond, Metal Base, 23 In.	1100.00
Lamp, Reverse Painted, Landscape, Wooden Bridge, Metal Base, 23 In.	990.00
Plate, Bird Of Paradise, White, 12 In.	50.00
Plate, Bird Of Paradise, Green, 12 In.	75.00
Plate, Bittersweet, Red, Brown, Green & White, 9 1/2 In.	125.00
Plate, Bluebell, Brown & White, 7 In.	85.00
Plate, Burgundy & Pearlized White, 6 In.	100.00
Plate, Chrysanthemums, Yellow, Green & White, 6 1/4 In.	75.00
Plate, Dancing Nymph, Frosted, 8 In.	70.00
Plate, Dragonfly & Cattails, White Frosted, 6 In.	75.00
Plate, Fern, Green & White, 6 In.	95.00
Plate, Starflower, Yellow & White, 7 In.	95.00
Platter, Jonquil, White Stain On Satin Crystal, 14-In. Diam.	300.00
Vase, Bluebells, Pink Flowers, Green Vines, White Ground, Label, 7 In.	210.00
Vase, Chrysanthemum, Tricolor On Custard	90.00
Vase, Cosmos, Sky Blue Pearl, Sticker	185.00
Vase, Dancing Nudes, Veils, Pan At Center, Cream Ground, 11 In.	525.00
Vase, Dogwood, Red, Brown, Green & White, 10 1/2 In.	150.00
Vase, Fan, Catalonian, Yellow, 7 In.	20.00
Vase, Fan, Katydid, White Frosted, 8 In.	90.00
Vase, Fan, Pink, Bown & Custard, 11 1/2 In.	200.00
Vase, Fern, Green, 7 In.	50.00
Vase, Figural, Tan & Milk, 6 In.	95.00
Vase, Freesia, Yellow, Tan Wash, 8 1/4 In.	170.00
Vase, Hummingbird, Brown & White, 5 1/2 In.	60.00
Vase, Katydid, Ovoid, Purple Wash, 8 1/2 In.	180.00
Vase, Le Fleur, Green Frosted, 10 1/2 In.	170.00
Vase, Madonna, Light Blue On Milk Glass.	130.00
Vase, Philodendron, Light Blue, Pearlized, 11 1/2 In.	145.00
Vase, Porcelain Medallion, Star Flower, Brass Trim, Handles, 14 In.	395.00
Vase, Ruba Rombic, Smoky Topaz, 6 1/2 In.	700.00
Vase, Seagull, Aqua Ground, White Gulls, 11 In.	200.00
Vase, Wild Geese, 9 1/4 In.	275.00
Vase, Wild Geese, Blues On Satin, 10 In.	140.00
Vase, Wild Rose, Aqua Wash, Silver Label, 10 1/2 In.	190.00
Vase, Wild Rose, Brown Shadow, 10 1/2 In.	95.00
Vase, Zodiac, White Figures, Peach, 10 1/2 In.	875.00

PHONOGRAPHS, invented by Thomas Edison in the 1880s, have been made by many firms. This category also includes other items associated with the phonograph. Jukeboxes and records are listed in their own categories.

Bing Pigmy	495.00
Brunswick, AM/FM, Console, Gold Inlaid	150.00
Brunswick, Mahogany, Crank Type, Floor Style	38.00
Cheney, Mahogany, Floor Style	66.00
Columbia, Bf Cylinder, Original Aluminum Horn	650.00
Columbia, Mahogany, Crank Type, Table Model	100.00 to 132.00
Columbia, Oak, Table Model	132.00
Edison, 8-Panel Wooden Horn, 1900	815.00
Edison, Amberola	300.00
Edison, Amberola, Model 30	345.00
Edison, Amberola, Model 30, 100 Cylinders, Box	675.00
Edison, Amberola, Model A, Mahogany, Floor Model	1800.00
Edison, Diamond Disc, 1927	800.00
Edison, Gramophone, Standard, Oak Case	515.00
Edison, Home, Oak, Cylinder	302.00
Edison, Horn, 17 In. Bell	200.00
Edison, Model 46904, Cylinder, Wooden Marquee, 1 Cent, 72 In.	5750.00
Edison, Morning Glory Horn, Oak Case	450.00
Edison, Oak, Horn Cylinder	412.00
Edison, Opera, Mahogany	5850.00
Edison, Standard, Cygnet Horn	800.00

Edison, Standard, Model B 110.00
Edison, Triumph, Model B .... 200.00 to 550.00
Edison, Triumph, Morning Glory Horn 200.00
Fairy, Lamp Shape, Fringed Shade, Ohio, 1920 .... 1000.00
General Electric, Model S-22 .... 145.00
Gramophone, Berliner, Disc, 1898.. 4300.00
Lambert, White, Celluloid Cylinder, Signed & Dated On Grooves...................... 2000.00
RCA Victor Special, Portable, John Vassos, Aluminum Case, 17 x 15 x 8 In. 2750.00
Standard, Model A, Blue Horn 850.00
Talk-O-Phone, Parrot Decal 800.00
Thomas Mfg., Portophone, Windup 500.00
U.S. Opera, Cylinder, Brass Horn, Mahogany.. 6500.00
United, Victor VV-VI, Mahogany, Crank Type 60.00
Victor, Copper Horn, c.1915... 600.00
Victor, Gramophone, Table Model, Mahogany Case, Internal Horn, 1920 .... 575.00
Victor, Model II, Petunia-Shaped Horn, Plays 78 RPM Records 1000.00
Victor, Model R, Outside Horn 1375.00
Victor, Model VI, Brass Horn, Interchangeable Mahogany Horn 4700.00
Victor, Model VV-210, Oak, Veneered, Cabriole Legs 110.00
Victor, Model VV-90, Mahogany, Floor Style 165.00
Victor, Model VV-IX, Mahogany, Table Model... 165.00
Victor, Oak Horn, c.1900... 2530.00
Victor, Orthophonic, Spring Wound 550.00
Victor, Painted Brass Horn, Oak Case 2000.00
Victor, School House, Oak Horn, Floor Model, Oak 2700.00
Victor, Type E, Brass Bell Horn 1550.00
Victrola, Cabinet, 3-Slot Vertical Rack 65.00
Victrola, Internal Horn, Wood, Phonola Co., Canada, 1930s................................ 375.00
Victrola, Model 50.. 225.00
Victrola, Spring Wound, 1920-1930 .... 495.00
Zon-O-Phone, Brass Horn, Universal Talking Machine Mfg. Co., Rear Bird 650.00
Zon-O-Phone, Model D, Case, Motor & Turntable... 600.00

PHOTOGRAPHY items are listed here. The first photograph was a view from
a window in France taken in 1826. The commercially successful photograph
started with the daguerreotype introduced in 1839. Today all sorts of photographs and photographic equipment are collected. Albums were popular in
Victorian times. Cartes de visite, popular after 1854, were mounted on 2 1/2-
by-4-inch cardboard. Cabinet cards were introduced in 1866. These were
mounted on 4 1/4-by-6 1/2-inch cards. Stereo views are listed under Stereo
Card. The cases for daguerreotypes are listed in the Gutta-Percha category.

Album, Tintype, Mother-Of-Pearl, Miniature 145.00
Ambrotype, Civil War Soldier, Full Dress Uniform, Case 195.00
Ambrotype, Civil War Soldier, Half Case 215.00
Ambrotype, Cobbler, 6th Plate 445.00
Ambrotype, Confederate Sergeant, Seated In Chair, Isaac Robinson 300.00
Ambrotype, Women, Advertising On Back 20.00
Beaker, Eastman, Glass... 22.00
Cabinet, Black Trumpet Player, Band Uniform, Lancaster, Pa.............................. 50.00
Cabinet, Boy With Toy Rifle, Gilmartin, St. Paul, 1888 .... 15.00
Cabinet, Drumming Musical Family, American Flags, York, Neb. 40.00
Cabinet, Farmers On Tractors, Harvest Time, Braddyville, Iowa, 1890s 25.00
Cabinet, Georgetown, Co., Mining Boomtown, Overview, 1880s 35.00
Cabinet, Hon. William McKinley, Before Being President, Launey, N.Y................ 20.00
Camera, Argus, No. 6, C3, Flash, Case, Directions.. 75.00
Camera, Bolsey, CZZ, 35 mm 39.00
Camera, Bugs Bunny, Instant Load, Green, Figural, Plastic, 5 In., 1976 .... 65.00
Camera, Coronet Midget, Case, Miniature.. 125.00
Camera, Fingerprint, Graflex, Film Holders, Adapter, Wooden Case 200.00
Camera, Fingerprint, Portable, Built-In Lights.. 175.00
Camera, Jiffy Kodak, Twindar Lens 45.00
Camera, Kodak, Brown Bellows, Lowey Design, Gift Box 575.00
Camera, Kodak, Brownie Bull's-Eye, Kodalite Flash Holder, Case........................ 25.00

Camera, Kodak, Medalist II, Supermatic, c.1950, 2 1/4 x 3 1/4 In. 150.00
Camera, Kodak, Model B, Autographic Folding Cartridge, 1920s 110.00
Camera, Kodak, No. 6-16, Chrome Design, Brown Enameled 85.00
Camera, Kodak, Rainbow Hawkeye, 2A, Model B, Instructions, Box 85.00
Camera, Kodak, Retina Reflex IIA 90.00
Camera, Kodak, Retina Reflex III 110.00
Camera, Kodak, W.D. Teague, Geometric Design, c.1930, Box 1090.00
Camera, Kunik, Petite, Vanity, 16 mm, Compact, Lipstick & Film Holder, Case 770.00
Camera, Leica, M2, Black, c.1950 .... 440.00
Camera, Minolta, 16 mm, Box 125.00
Camera, Minox B, Case, Chain 75.00
Camera, Minute, No. 16, Miniature 15.00
Camera, Motion Picture, Williamson, Mahogany, Hand Crank, c.1909 .... 1100.00
Camera, Norton, Bakelite, Miniature 45.00
Camera, Russia, Marked NKVD, Lens Cap, Case 225.00
Camera, Stereo, Wirgin 140.00
Camera, Univex, Model A, Box 25.00
Camera, Vario, Folding, Germany 50.00
Carte De Visite, Children Of The Regiment 85.00
Carte De Visite, Civil War, Hospital Scene 357.00
Carte De Visite, Death Of Lincoln 75.00
Carte De Visite, George Washington 60.00
Carte De Visite, Katrina-Karl Wohmans, Hermaphrodite, c.1875 .... 330.00
Carte De Visite, Le Pape Pie IX, Full Regalia, Paris 20.00
Carte De Visite, Man With 1 Leg Holding Crutches 45.00
Carte De Visite, Mulatto Girl, Case 55.00
Carte De Visite, New School At Avondale, Ohio, Large Brick Building, c.1870 .... 35.00
Carte De Visite, Palace Railroad, Young Girl 17.00
Carte De Visite, Stanton's Store, Wells Fargo Office, Roseburg, Ore., c.1865, Large ... 110.00
Carte De Visite, Street Scenes, Minneapolis, c.1875 .... 50.00
Carte De Visite, Young Man, Writing With Quill Pen, 1870s 20.00
Daguerreotype, James Monroe Ruggles, Ill. Militia Uniform, 1850s 1100.00
Daguerreotype, Man With Sailing Scene In Background, 3 1/2 x 2 1/2 In. 63.00
Daguerreotype, Melissa Payne, Maine, Gutta-Percha Frame, 1 1/2 In. 55.00
Daguerreotype, Stag & Cupid, 1/4 Plate 339.00
Daguerreotype, Young Husband & Wife 75.00
Film, Baseball Form, Pathex, 1920s 50.00
Film, Bashful, Harold Lloyd, Pathex, 2 Reels 100.00
Film, Bullfight, Will Rogers, Pathex 50.00
Lamp, Darkroom, Kodak 30.00
Photograph, Abraham Lincoln, Brady 450.00
Photograph, Abraham Lincoln, Half-Length Portrait, George B. Ayres, 9 x 6 In. 403.00
Photograph, Birch Road, Fred Thompson, 7 7/8 x 14 3/8 In. 65.00
Photograph, Civil War Soldier, Blue Coat, Colored, Frame, 16 x 20 In. 302.00
Photograph, Faneuil Hall Market, Parade, Black Photographer, c.1876, 20 In. 85.00
Photograph, Railroad & Wagon Troop Movement, World War I, 1918 .... 15.00
Photograph, Robert E. Lee, Brady 400.00
Photograph, Steamship, Robert E. Lee, Wooden Frame, 9 3/4 x 13 3/4 In. 440.00
Photograph, Ulysses S. Grant, Brady 150.00
Photograph, Young Lizzie Borden, c.1890, 3 1/2 x 4 1/2 In. 20.00
Projector, Bell & Howell, 16 mm, c.1926 .... 35.00
Projector, Magic Lantern, 3 Circular Slides, Box 100.00
Projector, Magic Lantern, 11 Hand Painted Slides, Germany, Box 350.00
Projector, Magic Lantern, 22 Slides, Colored, Wooden Case, Lithograph, 6 x 6 In. 265.00
Projector, Magic Lantern, Brass, Tin, Round, Wooden Base, c.1870 .... 125.00
Projector, Magic Lantern, Perfek & J. S. , Tin, Gilt Trim, Wooden Box, 11 Slides 82.00
Projector, Magic Lantern, Wooden Base, Brass & Tin, c.1870 .... 125.00
Projector, Movie, Edison, Crank, 1903 .... 600.00
Projector, Radiopticon, Postcard 50.00
Tintype, 116th Ohio Regiment, Civil War 250.00
Tintype, 3 Young Armed Men, 2 With Revolvers, All Wearing City Clothes 125.00
Tintype, Civil War Union Soldier, Armed, 1/6 Plate 303.00
Tintype, Civil War Union Soldier, Full Uniform, Rifle 150.00

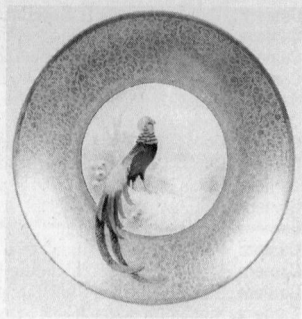

Pickard, Pitcher, Lemonade,
Purple Grapes, A. Coufall, 6 In.

Pickard, Platter, Landscape & Bird,
Gilded, Round, 12 In.

Tintype, Confederate Military School Cadet, Will W. Harris, 3 1/2 In.	265.00
Tintype, Cowboy On Horseback, 1/6 Plate	120.00
Tintype, Gentleman Wearing GAR Badge	50.00
Tintype, Girl With Large Dog, Civil War, Case	32.00
Tintype, Gunfight With Pinkertons In Chicago, 1/6 Plate	35.00
Tintype, Mrs. Jefferson Davis, 1 1/4 x 1 3/4 In.	100.00
Tintype, Street Car Conductor & Little Girl, 2 1/4 x 3 1/4 In.	85.00
Tintype, Streetcar Conductor	55.00
Tintype, Union Sergeant, Gutta-Percha Case	350.00
Tray, Developing	30.00

PIANO BABY is a collector's term. About 1880, the well-decorated home had a shawl on the piano. Bisque figures of babies were designed to help hold the shawl in place. They range in size from 6 to 18 inches. Most of the figures were made in Germany. Reproductions are being made. Other piano babies may be listed under manufacturers' names.

Boy, On Stomach, 4 3/4 In.	80.00
Crawling, Heubach, 5 1/2 In.	165.00
On Back, Heubach, 10 In.	250.00
On Back, Playing With Toes, Heubach, 4 In.	150.00
On Stomach, Bisque, Molded Dress & Bonnet, Karl Schneider, 7 In.	170.00
On Stomach, Heubach, 7 In.	350.00
On Stomach, Playing With Toes, Gown & Bonnet, Heubach, 7 In.	375.00
Sitting, Bisque, Molded White Slip & Left Sock, Germany, 4 1/2 In.	95.00
Sitting, Holding Foot, Molded White Dress, Blue Ribbon On Collar, Germany, 6 In.	185.00
Sitting, Ribbon Around Dress, Holding Cup, 14 x 12 x 9 In.	535.00

PICKARD China Company was started in 1898 by Wilder Pickard. Hand-painted designs were used on china purchased from other sources. In the 1930s, the company began to make its own china wares in Chicago, Illinois. The company now makes many types of porcelains, including a successful line of limited edition collector plates.

Berry Set, Hand Painted, Blackberry Design, 9 1/2-In. Bowl, 7 Piece	895.00
Bowl, Desert Garden Scene Border, Gold Center, 2 Handles, 8 1/2 In.	155.00
Bowl, Etched Gold, Ring Handle, 6 In.	20.00
Bowl, Fruit, Green Leaves & Fruits Exterior & Interior, Signed, 10 1/2 In.	350.00
Bowl, Fruit, Leaves & Melons, Inside & Outside Design, Gold Border, 10 x 8 In.	395.00
Bowl, Lemons, Cherries, Gold, 13 x 3 In.	495.00
Bowl, Scalloped, Handle, Iridescent, Pastels, Poppies, Buds, c.1900, 8 1/4 In.	255.00
Bowl, Schooner, 10 1/4 In.	495.00
Cake Plate, Open Handle, 11 1/2 In.	395.00
Charger, Red Poppies, Gold Border, 12 1/2 In.	225.00

Pickard, Vase, Deserted Garden, Gilding, Ring Handles, Yeschek, 12 In.

Pickard, Vase, Floral Panel, Allover Gilding, E. Challinor, 9 In.

Coffeepot, Creamer & Sugar, Peacock Medallions, Green, Gold Over Design	310.00
Compote, Floral, Handle, c.1905, 6 1/2 In.	65.00
Compote, Violet & Pink Floral, Fisher, c.1905, 10 1/2 In.	345.00
Cup & Saucer, Floral, Gold	35.00
Cup & Saucer, Flowers, Gold, Jumbo	45.00
Ginger Jar, Cover, Horizontal Bands, Floral Band, Mottled, c.1915, 8 5/8 x 6 In.	75.00
Mustard, Florals, Gold, c.1912	32.00
Pitcher, Cider, Band Of Roses, Gold Etched, Signed, F. Vober, 1922, 5 1/2 In.	350.00
Pitcher, Lemonade, Lemons With Blossoms, Leaves, Artist Schoner, 6 1/2 In.	725.00
Pitcher, Lemonade, Purple Grapes, A. Coufall, 6 In. .... *Illus*	300.00
Pitcher, Lemonade, Red Currents, Gilded, Artist Reaury, 6 3/4 In.	250.00
Plate, Clover Center, Abstract Designs, Allover Gold, Shield Mark, 10 3/4 In.	65.00
Plate, Dutch Girls, Windmills & Tulips, Matte Finish, Signed Rawlins, 8 1/2 In.	175.00
Plate, Flower Basket, Gold, 11 In.	95.00
Plate, Gold Plaid & Lions, Signed, c.1912, 9 In.	95.00
Plate, Iris, Signed Locke	95.00
Plate, Landscape Scene, Matte Finish, Signed, 7 In.	250.00
Plate, Lilies, Marked, 8 1/2 In.	138.00
Plate, Maple Leaf, Poinsettias, Nessy, 8 3/4 In.	145.00
Plate, Orchids, Signed, 8 1/2 In.	138.00
Plate, Peaches, c.1898, 8 1/2 In.	125.00
Plate, Pink Daffodils, Florence James, 8 1/2 In.	125.00
Plate, Poppies, Florence James, 9 In.	138.00
Plate, Wildwood, Signed, 8 1/4 In.	155.00
Plate, Yosemite Scene, Signed, c.1905, 8 1/2 In.	175.00
Platter, Challinor, 16 In.	575.00
Platter, Landscape & Bird, Gilded, Round, 12 In. .... *Illus*	450.00
Salt & Pepper, Gold, Signed King, 6 In.	95.00
Service For 10, Brocade Pattern	950.00
Sign, Advertising, Triangular, Gold Lion With Shield, Free Standing, 5 In.	95.00
Sugar & Creamer, Pilgrims & Sailing Ship Mayflower, c.1912	225.00
Sugar & Creamer, Scenic, Heavy Gold Trim	295.00
Sugar & Creamer, Violets	250.00
Tankard, Purple & Pink Iris, Gold Trim, Fuchs, 11 In.	695.00
Tea Set, Dutch Design, 3 Piece	475.00
Tea Set, Teapot, Sugar, Cover, 8-Sided Bowl, Tray, Gold Leaf Mark, 1895, 4 Piece	285.00
Tile, Tea, Turquoise & Gold, Band At Rim, Mark, 1910	135.00
Tray, Dresser, Italian Garden, Handles, Gasper, 16 1/2 x 10 1/4 In.	300.00
Vase, Carnation Pattern, Signed, 1908, 14 In.	950.00

Vase, Deserted Garden, Gilding, Ring Handles, Yeschek, 12 In. ....*Illus* 1350.00
Vase, Floral Panel, Allover Gilding, E. Challinor, 9 In. ....*Illus* 280.00
Vase, Portrait, 9 1/4 In. 795.00

PICTURES, silhouettes, and other small decorative objects framed to hang on
the wall are listed here. Some other types of pictures are listed in the Print and
Painting categories.

Calligraphy, Sailing Yacht, Lake Monnitonka, Small 150.00
Charcoal & Pencil, A Venture In Beans, George Wright, 9 3/4 x 24 In. 35.00
Charcoal & Watercolor On Paper, Profile, Woman, Bonnet, Frame, Round, 6 In. 330.00
Cutwork, Valentine, Birds & Tulips, Round, Pa., 1833 .... 620.00
Diorama, Maritime, Ships Scene, Lighted, Shadowbox 600.00
Embroidered, Silk, Basket Of Flowers, Frame, Roxa Downs, Age10 Years 250.00
Embroidered, Silk, Eagle, Blossoms, Gold Ground, Framed, China, 62 x 85 In. 1035.00
Embroidered, Silk, Floral, Grapes, Blessed Are The Pure, Framed, 17 1/4 x 17 1/2 In. . 517.00
Embroidered, Silk, Memorial, J. G. Hillhouse, Died Oct. 9, 1806, Frame, 16 x 20 In. 460.00
Embroidered, Woman & Child, Pink, Green, Yellow & Beige Silk, Frame, Oval, 10 In. 750.00
Hair Wreath, Burgundy Velvet Trim, Large Ornate Gilt Frame.............................. 375.00
Hair Wreath, Frame, Dated 1852, 9 x 10 In. 270.00
Ink On Paper, 2 Horses, Signed G.E.L. Hensel, Frame, 27 x 32 In. 175.00
Ink On Paper, Horse & Snake, Spencerian Type, Frame, 21 x 25 3/4 In. 120.00
Ink On Paper, Mother & Child, Charles Campbell, 12 x 9 In. 50.00
Ink On Paper, Stylized Bird, Blue Ink, Maple Frame, 1860, 4 x 5 In. 401.00
Needlepoint, Biblical Scene, Victorian, Giltwood Frame, 1860, 25 x 32 In. 220.00
Needlepoint, Girl, With Dog, Gilt Frame, 30 x 24 In. 358.00
Needlepoint, Panel, Still Life, Fruit, Game Birds, Wool, Frame, 22 1/4 x 48 In. 220.00
Needlepoint, Ship, White Swallow, Frame, 15 x 21 In. 46.00
Needlepoint, Woman Spinning, Wool & Silk, Green, Blue & Red, Initialed, 15 x 13 In. 44.00
Needlework, British Flags, Lion & Unicorn With Banner, Verse, 15 1/2 x 19 In............. 105.00
Needlework, Columned Building, Birds & Flowers, Mid-19th Century, 21 In. 150.00
Needlework, Family Record, Barnard, By Maria Barnard, Oct. 1824, 22 1/2 In. 500.00
Needlework, King Ahasuerus & Queen Esther, 1640s, 17 5/8 x 21 In. 5175.00
Needlework, Lion, Motto, God Is Love, Wool, Silk, Linen Ground, c.1829, 16 3/4 x 13 In. 1495.00
Needlework, Man & Woman, Playing Cards, Frame, 27 1/2 x 23 In. 1725.00
Needlework, Memorial, John Auley, April 23, 1813, Country Scene, Frame, 23 x 28 In. 1100.00
Needlework, Memorial, Oval Scene, Frame, 26 In. 2750.00
Needlework, Memorial, Silk, Abby Frances Moshes, c.1819, 16 1/2 x 22 In. 2530.00
Needlework, Memorial, Silk, Mourning Figures, 19th Century, 21 x 18 1/2 In. 920.00
Needlework, Orpheus, Playing Lyre, Floral Border, 1570s, 12 x 18 In. 5175.00
Needlework, Panel, Classic Woman, Sheep, Silk, Watercolor, Glass, Frame, 25 x 21 In. 2145.00
Needlework, Romeo & Juliet, Silk, Eglomise, Gold Leaf Frame, c.1870, 18 x 18 In...... 800.00
Needlework, Silk On Silk, Trees, Perched Birds & Butterflies, 15 x 27 3/4 In. 748.00
Needlework, Silk On Silk, Woman, Holding Basket, Garden, 19th Century, 11 x 9 In... 633.00
Needlework, Silk, Moses In The Bull Rushes, 19th Century, 13 x 15 In. 546.00
Pencil On Paper, Landscape, Ruined Abbey, Primitive, Frame, 12 x 17 In. 72.00
Pencil On Paper, Smiling Man, J.C. Beckwith, c.1885, 5 x 4 In. 125.00
Petit Point, 2 Girls, Floral Border, Late 19th Century, Round, Frame, 10 1/2 In. 44.00
Petit Point, Flowers In Vase, Frame, 5 1/8 x 6 1/8 In. 30.00
Petit Point, Landscape, Woman Picking Cherries, Victorian, 17 3/4 x 19 3/8 In. 288.00
Pinprick, Family, Country Scene, France, Frame, 19th Century, 14 1/2 x 10 In. 800.00
Pinprick & Lithograph, River Scene, France, Frame, 19th Century, 4 3/4 x 9 In., Pair.. 900.00
Pinprick & Watercolor, Aged Man With Hourglass, 9 1/2 x 6 1/2 In. 220.00
Pinprick & Watercolor, Elderly Lady, 10 x 8 In. 440.00
Pinprick & Watercolor, Figure With Staff, Boy Along Side, 8 1/2 x 7 1/2 In. 247.00
Pressed Flowers, Oval, Metal Frame... 40.00
Punched Paper, Embroidered, In God We Trust, Pastel, Walnut Frame, Victorian 125.00
Reverse On Glass, Seashore, Cliffs, Rolling Waves, 7 x 15 In. 25.00
Reverse On Glass, The White House, Multicolor, Brass Floral Frame, c.1880, 3 1/2 In. 225.00
Sandpaper, 2 Horses, In Storm, Signed, Frame, 20 x 29 In. 195.00
Sandpaper, Hudson River Scene, c.1880, Frame, 19 1/2 x 21 1/4 In. 245.00
Sandpaper, Hudson River View, Marey E. Folsom, Frame, 19 x 28 In. 690.00
Sandpaper, Landscape, Federal House, Trees, Frame, 13 x 16 In. 187.00
Shell Art, My Brothers, Blue Hill, Maine, Mid-Victorian 495.00

Silhouette, 4 Figures, Palm Trees, Birds, On Fabric, Framed, c.1900, 9 x 13 In. 137.00
Silhouette, Black Paper, Landscape, Wax Highlighted, Frame, 7 x 9 In. 170.00
Silhouette, Child, Standing, Penciled Hair, Brass Frame, 3 3/8 x 2 5/8 In. 460.00
Silhouette, Gentleman Portrait, Gilded Liner, Rosewood Frame, 15 3/4 x 12 In. 220.00
Silhouette, Gentleman With Top Hat, Bronzed, Frame, 11 x 8 In. 172.00
Silhouette, Gentleman, Gilt Trim, Ink, Black Lacquered Frame, 6 x 4 5/8 In. 715.00
Silhouette, Gentleman, Master Hubard, 13 Years, Frame, 5 x 4 1/4 In. 412.00
Silhouette, Gentleman, With A Cane, Frame, 10 1/2 x 6 1/2 In. 115.00
Silhouette, Lady, Seated, Open Window, Lithograph, c.1830, 13 1/2 x 10 In. 495.00
Silhouette, Male Bust, Hollow Cut, Original Frame, c.1860 .... 150.00
Silhouette, Mourning Figures, Bird's-Eye Maple Frame, 4 1/2 x 3 1/2 In. 137.00
Silhouette, Woman & Man, Hollow Cut, Frame, Mid-19th Century, 3 In., Pair 93.00
Silhouette, Woman, Bonner, London, Frame, 5 1/4 x 4 1/2 In. 220.00
Silhouette, Woman, In Chair, August Edouart, Frame, 10 x 8 1/4 In. 220.00
Silhouette, Woman, In Cloak, Bronzed, Watercolor Ground, Frame, 9 1/2 x 7 In. 144.00
Silhouette, Woman, Offering A Fig, Bronzed, Frame, 11 x 7 In. 115.00
Silhouette, Woman, Penciled Detail, Gilded Frame, 4 3/4 x 4 1/8 In. 352.00
Silhouette, Young Woman, Printed Bodice, Gilt Frame, 5 5/8 x 4 3/4 In. 550.00
Tapestry, Silk Chenille, Castle Scene, 1900, Oval, Frame.. 325.00
Theorem, Basket Of Strawberries, Gilt Frame, 11 x 9 In. 1760.00
Theorem, Compote Of Flowers, Mahogany Veneer Frame, 2 3/4 x 22 3/4 In. 935.00
Theorem, Compote Of Fruit, Watercolor On Paper, Frame, 14 1/2 x 11 1/2 In. 805.00
Theorem, Fruit, Floral Wreath Around, Eglomise, Gilt Frame, 20 x 20 In. 495.00
Wax, Woman's Profile, Oval Frame, Georgian, 7 1/2 x 6 1/2 In. 187.00

PIERCE, see Howard Pierce

PILKINGTON Tile and Pottery Company was established in 1892 in England. The company made small pottery wares, like buttons and hatpins, but soon started decorating vases purchased from other potteries. By 1903, the company had discovered an opalescent glaze that became popular on the Lancastrian pottery line. The manufacture of pottery ended in 1937 but decorating continued until 1948.

Vase, Blue Textured Glaze, Impressed Logo, 1913, 5 1/4 In. 220.00
Vase, Medieval Goat Design Mold, Luster, 8 In. 3900.00
Vase, Stylized Feathers, Orange & Yellow Ground, Signed, 13 1/4 In. 990.00
Vase, Textured & Mottled Orange Glaze, Marked, 1913, 5 2/3 In. 275.00

PINCUSHION DOLLS are not really dolls and often were not even pincushions. Some collectors use the term *half-doll*. The top half of each doll was made of porcelain. The edge of the half-doll was made with several small holes for thread, and the doll was stitched to a fabric body with a voluminous skirt. The finished figure was used to cover a hot pot of tea, powder box, pincushion, whisk broom, or lamp. They were made in sizes from less than an inch to over 9 inches high. Most date from the early 1900s to the 1950s. Collectors often find just the porcelain doll without the fabric skirt.

Arms Away, Playing Cards, Colored Plumes In Hair 195.00
Arms Crossed In Front, Painted Gray Hair, Bun & Blue Bow, 4 1/2 In. 70.00
Arms Outstretched, Dressel & Kister, 3 1/2 In. 135.00
Flapper, 6 In. 40.00
Flapper, Arms Away From Body, Painted Eyes & Bobbed Hair, 3 3/4 In. 120.00
Flapper, Clothes Brush, Japan 55.00
Flapper, Holds Powder Puffs & Compact, Blue Cloche, 5 In. 45.00
Molded Hat, Arms Away From Body, Holding Flowers, Lace Dress, 4 In. 95.00
Nude, Arms Away 295.00
Painted Blue Eyes, Legs On Base, Some Original Clothing, Goebel, 6 1/2 In. 120.00
Playing Cards, Arms Away 195.00
Queen Stitched, Square, Signed J.S., 18th Century, 7 In. 4600.00
Strapless Camisole, Goebel... 195.00
Sunflower, 4 In. 25.00
Taffeta Dress, Long Arms, c.1920, 8 1/2 In. 27.00
Tea Cozy, Lace, 14 In. 250.00
Toby Figure, Clothes Brush, Japan 55.00

White Bodice, Blue Ribbon In Hair, Gold Shoes, 2 Piece, Germany 40.00
Wolf, Clothes Brush, Germany 48.00
Woman, Blond, In Bathing Suit... 30.00
Woman, Carved Hands, 4 In... 450.00
Woman, Long Hair, Arms Folded To Neck... 45.00

PIPES have been popular since tobacco was introduced to Europe by Sir
Walter Raleigh. Meerschaum pipes are listed under Meerschaum.

Blown Glass, Opaque White Stem, Bowl, Red Threaded Design, 19th Century, 14 In. ... 345.00
Cigar, Sparkless, Silver Cap, Italian Briar, c.1900, 5 1/4 In. 75.00
Happy Hooligan & Cop, Red Clay, Painted 135.00
Redware, Admiral Dewey's Head, 1890s...95.00 to 135.00

PISGAH FOREST pottery was made in North Carolina beginning in 1926.
The pottery was started by Walter R. Stephen in 1914, and after his death in
1941, the pottery continued in operation. The most famous kinds of Pisgah
Forest ware are the cameo type with designs made of raised glaze and the turquoise crackle glaze wares.

Humidor, Streaked Green Glaze, 4 In. 75.00
Jar, Pink Satin Glaze, 2 Handles, W. Stephen, 1934, 6 x 5 In. 110.00
Lamp Base, Crystalline, 13 1/4 In. 895.00
Pitcher, Forest Green & Pink, 4 In.. 40.00
Pitcher, Streaked Glaze, 6 1/2 In... 95.00
Sugar & Creamer, Pink, 1965.. 25.00
Tea Set, Beige, Pink Interior, 1940, 3 Piece.. 485.00
Tea Set, White Conestoga Wagon, Oxen, Green Ground, Signed, 1953, 3 Piece........... 935.00
Vase, Allover White Crystalline Glaze, Yellow Ground, Signed, 7 In. 660.00
Vase, Blue & Green Crystalline Over Cream, Bulbous, 1948, 6 x 6 In............................ 467.00
Vase, Blue & White Crystalline Over Caramel, 1941, 7 In.. 715.00
Vase, Blue High Crackle Glaze, White Interior, 8 1/2 In.. 55.00
Vase, Brown Crystalline Glaze, Flared, Bulbous, 1936, 6 1/2 x 5 In. 330.00
Vase, Caramel Crystalline Over White High Glaze, 8 In.. 715.00
Vase, Crystalline Glaze, 5 In.. 495.00
Vase, Dog, 2 Deer, Olive Green Ground, Walter Stephen, 1938, 6 In. 500.00
Vase, Grape High Glaze, 1950, 8 In. ....66.00 to 100.00
Vase, Horizontal Ribbed, Blue & Wine, Crackled Pink Interior, 1942, 10 In. 220.00
Vase, Indian Camp, Olive Green Ground, Green High Glaze, 1931, 9 1/2 In. 1320.00
Vase, Light Green, 1926, 4 3/4 In.. 120.00
Vase, Turquoise, 1941, 6 In.. 100.00
Vase, Turquoise, Gray Interior, Bulbous, 1928, 8 In. 150.00

PLANTERS PEANUTS memorabilia is collected. Planters Nut and Chocolate
Company was started in Wilkes-Barre, Pennsylvania, in 1906. The Mr. Peanut figure was adopted as a trademark in 1916. National advertising for Planters Peanuts started in 1918. The company was acquired by Standard Brands,
Inc., in 1961. Standard Brands merged with Nabisco in 1981. Some of the
Mr. Peanut jars and other memorabilia have been reproduced and, of course,
new items are being made.

Bank, Mr. Peanut, Black & Gold, Plastic, 1990 .... 25.00
Bank, Mr. Peanut, Cast Iron, 11 In. 95.00
Bank, Mr. Peanut, Plastic 18.00
Bank, Mr. Peanut, Yellow, Box, 1938 .... 530.00
Bank, Peanut Can, Mr. Peanut, Tin, Slot For Coins 25.00
Book, Coloring, Presidents, 1953 .... 15.00
Book, Painting, With Story, 1935 .... 58.00
Bookmark, Mr. Peanut 17.00
Bowl, Mr. Peanut, Ceramic.. 17.00
Bracelet, Charm, Mr. Peanut, 1940s 30.00
Butter Knife, Mr. Peanut, Red Plastic 18.00
Butter Knife, Mr. Peanut, Yellow 12.00
Car, Racing, Mr. Peanut, Friction, Peanut Shell Shape, Plastic, 5 1/4 In. 110.00
Carafe, Wine, Mr. Peanut 75th Birthday 40.00

Card, Playing, Mr. Peanut, Sealed 8.00
Clock, Alarm, Mr. Peanut, Red, Yellow Face 85.00
Clock, Battery Operated, 13 x 17 In. 55.00
Clock, Mr. Peanut, Lifesaver Logo, Battery Operated, 12 In. 125.00
Clock, Mr. Peanut, Orange, 13 x 17 In. 85.00
Coin-Operated Machine, Dry Roasted, 10 Cents 500.00
Cookie Jar, Box 79.00
Cookie Jar, Mr. Peanut, Ceramic 125.00
Dart Board, Mr. Peanut 45.00
Display, Bowl, Mr. Peanut, Plastic, Yellow, Counter 50.00
Display, Head, Mr. Peanut, Yellow & Blue, Plastic, Counter 40.00
Doll, Mr. Peanut, Bendy, Vinyl, 6 In. .... 10.00 to 12.00
Doll, Mr. Peanut, Cloth, 15 In. 15.00
Doll, Mr. Peanut, Jointed, Wooden .... 185.00 to 240.00
Doll, Mr. Peanut, Stuffed, 1967, 20 In. .... 20.00 to 25.00
Figurine, Mr. Peanut, Bendy, 6 In. 10.00
Figurine, Mr. Peanut, Cloth, Diecut, Iron On, 1950s, 2 1/2 In. 2.00
Figurine, Santa Claus, Germany, 8 In. 75.00
Figurine, Santa Claus, On Reindeer, Germany, 6 In. 225.00
Glass, Cocktail, Mr. Peanut, Green, Plastic 27.00
Glass, Martini, Mr. Peanut, Plastic 30.00
Glass, Mr. Peanut 75th Birthday, Pilsner Beer 30.00
Glass, Mr. Peanut, Black & Tan 20.00
Glass, Mr. Peanut, Canada 20.00
Glass, Mr. Peanut, Yellow 40.00
Jar, 8 Sides, Cover 325.00
Jar, Barrel, Mr. Peanut, Cover 375.00
Jar, Embossed, Peanut Handle Cover, Square 175.00
Jar, Fishbowl, Mr. Peanut, Rectangular Label 175.00
Jar, Knobbed Cover, Red, White & Yellow Label, Round, 1960s 45.00
Jar, Mr. Peanut 75th Birthday, Glass Apothecary 40.00
Jar, Mr. Peanut, Label 175.00
Jar, Mr. Peanut, White Metal Screw On Cover, Canada 110.00
Jar, Peanut Corners, Cover 340.00
Jar, Store, Mr. Peanut, White Tin Cover, Black Letters 110.00
Marbles, 1960 .... 20.00
Marbles, Mr. Peanut, In Plastic Bag, 1960s 18.00
Mechanical Pencil, Mr. Peanut, Black, Gold, 1 3/8 In. 18.00
Mechanical Pencil, Mr. Peanut, Red, Cream 50.00
Mechanical Pencil, Mr. Peanut, Yellow, Blue 18.00
Mug, Mr. Peanut, Glass, Yellow 60.00
Mug, Mr. Peanut, Pewter, 1983 .... 38.00
Mug, Mr. Peanut, Plastic 10.00
Mug, Mr. Peanut, White Ceramic, Yellow & Black Logo, 1960 .... 75.00
Napkin Holder, Mr. Peanut, Ceramic 17.00
Nut Bowl Set, Mr. Peanut, Tin, 5 Piece 18.00
Paper, Gift Wrap, Mr. Peanut, Hallmark 30.00
Paperweight, Paper Insert, Mr. Peanut, Tennis Player, Glass, 1938 .... 75.00
Patch, Iron On, Mr. Peanut, 1950s 2.00
Peanut, Papier-Mache, Large 30.00
Peanut Butter Maker, Box 30.00
Pen & Pencil Set, 14K Gold 100.00
Pen & Pencil Set, Mr. Peanut 75th Birthday, Box 225.00
Pen & Pencil Set, Mr. Peanut, Cross Gold On Clip 150.00
Pencil, Mr. Peanut, 1950s 15.00
Pencil, Mr. Peanut, Mechanical, Blue, Gold 15.00
Pin, Mr. Peanut, 1 1/4 In. 2.00
Plate, Mr. Peanut Center, Metal, Numbered, Wilton Armetale Co., 6 In. 35.00
Poster, Our Hit Parade, Mr. Peanut Leading Parade, 1960s, 28 x 21 In. 50.00
Punchboard, Mr. Peanut, Can .... 95.00 to 125.00
Punchboard, Mr. Peanut, Win Tin Cocktail Peanuts, 2 Cents, 1940s 125.00
Salt & Pepper, Mr. Peanut, Black & Tan .... 12.00 to 20.00
Salt & Pepper, Mr. Peanut, Ceramic .... 50.00 to 95.00

Plastic, Placecard, Animal, 1 In.,
12 Piece, Box (4 shown)

Plastic, Sugar & Creamer, Cover,
Cream Blue, Red Speckled, Kenro, 2 In.

Salt & Pepper, Mr. Peanut, Green	18.00
Salt & Pepper, Yellow	6.00
Sign, Car, 11 x 21 In.	88.00
Sign, Cardboard, Radio Show, Mr. Peanut, 9 3/4 x 14 3/4 In.	18.00
Sign, Mr. Peanut, Carved Wood, Green & Yellow, 2 x 3 Ft.	595.00
Sign, Trolley, Pictures Mr. Peanut	675.00
Spoon, Mr. Peanut, Gold Wash	20.00
Spoon, Nut, Mr. Peanut, Red Plastic	15.00
Spoon, Serving, Mr. Peanut, Gold	25.00
Spoon, Serving, Mr. Peanut, Silver	20.00
Spoon Rest, Mr. Peanut, Ceramic	15.00
Tankard, Beer, Mr. Peanut, 75th Birthday	40.00
Tin, Mr. Peanut, Rare Novola, Yellow & Green, 5 Gal.	225.00
Tool Holder, Mr. Peanut, Ceramic	25.00
Toy, Truck, Mr. Peanut's Express, Plastic, Pyro, 5 In.	45.00
Watch, Mr. Peanut, Red, Yellow & Blue Logo	90.00
Watch, Mr. Peanut, White Face, Yellow & Black	90.00
Watch, Mr. Peanut, Yellow Face, Date Window, Blue Band	125.00

PLASTIC objects of all types are being collected. Some pieces are listed in other categories; gutta-percha cases are listed in photography, celluloid in its own category.

Creamer, Moo-Cow, Cow's Head Top, Yellow		6.00
Placecard, Animal, 1 In., 12 Piece, Box	*Illus*	65.00
Sugar & Creamer, Cover, Cream Blue, Red Speckled, Kenro, 2 In.	*Illus*	35.00

POLITICAL memorabilia of all types, from buttons to banners, is collected. Items related to presidential candidates are the most popular, but collectors also search for material related to state and local offices. Many reproductions have been made. A jugate is a button with photographs of both the presidential and vice presidential candidates. In this list a button is round, usually with a straight pin or metal tab to secure it to a shirt. A pin is brass, often figural, sometimes attatched to a ribbon.

Ashtray, Elephant, Everett Dirksen	15.00
Ashtray, President Kennedy & Mrs. John F. Kennedy Picture, c.1962, 4 x 4 1/2 In.	27.00
Badge, Republican Delegate, National Convention, 1908	125.00
Badge, Win With MacArthur, Hard Plastic, Figural	45.00
Balloon, Wallace For President, Unused, c.1972	8.00
Ballot, Election, Franklin D. Roosevelt, 1936	5.00
Bank, Eisenhower, Figural, Pot Metal	55.00

Bank, Land On Roosevelt, Cast Iron, c.1936, 5 1/2 In.	275.00
Banner, Claremont, N.H., Keene Republicans, Silk, c.1860, 48 In.	1800.00
Banner, Ike & Nixon, Stevenson & Sparkman, Cloth, Pair	1000.00
Banner, U.S. Grant, Schuyler Colfax, 36 Stars	6600.00
Banner, William McKinley, Inauguration, Brass Pin With Profile, c.1897	225.00
Blotter, Hughes For President, 1916	33.00
Booklet, Democratic Convention, Delegates Of Chicago, c.1968	40.00
Booklet, Kennedy For President, Leadership For 60s, Pictures, 11 x 14 1/4 In.	125.00
Booklet, Song, Republican Campaign, c.1912	12.00
Bookmark, Lincoln, Picture, c.1914	12.00
Box, Cigar, Roosevelt On Horse, Rough Rider, Cardboard, England, c.1910	18.00
Box, Cigarette, Bush For President, Full Pack, c.1988	35.00
Box, Cigarette, Dukakis For President, Full Pack, c.1988	35.00
Box, Cigarette, I Like Ike, c.1952	75.00
Bumper Sticker, Goldwater & Miller	6.00
Bumper Sticker, Roosevelt	20.00
Button, A Choice Not An Echo, Goldwater & Miller, Picture	7.00
Button, Adlai Stevenson, Picture, Rubber, 3/4 x 3/4 In.	14.00
Button, Alf Landon Photograph Center, Flower Pots Around	200.00
Button, Anti-Willkie Slogan, Green On Yellow, c.1940, 1 1/4 In.	9.00
Button, Bury Barry, Black & White, 1 1/4 In.	6.00
Button, Campaign, Abraham Lincoln, c.1860	240.00
Button, Carter Is Out Of Gas, Printed On Flag, 1 1/4 In.	5.00
Button, Carter, Full Face, Black & White, 5/8 In.	3.00
Button, Dick & Spiro In 1988, 2 Pictures, 1 In.	6.00
Button, Draft Ted In 1980, Photograph	5.00
Button, Dukakis & Bentsen, Over Draped Flag, 3 In.	2.00
Button, Dukakis & Nunn, 1 1/2 In.	2.00
Button, Dump Humph, Blue & Green, 1 1/4 In.	9.00
Button, Face Of Reagan, Reagan Hood, Feathered Hat, Rob The Poor, 3 In.	17.00
Button, Flasher, Kennedy, Front Facing, 7/8 In.	25.00
Button, Flasher, Ribbon, Welcome Mr. President, Eisenhower, Inauguration, c.1953	15.00
Button, For President, Lyndon B. Johnson, Picture, 3 In.	8.00
Button, Ford & Dole In '76, 2 Pictures, 3 1/2 In.	6.00
Button, Franklin Delano Roosevelt, Photograph, Flag Border, 1 1/4 In.	32.00
Button, Go Forward With Stevenson/Sparkman, Color Lithograph, 1 1/4 In.	58.00
Button, Harry S. Truman For President, Face In Center, 3/4 In.	19.00
Button, Harry Truman, Picture, Celluloid, 1940s, 1 In.	25.00
Button, Help Hoover Help Business, 7/8 In.	88.00
Button, Herbert Hoover, Brass	10.00
Button, I Want FDR Again	10.00
Button, I'm For Dick Nixon, Photograph Center, 1 In.	5.00
Button, I'm Voting For Nixon, J.F.K. Plays Poker With Your Money, Celluloid, 6 In.	425.00
Button, Ike & Mamie Eisenhower, Dick & Pat Nixon, 43rd Inauguration, Pictures	22.00
Button, John L. Lewis, Portrait	30.00
Button, Jugate, Kennedy & Johnson, Pictures, 1 1/4 In.	95.00
Button, L. B. J. All The Way, Face In Center, 1 3/8 In.	6.00
Button, MacArthur For America, Celluloid, c.1948	15.00
Button, Make Ross Boss, Battery Light, 5/8 In.	15.00
Button, McGovern, Happy Face With Name Underneath Smile, 1 In.	4.00
Button, Mondale & Ferraro, 1984, 1 3/4 In.	10.00
Button, Need Nixon Now, Blue & White, 1 1/2 In.	4.00
Button, Nixon & Agnew, Pictures, Full Color, 1 1/8 In.	3.00
Button, Nixon, Lodge, Red, White & Blue, 11/16 In.	15.00
Button, Photo-Flasher, John F. Kennedy	25.00
Button, Plant A Tree & Throw Out The Bush, Protect Our Environment, 2 In.	4.00
Button, Reagan & Bush, Shape Of Texas	4.00
Button, Ronald Reagan, Inauguration Day, c.1981, Picture, 2 1/2 In.	3.00
Button, S.W. Pulley, Black Candidate For President	20.00
Button, Shirley Chisholm, President, Catalyst For Change	20.00
Button, SOB, Sons Of Business, Anti-Kennedy, 1 1/4 In.	18.00
Button, Stevenson, Black & White Photograph, White Letters, Red Ground, 7/8 In.	12.00
Button, Thomas Dewey, Picture, Celluloid, 1 1/4 In.	95.00

Button, Truman Inauguration, Photograph, Red, White & Blue Rim, 1 3/4 In. 35.00
Button, Truman Memoriam, Photograph, White Letters, Purple Rim, 3 1/2 In. 8.00
Button, Truman, Civil Rights, 2 In. 350.00
Button, Union Of Democratic Clubs, Roosevelt Deputy, Red, White & Blue, 1 1/8 In. .. 8.00
Button, Vote Kennedy President, 1 In. 20.00
Button, Vote Libertarian Party, Oval, 3/4 x 1 In. 9.00
Button, Vote Truman & Barkley In '48, Lithographed 75.00
Button, Wallace & Roosevelt, Red Printed, White Ground, 1 1/4 In. 15.00
Button, We R For Rockefeller, 6 In. 28.00
Button, We Want Willkie, 1 In. 7.00
Button, Win With Goldwater, Red, White & Blue 12.00
Button, Youth For Quayle, Indiana Senate Campaign, 1 1/2 In. 26.00
Calendar, John F. Kennedy, Jackie & Children Picture, c.1963 .... 12.00
Calendar Plate, 1909, Bryan, 9 1/4 In. 55.00
Certificate, Membership, Teddy Roosevelt, Progressive Party, c.1912 .... 25.00
Cigar Band, William H. Taft Picture, 4 1/2 In. 30.00
Clock, At The Wheel For New Deal, Franklin D. Roosevelt 120.00
Cuff Links, Nixon & Agnew, Inaugural Ball, c.1973, Box 75.00
Decal, California Nixon For Governor, Blue, Yellow, c.1962 .... 23.00
Decal, Franklin D. Roosevelt, Hee, Haw! We're Coming Back, Happy Days, 7 x 5 In. ... 23.00
Decal, JFK For Senator, Red, White & Blue, 3 1/2 x 10 In. 29.00
Doll, Barry Goldwater, Remco, Box, 1964 .... 60.00
Fan, I'm A Republic Fan 5.00
Football, Nixon, Agnew, Car Aerial Attachment, Styrofoam, Red & White 25.00
Gallery Pass, U.S. Senator, c.1929 .... 55.00
Glass, Honoring Governor & Mrs. O'Neal, Ohio Inaugural Ball, 1957 .... 12.00
Handbag, Elephant Heads & I Like Ike, Both Sides, Cloth, Large 45.00
Key Chain, Jimmy Carter 10.00
Knife, Reagan & Bush, Pocket 18.00
Knife & Key Chain, Nixon Now 12.00
Lighter, Hot Seat, Bush Cartoon 8.00
Lighter, Lite The Light For Goldwater, Portrait 39.00
Lighter, Stevenson & Kefauver, Picture 25.00
Mirror, I Like Ike On Reverse, 1 In. 48.00
Mirror, I'm For Ike On Reverse, 2 In. 58.00
Mirror, John F. Kennedy For President, 2 In. 250.00
Mirror, Theodore Roosevelt, Full Color, Red Letters Lower Rim, 2 In. 325.00
Mug, Assassination, Of Lincoln & Garfield 65.00
Mug, Bobby Kennedy For President, Japan, c.1960 .... 30.00
Mug, Dwight Eisenhower, Yellow Flat Glaze, Porcelain, c.1952, 5 In. 89.00
Mug, McKinley, Protection, Prosperity, Cover, Glass 85.00
Newspaper, Globe, Congressional, 1867-1968 .... 28.00
Nodder, Eisenhower 90.00
Paperweight, McKinley, Full Bust, Glass 120.00
Pen, Richard Nixon, With Autograph 35.00
Pencil, Hoover For President, Eraser Is Head, Dated 1929, Unused 85.00
Pencil, Roosevelt, Landon, Bullet Shape 22.00
Pencil Sharpener, John F. Kennedy 2.00
Pennant, Franklin D. Roosevelt Commissioning Aircraft Carrier, 1940s 45.00
Pennant, I Like Ike, Gettsburgh, Pa., Felt, Portrait 40.00
Pennant, Kennedy & Johnson, Red, White & Blue 48.00
Pennant, Thomas Dewey For President, Felt, Picture 60.00
Pennant, Your Best Bet In '52, Jugate Photograph Of Ike & Dick 75.00
Perfume Bottle, Goldwater Campaign, 3 1/4 In. 10.00
Photograph, Gerald Ford, Autographed, Frame, 8 x 10 In. 65.00
Pin, Lapel, Nixon, Lodge, Enamel On Gold Metal, c.1960 .... 12.00
Pin, McKinley & Roosevelt, Red, White & Blue Bow, Gold Ground, c.1900, 7/8 In. 35.00
Pin, Teddy Roosevelt, Brass Plated, c.1904 .... 650.00
Ping-Pong Paddles, Tricky Dick & Mao Tse-Tung, c.1960 .... 35.00
Plate, Fish, Presidential Service, Rutherford B. Hayes, c.1880, 8 1/3 In., 3 Piece 1150.00
Plate, Inaugural, President Kennedy, Gray Border, c.1960 .... 35.00
Plate, Republican Convention, c.1968 .... 18.00
Pocket Knife, Jimmy Carter, Peanut Shape, c.1976 .... 25.00

Postcard, Gerald Ford, Congressman, Autographed, c.1964	150.00
Postcard, Nixon & Lodge, Oregon For Nixon, c.1960	29.00
Postcard, President Gerald R. Ford, Autographed	115.00
Postcard, President Harry S. Truman, Gray, Blue & White	35.00
Postcard, Taft & Sherman, Portraits, The Nation's Choice, c.1908	16.00
Postcard, William H. Taft, Ohio, Presidential Campaign, c.1908	425.00
Postcard, William Taft For President, 1908	425.00
Poster, A Time For Greatness, John F. Kennedy Campaign, 1960, 19 x 28 In.	35.00
Poster, Cox, Picture, Frame, 17 x 11 In.	195.00
Poster, John Davis, Sepia, 21 x 15 In.	125.00
Poster, Kennedy & Johnson, Red, White & Blue, Cardboard, 22 x 13 1/2 In.	225.00
Poster, Robert F. Kennedy, Paper, 18 x 12 In.	20.00
Poster, Willkie, McNary, Indiana Rep. Candidates Photographs, c.1940, 21 x 14 In.	125.00
Poster Set, Carry On With Franklin D. Roosevelt, Vice President, Wallace, 21 x 14 In.	40.00
Ribbon, Winfield Scott, William A. Graham, c.1852	3850.00
Ring, Flasher, John F. Kennedy, 1960s	18.00
Sheet Music, A March To Eisenhower, Inaugural Souvenir, 1953	24.00
Sheet Music, Bull Moose March, National Progressive Party Convention, c.1912	78.00
Sheet Music, Hurrah For Hoover & White	45.00
Sheet Music, Laughing Waters, Clinton B. Fisk, Prohibition Party	26.00
Sheet Music, McKinley Victory Song	55.00
Sheet Music, President Cleveland's Grand March, c.1885	20.00
Sheet Music, President Cleveland, Inauguration March	25.00
Sheet Music, Road Is Open Again, Franklin Delano Roosevelt Cover, c.1933	15.00
Sheet Music, Tippicanoe Or Log Cabin Quick Step, Whig Convention, 1841	58.00
Spoon, Kennedy, Friendship, 1961-1963	8.00
Stickpin, Al Smith, Celluloid	65.00
Textile, W.H. Taft, Portrait, Flags, Guns, Cowboys, 57 x 18 In.	295.00
Thimble, Nixon For Governor, Plastic	32.00
Thimble, Nixon For U.S. Senator, Plastic	37.00
Tie, I Like Ike, Silk, White & Purple	35.00
Tie Tack, Flag, Nation For Nixon, On Card, c.1960	23.00
Tie Tack, Nixon, On Picture Card, c.1960	20.00
Token, Campaign, Lincoln & Hamlin, Ferrotype Portraits	475.00
Torch, Campaign, Used For Lincoln & Grant	195.00
Voting Machine, Wooden, Miles J. Shinn, Richmond, Ind., 1860, 12 In.	350.00
Watch Fob, Cox & Roosevelt	100.00
Watch Fob, Taft & Sherman, c.1908	45.00
Wristwatch, Bill Clinton, Runs Backwards	20.00
Wristwatch, Nixon, I'm Not A Crook, Moving Eyes, 1973	125.00
Wristwatch, Spiro Agnew, Dirty Times, c.1970	65.00

POMONA glass is a clear glass with a soft amber border decorated with pale blue or rose-colored flowers and leaves. The colors are very, very pale. The background of the glass is covered with a network of fine lines. It was made from 1885 to 1888 by the New England Glass Company. First grind was made from April 1885 to June 1886. It was made by cutting a wax surface on the glass, then dipping it in acid. Second grind was a less expensive method of acid etching that was developed later.

Bowl, Etched Cornflower, 2nd Grind, 16 1/4 In.	77.00
Bowl, Fluted, Footed, 1st Grind, 10 In.	125.00
Jar, Ribbed Swirl, Amber Trim, Cover, 6 In.	70.00
Pickle Castor, Cornflower Design Insert, Frame & Tongs	395.00
Pitcher, Bluebird & Flowers, Ice Lip	325.00
Pitcher, Cornflower, 1st Grind, 7 In.	825.00
Toothpick, Rigaree	235.00
Tumbler, Cornflower, 1st Grind	90.00

PONTYPOOL, see Tole

POPEYE was introduced to the Thimble Theater comic strip in 1929. The character became a favorite of readers. In 1932, an animated cartoon featuring Popeye was made by Paramount Studios. The cartoon series continued and became even more popular when it was shown on television starting in

the 1950s. The full-length movie with Robin Williams as Popeye was made in 1980.

Ashtray, Chalkware, Carnival	145.00
Bank, American Bisque Co.	495.00 to 950.00
Bank, Daily Dime	150.00
Bank, Dime Register	50.00
Bank, Dime Register, 1929	75.00
Bank, Figural, Seated, Vinyl, Stopper	35.00
Bank, Mechanical, Popeye Knockout, Tin	990.00
Bank, Popeye, American Bisque Co.	950.00
Book, Big Little Book, Popeye The Sailor Man, 1937	20.00
Book, Big Little Book, Queen Olive Oyl, 1949	20.00
Book, Comic, No.130, 1975	4.00
Box, Bubble Bath, Woolfoam Co., Popeye & Olive, 1950s	58.00
Box, Crayon, Tin, King Features, 1933	30.00
Box, Pencil, Complete, 1933	75.00
Box, Pencil, Truck, Tin, Green, Popeye On Sides, Brutus Driving, Box, 7 1/2 In.	19.00
Candy Container, PEZ, Red Hat	40.00
Card, Christmas, Hallmark, 1934	20.00
Card, Christmas, Popeye, Engineer's Clothes, On Train, Unused, 1951	30.00
Case, Pencil, School Bus, Spinach	25.00
Christmas Light Shades, 1930s, Box	145.00
Colorforms, 1957	40.00
Cookie Jar, Olive Oyl	2875.00
Cookie Jar, Olive Oyl, American Bisque Co.	800.00 to 1500.00
Cookie Jar, Popeye, American Bisque	595.00
Cookie Jar, Popeye, Vandor	400.00
Cookie Jar, Vandor	375.00 to 750.00
Costume, Motorola TV Giveaway, 1953	45.00
Costume, Popeye, Collegeville, Box	58.00
Doll, Cloth Body, Rubber Head, Original Clothes, 1930s, 17 In.	350.00
Doll, Molded Vinyl Head & Arms, Cloth, Uneeda, 1975, Box	90.00
Doll, Swee'pea, Cloth & Vinyl, Uneeda, 1979, 8 In.	45.00
Figurine, Chalkware, 14 In.	125.00
Figurine, Composition, 1935, 13 In.	895.00
Figurine, Olive Oyl, Rubber, On Marx Hand Car, Windup, 1930s	850.00
Figurine, Popeye & Wimpy, Chalkware, Pair	135.00
Figurine, Sitting On Rope, King Features	100.00
Game, Ball Toss	45.00
Game, Magnetic Make A Face, Larami, 1979	23.00
Game, Ring Toss, Popeye & Olive Oyl, Standing Figures, Box, 1919	145.00
Game, Ring Toss, Popeye, With Pipe, Olive Oyl, Standing Figures, Box, 1933	95.00
Game, Target, Box	250.00
Glass, Popeye's Pals, Swee' Pea, Popeye's Famous Fried Chicken	28.00
Hairbrush, Czechoslovakia, 1930s	45.00
Lamp, Table, Slush Cast, Late 1940s, 11 1/4 In.	172.00
Lantern, Figural, Tin, Battery Operated	435.00
Lunch Box, With Thermos, 1964	65.00 to 160.00
Nodder, Popeye & Olive Oyl, Ceramic, Japan, 1950s, Pair	925.00
Paint Set, Unused	75.00
Pencil, Mechanical, Eagle, Box	40.00
Postcard, Patriotic, World War II, 1940s, 2 Piece	30.00
Puppet, Finger, Card	25.00
Puzzle, Sailboat, Wimpy, Olive, Swee'pea, Brutus, Frame Tray, 1960s, 10 x 12 1/2 In.	23.00
Puzzle, Treasure Chest, No. 35, Jamar, 1950s	35.00
Record, Never Pick A Fight With Popeye, No. 587, 78 RPM, Little Golden Record, 1959	32.00
Ring, Flicker, Package	10.00
Salt & Pepper, Popeye & Olive Oyl, Figural, Vandor, 1980, 7 In.	45.00 to 65.00
Sheet Music, Theme Song, 1930s	20.00
Soap, Figural, 3 In.	75.00
Soap, Head, On A Rope	45.00
Toy, Banjo	70.00

Toy, Basketball Player, Windup 2000.00
Toy, Boxing Popeye, Chein 2600.00
Toy, Bubble Blower, Battery Operated 750.00
Toy, Carrying Parrot, Windup, Marx 180.00
Toy, Dart Gun, Plastic, Wannatoy, Card.. 25.00
Toy, Jigger, With Olive Oyl, On Roof, Windup, 9 In... 1100.00
Toy, Motorcycle, Cast Iron, Original Paint & Tires, Hubley, 8 In............................ 4500.00
Toy, On Tricycle, Tin & Celluloid, Windup, Linemar.. 1100.00
Toy, Paddle & Ball, 1929 .... 129.00
Toy, Popeye & Parrots, Marx 385.00
Toy, Popeye Express, Windup, Marx 650.00
Toy, Popeye The Acrobat, Swings On Rocking Platform, Linemar........................... 3200.00
Toy, Puncher, Windup, Chein.. 2600.00
Toy, Shadow Boxer, Windup, Marx, 1930s 850.00
Toy, Spinach Can, Head Pops Out 35.00
Toy, Swinging Can Of Spinach & Bell, Pull Toy, Wooden, 9 1/2 x 11 1/2 In.......... 27.00
Toy, Tank, Rollover, Linemar, 4 In. 325.00
Toy, The Popeye Getar, Crank Wind, Musical, Mattel, 1950s................................. 125.00
Toy, Walks With Parrot Cages, Tin Lithograph, Windup, 8 1/4 In.......................... 270.00
Tray, Lap 20.00
Umbrella 25.00
Watch, Binky, Flicker, 1960s 11.00

PORCELAIN factories that are well known are listed in this book under the factory name. This category lists pieces made by the less well-known factories.

Bowl, Cupid, 3 Putti Holding Seashell, Sitzendorf, 12 x 20 In.. 2200.00
Bowl, Nabeshima, Japan, 13 1/4 x 9 1/4 In. 550.00
Box, Cover, Applied Rose, Flowers, Sitzendorf, 3 1/2 In... 25.00
Box, Cover, Italian Scenes, Enameled, Green Ground, England, 3 1/2 In. 330.00
Box, Leg Form, White Stocking, Gilt Tasseled Garter, Vienna, 1765, 4 1/4 In. 805.00
Cache Pot, Armorial, Flared, Removable Flower Frog, China, 8 1/2 In., Pair 2860.00
Centerpiece, Figural, Youth Supporting Reticulated Bowl, Germany, c.1900, 21 In. 715.00
Centerpiece, Louis XV Style, Gilt Bronze, Cherubs, Floral Sprays, 11 x 22 In. 3740.00
Clothes Brush, Figural, German Shepherd Dog, Germany.. 65.00
Coffee & Tea Set, Center Monograms, Gilt Swags, Green, Wallendorf, 10 Piece 490.00
Coffeepot, Cover, Pear Shape, Floral Bouquet, Bow, c.1765, 8 3/8 In. 1035.00
Compote, 3 Raised Faces Around, 3-Footed... 85.00
Compote, Reticulated Bowl, Green & Gold Stripes, 9 x 7 1/2 In. 71.00
Creamer, Calico Cat, Figural, Brayton Laguna.. 45.00

Porcelain, Figurine, God, Animal Pelts,
Bow, c.1780, 9 In.

♦♦♦♦♦♦♦♦♦♦♦♦♦♦♦♦♦♦♦♦♦♦♦♦

You can check to see if the light intensity is too strong for your antique pictures and fabrics. Take a light meter used with a camera and check the exposure values (EV) and lux. The maximum level for watercolors, paper, and other easily damaged items is 50 lux. Glass, stone, and metal is safe up to 300 lux.

♦♦♦♦♦♦♦♦♦♦♦♦♦♦♦♦♦♦♦♦♦♦♦♦

Glass plates that are cloudy may clean with silver polish and a plastic scouring pad. If the problem is a stain, it might clean. If it is damage from small scratches, it might look better for display if it is coated with a non-yellowing floor wax and then lightly buffed.

Porcelain, Pitcher, Lemonade,
Strawberries, Gilded Handle, S. Heap, 6 In.

Cup & Saucer, Gilt & Blue Highlights, Ivory Ground, 19th Century, 4 1/2 In.	35.00
Cup & Saucer, Orange Floral, Gold Trim, Royal Chelsea	35.00
Custard Cup, Cover, Boston State House, Rogers	395.00
Dessert Set, Forget-Me-Not, Pierced Border, Schumann, 46 Piece	1150.00
Dish, Blue & White, Molded Vines, Bow, c.1765, 8 7/16 In.	345.00
Dish, Ship, Gilt Trim, Carl Hans Tuppack, Tiefenfurth, Germany, 8 In.	132.00
Dish, Square, Blue On White, Dragons, 19th Century, Japan, 11 1/4 In.	109.25
Easter Egg, Painted Man Holding Candle, Russia, Late 19th Century, 4 1/2 In.	862.00
Eggcup, Eagle, Bisque, Polychrome & White, 4 1/4 In.	22.00
Figurine, 3 Choir Boys Singing, Japan, 5 1/2 In.	10.00
Figurine, Bird, Bunting, Low Stump, Bow, c.1760, 4 1/4 In. & 4 1/8 In., Pair	1955.00
Figurine, Bird, Flycatcher, Moussalli	100.00
Figurine, Bird, Hummingbird, Moussalli	20.00
Figurine, Bird, Ring Plover, Moussalli	30.00
Figurine, Bust, Woman's, Stone Base, Lenci, Italy, 14 In.	467.00
Figurine, Dancer, Outstretched Arms, Longton Hall, c.1754, 5 In.	575.00
Figurine, Dolphins, Kaiser	33.00
Figurine, Elephant, Trunk Curled Under To Mouth, Turquoise Glaze, 4 In.	402.00
Figurine, God, Animal Pelts, Bow, c.1780, 9 In. ....*Illus*	1650.00
Figurine, Hound, Seated, Black & Red Eyes, Bow, c.1760, 2 7/16 In.	5175.00
Figurine, Immortal, Holding Fan, 2 Horses On Head, Blue & White, 11 1/4 In.	1150.00
Figurine, Peasant Woman, Brayton Laguna	60.00
Figurine, Polar Bear, Sitzendorf, Marked, 8 1/2 In.	295.00
Figurine, Ram, Recumbent, Allover White Glaze, Black Eyes, 7 1/2 In.	230.00
Figurine, Satyr, Seated, Playing Flute, 5 1/2 In.	410.00
Figurine, Skater, Stamped Schau, Germany, 7 1/2 In.	95.00
Figurine, Slipper, Germany, 3 1/2 In.	40.00
Figurine, Terrier, Gray, White, Royal Heidelberg, 10 In., Pair	467.00
Figurine, Woman, Black Matte Enameled, Blue Stripes, Gilt, L'Industrie, 11 In.	71.00
Figurine, Young Man, Holding Cluster Of Grapes, Continental, 19th Century, 5 In.	24.00
Finger Bowl, Underplate, Pink Roses, Gold Trim, Royal Austria, 6 Piece	250.00
Group, 4 Children Playing With Goat, Continental, 19th Century, 14 1/4 In.	860.00
Group, Allegory Of Seasons, Carl Thieme Potschappel, Late 19th Century	69.00
Group, Parlor Scene, Man & Woman Holding Mandolin, Felix Zeh, 14 In.	465.00
Humidor, Clipper Ship, Crown Devon	65.00
Jar, Basket Shape, Applied Full-Relief Crabs, Hirado, Early 19th Century, 10 1/4 In.	770.00
Jar, Cover, Dog Design, Signed, Blue & White, 10 1/2 In.	330.00
Jar, Cover, Egyptian Revival, Figural Reserve, 13 In., Pair	1725.00
Jar, Hummingbird Design, Native Wood Stand, Victorian, 9 1/4 In.	23.00
Jar, Oriental, Blue, Red & White, Celadon Ground, 29 1/4 In.	82.00
Jar, Potpourri, Cover, Pink Flowers, Gold Leaves, 9 In.	60.00
Jardiniere, Gilt, Floral Painted, Footed, Continental, Late 19th Century, 7 In.	248.00
Jug, Geometric Design, Blue & White, Metal Cover, Bulbous, China, 9 1/4 In.	345.00

Jug, Milk, Branches Of Flowering Prunus, St. Cloud, c.1735, 5 3/8 In. 1955.00
Max & Moritz, Character, Kaiser, Germany, 7 1/2 In. 95.00
Menu Holder, Full-Bodied Putti, Crowns, Austria, Pair 270.00
Mug, 19th Century, R. Samish, San Francisco, 4 In. 42.00
Napkin Holder, Poodle, Winton 60.00
Night-Light, Windmill Shape, Beige, Roof Cover, Painted Base, France, 11 In. 660.00
Pipe Bowl, Military Scene, Germany, c.1902, 6 In. 52.00
Pipe Bowl, Painted Shaking Hands, Jan Hlaving, Germany, 5 1/2 In. 40.00
Pitcher, Lemonade, Strawberries, Gilded Handle, S. Heap, 6 In .... *Illus* 250.00
Plant Stand, Pagoda Shape, Bat & Insect Design, Oriental, 1900s, 14 x 28 1/2 In. 317.00
Plaque, 2 Small Boys, Giltwood Frame, Wagner, 5 13/16 x 4 In. 978.00
Plaque, Juno, Seated, Scepter, Peacock, Georgian Frame, China, 3 1/2 In. Diam. 610.00
Plaque, Mary, Mother Of Christ, Enameled, Gilt Ground, 8 1/8 x 4 In. 38.00
Plaque, Painted Flowers, Giltwood Frame, Late 19th Century, 12 1/4 In. 260.00
Plaque, Portrait Of Queen Louise Of Prussia, Frame, Wagner, 5 3/4 x 9 3/8 In. 633.00
Plate, Elk & Pheasant Reserve Scenes, Magenta Border, 10 In., Pair 33.00
Plate, Grass Design Rim, Pine Design In Center, Japan, 7 3/4 In., 8 Piece 675.00
Plate, Trompe-L'Oeil Wood Grained, Fornasetti, 10 In., 8 Piece 198.00
Plate, Woman & Angels, Gold Border, Hanging, Victoria, Austria, 10 In. 55.00
Sauceboat, Painted Floral Sprigs, Scalloped Rim, Vauxhall, c.1760, 6 3/4 In. 3162.00
Sugar, Cover, Newhall Type, Ovoid Form, Polychrome Chinoiserie Design, 5 In. 201.00
Sugar, Mushroom Knob, Blossoms & Scrolls Border, St. Cloud, c.1730, 3 9/16 In. 345.00
Sugar & Creamer, Royal Winton, Victorian 90.00
Sugar & Creamer, Royalty, Royal Winton 170.00
Tea Service, Multiflowers Band, Fired-Gold Trim, Royal Albert, 22 Piece 287.00
Tea Set, Child's, Children Playing With Dolls, 4 Designs, Germany, 1910, 15 Piece.... 450.00
Tea Set, Child's, Indian Picture, Germany 150.00
Tea Set, Child's, Red Checkered, Japan 350.00
Tea Set, Oak Leaf & Floral Design, Imari Palette, Gilt Trim, England, 3 Piece............. 259.00
Teapot, Floral Sprigs, Repeated On Cover, Artichoke Knop, c.1785, 5 In. 5462.00
Tray, Dresser, Colonial Courting Scene, Scalloped Diamond, France, 11 1/5 In. 132.00
Tureen, Cover, Melon Form, Gnarled Stem Knop, Longton Hall, c.1754, 4 5/8 In. 3162.00
Urinal, Floral Design, England 690.00
Urn, Classic Maidens, Digging For Diamonds, Green, Gilt, France, 10 3/4 In., Pair 165.00
Vase, Bacchic Masks On Supports, Ormolu Mounted, China, 10 In., Pair.................... 8625.00
Vase, Beaker, Floral Bouquet, Scattered Sprigs, Plymouth, c.1768, 7 3/16 In. 1725.00
Vase, Black Enamel At Neck, Medallion On Front, Robj, 9 In. 805.00
Vase, Blue & White, Foo Dog Handles, Lizard Trim, China, 15 1/2 In., Pair 805.00
Vase, Coral Carp Design, Ivory Ground, Wooden Stand, Oriental, 10 In., Pair............. 69.00
Vase, Cornucopia, Rectangular Plinth, Hand Painted Flowers, J. Petit, 11 In., Pair 860.00
Vase, Dragon Handle, Cloud & Bat Design, Baluster, China, 7 3/4 In., Pair 345.00
Vase, Flared Mouth & Foot, Allover Mirror Black Glaze, 17 In. 4025.00
Vase, Gilt & Black Design, Blue Ground, 14 1/4 In., Pair 220.00
Vase, Hourglass Shape, Pastel Graphic, Germany, 1950s, 22 In. 116.00
Vase, Lallemant, Cylinder Shape, Geometrics, France, 9 5/8 In., Pair 805.00
Vase, Neo-Baroque Ormolu, Marble Base, Deep Blue, Continental, 30 In. 2310.00
Vase, Palace, Hand Painted, Enamel, Gilt, Pink Luster, France, c.1885, 29 1/2 In. 2760.00
Vase, Shoe Shape, Full-Bodied Cupids, Blue & White, Sitzendorf, Pair 210.00
Vase, Shouldered Animal Mask, Ring Handles, Woman, Children, 30 In. 115.00
Vase, Square, Figures Standing On Animals, China, c.1840, 10 3/4 In. 403.00
Vase, Trumpet Shape, Dragon Form Handles, Lamp Mounted, Hirado, 11 In., Pair 3080.00
Vase, Urn, Floral, Silver & Gold, Ram's-Head Handles, 10 1/2 In. 192.00
Wall Pocket, Yellow, Pink Rosebuds, Royal Winton, Grimwades 165.00
Washbowl & Pitcher Set, Clover Pattern, John Maddock & Sons, 7 Piece.................... 875.00

POSTCARDS were first legally permitted in Austria on October 1, 1869. The
United States passed postal regulations allowing the card in 1872. Most of the
picture postcards collected today date after 1910. The amount of postage can
help to date a card. The rates are: 1872 (1 cent), 1917 (2 cents), 1919 (1 cent),
1925 (2 cents), 1928 (1 cent), 1952 (2 cents), 1959 (3 cents), 1963 (4 cents),
1968 (5 cents), 1973 (8 cents), 1975 (7 cents), 1976 (9 cents), 1978 (10
cents), 1981 (12 cents), 1981 (13 cents), 1985 (14 cents), 1988 (15 cents),
1991 (19 cents), 1995 (20 cents).

Autocar, Photograph, 1910 Truck, New York City	575.00
Boy In Tattered Clothing, But Elgin Watch Survived, 1914	40.00
Capitol Theater, Major Edward Bowes & His Family, New York City	35.00
Chevron Service Station, Thank You, 1964 Mustang, Unused	15.00
Christmas, C.W. Parker, Maker Of Carousels, c.1935	65.00
Christmas, Santa Claus In Green Outfit	65.00
Colorado Springs Resort Hotel, Maxfield Parrish, Broadmoor, 1937	40.00
Coney Island, c.1950, 6 Piece	15.00
Cruise Ships, 5 x 7 In., 6 x 8 In. & 4 x 6, 100 Piece	40.00
Dickens Character, Tuck	8.00
Doe-Wah-Jack	35.00
Fishing Gear, Conroy & Bissett, Importers & Manufacturers, 1883	50.00
Flying Fortress, Over Mountains, Tennessee, 1944	13.00
German Soldier's Mail, In Galicia, 1918	40.00
Geronimo, 1940s	8.00
Gold Miners At Perins Peak, At Mine Entrance, Lunch Buckets, c.1900	20.00
Hood's Sarsaparilla Factory, Unused	4.00
Hostettler's Stomach Bitters, Map Of Panama Canal	35.00
Hot Water Paint, Saxton's River, Vermont, 1892	40.00
I Should Worry If My Wife Is A Suffragette, Man With Crying Baby	30.00
Imperial Airways, Haviland Albatross, Germany, c.1940	35.00
Inland Steamers, Great Lakes, New York, Pre-1940, 50 Piece	80.00
International Hunting Exposition, Vienna, Austria, 1910	85.00
Jewish Midget, Greetings From Joh. Behnke, Little Cohn, 35 Inches Tall, Germany	60.00
Jewish New Year, Hebrew & German, Cloth Pattern	50.00
John Reed, Journalist, Poet & Revolutionary, Buried In Kremlin, 1919	800.00
Kellogg's Corn Flakes, Box With Rhyme	35.00
Kupferberg Gold Champagne, For Your Birthday, Germany	65.00
Mallory Gavenette Hat, Got Through Rainy Season O.K. 1909	35.00
Mariani Wine, Art Nouveau, Alphonse Mucha	1250.00
Master's Command, Raise Funds For Roerich Museum	25.00
Medical Students, Well-Used Cadaver	50.00
Midget Girl, Posed On Stairs, Indiana, c.1919	15.00
Military Hospital, Verona, Italy	40.00
Modern Art In New York City, Commemorative, 1913	400.00
Mutt & Jeff, Radio Advertising, 1935	35.00
Mysteries Of The Monastery, Drunken Monk With Girl, c.1907	17.00
N.Y. City Post Office Building, Depero	375.00
National Cash Register, 1913	50.00
National Women's Trade Union League, 1903	75.00
Nebraska State Prison, Electric Chair, 1920s, 16 Piece	65.00
New Year, Bavarian Red Cross, 1914	50.00
New York City, 34th St. & Broadway, Photograph	20.00
Nurses, Composite Of 3, Nightingale, Noyes, Delano, On Staircase	48.00
Philip Morris, Autographed Johnny, 1940's	38.00
Postcard Store, Perugia, Italy	35.00
Ray (Boom Boom) Mancini	12.00
Red Cap Wine, Chromolithograph, Town Of Freyburg, Germany, 1913	50.00
Saloon Smasher, Hatchet-Wielding Carrie Nation, Envelope, 6 Piece	300.00
Savoy Hotel, Soldiers, Wagon, Horses, 1916	65.00
Shopper, Woman Viewing New Corset, Art Nouveau	75.00
Shrimp Peddler, Charleston, South Carolina	35.00
Silver Slippers Saloon, Las Vegas, 1850s	7.00
Socialist Pyramid	79.00
Spanish American War, Capturing Signal Station On Cuban Soil, 1898	65.00
Tarzan & Boy, Johnny Weismuller	10.00
Thanksgiving, Black Chef	15.00
Three Wise Men, Christmas Theme, Bruder Kohn, Vienna, 1901	75.00
To The Red Cross Nurses, Text From Bible, 1918	25.00
Tournament Of Roses, Folio, 1924	20.00
Tournament Of Roses Parade, Pasadena, Ohio President Float, Leather, 1908	15.00
Valentine, Cherub, 1912, Pair	4.00
Victorian Women Driving Automobile, 1908	30.00

View Of Schoenfels Resort, Zugerberg, Switzerland, Woven Silk.................................. 65.00
Where Dice Are Legal, Bank Club, Reno, Nevada, 1941 .... 75.00
Wirl-Fly Ride, Coney Island 85.00
Woman Buying Postcards At Store, Germany.. 65.00
Yellow Kid, All Over, Buster Brown & His Bubble, Outcault 40.00
Yellow Kid, Pictures Kid & Shamrocks, March, 1912....................................... 35.00
Yellow Kid, Pictures Kid, Hatchet, Cherry Tree, February, 1912 .... 35.00

POSTERS have informed the public about news and entertainment events
since ancient times. Nineteenth-century advertising or theatrical posters and
twentieth-century movie and war posters are of special interest today. The
price is determined by the artist, the condition, and the rarity. Other posters
may be listed under Movie, Political, and World War I and II.

3-Dog Night Concert, 1970s 18.00
Advertising, The Designer Magazine, Colorful, 1920, 12 x 18 In.......................... 20.00
Allen-A Union Suit, Lithographed, She Won't Go Home To Mother, 30 x 20 In........... 72.00
American Tobacco Company, Stock Certificate With Indian Head 4.00
Barnum & Bailey Circus, 1950s 150.00
Beatty's California Grapevine, Girl Smelling Rose, Frame, Paper, 20 x 15 In. 165.00
Bert & Harry, Piels Light Beer, 1975, 20 x 32 In... 7.00
Boeing Jet, Sabena.. 65.00
Bonnie & Clyde, Wanted, 2 Photographs, Government Information, 9 x 7 In. 300.00
British Blond Burlesque Troupe, Playing Cards, Linen Backed, 1870, 44 x 60 In........ 880.00
Buffalo Bill, Strobridge, 1907 .... 4000.00
Burlesque, Tempest Storm, Striptease Girl, 1950s, 42 x 27 In. 85.00
Carter The Great, Magician Playing Cards With Devil, 1920s, 14 x 22 In. 125.00
Christmas Scribner's, Man In Burgundy Coat, Green Ground, 22 x 14 In. 375.00
Corvair, Aluminum Frame, 1965 .... 130.00
Dave Brubeck Quartet, Jazz, Sports Arena, Toledo, Ohio, 1959, 22 x 14 In. 690.00
Egyptienne Luxury Cigarettes, Frame.. 154.00
Enlist In The Navy, To Arms, U.S. Navy Recruiting Stations, 41 x 28 In. Mall Folio.... 250.00
Exposition Polonaise, Profiles, Black & Pink Ground, 39 x 27 In. 575.00
FBI Wanted, Patty Hearst, Bill & Emily Harris, 1975, 14 x 9 1/2 In. 85.00
Fly There By Swissair, Couple In Winter Wear, Carrying Skis, 40 x 25 In. 200.00
Garfield, Halloween, 1978, 20 x 28 In. 6.00
Graf Zeppelin, German Blimp, Photograph, 1930s.. 20.00
Grand Prix De France, Race Cars, Red & White Ground, 1952, 23 1/2 x 15 In. 545.00
Green River Whiskey, She Was Bred In Old Kentucky, Horse, 1899, 20 x 16 In. 125.00
Gulf Oil Co., Open For Business, Gulf Disc Logo, Orange Ground, c.1958, 46 x 28 In.. 25.00
Harper's May, Woman In Blue Dress, White Sheep, 1895, 17 x 13 1/2 In. 258.00
Holland For The Holidays, Ship & Dock, 39 1/2 x 25 In. 287.00
Hooside Tunnel, 1870s Train Entering & Leaving, Paper, Frame, 29 x 22 In. 550.00
Houdini, c.1925, 6 x 8 Ft.. 8500.00
I Want You For The Navy, Windblown Woman, 1917, 41 1/4 x 27 In. 690.00
Imperial Airways, Golden Lion, Blue & White Ground, 37 1/2 x 25 In. 200.00
Jim Morrison, Billboard Display, LA Radio Station KSRR, 1967, 14 x 16 In. 920.00
John Bull, Beer... 59.00
Kendall's Spavin Cure, Image Of Woman With Horse, Paper, 28 x 21 1/2 In. 715.00
King's Lemonade, Boy & Lemonade Bottle, 20 x 12 In. 287.00
Lefe'vre Utile Biscuits, Young Woman, France, 1907, 27 x 20 In. 330.00
McDonald's, Glasses, Don't Drink Water, Drink 7-Up 60.00
MG-Safety Fast, Green MG Racing On Dirt Road, 1953, 25 x 34 1/2 In. 630.00
Michelob, Bottle.. 39.00
Monte Carlo Beach, Adam & Eve, Water Skiing, 32 x 47 In. 805.00
Mrs. Pankhurst, Vote For Women, Mass., Nov. 15, 1912, Purple & Green, Frame 893.00
National Child Welfare Association, Girls' Basketball, 1918, 30 x 20 In. 24.00
New York Herald, Winged Woman, Blue & Orange Ground, 1896, 46 x 30 In. 488.00
Newell Clever Juggler, 3 Jugglers With Indian Clubs, Frame, 27 x 17 In. 1035.00
Opera, Forget-Me-Not, Genevieve Ward, W.H. Vernon, Rand Opera House, 24 x 38 In. 45.00
Orange Crush, Hootenanny Party Kit, 1960s, 18 x 24 In. 9.00
Peters Ammunition, Antlered Moose, Paper, 29 x 17 3/4 In................................... 770.00
Piedmont, Cigarette Of Quality, Woman, Egret Feathers, Frame............................ 154.00
Ping Proff Petrol, Better Gasoline, Earl Moran, Framed, 14 x 21 In......................... 165.00

Potlid, Bazin's Shaving Cream,
Red Ink, 2 3/4 x 1 1/2 In.

Potlid, Burgess Anchovy Paste,
3 1/2 x 1 3/4 In.

River Cruises, Golden Eagle, Cardboard, 27 x 21 In.		128.00
Robots Are Coming, Clayton Bailey, Laser War, 1983, 18 x 18 In.		15.00
Schlitz, Beer, Bluebird, 24 x 36 In.		89.00
Smokey The Bear, 1947, 18 x 26 In.		30.00
Student Mobilization Committee, N.Y., Student Strike, Purple, Green, 17 x 11 In.		95.00
Sweet Caporal Cigarettes, Man At Dinner Table, c.1898, Paper, 27 1/2 x 16 In.		385.00
Texaco Fire Chief, Hat, 34 x 18 In.		95.00
The 5 Sullivan Brothers, They Did Their Part, 1943, 28 x 22 In.		40.00
U.S. Marine Reserve, Recruiting, 1950s		25.00
Uncle Tom's Cabin, Bearded Black Man, c.1910, 88 1/2 x 40 In., Three Sheet		920.00
WAC, She's Ready To Buy War Bonds, 1942, 14 x 11 In.		45.00
Wrangler Rodeo Guide, Sam Savitt Picture, 1977, 24 x 37 In.		75.00

POTLIDS are just that, lids for pots. Transfer-printed potlids had their heyday
from the 1840s to the early 1900s. The English Staffordshire potteries made
ceramic containers with decorative lids for bear's grease, shrimp or meat
paste, cold cream, and toothpaste. Printed advertising and pictures of historical events, portraits of famous people, or scenic views were designed in black
and white or color. Reproductions have been made.

Bazin's Shaving Cream, Red Ink, 2 3/4 x 1 1/2 In.	*Illus*	125.00
Burgess Anchovy Paste, 3 1/2 x 1 3/4 In.	*Illus*	60.00
Bust Of Benjamin Franklin, Jules Hauel Perfumer, Ambrosial Cream, 3 In.	385.00 to	465.00
Chlorine Detergent & Orris Dentifrice, Royce & Esterly's, c.1860, 2 7/8 In.		385.00
Dr. Allports Dentifrice, Cleansing, Beautifying & Preserving Teeth & Gums, c.1850		577.00
Edward Cook's Hygienic Tooth Soap, c.1850, 1 3/4 x 2 3/8 In.		99.00
Eugene Roussel Odontine Of Rose Tooth Paste, Square, c.1850, 2 3/4 In.		192.00
General George Washington Preparing To Cross Delaware River, c.1850, 5 In.		5940.00
Independence Hall, Worsley's Saponaceous Shaving Compound, 4 In.		550.00
Jar, Battle Of The Nile.		132.00
Occidental Tooth Paste & Unrivaled Preparation, c.1850, 3 1/4 In.		300.00
Shakespeare House, Henley Street, Stratford On Avon, 4 1/4 In.		245.00
Swinton's English Primrose Tooth Paste, Floral Transfer, c.1850, 2 5/8 In.		200.00
Taylors Saponaceous Compound, Black Transfer, Man Shaving, c.1850, 3 3/4 In.		412.00
Taylors Saponaceous Compound, Blue Transfer, c.1860, 4 In.		440.00
Taylors Saponaceous Compound, Lavender Transfer, Man Shaving, c.1850, 4 In.		495.00
Taylors Saponaceous Compound, Purple Transfer, c.1850, 3 1/4 In.		300.00
W.A. Batchelor's Dentifrice, c.1860, 2 3/8 x 3 5/8 In.		467.00
Williams' Swiss Violet Shaving Cream, c.1880, 3 3/4 In.		210.00

POTTERY and porcelain are different. Pottery is opaque; you can't see through it. Porcelain is translucent. If you hold a porcelain dish in front of a strong light, you will see the light through the dish. Porcelain is colder to the touch. Pottery is softer and easier to break and will stain more easily because it is porous. Porcelain is thinner, lighter, and more durable. Majolica, faience, and stoneware are all pottery. Additional pieces of pottery are listed in this book in the Art Pottery category and under the factory name.

Bowl, Abstract Curved Shape, Pink, Green, Lavender Ground, Gambone, Italy, 9 In.....	125.00
Bowl, Copper Crystalline Flambe Glaze, Footed, Scheier, 3 1/2 x 7 In...........................	275.00
Bowl, Flared, Red & Green Metallic Glaze, Blue Center, Beatrice Wood, 6 In..............	550.00
Bowl, Flowing Verdigris Glaze, Footed, Gertrud & Otto Natzler, c.1965, 3 3/4 In...........	4025.00
Bowl, Metallic Flake Crystalline, Brown, Black, Folded, Footed, Natzler, 1 3/4 x 5 In. .	495.00
Bowl, Multicolored High Glaze, Natzler, 4 In...	275.00
Bowl, Pedestal, Faces, Scheier, 9 1/2 In...	475.00
Bowl, Pedestal, Tan & Brown Speckled Glaze, Scheier, 5 1/2 In..................................	99.00
Bowl, Round, Silver Gilt Interior, Gold & Silver Exterior, Waylande Gregory, 6 In.	132.00
Bowl, Speckled Satin Brown Glaze, Footed, Flared, Scheier, 3 1/2 x 6 1/4 In.	193.00
Bowl, Speckled Satin Brown, Speckled Pink Interior, Scheier, 4 1/2 x 5 In.	193.00
Bowl, Turquoise, Ginter, Broadmoor, 8 1/2 In.	40.00
Bowl, Woman, Rooster & Horse, Bright Colors, Pillin, 3 1/2 x 5 In.	512.00
Bust, Oriental Man & Woman, Italy, 7 1/2 In., Pair	60.00
Candlestick, Twisted Stem & Handle, Flat Base, Wannopee, No. 1, 13 In.	60.50
Chalice, Turquoise Interior, Silver Glazed Exterior, Howard Kottler, 5 1/2 In..............	495.00
Cradle, Brown Sponging, Ohio Buff Clay, 4 In..	39.00
Dish, Basket Handle, Hand Painted Grapes, Taylor, 13 x 5 1/2 In.	15.00
Dish, Cat Shape, L. A. Potteries	15.00
Dish, Cover, Roses, Black & Green Leaves, Handle, Finial, 3 Sections, Moriyama	18.00
Doorstop, Elf, Sitting, Reading Book, Norweta, 9 x 5 In.	385.00
Figurine, Camel, Multicolored Glaze, Gambone, Italy, 6 In.	330.00
Figurine, Chinese Coolie, Kaye	22.00
Figurine, Dog, Sitting, Dark Green Glaze, Ohio, 6 1/2 In...	385.00
Figurine, Dove, White, Silver Beak, Etched Wings, Waylande Gregory, 13 x 10 In.	825.00
Figurine, Flamingo, Brad Keeler, 7 In.	50.00
Figurine, Flamingo, Brad Keeler, 10 In.	45.00
Figurine, Hagenrenaker, Basset Hound...	50.00
Figurine, Lion, Glass Eyes, Bonibisse, 1890, Pair	895.00
Figurine, Man, With Dog, 2-Tone Green, Devonware	35.00
Figurine, Nude Woman, Running, With Torch, Art Deco, Schaw, Bach, Kunst, 9 In.....	245.00
Figurine, Peasant Woman, Brayton Laguna	65.00
Figurine, Pierrot Clown, Head Thrown Back, Guitar, Roses, Hertwig, 1932, 11 In........	175.00
Figurine, Raggedy Ann & Andy, Vallona Starr, Pair...	80.00
Figurine, Spaniel, Sitting, Rockingham Glaze, 19th Century, Ohio Pottery, 11 In.	345.00
Figurine, The Shawl, Woman Selling Violets, Charles Vyse, 1925, 10 1/2 In...............	345.00
Figurine, Warrior, Kneeling, Oriental, 7 In...	38.00
Figurine, Woman, Sitting, Applying Lipstick, Guiraud Riviere, France, 15 1/2 In.........	1150.00
Goblet, Abstract Linear, Under White, Brown Clay, Footed, Maija Grotell, 4 1/2 In.	413.00
Group, Punch & Judy, Puppet Show, Dog, Musician, Charles Vyse, 12 In.....................	575.00
Group, Reclining Female Nude & Swan, Guiraud Riviere, France, 10 x 27 In.	1725.00
Incense Burner, Dog Shape, Handle On Back, Pre-Columbian, 5 7/8 x 8 In.	292.00
Jar, Bird-Shaped Rim & Handle, Brown Clay, South America, 5 3/8 x 4 5/8 In.............	60.00
Jar, Crescent Shape, Wavy Line Design, Black & White Slip, Red Clay, 6 x 5 In.........	115.00
Jar, Fu Lion Finial Cover, Floral, Baluster, 6 Tusk Ring Handles, Japan, 15 3/4 In.	317.00
Jar, Holloway, For Cure Of Gout, England, c.1890	50.00
Jar, Storage, Horizontal Ring Design, Han Dynasty, 14 1/2 In.......................................	345.00
Jardiniere, Crackled Oatmeal Glaze, Stoneware, c.1960, Hans Coper, 29 1/2 In.	5430.00
Jug, Grotesque, Reinhard Pottery, Vale, N.C., June 1993, 11 1/2 In..............................	85.00
Jug, Slipware Flowers, Urns & Name Plates, Meacham, 1890, 8 1/4 In.	395.00
Mug, Fox Hunting, Silver Rim, Bronzed Trim, Turner, c.1800, 5 1/8 In.	430.00
Napkin Holder, Woman, Kneiss	35.00
Pitcher, Bird Shape, Stewart McCullock, Green, 6 In. .... *Illus*	20.00
Pitcher, Double Handle, R. Cole, 12 1/2 In.	595.00
Pitcher, Highwaymen, Leaf Borders, Turner, 8 In..	485.00

Pottery, Vase, Tea, Teal & Orange Swirl, Nemadii Pottery, 5 In.; Pottery, Vase, Green, Rust & Cream Swirl, Silver Springs, 2 1/2 In.

Pottery, Pitcher, Bird Shape, Stewart McCullock, Green, 6 In.

Pottery, Planter, Dove & Tree, Green, Orange Glaze, EHS, 1916, 3 In.

Pottery, Urn, Vase, Blue Green Glaze, 1930s, 6 In.

Pottery, Vase, Wheat Design, Green, Catalina, 7 In.

Pitcher, Milk, Flower & Berry Design, France, 6 In.	11.00
Pitcher, Tulip Design, Shenandoah Valley, 12 In.	690.00
Planter, Dove & Tree, Green, Orange Glaze, EHS, 1916, 3 In. ....*Illus*	45.00
Planter, Figural, Mack Truck, Bulldog, All Gold	75.00
Plate, Plum Tree, Muted Metallic Glazes, Handles, John Glick, 12 1/4 In.	488.00
Pot, Octopus, Barnacle Encrusted, Japan	350.00
Pot, Water, Aubergine Glaze, Ming Dynasty, 10 1/2 In.	575.00
Rose Bowl, Speckled Brown, M. Cardew, Wenford Bridge, c.1975, 13 In.	795.00
Teapot, House Form, Price Brothers, 20th Century, 6 In.	33.00
Teapot, Petals, 6-Cup, Purinton	90.00
Tureen, Soup, Chicken, Blue, Ladle, Morton	125.00
Urn, Vase, Blue Green Glaze, 1930s, 6 In. ....*Illus*	123.00
Vase, Animal Band On Shoulder, Han Dynasty, Green Glaze, 14 1/2 In.	920.00
Vase, Band Of Black Gazelles, Jean Mayodon, c.1935, 8 3/8 In.	1150.00
Vase, Black, Gouda Type Design, 10 In.	185.00
Vase, Blue Crystalline Glaze, Mustard Ground, Squatty, Thomas Gotham, 10 In.	192.00
Vase, Bottle Shape, Incised Bands, Buff, c.1958, Hans Coper, 19 3/4 In.	7300.00
Vase, Brown Crystalline Glaze, Bulbous, Cylindrical Neck, Pillin, 8 1/2 In.	297.00
Vase, Brown, Blue & White Clays, Ozark, Eureka Springs, Arts & Crafts, 4 3/4 In.	275.00
Vase, Brown, Rust & Cream Swirls, Ozark, Incised Eureka Springs, Ark., 11-5-27, 5 In.	192.00
Vase, Bulbous Bottom, Angular Shoulder, Incised Figures Inside Fish, Scheier, 5 In.	495.00
Vase, Bulbous, Apple Green & Gunmetal, Rose Cabat, 3 1/2 In.	275.00
Vase, Bulbous, Flared Lip, Blue & Gold Crystalline, Natzler, 4 1/2 In.	770.00
Vase, Bulbous, Pedestal Foot, Multitoned Blue High Glaze, Scheier, 5 In.	275.00
Vase, Canteen Form, Japanesque Vignettes, American Pottery Co., 9 1/4 In.	575.00
Vase, Cylindrical, White Crackle Glaze, Maija Grotell, 8 1/2 In.	2200.00
Vase, Dark Green Abstract Figures, Blue, Spherical, Maija Grotell, 9 1/2 In.	1725.00
Vase, Footed, Blue & Orange Geometrics, Wiener Werkstatte, No. 229, 8 In.	1045.00
Vase, Green, Rust & Cream Swirl, Silver Springs, 2 1/2 In. ....*Illus*	25.00
Vase, Incised Leaping Salmon & Birds, Squatty, B. Leach, St. Ives, c.1960, 8 1/2 In.	1885.00
Vase, Inverted Rim, Textured, Gertrud & Otto Natzler, c.1965, 4 3/4 In.	2990.00
Vase, Light To Dark Green High Glaze, Bulbous, Pillin, 6 1/2 In.	220.00

Vase, Mottled Matte Chartreuse Glaze, 4 Sides, G.R. Wall, 7 1/2 x 5 In. 315.00
Vase, Multicolored Exterior, Brown Flecked Interior, Peter Voulkos, 21 1/2 In. 1035.00
Vase, Ochre & Brown Mottled Matte Glaze, John Mason, 7 x 7 In. 660.00
Vase, Oviform, Green, Black Enameled Neck, Multicolored Medallion, Robj, Paris, 9 In. 800.00
Vase, Pear Shape, Footed, Brown Flecked Interior, Peter Voulkos, 21 1/2 In. 1035.00
Vase, Peasant Woman, Catalina Pottery, 6 1/2 In. 22.00
Vase, Rocket, Catalina, 6 In. 150.00
Vase, Tan & Maroon Mottled Design, Reuss, 6 7/8 In. 48.00
Vase, Tea, Teal & Orange Swirl, Nemadii Pottery, 5 In. .... *Illus* 35.00
Vase, Teco Form, Open Handles Joined At Rim, Spotted, Arts & Crafts, 6 In. 210.00
Vase, Triple, Female Nude, Metlox, C. Romanelli, 9 In. 150.00
Vase, Wheat Design, Green, Catalina, 7 In. .... *Illus* 40.00
Vase, White & Blue Over Violet High Glaze, Natzler, 5 x 8 1/2 In. 2860.00
Wall Pocket, Rooster, Jewel Eyes, California, Pair 50.00
Washstand Set, Brick Red, Taylor, Smith & Taylor, 8 Piece 880.00
Whistle, Bird, 19th Century, 2 1/4 In. 69.00

POWDER FLASKS AND POWDER HORNS were made to hold the gunpowder used in antique firearms. The early examples were made of horn or wood;
later ones were of copper or brass.

POWDER FLASK, Brass, Embossed Floral Design, 6 3/4 In. 55.00
  Brass, Fleur-De-Lis, 8 In. 45.00
  Copper, 2 Birds, Reclining Dog, 6 In. 55.00
  Copper, Black, Dram Measure, American Cap & Flask Co., 1840s 95.00
  Copper, Dead Game Scene, Scrollwork, Dixon & Sons, 8 1/2 In. 160.00
  Copper, Dog In Inverted Heart 75.00
  Copper, Embossed Basketweave & Leaf Design, Measuring Spout, 8 In. 70.00
  Copper, Embossed Indian Hunter Scene, 7 1/2 x 3 1/4 In. 165.00
  Copper, Hanging Game, Brass Trim, 7 3/8 In. 71.00
  Copper, Oak Leaves, Acorns & Stag's Head, Brass Trim, 8 7/8 In. 127.00
  Copper, Quail, Brass Trim, 7 In. 82.50
  Copper, Shell & Bush Design, Brass Spout, Dixon & Sons, 8 1/8 In. 82.00
  Copper, Treed Bear, Brass Trim, 8 3/8 In. 137.00
  Cow Horn, Flattened Triangular Body, Gilt-Bronze Mounts, Austria, c.1750 .... 1955.00
  Medallion With Hunter, Horse & Dog, Dixon & Sons On Spout 95.00
  Rifle, Leaf Designs, Deer Horns, 9 1/2 x 5 In. 165.00
  Steel, Triangular, Coat Of Arms, Cartouches, Italy, 17th Century, 8 1/2 In. 2587.00
  U.S. Navy, Fouled Anchor, Mid-19th Century 402.00
POWDER HORN, 2 Coat Of Arms Crests, Floral Borders, Bone Stopper, 6 3/4 In. 467.00
  Arm & Wreath, William Paulding, 1763 Signed 2190.00
  Carved Fish, Deer, Flintlock Muskets, Twice Dated 1761, 14 In. 675.00
  Carved Fish-Shaped Spout, Engraved Masonic Symbol, Alligator, 11 In. 495.00
  Cherry Plug, James McIntyre, Derry Twp., 1816, 10 1/2 In. 907.00
  Crown Point, Dan Leonard, Pay Document, 1760, 15 In. 2035.00
  Dark Horn Body, Pivoting Horn Stopper, Brass Chain, Batik, c.1800 .... 350.00
  Engraved, 3-Masted Ship & Schooner, 18th Century, 13 1/2 In. 517.00
  Engraved, Winthrop Chandler, His Horne, 10 1/2 In. 1265.00
  Engraved Geometric & Vine Design, Palitar Crooker, 18th Century, 11 In. 431.00
  Engraved WA, Circles, Flowers, 19th Century, 11 In. 115.00
  Flattened, Boar Hunting Scenes, Scrimshaw, 19th Century 375.00
  Independence, Metal Powder Measure, Carved 90.00
  Leather, Brass Hardware 47.00
  Raised Carved Intertwining Leaves, Wooden Plug, F.K.X., 1838, 7 3/4 In. 467.00
  Relief Carved Name & Date, Domed Pine Plug, Rings At Spout, 11 1/4 In. 330.00
  Screw Tip, Nailed Flat Pine Plug, Turned Designed Spout, 11 In. 71.00
  Storage, Primitive Engraved Dog, Stars & Shaw, Cork Stopper, 16 In. 82.00

PRATT ware means two different things. It was an early Staffordshire pottery,
cream-colored with colored decorations, made by Felix Pratt during the late
eighteenth century. There was also Pratt ware made with transfer designs during the mid-nineteenth century in Fenton, England. Reproductions of the
transfer-printed Pratt are being made.

PRATT
FENTON

Box, Scenic Cover, Royal Harbor, Ramsgate, England, c.1880, 5 In. 225.00

Creamer, Pearlware, Molded Satyr's Head, Silver Luster, 4 1/2 In.	121.00
Jar, Pomade, Cover, Volunteers, 2 7/8 In.	160.00
Jar, Pomade, Shakespeare's Birthplace	165.00
Jug, Lord Wellington & General Hill, c.1810, 5 1/4 In.	431.00
Jug, Medieval Print, Terra-Cotta, British Registry Mark, Aug. 5, 1859	525.00
Jug, Miser, 19th Century, 8 3/4 In.	374.00
Jug, Royal Sufferers & Duke Of York, Hawley, c.1795, 7 1/2 In.	690.00
Pitcher, Figure Of Blue Uniformed Soldier, Leaning On Rifle, 7 In.	175.00 to 195.00
Teapot, Eagle Spout	975.00
Toby Jug, Hearty Good Fellow, 11 In.	750.00
Toby Jug, Hearty Good Fellow, Tricorner Hat, Pipe In Left Hand, c.1820, 6 1/16 In.	3162.00

PRESSED GLASS was first made in the United States in the 1820s after the invention of glass pressing machines. Hundreds of patterns of pressed glass were made in complete table settings. Although the Boston and Sandwich Works was the most famous of the pressed glass factories, there were about sixteen other factories making pressed glass from 1830 to 1850, and still more from 1850 to 1900, when pressed glass reached its greatest popularity. It is now being widely reproduced. The pattern names used in this listing are based on the information in the book *Pressed Glass in America* by John and Elizabeth Welker. There may be pieces of pressed glass listed in this book in other categories, such as Lamp, Ruby, Sandwich, and Souvenir.

101 pattern is listed here as One-Hundred-One	
Acanthus pattern is listed here as Ribbed Palm	
Acme pattern is listed here as Butterfly With Spray	
Actress, Bowl, Miss Nielson, 5 x 8 In.	45.00
Actress, Butter, Cover	70.00
Actress, Cake Stand, 8 3/4 In.	145.00
Actress, Platter, H.M.S. Pinafore, Frosted Center, 7 x 11 In.	125.00
Actress, Sugar & Creamer	130.00
Admiral Dewey pattern is listed here as Spanish American	
Alabama, Bowl, 5 In.	20.00
Alabama, Butter, Cover	35.00
Alabama, Compote, Cover, 8 x 13 In.	150.00
Alabama, Creamer	30.00
Alabama, Relish, Oval, 3 3/4 x 8 1/2 In.	12.00
Alabama, Toothpick	70.00
Alaska, Pitcher, Water, Blue Opalescent	295.00
Alaska, Tumbler, Blue Opalescent, Enameled Flowers	75.00
Alaska, Tumbler, Vaseline	85.00
Almond Thumbprint, Goblet	18.00
Almond Thumbprint, Wine	10.00
Amazon, Butter, Cover	65.00
Amazon, Cruet	85.00
Amberette, Butter, Cover	130.00

Pressed Glass, Actress

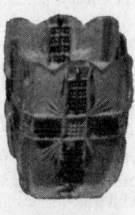
Pressed Glass, Amberette

Pressed Glass, Ashburton

Pressed Glass, Atlas

*Pressed Glass,
Barberry*

*Pressed Glass,
Beaded Grape Medallion*

*Pressed Glass,
Bellflower*

Amberette, Creamer	90.00
Amberette, Pitcher	260.00
Amberette, Punch Bowl, Pedestal	310.00
Amberette, Relish, Clear, 5 3/4 x 9 In.	16.00
Amberette, Sauce	68.00
Amberette, Sauce, Frosted	60.00
Amberette, Spooner	40.00
Amberette, Sugar, Cover	95.00
Amberette, Tumbler	100.00
Anthemion, Pitcher, 64 Oz.	45.00
Anthemion, Plate, 10 In.	20.00
Arabesque, Goblet	45.00
Arch & Forget-Me-Not Bands, Creamer	35.00 to 45.00
Arched Ovals, Goblet	19.00
Arched Ovals, Tumbler	14.00 to 25.00
Arched Ovals, Wine	12.00
Argent, Pitcher, 1/2 Gal.	25.00
Argent, Plate, 7 In.	8.00
Argus, Celery	95.00
Art, Banana Stand	88.00
Art, Bowl, 8 x 3 1/2 In.	32.00
Art, Cake Stand, 9 In.	65.00 to 85.00
Art, Celery Vase	48.00
Art, Compote, Open, 7 1/2 x 6 1/4 In.	48.00
Art, Compote, Scalloped Rim, 19 1/2 In.	95.00
Art, Sugar, Cover	48.00
Ashburton, Candy Dish, Pigeon Blood	125.00
Ashburton, Champagne, Flint	65.00
Ashburton, Creamer, Applied Handle, Flint	250.00
Ashburton, Eggcup, 10 Piece	121.00
Ashburton, Sugar, Cover, 7 1/4 In.	173.00
Ashburton, Tumbler, Ale, Flint	88.00
Ashburton, Tumbler, Water, Flint	125.00
Ashburton, Whiskey, Handle, Flint	125.00
Ashman, Cake Stand, 8 1/2 In.	60.00
Ashman, Celery Vase	45.00
Ashman, Compote, Cover, Square, 8 In.	125.00
Ashman, Relish, 4 x 8 In.	20.00
Atlanta, Compote, 8 3/8 x 8 1/2 In.	35.00
Atlanta, Compote, Jelly, 4 1/2 x 4 1/4 In.	32.00
Atlanta, Compote, Square, 1909, 6 In.	40.00
Atlanta, Spooner, Square, 7 In.	50.00
Atlas, Champagne	30.00
Atlas, Wine	20.00
Austrian, Creamer	35.00 to 60.00

Aztec, Punch Cup, Polished Bottom 5.00
Baby Thumbprint pattern is listed here as Dakota
Balder pattern is listed here as Pennsylvania
Balky Mule pattern is listed here as Currier & Ives
Ball & Bar, Tumbler, 4 In. 14.00
Baltimore Pear, Butter, Cover 55.00
Baltimore Pear, Compote, Cover, 8 In. 135.00
Baltimore Pear, Spooner 38.00
Banded patterns may also be listed under name of basic pattern: e.g., Banded Honeycomb is
called Honeycomb, banded
Banded Portland, Bowl, Cover, 8 In. 110.00
Banded Portland, Goblet, Pink Flashed 58.00
Banded Portland, Pitcher, Water 95.00
Banded Portland, Salt & Pepper 65.00
Banded Portland, Saltshaker, Pink Flashed.. 55.00
Banded Portland, Toothpick, Pink Flashed 25.00
Banded Portland, Vase, Pink Flashed, 6 In. 25.00
Banded Raindrop, Doughnut Stand 25.00
Banded Raindrop, Goblet, Blue... 65.00
Barberry, Cake Stand, Knob Stem, 10 3/4 In. x 6 1/4 In. 125.00
Barberry, Celery Vase 45.00
Barberry, Compote, Cover, Shell Finial 85.00
Barberry, Goblet 24.00
Barberry, Spooner 36.00
Barberry, Wine 30.00
Barley, Cake Stand, 9 1/2 In. 27.00
Barley & Oats pattern is listed here as Wheat & Barley
Barley & Wheat pattern is listed here as Wheat & Barley
Barred Forget-Me-Not, Bowl, Oval, Vaseline, 4 1/2 x 7 In. 38.00
Barred Forget-Me-Not, Pitcher, Milk 58.00
Barred Hobnail, Wine 12.00
Barred Oval, Cruet, Ruby Stained 300.00
Barreled Block pattern is listed here as Red Block
Basket Weave, Tray, Scenic, Blue, 12 In. 60.00
Beaded Band, Pitcher, Water.. 85.00
Beaded Bull's-Eye & Drape pattern is listed here as Alabama
Beaded Circle, Table Set, Green, Gold Trim, 4 Piece...................................... 350.00
Beaded Coarse Bars, Goblet 35.00
Beaded Dart Band, Goblet, Ruby Stained 90.00
Beaded Dewdrop pattern is listed here as Wisconsin
Beaded Fan, Bowl, Ruffled, Green 55.00
Beaded Grape, Celery Dish, Green, 5 x 10 1/2 In... 42.00
Beaded Grape, Compote, Square, 6 In... 25.00
Beaded Grape, Sugar 50.00
Beaded Grape Medallion, Compote, Cover, 8 x 10 In...................................... 95.00
Beaded Grape Medallion, Dish, Cable Rim, Star Base, 8 1/2 In. 28.00
Beaded Grape Medallion, Eggcup.. 30.00
Beaded Grape Medallion, Goblet 19.00
Beaded Grape Medallion, Pitcher, Water... 145.00
Beaded Grape Medallion, Spooner 32.00
Beaded Grape Medallion Banded, Compote, Cover, 8 In................................. 95.00
Beaded Loop, Bowl, Cover, 8 In.. 75.00
Beaded Loop, Bread Tray 22.00
Beaded Loop, Cake Stand, 7 3/4 In. 45.00
Beaded Loop, Compote, Open, 5 1/2 x 4 1/2 In. 16.00
Beaded Loop, Creamer 35.00
Beaded Loop, Goblet 35.00
Beaded Loop, Relish, Oval, 4 x 7 1/2 In. 14.00
Beaded Loop, Saltshaker 25.00
Beaded Loop, Sugar, Cover 22.00
Beaded Loop, Tumbler, Ruby Foot.. 45.00
Beaded Ovals In Sand, Cruet, Blue 145.00
Beaded Panels, Pitcher, Milk 65.00

Pressed Glass,
Bird & Strawberry

Pressed Glass,
Bleeding Heart

Pressed Glass,
Broken Column

Beaded Swirl & Disc, Relish, Triangular, Handle	10.00
Beaded Tulip, Goblet	30.00
Beaded Tulip, Pitcher, Milk	75.00
Bearded Man pattern is listed here as Queen Anne	
Beatty Rib, Finger Bowl, Blue, 4 1/4 In.	10.00
Beatty Rib, Spooner, Blue	20.00
Bellflower, Compote, 6 3/4 In.	58.00
Bellflower, Eggcup	25.00 to 35.00
Bellflower, Goblet, Rayed Base, Hexagonal Stem	40.00
Bellflower, Pitcher, Milk, Double Vine, Cut Flower, 8 1/2 In.	275.00
Bellflower, Syrup	600.00
Bellflower, Whiskey	125.00
Bellflower, Wine, 4 Piece	175.00
Belmont, Cake Stand, Amber, 10 In.	125.00
Bent Buckle pattern is listed here as New Hampshire	
Berkeley, Spooner, Frosted Leaves, 1893	30.00
Berry Cluster, Creamer	28.00
Bethlehem Star, Butter, Cover	42.00
Bethlehem Star, Compote, Cover, 6 1/4 x 9 1/2 In.	48.00
Bethlehem Star, Creamer	22.00
Bethlehem Star, Cruet	42.00
Bethlehem Star, Pitcher, Water	35.00
Bethlehem Star, Tumbler	26.00
Birch Leaf, Eggcup, Opalescent, Milk Glass, Flint	28.00
Birch Leaf, Spooner	28.00
Birch Leaf, Tumbler, Footed	22.00
Bird & Roses, Goblet, Etched	38.00
Bird & Strawberry, Butter	125.00
Bird & Strawberry, Butter, Cover	100.00 to 185.00
Bird & Strawberry, Compote, Open, 7 3/4 x 6 In.	125.00
Bird & Strawberry, Creamer	55.00
Bird & Strawberry, Pitcher, Water	350.00
Bird & Strawberry, Punch Cup	24.00
Bird & Strawberry, Water Set, 7 Piece	595.00
Bird & Strawberry, Wine	48.00
Bird In Ring pattern is listed here as Grace	
Blackberry, Goblet, 1870	30.00
Blaze, Spooner	42.00
Bleeding Heart, Cake Stand, 9 In.	75.00
Bleeding Heart, Cake Stand, 11 In.	95.00
Bleeding Heart, Compote, Cover, 8 1/2 x 9 1/2 In.	95.00
Bleeding Heart, Goblet, Knob Stem	38.00
Bleeding Heart, Spooner	38.00 to 45.00
Bleeding Heart, Sugar, Cover	55.00
Bleeding Heart, Wine, Knob Stem, Set Of 4	155.00

Block & Fan pattern is listed here as Romeo
Block & Star pattern is listed here as Valencia Waffle
Blockade pattern is listed here as Diamond Block With Fan
Blocked Arches pattern is listed here as Berkeley
Bluebird pattern is listed here as Bird & Strawberry
Bordered Ellipse, Spooner 28.00
Boy & Goose, Compote 225.00
Britannic, Cruet... 32.00
Britannic, Tumbler, Ruby Stained 45.00
Britannic, Wine, Ruby-Stained Ovals 55.00
Broken Column, Banana Stand 185.00
Broken Column, Cake Stand, 9 In. 95.00
Broken Column, Compote, Cover, Ruby Stained, 8 In. 450.00
Broken Column, Salt & Pepper, Pewter Tops 65.00
Broken Column, Tumbler, Ruby Stained Ovals .... 110.00 to 135.00
Brooklyn, Celery... 95.00
Brooklyn, Goblet, Flint... 95.00
Bryce pattern is listed here as Ribbon Candy
Bucket pattern is listed here as Oaken Bucket
Buckle, Goblet... 20.00
Buckle, Spooner 35.00
Buckle & Star, Goblet...28.00 to 45.00
Bulging Loops, Cruet, Yellow Cased 375.00
Bull's-Eye, Goblet, Flint 80.00
Bull's-Eye, Sugar 65.00
Bull's-Eye, Tumbler, 3 1/2 In. 50.00
Bull's-Eye & Buttons, Compote, Jelly, Green 40.00
Bull's-Eye & Buttons, Cruet, Gold Trim 55.00
Bull's-Eye & Daisy, Goblet, Green 30.00
Bull's-Eye & Fan, Creamer 18.00
Bull's-Eye & Fleur-De-Lis, Decanter, Stopper, Flint 350.00
Bull's-Eye & Fleur-De-Lis, Sugar, Flint.. 65.00
Bull's-Eye & Pillar, Wine 60.00
Bull's-Eye & Star, Toothpick 25.00
Bull's-Eye Variant, Tumbler, Footed 18.00
Bull's-Eye Variant, Wine.. 24.00
Bull's-Eye With Diamond Point, Spooner, Gold Band, Flint 95.00
Bullet, Creamer 125.00
Bullet Emblem, Creamer 165.00
Bunker Hill, Bread Plate... 65.00
Butterfly, Pitcher, Water 125.00
Butterfly & Fan pattern is listed here as Grace
Butterfly With Spray, Relish, Divided 38.00
Button Arches, Cake Stand, 9 1/4 x 4 1/2 In. 42.00
Button Arches, Creamer, Souvenir, Ruby Stained 30.00
Button Arches, Cup 20.00
Button Arches, Mug, 3 x 2 1/2 In. 15.00

Pressed Glass,
Bull's-Eye

Pressed Glass,
Classic

Pressed Glass,
Deer & Dog

Pressed Glass,
Delaware

Button Arches, Mug, Ruby Stained, 4 x 3 In. 28.00
Button Arches, Mug, Ruby Stained, Souvenir Pacific Grove............................... 35.00
Button Arches, Punch Cup 8.00
Button Arches, Toothpick, Marked 15.00
Button Arches, Toothpick, Opaque White 24.00
Button Arches, Tumbler, Ruby Etch, Souvenir 1st National Bank, 6 Piece 200.00
Button Arches, Wine 10.00
Button Band, Cake Stand 65.00
Button Panel, Sauce, Flat, 4 3/4 In... 8.00
Button Panel, Spooner 18.00
Button Panel, Vase, Gilded, 7 1/2 In... 30.00
Buzz Star, Toothpick 18.00
Cabbage Leaf, Sauce, Flat... 35.00
Cabbage Rose, Bowl, Oval, 5 x 7 1/2 In. 32.00
Cabbage Rose, Butter, Cover 68.00
Cabbage Rose, Cake Stand, 9 1/4 In. 42.00
Cabbage Rose, Compote, Cover, 7 1/2 x 10 In. 95.00
Cabbage Rose, Wine 40.00
Cable, Decanter, Stopper, 1 Qt. 209.00
Cable, Eggcup.. 33.00
Cable, Goblet, Water, 8 Piece 440.00
Cable, Pitcher, Syrup 308.00
Cable With Ring, Creamer, Flint 350.00
California pattern is listed here as Beaded Grape
Cameo is the name used for two different patterns listed here as Classic Medallion
Canadian, Bowl, Handle, 6 In.. 28.00
Canadian, Butter, Cover 35.00
Canadian, Compote, 6 3/4 x 4 1/2 In. 35.00
Canadian, Creamer, 5 In.. 110.00
Canadian, Plate, 6 In. 35.00
Canadian, Sugar, Cover 55.00
Canadian, Wine... 42.00
Candlewick as a pressed glass pattern is properly named *Banded Raindrop*. There is also a pattern called *Candlewick*, which has been made by Imperial Glass Corporation since 1936. It is listed in this book in the Imperial Glass category.
Candy Ribbon pattern is listed here as Ribbon Candy
Cane, Goblet, Amber 22.00
Cane, Waste Bowl, Amber... 35.00
Cannon Ball, Syrup Jug 103.00
Cannon Ball Pinwheel, Wine 10.00
Cape Cod, Compote, Cover, Large 125.00
Carmen pattern is listed here as Paneled Diamond & Finecut
Carolina, Goblet 18.00
Carolina, Plate, 7 1/4 In. 15.00
Carolina, Sauce, Flat... 10.00
Carolina, Wine.. 18.00
Cathedral, Cruet, Amber 135.00
Cayuga, Goblet 30.00
Celtic Cross, Creamer, Etched... 35.00
Celtic Cross, Goblet, Etched.. 42.00
Centennial, see the related patterns Liberty Bell and Washington Centennial
Chain With Diamonds pattern is listed here as Washington Centennial
Chain With Star, Creamer.. 20.00
Chandelier, Butter, Cover 75.00
Chandelier, Cake Stand 68.00
Chandelier, Celery...32.00 to 40.00
Chandelier, Compote, Open, Flared Rim, 7 x 7 In. 48.00
Chandelier, Creamer.. 15.00
Chandelier, Goblet, Etched.. 20.00
Chandelier, Inkwell 450.00
Chandelier, Pitcher 110.00
Chandelier, Spooner 42.00
Checkerboard, Pitcher 35.00

Checkerboard, Wine... 10.00
Chicken, Butter, Cover, Chicken Finial... 110.00
Chicken, Frosted, Compote, 7 In. 15.00
Church Windows pattern is listed here as Columbia
Classic, Berry Set, Log Feet, 7 Piece 345.00
Classic, Bowl, Footed, Hexagonal, 8 In. 125.00
Classic, Celery Vase, Collared Base.. 145.00
Classic, Creamer, Log Feet 210.00
Classic, Goblet, Log Feet, 8 Piece 290.00
Classic, Pitcher, Water 260.00
Classic, Spooner... 115.00
Classic, Spooner, Log Feet.. 110.00 to 150.00
Classic Medallion, Creamer.. 25.00
Clear Stork, Goblet 70.00
Coarse Cut & Block, Creamer... 12.00
Coin Spot pattern is listed in this book in its own category
Colonial, Celery Vase, Footed 50.00
Colorado, Banana Stand, Green... 30.00
Colorado, Butter.. 40.00
Colorado, Butter, Cover, Green 125.00
Colorado, Compote, 9 1/4 In. 85.00
Colorado, Nappy, Green, 7 1/4 In. 35.00
Colorado, Plate, Footed, Green, 6 3/4 In. 38.00
Colorado, Spooner, Green.. 85.00
Colorado, Spooner, Green, Gold Trim 60.00
Colorado, Sugar, Cover, Green... 68.00
Colorado, Tumbler, Souvenir, Gold Trim 30.00
Colossus, Cake Stand, 9 In. 35.00
Colossus, Goblet 35.00
Colossus, Sugar & Creamer 20.00
Columbia, Goblet 16.00
Columbia, Sugar, Cover, Rose Blush.. 60.00
Columbia, Sugar, Cover, Rose, Green, Vaseline Stain 52.00
Columned Thumbprints, Celery 9.00
Comet, Goblet 80.00
Compact pattern is listed here as Snail
Connecticut, Bowl, White Flowers, 7 1/2 In.. 32.00
Connecticut, Butter, Cover, White Flowers 85.00
Connecticut, Spooner, White Flowers 35.00
Cord & Tassel, Compote, Cover, Low Standard, 8 In. 75.00
Cord Drapery, Butter, Cover, 5 In. 37.00
Cord Drapery, Compote, Cover, 8 In. 225.00
Cord Drapery, Compote, Jelly.. 28.00
Cord Drapery, Punch Cup 16.00
Cord Drapery, Relish, 5 1/4 x 9 1/4 In. 32.00
Corona, Wine 10.00
Cosmos pattern is listed in this book as its own category
Cottage, Creamer 20.00
Cottage, Cup & Saucer.. 14.00
Crane pattern is listed here as Stork
Croesus, Butter, Cover, Green 95.00
Croesus, Butter, Cover, Green, Gold Trim 135.00
Croesus, Butter, Cover, Purple, Gold Trim 120.00
Croesus, Compote, Cover, 6 x 10 1/2 In. 95.00
Croesus, Compote, Jelly, Purple 295.00
Croesus, Creamer, Green 65.00
Croesus, Cruet, Green, Gold Trim 375.00
Croesus, Pitcher, Green, Gold Trim, 5 1/2 In.. 95.00
Croesus, Spooner, Green.. 70.00
Croesus, Sugar, Cover, Green 125.00
Croesus, Sugar, Cover, Purple .... 105.00 to 120.00
Croesus, Table Set, Green, Gold Trim, 4 Piece................................. 400.00 to 450.00
Croesus, Water Set, Green, Gold Trim, 5 Piece 650.00

Crowfoot, Cake Stand, 9 In. 48.00
Crowfoot, Creamer.. 16.00
Crown Jewels is a name used for two different patterns listed here as Chandelier or Queen's Necklace
Crystal Wedding, Banana Stand 125.00
Crystal Wedding, Bowl, Square, Frosted Loop, Scalloped Rim, 7 In. 48.00
Crystal Wedding, Cake Stand, Square, 9 In. 95.00
Crystal Wedding, Compote, Cover, Square, 5 In. 35.00
Crystal Wedding, Compote, Square, 9 x 7 In. 50.00
Crystal Wedding, Creamer 58.00
Crystal Wedding, Lamp, 9 In. 275.00
Crystal Wedding, Spooner, Ruby Stained 95.00
Crystal Wedding, Sugar, Cover 58.00
Cube, Goblet...15.00 to 18.00
Cupid & Psyche pattern is listed here as Psyche & Cupid
Cupid & Venus, Celery, Scalloped Rim 55.00
Cupid & Venus, Compote, Cover, 8 In. 125.00
Cupid & Venus, Pitcher, 7 1/2 In. 65.00
Cupid's Hunt, Sauce, Footed, 4 In. 10.00
Currant, Cake Stand, 10 3/4 x 6 1/4 In. 65.00
Currant, Wine 35.00
Currier & Ives, Creamer 4.00
Currier & Ives, Goblet, Amber 55.00
Currier & Ives, Pitcher, Milk 50.00
Currier & Ives, Pitcher, Water, Amber 150.00
Currier & Ives, Pitcher, Water, Blue 195.00
Currier & Ives, Plate, 7 In. 8.00
Currier & Ives, Sugar, Cover 4.00
Currier & Ives, Tray, Water, Balky Mule 40.00
Currier & Ives, Water Set, 7 Piece 250.00
Curtain, Creamer 26.00
Cut Log, Bowl, Footed, 10 In. 70.00
Cut Log, Cake Stand, 10 In. 62.00
Cut Log, Compote, Scalloped Rim, 8 3/4 In. 75.00
Cut Log, Cruet, 5 1/2 In. 50.00
Cut Log, Wine 16.00
Cyclone, Creamer, Etched... 35.00
Dahlia pattern is listed here as Square Fuchsia
Daisies In Oval Panels pattern is listed here as Bull's-Eye & Fan
Daisy & Button, Compote, Scalloped, 8 3/8 x 9 5/8 In. 38.00
Daisy & Button , see also the related pattern Paneled Daisy & Button
Daisy & Button, Ashtray, 3-Footed, Kettle Style, 3 3/4 x 2 In. 4.00
Daisy & Button, Bowl, 6 Sides, Pointy Rim, 8 3/4 x 3 1/4 In. 30.00
Daisy & Button, Bowl, Triangular, 8 In. 65.00
Daisy & Button, Dish, Fan 8.00
Daisy & Button, Goblet, Vertical Blue Thumbprint Panels 85.00
Daisy & Button, Plate, Amberina, 5 x 5 In. 150.00
Daisy & Button, Platter, Oval, Handles 26.00
Daisy & Button, Saltshaker, Pewter Top, Flint, Pair 60.00
Daisy & Button, Sugar, Cover 45.00
Daisy & Button, Sugar, Cover, Amber Panel... 145.00
Daisy & Button, Toothpick, Amber 9.00
Daisy & Button, Toothpick, Cube, Blue 15.00
Daisy & Button, Tumbler, Amber Panels 45.00
Daisy & Button With Crossbar, Bowl, Amber, 8 x 4 1/2 In......................... 15.00
Daisy & Button With Crossbar, Pitcher, Water, Amber 65.00
Daisy & Button With Crossbar, Sugar & Creamer, Amber...................... 40.00
Daisy & Button With Narcissus, Tray, Water, Gold Trim.......................... 25.00
Daisy & Button With Thumbprint, Celery 25.00
Daisy & Button With Thumbprint, Creamer 26.00
Daisy & Button With V-Ornament, Celery Vase.......................26.00 to 35.00
Daisy & Button With V-Ornament, Sauce, Flat, 4 1/2 In. 10.00
Daisy & Fan, Goblet, Scalloped, Green, Gold Trim & Base 40.00

Pressed Glass,   Pressed Glass,
Diamond   Egyptian
Thumbprint

Pressed Glass,
Frosted Circle

Pressed Glass,
Frosted Dolphin

Daisy & Plume, Compote, Candy, Green	48.00
Dakota, Cake Basket, Metal Handle	245.00
Dakota, Celery Vase, Pedestal, Etched	45.00
Dakota, Compote, Cover, 7 3/4 x 12 In.	65.00
Dakota, Compote, Etched, 6 x 6 1/2 In.	38.00
Dakota, Compote, Golf Ball Standard, 8 x 8 In.	34.00
Dakota, Compote, Jelly, Oak-Leaf Etching	28.00
Dakota, Creamer, Etched	55.00
Dakota, Goblet, Etched	22.00 to 28.00
Dakota, Goblet, Ruby Stained	95.00
Dakota, Jug, 1 Qt.	80.00
Dakota, Pitcher, Ruby Stained	250.00
Dakota, Pitcher, Water, Etched	95.00
Dakota, Spooner, Etched	38.00
Dakota, Sugar, Cover	30.00
Dakota, Sugar, Cover, Etched	60.00
Dakota, Wine, Ruby Stained	60.00
Dart, Compote, Cover, 8 x 12 In.	32.00
Deer & Doe With Lily-Of-The-Valley, Goblet	180.00
Deer & Dog, Goblet, U-Shaped	70.00
Deer & Oak Tree, Pitcher, Water	195.00
Deer & Pine Tree, Bread Plate, Amber	45.00
Deer & Pine Tree, Bread Plate, Canary	75.00
Deer & Pine Tree, Bread Plate, Green	70.00
Deer & Pine Tree, Bread Tray, Blue	125.00
Deer & Pine Tree, Cake Stand, 9 In.	125.00
Deer & Pine Tree, Compote, Cover, 9 x 7 x 12 1/2 In.	70.00
Deer & Pine Tree, Jam Jar	275.00
Deer & Pine Tree, Mug, Child's	40.00
Deer & Pine Tree, Pitcher	125.00 to 135.00
Deer & Pine Tree, Tray, Green	110.00
Deer & Pine Tree, Waste Bowl	125.00
Delaware, Bowl, Green, 8 In.	18.00
Delaware, Bowl, Green, Gold Trim, 8 In.	47.00
Delaware, Bowl, Green, Gold Trim, 9 In.	40.00
Delaware, Celery Vase, Rose, Gold Trim	38.00
Delaware, Cup	8.00
Delaware, Pitcher, Gold Trim	110.00
Delaware, Pitcher, Green, Gold Trim	125.00
Delaware, Pitcher, Green, Gold Trim, Jug Shape	150.00
Delaware, Punch Cup, Green, Gold Trim	35.00
Delaware, Spooner, Rose, Gold Trim	65.00
Delaware, Tankard, Water, Green, Gold Trim, 9 1/4 In.	100.00
Delaware, Toothpick, Green, Gold Trim	95.00

Delaware, Tumbler, Rose, Souvenir, Atlantic City, 1908 .... 25.00
Delaware, Water Set, Green, Gold Trim, 7 Piece 260.00
Dewdrop, Butter, Domed Cover 35.00
Dewdrop, Goblet, Amber 22.00
Dewdrop, Goblet, Vaseline 22.00
Dewdrop, Relish, Double, Leaf Handles 8.00
Dewdrop, Tumbler, Vaseline 14.00
Dewdrop In Points, Creamer 28.00
Dewdrop In Points, Pitcher, Water 45.00
Dewdrop With Star, Cheese Dish 125.00
Dewdrop With Star, Cheese Dish, Cover 125.00
Dewdrop With Star, Plate, 6 In. 7.00
Dewdrop With Star, Sauce, Footed, Scalloped Edge, 3 In. 5.00
Dewdrop With Star, Sugar, Cover 22.00
Dewey, see also the related pattern Spanish American
Dewey, Pitcher, 9 In. 22.00
Diagonal Band, Bread Plate 25.00
Diagonal Band, Compote, Cover, 8 In. 85.00
Diagonal Band, Goblet 28.00
Diagonal Block With Fan, Compote, Flared In, 7 x 6 1/4 In. 20.00
Diamond & Bull's-Eye Band, Bowl, Piecrust Edge, 7 1/4 .... 38.00
Diamond & Bull's-Eye Band, Cake Stand, 9 1/2 In. 95.00
Diamond & Bull's-Eye Band, Compote, Fruit, 8 In. 110.00
Diamond & Bull's-Eye Band, Pitcher 225.00
Diamond & Bull's-Eye Band, Sauce Dish, 3 3/4 In. 18.00
Diamond & Bull's-Eye Band, Tankard, Water, Etched Leaf & Flower, 12 In. 225.00
Diamond Medallion pattern is listed here as Grand
Diamond Point, Bar Bottle, Flint, 1 Qt. 125.00
Diamond Point, Champagne, Flint 125.00
Diamond Point, Compote, Flint, 8 In. 55.00
Diamond Point, Goblet 40.00
Diamond Point, Goblet, Flint 58.00
Diamond Point, Jar, Pomade, Cover, Knob Stem, Flint 45.00
Diamond Point, Pitcher, Flint 145.00
Diamond Point, Plate, 3 1/4 In. 14.00
Diamond Point, Sugar, Cover, Footed, Flint 75.00
Diamond Quilted, Celery Vase, Amethyst 68.00
Diamond Quilted, Cordial, Amber 25.00
Diamond Quilted, Pitcher, Water, Amber 55.00
Diamond Quilted, Sugar, Cover, Amber 68.00
Diamond Quilted, Waste Bowl, Blue 38.00
Diamond Spearhead, Toothpick 65.00
Diamond Sunburst Variant, Goblet 16.00
Diamond Thumbprint, Compote, 11 In. 160.00
Diamond Thumbprint, Honey Jar, Flint, 3 1/2 In. 20.00
Dog With Rabbit In Mouth, Plate, Scene 2, Clear 95.00
Dog With Rabbit In Mouth, Plate, Scene 3, Frosted 95.00
Doric pattern is listed here as Feather
Dot & Dash, Goblet 28.00
Double Loop pattern is listed here as Ribbon Candy
Double Ribbon, Bread Tray 65.00
Double Spear, Compote, Cover, 8 In. 180.00
Double Wedding Ring pattern is listed here as Wedding Ring
Doyle's Shell, Water Bottle 20.00
Drapery, Creamer 45.00
Drum, Creamer, Miniature 50.00
Drum, Mug, Opalescent 95.00
Drum, Mustard, Child's 100.00
Dynast pattern is listed here as Radiant
Egyptian, Creamer ....48.00 to 50.00
Egyptian, Goblet ....35.00 to 55.00
Egyptian, Pitcher, Water 255.00
Egyptian, Sauce, Footed, 4 1/2 In. 16.00

Egyptian, Spooner 42.00
Elaine, Plate, Swan Handles, Frosted 85.00
Emerald Green Herringbone, Cruet 95.00
Emerald Green Herringbone, Tumbler .... 18.00 to 22.00
Emerald Green Herringbone, Vase, 6 In. 160.00
Empire Colonial, Goblet, Flint 145.00
English Hobnail Cross pattern is listed here as Amberette
Esther, Celery, Amber Stained 85.00
Esther, Goblet, Enamel, Yellow Stained 50.00
Esther, Goblet, Etched, Amber Stained 145.00
Esther, Pitcher, Green .... 350.00 to 375.00
Esther, Sugar, Cover, Emerald, Gold Trim .... 85.00 to 135.00
Esther, Table Set, Green, 4 Piece 395.00
Etched Dakota pattern is listed here as Dakota
Eureka, Bread Plate 25.00
Eureka, Goblet, Flint 34.00
Eureka, Tumbler, Footed, Flint 25.00
Everglades, Sauce, Blue 25.00
Excelsior, Mug, Applied Handle, Flint 65.00
Excelsior, Spooner, 4 3/4 In. 35.00
Excelsior, Sugar, Cover, 6 1/2 In. 173.00
Excelsior, Sugar, Cover, 9 1/2 In. 230.00
Excelsior, Sugar, Pagoda Cover, Flint 110.00
Excelsior Variant, Creamer 30.00
Eyewinker, Compote, Pedestal, 8 1/2 x 9 1/2 x 5 In. .... 175.00 to 185.00
Eyewinker, Fruit Stand, Folded Edge, 7 In. 115.00
Eyewinker, Toothpick 20.00
Fan & Flute, Celery Vase 35.00
Fan & Flute, Creamer, Ruby Stained 55.00
Fan Band, Wine 42.00
Fan With Diamond pattern is listed here as Shell
Feather, Bowl, Oval, 6 1/2 x 9 In. 24.00
Feather, Cake Stand, 8 In. .... 32.00 to 40.00
Feather, Cake Stand, 9 1/2 In. 55.00
Feather, Compote, 8 In. 38.00
Feather, Compote, Cover, 7 In. 190.00
Feather, Pitcher, Water .... 48.00 to 55.00
Feather, Pitcher, Water, Green 175.00
Feather, Plate, 10 In. 55.00
Feather, Relish, 8 In. 18.00
Feather, Sugar, Cover 45.00
Feather, Wine, Scalloped 30.00
Feather Duster, Creamer 16.00
Fern Garland, Butter Pat 2.00
Festoon, Berry Bowl, Round, 9 In. 18.00
Festoon, Cake Plate, Pedestal, 9 In. 55.00
Festoon, Creamer 25.00
Festoon, Sugar, Cover .... 22.00 to 65.00
Festoon, Tumbler 30.00
Festoon, Waste Bowl 38.00
Festoon, Water Set, 6 Piece 200.00
Festoon & Grape pattern is listed here as Grape & Festoon
Fickle Block, Wine 10.00
Fine Cut, Wine 25.00
Fine Cut & Feather pattern is listed here as Feather
Fine Cut & Panel, Compote, 8 In. 35.00
Fine Cut & Panel, Goblet .... 12.00 to 20.00
Fine Cut & Panel, Goblet, Blue, 5 3/8 In. 40.00
Fine Rib, Claret, Flint, 5 In. 250.00
Fine Rib, Decanter, Flint 85.00
Fine Rib, Whiskey Taster, Crimped Handle, Flint 60.00
Fishscale, Cake Stand, 8 3/4 In. 25.00
Fishscale, Celery Vase 35.00

Pressed Glass,
Frosted Eagle

Pressed Glass,
Holly

Pressed Glass,
Horseshoe

Fishscale, Mug	95.00
Fishscale, Pitcher, 1 Gal.	55.00
Fishscale, Plate, Square, 9 In.	36.00
Fishscale, Sauce, Flat	10.00
Fishscale, Spooner	30.00
Flamingo Habitat, Celery	45.00
Flamingo Habitat, Creamer	48.00 to 50.00
Flamingo Habitat, Finger Bowl	55.00
Flamingo Habitat, Pickle Jar, Mushroom Stopper	115.00
Flamingo Habitat, Sugar, Cover	55.00
Flat Diamond, Goblet, Flint	195.00
Flat Diamond, Punch Bowl, Child's, Sunburst	24.00
Flattened Hobnail, Pitcher, 64 Oz.	55.00
Flattened Sawtooth, Bowl, 5 In.	30.00
Fleur-De-Lis, Sugar	65.00
Fleur-De-Lis & Drape, Celery Vase, Green	42.00
Fleur-De-Lis & Drape, Creamer	18.00
Fleur-De-Lis & Drape, Plate, Green, 8 In.	24.00
Flora, Cruet, Green, Gold Trim	295.00
Florida pattern pieces are listed here as Sunken Primrose if made of clear class and as Emerald Green Herringbone if made of green glass	
Flower & Honeycomb, Tumbler	16.00
Flower Flange pattern is listed here as Dewey	
Flower With Cane, Goblet	22.00
Flower With Cane, Mug, 3 3/4 In.	8.00
Flute, Berry Set, Childs's, 7 Piece	47.00
Flying Robin pattern is listed here as Hummingbird	
Forget-Me-Not In Scroll, Sugar	16.00
Four Petal, Sugar, Cover	45.00
Four Petal, Sugar, Cover, Flint	55.00
Frosted patterns may also be listed under name of main pattern	
Frosted Circle, Butter, Cover, Clear Circles	48.00
Frosted Circle, Goblet, Water	28.00
Frosted Circle, Sauce, Ruby Stained	35.00
Frosted Crane pattern is listed here as Frosted Stork	
Frosted Dolphin, Compote, 4 3/4 In.	125.00
Frosted Eagle, Celery Vase, Engraved Roses Design	75.00
Frosted Eagle, Compote, 6 x 6 In.	75.00
Frosted Eagle, Sugar, Cover, Dog Handle	90.00
Frosted Leaf, Eggcup, Flint	95.00
Frosted Leaf, Salt, Master, Flint	125.00
Frosted Leaf, Sugar	85.00
Frosted Leaf, Sugar, Flint	85.00
Frosted Ribbon, Butter	45.00
Frosted Ribbon, Celery Vase	38.00

Frosted Ribbon, Compote, Cover, 8 x 11 In. 95.00
Frosted Ribbon, Goblet.. 27.00
Frosted Ribbon, Spooner 34.00
Frosted Stork, Platter, 101 Border 65.00
Frosted Waffle pattern is listed here as Hidalgo
Fuchsia, Creamer, Applied Handle 45.00
Fuchsia, Spooner.. 32.00
Galloway, Bowl, Maiden's Blush, Flared Out, 7 3/4 In. 48.00
Galloway, Butter, Cover.. 55.00
Galloway, Castor, Pickle... 95.00
Galloway, Goblet, Gold Trim.. 85.00
Galloway, Relish, 8 1/2 x 6 3/4 In. 20.00
Galloway, Sauce, Maiden's Blush, Flared Out, 4 3/4 In. 22.00
Galloway, Vase, Green, 9 In. 30.00
Galloway, Wine 55.00
Galloway, Wine, Gold Trim.. 38.00
Garden Fruits, Goblet, Etched.. 38.00
Garden Of Eden, see also the related pattern Lotus & Serpent
Garden Of Eden, Goblet, Serpent... 475.00
Garfield Drape, Plate, We Mourn Our Nation's Loss 50.00
Georgia, Compote, 6 In. 18.00
Giant Bull's-Eye, Cheese Dish, Cover 95.00
Giant Bull's-Eye, Goblet... 35.00
Giant Bull's-Eye, Tray, 7 In. 32.00
Giant Prism With Thumbprint Band, Celery Vase, Flint 125.00
Giant Prism With Thumbprint Band, Tumbler, Flint.. 55.00
Gonterman Swirl, Celery, Amber.. 95.00
Gonterman Swirl, Toothpick, Amber, Frosted Base.. 195.00
Good Luck pattern is listed here as Horseshoe
Gooseberry, Creamer 45.00
Gooseberry, Mug, Handle 45.00
Gothic, Sugar.. 40.00
Gothic, Wine 100.00
Gothic Arch, Sugar, Cover, Canary Lace, 5 1/4 In. 605.00
Grace, Bowl, 7 In... 42.00
Grace, Compote, 7 1/2 x 6 1/4 In. 38.00
Grace, Creamer 55.00
Grace, Sauce, Footed, 4 1/2 In. 20.00
Grand, Cake Plate 15.00
Grand, Celery Vase 26.00
Grand, Compote, 7 x 5 1/2 In. 18.00
Grand, Creamer 20.00
Grand, Goblet 26.00
Grant, U. S., Plate, Green, Born 1822, Died 1885, 10 1/4 In. 270.00
Grant, U.S., Let Us Have Peace Plate, Amber... 65.00
Grape, see also the related patterns Beaded Grape, Beaded Grape Medallion, and Magnet &
Grape
Grape & Festoon, Compote, Cover, Acorn Finial 80.00
Grape & Festoon With Shield, Goblet.. 38.00
Grape Band, Tumbler 20.00
Grape With Vine, Plate, 6 3/4 In. 10.00
Grasshopper, Casserole, Cover, 7 In... 65.00
Grasshopper, Nappy, Footed, 4 3/4 In. 14.00
Grasshopper, Plate, 7 1/2 In. 18.00
Greek Key, Goblet, Frosted, Flint.. 65.00
Gridley, Pitcher, Water 135.00
Halley's Comet, Goblet 26.00
Halley's Comet, Wine 18.00
Hamilton, Compote, Pair 210.00
Hamilton, Compote, Scalloped Rim, 7 In. 46.00
Hamilton, Eggcup, Flint 35.00
Hamilton, Goblet, Flint 45.00
Hamilton, Pitcher, Peerless, c.1875 .... 100.00

Hand, Jam Jar... 45.00
Hand, Platter, Oval 25.00
Harvard Yard, Plate, 10 In.. 10.00
Harvard Yard, Sugar, Breakfast, 2 Handles, Open 10.00
Harvard Yard, Wine 10.00
Heart Stem, Celery Vase 60.00
Heart Stem, Celery Vase, Amber 125.00
Heart Stem, Sugar, Cover... 65.00
Heart With Thumbprint, Banana Stand, Flat, 10 In... 110.00
Heart With Thumbprint, Berry Set, 6 Piece 145.00
Heart With Thumbprint, Carafe 100.00
Heart With Thumbprint, Celery 95.00
Heart With Thumbprint, Compote, Ruffled Rim, 8 In. 225.00
Heart With Thumbprint, Cruet 80.00
Heart With Thumbprint, Goblet... 65.00
Heart With Thumbprint, Nappy, 6 1/4 In... 8.00
Heart With Thumbprint, Rose Bowl, 2 1/2 In. 58.00
Heart With Thumbprint, Wine ....30.00 to 50.00
Hearts Of Loch Laven pattern is listed here as Shuttle
Heavy Paneled Grape, Wine 22.00
Heron, Pitcher... 175.00
Herringbone, Goblet.. 12.00
Herringbone Band, Goblet.. 8.00
Hexagon Block, Pitcher, Ruby Stained, Leaf Etched... 225.00
Hexagon Block, Water Set, 6 Piece 325.00
Hickman, Cake Stand, 7 3/4 In. 18.00
Hickman, Compote, Cover, 5 x 7 1/2 In. 42.00
Hickman, Ice Bucket.. 45.00
Hickman, Pitcher, Water, Blue 95.00
Hickman, Punch Cup, Footed 25.00
Hickman, Relish, Green, 4 x 8 In. 14.00
Hickman, Toothpick 42.00
Hickman, Vase, 8 In. 18.00
Hickman, Wine 8.00
Hidalgo, Compote, Cover, Flowers, 7 1/2 x 12 In. 52.00
Hidalgo, Cruet, Amber Stained 195.00
Hidalgo, Goblet.. 12.00
Hidalgo, Goblet, Frosted...16.00 to 24.00
Hidalgo, Sugar Shaker, Frosted.. 35.00
Hobnail pattern is in this book as its own category
Hobnail & Bars pattern is listed here as Barred Hobnail
Holly, Creamer 115.00
Honeycomb, Bar Bottle, Stopper, Flint 110.00
Honeycomb, Celery Vase, Flint, Grapes On Vine Etching 45.00
Honeycomb, Compote, Flint, 10 x 7 1/4 In. 48.00
Honeycomb, Goblet, Etched, Flint.. 38.00
Honeycomb With Pillar, Goblet 10.00
Hops Band, Butter, Cover.. 35.00
Horn Of Plenty, Bottle, Bar... 95.00
Horn Of Plenty, Cake Stand, Frosted, 9 1/2 In. 85.00
Horn Of Plenty, Celery Vase 125.00
Horn Of Plenty, Compote, Cover, 13 In. 135.00
Horn Of Plenty, Goblet, Flint... 85.00
Horn Of Plenty, Lamp, Table, 15 In. 130.00
Horn Of Plenty, Plate, Flint, 6 In. 110.00
Horn Of Plenty, Sauce, Flint, 5 1/4 In. 20.00
Horn Of Plenty, Spooner.. 50.00
Horn Of Plenty, Tumbler, Flint... 75.00
Horn Of Plenty, Wine 175.00
Horseshoe, Bowl, Oval, 5 x 8 In. 28.00
Horseshoe, Bread Tray 48.00
Horseshoe, Butter, Cover 110.00
Horseshoe, Cake Stand, 7 3/4 In. 95.00

Horseshoe, Compote, Cover, 6 1/4 x 10 1/2 In.	95.00
Horseshoe, Pitcher, Milk	165.00
Horseshoe, Pitcher, Water	110.00
Horseshoe, Relish	25.00
Horseshoe, Sauce, Footed, 4 In.	15.00
Horseshoe, Spooner	35.00
Horseshoe, Sugar Shaker, Amber	80.00
Horseshoe, Tray, Double Handles	85.00
Huckle pattern is listed here as Feather Duster	
Hummingbird, Butter, Cover, Blue	110.00
Hummingbird, Pitcher, Water, Amber	125.00
Hummingbird, Sugar, Cover, Blue	110.00
Hummingbird, Sugar, Open, Blue	75.00
Hummingbird, Tumbler, Blue	45.00
Humpty-Dumpty, Mug, Amber	10.00
Hundred Eye, Wine	10.00
Ida pattern is listed here as Sheraton	
Idyll, Toothpick	45.00
Illinois, Berry Bowl, Individual	18.00
Illinois, Compote, Square	140.00
Illinois, Creamer	35.00
Illinois, Cruet, Stopper	120.00
Illinois, Sugar, Cover	48.00
Illinois, Toothpick	32.00
Indiana Swirl pattern is listed here as Feather	
Intaglio, Creamer	55.00
Inverted Fan & Feather, Creamer, Blue, Gold Trim	115.00
Inverted Fern, Sugar, Cover, Flint	60.00
Inverted Thistle, Tumbler	25.00
Inverted Thumbprint, Pitcher, Amber	40.00
Inverted Thumbprint, Pitcher, Blue, Ruffled Top	48.00
Inverted Thumbprint, Pitcher, Reeded Handle	185.00
Inverted Thumbprint, Tumbler, Blue	22.00
Inverted Thumbprint, Wine	10.00
Ionia, Goblet	18.00
Iowa, Saltshaker, Gilded Zippers	16.00
Iowa, Wine, Gold Trim	26.00
Ivy In Snow, Cake Stand, 8 In.	32.00
Jacob's Ladder, Bowl, Oval, 7 1/4 x 10 3/4 In.	26.00
Jacob's Ladder, Cake Stand, 9 1/4 In.	48.00
Jacob's Ladder, Celery	35.00
Jacob's Ladder, Celery Vase, 9 In.	38.00
Jacob's Ladder, Compote, Scalloped Rim, 9 3/4 x 5 In.	42.00
Jacob's Ladder, Creamer	8.00
Jacob's Ladder, Cruet	75.00
Jacob's Ladder, Dish, Oval, 8 3/4 x 6 In.	15.00
Jacob's Ladder, Plate, 6 1/4 In.	28.00

Pressed Glass,
Jacob's Ladder

Pressed Glass,
Jeweled Heart

Pressed Glass,
Jumbo

Pressed Glass,
Leaf and Dart

Jacob's Ladder, Sauce, Footed, 4 1/2 In.	12.00
Jacob's Ladder, Spooner, 6 In.	32.00
Jacobs Ladder, Wine	25.00
Japanese, Platter, 11 In.	30.00
Japanese, Sauce, Footed, 4 1/2 In.	25.00
Jefferson Optic, Creamer	75.00
Jewel, Creamer, Child's	55.00
Jewel, Spooner, Child's	42.00
Jewel & Dewdrop, Bread Plate	45.00
Jewel & Dewdrop, Cake Stand, 9 x 4 In.	58.00
Jewel & Dewdrop, Compote, Scalloped Rim, 6 1/4 In.	48.00
Jewel & Dewdrop, Relish, 8 1/2 In.	23.00
Jewel & Dewdrop, Spooner	75.00
Jewel & Dewdrop, Wine	95.00
Jewel & Festoon pattern is listed here as Loop & Jewel	
Jewel Band, Celery	18.00
Jewel Band, Eggcup	20.00
Jeweled Heart, Cruet, Green	150.00
Jeweled Heart, Tumbler, Blue, Gold Trim	45.00
Jeweled Heart, Water Set, Green, Gold Trim, 6 Piece	250.00
Jeweled Moon & Star pattern is listed here as Moon & Star	
Job's Tears pattern is listed here as Art	
Jubilee pattern is listed here as Hickman	
Jumbo, Butter, Cover, Rectangular	650.00
Jumbo, Creamer	285.00
Jumbo, Mug, Novelty, 5 1/4 In.	60.00
Kamoni pattern is listed here as Pennsylvania	
Kansas pattern is listed here as Jewel & Dewdrop	
Kentucky, Celery Dish	25.00
Kentucky, Punch Cup, Green	28.00
Kentucky, Wine	20.00
Keystone Grape, Goblet	26.00
King Arthur, Pitcher, Water, 10 1/2 In.	52.00
King's 500, Salt & Pepper, Blue, Gold Trim	145.00
King's Crown, see also the related pattern Ruby Thumbprint	
King's Crown, Banana Stand	75.00
King's Crown, Cake Stand, 9 In.	85.00
King's Crown, Compote, Scalloped Edge, 7 1/4 x 7 In.	42.00
King's Crown, Compote, Scalloped Edge, 8 In.	65.00
King's Crown, Creamer, Ruby-Stained, Individual	35.00
King's Crown, Cup	18.00
King's Crown, Goblet, Water, Ruby Flashed, 12 Piece	140.00
King's Crown, Mustard	30.00
King's Crown, Tankard, Water, 12 3/4 In.	195.00
King's Crown, Toothpick	25.00
King's Crown, Toothpick, Etched, Ruby Stained	45.00
King's Crown, Toothpick, Ruby Stained	42.00
King's Crown, Water Set, Cobalt Blue, Gold Trim, 7 Piece	850.00
King's Curtain, Goblet	14.00

Pressed Glass,
Liberty Bell

Pressed Glass,
Maine

Pressed Glass,
Lincoln Drape

Klondike pattern is listed here as Amberette

Lace, Goblet	28.00
Lacy Dewdrop, Mug, 3 x 3 In.	18.00

Lacy Medallion, see also the related pattern Princess Feather

Lacy Medallion, Creamer, Tankard Shape	28.00

Lacy Spiral pattern is listed here as Colossus

Ladder With Diamond, Plate, 5 1/2 In.	5.00
Ladder With Diamond, Wine	10.00
Late Butterfly, Butter, Cover	75.00
Late Butterfly, Pitcher, Milk, Tankard Shape	75.00
Late Paneled Grape, Goblet	15.00

Late Thistle pattern is listed here as Inverted Thistle

Leaf & Dart, Eggcup	15.00
Leaf & Dart, Tumbler, Footed	22.00
Leaf & Rib, Pitcher, Water, Amber	48.00
Leaf & Star, Pitcher	250.00
Leaf Medallion, Creamer, Cobalt Blue, Gold Trim	135.00
Leaf Medallion, Table Set, Green, Gold Trim, 4 Piece	600.00
Leaf Medallion, Water Set, 6 Piece	600.00
Leaf Rosette, Butter, Cover, Frosted	125.00

Lens & Star pattern is listed here as Star & Oval

Leverne pattern is listed here as Star in Honeycomb

Liberty Bell, Bowl, Footed, 8 In.	75.00
Liberty Bell, Bread Plate	95.00
Liberty Bell, Creamer, Reeded Handle	110.00
Liberty Bell, Goblet	35.00
Liberty Bell, Mug, Snake Handle	550.00
Liberty Bell, Relish, Oval	45.00
Liberty Bell, Sugar, Cover	105.00
Lily Of The Valley, Celery Vase	65.00
Lily Of The Valley, Compote, Cover, Large	125.00
Lincoln Drape, Eggcup, Flint	65.00
Lincoln Drape, Goblet	135.00
Lincoln Drape, Sweetmeat, Flint	375.00
Lincoln Drape, Syrup, Applied Handle, Pewter Cover	100.00
Lined Smocking, Sugar, Cover, Flint	85.00
Lion, Cocktail, Green Stem	28.00
Lion, Creamer	63.00
Lion, Spooner	55.00
Lion, Tobacco Jar, Frosted Cover, 6 3/4 In.	46.00
Lion & Baboon, Butter, Cover	190.00
Lion Frosted, Butter	195.00
Lion Frosted, Compote, 4 1/2 x 7 3/4 In.	145.00
Lion Frosted, Compote, 8 x 7 1/2 In.	70.00
Lion Frosted, Compote, Cover, 7 x 6 In.	150.00
Lion Frosted, Compote, Cover, Head Finial, 7 x 10 In.	175.00
Lion Frosted, Compote, Cover, Oval, 7 3/4 x 4 1/2 In.	145.00
Lion Frosted, Dish, Oval, 4 X7 In.	50.00
Lion Frosted, Sauce, Footed	18.00
Lion Frosted, Spooner, 5 1/2 In.	70.00
Lion's Head, Butter, Cover, Frosted	75.00

Lion's Leg pattern is listed here as Alaska

Lippman pattern is listed here as Flat Diamond

Locket On Chain, Cake Stand, 9 1/4 In.	150.00 to 225.00
Locket On Chain, Wine	70.00
Log & Star, Mug	20.00
Log Cabin, Compote, Cover, 6 x 4 1/4 x 9 In.	230.00
Log Cabin, Creamer	150.00
Log Cabin, Spooner	135.00
Log Cabin, Sugar, Open	75.00
Log Cabin, Tobacco Jar, 6 7/8 In.	126.00
Loop, Celery	65.00
Loop, Sugar	52.00

Loop, Vase, Stepped Hexagonal Base, Emerald Green, 10 In. 770.00
Loop & Block, Water Set, Ruby Stained, 7 Piece 25.00
Loop & Dart, Celery Vase 32.00
Loop & Dart, Sugar 30.00
Loop & Dart With Diamond Ornaments, Goblet 30.00
Loop & Jewel, Nappy, 5 In. 22.00
Loop & Pyramid, Goblet 15.00
Loops & Drops pattern is listed here as New Jersey
Lotus, Compote, Cover 125.00
Lotus & Serpent, Butter, Cover 75.00
Louisiana, Compote, 5 1/4 x 4 In. 18.00
Louisiana, Goblet 48.00
Lustre Rose, Compote, Jelly 40.00
Magnet & Grape, Sauce Dish 28.00
Maiden Blush, see pink flashed Banded Portland pieces
Maine, Compote, Jelly 28.00
Maine, Wine .... 30.00 to 38.00
Manhattan, Dish, Gold Trim, Scalloped, Oval, 6 x 7 1/2 In. 22.00
Manhattan, Ice Bucket, Cranberry Stained 50.00
Manhattan, Punch Set, 15 Piece 225.00
Maple Leaf, Bowl, 6 1/2 x 10 1/2 In. 22.00
Maple Leaf, Butter Chip 25.00
Maple Leaf, Compote, Cover, Frosted Cover, Leaf Finial, 8 In. 125.00
Mardi Gras, Butter Pat 16.00
Mardi Gras, Cake Stand, 10 1/2 In. 65.00
Mardi Gras, Champagne 25.00
Mardi Gras, Goblet 45.00
Mardi Gras, Pitcher 75.00
Mardi Gras, Pitcher, Gold Trim 145.00
Mardi Gras, Pitcher, Thumbprints, Tankard Shape 75.00
Mardi Gras, Punch Cup 10.00
Mardi Gras, Toothpick, Clear 25.00
Marquisette, Champagne 55.00
Marquisette, Goblet 16.00
Marquisette, Spooner 35.00
Marsh Fern, Cake Stand, Pedestal 65.00
Marsh Fern, Compote, 7 In. 45.00
Marsh Fern, Goblet, Etched 37.00
Marsh Fern, Pitcher 50.00
Marsh Pink, Plate, Square, 10 In. 62.00
Marsh Pink, Saltshaker, Pewter Top, Square 32.00
Maryland, Sugar 15.00
Mascotte, Compote, Cover, 8 In. 75.00
Mascotte, Compote, Cover, 12 1/2 In. 110.00
Mascotte, Compote, Cover, Etched, 8 x 11 1/4 In. 130.00
Mascotte, Creamer 35.00
Mascotte, Goblet 30.00
Mascotte, Pitcher, Water 160.00
Mascotte, Spooner, Etched 28.00
Massachusetts, Banana Stand, Flat, Up-Turned Sides 55.00
Massachusetts, Bonbon, Handle, 5 In. 20.00
Massachusetts, Butter, Cover 85.00
Massachusetts, Champagne, Saucer 45.00
Massachusetts, Jug, Rum, 5 In. 110.00
Massachusetts, Plate, 8 1/4 In. 18.00
Master Argus, Tumbler, Footed, Flint 36.00
McKinley, Tumbler, Etched Our President, 1896-1900 .... 38.00
McKinley Memorial, Bread Plate .... 45.00 to 60.00
Medallion, Goblet, Amber 35.00
Medallion, Pitcher, Water, Blue 85.00
Melton, Celery 55.00
Memphis, Punch Cup 5.00
Menagerie, Creamer, Owl 30.00

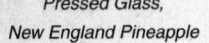

Pressed Glass,
New England Pineapple

Pressed Glass,
Moon and Star

Pressed Glass,
Pleat & Panel

Menagerie, Spooner, Fish, Blue	125.00
Mephistopheles, Mug	140.00
Michigan, Bowl, 8 1/2 In.	28.00
Michigan, Butter, Cover, Child's	60.00
Michigan, Creamer, Ruby Flashed	75.00
Michigan, Cup	10.00
Michigan, Goblet, Gold Trim	38.00
Michigan, Pitcher, Maiden's Blush, Gold Trim	250.00
Michigan, Pitcher, Tankard Shape, Child's	35.00
Michigan, Punch Cup, Enameled Design	25.00
Michigan, Sauce Dish, Handles, 5 x 6 In.	12.00
Michigan, Sugar, Individual	22.00
Mikado Fan, Creamer	18.00
Minerva, Goblet	95.00
Minerva, Relish, Loves Request	30.00
Minnesota, Biscuit Jar, Cover	50.00
Minnesota, Bowl, 7 1/2 In.	26.00
Minnesota, Bowl, Square, 5 3/4 In.	32.00
Minnesota, Bowl, Square, 8 In.	32.00
Minnesota, Carafe	48.00
Minnesota, Creamer, Gold Trim, Individual	18.00
Minnesota, Goblet, Gold Trim	15.00
Minnesota, Mug, Barrel Shape, Gold Trim	22.00
Minnesota, Plate, 8 In.	15.00
Minnesota, Relish, 6 1/2 x 8 3/4 In.	22.00
Minnesota, Rose Bowl	48.00
Minnesota, Toothpick	29.00
Minnesota, Wine	22.00
Missouri is listed here as Palm & Scroll	
Mitered Prisms, Celery	12.00
Mitered Prisms, Goblet	22.00
Moon & Star, Ashtray, 8 In.	25.00
Moon & Star, Celery	20.00
Moon & Star, Compote, Cover, Blue	55.00
Moon & Star, Compote, Cover, Green	50.00
Moon & Star, Lamp Shade, 4 In.	22.00
Moon & Star, Lamp, Hand, 4 In.	110.00
Moon & Star, Toothpick	20.00
Moon & Star, Wine	42.00
Moon & Stork pattern is listed here as Ostrich Looking At The Moon	
Morning Glory, Salt	110.00
Morning Glory, Sugar, Sandwich Glass, Flint	160.00
My Lady's Work Box, Goblet	15.00 to 18.00
Nail, Goblet, Ruby Stained	95.00
Nail, Salt, Ruby Stained, Says Annie	75.00
Nailhead, Cake Stand, 9 In.	25.00

Nailhead, Sugar, Cover... 20.00
Nestor, Spooner, Blue, Gold & White Enameled.............................. 60.00
Nestor, Tumbler, Green, Gold Trim 45.00
Netted Swan, Pitcher... 245.00
Nevada, Biscuit Jar, Cover... 23.00
Nevada, Butter, Cover.. 32.00
Nevada, Creamer 13.00
Nevada, Sauce, Frosted Flower Band, 4 1/2 In. 14.00
Nevada, Spooner... 16.00
Nevada, Sugar, Cover.. 16.00
Nevada, Sugar, Frosted, Painted Flowers 14.00
Nevada, Tumbler 7.00
Nevada, Water Set, Gold Trim, 5 Piece 95.00
New England Centennial, Goblet... 220.00
New England Pineapple, Creamer, 6 1/2 In. 38.00
New England Pineapple, Eggcup, Flint 65.00
New England Pineapple, Spooner, Flint 125.00
New England Pineapple, Sugar, Cover, Flint.............121.00 to 165.00
New England Pineapple, Sugar, Flint 50.00
New Hampshire, Butter, Cover, Maiden's Blush.............................. 150.00
New Hampshire, Creamer.. 30.00
New Hampshire, Goblet, Gold Trim.. 30.00
New Hampshire, Saltshaker... 22.00
New Hampshire, Sugar, Breakfast, Gold Trim 12.00
New Hampshire, Sugar, Maiden's Blush 14.00
New Jersey, Berry Set, Gold Trim, 7 Piece...................................... 175.00
New Jersey, Bowl, 9 1/4 In. 30.00
New Jersey, Compote, Shallow, 8 x 4 1/2 In. 24.00
New Jersey, Goblet, Gold Trim ....12.00 to 26.00
New Jersey, Plate, 11 In.. 25.00
New Jersey, Sugar, Cover, Gold Trim 36.00
New Jersey, Toothpick..60.00 to 75.00
New Jersey, Tumbler, Gold Trim..6.00 to 10.00
New Jersey, Water Set, 7 Piece 175.00
New Jersey, Wine 37.00
Nicotiana, Goblet, Etched... 25.00
Nursery Tales, Butter, Cover, Child's.. 75.00
Nursery Tales, Punch Set, Child's, 7 Piece 200.00
Nursery Tales, Sugar, Cover, Child's.......................................45.00 to 55.00
Nursery Tales, Water Set, Child's 7 Piece.........................175.00 to 285.00
Oak Leaf Band, Sugar, Cover, Flint 50.00
Oaken Bucket, Creamer, Amethyst 40.00
Oaken Bucket, Pitcher, Amethyst 165.00
Oaken Bucket, Pitcher, Blue 120.00
Odd Fellow's, Goblet 37.00
Ohio Star, Toothpick 45.00
Old Abe pattern is listed here as Frosted Eagle
Old State House, Tray, Bread..55.00 to 75.00
One-Hundred-One, Bread Plate, Implement Center, 11 In.............. 68.00
One-Hundred-One, Goblet, Amber.. 15.00
One-Hundred-One, Plate, 7 In. 16.00
One-O-One pattern is listed here as One-Hundred-One
One-Thousand Eye pattern is listed here as Thousand Eye
Open Rose, Eggcup 12.00
Opposing Pyramids, Goblet.. 22.00
Opposing Pyramids, Wine 10.00
Orange Peel, Goblet 14.00
Oregon, see the related patterns Beaded Loop and Skilton
Orion pattern is listed here as Cathedral
Ostrich Looking At The Moon, Goblet... 95.00
Oval Loop pattern is listed here as Question Mark
Oval Panels, Goblet, Vaseline 24.00
Owl & Possum, Goblet 145.00

Paddlewheel, Toothpick, Clear 25.00
Palm & Scroll, Bowl, 7 3/4 In. 22.00
Palm & Scroll, Cake Stand, 10 In. 65.00
Palm & Scroll, Compote, 6 x 4 In. 28.00
Palm & Scroll, Pitcher, Green 125.00
Palm Leaf, Celery Vase 78.00
Palm Leaf Fan, Goblet 22.00
Palm Leaf Fan, Spooner 38.00
Palm Stub, Goblet 16.00
Palmette, Creamer, Applied Handle 58.00
Palmette, Cup Plate 45.00
Panama, Wine 10.00
Panel & Rib, Goblet, Footed 9.00
Paneled 44, Bowl, Oval, 4 1/4 x 6 1/4 In. 22.00
Paneled 44, Compote, Handles, 5 1/2 x 4 In. 32.00
Paneled 44, Compote, Jelly, Platinum Trim, 6 In. 58.00
Paneled 44, Cruet 95.00
Paneled Acorn Band, Spooner 42.00
Paneled Daisy & Button, Berry Set, Amberette, 8 Piece 95.00
Paneled Daisy & Button, Tumbler, Amber Panels 45.00
Paneled Dewdrop, Goblet 25.00
Paneled Diamond & Finecut, Compote, Jelly 24.00
Paneled Diamond & Finecut, Wine, 5 In. 28.00
Paneled Diamond Block, Sugar & Creamer 85.00
Paneled Diamonds & Flowers, Goblet 45.00
Paneled Dogwood, Banana Boat, Green, 12 x 7 1/4 In. 36.00
Paneled Dogwood, Bowl, Green, Gold Trim 35.00
Paneled Forget-Me-Not, Cake Stand, 10 In. .... 38.00 to 48.00
Paneled Forget-Me-Not, Celery Vase 38.00
Paneled Forget-Me-Not, Compote, Cover, 7 In. 85.00
Paneled Forget-Me-Not, Goblet .... 28.00 to 35.00
Paneled Forget-Me-Not, Pitcher, Milk 60.00
Paneled Hexagons, Goblet 12.00
Paneled Holly, Butter, Cover 40.00
Paneled Holly, Creamer, Green, Gold Trim 50.00
Paneled Jewels, Goblet, Amber 28.00
Paneled Nightshade, Goblet 28.00
Paneled S, Compote, 8 In. 15.00
Paneled Sprig, Sugar Shaker, Opalescent, Green & Gold Enameled 95.00
Paneled Star & Button, Sauce Dish 3.00
Paneled Star & Square, Banana Boat, Gold Trim 8.00
Paneled Sunflower, Goblet 14.00
Paneled Thistle, Plate, 6 In. 37.00
Paneled Thistle, Sugar 30.00
Paneled Thumbprint, Goblet, Gold Trim 14.00
Paneled Wheat, Creamer 28.00
Paneled Wheat, Spooner 38.00
Pavonia, Butter, Cover 85.00
Pavonia, Celery, Etched 44.00
Pavonia, Creamer 38.00
Pavonia, Goblet .... 28.00 to 32.00
Pavonia, Pitcher, Etched Oak Leaf & Bird 145.00
Pavonia, Sugar, Cover, Ruby Stained 55.00
Pavonia, Waste Bowl 58.00
Peacock Feathers, Butter, Cover 35.00
Peacock Feathers, Compote, Low Standard, 6 3/4 In. 20.00
Peacock Feathers, Pitcher 65.00
Peacock Feathers, Relish, 4 x 8 1/2 In. 18.00
Peacock's Eye pattern is listed here as Peacock Feathers
Pennsylvania, see also the related pattern Hand
Pennsylvania, Butter, Cover, Green 150.00
Pennsylvania, Carafe, Water 65.00
Pennsylvania, Goblet .... 15.00 to 20.00

Pennsylvania, Goblet, Gold Trim 18.00
Pennsylvania, Punch Cup 8.00
Pennsylvania, Spooner 20.00
Pennsylvania, Wine 9.00
Pennsylvania, Wine, Gold Trim 12.00
Persian, Compote, Cover, 4 1/2 x 8 1/4 In. 38.00
Petal & Loop, Bowl 135.00
Petal & Loop, Compote, Flint, 9 1/2 x 6 1/2 In. 115.00
Picket, Compote, 7 x 71/4 In. 40.00
Picket Band, Goblet 12.00
Pigs In Corn, Goblet 550.00
Pillar, Bowl, 4 1/4 In. 10.00
Pillar & Bull's-Eye pattern is listed here as Thistle
Pillow Encircled, Tumbler, Ruby Flashed 32.00
Pinafore pattern is listed here as Actress
Pineapple, Goblet 65.00
Pineapple, Goblet, Flint 90.00
Pineapple, Spooner 30.00
Pineapple & Fan, Sugar, Cover 40.00
Pioneer, Bowl, Cover, 8 x 11 1/2 In. 230.00
Pioneer, Bread Tray, Frosted, 13 x 9 In. 105.00
Pioneer, Compote, Cover, 11 1/4 In. 105.00
Pioneer, Goblet, 6 5/8 In. 35.00
Pioneer, Pitcher, Frosted, 9 5/8 In. 58.00
Pioneer's Victoria, Tray, Wine, Ruby Flashed 70.00
Pitman, Goblet 16.00
Pittsburg, Bar Bottle, Pillar Mold, Applied Lip & Ring, Flint, 9 1/2 In. 50.00
Pittsburg, Decanter, Pillar Mold, Handle, Pewter Cap, Flint, 9 3/4 In. 143.00
Pittsburg, Vase, Pillar Mold, Baluster Stem, Flint, 9 3/4 In. 258.00
Plaid, Plate, 8 In. 55.00
Pleat & Panel, Bowl, Cover, 5 x 8 In. 75.00
Pleat & Panel, Bowl, Footed, 5 x 8 In. 32.00
Pleat & Panel, Cake Stand, Square, 10 In. 85.00
Pleat & Panel, Celery Vase 28.00
Pleat & Panel, Plate, Square, 5 In. 18.00
Pleat & Panel, Relish, Open Handle 15.00
Pleat Band, Tumbler, Etched 55.00
Pleating, Spooner, Ruby Stained 32.00
Pleating, Toothpick, Ruby Stained 75.00
Plume, Butter, Cover 35.00
Plume, Compote, Cover, 7 In. 48.00
Plume, Goblet 32.00
Plume, Relish, 4 x 8 In. 22.00
Pogo Stick, Cake Stand ....45.00 to 50.00
Pointed Jewel, Creamer, Child's 55.00
Pointed Panel Daisy & Button pattern is listed here as Paneled Daisy & Button
Pointed Thumbprint pattern is listed here as Almond Thumbprint

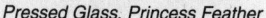

Pressed Glass, Princess Feather

Pressed Glass, Queen Anne

Polar Bear, Goblet 110.00
Polar Bear, Goblet, Frosted 125.00
Polar Bear, Pitcher, Water 490.00
Polar Bear, Tray, Frosted 225.00
Popcorn, Cake Stand 30.00
Popcorn, With Ears, Creamer 45.00
Pope Leo XIII, Plate 75.00
Portland, Basket, Rope Handle 90.00
Portland, Bowl 30.00
Portland, Compote, Cover, 7 1/4 x 10 In. 100.00
Portland, Cruet 45.00
Portland, Goblet 50.00
Portland, Goblet, Frosted, Flint 65.00
Portland, Goblet, Gold Trim 28.00
Portland, Punch Cup 12.00
Portland, Sugar, Cover 40.00
Portland, Toothpick 20.00
Portland With Diamond Point Band pattern is listed here as Banded Portland
Post, Goblet 45.00
Post, Lamp, 9 In. 125.00
Post, Tray, Bible 72.00
Powder & Shot, Goblet, Flint 55.00
Prayer Rug pattern is listed here as Horseshoe
Pressed Leaf, Eggcup, Flint 30.00
Pressed Leaf, Wine, Flint 48.00
Primrose, Pitcher, Milk, Amber 60.00
Princess Feather, Compote, Lacy Ribbed Base, 4 1/8 x 6 1/2 In. 275.00
Princess Feather, Goblet 32.00
Princess Feather, Spooner 25.00
Princess Feather, Wine 10.00
Priscilla, Berry Bowl, 10 In. 38.00
Priscilla, Cake Stand, 10 In. 65.00
Priscilla, Compote, Jelly, 4 3/4 x 4 3/4 In. 28.00
Priscilla, Toothpick 28.00
Prism & Block Band, Goblet 15.00
Prism & Broken Column, Goblet 16.00
Prism & Diamond Band, Goblet 16.00
Prize, Creamer, Ruby Stained 85.00
Prize, Salt & Pepper, Ruby Stained 145.00
Prize, Tumbler, Ruby Stained 45.00
Prize, Wine 30.00
Psyche & Cupid, Spooner 35.00
Queen, see also the related pattern Paneled Daisy & Button
Queen, Compote, Cover, Amber, 8 x 11 1/2 In. 95.00
Queen, Goblet, Amber 25.00
Queen Anne, Bread Plate 80.00
Queen Anne, Butter, Original Drainer 155.00
Queen Anne, Compote, Cover, 9 In. 225.00
Queen Anne, Creamer 36.00
Queen Anne, Mug 70.00
Queen Anne, Pitcher, Water, Face Under Spout, Frosted 175.00
Queen Anne, Spooner 42.00
Queen Anne, Sugar, Cover, Footed 38.00
Queen's Necklace, Saltshaker 25.00
Queen's Necklace, Vase, 9 In. 60.00
Question Mark, Bowl, 5 x 8 In. 14.00
Quintec, Compote, 6 1/2 x 6 1/4 In. 26.00
Rabbit Tracks, Pitcher, Milk 48.00
Racing Deer, Pitcher, Water, Scalloped 185.00
Radiant, Goblet 30.00
Radiant, Wine, Etched 22.00
Rail Fence Band, Goblet 18.00
Raindrop, Tray, Water, Blue, Round 48.00

Pressed Glass,
Ribbon Candy

Pressed Glass,
Roman Rosette

Pressed Glass,
Romeo

Pressed Glass,
Rose In Snow

Recessed Ovals With Block Band pattern is listed here as Melton

Red Block, Goblet	38.00 to 40.00
Red Block, Wine	25.00
Regent pattern is listed here as Leaf Medallion	
Remember The Maine, Tumbler, Etched Eagle & Flags	55.00
Remember The Maine, Tumbler, Etched Ship & Motto	65.00
Reverse 44 pattern is listed here as Paneled 44	
Reverse 44, Paneled 44, Platinum Trim	125.00
Reverse Swirl, Toothpick, Vaseline Opalescent	60.00
Reverse Torpedo pattern is listed here as Diamond & Bull's-Eye Band	
Rib & Bead, Toothpick, Ruby Stained	30.00
Ribbed Acorn, Compote, Flint	95.00
Ribbed Droplet Band, Compote, Etched, 7 x 5 3/4 In.	28.00
Ribbed Grape, Bowl, Flint	75.00
Ribbed Grape, Compote, Bellflower Base, Flint, 8 In.	87.00
Ribbed Opal pattern is listed here as Beatty Rib	
Ribbed Palm, Eggcup	35.00
Ribbed Palm, Goblet	35.00
Ribbed Palm, Goblet, Flint	42.00
Ribbon, Compote, Cover, 10 7/8 In.	60.00
Ribbon, Compote, Dolphin Base, 8 In.	145.00
Ribbon, Goblet	35.00
Ribbon Candy, Cake Stand, Green, 6 In.	125.00
Ribbon Candy, Creamer	35.00
Ribbon Candy, Plate, 7 1/4 In.	28.00
Ribbon Candy, Plate, 8 1/4 In.	32.00
Richards & Hartley No. 900, Compote, Cover, Large	100.00
Ripple, Goblet	32.00
Ripple Band pattern is listed here as Ripple	
Rising Sun, Goblet	28.00
Rising Sun, Sugar, Handle, Maiden's Blush	18.00
Robin Hood, Sugar, Cover	22.00
Rochelle pattern is listed here as Princess Feather	
Roman Key, Goblet, Flint	45.00
Roman Rosette, Butter, Cover	55.00
Roman Rosette, Pitcher, 5 1/4 In.	24.00
Roman Rosette, Platter	25.00
Romeo, Butter, Cover	38.00
Romeo, Celery	45.00
Romeo, Creamer	42.00
Romeo, Spooner	32.00
Rope Bands pattern is listed here as Argent	
Rose In Snow, Bottle, Stopper, 6 In.	85.00
Rose In Snow, Compote, Cover, 7 3/4 In.	42.00
Rose In Snow, Goblet, Amber	55.00
Rose In Snow, Goblet, Blue	85.00
Rose In Snow, Mug, Handle, Blue	125.00
Rose In Snow, Plate, 5 In.	28.00

Rose In Snow, Plate, 9 1/4 In. 20.00
Rose In Snow, Sauce, Blue, 4 In. 20.00
Rose Sprig, Cake Stand, Blue 125.00
Rose Sprig, Celery Vase 38.00
Rose Sprig, Compote, 9 x 10 x 4 1/4 In. 22.00
Rose Sprig, Goblet 35.00
Rose Sprig, Tray, Handles, 5 3/4 x 11 1/4 In. 32.00
Rosette, Pitcher, Water, 9 1/2 In. 54.00
Rosette Band, Compote, Cover, 7 1/2 In. 95.00
Rosette Medallion pattern is listed here as Feather Duster
Royal Ivy, Creamer, Frosted 85.00
Royal Ivy, Cruet, Clear & Frosted 55.00
Royal Ivy, Cruet, Rainbow Cracquelle 725.00
Royal Ivy, Pitcher, Water, Frosted 175.00
Royal Ivy, Salt, Rainbow Spatter 80.00
Royal Ivy, Sugar Shaker 185.00
Royal Ivy, Water Set, Frosted, 6 Piece .... 225.00 to 750.00
Royal Lady, Butter, Cover 52.00
Royal Lady, Cheese, Cover 115.00
Royal Lady, Compote, Cover, Ball Feet, 7 1/4 In. 85.00
Royal Lady, Creamer 32.00
Royal Oak, Sugar, Cover, Frosted 85.00
Ruby Thumbprint, see also the related pattern King's Crown
Ruby Thumbprint, Goblet, Red Stained 35.00
Ruby Thumbprint, Toothpick 25.00
Ruby Thumbprint, Toothpick, Red Stained 40.00
S-Repeat, Cruet 40.00
Sawtooth, Bowl, 5 In. 10.00
Sawtooth, Butter, Cover 65.00
Sawtooth, Celery Vase 40.00
Sawtooth, Celery Vase, 9 3/8 In. 48.00
Sawtooth, Celery, Knob Stem 45.00
Sawtooth, Compote, Deep, 8 x 8 In. 40.00
Sawtooth, Creamer, Handle, 6 1/4 In. 29.00
Sawtooth, Creamer, Handle, Bulbous, 6 1/2 In. 68.00
Sawtooth, Dish, Footed, Oval, 7 x 4 3/4 In. 14.00
Sawtooth, Goblet, 5 5/8 In. 34.00
Sawtooth, Jar, Pomade, Cover, Acorn Finial, Flint 95.00
Sawtooth, Salt, Footed 20.00
Sawtooth, Spooner, 5 1/2 In. 28.00
Sawtooth, Sugar, Cover 40.00
Sawtooth, Tumbler, 3 5/8 In. 22.00
Sawtooth Band pattern is listed here as Amazon
Saxon, Sugar, Scalloped, Ruby Stained 18.00
Scallop Shell, Pitcher 48.00
Scalloped Daisy & Fans, Goblet, Gold Trim 12.00
Scalloped Tape pattern is listed here as Jewel Band
Scroll With Cane Band, Bowl, Amber Stained, 8 In. 25.00
Scroll With Cane Band, Sugar & Creamer 150.00
Scroll With Cane Band, Tumbler, Amber Stained 45.00
Scroll With Flowers, Creamer 32.00
Scroll With Flowers, Plate, Handles, 10 In. 28.00
Seashell, Celery Vase, Etched 38.00
Seashell, Creamer, Clear Base 65.00
Sedan pattern is listed here as Paneled Star & Button
Seed Pod, Pitcher, Blue, Gold Trim 225.00
Seed Pod, Pitcher, Green, Gold Trim 200.00
Seed Pod, Spooner, Green, Gold Trim 90.00
Serrated Band & Prisms, Goblet 8.00
Sheaf & Diamond, Relish, Rectangular 12.00
Sheaf Of Wheat pattern is listed here as Wheat Sheaf
Shell, Relish 20.00
Shell & Jewel, Pitcher, Emerald Green 95.00

Pressed Glass,   Pressed Glass,   Pressed Glass,   Pressed Glass,
Shell & Tassel   Rose Sprig   Sawtooth   Squirrel

Shell & Jewel, Pitcher, Sapphire Blue 75.00
Shell & Jewel, Tumbler 45.00
Shell & Jewel, Water Set, 7 Piece 150.00
Shell & Tassel, Bowl, 6 In. 55.00
Shell & Tassel, Bride's Basket, Blue 350.00
Shell & Tassel, Butter Pat 20.00
Shell & Tassel, Butter Pat, 8 Piece 85.00
Shell & Tassel, Celery 115.00
Shell & Tassel, Compote, Cover, 7 In. 125.00
Shell & Tassel, Creamer, Square 55.00
Shell & Tassel, Goblet, Knob Stem 45.00
Shell & Tassel, Pitcher, Water, Round 145.00
Shell & Tassel, Platter, Oval, 9 x 13 In. 52.00
Shell & Tassel, Saltshaker 110.00
Shell & Tassel, Spooner 20.00
Sheraton, Goblet ....22.00 to 28.00
Sheraton, Spooner 18.00
Sheraton, Wine 12.00
Short Ribs, Wine 10.00
Short Teasel pattern is listed here as Teasel
Shoshone pattern is listed here as Victor
Shrine, Compote, Jelly 30.00
Shrine, Goblet 60.00
Shrine, Pitcher, Water, 8 1/2 In. 47.00
Shrine, Relish 32.00
Shuttle, Cake Stand 85.00
Shuttle, Wine .... 8.00 to 10.00
Skilton, Sugar, Cover 22.00
Snail, Banana Stand 85.00
Snail, Bowl, Cover, 8 In. 125.00
Snail, Cake Stand, 9 1/2 In. 95.00
Snail, Compote, Cover, 7 In. 145.00
Snail, Compote, Cover, 8 In. 135.00
Snail, Compote, Cover, 11 1/2 In. 135.00
Snail, Sauce, 4 In. 14.00
Snail, Sugar, Cover, Gold Trim, Individual 58.00
Snakeskin With Dot, Plate, 9 In. 35.00
Spanish American, Pitcher, Water 75.00
Spearhead, Goblet 22.00
Sprig, Butter, Cover 85.00
Sprig, Celery Vase 47.00
Sprig, Sauce, Footed, 4 In. 14.00
Square Fuchsia, Goblet 34.00
Square Fuchsia, Pitcher, Water 38.00
Square Fuchsia, Pitcher, Water, Footed, 9 In. 22.00
Square Fuchsia, Plate, Handle, Green, 9 In. 32.00
Square Fuchsia, Plate, Yellow, 9 In. 32.00
Square Fuchsia, Wine, Amber 58.00

Square Waffle, Goblet 20.00
Squirrel, Pitcher, Water 175.00
Star & Bar, Saltshaker, Pewter Top, Blue 28.00
Star & Buckle, Pitcher, Flared Mouth, Hollow Handle, 6 1/8 In. 150.00
Star & Crescent, Pitcher, Cranberry Stained 50.00
Star & Crescent, Tumbler, Cranberry Stained 20.00
Star & Oval, Celery Vase 28.00
Star & Punty pattern is listed here as Moon & Star
Star In Bull's-Eye, Creamer, Ruby 18.00
Star In Honeycomb, Wine 8.00
Star Medallion, Bowl, 5 x 2 1/2 In. 9.00
Star Rosetted, Goblet 20.00
Starred Cosmos, Creamer 30.00
States pattern is listed here as The States
Stedman, Sugar 16.00
Stippled Bar, Plate, 9 1/2 In. 81.00
Stippled Cherry, Bowl 75.00
Stippled Double Loop, Creamer 35.00
Stippled Fans, Plate, Blue, 10 In. 24.00
Stippled Fans, Toothpick 18.00
Stippled Forget-Me-Not, Cake Stand, 10 x 6 1/2 In. 68.00
Stippled Forget-Me-Not, Plate, Baby Center, 7 In. 58.00
Stippled Forget-Me-Not, Plate, Star Center, 7 In. 30.00
Stippled Fuchsia, Goblet .... 25.00 to 38.00
Stippled Grape & Festoon, Pitcher, Water, Clear Leaf, Applied Handle 95.00
Stippled Grape & Festoon, Sugar, Cover, Acorn Finial 65.00
Stippled Medallion, Sugar 30.00
Stippled Paneled Flower pattern is listed here as Maine
Stippled Peppers, Sugar, Buttermilk 26.00
Stork, Creamer 50.00
Stork, Plate, Frosted 95.00
Stork Looking At The Moon pattern is listed here as Ostrich Looking At The Moon
Strawberry, Goblet 38.00
Sunbeam, Creamer, Individual 10.00
Sunbeam, Wine 35.00
Sunburst, Cake Stand, 5 5/8 x 11 1/2 In. 30.00
Sunburst, Compote, Fruit, 9 1/2 x 8 In. 28.00
Sunburst, Sugar & Creamer 36.00
Sunburst, Toothpick, Oval, Clear 80.00
Sunk Honeycomb, Bowl, Ruby Stained, Hand Painted Floral, 8 1/4 In. 75.00
Sunk Honeycomb, Decanter, Wine, Ruby Stained 110.00
Sunk Honeycomb, Mug 45.00
Sunk Honeycomb, Mug, Ruby Stained 42.00
Sunk Honeycomb, Sugar, Cover, Ruby Stained 85.00
Sunk Honeycomb, Wine, Ruby Stained 35.00
Sunken Primrose, Mustard, Open, Attached Plate 12.00
Sunken Primrose, Plate, Square, 9 In. 10.00
Swag With Brackets, Berry Set, Green, 5 Piece 150.00
Swag With Brackets, Cruet 450.00
Swag With Brackets, Spooner, Blue Opalescent 32.00
Swan, Pitcher 135.00
Tacoma, Bowl, Ruby Stained, 8 1/2 In. 47.00
Tacoma, Sauce Boat, Ruby Stained 24.00
Tacoma, Water Set, Ruby Stained, 3 Piece 225.00
Tandem Bicycle 25.00
Tandem Diamonds & Thumbprint, Spooner 28.00
Tarentum Thumbprint, Pitcher, Water, Etched 52.00
Tarentum's Atlanta, Bowl, Flared, 8 In. 12.00
Tarentum's Atlanta, Cake Stand, 8 In. 25.00
Teardrop pattern is listed here as Teardrop & Thumbprint
Teardrop & Thumbprint, Pitcher, Blue 250.00
Teardrop & Thumbprint, Tumbler, Blue 35.00
Teasel, Goblet 22.00

Tennessee, Butter, Cover 90.00
Tennessee, Celery Vase ....75.00 to 95.00
Tennessee, Compote, 7 3/4 x 6 In. 48.00
Tepee, Champagne... 12.00
Tepee, Toothpick... 29.00
Texas, Compote, Scalloped Rim, 6 In.. 235.00
Texas, Creamer, Gold Trim 20.00
Texas, Creamer, Individual 15.00
Texas, Nappy, Oval, 4 1/4 x 5 3/4 In. 18.00
Texas, Sherbet, Footed, Gold Trim.. 12.00
Texas, Tray, Maiden's Blush, 6 1/2 x 11 1/4 In. 58.00
Texas, Vase, 7 3/4 In. 30.00
Texas Bull's-Eye pattern is listed here as Bull's-Eye Variant
Texas Star, Berry Set, Frosted, 7 Piece 120.00
Texas Star, Table Set, Frosted, 4 Piece 240.00
Texas Star, Toothpick 85.00
Texas Star, Water Set, Frosted, 7 Piece 285.00
The States, Creamer, Gold Trim 26.00
The States, Goblet, Gold Rim 35.00
The States, Plate, 9 In. 24.00
The States, Punch Cup 15.00
Theodore Roosevelt, Bread Plate, Bear, Frosted Center.. 145.00
Thistle, Bottle 120.00
Thistle, Bowl, Oval, 6 x 9 In. 32.00
Thistle, Goblet 65.00
Thistle, Goblet, Flint 80.00
Thistle, Tumbler, Footed.. 58.00
Thistleblow, Wine, 4 1/2 In. 9.00
Thousand Eye, Celery Vase, Variant.. 42.00
Thousand Eye, Goblet, Amber 26.00
Thousand Eye, Plate, Amber, 5 3/4 In. 25.00
Thousand Eye, Plate, Square, Blue, 7 3/4 In. 22.00
Thousand Eye, Spooner, Green 35.00
Thousand Eye, Tray, Water, Oval, Blue 75.00
Three Deer, Goblet... 225.00
Three Face, Butter.. 195.00
Three Face, Cake Stand.. 175.00
Three Face, Compote, Cover, 8 In. 285.00
Three Face, Compote, Low Standard 195.00
Three Face, Creamer, Face Under Spout.. 160.00
Three Face, Humidor, Marked mmAA.. 55.00
Three Face, Pitcher 650.00
Three Face, Spooner.. 80.00
Three Graces, see also the related pattern Three Face
Three Panel, Bowl, Footed, Blue, 5 1/2 In. 22.00
Three Panel, Bowl, Vaseline, Low, 10 1/2 In... 35.00
Three Panel, Compote, Amber, 7 1/4 x 4 In. 32.00
Three Panel, Creamer, Vaseline 32.00
Three Panel, Goblet, Amber 38.00
Three Presidents, Bread Plate... 85.00
Three Sisters pattern is listed here as Three Face
Thumbprint, Compote, Hobnail Base, 8 1/2 In. 25.00
Thumbprint, Goblet 14.00
Thumbprint, Lamp, 10 In. 55.00
Thumbprint, Vase, Yellow, 9 1/2 In., Pair.. 495.00
Tobin pattern is listed here as Leaf & Star
Toltec, Spooner... 27.00
Toltec, Toothpick.. 27.00
Tom Thumb pattern is listed here as Humpty-Dumpty
Torpedo, Bowl, 7 In... 32.00
Torpedo, Compote, Cover, 8 x 13 In.. 110.00
Torpedo, Lamp, Large 95.00
Torpedo, Pitcher, Milk... 95.00

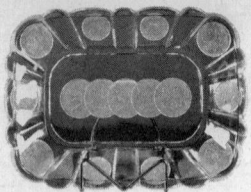 

Pressed Glass, U.S. Coin   *Pressed Glass, Washington*

Torpedo, Pitcher, Water 60.00
Torpedo, Tankard 85.00
Torpedo, Wine, Ruby Stained 110.00
Tree, Creamer 24.00
Tree Of Life, Compote, Hand Stem, 9 In. 65.00
Tree Of Life, Goblet 50.00
Tree Of Life, Goblet, Lemonade 30.00
Tree Of Life, Plate, Sugar 9.00
Tree Of Life, Salt 35.00
Tree Of Life, Salt, Blue 85.00
Tree Of Life, Salt, Green 85.00
Tree Of Life, Syrup, Brass Top 45.00
Tree Of Life, Tumbler, Lemonade, Applied Handle 135.00
Tree Of Life With Hand, Cake Stand, Frosted, 10 In. 40.00
Tree Of Life With Hand, Compote 55.00
Triangular Prism, Cruet 65.00
Trilby, Goblet 175.00
Triple Thumbprints, Sugar, Cover, Gold Thumbprints 32.00
Tulip Petals, Spooner 36.00
Tulip With Sawtooth, Celery Vase 75.00
Tulip With Sawtooth, Spooner 18.00
Twinkle Star pattern is listed here as Utah
Two Band, Compote, 7 1/2 In. 15.00
Two Band, Sugar, Amber 38.00
Two Panel, Bowl, Oval, 7 x 8 1/2 In. 6.00
Two Panel, Sauce, Apple Green, Pedestal, Oval 15.00
U.S. Coin, Cake Stand 265.00
U.S. Coin, Celery Vase, Frosted Coins 375.00
U.S. Coin, Spooner, Frosted Coins .... 150.00 to 325.00
U.S. Coin, Tobacco Jar, Cover, 6 3/4 In. 173.00
U.S. Coin, Tumbler, Frosted, Coins 250.00
Utah, Sugar & Creamer 15.00
Valencia Waffle, Compote, Cover, Blue, 8 In. 125.00
Valencia Waffle, Goblet .... 12.00 to 16.00
Valencia Waffle, Syrup, Amber 195.00
Valentine pattern is listed here as Trilby
Vermont, Goblet, Emerald, Gold Trim 48.00
Vermont, Relish, Green, Gold Trim, 4 x 8 1/2 In. 28.00
Victor, Cake Stand, Green .... 45.00 to 60.00
Victor, Celery Vase, Ruby Stained 95.00
Victor, Compote, Cover, 7 x 9 In. 35.00
Victor, Cruet 60.00
Victor, Plate, Green, 7 In. .... 10.00 to 20.00
Victoria, Goblet 35.00
Waffle, Celery Vase, Flint .... 80.00 to 85.00
Waffle, Goblet, Flint 65.00
Waffle & Thumbprint, Compote, Flint 85.00
Waffle & Thumbprint, Goblet, Flint 85.00
Waffle & Thumbprint, Wine, Flint 95.00
Washboard, Bowl, Oval 12.00
Washington, Cake Stand, 9 In. 55.00

Pressed Glass,
Waffle & Thumbprint

Pressed Glass,
Westward Ho

Pressed Glass,
Wedding Ring

Washington, Celery	80.00
Washington, Eggcup	60.00
Washington, Goblet	70.00
Washington, Sauce, 3 1/2 In.	12.00
Washington, Spooner, Frosted Flower Band	35.00
Washington, Sugar, Cover, Frosted Flower Band	55.00
Washington Centennial, Bread Tray, Clear Face	100.00
Washington Centennial, Relish	12.00
Washington Centennial, Relish, Bear Handles	35.00
Wedding Bells, Creamer, Cranberry Flashed	65.00
Wedding Bells, Water Set, Gold Trim, 5 Piece	85.00
Wedding Ring, Cologne Bottle, Stopper, Flint, 7 1/4 In.	175.00
Wedding Ring, Syrup	125.00
Wedding Ring, Wine, Flint, 4 1/4 In.	75.00
Wellington, Toothpick	25.00
Westward Ho, Compote, Jelly, Cover	82.00
Westward Ho, Creamer	120.00
Westward Ho, Pitcher, Water	360.00
Westward Ho, Sauce, 7 Piece	28.00
Wheat & Barley, Compote Jelly, Amber, 4 1/2 In.	28.00
Wheat & Barley, Goblet, Amber	45.00
Wheat & Barley, Goblet, Blue	65.00
Wheat & Barley, Pitcher, Amber	55.00 to 80.00
Wheat & Barley, Water Set, Amber, 7 Piece	225.00
Wheat In Shield, Sauce, 4 In.	10.00
Wheat Sheaf, Punch Cup, 2 1/2 In.	175.00
Whirligig pattern is listed here as Buzz Star	
Wild Bouquet, Condiment Set, 3 Piece	225.00
Wild Bouquet, Creamer	35.00
Wild Rose, Butter	75.00
Wildflower, Bowl, Amber, 7 1/2 In.	38.00
Wildflower, Cake Stand, 8 1/2 In.	45.00
Wildflower, Creamer	18.00
Wildflower, Creamer, Blue	55.00
Wildflower, Creamer, Footed, Amethyst	25.00
Wildflower, Goblet, Amber	35.00
Wildflower, Goblet, Blue	35.00
Wildflower, Plate, Square, 9 3/4 In.	20.00
Wildflower, Spooner, Amber	30.00
Wildflower, Tumbler, Amber	35.00
Wildflower, Tumbler, Blue	45.00
Willow Oak, Bowl, Amber, 7 In.	14.00
Willow Oak, Cake Stand, Blue, 8 3/4 In.	60.00
Willow Oak, Creamer, Amber	28.00
Willow Oak, Goblet, Amber	55.00
Willow Oak, Pitcher, Milk	33.00
Willow Oak, Plate, Amber, Handle, 9 In.	38.00
Willow Oak, Sugar	22.00
Windflower, Creamer	32.00
Winged Scrolls, Creamer, Green	110.00

Winged Scrolls, Spooner, Green	110.00
Winged Scrolls, Sugar, Cover	150.00
Winona pattern is listed here as Barred Hobnail	
Wisconsin, Berry Bowl, 7 1/2 In.	29.00
Wisconsin, Goblet	58.00
Wisconsin, Punch Cup	30.00
Wisconsin, Sauce, Beaded Rim, Flat	10.00
Wisconsin, Sugar, Individual	25.00
Wisconsin, Wine	95.00
Wooden Pail pattern is listed here as Oaken Bucket	
Wreath & Shell, Salt, Blue	80.00
Wreathed Cherry, Creamer, Blue	55.00
Wyoming, Bowl, Barrel Shape, Scalloped Feet, 7 In.	38.00
Wyoming, Cake Stand, 8 1/4 In.	58.00
Wyoming, Cake Stand, 9 1/2 In.	65.00
Wyoming, Compote, 8 x 5 1/2 In.	38.00
Wyoming, Creamer, Tankard Shape, 5 In.	32.00
Wyoming, Pitcher, Water	85.00
X-Ray, Celery Vase, Green	35.00
X-Ray, Celery Vase, Green, Gold Trim	90.00
X-Ray, Creamer, Green, Gold Trim	65.00
X-Ray, Toothpick, Green, Gold Trim	75.00
Yale pattern is listed here as Crowfoot	
Yoke Band, Goblet	10.00
York Herringbone, Syrup, Metal Cover	110.00
Zipper Slash, Champagne, 5 In.	22.00
Zipper Slash, Sherbet	14.00
Zippered Block, Goblet, Etched	35.00

PRINT, in this listing, means any of many printed images produced on paper by one of the more common methods, such as lithography. The prints listed here are of interest primarily to the antiques collector, not the fine arts collector. Many of these prints were originally part of books. Other prints will be found in the Advertising, Currier & Ives, Movie, and Poster categories.

Audubon bird prints were originally issued as part of books printed from 1826 to 1854. They were issued in two sizes, 26 1/2 inches by 39 1/2 inches and 11 inches by 7 inches. The quadrupeds were issued in 28-by-22-inch prints. Later editions of the Audubon books were done in many sizes, and reprints of the books in the original size were also made. The bird pictures have been so popular they have been copied in myriad sizes by both old and new printing methods. This list includes originals and later copies because Audubon prints of all ages are sold in antiques shops.

J.W.Audubon

Audubon, American Coot, Havell, 1835, 12 x 19 In.	660.00
Audubon, Burrowing Owl, Color, Reprint, 26 3/8 x 39 3/8 In.	225.00
Audubon, Clay Coloured Finch, Reprint, 23 1/2 x 17 1/2 In.	165.00
Audubon, Double Breasted Cormorant, Color, Reprint, 26 3/8 x 39 3/8 In.	195.00
Audubon, Little Owl, Color, 26 3/8 x 39 3/8 In.	138.00
Audubon, Pigeon Hawk, 1837, 34 x 24 7/8 In.	3900.00
Audubon, Red-Winged Starling Or Marsh Blackbird, 1860, 37 3/8 x 26 In.	2100.00
Audubon, Rose-Breasted Grosbeak, 1860, 35 x 24 In.	1900.00
Audubon, Surf Duck, Color, Reprint, 26 3/8 x 39 3/8 In.	275.00
Audubon, Tengelman's Owl, Color, Reprint, 26 3/8 x 39 3/8 In.	140.00
Audubon, White Nun, Color, Reprint, 26 3/8 x 39 3/8 In.	250.00
Audubon, Wild Turkey, Havell, Frame, 32 x 42 In.	750.00
Bartlett, Two Lakes & Catskill Mountain House	140.00
Buttmann, Message Of The Roses	265.00
Fisher, A Morning Greeting, Original Backing	85.00
Fisher, Final Instructions, Original Backing	85.00
Fox, Cows, 8 x 10 In.	95.00
Fox, June Moon, Frame, 18 x 10 In.	200.00
Fox, Magic Pool, 7 1/2 x 10 In.	75.00
Fox, Off Treasure Island, 7 1/2 x 10 In.	60.00

Gutmann, Excuse My Back, Frame, 12 x 8 In.	65.00
Gutmann, Happy Dreams, Frame, 9 x 11 In.	30.00
Gutmann, In Slumberland, 21 x 14 In.	45.00
Gutmann, Lovers Blossom, 11 x 14 In.	35.00
Gutmann, Miss Flirt	80.00
Gutmann, Sense Of Hearing, Frame	195.00
Gutmann, Sense Of Smell, Frame	195.00
Humphrey, Book, Baby Record, 12 Color Plates, Box, 1898	695.00
Icart, Don Juan, 1928, 20 1/4 x 13 1/4 In.	2000.00
Icart, Gay Senorita, Frame, 1939, 17 1/2 x 21 1/2 In.	3200.00
Icart, Green Robe, Signed, 1924.13 x 17 In.	1435.00
Icart, Japanese Gardens, Drypoint Etched, 1925, 14 1/4 x 17 3/8 In.	1320.00
Icart, La Lamp, 15 9/16 x 19 9/16 In.	1600.00
Icart, Lady Of The Camilias, 1907, 13 1/16 x 21 1/16 In.	1100.00 to 1750.00
Icart, Leda & The Swan, 1934, 19 5/8 x 30 7/8 In.	7000.00
Icart, Smoke, Drypoint Etch, 1926, 14 1/8 x 19 3/8 In.	1210.00

Japanese woodblock prints are listed as follows: Print, Japanese, name of artist, title or description, type, and size. Dealers use the following terms: Tate-e is a vertical composition. Yoko-e is a horizontal composition. The words Aiban (13 by 9 inches), Chuban (10 by 7 1/2 inches), Hosoban (12 by 6 inches), Oban (15 by 10 inches), and Koban (7 by 4 inches) denote size. Modern versions of some of these prints have been made.

Japanese, Generals Around Table, Meiji, Triptych, Frame	1150.00
Japanese, Helen Hyde, Oriental Girl, Flowing Robe, Butterflies, 1908, 2 1/2 x 7 In.	245.00
Japanese, Hokkel, Samurai With Lantern, Frame	300.00
Japanese, Kiyoshi Nagai, Butterfly, 10 x 14 1/2 In.	60.00
Japanese, Kunihiro Amano, Silence, 1965, 14 1/4 x 22 In.	125.00
Japanese, Kunisada, Samurai With Bloodied Prisoner, Frame	375.00
Japanese, Kuniyoshi, Wrestler, Triptych, 1850	3737.00
Japanese, Sahahide, Giant Straddling Harbor, Triptych, 1860	10350.00
Japanese, Shunko, Portrait Of Actor, 1790	865.00
Japanese, Torii Tadamasa, Kabuki Actor Portrait, Oban, 16 x 10 1/2 In.	165.00
Japanese, Toyokuni, Kabuki Theater Actors, 14 1/4 x 19 1/2 In.	80.00
Japanese, Toyokuni, Kabuki Theater Scene, 14 1/4 x 19 1/2 In.	80.00
Japanese, Toyokuni, Samurai Struggling, Frame	350.00
Japanese, Toyokuni, Subject Pays Tribute To His Master, Framed	290.00
Japanese, Utagawa Kunisada, Sano-Ki, Kiwame Seal, Warrior, Oban, 14 1/2 x 9 3/4 In.	110.00
Japanese, Utagawa Kuniyoshi, Warrior, Y. Sakujiro, Chuban, 9 1/2 In.X 6 3/4 In.	205.00
Japanese, Watanabe, Crucifixion, Dated 1973, 13 1/4 x 9 In.	38.00
Japanese, Watanabe, Jesus & Mary, Dated 1972, 12 x 9 In.	38.00
Japanese, Yoshiro Kanamori, Mountain & Lake, Moon & Butterfly, 24 x 18 In.	200.00
Kloss, Christmas Eve & Christmas Processional At Taos, Frame, 20 x 24 1/2 In., Pair	1300.00
Knuth, Winter Landscape, Doe, Frame, 21 1/2 x 23 1/2 In.	125.00
Mourning, Cross, Rock Of Ages, Flowers, Ribbon, Black Ground, Victorian, 8 x 20 In.	13.00
Neale, Black-Headed Gull, Medium Folio	85.00
Neale, Gray Phalarope, Adult Plumage, Medium Folio	85.00
Neale, Raven, With Rabbit, Medium Folio	75.00

Nutting prints are now popular with collectors. Wallace Nutting is known for his pictures, furniture, and books. Nutting *prints* are actually hand colored *Wallace Nutting* photographs issued from 1900 to 1941. There are over 10, 000 different titles.

Nutting, Bridge Of Sighs	198.00
Nutting, Chair For John, 16 x 12 In.	120.00
Nutting, Checkerings	495.00
Nutting, Comfort & A Cat	240.00
Nutting, Dahlia Jar	743.00
Nutting, Dixie Apple Blossom	50.00
Nutting, Entering The Old Bridge	605.00
Nutting, Favorite Corner	550.00
Nutting, Heifers By The Stream	495.00
Nutting, Hepatica	743.00
Nutting, Knickerbocker Fireplace	185.00

Nutting, Little Helper	715.00
Nutting, Meeting Place	2035.00
Nutting, Nap Time Stories	605.00
Nutting, Nashua Asleep, 9 x 11 In.	95.00
Nutting, Orchard Shadows	55.00
Nutting, Patchwork Siesta	605.00
Nutting, Street Border	198.00
Nutting, Towards Slumberland	798.00
Nutting, True D.A.R.	310.00
Nutting, Vanity & Constancy	715.00
Nutting, Water Garden In Venice	605.00
Nutting, Wine Carrier, Ravello	1705.00
Nutting, Winter Welcome Home	1430.00
Nutting, Yosemite Waters	280.00

Parrish prints are wanted by collectors. Maxfield Frederick Parrish was an illustrator who lived from 1870 to 1966. He is best known as a designer of magazine covers, posters, calendars, and advertisements.

Parrish, Canyon, Framed, 12 x 15 In.	195.00
Parrish, Cleopatra, Medium Folio	850.00
Parrish, Cleopatra, Small Folio	250.00
Parrish, Daybreak, 18 x 30 In.	225.00
Parrish, Dinkey Bird, Framed, 11 x 16 In.	200.00
Parrish, Dreaming, Medium Folio	450.00
Parrish, Garden Of Allah, 9 x 18 In.	125.00
Parrish, Hilltop, 8 x 10 In.	75.00
Parrish, Lute Players, 12 x 18 In.	175.00
Parrish, Old Glen Mill, Frame, 11 x 14 In.	225.00
Parrish, Prince Agib	150.00
Parrish, Reveries, Frame, 14 x 22 In.	450.00
Parrish, Reveries, Large Folio	575.00
Parrish, Rubaiyat, Frame, 36 x 13 In.	595.00
Parrish, Spirit Of Transportation, Frame, 16 x 20 In.	475.00 to 500.00
Parrish, Stars, Frame, 12 x 20 In.	400.00
Parrish, Waterfall, Frame, Large Folio	575.00
Parrish, Waterfall, Small Folio	195.00
Parrish, Young Girl, 1929, 22 1/4 x 16 1/4 In.	192.00
Philip Boileau, Girl, Large Hat, Frame, 18 x 15 In.	85.00
Prang, Whittier's Barefoot Boy, Frame, 13 1/2 x 10 In.	50.00
Yard Long, American Girl	190.00
Yard Long, Carnation Symphony	110.00
Yard Long, Easter Morning	295.00
Yard Long, Honeymoon Alps, Pressler	125.00
Yard Long, Puppies	295.00
Yard Long, White & Lavender Lilacs	130.00

PURSES have been recognizable since the eighteenth century, when leather and needlework purses were preferred. Beaded purses became popular in the nineteenth century, went out of style, but are again in use. Mesh purses date from the 1880s and are still being made. How to carry a handkerchief and lipstick is a problem today for every woman, including the Queen of England.

Alligator, Mark Cross, 7 3/4 x 9 1/4 In.	55.00 to 60.00
Bag, Alligator, Mark Cross, 7 3/4 x 9 1/4 In.	55.00
Basket, Nantucket, Swing Handle, Carved Ivory Whale On Cover, 6 x 9 1/2 In.	440.00
Basket Weave, Clear Etched & Cut Lucite Top & Handle, Chrome	47.00
Beaded, Black Hearts On Black Satin, Chain Handle, Top Frame, 6 1/2 x 5 In.	7.00
Beaded, Black, Gilt Frame, France, c.1940	34.00
Beaded, Blue, Vandyke Beaded Fringe	115.00
Beaded, Caron	22.00
Beaded, Clutch, Pearls, Zipper, Scalloped Top, 7 1/2 x 5 In.	10.00
Beaded, Coin, 3 Flying Horses On Cover	65.00
Beaded, Coin, Sequins, Jet Black, 1930s	30.00
Beaded, Drawstring Pouch, Flowers, Blue Ground	45.00

◆◆◆◆◆◆◆◆◆◆◆◆◆◆◆◆◆◆◆◆◆◆◆◆

An old leather purse will look better after it has been rubbed with leather cleaner, then leather conditioner. Your shoe repair shop will have several brands.

◆◆◆◆◆◆◆◆◆◆◆◆◆◆◆◆◆◆◆◆◆◆◆◆

Purse, Evening Bag,
Gold Mesh, Emeralds
& Diamonds

Beaded, Drawstring, Allover Design, Ball & Tassel Bottom	75.00
Beaded, German Silver, Leather Lining	85.00
Beaded, Gold Seed Bead Dots, Embroidered Portrait, Rhinestone Closure	210.00
Beaded, Jade Rectangles, White Flowers, France, c.1920, 6 In.	69.00
Beaded, Pearls, Bead Flower, Pearl Handle, Zipper	28.00
Beaded, Seed Pearl, White Front, White & Silver Bugle Beads, 5 3/4 x 3 1/2 In.	10.00
Beaded, Sequins, 1950s, 6 x 10 In.	35.00
Beaded, Silver, Swirled Patterns, Beaded Rope Handle, Snaps Beaded Clasp	40.00
Beaded, Steel, Carpet Design, Fringed	95.00
Beaded, Taj Mahal, Black Velvet	45.00
Brass & Copper, Shoulder Chain, Pillow Shape, Velvet Lining, Embossed, 1920s	80.00
Brocade, Gold-Filled Frame, Art Deco	75.00
Canvas Work, Stitched Bargello Pattern, 18th Century, 9 1/2 x 8 1/2 In.	1955.00
Cloth, 3 Standing Penguins, Grenfell, Label	500.00
Crocheted, Drawstring, Ireland	30.00
Crocodile, Gray, Hermes	2875.00
Enameled, Mandalian Mfg. Co.	350.00
Enameled, Multicolored, Rose Diamond Clusters, Glass Dove Finial, France, Art Deco	1955.00
Evening Bag, Gold Mesh, Emeralds & Diamonds .... *Illus*	2250.00
Gold Mesh, 14K, Scroll Diamond, Sapphire Frame, Cabochon Sapphire Thumbpiece...	2465.00
Gold Mesh, Coin, Accordion Closure	24.00
Gold Metallic Basket Weave, Box, Rust Cover, Brass Handle, Striped Lining	25.00
Leather, Shoulder, Saddle Form, Stirrups	145.00
Leather, Umbrella Shape, Coral, 4 1/2 In.	35.00
Leather & Brass, Reims Champagne	2000.00
Lucite, Alligator Trim	48.00
Mesh, 14K Gold, Engraved Owner's Name, 1920	800.00
Mesh, 14K Gold, Sea God, Dolphins, 6 In.	1610.00
Mesh, Brass Hinge, Exotic Bird & Floral, Yellow Ground, Mandalian Mfg. Co., 1900.	145.00
Mesh, Enameled Fringe, Mandalian Mfg. Co.	245.00
Mesh, Enameled, Floral Design, Flower Frame, Mandalian Mfg. Co.	115.00
Mesh, Enameled, Scenic, Whiting & Davis ....135.00 to	155.00
Mesh, Enameled, White, Whiting & Davis	30.00
Mesh, France, 4 x 3 3/4 In.	35.00
Mesh, Glass Studded Catch, Sterling Silver, 5 3/4 In.	75.00
Mesh, Gold, Designed Frame, 32 In. Chain, Annabelle, 9 1/2 x 12 In.	165.00
Mesh, Gold, Diamonds & Sapphires Frame, Sapphire Thumbpiece, England	2465.00
Mesh, Gold, Whiting & Davis, 5 In.	15.00
Mesh, Pastel Peacock Design, Whiting & Davis, 1920s	55.00
Mesh, Purple & Green, Whiting & Davis	55.00
Mesh, Silver, Accordion Closure	75.00
Mesh, Silver, White Whorls, Whiting & Davis	70.00
Miser's, Burgundy & Gold, 1860s	45.00
Needlepoint, Christine Custom Bags Of Detroit, 1925	105.00
Petit Point, Ballroom Party Scene, Vienna	290.00

Quezal, Vase,
Gourd Shape,
Double Handle,
Signed

◆◆◆◆◆◆◆◆◆◆◆◆◆◆◆◆◆◆◆◆◆◆◆◆

If you are the victim of a theft, be sure to give the police complete information about your antiques. You should have a good description, a photograph, and any known identifying marks. You might want to send information about the stolen antiques to the antiques papers.

◆◆◆◆◆◆◆◆◆◆◆◆◆◆◆◆◆◆◆◆◆◆◆◆

Petit Point, Coin, Flowers, Silk Lining, 1920, Austria	45.00
Petit Point, Marcasite & Enamel, Czechoslovakia	65.00
Petit Point, Multicolored Floral & Butterfly, Metal Frame, Maria Stransky, Box	578.00
Plastic, Clutch, Rhinestone Design, Gold Marble	45.00
Plastic, Double Buckle, Rust, Gold Flecks	65.00
Plastic, Gray Swirled Pearlized, Rialto	25.00
Rhinestones, Clear Plastic	45.00
Rhinestones & Black Silk	140.00
Seed Bead, Pouch, Crocheted, Floral Design, Tassel, 1920, Austria	60.00
Sequin Brocade, Silvered Frame, France, 1920, 6 In.	80.00
Silver Brocade, Gold Tone Filigree, Compact & Lipstick Holder	105.00
Steel Beaded, Envelope Style, Fringed	68.00
Sterling Silver, Cone Shape, Chased Ornaments, Malachite Clasp, Israel, 7 In.	110.00
Sterling Silver, Hammered Coin, With Compact	95.00
Tapestry, French Label	16.00
Tortoise Lucite, Suitcase Type, Brass, France, 8 x 4 x 6 In.	40.00
Velvet, Art Deco, Gray, Black & Wine, Tortoise-Like Plastic Handles	35.00
Woven, Indian Design, Wooden Handle, Ganscraft	50.00

QUEZAL glass was made from 1901 to 1920 by Martin Bach, Sr., in Brooklyn, New York. Other glassware by other firms, such as Loetz, Steuben, and Tiffany, resembles this gold-colored iridescent glass. After Martin Bach's death in 1920, his son continued the manufacture of a similar glass under the name *Lustre Art Glass.*

Quezal

Bowl, Gold, Ribbed, Shouldered To Flared Rim, Signed, 5 1/2 x 2 In.	165.00
Bowl, Ruffled Rim, Gold, Signed, 6 In.	250.00
Centerpiece, Gold, Inverted Pear Shape, Signed, 6 In.	440.00
Chandelier, 7-Light	3080.00
Lamp, Iridescent Blue, Pulled Feather Technique	2200.00
Punch Bowl, Signed, c.1900, 13 In.	1595.00
Salt, Ribbed, Scalloped Lip, Gold Iridescent, 1 3/4 In.	110.00
Shade, Brass Gooseneck On Weighted Base, Signed, 20 1/2 In.	275.00
Shade, Gold & Green Hooked & Pulled Feather, Gold Interior, 5 1/2 In.	110.00
Shade, Green Hooked Feather, Gold Outlining On Opaline, 5 In.	185.00
Shade, Green Pulled Feathers, Gold Interior, Signed, 13 1/2 In.	410.00
Shade, Hooked & Pulled Feather, Iridescent Green, 6 1/2 In.	4950.00
Shade, Pebbled Surface, Orange, Gold Iridescent, Signed, 5 1/4 In., Pair	632.00
Shade, Pulled Feather, Bulbous, Pair	1430.00
Shade, Ribbed, Gold Iridescent, 6 1/2 In., Pair	225.00
Shade, Tulip, Ribbed, Ruffled, Signed, 2 1/4 In. Fitters, Pair	180.00
Vase, Blue Iridescent, Signed, 7 In.	450.00
Vase, Blue Pulled Feathers & Scroll, Green Ground, Squatty, 5 1/2 In.	4719.00
Vase, Blue Pulled Feathers, Scroll On Green Ground, 5 1/2 In.	3900.00
Vase, Floriform, Iridescent, Signed, c.1915, 5 1/2 In.	1050.00
Vase, Floriform, Pulled Green Feathering, Amber Interior, Signed, 1900, 6 3/16 In.	1380.00

Vase, Gold Iridescent, Ruffled & Stretched Rim, Signed, 4 1/2 In.	375.00
Vase, Gold, Purple, Blue Iridescent, Flared, Ruffled, Signed, 3 x 5 In.	750.00
Vase, Gourd Shape, Double Handle, Signed .... *Illus*	1815.00
Vase, Green Pulled Leaves, Opalescent Ground, 7 In.	3500.00
Vase, Jack-In-The-Pulpit, Amber, c.1920, 13 1/2 In.	3162.00
Vase, Jack-In-The-Pulpit, Crackled Gold Iridescent, Pulled Feathers, 16 In.	5520.00
Vase, Jack-In-The-Pulpit, Gold & Green Pulled Feathers, Signed, 16 In.	5520.00
Vase, Jack-In-The-Pulpit, Gold Ruffled, Floral Fold Down Rim, Green & Opal, 15 In.	6958.00
Vase, Jack-In-The-Pulpit, Rose, Blue & Yellow, Gold Ground, No. 971, 11 1/2 In.	2640.00
Vase, Lily Pad Pulls, Gold Iridescent, 10 1/2 In.	2530.00
Vase, Pulled Leaves, Green Hooked Swirls, Gold Body, Signed, 10 1/4 In.	2200.00
Vase, Silver, Gold Iridescent Surface, Signed, 8 In.	575.00
Vase, Tapered, Gold & Platinum Hooked & Pulled Feathers, Green, Gold, 10 In.	2970.00
Vase, Trifold-Down Rim, Tapered, Signed, 6 In.	2950.00
Vase, Trumpet, Agate-Like Streaks Of Amber, Blue & Aqua, Signed, 6 In.	1610.00
Vase, Trumpet, Ruffled Rim, Ribbed Body, Bulbous Feet, Signed, 8 In.	230.00

QUILTS have been made since the seventeenth century. Early textiles were very precious and every scrap was saved to be reused. A quilt is a combination of fabrics joined to a filler and a backing by small stitched designs known as quilting. An appliqued quilt has pieces stitched to the top of a large piece of background fabric. A patchwork, or pieced, quilt is made of many small pieces stitched together. Embroidery can be added to either type.

Amish, Diamond-In-The-Square, Red, Indigo Blue Border, 78 x 77 3/4 In.	2185.00
Amish, Patchwork, Baskets, Black Ground, Lavender Edge, 60 x 83 In.	495.00
Amish, Patchwork, Lonestar, Multicolored, Navy Ground, 1931, 84 In.	1380.00
Amish, Purple & Black Basket Design, Crib, 48 x 36 In.	230.00
Amish, Snail's Trail, Blue Ground, Black Binding, 1910, 84 1/4 x 83 In.	1150.00
Appliqued, 3-Part Flower, Green, Red & Yellow, White Ground, Frame, 22 x 22 In.	27.00
Appliqued, 4 Floral Wreaths, Red Binding, Feather Quilted Border, 71 x 73 In.	385.00
Appliqued, 4 Leaf Pinwheels, Red, White Ground, 73 1/2 x 79 In.	522.00
Appliqued, 4 Open Pineapple, Green, Red & Orange Calico, White, 91 x 81 In.	1035.00
Appliqued, 4 Stylized Urns Of Flowers, Puffed Berries, 75 x 78 In.	635.00
Appliqued, 12 Wreath Blocks, Red & Green Calico, 19th Century, 90 1/2 x 70 In.	1265.00
Appliqued, 25 Block Crown, Red & Green Print Field, Late 19th Century, 77 x 80 In. .	300.00
Appliqued, Autumn Wheels, Oak Leaf & Acorn Quilting, c.1860, 90 x 74 In.	485.00
Appliqued, Basket, Yellow, White Ground, 68 x 84 In.	357.00
Appliqued, California Rose, Mid-19th Century, 74 x 74 In.	632.00
Appliqued, Cathedral, Multi-Colored, White Field, 98 x 90 In.	600.00
Appliqued, Coxcomb, Mid-19th Century, 81 x 81 In.	546.00
Appliqued, Feathered Pinwheel, Red & White, Waffle Quilted, 66 x 67 In.	675.00
Appliqued, Gold Diamond, More Than 4000 Pieces, 90 x 84 In.	400.00
Appliqued, Irish Chain, Green Calico, E.Z.C. 1884, 86 1/2 x 87 In.	660.00
Appliqued, Lily & Star, Red, White & Blue, Centennial Period, 89 x 72 In.	172.00
Appliqued, Lone Star, 72 x 78 In.	247.00
Appliqued, Maple Leaf, Yellow & White Calico, Cotton, 2 Pillow Shams, 74 x 84 In.	160.00
Appliqued, Nine Floral Medallions, Tan, Green, Brown, Pink Calico, 87 x 87 In.	165.00
Appliqued, Oak Leaves, Yellow & Green Inner Border, 78 x 66 In.	230.00
Appliqued, Patchwork, Black & Cross, Blue & White Calico, 74 x 67 In.	575.00
Appliqued, Patchwork, Double Irish Chain, Blue & White, Late 19th Century, 78 x 75 In.	230.00
Appliqued, Patchwork, Flying Geese, Light & Dark Green, Pink, Brown, 40 x 41 In.	35.00
Appliqued, Patchwork, Mosaic Star Variation, Red Inner Border, Penna., 85 x 84 1/2 In.	400.00
Appliqued, Patchwork, Oak Leaf Variation, L.B. Newman, 1930, 81 1/2 x 81 In.	345.00
Appliqued, Patchwork, Star Of Bethlehem, Calico Ground, Red, 83 3/4 x 81 In.	400.00
Appliqued, Patchwork, Star Variation, Calico Ground, M. Swab, 1905, 79 x 81 In.	345.00
Appliqued, Patchwork, Tree Of Life, Calico, 74 x 82 In.	920.00
Appliqued, Pineapple Leaves, Pink, Green & Yellow, Flowers, Cotton, 72 x 72 3/4 In.	690.00
Appliqued, Red & Green Patches, White Ground, 19th Century, 90 x 90 In.	1840.00
Appliqued, Red & Green Printed Patches, Cotton, 19th Century, 91 x 80 In.	747.00
Appliqued, Rose Of Sharon, 19th Century, 95 x 96 In.	920.00
Appliqued, Rose Pattern, Green, Orange, Red & Pink, 19th Century, 84 x 86 In.	172.00
Appliqued, Rose Wreath Friendship, Cotton, 84 x 84 In. .... *Illus*	2587.00
Appliqued, Star & Compass, Tenn., 1850-1860, 78 x 97 In.	4200.00

◆◆◆◆◆◆◆◆◆◆◆◆◆◆◆◆◆◆◆◆◆◆◆

Black buttonhole stitching outlining an applique on a quilt was popular from 1925 to 1950. Earlier quilts sometimes had tan or white buttonhole trim for the applique.

◆◆◆◆◆◆◆◆◆◆◆◆◆◆◆◆◆◆◆◆◆◆◆

Quilt, Appliqued, Rose Wreath Friendship,
         Cotton, 84 x 84 In.

Appliqued, Star Of Bethleham, Pieced, Red, Orange & Green, 91 x 90 In.	690.00
Appliqued, Star Of Bethlehem, 19th Century, 86 In.	3300.00
Appliqued, Star Of Bethlehem, 19th Century, 87 x 89 In.	1035.00
Appliqued, Star Of Bethlehem, Red Field, Mennonite, c.1880, 78 x 79 In.	1700.00
Appliqued, Stylized Black Children, Calico, Diamonds, Child's, Frame, 32 1/2 x 25 In.	302.00
Appliqued, Stylized Floral Medallions, Bowtie Grid, Green Calico, Red, 91 x 91 In.	275.00
Appliqued, Sun Bonnet Sue, Pinks, Blue, Muslin, Full Size	150.00
Appliqued, Triangles, Blue, White, Triangle Border, 90 x 92 In.	595.00
Appliqued, Trip Around The World, Scalloped, 1918, 72 x 98 In.	200.00
Appliqued, Tulip, Flower Leaves, Calico Binding, 102 x 83 In.	173.00
Appliqued, Tulips, Pastel Print, Pink & Green Grid, 74 x 93 In.	302.00
Appliqued, Vining Floral Grid, Meandering Border, 83 x 87 In.	220.00
Appliqued, Wreaths Of Lilies, Mid-19th Century, 91 x 77 In.	690.00
Crazy, Embroidered, Silk & Velvet, Late 19th Century, 65 x 93 In.	172.00
Crazy, Patchwork, Crib, 47 x 58 In.	125.00
Crib, Amish, Blazing Star, Cotton, Rayon, Square, Lancaster Co., 40 In.	220.00
Mennonite, Reversible, Crib, 42 x 37 1/2 In.	287.00
Patchwork, 4 Round Medallions, Tulips, Meandering Border, 83 x 83 In.	137.50
Patchwork, 4 Sawtooth Sunbursts In Grid, 82 x 82 In.	220.00
Patchwork, 9 Patch, Late 19th Century, 72 x 66 In.	115.00
Patchwork, 9 Pots Of Tulips, 3-Stripe Border, Feather Wreaths, 84 x 85 In.	465.00
Patchwork, 20 Baskets, Calico, Red Polished Cotton Ground, 75 x 93 In.	137.00
Patchwork, 20 Stars, Pink Calico, White, Mounted On Stretcher, 34 x 41 In.	220.00
Patchwork, 21 Red Medallions, 4-Part Fleur-De-Lis Design, 67 x 79 In.	165.00
Patchwork, 24 Baskets, White & Red Calico, Blue Squares, 64 x 83 In.	137.00
Patchwork, Alternating Squares, Blue, Green, Red & White, Calico Border, 85 x 65 In.	575.00
Patchwork, Amish, Bar Pattern, Solid Colors, Wool, Sarah Shelft, 1960s, 72 x 72 In.	165.00
Patchwork, Basket Design, Green & Magenta, White Ground, 80 x 96 In.	440.00
Patchwork, Blue & Pink, Prints, Crib	65.00
Patchwork, Bow Tie, Prints & Solids, Wool & Cotton, 72 x 74 In.	50.00
Patchwork, Calico Stars On White Ground, Crib, 31 x 42 In.	330.00
Patchwork, Carpenter's Square, Red & White, 78 x 78 In.	550.00
Patchwork, Chain Pattern Variation, 50 1/4 x 33 1/2 In.	403.00
Patchwork, Dresden Plate, Multicolored Prints, 82 x 106 In.	105.00
Patchwork, Drunkard's Path, Red & White, 69 x 85 In.	330.00
Patchwork, Feather Quilted Wreaths, Khaki & Red, White Ground, 70 x 85 In.	275.00
Patchwork, Flower Basket, Mary Chappell, South Carolina, 1848, 100 x 104 In.	3450.00
Patchwork, Flower Garden, Multicolored Print, Hexagon Shape, 70 x 84 In.	165.00
Patchwork, Flying Geese Pattern, Green & White Calico, 83 x 92 In.	28.00
Patchwork, Four Patch, Calico, Print On Reverse, 64 x 88 In.	172.00
Patchwork, Friendship, 1887, 83 x 84 In.	440.00
Patchwork, Friendship, Centennial Methodist Church, 1901, 72 x 80 In.	71.50
Patchwork, Indiana Meadows, 80 x 69 In.	765.00

Patchwork, Inscribed Names, 42 Stars, 1854, 96 x 87 In. 3100.00
Patchwork, Irish Chain, Crib, 28 x 30 In. 230.00
Patchwork, Irish Chain, Pink & White, Crib, 48 x 48 In. 38.50
Patchwork, Lady Of The Lake, Sawtooth Border, 1880s, 72 x 88 In. 747.00
Patchwork, Log Cabin With Courthouse Steps, c.1870, 83 x 71 In. 230.00
Patchwork, Log Cabin, Calico, Crib, 36 x 36 In. 11.00
Patchwork, Lone Star, Surrounded By 12 Small Stars, Pink Calico, 89 x 89 In. 1155.00
Patchwork, Medium Green, Pinkish Lavender, Ohio Amish, 67 x 80 In. 192.00
Patchwork, Morning Star Variant, Calico, 74 x 80 In. 165.00
Patchwork, Multicolored Circles On Brown, Seamstress Document, 1820, 72 x 72 In. .. 132.00
Patchwork, Nine Patch With Sawtooth, Bar Border, Crib, 48 x 52 In. 105.00
Patchwork, Nine Patch, Calico & Chintz, Herringbone In Squares, 100 x 100 In. 545.00
Patchwork, Nine Stars, Blue & White, Meandering Feather Designs, 75 x 77 In. 440.00
Patchwork, Poppies, 1930s, 94 x 76 In. 410.00
Patchwork, Printed Calico Alternating With White Patches, 96 x 96 In. 690.00
Patchwork, Robbing Peter To Pay Paul, 19th Century 144.00
Patchwork, Rolling Pinwheel & Star, 36 Medallions, 96 x 96 In. 165.00
Patchwork, School House, 74 1/2 x 63 In. 201.00
Patchwork, Signature, Quaker, Delaware Valley, 85 Names 4600.00
Patchwork, Star Of Bethlehem, 72 x 71 In. 1500.00
Patchwork, Star, 19th Century, 77 x 65 In. 431.00
Patchwork, Stylized Basket, Red & Blue Calico, White Ground, 68 x 79 In. 192.00
Patchwork, T Pattern, Red, White, c.1920, 80 x 64 In. 165.00
Patchwork, Trip Around The World, c.1918, 72 x 98 In. 200.00
Patchwork, White & Orange Cotton, Late 19th Century 82.50
Patchwork, Zigzag & Sawtooth Borders, Panels, Stars & Squares, 81 x 83 In. 192.50

QUIMPER pottery has a long history. Tin-glazed, hand-painted pottery has been made in Quimper, France, since the late seventeenth century. The earliest firm, founded in 1685 by Jean Baptiste Bousquet, was known as HB Quimper. Another firm, founded in 1772 by Francois Eloury, was known as Porquier. The third firm, founded by Guillaume Dumaine in 1778, was known as HR or Henriot Quimper. All three firms made similar pottery decorated with designs of Breton peasants and sea and flower motifs. The Eloury (Porquier) and Dumaine (Henriot) firms merged in 1913. Bousquet (HB) merged with the others in 1968. The group was sold to a United States family in 1984. The American holding company is Quimper Faience Inc., located in Stonington, Connecticut. The French firm has been called Societe Nouvelle des Faienceries de Quimper HB Henriot since March 1984.

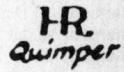

Ashtray, Peanuts Design, 1930s, 5 Piece 80.00
Ashtray, Peasant Women & Man 15.00
Butter Pat, Man In Hat 125.00
Cake Plate, Open Handle, 11 3/4 In. 75.00
Coaster, Rooster, Pair 58.00
Figurine, Breton Couple, Signed, 10 In. 375.00
Figurine, Colacq, 13 In. 475.00
Figurine, Marick, 13 In. 475.00
Plaque, Various Towns In Brittany, Lobate Shape, Marked, 18 In. 495.00
Plate, Leaf, Handle, Blue Ridge, 6 1/4 x 10 1/4 In. 52.00
Platter, Wedding Procession Of 10, Musicians, Chapel, Signed PBX 3250.00
Soup, Dish, Cover, 1 Qt. 350.00
Tray, Blue Floral, 12 1/4 x 6 In. 60.00
Vase, Couple, 2 Handles, Henriot, 13 In. 575.00

RADIO broadcast receiving sets were first sold in New York City in 1910. They were used to pick up the experimental broadcasts of the day. The first commercial radios were made by Westinghouse Company for listeners of the experimental shows on KDKA Pittsburgh in 1920. Collectors today are interested in all early radios, especially those made of Bakelite plastic or decorated with blue mirrors. Figural advertising radios and transistor radios are also collected.

Addison, Model 5, Catalin 1250.00
Addison, Model 5, Marbleized, Yellow Trim 1500.00

Advertising, Amoco Gas Pump	75.00
Advertising, Avon Skin So Soft, Bottle Shape	45.00
Advertising, B.F. Goodrich, Mantola, Wooden, Bakelite Grill & Handle, 1940s	70.00
Advertising, Chevron Custom Motor Oil, Figural Quart Of Oil, White, Gold	54.00
Advertising, Firestone Air Chief, Wooden Case, 1946	95.00
Advertising, Getty Gasoline, Gasoline Pump Shape, Transistor, Box	75.00
Advertising, Gulden's Mustard, Bottle Shape	75.00
Advertising, Heinz Ketchup, Bottle Shape	75.00
Advertising, Keen Tone, Keen Kutter, Magic Eye	300.00
Advertising, Marlboro Cigarette Pack, Battery Operated, 2 Ft.	450.00
Advertising, McDonald's Box, Big Mac, Battery Operated	65.00
Advertising, Mobil 1, Battery Operated, Can Shape, AM	35.00
Advertising, Motorola, Tabletop, Wooden Case	40.00
Advertising, Oreo Cookie, On Card, 1977	35.00
Advertising, Scrubbing Bubbles, Transistor, Mailer Box	20.00
Advertising, Teacher's Whiskey, Bakelite, Box, 1950s	350.00
Advertising, Texaco Oil Filters	50.00
Advertising, Tropicana Orange	25.00
Air King, Box	175.00
Airline, Table, Bakelite, c.1940	135.00
Arvin, Portable, c.1950	30.00
Arvin, Transistor, Red, Black Leather Case	50.00
Atwater Kent, Model 40	57.00
Atwater Kent, Speaker	50.00
Bendix, Model 115, Art Deco	115.00
Crosley, Model 11-102U, Bull's-Eye, Dark Green	85.00
Crosley, Model 11-102U, Dark Green Plastic	65.00
Detrola, Clock, triangular Shape, Wooden Case, 1930s	225.00
Detrola, Model 302, Dome Shape, Wooden, 1938	225.00
DeWald, Catalin	300.00
Emerson, Art Deco, Butterscotch Swirls, Catalin, 1938	1200.00
Emerson, Model 560, Portable, Plastic, 1940s, 9 x 7 In.	75.00
Emerson, Model AX-235, Tomato Red	2800.00
Emerson, Patriot, Blue Cabinet	1500.00
Emerson, Snow White & 7 Dwarfs, 1937	975.00
Fada, Bullet, Butterscotch Catalin	585.00
Fada, Model 1000, Maroon & Caramel	860.00
Farnsworth, Table Model, 1945	125.00
Figural, 1917 Model Automobile, Transistor, Side Dial, Metal, 1960s	125.00
Figural, Beetle Bailey	60.00
Figural, Big Bird, Transistor	20.00
Figural, Champagne Bottle	475.00
Figural, Cheeseburger	25.00
Figural, Football, 1950s	500.00
Figural, Fred Flintstone, Hanna-Barbera, 1973	55.00
Figural, Hamburger, 1960s	28.00
Figural, Jimmy Carter Head, Peanut Body, Battery Operated, Box	45.00 to 55.00
Figural, John Wayne, Battery Operated, Box	100.00
Figural, Race Car, John Player, Transistor	30.00
Figural, Smurf's Head	15.00
Figural, Tom & Jerry, Tom's Head, Figural Jerry, Battery Operated, Marx	65.00
Figural, Tom Thumb, Tomato Red, Square, Catalin, 6 1/2 In.	4250.00
Figural, Wooden Keg, Tube Type, 1930s	235.00
General Electric, Model 678 Transistor, Aqua	50.00
General Electric, Transistor, Sports Mate, 1964	40.00
Huckleberry Hound, Transistor, Box	65.00
Kolster, Remote Speaker	90.00
Majestic, Model 1, Charlie McCarthy	850.00
Majestic, Model 104, Fruit Salad, 1951	1250.00
Marlboro, Transistor, Box	15.00
McDonald's French Fries, 1977	40.00
Mitchell, Lumitone, Lamp, Art Deco, 1940s	135.00
Morse Brand, Transistor, Desk Set, Box	90.00

Philco, Model 37-610	80.00
Philco, Model 70-B	250.00
Philco, Portable, Flexible Plastic Carrying Handle, Wooden, 1946	50.00
Philco, Transistor, Model 7-124	75.00
Phillips, Push Buttons, Short Wave, Adjustable Volt, England	60.00
RCA, Model 12, Tubes	200.00
RCA, Model 3RH10, Transistor, 2 1/2 x 4 In.	50.00
Silvertone, Model 1202, Transistor, 1961	20.00
Silvertone, Model 2205, Transistor, 1962	12.00
Silvertone, Tombstone	65.00
Sony, Model TR-620, Transistor, 1961	40.00 to 60.00
SounDesign, Transistor, Red	50.00
Sparton, Blue Mirror, Chrome Plated Metal, Wooden Case, 17 x 8 In.	1150.00
Spica, Transistor, Leather Case	50.00 to 65.00
Stewart-Warner, Model 3044A, Bird's-Eye Maple Case, Grill Dial, 7 1/2 x 12 In.	258.00
Stewart-Warner, Short-Wave Band, Floor Model	245.00
Stromberg Carlson, Art Deco	80.00
Toshiba, Model 7th-425, Transistor, Wall Mount, 1961	150.00
Trancel, Transistor	35.00
Transistor, Minivox, Reverse Painted, Clock	80.00
Troy, Blue Mirror, 1938	1950.00
Zenith, Long Distance, Tabletop	70.00
Zenith, Model H511G, Console Tone	35.00
Zenith, Model L515F, Clock, Green Oblong Plastic Case	15.00
Zenith, Royal 50, Transistor, 1962	15.00 to 35.00
Zenith, Royal 250, Transistor, 1969	15.00 to 35.00
Zenith, Royal 500E, Transistor, 1960	30.00 to 50.00
Zenith, Table Model, Black Dial, Wooden Case, 1954	125.00
Zenith, Table Model, Green	25.00
Zenith, Tranoceanic	100.00
Zenith, Tranoceanic, Wave Magnet	60.00

RAILROAD enthusiasts collect any train memorabilia. Everything is wanted, from oilcans to whole train cars. The Chessie system has a store that sells many reproductions of their old dinnerware and uniforms.

Adz, Sante Fe RR	30.00
Ashtray, Chessie, Baltimore & Ohio, 3 1/2 In.	60.00
Badge, Patrolman, CRI & PR	110.00
Badge, Veteran Employee, Pittsburgh Railroad, Celluloid, Round	12.00
Bell, Capitol Limited, Diesel Locomotive	80.00
Bell, Engine, Iron Mounting Bracket, Bronze, 14 In.	330.00
Bench, C & M & R & M RR Pierced In 4 Seat Backs, 92 In.	440.00
Bill Of Lading, Lehigh Valley Railroad, 1914	4.00
Blotter, Ozark Zephyr, Burlington Route	9.00
Booklet, Southern Pacific RR, 16 Color Prints, 1942	35.00
Booklet, Union Pacific, Settling Western Lands, German Language, Map, 1871	425.00
Booklet, Where Gush The Geysers, Oregon Shorline Railway, 1910	10.00
Butter Chip, Baltimore & Ohio	42.00
Butter Chip, Milwaukee RR, Olympian	85.00
Butter Chip, RI Lines, 1924, 3 In.	50.00
Buttons, Uniform, C & O Railroad	15.00
Candleholder, Grand Trunk RR, Gold Trim, White, Limoges	130.00
Card, Trainmen Traveling, Brotherhood Of Railway, June 5, 1917	9.00
Card, Watch Inspection, Pennsylvania Railroad, 1916	10.00
Certificate, Stock, Baltimore & Ohio RR, 1841	65.00
Coffee Cup, Union Pacific, Pottery	15.00
Coffeepot, Santa Fe, Beehive Shape, Silver Plated	55.00
Container, Cover, B & O, Wonder Drink, Train Picture	40.00
Creamer, Hinged Cover, UPRR, 1910	95.00
Creamer, Orange, NY C & HR, 2 Oz.	95.00
Crumber, Burlington Route	55.00
Cup, Bouillon, Pullman	225.00
Cup & Saucer, Baltimore & Ohio	70.00

Cup & Saucer, Milwaukee RR, Traveler Pattern, After Dinner 120.00
Cuspidor, Union Pacific 50.00
Eggcup, Pullman 200.00
Extinguisher, Baltimore & Ohio RR 35.00
Fan, Hand, Missouri Pacific Lines, Train Picture, Wooden Handle 2.00
Hat, Brakeman's, C & O Railroad 50.00
Hat, Conductor's, Sante Fe RR.. 325.00
Kit, First Aid, Milwaukee RR, Tin.. 15.00
Lamp, Globe Switch, Sante Fe RR 150.00
Lamp, Wall, Original Bracket, France, 1880, Pair... 145.00
Lantern, Grand Trunk Railway, Bell Bottom, 1890s 225.00
Lantern, Salesman's Sample, 1870-1890 .... 750.00
Lantern, Target Light, Yellow Lenses, Back Of Caboose 175.00
Lock, Keen Kutter On Front, C & A RR On Back 525.00
Map, Ohio Railway, Folding, Linen Back, 1900 .... 45.00
Map, Pull Down, Showing All Lines In State Of Wisconsin, 1898 .... 40.00
Menu, Union Pacific RR, Bryce Canyon Cover, 1954.. 9.00
Padlock, MP & L 15.00
Pin, Railroad Car Shape, AA Of S & E Railroad, Gold Color, 1 In. 17.00
Plate, B & O, 9 In.. 80.00
Plate, B & O, Incline, Enoch Wood, 9 In.. 825.00
Plate, Baltimore & Ohio, Dark Blue Transfer, 10 1/4 In.. 495.00
Plate, Baltimore & Ohio, Thomas Viaduct, 7 In. 65.00
Plate, Dark Blue Transfer, Baltimore & Ohio, 10 1/4 In. 1045.00
Plate, Mercury, 9 In. 45.00
Plate, Missouri Pacific Lines, 10 1/2 In. 50.00
Plate, New York Central, Dewitt Clinton, 9 In... 45.00
Plate, Pennsburg, B & O RR 48.00
Plate, Pennsylvania RR, Mountain Laurel, 9 1/4 In. 45.00
Plate, Southern Pacific Lines, Prairie Mountain Wild Flower, 7 1/4 In. 40.00
Plate, Southern Pacific Lines, Prairie Mountain Wild Flower, 9 1/2 In. 90.00
Plate, Union Pacific, Flying Streamliner, 6 1/2 In.. 25.00
Platter, Atchison Topeka & Sante Fe, Adobe, 9 x 7 In. 65.00
Platter, Baltimore & Ohio, Oval, 11 1/2 In. 45.00
Platter, Pullman, 10 1/2 In... 155.00
Platter, Pullman, 12 1/2 In. 180.00
Platter, Southern Peach Blossom, 11 1/4 In. 135.00
Puzzle, Santa Fe & Baltimore & Ohio, Box, 1950s, 2 Piece.. 40.00
Saucer, Southern Pacific Lines, Prairie Mountain Wild Flower....................................... 35.00
Saucer, Texas Pacific, Eagle... 20.00
Sign, Capitol Limited, Observation Platform, Blue With Yellow Neon 550.00
Step, Conductor's, Burlington Railroad 80.00
Step, Conductor's, Canadian Pacific, Aluminum 60.00
Step Stool, Atchison, Topeka & Santa Fe, Steel 225.00
Step Stool, New York Central... 150.00
Syrup, Attached Plate, Silver Plate, Seaboard SMBM, SAL, 1925 .... 95.00
Teapot, Baltimore & Ohio... 90.00
Teapot, Rio Grande RR 55.00
Teapot, Verde Green, Pullman 225.00
Timetable, Boston & Maine RR, 1896 .... 30.00
Timetable, Colorado Midland Railway, Pikes Peak Route, 1891..................................... 400.00
Timetable, Pennsylvania RR, New York To Washington, 1912.. 28.00
Timetable, Piedmont, Richmond & Danville RR, 1889 .... 60.00
Torch, Great Western RR, No. 8, Bronze, Wall Mount, 6 x 6 1/4 In. 150.00
Torch, N & WRY, Cast Iron, Dayton Malleable Iron Co., 10 In. 95.00
Wrench, Baltimore & Ohio, Adjustable, Early 1900s, 18 In. 50.00

RAZORS were used in ancient Egypt and subsequently wherever shaving was in fashion. The metal razor used in America until about 1870 was made in Sheffield, England. After 1870, machine-made hollow-ground razors were made in Germany or America. Plastic or bone handles were popular. The razor was often sold in a set of seven, one for each day of the week. The set was often kept by the barber who shaved the well-to-do man each day in the shop.

Bank, Burma Shave, Used Razor Blades, Tin & Glass, 1920s 40.00
Bank, Donkey, Listerine Shaving Blades, Ceramic, For Used Blades........................ 45.00
Bank, Frog, Listerine Shaving Cream, Used Razor Blades 20.00
Blade Bank, Listerine, Elephant 22.00
Blade Bank, Man's Head, Cleminson 10.00
Boight, Straight, Spirit Of St. Louis, Inlaid Brass Biplane On Handle, Box 425.00
Box, 4 Aces Razor Blades, Cardboard, Some Blades, 1940, 1 x 2 In. 11.00
Durham Duplex, Straight, Box 35.00
Graef & Schmidt, Straight, Germany, 5 3/8 In. 115.00
H. Boker Co., Straight, Wooden Box 65.00
Hone, Keen Kutter, Aluminum Box 50.00
Little Joe, Straight, Box 35.00
Outdoor Scene, Stag & Trees Handle, Straight... 45.00
Peacock, Straight 45.00
Silver Inlaid Horn Handle, Straight, Late-1700s 48.00
Strap, Kriss Kross, Box, June 30, 1921 .... 35.00
Strap, Little Imp, Devil 37.00
Wade & Butcher, Civil War 25.00
Weck, Folding, Safety, Marked Trade Sample.. 18.00
Wilkinson, Safety, 7 Wedge Blades In Box, Strop... 110.00

REAMERS, or juice squeezers, have been known since 1767, although most of those collected today date from the twentieth century. Figural reamers are among the most prized.

Clown's Head, Japan.. 18.00
Crisscross, Sapphire Blue, Fire-King 300.00
Delphite, McKee, Small... 89.00
Duck, Pottery 20.00
Figural, Pig Clown 150.00
Grapefruit, Jadite 45.00
Grapefruit, Yellow, Seed Depression Top 295.00
Jadite, Green 30.00
Jennyware, Pink, Fire-King 90.00
Jennyware, Ultramarine, Fire-King ....75.00 to 125.00
Juice King 47.00
Lemon, Aluminum, No. 453 .... 20.00
Puddinhead, Red Top.. 80.00
Skillet Shape, Aluminum, Seed Guard, No-Slip Rubber Foot, Kwicky Juicer 5.00
Smiley, Orange... 49.00
Sunkist, Chaline, Glass... 198.00
Sunkist, White 27.00
Swan, Flowers... 78.00
Valencia 50.00
Vaseline, 7 1/2 In... 65.00
Wagner Ware, Lemon, No. 453, Cast Aluminum... 50.00

RECORDS have changed size and shape through the years. The cylinder-shaped phonograph record for use with the early Edison models was made about 1889. Disc records were first made by 1894, the double-sided disc by 1904. High-fidelity records were first issued in 1944, the first vinyl disc in 1946, the first stereo record in 1958. The 78 RPM became the standard in 1926 but was discontinued in 1957. In 1932, the first 33 1/3 RPM was made but was not sold commercially until 1948. In 1949, the 45 RPM was introduced. Compact discs became available in the U.S. in 1982 and many companies began phasing out the production of phonograph records.

6 Million Dollar Man, Vol. 1, Comic Book, Peter Pan Records, 1977, Original Wrap ... 8.00
After The Flood, Billy Joel, Germany.. 40.00
Album, 3 Stooges, Christmastime, 33 1/3 RPM, 1983 .... 12.00
Album, 52nd Street, Billy Joel, CBS, 1978 .... 9.00
Album, 7800 Fahrenheit, Bon Jovi, Autographed.. 125.00
Album, Alice In Wonderland, Magilla Gorilla, 33 1/3 RPM, 1977 .... 13.00
Album, Barbra Streisand, CBS 25.00
Album, Best Of Beach Boys, Dennis Wilson, Autographed 400.00

Album,	Best Of Doobies, Entire Band, Autographed	200.00
Album,	Close Encounters Music, 33 1/3 RPM	10.00
Album,	Don't Look Back, Boston, Autographed	175.00
Album,	Endless Wire, Gordon Lightfoot, Gold Floater	200.00
Album,	For Teen Twisters Only, Chubby Checker, 33 1/3 RPM, 1962	15.00
Album,	Four Lads, Breezin Along, 1959	10.00
Album,	Girl Happy, Judy Garland & Mickey Rooney	25.00
Album,	God Bless The Child, Billie Holiday, Columbia	50.00
Album,	Goldilocks & The 3 Bears, 33 1/3 RPM, 1963	12.00
Album,	Greatest Hits II, Bob Dylan, Columbia, 33 1/3 RPM	10.00
Album,	Greatest Hits, Janis Joplin, Columbia, 33 1/3 RPM	5.00
Album,	Greatest Hits, Joe Cocker, 33 1/3 RPM	8.00
Album,	Hans Brinker & The Silver Skates, 33 1/3 RPM, 1961	15.00
Album,	Jack & The Beanstalk, Shari Lewis, 33 1/3 RPM	10.00
Album,	Kaptain Kool & Kongs, Sid & Marty Kroft	45.00
Album,	Little Red Riding Hood, 33 1/3 RPM, 1968	12.00
Album,	Mirage, Fleetwood Mac	375.00
Album,	My Love, Petula Clark	17.00
Album,	My Way, Frank Sinatra, 33 1/3 RPM, 1969	15.00
Album,	Now, Rolling Stones, Brian Jones, Autographed	650.00
Album,	Pattie Page, The Waltz Queen, 33 1/3 RPM	20.00
Album,	Remember When, The Platters, 33 1/3 RPM, 1959	20.00
Album,	Season's Greetings From Barbra Streisand, Columbia	20.00
Album,	Shadow Dancing, Andy Gibb, Autographed	350.00
Album,	Southern Roots, Jerry Lee Lewis, Mercury, Stereo	20.00
Album,	Star Wars Soundtrack, 33 1/3 RPM	15.00
Album,	Study In Blue, Vogue Picture, Box, 2 Records	135.00
Album,	Surf City, Jan & Dean, 33 1/3 RPM, 1963	8.00
Album,	Tommy Dorsey Orchestra, Frank Sinatra, 33 1/3 RPM	10.00
Album,	Toys In The Attic, Aerosmith, Autographed	200.00
Album,	Tumbleweed Trails, Sons Of The Pioneers, Vocation, Stereo	18.00
Album,	Where Did Our Love Go, Supremes, Motown	25.00
Album,	Woody Woodpecker & Friends, 33 1/3 RPM, 1959	6.00
Album,	Yes Indeed, Pat Boone, 1958	10.00
Babalu,	Desi Arnaz, Boxed Set, 1950s	30.00
Boys From Yesterday,	Eagles	40.00
Captain Kangaroo,	Golden, 1957	12.00
Captain Kangaroo,	No. 471, 45 RPM, Little Golden Record, c.1960	25.00
Conway Twitty Sings,	Conway Twitty, MGM	50.00
Cylinder,	Always Take A Girl Named Daisy, Campell & Gillette, Blue Amberol	6.00
Cylinder,	An Old Sweetheart Of Mine, Harry E. Humphrey, Blue Amberol	7.00
Cylinder,	Casey Jones, Billy Murray, Blue Amberol No. 1550	15.00
Cylinder,	Dancing Down In Dixie Land, American Symphony Orchestra, Blue Amberol	6.00
Cylinder,	I'm Crying Just For You, Ada Jones, Billy Murray, Blue Amberol	10.00
Cylinder,	Jesse James, Vernon Dalhart, Edison, Blue Amberol No. 5057	25.00
Cylinder,	Mammy Jinny's Jubilee, Collins & Harlan, Blue Amberol	15.00
Cylinder,	My Uncle's Farm, Golden & Hughes, Blue Amberol	10.00
Cylinder,	Preacher & The Bear, Edison, Blue Amberol, No. 1560	50.00
Cylinder,	Roamin' In The Gloamin', Harry Lauder, Blue Amberol	6.00
Cylinder,	Shake, Rattle & Roll, Al Bernard & E. Hare, Blue Amberol	10.00
Cylinder,	Take Me To That Swanee Shore, Collins & Harlan, Blue Amberol	10.00
Doris Day's Greatest Hits,	33 1/3 RPM, 1962	10.00
Folk Concert,	Stanley Brothers	40.00
From The Pages Of My Mind,	Ray Charles, Columbia	12.00
Gone With The Window,	RCA, 1954, 10 In	40.00
His Own Songs,	Willie Nelson, RCA, Stereo	25.00
Hymns Of The Cross,	Stanley Brothers	35.00
Kojak,	Comic Book, Peter Pan Records, 1977, Original Wrap	8.00
LaBrea,	Buck Owens, 1st LP	60.00
Little Fireman, 1948		6.00
Martin Luther King,	I Have A Dream, Mountaintop Speeches, 1968, 45 RPM, Casino	25.00
Monkey & The Donkey, 1949		3.00
Now & Then,	Pretenders, London, 1981	20.00

Planet Of The Apes, Comic Book, Late 1970s, 45 RPM, Plastic Wrap 10.00
Star Wars Theme, 1977, 45 RPM 6.00
The Buddy Holly Story, Vol. II, Buddy Holly, Coral 60.00
Wish You Were Here Tonight, Ray Charles, Columbia 12.00
Your Twist Party, Chubby Checker, 33 1/3 RPM, Early 1960s 25.00

RED WING Pottery of Red Wing, Minnesota, was a firm started in 1878. The
company first made utilitarian pottery. In the 1920s art pottery was made.
Many dinner sets and vases were made before the company closed in 1967.
Rumrill pottery was made for George Rumrill by the Red Wing Pottery and
other firms. It was sold in the 1930s. For more information, see *Kovels'
Depression Glass & American Dinnerware Price List.*

Ashtray, Minnesota, Land Of 10, 000 Lakes, 3 Fish, Star Mark 140.00
Beater Jar, Dundee-Minn 165.00
Beater Jar, Spongeware, Akkerman Store, Rushmore, Mn. 975.00
Beverage Server, Smart Set, Stand 90.00
Birdbath, Salesman Sample 475.00
Bowl, A.E. Kelly, Genera Merchandise, Farley, Iowa, Greek Key, 8 In. 175.00
Bowl, Blossom Time, Concord Shape, 8 1/2 In. 9.00
Bowl, Greek Key, No. 6 .... 85.00
Bowl, Greek Key, No. 10 .... 90.00
Bowl, It Pays To Mix With Weisensels Sun Prairie, Blue & Red, 7 In. 175.00
Bowl, Magnolia, Square, 5 1/4 In. 4.00
Bowl, Saffron, Red & Blue Spongeware, Advertising, 8 In. 105.00
Bowl, Shoulder, 2 Blue Bands, No. 7 .... 50.00
Bowl, Spongeware, Panel, 7 In. 120.00
Bowl, Stoneware, White, 10 In. 23.00
Bowl, Vegetable, Pompeii, 2 Sections 17.00
Bowl, Vegetable, Starburst, Oval, 8 In. 10.00
Bowl, Vegetable, Tampico, 2 Sections 25.00
Bowl & Salt & Pepper, Round-Up, 9 3/8 In. Bowl, 3 Piece 200.00
Bread Plate, Bob White 5.00
Bread Plate, Random Harvest 4.00
Bread Plate, Tampico 5.00
Butter, Cover, Frontenac 15.00
Butter, Starburst 25.00
Cake Stand, Tampico 37.00
Candy Jar, Thou Shalt Not Steal 140.00
Casserole, Black Cover, Smart Set, 2 Qt. 70.00
Casserole, Compliments Of Dyste & Dyste, North Dakota, White 100.00
Casserole, Cover, Gray Line, 7 1/2 In. 370.00
Casserole, Iris 40.00
Chicken Drinking Fount, Klondike, Circle Stamp On Back 75.00
Chicken Waterer ....50.00 to 100.00
Churn, Blue Cobalt Leaf, Salt Glaze, Stamped Red Wing Stoneware Company, 4 Gal. .. 800.00
Churn, Large Wing, 6 Gal. 275.00
Console, Feathery Leaves, Tan Patina, Cream, 15 1/2 x 10 x 2 In. 24.00
Cookie Jar, Bob White 145.00
Cookie Jar, Chef, Blue 60.00
Cookie Jar, Chef, Yellow 120.00
Cookie Jar, Cover, Round-Up 300.00
Cookie Jar, Dutch Girl, 2 Shades Of Blue 150.00
Cookie Jar, Dutch Girl, Yellow 60.00
Cookie Jar, Jack Frost, Short ....575.00 to 725.00
Cookie Jar, Jack Frost, Tall 725.00
Cookie Jar, King Of Tarts, Blue Speckled 795.00
Cookie Jar, King Of Tarts, Multicolor 925.00
Cookie Jar, King Of Tarts, Pink 395.00
Cookie Jar, Round-Up 485.00
Cookie Jar, Spongeware 95.00
Cooler, Water, Bob White, Cover, Stand 600.00
Creamer, Magnolia 5.00
Creamer, Rose 7.00

Crock, 2 Small Wings, Upside Down, 1 Gal. 1075.00
Crock, Birch Leaf, 5 Gal. 85.00
Crock, Butterfly, Red Wing Stoneware Co., 20 Gal. 525.00
Crock, Elephant Ears, 20 Gal. 600.00
Crock, Large Wing, 4 Gal. 45.00
Crock, Large Wing, 12 Gal. 85.00
Crock, Large Wing, 20 Gal. 65.00
Crock, Large Wing, Spigot At Base, 50 Gal. 600.00
Crock, Large Wing, Water Cooler Spigot Hole, Oval, 2 Gal. 550.00
Crock, Long Turkey Dropping, Under Leaf, Minnesota Stoneware Co., 15 Gal. 1250.00
Crock, Minne-Ha-Ha Brand, M.A. Gedney Pk'lg Co., 3 Gal. 2200.00
Crock, No. 6 .... 33.00
Crock, Red Wing Union Stoneware, Blue Birch Leaf, 40 Gal. 450.00
Crock, Salt Glaze, Target, 2 Gal. 30.00
Crock, Small Wing, 2 Gal. 20.00
Crock, Union Stoneware Co., Oval, 1 Gal. 300.00
Crock, With Wing, 1 Gal. 365.00
Cruet, Round-Up, Pair 225.00
Cup & Saucer, Blossomtime, Concord Shape, Green 400.00
Cup & Saucer, Bob White 12.00
Cup & Saucer, Kermis, 12 Piece 100.00
Cup & Saucer, Random Harvest 10.00
Cup & Saucer, Rose 6.00
Cup & Saucer, Tampico 10.00
Dish, Baking, Spongeware, Hahns For 52 Years 270.00
Dish, Deer Insert 110.00
Feeder, Ko-Roc, 1 Gal. 40.00
Figurine, Bulldog, Brown 500.00
Flour Sack, Milling Co. 130.00
Flower Frog, Deer, 10 In. 22.00
Flower Frog, Seahorse 20.00
Gravy Boat, Tampico 20.00
Jar, Applesauce, Large Wing, 3 Gal. 170.00
Jar, Beater, Blue Banded 130.00
Jar, Beater, Gray Line, 3 Lb. 250.00
Jar, Beater, Redfiled 250.00
Jar, Canning, Marked MUSC, 1/2 Gal. 190.00
Jar, Mason, Black, 1 Qt. 185.00
Jar, Pantry, Cover, Spongeware 250.00
Jug, Albany Slip, 5 Gal. 1500.00
Jug, Albany Slip, Stylized Bird Base, 2 Gal. 140.00
Jug, Beehive, Albany Slip Top, Salt Glazed, Orange, Double Dipped, 4 Gal. 1750.00
Jug, Beehive, Colfax, Iowa, 5 Gal. 425.00
Jug, Bender-Fergus Falls, 1/2 Gal. 180.00
Jug, Brown & White, Advertising, 1 Qt. 90.00
Jug, Eddy Bros. 225.00
Jug, Elk, Aug. 22-24, 1929 .... 500.00
Jug, Large Wing, 5 Gal. 40.00
Jug, Noon Hour, George E. Ericson, 1 1/16, 7/8, 3/4, 11/16 & 9/16 In., 1888, 5 Piece ... 275.00
Jug, S.G. North Star, Signed, 1 Gal. 200.00
Jug, Souvenir, Farmington, Mn, 1/8 Pt. 110.00
Jug, Syrup, Signed, 1 Gal. 85.00
Jug, Whiskey, Ladner Brothers Wines & Liquors, White Shoulder, 1 Qt. 1150.00
Jug, Wing, 1/2 Gal. 175.00
Koverwate, 5 Gal. 175.00
Mug, Gray Line 1750.00
Pitcher, Charlie Wants To See You, Rush City, Mn., Cherry Band 185.00
Pitcher, Cherry Band 145.00
Pitcher, Saffron, Hahn Advertising 70.00
Pitcher, Spongeware, Hull, Iowa 1550.00
Place Setting, Capistrano, 5 Piece 90.00
Planter, Piano, Cover, Brown, M-1525 .... 110.00
Planter, Speckled Gold, Vertical Flute, 12 x 4 1/2 x 2 3/4 In. 12.00

Plate, Blossom Time, Concord Shape, 6 In.	2.00
Plate, Blossom Time, Concord Shape, 7 In.	4.00
Plate, Blossom Time, Concord Shape, 10 1/2 In.	5.00
Plate, Bob White, 6 1/2 In.	4.00
Plate, Bob White, 7 3/4 In.	8.00
Plate, Bob White, 11 In.	8.00
Plate, Capistrano, 6 1/2 In.	3.00
Plate, Dessert, Random Harvest	4.00
Plate, Dinner, Brittany	7.00
Plate, Dinner, Frontenac	7.00
Plate, Dinner, Random Harvest	7.00 to 10.00
Plate, Dinner, Rose	7.00
Plate, Dinner, Tampico	10.00
Plate, Lute Song, 10 In.	8.00
Plate, Magnolia, 7 In.	5.00
Plate, Magnolia, Green Leaves, 10 In.	5.00 to 10.00
Plate, Tampico, 11 1/2 In.	10.00
Platter, Bob White, 20 In.	95.00
Platter, Round-Up	110.00
Poultry Feeders & Drinking Founts, 2 Gal.	65.00 to 75.00
Relish, Tampico, 13 In.	23.00
Salt, Hanging, Gray Line, No. 3, Lid	1300.00
Salt & Pepper, Hourglass, Hamm's Brewery	150.00
Salt & Pepper, Schmoo	110.00
Salt & Pepper, Town & Country, Chartreuse	75.00
Salt Bowl, Cattle	75.00
Saltshaker, Brittany	5.00
Saltshaker, Gray Line	525.00
Saucer, Bob White	4.00
Saucer, Capistrano	2.00
Sheet Music, Kerry Mills, Matted & Framed	130.00
Soup, Cream, Lexington Rose	16.00
Sugar, Cover, Morning Glory, Pink Flowers	4.00
Sugar & Creamer, Crazy Rhythm	25.00
Sugar & Creamer, Lotus	22.00
Tea Set, Capistrano, 3 Piece	45.00
Teapot, Bob White	75.00
Teapot, Town & Country, Eva Ziesel	350.00
Tidbit, Normandy, 2-Tier	11.00
Tray, French Bread, Bob White	95.00
Trivet, Frontenac	55.00
Umbrella Stand, Blue & Red Spongeware	875.00
Umbrella Stand, Blue Bands, Blue & White Spongeware	1100.00
Umbrella Stand, Spongeware	1425.00
Vase, Antique White, 7 In.	4.00
Vase, Cattail, Green Brushware	100.00
Vase, Green, Molded Forest Scene, Lion, 7 In.	110.00
Vase, Leaves, Brushware	45.00
Vase, White, 7 In.	40.00
Vase, Yellow & Green Glazed, 17 1/2 In.	475.00
Water Cooler, 5 Gal.	450.00
Water Cooler, Birch Leaf, Straight Sides, 1 Gal.	3400.00
Water Cooler, Bob White, Cover, Spigot, Marked	375.00
Water Cooler, Large Wing, Hand Turned, 3 Gal.	975.00
Water Cooler, Large Wing, Union Oval, 4 Gal.	1500.00

REDWARE is a hard, red stoneware that originated in the late 1600s and continues to be made. The term is also used to describe any common clay pottery that is reddish in color.

Bank, Ovoid, Brown Running Glaze, 4 1/4 In.	275.00
Bottle, Dark Olive Amber Glaze, Paper Label, 1882, 7 7/8 In.	77.00
Bottle, Narrow Neck, 2 Faces Protruding From Shoulders	395.00
Bottle, Tan Glaze, Green Highlights, Ovoid, 6 3/4 In.	220.00

Redware, Bowl, Brown Squiggle,
18th Century, 12 7/8 In.

Redware, Bowl, Stylized Flowers,
Yellow & Green Bands, 1790s, 15 In.

Bowl, Brown Squiggle, 18th Century, 12 7/8 In. ....*Illus* 7130.00
Bowl, Stylized Flowers, Yellow & Green Bands, 1790s, 15 In. ....*Illus* 2530.00
Bowl, Yellow Slit Straight & Wavy Lines, Dark Brown Sponging, 7 3/4 In. 467.00
Charger, Crimped, Center Inscription In Yellow Slip, 19th Century, 13 1/2 In. 460.00
Charger, Sgraffito, Cream-White Slip, 1700s, 14 5/8 In. 320.00
Cradle, Slip Design, 1844 .... 1000.00
Creamer, American Eagle, Pointed Spout, Strap Handle, c.1820, 4 1/4 In. 315.00
Creamer, Inscribed Bottom, P.M.S., Jamestown Colony, 1935, 3 /58 In. 17.00
Creamer, Mottled Olive & Brown Glaze, 4 1/4 In. 330.00
Dish, Incised Tulips Interior, Sgraffito Design, c.1800, 11 1/4 In. 1840.00
Dish, Loaf, Mary's Dish In Script 4830.00
Figurine, Goddess, Holding Vessel, Hollow Case, Green Glaze, 15 3/4 In. 8625.00
Figurine, Lion, Reclining, Glazed, Late 19th Century, 7 1/2 In. 3737.00
Figurine, Rooster, Blue & White Glaze, Stahl Pottery, 1940, 4 1/4 In. 55.00
Flask, Brown & Yellow Glaze, 9 3/4 x 4 3/8 In. 200.00
Flask, Slip Design, Mottled Green & Yellow, 18th Century, 8 1/2 In. 115.00
Flowerpot, Attached Saucer, Glaze, Brown Splotches, Yellow Slip Dots, 3 1/2 In. 44.00
Flowerpot, Incised Eagle, Black Manganese Designs 3860.00
Flowerpot, Pie-Crust Edge, c.1860 .... 65.00
Jar, 3 Tulips, Slip Design, Bulbous, Handles 13800.00
Jar, Cover, Barrel Shape, 8 In. 150.00
Jar, Greenish Orange Glaze, Applied Ear Handles & Tooling, 19 1/2 In. 72.00
Jar, Incised Lines, Unglazed Exterior, Brown Slip At Shoulders, John Bell, 13 3/4 In. .. 330.00
Jar, Interior Glaze, Egg Shape, 8 1/4 In. 85.00
Jar, Tooled Lines, Dark Glaze, Brown Splotches, Strap Handle, 5 3/4 In. 70.00
Jug, 4 Pierced Carrying Handles, 1774, 8 In. 1610.00
Jug, Applied Seal, C.W., Dark Brown Glaze, Ribbed Strap Handle, 10 3/4 In. 60.00
Jug, Clear Shiny Glaze, Strap Handle, Egg Shape, 6 1/2 In. 190.00
Jug, Incised Shoulder Rings, Green & Amber Spots, Strap Handle, 7 3/4 In. 110.00
Jug, Puzzle, Verse, Yellow Slip, England, 1791, 8 In. 800.00
Mug, 2-Tone Green Glaze, Incised Label, Made By I.S. Stahl, 4/20/1938 .... 60.00
Pie Plate, 3-Line Yellow Slip, Coggled, 8 In. 330.00
Pie Plate, 3-Line Yellow Slip, Coggled, 8 7/8 In. 360.00
Pie Plate, Coggled Edge, 3-Line Yellow Slip Design, 9 3/4 In. 275.00
Pipe, Admiral Dewey's Head .... 125.00 to 135.00
Pitcher, Brown Design, Light Green Glaze 1150.00
Pitcher, New Geneva, Design 835.00
Pitcher, Unglazed Bottom Quarter, Pinched Spout, Late 18th Century 210.00
Pitcher, Yellow Slip Interior, Ovoid, Strap Handle, 7 In. 126.00
Plaque, Jean Nermoz, C. Granger, 19 1/2 In. 192.00
Plate, 3-Line Yellow Slip, Coggled, 8 7/8 In. 330.00
Plate, 3-Line Yellow Slip, Coggled, 9 3/4 In. 357.00

Ridgway, Plate, Black & White,
1950s Design, 5 1/2 In.

♦ ♦

When you move, pack plates
on their side with a pad under
and between the plates. The
weight of a stack of plates can
crack the bottom plates.

♦ ♦

Plate, 4 Birds, On Branch, Sgraffito	7475.00
Plate, Green, Daisies, Jack Field, 1870-1880	395.00
Plate, Herstine, Impressed Tulip & Initials DH, 10 1/4 In.	1150.00
Plate, Orange-Red Glaze, Brown Design Border, Late 18th Century, 8 1/2 In.	275.00
Plate, Polychrome Slip Design, White, Brown & Green, Coggled, 8 1/2 In.	5060.00
Plate, Slip Design, 19th Century, 8 In.	632.00
Plate, Yellow Slip Design, Coggled, 11 1/4 In.	495.00
Porringer, New England, 19th Century, 3 5/8 In.	125.00
Pot, Stew, Green Glaze, Ribbed Body, 8 1/2 In.	402.00
Tankard, Brown Manganese Splotches, Green Ground, 1770, 5 3/4 In.	4025.00
Water Set, Brown, White Interior, Buckeye, Pitcher, 6 Mugs	125.00

REGOUT, see Maastricht

RICHARD was the mark used on acid-etched cameo glass vases, bowls, night-lights, and lamps made in Lorraine, France, during the 1920s. The pieces were very similar to the other French cameo glasswares made by Daum, Galle, and others.

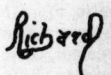

Vase, Cobalt Blue Flowers, Orange Ground, 3 3/4 In.	350.00
Vase, Double Overlay, Etched, Mountain Village Scene, 15 3/4 In.	920.00
Vase, Overall Iridescent Floral, Blue Ground, Cameo, 8 1/2 In.	445.00
Vase, Overlaid Orange & Brown, Etched Mountainous Village, Signed, 15 3/4 In.	920.00

RIDGWAY pottery has been made in the Staffordshire district in England since 1808 by a series of companies with the name Ridgway. The transfer-design dinner sets are the most widely known product. They are still being made. Other pieces of Ridgway are listed under Flow Blue.

Berry Bowl, Osborne, Flow Blue	35.00
Bowl, Burns & Highland Mary, Deep, 9 In.	45.00
Mug, Coaching Days, Silver Luster	35.00
Plate, Black & White, 1950s Design, 5 1/2 In. .... *Illus*	40.00
Plate, Chiswick, Flow Blue, 7 1/4 In.	37.00
Plate, Dundee, Flow Blue, 9 In.	50.00
Plate, Library, Philadelphia, 8 1/4 In.	25.00
Plate, New York City Hall, 10 In.	225.00
Plate, Robert Burns, Black Transfer, 9 In.	50.00
Plate, Valley Of The Shenandoah, New Hampshire, 6 7/8 In.	95.00
Platter, Danish Lace, Blue, 14 In.	125.00
Platter, Danish Lace, Blue, 16 In.	150.00
Platter, Narrows From Fort Hamilton, Purple, 17 1/2 In.	350.00
Soup, Dish, Church, Octagonal, 9 3/4 In.	425.00
Sugar, Canton, Cover, Flow Blue, Octagonal	250.00
Tureen, Soup, Ladle, Burlington, Blue & White	350.00 to 475.00

RIFLES that are firearms are not listed in this book. BB guns and air rifles are listed in the Toy category.

RIVIERA dinnerware was made by the Homer Laughlin Co. of Newell, West Virginia, from 1938 to 1950. The pattern was similar in coloring and in mood to Fiesta and Harlequin. The Riviera plates and cup handles were square. For more information, see *Kovels' Depression Glass & American Dinnerware Price List*.

Bowl, Oatmeal, Green	30.00
Butter, Cobalt Blue, 1/2 Lb.	295.00
Butter, Ivory, 1/2 Lb.	155.00
Butter, Turquoise, 1/4 Lb.	345.00
Casserole, Ivory	75.00
Casserole, Red	100.00
Pitcher, Juice, Mauve	275.00 to 325.00
Pitcher, Juice, Yellow	145.00
Plate, Cobalt Blue, 10 In.	55.00
Plate, Ivory, 10 In.	65.00
Plate, Red, 10 In.	65.00
Syrup, Cover, Red	150.00 to 160.00
Syrup, Ivory	125.00
Teapot, Ivory	180.00
Tumbler, Handle, Green	45.00

ROCKINGHAM, in the United States, is a pottery with a brown glaze that resembles tortoiseshell. It was made from 1840 to 1900 by many American potteries. Mottled brown Rockingham wares were first made in England at the Rockingham factory. Other types of ceramics were also made by the English firm. Related pieces may be listed in the Bennington category.

Bank, Ram's Head, 3 In.	71.00
Bedpan	90.00
Bedpan, Tortoiseshell Glaze	40.00
Bottle, Coachman, Brown, Yellow & Olive Green, Mark Of 1849, 10 1/2 In.	1100.00
Bottle, Fish, 11 In.	385.00
Casserole, Fruit Finial, 10 1/4 x 12 In.	264.00
Creamer, Cow	632.00
Creamer, Toby, 5 In.	92.00
Crock, Butter, Recessed Knob In Lid, Peacock At Fountain, 5 x 6 1/2 In.	225.00
Cuspidor, Industrial Size, 14 1/2 In.	115.00
Figurine, Cat, Oval Base, Streaks Of Green, 13 3/4 In.	3300.00
Figurine, Cat, Sitting, East Liverpool, Ohio	325.00
Figurine, Dog, Recumbent, 4 1/2 In., Pair	70.00
Figurine, Dog, Seated, Molded Hunting Dogs At Base, 12 1/2 In.	855.00
Figurine, Spaniel, Seated, Glazed, 9 1/2 In.	395.00
Flask, Mermaid, 8 In.	302.00
Pitcher, Batter, Cover, Figural Design, 9 In.	55.00
Pitcher, Christmas	175.00
Pitcher, Hound Handle, Hunting Scenes	55.00
Pitcher, Peacocks	110.00
Teapot, Final Cover	75.00
Teapot, Rebecca At The Well	75.00
Toby Jug, 1850, 9 In.	60.00
Toby Jug, Colonial Man	95.00
Whistle, Bird	275.00
Whistle, Figural, Frog	50.00
Window Stop, Grotesque Face, 5 1/4 In.	55.00

ROGERS, see John Rogers

ROOKWOOD pottery was made in Cincinnati, Ohio, from 1880 to 1960. All of this art pottery is marked, most with the famous flame mark. The R is reversed and placed back to back with the letter P. Flames surround the letters. After 1900, a Roman numeral was added to the mark to indicate the year. The name and some of the molds were purchased in 1984. A few new pieces were made, but these were glazed in colors not used by the original company.

Ashtray, Boss Stoves, 1946.. 125.00
Ashtray, Devil's Head, Figural 300.00
Ashtray, Frog.. 200.00
Ashtray, Frog, Open-Mouthed, Black High Glaze, No. 6097, 1929, 3 In. 187.00
Ashtray, Painted Bird, Signed... 100.00
Ashtray, Rook, Green High Glaze, No. 1139, 1950, 8 x 4 In. 110.00
Bookends, Collie, Gray Matte, No. 2778, 1929, 6 In.. 468.00
Bookends, Crows, Figural, Blue Glaze, Maker's Mark, 1926, 5 In. 422.00
Bookends, Elephant, Charcoal, 1925 .... 395.00
Bookends, Elephant, Ivory Ground, 1931 .... 255.00
Bookends, Hound, Green High Glaze, No. 2998, 1946, 6 In..................................... 132.00
Bookends, Owl, Figural, Logo, Dated 1940, 5 3/4 In. 55.00
Bookends, Owl, Ivory, 1938, 6 In. 275.00
Bookends, Owl, Matte Ivory 300.00
Bookends, Owl, On Book, Blue-Gray Matte Glaze, W. McDonald, 1933, 6 x 3 3/4 In.. 330.00
Bookends, Peacock.. 75.00
Bookends, Peacock On Throne, Yellow, No. 3345, 1924, 5 In. 358.00
Bookends, Peacock, McDonald, 7 In. 425.00
Bookends, Rook, High Glaze, MacDonald, 1950 .... 350.00
Bookends, Rook, Seated, Mint Green, No. 2275, 1927, 5 In. 193.00
Bookends, Ship, Blue 350.00
Bookends, Victorian Woman, Yellow, No. 2185, 1919.. 350.00
Bookends, Women, With Fans 189.00
Bowl, 3-Handled Form, Green Glaze, 1930, 3 1/3 In. 195.00
Bowl, 5-Footed, Oriental Design, Matte Yellow, No. 2802, 1929, 8 In...................... 176.00
Bowl, Arts & Crafts, Brown Vellum, Inverted Rim, No. 214, Duell, 1908, 3 x 6 In. 500.00
Bowl, Bird & Floral Design, 1884, 9 3/4 In. 550.00
Bowl, Bird & Floral Design, Signed MR, 9 1/4 In... 550.00
Bowl, Blue Berries, Yellow Leaves, Boat Shape, A.R. Valentien, 1888, 13 1/2 In. 1100.00
Bowl, Console, 1926, 10 In. 130.00
Bowl, Continuous Deer & Berry Design, Blue & Yellow Matte, 1929, 5 1/4 In. 300.00
Bowl, Corinthian Pink, Matte Glaze, 1921, 4 1/2 x 1 7/8 In....................................... 85.00
Bowl, Flower Frog, Art Deco Stylized Rose Border, 1918, 10 In............................... 295.00
Bowl, Flower Frog, Molded Arts & Crafts Design, Matte Blue, 4 1/2-In. Bowl............ 280.00
Bowl, Lincoln, Matte, 1904, 3 In. 350.00
Bowl, Lines Under Speckled Glaze, 1901, 1 1/2 x 5 In. 385.00
Bowl, Porridge, Blue Butterfly, Creamy Brown, Mary Taylor, 1884, 1 1/4 x 5 1/4 In. ... 220.00
Bowl, With Owl, Blue, No. 1084, c.1930 .... 375.00
Bust, Virgin Mary, Light Blue & Ivory Glaze, Flame Mark, 1946, 9 3/4 In. 247.00
Candleholder, Freeform, Alligatored Silver Green Glaze, Flame Mark, 1901, 6 In. 220.00
Candlestick, Blue-Gray Glaze, Drilled Hole Base, Curled Handles, 1923, 5 1/2 In. 247.00
Candlestick, Geometric Design, Carmel Glaze, 1947, 3 1/2 In., Pair........................... 172.00
Candlestick, Semi-Glaze, Blue, 1923, Pair.. 25.00
Chocolate Pot, Holly, Standard Glaze, Fechheimer, 1899, 9 In. 850.00
Chocolate Pot, Iris Glaze, Emma D. Foertmeyer, 1891 .... 1500.00
Clock, Black Panther, Glossy, No. 7039, 1950, 8 x 7 x 6 In. 550.00
Creamer, Holly Berries & Leaves, Mary Nourse, 1892, 4 1/4 In................................ 195.00
Decanter, Matte Green, Handle, Stopper, 1901, 6 3/4 x 5 1/2 In................................. 220.00
Dish, Candy, Rook, Green... 150.00
Dish, Cover, Stylized Petal Design, Carved, 3 Feet, Gray-Brown, 1912, 2 1/2 x 4 In. 357.00
Dish, Shell Shape, Painted Birds, Flowers, Grass, No. 222, M.H.P., 1882, 8 1/2 In. 90.00
Ewer, Floral Design, K.H., 1896 .... 400.00
Ewer, Matte Brown Exterior, High Glaze Interior, H. Wenderoth, 1882, 7 1/2 In. 187.00
Ewer, Scene, Blue Glaze, 10 3/4 In.. 175.00
Ewer, Standard Glaze, E. Diers, 1900, 9 In. 775.00
Figurine, Dog, White Matte, No. 277, 1924, 5 In. 360.00
Figurine, Donkey, Gun Metal, No. 6241, 1934, 6 In. 220.00
Figurine, Donkey, Matte White, No. 6216, M.H. McDonald, 1941, 6 In...................... 440.00
Figurine, Duck, Caramel, High Glaze, No. 6064, 1946, 3 In. 110.00
Figurine, Duck, White Matte, No. 6064, 1940, 3 1/2 In... 110.00
Figurine, Fruit Basket, Multicolored, No. 6020, 1928, 3 1/2 In. 235.00
Figurine, Nude, Seated, White Matte, No. 2868, 1928, 4 1/2 In. 470.00
Figurine, Pelican, Blue, 1950... 90.00

Figurine, Pelican, Matte White, No. 6149, 1939, 6 In. 248.00
Figurine, Polar Bear, Matte White, No. 6484, 1949, 4 In. 468.00
Figurine, Turtle, Matte White, No. 1686, 1939, 4 1/2 In. 330.00
Figurine, Woman's Bust, Greenware, Stand, No. 2026, 1930, 7 1/2 In. 220.00
Flask, Pilgrim, Incised Angels' Heads, Ivory Bisque, No. 35, E.P. Cranch, 1891, 6 In. ... 440.00
Flower Frog, Bird On Stump, Leaves, Aqua High Glaze, No. 2710, 1926, 6 In. 138.00
Flower Frog, Designs Between Holes, Blue, 2 x 3 3/4 In. 65.00
Jar, Coromandel Glaze, Green, Abel, 5 In. 275.00
Jar, Cover, Blue Matte Glaze, 1936, 5 3/4 In. 115.00
Jar, Cover, Relief Designs On Shoulder, Kataro Shirayamadani, 4 1/2 In. 1200.00
Jar, Round Lip, Matte Brown Drip Over Dark Brown, c.1905, 28 In. 770.00
Jardiniere, Blueberries & Foliage, Albert Valentien, c.1888 .... 1195.00
Jug, Butterfly & Florals, Signed A.R.V., 1884 .... 950.00
Jug, Carved & Painted Fruit, Matte Green, No. 512C, A. Pons, 1906, 5 1/2 In. 358.00
Jug, Leaves & Berries, Stopper, H. Altman, 1899 .... 495.00
Lamp, Carved Iris, Leaves Form Open Buttresses, Shirayamadani, 1906, 10 In. 4000.00
Lamp, Carved Pine Needles, Matte Green, No. 1134P, 1918, 14 In. 825.00
Lamp, Moon Flask, Yellow Glaze, Magnolia Design, 1938, Pair 1500.00
Loving Cup, Z Line, Geometric Designs, Dark Green Matte Glaze, 7 In. 350.00
Mug, Ear Of Corn & Husk, Elizabeth H. Lincoln, 1899, 4 5/8 In. 772.00
Mug, Encrusted Silver Overlay, Clover Blossoms, E.T. Hurley, 1905, 5 1/4 In. 1300.00
Mug, Falls City Logo, Brown, 1948 .... 60.00
Mug, Indian Design, Green, 1903, 4 x 3 In. 150.00
Mug, Owl, Figural, Oak Leaves, 1905 .... 265.00
Mug, Twisted Handle, Slip Decorated Boy, No. 328B, A.M. Valentien, 1890, 6 In. 715.00
Pin Tray, Molded Acorns & Leaves, Green, 1904, 5 1/2 In. 110.00
Pitcher, Ale, Brown Shading To Green, J.D. Wareham, 9 1/4 In. 650.00
Pitcher, Butterfly, Bullrushes, Gold & Brown Bisque, W. McDonald, 1885, 6 1/2 In. ... 550.00
Pitcher, Carved & Gilded Florals, Brown Matte, Signed W.B., 1882, 6 1/2 In. 300.00
Pitcher, Claret, Fannie Auckland, 1882 .... 995.00
Pitcher, Mushrooms, Frogs & Dragonflies, Limoges Style, 1881, 9 1/2 x 7 In. 1800.00
Pitcher, Yellow & Orange Flowers, No. 838F, E.R. Felton, 1899, 5 In. 115.00
Pitcher, Yellow Flowers, Gorham Silver Arabesques, S. Toohey, 1891, 5 1/2 In. 1875.00
Plaque, Mountainous Landscape, Lake, Trees, E.T. Hurley, 1946, 8 3/4 In. 3450.00
Plaque, Vellum, Landscape, River Bank, Trees, L. Asbury, 1922, 13 x 10 3/4 In. 6250.00
Plate, Wax Matte Floral, Katherine Jones, 1923, 8 In. 650.00
Stein, African American Portrait 4400.00
Stein, Wiedemann Brewing Co., Embossed Logo, Eagle On Shield, 5 1/2 In. 140.00
Sugar & Creamer, Blue Ships Around Bottom, White 75.00
Table, Demilune, Schmeig & Kotzian, N.Y., Marquetry Inlaid, Label, Pair 5500.00
Teapot, Ship Design, Blue & White, No. M-21, 5 1/2 In. 180.00
Tile, 2 Geese On Road To House, 1915 .... 805.00
Tile, Bird, Roses, Pinks And Purple, No. 3124, 1925, Square, 6 In. 330.00
Tile, Dove, White Trellis, Roses, Trivet, Flame Mark, 1928, 5 3/4 In. 315.00
Tile, Excised Galleon, Ochre Sails, Brown Ground, Signed, Square, 8 In. 500.00
Tile, Faience, Cutout Sea Horses & Seaweed, Green Matte, c.1905, 9 In. Square 1100.00
Tile, Faience, Oak Tree Landscape, Hanging Moss, Oak Frame, c.1910, 12 x 12 In. 4675.00
Tile, Galleon Ship, 2-Tone Brown Glaze, Frame, Square, 9 In. 335.00
Tile, Gulls, Yellow, Round 135.00
Tile, Landscape Of Trees, Riverbank, Faience, Frame, c.1904, Square, 12 In. 2970.00
Tile, Lily Blossom & Buds, Teal Stem, Blue, Frame, Signed, 5 x 3 1/2 In. 775.00
Tile, Memorative, Leaf Design, 1954, 5 1/2 In. 90.00
Tile, Oval, Raised Cherub, Pink & Blue Flowers, No. 93 W2, 2 x 1 1/2 x 14 In. 1760.00
Tile, Red Cherries, Black Outlining, Dark Blue Ground, Faience, 6 In. 275.00
Tile, Rose Design, Leaves, Dark Oak Frame, c.1905, 5 1/2 In. Square 530.00
Tile, Tea, Dutch Woman & Children, 1927 .... 350.00
Tile, Tea, Flower Basket, No. 3206 .... 250.00
Tile, Tree & Leaves, Swirling Roots, Blue, Cream, Oak Frame, 6 In. Square 1100.00
Tile, Wax Matte Poppy Blossom & Bud, Brown Centers, Signed, 5 x 3 1/2 In. 1650.00
Tray, Triangular, Frog On Edge, Matte Ivory, No. 2765, 1935, 6 In. 220.00
Trivet, Bird On Branch, Turquoise Ground, No. 2349, 1922, 6 In. 245.00
Trivet, Dutch Scene, Woman & Child, Signed, 1924, Square, 6 In. 225.00
Trivet, Floral Design, No. 1621, 1920 .... 140.00

Trivet, Parrot, Exotic Plumage, 1930, Square, 5 1/2 In. 275.00
Trivet, Rook, Blue... 110.00
Trivet, Star Burst, Matte Triochrome 250.00
Vase, 2 Carp Amid Underwater Foliage, Matthew A. Daly, c.1885, 10 1/2 In. 2875.00
Vase, Arabesques, Under Metallic Blue-Gray Ground, 1925, 9 x 3 3/4 In. 165.00
Vase, Arts & Crafts Design, Matte Brown, Handles, No. 1807, 1911, 4 1/2 In. 143.00
Vase, Astrological Design, Stylized, Signed, 1947, 9 In. 120.00
Vase, Aventurine Drip, 4 Colors, Flambe Glaze, 1930s, 3 x 3 In. 135.00
Vase, Aventurine Porcelain, Sparkling Brown Glaze, 1940, 7 1/2 In. 355.00
Vase, Band Of Stylized Flowers, Green To Maroon Matte, No. 704, 1914, 8 1/2 In. 413.00
Vase, Bearded Iris, Schmidt, 1911, 11 In. 4500.00
Vase, Birds On Tree Limbs, Dark Blue Matte, Mottled, No. 2481, 1919, 9 1/2 In. 302.00
Vase, Black & Blue Wisteria, Wax Matte, Jensen, 1929, 8 In. 2200.00
Vase, Black Dragon, Medium Brown Ground, A.R. Valentien, 1884, 6 1/4 In. 550.00
Vase, Black To Green Ground, Shirayamadani, 16 In. .... *Illus* 19800.00
Vase, Blossoming Trees, Birds, E.T. Hurley, 1933, 7 1/2 In. 1500.00
Vase, Blue & Red Drip Abstract Floral, Apple Green, Sax, 1931, 9 In. 1900.00
Vase, Brown & Green Landscape, Blue & Violet, Ovoid, F. Rothenbusch, 12 In. 880.00
Vase, Brown Circles, Repeated Pattern, Barrett, 1931, 7 In. 1700.00
Vase, Bulbous, Flared Neck, Raised Deer And Flora, Green High Glaze, 7 1/2 In. 88.00
Vase, Bulbous, Flared Neck, Raised Leaves & Blossoms, Blue High Glaze, 6 In. 187.00
Vase, Bulbous, Long Flaring Neck, Matte Ivory, No. 778, 1940, 10 In. 88.00
Vase, Cabinet, Purple, Blue & Brown Flambe Glaze, 1931, 3 3/4 x 2 1/2 In. 247.00
Vase, Canterbury Bells, Wax Matte, McDonald, 1937, 9 In. 2500.00
Vase, Cardinal & Butterflies, Green, 4 1/2 In. 95.00
Vase, Carved Florals, Vellum, Lincoln, 1920, 11 1/2 In. 1900.00
Vase, Carved Matte Green, C.S. Todd, 1913, 11 In. 10175.00
Vase, Carved Matte, Leaves & Red Berries, K. Shirayamadani, 1904, 5 1/2 In. 2090.00
Vase, Carved Red Flowers, Green Ground, No. 1126C, S.E. Coyne, 1905, 9 In. 248.00
Vase, Carved, Matte Green, Stylized Trees, Marianne Mitchell, 1905, 9 In. 990.00
Vase, Cattail-Tip Design, Stylized, Green Over Matte Pink Glaze, 1917, 6 3/4 In. 165.00
Vase, Cherry Blossoms, White To Pink To Green To Black, Iris Glaze, 1911, 6 1/4 In. 385.00
Vase, Cherry Cluster, Brown Glaze, Vreeland, 1900, 3 In. 200.00
Vase, Clover Blossoms, Leaves, Edith Noonan, 1905, 6 In. 357.00
Vase, Dark Blue, Feather Design, 1923, 6 In. 110.00
Vase, Dark Floral, C. Klinger, 1925, 9 1/2 In. 650.00
Vase, Dogwood Blossoms, Feathered Ground, Elizabeth Lincoln, 1921, 9 In. 660.00
Vase, Dogwood Blossoms, Mottled Green Glaze, Signed, 1911, 7 1/4 In. 495.00
Vase, Dogwood, Sallie Toohey, 1901, 8 1/2 In. 575.00

Rookwood, Vase,
Black To Green
Ground, Shiraya-
madani, 16 In.

Rookwood, Vase, Incised
Floral, French Red,
Sara Sax, 1923,
14 In.

Rookwood, Vase, Iris
Glaze, Valentien,
1903, 13 3/8 In.

Rookwood, Vase,
Lotus, Black Opal,
Sara Sax, 1927,
17 1/8 In.

Vase, Dragonflies, Pink & Green Matte Glaze, No. 1894, 1924, 6 1/2 In. 440.00
Vase, Elongated Flaring Neck, Geometric Border, 1927, 20 In. 665.00
Vase, Embossed Ravens & Trees, Pentagonal, 1910, 4 3/4 In. 385.00
Vase, Everted Rim, Flowering Chrysanthemums, A.B. Sprague, 1899, 14 1/2 In. 1380.00
Vase, Experimental Glaze, Green Flambe Over Mirror Black, 6 In. 400.00
Vase, Flared Neck, Black High Glaze, R.E. Menzel, 1953, 7 In. 285.00
Vase, Floral Design, Blue Vellum, 7 1/4 In. 800.00
Vase, Floral Vellum, Yellow & White Windswept Flowers, Elizabeth Lincoln, 7 In. 1540.00
Vase, Floral, Lawrence, 1901, 11 In. 975.00
Vase, Floral, No. 6870, Shirayamadani, 12 In. 450.00
Vase, Floral, Standard Glaze, No. 941D, Laura Lindeman, 1905, 8 In. 400.00
Vase, Floral, Stylized, Vellum Wax Matte, Lincoln, 1920, 9 In. 2200.00
Vase, Floral, Vellum, Diers, 1907, 9 x 6 In. 2400.00
Vase, Flowers, Stylized, Burgundy Matte, 1911, 7 1/2 x 3 1/2 In. 275.00
Vase, Fluted, Long Handles, Blue, 1931, 5 1/4 In. 115.00
Vase, Flying Bird, Flowers, High Glaze, No. 6459, 1914, 4 1/2 In. 385.00
Vase, Flying Geese, Full Moon, Matthew A. Daly, c.1886, 14 In. 2300.00
Vase, Forest Scene, Mountains In Background, Rothenbusch, 1916, 9 In. 3500.00
Vase, Geese In Flight, Orange & Brown Ground, Matthew Daly, 1900, 11 In. 3300.00
Vase, Geometric Shaped, Ridges, Green To Raspberry, Bottle Shape, 1909, 10 In. 360.00
Vase, Glazed, Carl Schmidt, 8 1/2 In. 4950.00
Vase, Green Leaf, Red Ground, Carved, Sara E. Coyne, 1904, 5 3/4 In. 660.00
Vase, Green Turtles, Swirling Ground, Kataro Shirayamadani, 1898, 10 1/2 In. 2100.00
Vase, Hunters With Bow & Arrow, On Horses, 1945, 12 In. 450.00
Vase, Incised Floral, French Red, Sara Sax, 1923, 14 In. ....*Illus* 31900.00
Vase, Incised Flowers, Ochre & Burnt Orange, Bulbous, A.M. Bookprinter, 5 3/4 In. 394.00
Vase, Incised Geometrics, Red-Brown Matte, No. 1658F, 1913, 6 In. 467.50
Vase, Incised Peacock Feathers, Blue To Pink Ground, E. Lincoln, 1920, 9 1/4 In. 1200.00
Vase, Iris Design, Lincoln, 1920, 6 In. 1500.00
Vase, Iris Glaze, 3 Painted Leaves, Brown, Green & Blue Glaze, 1903, 5 1/2 In. 440.00
Vase, Iris Glaze, Ovoid, E. Diers, 1904, 10 1/2 In. 1760.00
Vase, Iris Glaze, Valentien, 1903, 13 3/8 In. ....*Illus* 20900.00
Vase, Iris Glaze, Wax Matte, Lincoln, 1920, 6 In. 1500.00
Vase, Jewel Porcelain, Row Of Flowers, A. Conant, 1917, 5 x 5 3/4 In. 1045.00
Vase, Leaves & Flowers Band Top, Dark Blue Glaze, Flame Mark, 1919, 9 3/4 In. 165.00
Vase, Leaves & Stems, Yellow Flowers, N. Nourse, 1898, 9 In. 468.00
Vase, Lotus, Black Opal, Sara Sax, 1927, 17 1/8 In. ....*Illus* 17600.00
Vase, Matte Green And Pink, Handles, No. 77, 1927, 5 1/2 In. 138.00
Vase, Mistletoe, Celadon To Black Ground, Lenore Asbury, 1907, 7 In. 1700.00
Vase, Molded Flowers, Long Neck, Tan Over White, No. 2478, 1919, 7 1/2 In. 145.00
Vase, Molded Geometrics, Handles, Matte Blue, No. 2768, 1925, 4 In. 110.00
Vase, Molded Lotus Pattern, Caramel Color, High Gloss, 6 1/2 In. 210.00
Vase, Molded Zebras, Brown High Glaze, No. 6739, 1944, 10 1/2 In. 176.00
Vase, Molded, Matte Purple, No. 2493, 1919, 11 1/2 In. 248.00
Vase, Nudes, Stylized, Swan, Jens Jensen, 1913, 7 3/4 In. 4225.00
Vase, Orange & Yellow Flowers, Crimped Top, No. 216, M. Daly, 1887, 13 In. 110.00
Vase, Orange Floral Design, 12 In. 450.00
Vase, Oxblood Glaze, 1937, 4 1/2 In. 160.00
Vase, Painted Flowers, Green, Rose, Blue Ground, No. 1870, C.S. Todd, 1911, 6 In. 1210.00
Vase, Palm Leaves, M. Daly, 1902, 17 In. 1600.00
Vase, Pink To Gray Matte, 1921, 6 1/4 In. 88.00
Vase, Pink Wild Roses, Hearts, Blue To Pink Ground, E. Diers, 1930, 6 1/4 In. 357.00
Vase, Poppies, Painted, Matte, H.E. Wilcox, 1905, 9 In. 7150.00
Vase, Portrait, 2 Handles, Brown, G. Young, 1902, 11 1/2 In. 5500.00
Vase, Purple, Blue And Brown Flambe Glaze, 1931, Paper Label, 3 3/4 In. 225.00
Vase, Raised Leaf Design, Celadon Green Glaze, 1946, 8 3/4 In. 58.00
Vase, Raspberry Stylized Flowers, Purple, Jewel Porcelain, S. Sax, 1922, 5 1/2 In. 825.00
Vase, Red Dogwood Blossoms, Green Leaves, Sara Sax, 1924, 12 In. 2530.00
Vase, Red Flowers, Matte Wax, 24 In. 4500.00
Vase, Sang De Bouef High Glaze, No. 6197F, 1948, 5 In. 182.00
Vase, Sang De Bouef, Flambe Glaze, Turquoise Foot, Signed, 8 In. 305.00
Vase, Scenic, Mountains In Background, Rothenbusch, 1916, 9 In. 3500.00
Vase, Seascape, Fishing Boats, Sara Coyne, 1914, 5 In. 865.00

Vase, Seashells, Celadon, No. 6611, 1942, 8 In.	275.00
Vase, Shaded Brown Slip Ground, S. Coyne, 1899, 2 1/4 In.	475.00
Vase, Shamrock, Bulbous, Turquoise, 1945, 3 In.	85.00
Vase, Stylized Floral Design, 3 Panels, Matte Yellow, 5 1/2 x 3 1/4 In.	104.00
Vase, Stylized Flowers & Leaves, 6 Panels, No. 6147, 1930, 6 1/2 In.	275.00
Vase, Tapered Form, Black Glaze, 1920, 13 1/2 x 5 1/2 In.	220.00
Vase, Tulip, Blue, Red, Green Ground, 1912, 3 1/2 In.	385.00
Vase, Tulip, Stylized, Green Ground, W. Hentschel, 1912, 3 1/2 In.	385.00
Vase, Vellum Glaze, Red Rose, Dark Rose Ground, Sara Sax, 1913, 14 1/2 In.	1750.00
Vase, Vellum, Pink Nasturtium Blossoms, Rothenbusch, 1905, 8 1/2 In.	825.00
Vase, Velum, Floral Design, Blue, 1927, 7 1/4 In.	800.00
Vase, Vertical Leaves, Green Matte Over Pink, No. 2091, 1928, 6 1/2 In.	220.00
Vase, Vertical Leaves, Green Over Pink Matte Glaze, No. 1822, 1922, 6 In.	245.00
Vase, Water Lily Relief, Pink, 1949, 6 1/2 In.	145.00
Vase, Wax Matte, Pink & Green Gooseberries, M.H. McDonald, 1934, 10 1/4 In.	1760.00
Vase, Western & Southern Life Ins. Co., 1943, 7 1/4 In.	95.00
Vase, White & Gold Daisies, Cream To Gray, Vellum, E. Noonan, 1908, 7 1/4 In.	600.00
Vase, White & Gray Flowers, White Ground, Porcelain, Crazed, E. Barrett, 12 x 4 In.	525.00
Vase, White Lilies, Green Stems, Shaded Ground, Sallie Toohey, 1900, 10 1/2 In.	1320.00
Vase, White Lilies, Pink To Cream Ground, M.H. McDonald, 191, 8 1/2 In.	935.00
Vase, White Roses, Blue Ground, E. Diers, 1925, 5 1/2 In.	440.00
Vase, Winter Sunset, Snowy Foreground, Sallie Coyne, 1918, 8 In.	2185.00
Vase, Wisteria, Jensen, 1929, 8 In.	2200.00
Vase, Woodland Scene At Bawn, Shirayamadani, 1911, 10 In.	6300.00
Vase, Yellow 4-Petal Blossoms, Adeliza D. Schon, 1901, 6 3/4 In.	410.00
Vase, Z-Line, Rolled Rim, Incised Geometric Design, 7 In.	550.00
Wall Pocket, Molded Arts & Crafts Design, Matte Rose, No. 2008, 1920, 7 1/2 In.	220.00
Wall Pocket, Winged Insect Form, Feathered Green & Blue Matte, 1922, 9 x 4 In.	770.00

ROSALINE, see Steuben category

ROSE BOWLS were popular during the 1880s. Rose petals were kept in the open bowl to add fragrance to a room, a popular idea in a time of limited personal hygiene. The glass bowls were made with crimped tops, which kept the petals inside. Many types of Victorian art glass were made into rose bowls.

Blue & White Spatter Glass	75.00
Cabbage Leaf, Purple, 4 In.	265.00
Dark Green Satin Glass, Embossed Seashells	195.00
Rubina Overshot, Applied Tooled Rigaree, 3 1/2 In.	110.00
Satin Glass, Blown, Rose, White Lining, Crimped, 5 x 3 1/2 In.	68.00
Satin Glass, Blue, 4 In.	65.00

ROSE CANTON china is similar to Rose Medallion, except no people are pictured in the decoration. It was made in China during the nineteenth and twentieth centuries in greens, pinks, and other colors.

Mug, 18th Century, 4 3/4 In.	345.00
Plate, Exotic Birds & Butterflies, 8 In., Pair	94.00
Plate, Floral, 10 In.	88.00
Platter, Oval, 16 In.	302.00
Platter, Well & Tree, Oval, 16 1/4 In.	860.00
Teapot, Domed Cover, 9 1/2 In.	308.00
Teapot, Wicker Cozy, 7 In.	220.00
Vase, 5 In.	28.00
Vase, Bottle Form, Figural Reserves, Mounted As Lamp, 16 In.	575.00
Vase, Scalloped, Applied Dragons, 18 In., Pair	2340.00

ROSE MEDALLION china was made in China during the nineteenth and twentieth centuries. It is a distinctive design picturing people, flowers, birds, and butterflies. Pieces are colored in greens, pinks, and other colors. It is similar to Rose Canton.

Bottle, Water, c.1840, 15 1/2 In.	1595.00
Bough Pot, Cover, 19th Century, 8 In.	1265.00
Bowl, 10 x 4 In.	28.00

Bowl, 11 In.	385.00
Bowl, 16 In.	605.00
Bowl, 1850, 12 In.	1295.00
Bowl, 3 Figures, Deep, 7 1/2 In.	65.00
Bowl, 4 Panels, Figures In 2, Flowers In 2, 9 In.	285.00
Bowl, Acorn Knop Cover, Scalloped, Oval, 9 1/4 & 10 1/2 In., 2 Piece	748.00
Bowl, Chop, 19th Century, 15 1/2 In.	402.00
Bowl, Cover, Pineapple Finial, Square, 4 1/2 x 8 1/2 In.	220.00
Bowl, Native Wood Stand, 10 1/4 x 4 1/2 In.	126.00
Bowl, Shaped Corners, 10 In.	105.00
Bowl, Vegetable, Cover	650.00
Brush Box	525.00
Candlestick, Circular Form, 1920s, 8 In., Pair	145.00
Charger	412.00
Compote, Early 20th Century, 3 3/4 x 10 1/4 In.	82.00
Creamer, 19th Century, 3 1/2 In.	72.00
Creamer, 3 1/2 In.	55.00
Cup, Cover, 24 Piece	165.00
Cup & Saucer, Birds, People	38.00
Cup & Saucer, Wishbone Handle	75.00
Dish, Soap, Insert, 2 1/2 x 6 In.	358.00
Dish, Underplate, Reticulated	715.00
Jardiniere, 4 In.	220.00
Lamp, Oil, Electrified	795.00
Mug, Handle, Figural Decorations, 5 In.	385.00
Pitcher & Bowl, 13 In. Pitcher	3600.00
Plate, 7 In.	50.00
Plate, 8 1/2 In., Pair	65.00
Plate, Birds, Figures, 6 In.	20.00
Plate, Figures, Birds, 7 1/2 In.	36.00
Plate, Figures, Birds, 9 1/2 In.	56.00
Plate, Fluted, 8 1/2 In., Pair	100.00
Plate, Hot Water, 19th Century, 10 1/4 In.	345.00
Platter, 15 In.	330.00
Platter, Footed, Shaped Edge, Oval, 13 7/8 In.	373.00
Platter, Oval, 1920s, 12 In.	58.00
Platter, Oval, 1920s, 17 1/2 In.	285.00
Platter, Oval, Reticulated Insert, 19th Century, 20 x 13 1/2 In.	1035.00
Platter, Well & Tree, 19th Century, 19 In.	748.00
Platter, Well & Tree, Oval, 19th Century, 17 In.	488.00
Pot, Cover, Cylindrical, 3 In.	121.00
Punch Bowl, 14 1/2 x 5 7/8 In.	550.00
Punch Bowl, 19th Century, 15 5/8 In.	1380.00
Sugar, Cover, Bulbous, Birds, People, Handles, 4 x 6 In.	98.00
Sugar & Creamer, Cover, People On Porch, Flowers, Butterfly, 5 1/2 In.	145.00
Sweet Meat Set, Square Chinese Lacquer Box, 1920s, 13 1/2 In.	460.00
Tea Set	770.00
Teapot, Canister Form	110.00
Teapot, Insulated Basket, Brass Fittings, 19th Century	315.00
Teapot & Cup, Drum Shape, Figural Panels, Wicker Cozy, 5 In. Teapot	138.00
Tureen, Domed Cover, Bombe, Handles, 19th Century, 14 1/2 In.	3500.00
Tureen, Soup, Cover, 19th Century, 15 1/2 In.	2587.00
Vase, 19th Century, 18 In., Pair	2600.00
Vase, 9 In.	110.00
Vase, Circular, 12 1/4 In., Pair	575.00
Vase, Figural & Floral Scenes, Knopped Form, 15 1/2 In., Pair	2415.00
Vase, Spill, 7 1/4 In., Pair	690.00

ROSE O'NEILL, see Kewpie category

ROSE TAPESTRY porcelain was made by the Royal Bayreuth factory of Tettau, Germany, during the late nineteenth century. The surface of the porcelain was pressed against a coarse fabric while it was still damp, and the impressions remained on the finished porcelain. It looks and feels like a textured

cloth. Very skillful reproductions are being made that even include a variation of the Royal Bayreuth mark, so be careful when buying.

Basket, Roses On Rim, Bouquets On Each Side, Rope Handle, Blue Mark, 8 In.	325.00
Bowl, Victorian Lovers Scene, 7 In.	275.00
Box, Cover, 3 Small Gold Feet, 2 1/2 x 4 In.	250.00
Box, Cover, Dresser, Blue Mark, 4 x 6 In.	450.00
Box, Cover, Rose Pattern, 3 Small Gold Feet, 2 1/2 x 4 In.	250.00
Box, Cover, Shell Shape, Blue Mark, 5 1/2 x 3 In.	350.00
Cake Plate, Pierced Handle, 10 In.	245.00
Cake Plate, Reflecting Poppies, Gold Trim, Marked	475.00
Creamer, Corset Shape, Pink	195.00
Creamer, Pinched Spout	225.00
Dresser Set, Tray, Hair Receiver & Powder Box	1025.00
Hair Receiver, Blue Mark, 3 In.	275.00
Match Holder, Hanging, Lady Portrait, Blue Mark	300.00
Match Holder, Hanging, Musicians, Blue Mark	220.00
Nappy, Large Apricot, Roses, Gold Trim, Blue Mark	335.00
Nappy, Yellow Roses, Leaf Shape, 2 Handles, Blue Mark	175.00
Plate, 10 1/2 In.	495.00
Powder Box, Cover, Blue Mark	395.00
Sugar & Creamer, Pink & White	650.00
Toothpick, Portrait, Royal Bayreuth	355.00
Tray, Dresser	225.00
Tray, Dresser, Blue Mark, 11 x 8 In.	170.00
Vase, Blue Mark, 4 3/4 In.	250.00
Vase, Globular Shape, 5 In.	209.00

ROSEMEADE Pottery of Wahpeton, North Dakota, worked from 1940 to 1961. The pottery was operated by Laura A. Taylor and her husband, R.I. Hughes. The company was also known as the Wahpeton Pottery Company. Art pottery and commercial wares were made.

Rosemeade

Ashtray, Chick On Front	125.00
Ashtray, Illinois	30.00
Ashtray, Washburn, Wisconsin	20.00
Bank, Hippopotamus	2450.00
Bookends, Wolfhound	65.00 to 120.00
Creamer, Corn Design, Small	45.00
Dish, Rolled Edge, Blue	22.00
Figurine, Cock Pheasant	25.00
Figurine, Elephant	55.00
Figurine, Mountain Goat	135.00 to 200.00
Figurine, Pheasant, 10 In.	120.00 to 130.00
Figurine, Pheasant, 12 In.	150.00 to 200.00
Figurine, Pheasant, 14 In.	225.00
Figurine, Robin, Perching	150.00
Flower Frog, Bird	58.00
Flower Frog, Frog	30.00
Flower Frog, Turkey	90.00
Lamp, Television, Cougar	550.00
Lamp, Television, Pheasant	525.00
Salt & Pepper, Bear Cubs, Seated	65.00
Salt & Pepper, Bear, Brown	32.00
Salt & Pepper, Bloodhounds	40.00
Salt & Pepper, Buffalo	65.00
Salt & Pepper, Cactus	55.00
Salt & Pepper, Cat, Black	30.00
Salt & Pepper, Chihuahua	19.00
Salt & Pepper, Chow Dog	20.00
Salt & Pepper, Coyote Pups	125.00
Salt & Pepper, Deer, Jumping	55.00 to 65.00
Salt & Pepper, Donkey Heads, Paper Label	55.00
Salt & Pepper, Drake & Hen	45.00

Salt & Pepper, Egyptian Woman & Dog, Green	350.00
Salt & Pepper, Fawns	50.00
Salt & Pepper, Goat	85.00
Salt & Pepper, Mice	30.00
Salt & Pepper, Oxen	55.00
Salt & Pepper, Paul Bunyan & Babe	60.00
Salt & Pepper, Pheasant	25.00
Salt & Pepper, Prairie Dogs, 3 1/2 In.	65.00
Salt & Pepper, Scotty Dogs, Black	45.00
Salt & Pepper, Skunks, Large	55.00
Salt & Pepper, Turkeys	45.00
Spoon Rest, Cactus	55.00
Spoon Rest, Desert Rose	15.00
Spoon Rest, Lily	35.00
Spoon Rest, Pig	30.00
Sugar, Cover, Turkey	55.00
Sugar & Creamer, Blue, Individual, 2 1/4 In.	6.00
Sugar & Creamer, Tulip	28.00
Toothpick, Pheasant	25.00
Vase, Swan, Aqua	30.00

ROSENTHAL porcelain was made at the factory established in Selb, Bavaria, in 1880. The factory is still making fine-quality tablewares and figurines. A series of Christmas plates was made from 1910. Other limited edition plates have been made since 1971.

Cigarette Set, Rosebuds, Leaves, Scalloped, Underplate, Oval, 2 1/2 x 4 In.	25.00
Coffeepot, Grasses	40.00
Cup & Saucer, Grasses	15.00
Dinner Set, Colonial Rose, 1950s, 92 Piece	395.00
Figurine, Angelfish, Yellow, Black Stripes, Signed, 10 x 14 In.	595.00
Figurine, Beaver, White, Professor Gaul, 15 In.	375.00
Figurine, Boy, Running With Lamb, 6 1/2 In.	95.00
Figurine, Cat, White, Gray Tabby Markings On Face & Tail	295.00
Figurine, Cocker Spaniel, Puppy, Sad Face, Brown, Rospert, 4 In.	145.00
Figurine, Dachshund Puppy, Seated, 6 x 6 In.	275.00
Figurine, Doe & Baby, Textured White Base, Roehring, c.1954, 12 In.	575.00
Figurine, Great Dane, Brindle, 8 3/4 x 9 In.	400.00
Figurine, Hopfner Sisters, Dancing, c.1925, 12 In.	3162.00
Figurine, Island Woman, 6 In.	210.00
Figurine, Nude Boy, Sitting On Cello, 8 In.	375.00
Figurine, Pigeons, White, Pair	750.00
Figurine, Pigs, A. Cassman, Dated 1918, 7 In., Pair	595.00
Figurine, Poodle, Gray, Karner, 8 1/2 In.	150.00
Figurine, Rabbit, Laughing, Sitting Up, White, 5 1/4 In.	75.00
Figurine, Squirrel, 6 In.	395.00
Figurine, Two Lovers Kissing, Marked, 14 In.	195.00
Fish Service, Blue And White, 20 Piece	550.00
Mug, Grapes, Green Leaves & Vines, Gold & Cream Ground, 5 1/2 In.	150.00
Plate, Christmas, 1910, Winter Peace, 8 1/2 In.	550.00
Plate, Christmas, 1913, Christmas Lights, 8 1/2 In.	235.00
Plate, Christmas, 1930	65.00
Plate, Christmas, 1931	65.00
Plate, Christmas, 1955, Christmas In A Village, 8 1/2 In.	190.00
Plate, Christmas, 1971, Christmas In Garmisch, 8 1/2 In.	100.00
Plate, Fruit Center, Scalloped, Gold Trim, 8 In., 6 Piece	125.00
Plate, Fruit, Gold Trim, 8 In., 8 Piece	120.00
Plate, Michio, Edna Hibel, Box, 1979	300.00
Plate, Mr. Obata, Edna Hibel, Box, 1977	350.00
Plate, Pierrot, Commedia Dell'Arte, LeRoy Neiman, 1975, 10 1/4 In.	125.00
Plate, Punchinello, Commedia Dell'Arte, LeRoy Neiman, 1978, 10 1/4 In.	125.00
Plate, Sakura, Edna Hibel, Box, 1978	300.00
Tankard, Kneeling Nude, Hand Painted, 6 In.	175.00
Tea Set, Pastel Floral Enameled, Ivory Ground, Demitasse, 15 Piece	82.00

Tea Set, Silver Overlay, Porcelain, 3 Piece ....295.00 to 395.00
Teapot, Charcoal, White Cover, Loewey 50.00
Vase, Birds, Abstract Ground, Green, Ovoid, Signed, 5 3/4 x 5 3/4 In. 120.00
Vase, Cylindrical, Studio Line, Emillio Pucci, 1960s, 14 In. 265.00
Vase, Gold & Ebony Birds, Iridescent Lavender, Selb Bavaria, 10 1/2 In. 460.00
Vase, Gold & Green Floral Design, Off-White, 9 In.. 115.00
Vase, Organic Shape, Brown, Yellow, Studio-Line, c.1960, 6 In. 330.00
Vase, Stylized Trees, Clouds, Blue, Gold Tracery, 4 In.................................... 45.00

ROSEVILLE Pottery Company was organized in Roseville, Ohio, in 1890.
Another plant was opened in Zanesville, Ohio, in 1898. Many types of pottery were made until 1954. Early wares include Sgraffito, Olympic, and
Rozane. Later lines were often made with molded decorations, especially
flowers and fruit. Pieces are marked *Roseville*.

Roseville
U.S.A.

Ashtray, Autumn... 325.00
Ashtray, Bushberry, Brown... 75.00
Ashtray, Capri, Green 25.00
Ashtray, Capri, Turquoise.. 28.00
Ashtray, Hyde Park, Palette Shape, Green 30.00
Ashtray, Magnolia, Green... 75.00
Ashtray, Peony, Green.. 40.00
Ashtray, Pine Cone, Blue ....95.00 to 135.00
Ashtray, Pine Cone, Green ....95.00 to 120.00
Bank, Pig, 4 In.. 198.00
Bank, Uncle Sam 125.00
Basket, Apple Blossom, Blue, 10 In.. 195.00
Basket, Apple Blossom, Pink, 12 In.. 325.00
Basket, Bittersweet, Green, 10 In... 105.00
Basket, Bittersweet, Yellow, 10 In...185.00 to 195.00
Basket, Clematis, Green... 95.00
Basket, Columbine, Blue, 7 In... 160.00
Basket, Columbine, Blue, 12 In.. 240.00
Basket, Cosmos, Brown, 10 In.. 250.00
Basket, Dogwood II, 9 In.. 130.00
Basket, Dogwood II, Green Ground, White & Black Flowers, 5 In.............................. 138.00
Basket, Dogwood, Hanging, Green, 10 In.. 143.00
Basket, Foxglove, Green, 10 In.. 250.00
Basket, Freesia, Blue, 7 In...80.00 to 145.00
Basket, Freesia, Green, 1945, 7 In.. 50.00
Basket, Gardenia, Gray, 12 In... 275.00
Basket, Hanging, Apple Blossom, Blue.. 190.00
Basket, Hanging, Apple Blossom, Rose ....175.00 to 190.00
Basket, Hanging, Bittersweet, Green...215.00 to 250.00
Basket, Hanging, Bleeding Heart, Blue... 325.00
Basket, Hanging, Bleeding Heart, Green.. 290.00
Basket, Hanging, Bushberry, Brown... 340.00
Basket, Hanging, Clematis, Brown.. 140.00
Basket, Hanging, Columbine, 9 1/2 In.. 225.00
Basket, Hanging, Cosmos, Brown.. 250.00
Basket, Hanging, Donatello, 10 x 6 1/2 In... 165.00
Basket, Hanging, Donatello, 7 1/2 In. ....165.00 to 185.00
Basket, Hanging, Florentine, Tan..140.00 to 155.00
Basket, Hanging, Foxglove, Green..250.00 to 280.00
Basket, Hanging, Freesia, Brown... 202.00
Basket, Hanging, Fuchsia, Rose.. 425.00
Basket, Hanging, Futura, Stylized Leaves 310.00
Basket, Hanging, Imperial I, 7 1/2 x 4 In... 125.00
Basket, Hanging, Iris, Pink... 350.00
Basket, Hanging, Ixia, Yellow 250.00
Basket, Hanging, Normandy, Cream & Green, 7 In. 198.00
Basket, Hanging, Pine Cone ....245.00 to 350.00
Basket, Hanging, Primrose, Blue... 265.00
Basket, Hanging, Silhouette, Maroon, Ivy.. 125.00

Basket, Hanging, Snowberry, Pink 200.00
Basket, Hanging, Thorn Apple, Brown 275.00
Basket, Hanging, Velmoss Scroll 350.00
Basket, Hanging, White Rose, Rose & Green 200.00
Basket, Hanging, Zephyr Lily, Brown 120.00
Basket, Hanging, Zephyr Lily, Green .... 175.00 to 195.00
Basket, Iris, Blue 395.00
Basket, Magnolia, Blue, 10 In. 275.00
Basket, Magnolia, Green 95.00
Basket, Mock Orange, 10 In. 160.00
Basket, Monticello, Brown, 6 1/2 In. 450.00
Basket, Pine Cone, Brown 475.00
Basket, Snowberry, Blue, 8 In. 180.00
Basket, Snowberry, Green, 8 In. 120.00
Basket, Snowberry, Green, 10 In. 175.00
Basket, Snowberry, Pink, 12 In. 200.00
Basket, Water Lily, Aqua, 12 In. 275.00
Basket, Water Lily, Pink, 12 In. 250.00
Basket, Wincraft, Brown 135.00
Basket, Windsor, Brown, 5 In. 415.00
Basket, Woodland, Glossy, 10 1/2 In. 265.00
Bookends, Bleeding Heart 285.00
Bookends, Bleeding Hearts, Blue 120.00
Bookends, Clematis, Blue 145.00
Bookends, Ming Tree, Blue 140.00
Bookends, Ming Tree, White 155.00
Bookends, Snowberry, Blue 75.00
Bookends, Snowberry, Green 175.00
Bookends, White Rose, Brown 165.00
Bookends, Wisteria, Blue 350.00
Bookends, Zephyr Lily, Green 225.00
Bowl, Artcraft, Blue, Green, Brown, 4 In. 247.50
Bowl, Baneda, Rose, 8 1/2 In. 245.00
Bowl, Blackberry, 4 x 9 In. 475.00
Bowl, Cereal, Child's, Ducks, With Shoes 150.00
Bowl, Cereal, Juvenile, Sunbonnet Girl, 6 In. 154.00
Bowl, Cherry Blossom, Brown, 5 In. 225.00
Bowl, Cherry Blossom, Handles, 7 In. 385.00
Bowl, Corinthian, 8 1/2 x 3 1/2 In. 45.00
Bowl, Cornelian, 3 x 8 1/2 In. 55.00
Bowl, Cremona, Pink, Blue, Green, Oval, 10 In. 66.00
Bowl, Dahlrose, 10 In. 250.00
Bowl, Donatello, 7 In. 85.00
Bowl, Earlam, 2 Handles, Blue, Green, Brown, 4 In. 176.00
Bowl, Egypto, Matte Green, 4 Sides, 3 1/4 x 8 3/4 In. 275.00
Bowl, Ferrella, 12 In. 650.00
Bowl, Freesia, Green, No. 465, 8 In. 230.00
Bowl, Gardenia, Gray, No. 629, 10 In. 66.00
Bowl, Imperial, Handles, 10 1/2 In. 62.00
Bowl, Imperial, Ring Handles, 8 x 3 1/2 In. 110.00
Bowl, Ixia, Pink, No. 331, 9 In. 88.00
Bowl, Jonquil, 3 In. 125.00
Bowl, Jonquil, 4 In. 115.00
Bowl, Luffa, Yellow Flowers, 8 x 12 In. 250.00
Bowl, Ming Tree, Oblong, White, 9 In. 85.00
Bowl, Mock Orange, Footed 70.00
Bowl, Moderne, Paneled, White Matte Over Brown Glaze, Signed, 10 1/2 In. 60.00
Bowl, Moss, 6 In. 125.00
Bowl, Mostique, Floral Design, Berries & Leaves, Caramel Border, 6 1/2 In. 175.00
Bowl, Mostique, Tan, 6 1/2 In. 75.00
Bowl, Pauleo, Blue 250.00
Bowl, Pauleo, Curved Rim, Footed, 1916 .... 350.00
Bowl, Pine Cone, Brown, Oval, No. 322, 12 In. 175.00

Bowl, Poppy, Flat, Gray, 5 In.	75.00
Bowl, Rosecraft, 9 In.	85.00
Bowl, Silhouette, Nude, Blue, Green, 8 1/2 In.	550.00
Bowl, Teasel, Green Flower, Tan & Brown, 10 In.	85.00
Bowl, Utility, Lily Of The Valley, Large	30.00
Bowl, Windsor, Blue, 3 1/4 x 10 1/4 In.	295.00
Candlestick, Apple Blossom, 3 In.	85.00
Candlestick, Bittersweet, 3 In.	35.00
Candlestick, Clematis, 4 1/2 In., Pair	95.00
Candlestick, Columbine, 2 1/2 In.	28.00
Candlestick, Freesia, Blue, Pair	65.00
Candlestick, Freesia, Green, 4 1/2 In.	30.00
Candlestick, Futura, Blue, Green, Tan, No. 1073, 4 1/2 In., Pair	275.00
Candlestick, Gardenia, Green, Pair	65.00
Candlestick, Good Night, Green Ivy, Handle, 7 In.	413.00
Candlestick, Jonquil, 10 In., Pair	425.00
Candlestick, Luffa, Green, Pair	290.00
Candlestick, Magnolia, Blue, 4 1/2 In., Pair	150.00
Candlestick, Pine Cone, Blue, 2 1/2 In.	180.00
Candlestick, Pine Cone, Blue, 4 1/2 In., Pair	185.00
Candlestick, Pine Cone, Brown, 2 Handles, Pair	195.00
Candlestick, Rozane, Cone Shape, Ivory, 7 3/4 In.	70.00
Candlestick, Tuscany, Gray, 3 1/2 In., Pair	48.00 to 80.00
Candlestick, White Rose, Blue	30.00
Candlestick, Zephyr Lily, Brown, 2 In., Pair.	78.00
Candlestick, Zephyr Lily, Brown, 4 1/2 In., Pair.	45.00
Candlestick, Zephyr Lily, Green, 4 1/2 In.	30.00
Casserole, Cover, Raymor, Dark Green Lizard, 11 In.	45.00
Cider Set, Magnolia, 10 Piece	880.00
Compote, Florentine, Brown, Footed, 4 1/2 x 6 1/2 In.	50.00
Compote, Orian	60.00
Compote, Velmoss Scroll, Cream Ground, Red & Green Roses, 9 In.	110.00
Conch Shell, Water Lily, Blue, 8 In.	155.00
Console, Carnelian, Aqua, 17 In.	100.00
Console, Clematis, Green	30.00
Console, Falline, Silver Paper Labels	465.00
Console, Freesia	145.00
Console, Gardenia, Gray, 14 In.	135.00
Console, Mock Orange, Green	85.00
Console, Monticello, Brown	350.00
Console, Moss, Pink, 13 In.	195.00
Console, Pine Cone, Brown, 10 In.	195.00
Console, Pine Cone, Brown, 11 In.	310.00
Console, Sunflower, 12 1/2 In.	500.00
Console, Topeo, Red	185.00
Console, Wisteria, Blue	450.00
Console, Zephyr Lily, Footed, Blue	100.00
Console, Zephyr Lily, Green, 12 In.	65.00
Console Set, Cremona, Aqua, 3 Piece	130.00
Console Set, Silhouette, Turquoise Leaves, White, 3 Piece	175.00
Console Set, Zephyr Lily, Bowl, 12 In.	225.00
Console Set, Zephyr Lily, Green, 3 Piece	105.00
Cookie Jar, Clematis, Brown	250.00
Cookie Jar, Freesia	285.00
Cookie Jar, Magnolia, Brown	275.00
Cookie Jar, Magnolia, Tan	325.00
Cornucopia, Apple Blossom, Green, 6 In.	70.00
Cornucopia, Apple Blossom, Pink.	75.00
Cornucopia, Capri, Black, No. 556, 6 In.	33.00
Cornucopia, Clematis, Brown, 6 In.	55.00
Cornucopia, Clematis, Green	55.00
Cornucopia, Foxglove, Green.	75.00
Cornucopia, Iris, 8 In.	125.00

Cornucopia, Russco, 9 In. 100.00
Cornucopia, Snowberry, Blue, 6 In. 55.00
Creamer, Child's, Ducks 90.00
Creamer, Medallion 80.00
Creamer, Peony, Yellow 55.00
Crocus Pot, Jonquil.. 245.00
Cup & Saucer, Juvenile, Hooded Girl 115.00
Dish, Feeding, Chicks, Rolled Edge 75.00
Dish, Feeding, Dutch, Rolled Edge, 8 In. 100.00
Dish, Juvenile, Sunbonnet... 125.00
Eggcup, Juvenile, Chick, 4 In. 165.00
Ewer, Bittersweet, Green, 8 In. 135.00
Ewer, Bleeding Heart, Pink 225.00
Ewer, Blended, Brown, Green, 9 In. 55.00
Ewer, Clematis, Green, 10 In. 105.00
Ewer, Columbine, Brown & Aqua 120.00
Ewer, Egypto, Matte Green, 7 1/2 x 4 In. 330.00
Ewer, Freesia, Blue, 6 In. 125.00
Ewer, Gardenia, Gray, 10 In. 130.00
Ewer, Pine Cone, Blue, 14 In. 595.00
Ewer, Pine Cone, Green, No. 416 .... 650.00
Ewer, Pink & White Roses, 6 In. 95.00
Ewer, Scene, Blue Glaze, 10 3/4 In.. 175.00
Ewer, Silhouette, Aqua 95.00
Ewer, Silhouette, Rust, 10 In. 165.00
Ewer, Snowberry, Pink, 10 In. 175.00
Ewer, White Rose, Blue 120.00
Ewer, Zephyr Lily, Brown, 10 In. 135.00
Figurine, Dog, White Matte Glaze 300.00
Flower Frog, Clematis, Blue 45.00
Flower Frog, Cosmos, Green 135.00
Flower Frog, Donatello, 4 In. 22.00
Flower Frog, Iris, Brown 115.00
Flower Frog, Peony, No. 47... 70.00
Flower Frog, Poppy, Brown 110.00
Flower Frog, Tourmaline, Green, 4 1/2 x 1 3/4 In. 10.00
Flower Frog, White Rose, Blue 70.00
Flower Pot, Dahlrose, 4 In. 150.00
Flower Pot, Donatello, Attached Saucer.. 130.00
Flower Pot, Freesia, Brown, No. 670, 5 In. 88.00
Flower Pot, Saucer, Donatello, Impressed Mark 145.00
Flower Pot, Saucer, Water Lily, Blue.. 155.00
Flower Pot, Saucer, White Rose, Blue 175.00
Flower Pot, Snowberry, Pink 70.00
Flower Pot, Thorn Apple, Pink.. 150.00
Incense Burner, Donatello.. 575.00
Jar, Sand, Pine Cone, Green 1650.00
Jardiniere, Apple Blossom, Pedestal, Pink, Brown, White Flowers, 24 1/2 In. .... 415.00 to 900.00
Jardiniere, Apple Blossom, Pink, 5 In.. 125.00
Jardiniere, Apple Blossom, Pink, 8 In. 395.00
Jardiniere, Bittersweet, Yellow, 4 In... 68.00
Jardiniere, Blackberry, 7 In... 625.00
Jardiniere, Bushberry, Brown, 8 In. 520.00
Jardiniere, Cherry Blossom, Pink & Blue, 10 In. 1200.00
Jardiniere, Columbine, Rose, Green, Pedestal, 8 In. 975.00
Jardiniere, Corinthian, 6 x 9 In. 170.00
Jardiniere, Dahlrose, 8 In... 235.00
Jardiniere, Dahlrose, 10 In. 650.00
Jardiniere, Dahlrose, Pedestal, Brown, Green, White Flowers, 24 1/2 In. 660.00
Jardiniere, Donatello, Pedestal.. 885.00
Jardiniere, Freesia, Pedestal, Dark Brown, Orange, Cream Flowers, 24 In. ... 550.00
Jardiniere, Futura, Pedestal, 29 x 15 In. 990.00
Jardiniere, Gardenia, Gray, 6 In... 95.00

Jardiniere, Mock Orange, Pedestal, 31 In.. 495.00
Jardiniere, Mostique, 10 In... 125.00
Jardiniere, Mostique, Pedestal, Tan, Brown, Green, 28 In. 303.00
Jardiniere, Normandy, 7 In...175.00 to 180.00
Jardiniere, Normandy, 8 In... 132.00
Jardiniere, Normandy, Pedestal, Green, White, 28 In. 770.00
Jardiniere, Pine Cone, Green, 2 Handles, No. 632, 9 1/2 x 6 1/4 In. 330.00
Jardiniere, Pine Cone, Green, 6 In.. 155.00
Jardiniere, Pine Cone, Pedestal, Green, No. 402, 18 In. ....750.00 to 1500.00
Jardiniere, Pink Moss, 10 In... 1000.00
Jardiniere, Poppy, Green, 5 1/2 In.. 185.00
Jardiniere, Primrose, Pedestal, Rose...1350.00 to 1725.00
Jardiniere, Rosecraft, Blue, 9 In... 365.00
Jardiniere, Snowberry, Green.. 475.00
Jardiniere, Stand, Magnolia, Orange 585.00
Jardiniere, Sylvan, 11 1/2 In.. 700.00
Jardiniere, Vista, Pedestal, 27 In... 440.00
Jardiniere, Water Lily, 10 In... 450.00
Jardiniere, White Rose, 2 Handles, Green, Brown, No. 653, 9 x 6 In............ 110.00
Jardiniere, White Rose, Brown.. 85.00
Jardiniere, White Rose, Pedestal, Brown.. 950.00
Jardiniere, Wisteria, Deep Blue Ground, 2 Handles, 9 x 12 1/2 In. 440.00
Jardiniere, Zephyr Lily, Blue, 8 In... 650.00
Jug, Thorn Apple, Blue 135.00
Juvenile, Rabbit, 3 Piece 400.00
Lamp, Corinthian 700.00
Lamp, Egypto, Thick Matte Green Finish, Oil, Signed, 5 x 6 In. 300.00
Lamp, Ferella, Pink Base 1500.00
Lamp, Freesia, Brown, No. 145 .... 495.00
Lamp, Mostique, 6 In. 150.00
Lamp, Primrose, Blue 343.00
Mug, Dutch ....48.00 to 85.00
Mug, Eagle 80.00
Mug, Eight Feather, Creamware.. 225.00
Mug, Pine Cone 200.00
Mug, Pine Cone, Brown 250.00
Mug, Raymor, Light Brown 30.00
Mug, Star Flower 135.00
Pitcher, Bleeding Heart, Green, 3 1/2 In. 450.00
Pitcher, Blended, Blue-Green.. 90.00
Pitcher, Blossom Flite, 7 In.. 65.00
Pitcher, Cider, Bushberry, Blue, 8 1/2 In... 325.00
Pitcher, Cow, 1916, 6 1/2 In... 165.00
Pitcher, Donatello, 6 1/2 In.. 295.00
Pitcher, Egypto, Geometric, Matte Green Glaze, Handle, 10 1/2 x 5 In. 413.00
Pitcher, Juvenile, Side Pout, Ducks.. 200.00
Pitcher, Landscape Scene, Bridge, Stream & Trees, Blue, Green & Cream ... 475.00
Pitcher, Mayfair, Brown, 10 In.. 75.00
Pitcher, Mayfair, Green.. 35.00
Pitcher, Orchid, 13 In. 695.00
Pitcher, Turtle Skin 150.00
Pitcher, White Rose, 10 In. 225.00
Planter, Burmese, Green.. 65.00
Planter, Bushberry, Blue 130.00
Planter, Donatello, 9 In. 60.00
Planter, Freesia, Green 90.00
Planter, Magnolia, Brown 85.00
Planter, Mock Orange, Pink, No. 952, 5 In. 120.00
Planter, Morning Glory, Green Ground, Purple & Yellow Flowers, 13 1/2 In. ... 319.00
Planter, Persian, Hanging.. 185.00
Planter, Pine Cone, Brown, Footed, Side Handle, 5 In.................................. 200.00
Planter, Pine Cone, Witch's Pot Shape, Handles, 3 Ft. 6 In. 195.00
Planter, Silhouette, Green, 8 In.. 50.00

Planter, Sunflower, Dark Blue & Green, Label.. 150.00
Planter, Tuscany, Gray 80.00
Planter, Wildflower 65.00
Planter Bookends, Columbine, Pink 350.00
Plate, Catalina, Green, 10 In. 45.00
Plate, Juvenile, 4 Rabbits, 6 1/2 In. 95.00
Plate, Juvenile, Nursery Rhyme 155.00
Plate, Juvenile, Peter Rabbit 75.00
Plate, Rosecraft, Blue, 5 In. 10.00
Pot, Strawberry, Jonquil, 6 1/2 In. 395.00
Powder Jar, Donatello.. 350.00
Shell, Ming Tree, White, 7 1/2 In. 85.00
Sign, Dealer, Pink, 2 x 6 In. 1000.00
Sugar, Clematis, Green 45.00
Sugar, Cover, Snowberry, Pink 40.00
Sugar, Snowberry, Pink.. 40.00
Sugar & Creamer, Snowberry, Green 75.00
Tankard, Holland 315.00
Tankard Set, Elk, Creamware, 8 Piece 385.00
Tea Set, Apple Blossom, 3 Piece.. 125.00 to 325.00
Tea Set, Dutch, 5 Piece 180.00
Tea Set, Peony, Yellow, 3 Piece 325.00
Tea Set, Zephyr Lily, Brown, 3 Piece 385.00
Teapot, Peony, Pink 185.00
Teapot, Peony, Tan 95.00
Teapot, Snowberry, Green 195.00
Teapot, Windcraft 185.00
Trivet, Raymore, Light Gray, 3-Footed 35.00
Urn, Ferella, Red, 6 In. 450.00
Urn, Ferella, Red, Green, 6 1/2 In. 360.00
Urn, Ixia, Green, 5 In. 85.00
Urn, Laurel, Gold... 145.00
Urn, Laurel, Yellow, Orange, Black, 6 1/2 In. 210.00
Urn, Silhouette, Red, 8 In. 375.00
Urn, White Rose, Blue, Bulbous, 7 In. 100.00
Vase, Amaco, Wine, 8 In. 75.00
Vase, Apple Blossom, 10 In. 145.00
Vase, Apple Blossom, Blue, 12 In. 210.00
Vase, Apple Blossom, Green, 15 In. 350.00
Vase, Apple Blossom, Green, No. 382, 7 In. 143.00
Vase, Apple Blossom, Green, Side Handles, 7 1/4 In. 85.00
Vase, Baneda, 2 Handles, Red, 6 In. 220.00
Vase, Baneda, Green, 6 In. 250.00
Vase, Baneda, Green, 7 In. 350.00
Vase, Baneda, Red, 5 In. 350.00
Vase, Baneda, Red, 12 1/2 In. 850.00
Vase, Blackberry, 2 Handles, Squatty, 4 1/2 x 6 In. 275.00
Vase, Blackberry, 6 In. 350.00
Vase, Blackberry, Pear Shape, 2 Small Top Handles, 5 x 4 In........................... 330.00
Vase, Bleeding Heart, Blue, 18 In.. 550.00
Vase, Bleeding Heart, Handles, Blue, 5 In. 70.00
Vase, Bleeding Heart, Handles, Green, 10 In. 325.00
Vase, Bushberry, 2 Branch Handles, Green, No. 35-9, 9 1/4 In. 220.00
Vase, Bushberry, Blue, 4 In. 79.00
Vase, Bushberry, Brown, 7 In. 105.00
Vase, Bushberry, Green, Double, Bud, No. 158, 4 1/2 In. 143.00
Vase, Carnelian II, Rose, Black, Bud, 6 In. 135.00
Vase, Carnelian, Burgundy, 4 x 6 In.. 90.00
Vase, Carnelian, Fan, 7 In. 125.00
Vase, Carnelian, Stylized Handles, Green Drip, Signed, 10 1/2 In. 165.00
Vase, Cherry Blossom, 2 Handles, Brown, 10 1/2 x 7 In. 413.00
Vase, Cherry Blossom, Brown, 2 Handles, 4 x 5 3/4 In..................................... 220.00
Vase, Cherry Blossom, Brown, 2 Handles, 5 x 6 In... 248.00

Vase, Cherry Blossom, Brown, 7 In. 325.00
Vase, Cherry Blossom, Brown, 8 1/2 In. 395.00
Vase, Clematis, Green, 7 In. 95.00
Vase, Clematis, Green, 8 In. 135.00
Vase, Clematis, Green, 9 In. 90.00
Vase, Columbine, Blue, 8 In. 100.00
Vase, Dahlrose, 8 In. 135.00
Vase, Dahlrose, 12 In. 495.00
Vase, Dahlrose, Bulbous, Handles, 8 1/2 In. 120.00
Vase, Dahlrose, Square, 10 In. 175.00
Vase, Dogwood, Green, 8 In. 135.00
Vase, Donatello, Bud, 8 In. 50.00
Vase, Donatello, Footed, 7 In. 45.00
Vase, Donatello, Torch Shape, 8 1/2 In. 130.00
Vase, Egypto, Rozane, Double Overlapping Leaves, Iris, F. Rhead, 13 In. 4950.00
Vase, Falline, Brown, 6 In. ....275.00 to 475.00
Vase, Fan, Deco, 6 In. 215.00
Vase, Ferella, Brown Pink Matte Glaze, 2 Handles, Reticulated, 9 1/2 In. 413.00
Vase, Florentine, Double, 6 In. 85.00
Vase, Foxglove, 1942, 12 1/2 In. 325.00
Vase, Foxglove, Blue, 4 In. 40.00
Vase, Foxglove, Blue, 10 In. 220.00
Vase, Foxglove, Double Handles, Green & Pink, 7 In. 85.00
Vase, Foxglove, No. 161, 6 In. 58.00
Vase, Foxglove, Pink, 16 In. 231.00
Vase, Freesia, Brown, 8 In. 105.00
Vase, Fuchsia, Fan, 8 In. 150.00
Vase, Fuschia, Blue, 6 In. 135.00
Vase, Futura, 13 In. 900.00
Vase, Futura, 15 In. 750.00
Vase, Futura, Arrow-Shaped Art Deco Design, 7 In. 770.00
Vase, Futura, Bulbous Form, Terraced Tapered Neck, Label, 12 In. 825.00
Vase, Futura, Bulbous, Stepped Body, Triangular Top, Arched Handles, 14 In. 880.00
Vase, Futura, Fan, 1928, 6 In. 525.00
Vase, Futura, Green, 8 In. 850.00
Vase, Futura, Green, 12 1/2 In. 1195.00
Vase, Futura, Stemmed Globe, Irregular Diamond Base, Blue, Green, Gray, 8 In. 935.00
Vase, Futura, Terraced Tapered Neck, Gunmetal To Green High Glaze, 12 In. 550.00
Vase, Gardenia, Brown, Waist Handles, 6 1/4 In. 46.00
Vase, Gardenia, Gray, 6 In. ....65.00 to 95.00
Vase, Grapes & Leaves, Brown Matte Ground, Binocular, 4 3/4 x 8 In. 66.00
Vase, Imperial II, Aqua, 5 1/2 In. 125.00
Vase, Imperial, Shoulder Handles, 8 In. 75.00
Vase, Iris, Blue, 5 In. 75.00
Vase, Iris, Brown, 6 In. 135.00
Vase, Ixia, Green, Pillow, 10 In. 135.00
Vase, Ixia, Yellow & Brown, 12 In. 375.00
Vase, Jonquil, 8 In. High...235.00 to 325.00
Vase, Jonquil, Brown, 2 Handles, 8 1/2 x 8 In. 275.00
Vase, Knifewood, Owls All Around, Green, 9 In. 475.00
Vase, Laurel, Yellow, 12 In. 385.00
Vase, Lotus, Brown, Tan, Pillow, 7 5/8 x 2 5/8 x 10 1/2 In. 125.00
Vase, Luffa, Brown, 6 In. 115.00
Vase, Luffa, Green, 7 In. 100.00
Vase, Luffa, Green, 9 In. 325.00
Vase, Ming Tree, 8 In. 60.00
Vase, Moderne, White & Tan, 6 In. 75.00
Vase, Mongol, Pillow, 5 In. 675.00
Vase, Monticello, 6 In. ....225.00 to 300.00
Vase, Morning Glory, Cream, 12 In. 795.00
Vase, Mostique, 5 In. 60.00
Vase, Mostique, 10 In. 195.00
Vase, Mostique, Flaring Neck, Small Handles, Arts & Crafts Design, 8 1/2 In. 275.00

Vase, Nude Silhouette, Embossed 350.00
Vase, Orian, Beige & Aqua, 10 1/2 In. 215.00
Vase, Orian, Matte Blue, Experimental Glaze, 9 In. 358.00
Vase, Panella, 3-Footed, Green, 5 1/2 In. 44.00
Vase, Peony, Green, 20 In. 475.00
Vase, Peony, Tan, 10 In. 95.00
Vase, Pine Cone, 18 In. 600.00
Vase, Pine Cone, Blue 7 In. 220.00
Vase, Pine Cone, Blue Label, 7 In. 100.00
Vase, Pine Cone, Blue, Cone Shape, 8 In. 385.00
Vase, Pine Cone, Brown, 7 In. 175.00
Vase, Pine Cone, Brown, 14 In. 425.00
Vase, Pine Cone, Brown, Cut-Out Top, 10 In. 365.00
Vase, Pine Cone, Glossy Green & Brown, 8 In. 115.00
Vase, Pine Cone, Gold & Brown Ground, Marked, 6 In. 125.00
Vase, Pine Cone, Green, 7 In. 130.00
Vase, Pine Cone, Green, 8 In. 300.00
Vase, Pine Cone, Green, 10 1/2 In. 400.00
Vase, Pine Cone, Green, 18 In. 1350.00
Vase, Pocket, Wincraft, Brown, No. 272, 6 In. 55.00
Vase, Poppy, Green, 15 In. 425.00
Vase, Poppy, Pink, 6 In. 140.00
Vase, Primrose, Pink, 8 In. 165.00
Vase, Rosecraft, Black, 2 Handles, Classical, 12 x 9 In. 358.00
Vase, Rozane Fuji, Stylized Enamels, Tan Bisque Ground, 10 1/2 In. 1210.00
Vase, Rozane Royal, 10 In. 195.00
Vase, Rozane, Floral, 7 In. 125.00
Vase, Rozane, Glossy Deep Red Glaze, Corseted, 14 In. 700.00
Vase, Rozane, Pillow, Green High Glaze, White Flower, Timberlake, 10 x 11 In. 770.00
Vase, Rozane, Portrait Of Charles Dickens, A. Dunlavy, Signed, 14 In. 495.00
Vase, Rozane, Silver Overlay, Flowers, Orange & Olive Ground, No. 580, 5 In. 522.00
Vase, Rozane, Spaniel, Claude Leffler, Signed, Pillow, 9 x 11 In. 1210.00
Vase, Russco, Gold, Crystalline, 7 In. 150.00
Vase, Russco, Turquoise, 12 1/2 In. 115.00
Vase, Silhouette, Nude, White, Aqua, 7 In. 185.00
Vase, Snowberry, Blue, 9 In. 130.00
Vase, Snowberry, Pink, 12 In. 275.00
Vase, Snowberry, Tan Shaded To Brown, 12 In. 105.00
Vase, Sunflower, 2 Handles, 9 1/2 x 7 In. 880.00
Vase, Sunflower, 5 In. 150.00
Vase, Sunflower, 6 In. 375.00
Vase, Sunflower, 7 In. 595.00
Vase, Sunflower, 8 1/4 x 7 In. 880.00
Vase, Teasel, 6 In. ....55.00 to 95.00
Vase, Thorn Apple, Brown, 15 1/4 In. 420.00
Vase, Thorn Apple, Pink, 8 In. 135.00
Vase, Topeo, Blue, 6 In. 280.00
Vase, Topeo, Silver Paper Label, 8 In. 210.00
Vase, Tourist, Landscape With Automobiles, 22 In. 1540.00
Vase, Tourmaline, Blue, 4 1/2 In. 70.00
Vase, Tourmaline, Blue, Green, Bulbous, 12 1/2 In. 150.00
Vase, Tourmaline, Handles, Blue, 5 3/4 x 6 1/2 In. 85.00
Vase, Van, Carnelian I, Green On Green, 8 In. 55.00
Vase, Victorian Art Pottery, Yellow & Blue Fruit, Blue-Gray Ground, 11 x 7 1/2 In. 413.00
Vase, Vista, 10 In. 395.00
Vase, Vista, Green Tree Trunks & Foliage, 12 In. 495.00
Vase, Volpato, Ivory, Fluted, 7 1/4 x 4 In. 115.00
Vase, Water Lily, Blue, 9 In. 95.00
Vase, Water Lily, Blue, 15 In. 230.00
Vase, Water Lily, Brown, 12 In. 135.00
Vase, White Rose, 12 In. 155.00
Vase, White Rose, Brown 485.00
Vase, Wincraft, Peach, Orange, No. 282, 8 In. 55.00

Vase, Wisteria, 8 1/2 In. 325.00
Vase, Wisteria, 9 1/2 In. 495.00
Vase, Wisteria, 10 In. 475.00
Vase, Wisteria, Handles, 6 In. 210.00
Vase, Wisteria, Tan, 12 In. 695.00
Vase, Woodland, Enameled Tulips, Buff Ground, 6 1/2 In. 600.00
Vase, Zephyr Lily, Blue, 6 In. 49.00
Vase, Zephyr Lily, Blue, 7 In. 80.00
Vase, Zephyr Lily, Blue, 15 In. ....325.00 to 350.00
Vase, Zephyr Lily, Pillow 130.00
Wall Pocket, Apple Blossom, Green ....145.00 to 250.00
Wall Pocket, Apple Blossom, Pink... 140.00
Wall Pocket, Apple Blossom, Rose ....165.00 to 175.00
Wall Pocket, Bittersweet, Gray, 7 In. 155.00
Wall Pocket, Bushberry, Green 200.00
Wall Pocket, Carnelian I, Blue 185.00
Wall Pocket, Corinthian 155.00
Wall Pocket, Dahlrose 170.00
Wall Pocket, Donatello, 9 3/4 In. ....140.00 to 150.00
Wall Pocket, Donatello, 11 1/2 In. 175.00
Wall Pocket, Donatello, 12 In. 150.00
Wall Pocket, Florentine, 7 In... 140.00
Wall Pocket, Florentine, 9 In. 140.00
Wall Pocket, Freesia, Blue 150.00
Wall Pocket, Freesia, Green 140.00
Wall Pocket, Freesia, Orange 235.00
Wall Pocket, Futura, Orange & Blue, No. 1261, 8 1/2 In. 319.00
Wall Pocket, Jonquil, Droopy Handles, 4 In. 100.00
Wall Pocket, Magnolia, Blue.. 185.00
Wall Pocket, Ming Tree, Blue 175.00
Wall Pocket, Ming Tree, White 240.00
Wall Pocket, Mostique, Gray 143.00
Wall Pocket, Pine Cone, Brown, Bucket ....650.00 to 675.00
Wall Pocket, Pine Cone, Double, Brown 285.00
Wall Pocket, Rosecraft, Aqua, 10 In. 125.00
Wall Pocket, Silhouette, Maroon... 195.00
Wall Pocket, Snowberry, Blue, 7 In. 110.00
Wall Pocket, Snowberry, Brown 85.00
Wall Pocket, Snowberry, Green 145.00
Wall Pocket, Snowberry, Rose 150.00
Wall Pocket, Tuscany, Gray... 155.00
Wall Pocket, Vista.. 600.00
Wall Pocket, White Rose, Green 150.00
Wall Pocket, Wincraft 75.00
Wall Pocket, Zephyr Lily, Green, 8 In. 175.00
Wall Pocket, Zephyr Lily, Tan, No. 1297 .... 177.00
Window Box, Bittersweet, Gray... 95.00
Window Box, Cosmos, Blue, 9 In.. 195.00
Window Box, Dahlrose, 12 In. 250.00
Window Box, Freesia, Brown... 70.00
Window Box, Velmoss II, Green, 12 In. 120.00
Window Box, Velmoss, Green, 12 In. 120.00

ROY ROGERS was born in 1911 in Cincinnati, Ohio. In the 1930s, he made a
living as a singer; in 1935, his group started work at a Los Angeles radio station. He appeared in his first movie in 1937. From 1952 to 1957, he made 101
television shows. The other stars in the show were his wife, Dale Evans, his
horse, Trigger, and his dog, Bullet. Roy Rogers memorabilia is collected,
including items from the Roy Rogers restaurants.

Bandanna, Roy & Trigger, Red With Lariat Design, Rope-Print Script........................ 75.00
Bank, Wall, Tin Lithograph, 1950s.. 135.00
Bedspread, Gray Cotton Poplin, Embroidered Scenes, Twin Size 325.00
Bedspread, Roy Rogers & Dale Evans, Riding In Jeep.................................. 175.00

Bedspread, Tan & Red Design, Twin 210.00
Binoculars, 3 Power, Box 175.00
Binoculars, Black, 1950s 95.00
Book, Big Little Book, Robin Hood On Range 65.00
Book, Enchanted Canyon, Whitman, 1954 .... 20.00
Book, Favorite Cowboy Songs 10.00
Book, Roy Rogers & Raiders Of Sawtooth Ridge, Cover, Whitman, 1946 .... 20.00
Book, Roy Rogers & Rimrod Renegades, Whitman, 1952 .... 10.00
Book, Surprise, For Donnie, Whitman, 1954 .... 28.00
Book, The Sure 'Nough Cowpoke, Tell-A-Tale, Whitman, 1952 .... 29.00
Book Bag, Leatherette, Brown, 13 x 10 In. 145.00
Book Binder, Loose Leaf, Roy & Trigger On Front Cover 125.00
Box, Crayon, Tin Lithograph 65.00
Cap Gun, Die Cast, Leslie-Henry, c.1950, 9 In., Box 375.00
Clock, Alarm, Animated, Ingraham .... 145.00 to 250.00
Coloring Book, 1951 .... 40.00
Coloring Book, Unused, 1966 .... 35.00
Comic Book Holder 145.00
Container, Quick Quaker Oats, Autographed Cup 48.00
Dress-Up Kit, Colorforms, Dale Evans Western, 1969 .... 60.00
Game, Horseshoe Set, Ohio Art, 7 1/4 x 14 In., Box .... 120.00 to 145.00
Gloves, Leather, 2 Tone, Tan, Fringe 125.00
Guitar, Graphic, Red 225.00
Harmonica, Original Card 95.00
Hat, Secret Compartment, Holding Mechanical Snap Out Gun 375.00
Holster, 1950s 59.00
Key Chain, Pocket Knife, Diamond Shape, Roy In Horseshoe 6.00
Knife, Pocket 32.00
Lamp, Dale Evans On Rearing Buttermilk, Signed, Composition 275.00
Lamp, Display, Chuck Wagon, 2 Horses, Driver 175.00
Lamp, Figural, Composition, Pastel 145.00
Lamp, Roy On Rearing Trigger 175.00
Lobby Card, Heart Of The Rockies, 1951, 11 x 14 In. 25.00
Lunch Box, Dale Evans, Double R Bar Ranch, Metal, 1955 .... 150.00
Lunch Box, Dome Top 125.00
Lunch Box, Saddlebag, American Thermos Prod., 1960 .... 375.00
Marble, Picture, 1 In. 2.00
Movie Poster, Roll On Texas Moon, Linen Back, 1946, One Sheet, 27 x 41 In. 225.00
Mug, Box, F & F, Shipping Carton 85.00
Nodder, Box .... 175.00 to 275.00
Nodder, Figural, Bull, Composition, 7 1/2 In. 195.00
Paper Doll, Roy Rogers Corral, Uncut 95.00
Pencil, King Of The Cowboys 1.00
Pencil Box, Light Brown 75.00
Photograph, Roy & Dale Evans, Color, 11 x 14 In. 4.00
Pin, Post Grape Nuts, c.1956, 1 In. 16.00
Pin, Roy Rogers & Dale Evans, Color, Photograph, Pinback, 1 3/4 In., Pair 5.00
Play Set, Rodeo, Marx, Complete, Box 175.00
Poster, Movie, Man From Oklahoma, 1945, Linen Backed, One Sheet, 27 x 41 In. 575.00
Poster, Movie, Song Of Nevada, Roy & Dale, Re-Release 1994, Half Sheet, 22 x 28 In. ... 75.00
Puzzle, Photo, Rohr, 1950 .... 55.00
Raincoat & Hat 175.00
Record, Lord's Prayer/Ava Maria, 45 RPM, Little Golden Record, 1950s 20.00
Rifle, Clicker 110.00
Rifle, Silver, Marx .... 95.00 to 175.00
Ring, Gabby Hayes, Shooting Cannon, Brass Barrel 195.00
Ring, Roy & Trigger, Oval Face, Sterling Silver 250.00
Ring, Saddle, Sterling Silver, Signed 250.00
Sheet Music, Bible Tells Me So, Roy Rogers & Dale Evans On Cover, 1955 .... 5.00 to 7.00
Sticker Book, Roy, Dale, Trigger & Bullet, Uncut 75.00
Towel & Washcloth Set, 3 Piece 60.00
Toy, Horse Trailer, Tin Lithograph, Yellow, Blue, Red, 10 In. 145.00
Toy, Stage Coach, Fix-It, Ideal, 1955, Box 200.00

Toy, Trailer, Semi-Tractor, Moving Doors, Roy & Trigger, Marx	150.00
View-Master Reel, No. 945	15.00
Wristwatch, Dale Evans, Box	350.00 to 425.00
Wristwatch, Dale Evans, Silver, Dale On Buttermilk, Box	295.00
Wristwatch, Goldtone Case, Matching Band, Bradley, 1951	375.00
Yo-Yo, 1940s	10.00
Yo-Yo, Roy Rogers Picture, 1950s	11.00

ROYAL BAYREUTH is the name of a factory that was founded in Tettau, Bavaria, in 1794. It has continued to modern times. The marks have changed through the years. A stylized crest, the name *Royal Bayreuth*, and the word *Bavaria* appear in slightly different forms from 1870 to about 1919. Later dishes may include the words *U.S. Zone*, the year of the issue, or the word *Germany* instead of *Bavaria*. Related pieces may be found listed in the Rose Tapestry, Sand Babies, Snow Babies, and Sunbonnet Babies categories.

Ashtray, Dutch Woman, With Basket, 5 1/2 In.	48.00
Ashtray, Elk, 6 1/2 x 4 1/2 In.	185.00 to 275.00
Ashtray, Shell, Blue Mark, 4 1/2 In.	45.00
Basset Hound, Blue Mark	450.00
Bell, Ocean Liner Scene, Tugboats Wooden Clapper	235.00
Bell, Peacock	245.00
Bowl, Embossed, Bird & 2 Turkeys & Man, 10 In.	220.00
Bowl, Full-Size Woman, Florals Around Rim, 10 In.	250.00
Box, Hunt Scene, Olive Green, Footed, Octagonal, 4 x 2 In.	155.00
Box, Little Jack Horner, Shell Shaped, Cover, 5 1/2 In.	250.00
Box, Spade Shape, Hunt Scene, Blue Mark, Pair	150.00
Box, Stamp, Devil & Cards, Blue Mark	880.00
Cake Plate, Pink & White Roses	95.00
Cake Plate, Poppy, Pink, 10 1/2 In.	395.00
Candleholder, Corinthian, Black, Blue Mark, 4 In.	50.00
Celery Tray, Lobster	125.00
Celery Tray, Roses, Open Handles, 12 In.	125.00
Compote, Reticulated Bowl & Base, Pearl Finish, 4 1/2 x 4 1/2 In.	125.00
Compote, Rose, Small	39.00
Creamer, Arab On Horse, 4 1/2 In.	120.00
Creamer, Bathers	285.00
Creamer, Black Cat, Blue Mark	210.00
Creamer, Black Crow, Blue Mark	125.00
Creamer, Butterfly, Open Wings	250.00 to 275.00

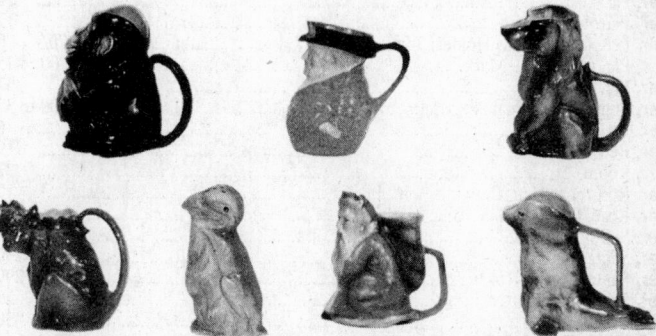

Royal Bayreuth, Creamer, Chimpanzee, 4 1/4 In.; Royal Bayreuth, Creamer, Coachman, 4 In.; Royal Bayreuth, Creamer, Dachshund, 4 In.; Royal Bayreuth, Creamer, Monkey, Green, 4 1/4 In.; Royal Bayreuth, Creamer, Penguins Hatpins Holder, 5 In.; Royal Bayreuth, Creamer, Santa Claus, 4 1/4 In.; Royal Bayreuth, Creamer, Seal, 4 In.

Creamer, Butterfly, Orange, Gray 395.00
Creamer, Cat 190.00
Creamer, Cat Handle, Blue 385.00
Creamer, Cat, Black 175.00
Creamer, Chimpanzee, 4 1/4 In. ....*Illus* 425.00
Creamer, Chimpanzee, Blue Mark 600.00
Creamer, Chinese Pheasant, Deponiert, Germany Mark 4000.00
Creamer, Clown 200.00
Creamer, Coachman, 4 In. ....*Illus* 150.00
Creamer, Colonial Curtsy Scene, 4 In. 265.00
Creamer, Corinthian, Green 40.00
Creamer, Cows, Trees & Pasture, Blue Mark.................................... 55.00
Creamer, Crow, Black, 4 3/4 In. 200.00
Creamer, Dachshund, 4 In. ....*Illus* 210.00
Creamer, Devil.. 210.00
Creamer, Devil & Cards... 125.00
Creamer, Devil & Cards, Blue Mark .... 175.00 to 195.00
Creamer, Eagle .... 140.00 to 150.00
Creamer, Elk... 80.00
Creamer, Fish.. 135.00
Creamer, Fish Head 210.00
Creamer, Girl & Horse.. 275.00
Creamer, Goat... 325.00
Creamer, Green Parrot Handle, Blue Mark 325.00
Creamer, Highland Goats.. 355.00
Creamer, Highland Sheep 295.00
Creamer, Highland Sheep, Left Handled 125.00
Creamer, Ibex 300.00
Creamer, Jack Horner, Blue Mark.. 110.00
Creamer, Lamplighter 300.00
Creamer, Lobster, Blue Mark, 5 In. ....60.00 to 135.00
Creamer, Lobster, Green Mark 65.00
Creamer, Maple Leaf .... 190.00 to 250.00
Creamer, Miss Muffet... 75.00
Creamer, Monk 550.00
Creamer, Monkey, Green, 4 1/4 In..*Illus* 450.00
Creamer, Multicolored Floral Spray, Gadroon Border, Footed 9.00
Creamer, Orange, Blue Mark .... 165.00 to 295.00
Creamer, Owl.. 295.00 to 300.00
Creamer, Pansy, Green Mark 225.00
Creamer, Parakeet... 225.00
Creamer, Parrot Handle 170.00
Creamer, Penguins Hatpins Holder, 5 In.............................*Illus* 700.00
Creamer, Pig, Gray, Blue Mark............................... 600.00 to 750.00
Creamer, Pig, White.. 575.00
Creamer, Poppy, Individual .... 200.00 to 375.00
Creamer, Raven Crow.. 60.00
Creamer, Red Poppy 195.00
Creamer, Robin.. 225.00
Creamer, Rooster & Hen, Crowing, 4 1/2 In. 125.00
Creamer, Rose, Pink & White, Blue Mark 325.00
Creamer, Sailing Ship 60.00
Creamer, Santa Claus... 2300.00
Creamer, Santa Claus, 4 1/4 In..*Illus* 2900.00
Creamer, Seal.. 200.00
Creamer, Seal, 4 In. ....*Illus* 300.00
Creamer, Shell, Coral, Handle 60.00
Creamer, Shell, Pearlized, Green Mark.. 30.00
Creamer, Tomato, Blue Mark, 3 In. 65.00
Creamer, Tomato, Footed 40.00
Creamer, Troubadour Scene, Brown Ground, Gold Handle, 3 In......... 75.00
Creamer, Trout... 170.00
Creamer, Water Buffalo... 110.00

Cup, 2 Handles, Grazing Sheep, 3 In. 38.00
Cup & Saucer, Devil & Cards, Demitasse 185.00
Dish, Little Bo Peep, Club 95.00
Dish, Little Dutch Girl, Blue Mark, 4 1/4 In. 110.00
Ewer, Babes In Woods, 6 In. 585.00
Ewer, Hunter With Dogs, 4 1/2 In. 180.00
Gravy, Liner, Multicolored Floral Spray, Gadroon Border, Gold Trim 18.00
Hair Receiver, Farmer With Turkeys, Blue Mark 265.00
Hair Receiver, Storks, Green 150.00
Inkwell, Hunting Scene, Ball Shape 315.00
Jug, Fox Hunter 145.00
Jug, Hunt Scene, Green 85.00
Jug, Hunt Scene, Squat, 5 x 5 In. 75.00
Match Holder, Chimpanzee, Hanging, Blue Mark 1250.00
Match Holder, Clown, Hanging, Pearlized, Blue Mark 600.00
Match Holder, Clown, Hanging, Red 450.00
Match Holder, Cows In Pasture, Scenic, Hanging, Blue Mark 200.00
Match Holder, Desert Scene, Hanging, Blue Mark 175.00
Match Holder, Devil & Cards, Hanging, Blue Mark 425.00
Match Holder, Elk 450.00
Match Holder, Jester, Hanging, Blue Mark 350.00
Match Holder, Little Jack Horner, Hanging, Blue Mark 400.00
Match Holder, Mountain Goat, Scene, Hanging, Blue Mark 525.00
Match Holder, Oyster & Pearl, Gloss Finish, Hanging, Blue Mark 700.00
Match Holder, Red, Scalloped Mold, Footed 295.00
Match Holder, Solid Green, Hanging, Blue Mark 40.00
Match Holder, Spiky, Hanging, Shell 250.00
Match Holder, Storks, Green, Hanging, Blue Mark 275.00
Mug, Beer, Elk, Tall, Blue Mark 495.00
Mug, Scuttle, Elk 435.00
Mustard, Cover, Leaf Underplate ....85.00 to 95.00
Mustard, Grapes, Yellow 150.00
Mustard, Green Ladle, Blue Mark 250.00
Mustard, Spoon, Lobster, Blue Mark, 4 In. 145.00
Mustard, Tomato, Blue Mark 56.00
Nappy, Little Miss Muffet 195.00
Pincushion, Elk, Blue Mark ....300.00 to 325.00
Pitcher, Angora Goats, 6 1/4 In. 220.00
Pitcher, Apple, Blue Mark, 6 In. 495.00
Pitcher, Arab On Horse, 3 1/2 In. 75.00
Pitcher, Babes In Woods, Blue Mark, 5 In. 175.00
Pitcher, Bear, 7 1/2 In. 825.00
Pitcher, Cat, Blue Mark, 5 In. 285.00
Pitcher, Clown, 4 1/2 In. 280.00
Pitcher, Crow, 5 In. 165.00
Pitcher, Devil & Cards 600.00
Pitcher, Duck, 5 In. 250.00
Pitcher, Eagle, 5 In. 400.00
Pitcher, Fish Head, 5 1/2 In. 375.00
Pitcher, Goose Girl, Blue Mark, 5 In. 110.00
Pitcher, Lamplighter, Blue Mark, 5 1/2 In. 495.00
Pitcher, Lobster, Marked 125.00
Pitcher, Musicians, 5 In. 80.00
Pitcher, Pearlized, Conch Shell, 7 In. 175.00
Pitcher, Rooster, Blue Mark, Miniature 50.00
Pitcher, Tomato, 6 1/4 In. ....350.00 to 500.00
Pitcher, Tomato, Blue Mark 225.00
Pitcher, Troubadour Scene, Olive-Green Base, Dixon, 6 1/2 x 5 In. 160.00
Pitcher, Watermelon, 5 In. 475.00
Planter, Corinthian, Red 75.00
Plate, African Boy On Donkey, Green Mark, 9 In. 60.00
Plate, Edwardian Woman Portrait, Crown Mark, 10 1/2 In. 100.00
Plate, Girl Walking Dog, 7 In. 75.00

Plate, Jack & The Beanstalk	80.00
Plate, Lettuce, Ring Handles, Blue Mark, 4 1/4 In.	18.00
Plate, Little Bo Peep, Signed, 7 1/2 In.	55.00
Plate, Man Fishing, 8 1/2 In.	95.00
Plate, Man Hunting, 8 1/2 In.	95.00
Relish, Underplate, Cover, Blue Mark	95.00
Salt & Pepper, Lobster	90.00 to 150.00
Salt & Pepper, Spiky Shell	75.00
Saltshaker, Farmer With Chickens	22.00
Shaving Mug, Elk, Blue Mark	550.00
String Holder, Rooster	220.00 to 395.00
Sugar, Cover, Two-Headed Rooster	450.00
Sugar, Jack & Jill	75.00
Sugar & Creamer, Apple	295.00
Sugar & Creamer, Boy With Donkey	150.00
Sugar & Creamer, Cover, Brittany Girls, Blue Mark	85.00
Sugar & Creamer, Goose Girl Creamer, Alpine Village Sugar	575.00
Sugar & Creamer, Tomato, Blue Mark, 4 In.	85.00 to 125.00
Tankard, Cows, Matte Finish, 9 1/2 In.	700.00
Tea Set, Tomato, 3 Piece	265.00
Toothpick, 2 Maidens With Sheep, Hills & Mountains	165.00
Toothpick, 3 Handles, Blue Mark	105.00
Toothpick, Arabs On Horseback, Ball Shape, 3 Ball Feet	195.00
Toothpick, Clown, Standing, Mother-Of-Pearl, Blue Mark	300.00
Toothpick, Elk	105.00
Toothpick, Lobster Claw	150.00
Toothpick, Man & Woman On Horseback, Dogs	175.00
Toothpick, Man With Staff, Turkeys	160.00
Toothpick, Musicians, Coal Hod Shape, Overhead Handle, Blue Mark	165.00
Toothpick, Spiky Shell, Iridescent Gray	135.00 to 150.00
Toothpick, Storks, White & Green, 3 Handles	85.00
Toothpick, Sunset Design	165.00
Toothpick, Tricorn, Musicians	130.00
Toothpick, Wedding Cup, 3 Roses, Lavender Handles	225.00
Toothpick, Woman With Horse	410.00
Toothpick/Match Holder, Elk Head, Blue Mark	450.00
Tray, Dresser, Sheep In The Meadow, Blue Mark, 8 x 11 In.	225.00
Tray, Pin, Hand Painted Little Girl	110.00
Vase, Babes In Woods, Handles, Girl Curtsying, No. 154	310.00
Vase, Bathing Scene, 9 1/4 In.	325.00
Vase, Black Clown, Tan Clown, Stick Spout	400.00
Vase, Bud, Double, Dutch Children Scene	105.00
Vase, Castle By Lake, 5 In.	350.00
Vase, Children, St. Bernard, 3 In.	85.00
Vase, Courting In Park, Scene Front & Back, 4 1/4 In.	475.00
Vase, Draft Horses, 6 In.	525.00
Vase, Fishing Scene, Base Handles, 2 3/4 In.	125.00
Vase, Sheep, 9 In.	275.00
Wall Pocket, Apple	450.00
Wall Pocket, Grapes, Yellow	260.00
Wall Pocket, Tomato	230.00

ROYAL BONN is the nineteenth- and twentieth-century trade name for the Bonn China Manufactory. It was established in 1755 in Bonn, Germany. A general line of porcelain was made. Many marks were used, most including the name *Bonn*, the initials *FM*, and a crown.

Clock, Ansonia, Enamel Face, Open Escapement, 11 x 14 In.	395.00
Clock, Ansonia, Paper Face, 9 x 11 In.	375.00
Ewer, Rose, Pink Flowers, Leaves, Raised Gold Design, Red Stamp	125.00
Mug, Cricket Players, Blue & White, Marked	75.00
Urn, Portrait, Handles, Signed, 14 In.	450.00
Vase, Dutch Women, Gleaners Series, Signed, 6 1/4 In.	595.00
Vase, Floral, Narrow Neck, Bulbous, 10 1/2 In.	135.00

Vase, Hand Painted Floral And Gilt Decoration, 8 1/2 In. 110.00
Vase, Multicolored Floral Spray, Bands, Neck Handles, Footed, Red Crown, 20 In. 310.00
Vase, Painted Roses, 9 1/2 In. 50.00
Vase, Pink & Yellow Roses, Gold Trim, Marked, c.1900, 11 1/4 In. 250.00
Vase, Pink Lilies, Aqua Ground, Gold Trim, 7 1/4 In. 150.00
Vase, Portrait, Bust Of Woman, Green, Brown & White, Signed, 5 1/2 In. 395.00
Vase, Roses, Green, 8 1/2 In. 275.00
Vase, Woman In Reserve, 8 1/4 In. 378.00
Vase, Woman, Full Length, Raised Gold Work, Blue Ground, Signed, 8 1/4 In. 595.00

ROYAL COPENHAGEN porcelain and pottery have been made in Denmark
since 1772. The Christmas plate series started in 1908. The figurines with
pale blue and gray glazes have remained popular in this century and are still
being made. Many other old and new style porcelains are made today.

Bowl, Vegetable, Cover, Henriette 500.00
Cup & Saucer, Flora Danica, 24 Piece 4125.00
Decanter, Stopper, Egeskov Castle, Blue & White, 12 1/4 In. 45.00
Decanter, Stopper, Rosenburg Castle, Blue & White, 9 3/4 In. 45.00
Dinner Set, Blue Flowers, 75 Piece 1600.00
Dinner Set, Blue, Fluted, 57 Piece 1550.00
Dish, Flora Danica, Triangular, 8 In. 775.00
Dish, Pickle, Flora Danica, 9 5/8 In. 460.00
Dish, Storks, Nesting, Square, 5 In. 45.00
Eggcup, Flora Danica, Domed Ovoid Base, Gilt Rim, 20th Century, Pair 345.00
Figurine, 2 Ducks, No. 516 .... 175.00
Figurine, Bear Family, Brown Glaze, 3 Piece 345.00
Figurine, Bear, White, No. 729, 4 1/2 In. 85.00
Figurine, Boy, With 2 Geese, No. 2139 .... 275.00
Figurine, Boy, With Calves, No. 1858, 7 1/2 x 9 In. 475.00
Figurine, Boy, With Pig, No. 848 .... 395.00
Figurine, Cat, Curled Up, Sleeping, White 125.00
Figurine, Chicken, No. 1024 .... 110.00
Figurine, Children Playing, No. 1568, Green Castle, 4 1/2 In. 200.00
Figurine, Children Reading, No. 1567, Green Castle, 3 7/8 In. 150.00
Figurine, Crawling Baby, 6 In. 40.00
Figurine, English Squirrels, No. 416, 8 x 7 In. 500.00
Figurine, Girl & Boy Hugging, No. 707 .... 400.00
Figurine, Girl Sewing, No. 1314, 6 In. 340.00
Figurine, Girl With Calf, No. 779, 6 In. 172.00
Figurine, Girl With Doll, No. 1938, 5 In. 325.00
Figurine, Girl With Goose, No. 528, 7 1/2 In. ....200.00 to 365.00
Figurine, Girl With Teddy Bear, No. 1879, 5 1/8 In. 475.00
Figurine, Girl, Braiding Hair, No. 1323, 8 In. 275.00
Figurine, Girl, Knitting, No. 1314, 6 In. 300.00
Figurine, Girl, Sewing, No. 1314, 6 In. 225.00
Figurine, Nude On Rock, No. 4027 .... 165.00
Figurine, Oriental King, No. 4382, 12 In. 500.00
Figurine, Pigs, 2 Lying Down, No. 683 .... 135.00
Figurine, Pinto Foal, Standing, 1925, 4 3/4 In. 17.00
Figurine, Seated Satyr, 5 1/2 In. 187.00
Figurine, Whetan Terrier, 3 3/4 In. 80.00
Figurine, Woman, Sewing, No. 1317, 9 In. 275.00
Figurine, Young Pan With Goat, No.1012 .... 190.00
Harvest, No. 1352, 16 In. 690.00
Mustard, Square Underplate, Flora Danica 300.00
Plaque, Cherub 98.00
Plaque, Relief Angel, 2 Slumbering Babes, Owl, White Parian, 6 In. 25.00
Plate, Christmas, 1908, Madonna & Child 2475.00
Plate, Christmas, 1909, Danish Landscape, 6 In. ....140.00 to 150.00
Plate, Christmas, 1912, Elderly Couple 124.00
Plate, Christmas, 1914, Sparrows In Tree 150.00
Plate, Christmas, 1916, Shepherd In Field 113.00
Plate, Christmas, 1917, Tower Of Our Saviour's Church, Copenhagen, 7 In. 90.00

Plate, Christmas, 1920, Mary With The Child Jesus, 7 In. 75.00
Plate, Christmas, 1922, Three Singing Angels 83.00
Plate, Christmas, 1925, Street Scene, Copenhagen 90.00
Plate, Christmas, 1928, Vicar's Family........................... 90.00
Plate, Christmas, 1931, Mother & Child, 7 In. 90.00
Plate, Christmas, 1932, Frederiksberg Gardens, 7 In. 90.00
Plate, Christmas, 1935, Fishing Boat, Castle..................... 188.00
Plate, Christmas, 1939, Expeditionary Ship 356.00
Plate, Christmas, 1941, Danish Village Church 319.00
Plate, Christmas, 1945, Peaceful Motif, 7 In. 325.00
Plate, Christmas, 1948, Nodebo Church At Christmas Time............... 155.00 to 190.00
Plate, Christmas, 1949, Church Of Our Lady............... 175.00 to 210.00
Plate, Christmas, 1959, Christmas Night..................... 89.00
Plate, Christmas, 1960, The Stag .... 80.00 to 99.00
Plate, Christmas, 1961, Training Ship Danmark .... 80.00 to 109.00
Plate, Christmas, 1962, Little Mermaid At Wintertime..................... 139.00
Plate, Christmas, 1963, Hojsager Mill 49.00
Plate, Christmas, 1965, Little Skaters 39.00
Plate, Christmas, 1966, Blackbird At Christmas Time 23.00
Plate, Christmas, 1971, Hare In Winter, 7 In. 80.00
Plate, Christmas, 1975, Marselisborg Palace 55.00
Plate, Christmas, 1994, Christmas Shopping 72.00
Plate, Cupid, Classically Dressed Figures, Gilt Trim, 13 1/2 In., Pair 275.00
Plate, Dinner, Flora Danica, 10 In., 12 Piece 5500.00
Plate, Fruit, Flora Danica, 9 In., 12 Piece 6600.00
Plate, Grape, 6 Piece 150.00
Plate, Hare, 1970..................... 55.00
Plate, Luncheon, Flora Danica, 9 In., 14 Piece 7150.00
Plate, Mermaid..................... 95.00
Plate, Mother's Day, 1971, American Mother 125.00
Plate, Mother's Day, 1972, Oriental Mother 39.00
Plate, Mother's Day, 1973, Danish Mother..................... 60.00
Plate, Mother's Day, 1975, Bird In Nest 55.00
Plate, Mother's Day, 1976, Mermaids 33.00
Plate, Mother's Day, 1978, Mother & Child 26.00
Plate, Service, Flora Danica, Reticulated, 10 3/4 In..................... 880.00
Plate, Serving, Flora Danica, Reticulated, 13 1/4 In. 990.00
Plate, Walk On The Moon, 1969..................... 75.00
Platter, Flora Danica, Oval, 14 1/4 In..................... 990.00
Platter, Flora Danica, Oval, 15 3/4 In..................... 1210.00
Sauceboat, Flora Danica, 5 1/4 In. 495.00
Tray, Flora Danica, Flowering Lady's Slipper, Oval, Signed, 14 1/4 In. 1725.00
Vase, 4 Sides, Pink Roses, Dark Gray Fence Border, 10 1/2 In..................... 412.00
Vase, Continuous Scene Of Geese In Meadow, 9 13/16 In..................... 230.00
Vase, Dogwood, 9 x 6 In. 160.00
Vase, Dogwood, Butterflies, 9 1/2 In..................... 450.00
Vase, Flowering Raspberries 50.00
Vase, Narcissus, Pale Blue Ground, 8 In. 85.00

ROYAL COPLEY china was made by the Spaulding China Company of
Sebring, Ohio, from 1939 to 1960. The figural planters and the small figurines, especially those with Art Deco designs, are of great collector interest.

Ashtray, Duck.. 5.00
Ashtray, Pink Bird On Green Flower, 5 In. 3.00
Figurine, Bird, Birdhouse 48.00
Figurine, Blackamoor 20.00
Figurine, Blackamoor, Gold 40.00
Figurine, Dog, With Wagon 15.00
Figurine, Dove..................... 18.00
Figurine, Hen, Priolo 60.00
Figurine, Kitten & Boot..................... 45.00
Figurine, Mallard Duck, Small..................... 52.00
Figurine, Mallard, Priolo, Pair..................... 150.00

Figurine, Poodle, Pink	22.00
Lamp, Doe & Fawn	90.00
Mailbox, Duck	50.00
Planter, Bear By Tree	25.00
Planter, Cat With Ball	20.00
Planter, Cub On Stump	15.00
Planter, Duck Eating Grass, 5 In.	12.00
Planter, Fawn, 7 In.	15.00
Planter, Kitten, Black & White	40.00
Planter, Pouter Pigeon, 5 3/4 In.	15.00
Planter, Rooster, Black & White	45.00
Planter, Yellow, Oriental Girl Beside Planter, Hat, Jacket, Pantaloons, 7 3/4 In.	5.00
Vase, Doe & Fawn, Figural, 9 In.	18.00
Vase, Essex, Deer	24.00
Wall Pocket, Boy & Girl, Wide Brim Hats, Pair	20.00
Wall Pocket, Pirate Head, 8 In.	45.00

ROYAL CROWN DERBY Company, Ltd., was established in England in 1890. There is a complex family tree that includes the Derby, Crown Derby, and Royal Crown Derby porcelains. The Royal Crown Derby mark includes the name and a crown. The words *Made in England* were used after 1921. The company is now a part of Royal Doulton Tableware Ltd.

Creamer, Blue On White, Oriental Figures, Landscape, 3 1/8 In.	22.00
Cup, Floral Spray, Gold Trim, Fluted & Scalloped, Posie	7.00
Cup & Saucer, Bouillon, Pink Flowers, White Ground, c.1912	65.00
Dinner Set, Golden Vine, 108 Piece	1760.00
Lighter, Cigarette, Old Imari	95.00
Lighter, Table, Imari	65.00
Plate, Floral Center, Gilded Grapes & Vines, Ruffled Border, 9 In., 5 Piece	60.00
Plate, Mikado, Blue & White, 10 1/2 In.	30.00
Sugar & Creamer, Gold Trim	45.00
Toothpick, Handles, Orange Flowers, Gold Trim	110.00
Vase, Dome Cover, Floral Molded Neck, Signed, c.1889, 12 In.	920.00
Vase, Flowers & Berries, Gilt, Yellow Ground, Handle, Marked, 7 1/4 In.	138.00
Vase, Imari, Footed, 2 1/2 In.	295.00
Vase, Nightingale, Polychrome, 9 3/4 In.	192.00

ROYAL DOULTON is the name used on Doulton and Company pottery made from 1902 to the present. Doulton and Company of England was founded in 1853. Pieces made before 1902 are listed in this book under Doulton. Royal Doulton collectors search for the out-of-production figurines, character jugs, and series wares.

Animal, Bear, Brown, HN 2659	295.00
Animal, Bird, Cockatoos, HN 885	175.00
Animal, Dog, Airdale, HN 1023	195.00
Animal, Dog, Cocker & Pheasant, HN 1028	225.00
Animal, Dog, Cocker Spaniel, Black & White, HN 1078	104.00
Animal, Dog, Cocker Spaniel, HN 1036	145.00
Animal, Dog, Cocker, HN 1001	350.00
Animal, Dog, Collie, Ashstead Applause, HN 1059	219.00
Animal, Dog, Doberman Pinscher, HN 2645	135.00
Animal, Dog, English Setter, HN 1050	150.00
Animal, Dog, Greyhound, HN 1077	259.00
Animal, Dog, Pekinese, HN 1012	65.00
Animal, Dog, Rough-Haired Fox Terrier, HN 1014	200.00
Animal, Dog, Welsh Corgi, HN 2558	275.00
Animal, Dog, Yawning, HN 1099	85.00
Ash Pot, Auld Mac	100.00
Ash Pot, Old Charley	65.00
Ashtray, Hamlet	75.00
Ashtray, Parson Brown	95.00
Ashtray, Ships, Profile View, Polychrome, D 2872, Square, 5 1/4 In.	75.00
Ashtray, Winston Churchill, This Was Their Final Hour, Commemorative, 4 5/8 In.	45.00

Bank, Bunnykins, Money Ball, Box 20.00
Bottle, Sherry, Sandeman, 4 3/4 In. 99.00
Bowl, Art Union Of London, Pineapple Design, c.1900, 7 3/4 In. 288.00
Bowl, Gallant Fishers, Jedo Border, Noke, 3 1/2 x 7 In. 185.00
Bowl, Monks, 7 In. 90.00
Bowl, Sung Ware, Mottled Glazed, Noke, c.1930, 6 1/8 In. 345.00
Bust, Jug, Mr. Pickwick, Miniature.. 110.00
Bust, Mr. Micawber, Miniature 100.00
Bust, Tony Weller, Miniature 100.00
Candlestick, 2 Knights, D 1961, Dated 1924, 6 1/2 In. 105.00

Royal Doulton character jugs depict the head and shoulders of the subject. They
are made in four sizes: large, 5 1/4 to 7 inches; small, 3 1/4 to 4 inches; miniature,
2 1/4 to 2 1/2 inches; and tiny, 1 1/4 inches. Toby jugs portray a seated, full figure.

Character Jug, 'Arriet, 1947 .... 5800.00
Character Jug, 'Arriet, Tiny 140.00
Character Jug, 'Arry, Small.. 200.00
Character Jug, Anne Boleyn, Miniature 63.00
Character Jug, Antique Dealer, Large 135.00
Character Jug, Antony & Cleopatra, Large 125.00
Character Jug, Apothecary, Large ....75.00 to 150.00
Character Jug, Apothecary, Small 50.00
Character Jug, Aramis, Miniature 38.00
Character Jug, Athos, Miniature.. 45.00
Character Jug, Bacchus, Miniature.. 48.00
Character Jug, Beefeater, Large 90.00
Character Jug, Benjamin Disraeli, Commemorative, Silver Top & Bottom 400.00
Character Jug, Benjamin Franklin, Small... 78.00
Character Jug, Bootmaker, Small 65.00
Character Jug, Buz Fuz, Miniature.. 100.00
Character Jug, Buz Fuz, Small... 125.00
Character Jug, Cardinal, A Mark, Minature 55.00
Character Jug, Cardinal, Miniature 45.00
Character Jug, Catherine Of Aragon, Miniature 95.00
Character Jug, Cavalier, Small.. 50.00
Character Jug, Charlie Chaplin, 1918.. 2500.00
Character Jug, Chelsea Pensioner, Large 95.00
Character Jug, City Gent, Large 90.00
Character Jug, Clown, Red Hair, 1988, Large.. 1500.00
Character Jug, Collector, Small... 100.00
Character Jug, Dick Turpin, Large 110.00
Character Jug, Doc Holliday, Medium 100.00
Character Jug, Elephant Trainer, Large 175.00
Character Jug, Falstaff, Large 115.00
Character Jug, Falstaff, Small 50.00
Character Jug, Gaoler, Large... 105.00
Character Jug, Gaoler, Small... 55.00
Character Jug, Gardener, Minature 45.00
Character Jug, George Washington, Large...125.00 to 130.00
Character Jug, Gone Away, Small 50.00
Character Jug, Granny, Large.. 95.00
Character Jug, Granny, Toothless 1050.00
Character Jug, Grant & Lee, Double Faced, Large... 225.00
Character Jug, Guardsman, Small 50.00
Character Jug, Henry V, Large 125.00
Character Jug, Henry VIII, Small... 60.00
Character Jug, Izaac Walton, Large 75.00
Character Jug, Jane Seymour, Small 85.00
Character Jug, John Barleycorn, Small.. 45.00
Character Jug, John Peel, Orange Band Handle, Miniature............................ 85.00
Character Jug, London Bobby, Large... 85.00
Character Jug, Long John Silver, Large 110.00
Character Jug, Lord Nelson, Large... 400.00

Character Jug, Louis Armstrong, Large 150.00
Character Jug, Lumberjack, Canadian Backstamp, Large 200.00
Character Jug, Mad Hatter, Large 1000.00
Character Jug, Mae West, Large 140.00
Character Jug, Mark Twain, Large 115.00
Character Jug, Mark Twain, Small 75.00
Character Jug, Merlin, Small 60.00
Character Jug, Mine Host, Large 75.00
Character Jug, Mr. Pickwick, Jim Beam Handle, 1981, Small 115.00
Character Jug, Mr. Pickwick, Small 125.00
Character Jug, Night Watchman, Large 105.00
Character Jug, Old Charley, Large 140.00
Character Jug, Old Salt, Large 95.00
Character Jug, Parson Brown, Large 95.00
Character Jug, Parson Brown, Small 63.00
Character Jug, Pearly Boy, Blue, White Buttons, Small 3200.00
Character Jug, Pearly Boy, Brown With White Buttons, Large 4600.00
Character Jug, Pearly Girl, Small 3800.00
Character Jug, Pearly King, Small 63.00
Character Jug, Pied Piper, Large 95.00
Character Jug, Red Queen, Large 110.00
Character Jug, Red Queen, Miniature 40.00
Character Jug, Robin Hood, Bow Handle, Miniature 43.00
Character Jug, Robin Hood, Bow Handle, Small 95.00
Character Jug, Ronald Reagan, Large 400.00
Character Jug, Sairey Gamp, Large 95.00
Character Jug, Scaramouche, Small 500.00
Character Jug, Simon The Cellarer, Small 40.00
Character Jug, Sleuth, Miniature 45.00
Character Jug, Tam O'Shanter, Minature 55.00
Character Jug, The Cavalier, Large 90.00
Character Jug, Toby Gillette, 1984, No. 1 .... 10000.00
Character Jug, Toby Philpots, Small .... 40.00 to 65.00
Character Jug, Tony Weller, Large .... 75.00 to 125.00
Character Jug, Tony Weller, Small 78.00
Character Jug, Touchstone, Large 225.00
Character Jug, Trapper, Large 60.00
Character Jug, Viking, Small 110.00
Character Jug, W.C. Fields, Large 175.00
Character Jug, William Shakespeare, Large .... 130.00 to 380.00
Coffeepot, April Showers 25.00
Compote, Gilded Flower Pattern, Luscian Are, Burslem, 1891, 2 1/2 x 11 In. 140.00
Creamer, George V Coronation 435.00
Cup & Saucer, Granthan, Demitasse 15.00
Cup & Saucer, Gum Trees With House, Australia, D 5506 .... 70.00
Decanter, Old Crow Bourbon, Crow Wears Tophat & Tuxedo, 14 In. 175.00
Dish, Art Deco Bird Amid Foliage, Hearts, Green Ground, 13 In. 145.00
Figurine, A 'Courting, HN 2004 .... 450.00
Figurine, Adornment, HN 3015 .... 750.00
Figurine, Adrienne, HN 2304 .... 315.00
Figurine, Affection, HN 2236 .... 55.00
Figurine, Afternoon Tea, HN 1747 .... 288.00 to 400.00
Figurine, Alexandra, HN 2398 .... 120.00 to 235.00
Figurine, All Aboard, HN 2940 .... 155.00
Figurine, Apple Maid, HN 2160 .... 325.00
Figurine, Aragorn, HN 2916 .... 27.00
Figurine, Artful Dodger, M 55 .... 65.00
Figurine, Autumn Breezes, HN 1911 .... 175.00 to 195.00
Figurine, Autumn Breezes, HN 1934 .... 95.00 to 255.00
Figurine, Autumntime, HN 3231 .... 195.00
Figurine, Bachelor, HN 2319 .... 215.00
Figurine, Ballad Seller, HN 2266 .... 275.00
Figurine, Ballerina, HN 2116 .... 220.00

Figurine, Balloon Man, HN 1954 ....95.00 to 115.00
Figurine, Bather, HN 597 .... 2100.00
Figurine, Bedtime Story, HN 2059 ....212.00 to 250.00
Figurine, Bell O' The Ball, HN 1997 ....265.00 to 400.00
Figurine, Biddy Penny Farthing, HN 1843 .... 275.00
Figurine, Blithe Morning, HN 2065 ....150.00 to 175.00
Figurine, Bluebeard, HN 2105 .... 350.00
Figurine, Bo-Peep, HN 1810 .... 700.00
Figurine, Boatman, HN 2417 .... 160.00
Figurine, Bobby, HN 2778 .... 115.00
Figurine, Boy Evacuee, HN 3202 .... 300.00
Figurine, Bride, HN 1762 .... 995.00
Figurine, Bride, HN 2166 .... 145.00
Figurine, Bridesmaid, HN 2196 .... 150.00
Figurine, Bridget, NH 2070 .... 275.00
Figurine, Bunnykins, Rise & Shine 39.00
Figurine, Bunnykins, School Days 24.00
Figurine, Calumet, HN 2068 .... 650.00
Figurine, Camella, HN 2222 .... 275.00
Figurine, Captain, HN 2260 .... 180.00
Figurine, Carolyn, HN 2112 ....235.00 to 275.00
Figurine, Carpet Seller, HN 1464 .... 350.00
Figurine, Charlotte, HN 2423 .... 195.00
Figurine, China Repairer, HN 2943 .... 350.00
Figurine, Choir Boy, HN 2141 .... 85.00
Figurine, Christmas Morn, HN 1992 ....126.00 to 245.00
Figurine, Christmas Tree, HN 2110 .... 300.00
Figurine, Cissie, HN 1809 ....110.00 to 120.00
Figurine, Clarinda, HN 2724 .... 150.00
Figurine, Clockmaker, HN 2279 .... 225.00
Figurine, Clothilde, HN 1599 .... 775.00
Figurine, Coachman, HN 2282 .... 276.00
Figurine, Cobbler, HN 1706 .... 225.00
Figurine, Country Lass, HN 1991 .... 145.00
Figurine, Country Rose, HN 3221 .... 245.00
Figurine, Cup Of Tea, HN 2322 .... 150.00
Figurine, Curly Knob, HN 1627 .... 485.00
Figurine, Daffy Down Dilly, HN 1712 ....220.00 to 300.00
Figurine, Dainty May, HN 1639 .... 700.00
Figurine, Darby, HN 1427 .... 275.00
Figurine, David Copperfield, M 88 .... 80.00
Figurine, Daydreams, HN 1731 ....140.00 to 160.00
Figurine, Delight, HN 1773 .... 750.00
Figurine, Detective, HN 2359 .... 175.00
Figurine, Diane, HN 3604 .... 190.00
Figurine, Dinky Do, HN 1678 ....55.00 to 65.00
Figurine, Doctor, HN 2858 ....160.00 to 210.00
Figurine, Dragon, Flambe, Veined Ware, c.1973, 10 1/2 In. 920.00
Figurine, Dreamweaver, HN 2283 .... 310.00
Figurine, Drummer Boy, HN 2679 .... 400.00
Figurine, Easter Day, HN 2039 ....295.00 to 435.00
Figurine, Elegance, HN 2264 ....115.00 to 170.00
Figurine, Elephant, Flambe, 7 1/2 In. 170.00
Figurine, Elizabeth I, HN 3099 .... 300.00
Figurine, Ellen, HN 3020 .... 450.00
Figurine, Enchantment, HN 2178 ....165.00 to 235.00
Figurine, Ermine, Coat, HN 1981 .... 405.00
Figurine, Esmerelda, HN 2168 ....260.00 to 275.00
Figurine, Fair Maiden, HN 221 .... 175.00
Figurine, Family Album, HN 2321 ....225.00 to 330.00
Figurine, Female, Art Nouveau, Doris Johnson, c.1930, 13 3/4 In. 1150.00
Figurine, Fiona, HN 2694 ....137.00 to 165.00
Figurine, Fleur, HN 2368 .... 160.00

Figurine, Foaming Quart, HN 2162 ....120.00 to 260.00
Figurine, Forty Winks, HN 1974 .... 220.00
Figurine, French Peasant, HN 2075 .... 400.00
Figurine, Frodo, HN 2912... 80.00
Figurine, Genevieve, HN 1962 .... 225.00
Figurine, Geraldine, HN 2348.. 97.00
Figurine, Girl Evacuee, HN 3203 .... 300.00
Figurine, Giselle, Forest Glade, HN 2140... 300.00
Figurine, Giselle, HN 2939.. 298.00
Figurine, Gollywog, HN 1979 .... 450.00
Figurine, Gollywog, HN 2040 .... 205.00
Figurine, Good Morning, HN 2671.. 25.00
Figurine, Gossips, HN 2025...285.00 to 425.00
Figurine, Grace, HN 2318.. 150.00
Figurine, Granny's Shawl, HN 1642 .... 595.00
Figurine, Groucho Marx, HN 2777... 350.00
Figurine, Harmony, HN 2824 .... 235.00
Figurine, Heart To Heart, HN 2276 .... 495.00
Figurine, Heather, HN 2956.. 65.00
Figurine, Her Ladyship, HN 1977... 350.00
Figurine, Honey, HN 1910... 316.00
Figurine, Jacqueline, HN 2000 .... 325.00
Figurine, Janet, HN 1537...85.00 to 175.00
Figurine, Janet, M 75 .... 525.00
Figurine, Janine, HN 2461 .... 176.00
Figurine, Jennifer, HN 3447 .... 135.00
Figurine, Jester, HN 2016 ....120.00 to 345.00
Figurine, Jill, HN 2061 .... 190.00
Figurine, Jovial Monk, HN 2144 .... 175.00
Figurine, Judge, HN 2443 ....115.00 to 225.00
Figurine, Julia, HN 2705.. 215.00
Figurine, Juliet, HN 2968 .... 275.00
Figurine, Kathy, HN 2346 .... 115.00
Figurine, Kelly, HN 2478 .... 95.00
Figurine, Lady Charmain, HN 1948...126.00 to 200.00
Figurine, Lady Charmain, HN 1949.. 100.00
Figurine, Laird, HN 2361 .... 175.00
Figurine, Lambing Time, HN 1890..150.00 to 190.00
Figurine, Lavinia, HN 1955... 90.00
Figurine, Leading Lady, HN 2269 .... 247.00
Figurine, Legolas, HN 2917...50.00 to 100.00
Figurine, Leisure Hour, HN 2055 .... 475.00
Figurine, Lights Out, HN 2262 .... 125.00
Figurine, Lisa, HN 2310 .... 135.00
Figurine, Lisa, HN 2394 .... 160.00
Figurine, Little Boy Blue, HN 2062.. 95.00
Figurine, Little Lady Make Believe, HN 1870... 280.00
Figurine, Lobster Man, HN 2317 ....150.00 to 275.00
Figurine, Loretta, HN 2337... 150.00
Figurine, Love Letters, HN 2149 .... 325.00
Figurine, Lynne, HN 2329 .... 135.00
Figurine, Marie, HN 1370...60.00 to 80.00
Figurine, Marigold, HN 1447 ....425.00 to 575.00
Figurine, Mary Had A Little Lamb, HN 2048.. 110.00
Figurine, Masquerade, HN 2251 .... 190.00
Figurine, Master, HN 2325 .... 240.00
Figurine, Maureen, HN 1770 ....185.00 to 295.00
Figurine, May Time, HN 2113... 400.00
Figurine, Melanie, HN 2271 ....145.00 to 155.00
Figurine, Mendicant, HN 1365 .... 245.00
Figurine, Merry Christmas, HN 3096 .... 121.00
Figurine, Midinette, HN 2090.. 275.00
Figurine, Midsummer Noon, HN 2033 ....495.00 to 595.00

Figurine, Milkmaid, HN 2057 .... 175.00
Figurine, Minuet, HN 2019 .... 180.00
Figurine, Mirabel, HN 1743 .... 1450.00
Figurine, Miss Demure, HN 1402 .... 225.00 to 235.00
Figurine, Miss Muffet, HN 1936 .... 190.00
Figurine, Mountie, HN 2555 .... 800.00
Figurine, Mr. Micawber, HN 2097 .... 350.00
Figurine, Nana, HN 1766 .... 445.00
Figurine, Nicola, HN 2804 .... 195.00
Figurine, Nicola, HN 2839 .... 260.00
Figurine, Nina, HN 2347 .... 135.00
Figurine, Ninette, HN 2379 .... 115.00
Figurine, Old Balloon Seller, HN 1315 .... 92.00 to 110.00
Figurine, Old Meg, HN 2494 .... 185.00
Figurine, Old Mother Hubbard, HN 2314 .... 225.00 to 265.00
Figurine, Olga, HN 2463 .... 185.00
Figurine, Orange Lady, HN 1759 .... 165.00 to 230.00
Figurine, Orange Lady, HN 1953 .... 350.00
Figurine, Paisley Shawl, HN 1988 .... 185.00
Figurine, Patchwork Quilt, HN 1984 .... 525.00
Figurine, Patricia, HN 3365 .... 135.00
Figurine, Paula, HN 2906 .... 285.00
Figurine, Peace, HN 2470 .... 60.00
Figurine, Pearly Boy, HN 2767 .... 115.00
Figurine, Pecksniff, HN 2098 .... 250.00
Figurine, Peggy, HN 2038 .... 95.00
Figurine, Penelope, HN 1901 .... 210.00 to 365.00
Figurine, Picnic, HN 2308 .... 83.00
Figurine, Pinkie, HN 1553 .... 1100.00
Figurine, Poacher, HN 2043 .... 195.00
Figurine, Polka, HN 2156 .... 110.00 to 325.00
Figurine, Potter, HN 1493 .... 250.00
Figurine, Professor, HN 2281 .... 165.00 to 175.00
Figurine, Puppetmaker, HN 2253 .... 385.00
Figurine, Rachel, HN 2919 .... 154.00
Figurine, Repose, HN 2272 .... 187.00 to 225.00
Figurine, Rhinoceros, Flambe, c.1973, 17 In. 405.00
Figurine, Rosalind, HN 2393 .... 175.00
Figurine, Rose, HN 1368 .... 98.00
Figurine, Roseanna, HN 1926 .... 265.00 to 375.00
Figurine, Royal Governor's Cook, HN 2233 .... 275.00
Figurine, Ruby, HN 1724 .... 650.00
Figurine, Ruby, HN 1725 .... 695.00
Figurine, Sabbath Morn, HN 1982 .... 295.00
Figurine, Sailor's Holiday, HN 2442 .... 180.00
Figurine, Sam Weller, M 48 .... 65.00
Figurine, Sea Farer, HN 2455 .... 115.00
Figurine, Secret Thoughts, HN 2382 .... 285.00
Figurine, Sharon, HN 3603 .... 160.00
Figurine, Shepherd, HN 1975 .... 225.00
Figurine, Silversmith, Williamsburg, HN 2208 .... 215.00
Figurine, Skater, HN 2117 .... 520.00
Figurine, Sleepyhead, HN 2114 .... 1500.00
Figurine, Southern Belle, HN 2229 .... 110.00
Figurine, Spring Flowers, HN 1807 .... 220.00
Figurine, Spring Morning, HN 1922 .... 225.00
Figurine, Spring Morning, HN 1923 .... 285.00
Figurine, St. George, HN 2051 .... 500.00
Figurine, Stop Press, HN 2683 .... 175.00
Figurine, Suitor, HN 2132 .... 184.00 to 522.00
Figurine, Summer's Day, HN 2181 .... 250.00
Figurine, Sunday Best, HN 2206 .... 150.00

Figurine, Sunday Morning, HN 2184 .... 250.00
Figurine, Sweet & Twenty, HN 1298 .... 200.00 to 265.00
Figurine, Sweet Anne, HN 1496 .... 235.00
Figurine, Symphony, HN 2287 .... 126.00
Figurine, Taking Things Easy, HN 2677 .... 175.00
Figurine, Thanksgiving, HN 2446 .... 110.00 to 225.00
Figurine, Tinkle Bell, HN 1677 .... 95.00
Figurine, Tinsmith, HN 2146 .... 250.00
Figurine, Tom, HN 2864 .... 375.00
Figurine, Top O' The Hill, HN 1833 .... 160.00
Figurine, Top O' The Hill, HN 1834 .... 165.00 to 195.00
Figurine, Top O' The Hill, HN 1849 .... 175.00 to 195.00
Figurine, Toymaker, HN 2250 .... 350.00
Figurine, Tuppence A Bag, HN 2320 .... 325.00
Figurine, Twilight, HN 2256 .... 260.00
Figurine, Uncle Ned, HN 2094 .... 350.00
Figurine, Valeria, HN 2107 .... 105.00 to 200.00
Figurine, Veronica, HN 1517 .... 295.00 to 325.00
Figurine, Victoria, HN 2417 .... 195.00
Figurine, Winston S. Churchill, HN 3433 .... 300.00
Figurine, Wintertime, HN 3060 .... 195.00
Flagon, Bell's Of Perth, Scotch, Brown & Tan, Cork, Stoneware, 1957, 9 In. 325.00
Flagon, Special Highland Whiskey, Stoneware, 7 In. 475.00
Flask, Golfers, Kingsware 650.00
Jar, Cover, Titanian Ware, Oriental Figural Finial, Signed, c.1925, 4 In. 315.00
Jug, Cardinal Lord Archbishop Of Rheims, Jackdaw Of Rheims, D 2532, 4 In. 195.00
Jug, Knights, Charging With Lances, Eglington Tournament, D 2792, 13 1/2 In. 525.00
Jug, Men & Women Figures, Red Ground, Egyptian, D 3619, 7 1/2 In. 325.00
Jug, Monks In Cellar, 7 1/2 In. 185.00
Lamp, Rouge Flambe, Noke, No. 1658 .... 750.00
Lighter, Bacchus 215.00
Lighter, Beefeaters 175.00
Lighter, Long John Silver 39.00
Lighter, Old Charley 275.00
Mug, Golfing 495.00
Music Box, Old King Cole, Yellow Crown, 1939 .... 1900.00
Pitcher, Geneva, 6 3/4 In. 120.00
Pitcher, Oliver Twist, 5 1/2 In. 175.00
Pitcher, Painted Bellflower & Bow, Ivory, Loop Handle, Cylindrical, 12 1/2 In. 140.00
Pitcher, Titanian Ware, Long-Tailed Bird, Signed, c.1925, 7 1/4 In. 175.00
Plate, 2 Barges Unloading In Front Of Stone Pier, Rack, W.E. Grace, 8 1/4 In. 60.00
Plate, 3 Ladies Galloping With Man & Falcon, Falconry, 10 1/4 In. 125.00
Plate, Bunnykins, Gardening 25.00
Plate, Canterbury Cathedral, England, 3 3/4 x 5 1/4 In. 25.00
Plate, Child's, My Pretty Maid 75.00
Plate, Kings Head, Chigwell, Old English Inns, 10 1/2 In. 75.00
Plate, Koala Bears, Photograph, Australian Views, 10 3/8 In. 80.00
Plate, Lake Louis & Victoria, Canadian Views, 10 1/2 In. 60.00
Plate, Madras, Flow Blue, 9 1/2 In. .... 85.00 to 110.00
Plate, Mr. Pickwick, Dickens Ware, 10 1/2 In. 155.00
Plate, Poor Jo, 1923, D3020, 9 3/8 In. 225.00
Plate, Portia, Polychrome, Sepia Ground, Shakespeare, 7 3/8 In. 105.00
Plate, Reunion, Grandest Gift Series 250.00
Plate, Robert Burns, 10 1/2 In. .... 70.00 to 75.00
Plate, Sam Weller, Dickens Ware, D 2973, 6 1/2 In. 65.00
Plate, Sir Roger Playing Bowls, 10 1/2 In. 150.00
Plate, Skaters 250.00
Plate, The Mayor 40.00
Plate, Windsor Castle, Lithograph, Castles & Churches, 10 3/8 In. 155.00
Sandwich Tray, A Village, Countryside, D 3467, 6 1/4 x 14 1/2 In. 195.00
Stein, Night Watchman, Front View, D 4746, 5 In. 85.00
Sugar, Tony Weller 395.00

Tankard, Christmas, 1979	80.00
Teapot, Berkis, Dickens Ware	300.00
Teapot, Old Salt	160.00
Tobacco Jar, Izaak Walton, Wooden Lid, 4 1/4 In.	150.00
Toby Jug, Albert Sagger, Doultonville, D 6745, Small	93.00
Toby Jug, Cap'n, D6266, Small	150.00
Toby Jug, Cliff Cornell, Large	300.00 to 380.00
Toby Jug, Falstaff, D 6062, Large	115.00
Toby Jug, George Robey, Detachable Hat	2295.00
Toby Jug, Mr. Tonsil, Town Crier, D 6713, Small	275.00
Toby Jug, Old Charley, D 6030, Large	358.00
Toby Jug, Sairey Gamp, D 6263, Small	65.00
Toby Jug, Sam Weller, D 6265, Small	150.00
Toby Jug, Sgt. Peeler, The Policeman	190.00
Toby Jug, Sherlock Holmes, D 6661, Large	110.00
Toby Jug, Winston Churchill, D 6175, Small	58.00 to 128.00
Toothpick, 2 Cottages & Church, Woodland, D 5815, 1938, 2 1/2 In.	105.00
Toothpick, Dickens Ware, Mr. Pickwick	135.00
Toothpick, Fox Hunting	115.00
Vase, Art Nouveau Design, Mottled Blue Ground, Stamped, 10 x 4 In., Pair	605.00
Vase, Babes In Woods, Girl With Basket, Picking Flowers, 3 3/4 In.	310.00
Vase, Babes In The Woods, Children Playing Blind Man's Bluff, 6 1/4 In.	435.00
Vase, Babes In Woods, 7 1/4 In.	500.00
Vase, Changware, Crackled Glaze Over Flambe Body, 1925, 7 3/4 In.	1495.00
Vase, Chinese Jade, Floral Relief, Streaked White & Green Glaze, 9 3/4 In., Pair	1880.00
Vase, Rouge Flambe, Black Ship, Marked, 8 In.	195.00
Vase, Stylized Grapes Band, Periwinkle Ground, Marked, 6 3/4 x 5 In.	313.00
Vase, Titanian Ware, Long-Tailed Bird, Signed, c.1925, 6 1/4 In.	230.00

ROYAL DUX is the more common name for the Duxer Porzellanmanufaktur, which was founded by E. Eichler in Dux, Bohemia, in 1860. By the turn of the century, the firm specialized in porcelain statuary and busts of Art Nouveau-style maidens, large porcelain figures, and ornate vases with three-dimensional figures climbing on the sides. The firm is still in business.

Bust, Woman, c.1900, 13 1/2 In.	515.00
Centerpiece, Maiden, Shell, Art Nouveau, No. 1776, 12 In.	495.00
Figurine, Elephant, 2 1/2 In.	70.00
Figurine, Elephant, Gray Head, Tusk & Trunk, No. 736, 13 x 16 In.	110.00
Figurine, Elephant, Pink Triangle, 10 x 15 In.	175.00
Figurine, Girl, Holding Hat, Windswept Dress, Cobalt Blue, Gold Trim, 8 In.	195.00
Figurine, Horse, Rearing, 8 In.	125.00 to 140.00
Figurine, Rebecca, Holding Jugs, Marked, 16 In.	300.00
Figurine, Retriever, Carrying Duck, Porcelain, 16 In.	475.00
Figurine, Spanish Woman, Cobalt Blue Dress	750.00
Figurine, Woman In Sedan Chair, 2 Courtiers & Hound, 15 1/2 In.	970.00
Group, Classical Lovers, No. 1559, Pink Triangle, 19 In.	825.00
Group, Peasant Couple, Woman, Kettle & Man, Grain, No. 2445-2446, 13 In., Pair	575.00
Group, The Hunt, 19 In.	1250.00
Salt & Pepper, Prayer Lady, Pink	12.00
Vase, Art Nouveau, Applied Leaves, Matte Finish, 16 1/2 In.	250.00
Vase, Art Nouveau, Raspberry Clusters, Neck Handles, Figural Rim, 16 In., Pair	750.00
Vase, Draped Woman, 16 In., Pair	2200.00
Vase, Woman's Portrait, Branch Handles, 7 In.	125.00

ROYAL FLEMISH glass was made during the late 1880s in New Bedford, Massachusetts, by the Mt. Washington Glass Works. It is a colored satin glass decorated with dark colors and raised gold designs. The glass was patented in 1894. It was supposed to resemble stained glass windows.

Biscuit Jar, Gold Outlined Sections, Marked	3950.00
Biscuit Jar, Medallions Of Scrolls, Flowers, Gold Enamel Leaves	3025.00
Lamp, Griffin, Raised Gold, Dragon On Back	1450.00

ROYAL HAEGER, see Haeger category

ROYAL NYMPHENBURG is the modern name for the Nymphenburg porcelain factory, which was established at Neudeck-ob-der-Au, Germany, in 1753 and moved to Nymphenburg in 1761. The company is still in existence. Marks include a checkered shield topped by a crown, a crowned *CT* with the year, and a contemporary shield mark on reproductions of eighteenth-century porcelain.

Dessert Set, Green & Yellow Flowers, Fish Scale Border, 72 Piece	2200.00
Seau A Glace, Hand Painted Floral Swags, Beadwork, 8 In., 3 Piece	1100.00
Tankard, Spray Of Flowers On Front, Sprigs On Back, 1780, 6 7/8 In.	4887.00

ROYAL RUDOLSTADT, see Rudolstadt

ROYAL VIENNA, see Beehive category

ROYAL WORCESTER is a name used by collectors. Worcester porcelains were made in Worcester, England, from about 1751. The firm went through many different periods and name changes. It became the Worcester Royal Porcelain Company, Ltd., in 1862. Today collectors call the porcelains made after 1862 *Royal Worcester*. In 1976, the firm merged with W. T. Copeland to become Royal Worcester Spode. Some early products of the factory are listed under Worcester.

Biscuit Jar, c.1893, 6 1/2 In.	425.00
Biscuit Jar, Hand Painted Flowers, Cream Ground, Ribbed, 6 1/4 x 6 1/2 In.	195.00
Biscuit Jar, Raised Gilded Border, Enameled Floral, 1890, 7 3/4 In.	316.25
Bowl, Cover, Pedestal, No. 7, Mark, 6 In.	325.00
Bowl, Queen & Duke Edinborough, 1972, Silver Wedding, 10 x 5 3/4 In.	105.00
Bowl, Reticulated Rim, Floral With Butterflies, Hadley Faience, 4 In.	295.00
Bowl, Vegetable, Portia, Oval	55.00
Candlestick, Column Shape, Flower Festoons, Square Base, 10 1/2 In., Pair	431.25
Candlestick, Figural, Ivory Ground, Gilt, James Hadley, c.1899, 8 In., Pair	1035.00
Cornucopia, Flower, Leaf Base, Satin Gold Finish, 3 3/4 x 4 In.	115.00
Creamer, Gold Handle, Yellow, 6 In.	75.00
Creamer, Seascape, Lighthouse, c.1880, 4 In.	115.00
Cup, Floral, 5 In.	66.00
Cup & Saucer, Portia	20.00
Dish, Melon, Hand Painted Floral, Gilt Trim, c.1886, 14 3/4 In.	145.00
Ewer, Floral & Gilt Design, 8 In.	90.00
Ewer, Flowers, Butterfly, Yellow Ground, 7 3/4 In.	125.00
Ewer, Ram Head Handle, 9 In.	325.00
Figurine, Amaryllis, No. 3108	350.00
Figurine, April, No. 3416	225.00
Figurine, At The Meet, No. 3114	495.00
Figurine, Bulldog, No. 2945	250.00
Figurine, Dachsund, No. 3294, 4 In.	150.00
Figurine, Eastern Water Carrier, c.1895	395.00
Figurine, Female Water Carrier, 5 1/2 In.	275.00
Figurine, First Dance, No. 3629, F.G. Doughty, 7 1/2 x 4 In.	165.00
Figurine, Girl, Dancing, Ivory Ground, Gilt, James Hadley, c.1885, 9 1/2 In.	517.00
Figurine, Girl, With Tambourine, Tree, Kate Greenaway, 9 In.	440.00
Figurine, Goosey Goosey Gander, No. 3304, 5 1/2 In.	195.00
Figurine, Grandmother's Dress, No. 3081	95.00 to 185.00
Figurine, Happy Days, No. 3435	1250.00
Figurine, Horse, Clydesdale Stallion, No. 25, Doris Lindner, 1976	1035.00
Figurine, Horse, Fox Hunter & Lt. Col. H.M. Llewellyn, Doris Lindner, 1960	920.00
Figurine, Jar, Hound, No. 2925	235.00
Figurine, Kingfisher, No. 3235	65.00
Figurine, L'Allegro, Parian, 1880s, 16 In.	675.00
Figurine, Mischief, No. 2914	240.00
Figurine, Mother MacHree, No. 2924	225.00
Figurine, Noel, No. 2905	175.00
Figurine, Orange Blossom & Butterflies, 8 In.	920.00
Figurine, Shorthorn Bull, Doris Lindner	800.00
Figurine, Sister, No. 3149, F.G. Doughty, 7 x 4 In.	175.00

Figurine, Sunday Morning	95.00
Figurine, Sweet Anne, No. 3630	95.00
Figurine, Young Foxes, No. 3131	350.00
Jardiniere, Gold Tones To Ivory Ground, c.1888, 7 1/8 In.	431.00
Jug, Bicentenary Commemorative, Mask Spout, 4 7/8 In.	75.00
Jug, Mask Spout, Hand Painted Floral, Gilt Trim, Signed, 9 3/4 In.	460.00
Jug, Owl On Branch, Moonlit Sky, Serpent Handle, c.1885, 11 1/4 In.	930.00
Jug, Pink & Blue Floral, Gold Gilt, Bamboo-Type Handle, 10 1/4 In.	250.00
Pitcher, Flowers & Butterflies, 7 3/4 In.	165.00
Pitcher, Leaf Handle, 6 In.	40.00
Plate, Bird In Flowering Branch Transfer, 4 1/2 In.	10.00
Plate, Dessert, Painted Insects, Blossoms, c.1885, 9 3/16 In., 10 Piece	3163.00
Plate, Gilt Foliate Design, Mottled Green Border, 10 1/2 In., 6 Piece	402.00
Plate, Lobster Design, 9 In., 11 Piece	410.00
Plate, Service, Gilt Foliate Design, 10 1/2 In., 12 Piece	920.00
Plate, Spiral Rosette Within Husk Wreath, c.1932, 8 3/8 In., 10 Piece	805.00
Plate, St. Augustine, Fla., Blue & White	60.00
Platter, Portia, Square, 12 In.	85.00
Rose Bowl, Brown Bird, Gold Enameled Branches, c.1897, 2 1/2 In.	195.00
Salt, Leaf	45.00
Sauce, Engadine	12.00
Snuffer, Candle, Monk	75.00
Sugar, Portia	25.00
Sugar & Creamer, Pink & Gilt Outlined Floral, 3 1/4 In.	225.00
Sugar Shaker, Figure Of Boy, Cream, Gold Trim	400.00
Tea Set, Cream Ground, Floral Design, 3 Piece	632.00
Teapot, Cobalt Bird & Butterflies, Lid, 1869 Mark	150.00
Toothpick, Hand Painted Flowers, 2 Handles, 1890s, 1 1/2 In.	89.00
Vase, Bottle Shape, Ivory Ground, Enamel Butterflies, Gilt Grass, 9 1/2 In.	230.00
Vase, Cover, Egg Shaped Body, 3 Hoofed Feet, c.1910, 6 In.	565.00
Vase, Fan Form, Blue-Green, Floral, Sprays, Hand Painted, c.1881, 7 In.	632.00
Vase, Gilt & Enamel, Bird & Floral Design, Handles, c.1885, 10 7/8 In.	546.00
Vase, Hand Painted Floral, Pierced Handles & Rim, c.1890, 10 3/4 In.	690.00
Vase, Hand Painted Lilacs, Gold Leaves, 2 Handles, Bulbous, 13 1/2 x 7 In.	1075.00
Vase, Hand Painted, Chalice Shape, Circle & Crown Mark, 10 In.	1000.00
Vase, Ivory, Raised Gold Jeweling & Landscape Panels, c.1892, 4 In.	690.00
Vase, Nautilus, 1890s, 9 In.	500.00
Vase, Portrait, Satyr Mask Handles, Blue Ground, c.1862, 6 In., Pair	632.00
Vase, Reticulated, Supported On A Hawk, Cherubs Mask, Cover, 9 In.	495.00
Vase, Sack Shape, Crimped Neck, Flowers, Leaves, Hand Painted, 1886, 6 x 5 In.	185.00
Vase, Tropical Bird, Gilt Handles, Silver Trim Rings, Marked, c.1881, 11 In.	632.00

ROYCROFT products were made by the Roycrofter community of East Aurora, New York, in the late nineteenth and early twentieth centuries. The community was founded by Elbert Hubbard, famous philosopher, writer, and artist. The workshops owned by the community made furniture, metalware, leatherwork, embroidery, and jewelry. A printshop produced many signs, books, and the magazines that promoted the sayings of Elbert Hubbard. Furniture by the Roycroft community is listed in the Furniture category.

Andirons, Iron, Spiral-Twisted, Hand Forged, No. 069, 27 x 13 1/2 x 20 In.	1760.00
Bookends, Copper, Hammered, Crimped Edge, Raised Leaf Design, 4 x 5 In.	302.00
Bookends, Embossed Floral Design, Hammered, Orb Mark, 4 1/2 x 4 3/4 In.	193.00
Bookends, Hinged Pulls, Riveted Straps, Signed, 5 1/4 In.	300.00
Bookends, Medallion Of Leather Framed As Braided Border, Copper, 4 3/4 In.	200.00
Bookends, Poppy, Riveted Rim, Signed, Hammered Copper, 5 1/2 x 5 In.	475.00
Bookstand, Little Journeys, Overhanging Top, 2 Shelves, Dark Finish, 26 In.	700.00
Box, Hammered Copper, Tooled Linear Design, Wood Lined, 5 1/2 x 4 In.	412.00
Calendar, Desk, Hammered Copper, Continuous Revolving Dates, 3 3/4 x 4 1/4 In.	220.00
Candlestick, Princess, 4-Sided Stem, Pyramid Base, Signed, 7 3/4 In., Pair	650.00
Catalog, 1908	75.00
Inkwell, Hammered Copper, Applied Knob, Signed, 5 x 3 1/2 In.	232.00
Lamp, Mica Panels, Hammered Wood-Grained Copper, Marked, 14 x 7 In.	995.00

◆◆◆◆◆◆◆◆◆◆◆◆◆◆◆◆◆◆◆◆◆◆◆◆◆

If you have a lightweight vase that tips easily, fill it with sand.

◆◆◆◆◆◆◆◆◆◆◆◆◆◆◆◆◆◆◆◆◆◆◆◆◆

Roycroft, Vase, Hammered Copper, Floral Design, 10 In.; Roycroft, Vase, Hammered Copper, Original Patina, 6 In.

Napkin Holder, Silver Plated On Copper, Sheffield Finish, Clip Style, 1/2 x 3 In.	95.00
Salt & Pepper, Buffalo	300.00
Tray, Card, Oval, 7 In.	75.00
Tray, Hammered Copper, 2 Handles, Impressed Orb, 12 x 10 In.	248.00
Tray, Hammered Copper, Crimped Ends, Oval, 13 1/2 x 6 In.	220.00
Tray, Hammered Copper, Green Tooled Edge, 6 In.	104.00
Vase, American Beauty, Collared Neck, Signed, 12 In.	1320.00
Vase, American Beauty, Hammered Copper, 8 x 21 In.	1760.00
Vase, Bud, Hammered Copper, Glass Tube, Brown Patina, Signed, 8 In.	285.00
Vase, Compressed Body, Everted Rim, Copper, Marked, 18 3/4 In.	2760.00
Vase, Cylinder, Hammered Copper, Applied Silver Design, 6 1/4 In.	2090.00
Vase, Everted Rim, Foot Rising To Cylindrical Neck, Marked, 19 1/2 In.	1725.00
Vase, Flared Top, Acid Etched, 10 In.	330.00
Vase, Geometric Overlay, Hammered Copper & Nickel Silver, Signed, 6 In. ...	650.00
Vase, Green Enameled Band, Stylized Quatrefoils, Copper, Signed, 5 In.	325.00
Vase, Hammered Copper, Floral Design, 10 In. .... *Illus*	2200.00
Vase, Hammered Copper, Flowers, Green Wash, 10 In.	2200.00
Vase, Hammered Copper, Original Patina, 6 In. .... *Illus*	385.00
Vase, Hammered Copper, Round Foot, Flared, Impressed Orb, 6 3/4 x 3 In. ...	165.00
Vase, Hammered, Stylized Flowers & Bells, Cylindrical Orb & Cross Mark, 9 3/4 In. ..	495.00
Vase, Hand Hammered Copper, 6 1/2 In.	605.00
Watch Fob, Glasgow Rose, Silver Link Chain, Signed, 10 In.	950.00

ROZANE, see Roseville category

ROZENBURG worked at The Hague, Holland, from 1890 to 1914. The most important pieces were earthenware made in the early twentieth century with pale-colored Art Nouveau designs.

Bowl, Art Nouveau Floral, Pale Green Ground, 7 1/4 In.	425.00
Pitcher, Exotic Birds, Terra-Cotta Ground, Bulbous, Incised, 7 1/2 x 6 1/2 In.	357.00

RRP is the mark used by the firm of Robinson-Ransbottom. It is not a mark of the more famous Roseville Pottery. The Ransbottom brothers started a pottery in 1900 in Ironspot, Ohio. In 1920, they merged with the Robinson Clay Product Company of Akron, Ohio, to become Robinson-Ransbottom. The factory is still working.

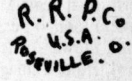

Cookie Jar, Dutch Boy	225.00
Cookie Jar, Dutch Boy & Dutch Girl, Pair ....396.00 to 550.00
Cookie Jar, Dutch Girl, Gold Trim	485.00
Cookie Jar, Hi Diddle Diddle, Gold ....290.00 to 495.00
Cookie Jar, Hi Diddle Diddle, Plain	265.00
Cookie Jar, Jocko The Monkey	285.00
Cookie Jar, Whale	850.00
Figurine, Ol' King Cole	225.00

RS GERMANY is part of the wording in marks used by the Tillowitz, Germany, factory of Reinhold Schlegelmilch from about 1869 until about 1956. The porcelain was sold decorated and undecorated. The Schlegelmilch families made porcelains marked in many ways. See also ES Germany, RS Poland, RS Prussia, RS Silesia, RS Suhl, and RS Tillowitz.

Bowl, Handles, Scene Of Woman With Cows Near Cottage, 10 In.	235.00
Bowl, Lettuce, Pearl Luster, Floral	200.00
Bowl, Nut, Pink Roses, Footed, Set, 6 Piece	75.00
Bowl, Roses, 12 Sides, 10 In.	75.00
Bowl, Summer Season, Oval, 8 1/2 x 13 In.	1700.00
Cake Plate, Carnation Mold, Gold Flowers & Trim, White, Marked	250.00
Celery, Roses, Open Handles, 12 5/8 In.	95.00
Console Set, All Gold, 3 Piece	185.00
Creamer, Cottage Scene	35.00
Dish, Olive, Rose Spray, Stylized Floral Rim, Loop Handles, Green Wreath, 9 x 4 In.	30.00
Hatpin Holder, Calla Lily, 4 In.	103.00
Hatpin Holder, Roses, 4 3/8 In.	125.00
Plate, Floral, 7 1/2 In.	35.00
Plate, LeBrun, Marked, 8 1/2 In.	395.00
Plate, Lilacs On White, Gold Trim, Gold Border, 11 1/4 In.	110.00
Plate, Red & Yellow Roses, Pastel Ground, Gold Trim, 6 1/4 In.	12.00
Plate, White Orange Blossoms, Muted Green & Rose, 8 1/2 In.	20.00
Relish, Peach & White Roses, Openwork, 4 x 9 In.	55.00
Sugar & Creamer, Cover, White Flowers, Blue Ground	40.00

RS POLAND (German) is a mark used by the Reinhold Schlegelmilch factory at Tillowitz from about 1946 to 1949, although the factory continued production until 1956. This is one of many of the RS marks used. See also ES Germany, RS Germany, RS Prussia, RS Silesia, RS Suhl, and RS Tillowitz.

Server, Center Handle, Lavender & Orange Roses, 11 In.	515.00
Vase, 1 Brown Cranes, Other Black Geese, 4 1/2 In., Pair	1200.00

RS PRUSSIA appears in several marks used on porcelain before 1915. Reinhold Schlegelmilch started his porcelain works in Tillowitz, Germany, in 1869. See also ES Germany, RS Germany, RS Poland, RS Silesia, RS Suhl, and RS Tillowitz.

Basket, Florals, Gold Trim, Oval, Red Mark	175.00
Berry Bowl, Dogwood, Light To Dark Green, 5 1/2 In.	215.00
Berry Set, Dark To Light Pink Roses, 7 Piece	350.00
Berry Set, Leaf Mold, Pink Roses, Lily Of The Valley Buds, 7 Piece	495.00
Berry Set, Pink & Yellow Roses, Carnation Mold, 6 Piece	495.00
Berry Set, Pink Carnations, 7 Piece	475.00
Berry Set, Point & Clover Mold	475.00
Berry Set, Rose & Carnation, 7 Piece	775.00
Biscuit Jar, Beige Ground, Pink Roses	285.00
Biscuit Jar, Carnation Mold, Floral Finial, Red Mark	495.00
Bowl, 3 Footed, Roses, Wildflowers, 6 3/4 In.	95.00
Bowl, 4 Portrait Medallions, Green & Gold Border, Altenberg, 9 In.	450.00
Bowl, Dice Players, Ribbon & Jewel, 10 1/2 In.	1450.00
Bowl, Fish Scale Mold, White Lilies, Purple & Orange Luster, c.1880, 11 x 3 In.	395.00
Bowl, Floral, 4 Seasons Medallions, Daisy Mold, 10 In. ....*Illus*	2700.00
Bowl, Flowers, Icicle Border, Pearl Finish	395.00
Bowl, Hidden Image, Hidden House	1600.00
Bowl, Lion, 10 In.	5000.00
Bowl, Madame LeBrun, 10 1/2 In.	1000.00
Bowl, Madame LeBrun, Lily Mold, 9 1/2 In.	850.00
Bowl, Madame Recamier, 10 In.	1000.00
Bowl, Pearlized, Multicolor Florals, 10 1/2 In.	250.00
Bowl, Pink Roses, Blue Border, Red Star Mark, 10 In.	115.00
Bowl, Potocka Portrait, Daisy, Lily Mold, Red, Gold, 10 In. ....*Illus*	1850.00
Bowl, Potocka, Tiffany Border, 8 In.	650.00
Bowl, Reflecting Poppies & Daisies, 10 In.	195.00

Bowl, Schooner, Red Mark, 10 3/4 In. 750.00
Bowl, Snowball & Roses, 9 In. 175.00
Bowl, Stag, Red Mark, 9 In. 600.00
Bowl, Swan & Gazebo, 10 3/4 In. ....595.00 to 625.00
Bowl, Swan Scene, Red Mark, 11 In. 595.00
Bowl, Vegetable, Rose Pattern, 11 In. 165.00
Bowl, Winter Season, Iris Mold, Satin, White, 10 1/2 In. .... *Illus* 2400.00
Bowl, Woman With Fan, Hexagon Mold, 10 3/4 In. 925.00
Box, Dresser, Hidden Image, 4 In. 300.00
Bread Plate, Rose Pattern 45.00
Cake Plate, 6 Iris, 11 In. 215.00
Cake Plate, Basket Of Roses, White & Gold, Marked 250.00
Cake Plate, Dice Players, Open Handles, Red Mark, 10 1/2 In. 750.00
Cake Plate, Flowers, Pink, White 35.00
Cake Plate, Hummingbird, 10 In. 2500.00
Cake Plate, Iris Mold, Scattered Pink Poppies, Lavender & Peach 600.00
Cake Plate, Old Man In The Mountain, Icicle Mold, 11 In. 650.00
Cake Plate, Old Man In The Mountain, Red Mark, Square 295.00
Cake Plate, Pearlized, Open Handles, Roses & Gold, 10 1/2 In. 165.00
Cake Plate, Scalloped, Pink & Peach Tulips & Lilies, 12 In. 160.00
Cake Plate, Snow Scene, Birds, Pierced Handles, Red Star Mark, 11 In. 1320.00
Cake Plate, Stippled Floral, Pierced Handles, 11 In. 200.00
Cake Plate, Sunflower Mold, Red Mark, 11 In. 250.00
Cake Plate, Swallows, Chickens & Ducks, Water Lilies, 10 In. 1010.00
Cake Plate, Swans, Evergreens, Handles, 10 In. 260.00
Celery, Floral, 12 In. 65.00
Celery, Grape Design, 13 1/2 In. 295.00

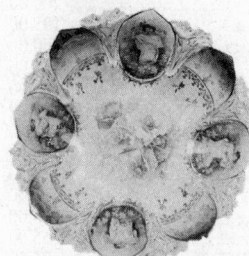

RS Prussia, Bowl, Floral, 4 Seasons Medallions, Daisy Mold, 10 In.

RS Prussia, Bowl, Potocka Portrait, Daisy, Lily Mold, Red, Gold, 10 In.

RS Prussia, Bowl, Winter Season, Iris Mold, Satin, White, 10 1/2 In.

RS Prussia, Plate, Spring, Woman Center, Keyhole, 9 In.

RS Prussia, Plate, Birds, Snow Scene, Gold Trim, 11 In.

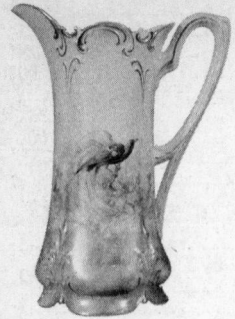 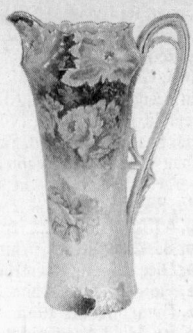

RS Prussia, Tankard, Bird Of Paradise,
Satin Gold Trim, 12 In.

RS Prussia, Tankard,
Floral Design, 13 In.

Celery, Hidden Image Woman	225.00
Celery, Melon Eaters, Point & Clover Mold, Open Handle, 9 x 4 In.	695.00
Chocolate Pot, Green, With Pink Roses, 9 In.	295.00
Chocolate Pot, Hummingbird	2750.00
Chocolate Pot, Swans In Pine Tree	1100.00
Chocolate Set, Green, Gold Bands, Rose Decoration, 11 Piece	302.00
Chocolate Set, Ostrich, 13 Piece	3900.00
Coffeepot, Drapery Mold, Pearlized, White With Pink Roses, Demitasse 13 Piece	2700.00
Compote, Ostrich, Gold, Beehive, 5 1/2 In.	2000.00
Cracker Jar, Green Foliage, White Ground	200.00
Creamer, Dachshund	195.00
Creamer, Hummingbird, Browns	350.00
Cup & Saucer, Swan, Satin Finish, Red Mark	425.00
Hair Receiver, Cover, Icicle Mold, Red Mark	150.00
Hair Receiver, Floral & Gilt Design, 2 1/4 In.	40.00
Hatpin Holder, Attached Open Trinket Box, Blue & Gold Trim, Red Mark	125.00
Hatpin Holder, Basket	200.00
Holder, Canned Milk, Blossom Lid, Bulging Ribs, Petals, Morning Glory Mold	195.00
Mustache Cup, Tulip Mold, Gold & Blue	275.00
Mustard, Snowbird	300.00
Mustard, Underplate, Lily Of The Valley	65.00
Pitcher, Tankard Shape, Yellow & Pink Roses, Red Star Mark, 10 1/2 In.	605.00
Plate, Birds, Snow Scene, Gold Trim, 11 In. *Illus*	1200.00
Plate, Cobalt, Raised Gold Border, Hand Painted Roses, Gold Steeple Mark, 9 In.	25.00
Plate, Cottage, Shepherd & Sheep Scene, 8 1/2 In.	850.00
Plate, Dice Players, 7 1/2 In.	395.00
Plate, Hummingbird, Red Mark, 7 3/4 In.	900.00
Plate, Mill Scene, 7 In.	250.00
Plate, Red Roses, Gold & Blue, 10 In.	150.00
Plate, Silesia, Handle, Oval, 10 In.	12.00
Plate, Snowbird, Icicle Mold, Red Mark, 8 In.	600.00 to 1075.00
Plate, Spring, Woman Center, Keyhole, 9 In. *Illus*	1300.00
Plate, Woman With Gold Hair, Hidden Image, Lavender, 11 In.	875.00
Radish, 2 Piece	75.00
Relish, Melon Eaters, Point & Clover Mold, Green	695.00
Relish, Melon Eaters, Red Mark, 9 1/2 In.	695.00
Relish, Open Handled, Pink & White Carnations, 4 x 10 1/2 In.	100.00
Shaving Mug, Mill Scene, Browns	395.00
Shaving Mug, Purple & Pink Flowers	275.00
Sugar, Cover, Mill Scene	125.00
Sugar, Swans	185.00
Sugar & Creamer, Dogwood, Pearlized	145.00
Sugar & Creamer, Pink Flowers, Red Star Mark	144.00

RS Prussia, Tray, Dresser,
Autumn Scene, Woman Center, 11 x 7 In.

RS Prussia, Vase, Pillow,
Melon Eaters, Jeweled, Tin

Sugar & Creamer, Snowball & Roses	125.00
Sugar & Creamer, Swan, Raised Gold, Satin	450.00
Sugar & Creamer, Swans, Pedestal Foot, Satin Finish, 6 In.	200.00
Sugar & Creamer, Winter Scene, Satin Finish, Red Mark	550.00
Sugar Shaker, Pink Roses, Gold Garlands, 4 3/4 In.	260.00
Tankard, Bird Of Paradise, Satin Gold Trim, 12 In. .... *Illus*	16000.00
Tankard, Carnation Mold, Red & Yellow Roses, 13 1/2 In.	895.00
Tankard, Fleur-De-Lis Mold, Colored Flowers, 10 1/4 In.	425.00
Tankard, Floral Design, 13 In. .... *Illus*	1100.00
Tankard, Hanging Basket Design, 13 In.	900.00
Tankard, Stipple Mold, Red & Yellow Roses, Blue-Green Ground, 13 1/4 In.	495.00
Tankard, Tiger, Scroll Handle	4100.00
Tea Set, Hidden Image, 3 Piece	1500.00
Thermometer, Desk, Stag On Base	150.00
Toothpick, 3 Handles, Floral, Red Mark	295.00
Toothpick, Blue Roses	100.00
Toothpick, Mold No. 509, 3 Handles	215.00
Toothpick, Stipple Mold, 2 1/4 In.	155.00
Toothpick, Stipple Mold, Floral	145.00
Toothpick, Water Lilies, Green Ground, Double Handles, 2 1/4 In.	65.00
Tray, Bun, Roses, 14 x 6 1/4 In.	300.00
Tray, Dresser, 6 Portrait Medallions, Red Mark	1075.00
Tray, Dresser, Autumn Scene, Woman Center, 11 x 7 In. .... *Illus*	1000.00
Tray, Dresser, Dice Players, Open Handles, 10 In.	895.00
Tray, Dresser, Oval, Scalloped Edges, Pink & White Flowers, 12 1/4 x 9 In.	125.00
Tray, Portrait Medallion, Cobalt Blue, Roses Center, Red Mark, 10 x 5 In.	695.00
Urn, Mill Scene, Castle Scene, 11 3/4 In., Pair	3475.00
Vase, 2 Ostriches, Red Mark, 9 In.	1350.00
Vase, Cottage Scene, Gold & Brown Tones, Red Mark, 6 1/2 In. ....495.00 to 600.00	
Vase, Lion, 12 In.	5000.00
Vase, Melon Eaters, 16 Jewels, Shades Of Green, Red Mark, 6 In.	2100.00
Vase, Mill Scene, Jeweled Pedestal, Double Handles, 10 In.	795.00
Vase, Parrot, 9 In.	900.00
Vase, Pedestal, Jeweled Bottom & Top, Mill Scene, 9 x 6 In.	475.00
Vase, Pillow, Dice Players, Jewels, 7 In.	2300.00
Vase, Pillow, Jewels, Lavender, Red Mark, 7 In.	2400.00
Vase, Pillow, Melon Eaters, Jeweled, Tin .... *Illus*	1425.00
Vase, Tiger, 11 1/2 In.	5750.00

RS SUHL is a mark used by the Erdmann Schlegelmilch factory in Suhl, Germany, before 1917. The Schlegelmilch families made porcelains in many places. See also ES Germany, RS Germany, RS Poland, RS Prussia, RS Silesia, and RS Tillowitz.

RLS

Suhl.

Coffee Set, Figural Scenes Each Piece, Gold Trim, 15 Piece 1675.00

RS TILLOWITZ was marked on porcelain by the Reinhold Schlegelmilch factory at Tillowitz in the 1930s and 1940s. Table services and ornamental pieces were made. See also ES Germany, RS Germany, RS Poland, RS Prussia, RS Silesia, and RS Suhl.

Bowl, Double Pierced Ends, Turquoise, Tray Ground, Gold Trim, 6 x 8 In. 95.00
Plate, Poppies, Green Ground, 6 In. 25.00

RUBENA is a glassware that shades from red to clear. It was first made by George Duncan and Sons of Pittsburgh, Pennsylvania, about 1885. This coloring was used on many types of glassware. The pressed glass patterns of Royal Ivy and Royal Oak are listed under Pressed Glass.

Claret Set, Embossed French Pewter, Stemmed Wines, Pewter Bases, 5 Piece 475.00
Cruet, Stopper, 10 In. 55.00
Perfume Bottle, Bands Of Leaves, Squatty, Bulbous, Clear Stopper, 4 1/2 x 3 1/2 In. 110.00
Pitcher, Threaded, Clear Handle, Gold Trim, 2 In. 85.00

RUBENA VERDE is a Victorian glassware that was shaded from red to green. It was first made by Hobbs, Brockunier and Company of Wheeling, West Virginia, about 1890.

Cruet, Inverted Thumbprint, Stopper, Round, 4 In. 535.00
Pitcher, Floral, Enamel, 7 1/2 In. 550.00

RUBY GLASS is the dark red color of the precious gemstone known as a *ruby*. It was a popular Victorian color that never went completely out of style. The glass was shaped by many different processes to make many different types of ruby glass. There was a revival of interest in the 1940s when modern-shaped ruby table glassware became fashionable. Sometimes the red color is added to clear glass by a process called flashing or staining. Flashed glass is clear glass dipped in a colored glass, then pressed or cut. Stained glass has color painted on a clear glass. Then it is refired so the stain fuses with the glass. Pieces of glass colored in this way are indicated by the word *stained* in the description. Related items may be found in other categories, such as Cranberry Glass, Pressed Glass, and Souvenir.

Goblet, Geometric Swirl Pattern, 6 Piece 460.00
Toothpick, Gold Design 20.00
Vase, Polychrome Floral And Gilt Design, Enameled, 11 3/4 In. 137.00
Vase, White Overlay Design, Victorian, 11 1/4 In., Pair 66.00

RUDOLSTADT was a faience factory in the Thuringia region of Germany from 1720 to about 1791. In 1854, Ernst Bohne began working in the area. From about 1887 to 1918, the New York and Rudolstadt Pottery made decorated porcelain marked with the RW and crown familiar to collectors. This porcelain was imported by Lewis Straus and Sons of New York, which later became Nathan Straus and Sons. The word *Royal* was included in their import mark. Collectors often call it *Royal Rudolstadt*. Most pieces found today were made in the late nineteenth or early twentieth century. Additional pieces may be listed in the Kewpie category.

Biscuit Jar, Fluted Body, Pastel Floral Design, Cream Ground, 7 In. 195.00
Chop Plate, White Roses 65.00
Cup & Saucer, Forest, Kewpies In Trees, Royal, 2 1/4 In. 90.00
Dish, Cheese, Flowers, Matte 95.00
Hatpin Holder, Roses, Pearl Finish, Hexagonal 145.00
Kewpie, Plate, Forest, 6 Kewpies Around, Royal, 7 3/4 In. 170.00
Mug, Forest, 5 Kewpies, Royal, 3 1/4 In. 80.00
Plate, Astor Hotel Picture, New York City, 9 In. 59.00
Plate, Christmas, Holly, Yellow Roses, 9 In. 65.00
Plate, Daisies & Foliage, Gold Rim, Hand Painted, Signed, 8 1/2 In. 16.00
Sugar & Creamer, Roses, Gold Trim 28.00
Tea Set, Child's, Golliwogs, 21 Piece 225.00
Tea Set, Child's, The Golliwogs, Royal Teapot, Sugar, Creamer, 6 Cups & Saucer 240.00
Tray, Dresser, Hand Painted Roses, 8 x 11 1/2 In. 60.00

Vase, Neptune, 7 x 20 In... 495.00

RUGS have been used in the American home since the seventeenth century. The oriental rug of that time was often used on a table, not on the floor. Rag rugs, hooked rugs, and braided rugs were made by housewives from scraps of material.

Afshar, 3 Ft. 8 In. x 5 Ft. 2 In.	440.00
Afshar, Concentric Medallions, Abrashed Blue Field, 6 Ft. x 4 Ft. 2 In.	977.50
Amish, Braided, Reds, Blues & Browns With Black, 39 In.	165.00
Anatolian, Rust, Beige, 3 Ft. 8 In. x 4 Ft. 9 In.	403.00
Anatolian Kilim, Rows Of Double Diamonds, Ivory Field, 4 Ft. 10 In. x 3 Ft. 4 In.	259.00
Anatolian Yastik, 3 Medallions, Red Field, 3 Ft. 2 In. x 2 Ft. 2 In.	103.00
Anatolian Yastik, Serrated Flower Heads, Red Field, 3 Ft. 2 In. x 1 Ft. 10 In.	115.00
Anauli, c.1940, 4 Ft. 10 In. x 6 Ft. 9 In.	3600.00
Aubusson, Central Floral Bouquet, Blossom Border, 1870s, 90 In. x 58 In.	6900.00
Aubusson, Central Floral Cartouche, Baskets, Vines, France, 9 x 7 Ft.	5750.00
Aubusson, Chinese Style, Pastel Floral, Cameo Medallion, On Ivory, 9 x 12 Ft.	577.00
Aubusson, Cream Medallion, Floral Bouquet, France, 14 x 11 Ft.	2415.00
Aubusson, Louis-Philippe, Floral Medallion, Damask, France, 7 x 6 Ft.	5462.00
Aubusson, Louis-Phillippe, Ebony, Floral Sprays, 12 Ft. 8 In. x 9 Ft. 5 In.	7475.00
Aubusson, Oval Floral Medallion, Cream Ground, France, 6 x 4 Ft.	5175.00
Aubusson, Oval Medallion Enclosing Floral Bouquet, 6 x 4 Ft.	5750.00
Aushak, Overall Palmettes, Palmette Border, 1920s, 11 Ft. 4 In. x 11 Ft.	4887.00
Azbekistan, Embroidered, Overall Flowering Vines, 8 Ft. 1 In. x 5 Ft. 10 In.	3450.00
Bakhtiari, 2 Hexagonal Medallions, Red Field, 7 Ft. 4 In. x 5 Ft. 8 In.	690.00
Bakhtiari, Square Grid, Floral, Geometric Motifs, Pinwheel Border, 1909, 72 x 52 In. .	316.00
Bakhtiari, White Medallion, Brownish-Red Ground, 8 Ft. 7 In. x 12 Ft. 6 In.	1760.00
Bakshaish, Tree Of Life Design, Camel Field, 4 Ft. 6 In. x 2 Ft. 7 In.	1092.00
Baluchi, Hexagonal Lattice, Red, Navy, Brown, Geometric Motifs, 54 x 34 In.	460.00
Baluchi, Medallions, Projections, Navy Field, Diagonal Stripe Border, 6 x 4 Ft.	230.00
Baluchi, Midnight Blue Ground, 3 Ft. 8 In. x 6 Ft. 1 In.	275.00
Baluchi, Multiple Borders, Central Diamond & Flowers, 3 Ft. 9 In. x 5 Ft. 4 In.	121.00
Baluchi, Octagonal Lattice, Hooked Squares, Blue Field, Red Border, 69 x 40 In.	546.00
Baluchi, Octagonal Lattice, Rosettes, Navy Field, Boat Border, 4 x 3 Ft.	230.00
Baluchi, Prayer, Rows Of Flower Heads, Camel Field, Red Border, 58 x 30 In.	431.00
Baluchi, Prayer, Trees, White Ground, 5 Ft. 3 In. x 3 Ft. 2 In.	143.00
Baluchi, Red, Tan & Purple, 5 x 9 Ft.	275.00
Baluchi, Serrated Diamond Lattice, Flowering Plants, Camel Field, 5 x 3 Ft.	2760.00
Bergama, Floral Designs, Blue-Green Field, 5 Ft. 6 In. x 4 Ft. 4 In.	460.00
Bergama, Ivory & Mandarin Medallions, Linked S Border, 82 x 59 In.	2875.00
Bidjar, Brick Field, Central Medallion, 3 Ft. x 5 Ft. 2 In.	165.00
Bidjar, Hexagonal Medallion On Blue Field, 6 Ft. 9 In. x 4 Ft. 6 In.	403.00
Bidjar Style, Floral, Central Medallion, 5 Ft. 9 In. x 8 Ft. 9 In.	715.00
Bigelow, Machine Woven, Art Deco Geometric Design, 1930s, 108 x 142 In.	1100.00
Bokhara, Black & Tan, Central Geometric Designs, Red Field, 1 Ft. 7 In. x 4 Ft.	77.00
Bokhara, Brown Ground, Orange & Blue Geometric, 4 Ft. 6 In. x 5 Ft. 1 In.	2090.00
Bokhara, Deep Pink Ground, 4 Ft. 1 In. x 5 Ft. 9 In.	137.00
Bokhara, Overall Gul Design, Red Field, 8 Ft. 2 In. x 11 Ft. 4 In.	690.00
Bokhara, Red & Blue Geometric, Brown Ground, 4 Ft. 2 In. x 5 Ft. 8 In.	220.00
Bokhara, Red Ground, Blue & Tan Geometrics, 3 Ft. 10 In. x 4 Ft. 7 In.	412.00
Caucasian, Multicolored Geometric, Orange Ground, 4 Ft. 7 In. x 10 Ft. 2 In.	4125.00
Caucasian, Multicolored Stylized Animal & Geometric, Rust Ground, 3 x 6 Ft.	275.00
Chain Stitch, Floral & Diamond Design, Black Ground, 8 x 10 Ft.	55.00
Chichi, Hooked Polygons, Midnight Blue Field, 5 Ft. 2 In. x 4 Ft.	920.00
Chichi, Rows Of Memling Guls, Navy Field, Striped Border, 9 Ft. 6 In. x 4 Ft.	690.00
Chinese, Floral Medallion, Navy Field, Ivory Floral Border, 5 x 3 Ft.	1035.00
Chinese, Round Medallion, Open Blue Field, Ivory Border, 4 Ft. 3 In. x 2 Ft. 7 In.	517.00
Craftsman, Honeycomb & Diamond Center, Green Border, Fringed, 20 x 36 In.	495.00
Craftsman, Honeycomb Center, Greek Key Border, G. Stickley, 110 x 140 In.	2750.00
Daghestan, Cruciform Geometric Design, Gold Field, 7 Ft. x 4 Ft. 10 In.	1840.00
Donegal, Arts & Crafts, Border Of Tulips, Gold Ground, 12 Ft. x 14 Ft. 6 In.	715.00
Donegal, Smyrna Design, Floral & Ribbon Border, 18 Ft. 5 In. x 12 Ft. 11 In.	3220.00
Donegal, Wool, Arts & Crafts, Morton & Robertson, c.1900, 7 Ft. x 6 Ft. 11 In.	3220.00

Rug, Grenfell, Floral & Geometric Design,
20th Century, 37 x 25 In.

◆◆◆◆◆◆◆◆◆◆◆◆◆◆◆◆◆◆◆◆◆◆◆◆

Oriental rugs are graded for quality by dealers. In most cases the quality is determined by the knot count over a measured distance on the width of a rug. A 90 line count for a Chinese rug means if 1 foot of the width is marked off there will be 90 knots. Pakistani rugs have quality measured by counting knots on 1 inch of the width and 1 inch of the length, so it might be 16/18.

◆◆◆◆◆◆◆◆◆◆◆◆◆◆◆◆◆◆◆◆◆◆◆◆

Drugget, Nile Pattern Border, Crisscross Checkerboard Center, 39 x 72 In. 330.00
Dutch, Art Nouveau, 1930s, 13 Ft. x 9 Ft. 7 In. 9200.00
Fereghan, Blue Ground, Floral Design, 7 Borders, 8 Ft. 9 In. x 11 Ft. 3960.00
Fereghan, Floral & Geometric Design, 4 x 6 1/2 Ft. 3500.00
Fereghan, Multicolored Floral & Geometric Design, On Red, 12 x 13 Ft. 9500.00
Fereghan, Multicolored Geometric, Floral & Paisley Design, 4 Ft. x 6 Ft. 5 In. 350.00
Fereghan, Red Ground, Floral & Geometric Design, 12 x 13 1/2 Ft. 9500.00
Floor Cloth, Log Cabin, Hand Woven, Blue, Ivory, Rose, 6 Ft. 8 In. x 13 Ft. 145.00
Grenfell, 3 Sled Dogs, Eskimo, 18 x 12 In. 165.00
Grenfell, Eskimo Design, 10 x 8 In. 489.00
Grenfell, Eskimos Pulled By Dog Sled, 38 x 26 In. 977.00
Grenfell, Floral & Geometric Design, 20th Century, 37 x 25 In. ....*Illus* 920.00
Grenfell Missions, Polar Bear On Iceberg, 24 1/2 x 31 In. 935.00
Hamadan, 3 Medallions, 4 Ft. 9 In. x 8 Ft. 6 In. 578.00
Hamadan, Brick Ground, Multiple Borders, Geometrics, 3 Ft. x 4 Ft. 4 In. 193.00
Hamadan, Camel Ground, Blue & Red Central Medallion, 3 Ft. 3 In. x 6 Ft. 330.00
Hamadan, Circular Medallions, Herati Blue Field, 10 Ft. 10 In. x 4 Ft. In. 863.00
Hamadan, Floral Cobalt Blue Border, Pink Ground, 11 Ft. 1 In. x 9 Ft. 990.00
Hamadan, Kirman Design, Medallion, Red, Floral Border, 9 Ft. 8 In. x 15 Ft. 4 In. 550.00
Hamadan, Multicolored Floral & Geometric, Red Ground, 2 Ft. 8 In. x 4 Ft. 2 In. 110.00
Hamadan, Overall Pattern, 9 Ft. x 3 Ft. 4 In. 303.00
Hamadan, Red Ground, 4 Ft. 1 In. x 6 Ft. 3 In. 180.00
Hamadan, Runner, 2 Ft. 6 In. x 9 Ft. 5 In. 525.00
Hamadan, Runner, Blue & Cranberry Floral Design, On Rose, 3 x 9 Ft. 357.00
Hamadan, Violet Ground, 4 Ft. 7 In. x 7 Ft. 8 In. 247.00
Hand Knotted, Hammersmith, Morris & Co., Florals, c.1880, 17 x 5 Ft. 8350.00
Heriz, Blue Ground, Palmettes, Turtle Border, 7 Ft. 6 In. x 11 Ft. 1 In. 3740.00
Heriz, Blues, Green, Raspberry, Brown, Beige, Red Ground, 27 In. x 2 Ft. 10 In. 770.00
Heriz, Brick Red Field, 9 Ft. 3 In. x 12 Ft. 4730.00
Heriz, Central Medallion, Red Field, 2 Ft. 3 In. x 4 Ft. 6 In. 88.00
Heriz, Cruciform, Medallion, Red Field, Spandrels, Turtle Border, 11 Ft. x 8 Ft. 2070.00
Heriz, Diamond Medallion, Serrated Leaves, Red Field, Navy Border, 110 x 88 In. 2990.00
Heriz, Gabled Square Medallion, Terra-Cotta Field, Blue Spandrels, 141 x 92 In. 1610.00
Heriz, Geometrics, Blue Ground, 5 Ft. 7 In. x 8 Ft. 3 In. 715.00
Heriz, Light Blue, Cobalt, Green & Cream Design, On Red, 9 Ft. x 11 Ft. 8 In. 1375.00
Heriz, Medallion On Red Angular Vinery, Ivory Ground, 78 x 57 In. 3737.00
Heriz, Medallion, Pendants, Rust Field, Spandrels, Turtle Border, 12 x 9 Ft. 1840.00
Heriz, Medallion, Terra-Cotta Field, Blue Border, Persia, 11 Ft. x 9 Ft. 8 In. 1500.00
Heriz, Red Field, 10 Ft. 6 In. x 13 Ft. 8 In. 2090.00

Rug, Hooked, 2 Yawls Racing, 37 x 67 In.

Rug, Hooked, Cat, Black & White, 20th Century,
21 1/2 x 40 In.

Homespun, Runner, Blue & White, 26 x 79 In.		110.00
Homespun, Whirling Log, J.B. Moore, 1920, 53 x 86 In.		1950.00
Hooked, 2 Men At Table, Cotton & Wool, Frame, 19 x 30 1/2 In.		173.00
Hooked, 2 Rabbits & Sheep, 22 x 37 In.		2090.00
Hooked, 2 White Cats, Black Collars, Wool, Cotton, Brown & Green, 30 x 51 In.		1840.00
Hooked, 2 White Cats, Facing, Wool, Brown & Black Ground, 31 1/4 x 53 1/2 In.		1955.00
Hooked, 2 Yawls Racing, 37 x 67 In.	*Illus*	6325.00
Hooked, American, Mid 19th Century, 12 Ft. 3 In. x 8 Ft. 3 In.		9200.00
Hooked, Animals, Stars, Flowers, Patchwork Field, 1893, 30 x 46 In.		1092.00
Hooked, Beige & Coral, House, 21 x 33 In.		578.00
Hooked, Blue Floral, 2 x 4 Ft.		195.00
Hooked, Cat, Black & White, 20th Century, 21 1/2 x 40 In.	*Illus*	1495.00
Hooked, Center Houses, Animal Corners, 62 x 76 In.		5400.00
Hooked, Central Diamond, Floral Border, 19th Century, 39 x 91 In.		575.00
Hooked, Clipper Ship, American Flag, Floral Border, 46 x 25 In.		525.00
Hooked, Dog & Cat, Hearts Ground, 20th Century, 20 x 37 In.	*Illus*	2530.00
Hooked, Dog, Floral Border, 17 1/2 x 36 In.		110.00
Hooked, Drum, Red, White & Blue, c.1930, 23 x 36 In.		325.00
Hooked, Eagle, Olive Ground, 40 x 57 In.		28.00
Hooked, Elk & Deer, Striped Block Border, Wool, Felt Canvas Mounted, 32 x 52 In.		173.00

Hooked, Floral, Cream Field, Variegated Scalloped Edge, 19th Century, 108 x 105 In. .   115.00
Hooked, Floral, Rose, Ivory & Green Shades, 4 x 6 Ft..   65.00
Hooked, Flower Basket, Primary Colors, Black Ground, Oval, 1950s, 38 In. 85.00
Hooked, Flower Pot, Wool, Multicolor, Border, 28 1/2 x 44 In. 920.00
Hooked, Folksy Peacock, Red, Blue & Yellow, Black Ground, 32 x 38 In. 55.00
Hooked, Frost Lion Pattern, 19th Century, 54 x 27 In. 488.00
Hooked, Geometric Design, Blue, Gray, Black, Purple, 31 x 49 In. 72.00
Hooked, Geometric Design, Mauve, Purple & Neutral Colors, 4 Ft. 6 In. x 2 Ft. 55.00
Hooked, Geometric, Mounted, 19th Century, 23 x 36 In. 431.00
Hooked, Grenfell, Canada Geese In Flight, Labrador Industries, 26 1/2 x 40 In. 550.00
Hooked, Happy Homestead, God Bless Our Home, Yarn Sewn, Fringed......................   3300.00
Hooked, Hearth, Central Diamond, Floral Border, 19th Century, 39 1/2 x 91 In............   575.00
Hooked, Hearts, Diamonds, Circles, 22 1/2 x 39 3/4 In...   413.00
Hooked, Home Scene, Roxbury, Maine, 1920, 3 x 5 Ft..   4500.00
Hooked, Horse, Bird, Stars, Flowers, Patchwork Field, 1893, 30 x 46 In......................   1092.00
Hooked, House & Chicken, Gagetown, 39 x 21 1/2 In. 345.00
Hooked, Ivy Trellis, Roses, 2-Tone Gray Ground, 22 x 37 In. 138.00
Hooked, Leaves In Zigzag Diamonds, Art Deco, Charles Cochrane, 106 x 144 In. 440.00
Hooked, Lion, Wool, Yellow, Brown, Green, Red, Black, 28 x 61 In. ....*Illus*   1495.00
Hooked, Multicolored Flowers, Wheat Ground, Art Deco, c.1930, 36 x 59 In..............   77.00
Hooked, Multicolored Primitive Design, Mid-1800s, 38 1/2 x 79 In..............................   180.00
Hooked, Oriental Design, Blue, 39 x 72 In..   1250.00
Hooked, Penny, Multicolored, c.1920, 42 x 21 In. 298.00
Hooked, Pictorial, 2 Rabbits & Sheep, Tan & Cream, 36 x 22 In..................................   2090.00

Rug, Hooked, Dog & Cat, Hearts Ground,
20th Century, 20 x 37 In.

Rug, Hooked, Lion, Wool, Yellow, Brown, Green, Red, Black, 28 x 61 In.

Hooked, Pineapple Design, Yellow & Green Border, Beige Field, 102 x 70 In. 115.00
Hooked, Rag & Yarn, Basket Of Flowers, Pastel Colors, Reed Frame, 27 x 41 In. 220.00
Hooked, Rag, 4 Medallions, Red, Purple, Black, With Gray Ground, 22 x 43 In. 170.00
Hooked, Rag, Dog, Brown, Gray, Beige, Maroon Ground, Stretcher, 33 x 38 1/2 In...... 660.00
Hooked, Rag, Dog, Spotted, Brown, Ivory Ground, Flowers, 28 1/2 x 46 1/2 In. 94.00
Hooked, Rag, Gray Cat, Blue & Black Diamond Border, Purple Ground, 17 x 36 In. 385.00
Hooked, Rag, Oriental Design, Medallions, Several Borders, 30 x 47 In. 137.00
Hooked, Rag, Ship, American Flag, Border Design, 40 x 60 In.. 1540.00
Hooked, Rag, Tumbling Blocks, Multicolored, Solids & Stripes, 27 x 52 In.................. 137.00
Hooked, Rag, Vining Floral Design, Banded Border, 39 x 63 In. 495.00
Hooked, Rag, Vining Floral Design, Brown Ground, 35 x 56 In. 55.00
Hooked, Reclining Gray Cat, Floral, Green Ground, 37 x 29 In. 250.00
Hooked, Rooster In Farm Yard, Barbara Merry, 14 x 20 In. 385.00
Hooked, Row Houses, Bright Colors, Mid-20th Century, 3 x 5 Ft. 1295.00
Hooked, Row Of Buildings, Animals, Barbara Merry, 40 x 50 In. 1100.00
Hooked, Runner, Stairway, Multicolored Wool, Burlap Edge, 17 1/2 x 11 1/2 Ft. 265.00
Hooked, Running Horse, Variegated Ground, 44 x 32 In. 977.00
Hooked, Sailing Ship, 32 x 44 In. 305.00
Hooked, Sleigh Ride Through Village, Barbara Merry, 25 x 40 In. 385.00
Hooked, Stair Treads, Each With Different Scene, 8 Piece.. 605.00
Hooked, Sugaring Scene, Horse, Man, Woolen, Vermont, 1920-1930, 17 x 35 1/2 In. .. 850.00
Hooked, Terrier, Primarily Green, c.1930, 23 x 36 In. 350.00
Hooked, Tree Of Life, Butterfly & Squirrel, Vine Border, 1940s, 61 x 88 In. 1935.00
Hooked, Trees, Animals, Mustard Ground, 1900, 32 x 65 In.. 4200.00
Hooked, Waldoboro, Floral, 19th Century, 45 1/2 x 22 In. 230.00
Hooked, Waldoboro, Flowers, Green Field, Black Border, 19th Century, 42 x 22 In. ... 1200.00
Indo Bidjar, Multicolored Borders, Central Geometric, 4 x 6 Ft.. 220.00
Indo Kashan, Cranberry Ground, Multicolored Geometric, 2 Ft. 6 In. x 5 Ft................. 143.00
Isfahan, Arabesque Formed Floral Medallion, c.1930, 11 Ft. 10 In. x 8 Ft. 7 In. 9775.00
Isfahan, Overall Scrolling Floral Vinery, Magenta Field, 4 Ft. 6 In. x 8 Ft.................... 575.00
Karabagh, Overall Floral Cartouches, Burgundy Field, 18 Ft. 2 In. x 6 Ft. 8 In. 6900.00
Karabagh, Rose Blossoms Overall, Indigo Flora Border, 9 Ft. 1 In. x 4 Ft. 9 In. 2300.00
Karadja, 2 Square Medallions, Blue, Rose, Gold, Terra-Cotta Red Field, 56 x 38 In. 748.00
Karastan, Floral, Wine Ground, 9 x 3 Ft. 99.00
Karastan, Lotus Blossom, Ivory Ground, With Scrolling Foliate & Floral, 6 x 9 Ft. 132.00
Karastan Sarouk, Geometric, Red Ground, 10 x 14 Ft. 550.00
Kashan, Blue Ground, Red Central Medallion, 11 Ft. 11 In. x 9 Ft. 3 In........................ 8140.00
Kashan, Floral Medallion, Palmette & Vine Border, c.1920, 14 Ft. x 10 Ft. 5 In. 9200.00
Kashan, Geometric, Floral & Paisley Design, 10 x 13 Ft. 3500.00
Kashan, Oval Floral Medallion, Blue, Rose Gold, Burgundy, 10 Ft. x 7 Ft. 8 In. 1840.00
Kashan, Overall Arabesques & Flowering Vines, c.1920, 14 Ft. x 10 Ft. 5 In. 9775.00
Kashan, Prayer, Tan Ground, Flowers & Trees, 4 Ft. 3 In. x 6 Ft. 9 In. 1650.00
Kashmir, Wool, Needlework, Ivory Ground, Floral, 6 Ft. x 3 Ft. 11 In. 248.00
Kasvin, Center Medallion On Floral Field, 10 Ft. 11 In. x 12 Ft. 4 In............................. 880.00
Kasvin, Lobed Medallions, Floral Sprays, Red Field, 5 Ft. x 3 Ft. 4 In. 545.00
Kasvin, Small Medallions, Blue Field, Red Border, 6 Ft. 9 In. x 4 Ft. 6 In. 460.00
Kazak, 3 Stepped Diamond Medallions, Red Field, 6 Ft. 2 In. x 3 Ft. 2 In. 920.00
Kazak, Geometrics, Yellows, Brown, Blue, Red, Green, Beige, 4 Ft. x 5 Ft. 8 In........... 825.00
Kazak, Prayer, Gabled Medallions, Blue Field, Cross Border, 5 Ft. x 3 Ft. 4 In. 345.00
Kazak, Staggered Rows Of Boteh, Red Field, 4 Ft. x 3 Ft. 2 In. 1150.00
Kazak, Stylized Animal & Geometric, Blue & Red Ground, 6 x 8 Ft. 5775.00
Kerman, Blue Floral Diamond Medallion, Persia, c.1930, 12 Ft. 8 In. x 10 Ft. 1840.00
Kerman, Central Medallion, Rose Field, Blue & Beige Borders, 11 x 14 Ft. 550.00
Kerman, Deer, Birds, Shrubs Within Medallions, 8 Ft. 1 In. x 5 Ft. 2 In. 5750.00
Kerman, Floral Medallion Center, 6 Ft. 3 In. x 4 Ft. 880.00
Kerman, Floral Tree, Ivory Ground, 3 x 5 Ft. 192.00
Kerman, Floral, Ivory Field, Blue & Rose Trim, 8 Ft. 9 In. x 12 Ft. 1 In. 220.00
Kerman, Pictorial, Nicholas & Alexandra, Prince Of Wales, 7 Ft. 4 In. x 4 Ft. 3738.00
Kerman, Pink Floral Sprays, Ogival Arches, Beige, 11 x 15 Ft. 990.00
Kerman, Red & Blue Foliate & Geometric, Ivory Ground, 8 Ft. 8 In. x 12 Ft. 5 In........ 715.00
Kerman, White Ground, c.1950, 8 Ft. 10 In. x 11 Ft. 10 In. 385.00
Khamseh, Hooked Hexagonal Medallions, Blue Field, 9 Ft. x 5 Ft. 6 In......................... 489.00
Khorossan, Allover Herati Design, Floral Border, 19 Ft. 7 In. x 13 Ft. 7 In. 3220.00

Kilim, 5 Cranes, Tan Field, 10 Ft. 8 In. x 4 Ft.. 517.00
Kilim, Cranberry Ground, Blue Medallion, c.1900, 12 Ft. 4 In. x 6 Ft. 3 In.................. 3220.00
Kilim, Flowering Vase Within Floral Vinery Border, c.1900, 7 x 5 Ft....................... 2875.00
Kilim, Geometrics, Beige Ground, 6 x 9 Ft.. 650.00
Kilim, Multicolored Checkerboard Design, 3 Ft. 4 In. x 7 Ft. 6 In............................... 85.00
Kilim, Overall Flowering Shrubs, Narrow Border, 8 Ft. 7 In. x 6 Ft. 2 In.................. 5462.00
Kilim, Overall Geometric Design, 5 Ft. 6 In. x 8 Ft. 4 In.. 145.00
Kilim, Tan, Green & Gray Geometrics, 4 x 8 Ft... 120.00
Konaghend, Arabesque Lattice, Dark Blue Field, Ivory Octagon Border, 66 x 43 In. 201.00
Kuba, 3 Lesghi Guls, Brown Field, Double Dragon Border, 3 Ft. 3 In. x 3 Ft............... 575.00
Kuba, Blue Ground, Red & Tan Geometric, 3 Ft. 5 In. x 8 Ft. 2 In............................. 248.00
Kuba, Columns, Blooming Plants, Navy Field, Red Border, 11 Ft. 5 In. x 4 Ft............. 690.00
Kuba, Diamond Medallions, Octagons, Leaves, Ivory Border, Navy Field, 68 x 42 In. .. 287.00
Kuba, Geometric Elements On Brown Ground, 4 Ft. 2 In. x 6 Ft. 9 In........................ 275.00
Kuba, Hooked Diamonds, Royal Blue Field, 6 x 3 Ft.. 1092.00
Kuba, Rows Of Carnation Blossoms, Navy Field, Rose Border, 57 x 31 In................. 747.00
Kuba, Tan Ground, Multiple Borders, Red, Green, Blue, 3 Ft. 4 1/2 In. x 4 Ft. 11 1/2 In. 1375.00
Kurd, Birds, Blue & Red Ground, 4 Ft. 3 In. x 6 Ft. 1 In.. 550.00
Kurd, Column Of 9 Memling Guls, Navy Blue Field, Ivory Border, 132 x 44 In. 517.00
Kurd, Floral Design, 7 Ft. 9 In. x 4 Ft. 4 In.. 825.00
Kurd, Geometric Medallion On Brown Field, 3 Ft. 6 In. x 5 Ft. 9 In........................... 193.00
Kurd, Herati Design, Midnight Blue Field, Flower Head Border, 12 x 4 Ft................. 374.00
Kurd, Oval Medallion, Boteh, Floral Motifs, Blue Field, Ivory Border, 10 x 6 Ft. 805.00
Lenkoran, Calyx Medallions, Dark Brown Field, 8 Ft. 8 In. x 4 Ft. 3 In..................... 1380.00
Lesghi, Geometric Design, Ivory & Tan Ground, 3 Ft. 6 In. x 4 Ft. 8 In..................... 115.00
Lilihan, Floral Sprays, Rust-Red Field, 10 Ft. 9 In. x 7 Ft. 6 In................................. 805.00
Lilihan, Herati Style Pattern, Gold Field, 6 Ft. 9 In. x 4 Ft. 3 In................................ 862.00
Lilihan, Paisley, Floral & Foliate, Blue Ground, 4 Ft. 2 In. x 6 Ft. 3 In..................... 900.00
Luri, Columns, Stylized Plants, Midnight Blue Field, Ivory Border, 84 x 46 In. 402.00
Luri, Hexagonal Medallions, Midnight Blue Field, 7 Ft. x 6 Ft. 4 In......................... 460.00
Luri, Polychrome Latch Hooked Diamonds, 9 Ft. 8 In. x 4 Ft.................................. 2588.00
Mahal, Diamond Medallion, Ivory Spandrels, Navy Field, Floral Border, 78 x 54 In. 747.00
Mahal, Diamond Medallion, Spandrels, Midnight Blue Field, Red Border, 79 x 50 In. .. 575.00
Mahal, Floral Design, Red Ground, 10 Ft. 6 In. x 7 Ft. 6 In..................................... 6500.00
Mahal, Floral Medallion, Red Field, Blue Border, 12 Ft. x 8 Ft. 9 In.......................... 690.00
Mahal, Multiple Gordes, Central Geometric Diamond Design, 2 Ft. 9 In. x 5 Ft. 3 In. ... 77.00
Mahal, Overall Palmettes, Rosettes, Vines, Red Field, 11 Ft. 8 In. x 9 Ft. 6 In.......... 2990.00
Mahal, Overall Stylized Herati Design, c.1900, 6 Ft. x 3 Ft. 11 In........................... 1725.00
Mahal, Palmettes, Medallions, Floral Motifs, Red Field, Blue Border, 144 x 112 In. 2415.00
Makri, 2 Elongated Panels, Diamond Border, 19th Century, 50 x 36 In...................... 172.00
Malayer, Geometric Design, Orange-Red Ground, 4 Ft. 4 In. x 6 Ft. 5 In.................... 230.00
Malayer, Multicolored Floral, Geometric, Red Ground, 4 Ft. 11 In. x 5 Ft. 8 In.......... 880.00
Malayer, Orange-Red Ground, 4 Ft. 4 In. x 6 Ft. 5 In... 230.00
Marasali, Prayer, Row, Serrated Boteh, Dark Blue Field, Ivory Border, 58 x 48 In........ 1035.00
Melas, Prayer, Floral, Ivory Spandrels, Apricot Border, Palmettes, 57 x 44 In. 632.00
Needlepoint, Floral Bouquet Within Floral Border, English, 8 Ft. 4 In. x 4 Ft. 3680.00
Needlepoint, Floral Bouquet, Blossom & Leaf Border, 1970, 56 x 43 In....................... 977.00
Needlepoint, Floral Filled Cartouches, 3 Ft. 3 In. x 3 Ft. 3 In................................... 3162.00
Needlepoint, Floral Trellis, Shell-Filled Border, France, 7 Ft. x 2 Ft. 8 In. 2875.00
Needlepoint, Overall Design, Floral Bouquets, French, 10 Ft. 3 In. x 6 Ft.................. 4600.00
New England, Reed Stitch, Flower Filled Bowl, Wool, 19th Century, 57 x 34 In. 6900.00
Ning-Hsia, Floral Roundels, Peony Blossoms, Butterflies, 7 Ft. 8 In. x 5 Ft............... 4600.00
Oriental, 3 Central Stars, Red Field, Blue, Green & Tan Border, 28 x 56 In. 330.00
Oriental, Floral, Vine, Blue, Red & Ivory, On Red, Signature In Border, 10 x 13 Ft. 2750.00
Oriental Style, Olive & Salmon, Ivory Ground, 6 x 9 Ft... 82.00
Oushak, Central Melon Medallion, Palmette Border, c.1900, 7 x 4 Ft. 977.00
Oushak, Overall Floral Vinery, Pale Rose Field, c.1900, 13 x 10 Ft........................... 4312.00
Perpedil, Ram's Horn Design, Ivory Field, Wine Glass Border, 5 Ft. x 4 Ft. 2 In. 2185.00
Persian, 3 Stacked Diamonds, Animal Motifs, Blue Field, 7 Ft. 3 In. x 4 Ft. 10 In. 688.00
Persian, Cream Ground, Stylized Geometric Florals, Pastels, 9 x 12 Ft. 798.00
Persian, Diamond Medallion, Anchor, Bird Motif, On Red, Ivory Border, 62 x 42 In. .. 431.00
Persian, Ivory Ground, Animals & Birds, 5 Ft. 8 In. x 8 Ft. 10 In............................... 908.00
Persian, Mina Khani Floral Lattice, Red Field, Abrashed Border, 82 x 48 In................. 460.00

Persian, Multicolored Floral Design, Cranberry Field, 4 Ft. 3 In. x 6 Ft. 8 In. 605.00
Persian, Ornamental Borders, Cut Corners, 3 Ft. 4 In. x 4 Ft. 8 In. 825.00
Persian, Overall Palmettes, Multiple Border, c.1900, 13 Ft. 9 In. x 11 Ft. 6 In. 9775.00
Persian, Runner, Floral Design, On Blue, Salmon Rose Border, 2 Ft. 6 In. x 10 Ft. 275.00
Qashgai Kilim, Red, Blue, Green & Cream Diamonds, Brown Field, 5 x 8 Ft. 220.00
Saraband, Allover Boteh Design, Navy Field, 6 Ft. 6 In. x 8 Ft. 374.00
Sarouk, 4 Cypress Trees, Flowers, Palmette Border, 11 Ft. 8 In. x 9 Ft. 2 In. 4888.00
Sarouk, Blue Floral Sprays, Burgundy Field, 14 Ft. 8 In. x 10 Ft. 8 In. 2645.00
Sarouk, Blue Medallion On Cream Field, 6 Ft. 5 In. x 4 Ft. 6900.00
Sarouk, Broken Border At Corners, 6 Ft. 2 In. x 4 Ft. 4 In. 633.00
Sarouk, Diamond Medallion, Florals, West Persia, c.1940, 5 Ft. x 3 Ft. 4 In. 518.00
Sarouk, Floral Sprays, Blue Field, 14 Ft. 4 In. x 10 Ft. 4 In. 9775.00
Sarouk, Floral Sprays, Midnight Blue Field, 11 Ft. 2 In. x 8 Ft. 9 In. 3450.00
Sarouk, Floral Sprays, Rose Field, Gold & Tan Border, 4 Ft. 2 In. x 3 Ft. 5 In. 403.00
Sarouk, Floral Sprays, Rose Field, Palmette Border, 16 Ft. 4 In. x 12 Ft. 8 In. 2875.00
Sarouk, Floral Sprays, Rust-Red Field, 12 Ft. x 9 Ft. 2 In. 2070.00
Sarouk, Geometric & Floral, Red Ground, 2 Ft. 5 In. x 4 Ft. 10 In. 330.00
Sarouk, Medallion, 5 Ft. 1 In. x 2 Ft. 7 In. 800.00
Sarouk, Multicolored Geometric, Maroon Ground, 2 Ft. 1 In. x 4 Ft. 1 In. 495.00
Sarouk, Pictorial, Equestrians In Landscape, 7 Ft. x 4 Ft. 4 In. 3162.00
Sarouk, Red Ground, 3 Ft. 2 In. x 4 Ft. 10 In. 165.00
Sarouk, Runner, 11 Ft. 8 In. x 2 Ft. 10 In. 1540.00
Saryk, 5 Columns Of Guls, Rust Field, 8 Ft. 6 In. x 7 Ft. 4 In. 1150.00
Savonnerie, Bold Blossoms, Ribbon Border, c.1900, 6 Ft. 5 In. x 2 Ft. 9 In. 2875.00
Savonnerie, Golden Scrollwork & Acanthus, Slate Blue Border, 8 x 5 Ft. 5750.00
Savonnerie, Pale Blue & Cream Damask Field, Floral, 1900, 6 Ft. 8 In. x 3 Ft. 2300.00
Senneh, Medallion Within Crimson Medallion, 6 Ft. 11 In. x 4 Ft. 2 In. 8050.00
Senneh, Radiating Medallions, Blue Field, 6 Ft. 8 In. x 4 Ft. 4 In. 8625.00
Shiraz, Geometric, Orange Ground, 3 Ft. 4 In. x 6 Ft. 4 In. 165.00
Shirvan, 2 Hexagonal Medallions, Flower Heads, Blue Field, 7 Ft. x 3 Ft. 9 In. 805.00
Shirvan, 2 Serrated Diamond Medallions, Ivory Pinwheel Border, 57 x 44 In. 805.00
Shirvan, 3 Diamond Medallions, Navy Field, Wineglass Border, 56 x 39 In. 172.00
Shirvan, 3 Lesghi Stars, Red Field, Ivory Crab Border, 4 Ft. 9 In. x 3 Ft. 6 In. 1035.00
Shirvan, 4 Flower Heads, Blue Field, Wine-Cup Border, 19th Century, 58 x 38 In. 374.00
Shirvan, Blue Ground, Multiple Border, Tan, Rust, Green, 3 Ft. 7 In. x 5 Ft. 1650.00
Shirvan, Diamond Lattice, Octagons, Diamonds, Arrowhead Border, 64 x 40 In. 230.00
Shirvan, Grid, Branching Plants, Blue, Red, Gold, Meander Border, 60 x 44 In. 1495.00
Shirvan, Horizontal Bands, Geometric Motifs, Bar Border, 4 Ft. x 3 Ft. 10 In. 920.00
Shirvan, Ivory Octagons, Geometrics, Red, Gold, Blue-Green, On Blue, 57 x 42 In. 10353.00
Shirvan, Octagonal Medallions, Geometric Motifs, Tan Field, 68 x 48 In. 690.00
Shirvan, Octagonal Medallions, Motifs, Navy Field, Red Border, 6 Ft. x 3 Ft. 6 In. 316.00
Shirvan, Octagons, Hexagons, Sky Blue Field, S Motif Border, 6 Ft. x 3 Ft. 10 In. 201.00
Shirvan, Tan Ground, Red & Brown Design, 3 Ft. 3 In. x 4 Ft. 8 In. 743.00
Soumak, 2 Diamond Medallions, Rust Field, Black Border, 13 Ft. x 8 Ft. 8 In. 2070.00
Soumak, 4-Hooked Diamond Medallions, Blue Field, Ivory Border, 102 x 51 In. 1495.00
Sultanbad, Navy, Flowers, Vines, Turtle Border, 12 Ft. 5 In. x 16 Ft. 5 In. 4510.00
Tabriz, Floral Medallion, Floral Spandrels, Floral Border, 5 Ft. 4 In. x 4 Ft. 2 In. 3738.00
Tabriz, Hanging Lanterns, 4 Ft. 1 In. x 6 Ft. 1 In. 165.00
Tabriz, Hunt Pattern, Wool, Oriental, Blue, Green, Brown, Ivory, Handmade, 8 x 10 Ft. 907.00
Tabriz, Maroon Ground, Cobalt Blue & Seafoam Borders, 9 x 12 Ft. 660.00
Tabriz, Open Madder Field, Floral Medallion, c.1910, 5 Ft. 4 In. x 3 Ft. 11 In. 1035.00
Tabriz, Runner, Brick, Multicolored Borders, Flower & Bird, 2 Ft. 8 In. x 10 Ft. 550.00
Tabriz, Scalloped Cruciform Medallion & Palmettes, Blue Field, 13 x 10 Ft. 1495.00
Talish, Blossoms Within Ivory Rosette, c.1875, 7 Ft. 9 In. x 3 Ft. 4 In. 1955.00
Teheran, Overall Floral Trellis, Bird & Animal Border, c.1900, 7 x 5 Ft. 4600.00
Tekke, 4 Rows Of Guls, Serrated Diamond End Panels, 9 Ft. 11 In. x 7 Ft. 5 In. 8338.00
Tekke, 5 Columns Of Guls, Rust Field, 8 Ft. 6 In. x 6 Ft. 10 In. 1265.00
Tekke Ensi, Quartered Garden Design, Rust Field, 4 Ft. 6 In. x 4 Ft. 1380.00
Tibetan, Overall Peony Trellis Within Mazework Border, 8 Ft. 5 In. x 4 Ft. 7 In. 3738.00
Timurid, Prayer, Tree Of Life, Navy Field, Matching Hand Panels, 56 In. x 45 In. 374.00
Turkoman, Blue & Ivory, Brick Red Field, 3 Ft. 4 In. x 3 Ft. 2 In. 275.00
Turkoman, Blue, Ivory, Brick Red Field, 3 Ft. 5 In. x 3 Ft. 2 In. 187.00
Turkoman, Chuval, 16 Guls, Light Rust Field, 3 x 2 Ft. 460.00

Turkoman Pattern, Ivory Ground, Handmade, Wool, 3 Ft. 6 In. x 5 Ft.	55.00
Ushak, 4 Vases Of Flowers, Rose Field, 11 Ft. 6 In. x 9 Ft..	920.00
Woven, Solid Colors, Wool, Rastetters Woolen Mill, Ohio, 9 x 12 Ft............................	770.00

RUMRILL Pottery was designed by George Rumrill of Little Rock, Arkansas. From 1933 to 1938, it was produced by the Red Wing Pottery of Red Wing, Minnesota. In 1938, production was transferred to the Shawnee Pottery in Zanesville, Ohio. Production ceased in the 1940s.

Jug, Orange Ball, Underplate, No. 547	28.00
Planter, Double Swans, White	45.00
Vase, Fish Handle, 10 1/2 In.	40.00
Vase, Loving Cup Style	45.00

RUSKIN is a British art pottery of the twentieth century. The Ruskin Pottery was started by William Howson Taylor and his name was used as the mark until about 1899. The factory, at West Smethwick, Birmingham, England, stopped making new pieces in 1933 but continued to glaze and sell the remaining wares until 1935. The art pottery is noted for its exceptional glazes.

Bowl, Speckled Beige & Ivory Glaze, Footed, Die Stamped, 2 x 5 In.	55.00
Inkwell, Mauve Flambe Glaze, Round, Oval Mark, 2 x 3 In.	193.00
Vase, Green Dripping, Gunmetal Mottled Glaze, Flat Shoulders, Oval Mark, 8 x 4 In. ...	220.00
Vase, Orange Lustre, 1913, 10 In.	550.00
Vase, Smooth Lustered Cobalt Blue Glaze, Flat Shoulders, Oval Mark, 1905, 6 In.	83.00

RUSSEL WRIGHT designed dinnerwares in modern shapes for many companies. Iroquois China Company, Harker China Company, Steubenville Pottery, and Justin Tharaud and Sons made dishes marked *Russel Wright*. The Steubenville wares, first made in 1938, are the most common today. Wright was a designer of domestic and industrial wares, including furniture, aluminum, radios, interiors, and glassware. Dinnerwares and other pieces by Wright are listed here. For more information, see *Kovels' Depression Glass & American Dinnerware Price List.*

Bowl, American Modern, Berry, Gray	7.00
Bowl, Cereal, Iroquois, Avocado, 5 In..	5.00
Bowl, Cereal, Iroquois, Cover, Ice Blue...	14.00
Bowl, Cereal, Iroquois, Pink, 5 In...|	6.00
Bowl, Divided, Iroquois, Pink, 10 In..	30.00
Bowl, Fruit, Iroquois, Ice Blue, 5 3/4 In...	3.00
Bowl, Iroquois, Divided, Ice Blue, 10 In.	18.00
Bowl, Iroquois, Ice Blue, 8 In. .... 12.00 to 15.00
Bowl, Iroquois, Pink, 5 In.	6.00
Bowl, Salad, Parsley Green, 10 In...	28.00
Bowl, Vegetable, American Modern, Chutney	25.00
Bowl, Vegetable, American Modern, Divided, Chutney	115.00
Bowl, Vegetable, Divided, Ripe Apricot..	40.00
Bowl, Vegetable, Iroquois, Divided, Avocado...	14.00
Bowl, Vegetable, Iroquois, Divided, Cover, Ice Blue	35.00
Butter, Casual, Pink	65.00
Butter, Casual, White	75.00
Butter, Iroquois, Half Pound, Pink..	52.00
Carafe, American Modern, Bean Brown	225.00
Carafe, Casual, Brown...	125.00
Carafe, Coral	120.00
Carafe, Ice Blue.. 95.00 to 110.00
Carafe, Iroquois, Ice Blue	115.00
Carafe, Pink	95.00
Carafe, Seafoam	120.00
Casserole, American Modern, Cantaloupe	250.00
Casserole, American Modern, Cover, Coral	45.00
Casserole, Cover, American Modern, Chutney..	45.00
Casserole, Cover, Iroquois, Avocado, 2 Qt..	35.00

Casserole, Cover, Iroquois, Pink, 4 Qt.	55.00
Casserole, Iroquois, Ice Blue, 4 Qt.	40.00
Celery, American Modern, Gray, 13 In.	24.00
Celery, American Modern, Seafoam	12.00
Celery, American Modern, White	35.00
Chop Plate, Iroquois, Ripe Apricot, 13 In.	22.00
Clock, General Electric, Wall	60.00
Coaster Ashtray, American Modern, Chartreuse	12.00
Coffee Bottle, Sterling Ivy, Individual	85.00
Coffeepot, American Modern, Chartreuse, After Dinner	65.00
Coffeepot, Casual, Ice Blue, After Dinner	135.00
Cup & Saucer, Iroquois, Avocado	5.00 to 9.00
Cup & Saucer, Iroquois, Ice Blue	6.00
Cup & Saucer, Iroquois, Pink	9.00
Cup & Saucer, Theme Informal	100.00
Cup Plate, American Modern, Hostess, Cedar Green	65.00
Dish, Wooden, Oceana, Spiral, Label, Signed, 11 In.	715.00
Lazy Susan, Wooden, Oceana	750.00
Pitcher, American Modern, Coral	65.00 to 85.00
Pitcher, American Modern, Pink, Restyled	350.00
Pitcher, Water, American Modern, Coral	68.00
Plate, American Modern, Gray, 6 1/2 In.	4.00
Plate, American Modern, Gray, 8 In.	9.00
Plate, Iroquois, Avocado, 6 1/2 In.	2.00
Plate, Iroquois, Avocado, 9 In.	5.00
Plate, Iroquois, Avocado, 10 In.	8.00
Plate, Iroquois, Cantaloupe, 10 In.	16.00
Plate, Iroquois, Lettuce Green, 10 In.	8.00
Plate, Iroquois, Pink, 6 1/2 In.	1.00
Plate, Iroquois, Pink, 10 In.	6.00
Plate, Salad, American Modern, Coral, 8 In.	3.00
Platter, Iroquois, Avocado, 14 In.	14.00 to 16.00
Platter, Iroquois, Brown, 12 1/2 In.	15.00
Platter, Iroquois, Pink, 14 1/2 In.	18.00 to 22.00
Platter, Sterling, Yellow, 7 1/2 In.	18.00
Relish, American Modern, Rosette, Gray	125.00
Salt & Pepper, American Modern, Gray	12.00
Salt & Pepper, Iroquois, Ice Blue, Stacking	8.00
Salt & Pepper, Iroquois, Parsley, Stacking	14.00
Salt & Pepper, Iroquois, Pink, Stacking	8.00
Saucer, American Modern, Coral	2.00
Soup, Gumbo, Casual, Pink	35.00
Soup, Lug, American Modern, Gray	15.00
Stack Set, American Modern, Cedar Green, 3 Piece	125.00
Sugar & Creamer, Iroquois, Pink, Stacking	15.00 to 25.00
Teapot, American Modern, Coral	85.00
Teapot, Casual, Lettuce Green	85.00
Torchere, Spun Aluminum, Lucite Trim, c.1940, 67 In., Pair	990.00
Torchere, Spun Aluminum, Wrapped Rope Trim, c.1940, 65 In., Pair	935.00
Tumbler, Iced Tea, Eclipse	15.00
Vase, Pillow, Flattened Form, Mottled Gray Glaze, 8 x 10 In.	520.00
Vegetable, American Modern, Divided, Chartreuse	45.00
Vegetable, Open, Iroquois, Nutmeg, 10 In.	16.00

SABINO glass was made in the 1920s and 1930s in Paris, France. Founded by Marius-Ernest Sabino (1878–1961), the firm was noted for Art Deco lamps, vases, figurines, and animals in clear, colored, and opalescent glass. Production stopped during World War II but resumed in the 1960s with the manufacture of nude figurines and small opalescent glass animals. The new pieces are a slightly different color and can be recognized.

Sabino
France

Figurine, Nude Woman With Doves, 6 1/2 In.	137.00
Figurine, Owl, Signed	75.00
Night-Light, 2 Nude Maidens, Scarf Draped, c.1930, 11 3/4 In.	203.00

Vase, Bumblebees Over Art Deco Designs, Signed, 8 In. 465.00
Vase, Flared Trumpet Form, Art Deco Design, Signed, 6 In. 345.00

SALOPIAN ware was made by the Caughley factory of England during the eighteenth century. The early pieces were blue and white with some colored decorations. Another ware referred to as *Salopian* is a late nineteenth-century tableware decorated with color transfers.

Salopian

Basin, c.1774, 12 3/4 In.. 385.00
Cup & Saucer, Bird, Miniature 550.00
Eye Bath, Blue & White, Lozenge-Shaped Bowl, Baluster Stem, c.1790, 2 1/16 In. 1150.00
Mustard, Cover, 3 Flowers, Blue & White, c.1780, 3 13/16 In. 230.00
Plate, c.1774, 8 In., Pair... 220.00

SALT AND PEPPER SHAKERS in matched sets were first used in the nineteenth century. Collectors are primarily interested in figural examples made after World War I. *Huggers* are pairs of shakers which appear to embrace each other. Many salt and pepper shakers are listed in other categories and can be located through the index at the back of this book.

Andy & Miranda, Ceramic, 1958.. 225.00
Aunt Jemima, Pearl China... 98.00
Aunt Jemima, Plastic, F & F 35.00
Aunt Jemima & Uncle Mose, 3 1/2 In.. 40.00
Aunt Jemima & Uncle Mose, 5 1/2 In.. 60.00
Aunt Jemima & Uncle Mose, F & F, Small .... 35.00 to 45.00
Aunt Jemima & Uncle Mose, Plastic, Small 30.00
Ball Perfect Mason Jar, Blue & White, Aluminum Screw Cap, Box 175.00
Bear, Playing Music, Japan... 7.00
Bears, Huggers, Van Tellingen .... 85.00 to 95.00
Bears, Yellowstone, Chalkware, 1930s 15.00
Beer Bottle, Falstaff.. 30.00
Beer Bottles, Miniature, Schlitz, Metal Tops, 1940s 20.00
Black Boy, Holding Watermelons 100.00
Black Boy & Watermelon, Japan 75.00
Black Cat, Shafford, 3 3/4 In. 24.00
Black Child, Washtub.. 25.00
Black Girl & Boy, Legs Up, Arms Out To Front, Ceramic 45.00
Blatz Beer 25.00
Blowfish, Treasure Craft... 8.00
Boy & Dog, Huggers, Van Tellingen .... 85.00 to 125.00
Boy & Dog, White, Van Tellingen 65.00
Bride & Groom, On Bench 10.00
Budman, Box .... 10.00 to 12.00
Budweiser, Bud Man, Old Style.. 275.00
Bust, Women, Black Top Hats, White Ruffled Cowl, Red Shawl, Blue Dress, 3 In. 16.00
Cat, Dressed As Person, Japan 12.00
Cat & Milk 55.00
Charlie Tuna 35.00
Chicks In Nest, Vallona Starr 35.00
Churn, Red, Gold Trim, Regal China .... 35.00 to 40.00
Cool Joe 45.00
Covered Wagon, Japan.. 8.00
Cowboy, Bronco.. 20.00
Cranberry Glass, White Opalescent Dots, Gargoyle Shape 58.00
Dairy Queen, Figural, Ceramic 189.00
Dog, Occupied Japan 12.00
Dog & Cat, Ken-L-Ration... 15.00
Donald Duck & Ludwig Von Duck 35.00
Donkey, Japan... 12.00
Donkey & Cart 55.00
Ducks, Huggers, Van Tellingen... 20.00 to 40.00
Dumbo 25.00
Dutch Boy & Girl, Huggers, Van Tellingen .... 35.00 to 45.00
Elsie, Holding Calf, Borden Co. 120.00

Flintstone Kids, Vandor	85.00
Funfetti	12.00
Gas Pump, Cities Service, 1950s	65.00
Gas Pump, Esso	20.00
Gas Pump, Phillips 66	40.00
Gas Pump, Standard Red Crown, 1950s	95.00
George & Martha Washington	15.00
German Bakers, Bisque	38.00
Goldilocks, Royal China	250.00
Goofy & Car, 1930s	195.00
Goose, With Egg	7.00
Green Giant Sprout	39.00
Greyhound Bus, Metal, Die Cast	40.00
Gun & Holster, Vandor	17.00
Halloween Ghost, Holding Pumpkin	8.00
Happy Bull	55.00
Harley-Davidson	75.00
Humpty Dumpty	65.00
Humpty Dumpty, Plastic, Red	60.00
Humpty Dumpty, Purinton	350.00
Humpty Dumpty, Regal China	110.00 to 150.00
Indian & Teepee, Vallona Starr	45.00
John F. Kennedy, Rocking Chair	45.00
Jonah & Whale, Huggers, Van Tellingen	95.00 to 115.00
Ken-L-Ration, Plastic	25.00
Keystone Cop, Twin Winton	80.00
Kitten, Winking, Enesco	20.00
Kittens, In Trousers, Kliban	275.00
Laurel & Hardy, Tray, Beswick	150.00
Little Bopeep	40.00
Looney Tunes, Box	20.00
Love Bugs, Huggers, Black, Bendel	70.00
Love Bugs, Huggers, Green, Bendel	65.00
Lovebirds, Bendel	45.00
Lulu & Tubby	125.00
Maggie & Jiggs, Japan	80.00 to 125.00
Magic Chef, Ceramic	90.00
Mammy, Polka Dot, Negatha	50.00
Mammy & Butler	125.00
Mammy & Chef	150.00
Mammy & Chef, Brayton, Red & Blue	115.00
Mammy & Rastus, Painted, Chase, Large	245.00
Mammy & Winking Chef	75.00
Man In The Moon, Stacking	102.00
Mary & Lamb	40.00
Mermaid & Sailor, Huggers, Van Tellingen	125.00 to 155.00
Monk, Kreiss	35.00
Moon Mullins & Kayo	35.00
Moon Mullins & Kayo, Chalkware	25.00
Mother Goose, Twin Winton	85.00
Nikolai Vodka	65.00
Noritake Buildings, On Tray, Delaware Water Gap	65.00
Old MacDonald & Feed Sack, Regal China	225.00
Old MacDonald & Girlfriend, Regal China	85.00
Old McDonald, Boy & Girl, Regal China	70.00
Old McDonald, Regal China	40.00
Orange, Wooden Crate	15.00
Owl & Pussycat In Boat	5000.00
Palm Tree, Purinton	400.00
Park Bench & Lamppost	55.00
Peek-A-Boo, Love Bug, Van Tellingen	175.00
Peek-A-Boo, Rabbit, Van Tellingen	175.00 to 195.00
Peek-A-Boo, Van Tellingen, Small	120.00

Pig, Regal China 195.00
Pigs, Huggers, Bendel 450.00
Pillsbury Doughboy, Range, Box 18.00
Pomeroy & Prunella, Enesco 65.00
Poodle, Japan 8.00
Queen City Brewing Co., Cumberland, Md., 7 In........................... 70.00
Raggedy Ann & Andy, Terrace 155.00
Rocket, World War II, Red, White & Blue 35.00
Rooster, Metlox 30.00
Royal Oak, Glossy Rubina 165.00
Salty & Peppy, Pearl China, Large 250.00
Santa Claus, Germany 26.00
Siam Boy & Girl, Nodder 45.00
Skiing Couple, Sorcha Boru 18.00
Skunk .... 8.00 to 40.00
Smokey The Bear 125.00
Sniffles The Mouse, Shaw Pottery, 1940, Pair............................... 195.00
Snow White & Dopey 350.00
Snowman & Snowwoman 25.00
Snuffy Smith & Brother, Japan, 3 3/4 In. 95.00
Stove & Icebox 55.00
Strawberry Shortcake 8.00
Sylvester & Tweety 15.00
Tappan Chef 20.00
Tulip, Pink, Brown Rubber Stopper 12.00
Turkey, Japan 8.00
Washing Machines, Westinghouse, Plastic 10.00
Willie & Millie 8.00
Winnie The Pooh & Rabbit 280.00
Witch, Polkadot, F & F... 150.00

SALT GLAZE has a grayish white surface with a texture like an orange peel. It is a method of decoration that has been used since the eighteenth century. Salt-glazed pieces are still being made.

Churn, Galesburg Pottery Co., 5 Gal. 550.00
Coffeepot, Cover, Pear Shape, Floral Bouquet, Sprigs, Staffordshire, c.1760, 8 In........ 920.00
Crock, Cobalt Blue 2, 4 Lines, 2 Gal. 27.50
Crock, Cobalt Blue Factory Name & Wreath, Dark Gray 70.00
Crock, J.A. & C.W. Underwood, Fort Edward, N.Y., Cobalt Blue Floral, 1 1/2 Gal....... 250.00
Cuspidor, Woman's 105.00
Dish, Vegetable, Cover, Tray, 14 In. 1650.00
Jug, Milk, Pear Shape, S-Scroll Handle, Staffordshire, 2 3/16 In. ... 402.00
Jug, Water, Cobalt Blue Design, F.H. Cowden 800.00
Mug, Child's, Ring Turnings, Reeded Strap Handle, Staffordshire, 2 3/16 In. 805.00
Pitcher, Hunt Scene 995.00
Plate, Reticulated Panels, Molded Surface Design, 11 7/8 In. 440.00
Puzzle Jug, Baluster Shape, Ring-Turned Neck, Shoulder & Foot, England, c.1743 ...... 1438.00
Salt Cellar, Man Wearing Curly Wig, Frock Coat, Germany, 7 5/8 In. 1955.00
Teapot, Cover, Enameled, King Of Prussia, Staffordshire, c.1760, 4 3/8 In. 575.00
Teapot, Fruiting Grapevines Issuing From Handle, Staffordshire, c.1740, 4 1/8 In. 1495.00
Vase, Wall, Cornucopia, Naked Boy Amid Vines, Staffordshire, 9 In., Pair 2185.00

SAMPLERS were made in America from the early 1700s. The best examples were made from 1790 to 1840. Long, narrow samplers are usually older than square ones. Early samplers just had stitching or alphabets. The later examples had numerals, borders, and pictorial decorations. Those with mottoes are mid-Victorian. A revival of interest in the 1930s produced simpler samplers, usually with mottoes.

ABC, Floral, Lovina Bixby, Age 11, 1829 .... 625.00
Adam & Eve, Apple Tree, Serpent, Silk On Homespun, Cord Ties, Frame, 6 x 5 In. 475.00
Adam & Eve, Serpent, Ann Symes, Aged 8 Years, 1831, Frame, 19 x 15 3/4 In. 550.00
Alphabet, Baskets, Mary Hawken, Allentown, 1857, 8 1/2 x 5 1/2 In...... 150.00

Alphabet, Eleanor Potter, Lincoln Maine, April, 1823 .... 595.00
Alphabet, Needlepoint, Barbara Richter 1861, Sewn To Card, Frame, 19 1/2 x 31 In. 525.00
Alphabet, Numbers, Basket Of Flowers, Birds, Dog, Red Border, Silk, Frame, 6 x 5 In. 990.00
Alphabet, Numbers, Inscription, Becca Bixby, Age 10, Boxford, Mass, 1791, 11 x 7 In. 805.00
Alphabet, Red Silk, Homespun, Gilt Frame, 7 1/4 x 8 3/4 In. 220.00
Alphabet, Verse, Charlotte P. Smith, Born Dec. 23, 1811, 12 1/2 x 8 In. 230.00
Alphabet, Verse, Urn With Flowers, Sarah Ann Tyson, 1833, 18 x 20 In. 495.00
Alphabet, Verses, Inscription, Philinda Burges, Age 12, 1831, 17 x 13 In. 690.00
Alphabet & Numbers, Elizabeth Wadsworth, Frame, 10 x 10 In. 140.00
Alphabet & Numbers, Martha Guite, 1882, Frame, 9 x 8 In. 135.00
Alphabet & Verse, Garden Scene, Jean Burrell, 17 1/2 x 12 3/4 In. 247.00
Alphabet & Verse, Maria Gurson, June 18, 1823, Silk On Linen, Frame, 14 x 9 1/2 In. 360.00
Alphabets, Church, Dog, House, Eliza Jane Houston, 7 Years, Ohio, 1828, 19 x 21 In. 3905.00
Alphabets, Compote Of Flowers, Birds, Silk Thread On Linen, 19th Century, 9 x 9 In. 287.00
Alphabets, Eliza Ann Green, 1841, Frame, 21 3/4 x 22 1/4 In. 775.00
Alphabets, Gingerbread, Apple Trees, Verse, Emma Vincent, Age 9 Yrs., 1872, 10 In. 300.00
Alphabets, House, Nancy Moncrief, 1836, Silk On Linen, Ohio, Frame, 26 x 19 In. 330.00
Alphabets & Flowers, Mary Dannelis, August, 1835, Linen, Frame, 19 1/4 x 18 In. 302.00
Alphabets & Numbers, Silk On Homespun, Mary Lewington, 1812, Frame, 15 x 10 In. 467.00
Alphabets & Verse, Silk On Linen, Lavina L. Wise, Age 9, 1834, Frame, 22 x 22 In. .. 1100.00
Animals, Ann Elizabeth Beirer, 1833, 16 1/2 x 21 In. 385.00
Animals & Birds, Art Deco Image Of Woman, WPA, Frame, 26 x 20 In., Pr. 255.00
Basket Of Flowers, Trees, Wrought By A. Welch, Frame, 12 x 8 1/2 In. 345.00
Birds, Flowers, Margaret Lind, 13th Year, 1841, Silk & Wool, Frame, 17 x 9 1/2 In. ... 445.00
Birds, Trees, Mary Ann Ashelford, 1843, 14 x 16 In. 495.00
Border, Deerfield School Petticoat, Embroidered, Lydia Safford, 1793, 96 In. 2645.00
Cross-Stitched, Hannah Lippincott, 1785, Frame, 8 x 16 In. 520.00
Cross-Stitched, Margret Hains, Aged 7 Years, 2 Months, 12 Days, 7 1/2 x 9 1/2 In. 220.00
Crowns, Flowers, Sarah Jane Charlton, 12 Years, 1843, Frame, 19 1/2 x 18 3/4 In. 660.00
Deer Amid Flowers, Anna Maria Champerlain, 1846, 8 1/2 x 8 1/2 In. 550.00
Drawing, J.W. Champney, Dated & Signed, 1874, Frame, 5 x 7 In. 395.00
English Is My Nation, Christ Is My Salvation, Maracia Turner, Frame, 23 x 10 In. 1550.00
Family Record, Collins Family, 1784, Gilt Frame, 17 3/4 x 17 3/4 In. 175.00
Family Record, Elizabeth Leek's Work, Aged 10 Years, 16 x 17 In. 440.00
Family Records, Wrought By Eliza A. Bryant, Aug. 1829, Frame, 22 x 19 3/8 In. 2695.00
Family Register, Births, Abigail F. Breed, Age 15, 1812, 25 1/2 x 25 1/2 In. 220.00
Floral, Sarah Ann Locock, Age 9 Years, Frame, 17 x 15 In. 990.00
Floral, Silk On Linen, Elizabeth Maria Robinson, 9 Years, 1824, Frame, 23 1/2 x 23 In. 885.00
Floral Border, Building, Eliza Wainwright, Aged 16, Frame, 17 1/2 x 18 1/2 In. 990.00
Floral Border, Verse, Mary A. Fairbairn Age 12, New York, 1836, Frame, 18 x 18 In. 2300.00

Sampler, Needlepoint, Farmhouse,
Farmer, Field, 1821, 13 x 15 In.

✦✦✦✦✦✦✦✦✦✦✦✦✦✦✦✦✦✦✦✦✦✦✦

Test a small piece of the fabric before you try this. To remove yellowing and stains from old textiles, soak them in dental cleaner and water mixed according to the directions on the package. Rinse several times.

✦✦✦✦✦✦✦✦✦✦✦✦✦✦✦✦✦✦✦✦✦✦✦

Floral Border, Wrought By Diana Paine, 1826, Frame, 17 3/8 x 18 1/2 In. 9800.00
Flowers, Brick House, Silk On Homespun Linen, Sarah Alice Devoe, 13 x 18 In. 2900.00
Flowers, Geometric, Rachel W. Wife, Wool, On Canvas, Frame, 25 3/4 x 20 3/4 In. 330.00
Flowers, Mary McCloud, Her Work, 1795, Silk On Linen, Frame, 13 3/4 x 12 In. 1450.00
House, Weeping Willow, Trust In Lord, Linen, Emily Ohrt, 1835, 6 x 9 In. 175.00
Hunter, Birds, Flowers, Verse, Mary C. Phillips, 1861, Frame, 15 x 22 In. 120.00
Lace Upper Section, Flowers & Alphabet Below, E.C. 1664, 29 x 6 1/2 In. 1650.00
Landscape, House, Mary L. Whittelsey, Aged 8 Years, 1809, 13 1/4 x 15 1/4 In. 2200.00
Needlepoint, Farmhouse, Abagail Knowlton, Age 12, 1821, 10 x 17 In. 2500.00
Needlepoint, Farmhouse, Farmer, Field, 1821, 13 x 15 In. ....*Illus* 2750.00
Silk On Homespun, Frances E. Stone, Black Frame, 10 x 11 In. 275.00
Silk On Linen, Abigail Treats, In 10th Year, 1819, Frame, 12 3/4 x 10 In. 220.00
Silk On Linen, All Red, T.E. Spalteholzin, 1819, Frame, 12 1/2 x 23 3/4 In. 275.00
Silk On Linen, Ann Lunn, Aged 6 Years, 1798, Frame, 12 3/4 x 11 In. 525.50
Silk On Linen, Anna Briggs, 1841, Gilt Frame, 4 x 9 3/4 In. 415.00
Silk On Linen, Berlin Inn, N.H., Berlin 1818, Frame, 27 x 29 1/2 In. 770.00
Silk On Linen, Betty Little, Finished May 22nd, 1814, Walnut Frame, 23 x 19 In. 775.00
Silk On Linen, Caroline Frances Kevill, July 8, 1841, Frame, 14 x 9 3/4 In. 300.00
Silk On Linen, Eliza Walker Kaatin, 12 Years, Born 1779, Frame, 10 3/8 x 8 3/8 In. 440.00
Silk On Linen, Elizabeth Brown In 12 Year Of Age 1814, Frame, 12 1/2 x 10 3/4 In. 250.00
Silk On Linen, Ellen Dowling, Oct. 24, 1940, Frame, 17 1/4 x 8 3/4 In. 250.00
Silk On Linen, Fait Par Anna Barset Aged De 15 Ans, 1844, Frame, 13 3/4 x 13 1/4 In. 220.00
Silk On Linen, Horizontal Lines, Rebekah Chaces, 9 Years, Frame, 8 3/8 x 7 In. 660.00
Silk On Linen, Lucy Wheelock Beaman, Aged 8 Years, 1811, 21 1/4 x 14 1/2 In. 550.00
Silk On Linen, Priscilla Blair's Work, Blue & Brown, 6 3/4 x 9 In. 165.00
Silk On Linen, Rosamond Lamb In The Year Of Our Lord 1799, 15 x 13 In. 1050.00
Silk On Linen, Roxanna Seward, Aged 10, Frame, 18 1/4 x 17 3/4 In. 2750.00
Silk On Linen, Sarah Willits, 1832, Frame, 10 x 19 1/4 In. 385.00
Silk On Linen, Vining Border, Elisabeth Thatcher, 1828, Frame, 12 x 10 In. 340.00
Silk On Linen Homespun, Eliza Hand, November 1812, Frame, 14 1/4 x 12 1/2 In. 715.00
Silk On Linen Homespun, Sally Blish, Age 13, 1826, Frame, 17 3/4 x 13 3/4 In. 600.00
Silk On Wool, 2 Figures, Turkey, Butterfly, Catherine Taylor, Frame, 9 1/2 x 9 1/2 In. . 550.00
Silk On Wool, Floral Border, Building Scene, Frame, 17 x 18 1/2 In. 3400.00
Silk Thread, Abigail Whiting, September AD 1821, 18 1/2 x 11 3/4 In. 1100.00
Silk Thread, House, Trees, Jessy Alexander, 1811, 11 x 8 1/4 In. 460.00
Stylized Floral, WPA, Frame, 26 x 20 In., Pair 110.00
Swag Tassels Border, Thankful Bright, 11 Th Year, 1819, 17 3/4 x 12 In. 1045.00
Ten Commandments, Catherine Chittenden, Ninth Year Of Age, 21 1/4 x 17 In. 247.00
The House May Be Wee, But The Welcome Big, 1930s, Frame, 10 x 12 In. 55.00
Urn With Flowers, Sarah Ann Tyson, 1833 .... 495.00
Urns, Trees, Deer, Frances Brown, 1841, 14 x 14 In. 795.00
Verse, Floral, House, Trees, Diana Paine Stockbridge, 1826, Frame, 17 3/8 x 18 1/2 In. 9800.00
Verse, Margaret Rimmington 1842, Frame, 16 1/2 x 12 1/2 In. 1150.00
Verse, Margaret Warnes, 14th Year Of Her Age September 14, 1822, 18 x 17 In. 1380.00
Vining Border, Lions, Birds, Dog, Nancy Maxey, Frame, 13 1/2 x 15 1/2 In. 690.00
Vining Border, Sundial & Verse, Inlaid Frame, 17 1/4 x 20 In. 3570.00
Wool On Canvas, Elizabeth Hohmann, 11 Years, 1862, Frame, 26 3/4 x 8 In. 1700.00
Wool On Canvas, Kunie G. Hohmann, July 16, 1862, Gilt Frame, 13 1/4 x 10 In. 770.00
Wool On Cotton, Mary Calvert's Work, Aged 64, 1895, Frame, 25 x 24 1/4 In. 45.00

SAMSON and Company, a French firm specializing in the reproduction of
collectible wares of many countries and periods, was founded in Paris in the
early nineteenth century. Chelsea, Meissen, Famille Verte, and Chinese
Export porcelain are some of the wares that have been reproduced by the
company. The firm uses a variety of marks on the reproductions. It is still in
operation.

Inkwell, Armorial Design, Brass Trim, Porcelain, Accessories, 4 x 5 In. 250.00
Mug, Oriental Style, Porcelain, 5 In. 165.00
Urn, Cover, Neoclassical, Geometric, Floral, Lowestoft, Chinese Mark, 16 In., Pair 805.00
Vase, Cover, Famille Rose, Armorial, 8 In. 195.00
Wine Cooler, Enameled Royal Arms Of England, Gilt Bands, 7 3/4 In. 520.00
Wine Cooler, Exotic Birds, Gilt Border, Ram's Head Handles, 7 In. 825.00

SAND BABIES were used as decorations on a line of children's dishes made by the Royal Bayreuth China Company. The children are playing at the seaside. Collectors use the names *Sand Babies* and *Beach Babies* interchangeably.

Match Holder, Hanging, Blue Mark, Royal Bayreuth 220.00

SANDWICH GLASS is any of the myriad types of glass made by the Boston and Sandwich Glass Works in Sandwich, Massachusetts, between 1825 and 1888. It is often very difficult to be sure whether a piece was really made at the Sandwich factory because so many types were made there and similar pieces were made at other glass factories. Additional pieces may be listed under Pressed Glass and in related categories.

Candlestick, Crucifix Form, White Opaque, 8 1/2 In., Pair 175.00
Candlestick, Dolphin, Clambroth & Blue, 10 1/2 In., Pair 2000.00
Candlestick, Hexagonal, Opalescent, Pressed, 9 1/4 In. 460.00
Candlestick, Loop & Petal, Pair 150.00
Candlestick, Loop & Petal, Vaseline, Flint, Pair 350.00
Candlestick, Opaque Light Blue, Wafer Joined, 2 Petals, Pair 1750.00
Celery Vase, Gothic Arch, Flint 65.00
Celery Vase, Pink Rim, Silver Plated Holder, 8 In. 115.00
Chamber Set, Cobalt, Paneled Pitcher, 2 1/2 In. 400.00
Cup Plate, Bigler, Amethyst, Pressed, 1835-1855, 6 1/8 In. 345.00
Cup Plate, Heart Border, Light Blue, Pressed, 3 3/4 In. 316.00
Decanter, Blown, Molded Sunburst, Clear, 1825-1835, 3 3/4 In. 290.00
Dish, Pekinese Cover, Diamond & Stippled Base 800.00
Epergne, Pink Rim, Clear & Frosted, Cut & Wheel Design, 17 1/4 In. 750.00
Jug, Blown, Molded, Miniature Diamond, 1825-1835 .... 287.00
Lamp, Hurricane, 3 Clambroth Dolphin Base, Pair .... *Illus* 13200.00
Lamp, Oil, Ellipse & Bull's-Eye, Square Block Base, 11 In., Pair 115.00
Lamp, Overlay, Star & Quatrefoil Cut, White To Red, 12 In. 865.00
Lamp, Pressed, Cobalt Blue, Hexagonal Fonts, c.1850, 10 In., Pair 1725.00
Lamp, Pressed, Star & Punty, Clambroth, c.1850, 11 In., Pair 920.00
Shade, 3 Egyptian Transfers In Gold Oval, 10 1/8 In. 195.00
Shade, Clusters Of Leaves, White Outlining, 10 In., Pair 385.00
Shade, Leaf Design, Double Ring Top, 10 1/2 In. 220.00
Shade, Mountain Scene, Leaves & Butterfly, 9 3/4 In. 220.00
Spooner, Star & Punty, Cobalt Blue, 1840, 4 1/4 In. 1500.00
Tie Back, Opalescent, 3 In., Pair 35.00
Tumbler, Paneled, Flint, Miniature 20.00

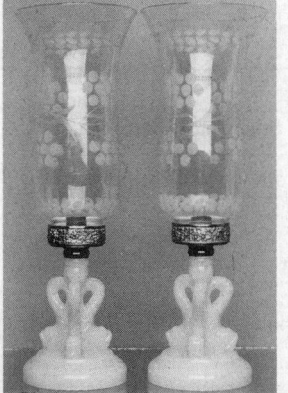

◆◆◆◆◆◆◆◆◆◆◆◆◆◆◆◆◆◆◆◆◆◆◆◆◆

When cleaning old hairbrushes backed with celluloid, do not plunge the brushes in a sink full of water. If water collects between the brush and the plastic, it will cause damage. Never keep in direct sunlight. Celluloid, or cellulose nitrate, is flammable.

◆◆◆◆◆◆◆◆◆◆◆◆◆◆◆◆◆◆◆◆◆◆◆◆◆

Sandwich Glass, Lamp, Hurricane,
3 Clambroth Dolphin Base, Pair

Vase, Green Loop, Gauffered Rim, Pressed, 10 In.	1095.00
Vase, Loop, Amethyst, Gauffered Rim, Pressed 9 1/2 In.	1495.00
Vase, Tulip, Amethyst, Pair	2350.00
Vase, Tulip, Emerald, 10 In., Pair	2645.00

SARREGUEMINES is the name of a French town that is used as part of a china mark. Utzschneider and Company, a porcelain factory, made ceramics in Sarreguemines, Lorraine, France, from about 1775. Transfer-printed wares and majolica were made in the nineteenth century. The nineteenth-century pieces, most often found today, usually have colorful transfer-printed decorations showing peasants in local costumes.

Basket, Strawberry, Majolica	125.00
Box, Cover, Four-Leaf Clovers, Round, 3 1/2 In.	65.00
Candlestick, Yellowware, Silver Luster, 8 In., Pair	300.00
Charger, Nanny Holding Baby, Parents Looking On, 1870s, 14 In.	450.00
Ewer, Crystalline Glaze, Brown, 1880s, 12 In.	850.00
Humidor, French Peasants, 1870s, 7 In.	285.00
Pitcher, Metallic Silver Crystalline Glaze, Brown, Ink Mark, 12 x 3 1/2 In.	195.00
Plate, Bryonia, Mulberry, 9 1/2 In.	45.00
Plate, Lobster, Olive Green Ground, Large	445.00
Plate, Pears, Majolica, 7 1/2 In.	30.00
Platter, Serving, Boar's Head Cover, 18 In.	620.00
Vase, Triple, Art Nouveau, Oxblood, Turquoise & Purple, Gold Trim, 7 1/2 In.	250.00

SASCHA BRASTOFF made decorative accessories, ceramics, enamels on copper, and plastics of his own design. He headed a factory, Sascha Brastoff of California, Inc., in West Los Angeles, from 1953 until about 1973. He died in 1993.

Ashtray, Alaska, Domed	45.00
Ashtray, Eskimo Dome, Yellow	45.00 to 60.00
Ashtray, Freeform House	55.00
Ashtray, Gold Bird, Chimney, 6 In.	30.00
Ashtray, Horse Design, 6 1/4 x 5 In.	40.00
Ashtray, Horse Design, Shaded Gray, 6 3/4 x 5 In.	42.00
Ashtray, Houses, Signed, 9 x 12 In.	32.00 to 45.00
Ashtray, Stylized Floral, Greenish-Gold Ground, Metal, 6 1/4 In.	30.00
Ashtray, Teepee Shape, 7 In.	35.00
Ashtray, Walrus Dome	75.00
Ashtray & Cigarette Holder, Ceramic, Houses, 2 Piece	95.00
Bowl, 3 Houses	50.00
Bowl, 6 1/2 In.	18.00
Bowl, 8 1/2 In.	26.00
Bowl, Abstract Flowers, Enameled, 14 In.	55.00
Bowl, Horse & Trainer, 12 In.	95.00
Bowl, Star Horse, Free-Form, 9 x 8 In.	150.00
Charger, Abstract, Gold, 17 In.	65.00
Charger, Enamel, 17 In.	145.00
Cigarette Box, Cover, Free-Form Bowl, Matte Black, Multicolored, 2 Piece	55.00
Coffee Set, 3 Piece	60.00
Compote, 8-Footed, 9 In.	125.00
Compote, Green Grapes, Enamel	35.00
Compote, Metal-Footed, 9 In.	85.00
Dish, Enamel, Green, Orange, Flowers, 4 In.	18.00
Dish, Horse Design, Shaded Gray, 6 3/4 In.	42.00
Dish, Pipe Shape	60.00
Figurine, Owl, Gold Resin, 14 In.	350.00
Figurine, Rooster, Signed, 17 In.	395.00
Lamp, Multicolored Mosaic, 36 In.	200.00
Lighter & Cigarette Box, Enamel, Flowers	55.00
Mug, Bird, White, Gold Trim	30.00
Pitcher, Gray Specks Over Ivory, Bulbous, 3 3/4 In.	60.00
Plate, Stylized Rooster	15.00
Plate, White Fruit, Hunter Green, 10 In.	40.00

Plate, White Fruit, Hunter Green, 12 In.	45.00
Platter, Blue Grapes, Enamel, 15 In.	95.00
Vase, Alaska, 8 1/2 In.	70.00
Vase, Alaskan Igloo	65.00
Vase, Blue, Inscribed Lion, No. HB, 6 x 5 1/2 In.	110.00
Vase, Copper & Enamel, 5 In.	55.00
Vase, Rearing Stallion, 9 1/4 In.	100.00

SATIN GLASS is a late nineteenth-century art glass. It has a dull finish that is caused by hydrofluoric acid vapor treatment. Satin glass was made in many colors and sometimes has applied decorations. Satin glass is also listed by factory name, such as Webb, or in the Mother-of-Pearl category in this book.

Biscuit Jar, White, Flowers, Silver Plated Top & Bail, 9 In.	90.00
Box, Dresser, Mother-Of-Pearl, Enameled Chrysanthemums, 5 x 3 In.	275.00
Cookie Jar, Shell & Seaweed Overlay, Silver Plated Top, 8 x 5 In.	395.00
Ewer, Flowers, Rose Ground, Frosted Applied Handle, White Lining, 6 In.	85.00
Ewer, Rainbow, Pink, Blue & Yellow Stripes, Swirl Over White, 8 1/2 In.	580.00
Fairy Lamp, Blue & White Swirl, Ruffled Edge, 6 1/2 In.	635.00
Fairy Lamp, Pink Swirl, Ruffled Base & Shade, 5 In.	525.00
Perfume Bottle, Lay-Down, Light Green, Flowers, Sterling Screw Top, 4 3/4 In.	385.00
Rose Bowl, Cut Velvet, Egg Shape, White Lining, 4 1/2 x 3 1/2 In.	165.00
Rose Bowl, Mother-Of-Pearl, White Lining, 9-Crimp Top, 2 5/8 x 3 1/2 In.	265.00
Rose Bowl, Orange Enameled Flowers, Crimped	120.00
Rose Bowl, Pinwheel Pattern, Mother-Of-Pearl, White Lining, 6 In.	225.00
Sugar, Diamond-Quilted, Silver Plated Handles, Rose Ground, Lining, 3 1/2 In.	85.00
Sugar Shaker, Leaf Mold, Blue, 4 In.	315.00
Syrup, Cone Pattern, Pink	235.00
Table Set, Pink To Opalescent, Silver Plated Trim & Cover, c.1850, 4 Piece	575.00
Tumbler, Quilted, Pale Blue To White	40.00
Vase, Coralene Wheat, Blue, 12 In.	1200.00 to 1250.00
Vase, Coralene, White Lining, Gold Trim, Bulbous, Blue Overlay, 4 1/2 x 3 7/8 In.	395.00
Vase, Diamond-Quilted, Mother-Of-Pearl, Butterscotch, Ruffled, 5 1/2 x 4 In.	195.00
Vase, Iris, Black, 6 In.	38.00
Vase, Pale Pink To Apricot, Clear Frosted Handle, 8 1/2 In.	115.00
Vase, Prunus & Pine Needles, Butterfly, Shaded Brown, 5 1/2 x 5 1/4 In.	550.00

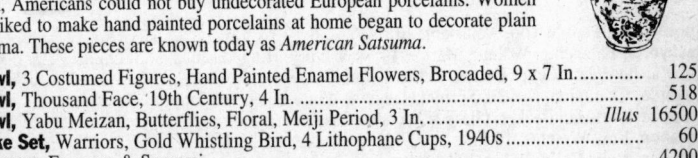

SATSUMA is a Japanese pottery with a distinctive creamy beige crackled glaze. Most of the pieces were decorated with blue, red, green, orange, or gold. Almost all Satsuma found today was made after 1860. During World War I, Americans could not buy undecorated European porcelains. Women who liked to make hand painted porcelains at home began to decorate plain Satsuma. These pieces are known today as *American Satsuma*.

Bowl, 3 Costumed Figures, Hand Painted Enamel Flowers, Brocaded, 9 x 7 In.	125.00
Bowl, Thousand Face, 19th Century, 4 In.	518.00
Bowl, Yabu Meizan, Butterflies, Floral, Meiji Period, 3 In. *Illus*	16500.00
Cake Set, Warriors, Gold Whistling Bird, 4 Lithophane Cups, 1940s	60.00
Charger, Emperor & Samurai	4200.00
Dish, Figural & Landscape Design, 1880s, 8 3/4 In.	315.00
Dish, Potpourri, 3 Rows Of Figures, Fired-Gold Trim, Footed, 6 In.	980.00
Ewer, Black Dragon, Floral Texture, Smoke Swirls, 13 x 10 In.	595.00
Incense Burner, Cover, 3 Panels Of Landscape, Woman, Signed, 4 1/2 In.	115.00
Incense Burner, Foo Dog, Finial, Handles, Cobalt Blue, Flowers, c.1900, 10 In.	125.00
Jar, Garden & Scenic Design, Figures, Square, Pierced Lip, 4 In.	465.00
Jar, Ginger, Figural Finial, Dragons Surround Figures In Landscape, 10 1/2 In.	1610.00
Jar, Potpourri, Figural & Landscape Design, Ivory Ground, 1910s, 4 1/2 In.	460.00
Plate, Figural & Landscape Design, 8 1/2 In., 12 Piece	145.00
Saki Pot, Autumn Leaves, Wire Handle, c.1940	100.00
Tea Caddy, Figural Design, Diamond Form, 4 In.	465.00
Tea Set, Baluster Shape, 8 Immortals, Geometrics, 15 Piece	550.00
Tea Set, Peacocks & Flowers, 13 Piece	160.00
Toothpick, Butterflies, Kinko, c.1880, 1 3/4 In.	247.00
Urn, Baluster Shape, Lizard Handles, Stick Neck, Socle Foot, 9 In.	260.00
Urn, Foo Dog Finial, Arahats & Scholars In Garden, Children Form Feet, 16 In.	805.00

◆◆◆◆◆◆◆◆◆◆◆◆◆◆◆◆◆◆◆◆◆◆◆

Have your chimney cleaned if you move into an old house or if you burn wood regularly. A creosote buildup can cause an explosion. Nesting animals can cause fire or smoke.

◆◆◆◆◆◆◆◆◆◆◆◆◆◆◆◆◆◆◆◆◆◆◆

Satsuma, Bowl, Yabu Meizan, Butterflies,
Floral, Meiji Period, 3 In.

Vase, Arahats In Garden Landscape, Floral Border At Neck & Base, 5 In.	805.00
Vase, Eagle Design, Butterflies On Handles, c.1890	1900.00
Vase, Family, Watching Carp, Birds & Flowers, Kinkozan, Baluster, c.1890, 3 3/4 In.	275.00
Vase, Figural & Landscape Design, Ivory Ground, 5 3/4 In.	92.00
Vase, Figural Reserves, Floral Ground, 10 1/2 In.	220.00
Vase, Figural Reserves, Shouldered Ovoid Form, 36 In.	632.00
Vase, Gathering Of Arahats, Wooden Base & Cover, 19 In.	2185.00
Vase, Male Figures, 2 Panels, 8 1/2 In.	165.00
Vase, Oriental Maidens & Children, Cobalt Blue Borders, c.1890, 12 In., Pair	550.00
Vase, Polychrome & Beaded Enamel, 16 In.	71.00
Vase, Teardrop Shape, Peach-Shaped Medallions, Figures, c.1885, 5 In., Pair	330.00
Vase, Thousand Butterflies, Gold Elephant Handles, Signed, 3 1/2 In.	150.00
Vase, Thousand Flowers Ground, Figural Panels, Cylinder, c.1880, 3 1/2 In.	165.00
Vase, Warrior Cartouches, Signed Shimazu Mon, 19th Century, Hexagonal, 4 3/4 In.	385.00
Vase, Woman In Reserve, 2 Handles, c.1890, 19 In.	357.00

SATURDAY EVENING GIRLS, see Paul Revere Pottery

SCALES have been made to weigh everything from babies to gold. Collectors search for all types. Most popular are small gold dust scales and special grocery scales.

Apothecary, Marble Top, Adjustable Brass Pans, 6 x 13 x 5 In.	90.00
Assayer's, Balancing, Walnut, Marble, Brass & Ivory, Hinged Lid	300.00
Baby's, Jay-Bee, Wicker Basket, Yellow Paint	25.00
Balance, Champion, No. 30, Spring, Hanging, White Enameled Tray	95.00
Balance, Christian Becker, Glass & Wooden Case	350.00
Balance, Iron, Weights, 19 In.	24.00
Balance, Nude Child, Brass, 30 In.	175.00
Balance, Scoop, Jacob Bros.	65.00
Buffalo Hide, H. Boker & Co., Germany	110.00
Candy, Brandford, Visible Mechanism, 3 Lb.	250.00 to 300.00
Candy, Computing Scale Co.	160.00
Candy, Jones Of Binghamton, New York, Cloverleaf	265.00
Candy, Norvell-Shapleigh, Countertop, 1906	375.00
Candy, Tin Scoop	125.00
Candy, Toledo, Honest Weight-No Springs, 15 x 14 1/2 In.	198.00
Charlie The Tuna, Sorry Charlie, 13 In.	40.00
Chatillon, Hanging, Chain Held Tray, 25 Pound Capacity, 1900s	150.00
Computing, Dayton, 32 x 19 In.	2310.00
Computing Scale Co., Brass Trim, 5 Lb.	200.00
Egg, Jiffy Way	30.00
Fairbanks, Cast Iron, Brass, Pat. Apr. 28, 1878, Small	192.00
Fairbanks, Cast Iron, Red Paint, Gold Design, Weights, 19th Century	95.00
Fairbanks, Fishtail, Cast Iron, Brass, Dark Red & Gilt Paint	110.00

Family Type, Pelouze	75.00
Fortune Telling, Watling, Porcelain, Front Mirrored Marquis, 66 1/2 In.	247.00
Fruit, Cast Iron, Brass Tray, Pair	75.00
Gold, Hand-Held, Pan, Brass	72.00
Henry Troemner, Nickeled Brass Trays, Wooden Case, 5 Lbs.	125.00
Henry Troemner, Wooden Base, Porcelain Knobbed Drawer	95.00
Jennings, Lollipop Form	895.00
Jeweler's, Henry Troemner, Glazed Case, Patinated Metal, Maple, 16 x 17 In.	230.00
Jeweler's, Kodak, 6 Weights, Avoirdupois Weight	95.00
Nursery, Overlay On Dial, 36 Lbs., 8 x 8 In.	27.00
Pendulum, Nickel Plated Brass, Cross Pen Co., Boston, 0-12 Oz., 3 1/4 In.	65.00
Postage, National, Patent 1896	35.00
Postal, 2 Cents For 1 Oz., Rexall	35.00
Postal, 3 Cents	22.00
Postal, Liberty	15.00
Postal, Sterling Silver, Gorham, 6 1/2 In.	745.00
Precision, Sartourius Werke, Oak & Glass Case	750.00
Reading, Pennsylvania, Marked, Weights, Pans	225.00
Salter's, Hanging, To 24 Lbs.	10.00
Spring, Hanson, Model 8920, 200 Lbs.	38.00
Step-Up, American Accurate, 46 In.	93.00
Store, National, Specialty, Brass Pan, Up To 3 Lbs., 16 x 16 In.	385.00
Talking, I Speak Your Weight, Phonograph Disc Within, United, 5 Cents, 84 In.	7475.00
Toledo, Porcelain, 3 Lbs.	65.00
Voland & Sons, Glass & Cherry Case	250.00
Watling, Lollipop Form, Porcelain & Enamel, Etched See-Through Glass, 24 x 72 In.	1870.00
Weighing, Caille, George Washington, Wooden Case, Tin Dial Cent, 69 1/2 In.	3162.00
Weighing, Caille, Iron, Cast Marquee, 1 Cent, 66 In.	1035.00
Weighing, Check Your Weight, Peerless, 1 Cent, 60 In.	1380.00
Weighing, Mills, Lollipop Form, Porcelain Body, Mirrored Center, 1 Cent, 74 In.	460.00
Weighing, Weight 1 Cent, National, Cast Iron, 70 In.	920.00

SCHAFER & VATER, makers of small ceramic items, are best known for their amusing figurals. The factory was located in Volkstedt-Rudolstadt, Germany, from 1890 to 1962. Some pieces are marked with the crown and R mark, but many are unmarked.

Bottle, Egyptian Woman Kneeling, Jug On Shoulder, Stopper, 9 In.	185.00
Bottle, Fire Water	160.00
Bottle, Skeleton, 8 In.	165.00
Bottle, Troubadour & Lady Toasting Each Other, Green, 6 1/2 In.	175.00
Bottle, What A Night	160.00
Box, Cameo Lady, Jewels, Triangular, 4 In.	85.00
Creamer, Maid With Keys, Blue & White, 3 3/4 In.	85.00
Creamer, Smiling Girl, With Jug & Basket	75.00
Creamer, Smiling Orange, 4 In.	35.00
Creamer, Witch, Blue	75.00
Decanter, Figural, Scotsman, Blue & White	150.00
Figurine, Golfer, Comical	225.00
Flask, Drinkometer	35.00
Flask, Skeleton, 8 In.	175.00
Hatpin Holder, Woman Playing Pipes, Ivory	25.00
Humidor, Place Under Cover For Moistener	40.00
Match Holder, Scratch My Back, 2 Monkeys, Bisque	165.00
Pitcher, Multicolored Maid, Jug & Keys, 3 1/2 In.	85.00 to 98.00

SCHNEIDER Glassworks was founded in 1903 at Epinay-sur-Seine, France, by Charles and Ernest Schneider. Art glass was made between 1903 and 1930. The company still produces clear crystal glass.

Bowl, Bubbled Colorless Crystal, Pink Mottling, Signed, 12 In.	345.00
Bowl, Double Knobbed Amethyst Pedestal, Signed, 8 1/2 In.	550.00
Bowl, Red To White, Inverted Rim, Mottled, 2 3/8 x 4 1/4 In.	275.00
Bowl, Tangerine To Lemon, Mottled, Signed, 2 3/8 x 4 3/4 In.	250.00

Compote, White To Pink, Black Amethyst Stem, Mottled Interior, 12 1/4 In. 633.00
Night-Light, Red Glass Shade 400.00
Pitcher, Colored Interior, Pulled Design, Amethyst Handle, Signed, 15 In. 748.00
Planter, Turquoise, Acid Etched Blossom Overlay, Mottled, Signed............................ 460.00
Vase, Green Shading To Yellow, Iron Mounted, 10 In. 575.00
Vase, Milky Turquoise & Green, Maroon Splotches, Signed, 5 1/4 In. 290.00
Vase, Optic Ribbed, Green Shaded To Orange Overlay, 8 In. 375.00
Vase, Tango, Blown-Out, Ribbed Wrought Iron Cage, Signed, 8 3/8 In. 690.00

SCIENTIFIC INSTRUMENTS of all kinds are included in this category. Other categories such as Barometers, Binoculars, Dental, Medical, Nautical, and Thermometer may also price scientific apparatus.

Altazimuth, 1. Casella, London, Pocket, Case, Instructions, 6 In. 172.00
Altimeter, Russian Soyuz Flight, Oct. 26-30, 1968 ....*Illus* 3450.00
Calculator, Canon 163, Desk-Top, Nixie-Tube.. 30.00
Calculator, Curta, Model I, Mechanical, Metal Case 575.00
Calculator, Fowler's Magnum, Long Scale, Leather Case 325.00
Calculator, Otis King, Model K, Original Box, Patent 150.00
Calculator, Thacher's, 4012, Keuffel & Esser, Box 1850.00
Compass, Alexander Magarey, New York, Surveyor's, Brass, Pine Case.................... 805.00
Compass, B. Pike & Sons, New York, Surveyor's, Mahogany Case............................ 546.00
Compass, Benj. Pike & Son, Surveyor's, Brass, New York, 15 In. 115.00
Compass, Cary, London, Level & Sundial, c.1815, 6 In. 675.00
Compass, Circumferentor, Mining, 4 Sight Vane, American, c.1890 .... 2200.00
Compass, Circumferentor, Wissler, Mining, c.1890 .... 2800.00
Compass, Ellio Bros., London, Prismatic, Brass, Card, 3 In. 230.00
Compass, Gurley, Pocket, Wooden Case, 1918, 3 In. 150.00
Compass, Gurley, Wooden Case, Pocket 150.00
Compass, J.W. Hagger, Baltimore, Large Plane 1600.00
Compass, K & E, Sight Vanes, Leveling Head, c.1895, 12 In. 550.00
Compass, Surveyor's, Brass, Continental, Case, 19th Century, 8 In. 172.00
Compass, W. & L.E. Gurley, Troy N.Y., Brass Dip, 19th Century 287.00
Compass, Waltham, Brass, Marked U.S. 65.00
Counterfeit Detector, Heath's, Magnifier, Nickel Plated, Dec. 25, 1877 .... 295.00
Gauge, Wind Velocity, Case 75.00
Hydrometer, Casartelli, Mahogany Box, 10 In.. 88.00
Hydrometer, Sike, Inlaid Ivory, Mahogany Box 195.00
Magnifier, Table Type, Adjustable, Iron Stand, Victorian, 13 1/4 In. 110.00
Microscope, Bausch & Lomb 150.00
Microscope, Bausch & Lomb, Physician's, Case & Accessories 1250.00
Microscope, Bockett, Adjustable Condenser, 9 In. 280.00
Microscope, Brass, 2 Lenses, Case, Pocket 25.00
Microscope, Bulloch, Meyrowitz, Histological No. 104, c.1890 .... 2200.00
Microscope, Craig Style, Pivoting Mirror, 4 1/2 In. 60.00
Microscope, Field, Brass, Wooden Case, c.1860 .... 150.00

Scientific Instrument, Altimeter,
Russian Soyuz Flight, Oct. 26-30, 1968

• •

Metal polish paste or cream cleans better than polish-impregnated cloth if you have a very tarnished piece. Cloths are good for small metal parts with little tarnish.

• •

Microscope, Spencer, No. 25965, Brass, Wooden Case, c.1900, 13 In.	585.00
Microscope, T.H. McAllister, New York, Iron & Brass	175.00
Microscope, Tighe, Detroit, Swing Mirror, Optical Substage, Case	900.00
Orrery, Glass & Wood Teaching Slides, Labeled, Case, c.1875	1450.00
Orrery, Trippensee Planetarium, Detroit, Michigan, 14 x 25 1/2 In.	1495.00
Pedometer, A. LaFontaine, Paris, Case, Instructions, 19th Century, 2 In.	230.00
Planetarium, Laing Planetarium Co., Box, Literature, 1900s, 19 x 12 In.	6100.00
Refractometer, Bausch & Lomb, 1920s	175.00
Register, Telegraph, L.M. Ericsson, Clockwork, c.1880	1350.00
Sextant, Rosewood, Brass & Ivory Trim, Wm. Williams, c.1785	1870.00
Slide Rule, Ivory & Wood, c.1944	45.00
Slide Rule, Leather Case, c.1962	25.00
Telescope, Andrew J. Lloyd Co., Brass, Wooden Tripod, Case, 40 In.	1955.00
Telescope, Bardou & Son, Paris, Brass, 19th Century, 36 In.	4070.00
Telescope, Bardou & Son, Wooden Tripod Stand, Brass, 60 In.	990.00
Telescope, Brass, 2 Draw, 19th Century	192.00
Telescope, Brass, 2 Draw, England, 36 In.	65.00
Telescope, Brass, Wooden, c.1795	395.00
Telescope, J. Pillischer, Brass, Leather Covering, Extends 28 In.	110.00
Telescope, Jesse Ramsden, Hand-Held, 18th Century	1320.00
Telescope, Salmon Co., Edinburgh, Brass, Leather Case, Cap	176.00
Telescope, Transit Circle, Ainsworth, Leather Case, Pocket, c.1930	150.00
Telescope, Transit Circle, H. Ware, Tripod Stand, Brass, 66 In.	907.00
Telescope, W. & T. Tulley, London, Library, Brass	1760.00
Telescope, W. Ashmore Of London, Brass, 37 In.	90.00
Telescope, Watson, Terrestrial, Brass, Tripod, 4 Ft. 6 In.	1775.00
Telescope, Watson, Terrestrial, Mahogany Tripod, c.1885, 4 Ft. 6 In.	4170.00
Tellurium, Trippensee, Bakelite Sun & Arm	800.00
Trippensee Planetarium, Pat. Date, Mar. 10, 1908	1500.00
Vernier, Knox & Shain, Case, Philaplhia, 1855-1891	1100.00
Vise, Brass, Jaws, Screw Driven Beveled Slide, 2 x 1 3/4 In.	45.00

SCRIMSHAW is bone or ivory or whale's teeth carved by sailors and others for entertainment during the sailing-ship days. Some scrimshaw was carved as early as 1800. There are modern scrimshanders making pieces today on bone, ivory, or plastic. Other pieces may be found in the Ivory and Nautical categories.

Basket, Sewing, Openwork, 19th Century, 9 1/4 x 6 3/4 In.	1650.00
Bed, Doll's, Whalebone, Engraved Designs, 1858	3410.00
Cup, Engraved Ship & Eagle, American Shield, New Bedford, 1859, 3 In.	880.00
Dipper, Water, Coconut, Wooden Exotic Wood, Scrimshaw Band Around Bowl	935.00
Snuffbox, Whalebone, Carved, Flower Pot, 3 1/2 x 3/4 x 3 1/2 In.	260.00
Stand, Jewelry, Whalebone, Center Handle, 6 Carved Panels, Acorn Finials, 8 In.	2300.00
Stand, Whatnot, Whalebone, 8 In.	2310.00
Swift, Whalebone, Table Clamp Thumb Screw, 18 In.	360.00
Tooth, Whale's, American Whale Ship & Whale, 6 In.	770.00
Tooth, Whale's, Clipper Ship, Morning Star, Palmer Martin, 1856, 5 3/4 In.	690.00
Tooth, Whale's, Eagle's Head, Oval Wooden Base, 6 1/4 In.	920.00
Tooth, Whale's, Erotic Scene, 6 In.	2200.00
Tooth, Whale's, Man, Playing Cards, Skeletons, 1870-1890, 5 1/2 In.	250.00
Tusk, Walrus, Bella Union Saloon, 5 Playing Cards, San Francisco, 1850s, 17 In.	1760.00
Tusk, Walrus, Full-Rigged Ship Dakota, Reverse, Nantucket, 1860	60.00
Tusk, Walrus, Salt & Pepper	60.00
Tusk, Walrus, Woman Riding Dolphin, Reverse, Praying For Good Whaling	225.00
Whale Rib, Small Boat Bay Whaling, 1868	120.00
Whale Rib, U.S. Whaler, Full Sail, 1834	120.00

SEBASTIAN MINIATURES were first made by Prescott W. Baston in 1938 in Marblehead, Massachusetts. More than 400 different designs have been made and collectors search for the out-of-production models. The mark may say *Copr. P. W. Baston U.S.A.,* or *P. W. Baston, U.S.A.,* or *Prescott W. Baston.* Sometimes a paper label was used.

Boy On Sled	25.00

Conestoga Wagon	15.00
Cow Jumped Over The Moon	250.00
First House, Plymouth Plantation	75.00
Howard Johnson Pieman	200.00
Huckleberry Finn	50.00
Lobsterman	55.00
Lost In The Kitchen, Now's The Time For Jell-O,	200.00
Mrs. Cratchit	25.00
Parade Rest, 1955	25.00
Plaque, Dealer's, Figure	85.00
Robert E. Lee	90.00
Sampling The Stew	45.00
Sistine Madonna, 1955, 4 In.	35.00
Snow Days, Boy, 1979	40.00
Snow Days, Girl, 1979	40.00
Songs At Cratchits	18.00
Swan Boat, Boston Public Garden	150.00
Yankee Sea Captain	42.00

SEG, see Paul Revere Pottery category

SEVRES porcelain has been made in Sevres, France, since 1769. Many copies of the famous ware have been made. The name originally referred to the works of the Royal Porcelain factory. The name now includes any of the wares made in the town of Sevres, France. The entwined lines with a center letter used as the mark is one of the most forged marks in antiques. Be very careful to identify Sevres by quality, not just by mark.

Bottle, Volcanic Gunmetal & Sang-De-Boeuf Glaze, Labels, 1905, 5 In.	2100.00
Box, Dresser, Floral Interior, 1840, 5 In.	595.00
Box, Egg Shape, Hinged Cover, Lavender, Green & Gilt, Marked, 4 1/2 In.	415.00
Bust, Marshall Of France, Military Clothes, Gilded Socle Base, 1874 Mark, 13 3/4 In.	715.00
Cachepot, Painted Reserves Of Rustic Lovers, Blue Ground, 6 3/4 In., Pair	1265.00
Candlestick, Royal Blue, 19th Century, 9 In.	275.00
Centerpiece, Figure & Floral Panel, Scrolled Handles, Bronze Mounted, 17 In.	3162.00
Clock, Bronze, Cupids, 19th Century, 34 3/4 In. ....*Illus*	21000.00
Clock, Cherub Chasing Butterflies, Ormolu	385.00
Figurine, Cat, Signed, 8 1/2 In.	595.00
Inkstand, Bronze Mounted, Green Enamel Ground, Gilt Borders, 10 In.	1840.00
Plate, Chateau De Tuilleries, Battle Scene, Cobalt Blue Rim, c.1884, 9 1/2 In.	286.00
Plate, Flowers, Gilt, Allover Floral Border, Marked, 10 In., Pair	468.00

Sevres, Clock, Bronze, Cupids, 19th Century, 34 3/4 In.

Sevres, Urn, Cover, Dore Bronze, Handles, 19th Century, 28 In., Pair

Plate, Louis-Philippe, Blue, Central Cartouche, Gilt Monogram, 9 1/2 In., 12 Pc. 920.00
Plate, Marie Antoinette, Flowers, Gold Enameling On Pink, c.1844, 9 1/2 In. 325.00
Plate, Old Woman & Man, Cobalt Blue Border, Floral Panels, c.1844, 9 1/2 In. 748.00
Plate, Romantic Scenes Of Figures, 18th-Century Costumes, 9 1/2 In., 12 Piece........... 2860.00
Pomander, Domed Cover, Woman's Bust Handles, 28 In. 7650.00
Teapot, Cover, Bird In Flight Spout, Egg Shape, 1760, 4 In. 805.00
Tray, Perfume, Cobalt Blue, Gilt, Serpentine Shape, Painted Reserve, 13 1/4 In. 385.00
Urn, Cherub Finial Cover, Bisque, White, c.1896, 33 In. 5500.00
Urn, Cover, Courting Scene, Landscape, Yellow Ground, Bird Handle, 7 In., Pair 575.00
Urn, Cover, Dore Bronze, Handles, 19th Century, 28 In., Pair.............................. *Illus* 14300.00
Urn, Cover, Figural Scene, Reverse Landscape, Bronze Mounted, 48 In. 6900.00
Urn, Cover, Lion Masks Holding Rings, Foliate Swags, Paw Feet, Signed, 12 1/4 In. ... 1726.00
Urn, Lovers, Castle Scene, Oxblood, 21 1/2 In,, Pair 2530.00
Vase, Band Of Flowers, Gilt Foot & Neck, Mounted As Lamp, 22 1/2 In. 975.00
Vase, Cover, Flower, Blue Borders, Ormolu Mounts, 6 1/2 In. 660.00
Vase, Cover, Reserves, Seated Maiden, Satyr, Ram's Horn Handles, 20 1/4 In............. 770.00
Vase, Feathered Black & Amber Glaze, 2 Handles, Stamped, 10 1/2 x 5 In., Pair......... 313.00
Vase, Floral Reserves, Gilt Traced Shoulder & Foot, 1809, 13 In. 2200.00
Vase, Hand Painted Floral Panels, Yellow Ground, Gilt Mounted, 18 In., Pair 1100.00
Vase, Marseille's & Lyon Commemoration, Polychrome, 10 In................................. 1155.00
Vase, Paneled Sides, Figures & Floral, Blue Ground, 11 In.. 2760.00
Vase, Tapered, 3 Applied Snakes, Circular Mark, 9 In. 1980.00

SEWER TILE figures were made by workers at the sewer tile and pipe factories in the Ohio area during the late nineteenth and early twentieth centuries.
Figurines, small vases, and cemetery vases were favored. Often the finished
vase was a piece of the original pipe with added decorations and markings.
All types of sewer tile work are now considered folk art by collectors.

Bank, Pig, Seated, 9 3/4 In. ....330.00 to 385.00
Birdhouse, Tree Trunk Form, Wooden Lid 230.00
Cat, Seated, 7 1/2 In... 302.00
Dog, Red Paint, Marked UBCW, Small 375.00
Dog, Seated, 9 /12 In... 93.00
Dog, Seated, 10 In.. 82.00
Dog, Seated, Coin Slot In Back Of Head, 10 1/2 In.. 104.00
Dog, Seated, Molded & Tooled, 11 In.. 192.00
Dog, Seated, Oval Base, 8 In... 247.00
Dog, Spaniel, Signed Henry, 8 1/4 In.. 225.00
Figurine, Puppy, Incised Nobody Loves Me, 4 In... 137.00
Lamp Base, Tree With Dog, Stump & Woodpecker, 12 In. 715.00
Planter, 1924 .... 385.00
Rabbit, Pair, 9 In... 440.00
Roof Vent, Eagle Finial, 12 x 12 x 15 1/4 In... 385.00
Urn, Garden, Tree Trunk Base, Oak Leaf Design, Impressed Label, 42 In., Pair 990.00

SEWING equipment of all types is collected, from sewing birds that held the
cloth to old wooden spools.

Basket, Cover, Painted Wicker, Round, 7 In. 30.00
Basket, Lower Tray, Wicker, Green.. 145.00
Bias Tape, Matching Thread, On Round Bobbin, Card, 2 1/2 x 6 1/2 In. 9.00
Bird, Brass, 1855.. 250.00
Book, Needle, Navy & Army, 1918.. 20.00
Box, Anglo-Indian Horn, Fitted Interior, 19th Century, 5 1/2 x 11 1/2 In. 632.00
Box, Center Figure Within Wreath, Quill Work, Quilted Interior, 16 1/2 In. 920.00
Box, Child's, Paper Cover, Fitted, France, 1900, 10 x 6 In. 400.00
Box, Daguerreotypes & Tintype Portraits In Cover, Compartments, Trays, 16 x 12 In... 1725.00
Box, Gilt Lacquer, Chinese Export, 19th Century, 8 x 12 In. 327.00
Box, Hanging, Chip Caved, Lift Lid, 2 Shelves & Pincushion, Poplar, 20 1/2 In. 467.00
Box, Monarch Silk Thread, 12 Unused Spools, Chart, Early 1900s 75.00
Box, Needle, Darner On Cover, Staffordshire 120.00
Box, Oak, 2 Drawers, 7 x 20 x 14 In... 48.00
Box, Pincushion Top, Wallpaper Covered, Miniature 660.00
Box, Regency, Wooden, Fitted Sections, Handle, 13 In....................................... 895.00

Box, Scalloped & Sawtooth Moldings, Applied Knobs, Pine, 5 1/4 x 11 1/4 In. 105.00
Box, Serpentine Edge, Fitted Interior, Divided Tray, Mahogany, 11 1/2 In. 70.00
Box, Wallpaper Covered, 19th Century, 3 3/4 x 11 In. 201.00
Box, Walnut, Peaked Top, Natural, Mirror, Velvet, 9 1/4 x 5 3/4 x 4 3/8 In. 185.00
Braid, Middy, On Card 3.00
Cabinet, Spool, see Advertising category under Cabinet, Spool
Caddy, Lift-Top, Pincushion, Ivory Thread Guides For 6 Spools 165.00
Caddy, Pincushion, Peaseware 65.00
Caddy, Thread, Green Velvet Pincushion, Pease, 6 1/4 In. 385.00
Caddy, Thread, Spool Rods Inside With Holes For Thread, Pease, 6 1/2 In. 203.50
Darner, Amethyst Glass 65.00
Darning Egg, Cleminson 18.00
Darning Egg, Ivory, Vegetable, Victorian 50.00
Display Card, Needles, Dixieland, 6 x 8 In., 24 Packs 18.00
Display Card, Needles, Vogue, 6 3/4 x 8 1/2 In., 24 Packs 15.00
Dress Fasteners, Card, Eversnap, 3 x 4 1/2 In. 4.00
Gauge, Hem, Sterling Silver Tip 95.00
Hooks & Loops, Card, Eldorado, 2 1/2 x 2 1/8 In. 3.00
Hooks & Loops, Card, Maple Wood, 2 1/2 x 4 3/4 In. 3.00
Hoop, Embroidery, Frame, Attached To Tool Box, Sliding Lid, Wooden, 11 1/2 In. 550.00
Kit, Doll, Simplicity, Original 135.00
Kit, Metal Box, Red Velvet Mirrored Top, Occupied Japan 20.00
Kit, Music Box, Grand Piano Shape, Mother-Of-Pearl Handled Tools, 1850s................. 1500.00
Kit, Silver Tools, Painted Girl Scene Box Top, Mid-19th Century 825.00
Machine, Black Metal, Painted Design, Eagle Mark, Germany, 6 In. 145.00
Machine, Child's, Singer.. 77.00
Machine, Child's, Singer, 1930s 110.00
Machine, Red Metal, Miniature, 7 In. 78.00
Machine, Singer, Double Pedestal Cabinet, Treadle 80.00
Machine, Singer, Egyptian Design On Machine 60.00
Machine, Singer, Featherweight, Black, Model 222-1, Case, No Accessories 395.00
Machine, Singer, Featherweight, Case, Attachments, Book 275.00
Machine, Singer, Featherweight, Model 221, Accessories 290.00
Machine, Singer, Oak Veneered, Treadle Type.. 100.00
Machine, Smith, Folding, 1884 .... 250.00
Machine, Wilcox & Gibbs .... 125.00 to 135.00
Mannequin, Tape Measure In Base, Thimble Head, Pincushion Body.......................... 65.00
Needle, Book, Navy & Army, Contents, Colorful, 1918 .... 20.00
Needle, Book, Sew Smart, 5 x 3 3/4 In... 6.00
Needle, Knitting, Ebony & Whalebone, Pair, 12 1/2 In.. 165.00
Needle, Pack, Deans 3.00
Needle, Threader, Magic, Woman's Head On Front 3.00
Needle Case, Egg Shape, Vegetable Ivory, Pierced Design 48.00
Needle Case, Embroidered, Ribbons With Needles, 1900s, 3 1/2 x 5 In. 25.00
Needle Case, Tin Lithograph, 16 In. 45.00
Needle Pack, Dix & Rand, Gold Ink.. 3.00
Needle Pack, Laundry Advertising, Woman Sewing, c.1920, 3 1/4 x 5 In. 10.00
Needle Pack, Rockford's Best Gold Eye 3.00
Needle Pack, Shrimptons 3.00
Needle Pack, Watson's Church Brand 4.00
Needle Pack, Worcester Iodized Salt, Paper, Elephant Lithograph, 1 1/2 x 3 In. 21.00
Pattern, 1930s, Pair 15.00
Pincushion, Basket, Woven Celluloid, 1930s 15.00
Pincushion, Elephant, Sterling Silver 90.00
Pincushion, Flattened Ball Form, Silk Damask Cover, Silvered Chain, 18th Century. ... 2070.00
Pincushion, Frog, Silver Plate, Miniature 26.00
Pincushion, Hedgehog, Silver Plate 45.00
Pincushion, Indian Bark, 19th Century, 2 Piece... 135.00
Pincushion, Lady's Slipper, Bronze Patinated Spelter, 6 x 3 In. 40.00
Pincushion, Oriental Couple, Brown Bucket Pincushion On Back Of Man, 6 In. 50.00
Pincushion, Pease Brown Sticker 300.00
Pincushion, Strawberry, Green Felt Leaves, 4 3/4 In... 85.00
Pincushion Dolls are listed in their own category

Repair Kit, Bra, Beltz, 15 Cents, 3 x 6 In. 5.00
Safety Pin, Card, Clinton, 2 1/4 x 4 1/2 In. 3.00
Safety Pin, Card, Gem, 2 1/2 x 7 1/2 In. 4.00
Scissors, Sterling Silver 38.00
Shuttle, Tatting, Sterling Silver 85.00
Snap Fasteners, Card, Nobility, 3 5/8 x 4 5/8 In. 4.00
Snap Fasteners, Card, Prims, 2 3/8 x 3 1/2 In. 4.00
Snap Fasteners, Card, Shurlock, 1916, 4 1/4 x 3 1/4 In. 8.00
Snap Fasteners, Card, Stars 20.00
Snap Fasteners, Card, Waldes Koh-Noor, Box, 2 3/4 x 5 In. 15.00
Snap Fasteners, Eldorado, Castle, 3 1/2 x 4 3/4 In. 4.00
Snap Fasteners, Round, Card, Guardian, 4 3/8 x 3 3/8 In. 4.00
Spool Cabinets are in the Advertising category under Cabinet, Spool
Spool Holder, Walnut, Cast Iron, Black Paw Feet, Victorian, 10 In. 230.00
Tape Measure, Abbott's Ice Cream 50.00
Tape Measure, Baseball Player, Celluloid, Japan 265.00
Tape Measure, Bear, On All Fours 67.00
Tape Measure, Black Man's Head, Alligator, Celluloid 65.00
Tape Measure, Chariot, Celluloid, Germany 195.00
Tape Measure, Coffee Grinder, Metal, Germany 95.00
Tape Measure, Cottage 78.00
Tape Measure, Diamond Boot & Shoe 40.00
Tape Measure, Donald Duck, Celluloid, Japan 450.00
Tape Measure, Donkey 85.00
Tape Measure, Donkey, Metal, Germany 210.00
Tape Measure, Dressmaker's Form, Wooden Stand, Brass Thimble Topper, 6 In. 95.00
Tape Measure, E-Z, 20 Cents 3.00
Tape Measure, Egg Shape, Chicago World's Fair, 1933 .... 75.00
Tape Measure, Egg Shape, Fly Pull 65.00
Tape Measure, Elephant, Sitting, Celluloid, Germany 265.00
Tape Measure, Frigidaire, Celluloid 40.00
Tape Measure, Frog, F.O. Corsets, Pull My Head Not My Leg 225.00
Tape Measure, Fruit Basket 57.00
Tape Measure, Fruit Basket, Celluloid, Japan 8.00
Tape Measure, General Electric, Shows 1920 Refrigerator 30.00
Tape Measure, Girl, With Muff, Celluloid, Japan 125.00
Tape Measure, Hat, Metal, Germany 140.00
Tape Measure, Hoover Vacuum Cleaner 40.00
Tape Measure, Indian Boy 115.00
Tape Measure, Indian Head, Celluloid, Japan 110.00
Tape Measure, Jon Deere, Celluloid, Running Deer Logo 88.00
Tape Measure, Kangaroo & Joey 50.00
Tape Measure, Kangaroo, Celluloid, Japan 65.00
Tape Measure, Lafayette South Side Bank, Pretty Girl, Claith 45.00
Tape Measure, Lewis Lye ....25.00 to 40.00
Tape Measure, Mammy 165.00
Tape Measure, Owl, Glass Eyes, Brass, Chrome Case, Germany 40.00
Tape Measure, Parrot's Head, Celluloid, Germany 190.00
Tape Measure, Pig, Celluloid, Japan 85.00
Tape Measure, Pig, Pink, Celluloid 42.00
Tape Measure, Poodle, Metal, Germany 300.00
Tape Measure, S & H Green Stamps 65.00
Tape Measure, Sadiron Shape, Pincushion Top 35.00
Tape Measure, Sears Roebuck Plows, Celluloid ....60.00 to 85.00
Tape Measure, Ship, Red, Celluloid, Japan 115.00
Tape Measure, Shoe Worker's Union, Celluloid 42.00
Tape Measure, Squirrel, With Nut, Celluloid, Japan 95.00
Tape Measure, Star Drilling Machine Co., Akron, Ohio, Lufkin, 60 In. 35.00
Tape Measure, Turtle, Brass 50.00
Thimble, 10K Gold, Fancy 55.00
Thimble, Brass, Thread Cutter Top, Patent May 15, 1900, Size 10 .... 5.00
Thimble Holder, Cherub Reclining, For A Good Girl 110.00
Yarn Winder, Reel Type, Primitive 135.00

SHAKER items are characterized by simplicity, functionalism, and orderliness. There were many Shaker communities in America from the eighteenth century to the present day. The religious order made furniture, small wooden pieces, and packaged medicines, herbs, and jellies to sell to *outsiders*. Other useful objects were made for use by members of the community. Shaker furniture is listed in this book in the Furniture category.

Basket, Apple, Squared Bottom, New Lebanon, N.Y., Brown, Ash, c.1870, 15 x 13 In.	1725.00
Basket, Brown, Ash, Oval, Mount Lebanon, c.1840, 13 1/2 x 12 In.	2300.00
Basket, Laundry, Black Ash Splint, 2 Handles, New Lebanon, c.1840, 23 x 29 In.	1320.00
Basket, Market, Splint	200.00
Basket, Oyster, Yellow & Red, Stenciled	275.00
Basket, Sewing, 4 Smaller Baskets Inside, Handles	495.00
Basket, Swing Handle	575.00
Basket, Work, Maple & Hickory, 15 In.	440.00
Bench, Apple, Pine, Maple, Paring Mechanism, 3 Legs, 1827, 26 x 18 x 22 In.	770.00
Bonnet, Adult	175.00
Bonnet, Doll's, Blue Silk Collar, Poplar Ware Box, J. Fairbanks, Harvard, Me., 6 In.	220.00
Book, Golden Rule, Mother Lucy's, Paper Wrap, Signed, Amelia J. Calver, c.1840	3960.00
Bookmark, E.J. Neale & Co. Mt. Lebanon, N.Y., Woven Silk, Olive Green	185.00
Boot Scraper, Cast Iron, 3 Upright Wedges, 10 1/2 x 24 1/2 In.	140.00
Bottle, Extract Of Wormwood, Hand Blown, Contents, Wax Sealed, Aqua, 6 In.	275.00
Box, 1-Finger, Copper Tacks, Harvard, Me., Oval, 6 1/2 In.	165.00
Box, 2-Finger, 6 In.	275.00
Box, 2-Finger, Oval	395.00
Box, 3-Finger, 12 In.	660.00
Box, 3-Finger, Candy Apple Red	1500.00
Box, 3-Finger, Oval, Maple & Pine, Gray Paint, 7 1/8 In.	385.00
Box, 3-Finger, Oval, Maple & Pine, Varnish Finish, 4 1/2 In.	495.00
Box, 4-Finger, Maple, Pine, Red Paint, 4 3/4 x 11 In. ....*Illus*	330.00
Box, 4-Finger, Oval, Maple, Pine, 8 7/8 In.	275.00
Box, Bentwood, Finger, Old Varnish, Oval, 6 1/2 In.	94.00
Box, Bentwood, Harvard Type Construction, Iron Tacks, Oval, 5 1/4 In.	82.00
Box, Bentwood, Harvard Type, Single Finger Construction, Iron Tacks, Gray Paint	220.00
Box, Bentwood, Lapped Nailed Seam, Red Traces, 10 5/8 In.	275.00
Box, Bentwood, Oval, Single Finger Construction, Copper Tacks, 6 1/4 In.	192.00
Box, Candle, Sliding Lid, Maple, Birch, Canterbury, N.H., c.1840, 6 3/4 x 10 3/4 x 9 In.	440.00
Box, Candy, Flagroot, East Canterbury, N.H., Unused	30.00
Box, Collection, Mahogany, Dovetailed, Turned Handle, 6 x 6 In.	275.00
Box, Cover, Pumpkin Orange Paint, Oval, 4 1/8 x 10 1/8 In.	6600.00
Box, Document, Poplar, Red Stain Varnish, Brass Hinges, c.1840, 8 x 14 1/2 x 9 In.	440.00
Box, Finger Construction, Iron Tacks, Oval, 5 1/2 In.	248.00
Box, Fitted Lid, 4 Tucked Fingers, Brown, Maple & Pine, 10 In.	1150.00
Box, Fitted Lid, Oval, Jennet Angus, Watervliet, N.Y., c.1844, 3 1/2 x 8 1/4 In.	8625.00
Box, Garden Seed, Pine, Shaker's Seeds, Mount Lebanon, N.Y., 3 x 23 x 11 1/2 In.	1375.00
Box, Garden Seed, Raised By The Society Of Shakers, Near Albany, N.Y., Pine, Label	1155.00
Box, Inscribed, Amanda Surman T.B. 1864, 4 5/8 In.	460.00
Box, Letter, Tiger Maple, Dovetailed, Diamond Escutcheon, Ivory, Signed, 4 x 11 In.	1100.00

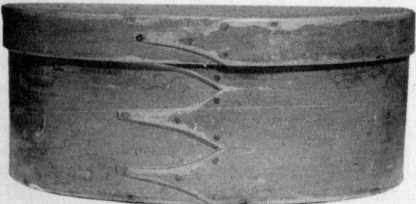

Shaker, Box, 4-Finger, Maple,
Pine, Red Paint, 4 3/4 x 11 In.

◆ ◆ ◆ ◆ ◆ ◆ ◆ ◆ ◆ ◆ ◆ ◆ ◆ ◆ ◆ ◆

A two-finger Shaker box
really has three. Two are
on the bottom, one is on
the lid.

◆ ◆ ◆ ◆ ◆ ◆ ◆ ◆ ◆ ◆ ◆ ◆ ◆ ◆ ◆ ◆

Box, Mirror Set Into 1-Finger Cover, 2 Fingers On Base, 7 3/4 In. 550.00
Box, Oval, Inscribed Cover, 1821, 11 1/2 In. 632.00
Box, Oval, Miniature, 19th Century, 3 3/4 In. 690.00
Box, Salmon Brown, 13 1/2 In. 3000.00
Box, Salmon Stain, Poplar, 2-Tier Interior, 3 Drawers, c.1840, 9 x 34 x 9 In. 1150.00
Box, Seed, Pine, Natural, 2 Hinged Cover, Japan Musk Melon, Mt. Lebanon, 5 x 18 In. 385.00
Box, Sewing, Poplar Ware, Felt Top, Tomato Pincushion, 5 1/2 In. 350.00
Box, Sewing, Poplar Ware, Silk Lining, Needle Case, Beeswax, Scissors, Hexagonal ... 440.00
Box, Storage, Ivory Heart Escutcheon, Enfield, N.H., 4 1/4 x 10 In. 1705.00
Box, Yellow, Oval, 13 In. 775.00
Bucket, Green Paint, Signed Cotton Hersey, Pair 4300.00
Carrier, Sewing, 3-Finger, Maple & Pine, Swing Handle, Silk Lining, 5 1/2 x 8 In. 385.00
Carrier, Sewing, 4-Finger, Maple & Cedar, Orange Shellac, Satin Lining, 7 1/2 x 9 In. 495.00
Carte De Visite, 5 Women, Dressed In Shaker Clothes, Churchill & Denison, Civil War 200.00
Carte De Visite, Malinda Hubbard 110.00
Carte De Visite, Rosalinda Allard 100.00
Churn, Cover, Stand, Wooden, 1780s 525.00
Cloak, Gray Wool, 2 Interior Pockets, Sabbathday Lake, Me. 357.00
Cloak, Sister's, Red Wool, Red Silk Lining, Blue Label, E. Canterbury, N.H. 990.00
Colander, Tin, Ring, E. Canterbury, N.H., 4 x 11 1/4 In. 193.00
Counter, Pine, White Painted, Ends, Missing 4 Drawers, c.1850, 37 x 60 x 26 In. 385.00
Cushion, Bureau, Red Velvet, Basketry Base, Doily Top, Mt. Lebanon N.Y., 5 In. 137.00
Dipper, Maple, Pine & Hickory, Worn Gray Paint, c.1850, 8 1/4 x 6 In. 165.00
Doll, Bisque, Glass Eyes, Gray Hooded Cloak & Dress, Lace Trim, 12 1/2 In. 825.00
Door Latch, Strap Hinge 80.00
Dough Box, Poplar, Yellow Varnish Finish, Shaped Handles, 12 x 30 x 14 In. 550.00
Dust Pan, Tin, Steel Bands Reinforced, Loop, 16 1/2 x 17 In. 110.00
Flax Wheel, Maple & Oak, Natural, Stamped FW, 44 1/4 x 36 In. 413.00
Flax Wheel, Maple, Oak, Natural Patina, Stamped SR-AL, c.1840, 34 In. 550.00
Fruit Press, Oak, Maple, Steel Colander, Groveland, N.Y., c.1840, 36 x 30 x 14 In. ... 440.00
Hanger, Cloak, Brass Wire Hook, Long Handled, Ash & Chestnut, 60 3/4 In. 77.00
Hat, Brothers 595.00
Herb Bed, Pine, 7 Slat, Rectangular Rack, New Lebanon, N.Y., c.1840, 75 1/2 x 47 In. 440.00
Holder, Spool, Clamp 398.00
Ironing Board, Pine, Varnish, Portable, Iron Braces, Watervliet, N.Y., 30 x 56 x 14 In. 132.00
Label, Corbett's Shakers' Compound Syrup, Sarsaparilla, June 30, 1906 .... 75.00
Label, Preserved Peaches Ready For Table, Harvard Shakers, Red, Frame, 5 x 6 In. 330.00
Label, Shaker's Apple Sauce, Mount Lebanon, N.Y., Yellow, 4 3/4 x 6 1/4 In. 75.00
Lap Board, Hand Numbered, 1 To 36 In., Esther L. Bishop, Hancock, Mass., 36 x 18 In. 357.00
Manuscript, Journal, July 9, 1852-November 30, 1858, 118 Pages 3105.00
Measure, Maple, Hickory Rim, Steel Braces, ND, Enfield, N.H., c.1850, 6 x 12 In. 165.00
Mop, Maple, Cotton, Natural Patina, 40 In. 137.00
Pail, Blue Paint, White Interior, Handle, 19th Century, 7 1/2 In. 575.00
Pail, Cheese, Blue, c.1880 .... 350.00
Pail, Cover, Pine, Blue Paint, Stamped No. 31, Eliza. Sterling, Canterbury, N.H., 10 In. 880.00
Pail, Cover, Pine, Iron Diamond Bail Plates, Turned Knob, Bail Handle, 12 x 9 In. 1980.00
Pail, Cover, Pine, Steel Bands, Swing Handle, Enfield, N.H., 13 1/4 x 9 3/4 In. 357.00
Pamphlet, Shakers & Shakerism, Giles Avery, Albany N.Y., c.1884, Paper Cover 137.00
Photograph, Anna Case & Isabella Graves, Sabbathday Lake, Creased 110.00
Photograph, Elder H. Green, Horse, Wagon, Alfred, Me., Frame, c.1895, 6 x 8 In. 275.00
Photograph, Laura Love, Sabbathday Lake, Me. 95.00
Pincushion, Small 195.00
Postcard, Shaker Village, Harvard, Mass., 1970s 20.00
Postcard, View, Eldress Bertha Lindsay & Sister, Making Poplar Boxes 20.00
Postcard, View, Painted, Sister Helena Sarle, c.1950 .... 20.00
Print, Dance, Shakers Near Lebanon, Engraved, Frame, 8 1/2 x 12 1/2 In. 440.00
Print, Elder Fred Evans At Home, Harper's Weekly, Sept., 1871, Frame, 9 1/2 x 12 In. 137.00
Rack, Drying, Birch, Red Paint Traces, Pegged & Mortised, Shoe Footed, 24 x 21 In. ... 220.00
Rake, Maple & Oak, Green Paint, Bent Hickory Wooden Brace, 50 x 16 1/4 In. 220.00
Rug, Cotton, Red, Blue, Gray & Olive Graduating Oval Stripes, 65 x 44 In. 715.00
Rug, Mottled Red, Olive & Cream Side, Stripes, Cotton, Wool, 6 Ft. 11 In. x 4 Ft. 8 In. 440.00
Rug, Wool, Multicolored, 49 In. 770.00
Rug, Wool, Ravel-Knit, Shirred, Blue, Gray, Red, Green, Black, 19th Century, 27 x 43 In. 748.00

Shaker, Wool Winder, Maple, Red Repaint, 47 3/4 In.

◆ ◆

To remove the odor from a wooden bowl, try washing it with baking soda or vinegar and then airing it in sunlight. As a last resort, use diluted household bleach. Soak the bowl for about 15 minutes, then rinse with full-strength vinegar, then clear water. If this does not remove the odor, repeat the process with a stronger solution of bleach.

◆ ◆

Rug, Wool, Ravel-Knit, Shirred, Burgundy, Black, Green, Brown, 19th Century, 50 In.	633.00
Rug Whip, Maple, Steel Wire, Label, Levi Shaw, Mt. Lebanon, N.Y., 27 1/2 In.	303.00
Ruler, Tiger Maple, Drilled Hole, c.1840, 2 Ft.	110.00
Scoop, Bentwood, Copper Tack, Worn Varnish, 5 3/4 x 7 1/2 In.	77.00
Scoop, Horehound, White Hellibore Label, Cherry, New Lebanon, N.Y., 9 In., 1 Piece	357.00
Shovel, Maple, Red Stained, 1 Piece Carved Handle, Shaft & Scoop, 41 x 12 In.	495.00
Sieve, Herb, Pink, Natural Patina, Plaid Design, Dyed Horse Hair	385.00
Sieve, Herb, Red & Yellow, Horsehair Woven Into Plaid Design	385.00
Sieve, Horsehair	225.00
Sieve, Woven Horsehair, Herringbone Pattern, Pleasant Hill, Ky.	300.00
Sign, Short, Comprehensive Definition Of Shakerism, O.C. Hampton, Frame, 12 x 8 In.	275.00
Sock Form, Poplar, Canterbury, N.H., Set Of 5	137.00
Spool, Red, Thread	550.00
Spool Holder, Maple, Velvet Tomato Pincushion, Needle Case, 6 In.	275.00
Stereo Card, Church Family, From South, Canterbury	65.00
Stereo Card, Elders & Eldresses Of Canterbury, N.H., WGC Kimball, Concord, N.H...	220.00
Stereo Card, Reat Barn, 240 x 45 Ft., H.A. Kimball, Concord, N.H.	65.00
Stereo Card, Shaker Village, Mt. Lebanon, N.Y., Before Fire, Mid-1870s	80.00
Stereoscope, Chase's Pocket, 2 Cards, 1 Elder & Sister Saxton, Pat. 1872, 3 Piece	770.00
Swift, Table Clamp, Thumbscrews, Maple, Hancock, Me., c.1870, 22 In.	302.00
Tool Carrier, Birch, Natural, Varnished, 3-Finger Hole Handle, 6 x 26 x 9 3/4 In.	385.00
Trunk, Domed Top, Black Painted Leather, Brass, New Lebanon, N.Y., c.1860, 27 In.	220.00
Wood Bin, Poplar, Turned Pegs On Each Side, Worn Paint, 35 x 19 x 38 1/4 In.	495.00
Wool Wheel, Birch, Maple & Hickory, Washed, Signed F.W., 60 x 80 In.	275.00
Wool Winder, Maple, Hand-Held, 4 Extendible Arms, Circular Disc	220.00
Wool Winder, Maple, Red Repaint, 47 3/4 In. ....*Illus*	440.00
Work Stand, Cherry, Butternut, 2 Graduated Drawers, New Lebanon, N.Y., c.1830	6050.00

SHAVING MUGS were popular from 1860 to 1900. Many types were made, including occupational mugs featuring pictures of men's jobs. There were scuttle mugs, silver-plated mugs, glass-lined mugs, and others.

Beaded & Scrolled, Roses, Gray Lustre, Melon Ribbed, Castle Mark, Germany	48.00
Eagle, Flags, Shield & World Globe, Name In Gold, Limoges	110.00
Elk, Hand Painted, Barber's Furniture & Supplies, St. Louis, Mo.	24.00
Flowers, Gold Trim, Name Elmer Olson	65.00
Foresters Of America, Flags, Shield, Deer, Eagle	135.00
Harp On Front, Green, Gold Trim	250.00
Milk Glass, Hazel Atlas	18.00
Multicolored Floral Spray, Scalloped Blank & Handle	35.00
Occupational, 2 Lions & Loaf Of Bread	250.00
Occupational, Baker's Emblem	250.00
Occupational, Black Jack	435.00
Occupational, Blacksmith & Anvil	550.00

Occupational, Brick Layer, 5 Men 575.00
Occupational, Butcher 75.00
Occupational, Butcher, Gutting Cow 275.00
Occupational, Cabinet Maker & Bench 550.00
Occupational, Carpenter, In Workshop, Chas. Kraushaar, Limoges 450.00
Occupational, Cornet Player, Blue Asters, Green Ferns & Leaves 425.00
Occupational, Crossed Wooden Hammers 250.00
Occupational, Electric Motor 375.00
Occupational, Engineer & Fireman, Steam Engine, Coal Car, L. Cooley 395.00
Occupational, Farmer, Man With Plow & Horse 450.00
Occupational, Leather Tanner's Tools 200.00
Occupational, Lit Cigar 300.00
Occupational, Locomotive, Tender, F.C. Fennings, Limoges 395.00
Occupational, Musician, Yellow Horn, Name In Gold & Florals 235.00
Occupational, Photographer's Flash Pan 250.00
Occupational, Railroad Locomotive 200.00
Occupational, Sailboat, Name Gold 225.00
Occupational, Tailor, Cutting Cloth, Gold Name 145.00
Occupational, Telegrapher 300.00
Occupational, Telegrapher At Key, Message 250.00
Occupational, Wild Horse 250.00
Scuttle, Hand Painted Violets, Green Ground, Dated 1901 .... 60.00
Sheaves Of Wheat, Limoges, c.1900 .... 85.00
Tea Leaf Ironstone, Lily-Of-The-Valley Mold, Copper Luster, Shaw 155.00
Train On Front 250.00

SHAWNEE POTTERY was started in Zanesville, Ohio, in 1937. The company made vases, novelty ware, flowerpots, planters, lamps, and cookie jars. Three dinnerware lines were made: Corn, Lobster Ware, and Valencia (a solid color line). White Corn pattern utility pieces were made in 1945. Corn King was made from 1946 to 1954; Corn Queen, with darker green leaves and lighter colored corn, from 1954 to 1961. Shawnee produced pottery for George Rumrill during the late 1930s. The company closed in 1961.

Bank, Bulldog, 4 1/2 In. 165.00
Bank, Tumbling Bear, 4 1/2 In. 185.00
Bookends, Dog Heads 75.00
Bowl, Confetti, Kenwood, Pink, 15 x 5 x 3 In. 25.00
Bowl, Mixing, Corn King, 6 1/2 In. 40.00
Butter, Cover, Corn King ....30.00 to 70.00
Casserole, Corn King, Individual 45.00
Casserole, Cover, Corn King, Large 50.00
Casserole, Lobster Ware 30.00
Casserole, Sundial, Pink 25.00
Coffeepot, Pennsylvania Dutch, Blue 150.00
Cookie Jar, Cookie, Gold ....245.00 to 325.00
Cookie Jar, Corn King ....65.00 to 110.00
Cookie Jar, Cottage 2000.00
Cookie Jar, Drum Major ....285.00 to 495.00
Cookie Jar, Dutch Boy 400.00
Cookie Jar, Dutch Girl 65.00
Cookie Jar, Dutch Girl, Blond, With Gold 285.00
Cookie Jar, Dutch Girl, Tulip 140.00
Cookie Jar, Elephant 80.00
Cookie Jar, Farmer Pig, Shamrock 245.00
Cookie Jar, Gold Elephant 850.00
Cookie Jar, Great Northern Girl, Green Dress 350.00
Cookie Jar, Happy, Striped Pants 250.00
Cookie Jar, Jack Tar 140.00
Cookie Jar, Jojo Clown ....375.00 to 450.00
Cookie Jar, Jojo Clown, Gold 600.00
Cookie Jar, Little, Chef, Caramel ....110.00 to 145.00
Cookie Jar, Muggsy ....360.00 to 425.00
Cookie Jar, Owl 130.00

Cookie Jar, Pennsylvania Dutch Jug 165.00
Cookie Jar, Pink Elephant .... 65.00 to 115.00
Cookie Jar, Puss 'n Boots .... 85.00 to 225.00
Cookie Jar, Puss 'n Boots, Gold 295.00
Cookie Jar, Puss 'n Boots, White Bow, Gold Trim 595.00
Cookie Jar, Smiley, Blue Collar, Gold Trim 475.00
Cookie Jar, Smiley, Blue, Yellow Kerchief, Gold Trim..*Illus* 115.00
Cookie Jar, Smiley, Chrysanthemum .... 275.00 to 365.00
Cookie Jar, Smiley, Gold 425.00
Cookie Jar, Smiley, Shamrocks.. 245.00
Cookie Jar, Smiley, Shamrocks, Gold Trim .... 325.00 to 495.00
Cookie Jar, Smiley, Tulips 250.00
Cookie Jar, Smiley, Unpainted... 75.00
Cookie Jar, Smiley, Yellow Bib... 320.00
Cookie Jar, Smiley, Yellow Bib, Gold Trim, Decals... 495.00
Cookie Jar, Winnie, Blue Collar.. 250.00 to 350.00
Cookie Jar, Winnie, Green Collar 365.00
Cookie Jar, Winnie, Red & Gold 395.00
Cookie Jar, Winnie, Shamrocks 295.00
Cookie Jar, Winnie, Shamrocks, Green Collar .... 175.00 to 300.00
Creamer, Corn King, No. 70... 15.00
Creamer, Elephant .... 15.00 to 48.00
Creamer, Elephant, Gold, Decals.. 250.00
Creamer, Elephant, Red & Gold 125.00
Creamer, Pekinese 40.00
Creamer, Pennsylvania Dutch, Ball 50.00
Creamer, Puss 'n Boots, Yellow 48.00
Creamer, Puss 'n Boots, Gold Trim .... 150.00 to 225.00
Creamer, Puss 'n Boots, Yellow & Green... 50.00 to 62.00
Creamer, Smiley, Clover Bud 150.00
Creamer, Smiley, Gold 225.00
Creamer, Smiley, Peach & Gold.. 90.00 to 110.00
Creamer, Sunflower .... 25.00 to 40.00
Creamer, Tulip.. 110.00
Cup & Saucer, Corn King.. 35.00
Cup & Saucer, Corn King, 4 Sets 140.00
Figurine, Bear 21.00
Figurine, Pekinese .... 45.00 to 75.00
Figurine, Rabbit 21.00
Figurine, Raccoon 60.00
Flower Frog, Sea Horse, 3 1/2 In. 30.00
Flower Frog, Snail, 4 x 5 In.. 20.00
Flower Frog, Swan, 4 1/4 In... 30.00
Flower Frog & Bowl, Dolphin, Light Blue 18.00
Hors D'Oeuvre, Lobster 129.00

Shawnee, Cookie Jar, Smiley,
Blue, Yellow Kerchief, Gold Trim

♦♦♦♦♦♦♦♦♦♦♦♦♦♦♦♦♦♦♦♦♦♦♦♦

The average burglar spends
60 seconds breaking into a
house. If you can delay them
with bars, locks, or other
security measures, they may
become impatient and leave.

♦♦♦♦♦♦♦♦♦♦♦♦♦♦♦♦♦♦♦♦♦♦♦♦

Jug, Valencia, Green 35.00
Matchbox Holder, Fern 95.00
Pepper Shaker, Owl 14.50
Pie Bird, Pink..35.00 to 75.00
Pitcher, Bo Peep, Gold, Decals 275.00
Pitcher, Bo Peep, No. 47 .... 90.00
Pitcher, Bo Peep, Small... 88.00
Pitcher, Bo Peep, White, Yellow, Green 155.00
Pitcher, Boy Blue ....50.00 to 125.00
Pitcher, Chanticleer ....45.00 to 125.00
Pitcher, Juice, Fruit, Tilt, Round 50.00
Pitcher, Milk, Bo Peep, Heavy Gold 175.00
Pitcher, Pennsylvania Dutch, Tilt.. 78.00
Pitcher, Rooster, Gold Sponge, Gold Lines.. 230.00
Pitcher, Smiley 125.00
Pitcher, Smiley, Gold Trim 425.00
Pitcher, Smiley, Peach.. 120.00
Pitcher, Stars & Stripes 18.00
Planter, Auto, Gold 25.00
Planter, Bicycle Built For Two... 10.00
Planter, Canopy Bed.. 125.00
Planter, Chantilly, Label 10.00
Planter, Chihuahua & Doghouse 25.00
Planter, Clown, Flowerpot Type, Gold.. 40.00
Planter, Clown, No. 607 .... 25.00
Planter, Clown, No. 619 .... 30.00
Planter, Covered Wagon 30.00
Planter, Deer & Fawn... 25.00
Planter, Dog In Boat.. 10.00
Planter, Dutch Mill, Gold Trim 24.00
Planter, Elf & Shoe, Gold Trim.. 35.00
Planter, Fox & Bag... 40.00
Planter, Girl & Mandolin, No. 576... 15.00
Planter, Hobby Horse... 12.00
Planter, House 45.00
Planter, Queenie Dog 20.00
Planter, Rabbit & Wheelbarrow 225.00
Planter, Ram... 33.00
Planter, Rooster.. 33.00
Planter, Sleepy Owl.. 45.00
Planter, Squirrel & Nut 35.00
Planter, Teddy & Wagon.. 58.00
Planter, Tractor Trailer...25.00 to 80.00
Planter, Wishing Well 60.00
Plate, Corn King, 10 In... 37.00
Plate, Corn King, No. 68 .... 30.00
Platter, Corn King, 12 In.. 45.00
Salt & Pepper, Bo Peep & Sailor Boy ....14.00 to 125.00
Salt & Pepper, Chanticleer.. 48.00
Salt & Pepper, Chef ....15.00 to 17.00
Salt & Pepper, Cookie House.. 395.00
Salt & Pepper, Corn King, 3 1/4 In.. 20.00
Salt & Pepper, Corn King, 5 1/4 In...25.00 to 28.00
Salt & Pepper, Cottage.. 425.00
Salt & Pepper, Dutch Boy & Girl ....55.00 to 75.00
Salt & Pepper, Dutch Boy & Girl, Gold, Decals..................................... 175.00
Salt & Pepper, Farmer Pig ....30.00 to 40.00
Salt & Pepper, Fruit..27.00 to 28.00
Salt & Pepper, Milk Can...12.00 to 20.00
Salt & Pepper, Muggsy, 3 1/4 In...48.00 to 55.00
Salt & Pepper, Muggsy, 5 1/2 In...60.00 to 175.00
Salt & Pepper, Muggsy, Gold Trim, 5 1/4 In. 80.00
Salt & Pepper, Owl, Blue Eyes ....10.00 to 20.00

Salt & Pepper, Owl, Gold, 3 1/4 In. 70.00
Salt & Pepper, Peek A Boos, Small 250.00
Salt & Pepper, Puss 'n Boots .... 30.00 to 45.00
Salt & Pepper, Smiley 35.00
Salt & Pepper, Smiley, Green 125.00
Salt & Pepper, Smiley, Green Bib 110.00
Salt & Pepper, Smiley, Peach 50.00
Salt & Pepper, Smiley, Pink Scarf 90.00
Salt & Pepper, Swiss Boy & Girl, Gold Trim 85.00
Salt & Pepper, Watering Cans .... 8.00 to 20.00
Salt & Pepper, Winnie & Smiley, 3 In. .... 25.00 to 55.00
Salt & Pepper, Winnie & Smiley, Clover Bud .... 55.00 to 155.00
Salt & Pepper, Winnie & Smiley, Heart, Range .... 135.00 to 145.00
Saltshaker, Lobster 46.00
Saltshaker, Muggsy, 5 1/2 In. 135.00
Saltshaker, Puss 'n Boots 14.00
Saltshaker, Smiley, Green, 5 1/2 In. 125.00
Saltshaker, Smiley, Peach, 3 1/4 In. 60.00
Saltshaker, Smiley, Peach, 5 1/2 In. 125.00
Sugar, Cover, Corn King 35.00
Sugar & Creamer, Flower & Fern 22.00
Teapot, Blue Flower .... 40.00 to 45.00
Teapot, Blue Flower, Gold 50.00
Teapot, Blue Snowflake, Individual 55.00
Teapot, Corn King, 10 Oz. .... 82.00 to 250.00
Teapot, Corn King, 30 Oz. 90.00
Teapot, Corn Queen, 10 Oz. 250.00
Teapot, Elephant 250.00
Teapot, Embossed Rose, Green 18.00
Teapot, Embossed Rose, Peach 15.00
Teapot, Floral, Gold 50.00
Teapot, Granny Ann .... 70.00 to 135.00
Teapot, Granny Ann, Gold, Decals 275.00
Teapot, Granny Ann, Green Shawl 165.00
Teapot, Granny Ann, Peach, Blue Apron .... 90.00 to 110.00
Teapot, Pennsylvania Dutch, 18 Oz. 75.00
Teapot, Pennsylvania Dutch, Yellow, 10 Oz. 20.00
Teapot, Red Flower 25.00
Teapot, Snowflake, 10 Oz. 6.00
Teapot, Snowflake, Blue, 10 Oz. 55.00
Teapot, Sunflower .... 70.00 to 75.00
Teapot, Tom The Piper's Son, White 75.00
Utility Jar, Corn King 35.00
Vase, Philodendron, Gold Trim, No. 805 .... 35.00
Wall Pocket, Birds On Roof 15.00
Wall Pocket, Little Bo Peep 25.00
Wall Pocket, Mantel Clock 25.00
Wall Pocket, Scotty .... 17.00 to 50.00
Wall Pocket, Telephone, Gold 45.00

SHEARWATER pottery is a family business started by Mr. and Mrs. G. W. Anderson, Sr., and their three sons. The local Ocean Springs, Mississippi, clays were used to make the wares in the 1930s. The company is still in business.

Lamp, Black Minstrel Player, White 175.00
Plate, Pirate Holding Sword, Black Beard & Eyebrows, Signed, 6 In. 45.00
Pot, Gunmetal Green, Peter Anderson, 1930, 3 x 5 In. 475.00
Vase, Aqua, Gunmetal & Pale Green Glaze, Signed, 6 In. 175.00
Vase, Crimped, Turquoise, 9 1/2 In. 75.00
Vase, Hat Shape, Flaring Rim, Metallic Olive Green Glaze, 2 1/2 x 5 In. 150.00

SHEET MUSIC from the past centuries is now collected. The favorites are examples with covers featuring artistic or historic pictures. Early sheet music covers were lithographed, but by the 1900s photographic reproductions were

used. The early music was larger than more recent sheets and you must watch
out for examples that were trimmed to fit in a twentieth-century piano bench.

A White Sport Coat, Marty Robbins	15.00
Alcoholic Blues, 1919	10.00
Amelia Earhart's Last Flight	25.00 to 35.00
Animal Crackers, Marx Brothers	25.00
Barney Google, Barney & Sparkplug Cover, 1923	15.00 to 22.00
Be Careful, It's My Heart, 1942	35.00
Be My Love, Mario Lanza	10.00
Bewitched, Television Series, 1964	20.00
Bidin' My Time, J. Garland, M. Rooney, T. Dorsey, 1930	14.00
Christmas Holiday, Deanna Durbin, 1943	8.00
Conquered Banner, Confederate Flag In Sunset, New Orleans, 1866	85.00
Daddy Don't You Walk So Fast, Wayne Newton, 1970	4.00
Diana, Paul Anka	15.00
Down Argentina Way, B. Grable, D. Ameche, C. Miranda, 1940	16.00
Easter Parade, J. Garland, F. Astaire, 1947	14.00
Friendly Persuasion, Gary Cooper, Dorothy McGuire On Cover, 1968	5.00
Hers To Hold, Deanna Durbin, 1943	8.00
I Get The Neck Of The Chicken, Victor Mature & Ginny Simms, 1942	4.00
I Have But One Heart, Frank Sinatra	25.00
I'm A Jonah Man, Black Minstrels	50.00
I'm Getting So Now I Don't Care, Rudolph Valentino, 1924	20.00
I'm Nobody's Baby, Andy Hardy Meets Debutante, J. Garland, M. Rooney, 1940	20.00
Indian Fable, Red Wing	20.00
It's A Hap-Hap-Happy Day, 1939	12.00
Jenny Lind's Songs, Full Length Portrait Of Swedish Nightegale, 1860s	45.00
Last Train To Clarksville, Monkees, 1966	18.00
Little Orphan Annie, 1931	10.00
Mad About Music, Deanna Durbin, 1938	8.00
Mr. Sandman, Chordettes	8.00
My Own True Love, Gone With The Wind, C. Gable, V. Leigh	12.00
Oh! Gee, Oh! Gosh, Oh! Golly, I'm In Love, Eddie Cantor On Cover, 1923	8.00
Oh! Your Circus Day, Girl On Tiger's Foot, Clown	95.00
On The Atchison, Topeka & Santa Fe, Judy Garland, 1945	20.00
Over There, Norman Rockwell Cover	35.00
Perfect Song, Featuring Amos 'n Andy, Pepsodent Hour, 1939	35.00
Ragtime Cowboy	40.00
Re-Enlistment Blues, From Here To Eternity, B. Lancaster, D. Kerr, M. Clift, 1953	15.00
Roses In December, Harriet Hillard, 1937	4.00
Saint Louis Blues, Louis Armstrong On Cover, 1942	4.00
Stars & Stripes Forever	35.00
Swinging On The Swanee Shore, 1935	10.00
The Stroll, Diamonds	20.00
They're On Their Way To Mexico, Irving Berlin, 1914	20.00
Trinity Chimes, Lincoln, 1909	7.00
Trolley Song, Judy Garland On Cover	10.00
Venus, Frankie Avalon	12.00
When The Moon Comes Over The Mountain, Kate Smith, 1931	10.00
White Christmas, Irving Berlin, 1943	14.00
Wizard Of Oz, Stars On Cover, 1939	15.00 to 50.00
Wreck Of The Titanic, 1912	30.00
Yale, Football, 1906	19.00
You'll Always Be The One I Love, Frank Sinatra Cover, 1946	15.00
You're Sensational	11.00
Your Cheatin' Heart, Hank Williams On Cover, 1952	5.00

SHELLEY first appeared on English ceramics about 1912. The Foley China
Works started in England in 1860. Joseph Ball Shelley joined the company in
1862 and became a partner in 1872. Percy Shelley joined the firm in 1881.
The company went through a series of name changes and in 1910 the then
Foley China Company became Shelley China. In 1929 it became Shelley Pot-
teries. The company was acquired in 1966 by Allied English Potteries, then

merged with the Doulton group in 1971. The name *Shelley* was put into use again in 1980.

Ashtray, Blue Rock	30.00
Bowl, Japanese Lake Scene, Octagonal, 8 In.	350.00
Bowl, Vegetable, Wildflower, Oval	199.00
Breakfast Set, Indian Peony, Green, 3 Piece	75.00
Cake Plate, Blue Rock	85.00
Cake Plate, Crochet, 2 Handles, Yellow	105.00
Candy Dish, Rose Spray, 6 Flutes	60.00
Cheese Dish, Domed Cover, Dainty Orange, Oval, 6 Flutes	375.00
Coffeepot, Colonial Bouquet	359.00
Coffeepot, Lily Of The Valley, 6 Flutes	235.00
Coffeepot, Lily Of The Valley, Demitasse	155.00
Coffeepot, Wildflower	370.00
Creamer, Bridal Rose	45.00
Creamer, Silver Art Deco Design, Black Ground	45.00
Cup & Saucer, Begonia	35.00 to 50.00
Cup & Saucer, Blue Poppy, Demitasse	40.00
Cup & Saucer, Bridal Rose	45.00 to 48.00
Cup & Saucer, Celandine, 6 Flutes, Demitasse	45.00
Cup & Saucer, Charm, Blue, 6 Flutes	65.00
Cup & Saucer, Dainty White	30.00
Cup & Saucer, Harebell, Petal	48.00 to 65.00
Cup & Saucer, Heather	45.00 to 48.00
Cup & Saucer, Lily Of The Valley	40.00 to 48.00
Cup & Saucer, Maytime	45.00 to 50.00
Cup & Saucer, Ovington	48.00
Cup & Saucer, Primrose, 14 Flutes	68.00
Cup & Saucer, Regency	45.00
Cup & Saucer, Rock Garden	35.00 to 70.00
Cup & Saucer, Rose & Red Daisy, Demitasse	45.00
Cup & Saucer, Rose Spray, Green Border	50.00
Cup & Saucer, Rosebud	48.00
Cup & Saucer, Rosebud, 16 Flutes, Demitasse	45.00
Cup & Saucer, Summer Glory	48.00
Cup & Saucer, Wild Anemone	48.00
Cup & Saucer, Woodland, Blue Foot & Handle, Demitasse	50.00 to 65.00
Cup & Saucer, Yellow Flowers, White Ground, 6 Flutes	15.00
Eggcup, Blue Flowers	30.00
Eggcup, Regency, 6 Flutes	50.00
Jam Pot, Orange, Beige	65.00
Pitcher, Cranes, England	50.00
Plate, Begonia, 6 Flutes, 6 1/4 In.	50.00
Plate, Begonia, 6 Flutes, 9 In.	65.00
Plate, Duchess, Blue, 11 In.	75.00
Plate, Harebell, 8 In.	50.00
Plate, Lakeland, Square, Signed, 5 1/2 In.	20.00
Plate, Luncheon, Birds, Scene, Old Sevres, 8 Piece	375.00
Plate, Niagara, 10 In.	18.00
Plate, Pink Flowers, Square, 5 1/2 In.	20.00
Plate, Regency, 6 In.	25.00
Plate, Rose Spray, 8 In.	150.00
Plate, Shereton, Green, 8 In.	35.00
Plate, Wild Flower, 6 Flutes, 6 In.	35.00
Platter, Blue Rock, 17 In.	200.00
Saucer, Dainty Blue	20.00
Set, Demitasse, Phlox, Blue, Pink, 20 Piece	750.00
Sugar, Bridal Rose	45.00
Sugar, Creamer & Tray, Rose Spray, 3 Piece	150.00
Sugar & Creamer, Blue Rock	60.00
Sugar & Creamer, Crochet, Yellow & Beige	110.00

Sugar & Creamer, Dainty Blue	95.00
Sugar & Creamer, Georgian	100.00
Sugar & Creamer, Mixed Flowers	125.00
Sugar & Creamer, Rock Garden	69.00
Tea Set, Flute, Blue, 15 Piece	695.00
Teapot, Rosebud, 6 Flutes	250.00
Vase, Balloons & Flashes, 5 In.	325.00
Vase, Black, Violets, 5 In.	175.00
Vase, Bud, Orange, Storks, 6 1/2 In.	165.00
Vase, Bud, Twin, Fruit, Black & Orange, 3 In., Pair	125.00
Vase, Cloissello, 10 In.	475.00
Vase, Harmony, 9 In.	165.00
Vase, Japanese Fruit, Luster, 10 In.	350.00
Vase, Storks, Orange, 6 1/2 In.	195.00

SHIRLEY TEMPLE, the famous movie star, was born in 1928. She made her first movie in 1932. Thousands of items picturing Shirley have been and still are being made. Shirley Temple dolls were first made in 1934 by Ideal Toy Company. Millions of Shirley Temple cobalt blue glass dishes were made by Hazel Atlas Glass Company and U.S. Glass Company from 1934 to 1942. They were given away as premiums for Wheaties and Bisquick. A bowl, mug, and pitcher were made as a breakfast set. Some pieces were decorated with the picture of a very young Shirley, others used a picture of Shirley in her 1936 *Captain January* costume. Although collectors refer to a cobalt creamer, it is actually the 4 1/2-inch-high milk pitcher from the breakfast set. Many of these items are being reproduced today.

Album, Song, No. 2, Movietone Corp, 1936, 8 Songs	28.00
Book, Big Little Book, The Littlest Rebel	17.00
Book, Poor Little Rich Girl	39.00
Calendar, Starlight Trail, 1938, 36 In.	45.00
Card, Playing, Bridge, Shirley With Sunbonnet, Blue, 1940	60.00
Card, Playing, Shirley's Picture, Yellow, 1940	110.00
Carriage, Baby's, Wicker, Hooded	523.00
Doll, 1950, 12 In.	150.00
Doll, 5 Piece Composition Body, Hazel Sleep Eyes, Dress, 13 In.	305.00
Doll, Baby, Composition, Bent Limb Cloth Body, White Dress, 16 In.	850.00
Doll, Composition, Dress, Tag, 22 In.	750.00
Doll, Composition, Flirty Sleep Eyes, Mohair Wig, Ideal, Box, 25 In.	1600.00
Doll, Composition, Original Hair, Pink Organdy Dress, 17 In.	1350.00
Doll, Composition, Tagged Dress, 18 In.	245.00
Doll, Hawaiian, Original Clothes, Ideal, 13 In.	210.00
Doll, Ideal, 1940s, 18 In.	440.00
Doll, Ideal, Composition Box, 17 In. .... *Illus*	632.00
Doll, Original Clothes, Label & Pin, 16 In.	895.00
Doll, Original Clothes, Pin, 18 1/2 In.	995.00
Doll, Socket Head, Open Mouth, Teeth, Dress, Reliable, 1935, 22 In.	1200.00
Doll, Stand Up & Cheer Outfit, 1972	69.00
Doll, Starburst Design Dress, Ideal, 22 In.	995.00
Fan, RC Cola, Hand	45.00
Figurine, Chalkware	55.00
Mirror, Pocket, 1937	30.00
Mug	46.00
Paper Doll, Movie Outfits, Tom Tierney, Black & White, Uncut	60.00
Paper Doll, Whitman, 1986, Uncut	20.00
Picture, Sepia, 11 x 14 In.	75.00
Pitcher, Cobalt Blue	42.00 to 65.00
Pitcher, Cobalt Blue, 4 1/2 In.	40.00
Plate, Baby Takes A Bow	75.00
Poster, Bright Eyes, 1934	20.00
Sheet Music, Stowaway, 1936	15.00
Trunk, Brown Wood, 17 In.	180.00

SHRINER, see Fraternal category

SILVER DEPOSIT glass was made during the late nineteenth and early twentieth centuries. Solid sterling silver was applied to the glass by a chemical method so that a cutout design of silver metal appeared against a clear or colored glass. It is sometimes called silver overlay.

Decanter, Game Cocks, Pinched, Stopper	125.00
Decanter, Green, Design	25.00
Decanter, Scotsman	20.00
Decanter, Whiskey, Game Cocks, Pinched	125.00
Dish, Etched	35.00
Pitcher, Grape & Vine Design, Pear Shape, 4 1/2 In.	95.00
Plate, Rounded Corners, Square 10 In.	45.00
Punch Set, Peacocks, Orange, Czechoslovakia, 8 Piece	395.00
Sugar & Creamer, Cambridge	35.00
Vase, Crane, Orange, 11 In.	65.00
Vase, Jack-In-The-Pulpit, 9 In.	310.00

SILVER FLATWARE includes many of the current and out-of-production silver and silver-plated flatware patterns made in the past eighty years. Other silver is listed under Silver-American, Silver-English, etc. Most silver flatware sets that are missing a few pieces can be completed through the help of one of the many silver matching services listed in *Kovels' Guide to Selling, Buying, and Fixing Your Antiques and Collectibles.*

SILVER FLATWARE PLATED, Alhambra, Cold Meat Fork	7.00
Alhambra, Food Pusher, Wallace	45.00
Alhambra, Pickle Fork, Twisted, 8-In. Long Handle	4.00
Alhambra, Soup Ladle, Wallace, 10 1/2 In.	135.00
Alhambra, Teaspoon	1.00
Allure, Teaspoon	1.00
Ambassador, Dinner Fork, Notched Handle	2.00
Ancestral, Dinner Knife, Solid Handle	2.00
Anniversary, Soup Spoon, Round	3.00
Anniversary, Sugar Spoon	2.00
Baroque, Bread Knife, Wallace, 13 1/2 In.	195.00
Burlington, Bouillon Spoon	2.00
Charter Oak, Dinner Fork	40.00
Charter Oak, Dinner Place Setting, Moselle, 4 Piece	125.00
Charter Oak, Soup Spoon, Rogers	40.00
Chatham, Soup Spoon	8.00
Columbia, Salad Fork, Rogers	45.00
D'Orleans, Serving Spoon, Towle, Large	45.00

*Shirley Temple, Doll, Ideal,
Composition Box, 17 In.*

♦ ♦

If your doll's body leaks sawdust, try patching the hole by putting a few drops of clear glue in the hole. If the hole is too large, patch it with a piece of muslin or kid cut from an old glove. Cut a circular patch and glue in place.

♦ ♦

Daisy, Gravy Ladle 40.00
Elite, Soup Spoon, Oval 10.00
Enchantment, Butter Knife, Master 6.00
Enchantment, Dinner Fork 8.00
Fiddle Thread, Salad Fork, F. Smith 20.00
Fiddle Thread, Teaspoon, F. Smith 15.00
Fleur De Luce, Dinner Fork, Community 20.00
Fleur De Luce, Dinner Knife, Community 20.00
Floral, Pie Server, Wallace 75.00
Floral, Salad Fork, Wallace, 1903 .... 25.00
Floral, Soup Spoon, Wallace 15.00
Glenrose, Butter Spreader, Rogers 18.00
La Vigne, Citrus Spoon, Rogers 25.00
La Vigne, Strawberry Fork, Rogers 60.00
La Vigne, Sugar Tongs, Rogers 90.00
Lyonaise, Soup Ladle, Eastlake 75.00
Martha Washington, Teaspoon, F. Smith 10.00
Martinique, Soup Spoon, Oval 7.00
Martinque, Vegetable Serving Spoon 12.00
Old Colonial, Gravy Ladle, Towle 45.00
Old Colonial, Luncheon Fork, Towle 25.00
Old Colony, Ice Cream Spoon, Rogers 35.00
Old English, Luncheon Fork, Towle 20.00
Old English, Teaspoon, Towle 12.00
Princess Mary, Dinner Knife, Wallace 18.00
Princess Mary, Salad Fork, Wallace 18.00
Rhythm, Dinner Knife, Wallace 18.00
Rhythm, Sauce Ladle, Wallace 18.00
Rhythm, Spoon, Iced Tea, Wallace 18.00
Unique, Demitasse Spoon, Reed & Barton 15.00
Vintage, Carving Set, Rogers, 3 Piece 135.00
Vintage, Cream Soup Spoon, Rogers 25.00
SILVER FLATWARE STERLING, Abbotsford, Berry Spoon, International 75.00
Abbottsford, Luncheon Fork, International 20.00
Acorn, Pickle Fork, Georg Jensen 125.00
Aegean Wave, Knife, Wallace 25.00
Afterglow, Place Setting, Oneida, 4 Piece 65.00
Afterglow, Sugar Spoon, Oneida 15.00
Afterglow, Teaspoon, Oneida 14.00
Ailanthus, Cold Meat Fork, Tiffany 375.00
Ailanthus, Olive Fork, Tiffany 225.00
Alhambra, Egg Spoon, Whiting 25.00
Alhambra, Mustard Ladle, Whiting 35.00
Alhambra, Sauce Ladle, Whiting 75.00
American Chippendale, Horseradish Spoon, Frank Smith 50.00
American Chippendale, Olive Spoon, Frank Smith 45.00
American Classic, Butter Knife, Master 25.00
Angelo, Berry Spoon, Wood & Hughes 235.00
Angelo, Fish Knife, Knowles 30.00
Angelo, Sugar Sifter, Gorham 125.00
Arabesque, Mustard Ladle, Whiting 90.00
Arabesque, Teaspoon, Whiting 22.00
Audubon, Coffee Spoon, Tiffany, 6 Piece 455.00
Audubon, Ice Cream Server, Tiffany, 12 In. 975.00
Audubon, Ice Cream Spoon, Gold Wash, Tiffany 165.00
Avalon, Olive Spoon, International 65.00
Baronial, Chocolate Muddler, Gorham 80.00
Baronial, Mustard Ladle, Gorham 50.00
Baronial, Salad Fork, Gorham 30.00
Beacon Hill, Salad Fork, International 15.00
Ben Franklin, Bonbon Spoon, Towle 30.00
Ben Franklin, Salt Spoon, Towle 11.00
Ben Franklin, Strawberry Fork, Towle 28.00

Bird, Teaspoon, Whiting 20.00
Blossom, Ladle, Georg Jensen, 13 In. 880.00
Bridal Rose, Berry Spoon, Alvin 175.00
Bridal Rose, Chocolate Spoon, Alvin 65.00
Bridal Rose, Cream Ladle, Alvin 85.00
Bridal Rose, Dinner Fork, Alvin 65.00
Bridal Rose, Gravy Ladle, Alvin 225.00
Bridal Rose, Olive Spoon, Alvin .... 75.00 to 195.00
Bridal Rose, Sardine Fork, Alvin .... 75.00 to 150.00
Broom Corn, Chicken Claw Tongs, Tiffany 675.00
Broom Corn, Punch Ladle, Tiffany 850.00
Broom Corn, Stuffing Spoon, Tiffany 575.00
Buckingham, Soup Spoon, Gorham, 6 3/4 In. 23.00
Buckingham, Tomato Server, Gorham, 7 1/2 In. 110.00
Buttercup, Bonbon, Pierced, Gorham 45.00
Buttercup, Fork, Gorham, 7 1/2 In. 50.00
Buttercup, Pasta Scoop, Gorham 25.00
Buttercup, Pastry Tongs, Gorham, 6 In. 295.00
Buttercup, Punch Ladle, Gorham 27.00
Buttercup, Salad Set, Gold Wash, Gorham 325.00
Buttercup, Stuffing Spoon, Gorham, 12 1/4 In. 85.00
Buttercup, Teaspoon, Gorham 20.00
Cactus, Salad Fork & Spoon, Georg Jensen 330.00
Cactus, Spoon, Iced Tea, Georg Jensen, 6 Piece 192.00
Cambridge, Lemon Fork, Gorham 30.00
Cambridge, Mustard Ladle, Gorham 60.00
Cambridge, Salad Fork, Gorham 35.00
Candlelight, Cheese Cleaver, Towle 19.00
Candlelight, Punch Ladle, Double Lip, Towle 375.00
Candlelight, Sugar Spoon, Towle 18.00
Candlelight, Tomato Server, Towle 50.00
Carthage, Salad Fork, Wallace 32.00
Castle Rose, Dinner Service, Chest, 36 Piece 625.00
Castle Rose, Teaspoon, Gorham 10.50
Celeste, Cream Ladle, Gorham 20.00
Celeste, Teaspoon, Gorham 11.00
Celestial, Ice Cream Spoon, Wood & Hughes 55.00
Century, Fruit Spoon, Dominick & Haff 20.00
Century, Tea Infuser, Dominick & Haff 110.00
Chambord, Meat Fork, Reed & Barton 75.00
Chantilly, Asparagus Tong, Gorham 165.00
Chantilly, Butter Knife, Gorham 21.00
Chantilly, Gravy Ladle, Gorham 65.00
Chantilly, Luncheon Fork, Gorham 18.00
Chantilly, Vegetable Serving Spoon 70.00
Charter Oak, Cocktail Fork, Rogers, 6 Piece 125.00
Chateau Rose, Service For 11, 65 Piece 2300.00
Chippendale, Cheese Cleaver, Towle 21.00
Chippendale, Lettuce Fork, Alvin 85.00
Chippendale, Soup Ladle, Gorham 275.00
Chrysanthemum, Chocolate Spoon, Durgin, 4 In. 45.00
Chrysanthemum, Grapefruit Spoon, Durgin 55.00
Chrysanthemum, Sardine Fork, Durgin 125.00
Cloud, Cocktail Fork, Gorham 65.00
Cluny, Fish Slice, Gorham, 11 1/2 In. 475.00
Colonial, Cake Knife, Bright Cut Blade, Gorham 225.00
Continental, Service For 2, Georg Jensen, 12 Piece 825.00
Coronet, Salad Set, Lunt 65.00
Cortland, Salad Fork, International 25.00
Cortland, Salad Fork, Lunt 20.00
Cotillion, Pastry Fork, Federal, 6 Piece 200.00
Craftsman, Gravy Ladle, Towle 35.00
Craftsman, Salt Spoon, Towle 11.00

Craftsman, Teaspoon, Towle	14.00
Damask Rose, Teaspoon, Oneida	13.00
Devon, Service For 6, Reed & Barton, Chest, 1911, 24 Piece	900.00
Diamond, Mustard Ladle, Shiebler	65.00
Diamond, Salt Spoon, Polhemus	25.00
Douvaine, Master Butter Knife, Unger	75.00
Douvaine, Mustard Ladle, Unger	125.00
Douvaine, Nut Scoop, Unger	165.00
Douvaine, Sardine Fork, Unger	175.00
Douvaine, Sugar Spoon, Unger	60.00
Douvaine, Sugar Tongs, Unger	65.00
Dresden, Asparagus Fork, Whiting	295.00
Du Barry, Lettuce Spoon, Durgin	110.00
Du Barry, Salad Set, Durgin	350.00
Du Barry, Tomato Server, Durgin	225.00
Duchess, Sauce Ladle, Whiting	35.00
Duke Of York, Fork, Whiting	19.00
Easter Lily, Salad Set, Alvin	600.00
Eloquence, Salad Set, Lunt, 2 Piece	175.00
Eloquence, Sugar Spoon, Lunt	35.00
Empire, Teaspoon, Buccelati	30.00
Enchantress, Salad Fork, International	21.00
Enchantress, Sugar Spoon, International	15.00
Enchantress, Teaspoon, International	14.00
Engagement, Cream Soup Spoon, Oneida	16.00
Engagement, Luncheon Fork, Oneida ..:	20.00
Engagement, Teaspoon, Oneida	13.00
English King, Lobster Fork, Gold Wash Bowl, William Gale	400.00
English Shell, Butter Spreader, Lunt, Individual	16.00
English Shell, Luncheon Fork, Lunt	22.00
English Shell, Salad Fork, Lunt	21.00
Etruscan, Dinner Fork	25.00
Etruscan, Salad Fork, Gold Wash, Gorham	32.00
Etruscan, Teaspoon, Gorham	12.00
Fairfax, Lasagna Server, Gorham	25.00
Fairfax, Pie Server, Durgin	150.00
Fairfax, Salad Fork, Gorham	22.00
Fairfax, Steak Carving Set, Gorham	65.00
Fairfax, Sugar Tongs, Durgin	26.00
Fairfax, Tablespoon, Durgin	25.00
Feather Edge, Tablespoon, Buccelati	65.00
Federal Cotillion, Cold Meat Fork, Frank Smith	95.00
Federal Cotillion, Cream Soup Spoon, Frank Smith	45.00
Federal Cotillion, Pickle Fork, Frank Smith	45.00
Fiddle Shell, Cake Server, Frank Smith	29.00
First Frost, Cocktail Fork, Oneida	19.00
First Frost, Pickle Fork, Oneida	18.00
First Frost, Place Setting, Oneida, 4 Piece	80.00
First Frost, Tablespoon, Oneida	40.00
Fleetwood, Butter Spreader, Manchester, Individual	13.00
Fleetwood, Sugar Spoon, Manchester	15.00
Fleetwood, Teaspoon, Manchester	12.00
Fleur-De-Lis, Soup Ladle, Alvin	255.00
Fleury, Olive Spoon, Gorham	48.00
Florentine, Cheese Knife, Wendt	85.00
Florentine, Fish Fork, Gorham	55.00
Florentine, Pie Server, Wendt	125.00
Florentine, Sardine Fork, International	45.00
Fontaine, Tablespoon, International	16.00
Fontainebleau, Sardine Fork, Gorham	125.00
Fontainebleau, Soup Ladle, Gorham	350.00 to 475.00
Fontainebleau, Sugar Spoon, Gorham	35.00

Fontana, Salt Spoon, Towle 11.00
Francis I, Baby Set, Reed & Barton, 2 Piece 45.00
Francis I, Fish Knife, Reed & Barton 295.00
Francis I, Gravy Ladle, Reed & Barton 70.00
Francis I, Jelly Roll Server, Reed & Barton 150.00
Francis I, Meat Fork, Alvin 45.00
Francis I, Pie Server, Reed & Barton 125.00
Francis I, Tomato Server, Reed & Barton 80.00
French Provincial, Strawberry Fork, Towle 19.00
French Provincial, Teaspoon, Towle 12.00
French Provincial, Youth Set, Towle, 3 Piece 50.00
French Renaissance, Gravy Ladle, Reed & Barton 35.00
French Renaissance, Pickle Fork, Reed & Barton 25.00
French Renaissance, Teaspoon, Reed & Barton 15.00
Frontenac, Dinner Knife, International 45.00
Frontenac, Salad Fork, International 70.00
Frontenac, Sauce Ladle, International 85.00
Frontenac, Tablespoon, International 65.00
Fuchsia, Demitasse Spoon, Georg Jensen 25.00
George III, Fish Fork, Whiting 30.00
George III, Jelly Server, Whiting 30.00
Georgian, Nut Spoon, Gilt, Towle 235.00
Georgian, Salt Spoon, Towle 11.00
Georgian, Steak Knife, Towle 34.00
Georgian Bead, Oyster Fork, Amston 22.00
Golden Calvert, Salad Fork, Kirk 12.00
Golden Calvert, Teaspoon, Kirk 7.00
Golden Columbine, Butter Knife, Lunt 9.00
Golden Columbine, Knife, Lunt, 9 In. 17.00
Golden Scroll, Cold Meat Fork, Gorham 44.00
Golden Scroll, Dinner Fork, Gorham 22.00
Golden Tradewinds, Salad Fork, International 17.00
Golden Tradewinds, Teaspoon, International 13.00
Gossamer, Citrus Spoon, Gorham 18.00
Gossamer, Ice Cream Fork, Gorham 18.00
Gossamer, Teaspoon, Gorham, 6 In. 9.00
Governor's Lady, Salad Fork, Gorham 2200.00
Grand Baroque, Baked Potato Server, Wallace 38.00
Grand Baroque, Ice Cream Fork, Wallace, 8 Piece 105.00
Grand Colonial, Citrus Spoon, Wallace 19.00
Grand Colonial, Cream Soup Spoon, Wallace 16.00
Grand Colonial, Ice Cream Fork, Wallace 17.00
Grand Colonial, Knife, Wallace, 9 3/4 In. 12.00
Grecian, Berry Spoon, Gorham .... 95.00 to 225.00
Grecian, Gravy Ladle, Gorham 95.00
Greenbrier, Butter Fork, Gorham 7.00
Greenbrier, Cream Soup Spoon, Rogers 15.00
Greenbrier, Luncheon Fork, Gorham 17.00
Greenbrier, Sugar Spoon, Gorham 12.00
Greenbrier, Teaspoon, Gorham 10.00
Hanover, Lettuce Fork, Gorham 55.00
Heiress, Baked Potato Server, Oneida 19.00
Helene, Citrus Spoon, Easterling 11.00
Helene, Dessert Spoon, Easterling 13.00
Helene, Ice Cream Spoon, Easterling 11.00
Helene, Salad Fork, Easterling 11.00
Hepplewhite, Ladle, Reed & Barton, 11 In. 100.00
Heraldic, Cheese Scoop, Whiting 175.00
Heraldic, Fruit Spoon, Whiting 35.00
Heraldic, Mustard Ladle, Whiting 80.00
Homewood, Gumbo Soup Spoon, Stieff 35.00
Honeysuckle, Gravy Ladle, Whiting 150.00
Hyperion, Demitasse Spoon, Whiting 20.00

Hyperion, Salad Set, Whiting.. 325.00
Imperial Chrysanthemum, Berry Spoon, Durgin, 7 1/4 In............................ 110.00
Imperial Chrysanthemum, Dinner Fork, Gorham....................................... 55.00
Imperial Chrysanthemum, Fish Knife & Fork Server, Durgin 425.00
Imperial Chrysanthemum, Ice Cream Fork, Gorham, 6 Piece 260.00
Imperial Chrysanthemum, Pea Spoon, Gorham 350.00
Imperial Queen, Gravy Ladle, Whiting 95.00
Imperial Queen, Ice Tongs, Whiting 275.00
Imperial Queen, Sardine Fork, Gold Wash, Whiting 65.00
Imperial Queen, Sugar Tongs, Whiting... 40.00
Imperial Queen, Tablespoon, Whiting... 55.00
Intaglio, Berry Spoon, Reed & Barton, 9 1/2 In... 175.00
Ionic, Dessert Spoon, Gorham 55.00
Iris, Dinner Fork, Durgin, 6 Piece 220.00
Ivory, Cocktail Fork, Gold Wash, Whiting, 12 Piece 575.00
Ivy, Gravy Ladle, Gorham.. 65.00
Japanese, Gravy Ladle, Gorham 275.00
Japanese, Mustard Ladle, Whiting... 125.00
Japanese, Salad Set, Whiting, 12 1/2 In... 695.00
Japanese, Serving Spoon, Large, Whiting.. 200.00
Japanese, Soup Ladle, Whiting.. 475.00
Jenny Lind, Dessert Spoon, Albert Coles 30.00
Josephine, Fish Slice, Whiting... 175.00
Jubilee, Jelly Server, Reed & Barton 28.00
Kenilworth, Soup Ladle, Albert Coles 275.00
King, Macaroni Spoon, Knowles.. 235.00
King Cedric, Luncheon Knife, Oneida 13.00
King Cedric, Sugar Spoon, Oneida 15.00
King Edward, Citrus Spoon, Whiting.. 35.00
King Edward, Lettuce Fork, Whiting 195.00
King Edward, Teaspoon, Gorham 30.00
King George, Bouillon Spoon, Gorham 25.00
King George, Dinner Fork, Gorham... 45.00
King George, Fish Fork, Gorham.. 55.00
King Richard, Carving Set, Towle, 2 Piece 65.00
King Richard, Cocktail Fork, Towle.. 24.00
King Richard, Master Butter Knife, Towle.. 28.00
King Richard, Salt Spoon 10.00
King Richard, Tomato Server, Towle.. 65.00
Kings, Fork, Dominick & Haff, 7 1/2 In., 6 Piece.. 385.00
L'Elegante, Ice Cream Spoon, Gilt Bowl, Reed & Barton, 5 In. 17.00
La Modele, Olive Spoon, Gorham 45.00
La Modele, Salad Fork, Gorham 25.00
La Modele, Salad Set, Long Handles, Gorham 200.00
La Parisienne, Salad Set, Reed & Barton, 10 In.. 700.00
La Rochelle, Butter Pick, Wilcox & Evertsen... 28.00
La Rochelle, Olive Fork, Wilcox & Eversten 26.00
La Rochelle, Spoon, Iced Tea, Wilcox & Evertsen 28.00
La Rochelle, Tablespoon, Wilcox & Eversten... 38.00
Lace Point, Teaspoon, Lunt.. 12.00
Lady Washington, Cake Saw, Gorham 200.00
Lafayette, Pie Server, Manchester 200.00
Lambeth Manor, Sugar Shell, International 25.00
Lancaster, Asparagus Fork, Gorham.. 225.00
Lancaster, Bouillon Ladle, Gorham 115.00
Lancaster, Butter Pick, Gorham 75.00
Lancaster, Cracker Scoop, Pierced, Gorham 275.00
Lancaster, Fish Fork, Gorham.. 45.00
Lancaster, Poached Egg Server, Gorham.. 155.00
Lasting Spring, Sugar Spoon, Oneida 15.00
Leonore, Citrus Spoon, Manchester 15.00
Leonore, Cream Soup Spoon, Manchester 12.00
Leonore, English Server, Manchester... 22.00

Leonore,	Fruit Knife, Manchester	16.00
Leonore,	Steak Knife, Manchester	19.00
Les Six Fleurs,	Salad Set, Reed & Barton, 2 Piece	345.00
Lexington,	Bouillon Spoon, Dominick & Haff	9.00
Lexington,	Croquette Server, Knowles	85.00
Lexington,	Dessert Spoon, Dominick & Haff	12.00
Lexington,	Horseradish Spoon, Knowles	36.00
Lily,	Lettuce Fork, Whiting	200.00
Lily,	Pie Server, Pierced, Gorham	250.00
Lily,	Sauce Ladle, Gorham	75.00
Lily,	Serving Spoon, Pierced, Whiting, 8 3/4 In.	358.00
Lily,	Teaspoon, Whiting	20.00
Lily Of The Valley,	Butter Fork, Whiting	175.00
Lily Of The Valley,	Cold Meat Fork, 3 Prong, Whiting, 6 1/2 In.	145.00
Lily Of The Valley,	Gravy Ladle, Gorham	30.00
Lily Of The Valley,	Gravy Ladle, Scalloped Rim, Whiting, 7 1/4 In.	150.00
Lily Of The Valley,	Lettuce Fork, Whiting	125.00
Lily Of The Valley,	Place Setting, Luncheon, Whiting, 3 Piece	135.00
Lily Of The Valley,	Sifter, Gold Wash, Whiting	375.00
Lily Of The Valley,	Teaspoon, Gorham	20.00
Lincoln,	Cocktail Fork, F. Smith	8.00
Lincoln,	Gumbo Spoon, F. Smith, 6 3/4 In.	14.00
Livingston,	Berry Spoon, Whiting	70.00
Livingston,	Ice Cream Slice, Whiting	105.00
Louis XIV,	Butter Fork, Towle	12.00
Louis XIV,	Dinner Fork, Gorham	45.00
Louis XIV,	Sugar Tongs, Towle	25.00
Louis XIV,	Tablespoon, Gorham	55.00
Louis XIV,	Tablespoon, Towle	30.00
Louis XIV,	Teaspoon, Dominick & Haff	11.00
Louis XV,	Berry Spoon, Whiting	80.00
Louis XV,	Butter Fork, Durgin	20.00
Louis XV,	Cheese Scoop, Whiting	65.00
Louis XV,	Dessert Spoon, Wood & Hughes, 8 In.	28.00
Louis XV,	Dinner Fork, Whiting	35.00
Louis XV,	Ice Cream Slice, Whiting, 10 1/2 In.	165.00
Louis XV,	Salad Fork	40.00
Louis XV,	Teaspoon, Wood & Hughes, 5 /38 In.	16.00
Louvre,	Citrus Spoon, Wallace	17.00
Louvre,	Dessert Spoon, Wood & Hughes	22.00
Love Disarmed,	Cake Server, Reed & Barton	185.00
Love Disarmed,	Cold Meat Fork, Reed & Barton	90.00
Love Disarmed,	Fish Slice, Reed & Barton	225.00
Love Disarmed,	Gravy Ladle, Reed & Barton	90.00
Love Disarmed,	Toast Server, Whiting	310.00
Love Disarmed,	Tomato Server, Reed & Barton	90.00
Luxembourg,	Master Butter Knife, Gorham	30.00
Luxembourg,	Sardine Fork, Gorham	55.00
Lyric,	Grapefruit Knife, Gorham	12.00
Lyric,	Gravy Ladle, Gorham	30.00
Lyric,	Potato Serving Fork, Gorham	21.00
Madam Jumel,	Fried Egg Server, Whiting	190.00
Madame Royal,	Ice Cream Spoon, Durgin	35.00
Madame Royal,	Salad Fork, Durgin	45.00
Madison,	Gravy Ladle	40.00
Madrigal,	Sugar Spoon, Lunt	13.00
Majestic,	Lettuce Fork, Alvin	65.00
Marechal Niel,	Ice Cream Fork, Gilt Tines, Durgin	55.00
Margaret,	Cucumber Server, International	35.00
Margaret Rose,	Cream Soup Spoon, National	12.00
Margaret Rose,	Salad Fork, National	17.00
Margaret Rose,	Teaspoon, National	10.00
Marguerite,	Cucumber Server, Gorham	65.00

Marie Antoinette, Fish Slice, Gorham	150.00
Marie Antoinette, Pea Spoon, Gorham	225.00
Marine Design Handle, Tea Caddy Spoon, Gorham	125.00
Marlborough, Dessert Fork, Watson	20.00
Maryland, Spoon & Fork, Child's, Gorham	25.00
Mayflower, Egg Spoon, Kirk	25.00
Medici, Cocktail Fork, Gorham	14.00
Medici, Fruit Knife	20.00
Medici, Gravy Ladle, Gorham	60.00
Medici, Soup Ladle, Kirk	295.00
Medici, Teaspoon, Gorham	16.00
Melrose, Dinner Knife, Gorham	30.00
Melrose, Tomato Server, Gorham	70.00
Milano, Cream Soup Spoon, Buccelati	85.00
Modern Victorian, Salad Set, Lunt, 2 Piece	135.00
Monticello, Berry Spoon, Lunt, 8 3/4 In.	75.00
Monticello, Butter Knife, International	22.00
Monticello, Master Butter, Lunt	30.00
Monticello, Salad Fork, Lunt	45.00
Monticello, Tablespoon, Lunt	48.00
Mount Vernon, Asparagus Server, Watson, 5 In.	145.00
Mount Vernon, Fruit Spoon, Lunt	30.00
Mount Vernon, Soup Ladle, Lunt	350.00
Mythologique, Citrus Spoon, Gorham	45.00
Mythologique, Serving Spoon, Gorham	154.00
Napoleon, Asparagus Shovel, Wilcox & Evertsen	225.00
Napoleon, Dinner Knife, International, 6 7/8 In.	25.00
Narcissus, Citrus Spoon, Fessenden, 6 Piece	150.00
Narcissus, Dessert Spoon, Fessenden	35.00
Narcissus, Gravy Ladle, Fessenden	65.00
New Art, Asparagus Fork, Durgin	575.00
New Art, Salad Set, Durgin	875.00
New Queens, Fish Set, Durgin	185.00
Newport Scroll, Soup Ladle, Gorham	25.00
Nuremburg, Pierced Server, Alvin, 6 In.	155.00
Nuremburg, Teaspoon, Alvin	30.00
Old Atlanta, Oval Spoon, Wallace	20.00
Old Baronial, Salad Fork, Gorham, 12 Piece	360.00
Old Colonial, Fruit Spoon, Towle	30.00
Old Colonial, Lettuce Fork, Towle	150.00
Old Colonial, Luncheon Fork, Towle	25.00
Old Colonial, Tablespoon, Towle	55.00
Old English, Cocktail Fork, Towle	15.00
Old English, Lettuce Fork, Towle	55.00
Old English, Salad Fork, Towle	32.00
Old English, Spoon, Iced Tea, Towle	32.00
Old French, Place Spoon, Gorham	27.00
Old Italian, Cold Meat Fork, Buccelati	145.00
Old Italian, Fish Slice, Buccelati	140.00
Old Italian, Spaghetti Server, Buccelati	320.00
Old Maryland, Seafood Fork, Kirk	25.00
Old Newbury, Sugar Tongs, Towle	30.00
Olive, Strawberry Ladle, William Gale	350.00
Onslow, Salad Set, Tuttle	395.00
Orange Blossom, Lettuce Fork & Spoon, Alvin	350.00
Orange Blossom, Tomato Server, Alvin, 6 1/4 In.	185.00
Oval Twist, Berry Spoon, Whiting	55.00
Paul Revere, Baked Potato Fork, Towle	65.00
Paul Revere, Bonbon Scoop, Towle	95.00
Paul Revere, Ice Cream Spoon, Towle	25.00
Paul Revere, Mustard Ladle, Towle	45.00
Plymouth, Asparagus Fork, Gorham	195.00
Pompadour, Bouillon Ladle, Whiting	225.00

Pompadour, Cake Fork, 3 Tines, Whiting, 6 1/2 In. 50.00
Poppy, Salad Server, Gorham, 2 Piece 187.00
Poppy, Sugar Spoon, Gorham 40.00
Princess, Sugar Spoon, Towle 20.00
Princess Elizabeth, Sugar Spoon, National 16.00
Princess Elizabeth, Teaspoon, National 13.00
Promise, Cream Soup Spoon, Royal Crest 14.00
Promise, Teaspoon, Royal Crest 12.00
Quintessence, Soup Ladle, Lunt 175.00
Radiant, Cracker Scoop, Whiting 295.00
Radiant, Fish Slice, Whiting, Small 125.00
Radiant, Salad Fork, Whiting 50.00
Radiant, Teaspoon, Whiting 20.00
Raleigh, Berry Spoon, Scalloped, Alvin, 9 1/4 In. 95.00
Raphael, Bonbon Spoon, Alvin, 1902, Large 325.00
Raphael, Sauce Ladle, Gorham 45.00
Renaissance, Butter Knife, Master, Dominick & Haff 65.00
Renaissance, Cocktail Fork, Dominick & Haff 20.00
Renaissance, Dessert Fork, Dominick & Haff, 6 Piece 230.00
Repousse, Asparagus Fork, Kirk 170.00
Repousse, Baby Set, Kirk, 2 Piece 40.00
Repousse, Food Pusher, Kirk 21.00
Repousse, Lobster Shears, Kirk 120.00
Rhapsody, Sugar Shell, International 25.00
Rhondaoa, Teaspoon, Gorham 15.00
Roman, Soda Spoon, Knowles 45.00
Romantique, Demitasse Spoon, Alvin 20.00
Rose Point, Cold Meat Fork, Wallace 85.00
Rose Point, Gravy Ladle, Wallace 56.00
Rose Point, Salad Fork, Wallace 28.00
Rose Point, Teaspoon, Wallace 18.00
Royal Danish, Jelly Server, International 25.00
Saratoga, Oyster Ladle, Reed & Barton 450.00
Saxon, Dinner Set, Wallace, 72 Piece 660.00
Sculptured Rose, Luncheon Fork, Towle 21.00
Sculptured Rose, Sugar Spoon, Towle 16.00
Sculptured Rose, Teaspoon, Towle 14.00
Serenity, Sugar Spoon, International 15.00
Silver Spray, Cold Meat Fork, Towle 34.00
Southern Rose, Dinner Fork, Manchester 15.00
Southern Rose, Soup Spoon, Oval, Manchester 15.00
Sovereign, Cream Soup Spoon, Gorham 24.00
Sovereign, Salad Fork, Gorham 29.00
Sovereign, Sugar Spoon, Gorham 23.00
Spanish Provincial, Teaspoon, Towle 15.00
Spring Glory, Sugar Spoon, International 24.00
Spring Glory, Tablespoon, International 45.00
Spring Glory, Teaspoon, International 11.00
St. Cloud, Dessert Fork, Gorham 45.00
St. Cloud, Gravy Ladle, Gorham 175.00
St. Cloud, Sugar Tongs, Georg Jensen 125.00
Stardust, Pickle Fork, Gorham 15.00
Stardust, Place Setting, Gorham, 4 Piece 60.00
Stardust, Spoon, Iced Tea, Gorham 18.00
Strasbourg, Berry Spoon, Gorham 85.00
Strasbourg, Cream Soup Spoon, Gorham 24.00
Strasbourg, Dessert Spoon, Gorham 36.00
Strasbourg, Dinner Fork, Gorham 45.00
Strasbourg, Fish Set, Gorham 250.00
Strasbourg, Pie Server, Gorham .... 38.00 to 195.00
Strasbourg, Soup Ladle, Gorham 195.00
Stratford, Cold Meat Fork, International 65.00
Stratford, Olive Spoon, International 50.00

Strawberry, Pie Cutter, Serrated Edge, William Gale 450.00
Stuart, Pie Knife, Whiting 110.00
Sweetheart Rose, Gravy Ladle, Lunt 26.00
Sweetheart Rose, Sugar Spoon, Lunt 15.00
Symphony, Cream Soup Spoon, Towle 14.00
Symphony, Teaspoon, Towle 11.00
Theseum, Berry Spoon, International, 8 /14 In. 85.00
Tiber, Gravy Ladle, Buccelati 130.00
Tiber, Ice Tongs, Buccelati 200.00
Tulip, Teaspoon, Durgin 22.00
Vergennes, Sardine Fork, F. Smith 25.00
Versailles, Gravy Ladle, Gorham 130.00
Versailles, Sauce Ladle, Gorham 95.00
Violet, Dessert Spoon, Wallace 25.00
Violet, Fork, Wallace 24.00
Violet, Mustard Ladle, Wallace 55.00
Violet, Soup Ladle, Wallace 165.00
Violet, Teaspoon, Wallace 12.00
Virginia, Sardine Fork, Alvin 65.00
Warwick, Butter Knife, International 25.00
Watteau, Ice Cream Slice, Alvin 200.00
Watteau, Ice Cream Spoon, Alvin 35.00
Watteau, Pie Server, Durgin 125.00
Waverly, Cold Meat Fork, Wallace 44.00
Waverly, Horseradish Spoon, Wallace 50.00
Waverly, Ice Cream Knife, Wallace 165.00
Waverly, Tea Strainer, Wallace 250.00
Wedgwood, Salad Fork, International, 12 Piece 978.00
Wild Flower, Butter Knife, Royal Crest, Individual 12.00
William & Mary, Cocktail Fork, Lunt 13.00
William & Mary, Salad Set, Lunt, 2 Piece 135.00
Windsor Castle, Bar Spoon, Attached Shot Glass, Tuttle 75.00

SILVER PLATE is not solid silver. It is a ware made of a metal, such as nickel
or copper, that is covered with a thin coating of silver. The letters *EPNS* are
often found on American and English silver-plated wares. Sheffield is a term
with two meanings. In this section, Sheffield refers to a type of silver plate,
usually English.

Basket, Glass Insert, Wiener Werkstatte, 3 1/2 x 10 In. 1840.00
Basket, Swing Handle, Oval Pierced Form, 11 1/2 x 14 1/2 In. 155.00
Beaker, Horn, Engraved Plated Rim & Foot Bands, 5 3/4 In. 210.00
Bottle Cooler, Repeating North Wind Faces, Handles, Sheffield 2640.00
Bowl, 2 Large Winged Cherubs Base 2000.00
Box, Cigarette, Queen Of Spades, 1920 .... 66.00
Box, Letter, Chased, Engraved, Asymmetrical Panels, 6 x 9 x 4 3/4 In. 300.00
Bucket, Champagne, Applied Ribbing, Gorham, 8 In. 225.00
Butter, Cover, Frame With Notch, Rogers 200.00
Cachepot, Chased Laurel Swags, Cardailhac, c.1900, 12 In., Pair 6612.00
Caddy, Hobnail Insert, Cranberry Glass, Clear Finial, 4-Footed, 11 1/4 In. 155.00
Candelabrum, 2-Light, Low Baluster Shape, Square Bobeches, 8 1/2 In., Pair 115.00
Candelabrum, 3-Light, Matthew Boulton Plate Co., c.1810, 22 In., Pair 3162.00
Candelabrum, George III, Matthew Boulton, c.1805, 24 1/4 In. 6900.00
Candelabrum, Quadruple Plate, 13 1/4 In. 88.00
Candelabrum, Victorian, Reed & Barton, 15 1/2 In. 302.00
Candlestick, Detachable Nozzle, Henry Tudor, c.1770, 9 7/8 In., 4 Piece 2185.00
Candlestick, Rococo, Baluster, Rose Vine Design, England, 10 1/2 In., Pair 220.00
Chamberstick, Art Deco Figural Art, Wilcox 120.00
Charger, Plated Copper, Zodiac Signs, Man & Woman In Garden, 19 In. 88.00
Cocktail Shaker, Hammered 11 In. 55.00
Coffee Set, Ball Feet, Squatty Bulbous Form, c.1868, 4 Piece 200.00
Coffee Set, Heritage, With Tray, Rogers, 21 x 14 1/2 In., 4 Piece 175.00
Coffeepot, Pedestal Base, Wooden Handle, Sheffield, England 405.00
Coffeepot, Sheffield, Walker & Hall 195.00

Coffeepot, Sphinx Finial, Deer Head, Hall Elton Co., 10 1/2 In. 135.00
Compote, Art Nouveau, Berries, Tripod Legs, WMF, 9 1/2 In. 460.00
Compote, Triangles Enclosing Grape Clusters On Rim, D. Peche, 1925, 6 In. 1380.00
Cooler, Wine, Staved Bucket Shape, Lion Head Handles, 5 1/2 In. 48.00
Dish, Cover, Armorial Crest, Folite Handle, Sheffield, 8 x 14 In. 202.00
Dish, Entree, Telescoping, Hand Holding Baton Cover, Legs, England, 12 In. 248.00
Dish, Flowers & Peacock, Tail Forms Bowl, 7 1/2 In. 38.00
Epergne, 4 Arms, Crystal Inserts & Center Bowl, Sheffield 1800.00
Epergne, 4 Scroll Arms, Cut Glass Bowls, Gadrooned Beading, 20 x 11 In. 1100.00
Fish Service, Engraved Foliage, Oak Case, England, c.1900, 24 Piece 358.00
Fish Slice, Peerless 32.00
Food Dome, Sheffield, 15 3/4 In. 93.00
Fruit Set, Mother-Of-Pearl Handles, Sterling Bands, c.1860, 12 Piece 143.00
Goblet, Band Of Beading On Bowl, Derby, 6 In., Pair 125.00
Holder, Wine Bottle, Honeycomb Design, Meriden Britannia 125.00
Inkstand, England, 1890s, 3 1/2 x 11 In. 55.00
Inkstand, Golfer, 2 Ink Pots, England, 12 In., 3 Piece 695.00
Jug, Claret, Drop-Shape Body, Bird Feet, Dresser, c.1879, 9 3/8 In. 3450.00
Kettle, Stand, Flower Finial, Engraved Flowers & Scrolls, Cristofle, 15 1/2 In. 435.00
Kettle, Stand, Fluted Form, Flowers & Scrolls, Flower Finial, 15 1/2 In. 575.00
Knife Rest, 2 Swans 40.00
Lamp, Coach, Ribbon Bows, Coronet Finial, Electrified, 29 1/2 In., Pair 3165.00
Lamp, Oil, Corinthian Column Form, Cut Glass Font, Electrified, 38 1/2 In. 2070.00
Mustache Cup, Saucer, Engraved Flowers, Pairpoint 60.00
Napkin Rings are listed in their own category
Pitcher, Milk, Reserves Of Country Folk, Florals, Holland, 6 3/4 In. 110.00
Planter, Pedestal, Reticulated Rim & Base, Liner, Ornate, 7 1/2 x 12 3/4 In. 40.00
Plate, Cold Meat, Royal 25.00
Plate, Raised Leaves, Wallace, 12 In., Pair 38.00
Platter, Cover, Gadrooned Edge, Foliate Handle, Sheffield, 15 1/2 x 17 1/2 In. 748.00
Punch Ladle, Holly, Rogers 195.00
Punch Set, Oneida, 15 Piece 250.00
Punch Set, Sheffield, c.1870, 12 Piece 975.00
Rattle, Baby's, Humpty-Dumpty, Marked Victor Hayes, 1864 .... 88.00
Salt, Attached Heart Tray, Round 32.00
Salver, Piecrust Edge, Hand Chased, Footed, Sheffield, 14 1/2 In. 220.00
Server, Swivel Domed Top, Oval, 13 3/4 In. 148.00
Smoking Set, Cut Glass, Center Handle, Sheffield, 19th Century, 11 In. 425.00
Snuffer, Candle, Tray, Sheffield, c.1840 .... 135.00
Spoon, Demitasse, Berkley Square 7.00
Spoon, Souvenir, see Souvenirs category
Spooner, Pointed Rims, Etched, Bell Inside Handle, Wilcox 295.00
Sugar & Spoon Holder, Dimpled Blue Insert, With 12 Spoons, 8 3/4 In. 520.00
Sugar Shaker, Floral Design, Tufts, 3 1/2 In. 95.00
Tazza, Faux Ivory Handle, 6 1/4 x 5 1/4 In., Pair 66.00
Tea & Coffee Set, Repousse Honeycomb Pattern, Meriden, 5 Piece 110.00
Tea & Coffee Set, Wilcox, 5 Piece 140.00
Tea Caddy, Allover Aesthetic Die Cut, Tufts 95.00
Tea Service, Van Bergh Silverplate Co., 4 Piece 77.00
Tea Set, Chased & Repousse Florals, Simpson, Hall, Miller & Co., 6 Piece 1100.00
Tea Set, King Francis, Matching Tray, Reed & Barton, 4 Piece 995.00
Tea Set, Rose Design, Square Shape, Reed & Barton, 5 Piece 145.00
Teapot, Die Cut Band, Spider Webs, Snails, Pairpoint 125.00
Teapot, Griffin Finial, Victorian, Reed & Barton, 6 7/8 In. 50.00
Toothpick, Lee's Headquarters 50.00
Tray, Breakfast, Bamboo & Oriental Design, Handles, American, 28 x 17 1/2 In. 460.00
Tray, Engraved Design & Crest, 1880s, 19 1/4 In. 345.00
Tray, Foliate Design, Serpentine Edge, Scrollwork Handle, 30 1/2 In. 190.00
Tray, Full-Blown Irises, Poppies, Initialed, Dominick & Haff, c.1901, 32 In. 5462.00
Tray, Stylized Bouquet, Whiplash Handles, Paul Follot, c.1900, 24 1/2 In. 4312.00
Tureen, Beaded Handle On Cover, Pistol Handles, England, c.1850, 11 In. 625.00
Tureen & Ladle, Loop Handles, Gadroon Moldings, Gorham, c.1900, 13 In. 345.00
Urn, Cover, Ram's Head Handles, Swags Of Fruit, 29 1/2 In. 3737.00

Vase, Winged Cherubs Feet, Floral Etching On Body, Meriden, 6 In............................ 155.00
Watch Holder, Cherub Holder.. 175.00
Wax Jack, 6 1/4 In. 121.00
Wine Cooler, Fenton, Creswick & Co.. 1840.00
Wine Cooler, Floral Sprays, Liner, Sheffield, c.1830, 11 1/4 In., Pair........................... 1035.00
Wine Cooler, Georgian Style, Campana Shape, Lion Mask Handle, 9 1/2 In., Pair........ 385.00

SILVER, SHEFFIELD, see Silver Plate; Silver-English

SILVER-AMERICAN. American silver is listed here. Most of the sterling silver listed in this book is subdivided by country. There are also other pieces of silver and silver plate listed under special categories, such as Napkin Ring, Silver Flatware, Silver Plate, Silver-Sterling, and Tiffany Silver.

SILVER-AMERICAN, Basket, 4 Sections, Pierced Handle, Monogram, Lebolt & Co., 9 In. 1350.00
Basket, Gadrooned Lip, Monogrammed Medallion, Dominick & Haff.......................... 805.00
Basket, Reticulated, Oval, Pierced Sides, Flowers & Leaves, Whiting, 13 1/2 In. 345.00
Basket, Swing Handle, Repousse Floral, Pedestal, Coin Silver..................................... 220.00
Beaker, Coin, Hyde & Goodrich, 1850s, 3 In.. *Illus* 468.00
Berry Bowl, Wavy Rim, Chased Chrysanthemum, Gorham, c.1902, 11 In. 3737.00
Bowl, 2 Angular Ebony Handles, Fisher Silversmiths, 2 1/2 x 16 In............................. 425.00
Bowl, Alternating Flowers & Reticulated Rim, Black, Starr & Frost, 11 In. 575.00
Bowl, Applied Floral & Scroll Rim, Dominick & Haff, 11 In. 285.00
Bowl, Applied Floral Swags, Scrolling Rim, Whiting, 9 In... 345.00
Bowl, Chased Pappy Design, Shiebler, c.1900, 8 5/8 In... 517.00
Bowl, Chased Spiral Pattern, Gorham, c.1902, 6 7/16 In.. 145.00
Bowl, Chased Tudor Rose, Classic Form, 1918, Arthur J. Stone, 1 1/2 x 3 In.................. 1100.00
Bowl, Chased Violets, Classic Form, Footed, Arthur J. Stone, 3 1/2 x 8 In..................... 5000.00
Bowl, Chowder, Spoon, Flared Fluted Rim, Applied Fishing Nets, Whiting................... 2990.00
Bowl, Classic Greek Kantharos, 2 Handles, A.J. Stone, 4 1/4 x 7 1/8 In. 695.00
Bowl, Cylindrical, Chased Floral Rim, S. Kirk & Son, 9 3/4 In. 345.00
Bowl, Flaring Form, Stieff, 9 In. 175.00
Bowl, Floriform, Rolled Rim, Kalo Shop, c.1928, 2 x 7 In. 315.00
Bowl, Fluted, Pointed Panels, Applied Monogram, Novick, 1 1/2 x 10 In. 900.00
Bowl, Footed, Chased Pods & Berries, Arthur J. Stone, 1918, 2 1/8 x 4 In..................... 1600.00
Bowl, Francis I, Reed & Barton, 11 1/2 In. 400.00
Bowl, Fruit, Francis I, Reed & Barton... 850.00
Bowl, Fruit, Normandie, Wallace 175.00
Bowl, Fruit, Pedestal, Chased Flowers, Martele, Gorham, 14 In. 6900.00
Bowl, Fruit, Poppy, Square Corners, Gorham, c.1906, 10 1/2 In.................................... 373.00
Bowl, Hand Hammered, Five Lobes, No. M325, Kalo, 9 1/2 In..................................... 660.00
Bowl, Irish Pattern, Everted Rim, Whiting, 11 In.. 175.00
Bowl, Oval, Undulated Everted Rim, Chased Hollyhocks, Whiting, 12 1/2 In. 460.00
Bowl, Overlapping Geometric & Linear Design, T. Tuttle, c.1938, 6 1/2 In. 115.00
Bowl, Paul Revere, Lunt, 8 In. 130.00
Bowl, Pierced Border, Shield & Swirl, Dominick & Haff, 18 In. 990.00
Bowl, Pine Needles & Cones, Hammered, Marshall Field, 3 x 9 1/4 In. 1500.00

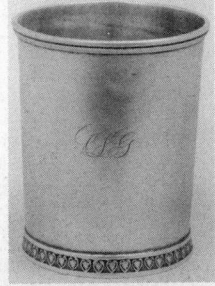

Silver-American, Beaker, Coin,
Hyde & Goodrich, 1850s, 3 In.

Silver-American, Cup, Coin, Gorham, 1860, 4 In.

Silver-American, Cup, Script Initials, Coin, H. Buckley, c.1855, 4 In.

Bowl, Raised Edge, Repousse Strawberries, Woodside Silver Co., 8 3/4 In. 248.00
Bowl, Repousse Pattern, Serving Spoon, Gorham 850.00
Bowl, Revere Style, S. Kirk & Son, 9 In. 165.00
Bowl, Rope Edge, Handles, William Gale & Sons, c.1856, 14 In. 625.00
Bowl, Scroll Design, Ring Foot, Circular, Joseph Loring, c.1790, 5 3/4 In. 1850.00
Bowl, Serving, Pierced Leaf Border, C Scrolls, Frank W. Smith, c.1900, 9 3/4 In. 550.00
Bowl, Shaped Reserve, John P. Kohler, c.1915, 6 1/4 In. 460.00
Bowl, Undertray, Fluted, Raised Border, Kalo, 1 5/8 x 4 5/8 In. 800.00
Bowl, Vasiform, Rolled Rim, Spread Foot, Shreve, Crump & Low, 8 In. 920.00
Bowl, Wide Rim, Hammered, Kalo Shop, 4 x 7 In. 880.00
Box, Cigarette, Inscribed Top, Wooden Liner, Gorham, 5 1/2 x 3 1/2 In. 90.00
Box, Domed Coral Cabochon On Cover, Hammered, Kalo, 2 x 3 In. 2800.00
Box, Domed Cover, Smooth, Geo. Porter Blanchard, Oval, 1 x 3 x 2 3/8 In. 495.00
Box, Repousse Floral Garland & Ribbon, Gorham, c.1882, 2 1/4 In. 195.00
Bread Basket, Rose Repousse Rim, Bigelow, Kennard & Co., c.1881, 13 In. 660.00
Bread Tray, Oval, Repousse Floral Border, Gorham, c.1900, 15 3/4 In. 330.00
Bread Tray, Oval, Scalloped Edges, Floral Repousse, Whiting, 11 1/2 In. 220.00
Bread Tray, Reticulated, Gorham, 16 In. 460.00
Butter, Cover, Cow Finial, William Gale 600.00
Butter, Dome Cover, Coin, Panels, Beaded Border, Footed, 7 1/2 In. 825.00
Cake Basket, Foliage, Hoop Handles, John Targee, c.1810, 17 1/4 In. 3450.00
Cake Breaker, C. & A.A.W. Johnson, c.1830 .... 450.00
Cake Knife, Server, Karen Pattern, Mar. 19, 1966, Ole Newbury Crafters 375.00
Cake Plate, Chased Fruit Design, Watson, 1920s, 10 3/4 In. 175.00
Cake Plate, Roger Williams, Pierced, Gorham, c.1901, 11 In. 201.00
Candle Snuffer, Bigelow, Kennard & Co. 330.00
Candlestick, Baluster Shape, Footed Rim, Scrolls, Towle, 10 1/2 In., Pair 460.00
Candlestick, Buds, Ribbons Openwork Stem, Wm. Dematteo, 10 In., Pair 1955.00
Candlestick, Hammered Raised Border, Shreve, 11 In., Pair 410.00
Chalice, Portrait Medallions, Inscription, Toledo, Ohio, July 9, 1869, 7 1/8 In. 236.00
Child's Set, Nursery Rhyme On Each Piece, Gorham, c.1881, 3 Piece 800.00
Chocolate Set, Oak & Sterling Tray, Shreve & Co., 12 Piece 825.00
Chocolate Set, Repousse Pattern, Tray, Monogram D, Stieff, 4 Piece 2000.00
Coffee & Tea Set, Gorham, c.1906, 4 Piece 300.00
Coffee Set, Baluster Form, Gorham, c.1929, 3 Piece 402.00
Coffee Set, Demitasse, Georgian Style, Rosewood, c.1911, Gorham, 3 Piece 375.00
Coffeepot, Demitasse, Bixby Silver Co., c.1900 .... 132.00
Coffeepot, Fluted, Fluted Lower Half, Leinonen, 8 1/2 In. 975.00
Comb, Mustache, Etched Nude, Unger Brothers 135.00
Compote, Fluted, Pedestal, Applied Wire Rim, Hammered, J.O. Randahl, 6 In. 575.00
Compote, Fluted, Pedestal, Hammered, Kalo, 6 x 7 In. 900.00
Compote, Fluted, Short Pedestal, Turned-In Rim, Lebolt & Co., 9 In. 950.00

Compote, Hammered, Lebolt, 5 x 6 1/2 In.	220.00
Compote, Hand Hammered, 5 Lobes, Flaring Base, Lebolt, 6 In.	470.00
Compote, Hand Hammered, Applied Initials MAR, Lebolt, 6 1/2 In.	360.00
Compote, Hinged Handles, Wood & Hughes, 13 In.	1400.00
Compote, Pedestal, Fluted, MM Monogram, Clemens Friedell, 7 x 6 In.	1100.00
Compote, Putti & Swags Handles, Human Feet, Gorham, c.1865, 13 In.	1150.00
Compote, Reticulated Floral Rim & Base, Howard & Co., 12 1/4 In.	545.00
Console Set, Celeste, 8-In. Bowl, 10-In. Candelabrum, Gorham, 3 Piece	135.00
Creamer, Flower & Fruit Sprays, Thomas Dane, c.1760, 3 1/8 In.	4325.00
Creamer, Pear Form, 3 Hoof Feet, Tobias Stoutenburgh, c.1740, 4 In.	6000.00
Creamer, Rolled Rim, Arthur Stone, c.1920, 3 1/4 In.	345.00
Creamer, Scroll Handle, Gadrooned Rim, R. Humphreys, c.1775, 5 In.	2587.00
Cup, Baby's, Repousse Duck & Duckling, Strap Handle, Kalo, 2 x 3 1/2 In.	625.00
Cup, Baby's, Thumb Rest Handle, Engraved Name, 1916, A.J. Stone, 2 In.	575.00
Cup, Coin, Gorham, 1860, 4 In. .... *Illus*	225.00
Cup, Hammered, Curved Handle From Rim To Base, Kalo Shop, 2 1/2 In.	65.00
Cup, Julep, Engraved, Coin Silver, Hildeburn & Bros., 3 3/8 In.	220.00
Cup, Julep, Tooled Design, Coin Silver, Blynn & Baldwin, 3 3/4 In.	440.00
Cup, Repousse & Chase, Coin Silver, A. Tyler, c.1850, 3 7/8 In.	350.00
Cup, Script Initials, Coin, H. Buckley, c.1855, 4 In. .... *Illus*	275.00
Cup & Saucer, Applied Rose & Scroll Rim, No Handles, Shreve, 12 Piece	345.00
Cup & Saucer, Lenox Liner, After Dinner, Whiting, 8 Sets	220.00
Curling Iron, Heater Box, J.E. Caldwell, Monogram, 1896	400.00
Cutter, Angel Food Cake, Hammered Handle, Allan Adler, 11 In.	265.00
Demitasse Set, Vase Shape, Engraved Flowers, Matthews, 3 Piece	345.00
Dessert Spoon, Kent & Michie, 6 Piece	150.00
Dish, Hammered, Stylized Lobes, Signed, Kalo Shop, 5 x 9 In.	715.00
Dish, Low Footed, Applied Wire Rim, Frans J.R. Gillenberg, 9 1/2 In.	525.00
Dish, Oblong, Shaped Sides, Gorham, 10 1/2 In.	154.00
Dish, Oval, Hammered, 14th-Century Pattern, R.W. Edwards, 1 3/4 x 11 1/2 In.	192.00
Dish, Shell Shape, Fluted Scallop Shell, Hammered, Cellini Craft, 8 3/8 In.	495.00
Dish, Vegetable, Divided, Center Handles, Cellini Craft, 10 3/8 In.	1100.00
Dish, Vegetable, Oval Lobed Form, Arthur J. Stone, 10 1/4 x 7 5/8 In.	260.00
Dresser Set, Engraved, Monogram, Theodore B. Starr, 7 Piece	230.00
Dresser Set, Mirror, Brush & Comb, International, 3 Piece	35.00
Epergne, Reticulated, Engraved Flowers, Roger Williams, c.1900, 14 1/2 In.	5175.00
Ewer, Gilmor, Samuel Kirk, Daniel Webster Previous Owner	6600.00
Ewer, Rococo Revival, Vasiform, Chased & Repousse Vines, P.L. Krider	2310.00
Flagon, Leaf & Floral Design, Fletcher & Gardiner, 1820s, 11 3/4 In.	1380.00
Frame, Blossom Repousse, Hammered, Clemens Friedell, 13 x 9 7/8 In.	2400.00
Goblet, Applied Monogram, Stemmed, Lebolt & Co., 6 1/4 In.	350.00
Goblet, Campana Form, Beaded Border, Kirk, 7 In., 12 Piece	8912.00
Goblet, Cocktail, Vase-Form Bowl, Coat Of Arms, Reed & Barton, 18 Piece	4830.00
Goblet, Presentation, Baluster Form, William Adams, c.1840, 6 In.	345.00
Goblet, Wine, Blossom Form Bowl, Gorham, 8 Piece	660.00
Gravy Boat, Undertray, Fluted, Low Strap Handle, Kalo, 9 1/8 x 5 1/4 In.	1400.00
Holder, Matchbox, Beaded Border, Gorham	20.00
Holder, Stamp, Raised Border Design On Lid, Shreve & Co., 4 1/2 In.	185.00
Infuser, Tea, Dominick & Haff	110.00
Jar, Ivory Finial Cover, Tusk Ivory, Chinese Village, Potter Studio, 7 In.	1600.00
Jug, Hot Water, Hammered, Carved Ebony Handle, Leinonen, 7 3/4 In.	875.00
Knife, Butter, Jenny Lind, Twist Handle, Albert Cole, c.1860	55.00
Knife, Letter, Curved, Chased Diamond & Lines, A.J. Stone, 5 3/4 In.	650.00
Ladle, Coin, Diamond Pattern, John Polhemus, c.1867, 13 In.	495.00
Ladle, Coin, Engraved Monogram Handle, E. Kinsey, 8 In.	225.00
Ladle, Coin, Mercury Head, Oval Medallion, Monogram, Duhme Co., 13 In.	425.00
Ladle, Gilt Bowl, William Gale, c.1855, 14 In.	450.00
Ladle, Inverted Whale Shape Bowl, Ebony Handle, Leinonen, 10 3/4 In.	695.00
Ladle, Punch, Ball, Tompkins & Black, 20 In.	395.00
Ladle, Punch, Baltimore Rose, Schofield	270.00
Ladle, Punch, Kirk & Son	345.00
Ladle, Punch, Persian Design, Embossed Bell Flowers, Wood & Hughes	358.00
Ladle, Punch, Wood Extension, Thomas Edwards, c.1750, 4 3/8-In. Bowl	8337.00

Ladle, Scalloped Bowl, Embossed Floral, Wooden Handle, Parker, c.1750 .... 550.00
Ladle, Scenes Of Columbus, Gorham, 13 In. 1045.00
Ladle, Scroll & Leaf Pattern, Bigelow, Kennard, 13 3/4 In. 140.00
Ladle, Soup, Coin, Cut Designs, Coffin Cover Handle, Initials, 1799-1882 .... 373.00
Ladle, Soup, Fiddle Thread, William Thomson, c.1820, 13 5/8 In. 675.00
Ladle, Toddy, Whalebone Handle, 1775 .... 450.00
Loving Cup, Goodnow & Jenks, Monogram, 8 In. 402.00
Match Safe & Case, Cigarette, Admiral Robert E. Peary, 2 1/2-In. Safe 550.00
Mayonnaise, Attached Undertray, Lotus Pattern, Porter Blanchard, 3 x 7 In. 875.00
Measure Shot, Roseville Handle, Wallace 85.00
Mirror, Hand, Repousse, Square Shape, Chased Flowers & Leaves, 11 In. 172.00
Mug, Baby's, Mitchell & Tyler, c.1860 .... 275.00
Mug, Baluster Shape, Double Scroll Handle, Reed & Barton, 5 3/4 In. 260.00
Mug, Christening, Barrett & Sherwood, c.1860, 3 1/4 In. 8050.00
Mug, Coin, Lincoln & Foss, Boston, c.1850, 3 1/2 In. 259.00
Mug, Handle, Oscar J.H. Dibble, Savannah, 3 1/2 In. 1650.00
Nut Scoop, Howard, 1776 .... 65.00
Nut Set, Bushel Basket Shape, Ring Handles, Gorham, c.1869, 5 Piece 400.00
Pastry Server, Twist Handle, R. & W. Wilson, c.1850 .... 150.00
Pitcher, B. Gardiner, c.1820 .... 2300.00
Pitcher, Bulbous Cylindrical Form, Open Handle, International, 8 1/4 In. 150.00
Pitcher, Hammered, Riveted Straps, Monogram, Shreve & Co., 10 In. 1430.00
Pitcher, Oak Branches, Eagle Spout, Lincoln & Foss, c.1850, 10 In. 1840.00
Pitcher, Village Scenes, Scrolling Border, Grape Finial, Kirk, 11 Oz. 2530.00
Pitcher, Water, Art Deco, Durgin, Gorham, 4 1/2 Pt. 402.00
Pitcher, Water, Baluster, Monogram, Watson, 9 1/4 In. 287.00
Pitcher, Water, Baluster, Scrolled Handle, R. Wallace & Sons, 9 In. 260.00
Pitcher, Water, Egg Shape, Classic Greek, Kalo, 8 1/2 x 6 1/2 In. 2000.00
Pitcher, Water, Engraved, 1911, Kalo, 8 3/4 x 8 In. 2700.00
Pitcher, Water, Half-Reeded Vase, Chased, Lebkeucher & Co., c.1900, 11 In. 805.00
Pitcher, Water, Hammered, Porter Blanchard 300.00
Pitcher, Water, Monogram, Gorham, 4 1/2 In. 330.00
Pitcher, Water, Repousse Grape Clusters, Leaves, Gorham, 19th Century 2070.00
Pitcher, Water, Richard Dimes, c.1751, 8 1/2 In. 440.00
Pitcher, Water, Tapering Body, Scroll Handle, Gorham, c.1923, 8 In. 330.00
Pitcher, Water, Wallace, 4 Pt. 225.00
Plate, Edgeworth, Gorham, 6 1/4 In., 12 Piece 600.00
Plate, Footed, Antique Pattern, Monogram, Wallace, 10 In. 121.00
Plate, Hand Hammered Shield & Swag, Rogers Brothers, 11 In., 12 Piece 195.00
Plate, Shaped Rim, Richard Dimes, 6 1/4 In., 6 Piece 175.00
Platter, Floral Sprays On Rim, Theodore B. Starr, 20 In. 750.00
Platter, Meat, Oval, Gorham, 20 In. 440.00
Porringer, Coin, Cast Handle, 5 1/4 In. 605.00
Porringer, Coin, John B. Jones & Co., 5 1/2 In. 862.00
Porringer, Pierced Keyhole Handle, Benjamin Burt, c.1785, 8 1/4 In. 2300.00
Punch Bowl, Embossed Hearts, Foliage, Gorham, c.1905, 14 3/4 In. 2875.00
Punch Bowl, Green Enamel Liner, Towle, c.1940, 12 In. 632.00
Punch Cup, Orange With Twig Stalk Handle, Gorham, c.1886, 12 Piece 3165.00
Salt, Key Pattern Rim, Loop Handles, Gorham, c.1865, 3 3/8 In., 4 Piece 690.00
Salt, Open Curling Leaf Form, Spider Forms Handle, Shiebler, Pair 1725.00
Salt Cellar, Spoon, Green Enameled, Mildred G. Watkins, 3/4 x 2 1/2 In. 1350.00
Salt Set, Hammered Bowls, Turquoise Enameled Lining, Spoon, 4 Piece 100.00
Salver, Embossed Rim, Multiple Moldings, Edward Webb, c.1700, 6 In. 9200.00
Sauceboat, Engraved, Acanthus Leaf Handle, Jones, Ball & Co., c.1850 .... 345.00
Sauceboat, Ladles, Foliate Arabesque Stem & Rim, Gorham, c.1875, Pair 2300.00
Sauceboat, Stand, Hand Hammered, Double Lip, Handles, Redlich, 8 In. 287.00
Sauceboat, Undertray, Classic Style, Planished, A.J. Stone, 2 x 5 In. 975.00
Serving Spoon, Applied Flowers, Chased Bowl, Gorham, Box, 9 In. 230.00
Serving Spoon, Leaf-Shaped Gilded Bowl, Branch-Like Handle, Gorham 525.00
Spoon, Down-Turned Fiddle Handle, William G. Forbes, 9 1/4 In., 6 Piece 248.00
Spoon, Iced Tea, Teardrop Bowl, Hammered, G. Porter Blanchard, 8 In. 68.00
Spoon, Martini, Engraved E.G. Overn, David Carlson, 12 1/4 In. 135.00
Spoon, Salt, Hammered Handle, Gaylord-Craft, 2 1/2 In. 45.00

Silver-American Tankard, Scrolled
Thumb Lattice, J. Edwards, 6 1/2 In.

◆◆◆◆◆◆◆◆◆◆◆◆◆◆◆◆◆◆◆◆◆

Felt gives off hydrogen sulphide, which tarnishes silver. Do not use felt liners in drawers or felt bags to store silver unless they are the specially treated tarnish-preventive cloths.

◆◆◆◆◆◆◆◆◆◆◆◆◆◆◆◆◆◆◆◆◆

Spoon, Serving, Ball, Black & Co., Leather Case	95.00
Spoon, Serving, Hammered Handle, Monogram EP, Kalo Shop, 10 1/4 In.	325.00
Spoon, Stuffing, Twist Handle, R. & W. Wilson, c.1850, 13 1/4 In.	275.00
Spoon, Sugar, Norman Pattern, Pierced Initial L, Shreve & Co., 5 7/8 In.	95.00
Spoon, Tea Caddy, Pierced Heart Handle, Potter Studio, 5 5/16 In.	1400.00
Stamp Box, Barrel Shape, Flat Top, Shreve & Co., 4 x 1 In.	302.00
Sucrier, Coin, F. Marquand, Savannah, Ga., c.1825	5600.00
Sugar & Creamer, Bateau Shape, Repousse Cartouche, R. Richardson, c.1778	880.00
Sugar & Creamer, Hammered Interior, Sinuous Handles, A.J. Stone, 4 In.	750.00
Sugar & Creamer, Tray, Hammered, Square-Top Handles, Marshall Field	595.00
Sugar Castor, Colonial Revival Style, Smooth, Frans J.R. Gyllenberg, 6 1/2 In.	525.00
Sugar Sifter, Fiddle Thread, W. Gale & Son, c.1850	100.00
Syrup, Egg Shape, Low Footed, Strap Handle, Ivory Finial, Kalo, 6 x 5 1/4 In.	1100.00
Tablespoon, Joseph Moulton, c.1790	125.00
Tablespoon, Joseph Warner, c.1830	55.00
Tablespoon, W. Kendrick, c.1840	30.00
Tankard, Cover, Corkscrew Handle, Rattail Handle, Marked AC, 7 1/4 In.	1600.00
Tankard, Detachable Lid, Beaded Borders, T. Shields, c.1780, 8 5/8 In.	2075.00
Tankard, Scrolled Thumb Lattice, J. Edwards, 6 1/2 In. ....*Illus*	5500.00
Tazza, Footed, Stylized Swans' Heads Handles, Marcus & Co., 4 3/8 x 12 In.	2300.00
Tea & Coffee Set, Cartouche & Shell Panels, Durgin, 5 Piece	2500.00
Tea & Coffee Set, Engraved Design, R. & W. Wilson, c.1825, 4 Piece	2415.00
Tea & Coffee Set, Georgian Rose, Reed & Barton, 5 Piece	1900.00
Tea & Coffee Set, Girdles Of Grapevines, T. Fletcher, c.1825, 4 Piece	2070.00
Tea & Coffee Set, Princess Mary, Wallace, 4 Piece	660.00
Tea & Coffee Set, Rococo, Pear Shape, Shell & Scroll Border, Gorham, 5 Pc.	1210.00
Tea & Coffee Set, Vase Form, Shreve, Oak Tray, c.1915, 5 Piece	1380.00
Tea Set, Bands Of Flowers, Scroll Handles, Foliate Trim, F. Whiting, 4 Piece	920.00
Tea Set, Canted Sides, Foliate Scrolling, Durgin, 3 Piece	545.00
Tea Set, Diamond, Reed & Barton, 6 Piece	2300.00
Tea Set, Fluted, Vase Shape, Monogram, Howard & Co., c.1904, 4 Piece	745.00
Tea Set, Gadrooned Lower Half, Dominick & Haff & Howard, c.1880, 3 Piece	460.00
Tea Set, Georgian Style, Raised Pad Feet, Gorham, 3 Piece	413.00
Tea Set, Hammered Surface, Reed & Barton, c.1928, 4 Piece	575.00
Tea Set, Hampton Court, Reed & Barton, 3 Piece	2400.00
Tea Set, Repousse, Whiting Division Of Gorham, 5 Piece	1980.00
Tea Set, Towle, 3 Piece	467.00
Tea Strainer, Repousse Lily, Merrill Shops, N.Y., 6 1/2 In.	172.00
Tea Strainer, Star Pierced Bowl, A.J. Stone, 6 1/2 In.	375.00
Teapot, Acanthus Scroll, Floral Chased, 4 Paw Feet, 5 3/4 In.	172.00
Teapot, Gift To Wife Lydia, Gorham, Dated 1857	825.00
Teapot, Repousse Diamonds & Flowers, Ivory Banded Handle, Wallace	385.00
Teapot, Repousse Flowers & Foliage, Ovoid Form, 7 1/2 In.	515.00
Teapot, Stand, Ribbed Ovoid Form, Gorham, Engraved Date, 1891, 12 In.	805.00
Teapot, Stieff, c.1900, 7 In.	635.00

Teapot, William G. Forbes, New York, Marked Base, c.1800, 8 1/2 In. 805.00
Teaspoon, Bead Pattern, M.W. Galt & Bros., c.1850, 6 Piece 110.00
Teaspoon, G.W. Wolf, c.1790, Pair 100.00
Teaspoon, George Gordon 380.00
Teaspoon, Paul Revere, c.1780 .... 1350.00
Teaspoon, Pointed End, Engraved M. Porter Blanchard, 6 In. 45.00
Teaspoon, W.S. Pelletreau, c.1820 .... 25.00
Tongs, M. Pelletreau, c.1815 .... 175.00
Tongs, Sugar, H.B. Myer 120.00
Tongs, Sugar, Hammered, Marshall Field Craft, 2 7/8 In. 65.00
Tongs, Sugar, Lotus Pattern, G. Porter Blanchard, 2 3/4 In. 55.00
Tray, 3-Footed, Beaded Border, Goodnow & Jenks, Boston, 13 1/2 In. 475.00
Tray, Applied Floral Border, Unger Bros., 12 1/2 In. 410.00
Tray, Chippendale, Reed & Barton, 12 In. 245.00
Tray, Enameled Design, Punch Work, Mary Knight, 7 3/4 In. 2200.00
Tray, Fluted, Applied Monogram Each Side, Kalo, 16 1/4 x 10 1/4 In. 1800.00
Tray, Liqueur, Art Deco, Gorham, 13 In. 125.00
Tray, Pierced Borders, Ring Foot, Gorham, c.1910, 11 1/2 In. 230.00
Tray, Raised Boarder, Applied Wire Rim, Katharine Pratt, Round, 14 In. 975.00
Tray, Reeded Edge, Oval, Gorham, 28 1/2 In. 1610.00
Tray, Round, Engraved, Cowell & Hubbard, 13 In. 250.00
Tray, Square, Reticulated Gallery, 4-Footed, Howard & Co., c.1900, 9 In. 460.00
Trophy, Yacht, Anchor & Rudder Handles, Shreve, Crump & Low, c.1865 .... 5750.00
Tureen, Cover, Engraved Flowers & Scrolls, Meriden Britannia, 12 In. 1035.00
Tureen, Soup, Cover, Stag Finial, Ring Handles, Vanderslice, c.1870, 15 In. 4312.00
Urn, Sugar, Cover, Baluster Form, Beaded Rim, Monogram, c.1790, 9 In. 1840.00
Vase, Amphora Form, Snake On Book, Handles, Marcus & Co., 12 x 5 1/2 In. 2500.00
Vase, Chased Large Poppy Plants, G.W. Shiebler, c.1900, 23 In. 8050.00
Vase, Engraved, Flared Top, Columnar, 24 1/2 In. 2310.00
Vase, Flared Lip, Pairpoint Ruby Liner, Dominick & Haff, 14 1/4 In. 925.00
Vase, Hand Hammered, Bulbous Base, Tapered Neck, Kalo Shop, 7 In. 1210.00
Vase, Hand Hammered, Flaring Ribs, Pedestal Footed, Kalo Shop, 6 x 7 In. 880.00
Vase, Trumpet Shape, Monogram, Watson Co., 24 In. 247.00
Vase, Trumpet, Allover Chased Bellflowers, Conical, International, 18 1/4 In. 1495.00
SILVER-AUSTRIAN, Basket, Art Nouveau, Swing Handle, Floral, Oval, Vienna, 5 x 4 x 6 In. 260.00
Bowl, Chased Floral Design, 19th Century, 6 In. 86.00
Bowl, General Bandholtz, To R. Sig. Gorton, Dec. 18, 1919, 9 1/2 In. 70.00
Bowl, Grape Leaf & Vine Rim, Handles, 19th Century, 13 In. 201.00
Inkwell, Waved & Fluted, Matching Tray, J. Hoffman, c.1910, 7 1/4 In. 2760.00
Tea Caddy, Turkey Finial, Egg Shape, 19th Century, 5 1/2 In. 489.00
Tray, Running Floral Rim, Center Garland, Eduard Friedmann, c.1900, 22 In. 1725.00
SILVER-CHINESE, Box, Raised & Applied Dragon & Cloud, 2 x 4 5/8 In. 57.00
Candlestick, Baluster Form, Scroll Design, 1870s, 10 3/8 In., Pair 747.00
Dish, Meat, Oval, Cyma Edges, c.1935, 18 1/2 In., Pair 770.00
Pitcher, Water, c.1935 .... 385.00
Tea Set, Dragon Design, Tongs, Fitted Wooden Case, Shanghai, 4 Piece 1092.00
Teapot, Enamel Medallion, 5 1/4 In. 900.00
Tray, Engraved Dragon Design, Fitted Wooden Case, Shanghai, 22 5/16 In. 1265.00
SILVER-CONTINENTAL, Basket, Swing Handle, Figural Pierced Design, Glass Liner, 10 In. 402.00
Bowl, Figural Medallions, Floral Swags, Lobed Oval Form, 16 In. 920.00
Charger, Saint Ambrosius, Polished Stones Border, 17 1/2 In. 575.00
Goblet, Putti & Dolphin Standard, Frog Pond Base, 6 In. 97.00
Lantern, Tooled Stars & Bosses, Pierced Cover, 1850s, 13 1/2 In. 3220.00
Salt, 4 Silver Horses, Pulling Double Cart, Cobalt Blue Glass Liner 400.00
Spoon, Apostle, Gold Washed Bowl, 7 1/4 In., Pair 115.00
Tureen, Soup, Cover & Stand, Shell Handles, 1920s, 21 3/4 In. 4300.00
SILVER-DANISH, Bank, Hinged Lid, Double Globular Form, Georg Jensen, c.1930, 4 In. 920.00
Berry Spoon, Acanthus Pattern, Georg Jensen 275.00
Bottle Opener, Lemon Spear, Georg Jensen 69.00
Bowl, Caviar, Domed Cover, Enameled, Georg Jensen, 7 1/2 In. 2550.00
Bowl, Flared Rim, Openwork Leaves, Berries, J. Rohde For Georg Jensen, 7 In. 4600.00
Bowl, Flaring Rim, Foliate & Bead Openwork Support, Georg Jensen, 6 In. 1495.00
Bowl, Grapevine Pattern, Georg Jensen, c.1919, 7 3/4 In. 5750.00

Silver-Danish, Tea Set, Blossom,
Ivory Handles, Georg Jensen, 4 Piece

◆◆◆◆◆◆◆◆◆◆◆◆◆◆◆◆◆◆◆◆

Clean silver with gilt, like berry spoons or salt dishes, with soap, warm water, and a sponge. Do not use abrasive polish.

◆◆◆◆◆◆◆◆◆◆◆◆◆◆◆◆◆◆◆◆

Bowl, Grapevine, Georg Jensen, c.1945, 11 In. 6900.00
Bowl, Openwork Stem, Berries, Leaves, Scalloped, Georg Jensen, 6 5/8 In. 2530.00
Bowl, Scalloped, No. 856, S. Bernadotte For Georg Jensen, 8 1/2 In. 1495.00
Bowl, Stand, Art Nouveau, Georg Jensen, 6 1/2 In. 852.00
Bowl, Stylized Branch Support, c.1937, Georg Jensen, 6 1/2 In. 2300.00
Bowl, Stylized Leaves Open Standard, Round, Georg Jensen, 7 5/8 In. 4600.00
Box, Cover, Stylized Bird Shape, Allan Scharff, c.1980, 4 1/2 In. 800.00
Cake Server, Acorn Pattern, Georg Jensen 175.00
Candelabrum, 3-Light, Stylized Foliage, Georg Jensen, 6 1/8 In. 3162.00
Candlestick, 2-Light, Georg Jensen, Pair 2200.00
Candlestick, Ribbed Baluster Form, Georg Jensen, c.1945, 7 3/8 In., Pair 2875.00
Cheese Slice, Acorn Pattern, Georg Jensen 95.00
Cocktail Shaker, Berry Cluster Finial, Georg Jensen, c.1930, 12 In. 1850.00
Coffeepot, Ebony Handle & Finial, Georg Jensen, 6 1/2 In. 1725.00
Compote, Flared Bowl, Petal Form Stem, C.G. Hermann, 6 7/8 In., Pair 635.00
Compote, Grape Pattern, Hand Hammered, No. 263B, Georg Jensen, 7 In. 1500.00
Compote, Grape, Spiral Fluted Stem, No. 263B, Georg Jensen, 7 3/8 In. 2185.00
Compote, No. 97A, George Jensen, 7 3/4 In. 2475.00
Cordial, Inverted Bell Form, Floral Pedestal, Georg Jensen, Box, 8 Piece 374.00
Dish, 3 Sections, Beaded Borders, Bud Finial, Georg Jensen, 1945, 10 In. 1725.00
Dish, Meat, Acorn Rim, No. 642P, J. Rohde For Georg Jensen, 16 In. 4600.00
Dish, Preserve, Cover, Ebony Finial, Georg Jensen, c.1945, 6 7/8 In. 3100.00
Grape Shears, Georg Jensen 660.00
Inkstand, Domed Cover, Rectangular, Georg Jensen, 12 3/16 In. 2875.00
Ladle, Soup, Overlapping Leaves Rim, Georg Jensen, 16 In. 4600.00
Pitcher, Ebony Handle, Leaf & Berry Cluster, No. 385a, Georg Jensen, 7 In. 2070.00
Pitcher, Grapevine Pattern, Ebony Handle, Georg Jensen, c.1945, 9 In. 3160.00
Pitcher, Triangular, Openwork Spout, Ebony Handle, S. Bernadotte, 6 In. 3680.00
Pitcher, Water, Rounded Shoulders, Grapes, No. 407B, Georg Jensen, 8 3/4 In. 4850.00
Platter, Interval Acorn Rim, Georg Jensen, Oval, 16 In. 4600.00
Salt, Leaf Design Stems, Faceted Foot, Georg Jensen, c.1930, 3 7/8 In., 4 Piece 920.00
Sugar Tongs, Blossom Pattern, Georg Jensen 195.00
Tankard, Hinged Cover, 3 Lion & Ball Supports, 8 1/2 In. 4370.00
Tea & Coffee Set, Cosmos, Georg Jensen, c.1925, 5 Piece 8100.00
Tea Set, Blossom Pattern, Georg Jensen, c.1937, 3 Piece 3700.00
Tea Set, Blossom, Ivory Handles, Georg Jensen, 4 Piece .... *Illus* 5500.00
Toothpick, Georg Jensen, 2 1/4 In. 375.00
Tray, Openwork Foliate, Flower Handles, Georg Jensen, c.1945, 13 1/2 In. 2300.00
Tray, Raised Bead & Reel Rim, Ebony Handles, Georg Jensen, 20 3/4 In. 4315.00
Tray, Tea, Ivory Handles, Georg Jensen, 21 In. 3850.00
Vase, Embossed & Chased Clover Plants, A. Michelsen, c.1905, 10 3/8 In. 3165.00
SILVER-DUTCH, Bell, Table, Baluster Handle, Cornelis Knuysting, c.1784, 5 3/4 In. 4025.00
   Bowl, Chased Figure And Animals, Ornate Tab Handles, 4 5/8 In. 200.00

Bowl, Floral Form, Rim Foot, Handles, 10 1/4 In. 345.00
Box, Footed, Chased Genre Decoration, 3 1/2 x 4 In. 470.00
Box, Sewing, Figures In Cartouches, 19th Century, 2 1/2 x 4 3/8 In. 230.00
Box, Tobacco, Engraved Windmills Interior & Exterior, Rectangular, 5 In. 460.00
Mustard, Initialed Cover, Forked Thumbpiece, Marked, 4 5/8 In. 2530.00
Tea Caddy, Courting Scene, Ball Feet, Rectangular, 4 1/2 In. 200.00
Tobacco Jar, Cover, Octagonal Bombe, Bastiaan Havelaar, c.1741, 5 1/2 In. 8625.00

SILVER-ENGLISH. English silver is marked with a series of four or five small
hallmarks. The standing lion mark is the most commonly seen sterling quality
mark. The other marks indicate the city of origin, the maker, and the year of
manufacture. These dates can be verified in many good books on silver.

SILVER-ENGLISH, Basket, Applied Birds, Flowers, Handle, C. Crichton, c.1909, 6 5/8 In. 316.00
Basket, Cake, Georgian, Wirework, Vine Handle, Samuel Herbert, c.1762, 15 In. 5500.00
Basket, George III, Wirework Sides, Oval, John Schofield, c.1793, 12 In., Pair 6900.00
Basket, Scalloped Shell Form, 3 Dolphin Feet, L.A. Crichton, c.1917 .... 6050.00
Basket, Sweetmeat, London, c.1895, 3 1/2 In., Pair.. 260.00
Basket, Swing Handle, Geometric Pear Design, William Plummer, 17 In. 6275.00
Beaker, Engraved Foliate Cartouche, F. Brown, c.1876, 4 In., 5 Piece 2760.00
Bell, Table, George III, Ivory Handle, Phipps & Robinson, c.1794, 5 1/8 In................. 2070.00
Bell, Table, George III, Stylized Bud Finial, Joseph Angell, c.1814, 4 3/4 In. 2415.00
Belt, Woman's, Edwardian, Cherub Design, Marked 695.00
Bowl, Punch, Sheffield, 1904-05, 12 x 9 In. ....*Illus* 1760.00
Bowl, Stylized Ribbon Bows, 5 Trifid Feet, Liberty & Co., c.1902, 9 In........................ 5460.00
Box, Cigarette, Gold Trim, Reeded, Rectangular, Cartier, c.1936, 6 7/16 In. 4370.00
Box, Cover, Cylindrical, Engraved Crest, George IV, 4 x 4 3/4 In. 800.00
Cake Basket, Scrollwork Pierced Panels, S. Herbert, c.1763, 13 3/4 In. 2990.00
Candelabrum, 4-Light, Drip Pans, Fluted Sconces, Naylor Bros., c.1961, 14 In. 3740.00
Candlestick, George II, Floral Design, John Priest, c.1752, 4 Piece 7200.00
Candlestick, George III, Corded Borders, Ebenezer Coker, c.1711, 8 In., Pair............. 3450.00
Candlestick, George III, Corinthian Capitals, William Cafe, c.1760, 12 In., Pair 3450.00
Candlestick, John Crouch, c.1772, 9 3/4 In., Pair 4100.00
Card Case, Foliate Scrollwork, Windsor Castle, Birmingham, c.1837, 4 In. 330.00
Card Case, Victorian, Chased, Marked Y & W, Leather Case, 4 In. 287.00
Centerpiece, 2 Back-To-Back Swans, Asprey & Co., 20 1/2 In................................... 6900.00
Centerpiece, James Crichton & Co., 1892, 12 3/4 In. 2500.00
Coaster, Wine, Pierced Sides, Peter, Ann & William Bateman, c.1803, Pair.................. 1840.00
Coffeepot, Baluster Shape, Wooden Handle, Crichton Bros., c.1931, 7 1/4 In.............. 255.00
Coffeepot, George II, Scrolling Spout, John Swift, c.1758, 10 3/4 In. 2100.00
Creamer, George III, Chased Florals & Swag, P. & A. Bateman, c.1797, 5 In. 2875.00
Creamer, Repousse, Chased Floral Decorations, Samuel Wheat, c.1756, 4 In............... 155.00

Silver-English, Bowl, Punch, Sheffield,
1904-05, 12 x 9 In.

Silver-English, Water Kettle,
Revolving Handle,
George III, 1764, 11 In.

Silver-English, Tea Service, Melon Pattern,
c.1834, Sterling, 4 Piece

Cruet Set, 5 Cut Glass Bottles, Hester Bateman, c.1786, 10 1/2 In.	2300.00
Cup, Caudle, Baroque Cartouche, Leaf Rows, Thomas Parr I, c.1703, 4 1/2 In.	2530.00
Dish, Entree, Engraved Arms On Cover, Paul Storr, c.1805, 11 In., Pair	9200.00
Epergne, George II, William Cripps, c.1758	8625.00
Fish Slice, George III, 1811-1812, HS Mark, 12 In.	182.00
Flask, Hinged Cover, Lion Touch Marks, Maker H. & T., 4 In.	145.00
Flask, Whiskey, Bottom Becomes Cup, London, c.1902	155.00
Gravy Boat, Scimitar, Double-Winged Flank, c.1755, 7 In.	715.00
Inkwell, Pond Form, Lily Supports, Heath & Middleton, c.1886, 6 3/4 In.	1150.00
Kettle, On Lampstand, Flower Spray Finial, R. & S. Garrard, c.1859, 15 1/2 In.	2415.00
Knife, Pastry, Lunch, Elizabeth & John Eaton, c.1863	50.00
Ladle, Engraved Horsehead & Wings, London, 13 1/4 In.	165.00
Letter Opener, Chased Design, 2 Children In Landscape, c.1896, 11 1/4 In.	345.00
Magnifying Glass, Hallmarked Handle	65.00
Page Turner, Ivory Blade, Amorous Couple, W. Comyns, 17 5/8 In.	200.00
Pitcher, Sauce, Repousse Floral Decoration, Footed, London, c.1758	300.00
Plate, George III, Crest, Baron's Coronet, C. Wright, c.1782, 9 In., 12 Piece	6037.00
Platter, Gadroon Rim, Engraved Crest, Frederick Kandler, c.1766, 17 1/2 In.	1955.00
Platter, Well & Tree, George III, George Ashworth, c.1806	2760.00
Potato Fork, Fiddle Head, Mary Chawner, c.1838	150.00
Salt, Master, Shell Shape, Dolphin Feet, Robert Hennell, 2 1/4 In., Pair	345.00
Salver, Edwardian, Shaped Rim, WA Maker, 12 5/8 In.	345.00
Salver, Molded Rim, 4 Scroll Feet, Cheltenham, 16 1/8 In.	805.00
Salver, Oval, Gadrooned Rim, Shells, Flowers, Paul Storr, c.1813, 12 1/2 In.	2185.00
Salver, Square, Molded Rim, Footed, Goldsmiths & Silversmiths, c.1903	1150.00
Spoon, A.W. Initial, Jacob Marsh, 8 In., Pair	395.00
Spoon, Berry, George III, Gold Washed Fruit, 8 7/8 In., 4 Piece	290.00
Spoon, Master Salt, Prince Of Wales Feathers, Hester Bateman, c.1786, Pair	110.00
Sugar Castor, Elizabeth II, Gadrooned Detail, C. & Co., c.1953	400.00
Sugar Castor, Pierced Cover, Marked CE, 9 1/4 In.	165.00
Sugar Shaker, George II	275.00
Tablespoon, W. Godbehere & E. Wigan, c.1796	65.00
Tankard, Charles II, Coat Of Arms, Frances Leake, c.1660	5175.00
Tankard, Engraved Crest, George III, Walter Brind, London, c.1775, 8 In.	2415.00
Tankard, Low Girdle, Flat Cover, Leaf Thumbpiece, W. Gamble, c.1703, 7 1/8 In.	5175.00
Tea & Coffee Set, Chased Flowers & Shells, J.E. Terry, c.1828, 4 Piece	3100.00
Tea & Coffee Set, Lampstand, Trellis Strapwork, E. Barnard, c.1863, 5 Piece	6900.00
Tea & Coffee Set, Oak Branch Handles & Spout, Paul Storr, c.1838, 4 Piece	6325.00
Tea Caddy, Edward VII, Cylinder, Spoked Wheels, c.1910, 3 1/2 In.	200.00
Tea Caddy, Floral & Leaf Design, Bombe Form, Newcastle, 5 3/4 In.	345.00
Tea Service, Melon Pattern, c.1834, Sterling, 4 Piece .... *Illus*	5175.00
Tea Set, Melon Pattern, Squash Finials, London, c.1835, 4 Piece	5175.00
Tea Set, Neoclassical Form, Meriden Britannia, 4 Piece	400.00

Teapot, Beaded Borders, Peter & Jonathan Bateman, c.1790, 5 1/2 In. 2100.00
Teapot, Drum Shape, Wooden Finial & Handle, P. & W. Bateman, c.1801 .... 460.00
Teapot, Ivory Fittings, Scroll Handle, Marked, c.1933, 6 x 9 1/2 In. 300.00
Teapot, Oval, Chased Florals, Flower Finial, John Wakefield, c.1840, 12 1/2 In. 690.00
Teapot, Wooden Handle & Finial, London Hallmark, c.1929, 7 7/8 In. 100.00
Teaspoon, Fiddle, William Bateman, c.1814 .... 90.00
Teaspoon, George III, Old English Pattern, 1802, 6 Piece 160.00
Teaspoon, Old English Pattern, William Eley & William Fearn, 5 In., 6 Piece 230.00
Teaspoon, Sheaf Of Wheat Back Of Bowl, W. Haverstick, c.1790 .... 70.00
Tongs, Bright Cut, Paul & Ann Bateman, c.1792 .... 125.00
Tray, Knife, Incurved Sides, British Isles Emblems, R. Sharp, c.1801, 16 1/2 In. 7187.00
Tray, Pen, Egg Shape, Hinged Cover, Reeded Rim, RH/DH, London, c.1835 .... 220.00
Tray, Rim With Shells & Flowers, Langley Archer, c.1900, 29 1/2 In. 4600.00
Tray, Well & Tree, Domed Cover, Hot Water Base, P. Storr, c.1818, 26 3/8 In. 5750.00
Tureen, Sauce, Bombe, Acanthus Supports, Cradock & Reid, c.1819, Pair 6325.00
Urn, Tea, Glove Form Body, Ebony Handle, Sheffield, c.1790 .... 885.00
Water Kettle, Revolving Handle, George III, 1764, 11 In. ....*Illus* 1100.00
SILVER-FRENCH, Bottle Opener & Stopper, Cartier, Case 100.00
Bowl & Mirror Plateau, Boat Form, Ivory Block Handles, c.1925, 20 1/2 In. 4600.00
Box, Cartouche Form, Figural & Scroll Repousse, 18th Century, 3 1/2 In. 120.00
Castor, Chased Flower & Shell Design, 7 1/4 In. 375.00
Coffeepot, George II, Lighthouse Shape, Jacob Margas, c.1737 .... 6900.00
Dressing Table Set, Leaf Wrapped Borders, Traveling Case, G. Keller, c.1900............. 8050.00
Fish Server, Wooden Handle, Engraved Dolphin, Marked, 14 1/4 In. 65.00
Gravy Boat, Double Lip, Ribbed Borders, 1880s.. 150.00
Jug, Claret, Spiral Shell Form, Conch Finial, Puiforcat, 1870s, 12 1/2 In. 3335.00
Mustard, Handled Lift Lid, Cut Glass Liner, Ladle, 4 1/2 In. 50.00
Sauceboat, Attached Tray, Leafy Scroll Rim & Handle, 9 1/2 In. 400.00
Sugar Basket, Urn Shape, Swing Handle, Cartouches, Openwork, 6 In. 165.00
Tea & Coffee Set, Quadrangular Bombe Form, Tetard Freres, c.1925, 5 Piece 4025.00
Vase, Chased Branches, Nymph At Waterfall, Boucheron, c.1880, 6 3/8 In. 1150.00
Vase, Chased Peonies, Marked AR, c.1900, 16 1/4 In.. 2650.00
Vase, Spreading Circular Base, Cartier, 14 In.. 1095.00
SILVER-GERMAN, Basket, Hammered, Ivory Handle, German Mark, 4 1/2 x 6 1/4 In...... 725.00
Basket, Reticulated, Round, Spread Foot, Pierced, Chased, Birds, 10 1/4 In. 345.00
Beaker, Engraved Floral, Marked, c.1709, 3 In. 1265.00
Beaker, Spirally Lobed & Fluted, Fournier, c.1760, 7 7/8 In. 3105.00
Bowl, Dessert, Shell Dolphin Supports, Putto At Top, c.1900, 10 3/4 In.......................... 2587.00
Bowl, Footed, Round, Chased Scrolls, Monogram, Dresden, 6 In. 140.00
Bowl, Pierced Panels, Figural, Floral & Bird, Half Spherical, 6 3/4 x 4 1/4 In. 262.00
Box, Pierced & Rose Design, Oval, Early 20th Century, 6 x 10 1/2 In. 35.00
Candelabrum, 5-Light, Scrolling Arms, Bacchian Figure Center, 14 1/2 In. 255.00
Coffee & Tea Set, Monogrammed, N.K. Rischer, 6 Piece 1275.00
Coffeepot, Spiraled Ribbons, Rose Spray Finial, G.N. Gierfreund, c.1760.................... 4600.00
Cup, Stirrup, Fox Head, Tooled Fur, Pointed Snout, 5 1/2 In., Pair................................. 1610.00
Dance Card, 2 Embossed Cards Holding Horn Paper, Finger Chain............................... 200.00
Dish, Muffin, 3 Shell-Form Compartments, Putti Finial, Hoof Feet, 10 In....................... 2587.00
Figurine, Knight, Medieval Dress, Ivory Face, Openwork, 8 1/8 In., Pair 2760.00
Jug, Cover, Rococo Shell & Scroll Supports, G. Haase, c.1770, 11 5/8 In. 2760.00
Nef, Wooden Plinth, 19 x 19 3/4 In., 2 Piece.. 1435.00
Snuffbox, Slip-On Cover, Landscape, Martin Roth, c.1730, 3 1/2 In. 3737.00
Sugar Box, Bombe, Hinged Cover, Floral Top, 1780, 5 3/4 In.. 3190.00
Tazza, Dolphin Stem, Ruby Crystal Bowl, 5 In., Pair.. 460.00
Tea & Coffee Set, Repousse Floral Swags, 4 Piece 1610.00
Tea & Coffee Set, Rococo, Domed Cover, Pear Shape, Eugen Ferner, 4 Piece 1320.00
Teapot, Pear Form, Swan Neck Spout, Esaias Busch III, 1735, 5 In............................... 6900.00
Tray, Oval, Chased & Engraved Ribbon-Tied Swags, Canted Edge, 23 x 19 In. 1100.00
SILVER-HUNGARIAN, Ewer, Leaf & Berry Finial, Engraved, A. Kolbany, 1785, 8 3/4 In. 1725.00
SILVER-INDIAN, Bowl, Tiger & Wild Boar Hunting Scene, 7 3/4 In. 1150.00
Box, Spice, Floral Finial, 6 Radiating Hinged Compartments, 6 In. 1380.00
SILVER-IRISH, Bowl, Bright Cut Swags Of Flowers, Joseph Jackson, c.1780, 7 1/4 In...... 1150.00
Bowl, George III, Flared Rim, Engraved Crest, Matthew West, c.1776, 5 1/2 In. 1610.00
Coffeepot, Repousse Birds & Branch, Richard Tudor, Bone Handle, 30 Oz. 1700.00

Creamer, Allover Leaf & Floral Design, Samuel Walker, c.1759, 4 Oz. 600.00
Cup, Beaded Girdles, Leaf-Capped Handles, Richard Tudor, c.1783, 5 In., Pair. 2070.00
Egg Spoon, Dublin, c.1812 .... 45.00
Tongs, M. West & Son, c.1827 .... 75.00
Tureen, Sauce, Fruit & Vine Finial, 4 Hoofed Feet, John Craig, c.1779, Pair 5520.00
Waiter, Leafy Scrolls, 3 Hoof Feet, Samuel Walker, c.1745, 6 In. 2415.00
SILVER-ITALIAN, Bell, Table, Baluster Handle, Square, Vincenzo Belli I, 4 3/4 In. 2875.00
Bookbinding, Lion Of Judea Reserves Front & Back, A. Geinnotti, c.1840, 7 In. 3450.00
Box, Dresser, Oval, 4 Leaf-Shaped Feet, Domed Cover, Floral Finial, c.1900, 5 In. 220.00
Box, Engraved Floral & Scrolling Acanthus, Wood Lined, 7 x 4 1/4 In. 115.00
Box, Sugar, Bird Finial, Draped Repousse Design, 17 x 6 1/2 In. 1035.00
Candelabrum, 2-Light, Lion Masks & Swags, Paw Feet, D. Massotti, c.1830, Pair 8050.00
Case, Lipstick, Etched Enamelwork, Turquoise Oval Stone 80.00
Dish, Meat, Cover, Figural, Hog 1100.00
Lamp, Oil, 3 Spouts, Chain Attached Handles, Snuffers, 25 In., Pair 9775.00
Pitcher, Triangular Spouts, Cylindrical, Mario Botta, 11 3/4 In. 5750.00
Sugar, Cover, Ecclesiastical Coat Of Arms, G. Romanelli, c.1840, 7 1/4 In. 2300.00
Tea & Coffee Set, Geometric Form, Strapwork Handles, Cleto Munari, 5 Piece 3680.00
SILVER-JAPANESE, Bowl, Raised Dragon Design, Hammered Surface, 10 1/8 In. 205.00
Box, Raised Dragon Design, Hammered Surface, Wood Liner, 6 x 9 1/2 In. 975.00
Coffee Set, Chrysanthemum Repousse, Bamboo Handles, 3 Piece 550.00
Figurine, Tiger, Prowling, Akichika, Mid-19th Century, 5 1/4 In. 4400.00
Figurine, Waves, Tossing 3 Crystal Spheres, Yamanaka, 7 7/8 In. 3080.00
Model Fighter Plane, 1930 Nakijima Type, 1:24 Scale, c.1930, 12 In. 6900.00
Saki Set, 7 Piece 175.00
Tea Set, Dragon Handles, 6 1/2-In. Teapot, 3 Piece 977.00
Tea Set, Raised Floral Design, Tray, 6 Piece 6325.00
Tray, Engraved Birds On Flowering Branches, Bamboo Design, 18 In. 3737.00
Vase, Cherry Blossom Branch Feet, Wooden Base, 1890s, 5 In. 977.00
SILVER-MEXICAN, Bowl, Dragon-Shaped Handles, Undulating Rim, Oval, 19 1/2 In. 460.00
Bowl, Round, Circular Foot, Applied Blossoms, 4 3/4 In. 370.00
Bracelet, Oval Blue Stones, Free-Form Links 170.00
Brandy Warmer, Turned Wooden Handle 110.00
Candelabrum, Scrolled Supports, Rectangular Base, 11 In., Pair. 345.00
Dish, Vegetable, Cover, Scrolled Rim, Divided, Conquistador, 16 In. 287.00
Lamp, Oil, Classical, Leopard's-Head Scroll Handle, Sanborn's Factory, 4 In. 192.00
Pendant, Aztec Calendar Form 115.00
Pin, Butterfly 35.00
Pin, Circle, Black Stone, Silver Figure Inlay, Los Castillo, 1 1/2 In. 65.00
Pitcher, Stylized Eagle Head, Wooden Handle, W. Spratling, c.1940, 6 In. 2300.00
Pitcher, Water, Vase Shape, Applied Blossoms, 11 1/4 In. 745.00
Salad Set, Large Blossom Handle, Stamped, 11 In. 247.00
Spurs, 1940s 275.00
Sugar & Creamer, Tray, 3 Piece 460.00
Tea & Coffee Set, Domed Cover, Ball Finial, Tray, 1960s, 5 Piece 3600.00
Tea & Coffee Set, Turquoise, 4 3/4-In. Tray, Miniature 82.00
Tea Set, Melon Form, Foliate Feet, 4 Piece 485.00
Tea Set, Oval Tray, Candelabrum, 6 Piece 1210.00
Tray, Embossed Border & Handle, Oval, Taxco 925, 27 3/4 In. 355.00
Tray, Shell Form, Floral, Geometric Chasing Overall, Sanborn, 7 1/2 In. 60.00
Tray, Wide Border, Repousse Roses, Oval, 12 In. 80.00
Vase, Gourd Shape, Squatty Base, Signed, 10 1/4 x 6 In. 325.00
SILVER-NORWEGIAN, Centerpiece, Viking Ship, Andersen, Oslo, c.1906, 10 1/2 In. 9200.00
SILVER-POLISH, Candlestick, Neoclassical, Lamp Mounted, 19th Century, 12 3/4 In., Pair . 172.00
SILVER-PORTUGUESE, Basin, Flowers On Rim, Festoons Of Flowers, 20 1/2 In. 2070.00
Model, Ship, Gilt Filigree, Plexiglas Case, 19 x 17 In. 630.00

SILVER-RUSSIAN. Russian silver is marked with the Cyrillic, or Russian, alphabet. The numbers 84, 88, or 91 indicate the silver content. Russian silver may be higher or lower than sterling standard. Other marks indicate maker, assayer, or city of manufacture. Many pieces of silver made in Russia are decorated with enamel. Faberge pieces are listed in their own category.

SILVER-RUSSIAN, Box, Cigarette, Hinged Cover, Match Safe On End, Ribbed Design, 4 In.   200.00

Box, Cover, Oval, Ribbed, Scroll Feet, Double-Headed Eagle Mark, 4 3/4 In. 290.00
Cake Basket, Grapevine Border, Swing Handle, c.1885, 11 3/4 In. 2760.00
Candlestick, Baluster Stem, Chased, C. Heine, c.1825, 11 3/8 In., Pair 4850.00
Candlestick, Chased, Ribbon-Tied Borders, c.1830, 9 3/8 In., Pair 1400.00
Cane, Silver & Shaded Enamel Handle, c.1910, 4-In. Handle. 2415.00
Dish, Cover, Stand, 2 Handles, Applied Shell & Scroll Rim, Flower Finial 460.00
Egg, Chased & Engraved Basket Work, P. Ovchinnikov, c.1900, 4 1/2 In. 1320.00
Fish Service, Fish Decorated, Hempel, St. Petersburg, c.1900, 26 Piece 3737.00
Jar, Relief Decorated, Fish, Insects, Plants, 3 In. 260.00
Tray, Footed, Square, c.1774, 9 In. 412.00
SILVER-SCOTTISH, Bonbon Spoon, St. Giles On Handle, Cathedral In Bowl, c.1898 ...... 95.00
  Spoon, Stuffing, Fiddle, Peter Aiken, c.1831 .... 195.00
  Tablespoon, George III, Engraved Crests, 1749-1772, 12 Piece 375.00

SILVER-STERLING. Sterling silver is made with 925 parts silver out of 1,000
parts of metal. The word *sterling* is a quality guarantee used in the United
States after about 1860. The word was used much earlier in England and Ireland. Pieces listed here are not identified by country. Other pieces of sterling
quality silver are listed under Silver-American, Silver-English, etc.

SILVER-STERLING, Basket, Fruit, Reticulated, Oval, 1890s, 11 1/2 In. 635.00
Beaker, Country Club Trophy, Kalo Shops, 1916, 4 3/4 In. 110.00
Box, Hinged Cover, Flower Finial, 4 Scrolled Feet, Gilt Interior 495.00
Box, Repousse, Oval, High Relief Cherub, Floral Garlands, c.1900, 6 In. 770.00
Bud Vase, Art Nouveau, Bust Of Woman, Floral Petals, 10 3/4 In. 1870.00
Candelabrum, 3-Light, Weighted, 13 In., Pair 495.00
Candlestick, Colonial Revival, c.1926, 11 3/4 In., Pair 947.00
Case, Cigarette, Engraved Dragon & Scroll, Monogram TSD 60.00
Centerpiece, Hammered, Elliptical, Loop Handles, Sciarrotta, 14 1/2 x 7 In. 460.00
Cigarette Box, Royal Flush, Hearts, Enamel, c.1890 ....*Illus* 935.00
Cigarette Case, Diamond & Spade, c.1880, 3 1/2 In. ....*Illus* 440.00
Cigarette Case, Enameled Roulette Wheel ....*Illus* 880.00
Coffee Set, Signed Toshikazu, 3 Piece 985.00
Coffeepot, Art Nouveau, Demitasse, 8 In. 275.00
Compote, Hammered, Footed, Scalloped & Flared Rim, Jessop, 7 1/2 In. 220.00
Cup, Bouillon, Lenox Liner, Methews Co., Fitted Box, Pair 460.00
Dish, Leaf Shape, 2 Sections, Handle, 8 3/4 In. 80.00
Dish, Muffin, Pierced Oak Leaf Bands, 7 Sided Base, Woodside, 1910s, 10 In. 425.00
Dresser Set, 2 Perfume Bottles, Powder Jar, Rouge Pot, 15 Piece 1500.00
Dresser Set, Lady's Face Motif, Flowing Hair, Art Nouveau, c.1902, 8 Piece 800.00
Dresser Set, Monogram B, Mauser, 5 Piece 60.00
Flask, Garden Flower Design On Face, 5 1/4 In. 250.00
Flask, Whiskey, Incised Pierced Floral Overlay, 6 1/2 In. 245.00
Flask, Whiskey, Undecorated, 3 Pt. 175.00
Ladle, Magnolia Blossom, Scrolled Handle, Peterson 230.00
Miniature Settee, Armchair & Side Chair, 20th Century, 1 3/4 In., 3 Piece 176.00

Silver-Sterling, Cigarette Box, Royal Flush, Hearts, Enamel, c.1890

Silver-Sterling, Cigarette Case, Diamond & Spade, c.1880, 3 1/2 In.

Silver-Sterling, Cigarette Case, Enameled Roulette Wheel

Muffineer, 7 1/8 In.	26.00
Pill Box, Engraved Ace Of Diamonds, July 14, 1893, 1 x 1 1/4 In.	121.00
Pitcher, Ribbed Banded Design, International, 7 In.	200.00
Pitcher, Water, Tray, Initial G, Bunkirk, 1940s, 2 Piece	350.00
Plate, Fluted & Scalloped Rim, 10 In., 12 Piece	1725.00
Rattle, Humpty Dumpty, Victoria Hayes, Born 3rd June, 1948	165.00
Shaving Mug, Brush Handle, Floral Repousse, Monogram, 3 1/4 In.	220.00
Spoon, Souvenir, see Souvenir category	
Tea & Coffee Set, Colonial, Octagonal, 4 Piece	1200.00
Tea Service, Bird & Floral Design, 4 Piece	825.00
Tea Set, Neoclassical, Urn-Shaped Bowls, Monogram, 5 Piece	1045.00
Tea Strainer, Lily Pads, Turned Wooden Handle	82.00
Tongs, Flying Geese Design	110.00
Tray, 2 Handles, Rectangular, Fenton Brothers, 1918	1250.00
Tray, Card, Scalloped Hammered Border, Shreve & Co., Round, 6 In., Pair	165.00
Tray, Hand Hammered, Double Handles, 28 In.	1485.00
Trophy, Yachting, Chicago Yacht Club, c.1912, 5 1/2 x 9 1/2 In.	330.00
Urinal, c.1880.	1035.00
Vase, Trumpet, Reticulated Collar, Floral Design, G. Henckel, 20 In.	345.00
SILVER-SWEDISH, Coffeepot, Fluted Barrel Form, Blomsterwall, c.1829, 8 1/4 In.	1610.00
Ladle, Punch, Turned Ebony Handle, c.1850, 15 In.	395.00
Sugar Box, Cover, Baluster Shape, Flower Finial & Feet, 5 1/2 x 4 1/4 In.	285.00
Sugar Box, Spaniel Finial, Swing Handle, Bombe Form, Isberg, c.1809, 8 In.	2300.00

SINCLAIRE cut glass was made by H. P. Sinclaire and Company of Corning, New York, between 1905 and 1929. He cut glass made at other factories until 1920. Pieces were made of crystal as well as amber, blue, green, or ruby glass. Only a small percentage of Sinclaire glass is marked with the S in a wreath.

Candlestick, Amber, Ribbed Mushroom Top, 10 In., Pair	235.00
Candlestick, Amber, Twisted Stem, Dome Footed, 10 In., Pair	275.00
Candlestick, Turned-Down Rim, Engraved Flower, Amber, 9 1/2 In.	75.00
Compote, ABC, Flower Design, White Rim, 6 In.	295.00
Compote, Stem, Amber, 6 1/2 In.	50.00
Decanter, Etched, No Stopper, Signed, 8 In.	138.00
Vase, Bud, Floral, 10 In.	100.00
Vase, Colonial Blue, 7 1/4 In.	90.00
Vase, Hobstars & Flutes, Hobstar Cut Foot, Signed, 12 In.	580.00
Vase, Olive Green, 12 In.	60.00

SKIING, see Sports category

SLAG GLASS resembles a marble cake. It can be streaked with different colors. There were many types made from about 1880. Pink slag was an American Victorian product of unknown origin. Purple and blue slag were made in American and English factories. Red slag is a very late Victorian and twentieth-century glass. Other colors are known but are of less importance to the collector. New versions of chocolate glass and colored slag glass are being made.

Blue, Animal, Elephant, 4 In.	35.00
Blue, Creamer, Marquis Of Lorne	285.00
Caramel slag is listed in the Chocolate Glass category	
Pink, Salt & Pepper, Tapered Scroll	75.00
Pink, Sauce, Inverted Fan & Feather, Shell Feet, 2 3/8 In.	300.00 to 450.00
Pink, Sugar, Cover, Opalescent, 7 1/4 x 4 In.	1050.00
Pink, Tumbler, Inverted Fan & Feather, 4 In.	475.00
Purple, Animal, Owl, Imperial	85.00
Purple, Cup, 3 Handles, Monogram, 1850s, 2 x 2 In.	45.00
Purple, Dish, Lion Cover	118.00
Purple, Plate, Pierced Rim, 10 In.	40.00
Purple, Vase, Argonaut Shell, 4 In., Pair	90.00
Red, Dish, Rabbit On Nest Cover	525.00
Red, Rose Bowl, Crimped, 8 1/2 In.	75.00
Red, Toothpick, Witch's Head	6.00

SLEEPY EYE collectors look for anything bearing the image of the nine-teenth-century Indian chief with the drooping eyelid. The Sleepy Eye Milling Co., Sleepy Eye, Minnesota, used his portrait in advertising from 1883 to 1921. It offered many premiums, including stoneware and pottery steins, crocks, bowls, mugs, and pitchers, all decorated with the famous profile of the Indian. The popular pottery was made by Western Stoneware and other companies long after the flour mill went out of business in 1921. Reproductions of the pitchers are being made today. The original pitchers came in only five sizes: 4 inches, 5 1/4 inches, 6 1/2 inches, 8 inches, and 9 inches. The Sleepy Eye image was also used by companies unrelated to the flour mill.

Bowl, Salt	560.00
Calendar, 1903	250.00
Calendar, 1904	190.00
Cookbook	125.00 to 225.00
Crock, Butter	850.00
Fan, 12 1/4 In.	200.00 to 280.00
Label, Barrel, Trademarked Image, Round, 16 In.	275.00
Letter Opener, Bronze	925.00
Mug, Blue & Gray	360.00
Mug, Blue On White, 4 1/2 In.	145.00
Mug, Chestnut, 1952	230.00
Mug, Left Handled, Blue & Gray, 1952	500.00
Paperweight, Bronze	400.00
Paperweight, Metal	185.00
Pillow Top, Monroe, Square, 22 In.	700.00 to 925.00
Pitcher, No. 1, Blue & Gray, 4 In.	250.00 to 270.00
Pitcher, No. 2, Blue & White	250.00
Pitcher, No. 3, Blue & White	1300.00
Pitcher, No. 4, Blue & Gray, 8 In.	200.00
Pitcher, No. 5, Blue & White, Sprayed, 9 In.	4850.00
Pitcher, Oak Barrel	4500.00
Rose Jar, 9 In.	400.00
Sheet Music, Frame	300.00
Stein, Blue & Gray, 7 3/4 In.	600.00
Stein, Brown & White	1100.00
Stein, Chestnut Brown, 1952	190.00 to 350.00
Stein, Flemish	650.00
Stein, Koehler & Hinrichs, Blue & White	410.00
Sugar, Blue On White	675.00
Teapot, White	3150.00
Vase, Cattail, Brown & Yellow, 8 1/2 In.	350.00
Vase, Cobalt Blue, 8 1/2 In.	1450.00
Vase, Solid Green	4000.00

SLIPWARE is named for *slip*, a thin mixture of clay and water, about the consistency of sour cream, which is applied to pottery for decoration. It is a very old method of making pottery and is still in use.

Chamber Pot, 2 Rows Of Dots, Everted Rim, Border Of Smaller Dots, 7 1/2 In.	1495.00
Jug, Rows Of Dots, Red Ground, Handle, Powell Buckley, c.1909	295.00

SMITH BROTHERS glass was made after 1878. Alfred and Harry Smith had worked for the Mt. Washington Glass Company in New Bedford, Massachusetts, for seven years before going into their own shop. They made many pieces with enamel decoration.

Smith Bros. Co.

Biscuit Jar, Daisies, Sterling Lid & Bale	415.00
Box, Melon Ribbed Pansies, 5 1/2 In.	385.00
Cracker Jar, Silver Plated Cover, Pansies, Gold Outlined, Ribbed, 6 1/2 In.	400.00
Dish, Sweetmeat, Blue Flowers, Matching Lid, Marked, 5 1/4 In.	640.00
Salt Dip, Blue Florals	85.00
Shaker, Egg, Lay Down, Violets, Signed In Gold, 3 In.	330.00
Vase, Birds, Leaves, Front & Back, c.1885, 7 3/4 In.	595.00

Vase, Daisy Design, Melon Ribbed, Rope Rim, 6 1/4 In. 55.00
Vase, Swirl Mold, Irises, Marked, 7 In. 565.00

SNOW BABIES, made from bisque and spattered with glitter sand, were first
manufactured in 1864 by Hertwig and Company of Thuringia. Other German
and Japanese companies copied the Hertwig designs. Originally, Snow
Babies were made of candy and used as Christmas decorations. There are also
Snow Babies tablewares made by Royal Bayreuth. Copies of the small Snow
Babies figurines are being made today and can easily confuse the collector.

Candleholder, Handle.. 250.00
Figurine, 2 Googly-Eyed, Painted, 1915, 2 1/2 x 3 In., 3 Piece 1050.00
Figurine, Bisque, Various Models, Germany, c.1915, 2 1/2 To 5 In., 10 Piece 1600.00
Figurine, On Sled, Pulled By 2 Huskies.. 275.00
Figurine, Prone On Red Sled, Germany, 1 1/2 In. 55.00
Figurine, Seated Boy, Pink Scarf, Blue Pants, 1 1/2 In. 90.00
Figurine, Seated, Arms & Legs Outspread, 1 1/4 In. 40.00
Figurine, Sitting, Hat & Jacket, Scarf, Knickers, Leggings, 1 1/4 In. 115.00
Figurine, Standing On Snowball, Chile, 2 1/8 In. 35.00
In Sleigh, Pulled By Reindeer, Germany 200.00
On Sled, Waving, 1 1/4 In...35.00 to 55.00
Ornament, Children On Sled, Bisque 225.00
Ornament, Skiers, Male & Female, 1 1/2 In. 75.00
Paperweight, Snow Dome, 1940s 75.00

SNUFFBOXES held snuff. Taking snuff was popular long before cigarettes
became available. The gentleman or lady would take a small pinch of the
ground tobacco or snuff in the fingers, then sniff it and sneeze. Snuffboxes were
made of many materials, including gold, silver, enameled metal, and wood.
Most snuffboxes date from the late eighteenth or early nineteenth centuries.

Black, Animal Dancing On Hinged Cover, 3 In.. 40.00
Bottle Of Lobositz On Cover, Maps Of Region On Sides, Germany, c.1756, 4 In. 1150.00
Burled Wood, Humorous Interior Scene, Germany, 2 3/4 x 4 In. 430.00
Burr Fruitwood, Tortoiseshell Lined, Watercolor Bust Of Lady Top, Round, 3 In. 198.00
Classical Scene On Cover, Royal Crown, John Jones III, London, c.1838, 4 In............. 1035.00
Copper, Dragon On Cover 65.00
Copper, Engraved Eagle & 1802, Brass Hinge, 3 In. 675.00
Enamel, Painted Insects & Flowers, Rectangular, Germany, c.1755, 2 9/16 In. 2300.00
Enamel, Translucent Border Of Leaves & Dots, Louis VI, Paris, c.1783 .... 6325.00
Enamel & Diamond, Trophy With Flowers, Gentleman Cover, Switzerland, 1830 .... 7800.00
Gold, Enamel, Hexagonal Cover Plaque, Holy Family, Geneva, c.1810, 3 1/2 In. 7187.00
Gold, Enamel, Rectangular, Miniature Portrait, Woman, Diamond Border, c.1900 .... 4887.00
Gold, Enamel, Rectangular, Rounded Corners, Chased Cover, Switzerland, 2 1/2 In. 1725.00
Gold, Enamel, Sailing Ships, Bautte & Moynier, Geneva, c.1825, 3 1/8 In. 3450.00
Gold, Soldiers At Camp Site On Cover, Secret Compartment, Germany, 3 1/8 In. 4300.00
Gold & Enamel, Children Playing In Garden On Lid, Switzerland, c.1810 .... 7475.00
Gold & Enamel, Painted Venus On Lid, Cloudy Sky, Switzerland, c.1800, 2 5/8 In. 9775.00
Ivory, Carved, Pug's-Head Shape, Jeweled Eyes, c.1765, 1 7/8 In................................. 1380.00
Lady, With Military Officer, Paper Lithograph, Brass Box, 2 1/4 In............................... 110.00
Memorial, Memory Of Mother, Baleen Hair, Gold Plate, June 12, 1853, 3 3/8 In.......... 175.00
Papier-Mache, Boys Playing, 3 In.. 120.00
Papier-Mache, Grecian Type Woman, Instrument, Oil Painted, c.1830, 3 In. Diam...... 130.00
Papier-Mache, Inlaid Pewter Design, 2 In. 38.00
Papier-Mache, Lady With Lyre, 3 In. 145.00
Papier-Mache, Praying Angel, 2 1/8 In. 155.00
Papier-Mache, Printed Battle Scene On Top, New Orleans Defence, 3 1/2 In. 165.00
Pewter Flower & Bands Inset, Revolutionary War, 1 4/5 In. 140.00
Rosewood, Brass Inlay, 2 1/4 In. 85.00
Shoe Shape, Wooden, Paris 89.00
Silver, Applied Rococo Design, George II, London, c.1745, 2 3/4 In. 230.00
Silver, Hinged Cover, Gilt Interior, Rectangular, Vienna, 1847, 3 1/2 In. 315.00
Silver, Scrolled Engraving, Marked CC, Birmingham, c.1855, 3 3/4 In.......................... 302.50
Sterling Silver, Floral Chased Hinged Lid, Oval, Monogram..................................... 110.00

Tin, Prince & Princess, Edward VII & Alexandria, c.1860, 2 In.	130.00
Tortoiseshell, Lecoultre	2680.00
Tortoiseshell, Musical, Nicole	3080.00
Tortoiseshell & Bone, Rectangular, 2 In.	55.00
Walnut, Carved, c.1860	195.00
Whale's Tooth, Cover At End Of Tooth, Georgian Lovers, Monks, 6 1/2 In.	2100.00
Wood, Carved, 3 Male Figures, Scroll-Shaped Cover, France, 2 1/2 x 3 1/2 In.	287.50
Yellow Gold, Diamond, Continental	1430.00

SOAPSTONE is a mineral that was used for foot warmers or griddles because of its heat-retaining properties. Soapstone was carved into figurines and bowls in many countries in the nineteenth and twentieth centuries. Most of the soapstone seen today is from China or Japan. It is still being carved in the old styles.

Box, Monkey & Bear, Small	135.00
Figurine, Eskimo, Child On Back, 11 In.	3740.00
Figurine, Quan Yin, Lotus Base, 16 In.	35.00
Figurine, Standing Maiden, Carved Plinth, Oriental, 10 In.	35.00
Figurine, Walrus, Ivory Tusks, Eskimo, 7 In.	77.00
Foo Dogs & Birds, Dark Browns, 10 In.	225.00
Vase, Double, Joined By Floral Carving	50.00

SOFT PASTE is a name for a type of pottery. Although it looks very much like porcelain, it is a chemically different material. Most of the soft-paste wares were made in the early nineteenth century. Other pieces may be listed under Gaudy Dutch or Leeds.

Coffeepot, King's Rose	880.00
Dish, Vegetable, Cover, Octagonal, Strawberry	375.00
Platter, Landscape Design, Blue & White, 19th Century	385.00
Platter, Polychrome Design, Staffordshire, 19 In.	230.00
Sugar, Cover, Classical Figure, Acanthus Panel, Blue Border, Enamel Bands	270.00
Teapot, Child's, Yellow Banding, 4 1/4 In.	121.00

SOUVENIRS of a trip—what could be more fun? Our ancestors enjoyed the same thing and souvenirs were made for almost every location. Most of the souvenir pottery and porcelain pieces of the nineteenth century were made in England or Germany, even if the picture showed a North American scene. In the twentieth century, the souvenir china business seems to have gone to the manufacturers in Japan, Taiwan, Hong Kong, England, and America. Another popular souvenir item is the souvenir spoon, made of sterling or silver plate. These are usually made in the country pictured on the spoon. Related pieces may be found in the Coronation and World's Fair categories.

Apron, N.Y. Daily Mirror	90.00
Ashtray, Las Vegas, Working Roulette Wheel, Copper	35.00
Ashtray, Vanderbilt University Football, With Music Box	32.00
Bowl, Brooklyn Bridge, Carnival Glass, Marigold	495.00
Cup & Saucer, There Will Always Be An England, World War II Series, Paragon	98.00
Figurine, Apollo II Moon Walk Astronaut, Flag, Marx, 1970	22.00
Hatpin, Snoqualmie Falls, Sterling Silver, 10 1/4 In.	65.00
Kennedy Space Center, Rocket On Base, Apollo-Saturn, Plastic	16.00
Mirror, Niagara Falls, Boat, Oval, Pocket	10.00
Mirror, U.S.S. Enterprise & Star Trek Crew, Color, 2 x 3 In.	2.00
Napkin, Silk, Hotel Royal, Boston, 1854 Continental Guards, 1894	22.00
Necklace, Zeppelin Hindenberg Movie, On Card, 1975	45.00
Pennant, Felt, Great Lakes Exposition, 1937	15.00
Pin, Astronaut's Picture, Dated July 20, 1969, 6 In.	19.00
Pin, Protected By Women's National Weekly, Suffrage Newspaper	110.00
Plate, Dessert, Graf Zeppelin, Heinrich & Co., 1928, 8 In.	1080.00
Plate, Elks Street Carnival, East Liverpool, Ohio, Boat Scene, July, 1899	40.00
Plate, Indian River, Mich., White Opalescent Glass, Hand Painted, 5 1/4 In.	15.00
Plate, Pioneer Flour Mills	90.00
Ribbon, Knights Of Labor, Labor Day, Sept. 1, 1890, Blue Silk, 5 1/2 In.	388.00

Scarf, Delta Air Lines, DC-6, Florida Service, 1950s 27.00
Spoon, Demitasse, Head Of Black Man Top, Natural Bridge, Virginia, Alvin, 4 In. 150.00
Spoon, Grand Army Of Republic, National Encampment, 1892 .... 55.00
Spoon, Silver Plate, Green Hornet, 1966 .... 22.00
Spoon, Silver Plate, Harlem Opera House, Embossed Early Jointed Bear 95.00
Spoon, Silver Plate, Le Casino Municipal Nice, Roulette Wheel, c.1890 .... 475.00
Spoon, Silver Plate, Monte Carlo, Red Enamel, 3 Cards Leaf Cover, c.1890 .... 400.00
Spoon, Silver Plate, Monte Carlo, Roulette Wheel, c.1890 .... 375.00 to 475.00
Spoon, Silver Plate, Roulette Layout, Pig Over Roulette Wheel, c.1890 .... 650.00
Spoon, Sterling Silver, Buffalo Exposition 12.00
Spoon, Sterling Silver, Cincinnati Fountain, Duhme 42.00
Spoon, Sterling Silver, Cincinnati, Ohio, Rookwood Handle 75.00
Spoon, Sterling Silver, Columbus, Standing On World Handle 35.00
Spoon, Sterling Silver, Denver, Capital In Bowl 15.00
Spoon, Sterling Silver, Dodge Center, Cutout Handle 20.00
Spoon, Sterling Silver, Enameled, Ace Of Diamonds, 1900 .... 50.00
Spoon, Sterling Silver, GAR, Civil War Musket Handle, 1894 .... 65.00
Spoon, Sterling Silver, Geneva, Wisconsin, Sailboats, Flowers, YMCA Camp 32.00
Spoon, Sterling Silver, Glacier Park, Indian On Handle 25.00
Spoon, Sterling Silver, Grand Junction, Co., Cutout Flower Handle 20.00
Spoon, Sterling Silver, Kansas City, Mo., Oval Bowl, Sword Handle 27.00
Spoon, Sterling Silver, Lorain, Ohio, 1905 .... 20.00
Spoon, Sterling Silver, Minnesota, Cutout Handle 20.00
Spoon, Sterling Silver, Monte Carlo, Enameled, 1890 .... 176.00
Spoon, Sterling Silver, Oklahoma City, Indian Head, Demitasse 32.00
Spoon, Sterling Silver, Palm Beach, Florida, Alligator Handle, Citrus, 6 Piece 165.00
Spoon, Sterling Silver, Pan American Exposition, President McKinley, 1901 .... 30.00
Spoon, Sterling Silver, Park Rapids, Cutout Handle 20.00
Spoon, Sterling Silver, Peoria, Illinois, Courthouse & Soldiers Monument 40.00
Spoon, Sterling Silver, Pisces, Carnation Design 32.00
Spoon, Sterling Silver, Soldiers & Sailors Monument, Cleveland, Ohio 10.00
Spoon, Sterling Silver, South Haven, Mi., 1897 Embossed Each Side 28.00
Spoon, Sterling Silver, St. Paul, Cutout Skyline 18.00
Spoon, Sterling Silver, St. Paul, Minn., Scenes 35.00
Spoon, Sterling Silver, Statue Of Liberty, Brooklyn Bridge 55.00
Spoon, Sterling Silver, Steel Pier, Atlantic City 45.00
Spoon, Sterling Silver, Sugarloaf, Michigan, 1909 .... 38.00
Spoon, Sterling Silver, Tupper Lake, Indian Handle 30.00
Spoon, Sterling Silver, Utah State, Indian Corn On Handle 20.00
Spoon, Sterling Silver, Vancouver, Figural Miner Handle, 5 In. 38.00
Spoon, Sterling Silver, Waukesha, Wisconsin, Gorham 35.00
Spoon, Sterling Silver, WCTU, Tulip & Scrolls, 1904, 6 In. 35.00
Token, Good For 1 Sea Bath, San Francisco 69.00

SPANGLE GLASS is multicolored glass made from odds and ends of colored
glass rods. It includes metallic flakes of mica covered with gold, silver,
nickel, or copper. Spangle glass is usually cased with a thin layer of clear
glass over the multicolored layer. Similar glass is listed in the Vasa Murrhina
category.

Creamer, Cobalt Blue, Silver Flakes, Clear Handles 110.00
Pitcher, Pink 100.00
Vase, Mica Inner Layer, Outer Green Layer, Enamel Design, 12 In. 310.00

SPANISH LACE is a type of Victorian glass that has a white lace design.
Blue, yellow, cranberry, or clear glass was made with this distinctive white
pattern. It was made in England and the United States after 1885. Copies are
being made.

Lamp, White Opalescent, Square, Clear Handle 225.00
Pitcher, Blue, 9 In. 400.00
Rose Bowl, Yellow, Stand 58.00
Saltshaker, Vaseline 95.00
Sugar Shaker, Vaseline, Metal Top .... 200.00 to 235.00
Tumbler, Blue, 3 In. 30.00

SPATTER GLASS is a multicolored glass made from many small pieces of different colored glass. It is sometimes called *End-of-Day* glass. It is still being made.

Basket, Light Green, Thorny Applied Handle, Ruffled Edge, 6 x 5 In.	165.00
Bowl, Yellow, Orange & Red, Czechoslovakia	195.00
Pitcher, Red & White Cased In Clear, Applied Ribbed Handle, 8 1/4 In.	66.00
Vase, Ruffled Top, Opaque Blue, 11 In., Pair	395.00

SPATTERWARE is the creamware or soft paste dinnerware decorated with colored spatter designs. The earliest pieces were made in the late eighteenth century, but most of the spatterware found today was made from about 1800 to 1850, or it is a form of kitchen crockery with added spatter designs made in the late nineteenth and twentieth centuries. The early spatterware was made in the Staffordshire district of England for sale in America. The later kitchen type is an American product.

Bowl, Blue, 4 7/8 In.	50.00
Bowl, Castle	485.00
Bowl, Waste, Christmas Balls, Green, 2 3/4 x 4 7/8 In.	1595.00
Bowl & Plate, Mush, 8 1/2 In.	137.00
Coffeepot, Peafowl, 19th Century, 9 1/2 In.	690.00
Creamer, Adam's Rose, Blue, 5 1/2 In.	275.00
Creamer, Blue & White, Blueberry Design, 4 1/2 In.	1072.00
Creamer, Cow, Brown & Black Stripes, Green Base, 5 In.	467.00
Creamer, Paneled, Red & Blue Rainbow, 5 5/8 In.	137.00 to 275.00
Creamer, Peafowl, On Leafy Branch, Paneled, Red, 6 In.	522.50
Cruet, Spatter Lining, Clear Handle, Heart-Shaped Stopper, Blue, 8 3/4 In.	135.00
Cup, Handless, Rainbow, Red & Yellow	38.00
Cup & Saucer, Bull's-Eye Center, Rainbow, Maroon & Blue	110.00
Cup & Saucer, Handleless, Red	94.00
Cup & Saucer, Handleless, Red & Blue	82.00
Cup & Saucer, Handleless, Red Peafowl, Blue, Yellow, Green, Black	467.00
Cup & Saucer, Handleless, Rooster Red	1375.00
Cup & Saucer, Mauve & Red	775.00
Cup & Saucer, Peafowl	475.00
Cup & Saucer, Peafowl, Green & White	176.00
Cup & Saucer, Peafowl, Red	220.00
Cup & Saucer, Thistle, Deep Maroon	412.00
Mug, Blue Handle, 4 1/4 In.	121.00
Pitcher, Four-Part Flower, Paneled, Blue, 11 1/4 In.	330.00
Pitcher, Peafowl, Blue, Yellow Green & Black, Red Ground, 5 3/8 In.	345.00
Pitcher, Peafowl, Pink & White, 3 1/2 In.	198.00
Pitcher, Water, Peafowl, Blue & White, 20 In.	1045.00
Pitcher & Bowl, Blue, 9 1/2 x 12 In.	385.00
Plate, Adam's Rose, Blue, 9 1/4 In.	110.00

Spatterware, Plate, Green Floral,
Yellow Border, Pair

◆◆◆◆◆◆◆◆◆◆◆◆◆◆◆◆◆◆◆

When stacking dinner plates, put a piece of felt or paper between each plate. Never put more than 24 in one stack.

◆◆◆◆◆◆◆◆◆◆◆◆◆◆◆◆◆◆◆

Spelter, Figurine, Hunter First Over,
   Green Patina, 15 x 14 x 7 In.

Plate, Adam's Rose, Rainbow, 8 In.	330.00
Plate, Blue, Tulip, Red, Blue, Green, Black, 8 1/4 In.	605.00
Plate, Dahlia Center, Blue, 8 /14 In.	220.00
Plate, Flowers, Red, Blue, Green, Adams, Tunstall, 9 1/2 In.	60.00
Plate, Green & Red Berries, Blue Border, 8 1/2 In., Pair	577.00
Plate, Green Floral, Yellow Border, Pair. *Illus*	10000.00
Plate, Peafowl, Leafy Branch, Red, 8 3/4 In.	660.00
Plate, Peafowl, Red, 8 1/4 In.	137.00
Plate, Red Rim, Blue Stripe, Viola In Purple, 6 5/8 In.	203.00
Plate, Schoolhouse, Green, Red & Dark Brown, 8 3/8 In.	330.00
Plate, Tulips, Thos. Walker, Blue, 8 /58 In.	185.00
Soup, Dish, Bull's-Eye Center, Rainbow, 10 1/2 In.	925.00
Soup, Dish, Floral Design, Red	400.00
Sugar, Black & Yellow	1600.00
Sugar, Blue & Purple Bands, Cover, 4 1/4 In.	330.00
Sugar, Cover, Blue & White, Green & Red Berries, 4 1/2 In.	632.00
Sugar, Cover, Peafowl, Red, 4 1/4 In.	247.00
Sugar, Cover, Peafowl, Red, 7 1/4 In.	357.00
Sugar, Cover, Red Rooster, 4 3/4 In.	385.00
Sugar, Paneled, Rainbow, 7 /14 In.	275.00
Sugar, Peafowl, Blue, 8 1/4 In.	385.00
Tea Set, Child's, Blue Flower, Leaves, Stick, 17 Piece	200.00
Tea Set, Child's, Peafowl, 19th Century, 6 Piece	632.00
Tea Set, Child's, Rainbow, 19th Century, 14 Pieces	1840.00
Teapot, Rainbow	895.00
Teapot, Sponged Leaf Design	230.00
Vase, Jack-In-The-Pulpit, Vase, White, Green, Cranberry, 8 1/2 In.	110.00

SPELTER is a synonym for a zinc alloy. Figurines, candlesticks, and other pieces were made of spelter and given a bronze or painted finish. The metal has been used since about the 1860s to make statues, tablewares, and lamps that resemble bronze. Spelter is soft and breaks easily. To test for spelter, scratch the base of the piece. Bronze is solid; spelter will show a silvery scratch.

Ashtray, Figure Of Girl, On Green Onyx, 8 1/2 In.	200.00
Bookends, Leaping Gazelle, Onyx Base, 5 3/8 x 5 1/4 In.	190.00
Clock, Figural, Cupid, Holding Basket, Green Onyx Base, Marked JBC, 19 In.	350.00
Epergne, Young Girl Standard, Yellow & White Glass, Trumpet Vase, 33 1/2 In.	605.00
Figurine, Arab Warrior, On Horseback, Painted	1093.00
Figurine, Clown, Woman, Art Deco	300.00
Figurine, Hunter First Over, Green Patina, 15 x 14 x 7 In. *Illus*	143.00
Lamp, Figural, Nude Man, Draped Cloth, Vines, Flowers, 4-Light, 41 In.	1265.00

Lamp, Newel Post, Bride Of The Sea 2800.00

SPINNING WHEELS in the corner have been symbols of earlier times for the past 100 years. Although spinning wheels date back to medieval days, the ones found today are rarely more than 200 years old. Because the style of the spinning wheel changed very little, it is often impossible to place an exact date on a wheel.

Flax 300.00
Hardwoods, Turned & Chip Carved, 37 1/2 In. 176.00
Pedal & Spindle, Small 275.00
Shaker, Wooden Wheel, Stamped And Dated 1826 .... 1000.00
Signed AB Within Diamond, Late 19th Century, 45 3/4 In. 175.00
Wool, Hardwoods, Bobbin Says A. Minor's Wheel Heads, 45 In. 104.00

SPODE pottery, porcelain, and bone china were made by the Stoke-on-Trent factory of England founded by Josiah Spode about 1770. The firm became Copeland and Garrett from 1833 to 1847, then W. T. Copeland or W. T. Copeland and Sons until 1976. It then became Royal Worcester Spode Ltd. The word *Spode* appears on many pieces made by the factories. Most collectors include all the wares under the more familiar name of Spode. Porcelains are listed in this book by the name that appears on the piece. Related pieces are listed under Copeland and Copeland Spode.

Basket & Underplate, Pearlware, Reticulated, 1800, 9 3/4 In. 700.00
Cache Pot, Covered, Tower, Blue & White, 2 Handles, 10 In., Pair 1650.00
Dish, 1166 Pattern, Gilt Scalework, Medallion Center, c.1807, 11 3/8 In., Pair 2645.00
Dish, Japan Pattern, Imari Palette, Twig Handles, Signed, 13 1/2 In. 1265.00
Jar, Potpourri, Pierced Cover, White Cameo Cupids, Lizard Handles, 4 1/2 In. 325.00
Plate, Blue & White, Camel With Rider, Palace, 9 3/4 In. 90.00
Plate, Gilt & Enamel Tree & Floral, Signed, c.1799, 9 3/4 In. 345.00
Plate, Hot Water, Tower, Blue & White, 10 In. 220.00
Plate, Pie, Tower 45.00
Plate, Pink Border, Tooled Gilt Rim, 10 1/2 In., 12 Piece 575.00
Plate, Tower, Pink, 10 1/2 In. 38.00
Plate, Transfer, Gilt, Central Coat Of Arms, 19th Century, 12 Piece 215.00
Plate, Warming, Blue Stenciled Village Scene, Marked, 11 In. 225.00
Platter, Buffalo Pattern, 22 In. 795.00
Platter, Green Floral Transfer, 21 In. 330.00
Platter, Octagonal, Ironstone, Painted Oriental Design, Scalloped Border, 22 1/2 In. 665.00
Sign, Dealer, Small 10.00
Soup, Cream, Wickerlane 89.00
Teapot, Tower, Blue, New Mark 125.00
Tile, Tower, Flow Blue 95.00
Urinal, Blue Transfer, Landscape 345.00

SPONGEWARE is very similar to spatterware in appearance. The designs were applied to the ceramics by daubing the color on with a sponge or cloth. Many collectors do not differentiate between spongeware and spatterware and use the names interchangeably. Modern pottery is being made to resemble the old spongeware, but careful examination will show it is new.

Bowl, Blue & White, 11 In. 143.00
Bowl, Blue On Cream, 7 1/2 In. 65.00
Bowl, Vertical Bands, Red & Green, Staffordshire, 19th Century, England, 7 In. 115.00
Bowl, Wisconsin Advertising, Brown & Blue, 8 In. 85.00
Cookie Jar, Multicolor 225.00
Creamer, Blue On Cream, 8 Grape & Leaf Panels, Octagonal, 3 In. 54.00
Mustard Pot, Cover, Banded, 19th Century, 3 1/2 In. 316.00
Pie Plate, Blue & White, Sanitary, The Pure Food 140.00
Pitcher, Blue & White, 9 In. .... 330.00 to 412.00
Pitcher, Blue, Rust & Yellow, 9 1/2 In. 125.00
Pitcher, Blue-Gray, 8 1/2 In. 195.00
Pitcher, Embossed Trellis, Flowers, Gold Spattered, Yellow & Green, 9 In. 145.00
Pitcher & Bowl, Child's, Blue 95.00

SPORTS equipment, sporting goods, brochures, and related items are listed here. Other categories of interest are Bicycle, Card, Fishing, Sword, and Toy.

Auto Racing, Box, Auto Brand Shirts, Made By Lewis Meier & Co., Indianapolis........	185.00
Auto Racing, Glass, Indy 500 Golden Anniversary, 1962	23.00
Auto Racing, Glass, Winner, Indianapolis Speedway, 7 Piece	45.00
Auto Racing, Keg, Indianapolis Speedway Motor Oil, Wooden	450.00
Auto Racing, Menu, 10th Annual Banquet, Automobile Club Of America, 1909..........	475.00
Auto Racing, Photograph, Lineup Of 2nd Indy 500, Yard Long, 1912.......................	500.00
Auto Racing, Pit Shirt, Valvoline, Neil Bonnett's Crew, 1 Piece.................................	250.00
Auto Racing, Program, Indianapolis Motor Speedway, 1911	1000.00
Auto Racing, Program, Scorecard, Ontario Speedway, 1974.......................................	20.00
Auto Racing, STP Motor Oil Container, Parnelli Jones, Autographed	25.00
Auto Racing, Suit, Kyle Petty's Crew..	395.00
Auto Racing, Whiskey, Indy 500, 2 3/8 In.	10.00
Baseball, Autographed, Glove, Steve Garvey Model, Rawlings, FJ6, 1 Lb..................	115.00
Baseball, Autographed, Shoes, Joe DiMaggio Little League, Endicott Johnson Co.	475.00
Baseball, Ball, American Assoc.	25.00
Baseball, Ball, Autographed, Babe Ruth, Cincinnati, Box..	2750.00
Baseball, Ball, Autographed, Babe Ruth, Red & Black Stitches, 1930s	407.00
Baseball, Ball, Autographed, Charlie Gehringer, Bobby Brown American League Ball	70.00
Baseball, Ball, Autographed, Cy Young, Ed Walsh, All-Star Reunion, 1920s	1975.00
Baseball, Ball, Autographed, Detroit Tigers, Plexiglas Box, 1968	92.00
Baseball, Ball, Autographed, Jackie Robinson, Signed On Sweet Spot	2760.00
Baseball, Ball, Autographed, Rabbit Maranville, Signed On Sweet Spot.....................	3450.00
Baseball, Ball, Autographed, Roger Maris, 1962	633.00
Baseball, Ball, Autographed, Yankees, Signed By Team, 1929	2550.00
Baseball, Ball, Dated June 19, 1857..	6775.00
Baseball, Ball, Reggie Smith's 255th Home Run, 1978..	195.00
Baseball, Ball, World Series, 1903..	4919.00
Baseball, Bank, Cleveland Indians, Baseball Player, Stafford Pottery, 1950s	135.00
Baseball, Bank, Los Angeles Dodgers, Ceramic, 1969..	90.00
Baseball, Banner, Pittsburgh Pirates, Clemente's Name, Team Members, 1960	50.00
Baseball, Bat, Eric Davis, Game-Used, Louisville Slugger Model C271	125.00
Baseball, Bat, Ernie Banks, Game-Used, Hillerich & Bradsby....................................	4025.00
Baseball, Bat, Kent Hrbek, Game-Used, Louisville Slugger ..:....................................	95.00
Baseball, Bat, Negro League, Signed By 90 Former Players..	1840.00
Baseball, Bat, Spalding T-5, 1900s..	95.00
Baseball, Bottle, Whiskey, Commemorative, Kansas City Royals, McCormick, 1971...	75.00
Baseball, Candy Container, Jackie Robinson, 1954, 5 In.	295.00
Baseball, Catalog, Rawlings Sports, 1927	45.00
Baseball, Catcher's Mitt, Gabby Hartnett Model, 1930...	200.00
Baseball, Christmas Card, Signed Honus Wagner...	880.00
Baseball, Cigar Box, Joe Tinker, 50 Cigars, Unopened..	1803.00
Baseball, Clock, Desk, Figural, Ball, Brass, Welby, U.S. Zone, Germany	125.00
Baseball, Commissioner's Chair, Oakland A's World Series, 1989	1500.00
Baseball, Contest Coupon, Babe Ruth Boys Club, Esso, 1930s..................................	45.00
Baseball, Figurine, Babe Ruth, Red-Top Beer, Metal, 1957.......................................	15.00
Baseball, Figurine, Batter, Catcher & Umpire, Composition, L.L. Rittgers, 1941..........	275.00
Baseball, Figurine, Ernie Banks, Hartland...	145.00
Baseball, Figurine, Mickey Mantle, Hartland..	350.00
Baseball, Figurine, Warren Spahn, Hartland ....100.00 to 175.00
Baseball, Flannel, Harry Coveleski, Detroit, Frame, 5 x 5 In.	27.50
Baseball, Game Pinball, Jackie Robinson, Gotham Pressed Steel Corp., 1947	2240.00
Baseball, Game, Carl Yastrzemski Action Baseball	50.00
Baseball, Game, Electric, Jim Prentice, Battery Operated...	125.00
Baseball, Game, Four Bagger, Mickey Mantle, Autographed	1150.00
Baseball, Game, Major League Indoor Game, 1910, Philadelphia Game Co.	5040.00
Baseball, Glass, 7-Eleven, Hank Aaron, 1972, Atlanta Braves Logo	22.00
Baseball, Glass, Gold Star Chili, Pete Rose..	6.00
Baseball, Glass, Mississippi State University, 4 In.	3.00
Baseball, Glass, Montreal Expos, Andre Dawson, 1984...	5.00
Baseball, Glass, New York Mets, 1969	15.00

Sports, Baseball, Schedule, Toronto Blue Jays, Pocket, 1980

Sports, Baseball, Score Book, All Star Game, Comiskey Park, 1933

Sports, Baseball, Wheaties Box, Jimmie Cox, 1935

Baseball, Glove, Babe Ruth Model, Spaulding	350.00
Baseball, Glove, Bill Doak, Fielder's, Rawlings, Split Finger, Improved Model 5bd	105.00
Baseball, Glove, Billy Martin Model	20.00
Baseball, Glove, Christy Mathewson, Game-Used, A.J. Reach, 1910	5952.00
Baseball, Glove, Frank Pytlak Model, Goldsmith C31	125.00
Baseball, Glove, Jim Bottomley Model, Rawlings, 1920s	349.00
Baseball, Glove, Moose Skowran Model	17.00
Baseball, Glove, Wally Berger, Game-Used, D & M Buckle Back, 1930-1940	225.00
Baseball, Glove, Warren Spahn Model, MacGregor	75.00
Baseball, Gloves, Al Kaline Model	35.00
Baseball, Jersey, Gary Sheffield, Milwaukee Brewers, Game-Worn	605.00
Baseball, Jersey, Home, Carl Yaztremski, Game-Worn, 1976	978.00
Baseball, Jersey, Home, Don Drysdale, Flannel, Game-Worn, Size 46	5750.00
Baseball, Jersey, Home, Reggie Jackson, Game-Worn, Autographed On Front	1150.00
Baseball, Lid, Topps Candy, Carlton Fisk, 1973	75.00
Baseball, Magazine, Life, Mickey Mantle Cover, 1956	30.00
Baseball, Magazine, Top-Notch, Joe Jackson Cover, 1914	495.00
Baseball, Mask, Steve Yeager	110.00
Baseball, Menu, Johnny Bench's Home Plate Restaurant	40.00
Baseball, Model Kit, Willie Mays, Running To Catch Fly Ball, Plastic, 1965	330.00
Baseball, Nodder, Chicago Cubs, 4 In.	150.00
Baseball, Nodder, Roger Maris	140.00
Baseball, Pass, Gold, Kenesaw Mountain Landis, 1919-1933	3220.00
Baseball, Pencil, Yankees, Wooden Bat	8.00
Baseball, Pendant, Brooklyn Baseball Club, Gold, 1886	150.00
Baseball, Pennant, Grand Opening Of Dodger Stadium, April 9, 1962	50.00
Baseball, Photograph, Cardinals, Frisch, Hafey, 1928	60.00
Baseball, Photograph, Cleveland Indians, 1913	1840.00
Baseball, Photograph, Cleveland Indians, 1955, 19 x 14 1/2 In.	518.00
Baseball, Photograph, Hank Aaron, Color, Signed, 10 x 8 In.	50.00
Baseball, Photograph, Jimmie Foxx, From Newspaper, Signed, 3 x 5 In.	195.00
Baseball, Photograph, N.Y. Baseball Club, National League Champions, 1913, Frame	120.00
Baseball, Pin, Babe Ruth, Never Forgotten, Brown, 1 1/4 In.	2.00
Baseball, Pin, Ted Williams, Red Sox, Black & White, 1 1/4 In.	1.00
Baseball, Placemat, Detroit Tigers World Series, Big Boy, 1984	5.00
Baseball, Playing Cards, Player On Box, Willis Russell, 1905	385.00
Baseball, Postcard, Hall Of Fame, Gold Plaque, Rock Averill, Autographed	28.00
Baseball, Postcard, Hall Of Fame, Gold Plaque, Max Carey, Autographed	50.00
Baseball, Postcard, Hall Of Fame, Gold Plaque, Hank Greenberg, Autographed	75.00
Baseball, Postcard, Hall Of Fame, Gold Plaque, Carl Hubbell, Autographed	25.00

Baseball, Poster, White Sox, Pabst Premium, 1930 .... 110.00
Baseball, Press Pin, Pittsburgh Pirates World Series, 1925 .... 1695.00
Baseball, Program, Bob Feller's All Stars Vs. Satchel Paige's Negro League 368.00
Baseball, Program, Cleveland At Yankees, Vic Raschi, 1949 .... 20.00
Baseball, Program, Women's Team, Daisies, Fort Wayne, Ind., 1950s 4.00
Baseball, Program, Yankees Vs. Cubs, Wrigley Field, Unscored, 1938 .... 295.00
Baseball, Puzzle, Cleveland Indians Sport Stars Poster 12.00
Baseball, Puzzle, Willie Mays, American Publishing Co., 1972 .... 50.00
Baseball, Ring, Pittsburgh Pirates, 1-Carat Center Diamond, Mr. Abrams, Writer 3450.00
Baseball, Schedule, Folder, Princeton, 1913 .... 25.00
Baseball, Schedule, Toronto Blue Jays, Pocket, 1980 .... *Illus* 2.00
Baseball, Score Book, All Star Game, Comiskey Park, 1933 .... *Illus* 2530.00
Baseball, Scorecard, Baltimore Orioles, 1972 .... 20.00
Baseball, Scorecard, Boston Vs. Philadelphia, 1875 .... 1265.00
Baseball, Scorecard, Cardinals, 1942 .... 30.00
Baseball, Stadium Seat, Crosley Field, Red, Cast Iron Sides, Cherry Wood, 1930s 750.00
Baseball, Tape Measure, Baseball Player, Celluloid, Japan.. 265.00
Baseball, Ticket Stub, World Series, 1931, Shibe Park, Philadelphia A's..................... 135.00
Baseball, Tintype, 2 Baseball Players, 1880 .... 400.00
Baseball, Tray, All Star Game, Minnesota, Red Wing Pottery Co., 1965...................... 179.00
Baseball, Trunk, Pie Traynor, Pittsburgh Pirates, Brass Tag, Large.............................. 690.00
Baseball, Uniform, Buffalo Bison, Farm Team, 1920s 695.00
Baseball, Uniform, Cal Ripkin Jr., Game-Worn, 1990 .... 2070.00
Baseball, Uniform, Road, Flannel, Gary Gentry, Mets, 1971 .... 2300.00
Baseball, Wheaties Box, Jimmie Cox, 1935.. *Illus* 805.00
Baseball, Window Decal, National Hall Of Fame, Museum, Cooperstown, N.Y., 1940s 20.00
Baseball, Yearbook, Mets, 1970-1973, 4 Books... 95.00
Basketball, Ball, 13 Autographs, Los Angeles Lakers, 1982... 320.00
Basketball, Glass, Detroit Pistons, 6 In. 6.00
Basketball, Jacket, Geo. Gervin, Game-Worn, San Antonio Spurs, Rawlings, 1985 ..... 405.00
Basketball, Jacket, Mike Gminski, New Jersey Nets, 1982-83 .... 300.00
Basketball, Jersey, David Robinson, San Antonio Spurs 199.00
Basketball, Jersey, Home, Alex English, 1980s 863.00
Basketball, Jersey, Home, Magic Johnson, 1991 .... 300.00
Basketball, Jersey, Home, Maurice Lucas, Phoenix Suns 288.00
Basketball, Jersey, Larry Bird, Not Game-Used.. 150.00
Basketball, Movie Poster, Go Man Go, Harlem Globetrotters & Sidney Poitier, 1954 .. 55.00
Basketball, Press Guide, Oscar Robertson Cover, University Of Cincinnati, 1958 .... 30.00
Basketball, Press Pass, Boston Celtics, 1946-1947 .... 125.00
Basketball, Program, 4th Annual World Series Of Basketball, March 28, 1929 .... 575.00
Basketball, Program, Globetrotters Vs. All Stars, Photographs, Biographies................ 175.00
Basketball, Program, NBA All Stars, Philadelphia, 1976.. 35.00
Basketball, Program, New York Knicks, First Game, Against Chicago Stags 863.00
Basketball, Record Album, The Globetrotters, Fold-Out Jacket, 1970 .... 50.00
Basketball, Record, Harlem Globetrotters, 45 Rpm, Original Jacket, 1950s................. 25.00
Basketball, Rulebook, Official NCAA, 1951 .... 15.00
Basketball, Schedule, Scorecard, Colgate University, 1910, 32 Pages.......................... 24.00
Basketball, Shoes, Autographed, Tim Hardaway, Size 14 .... 195.00
Basketball, Shoes, Autographed, Vinnie Johnson 85.00
Basketball, Shoes, Kevin McHale, Game-Used, Converse, Signed, 1991 .... 230.00
Basketball, Uniform, Dominique Wilkins, Game-Worn, Atlanta Hawks 1030.00
Billiards, Rack, Cue, Mahogany 450.00
Billiards, Rack, Cue, Oak, Floor Model.. 3500.00
Billiards, Table, Eclipse, Inlaid Ebony 20000.00
Billiards, Table, Eclipse, Inlaid Rosewood 18000.00
Billiards, Table, Neo-Grec Marquetry Panels, 1870s 2000.00
Billiards, Table, Oak, Fancy Legs, 1880s, 9 Ft. 7500.00
Bowling, Medal, August Hermann, Celluloid Disc On Ribbon, 1908 .... 230.00
Boxing, Baby Shoes, Bronzed, Rocky Marciano, Bookends.. 715.00
Boxing, Book, Rocky Graziano, Somebody Down Here Likes Me Too, 1981 .... 40.00
Boxing, Book, The Art Of Boxing Made Easy, Hurst Company, 1883, 100 Pages 95.00
Boxing, Clock, Joe Lewis, Figural 750.00
Boxing, Gloves, 21 Signatures, Includes Jack Dempsey, Gene Tunney, Joe Louis......... 2200.00

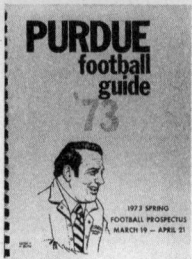

Sports, Football, Media Guide,
Purdue University, West Lafayette, Ind., 1973

◆◆◆◆◆◆◆◆◆◆◆◆◆◆◆◆◆◆◆◆◆◆◆◆

Wash your hands before handling old paper collectibles. The oil from your hands will cause damage. Museum personnel wear white cotton gloves.

◆◆◆◆◆◆◆◆◆◆◆◆◆◆◆◆◆◆◆◆◆◆◆◆

Boxing, Gloves, Bobo Olson, Everlast, 12 Oz., Signed	375.00
Boxing, Gloves, Gene Tunney, TruSports, Brown, 8 Oz., 1920s	485.00
Boxing, Gloves, Ingemar Johansson, Autographed, Everlast, 12 Oz.	75.00
Boxing, Gloves, Rocky Marciano, Red Leather, Autographed	1500.00
Boxing, Gloves, Vito Antuofermo Vs. Marvin Hagler Fight, 1981	748.00
Boxing, Hair Conditioner, Knockout, Muhammad Ali Picture, Contents, 8 Oz.	20.00
Boxing, Magazine, Ring, Jake LaMotta Cover, Oct. 1949	15.00
Boxing, Model Kit, Great Moments In Sports, Jack Dempsey Vs. Luis Firpo	115.00
Boxing, Photograph, Jim Corbett, Signed, Best Friend Christy Walsh, 8 x 11 In.	805.00
Boxing, Postcard, Jack Dempsey's Restaurant, Autographed, 1951	55.00
Boxing, Poster, Evander, Holyfield, Autographed	150.00
Boxing, Poster, Jack Johnson, 1st Black Heavy Weight Champion, 1909, 20 x 16 In.	225.00
Boxing, Poster, Jack Johnson, Heavyweight Champion, 1909, 20 x 16 In.	225.00
Boxing, Press Pass, Leon Spinks Vs. Mike Tyson, Trump Plaza, June 27, 1988	35.00
Boxing, Program, Jack Sharkey Vs. Primo Carnera, Oct. 12, 1931	288.00
Boxing, Program, Mike Tyson, March 6, 1985, Black & White Photograph	235.00
Boxing, Program, Sugar Ray Leonard Vs. Thomas Hearns, 1981	20.00
Boxing, Program, Tunney Vs. Dempsey, 1927	690.00
Boxing, Sheet Music, Jim Jeffries, Jim-A-Da-Jeff, 1909	175.00
Boxing, Striking Bag, Black Leather, Reach, 1920s	125.00
Boxing, Suitcase, Joe Louis, Brown Leather, Towne	345.00
Boxing, Ticket, Full, Bob Fitzsimmons Vs. Gus Ruhlin, August 10, 1900	4140.00
Boxing, Ticket, Full, Joe Louis Vs. Arturo Godoy, Heavyweight Championship, 1940	200.00
Boxing, Ticket, Full, Larry Holmes Vs. Gerry Cooney, June 11, 1982	65.00
Boxing, Trophy, Archie Moore, 1971, 19 In.	230.00
Boxing, Trophy, Chuck Wepner Vs. Ernie Terrell, Victory, 1973, 15 In.	490.00
Boxing, Yearbook, Sugar Ray Robinson, Autographed, 1952	250.00
Football, Award, Dan Marino, Player Of Year, Florida State Form, 11 In.	45.00
Football, Bag, Equipment, Washington Redskins, Cosby, 1960	300.00
Football, Ball, Green Bay Packers, 1961-1962	978.00
Football, Ball, Sid Luckman, Autographed, Plexiglas Case	460.00
Football, Blanket, Sideline, Green Bay Packers, Paul Horning's, 1959	550.00
Football, Charm Bracelet, NFL, Box, 1960	75.00
Football, Figurine, Los Angeles Rams, Hartland	75.00
Football, Game, Pro Draft, 50 Topps Cards, 1974, Parker Bros.	75.00
Football, Glass, Cincinnati Bengals, Rocks, 4 In.	4.00
Football, Glass, Old-Fashioned, Army-Navy, Penn. Railroad, 1962	50.00
Football, Glass, Pittsburgh Steelers, Andy Russell, 1976	7.00
Football, Glass, Pittsburgh Steelers, Glen Edwards, 1976	9.00
Football, Glass, Pittsburgh Steelers, Ray Mansfield, 1976	7.00
Football, Helmet, Leather, Michigan Style, Adult, 1940s	215.00
Football, Helmet, Leather, Victor, Wright & Ditson, Chin Strap, 1920	350.00
Football, Helmet, New Orleans Saints, Eugene Goodlow, Game-Used, 1983	395.00
Football, Helmet, Standard Collegiate, Leather, 24 Air Holes, Chin Strap, 1920s	350.00
Football, Jersey, Keith Byars, Philadelphia Eagles, Game-Worn, 1980	700.00
Football, Lunch Box, NFL, Metal, King Seeley Thermos, 1978	25.00

Football, Lunch Box, NFL, Players On Sides, Metal, King Seeley Thermos, 1976 .... 20.00
Football, Lunch Box, NFL, Quarterback, Metal, Aladdin, 1964 .... 125.00
Football, Magazine, Cover, Roger Staubach, Autographed, 1977 .... 22.00
Football, Media Guide, New York Giants, 1944 .... 169.00
Football, Media Guide, Purdue University, West Lafayette, Ind., 1973 .... *Illus* 4.00
Football, Model Kit, Jimmy Brown, Running To Goal Line, Aurora, 1965 .... 240.00
Football, Model Kit, Johnny Unitas, With 2 Action Players, Plastic, 1965 .... 230.00
Football, Mug, Notre Dame, Figural Handle, 1940s 75.00
Football, Mug, Slim Jim Browns 3.00
Football, Mug, Slim Jim Steelers 8.00
Football, Pin, Photograph, Red Grange, Chicago Bears Uniform, 1920s 230.00
Football, Premium, Fatima Cigarettes, Harvard Insignia, 1910, 13 x 26 In. 250.00
Football, Program, Southern Calif. Vs. Washington State, J. Wayne, Oct. 9, 1926 .... 175.00
Football, Puzzle, Joe Namath, 500 Pieces, American Publishing, 1972, Sealed 40.00
Football, Ring, National Championship, Salesman's Sample, 10K Gold, 1980 .... 1076.00
Football, Scarf, Rose Bowl, 1937 .... 125.00
Football, Sheet Music, Movie The Forward Pass, Douglas Fairbanks, Jr. 40.00
Football, Toy, Van, Dallas Cowboys Cheerleaders, Snap-Together, Revell, 1970s 122.00
Football, Watch, Super Bowl XIX, Presented To The 49ers, Vince Lombardi Face 1495.00
Football, Yearbook, Roger Staubach's High School, Purcell High, 1957 .... 295.00
Golf, Ashtray-Pipe Holder, Caddie Laddie 18.00
Golf, Autograph, Ben Hogan, Personal Note Paper 200.00
Golf, Bag, Canvas & Leather, 1930 .... 125.00
Golf, Bag, Canvas & Leather, c.1935 .... 150.00
Golf, Bag, Canvas, Drawstring, Holds Spalding Balls, c.1925 .... 50.00
Golf, Ball, Fred Couples, Autographed 35.00
Golf, Ball, Wilson Sporting Goods Hol-Hi Dimple, Stamped Gene Sarazen, 1932 .... 220.00
Golf, Caddie Badge, First Class Caddie, Park Hill Golf Club, 1935, 1 3/4 In. 55.00
Golf, Card Game, Par Golf, Invented By Bert Wheeler Moorman, 1926 .... 45.00
Golf, Club, Iron, Chi Chi Rodriguez Autographed 105.00
Golf, Club, No. 7 Mashie Niblick, Archie MacDonald, Hickory Shaft 35.00
Golf, Club, Putter, A.G. Spalding & Bros., Model M-18 .... 80.00
Golf, Club, Putter, Willie Park, Stamped Head, c.1894 .... 110.00
Golf, Club, Robroy Mashie, Hickory Shaft 25.00
Golf, Club, Spade Mashie, Ernest Jones Special 200.00
Golf, Club, Tabletop Range, Yellow, Green, Red, Miniature 1050.00
Golf, Club, Wooden-Shaft Mashie 45.00
Golf, Game, Arnold Palmer's Indoor Golf Course, Marx, 1968 .... 50.00
Golf, Glass, Rock, Julius Boros, 3 3/4 In. 6.00
Golf, Plate, Babe Didrikson 9.00
Golf, Program, Metropolitan Golf Writer's Assoc. National Awards Dinner, 1962 .... 300.00
Golf, Tool, Divot, Tiffany Silver 43.00
Golf, Trophy, Ayer Tournament, Nickel-Plated Brass, Man, Club Overhead, 1962, 13 In. 125.00
Golf, Whiskey, Hole In One, Eagle, Birdie, Par, Box, 4 Piece 45.00
Golf, Wristwatch, Ben Hogan Model, Timex, Gray Band 375.00
Hockey, Goalie Glove, Jay Wells, Philadelphia Flyers, Autographed 195.00
Hockey, Jersey, Kelly Kisio, New York Rangers, 1987 .... 495.00
Hockey, Jersey, St. Paul Saints, Game-Worn, O'Shea Knitting Mills, 1930 .... 895.00
Hockey, Lunch Pail, Bobby Orr, Black & Yellow Vinyl 150.00
Hockey, Mug, Phil Esposito, White Milk Glass, Caricature, 1971 .... 40.00
Hockey, Program, Boston Bruins Vs. Toronto Maple Leafs, 1941 .... 460.00
Hockey, Program, Madison Square Garden, Rangers, 1942 .... 150.00
Hockey, Program, Madison Square Garden, Opening, December 15, 1925 .... 575.00
Hockey, Program, Stanley Cup, Montreal Canadiens Vs. Detroit Red Wings, 1937 .... 125.00
Hockey, Puck, Fight Saints, Game-Used, Orange Logo Inside Shield 45.00
Hockey, Puck, Seattle Breakers, Game-Used, 1980 .... 30.00
Hockey, Skate Sharpener, Bobby Hull, By McIntyre 30.00
Hockey, Skates, Kevin Stevens, Pittsburgh Penguins, 1989 .... 350.00
Hockey, Stick, Bobby Orr, Game-Used 1380.00
Hockey, Stick, Gordie Howe, Game-Used, 1974-75 Season 1955.00
Hockey, Stick, Henri Richard, Game-Used, Louisville Slugger Mfg., 1970s 402.00
Hockey, Stick, Larry Robinson, Game, Koho K9, Montreal Canadiens, Autographed ... 350.00
Hockey, Stick, Montreal Canadiens, 18 Autographs, 1956-1957 .... 1500.00

Hockey, Stick, Sergei Fedorov, Autographed, 1991 .... 125.00
Horse Racing, Glass, Kentucky Derby 100th Anniversary, 1974.................................. 12.50
Horse Racing, Glass, Kentucky Derby, 1945... 300.00
Horse Racing, Glass, Kentucky Derby, 1948..115.00 to 135.00
Horse Racing, Glass, Kentucky Derby, 1955..70.00 to 100.00
Horse Racing, Glass, Kentucky Derby, 1956..40.00 to 115.00
Horse Racing, Glass, Kentucky Derby, 1957..35.00 to 70.00
Horse Racing, Glass, Kentucky Derby, 1959... 38.00
Horse Racing, Glass, Kentucky Derby, 1961..22.00 to 80.00
Horse Racing, Glass, Kentucky Derby, 1963... 20.00
Horse Racing, Glass, Kentucky Derby, 1964... 25.00
Horse Racing, Glass, Kentucky Derby, 1975... 16.00
Horse Racing, Glass, Kentucky Derby, French Lick, Aluminum, 1940...................... 400.00
Horse Racing, Glass, Preakness, 1975... 50.00
Horse Racing, Glass, Preakness, 1977... 40.00
Horse Racing, Glass, Preakness, 1978... 40.00
Horse Racing, Plate, Dan Patch, Christmas Greetings, Harry Luechtefeld 200.00
Horse Racing, Program & Menu, Kentucky Derby, 1940.. 125.00
Horse Racing, Program, 67th Kentucky Derby, Churchill Downs, 1941 .... 125.00
Horse Racing, Program, First Hembletonian, Signed By Howard Cosell, 1981............. 45.00
Horse Racing, Program, Kentucky Derby Diamond Jubilee, 1949 .... 150.00
Horse Racing, Program, Kentucky Derby, 1954..35.00 to 42.00
Hunting, Bag, Deer Hooves On Front Flap, Leather, 12 x 14 1/2 In. 165.00
Hunting, Game Call, Deer, Herters, Box 20.00
Hunting, Goose Call, Herters.. 15.00
Hunting, Knife, Randall, Brown Leather Scabbard, Orlando, Fla., 10 In. 275.00
Hunting, Knife, Skinning, Leather Sheath, Herters 45.00
Hunting, Launcher, Clay Pigeon, Chamberlin Cartridge & Target Co., Pat. 1882.......... 110.00
Hunting, License, Arkansas 1929-1930, On Linen 35.00
Hunting, License, Montana, 1920... 22.00
Hunting, License, Pennsylvania, 1933... 20.00
Hunting, License, Pennsylvania, Tin, 1934 .... 14.00
Hunting, License, Signed By Clark Gable, 1938, 12 x 15 In. 2300.00
Pool, Cue, Willie Mosconi, Autographed 195.00
Pool, Table, Mother-Of-Pearl & Ivory Inlay, Brunswick, Kling................................ 4950.00
Pool, Table, Slate Top, Carved Wood, Brunswick Balke, Collender & Co., c.1890 .... 5000.00
Sheet Music, Babe, Babe Ruth Picture, 1947... 75.00
Shuffleboard, Puck, Heywood Wakefield.. 30.00
Skating, Ice Skates, Keen Kutter 30.00
Skating, Ice Skates, Wooden, Leather Bindings.. 75.00
Skating, Ice, Program, Skating Vanities, Varga Cover, 1948...................................... 22.00
Skating, Ice, Skates, Lace-Up Fronts, Buckle Straps, Winchester Logo, 1920s............. 199.00
Skating, Ice, Skates, Large Curved Wooden Fronts... 275.00
Skating, Ice, Skates, Sonja Henie, Original Box, 1930s... 175.00
Skating, Ice, Skates, Swan Terminal, Not A Pair 2300.00
Skating, Roller Skates, Winchester 35.00
Skating, Roller Skates, Winchester, Box 42.00
Snooker Table, Brunswick, 1893 .... 5500.00
Snowshoeing, Key, Wooden, Convention Intl. Des Raquetteurs, Quebec, 1936, 8 Ft..... 302.00
Snowshoes, Mellie Dunham, Made For Peary's Son, 33 In. 578.00
Snowshoes, Military Style, Toe Curl, Boot Harness, 54 In. 110.00
Soccer, Jersey, Pele, New York Cosmos, Number 10 Front & Back 3220.00
Soccer, Medal, Major Indoor Soccer League Championship, 1988 .... 275.00
Tennis, Ball, Arthur Ashe, Autographed 138.00
Tennis, Ball, Autographed, Martina Navratilova 25.00
Tennis, Program, U.S. Open, 1977, Forest Hills, Evert, Borg, Connors, McEnroe, Lendl .. 45.00
Tennis, Racket, F.J. Bancroft, Humdinger Model, 1915.. 40.00
Tennis, Racket, Parlor, Bamboo Frame, Goat Skin, A.G. Spalding, 1910 .... 55.00
Tennis, Racket, Wooden, Metal, 1920s 115.00
Tennis, Racket, Wright & Ditson, 1870s.. 70.00
Tennis, Racket, Wright & Ditson, 1880s.. 70.00
Trophy, Penn Relay Races, 1898, Simons Bros., Philadelphia, Silver, 3 1/4 x 4 1/2 In. .. 245.00
Weight Lifting, Medicine Ball, 1920s... 185.00

STAFFORDSHIRE, England, has been a district making pottery and porcelain since the 1700s. Hundreds of kilns are still working in the area. Thousands of types of pottery and porcelain have been made in the many factories that worked and still work in the area. Some of the most famous factories have been listed separately, such as Adams, Davenport, Ridgway, Royal Doulton, Royal Worcester, Spode, Wedgwood, and others. Some Staffordshire pieces are listed under categories like Fairing, Flow Blue, Mulberry, Shaving Mug, etc.

Bank, Cottage, Orange & Cream	225.00
Bank, Dog's Head, Pair	345.00
Bank, Spaniel Dog Head, Gold Locket & Chain, 1860s, 4 In.	235.00
Bowl, Cover, Liberty Blue, 1976, 8 1/2 In.	45.00
Bowl, Liberty Blue, Oblong, 1976, 9 x 7 In.	45.00
Bowl, Vegetable, Cover, American Marine, Brown Transfer	195.00
Box, Cover, Figural, Mirror Frame	110.00
Box, Trinket, Fruit & Foliage Cover	110.00
Bulbpot, Cover, Couple Strolling With Dog, c.1805, 8 1/4 In.	2415.00
Burner, Pastille, Cottage Shape	138.00
Bust, George Washington, Enoch Wood, 19th Century, 8 1/2 In.	545.00 to 675.00
Carpet Ball, White & Black, 3 In.	82.00
Castor, Landing Of Gen. Lafayette, Blue, c.1824, 4 1/2 In.	862.00
Chimney Piece, Shakespeare, Gilt, 10 3/4 In.	247.00
Coffeepot, Commodore MacDonnough's Victory, 10 In.	880.00
Cooler, Wine, Japan, Flower Heads, Shell Handles, c.1815, 6 11/16 In.	460.00
Cup & Saucer, Handleless, Carnelia, Challinor	55.00
Cup & Saucer, Handleless, Couple, Woods, Black & White	35.00
Cup & Saucer, Handleless, Horse Drawn Sleigh, Dark Blue Transfer, Woods	330.00
Cup & Saucer, Handleless, Vase Of Flowers, Medium Dark Blue Transfer	110.00
Cup & Saucer, Royal Family, Victoria & Albert With Children, c.1848	275.00
Custard Cup, Boston State House, Beauties Of America Series, Blue, 2 3/4 In.	143.00
Dish, Cheese, Bull's Head, Large	975.00
Dish, Cover, Blue Transfer, 11 1/4 In.	632.00
Dish, Cover, Brown Basket Weave, Oval, 6 x 5 1/2 In.	245.00
Dish, Scenic River, Town, Blue & White, 12 In.	132.00
Dish, Serving, Cover, Peaches & Grape Design, 11 1/2 In.	900.00
Dish, Vegetable, Masted Ship, Square	750.00
Figurine, 2 Poodles, 4 1/2 In., Pair	285.00
Figurine, Boy In Sailor Suit, 6 1/2 In.	220.00
Figurine, Cat, On Pillow, 20th Century, 6 In.	247.00
Figurine, Cat, Seated, Black, 7 In., Pair	1100.00
Figurine, Cat, Sitting, Cream, Red Brown, 7 1/4 In. *Illus*	110.00
Figurine, Cat, Sitting, White, 7 1/2 In. *Illus*	100.00
Figurine, Children Reading, On Crotch Of Tree, c.1810, 7 1/8 In., Pair	925.00
Figurine, Cobbler & Wife, c.1840, Pair	400.00
Figurine, Cockatoo, 9 In.	165.00
Figurine, Courting Couple Seated Beneath Tree, 19th Century, 7 1/2 In.	126.00

Staffordshire, Figurine, Cat,
Sitting, Cream,
Red Brown, 7 1/4 In.;
Staffordshire, Figurine, Cat,
Sitting, White, 7 1/2 In.

Figurine, Dog & Deer, 9 In. 330.00
Figurine, Dog, Copper Luster Spots & Chain, 9 1/2 In. 225.00
Figurine, Dog, Greyhound, Standing, 7 1/2 In. 236.00
Figurine, Dog, Light Brown, 8 In., Pair 138.00
Figurine, Dog, Poodle With Flower Basket, 5 In. 340.00
Figurine, Dog, Poodle, 3 1/2 In., Pair 300.00
Figurine, Dog, Poodle, 5 In., Pair 165.00
Figurine, Dog, Poodle, Laying, c.1840, 5 In., Pair 500.00
Figurine, Dog, Seated, 7 1/2 In. 325.00
Figurine, Dog, Seated, Black, Gilt, 5 1/8 In. 104.00
Figurine, Dog, Seated, Red Spots, Black & Yellow, 3 5/8 In. 38.00
Figurine, Dog, Spaniel, 1910, Pair 200.00
Figurine, Dog, Spaniel, Black Glaze, 9 1/2 In., Pair 230.00
Figurine, Dog, Spaniel, Brown & White, 12 In., Pair 685.00
Figurine, Dog, Spaniel, Brown Muzzle, White, 10 In. 440.00
Figurine, Dog, Spaniel, Glass Eyes, 11 3/8 In. 275.00
Figurine, Dog, Spaniel, Seated, Gold Lustre Detail, 9 1/8 In., Pair 172.00
Figurine, Dog, Standing, Tan, White Feet, 11 In., Pair 475.00
Figurine, Dog, Whippet, 5 In. 230.00
Figurine, Dog, Whippet, 6 In. 235.00
Figurine, Dog, Yellowware, Cobalt Blue Glaze 1350.00
Figurine, Drummer Boy, Goat On Mountain Above, 12 In. 154.00
Figurine, Fruit Seller, 5 In., Pair 38.00
Figurine, Girl With Lamb, 4 In. 80.00
Figurine, Hen On Nest, 10 In. 360.00
Figurine, Herdsman, With Cow, 6 1/2 In. 250.00
Figurine, Lion, Crouched, Glass Eyes, 13 In., Pair .... 600.00 to 900.00
Figurine, Lion, Yellow, Brown & Black, 3 1/4 In. 60.00
Figurine, Little Red Riding Hood, 4 1/4 In. 27.00
Figurine, Little Red Riding Hood, Basket, Wolf, 15 In. 800.00
Figurine, Little Red Riding Hood, Wolf, c.1850, 11 In. 275.00
Figurine, Man, On Bicycle, Green, Red & Black, 3 3/8 In. 110.00
Figurine, Market Fruit Seller, 15 In. 286.00
Figurine, Milkmaid & Cow, 10 In. 650.00
Figurine, Napoleon Bonaparte, c.1850, 8 1/2 In. 650.00
Figurine, Parrot, On Branch, Multicolored, 4 In. 175.00
Figurine, Prince & Princess Of Wales, 19th Century, 5 1/2 In., Pair 415.00
Figurine, Princess On Goat, c.1850, 4 In. 250.00
Figurine, Rabbit, Black & White, 3 1/4 In. 275.00
Figurine, Sampson With Lion, 10 In. 750.00
Figurine, Scotsman, 12 In. 220.00
Figurine, Scotsman, With Dog, Gilt, 7 In. 220.00
Figurine, Sheep, 4 In. 115.00
Figurine, Sheep, Recumbent, 3 1/2 In. 190.00

◆ ◆

Recycle your unused ashtrays
as drip-catching candleholders,
as holders for change on your
bedroom dresser, or as holders
for imitation sweeteners.

◆ ◆

Staffordshire, Figurine,
Uncle Tom, Holding Girl On Knee,
10 1/4 In.

Figurine, Shepherd & Shepherdess, Bench, Trees, 6 In.		145.00
Figurine, Shepherdess, Petting Small Lamb, c.1790, 6 1/2 In.		805.00
Figurine, Shepherdess, Sheep, Flowering Tree, 5 3/4 In.		275.00
Figurine, Shoemaker, c.1790, 4 1/2 In.		330.00
Figurine, Stout Man, On Stool, 5 3/8 In.		50.00
Figurine, Turk, 5 In.		115.00
Figurine, Uncle Tom, Holding Girl On Knee, 10 1/4 In.	*Illus*	800.00
Figurine, Vicar & Moses, 9 3/4 In.		345.00
Figurine, Village Maid, Seated On Tree Stump, 10 3/8 In.		175.00
Figurine, Woman, Seated, With Dog, 6 In.		66.00
Figurine, Young Man, Playing Bagpipe, 11 1/2 In.		115.00
Figurine, Zebra, Pair		250.00
Incense Burner, Cottage Form, Bay, Dormer, Oriel Windows, c.1860, 11 In.		1725.00
Jar, Tobacco, Woman, Large		475.00
Jug, Lord Nelson, Cannon, Figural, 11 1/2 In.		495.00
Jug, Milk, Cover, Creamware, Flowers & Fruit, Basket Weave Rim, c.1780, 5 In.		805.00
Jug, Peace, Plenty & Independence, 10 In.		2400.00
Jug, Weaver, Polychrome Enamel, 19th Century, 6 In.		172.00
Lazy Susan Set, Landscape, Midwinter, Blue & White, Wooden Base, 9 Pc.		935.00
Loving Cup, Robert Hill, Figural Handles, Colors, Gaudy, 7 In.		275.00
Mug, Black Transfer, Black Man & Boy, Subtraction, 2 3/4 In.		192.00
Mug, Child's, A Present For William, Horse Design		495.00
Mug, Child's, George, Green Flowers Border, Shell At Top		525.00
Mug, Child's, Joseph, Brown, Scroll Design		495.00
Mug, Child's, Nursery Rhyme, Child In Nightcap & Gown, Sugarplums		85.00
Mug, Child's, Prosper Freedom, Purple Transfer, 2 1/2 In.		175.00
Mug, Child's, Washington, 19th Century, 2 1/2 In.		489.00
Mug, Landing Of Gen. Lafayette, c.1824, 4 3/4 In.		862.00
Pipe, Creamware, Curved Stem, Wide Stripes, c.1760, 5 3/4 In.		575.00
Pitcher, American Naval Heroes, Blue, 6 In.		690.00
Pitcher, Arms Of The United States, Free Trade & Sailors Rights		2650.00
Pitcher, Cottage, Polychrome Enamel, 6 5/8 In.		137.00
Pitcher, Cream, Cow Shape, 19th Century, 6 1/2 In.		385.00
Pitcher, George Peabody, Rope Twist Handle, 1870, 7 3/4 In.		125.00
Pitcher, Gilded Scrollwork, Garden Flowers, J. Venables, 12 1/2 In.		132.00
Pitcher, House Shape, Grapevine Design, 3 1/2 In.		75.00
Pitcher, Lafayette At The Tomb Of Franklin, Dark Blue Transfer, 7 1/4 In.		605.00
Pitcher, Lafayette At The Tomb Of Franklin, Blue, 19th Century, 7 In.		750.00
Pitcher, Lafayette At The Tomb Of Washington, 9 In.		1210.00
Pitcher, Ming, Black Transfer, 6 In.		50.00
Pitcher, New York City Hall & Boston State House, Stubbs, 6 1/2 In.		695.00
Pitcher, Night Watchman With Lantern Shape, 9 In.		247.00
Pitcher, Northern Scenery, Loch Awe, Blue & White, 7 1/4 In.		374.00
Pitcher, Pastoral Landscape, Blue Transfer, Copper Banding, 6 In.		66.00
Pitcher & Bowl, New York, Almhouse, Stevenson		3500.00
Plate, America & Independence, Blue, 8 /12 In.		165.00
Plate, America & Independence, Dark Blue Transfer, 8 In.		357.00
Plate, Arms Of Rhode Island, Mayer, 8 3/4 In.		750.00
Plate, Arms Of Rhose Island, Blue Transfer, c.1829, 8 1/2 In.		460.00
Plate, Asiatic Pheasants, Blue, Signed, Podmore Walker, c.1850, 10 In.		165.00
Plate, Baker's Falls, Black Transfer, 9 In.		105.00
Plate, Baltimore Exchange, Dark Blue Transfer, 9 3/4 In.		440.00
Plate, Bank Of The United States, Philadelphia, Blue, Marked, 10 In.		345.00
Plate, Black Transfer, Gentlemen's Cabin, Boston Mails, Ironstone, 8 1/4 In.		85.00
Plate, Boston State House, Blue Transfer, Enoch Wood, 10 1/4 In.		137.00
Plate, Boston State House, Medium Blue Transfer, 8 3/4 In.		165.00
Plate, British Scenery, Dark Blue Transfer, 9 7/8 In.		165.00
Plate, British Scenery, Dark Blue, 9 In.		200.00
Plate, Cadmus, Enoch Wood, 10 In.		595.00
Plate, Canova, Pink & Green Transfer, 9 1/4 In.		65.00
Plate, Capitol Washington, Blue, 7 1/2 In.		374.00
Plate, Catholic, Cathedral, N.Y., Stevenson, 6 1/2 In.		1650.00
Plate, Catskill House, Hudson, Red & White, 10 1/4 In.		195.00

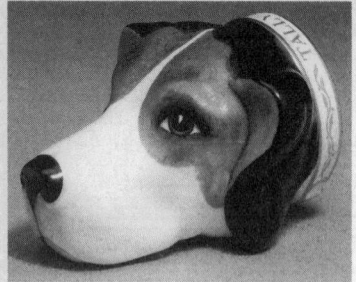

◆ ◆

Dental wax (ask your orthodontist about it) is a good adhesive to keep figurines on shelves, or lids on teapots.

◆ ◆

Staffordshire, Stirrup Cup,
Hound's Head, 1825-1835

Plate, City Of Albany, State Of New York, Blue, 10 1/8 In. 460.00
Plate, City Of Montreal, Red & White, 9 In. 160.00
Plate, City Series, Hobart Town, Blue, 9 In. 145.00
Plate, Columbia College, N.Y., Stevenson, 8 In. 650.00
Plate, Commodore MacDonnough's Victory, Blue, Marked, 10 In. 345.00
Plate, Cupid Series, Dark Blue, 10 In. 210.00
Plate, Dam & Water Works, Philadelphia, Dark Blue Transfer 440.00
Plate, Dartmouth, Dark Blue Transfer, 8 1/8 In. 247.00
Plate, Dessert, Floral Sprigs, c.1840, 12 In. 1725.00
Plate, Fairmount Near Philadelphia, Medium Dark Blue Transfer, 10 3/8 In. 115.00
Plate, Fall Of Montmorenci, Near Quebec, Enoch Wood, 9 In. 275.00
Plate, Fisherman's Family, Hut, 6 1/2 In. 125.00
Plate, Fruit Design, Blue Transfer, 10 In. 99.00
Plate, Hartford, Connecticut, Black, Jackson, 10 1/4 In. 85.00
Plate, Historical Scenes, Blue, Late 19th Century, 9 3/4 In., 8 Piece 144.00
Plate, Horse Racing Scene, c.1880. .... 45.00
Plate, Landing Of Fathers At Plymouth, Blue Transfer, 10 1/4 In. 105.00
Plate, Landing Of Gen. Lafayette, Dark Blue Transfer 385.00
Plate, Millennium, Brown, Stevenson, 10 1/2 In. 110.00
Plate, Monte Video, Black, 7 In. 125.00
Plate, Monte Video, Red & White, 7 In. 125.00
Plate, Nahant Hotel, Near Boston, Eagle Border, Blue, 9 In. .... 325.00 to 374.00
Plate, New York, Battery, Stevenson, 7 In. 450.00
Plate, Palestine Series, Bethlehem, 7 In. 40.00
Plate, Pine Orchard House, Catskill Mountains, Enoch Wood, 9 1/4 In. 725.00
Plate, Pittsburgh, Pennsylvania, Steamboat, Marked, Maroon, 10 1/2 In. 258.00
Plate, Polychrome, Chinoiserie Design, 8 In., Pair 154.00
Plate, Race Bridge, Philadelphia, Black Transfer, 9 In. 60.00
Plate, Race Bridge, Philadelphia, Brown, 9 In. 165.00
Plate, Rapids Above Hadley's Falls, Brown, 7 In. 125.00
Plate, Shannondale Springs, Va., Red & White, 8 In. 135.00
Plate, St. Paul's Chapel, New York, Stevenson, 6 1/2 In. 975.00
Plate, Striped Bass, Hayes, 8 3/4 In. 950.00
Plate, Table Rock, Niagara, Enoch Wood, 10 In. 550.00
Plate, Tivoli, Blue & White. 55.00
Plate, Toddy, Beehive, Stevenson, 5 1/4 In. 195.00
Plate, Uncle Tom's Cabin, c.1860, 8 In., 2 Piece 265.00
Plate, Upper Ferry Bridge Over The River Schuylkill, Stubbs, 8 7/8 In. 325.00
Plate, View Near Conway, Red & White, 9 In. 125.00
Plate, View Near Fishkill, Hudson River, 10 1/2 In. 120.00
Plate, View Of Liverpool, Dark Blue, 10 In. 425.00
Plate, View Of Trenton Falls, Blue, 7 1/2 In. 210.00
Plate, William IV, Raised Fruit, Figural Border, c.1831, 6 3/4 In. 460.00
Platter, Arms Of Delaware, Mayer, 16 3/4 In. 3500.00
Platter, Blue & White Floral Design, 19th Century, 15 In. 345.00

Staffordshire, Teapot,
Salt Glaze, White Camel

◆◆◆◆◆◆◆◆◆◆◆◆◆◆◆◆◆◆◆◆◆◆◆◆◆◆
Cups are best stored by
hanging them on cup hooks.
Stacking cups inside each
other can cause chipping.
◆◆◆◆◆◆◆◆◆◆◆◆◆◆◆◆◆◆◆◆◆◆◆◆◆◆

Platter, Boston State House, Stubbs, 14 1/4 In. 1200.00
Platter, Canova, Red Transfer, 15 1/2 In. 160.00
Platter, Castle Garden, Battery, New York, Blue, 15 In. 460.00
Platter, Chesapeake & Shannon, Blue Transfer, 21 1/2 In. 1540.00
Platter, Fairmount Near Philadelphia, Dark Blue Transfer 203.00
Platter, Game Birds, Blue Transfer, 19th Century, 14 5/8 In. 805.00
Platter, Gyrn Flintshire Wales, Blue, Mid-19th Century, 17 In. 690.00
Platter, Horses Grazing, Blue Transfer, Marked, 11 In. 862.00
Platter, Indian Design, Elephants, Building, Blue & White, 19 In. 135.00
Platter, Lake George, Blue, Shell Border, Enoch Wood, 15 1/2 In. 852.00
Platter, Pastoral Scene, Floral Border, 19th Century, 23 In. 575.00
Platter, Polar Bear Hunt, Blue, 19th Century, 16 3/4 In. 862.00
Platter, Solar Rays, Brown Transfer, 19 5/8 In. 187.00
Platter, Tower, Blue & White, 16 1/2 In. 330.00
Platter, Upper Ferry Bridge, Dark Blue Transfer, 19 In. 1100.00
Platter, View Of Dublin, Enoch Wood, 15 In. 1200.00
Platter, Winter View Of Pittsfield, Mass., Dark Blue Transfer 715.00
Platter, Woodlands 522.00
Salt & Pepper, Liberty Blue, c.1976 .... 25.00
Soup, Dish, Boston State House, 9 3/4 In. 225.00
Stirrup Cup, Hound's Head, 1825-1835 ....*Illus* 1380.00
Stirrup Cup, Pearlware, Head Of Bearded Man, c.1790, 4 3/8 In. 1380.00
Sugar, 2 Men Fishing, Medium Blue, 5 1/2 In. 250.00
Sugar, Cover, American Eagle, Shield, Harbor, Blue, c.1830, 7 3/4 In. 285.00
Sugar, Cover, Liberty Blue, c.1976 .... 30.00
Sugar, Cover, Mt. Vernon, Seat Of The Late Gen. Washington, Blue, 7 In. 172.00
Sugar, Floral Design, Red, Blue, Green, Black, 4 7/8 In. 50.00
Tankard, View Of Liverpool, 6 In. 1200.00
Tea Strainer, Under Cup, Blue & White 118.00
Teapot, Canova, Pink & Green, White Ground, Mayer, 6 In. 303.00
Teapot, Chinese Figures, Garden, Salt Glaze, Polychrome Enamel, c.1755, 6 In. 977.00
Teapot, Domestic Animals, Blue, Large 495.00
Teapot, Dragon Handle 775.00
Teapot, Engine Turned Design, Red Stoneware, c.1770, 3 In. 1100.00
Teapot, Floral Design, 6 1/2 In. 158.00
Teapot, Landing Of Gen. Lafayette 330.00
Teapot, Paneled Sides, Cobalt Pectin Shells, Salt Glaze, c.1745, 5 1/4 In. 635.00
Teapot, Pink, 6 In. 260.00
Teapot, Salt Glaze, White Camel..*Illus* 1725.00
Teapot, Stand, Tortoiseshell Glaze, Loop Handle, c.1765, 4 In. 575.00
Teapot, Toby 425.00
Toby Jugs are listed in their own category
Tureen, Sauce, Boston State House, Blue, 8 In. 345.00
Tureen, Soup, Cover, Blue-Black Transfer, 1850s, 14 1/4 In. 430.00
Tureen, Soup, Persian, Matching Underplate & Ladle, Signed, 11 x 14 In. 675.00

Tureen, Soup, Schenectady On Mohawk River, Brown, Jackson 1650.00
Tureen, Soup, Village Of Cedars, St. Lawrence Morley & Co., 11 In. 1000.00
Underplate, Chillicothe, Medium Blue Transfer, 9 5/8 In. 4345.00
Underplate, Rice Molded Border, 18th Century, 10 In. 402.00
Urinal, Pastoral Scene.. 345.00
Vase, 3 Dogs, Stump & Scottish Lass, Gilt, 8 1/8 In. 225.00
Vase, Bottle, Famille Rose, Willow Tree, Peonies, c.1752, 5 3/16 In. 1380.00
Vase, Cow & Calf, Polychrome & Gilt, 12 In. 395.00
Vase, George V & Mary, 1935, 4 In. 30.00
Vase, Spill, Girl, Seated, With Dog, 6 In. 138.00
Vase, Spill, Sheep Shape, Pebbled-Wool Finish, Trees, 19th Century, Pair 412.00
Vase, Tree Stump, Stag In Front, Rust, 11 1/2 In., Pair... 750.00
Watch Holder, Castle Form, c.1840 .... 550.00
Watch Holder, Form Of Couple, 11 In. 135.00

STANGL Pottery traces its history back to the Fulper Pottery of New Jersey.
In 1910, Johann Martin Stangl started working at Fulper. He bought into the
firm in 1913, became president in 1926, and in 1929 changed the company
name to Stangl Pottery. The pottery made dinnerwares and a line of limited-
edition bird figurines. The company went out of business in 1978.

Ashtray, Cosmos, Pink, 5 1/2 In. 20.00
Ashtray, Dog Hunting, 8 1/4 In. 50.00
Ashtray, Golfer.. 95.00
Ashtray, Mallard, Sportsman's Ware, Oval, No. 3926, 10 5/8 In. 38.00
Ashtray, Pansy, Multicolor, 5 Piece 75.00
Ashtray, Pheasant, No. 3926, 10 1/2 In. 35.00
Ashtray, Quail ....16.00 to 35.00
Ashtray, Tulip 16.00
Bank, Pig, Animalware, Green 95.00
Bank, Pig, Tulips, Sticker.. 80.00
Bean Pot, Tulip On Town & Country, Yellow... 60.00
Berry Bowl, Magnolia.. 15.00
Berry Bowl, Star Flower.. 15.00
Bird, Bird Of Paradise, No. 3408 ....85.00 to 100.00
Bird, Blue Jay, No. 3716...450.00 to 700.00
Bird, Blue-Headed Vireo, No. 3448.. 60.00
Bird, Bluebird, No. 3276S ....78.00 to 100.00
Bird, Bluebirds, Double, No. 3276D..135.00 to 195.00
Bird, Broadbill Hummingbird, No. 3629 ....115.00 to 125.00
Bird, Broadtail Hummingbird, No. 3626 .... 130.00
Bird, Cardinal, No. 3444...44.00 to 135.00
Bird, Chestnut-Backed Chickadee, No. 3811 .... 85.00
Bird, Cockatoo, No. 3405S 120.00
Bird, Cockatoos, Double, No. 3405D 125.00
Bird, Cockatoos, Double, No. 3580D 165.00
Bird, European Finch, No. 3722 .... 800.00
Bird, Evening Grosbeak, No. 3813 ....95.00 to 120.00
Bird, Flying Duck, No. 3443 ....225.00 to 285.00
Bird, Golden-Crowned Kinglet, No. 3848 .... 88.00
Bird, Gray Cardinal, No. 3596 ....60.00 to 62.00
Bird, Hen, No. 3446.. 150.00
Bird, Indigo Bunting, No. 3589 .... 70.00
Bird, Kentucky Warbler, No. 3598 .... 45.00
Bird, Key West Quail Dove, No. 3454 ....238.00 to 325.00
Bird, Kingfishers, Double, No. 3406D 105.00
Bird, Love Bird, No. 3400 .... 55.00
Bird, Magpie-Jay, No. 3758... 900.00
Bird, Nuthatch, No. 3593 .... 66.00
Bird, Oriole, No. 3402S 48.00
Bird, Orioles, Blue Beak, Double, No. 3402D 90.00
Bird, Owl, No. 3407 .... 330.00
Bird, Parakeets, Double, No. 3582D ....155.00 to 175.00
Bird, Parula Warbler, No. 3583 ....45.00 to 85.00

Bird, Penguin, No. 3274	500.00
Bird, Redstarts, Double, No. 3490D	90.00 to 155.00
Bird, Rooster, No. 3445	44.00
Bird, Rooster, Yellow, No. 3446	125.00
Bird, Running Duck, No. 3432	380.00 to 425.00
Bird, Titmouse, No. 3592	45.00 to 50.00
Bird, Turkey, No. 3275	550.00
Bird, Western Blue Bird, No. 3815	165.00
Bird, Wild Duck, No. 3250	100.00
Bird, Wilson Warbler, No. 3597	50.00 to 80.00
Bird, Wren, No. 3401S	200.00
Bird, Yellow Warbler, No. 3447	68.00 to 75.00
Bird, Yellow Warbler, No. 3850	100.00
Bowl, Apple Delight, 5 1/2 In.	10.00
Bowl, Apple Delight, Lug Handles, 5 1/4 In.	12.00
Bowl, Cereal, Blueberry	8.00
Bowl, Cereal, Star Flower	10.00
Bowl, Cereal, Town & Country, Green	16.00
Bowl, Country Garden, 8 In.	30.00
Bowl, Eggplant, Black, Gold, No. 3783	8.00
Bowl, Fruit, Golden Harvest, 12 In.	40.00
Bowl, Fruit, Thistle, 5 1/2 In.	12.00
Bowl, Gold Leaf, Basket Handle, 13 1/4 x 4 1/4 In.	35.00
Bowl, Golden Blossom, 8 In.	30.00
Bowl, Little Boy Blue	85.00
Bowl, Pony Trail, Kiddieware	125.00
Bowl, Salad, Golden Harvest	35.00
Bowl, Thistle, 5 1/2 In.	10.00
Bowl, Town & Country, 5 1/2 In.	17.50
Bowl, Vegetable, Amber Glo, 2 Sections	33.00
Bowl, Vegetable, Amber Glo, Round	25.00
Bowl, Vegetable, Fruit & Flowers	25.00
Bowl, Vegetable, Golden Harvest, 2 Sections	35.00
Bowl, Vegetable, Magnolia, 10 In.	25.00
Bowl, Vegetable, Star Flower, 8 In.	25.00
Bowl, Wild Rose, Round, 8 In.	37.50
Butter, Cover, Country Garden	30.00
Candleholder, Town & Country, Blue, Pair	50.00
Candy, Terra Rose	18.00
Candy Dish, Thistle, 11 In.	15.00
Carafe, Colonial, Blue	30.00
Charger, Garden Flower, 14 In.	20.00
Chop Plate, Colonial, Blue, 12 1/2 In.	12.00
Chop Plate, Fruit & Flowers, 12 In.	27.00
Chop Plate, Thistle, 12 1/2 In.	28.00
Chop Plate, Town & Country, Blue	45.00
Chop Plate, Tulip, 14 In.	30.00
Clock, Rooster, Plate Type	28.00 to 40.00
Coaster, Orchard Song, 5 In.	5.00
Coffee Warmer, Golden Harvest	12.00
Coffeepot, Cactus, Donkey, Porcelier	35.00
Coffeepot, Florentine	40.00
Coffeepot, Star Flower, Individual	45.00
Coffeepot, Town & Country, Blue	130.00
Creamer, Country Life	80.00
Creamer, Holly	18.00
Cruet, Oil & Vinegar, Blueberry	90.00
Cup, Apple Delight	6.00
Cup, Chicory	10.00
Cup, Cosmos	3.00
Cup, Country Life	50.00
Cup, Dahlia	3.00
Cup, Golden Harvest	5.00

Cup, Magnolia	3.50
Cup, Peter Rabbit, Kiddieware	85.00
Cup, Saucer, Plate, Ducky Dinner, Kiddieware	80.00
Cup, Thistle	7.00
Cup, Town & Country, Green	22.00
Cup & Saucer, Apple Delight	13.00
Cup & Saucer, Country Garden	2.00
Cup & Saucer, Dahlia, Blue, Green, White	5.00
Cup & Saucer, Fruit & Flowers	15.00
Cup & Saucer, Garland	14.00
Cup & Saucer, Golden Harvest	6.00 to 11.00
Cup & Saucer, Magnolia	5.00 to 15.00
Cup & Saucer, Rooster	9.00
Cup & Saucer, Star Flower	15.00
Eggcup, Double, Thistle	12.00
Eggcup, Golden Harvest	8.00
Eggcup, Thistle	6.00
Figurine, Draft Horse	190.00
Flowerpot, Red Flower, 5 x 5 1/2 In.	14.00
Flowerpot, Tulip, 3 In.	10.00
Flowerpot, Yellow Tulip, 5 x 5 3/4 In.	14.00
Ginger Jar, Cover, Green, Mason's, Willow	65.00
Gravy Boat, Fruit	20.00
Gravy Boat, Magnolia	20.00
Gravy Boat, Thistle	18.00
Mold, Jell-0, Town & Country, Green	45.00
Mug, Holly	35.00
Mug, Jack & Jill, Musical, Porcelain	295.00
Mug, Town & Country, Blue, 14 Oz.	35.00
Mug, Town & Country, Green, 12 Oz.	23.00
Mug, Town & Country, Yellow, 12 Oz.	25.00
Pitcher, Country Garden, 1 1/2 Pt.	25.00
Pitcher, Country Garden, 1 Pt.	20.00
Pitcher, Garden Flower	12.00
Pitcher, Provincial	25.00
Pitcher, Tickled Pink, 9 1/2 In.	14.00
Pitcher, Town & Country, Blue, 6 1/2 In.	40.00
Plate, Amber Glo, 10 In.	12.00
Plate, Amber Glo, 12 1/2 In.	20.00
Plate, Apple Delight, 6 In.	5.00
Plate, Apple Delight, 10 In.	15.00
Plate, Blueberry, 6 In.	7.00
Plate, Blueberry, 10 In.	16.00
Plate, Country Garden, 8 In.	3.00
Plate, Country Life, Pig, 8 In.	50.00
Plate, Dahlia, 6 In.	2.00
Plate, Dessert, Fruit & Flowers	7.00
Plate, Deviled Egg, Golden Blossom	40.00
Plate, Deviled Egg, Hen Figurine	65.00
Plate, Deviled Egg, With Saltshaker	108.00
Plate, Fish, 8 1/2 In.	35.00
Plate, Fruit & Flowers, 10 In.	13.00
Plate, Fruit, 10 In.	8.00
Plate, Garden Flower, 10 In.	10.00
Plate, Garland, 8 In.	10.00
Plate, Golden Blossom, 8 In.	5.00
Plate, Golden Blossom, 10 In.	5.00
Plate, Golden Harvest, 6 In.	6.00
Plate, Golden Harvest, 8 In.	7.00
Plate, Golden Harvest, 10 In.	12.00
Plate, Humpty-Dumpty, Kiddieware	85.00
Plate, Humpty-Dumpty, Kiddieware, Green	165.00
Plate, Little Bo Peep, Kiddieware	115.00 to 135.00

Plate, Little Boy Blue, Kiddieware ....55.00 to 135.00
Plate, Little Quackers, Kiddieware 115.00
Plate, Magnolia, 10 In. 8.00
Plate, Orchard Song, 6 In. 5.00
Plate, Peter Rabbit, Kiddieware 185.00
Plate, Rooster, 10 In. 12.00
Plate, Salad, Garden Flower 8.00
Plate, Snack, Apple Delight, 8 1/4 In. 3.00
Plate, Star Flower, 6 In. 2.00
Plate, Star Flower, 10 In. 11.00
Plate, Thistle, 6 1/4 In. 6.00
Plate, Thistle, 14 In. 25.00
Plate, White Dogwood, 8 In. 10.00
Platter, Tickled Pink, 13 1/2 In. 10.00
Platter, White Dogwood, 14 3/4 In. 35.00
Relish, Bittersweet .... 24.00 to 25.00
Relish, Country Garden 30.00
Salt & Pepper, Bittersweet 20.00
Salt & Pepper, Daisy, Figural, Blue & Yellow 35.00
Salt & Pepper, Pig 195.00
Salt & Pepper, Ranger 495.00
Saucer, Apple Delight 3.00
Saucer, Country Garden 1.00
Saucer, Garden Flower 5.00
Server, Bella Rose, Center Handle 10.00
Server, Orchard Song, Center Handle 14.00
Shaving Mug, Yellow 18.00
Soup, Cream, Americana, Orange 4.00
Soup, Lug, Blueberry 15.00
Spoon Rest, 4 Pansy Trays, Town & Country 50.00
Sugar, Country Life 125.00
Sugar, Cover, Thistle 15.00
Teapot, Field Daisy, Blue Ground 75.00
Teapot, Town & Country, Blue 75.00
Tidbit, First Love 9.00
Tray, Bread, Orchard Song 25.00
Vase, Applied Bands, White, 8 In. 45.00
Vase, Cabbage, Green 22.00
Vase, Leaping Fish, 9 1/2 In. 125.00
Vase, Rainbow Ware, Handles, 12 In. 250.00
Vase, Rainbow Ware, Yellow Rim, Green & Yellow Interior, Marked, 7 In. 125.00
Vase, Terra Rose, 7 In. 27.00
Wall Pocket, Golden Harvest, Geisha With Parasol, Unglazed Face & Hands, 9 1/2 In. 48.00
Wig Stand, Blond Head 275.00
Wig Stand, Brunette Head .... 285.00 to 350.00

STEINS have been used by beer and ale drinkers for over 500 years. They
have been made of ivory, porcelain, stoneware, faience, silver, pewter, wood,
or glass in sizes up to nine gallons. Although some were made by Mettlach,
Meissen, Capo-di-Monte, and other famous factories, most were made by
less important German potteries. The words *Geschutz* or *Musterschutz* on a
stein are the German words for *patented* or *registered design*, not company
names. Steins are still being made in the old styles. Lithophane steins may be
found in the Lithophane category.

2 Women, Painted, White, Lithophane Base, 1 Liter 95.00
Bowling Pin Shape, Scene With Pin Setter, 1/2 Liter 200.00
Brass Log Of 24-Karat Club, New York City, Pewter, 1/2 Liter, 1904 .... 25.00
Brewmeister, Instruments, Cherubs, Cobalt Ground, Dome Lid, Early 1900s, 1 Liter... 275.00
Budweiser, 15th Winter Olympic Games, Calgary, 7 1/2 In. 150.00
Budweiser, Basketball, Heroes Of Hardwood, Gift Box 16.00
Budweiser, Fore!, Logo On Black Golf Bag, 6 3/4 In. 14.00
Budweiser, Golf, Par For The Course, Gift Box 16.00
Budweiser, Holiday Series, Cameo Wheatland, 1983, 6 1/2 In. 25.00

Budweiser, Holiday Series, Champion Clydesdales, 1980 .... 95.00
Budweiser, National Historical Landmark, 7 1/2 In. 150.00
Cat On A Book, 1/2 Liter.. 2310.00
Cavalier, Holding Stein & Sword, Hand Painted, Pewter, Germany, 1/2 Liter, 6 1/4 In. 295.00
Enameled Sprays & Scrolls, Stained Glass, Champagne Color, Pewter Top, 1/2 Liter.. 265.00
Figural, Polychrome, Gesetzlich Geschutzt, Pewter Lid, 7 1/4 In. 220.00
G. Heileman Brewery, LaCross, Wisconsin, 1981 .... 65.00
Golfer, Wearing Knickers, Porcelain, 5 In. 895.00
Grand Army Of Republic, Eagle, Flag, 1861-Veteran-1866, Mellor & Co., 6 In. 282.00
Ivory, Roman Figures, Silver & Silver-Gilt Mounted, 8 4/8 In. 4715.00
Low Relief Reserve Of Monkeys, Monkey Thumb Rest, Germany, c.1920, 16 In. 495.00
Man With Pipe, Die Kehl Kost Veel, Germany, 6 In. 185.00
Markelbach, Blue & Brown Designs, Pewter Lid, 25 In. 295.00
Mettlach steins are listed in the Mettlach category.
Monkey, E. Bohne Sohne, Brown 2310.00
Monkey, E. Bohne Sohne, White.. 3630.00
O'Hara Dial Co., Ceramic, Metal Watch Dial Top, 1 Liter, 1890................................. 467.00
Raised Genre Scene, Germany, 2 Liter, Pair.. 77.00
Regimental, 111th Infantry, Germany, 1 Liter, 1895... 595.00
Regimental, Lithophane Canon Finial, Names Of Gun Crew, 1 Liter, 1899-1901 .... 450.00
Regimental, Lithophane In Base, Pewter Lid, Cannon Finial, 1 Liter............................. 350.00
Regimental, Roster Back, Dated 1903, 1 Liter.. 325.00
Schlitz Brewery, 125th Anniversary, Raised Brewery, 1849-1974, 7 3/4 In. 50.00
Stroh's, Heritage Series II, Ceramart, 1 Liter.. 35.00

STEREO CARDS that were made for stereoscope viewers became popular after 1840. Two almost identical pictures were mounted on a stiff cardboard backing so that, when viewed through a stereoscope, a three-dimensional picture could be seen. Value is determined by maker and by subject. These cards were made in quantity through the 1930s.

Blacks Eating Sugar Cane 40.00
Middle East, Convent, Arab Girls, Desert Scene, 1882, 5 Piece 40.00
New Orleans International Expo., 7 Imperial Cards, Edward L. Wilson, 1884.............. 45.00
Pennsylvania Oil Fields, 26 Piece... 1090.00
Spotted Tail Portrait, 1860s 225.00
Stage Coach, Fort William Henry Hotel, Lake George, 1870.. 75.00

STEREOSCOPES were used for viewing stereo cards. The hand viewer was invented by Oliver Wendell Holmes, although more complicated table models were used before his was produced in 1859. Do not confuse the stereoscope with the stereopticon, a magic lantern that used glass slides.

Oculist 20.00
Wooden, St. Louis, 30 Views, 1904 .... 95.00

STERLING SILVER, see Silver-Sterling category

STEUBEN glass was made at the Steuben Glass Works of Corning, New York. The factory, founded by Frederick Carder and T. G. Hawkes, Sr., was purchased by the Corning Glass Company. They continued to make glass called *Steuben*. Many types of art glass were made at Steuben. The firm is still making exceptional quality glass but it is clear, modern-style glass. Additional pieces may be found in the Aurene and Cluthra categories.

Ashtray, Tooled Tricon, Central Hooked Holder, Marked, 5 In. 260.00
Bowl, 4 Scrolled Feet, 7 3/4 In. 220.00
Bowl, Asymmetrical, Applied Flower Petals, 9 1/2 In. 195.00
Bowl, Calcite, Footed, 13 3/4 In. 330.00
Bowl, Clear, Signed, 12 x 6 3/4 In., Pair.. 413.00
Bowl, Coronet, No. 8039, Signed, 12 3/4 In. 315.00
Bowl, Foliated Base, James McNaughton, 1937, 8 1/4 In. 460.00
Bowl, Grotesque, Carder Mold, 4 Pillar Design, Signed, 6 1/2 x 7 In. 387.00
Bowl, Grotesque, Green Rim Shading To Colorless Crystal, Signed, 12 1/4 In. 375.00
Bowl, Grotesque, Ivory, 5 1/4 x 9 1/2 In. 110.00
Bowl, Oriental Pattern, Black Jade On Flint White Double Etched Bowl, 10 In. 1850.00

Bowl, Ovoid, Applied Petal Base, 11 In.	412.00
Bowl, Pomona Green, 11 In.	125.00
Bowl, Pomona Green, Signed, 10 In.	125.00
Bowl, Rosaline, Design 2687, 7 3/4 x 4 In.	275.00
Bowl, Rouge Flambe, 16 In.	6000.00
Bowl, Talisman, 7 In.	192.00
Box, Dresser, Seated Cover, Pomona Green Random Threads, 4 1/4 In.	172.50
Candleholder, Self-Reeding On Foot, Ruffled Rim, Signed, Blue, 5 1/2 In., Pair	300.00
Candleholder, Venetian Style, Selenium, Engraved Floral, 6 3/4 In., Pair	920.00
Candlestick, 2-Arm, Random Bubbles With Base, Spanish Green, 5 1/2 In., Pair	172.00
Candlestick, Double Twisted Stem, Amber, Signed, 10 In., Pair	495.00
Candlestick, Double Wafer & Baluster Shape, Teardrop, D. Pollard, c.1955, 14 In.	1650.00
Candlestick, Leaf Shape, Nozzle Top, Pale Green Spiral, Air Bubbles, 3 1/2 In., Pair	110.00
Candlestick, Pale Green Nozzles & Twist Stem, Clear Handles, 5 3/4 In., Pair	55.00
Candlestick, Rippled Base, 3 1/2 In., 3 Piece	715.00
Candlestick, Yellow Threading Top & Bottom, Bubbly Crystal, 5 In., Pair	310.00
Centerpiece, Ivrene Bowl, Amethyst Domed Foot, Design 5068, 13 7/8 x 3 3/4 In.	1045.00
Centerpiece, Topaz Bowl, Pale Green Conical Vase, Design 6044, 11 3/4 x 6 1/4 In.	440.00
Champagne, Air Twist, 12 Piece	990.00
Champagne, Swirl, Amber, 7 Oz.	49.00
Compote, Amber, Hollow Stem & Ball Connector, No. 6002, 6 x 6 In.	50.00
Compote, Blue Stem, Mica Flecks, Amber Foot, Swirl Optics, 8 1/4 In.	450.00
Compote, Controlled Bubbles, Topaz Threading, 4 1/2 x 7 In.	65.00
Compote, Rosaline Bowl, Alabaster Hollow Turned Standard, 8 1/2 x 6 In.	357.00
Console, Bristol Yellow, Optic Design, Rolled Edge, Signed, 13 In.	175.00
Cordial, Alabaster, Conical Bowls, Design 3070, 6 In., 4 Piece	66.00
Cordial Set, Teardrop Decanter, Signed, 7 Piece	373.00
Decanter, Liqueur, Air Twist Stopper, 9 1/4 In.	275.00
Dessert Set, Rosaline, Alabaster, Carved, 16 Piece	2000.00
Dish, Apple Form, Signed, 9 In.	330.00
Figurine, Apple, 4 In.	165.00
Figurine, Bird In Flight, Resting On Sphere, Signed, 7 In.	315.00
Figurine, Diving Nymph, Blue	1450.00
Figurine, Giraffe, 15 In.	150.00
Figurine, Lion, Reclining, Walnut Stand, Leather & Velvet Case, 8 1/4 In.	1380.00
Figurine, Pear, 3 In.	143.00
Figurine, Pelican, 6 1/2 In.	1100.00
Figurine, Pheasant, Stylized Feathers, Frederick Carder, c.1932, 6 1/2 In., Pair	2558.00
Figurine, Pouter Pigeon, No. 7729, 7 In.	630.00
Figurine, Rooster, Plinth Base, Signed, 10 In.	760.00
Figurine, September Morn Nymphs, Rosaline, With Base	95.00
Figurine, Snail, 1949, 1 x 2 1/2 In.	105.00
Flower Frog, 2 Tiers, Blue, 1 3/4 x 4 In.	55.00
Glass, Old Fashioned, Donald Pollard Design, 9 Oz., 9 Piece	190.00
Goblet, Crystal & Gold Ruby, 10 In.	1050.00
Goblet, Crystal Teardrop	39.00
Goblet, Curved Handle, Leaping Trout, F. Carder, 1990	1600.00
Goblet, Foliate Pattern, Engraved Black Over Crystal, 9 In.	920.00
Goblet, Gold & Ruby, 10 In.	1050.00
Goblet, Rosaline, Footed	50.00
Goblet, Water, Air Twist, 10 Piece	1100.00
Lamp, Acid Etched, Roycroft Silvered Mount, 24 In., Pair	1705.00
Lamp, Desk, Gilt Metal Harp, Swing Socket, Cluthra Shade, Signed, 14 In.	1725.00
Lamp, Double Cut-Back, Quartz, 25 In.	750.00
Lamp, Floor, Grapevine, Red Over Black Shade, Bronze, 69 In.	2185.00
Lemonade Set, Jade Green, 9 Piece	3500.00
Letter Opener, Crystal Handle, Red Leather Case, Signed	440.00
Night-Light, Greek Wrestlers, Chrome Plated Base, Electric, 9 1/2 x 11 In.	4300.00
Parfait, Oriental Jade, White Pedestal Foot, 6 3/8 In.	373.00
Plate, Audubon, Copper Engraved Parakeet	1150.00
Plate, Audubon, Copper Engraved Pelican	1150.00
Plate, Engraved Flower Center	375.00
Plate, Garland & Swag Design, Jade Over Clear, 8 3/4 In., Pair	330.00

Plate, Rosaline, Engraved 195.00
Rose Bowl, F. Carder... 1300.00
Shade, Gold Gilded Feather Design, Cream Ground, Signed, 4 3/8 In............... 195.00
Sherbet, Rosaline.. 300.00
Sherbet, Rose Highlights, Gold Aurene, Engraved No. 2680, 3 7/8 In. 110.00
Sherbet, Underplate, Blue Calcite 375.00
Sherbet & Underplate, Gold Aurene On Calcite, Gold Label, 2 Piece 225.00
Smoke Set, Cigarette Urn & Ashtray, Signed 235.00
Stemware Set, Trumpet Shape, S. Waugh, 1935, 8 Water, 8 Martini, 16 Piece............. 1495.00
Tumbler, Swirl, Amber, 10 Oz. 59.00
Urn, Federal Pattern, Engraved Eagle, 2 Handles, 13 In...................................... 5500.00
Vase, 3-Part, Thorn, Blue Highlights, Gold Aurene, Engraved, c.1744, 6 1/4 In........... 605.00
Vase, 4 Pulled Feathers, Double Gored Body, Double Hooked Aurene, 5 3/4 In. 3335.00
Vase, 10 Pillar Trumpet Form, Blue Jade, Signed, 5 In. 1495.00
Vase, Acid Cut Back, Pussy Willows, Oviform, Blue Over Frosted White, 6 1/4 In. 3105.00
Vase, Acid Etched, 2 Balancing Acrobats, Footed, Inscribed, 1939, 13 1/2 In. 7475.00
Vase, Bird Design, Acid Cut, 7 In. 1200.00
Vase, Blue Applied Threads, Raindrop, 7 In. 155.00
Vase, Bouquet Vase, George Thompson, Flannel Bag, 1949, 5 1/4 In. 195.00
Vase, Bristol Yellow, Fleur-De-Lis Mark, 10 In. 125.00
Vase, Bubbly Crystal, Green Reeding, 6 In. 85.00
Vase, Bud, Teardrop, Inscribed Chance Cannot Change My Love Nor Time Impair 165.00
Vase, Bud, Trumpet Form, Flat Foot, Pale Green, Acid Etched, 1920s, 10 In................. 275.00
Vase, Calcite, Design 2081, Flared Ribbed Shape, Ring Foot, 8 In...................... 660.00
Vase, Cintra, Green, White & Gray, 7 In.. 550.00
Vase, Clear, Blue Threading, Flared, 5 3/4 x 8 In... 85.00
Vase, Cornucopia, Signed.. 125.00
Vase, Cornucopia, Square Pedestal, Crystal, Signed, 6 In................................... 235.00
Vase, Cyprian, White To Blue Iridescent, Blue Lip, c.1920, 5 In......................... 195.00
Vase, Diamond Quilted Body, Pink Reeding At Top, 7 x 6 In.............................. 165.00
Vase, Double Gourd Shape, Yellow Iridescent, Applied Leaves & Berries, 11 In. 920.00
Vase, Fan, Green, Ball Stem, Diamond Optic, Signed, 8 x 7 In., Pair 450.00
Vase, Fan, Spanish, Green, Random Bubbles, Signed, No. 6287, 8 In. 175.00
Vase, Flared, Crimped Lip, Verre De Soie, 4 In... 120.00
Vase, Florentia, Pink Blossom, Ruffled Rim, Gold Iridescence, Signed, 7 1/2 In. 2100.00
Vase, Fluted Floriform, Pulled Feathering, c.1910, 5 7/8 In................................ 5175.00
Vase, Frosted White Ground, Etched Pussy Willow Trees, Egg Shape, 6 1/4 In. 3100.00
Vase, Grotesque, Amethyst To Clear, Signed, 9 In... 330.00
Vase, Grotesque, Amethyst, c.1920, 11 In.. 575.00
Vase, Grotesque, Pillar Ribbed, Quatraform, White Ivrene, Signed, 6 1/2 In. 690.00
Vase, Grotesque, Pomona Green Top, Clear, Pinched Flared, Ring Foot, Signed, 11 In. 690.00
Vase, Intarsia, Interior Repeating Leaf & Vine, 6-Sided Base, Carder, 7 1/8 In. 8625.00
Vase, Ivrene, Grotesque, Pinched Flared, Ring Footed, 12 In. 580.00
Vase, Ivrene, Iridescent Satin Surface, Signed, 6 In... 800.00
Vase, Jack-In-The-Pulpit, 3 Trumpet, Ivrene, Signed, 12 1/2 In. 1265.00
Vase, Modern Style, Flaring Ribbed Edge, Conical Base, 9 In............................ 120.00
Vase, Pedestal, Light Blue Jade, 7 In. 950.00
Vase, Pink Exterior, Gold Lines & Crackle, Peacock Eyes, Signed, 5 In. 5750.00
Vase, Poppy, Iridized Surface, Ribbed Pink, Carder, 5 x 6 In. 2185.00
Vase, Ribbed Ivory Oval, Black Pedestal Foot, 7 3/4 In..................................... 260.00
Vase, Rosaline Threading, 12 x 7 In. 250.00
Vase, Rose, Applied Lobes, George Thompson, 1959, 10 3/4 In. 315.00
Vase, Stylized 2 Balancing Acrobats, Signed, 1939, 13 1/2 In. 7475.00
Vase, Stylized Figure Of Circe, Sailing Ship, Horse, Signed, 1939, 11 7/8 In. 9200.00
Vase, Tapered Sides, Applied Swirl At Base, 6 1/2 In.. 402.00
Vase, Tyrian, Silver-Blue Trailings, Heart Shaped Leaves, c.1916, 6 3/8 In. 3450.00

STEVENGRAPHS are woven pictures made like fancy ribbons. They were
manufactured by Thomas Stevens of Coventry, England, and became popular
in 1862. Most are marked *Woven in silk by Thomas Stevens* or were mounted
on a cardboard that tells the story of the Stevengraph. Other similar ribbon
pictures have been made in England and Germany.

Bookmark, Unchanging Love, Frame 85.00

Bookmark, Washington Centennial 95.00
Crystal Palace, London, May 10, 1854, 10 x 2 1/4 In. 175.00
Home Sweet Home, Beehives, Cottage, Woman, 12 In. 285.00
Present Time 285.00
Wellington & Blugher, Meeting After Waterloo 275.00

STEVENS & WILLIAMS of Stourbridge, England, made many types of glass,
including layered, etched, cameo, and art glass, between the 1830s and
1930s. Some pieces are signed *S & W*. Many pieces are decorated with flowers, leaves, and other designs based on nature.

Basket, Draped Leaves, Amber Feet, Thorn Handle, 13 1/2 In. 985.00
Bell, Pink & White Overlay, 6 1/2 In. 395.00
Biscuit Jar, Ruffled Glass Leaves, Silver Top, Pink Lined, 7 1/2 In. 395.00
Bowl, Bubbly, Yellow, Late 19th Century, 8 3/4 In. 225.00
Bowl, Rose & Pink Swirled Design, Leaf Shape Base, 5 3/4 In. 450.00
Bowl, Ruffled, Robin's Egg Blue Lining, Shaded Gold, 7 1/2 In. 895.00
Box, Pleated Top, 3 1/2 x 5 1/4 In. 435.00
Fairy Lamp, Stripes, Ruffled Rim On Base, Clarke Cup, 5 1/4 In. 815.00
Pitcher, Silver Rim, Branch Handle, Alternating Stripes, 9 1/2 In. 325.00
Rose Bowl, Acanthus Leaves Form Loop Feet, 4 1/2 In. 385.00
Rose Bowl, Airtrap Swirl 225.00
Rose Bowl, Box-Pleated Top, Opalescent Stripes, 4 1/4 In. 125.00
Rose Bowl, Coral Exterior, Rose Interior, Applied Acanthus Leaf, 4 In. 225.00
Rose Bowl, Quadraform Rim, Pink Liner, Acanthus Leaf Feet, 4 1/2 In. 385.00
Rose Bowl, Rose & Pink Swirled Design, Attached Base, 5 3/4 In. 450.00
Rose Bowl, Thumbprint Pattern, Blue Jewel Glass, 2 1/4 In. 180.00
Vase, Glass Fruit, Horn Shape, Amber Crimped Rim, 13 1/2 In. 275.00
Vase, Intaglio Cut, White Lining, Ruffled Top, 4 1/4 In. 225.00
Vase, Jack-In-The-Pulpit, Pink & White, 15 1/4 In. 300.00
Vase, Pear & Plum Branches, Blue Feet, 6 In. 385.00
Vase, Petal Top, 23 Panels, Greens At Top, Leaves, 2 x 4 In. 205.00
Vase, Pillow, Floral Design, Amber Handles, Pair 700.00
Vase, Pink Flowers, Thorny Feet & Branches, 13 1/2 In. 595.00
Vase, Ruffled Rim, Amber & Cranberry Flower, c.1860, 11 1/2 In. 375.00
Vase, Ruffled, Amber Rim, Applied Leaves, Pink Lining, 4 In. 115.00
Vase, Ruffled, Applied Leaves, Flower Prunt, White Ground, 7 1/2 In. 265.00
Vase, Swirl, Mother-Of-Pearl, Reverse Rubena Verde, 10 In. 468.00
Vase, White Flowers, Leaves, Bands Of Dots, 4 In. 245.00

STONEWARE is a coarse, glazed, and fired potter's ceramic that is used to
make crocks, jugs, bowls, etc. It is often decorated with cobalt blue decorations. Stoneware is still being made.

Barrel, Water, Cobalt Blue Floral, Haxstun, Ottman & Co., 6 Gal. 550.00
Batter Jar, Cobalt Flowers, 9 1/2 In. 264.00
Bottle, C.F. Washburn, 9 In. 50.00
Bottle, Continental, Glazed, 18th Century, 7 1/4 In. 86.00
Bottle, Ginger Beer, Cobalt Blue Advertising, 8 In. 45.00
Bottle, Keller's Inks, Blue & White 200.00
Bottle, Pewter Screw Lid, Ivy, Flowers, Women With Dogs, Brown Glaze, 6 1/2 In. 55.00
Bottle, Salt Glazed, Continental, 18th Century, 7 1/2 In. 86.00
Bowl, Bail Handle, Daisy, Blue & White 110.00
Bowl, Cosmos, Blue & White, 5 In. 58.00
Bowl, Marked 2, Cobalt Blue Flower Both Sides, Flowerpot Shape, 10 1/4 In. 220.00
Bowl, Mixing, Inverted Picket Design, White, 10 In. 12.00
Bowl, Raised Design, Green Glaze, 9 1/2 In. 45.00
Bowl, Wildflower, Blue & White, 6 In. 100.00
Butter, Cover, Swastika 125.00
Butter, Freehand Feather Design, Stencil, James Hamilton 325.00
Canteen, White's Utica Pottery, Miniature 660.00
Cask, Vinegar, Cobalt Blue Design, Legs, 19th Century 650.00
Churn, Brown & White, Cover, Dasher, 2 Gal. 60.00
Churn, Cobalt Blue Design, J. & E. Norton, Bennington, Vt., 18 1/2 In. 132.00
Churn, Cobalt Blue Quill Work Flower, Impressed Label, Ovoid, 18 1/4 In. 220.00

Churn, Cobalt, White & Wood, Binghampton, New York, 1883-1887, 5 Gal. 4600.00
Churn, Foliage Design, Shoulder Handles, F. Fowler 3, 12 1/2 In. 600.00
Churn, Free Hand & Stenciled Label, Williams & Reppert, Pa 5, 17 1/4 In. 300.00
Churn, S. Purdy 4, Spots Of Blue At Handles, 17 3/4 In. 357.00
Churn, Salt Glazed, Stenciled Eagle, 6 Gal. 140.00
Churn, White Hall Sewer Pipe & Stoneware Co., 1 Gal. 450.00
Coffeepot, Horizontal Bands, Staffordshire, Gilded Date, 1747, 10 In. 460.00
Colander, Straight Sides, Dated July 1895 .... 1300.00
Cookie Jar, Hand Painted Pears, Leaves, Blossoms, Applied Handles 125.00
Cooler, Admiration Ice Tea, Cover 195.00
Cooler, Barrel Form 715.00
Cooler, Barrel Shape, Basket Of Flowers, Cobalt Blue, Impressed 10, 21 In. 3850.00
Cooler, Cobalt Florals Each Side, Lambright 8 Westhope, 1865 .... 3750.00
Cooler, Cover, Blue Gray, 8 Blue Narrow Bands, Barrel Shape, 2 Gal. 250.00
Cooler, Incised & Blue Willow Tree, Grazing Cow, 10 Gal. 9350.00
Cooler, Maxwell House Iced Tea, Blue Banded, Contents 400.00
Cooler, Nestea, Green 175.00
Cooler, Western, 4 Gal. 140.00
Creamer, Molded Lilies & Daffodils, Blue & White, 6 3/8 In. 195.00
Crock, 2 Birds, Ottman Bros. & Co., Fort Edward, 1870, 6 Gal. ....*Illus* 1155.00
Crock, A. Conrad, Eagle Stencil, 4 Gal. 550.00
Crock, Backwards Looking Bird, Cobalt Blue Quill Work, N. Clark, 10 1/2 In. 1155.00
Crock, Basket Of Flowers, F.E. Norton, 3 Gal. 1700.00
Crock, Bird & Flower, N.A. White & Son, Utica, N.Y., 6 Gal. ....*Illus* 1815.00
Crock, Bird Decoration, F.E. Norton & Co., Worcester, Mass., 4 Gal. 495.00
Crock, Bird In Wreath, Fort Edward, N.Y., c.1870, 5 Gal. 2550.00
Crock, Bird On Plume, Slip Decorated, N.A. White Co., Binghamton, c.1867, 4 Gal. 440.00
Crock, Blue & White, Lovebirds 495.00
Crock, Blue Bird, Hauxton Ottman & Co., 2 Gal. 395.00
Crock, Blue Design, Ear Handles, No. 3, 11 1/4 In. 200.00
Crock, Blue Flower, Ear Handles, Lid, 7 x 6 In. 175.00
Crock, Blue Indian, 1/2 Gal. 50.00
Crock, Blue Leaf & Wing, Burger & Co., New York, No. 4, 12 In. 350.00
Crock, Blue Lines, Stenciled Label, Dillard, 13 1/2 In. 165.00
Crock, Blue Plume Design, C. Boynton & Co., c.1829, 2 Gal. 275.00
Crock, Chicken Pecking Corn, Ottman Bros. & Co., c.1875, 3 Gal. 635.00
Crock, Chicken, Frank Norton Pottery 4730.00
Crock, Clarkson Crolius, c.1840, 17 In. 525.00
Crock, Cobalt Blue Design, Applied Handles, 11 x 6 In. 495.00
Crock, Cobalt Blue Design, Brown Albany Slip, 8 x 4 3/4 In. 390.00
Crock, Cobalt Blue Design, Bullard & Scott, 2 Gal. 220.00
Crock, Cobalt Blue Design, Handles, Early 19th Century, 3 Gal. 143.00
Crock, Cobalt Blue Flower & 3, 10 In. 214.00
Crock, Cobalt Blue Flower, Whites, Utica, N.Y. Label, 7 1/2 In. 187.00

*Stoneware, Crock, Flower,
John Burger, Rochester,
c.1855, 4 Gal.*

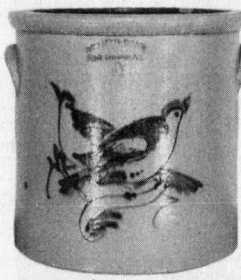

*Stoneware, Crock, 2 Birds,
Ottman Bros. & Co., Fort
Edward, 1870, 6 Gal.*

*Stoneware, Crock, Bird &
Flower, N.A. White & Son,
Utica, N.Y., 6 Gal.*

Crock, Cobalt Blue Stenciled Label, Ovoid, 6 In.	192.00
Crock, Cobalt Blue Stylized Bowtie, A.K. Ballard, Vermont, 1880, 2 Gal.	235.00
Crock, Cobalt Leaf, Gray Salt Glaze, Side Handles, 8 x 7 In.	45.00
Crock, Cobalt Peacock, J. & E. Norton, Bennington, Vermont, 1850s, 11 1/2 In.	7975.00
Crock, Cobalt Stenciled Rooster, 2 Gal.	310.00
Crock, Consumer Exchange, Paris, Illinois	35.00
Crock, Cottage Cheese, Victory Cheese Co., 10 Lb.	125.00
Crock, Cover, Blue & White, 5 x 7 In.	22.00
Crock, E. & L. P. Norton, Bennington, Vt., Cobalt Blue Leaf Design, 7 In.	247.00
Crock, E. & L.P. Norton, Bennington, Vt., 3 Label, Floral Design, 10 1/4 In.	275.00
Crock, Eagle & Roses, A. Conrad, New Geneva, Fayette Co., 3, Label, 11 1/4 In.	412.00
Crock, Elephant Ear Leaves, Union Stoneware Co., 5 Gal.	225.00
Crock, Floral Design, Slip Design, Haxstun & Co., Fort Edward N.Y., c.1880, 4 Gal.	160.00
Crock, Flower, John Burger, Rochester, c.1855, 4 Gal. .... *Illus*	1430.00
Crock, Fuchsia Flower, Offord & Federer, Brownsville, Pa., 4 Gal.	5500.00
Crock, H.J. Heinz Co.	385.00
Crock, Handles, Salt Glaze, Haxstun Co., Fort Edward, N.Y., 1880s, 11 In., 4 Gal.	4675.00
Crock, Impressed Boston, Early 19th Century, 12 1/2 In., 2 Gal.	287.00
Crock, J. Burger Jr., Rochester, N. Y., 2, Cobalt Blue Foliage Design, 9 In.	220.00
Crock, Maxwell House Iced Tea, Blue Banded.	400.00
Crock, Monmouth Pottery Co., Illinois, 4 Gal.	100.00
Crock, Monmouth Pottery, Women In A Crock Stamp, 15 Gal.	360.00
Crock, P.H. Smith, 4 Gal.	185.00
Crock, Shepherdess, Under Pear Tree, 2 Ear Handles, Monongahela River	4100.00
Crock, Straight Sides, A. Conrad	275.00
Crock, Triple Bird Design, West Troy, N.Y. Pottery, c.1880, 12 In. 5 Gal.	963.00
Crock, Wm. Haslage, Pittsburgh, 1 Gal.	180.00
Dish, Soap, Wildflower	250.00
Figurine, Cat, Dark Mustard Glaze, Mogadore, Ohio, 20 In.	2350.00
Figurine, Dog, On Pedestal, 30 In.	880.00
Figurine, Dog, Red Painted, Uhrichsville	375.00
Figurine, Girl On Man's Shoulder, Telcse, 24 1/2 In.	1650.00
Figurine, Head Of Buddha, 17 In.	1100.00
Figurine, Head Of Venus, Socle Base, 15 In.	3520.00
Flagon, Chivas Brothers Ltd., Cork, Queen Elizabeth II Coronation, 1953	200.00
Flask, Figure Of Apostle Over Cluster Of Grapes, Pewter Mounted, 8 1/2 In.	1380.00
Flask, Incised 4 Leaf Clover, Salt Glaze, New York, New Jersey, 6 1/2 In.	1430.00
Foot Warmer, Blue, Brown, Mottled, Portland Stoneware, 1870-1880, 11 1/2 In.	115.00
Fruit, 3 Bunches Of Grapes	60.00
Fruit, Peach, Pear, Orange & Apple	132.00
Funnel, Albany Brown Glaze, Ribbed, 9 x 7 1/2 In.	175.00
Head, Folk Art, Tooled Detail, Greenish-Gray Glaze, Initialed, 4 3/4 In.	38.00
Jar, Basket Of Flowers Stencil, 1/2 Gal.	160.00
Jar, Black Glaze, Ovoid, Impressed Label, S. Robson, Wooster, O., 9 1/4 In.	357.00
Jar, Blue Quill Design, Ovoid, Fort Edward, N.Y., 8 3/4 In.	80.00
Jar, Blue Stenciled & Freehand Label, L.B. Dilliner, New Geneva, Pa., 5, 17 In.	330.00
Jar, Brown, Orange Peel Look, Hewitt, 9 Gal.	325.00
Jar, Butter, Lambrecht, Chicago & Milwaukee	50.00
Jar, Canning, Cobalt Blue Stencil, A. Conrad New Geneva, Fayette, Co., Pa., 8 In.	165.00
Jar, Canning, Cobalt Blue Stencil, A.P. Donagho, Fredericktown, Pa., 9 In.	600.00
Jar, Canning, Cobalt Blue Stencil, Stars, New Geneva Pottery, 8 In.	105.00
Jar, Canning, Cobalt Blue Stenciled Label, 6 1/4 In.	415.00
Jar, Canning, Cobalt Blue Stenciled Label, Pear, Palantine Pottery Co., 8 In.	220.00
Jar, Canning, Cobalt Blue Stenciled Label, Hamilton & Jones, 9 1/2 In.	165.00
Jar, Canning, Cobalt Blue Stenciled Label With Rose, Jas. Hamilton & Co., 10 In.	250.00
Jar, Canning, Crown, Brown Over White, 2 Gal.	12.00
Jar, Canning, Freehand Foliage & Leaves, Gray	125.00
Jar, Canning, Stenciled Label With Shield, Wilton & Jones, 8 1/4 In.	192.00
Jar, Canning, Stenciled Label, W.F. McCoy, Wholesale Dealer, 9 1/4 In.	105.00
Jar, Canning, Stenciled, Hamilton & Jones, Greensboro, Pa.	110.00
Jar, Canning, Three Line, Tin Lid	95.00
Jar, Cobalt Blue Floral Design, Impressed Label, 8 1/4 In.	302.00
Jar, Cobalt Blue Floral Design, Impressed 3, Applied Handles, 13 1/2 In.	93.00

Jar, Cobalt Blue Flower, Handles, Impressed, Golden-Gray Glaze, 12 In. 1210.00
Jar, Cobalt Blue Flower, Impressed Evan B. Jones, Pittston, Pa., 7 7/8 In. 330.00
Jar, Cobalt Blue Foliage, Ovoid, Applied Handles, 9 1/2 In. 385.00
Jar, Cobalt Blue Foliage, Shoulder Handles, Tooled Ridges, 13 1/2 In. 385.00
Jar, Cobalt Blue Handles & Label, Ovoid, Ohio, 9 1/2 In. 192.00
Jar, Cobalt Blue Quill Work Label, T. Reed Newport, Ohio, 6, 15 In. 236.00
Jar, Cobalt Blue Stenciled & Free Hand Label, Hamilton & Jones, 8 /12 In. 357.00
Jar, Cobalt Blue Stenciled & Free Hand Label, I. McCurdy, New Castle, Ohio, 16 In. 715.00
Jar, Cobalt Blue Stenciled Label, Hamilton & Jones, Greenboro, Pa. 6, 16 1/2 In. 429.00
Jar, Cobalt Blue Stenciled Label, Ovoid, James Hamilton & Co., Pa., 9 3/4 In. 105.00
Jar, Cobalt Blue Stenciled Label, T.S. Reppert, 13 1/2 In. 300.00
Jar, Cobalt Blue Stenciled, Hamilton & Jones, Greensboro, Pa., 9 In. 305.00
Jar, Cobalt Blue Vining Tulip, Impressed, 11 3/4 In. 193.00
Jar, Cobalt Blue, Stenciled Label, Ovoid, A. Conrad New Geneva, Pa., 6 1/2 In. 155.00
Jar, Cobalt Blue, Stenciled Label, Sibb J. Beighel, Pleasant Unity, Pa., 9 1/4 In. 385.00
Jar, Cobalt Blue, Stenciled Label, Stripes, Jas. Hamilton & Co., Greensboro, 8 In. 95.00
Jar, Cobalt Stencil, Label, Jas. Hamilton & Sons, Greensboro, Pa., 3, 13 1/2 In. 440.00
Jar, Excelsior Works, Straight Sides, 1/2 Gal. 350.00
Jar, Floral Design, J. & E. Norton, Bennington, Vt., 2, 11 1/2 In. 275.00
Jar, Free Hand Tulips & Stencil, Isaac Hewitt Jr., 4 Gal. 160.00
Jar, Handles At Neck, Amber Glaze Over Slip On Sides, Liang Dynasty, 5 In. 1840.00
Jar, Impressed Boston 2, Brown, Gray Band, Applied Handles, Ovoid, 12 In. 300.00
Jar, Incised Shoulder Wave Design, Tambo, 19th Century, 11 1/2 In. 330.00
Jar, Open Handle, Crolius, Large 880.00
Jar, R.T. Williams, New Geneva, Pa., 6 Gal. 230.00
Jar, Salt Glaze, Impressed S. Amboy, N. Jersey, c.1810, 1 Gal. 2970.00
Jar, Shoulder Handles, Cobalt Blue Floral Wreath, Impressed 4, 10 3/4 In. 420.00
Jar, Tooled Band, Applied Shoulder Handles, Reddish Brown Glaze, 20 In. 75.00
Jardiniere, Daisies In Medallion, Blue & White 389.00
Jug, 2 Birds, Number 3 In Cobalt Blue Quill Work, S. Hart, 14 In. 825.00
Jug, Bird On Branch, Cobalt Blue Slip, Impressed No., 15 5/8 In. 440.00
Jug, Bird On Nest, Cowden & Wilcox, 2 Gal. 2640.00
Jug, Blue & White Bands, John M. Connelly, Elmira, N.Y., 1 Gal. 125.00
Jug, Blue Bird Design, Edmunds & Co., 14 In. 300.00
Jug, Blue Bird Design, New York, Stoneware Co., 14 In. 300.00
Jug, Blue Maple Leaf, E. & L.P. Norton, Bennington, Vt., 11 In. 200.00
Jug, Blue Stenciled & Freehand Label, Hamilton & Jones, Pa., 2, 14 In. 165.00
Jug, Bluebird On Branch, Fort Edward Co., 2 Gal. 1200.00
Jug, Boston 2, Gray Salt Glaze, Olive Highlights, Strap Handle, Ovoid, 15 In. 220.00
Jug, Brown & White, Peekskill Wine & Liquor Co., N.Y., 1/2 Gal. 45.00
Jug, Brown Albany Slip, Spout, E. & L. P. Norton, Bennington, Vt. 2, 12 In. 165.00
Jug, Charlestown 2, Cobalt Blue Highlights, Ovoid, 13 1/2 In. 220.00
Jug, Cobalt Blue Codfish, Ovoid-Form, Marked Charlestown, c.1800-1810, 17 In. 1870.00
Jug, Cobalt Blue Design, Impressed 3, 16 1/2 In. 95.00
Jug, Cobalt Blue Design, Label, D.W. Graves, Westmoreland 2, 13 1/4 In. 193.00
Jug, Cobalt Blue Floral & 2, Impressed S., Hart Fulton, 12 In. 330.00
Jug, Cobalt Blue Floral Design, Ovoid, Strap Handle, 13 1/4 In. 220.00
Jug, Cobalt Blue Floral Design, Whites, Utica, 15 1/2 In. 165.00
Jug, Cobalt Blue Floral, Marked 2, Ovoid, 13 1/2 In. 220.00
Jug, Cobalt Blue Flower, No. 3, 1850s 180.00
Jug, Cobalt Blue Flower, Ovoid, Strap Handle, 14 In. 138.00
Jug, Cobalt Blue Leaf, Fort Edward, New York, 11 1/4 In. 225.00
Jug, Cobalt Blue Name, Louis J. Miller & Co., Boston, Mass., 1 Gal. 90.00
Jug, Cobalt Blue Stencil Label, Hamilton & Jones, Greensboro, Pa., 9 5/8 In. 115.00
Jug, Cobalt Blue Turkey, Strap Handle, Ovoid, 13 1/2 In. 1100.00
Jug, Cobalt Blue Woman, Bending Over, Looking Through Legs, N.Y., 1810, 3 Gal. 10350.00
Jug, Cobalt Blue, Cylindrical, Jones & Co., 11 1/4 In. 115.00
Jug, Cobalt Blue, Stenciled Label, A. Conrad, New Geneva, Pa., 11 1/4 In. 247.00
Jug, Cobalt, Incised, Royal Cipher, GR, 17th Century, Germany, Westerwald, 10 In. 690.00
Jug, Daniel Nooman Dealer In Groceries, New York, Floral, Blue Slip, 13 In. 132.00
Jug, Eat, Drink & Be Merry, Brown & White, Miniature 32.50
Jug, EE Hall & Co., Boston, Mass., 2 Gal. 595.00

♦♦♦♦♦♦♦♦♦♦♦♦♦♦♦♦♦♦♦♦♦♦♦♦♦

Light can damage many types of antiques. Furniture finish will fade, and textiles and paper will fade or darken. Light will also weaken wood and fabric.

♦♦♦♦♦♦♦♦♦♦♦♦♦♦♦♦♦♦♦♦♦♦♦♦♦

Stoneware, Syrup, Fern Leaf Design, Cream, Black Interior & Rim, 1850

Jug, Egyptian Design, Brown, Tan Frieze, Oviform, Lambeth, 1884, 8 In.	495.00
Jug, Floral Design, Slat Glaze, 2 Gal.	200.00
Jug, Gray Design, Noah White, Utica, N.Y.	140.00
Jug, Handles, Impressed A.K. Ballard, Burlington, Vt., 1860s, 3 Gal.	3575.00
Jug, Heron, Beak In Gin Bottle, Label In Banner, Timothy McCarty, 11 In.	600.00
Jug, Hollister Wilson Laboratories, Chicago, 1 Gal.	75.00
Jug, Huntingware Design, Brown & Tan Panels, Lambeth, 1869-1872, 7 1/2 In.	475.00
Jug, Impressed Label, S. Purdy 2, Ohio, 14 1/4 In.	330.00
Jug, Incised Cobalt Blue Design, Impressed S.D.R., 19th Century, 4 1/2 In.	6325.00
Jug, James Bell, 105 Market Street, Paterson, N.J., 2 Gal.	135.00
Jug, Jas. J. Donnelly, Paterson, N.J.	198.00
Jug, Jugtown Ware, Green Glaze, 4 1/2 In.	193.00
Jug, Man In The Moon, Cowden & Wilcox, 2 Gal.	5225.00
Jug, Milk, Cover, Diamond & Chevron Pattern, Staffordshire, 1765, 6 1/4 In.	345.00
Jug, No. 4, Ballard & Brothers, Burlington, Vt.	240.00
Jug, Sour Mash, Blue & White Bands, Geo. A. Dickel & Co., c.1888, 1 Gal.	125.00
Jug, Star Liquor Co., Buffalo, N.Y., 1/2 Gal.	65.00
Jug, Utility, Mustard & Beige Panels, Lambeth, 1858, 1890, 5 1/2 In.	95.00
Jug, Wine, Swan, D. Breeze	150.00
Keg, Brandy, Blue Open Mouthed Pike, Wooden Spigot	8800.00
Mug, Horizontal Ring Turnings, Flared Foot, England, 3 5/8 In.	1495.00
Pitcher, Apricot, Blue & White	140.00
Pitcher, Basket Weave & Flower, Blue & White, 9 In.	125.00
Pitcher, Blue & White, Northstar, Grapes	90.00
Pitcher, Brown, No Design, 1 Qt.	55.00
Pitcher, Castle, Fishscale, Blue & White	225.00
Pitcher, Cobalt Blue Quilled Work Design, Ovoid, Impressed 1 1/2, 11 In.	220.00
Pitcher, Dutch Farm	180.00 to 190.00
Pitcher, Eagle, American Pottery Co.	3400.00
Pitcher, Fannie Flagg, Blue & White	275.00
Pitcher, Huntsman, Stag, Blue & Gray	300.00
Pitcher, Leaping Deer, Blue & White	175.00
Pitcher, Milk, Cow, Girl, Don't Cry Over Spilled Milk, Trenton Potteries	95.00
Pitcher, Molded Busts, Dog's Head, Spout, Blue & White, 10 1/2 In.	100.00
Pitcher, Morning Glory, Blue & White	150.00
Pitcher, Rockingham Glaze, Peoria Pottery Co.	500.00
Pitcher, Rose Decal, Blue & White, 7 In.	100.00
Pitcher, Sponge Band Top & Base, Blue Bands Around Middle, White	395.00
Pitcher, White's Pottery, Embossed Deer, Inscription, Bristol Glaze	265.00
Plate, Grey Portrait, Peter Voulkos, c.1955, 15 In.	1035.00
Roaster, Cover, Wildflower, Blue & White	245.00
Rolling Pin, Brown & White, Advertising	100.00
Rolling Pin, Wildflower	195.00
Ruler, Western Stoneware	55.00

Sugar & Creamer, Hunt Scene, Sterling Silver Rims 165.00
Syrup, Fern Leaf Design, Cream, Black Interior & Rim, 1850 ....*Illus* 125.00
Talcum, Baseball Shape, Batter Up 35.00
Teapot, Bulbous, 3 Paw Feet, Blue Salt Glaze, Littler's, c.1750, 3 1/2 In. 489.00
Teapot, Hinged Cover, Fretwork Panels, Dutch Silver Spout, 5 In. 2300.00
Teapot, Pear Shape, Chrysanthemum Plants, Dragons, Chinese Red, 5 In. 4312.00
Umbrella Stand, Impressed Floral Bands 400.00
Vase, Cardew Abuja, 11 In. 1200.00
Water Cistern, Blue Band Of Flowers, Plaque, Ice Water, Spigot, 18 1/2 In. 205.00
Whimsy, Heart, Applied Flowers, Clasped Handles, Blue, Gray, E. Smallsreed, 1904 ... 575.00

STORE fixtures, cases, cutters, and other items that have no advertising as
part of the decoration are listed here. Most items found in an old store are
listed in the Advertising category in this book.

Back Bar, Mirrors, Oak, 16 Ft. 2500.00
Barrel, Brass Tap, Says Rum, Brandy & Gin, 3 Piece 660.00
Bin, Pine, Divided, Lift Lid, 45 x 17 x 35 In. 193.00
Cabinet, Bolt, Revolving Octagonal Form, 80 Drawers, Glass Knobs, 63 x 31 In. 3800.00
Cabinet, Display, 2 Shelves, 1 Long Over 2 Drawers, Lighted 50.00
Cabinet, Seed, Grain Painted, 20 Drawers, 5 x 5 Ft. 2800.00
Cabinet, Seed, Individual Glass Front Compartments, Oak, 12 Ft. 3500.00
Case, Display, 3 Glass Sides, Top & 4 Mirrored Back Doors, 43 x 103 In. 725.00
Case, Display, Beveled Doors & Sides, Lighted, Henredon, 31 x 15 x 82 In., Pair 1610.00
Case, Display, Counter, Aluminum Base, Rounded Front, 13 x 24 x 24 In. 198.00
Case, Display, Counter, Oak, Metal Corners, 15 x 34 x 27 In. 257.00
Case, Display, Mahogany, Glass Doors, Wooden Shelves, 50 x 36 x 14 In. 275.00
Case, Display, Oak, Glass, 7 x 47 x 12 In. 264.00
Case, Display, Oak, Slant Front, Glass Shelves, 54 x 25 x 24 In. 257.00
Case, Display, Poplar, 3 Glass Slides, Hinged Door, 2 Glass Shelves, 34 In. 148.00
Case, Pharmacy, 5 Drawers For Various Items 120.00
Chest, Apothecary, 29 Drawers, Gray Painted, 69 In. 3295.00
Chest, Wooden, Painted, 18 Short Over 4 Medium Over 3 Large Drawers, 29 x 55 In... 2990.00
Coffee Grinders are listed in their own category
Dispenser, Tape, Counter, Ornate, Victorian, Cast Iron 85.00
Form, Display, Bras 22.00
Freezer, Ice Cream, Drugstore, 3 Doors, Brass Hardware, Oak, 8 Ft. 1400.00
Hat Stand, Child's Head Base 95.00
Hat Stand, Fashion Model's Head Base 140.00
Holder, Postcard, Ferris Wheel 1500.00
Humidor, Cigar, Glass, Pat. Dec. 7, 1915 .... 50.00
Malt Machine, Arnold No. 15 .... 155.00
Mannequin, Child, 25 In., Pair 60.00
Milk Shake Machine, Hamilton-Beach, Soda Fountain, Brass, 14 In. 440.00
Nail Cup, Hardware, Rotating, Cast Iron, Rotating, 8 Pie-Shaped Sections, 1860 .... 175.00
Safe, Victorian, Hall's Safe & Lock Co., Painted, 27 x 17 1/2 In. 475.00
Showcase, Mahogany, U-Form, Paneled Fronts, Glass Top, Victorian, 45 x 92 x 81 In. 2530.00
Stand, Shoeshine, Flip Top, Shoe Holder, Front Opens To Supplies, Pine, 9 x 18 In. 195.00
String Holder, Countertop, Cast Iron 20.00
String Holder, Wood, Brass & Iron Cutting Blade Finial, Pease, 5 In. 270.00
Tin, General Store, Slanted Hinged Cover, Gold Design, Black, W. Pepper, 8 x 10 1/2 In. 95.00

STOVES have been used in America for heating since the eighteenth century
and for cooking since the nineteenth century. Most types of wood, coal, gas,
kerosene, and even some electric stoves are collected.

Acorn, Nickleled, Isinglass 1000.00
Backpack, Coleman, Model 530, Aluminum Cup Container 25.00
Backpack, Seva, Model 106, Sweden, Brass 75.00
Camp, Coleman, Model 425, 2 Burner, Self-Contained, Folding Stand, 1930s 75.00
Camp, Winchester 100.00
Cook, Majestic, Wood Burning, 1895 .... 2500.00
Cook, Marklin, Copper Containers 1850.00
Glenwood, Enamel & Chrome, Double Back Shelves, 1812 .... 695.00

Home Comfort, Wrought Iron Range Co., St. Louis 200.00
Kitchen, Glenwood, 1937 .... 650.00
Kitchen, Roper, Porcelain, 1910, 48 x 36 In. 1420.00
Parlor, 10 Ceramic Tiles In Frame Over Top, Cast Iron, 1925 .... 995.00
Parlor, Morrison & Manning, Anthemion & Drapery Swags 1700.00
Parlor, Summit, Base Burner, c.1905 .... 3950.00
Portable, Isinglass Chimney, Whale Oil Burner, Patent 1854, 8 In. 55.00
Railroad, Caboose, Denver & Rio Grande 3000.00
Sylvan, No. 5, Cast Iron 82.00
Universal, Circular, Silver Gilt Urn Finial, Cast Iron, 1912, 78 In. 770.00

SUMIDA, or Sumida Gawa, is a Japanese pottery. The pieces collected by that name today were made about 1895 to 1970. There has been much confusion about the name of this ware, and it is often called *Korean Pottery*. Most pieces have a very heavy orange-red, blue, or green glaze, with raised three-dimensional figures as decorations.

Bowl, Geometric & Foliate Design, Blue On Celadon, 7 1/4 In., Pair 58.50
Figurine, Bearded Elder, Seated, Kneeling Woman 375.00
Figurine, Young Man, Walking, Backpack 275.00
Mug, Applied Monkey, Enamel Drip At Top, 4 1/2 In. 90.00
Mug, Child About To Throw Ball, Dog Watching, 5 1/2 In. 225.00
Mug, Man With Plant Front, Enamel Drip Border, 5 1/4 In. 225.00
Mug, Wise Man At Center, Black Ground, Enamel Border & Handle, 5 1/2 In. 150.00
Pitcher, Red & Blue Porcelain Top, Leopards Crouching On Limbs, 10 In. 500.00
Tankard, 2 Boys, Drip Glaze, Signed, Impressed Mark, 9 1/4 In. 275.00

SUNBONNET BABIES were first introduced in 1900 in the book *The Sunbonnet Babies.* The stories were by Eulalie Osgood Grover, illustrated by Bertha Corbett. The children's faces were completely hidden by the sunbonnets. The children had been pictured in black and white before this time, but the color pictures in the book were immediately successful. The Royal Bayreuth China Company made a full line of children's dishes decorated with the Sunbonnet Babies. Some Sunbonnet Babies plates have been reproduced, but are clearly marked.

Bell, Cleaning 300.00
Bowl, Feeder 85.00
Box, Washing 488.00
Cake Plate, Handled, Blue Mark 275.00
Candleholder, 4 In. 95.00
Candleholder, Washing, 5 x 1 3/4 In. 225.00
Chocolate Pot, Fishing 1035.00
Compote, Sweeping 345.00
Creamer, Washing, Blue Mark 145.00
Dish, Nut, Mending 200.00
Hatpin Holder 980.00
Pitcher, Fishing, 4 In. 175.00
Pitcher, Washing, Square Base, Ruffled Rim 345.00
Plate, Baking, Handle, 1974 .... 40.00
Plate, Ironing, Harker, 7 In. 90.00
Plate, Mending, 6 1/2 In. 165.00

SUNDERLAND luster is a name given to a special type of pink luster made by Leeds, Newcastle, and other English firms during the nineteenth century. The luster glaze is metallic and glossy and appears to have bubbles in it. Other pieces of luster are listed in the Luster category.

Bowl, Masonic, Luster, 1800-1820, 8 1/4 In. 715.00
Mug, Ship, Enamel, Here's To The Wind That Blows, 19th Century, 4 1/2 In. 287.00
Pitcher, An East View Of New Bridge, Sunderland, 9 In. 550.00
Pitcher, Black Transfer, Crimea, Verse, Polychrome Enamel, 7 1/2 In. 330.00
Pitcher, Milk, British Warship Northumberland, Masonic Poem, 7 In. 245.00
Plate, Ship Under Sail, Drilled For Hanging, 8 In. 175.00
Watch Holder, Tall Case, Pink Luster, England, 1825, 11 In. .... *Illus* 920.00

Sunderland, Watch Holder,
Tall Case, Pink Luster,
England, 1825, 11 In.

◆◆◆◆◆◆◆◆◆◆◆◆◆◆◆◆◆◆◆◆◆◆◆

If you live in an old house and the locks are old, check the new types. There have been many improvements, and new locks provide much better security.

◆◆◆◆◆◆◆◆◆◆◆◆◆◆◆◆◆◆◆◆◆◆◆

SUPERMAN was created by two seventeen-year-olds in 1938. The first issue of *Action* comics had the strip. Superman remains popular and became the hero of a radio show in 1940, cartoons in the 1940s, a television series, and several major movies.

Airplane, Corgi, 1930s	25.00
Bank, Bust, Plastic, Mego, 1974	65.00
Belt Buckle, Signed, Lee Company, 1950	98.00
Card, Membership Club, 1940s	120.00
Clock, Alarm, Westclock, 1939	1500.00
Coloring Book, The Missile Base Mystery, Whitman, 1977	6.00
Cookie Jar, Silver, California Originals	300.00 to 675.00
Costume, Captain Action	150.00
Cup, Superman Figure Hands Attached, White, R. Rumars, DC Comics, 1985	2.00
Doll, Energized, Remco, 12 In., Box	70.00
Game, Board, Hasbro, 1978	25.00
Game, Card, Whitman, 1966	30.00
Game, Flying Bingo	17.00
Game, Quoit Set, Box	65.00
Glass, Supergirl, Moon Superheroes	11.00
Glass, Superman The Movie, Lois Lane, Moon Superheroes	5.00
Gum Wrapper, 1966	27.00
Jigsaw Puzzle, No. 1540, American Publishing, 1973, 81 Piece	17.00
Lunch Box, Metal, King Seeley Thermos, 1967	125.00
Lunch Box, Metal, Universal, 1954	150.00
Lunch Box, Thermos Only, 1967	50.00
Nutcracker, Figural, DC Comics, 1979, 10 In.	38.00
Paddle Ball, Blue Transparent Plexiglas, Yellow Logo, 1966	65.00
Pen, Fountain, 1947	250.00
Pillowcase, Graphics, 1930s	125.00
Pin, Club, Superman Of America, Bright Colors, 1950s	85.00
Pin, Official Member Superman Club, Pinback, 1966, 3 1/2 In.	25.00
Pin, Read Superman Action Comics Magazine, Tin Lithograph, 1940	75.00
Pin, Superman Club Membership, Pinback, Color, 1965	1.00
Play Set, Play City, 19 Figures, Vinyl, 1970s, Box	85.00
Puppet, Marionette	25.00
Puzzle, Jigsaw	35.00
Puzzle, Sliding, American Publishing, 1978	12.00
Ray Gun, 1950s	100.00
Record Player, DC Comics, 1978	125.00
Ring, Crusader's	250.00
Ring, Gold Metal, Nestle's, DC, 1976	35.00

Soaky	45.00
Swim Fins, Official	95.00
Thermos, England, 1971	75.00
Toy, Turn Over Tank, Chrome, 1940, 4 In.	850.00
Valentine Card, Fold-Out, Little Boy Saying I'm No Superman, 1940	75.00
Van, Die Cast, Corgi, 1979	20.00
View-Master, 3 Reels, 1938, Box	75.00
Whistle, Tin Lithograph, Blond Hair, Japan, 1950s, 2 3/4 x 1 1/2 In.	85.00

SUSIE COOPER began as a designer in 1925 working for the English firm A.E. Gray & Company. In 1932 she formed Susie Cooper Pottery, Ltd. In 1950 it became Susie Cooper China, Ltd., and the company made china and earthenware. In 1966 it was acquired by Josiah Wedgwood & Sons, Ltd. The name Susie Cooper appears with the company names on many pieces of ceramics.

Cup & Saucer, Brown, Tan Rings	20.00
Dish, Baby's	125.00
Plate Set, Hand Painted, 12 Piece	195.00

SWANKYSWIGS are small drinking glasses. In 1933, the Kraft Food Company began to market cheese spreads in these decorated, reusable glass tumblers. They were discontinued from 1941 to 1946, then made again from 1947 to 1958. Then plain glasses were used for most of the cheese, although a few special decorated Swankyswigs have been made since that time. A complete list of prices can be found in *Kovels' Price Guide to Depression Glass & American Dinnerware*.

Atlantic City, Cobalt Blue, 5 In.	25.00
Band, No. 2, 4 3/4 In.	7.00
Bank, No. 2, Black & Red, 3 3/8 In.	4.00
Bustlin' Betsy, Yellow, 3 3/4 In.	4.00
Checkerboard, Green	27.00
Checkerboard, Red	25.00
Circles & Dot, Blue, 4 3/4 In.	8.00
Circles & Dot, Green, 3 1/2 In.	5.00
Cornflower, No. 1, Light Blue, 3 1/2 In.	5.00
Cornflower, No. 2, Yellow	3.00
Forget-Me-Not, Dark Blue, 3 1/2 In.	3.00
Forget-Me-Not, Red, 3 1/2 In.	3.00
Forget-Me-Not, Yellow	3.00
Kiddie Cup, Duck & Horse, Black	10.00
Lily Of The Valley, Red & Black, 4 3/4 In.	10.00
Posy, Cornflower, No. 1, Blue, 4 5/8 In.	12.00
Posy, Daffodil, Yellow	4.00
Posy, Jonquil, Yellow, 3 1/2 In.	4.00
Posy, Tulip, Red, 4 5/8 In.	12.00
Posy, Violet, Purple, 3 1/2 In.	5.00
Sailboat, Red, 4 1/2 In.	15.00
Sailboat, White, 4 3/4 In.	25.00
Stars, Green, 3 1/2 In.	4.00
Tavern, Silver, 4 3/4 In.	15.00
Texas Centennial, Green	22.00
Tulip, No. 1, Black, 3 1/2 In.	4.00
Tulip, No. 1, Red, 3 1/2 In.	4.00
Tulip, No. 3, Light Blue, 3 3/4 In.	3.00
Tulip, No. 3, Yellow, 3 3/4 In.	3.00
Tulip, Red	25.00

SWORDS of all types that are of interest to collectors are listed here. The military dress sword with elaborate handle is probably the most wanted. Be sure to display swords in a safe way, out of reach of children.

Army Officer, Nazi, Bird-Head Pommel, Swastika In Eagle's Claw, 35 In.	165.00

Bayonet, 45/70, Scabbard, 1874	95.00
Bayonet, Civil War, Metal Scab, New Jersey, U.S. Springfield	155.00
Bayonet, Mauser	30.00
Bayonet, Ramrod, For 45/70 Rifle	48.00
Bayonet, Revolutionary War, England, 23-In. Blade, 28 In.	88.00
Brass Hilt, Ebony Grip, War Of 1812, 29 In.	375.00
Cavalry Officer's, Lion Head Pommel, Napoleonic Period, 30 In.	450.00
Child's, D-Guard, Metal Scabbard, Wire & Leather Wooden Hilt, 1800	220.00
China, Inlaid Figural Design On Blade, Ivory & Bronze Handle, 42 1/2 In.	287.00
Civil War Officer's, Etched U.S., Eagle, Flags On Blade, Horsstmann & Son, 37 In.	660.00
Crescent Terminal Edge, Black Scale Finish, Konda, 15 1/2 In.	365.00
Cutlass, Revolutionary War, Stamped R, 28 3/4 In.	290.00
Dagger, Carved Woman's Head, African Ivory, 15 1/2 In.	40.00
Dagger, Officer's, Japanese, Sharkskin Handle	150.00
Dagger, Officer's, Luftwaffe	350.00
Dirk, Scottish Highland, Silver Mounted, Victorian, Notch-Pierced Back, 17 1/4 In.	920.00
Fighting, Foliage Form Grip, Brass Hilt, c.1850, 31 In.	250.00
Gauntlet, Medieval Style	375.00
Georgian, Serrated Edge, Wilkinson	143.00
Hunter's, Stag Hilt, Brass Shell & Mountings, Revolutionary War, 18 1/2 In.	285.00
Infantry, Brass & Wooden Hilt, England, c.1750, 24 3/4 In.	475.00
Ivory Scabbard, Carved, Japan, 30 In.	350.00
Japan, Military, Metal Handle, Machine Made	220.00
Knights Golden Eagle, Gilded, Ceremonial, 36 1/2 In.	95.00
Musician's, Model 1840, C. Roby, 28-In. Blade, Gilded Brass Hilt	192.00
Officer's, Confederate, Leather Grip, Wire Wrap, 31 1/2-In. Blade, 37 In.	3300.00
Officer's, German, W.K. & C., c.1900, 31-In. Blade	126.00
Officer's, Imperial German, Brass Hilt, Silver Wire Wrapped, 27 In.	180.00
Officer's, Naval, Germany, World War I, Folding Anchor Guard, Carl Eickhorn	770.00
Officer's, Naval, Lion-Head Pommel, Crown Of Spain, c.1898, 36 In.	1265.00
Officer's, Naval, Seki Tang, Shark-Skin Case, Yoshimitsu, Japan, 26 1/4 In.	747.00
Saber, Cavalry, Gilded Brass Hilt, Steel Scabbard, 1860	632.00
Saber, Cavalry, Sheble & Fisher, Phila., Leather Handle, Scabbard, 1860, 35 In.	495.00
Saber, English Horseman's, Wired Wrapped Grip, 1700, 33 3/4 In.	975.00
Saber, Lion Pommel, Branch Guard, Engraved Blade, American, Short	2200.00
Saber, Officer's, Western, Engraved Blade, Horn Handle, Scabbard, 1902	200.00
Saber, Revolutionary War, Brass Hilt, 10-In. Blade, 33 1/2 In.	935.00
Saber, Scabbard Of War Of 1812, Brass Guard, Carved Hilt, 27 1/2 In.	310.00
Saber, Silver Hilt, Gold Filled Engraving, Eagle & Soldier, c.1810	1485.00
Sailor Made, Carved, Inlaid Band Of Exotic Wood, 19th Century, 42 3/4 In.	345.00
Samurai, Cloth Wrapped Sharkskin Handle, 30 1/2 In.	1760.00
Samurai, Navy, Military, World War II	250.00
Scabbard, Officer's, Schuller Hartley & Graham, New York	550.00
Short, D-Guard, Black Painted Oak Hilt, Forged Blade & Guard, American, 24 In.	300.00
Silver Hilt, Chased Putti, Heroic Figures, France, c.1730, 30 1/4-In. Blade	4140.00
Stiletto, Wooden Case, 13 In.	75.00
U.S. Army, Non-Commissioned Officer, Model 1840, 32-In. Blade, 37 In.	220.00

SYRACUSE is a trademark used by the Onondaga Pottery of Syracuse, New York. The company was established in 1871. It is still working. The name became the Syracuse China Company in 1966. It is known for fine dinnerware and restaurant china.

SYRACUSE
iïïi *China*

Compote, Floral Garland, Green Border, Portrait Medallions, 7 x 4 In.	15.00
Cup & Saucer, Jefferson	15.00
Cup & Saucer, Roses, Leaves, Molded Scrolls, Sprayed Gold	12.00
Dinner Set, Calypso, Blue & Green, 44 Piece	175.00
Dish, Olive, Floral Quadruple Border, 4 Urn Medallions	6.00
Pitcher, Figural Herbert Hoover, Cream, No. 1390, 6 x 7 In.	80.00
Plate, Indian Standing In Canoe, 10 In.	35.00
Soup, Dish, Jefferson	7.00

TAPESTRY, PORCELAIN, see Rose Tapestry category

Tea Leaf Ironstone, Relish, Elsmore Forster Ceres;
Tea Leaf Ironstone, Relish, Shaw Niagara Fan;
Tea Leaf Ironstone, Relish, Teaberry

TEA CADDY is the name for a small box made to hold tea leaves. In the eighteenth century, tea was very expensive and it was stored under lock and key. The first tea caddies were made with locks. By the nineteenth century, tea was more plentiful and the tea caddy was larger. Often there were two sections, one for green tea, one for black tea.

Brass Scrollwork, Incised Escutcheon Plates, Victorian, 4 1/4 In.	125.00
Copper, Russia, 4 1/2 In., Pair	150.00
Ivory, Knobbed Cover, Fitted, 1850, 5 1/2 In.	1050.00
Lacquerware, Boat, Side-Wheel, Figural, 1st Voyage On Pearl River, Gilt, 21 In.	13200.00
Mahogany, Bands Of Marquetry, 2 Compartments, Lock With Key, 10 In.	210.00
Mahogany, Georgian, 8 In.	125.00
Mahogany, Inlaid, Fitted Interior, Hepplewhite	495.00
Mahogany, Inlaid, Hinged Top, Fitted With 2 Compartments, 6 x 12 x 6 In.	175.00
Mahogany, Regency, Bun Feet, Flaring Sides, 9 x 14 x 7 1/2 In.	440.00
Mahogany, Sarcophagus Shape, 12 In.	192.00
Mahogany & Satinwood, Floral Inlay, Victorian, 6 1/8 x 12 1/8 In.	115.00
Mahogany Inlay, Tin Fitted Interior, English	440.00
Mahogany Veneer, 3 Sections, Metal Foil Traces, 9 1/2 In.	275.00
Moorish Style, Chamfered Cover, W.R. Nutt & Co., Repousse Panels, 4 1/2 In.	155.00
Porcelain, Hand Painted, Sabinerraub, Vienna, 19th Century, 5 In.	450.00
Rosewood, Hinged Top, Inner 2 Canisters & Glass Dish, Incurving Sides	500.00
Rosewood, Mother-Of-Pearl Swans & Birds, Regency, 13 In.	440.00
Rosewood, Pressed Glass Mixer, 1835, 12 1/2 x 6 x 6 3/4 In.	385.00
Rosewood, Veneered, Ivory Inlay, Regency, 1810-1820, 5 3/4 In.	330.00
Silver, Dragonflies & Insects, Inverted Pyriform, Cover, Dominick & Haff, 4 In.	2100.00
Silver Plate, Barrel Form, Chased Floral & Scroll Waist Band, Whiting, 4 In.	375.00
Silver Plate, Equestrian Scenes, English, 4 1/2 In.	345.00
Silver Plate, Oval, Embossed Figures, Continental, 5 In.	154.00
Stumpwork, England	600.00
Tortoiseshell, Molded Chinoiserie Designs	4400.00
Tortoiseshell, Regency, Hinged Top, 2 Lidded Compartments, 8 In.	1150.00
Tortoiseshell & Ivory, Regency, Domed Lid, Ring Handles, 11 In.	1265.00
Wood, Apple Shape, England	4750.00
Wood, Lacquered, Dome Top, 2 Sections With Covers, Olive, 8 In.	220.00

TEA LEAF IRONSTONE dishes are named for their decorations. There was a superstition that it was lucky if a whole tea leaf unfolded at the bottom of your cup. This idea was translated into the pattern of dishes known as *tea leaf*. By 1850, at least twelve English factories were making this pattern, and by the 1870s, it was a popular pattern in many countries. The tea leaf was always a luster glaze on early wares, although now some pieces are made with a brown tea leaf.

◆ ◆ ◆ ◆ ◆ ◆ ◆ ◆ ◆ ◆ ◆ ◆ ◆ ◆ ◆ ◆ ◆ ◆

Rinse food off plates as soon as possible after use to avoid stains.

◆ ◆ ◆ ◆ ◆ ◆ ◆ ◆ ◆ ◆ ◆ ◆ ◆ ◆ ◆ ◆ ◆ ◆

Tea Leaf Ironstone, Soup Tureen,
Brocade Pattern, Cover, Ladle

Bowl, Mellor, Taylor, 10 In.	85.00
Butter, Cover, Square	75.00
Butter, Cover, Tea Leaf Drainer, Square, Meakin	165.00
Butter Chip, Chelsea, Johnson Bros., 6 Piece	60.00
Casserole, Cover, Pedestal Base, 6 1/2 x 11 In.	250.00
Chamber Pot, Cover	75.00
Chamber Pot, Cover, Cable, Shaw	175.00
Chamber Pot, Cover, Square, Ridged, Wedgwood	175.00
Chamber Pot, Flower Finial, Copper Luster	325.00
Chamber Pot, Lionshead, Mellor, Taylor	185.00
Chamber Pot, Square, Ridged, Powell & Bishop	90.00
Coffeepot, Fishhook, Meakin	120.00
Coffeepot, Lily Of The Valley, Shaw	500.00
Compote, Square, Red Cliff	110.00
Creamer, Square, Ridged, Wedgwood	110.00
Cup, Handleless, Morning Glory, Elsmore & Forster	65.00
Cup & Saucer, Anthony Shaw	35.00
Cup & Saucer, Morning Glory, Wileman	65.00
Cuspidor, Figural Head Spout Each Side, 8 In.	595.00
Cuspidor, Shaw	1100.00
Demitasse Set, Gray's Pottery, 11 Piece	120.00
Dish, Vegetable, Cover, Square, Wilkinson	90.00
Dish, Vegetable, Cover, Sunburst, Wilkinson	60.00
Eggcup, Boston, Meakin	325.00
Gravy Boat, Fishhook, Meakin	55.00 to 60.00
Holder, Toothbrush	200.00
Mug, Child's, Pepperleaf, Elsmore & Forster	350.00
Pitcher, Square, Shaw, 8 In.	150.00
Pitcher, Tall	150.00
Pitcher, Teaberry, Clementson, 7 1/2 In.	610.00
Pitcher, Wash, Teaberry, Clementson, 13 In.	300.00
Plate, Gothic Pinwheel, Walley, 8 1/2 In., 4 Piece	125.00
Platter, 13 In.	55.00
Platter, Cold Cuts, Meakin, 10 x 6 In.	55.00
Platter, Copper Luster, Meakin, 10 x 6 In.	35.00
Platter, Meakin, 13 x 9 1/2 In.	45.00
Relish, Elsmore Forster Ceres *Illus*	225.00
Relish, Mitten Shape, Teaberry	510.00
Relish, Shaw Niagara Fan *Illus*	400.00
Relish, Sunburst, Wilkinson	65.00
Relish, Teaberry *Illus*	510.00
Shaving Mug, Chinese, Shaw	80.00 to 180.00
Shaving Mug, Lily Of The Valley, Hotel, Copper Luster Room Number	135.00
Shaving Mug, Lily Of The Valley, Shaw	110.00

Shaving Mug, Teaberry, Clementson, 3 1/2 In. 2000.00
Soap Dish, Cover, Insert, Teaberry, Clementson, Oval, 6 In. 1800.00
Soup Tureen, Brocade Pattern, Cover, Ladle .... *Illus* 1700.00
Soup Tureen, Square, Ridged, Mellor, Taylor.. 160.00
Sugar, Bamboo, Meakin 90.00
Sugar, Fishhook, Meakin 50.00
Sugar, Hexagon, Shaw 165.00
Tea Set, Hexagon, Shaw, 3 Piece 425.00
Tea Set, Round, Wilkinson, 3 Piece 275.00
Tea Set, Square, Ridged, Powell & Bishop, 3 Piece 190.00
Teapot, Bamboo, Meakin 140.00
Teapot, Square, Burgess 155.00
Toothbrush Holder, Teaberry, Clementson, 4 1/2 In. 650.00
Tureen, Sauce, Cover, Underplate, Ladle, Meakin, 4 Piece 285.00
Tureen, Sauce, Ladle, Square, Ridged, Mellor, Taylor 205.00
Vegetable Dish, Cover, Fishhook, Meakin 85.00
Washbowl, Lily Of The Valley 185.00
Washbowl, Meakin 125.00
Waste Bowl, Hanging Leaves, Shaw 110.00

TECO is the mark used on the art pottery line made by the American Terra Cotta and Ceramic Company of Terra Cotta and Chicago, Illinois. The company was an offshoot of the firm founded by William D. Gates in 1881. The Teco line was first made in 1885 but was not sold commercially until 1902. It continued in production until 1922. Over 500 designs were made in a variety of colors, shapes, and glazes. The company closed in 1930.

Ashtray, Crimped, Flared Sides, Green, W.D. Gates, 4 1/2 In. 275.00
Ashtray, Grumpy Old Man 200.00
Bowl, Matte Green & Black Glaze, Scalloped, Stamped, 2 1/2 x 8 In. 440.00
Bowl, Nested Flower Frog, Green, 3 x 9 In. 895.00
Bowl, No. 80, Squat, Flared Rim, Matte Green, Impressed Mark, 2 1/2 x 7 In. 440.00
Bowl, No. 372, Notched Rim, Matte Green, Mark, 2 x 9 In. 330.00
Bowl, Sculpted Design Of Leaves, Berries, Green, Matte Glaze, Signed, 9 In. 330.00
Candlestick, Handle, Green Matte, W.D. Gates, 6 1/2 In. 330.00
Chamberstick, Handle, Organic Decoration, Green Matte, Fritz Albert, 10 1/2 In. 880.00
Charger, No. 511, Green Matte, Embossed Initials, W.D. Gates, 10 1/2 In. 550.00
Dish, Pinched Rim, Green Glaze, 1 x 4 1/2 In. 165.00
Vase, 3 Sides, Green Matte, Fritz Albert, 8 In. 705.00
Vase, 3 Squat Feet, Medium Gray Glaze, Signed, 3 1/2 x 7 1/2 In. 320.00
Vase, 4 Broad Handles At Shoulder, Yellow Glaze, Marked, 14 In. 2530.00
Vase, 4 Lobes, Organic Molded Design, Green, Fritz Albert, 10 In. 880.00
Vase, Broad Shoulder, Flared Neck, Medium Gray Matte Glaze, Signed, 11 1/2 In. 715.00
Vase, Bulbous Form, Flared, Adventurine Glaze, Rim, Impressed Mark, 4 x 3 3/4 In. ... 495.00
Vase, Bulbous, Matte Green, 4 1/2 In. 66.00
Vase, Buttressed Handles, Hourglass Shape, Signed, 7 1/2 In. 1750.00
Vase, Charcoaling Over Organic Tulip Design, Signed, 12 In. 3850.00
Vase, Classic Form, Green Matte Glaze, Signed, 9 In. 825.00
Vase, Conical, Bulbous Neck, Light Green Matte Glaze, Stamped, 9 1/4 x 4 1/2 In. 770.00
Vase, Cylindrical, Mottled Dark Green & Gun-Metal Glaze, 17 In. 1430.00
Vase, Ginger Jar Shape, Green, 5 1/4 In. 850.00
Vase, No. 43, Green Matte & Gun-Metal Glaze, W. Gates, 7 1/2 In. 1980.00
Vase, No. 52, Bulbous, Charcoaling, Matte Green, W.D. Gates, 4 x 4 In. 495.00
Vase, No. 60B, Cylindrical Shape, Stylized Grass Blades & Flowers, Green, 9 x 4 In. ... 825.00
Vase, No. 111, Baluster, Everted Rim, Carved Lotus Blossoms, Green, 30 In. 9200.00
Vase, No. 182, 4-Sided, Wide Bottom, Flared Neck, Matte Green, Mark, 16 x 7 In. 1100.00
Vase, No. 182, Matte Green Glaze, Marked, 16 In. 373.00
Vase, No. 201, Bulbous Form, Flared Rim, Matte Green, Impressed Mark, 3 x 3 In. 247.00
Vase, No. 233, Bulbous Base, Scalloped & Flared Rim, Matte Green, Mark, 5 x 4 In. 440.00
Vase, No. 233, Bulbous, Scalloped Top, Green, F. Albert, 5 In. 357.00
Vase, No. 362, Bulbous, Straight Neck, Matte Green, Impressed Mark, 3 1/2 x 3 In. 302.00
Vase, No. 363, Cylinder, Flared Base, Charcoaling, Green Matte, W.D. Gates, 3 x 5 In. .. 302.00
Vase, No. 405, 4 Long Square Handles, Matte Green, Impressed Mark, 7 x 3 1/4 In. 935.00

Vase, No. 407, 2 Round Handles, Flared Rim, Matte Green, Impressed Mark, 8 x 4 In.. 1430.00
Vase, No. 434, 4 Body Length Handles, Matte Brown, Mark, 7 1/4 x 4 1/4 In. 1650.00
Vase, No. 447A, 2 Body Length Buttress Handles, Matte Brown, Mark, 6 x 2 In. 715.00
Vase, Ribbed Design Rising To Fluted Rim, Leaves Attached At Waist, Signed, 12 In.. 2750.00
Vase, Stovepipe Neck, Buttressed Handles, Green & Silver Glaze, 3 1/2 In. 465.00
Vase, Wide Tapered Shape, Green, 5 1/2 x 4 In. 468.00
Wall Pocket, Spiked Leaves, Mottled Green & Black Glaze, Signed, 15 x 6 1/2 In. 500.00

TEDDY BEARS were named for a president of the United States. The first
teddy bear was a cuddly toy said to be inspired by a hunting trip made by
Teddy Roosevelt in 1902. Morris and Rose Michtom started selling their
stuffed bears as *teddy bears* and the name stayed. The Michtoms founded the
Ideal Novelty and Toy Company. The German version of the teddy bear was
made about the same time by the Steiff Company. There are many types of
teddy bears and all are collected. The old ones are being reproduced. Other
bears are listed in the Toy section.

Andy Panda, Tag, 21 In.. 158.00
Bing, Cinnamon, Black Button Eyes, Hump, Swivel Head, c.1910, 15 In. 1840.00
Chad Valley, Mohair Gold, 1940s 395.00
Knickerbocker, Mohair, Brown, Glass Eyes, Tag, 12 In. 275.00
Mohair, Beige, 2 Tone Brown, Straw Stuffing, Articulated Limbs, Glass Eyes, 17 In. ... 72.00
Mohair, Blond, Fully Jointed, Embroidered, Steel Eyes, c.1906, 16 In. 2760.00
Mohair, Brown, Articulated Limbs, Bead Eyes, 10 1/2 In. 93.00
Mohair, Brown, Cotton Batting Stuffing, Embroidered Face, Glass Eyes, 18 In. 220.00
Mohair, Embroidered, Excelsior Stuffing, Fully Jointed, Steel Eyes, c.1910, 12 In. 144.00
Mohair, Excelsior Stuffed, Swivel Head, Hump, 22 In. 1450.00
Mohair, Gold, Articulated Limbs, Glass Eyes, 18 In. 192.00
Mohair, Gold, Excelsior Stuffed, Jointed, Glass Eyes, 13 In. 100.00
Mohair, Gold, Straw Stuffed, 1920, 14 In. 245.00
Mohair, Gold, Swivel Head & Body, Plaid Bow, Glass Eyes, 20 In. 150.00
Mohair, Light Blue, Jointed, Glass Eyes, 12 In. 225.00
Mohair, Pink, Articulated Limbs, Felt Paw Pads, Glass Eyes, 19 In. 55.00
Mohair, Silver, Soft Stuffed, 1930, 18 In. 195.00
Mohair, Yellow, Embroidered Features, Steel Eyes, 1920s, 13 In. 403.00
Schuco, 1910, 2 In. 435.00
Schuco, Tan, 2 1/2 In. 300.00
Schuco, Yes/No Bear, Golden, Glass Eyes, Pull Tail, 9 In. 805.00
Steiff, Amber Plush, Snout Nose, Felt Paws, Jointed, Beaded Eyes, 1915, 13 In. 1100.00
Steiff, Amber Plush, Straw Filled, Felt Paws, Jointed, 1945, 9 In. 1300.00
Steiff, Champagne Colored Plush, Jointed, Beaded Eyes, 1920, 11 In. 1400.00
Steiff, Dark Brown, 14 In. 635.00
Steiff, Golden, Stitched Nose, Swivel Head, Black Boot Eyes, 1905, 12 In. 1495.00
Steiff, Growler.. 42.00
Steiff, Horizontal Stitched Nose, Black Button Eyes, Squeaker, 1905, 12 In. 1495.00
Steiff, Mohair, Blond, Embroidered Features, In Basket, c.1920, 19 In. 230.00
Steiff, Mohair, Blonde, Embroidered, Fully Jointed, Ear Button, 1920s, 18 In. 2185.00
Steiff, Mohair, Chocolate, Shaved Muzzle, Velour Pads, Growler, 19 In. 140.00
Steiff, Mohair, Cinnamon, Excelsior Stuffing, Steel Eyes, c.1906, 13 In. 805.00
Steiff, Mohair, Gold, Embroidered Nose & Mouth, Glass Eyes, c.1910, 12 In. 690.00
Steiff, Mohair, Gold, Turned Up Feet, Felt Pads, Floss Nose, Jointed, 6 1/2 In. 275.00
Steiff, Mohair, White, Straw Filled, 1950s, 3 1/4 In.. 150.00
Steiff, Mohair, White, Straw Filled, Button In Ear, c.1910, Bead Eyes, 10 In. 1500.00
Steiff, Mohair, White, Straw Filled, Snout Nose, Swivel Neck, Bead Eyes, 10 In. 1100.00
Steiff, Mohair, Yellow, 1904, 15 In.. 5465.00
Steiff, Mohair, Yellow, Embroidered Features, Jointed, Button, Eyes, 1904, 29 In. 5462.00
Steiff, Musical, Yellow, 1928, 12 In. 285.00
Steiff, U.S. Zone, 1940, 9 In. 425.00
Steiff, White, Muzzle, Box, 18 In. 350.00
Steiff, White, Muzzle, Box, 22 In. 550.00
Steiff, Zotty, Mohair, Platinum, Open Mouth, Felt Pads, Jointed, 9 In. 320.00
Voice Box, Shoebutton Eyes, Straw Filled, c.1915, 14 In. 435.00
White Mohair, Glass Eyes, Velvet Pads, 1930s, 23 In. 275.00
Zotty, Herman, Shaggy Mohair, Brown, Excelsior Stuffed, Open Mouth, 19 In. 110.00

TELEPHONES are wanted by collectors if the phones are old enough or unusual enough. The first telephone may have been made in Havana, Cuba, in 1849, but it was not patented. The first publicly demonstrated phone was used in Frankfurt, Germany, in 1860. The phone made by Alexander Graham Bell was shown at the Centennial Exhibition in Philadelphia in 1876, but it was not until 1877 that the first private phones were installed. Collectors today want all types of old phones, phone parts, and advertising. Even recent figural phones are popular.

A.T.T., Candlestick, Brass & Black, Patent 1920	125.00
American Electric, Wall, Dial	27.00
American Electric, Wall, Pre-Dial	25.00
Art Deco, Chrome Trim	75.00
Art Deco, Streamline Design, Hard Black Plastic, Monophone, 5 x 8 In.	35.00
Bell System, Test Set, Lineman's, Rotary, Piecing Clips	30.00
Booth, Oak, Beveled Glass	2150.00
Booth, Oak, Double Wall Construction	750.00
Bozo The Clown, Box	48.00
Bozo The Clown, Nose Lights With Rings	95.00
Brass, Oriental Style, Standing, 41 1/2 In.	69.00
Budweiser Beer, Beer Can Shape	55.00
Bugs Bunny	75.00
Candlestick, Pulse Dial, Brass	100.00
Charlie The Tuna, Box, 1987	48.00 to 85.00
Chicago North Western Railroad, Ringer Box, c.1920	100.00
Cradle, Dial Base, Brass, 6 x 9 1/2 In.	120.00
Crest Sparkle, Box	42.00
European, Hi-Boy, Brass Finger Wheel	130.00
Garfield, Talking 11 Different Wisecrack Phrases	51.00
Golf Bag, Golf Balls For Keys On Dial Pad, Rubber Feet	45.00
Harley-Davidson, Pulse Dialing & Redial	65.00
Hawaiian Punch, Plastic	195.00
Heinz Ketchup, Figural, Box	45.00 to 50.00
Keebler Elf	85.00
Kellogg, Desk	15.00
Kellogg, Wall, Redbar	80.00
Kellogg Switchboard Supply, Oak, Wall, Black Bells, Crank	90.00
Kermit The Frog	110.00
Kettle, Gold Decal, Brass Carrying Handle, Black	140.00
Leich, Desk, Hand Crank	35.00
Locomotive, Crescent Rain, 1925 Model	35.00
Mickey Mouse, Yellow Receiver	125.00
Oscar Mayer, Hotdog Shape, Box	65.00
Paperweight, Bell, Cobalt Blue Glass	115.00
Plane, Alexander Graham, 2-Tone Orange Plane	150.00
Raid Bug, Box, 52 In.	225.00
Sears, Wall, Chestnut	275.00
Snoopy	125.00 to 150.00
Sprout, Box	125.00
Stromberg Carlson, Brass Finger Wheel	142.00
Stromberg Carlson, Dial, Black	20.00
Stromberg Carlson, Wall, Oak Case	385.00
Stromberg Carlson, Wall, Oak, 33 In.	115.00
Stromberg Carlson, Wall, Pink, 1950s	245.00
Wall, Skyscraper, Art Deco	400.00
Western Electric, Candlestick, Brass	250.00
Western Electric, Candlestick, Gray, Pay Phone, 1898-1910	720.00
Western Electric, Cradle	50.00
Ziggy	35.00

TELEVISION sets are twentieth-century collectibles. Although the first television transmission took place in England in 1925, collectors find few sets which pre-date 1946. The first sets had only five channels, but by 1949 the additional VHF channels were included. The first color television set became available in 1951.

Emerson, 7 In.	250.00
Philco, Predicta, Stand, 1960, 24 3/4 In.	405.00
Philco, Table Model, 17 In.	425.00
Philco Predicta, 17 In.	150.00
Sony, Trinatron, 19 In.	55.00
Zenith, Small	27.00

TEPLITZ refers to art pottery manufactured by a number of companies in the Teplitz-Turn area of Bohemia during the late nineteenth and early twentieth centuries. The Amphora Porcelain Works and the Alexandra Works were two of these companies.

Ashtray, Blue Willow, Amphora	14.00
Bowl, Stylized Grapevine, 2 Applied Parrots On Rim, 11 1/2 In.	200.00
Creamer, Drummer Boy With House, Fence & Trees, Stellmacher, 3 3/4 In.	70.00
Cup, 3 Handles, Amphora, 6 3/4 In.	143.00
Figurine, Rising Stallion, Green & Gold Base, Amphora, 15 3/4 In.	385.00
Figurine, Woman, Cream Ground, Marked E. Stellmacher, Amphora, c.1904, 28 In.	2200.00
Group, Arab On Camel, Late 19th Century, 18 3/4 x 12 3/4 In.	460.00
Pitcher, Floral & Gold Tilt Design, Snake Entwined Handle, 9 1/4 In.	165.00
Vase, 2 Scenic Panels, Stylized Floral Banding, Amphora, 6 In.	258.00
Vase, 3 Full-Figured Crested Parrots, Gold Matte Glaze, Amphora, 12 In.	725.00
Vase, Applied Purple Berries, Iridescent Purple, Amphora, Signed, 8 3/4 In.	285.00
Vase, Art Nouveau Shape, Stylized Tulip-Shaped Neck, Landscape, Amphora, 6 In.	605.00
Vase, Bird Pursuing Spider, Snake Handles, Amphora, 9 In.	650.00
Vase, Blue Ground, Landscape Panels, Gilt, 6 In.	86.00
Vase, Floral, Swirled Handles, c.1890, 10 In.	225.00
Vase, Flowers, Pearlized Jewel Centers, Double Handle, Amphora, 6 1/4 In.	295.00
Vase, Gold Leaves & Vines, Cobalt & Green, Gold Top, Bulbous, Amphora, 6 x 6 In.	325.00
Vase, Gold Pinecones, Reddish Leaves, Green Vines, Amphora, 6 1/2 In.	350.00
Vase, Incised Greek Water Vessel Design, Amphora, Large, Pair	370.00
Vase, Japanese Style Flowering Branches, Pierced, Handles, Bombe, Wahliss, 6 x 9 In.	550.00
Vase, Jeweled Flowers, Salamander Handles, Gray & Green Ground, Amphora, 9 In.	395.00
Vase, Luster Design Around Middle, Amphora, 8 In.	150.00
Vase, Multicolored Flowers, Cobalt Ground, Amphora, 7 1/4 In.	60.00
Vase, Peacock Feather, Bulbous Base, Amphora, 12 In.	285.00
Vase, Portrait Of Girl, Long Hair, Holding Flowers, Marked, 6 3/4 In.	495.00
Vase, Portrait Of Woman, Long Hair, Helmet, Eagle On Visor, Signed, 9 In.	1050.00
Vase, Portrait Of Woman, Long Hair, Jeweling, Amphora, 6 In.	950.00
Vase, Portrait Of Young Man, 1 Side, Swan Opposite Side, Signed, 10 1/2 In.	245.00
Vase, Purple Iris, Reticulated Floral Top, Gold Nouveau Handles, 9 In.	250.00
Vase, Tapered, Drip Design, 4 Handles, Tan, Green, Pink Iridescent, Amphora, 7 In.	330.00
Vase, Twisted, Applied Yellow, Red & Black Cherries, Iridescent Blue Ground, 5 In.	130.00
Vase, White Enameled Flowers, Butterflies, Cobalt Blue, E. Wahliss, 15 In.	575.00
Vase, Woman Figures, Iridized, Red Ground, 24K Gold, Amphora, Nouveau Mark	2500.00
Vase, Woman's Head, Jeweled & Enameled, Amphora, 6 In.	895.00

TERRA-COTTA is a special type of pottery. It ranges from pale orange to dark reddish-brown in color. The color comes from the clay, which is fired but not always glazed in the finished piece.

Amphora Jar, Neoclassical, Angular Handles, Polychromed, Italy, 16 1/8 In., Pair	5175.00
Bowl, Children Figural Handles, 8 In.	330.00
Bust, Curls, Wide Eyes, From Building, 20 In.	1850.00
Bust, Eros, Faux Marble, Plinth Base, G. Ruggeri, 15 In.	135.00
Bust, Louis XIV, Long Hair, Draped Cape, Socle Base, 26 In.	1875.00
Bust, Othello, 19th Century, 24 In.	1800.00
Bust, Woman, A. Carrier Belleuse, 23 3/4 In.	1725.00
Corbel, Neoclassical Style, Reeded, Scrolled Shape, Acanthus Design, 29 In., Pr.	1615.00
Figurine, Classical Woman, Holding Lyre, Stepped Plinth, Italy, 43 In.	6325.00
Figurine, Female, Holding Peach, Straw Glaze, Tan, 10 In.	115.00

Figurine, Horse, Black Metallic Mane, Tail & Hooves, Nicodemus, 11 7/8 In.	225.00
Figurine, Hunter, Loin Cloth, Marked India, 9 1/4 In.	95.00
Figurine, Lamb, Lying, Limaville Terra-Cotta & Stoneware Works, 24 In.	375.00
Figurine, Maiden, Pierre LeFaguays, 20 In.	2300.00
Figurine, Nude Woman, Draped, Bouquet In Hand, Craggy Pedestal, 34 In.	1430.00
Figurine, Reclining Woman, Raoul Francois Larche, c.1900, 28 1/2 In.	3737.00
Fountain Head, 2 Children, Animal, A. St. Gaudens, 16 In.	825.00
Paperweight, Brick, Frog 1 Side, Washington BrimLine Building Co., 1 x 3 In.	82.00
Pitcher, Enameled, Small	225.00
Plaque, African Woman's Head, Relief, A. St. Gaudens, Square, 17 In.	880.00
Plaque, Classical Urn Flanked By Griffins, 19th Century, 36 1/2 In.	1430.00
Plaque, Woman Nude, Relief, A. St. Gaudens, 6 x 14 In.	550.00
Sign, Ram's Head, 10th Windsor Farmer's Market, Reading, 24 In.Diameter	950.00
Urn, Faces, 60 In., Pair	2500.00
Urn, Garden Gate, 19th Century, 5 Ft. 4 In. x 4 Ft.	3300.00
Urn, Neoclassical, Campana Shape, Egg & Dart Rim, Mask Handles, 29 In., Pair	7475.00

TEXTILES listed here include many types of printed fabrics and table and household linens. Some other textiles will be found under Clothing, Coverlet, Rug, Quilt, etc.

Banner, Patriotic, America, c.1830-1850, 28 x 29 In.	489.00
Bedspread, Chenille, Twin Peacocks, Full Size	175.00
Bedspread, Crocheted Lace, Off-White, 82 x 90 In.	60.00
Bedspread, Crocheted, Diamond Pattern, Swirling Design, Border, Ivory, 81 x 72 In.	248.00
Bedspread, Crocheted, Medallions, Green, Double-Bed Size	250.00
Bedspread, Crocheted, Now I Lay Me, Children & Teddy Bear Squares, 52 x 96 In.	195.00
Bedspread, Crocheted, Popcorn Stitch, Double Bed Size	200.00
Bedspread, Embroidered Silk, Pheasant, Birds, Flowers, Tasseled Fringe, 92 x 75 In.	345.00
Bedspread, Woven, Embroidery On Canvas, Birds & Geometric Design, 88x 94 In.	137.00
Bell Pull, Needlepoint, Black Ground, Floral & Rope Twist Design	236.00
Bell Pull, Needlepoint, Light Blue Ground, Flowers, Beadwork, Brass Pendant	110.00
Canopy Bed Cover, Net Work, Signed Jeanne Orndorff, 1900, 77 1/2 x 62 In.	300.00
Chair Seat, Needlepoint, Rose Sprays & Flowers, Dark Green	35.00
Cocktail Napkins, Designed By Georges Briard, Set Of 8, Boxed	20.00
Coverlet, Jacquard, 4 Rose Medallions, Wool, Fringed, J. Schnee, 79 x 96 In.	192.00
Coverlet, Jacquard, Floral Medallions, Bird Borders, J. Mellinger, 1839, 81 x 96 In.	495.00
Coverlet, Jacquard, Geometric Floral Medallion, Navy, Natural, 1842, 76 x 91 In.	192.00
Coverlet, Jacquard, Medallion, Border, Pheasant Corners, Red, Natural, 84 x 93 In.	357.00
Coverlet, Overshot, Mauve, Black, Blue & Natural, 70 x 97 In., 2 Piece	148.00
Coverlet, Overshot, Optical Pattern, 2 Tone Brown, Natural, 64 x 88 In., 2 Piece	104.00
Coverlet, Overshot, Snowflake & Pine Tree, Navy & Natural, 70 x 96 In.	220.00
Coverlet, Red & White, Asbury 1841, C. Van Northwic, Fancy Weaver, 93 x 80 In.	225.00
Cushion, Brussels Tapestry Covered, Courtly Figures, Square, 16 In., Pair	2990.00
Cushion, Crewel, Blossoming Foliage, 14 x 12 1/2 In., Pair	322.00
Flag, American, 13 Stars, Hand Sewn, Wool, Civil War Gunboat Type, 22 x 33 In.	133.00
Flag, American, 32 Stars, Hand Stitched	635.00
Flag, American, 35 Stars, Silky Material, 31 x 46 In.	57.00
Flag, American, 46 Stars, 60 x 96 In.	80.00
Flag, American, 46 Stars, Printed Silk, Frame, 11 1/2 x 16 1/2 In.	145.00
Flag, American, 48 Stars, 5 Ft. x 9 1/2 Ft.	21.00
Flag, American, 48 Stars, Nylon, 4 x 5 Ft.	85.00
Flag, Red Cross, Destination, WWII, 20 x 36 In.	17.00
Gloves, Sleigh, Horsehair	30.00
Homespun, Blue & Black, Ellsworth, Ohio, 75 x 91 In.	120.00
Lap Robe, Mohair, Colorful	30.00
Mat, Brown & Blue Shades, Grenfell, 10 In. Diam.	245.00
Mat, Table, Sarouk, Fereghan, 33 x 31 In.	925.00
Napkin, Linen, Damask, Wreaths, 20 In., 4 Piece	20.00
Needlework, Shepherdess, Silk Embroidered, Paint, Rhoda Whiting, Frame, 21 x 17 In.	460.00
Panel, Embroidered, 4 Dragons, Gold Metallic Thread, Blue Silk Ground, 42 x 47 In.	60.00
Panel, Embroidered, Ducks In River Landscape, Oriental, 35 1/2 x 50 1/2 In.	115.00
Panel, Embroidered, Iris & Scrolls, Frame, 26 x 26 In.	30.00

Panel, Hanging, Embroidered Oriental Landscape, 19th Century, 57 x 71 In. 143.00
Panel, Needlework, Memorial, Watercolor & Ink, On Silk, 18th Century, 16 x 19 In. 3737.00
Panel, Needlework, Shepherd, 1 Sheep, Floral Border, American, Framed 885.00
Panel, Needlework, Wool, Church & Tree, Frame, 17 1/4 x 16 In. 100.00
Panel, Petit Point, Floral Still Life, Framed, Square, 16 In. 172.00
Pillow, Aubusson Cover, Late 19th Century, 27 x 18 In. 1035.00
Pillow, Embroidered Blossoms, Stylized Leaves, Arts & Crafts, 14 x 18 In. 195.00
Pillow, Embroidered Floral Design, Natural Ground, Arts & Crafts, 14 x 18 In. 137.00
Pillow, Embroidered Red Roses, Dark Brown Linen, Arts & Crafts, 23 x 17 In. 220.00
Pillow, Needlework, Embroidered, Stark County, Ohio, 1842, 8 x 9 In. 292.00
Pillow Cover, Homespun, Blue & White, Woven Tape Ties, Embroidered Initials 165.00
Pillow Sham, Red Embroidered Turkey In Wreath, Red Floral Edge, 27 1/2 x 30 In., Pair 115.00
Pillowcase, Lace Edge, Cherubs, 1925 .... 85.00
Place Mat, Crocheted, Ecru, Basket Of Flowers, 1920s, 12 Piece 75.00
Runner, Embroidered, Stylized Brown & Green Silk Flower Design, 47 x 16 In. 247.00
Runner, Table, Tapestry, Figural Pattern, Dark Green & Brown, 78 In. 65.00
Scarf, Piano, Coral, Blue Embroidered Flowers, Fringed, 30 In. 90.00
Scarf, Piano, Embroidered, Ecru, Silk, Fringe, 64 x 61 In. 250.00
Scarf, Piano, Embroidered, Fringed, Square, 30 In. 45.00
Scarf, St. Andrews Golf Club, Silk 9.00
Scarf, Table, China Tree Embroidered Ends, Gustav Stickley, Linen, 68 x 15 In. 2070.00
Scarf, Table, Stylized Blossoms, Natural, Fringed, Arts & Crafts, 32 x 74 In. 220.00
Sham, Pillow, Pieced, Calico, Yellow & Green Squares, Ruffle, Chintz Back, 14 x 34 In. 27.00
Shawl, Kashmir, Patchwork, Mid-19th Century, 77 1/2 x 77 1/2 In. 800.00
Shawl, Paisley, France, 19th Century, Square, 69 In. 172.00
Shawl, Paisley, Wool, Embroidered Pieced Border, 72 x 80 In. 412.00
Shawl, Table, Cashmere, Red, 72 x 72 In. 96.00
Sheet, Homespun, Center Seam, Embroidered Initials, E.O.S., 65 x 82 In. 65.00
Silkwork, In Memory Of My Cruise In Orient, Mar., 1896, 19 x 22 In. 247.00
Table Cover, Card, Blue Needlepoint, Dice, Chips, Poker Hands, 1920, 30 x 30 In. 132.00
Tablecloth, Banquet, Lace, Pierced Grape Cluster, Floral & Figural, 68 x 135 In. 247.00
Tablecloth, Battenberg Lace, 48 x 48 In. 125.00
Tablecloth, Battenberg Lace, 132 x 63 In. 250.00
Tablecloth, Brocade, Orchids, Cream, Rust, Gold To Rose, 19th Century, 49 x 116 In.. 125.00
Tablecloth, Calico Print, Playing Cards, Oriental Print Works, 1850, 96 x 120 In. 303.00
Tablecloth, Crocheted, Filet Work, Cornucopia Design, 44 x 60 In. 225.00
Tablecloth, Cutwork, Linen, 12 Napkins, 1950, 71 x 102 In. 150.00
Tablecloth, Damask, Banquet, 12 Napkins, 62 x 100 In. 55.00
Tablecloth, Damask, Cherry Design, 84 x 69 In. 22.00
Tablecloth, Lace Inserts, 80 x 60 In. 105.00
Tablecloth, Linen, Embroidered Chrysanthemums, Arts & Crafts, 32 In. Diam. 88.00
Tablecloth, Linen, Richelieu, Cutwork & Embroidery, 68 x 100 In. 575.00
Tablecloth, Napkins, Linen, Alencon Lace Trim, Compotes, Urns, 204 x 82 In., 19 Pc. 2300.00
Tablecloth, Scalloped Edge, Embroidered Pink Roses, Round, 32 In. 120.00
Tablecloth, White On White, Washington On Horseback, 11 Napkins, 87 x 104 In. 55.00
Tapestry, Alter Cloth, Gothic, Gold Threads 500.00
Tapestry, Aubusson, Castle Framed By Two Trees, 5 Ft .9 In. x 6 Ft. 9 In. 6325.00
Tapestry, Aubusson, Fish In Woodland, 1950s, 8 Ft. 3100.00
Tapestry, Aubusson, Poppies & Leaves, 10 Ft. x 2 Ft. 11 In. 2760.00
Tapestry, Aubusson, Shaped To Ascend Staircase, 19 Ft. 9 In. x 6 Ft. 8625.00
Tapestry, Aubusson, Silk, Wool, Landscape, Floral Border, France, 10 x 4 Ft. 5750.00
Tapestry, Bacchus Served Wine By Female Attendant, Franco-Flemish, 39 In. 1955.00
Tapestry, Jacquard, Floral Garlands, Trellis Panel, Birds, Gods, 76 x 57 In. 825.00
Tapestry, Landscape, Bird In Tree, Chateau & River In Distance, 84 x 86 In. 1030.00
Tapestry, Organists In Wooded Setting, Unicorn, Lion, Wool, 72 x 57 In. 435.00
Tapestry, Throw, Floral Design, Earth Colors, Knotted Fringe, 57 x 96 In. 181.00
Tapestry, Verdure, Crane, Trees, France, 19th Century, 7 Ft. x 7 Ft. 6 In. 7475.00
Tapestry, Washington, On Horseback, Cannons, Ships, Fringed, 43 x 20 In. 35.00
Tea Cozy, Allover Beading, Velvet 145.00
Tea Cozy, Doll, Felt, Bead Eyes, Lenci, 16 In. 245.00
Throw, Bargello, Shepherd & Shepherdess, Animals, Red Ground, 84 x 67 In. 550.00
Throw, Red Plaid Wool, Scotland, 54 x 62 In. 50.00

Tie & Handkerchief, Paisley	25.00
Towel, Hand, Chain Stitched Eagles, Wool, Frame, Anna Roland, 1846	1050.00
Towel, Homespun, Blue & White, Fringe On One End, 19 x 26 In.	60.00
Towel, Show, Embroidered Linen, Anna Reist, Lancaster County, 60 x 17 3/4 In.	3737.00
Towel, Show, Strips Of Birds & Trees, Alphabet On Bottom, Maria Diller, 1825	1700.00
Valance, Handmade Lace, Graduated Gladiator Points, Tassels, 1900	75.00

THERMOMETER is a name that comes from the Greek word for heat. The thermometer was invented in 1731 to measure the temperature of either water or air. All kinds of thermometers are collected, but those with advertising messages are the most popular.

7-Up, Porcelain	85.00
7-Up, Porcelain, Pictures Bottle, French, 6 x 16 In.	100.00
7-Up, Red, Black & Green, Round, 1960, 12 In.	150.00
7-Up, Round, Pam, 1950	100.00
AC Oil Filter	85.00
Alka-Seltzer, Speedy, Round, Missing Glass	195.00
American Fence & Posts, Porcelain, 19 In.	135.00
Amphora Pipe Tobacco	40.00
Arbuckle Coffee	210.00
Auto Light, Tin Lithograph, 27 In.	37.00
Banner Milk, Red & White, Porcelain, 24 x 14 In.	75.00
Baugh's Fertilizer, Wooden, 15 x 4 In.	60.00
Bronze, On Ladder, Figural Woman Top, 19th Century, 7 1/8 In.	385.00
Camel Cigarettes, Metal, 14 1/2 x 18 1/2 In.	40.00
Campbell Kids, Tin	35.00
Clark Bar, 21 1/4 x 5 1/2 In.	440.00
Cloverdale, Round, 12 In.	90.00
Delco Batteries, Metal, 39 x 8 In.	100.00
Dr Pepper, Hot & Cold, Round	125.00
Dreikorns Bread, Barometer, Colored Loaf	295.00
Drink Dr Pepper, Good For Life, Metal	225.00
Dry-Slitz, Smoke Dry-Slitz, 2 For 5 Cents, Leader For 35 Years	115.00
Enjoy RC, Tin, 3 x 13 In.	95.00
Eskimo Anti-Freeze, Head Of Eskimo, Round	65.00
Ex-Lax, 7 3/4 x 38 In.	85.00
Ex-Lax, Metal, 39 x 8 In.	120.00
Fisherman, Figural, Chalkware	25.00
Five Roses Flour, Porcelain, 39 In.	225.00

Thermometer, Moxie, Drink Moxie, Good At Any Temperature

◆◆◆◆◆◆◆◆◆◆◆◆◆◆◆◆◆◆◆◆◆

Musty odors in trunks seem to be a constant problem. Try this system. Fill the trunk with wrinkled, crushed newspaper, close the lid for a week, remove and replace the papers. Repeat the process until the musty odor is gone. This system also helps with car interiors for tobacco odors, musty books if kept in a closed paper bag, and suitcases.

◆◆◆◆◆◆◆◆◆◆◆◆◆◆◆◆◆◆◆◆◆

Fram Filter Service, Oil Filters, c.1950, 39 x 8 In. 95.00
Genesee Beer, Wall, 6 In. 5.00
Gulf Motor Oil, 27 x 8 In. 245.00
Hires Root Beer, Bottle Shape, Tin, 1950s, 28 1/2 In. .... 150.00 to 175.00
Hires Root Beer, Bottle Shape, Tin, c.1940, 27 x 8 In. 125.00
International Paint Co., Man Holding Can Of Paint, Round.................................... 90.00
International Stock Food, Dan Patch Portrait, Wooden 4400.00
International Tailoring Co., Lion, King Of Tailors, Wooden, 23 In. 148.00
Kool-Winston, Standard, 1960. .... 35.00
Lash's Bitters, Wooden 150.00
Little Debbie, Picture Of Debbie.. 48.00
Mail Pouch, Treat Yourself To The Best, Porcelain 90.00
Mail Pouch Tobacco, Chew, Smoke, Blue Porcelain, 12 x 3 In. 175.00
Mail Pouch Tobacco, Chew, Tin Lithograph, 1920s, 3 x 9 In. 210.00
Mail Pouch Tobacco, Metal, 39 x 8 In. 110.00
Mapco Pipeline Systems 40.00
McKesson's Aspirin 475.00
Mirror, Anvil Brand Work 'n' Play Clothes 75.00
Morton Salt 75.00
Motorola Radio, For Home & Car, 39 x 8 In. 235.00
Moxie, Drink Moxie, Good At Any Temperature ....*Illus* 150.00
Nesbitt's California Orange, 1938. .... 90.00
Nu-Grape, Have Fun With Nu-Grape, Pictures Bottle, Tin 85.00
Occident Flour, Wooden.. 90.00
Oilzum, Metal, 15 x 8 In. 100.00
Osh-Kosh-B'Gosh 95.00
Pabst, Picture, Tin, 14 x 17 In. 95.00
Packard, 1948, 38 In. 300.00
Pam, Sign Of Good Taste, 1950 .... 200.00
Pepsi-Cola, 27 x 7 In. 65.00
Permazone Freesone, Mobil Gasoline, Metal, Glass Dial, Round, 12 In. 100.00
Prestolite, Battery, Vibration Proof, Tin.. 95.00
Prestone, Porcelain, 36 x 8 In. .... 115.00 to 150.00
Quaker State Oil, Round, 12 In. 60.00
Ramon's Liver Pills, Wooden 75.00
Red Crown Polarine, 5 Ft. 925.00
Regal Flour, Porcelain, Red & White On Green, 30 x 8 In. 225.00
Reliable Batteries 85.00
Remington, Porcelain.. 575.00
Robin Hood Flour, Red On White, Porcelain, 20 x 9 In. 110.00
Roseberg Oregon Timber 40.00
Royal Crown Cola, Mounted In Metal Plaque 20.00
Royal Crown Cola, Tin 85.00
Sauer's Vanilla, Wooden, 8 x 4 In. 600.00
Standard Oil, 1940s 25.00
Sun-Crest 85.00
Teem Soda, Pictures Bottle, Tin, 9 x 27 In. 175.00
Tycos-Taylor 125.00
Westinghouse, Betty Furness, Box 6.00
Wilkinson Lumber Co., Tin 11.00
Winchester, Tin 85.00

TIFFANY is a name that appears on items made by Louis Comfort Tiffany, the American glass designer who worked from about 1879 to 1933. His work included iridescent glass, Art Nouveau styles of design, and original contemporary styles. He was also noted for stained glass windows, unusual lamps, bronze work, pottery, and silver. Other types of Tiffany are listed under Tiffany Glass, Tiffany Pottery, or Tiffany Silver. The famous Tiffany lamps are listed in this section. Tiffany jewelry is listed in the jewelry and wristwatch categories. Reproductions of some types of Tiffany are being made.

Ashtray, Bronze, Gold Dore, 2 Handles, Round, Signed, 4 x 1 In. 95.00
Ashtray, Match Safe, Bronze, Red & Pink Enameled Geometric, Square, 5 x 4 In. 275.00
Blotter, Hand, Grapevine, Dark Patina, Green Glass, Beaded Edge, 3 x 6 In. 300.00

Blotter, Hand, Heraldic Pattern, Green Enameled, Silver Hobnail, 5 1/4 x 2 3/4 In. 300.00
Blotter Ends, Grapevine, Bronze, Dark Patina, 19 x 2 In., Pair 350.00
Bookends, Grapevine, Bronze, Amber Slag Glass, Gold Dore, 5 1/2 In. 900.00
Bookends, Ninth Century, Bronze, Blue & Green Jewels, 4 1/2 x 6 In. 900.00
Box, Abalone Discs, Gold Dore, Hinged Cover, Bronze, 5 1/2 x 3 1/2 x 1 1/4 In. 550.00
Box, Blue-Violet Enameled Fleur-De-Lis Each Corner, Bronze, 6 x 3 3/4 x 2 In. 950.00
Box, Geometric Enamel Design, Bronze Dore, No. 350, 6 1/2 x 2 1/2 In. 770.00
Box, Jewelry, Grapevine, Green Favrile Glass, Bronze, Signed, 9 1/2 In. ....978.00 to 1800.00
Box, Pine Needle, Glass Panels, Bronze, 6 In. 350.00
Calendar, Perpetual, Triform Frame, 3 Windows, Day, Date & Month, 1889, 8 In. 3737.00
Candelabrum, 2-Light, Green Glass Inserts, Bronze, 12 In. 1450.00
Candelabrum, Bronze, 6-Light, Signed, 15 In. 2500.00
Candle Snuffer, Brown & Green Patina, Bronze, 6 In. 250.00
Candlestick, Bronze, 3 Ball Feet, Favrile Gold Iridescent Ball, Signed, 8 In. 2000.00
Candlestick, Bronze, 6 Leaf Arms, 10 In., Pair 2500.00
Candlestick, Bronze, Amber Glass Shade, Signed, 1899, 15 3/4 In. 2013.00
Candlestick, Bronze, Bamboo, Green Feathering, 1918, 13 In., Pair 6325.00
Candlestick, Bronze, Cobra, 4-Sided Leaf Form, Crook Neck, Signed, 7 3/4 In. .....750.00 to 1400.00
Candlestick, Bronze, Pierced Candle Cup, Bobeche, Signed, 19 3/4 In. 2300.00
Candlestick, Bronze, Prong Supports, 3 Legs, Ovoid Bobeche, 8 3/4 In., Pair 1150.00
Candlestick, Bronze, Round Foot, 6-Pronged Standard, No. 1210, 10 1/2 In., Pair 1380.00
Candlestick, Copper, Pear-Shaped, Hammered, Silver Beads, c.1900, 11 In., Pair 4125.00
Candlestick, Floral Form, Brown & Green Patina, Marked, 17 1/2 In., Pair 1725.00
Candlestick, Gilt-Bronze, Urn-Shape Socket, 4 Legs, Bobeche, No. 1201, 11 In., Pair . 1035.00
Candlestick, Root Base, Jeweled Bowl, No. 1200, 12 1/2 In., Pair 4125.00
Chandelier, Beaded Border, 2 Rows Of Jewels, Chandelier Stalactite Shade, 22 In. 6900.00
Chandelier, Bronze, 6-Light, Lily Shades, Prisms, Beaded Chain, 27 In. 10350.00
Clock, Alarm, Chronograph 725.00
Clock, Boulle Style, c.1890 .... 2100.00
Clock, Desk, Bronze, Adam Pattern, 4 x 4 1/4 x 2 In. 1800.00
Clock, Desk, Gilt Bronze, Enameled, Square, 4 Ball Feet, Burgundy Enamel, 4 1/2 In. .. 1150.00
Clock, Grapevine, Beaded Etched Metal, Green Case, Signed, 10 1/2 In. 2750.00
Clock, Tall Case, Sheraton Style, Satinwood Inlay, 4 Chimes, Works By Dufrey 4600.00
Clock, Wall, Enamel Dial & Pendulum, Ribbon Back Plate, c.1900, 16 3/4 In. 1850.00
Compote, Bronze & Glass, Abalone, Signed, 7 In. 225.00
Compote, Bronze, Abalone Discs In Leaf Pattern, Gold Dore, 6 3/4 x 3 1/2 In. 250.00
Desk Set, American Indian, Gilt-Bronze, 7 Piece 1100.00
Desk Set, Bronze, Amber Opalescent Glass, Gilt Metal Frame, 3 Piece 440.00
Desk Set, Bronze, Modeled, Bronze, Alligator Finish, 11 Piece 920.00
Desk Set, Zodiac, Bronze, 5 Piece 1000.00
Desk Set, Zodiac, Signed, 6 Piece 460.00
Frame, Abalone, Discs Set In Floral Design, Signed, 7 x 14 In. 2200.00

Tiffany, Lamp, Acorn Domed Shade, 23 In.

◆◆◆◆◆◆◆◆◆◆◆◆◆◆◆◆◆◆◆◆◆◆◆

Old linens should be rolled,
not folded. Creases weaken
the fabric. If storing over a
long period, do not starch.
Starch attracts silverfish. Quilts
can be folded.

◆◆◆◆◆◆◆◆◆◆◆◆◆◆◆◆◆◆◆◆◆◆◆

Tiffany, Lamp, Desk,
Gold & Green Shade, 13 In.

Frame, Arms & Armor Border, Bronze, Easel Style, Signed, 10 x 12 In.	1500.00
Frame, Calendar, Grape, Caramel Glass, 7 x 6 In.	595.00
Frame, Chinese, Bronze, Symbols Border, Easel Style, 6 3/4 x 8 3/4 In.	950.00
Frame, Grapevine, Bronze Openwork, Signed, 14 In.	4600.00
Frame, Grapevine, Green Glass Overlay, Bronze Openwork, 8 x 9 1/2 In.	90.00
Frame, Grapevine, Mottled Green & White, Bronze Openwork, No. 919, 14 In.	4600.00
Frame, Pine Needle Pattern, Bronze, Easel Style, Signed, 7 x 8 1/4 In.	1800.00
Frame, Pine Needle, Bronze, Amber Slag Glass, Beading, 9 3/4 x 12 In.	2500.00
Frame, Pine Needle, Mottled Green, Bronze Openwork, No. 917, 14 In.	3680.00
Frame, Triple, 14K Gold Borders, 6 1/2 In.	3450.00
Frame, Wooden Back & Strut, 14K Gold, c.1930, 7 3/4 In.	2300.00
Frame, Zodiac, Bronze, Signed, 8 In.	865.00
Frame, Zodiac, Gilt-Bronze, No. 942, 8 In.	860.00
Frame, Zodiac, No. 912, 8 x 7 In.	470.00
Humidor, Sunburst Design, Cedar Lined, Bronze, 9 x 6 x 2 1/2 In.	3500.00
Inkstand, Crab, Hinged Cover, Seashell Covered Well, Bronze, 8 In.	4315.00
Inkstand, Grapevine, Gilt Finish, Bronze, Signed	400.00
Inkstand, Turtleback Tile, 6 Jewels, Hinged Cover, Signed, 4 x 4 In.	3450.00
Inkstand, Wild Carrot, Hinged Cover, Bronze, Signed, 3 3/4 x 5 1/4 In.	6900.00
Inkwell, Brickwork Tiles, Mosaic & Bronze, Cover Cast As Rose, 2 7/8 In.	5750.00
Inkwell, Byzantine, Inset Cabochon & Hard Stones At Top, Signed, 4 1/2 In.	1725.00
Inkwell, Carved & Hammered Design, Bronze, No. 1112, 5 1/2 x 4 In.	600.00
Inkwell, Grapevine Pattern, Green Slag Glass Insert, Bronze, 7 x 3 In.	1500.00
Inkwell, Heraldic Pattern, Canister Shape, Leather, Enameled, Silver Shield, 3 1/2 In.	650.00
Inkwell, Pine Needle, Green Glass, Bronze, 6 In.	695.00
Inkwell, Square, Glass Insert, Marked, Bronze	4000.00
Jam Jar, Silver Rim, Cover & Automatic Handle, Signed, 3 1/2 In.	635.00
Jardiniere, Cyclamen Blossoms, Gilt-Bronze, Signed, 1918, 10 3/4 In.	2875.00
Lamp, 2-Light, Gold Dore Finish, Favrile, Red, Iridescent, Bronze, Signed, 13 In.	2800.00
Lamp, 3-Light, Tapering Gold Shades, No. 419, 21 In.	3450.00
Lamp, 4-Light, Bronze, 21 1/2 In.	2650.00
Lamp, Acorn	9775.00
Lamp, Acorn Domed Shade, 23 In. ....*Illus*	9000.00
Lamp, Acorn Cap, Bronze Base, Green & White Glass, No. 1485, 22 In.	6000.00
Lamp, Adam, Bronze, Pale Green & Yellow Shade, Signed, 17 In.	5000.00
Lamp, American Indian, Favrille Shade, 16 In.	5200.00
Lamp, Bridge, Bronze, Gold Favrile, Base No. 670, 54 In.	4025.00
Lamp, Candlestick, Electric, Favrile	470.00
Lamp, Candlestick, Favrile, Glass Bead Fringe, Twisted Cylinder Base	550.00
Lamp, Candlestick, Favrile, Gold, Iridescent, Signed, 12 In.	1400.00
Lamp, Candlestick, Signed, 12 3/4 In., Pair	2295.00
Lamp, Chandelier, 6-Light, Lily Shades, Rainbow Iridescent, Gilt Bronze, 27 In.	10350.00
Lamp, Chandelier, Jeweled, Beaded Borders, Stalactite Shade, No. 5854, 21 In.	6900.00
Lamp, Daffodil, Gold, 14 In.	9000.00
Lamp, Damascene, Amber Glass, Bronze, 1928, 24 1/4 In.	5750.00
Lamp, Damascene, Carved Dragonflies, Butterfly, 9-In. Shade, No. 369, 15 In.	4675.00

Lamp, Desk, Gold & Green Shade, 13 In.. *Illus* 3750.00
Lamp, Gold Iridescent Zipper Design, Favrile, Emerald Green Base, Signed, 15 In. 3000.00
Lamp, Grapevine, 16 In. 8500.00
Lamp, Leaded Striated Green Domed Shade, Bronze, 65 In. .... *Illus* 2750.00
Lamp, Lemon Leaf, Domed Shade, Bronze, 21 1/2 In. .... *Illus* 8000.00
Lamp, Lily, 3-Light, 4 Stem Arms, Bronze Platform Base, Signed, 9 1/4 In. 2645.00
Lamp, Lily, 3-Light, Favrile, Signed Base & Shade 2500.00
Lamp, Lily, 3-Light, Gold Dore, Piano Style Base, Signed 3995.00
Lamp, Lily, 7-Light, Favrile, Gilt-Bronze, No. 385, 20 1/2 In. 3680.00
Lamp, Linen Fold, Leaded Glass, 12 Panels, Bronze, No. 686, 15 In. 925.00
Lamp, Mesh, Bronze, Floral Of Green Leaves, Yellow Beads, Red Enamel, Signed...... 1100.00
Lamp, Nautilus, Bronze & Shell, Signed, 1918, 13 1/2 In. 4600.00
Lamp, Nautilus, Bronze Platform, Shell Shade, Signed, 13 1/2 In. 3225.00
Lamp, Nautilus, Bronze, Emerald To White Glass Shade, 5 Ball Feet, Signed, 13 1/2 In. 7500.00
Lamp, Nautilus, Curving Shell Mounted To Bronze Base, Signed, 14 In. 3850.00
Lamp, Pine Needle, Bronze, Green Glass Shade, 13 1/2 In.. 2200.00
Lamp, Pomegranate, Emerald Green Shade, Gold, Bronze, Signed, 21 In. 9000.00
Lamp, Ribbed Iridescent Shade, 10-In. Shade, 4-Footed, Bronze Base, 56 1/2 In. 6050.00
Lamp, Sconce, Wall, Spherical, 1 Arm, Acanthus Leaves, Pulled Feather, 12 1/ In., Pr. 3150.00
Lamp, Spanish, Bronze, Adjustable Shade, Signed, 14 In.. 2800.00
Lamp, Student, Acorn, Domed Circular Foot, Gadroon Border, 24 x 12 In. 6000.00
Lamp, Turtleback Glass Tile, Favrile, Bronze, 1888, 14 1/2 In. 3738.00
Lamp, Turtleback Tile Shield, Favrile, Signed, 1899, 15 1/2 In. 3220.00
Lamp, Turtleback, Favrile Leaded Glass Shade, Bronze, 18 In.. 9350.00
Lamp, Turtleback, Tile Shield, Bronze, 16 Iridescent Jewels, Leaf Design, 14 1/2 In.... 5000.00
Lamp, Weight-Balance, Bronze, Green & Gold Shade, Favrile, 15 3/8 In. 5225.00
Lamp, Weight-Balance, Dimpled Design, Favrile, Bronze, 1920, 14 In. 2875.00
Lamp, Weight-Balance, Floor, Bronze, Signed Murano, 10 In. Shade............................ 4450.00
Lamp, Weight-Balance, Green Glass Shade, Gold Trailings, Bronze, 1899, 15 1/2 In. .. 4600.00
Lamp, Weight-Balance, Murano, 10 In. Shade, Signed, Floor.. 5385.00
Letter Holder, Bookmark, Bronze, Gold Dore, Tall Divider, 6 x 4 1/2 In. 500.00
Letter Holder, Pine Needle, Bronze, Green Glass 395.00
Letter Opener, American Indian Pattern, Bronze, Gold Dore, Signed, 10 1/2 In. 200.00
Letter Opener, Entwined Design, Bronze, Gold Dore, Signed, 9 In. 225.00
Letter Opener, Entwined Design, Gold Dore Finish, Signed, 9 In. 225.00
Letter Opener, Geometric, Bronze, Gold Dore, Enameled, Signed, 11 In. 350.00
Letter Opener, Graduate, Bronze, Gold Dore, Signed, 9 In.. 200.00
Letter Opener, Grapevine, Bronze, Green Glass, Signed, 9 1/4 In. 275.00
Letter Opener, Grapevine, Gold Dore Finish, Amber Slag Glass Handle, 9 In. 275.00
Letter Opener, Spanish, Bronze, Gold Dore, Signed, 9 In... 250.00

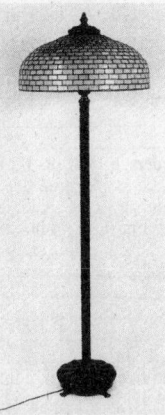

♦ ♦

When removing a lock on an old piece of furniture, make a diagram of the lock. Tape each screw on the proper place on the diagram so you can return each one to its original hole. Old screws may be different lengths and putting a long screw in a short hole could cause damage.

♦ ♦

Tiffany, Lamp, Leaded Striated Green
Domed Shade, Bronze, 65 In.

Tiffany, Lamp, Lemon Leaf, Domed Shade,
Bronze, 21 1/2 In.

♦♦♦♦♦♦♦♦♦♦♦♦♦♦♦♦♦♦♦♦♦♦♦♦

When polishing silver, first remove all detachable parts like screw-on handles or finials. Rest the silver piece on a cloth in your lap, never on the table or other hard surface. Polish by rubbing in circles. If there are wooden handles or other parts, these should be waxed when the silver is cleaned.

♦♦♦♦♦♦♦♦♦♦♦♦♦♦♦♦♦♦♦♦♦♦♦♦

Letter Rack, Grapevine, Etched Metal, Green Slag Glass, 10 x 6 1/2 In.	950.00
Letter Rack, Heraldic, Bronze, Leather Enameled, Silver Shield, 9 1/2 In.	750.00
Lighter, Leopard Head Shape, Niello, 14K Gold	1760.00
Magnifying Glass, Grapevine, Green Glass, 3 1/2 x 8 In.	1200.00
Match Safe, Zodiac	195.00
Mirror, Turtleback, 16 x 20 In.	4500.00
Paper Clip, Pine Needle, Dore, Caramel Slag Glass, No. 971	195.00
Paper Clip, Zodiac, Dark Patina, 2 1/4 x 3 3/4 In.	250.00
Paperweight, Boston Bull, Bronze, Gold Dore, Signed	600.00
Paperweight, Bulldog, Sitting, Bronze, Dark Patina Finish, No. 933, Signed, 2 1/2 In.	475.00
Paperweight, Lion, Bronze, 5 In.	675.00
Paperweight, Turtleback, Blue Iridescent, Bronze, Signed	625.00
Pen Tray, Grapevine, Bronze, Green Slag Glass, 3 Sections, 9 1/2 x 2 3/4 In.	250.00
Pen Tray, Heraldic Pattern, Green Enameled, 3 Sections, Shield Center	250.00
Planter, Bronze, Insert, Signed, 4 x 11 In.	440.00
Planter, Geometric Design, Gold Dore Finish, Liner, Signed, 8 1/2 x 2 1/2 In.	650.00
Planter, Venetian Border, Etched Surface, Gilt Metal, Signed, 10 1/2 In.	632.00
Plaque, Butterfly Nymph, Nude Figure, Amber, Bronze, c.1903, 11 In.	6900.00
Plate, Pastel, Deep Turquoise, Signed, 11 In.	425.00
Scale, Postage, Zodiac, Signed, 1 1/2 x 3 1/4 In.	550.00
Sconce, Acanthus Leaves & Scrolls, 1-Light, Tulip Shade, Bronze, 12 1/2 In., Pair	3450.00
Screen, Tea, Grapevine, 3-Panel, Favrile Glass, Bronze, 1928, 8 x 13 In.	2300.00
Shade, Candle, Stretched Border, Gold Iridescence, Signed	400.00
Shot Glass, Gold Favrile, Monogrammed, Signed, C771	375.00
Stamp Box, Grapevine, Green Slag Glass, 4 Ball Feet, 3 Section Tray, 4 x 2 x 1 In.	550.00
Sundial, Monogram G.E.D., Bronze, 1910, 12 3/4 In.	2760.00
Tazza, Venetian, Bronze, 6 1/2 In.	600.00
Thermometer, Kingwood, Ormolu, Ribbon Crest, Beaded Borders, c.1900, 10 1/2 In.	355.00
Tray, Bronze, Geometric Border, Gold Dore, 12 In. Diam.	300.00
Tray, Geometric Border, Bronze, Gold Dore, Signed, 9 In. Diam.	225.00
Tray, Geometric Design Outer Edge, Short Pedestal, Gold Dore Finish, 9 3/4 In.	225.00
Tray, Pen, Mosaic Gold Glass, Bronze, Signed, 1918, 7 3/4 In.	3450.00
Trivet, Zodiac, Bronze, Gold Dore, Signed, 8 x 7 In.	550.00
Vase, Berry Clusters, Green Glaze, Signed, 1910, 2 In.	1325.00
Vase, Bronze, Green Glass Insert, Monogrammed Base, Signed, 11 In.	950.00
Vase, Favrile, Bronze Mount, Flower Shape, No. 1743, 15 In.	3225.00
Vase, Green Striations, Floral Body, Bronze Mounted, Signed, 15 In.	3220.00
TIFFANY GLASS, Bonbon, Favrile, Gold Iridescent, Applied Tear Drop, Signed, 2 In.	225.00
Bonbon, Favrile, Short Pedestal, Gold Iridescent, Signed, 2 x 4 3/4 In.	275.00
Bowl, Blue Rim, Gold, 3 Scrolled Feet, Signed, 2 1/2 x 8 In.	800.00
Bowl, Butterscotch Opalescent, Raised Diamond Quilting, Signed, 6 In.	575.00

◆◆◆◆◆◆◆◆◆◆◆◆◆◆◆◆◆◆◆◆◆◆◆◆

Never use mending tape or transparent tape on a book. It will eventually permanently damage the paper. Even Post-its will eventually leave a spot.

◆◆◆◆◆◆◆◆◆◆◆◆◆◆◆◆◆◆◆◆◆◆◆◆

Tiffany Glass, Vase, Favrile, 13 1/2 In.;
Tiffany Glass, Vase, Floriform, 8 In.

Bowl, Favrile, Blue Iridescent, Deep, Ruffled Edge, Signed, 3 1/4 In. Diam.	850.00
Bowl, Favrile, Blue, Gold Iridescent, Raised Rim, Signed, 5 1/4 In. Diam.	650.00
Bowl, Favrile, Gold Iridescent, Ruffled, Signed, 7 1/4 x 3 1/4 In.	650.00
Bowl, Gold Favrile, Undulating Rim, 6 1/2 In.	605.00
Bowl, Gold Iridescent Violet Tones, Ruffled Rim, Signed, 6 In. Diam.	650.00
Bowl, Inverted Bell Form, Green Feathers, Signed, c.1927, 6 3/4 In.	518.00
Bowl, Purple Shading To White, Signed, 8 1/4 In.	995.00
Bowl, Silver-Gold Egyptian Chain Pattern, Signed, c.1895, 9 In.	2300.00
Bowl & Flower Frog, Heart Shaped Leaves, Vines, c.1917, 10 1/2 In.	2300.00
Box, Favrile, Blue, Leaves & Vines, Domed Openwork Cover, No. 7836, 6 1/2 In.	2100.00
Candlestick, Favrile, Swirled Design, Ribbed, 10 1/2 In.	385.00
Candlestick, Favrile, White Foot, Bulbous Candle Cup, Aquamarine, 14 1/2 In.	1150.00
Candy Dish, Ruffled & Rubbed, Footed, Blue Iridescent, Signed, 4 In.	575.00
Charger, Peacock, Silver Pea Eyes, Signed, 20 In.	3450.00
Compote, Favrile, Gold Iridescent, Ruffled, Pedestal, 2 1/2 x 4 In.	450.00
Compote, Pulled Feather Design On Stem & Body, Gold Interior, 4 1/2 In.	965.00
Cordial, Gold, Purple Highlights, Pinched Sides, Label, 2 In.	150.00
Cordial, Iridescent Amber, Signed, 1892, 10 Piece	2600.00
Decanter, Swirled & Pulled Ribbed Design, Pulled Stopper, Signed, 10 1/2 In.	495.00
Dish, Favrile, Signed, 6 In.	300.00
Finger Bowl, Underplate, Favrile, Platinum Highlights, 4-In. Bowl, 6 In. Plate	285.00
Frame, Cypriote, Iridescent Aubergine, Swirls, Leaded, 15 1/2 x 17 3/4 In.	1725.00
Frame, Cypriote, Swirls, Aubergine Glass, Leaded Frame, 15 1/2 x 18 In.	1725.00
Jar, Cover, Intaglio Cut Knob, Gold Iridescent, Red & Violet Highlights, 8 x 5 In.	1500.00
Paperweight, Scarab, Favrile	485.00
Plate, Pink & Green Iridescence, Gold, Pulled Design, No. T6520, 5 1/2 In.	120.00
Punch Bowl, Blue, Gold, Ribbed, Scalloped Rim, Signed, 2 Part	5445.00
Punch Bowl, Ribbed Body, Scalloped Edge, Signed	4500.00
Punch Cup, Favrile, Gold, Scroll Handle, Green Leaves, 2 1/2 In., Pair	520.00
Salt, Favrile, Gold Iridescent, All Around Twists, Signed, 1 1/8 x 2 In.	375.00
Salt, Favrile, Gold Iridescent, Flared, 4 Footed, Signed, 1 1/2 x 2 In.	250.00
Salt, Peacock Blue Iridescent, Ruffled Edge	650.00
Salt, Ruffled, Signed, 1 x 2 1/2 In.	130.00
Shade, Full Feather Style	3525.00
Sherbet, Gold Iridescence, Blue & Violet Highlights, Signed, 2 1/2 In. Diam.	225.00
Tile, Stylized Quatrefoil In Relief, Mottled Red & Yellow, 3 In., 4 Piece	300.00
Tumbler, Favrile, Gold, Blue Highlights, Marked, 3 1/4 In.	330.00
Vase, Blue Lava Ground, Gold Wavy Line Design, Signed, 5 In.	5500.00
Vase, Blue, Handles, Bottom Base Dark Blue Purple, Signed	1800.00
Vase, Bud, Favrile, Amber Striated Feathering On Lower Half, 1900, 9 In.	3165.00
Vase, Bud, Gold Iridescent, Footed, Signed, 8 1/4 In.	350.00
Vase, Bulb, Favrile, Fluted, Signed, 4 3/4 In.	725.00
Vase, Cased Green Leaves, Gold Dore, Mushroom Base, 12 In.	650.00

Vase, Double Gourd Form, Bands Of Gold Swags, Signed, 13 In.	3450.00
Vase, Favrile, 13 1/2 In. ....*Illus*	550.00
Vase, Favrile, 2 Handles, Ivory & Pale Gold, Blue & Pink Iridescence, 3 In.	415.00
Vase, Favrile, Black To Blue Lava Ground, Gold Waves, No. 8408J, 3 In.	3000.00
Vase, Favrile, Blue, Baluster, Black Foot & Everted Rim, No. 1263, 10 1/2 In.	2125.00
Vase, Favrile, Blue, Blossom Shape, No. 5460C, 4 3/4 In.	660.00
Vase, Favrile, Blue, Raised Ruffled Edge, Cut Leaf, Signed, 4 In.	1200.00
Vase, Favrile, Blue, Round Body, Silver Overcast, 4 In.	800.00
Vase, Favrile, Brick Red Feathered Trailing, 1892, 10 3/4 In.	2300.00
Vase, Favrile, Carved Leaves & Vines, Gold Ground, No. 5-8132N, 8 1/2 In.	4125.00
Vase, Favrile, Circular Foot, Bulbous Bowl, Gold Iridescence, No. 2942, 7 2/3 In.	975.00
Vase, Favrile, Double Gourd, Rainbow Iridescent, No. 5267816, 13 In.	3450.00
Vase, Favrile, Gold Iridescent Leaf Pattern, Green Outlining, Signed, 5 In.	1400.00
Vase, Favrile, Gold Iridescent, Deep Violet & Red, Stretch Edge, Signed, 4 In.	850.00
Vase, Favrile, Gold Iridescent, Trifold Shape, Straight Neck, Signed, 2 1/4 In.	500.00
Vase, Favrile, Gold Top, Gray-Blue Base, Signed, 6 In.	265.00
Vase, Favrile, Gold, With Green Leaves, Millefiori White, Signed, 2 In.	1800.00
Vase, Favrile, Iridescent Gold, Millefiori Floral, Green Leaves, 2 1/2 In.	1800.00
Vase, Favrile, Millefiori Blossoms, Heart-Shaped Leaves, Label, 6 3/8 In.	2990.00
Vase, Favrile, Oviform, Green Iridescent, Silver Rainbow, No. 980 IX, 8 In.	2185.00
Vase, Favrile, Peacock Blue, Flattened Top, Ribbed, Footed, Signed, 6 In.	2800.00
Vase, Favrile, Purple Bands, Pinched Shoulder, Green Ground, c.1900, 3 1/2 In.	550.00
Vase, Favrile, Red, Bulbous Neck, Signed, 1918, 6 3/4 In.	2875.00
Vase, Favrile, Ruffled Top, Gold Interior, Pink Highlights, No. 7856E, 5 1/2 In.	1320.00
Vase, Favrile, Silver-Gold Iridescent, Green Lines, Flower Form, 4 3/4 In.	1100.00
Vase, Favrile, Squat Bulbous Shape, Gold Iridescent Swirl, No. 8045A, 3 In.	2875.00
Vase, Floriform, 8 In. ....*Illus*	2750.00
Vase, Flower Form, Green Striations, Pulled Feather, Signed, 11 1/4 In.	8625.00
Vase, Flower Shape, Gold Design, Signed, 14 1/2 In.	3000.00
Vase, Flower Shape, Gold Iridescent, Green, Marked, 5 1/2 x 4 In.	635.00
Vase, Flower Shape, White & Green Step, Green Striations, No. T312, 11 In.	8625.00
Vase, Flowering Lily Stems, Mottled Green Glaze, Signed, 15 In.	3450.00
Vase, Gold Iridescent, Ribbed, Experimental, Signed, 7 1/2 In.	450.00
Vase, Gold Iridescent, Ruffled Edge, Ribs, Signed, Numbered, 18 In.	2500.00
Vase, Green Leaves & Vines, White & Red Millefiori, Signed, 6 1/2 In.	4125.00
Vase, Iridescent Design, Turquoise Ground, Signed, 6 In.	7150.00
Vase, Jack-In-The-Pulpit, Internal Ribbed Stem, Signed, 17 In.	5465.00
Vase, Jack-In-The-Pulpit, Signed, 19 In.	2425.00
Vase, Onion Shape, Ribbed, Purple, Green, Silver, Favrile, 1917, 9 In.	345.00
Vase, Pulled Green Leaves, Amber & Opalescent, Signed, 18 In.	7000.00
Vase, Pulled Green Leaves, Opalescent Shoulder, Signed, 12 3/4 In.	4000.00
Vase, Red Ground, Gold Swirl Design, Squat, Signed, 3 2/3 In.	2875.00
Vase, Reddish Gold Pod Leaves, Signed, 10 1/4 In.	3700.00
Vase, Repeating Gold Iridescent Pulled Feathers, Signed, 6 1/2 In.	978.00
Vase, Shoulder Dimples, Collar Fold, Gold Iridescent, Signed, 7 1/4 In.	1495.00
Vase, Silver Rainbow Pulled Feather, Green Ground, Label, 8 In.	2185.00
Vase, Tel Al Amarna, Iridescent Green, Gold Band, No. 3624L, 15 1/4 In.	3220.00
Vase, Tel El Amarna, Heart-Shaped Leaves, Favrile, 1918, 12 1/2 In.	6900.00
Vase, Vertical Blue & Gold Dots, Amber Ground, Cylindrical, Signed, Large	9982.00
TIFFANY GOLD, Cigarette Case, Hand Hammered 14K	2000.00
Cufflinks, Man's, Love Knot Design, 14K Gold	635.00
Necklace, Fox Link Chain, 19 Graduated Brilliant Cut Diamonds	690.00
Powder Jar, Glass, 18K Gold Cover & Handle, Puff, 4 In. Diam.	2500.00
Watch, Pocket, Yellow Gold, Dated 1907	360.00
TIFFANY POTTERY, Vase, Allover Brown Raised Stalks Pattern, Yellow, 7 x 5 1/4 In.	3500.00
Vase, Beaded Egyptian Style Lions Around Body, Signed, 6 1/2 In.	825.00
Vase, Bud, Raised Vines & Hanging Pods, Yellow-Green & Blue, 5 In.	2200.00
Vase, Bud, Vines & Hanging Pods, Green-Yellow & Blue, Glazed, 5 In.	2200.00
Vase, Chocolate Brown, Eggplant Shape, Raised Leaves, 4 1/2 x 4 In.	2800.00
Vase, Classical Figures, Raised Relief Grecian Dress, Unglazed, 8 In.	750.00
Vase, Favrile, Gourd Shape, Lily Stem, Mottled Green, No. PG21, 15 In.	3450.00
Vase, Hanging Pods, Leaves, Blue-Green Speckled Finish, Tan Rim, 6 1/2 In.	2200.00

Vase, Shades Of Green, Raised Leaves & Branches, Glazed, 8 x 6 In. 2500.00
Vase, Swirl Design, Mottled Amber Glaze, L.C.T., 7 In. 2185.00
Vase, White Low Relief Floral Design, Signed, c.1905, 3 1/4 In. 1150.00
TIFFANY SILVER, Basket, Reticulated Footed, 2 U-Shaped Handles, 3 x 6 1/2 In. 250.00
Bowl, Child's, Chased Bunnies, Inscribed, Wee MacGregor 660.00
Bowl, Moderne Style, Tapering, Small Ring Footed, 2 1/2 x 5 1/2 In., Pair 275.00
Box, Pill, Fox Head Finial, Cubed 3/4 In. 70.00
Carving Set, Olympian, 1878, 3 Piece 1900.00
Cigar Box, Book Shape, Gilt Imitation Page Edges, 12 x 9 1/2 x 2 In. 2300.00
Coffeepot, Mask & Blind Lattice Work, Ivory Insulators, 8 3/4 In. 2100.00
Compote, Chased Herbaceous Border, Monogram, 7 3/16 In., Pair 1400.00
Compote, Scroll & Flower Rim, Foliate Handles, c.1875, 15 3/4 In., Pair 6325.00
Cup, Infant's, Children & Dogs Playing 182.00
Demitasse Service, Fluted, Tapering Shape, Engraved, c.1910, 3 Piece 1265.00
Dish, Leaf Shape, 8 In. 330.00
Dresser Set, Chased Putto, Cherub, Florals, c.1900, 3 Piece 1150.00
Dresser Set, Molded Edge, c.1930, 7 Piece 315.00
Flask, Scene Of Hunters With Rifles, Standing Over Fallen Bear, 5 1/2 In. 2300.00
Flask, Sterling, Grasses Design, Egg Shape 520.00
Fork, Breakfast, Winthrop, 6 3/4 In. 45.00
Fork, Cold Meat, San Lorenzo 150.00
Fork, Dinner, English King 80.00
Fork, Luncheon, Audubon 95.00
Fork, Sardine, Holly Berry 225.00
Fork, Serving, Narcissus, 1880 .... 520.00
Fork, Vine, 9 In. 201.00
Ice Cream Slice, 11 3/4 In. 375.00
Kettle, Hot Water, On Stand 2200.00
Ladle, Soup, Chrysanthemum 1495.00
Ladle, Soup, Corn, Broom 550.00
Match Safe, Playing Cards Design, 1890 .... 990.00
Money Clip, Engraved CBL, Marked 55.00
Money Clip, Sterling 225.00
Pitcher, Leafy Straps Rising From Agee Lobes, c.1915, 8 1/8 In. 1955.00
Porringer, Arts & Crafts Design, Reticulated Handle, 1917, 4 1/2 In. 175.00
Salt, Neoclassical, Greek Key Border, 3 Ram Head Feet, Signed, 3 1/2 In., Pair 230.00
Salt & Pepper, Prelude 82.00
Salver, Chrysanthemum, c.1885, 13 In. 2875.00
Sauce Boat & Stand, Circular, Ebony Handle, 6 1/8-In. Stand 288.00
Sewing Tool, Scissor-Type, Stork Form, Beak Opens, 5 In. 385.00
Shears, Lobster, English Kings 135.00
Spoon, Demitasse, Audubon 50.00
Spoon, Ice Cream, Beekman 50.00
Spoon, Serving, Pierced, Broom Corn 415.00
Tablespoon, Wave Edge 70.00
Tea & Coffee Set, Engraved & Applied Ivy, Putti Finials, c.1860, 5 Piece 6325.00
Tea Caddy, Holly Berry 125.00
Tray, Canted Corners, Reeded Edge, 19 /12 In. 1265.00
Vase, Pierced Floral Design, Serpentine Rim, 9 3/4 In. 715.00
Vase, Reeded Stem, Fluted, 1898, 11 1/2 In. 810.00
Vase, Trumpet, Molded Border, c.1920, 15 3/4 In., Pair 4900.00

TIFFIN Glass Company of Tiffin, Ohio, was a subsidiary of the United States
Glass Co. of Pittsburgh, Pennsylvania, in 1892. The U.S. Glass Co. went
bankrupt in 1963, and the Tiffin plant employees purchased the building and
the inventory. They continued running it from 1963 to 1966, when it was sold
to Continental Can Company. In 1969, it was sold to Interpace, and in 1980,
it was closed. The black satin glass, made from 1923 to 1926, and the stemware of the last twenty years are the best-known products.

Bowl, Center, Blue Satin, 9 1/4 In. 12.00
Candlestick, Satin Amberina, Twisted, 8 1/2 In. 42.00
Champagne, Flanders 25.00

Champagne, Saucer, Flanders.. 15.00
Cocktail, Cerise, Crystal.. 18.00
Cocktail, Flanders 15.00
Console Set, Twisted Pedestal Stems, c.1930s 200.00
Cordial, June Night.. 45.00
Cordial, Trousseau... 35.00
Goblet, Byzantine 25.00
Goblet, Cerise, Crystal, 8 In. 24.00
Goblet, Cherokee, Low Stem.. 15.00
Goblet, Flanders, Yellow 25.00
Goblet, Fuchsia.. 22.00
Goblet, Laurel, Gold Trim, 7 1/2 In. 15.00
Iced Tea, Classic, 12 Oz.. 60.00
Lamp, Owl, Figural, 1920s 450.00
Mayonnaise Set, Cherokee Rose, 3 Piece... 40.00
Nappy, Twilite, Handle.. 75.00
Pilsner, Classic.. 47.00
Plate, Empire, Pink, 6 In. 20.00
Plate, Empire, Pink, 8 In. 30.00
Plate, Flanders, Pink, 6 In. 13.00
Sherbet, Byzantine.. 20.00
Sherbet, Cherokee Rose, Footed 15.00
Sherbet, Coronada 18.00
Sherbet, Fuschia, Crystal, 5 3/8 In.. 24.00
Sherbet, Pink 27.00
Tumbler, Fuchsia, Footed 18.00
Tumbler, June Night, Iced Tea 15.00
Vase, Cherokee Rose, 8 In.. 45.00
Vase, Fuchsia, Handles, 9 In. 75.00
Wine, Byzantine 35.00
Wine, Flanders, Pink.. 60.00

TILES have been used in most countries of the world as a sturdy building material for floors, roofs, fireplace surrounds, and surface toppings. Many of the American tiles are listed in this book under the factory name.

Benjamin Franklin Profile, Deep Brown Majolica Glaze, Trent, Frame, 4 In. 248.00
Carved Tree Landscape, Mountain, Green, Blue & Purple, Walrich, 5 1/2 In. 616.00
Celadon Peacock, Brown Trellis, Grapes, California Art, 11 3/4 x 7 3/4 In. 688.00
Cuenca, White Outlined Link Pattern, Green Ground, Walrich, 4 x 8 In. 275.00
Desert Scene, White Clouds, Mountain, Trivet, California Faience, Round, 5 1/2 In. ... 495.00
Dog Of Nuremberg, Silhouette, Green, Ivory Ground, Moravian Pottery, 4 1/2 In. 105.00
Dragonfly, Cobalt Blue Morning Glory, A. Rice, Wheeling, Round, 6 In. Diam. 94.00
Dutch Woman, Selling, Dog-Pulled Cart Transfer, Pardee, 6 In. 94.00
Fireplace, 2 Flying Putti, Amber Majolica Glaze, J. & J.G. Low, 1883, 6 In. 248.00
Floral, Hand Painted, Ramona, Signed Ramsey 40.00
Flying Putti, Holding To Arabesque Grid, Teal Majolica Glaze, J. & J.G. Low, 4 In. 165.00
George Washington Profile, Commemorative, 1732-1932, Robertson, 6 In. 72.00
Girl, Dutch Clothes, Old Man, Smoking Pipe, Self Framed, Franklin Label, 6 In. 210.00
Hispano-Moresque, Blue, Green, Orange & Yellow Pattern, Kraftile, 6 In. 121.00
Juggler, Brown, Moravian Pottery, 1977, 4 In. 25.00
Man & Woman, Dutch Renaissance Clothes, Trent, Frame, 6 In., Pair....................... 522.00
Man & Woman, Dutch Renaissance Style, Olive Majolica, Isaac Broome, 6 In., Pair.... 495.00
Man Profile, Dutch Renaissance Clothes, Green Majolica, J. & J.G. Low, 1882, 8 In.... 435.00
Mexican Style, Gladding McBean, 6 In. 45.00
Moravian Musician Brocades, Under Acanthus Leaf, 6 1/2 In., 8 Piece.................... 128.00
Nathan Hale Portrait, Yellow Majolica Glaze, Frame, J.G. & J.F. Low, 7 x 5 In. 264.00
Olive Stylized Tulips, Ochre Ground, Trivet, California Faience, Round, 4 1/2 In. 325.00
Panel, Face, Buildings, Cubist, Yellow, Black, Turquoise, Harris Strong, 43 x 11 In..... 990.00
Panel, Galleon Ship, Teal Sea, Turquoise & Gray Sky, Arts & Crafts, 4 1/4 In., 6 Piece 385.00
Pine Branch, Needles & Pine Cones, Caramel Majolica Glaze, Hamilton, 6 In. 138.00
Polychrome Flamingoes, Green Water Pool, San Jose Potteries, 8 In. 412.00
Roof, Horse Sitting On Haunches, Black Glaze, Green Eyes, Chinese, 15 In. 345.00

Round Stove, Man, Blue Majolica Glaze, B.F.A.T. Co., Artist, 4 1/4 In. 325.00
Scales, Brown & Blue, Moravian Pottery, 1979, 4 In. 25.00
Shepherdess, Sheep, Light Burgundy Majolica Glaze, Trent, 17 3/4 x 5 3/4 In. 412.00
Silhouette, Norcraft, Square, 4 1/4 In. 35.00
Single Tulip, Stove, Mottled Ivory & Caramel Glaze, Moravian Pottery, 6 3/4 x 5 1/2 In. 325.00
Spanish Cross, Tulip Design, Yellow & Green Glaze, Moravian Pottery, 7 x 5 3/4 In.. 275.00
St. Sebastian, Oil Hand Painted, Wood Baked, Hanger, Sgraffito Style, 11 1/2 x 12 In. 220.00
Stylized Blue Griffin, Yellow Ground, Red Clay Outline, California Faience, 5 In........ 468.00
Stylized Woman, Foliage, Crackle Glaze, Primavera, Longwy, France, 1920s, 8 In. 165.00
Tea, Chintz, Marguerite, Royal Winton 125.00
Ulysses Grant Portrait, Teal Majolica Glaze, Frame, J.G. & J.F. Low, 1885, 6 x 4 In.. 204.00
Winged Griffin, Painted Dark Blue, Green-Yellow Glaze, California Faience, 3 In. 330.00
Woman, Sitting At Spinning Wheel, Industry, Transfer, International Tile Co., 6 In. 192.00
Woman Profile, Bonnet, Overcoat, Burgundy Majolica Glaze, Trent, 6 In. 193.00

TINWARE containers for household use have been made in America since the
seventeenth century. The first tin utensils were brought from Europe, but by
1798, tin plate was imported and local tinsmiths made the wares. Painted tin
is called *tole* and is listed separately. Some tin kitchen items may be found
listed under Kitchen. The lithographed tin containers used to hold food and
tobacco are listed in the Advertising category under Tin.

Basket, Double Hinged Cover, Floral & Kittens, Handle, Germany, 1900, 2 1/2 In. 175.00
Boiler, Coffee, Wood Handle, James Heckin & Co., Ohio, c.1906 .... 110.00
Box, Document, Country, Painted, U.S., 19th Century 220.00
Box, Tinder, Double Candleholder & Striker In Cover 550.00
Box, Tinder, Finger Ring, Flint & Striker, 1 3/4 x 4 5/16 In. 265.00
Box, Tinder, With Candleholder, Finger Holder, 1 3/4 x 4 5/16 In. 215.00
Candleholder, Saucer, Thumb Loop 20.00
Chamberstick, 3 1/4 x 5 In. 45.00
Chamberstick, With Match Holder & Striker, Mid-1800s, 6 3/4 x 1 1/8 In. 120.00
Chandelier, 16 Arm, 33 1/2 In. 4025.00
Coddler, 1 Dozen Eggs, Side By Side Lids, Victorian, 19th Century, 2 Piece 185.00
Coffeepot, Punched, P. Shade, c.1800, 11 In. 2500.00
Foot Warmer, Punched, Mortised Cherry Frame, Turned Posts, 9 In. 105.00
Mold, Candle, 4 Tube, Handle, 10 In. 75.00
Mold, Candle, 12 Tube, 10 1/2 In. 50.00
Mold, Candle, 12 Tube, 2 Ear Handles 120.00
Mold, Candle, 12 Tube, Handle 95.00
Mold, Candle, 18 Tube, 10 3/4 In. 100.00
Rattle, Embossed, 8 1/2 In. 90.00
Rattle-Whistle, Embossed, Blue Traces, 4 3/4 In. 60.00
Sconce, Candle, Circular Reflector, Late 18th Century, 9 3/4 In. 350.00
Sconce, Concave Mirrored Reflector Back, Crimped Cockets, Tin, 10 In., Pair 550.00
Sconce, Continental, Crown & Heart Design, 19th Century, 6 In. 431.00
Spoon, Curved, For Dipping Cream From Bottles 16.00
Sugar Shaker, English, 5 In. 25.00

TOBACCO JAR collectors search for those made in odd shapes and colors.
Because tobacco needs special conditions of humidity and air, it has been
stored in special containers since the eighteenth century.

Emperor Franz Joseph, Porcelain 900.00
Figural, Sailor On Lid, Minton, 1864 .... 1955.00
Pipe Handle, Drinking Scene, 3 Men & Woman, Porcelain, 7 3/4 In. 145.00
Whimsical Portrait Of Long-Haired Dog, Mahogany, 8 In. 575.00

TOBY JUG is the name of a very special form of pitcher. It is shaped like the
full figure of a man or woman. A pitcher that shows just the top half of a person is not correctly called a toby. More examples of toby jugs can be found
under Royal Doulton and other factory names.

Betsy, Wood & Son, 6 1/2 In. 68.00
Frowning Man, Head, Blue Curls, Brown Hat, Green Collar, Mustache, 3 In. 24.00
Mamie Eisenhower 50.00

Sailor, 19th Century, Staffordshire, 10 1/2-In.	345.00
Toby Philpots, Wood & Son, 6 1/2 In.	85.00
Tricorner Hat, Brown Hair, Creamware, Staffordshire, c.1785, 7 1/4 In.	345.00

TOLE is painted tin. It is sometimes called *japanned ware, pontypool,* or *tole-ware.* Most nineteenth-century tole is painted with an orange-red or black background and multicolored decorations. Many recent versions of toleware are made and sold. Related items may be listed in the Tinware category.

Basket, Bread, Painted, Floral Sprays, Maroon Ground, 21 1/2 x 19 x 21 In.	330.00
Bowl, Apple, Oil Paint Design, Square, 11 In.	110.00
Box, Cutlery, Marked Knives-Forks, 13 In.	110.00
Box, Deed, Floral, Black Ground, Red Interior, Coin Slot In Lid, 8 In.	94.00
Box, Document, Domed Lid, Ring Handle, Swag Design, 1836, 6 1/4 x 8 x 4 In.	230.00
Candle Sconce, Hanging, 14 x 4 In., Pair	550.00
Canister, Tea, Flower, Black Ground	25300.00
Canister, Tea, Painted Oriental Figures, Black Surface	88.00
Canister, Tea, Painted, Crown Store Pure Teas, 17 1/2 In., 4 Piece	1955.00
Chandelier, 3-Light, Empire Style, Gilt Metal Ornament, Electrified, 16 x 12 In.	935.00
Coffeepot, Black Japanning, Fruit, Flowers & Foliage, 10 1/4 In.	600.00
Coffeepot, Hinged Cover, Red Paint, Spout, Brown, 8 5/8 In. ....*Illus*	36800.00
Coffeepot, Red Paint, Gold Stenciling, 2 3/4 In.	100.00
Coffeepot, Wriggle Work Design, Gold Leaf Engraving	7500.00
Coffeepot, Wriggled, Tulips & Vines, c.1840, 12 1/2 In.	4312.00
Container, Coffee, French Roast, Red Paint, Flowers, 25 x 32 x 18 In.	220.00
Cream Can, Sage Paint, 18 In.	44.00
Jardiniere, Flared, Chinoiserie Motifs, Acanthus Feet, Gilded, 11 1/4 x 13 1/4 In.	1850.00
Lamp, Victorian, Urn Form, Gilt, 25 In.	60.00
Lantern, Barn, Paneled Mirrored Reflector, Green Paint, 19th Century, 19 x 11 x 11 In.	287.00
Mug, Child's, Blue Grapes & Leaves, Cream Ground, Rattle In Base, 3 x 3 1/2 In.	45.00
Mug, Gold Stenciled My Boy, Red Paint, 2 In.	50.00
Planter, Oval Scene, Teal & Gold, France, 1815, 8 In.	375.00
Shaving Cup, Left-Handed, Black	100.00
Sugar, Finial Cover, Black Paint	920.00
Sugar, Red Floral Design, Dark Japanned Ground, 3 3/4 In.	192.00
Tea Caddy, Brown & Gold Painted Design, Mounted As Lamps, 18 In., Pair	545.00
Tea Caddy, Polychrome Floral, Black Paint, 7 1/2 In.	50.00
Tea Set, Flamingoes, Green, 7 Piece	30.00
Tray, 19th Century, 24 x 17 1/2 In.	58.00
Tray, Alternating Panels Of Wriggle Work Border, Medallions, 28 x 20 1/2 In.	201.25
Tray, Bird & Flower Design, 29 x 21 1/2 In.	96.00
Tray, Catherine The Great, Angels, Reticulated Gallery, Russia	605.00
Tray, Charles X, Allegorical Scene, Greek Key Border, Multicolored, 30 In.	1035.00

Tole, Coffeepot, Hinged Cover, Red Paint, Spout, Brown, 8 5/8 In.

♦ ♦

Pen collectors look for quality workmanship. A gold pen nib is good. The iridium ball fused to some nibs should be intact. The filling system should work or have only a minor problem like a bad ink sac. Replacement sacs are available. Large pens usually bring higher prices than small pens.

♦ ♦

Tray, Early Train In Landscape, People, Bronze Powder, Black Paint, 20 x 28 In. 275.00
Tray, Empire Style, Oval, Everted Rim, Swans, Fountain, Vines, Gilding, 23 1/4 In. 1810.00
Tray, Exotic Birds, In Garden, 25 x 19 In. 72.00
Tray, Fruits & Flowers, Octagonal, 26 x 18 In. 110.00
Tray, Gold Stencil & Freehand Floral Design, Black Ground, 28 1/4 x 20 3/4 In. 58.00
Tray, Hand Painted Floral, Oval, 20 In. 33.00
Tray, Late Faux Bas Design, France, Oval 550.00
Tray, Ocean Ships Scene, Cut Corners, Red, Black, Pair 2400.00
Tray, Oval, Interior Genre Scene, Continental, c.1800, 30 In. 2185.00
Tray, Painted Kittens At Play 225.00
Tray, Paris & Napoleon, Peach Ground, France, Rectangular 495.00
Tray, Red Berries, Green Leaves, Yellow Border, New York, Octagonal, 12 x 8 3/4 In. 115.00
Tray, Regency, Ceres In Center, Pierced For Handles, Yellow, Black, Stand, 25 1/4 In. 3450.00
Tray, Scene Of Figures By Sea, Red Ground, Pierced Handles, 32 1/4 x 24 In. 2875.00
Tray, Stand, Oval, Chinoiserie Motif, Trellis Border, X-Form Stand, 19 x 28 3/4 In. 3450.00
Tray, Tavern, Playing Cards, Black Ground, Hand Painted, 1880, 16 x 22 In. 245.00
Tray, Theorem Watermelon, Basket Of Strawberries, Yellow Bird, 19 x 22 In. 4840.00
Urn, Flared Tapered Shape, Chinoiserie Motifs, Acanthus Feet, 11 1/4 In., Pair 2300.00
Urn, Tea, Pear Shape, 3 Legs, Ball Feet, France, 1800, 16 In. 70.00
Vase, Continental, Mountain Peasants, 15 1/2 In., Pair 3900.00
Wash Set, Reserves Of Birds, Fans & Day Lilies, 4 Piece 220.00
Washstand, Tilting Round Mirror, Original Bowl, Lower Shelf 1350.00

TOM MIX was born in 1880 and died in 1940. He was the hero of over 100
silent movies from 1910 to 1929, and 25 sound films from 1929 to 1935. There
was a Ralston Tom Mix radio show from 1933 to 1950, but the original Tom
Mix was not in the show. Tom Mix comics were published from 1942 to 1953.

Arrowhead, Lucite Signal 45.00
Bandanna, Straight Shooters, Ralston Premium 75.00
Book, Big Little Book, Tom Mix And His Circus On The Barbary Coast 55.00
Book, Comic, 1949 .... 20.00
Book, Comic, Ralston Premium 26.00
Bracelet, ID, Ralston Straight Shooters ....35.00 to 60.00
Compass, Bullet, With Bird Call 400.00
Compass, Glow In The Dark 55.00
Label, Photograph, Black & White, Diamond Shape, 1930s, 4 x 2 In. 2.00
Label Set, Tom Mix Cigar Box, 6 x 10 In. & 2 Smaller, 4 Piece 35.00
Manual, Secret Ink Writing Set, 1938 .... 65.00
Medal, Ribbon, Glow In Dark 125.00
Parachute, Rocket, Mailer, Instructions ....120.00 to 145.00
Pistol, Wooden Cylinder Spins 95.00
Poster, Safety, Color, 1947, 17 x 22 In. 4.00
Ring, Magnet 65.00
Ring, Mystery 300.00
Ring, Sliding Ring 125.00
Toy, Clicker 30.00
Watch Fob, Gold Ore 60.00
Whistle Ring, Premium ....75.00 to 95.00

TOOLS of all sorts are listed here, but most are related to industry. Other tools
may be found listed under Iron, Kitchen, Tinware, and Wooden.

Anvil, Shoemaker's, Iron, 9 1/2 x 3 1/2 x 10 In. 15.00
Auger, Sugar 75.00
Auger Bits, Russell Jennings, No.100, 1940s, Box, 3 Piece 35.00
Ax, Modern Woodsmen, Promotional, Box 15.00
Ax, Pole, Side Stamped Irnest, Iron, 18th Century, 7 In. 195.00
Back Saw, Adjustable, Keen Kutter, No. KK97, Apple Wood Carved Handle 130.00
Back Saw, Wood & Metal Cutting, 3/4 Hsp., Cast Iron Stand, Delta Rockwell, 14 In. .. 875.00
Beader, Stanley, No. 66, 6 Cutters, 1920s 125.00
Bee Smoker 9.00
Bench, Cobbler's, Dovetailed Drawer, Leather Seat, Pine, 36 1/2 In. 220.00
Bench, Cobbler's, Drawers, 29 x 48 In. 440.00
Bench, Cobbler's, Pine, 2 Drawers, Tools, 21 x 44 x 18 In. 220.00

Bit Brace, Stanley, No. 923, Rosewood Handles, 1930s, 10-In. Sweep 150.00
Blasting Machine, Atlas Powder Co., No. 3, Dovetailed, Early 1900s, 6 x 8 x 13 In. 270.00
Block, Squirrel Tail, Strong Boy, 100. .... 26.00
Blow Torch, Brass 75.00
Board Stick, Stanley No. 43 1/2, 1900, 36 In. 145.00
Board Stick, Stanley No. 46, 1900, 24 In. 225.00
Box, Fordson Tractor 9.00
Box, Machinist's, Oak, 3 Drawers, 1930s 215.00
Box, Weatherstrip Plow, Stanley, No. 248, 1/8-In. Cutter, 1940s 110.00
Brace, Carpenter's, Wooden, Stamped F.W.T. 1846 .... 215.00
Brace, Ebony & Brass Bound, English 375.00
Brace, Shefield, Brass Plated, H. Brown 155.00
Broadax, Ash Handle, 11-In. Blade 72.00
Broadax, Wm. Beatty & Son, Chester, Pa., 13-In. Blade 72.00
Butter Table, Original Green Paint, Turned Legs & Wooden Plug 200.00
Buttoner, Shoe, Advertising 25.00
Caliper, Double, Heart Shape, Smith Made, 15 3/4 x 5 In. 135.00
Caliper, Forged Iron, 18th Century, Opens To 15 1/4 In. 95.00
Caliper, Inside, Athol, Mass., 1885, 5 In. 15.00
Caliper, Leg 65.00
Caliper, Log, Measures Size Of Timber, Wooden, Primitive 150.00
Caliper Rule, Forged Iron, Red Paint, 1850-1860, Opens To 33 1/4 In. 85.00
Caliper Rule, Metric, Stanley, No. 3, 4 Fold, 1 Ft. 695.00
Caliper Rule, SR & L Co., Special, 1900, 6 In. 1495.00
Caliper Rule, Stanley No. 12, 4 Fold, 1 Ft., 1910 .... 245.00
Candleholder, Miner's, Cast Iron, Points Were Driven Into Mine Wall, Pair 120.00
Carrier, Bucket, Wooden Frame, Green, 11 x 33 In. 150.00
Chain, Measuring, Surveyor's, Handles, 30 Ft. 55.00
Chain, Surveyor's, Brass Handles, Steel Links & Rods, c.1880, 100 Ft. 210.00
Chain Breaker, Harley 225.00
Check Writer, Defiance, 1880s 1000.00
Check Writer, Safe Guard, Iron, c.1900 .... 13.00
Chest, Carpenter's, Lift Top, 25 1/2 x 40 In. 110.00
Chest, Carpenter's, Paneled Front & Ends, 33 1/2 In. 115.00
Chest, Machinist's, Lift Top, 10 Drawers 200.00
Chest, Mechanic's, Lift Top, 3 Drawers, Bird's-Eye Maple, 15 x 22 In. 135.00
Chest, Pine, 17 x 39 x 14 In. 134.00
Chest, Ship Carpenter's, 3 Drawers, Original Beckets, 20 x 39 In. 305.00
Chisel, Stanley, No. 720, 1940s, 1 1/2 In. 20.00
Chisel, Winchester, Set Of 5 .... 210.00
Clamp, Glue, Signed, Stanley Tool Co., Connecticut, 8 1/2 In. 35.00
Comb, Flax, Square Handle, 18th Century, 8 1/2 x 12 In. 325.00
Combination Glass Cutter, Knife Sharpener & Can Opener, Andress, 1875, 5 1/2 In. .. 35.00
Cork Puller, Brass & Wooden, 1898 .... 25.00
Counter, Bean, Oak, 12 Ft. 1200.00
Cutter, Glass, Diamond Point, Marked Leather Case 75.00
Cutter, Plug Tobacco, Griswold 75.00
Cutter, Shave, Double, Stanley, No. 60 .... 50.00
Cutter, Side, Winchester 50.00
Douters, With Wick Trimming Blades, Blacksmith Made, Marked M, 6 1/2 In. 235.00
Draftman's Set, Lift-Out Tray, Brass Angles, Brass Tools, Wood Box, 11 Piece 125.00
Drying Rack, 3 Sections, Pine, Each Section 66 1/2 x 40 In. 55.00
Fence Stretcher, Wooden 18.00
File, Cooper's, Convex, Coarse, On Wood 45.00
Flashlight, Eveready, Masterlite, Ball Top 35.00
Flax Comb, Pierced Handles, Primitive, Dated 1816 .... 80.00
Fork, Potato Digger 6.00
Gaslighter, Kerosene, Brass Plated, 21 1/8 In. 130.00
Gauge, Double, Stanley, No. 74, Boxwood, Type 1, Pat. Oct. 22, 1872 .... 135.00
Gauge, Height, Chesterman, Precision Tool Co., Wooden Box 450.00
Gauge, Marking, Stanley, No. 64 1/2 .... 25.00
Gauge, Rope 85.00
Gauging Rod, Wine Barrel, Stanley, No. 45 .... 150.00

Grinder, Keen Cutter... 30.00
Gun, Bug Spray, Copper.. 45.00
Hackle, Fine Nails Mounted On Tin Covered Block, 4 x 18 In................................ 70.00
Hackle, Hand Forged Spines, Maple, 1796, 6 3/4 x 16 1/2 In.................................. 220.00
Hackle, Star Pattern, Beveled, Tin Clad & Punched, Aron Maning, 5 1/8 x 10 1/4 In. ... 180.00
Hacksaw, Keen Kutter.. 90.00
Hairdryer, Wahl Clipper, 1949 .... 45.00
Hammer, Claw, 11 Oz. 50.00
Hammer, Fulcrum, Keen Kutter 200.00
Hammer, Rooting, Keen Kutter 35.00
Hammer, Upholsterer's, Magnetic Tack, Stanley, No. 6020, Made With No Claw, 1934 50.00
Hammer, Upholsterer's, Stanley, No. 603, Decal On Handle, Early 1940s 50.00
Handcuffs, Tower Bean Pattern, With Key 185.00
Hatchet, Keen Kutter.. 65.00
Hatchet, Keen Kutter, Sportsman.. 125.00
Hatchet, Winchester, With Hammer Head & Nail Puller 65.00
Haystack Measure, Copper, Dovetailed, England, 1 Qt., 6 1/2 In............................. 165.00
Hone, Razor, Keen Kutter.. 48.00
Ice Chipper, Iron Head, Oak Shaft, c.1890, 25 1/2 In. 65.00
Ice Chipper, Peerless, Dana & Co., Iron, Jagged Teeth, Wooden Handle, 2 1/2 x 21 In. 12.00
Ice Shaver, Nickel Plated, Zeppelin On Front 2600.00
Ice Tongs, Forged Iron, Large 25.00
Ice Tongs, Polar Ice & Fuel Co., Wooden Handle.. 10.00
Iron, Branding, Double B... 20.00
Jack, Conestoga, 1866 .... 135.00
Jack, Defiance, Bailey Tool Co. Logo, No Adjustment, 1880s................................. 380.00
Jack, Wagon 45.00
Key, Sending, Telegrapher's, A.T. & T. S.F, Brass Plate 140.00
Knife, Draw Shave, Handles Fold Back, Wilkinson, 1895 .... 55.00
Knife, Farrier's, Hoof, Iron Handle 9.00
Lathe, Turning, Foot Powered, Wood Ends & Base, 24 In. 350.00
Leader, Bull, With Nose Clamp... 4.00
Level, Abney, Watson & Son, Leather Case, c.1900.. 150.00
Level, Carpenter's, Stanley, No. 347n, Embossed Wood, 1930s, 24 In........................ 50.00
Level, Case Farm Equipment, 6 In... 50.00
Level, Dandy, Wood & Brass, Stratton 28.00
Level, Davis, Pat. September 17, 1867, 7 In.. 350.00
Level, Machinist's, Stanley, No. 34, 6 In. ....50.00 to 125.00
Level, Machinist's, Stanley, No. 45, Type 1, 1859, 6 In. 300.00
Level, Nicholson's, No. 13, Brass Cover Plate, Brass Plate Stamped SR & L Co. 1860 . 225.00
Level, Pocket, Stanley, No. 40, 3 In. 25.00
Level, Torpedo, Stanley, No. 264... 18.00
Level, Transom, Stanley, 3 In... 5.00
Level, Trim, Brass, Stanley, No. 04.. 40.00
Level, Winchester, Cast Iron, 12 In.. 325.00
Log Cane, Stanley No. 48 1/2, 36 In... 400.00
Loom, Ruffle, Wooden, Spring Steel Reeds, 16 x 10 x 1 In. 190.00
Machine, Broom Making, Vise... 250.00
Machine, Doweling, Stanley, No. 77, 8 Cutter Heads, 1930s, 1/4 To 11/16 In. 950.00
Machine, Rope, Hawkeye.. 185.00
Measure, Stanley, No. 66, 4 Fold, 1900, 3 Ft... 275.00
Micrometer, Starret, No. 231, 1 In. 25.00
Micrometer, Starrett, Box, 1 In. 25.00
Micrometer, Watch, Brass Front, Wooden Base, Germany, 6 1/2 In........................... 65.00
Miter Box, Stanley, No. 246, With 7 x 17-In. Poster, Wooden Shipping Box, 1930s 395.00
Miter Square, Stanley, No. 16, 1905, 10 In. Blade... 75.00
Mold, Spoon, Bronze, 8 1/2 In. 285.00
Niddy Noddy, 18 In. 154.00
Niddy Noddy, Cherry & Hickory, Hand-Held, 18th Century, 12 x 17 1/2 In. 120.00
Ox Goad, Spanish Colonial 150.00
Padlock, 6 Lever, Winchester...100.00 to 110.00
Padlock, Violin Shape, Iron, Blacksmith Made.. 1400.00
Pitchfork, 4 Prongs, Wooden... 135.00

Plane, Bedrock Fore, Stanley, No. 606, Type 7-A, 1925 .... 275.00
Plane, Bedrock Smooth, Stanley, No. 604-1/2, Type 8, 1927 .... 315.00
Plane, Belt Maker's, Stanley, No. 11, 1910 .... 185.00
Plane, Bench, Keen Kutter 335.00
Plane, Block, Cabinetmaker's, Stanley, No. 9, Type 2, Screw Adjustment, 1870s 1200.00
Plane, Block, Stanley, No. 9 1/4, Christmas Box, 1940s 200.00
Plane, Block, Stanley, No. 65, Box 45.00
Plane, Block, Stanley, No. 203, 1940s 125.00
Plane, Block, With Side Plane, Keen Kutter 175.00
Plane, Bull Nose Rabbet, Stanley, No. 75 .... 25.00
Plane, Carpenter's, Shaker, Maple, Paper Tag, Canterbury, N.H., c.1850, 7 x 22 In. 165.00
Plane, Chamfer, Stanley, No. 72, Cap Screw, 1890s 285.00
Plane, Circular, Stanley, No. 20, Box, 1940s 395.00
Plane, Circular, Victor, No. 20 .... 233.00
Plane, Compass, Keen Kutter, No. KK 115, Nickel Plated 530.00
Plane, Corner Rounding, Stanley, No. 144, Pat.10-6-25, 1/2 Inside 425.00
Plane, Crown Molding, Birch, 14 In. 400.00
Plane, Crown Molding, M. Eisenhauer 250.00
Plane, Dado, Greenfield 30.00
Plane, Dado, Stanley, No. 39-3/8 .... 100.00
Plane, Dado, Stanley, No. 46, Type 1, 1873 .... 1495.00
Plane, Dovetail, Stanley, No. 444, 2 Spur Blocks, Cutters, Pat. 8-28-1910, Box 1450.00
Plane, Fiberboard, Stanley, No. 193a, Extra Blades 210.00
Plane, Fiberboard, Stanley, No. 194 .... 65.00
Plane, Finger, Brass, 1 1/8 In. 195.00
Plane, Finger, Brass, 1 3/4 In. 225.00
Plane, Floor, Stanley, No. 74 .... 310.00
Plane, Flooring, Stanley, No. 11-1/2, T On Cutter 550.00
Plane, Gage, Stanley, No. G5c 140.00
Plane, Jack, Junior, Stanley, No. 5 1/4 .... 65.00
Plane, Jack, Stanley, No. 104, Stamped Oct. 5, 1875 .... 125.00
Plane, Jack, Stanley, No. 5c, Type 18, Box 85.00
Plane, Jack, Wooden, Chapin Stephen Co., 16 In. 45.00
Plane, Jointer, Stanley, No. 8, c.1891 .... 74.00
Plane, Light Plow & Rabbet, Stanley, No. 54, WWII, 7 Cutters 925.00
Plane, Maple, Hand Made, Blade, 7 1/2 In. 35.00
Plane, Patent Pattern, Phelp's Co. 600.00
Plane, Plough, Boxwood & Ivory, Brass Reinforced To Top & Bottom 750.00
Plane, Plough, Stanley, No. 50s, 8 Cutters, Box 425.00
Plane, Rabbet, Stanley, No. 45, Box, 21 Bits 95.00
Plane, Rabbet, Stanley, No. 181 .... 50.00
Plane, Roughing, Iron, Sargent, No. 160 .... 122.00 to 150.00
Plane, Roughing, Stanley, No. 40, Rosewood Handle & Knob, 1940s 85.00
Plane, Side Rabbet, Type 1, Stanley, No. 79 .... 65.00
Plane, Side Trimming, Stanley, No. 95, 1940s 145.00
Plane, Smooth, Stanley, No. 21, Type 4, Eagle Mark, 1871-1872 .... 195.00
Plane, Smooth, Stanley, No. 1203, 1940s, Box 200.00
Plane, Smooth, Union, No. X3 .... 135.00
Plane, Stanley, No. 2, Smooth 225.00
Plane, Stanley, No. 10 .... 125.00
Plane, Stanley, No. 55 .... 500.00
Plane, Stanley, No. 62 .... 250.00
Plane, Stanley, No. 95, Edge Trimmer 160.00
Plane, Stanley, No. 113, Curved Wood, 1897 .... 75.00
Plane, Stanley, No. 444, 1 Cutter 600.00
Plane, Wood, Sawtooth Logo, Keen Kutter 65.00
Plane, Wood, Winchester 60.00
Planter, Corn, American Seeding Machine Co., 1896 .... 1200.00
Planter, Corn, Hoosier, Horse Drawn, American Seeding Machine Co., Patent 1896 .... 975.00
Pliers, Winchester, No. 2108-8 .... 55.00
Plumb, Mason's, Keen Kutter, No. KK25, Softwood 90.00
Plumb & Level, Brass Bound, Stratton, No. 1, 28 In. 50.00
Plumb & Level, Keen Kutter, No. K000-28, Wooden 25.00

Punch, Paper, Keen Kutter 35.00
Push Drill, Keen Kutter 95.00
Router, Stanley, No. 71, Throat Closing Attachment, 3 Cutters, Type 10, 1925, Box 175.00
Rule, 2 Fold, Winchester, No. 9518 .... 110.00
Rule, 4 Fold, Metric, Stanley, 40 Cm., 1870s 795.00
Rule, Carpenter's Caliper, 1 Foot, 4 Fold, c.1910 .... 275.00
Rule, Carpenter's, Stanley No. 6, Folding, Ivory 525.00
Rule, Carpenter's, Stanley No. 30, 1877-1879, 4 Fold 695.00
Rule, Carpenter's, Stanley, No. 63 .... 36.00
Rule, Desk, Stanley No. 98, 1910, 12 In. 150.00
Rule, Folding, Keen Kutter, K320, Brass Bound, With Caliper 45.00
Rule, Folding, Stanley, 62 1/2 In. 35.00
Rule, Scholar's, Stanley, No. 50, 1860s, 12 In. 235.00
Rule, Shrink, Pattern Makers, 3301/2, c.1900 .... 60.00
Rule, Spiral, Fuller's, Bakelite, Model 2, Stanley, Box 475.00
Rule, Spiral, Fuller's, Model 1, Mahogany, Stanley, Original Box 575.00
Rule, Stanley No. 86, 1880, 24 In. 450.00
Saw, Crosscut, 2 Handles 9.00
Saw, Hand, Simonds Saws Are The Best, On Blade 65.00
Saw, Hand, Winchester, No.W8, As Good As The Gun On Blade 100.00
Saw, Keyhole, Keen Kutter 18.00
Saw, Stanley, 1930s, 23 In. 95.00
Saw, Tread 24.00
Scissors, Grape, Italy, Brass 70.00
Scissors, Keen Kutter, 9 In. 40.00
Scissors, Wick Trimmer, In Stand, Brass, 7 1/2 In. 275.00
Scoop, Grain, Shovel Size 115.00
Scraper, Cabinet, Stanley, No. 80, Unused, Box 75.00
Scraper, Keen Kutter, No. K70 .... 45.00
Scraper, Stanley, No. 12 1/2, Japanned, 1920 .... 125.00
Scraper, Stanley, No. 112, Japanned, 1900 .... 195.00
Screwdriver, Stanley, No. 88, 3 Interchangeable Bits, Fit Into Handle, 1940s 50.00
Screwdriver, Winchester, No. 7103, 3 In. 28.00
Shaper, Wood, Delta Homecraft, Retractable Caster 325.00
Shoe Stretcher, Screw Type, Wooden, Watt's Pat., England, 1880 .... 50.00
Shoehorn, Blacksmith Made, Iron, 7 In. 175.00
Shoemaker's Kit, Lasts, Stand & Tools 30.00
Shovel, Grain, Wooden, 36 x 12 In. 198.00
Sifter, Sliding, Dovetailed, 2 Piece, 10 In. 205.00
Slate Roof Remover, Bangor Slate Company, Easton, PA., c.1850, 32 In. 75.00
Slide Rule, Pickett, Leather Case, 1962 ....20.00 to 25.00
Spokeshave, Keen Kutter 48.00
Spokeshave, Rabbet, Stanley, No. 68, 1910 .... 125.00
Spokeshave, Stanley, No. 60, Double Cutter, 1910 .... 75.00
Spotlight, Bakelite Handle, Side Mount, Keen Kutter 18.00
Spray, Insect, Hudson, Hand 30.00
Square, Winchester, No. 14, Steel, 24 x 16 In. 85.00
Staking Tool Set, Watchmaker's, E. Rivette, Fitted Wooden Case 100.00
Still, Brass 140.00
Stretcher, Barbed Wire Fence 12.00
Stretcher, Glove, Hard Pink Plastic 18.00
Stump Puller 2500.00
T Square, Sliding Stanley, No. 25, 8 In. 10.00
T-Bevel, Sliding, 1871-1872 .... 75.00
Table, Butchering, Hog, Primitive, 2 12-In. Ash Boards, Short Legs 700.00
Table, Butter Working 325.00
Tape, Surveyor's, Hand-Wound, Lufkin Rule 50.00
Ticker Tape, Glass Domed, New York Quotation Company 5720.00
Tongs, Blacksmith's 5.00
Tongs, Wrought Iron, Tobacco Press, Pipe Cleaner, 1750-1800, 22 In. 7575.00
Tote, Tool & Hardware, 12 Compartments, Handle, Hand Made, 1930s 95.00
Trammel, Forged Iron, Large Rod, 1750-1800, 32 To 53 1/2 In. 225.00
Trammel, Forged Iron, Small Rod, 1750-1800, 16 1/2 To 24 In. 200.00

Transit, Engineer's, Brass Plumb Bob, Case, Tripod, Brass & Wood	995.00
Traveler, Wheelwright's, Forged Spokes	135.00
Tray, Carpenter's, Wooden, 24 In.	35.00
Trimmer, Hoof, Horse, Compound	125.00
Trimmer, Wick, Wide Blade Catches Trimmings, Cast Iron	42.00
Try Square, Stanley, No. 12, Logo In Border, 1905, 2-In. Blade	175.00
Vernier/Arm Protractor, Brass, Signed, Messer, London, 6 In.	144.00
Vise, Clockwork, Cast Iron, Hand Wheel Adjustment, 14 In.	75.00
Vise, Springfield Rifle Spring	70.00
Wheelbarrow, Wooden Wheel, Runner-Like Arrangement Underneath	300.00
Winder, Yarn, Brass, English, 21 x 28 In.	220.00
Wrench, Alligator, Double Ended	50.00
Wrench, Alligator, Keen Kutter	30.00
Wrench, Bicycle, Keen Kutter, 4 In.	65.00
Wrench, Pipe, Winchester, No. 1021, 8 In.	65.00
Wrench, Triplet, 1910	245.00
Yoke, Calf Ox, Training, Single, Pine, Hickory Bow, c.1820, 17 1/2 x 16 x 4 In.	140.00
Yoke, Oxen Calf, Double, Maple, Hickory Bows, 44 x 21 In.	250.00

TOOTHPICK HOLDERS are sometimes called *toothpicks* by collectors. The variously shaped containers used to hold small wooden toothpicks are made of glass, china, or metal. Most of the toothpick holders are Victorian. Additional items may be found in other categories, such as Bisque, Silver Plate, Slag Glass, etc.

Atlantic City, Souvenir	20.00
Aunt Jemima	15.00
Beaded Grape, Green, Pressed Glass	45.00
Beaded Swag, Ruby Glass	55.00
Bees On Basket, Blue Opaque	50.00
Beggar's Hand, Milk Glass	15.00
Bird's Basket, Carnival Glass, Amber	30.00
Box In Box, Green	60.00
Boy, With Pack, Amber	55.00
Brittanic, Amber Flashed	135.00
Buckingham, Green, Pink & Gold	85.00
Cat, On Pillow, Amber	70.00
Cat, On Pillow, Blue	90.00
Cranberry, Gold, Bohemian	225.00
Cuspidor, Flare, Amethyst	30.00
Cut Block, Red Flashed	60.00
Daisy & Button, Amber, Flared	40.00
Daisy & Button, Green, Metal Rim	29.00
Delaware, Green, Gold Trim	38.00
Delaware, Rose, Gold	90.00
Diamond & Button, Hat, Blue	35.00
Diamond Panels, Green	36.00
Diamond Spearhead, Vaseline, Opalescent	85.00
Dog & Bone, Basket, Silver Plated, Marked James Tufts, 3 x 2 1/8 In.	165.00
Figural, Porcupine, Silver Plate, Meridan	95.00
Flute, Purple Carnival	44.00
Frog, Standing, Silver Plate	150.00
Georgia Gem, Custard, Souvenir Maine	49.00
Harvard, Yellow Custard	35.00
Illinois	20.00 to 35.00
Inverted Thumbprint, Enameled Flowers, Ring Base, Sapphire Blue	110.00
Iris With Meander, Blue, Opalescent	49.00 to 80.00
Iris With Meander, Green	29.00
Jefferson Colonial, Green	29.00
Jefferson Optic, Green, Gold, Enameled Flowers	50.00
Jeweled, Floral Design, Red Stones, Brass Finish, 1 3/4 In.	20.00
Lacy Medallion, Green	19.00
Man, Barrel On Back, Silver Plate, Tufts	425.00
Manhattan, Green Stained	29.00

National Eureka, Clear	25.00
New Hampshire, Blush	30.00
Nickel Swirl, Blue, Opalescent	150.00
Palm Leaf, Pink & White	65.00
Paneled Sprig, White, Opalescent	85.00
Pansy, Blue	45.00
Parrot, Silver Plate	80.00
Peek-A-Boo, Milk Glass	15.00
Pig, Laying Against Green Sheaf Of Wheat, Porcelain	95.00
Plain Scalloped Panel, Green	20.00
Pleat & Bow, Blue Flowers	28.00
Pomona, Amber Band, Applied Rigaree	85.00
Porcupine Quill, Silver Plate, Wilcox	50.00
Punty Band, Red Flashed	30.00
Reverse Swirl, White, Opalescent	85.00
Ribbed, Apple Green	30.00
Ribbed Enamel Flowers, Cobalt Blue	45.00
Ribbed Lattice, Blue, Opalescent	125.00
Ribbed Lattice, Cranberry, Opalescent	295.00
Ribbed Spiral, Blue, Opalescent	95.00
Rising Sun, Blush	35.00
Ruby Thumbprint, Etched	40.00 to 45.00
Santa Claus, St. Clair, Red	60.00
Saving Rock Conn., Bean Pot, White Bear Handle, Germany, 1920-1930, 2 x 4 In.	75.00
Scrolled Shell	30.00
Shamrock, Green	45.00
Six Point, Scalloped	25.00
Swag, With Brackets, Amethyst	55.00
Swan Scene, China	39.00
Swinger, Ruby	24.00
Swirl, 2-Ply, Clear With Gold	30.00
Texas, Clear, Gold Trim	23.00
Twist, Blue, Opalescent	450.00
Utility Boot, Blue	27.00
Vaseline Glass, Opalescent Hobnail, 3-Footed, Scalloped Rim	15.00
Waldorf Astoria, Clear	95.00
Windsor Anvil, Amber	26.00
Wolf, Porcelain	70.00
Wreath & Shell, Blue, Opalescent	275.00
Wreath & Shell, Yellow, Opalescent	75.00
X-Ray, Amethyst, Gold Trim, Opalescent	235.00

TORQUAY is the name given to ceramics by several potteries working near Torquay, England, from 1870 until 1962. Until about 1900, the potteries used local red clay to make classical-style art pottery vases and figurines. Then they turned to making souvenir wares. Items were dipped in colored slip and decorated with painted slip and sgraffito designs. They often had mottoes or proverbs, and scenes of cottages, ships, birds, or flowers. The *Scandy* design was a symmetrical arrangement of brushstrokes and spots done in colored slips. Potteries included Watcombe Pottery (1870–1962); Torquay Terra-Cotta Company (1875–1905); Aller Vale (1881–1924); Torquay Pottery (1908–1940); and Longpark (1883–1957).

TORQUAY

Ashtray, Black Cockerel, A Place For Ashes, 3 1/4 x 4 3/4 In.	45.00
Bean Pot, Lucky Devon Pixie, 3 x 3 1/4 In.	65.00
Candlestick, Scandy	125.00
Chamberstick, Last In Bed, Put Out Light, 4 1/2 x 4 In.	155.00
Chamberstick, Sailboat	98.00
Creamer, Cottage, Motto Ware	35.00
Creamer, Metal Rim	250.00
Creamer, Scandy, Miniature	40.00
Cup & Saucer, Motto Ware, Scandy, Aller Vale	30.00 to 55.00
Eggcup, Cottage	45.00
Jam Dish, Cottage, Take A Little Jam, Fluted Edge, Handle, 2 x 4 1/2 In.	45.00

Jam Jar, Cottage, Go Aisy Wi' It Now, 4 1/4 x 3 In.	50.00
Jam Jar, Lucky Wiltshire Pixie, 4 In.	90.00
Mug, Cottage, Haste Makes Waste, 3 x 2 3/4 In.	35.00
Mug, Sailing Ship, 3 Handles	85.00
Mustard, Saltbun By-The-Sea, Hot & Strong, 1 3/4 In.	50.00
Pitcher, Barrel Shape, Motto Ware, 3 1/2 In.	50.00
Pitcher, Cockerel, Green & Blue, Motto Ware, Aller Vale, 6 In.	150.00
Pitcher, Cockerel, Green & Blue, Motto Ware, Allervale, 6 In.	175.00
Pitcher, Cottage, Motto Ware, 4 In.	45.00
Pitcher, Milk, Men Know, Women Know Better	95.00
Plate, Cottage, Motto Ware, 10 In.	40.00
Pot, Hasty Climbers, Motto Ware, 2 1/2 In.	45.00
Relish, Triangular Shape	75.00
Salt & Pepper, Cottage, Egg Shape, Verse, 2 3/4 x 1 3/4 In.	60.00
Server, Cottage, 2 Sections, Motto Ware.	115.00
Spooner, Metal Rim	250.00
Sugar, Cover, Ruby	225.00
Sugar, Metal Rim	250.00
Teapot, Cottage	130.00
Teapot, Hinges Of Friendship, Motto Ware	125.00
Tray, Motto Ware, 5 1/2 x 2 1/2 In.	35.00

TORTOISESHELL is the shell of the tortoise. It has been used as inlay and to make small decorative objects since the seventeenth century. Some species of tortoise are now on the endangered species list, and objects made from these shells cannot be sold legally.

Box, Brass Inlaid, Boulle Type, Asprey & Co., London, Round	468.00
Box, Cigarette, 6 In.	88.00
Box, Inlaid Silver Shield Cover, 10 In.	550.00
Box, Rectangular, Silk Lined, 19th Century, 8 In.	575.00
Box, Trinket, 6 x 5 In.	220.00
Case, Dome Top, Scent Bottle, 3 In.	237.00
Case, Lorgnette, c.1880	485.00
Cigar Case, 7 In.	170.00
Desk Set, Boulle, 2 Pen Trays, 2 Ink Pots, Bronze Lids, France, c.1900, 15 1/4 In.	920.00
Figurine, Mandolin, Ivory, 8 In.	121.00
Figurine, Violin, Shell & Ivory, 5 1/2 In.	44.00
Jewel Chest, Boulle, Canted Corners, Inlaid, 19th Century, 12 x 6 1/2 x 6 In.	632.00
Powder Box, Round, 4 In.	99.00
Snuffbox, Carved, Silver Frame, 19th Century, 3 x 2 In.	345.00
Tea Caddy, Fitted Interior, 19th Century, 4 1/2 x 6 1/4 In.	1305.00

TORTOISESHELL GLASS was made during the 1800s and after by the Sandwich Glass Works of Massachusetts and some firms in Germany. Tortoiseshell glass is, of course, named for its resemblance to real shell from a tortoise. It has been reproduced.

Compote, 1880, 6 1/2 In.	350.00
Pitcher, Water, Tri-Shape, Ruffled Top, Amber Handle, 8 In.	125.00
Platter, Round, 16 In.	95.00

TOY collectors have special clubs, magazines, and shows. Toys are designed to entice children, and today they have attracted new interest among adults who are still children at heart. All types of toys are collected. Tin toys, iron toys, battery operated toys, and many others are collected by specialists. Dolls, Games, Teddy Bears, and Bicycles are listed in their own categories. Other toys may be found under company or celebrity names.

Accordion, Germany, 7 In.	65.00
Acrobat, Ajax, Somersaults, Windup, Lehmann	1475.00
Acrobat, Barrel Walker, Windup, Tin Lithograph, Chein, 1930s	375.00
Acrobats, 2 Dancing Figures, Bells, 4-Wheel Platform, Cast Iron, 6 1/2 In.	460.00
Acrobats, Big 3 Aerial, Windup, Marx, 1920s	225.00
Air Ship, Pull Toy, Cast Iron, 5 1/2 In.	55.00
Airplane, 2 Pilots, Windup, Prewar, CK, Japan	620.00

Airplane, Aero, Flip Over, Tin Lithograph, Windup, U.S. Zone, 5-In. Wingspan 225.00
Airplane, Aeroplane, No. 68, Dinky 2340.00
Airplane, Air France Transatlantic, 4-Engine Carrier, Fany 4070.00
Airplane, Air France, Clockwork, Tin, 24 In. 700.00
Airplane, Airliner, 3-Motor, Farman, Box 1650.00
Airplane, Airmail, Monoplane, Kenton, 1920s, 6 1/4-In. Wingspan 450.00
Airplane, Airmail, Pressed Steel, Mail Bag, Keystone, Late 1920s, 24 In. 575.00
Airplane, Airmail, Pressed Steel, Tri-Motor, Late 1920s, 24 In. 545.00
Airplane, American Airlines, Battery Operated, Marx, Japan, 19 1/2 In. 295.00
Airplane, American Airlines, Jet Of The Soaring '60s, Marx, Japan, 13 1/2 In., Box 175.00
Airplane, B-50, Etco, Box 500.00
Airplane, Bi-Wing Jenny, Friction, Japan, 15-In. Wingspan 285.00
Airplane, Boeing 747, Blinking Wing Lights, Windup, Box 75.00
Airplane, Boeing B-50, 4 Motors, Friction, Japan, 15-In. Wingspan 385.00
Airplane, Boeing Stratocruiser, 4 Motors, Metal, 13-In. Wingspan 125.00
Airplane, Bomber, P35, 2 Engines, Marx, 16-In. Wingspan 120.00
Airplane, British Army, Tin Lithograph, Windup, Mettoy, 10-In. Wingspan 295.00
Airplane, Capital Airlines, 4 Motors, Japan, 17-In. Wingspan 275.00
Airplane, Driver, Windup, Collapsible Wings, Orobr Co., Germany, 1905, 11 In. 1450.00
Airplane, Fighter Jet, Red & Silver, All Metal, Hubley 75.00
Airplane, Flying Tiger, Battery Operated, Marx 150.00
Airplane, Glider, Loop The Loop, Ideal, 1916, Box 155.00
Airplane, Globe Master Transport, Box 1200.00
Airplane, Go-Round, Lever Action, Tin Lithograph, 3 Planes, U.S. Zone Germany 195.00
Airplane, Hangar, Spirit Of St. Louis, Metalcraft, No. 890, Box 695.00
Airplane, Jet, F-14, Battery Operated, Wings & Canopy Open, Tin Lithograph, 12 In... 10.00
Airplane, Key Wind, Red, White, Blue, c.1930, 6 1/2 In. 77.00
Airplane, Lindy Glider, Detroit Gull On Tail, Hubley, 1930s, 9 7/8 In. 605.00
Airplane, Lindy, Gear Drive, 10 In. 3200.00
Airplane, Lockheed Sirius, Steelcraft 700.00
Airplane, Lucky Stunt Flyer, New York To Paris, Marx 925.00
Airplane, Martin Matador, Pilot & Cockpit, Japan 275.00
Airplane, Messerschmitt, Dinky, No. 724, Sahara Camouflage, Box 154.00
Airplane, Military, Rollover, Linemar, Box 195.00
Airplane, Mono, Single Engine, Mettoy 770.00
Airplane, Navy Hell Fighter, Cox, Gas Powered 400.00
Airplane, P-35, Marx, 13 1/2-In. Wingspan 95.00
Airplane, Pan Am See-Through Jet, Plastic, Battery Operated, 15 In. 125.00
Airplane, Pan Am, Battery Operated, Box 75.00
Airplane, Penny Toy, Tin, Windup, Rear Propeller, 5 1/2 x 4 In. 400.00
Airplane, Piper Cub, Red, 8 In. 75.00
Airplane, Piper Cub, Yellow Paint, Missing Prop, Monogram, 24 In., 35-In. Wingspan ... 95.00
Airplane, Pontoon, Sea Patrol, Red, Yellow & Blue, Windup 80.00
Airplane, Red Baron, Tri-Wing, Tootsietoy, Box 175.00

Toy, Baby Quieter, J. & E. Stevens,
Bell, Painted, Cast Iron, 8 In.

◆◆◆◆◆◆◆◆◆◆◆◆◆◆◆◆◆◆◆◆◆◆◆◆

When polishing the metal hardware on old chests of drawers, take a piece of stiff paper and slide it under the brass plate. This will protect the wood near the brass.

◆◆◆◆◆◆◆◆◆◆◆◆◆◆◆◆◆◆◆◆◆◆◆◆

Airplane, Rollover Plane, Marx 125.00
Airplane, Seaplane, Spinning Propellers, Key Wind, Tin, Paya, 13 In. 185.00
Airplane, Seaplane, Tin Windup, Chein, Box 250.00
Airplane, Silver Eagle, Twin Engines, Aluminum, Automatic Toy Co., 13-In. Wingspan   180.00
Airplane, Single Prop, Windup, Tin, Girard, 1920s 285.00
Airplane, Spinning Propeller, Friction, Tin, 16-In. Wingspan 135.00
Airplane, Spirit Of '76, Box, Metalcraft, Box, 1920s 350.00
Airplane, Spirit Of America, Tin Lithograph, Windup, 1920s, 6 5/8-In. Wingspan 200.00
Airplane, Spirit Of St. Louis, Cereal Premium, Cellophane Package 25.00
Airplane, Stratojet, Friction, Marx, Box 75.00
Airplane, Super Sonic Jet, Friction & Battery Operated, Tin, 24 In. 295.00
Airplane, Tin Lithograph, Indian Decoration, Pioneer, Marx, c.1920, 25 x 24 In. 230.00
Airplane, Topflite, Hellcat, Balsa, 1960s 30.00
Airplane, Tri-Motor, Cast Iron, Arcade 150.00
Airplane, Tri-Motor, Green & Orange, Pressed Steel, 18-In. Wingspan 595.00
Airplane, U.S. Army, No. 712, Sparking Guns, Windup, Tin, Marx 295.00
Airplane, U.S. Mail, Wheels Turn Prop, 23-In. Wingspan 485.00
Airplane, Voo Doo Jet, U.S. Air Force, Friction & Battery Operated, 19 In. 285.00
Airplane, Wooden, Dr. Barton, Rochester, N.Y., 1832 .... 25.00
Airplane, Woody Woodpecker, Windup, Box, 1960s 45.00
Airplane, Yankee Scout, Wheels Turn Prop, Ideal, 20-In. Wingspan 485.00
Alabama Coon Jigger, Lehmann, Box 810.00
Alligator, Painted Eyes & Teeth, Leather Feet, Schoenhut, 12 1/2 In. 165.00
Alligator, Steiff, 12 In. 125.00
Ambulance, Emergency Medical Service, Matchbox, No. 41, 1976 .... 12.00
Ambulance, Ford, Friction, Japan, 1963, 10 In. 39.00
Ambulance, Matchbox 28.00
Amos 'n' Andy, Walker, Marx, 11 1/2 In. 1895.00
Amusement Park & Circus, Merry Go Round, Battery Operated, Chein 495.00
Armchair, Doll's, Ladder Back, Woven Splint Seat, 13 In. 60.00
Armoire, Doll's, French Fashion, Mirrored Door, Base Drawer, 19th Century 155.00
Artie The Clown, In His Crazy Car, Tin, Unique Art 270.00
Astronaut, Crank Operated, Red, Cragstan 1650.00
Astronaut, Rotate-O-Matic 225.00
Autobus, Windup, Lehmann, c.1910 .... 375.00
Baby Beth, Fisher-Price, My Sleepy Baby, Box 435.00
Baby Quieter, J. & E. Stevens, Bell, Painted, Cast Iron, 8 In. ....*Illus* 2070.00
Back Hoe, Nylint 85.00
Backpack, Good 'n' Plenty, Canvas 28.00
Badge, Dick Steel, News Service Reporter 25.00
Badge, Lee Riders Deputy Sheriff, Silver Metal, 1950s 5.00
Badge, Sky Riders Club, Lieutenant 15.00
Baking Set, Comicooky, Pillsbury, 1937 .... 135.00
Balloon Blower, Gineo-Neapolitan, Battery Operated, Tomiyama Co., Box 175.00
Barber Shop Quartet, Automaton, 25 x 15 In. 3575.00
Barney Google & Spark Plug, Scooter Base, Pull Toy, 1920s 2250.00
Bartender, Blushing Willy, Battery Operated 105.00
Bartender, Pours Drink, Smoke From Ears, Battery Operated, Rosco, Box 95.00
Basket, Sewing, Doll's, Straw, Hinged Lid, Silk Ribbons, Furnishings, c.1920, 15 In... 375.00
Bears are also listed in the Teddy Bears category
Bear, Andy The Panda, Pull Toy, Wooden, Gong Bell, 1930s 75.00
Bear, Balloon Blowing, Alps Of Japan, c.1950s, Light-Up Eyes 185.00
Bear, Bell Toy, 2 Bears Ring Bells, Steel Frame, 10 In. 795.00
Bear, Drumming, Tin, Rubber Drumsticks, Japan, 9 In. 395.00
Bear, Mama Bear Feeding Baby Bear, Battery Operated, Japan 225.00
Bear, Panda, Drinking, Light-Eyes 225.00
Bear, Picnic, Light-Up Eyes, Battery Operated, Alps Co. 285.00
Bear, Red Leatherette Muzzle, Fur Cover, Windup, Begging 195.00
Bear, Ride-On, Blond, Steel Frame, Embroidered Nose, c.1950, 25 1/2 In. 230.00
Bear, Shooting, Battery Operated, San Co., Box 300.00
Bear, Skater, Windup, Japan, Box 125.00
Bear, Smoking, Battery Operated, Japan 185.00
Bear, Spanking, Battery Operated, Box 575.00

Bear, Walking, Pole Behind Head, Twisting Motion Walker, Windup, Tin, 8 1/2 In. 145.00
Beaver, Steiff, 6 In. 125.00
Bed, Doll's, Angels & Birds On Sides, Cast Iron, c.1880 .... 2250.00
Bed, Doll's, Hidden Drawer, Carved Wood, 20 x 12 1/2 x 18 In. 165.00
Bedroom Set, Doll's, White, Painted Design, 3 Piece 3400.00
Bee, Queen Buzzy Bee, Pull Toy, Fisher-Price 5.00
Beetle, Peplex, Spins & Lurches, Windup, Germany 75.00
Beetle, Walking, Tin Lithograph, Windup, Japan, Box 65.00
Bell Ringer, Cast Iron, Ding Dong Bell, Pussy's Not In The Well, 1890s 1250.00
Bell Ringer, Clockwork, Standing Pig, Bell Rings When Tail Pulled, Germany, 6 In. ... 488.00
Bell Ringer, Clown & Poodle, Wheeled Platform, Painted, Cast Iron, 8 In. 1150.00
Bell Ringer, Little Nemo, Cast Iron, 1880s 950.00
Bell Toy, Clown & Trick Poodle, Gong Bell Co. 2300.00
Betty's Pastry Set, Box 20.00
Bicycles are listed in their own category
Bicycle Horn, Machine Gun, Battery Operated, Box 295.00
Bicyclist, Duett, 2 Clowns Riding, Tin Lithograph, Yellow, DBS, Germany, 8 In. 110.00
Bird, Chirping, Tin, Windup, Japan, 3 1/2 x 4 3/4 In. 50.00
Bird, Flapping Lovebird, Moving Wings, Tin Lithograph, Japan, Box 65.00
Bird, Flying, Tin Lithograph, Windup, Tree Base 437.00
Bird, Pecking, Windup, Lindstrom 50.00
Bird, Raven, Black, Metal Feet, Steiff, 7 In. 185.00
Birds, Pecking, Pull Toy, Handmade, Painted, 1920s 185.00
Black Boy, Waddles, Holding Watermelon, Dog Biting Pants, Celluloid, 1930s 650.00
Blocks, ABC & Victorian Pictures, Stacking, 4 1/4 In., 7 Piece 425.00
Blocks, Alphabet, Lithographed Children, Animals, Schoenhut, 1916, 26 Pc. 1250.00
Blocks, Alphabet, McLoughlin, Set 1575.00
Blocks, Mother Goose, McLoughlin, 1895, 20 Piece 525.00
Boat, Aircraft & Carrier, Twin Screw, Key Wind, World War II Model, 20 In. 550.00
Boat, Battleship, Black Superstructure, Painted Tin & Wood, Orkin, 25 In. 465.00
Boat, Battleship, The Maine, Tin, 11 In. 145.00
Boat, Cabin Cruiser, Painted Tin, Detailed Controls, Orkin, 32 In. 495.00
Boat, Destroyer, 2 Stacks, Two-Tone Gray, Windup, Painted Tin, Ives, 13 In. 550.00
Boat, Ferry, Tin Lithograph, Windup, Lindstrom, 7 In. 135.00
Boat, Fireboat, Deck Mounted Hose Reel & Boiler, Pumps Water, Tin, 12 In. 825.00
Boat, Firefighter, Hatch On Rear Deck Lifts For Access To Windup Mechanism, 26 In. 990.00
Boat, Gun, Big Bang, Fires Carbide Charge, Conestoga Mfg. Co., Cast Iron, 9 1/2 In. .. 70.00
Boat, Gun, Fires Caps, Tin Lithograph, Battery Operated, c.1950, Box 275.00
Boat, Gun, Single Stack, Painted Tin, Bing, 16 1/2 In. 330.00
Boat, Liberty Scout, Windup, Tin 385.00
Boat, Mary Jane, Yellow, Red, White & Blue, Windup, Chein, 14 In. 150.00
Boat, Motor, Outboard, Mercury, Model MK55 .... 300.00
Boat, Motor, Outboard, Mercury, Model MK78 .... 400.00
Boat, Navy PT, Package, Cereal Premium 15.00
Boat, Ocean Liner, Carmania, 2 Stacks, 6 Life Boats, Germany, 24 In. 2035.00
Boat, Ocean Liner, Red, Black, White Hull, 4 Stacks, Painted Tin, Carrette, 13 1/2 In.. 385.00
Boat, Paddlewheeler, City Of New York, Floor Toy, Working Beam, Cast Iron, 15 In.. 385.00
Boat, Peggy Jane, Tin, Windup, Box, Chein, 13 In. 125.00
Boat, Penny, Fisher, Germany, 4 1/2 In. 425.00
Boat, Pond Yacht, Hardwood, England, 24 In. 150.00
Boat, River, Metal Party Of Figures Under Canopy, Windup, Tin, Carrette, 22 In. 575.00
Boat, River, Sightseeing, Metal Captain, Windup, Tin, Bing, 20 In. 2420.00
Boat, Rowboat, Tin Lithographed Figure Rows, Key Wind, Tin, Paya, 14 In. 130.00
Boat, Sailboat, Tin, Painted, Lutz, c.1900, 16 In. 1035.00
Boat, Sand-O-Land, Wyandotte, Tin 125.00
Boat, Sea Hawk, Battery Operated, Tin, Straits Co., Box, 1920s, 20 In. 490.00
Boat, Side-Wheeler, Adirondack, Working Beam, Cast Iron, 15 In. 495.00
Boat, Side-Wheeler, Clockwork, Wood, Metal, Steam-Type Sidewinder, c.1870, 26 In. 6500.00
Boat, Side-Wheeler, Embossed Tin, Cast Wheels, Fallows, 8 1/2 In. 550.00
Boat, Side-Wheeler, Mermaid Figurehead, Painted Tin, Windup, Falck, 9 In. 905.00
Boat, Side-Wheeler, N.Y. Ferry Co., Paper Lithograph, Reed, 19th Century, 13 In. 3737.00
Boat, Side-Wheeler, Puritan, White, Moving Beam, Cast Iron, 11 In. 550.00
Boat, Side-Wheeler, Twin Stacks, Windup, Fleischmann, 8 1/2 In. 330.00

Boat, Siren Sound, Windup, Tin, 1950s, 9 In. 135.00
Boat, Speed, Flying Yankee, Wooden Hull, Cable Rigged Steering, Windup, 20 In. 240.00
Boat, Speed, Miss Liberty, Brass Boiler, Single Engine, Tin, Japan, 14 In. 355.00
Boat, Speed, Pollywog, Live Steam, Brass Boiler, Wooden, Boucher, 24 1/2 In. 605.00
Boat, Speed, Putt-Putt, Impulse Steam Powered, Alden Novelty Co., 9 In. 105.00
Boat, Speed, Tin, Red, Blue, Battery Operated, Jouet Gil, France, c.1930, 19 In., Box .. 77.00
Boat, Speed, Toc-Toc, Impulse Steam Powered, Tin Driver, Abbey, Box, 9 In. 88.00
Boat, Speed, Vixen, Green & White, Open Cockpit, Seats, Tin, Windup, Ives, 13 In. 1015.00
Boat, Speed, Whiz, Brass Engine Cover, Painted Tin, Windup, Boucher, 21 In. 465.00
Boat, Station Wagon, Trailer, Friction, Cragstan, Japan, Box 250.00
Boat, Steamship, America, Live Steamer, Oscillating Engine, Painted Copper, 25 In. ... 8250.00
Boat, Steamship, Lithograph, Windup, Germany, 1930 .... 100.00
Boat, Submarine, Carries 2 Flags, Painted Tin, Windup, Bing, 10 1/4 In. 210.00
Boat, Submarine, Corgi, No. 803, Yellow, Red Caps, Water Box Insert, Box 385.00
Boat, Tanker, Esso, Red & Black Hull, Masts, Life Boats, Fleischmann, 19 1/2 In. 550.00
Boat, Tanker, Texaco, 24 In. 90.00
Boat, Tin, Alcohol Burning 55.00
Boat, Torpedo, 2 Deck Guns, Painted Tin, Windup, Carrette, 15 1/2 In. 605.00
Boat, Torpedo, Twin Tubes In Bow, Painted Tin, Windup, France, 19 In. 1650.00
Boat, Tug, Windup & Battery Operated, Tin, Japan, 12 1/2 x 5 1/2 In. 110.00
Boat, U-25 Patrol, Electric Drive, Hatch Access Cover, Painted Tin, France, 21 In. 135.00
Boat, U-Boat, Marklin 8625.00
Boat, U.S.S. Enterprise, On Wooden Wheels, Wyandotte 125.00
Boat, War, Sparking, Tin, Keywind, Arnold, Germany, Box, 9 In. 95.00
Bombo The Monk, Windup, Tin, 1930s, Unique 185.00
Boxers, Celluloid, Tin, Windup 95.00
Boxers, Clowns & Kangaroo, Cast Metal, All With Boxing Gloves, Britains, 2 1/4 In. ... 60.00
Boy, On Sled, Articulated Arms, Steer Sled, Windup, Germany, 6 3/4 In. 495.00
Boy, On Steer, Rocking, Tin, Windup, Gunthermann, c.1910, 6 1/2 x 7 1/2 In. 546.00
Boy, Ringing Bell, Japan.. 235.00
Boy On Bike, Balance Toy, Tin 275.00
Boy On Sled, Friction, Dayton.. 675.00
Brer Rabbit, Fun On Wheels, Plastic, 1960s, 3 In. 20.00
Bronco Cowboy On Slinky Horse, Pull Toy, James Industries 40.00
Bubble Blower, Blo Bubbles, Fish-Shaped Pipe, Plastic, Knickerbocker, 1950s 40.00
Bubble Pipe, Bird, Figural 6.00
Buffalo, Steiff, 10 x 14 In. 300.00
Buggy, 2 Horses, Driver, Passenger, Fringed Cloth Top, Cast Iron, Stanley, Pair 99.00
Bugle, Music-Tone Mouthpiece, Metal, c.1915.. 65.00
Building, American Railway Express, Tin, Chein 35.00
Building Set, Romper Room Magic, Wood, Canister, Gem Color Co., 1957, 10 In........ 24.00
Building Set, Tin, Drug Store, Firehouse, School, Green House, Tin, West Bros., 1914 100.00
Bulldozer, Hubley, 10 In. 120.00
Bulldozer, Plastic, Windup, Marx, Box 65.00
Bullwinkle, Windup, Box.. 75.00
Bureau, Doll's, Oak, Attached Mirror, 10 x 6 x 18 In. 165.00
Burro, Painted Eyes, Leather Ears, Twine Tail, Schoenhut, 7 In., Pair 230.00
Bus, Airport Service, Tin, Friction, 9 In. 65.00
Bus, Around The World, Friction, Daiya, Japan, c.1950, 13 In. 90.00
Bus, Coast-To-Coast, GMC, Arcade, 1937, 7 1/2 In. 275.00
Bus, Coast-To-Coast, GMC, Arcade, 1937, 9 In.. 375.00
Bus, Continental Trailways, Tin, Friction... 50.00
Bus, Deluxe, No. 105, Chauffeur, Seats, Tin Lithograph, Strauss, 13 1/2 In. 1380.00
Bus, Double Decker, 3 Figures, Cast Iron, Kenton, 10 In. 990.00
Bus, Double Decker, 8 Passengers, 1 Child, Cast Iron, c.1920, 9 1/2 In. 745.00
Bus, Double Decker, Clockwork, Minic, Box 150.00
Bus, Double Decker, Kenton... 2090.00
Bus, Double Decker, Tin Lithograph, Penny Toy, 4 1/2 In. 300.00
Bus, Double Decker, Triumph 50.00
Bus, Double Decker, Wells "O" London, England... 325.00
Bus, Double Decker, Yellow Coach, Iron, AR260, Arcade, 14 In. 5000.00
Bus, Great Lakes Exposition, Arcade, 1936, 6 3/4 In.. 875.00
Bus, Greyhound, Coast To Coast, Arcade 460.00

Bus, Greyhound, Friction, Tin, 14 In. 125.00
Bus, Greyhound, GMC, Pea Green, Arcade 5720.00
Bus, Greyhound, Scenic Cruiser, Tin, Friction, Japan, 11 In. 65.00
Bus, Greyhound, Scenic Cruiser, Tootsie Toy 40.00
Bus, Greyhound, Tin, Friction, Japan, 5 In. 75.00
Bus, Jackie Gleason, Push-Down Action, Tin, 1955, 14 1/2 In. 395.00
Bus, Motor Coach, Windup, Lehmann, 5 In. 600.00
Bus, Public Service, Dent 6270.00
Bus, Remote Control, Radicon, T.M., Japan, 14 In., Box 275.00
Bus, Royal Blue Line, Chein, 1920s, 18 In. 1400.00
Bus, Speedway, Windup, Wolverine, Box, 14 In. 195.00
Bus, Touring, 999 Seeing New York, Kenton 3850.00
Bus, Twin Coach, Niagara Lines, A.C. Williams, 1930 .... 5500.00
Bus, United Airport Limousine, Ringing Bell, Opening Door 75.00
Bus, Volkswagen, Micro, White Top, Red Body, Box 175.00
Camel, Mohair, On Wheels, Glass Eyes, Steel Frame, Steiff, 1930, 21 1/2 x 25 In. 805.00
Camel, On Wheels, Felt & Mohair, Steel Eyes, Steiff, 1913, 9 1/2 In. 745.00
Camera, Sesame Street, Big Bird, 3D, 1970s... 40.00
Camera, Shutterbug, Battery Operated, T-N Co., Box 750.00
Cannon, Big Bang, No. 15, 24 In. 85.00
Cannon, Parade, Winchester 1250.00
Cannon, Wooden, Painted Red & Blue 280.00
Canoe Ride, Bisque Passengers, Propeller Driven, Muller & Kadeder 3300.00
Cap Gun, 2 In 1, Long & Short Barrels, Box, Die Cast, Hubley, 1950s 165.00
Cap Gun, 50-Shot Repeater, Kilgore, 1936, 3 7/8 In. 110.00
Cap Gun, American Bulldog 65.00
Cap Gun, Atomic Disintegrator, No. 270, Hubley, 1954 .... 385.00
Cap Gun, Big Scout, Cast Iron, 1930s 125.00
Cap Gun, Billy The Kid, J. & E. Stevens, 8 In., Box 160.00
Cap Gun, Buffalo Bill, 1890s, 12 In. 275.00
Cap Gun, Buffalo Bill, Cast Iron, 1930s 125.00
Cap Gun, Buffalo Bill, Die Cast, See-Through Plastic Grips, c.1950s, 7 In. 65.00
Cap Gun, Buffalo Bill, Plastic Handle, Portrait Of Buffalo Bill, Metal, 1950s 65.00
Cap Gun, Buffalo Rifle, Hubley, 24 In. 150.00
Cap Gun, Camera, Agent Zero M, Box 80.00
Cap Gun, Chief, Hubley... 25.00
Cap Gun, Cody Colt 165.00
Cap Gun, Cupid 325.00
Cap Gun, Detective Special, Hubley, Box 50.00
Cap Gun, Double Barrel, 1880s 275.00
Cap Gun, Eagle, 1890 .... 2140.00
Cap Gun, Fanner 50, Box... 185.00
Cap Gun, Federal, No. 1 .... 65.00
Cap Gun, Figural, Camera, Chein, Box 35.00
Cap Gun, G-Men, Cast Iron, Kilgore, 1935, 6 In. 115.00
Cap Gun, Galaxy, Cast Iron & Plastic, Box 25.00
Cap Gun, Gunsmoke 65.00
Cap Gun, Gunsmoke, Matt Dillon Holster, 1950s.. 150.00
Cap Gun, Ivory Handle, Black Steer Head, 9 In. 22.00
Cap Gun, King 275.00
Cap Gun, Lawmaker, Kenton 115.00
Cap Gun, Lone Star, Moonraker, Ox, 11 x 17 In. 70.00
Cap Gun, Long Boy, Cast Iron, Holster, 1910 .... 160.00
Cap Gun, Magazine Peashooter, 1890 .... 375.00
Cap Gun, Maverick 85.00
Cap Gun, Monkey & Coconut, Animated, Cast Iron, Stevens, c.1882, 4 In. 875.00
Cap Gun, Peacemaker, Steven's 65.00
Cap Gun, Pioneer, Die Cast, 1950s 85.00
Cap Gun, Pirate, Cast Iron 50.00
Cap Gun, Ranger, Kilgore, Box 30.00
Cap Gun, Restless, Actoy 125.00
Cap Gun, Ric-O-Shey, Hubley.. 150.00
Cap Gun, Rifle, Wild West, Marx, 30 In.. 100.00

Cap Gun, Secret Agent Hideaway, Box, 1960s	75.00
Cap Gun, Sheriff, Cast Iron, 1930s	125.00
Cap Gun, Shootin' Shell, Snub Nose, 38 Cylinder, Mattel	95.00
Cap Gun, Smoky, Aluminum, 5 1/2 In.	10.00
Cap Gun, Stub Nose, Kusan	50.00
Cap Gun, Tex, Gold Plated, Hubley	225.00
Cap Gun, Texas Jr., Hubley	35.00
Cap Gun, Texas Ranger, Leslie Henry, Bronze	45.00
Cap Gun, Thundrgun, Box, Caps, Marx	300.00
Cap Gun, Wagon Train, Original Holsters, 1950s	150.00
Car, 348, Andy Gump, Roadster, Cast Iron, Red, Green, White, Arcade, c.1923, 7 In....	2990.00
Car, Angeleno M70, Green, Sizzlers, Hot Wheels, Box	65.00
Car, Armored, 1915	1200.00
Car, Armored, Windup, Steel, Marklin	550.00
Car, Army Headquarters Staff, Marx, 1930s	375.00
Car, Aston-Martin, Gold Plated, Corgi	600.00
Car, Aston-Martin, James Bond 007, 12 In.	250.00
Car, Benz, 1956 Model, Friction, Sound, 1980s	30.00
Car, Blondie's Jalopy, Windup, Marx	2860.00
Car, Buick, Red, Arcade	5800.00
Car, Buick, Stock Car, Red, White, Black, Cragstan, 1963, 11 1/2 In.	1122.00
Car, Bump 'n' Go, 2 Metal Passengers, Windup, Germany, c.1940, 9 In.	250.00
Car, Cabriolet Convertible, Key Wind, Tin, Opening Doors & Trunk, Box, Paya	325.00
Car, Cadillac, 1950 Model, Black, Tin, Friction, Rubber Tires, Box, 11 In.	24.00
Car, Cadillac, 1952 Model, Sedan, Dinky, Box	95.00
Car, Cadillac, Convertible, Electromobile, Black, T.N., 1950s, 13 1/4 In.	880.00
Car, Cadillac, Remote Control, Plastic, Box, 10 In.	125.00
Car, Cadillac, Sedan, Tin, Gray, Friction, Japan, 1950, 11 In., Box	1750.00
Car, Cadillac, Stunt, Rollover, Battery Operated, Japan	150.00
Car, Cadillac, White, Bandai, 1960, 11 1/2 In.	200.00
Car, Camaro, Red, Hot Wheels, Mattel, Unopened, 1968	403.00
Car, Carette Town Car, Tinplate, Clockwork, 16 In.	3740.00
Car, Chaparral 2Z, Silver, Gran Toros, Hot Wheels	180.00
Car, Chevrolet Citation, White, Black Walls, France, Box	25.00
Car, Chevrolet, 1955 Model, Friction, Asahitoy, 7 In.	130.00
Car, Chevrolet, Impala, 1960 Model, Two-Tone Blue, Alps, 9 In.	235.00
Car, Chevrolet, Nickled Tires, Painted, Arcade, 8 In.	715.00
Car, Chitty Chitty Bang Bang, No. 266, Corgi	200.00
Car, Chrysler, Imperial, Promo Car, Friction Drive, S.M.P., 1960	65.00
Car, Chrysler, Kingsbury, Airflow	750.00
Car, Circus, Windup, KO, Box	95.00
Car, Clown, Articulated Driver, Gunthermann	2310.00
Car, Convertible, Packard, Friction, Tin, Paya, Tin, Box, 13 1/2 In.	100.00
Car, Convertible, Packard, No. 132, Brown, Red Interior, Dinky	125.00
Car, Convertible, Remote Controlled, 4 On The Floor, Distler, 10 In.	825.00
Car, Coo-Coo, Man Bounces Up & Down, Windup, Marx, Box, 8 1/2 In.	935.00
Car, Corvette, Hubley	295.00
Car, Crash, Hubley	325.00
Car, Crazy, Milton Berle, Box	695.00
Car, Dodge, Command, FR810, Dinky, Box	187.00
Car, Dodgem, Bumper, 1940s	3395.00
Car, Ferrari, 312P, Red, Hot Wheels, Blister Pack	45.00
Car, Ferrari, Can Am, Red, Gran Toros, Hot Wheels, Box	100.00
Car, Ferrari, Driver, Sliding Roof, Red & Cream, Battery Operated, 12 In.	475.00
Car, Fire Chief, Elmer Fudd, Pull Toy, Wooden, Brice	150.00
Car, Fire Chief, Ford, Friction, 1958, Tin, Box	65.00
Car, Fire Chief, Hudson, Marx	185.00
Car, Fire Chief, Siren, Windup & Battery Operated, 1930s, 14 1/2 In.	675.00
Car, Firebird Trans AM, Silver, Sizzlers, Hot Wheels, Box	50.00
Car, Flivver, Roadster, Buddy L	1475.00
Car, Ford, 1957 Model, Green & White, Ichiko, 10 In.	1250.00
Car, Ford, Convertible, Light Green, Haji, 1950s, 7 1/2 In.	2100.00
Car, Ford, Fairlane 500, Retractable Top, Remote Control, Cragstan, Box	295.00 to 350.00

Toy, Car, Moxie Mobile, Blue,
Horse & Rider, 1917, 8 1/2 x 6 1/2 In.

Toy, Car, Old Jalopy, Red Tin,
Lithographed Paper, Friction, Linemar, 9 In.

Car, Ford, Fairlane, Two-Tone Blue, Yonezawa, 1956, 12 1/4 In. 5500.00
Car, Ford, Falcon, Blue, Bandai, 8 In. 55.00
Car, Ford, Galaxie, 1966 Model, Blue, Promotional 95.00
Car, Ford, GT, White, Matchbox 30.00
Car, Ford, Light Green, White Top, Ichiko, 1957, 10 In. 1250.00
Car, Ford, Mark IV, Red, Hot Wheels 45.00
Car, Ford, Mustang, Fastback, White, Tomica Dandy, Box 50.00
Car, Ford, Thunderbird, 1956 Model, Battery Operated, TN, 11 In. 265.00
Car, Ford, Thunderbird, 1960 Model, Friction, Bandai, 8 In. 105.00
Car, Ford, Touring, Cast Iron, Arcade, 6 1/2 In. 300.00
Car, Ford, White Trailer, Pressed Steel, Windup, Kingsbury, 1937 .... 500.00
Car, Gerry Anderson Armoured Command Car, Box 135.00
Car, Hill Climber, Flywheel Friction, Pressed Steel, Lithograph Man Inside 450.00
Car, House Trailer, Friction, 5-In. Car, 7-In. Trailer, Box 195.00
Car, House Trailer, Friction, SSS Toys, Japan, 1950s, Box 195.00
Car, Jaguar, E-Type, No. 120, Metallic Blue, Cream Interior, Plastic Roof, Dinky 1520.00
Car, Jaguar, Remote Control, Japan, Box, 7 In. 95.00
Car, Johnny Lightning Commemorative, Series B, On Card, 8 Piece 50.00
Car, Joy Rider, Windup, Tin, Marx, 9 x 6 In. 135.00
Car, Kissing Couple, Just Married, Tin Lithograph, Ichida, 1950s, 11 In., Box 225.00
Car, Knight Rider, Talking, Figure, Large 32.00
Car, Lamborghini Miuara, Red, Gran Toros, Hot Wheels, Box 100.00
Car, Land Rover, Circus, & Elephant Trailer, GS19, Corgi, Box 132.00
Car, Lasalle, Sedan, Trailer, White Rubber Tires, Green Paint, Pressed Steel, 26 In. 850.00
Car, Leaping Lena, Tin, Windup, Black, Gray, Strauss, c.1930, 8 In. 305.00
Car, Learn To Drive, Windup, Marx, 6 1/2 In. 95.00
Car, Limousine, Penny Toy, Tin Lithograph, Meier, Germany, 4 1/4 In. 195.00
Car, Lincoln, Convertible, Remote Control, Box, Japan, 11 1/2 In. 550.00
Car, Lotus Europa, Green, Hot Wheels, Large 45.00
Car, Lucky, Occupied Japan, Box 65.00
Car, Mercedes-Benz, 190SL, Dux, Germany, Box 1700.00
Car, Mercedes-Benz, Blinking Rear-Window Lights, Battery Operated, Box 125.00
Car, Mercedes-Benz, Convertible, Windup, Distler, 10 In. 245.00
Car, Mercedes-Benz, Dark Red, Matchbox 35.00
Car, Mercedes-Benz, Model III, Battery Operated, Schuco, Box 200.00
Car, Mercedes-Benz, Rollover, Windup, Box 125.00
Car, Mercedes-Benz, Sedan, Red, Blinking Rear Lights, Battery Operated 95.00
Car, Mercedes-Benz, Sports Car, Battery Operated, Dashboard Controller, 11 In., 1950s 650.00
Car, Mercury Cougar Fire Chief, Battery Operated, 1970, 10 In. 75.00
Car, Mercury, Cougar, Blue 65.00
Car, Model A Ford, Coupe, Rumble Seat, Arcade, 1928, 6 3/4 In. 650.00
Car, Model T Ford, Coupe, 1925 Model, Sun Visor, Arcade, 6 1/4 In. 475.00
Car, Model T Ford, Coupe, Driver, Windup, Germany, 1920s 750.00

Car, Model T Ford, Gasoline Powered, 1952 .... 2950.00
Car, Moonbuggy 811, Corgi 195.00
Car, Moxie Mobile, Blue, Horse & Rider, 1917, 8 1/2 x 6 1/2 In. ....*Illus* 2200.00
Car, Mystery, Tin, Windup, Red, Black, Wolverine, c.1930, 13 In. 110.00
Car, Old Jalopy, Key Wind, Marx, 1950, 7 In. 180.00
Car, Old Jalopy, Linemar, 5 In. 75.00
Car, Old Jalopy, Red Tin, Lithographed Paper, Friction, Linemar, 9 In. ....*Illus* 159.00
Car, Old Jalopy, Windup, Tin Lithograph, Phrases On Hood, Marx, 7 In. 184.00
Car, Oldsmobile, 1958 Model, Ichiko, Box, 8 In. 450.00
Car, Opel, Two-Tone, Marusan, Japan, 1950s 750.00
Car, Packard, Conway Co., 12 In. 175.00
Car, Peugeot, 505, Brown, Black Walls, Hot Wheels, France, Box 35.00
Car, Plymouth, Valiant, Green, Tin, 8 In. 145.00
Car, Police Patrol, Battery Operated, Japan, Box, 9 1/2 In. 250.00
Car, Police Wagon, Ford, Friction, Tin, 1958, Box 65.00
Car, Police Wagon, Patrolmen & Driver, Cast Iron, 16 In. 440.00
Car, Police, Friction, Tin, Japan, 7 In. 10.00
Car, Police, Lincoln, Battery Operated, 1960, 12 In. 140.00
Car, Pontiac, Arcade 325.00
Car, Pontiac, Firebird, Battery Operated, Japan, Box, 11 1/2 In. 250.00
Car, Porsche, 911, No. 6, Schuco 250.00
Car, Porsche, 911, Tin Friction, Blue, Chrome Trim, Yone, Japan, 8 1/2 In. 50.00
Car, Porsche, Electromatic 7500, Gear Shift, White Walls, Distler, 1950s 750.00
Car, Postal Delivery, Buick, Roadmaster, Cast Metal, West Germany 1730.00
Car, Racing Set, Hot Strip Track, Super Pack, Hot Wheels, 1970 .... 29.00
Car, Racing Set, Mongoose & Snake, Wild Wheelie, Hot Wheels, 1970 .... 950.00
Car, Racing, 12-Cylinder, Cast Iron, Hubley, 10 1/2 In. 1540.00
Car, Racing, Alfa Romeo, Tin, Key Wind, Red, CJI, France, 21 In. 3900.00
Car, Racing, Bearcat, No. 8, Windup, Tin 250.00
Car, Racing, Camero, Lightning Star, Battery Operated, 10 In. 100.00
Car, Racing, Champion's, Red, White, Yonezawa, 1950s, 18 In. 1210.00
Car, Racing, Cox Thimble Drome, Gas Powered, TLC 400.00
Car, Racing, Driver, Hood Opens, Hubley, 1927, 9 1/2 In. 1850.00
Car, Racing, Driver, Hubley, Cast Iron, 1930s, 7 In. 375.00
Car, Racing, Driver, Hubley, Cast Iron, 7 In. 350.00
Car, Racing, Hessmobile, Driver, Front Crank, Germany, 1915, 8 In. 850.00
Car, Racing, High Fin, Silver, Hubley 1540.00
Car, Racing, King Racer, Windup, Marx, c.1920, 9 In. 750.00
Car, Racing, Kingsbury, Windup, 20 In. 385.00
Car, Racing, McCoy, Gas Powered, TLC 300.00
Car, Racing, Mercedes-Benz, Blue, Red, Battery Operated, Homura, 11 In. 285.00
Car, Racing, Micro Racer, Green, Brown Interior, Schuco 50.00
Car, Racing, No. 2, Red, Alpha 3850.00
Car, Racing, No. 2, White, Alpha 4500.00
Car, Racing, No. 55, Friction, Banai, 6 In. 165.00
Car, Racing, Porch, Y Toys, Japan, 1960s, 5 In. 20.00
Car, Racing, Racing Champions, Chad Little, No. 66 .... 50.00
Car, Racing, Racing Champions, Kulwicki, 87th Premier Hauler 60.00
Car, Racing, Racing Champions, R. Petty, Blue Wheels 37.00
Car, Racing, Red, Rubber Wheels, Electric Lights, Battery Operated, Marx, 8 1/2 In. ... 165.00
Car, Racing, Rocket Racer, Driver, Windup, Marx, 1930s, 16 1/2 In. 350.00
Car, Racing, Rocket Racer, Tin, Windup, Marx, 16 1/2 In. 99.00
Car, Racing, Roy Cox, Gas Powered, 1940s 550.00
Car, Racing, Shark, Remco, 1961 .... 125.00
Car, Racing, Speed King, No. 16, Tin Lithograph, Friction, Japan, 1950s, 8 In. 230.00
Car, Racing, Switch 'n' Go, Custom GT4, Mattel, 1965, Box 55.00
Car, Racing, T.N. Toys, 1950s, 6 In. 225.00
Car, Racing, Tin Lithograph, 6 In., 1950s 135.00
Car, Racing, Windup, Marklin, 1920s, 14 In. 950.00
Car, Racing, Windup, Tin, 1949, Marx 175.00
Car, Red Baron, Red, Hot Wheels, Blister Pack 55.00
Car, Roadster, Flivver, Buddy L 1475.00
Car, Roadster, Red Seats, Multi-Speed, Shift Reverse, Brakes, Windup, Schuco 130.00

Car, Roadster, Tin, Windup, Green, Yellow, Red, Marx, c.1930, 8 In. 99.00
Car, Rolls-Royce, 1912 Model, Matchbox 45.00
Car, Rolls-Royce, Corgi 19.00
Car, Rolls-Royce, Silver Cloud, Convertible, Red, 12 In., Box 485.00
Car, Rolls-Royce, Tin, Linemar 85.00
Car, Sedan, 2-Door, Pressed Steel, Green, Rubber Tires, Kingsbury Airflow, 14 In. 305.00
Car, Sedan, Delivery, Standard Coffee, Galaxie, 1960s, 11 1/2 In. 1210.00
Car, Sedan, Driver, Opening Doors, Windup, Orobr, 1915 .... 1125.00
Car, Sedan, Green, Windup, Lehmann 550.00
Car, Sedan, Model T, Driver, Tin, Windup, Bing, Germany, 1920s, 6 1/4 In. 402.00
Car, Sedan, Streamlined, Battery-Operated Headlights, 1930s 852.00
Car, Sedan, Streamlined, Light Blue, Yellow Wheels, No. 59, Renwal 20.00
Car, Sedan, Tin Lithograph, Windup, Two Tone Brown & Cream, Tipp Co., 1930s, 9 In. 374.00
Car, Sedan, Tin, Windup, Blue, Yellow, Black, Orange, Marke Hess, c.1930, 8 In. 154.00
Car, Sedan, Windup, Plastic, Silver Trim, Reliable, 1950s, 7 In. 85.00
Car, Snoopy & Friends, Battery Operated, Mystery Action, Flashing Lights, 1972 .... 100.00
Car, Sports, Examico, 2 Keys, Schuco, 1960s, 5 3/4 In. 330.00
Car, Station Wagon, Ford, Tin Lithograph, Blue & White, 1950s 125.00
Car, Station Wagon, Woodie, Buddy L, c.1940, 19 In. 395.00
Car, Studebaker, Lark On Plate, Friction, Japan, 5 1/2 In. 165.00
Car, Supercar, Pull Toy, Tin, American, 1930s, 9 In. 145.00
Car, Thunderbird, 1956 Model, Friction, Tin, Box, 1950s, 11 1/2 In. 150.00
Car, Thunderbird, Promotional Model, Light Green, Friction, 1967 .... 50.00
Car, Tin, Windup, Red, White, Blue, Rico, c.1930, 7 In. 55.00
Car, Tin, Windup, Red, Yellow, Black, Guntherman, c.1930, 10 In. 550.00
Car, Touring, Open, Driver, Windup, Richter, 1908, 7 1/2 In. 1750.00
Car, Toyota, 2000 GT, Blue, Gran Toros, Hot Wheels 90.00
Car, Tricky Fire Chief, Marx 85.00
Car, Trikauto, Tin, Windup, Orange & Yellow, Strauss, c.1930, 7 In. 77.00
Car, Tut-Tut, Windup, White & Red, Lehmann, c.1903, 6 3/4 In. 660.00
Car, Volkswagen Rabbit, Metal, Tootsietoy, 4 In. 6.00
Car, Volkswagen, Battery Operated, Tin, Modern Toys 55.00
Car, Volkswagen, Bug, Blue, Friction, Bandai, 8 In. 65.00
Car, Volkswagen, Challenger, Tin Lithograph, Rubber Tires, Battery Operated 85.00
Car, Volkswagen, Gray, TN, Japan, Box 200.00
Car, Volkswagen, Herbie, Bump, Taiyo, Box 170.00
Car, Volkswagen, Transparent, Japan 45.00
Car, Whoopie, Marx 550.00
Car, Wild Wheelie Set, Mongoose & Snake, Hot Wheels, Box, 1971 .... 275.00
Carousel, Animals, Metal Poles, Motorized, R.M. Schafer, 22 In. 2875.00
Carousel, Circus, Children Riding Horses, Pipe Organ, Ticket Kiosk, 9 x 6 In. 4450.00
Carousel, Horses & Riders, People In Gondolas, Tin Flags, Germany, 18 x 13 In. 6950.00
Carousel, Penny Toy, Tin Lithograph, Meier, Germany, 2 1/2 In. 230.00
Carousel, Tasseled Canopy, Tin Flags, 8 Horses, Gondolas, Germany, 18 In. 6930.00
Carousel, Tin Lithograph, Painted, Windup, Gunthermann, 9 In. 845.00
Carousel, Tin, Windup, 3 Children On 3 Horses, Multicolored, Germany, 12 1/2 In. 220.00
Carousel, Windup, Tin, Paya, 6 1/2 In. 100.00
Carriage, Doll's, 3 Wheels, Canvas Canopy, Iron Fittings, Leather Upholstery, 21 In. ... 180.00
Carriage, Doll's, Chrome Fenders, Wicker 250.00
Carriage, Doll's, Painted & Stenciled Tinplate, Germany, c.1915, 8 In. 4025.00
Carriage, Doll's, Push, Almond & Orange Striping, White Flourishes, 31 In. 185.00
Carriage, Doll's, Steel-Spoke Wheels, 25 1/2 In. 250.00
Carriage, Doll's, Wicker, 19th Century, 27 x 14 x 25 1/2 In. 110.00
Carriage, Doll's, Wicker, Canopy, White Paint 235.00
Carriage, Doll's, Wooden, Canopy, Metal Springs, Red Oilcloth Cushion, 24 x 29 In. . 300.00
Carriage, Doll's, Wooden-Spoke Wheels, Convertible Cloth Top, c.1870, 35 In. 200.00
Carriage, Doll's, Wooden-Spoke Wheels, Leather Sunshade, 1875, 33 In. 1100.00
Carriage, Stroller, Doll's, Dagwood & Blondie, Tin Lithograph, 1949 .... 65.00
Carriage, Stroller, Doll's, Wicker, 4 Large Wheels, Victorian 395.00
Carriage, Wooden, Knotted Design, Spoke Wheels, Curved Handle, 25 x 34 In. 200.00
Cart, Baggage Handler, Windup, Unique 275.00
Cart, Bell Toy, Galloping Horse, Woman In Plumed Hat, Cast Iron, 9 1/2 In. 1595.00
Cart, Farmer, Pulled By Zebra, Zikra, Windup, Lehmann, Box 1250.00

Cart, Maggie & Jiggs, Windup, Tin, Germany, 7 x 5 1/2 In.. 550.00
Cart, Push-Pull, Foldover Leather Seat, Spoked Rubber Wheels, Geneva Co., 59 In...... 115.00
Cart, Shopping, 1950.. 250.00
Cash Register, American Flyer, Play Money, 1930s ....25.00 to 65.00
Cat, Black, Tartan Dress, Steiff, 3 In... 75.00
Cat, Chases Mouse In Cage, Windup, Guntherman, 1900 .... 850.00
Cat, Felix, Felt Covered, Glass Eyes, Metal Nose, Bendable Limbs, 15 1/2 In. 82.00
Cat, Felix, Laying Violin, Celluloid, 6 In. 375.00
Cat, Felix, On Scooter, Tin Lithograph, Windup, Nifty, 7 1/2 In. 747.00
Cat, Felix, Pull Toy, Nifty Toy Co. 1200.00
Cat, Felix, Rubber, Squeeze, Blue, 6 In. 95.00
Cat, Felix, Wooden, Jointed, Leather Ears, Schoenhut, 1925, 8 In. 500.00
Cat, Housekeeper Cat, Tin, Cloth Body, Windup, Japan, Box 125.00
Cat, Kitten, Tabby, Bell, Silk Bow & Whiskers, Steiff.. 145.00
Cat, Minka, Tags, Steiff, 14 In. 150.00
Cat, With Turning Ball, Mechanical, Metal, Japan, 6 In. 15.00
Chair, Doll's, Ebony Wood, Bamboo, Arms, Toile Seat, France, 1885, 9 In., Pair 325.00
Chair, Doll's, Rawhide Seat, Square Nails, Peg Jointed, 1800s 145.00
Chalk Board, Alphabet, Tin, 1917 .... 45.00
Chariot, Bell, Cinderella's, Horse, Cast Iron, c.1890, 9 1/2 In. 374.00
Chariot, Lost In Space 225.00
Chariot, Swan-Shaped, Seated Girl, Moving Wings, Spoked Wheels, c.1885, 10 1/2 In. 6900.00
Charleston Trio, Black Dancer, Fiddler, Dog, Windup, Marx, 1920s 925.00
Chemistry Set, Gilbert, No. 1, 1943... 65.00
Chest, Doll's, 4 Drawers, Porcelain Knobs, Wooden, 9 x 9 In. 60.00
Chest, Metal Dome, Pirates & Buccaneer, Ohio Art, c.1960, 25 x 18 x 18 In. 185.00
Chick-Mobile, Peter Rabbit, Clockwork, Lionel, Box, 1935, 8 1/2 In. 1210.00
Chicken, Little Red Hen, Cackles, Lays Eggs, Windup, Baldwin, Tin............................. 150.00
Chicken, Mother Hen, Chicks, Cast Iron, White Hen, Pulls Cage, Yellow Chicks, 8 In. 345.00
Chicken, Pecking, Windup, Tin, Haji, 2 In... 35.00
Chicken, With Worm, Windup, Tin 100.00
Children On Teeter-Totter, Polychrome, Tin, Gibbs Toys, 14 1/2 In. 300.00
Chop-Cycles Speed Pack, 2 Tricycles, Recharger, Mattel, 1975, Box 30.00
Circus, Cage, Cast Iron, Kenton, Box, 14 In. 1600.00
Circus, Carnival Shooting Gallery, Tin, Windup, Ohio Art, Box, 11 x 17 In. 145.00
Circus, Clockwork, Electric Power Unit, Elgin Toy Co., 1920s 8250.00
Circus, Overland, Kenton, Cast Iron, Box, 14 In. 495.00
Circus, Rider, Pull Toy, Rider, 4 Composition Horses, 19th Century, 16 1/2 In. 1800.00
Circus, Ring-A-Ling, Windup 850.00
Circus, See-Saw, Windup, Tin, Lewco, 1930s, Box 175.00
Circus, Shooting Gallery, Moving Ducks, Rotating Disk, Battery Operated, Ohio Art... 175.00
Circus, Train, Windup, Linemar, 4 Cars... 50.00
Circus Wagon, Cage, Driver, Horses, Wooden Wagon, Cast Iron, 14 In. 220.00
Circus Wagon, Cage, Gray Bars & Wheels, Stenciling, Wooden, Schoenhut, 9 3/4 In... 245.00
Circus Wagon, Overland Circus, Team, Animal Wagon, Kenton, Cast Iron, 1941 .... 260.00
Circus Wagon, Overland, Musicians, Cast Iron, Kenton.. 650.00
City, 3 Clockwork Vehicles, Tinplate 225.00
Clock, Tall Case, Plymires Cafe, Elgin Pocket Watch Top, Dark Finish, 20 In............... 150.00
Clothespins, Wooden, For Doll Clothes, Box, 36 Pieces, 1930s..................................... 16.00
Clown, Acrobat, Windup 95.00
Clown, Artie, Windup, Unique 395.00
Clown, ATM Rocket, Tin Lithograph, Windup, 1950s ....:....... 395.00
Clown, Balloon Vendor, Windup, Box.. 275.00
Clown, Bell, Pull Toy, 2-Clowns, Cast Iron, Metal Platform, 3 Bells, Watrous, 10 In..... 316.00
Clown, Charlie, Drumming, Battery Operated, Cragston, Box... 325.00
Clown, Circus, Big Top Champ, Battery Operated, Alps 295.00
Clown, Clarabell, Push-Up, Wooden, Kohner.. 225.00
Clown, Cymbals, Windup, Box 175.00
Clown, Dandy Jim The Clown Dancer, Windup, Unique Art Co., 1922 .... 700.00
Clown, Driving Car, Lithographed, Unique Art, 1930s, 7 3/4 In. 230.00
Clown, Fiddler, Schuco, Windup 195.00
Clown, Happy 'n' Sad Magic Face, Battery Operated, Box 285.00
Clown, Hi-Jink Circus Clown, Battery Operated, Box 300.00

Clown, Juggler, Windup, Alps..	345.00
Clown, Juggler, Windup, Schuco, 4 3/4 In.	130.00
Clown, Monkey, Hi-Jinx, With Cymbals, Battery Operated, TN Co., 1950s...................	195.00
Clown, On Cycle, Tin Lithograph, Windup, Japan...	33.00
Clown, On Skates, Windup, Japan, Celluloid, Box...	280.00
Clown, On Tricycle, Schuco...	1390.00
Clown, Walking Tightrope, Hand Over Head, Windup, U.S. Zone, Germany, Box	145.00
Clown, With 2 Horses, Clown Somersaults, Horses Jump, Cast Iron, Hubley, 6 In.	805.00
Coach, Coronation, Horse, Britains, 20 In.	300.00
Coach, Fageol Safety, Yellow Boyd, Cream Upper Panel, Arcade, 12 In.	1925.00
Coffee Grinder, Penny Toy, Germany	135.00
Colorforms, Captain Kangaroo's Treasure House, Die-Cut, 1961	49.00
Colorforms, Nanny & The Professor, 1970, 8 x 12 In.	24.00
Colorforms, Play Set 31, Unused, 1986	2.00
Colorforms, Tarzan, 1966...	14.00
Colorforms, Welcome Back Kotter, 1976..	18.00
Comb, Flipper, Figural, Plastic, 1966, 8 In.	12.00
Construction Set, Lionel, No. 444, Metal Case, 1945..	165.00
Construction Set, Orange, Pressed Steel, Marx, 3 Piece	295.00
Coon Jigger, Dapper Dan..	450.00
Costume, Cowboy, Lassoin' Bill's, Red & White	85.00
Covered Wagon, Cloth Wagon Cover, Cast Iron, Kenton, Box, 15 In.	990.00
Cow, Pull Toy, Hide Covered, Moos, Milking Reservoir, Germany, 11 In.	345.00
Cow, Pull Toy, Hide Covered, Platform	45.00
Cow, Pull Toy, Papier-Mache, Wooden Platform, Steel Wheels, Germany, 7 In.	230.00
Cowboy, On Horse, Tin, Painted Features, Mechanical, Key Wind, Marx	95.00
Cradle, Doll's, Art Deco, 12 x 24 In.	40.00
Cradle, Doll's, Hooded, Oak, Black Paint, Painted Birds, 13 x 23 In.	185.00
Cradle, Doll's, Pine, White Paint, 14 1/2 In.	94.00
Cradle, Doll's, Red Paint, Stylized Floral, Black & White Striping, 15 In.	192.00
Cradle, Doll's, Twisted Spiral Design Metal, Swinging, c.1885, 23 In.	375.00
Cradle, Doll's, Wicker...	195.00
Crane, Giant, Plastic, Battery Operated, Box..	100.00
Crane, Overhead, Traveling, Pressed Steel, Buddy L, 45 In.	1045.00
Crapshooter, Battery Operated, Cragstan..	120.00
Crazy Car, Mortimer Snerd, Marx, c.1939...	700.00
Cupboard, Doll's, Art Nouveau, Wooden, 6 Drawers, Door, France, 1890, 12 x 18 In..	750.00
Cuzner Trotter, Ives, 11 1/2 In.	3700.00
Dairy Wagon, Borden's, Wooden, Horse Drawn, Rich Toy, 1920s, 29 1/2 In.	632.00
Dairy Wagon, Toytown, Horse Drawn, Pull Toy, Tin Lithograph, Wood, Marx, 10 In. .	167.00
Dancer, Be-Bop Jigger, Windup, Tin..	325.00
Dancer, Black Man, Clockwork, Ives	1500.00
Dancer, Hackie The Hornpipe Dancer, Strauss..	750.00
Dancer, Strutting Sam, On Pedestal, Box	575.00
Dancers, Clockwork, Wood Lithograph, Theater, 1865, 9 3/4 In.	1725.00
Dancing Couple, Prince & Cinderella, Windup, Plastic	175.00
Dancing Couple, Windup, Celluloid, Occupied Japan, 5 In.	95.00
Dancing Men, Minstrel, Black, c.1920s, 8 In.	260.00
Dancing Sambo, c.1940s, 10 In..	30.00
Dandy Dobbin, Riding, Fisher-Price, 1941	375.00
Dapper Dan, Dances On Box, Tin, Windup, Marx, 1920s...	1250.00
Deer, Bambi, Button & Tag, Steiff, 6 In.	65.00
Delivery Wagon, Double Team, Black Driver, Iron, Kenton, c.1929, 14 3/4 In.............	453.00
Destroyer, Taku, Tin Lithograph, Windup, Floor Toy, Lehmann, 9 1/2 In.	110.00
Dinner Set, Barbie's 25th Anniversary, Pottery, Box	35.00
Dinner Set, Green Hornet, On Original Store Card, 1966..	200.00
Dino The Dinosaur, Tin, Fred, Plush, Battery Operated, Marx, 16 In..................... *Illus*	385.00
Dinosaur, Dino, Tin, Windup, Linemar, Box...	1500.00
Dinosaur, Tyrannosaurus, Remote Control, Toy Town, Box	100.00
Dirigible, Akron, Steelcraft	695.00
Dirigible, U.S.A. Los Angeles, Tootsietoy..	95.00
Dog, Basset, Lady Gaylord, Pull Toy, Ideal, 1964	125.00
Dog, Black Caracul, Stuffed, Link Chain Collar, 5 x 11 In.	120.00

Toy, Dino The Dinosaur, Tin, Fred, Plush,
Battery Operated, Marx, 16 In.

Wave and call good-bye to "Grandma and the kids" when leaving in a cab for the airport. Make it sound as if the house will be occupied.

Dog, Boston Terrier, Bonzo, Cast Iron, Painted, 1920, Small	450.00
Dog, Bulldog Mascot, Nodder, Wheels Under Paws, Mouth Moves, Growls	2650.00
Dog, Bulldog, Leather Muzzle & Leash, Jointed, Steiff, 9 x 13 In.	295.00
Dog, Dachshund, Long Hair, Gold, Button & Tag, Steiff, 8 x 13 In.	165.00
Dog, Dalmatian, Sitting, Steiff, 4 In.	120.00
Dog, Fox Terrier, Cloth, Lithograph, 1911	125.00
Dog, Fur Cover, Curly Blond, Excelsior Stuffed, 13 x 19 In.	75.00
Dog, Hassan, Afghan Hound, Steiff, Button & Tag	446.00
Dog, Mopsy, Tan Mohair, Glass Eyes, Steiff, 5 In.	45.00
Dog, On Motorcycle, Bonzo, Tin Windup, Germany	1100.00
Dog, On Tricycle, Lever Action, Germany, 1930s	210.00
Dog, On Tricycle, Lever-Action, Germany, Pre-War, 1930s	225.00
Dog, RCA Nipper, Stuffed, Original Tag & Collar, 1940, 9 In.	150.00
Dog, Seated, Mohair, Joint, Embroidered, Glass Eyes, 1930s, 11 1/2 In.	126.00
Dog, Shepherd, Reclining, Steiff, 10 In.	120.00
Dog, Smoking, Tin, Box, Japan	20.00
Dog, Tippy Scotty Dog, Windup, Schuco, Box	145.00
Dog, Walks With A Rolling Ball, Arms Move, Tin, Paya, Box, 4 1/2 In.	50.00
Dolls are listed in their own category	
Doll, Case, Barbie, Vinyl, 1961, 3 x 10 x 12 In.	25.00
Dollhouse, 1 Room, Latched Door Covering The Back	285.00
Dollhouse, 2 Story, 2 Room, Attic, Bliss, Early 1900s, 17 x 11 In.	900.00
Dollhouse, 2 Story, 2 Room, Attic, Wooden, Converse, c.1915, 11 x 8 In.	525.00
Dollhouse, 2 Story, 3 Chimneys, Gottschalk Kitchen Ware, 1900, 56 x 45 In.	1900.00
Dollhouse, 2 Story, 4 Room, Attic, Bliss, 1900s, 23 x 21 In.	1525.00
Dollhouse, 2 Story, 4 Rooms, 6 Windows, Fireplace In Each Room, Scotland, 32 In.	3000.00
Dollhouse, 2 Story, Bay Window, Pennsylvania, Late 19th Century	1150.00
Dollhouse, 3 Story, Faux-Brick Exterior, 8 Windows, Balcony, 4 Fireplaces, 56 In.	2400.00
Dollhouse, 3 Story, Wooden, Painted, Hinged, Victorian, 1900, 56 x 40 x 27 In.	1150.00
Dollhouse, Annie, Furniture & Figures	150.00
Dollhouse, Baby House, 2 Story, 18th Century Style, England, 72 x 54 In.	2070.00
Dollhouse, Brass, 2 Story, Opening Facade, Wood Lithograph, 9 In.	495.00
Dollhouse, Dutch Colonial, 3 Rooms, 1920s, 17 x 17 In.	85.00
Dollhouse, English Boudoir, Signed Mrs. James Ward Thorne, c.1930, 9 x 12 In.	495.00
Dollhouse, Farm, Opens 2 Sides, 2 Story Gable, 4 Furnished Rooms, 1890, 28 In.	1800.00
Dollhouse, Furnishings, Presentation Box, Couple, Wooden, 12 x 16 In.	1000.00
Dollhouse, Furniture, Bathroom Sink, Toilet & Tub, Room Setting	65.00
Dollhouse, Furniture, Bed, Half-Tester, Rosewood	2200.00
Dollhouse, Furniture, Bed, Sheraton, Maple & Bird's-Eye Maple, 16 1/8 In.	370.00
Dollhouse, Furniture, Chair, Shaker, Ladder Back, 5 1/2 x 7 x 15 In.	45.00
Dollhouse, Furniture, Cradle, Soap Hollow, Grain Painted Brown & Mustard	1700.00
Dollhouse, Furniture, Kitchen, Accessories, Painted Tin, Bergmann, 1875, 19 In.	150.00
Dollhouse, Furniture, Kitchen, Tin, 15 x 21 In.	155.00
Dollhouse, Furniture, Maids, Tied Into Box, c.1895, 16 x 12 In., 10 Piece	1200.00
Dollhouse, Furniture, Refrigerator, White & Red, Wolverine	55.00
Dollhouse, Furniture, Sink, White & Red, Wolverine	65.00

Toy, Drinking Bird, Plastic, Tin, Red, Yellow, Green, 1970s

◆ ◆

If you have an instant-on television set, beware! The instant-on works because a current is always running through the set, even when it is off. This means more power is used, the set wears out faster, and, most serious for the collector, there is a greater risk of fire. Next time the set needs repair, ask the serviceman to remove the instant-on feature. If you use a remote unit to turn off the set, the same dangers exist.

◆ ◆

Dollhouse, Furniture, Table, Folding, Early 1900s, 16 x 10 In.	65.00
Dollhouse, Furniture, Toilet, Metal, Gray, Cast Iron, Hinged Cover, 1 3/4 x 1 In.	10.00
Dollhouse, Furniture, Washing Machine, White & Red, MAR	45.00
Dollhouse, Furniture, Wood Lithograph, Furnished, Bliss	425.00
Dollhouse, Little Kiddles, 3 Story, Plastic, With Furniture, Box, 1968	70.00
Dollhouse, Mansard Roof, 2 Story, Balcony, 19th Century, 26 x 25 In.	4800.00
Dollhouse, Play Time, Paper, Brown & Red, c.1940, 10 1/2 x 12 1/2 In., Box	800.00
Dollhouse, San Francisco Row House, 2 Rooms, Attic, Basement, c.1920s, 48 x 22 In.	1430.00
Dollhouse, Townhouse Style, 4 Rooms, Wallpaper, Gables, England, 1900, 20 x 17 In.	690.00
Dollhouse, Tudor Style, Wooden, Early 1900s, 16 x 19 In.	685.00
Dollhouse, Victorian Style, 2nd & 3rd Story Balcony, Side Gables, Bliss, 24 In.	3000.00
Dollhouse, Wood, c.1900, Wood Lithograph, 20 x 13 In.	790.00
Dollhouse, Wooden, Sliding Glass Windows, Tongue-And-Groove Floors, 1930s	52.00
Donkey, Button Eyes, Black Mane, Steiff, 11 1/2 In.	225.00
Donkey, Mohair, Black Main, Straw Stuffed, Steiff, 8 1/2 x 11 In.	175.00
Donkey Cart, Driver, Tin, Windup	65.00
Donkey Cart, Mechanical, Marx	295.00
Dresser, Doll's, 2 Drawers, Mirror, Victorian, Large	110.00
Drinking Bird, Plastic, Tin, Red, Yellow, Green, 1970s .... *Illus*	35.00
Drive-In Theater, Movieland, Remco, Box	175.00
Drum, Charlie Brown, Lithograph	45.00
Drum Major, Tin Lithograph, Windup, Chein	200.00
Duck, Pull Toy, Hubley	3200.00
Duck, Pull Toy, Papier-Mache, Glass Eyes, Wooden Platform & Wheels, c.1930	155.00
Duck, Windup, Tin, Chein, 1930s, 4 In.	55.00
Dune Buggy, Gas Powered, Cox, Box	75.00
Dust & Sweep Kit, Cinderella, Box, 1950s	55.00
Dust Pan, Dressed Boy At Seashore, Victorian Clothes, Tin	95.00
Eagle, Pull Toy, Bell In Beak, Moves On Green Cart, No. 30, Cast Iron, 5 3/4 In.	410.00
Elephant, Horton, Dr. Seuss, Coleco, 1983	69.00
Elephant, Howdah, Children, Metal, Britains, Box, 4 1/2 In.	495.00
Elephant, Jumbo, Windup, Tin	250.00
Elephant, On Bike, Windup, Tin, Spinning Propeller On Bike, Paya, 5 1/2 In.	60.00
Elephant, On Wheels, Bellows, Steiff	995.00
Elephant, On Wheels, Pulling Calliope Wagon, Steiff	1500.00
Elephant, Pull Toy, Iron Wheels, 19th Century, 15 In.	250.00
Elephant, Tin, Windup, Spins 3 Blades On Trunk, Balances Log, U.S. Zone Germany	235.00
Elephant, Walker, Windup, Tin, Occupied Japan, Box	225.00
Elf, Gucki, Paper Tag & Button, Steiff, 5 In.	85.00
Eras-O-Board Set, Captain Kangaroo, 1956	100.00
Erector Set, Assembled Hudson Locomotive & Tender	2400.00
Erector Set, Assembled Zeppelin	2200.00
Erector Set, Gilbert, No. 6 1/2, Electric, Box, 1950s	55.00

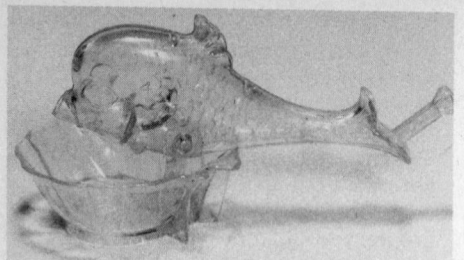

Toy, Fish, Bubble Blower, Pink & Yellow,
Knickerbocker, 4 3/4 In.

◆◆◆◆◆◆◆◆◆◆◆◆◆◆◆◆

Rusted   toys   have
very low value.

◆◆◆◆◆◆◆◆◆◆◆◆◆◆◆◆

Erector Set, Gilbert, No. 10, Ferris Wheel	95.00
Ewe & Lamb, Pull Toy, Wood, Papier-Mache, Woolly Coats, Tin Wheels, 5 In.	302.00
Expert Motor Cyclist, T.M., Japan, Box	1870.00
Fainting Couch, Doll's, Original Tufted Leather Upholstery	230.00
Fainting Couch, Doll's, Tapestry	120.00
Farm, 2 Story, Painted Stone, Fishscale Shingled Roof, Open Back, Germany	320.00
Farm Set, Auburn, 42 Piece	170.00
Farm Set, Carved Wood, Buildings, People, Animals, Germany, 6 3/4-In. Barn	330.00
Farm Set, Tractor & Mower, Windup, Marx	225.00
Farm Wagon, Horse Team, Cast Iron	250.00
Farm Wagon, With Grain Box, John Deere	500.00
Ferdinand The Bull, Ideal, Jointed, 1930s, 9 x 9 In.	80.00
Ferris Wheel, 6 Gondolas, Tinplate, Painted, Steam, Superb Doll & Co., 15 1/2 In.	4250.00
Ferris Wheel, Clockwork	1485.00
Ferris Wheel, Giant Ride, Ohio Art	250.00
Ferris Wheel, Hercules, Chein, 1930s	390.00
Ferris Wheel, Iron Passengers, Clockwork, Steel, 17 In.	385.00
Ferris Wheel, Tin Lithograph, Windup, Chein, 16 1/2 In.	172.00
Finnegan The Porter, Tin, Windup, Unique Art, 13 In.	325.00 to 475.00
Fire Chief, Siren, Windup, Marx, 14 1/2 In.	145.00
Fire Patrol, 2 Horses, Cast Iron	990.00
Fire Pumper, 2 Horses, 2 Firemen, Painted, Cast Iron, Wilkens, 18 In.	3450.00
Fire Pumper, Horse Drawn, Driver, Cast Iron, c.1939, 9 1/2 In.	175.00
Fire Pumper, Label, Hubley, 8 1/2 In.	375.00
Fire Station, Wood Lithograph, Bliss, c.1880, 12 1/2 x 10 x 5 In.	1430.00
Fire Truck, Aerial Ladder, American La France	235.00
Fire Truck, Aerial Ladder, Big Boy, Hard Rubber Tires, Kelmet, 29 In.	990.00
Fire Truck, Aerial Ladder, Red Paint, Keystone, 32 In.	825.00
Fire Truck, Aerial Ladder, Schuco	2000.00
Fire Truck, Bump & Go Action, Siren Sound, Battery Operated, Box	110.00
Fire Truck, Cast Iron, Iron Art, 10 In.	125.00
Fire Truck, Cast Steel, Hill Climber, Red, c.1920, 11 In.	220.00
Fire Truck, Erzgebirger, 4 1/2 In.	50.00
Fire Truck, Fire Pumper, 2 Firemen, 3 Horses, Kenton, 1911, 20 In.	1450.00
Fire Truck, Fire Pumper, 2 Firemen, Hoses, Kenton, 1930, 14 In.	950.00
Fire Truck, Hess, Box, 1989	70.00
Fire Truck, Hydraulic Aerial, Brass Bell & Wheel, Pressed Steel, Buddy L, 39 In.	1495.00
Fire Truck, Ladder, Battery Operated, Tin Lithograph, 1960s	195.00
Fire Truck, Ladder, Kingsbury, 36 In.	900.00
Fire Truck, Ladder, Windup, Tin Lithograph, Friction Motor, Japan, 11 1/2 In.	920.00
Fire Truck, Ladders & Lantern, American National Giant Chemical, 28 In.	2700.00
Fire Truck, No. 79, Keystone	850.00
Fire Truck, Pressed Steel And Tin Lithograph, Wyandotte, 1940s	195.00
Fire Truck, Pressed Steel, Red Body, Buddy L, 23 In.	660.00
Fire Truck, Pumper, Double Horse, Cast Iron	635.00
Fire Truck, Pumper, Hubley, 6 In.	225.00

Fire Truck, Pumper, Hubley, Label, 8 1/2 In. 375.00
Fire Truck, Pumper, Tonka 150.00
Fire Truck, Pumper, Vertical Boiler, Painted Steel, Buddy L, 1929, 23 In. 392.00
Fire Truck, Pumper, Wagon, 3 Horses, Driver, Cast Iron, 10 1/4 In. 115.00
Fire Truck, Riding, Marx 125.00
Fire Truck, Short Ladder, Steelcraft 855.00
Fire Truck, Siren, Marx, 14 In. 165.00
Fire Truck, Steel Ladders, Bing, 1920s 1265.00
Fire Truck, Tin, Windup, 3 Firemen, Red, White, Germany, 13 In. 88.00
Fire Truck, Water Tower, Hoses, Pressed Steel, Sturditoy, 34 In. 525.00
Fire Wagon, Chemical Tank, Horses, Ladders, Cast Iron, Painted, Wilkins, 19 In. 3220.00
Fire Wagon, Ladder, 3 Horses, Kenton, 1940-1950s, 16 In. 287.00
Firehouse, Cast Iron, Wood, Ives, c.1890 .... 4500.00
Fish, Bubble Blower, Pink & Yellow, Knickerbocker, 4 3/4 In. .... *Illus*   20.00
Flashlight, Felix The Cat, Pocket, 1950s 45.00
Flying Saucer, Jupiter 077, Battery Operated 75.00
Footstool, Raggedy Ann, Knickerbocker, 1965 .... 195.00
Fort, Wood & Paper Lithograph, 23 Piece 585.00
Frankenstein, Battery Operated, 1960s 925.00
Fred Flintstone, On Tricycle, Windup, Marx, 4 In. 525.00
Fred Flintstone, Riding Dino, Windup, Linemar, 8 In. 200.00
Frisbee, Empire Strikes Back 40.00
Frisbee, Star Wars 40.00
G.I. Joe, Action Pilot, 1964 .... 322.00
G.I. Joe, Action Soldier, Painted Black Hair, Brown Suit 55.00
G.I. Joe, Black Commander Adventure Team, Talking, 1974 .... 220.00
G.I. Joe, British Commandos, 1964 .... 575.00
G.I. Joe, Combat Set, No. 7501, On Card, 12 In. 325.00
G.I. Joe, Dress Parade Set, No. 7619, On Card, 12 In. 95.00
G.I. Joe, Frogman Equipment Set, 1964 .... 322.00
G.I. Joe, Green Beret Set, 1966 .... 230.00
G.I. Joe, Helicopter 70.00
G.I. Joe, Hidden Treasure Outfit 35.00
G.I. Joe, Jouncing Jeep, Unique Art, 1940s ....225.00 to 240.00
G.I. Joe, Jungle Fighter Set, 1967 .... 437.00
G.I. Joe, Land Adventurer, Brown Flocked Hair & Beard 45.00
G.I. Joe, Machine Gun, On Card, Sticker 40.00
G.I. Joe, Marine Dress Uniform 95.00
G.I. Joe, Marine Jungle Fighter 850.00
G.I. Joe, Marine Medic, Accessories 375.00
G.I. Joe, Medic, 1983 .... 70.00
G.I. Joe, Military Police Set, 1964 .... 220.00
G.I. Joe, Navy Attack Set, No. 7610, On Card, 12 In. 110.00
G.I. Joe, Pole Explorer Set, 1960s 437.00
G.I. Joe, Police Officer, 1967 .... 345.00
G.I. Joe, Ranger, 1982 .... 80.00

Toy, Gift Set, Barbie & Ken, Boxed, 1962

G.I. Joe, Russian Infantryman Set... 345.00
G.I. Joe, Search For Stolen Idol, Box 100.00
G.I. Joe, Shore Patrol, M-L Rifle 375.00
G.I. Joe, Shore Patrol, Painted Hair 160.00
G.I. Joe, Space Capsule 145.00
G.I. Joe, Talking, Brown Flocked Hair, Green Shirt, Camouflage Shorts...................... 45.00
G.I. Joe, Talking, Foot Locker, Communication Box, 1967 .... 200.00
G.I. Joe, Test Pilot Parachute Set, 1969, Pair 275.00
G.I. Joe, West Point Cadet, Painted Hair, 1967 .... 195.00 to 350.00
G.I. Joe & Headquarters Command Center, Box, 4- In.Figure, 1983......................... 45.00
G.I. Joe & K-9 Pups, Tin, Windup, Unique Art, 1941, 9 In. .... 250.00 to 375.00
Games are listed in their own category
Garage, Accessory Pack, Matchbox 45.00
Gardener, Sam, Windup Figure Pushing Wheelbarrow, Tools, Marx 375.00
Gas Station, Studebaker, Distler, Box.. 375.00
Gas Station, Texaco, Buddy L, Box... 750.00
Gift Set, Barbie & Ken, Boxed, 1962 .... *Illus* 1050.00
Giraffe, Steiff, 8 Ft. 1850.00
Girl, Hula Hoop, Tin, Windup, 1950s 225.00
Girl, Riding Velocipede, Clockwork, Painted Tin, Brown & Stevens, 1875 .... 1760.00
Go-Cart, Tom & Jerry, Friction, Marx, Box 100.00
Go-Cart, Wicker, Side Pockets, Parasol... 450.00
Go-Cart, Wooden... 88.00
Goat, Pull Toy, Hide Covered, Nodding Head, Squeaker, Platform, 10 1 /2 In. 770.00
Good Time Charley, 7 Actions, Windup, Japan... 145.00
Goose, Pip-Squeak, Papier-Mache, Spring Legs, Bellows, 7 1/ 2 In. 280.00
Gorilla, Battery Operated, Tin, Japan, Box, 9 1/2 In... 340.00
Gorilla, Magilla, Rubber, Ideal, 7 In. 35.00
Gorilla, Pounds Chest, Roars, Windup, Marx, Box... 450.00
Gorilla, Roaring, Battery Operated, Box.. 225.00
Gorilla, Roaring, Push Button, He Roars, Raises Arms, Eyes Light, Battery Operated ... 175.00
Grandpa, Smoking, Battery Operated, S.A.N., Japan, c.1950s.. 375.00
Granny Doodle, Fisher-Price, 1930s.. 950.00
Graphophone, Cast Iron, Tin & White Metal, Box 72.00
Grocery Store, Shelves & Drawers, Ebony Trim, Food, Wooden, c.1880, 33 In. 4000.00
Guitar, Musical, Bugs Bunny, 1962.. 97.00
Gun, Air Pistol, Benjamin, Model 112 .... 110.00
Gun, Air Pistol, Benjamin, Model 122, Front Pump 95.00
Gun, Air Pistol, Benjamin, Model 132, Gray Grips, Holds Air.. 45.00
Gun, Air Pistol, Benjamin, Model 137, Wooden Grips... 65.00
Gun, Air Pistol, Benjamin, Model 3030 .... 45.00
Gun, Air Pistol, Benjamin, Model HW97 .... 90.00
Gun, Air Pistol, Crosman, Model 38T 80.00
Gun, Air Pistol, Crosman, Model 102 .... 60.00
Gun, Air Pistol, Crosman, Model 106 .... 90.00
Gun, Air Pistol, Crosman, Model 130, Custom Carbine 125.00
Gun, Air Pistol, Crosman, Model 600, Open Cap Type, Papers, Box 92.00
Gun, Air Pistol, Daisy, Model 99, Shooter's Edition... 50.00
Gun, Air Pistol, Daisy, Model 100-38, Plymouth, 1947 .... 45.00
Gun, Air Pistol, Daisy, Model 111 .... 30.00
Gun, Air Pistol, Daisy, Model 160.. 40.00
Gun, Air Pistol, Daisy, Model 177, Target Special.. 15.00
Gun, Air Pistol, Daisy, Model 747 .... 100.00
Gun, Air Pistol, Daisy, Red Ryder, 1938 .... 45.00
Gun, Air Pistol, Healthways Sharpshooter.. 35.00
Gun, Air Pistol, Hy-Score, Model 800.. 65.00
Gun, Air Pistol, Hy-Score, Model 803, Sportster.. 163.00
Gun, Air Pistol, Marksman, Model 1050, GAT, Great Britain... 50.00
Gun, Air Pistol, Quackenbush, Model 1, Nickel 250.00
Gun, Air Pistol, Quackenbush, Model 5, 22 Cartridge Adapter, Target Sights, Nickel.... 700.00
Gun, Air Pistol, Sears, Model 150 .... 130.00
Gun, Air Pistol, Slavia, Model 618 .... 50.00
Gun, Air Pistol, Smith & Wesson, Model 79G 50.00

Gun, Air Pistol, Webley, Premier... 140.00
Gun, Air Pistol, Webley, Vulcan... 90.00
Gun, Air Rifle, Benjamin, Model 300, Bicycle Pump Style 100.00
Gun, Air Rifle, Benjamin, Model 342, Wooden 62.00
Gun, Air Rifle, Benjamin, Model 710.. 80.00
Gun, Air Rifle, Benjamin, Model F, Nickel, Complete 88.00
Gun, Air Rifle, Crosman, Model 102, Repeater, Walnut... 63.00
Gun, Air Rifle, Daisy, Model 25 .... 65.00
Gun, Air Rifle, Daisy, Model 95B... 28.00
Gun, Air Rifle, Daisy, Red Ryder, Anniversary Special, 1988..................................... 45.00
Gun, Air Rifle, Daisy, Red Ryder, Model 111 .... 85.00
Gun, Air Rifle, Daisy, Red Ryder, Wooden Stock 45.00
Gun, Air Rifle, Smith & Wesson, Model 80, Box ....80.00 to 84.00
Gun, Air, Daisy, Red Ryder, Box 150.00
Gun, Atomic, Working, Jahl, 1957, 9 In. 75.00
Gun, BB, Red Ryder, 1950s 50.00
Gun, Coastal Defense, Brass Barrel, Painted Metal, Marklin, 10 In. 770.00
Gun, Dart, Captain Commando, Box 75.00
Gun, Flashy Flickers Magic Picture Gun, Marx, 1960s, Box 90.00
Gun, I Spy Camera Gun, On Card.. 225.00
Gun, Pom-Pom, Air Defense, Lights, Linemar, 14 In. 235.00
Gun, Pop Gun, Daisy, Double Barrel 95.00
Gun, Pop Gun, U.N.C.L.E., Plastic, 1965 .... 15.00
Gun, Pop, Daisy, Double Barrel 65.00
Gun, Popeye, Auto Magic Picture, Projects Image On Wall, Metal, 1930s.................... 210.00
Gun, Ray, Plazer, Box 700.00
Gun, Ray, Sparking, Tom Corbett, Space Cadet, Tin & Plastic, 1950s, 22 In. 325.00
Gun, Space Pistol, Flashlight, Clicker.. 145.00
Gun, Space, Atomic Disintegrator, Nickel Plated, Hubley 475.00
Gun, Space, Hero, 1960, 7 In. 65.00
Gun, Space, Red Plastic, 1950s.. 25.00
Gun, Space, Tommy-Ray, Box 190.00
Gun, Squirt, Big Squirt, Box, 1940s.. 75.00
Gun, Squirt, Daisy, Rocket Dart, Lithograph 95.00
Gun, Squirt, Water, Cowboy, 10 In. 8.00
Gun, Squirt, Water, Junior Ranger 23.00
Gun, Stallion 38, 6-Shooter, Unused, Nichols, Box 200.00
Gun, Sub-Machine Gun, Thompson Automatic, Plastic, Fires Balls, Wes-Ko, 26 In. 185.00
Gun, Tom Corbett, Space Cadet, Clicker... 110.00
Gun, Wagon Tray, Holster, Hubley.. 65.00
Gun & Holster Set, Wyatt Earp, Frontier Marshall, Box 95.00
Gypsy, Fortune Teller, Battery Operated, 10 Cards 1400.00
Hair Dryer, Suzy Homemaker, Topper, Box, 1971 .... 20.00
Ham & Sam, Minstrel Team, Windup, Tin, Strauss, c.1921, 6 1/2 In. ....515.00 to 770.00
Hansom Cab, Cast Iron, Kenton, 15 1/2 In., Box 770.00
Hansom Cab, Kenton, Cast Iron, Box, 16 In. 550.00
Harmonica, Figural, Woody Woodpecker, Red Plastic, 1960s 85.00
Harvester, McCormick Deering, Arcade, 9 In. 350.00
Hearse, Adams Family, Take-Apart, Williams.. 275.00
Helicopter, Chop Chop, Air Force, Plastic, Battery Operated, Marx, 1967, 17 In. 85.00
Helicopter, Moon Scout, Battery Operated, Box 145.00
Helicopter, Police Department Patrol, Tin, Friction, Japan, 10 In. 35.00
Helicopter, Rescue, Tin, Windup, Japan, 8 In. 150.00
Helicopter, Sikorsky, Friction, Tin, Alps... 125.00
Helicopter, Smokey Bear Forest Patrol, Box 135.00
Helicopter, Windup, Japan 155.00
Helicopter, Windup, Tin, Chein, 12 In. 300.00
Helmet, Robocop, Removable Faceplate, Fiberglass 325.00
Helmet, Space Patrol, Inflatable Collar, 1950s 250.00
Helmet, Space Pilot, Box 295.00
Helmet, Space, Colonel Ed McCauley, Visor, 1960 .... 45.00
Helmet, Space, Radar Goggles, Box 550.00
Hi-Way Henry, Tin Windup, 1920s.. 4600.00

High Chair, Convertible, Penny Toy, Tin Lithograph, Meier, c.1900, 3 In. 144.00
High Chair, Doll's, Spindle Back, Dowel Arms, Decal Back, Off White Paint, 21 In. :.... 75.00
Hippo, Fisher-Price, No. 151 .... 80.00
Hobbyhorse, Dapple Gray Paint, Ears, Mane & Tail Missing, Red Base 650.00
Hobbyhorse, On Stick, Schoenhut, 25 In. 60.00
Hobo, Skating, Windup, Linemar 295.00
Honeymoon Express, With Airplane, Windup, Tin, Marx, 1940s..................... 135.00 to 170.00
Hoosier Cabinet, Boone Brand, Doors Open, Cutting Board, Cast Iron, 8 In................. 1000.00
Horse, Breyer 10.00
Horse, Horsehide Body & Mane, Head Turns, Pedals, On Wheels, 33 In. 825.00
Horse, On Platform, Wheels, Mohair, Horsehair Tail, Reins, Bridle, Saddle, 10 1/2 In. . 215.00
Horse, On Platform, With Milk Cart, Cloth-Covered Horse, Milk Cans, Wooden, 33 In. 900.00
Horse, Pony, Ride-On, Mohair, Cream & Tan Spots, Glass Eyes, Steiff, 24 1/2 In. 145.00
Horse, Pony, Steiff, 5 1/2 In. 55.00
Horse, Pony, Trick, Bell Ringer, 4-Wheel Platform, Painted, Cast Iron, 8 In. 575.00
Horse, Pull Toy, Burlap Body, Pine Base, Red Iron Wheels, 26 x 26 In. 135.00
Horse, Pull Toy, Felt Covered, Glass Eyes, Wooden Wheels, Steiff, 1930s, 15 In. 546.00
Horse, Pull Toy, Mohair, Bells, Germany, 1890 .... 995.00
Horse, Race Horse, Rider, Windup, Tin, Germany 100.00
Horse, Ride-On, 4 Wheels In Tripod Shape, Head Turns To Steer 450.00
Horse, Rocking, Burlap Body, Glass Eyes, Wooden Rockers, 27-In. Tall. 350.00
Horse, Rocking, Canvas Cover, Excellior, c.1905 .... 245.00
Horse, Rocking, Cutout Horse Silhouettes, Upholstered Seat, 42 1/2 In. 65.00
Horse, Rocking, Dapple Gray Paint, Blue Rockers, Wooden, 45 In. 440.00
Horse, Rocking, Dapple Gray, Carved Wood, Leather Tack, Red Rockers, 51 In. 517.00
Horse, Rocking, Dapple Gray, Laminated Wood, Horsehair Mane, Tail, Red Base, 37 In. 330.00
Horse, Rocking, Dapple Gray, Leather & Cloth Tack, Red Rockers, 48 In. 365.00
Horse, Rocking, Gesso On Wood Body, Cast Iron Head, 3 x 2 Ft. 3630.00
Horse, Rocking, Hide Covered, Crandall's Spring Horse Velocipede, 39 In. 550.00
Horse, Rocking, Hollow Body, Horsehair Mane, Original Paint 575.00
Horse, Rocking, Leather Saddle & Bridle, Horsehair Mane, Tail, c.1870, 42 In. 1760.00
Horse, Rocking, Leather Saddle, American, 32 1/2 x 47 1/2 In. 195.00
Horse, Rocking, Natural Finish, Restored Tack, England, 1910, Small 395.00
Horse, Rocking, Paper Lithograph On Wood, Tin Legs, Wooden Rockers, Gibbs, 9 In. 265.00
Horse, Rocking, Pull Toy, Burlap Body, Horsehair Tail, c.1920, 30 x 36 In. 150.00
Horse, Rocking, Pull Toy, Leather Harness & Saddle, Fabric Cover, c.1890, 32 In. 1800.00
Horse, Rocking, Rattan 115.00
Horse, Rocking, Seat Between 2 Horse Silhouettes, 44 In. 192.00
Horse, Rocking, Seat In Glider Frame, Silhouettes Of White Horses, 34 In. 55.00
Horse, Rocking, Stenciled Runners, Original Saddle 2530.00
Horse, Rocking, Victorian, Leather Seat, Wooden, 28 x 37 In. 400.00
Horse, Rocking, Whitney-Reed, 1880 .... 995.00
Horse, Rocking, Wooden Head, Burlap Body, Painted Red, Germany, 34 In. 975.00
Horse, Spark Plug, Floor Toy, Tin, 9 x 6 1/2 In. 1815.00
Horse, Trick Pony, Cast Iron, Bell Toy, Gong Bell Co., 1880s 950.00
Horse, Wooden, Sheepskin, Braided Leather Tail, Wheeled Platform, 1900s, Folk Art.. 1075.00
Horse & Jockey, Pull Toy, Hull & Stafford, 1870s, 6 5/8 In. 373.00
Horse & Rider, Bell Toy, Jumps Over Fences Ringing A Bell, Orange, Cast Iron, 6 In.. 230.00
Horse & Rider, Pull Toy, Tin, 8 In. 1430.00
Horse Racers, Push Toy, Tin Lithograph, Chein, 7 In. 195.00
Horse-Drawn Wagon, Sand & Gravel, Driver, 2 Horses, Kenton 350.00
Hula Girl, Windup, Celluloid, 1930s, 7 In. 150.00
Ice Box, Alaska, Glass Ice Cubes, 3-Hinged Operating Door, Cast Iron, 1920s............. 475.00
Ice Cream Vendor, Windup, M.T., Japan, 7 In., Box 975.00
Indian, Crawling, Holding Tomahawk, Clockwork, Ohio Art, c.1950, 8 In. 83.00
Indian, Drummer, Battery Operated, 6 x 12 In. 88.00
Indian Village Set, Wigwams, Canoes, Figures, 1920, Germany, 16 Piece 300.00
Iron, Box 75.00
Iron, Detachable Handle, Pat. 5/30/1900, 2 Parts, 4 3/4 x 2 1/4 In. 49.00
Iron, Dolly, 1930s 15.00
Iron, Lady Dover 28.00
Iron, Raggedy Ann, Tin ....8.00 to 15.00
Iron, Removable Wooden Handle, Potts, 3 3/4 In. 75.00

Iron, Skillet, Griswold No. 0, Chrome Finish 65.00
Iron, Steam, Westinghouse, Box, 1950s 35.00
Iron, Sunny Suzy, Electric 25.00
Iron, The Pearl, With Trivet 125.00
Iron, Wolverine, Electric 15.00
Ironing Board, Renwal 10.00
Jack-In-The-Box, Bugs Bunny, Tin, Original Box 225.00
Jack-In-The-Box, Clown, Papier-Mache Head, Chromolithograph Paper Covering, 11 In.   55.00
Jack-In-The-Box, Germany, 19th Century, 2 1/2 In. 430.00
Jack-In-The-Box, Jolly Tune, Box, Mattel 95.00
Jack-In-The-Box, Papier-Mache Pig, Cloth Ruff, Germany, 1904, 4 x 3 3/4 In. 270.00
Jack-In-The-Box, Wizard Of Oz, Bisque Head, Large, Box 195.00
Jazzbo Jim, Marx, Box 795.00
Jazzbo Jim, Strauss, 1921 .... 375.00
Jazzbo Jim, Unique Art Co. 550.00
Jeep, Gumby, 1966, Box 100.00
Jeep, Jumpin' Jeep, Marx 325.00
Jeep, Jumping Jeep, Windup, Tin, Marx, 5 1/2 x 4 1/4 In. 100.00
Jeep, Military, Turn-O-Matic, Gun Fires, Lights, 11 In. 225.00
Jeep, Steer Horns On Hood, Windup, Marx 425.00
Jeep, Surrey, Tonka, Box 175.00
Jeep, Tonka, 1964, 10 x 5 In. 39.00
Jeep, Willys, Headlights, Tin Wheels, Battery Operated, Marx, 11 In. 85.00
Jester, Mechanical, Pulls Long Length Of Ribbons From Mouth 495.00
Jewelry Set, Josie & The Pussycats, Plastic, Blister Card, Larami Corp., 1973 .... 50.00
Jiminy Cricket, Plush, Knickerbocker 30.00
Jolly Penguin, Windup, Beaded Eyes, Fur Covered, MT Toys 225.00
Jumbo Jitterbug, Wooden, Pop-Up, Fisher-Price, 1930s 190.00
Kaleidoscope, Million Design, Hobby Products, 1940s 45.00
Kazoo, Woody Woodpecker, Cereal Premium, With Directions, 1950s 45.00
Kico Man, Shoots Billiards, Windup, Germany, 1915 .... 380.00
Kiddie Kampers, Windup, Wolverine 475.00
Kiddy Cyclist, Unique Art, 1930s 250.00
Kitchen Counter, Campbell's Soup, Working, 1949 .... 150.00
Kitchen Set, Table & 4 Chairs, Renwal, Green 30.00
Kite, Reddy Kilowatt 72.00
Kitty Puss, Drayton 795.00
Krazy Kat, Pop-Up, Souvenir Great Lakes Exposition Cleveland Ohio, Fisher-Price 350.00
Lab Set, Microscope, Gilbert, 1950s 75.00
Lady Bugs, Tin, Windup, TPS, Box 225.00
Lamb, Head Turns, Knickerbocker, 22 In. 16.00
Lamb, Pull Toy, Lambskin Cover, Glass Eyes, Wool Twill Face, Germany, 22 1/2 In. .. 1121.00
Leaping Lena, Windup 950.00
Li'l Abner Dogpatch Band, Tin Lithograph, Windup, Unique Art, 10 In. ....550.00 to 690.00
Lion, On Wheels, Mohair, Steel Eyes, Embroidered Muzzle, Steiff, c.1908, 9 x 9 In. 316.00
Lion, Walking, Windup, Occupied Japan, Box 90.00
Lite, Blinker Code, Navy, Hasbro, Box 40.00
Little Helper Laundry Set, Ironing Board, Newton & Thompson Mfg., Box 200.00
Little Jim Rooster, Pull Toy, J.C. Penney 85.00
Living Room Set, Doll's, Wicker, 1920s, 3 Piece 300.00
Louis Armstrong, Trumpet Playing, Windup 425.00
Maggie & Jiggs, Windup, Wheeled Platform, Nifty, Germany 1350.00
Magic Slate, Atom Ant, Watkins, 1964 .... 65.00
Magic Slate, Felix The Cat, No. 3040, Lowe, 1950s 65.00
Magic Slate, Space Kidettes, Watkins, 1968 .... 35.00
Mammie's Boy, Marx, 1930, 11 In. 700.00
Man, Dancing, Top Hat, Green Suit, Painted Tin, 19th Century, 16 In. 402.00
Man, On Motorcycle, Arnold, Red, Box, Germany 1280.00
Man, On Motorcycle, Cruvo-1000, Schuco, Box ....880.00 to 1100.00
Man, Playing Xylophone, Wolverine, Windup, 6 Discs 420.00
Man, Smoking Cigarette, Puffy Morris, Battery Operated, Box 195.00
Man, Trapeze, Wolverine 300.00
Mary Kornman, Our Gang Series, Dances In Circle, Windup, 1926, 12 In. 450.00

Mask, Yogi Bear, Hanna-Barbera, Cereal Premium, 1961 .... 50.00
Merry Makers, Tin Lithograph, Windup, Marx, 9 1/4 x 9 In. 1380.00
Merry-Go-Round, 4 Airplanes, 2 Swans, Tin Lithograph, Windup, Wyandotte, 5 In. 335.00
Merry-Go-Round, 4 Flags, 4 Airplanes, Windup, Wolverine, 1930s .... 450.00 to 495.00
Merry-Go-Round, Playland, No. 385, Chein 1050.00
Merry-Go-Round, Swan Boats, Windup, Chein, Box 895.00
Microscope, A.C. Gilbert 40.00
Microscope & Lab Set, Gilbert, Test Tube Container 40.00
Microscope Jr., Medical Slides, Newman Sterns, Cast Iron 65.00
Mighty Kong, Battery Operated, Inserts 750.00
Milk Wagon, Borden's, Cart & Horse, Wood & Metal, Pull Toy, 1930s 495.00
Milk Wagon, Four Wheels, Blue & Gold, Driver Seat, Brown & Co., 13 In. 322.00
Milk Wagon, Horse, Wooden, Sheffield Farms Milk, 23 In. 750.00
Mine Sweeper, Personnel Carrier 750.00
Model, U.S. Navy Frogmen Demolition Team, Boat, Monogram, 1959, Box 225.00
Model, U.S. Navy Hospital Ship, Haven, S Kit, Revell, 1955, Box 165.00
Model Kit, Bertram The Stag Beetle, Science Series, No. 516, Hawk, 1959 .... 48.00 to 50.00
Model Kit, Bride Of Frankenstein, Bride Lying On Lab Table, Aurora, Box, 1965 .... 995.00
Model Kit, Chicken Little, The Miracle Of Life In An Eggshell, Revell, 1961 .... 65.00
Model Kit, Competition Dragster, Hawk, 1961 .... 29.00
Model Kit, Cord Super Charge, 1937, 812 Convertible Coupe, By AMT, Plastic............ 59.00
Model Kit, Creature Of Black Lagoon, Reptile & Snake, Plastic, 1963, Box 498.00
Model Kit, Creature Of The Black Lagoon, Underwater Scene, Aurora, 1975 .... 240.00
Model Kit, Davey Weird-Ohs, Hawk, 1963 .... 125.00
Model Kit, Dracula, Aurora, 1962 .... 379.00
Model Kit, Duesenberg, Hubley 65.00
Model Kit, Flying Sub, Monogram, 1964 .... 80.00
Model Kit, Frankenstein Monsters Of The Movies, Aurora, 1975 .... 279.00
Model Kit, Godzilla's Go-Cart, Aurora 5700.00
Model Kit, Grumman Gulfhawk 125.00
Model Kit, Harley-Davidson, Evel Knievel's Wheelie, 1/12 Scale, No. 153, Addar 98.00
Model Kit, Hunchback Of Notre Dame, Aurora, 1964 .... 439.00
Model Kit, King Arthur Of Camelot, No. 825, Aurora, 1967 .... 80.00
Model Kit, King Kong, Aurora, 1964, Box 1400.00
Model Kit, Land Of The Giants, 3 People Fighting Rattlesnake, Box, 1968.................... 490.00
Model Kit, Lindberg Satellite, 3-Stage Rocket, 1950s, Box 250.00
Model Kit, Lost In Space 4220.00
Model Kit, Messerschmitt ME 109, Propeller, Stand... 66.00
Model Kit, Mummy, Glow-In-The-Dark, Plastic, Aurora, 1972, 8 x 8 In., Box 89.00
Model Kit, Paddy Wagon, Motorized, Remco, Unassembled 295.00
Model Kit, Phantom Of The Opera, Billiken, 1982 .... 229.00
Model Kit, Phantom Of The Opera, Glow Model, 1969 .... 87.00
Model Kit, Planet Of The Apes, General Aldo, Addar, 1973... 35.00
Model Kit, Pontiac Firebird, No. 565, Aurora, 1961... 225.00
Model Kit, Rhinoceros Beetle, Motorized, Plastic, Natural Science, Banda, 1960s........ 75.00
Model Kit, Rocket, Jupiter "C" U.S. Army Missile, No. 804, Comet, 1950s.................. 160.00
Model Kit, Self-Propelled Howitzer, No. M551, Military Blueprint Series, Renwal 85.00
Model Kit, Star Trek, Bridge, 1975 .... 40.00
Model Kit, The Black Knight Of Aurnberg, Aurora, Box, 1963 .... 25.00
Monkey, Battery Operated, Alps, Box 75.00
Monkey, Bell Boy, Windup 120.00
Monkey, Bongo, Windup, Plays Drums, Box 250.00
Monkey, Bubble Blowing, Battery Operated, Japan, 11 In. 75.00
Monkey, Climbing, Lehmann 250.00
Monkey, Climbing, Pull Cord, Metal Lithograph, Fully Jointed, Germany, 8 1/2 In. 85.00
Monkey, Drummer, Windup, Schucco 95.00
Monkey, Frankie, Roller Skating, Battery Operated, Box.. 145.00
Monkey, Glass Eyes, Brown & Tan, Steiff, c.1900, 11 1/2 In. 99.00
Monkey, Hula Hoop, Windup, Tin 125.00
Monkey, Jocko, Drinking, Battery Operated, Linemar, Box 100.00
Monkey, Jocko, Drinking, Light-Up, Linemar, Japan... 145.00
Monkey, Jolly Guitarist, Windup, Tin 165.00
Monkey, Licking Lollipop, Windup, Tin, 5 In.. 65.00

Monkey, Mohair Over Metal, Shuco, 5 In.	295.00
Monkey, Mohair, Straw Stuffed	295.00
Monkey, Mr. Chimp, Battery Operated, Flips, Tumbles, Marx, 1969, Box	225.00
Monkey, Musical, Celluloid, Tin, Windup, Japan, 8 In.	245.00
Monkey, On Velocipede, Bell, Pedals When Pulled, Cast Iron, J. & E. Stevens, 8 In.	3680.00
Monkey, On Velocipede, Tin Tricycle, Stuffed Animal, Windup, Bing, c.1890, 10 In.	3500.00
Monkey, Porter, Battery Operated, 1960, Box	75.00
Monkey, Shooting Pool, Tin, Windup, Box, Japan	395.00
Monkey, Talking, Black, Molded Vinyl Head, Pull String, Mattel, 1960s, 14 In.	125.00
Monkey, Tippee Tim Dancing Monkey Music Box, Mattel	25.00
Monkeys, Acrobatic, Wyandotte	245.00
Monoplane, Airmail, Decals, Pressed Steel, Keystone	750.00
Monoplane, Empire Express 550, USA	550.00
Monoplane, Right Plane, Belt Driven Propeller, Scheible, 29 In.	575.00
Moonraker Set, James Bond, Box	190.00
Mortimer Snerd, Walker, Marx	325.00
Motor Scooter, Vespa, Tin, Bandai, 9 In.	235.00
Motorbike, Rider Moves Up & Down, Friction, Tin, Japan, 7 1/2 In.	200.00
Motorcycle, Arnold, 1935	675.00
Motorcycle, Atom, Rolls, Stops, Driver Dismounts, Climbs Back & Takes Off, Battery	520.00
Motorcycle, Bobbing Rider, Friction, Tin, Box, 8 In.	40.00
Motorcycle, Daredevil Stunt, Battery Operated, Tin, Cragston, 10 1/2 In., Box	475.00
Motorcycle, Dinky, c.1936	45.00
Motorcycle, Echo Clockwork, Painted Tin, Lehman, 1903-1907	1760.00
Motorcycle, Flying Spaceman, Box	7975.00
Motorcycle, Harley-Davidson, Hubley, 1930s	250.00
Motorcycle, Harley-Davidson, Orange, Hubley, 9 In.	1600.00
Motorcycle, Harley-Davidson, Swirl Head, Hubley	575.00
Motorcycle, Indian, Red, Hubley, 9 1/4 In.	1100.00
Motorcycle, Police Patrol, Policeman, Tin, Battery Operated, Japan..................*Illus*	83.00
Motorcycle, Police, Renwal, c.1954, 9 In.	65.00
Motorcycle, Police, Tin, Battery Operated	495.00
Motorcycle, Policeman, Cast Iron, 1930s, 6 1/4 In.	275.00
Motorcycle, Policeman, Sidecar No. 3, Tin, Windup, Yellow, Marx, c.1940, 8 In.	275.00
Motorcycle, Policeman, Tin Lithograph, Windup, Marx, 8 1/2 In.	259.00
Motorcycle, Red, Cast Iron, 6 1/2 In.	395.00
Motorcycle, Rider, Sparking Front Headlight, CKO	495.00
Motorcycle, Rubber, Auburn, 6 In.	55.00
Motorcycle, Sidecar, Box	450.00
Motorcycle, Sidecar, Indian Lithograph On Tank, Marx, Windup, 6 1/2 In.	250.00
Motorcycle, Space Patrol Super, Box	3740.00
Motorcycle, Speed Boy Delivery Cycle, Windup, Marx, 1930s, Box	750.00
Motorcycle, Tin Lithograph, Rolling Wheels, JMI, 1950s, 6 1/2 In.	295.00
Motorcycle, Tin, Red & Blue, JML, France, 1940	535.00
Motorcycle, Tinplate, Key Wind, Side Car, Driver, 2 Passengers, Germany, 11 In.	980.00

Toy, Motorcycle, Police Patrol, Policeman,
Tin, Battery Operated, Japan

Motorcycle, U-Turn, Windup, Box 175.00
Motorcycle, Windup, Nickel Plated, Japan, 10 In. 2450.00
Motorcycle, Windup, Tin, Technofix, Germany, 7 In. 190.00
Motorcyclist, Lithograph, Painted Metal, Germany, 1914, 8 1/8 In. 665.00
Mountain Climber, Mechanical, Windup, Marx, Box 275.00
Mr. & Mrs. Potato Head, Deluxe Set, 1950s, Box 95.00
Mr. Machine, Ideal 65.00
Mr. Magoo Ring Set, Plastic, Magoo Head 24.00
Mr. Mercury, Walks, Bends, Lifts, Remote Control, Marx, 13 In. 275.00
Mr. Potato Head, Hasbro, 1972, Box 30.00
Music Box, Cat In The Hat, Mattel, Box 68.00
Music Box, Pink Panther 25.00
Music Box, Tick Tock Clock, Fisher-Price 65.00
Music Maker, Man With Jocko, Mattel, Box 150.00
Native On Turtle, Chein 495.00
Navy Frogman, Mechanical, Chein, Box 235.00
Noah's Ark, Bliss 450.00
Noah's Ark, Wooden, Carved, Painted, Noah, Wife, Animals, 15 Pairs, c.1900, 18 In. .. 460.00
Noisemaker, Safety Cracker, Red, White & Blue, Patent Date 1918 .... 25.00
Omnibus, Horse Drawn, 2 Horses, Bench Seats, Rear Door, c.1870s, 13 1/2 In. 489.00
Orangutan, Baby, Yes-No, Schuco, 8 In. 225.00
Organ, Magnus Harmonica Corp., Bakelite, c.1930, 7 In. 475.00
Organ, Mechanical, Tin Lithograph, Germany, 1900, 5 In. 500.00
Organ Grinder, Automaton, 25 x 21 In. 2300.00
Organette, Melody Player, 3 Music Rolls, Chein, 1950s 350.00
Ostrich, Painted Eyes, Schoenhut, 20th Century, 8 7/8 In. 172.00
Oven, Doll's, Sheet Metal, Nickel-Plated Trim, Accessories, Karr Range Co., 21 In. 3300.00
Pail, Boy On Sea Horse, Ohio Art 50.00
Pail, Circus Animals, Shovel, Tin, Chein, 1950s, 5 1/4 In. 30.00
Pail, Girl On Swan, Ohio Art 50.00
Pail, Story Of Three Bears, Chein 25.00
Pail, Tin Lithograph, Seashore, Children & Battleship, Remember The Maine, 3 1/4 In. 93.00
Pail, Tin, Flowers, With Tools, Ohio Art 25.00
Paint By Number, Flintstones, Watercolor, 1961 .... 150.00
Paint Set, Easel, Palette, Tools, France, 11 x 12 In., Box 200.00
Parasol, Doll's, Ivory Handle, Corded Tassel, Coffee Silk Twill, Early 20th Century ... 165.00
Parasol, Doll's, Ivory Handle, Ivory Silk Cover, Scalloped, Mid-19th Century 550.00
Parrot, Talking, Battery Operated, Repeats What Is Said, 17 In. 275.00
Peacock, Strutting, Windup, Germany, 5 x 4 In. 38.00
Pedal Boat, Built As Chris Craft, Rear Storage Compartment, Windshield, 1940s 3800.00
Pedal Car, 501 Jet Sweep, AMF, 1950s 375.00
Pedal Car, AF Fire Chief, No. 506, All Original 125.00
Pedal Car, Airplane Hood Ornament, 1940s 800.00
Pedal Car, Airplane, Pursuit, 1940s, 46 In. 2750.00
Pedal Car, Airplane, Red Wing, Pressed Steel, American National, c.1930, 30 x 50 In. 1955.00
Pedal Car, Aluminum Body, Upholstered, Simulated Fuel Pump, Lion Head Special.... 4900.00
Pedal Car, Battery-Powered Headlights, Heavy Gauge Tin, Russia, 44 In. 230.00
Pedal Car, Black, Red Fenders, 38 x 20 x 20 In. 550.00
Pedal Car, Bugatti, Type 35, Metal Body & Chassis, Hand Brake, 6 Ft. 7500.00
Pedal Car, Buick Roadster, American National, Restored, 1927 .... 5720.00
Pedal Car, Buick, American National, Pedestal For Barber Shop, 1926 ...... 5500.00
Pedal Car, Buick, Roadster, Rumble Seat, American National, 1927 .... 5720.00
Pedal Car, Buick, Steelcraft, 1940s 2995.00
Pedal Car, Cadillac, Spring Suspension, Open Hood, American National, 1920 .... 5500.00
Pedal Car, Caterpillar, Diesel Crawler, 1950s 2195.00
Pedal Car, Champion Jet-Flow, Blue & White, 1940s 495.00
Pedal Car, Champion, Dip Side, Restored, 1950s 450.00
Pedal Car, Champion, Original Paint 400.00
Pedal Car, Chrysler Airflow, Original Paint, 1935 .... 12650.00
Pedal Car, Chrysler Convertible, Steelcraft, Original Paint, 1933 .... 7700.00
Pedal Car, Comet, 1948 Model, Murray 675.00
Pedal Car, Comet, Murray, 1949 .... 1000.00
Pedal Car, Dan Patch, Brass Lights, Rear Drive Mechanism, 1920 .... 2900.00

Pedal Car, Dolphin Boat, Murray, 1958 .... 695.00
Pedal Car, Dude-Ranch Wagon, Murray, 1959 .... 595.00
Pedal Car, Earth Mover, Murray, 1959 .... 595.00
Pedal Car, Fire Chief, Murray, 1959 .... 495.00
Pedal Car, Fire Chief, Murray, 1960 .... 395.00
Pedal Car, Fire Chief, Murray, 1962 .... 295.00
Pedal Car, Fire Chief, Pressed Steel, American National, 1920s............................... 7700.00
Pedal Car, Fire Chief, Tool Box, Gendron, 1927 .... 2200.00
Pedal Car, Fire City Battalion, No. 1, Murray, 1960 .... 395.00
Pedal Car, Fire Hose Cart, Gendron 7800.00
Pedal Car, Fire Patrol, Wooden Sides, Tin Hood & Wheels, Stegar, 1940s 300.00
Pedal Car, Fire Truck, 1950s.. 450.00
Pedal Car, Fire Truck, AMF, 1962 .... 175.00
Pedal Car, Fire Truck, Hose & Reel, Gendron Co., Toledo, Ohio, c.1930 .... 7800.00
Pedal Car, Fire Truck, Pontiac, Murray, 1947... 995.00
Pedal Car, Fire Truck, Red, Mors.. 900.00
Pedal Car, Fire Truck, Steelcraft, 1930s.. 6500.00
Pedal Car, Fire Truck, Water Tower, Lights & Horn, American National, 1930, 86 In. 8250.00
Pedal Car, Gendron, Cole On Grille, 1932 .... 6000.00
Pedal Car, Gendron, Green, c.1935 .... 1395.00
Pedal Car, Graham, Shark-Nosed, American National, 1938 .... 4400.00
Pedal Car, Keystone Butterfly Fender, 1915, 43 In. 3300.00
Pedal Car, Metal Chassis & Wheels, Painted Steel, Keystone, 1920s, 32 In. 905.00
Pedal Car, Mustang, 1965 .... 550.00
Pedal Car, Mustang, 1966 .... 525.00
Pedal Car, Oldsmobile, 1913 Model, Tin Body, Wooden Chassis, Green, 40 In. 1155.00
Pedal Car, Packard, De Luxe Roadster, Rumble Seat, Gendron, 1928 .... 6270.00
Pedal Car, Pontiac, Steelcraft, 1940s.. 2995.00
Pedal Car, Pony, 1930s 350.00
Pedal Car, Racer, No. 6, Gendron, c.1924.. 3960.00
Pedal Car, Sad Face Dump Truck, Murray... 695.00
Pedal Car, Spirit Of St. Louis, American National, 1932 .... 4950.00
Pedal Car, Spirit Of St. Louis, Steelcraft, 1928 .... 3520.00
Pedal Car, Sunbeam Racer No. 8, Gendron, Restored, 1932 .... 5500.00
Pedal Car, Tin Lizzy, Garton, 1960.. 795.00
Pedal Car, Torpedo, Yellow, Steel, Rubber Wheels, Murray, 1953, 40 In. .... *Illus* 3220.00
Pedal Car, Tractor & Grader, Heavy Duty Senior, 1950s.. 650.00
Pedal Car, Tractor, AMF, No. 4 .... 225.00
Pedal Car, Tractor, Big 4, Murray.. 125.00
Pedal Car, Tractor, Ertl 85.00
Pedal Car, Tractor, Eska, Small H, Restored, 1949... 450.00
Pedal Car, Tractor, John Deere, No. 4430, Restored... 175.00
Pedal Car, Tractor, Red Wheels, Spark Plug, Exhaust Graphics, Murray Ohio, 1949.... 295.00

Toy, Pedal Car, Torpedo, Yellow, Steel,
Rubber Wheels, Murray, 1953, 40 In.

Dirty or warped cards should be wiped with a sponge dipped in a mild solution of detergent and water. The detergent will help make the cards cleaner and more pliable. Warped cards should be wiped, dried, then put under a heavy weight for a few days.

Pedal Car, Transport Truck, AMF, 1950s 895.00
Pedal Car, Triang Jeep, 1950 Model, England 475.00
Pedal Car, Volkswagen, Red, Fiberglass 150.00
Pedal Car, Wood, Steel, Sheet Metal, Olds Stenciled On Radiator, 37 In. 825.00
Penguin, Skier, Plush Over Tin, Windup, Box, Japan 125.00
Penguin, Walking, Windup, Tin, Chein, 4 In. 75.00
Phaser, Star Trek, 1970s 55.00
Phonograph, Electric, Marx, Box 145.00
Phonograph, Polly Parrot, Portable 205.00
Piano, Player, Roll, Chein 125.00
Piano, Schoenhut, 16 In. 185.00
Piano, Stool, Grand, Tootsietoy 100.00
Pig, Clown Rider, Bell Ringer, 3 Wheels, Painted, Cast Iron, 6 In. 1035.00
Pig, Windup, U.S. Zone Germany, 4 In. 95.00
Pinball Machine, Young Clark Gable Dealing Cards, Marx, 27 x 12 1/2 In. 60.00
Ping Pong, Parker, 1930, Box 65.00
Pink Panther, On Racing Cycle, On Card, Corgi Toy, 4 x 5 1/4 In. 14.00
Pip-Squeak, Chicken, Pops Out Of Wooden Coop, Lithographed Roof, Plaster, 5 In. 35.00
Pip-Squeak, Eeyore, Rubber, 1966 .... 15.00
Pip-Squeak, Mighty Mouse, In Package 15.00
Pip-Squeak, Parrot, Papier-Mache, Polychrome Paint, 6 5/8 In. 50.00
Pip-Squeak, Rabbit, 2 Eggs On Bellows Base, Composition, 3 1/4 In. 70.00
Pip-Squeak, Rooster, Crowing, Papier-Mache 75.00
Pip-Squeak, Rooster, In Cage, Wood & Printed Paper, 6 3/4 In. 38.00
Pipe, Bubble, Tin, 19th Century, 5 7/8 In. 45.00
Pipe, Happy Hooligan, Molded Figure Against Bowl, Policeman On Stem 175.00
Play Golf, Mechanical, Strauss, Box 700.00
Play Set, Atom Ant Play Fun, No. 4756, Whitman, 1966 .... 65.00
Play Set, Circus, Marx 750.00
Play Set, Fairykins, Marx, Box 135.00
Play Set, Flintstones, Marx, Canada, 1980 .... 395.00
Play Set, Fort Dearborn, Marx, Box 135.00
Play Set, M*A*S*H, Box 100.00
Play Set, Pan American Airways, No. 4310, Tootsietoy, Box 895.00
Play Set, Tom Corbett, Space Academy, Marx, 1950s 550.00
Play-Doh Fun Factory, Rainbow Crafts, 1960 .... 39.00
Playasax, 6 Rolls 200.00
Polyphone, Flowers On Lid, Interior Music Box, 19th Century, 8 x 7 In. 2700.00
Porpoise, Swimming, Brass, Powered By Moving Tail, Windup, 15 In. 110.00
Preacher, Black Man, Clockwork, Ives, c.1870 .... 5720.00
Presto Slate, Capt. Kangaroo, Mr. Green Jeans 20.00
Projector, Flintstones, Give-A-Show, 1963 .... 55.00
Projector, Movie, Hand Crank, Bobby Bumps Film, Keystone 50.00
Puppet, Fritzi, Pelham, Box, 1950s 65.00
R2-D2, Windup, Takara, Box 50.00
Rabbit, 2 Cymbals, Windup, Tin, Guntherman, 9 1/2 In. 410.00
Rabbit, In Carriage, Windup, Box 450.00
Rabbit, Nikili, Dressed, Stitched On Orange Felt Shoes, Steiff, 1950, 11 In. 400.00
Rabbit, Peter Rabbit, Steiff 175.00
Rabbit, Peter The Drumming Rabbit, Box 95.00
Rabbit, Riding Bicycle, Balloon, Windup, Tin 30.00
Rabbit, Skiing, Brown Mohair, Red Plush Ski Suit, Incised Button, Steiff, 14 In. 320.00
Rabbit, Skiing, Key Wind, Tin, Celluloid Head, Japan 175.00
Rabbit, Windup, Tin, 7 In. 895.00
Railroad Set, Lionel, Santa Fe, 5 Cars & Engine, 1971 .... 285.00
Ramp Walker, Black, On Animal, Marx, Package, 1960s 50.00
Ramp Walker, George Jetson & Astro, Marx, 1963 .... 95.00
Ramp Walker, Pillsbury Funny Face, 4 Figures 245.00
Ramp Walker, Sailor, With Tin Lithographed Ramp 95.00
Ramp Walker, Space Men, Package, 1960s 20.00
Ramp Walker, Walking Space Dog, Package, 1950s 35.00
Rapid Fire Cannon, Bullets & Soldiers, Bradley, Box 100.00
Rattle, Twisted Wire, 6 Bells, Glass Beads, Wooden Handle, 7 1/2 In. 140.00

Red The Iceman, Marx, Box 3300.00
Ride A Rocket, Tin, Chein, 18 In. 690.00
Rifle, Colt, 6 Shooter, Mattel, 1960 .... 325.00
Rifle, Cork, Daisy, No. 25, Wooden Handle, 37 In. 100.00
Rifle, Scout, Hubley, c.1960 .... 115.00
Ring, Compass, Silver Metal, 1950s 25.00
Ring, Cowboy, Riding Horse, Metal, 1950s 10.00
Ring, Gunsmoke, Flasher, Color, 1960s 2.00
Ring, James Bond, Flicker, 1965, Set Of 6 Different Rings 45.00
Ring, Road Runner, Flasher, Chrome, 1960s 45.00
Ring, Siren, Elephant Base, Metal 20.00
Ring, Wonder Woman, Gold Metal Logo, D.C., 1976 .... 35.00
Ring, Zorro, Logo, Black Plastic, 1960s 35.00
Robot, Astronaut, Friction, Red, Cragstan 450.00
Robot, Atomic Man, Windup 775.00
Robot, Big Max, Electronic Conveyor, Remco, Box 265.00
Robot, Captain, Walking, Tin & Plastic, Korea, Box, 1960s 65.00
Robot, Dino, Battery Operated, Box 1275.00
Robot, Directional, Bump & Go Action, Battery Operated, Tin, Japan, 11 In. 2600.00
Robot, Dog, Friction, Red 295.00
Robot, Galaxy 195.00
Robot, Jetsujin 795.00
Robot, Jupiter, Box 6000.00
Robot, Machine Robot, Battery Operated, S.H., Japan, Box 575.00
Robot, Marline, Windup, 1950s 325.00
Robot, Monster Of The Empire, Battery Operated, Lights, Sounds, Box 200.00
Robot, Monster, Head Opens To Growling Dragon, Flashing Lights, Windup, Japan 495.00
Robot, Monster, Helmet Opens, Red Lighted Dragon, Walks, Battery Operated 95.00
Robot, Moon, Mechanical, Yonezowa, Box 3300.00
Robot, Mr. Mercury, Box 750.00
Robot, Mr. Rembrandt The Drawing Robot, Ideal, Box 30.00
Robot, Mr. Robot The Mechanical Brain, Windup, Battery-Operated Lights, Box 1275.00
Robot, New Space Explorer, Battery Operated, Box 145.00
Robot, Piston, Japan 175.00
Robot, Planet 395.00
Robot, Radar, Tin, Walks, Eyes Light, Antenna, Wrench In Hand 2150.00
Robot, Radicon, Box 7500.00
Robot, Ratchet, Windup, Box 1175.00
Robot, Robbie, Chrome 795.00
Robot, Robby, Box 1250.00
Robot, Rocket Control Center, Battery Operated, Box 515.00
Robot, Smoking 695.00
Robot, Space Explorer, Japan, 11 In. 190.00
Robot, Space Radio, Face Flashes, 1977 .... 75.00
Robot, Sparky, Windup, Box 299.00
Robot, Star Strider, Blue, Battery Operated, Box 80.00
Robot, Super Giant, Box, 17 In. 290.00
Robot, Tobor, Promotional, Robots International, Tape Deck, 1970s, 56 1/2 In. 1250.00
Robot, Transparent, Taiwan, 1970s 65.00
Robot, Wheel-A-Gear, Battery Operated, Box 1600.00
Robot, YM-3, Talking, Vinyl, Flashing Lights, Masudaya, Japan, 1985 .... 89.00
Robot, Zoomer, Battery Operated, Box 1295.00
Rocker, Doll's, Wicker, Upholstered Seat, Victorian, 9 In. 300.00
Rocket, Amusement Park, Tin Windup, 1960s, Box 175.00
Rocket, Apollo Moon 295.00
Rocket Fighter, Marx, 1930s 325.00
Rocket Ride, No. 260, Lever Windup, Chein, 9 In. 695.00
Rocket Ride, No. 400, Chein 1500.00
Rocket Ship, Buck Rogers, Box 2500.00
Rocket Ship, Buck Rogers, Marx, 1921 .... 550.00
Roller Coaster, 2 Cars, Battery Operated, Chein, 1930s 475.00
Roller Coaster, 2 Cars, Chein, 1960s 295.00
Roller Coaster, No. 275, Chein 450.00

Roller Coaster, Tin, Chein, 1930s 295.00
Roly Poly, Clown, Composition, Movable Eyes, 1900, 15 1/2 In. 950.00
Roly Poly, Dutch Girl, Schoenhut, 8 In. 750.00
Roly Poly, Rabbit, Orange, Tan & White Lithograph, Chein, 6 1/2 In. 165.00
Roly Poly, Scottish Boy, Celluloid, 3 1/2 In. 95.00
Rooster, Cock-A-Doodle, Battery Operated, Tin, Felt Tail, Box 150.00
Rooster, Pull Toy, Papier-Mache, Spring Legs, Wooden Base, Ultrahart, 8 1/4 In. .. 687.00
Rooster, Push Toy, Wood, Wire, Cast Iron & Tin, Chromolithograph, 25 In. 385.00
Sadiron, Lady Dover 22.00
Sailor, Walking, Columbia Hat, Windup, Lehmann, 7 1/2 In. 355.00
Sam The Gardener, Wheelbarrow, Tools, Windup, Marx 375.00
Sand, Busy Mike Sea-Saw, Chein 200.00
Sand, Speedy Hoist, Tin, Wolverine, Windup 200.00
Saw Mill, Automaton, 23 x 14 1/2 In. 825.00
Scale, Baby, Tin Lithograph, Pink, 1950s 35.00
Schoolhouse, Fisher-Price, Box 45.00
Scissors, Snippy, Fish Shape, Electric, Ungar Electric Tools, 1940s 22.00
Scissors Grinder, Windup, Germany 425.00
Scooter, Smitty, Windup, Marx 1850.00
Scooter, Two Riders, Friction, Yellow & Green, Technoflex, 6 1/2 In. 285.00
Scrappy & Margy, Pull Toy, Wooden, 1930s 100.00
Sea Lion, Steiff, 6 In. 95.00
Seal, With Ball, Windup, Celluloid, 1950 .... 79.00
Seesaw, 2 Men, Zigzag, Tin, Windup, Lehmann, 1907 .... 1200.00
Seesaw, Clockwork, Albert Dean 5775.00
Seesaw, Ives 5775.00
Seesaw Circus, Windup, Tin, Lewco, 1930s 175.00
Service Station Set, Lionel, 1978, Box 295.00
Sewing Machine, Betsy Ross 150.00
Sewing Machine, Chain Driven, Wooden Base 120.00
Sewing Machine, F. & W. Automatic Sewing Machine, Dovetailed Box, 1911 .... 325.00
Sewing Machine, Foley & Williams, A Perfect Chain Stitch Machine 325.00
Sewing Machine, Kay An Ee, U.S. Zone Germany, Box 50.00
Sewing Machine, Little Miss 125.00
Sewing Machine, Lucky Baby, Celluloid Doll At Machine, Tin, Box, Marusan, 5 In. ... 520.00
Sewing Machine, Martha Washington, Sotoy, Metallogram Corp. 150.00
Sewing Machine, Singer, Black Paint, Iron, 6 1/2 In. 69.00
Sewing Machine, Singer, Lock Stitch 35.00
Sewing Machine, Singer, No. 20, Box, Instructions 120.00
Sewing Machine, Singer, No. 22, SewHandy, Case 67.00
Shark, Tin, Windup, Chein, 11 In. 65.00
Shaver, Tripleheader Speadshaver, Battery Operated, Norelco, c.1960 .... 15.00
Sheep, Pull Toy, Wood, Papier-Mache, Wooly Coat, Pewter Wheels, Germany, 7 In. 632.00
Sheriff, 2 Guns, Weaves Side To Side, Shoots Guns, Battery Operated, Cragstan, Box .. 195.00
Shoeshine Joe, Battery Operated, Box 200.00
Shooting Gallery, Battery Operated, Windup, Traveler Target, Marx 195.00
Shooting Gallery, Carnival, Windup, Tin, Ohio Art, Box 145.00
Shotgun, Johnny Eagle Skeet Shooter, Launcher, Topper, Box 85.00
Showboat, Floor Toy, White Rubber Tires, Arcade, Cast Iron, 10 3/4 In. 465.00
Signalscope, Sky King, Directions 20.00
Silversmith Shop, 40 Pieces Of Silver, Eugene Kupjack, 11 1/2 x 17 In. 1900.00
Skating Chef, Tin & Cloth, Dressed, Windup, TPS, Japan 275.00
Skillet, Griswold, Erie 85.00
Skillet, Iron, Black, Wagner 40.00
Skunk, Plush, Windup, 3 In. 33.00
Slate, Magic, The Impossibles, Hanna-Barbera, 1967 .... 30.00
Sled, Black Striping, Stenciled Tiger, Steel Runners, Wooden, 38 1/4 In. 385.00
Sled, Dog's Head Design, Wooden Runners Tipped With Tin, 32 In. 412.00
Sled, Flexible Flyer, No. 47 .... 110.00
Sled, Flexible Flyer, Original Paint & Designs, 1920s 175.00
Sled, Front & Back Steel Banded Runners, Wood Rails, 1870s, 10 Ft. 172.00
Sled, Painted Wood, Red, Stenciled Design, Curved Runners 425.00
Sled, Platform, Central Scene, Friendship Stenciled Runners, Wooden, 42 In. 1100.00

Sled, Sno-Plane, Art Deco, Red Metal Runners, Black Top, 48 x 13 x 7 In. 143.00
Sled, Snow Rocket.. 185.00
Sled, Steel Topped Runners, Black Paint, 35 In. 60.00
Sled, Stenciled & Painted Flowers, Red Ground, Enola M. Brownell, 1909, 33 In. 385.00
Sled, Stenciled Indian Head, Green, Pine, c.1920, 36 In. 135.00
Sled, Stenciled Red Seat, Swan Neck Handles, Wooden & Iron, 19th Century, 39 In. ... 75.00
Sled, Upholstered, South Paris.. 625.00
Sled, Victorian, Wooden, Platform, Stenciled Runners, 42 In. 1100.00
Sled, Yellow Striping, Black Stenciled Design, Metal Runners, Wooden, 33 In. 192.00
Smitty Scooter, Marx 2195.00
Smoking Grandpa, Battery Operated 175.00
Snail, Mobo, Riding, Inch-Along Motion 300.00
Snoopy, Windup, Walking, Jointed Feet, Plastic, Aviva Enterprises, 1970s, 3 In. 12.00
Snowmobile, Tin & Plastic, Bandai, Japan, 10 In. 175.00
Soccer Team, Officials, Markers, Ball, Britains, Box, 12 1/4 .... 825.00
Soldier, 2nd Dragoons, Mounted With Lances, Bugler, Britain, c.1945, 5 Piece 215.00
Soldier, Arabs Of The Desert, Camels, Riders, Britains, 14 Piece 310.00
Soldier, Bahamas Police Drum & Bugle Corp, 16 Piece 93.00
Soldier, Band Of The Berkshire Regiment, No. 1, 19 Piece 500.00
Soldier, Band Of The Line, 12 Marchers, No. 27, Britains Box 315.00
Soldier, Bedouin Racing Warrior, On Horse, Weapons, Britains, Box, 5 Piece 180.00
Soldier, Changing Of The Guard At Buckingham Palace, Box, 83 Piece 785.00
Soldier, Cold Royal Scots Grays & Grenadiers, No. 41, Britains, 12 Piece, Box........... 145.00
Soldier, Cold Stream Guards, No. 90, Britains, c.1950, 21 Piece, Box 145.00
Soldier, Last Stand Of Seaforths, 38 Piece 303.00
Soldier, Middlesex Regiment, No. 439, 9 Marchers, Britains, Parade Series Box 747.00
Soldier, Royal Artillery Gun No. 2, 4 Piece.. 77.00
Soldier, Walking Guards, 10 Men & Horses, Coach, Britains 450.00
Soldier, Windup, Crawls, Shoots, Turns Head, Celluloid, Tin, Box, Alps 285.00
Space Capsule, Astronaut, Tin Lithograph, Friction, Kanto, Japan, 1960s, 6 In. 115.00
Space Dog 395.00
Space Scout 495.00
Space Station, Tin Lithograph, Battery Operated 195.00
Space Vehicle, Moon Explorer, Ideal, 1960 .... 65.00
Spaceman, Fighting 525.00
Spaceman, Tin, Walks, Smokes, Revolving Kaleidoscope Top, Linemar, 12 1/2 In. 4100.00
Spaceman, Vinyl Head, Tin, Windup, Marx, 7 In. 50.00
Speed Shop, Hot Wheels, 1969 .... 85.00
Spic Coon Drummer, Tin, Windup, Marx, c.1924, 8 1/2 In. 360.00
Spinner, Paddy & Pig, Tiny Curly Tail, Windup, 1910s... 790.00
Spinning Hat, Koo-Lee, Molded Green Vinyl, Late 1950s, 9 In. 95.00
Spy Set, 007 James Bond, Box 49.00
Stamping Kit, Sky King, Name & Address 15.00
Star Wars Leia, White Dress, Molded Accessories, Kenner 80.00
Star Wars Luke, White Shirt, Tan Pants, Molded Accessories, Kenner........................... 75.00
Station, Railroad, Gare Centrale, Tinplate, Marklin, 21 1/2 In.. 5462.00
Steam Engine, 2 Cylinder, Working Model 295.00
Steam Engine, Cast Iron, Avery, Black, Red & Gold, Cast Iron 205.00
Steam Roller, Clockwork, Marklin.. 1900.00
Steam Roller, Keystone, 1920s 350.00
Steam Roller, Orange, Driver, Cast Iron, Nickeled Wheels, Huber, 7 3/4 In. 403.00
Steam Shovel, Keystone, Extended Arm, 34 1/2 In. 250.00
Steam Shovel, Ride-On, Red & Black, Decal On Side, Keystone, 1920s, 26 In. 115.00
Steamboat, Double Bells, Tin, George W. Brown, 11 3/4 In. 825.00
Steamboat, Single Piston, Brass Funnel, H.E. Boucher, Box, 28 In............................... 325.00
Store, Confectionery, Presentation Box, 60 Packages, France, c.1890.18 x 12 In. 2700.00
Stork, Lenci, 54 In. 875.00
Stove, A1, Gold Gilt Finish, J. & E. Stevens 235.00
Stove, Baby, Cast Iron, 6 Cast Iron Utensils 440.00
Stove, Betty Crocker 12.00
Stove, Brass Doors, Enameled Ceramic Sides, 5 Burners, Metal, 18 In........................ 110.00
Stove, Cast Iron, Gray, Black, White & Silver, Arcade, c.1930, 6 In............................... 66.00
Stove, Cast Iron, Royal, 4 1/2 In.. 55.00

Stove, Coal, Cast Iron, Cooking Utensils, Miniature 100.00
Stove, Coal, Cast Iron, Drop-Down Oven Doors, Cast Iron Cooking Set 35.00
Stove, Cook, 5 Pots, Waffle Iron, Skillet, Iron, Acme, 13 1/2 In. 210.00
Stove, Crescent, 4 Pots, Cast Iron, 13 In. 27.00
Stove, Crescent, Cast Iron 325.00
Stove, Eagle, Cast Iron 50.00
Stove, Electric, Empire, 1930 .... 95.00
Stove, Electric, Green & Marbelized Cream, 15 In. 375.00
Stove, Electric, Little Lady, White, 15 x 10 In. 90.00
Stove, Green & White, Wolverine, 11 x 8 In. 75.00
Stove, Hoist & Wagon, Cast Iron, Arcade, 6 Ft. 200.00
Stove, Li'l Bopeep, Tin Lithograph, Wolverine, Box, 12 In. 60.00
Stove, Little Eva, Cast Iron, T. Southard 275.00
Stove, Little Willie, Cast Iron, 3 Cast Iron Utensils 175.00
Stove, Marklin, 1910 .... 2450.00
Stove, Perfection, Warming Shelf, Brass Plated, 8 1/2 x 10 In. 260.00
Stove, Queen, Cast Iron 125.00
Stove, Rival, J. & E. Stevens, 1895, 14 1/2 x 15 In. 775.00
Stove, Royal, Cast Iron, c.1920, 4 1/2 In. 85.00
Stove, Spark, Cast Iron, Gray 335.00
Stove, Sunny Suzy, Tin 15.00
Stove, Uncle Sam, Cast Iron 600.00
Stunt Kit, Sky Command, Remote Control, Remco, 1969 .... 22.00
Submarine, Diving Dolphin, Rubber-Band Mechanism, 1950s, Box 195.00
Submarine, Diving, Windup, No. S-87, Wolverine 200.00
Submarine, Nautilus, Lighted Ventilator Towers, Battery Operated, Box, 16 In. 105.00
Submarine, Propulsion System, Handrails, Painted Tin, 20 In. 275.00
Submarine, String-Ray, Matchbox, 45 In. 55.00
Submarine, Unda-Wunda, Windup, Tin, Sutcliffe, 9 In. 95.00
Submarine, Windup, Wolverine 110.00
Sulky, Shuttle Legged, Wooden, Germany 220.00
Sunny Andy Kiddie Kampers, Mechanical, Tin, 5 Figures 140.00
Sunny Andy Rabbit Chase, Lithographed Tin, Windup, Wolverine, 9 3/4 In. 300.00
Super Space Capsule 495.00
Sweeper, Carpet, Bissell Junior, Wooden 55.00
Sweeper, Little Jewel, Bissel 65.00
Switching Station, Tinplate, Windup, Clockwork, Carette, Germany, c.1880 .... 1250.00
Table & Chair, Doll's, Red, Green, 1930s, Large, 3 Piece 110.00
Tank, Army, Green, Red, Turret Rotates Searchlight, Structo, c.1930 .... 295.00
Tank, Casper The Ghost, Turnover, Windup 425.00
Tank, Doughboy, Windup, Marx 295.00
Tank, Driver, Windup, Marx 287.00
Tank, Jetsons, Blue, Key Wind, Tin Lithograph, Marx, 2 1/2 x 4 x 2 1/2 In. 506.00
Tank, M-27, Armored, Tin Friction, Sparks, Japan, 8 In. 65.00
Tank, Rex Mars Space Patrol, Windup, Marx 265.00
Tank, Robotank-Z, Battery Operated, Box 495.00
Tank, Rollover, Marx, 1940s 110.00

Toy, Taxi, Amos 'n' Andy, Fresh-Air,
Marx, c.1930, 8 In.

◆◆◆◆◆◆◆◆◆◆◆◆◆◆◆◆◆◆◆◆◆◆◆◆◆

Snow domes are liquid-filled paperweights. They should not be stored in the dark. Exposure to the light is necessary to keep the liquid clear. Do not keep the snow domes in direct sunlight. They can magnify the rays and start a fire.

◆◆◆◆◆◆◆◆◆◆◆◆◆◆◆◆◆◆◆◆◆◆◆◆◆

Tank, Soldier, Bing	800.00
Tank, Sparking, Pop-Up Soldier, Max, 1930s	185.00
Tank, Sparking, Windup, No. 3, Marx, 8 In.	385.00
Tank, Strange Explorer, Rollover, Battery Operated, Flips Over, 1960s	195.00
Tank, U.S. Army, Rollover, Marx	450.00
Target Set, Huckleberry Hound, 1959	65.00
Target Set, Planet Of The Apes, 2 Rubber Darts, Box	35.00
Tattoos, Archies, Topps, 1969, Unopened	20.00
Taxi, Amos 'n' Andy, Fresh-Air, Marx, c.1930, 8 In. .... *Illus*	750.00
Taxi, Checkered Cab, Tin, Battery Operated, 1950s	30.00
Taxi, Hansom Cab, Lila, 2 Women, Dog, Driver, Lehmann	1900.00
Taxi, Hansom Cab, Pulled By 1 Horse, Driver, Moveable Arms, Cast Iron, 11 In.	495.00
Taxi, Hansom Cab, Tin Lithograph, Penny Toy, 4 1/2 In.	330.00
Taxi, Plymouth, Super King, Matchbox, Box	25.00
Taxi, Tin Lithograph Driver, Windup, Paya, Box, 8 1/2 In.	100.00
Taxi, Tricky Taxi, Street Plate, Marx, Box	495.00
Taxi, Wacky Taxi, Marx	250.00
Taxi, Yellow, Arcade	1705.00
Taxi, Yellow, Lithograph, Distler	2700.00
Tea Set, Alice In Wonderland, Red, Box, 1933, 16 Piece	125.00
Tea Set, Bunny's Birthday, Tin Lithograph, Fern Bisell Peat, 7 Piece	800.00
Tea Set, Buster Brown, Foliated Scroll Handles, 3 Piece	495.00
Tea Set, Cinderella, Happynak, Tin, Box, 15 Piece	400.00
Tea Set, Dutch Ice Skaters, Tin Lithograph, Fern Bisell Peat, 15 Piece	175.00
Tea Set, Garden Girl, Tin Lithograph, Fern Bisell Peat, 15 Piece	275.00
Tea Set, Geisha Women, Tin Lithograph, Ohio Art, Box, 8 Piece	250.00
Tea Set, Girls Dressed As Kittens, Tin Lithograph, Fern Bissell Peat, 15 Piece	275.00
Tea Set, Humpty Dumpty, Tin Lithograph, Ohio Art, Box, 15 Piece	225.00
Tea Set, Kittens, Tin Lithograph, Ohio Art, Box, 1930s, 6 Piece	250.00
Tea Set, Little Bopeep, Tin Lithograph, Ohio Art, Box, 7 Piece	225.00
Tea Set, Mary Poppins, Box, 13 Piece	250.00
Teapot, Wagner, Aluminum, 4 In.	95.00
Teddy Bears are also listed in the Teddy Bear category	
Teddy Zilo, Fisher-Price, 1964	39.00
Telephone, Snoopy, Romper Room, Plastic	30.00
Telephone, Walkie-Talkie, Planet Of The Apes, 1979	20.00
Tell-A-Tale, Gumby & Pokey, 1968	10.00
Tell-A-Tale, Ricochet Rabbit, 1965	17.00
Tent, Circus, Flags, Schoenhut	1250.00
Thingmaker, Creepie People, Box, Mattel	100.00
Thingmaker, Fright Factory, Mattel, Box	150.00
Tiger, Reclining, Orange Mohair, Airbrushed Stripes, Steiff, 15 In.	130.00
Tiger, Walking, Windup, Marx, Box, 8 In.	125.00
Tin Lizzie, 4 Passengers, Cable, Mechanical, Arnold Co., Germany, 1940s	750.00
Tip Top Porter, Black Man Pushing Cart, Strauss, 1920s, Box .... 595.00 to 895.00	
Tom & Jerry, Riding On Scooter, Friction Motor, Plastic, Box	125.00
Top, Charlie Brown & Snoopy, Tin, Ohio Art, 11 In.	40.00
Top, Humming, Chad Valley Co.	30.00
Top, Windup, Colorful, Tin, 5 1/2 In.	28.00
Townhouse, Little Kiddles, Mattel, 1968, Large	65.00
Tractor, 6 Wheels, Windup, Marx, 12 In.	245.00
Tractor, Army, Tonka, 1964	120.00
Tractor, Caterpillar, Diesel, Road Contractor's, Yellow	3850.00
Tractor, Climbing, Prewar, Marx, Box	225.00
Tractor, Crawler, John Deere	1450.00
Tractor, Driver, Cast Iron, Kilgore, 4 1/2 In.	395.00
Tractor, Farm, Frontend Loader, Tin Lithograph, Marx, 1940	140.00
Tractor, Farmall, Model M, Hard Plastic	100.00
Tractor, Ford, Model 9N, Rubber Tires, 1939, Box	4180.00
Tractor, Fordson, Gray & Red, Williams	200.00
Tractor, Grain Cart, Red, Hubley, c.1950, 17 In.	55.00
Tractor, John Deere, Model	1000.00
Tractor, Marvelous Mike, Battery Operated, Sanders, Box	220.00

Tractor, McCormick Deering, Cast Iron, Gray, Decal, Arcade, 7 In. 275.00
Tractor, No. 948, McLeans, Decal, Dinky, Box 198.00
Tractor, Oliver, Cast Iron, 1948, 9 In. 795.00
Tractor, Oliver, Driver, Cast Iron, 2 3/4 In. 100.00
Tractor, Oliver, Orchard, Cast Iron, 5 1/2 In. 300.00
Tractor, Oliver, With Bottom Dump Wagon, Arcade... 100.00
Tractor, Plow, Tin Driver, Key Wind, Marx 175.00
Tractor, Windup, Tin, Mettoy, England, 7 1/2 In. 100.00
Tractor, With Bucket, Hubley, 13 In. 110.00
Trailer, Mercedes, Gold, Pumpkin Canopy, Die Cast, Matchbox, 1967 .... 12.00
Train, American Flyer, Freight 290.00
Train, Bing, Coal Car, Tin-Plate, Gray, 12 In. 150.00
Train, Cable, Tin, Electric, Japan, 1940s, 2 Piece Box 125.00
Train, Caboose, Marklin, No. 1 Gauge Wheels, Painted Tin, 7 1/4 In. 355.00
Train, Coffee Tins, Tasty Food Limited, c.1928, 4 Cars.. 2000.00
Train, Dinky, Tanker, No. 504, Red & Gray, Box 220.00
Train, Exploration, Battery Operated, Box 675.00
Train, Flat Car, Gray, Pressed Steel, Buddy L, 20 In. 82.00
Train, Freight Station, Lionel, No. 155.. 522.00
Train, Gilbert, Engine, Tender, No. 31005, New York Central 92.00
Train, Guntermann, Metropolitan 660, c.1920... 400.00
Train, Honeymoon Express, Tin, Windup, Marx, c.1927, 9 In. .... 110.00 to 175.00
Train, Huffy Puffy, Fisher-Price, 1963 .... 19.00
Train, Huffy Puffy, Pull Toy, Fisher-Price 75.00
Train, Iron Horse, Japan, Box 35.00
Train, Ives, Caboose, No. 7546, Tinplate, Red, 12 In. 184.00
Train, Ives, Cattle Car, No. 65, Gray Lithograph Sides, Butterscotch Roof & Doors 1540.00
Train, Ives, Coal Car, No. 7648, Pennsylvania Coal & Coke Co., Dark Green, 12 In. 58.00
Train, Ives, Gondola, No. 63, Black & Yellow Vertical Stripes 770.00
Train, Lionel Set, No. 736, Berkshire, Box... 950.00
Train, Lionel, Boxcar, No. 3494-625, Box 468.00
Train, Lionel, Boxcar, No. 6464-375, Central Of Georgia, Silver 176.00
Train, Lionel, Boxcar, Baltimore & Ohio, Lionel, Box, 1956.. 605.00
Train, Lionel, Boxcar, Western Pacific, Box 165.00
Train, Lionel, Engine, No. 8, Standard Gauge, Green, Gold, c.1950, 11 In. 121.00
Train, Lionel, Engine, No. 42, N.Y. Central, Standard Gauge, Pre-WW II, 16 In. 550.00
Train, Lionel, Engine, No. 58, Great Northern Railway Rotary Snow Plow Diesel, Box ... 750.00
Train, Lionel, Engine, No. 318, Super-Motor, Gray, Gold, Pre-WW II, 12 In. 360.00
Train, Lionel, Engine, No. 2020, O-Gauge, c.1950, 10 1/2 In. 88.00
Train, Lionel, Engine, No. 2321, Lackawanna 900.00
Train, Lionel, Engine, No. 8020, Santa Fe 125.00
Train, Lionel, Gang Car, No. 50, O-Gauge, 6 In., Box 55.00
Train, Lionel, Locomotive & Tender, No. 400E, Crackle Black.. 8200.00
Train, Lionel, Locomotive, No. 318, Standard Gauge, Gray 330.00
Train, Lionel, Log Loader, No. 164, Black Paint, Vermilion Roof...................................... 231.00
Train, Lionel, No. 2363, Diesel, Twin Motor, Illinois Central, 1954................................... 1200.00
Train, Lionel, Power Car, No. 3530, Long Stripe, Black Tanks, Box 275.00
Train, Lionel, Smoking Caboose, No. 6557, With Smoke Fluid, Box 302.00
Train, Lionel, Trolley, No. 100, Standard Gauge, Blue & Yellow, Box 2420.00
Train, Locomotive, Hill Climber, Cast Iron, 16 In. 155.00
Train, Locomotive, Piddler, Live Steam, Alcohol Fired, Holborn, 7 1/4 In...................... 355.00
Train, Locomotive, Riding, Electric Lights, Pressed Steel, Keystone, 26 1/2 In. 230.00
Train, Marklin, Logging Car, Set Of Logs, 12 In. 138.00
Train, Marx, Diesel, Santa Fe, Box... 310.00
Train, Mercury Flyer, Ride-On, Pressed Steel, 1939 .... 125.00
Train, Nosco, Amusement Park, Windup, Hard Plastic, Passengers.................................... 120.00
Train, Switcher, No. 227, Box 2100.00
Train, Western Express, Tin, Windup, Box, 11 In. 75.00
Train, Wilkins, Locomotive & Tender, Cast Iron, 21 In. 2750.00
Train Set, American Flyer, Clockwork, Repainted, Black Roof & Frames, 5 Piece........ 176.00
Train Set, American Flyer, Green, Black Roof, 4 Piece 231.00
Train Set, American Flyer, Locomotive, 3 Passenger Cars, Standard Gauge 675.00
Train Set, American Flyer, No. 282 .... 350.00

Train Set, American Flyer, No. 300 ....250.00 to 255.00
Train Set, American Flyer, No. 4220 Bridge, San Fran., Denver, Wooden, Box 770.00
Train Set, American Flyer, No. 484-5-6, Santa Fe ABA 1050.00
Train Set, American Flyer, Passenger, Standard Gauge, 1925 .... 650.00
Train Set, American Flyer, S Gauge, Activator & Control Mail Car, Coaches 330.00
Train Set, American Flyer, Statesman, Standard Gauge, Orange, Gray, 4 Piece 358.00
Train Set, Desert Storm, K-Line, Box 135.00
Train Set, Engine, Tender & Freight Car, Cast Iron, 1880s, 15 In. 58.00
Train Set, Hornby, No. 126 Southern Locomotive, Clockwork, 4 Piece 412.00
Train Set, Hornby, No. 616 Locomotive & Tender, Red & Black, Clockwork, Box 231.00
Train Set, Ives, Green, Gray Roof, 5 Piece 385.00
Train Set, Ives, Locomotive, 3 Passenger Cars, Standard Gauge, 1925 .... 700.00
Train Set, Ives, Tiger, Standard Gauge, Orange & Black, 3 Piece 880.00
Train Set, Jupiter, Green & Red Cars, Black & Red Engine, 5 Piece 978.00
Train Set, Lionel, Apple Green, Standard Gauge, Restored, 8 Piece 1430.00
Train Set, Lionel, Baby State, Standard Gauge, 4 Piece 660.00
Train Set, Lionel, Baltimore & Ohio, Smoking Locomotive, 1959 .... 140.00
Train Set, Lionel, Engine, No. 402, Standard Gauge, 7 Cars, Track & Box 2750.00
Train Set, Lionel, Flying Yankee, Chrome, Gunmetal, 4 Piece 275.00
Train Set, Lionel, Locomotive, 4 Freight, Transformer, Switches, Track, 1930 .... 500.00
Train Set, Lionel, No. 8, Engine, 2 Passenger Cars, 1920s 250.00
Train Set, Lionel, No. 97, Coal Elevator, Controller & 206 Coal Bag, Box 358.00
Train Set, Lionel, No. 253, Passenger, 1930s, 4 Piece 215.00
Train Set, Lionel, No. 259E, Freight, 1930s, 5 Piece 225.00
Train Set, Lionel, No. 400E, Blue Comet, Standard Gauge, Passenger Cars, Box, 1984 2950.00
Train Set, Lionel, No. 773, Letters NYC, Box, 1964 .... 1210.00
Train Set, Lionel, No. 2231W, Southern, F3 ABA 3600.00
Train Set, Lionel, No. 2331, Virginian FM 1500.00
Train Set, Lionel, Redwood Valley, Box 250.00
Train Set, Lionel, Southern Crescent, 8 Piece, Box 550.00
Train Set, Marklin, HO, 125th Anniversary, Box 385.00
Train Set, Marx, Army, Comm. Vanderbilt, Electric, 6 Piece 632.00
Train Set, Marx, Bunny Express, Clockwork, 3 Hoppers, 4 Piece 2090.00
Train Set, Marx, Comm. Vanderbilt Locomotive, Steam, Illuminated Cars 154.00
Train Set, Marx, No. 338 Hudson, 3/16 Scale, 7 Piece 154.00
Train Set, McCoy, Standard Gauge 385.00
Train Set, Pennsylvania, Freight, 1958 .... 140.00
Train Set, Pillsbury, HO 45.00
Train Set, Pride Lines, 7 Dwarfs Mining, Box 385.00
Train Set, Tyco, Santa Fe, 7 Cars, Track, Accessories 350.00
Train Station, Brick, Center Walk-Through, Awnings, Tinplate, Germany, 19 x 9 In. .. 805.00
Train Station, Goelring, Dual Staircases, Upper Platform, Germany, 19 x 15 In. 2185.00
Train Station, Gull-Winged, Ticket Booth, Benches, Tinplate, 14 x 12 In. 230.00
Train Station, Ives, No. 116, Label, Large 578.00
Train Station, Ives, No. 117 .... 1072.00
Tramp, Friction, Tin Lithograph, Linemar, 1950s, 3 1/2 In. 165.00
Tricycle, Wilma & Fred Flintstone, Pair 850.00
Troll, Witch Doctor, Cloth Outfit, Plastic, 3 In. 20.00
Trolley, Electric, O Gauge, Pole Line & Track, Germany, 1950 .... 200.00
Trolley, Floor Toy, Pressed Steel, Friction, 15 1/2 In. 250.00
Trolley, Horse Drawn, Tin Lithograph, Upper Deck, Germany, 12 1/2 In. 135.00
Trolley, Nifty Toonerville Trolley, Red & Yellow, Clockwork 935.00
Trolley, Tin Lithograph, Friction, German Advertising On Sides, Japan, 9 In. 145.00
Trolley, Toonerville, Hand Painted Aluminum, Dent, 1920s, Box 1150.00
Trolley, Toonerville, Tin Lithograph, Windup, Nifty, Germany, c.1922, 7 x 5 In. 750.00
Trolley, Toonerville, Windup, Tin, 5 x 7 In. 95.00
Trolley, Women Passengers, Lead-Weighted Tin, c.1890 .... 880.00
Truck, 5-Ton, Driver, Hubley, 17 In. 1450.00
Truck, Aerial, Buddy L, c.1930, 34 In. 470.00
Truck, Aerial, Ladder, Bell, Windup Siren, Doepke 300.00
Truck, Aerial, Ladders, Buddy L, 29 In. 795.00
Truck, Allied Van Lines, Semi, Tonka ....250.00 to 300.00
Truck, Army, Canvas Cover, Olive Drab, Pressed Steel, Keystone, 26 In. 275.00

Truck, Army, Canvas Top, Push, 1940s, Chein, 8 In.		150.00
Truck, Army, Khaki, Canvas Cover, Pressed Steel, Keystone, 26 1/2 In.		410.00
Truck, Army, Tin, Windup, Marx, c.1920		450.00
Truck, Bedford Coal, No. 425, Dinky, Box		121.00
Truck, Bell Telephone, Pole Wagon, Wench, Hubley, 10 In.		975.00
Truck, Big Job, Battery Operated, Plastic, 30 In.		225.00
Truck, Borden's Milk, Cast Iron, Hubley, 6 In.		1095.00
Truck, Borden's Milk, Nickel Radiator Grill & Wheels, Arcade		4950.00
Truck, Borden's Milk, Rubber Tires, Arcade, 5 3/4 x 3 1/4 In.		1320.00
Truck, Buddy L, Black, Steel Wheels		195.00
Truck, Burger King, Refrigeration, Matchbox, Box, 12 In.		70.00
Truck, Camper, Nylint, 1961		175.00
Truck, Car Carrier, 3 Austins, Cast Iron, A.C. Williams, 12 1/2 In.		995.00
Truck, Car Carrier, 4 Autos, Dent, Arcade		2420.00
Truck, Car Carrier, Buddy L		70.00
Truck, Carrier Refuse, Gray, No. 38, Matchbox		35.00
Truck, Cement Mixer, Bronze Body, White Mixer, 20 In.		85.00
Truck, Cement Mixer, Matchbox		14.00
Truck, Cement Mixer, Red, White, Green, Silver, Jaeger, c.1930, 6 x 6 In.		415.00
Truck, Cement Mixer, Tonka		150.00
Truck, Chevrolet, Stake, Black, Chromed Driver, White Walls, Cast Iron, 9 In.		633.00
Truck, Chevron, Pick-Up, With Barrels, Tonka		40.00
Truck, Chivers Jellies, Dinky		90.00
Truck, Circus, Pulling Trailer, Wyandotte, 1930s		850.00
Truck, Coal Delivery, Marx, 1930s, 13 In.		850.00
Truck, Coal, Kenton, 1920s, 6 1/4 In.		225.00
Truck, Coal, Mack-Type, Nickel Wheels, Cast Iron, 5 1/2 In.		330.00
Truck, Coal, Orange & Black, Pressed Steel, Sturditoy, 27 In.		1450.00
Truck, Concrete Mixer, Tin, Friction, Toy Master, Japan, c.1950s, 9 In.		135.00
Truck, Crane, Gama, West Germany, Early 1950s		250.00
Truck, Crane, Red, Blue, Spare Tire, Gama, 1950s		145.00
Truck, Crawler, Marx		85.00
Truck, Delivery, Air France, White, Hot Wheels, Box		10.00
Truck, Delivery, Beer, Barrels, Barclay		225.00
Truck, Delivery, Hardy's Salt, St. Louis, Metalcraft		495.00
Truck, Delivery, Ice, 6 Ice Cubes, Marx, 1930s		350.00
Truck, Delivery, Ice, Mack, Blue, Arcade		750.00
Truck, Delivery, Keg, Falstaff Brewing Co., General Motors, 1952		40.00
Truck, Delivery, Mountain Dew, Bottle, Green & White, 1951		35.00
Truck, Delivery, Red & Yellow, Buddy L, 1935		555.00
Truck, Delivery, Waldorf Lager Beer, Metalcraft		950.00
Truck, Die Cast, Penny Toy, France, 1920s, 3 1/2 In.		185.00
Truck, Dump, Battery Operated, Japan, 10 In.		140.00
Truck, Dump, Blue Mack, Arcade		1700.00
Truck, Dump, Chain Type, Red Chassis, Pressed Steel, Buddy L, 24 In.		550.00
Truck, Dump, Coal, Hubley, 1920s, 10 In.		750.00
Truck, Dump, Construction Company, Metal, Buddy L		11.00
Truck, Dump, Contractor's, Cast Iron, Arcade		200.00
Truck, Dump, Farm Supplies, Pressed Steel, Buddy L, 1930s		385.00
Truck, Dump, Foden, No. 949, Red Blade, Dinky, Box		176.00
Truck, Dump, Ford, Anthony, Mechanical, Arcade, 8 1/2 In.		2050.00
Truck, Dump, Hubley, 1932, 10 1/2 In.		950.00
Truck, Dump, Hydraulic Dump Mechanism, Dual Rear Wheels, Buddy L, 24 In.		935.00
Truck, Dump, Hydraulic, Structo, 20 1/2 In.		110.00
Truck, Dump, Keystone, Crank, Pressed Steel, Keystone, 26 In.		575.00
Truck, Dump, Mack Type, Lift Mechanism, Pressed Steel, Toledo, 27 In.		800.00
Truck, Dump, Mack, Cast Iron, Gray, Driver, Arcade, 1925, 12 x 5 1/2 In.		935.00
Truck, Dump, Mack, Driver, Rubber Tires, Spring Mechanism, Arcade, 1925, 12 In.		1250.00
Truck, Dump, Mack, Tin Lithograph, Windup, Marx, 1930, 9 1/2 In.		258.00
Truck, Dump, Muir Hill, Matchbox, King Size, No. 2, Red, Green Wheels		35.00
Truck, Dump, No. 201, Buddy L		475.00
Truck, Dump, Opening Doors, Hydraulic Lift, Pressed Steel, Russia, Box, 21 In.		70.00
Truck, Dump, Painted Pressed Steel, Sturditoy, 25 In.		440.00

Truck, Dump, Red Paint, Buddy L, 1950s, 14 x 5 1/2 In. 175.00
Truck, Dump, Red, Structo 100.00
Truck, Dump, Ride-On, Black Chassis, Red Body, Keystone, 1920s, 26 3/4 In. 315.00
Truck, Dump, Rider, International, Green & Yellow, Buddy L 100.00
Truck, Dump, Switch 'n' Go, Mattel, 1965 .... 65.00
Truck, Emergency Searchlight, White, Marx, 18 In. 225.00
Truck, Express Line, Steel, Black, Green Screen Top, Buddy L, 1930s, 24 1/2 In. 1725.00
Truck, Express, Key Wind, Germany, 5 1/2 In., Box 350.00
Truck, Express, Railway Express, Pressed Steel, Sturditoy, 26 In. 855.00
Truck, Farm Supplies, Blue & Yellow, Buddy L 275.00
Truck, Farm, Campbell's Kid, Fisher-Price 285.00
Truck, Fire, Mobil Oil, Red & White, Buffalo Refinery, 1957 .... 39.00
Truck, Firestone, 18-Wheeler, Nylint, Box 45.00
Truck, Flatbed, Foden, No. 902, Red, Green, Dinky, Box 250.00
Truck, Flatbed, Turn Crank & Chain, Structo, 1950s 145.00
Truck, Ford, Royal Crown Cola, With Bottles, Red, Yellow & Black, 1951 .... 36.00
Truck, Fork Lift, International, Driver, Tin, Bump & Go Action, Battery, 7 1/2 In. 120.00
Truck, Grain Hauler, Tonka, 1966 .... 150.00
Truck, Heinz Pickle, Battery-Operated Lights, Metalcraft 535.00
Truck, Hershey's Cocoa, GMC, Brown, Logo, 1952 .... 35.00
Truck, Hi-Way Express, Tin Lithograph, Marx 195.00
Truck, Hook & Ladder, No. 902, Structo, Box 125.00
Truck, Horse Trailer, Buddy L 70.00
Truck, Horse Trailer, Nylint 295.00
Truck, Livestock, Open Bed, Cast Iron, Blue & Maroon, c.1925, 8 In. 920.00
Truck, Livestock, Van, Red, No. 500, Tonka, 1953 .... 275.00
Truck, Loader, Front End, John Deere, Box 500.00
Truck, Log Hauler, Tonka 225.00
Truck, Low Loader & Steam Shovel, No. GS27, Corgi 165.00
Truck, Mack, Aerial Ladder, Smith Miller 750.00
Truck, Mack, Van, Pressed Steel, American National, 26 In. 495.00
Truck, Medical Corps, Wyandotte, Box 225.00
Truck, Mercedes, Gold, Orange Canopy, Die Cast, Matchbox, 1967 .... 13.00
Truck, Mercury Marine, Mack, White, Green Fenders, 1960 .... 70.00
Truck, Mike Mam, Buddy L, 1961 .... 225.00
Truck, Missile Carrier, Nylint 200.00
Truck, Model A, Stake, Arcade 390.00
Truck, Moving Van, Coast To Coast, Wyandotte, 8 In. 75.00
Truck, Moving Van, Greyline, Red & Silver, Wyandotte 150.00
Truck, Moving Van, Shipping & Storage, Marx 150.00
Truck, Moving Van, Son-Ny, Black, Large 475.00
Truck, Overland Freight Lines, Orange, Blue Cab, Structo, 21 In. 195.00
Truck, P*I*E, Motor Express, Hubley 650.00
Truck, Parcel Post, Orange Wheels, Pressed Steel, Sonny, 26 In. 680.00
Truck, Pathe News, 1930s 175.00
Truck, Pickup, Arcade, Black 650.00
Truck, Pickup, Ford Econoline, Nylint 65.00
Truck, Pickup, Horse Trailer, Tonka 48.00
Truck, Pickup, Hubley, 5 In. 175.00
Truck, Pickup, International Harvester, Yellow, Silver Striping 3080.00
Truck, Pickup, Red, Tonka, 1962 .... 95.00
Truck, Pickup, Tonka, 1961 .... 65.00
Truck, Police Patrol, Moon Mullins, Tootsietoy 350.00
Truck, Police Wrecker, Black, White, Gold Shield On Door, 1957 .... 40.00
Truck, Postal, Driver, Deutsche Reichspost, Windup, 1927, Lehmann 1750.00
Truck, Railway Express, 2-Piece Wheels, Pressed Steel, Keystone, 26 In. 550.00
Truck, Railway Express, Buddy L, 22 In. 770.00
Truck, Ranch, Horses, Buddy L, 1960s 145.00
Truck, Red & Yellow Logo, Windup, Structo, 12 In. 120.00
Truck, Riding Academy, Buddy L 75.00
Truck, Road Roller, Tin Lithograph, Windup, U.S. Zone Germany, 10 In. 185.00
Truck, Road, Grader, Yellow, Williams 300.00
Truck, Rocket Launching, Battery Operated, Ideal, 12 In., Box 350.00

Truck, Royal Mail, Tin Lithograph, Windup, Red & Beige, Lehmann, c.1927, 6 1/2 In.　2300.00
Truck, Sanitation, Crank Raises Bin, Opens To Dump, Structo, c.1940 ....　225.00
Truck, Searchlight, Battery Operated, Tommytoy, 1950s, 16 In. ....　125.00
Truck, Semitrailer, Consolidated Freight, 2 Trailers, Tin, Japan, 21 In. ....　145.00
Truck, Semitrailer, Continental Express, Structo..　85.00
Truck, Semitrailer, Star Newspaper, Navy Blue, Minnitoy, Canada, 29 In.....................　560.00
Truck, Sheffield Farm, Steelcraft ....　925.00
Truck, Sportsman, Tonka ....　160.00
Truck, Stake, Arcade, 7 In...　375.00
Truck, Stake, Red Paint, White Rubber Tires, Wyandotte, 1930s, 6 In. ....　80.00
Truck, Stake, Tonka ....　160.00
Truck, Stake, Wyandotte ....　325.00
Truck, Surry Jeep, Pink, Tonka ....　75.00
Truck, Tanker, B/A, Pressed Steel, Rubber Wheels, Minnitoy, Canada, 1950s, 29 In.....　395.00
Truck, Tanker, Esso, Dinky ....　35.00
Truck, Tanker, Funline, Pressed Steel, Red, White, Unique, 20 In...................................　295.00
Truck, Tanker, Gasoline, Headlights, Pressed Steel, Red, Sturditoy, 33 In. ....　2090.00
Truck, Tanker, Gasoline, Red, Cast Iron ....　295.00
Truck, Tanker, Hess, 1977, Box ....　143.00
Truck, Tanker, Mobilgas, Bedford, No. 1110, Corgi, Box...　187.00
Truck, Tanker, Mobilgas, Studebaker, No. 440, Dinky ....　218.00
Truck, Tanker, Oil & Gas, Silvered Wheels, Cast Iron, Kenton, 1927, 9 3/4 In. ....　920.00
Truck, Tanker, Pure Oil, Royal Blue, Steelcraft ....　850.00
Truck, Tanker, Shell Oil, Buddy L, 1940s ....　135.00
Truck, Tanker, Shell Oil, Minitoy, 27 In. ....　650.00
Truck, Tanker, Standard Oil, Tootsietoy ....　75.00
Truck, Tanker, Texaco, Plastic Wheels, Pressed Steel, Buddy L, 24 In............................　77.00
Truck, Telephone, 1947 Chevrolet, Green, Metal, Pole Trailer, Hubley ....　275.00
Truck, Texaco Fire Chief, Buddy L, 1950s, 25 x 7 In. ....　85.00
Truck, Texaco Fire Chief, Buddy L, 24 In. ....　170.00
Truck, Tow, Emergency, Tin, Strauss, 11 1/2 In. ....　375.00
Truck, Tow, Repair It, Diamond T, Red & White, Die-Cast Cab, Buddy L ....　735.00
Truck, Tow, Schuco ....　995.00
Truck, Tractor Trailer, Shady Glen Stock Ranch, Wyandotte, 1950s, 17 In....................　185.00
Truck, Transport, Racing Cars, Matchbox, Green ....　55.00
Truck, Turbine Aerial Ladder, Ladders, Tonka ....　175.00
Truck, Turbine Snorkel, Tonka ....　160.00
Truck, U.S. Army, Pressed Steel, Cor-Cor, 22 1/2 In. ....　395.00
Truck, Utility, Green Giant, Cast Iron, Tonka, 1959 ....　250.00
Truck, Weston's Biscuits, Metalcraft, 1930...200.00 to 325.00
Truck, Wrecker, 3 Spare Goodrich Tires, Pressed Steel, Metalcraft, 12 In. ....　275.00
Truck, Wrecker, Ford, Cast Iron, Arcade, 8 1/2 In. ....　1150.00
Truck, Wrecker, Packard, Keystone, 1920s...　475.00
Truck, Wrecker, Zephyr Petroleum, White Body, Red Wheels, Blue Cab......................　36.00
Trunk, Doll's, Lithographed Boy, Girl, Cat & Dog ....　95.00
Trunk, Doll's, Lithographed Hardware, Travel Scenes, Bliss, c.1890, 5 x 14 In. ....　475.00
Trunk, Doll's, Raggedy Ann, Metal ....　15.00
Trunk, Doll's, Wooden, Metal Trim, Brown Paint, 10 1/2 x 18 x 10 1/4 In. ....　66.00
Trunk, Humpback, Insert Tray, Wooden, c.1880..　140.00
Turkey, Gobbles, Windup..　55.00
Turnpike Set, No. 8, Girder & Panel Bridge, Kenner, Box ....　95.00
Turtle, On Wheels, Bell Rings When Pulled, Painted, Cast Iron, 6 1/4 In. ....　575.00
Turtle, Windup, Celluloid, Tin, Occupied Japan ....　200.00
Typewriter, Deluxe, Dial, Marx, Box ....60.00 to 65.00
Typewriter, Marx, 1940s, 8 In. ....　30.00
Typewriter, Tom Thumb, Box ....　40.00
Typewriter, Underwood, Tin ....　5.00
U-Boat, Clockwork Mechanism, Periscope, Lifeboat, Tinplate, Marklin, 30 In. ....　8625.00
UFO, X-7..　295.00
Umbrella, Raggedy Ann, 1950 ....　45.00
Utensils, Kitchen, Red Wood Handles, Display Cardboard, 5 Piece ....　65.00
Vac-U-Form Mold Kit, Animals, Mattel ....　25.00
Van, Adventure, Charlie's Angels, Hasbro, 1970s...　75.00

Toy, Washer Woman & Woman Ironing,
   China Heads, c.1880, 8 x 5 In.

When cleaning mother-of-pearl inlay, use a weak solution of detergent, never an acid.

Van, Camper, Weekender, Structo	145.00
Van, Moving, Pressed Steel, Buddy L, 1920s, 23 In.	489.00
View-Master, Baseball Stars Of The Major Leagues, 1953	65.00
View-Master, Beverly Hillbillies, No. B570, 1963, 3 Reels	65.00
View-Master, Fantastic Voyage	75.00
View-Master, Fotoreel, With Films	50.00
View-Master, James Bond, Live & Let Die	45.00
View-Master, James Bond, Moonraker	45.00
View-Master, Land Of The Giants	75.00
View-Master, Lost In Space	125.00
View-Master, Movie, Six Million Dollar Man, The Crash, 1973	25.00
View-Master, Partridge Family, No. B569, 1971, 3 Reels	65.00
View-Master, Star Trek	30.00
View-Master, Voyage To The Bottom Of Sea	75.00
View-Master Set, Partridge Family, 1971	45.00
Violinist, Tin, Windup, Japan, Linemar	395.00
Wagon, Big Four, Wooden, Child's	1650.00
Wagon, Buckboard & Driver, Pulled By 2 Goats, On Wheels, 13 1/2 In.	368.00
Wagon, Doll's, Western Express, Bliss, Wooden, Paper Lithograph, 10 In.	275.00
Wagon, Hand Drawn, Little Boss, Red & Black Letters, Wooden, 50 In.	155.00
Wagon, Heider Coaster, Wooden, 40 In.	110.00
Wagon, Janesville Ball Bearing Coaster, Wooden, Red Paint, Spoke Wheels	395.00
Wagon, Little Boss, Wooden, 50 In.	155.00
Wagon, Our Boy, Stenciled, Wooden, White Wagon Works, Patent 1919, 44 In.	195.00
Wagon, Red & Green Painted, 2 Large Back Wheels, Runners Convert To Snow Wagon	1430.00
Wagon, Shapleigh's Flyer, Metal	475.00
Wagon, Simmons Koaster, Wooden Bed	500.00
Wagon, Star Coaster, Stenciled Wood	170.00
Wagon, Studebaker Junior, Green Paint, Gilt Letters, Dog Or Goat Harness Frame	2250.00
Wagon, Studebaker Junior, Wooden, Stenciling, Late 1880s	2700.00
Wagon, Winchester, Metal	375.00
Wagon, Wooden Construction, Wooden Spoke Wheels, 18 x 30 In.	165.00
Wagon, Wooden, Metal Wheel Rims, Wooden Spokes, Early 1900, 14 In.	250.00
Waiter, Skating, Windup, Japan, 6 1/2 In.	65.00
Walkie-Talkie, Space Patrol, Tin Lithograph, J. & L. Randall, Box, 1955, 9 1/2 In.	135.00
Walkie-Talkie, Yogi Bear, Ranger, Box	80.00
Walking Stick, Doll's, Umbrella Shape, Curved Grip, Blue Body, 19th Century	66.00
Wallet, Snoopy, Whistling, Vinyl, 1965	10.00
Walrus, Paddy, Button & Chest Tag, Steiff, 6 In.	110.00
Walrus, Paddy, Button & Tag, 8 1/2 In.	200.00
Waltzing Couple, Windup, Spring Driven, Gunthermann, c.1890, 8 1/8 In.	545.00
Wardrobe, Doll's, Mirrored Door, 1 Base Drawer, Victorian	110.00
Wash Tub & Washboard, Doll's	85.00
Washer Woman & Woman Ironing, China Heads, c.1880, 8 x 5 In. *Illus*	10925.00

Toy, Whistle, Cat, Watching Bird In Cage, Germany, 6 In.;
Toy, Whistle, Motorcycle, Plastic, Red, Commonwealth Plastic, 4 In.

Washing Machine, Glass Body, Red Tin Base, Side Wringer, 8 3/4 In.	140.00
Washing Machine, Ideal	65.00
Washing Machine, Little Miss Toy, Marx, 1940	135.00
Washing Machine, Wolverine, No.12	115.00
Washing Machine & Dryer, Suzy Homemaker, Battery Operated, Topper	95.00
Whale, Swimming, Powered By Propeller In Rear, Windup, 12 In.	1100.00
Wheelbarrow, Paris Mfg.Co.	285.00
Whistle, Carved Bird, Red, Blue, White, Bead Eyes, 20th Century, 6 In.	60.00
Whistle, Cat, Watching Bird In Cage, Germany, 6 In. *Illus*	15.00
Whistle, Motorcycle, Plastic, Red, Commonwealth Plastic., 4 In. *Illus*	15.00
Whistle, Owl, Trecle Glaze	225.00
Whistle, Police, Sergeant Preston	40.00
Whistle, Red Rooster On End, Tin	30.00
Whistle, Snoopy, Figural, Plastic, 1970s, 3 In.	5.00
Whistle, Squirrel In Cage, Penny Toy	55.00
Whistle & Rattle, Felix The Cat, European	225.00
Woman, Pushing Sweeper, Mechanical, Tin Lithograph, 1910, 6 In.	550.00
Xylophone, Glass Tubes, Lithograph, Cardboard Frame, Wooden Mallet	48.00
Xylophone, Letters Impressed On Note, Cherubs Playing Bells & Horn	68.00
Yo-Yo, Captain Caveman, On Card	35.00
Yo-Yo, Duncan, Bowling Ball Shape, 1962	50.00
Yo-Yo, Football Shape	35.00
Yo-Yo, New York World Series, 1939	98.00
Yo-Yo, Sterling, Gorham	190.00
Yogi Bear, Plastic, Rubber Head, Hat Spins, Jointed Arms, c.1960, 8 In.	15.00
Zeppelin, Flying Air Ship, Strauss, 1920s, Box	475.00
Zeppelin, New York, Windup, Strauss	175.00
Zilotone, Clown With Hammer, Striking Xylophone, Windup, Tin Lithograph, 1930	520.00

TRAMP ART is a form of folk art made since the Civil War. It is usually made from chip-carved cigar boxes. Examples range from small boxes and picture frames to full-sized pieces of furniture.

Box, Jewelry, Paper Label, Dec. 24, 1932, 9 In.	140.00
Box, Writing, 1920s	425.00
Chest, 12 Glass Cutouts, 4 Mirrors, 14 1/4 x 7 1/2 In.	245.00
Chest, Made From Pine Crates, 5 Drawers, Miniature	192.00
Clock Case, 3 Story Building	950.00
Clock Case, Small	160.00
Cradle, Wooden, Steeple Type Corners	650.00
Dresser, Child's, Pivoting Mirror, Split Hickory Nuts Drawer Pulls	425.00
Figure, Eiffel Tower, Chip Carved, Paul George Keilberg, 1915	1750.00
Frame, Designed Crest, Over Fabric, Cloth Reserves, 32 1/2 x 25 1/2 In.	404.00
Frame, Old Varnish, Silver, Gold & Bronze Paint, 28 1/4 x 35 1/2 In.	715.00
Jewelry Box, Geometric & Heart Designs, 10 1/2 x 9 x 6 In.	298.00
Train, Boxcar, Tin Underpinnings & Wheels	125.00

TRAPS for animals may be handmade. One of the most unusual is the mouse-trap made so that when the mouse entered the trap, it was hit on the head with a mallet. Other traps were commercially manufactured and often are marked with the name of the manufacturer. Many traps were designed to be as humane as possible, and they would trap the live animal so it could be released in the woods.

Fly Catcher, Glass, Bale Handle, 5 In.	55.00
Mole, Nash	38.00
Mouse, Ayers, Wire Entrance Into Rotating Cage	45.00
Mouse, Catch Em Alive, Wooden, Tin, Red & Gold, 5 x 3 3/4 x 2 1/2 In.	120.00
Mouse, Peerless, Wooden & Tin	250.00
Mouse Exterminator, N.J. Wigginton, Glass, Winchester, Va., Pat. 1918	18.00 to 20.00
Roach, Screw-On-Cap, Glass	50.00

TREEN, see Wooden category

TRENCH ART is a form of folk art made by soldiers. Metal casings from bullets and mortar shells were cut and decorated to form useful objects, such as vases.

Lamp, Brass Shell Casing, 12 In.	55.00
Vase, Hammered, 7 In.	135.00

TRIVETS are now used to hold hot dishes. Most trivets of the late nineteenth and early twentieth centuries were made to hold hot irons. Iron or brass reproductions are being made of many of the old styles.

Brass, Circular Designs, England, 14 3/4 x 4 1/2 In.	125.00
Brass, Eagle	25.00 to 29.00
Brass, Folding, Attaches To Fire Grate, Brace, English, 1780s	325.00
Brass, Iron Frame, Footman, Cutout Sides & Top, England, 1840, 12 3/4 x 13 5/8 In.	370.00
Brass, President Adams	60.00
Brass & Wrought Iron, Hangs On Fender, Reticulated Ivy Design, 7 1/2 In.	110.00
Coffeepot, Griswold, 7 In.	145.00
Enamel On Iron, State Of Maine Center, Portland Stove Foundry, 7 5/8 x 9 1/2 In.	70.00
Iron, Favorite Stoves & Ranges	40.00
Iron, George Washington, 9 1/2 In.	35.00
Iron, Girl, Dog & Hat, 11 In.	22.00
Iron, Hearts & Birds	40.00
Iron, Parlor, Handle, 3 Tall Footed	450.00
Iron, Reddy Kilowatt	8.00
Iron, Star, Griswold	40.00
Warmer, Rotating, Wrought Iron, Black Paint, 18th Century, 21 x 7 In.	185.00
Wrought Iron, Scrolled Platform Feet, Handle, 19th Century, 9 x 19 1/2 x 9 In.	230.00

TRUNKS of many types were made. The nineteenth-century sea chest was often handmade of unpainted wood. Brass-fitted camphorwood chests were brought back from the Orient. Leather-covered trunks were popular from the late eighteenth to mid-nineteenth centuries. By 1895, trunks were covered with canvas or decorated sheet metal. Embossed metal coverings were used from 1870 to 1910. By 1925, trunks were covered with vulcanized fiber or undecorated metal.

Camphorwood, Brass Bound, Red Paint, Floral Design, 19th Century, 10 x 25 In.	1093.00
Camphorwood, Carved Figures & Man On Horseback, Oriental	250.00
Camphorwood, Carved Village Scenes, Horses & Trees, Stand, Tray, 32 x 47 x 22 In.	450.00
Humpback, Inserts, Small	200.00
Leather, Black, Brass Studs & Bale Handle, Wallpaper Lining, Nathan Neat, 10 In.	160.00
Leather, Brass Studded, 25 In.	465.00
Leather, Brass Tacks, Brass Ring Handle, 12 In.	140.00
Leather, Brass, Paper Label Inside, 7 x 14 x 9 In.	60.00
Leather, Dome Top, Brass Trim, 10 1/2 In.	85.00
Leather, Wicker, Canvas	290.00
Louis Vuitton, 28 x 24 In.	920.00
Louis Vuitton, Suitcase	360.00
Mahogany, Foliate & Scroll Carving On Body & Lid, 19th Century, 20 1/2 In.	1035.00
Pine, Black Paint, Dome Top, Red-Brown Ground, 19th Century, 12 1/2 x 24 1/2 In.	575.00
Pine, Camelback, Child's	250.00
Pine, Camelback, Child's, Brass Hardware	185.00

Pine, Dome Top, Bail Handle, Yellow & Brown On Yellow Ground, 8 3/4 x 18 In. 4025.00
Pine, Dome Top, Child's, Iron Bands, Original Handles, Tray, Refinished 250.00
Pine, Dome Top, Opening To Well, Painted Allover Stenciled Design, 23 In. 1265.00
Pine, Dome Top, Painted, Swags On Green Ground, 19th Century, 10 x 24 1/2 In........ 1092.00
Pine, Dome Top, Spotted Sponge Design, 20th Century 250.00
Pine, Dome Top, Vinegar Grained, Green Stripes, Ochre Ground, 13 1/2 x 30 In. 316.00
Pine, Immigrant's, Dome Top, Bear Trap Lock, Key, Till, 37 In. 220.00
Pine, Immigrant's, Igrant, 1811 .... 595.00
Pine, Immigrant's, Iron Banding, Iron Ball Handles, 1820s 850.00
Pine, Oil On Canvas Panels, Religious Scenes, Spanish, 20 1/2 In. 1090.00
Pine, Stagecoach, Iron Straps, 1800s.. 155.00
Saddle Harness, Inside Label, S. Nims, 1827 .... 350.00
U.S. Army, General Bandholtz's, Inscribed Name, 22 x 36 In. 172.00
Wallpaper Covered, 19th Century, 30 x 13 In. 546.00
Wood, European, Brass & Metal Flower Design, 13 x 18 1/8 x 9 3/4 In. 250.00

TUTHILL Cut Glass Company of Middletown, New York, worked from 1902 to 1923. Of special interest are the finely cut pieces of stemware and tableware.

Bowl, Fruit, Open Petal Hobstar, Open Petal Hobstar Base, 9 1/4 In.............................. 1375.00
Bowl, Intaglio Cut, Chrysanthemum Leaves & Blossoms, Signed, 9 In. 345.00
Bowl, Wild Rose, 10 In.. 375.00
Compote, Hobstars, Crosshatching, Fans, Signed, 6 x 3 1/4 In. 235.00
Compote, Intaglio, Florals, Signed, 6 In.. 215.00
Creamer, Grape Vine Pattern, Signed 55.00
Dish, Hobstars, Fans, Signed, 6 In.. 175.00
Mayonnaise Set, Hobstars, Fans, Crosshatching, Sawtooth Rim, 2 Piece 225.00
Nappy, Cosmos, Signed, 2 x 5 In.. 75.00
Nappy, Engraved Blackberries, Notched Handle, 7 In. 165.00
Plate, Wild Rose, Intaglio & Cut Design, 9 In. 925.00
Rose Bowl, Butterfly & Flower 235.00
Sugar & Creamer, Primrose.. 225.00
Sugar & Creamer, Wild Rose, Handled, Signed, 2 1/4 x 5 1/2 In. 100.00
Tray, Bread, Primrose, 13 x 6 In... 550.00
Tray, Cheese & Cracker, Blazed Leaf Design, Band Of Hobstars, Signed, 10 In............. 575.00
Tumbler, Cosmos, Signed, 3 1/2 In., 4 Piece 110.00
Vase, Violet, Horn Shape, Phlox Pattern, 4 In... 150.00

TYPEWRITER collectors divide typewriters into two main classifications: the index machine, which has a pointer and a dial for letter selection, and the keyboard machine, most commonly seen today. The first successful typewriter was made by Sholes and Glidden in 1874.

Blickensderfer, No. 5, Oak Case.. 225.00
Crandall, Engraved & Painted.. 4750.00
Folding Easel, Field Type, World War I, 7 In. 75.00
Mignon, Index, Model No. 4 .... 195.00
Simplex, Box, 1902 .... 50.00

UHL pottery was made in Evansville, Indiana, in 1854. The pottery moved to Huntingburg, Indiana, in 1908. Stoneware and glazed pottery were made until the mid-1940s.

Casserole, Tan, Ear Handles 65.00
Crock, 6 Gal. 22.50
Crock, No. 2 .... 25.00
Crock, Watering, With Tray 40.00
Crock, Wire Handles, No. 5 .... 60.00
Flowerpot, Ribbed, Blue, Attached Saucer, 2 In.. 180.00
Flowerpot, Small 69.00
Jar, Beater, Pink Lid 57.50
Jug, 1 Gal.. 17.50
Pitcher, Grape, Blue.. 150.00
Vase, Black Glaze, 8 1/2 In. 100.00

UMBRELLA collectors like rain or shine. The first known umbrella was owned by King Louis XIII of France in 1637. The earliest umbrellas were sunshades, not designed to be used in the rain. The umbrella was embellished and redesigned many times. In 1852, the fluted steel rib style was developed and it has remained the most useful style.

14K Yellow Gold, Diamond, Enameled, Handle Cap, Russia, 1 1/8 In.	660.00
Parasol, Exposition, 1936	18.00
Schiaparelli, Box, 14 In.	125.00
Tiffany Co., Union Square	100.00

UNION PORCELAIN WORKS was established at Greenpoint, New York, in 1848 by Charles Cartlidge. The company went through a series of ownership changes and finally closed in the early 1900s. The company made a fine quality white porcelain that was often decorated in clear, bright colors.

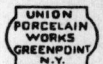

Oyster Plate, 5 Openings, Shell Shape, 8 1/2 In.	150.00
Oyster Plate, 6 Openings, Round	350.00
Oyster Plate, Black, Polychrome & Gilt, 10 1/4 In.	187.00
Water Cooler, Flowering Plants, 1889, 14 1/8 In. .... *Illus*	575.00

UNIVERSITY OF NORTH DAKOTA, see North Dakota School of Mines

VAL ST. LAMBERT Cristalleries of Belgium was founded by Messieurs Kemlin and Lelievre in 1825. The company is still in operation. All types of table glassware and decorative glassware have been made. Pieces are often decorated with cut designs.

Bowl, Cranberry Cut To Clear, 12 In.	450.00
Bowl, Round, Inverted Lip, 10 In.	86.25
Box, Blue Milk Glass, Fiery Opalescent Basket Weave Handle, 3 x 4 In.	85.00
Candlestick, 5 x 5 In., Pair	97.00
Candlestick, Column Shape, Crystal, 9 1/2 In., Pair	220.00
Dish, Swirled Design, Green-Yellow	135.00
Garniture Set, Cobalt Blue Cut To Clear, Gilded Bacchic Procession, 3 Piece	990.00
Liqueur, Teardrop Stem, Hexagonal Base, 9 Piece	97.75
Paperweight, Mountain Goat, 4 In.	128.00
Vase, Cameo, Floral, Red Cut To Yellow Cut To Clear, Signed, 9 In.	850.00
Vase, Green Top, Clear Base, Signed, 9 In.	60.00
Vase, Hammered Surface, Crystal Of Green Encased In Crystal, 5 1/2 x 7 In.	50.00
Wine, Teardrop Stem, Hexagonal Base, 7 Piece	109.25

Union Porcelain Works, Water Cooler,
Flowering Plants, 1889, 14 1/8 In.

♦ ♦

Most shaving mug reproductions are imaginative copies of old mugs that would not fool a serious collector. There is often no space for the owner's name. Some examples are marked Brandenburg. Copies include designs such as Currier and Ives prints, a hearse drawn by horses, and trade names such as Peddler, Fireman, or Painter.

♦ ♦

VALLERYSTHAL Glassworks was founded in 1836 in Lorraine, France. In 1854, the firm became Klenglin et Cie. It made table and decorative glass, opaline, cameo, and art glass. A line of covered, pressed glass animal dishes was made in the nineteenth century. The firm is still working.

Dish, Hunting Dog Cover, Blue Milk Glass, 5 x 4 1/2 In.	250.00
Plate, Thistle, 7 In.	65.00
Salt, Hen	35.00

VAN BRIGGLE pottery was made by Artus Van Briggle in Colorado Springs, Colorado, after 1901. Van Briggle had been a decorator at Rookwood Pottery of Cincinnati, Ohio. He died in 1904. His wares usually had modeled relief decorations and a soft, dull glaze. The pottery is still working and still making some of the original designs.

Ashtray, Kneeling Indian, Grinding Corn, Signed, 5 1/2 In.	62.00
Bookends, Squirrel	265.00
Bowl, 3 Dragonflies, Under Purple To Navy Glaze, Spherical, 1916, 3 x 4 3/4 In.	357.00
Bowl, 3-Frog Flower Frog, Turquoise, Dragon Fly Bowl, 8 3/8 x 2 1/2 In.	165.00
Bowl, Blue Pine Cones, Burgundy Ground, Closed In, 1930, 5 x 10 In.	385.00
Bowl, Butterfly, 3 In.	50.00
Bowl, Flower Frog, Oak Leaves, Turquoise, Square, 7 1/2 In.	75.00
Bowl, Ivy Leaves Under Blue Glaze, Squatty, 1903, 2 1/2 x 5 1/2 In.	495.00
Bowl, Matte Maroon, Blue Highlights, 1911, 9 In.	143.00
Bowl, Molded Dragonflies, Maroon & Blue, 1919, 8 x 2 1/2 In.	522.50
Bowl, Stylized Leaves, Deep Turquoise, 1920, 6 3/8 x 2 In.	135.00
Bowl, Swirled Leaves, Light & Dark Turquoise, 5 1/2 x 3 1/2 In.	70.00
Bowl, Turquoise Blue, Leaf Design, 5 x 8 In.	350.00
Bowl, Violet Embossed Leaves, Gray Ground, Squatty, 1907-1912, 4 x 7 In.	330.00
Candleholder, Persian Rose, 1917, 9 In.	150.00
Candlestick, Double, Tulip, Turquoise, 9 In.	30.00
Candlestick, Tapered, Flared Foot, Green To Dark Maroon, c.1920, 9 In., Pair	302.50
Centerpiece, Frog, Mermaid On Shell, Blue, 1930, 8 3/4 x 15 In.	825.00
Console, Swan Flower Frog	275.00
Creamer, Floral Band, Turquoise	20.00
Creamer, Neptune, Marked	90.00
Creamer, Sweetheart, 2-Tone Blue, 4 In.	40.00
Ewer, Persian Rose, Bowling Pin Shape, Buff Bottom, 7 x 3 1/4 In.	48.00
Figurine, Dragon Fly, Blue, 1917, 7 In.	125.00
Figurine, Elephant, Raised Trunk, Turquoise, 4 1/4 x 3 1/4 In.	35.00
Figurine, Girl, Reading Book, 6 In.	77.00
Figurine, Indian Maiden, Grinding Corn, White	143.00
Flower Frog, Cobalt Glaze, White On Top	60.00
Flower Frog, Duck On Water, Marked, 9 1/2 In.	75.00
Flower Frog, Persian Rose	65.00
Lamp, Blue, 2 Vine Handles, Shade, 8 In.	135.00
Lamp, Owl, Matte Blue & Brown, c.1915, 6 In.	275.00
Lamp, Pods, Long Stems, Blue Over Turquoise, Celluloid Shade, 8 In.	400.00
Mug, Gold Greek Letters, Fraternity, Purple Matte Ground, 1907-1912, 4 1/2 In.	313.00
Mug, Green-Gray, Matte, 1905, 5 In.	275.00
Mug, Signed Arteus Van Briggle, 4 1/2 In.	1950.00
Mug, Signed H. Wilcox, 4 1/2 In.	950.00
Night-Light, Overlapping Leaves, Mulberry, 6 In.	350.00
Paperweight, Rabbit, Figural, Turquoise Ming Matte Glaze, 2 3/4 x 3 1/4 In.	137.00
Pitcher, Melon Ribbed, 4 In.	30.00
Pitcher, Mottled Turquoise, c.1950s, 11 1/2 In.	60.00
Pitcher, Sweetheart, Turquoise, Heart Shaped Mouth, 3 1/2 x 3 3/4 In.	35.00
Pitcher, Water, Ice Lip, Blue, No. 5118, 9 In.	125.00
Plaque, Indian Brave, Persian Rose, A Yani, Big Buffalo, 6 x 4 3/8 In.	145.00
Plaque, Indian Squaw, Persian Rose, Oval, So Ya Zhe, Little Star, 5 1/2 x 3 5/8 In.	140.00
Plate, Arrow Root Leaves, Light Blue, 5 In.	225.00
Plate, Blue, Arrowhead Leaves, 1907, 6 In.	295.00
Plate, Embossed Poppy & Leaves Under Leathery Blue Glaze, 8 1/2 In.	440.00
Plate, Persian Rose, Hand Thrown, 4 1/4 In.	45.00

Plate, Raised Spider Design, Yellow Glaze, Incised Logo, 4 In.	550.00
Salt & Pepper, Persian Rose	65.00
Stylized Mistletoe, Speckled Matte Green, 1903, 5 1/2 In.	470.00
Tile, Ochre & Mauve Monarch Butterfly, Blue-Gray Ground, Marked, 4 In.	300.00
Vase, 2 Butterflies, Under Turquoise Glaze, Clay Body, 1907-1912, 3 1/2 In.	330.00
Vase, 2 Handles, Matte Blue, Incised Mark, 1916, 10 1/2 x 4 1/2 In.	440.00
Vase, 2 Handles, Sculpted Irises, Leaves, Brown & Green, No. 137, 1903, 13 1/2 In. ...	3850.00
Vase, 3 Color Design, Blossoms, Stems & Leaves, 1903, 8 In.	6900.00
Vase, 3 Dragonflies, Under Green To Brown Glaze, 1914, Spherical, 3 1/2 x 5 In.	440.00
Vase, 4 Vertical Leaves & Stems, Blue, No. 857, 1915, 5 In.	550.00
Vase, Art Nouveau Flowers, Two Handles, Maroon, No. 82, 1903, 8 x 7 1/2 In.	2750.00
Vase, Aztec Designs, Spider, Bird's Head, Matte Brown, 1902, 4 1/2 In.	2200.00
Vase, Bud, Persian Rose, Narrow, Corset Shape, 8 7/8 In., Pair	98.00
Vase, Carved Leaves, Organic Green Matte Glaze, 16 In.	6930.00
Vase, Dragonfly, Persian Rose With Blue, 1920s, 6 1/2 In.	175.00 to 250.00
Vase, Embossed Butterflies, Maroon Matte Glaze, Signed, 1915, 4 x 4 In.	410.00
Vase, Indian Heads At Top, Burgundy & Black Glaze, Signed, 11 In.	1200.00
Vase, Lorelei, Woman Wrapped Around Rim, Blue, 9 1/2 In.	750.00 to 1200.00
Vase, Maroon Glaze, Relief Floral & Foliate Design, 1904, 9 3/4 In.	1725.00
Vase, Maroon, 1916, 8 In.	850.00
Vase, Mistletoe Blossoms & Berries, Celadon Glaze, 1906, 3 3/4 In.	300.00
Vase, Molded Leaf Design, Bronze Green Glaze, Signed, 1907, 6 1/2 In.	475.00
Vase, Mountain Craig, Brown, 1920s, 4 1/2 In.	95.00
Vase, No. 833, Stylized Vertical Floral Design, Matte Blue, 1916, 6 x 3 In.	165.00
Vase, Ovoid, Burgundy Ground, Raised Flowers, 9 1/2 In.	172.50
Vase, Persian Rose, Blue, 1920, 8 In.	125.00
Vase, Poppy Pods At Shoulder, Textured Glaze, Signed, 1905, 9 In.	1800.00
Vase, Raised Leaf Design, 2 Handles, c.1920s, 13 In.	660.00
Vase, Raised Poppies, Maroon Matte, 3 1/2 x 4 In.	330.00
Vase, Stylized Flower Buds & Stems, Matte Glaze, Incised, 1915, 7 x 3 1/2 In.	110.00
Vase, Stylized Leaf Design, Matte Blue, Incised, 5 1/4 x 3 1/2 In.	165.00
Vase, Stylized Leaves, Green Matte Glaze, Signed, 1904, 5 1/2 In.	690.00
Vase, Swirling Arts & Crafts Design, Floral Accents, c.1918, 6 In.	275.00
Vase, Swirling Stems, Leaves & Blossoms, Blue Glaze, Signed, 3 1/2 In	358.00
Vase, Vertical Leaf Design, 2 Broad Handles, c.1920, 13 1/2 In.	660.00
Vase, Yucca Pattern, Persian Rose Glaze, Incised, 4 1/2 x 5 1/4 In.	77.00

VASA MURRHINA is the name of a glassware made by the Vasa Murrhina Art Glass Company of Sandwich, Massachusetts, about 1884. The glassware was transparent and was embedded with small pieces of colored glass and metallic flakes. The mica flakes were coated with silver, gold, copper, or nickel. Some of the pieces were cased. The same type of glass was made in England. Collectors often confuse Vasa Murrhina glass with aventurine, spatter, or spangle glass. There is uncertainty about what actually was made by the Vasa Murrhina factory. Related pieces may be listed under Spangle Glass.

Bottle, Mica Flakes, Butterflies, Screw-On Silver Dome Cap, 5 In.	395.00
Pitcher, Blue, Swirl Pattern, Embossed, Bulbous, 4 5/8 x 3 1/2 In.	195.00
Pitcher, Mica Flakes, Embossed Swirl Pattern, Clear Handle, 4 5/8 In.	195.00
Rose Bowl, 8-Crimp Top, Mica Flakes, White Lining, 3 3/8 In.	95.00
Rose Bowl, Blue, White & Silver Mica	95.00
Rose Bowl, Pink & Blue, Mottled Pastels	45.00
Rose Bowl, Silver Mica Flakes	120.00
Toothpick, Leaf Umbrella	225.00
Vase, Mica Flakes, 4-Fluted Rim, White Lining, Wishbone Feet, 6 1/4 In.	95.00
Vase, Mica Flakes, Clear Handle, Blue, 6 3/4 In.	65.00
Vase, Mica Flakes, Ruffled Rim, White Lining, Rose, 8 3/4 In.	75.00
Vase, Thorn Prunts, 10 In.	220.00

VASELINE GLASS is a greenish-yellow glassware resembling petroleum jelly. Some vaseline glass is still being made in old and new styles. Pressed glass of the 1870s was often made of vaseline-colored glass. Additional pieces of vaseline glass may also be listed under Pressed Glass in this book.

Basket, Hobnail, Ruffled Top, Opalescent, 6 3/4 In.	80.00
Bowl, Barred Forget-Me-Not, 4 1/2 x 7 In.	38.00
Bowl, Jam, Peacock Feather, Silver Plated Holder, Shell Trim, 5 In.	100.00
Bread Plate, General Ulysses S. Grant, Patriot & Soldier	65.00
Butter, Cover, Cherry	45.00
Butter, Cover, Hobnail, Opalescent	120.00
Candlestick, 9 1/4 In., Pair	402.00
Candlestick, Flint, c.1880, 10 1/4 In.	225.00
Candlestick, Petal & Loop, Flint, Pair	4250.00
Candlestick, Silver Overlay, c.1880, 9 1/2 In., Pair	295.00
Celery Vase, Embossed Rib, Footed, Scalloped Top, Opalescent, 7 3/8 In.	135.00
Celery Vase, Wildflower	110.00
Compote, Opalescent, 5 In.	44.00
Creamer, Hand Painted Flowers, Jewels, Individual	55.00
Creamer, Swag With Brackets	22.00
Creamer, Three Panel	32.00
Cruet, Dewey, Greentown	165.00
Cruet, Hobnail, Grooves, Opalescent, 5 In.	60.00
Cruet, Ranson, Stopper	175.00
Dish, Paneled Cane, Scalloped Edge, Opalescent, 6 1/2 x 8 1/2 In.	75.00
Fish Bowl, 7 x 13 1/2 In.	300.00
Mug, Pine & Deer, c.1880	100.00
Pitcher, Opalescent Hobnails, Square Mouth, Clear Ribbed Handle, 7 In.	93.00
Rose Bowl, Hobnail, Opalescent, Ruffled Top, 4 3/4 In.	58.00
Salt Dip, Bird With Cherry	10.00
Salt Dip, Swan, Open	10.00
Salt Dip, Turkey	10.00
Shoe, 6 In.	25.00
Spooner, Dewey, 3 Footed	30.00
Sugar & Creamer, Smocking, Cover, Flint	140.00
Toothpick, Basket Weave	10.00
Toothpick, Gypsy Pot	10.00
Toothpick, Heart	10.00
Toothpick, Michigan, Beaded Oval	10.00
Toothpick, Thousand Eye	40.00
Tumbler, Dewey, Greentown	75.00
Vase, Bud, Hobnail, Opalescent, 8 1/2 In.	65.00
Vase, Jack-In-The-Pulpit, Opalescent Stripes, 8 In.	110.00
Vase, Swirled Feather, Cranberry Ruffled Rim, 6 In.	95.00
Water Set, Petticoat, 6 Piece	495.00
Wine, Austrian, Greentown	85.00

VENETIAN GLASS, see Glass-Venetian

VENINI glass was first designed by Paolo Venini, who established his factory in Murano, Italy, in 1925. He is best known for pieces of modern design, including the famous *handkerchief* vase. The company is still working. Other pieces of Italian glass may be found in the Glass-Contemporary, Glass-Midcentury, and Glass-Venetian categories of this book.

Bottle, Blue Interior, Square Form, 1950s, 9 1/2 In.	440.00
Bottle, Giada, Opaque Orange, Twisted Threads, Tony Zuccheri, 1950, 9 In.	1650.00
Bottle, Green, Red Band, Fulvio Bianconi, 1950, 7 1/2 In.	155.00
Bowl, Clear Over White Over Yellow, 5 1/2 In.	350.00
Figurine, Rooster, Polychrome Variegato, F. Bianconi, c.1950, 7 1/2 In.	2200.00
Jar, Amber Cover, Opaque Olive Green, Signed, 4 3/4 In.	172.50
Obelisk, Internal Swirling Gold Leaf Canes, Ribbed Brass Base, 20 In.	525.00
Tumbler, Blue, Green, A. Canne, 1950, 5 1/2 In., 4 Piece	155.00
Vase, Acid Etched Surface, c.1935, 12 1/2 In.	920.00
Vase, Bollicine, Ovoid, Lime Green, Internal Bubbles, Scarpa, 1930, 7 In.	525.00
Vase, Fazzoletto, White Zanfirico, Rose Ground, F. Bianconi, 5 1/2 In.	660.00
Vase, Free Blown Patchwork, F. Bianconi, 8 /14 In.	5462.00
Vase, Handkerchief, Blue & White Latticino, Signed, 5 In.	350.00
Vase, Handkerchief, Slumped Design, Turquoise Cased To White, Signed, 6 In.	345.00

Vase, Internal Gray Veining & Purple Raffia, Signed, c.1960, 15 1/2 In. 2300.00
Vase, Multicolored Bands, Bottle, Signed Murano, 9 1/4 In. 1350.00
Vase, Paolo Venini, Inciso, Teardrop, Blue Interior, 1955, 8 In. 1210.00
Vase, Pezzati, Irregular Squares, Beaker Form, c.1951, 9 1/8 In. 5175.00
Vase, Pezzato, Multicolored Patches, Fulvio Bianconi, 1950, 9 1/2 In. 4400.00
Vase, Spherical Body, Square Sections Of Amber & Green, c.1960, 6 1/2 In. 4125.00
Vase, Translucent Blue, Ribbed Ball Stem & Foot, 1920s, 9 1/2 In. 220.00

VERLYS glass was made in France after 1931. It was made in the United States from 1935 to 1951. The glass is either blown or molded. The American glass is signed with a diamond-point-scratched name, but the French pieces are marked with a molded signature. The designs resemble those used by Lalique.

Bowl, Chrysanthemum, Etched, Signed, 6 1/4 x 10 1/8 In. 295.00
Bowl, Floral Design, 11 1/2 In. 33.00
Bowl, Poppy, Signed, 13 In. 145.00
Bowl, Seagull & Fish Design, Signed, 3 3/4 x 13 3/4 In. 110.00
Bowl, Tassels, Blue, Signed, 12 In. 350.00
Bowl, Water Lily, Signed, 15 In. 100.00
Console, Poppy, Signed, 14 In. 250.00
Vase, Summer & Winter, Signed, 8 1/4 In. 275.00

VERNON KILNS was the name used after 1958 by Vernon Potteries, Ltd. The company, which started in 1931 in Vernon, California, made dinnerware and figurines until it closed in 1958. Collectors search for the brightly colored dinnerware and the pieces designed by Rockwell Kent, Walt Disney, and Don Blanding. For more information, see *Kovels' Depression Glass & American Dinnerware Price List*.

Bowl, Divided, Organdie 18.00
Bowl, Mayflower, Tab Handle, 6 1/8 In. 10.00
Bowl, Mixing, Organdie, 7 In. 30.00
Bowl, Mushroom, 1940 .... 425.00
Bowl, Mushroom, Rectangular, 1940 .... 450.00
Bowl, Organdie, 7 In. 7.00
Bowl, Tam O'Shanter, 5 1/4 In. 14.00
Bowl, Vegetable, Orchard 30.00
Butter, Organdie 35.00
Carafe, Calico 95.00
Carafe, Stopper, Tam O'Shanter 60.00
Carafe, Tweed 95.00
Casserole, Cover, Homespun 20.00
Casserole, Cover, Tam O'Shanter, 2 Handles 49.00
Chop Plate, Blossom 55.00
Chop Plate, Cowboy Scene, Brown, 14 In. 110.00
Chop Plate, Frontier Days 180.00
Chop Plate, Hawaiian Flowers, Maroon, 14 In. 150.00
Chop Plate, Lei Lani, 12 In. ....75.00 to 95.00
Chop Plate, Lei Lani, 14 In. ....110.00 to 135.00
Chop Plate, Lei Lani, 17 In. 250.00
Chop Plate, Mayflower, 12 In. 38.00
Chop Plate, Moby Dick, Blue, 12 In. 160.00
Chop Plate, Moby Dick, Brown, 11 In. 145.00
Chop Plate, Moby Dick, Maroon, 12 In. 125.00
Chop Plate, Modern California, Ivory, 14 In. 65.00
Chop Plate, Organdie, 14 In. 24.00
Chop Plate, Salamina, 14 In. 450.00
Chop Plate, Salamina, 17 In. 575.00
Coaster, Homespun 35.00
Coffeepot, Hawaiian Flowers, After Dinner 195.00
Coffeepot, Mayflower 60.00
Creamer, Cover, Brown Eyed Susan 25.00
Creamer, Modern California, Ivory 20.00
Cup, Mayflower 12.00
Cup & Saucer, Gingham 8.00

Cup & Saucer, Moby Dick, After Dinner	100.00
Cup & Saucer, Mormon Temple, After Dinner	25.00
Cup & Saucer, Mt. Vernon, After Dinner	25.00
Cup & Saucer, Organdie	12.00
Cup & Saucer, Organdie, After Dinner	20.00
Dinner Set, Lei Lani, 4 Piece Setting, Serving Pieces, 32 Piece	1000.00
Eggcup, Homespun	16.00
Eggcup, Organdie	18.00
Figurine, Satyr, No. 3002	325.00
Fruit, Organdie, 5 1/2 In.	3.50
Mixing Bowl, Calico, 6 In.	30.00 to 50.00
Mixing Bowl, Calico, 7 In.	60.00
Mixing Bowl, Calico, 8 In.	40.00 to 70.00
Mixing Bowl, Tam O'Shanter, 6 In.	30.00
Mug, Homespun	20.00
Mug, Organdie, 3 1/2 In.	16.00
Pitcher, Brown Eyed Susan, 2 Qt.	30.00
Pitcher, Casual California	38.00
Pitcher, Gingham, 1 Qt.	38.00
Pitcher, Harvest, 1 Pt.	35.00
Pitcher, Homespun, 1 Qt.	30.00
Pitcher, Mexicana, Bulb Base	20.00
Pitcher, Organdie, Streamline, 2 Qt.	40.00
Plate, 100th Anniversary Wisconsin	5.00
Plate, Baltimore Harbor, Blue, 8 1/2 In.	11.00
Plate, Bits Of Old England, Multicolor, 8 1/2 In.	6.50
Plate, Brown Eyed Susan, 9 1/2 In.	10.00
Plate, Brown Eyed Susan, 10 1/2 In.	20.00
Plate, Calico, 7 In.	15.00
Plate, California, Multicolor, 10 1/2 In.	13.00
Plate, Capitol, California Centennial 1849-1949, White & Brown, 10 In.	8.50
Plate, Connecticut, Red, 10 1/2 In.	13.00
Plate, Early California, 7 In.	8.00
Plate, Early California, 10 In.	12.00
Plate, El Camino Rezel, 14 In.	80.00
Plate, Gingham, 10 In.	8.00
Plate, Homespun, Bread & Butter	2.00
Plate, Homespun, Dinner	6.00
Plate, Iowa State University	5.00
Plate, Long Beach, California, Blue, 10 1/2 In.	13.00
Plate, Mayflower, 10 1/4 In.	16.00
Plate, Moby Dick, Blue, 6 1/4 In.	25.00
Plate, Moby Dick, Blue, 9 1/2 In.	50.00
Plate, Modern California, Ivory, 10 In.	20.00
Plate, Old Shot Tower, Blue, 8 1/2 In.	11.00
Plate, Old South, Cypress Swamp, 8 In.	40.00
Plate, Old South, Tobacco Field, 8 In.	40.00
Plate, Organdie, 6 1/2 In.	3.00
Plate, Organdie, 7 1/2 In.	5.00
Plate, Organdie, 9 1/2 In.	9.00
Plate, Organdie, Bread & Butter	4.00
Plate, Our America, Rockwell Kent, 10 1/2 In.	95.00
Plate, Salad, Brown Eyed Susan, Individual	30.00
Plate, Salad, Mexicana, 10 In.	65.00
Plate, Salamina, 10 In.	125.00
Plate, Scenic Utah, Red, 10 1/2 In.	13.00
Plate, Tam O'Shanter, 6 1/4 In.	5.00
Plate, Tam O'Shanter, 9 3/4 In.	11.00
Plate, Vermont, Red, 10 1/2 In.	12.00
Plate, Williamsburg, Va., Multicolor, 10 1/2 In.	13.00
Plate Set, States Missionaries, Blue, 8 Piece	80.00
Platter, Brown Eyed Susan, 12 In.	20.00
Platter, Fruitdale, 14 In.	35.00

Platter, Organdie, 12 1/2 In.	12.00
Platter, Organdie, 14 In.	32.00
Relish, Cosmos, Leaf Shape, 4 Sections	95.00
Salt & Pepper, Hawaiian Flowers	45.00
Salt & Pepper, Tam O'Shanter	18.00
Saucer, Organdie	2.50
Shaker, Pepper, Mayflower	8.00
Soup, Dish, Chatalaine, Jade, 4 Piece	25.00
Soup, Dish, Early California, Lug Handle	10.00
Soup, Dish, Homespun	15.00
Soup, Dish, Organdie	15.00
Soup, Dish, Modern California, Ivory, Lug Handle	20.00
Sugar, Brown Eyed Susan	18.00
Sugar, Cover, Honolulu	95.00
Sugar, Homespun	12.00
Sugar & Creamer, Early California	18.00
Syrup, Organdie	45.00
Teapot, Barkwood, 11 In.	25.00
Teapot, Chintz	60.00
Teapot, Dolores	55.00
Teapot, Mayflower	40.00
Teapot, Mexicana	50.00
Tumbler, Brown Eyed Susan, 14 Oz.	15.00
Tumbler, Homespun	25.00
Tumbler, Organdie	20.00
Tumbler, Tam O'Shanter, 5 1/2 In.	16.00
Tureen, Hawaiian Flowers, Maroon	325.00
Vase, Gold Fish Bowl, 3 Fish, Bubbles, Solid Pink & Orange, 1940, 6 In.	450.00

VERRE DE SOIE glass was first made by Frederick Carder at the Steuben Glass Works from about 1905 to 1930. It is an iridescent glass of soft white or very, very pale green. The name means *glass of silk*, and it does resemble silk. Other factories have made verre de soie, and some of the English examples were made of different colors. Verre de soie is an art glass and is not related to the iridescent, pressed, white carnival glass mistakenly called by its name. Related pieces may be found in the Steuben category.

Compote, Spherical Turned Standard, Domed Foot, 8 x 5 3/4 In.	440.00
Goblet, Rosaline Band, Conical, 7 1/4 In.	121.00
Perfume Bottle, Engraved Florals, Mushroom Stopper, 5 In.	260.00
Rose Bowl, 8 x 5 In.	165.00

VIENNA, see Beehive category

VIENNA ART plates are round metal serving trays produced at the turn of the century. The designs, copied from Royal Vienna porcelain plates, usually featured a portrait of a woman encircled by a wide, ornate border. Many were used as advertising or promotional items and were produced in Coshocton, Ohio, by J. F. Meeks Tuscarora Advertising Co. and H. D. Beach's Standard Advertising Co.

Plate, Anheuser-Busch, Madonna Della Sedia, 1905, 10 In.	135.00
Plate, LaBelle Chocolatier, Walter Baker, Jeweled Border, 10 1/4 In.	410.00

VILLEROY & BOCH Pottery of Mettlach was founded in 1841. The firm made many types of wares, including the famous Mettlach steins. Collectors can be confused because although Villeroy & Boch made most of its pieces in the city of Mettlach, Germany, they also had factories in other locations. The dating code impressed on the bottom of most pieces makes it possible to determine the age of the piece. Additional items may be found in the Mettlach category.

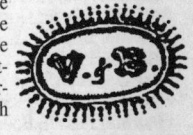

Charger, Flow Blue, Deer Scene, 15 In.	175.00
Charger, Rural Scene, 12 In.	65.00
Drink Set, Floral, Art Nouveau, 5 Piece	850.00
Plate, Blue Willow, 8 1/2 In.	50.00

Tray, Silver Plated Rim & Handles, Footed, 10 1/2 In... 125.00

VOLKMAR pottery was made by Charles Volkmar of New York from 1879 to about 1911. He was associated with several firms, including the Volkmar Ceramic Company, Volkmar and Cory, and Charles Volkmar and Son. Volkmar had been a painter, and his designs often look like oil paintings drawn on pottery.

VOLKMAR
Corona N.Y

Bowl, Fruit, Volcanic Purple Glaze, Pale Green Interior, Scalloped, 1916, 4 x 10 1/2 In.   440.00
Candlestick, Maroon Glaze, Durant, 1916, 10 x 3 1/4 In... 110.00
Tile, Duck Silhouette, Squeeze-Bag Outlining, Mottled Matte Green Glaze, 8 1/4 In. 644.00
Tile, Hispano-Moresque, Majolica-Glazed Floral, Marked, 6 In................................... 715.00
Tile, Rabbit Family, Yellow Incised, Green Ground, Frame, Incised V, 6 In. 963.00
Tile, Tree Landscape Painted Style, Blue & Green Matte Glaze, Incised V, 6 In. 875.00
Vase, Black Satin Glaze, Footed, Spherical, Incised Mark, 1933, 5 1/2 x 5 3/4 In. 183.00
Vase, Matte Green Glaze, Squatty, Bulbous Base, Incised V, 3 1/2 x 4 1/2 In. 165.00
Vase, Matte Green, 3 1/2 x 3 1/2 In.. 225.00
Vase, Speckled Matte Green Glaze, Marked, 7 3/4 In. 440.00
Vase, Waterfowl Scene, Signed, c.1900, 11 1/2 In.. 3737.00
Vase, White & Pink Blossoms, Scalloped, Barbotine, Mottled Black Ground, 6 1/2 In. .   357.00

VOLKSTEDT was a soft-paste porcelain factory started in 1760 by Georg Heinrich Macheleid at Volkstedt, Thuringia. Volkstedt-Rudolstadt was a porcelain factory started at Volkstedt-Rudolstadt by Beyer and Bock in 1890. Most pieces seen in shops today are from the later factory.

Vase, Putti & Roses, c.1884 .... 895.00

WADE pottery is made by the Wade Group of Potteries started in 1810 near Burslem, England. Several potteries merged to become George Wade & Son, Ltd. early in the twentieth century and other potteries have been added through the years. The best known Wade pieces are the small figurines given away with Red Rose Tea and other promotional items. The Disney figures are listed in this book in the Disneyana category.

WADE
Figures

c. 1936+

Bank, Fawn 35.00
Bank, Pig, Sister, Green Dress 55.00
Figurine, Bear 3.00
Figurine, Beaver 2.00
Figurine, Camel... 2.00
Figurine, Cat.. 2.00
Figurine, Chimp 2.00
Figurine, Crocodile, 1953-1959.. 60.00
Figurine, Elephant, 1953-1959 .... 50.00
Figurine, Fawn, 1953-1959 .... 38.00
Figurine, Frog 4.00
Figurine, Georgie Porgie 95.00
Figurine, Goat, 1950s... 60.00
Figurine, Humpty-Dumpty 3.00
Figurine, Jerry.. 98.00
Figurine, Kangaroo.. 4.00
Figurine, Koala Bear 3.00
Figurine, Lamb, 1953-1959 .... 44.00
Figurine, Lion... 4.00
Figurine, Miss Muffet.. 8.00
Figurine, Mother Goose 10.00
Figurine, Nod... 95.00
Figurine, Pegasus 90.00
Figurine, Polar Bear 3.00
Figurine, Poodle, 1950s... 40.00
Figurine, Puss In Boots 4.00
Figurine, Raccoon, 1953-1959 .... 40.00
Figurine, Scamp, With Hat Box 50.00
Figurine, Snow White.. 120.00
Figurine, Squirrel 5.00
Figurine, St. Bernard, 1953-1959 .... 55.00

Figurine, Three Bears 16.00
Figurine, Tom 98.00
Figurine, Yogi Bear 90.00
Frame, Cutout, Wade, 3 3/4 x 2 1/2 In. 24.00
House, Picture Palace, Whimsey-On-Why 25.00
Huckleberry Hound 108.00
Jug, Johnnie Walker, Gold Trim 15.00
Jug, Water, Bombay London Dry Gin 19.00
Jug & Ashtray, Cutty Sark 15.00
Jug & Ashtray, Dewar's 15.00
Pipe Rest, Cairn 22.00
Pipe Rest, Setter 22.00
Pitcher, Pub, Beefeater Gin, White 25.00
Shaving Mug, 1909 Rolls-Royce 24.00
Sugar, Cover, Bramble Ware, Autumn Tints 28.00
Sugar & Creamer, Copper Luster, Hand Painted Floral 55.00
Tankard, Cadillac, 1/2 Pt. 15.00
Teapot, China Shop 60.00
Teapot, Tetley 24.00

WAHPETON POTTERY, see Rosemeade category

WALLACE NUTTING photographs are listed under Print, Nutting. His reproduction furniture is listed under Furniture.

WALRATH was a potter who worked in New York City; Rochester, New
York; and at the Newcomb Pottery in New Orleans, Louisiana. Frederick
Walrath died in 1920. Pieces listed here are from his Rochester period.

Walrath
Pottery

Bowl, Matte Gray, 8 In. 110.00
Figurine, Reclining Nude, Brown Matte Glaze, Green Matte Base, 3 In. 495.00
Flower Frog, Crouching Nude, Reticulated Base, Incised Mark, 5 3/4 x 5 1/4 In. 330.00
Inkwell-Pen Holder, Winged Angel, Matte Greens, Incised Mark, 1914, 7 1/2 x 6 In.... 550.00
Tile, Stylized Floral, Dark Green & Red, Olive Ground, Beaver Falls, 6 In.................... 748.00
Vase, Green Snowflake Crystalline & Cream Flambe Glaze, 9 1/2 In. 4125.00
Vase, Red Flowers, Blue Leaves, Blue Ground, Crystalline, 1911, Marked, 6 3/4 In. 523.00

WALT DISNEY, see Disneyana

WALTER, see A. Walter

WARWICK china was made in Wheeling, West Virginia, in a pottery working
from 1887 to 1951. Many pieces were made with hand painted or decal decorations. The most familiar Warwick has a shaded brown background. The
name *Warwick* is part of the mark and sometimes the mysterious word *IOGA*
is also included.

IOGA

Cuspidor, Brown & Yellow Flowers, IOGA, 8 In. 150.00
Mug, Fat Man... 115.00
Mug, Monk 115.00
Pitcher, Friar 145.00
Pitcher, Hand Painted Flowers, Sponged Gold Rim & Handle, 7 1/4 In. 55.00
Pitcher, Poppies, Leaves, Brown To Beige, Relief Base & Spout, 9 1/2 In. 98.00
Tankard & Mug, Dickens, Man Playing Guitar 300.00
Vase, Amber & Brown, White Reserve Young Woman Portrait, IOGA, 10 1/2 In. 50.00
Vase, Cockatoo, Gray, White, IOGA, 10 In. 165.00
Vase, Portrait, Orchid, 10 1/2 In. 225.00
Vase, Portrait, Red, IOGA, 11 1/2 In. 185.00
Vase, Red & Pink Roses, Twig Handles 195.00
Vase, Red Poppies, Leaves, Gold To Brown, Twisted Double Handles, 10 x 4 In.......... 185.00
Vase, Woman With Roses & Pearls, 11 1/2 In. 250.00

WATCH pockets held the pocket watch that was important in Victorian times
because it was not until World War I that the wristwatch was used. All types
of watches are collected: silver, gold, or plated. Watches are arranged by
company name or by style. Pocket watches are listed here; wristwatches are a
separate category.

A.L. Brequet, Chased Hunting Case, Child, Dog, Landscape, 15 Jewel, 18K 345.00
Accutron, Quartz, 14K Gold, 1st Edition, Box 875.00
Accutron, Railroad, Stainless Steel 175.00
American Watch Co., Coin Silver, Hunting Case, P.S. Bartlett, Key Wind, c.1866 .... 200.00
Barnes Smith & Co., Monaco Salon Depose 850.00
Bueche Girard, Musical, Alarm, 2 1/8 In. 70.00
C.H. Meylan, Chronograph, Open Face, Split Second Hands, 14K Gold 1250.00
C.H. Meylan, Dress, 19 Jewel, Platinum, 1920s 525.00
Columbus, Hunting Case, Size 6, 1897 .... 150.00
Cromwell, Outer Roulette Wheel Spins, 17 Jewel, 1960 .... 121.00
Elgin, 1905 .... 200.00
Elgin, Buffalo, 1894 .... 365.00
Elgin, Chief Of Police, Larned, Kansas, 1882 .... 585.00
Elgin, Cowboy Shooting Buffalo, 1879 .... 485.00
Elgin, Engraved Heart & Horseshoe, 14K Gold 38.00
Elgin, Floral Engraving, Presentation, Enameled Face, 14K Gold, 1901 .... 115.00
Elgin, GM Wheeler, Key Wind, Size 18 .... 115.00
Elgin, Hunting Case, Chain & Fob 150.00
Elgin, Hunting Case, Gold 100.00
Elgin, Hunting Case, Key Wind, Coin Silver 260.00
Elgin, Hunting Case, Size 0, 1903 .... 115.00
Elgin, Indian, Kneeling, Shooting Buffalo, 1879 .... 485.00
Elgin, National, Gold, Size 18 .... 175.00
Elgin, Open Face, Engraved Stork, Sweep Second Hand, 18K Gold 825.00
Elgin, Open Face, White Porcelain, Arabic Numerals, 17 Jewel, 1898 .... 145.00
Elgin, Shorthorn Bull, 1905 .... 325.00
Elgin, Woman's, Engraved, Box 85.00
Elgin, Woman's, Key Wind, Key 150.00
Elgin, Woman's, Slide Chain & Pin, Box 425.00
English, Butterfield Overland Dispatch Stage, Smokie Hills Route, 1840s 1450.00
Geneva, No. 488, 18K Yellow Gold, Oval,.43-In. Turquoise & Enameled Chain 1958.00
Golay-Leresche-Atfis & Fils, Open Face, Lapis Seal, Chased Case, Geneve 920.00
Hamilton, Model 23, Military Chronograph, 1942 .... 375.00
Hamilton, Swing-Out, 17 Jewel 115.00
Hamilton, Wadsworth, 14K Gold, 17 Jewel, 1939 .... 375.00
Hampden, General Stark, Hunting Case, Engraved, Floral & Scenic 250.00
Hampden, John Hancock, Hunting Case, 21 Jewel, c.1900 .... 200.00
Hampden, Presentation, Engraved Date, 1903, 23 Jewel, 14K Gold 302.00
Howard, 19 Jewel, Silver, Chain 275.00
Howard, Carried By Admiral Perry To Arctic, 23 Jewel, Aluminum Case 2200.00
Howard, Hunting Case, Presentation, Inscription, 1872, 18K Gold 467.00
Howard, Open Face, Monogram, 17 Jewel, 14K Gold 192.00
Howard, Open Face, Tooled Face, 23 Jewel, 14K Gold 500.00
Illinois, 21 Jewel, 1906 Special 230.00
Illinois, 21 Jewel, Glass Back 275.00
Illinois, Bunn Special, 10K Gold Plate 275.00
John C. Heppert, Railroad, 21 Ruby Jewel, Lever Set 150.00
Lord Elgin, Open Face, 14K Gold, 17 Jewel, With Chain & 10K Gold Penknife 195.00
Marshal & Bragg, Pendant, Woman's, Gold-Filled 95.00
Monte Carlo, c.1890 .... 475.00
Monte Carlo At Home, Beveled Glass, Jeweled Stones 550.00
Omega, Open Face, Porcelain Dial, 14K Gold, Swing-Out Case 395.00
Patek Philippe, Open Face, White Enamel Dial, Arabic Numerals, No. 134777 .... 1495.00
Patek Philippe, Wolf Tooth Wind, Open Face, 18K Gold, Minute Repeating, c.1900 ... 8165.00
Ravina, 17 Jewels, Diamond Case, Diamond Band, 18K White Gold 920.00
Roulette, American Pedometer Co., Wheel Spins, Cardboard Dial, 1920 .... 121.00
Roulette, Monte Carlo At Home, Enameled Dial, Beveled Glass, 1890 .... 550.00
Roulette, St. Louis Expo, 1904 .... 520.00
Roulette, U.S.A., & 00 Slots, Cardboard Dial, Beveled Glass, 1900 .... 467.00
Universal Geneve, Man's, Leather Strap, 18K White Gold, 1950s 595.00
Vacheron & Constantin, Open Face, 18K Gold, Replaced Crystal 660.00
Vacheron & Constantin, Open Face, Circular White Enamel Dial, No. 213333 .... 2645.00
Waltham, Bucking Horse, 1908 .... 465.00

Waltham, Buffalo On Prairie, 1907 .... 365.00
Waltham, Hunting Case, 14K Gold 440.00
Waltham, Hunting Case, Coin Silver.. 82.00
Waltham, Hunting Case, White Circular Enamel Dial, Roman Numerals, 14K Gold..... 431.00
Waltham, Miner, Gold, 1976 .... 550.00
Waltham, Open Face, 17 Jewel, 14K Yellow Gold 230.00
Waltham, Open Face, Arabic Numerals, 17 Jewel, 1891............................ 175.00
Waltham, Panhandle, Dodge City, 1878 .... 495.00
Waltham, Pendant, Woman's, Gold Hunting Case, c.1903...................... 120.00
Waltham, Woman's, 14K Gold, Open Face, Stem Wind, No. 18058920 ...... 165.00
Waltham, Woman's, 14K Yellow Gold, Machine Engraved, Presentation.......... 82.00
Waltham, Woman's, Floral, Yellow Gold, Engraved Ruth Heseltine, Delaware, Ohio .. 38.00
Waltham, Woman's, Hunting Case, Allover Engraving, Chain With Slide, c.1892........ 295.00
Westclox, Scotty, Dollar.. 25.00
Woman's, Open Face, Silver, Gold, Monogrammed, Owl Stamp.................... 247.00

WATCH FOBS were worn on watch chains. They were popular during Victorian times and after. Many styles, especially advertising designs, are still made today.

Abraham Fur Co., St. Louis ....95.00 to 150.00
Adams Machinery 35.00
Allis Chalmers, Pictures Tractor..35.00 to 60.00
Armour Meats, Steer Head ....25.00 to 30.00
Babe Ruth, Celluloid, Scorekeeper, Strap Type 160.00
Bailey, Banks & Biddle, Woman's, Pave-Diamond, Platinum Pearl Chain.................... 4332.00
Baseball Diamond Shape 27.00
Beaded, Indian 45.00
Blatz Brewing, Chain With Spinner.. 145.00
Brass, Floral, Hammered Border, Leather Strap, 5 x 1 3/4 In......................... 125.00
Buffalo Bill, Busts Of Wild West Partners, Brass ....50.00 to 85.00
Bull Durham Cigars, Strap Type 150.00
Buster Brown Shoes 200.00
Case Eagle, Mother-Of-Pearl 250.00
Case Knives 57.00
Caterpillar, Brass & Leather.. 22.50
Caterpillar, Diesel Engines, Brass 55.00
Caterpillar, Tractor, Brass 45.00
Chased Foliate Frame, Angelic Female Busts, 14K Gold, Amethyst 1210.00
Colt Firearms, Horse ....145.00 to 195.00
Colt Firearms, Sterling Silver.. 240.00
Confederate, Biloxi, 1930... 150.00
Delaval 45.00
Dodge Brothers Motor Vehicles, 3-Color Enamel............................... 95.00
Dominion Cartridge Co., Presented As Trophy In Shooting Match 575.00
Dr Pepper, Strap Type.. 150.00
Dutch Cleanser, Brass, Strap Type.. 95.00
Dutch Cleanser, Porcelain, Strap Type 125.00
Elk's Tooth, 14K Gold Mount 90.00
Gallup Saddlery, Pueblo, Colo. 150.00
Gardner Denver Jackhammer 39.00
Green River Whiskey 50.00
Harley-Davidson ....55.00 to 125.00
Indian Motorcycle 125.00
John Deere, Mother-Of-Pearl 250.00
Levi Strauss, Celluloid, Mirror, Strap Type 250.00
Lima Shovels 35.00
Massye-Harris, 1950s.. 35.00
Oil Well Supply 95.00
Patton Brewing Co., Celluloid On Metal 45.00
Playing Card, 8 Enameled Suit Signs, Gold Plated, 1920, 6 In. 121.00
Saddle 95.00
Shapleigh Hardware 80.00
Spirit Of St. Louis & Airship 65.00

Tenison Saddle Co.	225.00
Texas Cowboy Reunion, Strap Type, 1930	150.00
United Commercial Travelers, Porcelain & Metal	35.00
Woman's, Hunter, 14K Gold, Enameled Cherub Other Side...........................	432.00

WATERFORD type glass resembles the famous glass made from 1783 to 1851 in the Waterford Glass Works in Ireland. It is a clear glass that was often decorated by cutting. Modern glass is being made again in Waterford, Ireland, and is marketed under the name *Waterford*.

Bowl, Lismore, 7 In.	143.75
Carafe, Lismore..	68.00
Carving Set, Sticker, Box, 2 Piece	200.00
Compote, Knobbed Stem, Scalloped & Lobed Rim, 9 In., Pair....................	402.50
Decanter, 10 In.	167.00
Decanter, Lismore .... 150.00 to 215.00
Decanter, Ship's, Signed, 10 x 7 1/2 In. .... 175.00 to 190.00
Decanter, Vodka..	128.00
Flute, Champagne, Curraghmore, 8 Oz.	110.00
Goblet, Ovoid Cut Bowl, Tapering Stem, 8 In., 8 Piece	258.00
Lamp, Kerosene, 18 In., 2 Piece	285.00
Paperweight, Pyramid..	42.00
Pitcher, Kylemore	150.00
Plate, Buzz Stars, Square, 8 1/2 In.	85.00
Pokal, Flutes & Diamond Point Band, 12 In.	195.00
Salt, Boat Shape, 2 1/2 x 3 1/2 In.	95.00
Urn, Cover, 19th Century, 15 In.	110.00
Vase, Ferns & Leaves, Frosted, 12 In.	375.00

WATT family members bought the Globe pottery of Crooksville, Ohio, in 1922. They made pottery mixing bowls and dishes of the type made by Globe. In 1935 they changed the production and made the pieces with the freehand decorations that are popular with collectors today. Apple, Starflower, Rooster, Red & Blue Tulip, and Autumn Foliage are the best-known patterns. Apple, the most popular pattern, can be dated from the leaves. Originally, the apples had three leaves; after 1958 two leaves were used. The plant closed in 1965. For more information, see *Kovels' Depression Glass & American Dinnerware Price List*.

Baker, Apple, No. 54..	250.00
Baker, Apple, No. 66..	35.00
Baker, Apple, No. 96..	35.00
Baker, Cover, Apple, No. 601	155.00
Baker, Rooster, Rectangular, No. 85	1100.00
Bean Cup, Apple, No. 75	225.00
Bean Pot, 3 Leaves, Apple, No. 76	165.00
Bean Pot, American Red Bud, No. 76..	85.00
Bean Pot, Teardrop, Yellow Over-Glaze	279.00
Bowl, 4-Petal Starflower, Tab-Handled, No. 18..	125.00
Bowl, 5-Petal Starflower, No. 7	45.00
Bowl, 5-Petal Starflower, No. 8	45.00
Bowl, Apple, No. 39, Slant Side, 13 In.	425.00
Bowl, Apple, No. 7	45.00
Bowl, Apple, No. 73	75.00
Bowl, Autumn Foliage, No. 39	150.00
Bowl, Dutch Tulip, No. 8, Advertising	165.00
Bowl, Pansy, No. 7..	20.00
Bowl, Salad, Kitch-N-Queen, No. 73	95.00
Bowl, Salad, Teardrop, No. 74	40.00
Bowl, Salad, Tulip, No. 73..	245.00
Bowl, Spaghetti, Apple, No. 24...	195.00
Bowl, Spaghetti, Apple, No. 39...	1000.00
Bowl, Spaghetti, Pansy, No. 39.. 45.00 to 65.00
Bowl, Starflower, No. 6	50.00

Bowl, Starflower, No. 18, Stick Handle 125.00
Canister, Apple, No. 72 ....495.00 to 550.00
Canister, Coffee, Black & White Stenciled Snowflake, No. 82 .... 75.00
Canister, Coffee, Starflower, No. 82 .... 350.00
Canister, Teardrop, No. 72 .... 550.00
Casserole, Cover, Moon & Star, 1940s 50.00
Casserole, Cover, Teardrop, Square 495.00
Casserole, Starflower 125.00
Chip And Dip Set, Double Apple, No. 120 .... 550.00
Cookie Jar, Apple & Pear, Wooden Cover 110.00
Cookie Jar, Apple, No. 21 .... 400.00
Cookie Jar, Apple, No. 503 ....435.00 to 450.00
Cookie Jar, Policeman ....1350.00 to 1850.00
Cookie Jar, Starflower, No. 21 .... 275.00
Cookie Jar, Starflower, No. 21, Missing Lid 65.00
Cookie Jar, Tulip, No. 503 ....350.00 to 425.00
Creamer, Apple, 2 Leaves, No. 62 .... 95.00
Creamer, Apple, 3 Leaves, No. 62 .... 125.00
Creamer, Autumn Foliage, No. 62 ....225.00 to 290.00
Creamer, Double Apple, No. 62 ....450.00 to 650.00
Creamer, Mason City 300.00
Creamer, Morning Glory 600.00
Creamer, Orchard Ware, No. 62, Brown, White Drip 475.00
Creamer, Rooster, No. 62 .... 225.00
Creamer, Teardrop 150.00
Creamer, Tulip, No. 62 ....230.00 to 275.00
Crock, Cheese, Cover, Dutch Tulip, No. 80 .... 575.00
Crock, Cheese, Dutch Tulip, No. 80 .... 900.00
Cup & Saucer, Pansy 95.00
Dutch Oven, Apple, No. 70 .... 235.00
Ice Bucket, Apple, 3 Leaves, No. 59 ....295.00 to 325.00
Ice Bucket, Apple, No. 59 ....200.00 to 350.00
Ice Bucket, Starflower, No. 59 .... 85.00
Jar, Grease, Apple, 3 Leaves, No. 47 .... 725.00
Jar, Grease, Starflower, No. 01 .... 100.00
Keg, Iced Nestea, No. 400-2 .... 235.00
Mixing Bowl, Apple, No. 5, Ribbed 55.00
Mixing Bowl, Apple, No. 64 .... 35.00
Mixing Bowl, Apple, No. 65 .... 35.00
Mixing Bowl, Basket Weave, Rose, No. 9 .... 25.00
Mixing Bowl, Kitch-N-Queen, Ribbed, No. 9 .... 65.00
Mixing Bowl, Tulip, No. 64 .... 90.00
Mixing Bowl, Tulip, No. 65 .... 90.00
Mixing Bowl Set, Apple, Nos. 63-65 .... 165.00
Mixing Bowl Set, Basket Weave, Nested, 5 Piece 120.00
Mixing Bowl Set, Double Apple, Nested, Nos. 4-7, 4 Piece 475.00
Mixing Bowl Set, Pansy, 3 Piece 100.00
Mug, Heirloom, No. 801 .... 15.00
Mug, Starflower 150.00
Mug, Starflower, No. 501 ....50.00 to 90.00
Nappy, Apple, No. 6 .... 45.00
Nappy, Double Apple, No. 07 .... 125.00
Pepper Shaker, Starflower 65.00
Pie Plate, Apple, 3 Leaves, No. 33, 10th Anniversary 1962 Georges Bakery 165.00
Pie Plate, Apple, Advertising 265.00
Pie Plate, Autumn Foliage, No. 33 .... 155.00
Pitcher, 4-Petal Starflower, No. 15 ....225.00 to 250.00
Pitcher, 5-Petal Starflower, No. 15 .... 75.00
Pitcher, Apple No. 15 ....65.00 to 75.00
Pitcher, Apple, 2 Leaves, No. 16 .... 140.00
Pitcher, Apple, 3 Leaves, No. 15 .... 100.00
Pitcher, Apple, 3 Leaves, No. 16 .... 120.00
Pitcher, Apple, Commemorative, 1994 .... 425.00

Pitcher, Apple, No. 16 .... 105.00 to 135.00
Pitcher, Apple, No. 17, Ice Lip 150.00
Pitcher, Apple, No. 17, No Ice Lip, 2 Leaves, Shaded .... 115.00 to 125.00
Pitcher, Apple, No. 69 .... 400.00
Pitcher, Apple, Rough Texture, Purple 650.00
Pitcher, Autumn Foliage, No. 15 .... 130.00
Pitcher, Autumn Foliage, Peshitco Feed Mill, No. 17 .... 195.00
Pitcher, Cherry .... 80.00 to 95.00
Pitcher, Cherry, No. 15 .... 145.00
Pitcher, Refrigerator, Rooster, No. 69 .... 400.00
Pitcher, Rio Rose, No. 15 .... 180.00
Pitcher, Rooster, No. 15 .... 175.00
Pitcher, Rooster, No. 16 .... 190.00
Pitcher, Rooster, No. 69 .... 695.00
Pitcher, Starflower, No. 15 .... 60.00
Pitcher, Starflower, No. 16 .... 45.00 to 85.00
Pitcher, Starflower, No. 17 .... 160.00
Pitcher, Teardrop, No. 15 .... 65.00 to 75.00
Pitcher, Tulip, No. 16 .... 165.00 to 210.00
Pitcher, Tulip, No. 17, Ice Lip 325.00
Plate, Apple, No. 49 .... 400.00
Platter, Autumn Foliage, No. 31 .... 185.00
Platter, Pansy, 15 In. 95.00
Platter, Pansy, Cut Leaf, 13 In. 85.00
Salt & Pepper, Apple, Hourglass 300.00
Salt & Pepper, Apple, Hourglass, Advertising 285.00
Salt & Pepper, Starflower 165.00
Salt & Pepper, Starflower, Barrel .... 125.00 to 150.00
Salt & Pepper, Starflower, Hourglass 205.00
Saltshaker, Apple, Hourglass, Advertising 150.00
Sugar, Apple, No. 98, Ackley Feed Mill, Ackley, Iowa 250.00
Sugar, Cover, Apple, 3 Leaves, No. 98 .... 600.00
Teapot, Bottle, Milk, Double Baby Face, Dairylee 52.00

WAVE CREST glass is a white glassware manufactured by the Pairpoint Manufacturing Company of New Bedford, Massachusetts, and some French factories. It was decorated by the C. F. Monroe Company of Meriden,
Connecticut. The glass was painted in pastel colors and decorated with flowers. The name *Wave Crest* was used after 1898.

**WAVE CREST
WARE**

Biscuit Jar, Hand Painted Violets, Veins & Leaves, Pink Ground 200.00
Biscuit Jar, Lilac Blossoms, Leaves & Branches 250.00
Biscuit Jar, Wild Rose, Egg Crate Shape 250.00
Bowl, 2 Handles, 1 1/2 In. 175.00
Box, Collar & Cuff, Egg Crate Shape, Cream Ground, 7 In. 950.00
Box, Puffy, Metal-Trim Top, 3 1/4 x 6 1/2 x 4 1/4 In. 450.00
Box, Robin On Lid, Hand Painted Floral Design On Sides, 5 x 5 3/4 x 6 1/2 In. 1850.00
Box, Round, Courting Scene, 4 1/2 x 6 In. 950.00
Box, Swirl Pattern, Enameled White & Blue Flowers, Leaves, Hinged Lid, 4 In. 275.00
Compote, 2 Handles, 3 In. 225.00
Fernery, Wild Roses, Veins, Beading, Lace Scallops, Marked, 11 x 8 In. 975.00
Humidor, Cigars, Blown Out Scrolls, Floral, Blue-Green Ground, Marked, 6 x 5 In. 895.00
Ice Bucket, Wild Roses, Light Blue Ground, 13 1/4 In. 1020.00
Jar, Dresser, Dancing Storks On Cover, Gilt Metal Rims & Clasp, 3 1/2 In. 1150.00
Jardiniere, Flowers, Hand Painted, Pink Ground, Footed, 8 1/2 In. 895.00
Pin Jar, Florals, Metal Band 88.00
Ring Box, Enameled Flowers, Original Lining 175.00
Sugar Shaker, Helmschmied Swirl 485.00
Tobacco Jar, Yellow, Tobacco In Gold, Embossing, Floral, 5 1/4 In. 675.00
Toothpick, Enameled Flowers, Satin Glass, Gilded Metal Base, 2 1/4 In. 220.00
Vase, Blue & Pink Floral, Green Enamel Scrolls, Beaded Top, Marked, 9 In. 275.00
Vase, Pink, White Dots, Blue Forget-Me-Nots, Metal Feet, 8 /34 In. 670.00
Vase, Trumpet Form, Floral Design, Mark, C.F.M. Co., 9 1/2 In. 1100.00
Water Set, Pink Apple Blossoms, Sailboat Scenes, 6 Piece 250.00

WEAPONS listed here include instruments of combat other than guns, knives, rifles, or swords. Firearms are not listed in this book. Knives and swords are listed in their own sections.

Lance, Revolutionary War, Iron Head, Wooden Haft	425.00
Spear, Dayak, Head Hunter, Tapered Wooden Handle, Iron Blade	275.00
Spear, Indonesian, Leaf Shape Blade, Upper Part In Brass, 10 3/4 In.	245.00

WEATHER VANES were used in seventeenth-century Boston. The direction of the wind was an indication of coming weather, important to the seafaring and farming communities. By the mid-nineteenth century, commercial weather vanes were made of metal. Today's collectors often consider weather vanes to be examples of folk art, even though they may not have been handmade.

2 Men In A Boat, Sperm Whale, Carved, Metal Base, 1925, 46 In.	2350.00
Arrow, Copper, Full-Bodied, 58 x 23 In.	431.00
Arrow, Stars Design	1650.00
Blacksmith, Shoeing Horse, Penna.	900.00
Bull, Gilt Copper, Mass., 40 In.	9500.00
Cow, Copper Spire, Zinc Figure, Cast Iron Arrow, Insulating Ball, 55 In.	165.00
Cow, Sheet Metal, Early 20th Century, 22 In.	460.00
Cow, Zinc, Cast Iron & Copper Arrow, Lightning Rod Base, 49 In.	195.00
Dove, On Ball, Arrow Base, 12 x 13 1/2 In.	8500.00
Eagle, Copper, 19 1/2 In.	460.00
Eagle, Iron & Bronze, 15-In. Wingspan	2250.00
Ewe, Standing, Iron	3190.00
Fireman's Pumper, Copper	19500.00
Fish, Wooden Body, Lead & Copper Fittings, 31 In.	205.00
Flying Eagle, Copper, 46-In. Wingspan	2145.00
Fox, Running, Directionals, Sheet Steel, 30 In.	550.00
Gabriel, Sheet Metal, 48 In.	3335.00
Globe, Bronze, Fluted Pedestal, Stone, 5 Ft.	1495.00
Goat Bucking & Farmer, Iron, 4 x 3 Ft.	4000.00
Goose, Flying, Iron	250.00
Hand Saw, Wooden, Copper Base, 19th Century, 23 1/2 In.	489.00
Hawk, Black, Copper, Stamped, Gilt Verdigris Surface, 24 1/2 In.	1840.00
Horse, 1 Front Leg Up, Cast Head, 14 In.	2750.00
Horse, 19th Century	2350.00
Horse, Copper, Cast Iron Head	2050.00
Horse, Copper, Snow Iron Works, Boston, Original Packing Crate, 30 1/2 In.	920.00
Horse, Galloping, Copper, Hollow, 29 In.	632.00
Horse, Molded Copper, Zinc Head, 1820s, 27 x 33 In.	8250.00
Horse, Painted, J.Howard & Co., Mass., c.1880, 18 In.	4000.00
Horse, Pine, Silhouette, Cutout, 33 x 36 1/2 In.	110.00
Horse, Running, Black Hawk, Gilt Copper, 19th Century, 24 1/2 In.	460.00
Horse, Running, Black Paint, Molded Copper, A.J. Harris & Co., Boston, 29 In.	575.00
Horse, Running, Gilt Copper, 19th Century, 29 1/2 In.	1265.00
Horse, Running, Zinc & Copper, 26 In.	2300.00
Horse, Standing, Copper Molded, Cast Zinc Head	8250.00
Horse, Trotting, Zinc, Hollow, Gold Paint	325.00
Horse, Zinc	235.00
Horse, Zinc, Cast Iron Directionals, 14 1/2 In.	325.00
Indian, On Rearing Horse, Spear, Iron, Painted Gray, 19th Century, 23 x 29 In.	403.00
Indian, Pontiac, 1950s, 55 In.	1200.00
Locomotive, Wrought Iron	470.00
Pig, Sheet Metal, Paint Decorated, 19th Century, 42 In.	2070.00
Plane, Green & Yellow Sprayed, Quebec, 1960	395.00
Polar Bear, Swell-Bodied, Metal Ears & Eyes, Gilded Copper, 19 In.	3450.00
Roadster, Zinc, Cast Iron & Copper Base, Arrow, On Wooden Base, 22 x 21 In.	77.00
Rooster, Cast Iron Body, Sheet Metal Tail, 22 1/2 In.	1000.00
Rooster, Copper, 19th Century, 24 In.	1495.00
Rooster, Full-Bodied, Copper, Gilt Verdigris Surface, 23 In.	1840.00
Ship, Painted, Carved, 39 In.	115.00
Silhouette, Indian In A Canoe, Riveted Sheet Zinc, Primitive, 39 In.	495.00

Swan, Wooden, White Paint, Hole Eyes, Open Beak, 1889, 15 x 70 In. 8300.00

WEBB glass is made by Thomas Webb & Sons of Stourbridge, England. Many types of art and cameo glass were made by them during the Victorian era. The factory is still producing glass. Webb Burmese and Webb Peachblow are special colored glasswares of the Victorian era. They are listed at the end of this section. Glassware that is not Burmese or Peachblow is included here.

Webb

Finger Bowl, Diamond Quilted, Raspberry To Pink, White Lining, Crimped 275.00
Flask, Bamboo, Silver Gilt Screw Lid, Signed, c.1890, 6 3/4 In. 690.00
Flask, Swan's Head, Silver Gilt Screw Lid, Signed, c.1884, 5 3/4 In. 3740.00
Perfume Bottle, Lay Down, Floral Sprays, Feather Border, Hinged Cover, 4 In. 978.00
Punch Cup, Rainbow Stain, Signed 85.00
Snuff Bottle, Deer Within Cloud Band, Landscape, Metal Stopper, c.1890, 3 In. 5460.00
Vase, Allover Carved White Flowers, Branches & Leaves, White On White, 4 3/4 In. 1250.00
Vase, Basket Weave, Mother-Of-Pearl, Satin Glass, Brown To Tan, 7 x 5 1/2 In. 850.00
Vase, Cut Trumpet Flowers, Red & White, Footed, Citron Ground, 6 In. 2850.00
Vase, Cut Trumpet Flowers, Red & White, Footed, Citron Ground, Marked, 6 In. 3438.00
Vase, Dimpled Each Side, Gold Prunus Blossoms, Cream Interior, 4 In. 245.00
Vase, Gold Florals, Gold Butterfly On Back, Ivory Glass, 3 3/8 In. 175.00
Vase, Gold Prunus & Butterfly, White Lining, 4 1/2 In. 110.00
Vase, Gold Prunus Blossoms, Gold Butterfly, Yellow Satin Glass, 3 x 4 1/2 In. 325.00
Vase, Holly, Cobalt Blue, Gilt Ground, Cameo, 6 3/4 In. 750.00
Vase, Oxblood, Raised Gold Decoration, White Liner, Signed, 8 In. 420.00
Vase, Raised Gold, Snowball On Leafy Branch, Butterflies, Turquoise, 8 In. 550.00
Vase, Red & White Over Yellow, Flowering Geranium, Butterfly, Footed, 9 In. 1150.00
Vase, Waisted Neck Shirt Trumpet Flowers & Grasses, Signed, 6 In. 225.00

WEBB BURMESE is a colored Victorian glass made by Thomas Webb & Sons of Stourbridge, England, from 1886.

Bowl, 5 Point Petal Top, 2 1/4 x 3 1/2 In. 165.00
Fairy Lamp, Clarke Base, 3 3/4 In. 105.00
Fairy Lamp, Vines, Leaves & Red Berries On Shade, Clarke Base, 4 3/4 x 4 In. 475.00
Lamp, Oil, Yellow Acorns, Fall Colored Oak Leaves, Miniature 9790.00
Perfume Bottle, Purple Flowers, Sterling Top, 3 1/2 In. 615.00
Rose Bowl, 8-Crimp Top, 2 5/8 x 2 7/8 In. 200.00
Vase, 7 Point Petal Top, Signed, 3 1/4 In. 220.00
Vase, 10 Vertical Ribs, 3 1/2 In. 135.00
Vase, Black Bands, Garland Of Flowers, 3 1/2 In. 275.00
Vase, Flower-Form, Foliage & Berries, Crimped Edge, 2 3/4 x 3 1/2 In. 625.00
Vase, Flowers & Butterflies, 9 In., Pair 4000.00
Vase, Ruffled, 3 7/8 x 2 7/8 In. 225.00
Vase, Ruffled, Salmon To Yellow, Acid-Finish, 3 3/4 x 3 In. 195.00
Vase, Salmon Pink To Yellow, Ruffled Rim, 3 3/4 In. 195.00

WEBB PEACHBLOW is a colored Victorian glass made by Thomas Webb & Sons of Stourbridge, England, from 1885.

Bowl, Acid Finish, Cream Lining, Oval, Rose To Pink, Pinched Middle, 3 x 5 In. 235.00
Rose Bowl, Gold Flowers & Butterfly, 2 1/2 In. 380.00
Vase, Bird & Flowers, Off-White Lining, Red To Pink, Gold Leaves, 5 x 3 1/2 In. 495.00
Vase, Gold Butterfly & Flowers, 5 1/4 In. 295.00
Vase, Owl Perched On Branch, Acorns, Flying Bat, 14 1/2 In. 2600.00

WEDGWOOD, one of the world's most successful potteries, was founded by Josiah Wedgwood, who was considered a cripple by his brother and was forbidden to work at the family business. The pottery was established in England in 1759. A large variety of wares has been made, including the well-known jasperware, basalt, creamware, and even a limited amount of porcelain. There are two kinds of jasperware. One is made from two colors of clay, the other is made from one color of clay with a color dip to create the contrast in design. The firm is still in business. Other Wedgwood pieces may be listed under Flow Blue, Majolica, or in other porcelain categories.

WEDGWOOD

Ashtray, Jasperware, Terra-Cotta 38.00

Biscuit Jar, Jasperware, Tricolor, Scrolled Banding, Signed, 5 In. 862.00
Bowl, Black Basalt, Foliated Band, Dancing Classical Maidens, 1872, 8 3/4 In. 1200.00
Bowl, Black Basalt, Half-Spherical, Ring Foot, 18th Century, 10 1/4 x 4 1/4 In............. 290.00
Bowl, Creamware, Black Transfer, Nautical & Military Subjects, c.1800, 9 1/2 In. 315.00
Bowl, Creamware, Leaf, Acorn & Berry Design, Oval, 19th Century, 12 1/4 In.............. 125.00
Bowl, Dragon Luster, 8 In. 900.00
Bowl, Dragon Luster, Mother-Of-Pearl Exterior, Signed, 1925, 8 3/4 In. 690.00
Bowl, Dragon Luster, Orange Outside, Blue Inside, 5 1/2 In. 425.00
Bowl, Fairyland Luster, Black, Leapfrogging Elves, Marked, c.1925, 3 7/8 In. 1150.00
Bowl, Fairyland Luster, Butterflies, Octagonal, 7 3/4 In. 415.00
Bowl, Fairyland Luster, Fiddler In Tree, Octagonal, Signed, c.1925, 8 In. 1400.00
Bowl, Fairyland Luster, Poplar Trees, Black Sky Exterior, Signed, c.1925, 11 In. 3700.00
Bowl, Flame Luster, Butterflies, 7 In. 925.00
Bowl, Hummingbird Luster, Flying Geese Border, Signed, 1925, 10 In. 430.00
Bowl, Lobster, Enamel Design, Ocean Foliage Transfer, Lobster Feet, c.1864, 10 In. ... 290.00
Bowl, Salad, With Servers, Yellow, Jasper Dip, 8 1/2 In. 635.00
Box, Cover, Round, 3 1/4 x 3 1/8 In... 145.00
Box, Jasperware, Dark Blue, 3 In. 65.00
Box, Jasperware, Scalloped, White On Solid Light Blue 65.00
Bust, David Garrick, Black Basalt, Raised Circular Base, Marked, 4 In. 490.00
Bust, George Moore, Carrara, c.1859, 14 1/4 In. 430.00
Bust, George Washington, Black Basalt, Impressed Title & Mark, 18 In. 1725.00
Bust, James Watt, Carrara, Signed, c.1859, 15 In. 290.00
Bust, Marcus Aurelius, Black Basalt, Wooden Base, c.1775, 15 3/8 In. 2600.00
Bust, Milton, Black Basalt, Signed, 1850s, 13 1/4 In. 920.00
Bust, Minerva, Black Basalt, 19th Century, Signed, 18 1/2 In. 1955.00
Bust, Minerva, Black Basalt, Marble & Silver Stand, 1830s, 3 1/2 In. 430.00
Bust, Robert Burns, Carrara, Signed, c.1859, 14 1/2 In. 518.00
Bust, Shakespeare, Black Basalt, Circular Base, 19th Century, 4 In. 375.00
Bust, Venus, Black Basalt, Marble Base, 19th Century, 3 3/4 In. 400.00
Candlestick, Black Basalt, Column Shape, Garlands, 11 In., Pair 850.00
Candlestick, Flaring Bobeche, Acanthus Leaves, Creamware, 1790, 10 In., Pair 1150.00
Canister, Cover, White Muses Below Florets, Signed, 5 In., Pair 485.00
Cann & Saucer, 3 Color, Running Laurel, Leaf Border, Signed, 2 1/2 In. 1610.00
Chop Plate, Creamware, Green Enamel Edge, 18th Century, 18 1/2 In. 475.00
Coffeepot, Bullfinch, Wellesley, No. 3217 .... 185.00
Compote, Blue & White, 1966.. 195.00
Compote, Pearlware, Nautilus Shell Form, 9 1/2 In. 385.00
Creamer, Dancing Cherubs, Animal-Head Spout 65.00
Cup & Saucer, Butterfly Luster, Blue, After Dinner 295.00
Cup & Saucer, Jasperware, Crimson, White Classical Relief, Signed, c.1920 .... 895.00
Cup & Saucer, Queensware, Shell Edge, Cream & Lavender 15.00
Cup & Saucer, Terra-Cotta, 1957 .... 195.00
Decanter, Shadow, White..45.00 to 50.00
Dessert Set, Dolphin Pedestal, Tortoiseshell Glaze, Reticulated Fret Borders............... 6037.00
Dessert Set, Strawberry Design, Cream Ground, 14 Piece.. 440.00
Dinner & Dessert Set, Creamware, Nursery, c.1820... 2800.00
Dish, Classical Figures, Heart Shape, c.1920, 4 1/2 In.. 395.00
Dish, Game, Drabware, Rabbit Handle, Liner, 12 In... 770.00
Dish, Inkstand Boat Shape, Viking Head, Swan Ends, 2 Ink Pots, Enamel, 10 1/4 In..... 805.00
Dish, Jasperware, Heart-Shaped, Crimson, Classical Relief, Floral Border, 4 1/2 In. 230.00
Dish, Jasperware, Lilac, Stilton Cheese, Stand, White Classical Relief, 10 1/2 In. 430.00
Dish, Stilton Cheese, White Classical & Floral Relief, Lilac, 10 1/2 In. 200.00
Figurine, Black Cat, Basalt, c.1913, 3 1/2 In... 550.00
Figurine, Cupid, Black Basalt, Rocky Circular Base, Signed, 8 In................................. 490.00
Figurine, Faun, Black Basalt, c.1860, 16 5/16 In. 1495.00
Figurine, Girl On Blue Base, Coat & Hat, Yellow Curls, 5 1/2 In. 165.00
Figurine, Infant, Head Resting On Basket Of Fruit, Black Basalt, Marked, 4 7/8 In....... 1495.00
Figurine, Infant, On Stomach, Black Basalt, Rectangular Base, c.1800, 4 7/8 In............ 865.00
Figurine, Mercury On A Rock, Black Basalt, c.1880, 18 1/2 In..................................... 2300.00
Figurine, Raven, Black Basalt, Free-Form Base, Signed, 4 1/4 In. 460.00
Finger Bowl, Butterfly Luster, Interior Flying Butterfly, 2 3/4 x 4 1/4 In. 165.00
Finger Bowl, Dragon Luster, Interior Dragon, 2 x 3 1/2 In. 165.00

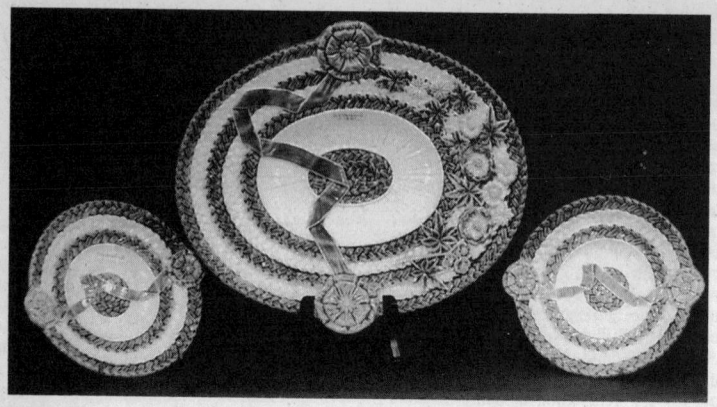

Wedgwood, Serving Set, Ribbon & Bow, Platter, 8 Dishes, Majolica

Flowerpot, Blue Jasper Dip, White Bands, Ring Handles, Impressed, 4 1/2 In.	80.00
Goblet, Moonlight Luster, Signed, c.1815, 3 5/8 In.	230.00
Inkstand, Classical Figures, Dark Blue, Marked, 1 1/4 x 2 In.	165.00
Jar, Black Basalt, Classical Figures, Marked, 4 1/2 In.	200.00
Jardiniere, White Classical Relief, Lilac, Signed, 6 1/4 In.	400.00
Jug, Classical Figures, Dark Blue & White, Portland, c.1840, 7 3/4 In.	395.00
Jug, Cream, Fallow Deer, 5 1/4 In.	103.00
Jug, Doric, White Classical Relief, Hinged Pewter Lid, Lilac, Signed, 6 In.	515.00
Lamp, Oil, Jasperware, Green, White Classical Relief, Brass, 15 1/2 In.	315.00
Letter Opener, Bust Of Christ, Black Basalt, Ivory Blade, Marked, 9 1/4 In.	230.00
Loving Cup, 3 Handles, Green, White Classical Decoration	90.00
Medallion, Bust, Catherine II & Michel Le Tellier, Jasperware, 4 1/4 In., Pair	319.00
Mug, Charles, Basalt, 1969	60.00
Pitcher, Chusan, Flow Blue, 9 In.	175.00
Pitcher, Cider, Band Of Acorn & Oak Leaves, Loop Handle, Signed, 4 1/2 x 6 In.	135.00
Pitcher, Classical Design, Jasperware, 1950s	60.00
Pitcher, Crimson Jasper, White Classical Relief, c.1920, 8 1/2 In.	345.00
Pitcher, Green Jasperware, Franklin & Washington Heads, 3 3/4 In.	325.00
Pitcher, Green Jasperware, Ladies & Cupids, Grapes At Rim, 6 1/2 x 4 In.	165.00
Pitcher, Jasper Dip, Crimson, Classical Relief, Rope Twist Handle, Marked, 5 In.	520.00
Pitcher, Jasperware, Blue, 1935, 2 1/2 In.	85.00
Pitcher, Jasperware, Crimson, Classical Figures	725.00
Pitcher, Silver Luster, Fallow Deer, Small	95.00
Plaque, Fairyland Luster, Elves In Pine Tree, 1917, 10 7/8 In.	4887.00
Plaque, Green Jasper, Dancing Hours, Wooden Frame, c.1840, 3 1/2 x 9 In.	520.00
Plaque, Tricolor Jasper, Discovery Of Achilles, Signed, 8 1/4 x 23 In.	2070.00
Plate, Black Knight Exchanges With Friar, 10 In.	65.00
Plate, Christmas, 1969, Windsor Castle, Jasperware	100.00 to 225.00
Plate, Christmas, 1970, Christmas In Trafalgar Square, Jasperware	25.00
Plate, Creamware, Black Transfer Flowers, Bird, 9 1/2 In.	50.00
Plate, Creamware, Pierced Border, Rope Twist Rim, Central Figure, 9 In., 8 Piece	880.00
Plate, J.C.J. Van Speyk, Dutch City Arms, 5 In.	75.00
Plate, Man On Moon	35.00
Plate, Mothers Day, 1972, Sewing Lesson, Jasperware	25.00
Plate, Nautilus, Black Basalt, Box, 10 In., 8 Piece	200.00
Plate, Railroad, New York Central, Limited Edition	55.00
Plate, Shell, Pearlware, 9 In., 3 Piece	405.00
Plate, Statue Of Liberty Centennial, 6 1/2 In.	75.00
Platter, Harvard, Blue, 20 In.	450.00
Platter, Transfer, Cows, 17 x 13 1/2 In.	230.00
Pot, Pierced Lid, Checkerboard Design, Terra-Cotta, D Form, 8 1/2 In.	1955.00

Powder Box, Queensware, Green & White	85.00
Salad Set, Neoclassic Figural Design, Blue Ground, 3 Piece	228.00
Salt, Open, Lady Templeton Style, Classical White Figures, Signed, 3 In.	245.00
Serving Set, Ribbon & Bow, Platter, 8 Dishes, Majolica .... *Illus*	1540.00
Soup, Dish, Emile Lessore, Pearlware, Enamel Border, c.1867, 10 1/4 In., Pair	230.00
Soup, Dish, Queensware, Ruffled Rim, White On Blue, c.1952	30.00
Sugar, Pearlware, Nautilus Shell Form Cover, 7 In.	500.00
Sugar, Shell, Pearlware, Pedestal, 19th Century, 6 In.	550.00
Sugar & Creamer, Canadian Coat Of Arms, Basalt	95.00
Sugar & Creamer, Cover, Classic Figures	145.00
Sugar & Creamer, Devon Sprays	45.00
Sugar & Creamer, Jasperware, Blue	135.00
Tea Set, Caneware, Signed, 3 Piece	690.00
Tea Set, Child's, Peter Rabbit, Beatrix Potter, Box, 10 Piece	110.00
Tea Set, Jasperware, Blue With White, 4 Piece	220.00
Tea Set, Lilac Jasper, White Classical Relief, 16 Piece	545.00
Tea Set, Pink & Copper Luster, 23 Piece	80.00
Tea Set, Yellow Buff, Black Bas Relief Work, 3 Piece	1200.00
Teapot, Black Basalt, Widow Finial, 6 In.	1095.00
Teapot, Blue Jasper Dip, White Classical Figures, Finial, Impressed, 6 1/2 In.	225.00
Teapot, Bullfinch, Wellesley	145.00
Teapot, Classical Figures, Blue With White, 7 x 4 1/4 In.	150.00
Teapot, Drabware, Widow Finial, Signed, 1830s, 7 In.	230.00
Teapot, Jasperware, Black	195.00
Teapot, Jasperware, Green..75.00 to	100.00
Teapot, Jasperware, Raised White Figures At Sides, 6 1/4 In.	295.00
Teapot, Lavender On Cream	95.00
Teapot, Month, August, Polychrome, Signed, c.1878, 6 3/4 In.	1725.00
Teapot, Month, October, Polychrome, Signed, c.1878, 6 1/2 In.	1725.00
Teapot, Queensware, Cream & Lavender	35.00
Toothpick, Queensware, Cream & Lavender	20.00
Tray, Jasperware, White On Blue, 3 1/4 x 6 In.	45.00
Tureen, Domed Cover, Handles, Ivory, 1780	695.00
Tureen, Lion Head Handles, Cream Glaze, 1935	95.00
Tureen, Pearlware, Shell Shape, Pedestal, 13 In.	850.00
Urn, Classical, Handles, 10 1/2 In.	195.00
Urn, Cover, Jasperware, Classic Figures On Lavender, 9 1/4 In.	1190.00
Urn, Cover, Jasperware, Classical Figures, 1968, 9 In.	695.00
Urn, Jasperware, Allegorical Figures, Tricolor, 7 1/2 In.	440.00
Vase, Black Basalt, White Allegorical Design, Marked, 10 1/2 In.	715.00
Vase, Cover, Black Basalt, Bronzed & Gilt, c.1875, 8 In.	1035.00
Vase, Cover, Creamware, Porphyry, Drapery Festoons, 5 1/4 In., Pair	805.00
Vase, Cover, Sacrifice To Hymen, Cupids Around Body, Signed, 19 1/2 In.	4025.00
Vase, Cover, White Classical Dancing Hours, Lilac, Signed, 6 3/4 In.	258.00
Vase, Dragonware, 8 In.	500.00
Vase, Fairyland Luster, Willow Pattern, Marks, Gilded Initials, c.1925, 8 In.	1610.00
Vase, Jasperware, Black, White Classical Relief, With Phrygian Cap, 10 1/2 In.	1840.00
Vase, Jasperware, Dark Blue, White Classical Relief, c.1877, 8 1/4 In.	345.00
Vase, Jasperware, Green, White Classical Relief, Portland, c.1920, 5 In.	545.00
Vase, Jasperware, Raised Classical Figures, Green, White, 5 x 3 1/2 In.	195.00
Vase, Pearlware, Blue Ribbed Band, Pierced Cover, c.1800, 9 3/4 In.	632.00
Vase, Potpourri, Caneware, Famille Rose, 2 Loop Handle, Disc Lid, c.1820, 8 In.	1265.00
Vase, Queensware, 8 1/2 In.	45.00
Vase, White, Raised Blue Grape & Leaf Banding, Reeded	55.00
Wash Set, Brown Transfer, Begonia, 8 Piece	180.00
Wine Cooler, Leaf & Medusa Head Panels, Lilac, Signed, 10 1/2 In.	690.00

WELLER pottery was first made in 1873 in Fultonham, Ohio. The firm moved to Zanesville, Ohio, in 1882. Art wares were introduced in 1893. Hundreds of lines of pottery were produced, including Louwelsa, Eocean, Dickens Ware, and Sicardo, before the pottery closed in 1948.

LOUWELSA
WELLER

Ashtray, Roma	40.00
Basket, Fruit, Woodcraft, 13 x 10 1/2 In.	75.00

Basket, Hanging, Parian.. 250.00
Basket, Melrose 110.00
Basket, Silvertone, 6 1/2 In.. 250.00
Bonbon, Coppertone, Frog On Blossom, Incised Mark, 4 1/4 x 5 1/2 In. 330.00
Bowl, Baldin, Blue, 4 In... 150.00
Bowl, Batter, Mammy .... 650.00 to 1250.00
Bowl, Blue Drapery, 5 1/2 In... 59.00
Bowl, Coppertone, Lily Pad, Bullfrog, Matte Green & Brown, Ink Stamp, 3 1/2 x 10 3/4 In. 358.00
Bowl, Flower Frog, Malverne 155.00
Bowl, Flower Frog, Warwick... 175.00
Bowl, Mixing, Pierre, Green, 10 1/2 x 5 1/2 In. 35.00
Bowl, Monochrome, Green-Yellow, 4 x 9 In. 125.00
Bowl, Muskota, 3 Flying White Geese, Grasses, 6 1/2 x 10 In. 465.00
Bowl, Patricia, Ducks, White, 13 In. 65.00
Bowl, Patricia, Goose-Head Handles, 4 In. 25.00
Bowl, Sabrinian, 9 In. 225.00
Bowl, Sabrinian, Shell, 4 x 5 In. 135.00
Bowl, Velva, Oval, Dark Green, Purple Flowers, 12 1/2 In. 110.00
Candelabrum, Triple, Roma, 9 In. 125.00
Candlestick, 2-Light, Woodcraft, Owl Perched On Apple Tree, 12 1/2 x 8 In. 358.00
Candlestick, Coppertone, 3 In., Pair 100.00
Candlestick, Silvertone, Pair... 325.00
Centerpiece, Coppertone, Frog On Rim, Green, Brown, Kiln Mark, 5 x 10 1/2 In. 385.00
Clock, Louwelsa, Floral, 12 In... 900.00
Clock, Louwelsa, Tall Case Shape, Flowers, 11 In... 650.00
Compote, Roma, Pedestal, 9 In. 100.00
Console Set, Ardsley, Cattail Bowl, Kingfisher Flower Frog, 2 Candleholders, Signed . 475.00
Cornucopia, Wild Rose, Green, 6 In. 32.00
Ewer, Aurelian, Signed, 6 In.. 235.00
Ewer, Barcelona, 6 1/2 In. 130.00
Ewer, Dickens Ware II, Carved Mermaids, Green & Blue Ground, 11 In. 605.00
Ewer, Louwelsa, Autumn Leaves, 7 In. 125.00
Ewer, Louwelsa, Floral, Elizabeth Ayers, 5 1/2 x 3 In... 148.00
Figurine, Dachshund 75.00
Figurine, Frog, Coppertone, 2 In. .... 175.00 to 225.00
Figurine, Frog, Coppertone, 4 In. .... 275.00 to 325.00
Figurine, Kingfisher, Brighton, 9 In... 275.00
Figurine, Kingfisher, Muskota, 9 In. 385.00
Figurine, Lovebirds, Brighton, On Curving Branch, Glossy Finish, 9 In. 1000.00
Figurine, Parakeet, Brighton, On Green Perch, Polychrome Colors, 7 1/2 In. 750.00
Figurine, Woodpecker, Brighton 300.00
Flower Frog, Boy On Large Green Rock, 4 1/4 x 4 1/4 In... 250.00
Flower Frog, Brighton, Kingfisher, 8 3/4 x 7 In. 275.00
Flower Frog, Coppertone, 2 In. 125.00
Flower Frog, Coppertone, 4 In. .... 275.00 to 300.00
Flower Frog, Coppertone, 8 Hole Tree Form Rock 30.00
Flower Frog, Kingfisher 170.00
Flower Frog, Muskota, Fisher Boy, 6 1/2 In. 235.00
Flower Frog, Muskota, Frog On Lily Pad, 4 In. 410.00
Flower Frog, Muskota, Small Girl With Watering Can, 6 3/4 x 4 In. 330.00
Flower Frog, Nude.. 250.00
Flower Frog, Sydonia, Blue 25.00
Flower Frog, White Rose, Green 75.00
Flower Frog, Woodcraft, Pheasant 495.00
Flower Frog, Woodcraft, Robin, Spread Wings, Signed, 5 x 6 1/4 In. 330.00
Flowerpot, Liner, Coppertone, 7 In. 125.00
Jar, Cover, Knifewood, Berries, Birds, Leaves, 8 In. 385.00
Jardiniere, Aurelian, Footed, Schneider, 12 In.. 600.00
Jardiniere, Aurelian, Pedestal, Signed, 38 In... 1210.00
Jardiniere, Blue Ware, Footed, Dancing Woman, 7 1/2 In. 220.00
Jardiniere, Burntwood, Dancing Satyrs, Cream Bisque, High Glaze Interior, 8 In. 286.00
Jardiniere, Claywood, Gladiators, 9 In.. 275.00 to 300.00
Jardiniere, Dickens Ware I, Green High Glaze, Yellow Flowers, 6 1/2 In........................... 176.00

Jardiniere, Embossed Hosta Leaves, Matte Green, 8 In.	250.00
Jardiniere, Flemish, 4 Lion Heads, Garlands, 11 In.	275.00
Jardiniere, Forest, 12 x 11 In.	650.00
Jardiniere, Forest, Kiln Mark, 6 1/2 In.	150.00
Jardiniere, Fruit, Paneled, Green & Ocher Brown, 7 In.	95.00
Jardiniere, Gardenware, Lion Heads, Garlands In Mouths, 12 1/2 In.	150.00
Jardiniere, Hand Painted Pansies, Dark Brown, Ruffled Rim, 10 x 8 5/8 In.	192.00
Jardiniere, Ivory, Floral Relief Panels, 9 1/2 x 8 In.	50.00
Jardiniere, Marvo, Green, 8 In.	125.00
Jardiniere, Pedestal, Blue Ware, 32 In.	440.00
Jardiniere, Pedestal, Flemish, Blue Parrots, Pink Cockatoos, 32 In.	1540.00
Jardiniere, Pedestal, Forest, 32 In.	1650.00
Jardiniere, Pedestal, Lattice, 27 1/2 In.	275.00
Jardiniere, Pedestal, Marvo, Orange & Green, 33 In.	303.00
Jardiniere, Pedestal, Matte Green, 26 In.	715.00
Jardiniere, Pedestal, Roma, 28 1/2 In.	605.00
Jardiniere, Roma, Incised Design On 4 Panels, Medium Brown Glaze, 8 3/4 In.	95.00
Jardiniere, Roma, Swags, 8 1/2 In.	75.00
Jardiniere, Sicard, Iridescent Peacock Feather, Bulbous, 8 x 10 1/2 In.	1210.00
Jardiniere, Sicard, Moorish Arabesques, Signed, 12 1/2 x 14 1/2 In.	1500.00
Jardiniere, Woodrose, 8 1/2 In.	150.00
Jug, Barcelona, Multicolored Stylized Flowers, Tan Ground, No. 5, 6 In.	165.00
Jug, Dickens Ware, Ear Of Corn, 4 1/2 In.	250.00
Jug, Syrup, Mammy, Script Mark, 6 3/4 In.	550.00
Lamp, Louwelsa, Blue, 10 In.	975.00
Mug, Dickens Ware, Deer Head, Hand Painted	95.00
Mug, Dickens Ware, Deer Head, Wave Crest, Cracker Jar, Blue Flowers	165.00
Mug, Dickens Ware, Portrait Of Tame Wolf, Anna Dautherty, 6 1/4 In.	625.00
Mug, Etna, Grape Cluster, 6 In.	125.00
Mug, Louwelsa, Fruit, White Ground, 4 1/2 In.	20.00
Mug, Louwelsa, Silhouette Portrait Of Monk, Signed, 6 In.	165.00
Mug, Monk Portrait	215.00
Pitcher, Bittersweet, Gray, 9 In.	75.00
Pitcher, Coppertone, Fish, Green Over Brown Glaze, c.1920, 11 In.	460.00
Pitcher, Dickens Ware, Portrait Of Monk, 10 1/2 In.	625.00
Pitcher, Flower, Twig Handle, 6 In.	75.00
Pitcher, Juvenile, Duck, 7 In.	85.00
Pitcher, Sabrinian, 10 1/2 In.	300.00 to 475.00
Pitcher, Zona, Kingfisher, 8 In.	165.00 to 225.00
Planter, Roba, Blue & White	65.00
Planter, Roma, Rectangular, 7 5/8 In.	35.00
Planter, Windowsill, Dupont	50.00
Plaque, Lincoln, Greenish-Gray, Cream Back, Relief Portrait, 4 5/8 In.	95.00
Plate, Baby's, Duck, 7 In.	85.00
Plate, White Rose, Blue, 6 In.	70.00
Tankard, Dickens Ware, Captain Cuttle Gave Them The Lovely Peg	725.00
Tea Set, Zona, 1916, 26 Piece	650.00
Teapot, Mammy	650.00
Tile, Leaping Gazelle In Medallion, Dark Brown, Orange Matte Mottled Ground, 4 In.	247.00
Tobacco Jar, Dickens Ware, Captain, 6 1/2 In.	660.00
Tobacco Jar, Dickens Ware, Turk, 7 1/2 In.	467.00
Umbrella Stand, Embossed Long-Stemmed Flowers, 20 1/4 In.	935.00
Umbrella Stand, Flemish, Earth Tones, Red Apples, 22 In.	308.00
Umbrella Stand, Zona, Women In Purple Dresses, Grape Vines, 20 In.	650.00
Urn, Bonit, Pansies, Cream Ground, Script Mark, 7 x 6 1/2 In., Pair	275.00
Urn, Chengtu, Cover, Orange Matte Glaze, Label, Signed, 12 In.	135.00
Vase, Alvin, 12 In.	125.00
Vase, Ardsley, 7 1/2 In.	35.00
Vase, Asymmetrical Poppy Design, 1930s, 9 1/2 In.	230.00
Vase, Atlas, Blue, White Interior, 13 1/2 In.	250.00
Vase, Aurelian, Berry & Leaf Design, c.1900, 15 In.	920.00
Vase, Aurelian, Brown & Green Roses, Yellow, Brown Ground, H. Mitchell, 5 1/2 In.	468.00
Vase, Aurelian, Multicolored Birds, Abstract Ground, No. 453C, Ed Abel, 11 In.	1540.00

Vase, Baldin, Blue, 11 In.. 395.00
Vase, Baldin, Brown, Red Apples, 6 In. 148.00
Vase, Barcelona, 6 In... 120.00
Vase, Barcelona, 9 1/4 In... 375.00
Vase, Besline, Orange Leaves, Gold Ground, 9 In. 250.00
Vase, Black Bat & Moon, Blue Matte Glaze, Incised Mark, 8 1/4 x 8 In............... 1540.00
Vase, Blo' Red, 4 1/2 In... 55.00
Vase, Bonit, 2 Handles, Cream Ground, 10 In... 220.00
Vase, Bouquet, Flower & Bud, Green Leaves, Ivory Ground, Footed, Handle, 9 x 5 In.. 35.00
Vase, Bud, Butterflies 300.00
Vase, Bud, Camelot, Yellow.. 145.00
Vase, Bud, Coppertone, Climbing Frog, Mottled Green, Brown Glaze, Kiln Mark, 9 In. 360.00
Vase, Bud, Coppertone, Fish, Green Over Brown Glaze, c.1920, 8 In. 3000.00
Vase, Bud, LaSa, Landscape, 6 1/2 In. 165.00
Vase, Bud, LaSa, Landscape, Metallic, 7 1/2 In. 412.00
Vase, Bud, Name Card, Butterflies 300.00
Vase, Bud, Triple, Roma, 7 1/2 In. 75.00
Vase, Bud, Woodcraft, 10 1/2 In. 65.00
Vase, Burntwood, Birds, 8 In... 175.00
Vase, Burntwood, Stylized Flowers, Chocolate Brown Ground, Stamped, 9 x 4 1/2 In... 220.00
Vase, Camelot, Bulbous Bottom, Flared Neck, White Geometrics, 7 1/2 In. 440.00
Vase, Cameo, Tan, Footed, 11 1/4 In... 38.00
Vase, Chengtu, 12 In... 125.00
Vase, Chengtu, 6 Sides, 10 In.. 150.00
Vase, Clarmont, 2 Handles, Roses, Browns & Green, 6 In. 110.00
Vase, Claywood, Oak Leaves, 8 1/2 In.. 45.00
Vase, Coppertone, Life-Size Frog Holding Water Lily, Signed, 4 x 4 /34 In. 275.00
Vase, Coppertone, Lily Pads, 12 In. 850.00
Vase, Darsie, Ivory, 7 x 6 1/2 In... 26.00
Vase, Dickens Ware I, Embossed Flowers, 11 In. 300.00
Vase, Dickens Ware II, Sgraffito Swamp Scene, Signed, 5 1/4 In.............................. 200.00
Vase, Dickens Ware, Chief Running Bear, Signed, 7 1/2 In. .... 1035.00 to 1125.00
Vase, Dickens Ware, Ghost Bull, Brown Bisque, 9 1/2 In. 525.00
Vase, Dickens Ware, Indian Chief, 6 In.. 100.00
Vase, Dickens Ware, Portrait Of American Indian, Ghost Bull, 8 1/2 In. 1210.00
Vase, Dresden, Dutch Girl, Windmills & Boats, Levi J. Burgess, 13 1/4 In. 825.00
Vase, Enameled Poppy, Yellow To Pink, Pastel, Hexagonal Shape, 8 1/2 In. 165.00
Vase, Eocean Rose, Green & Violet Leaves, Handles, Pink & Green Ground, 12 3/4 In. 880.00
Vase, Eocean, Canada Thistle, Dark Green To Lavender Ground, 12 In. 110.00
Vase, Eocean, Daisies, Gray, 10 1/2 In.. 150.00
Vase, Eocean, Mauve Wild Roses, Shaded Gray Ground, M.L., Incised, 12 x 4 In......... 330.00
Vase, Eocean, Painted Lily Of The Valley, Shaded Ground, Signed, 8 In..................... 375.00
Vase, Etched Male Golfer, 10 In. 1540.00
Vase, Etna, Pink Pansies, Blue-Gray, Die Stamped, 7 In... 95.00
Vase, Etna, Thistles, 11 In... 450.00
Vase, Fishes Swimming Amid Sea Grasses, 8 In.. 1210.00
Vase, Forest, Waisted, 12 In.. 200.00
Vase, Graystone, Fish, 18 In.. 300.00
Vase, Greenbriar, 9 In... 150.00
Vase, Hudson, Daisies, Black & Green Foliage, Hunter, 8 In................................... 305.00
Vase, Hudson, Floral, Handles, Signed Timberlake, 6 In. 400.00
Vase, Hudson, Iris, Cylindrical, 8 1/2 In. 435.00
Vase, Hudson, Morning Glories, Blue To Green Ground, Hester Pillsbury, 9 1/2 In. 550.00
Vase, Hudson, Pink & Yellow Flowers, Pink To Green Ground, Hood, 7 In. 330.00
Vase, Hudson, Pink Dogwood Blossoms, M. Ansel, 7 x 3 1/2 In. 313.00
Vase, Hudson-Perfecto, Iris, Hester Pillsbury, 10 1/2 In. 335.00
Vase, Impressed White Roses, Green Leaves, 4-Sided, Signed, 10 1/2 In.................. 135.00
Vase, Jap Birdimal, Geisha Girl, No. 471, Rhead, 13 In.................... 1750.00 to 3000.00
Vase, Juneau, Rose, 14 In.. 250.00
Vase, Kylro, Brown, 8 In.. 75.00
Vase, L'Art Nouveau, Embossed Woman & Flowers, Signed, 17 1/2 In...................... 550.00
Vase, L'Art Nouveau, Floral, 13 1/2 In. .... 325.00 to 425.00
Vase, LaMar, 7 In.. 150.00

Vase, LaMar, 8 In. ....175.00 to 200.00
Vase, LaMar, Mountain Landscape, Metallic Gray Details, 8 In. 220.00
Vase, LaSa, 5 1/4 In. 350.00
Vase, LaSa, Iridescent Landscape, Bulbous, Pinched Neck, Marked 247.00
Vase, LaSa, Landscape, 14 In. 1210.00
Vase, LaSa, Landscape, Iridescent Glaze, Signed, 7 1/2 In. 465.00
Vase, LaSa, Rainbow Iridescent Ground, Poppies, 9 In. 357.50
Vase, LaSa, Trees & Hills Landscape, 9 In. 400.00
Vase, Lavonia, Figural, Girl, Turquoise, 11 In. 275.00
Vase, Leathery Green To Terra-Cotta Glaze, Squatty Base, Stovepipe Neck, 11 x 10 In. 275.00
Vase, Leaves On Green Stems, Orange Matte Ground, Signed, 6 1/2 In. 410.00
Vase, Life-Sized Frogs, On Water Lilies, Paper Label, 8 1/4 x 9 In. 990.00
Vase, Louwelsa, Carnations, Foliage, Eugene Roberts, Signed, 24 x 8 3/4 In. 1100.00
Vase, Louwelsa, Daffodils, 9 In. 600.00
Vase, Louwelsa, Orange & Yellow Mums, No. 463, A. Haubrich, 16 In. 1650.00
Vase, Maiden & Windmill Scene, Grays, Blue-Greens, Levi J. Burgess, 14 x 4 In. 413.00
Vase, Marbelized, Red, Gray & Black, 10 1/2 In. 175.00
Vase, Marengo, 9 In. 225.00
Vase, Marvo, Chengtu Glaze, 6 1/2 In. 190.00
Vase, Mistletoe Branches, Multicolored Glaze, Signed, 5 In. 437.00
Vase, Nile, Green, 2 Handles, 13 In. 195.00
Vase, Nile, Handles, 7 1/2 In. 125.00
Vase, Paragon, Incised Flowers, Overlapping Leaves, Mustard Glaze, 6 3/4 x 5 1/2 In. 165.00
Vase, Paragon, Molded Art Deco Flowers, Blue High Glaze, 7 1/2 In. 120.00
Vase, Perfecto, Slip Roses Against Light Ground, Marked, 14 In. 1150.00
Vase, Pillow, Chase, Cameo Hunting Scene, Cobalt Blue, Incised Mark, 6 3/4 x 7 In.... 247.00
Vase, Pillow, Dickens Ware, Signed H.S. 350.00
Vase, Pillow, Dickens Ware, Water Fowl, 6 In. 250.00
Vase, Pillow, Louwelsa, Signed, 4 1/4 In. 150.00
Vase, Pillow, Sabrinian 295.00
Vase, Poppies, Butterflies, Silvertone, 12 In. 395.00
Vase, Poppies, C. Leffler, 20 In. 2000.00
Vase, Relief Owls, Squirrels & Oak Trees, Signed, 7 In. 185.00
Vase, Roba, Brown, 6 1/2 In. 25.00
Vase, Rolled Rim, Colored Roses In Blue Band, Ivory Ground, Signed, 13 In. 700.00
Vase, Roma, 2 Bands Of Leaves & Flowers, Cylinder, 7 5/8 x 3 1/4 In. 46.00
Vase, Roma, 6 In. ....45.00 to 125.00
Vase, Rose Blossoms, Foliate Silver Neck, Hattie Mitchell, 1898, 7 In. 1840.00
Vase, Rozaane, Fuji, Stylized Enamel Design, 8 1/2 In. 1210.00
Vase, Sicard, Baluster Shape, Multicolored Iridescence, Mistletoe, 5 In. 437.00
Vase, Sicard, Dandelion Leaves, Burgundy Luster Glaze, Signed, 4 In. 460.00

Weller, Vase, Sicard, Iridescent,
1904, 27 3/4 In.

◆◆◆◆◆◆◆◆◆◆◆◆◆◆◆◆◆◆◆◆◆

Lace handkerchiefs can be pressed the old-fashioned way. After washing the handkerchief, push it flat on a mirror or tile wall surface. Straighten it, and let the water run off and the handkerchief dry. It will need no further ironing. Avoid using an iron. It will flatten the lace.

◆◆◆◆◆◆◆◆◆◆◆◆◆◆◆◆◆◆◆◆◆

Vase, Sicard, Floral Design, 6 In. 500.00
Vase, Sicard, Iridescent Floral, Bulbous, Small Neck, Drilled, 17 1/2 x 11 In. 5500.00
Vase, Sicard, Iridescent Stylized Floral Design, Tapered, 4 3/4 x 2 3/4 In. 412.00
Vase, Sicard, Iridescent, 1904, 27 3/4 In. .... *Illus* 9625.00
Vase, Sicard, Ribbed Iridescent Form, 7 1/2 In. 1980.00
Vase, Sicard, Spotted Ground, Florals, 7 In. 650.00
Vase, Sicard, Trefoil Rim, Gold Arabesques, Signed, 3 1/4 x 5 3/4 In. 650.00
Vase, Sicard, Vertical Blades Of Grass, Abstract Swirls, Signed, 8 1/2 In. 1045.00
Vase, Silvertone, 7 In. 250.00
Vase, Silvertone, 8 1/2 In. 625.00
Vase, Silvertone, Calla Lilies, 15 In. 500.00
Vase, Silvertone, Handles, 7 1/2 In. 210.00
Vase, Silvertone, Iris, 5 In. .... 195.00 to 235.00
Vase, Silvertone, Multicolored Flowers, 8 In. 209.00
Vase, Softone, Blue, Large 35.00
Vase, Souevo, 14 1/2 In. 250.00
Vase, Stellar, Collar Rim, White Stars, Black Ground, Hester Pillsbury, 5 3/4 In. 450.00
Vase, Stylized Red Flower, Textured Blue Ground, Impressed Mark, 8 1/4 In. 495.00
Vase, Sydonia, Blue, Green Base, 9 1/2 In. 55.00
Vase, Triple Bud, Sydonia, 8 1/2 In. 95.00
Vase, Tulips, Black Outlined, Caramel Ground, F. Ferrell, 10 1/4 x 4 1/4 In. 413.00
Vase, Turada, Black, Blue, Yellow, Peach, c.1900, 11 In. 230.00
Vase, Tutone, Maroon, 6 In. 80.00
Vase, Wild Rose, 6 In. 50.00
Vase, Wild Rose, 8 In. 25.00
Vase, Wild Rose, 9 1/2 In. 65.00
Vase, Wild Rose, 14 In. 110.00
Vase, Wild Rose, Peach, 6 1/2 In. 60.00
Vase, Woodcraft, Plums, 12 In. 195.00
Vase, Xenia, Corset, Stylized Poppies, Gray-Blue Ground, Incised Mark, 10 3/4 In. 880.00
Vase, Xenia, Stylized Roses, Green Leaves, Signed, 11 In. 2860.00
Wall Hanging, Woodcraft, Climbing Squirrel, Signed, 13 1/2 In. 850.00
Wall Pocket, Colonial Woman, Glossy Blue 120.00
Wall Pocket, Colonial Woman, Matte Blue 95.00
Wall Pocket, Flowers & Columns 70.00
Wall Pocket, Klyro, Brown 120.00
Wall Pocket, Orris, Ivory 60.00
Wall Pocket, Woodcraft, Squirrel 225.00
Wall Pocket, Woodrose, Lavender, 6 1/2 In. 70.00

WEMYSS ware was made by Robert Heron in Kirkaldy, Scotland, from 1850
to 1929. It is a colorful peasant-type pottery.

Figurine, Pig, Signed, 6 1/2 In. 750.00

WESTMORELAND GLASS was made by the Westmoreland Glass Company
of Grapeville, Pennsylvania, from 1890 to 1984. They made clear and colored glass of many varieties, such as milk glass, pressed glass, and slag glass.

Ashtray, Old Quilt, Square, 4 In. 15.00
Basket, Paneled Grape, 8 In. 115.00
Basket, Split Handle, 4 1/2 In. 20.00
Basket, Split Handle, Oval, 6 1/2 In. 45.00
Bell, Beaded Bouquet, Almond Cameo 40.00
Bell, Soft Mist, Daisies, Brown 25.00
Bonbon, American Hobnail, Blue Mist, Daisies 30.00
Bowl, Cover, Beaded Grape, Square, 9 In. 38.00
Bowl, Cover, Golden Sunset, 7 In. 22.00
Bowl, Doric, Oval, 12 In. 23.00
Bowl, English Hobnail, Footed, 2 Handles, Amber, 8 In. 35.00
Bowl, Maple Leaf, Crimped, Rippled Rim, 7 1/2 In. 18.00
Bowl, Mayonnaise, Old Quilt, 4 1/2 In. 17.00
Bowl, Paneled Grape, Bowl, 9 /12 In. 60.00
Bowl, Paneled Grape, Milk Glass, Bell Footed, 9 In. 95.00

Bowl, Ring & Petal, Footed, Square, 7 In.. 35.00
Bowl, Rose & Lattice, Footed, Crimped Rim, 8 In. 21.00
Bowl, Shell & Dolphin, Large 120.00
Bowl, Spoke & Rim, Flared, 11 In. 18.00
Bowl, Wedding, Ruby Stained, 10 In. 42.00
Box, Beaded Grape, Square, 4 In. 37.00
Box, Jewelry, China Rose On Crystal Mist, 4-Footed 25.00
Box, Trinket, Pink Dogwood 30.00
Box, Trinket, Princess Feather, Almond.. 20.00
Butter, Cover, Milk Glass, Round 35.00
Butter, Cover, Paneled Grape, 1/4 Lb... 24.00
Butter, Cover, Red... 45.00
Cake Stand, Child's, Fan & File, Ruby 38.00
Cake Stand, Paneled Grape, Footed, 11 In. 60.00
Cake Tray, White Milk Glass... 45.00
Candelabrum, 3-Light, Paneled Grape, Milk Glass... 225.00
Candleholder, 4 In., Pair 25.00
Candleholder, Beaded Grape, 4 In., Pair 13.00
Candlestick, Green Marble, Label, Pair 50.00
Candlestick, Paneled Grape, 4 In., Pair 15.00
Candlestick, Starfish 10.00
Candlestick, Thousand Eye, Snow Ball, Pair 15.00
Candy, Cover, English Hobnail, 3-Footed, 6 In. 29.00
Candy Dish, Cover, Colonial, Green.. 40.00
Candy Dish, Paneled Grape, Footed.. 50.00
Candy Dish, Paneled Grape, Pedestal 15.00
Canister Jar, Paneled Grape, Cover... 300.00
Canister Set, Andrea West Rooster Decals, Crystal, 4 Piece 70.00
Celery, American Hobnail, Brandy Wine Blue Opalescent 30.00
Compote, Cover, Old Quilt, Square 14.00
Compote, Cover, Sawtooth, 10 1/2 In. 40.00
Compote, Open, Old Quilt, 8 In... 29.00
Cookie Jar, Almond Cherry 115.00
Cookie Jar, Milk Glass, No. 109 .... 250.00
Creamer, English Hobnail 15.00
Creamer, Old Quilt, 3 1/2 In...12.00 to 20.00
Cruet, Old Quilt, Label 30.00
Cruet, Paneled Grape, Stopper, 2 Oz. 22.00
Cup & Saucer, Paneled Grape ....21.00 to 27.00
Della Robia, Candy Dish, Cover, Footed 65.00
Dinner Set, Paneled Grape, Service For 8 .... 700.00
Dish, Candy & Planter, Cover.. 32.00
Dish, Cover, Footed, 5 In. 20.00
Dish, Eagle Cover, Purple Slag 265.00
Dish, Fox Cover, Purple Slag 265.00
Dish, Rooster Cover 20.00
Epergne, Paneled Grape, Milk Glass 195.00
Goblet, Della Robbia, Gold Trim, Trim & Stem, 8 Oz. 15.00
Goblet, Paneled Grape 18.00
Goblet, Water, Thousand Eye, Footed 12.00
Ladle, Punch Bowl, Paneled Grape.. 59.00
Nappy, Paneled Grape, Handle, 5 In. 20.00
Owl, Black, 5 1/2 In.. 95.00
Pitcher, Golden Sunset, Footed, 1 Qt. 75.00
Pitcher, Paneled Grape, 32 Oz.. 39.00
Pitcher, Tankard, Single Rose 75.00
Pitcher, Water, Old Quilt 43.00
Planter, Paneled Grape, Rectangular, 4 x 8 3/4 In.. 35.00
Planter, Paneled Grape, Square, 4 In. 30.00
Plate, Beaded Bouquet, Almond, 8 In.. 45.00
Plate, Dinner, Paneled Grape... 49.00
Plate, Green Mist With Daisy, 8 In... 22.00

Plate, Paneled Grape, 8 1/2 In.	22.00
Plate, Torte, Beaded Grape, 15 In.	100.00
Plate, White Dogwood, Ruby, 9 In.	35.00
Powder Box, American Hobnail	28.00
Punch Bowl, Paneled Grape, Stand, Ladle, 15 Piece	175.00
Punch Set, Child's, Ruby, Box	60.00
Punch Set, Paneled Grape, 14 Piece	600.00
Punch Set, Paneled Grape, Milk Glass	410.00
Robin, Pink, 5 1/8 In.	24.00
Salt & Pepper, English Hobnail	13.00
Salt & Pepper, Paneled Grape	21.00
Sherbet, Crystal	22.00
Sherbet, English Hobnail, Round Foot	9.00
Sherbet, Paneled Grape	12.00
Sherbet, Princess Feather, Green	20.00
Sugar & Creamer, Blackberry	51.00
Sugar & Creamer, Cherry	16.00
Sugar & Creamer, Child's, Fan & File, Ruby	30.00
Sugar & Creamer, Della Robbia	21.00
Sugar & Creamer, Maple Leaf, Ruby	16.00
Sugar & Creamer, Paneled Forget-Me-Nots, Milk Glass	55.00
Sugar & Creamer, Paneled Grape	26.00
Sugar & Creamer, Wings, Green	25.00
Sugar & Creamer, Wings, Pink	25.00
Sweetmeat, Colonial, Green Slag	32.00
Sweetmeat, Colonial, Purple Slag	32.00
Syrup, Old Quilt	21.00
Tray, Paneled Grape, 10 In.	115.00
Tumbler, Beaded Edge, Red Rim, Footed	8.00
Tumbler, Juice, Old Quilt, 5 Oz.	25.00
Vase, Bud, Beaded Bouquet, 9 In.	15.00
Vase, Bud, Paneled Grape, 8 In.	37.00
Vase, Bud, Paneled Grape, 9 In.	15.00
Vase, Christmas, Holly	43.00
Vase, Crimped Top, 9 In.	37.00
Vase, Fan, Old Quilt, 8 1/2 In.	17.50
Vase, Fan, Roses & Bows	55.00
Vase, Paneled Grape, Footed, 6 In.	40.00
Vase, Paneled Grape, Footed, Cupped, 4 1/2 In.	35.00
Vase, Paneled Grape, Hexagonal Base, 10 In.	42.00
Wine, Old Quilt	15.00
Wine Set, Paneled Grape, Decanter & 6 Wines	250.00
Wren, Crystal Mist, 2 1/2 In.	17.50
Wren, Red, 2 1/2 In.	22.50

WHEATLEY Pottery was established in 1880. Thomas J. Wheatley had worked in Cincinnati, Ohio, with the founders of the art pottery movement, including M. Louise McLaughlin of the Rookwood Pottery. Wheatley Pottery was purchased by the Cambridge Tile Manufacturing Company in 1927.

Bowl, Dogwood Blossoms & Leaves, Matte Green Glaze, Signed, 7 1/2 In.	350.00
Bowl, Leaf Design, Green Glaze, Signed, 7 1/2 In.	495.00
Bowl, Water Plant Design, Variegated Green Glaze, 8 In.	795.00
Sand Jar, Black Drip Glaze Over Light Blue, No. 610, 30 In., Pair	1450.00
Tile, Lion In Relief, Leather Brick Red Glaze, 8 In.	150.00
Urn, Monumental, Black Drip Glaze, Clay, c.1924, 31 In.	230.00
Vase, Applied Purple & White Flowers, Shaded Blue Ground, 1882, 13 In.	2200.00
Vase, Embossed Leaves & Pussy Willows, Flowing Green Glaze, Signed, 12 In.	1500.00
Vase, Flat Leaves, Green Buds, Feathered Green Matte Glaze, Signed, 19 1/2 In.	3000.00
Vase, Matte Green Glaze, Bulbous, Waisted Center, Flared, 5 1/2 x 6 In.	415.00
Vase, Matte Green, 24 In.	6050.00
Vase, Matte Green, Applied Grapevine Design, 11 1/2 x 6 1/4 In.	1200.00
Vase, Sculpted Vertical Lead Design, Buds At Rim, Yellow Glaze, 7 1/2 x 5 In.	1045.00

WHIELDON was an English potter who worked alone and with Josiah Wedgwood in eighteenth-century England. Whieldon made many pieces in natural shapes, like cauliflowers or cabbages.

Plate, Brown Tortoiseshell Glaze, Green & Yellow, Scalloped, 8 In.	110.00
Plate, Tortoiseshell Glaze, 10 1/4 In.	275.00
Teapot, Bird Finial, Brown Tortoiseshell Glaze, Paw Feet, 4 7/8 In.	1045.00
Teapot, Cauliflower, Glazed Florets, Green Leaves, Cover, 8 In.	345.00
Teapot, Squat Shape, Twist Handle & Finial, Blue, Green, Brown	140.00

WILLOW, see Blue Willow category

WINDOW glass that was stained and beveled was popular for houses during the late nineteenth and early twentieth centuries. The old windows became popular with collectors in the 1970s; today, old and new examples are seen.

Clerestory, Concentric Rectangles, Inset Triangles, Wright, 1912, 22 x 19 In.	4025.00
Frosted & Clear, Zinc Caned, Stylized Floral, Elmsley & Purcell, 51 In.	2600.00
Geometric Designs, Amber & Frosted On Clear, Prairie School, 52 1/2 In., Pair	1500.00
Leaded, Center Bead-Eyed Owl, Jeweled Border, Moon Medallion, 46 1/2 x 24 In.	1265.00
Leaded, Clear, Triangular Design, Frank Lloyd Wright, 1912, 21 x 14 In.	2070.00 to 2300.00
Leaded, Cliff Side Garden Overlooking Villa, 39 x 57 In.	5750.00
Leaded, Linear Abstract Design On Side, Frank Lloyd Wright, 1912, 43 x 15 In.	8625.00
Leaded Glass, Arts & Crafts, Green Jeweled Flowers In Corners, Ribbed, 28 x 28 In.	357.50
Leaded Glass, Central Stylized Floral, Clear Field, 48 x 19 3/4 In., Pair	315.00
Leaded Glass, Clear, Decorated, Geometric, Frank Lloyd Wright, 1912, 21 x 14 In.	3680.00
Leaded Glass, White, Red & Clear, Frank Lloyd Wright, c.1900, 32 x 14 In.	4370.00
Sash, Wooden, Double Hung, Brown Finish, Salesman's Sample, Pat. 1890, 26 x 12 In.	110.00
Skylight, Celtic Interlaced Design, Adler & Sullivan, Frame, 38 x 62 In.	6900.00
Stained Glass, 2 Life Size People, Chapel-Type, 1896	3500.00
Stained Glass, Art Nouveau Floral, Brussels, Belgium, Pair	450.00
Stained Glass, Landscape, c.1900, 80 x 87 In.	8320.00
Stained Glass, Landscape, Trees, 6 Section, 1900, 80 x 87 In. .... *Illus*	8625.00
Stained Glass, Pink, Yellow & White, 18 x 48 In.	120.00
Stained Glass, Schlitz Beer, Banner Circling Globe, 67 x 36 In.	1705.00

WOOD CARVINGS and wooden pieces are listed separately in this book. There are also wooden pieces found in other categories, such as Kitchen.

Angel, Wavy Hair, Arm Outstretched, Gilt, Silvered, Italy, c.1750, 57 1/4 In.	5750.00
Angel's Head, Late 19th Century, Mexico	450.00
Bear, Standing, 29 In.	1760.00
Bird, Blue & White Paint, Wire Legs, 4 In.	11.00
Bowl, Basswood, 25 In.	36.00

Window, Stained Glass, Landscape, Trees, 6 Section, 1900, 80 x 87 In.

Some collectors want carousel horses that have been completely restored. Some buy only pieces with original paint. This is one type of collectible that can be restored without a loss in value. The work should be done by an expert. This rule is true for a few other types of wooden, painted folk art, too.

Bowl, Figured Maple, 13 1/2 x 14 x 5 1/2 In. 962.00
Brackets, Wall, Rococo, Serpentine Top, Bellflowers, 19th Century, 16 In., Pair 770.00
Buddha, Head, 13 In. 385.00
Buddha, Seated, Polychrome, 13 In. 85.00
Bust, African Woman, Wiener Werkstatte, 14 In. 1325.00
Cherub's Head, Painted, Continental, c.1900 .... 495.00
Eagle, American, Half-Round, Gilded Pine, John H. Bellamy, 38 1/2 In. 2875.00
Eagle, Pine, Mass., 19th Century, 37 x 32 In. 3500.00
Eagle, War Spread, Gilt & Polychrome, Weathered 2850.00
Eagle, Wilhelm Schimmel, 12 3/4-In. Wingspan 19550.00
Eagle, Wings Spread, Full Bodied, Red Sphere, Gray, 19th Century, 38 In. 6325.00
Eagle, Wings Spread, Gesso, 1820, 18 In. 1350.00
Eagle, Wings Spread, Painted, 32 In. 3165.00
Eaglet, Wilhelm Schimmel, 7 In. 6325.00
Figure, Peasant Woman & Man, Colorful, Russia, 7 1/2 In., Pair 48.00
Figure, Pelican, Mahogany, 30 In. 165.00
Figure, Woman's Head, Henry Schonbauer 220.00
Frame, House Form, Walnut, Carved Cork Landscape, 22 x 19 In. 2530.00
Group, Madonna & Child, Gesso, Painted, 27 In. 4950.00
Headdress, Gazelle, African, Chip Carved, Mali, 37 1/4 In. 330.00
Horse, Circus, Painted, Joseph Brown, Salem, Mass., 10 1/4 In., Pair 1840.00
Mask, African, Black Finish, Incised Lines, 15 3/8 x 13 In. 65.00
Mask, African, Bush Cow, Crescent Horns, Painted, 25 In. 253.00
Model, London Coach & Team Of Horses, Working Door, Mid-19th Century, 23 In. 550.00
Nativity Scene, Music Box Manger, Italy, Anri Label, 1940s, 15 Piece 3800.00
Page Turner, Japan 65.00
Panel, Jousting Knight On Horse Back, Worn Paint, Primitive, 35 x 21 In. 27.50
Plaque, Diving Seagull, Benjamin Schmidt, 1933, 24 x 16 1 /2 In. 375.00
Plaque, Running Buck, Benjamin Schmidt, c.1933, 8 1/2 x 11 1/2 In. 230.00
Plaque, U.S. Grant Face, Walnut, Shield Shape, 1880, 6 x 8 1/4 In. 165.00
Rooster, Polychromed 1320.00
Rooster, Wilhelm Schimmel, 6 1/2 In. 4025.00
Santos, Continental, c.1800, 16 In. 800.00
Train Set, Engine & 3 Cars, Polychrome, Mennonite, c.1880 .... 2600.00
Trophy, Deer, Mahogany, Black Forest, Shield Plaque, Life Size 715.00
Urn Of Fruit & Flowers, Spain, 23 In. 525.00
Water Buffalo, Small Man, Oriental, 8 In. 50.00
Woman In Robes, Painted Wooden Base, 10 In. 1650.00

WOODEN wares were used in all parts of the home. Wood was used for many
containers and tools. Small wooden pieces are called *treenware* in England,
but the term *woodenware* is more common in the United States. Additional
pieces may be found in the Advertising, Kitchen, and Tool categories.

Barrel, Cover, Flour, Wooden Staves, 3 Ft. 50.00
Barrel, Gun Powder, Wound With 5 Barb Covered Branches, 15 x 11 In. 75.00
Bowl, Burl, Carved Handles, 19th Century, 16 In. 2760.00
Bowl, Burl, Raised Cutout Handles, 14 x 18 In. 1650.00
Bowl, Burl, Red Exterior, Scrubbed Interior, 5 x 16 1/2 In. 1760.00
Bowl, Pine & Hardwood, Dough, Table Top, Splayed Legs, 27 x 48 In. 715.00
Bowl, Relief Carved, Geometric Design, Men Sword Fighting, England, 10 x 10 In. 415.00
Bucket, Sugar, Cover, Bentwood Handle, 1870, 11 In. 115.00
Bucket, Sugar, Stave Constructed, Bale Handle, 14 x 15 In. .... 220.00 to 258.00
Bucket, Sugar, Stave Construction, Lid, Bentwood Handle, Blue Paint, 9 1/2 In. 368.00
Bucket, Tapered Staves, 2 Iron Hoops, Hand Wrought Handle, 12 x 11 In. 75.00
Canteen, Round, Leather Loops, White Star, Rosette Border, 6 1/2 x 2 In. 1265.00
Casket, Flower Heads & Acanthus, Tyrolean, 17th Century, 9 1/2 x 4 1/4 In. 1265.00
Chest, Jewelry, Teak, Brass Trim, Jadite Inlaid Panels, Intricate Lock, China 125.00
Chest, Treasure, Grained, Black Design, Fish-Tail Hinges, Dated 1724 On Lid 690.00
Egg, Village Design, Russia 10.00
Inkwell, Glass Inserts, Brown Graining, Gold Stenciled Design, 3 1/2 In. 140.00
Jar, Burl, Acorn Finial Cover, Dark Varnish, 10 In. 440.00
Jar, Lid, Pease, 6 3/4 In. 330.00

Jar, Red & Yellow Sponge Graining, Wire Reinforcement, 11 1/2 In. 3850.00
Jar, Rim Flange, Pease, 8 1/2 In. 115.00
Jar, Wire Bale Handle, Pease, 4 1/2 In. 258.50
Jar, Wire Bale Handle, Pease, 6 In. 192.50
Jardiniere, Mahogany, Georgian, Copper Lined, Molded Handles, 12 x 14 In., Pair 385.00
Keg, Pine, Stave Construction, Lid, Blue-Gray Paint, 17 x 14 3/4 In. 687.00
Plaque, Arabian Horse Heads, Burnt Wood, Flemish Art Co., Round, 14 1/2 In. 45.00
Sander, Ink, Pierced Star In Top, Maple, c.1810, 3 In. 85.00
Tray, Butterfly, Inlaid, Handle Opening, With 15 Butterflies, On Cotton, 20 1/2 x 13 In. ... 45.00
Tray, Mahogany, Shell Inlaid, Oval, 24 In. 248.00
Urn, Knife, Federal, Burl Walnut & Tiger Maple, Square Domed Cover, 1800, 28 In., Pair 5750.00
Wall Pocket, Hanging, Maple, Folksy Design, Heart & Scalloped Edge, 22 1/2 In. 165.00

WORCESTER porcelains were made in Worcester, England, from 1751. The
firm went through many name changes and eventually, in 1862, became The
Royal Worcester Porcelain Company Ltd. Collectors often refer to *Dr. Wall*,
Barr, Flight, and other names that indicate time periods or artists at the factory. It became part of Royal Worcester Spode Ltd. in 1976. Related pieces
may be found in the Royal Worcester category.

Basket, Oval, Pine Cone Pattern, Leaf Scroll Border, c.1775, 8 1/2 In. 800.00
Basket, Reticulated, Single Rose Sprig Center, Gilded Rim, 1760, 10 3/4 In. 575.00
Beaker, Lemonade, 3 Oval Landscape Panels, Flight & Barr, 1805, Pair 1035.00
Bough Pot, Venus & Cupid, Salmon Ground, Gilt Ovals & Diamonds, 7 In. 825.00
Butter Boat, Leaf Shape, Overlapping Leaves, 1756, 3 3/16 In. 690.00
Chamber Candlestick, Hilly Landscape, Malvern Church, c.1825, 4 1/4 In. 980.00
Egg Cup Tray, 6 Egg Cups, Queen Charlotte Pattern, c.1800, 8 In. 920.00
Fruit Cooler, Queen Charlotte Pattern, Liner, Cover, 2 Handles, c.1800, 10 3/4 In. 690.00
Inkstand, Kidney Shape, 3 Covers, Salmon Ground, Guilloche Border, c.1805 .... 2300.00
Jug, Cabbage Leaf, Molded Leaves, Gilt Scrolled Edge, c.1775, 7 7/8 In. 4000.00
Jug, Quail Pattern, Grooved Loop Handle, c.1765, 4 11/16 In. 2185.00
Mug, Jabberwocky Pattern, Trellis Panels, c.1770, 4 5/8 In. 1050.00
Pickle Dish, Leaf Shape, Kakiemon, c.1755, 3 1/4 In. 1725.00
Pitcher, Cabbage Leaf, Large 3200.00
Plate, Arms Of Giffard, Red Painted Mark, c.1820, 10 In. 200.00
Plate, Blind Earl, Rosebuds, Blossom, Sprays Of Leaves, 1765, 7 3/4 In., Pair 1725.00
Plate, Brocade Pattern, Scalloped, Signed, 8 1/2 To 8 9/16 In., 6 Piece 1495.00
Plate, Brocade, Dragons, Prunus, Trellis, Diaperwork, c.1772, 8 7/16 In. 1265.00
Plate, Dessert, Hand Enameled Flower, Chamberlain, 9 In., 12 Piece 2300.00
Plate, Dessert, Rosemary, Floral, Ivory Rim, Blue Trim, 6 Piece 22.00
Plate, Lyster Family Crest, Sky Blue & Gilt Border, 1810, Flight, Barr & Barr, Pair..... 730.00
Plate, Pavilion Pattern, Dragon Amid Clouds, c.1770, 8 13/16 In. 345.00
Plate, Pine Cone, Scalloped, c.1770, 9 1/4 In. 368.00
Sauceboat, Black Transfer, Seated Squirrel, Floral Sprays, 1755, 7 9/16 In. 1840.00
Sauceboat, Oriental Figures, Butterflies, Strapwork Body, 1770, 7 1/2 In. 1035.00

♦ ♦

Molded plastic parts of toys or computers or dishes will become brittle
and deteriorate when exposed to
ultraviolet light. Plastic often yellows
and although there are several products that may improve the appearance of discolored plastic, there has
been no major study to decide the
best type of care. For now, it is best
to keep plastic away from strong
lights and pollution.

Worcester, Vase, Dr. Wall,
Blue, White, 15 In., Pair

♦ ♦

Sugar, Floral Sprig Knop, Double Branch Of Hibiscus, 1755, 4 1/2 In.......................... 1265.00
Tea Strainer, Dr. Wall, Dark Blue, Gold, Crescent Mark, 3 3/4 In. 425.00
Teabowl, Saucer, Two Quails, c.1775, 3 1/6-In.Bowl, 4 7/8-In.Saucer 345.00
Teacup & Saucer, Quail, Fluted, Kakiemon, c.1770, 3 1/4-In. Cup, 5 3/8-In. Saucer 460.00
Teapot, Chinaman Amid Shrubbery, Loop Handle, c.1768, 5 3/8 In............................... 1850.00
Vase, Dr. Wall, Blue, White, 15 In., Pair...*Illus* 4125.00
Waste Bowl, King Of Prussia, Transfer Printed, c.1760, 6 1/8 In. 520.00

WORLD WAR I and World War II souvenirs are collected today. Be careful
not to store anything that includes live ammunition. Your local police will tell
you how to dispose of the explosives. See also Sword and Trench Art.

WORLD WAR I, Ashtray, German Imperial 20.00
Booklet, Job Book, For Men Leaving Service, Library War Service, 64 Pages, 1919..... 13.50
Ditty Bag, Eagle, Silk 165.00
Figure, Uncle Sam, Bond Display, Plaster, 26 In. 750.00
Label, Mailing, Buy War Bonds, Machine Gunners, Unused, 7 In. 6.00
Pillow, U.S. Army, Inflatable... 18.00
Poster, Americans All, Victory Liberty Loan, H.C. Christy, c.1919, 40 x 27 In............. 86.25
Poster, Fight Or Buy Bonds, Third Liberty Loan, H.C. Christy, c.1917, 40 x 30 In. 143.75
Poster, Greatest Mother In The World, Red Cross, c.1918, 37 1/2 x 27 In. 109.25
Sword & Scabbard, Officer's Dress Parade.. 75.00
Uniform, Balloon Corp Lieutenant, Sam Brown Belt... 2200.00
WORLD WAR II, Belt, Cartridge, U.S. Army, Web.. 18.00
Button, Kilroy Was Here-Buy War Bonds, 1 1/4 In.. 30.00
Canteen, U.S. Army, Cup & Cover... 15.00
Clock, Ship's, U.S. Navy 275.00
Dagger, Luftwaffe, Officer's Dress, G. Weyersberg & Sons, 19 1/2 In. 302.50
Dagger, SS Officer, Chained, Polished Blade With Motto, M36 Type........................... 2500.00
First Aid Pouch, U.S. Army, Web.. 6.00
Flare Pistol, Nazi, Black Leather Holster.. 495.00
Gas Mask, U.S. Army, Lightweight Service, With Bag 218.00
Gun Sight, Air Force, B-29 .... 85.00
Helmet, Aviator's, Leather 95.00
Helmet, Flying, Leather, Air Force, A-11 .... 95.00
Helmet, Mosquito Net, U.S. Army, Head Cover 12.00
Jacket, Dress, Navy Pilot, Bouillon Wings, Lieutenant Commander 70.00
Jacket & Pants, Navy, Bombardier, Fleece Lined 460.00
Knife, Dagger, Nazi Air Force, Engraved Blade, Case 565.00
Life Preserver, Mae West, Air Force, B-4, Dated 1944 .... 125.00
Life Preserver, U.S. Navy, Inflatable.. 55.00
Medal, Woman's Army Corp., Bronze 45.00
Mess Kit, Nazi, Marked Spoon.. 100.00
Mess Kit, U.S. Army 15.00
Monocular, Air Force, Case 45.00
Periscope, Trench, Case, Japanese, 5 x 10.. 175.00
Pin, George Patton, Celluloid, 1 1/4 In... 13.00
Pin, Lapel, Nazi SS, Round, Swastika, Enamel 125.00
Pin, Student Campaign Against The Nazis, 5 Arrows, 1 1/4 In. 7.00
Pin, Triple S, Save Material, Save Jobs, Serve Country, Black, 1 1/4 In. 16.00
Poster, United Nations Fight For Freedom, 30 UN Flags, c.1942, 29 x 40 In.................. 45.00
Radar Trainer, U.S. Navy, Ordnance, Case, Mark 5 .... 125.00
Ring, Sterling Silver, U.S. Air Corps.. 55.00
Saber, Army Officer's, F. Horster, Solingen, Spread Eagle Swastika, German 550.00
Skirt & Blouse, Service & Overseas Cap, WAAC 75.00
Toilet Paper, Hitler, 3 Sheets In Envelope 65.00
Vest, Flying, Air Force, Green Fabric, Alpaca Lining... 175.00
Wings, 1st Air Force, Bullion, Hand Made, Gold & Silver Threads............................... 13.50
Wings, 8th Air Force, Stubby Wing, Hand Made, Gold & Silver Threads 12.00

WORLD'S FAIR souvenirs from all of the fairs are collected. The first fair
was the Great Exhibition of 1851 in London. Other important exhibitions and
fairs include Philadelphia, 1876 (Centennial); Chicago, 1893 (World's
Columbian); Buffalo, 1901 (Pan-American); St. Louis, 1904 (Louisiana Pur-

chase); San Francisco, 1915 (Panama-Pacific); Philadelphia, 1926 (Sesqui-centennial); Chicago, 1933 (Century of Progress); Cleveland, 1936 (Great Lakes); San Francisco, 1939 (Golden Gate International); New York, 1939 (World of Tomorrow); Seattle, 1962; New York, 1964; Montreal, 1967; New Orleans, 1984; Tsukuba, Japan, 1985; Vancouver, B.C., 1986; Brisbane, Australia, 1988; Seville, Spain, 1992; and Genoa, Italy, 1992. Memorabilia of fairs include directories, pictures, fabrics, ceramics, etc.

Bandanna, 1939, New York, 19 x 20 In.	65.00
Bank, 1893, Ceramic, 4 3/8 In.	440.00
Bank, 1893, Mechanical, Cast Iron, Charles Bailey, 8 3/16 In.	805.00
Bank, 1939, New York, Tin, 12 1/4 In.	275.00
Bank, 1939, New York, White Metal, 5 In.	286.00
Bank, 1939, New York, White Metal, 8 1/2 In.	187.00
Bank, 1964, New York, Mechanical, White Metal 10 3/4 In.	99.00
Bobbin' Head, 1964, New York, Girl	30.00
Book, 1915, Panama Pacific International Expo., 70 Views, Paper Wrap	45.00
Book, 1939, New York, 60 Pages, 9 x 6 In.	15.00
Booklet, 1921, Paris Exposition, Map	15.00
Booklet, 1939, Recipes From Bordens, 32 Pages	27.00
Bottle, Vinegar, 1939, Milk Glass, A & P	35.00
Button, 1939, New York, 1/14 In.	12.00
Button, Flicker, 1964, New York, Package	20.00
Cane, 1934, Metal, Chicago	25.00
Chair, 1939, Folding, Can-O-Seat	60.00
Cigar Box, 1893, Chicago	25.00
Cigarette Lighter, 1939, New York, Clear Glass	60.00
Compact, 1934, Chicago, Century Of Progress, Federal Building	75.00
Compact, 1939, Blue & White Logo, Metal	65.00
Cookbook, 1964, Borden, New York	15.00
Doll, 1939, Dandy Goodwill, Composition, Joy Doll Products, 14 1/4 In.	287.00
Egg, 1904, Louisiana Purchase, Tin	50.00
Game, 1904, Down The Pike With Mrs.Wiggs, Milton Bradley	175.00
Glass, 1904, Ax With George Washington	100.00
Glass, 1936, Souvenir Great Lakes Expo	26.00
Glass, 1962, Seattle, 4 1/4 In.	4.00
Glass, 1964, New York	4.00
Guide Book, 1939, New York, Belgian Pavilion, 100 Pages	20.00
Hat Box, 1939, Adams, New York, Oval, 14 In.	65.00
Juicer, 1939, New York, Vita, Glass, With Cover, Box	10.00
Key Thermometer, 1933, Chicago, Century Of Progress, To City	25.00
Knife, 1933, Pocket, Century Of Progress, Steel, Pictures Planet & Chicago	85.00
Knife, 1982, Parker	11.00
Knife, Pocket, 1933	35.00
Map, 1904, St. Louis, Press & Publicity Dept, Folding, Color, 3 x 5 1/2 In.	12.00
Map, 1939, BMT Transit Line, Travel Guide	15.00
Map, 1939, New York	15.00
Mug, 1893, Quadruple	30.00
Mug, 1933, Chicago, Embossed Nudes, Nude Handle	50.00
Mug, 1964, New York, President Kennedy	25.00
Napkin Ring, 1893, Chicago, Metal	22.00
Paperweight, 1893, Chicago, Virginia State Building, Milk Glass, Libbey	45.00
Paperweight, 1904, St. Louis, Festival Hall	45.00
Paperweight, 1904, St. Louis, Observation Wheel	175.00
Paperweight, 1967, Montreal Expo, Plastic, Ramp, Fence, Monorail, Liquid, Glitter	3.00
Parasol, 1936, Great Lakes Expo, Cleveland	29.00
Pass, 1893, Columbia Exposition, Dedication Ceremonies, Sept. 17	45.00
Pencil Holder, 1933, Chicago, Painted Bulldog, Medallion Around Neck, 1 3/4 In.	37.50
Pennant, 1939, Golden Gate	15.00
Pillow Cover, 1939, Art Deco, Satin, Airplane Decoration	66.00
Pin, 1940, Scotty Dog, New York, Date On Chain	35.00
Pitcher, 1939, New York, George Washington, Bisque, 2 In.	35.00
Pitcher, 1939, Porcelier, 5 1/2 In.	80.00

Plaque, 1939, New York, Sweden, Costumed Dancers, Colorful, 7 In. 22.00
Plaque, 1964, New York 10.00
Plate, 1893, Columbian Exposition, Machinery Building, Wedgwood 65.00
Plate, 1904, Festial Hall & Cascade Gardens, Glass, Embossed Flower Border 85.00
Plate, 1939, Unisphere, Green & White 22.00
Plate, 1940, San Francisco Exposition, Homer Laughlin 175.00
Plate, 1964, New York, Blue & Orange 75.00
Playing Cards, 1933, Chicago, Century Of Progress 35.00
Postcard, 1933, Chicago & New York, Used & Unused, 50 Piece 50.00
Postcard, 1964, Reddy Kilowatt 9.00
Postcard, 1965, 4 Piece 15.00
Ribbon, 1893, Columbian Exhibition, Award To National Sewing Machine Co. 45.00
Salt & Pepper, 1893, Chicago, Condiment 275.00
Salt & Pepper, 1939 .... 25.00
Skillet, 1904, St. Louis, Home Comfort Ranges, Miniature 25.00
Spoon, 1901, Pan American Exposition Tower, Sterling Silver 22.00
Spoon, 1933, Chicago .... 12.00 to 18.00
Spoon, 1933, Chicago Century Of Progress, Sterling Silver 32.00
Spoon, 1939, New York, Textile Building 10.00
Tape Measure, 1933, Chicago 13.00
Thermometer, 1939, Golden Gate 15.00
Tin, 1904, St. Louis, Jack Daniels Whiskey 110.00
Toy, 1933, Chicago, Semi, Greyhound, Arcade 225.00
Toy, 1933, Trailer & Cab, 7 1/2 In. 250.00
Toy, 1939, 2-Piece Tractor Train, Driver, Arcade 350.00
Tray, 1967, Montreal Expo, Smoke Glass, Expo Scene, Gold, White, 4 x 4 3/4 In. 5.00
Tumbler, 1904, St. Louis 32.00
Tumbler, 1904, St. Louis, Carlsbad, China 50.00
Tumbler, 1939, New York, Marine Transportation Building, 5 1/4 In. 12.00
View-Master Reel, 1939, New York, No. 88 .... 30.00
View-Master Reel, 1964, New York, Package, 18 Piece 100.00
Watch, 1904, St. Louis, Chain & Pencil Fob 200.00
Watch Fob, 1893, Chicago, Columbian Exposition .... 45.00 to 95.00

WRISTWATCH came into use during World War I. Wristwatches are listed
here by manufacturer or as advertising or character watches. Pocket watches
are listed in the Watch category.

Advertising, Campbells, Battery Operated, Leather Band, Box 35.00
Advertising, Hush Puppies Shoes, Logo, Animated Dial, 1960s 160.00
Advertising, Ritz Crackers, Crackers Indicate Hour, Steel, 1960s 825.00
Advertising, Ronald McDonald, Woman's 40.00
Advertising, Star-Kist Tuna, Charlie, Gold Toned, Glow In Dark Numbers, 1971 .... 95.00
Bulova, 14K Gold Filled, 17 Jewel 90.00
Bulova, 14K White Gold Diamond, Diamond Band 650.00
Bulova, Tank Watch, 14K Pink Gold, Gold-Filled Band, 1940s 300.00
Bulova, Woman's, Gold Filled, Diamond Chips, 23 Jewel, c.1940 .... 140.00
Cartier, Tank, 18K Gold & Diamond, 17 Jewel, Black Dial 1840.00
Cartier, Woman's, 18K Yellow Gold, Oval Dial, Roman Numerals, Flexible Band 1042.00
Cartier, Woman's, Gold Washed, Marked .925 .... 350.00
Character, Abbott & Costello, Bradley, Box 60.00
Character, Barbie, Mattel, Box, 1964 .... 125.00
Character, Buffy & Jody, Family Affair 30.00
Character, California Raisins, Black Band, LED, 1988 .... 45.00
Character, Cinderella, 1950 .... 60.00
Character, Evil Knievel, 1976 .... 85.00
Character, Fred Flintstone, Flintstone Band, 1972 .... 160.00
Character, G.I. Joe, Gilbert 100.00
Character, Jackie Gleason, Ralph Kramden Face 45.00
Character, Morris The Cat 50.00
Character, Olympics, Los Angeles, Blue, LED, 1984 .... 30.00
Character, Pee Wee Herman, Package 18.00
Character, Roger Rabbit, White Band, Digitech 45.00
Character, Snoopy Time, Dial Face, Glossy Black Vinyl Strap 60.00

Character, Snoopy, Holding Tennis Racket, Animated, 1960s 90.00
Character, Star Trek, Mr. Spock, Box, 1979 .... 125.00
Character, Tony The Tiger, Woman's, Box 65.00
Character, Wonder Woman, Dabbs, Box, 1970s 175.00
Character, Zorro, Box 325.00
Corum, On $10 Gold Coin, 18K Gold Brick Textured Band 1840.00
Elgin, Woman's, Platinum & Diamond, Metal Expandable Band 175.00
Eterna, Woman's, Jeweled Movement, Stem Wind, 14K Yellow Gold 345.00
Fendi, Bracelet, Black Face, Second Hand, Date Window, 18K Gold, Box 2850.00
Geneve, Woman's, Platinum, Brilliant & Baguette Diamonds, Black Cord Strap 1035.00
Gruen, 4 Strand Seed Pearl Bracelet 95.00
Hamilton, 22 Jewel, 14K Gold, 1950 .... 500.00
Hamilton, Platinum & Diamond, 17 Jewel 315.00
Hamilton, Thin-O-Matic, 14K Gold, Sweep Second Hand 300.00
Hamilton, Woman's, 14K White Gold, Diamond Chevrons Frank Face 132.00
Hamilton, Woman's, 14K White Gold, Marquise-Shaped Case, Diamond Bezel 575.00
Hamilton, Woman's, Circular Hinged Cover, 14K White Gold, Diamond Bracelet 2645.00
Hamilton, Woman's, Cushion-Shaped Case, Platinum, Diamond Bracelet 1725.00
Hamilton, Woman's, Single-Cut Diamond Shoulders, Woven Mesh Bracelet 258.75
Henry Sandoz, Woman's, Platinum, Rectangular Case, Diamond Case & Bracelet 2070.00
Hinged Cover, Woman's, Brilliant & Single Cut Diamonds, Diamond Bracelet 1150.00
King Center, 4 Playing Card Signs, Game, 1920 .... 88.00
Longines, 14K Gold 168.00
Longines, 14K Gold, 1950s 250.00
Longines, 14K Gold, Round Lugs, Alligator Strap 350.00
Longines, Gold, Square Dial, Gilt Batons, Second Hands, Chevron Gold Band 518.00
Longines, Ruby & Diamonds, Double Rope-Link Bracelet, 14K Gold, c.1940 .... 747.50
Longines, Woman's, 10 Diamonds, Tiny Face, 14K White Gold, 17 Jewel, c.1940 .... 295.00
Longines, Woman's, 14K White Gold, Diamonds Around Dial, c.1940 .... 175.00
Longines, Woman's, Rectangular Case, Platinum, Diamonds, Black Cord Strap 1725.00
Louis Pierre, Woman's, Concealed In 14K Gold Mesh Band 750.00
Movado, Calendomatic, 14K Yellow Gold, Leather Strap 1092.50
Movado, Calendomatic, Stainless Steel 325.00
Movado, Calendomatic, Stainless Steel, Speidel Stretch Band, 1950s 375.00
Movado, Tank Watch, 14K Gold, Two-Tone Dial, 1940s 500.00
Movado, Two-Tone Dial, 14K Gold, Late 1930s 400.00
Movado, Woman's, Yellow Gold, Hinged Cover, Not Running 275.00
Omega, Automatic, Calendar, Stainless Steel, Mesh Bracelet 195.00
Omega, Constellation, 18K Gold, Satin White Dial, Day/Date 1800.00
Omega, Moon Phase, Calendar, 18K, Pink Gold, 17 Jewel, Silvered Dial, c.1945 .... 2587.00
Omega, Woman's, 14K Yellow Gold Oval Case, Diamond & Ruby Bracelet 805.00
Omega, Woman's, Brilliant Cut Diamonds, 18K Gold, Braided Mesh Strap 635.00
Patek Philippe, 18K Yellow Gold, Round Blue Dial, Textured Band 2465.00
Patek Philippe, Ellipse, Blue Matte Dial, 18K, Oval, 18 Jewel 3105.00
Patek Philippe, Gold, Micrometer Regulator, 18K Gold, 20 Diamonds 1760.00
Patek Philippe, Rose Gold Case & Dial, Gilt Roman Numerals, Leather Strap 2530.00
Patek Philippe, Woman's, 20 Full Cut Diamonds, 18K White Gold 1667.00
Pery, Platinum, 73 Single & Round Cut Diamonds, 17 Jewel 288.00
Piaget, 18K Gold, Rectangular Champagne Dial, Baton Chapters, Mesh Band 1150.00
Piaget, Woman's, 8K White Gold, Diamond Bezel 1000.00
Rolex, 12 Diamonds, Manual Wind, Gold Tone Dial 2495.00
Rolex, 18K Gold, Baton Numerals, Silvered Dial, 17 Jewel, c.1950 .... 1840.00
Rolex, Daytona, Chronograph, Stainless Steel, 1960s 6500.00
Rolex, Man's, 18K Gold 1400.00
Rolex, Model 1002, Two-Tone 14K Gold & Stainless Steal, Leather Band 875.00
Rolex, Oyster, Stainless Steel, Pink Gold, Silvered Dial, Self-Winding, c.1945 .... 2587.00
Rolex, Woman's, Pink Gold Bracelet, 18K, Silvered Dial, 17 Jewel, c.1945 .... 2875.00
Tissot, 14K Gold, 1950s 250.00
Tourneau, Circular Dial, Sweep Seconds, Date Aperture, Leather Strap 402.50
Ulysse Nardin, 18K Gold Rectangular Case, Silvered Dial, Leather Strap 517.50
Ulysse Nardin, Circular 14K Yellow Gold Case, Scrolled Lugs, Leather Strap 632.50
Universal, 14K Yellow Gold, Flexible Link Band, c.1957 .... 935.00
Vacheron & Constantin, 18K, Pink Gold, Silvered Dial, c.1950 .... 2185.00

Woman's, 14K Yellow Gold, Roman Numerals, Oval Dial, Rope Twist Band 805.00
Woman's, 18K Gold, Arabic Numerals, Diamond Set Bezel, Hinged Design, 1925 .... 2175.00
Woman's, Open Face, Key Wind, 18K Gold, Enamel Dial 82.00
Woman's, Piaget, 18K Yellow Gold, Roman Numerals, Diamonds, Mesh Band 2465.00

YELLOWWARE is a heavy earthenware made of a yellowish clay. It varies in
color from light yellow to orange-yellow. Many nineteenth- and twentieth-
century kitchen bowls and jugs were made of yellowware. It was made in
England and in the United States. Another form of pottery that is sometimes
classed as yellowware is listed in this book in the Mocha category.

Bank, Pig, Brown & Blue Sponging, 6 In. 132.00
Beater Jar, Folda, Minn. 85.00
Bedpan, Mocha, White Band, Blue Seaweed Design, Brown Stripes, 8 1/4 In. .. 100.00 to 110.00
Bowl, 3 White Bands, 4 1/4 x 2 In. 95.00
Bowl, Blue & White Bands, 7 In. 72.00
Bowl, Blue & White Bands, 8 In. 75.00
Bowl, Blue & White Bands, Large 45.00
Bowl, Blue Seaweed On White Band, Black Stripes, 11 3/4 In. 110.00
Bowl, Blue Seaweed On White Band, East Liverpool, 8 3/4 In. 192.50
Bowl, Blue Seaweed, White Band, Brown Stripes, 8 1/2 In. 241.50
Bowl, Blue Stripe, 10 In. 25.00
Bowl, Brown & White Bands, 14 x 7 In. 120.00
Bowl, Cobalt Blue Bands, Rust, 9 1/2 In. 35.00
Bowl, Cottage Scene, 10 In. 120.00
Bowl, Green & White Stripes, Marked Watt, 5 In. 30.00
Bowl, Green Foliage 100.00
Bowl, Mixing, Blue & White Stripes, 9 x 5 In. 25.00
Bowl, Mixing, Mocha, White Band, Blue Seaweed Design, 14 3/4 In. 165.00
Bowl, Mixing, White Band, Brown Stripes, Green Seaweed, 13 1/2 In. 155.00
Bowl, Mocha Design, Blue Seaweed On White Band, 8 3/4 In. 275.00
Bowl, Mocha Design, Green Seaweed, 4 In. 68.00
Bowl, Peacock & Fountain, Brown 575.00
Chamber Pot, Blue Spooning, 1 5/8 In. 82.00
Chamber Pot, Miniature 50.00
Chamber Pot, White Band, Blue Seaweed, Miniature 150.00
Cooler, Keg Shape, Price, Bristol, 20 In. 93.50
Jar, Spice, Ginger 175.00
Jar, Tobacco, Woman Finial Cover, Swags & Women's Heads, England, 6 1/2 In. 93.00
Mixing Bowl, Raised Design, Grip Stand, England, 13 x 6 In. 48.00
Mold, Food, Grapes ....85.00 to 95.00
Mold, Pineapple 60.00
Mold, Pudding, Rat Form, 10 In. 55.00
Mold, Rabbit 95.00
Mug, Black Transfer Cow Design, Silver Luster Rim, Leaf Handle, 2 5/8 In. 302.00
Mug, Blue Bands 175.00
Mug, Buckeye 22.50
Mug, White Band, Black Seaweed, Brown Stripes, 3 1/8 In. 523.00
Pepper Pot, Blue Seaweed Design 795.00
Pie Plate, Pumpkin Yellow, 10 In. 65.00
Pitcher, Brown & Green Spongeware, 1900, 7 1/4 In. 100.00
Pitcher, Brown, Black & Green Sponging, 6 3/4 In. 203.50
Pitcher, Cobalt Blue Band, Buff Color, 1880s, 9 1/4 In. 240.00
Pitcher, Dolphin Handle, 2 Qt. 95.00
Pitcher, Embossed Trees, 4 3/4 In. 25.00
Pitcher, Green Bark Type Exterior 80.00
Pitcher, Green Glaze, 10 In. 60.00
Pitcher, Herbert Hoover, c.1928, 6 1/4 In. 95.00
Pitcher, Molded Basket Weave, 1900, 8 7/8 In. 100.00
Rolling Pin, Wooden Axle 200.00
Salt Shaker, Blue Stripes, Footed, 2 1/8 In. 220.00
Wall Salt, Wood Cover, Hinged, Cobalt "salt, " 6 In. 120.00
Washboard, Toy 535.00

ZANE Pottery was founded in 1921 by Adam Reed and Harry McClelland in South Zanesville, Ohio, at the old Peters and Reed Building. Zane pottery is very similar to Peters and Reed pottery, but it is usually marked. The factory was sold in 1941 to Lawton Gonder.

Vase, Green & Cream Drip Over Light & Dark Speckled Brown, 8 In........................... 135.00

ZANESVILLE Art Pottery was founded in 1900 by David Schmidt in Zanesville, Ohio. The firm made faience umbrella stands, jardinieres, and pedestals. The company closed in 1962. Many pieces are marked with just the words *La Moro*.

LA MORO

Planter, Scotty, Large... 35.00

ZSOLNAY pottery was made in Hungary after 1862 and was characterized by Persian, Art Nouveau, or Hungarian motifs. A series of new Zsolnay figurines with green-gold luster finish is available in many shops today. Early Zsolnay was not marked, but by 1878, the tower trademark was used.

Ewer, Medallions Alternate With Reticulation, Green, Beige, Ornate Handle, 4 1/2 In..	90.00
Figurine, Buffalo	295.00
Figurine, Walking Bears, Green, Iridescent	245.00
Figurine, Wrestling Bears, Signed, 1911, 13 In.	1265.00
Jug, Reticulated, Double Walled, Openwork Handle, 5 3/4 In.	200.00
Vase, Baluster Shape, Mottled Silver-Red Iridescent, Flying Hawk, 10 1/4 In.	2300.00
Vase, Bulbous, Red To Purples, Swirl, Iridescent, 6 1/2 In.	325.00
Vase, Figural, 3 Lizards Peering Into Pierced Top, Signed, c.1900, 8 In.	8050.00
Vase, Iridescent Eggplant Glaze, Frogs, Pierced Pods, 4 5/8 In.	1610.00
Vase, Marbleized Luster Glaze, Signed, 13 In.	600.00
Vase, Red Poppy, Iridescent, 18 In.	3100.00
Vase, Reticulated Design, Scrollwork, Horizontal Bands, Handles, Tower Mark, 8 In...	275.00
Vase, Silver-Red Iridescent Ground, Stylized Hawk In Flight, Baluster, 10 1/4 In........	2300.00

INDEX

This index is computer-generated, making it as complete as possible. References in upper-case type are category listings. Those in lower-case letters refer to additional pages of the book where the piece can be found. There is also an internal indexing system used in the main part of the book, so if you look for a Kewpie doll in the doll section, you will be told it is in the Kewpie section. There is additional information about where to find prices of pieces similar to yours at the end of many paragraphs.

THE KOVELS' LIBRARY

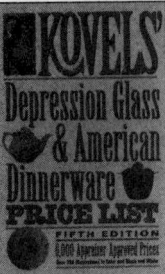

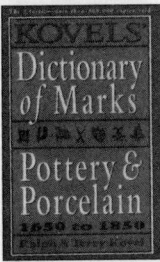
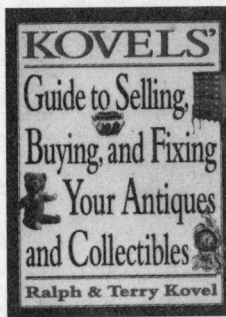

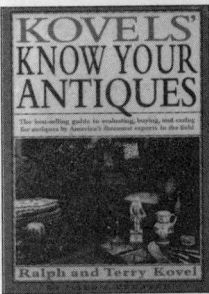

KOVELS' AMERICAN ART POTTERY
The Collector's Guide to Makers,
Marks, and Factory Histories

At last! *Kovels' American Art Pottery,* the book you have been waiting for. Here is information on 104 potteries and 95 tile factories. Fabulous color and black-and-white photographs show details of design, lists of makers with the identifying marks, factory marks with dating information, and hundreds of clues to help the collector identify all types of art pottery. More than 700 pictures of art pottery, from the $198,000 green Rookwood "fish" vase to the ordinary Weller bowl worth $50 are included. This is the book for the beginner or serious collector, with extensive history and production information written to aid you in identification of art pottery. Listed here from A to Z are the major potteries, such as Rookwood, Weller, Ohr, Roseville, Newcomb, Van Briggle, and Dedham, as well as the less well-known works of the North Dakota School of Mines, Arequipa, Avon, Ouachita, Roblin, or Walrath. Also included are tile companies, with marks, pictures, and histories. *Kovels' American Art Pottery* is a beautiful coffee-table color picture book that belongs in every collector's research library.

580128 336 pages / $60.00 hardcover

THE AMERICAN ENLIGHTENMENT
The Shaping of the American
Experiment and a Free Society

By Adrienne Koch

PHILOSOPHY FOR A TIME OF CRISIS

JEFFERSON AND MADISON:
The Great Collaboration

POWER, MORALS AND THE FOUNDING FATHERS

PHILOSOPHY OF THOMAS JEFFERSON

ADAMS AND JEFFERSON:
Posterity Must Judge

THE AMERICAN ENLIGHTENMENT

The Shaping of the American Experiment and a Free Society

SELECTED AND EDITED WITH INTRODUCTION
AND NOTES BY

Adrienne Koch

GEORGE BRAZILLER

NEW YORK

Acknowledgments

For permission to reprint the selections in this volume the editor is indebted to the following publishers and editors:

COLUMBIA UNIVERSITY PRESS—selections from *The Papers of Alexander Hamilton*, Harold C. Syrett, Editor, copyright 1961, 1962 by Columbia University Press.

HARVARD UNIVERSITY PRESS—selections reprinted by permission of the publishers from *Diary and Autobiography of John Adams* and *Family Correspondence*, Lyman H. Butterfield, Editor, Cambridge, Mass., The Belknap Press of Harvard University Press, copyright 1961, 1963, by The President and Fellows of Harvard College.

PRINCETON UNIVERSITY PRESS—selections from *The Papers of Thomas Jefferson*, Julian P. Boyd, Editor, copyright 1950, 1951, 1952 by Princeton University Press.

THE UNIVERSITY OF CHICAGO PRESS—selections from *The Papers of James Madison*, William T. Hutchinson and William M. E. Rachal, Editors, copyright 1962 by the University of Chicago.

YALE UNIVERSITY PRESS—selections from *The Papers of Benjamin Franklin*, Leonard W. Labaree, Editor, copyright 1959, 1960, 1961 by the American Philosophical Society.

To my mother

I wish to acknowledge with gratitude the grant extended to me by the Institute of Social Sciences of the University of California at Berkeley in support of research for this study.

It is a pleasure to say thanks to my graduate research assistant, William Derveniotes, for his good-natured and intelligent help; and to Renée Renouf Hall, for typing the manuscript and converting a routine task into an affair of friendly excitement, almost a lark. As for my husband, Lawrence Robert Kegan, I discovered long ago that his acute intellect and powers of logical organization were essential to me and I have continued to exploit him shamelessly and happily for the benefit of this book.

A. K.

Preface

Out of the classic period of American thought, the age of the Enlightenment, came a body of ideas which, incorporated in our constitutions and our political traditions, have served as fundamental guidelines for the nation throughout its history. These principles, embodied in such documents as the Declaration of Independence, the Constitution, and the Bill of Rights, have retained their cogency through the centuries.

The writings of the leading American exponents of Enlightenment thought still read with a resplendent freshness. Stylistic brilliance and a breadth of vision distinguish the diverse work of all five men represented in this volume, whether they were concerning themselves with government, economics, the arts, science, or questions involving human passions.

Yet, although there was much that was memorable in the thoughts of Benjamin Franklin, John Adams, Thomas Jefferson, James Madison, and Alexander Hamilton, it is possible for us today to be misled. These are not twentieth century men. They were men of their own time and they wrote as such; their attitudes at times differ markedly from those of later years. Hence the particular significance of of Adrienne Koch's selections and introductions. She has brought to them her own profound knowledge of the era and its thought, and has placed these writings in their proper context and interrelationships, providing an indispensable guide to those brilliant but very human eighteenth century figures who were the Founding Fathers.

Readers need not be alarmed by Professor Koch's warning that she writes of this age "con amore." Who would dispute her judgment that "the period of the American Enlightenment was an exceptional, indeed, a glorious, time of thought and human constructive effort," and that "the writings which were its products represent a rich vein of moral and political wisdom hard to match anywhere in the history of Western civilization"?

Frank Freidel

Contents

LETTERS

OTHER WRITINGS

PART V   ALEXANDER HAMILTON

AUTOBIOGRAPHY

LETTERS

OTHER WRITINGS

Introduction

Adrienne Koch

This volume on the American Enlightenment presents representative selections from the writings and papers of five memorable Americans: Benjamin Franklin, John Adams, Thomas Jefferson, James Madison, and Alexander Hamilton. The selections attempt to show the scope of their abilities and activities and the nature of the contributions they made to the formation of American society. In a very real sense, these are the men who pre-eminently fulfill the role of makers of the American political tradition. Their vision and their spirit provided the foundations for that free society which developed in subsequent years into the most flourishing democratic civilization in the modern world.

It is natural to expect that a historian will write of his chosen period of time and thought "con amore." For it would be a sad task to devote many years of a meager human life to the study of men, minds, actions and achievements that were devoid of the glitter and pull of deep human significance. The reader must therefore be on guard from the opening of this volume to its close for the implicit judgment of the editor, that the period of the American Enlightenment was an exceptional, indeed, a glorious, time of thought and human constructive effort; and that the writings which were its products represent a rich vein of moral and political wisdom hard to match anywhere in the history of Western civilization.

1

The period of the American Enlightenment spanned the half century from 1765 to 1815 and was, in the words of John Adams, "an age of revolutions and constitutions." It opened with the developing arguments

for separation from Great Britain, culminating with the Declaration of Independence. Efforts were then made to establish securely the new political order for which the revolution was fought. These creative inventions included the Articles of Confederation, state constitutions, and the Federal Constitution. The third and final phase embraced the first critical steps toward transforming a ratified paper constitution into a functioning representative government on a national scale.

Each of these three major phases were stages in a continuing revolution, maturing, unlike later revolutionary developments, in more effective democratic institutions. For this reason, the period of the American Enlightenment marked a new chapter in the history of man. The first revolutionary phase witnessed the making of an entirely new kind of revolution against imperial power which caught the imagination of the entire civilized world, with incalculable consequences for the redirection of thought and reconstruction of society. The second constitutional phase involved another unprecedented process: the creation of an "extensive republic" unlike any that existed before, both in terms of the process of deliberation by a group of enlightened men which produced and ratified the constitutions—state and federal—and in terms of the central human ethos reflected in the provisions of these organic laws. The third phase established the first new nation in the modern sense, a nation under a two-party system and in a setting of economic growth.

These claims for the significance of the American Enlightenment are not simply personal or parochial prejudices. They are supported by the judgments of political and philosophical critics the world over, in successive waves from the eighteenth century to our own day. For example, in the key year 1776, as far away as Naples, the Abbe Galiani addressed a friend in Paris in this revealing way: "The epoch has become one of the total fall of Europe, and of transmigration into America. All here turns into rottenness—religion, law, arts, sciences—and all hastens to renew itself in America. This is not a jest; nor is it an idea drawn from the English quarrels; I have said it. . . . for more than twenty years, and I have constantly seen my prophecies come to pass. Therefore, do not buy your house in the Chaussée d'Antin; you must buy it in Philadelphia."

It is well known that the enlightened philosophes in France outdid other Europeans in acclaiming and affiliating themselves with the American cause. Nor should we forget the famous young lords of the Queen's circle—Ségur, Noailles, the Dillons, Lafayette—who had, in the Count de Ségur's words, grown tired of the "gilded servitude" of the court and were ready to stake fortune and risk life serving in a far-away Revolutionary War that represented an ideal "cause." In addition, there were the French soldiers and sailors who tended to be enthusiastic gospelizers for American freedom and the American "ex-

ample" when they returned to France. And finally we must reckon with the innumerable friends of the adored Dr. Franklin who coalesced, as well they might, their reverence for him with his country's venture. The list of the illustrious Doctor's friends and admirers is too long to print here; but prominent among them were the intimates of Madame de Helvetius' brilliant salon—the Marquis de Condorcet, the Abbé Morellet, Cabanis, Volney, Destutt de Tracy. Other great and influential friends of America were Turgot, the Duc de la Rochefoucauld, Démeunier, the Abbés Mably, Chalut and Arnoux. Since for all well-wishers the American "example" of freedom was more than a question of detached study, myths and legends flourished. But one kernel of truth was apprehended by them all. It was most strikingly expressed by the Marquis de Chastellux, in his journals: "I firmly believe that Parliament has no right to tax America without her consent," he wrote, "and I also believe that when a noble people say "We want to be free" it is difficult to prove that they are in the wrong." So powerful, indeed, did the pro-American sentiment become in France that it must be counted one of the intellectual causes of the French Revolution.

Across the channel, English liberals and radicals too numerous to name were also eager students and advocates of the American cause. Richard Price, who spoke for so many of them, was an ardent friend who did not hesitate, in his published works, to celebrate what had been achieved in America and to recommend what he believed should be the next steps. As he wrote to Benjamin Rush in 1783: "The struggle has been glorious on the part of America; and it has now issued just as I wished it to issue: in the emancipation of the American States and the establishment of their independence. . . . I think it one of the most important revolutions that has ever taken place in the world. It makes a new opening in human affairs which may prove an introduction to times of more light and liberty and virtue than have been yet known."

So far, the views cited are those of the Italian, French and English liberal intellectuals in the late eighteenth century who contributed to the European Enlightenment. But the judgment that the work of the American Enlightenment constituted a momentous new chapter in Western civilization is reaffirmed by later commentators in the nineteenth century. Who is not familiar with Prime Minister Gladstone's pronouncement that the American Constitution was "the most remarkable work known to me in modern times to be produced by the human intellect at a single stroke (so to speak) in its application to political affairs"? Perhaps less familiar is the more memorable appreciation we owe to the French social philosopher, Alexis de Tocqueville, who wrote: "In that land the great experiment of the attempt to construct society upon a new basis was to be made by civilized man; and it was there, for the first time, that theories hitherto unknown, or deemed impracticable, were to

exhibit a spectacle for which the world has not been prepared by the history of the past."

The tenor of the foregoing appraisals is echoed by students of the American Enlightenment in our own time. Thus, we have the judgment of the late Harold Laski that this fruitful period was a veritable political and social renaissance in America, animated by "one of the most informed public debates on the nature of free institutions ever to grace the annals of any nation;" while even more recently Max Beloff, the Gladstone Professor of Politics at Oxford, wrote that the American and French Revolutions together precipitated "the most prolonged and far-reaching examination of the basis of society and government which had been attempted since the age of Plato and Aristotle."

Finally, one turns homeward for support of foreign estimates of the American Enlightenment movement. Here one evaluation suffices, that of the contemporary American philosopher, Herbert Schneider, who, in his *History of American Philosophy*, aptly said: "Never in America were philosophical thinking and social action more closely joined—Never was history made more consciously and conscientiously, and seldom since the days of classic Greece has philosophy enjoyed greater opportunity to exercise public responsibility." For this reason, he concludes: "It is impossible to read and write dispassionately of the American Enlightenment, for it contains the heart of our heritage as a people and our deepest ties to the rest of humanity."

2

These reflections on the American Enlightenment focus our attention on the greatest of all historical forces, the human agent. A social movement, and the democratic revolution above all, must be understood in terms of men who made it: the root is man. The developments in the three major phases of the American Enlightenment were not fated by divine intervention, as suggested by the nineteenth century American historian, George Bancroft; or forced by economic causes, as proclaimed early in the twentieth century by the inimitable Charles Beard. They were largely the outcome of multiple, often conflicting human acts and choices under eighteenth century American conditions and favored by chance elements which we may call "luck."

In the first revolutionary phase, the over-riding need to unite the colonies, to organize the men and materials for the bleak and extended trial of seven years of battle, bloodshed, flight and stand, demanded intellectual power, moral courage, and the intelligence to meet and master a thousand unexpected necessities and emergencies. The second or constitutional phase may not have been the "miracle" it was pronounced to be by Gladstone, but it was surely a miracle of everyday patience, negotiations, political sagesse and invention, to prevail over

the jealous sovereignties of the states. The period of political argument and reflection persisted through the third phase of launching the Republic, in the critical decade when the new instrument of popular will was tested in practice, to establish whether it would float or founder—whether President Washington could succeed in holding the contending party factions together in peacetime, under non-military auspices to assure a unique democratic succession.

Seen in this perspective, the American Enlightenment required genius from its leading men. And what leaders there were! From the opening of the movement for independence in the 1760's to the establishment of the federated republic and its first decade of administrative solidification on the threshold of a new century, there were men of superb ability: James Otis, Sam Adams, Patrick Henry, John Dickinson, Benjamin Franklin, George Mason, George Wythe, George Washington, Thomas Jefferson, John Jay, James Wilson, Alexander Hamilton, James Madison, Benjamin Rush, among others.

Since the age of democratic revolution had a rich supply of gifted leaders, the editor's decision about which men to take as "representative" was far from easy. Unlike other periods in the American past—or in the history of any modern Western nation—this one embarrasses us with its luxuriant supply of leadership. A word, then, is required to explain why an indisputably great man, George Washington, is not represented by selected writings in this volume; and why the five men chosen *are* representative of the American Enlightenment.

We may get at the key criterion by citing the judgment of an English historian to the effect that Washington was "not an architect in ideas; he was essentially a man of deeds." He surveyed unexplored land, travelled on military missions into Indian country, mastered the art of military command and organization, read enough books to know the special character of the age he lived in, and sensed the repeated needs of his country for fresh experiments in government and union. It is true that his contribution to the winning of independence extended far beyond the field of his military genius in the technical sense. Indeed, the enlightened philosophes and statesmen of Europe made a cult of the *virtues* of this heroic and wise revolutionary leader, who firmly spurned every person who approached him to use his military command to make himself a dictator, or as some preferred, a king! He rightly and dutifully became the first President of the Republic he had already done so much to bring about, and he proved anew that he was *the* critical man, uniting all the former colonies of the new United States and accepting the ardors of political life for a second term (at the urging of such powerful antagonists as Hamilton and Jefferson) to assure its continued national existence as a republic. In terms of the primary contribution Washington made to the success of the revolutionary war,

and through the magic of his name in the unification of the Americans—
North, South and West—to support "the great Experiment," one can
hardly question that he is entitled to his name as "father" of the country.

It is thus appropriate at the outset to quote Washington on the central
core of faith shared by all these men as conscious and conscientious
believers in the mission of Enlightenment. At the end of the War of
Independence, Washington, much concerned about its political outcome,
addressed a circular letter in June, 1783, to the governors of the thirteen
states with the hopeful prophecy that the future of the Republic would
be assured if the union of the states could be preserved. He wrote
these words not simply as the military commander of a successful war
effort, but as the statesman and political leader he was already becoming:

"The foundation of our Empire was not laid in the gloomy age of
ignorance and superstition, but at an Epoch when the rights of mankind were better understood and more clearly defined, than at any former
period; the researches of the human mind after social happiness, have
been carried to a great extent, the treasures of knowledge, acquired
by the labours of Philosophers, Sages and Legislators, through a long
succession of years, are laid open for our use, and their collected wisdom
may be happily applied in the establishment of our forms of Government. . . . At this auspicious period, the United States came into existence as a Nation, and if their Citizens should not be completely free
and happy, the fault will be entirely their own."

Yet it remains true that if one would uncover the intellectual aspects
of the American Enlightenment, one must turn to other American
statesmen than Washington for its deeper and more detailed meaning.
Like Washington, Franklin, Adams, Jefferson, Madison and Hamilton
were men whose deeds left their mark on the American political tradition. But, unlike Washington, they were architects of ideas, whose
thought and writings were crucial in formulating our goals and forming our political institutions. They were our first advocates and illustrious
representatives to the world at large. Much that is known, and will
ever be known, as "American" had to do with the impression that these
five statesmen were able—sometimes singly, sometimes as a group—to
inspire in the judgment of men who were their contemporaries. Yet it
is all-important to recognize that without a deep new vision, defined
in writing and productive of social and institutional programs, the rage
for "the American Experiment" would have been as insubstantial and
fleeting as a brightly-colored gas balloon! This vision flowed from the
conjunction of political philosophy and social engineering and formed a
new moral imagination that would take the American Experiment beyond the letter, beyond the technicalities of simply one new set of men
in power. The fact that there were areas of firm agreement and yet

sharp differences among them helps us to feel the shock of real alternatives in the formative years of the democratic experiment and thus more able to see history in other terms than a flat and fictive determinism. The event-making and thought-making roles that established these five statesmen as most representative of the American Enlightenment can be seen in their leadership in each of the major patterns of that densely-textured tapestry of events we call the American Experiment.

3

In the first, revolutionary phase, Franklin, Adams and Jefferson provided the intellectual leadership which defined the rights of British Americans and then argued philosophically, legally and politically, for independence. Franklin, the oldest and most prudential of the group, initially argued for reform. As early as 1754, he proposed a thorough plan of inter-colonial union for defense, the so-called Albany Plan of Union. Franklin's plan did not bear fruit at the time, but like other interesting, short-run defeats, this one was, in fact, far from total. It sharpened Franklin's own perception of the growing need for some form of federation. Even his famous political cartoon for the Albany Plan—the cartoon of the severed body of the snake, captioned "Join or Die"—corroborates the point. In the American Revolution, it was snatched up and given wide use, its shattered parts apparently glistening with the sap of life which the revolutionaries were determined to set a-flowing again! In Franklin's own development, the Albany Plan was a notable first step which led him in the second Continental Congress to compose a draft "Articles of Confederation and Perpetual Union," again in advance of others, but this time his was an idea that did not have long to wait for action.

The great legal philosopher of the trio, John Adams, for his part was employing the casual phrase "we Americans" in his Diary as early as 1763. He confided that he was thrown into whirlwind action in the fateful year 1765 when the news of the Stamp Act blew up a storm in Massachusetts and the other colonies. In Adams' first influential essay, "A Dissertation on Canon and Feudal Law," he wrote that "It was not religion alone as is commonly supposed; but it was a love of universal liberty, and a hatred, a dread, a horror, of the infernal confederacy (between the two tyrannical systems of the canon and the feudal law) that projected, conducted, and accomplished the settlement of America." From bold sentiments of colonial liberty which he voiced in his influential "Braintree Instructions," and from a set of powerful essays printed in the Boston Gazette in 1775, Adams was building the moral, legal and political justification for resistance. He was erudite, as he threaded his way in questions of Parliamentary statutes, royal proclamation, traditions

of natural law and political philosophy, and he was eloquent as he mar-shalled the grievances of the colonies into the logic of separation from the British Empire—all but! For, lawyer-like, he drew a tenuous line arguing for a voluntary recognition (based on custom and not much more) of loyalty to the King and reaffirming that the American Whigs "*still consented*" that Parliament should regulate the trade of the "do-minions." By the time Adams rode into Philadelphia to take his place in the first Continental Congress he was, as he promptly reported, a marked man, known for his radical sentiments.

Jefferson, the talented young Virginian, entered the lists in 1773, when he joined the group of bold new patriot leaders like Patrick Henry and Richard Henry Lee. Acting as a standing committee of the Virginia House of Burgesses, these patriots and their associates were responsible for the first effective call for an inter-colonial linkage of the Committees of Correspondence. After the Boston Tea Party and the passage of the Coercive Acts which closed the port of Boston in 1774, Jefferson wrote his *Summary View of the Rights of British America*, the most fundamental protest against the oppressive legislation of Parliament. Jefferson's paper was drafted to guide the Virginia delegates to the first Continental Congress and it argued that Parliament had *no* authority over the colonies, that America had simply the same executive chief but no other political tie that warranted taxation or legislation of any sort whatever. This attempt to urge the concept of a commonwealth of nations, an imperial partnership, was based on an uncompromising concept of free men, possessed of the natural right to emigrate and establish laws on the basis of choice and reason. It was considered too bold at the time because it suggested goodbye to compromise. Nevertheless, it was printed and won fame quickly as a "handsome" public paper. Its audacity and clean logic earned Jefferson, in the view of Adams and others, the repu-tation that justified his selection to draft the Declaration of Independ-ence.

As a result of their influential and effective intellectual leadership, Franklin, Adams and Jefferson were brought into close mutual contact in the second Continental Congress, and the three worked together for Independence. It seems natural that these three men were selected to serve together on the five-man Committee charged with producing a draft of the Declaration of Independence. The glory of authorship of this document unsurpassed in the history of human freedom is clearly Jefferson's. Only a few and small changes are due to Adams and Frank-lin, none to Sherman and Livingston, the other two Committee members. Changes were more extensively made when the document went before the Congress. But Jefferson himself viewed Adams' role as strategic in securing the vote for the Declaration. He often volunteered statements like: "He [Adams] was the pillar of its support on the floor of Congress,

its ablest advocate and defender against the multiple assaults it encountered." Thus, although Jefferson as the author of the Declaration comes first to mind, it is important to remember that all three men—Franklin, Adams and Jefferson—were associated in the processes of philosophical inquiry, political action, and sustaining sentiment that produced this central achievement of the heart and will of the American Enlightenment.

4

In the second constitutional phase that developed as the natural sequence of the logic of Independence craved by free men, these three Americans were joined by the younger statesmen, Madison and Hamilton, in fighting for and formulating a basic constitutional philosophy and the cognate institutions that would secure democratic liberties as the fruits of colonial revolution. The culminating work of this period of experimentation with state constitutions is surely the central achievement of the mind of the American Enlightenment—the Federal Constitution. Here Madison as the "father" of the Constitution comes first to mind. But this, too, was not a solo performance. If we look deeper and try to gain more insightful understanding of its place in the processes of philosophical inquiry, political action and sentiment which produced it, we are made aware of the fact that all five American statesmen played major roles.

Three of these eminent statesmen—Franklin, Adams and Jefferson—recognized that the issuing of such manifestoes as the Declaration of Independence represented only the beginning of their work. Freedom, not anarchy or a new tyranny, was the desired goal and for this it was necessary to do more than win the revolutionary struggle. Franklin himself, as we have seen, drafted articles for confederation that updated the Albany Plan of Union and helped in the consideration of the Articles of Confederation which were soon adopted. Under the Confederation system, Congress acted principally as a committee, with the basic powers for the processes of government left to the states. It was therefore essential to organize these state governments on a firm representative basis.

The whole object of the revolutionary effort, Jefferson said, was to draft good republican constitutions for the states: "for should a bad government be instituted for us in future, it had been as well to have accepted at first the bad one offered to us from beyond the water without the risk and expense of contest." Jefferson proceeded to the constructive phase of the program with the proposal of new and basic legislation. In the spring of 1776, from Congress where he was a delegate, Jefferson sent his draft of a constitution for Virginia to the Virginia Convention.

It arrived late in the Convention's work, but Jefferson's preamble was adopted in its entirety as well as several other features. This was important since Virginia's was the first of the state constitutions to be formulated in the period of independence.

But it was in another context, in the autumn of 1776, that Jefferson entered upon a program of political reform that must truly be described as Herculean: the task of the revisal of the laws of Virginia. His aim was to bring the accumulated laws of colonial Virginia into conformity with republican principles and the dignity of a self-governing modern state. In this vast work he was associated with some of the finest legal minds in America—especially George Wythe and Edmund Pendleton, but Jefferson by himself drafted 126 bills—a system, as he described it in his autobiography, "by which every fibre would be eradicated of ancient or future aristocracy; and a foundation laid for a government truly republican."

Even more urgent than Jefferson's perception of the need for constitutional anchors was John Adams' anguished conviction that independence could become *merely* a destructive movement—"Samson, pulling down, unless the people also—preferably first—build up the house in which they will live." Not content with the fact that Congress adopted his resolution recommending that the colonies assume all the powers of government, he hastened early in the year 1776 to compose a small dissertation, in the form of a letter originally addressed to George Wythe of Virginia. This letter was in fact an essay on republican government and on how to construct a permanent constitutional framework, providing for elective, limited and balanced government. The exhilaration Adams felt with his pioneer role as lawgiver, as philosophical legislator, is reflected in his outburst to George Wythe: "You and I, my dear friend, have been sent into life at a time when the greatest lawgivers of antiquity would have wished to live. How few of the human race have ever enjoyed an opportunity of making an election of government—more than of air, soil, or climate—for themselves or their children! When, before the present epoch, had three millions of people full power and a fair opportunity to form and establish the wisest and happiest government that human wisdom can contrive?" Adams' creative encounter with lawgiving proved to be extensively influential in the constitutions adopted by the various states. He later became the principal architect of the Massachusetts Constitution of 1780, which provided, in his words, "a social compact, by which the whole people covenants with each citizen, and each citizen with the whole people, that all should be governed by certain laws for the common good." He thus tended to find confirmation for his notion that he had a unique role to play as Solon for all America.

Having seen to these preliminary safeguards for a constitutional

order, the three older statesmen were each in turn called upon to secure foreign financial, commercial and ideological support for the cause of the new American nation. In this critical effort of diplomacy, much depended upon Franklin's mastery of satire, his adroit and mysterious *sang-froid* in the company of the most sophisticated and sometimes cynical Europeans, and his vital fund of animal spirits and playfulness that kept the curse of dry-as-dust plaintiveness out of his relentless campaign to win respect for the new American experiment. Much also depended, in turn, upon Jefferson, whose cultivated and urbane comportment never masked an inner void, as he avidly entered upon discussions of ideas, and tirelessly hand-picked books from the bulging book-stalls of Paris to send home to politically active friends for their enlightenment as well as for his extensive personal library. The esteem he won from the enlightened philosophes and statesmen of the French Revolution, especially in its early phase, brought him the affection and praise of leaders of government and opinion—men like Lafayette, Condorcet, the Abbé Morellet and the Marquis de Chastellux. These key men helped him in his task to establish the reputation of America as a new force for modern free society. In his distinctive style of blunt and more aggressive pressure, John Adams, too, earned the respect and cooperation of Dutch bankers, although he deliberately provoked the displeasure of French officials like Vergennes. In England, where Adams assumed the cruel office of America's first Ambassador, he achieved less than in the Netherlands, or even in France, in the immediate arena of diplomacy; but he made himself intimately welcome with the group of nonconformist ministers and constitutional reformers who were the daring liberals of that day. Amidst these friendly reformers, even his demurs and dissents from the political idealism of this circle were effective in inciting doubts about what had come to be dogma of a sort. They introduced a note of Yankee hard-headedness and caution in the highly emotional atmosphere of political debate and commitment that flourished in an age of impending revolution.

Madison and Hamilton, without leaving American shores, nonetheless managed to further America's influence throughout the entire world. Widespread dissatisfaction with the ineffectual Articles of Confederation had inspired these young statesmen to agitate for a strong national union. They employed every means at their disposal—detailed argument in person and in letters to influential people, active membership in the Continental Congress, skillful promotion of the Annapolis Convention, and, when that failed of its purpose, the Federal Convention in Philadelphia—all steps to secure more power for the national government.

Franklin was present when the momentous Federal Constitution finally opened in Philadelphia in the summer of 1787; an American Ulysses, returned from his many years of invaluable diplomacy abroad,

ready for one more service to his country. The fact that he was old, ill, and so greatly famed, that he was bringing his tested skills and philosophical temper to the deliberation of the Convention, satisfied the other members and, indeed, the country, that his wisdom and experience would protect them, as he scrutinized bold measures for a stronger and more lasting union. His final address to the delegates—a masterpiece of philosophical and political common sense—could hardly have failed to secure signatures for the document from wavering men.

Once the Constitution had been signed, Madison and Hamilton contributed more to its defense and survival through the dangerous stage of ratification by the states than any other two men in America. As part of this strategic campaign to gain ratification of the Constitution, Madison and Hamilton assumed the shining mask of "Publius" as they wrote the classic defense of the federal republic of the United States. If each of these statesmen had thought and accomplished nothing else but collaboration in this writing of *The Federalist Papers,* they would have achieved a world-wide reputation; for that series of political essays was quickly recognized at home and abroad as a major contribution to the theory of modern federalism and constitutional government. It also provided a deepened and deliberate emphasis upon the competition of numerous interests and the protection of individual liberty that gave to the structure of the constitutional republic being advocated an unmistakably free and popular spirit.

5

The leading roles which Adams, Jefferson, Madison and Hamilton played in the third and fulfilling phase of the American experiment are more the familiar stuff of history. Yet even so, few people realize that after the new government had been established, it was a touch-and-go affair—more precarious than it would ever be again. It obviously could not count upon precedent and tradition, and it could easily have taken one or another fatal turn. Madison declared that the men in Congress and in other offices in the new American Republic were "in a trackless wilderness without a single footstep to guide us." Their perplexities about infusing the Constitution with life under an effective working government cannot help but move us, even today. The American experiment in democratic human values under a constitutional Republic could have proved itself unsteady, unworkable, unworthy of a further trial. It might, for example, have been diverted into a forced and forceful materialism—or it might have become a variety of satellites in the orbit of a "big" European empire—or it might have simmered and seethed with bloody contests until a domestic or imported dictator put an end to commotion and riot by iron rule. That none of these tragic

losses of liberty actively came about is the extraordinary fact about the
first decade of political life under the Constitution.

Somehow, the contest and conjunction of the four political leaders—
Jefferson, Madison, Adams and Hamilton, under the popular command
of Washington—succeeded in establishing a strong national government, and yet in stubbornly winning increased commitment to the equal
rights of man! An important part of their success in this unique experiment was the discovery of certain basic and hard truths about a
free society. They came more or less reluctantly to see that a one-party
state is a dictatorship; that there is no monopoly on political right,
insight, ways and means; that, accordingly, there should be no monopoly
on political power; and that those who challenge the prevailing power,
so long as they conform to the fundamental rules of an open society,
are not conspirators to be silenced or crushed. The will of the majority
is something more than a dumb show; it is the spirit and real process of
political choice. In short, just as personal freedom necessitates the presence of real alternatives which can be scrutinized prior to intelligent
action, so political freedom requires the diversity of political groups
within parties and usually between or among parties to make "government by consent" an operational reality. These truths were won out of
the political battles in which the great statesmen of the early Republic
engaged. As a result of their efforts, three of them were called to the
highest office in the new government—Adams, Jefferson, and Madison—
while Hamilton played the role of a singularly powerful Cabinet member,
advising Washington on all matters, propounding a vast new program
for economic growth and leading one of the two first major political
parties.

It should be evident from this summary view that all our five American
statesmen made indispensable contributions in the thought and leadership of at least two of the three momentous phases of the American
Experiment. The calibre of these men, their memorable writings and
the record of their far-seeing policies and acts entitle them to be considered "the representative men" of the American Enlightenment.

6

The selections from the collected writings of these five statesmen
attempt to suggest the broad range of their abilities and activities.
It is sometimes forgotten that the kind of men they were, their manner
and style of living, and the ideal component of life which they tried to
serve have as much to do with the basic institutions of a free society
as do the mechanics of political events. American character is admittedly
a complex of rough as well as shiny traits. That aspect of our character,
however, which is persistently our "best" is the open-minded, experi-

Adam's penetrating suspicion; Madison's powerful logic; Hamilton's impatient realism.

It is also natural that readers will quickly see that these men do not all sound alike, nor write alike. Franklin and Madison may have enjoyed each other and shared some common beliefs—but only a man born deaf to diction would confuse the two. Franklin as printer, community organizer, business man, colonial politician, scientist, journalist— a rare combination of wit and sagacity—offers a different range of talents from that of the modest younger man, Madison, whose logical penetration was noted by the contemporaries who heard him speak and whose consummate skills of philosophical legislation are more responsible for the substance of the Federal Constitution than that of any other member of the Convention.

Nor can Jefferson be assimilated to Hamilton or even to his friend, John Adams. For Jefferson was an eighteenth-century man, who nonetheless held before himself the Renaissance ideal. He was as a person aristocratic, humanistic, and yet full of the insight and learning that favored political creation. He was superbly and notoriously versatile; mastery, originality, characterized his performance not only in political thought and leadership but in the fields of law, architecture, scientific farming and education. He was noted for his vast and choice private library, his remarkable circle of friends (including the ablest philosophes of Europe as well as men of distinctive intellectual calibre in America). His urbane manners, vast resources of information, and distinctive style of life won the envy of lesser men and the admiration of his peers. But his genius for getting to the heart of moral and political principles in cadenced and memorable prose was a lifelong trait. His countrymen could not then or ever forget that he had composed the Declaration of Independence. We now know, from the treasury of his enormous private correspondence and body of public papers that he was literally creating a complex literature of American politics in the midst of the rigorous duties that were his for half a century.

Adams and Hamilton, on the other hand, shared a consuming interest in the principles of government, though they brought a radically different vision to this majestic study. For Adams, all of human nature, all moral insight, was an essential foundation to the "laws" and basic elements of "the divine science" of politics. Working with this philosophically broad conception of government and law, Adams maintained a profound unifying perspective in all his highly-excited reports of new experience and in all his ironic reflections on that queer creature, man. Everything, from the oddities of behavior of his fellow "mites" and "worms" to his first-hand discoveries of the way the "old world" of European diplomacy works, was grist to his mill. Intellectual hunger

and passion characterized Adams' earthly pilgrimage and elevated even his fits of bad temper into luminous insights and prophetic hints.

Hamilton, on the other hand, was preoccupied with the organization of power for an efficient and productive state, and his lifelong quest was therefore stringently conceived. This boldly brilliant man was an endless fountain of ideas, ideas characteristically directed to questions of political power, governmental energy, and economic growth on a presumed basis of an unalterable human nature. Without remorseless inquiry into human nature itself, Hamilton lacked Adams' relish for the human drama, and even for the human comedy in its place. He was therefore less the philosopher-statesman than the other men of genius in this group. On the other hand, his powerful comprehension of the meaning and workings of law, of political debate and management, and of directed economic growth and his marked abilities as an administrator cannot be overlooked. Both his keen sense of governmental strength and activity and his powerful logic supporting a broad and flexible interpretation of the Constitution comprise one line of indispensable thought in the American Enlightenment, even as they challenge some of its distinctive ideals.

The only impregnable conclusion of these observations is that these leading representatives of the American Enlightenment were a cluster of extraordinary men such as is rarely encountered in modern history. They were not supermen, either by conscious will or supra-human immunities. On the contrary, they were recognizably human in their trials and tears, their efforts, disappointments and successes. They are unforgettable men because they brought more to these trials, and created more out of the surrounding welter of confusion and obstacles, than men ordinarily do. In this sense they were able to achieve a measure of timelessness. What they perceived truly about human growth, cooperation, negotiation and fulfillment—about the independent and unquenchable human spirit in a society that honors and promotes it—is worth study and reflection in our own troubled time, when men are still seeking, still groping to comprehend the art of common life and commonwealth.

These eighteenth century philosopher-statesmen are the human agents whose personal vision and mental and moral traits captured the imagination of followers in their time, and exerted continuing influence over successive generations of Americans who could share their vision. They show by their writings why they were capable of achieving such wide and enduring influence: they are men of acute mind and disciplined habit; their talents are joyously diverse; and they are at many points so aware of the deepest layers of human experience, that their reflections sound surprisingly modern—perhaps because their struggle for freedom and order is still the central challenge of human society.

The claim is here put forward that these five great men best represent the American Enlightenment precisely because they were both learned and politically inventive, competent in so-called "abstract" or general ideas and in their practical applications for human conduct. This much they shared as a group, and one thing more: Franklin, Adams, Jefferson, Madison and Hamilton each perceived that the historical imperative of their time was the advancement of human freedom, beyond what had been achieved anywhere in the world of their day. On so many matters they differed, in so many sensitivities, loyalties, interests and ideals they thought alone as proud men must. But since they loved their country, and were determined to protect and promote its interests, they realized that what they recommended for the United States must square with the simple truth that men, to be human, must be free. This shared understanding was enough to bind them together as a group, however emphatic their differences or disagreements as creative philosophical statesmen in the second-order problems of economic and political means to this great end.

7

Now, given these general observations on the thought and deeds of five highly creative American statesmen, we may turn to the question of the nature and temper of the American Enlightenment as they gave it definition in their works and by their own life-styles. At once, the question of what the American Enlightenment means implies the larger context of the Enlightenment in general. Let us agree, then, that for our purposes, the Enlightenment relates to that movement of thought in the eighteenth century when learned men in all of Europe sought to assimilate, popularize, extend and apply the scientific and philosophic heritage of the "new science" of the seventeenth century. The deepest influences were Bacon, Newton and Locke; the high places were London, Edinburgh, Paris and Geneva; and the greatest figures, perhaps, were Hume, Voltaire and Rousseau. In France where "le siècle des lumières" shone with special radiance, many philosophes of unquestioned genius must be remembered as Voltaire's friends, associates or followers. Thinkers of the order of Diderot, d'Alembert, and Condorcet are ignored at very great risk and under very strong pressure for a compressed story. Voltaire, who was the inspiration and the literary master of the age, must be taken as formulator of a basic doctrine which the younger philosophes concurred in, even though they naturally had their own resources to develop and express.

It is important to recognize that there is no fixed doctrine or comprehensive philosophy that unites all Enlightenment figures. There are significant variations among the major national movements in France and England, for example, and there are also deep or considerable variations

among the major figures within each national movement. Nevertheless, there is a broad consensus of orientation and attitude that seems to distinguish Enlightenment thought from preceding or succeeding thought. These elements revolve around three basic concepts—reason, experience and progress; and three major strands of thought: that one must turn to reason for whatever one believes; that experience, gained through personal life, through history, and through active discoveries of nature and of human conditions all over the globe, supplies the basic materials with which reason must work; that there is hope that man, enlightened by reason, and lightened by improved tools and inventions may entertain hope of progress to more humane conditions.

In this view, the Enlightenment moves beyond sixteenth century Humanism and seventeenth century Reformation, since it finds *light* in reasons and *lightens* men's necessary toil. Progress becomes linked with reasonable efforts, through the improvement of human knowledge and the improvement of human techniques. The nature of science as method joins with the role of science as technology to permit lifting the conditions of human existence, lightening man's burdens and permitting all men to have the intelligence and education to share in governmental choices through representation. Thus the technical aspect, the technocratic basis of Enlightenment humanism, goes beyond Renaissance humanism which was still élitist in its confinement of intellectual life to a small and special class. And the resort to reasons without recourse to revelation, the resort to justifications on avowedly and explicitly human bases, distinguished the Enlightenment from the Reformation. For the opposition was not only to popery and papal infallibility, as reflected in the crisis of modern science symbolized by the burning of Bruno and the trial of Galileo, but also to religious sectarianism of the Reformation variety. The Enlightenment thinkers did not form a sect. They viewed reasons as individual decisions which ultimately had to be justified on personal grounds. By opposing both revelation and sects, they not only committed themselves to the logic and practice of toleration. By making reason universal in man, the trait that distinguishes man from all the rest of nature, they introduced (or reintroduced) the notion of the human family, of mankind as the center of human concern. Thus, they considered philosophical legislation and introduced certain moral claims as "the rights of man." They believed that man, properly brought up, with the aid of reasonable, minimum means of livelihood and education, could share in the government. Thus no break was required between a permanent, small governing élite and all others. This new outlook implied the democratization of humanism.

If we now consider the specific character of the American Enlightenment, we are likely to encounter the inevitable iconoclast who denies that there was such a thing as "the American Enlightenment." He is

typically ready to concede that there were, of course, changes from
seventeenth century colonial patterns—changes that even encompassed
a revolution, the creation of a federal republic, and the establishment of
a durable constitutional system of popular government. Yet these vast
changes supposedly came about through an alchemy of "favorable conditions," spiced with sub-intellectual "know-how," and borrowing lavishly
from available English traditions of law and liberty. The moral and political thought of the founding fathers has been brushed off as "derivative"
and "unoriginal"—at once systematic importations and at the same time,
oddly enough, a tissue of inconsistencies, irrelevancies and rhetoric—a
"salad of illusions." Meanwhile ideological symbols and images are substituted for what the great and individual American statesmen had to
offer in their writings, or in their individual lives, in their actuality. The
real issues these philosopher-statesmen managed to face are evaded;
and the intellectual response they made to the root problems and crises
of their time are brewed into a homogeneous synthetic fluid dubbed
"reason" or "rationalism," or "innocence;" "mission" or "the cult of progress." What was distinctly philosophic in their formulations of a characteristic point of view is thus lost, just as what was modified over time in
their development as thinkers and statesmen—instructed by experience,
temperament and their original talent responding to the search for ever
wider understanding, is left unexplained and unexplored. This is only to
say that what some critics and their followers have done is to drain out
the human agents and human agencies, in all their grandeur, all their
comedy and share of tragedy, from the history of this intensively creative period of America's birth.

To get at something more like reality, we should insist upon a few
obvious and indispensable truths. First, the waves of Enlightenment
philosophy reached American colonial shores early in the eighteenth
century and would normally have had a coterie of believers and followers
no matter what the historic imperatives of the later part of that century
would prove to be. For example, John Wise, to defend the old Congre-
gational ways of the New England churches, virtually at the opening
of the eighteenth century, appealed to man's natural reason, to a "Noble
Democracy" that should be included in every wise Monarchy, and spoke
in terms of praise (borrowed, it seems, from Pufendorf's seventeenth-
century exposition of natural law systems) of the equal rights of men.
This liberal philosophy Wise put at the service of the movement to maintain the organizational independence and autonomy of the individual
churches. Doubtless, some such influence—if not in the churches, in
other and related areas of social and political life, would naturally have
reflected this current of European thought. Barring other factors, a meek
and mild school of enlightened thought might easily have been the outcome.

But the supreme fact of the American affiliation with this European and

British line of thought is that it was political. The temper of the Colonists, the reasons which they employed to question the authority of British Ministers and Parliament—especially in the decade before Independence—had the urgency of life and death. The moral-political crisis called for, and found, native genius! The distinctive American Enlightenment was born in this struggle—a moral and political struggle, *immediately*: *ultimately*, a struggle to come to grips with the overarching issues of a philosophy of man, nature and society, to meet the remorseless demands that a career of independence and experiment set up—to provide a sense of direction and commitment.

Thus, there is cohesion and a core of profound agreement about the basic tenets of the American Enlightenment that individuates it when we compare it with the English or French variety. The comparison with the English tradition is particularly important, since it was peculiarly true that "Whig principles" exercised a powerful sway over the minds of the colonial spokesmen who argued for American liberty. Nonetheless, Whig principles would prove not to be the whole story nor the whole achievement of the American Enlightenment. Locke's philosophy and its "real Whig" followers in eighteenth-century England would continue to agitate by pamphlet and newspaper opinion and a multiplicity of constitutional reform societies, but they would never engage in the anguished moral, political, legal and emotional search for identity that was precipitated by the need to ask what an American style and destiny would be if all ties were cut with the British Crown and realm.

On the other hand, the French Enlightenment, in all its brilliant achievements and rich profusion of doctrines and dogmas, did not cast up the kind of sagacious and flexible leadership that came to the highest places of power in the American Revolution and in the ensuing years of Confederation and Constitutional Republic. Moreover, by the time the French Revolution was to open, a veritable cult of America as the new world, the world of promise, the ideal Republic of liberty, would intervene between the original English Enlightenment heritage and the native varieties of qualified monarchism that had been propounded by great French philosophes like Montesquieu and Voltaire. Rousseau, as a conceivable exception, as an influential advocate of Republicanism, was in fact markedly different in political theory as well as personal mode of influencing society from the American philosopher-statesmen. It is tiresome to repeat again what is so widely known, but Rousseau's concept of "the general will" in its inherent unity and its imperial latitude over particular wills, is incompatible in spirit, root and branch, with the major traditions and procedures of American Enlightenment thought. In short, neither the *Encyclopédie* nor the salons, neither Socialists, liberal reformers, nor democrats and fanatical radicals who would come to brief power in the Jacobin and post-Jacobin phase of the Revolution, produced

statesmen capable of devising durable forms of government and exercising responsible power.

To put it differently, the American Revolution did not devour its own
leaders as did the French Revolution. Moreover, it was not merely an
incident of the *kind* of revolution that took place in each country that
encouraged a set of benign and creative leaders to achieve stable control
in America. At least part of this unique sequence of events in America
must be attributed to the temperate, philosophical and informed understanding of the leading men who mastered the intricate arts of peaceful
political leadership on the one hand, and who were able to formulate a
philosophy that eschewed extremes of doctrine precisely because they
appreciated the factor of experience and respected the spirit and equal
rights of each individual. We are impressed by the fact that they were
moved by the twin demands of life: thought *and* action; contemplation,
deliberation, and patient scrutiny of ideas *as well as* the fertile invention
of laws and institutions; theory *and* practice; political ideals and the
exercise of actual political power; mental and moral "science," and also
the devising of moral positions and attitudes that put basic notions of
good and right into a fresh and functional context. All these men of the
American Enlightenment admired Bacon and his experimental philosophy; yet none of them seemed to share Bacon's admitted unhappiness as
typified in his remark to Sir Thomas Bodley: "Knowing myself by inward
calling to be fitter to hold a book than to play a part, I have used my
life in civil causes, for which I was not very fit by nature, and more unfit
by the preoccupation of my mind." These great men of the American
Enlightenment, one can only observe, were "fit" for *their* special calling—
to think deeply and even profoundly of a new human ethos, to envisage
a new philosophy and role for man, and to carry on this stubborn inquiry
at the very time and in the midst of the pressures and urgent issues of
political leadership.

Perhaps the point is that the statesmen presented here were a special
kind of "architect of ideas"—their blueprints were essentially livable
and durable. They tried to design a vast republic—an "extensive" republic was Madison's phrase—to be inhabited by men whose worth and
judgment would bring them not only to the management of private life
(kept really private by the priceless "right to be let alone") but to responsible participation in public or political life. The common-wealth
was to be in their vigilant keeping. How easy it would have been to
design a wedding-cake affair, only to find out its perishability on first
trial! Or to strain and force the fancy into an "ideal" structure, forgetting
that "utopia" belongs in the skies for contemplation, otherwise literally
nowhere. Or, finally, to perfect a faithful copy, in detail, of the most
modish and celebrated of the established dwellings! Before we tire of
the metaphor, let us say plainly that these statesmen were inventive in

the most thoughtful and functional way. They were developing *relevant* ideas for a world partly formed, partly in the process of becoming. They were consciously mediating between the purely ideal and the needlessly narrow habits of their society. Their ideas issued in plans, their ideals in policies.

Meeting the twin demands of thought and creative action, our five Americans were, in sum, philosopher-statesmen. They accepted the responsibilities of political leadership and continuous action on the political scene, and yet they were profound and stubborn critics of government, of man, of society. It should be understood that they differed widely in type from the Philosopher-King, who plans and reveals only what he must to the "guardians" of the Republic, and manages paternally and on his sole responsibility the lives of the great producing class of society. Unlike the Platonic super-statesman, the American philosopher-statesmen regarded their share of power as entrusted, delegated, limited in tenure, dependent upon specific office, and inexorably committed to ultimate election and rejection by the people. But equally, the philosopher-statesmen should be sharply differentiated from the mere politician whose comprehension of human ends and goals is neither far-ranging nor serious, and whose concern is immediately and narrowly tied to his own political career as *summum bonum*. For the philosopher-statesmen the dimension of political thought, debate and program was a majestic and engrossing adventure. While not the crown of life, to that adventure they brought themselves—in the full service of men with strong hearts, clear heads, and the wisdom and patience to cope with tragic necessities without abandoning hope for significant human freedom.

8

We can now turn to the charge that the political philosophy of the American statesmen was merely derivative, a massive ritual, full of English liberal slogans, and signifying nothing new. We can appraise this charge by examining one aspect of the Declaration of Independence, since there is a general view that the Declaration is simply a copy of the political philosophy of John Locke.

The truth of the matter is that a wholly new element was introduced into natural rights philosophy in the American document. Its opening words cue us to the novelty of the case: the opinion of mankind is solicited, as a court of judgment on the justice of the American cause and the need to wage a revolutionary struggle to defend it. Recall that there was no precedent in history for such a document. No colony had ever advanced a reasoned statement of its need and decision to rebel from an imperial power.

The ensuing political philosophy is also irreducible to earlier models and discontinuous with earlier feelings and sentiments. Men are declared

to be born equal, with natural rights among which are specified the rights to "life, liberty, and the pursuit of happiness." No public document had ever employed language pointing to this kind of moral ideal—equal rights paired with the individual pursuit of happiness. *Property* had been invoked in the past; public happiness had been stated as the *theoretical* objective of a lawful or good government. But the individual right to pursue happiness, and to include in its scope the techniques and deliberations required for constant participation in self-government, envisaged a fuller meaning for the individual person. The free man, in this perspective, would grow towards real individuality by social partnership with others; the process of selecting officials, scrutinizing the rules of government, deciding when, why and how to alter or abolish them would promote self-government in a double sense: for the person, for the public. Also, unlike property, "the pursuit of happiness" has no class boundary. It is thus neither an exclusive privilege, nor is it a merely formal ideal. Franklin made "Poor Richard" say that an empty bag cannot stand upright: and men who set this strange new value on the public "pursuit of happiness" would not require the advent of Marxism to teach them that without means, without control over the laws (including the laws of property) men could be reduced to "mere automata" of servitude and suffering.

The upshot of the thinking that permeates the philosophical sections as well as the statement of particular and local "grievances" in the Declaration is a tough new political logic: government *by consent,* or government *without and possibly against* consent. In short, freedom or tyranny. This hard new political logic embodied what came to be called "the principles of 1776." It was not meant to imply that men were wholly free or wholly captive, nor did it call for utopias. It did argue in principle, however, that there could be no middle ground between government based on the consent of the governed, and government carried on *over* the people, without their consent. Political theorists in the past had toyed with doctrines of "tacit" consent, or of merely formal consent—sometimes even substituting coerced "consent" for the real thing. These were all subterfuges according to the philosophy of the Declaration. From antiquity on, and including Montesquieu, political philosophers had envisaged three basic models of government—monarchy, aristocracy, republics—and had assigned different principles and justifications for each. The new position made no compromise with monarchy or aristocracy. Governments were free if and only if they were ready to make good the promise of self-government— that is, ready to provide effective processes of consent. Such processes must be devised and maintained in order to permit the people to judge infringements of rights and suitable occasions to "alter and abolish" bad laws or despotic governments.

This notion of the people as the constituent power is realized in various instruments devised deliberately to create new governments. Most notable of these inventions, perhaps, was the calling of conventions to draft con-

stitutions which, in the demands of the American theory, were to be subject to ratification by the people. The use of this device was urgently proposed by Jefferson in his criticism of the wartime constitution of Virginia and call for a convention to draft a new constitution "when peace shall be established and leisure given us for entrenching within good forms, the rights for which we have bled." More weight must be given, however, to the example set with the Massachusetts Constitution of 1780, which followed upon the prior choice by the separate towns of delegates to a state convention expressly devoted to framing a new constitution and subjecting the constitution to ratification by the people. In this celebrated Massachusetts Constitution for the first time there appears the phrase, "We, the people . . . agree, hope, ordain and establish" whence it passed into the Federal constitution and later state constitutions. John Adams, who was the principal architect, reflected with pleasure that Massachusetts had turned to the people as sovereign source for fundamental law— "a phenomenon in the political world that is new and singular," he pointed out. He had often been angry with his fellow citizens in Massachusetts, dreading, as he had habitually confessed from 1776 on, their "rage for innovation" and their levelling tempers and moves. But he now loved them for being "the first people who have taken so much time to deliberate upon government—that have allowed such universal liberty to all people to reflect upon the subject, and to propose objections and amendments—and that have reserved to themselves at large the right of finally accepting or rejecting the form." This new and widespread consciousness of the real meaning of government by consent and self-government, Adams hailed as an "epoch in the history of the progress of society."

Whatever else one may conclude about these representative men of the American Enlightenment, as political leaders and thinkers they were in one profound sense unlike Marx, who in his conception of revolutionary strategy spoke contemptuously of the demand for plans for the society to come after revolution as a demand for kitchen "recipes." On the contrary, they found complete accord in the belief that to revolt without *constituting*, without planning the orderly transition to that "self-government" in whose name the revolution was being waged, was the road to needless turmoil, bloodshed and political servitude. The experiment in popular sovereignty, unless deliberately held to constitutional laws and parliamentary debates and popular discussions on legislation, might be foreclosed, perverted to a greater tyranny than the one they had known. However high the ideals of the philosopher-statesmen might reach, they were entirely realistic about the capacity of any slogan—including the slogan of freedom, liberty, self-government—to become a disguise for new oppressions. Out of loyalty to the free principles of '76, they tended carefully their kitchen recipes.

9

We turn finally to consider another major reason often cited for rejecting any serious philosophic thought in the American Enlightenment—the alleged fact that it produced no systematic treatises, no books of political theory. This charge proves to be indefensible when scrutinized, and on two main grounds. First, we have learned enough in the modern world from a variety of philosophical schools and movements, not to assume automatically that men who do not write "systematic treatises" in the high style, are conveniently to be read out of the ranks of serious and philosophical minds. What is clear, now more than ever, from the body of extensive writings of these five brilliant American political leaders is that there is indeed a *massive* literature which is the fruit of the American Enlightenment. The papers and writings of these enlightened Americans reflect their double role and capacity; they were deeply committed to humanistic learning and letters—and they were pressed to put that learning to the test of potential usefulness. Everything significant that had been said about human nature, forms of government, laws natural and civil, ideas of freedom and determinism, of sin, of doing good, education, scientific progress, the patterns of history in the rise and fall of nations, the characters of conquerors and the different aspirations of the moral heroes of mankind from Socrates to Voltaire—became for them a matter of study, reflection and revision. It is true that these men were working in the tradition of the European Enlightenment—at least in one or another line within the tradition. But they selected what they considered valuable in it, they responded favorably to some of the philosophy and not the rest, and they changed, expanded, or made themselves go beyond what was given. The papers and writings that comprise this book should confirm these observations.

Second, the writings of the philosopher-statesmen were not wholly confined to notes, manifestoes and specific papers dealing with immediate, therefore urgent, social and political problems. Even if we pass over the comprehensive analysis by Madison and Hamilton in the one undisputed political classic of the age, *The Federalist Papers,* Jefferson and John Adams (who seemed to anticipate by their own performance what Emerson would demand of the American scholar—that he be a "university of knowledges") must each be credited with at least one political treatise. Jefferson's *Notes on Virginia* and Adams' *Defence of the Constitutions of Government of the United States,* published when they were diplomats abroad, are interesting, original and important works, and, in the eighteenth century, were probably more widely influential than the justly famous classic, *The Federalist Papers,* which we all know by name at least. These unusual publications formulated two distinct visions and

versions of the political freedom and thereby set the range of American political views, values and measures into a new and deeper focus on both sides of the Atlantic.

Jefferson's *Notes* is full of the sense of the American terrain, its fertility and possible growth, and expounds a new American culture that he finds vigorous and promising in infancy and vast in its potential if mistakes are corrected and liberal principles courageously enacted. The *Notes* is a primer of the new country, the American version of free society. The *Notes* make it clear that Jefferson belongs to that select group of American patriots who took to heart the fully progressive sense of the revolutionary faith. Jefferson, in his adherence to this ideal, devised ways and means to introduce it in every sector affecting the well-being and happiness of man. To give only one important example: he argued for man's right to economic self-sufficiency as a human value which transcended the merely legal sanctity of property. Many of his provisions in the draft he drew for a constitution for Virginia in 1776 had envisaged a new type of economic justice, and attendant political participation. Thus, he had provided that free male adults who could not meet the small property qualifications for the franchise, be given "in free and absolute dominions" fifty acres of land by the state, and, thus, qualify for suffrage. Later, in Paris, with his sympathies deepened by the sight of widespread poverty, he formulated his sweeping principle that "the earth belongs to the living" for their use and sustenance.

Adams' *Defence*, composed late in the 1780's and taking stock of European and American developments, is a searching would-be "science" of politics, depicting man's inhumanity to man and the eternal cycle of rulers and ruled. Only the precious "balance" of orders in society and mixed government can contain runaway human nature, whether in the people or in the aristocrats and the rulers. The State governments in the United States are defended as conforming to natural truths about man in society and the implication is that these must hold in any future government for free man (whether for an extensive nation or a modest state).

If we now move our perspective to the larger scene of the eighteenth century world in the late 1780's, it must be said that Adams sensed very early that a vast movement of social and political revolution was gaining headway on the continent of Europe. He thus provided, through his elaborate work, a rehearsal of the arguments that would later erupt into the great controversy between Burke and Paine over the French Revolution and the rights of man. It was precisely in this sense that the *Defence* functioned, both in England and in France. In Paris, a democratic-republican *refutation* of his doctrine was read by French philosophes before the work itself was translated. An American pamphlet "Observations of Government, including some animadversion on Mr. Adams' *Defence* . . .

and Mr. De Lolme's Constitution of England" by "Farmer of New Jersey" (John Stevens, in reality) was translated into French in 1789 as "Examen du gouvernement d'Angleterre, comparé aux constitutions des États-Unis" (a revealing title) and accompanied by lengthy notes and commentary by Dupont de Nemours, Condorcet, and a few others. Thus, Lafayette, Condorcet, Dupont and many of their associates were fully apprised of the conservative case against democratic Republicanism, before they made their decision to advocate a liberal program of human rights. They continued to lead the "Patriot party" in proposals for the reform of the desperate evils of French society and for the substitution of a limited constitutional monarchy, bound by a bill of rights for the monarchy of Louis XVI. In these moves, Lafayette brought his group into close consultation with Jefferson, including one rather indiscreet dinner and discussion meeting at the American Minister's residence. Jefferson also advised Lafayette and made some changes in his draft of the French bill of rights. Ultimately, when the French Revolution moved far beyond these moderate reformers, Adams concluded self-righteously that he had predicted sooner even than Burke that it would devour its own children.

10

More than a century ago, George Bancroft confided to Jared Sparks: "The people of the United States will by degrees learn that theirs is a history worth knowing." Both of these early historians believed this so deeply that it sustained their arduous historical inquiries all through their lives. And yet the judgment remains little more than prophecy for us. Many Americans assume that modern industrial democracy is totally different from the small agricultural world which fashioned the American republic. They call that eighteenth century world "Arcadian," or the "lost world"—in any case it *is* lost to them! Others become converts to Zen Buddhism or "Existentialism" or theosophy and find they need not bother with anything so local, so close to home and presumably uninteresting as the democratic culture of which they are, consciously or not, a part. And on the whole, if Americans do discover in themselves some lively curiosity about the past, their reading about it tends to be drawn from second-hand accounts: magazine articles, fictionalized biography, historical accounts of varying degrees of excellence and accuracy which the readers rarely try to check against their own impressions of something first-hand.

In an animated epistolary discussion of the American Revolution, John Adams and Thomas Jefferson, both by then elder statesmen retired from public office, entertained some searching doubts about the historian's treatment of its meaning and worth. Jefferson, in the course of this ex-

change in 1815, permitted himself the following outburst: "On the subject of the history of the American Revolution, you ask who shall write it? Who can write it? And who will ever be able to write it? Nobody; except merely its external facts; all its councils, designs, and discussions having been conducted by Congress with closed doors, and with no members, as far as I know, having even made notes of them. These, which are the life and soul of history, must forever be unknown."

One notices Jefferson's vigorous distinction between the external facts, and the life and soul of history. Records of debates, of committee deliberations and motions, and evidences of conflict of various sorts of interests; the power to plan, solve problems and persuade by reason; or to influence by personal traits and social position; the evidence of political hostilities—all these he knew to be essential to the meaning of the American Revolution. Without recourse to the record of what men had thought and argued, designed and even tried to get accepted but failed—a record that would catch the thoughts and accents of the human agents who led the revolution, who, in infinite diversity, were moved by what they had learned and read as well as by what they reflected from their particular positions in colonial society—without that evidence, a historical account of the revolution would afford "merely its external facts."

Fortunately, our own era is witnessing the long overdue publication of documentary records of the American past. Especially is this true of the highly creative period of the American Enlightenment. In the past dozen years, and in the years to come, readers on at least two continents are in a new position to grasp something of "the life and soul of history" for that exhilarating era. Comprehensive new editions, superbly and faithfully edited, are in progress and will restore the papers of the five great early American statesmen to their friends everywhere. This vast program is giving us the Julian Boyd edition of *The Papers of Thomas Jefferson*, estimated to run 50 volumes; the Leonard Labaree edition of *The Papers of Benjamin Franklin*, projected at 40 volumes; the Lyman Butterfield edition of *The Adams Papers* (primarily collections of documents by and to John Adams, John Quincy Adams, and Charles Francis Adams) which may together amass 100 volumes; and 40 volumes each are anticipated for *The Papers of Alexander Hamilton* and *The Papers of James Madison*.

To introduce the reader to this growing and impressive library and thereby overcome the state of affairs which has confined our knowledge to second-hand sources, this volume of readings presents first-hand sources: letters, speeches, public papers, essays by the five greatest philosophical statesmen of the American Enlightenment. The readings have been selected in each case out of a gigantic collection of papers which each of these statesmen wrote, and the implicit wager of this book is that the men and their times will emerge more meaningfully than

through synthetic accounts, at second hand. The world these statesmen inhabit may no longer be mis-named "lost," "Arcadian," "abstract" or "simple;" for it is not likely to lack connections with the world of current experience—including its hopes, fears and crises. And as one senses the power of intelligence that emanates from these great men and catches glimpses of their wisdom, their vision and distinctive charm, one will naturally be "learning by degrees" that our history is worth knowing.

It is in this spirit that the present volume of readings has been prepared, to facilitate the meeting between twentieth century Americans and five of their surprisingly enlightened forebears. It also reflects the hope that the founders of the American political tradition who created our "deepest ties to the rest of humanity" will prove to be worth the friendly scrutiny of men and women anywhere in the world who continue to concern themselves with freedom, justice, order—and truth! Beyond these primary concerns, this American Enlightenment reader is offered simply to introduce or recall to mind five extraordinary men, who in an era of crisis proved themselves to be *philosophical* in their sustained reflections on moral and political issues; *practical* in their ability to formulate policies and wield political power in the interests of enlightened human goals; and wholly *individual* in their characteristic style of expression and conduct of life.

Today, as never before, the American world is charged with understanding and explaining to a world-wide community its revolutionary past, its federalism, its concern with freedom and equality, its ideas, ideals, institutions, and the great men who helped make its history. In this connection one might cite the aperçu of the irrepressible Denis Brogan, that the trend in American-British relations is from contempt to concern; and that these countries must learn the historical forces which shape their respective characters.

Americans who learn to read and comprehend the record may now have within their grasp the means to fulfill a cherished goal of James Madison:

"It has been the misfortune of history that a personal knowledge and an impartial judgment of things can rarely meet in the historian. The best history of our country therefore must be the fruit of contributions bequeathed by contemporary actors and witnesses, to successors who will make an unbiased use of them. And if the abundance and authenticity of the materials which still exist in private as well as in public repositories among us should descend to hands capable of doing justice to them, then American History may be expected to contain more truth, and lessons certainly not less valuable, than that of any Country or age whatever."

PART I

BENJAMIN FRANKLIN
(*1706–1790*)

This fabulous man, whose thought, inventions, wit, wisdom and charm made him the idol of the Enlightened world of Europe and America, was properly hailed by Thomas Jefferson as "the father of American philosophy." Richly sceptical all his life about conventional theology, metaphysics, and pompous formalism in all its guides, Franklin loved to call attention to his humble birth, his youthful poverty, his self-taught and self-made role. A youthful rebel against the proper Puritan Boston of his birth, his Autobiography *has made immortal the vivid image of his arrival in Philadelphia, hardly a penny in his jeans, walking along Market Street as he munched his puffy two-penny rolls. His rapid rise by dint of hard work, shrewd sense, artful connections with men who could afford to help him—so that his success as a printer, journalist, almanac maker, Philadelphia politician was rapidly assured—has been persistently and wilfully misunderstood as the "essence" of the real Benjamin Franklin—a man presumably the ideal type for the early Capitalist: the ascetic, penny-pinching, ledger-watching business creature, whose dream of tomorrow opens only another compulsive field for squeezing profits and engineering future expansion by investment of saved earnings. Perhaps the modern critic would do better to be guided by Franklin's contemporaries who knew him in quite other terms, as an indispensable man, the embodiment of that new man, the American.*

In truth, very uncommon talents drew the world to him. In France, in England, throughout Europe, his value as a great scientist and moral philosopher, and his personal traits of brilliance paired with benevolence, were the source of his fame. John Adams, who could not abide him, at least partly because of this very acclaim, once drew this estimate of his rival's reputation: "Franklin's reputation was more universal than that of Leibnitz or Newton, Frederick or Voltaire; and his character was more beloved and esteemed than any or all of them. His name was familiar to government and people, to kings, courtiers, nobility, clergy, and philosophers, as well as plebians, to such a degree that there was

51

scarcely peasant or citizen, a valet de chambre, coachman or footman, a lady's chambermaid or a scullion in a kitchen who was not familiar with it and who did not consider him a friend to humankind. When they spoke of him they seemed to think he was to restore the golden age." The good David Hume, a great friend of Franklin's, who knew after repeated encounters with the American that this man was not at all a façade, once wrote to him: "America has sent us many good things, gold, silver, sugar, tobacco, indigo, etc. but you are the first philosopher, and indeed the first great man of letters, for whom we are beholden to her."

Perhaps most interesting of all is the appraisal made of Franklin by a gentle young Bostonian, some thirty years after the celebrated printer's "book of life" had closed. Ralph Waldo Emerson, then in his twenties, wrote thus to his aunt: "Was Dr. Franklin (one of the most sensible men that ever lived) as likely to be born elsewhere as at Boston. . . . ? Don't you admire (I am not sure you do) the serene and powerful understanding which was so eminently practical and useful, which grasped the policy of the glove and the form of a fly with like facility and ease; which seemed to be a transmigration of the genius of Socrates—yet more useful, more moral, and more pure. . . . Franklin was no verbal gladiator, clad in complete mail of syllogisms, but a sage who used his pen with an effect which was new and had been supposed to belong to the sword. He was a man of that singular force of mind . . . which seems designed to affect by individual influence what is ordinarily accomplished by the slow and secret work of institutions and national growth. . . . Many millions have already lived and millions are now alive who have felt through their whole lives the powerful good effect of Franklin's actions and writings. His subtle observation, his seasonable wit, his proved reason, and his mild and majestic virtues made him idolized in France, feared in England and obeyed in America."

The selections from his writings reveal the extraordinary range of curiosity and mastery of subject-matter that was Franklin's benchmark. In his own time, Franklin's advancement of new theoretical discoveries in the field of electromagnetism placed him distinctly in the vanguard of the eighteenth century's typically modern rage for the extension and diffusion of science. A full study by I. B. Cohen of Franklin's contribution to science, theoretical as well as applied, bears the significant title: Franklin and Newton, and demonstrates from the perspective of the twentieth century the correctness of the eighteenth century's tribute to him as "the Newton" of their time. Thus, Franklin's work in science should be understood as one road toward that early ideal he had announced, "to love truth and to seek and serve it," rather than as a gadgeteer's merely practical invention of mechanical comforts. To be sure, Franklin did invent the Franklin stove, the lightning rod, bifocal lenses, and innumerable other improved instruments. It even followed from his understanding of the proper relationship of theory and practice

that "helps" and instruments should be the products of fruitful new concepts in basic research—though he fully appreciated the intrinsic value of knowledge as a supreme expression of human delight. Boswell's mention to Dr. Johnson of Franklin's remarkable definition of man as "a tool-making animal" is a reminder that Franklin, like his mentor, Sir Francis Bacon, saw human intelligence as experimental, active, and productive rather than as the comparatively rationalistic view that is implicit in the Aristotelian definition of man as a "rational animal."

If scientific originality brought Franklin the plaudits of the Royal Society and the community of scientific men, his political role made him a completer man and an historical agent of vast significance. For Franklin's political role was wholly unique. His own life provided the symbolism for his country's progress from subservient colonial status to independent creation of nationhood. As a youth, Franklin felt himself to be virtually in a position of slavery, as an indentured apprentice to his older brother. His response to that harsh treatment was flight to a new and self-sufficient life, and he wrote that he was thus early impressed "with that aversion to arbitrary power that has stuck to me through my whole life." Years of service to Philadelphia and to Pennsylvania as a powerful political leader and legislator, and his important missions to England where he became conspicuous as the colonial agent for Pennsylvania, Georgia, New Jersey and Massachusetts, and the chief advocate of the American cause, provided him with an experience of both the mother country and his own which none of his countrymen could parallel. Precisely because he had done his utmost to negotiate differences between the Colonies and the Ministry and Parliament of George III and concluded, sadly but wisely, that reconciliation was henceforth a coward's illusion, his decision to throw in his lot, at an advanced age, with the most active revolutionaries in the Continental Congress in 1775 was a momentous one. He brought his splendid talents and his reservoir of experience to the patriot side. One need only consider what it would have meant to the loyalists, to English morale, and conversely to the timid "olive branch" peace-petitioners in Congress had Franklin joined the other side instead, to begin to sense the importance of his initial revolutionary role.

Once embarked, Franklin mustered his energies for what Verner Crane has called "his busiest and most brilliant decade in public service." In recognition of his contribution to the success of the revolution and mindful of his other role as leader of the scientific enlightenment, Turgot penned his classic epigram: "He seized the lightning from the sky, and the sceptre from tyrants." This epigram became an international slogan testifying to Franklin's dual image, uniting the two predominant passions of the age: man as a new Prometheus, stealing fire from heaven by bold but ordered intelligence, and man ready and able to revolt against tyranny. Both drives were manifestations of the yearning for

emancipation, the first emancipating mankind from slavish fear and dread, the second from political oppression to a fuller freedom.

The "Prometheus," however, was also a quite lovable man, fond of good conversation, broad jokes and hoaxes, and the whole spectacle of life. His humanity as a moralist, satirist, and creative reformer endeared him to philosophers and men of letters; and his magnetic mind and serene temper drew to him a vast circle of friends throughout America and Europe. Conspicuous among these friends were children, for whom he reserved his most exquisite subtlety and unqualified enthusiasm. He was apparently uncomfortable living in a house without young company —his own children, then grandchildren, nephews, the children of friends and even the children of unfriendly associates (John Quincy Adams remembered the enchanting times spent at Franklin's home in Passy during the very years that his father was feuding with Franklin). It must also be said that Franklin would not have thought it worth existing without the excitement of attractive women in his life—"attractive" in the usual sense, of appearance, or in the special sense of distinctive mind, style or spirit. For these women, with whom Franklin's world seemed always plentifully supplied, he demonstrated an unconcealed and apparently inexhaustible sexual interest, more or less "elevated" by clever correspondence, witty conversation, and what we today call "fun and games."

As a master of American prose, Franklin's style is suggested by his brief statement about education: "Men should be taught as if you taught them not." So seasoned was Franklin's understanding of human nature that he never ventured to instruct men without appealing to their sense of shocked surprise, or enchantment with parables, maxims, artful forms that removed the sting of direct controversy and criticism. Even his early quarrel with Calvinist theologians reflected his own sense of "disgust" with the soured tempers their polemics produced. His preference for morality and virtue over official piety is born of his humanistic philosophy. Man's work and conduct must produce good on earth and not on an installment plan beyond human knowledge or experience. As he phrased it, man's saying, "Lord, Lord" gave them no title to salvation; only their "Doing" the heavenly will. Faith for him becomes a means of producing virtue and morality among men; and morality alone justifies a hope of salvation. This faith caused Franklin to spend his "long life. . . in meaning well," enjoying the human comedy that his journey provided. "All among us may be happy," he once wrote, "who have happy dispositions; such being necessary to happiness even in paradise."

Whatever the subject of his interest was, Franklin's lucid and adaptive prose served him unfailingly. "The most exquisite folly," he sagely observed, "is made of wisdom spun too fine." His wisdom always appeared like an ideal form of common sense, whether it was a question of exposing England's shortsighted and unjust policy towards the American Col-

onies (as in his brilliant satiric newspaper article, "Rules by Which a Great Empire May Be Reduced to a Small One") or of prodding the conscience of his own countrymen to appreciate human fallibility and the spirit of tolerant compromise (an attitude so perfectly defined in his "Speech in the Convention at the Conclusion of its Deliberations"). In his younger days, when he was in his youthful sixties, he had lightheartedly written playful bagatelles (like his marriage proposal to Madame Helvetius, in the form of a "dream" encounter with her dead husband in Elysium). Very different was the prudential mask he had assumed when he was in truth a young man and author of the "Poor Richard" almanacs, studding his pages with borrowed bits of folk wisdom and maxims from every land. The enormous success which Poor Richard's "Way to Wealth" achieved in France, where it was translated under the title La Science du Bonhomme Richard, has its amusing side. Misreading Father Abraham as a surrogate for Franklin himself, French critics and readers apparently read this summary of the proverbs compiled for the almanacs of the past quarter-century as serious moral and economic counsels, missing irony and satire in the piece altogether. This accident of over-evaluation converted "The Way to Wealth" into a primer of bourgeois moralism which doubtless influenced later misinterpretations—such as Max Weber's—of "the real" Franklin. One must never forget that Franklin, having made of himself the independent man, who was able to join the society of the free and easy, devoted the second half of his life to public service, arduous political leadership, and diplomatic service that gave Europe its first (and let us hope, not last) ambassadorial taste of American wit, art, skill and address conjoined with democratic and liberal sentiments.

Thus, Franklin, the Colonial turned American patriot, signer of the Declaration of Independence, and of the Constitution, was the first American to represent us personally and memorably face to face with the European world. He was in this experience indeed "the first American," creating the first impression of American character. He gave his new country a face, as well as a character, ideals as well as proverbs for business success. That he asked for the day when "a thorough knowledge of the rights of man, may pervade all the nations of the earth, so that a philosopher may set his foot anywhere on its surface, and say, 'This is my Country'" is one facet of his ardent, humanistic faith. Since he was not one to tilt at windmills, he did all he could with reason and common sense, meaning well and negotiating intelligently. The rest was the magic of human comedy, of the cosmic jest that dogs man's pursuit of goodness and truth.

Autobiography

1. *Reading and Writing*

From a Child I was fond of Reading, and all the little Money that came into my Hands was ever laid out in Books. Pleas'd with the Pilgrim's Progress, my first Collection was of John Bunyan's Works, in separate little Volumes. I afterwards sold them to enable me to buy R. Burton's Historical Collections; they were small Chapmen's Books and cheap, 40 or 50 in all.—My Father's little Library consisted chiefly of Books in polemic Divinity, most of which I read, and have since often regretted, that at a time when I had such a Thirst for Knowledge, more proper Books had not fallen in my Way, since it was now resolv'd I should not be a Clergyman. Plutarch's Lives there was, in which I read abundantly, and I still think that time spent to great ["Great" seems to have been deleted.] Advantage. There was also a Book of Defoe's, called an Essay on Projects, and another of Dr. Mather's, called Essays to do Good which perhaps gave me a Turn of thinking that had an influence on some of the principal future Events of my Life.

This Bookish inclination at length determin'd my Father to make me a Printer, tho' he had already one Son (James) of that Profession. In 1717 my Brother James return'd from England with a Press and Letters to set up his Business in Boston. I lik'd it much better than that of my Father, but still had a Hankering for the Sea.—To prevent the apprehended Effect of such an Inclination, my Father was impatient to have me bound to my Brother. I stood out some time, but at last was persuaded and signed the Indentures, when I was yet but 12 Years old.— I was to serve as an Apprentice till I was 21 Years of Age, only I was to be allow'd Journeyman's Wages during the last Year. In a little time I made great Proficiency in the Business, and became a useful Hand to my Brother. I now had Access to better Books. An Acquaintance with the Apprentices of Booksellers, enabled me sometimes to borrow a small one, which I was careful to return soon and clean. Often I sat up in my Room reading the greatest Part of the Night, when the Book was borrow'd in the Evening and to be return'd early in the Morning[,] lest it should be miss'd or wanted. And after some time an ingenious Tradesman Mr. Matthew Adams who had a pretty Collection of Books, and who fre-

quented our Printing House, took Notice of me, invited me to his Library, and very kindly lent me such Books as I chose to read. I now took a Fancy to Poetry, and made some little Pieces. My Brother, thinking it might turn to account encourag'd me, and put me on composing two occasional Ballads. One was called The *Lighthouse Tragedy*, and contained an Acc^t of the drowning of Capt. Worthilake with his Two Daughters; the other was a Sailor Song on the Taking of *Teach* or Blackbeard the Pirate. They were wretched Stuff, in the Grub-street Ballad Stile, and when they were printed he sent me about the Town to sell them. The first sold wonderfully, the Event being recent, having made a great Noise. This flatter'd my Vanity. But my Father discourag'd me, by ridiculing my Performances, and telling me Verse-makers were generally Beggars; so I escap'd being a Poet, most probably a very bad one. But as Prose Writing has been of great Use to me in the Course of my Life, and was a principal Means of my Advancement, I shall tell you how in such a Situation I acquir'd what little Ability I have in that Way.

There was another Bookish Lad in the Town, John Collins by Name, with whom I was intimately acquainted. We sometimes disputed, and very fond we were of Argument, and very desirous of confuting one another. Which disputacious Turn, by the way, is apt to become a very bad Habit, making People often extreamly disagreeable in Company, by the Contradiction that is necessary to bring it into Practice, and thence, besides souring and spoiling the Conversation, is productive of Disgusts and perhaps Enmities where you may have occasion for Friendship. I had caught it by reading my Father's Books of Dispute about Religion. Persons of good Sense, I have since observ'd, seldom fall into it, except Lawyers, University Men, and Men of all Sorts that have been bred at Edinborough. A Question was once some how or other started between Collins and me, of the Propriety of educating the Female Sex in Learning, and their Abilities for Study. He was of Opinion that it was improper, and that they were naturally unequal to it. I took the contrary Side, perhaps a little for Dispute['s] sake. He was naturally more eloquent, had a ready Plenty of Words, and sometimes as I thought bore me down more by his Fluency than by the Strength of his Reasons. As we parted without settling the Point, and were not to see one another again for some time, I sat down to put my Arguments in Writing, which I copied fair and sent to him. He answer'd and I reply'd. Three of [or] four Letters of a Side had pass'd, when my Father happen'd to find my Papers, and read them. Without ent'ring into the Discussion, he took occasion to talk to me about the Manner of my Writing, observ'd that tho' I had the Advantage of my Antagonist in correct Spelling and pointing (which I ow'd to the Printing House) I fell far short in elegance of Expression, in Method and in Perspicuity, of which he convinc'd me by several Instances. I saw the Justice of his Remarks, and thence grew more attentive to the *Manner* in writing, and determin'd to endeavour at Improvement.—

About this time I met with an odd Volume of the Spectator. It was the Third. I had never before seen any of them. I bought it, read it over and over, and was much delighted with it. I thought the Writing excellent, and wish'd if possible to imitate it. With that View, I took some of the Papers, and making short Hints of the Sentiment in each Sentence, laid them by a few Days, and then without looking at the Book, try'd to compleat the Papers again, by expressing each hinted Sentiment at length, and as fully as it had been express'd before, in any suitable Words, that should come to hand.

Then I compar'd my Spectator with the Original, discover'd some of my Faults and corrected them. But I found I wanted a Stock of Words or a Readiness in recollecting and using them, which I thought I should have acquir'd before that time, if I had gone on making Verses, since the continual Occasion for Words of the same Import but of different Length, to suit the Measure, or of different Sound for the Rhyme, would have laid me under a constant Necessity of searching for Variety, and also have tended to fix that Variety in my Mind, and make me Master of it. Therefore I took some of the Tales and turn'd them into Verse: And after a time, when I had pretty well forgotten the Prose, turn'd them back again. I also sometimes jumbled my Collections of Hints into Confusion, and after some Weeks, endeavour'd to reduce them into the best Order, before I began to form the full Sentences, and compleat the Paper. This was to teach me Method in the Arrangement of Thoughts. By comparing my work afterwards with the original, I discover'd many faults and amended them; but I sometimes had the Pleasure of Fancying that in certain Particulars of small Import, I had been lucky enough to improve the Method or the Language and this encourag'd me to think I might possibly in time come to be a tolerable English Writer, of which I was extreamly ambitious.

My Time for these Exercises and for Reading, was at Night, after Work or before it began in the Morning; or on Sundays, when I contrived to be in the Printing House alone, evading as much as I could the common Attendance on publick Worship, which my Father used to exact of me when I was under his Care: And which indeed I still thought a Duty; tho' I could not, as it seemed to me, afford the Time to practise it.

When about 16 Years of Age, I happen'd to meet with a Book, written by one Tryon, recommending a Vegetable Diet. I determined to go into it. My Brother being yet unmarried, did not keep House, but boarded himself and his Apprentices in another Family. My refusing to eat Flesh occasioned an Inconveniency, and I was frequently chid for my singularity. I made myself acquainted with Tryon's Manner of preparing some of his Dishes, such as Boiling Potatoes or Rice, making Hasty Pudding, and a few others, and then propos'd to my Brother, that if he would give me Weekly half the Money he paid for my Board I would board myself. He instantly agreed to it, and I presently found that I could save half

what he paid me. This was an additional Fund for buying Books. But I had another Advantage in it. My Brother and the rest going from the Printing House to their Meals, I remain'd there alone, and dispatching presently my light Repast, (which often was no more than a Bisket or a Slice of Bread, a Handful of Raisins or a Tart from the Pastry Cook's, and a Glass of Water) had the rest of the Time till their Return, for Study, in which I made the greater Progress from that greater Clearness of Head and quicker Apprehension which usually attend Temperance in Eating and Drinking. And now it was that being on some Occasion made asham'd of my Ignorance in Figures, which I had twice failed in Learning when at School, I took Cocker's Book of Arithmetick, and went thro' the whole by myself with great Ease. I also read Seller's and Sturmy's Books of Navigation, and became acquainted with the little Geometry they contain, but never proceeded far in that Science.—And I read about this Time Locke on Human Understanding, and the Art of Thinking by Messrs du Port Royal.

While I was intent on improving my Language, I met with an English Grammar (I think it was Greenwood's) at the End of which there were two little Sketches of the Arts of Rhetoric and Logic, the latter finishing with a Specimen of a Dispute in the Socratic Method. And soon after I procur'd Xenophon's Memorable Things of Socrates, wherein there are many Instances of the same Method. I was charm'd with it, adopted it, dropt my abrupt Contradiction, and positive Argumentation, and put on the humble Enquirer and Doubter. And being then, from reading Shaftsbury and Collins, become a real Doubter in many Points of our religious Doctrine, I found this Method safest for myself and very embarrassing to those against whom I us'd it, therefore I took a Delight in it, practis'd it continually and grew very artful and expert in drawing People even of superior Knowledge into Concessions the Consequences of which they did not foresee, entangling them in Difficulties out of which they could not extricate themselves, and so obtaining Victories that neither myself nor my Cause always deserved.—I continu'd this Method some few years, but gradually left it, retaining only the Habit of expressing myself in Terms of modest Diffidence, never using when I advance any thing that may possibly be disputed, the Words, *Certainly, undoubtedly;* or any others that give the Air of Positiveness to an Opinion; but rather say, I conceive, or I apprehend a Thing to be so or so, It appears to me, or I should think it so or so for such and such Reasons, or I imagine it to be so, or it is so if I am not mistaken. This Habit I believe has been of great Advantage to me, when I have had occasion to inculcate my Opinions and persuade Men into Measures that I have been from time to time engag'd in promoting.—And as the chief Ends of Conversation are to *inform,* or to be *informed,* to *please* or to *persuade,* I wish wellmeaning sensible Men would not lessen their Power of doing Good by a Positive assuming Manner that seldom fails to disgust, tends to create Opposition,

and to defeat every one of those Purposes for which Speech was given us, to wit, giving or receiving Information, or Pleasure: For if you would *inform,* a positive dogmatical Manner in advancing your Sentiments, may provoke Contradiction and prevent a candid Attention. If you wish Information and Improvement from the Knowledge of others and yet at the same time express yourself as firmly fix'd in your present Opinions, modest sensible Men, who do not love Disputation, will probably leave you undisturbed in the Possession of your Error; and by such a Manner you can seldom hope to recommend yourself in *pleasing* your Hearers, or to persuade those whose Concurrence you desire. . . .

My Brother had in 1720 or 21, begun to print a Newspaper. It was the second that appear'd in America, and was called *The New England Courant.* The only one before it, was *The Boston News Letter.* I remember his being dissuaded by some of his Friends from the Undertaking, as not likely to succeed, one Newspaper being in their Judgment enough for America.—At this time 1771 there are not less than five and twenty.—He went on however with the Undertaking, and after having work'd in composing the Types and printing off the Sheets, I was employ'd to carry the Papers thro' the Streets to the Customers.—He had some ingenious Men among his Friends who amus'd themselves by writing little Pieces for this Paper, which gain'd it Credit, and made it more in Demand; and these Gentlemen often visited us.—Hearing their Conversations, and their Accounts of the Approbation their Papers were receiv'd with, I was excited to try my Hand among them. But being still a Boy, and suspecting that my Brother would object to printing any Thing of mine in his Paper if he knew it to be mine, I contriv'd to disguise my Hand, and writing an anonymous Paper I put it in at Night under the Door of the Printing House. It was found in the Morning and communicated to his Writing Friends when they call'd in as usual. They read it, commented on it in my Hearing, and I had the exquisite Pleasure, of finding it met with their Approbation, and that in their different Guesses at the Author none were named but Men of some Character among us for Learning and Ingenuity.—I suppose now that I was rather lucky in my Judges: And that perhaps they were not really so very good ones as I then esteem'd them. Encourag'd however by this, I wrote and convey'd in the same Way to the Press several more Papers, which were equally approv'd, and I kept my Secret till my small Fund of Sense for such Performances was pretty well exhausted, and then I discovered it; when I began to be considered a little more by my Brother's Acquaintance, and in a manner that did not quite please him, as he thought, probably with reason, that it tended to make me too vain. And perhaps this might be one Occasion of the Differences that we began to have about this Time. Tho' a Brother, he considered himself as my Master, and me as his Apprentice; and accordingly expected the same Services from me as he would from another; while I thought he demean'd me too much in some he requir'd of

me, who from a Brother expected more Indulgence. Our Disputes were often brought before our Father, and I fancy I was either generally in the right, or else a better Pleader, because the Judgment was generally in my favour: But my Brother was passionate and had often beaten me, which I took extreamly amiss; and thinking my Apprenticeship very tedious, I was continually wishing for some Opportunity of shortening it, which at length offered in a manner unexpected.* . . .

2. Morals and Religion

Before I enter upon my public Appearance in Business it may be well to let you know the then State of my Mind, with regard to my Principles and Morals, that you may see how far those influenc'd the future Events of my Life. My Parent's [sic] had early given me religious Impressions, and brought me through my Childhood piously in the Dissenting Way. But I was scarce 15 when, after doubting by turns of several Points as I found them disputed in the different Books I read, I began to doubt of Revelation it self. Some Books against Deism fell into my Hands; they were said to be the Substance of Sermons preached at Boyle's Lectures. It happened that they wrought an Effect on me quite contrary to what was intended by them: For the Arguments of the Deists which were quoted to be refuted, appeared to me much Stronger than the Refutations. In short I soon became a thorough Deist. My Arguments perverted some others, particularly Collins and Ralph: but each of them having afterwards wrong'd me greatly without the least Compunction and recollecting Keith's Conduct towards me, (who was another Freethinker) and my own towards Vernon and Miss Read, which at Times gave me great Trouble, I began to suspect that this Doctrine tho' it might be true, was not very useful.—My London Pamphlet, which had for its Motto these Lines of Dryden

> Whatever is, is right. Tho' purblind Man
> Sees but a Part of the Chain, the nearest Link,
> His Eyes not carrying to the equal Beam,
> That poises all, above.

And from the Attributes of God, his infinite Wisdom, Goodness and Power concluded that nothing could possibly be wrong in the World, and that Vice and Virtue were empty Distinctions, no such Things existing: appear'd now not so clever a Performance as I once thought it; and I doubted whether some Error had not insinuated itself unperceiv'd, into my Argument, so as to infect all that follow'd, as is common in metaphys-

* I fancy his harsh and tyrannical Treatment of me, might be a means of impressing me with that Aversion to arbitrary Power that has stuck to me thro' my whole life. [Franklin's note.]

ical Reasonings.—I grew convinc'd that *Truth, Sincerity* and *Integrity* in Dealings between Man and Man, were of the utmost Importance to the Felicity of Life, and I form'd written Resolutions, (wch still remain in my Journal Book) to practice them everwhile I lived. Revelation had indeed no weight with me as such; but I entertain'd an Opinion, that tho' certain Actions might not be bad *because* they were forbidden by it, or good *because* it commanded them; yet probably those Actions might be forbidden *because* they were bad for us, or commanded *because* they were beneficial to us, in their own Natures, all the Circumstances of things considered. And this Persuasion, with the kind hand of Providence, or some guardian Angel, or accidental favourable Circumstances and Situations, or all together, preserved me (thro' this dangerous Time of Youth and the hazardous Situations I was sometimes in among Strangers, remote from the Eye and Advice of my Father) without any *wilful* gross Immorality or Injustice that might have been expected from my Want of Religion. I say *wilful,* because the Instances I have mentioned, had something of *Necessity* in them, from my Youth, Inexperience, and the Knavery of others. I had therefore a tolerable Character to begin the World with, I valued it properly, and determin'd to preserve it.—. . .

I had been religiously educated as a Presbyterian; and tho' some of the dogmas of that persuasion, such as *the eternal decrees of God, election, reprobation, etc.,* appeared to me unintelligible, others doubtful, and I early absented myself from the public assemblies of the sect, Sunday being my studying day, I never was without some religious principles. I never doubted, for instance, the existence of the Deity; that he made the world, and govern'd it by his Providence; that the most acceptable service of God was the doing good to man; that our souls are immortal; and that all crime will be punished, and virtue rewarded, either here or hereafter. These I esteem'd the essentials of every religion; and, being to be found in all the religions we had in our country, I respected them all, tho' with different degrees of respect, as I found them more or less mix'd with other articles, which, without any tendency to inspire, promote, or confirm morality, serv'd principally to divide us, and make us unfriendly to one another. This respect to all, with an opinion that the worst had some good effects, induc'd me to avoid all discourse that might tend to lessen the good opinion another might have of his own religion; and as our province increas'd in people, and new places of worship were continually wanted, and generally erected by voluntary contribution, my mite for such purpose, whatever might be the sect, was never refused.

Tho' I seldom attended any public worship, I had still an opinion of its propriety, and of its utility when rightly conducted, and I regularly paid my annual subscription for the support of the only Presbyterian minister or meeting we had in Philadelphia. He us'd to visit me sometimes as a friend, and admonish me to attend his administrations, and I was now and then prevail'd on to do so, once for five Sundays successively. Had he

been in my opinion a good preacher, perhaps I might have continued, notwithstanding the occasion I had for the Sunday's leisure in my course of study; but his discourses were chiefly either polemic arguments, or explications of the peculiar doctrines of our sect, and were all to me very dry, uninteresting, and unedifying, since not a single moral principle was inculcated or enforc'd, their aim seeming to be rather to make us Presbyterians than good citizens.

At length he took for his text that verse of the fourth chapter of Philippians, *"Finally, brethren, whatsoever things are true, honest, just, pure, lovely, or of good report, if there be any virtue, or any praise, think on these things."* And I imagin'd, in a sermon on such a text, we could not miss of having some morality. But he confin'd himself to five points only, as meant by the apostle, viz.: 1. Keeping holy the Sabbath day. 2. Being diligent in reading the holy Scriptures. 3. Attending duly the publick worship. 4. Partaking of the Sacrament. 5. Paying a due respect to God's ministers. These might be all good things; but, as they were not the kind of good things that I expected from that text, I despaired of ever meeting with them from any other, was disgusted, and attended his preaching no more. I had some years before compos'd a little Liturgy, or form of prayer, for my own private use (viz., in 1728), entitled *Articles of Belief and Acts of Religion.* I return'd to the use of this, and went no more to the public assemblies. My conduct might be blameable, but I leave it, without attempting further to excuse it; my present purpose being to relate facts, and not to make apologies for them.

It was about this time I conceiv'd the bold and arduous project of arriving at moral perfection. I wish'd to live without committing any fault at any time; I would conquer all that either natural inclination, custom, or company might lead me into. As I knew, or thought I knew, what was right and wrong, I did not see why I might not always do the one and avoid the other. But I soon found I had undertaken a task of more difficulty than I had imagined. While my care was employ'd in guarding against one fault, I was often surprised by another; habit took the advantage of inattention; inclination was sometimes too strong for reason. I concluded, at length, that the mere speculative conviction that it was our interest to be completely virtuous, was not sufficient to prevent our slipping; and that the contrary habits must be broken, and good ones acquired and established, before we can have any dependence on a steady, uniform rectitude of conduct. For this purpose I therefore contrived the following method.

In the various enumerations of the moral virtues I had met with in my reading, I found the catalogue more or less numerous, as different writers included more or fewer ideas under the same name. Temperance, for example, was by some confined to eating and drinking, while by others it was extended to mean the moderating every other pleasure, appetite, inclination, or passion, bodily or mental, even to our avarice and ambition.

I propos'd to myself, for the sake of clearness, to use rather more names, with fewer ideas annex'd to each, than a few names with more ideas; and I included under thirteen names of virtues all that at that time occurr'd to me as necessary or desirable, and annexed to each a short precept, which fully express'd the extent I gave to its meaning.

These names of virtues, with their precepts, were:

1. TEMPERANCE

Eat not to dullness; drink not to elevation.

2. SILENCE

Speak not but what may benefit others or yourself; avoid trifling conversation.

3. ORDER

Let all your things have their places; let each part of your business have its time.

4. RESOLUTION

Resolve to perform what you ought; perform without fail what you resolve.

5. FRUGALITY

Make no expense but to do good to others or yourself; *i.e.,* waste nothing.

6. INDUSTRY

Lose no time; be always employ'd in something useful; cut off all unnecessary actions.

7. SINCERITY

Use no hurtful deceit; think innocently and justly, and, if you speak, speak accordingly.

8. JUSTICE

Wrong none by doing injuries, or omitting the benefits that are your duty.

9. MODERATION

Avoid extreams; forbear resenting injuries so much as you think they deserve.

10. CLEANLINESS

Tolerate no uncleanliness in body, cloaths, or habitation.

11. TRANQUILLITY

Be not disturbed at trifles, or at accidents common or unavoidable.

12. CHASTITY

Rarely use venery but for health or offspring, never to dulness, weakness, or the injury of your own or another's peace or reputation.

13. HUMILITY

Imitate Jesus and Socrates.

My intention being to acquire the *habitude* of all these virtues, I judg'd it would be well not to distract my attention by attempting the whole at once, but to fix it on one of them at a time; and, when I should be master of that, then to proceed to another, and so on, till I should have gone thro' the thirteen; and, as the previous acquisition of some might facilitate the acquisition of certain others, I arrang'd them with that view, as they stand above. Temperance first, as it tends to procure that coolness and clearness of head, which is so necessary where constant vigilance was to be kept up, and guard maintained against the unremitting attraction of ancient habits, and the force of perpetual temptations. This being acquir'd and establish'd, Silence would be more easy; and my desire being to gain knowledge at the same time that I improv'd in virtue, and considering that in conversation it was obtain'd rather by the use of the ears than of the tongue, and therefore wishing to break a habit I was getting into of prattling, punning, and joking, which only made me acceptable to trifling company, I gave *Silence* the second place. This and the next, *Order*, I expected would allow me more time for attending to my project and my studies. *Resolution*, once become habitual, would keep me firm in my endeavours to obtain all the subsequent virtues; *Frugality* and Industry freeing me from my remaining debt, and producing affluence and independence, would make more easy the practice of Sincerity and Justice, etc., etc. Conceiving then, that, agreeably to the advice of Pythagoras in his *Golden Verses*, daily examination would be necessary, I contrived the following method for conducting that examination.

I made a little book, in which I allotted a page for each of the virtues. I rul'd each page with red ink, so as to have seven columns, one for each day of the week, marking each column with a letter for the day. I cross'd these columns with thirteen red lines, marking the beginning of each line with the first letter of one of the virtues, on which line, and in its proper column, I might mark, by a little black spot, every fault I found upon examination to have been committed respecting that virtue upon that day . . .

I determined to give a week's strict attention to each of the virtues successively. Thus, in the first week, my great guard was to avoid every the least offence against *Temperance*, leaving the other virtues to their ordinary chance, only marking every evening the faults of the day. Thus, if in the first week I could keep my first line, marked T, clear of spots, I suppos'd the habit of that virtue so much strengthen'd, and its opposite weaken'd, that I might venture extending my attention to include the next, and for the following week keep both lines clear of spots. Proceeding thus to the last, I could go thro' a course compleat in thirteen weeks,

and four courses in a year. And like him who, having a garden to weed, does not attempt to eradicate all the bad herbs at once, which would exceed his reach and his strength, but works on one of the beds at a time, and, having accomplish'd the first, proceeds to a second, so I should have, I hoped, the encouraging pleasure of seeing on my pages the progress I made in virtue, by clearing successively my lines of their spots, till in the end, by a number of courses, I should be happy in viewing a clean book, after a thirteen weeks' daily examination.

This my little book had for its motto these lines from Addison's *Cato:*

> Here will I hold. If there's a power above us
> (And that there is, all nature cries aloud
> Thro' all her works), He must delight in virtue;
> And that which he delights in must be happy.

Another from Cicero,

O vitæ Philosophia dux! O virtutum indagatrix expultrixque vitiorum! Unus dies, bene et ex præceptis tuis actus, peccanti immortalitati est anteponendus.

Another from the Proverbs of Solomon, speaking of wisdom or virtue:

Length of days is in her right hand, and in her left hand riches and honour. Her ways are ways of pleasantness, and all her paths are peace. —iii. 16, 17.

And conceiving God to be the fountain of wisdom, I thought it right and necessary to solicit his assistance for obtaining it; to this end I formed the following little prayer, which was prefix'd to my tables of examination, for daily use.

O powerful Goodness! bountiful Father! merciful Guide! Increase in me that wisdom which discovers my truest interest. Strengthen my resolutions to perform what that wisdom dictates. Accept my kind offices to thy other children as the only return in my power for thy continual favours to me. . . .

3. *Albany Plan of Union*

In 1754 war with France being again apprehended, a congress of commissioners from the different Colonies was by an order of the Lords of Trade to be assembled at Albany, there to confer with the chiefs of the six nations concerning the means of defending both their country and ours. Governor Hamilton having received this order, acquainted the House with it, requesting they would furnish proper presents for the Indians to be given on this occasion, and naming the Speaker (Mr.

Norris) and myself to join Mr. Thomas Penn and Mr. Secretary Peters as commissioners ... to act for Pennsylvania. The House approved the nomination, and provided the goods for the present, and though they did not much like treating out of the provinces; and we met the other commissioners at Albany about the middle of June.

In our way thither, I projected and drew a plan for the union of all the colonies under one government, so far as might be necessary for defense, and other important general purposes. As we passed through New York, I had there shown my project to Mr. James Alexander and Mr. Kennedy, two gentlemen of great knowledge in public affairs, and, being fortified by their approbation, I ventured to lay it before the Congress. It then appeared that several of the commissioners had formed plans of the same kind. A previous question was first taken, whether a union should be established, which passed in the affirmative unanimously. A committee was then appointed, one member from each colony, to consider the several plans and report. Mine happened to be preferred, and, with a few amendments, was accordingly reported.

By this plan the general government was to be administered by a president-general, appointed and supported by the Crown, and a grand council was to be chosen by the representatives of the people of the several colonies, met in their respective assemblies. The debates upon it in Congress went on daily, hand in hand with the Indian business. Many objections and difficulties were started, but at length they were all overcome, and the plan was unanimously agreed to, and copies ordered to be transmitted to the Board of Trade and to the assemblies of the several provinces. Its fate was singular: the assemblies did not adopt it, as they all thought there was too much *prerogative* in it, and in England it was judged to have too much of the *democratic*. The Board of Trade therefore did not approve of it, nor recommend it for the approbation of His Majesty; but another scheme was formed, supposed to answer the same purpose better, whereby the governors of the provinces, with some members of their respective councils, were to meet and order the raising of troops, building of forts, etc., and to draw on the treasury of Great Britain for the expense, which was afterwards to be refunded by an act of Parliament laying a tax on America. My plan, with my reasons in support of it, is to be found among my political papers that are printed.

Being the winter following in Boston, I had much conversation with Governor Shirley upon both the plans. Part of what passed between us on the occasion may also be seen among those papers. The different and contrary reasons of dislike to my plan makes me suspect that it was really the true medium; and I am still of opinion it would have been happy for both sides the water if it had been adopted. The colonies, so united, would have been sufficiently strong to have defended themselves; there would then have been no need of troops from England; of course, the subsequent pretense for taxing America, and the bloody contest it occa-

sioned, would have been avoided. But such mistakes are not new; history is full of the errors of states and princes.

"Look around the habitable world, how few
Know their own good, or, knowing it, pursue!"

Those who govern, having much business on their hands, do not generally like to take the trouble of considering and carrying into execution new projects. The best public measures are therefore seldom adopted from previous wisdom, but forced by the occasion.

Letters

4. *Freedom of Thought*

To Josiah Franklin

Philadelphia, April 13, 1738

Honoured Father,

I have your favours of the 21st of March, in which you both seem concerned lest I have imbibed some erroneous opinions. Doubtless I have my share; and when the natural weakness and imperfection of human understanding is considered, the unavoidable influence of education, custom, books, and company upon our ways of thinking, I imagine a man must have a good deal of vanity who believes, and a good deal of boldness who affirms, that all the doctrines he holds are true, and all he rejects are false. And perhaps the same may be justly said of every sect, church, and society of men, when they assume to themselves that infallibility, which they deny to the Pope and councils.

I think opinions should be judged of by their influences and effects; and, if a man holds none that tend to make him less virtuous or more vicious, it may be concluded he holds none that are dangerous; which I hope is the case with me.

I am sorry you should have any uneasiness on my account; and if it were a thing possible for one to alter his opinions in order to please another, I know none whom I ought more willingly to oblige in that respect than yourselves. But, since it is no more in a man's power to *think* than to *look* like another, methinks all that should be expected from me is to keep my mind open to conviction, to hear patiently and examine attentively, whatever is offered me for that end; and, if after all I continue in the same errors, I believe your usual charity will induce you to rather pity and excuse, than blame me. In the mean time your care and concern for me is what I am very thankful for.

My mother grieves, that one of her sons is an Arian, another an Arminian. What an Arminian or an Arian is, I cannot say that I very well know. The truth is, I make such distinctions very little my study. I think vital religion has always suffered, when orthodoxy is more regarded than

virtue; and the Scriptures assure me, that at the last day we shall not be examined what we *thought*, but what we *did;* and our recommendation will not be, that we said, *Lord! Lord!* but that we did good to our fellow creatures. See Matt. xxv.

As to the freemasons, I know no way of giving my mother a better account of them than she seems to have at present, since it is not allowed that women should be admitted into that secret society. She has, I must confess, on that account some reason to be displeased with it; but for any thing else, I must entreat her to suspend her judgment till she is better informed, unless she will believe me, when I assure her that they are in general a very harmless sort of people, and have no principles or practices that are inconsistent with religion and good manners. . . .

5. *Advice to a Young Man on the Choice of a Mistress*

June 25, 1745

My dear Friend,

I know of no Medicine fit to diminish the violent natural Inclinations you mention; and if I did, I think I should not communicate it to you. Marriage is the proper Remedy. It is the most natural State of Man, and therefore the State in which you are most likely to find solid Happiness. Your Reasons against entring into it at present, appear to me not well-founded. The circumstantial Advantages you have in View by postponing it, are not only uncertain, but they are small in comparison with that of the Thing itself, the being *married and settled.* It is the Man and Woman united that make the compleat human Being. Separate, she wants his Force of Body and Strength of Reason; he, her Softness, Sensibility and acute Discernment. Together they are more likely to succeed in the World. A single Man has not nearly the Value he would have in that State of Union. He is an incomplete Animal. He resembles the odd Half of a Pair of Scissars. If you get a prudent healthy Wife, your Industry in your Profession, with her good Œconomy, will be a Fortune sufficient.

But if you will not take this Counsel, and persist in thinking a Commerce with the Sex inevitable, then I repeat my former Advice, that in all your Amours you should *prefer old Women to young ones.* You call this a Paradox, and demand my Reasons. They are these:

1. Because as they have more Knowledge of the World and their Minds are better stor'd with Observations, their Conversation is more improving and more lastingly agreable.

2. Because when Women cease to be handsome, they study to be good.

To maintain their Influence over Men, they supply the Diminution of Beauty by an Augmentation of Utility. They learn to do a 1000 Services small and great, and are the most tender and useful of all Friends when you are sick. Thus they continue amiable. And hence there is hardly such a thing to be found as an old Woman who is not a good Woman.

3. Because there is no hazard of Children, which irregularly produc'd may be attended with much Inconvenience.

4. Because thro' more Experience, they are more prudent and discreet in conducting an Intrigue to prevent Suspicion. The Commerce with them is therefore safer with regard to your Reputation. And with regard to theirs, if the Affair should happen to be known, considerate People might be rather inclin'd to excuse an old Woman who would kindly take care of a young Man, form his Manners by her good Counsels, and prevent his ruining his Health and Fortune among mercenary Prostitutes.

5. Because in every Animal that walks upright, the Deficiency of the Fluids that fill the Muscles appears first in the highest Part: The Face first grows lank and wrinkled; then the Neck; then the Breast and Arms; the lower Parts continuing to the last as plump as ever: So that covering all above with a Basket, and regarding only what is below the Girdle, it is impossible of two Women to know an old from a young one. And as in the dark all Cats are grey, the Pleasure of corporal Enjoyment with an old Woman is at least equal, and frequently superior, every Knack being by Practice capable of Improvement.

6. Because the Sin is less. The debauching a Virgin may be her Ruin, and make her for Life unhappy.

7. Because the Compunction is less. The having made a young Girl *miserable* may give you frequent bitter Reflections; none of which can attend the making an old Woman *happy*.

8[thly and Lastly] They are *so grateful!!*

Thus much for my Paradox. But still I advise you to marry directly; being sincerely Your affectionate Friend.

6. *On Electricity*

To Peter Collinson

Philadelphia, July 11, 1747

Sir,

In my last I informed you that, in pursuing our electrical enquiries, we had observed some particular phenomena, which we looked upon to be new, and of which I promised to give you some account, though I apprehended they might possibly not be new to you, as so many hands are

daily employed in electrical experiments on your side the water, some or other of which would probably hit on the same observations.

The first is the wonderful effect of pointed bodies, both in *drawing off* and *throwing off* the electrical fire. For example,

Place an iron shot of three or four inches diameter on the mouth of a clean dry glass bottle. By a fine silken thread from the cieling, right over the mouth of the bottle, suspend a small cork ball, about the bigness of a marble; the thread of such a length, as that the cork ball may rest against the side of the shot. Electrify the shot, and the ball will be repelled to the distance of four or five inches, more or less, according to the quantity of Electricity. When in this state, if you present to the shot the point of a long slender sharp bodkin, at six or eight inches distance, the repellency is instantly destroy'd, and the cork flies to the shot. A blunt body must be brought within an inch, and draw a spark, to produce the same effect. To prove that the electrical fire is *drawn off* by the point, if you take the blade of the bodkin out of the wooden handle, and fix it in a stick of sealing-wax, and then present it at the distance aforesaid, or if you bring it very near, no such effect follows; but sliding one finger along the wax till you touch the blade, and the ball flies to the shot immediately. If you present the point in the dark, you will see, sometimes at a foot distance, and more, a light gather upon it, like that of a fire-fly, or glow-worm; the less sharp the point, the nearer you must bring it to observe the light; and, at whatever distance you see the light, you may draw off the electrical fire, and destroy the repellency. If a cork ball so suspended be repelled by the tube, and a point be presented quick to it, tho' at a considerable distance, 'tis surprizing to see how suddenly it flies back to the tube. Points of wood will do near as well as those of iron, provided the wood is not dry; for perfectly dry wood will no more conduct Electricity than sealing-wax.

To shew that points will *throw off* as well as *draw off* the electrical fire; lay a long sharp needle upon the shot, and you cannot electrise the shot so as to make it repel the cork ball. Or fix a needle to the end of a suspended gun-barrel, or iron rod, so as to point beyond it like a little bayonet; and while it remains there, the gun-barrel, or rod, cannot by applying the tube to the other end be electrised so as to give a spark, the fire continually running out silently at the point. In the dark you may see it make the same appearance as it does in the case before mentioned.

The repellency between the cork ball and the shot is likewise destroyed. 1, by sifting fine sand on it; this does it gradually. 2, by breathing on it. 3, by making a smoke about it from burning wood. 4, by candle-light, even though the candle is at a foot distance: these do it suddenly. The light of a bright coal from a wood fire; and the light of red-hot iron do it likewise; but not at so great a distance. Smoke from dry rosin dropt on hot iron, does not destroy the repellency; but is attracted by both shot and cork ball, forming proportionable atmospheres round them, making

them look beautifully, somewhat like some of the figures in *Burnet's* or *Whiston's Theory of the Earth.*

N. B. This experiment should be made in a closet, where the air is very still, or it will be apt to fail.

The light of the sun thrown strongly on both cork and shot by a looking-glass for a long time together, does not impair the repellency in the least. This difference between fire-light and sun-light is another thing that seems new and extraordinary to us.

We had for some time been of opinion, that the electrical fire was not created by friction, but collected, being really an element diffus'd among, and attracted by other matter, particularly by water and metals. We had even discovered and demonstrated its afflux to the electrical sphere, as well as its efflux, by means of little light windmill-wheels made of stiff paper vanes, fixed obliquely and turning freely on fine wire axes; also by little wheels of the same matter, but formed like water-wheels. Of the disposition and application of which wheels, and the various phaenomena resulting, I could, if I had time, fill you a sheet. The impossibility of electrising one's self (though standing on wax) by rubbing the tube, and drawing the fire from it; and the manner of doing it, by passing the tube near a person or thing standing on the floor, &c., had also occurred to us some months before Mr. Watson's ingenious *Sequel* came to hand, and these were some of the new things I intended to have communicated to you. But now I need only mention some particulars not hinted in that piece, with our reasonings thereupon; though perhaps the latter might well enough be spared.

1. A person standing on wax, and rubbing the tube, and another person on wax drawing the fire, they will both of them, (provided they do not stand so as to touch one another) appear to be electrised, to a person standing on the floor; that is, he will perceive a spark on approaching each of them with his knuckle.

2. But, if the persons on wax touch one another during the exciting of the tube, neither of them will appear to be electrised.

3. If they touch one another after exciting the tube, and drawing the fire as aforesaid, there will be a stronger spark between them, than was between either of them and the person on the floor.

4. After such strong spark, neither of them discover any electricity.

These appearances we attempt to account for thus: We suppose, as aforesaid, that electrical fire is a common element, of which every one of the three persons above mentioned has his equal share, before any operation is begun with the tube. *A*, who stands on wax and rubs the tube, collects the electrical fire from himself into the glass; and his communication with the common stock being cut off by the wax, his body is not again immediately supply'd. *B*, (who stands on wax likewise) passing his knuckle along near the tube, receives the fire which was collected by the glass from *A*; and his communication with the common stock being like-

wise cut off, he retains the additional quantity received. To *C*, standing on the floor, both appear to be electrised: for he having only the middle quantity of electrical fire, receives a spark upon approaching *B*, who has an over quantity; but gives one to *A*, who has an under quantity. If *A* and *B* approach to touch each other, the spark is stronger, because the difference between them is greater: After such touch there is no spark between either of them and *C*, because the electrical fire in all is reduced to the original equality. If they touch while electrising, the equality is never destroy'd, the fire only circulating. Hence have arisen some new terms among us: we say, *B*, (and bodies like circumstanced) is electrised *positively; A, negatively*. Or rather, *B* is electrised *plus; A, minus*. And we daily in our experiments electrise bodies *plus or minus*, as we think proper. To electrise *plus* or *minus*, no more needs to be known than this, that the parts of the tube or sphere that are rubbed, do, in the instant of the friction, attract the electrical fire, and therefore take it from the thing rubbing: the same parts immediately, as the friction upon them ceases, are disposed to give the fire they have received, to any body that has less. Thus you may circulate it, as Mr. *Watson* has shewn; you may also accumulate or subtract it upon, or from any body, as you connect that body with the rubber or with the receiver, the communication with the common stock being cut off. We think that ingenious gentleman was deceived when he imagined (in his *Sequel*) that the electrical fire came down the wire from the cieling to the gun-barrel, thence to the sphere, and so electrised the machine and the man turning the wheel, &c. We suppose it was *driven off*, and not brought on through that wire; and that the machine and man, &c., were electrised *minus, i.e.* had less electrical fire in them than things in common.

As the vessel is just upon sailing, I cannot give you so large an account of *American* electricity as I intended: I shall only mention a few particulars more. We find granulated lead better to fill the phial with, than water, being easily warmed, and keeping warm and dry in damp air. We fire spirits with the wire of the phial. We light candles, just blown out, by drawing a spark among the smoke, between the wire and snuffers. We represent lightning, by passing the wire in the dark, over a China plate, that has gilt flowers, or applying it to gilt frames of looking-glasses, &c. We electrise a person twenty or more times running, with a touch of the finger on the wire, thus: He stands on wax. Give him the electrised bottle in his hand. Touch the wire with your finger, and then touch his hand or face; there are sparks every time. We increase the force of the electrical kiss vastly, thus: Let *A* and *B* stand on wax; or *A* on wax, and *B* on the floor; give one of them the electrised phial in hand; let the other take hold of the wire; there will be a small spark; but when their lips approach, they will be struck and shock'd. The same if another gentleman and lady, *C* and *D*, standing also on wax, and joining hands with *A* and *B*, salute or shake hands. We suspend by fine silk thread a counterfeit spider, made of a small piece of burnt cork, with legs of linnen thread,

and a grain or two of lead stuck in him, to give him more weight. Upon the table, over which he hangs, we stick a wire upright, as high as the phial and wire, two or three inches from the spider: then we animate him, by setting the electrified phial at the same distance on the other side of him; he will immediately fly to the wire of the phial, bend his legs in touching it; then spring off, and fly to the wire on the table; thence again to the wire of the phial, playing with his legs against both, in a very entertaining manner, appearing perfectly alive to persons unacquainted. He will continue this motion an hour or more in dry weather. We electrify, upon wax in the dark, a book that has a double line of gold round upon the covers, and then apply a knuckle to the gilding; the fire appears everywhere upon the gold like a flash of lightning: not upon the leather, nor, if you touch the leather instead of the gold. We rub our tubes with buckskin, and observe always to keep the same side to the tube, and never to sully the tube by handling; thus they work readily and easily, without the least fatigue, especially if kept in tight pasteboard cases, lined with flannel, and sitting close to the tube. This I mention, because the *European* papers on Electricity, frequently speak of rubbing the tube, as a fatiguing exercise. Our spheres are fixed on iron axes, which pass through them. At one end of the axis there is a small handle, with which you turn the sphere like a common grindstone. This we find very commodious, as the machine takes up but little room, is portable, and may be enclosed in a tight box, when not in use. 'Tis true, the sphere does not turn so swift as when the great wheel is used: but swiftness we think of little importance, since a few turns will charge the phial, &c., sufficiently.

7. *The Albany Plan of Union*

To James Parker

Philadelphia, March 20, 1750

Dear Mr. Parker,

I have, as you desire, read the Manuscript you sent me; and am of Opinion, with the publick-spirited Author, that securing the Friendship of the *Indians* is of the greatest Consequence to these Colonies; and that the surest means of doing it, are, to regulate the *Indian* Trade, so to convince them, by Experience, that they may have the best and cheapest Goods, and the fairest Dealing from the *English;* and to unite the several Governments, so as to form a Strength that the *Indians* may depend on for Protection in Case of a Rupture with the *French;* or apprehend great Danger from, if they should break with us.

This Union of the Colonies, however necessary, I apprehend is not to be brought about by the Means that have hitherto been used for that

Purpose. A Governor of one Colony, who happens from some Circumstances in his own Government, to see the Necessity of such an Union, writes his Sentiments of the Matter to the other Governors, and desires them to recommend it to their respective Assemblies. They accordingly lay the Letters before those Assemblies, and perhaps recommend the Proposal in general Words. But Governors are often on ill Terms with their Assemblies, and seldom are the Men that have the most Influence among them. And perhaps some Governors, tho' they openly recommend the Scheme, may privately throw cold Water on it, as thinking additional publick Charges will make their People less able or less willing to give to them. Or perhaps they do not clearly see the Necessity of it, and therefore do not very earnestly press the Consideration of it: And no one being present that has the Affair at Heart, to back it, to answer and remove Objections, &c., 'tis easily dropt, and nothing is done. Such an Union is certainly necessary to us all, but more immediately so to your Government.* Now, if you were to pick out half a Dozen Men of good Understanding and Address, and furnish them with a reasonable Scheme and proper Instructions, and send them in the Nature of Ambassadors to the other Colonies, where they might apply particularly to all the leading Men, and by proper Management get them to engage in promoting the Scheme; where, by being present, they would have the Opportunity of pressing the Affair both in publick and private, obviating Difficulties as they arise, answering Objections as soon as they are made, before they spread and gather Strength in the Minds of the People, &c., &c. I imagine such an Union might thereby be made and established: For reasonable sensible Men, can always make a reasonable Scheme appear such to other reasonable Men, if they take Pains, and have Time and Opportunity for it; unless from some Circumstances their Honesty and good Intentions are suspected. A voluntary Union entered into by the Colonies themselves, I think, would be preferable to one impos'd by Parliament; for it would be perhaps not much more difficult to procure, and more easy to alter and improve, as Circumstances should require and Experience direct. It would be a very strange Thing, if *Six Nations* of ignorant Savages should be capable of forming a Scheme for such an Union, and be able to execute it in such a Manner, as that it has subsisted Ages, and appears indissoluble; and yet that a like Union should be impracticable for ten or a Dozen *English* Colonies, to whom it is more necessary, and must be more advantageous; and who cannot be supposed to want an equal Understanding of their Interests.

Were there a general Council form'd by all the Colonies, and a general Governor appointed by the Crown to preside in that Council, or in some Manner to concur with and confirm their Acts, and take Care of the Execution; every Thing relating to Indian Affairs and the Defence of the Colonies, might be properly put under their Management. . . .

* New York.

8. *On Education of Youth*

To Samuel Johnson

Philadelphia, August 23, 1750

. . . I think with you, that nothing is of more importance for the public weal, than to form and train up youth in wisdom and virtue. Wise and good men are, in my opinion, the strength of a state; much more so than riches or arms, which, under the management of ignorance and wickedness, often draw on destruction, instead of providing for the safety of the people. And though the culture bestowed on *many* should be successful only with a *few*, yet the influence of those few and the service in their power may be very great. Even a single woman, that was wise, by her wisdom saved the city.

I think also, that general virtue is more probably to be expected and obtained from the education of youth, than from the exhortation of adult persons; bad habits and vices of the mind being, like diseases of the body, more easily prevented than cured. I think, moreover, that talents for the education of youth are the gift of God; and that he on whom they are bestowed, whenever a way is opened for the use of them, is as strongly *called* as if he heard a voice from heaven; nothing more surely pointing out duty in a public service, than ability and opportunity of performing it. ⸱ . .

9. *The Kite Experiment*

To Peter Collinson

[Philadelphia] October 19, 1752

Sir,

As frequent mention is made in public papers from *Europe* of the success of the *Philadelphia* experiment for drawing the electric fire from clouds by means of pointed rods of iron erected on high buildings, &, it may be agreeable to the curious to be informed, that the same experiment has succeeded in *Philadelphia*, though made in a different and more easy manner, which is as follows:

Make a small cross of two light strips of cedar, the arms so long as to reach to the four corners of a large thin silk handkerchief when extended; tie the corners of the handkerchief to the extremities of the cross, so you

have the body of a kite; which being properly accommodated with a tail, loop, and string, will rise in the air, like those made of paper; but this being of silk, is fitter to bear the wet and wind of a thunder-gust without tearing. To the top of the upright stick of the cross is to be fixed a very sharp-pointed wire, rising a foot or more above the wood. To the end of the twine, next the hand, is to be tied a silk ribbon, and where the silk and twine join, a key may be fastened. This kite is to be raised when a thunder-gust appears to be coming on, and the person who holds the string must stand within a door or window or under some cover, so that the silk ribbon may not be wet; and care must be taken that the twine does not touch the frame of the door or window. As soon as any of the thunder-clouds come over the kite, the pointed wire will draw the electric fire from them, and the kite, with all the twine, will be electrified, and the loose filaments of the twine will stand out every way, and be attracted by an approaching finger. And when the rain has wet the kite and twine, so that it can conduct the electric fire freely, you will find it stream out plentifully from the key on the approach of your knuckle. At this key the phial may [be] charged; and from electric fire thus obtained, spirits may be kindled, and all the other electric experiments be performed, which are usually done by the help of a rubbed glass globe or tube, and thereby the sameness of the electric matter with that of lightning completely demonstrated.

10. *Good Works*

To Joseph Huey

Philadelphia, June 6, 1753.

Sir,

I received your kind Letter of the 2d inst., and am glad to hear that you increase in Strength; I hope you will continue mending, 'till you recover your former Health and firmness. Let me know whether you still use the Cold Bath, and what Effect it has.

As to the Kindness you mention, I wish it could have been of more Service to you. But if it had, the only Thanks I should desire is, that you would always be equally ready to serve any other Person that may need your Assistance, and so let good Offices go round, for Mankind are all of a Family.

For my own Part, when I am employed in serving others, I do not look upon myself as conferring Favours, but as paying Debts. In my Travels, and since my Settlement, I have received much Kindness from Men, to whom I shall never have any Opportunity of making the least direct

Return. And numberless Mercies from God, who is infinitely above being benefited by our Services. Those Kindnesses from Men, I can therefore only Return on their Fellow Men; and I can only shew my Gratitude for these mercies from God, by a readiness to help his other Children and my Brethren. For I do not think that Thanks and Compliments, tho' repeated weekly, can discharge our real Obligations to each other, and much less those to our Creator. You will see in this my Notion of good Works, that I am far from expecting [(as you suppose) that I shall ever] to merit Heaven by them. By Heaven we understand a State of Happiness, infinite in Degree, and eternal in Duration: I can do nothing to deserve such rewards: He that for giving a Draught of Water to a thirsty Person, should expect to be paid with a good Plantation, would be modest in his Demands, compar'd with those who think they deserve Heaven for the little good they do on Earth. Even the mix'd imperfect Pleasures we enjoy in this World, are rather from God's Goodness than our Merit; how much more such Happiness of Heaven. For my own part I have not the Vanity to think I deserve it, the Folly to expect it, nor the Ambition to desire it; but content myself in submitting to the Will and Disposal of that God who made me, who has hitherto preserv'd and bless'd me, and in whose Fatherly Goodness I may well confide, that he will never make me miserable, and that even the Afflictions I may at any time suffer shall tend to my Benefit.

The Faith you mention has doubtless its use in the World. I do not desire to see it diminished, nor would I endeavour to lessen it in any Man. But I wish it were more productive of good Works, than I have generally seen it: I mean real good Works, Works of Kindness, Charity, Mercy, and Publick Spirit; not Holiday-keeping, Sermon-Reading or Hearing; performing Church Ceremonies, or making long Prayers, filled with Flatteries and Compliments, despis'd even by wise Men, and much less capable of pleasing the Deity. The worship of God is a Duty; the hearing and reading of Sermons may be useful; but, if Men rest in Hearing and Praying, as too many do, it is as if a Tree should Value itself on being water'd and putting forth Leaves, tho' it never produc'd any Fruit.

Your great Master tho't much less of these outward Appearances and Professions than many of his modern Disciples. He prefer'd the *Doers* of the Word, to the meer *Hearers;* the Son that seemingly refus'd to obey his Father, and yet perform'd his Commands, to him that profess'd his Readiness, but neglected the Work; the heretical but charitable Samaritan, to the uncharitable tho' orthodox Priest and sanctified Levite; & those who gave Food to the hungry, Drink to the Thirsty, Raiment to the Naked, Entertainment to the Stranger, and Relief to the Sick, tho' they never heard of his Name, he declares shall in the last Day be accepted, when those who cry Lord! Lord! who value themselves on their Faith, tho' great enough to perform Miracles, but have neglected good

Works, shall be rejected. He profess'd, that he came not to call the Righteous but Sinners to repentance; which imply'd his modest Opinion, that there were some in his Time so good, that they need not hear even him for Improvement; but now-a-days we have scarce a little Parson, that does not think it the Duty of every Man within his Reach to sit under his petty Ministrations; and that whoever omits them [offends God. I wish to such more humility, and to you health and happiness, being your friend and servant,]

11. *Three Letters to Governor Shirley*

Concerning the Voice of the People in Choosing the Rulers by Whom Taxes are Imposed[1]

Tuesday Morning [December 17, 1754].

Sir,

I return you the loose sheets of the plan, with thanks to your Excellency for communicating them.

I apprehend, that excluding the *people* of the colonies from all share in the choice of the grand council will give extreme dissatisfaction, as well as the taxing them by act of Parliament, where they have no representative. It is very possible, that this general government might be as well and faithfully administered without the people, as with them; but where heavy burthens have been laid on them, it has been found useful to make it, as much as possible, their own act; for they bear better when they have, or think they have some share in the direction; and when any public measures are generally grievous, or even distasteful to the people, the wheels of government move more heavily.

On the Imposition of Direct Taxes upon the Colonies without Their Consent[2]

Wednesday Morning [December 18, 1754].

Sir,

I mentioned it yesterday to your Excellency as my opinion, that excluding the *people* of the colonies from all share in the choice of the grand council, would probably give extreme dissatisfaction, as well as the taxing them by act of Parliament, where they have no representative. In matters of general concern to the people, and especially where burthens are to be laid upon them, it is of use to consider, as well what they will be apt to think and say, as what they ought to think; I shall

therefore, as your Excellency requires it of me, briefly mention what of either kind occurs to me on this occasion.

First they will say, and perhaps with justice, that the body of the people in the colonies are as loyal, and as firmly attached to the present constitution, and reigning family, as any subjects in the king's dominions.

That there is no reason to doubt the readiness and willingness of the representatives they may choose, to grant from time to time such supplies for the defence of the country, as shall be judged necessary, so far as their abilities will allow.

That the people in the colonies, who are to feel the immediate mischiefs of invasion and conquest by an enemy in the loss of their estates, lives and liberties, are likely to be better judges of the quantity of forces necessary to be raised and maintained, forts to be built and supported, and of their own abilities to bear the expence, than the parliament of England at so great a distance.

That governors often come to the colonies merely to make fortunes, with which they intend to return to Britain; are not always men of the best abilities or integrity; have many of them no estates here, nor any natural connexions with us, that should make them heartily concerned for our welfare; and might possibly be fond of raising and keeping up more forces than necessary, from the profits accruing to themselves, and to make provision for their friends and dependants.

That the counsellors in most of the colonies being appointed by the crown, on the recommendation of governors, are often of small estates, frequently dependant on the governors for offices, and therefore too much under influence.

That there is therefore great reason to be jealous of a power in such governors and councils, to raise such sums as they shall judge necessary, by draft on the lords of the treasury, to be afterwards laid on the colonies by act of parliament, and paid by the people here; since they might abuse it by projecting useless expeditions, harassing the people, and taking them from their labour to execute such projects, merely to create offices and employments, and gratify their dependants, and divide profits.

That the parliament of England is at a great distance, subject to be misinformed and misled by such Governors and Councils, whose united interests might probably secure them against the effect of any complaint from hence.

That it is supposed an undoubted right of Englishmen, not to be taxed but by their own consent given through their representatives.

That the colonies have no representatives in parliament.

That to propose taxing them by parliament, and refuse them the liberty of choosing a representative council, to meet in the colonies, and consider and judge of the necessity of any general tax, and the quantum, shews suspicion of their loyalty to the crown, or of their regard for their country, or of their common sense and understanding, which they have not deserved.

That compelling the colonies to pay money without their consent, would be rather like raising contributions in an enemy's country, than taxing of Englishmen for their own public benefit.

That it would be treating them as a conquered people, and not as true British subjects.

That a tax laid by the representatives of the colonies might easily be lessened as the occasions should lessen, but being once laid by parliament under the influence of the representations made by Governors, would probably be kept up and continued for the benefit of Governors, to the grievous burthen and discouragement of the colonies, and prevention of their growth and increase.

That a power in Governors to march the inhabitants from one end of the British and French colonies to the other, being a country of at least 1500 square miles, without the approbation or the consent of their representatives first obtained, such expeditions might be grievous and ruinous to the people, and would put them on footing with the subjects of France in Canada, that now groan under such oppression from their Governor, who for two years past has harrassed them with long and destructive marches to Ohio.

That if the colonies in a body may be well governed by governors and councils appointed by the crown, without representatives, particular colonies may as well or better be so governed; a tax may be laid upon them all by act of parliament for support of government, and their assemblies may be dismissed as an useless part of the constitution.

That the powers proposed by the Albany Plan of Union, to be vested in a grand council representative of the people, even with regard to military matters, are not so great as those the colonies of Rhode Island and Connecticut are entrusted with by their charters, and have never abused; for by this plan, the president-general is appointed by the crown, and controls all by his negative; but in those governments, the people choose the Governor, and yet allow him no negative.

That the British colonies bordering on the French are properly frontiers of the British empire; and the frontiers of an empire are properly defended at the joint expence of the body of the people in such empire: It would now be thought hard by act of parliament to oblige the Cinque Ports or seacoasts of Britain to maintain the whole navy, because they are more immediately defended by it, not allowing them at the same time a vote in choosing members of the parliament; and if the frontiers in America bear the expence of their own defence, it seems hard to allow them no share in voting the money, judging of the necessity and sum, or advising the measures.

That besides the taxes necessary for the defence of the frontiers, the colonies pay yearly great sums to the mother-country unnoticed: For taxes paid in Britain by the land-holder or artificer, must enter into and increase the price of the produce of land and of manufactures made of

it; and great part of this is paid by consumers in the colonies, who thereby pay a considerable part of the British taxes.

We are restrained in our trade with foreign nations, and where we could be supplied with any manufacture cheaper from them, but must buy the same dearer from Britain; the difference of price is a clear tax to Britain.

We are obliged to carry a great part of our produce directly to Britain; and where the duties laid upon it lessen its price to the planter, or it sells for less than it would in foreign markets; the difference is a tax paid to Britain.

Some manufactures we could make, but are forbidden, and must take them of British merchants; the whole price is a tax paid to Britain.

By our greatly increasing the demand and consumption of British manufactures, their price is considerably raised of late years; the advantage is clear profit to Britain, and enables its people better to pay great taxes; and much of it being paid by us, is clear tax to Britain.

In short, as we are not suffered to regulate our trade, and restrain the importation and consumption of British superfluities (as Britain can the consumption of foreign superfluities) our whole wealth centers finally amongst the merchants and inhabitants of Britain, and if we make them richer, and enable them better to pay their taxes, it is nearly the same as being taxed ourselves, and equally beneficial to the crown.

These kind of secondary taxes, however, we do not complain of, though we have no share in the laying, or disposing of them; but to pay immediate heavy taxes, in the laying, appropriation, and disposition of which we have no part, and which perhaps we may know to be as unnecessary, as grievous, must seem hard measure to Englishmen, who cannot conceive, that by hazarding their lives and fortunes, in subduing and settling new countries, extending the dominion, and increasing the commerce of the mother nation, they have forfeited the native rights of Britons, which they think ought rather to be given to them, as due to such merit, if they had been before in a state of slavery.

These, and such kind of things as these, I apprehend, will be thought and said by the people, if the proposed alteration of the Albany plan should take place. Then the administration of the board of governors and councils so appointed, not having any representative body of the people to approve and unite in its measures, and conciliate the minds of the people to them, will probably become suspected and odious; dangerous animosities and feuds will arise between the governors and governed; and every thing go into confusion.

Perhaps I am too apprehensive in this matter; but having freely given my opinion and reasons, your Excellency can judge better than I whether there be any weight in them, and the shortness of the time allowed me, will, I hope, in some degree excuse the imperfections of this scrawl. . . .

On the Subject of Uniting the Colonies More Intimately with Great Britain, by Allowing Them Representatives in Parliament[3]

Boston, Dec. 22, 1754.

Sir,

Since the conversation your Excellency was pleased to honour me with, on the subject of *uniting the colonies* more intimately with Great Britain, by allowing them *representatives in parliament,* I have something further considered that matter, and am of opinion, that such a union would be very acceptable to the colonies, provided they had a reasonable number of representatives allowed them; and that all the old acts of Parliament restraining the trade or cramping the manufactures of the colonies be at the same time repealed, and the British subjects *on this side the water* put, in those respects, on the same footing with those in Great Britain, till the new Parliament, representing the whole, shall think it for the interest of the whole to reënact some or all of them. It is not that I imagine so many representatives will be allowed the colonies, as to have any great weight by their numbers; but I think there might be sufficient to occasion those laws to be better and more impartially considered, and perhaps to overcome the interest of a petty corporation, or of any particular set of artificers or traders in England, who heretofore seem, in some instances, to have been more regarded than all the colonies, or than was consistent with the general interest, or best national good. I think too, that the government of the colonies by a parliament, in which they are fairly represented, would be vastly more agreeable to the people, than the method lately attempted to be introduced by royal instructions, as well as more agreeable to the nature of an English constitution, and to English liberty; and that such laws as now seem to bear hard on the colonies, would (when judged by such a Parliament for the best interest of the whole) be more cheerfully submitted to, and more easily executed.

I should hope too, that by such a union, the people of Great Britain, and the people of the colonies, would learn to consider themselves, as not belonging to a different community with different interests, but to one community with one interest; which I imagine would contribute to strengthen the whole, and greatly lessen the danger of future separations.

It is, I suppose, agreed to be the general interest of any state, that its people be numerous and rich; men enough to fight in its defence, and enough to pay sufficient taxes to defray the charge; for these circumstances tend to the security of the state, and its protection from foreign power: But it seems not of so much importance, whether the fighting be done by John or Thomas, or the tax paid by William or Charles. The iron manufacture employs and enriches British subjects, but is it of any

importance to the state, whether the manufacturers live at Birmingham, or Sheffield, or both, since they are still within its bounds, and their wealth and persons still at its command? Could the Goodwin Sands be laid dry by banks, and land equal to a large country thereby gained to England, and presently filled with English inhabitants, would it be right to deprive such inhabitants of the common privileges enjoyed by other Englishmen, the right of vending their produce in the same ports, or of making their own shoes, because a merchant or a shoemaker, living on the old land, might fancy it more for his advantage to trade or make shoes for them? Would this be right, even if the land were gained at the expence of the state? And would it not seem less right, if the charge and labour of gaining the additional territory to Britain had been borne by the settlers themselves? And would not the hardship appear yet greater, if the people of the new country should be allowed no representatives in the parliament enacting such impositions?

Now I look on the colonies as so many counties gained to Great Britain, and more advantageous to it than if they had been gained out of the seas around its coasts, and joined to its land: For being in different climates, they afford greater variety of produce, and being separated by the ocean, they increase much more its shipping and seamen; and since they are all included in the British empire, which has only extended itself by their means; and the strength and wealth of the parts are the strength and wealth of the whole; what imports it to the general state, whether a merchant, a smith, or a hatter, grow rich in Old or New England? And if, through increase of people, two smiths are wanted for one employed before, why may not the *new* smith be allowed to live and thrive in the *new* country, as well as the *old* one in the *old*? In fine, why should the countenance of a state be *partially* afforded to its people, unless it be most in favour of those who have most merit? And if there be any difference, those who have most contributed to enlarge Britain's empire and commerce, increase her strength, her wealth, and the numbers of her people, at the risk of their own lives and private fortunes in new and strange countries, methinks ought rather to expect some preference. . . .

12. *The Art of Virtue*

To Lord Kames

London, May 3, 1760

My Dear Lord,
. . . I will shortly send you a copy of the Chapter you are pleased to mention in so obliging a manner; and shall be extremely obliged in

receiving a copy of the collection of *Maxims for the Conduct of Life,* which you are preparing for the use of your children. I purpose likewise a little work for the benefit of youth, to be called *The Art of Virtue.* From the title I think you will hardly conjecture what the nature of such a book may be. I must therefore explain it a little. Many people lead bad lives that would gladly lead good ones, but know not *how* to make the change. They have frequently *resolved* and *endeavoured* it; but in vain, because their endeavours have not been properly conducted. To expect people to be good, to be just, to be temperate, &c., without *shewing* them *how* they should *become* so, seems like the ineffectual charity mentioned by the Apostle, which consisted in saying to the hungry, the cold, and the naked, "Be ye fed, be ye warmed, be ye clothed," without shewing them how they should get food, fire, or clothing.

Most people have naturally *some* virtues, but none have naturally *all* the virtues. To *acquire* those that are wanting, and secure what we acquire, as well as those we have naturally, is the subject of *an art.* It is as properly an art as painting, navigation, or architecture. If a man would become a painter, navigator, or architect, it is not enough that he is *advised* to be one, that he is *convinced* by the arguments of his adviser, that it would be for his advantage to be one, and that he resolves to be one, but he must also be taught the principles of the art, be shewn all the methods of working, and how to acquire the habits of using properly all the instruments; and thus regularly and gradually he arrives, by practice, at some perfection in the art. If he does not proceed thus, he is apt to meet with difficulties that discourage him, and make him drop the pursuit.

My *Art of Virtue* has also its instruments, and teaches the manner of using them. Christians are directed to have faith in Christ, as the effectual means of obtaining the change they desire. It may, when sufficiently strong, be effectual with many: for a full opinion, that a Teacher is infinitely wise, good, and powerful, and that he will certainly reward and punish the obedient and disobedient, must give great weight to his precepts, and make them much more attended to by his disciples. But many have this faith in so weak a degree, that it does not produce the effect. Our *Art of Virtue* may, therefore, be of great service to those whose faith is unhappily not so strong, and may come in aid of its weakness. Such as are naturally well disposed, and have been so carefully educated, as that good habits have been early established, and bad ones prevented, have less need of this art; but all may be more or less benefited by it. It is, in short, to be adapted for universal use. I imagine what I have now been writing will seem to savour of great presumption: I must therefore speedily finish my little piece, and communicate the manuscript to you, that you may judge whether it is possible to make good such pretensions. I shall at the same time hope for the benefit of your corrections.

13. *On French Civility*

To Mary Stevenson

Paris, Sept. 14, 1767

... The Civilities we everywhere receive give us the strongest Impressions of the French Politeness. It seems to be a Point settled here universally, that Strangers are to be treated with Respect; and one has just the same Deference shewn one here by being a Stranger, as in England by being a Lady. The Customhouse Officers at Port St. Denis, as we enter'd Paris, were about to seize 2 doz of excellent Bordeaux Wine given us at Boulogne, and which we brought with us; but, as soon as they found we were Strangers, it was immediately remitted on that Account. At the Church of Notre Dame, where we went to see a magnificent Illumination, with Figures, &c., for the deceas'd Dauphiness, we found an immense Crowd, who were kept out by Guards; but, the Officer being told that we were Strangers from England, he immediately admitted us, accompanied and show'd us every thing. Why don't we practise this Urbanity to Frenchmen? Why should they be allowed to outdo us in any thing?

Here is an Exhibition of Paintings like ours in London, to which Multitudes flock daily. I am not Connoisseur enough to judge which has most Merit. Every Night, Sundays not excepted here are Plays or Operas; and tho' the Weather has been hot, and the Houses full, one is not incommoded by the Heat so much as with us in Winter. They must have some Way of changing the Air, that we are not acquainted with. I shall enquire into it.

Travelling is one Way of lengthening Life, at least in Appearance. It is but about a Fortnight since we left London, but the Variety of Scenes we have gone through makes it seem equal to Six Months living in one Place. Perhaps I have suffered a greater Change, too, in my own Person, than I could have done in Six Years at home. I had not been here Six Days, before my Taylor and Perruquier had transform'd me into a Frenchman. Only think what a Figure I make in a little Bag-Wig and naked Ears! They told me I was become 20 Years younger, and look'd very galante;

So being in Paris where the Mode is to be sacredly follow'd I was once very near making Love to my Friend's Wife. ...

14. *On Physiocratic Philosophy*

To Dupont de Nemours

London, July 28, 1768.

I received your obliging letter of the 10th May, with the most acceptable present of your *Physiocratie*, which I have read with great pleasure, and received from it a great deal of instruction. There is such a freedom from local and national prejudices and partialities, so much benevolence to mankind in general, so much goodness mixt with the wisdom, in the principles of your new philosophy, that I am perfectly charmed with them, and wish I could have stayed in France for some time, to have studied in your school, that I might by conversing with its founders have made myself quite a master of that philosophy. . . . I had, before I went into your country, seen some letters of yours to Dr. Templeman, that gave me a high opinion of the doctrines you are engaged in cultivating and of your personal talents and abilities, which made me greatly desirous of seeing you. Since I had not that good fortune, the next best thing is the advantage you are so good to offer me of your correspondence, which I shall ever highly value, and endeavour to cultivate with all the diligence I am capable of.

I am sorry to find that that wisdom which sees the welfare of the parts in the prosperity of the whole, seems yet not to be known in this country. . . . We are so far from conceiving that what is best for mankind, or even for Europe in general, may be best for us, that we are even studying to establish and extend a separate interest of Britain, to the prejudice of even Ireland and our colonies. . . . It is from your philosophy only that the maxims of a contrary and more happy conduct are to be drawn, which I therefore sincerely wish may grow and increase till it becomes the governing philosophy of the human species, as it must be that of superior beings in better worlds. I will take the liberty of sending you a little fragment that has some tincture of it, which, on that account, I hope may be acceptable. . . .

15. *Moral Algebra*

To Joseph Priestley

London, Sept. 19: 1772.

Dear Sir,

In the Affair of so much Importance to you, wherein you ask my Advice, I cannot for want of sufficient Premises, advise you *what* to determine, but if you please I will tell you *how*. When those difficult Cases occur, they are difficult, chiefly because while we have them under Consideration, all the Reasons *pro* and *con* are not present to the Mind at the same time; but sometimes one Set present themselves, and at other times another, the first being out of Sight. Hence the various Purposes or Inclinations that alternately prevail, and the Uncertainty that perplexes us.

To get over this, my Way is, to divide half a Sheet of Paper by a Line into two Columns; writing over the one *Pro,* and over the other *Con.* Then during three or four Days Consideration, I put down under the different Heads short Hints of the different Motives, that at different Times occur to me, *for* or *against* the Measure. When I have thus got them all together in one View, I endeavour to estimate their respective Weights; and where I find two, one on each side, that seem equal, I strike them both out. If I find a Reason *pro* equal to some two Reasons *con,* I strike out the three. If I judge some two Reasons *con,* equal to some three Reasons *pro,* I strike out the five; and thus proceeding I find at length where the Ballance lies; and if after a Day or two of farther Consideration, nothing new that is of Importance occurs on either side, I come to a Determination accordingly. And, tho' the Weight of Reasons cannot be taken with the Precision of Algebraic Quantities, yet, when each is thus considered, separately and comparatively, and the whole lies before me, I think I can judge better, and am less liable to make a rash Step; and in fact I have found great Advantage from this kind of Equation, in what may be called *Moral* or *Prudential Algebra.* . . .

16. *The Whistle*

To Madame Brillon

Passy, November 10, 1779.

. . . I am charmed with your description of Paradise, and with your plan of living there; and I approve much of your conclusion, that, in the mean

time, we should draw all the good we can from this world. In my opinion, we might all draw more good from it than we do, and suffer less evil, if we would take care not to give too much for *whistles*. For to me it seems, that most of the unhappy people we meet with, are become so by neglect of that caution.

You ask what I mean? You love stories, and will excuse my telling one of myself.

When I was a child of seven years old, my friends, on a holiday, filled my pocket with coppers. I went directly to a shop where they sold toys for children; and, being charmed with the sound of a *whistle*, that I met by the way in the hands of another boy, I voluntarily offered and gave all my money for one. I then came home, and went whistling all over the house, much pleased with my *whistle*, but disturbing all the family. My brothers, and sisters, and cousins, understanding the bargain I had made, told me I had given four times as much for it as it was worth; put me in mind what good things I might have bought with the rest of the money; and laughed at me so much for my folly, that I cried with vexation; and the reflection gave me more chagrin than the *whistle* gave me pleasure.

This however was afterwards of use to me, the impression continuing on my mind; so that often, when I was tempted to buy some unnecessary thing, I said to myself, *Don't give too much for the whistle*; and I saved my money.

As I grew up, came into the world, and observed the actions of men, I thought I met with many, very many, who *gave too much for the whistle*.

When I saw one too ambitious of court favour, sacrificing his time in attendance on levees, his repose, his liberty, his virtue, and perhaps his friends, to attain it, I have said to myself, *This man gives too much for his whistle*.

When I saw another fond of popularity, constantly employing himself in political bustles, neglecting his own affairs, and ruining them by that neglect, *He pays, indeed*, said I, *too much for his whistle*.

If I knew a miser, who gave up every kind of comfortable living, all the pleasure of doing good to others, all the esteem of his fellow-citizens, and the joys of benevolent friendship, for the sake of accumulating wealth, *Poor man*, said I, *you pay too much for your whistle*.

When I met with a man of pleasure, sacrificing every laudable improvement of the mind, or of his fortune, to mere corporeal sensations, and ruining his health in their pursuit, *Mistaken man*, said I, *you are providing pain for yourself, instead of pleasure; you give too much for your whistle*.

If I see one fond of appearance, or fine clothes, fine houses, fine furniture, fine equipages, all above his fortune, for which he contracts debts, and ends his career in a prison, *Alas!* say I, *he has paid dear, very dear, for his whistle*.

When I see a beautiful, sweet-tempered girl married to an ill-natured

brute of a husband, *What a pity*, say I, *that she should pay so much for a whistle!*

In short, I conceive that great part of the miseries of mankind are brought upon them by the false estimates they have made of the value of things, and by their *giving too much for their whistles.*

Yet I ought to have charity for these unhappy people, when I consider, that, with all this wisdom of which I am boasting, there are certain things in the world so tempting, for example, the apples of King John, which happily are not to be bought; for if they were put to sale by auction, I might very easily be led to ruin myself in the purchase, and find that I had once more given too much for the *whistle.* ...

17. *On Scientific Progress*

To Joseph Priestley

Passy, Feb. 8, 1780.

Dear Sir,

... I always rejoice to hear of your being still employ'd in experimental Researches into Nature, and of the Success you meet with. The rapid Progress *true* Science now makes, occasions my regretting sometimes that I was born so soon. It is impossible to imagine the Height to which may be carried, in a thousand years, the Power of Man over Matter. We may perhaps learn to deprive large Masses of their Gravity, and give them absolute Levity, for the sake of easy Transport. Agriculture may diminish its Labour and double its Produce; all Diseases may by sure means be prevented or cured, not excepting even that of Old Age, and our Lives lengthened at pleasure even beyond the antediluvian Standard. O that moral Science were in as fair a way of Improvement, that Men would cease to be Wolves to one another, and that human Beings would at length learn what they now improperly call Humanity!

I am glad my little Paper on the *Aurora Borealis* pleased. If it should occasion further Enquiry, and so produce a better Hypothesis, it will not be wholly useless. ...

18. *Homage to Washington*

To George Washington

Passy, March 5, 1780.

Sir,

I have received but lately the Letter your Excellency did me the honour of writing to me in Recommendation of the Marquis de la Fayette. His modesty detained it long in his own Hands. We became acquainted, however, from the time of his Arrival at Paris; and his Zeal for the Honour of our Country, his Activity in our Affairs here, and his firm Attachment to our Cause and to you, impress'd me with the same Regard and Esteem for him that your Excellency's Letter would have done, had it been immediately delivered to me.

Should peace arrive after another Campaign or two, and afford us a little Leisure, I should be happy to see your Excellency in Europe, and to accompany you, if my Age and Strength would permit, in visiting some of its ancient and most famous Kingdoms. You would, on this side of the Sea, enjoy the great Reputation you have acquir'd, pure and free from those little Shades that the Jealousy and Envy of a Man's Countrymen and Cotemporaries are ever endeavouring to cast over living Merit. Here you would know, and enjoy, what Posterity will say of Washington. For 1000 Leagues have nearly the same Effect with 1000 Years. The feeble Voice of those grovelling Passions cannot extend so far either in Time or Distance. At present I enjoy that Pleasure for you, as I frequently hear the old Generals of this martial Country, (who study the Maps of America, and mark upon them all your Operations,) speak with sincere Approbation and great Applause of your conduct; and join in giving you the Character of one of the greatest Captains of the Age.

I must soon quit the Scene, but you may live to see our Country flourish, as it will amazingly and rapidly after the War is over. Like a Field of young Indian Corn, which long Fair weather and Sunshine had enfeebled and discolored, and which in that weak State, by a Thunder Gust, of violent Wind, Hail, and Rain, seem'd to be threaten'd with absolute Destruction; yet the Storm being past, it recovers fresh Verdure, shoots up with double Vigour, and delights the Eye, not of its Owner only, but of every observing Traveller. . . .

19. *Religious Toleration*

To Richard Price

Passy, Oct. 9, 1780.

Dear Sir,

Besides the Pleasure of their Company, I had the great Satisfaction of hearing by your two valuable Friends, and learning from your Letter, that you enjoy a good State of Health. May God continue it, as well for the Good of Mankind as for your Comfort. I thank you much for the second Edition of your excellent Pamphlet. I forwarded that you sent to Mr. Dana, he being in Holland. I wish also to see the Piece you have written (as Mr. Jones tells me) on Toleration. I do not expect that your new Parliament will be either wiser or honester than the last. All Projects to procure an honest one, by Place Bills, &c., appear to me vain and Impracticable. The true Cure, I imagine, is to be found only in rendring all Places unprofitable, and the King too poor to give Bribes and Pensions. Till this is done, which can only be by a Revolution (and I think you have not Virtue enough left to procure one), your Nation will always be plundered, and obliged to pay by Taxes the Plunderers for Plundering and Ruining. Liberty and Virtue therefore join in the call, COME OUT OF HER, MY PEOPLE!

I am fully of your Opinion respecting religious Tests; but, tho' the People of Massachusetts have not in their new Constitution kept quite clear of them, yet, if we consider what that People were 100 Years ago, we must allow they have gone great Lengths in Liberality of Sentiment on religious Subjects; and we may hope for greater Degrees of Perfection, when their Constitution, some years hence, shall be revised. If Christian Preachers had continued to teach as Christ and his Apostles did, without Salaries, and as the Quakers now do, I imagine Tests would never have existed; for I think they were invented, not so much to secure Religion itself, as the Emoluments of it. When a Religion is good, I conceive that it will support itself; and, when it cannot support itself, and God does not take care to support, so that its Professors are oblig'd to call for the help of the Civil Power, it is a sign, I apprehend, of its being a bad one. But I shall be out of my Depth, if I wade any deeper in Theology, and I will not trouble you with Politicks, nor with News which are almost as uncertain; but conclude with a heartfelt Wish to embrace you once more, and enjoy your sweet Society in Peace, among our honest, worthy, ingenious Friends at the *London.*

20. *On Experimental Philosophy*

To Joseph Priestley

Passy near Paris, June 7, 1782.

Dear Sir,

. . . I have always great Pleasure in hearing from you, in learning that you are well, and that you continue your Experiments. I should rejoice much, if I could once more recover the Leisure to search with you into the Works of Nature; I mean the *inanimate,* not the *animate* or moral part of them, the more I discover'd of the former, the more I admir'd them; the more I know of the latter, the more I am disgusted with them. Men I find to be a Sort of Beings very badly constructed, as they are generally more easily provok'd than reconcil'd, more disposed to do Mischief to each other than to make Reparation, much more easily deceiv'd than undeceiv'd, and having more Pride and even Pleasure in killing than in begetting one another; for without a Blush they assemble in great armies at NoonDay to destroy, and when they have kill'd as many as they can, they exaggerate the Number to augment the fancied Glory; but they creep into Corners, or cover themselves with the Darkness of night, when they mean to beget, as being asham'd of a virtuous Action. A virtuous Action it would be, and a vicious one the killing of them, if the Species were really worth producing or preserving; but of this I begin to doubt. . . .

But to be serious, my dear old Friend, I love you as much as ever, and I love all the honest Souls that meet at the London Coffee House. I only wonder how it happen'd, that they and my other Friends in England came to be such good Creatures in the midst of so perverse a Generation. I long to see them and you once more, and I labour for Peace with more Earnestness, that I may again be happy in your sweet society.

I show'd your letter to the Duke de Larochefoucault, who thinks with me, the new Experiments you have made are extremely curious; and he has given me thereupon a Note, which I inclose, and I request you would furnish me with the answer desired.

Yesterday the Count du Nord was at the Academy of Sciences, when sundry Experiments were exhibited for his Entertainment; among them, one by M. Lavoisier, to show that the strongest Fire we yet know, is made in a Charcoal blown upon with dephlogisticated air. In a Heat so produced, he melted Platina presently, the Fire being much more powerful than that of the strongest burning mirror. . . .

21. *The Absurdity of Inherited Honors*

To Mrs. Sarah Bache

Passy, Jan. 26, 1784.

My Dear Child,

Your Care in sending me the Newspapers is very agreable to me. I received by Capt. Barney those relating to the *Cincinnati.* My Opinion of the Institution cannot be of much Importance; I only wonder that, when the united Wisdom of our Nation had, in the Articles of Confederation, manifested their Dislike of establishing Ranks of Nobility, by Authority either of the Congress or of any particular State, a Number of private Persons should think proper to distinguish themselves and their Posterity, from their fellow Citizens, and form an Order of *hereditary Knights,* in direct Opposition to the solemnly declared Sense of their Country! I imagine it must be likewise contrary to the Good Sense of most of those drawn into it by the Persuasion of its Projectors, who have been too much struck with the Ribbands and Crosses they have seen among them hanging to the Buttonholes of Foreign Officers. And I suppose those, who disapprove of it, have not hitherto given it much Opposition, from a Principle somewhat like that of your good Mother, relating to punctilious Persons, who are always exacting little Observances of Respect; that, *"if People can be pleased with small Matters, it is a pity but they should have them."*

In this View, perhaps, I should not myself, if my Advice had been ask'd, have objected to their wearing their Ribband and Badge according to their Fancy, tho' I certainly should to the entailing it as an Honour on their Posterity. For Honour, worthily obtain'd (as for Example that of our Officers), is in its Nature a *personal* Thing, and incommunicable to any but those who had some Share in obtaining it. Thus among the Chinese, the most ancient, and from long Experience the wisest of Nations, honour does not *descend,* but *ascends.* If a man from his Learning, his Wisdom, or his Valour, is promoted by the Emperor to the Rank of Mandarin, his Parents are immediately entitled to all the same Ceremonies of Respect from the People, that are establish'd as due to the Mandarin himself; on the supposition that it must have been owing to the Education, Instruction, and good Example afforded him by his Parents, that he was rendered capable of serving the Publick.

This *ascending* Honour is therefore useful to the State, as it encourages Parents to give their Children a good and virtuous Education. But the *descending Honour,* to Posterity who could have no Share in obtaining it, is not only groundless and absurd, but often hurtful to that Posterity, since it is apt to make them proud, disdaining to be employ'd in useful

Arts, and thence falling into Poverty, and all the Meannesses, Servility, and Wretchedness attending it; which is the present case with much of what is called the *Noblesse* in Europe. Or if, to keep up the Dignity of the Family, Estates are entailed entire on the Eldest male heir, another Pest to Industry and Improvement of the Country is introduc'd, which will be followed by all the odious mixture of pride and Beggary, and idleness, that have half depopulated [and *decultivated*] Spain; occasioning continual Extinction of Families by the Discouragements of Marriage [and neglect in the improvement of estates].

I wish, therefore, that the Cincinnati, if they must go on with their Project, would direct the Badges of their Order to be worn by their Parents, instead of handing them down to their Children. It would be a good Precedent, and might have good Effects. It would also be a kind of Obedience to the Fourth Commandment, in which God enjoins us to *honour* our Father and Mother, but has nowhere directed us to honour our Children. And certainly no mode of honouring those immediate Authors of our Being can be more effectual, than that of doing praiseworthy Actions, which reflect Honour on those who gave us our Education; or more becoming, than that of manifesting, by some public Expression or Token, that it is to their Instruction and Example we ascribe the Merit of those Actions.

But the Absurdity of *descending Honours* is not a mere Matter of philosophical Opinion; it is capable of mathematical Demonstration. A Man's Son, for instance, is but half of his Family, the other half belonging to the Family of his Wife. His Son, too, marrying into another Family, his Share in the Grandson is but a fourth; in the Great Grandson, by the same Process, it is but an Eighth; in the next Generation a Sixteenth; the next a Thirty-second; the next a Sixty-fourth; the next an Hundred and twenty-eighth; the next a Two hundred and Fifty-sixth; and the next a Five hundred and twelfth; thus in nine Generations, which will not require more than 300 years (no very great Antiquity for a Family), our present Chevalier of the Order of Cincinnatus's Share in the then existing Knight, will be but a 512th part; which, allowing the present certain Fidelity of American Wives to be insur'd down through all those Nine Generations, is so small a Consideration, that methinks no reasonable Man would hazard for the sake of it the disagreable Consequences of the Jealousy, Envy, and Ill will of his Countrymen.

Let us go back with our Calculation from this young Noble, the 512th part of the present Knight, thro' his nine Generations, till we return to the year of the Institution. He must have had a Father and Mother, they are two. Each of them had a father and Mother, they are four. Those of the next preceding Generation will be eight, the next Sixteen, the next thirty-two, the next sixty-four, the next one hundred and Twenty-eight, the next Two hundred and fifty-six, and the ninth in this Retrocession Five hundred and twelve, who must be now existing, and all contribute their

Proportion of this future *Chevalier de Cincinnatus.* These, with the rest, make together as follows:

$$2$$
$$4$$
$$8$$
$$16$$
$$32$$
$$64$$
$$128$$
$$256$$
$$512$$

Total   1022

One Thousand and Twenty-two Men and Women, contributors to the formation of one Knight. And, if we are to have a Thousand of these future knights, there must be now and hereafter existing One million and Twenty-two Thousand Fathers and Mothers, who are to contribute to their Production, unless a Part of the Number are employ'd in making more Knights than One. Let us strike off then the 22,000, on the Supposition of this double Employ, and then consider whether, after a reasonable Estimation of the Number of Rogues, and Fools, and Royalists and Scoundrels and Prostitutes, that are mix'd with, and help to make up necessarily their Million of Predecessors, Posterity will have much reason to boast of the noble Blood of the then existing Set of Chevaliers de Cincinnatus. [The future genealogists, too, of these Chevaliers, in proving the lineal descent of their honour through so many generations (even supposing honour capable in its nature of descending), will only prove the small share of this honour, which can be justly claimed by any one of them; since the above simple process in arithmetic makes it quite plain and clear that, in proportion as the antiquity of the family shall augment, the right to the honour of the ancestor will diminish; and a few generations more would reduce it to something so small as to be very near an absolute nullity.] I hope, therefore, that the Order will drop this part of their project, and content themselves, as the Knights of the Garter, Bath, Thistle, St. Louis, and other Orders of Europe do, with a Life Enjoyment of their little Badge and Ribband, and let the Distinction die with those who have merited it. This I imagine will give no offence. For my own part, I shall think it a Convenience, when I go into a Company where there may be Faces unknown to me, if I discover, by this Badge, the Persons who merit some particular Expression of my Respect; and it will save modest Virtue the Trouble of calling for our Regard, by awkward roundabout Intimations of having been heretofore employ'd in the Continental Service.

The Gentleman, who made the Voyage to France to provide the

Ribands and Medals, has executed his Commission. To me they seem tolerably done; but all such Things are criticis'd. Some find Fault with the Latin, as wanting classic Elegance and Correctness; and, since our Nine Universities were not able to furnish better Latin, it was pity, they say, that the Mottos had not been in English. Others object to the Title, as not properly assumable by any but Gen. Washington, [and a few others] who serv'd without Pay. Others object to the *Bald Eagle* as looking too much like a *Dindon*, or Turkey. For my own part, I wish the Bald Eagle had not been chosen as the Representative of our Country; he is a Bird of bad moral Character; he does not get his living honestly; you may have seen him perch'd on some dead Tree, near the River where, too lazy to fish for himself, he watches the Labour of the Fishing-Hawk; and, when that diligent Bird has at length taken a Fish, and is bearing it to his Nest for the support of his Mate and young ones, the Bald Eagle pursues him, and takes it from him. With all this Injustice he is never in good Case; but, like those among Men who live by Sharping and Robbing, he is generally poor, and often very lousy. Besides, he is a rank Coward; the little *King Bird*, not bigger than a sparrow, attacks him boldly and drives him out of the District. He is therefore by no means a proper emblem for the brave and honest Cincinnati of America, who have driven all the *Kingbirds* from our Country; though exactly fit for that Order of Knights, which the French call *Chevaliers d'Industrie.*

I am, on this account, not displeas'd that the Figure is not known as a Bald Eagle, but looks more like a Turk'y. For in Truth, the Turk'y is in comparison a much more respectable Bird, and withal a true original Native of America. Eagles have been found in all Countries, but the Turk'y was peculiar to ours; the first of the Species seen in Europe being brought to France by the Jesuits from Canada, and serv'd up at the Wedding Table of Charles the Ninth. He is, [though a little vain and silly, it is true, but not the worse emblem for that,] a Bird of Courage, and would not hesitate to attack a Grenadier of the British Guards, who should presume to invade his Farm Yard with a *red* Coat on.

I shall not enter into the Criticisms made upon their Latin. The gallant officers of America may [not have the merit of being] be no great scholars, but they undoubtedly merit much, [as brave soldiers,] from their Country, which should therefore not leave them merely to *Fame* for their *"Virtutis Premium,"* which is one of their Latin Mottos. Their *"Esto perpetua,"* another, is an excellent Wish, if they meant it for their Country; bad, if intended for their Order. The States should not only restore to them the *Omnia* of their first Motto, which many of them have left and lost, but pay them justly, and reward them generously. They should not be suffered to remain, with [all] their new-created Chivalry, *entirely* in the Situation of the Gentleman in the Story, which their *omnia reliquit* reminds me of. You know every thing makes me recollect some Story. He had built a very fine House, and thereby much impair'd his Fortune. He

had a Pride, however, in showing it to his Acquaintance. One of them, after viewing it all, remark'd a Motto over the Door, "Ōıa Vanitas." "What," says he, "is the Meaning of this Ōıa? it is a word I don't understand." "I will tell you," said the Gentleman; "I had a mind to have the Motto cut on a Piece of smooth Marble, but there was not room for it between the Ornaments, to be put in Characters large enough to be read. I therefore made use of a Contraction antiently very common in Latin Manuscripts, by which the *m*'s and *n*'s in Words are omitted, and the Omission noted by a little Dash above, which you may see there; so that the Word is *omnia*, omnia vanitas." "O," says his Friend, "I now comprehend the Meaning of your motto, it relates to your Edifice; and signifies, that, if you have abridged your *Omnia*, you have, nevertheless, left your vanitas legible at full length." I am, as ever, your affectionate father.

22. *On Cotton Mather*

To Samuel Mather

Passy, May 12, 1784

Rev⁴ Sir,

I received your kind letter, with your excellent advice to the people of the United States, which I read with great pleasure, and hope it will be duly regarded. Such writings, though they may be lightly passed over by many readers, yet, if they make a deep impression on one active mind in a hundred, the effects may be considerable. Permit me to mention one little instance, which, though it relates to myself, will not be quite uninteresting to you. When I was a boy, I met with a book, entitled *"Essays to do Good,"* which I think was written by your father. It had been so little regarded by a former possessor, that several leaves of it were torn out; but the remainder gave me such a turn of thinking, as to have an influence on my conduct through life; for I have always set a greater value on the character of a *doer of good*, than on any other kind of reputation; and if I have been, as you seem to think, a useful citizen, the public owes the advantage of it to that book.

You mention your being in your 78ᵗʰ year; I am in my 79ᵗʰ; we are grown old together. It is now more than 60 years since I left Boston, but I remember well both your father and grandfather, having heard them both in the pulpit, and seen them in their houses. The last time I saw your father was in the beginning of 1724, when I visited him after my first trip to Pennsylvania. He received me in his library, and on my taking leave showed me a shorter way out of the house through a narrow pas-

sage, which was crossed by a beam over head. We were still talking as I withdrew, he accompanying me behind, and I turning partly towards him, when he said hastily, "*Stoop, stoop!*" I did not understand him, till I felt my head hit against the beam. He was a man that never missed any occasion of giving instruction, and upon this he said to me, "*You are young, and have the world before you;* STOOP *as you go through it, and you will miss many hard thumps.*" This advice, thus beat into my head, has frequently been of use to me; and I often think of it, when I see pride mortified, and misfortunes brought upon people by their carrying their heads too high.

I long much to see again my native place, and to lay my bones there. I left it in 1723; I visited it in 1733, 1743, 1753, and 1763. In 1773 I was in England; in 1775 I had a sight of it, but could not enter, it being in possession of the enemy. I did hope to have been there in 1783, but could not obtain my dismission from this employment here; and now I fear I shall never have that happiness. My best wishes however attend my dear country. *Esto perpetua.* It is now blest with an excellent constitution; may it last for ever!

This powerful monarchy continues its friendship for the United States. It is a friendship of the utmost importance to our security, and should be carefully cultivated. Britain has not yet well digested the loss of its dominion over us, and has still at times some flattering hopes of recovering it. Accidents may increase those hopes, and encourage dangerous attempts. A breach between us and France would infallibly bring the English again upon our backs; and yet we have some wild heads among our countrymen, who are endeavouring to weaken that connexion! Let us preserve our reputation by performing our engagements; our credit by fulfilling our contracts; and friends by gratitude and kindness; for we know not how soon we may again have occasion for all of them. . . .

23. *On Luxury*

To Benjamin Vaughn

Passy, July 26, 1784

. . . You ask, "what Remedy I have for the growing Luxury of my Country, which gives so much *Offence* to all *English travellers* without exception." I answer, that I think it exaggerated, and that Travellers are no good Judges whether our Luxury is growing or diminishing. Our People are hospitable, and have indeed too much Pride in displaying upon their Tables before Strangers the Plenty and Variety that our Country affords.

They have the Vanity, too, of sometimes borrowing one another's Plate to entertain more splendidly. Strangers being invited from House to House, and meeting every Day with a Feast, imagine what they see is the ordinary Way of living of all the Families where they dine; when perhaps each Family lives a Week after upon the Remains of the Dinner given. It is, I own, a Folly in our People to give *such Offence to English Travellers*. The first part of the Proverb is thereby verified, that *Fools make Feasts*. I wish in this Case the other were as true, *and wise Men eat them*. These Travellers might, one would think, find some Fault they could more decently reproach us with, than that of our excessive Civility to them as Strangers.

I have not, indeed yet thought of a Remedy for Luxury. I am not sure, that in a great State it is capable of a Remedy. Nor that the Evil is in itself always so great as it is represented. Suppose we include in the Definition of Luxury all unnecessary Expence, and then let us consider whether Laws to prevent such Expence are possible to be executed in a great Country, and whether, if they could be executed, our People generally would be happier, or even richer. Is not the Hope of one day being able to purchase and enjoy Luxuries a great Spur to Labour and Industry? May not Luxury, therefore, produce more than it consumes, if without such a Spur People would be, as they are naturally enough inclined to be, lazy and indolent? To this purpose I remember a Circumstance. The Skipper of a Shallop, employed between Cape May and Philadelphia, had done us some small Service, for which he refused Pay. My Wife, understanding that he had a Daughter, sent her as a Present a new-fashioned Cap. Three Years After, this Skipper being at my House with an old Farmer of Cape May, his Passenger, he mentioned the Cap, and how much his Daughter had been pleased with it. "But," says he, "it proved a dear Cap to our Congregation." "How so?" "When my Daughter appeared in it at Meeting, it was so much admired, that all the Girls resolved to get such Caps from Philadelphia; and my Wife and I computed, that the whole could not have cost less than a hundred Pound." "True," says the Farmer, "but you do not tell all the Story. I think the Cap was nevertheless an Advantage to us, for it was the first thing that put our Girls upon Knitting worsted Mittens for Sale at Philadelphia, that they might have wherewithal to buy Caps and Ribbands there; and you know that that Industry has continued, and is likely to continue and increase to a much greater Value, and answer better Purposes." Upon the whole, I was more reconciled to this little Piece of Luxury, since not only the Girls were made happier by having fine Caps, but the Philadelphians by the Supply of warm Mittens.

In our Commercial Towns upon the Seacoast, Fortunes will occasionally be made. Some of those who grow rich will be prudent, live within Bounds, and preserve what they have gained for their Posterity; others, fond of showing their Wealth, will be extravagant and ruin themselves.

Laws cannot prevent this; and perhaps it is not always an evil to the Publick. A Shilling spent idly by a Fool, may be picked up by a Wiser Person, who knows better what to do with it. It is therefore not lost. A vain, silly Fellow builds a fine House, furnishes it richly, lives in it expensively, and in few years ruins himself; but the Masons, Carpenters, Smiths, and other honest Tradesmen have been by his Employ assisted in maintaining and raising their Families; the Farmer has been paid for his labour, and encouraged, and the Estate is now in better Hands. In some Cases, indeed, certain Modes of Luxury may be a publick Evil, in the same Manner as it is a Private one. If there be a Nation, for Instance, that exports its Beef and Linnen, to pay for its Importation of Claret and Porter, while a great Part of its People live upon Potatoes, and wear no Shirts, wherein does it differ from the Sot, who lets his Family starve, and sells his Clothes to buy Drink? Our American Commerce is, I confess, a little in this way. We sell our Victuals to your Islands for Rum and Sugar; the substantial Necessaries of Life for Superfluities. But we have Plenty, and live well nevertheless, tho' by being soberer, we might be richer.

By the by, here is just issued an *arrêt* of Council taking off all the Duties upon the exportation of Brandies, which, it is said, will render them cheaper in America than your Rum; in which case there is no doubt but they will be preferr'd, and we shall be better able to bear your Restrictions on our Commerce. There are Views here, by augmenting their Settlements, of being able to supply the growing People of America with the Sugar that may be wanted there. On the whole, I guess England will get as little by the Commercial War she has begun with us, as she did by the Military. But to return to Luxury.

The vast Quantity of Forest Lands we have yet to clear, and put in order for Cultivation, will for a long time keep the Body of our Nation laborious and frugal. Forming an Opinion of our People and their Manners by what is seen among the Inhabitants of the Seaports, is judging from an improper Sample. The People of the Trading Towns may be rich and luxurious, while the Country possesses all the Virtues, that tend to private Happiness and publick Prosperity. Those Towns are not much regarded by the Country; they are hardly considered as an essential Part of the States; and the Experience of the last War has shown, that their being in the Possession of the Enemy did not necessarily draw on the Subjection of the Country, which bravely continued to maintain its Freedom and Independence notwithstanding.

It has been computed by some Political Arithmetician, that, if every Man and Woman would work for four Hours each Day on something useful, that Labour would produce sufficient to procure all the Necessaries and Comforts of Life, Want and Misery would be banished out of the World, and the rest of the 24 hours might be Leisure and Pleasure.

What occasions then so much Want and Misery? It is the Employment of Men and Women in Works, that produce neither the Necessaries nor

Conveniences of Life, who, with those who do nothing, consume the Necessaries raised by the Laborious. To explain this.

The first Elements of Wealth are obtained by Labour, from the Earth and Waters. I have Land, and raise Corn. With this, if I feed a Family that does nothing, my Corn will be consum'd, and at the end of the Year I shall be no richer than I was at the beginning. But if, while I feed them, I employ them, some in Spinning, others in hewing Timber and sawing Boards, others in making Bricks, &c. for Building, the Value of my Corn will be arrested and remain with me, and at the end of the Year we may all be better clothed and better lodged. And if, instead of employing a Man I feed in making Bricks, I employ him in fiddling for me, the Corn he eats is gone, and no Part of his Manufacture remains to augment the Wealth and Convenience of the family; I shall therefore be the poorer for this fiddling Man, unless the rest of my Family work more, or eat less, to make up the Deficiency he occasions.

Look round the World and see the Millions employ'd in doing nothing, or in something that amounts to nothing, when the Necessaries and Conveniences of Life are in question. What is the Bulk of Commerce, for which we fight and destroy each other, but the Toil of Millions for Superfluities, to the great Hazard and Loss of many Lives by the constant Dangers of the Sea? How much labour is spent in Building and fitting great Ships, to go to China and Arabia for Tea and Coffee, to the West Indies for Sugar, to America for Tobacco! These things cannot be called the Necessaries of Life, for our Ancestors lived very comfortably without them.

A Question may be asked; Could all these People, now employed in raising, making, or carrying Superfluities, be subsisted by raising Necessaries? I think they might. The World is large, and a great Part of it still uncultivated. Many hundred Millions of Acres in Asia, Africa, and America are still Forest, and a great Deal even in Europe. On 100 Acres of this Forest a Man might become a substantial Farmer, and 100,000 Men, employed in clearing each his 100 Acres, would hardly brighten a Spot big enough to be Visible from the Moon, unless with Herschell's Telescope; so vast are the Regions still in Wood unimproved.

'Tis however, some Comfort to reflect, that, upon the whole, the Quantity of Industry and Prudence among Mankind exceeds the Quantity of Idleness and Folly. Hence the Increase of good Buildings, Farms cultivated, and populous Cities filled with Wealth, all over Europe, which a few Ages since were only to be found on the Coasts of the Mediterranean; and this, notwithstanding the mad Wars continually raging, by which are often destroyed in one year the Works of many Years' Peace. So that we may hope the Luxury of a few Merchants on the Seacoast will not be the Ruin of America.

One reflection more, and I well end this long, rambling Letter. Almost all the Parts of our Bodies require some Expence. The Feet demand

Shoes; the Legs, Stockings; the rest of the Body, Clothing; and the Belly, a good deal of Victuals. *Our* Eyes, tho' exceedingly useful, ask, when reasonable, only the cheap Assistance of Spectacles, which could not much impair our Finances. But *the Eyes of other People* are the Eyes that ruin us. If all but myself were blind, I should want neither fine Clothes, fine Houses, nor fine Furniture. . . .

24. *On Bifocals*

To George Whatley

Passy, May 23, 1785

. . . By Mr. Dollond's saying, that my double spectacles can only serve particular eyes, I doubt he has not been rightly informed of their construction. I imagine it will be found pretty generally true, that the same convexity of glass, through which a man sees clearest and best at the distance proper for reading, is not the best for greater distances. I therefore had formerly two pair of spectacles, which I shifted occasionally, as in travelling I sometimes read, and often wanted to regard the prospects. Finding this change troublesome, and not always sufficiently ready, I had the glasses cut, and half of each kind associated in the same circle, thus,

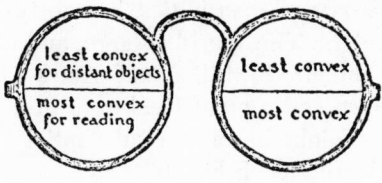

By this means, as I wear my spectacles constantly, I have only to move my eyes up or down, as I want to see distinctly far or near, the proper glasses being always ready. This I find more particularly convenient since my being in France, the glasses that serve me best at table to see what I eat, not being the best to see the faces of those on the other side of the table who speak to me; and when one's ears are not well accustomed to the sounds of a language, a sight of the movements in the features of him that speaks helps to explain; so that I understand French better by the help of my spectacles. . . .

25. *"We Are Making Experiments"*

To Jonathan Shipley

Philadelphia, Feb. 24ᵗʰ, 1786.

Dear Friend,

. . . My Reception here was, as you have heard, very honourable indeed; but I was betray'd by it, and by some Remains of Ambition, from which I had imagined myself free, to accept of the Chair of Government for the State of Pennsylvania, when the proper thing for me was Repose and a private Life. I hope, however, to be able to bear the Fatigue for one Year, and then to retire.

I have much regretted our having so little Opportunity for Conversation when we last met. You could have given me Informations and Counsels that I wanted, but we were scarce a Minute together without being broke in upon. I am to thank you, however, for the Pleasure I had after our Parting, in reading the new Book you gave me, which I think generally well written and likely to do good; tho' the Reading Time of most People is of late so taken up with News Papers and little periodical Pamphlets, that few now-a-days venture to attempt reading a Quarto Volume. I have admir'd to see, that, in the last Century, a Folio, *Burton on M(melancholly)*, went through Six Editions in about Twenty Years. We have, I believe, more Readers now, but not of such large Books.

You seem desirous of knowing what Progress we make here in improving our Governments. We are, I think, in the right Road of Improvement, for we are making Experiments. I do not oppose all that seem wrong, for the Multitude are more effectually set right by Experience, than kept from going wrong by Reasoning with them. And I think we are daily more and more enlightened; so that I have no doubt of our obtaining in a few Years as much public Felicity, as good Government is capable of affording.

Your NewsPapers are fill'd with fictitious Accounts of Anarchy, Confusion, Distresses, and Miseries, we are suppos'd to be involv'd in, as Consequences of the Revolution; and the few remaining Friends of the old Government among us take pains to magnify every little Inconvenience a Change in the Course of Commerce may have occasion'd. To obviate the Complaints they endeavour to excite, was written the enclos'd little Piece, from which you may form a truer Idea of our Situation, than your own public Prints would give you. And I can assure you, that the great Body of our Nation find themselves happy in the Change, and have not the smallest Inclination to return to the Domination of Britain. There could not be a stronger Proof of the general Approbation of the Measures, that promoted the Change, and of the Change itself, than has been given

by the Assembly and Council of this State, in the nearly unanimous Choice for their Governor, of one who had been so much concern'd in those Measures; the Assembly being themselves the unbrib'd Choice of the People, and therefore may be truly suppos'd of the same Sentiments. I say nearly unanimous, because, of between 70 and 80 Votes, there were only my own and one other in the negative. . . .

26. *Progress of Invention*

To Rev. John Lathrop

Philadᵃ, May 31, 1788.

Reverend Sir,

. . . I have been long impressed with the same sentiments you so well express, of the growing felicity of mankind, from the improvements in philosophy, morals, politics, and even the conveniences of common living, by the invention and acquisition of new and useful utensils and instruments, that I have sometimes almost wished it had been my destiny to be born two or three centuries hence. For invention and improvement are prolific, and beget more of their kind. The present progress is rapid. Many of great importance, now unthought of, will before that period be produced; and then I might not only enjoy their advantages, but have my curiosity gratified in knowing what they are to be. I see a little absurdity in what I have just written, but it is to a friend, who will wink and let it pass, while I mention one reason more for such a wish, which is, that, if the art of physic shall be improved in proportion with other arts, we may then be able to avoid diseases, and live as long as the patriarchs in Genesis; to which I suppose we should make little objection. . . .

27. *On the New Constitution*

To Dupont de Nemours

Philadelphia, June 9, 1788.

Sir,

. . . But seven States having, before it arrived, ratified the new constitution, and others being daily expected to do the same, after the fullest discussion in convention, and in all the public papers, till everybody was

tired of the argument, it seemed too late to propose delay, and especially the delay that must be occasioned by a revision and correction of all the separate Constitutions. For it would take at least a year to convince thirteen States, that the Constitutions they have practised ever since the Revolution, without observing any imperfections in them so great as to be worth the trouble of amendment, are nevertheless so ill formed as to be unfit for continuation, or to be parts of a federal government. And, when they should be so convinced, it would probably take some years more to make the corrections.

An eighth State has since acceded, and when a ninth is added, which is now daily expected, the constitution will be carried into execution. It is probable, however, that, at the first meeting of the new Congress, various amendments will be proposed and discussed, when I hope your *Ouvrage sur les Principes et le Bien des Républiques en général*, &c. &c., may be ready to put into their hands; and such a work from your hand I am confident, though it may not be entirely followed, will afford useful hints, and produce advantages of importance.

But we must not expect, that a new government may be formed, as a game of chess may be played, by a skilful hand, without a fault. The players of our game are so many, their ideas so different, their prejudices so strong and so various, and their particular interests, independent of the general, seeming so opposite, that not a move can be made that is not contested; the numerous objections confound the understanding; the wisest must agree to some unreasonable things, that reasonable ones of more consequence may be obtained; and thus chance has its share in many of the determinations, so that the play is more like *tric-trac* with a box of dice. . . .

28. *On French Revolution*

To David Hartley

Philadelphia, December 4, 1789

. . . The Convulsions in France are attended with some disagreable Circumstances; but if by the Struggle she obtains and secures for the Nation its future Liberty, and a good Constitution, a few Years' Enjoyment of those Blessings will amply repair all the Damages their Acquisition may have occasioned. God grant, that not only the Love of Liberty, but a thorough Knowledge of the Rights of Man, may pervade all the Nations of the Earth, so that a Philosopher may set his Foot anywhere on its Surface, and say, "This is my Country." . . .

29. *"On My Religion"*

To Ezra Stiles

Philadᵃ, March 9, 1790.

Reverend and Dear Sir,

I received your kind Letter of Jan'y 28, and am glad you have at length received the portrait of Gov'r Yale from his Family, and deposited it in the College Library. He was a great and good Man, and had the Merit of doing infinite Service to your Country by his Munificence to that Institution. The Honour you propose doing me by placing mine in the same Room with his, is much too great for my Deserts; but you always had a Partiality for me, and to that it must be ascribed. I am however too much obliged to Yale College, the first learned Society that took Notice of me and adorned me with its Honours, to refuse a Request that comes from it thro' so esteemed a Friend. But I do not think any one of the Portraits you mention, as in my Possession, worthy of the Place and Company you propose to place it in. You have an excellent Artist lately arrived. If he will undertake to make one for you, I shall cheerfully pay the Expence; but he must not delay setting about it, or I may slip thro' his fingers, for I am now in my eighty-fifth year, and very infirm.

I send with this a very learned Work, as it seems to me, on the antient Samaritan Coins, lately printed in Spain, and at least curious for the Beauty of the Impression. Please to accept it for your College Library. I have subscribed for the Encyclopædia now printing here, with the Intention of presenting it to the College. I shall probably depart before the Work is finished, but shall leave Directions for its Continuance to the End. With this you will receive some of the first numbers.

You desire to know something of my Religion. It is the first time I have been questioned upon it. But I cannot take your Curiosity amiss, and shall endeavour in a few Words to gratify it. Here is my Creed. I believe in one God, Creator of the Universe. That he governs it by his Providence. That he ought to be worshipped. That the most acceptable Service we render to him is doing good to his other Children. That the soul of Man is immortal, and will be treated with Justice in another Life respecting its Conduct in this. These I take to be the fundamental Principles of all sound Religion, and I regard them as you do in whatever Sect I meet with them.

As to Jesus of Nazareth, my Opinion of whom you particularly desire, I think the System of Morals and his Religion, as he left them to us, the best the World ever saw or is likely to see; but I apprehend it has received various corrupting Changes, and I have, with most of the present Dissenters in England, some Doubts as to his Divinity; tho' it is a ques-

tion I do not dogmatize upon, having never studied it, and think it needless to busy myself with it now, when I expect soon an Opportunity of
knowing the Truth with less Trouble. I see no harm, however, in its being
believed, if that Belief has the good Consequence, as probably it has, of
making his Doctrines more respected and better observed; especially as
I do not perceive, that the Supreme takes it amiss, by distinguishing the
Unbelievers in his Government of the World with any peculiar Marks of
his Displeasure.

I shall only add, respecting myself, that, having experienced the Goodness of that Being in conducting me prosperously thro' a long life, I have
no doubt of its Continuance in the next, though without the smallest Conceit of meriting such Goodness. My Sentiments on this Head you will see
in the Copy of an old Letter enclosed, which I wrote in answer to one
from a zealous Religionist, whom I had relieved in a paralytic case by
electricity, and who, being afraid I should grow proud upon it, sent me
his serious though rather impertinent Caution. . . .

P. S. Had not your College some Present of Books from the King of
France? Please to let me know, if you had an Expectation given you of
more, and the Nature of that Expectation? I have a Reason for the Enquiry.

I confide, that you will not expose me to Criticism and censure by
publishing any part of this Communication to you. I have ever let others
enjoy their religious Sentiments, without reflecting on them for those that
appeared to me unsupportable and even absurd. All Sects here, and we
have a great Variety, have experienced my good will in assisting them
with Subscriptions for building their new Places of Worship; and, as I
have never opposed any of their Doctrines, I hope to go out of the World
in Peace with them all.

Other Writings

30. *Rules for a Club Established for Mutual Improvement*

[1728]

Previous Question, To Be Answered At Every Meeting

Have you read over these queries this morning, in order to consider what you might have to offer the Junto touching any one of them? viz.

1. Have you met with any thing in the author you last read, remarkable, or suitable to be communicated to the Junto? particularly in history, morality, poetry, physic, travels, mechanic arts, or other parts of knowledge.

2. What new story have you lately heard agreeable for telling in conversation?

3. Hath any citizen in your knowledge failed in his business lately, and what have you heard of the cause?

4. Have you lately heard of any citizen's thriving well, and by what means?

5. Have you lately heard how any present rich man, here or elsewhere, got his estate?

6. Do you know of a fellow citizen, who has lately done a worthy action, deserving praise and imitation; or who has lately committed an error, proper for us to be warned against and avoid?

7. What unhappy effects of intemperance have you lately observed or heard; of imprudence, of passion, or of any other vice or folly?

8. What happy effects of temperance, of prudence, of moderation, or of any other virtue?

9. Have you or any of your acquaintance been lately sick or wounded? If so, what remedies were used, and what were their effects?

10. Whom do you know that are shortly going voyages or journeys, if one should have occasion to send by them?

11. Do you think of any thing at present, in which the Junto may be serviceable to *mankind*, to their country, to their friends, or to themselves?

12. Hath any deserving stranger arrived in town since last meeting, that you have heard of? And what have you heard or observed of his character or merits? And whether, think you, it lies in the power of the Junto to oblige him, or encourage him as he deserves?

13. Do you know of any deserving young beginner lately set up, whom it lies in the power of the Junto any way to encourage?

14. Have you lately observed any defect in the laws of your *country*, of which it would be proper to move the legislature for an amendment? Or do you know of any beneficial law that is wanting?

15. Have you lately observed any encroachment on the just liberties of the people?

16. Hath any body attacked your reputation lately? And what can the Junto do towards securing it?

17. Is there any man whose friendship you want, and which the Junto, or any of them, can procure for you?

18. Have you lately heard any member's character attacked, and how have you defended it?

19. Hath any man injured you, from whom it is in the power of the Junto to procure redress?

20. In what manner can the Junto, or any of them, assist you in any of your honourable designs?

21. Have you any weighty affair on hand, in which you think the advice of the Junto may be of service?

22. What benefits have you lately received from any man not present?

23. Is there any difficulty in matters of opinion, of justice, and in-justice, which you would gladly have discussed at this time?

24. Do you see any thing amiss in the present customs or proceedings of the Junto, which might be amended?

Any person to be qualified [as a member of the Junto], to stand up, and lay his hand upon his breast, and be asked these questions, viz.

1. Have you any particular disrespect to any present members? *Answer.* I have not.

2. Do you sincerely declare, that you love mankind in general, of what profession or religion soever? *Answer.* I do.

3. Do you think any person ought to be harmed in his body, name, or goods, for mere speculative opinions, or his external way of worship? *Answer.* No.

4. Do you love truth for truth's sake, and will you endeavour im-partially to find and receive it yourself, and communicate it to others? *Answer.* Yes.

31. *An Apology for Printers*

[From the *Pennsylvania Gazette*, June 10, 1731.]

Being frequently censur'd and condemn'd by different Persons for printing Things which they say ought not to be printed, I have sometimes thought it might be necessary to make a standing Apology for my self, and publish it once a Year, to be read upon all Occasions of that Nature. Much Business has hitherto hindered the execution of this Design; but having very lately given extraordinary Offence by printing an Advertisement with a certain N. B. at the End of it, I find an Apology more particularly requisite at this Juncture, tho' it happens when I have not yet Leisure to write such a Thing in the proper Form, and can only in a loose manner throw those Considerations together which should have been the Substance of it.

I request all who are angry with me on the Account of printing things they don't like, calmly to consider these following Particulars.

1. That the Opinions of Men are almost as various as their Faces; an Observation general enough to become a common Proverb, *So many Men so many Minds.*

2. That the Business of Printing has chiefly to do with Mens Opinions; most things that are printed tending to promote some, or oppose others.

3. That hence arises the peculiar Unhappiness of that Business, which other Callings are no way liable to; they who follow Printing being scarce able to do any thing in their way of getting a Living, which shall not probably give Offence to some, and perhaps to many; whereas the Smith, the Shoemaker, the Carpenter, or the Man of any other Trade, may work indifferently for People of all Persuasions, without offending any of them: and the Merchant may buy and sell with Jews, Turks, Hereticks and Infidels of all sorts, and get Money by every one of them, without giving Offence to the most orthodox, of any sort; or suffering the least Censure or Ill will on the Account from any Man whatever.

4. That it is as unreasonable in any one Man or Set of Men to expect to be pleas'd with every thing that is printed, as to think that nobody ought to be pleas'd but themselves.

5. Printers are educated in the Belief, that when Men differ in Opinion, both Sides ought equally to have the Advantage of being heard by the Publick; and that when Truth and Error have fair Play, the former is always an overmatch for the latter: Hence they chearfully serve all contending Writers that pay them well, without regarding on which side they are of the Question in Dispute.

6. Being thus continually employ'd in serving both Parties, Printers naturally acquire a vast Unconcernedness as to the right or wrong

Opinions contain'd in what they print; regarding it only as the Matter of their daily labour: They print things full of Spleen and Animosity, with the utmost Calmness and Indifference, and without the least Ill-will to the Persons reflected on; who nevertheless unjustly think the Printer as much their Enemy as the Author, and join both together in their Resentment.

7. That it is unreasonable to imagine Printers approve of every thing they print, and to censure them on any particular thing accordingly; since in the way of their Business they print such great variety of things opposite and contradictory. It is likewise as unreasonable what some assert, "That Printers ought not to print any Thing but what they approve;" since if all of that Business should make such a Resolution, and abide by it, an End would thereby be put to Free Writing, and the World would afterwards have nothing to read but what happen'd to be the Opinions of Printers.

8. That if all Printers were determin'd not to print any thing till they were sure it would offend no body, there would be very little printed.

9. That if they sometimes print vicious or silly things not worth reading, it may not be because they approve such things themselves, but because the People are so viciously and corruptly educated that good things are not encouraged. I have known a very numerous Impression of Robin Hood's Songs go off in this Province at 2s. per Book, in less than a Twelvemonth; when a small Quantity of David's Psalms (an excellent Version) have lain upon my Hands above twice the Time.

10. That notwithstanding what might be urg'd in behalf of a Man's being allow'd to do in the Way of his Business whatever he is paid for, yet Printers do continually discourage the Printing of great Numbers of bad things, and stifle them in the Birth. I my self have constantly refused to print anything that might countenance Vice, or promote Immorality; tho' by complying in such Cases with the corrupt Taste of the Majority I might have got much Money. I have also always refus'd to print such things as might do real Injury to any Person, how much soever I have been solicited, and tempted with Offers of Great Pay; and how much soever I have by refusing got the Ill-will of those who would have employ'd me. I have hitherto fallen under the Resentment of large Bodies of Men, for refusing absolutely to print any of their Party or Personal Reflections. In this Manner I have made my self many Enemies, and the constant Fatigue of denying is almost insupportable. But the Publick being unacquainted with all this, whenever the poor Printer happens either through Ignorance or much Persuasion, to do any thing that is generally thought worthy of Blame, he meets with no more Friendship or Favour on the above Account, than if there were no Merit in't at all. Thus, as Waller says,

> Poets lose half the Praise they would have got
> Were it but known what they discreetly blot;

Yet are censur'd for every bad Line found in their Works with the utmost Severity. . . .

I take leave to conclude with an old Fable, which some of my Readers have heard before, and some have not.

"A certain well-meaning Man and his Son, were travelling towards a Market Town, with an Ass which they had to sell. The Road was bad; and the old Man therefore rid, but the Son went a-foot. The first Passenger they met, asked the Father if he was not ashamed to ride by himself, and suffer the poor Lad to wade along thro' the Mire; this induced him to take up his Son behind him: He had not travelled far, when he met others, who said, they are two unmerciful Lubbers to get both on the Back of that poor Ass, in such a deep Road. Upon this the old Man gets off, and let his Son ride alone. The next they met called the Lad a graceless, rascally young Jackanapes, to ride in that Manner thro' the Dirt, while his aged Father trudged along on Foot; and they said the old Man was a Fool, for suffering it. He then bid his Son come down, and walk with him, and they travell'd on leading the Ass by the Halter; 'till they met another Company, who called them a Couple of senseless Blockheads, for going both on Foot in such a dirty Way, when they had an empty Ass with them, which they might ride upon. The old Man could bear no longer; My Son, said he, it grieves me much that we cannot please all these People. Let me throw the Ass over the next Bridge, and be no further troubled with him."

Had the old Man been seen acting this last Resolution, he would probably have been called a Fool for troubling himself about the different Opinions of all that were pleas'd to find Fault with him: Therefore, tho' I have a Temper almost as complying as his, I intend not to imitate him in this last Particular. I consider the Variety of Humors among Men, and despair of pleasing every Body; yet I shall not therefore leave off Printing. I shall continue my Business. I shall not burn my Press and melt my Letters.

32. *Dialogue Between Two Presbyterians*

Mr. Franklin,
You are desired by several of your Readers to print the following Dialogue. *It is between Two of the Presbyterian Meeting in this City. We cannot tell whether it may not be contrary to your Sentiments, but hope, if it should, you will not refuse publishing it on that Account: nor shall we be offended if you print any thing in Answer to it. We are yours,* &c. A.B.C.D.

S. Good Morrow! I am glad to find you well and abroad; for not having seen you at Meeting lately, I concluded you were indispos'd.

T. Tis true I have not been much at Meeting lately, but that was not occasion'd by any Indisposition. In short, I stay at home, or else go to Church, because I do not like Mr. H. your new-fangled Preacher.

S. I am sorry we should differ in Opinion upon any Account; but let us reason the Point calmly; what Offence does Mr. H. give you?

T. Tis his Preaching disturbs me: He talks of nothing but the Duties of Morality: I do not love to hear so much of Morality: I am sure it will carry no Man to Heaven, and I do not think it fit to be preached in a Christian Congregation.

S. I suppose you think no Doctrine fit to be preached in a Christian Congregation, but such as Christ and his Apostles used to preach.

T. To be sure I think so.

S. I do not conceive then how you can dislike the Preaching of Morality, when you consider, that Morality made the principal Part of their Preaching as well as of Mr. H's. What is Christ's Sermon on the Mount but an excellent moral Discourse, towards the End of which, (as foreseeing that People might in time come to depend more upon their *Faith* in him, than upon *Good Works,* for their Salvation) he tells the Hearers plainly, that their saying to him, *Lord, Lord,* (that is, professing themselves his Disciples or *Christians*) should give them no Title to Salvation, but their *Doing* the Will of his Father; and that tho' they have prophesied in his Name, yet he will declare to them, as Neglecters of Morality, that he never knew them.

T. But what do you understand by that Expression of Christ's, Doing the Will of my Father?

S. I understand it to be the Will of God, that we should live virtuous, upright, and good-doing Lives; as the Prophet understood it, when he said, *What doth the Lord require of thee, O Man, but to do justly, love Mercy, and walk humbly with the Lord thy God.*

T. But is not Faith recommended in the New Testament as well as Morality?

S. Tis true, it is. Faith is recommended as a Means of producing Morality: Our Saviour was a Teacher of Morality or Virtue, and they that were deficient and desired to be taught, ought first to *believe* in him as an able and faithful Teacher. Thus Faith would be a Means of producing Morality, and Morality of Salvation. But that from such Faith alone Salvation may be expected, appears to me to be neither a Christian Doctrine nor a reasonable one. And I should as soon expect, that my bare Believing Mr. Grew to be an excellent Teacher of the Mathematicks, would make me a Mathematician, as that Believing in Christ would of it self make a Man a Christian.

T. Perhaps you may think, that tho' Faith alone cannot save a Man, Morality or Virtue alone, may.

S. Morality or Virtue is the End, Faith only a Means to obtain that End: And if the End be obtained, it is no matter by what Means. What

think you of these Sayings of Christ, when he was reproached for conversing chiefly with gross Sinners, *The whole*, says he, *need not a Physician, but they that are sick;* and, *I come not to call the Righteous, but Sinners, to Repentance:* Does not this imply, that there were good Men, who, without Faith in him, were in a State of Salvation? And moreover, did he not say of Nathanael, while he was yet an Unbeliever in him, and thought no Good could possibly come out of Nazareth, *Behold an Israelite indeed, in whom there is no Guile!* that is, *behold a virtuous upright Man.* Faith in Christ, however, may be and is of great Use to produce a good Life, but that it can conduce nothing towards Salvation where it does not conduce to Virtue, is, I suppose, plain from the Instance of the Devils, who are far from being Infidels, *they believe*, says the Scripture, *and tremble.* There were some indeed, even in the Apostles' Days, that set a great Value upon Faith, distinct from Good Works, they meerly idolized it, and thought that a Man ever so righteous could not be saved without it: But one of the Apostles, to show his Dislike of such Notions, tells them, that not only those heinous Sins of Theft, Murder, and Blasphemy, but even *Idleness*, or the Neglect of a Man's Business, was more pernicious than meer harmless Infidelity, *He that neglects to provide for them of his own House*, says he, *is* WORSE *than an Infidel.* St. James, in his second Chapter, is very zealous against these Cryers-up of Faith, and maintains that Faith without Virtue is useless, *Wilt thou know, O vain Man*, says he, *that Faith without Works is dead;* and, *shew me your Faith without your Works, and I will shew you mine by my Works.* Our Saviour, when describing the last Judgment, and declaring what shall give Admission into Bliss, or exclude from it, says nothing of *Faith* but what he says against it, that is, that those who cry *Lord, Lord,* and profess to have *believed* in his Name, have no Favour to expect on that Account; but declares that 'tis the Practice, or the omitting the Practice of the Duties of Morality, *Feeding the Hungry, cloathing the Naked, visiting the Sick*, &c. in short, 'tis the Doing or not Doing all the Good that lies in our Power, that will render us the Heirs of Happiness or Misery.

T. *But if Faith is of great Use to produce a good Life, why does not Mr. H. preach up Faith as well as Morality?*

S. Perhaps it may [be] this, that as the Good Physician suits his Physick to the Disease he finds in the Patient, so Mr. H. may possibly think, that though Faith in Christ be properly first preach'd to Heathens and such as are ignorant of the Gospel, yet since he knows that we have been baptized in the Name of Christ, and educated in his Religion, and call'd after his Name, it may not be so immediately necessary to preach *Faith* to us who abound in it, as *Morality* in which we are evidently deficient: For our late Want of Charity to each other, our Heart-burnings and Bickerings are notorious. St. James says, *Where Envying and Strife is, there is Confusion and every evil Work:* and where Confusion and every evil Work is, *Morality* and Good-will to Men, can, I think, be no unsuita-

ble Doctrine. But surely *Morality* can do us no harm. Upon a Supposition that we all have Faith in Christ already, as I think we have, where can be the Damage of being exhorted to Good Works? Is Virtue Heresy; and Universal Benevolence False Doctrine, that any of us should keep away from Meeting because it is preached there?

T. *Well, I do not like it, and I hope we shall not long be troubled with it. A Commission of the Synod will sit in a short Time, and try this Sort of Preaching.*

S. I am glad to hear that the Synod are to take it into Consideration. There are Men of unquestionable Good Sense as well as Piety among them, and I doubt not but they will, by their Decision, deliver our Profession from the satyrical Reflection, which a few uneasy People of our Congregation have of late given Occasion for, to wit, That the Presbyterians are going to persecute, silence and condemn a good Preacher, for exhorting them to be honest and charitable to one another and the rest of Mankind.

T. *If Mr. H. is a Presbyterian Teacher, he ought to preach as Presbyterians use to preach; or else he may justly be condemn'd and silenc'd by our Church Authority. We ought to abide by the Westminster Confession of Faith; and he that does not, ought not to preach in our Meetings.*

S. The Apostacy of the Church from the primitive Simplicity of the Gospel, came on by Degrees; and do you think that the Reformation was of a sudden perfect, and that the first Reformers knew at once all that was right or wrong in Religion? Did not Luther at first preach only against selling of Pardons, allowing all the other Practices of the Romish Church for good? He afterwards went further, and Calvin, some think, yet further. The Church of England made a Stop, and fix'd her Faith and Doctrine by 39 Articles; with which the Presbyterians not satisfied, went yet farther; but being too self-confident to think, that as their Fathers were mistaken in some Things, they also might be in some others; and fancying themselves infallible in *their* Interpretations, they also ty'd themselves down by the Westminster Confession. But has not a Synod that meets in King George the Second's Reign, as much Right to interpret Scripture, as one that met in Oliver's Time? And if any Doctrine then maintain'd is, or shall hereafter be found not altogether orthodox, why must we be for ever confin'd to that, or to any, Confession?

T. *But if the Majority of the Synod be against any Innovation, they may justly hinder the Innovator from Preaching.*

S. That is as much as to say, if the Majority of the Preachers be in the wrong, they may justly hinder any Man from setting the People right; for a *Majority* may be in the wrong as well as the *Minority*, and frequently are. In the beginning of the Reformation, the *Majority* was vastly against the Reformers, and continues so to this Day; and, if, according to your Opinion, they had a Right to silence the *Minority*, I am sure the *Minority* ought to have been silent. But tell me, if the Presbyte-

rians in this Country, being charitably enclin'd, should send a Missionary into Turky, to propagate the Gospel, would it not be unreasonable in the Turks to prohibit his Preaching?

T. *It would, to be sure, because he comes to them for their good.*

S. And if the Turks, believing us in the wrong, as we think them, should out of the same charitable Disposition, send a Missionary to preach Mahometanism to us, ought we not in the same manner to give him free Liberty of preaching his Doctrine?

T. *It may be so; but what would you infer from that?*

S. I would only infer, that if it would be thought reasonable to suffer a Turk to preach among us a Doctrine diametrically opposite to Christianity, it cannot be reasonable to silence one of our own Preachers, for preaching a Doctrine exactly agreeable to Christianity, only because he does not perhaps zealously propagate all the Doctrines of an old Confession. And upon the whole, though the *Majority* of the Synod should not in all respects approve of Mr. H.'s Doctrine, I do not however think they will find it proper to condemn him. We have justly deny'd the Infallibility of the Pope and his Councils and Synods in their Interpretations of Scripture, and can we modestly claim *Infallibility* for our selves or our Synods in our way of Interpreting? Peace, Unity and Virtue in any Church are more to be regarded than Orthodoxy. In the present weak State of humane Nature, surrounded as we are on all sides with Ignorance and Error, it little becomes poor fallible Man to be positive and dogmatical in his Opinions. No Point of Faith is so plain, as that *Morality* is our Duty, for all Sides agree in that. A virtuous Heretick shall be saved before a wicked Christian: for there is no such Thing as voluntary Error. Therefore, since 'tis an Uncertainty till we get to Heaven what true Orthodoxy in all points is, and since our Congregation is rather too small to be divided, I hope this Misunderstanding will soon be got over, and that we shall as heretofore unite again in mutual *Christian Charity*.

T. *I wish we may. I'll consider of what you've said, and wish you well.*

S. Farewell.

33. *A Proposal for Promoting Useful Knowledge Among the British Plantations in America*

Philadelphia, May 14, 1743

The first drudgery of settling new colonies, which confines the attention of people to mere necessaries, is now pretty well over; and there are many in every province in circumstances that set them at ease, and af-

ford leisure to cultivate the finer arts and improve the common stock of
knowledge. To such of these who are men of speculation, many hints
must from time to time arise, many observations occur, which if well
examined, pursued, and improved, might produce discoveries to the
advantage of some or all of the British plantations, or to the benefit of
mankind in general.

But as from the extent of the country such persons are widely separated, and seldom can see and converse or be acquainted with each
other, so that many useful particulars remain uncommunicated, die with
the discoverers, and are lost to mankind; it is, to remedy this inconvenience for the future, proposed,

That one society be formed of *virtuosi* or ingenious men, residing in
the several colonies, to be called *The American Philosophical Society*,
who are to maintain a constant correspondence. . . .

34. *The Way to Wealth*

Preface to Poor Richard Improved: 1758.

Courteous Reader,

I have heard that nothing gives an Author so great Pleasure, as to find
his Works respectfully quoted by other learned Authors. This Pleasure I
have seldom enjoyed; for tho' I have been, if I may say it without Vanity,
an *eminent Author* of Almanacks annually now a full Quarter of a Century, my Brother Authors in the same Way, for what Reason I know not,
have ever been very sparing in their Applauses; and no other Author has
taken the least Notice of me, so that did not my Writings produce me
some solid *Pudding*, the great Deficiency of *Praise* would have quite discouraged me.

I concluded at length, that the People were the best Judges of my
Merit; for they buy my Works; and besides, in my Rambles, where I am
not personally known, I have frequently heard one or other of my Ad-
ages repeated, with, *as Poor Richard says*, at the End on't; this give me
some Satisfaction, as it showed not only that my Instructions were regarded, but discovered likewise some Respect for my Authority; and I
own, that to encourage the Practice of remembering and repeating those
wise Sentences, I have sometimes *quoted myself* with great Gravity.

Judge then how much I must have been gratified by an Incident I am
going to relate to you. I stopt my Horse lately where a great Number of
People were collected at a Vendue of Merchant Goods. The Hour of Sale
not being come, they were conversing on the Badness of the Times, and
one of the Company call'd to a plain clean old Man, with white Locks,

Pray, Father Abraham, *what think you of the Times? Won't these heavy Taxes quite ruin the Country? How shall we ever be able to pay them? What would you advise us to?*——Father *Abraham* stood up, and re-ply'd, If you'd have my Advice, I'll give it you in short, for a *Word to the Wise is enough,* and *many Words won't fill a Bushel,* as *Poor Richard* says. They join'd in desiring him to speak his Mind, and gathering round him, he proceeded as follows;

"Friends, says he, and Neighbours, the Taxes are indeed very heavy, and if those laid on by the Government were the only Ones we had to pay, we might more easily discharge them; but we have many others, and much more grievous to some of us. We are taxed twice as much by our *Idleness,* three times as much by our *Pride,* and four times as much by our *Folly,* and from these Taxes the Commissioners cannot ease or deliver us by allowing an Abatement. However let us hearken to good Advice, and something may be done for us; *God helps them that help themselves,* as *Poor Richard* says, in his Almanack of 1733.

It would be thought a hard Government that should tax its People one tenth Part of their *Time,* to be employed in its Service. But *Idleness* taxes many of us much more, if we reckon all that is spent in absolute *Sloth,* or doing of nothing, with that which is spent in idle Employments or Amusements, that amount to nothing. *Sloth,* by bringing on Diseases, absolutely shortens Life. *Sloth, like Rust, consumes faster than Labour wears, while the used Key is always bright,* as *Poor Richard* says. But *dost thou love Life, then do not squander Time, for that's the Stuff Life is made of,* as *Poor Richard* says.—How much more than is necessary do we spend in Sleep! forgetting that *The sleeping Fox catches no Poultry,* and that *there will be sleeping enough in the Grave,* as *Poor Richard* says. If Time be of all Things the most precious, *wasting Time* must be, as *Poor Richard* says, *the greatest Prodigality,* since, as he elsewhere tells us, *Lost Time is never found again;* and what we call *Time-enough, always proves little enough:* Let us then up and be doing, and doing to the Purpose; so by Diligence shall we do more with less Perplexity. *Sloth makes all Things difficult, but Industry all easy,* as *Poor Richard* says; and *He that riseth late, must trot all Day, and shall scarce overtake his Business at Night.* While *Laziness travels so slowly, that Poverty soon overtakes him,* as we read in *Poor Richard,* who adds, *Drive thy Business, let not that drive thee;* and *Early to Bed, and early to rise, makes a Man healthy, wealthy and wise.*

So what signifies *wishing* and *hoping* for better Times. We may make these Times better if we bestir ourselves. *Industry need not wish,* as *Poor Richard* says, and *He that lives upon Hope will die fasting. There are no Gains, without Pains;* then *Help Hands, for I have no Lands,* or if I have, they are smartly taxed. And, as *Poor Richard* likewise observes, *He that hath a Trade hath an Estate, and He that hath a Calling, hath an Office of Profit and Honour;* but then the *Trade* must be worked at, and

the *Calling* well followed, or neither the *Estate,* nor the *Office,* will enable us to pay our Taxes.—If we are industrious we shall never starve; for, as *Poor Richard* says, *At the Working Man's House* Hunger *looks in, but dares not enter.* Nor will the Bailiff or the Constable enter, for *Industry pays Debts, while Despair encreaseth them,* says *Poor Richard.*— What though you have found no Treasure, nor has any rich Relation left you a Legacy, *Diligence is the Mother of Good luck,* as *Poor Richard* says, *and God gives all Things to Industry.* Then *plough deep, while Sluggards sleep, and you shall have Corn to sell and to keep,* says *Poor Dick.* . . .

35. *Rules by Which a Great Empire May Be Reduced to a Small One*

Presented to a late Minister, when he entered upon his Administration

[From the *Gentleman's Magazine,* Sept., 1773.]

An ancient Sage boasted, that, tho' he could not fiddle, he knew how to make a *great city* of a *little one.* The science that I, a modern simpleton, am about to communicate, is the very reverse.

I address myself to all ministers who have the management of extensive dominions, which from their very greatness are become troublesome to govern, because the multiplicity of their affairs leaves no time for *fiddling.*

I. In the first place, gentlemen, you are to consider, that a great empire, like a great cake, is most easily diminished at the edges. Turn your attention, therefore, first to your *remotest* provinces; that, as you get rid of them, the next may follow in order.

II. That the possibility of this separation may always exist, take special care the provinces are never incorporated with the mother country; that they do not enjoy the same common rights, the same privileges in commerce; and that they are governed by *severer* laws, all of *your enacting,* without allowing them any share in the choice of the legislators. By carefully making and preserving such distinctions, you will (to keep to my simile of the cake) act like a wise ginger-bread-baker, who, to facilitate a division, cuts his dough half through in those places where, when baked, he would have it *broken to pieces.*

III. Those remote provinces have perhaps been acquired, purchased, or conquered, at the *sole expence* of the settlers, or their ancestors, with-

out the aid of the mother country. If this should happen to increase her *strength,* by their growing numbers, ready to join in her wars; her *commerce,* by their growing demand for her manufactures; or her *naval power,* by greater employment for her ships and seamen, they may probably suppose some merit in this, and that it entitles them to some favour; you are therefore to *forget it all, or resent it,* as if they had done you injury. If they happen to be zealous whigs, friends of liberty, nurtured in revolution principles, *remember all that* to their prejudice, and resolve to punish it; for such principles, after a revolution is thoroughly established, are of *no more use;* they are even *odious* and *abominable.*

IV. However peaceably your colonies have submitted to your government, shewn their affection to your interests, and patiently borne their grievances; you are to *suppose* them always inclined to revolt, and treat them accordingly. Quarter troops among them, who by their insolence may *provoke* the rising of mobs, and by their bullets and bayonets *suppress* them. By this means, like the husband who uses his wife ill *from suspicion,* you may in time convert your *suspicions* into *realities.*

V. Remote provinces must have *Governors* and *Judges,* to represent the Royal Person, and execute everywhere the delegated parts of his office and authority. You ministers know, that much of the strength of government depends on the *opinion* of the people; and much of that opinion on the *choice of rulers* placed immediately over them. If you send them wise and good men for governors, who study the interest of the colonists, and advance their prosperity, they will think their King wise and good, and that he wishes the welfare of his subjects. If you send them learned and upright men for Judges, they will think him a lover of justice. This may attach your provinces more to his government. You are therefore to be careful whom you recommend for those offices. If you can find prodigals, who have ruined their fortunes, broken gamesters or stock-jobbers, these may do well as *governors;* for they will probably be rapacious, and provoke the people by their extortions. Wrangling proctors and pettifogging lawyers, too, are not amiss; for they will be for ever disputing and quarrelling with their little parliaments. If withal they should be ignorant, wrong-headed, and insolent, so much the better. Attornies' clerks and Newgate solicitors will do for *Chief Justices,* especially if they hold their places *during your pleasure;* and all will contribute to impress those ideas of your government, that are proper for a people *you would wish to renounce it.*

VI. To confirm these impressions, and strike them deeper, whenever the injured come to the capital with complaints of maladministration, oppression, or injustice, punish such suitors with long delay, enormous expence, and a final judgment in favour of the oppressor. This will have an admirable effect every way. The trouble of future complaints will be prevented, and Governors and Judges will be encouraged to farther acts of oppression and injustice; and thence the people may become more disaffected, and at length desperate.

VII. When such Governors have crammed their rich coffers, and made themselves so odious to the people that they can no longer remain among them, with safety to their persons, *recall and reward* them with pensions. You may make them *baronets* too, if that respectable order should not think fit to resent it. All will contribute to encourage new governors in the same practice, and make the supreme government, *detestable*.

VIII. If, when you are engaged in war, your colonies should vie in liberal aids of men and money against the common enemy, upon your simple requisition, and give far beyond their abilities, reflect that a penny taken from them by your power is more honourable to you, than a pound presented by their benevolence; despise therefore their voluntary grants, and resolve to harass them with novel taxes. They will probably complain to your parliaments, that they are taxed by a body in which they have no representative, and that this is contrary to common right. They will petition for redress. Let the Parliaments flout their claims, reject their petitions, refuse even to suffer the reading of them, and treat the petitioners with the utmost contempt. Nothing can have a better effect in producing the alienation proposed; for though many can forgive injuries, *none ever forgave contempt.*

IX. In laying these taxes, never regard the heavy burthens those remote people already undergo, in defending their own frontiers, supporting their own provincial governments, making new roads, building bridges, churches, and other public edifices, which in old countries have been done to your hands by your ancestors, but which occasion constant calls and demands on the purses of a new people. Forget the *restraints* you lay on their trade for *your own* benefit, and the advantage a *monopoly* of this trade gives your exacting merchants. Think nothing of the wealth those merchants and your manufacturers acquire by the colony commerce; their encreased ability thereby to pay taxes at home; their accumulating, in the price of their commodities, most of those taxes, and so levying them from their consuming customers; all this, and the employment and support of thousands of your poor by the colonists, you are *intirely to forget.* But remember to make your arbitrary tax more grievous to your provinces, by public declarations importing that your power of taxing them has *no limits;* so that when you take from them without their consent one shilling in the pound, you have a clear right to the other nineteen. This will probably weaken every idea of *security in their property,* and convince them, that under such a government they *have nothing they can call their own;* which can scarce fail of producing the *happiest consequences!*

X. Possibly, indeed, some of them might still comfort themselves, and say, "Though we have no property, we have yet *something* left that is valuable; we have constitutional *liberty,* both of person and of conscience. This King, these Lords, and these Commons, who it seems are too remote from us to know us, and feel for us, cannot take from us our *Habeas Corpus* right, or our right of trial *by a jury of our neighbours;* they cannot

deprive us of the exercise of our religion, alter our ecclesiastical constitution, and compel us to be Papists, if they please, or Mahometans." To annihilate this comfort, begin by laws to perplex their commerce with infinite regulations, impossible to be remembered and observed; ordain seizures of their property for every failure; take away the trial of such property by Jury, and give it to arbitrary Judges of your own appointing, and of the lowest characters in the country, whose salaries and emoluments are to arise out of the duties or condemnations, and whose appointments are *during pleasure*. Then let there be a formal declaration of both Houses, that opposition to your edicts is *treason,* and that any person suspected of treason in the provinces may, according to some obsolete law, be seized and sent to the metropolis of the empire for trial; and pass an act, that those there charged with certain other offences, shall be sent away in chains from their friends and country to be tried in the same manner for felony. Then erect a new Court of Inquisition among them, accompanied by an armed force, with instructions to transport all such suspected persons; to be ruined by the expence, if they bring over evidences to prove their innocence, or be found guilty and hanged, if they cannot afford it. And, lest the people should think you cannot possibly go any farther, pass another solemn declaratory act, "that King, Lords, Commons had, hath, and of right ought to have, full power and authority to make statutes of sufficient force and validity to bind the unrepresented provinces IN ALL CASES WHATSOEVER." This will include *spiritual* with temporal, and, taken together, must operate wonderfully to your purpose; by convincing them, that they are at present under a power something like that spoken of in the scriptures, which can not only *kill their bodies,* but *damn their souls* to all eternity, by compelling them, if it pleases, *to worship the Devil.*

XI. To make your taxes more odious, and more likely to procure resistance, send from the capital a board of officers to superintend the collection, composed of the most *indiscreet, ill-bred,* and *insolent* you can find. Let these have large salaries out of the extorted revenue, and live in open, grating luxury upon the sweat and blood of the industrious; whom they are to worry continually with groundless and expensive prosecutions before the abovementioned arbitrary revenue Judges; *all at the cost of the party prosecuted,* tho' acquitted, because *the King is to pay no costs.* Let these men, *by your order,* be exempted from all the common taxes and burthens of the province, though they and their property are protected by its laws. If any revenue officers are *suspected* of the least tenderness for the people, discard them. If others are justly complained of, protect and reward them. If any of the under officers behave so as to provoke the people to drub them, promote those to better offices: this will encourage others to procure for themselves such profitable drubbings, by multiplying and enlarging such provocations, and *all will work towards the end you aim at.*

XII. Another way to make your tax odious, is to misapply the produce of it. If it was originally appropriated for the *defence* of the provinces, the better support of government, and the administration of justice, where it may be *necessary*, then apply none of it to that *defence*, but bestow it where it is *not necessary*, in augmented salaries or pensions to every governor, who has distinguished himself by his enmity to the people, and by calumniating them to their sovereign. This will make them pay it more unwillingly, and be more apt to quarrel with those that collect it and those that imposed it, who will quarrel again with them, and all shall contribute to your *main purpose*, of making them *weary of your government*.

XIII. If the people of any province have been accustomed to support their own Governors and Judges to satisfaction, you are to apprehend that such Governors and Judges may be thereby influenced to treat the people kindly, and to do them justice. This is another reason for applying part of that revenue in larger salaries to such Governors and Judges, given, as their commissions are, *during your pleasure* only; forbidding them to take any salaries from their provinces; that thus the people may no longer hope any kindness from their Governors, or (in Crown cases) any justice from their Judges. And, as the money thus misapplied in one province is extorted from all, probably *all will resent the misapplication.*

XIV. If the parliaments of your provinces should dare to claim rights, or complain of your administration, order them to be harrassed with *repeated dissolutions.* If the same men are continually returned by new elections, adjourn their meetings to some country village, where they cannot be accommodated, and there keep them *during pleasure;* for this, you know, is your PREROGATIVE; and an excellent one it is, as you may manage it to promote discontents among the people, diminish their respect, and *increase their disaffection.*

XV. Convert the brave, honest officers of your *navy* into pimping tidewaiters and colony officers of the *customs.* Let those, who in time of war fought gallantly in defence of the commerce of their countrymen, in peace be taught to prey upon it. Let them learn to be corrupted by great and real smugglers; but (to shew their diligence) scour with armed boats every bay, harbour, river, creek, cove, or nook throughout the coast of your colonies; stop and detain every coaster, every wood-boat, every fisherman, tumble their cargoes and even their ballast inside out and upside down; and, if a penn'orth of pins is found unentered, let the whole be seized and confiscated. Thus shall the trade of your colonists suffer more from their friends in time of peace, than it did from their enemies in war. Then let these boats crews land upon every farm in their way, rob the orchards, steal the pigs and the poultry, and insult the inhabitants. If the injured and exasperated farmers, unable to procure other justice, should attack the aggressors, drub them, and burn their boats; you are to call this *high treason and rebellion,* order fleets and armies into

their country, and threaten to carry all the offenders three thousand miles to be hanged, drawn, and quartered. *O! this will work admirably!*

XVI. If you are told of discontents in your colonies, never believe that they are general, or that you have given occasion for them; therefore do not think of applying any remedy, or of changing any offensive measure. Redress no grievance, lest they should be encouraged to demand the redress of some other grievance. Grant no request that is just and reasonable, lest they should make another that is unreasonable. Take all your informations of the state of the colonies from your Governors and officers in enmity with them. Encourage and reward these *leasing-makers;* secrete their lying accusations, lest they should be confuted; but act upon them as the clearest evidence; and believe nothing you hear from the friends of the people: suppose all *their* complaints to be invented and promoted by a few factious demagogues, whom if you could catch and hang, all would be quiet. Catch and hang a few of them accordingly; and the *blood of the Martyrs* shall *work miracles* in favour of your purpose.

XVII. If you see *rival nations* rejoicing at the prospect of your disunion with your provinces, and endeavouring to promote it; if they translate, publish, and applaud all the complaints of your discontented colonists, at the same time privately stimulating you to severer measures, let not that *alarm* or offend you. Why should it, since you all mean *the same thing?*

XVIII. If any colony should at their own charge erect a fortress to secure their port against the fleets of a foreign enemy, get your Governor to betray that fortress into your hands. Never think of paying what it cost the country, for that would look, at least, like some regard for justice; but turn it into a citadel to awe the inhabitants and curb their commerce. If they should have lodged in such fortress the very arms they bought and used to aid you in your conquests, seize them all; it will provoke like *ingratitude* added to *robbery.* One admirable effect of these operations will be, to discourage every other colony from erecting such defences, and so your enemies may more easily invade them; to the great disgrace of your government, and of course *the furtherance of your project.*

XIX. Send armies into their country under pretence of protecting the inhabitants; but, instead of garrisoning the forts on their frontiers with those troops, to prevent incursions, demolish those forts, and order the troops into the heart of the country, that the savages may be encouraged to attack the frontiers, and that the troops may be protected by the inhabitants. This will seem to proceed from your ill will or your ignorance, and contribute farther to produce and strengthen an opinion among them, *that you are no longer fit to govern them.*

XX. Lastly, invest the General of your army in the provinces, with great and unconstitutional powers, and free him from the controul of even your own Civil Governors. Let him have troops enow under his command, with all the fortresses in his possession; and who knows but (like

some provincial Generals in the Roman empire, and encouraged by the universal discontent you have produced) he may take it into his head to set up for himself? If he should, and you have carefully practised these few *excellent rules* of mine, take my word for it, all the provinces will immediately join him; and you will that day (if you have not done it sooner) get rid of the trouble of governing them, and all the *plagues* attending their *commerce* and connection from henceforth and for ever.

Q. E. D.

36. *A Parable Against Persecution* (1774)

1. And it came to pass after these things, that Abraham sat in the door of his tent, about the going down of the sun.

2. And behold a man, bent with age, coming from the way of the wilderness, leaning on a staff.

3. And Abraham arose and met him, and said unto him, Turn in, I pray thee, and wash thy feet, and tarry all night, and thou shalt arise early in the morning, and go on thy way.

4. But the man said, Nay, for I will abide under this tree.

5. And Abraham pressed him greatly; so he turned, and they went into the tent; and Abraham baked unleavened bread, and they did eat.

6. And when Abraham saw that the man blessed not God, he said unto him, Wherefore dost thou not worship the most high God, Creator of heaven and earth?

7. And the man answered and said, I do not worship thy God, neither do I call upon his name; for I have made to myself a god, which abideth always in mine house, and provideth me with all things.

8. And Abraham's zeal was kindled against the man, and he arose and fell upon him, and drove him forth with blows into the wilderness.

9. And God called unto Abraham, saying, Abraham, where is the stranger?

10. And Abraham answered and said, Lord, he would not worship thee, neither would he call upon thy name; therefore have I driven him out from before my face into the wilderness.

11. And God said, Have I borne with him these hundred and ninety and eight years, and nourished him, and cloathed him, notwithstanding his rebellion against me; and couldst not thou, who art thyself a sinner, bear with him one night?

12. And Abraham said, Let not the anger of the Lord wax hot against his servant; lo, I have sinned; lo, I have sinned; forgive me, I pray thee.

13. And Abraham arose, and went forth into the wilderness, and sought diligently for the man, and found him, and returned with him to

the tent; and when he had entreated him kindly, he sent him away on the morrow with gifts.

14. And God spake again unto Abraham, saying, For this thy sin shall thy seed be afflicted four hundred years in a strange land;

15. But for thy repentance will I deliver them; and they shall come forth with power, and with gladness of heart, and with much substance.

37. *Articles of Confederation and Perpetual Union*

Philadelphia May 10, 1775

ART. I.

The name of this Confederacy shall henceforth be The United Colonies of North America.

ART. II.

The said United Colonies hereby severally enter into a firm League of Friendship with each other, binding [on] themselves and their Posterity, for [their common] Defence against their Enemies, for the Security of their Liberties and Properties, the Safety of their Persons and Families, and their mutual and general Welfare.

ART. III.

That each Colony shall enjoy and retain as much as it may think fit of its own present Laws, Customs, Rights, Privileges, and peculiar jurisdictions within its own Limits; and may amend its own Constitution, as shall seem best to its own Assembly or Convention.

ART. IV.

That for the more convenient Management of general Interests, Delegates shall be annually elected in each Colony, to meet in General Congress at such Time and Place as shall be agreed on in the next preceding Congress. Only, where particular Circumstances do not make a Duration necessary, it is understood to be a Rule, that each succeeding Congress be held in a different Colony, till the whole Number be gone through; and so in perpetual Rotation; and that accordingly the next [Congress] after the present shall be held at Annapolis, in Maryland.

ART. V.

That the Power and Duty of the Congress shall extend to the Deter-

mining on War and Peace; the entring into Alliances, [sending and receiving ambassadors] (the reconciliation with Great Britain); the settling all Disputes and Differences between Colony and Colony, [about Limits or any other cause,] if such should arise; and the Planting of new Colonies; when proper. The Congress shall also make such general [ordinances] as, tho' necessary to the General Welfare, particular Assemblies cannot be competent to, viz. [those that may relate to our general] Commerce, or general Currency; the establishment of Posts; [and] the Regulation of [our common] Forces. The Congress shall also have the appointment of all General Officers, civil and military, appertaining to the general Confederacy, such as General Treasurer, Secretary, &c.

ART. VI.

All Charges of Wars, and all other general Expences [to be] incurr'd for the common Welfare, shall be defray'd out of a common Treasury, which is to be supply'd by each Colony in proportion to its Number of Male Polls between 16 and 60 Years of Age; the Taxes for paying that Proportion [are] to be laid and levied by [the] Laws of each Colony.

ART. VII.

The Number of Delegates to be elected and sent to the Congress by each Colony shall be regulated, from time to time, by the Number of [such] Polls return'd; so as that one Delegate be allowed for every 5000 Polls. And the Delegates are to bring with them to every Congress an authenticated return of the number of Polls in their respective Provinces, [which is] to be $\frac{\text{triennially}}{\text{annually}}$ taken for the Purposes above mentioned.

ART. VIII.

At every Meeting of the Congress, one half of the Members return'd, exclusive of Proxies, be necessary to make a Quorum; and each Delegate at the Congress shall have a Vote in all Cases, and, if necessarily absent, shall be allow'd to appoint [any other Delegate from the same Colony to be his] Proxy, who may vote for him.

ART. IX.

An executive Council shall be appointed by the Congress [out of their own Body,] consisting of 12 Persons; of whom, in the first appointment, [one third, viz.] (four,) shall be for one Year, (four) for two Years, and (four) for three Years; and as the said terms expire, the Vacancies shall be filled by appointments for three Years; whereby one Third of the Members will be changed annually. And each Person who has served the said Term [of three Years] as Counsellor, shall have a Respite of

three Years, before he can be elected again. This Council, [of whom two thirds shall be a Quorum] in the Recess of Congress, is to execute what shall have been enjoin'd thereby; [to] manage the general [Continental] Business and Interests; to receive applications from foreign Countries; [to] prepare Matters for the Consideration of the Congress; to fill up, [*pro tempore*,] [continental] offices, that fall vacant; and to draw on the General Treasurer for such Monies as may be necessary for general Services, and appropriated by the Congress to such Services.

ART. X.

No Colony shall engage in an offensive War with any Nation of Indians without the Consent of the Congress, or great Council above mentioned, who are first to consider the Justice and Necessity of such War.

ART. XI.

A perpetual Alliance, offensive and defensive, is to be entred into as soon as may be with the Six Nations; their Limits to be ascertain'd and secur'd to them; their Land not to be encroach'd on, nor any private [or Colony] Purchases made of them hereafter to be held good; nor any [Contract for Lands] to be made, but between the Great Council [of the Indians] at Onondaga and the General Congress. The Boundaries and Lands of all the other Indians shall also be [ascertain'd and] secur'd to them [in the same manner,] and Persons appointed to reside among them in proper Districts; who shall take care to prevent Injustice in the Trade with them; [and be enabled at our general Expence,] by occasional small supplies, to relieve their personal Wants and Distresses. And all Purchases from them shall be by the Congress, for the General Advantage and Benefit of the United Colonies.

ART. XII.

As all new Institutions may have Imperfections, which only Time and Experience can discover, it is agreed, that the General Congress, from time [to time,] shall propose such amendments of the Constitution as may be found necessary; which, being approv'd by a Majority of the Colony Assemblies, shall be equally binding with the rest of the Articles of this Confederation.

ART. XIII.

Any and every Colony from Great Britain [upon the continent of North America,] not at present engag'd in our Association, may, upon application [and joining the said Association,] be receiv'd into the Confederation, viz. [Ireland,] the West India Islands, Quebec, St. John's, Nova Scotia, Bermudas, and the East and West Floridas; and shall

[thereupon] be entitled to all the advantages of our Union, mutual Assistance, and Commerce.

These Articles shall be propos'd to the several Provincial Conventions or Assemblies, to be by them consider'd; and if approved, they are advis'd to impower their Delegates to agree to and ratify the same in the ensuing Congress. After which the Union thereby establish'd is to continue firm, till the Terms of Reconciliation proposed in the Petition of the last Congress to the King are agreed to; till the Acts since made, restraining the American Commerce [and Fisheries,] are repeal'd; till Reparation is made for the Injury done to Boston, by shutting up its Port, for the Burning of Charlestown, and for the Expence of this unjust War; and till all the British Troops are withdrawn from America. On the Arrival of these Events, the Colonies return to their former Connection and Friendship with Britain: But on Failure thereof, this Confederation is to be perpetual.

READ BEFORE CONGRESS JULY 21, 1775.

Whereas. It hath pleased God to bless these countries with a most plentiful harvest, whereby much corn and other provisions can be spared to foreign nations who may want the same, Resolved, That [after the expiration of Six Months] from . . . the [20th of July Instant,] . . . [being] the Day appointed by a late Act of the Parliament of Great Britain, for restraining the Trade of the Confederate Colonies, all Custom-Houses [therein] (if the Act be not first rescinded) shall be shut up, and all officers of the same discharged from the Execution of their several Functions, and all the Ports of the said Colonies are hereby declared to be thenceforth open to the Ships of every State in Europe that will admit of our Commerce and protect it; who may [*torn off*] and expose to sale free of all Duties their respective Produce and Manufactures, and every kind of Merchandize, excepting Teas, and the Merchandize of Great Britain, Ireland, and the British West India Islands.

Resolved, That we will to the utmost of our Power, maintain and support this Freedom of Commerce for [two] years certain after its Commencement, any reconciliation between us and Britain notwithstanding; and as much longer beyond that term, as the late Acts of Parliament for restoring the Restraining the Commerce and fisheries, and altering the Laws and Charters of any of the Colonies, shall continue unrepealed.

ENDORSED—No 2. (*Articles of Confederation*) A proposal for opening the ports of N. A. bro^t in by committee—read July 21, 1775—on motion postponed for future consideration.

38. *Morals of Chess*

[1779]

The Game of Chess is not merely an idle Amusement. Several very valuable qualities of the Mind, useful in the course of human Life, are to be acquir'd or strengthened by it, so as to become habits, ready on all occasions. For Life is a kind of Chess, in which we often have Points to gain, & Competitors or Adversaries to contend with; and in which there is a vast variety of good and ill Events, that are in some degree the Effects of Prudence or the want of it. By playing at Chess, then, we may learn,

I. *Foresight*, which looks a little into futurity, and considers the Consequences that may attend an action; for it is continually occurring to the Player, "If I move this piece, what will be the advantages or disadvantages of my new situation? What Use can my Adversary make of it to annoy me? What other moves can I make to support it, and to defend myself from his attacks?"

II. *Circumspection*, which surveys the whole Chessboard, or scene of action; the relations of the several pieces and situations, the Dangers they are respectively exposed to, the several possibilities of their aiding each other, the probabilities that the Adversary may make this or that move, and attack this or the other Piece, and what different Means can be used to avoid his stroke, or turn its consequences against him.

III. *Caution*, not to make our moves too hastily. This habit is best acquired, by observing strictly the laws of the Game; such as, *If you touch a Piece, you must move it somewhere; if you set it down, you must let it stand.* And it is therefore best that these rules should be observed, as the Game becomes thereby more the image of human Life, and particularly of War; in which, if you have incautiously put yourself into a bad and dangerous position, you cannot obtain your Enemy's Leave to withdraw your Troops, and place them more securely, but you must abide all the consequences of your rashness.

And *lastly*, we learn by Chess the habit of not being discouraged by present appearances in the state of our affairs, the habit of hoping for a favourable Change, and that of persevering in the search of resources. The Game is so full of Events, there is such a variety of turns in it, the Fortune of it is so subject to sudden Vicissitudes, and one so frequently, after long contemplation, discovers the means of extricating one's self from a supposed insurmountable Difficulty, that one is encouraged to continue the Contest to the last, in hopes of Victory from our own skill, or at least [of getting a stale mate] from the Negligence of our Adversary. And whoever considers, what in Chess he often sees instances of,

that [particular pieces of] success is [are] apt to produce Presumption, & its consequent Inattention, by which more is afterwards lost than was gain'd by the preceding Advantage, while misfortunes produce more care and attention, by which the loss may be recovered, will learn not to be too much discouraged by any present success of his Adversary, nor to despair of final good fortune upon every little Check he receives in the pursuit of it. . . .

39. Information to Those Who Would Remove to America

[1782]

Many Persons in Europe, having directly or by Letters, express'd to the Writer of this, who is well acquainted with North America, their Desire of transporting and establishing themselves in that Country; but who appear to have formed, thro' Ignorance, mistaken Ideas and Expectations of what is to be obtained there; he thinks it may be useful, and prevent inconvenient, expensive, and fruitless Removals and Voyages of improper Persons, if he gives some clearer and truer Notions of that part of the World, than appear to have hitherto prevailed.

He finds it is imagined by Numbers, that the Inhabitants of North America are rich, capable of rewarding, and dispos'd to reward, all sorts of Ingenuity; that they are at the same time ignorant of all the Sciences, and, consequently, that Strangers, possessing Talents in the Belles-Lettres, fine Arts, &c., must be highly esteemed, and so well paid, as to become easily rich themselves; that there are also abundance of profitable Offices to be disposed of, which the Natives are not qualified to fill; and that, having few Persons of Family among them, Strangers of Birth must be greatly respected, and of course easily obtain the best of those Offices, which will make all their Fortunes; that the Governments too, to encourage Emigrations from Europe, not only pay the Expence of personal Transportation, but give Lands gratis to Strangers, with Negroes to work for them, Utensils of Husbandry, and Stocks of Cattle. These are all wild Imaginations; and those who go to America with Expectations founded upon them will surely find themselves disappointed.

The Truth is, that though there are in that Country few People so miserable as the Poor of Europe, there are also very few that in Europe would be called rich; it is rather a general happy Mediocrity that prevails. There are few great Proprietors of the Soil, and few Tenants; most People cultivate their own Lands, or follow some Handicraft or Merchandise; very few rich enough to live idly upon their Rents or Incomes,

or to pay the high Prices given in Europe for Paintings, Statues, Architecture, and the other Works of Art, that are more curious than useful. Hence the natural Geniuses, that have arisen in America with such Talents, have uniformly quitted that Country for Europe, where they can be more suitably rewarded. It is true, that Letters and Mathematical Knowledge are in Esteem there, but they are at the same time more common than is apprehended; there being already existing nine Colleges or Universities, viz. four in New England, and one in each of the Provinces of New York, New Jersey, Pensilvania, Maryland, and Virginia, all furnish'd with learned Professors; besides a number of smaller Academies; these educate many of their Youth in the Languages, and those Sciences that qualify men for the Professions of Divinity, Law, or Physick. Strangers indeed are by no means excluded from exercising those Professions; and the quick Increase of Inhabitants everywhere gives them a Chance of Employ, which they have in common with the Natives. Of civil Offices, or Employments, there are few; no superfluous Ones, as in Europe; and it is a Rule establish'd in some of the States, that no Office should be so profitable as to make it desirable. The 36th Article of the Constitution of Pennsilvania, runs expressly in these Words; "As every Freeman, to preserve his Independence, (if he has not a sufficient Estate) ought to have some Profession, Calling, Trade, or Farm, whereby he may honestly subsist, there can be no Necessity for, nor Use in, establishing Offices of Profit; the usual Effects of which are Dependance and Servility, unbecoming Freemen, in the Possessors and Expectants; Faction, Contention, Corruption, and Disorder among the People. Wherefore, whenever an Office, thro' Increase of Fees or otherwise, becomes so profitable, as to occasion many to apply for it, the Profits ought to be lessened by the Legislature."

These Ideas prevailing more or less in all the United States, it cannot be worth any Man's while, who has a means of Living at home, to expatriate himself, in hopes of obtaining a profitable civil Office in America; and, as to military Offices, they are at an End with the War, the Armies being disbanded. Much less is it adviseable for a Person to go thither, who has no other Quality to recommend him but his Birth. In Europe it has indeed its Value; but it is a Commodity that cannot be carried to a worse Market than that of America, where people do not inquire concerning a Stranger, *What is he?* but, *What can he do?* If he has any useful Art, he is welcome; and if he exercises it, and behaves well, he will be respected by all that know him; but a mere Man of Quality, who, on that Account, wants to live upon the Public, by some Office or Salary, will be despis'd and disregarded. The Husbandman is in honor there, and even the Mechanic, because their Employments are useful. The People have a saying, that God Almighty is himself a Mechanic, the greatest in the Univers; and he is respected and admired more for the Variety, Ingenuity, and Utility of his Handyworks, than for the

Antiquity of his Family. They are pleas'd with the Observation of a Negro, and frequently mention it, that *Boccarorra* (meaning the White men) *make de black man workee, make de Horse workee, make de Ox workee, make ebery ting workee; only de Hog. He, de hog, no workee; he eat, he drink, he walk about, he go to sleep when he please, he libb like a Gentleman.* According to these Opinions of the Americans, one of them would think himself more oblig'd to a Genealogist, who could prove for him that his Ancestors and Relations for ten Generations had been Ploughmen, Smiths, Carpenters, Turners, Weavers, Tanners, or even Shoemakers, and consequently that they were useful Members of Society; than if he could only prove that they were Gentlemen, doing nothing of Value, but living idly on the Labour of others, mere *fruges consumere nati,** and otherwise *good for nothing,* till by their Death their Estates, like the Carcass of the Negro's Gentleman-Hog, come to be *cut up.*

With regard to Encouragements for Strangers from Government, they are really only what are derived from good Laws and Liberty. Strangers are welcome, because there is room enough for them all, and therefore the old Inhabitants are not jealous of them; the Laws protect them sufficiently, so that they have no need of the Patronage of Great Men; and every one will enjoy securely the Profits of his Industry. But, if he does not bring a Fortune with him, he must work and be industrious to live. One or two Years' residence gives him all the Rights of a Citizen; but the government does not at present, whatever it may have done in former times, hire People to become Settlers, by Paying their Passages, giving Land, Negroes, Utensils, Stock, or any other kind of Emolument whatsoever. In short, America is the Land of Labour, and by no means what the English call *Lubberland,* and the French *Pays de Cocagne,* where the streets are said to be pav'd with half-peck Loaves, the Houses til'd with Pancakes, and where the Fowls fly about ready roasted, crying, *Come eat me!*

Who then are the kind of Persons to whom an Emigration to America may be advantageous? And what are the Advantages they may reasonably expect?

Land being cheap in that Country, from the vast Forests still void of Inhabitants, and not likely to be occupied in an Age to come, insomuch that the Propriety of an hundred Acres of fertile Soil full of Wood may be obtained near the Frontiers, in many Places, for Eight or Ten Guineas, hearty young Labouring Men, who understand the Husbandry of Corn and Cattle, which is nearly the same in that Country as in Europe, may easily establish themselves there. A little Money sav'd of the good Wages they receive there, while they work for others, enables them to buy the Land and begin their Plantation, in which they are assisted by the Good-Will of their Neighbours, and some Credit. Multitudes of poor People from England, Ireland, Scotland, and Germany, have by this

---

* ". . . born merely to eat up the corn."—WATTS. [*Franklin's note.*]

means in a few years become wealthy Farmers, who, in their own Countries, where all the Lands are fully occupied, and the Wages of Labour low, could never have emerged from the poor Condition wherein they were born.

From the salubrity of the Air, the healthiness of the Climate, the plenty of good Provisions, and the Encouragement to early Marriages by the certainty of Subsistence in cultivating the Earth, the Increase of Inhabitants by natural Generation is very rapid in America, and becomes still more so by the Accession of Strangers; hence there is a continual Demand for more Artisans of all the necessary and useful kinds, to supply those Cultivators of the Earth with Houses, and with Furniture and Utensils of the grosser sorts, which cannot so well be brought from Europe. Tolerably good Workmen in any of those mechanic Arts are sure to find Employ, and to be well paid for their Work, there being no Restraints preventing Strangers from exercising any Art they understand, nor any Permission necessary. If they are poor, they begin first as Servants or Journeymen; and if they are sober, industrious, and frugal, they soon become Masters, establish themselves in Business, marry, raise Families, and become respectable Citizens.

Also, Persons of moderate Fortunes and Capitals, who, having a Number of Children to provide for, are desirous of bringing them up to Industry, and to secure Estates for their Posterity, have Opportunities of doing it in America, which Europe does not afford. There they may be taught and practise profitable mechanic Arts, without incurring Disgrace on that Account, but on the contrary acquiring Respect by such Abilities. There small Capitals laid out in Lands, which daily become more valuable by the Increase of People, afford a solid Prospect of ample Fortunes thereafter for those Children. The writer of this has known several Instances of large Tracts of Land, bought, on what was then the Frontier of Pensilvania, for Ten Pounds per hundred Acres, which after 20 years, when the Settlements had been extended far beyond them, sold readily, without any Improvement made upon them, for three Pounds per Acre. The Acre in America is the same with the English Acre, or the Acre of Normandy.

Those, who desire to understand the State of Government in America, would do well to read the Constitutions of the several States, and the Articles of Confederation that bind the whole together for general Purposes, under the Direction of one Assembly, called the Congress. These Constitutions have been printed, by order of Congress, in America; two Editions of them have also been printed in London; and a good Translation of them into French has lately been published at Paris.

Several of the Princes of Europe having of late years, from an Opinion of Advantage to arise by producing all Commodities and Manufactures within their own Dominions, so as to diminish or render useless their Importations, have endeavoured to entice Workmen from other

Countries by high Salaries, Privileges, &c. Many Persons, pretending to be skilled in various great Manufactures, imagining that America must be in Want of them, and that the Congress would probably be dispos'd to imitate the Princes above mentioned, have proposed to go over, on Condition of having their Passages paid, Lands given, Salaries appointed, exclusive Privileges for Terms of years, &c. Such Persons, on reading the Articles of Confederation, will find, that the Congress have no Power committed to them, or Money put into their Hands, for such purposes; and that if any such Encouragement is given, it must be by the Government of some separate State. This, however, has rarely been done in America; and, when it has been done, it has rarely succeeded, so as to establish a Manufacture, which the Country was not yet so ripe for as to encourage private Persons to set it up; Labour being generally too dear there, and Hands difficult to be kept together, every one desiring to be a Master, and the Cheapness of Lands inclining many to leave Trades for Agriculture. Some indeed have met with Success, and are carried on to Advantage; but they are generally such as require only a few Hands, or wherein great Part of the Work is performed by Machines. Things that are bulky, and of so small Value as not well to bear the Expence of Freight, may often be made cheaper in the Country than they can be imported; and the Manufacture of such Things will be profitable wherever there is a sufficient Demand. The Farmers in America produce indeed a good deal of Wool and Flax; and none is exported, it is all work'd up; but it is in the Way of domestic Manufacture, for the Use of the Family. The buying up Quantities of Wool and Flax, with the Design to employ Spinners, Weavers, &c., and form great Establishments, producing Quantities of Linen and Woollen Goods for Sale, has been several times attempted in different Provinces; but those Projects have generally failed, goods of equal Value being imported cheaper. And when the Governments have been solicited to support such Schemes by Encouragements, in Money, or by imposing Duties on Importation of such Goods, it has been generally refused, on this Principle, that, if the Country is ripe for the Manufacture, it may be carried on by private Persons to Advantage; and if not, it is a Folly to think of forcing Nature. Great Establishments of Manufacture require great Numbers of Poor to do the Work for small Wages; these Poor are to be found in Europe, but will not be found in America, till the Lands are all taken up and cultivated, and the Excess of People, who cannot get Land, want Employment. The Manufacture of Silk, they say, is natural in France, as that of Cloth in England, because each Country produces in Plenty the first Material; but if England will have a Manufacture of Silk as well as that of Cloth, and France one of Cloth as well as that of Silk, these unnatural Operations must be supported by mutual Prohibitions, or high Duties on the Importation of each other's Goods; by which means the Workmen are enabled to tax the home Consumer by greater Prices, while the higher Wages they receive

makes them neither happier nor richer, since they only drink more and work less. Therefore the Governments in America do nothing to encourage such Projects. The People, by this Means, are not impos'd on, either by the Merchant or Mechanic. If the Merchant demands too much Profit on imported Shoes, they buy of the Shoemaker; and if he asks too high a Price, they take them of the Merchant; thus the two Professions are checks on each other. The Shoemaker, however, has, on the whole, a considerable Profit upon his Labour in America, beyond what he had in Europe, as he can add to his Price a Sum nearly equal to all the Expences of Freight and Commission, Risque or Insurance, &c., necessarily charged by the Merchant. And the Case is the same with the Workmen in every other Mechanic Art. Hence it is, that Artisans generally live better and more easily in America than in Europe; and such as are good Œconomists make a comfortable Provision for Age, and for their Children. Such may, therefore, remove with Advantage to America. . . .

40. *Remarks Concerning the Savages of North America*

[1784]

Savages we call them, because their Manners differ from ours, which we think the Perfection of Civility; they think the same of theirs.

Perhaps, if we could examine the Manners of different Nations with Impartiality, we should find no People so rude, as to be without any Rules of Politeness; nor any so polite, as not to have some Remains of Rudeness.

The Indian Men, when young, are Hunters and Warriors; when old, Counsellors; for all their Government is by Counsel of the Sages; there is no Force, there are no Prisons, no Officers to compel Obedience, or inflict Punishment. Hence they generally study Oratory, the best Speaker having the most Influence. The Indian Women till the Ground, dress the Food, nurse and bring up the Children, and preserve and hand down to Posterity the Memory of public Transactions. These Employments of Men and Women are accounted natural and honourable. Having few artificial Wants, they have abundance of Leisure for Improvement by Conversation. Our laborious Manner of Life, compared with theirs, they esteem slavish and base; and the Learning, on which we value ourselves, they regard as frivolous and useless. An instance of this occurred at the Treaty of Lancaster, in Pennsylvania, *anno* 1744, between the Government of Virginia and the Six Nations. After the principal Business was settled, the Commissioners from Virginia acquainted the Indians by a Speech, that there was at Williamsburg a College, with a Fund for Ed-

ucating Indian youth; and that, if the Six Nations would send down half a dozen of their young Lads to that College, the Government would take care that they should be well provided for, and instructed in all the Learning of the White People. It is one of the Indian Rules of Politeness not to answer a public Proposition the same day that it is made; they think it would be treating it as a light matter, and that they show it Respect by taking time to consider it, as a Matter important. They therefore deferr'd their Answer till the Day following; when their Speaker began, by expressing their deep Sense of the kindness of the Virginia Government, in making them that Offer; "for we know," says he, "that you highly esteem the kind of Learning taught in those Colleges, and that the Maintenance of our young Men, while with you, would be very expensive to you. We are convinc'd, therefore, that you mean to do us Good by your Proposal; and we thank you heartily. But you, who are wise, must know that different Nations have different Conceptions of things; and you will therefore not take it amiss, if our Ideas of this kind of Education happen not to be the same with yours. We have had some Experience of it; Several of our young People were formerly brought up at the Colleges of the Northern Provinces; they were instructed in all your Sciences; but, when they came back to us, they were bad Runners, ignorant of every means of living in the Woods, unable to bear either Cold or Hunger, knew neither how to build a Cabin, take a Deer, or kill an Enemy, spoke our Language imperfectly, were therefore neither fit for Hunters, Warriors, nor Counsellors; they were totally good for nothing. We are however not the less oblig'd by your kind Offer, tho' we decline accepting it; and, to show our grateful Sense of it, if the Gentlemen of Virginia will send us a Dozen of their Sons, we will take great Care of their Education, instruct them in all we know, and make *Men* of them."

Having frequent Occasions to hold public Councils, they have acquired great Order and Decency in conducting them. The old Men sit in the foremost Ranks, the Warriors in the next, and the Women and Children in the hindmost. The Business of the Women is to take exact Notice of what passes, imprint it in their Memories (for they have no Writing), and communicate it to their Children. They are the Records of the Council, and they preserve Traditions of the Stipulations in Treaties 100 Years back; which, when we compare with our Writings, we always find exact. He that would speak, rises. The rest observe a profound Silence. When he has finish'd and sits down, they leave him 5 or 6 Minutes to recollect, that, if he has omitted any thing he intended to say, or has any thing to add, he may rise again and deliver it. To interrupt another, even in common Conversation, is reckon'd highly indecent. How different this is from the conduct of a polite British House of Commons, where scarce a day passes without some Confusion, that makes the Speaker hoarse in calling *to Order;* and how different from the Mode of Conversation in many polite Companies of Europe, where, if you do not deliver your Sentence with great Rapidity, you are cut off in the middle of it by the

Impatient Loquacity of those you converse with, and never suffer'd to finish it!

The Politeness of these Savages in Conversation is indeed carried to Excess, since it does not permit them to contradict or deny the Truth of what is asserted in their Presence. By this means they indeed avoid Disputes; but then it becomes difficult to know their Minds, or what Impression you make upon them. The Missionaries who have attempted to convert them to Christianity, all complain of this as one of the great Difficulties of their Mission. The Indians hear with Patience the Truths of the Gospel explain'd to them, and give their usual Tokens of Assent and Approbation; you would think they were convinc'd. No such matter. It is mere Civility.

A Swedish Minister, having assembled the chiefs of the Susquehanah Indians, made a Sermon to them, acquainting them with the principal historical Facts on which our Religion is founded; such as the Fall of our first Parents by eating an Apple, the coming of Christ to repair the Mischief, his Miracles and Suffering, &c. When he had finished, an Indian Orator stood up to thank him. "What you have told us," says he, "is all very good. It is indeed bad to eat Apples. It is better to make them all into Cyder. We are much oblig'd by your kindness in coming so far, to tell us these Things which you have heard from your Mothers. In return, I will tell you some of those we have heard from ours. In the Beginning, our Fathers had only the Flesh of Animals to subsist on; and if their Hunting was unsuccessful, they were starving. Two of our young Hunters, having kill'd a Deer, made a Fire in the Woods to broil some Part of it. When they were about to satisfy their Hunger, they beheld a beautiful young Woman descend from the Clouds, and seat herself on that Hill, which you see yonder among the Blue Mountains. They said to each other, it is a Spirit that has smelt our broiling Venison, and wishes to eat of it; let us offer some to her. They presented her with the Tongue; she was pleas'd with the Taste of it, and said, 'Your kindness shall be rewarded; come to this Place after thirteen Moons, and you shall find something that will be of great Benefit in nourishing you and your Children to the latest Generation.' They did so, and, to their Surprise, found Plants they had never seen before; but which, from that ancient time, have been constantly cultivated among us, to our great Advantage. Where her right Hand had touched the Ground, they found Maize; where her left hand had touch'd it, they found Kidney-Beans; and where her Backside had sat on it, they found Tobacco." The good Missionary, disgusted with this idle Tale, said, "What I delivered to you were sacred Truths; but what you tell me is mere Fable, Fiction, and Falshood." The Indian, offended, reply'd, "My brother, it seems your Friends have not done you Justice in your Education; they have not well instructed you in the Rules of Common Civility. You saw that we, who understand and practise those Rules, believ'd all your stories; why do you refuse to believe ours?" . . .

41. *The Internal State of America*

[1785]

Whoever has travelled through the various parts of Europe, and observed how small is the proportion of people in affluence or easy circumstances there, compared with those in poverty and misery,—the few rich and haughty landlords, the multitude of poor, abject, rack-rented, tithe-paying tenants, and half-paid and half-starved ragged laborers,—and views here the happy mediocrity that so generally prevails throughout these states, where the cultivator works for himself, and supports his family in decent plenty, will, methinks, see abundant reason to bless Divine Providence for the evident and great difference in our favor, and be convinced that no nation known to us enjoys a greater share of human felicity.

It is true that in some of the states there are parties and discords; but, let us look back, and ask if we were ever without them. Such will exist wherever there is liberty; and perhaps they help to preserve it. By the collision of different sentiments, sparks of truth are struck out, and political light is obtained. The different factions, which at present divide us, aim all at the public good: the differences are only about the various modes of promoting it. Things, actions, measures, and objects of all kinds, present themselves to the minds of men in such a variety of lights, that it is not possible we should all think alike at the same time on every subject, when hardly the same man retains at all times the same ideas of it. Parties are therefore the common lot of humanity; and ours are by no means more mischievous or less beneficial than those of other countries, nations and ages, enjoying in the same degree the great blessing of political liberty.

42. *The Art of Procuring Pleasant Dreams*

Inscribed to Miss [Shipley], being written at her request

[1786]

As a great part of our life is spent in sleep during which we have sometimes pleasant and sometimes painful dreams, it becomes of some consequence to obtain the one kind and avoid the other; for whether real or imaginary, pain is pain and pleasure is pleasure. If we can sleep without

dreaming, it is well that painful dreams are avoided. If while we sleep we can have any pleasing dream, it is, as the French say, *autant de gagné,* so much added to the pleasure of life.

To this end it is, in the first place, necessary to be careful in preserving health, by due exercise and great temperance; for, in sickness, the imagination is disturbed, and disagreeable, sometimes terrible, ideas are apt to present themselves. Exercise should precede meals, not immediately follow them; the first promotes, the latter, unless moderate, obstructs digestion. If, after exercise, we feed sparingly, the digestion will be easy and good, the body lightsome, the temper cheerful, and all the animal functions performed agreeably. Sleep, when it follows, will be natural and undisturbed; while indolence, with full feeding, occasions nightmares and horrors inexpressible; we fall from precipices, are assaulted by wild beasts, murderers, and demons, and experience every variety of distress. Observe, however, that the quantities of food and exercise are relative things; those who move much may, and indeed ought to eat more; those who use little exercise should eat little. In general, mankind, since the improvement of cookery, eat about twice as much as nature requires. Suppers are not bad, if we have not dined; but restless nights naturally follow hearty suppers after full dinners. Indeed, as there is a difference in constitutions, some rest well after these meals; it costs them only a frightful dream and an apoplexy, after which they sleep till doomsday. Nothing is more common in the newspapers, than instances of people who, after eating a hearty supper, are found dead abed in the morning.

Another means of preserving health, to be attended to, is the having a constant supply of fresh air in your bed-chamber. It has been a great mistake, the sleeping in rooms exactly closed, and in beds surrounded by curtains. No outward air that may come in to you is so unwholesome as the unchanged air, often breathed, of a close chamber. As boiling water does not grow hotter by longer boiling, if the particles that receive greater heat can escape; so living bodies do not putrefy, if the particles, so fast as they become putrid, can be thrown off. Nature expels them by the pores of the skin and the lungs, and in a free, open air they are carried off; but in a close room we receive them again and again, though they become more and more corrupt. A number of persons crowded into a small room thus spoil the air in a few minutes, and even render it mortal, as in the Black Hole at Calcutta. A single person is said to spoil only a gallon of air per minute, and therefore requires a longer time to spoil a chamber-full; but it is done, however, in proportion, and many putrid disorders hence have their origin. It is recorded of Methusalem, who, being the longest liver, may be supposed to have best preserved his health, that he slept always in the open air; for, when he had lived five hundred years, an angel said to him; "Arise, Methusalem, and build thee an house, for thou shalt live yet five hundred years longer." But Methusalem answered, and said, "If I am to live but five hundred years

longer, it is not worth while to build me an house; I will sleep in the air, as I have been used to do." Physicians, after having for ages contended that the sick should not be indulged with fresh air, have at length discovered that it may do them good. It is therefore to be hoped, that they may in time discover likewise, that it is not hurtful to those who are in health, and that we may be then cured of the *aërophobia*, that at present distresses weak minds, and makes them choose to be stifled and poisoned, rather than leave open the window of a bed-chamber, or put down the glass of a coach. . . .

Here, then, is one great and general cause of unpleasing dreams. For when the body is uneasy, the mind will be disturbed by it, and disagreeable ideas of various kinds will in sleep be the natural consequences. . . .

One or two observations more will conclude this little piece. Care must be taken, when you lie down, to dispose your pillow so as to suit your manner of placing your head, and to be perfectly easy; then place your limbs so as not to bear inconveniently hard upon one another, as, for instance, the joints of your ankles; for, though a bad position may at first give but little pain and be hardly noticed, yet a continuance will render it less tolerable, and the uneasiness may come on while you are asleep, and disturb your imagination. These are the rules of the art. But, though they will generally prove effectual in producing the end intended, there is a case in which the most punctual observance of them will be totally fruitless. I need not mention the case to you, my dear friend, but my account of the art would be imperfect without it. The case is, when the person who desires to have pleasant dreams has not taken care to preserve what is necessary above all things,

A GOOD CONSCIENCE.

43. *Speech in the Convention*

At the Conclusion of its Deliberations

[September 17, 1787]

Mr. President,

I confess, that I do not entirely approve of this Constitution at present; but, Sir, I am not sure I shall never approve it; for, having lived long, I have experienced many instances of being obliged, by better information or fuller consideration, to change my opinion even on important subjects, which I once thought right, but found to be otherwise. It is therefore that, the older I grow, the more apt I am to doubt my own judgment of others. Most men, indeed, as well as most sects in religion, think

themselves in possession of all truth, and that wherever others differ from them, it is so far error. Steele, a Protestant, in a dedication, tells the Pope, that the only difference between our two churches in their opinions of the certainty of their doctrine, is, the Romish Church is *infallible,* and the Church of England is *never in the wrong.* But, though many private Persons think almost as highly of their own infallibility as of that of their Sect, few express it so naturally as a certain French Lady, who, in a little dispute with her sister, said, "But I meet with nobody but myself that is *always* in the right." *"Je ne trouve que moi qui aie toujours raison."*

In these sentiments, Sir, I agree to this Constitution, with all its faults,—if they are such; because I think a general Government necessary for us, and there is no *form* of government but what may be a blessing to the people, if well administered; and I believe, farther, that this is likely to be well administered for a course of years, and can only end in despotism, as other forms have done before it, when the people shall become so corrupted as to need despotic government, being incapable of any other. I doubt, too, whether any other Convention we can obtain, may be able to make a better constitution; for, when you assemble a number of men, to have the advantage of their joint wisdom, you inevitably assemble with those men all their prejudices, their passions, their errors of opinion, their local interests, and their selfish views. From such an assembly can a *perfect* production be expected? It therefore astonishes me, Sir, to find this system approaching so near to perfection as it does; and I think it will astonish our enemies, who are waiting with confidence to hear, that our councils are confounded like those of the builders of Babel, and that our States are on the point of separation, only to meet hereafter for the purpose of cutting one another's throats. Thus I consent, Sir, to this Constitution, because I expect no better, and because I am not sure that it is not the best. The opinions I have had of its *errors* I sacrifice to the public good. I have never whispered a syllable of them abroad. Within these walls they were born, and here they shall die. If every one of us, in returning to our Constituents, were to report the objections he has had to it, and endeavour to gain Partisans in support of them, we might prevent its being generally received, and thereby lose all the salutary effects and great advantages resulting naturally in our favour among foreign nations, as well as among ourselves, from our real or apparent unanimity. Much of the strength and efficiency of any government, in procuring and securing happiness to the people, depends on *opinion,* on the general opinion of the goodness of that government, as well as of the wisdom and integrity of its governors. I hope, therefore, for our own sakes, as a part of the people, and for the sake of our posterity, that we shall act heartily and unanimously in recommending this Constitution, wherever our Influence may extend, and turn our future thoughts and endeavours to the means of having it *well administered.*

On the whole, Sir, I cannot help expressing a wish, that every member of the Convention who may still have objections to it, would with me on this occasion doubt a little of his own infallibility, and, to make *manifest* our *unanimity*, put his name to this Instrument.

[Then the motion was made for adding the last formula, viz. "Done in convention by the Unanimous Consent," &c.; which was agreed to and added accordingly.]

44. *Queries and Remarks*

Respecting Alterations in the Constitution of Pennsylvania

[The following "Queries and Remarks" are Franklin's marginal comments in reply to an article, "Hints for the Members of the Convention," published in the *Federal Gazette*, Nov. 3, 1789, when a revision of the Pennsylvania constitution was in view. Franklin's comments are printed in *roman type*, following extracts from the *Gazette* article which are printed in *italic type*.]

I. Of the Executive Branch.

"Your executive should consist of a single Person."

On this I would ask, Is he to have no council? How is he to be informed of the state and circumstances of the different counties, their wants, their abilities, their dispositions, and the characters of the principal people, respecting their integrity, capacities, and qualifications for offices? Does not the present construction of our executive provide well for these particulars? And, during the number of years it has existed, have its errors or failures in answering the end of its appointment been more or greater than might have been expected from a single person?

"But an individual is more easily watched and controlled than any greater number."

On this I would ask, Who is to watch and controul him? and by what means is he to be controuled? Will not those means, whatever they are, and in whatever body vested, be subject to the same inconveniencies of expence, delay, obstruction of good intentions, etc., which are objected to the present executive?

II. The Duration of the Appointment.

*"This should be governed by the following principles, the indepen-
dency of the magistrate, and the stability of his administration; neither
of which can be secured but by putting both beyond the reach of every
annual gust of folly and of faction."*

On this it may be asked, Ought it not also to be put beyond the reach
of every triennial, quinquennial, or septennial gust of folly and of faction,
and, in short, beyond the reach of folly and of faction at any period
whatever? Does not this reasoning aim at establishing a monarchy at
least for life, like that of Poland? or to prevent the inconveniencies such
as that kingdom is subject to in a new election on every decease, does it
not point to an hereditary succession? Are the freemen of Pennsylvania
convinced, from a view of the history of such governments, that it will
be for their advantage to submit themselves to a government of such
construction?

III. On the Legislative Branch.

*"A plural legislature is as necessary to good government as a single
executive. It is not enough that your legislature should be numerous; it
should also be divided. Numbers alone are not a sufficient barrier against
the impulses of passion, the combinations of interest, the intrigues of
faction, the haste of folly, or the spirit of encroachment. One division
should watch over and controul the other, supply its wants, correct its
blunders, and cross its designs, should they be criminal or erroneous.
Wisdom is the specific quality of the legislature, grows out of the number
of the body, and is made up of the portions of sense and knowledge
which each member brings to it."*

On this it may be asked, May not the wisdom brought to the legislature
by each member be as effectual a barrier against the impulses of passion, etc., when the members are united in one body, as when they are
divided? If one part of the legislature may controul the operations of the
other, may not the impulses of passion, the combinations of interest,
the intrigues of faction, the haste of folly, or the spirit of encroachment
in one of those bodies obstruct the good proposed by the other, and
frustrate its advantages to the public? Have we not experienced in this
colony, when a province under the government of the proprietors, the
mischiefs of a second branch existing in the proprietary family, countenanced and aided by an aristocratic council? How many delays and what

great expences were occasioned in carrying on the public business; and what a train of mischiefs, even to the preventing of the defence of the province during several years, when distressed by an Indian war, by the iniquitous demand that the proprietary property should be exempt from taxation! The wisdom of a few members in one single legislative body, may it not frequently stifle bad motions in their infancy, and so prevent their being adopted? whereas, if those wise men, in case of a double legislature, should happen to be in that branch wherein the motion did not arise, may it not, after being adopted by the other, occasion lengthy disputes and contentions between the two bodies, expensive to the public, obstructing the public business, and promoting factions among the people, many tempers naturally adhering obstinately to measures they have once publicly adopted? Have we not seen, in one of our neighbouring states, a bad measure, adopted by one branch of the legislature for want of the assistance of some more intelligent members who had been packed into the other, occasion many debates, conducted with much asperity, which could not be settled but by an expensive general appeal to the people? And have we not seen, in another neighbouring state, a similar difference between the two branches occasioning long debates and contentions, whereby the state was prevented for many months enjoying the advantage of having senators in the Congress of the United States? And has our present legislative in one assembly committed any errors of importance, which they have not remedied, or may not easily remedy; more easily, probably, than if divided into two branches? And if the wisdom brought by the members to the Assembly is divided into two branches, may it not be too weak in each to support a good measure, or obstruct a bad one? The division of the legislature into two or three branches in England, was it the product of wisdom, or the effect of necessity, arising from the preëxisting prevalence of an odious feudal system? which government, notwithstanding this division, is now become in fact an absolute monarchy; since the King, by bribing the representatives with the people's money, carries, by his ministers, all the measures that please him; which is equivalent to governing without a parliament, and renders the machine of government much more complex and expensive, and, from its being more complex, more easily put out of order.

Has not the famous political fable of the snake, with two heads and one body, some useful instruction contained in it? She was going to a brook to drink, and in her way was to pass thro' a hedge, a twig of which opposed her direct course; one head chose to go on the right side of the twig, the other on the left; so that time was spent in the contest, and, before the decision was completed, the poor snake died with thirst.

"Hence it is that the two branches should be elected by persons differently qualified; and in short, that, as far as possible, they should be made to represent different interests. Under this reasoning I would

establish a legislature of two houses. The upper should represent the property; the lower the population of the state. The upper should be chosen by freemen possessing in lands and houses one thousand pounds; the lower by all such as had resided four years in the country, and paid taxes. The first should be chosen for four, the last for two years. They should in authority be coequal."

Several questions may arise upon this proposition. 1st. What is the proportion of freemen possessing lands and houses of one thousand pounds' value, compared to that of freemen whose possessions are inferior? Are they as one to ten? Are they even as one to twenty? I should doubt whether they are as one to fifty. If this minority is to chuse a body expressly to controul that which is to be chosen by the great majority of the freemen, what have this great majority done to forfeit so great a portion of their right in elections? Why is this power of controul, contrary to the spirit of all democracies, to be vested in a minority, instead of a majority? Then is it intended, or is it not, that the rich should have a vote in the choice of members for the lower house, while those of inferior property are deprived of the right of voting for members of the upper house? And why should the upper house, chosen by a minority, have equal power with the lower chosen by a majority? Is it supposed that wisdom is the necessary concomitant of riches, and that one man worth a thousand pounds must have as much wisdom as twenty who have each only 999; and why is property to be represented at all?

Suppose one of our Indian nations should now agree to form a civil society; each individual would bring into the stock of the society little more property than his gun and his blanket, for at present he has no other. We know that when one of them has attempted to keep a few swine, he has not been able to maintain a property in them, his neighbours thinking they have a right to kill and eat them whenever they want provision, it being one of their maxims that hunting is free for all; the accumulation therefore of property in such a society, and its security to individuals in every society, must be an effect of the protection afforded to it by the joint strength of the society, in the execution of its laws. Private property therefore is a creature of society, and is subject to the calls of that society, whenever its necessities shall require it, even to its last farthing; its contributions therefore to the public exigencies are not to be considered as conferring a benefit on the publick, entitling the contributors to the distinctions of honour and power, but as the return of an obligation previously received, or the payment of a just debt. The combinations of civil society are not like those of a set of merchants, who club their property in different proportions for building and freighting a ship, and may therefore have some right to vote in the disposition of the voyage in a greater or less degree according to their respective contributions; but the important ends of civil society, and the personal securities

of life and liberty, these remain the same in every member of the society; and the poorest continues to have an equal claim to them with the most opulent, whatever difference time, chance, or industry may occasion in their circumstances. On these considerations, I am sorry to see the signs this paper I have been considering affords, of a disposition among some of our people to commence an aristocracy, by giving the rich a predominancy in government, a choice peculiar to themselves in one half the legislature to be proudly called the UPPER house, and the other branch, chosen by the majority of the people, degraded by the denomination of the LOWER; and giving to this upper house a permanency of four years, and but two to the lower. I hope, therefore, that our representatives in the convention will not hastily go into these innovations, but take the advice of the prophet, "*Stand in the old ways, view the ancient paths, consider them well, and be not among those that are given to change.*"

45. *An Address to the Public*

From the Pennsylvania Society for Promoting the Abolition of Slavery, and the Relief of Free Negroes Unlawfully Held in Bondage.

It is with peculiar satisfaction we assure the friends of humanity, that, in prosecuting the design of our association, our endeavours have proved successful, far beyond our most sanguine expectations.

Encouraged by this success, and by the daily progress of that luminous and benign spirit of liberty, which is diffusing itself throughout the world, and humbly hoping for the continuance of the divine blessing on our labours, we have ventured to make an important addition to our original plan, and do therefore earnestly solicit the support and assistance of all who can feel the tender emotions of sympathy and compassion, or relish the exalted pleasure of beneficence.

Slavery is such an atrocious debasement of human nature, that its very extirpation, if not performed with solicitous care, may sometimes open a source of serious evils.

The unhappy man, who has long been treated as a brute animal, too frequently sinks beneath the common standard of the human species. The galling chains, that bind his body, do also fetter his intellectual faculties, and impair the social affections of his heart. Accustomed to move like a mere machine, by the will of a master, reflection is suspended; he has not the power of choice; and reason and conscience have but little influence over his conduct, because he is chiefly governed by

the passion of fear. He is poor and friendless; perhaps worn out by extreme labour, age, and disease.

Under such circumstances, freedom may often prove a misfortune to himself, and prejudicial to society.

Attention to emancipated black people, it is therefore to be hoped, will become a branch of our national policy; but, as far as we contribute to promote this emancipation, so far that attention is evidently a serious duty incumbent on us, and which we mean to discharge to the best of our judgment and abilities.

To instruct, to advise, to qualify those, who have been restored to freedom, for the exercise and enjoyment of civil liberty, to promote in them habits of industry, to furnish them with employments suited to their age, sex, talents, and other circumstances, and to procure their children an education calculated for their future situation in life; these are the great outlines of the annexed plan, which we have adopted, and which we conceive will essentially promote the public good, and the happiness of these our hitherto too much neglected fellow-creatures.

A plan so extensive cannot be carried into execution without considerable pecuniary resources, beyond the present ordinary funds of the Society. We hope much from the generosity of enlightened and benevolent freemen, and will gratefully receive any donations or subscriptions for this purpose, which may be made to our treasurer, James Starr, or to James Pemberton, chairman of our committee of correspondence.

Signed, by order of the Society,
B. FRANKLIN, *President.*

Philadelphia, 9th of
November, 1789.

46. *A Printer's Epitaph* (1728)

The Body of
B Franklin Printer,
(Like the Cover of an old Book
Its Contents torn out
And stript of its Lettering & Gilding)
Lies here, Food for Worms.
But the Work shall not be lost;
For it will, (as he believ'd) appear once more,
In a new and more elegant Edition
Revised and corrected,
By the Author.

PART II

JOHN ADAMS

(*1735–1826*)

Some thirty years after the birth of Benjamin Franklin, another New Englander was born in a pleasant but plain farmhouse in Braintree, only a short distance from Boston. He was John Adams, one of the most learned and profoundly reflective of all American statesmen and one who must be credited with being a "founding father" in two senses. As a leader of the American revolutionary movement, and of the subsequent foundation of the American Republic, Adams proved himself as the greatest constitutional thinker and statesman of the period. And as one might almost say the deliberate founder of the illustrious Adams family he continued to influence the quality of his country's character and culture long beyond the period of his mortal journey. That Adams predetermined the dedication of the subsequent Adamses to his beloved America is clear from many indications. One may read as typical of his spirit the following prophetic peek into the future, which he wrote home from Paris to his adored and adoring wife Abigail in 1780: "The science of government is my duty to study, more than all other sciences; the arts of legislation and administration and negotiation ought to take place of, indeed to exclude in a manner all other arts. I must study politics and war that my sons may have liberty to study mathematics and philosophy, geography, natural history and naval architecture, navigation, commerce, and agriculture, in order to give their children a right to study painting, poetry, music, architecture. . . ."

Yet this ardent patriot, who once instructed a friend that he wished to be known as "John Yankee" to counter-distinguish himself from "John Bull," travelled an essentially lonely political path for the forty years of public service when he was conspicuously in the limelight of leadership. A man who could not be had for any price, but whose reputation for blunt and caustic dealings with associates was fully deserved, Adams felt that the American people had "repudiated" him when they did not return him to the Presidency in 1800. This feeling settled into something akin to a mood of persecution, as he proceeded in the years of his retire-

ment to review his own sacrifices and service for the American cause, and the signs he read that not he but others—Franklin, Washington and Jefferson—would be elevated to the Pantheon of Revolutionary gods and American culture heroes. Brooding over the "mean tricks and arti- fices" of the men he called his "fellow worms," Adams forecast that a dim portrait of himself would be transmitted to posterity. "Mausoleums, Statues, Monuments will never be erected to me," he bitterly confided to a friend. "Panegyrical romances will never be written, nor flattering ora- tions spoken to transmit me to Posterity in brilliant colors."

Sad to say, for something like a century after his death, these purple predictions appeared to be virtually self-fulfilling. Neither historians nor the American people he had so paternally looked after paid him tribute for his great statesmanship and his indispensable contribution to the logic of independence and republican government in the states. One could not find a statue to him in Washington, the city over which he had presided as the first occupant of the White House, nor in his native Massachusetts for whose interests he had fought as fiercely as a mother lion guards her cubs. Remembered only for his failings—his maladroit politicianship, his explosive temper and oft-confessed vanity—he was frequently described in the language of his political enemies as the "Duke of Braintree" or "His Rotundity;" supposedly, in any case, a dull dog and parochial Yankee, or a regular New England Puritan in the censorious, vindictive and narrow sense of the word.

Much of this malicious caricature and faulty understanding of Adams is at long last being exposed. In recent years he has emerged from the un- justified obscurity of the past and as the fuller and unvarnished record of his writings is being made available in print (in the new Butterfield edi- tion of his papers) his stock is rising at a rapid rate. Grave faults and superb virtues and talents co-existed in this engrossing man. But he and his ideas stubbornly resist standard labels and general descriptions. They have not yet been caught in all their shifting subtlety, comprehensive thrust, and concrete context. For Adams is in turn classicist, humanist, Puritan, child of the Enlightenment, sceptic, Biblical prophet and sage. But he is also angry and contemptuous of the "absurdities," pretensions, frauds and theological dogma in the Bible; while similarly he repudiated, or deliberately exposed, the shortcomings of every one of the other philo- sophic and intellectual traditions to which, on other occasions, he laid some claim. The same baffling uncertainty surrounds his political writings if one wishes to place them in a pattern. Thus he is both a revolutionary, a modernist; and an "ancient," a conservative with relatively rigid pre- scriptions about order and the containment of power. Actually, his imagination is captured by the world of Shakespearean creation: the boiling, seething dynamism, the plots and counterplots, the endemic tragedy and the gusty humor that exist there create resonances in Adams that one can trace without much trouble in his private and public writ-

ings and in what he himself reported about his behavior on numerous occasions. When these Shakespearean roles and moods come off well, Adams is majestic, irresistible; when they imperfectly cover a Yankee twang, a proper Bostonian myopia, a small and vain man's posturing and preaching, they render the protagonist almost ridiculous.

Three things in his crisis-ridden yet glorious life of ninety-one years he loved with unflagging ardor: his wife and children, his country, and "the divine science of politics." Mordant and devastating in his recurring doubts about virtually all else, these three ideal loyalties gave his life its deepest meaning. His marriage to Abigail Smith was not the product of love at first sight, though she was, as we may see in portraits, a sightly and spirited young woman when he courted her. Her courage and keen good sense must be joined to her husband's youthful habit of calling her "Miss Adorable" to suggest the formidable array of her satisfactory traits as a partner through life. John Quincy Adams, their eldest and favorite son, wrote of his mother after her death in 1818: "She had been fifty-four years the delight of my father's heart, the sweetener of all his toils, the comforter of all his sorrows, the sharer and heightener of all his joys. It was but the last time when I saw my father that he told me . . . that in all the vicissitudes of his fortunes, through all the good report and evil report of the world, in all his struggles and in all his sorrows, the affectionate participation and cheering encouragement of his wife had been his never-failing support, without which he was sure he should never have lived through them . . . Oh God! may I die the death of the righteous, and may my last end be like hers!"

This elegiac tribute acquires particular value as a counter-balance to the traumatic heart-burnings and agonies of Adams' long pilgrimage. These he sets forth in painful detail in his Diary and correspondence, engaging in remorseless self-scrutiny as well as pitiless execution of the characters of men who have crossed or disappointed him. The masochistic accusations he directed at himself take place and turn-about with exultant and equally immoderate estimates of his single-handed role in engineering the freedom, safety and power of the new American nation. A characteristic passage in his Diary gives us low man and tribal chief on the totem pole in one composite flash: "There is a feebleness and a languor in my nature. My mind and body both partake of this weakness. By my physical constitution, I am but an ordinary man. The times alone have destined me to fame—and even these have not been able to give me much. Yet some great events, some cutting expression, some mean hypocrisies, have at times thrown this assemblage of sloth, sleep and littleness into rage a little like a lion."

Actually, this constructive rage was manifest in the battles waged against men he believed to be misleading his country or betraying its true interests, as he had also gathered and used his vast powers in formulating the strongest intellectual case for "the liberty side" in his

*native Massachusetts Bay colony against the "prerogative side," which
was tied to the interests of the British Empire. Jefferson's judgment that
he was a "Colossus" in the debate on Independence, the "Atlas of Independence" in carrying the burden of its defense on the floor of the
Continental Congress, is echoed by the testimony of many others. Nor
was this the only great occasion for John Adams, lion. Other heroic
stands were his early campaign to instruct leaders in the various states as
the ends and means of "gliding" quickly and smoothly into orderly republican systems of government. His own detailed draft of a constitution
for Massachusetts in 1780 was a major political achievement, one which
has endured longer and served as a model for more state constitutions
than any other in the land. As a diplomat, Adams had to meet the merciless test of representing a beggarly new nation at the proudest and most
ornate courts of the pre-revolutionary European world. In Paris he was
checkmated by the universal prestige and enormous influence and skill of
Franklin—for which he never forgave his serene and secure older col-
league. But in Holland he literally conducted a campaign of publicity
and personal diplomacy on his own initiative and won the United States
sympathy, official recognition at The Hague, plus the golden boon of
substantial loans from Dutch banking houses. In London, he spent three
trying years in the unenviable role of first minister from the United States
to England, where, after a gracious reception by George III, he was
systematically treated with "dry decency and cold civility" in a deliberate
effort to freeze him out of significant diplomatic contact. Yet in this
hostile setting Adams made an unorthodox move, that in terms of hind-
sight at least appears a brilliant gamble—and which he won.*

*Since his official duties were perforce contained, and news of unrest
and Shays' Rebellion at home was alarming, Adams set to work on an
inquiry into the fundamentals of political science that would become his
three-volume masterpiece, A DEFENCE OF THE CONSTITUTIONS
OF GOVERNMENT OF THE UNITED STATES. He translated lengthy
sections from every work of political history and political philosophy that
he did not easily come to in an English version and he wove together
these proofs of the experience of men in other ages and climes with his
own distinctive criticisms and original reflections. He believed he had
uncovered the fundamental law of peaceful politics—the "political trinity
in unity" or in plainer words, the "balance" by which the several powers
of government would be carefully separated, and the eternal three orders
of society, faithfully represented in the Legislature, would each be
checked and balanced against the others. The grand objective of his
political "science" was to arrange republican government. Since Adams
referred in this book to the "gentlemen" and the "simplemen," and
warned of the evils flowing from popular democracy, as well as of the
corruptions masquerading under the banner of a pretended equality and
fraternity, he could be read at one and the same time as a conservative*

critic of the impending French Revolution and a reactionary would-be "Aristocrat" repudiating the faith of his own revolutionary principles of 1776.

His normal tendency to speak and write in excited and exaggerated terms only increased the ambiguity of the position he was taking in the Defence. On the whole, Adams was urging that America not abandon its republican constitutions and government for a sentimental pure majoritarian principle, on the ground that this "total" will in society would bring despotism or anarchy. Proud that something new under the sun had been launched in America, he thought it elementary prudence and wisdom to anticipate that it would not be free of the deterioration and degeneration of all previous political forms in history. He understood that he was preaching against the tide of sentiment and hope nourished by his countrymen; but he felt that his unwelcome mission might be the medicine that cures. There was self-deception perhaps on both sides of the equation—on the part of those who imagined that all men were born equal and could live as equals in all respects; and on the part of the author of this political treatise who believed that every device and symbol encouraging equality in a free society was nothing but a fraud and a covert bid for a new power alignment!

Some years later, John Adams confessed to his friend Benjamin Rush that he had become disgusted with the word "rebel," as he saw the rash theories and unruly practices which that honorific term often justified. The mob rule which he had always hated as a young lawyer, the repudiation of debts which outraged his sense of honesty and appeared to him to threaten the precious and universal right of property, and the dangerous illusion that liberty meant absolvement from responsibility were all compresent in what he detested in this snowballing movement towards more democracy and more rebellion. He therefore went to pains to make clear that he had never endorsed such principles of irresponsibility, and re-interpreted his revolutionary role. He wrote: "I was determined never to rebel, as much as I was to resist rebellion against the fundamental privileges of the Constitution, whenever British generals or governors should begin it."

Sentiments like these made his political fate in the critical decade of the 1790's and his lot was cast as one of the leaders of the Federalist Party. He and his good friend Thomas Jefferson, with whom he had become intimate in Paris, were now estranged. Yet Adams was far from being in accord with the other big men of his own party, and especially Alexander Hamilton. As Vice-President under Washington and as second President of the United States, Adams kept his own counsel. Many illiberal measures and attitudes while he was President he thought were dictated by the danger the country faced of war with France. Consequently, the stellar measure of his Administration that he said he wished to be remembered for was that he had brought about "peace with France

in 1800." His intense pride in this achievement was partly due to his knowledge that he had laid his political future on the line for the country's best interest. But Hamilton and his cohorts and supporters would not forgive his single-handed, successful olive-branch statesmanship and in effect they scuttled Federalist chances in the election rather than support candidate Adams.

Although Adams never became a well-tempered clavichord of a man, he mellowed and deepened in thought and spirit in the years he spent in retirement at Quincy. The re-opened friendship with Thomas Jefferson that enlivened the last fourteen years of his life provided the occasion for his most brilliant and memorable letters. Religion, friendship, politics, history, the classics, war and peace, revolution and non-violent evolution, aristocracy and democracy, the meaning of equality, shared experiences of all sorts, and the vast literature of their past and present reading were the subjects of this matchless correspondence. The sense of their common devotion to the American experiment and the American union, its glory unshaken by the severe trials it had passed through since the movement for independence, sustained the two old friends. Even the pungent reproofs that Adams continued to pen, almost to the last, in a mocking, satiric style—as when he reduced the old contests between the Republican and Federalist parties to the single preoccupation: "the fear that they shall lose the elections and consequently the Loaves and Fishes." In this vein he had tried earlier to minimize the real differences of principle that separated Jefferson and himself, scoffing that "Jefferson and Rush were for liberty and straight hair. I thought curled hair was as republican as straight." Yet in a more realistic mood, he challenged Jefferson with the statement: "Whether you or I were right, posterity must judge."

No judgment, however, need be rendered concerning their mutual dedication to the freedom, strength and creativity of America. Adams had once written in the margin of a book: "National pride is as natural as self-love, or family pride, the pride of one's city, country, or province . . . It is at present the bulwark of defense to all nations. When it is lost, a nation sinks below the character of man." This he knew, and knew surely. Of the more speculative concerns of philosophical inquiry, he grew progressively more sceptical. Deeply shaken after reading a ponderous study on comparative religions, he wrote to his son, John Quincy Adams, in the spirit of a dauntless seeker: "Let the human Mind loose. It must be loose. It will be loose. Superstition and despotism cannot confine. And the conclusion must be that Musquito's are not competent to dogmatise." Most poignant of all is the statement of this restless man who had set out to unlock the secrets of man's nature, human reason, and politics: "What is Philosophy but the study of the World and its cause? Man is a riddle to himself. The World is a riddle to him. He puzzles to find a Key and this puzzle is called Philosophy." The morality which now approved itself to him he said he could reduce to simple terms: "Be just and good."

By a coincidence that even a Shakespeare might fear to create, as the fiftieth anniversary of the Declaration of Independence approached, each of its two great sponsors was still clinging to the last days of his life. Naturally, each man was invited to say something about the momentous document. Adams, in a final recognition of the miraculous power that distinguished man from merely animal nature, wrote: "A memorable epoch in the annals of the human race; destined in future history to form the brightest or the blackest page, according to the use or the abuse of those political institutions by which they shall in time to come be shaped by the human mind." He was asked for a toast, by the committeeman who was deputed to visit him. "I give you," he said, "Independence Forever!" Urged to say something more, he refused another word. July fourth found Jefferson and Adams dying, each man humble in his pride, each, it appears, thinking of the other and of the community together they had served.

Autobiography

1. *Answers to a Biographical Questionnaire*

To Skelton Jones

Quincy, March 11, 1809

I received yesterday your favor of the month of August 1808, and if the following answers to your questions will be any gratification to your curiosity, or any aid to your work, they are at your service.

1. My father was John Adams, the son of Joseph Adams, the son of another Joseph Adams, the son of Henry Adams, who all lived independent New England farmers, and died and lie buried in this town of Quincy, formerly called Braintree, and more anciently still Mount Wollaston. My mother was Susanna Boylston, daughter of Peter Boylston, of Brookline, the oldest son of Thomas Boylston, a physician who came from England in 1656, and purchased a farm in that town near Boston.

2. I was born in Quincy, on the 19th of October 1735.

3. My early life and education were, first at the public Latin school in the then town of Braintree; then at a private academy under Mr. Joseph Marsh, within three doors of my father's house; then at Harvard College, in Cambridge, where, after four years' studies, I received a degree as bachelor of arts in 1755, and, after three years more, that of master of arts.

4. Among these accidents, the principal that I recollect were certain theological controversies, which were conducted, as I thought, with an uncharitable spirit of intolerance that convinced me I should be forever unfit for the profession of divinity, and determined me to the profession of the law. To this cause were added many compliments from my academical companions, who endeavored to make me believe that I had a voice and a tongue, as well as a face and front, for a public speaker, and that I was better fitted for the bar than the pulpit. For the faculty of medicine I never had any inclination, having an aversion to sickrooms and no fondness for rising at all hours of the night to visit patients.

5. Mr. Maccarty, a clergyman of Worcester, authorized by the select-

men, at the commencement at college, in 1755, happening to be pleased with the performance of my part in the public exhibition, engaged me to take the charge of the Latin school in that town, where in a few months I entered as a clerk in the office of Colonel James Putnam, a counsellor at law in very large practice and of very respectable talents and information. Here, as I boarded in his family, I had opportunities of conversing with all the judges, lawyers, and many others of the principal characters of the province, and heard their speculations upon public affairs. This was highly delightful to me, because my father, who had a public soul, had drawn my attention to public affairs. From my earliest infancy I had listened with eagerness to his conversation with his friends during the whole expedition to Cape Breton, in 1745, and I had received very grievous impressions of the injustice and ingratitude of Great Britain towards New England in that whole transaction, as well as many others before and after it, during the years 1754, 1755, 1756, and 1757. The conduct of Generals Shirley, Braddock, Abercrombie, Webb, and above all Lord Loudon, which were daily discussed in Mr. Putnam's family, gave me such an opinion and such a disgust of the British government that I heartily wished the two countries were separated for ever. I was convinced we could defend ourselves against the French, and manage our affairs better without, than with, the English. In 1758 and 1759, Mr. Pitt, coming into power, sent Wolfe, and Amherst, whom I saw with his army as they passed through Worcester, and these conquered Cape Breton and Quebec. I then rejoiced that I was an Englishman, and gloried in the name of Briton. But, alas! how short was my triumph in British wisdom and justice! In February 1761, I heard the argument in the council chamber in Boston upon writs of assistance, and there saw that Britain was determined to let nothing divert me from my fidelity to my country.

6. An inflexible course of studies and labors, to promote, preserve, and secure that independence of my country which I so early saw to be inevitable, against all parties, factions, and nations that have shown themselves unfriendly to it.

7. The 4th of March 1801. The causes of my retirement are to be found in the writings of Freneau, Markoe, Ned Church, Andrew Brown, Paine, Callender, Hamilton, Cobbett, and John Ward Fenno and many others, but more especially in the circular letters of members of Congress from the Southern and Middle States. Without a complete collection of all these libels, no faithful history of the last twenty years can ever be written, nor any adequate account given of the causes of my retirement from public life.

8. My life for the last eight years has been spent in the bosom of my family, surrounded by my children and grandchildren; on my farm, in my garden and library. But in all this there is nothing interesting to the public.

9. Five feet, seven or nine inches, I really know not which.

10. I have one head, four limbs, and five senses, like any other man, and nothing peculiar in any of them.

11. I have been married forty-four years.

12. To Miss Abigail Smith, on the 25th of October 1764, in her father's house at Weymouth, the next town to this, and by her father, who was a clergyman.

13. Three sons and a daughter. . . .

15. My temper in general has been tranquil, except when any instance of extraordinary madness, deceit, hypocrisy, ingratitude, treachery, or perfidy has suddenly struck me. Then I have always been irascible enough, and in three or four instances, very extraordinary ones, too much so. The storm, however, never lasted for half an hour, and anger never rested in the bosom. . . .

17. Under my first Latin master, who was a churl, I spent my time in shooting, skating, swimming, flying kites, and every other boyish exercise and diversion I could invent. Never mischievous. Under my second master, who was kind, I began to love my books and neglect my sports.

18. From that time I have been too studious. At college, next to the ordinary routine of classical studies, mathematics and natural philosophy were my favorite pursuits. When I began to study law, I found ethics, the law of nations, the civil law, the common law, a field too vast to admit of many other inquiries. Classics, history, and philosophy have, however, never been wholly neglected to this day.

19. Such persons are all dead, or so old as to be incapable of writing any long details.

20. I have no miniature, and have been too much abused by painters ever to sit to anyone again.

2. "My Public Life"

To Benjamin Rush

Quincy, April 12, 1809

I will give you a few hints among a thousand.

1. When I went home to my family in May 1770 from the town meeting in Boston, which was the first I had ever attended, and where I had been chosen in my absence, without any solicitation, one of their representatives, I said to my wife, "I have accepted a seat in the House of Representatives, and thereby have consented to my own ruin, to your ruin, and the ruin of our children. I give you this warning, that you may prepare your mind for your fate." She burst into tears but instantly cried

out in a transport of magnanimity, "Well, I am willing in this cause to run all risks with you, and be ruined with you, if you are ruined." These were times, my friend, in Boston, which tried women's souls as well as men's.

2. I saw the awful prospect before me and my country in all its horrors, and, notwithstanding all my vanity, was conscious of a thousand defects in my own character as well as health, which made me despair of going through and weathering the storms in which I must be tossed.

3. In the same year, 1770, my sense of equity and humanity impelled me, against a torrent of unpopularity, and the inclination of all my friends, to engage in defence of Captain Preston and the soldiers. My successful exertions in that cause, though the result was perfectly conformable to law and justice, brought upon me a load of indignation and unpopularity, which I knew would never be forgotten, nor entirely forgiven. The Boston newspapers to this day show that my apprehensions were well founded.

4. You can testify for me that in 1774 my conduct in Congress drew upon me the jealousy and aversion, not only of the tories in Congress, who were neither few nor feeble, but of the whole body of Quakers and proprietary gentlemen in Pennsylvania. I have seen and felt the consequences of these prejudices to this day.

5. I call you to witness that I was the first member of Congress who ventured to come out in public, as I did in January 1776, in my "Thoughts on Government, in a letter from a gentleman to his friend," that is, Mr. Wythe, in favor of a government in three branches, with an independent judiciary. This pamphlet, you know, was very unpopular. No man appeared in public to support it but yourself. You attempted in the public papers to give it some countenance, but without much success. Franklin leaned against it. Dr. Young, Mr. Timothy Matlack, and Mr. James Cannon, and I suppose Mr. George Bryan were alarmed and displeased at it. Mr. Thomas Paine was so highly offended with it that he came to visit me at my chamber at Mrs. Yard's to remonstrate and even scold at me for it, which he did in very ungenteel terms. In return, I only laughed heartily at him, and rallied him upon his grave arguments from the Old Testament to prove that monarchy was unlawful in the sight of God. "Do you seriously believe, Paine," I said, "in that pious doctrine of yours?" This put him in good humor, and he laughed out. "The Old Testament!" said he, "I do not believe in the Old Testament. I have had thoughts of publishing my sentiments of it, but, upon deliberation, I have concluded to put that off till the latter part of life." Paine's wrath was excited because my plan of government was essentially different from the silly projects that he had published in his "Common Sense." By this means I became suspected and unpopular with the leading demagogues and the whole constitutional party in Pennsylvania.

6. Upon my return from France in 1779, I found myself elected by my

native town of Braintree a member of the Convention for forming a Constitution for the State of Massachusetts. I attended that convention of near four hundred members. Here I found such a chaos of absurd sentiments concerning government that I was obliged daily, before that great assembly, and afterwards in the Grand Committee, to propose plans, and advocate doctrines, which were extremely unpopular with the greater number. Lieutenant-Governor Cushing was avowedly for a single assembly, like Pennsylvania. Samuel Adams was of the same mind. Mr. Hancock kept aloof, in order to be governor. In short, I had at first no support but from the Essex junto, who had adopted my ideas in the letter to Mr. Wythe. They supported me timorously, and at last would not go with me to so high a mark as I aimed at, which was a complete negative in the governor upon all laws. They made me, however, draw up the Constitution, and it was finally adopted, with some amendments very much for the worse. The bold, decided, and determined part I took in this assembly in favor of a good government acquired me the reputation of a man of high principles and strong notions in government, scarcely compatible with republicanism. A foundation was here laid of much jealousy and unpopularity among the democratical people in this State.

7. In Holland, I had driven the English party and the stockholders' party before me, like clouds before the wind, and had brought that power to unite cordially with America, France, and Spain against England. If I had not before alienated the whole English nation from me, this would have been enough to produce an eternal jealousy of me; and I fully believed that whenever a free intercourse should take place between Britain and America, I might depend upon their perpetual ill will to me, and that their influence would be used to destroy mine.

8. In all my negotiations in France and Holland in 1778, 1779, 1780, 1781, 1782, 1783, and 1784, I had so uniformly resisted all the arts and intrigues of the Count de Vergennes and M. de Sartine and all their satellites, and that with such perfect success, that I well knew, although they treated me with great external respect, yet in their hearts they had conceived an ineradicable jealousy and aversion to me. I well knew, therefore, that French influence in America would do all in its power to trip me up.

9. Dr. Franklin's behavior had been so excessively complaisant to the French ministry, and in my opinion had so endangered the essential interests of our country, that I had been frequently obliged to differ from him, and sometimes to withstand him to his face; so that I knew he had conceived an irreconcilable hatred of me, and that he had propagated and would continue to propagate prejudices, if nothing worse, against me in America from one end of it to the other. Look into Benjamin Franklin Bache's Aurora and Duane's Aurora for twenty years, and see whether my expectations have not been verified.

With all these reflections fresh in my mind, you may judge whether my anticipations in the good-humored conversation with Deodati were rash, peevish, or ill grounded.

In short, I have every reason to acknowledge the protecting providence of God, from my birth, and especially through my public life. I have gone through life with much more safety and felicity than I ever expected. With devout gratitude I acknowledge the divine favor in many instances, and among others for giving me a friend in you, who, though you would never follow me as a disciple, have always been my friend.

3. *Diary*

Early Entries[1]

February 1756

14 SATURDAY.

Good Weather. This afternoon took a Vomit of Tartar Emet. and Turbith mineral, that worked 7 Times, and wrecked me much.

15 SUNDAY.

Charming Weather. A.M. staid at home reading the Independent Whig. Very often Shepherds that are hired, to take care of their Masters sheep, go about their own Concern's and leave the flock to the Care of their Dog. So Byshops, who are appointed to oversee the flock of Christ, take the Fees themslves, but leave the Drudgery to their Dogs, alias i.e. curates and understrappers.

16 MONDAY.

A most beautiful morning. We have the most moderate Winter that ever was known in this country. For a long time together we have had serene and temperate Weather and all the Roads perfectly settled and smooth like Summer.—The Church of Rome has made it an Article of Faith that no man can be saved out of their Church, and all other religious Sects approach to this dreadfull opinion in proportion to their Ignorance, and the Influence of ignorant or wicked Priests. Still reading the Independent Whigg. Oh! that I could wear out of my mind every mean and base affectation, conquer my natural Pride and Self Conceit, expect no more defference from my fellows than I deserve, acquire that meekness, and humility, which are the sure marks and Characters of a great and generous Soul, and subdue every unworthy Passion and treat all men as I wish to be treated by all. How happy should I then be, in the favour and good will of all honest men, and the sure prospect of a happy immortality!

17 TUESDAY.

A clowdy Day. Dined at Mr. Greenes.

18 WEDNESDAY.

A charming morning. My Classmate Gardner drank Tea with me. Spent an Hour in the beginning of the evening at Major Gardiners, where it was thought that the design of Christianity was not to make men good Riddle Solvers or good mystery mongers, but good men, good majestrates and good Subjects, good Husbands and good Wives, good Parents and good Children, good masters and good servants. The following Question may be answered some time or other—viz. Where do we find a præcept in the Gospell, requiring Ecclesiastical Synods, Convocations, Councils, Decrees, Creeds, Confessions, Oaths, Subscriptions and whole Cartloads of other trumpery, that we find Religion incumbered with in these Days?

19 THURSDAY.

No man is intirely free from weakness and imperfection in this life. Men of the most exalted Genius and active minds, are generally perfect slaves to the Love of Fame. They sometimes descend to as mean tricks and artifices, in pursuit of Honour or Reputation, as the Miser descends to, in pursuit of Gold. The greatest men have been the most envious, malicious, and revengeful. The miser toils by night and Day, fasts and watches, till he emaciates his Body, to fatten his purse and increase his coffers. The ambitious man rolls and tumbles in his bed, a stranger to refreshing sleep and repose thro anxiety about a preferment he has in view. The Phylosopher sweats and labours at his Book, and ruminates in his closet, till his bearded and grim Countenance exhibit the effigies of pale Want and Care, and Death, in quest [of] hard Words, solemn nonsense, and ridiculous grimace. The gay Gentleman rambles over half the Globe, Buys one Thing and Steals another, murders one man, and disables another, and gets his own limbs and head broke, for a few transitory flashes of happiness. Is this perfection, or downright madness and distraction?—A cold day.

20 FRYDAY.

A dull Day. Symptoms of Snow. Writing Tillotson.

21 SATURDAY.

A Snowy day. Snow about ancle deep. I find by repeated experiment and observation, in my School, that human nature is more easily wrought upon and governed, by promises and incouragement and praise than by punishment, and threatning and Blame. But we must be cautious and sparing of our praise, lest it become too familiar, and cheap and so contemptible. Corporal as well as disgraceful punishments, depress the spirits, but commendation enlivens and stimulates them to a noble ardor and emulation.

22 SUNDAY.

Suppos a nation in some distant Region, should take the Bible for their only law Book, and every member should regulate his conduct by the precepts there exhibited. Every member would be obliged in Concience to temperance and frugality and industry, to justice and kindness and Charity towards his fellow men, and to Piety and Love, and reverence towards almighty God. In this Commonwealth, no man would impair his health by Gluttony, drunkenness, or Lust—no man would sacrifice his most precious time to cards, or any other trifling and mean amusement—no man would steal or lie or any way defraud his neighbour, but would live in peace and good will with all men—no man would blaspheme his maker or prophane his Worship, but a rational and manly, a sincere and unaffected Piety and devotion, would reign in all hearts. What a Eutopa, what a Paradise would this region be. Heard Thayer all Day. He preach'd well.

Spent the Evening at Coll. Chandlers, with Putnam, Gardiner, Thayer, the Dr. and his Lady, in Conversation, upon the present scituation of publick affairs, with a few observations concerning Heroes and great Commanders. Alexander, Charles 12th., Cromwel.

Schoolmaster[2]

March 1756

15 MONDAY.

I sometimes, in my sprightly moments, consider my self, in my great Chair at School, as some Dictator at the head of a commonwealth. In this little State I can discover all the great Genius's, all the surprizing actions and revolutions of the great World in miniature. I have severall renowned Generalls but 3 feet high, and several deep-projecting Politicians in peticoats. I have others catching and dissecting Flies, accumulating remarkable pebbles, cockle shells &c., with as ardent Curiosity as any Virtuoso in the royal society. Some rattle and Thunder out A, B, C, with as much Fire and impetuosity, as Alexander fought, and very often sit down and cry as heartily, upon being out spelt, as Cesar did, when at Alexanders sepulchre he recollected that the Macedonian Hero had conquered the World before his Age. At one Table sits Mr. Insipid foppling and fluttering, spinning his whirligig, or playing with his fingers as gaily and wittily as any frenchified coxcomb brandishes his Cane or rattles his snuff box. At another sitts the polemical Divine, plodding and wrangling in his mind about Adam's fall in which we sinned all as his primmer has it. In short my little school like the great World, is made up of Kings, Politicians, Divines, L.D. [LL.D.'s?], Fops, Buffoons, Fidlers, Sychophants, Fools, Coxcombs, chimney sweepers, and every other Character drawn in History or seen in the World. Is it not then the highest Pleasure my Friend to preside in this little World, to bestow the proper applause

upon virtuous and generous Actions, to blame and punish every vicious and contracted Trick, to wear out of the tender mind every thing that is mean and little, and fire the new born soul with a noble ardor and Emulation. The World affords no greater Pleasure. Let others waste the bloom of Life, at the Card or biliard Table, among rakes and fools, and when their minds are sufficiently fretted with losses, and inflamed by Wine, ramble through the Streets, assaulting innocent People, breaking Windows or debauching young Girls. I envy not their exalted happiness. I had rather sit in school and consider which of my pupils will turn out in his future Life, a Hero, and which a rake, which a phylosopher, and which a parasite, than change breasts with them, tho possest of 20 lac'd wast coats and £1000 a year. Methinks I hear you say, this is odd talk for J. Adams. I'll tell you, then the Ocasion of it. About 4 months since a poor Girl in this neighbourhood walking by the meeting H[ouse] upon some Ocasion, in the evening, met a fine Gentleman with laced hat and wast coat, and a sword who sollicited her to turn aside with him into the horse Stable. The Girl relucted a little, upon which he gave her 3 Guineas, and wished he might be damned if he did not have her in 3 months. Into the horse Stable they went. The 3 Guineas proved 3 farthings—and the Girl proves with Child, without a Friend upon Earth that will own her, or knowing the father of her 3 farthing Bastard.

The Law[3]

August 1756

22 SUNDAY

Yesterday I compleated a Contract with Mr. Putnam, to study Law under his Inspection for two years. I ought to begin with a Resolution to oblige and please him and his Lady in a particular Manner. I ought to endeavour to oblige and please every Body, but them in particular. Necessity drove me to this Determination, but my Inclination I think was to preach. However that would not do. But I set out with firm Resolutions I think never to commit any meanness or injustice in the Practice of Law. The Study and Practice of Law, I am sure does not dissolve the obligations of morality or of Religion. And altho the Reason of my quitting Divinity was my Opinion concerning some disputed Points, I hope I shall not give Reason of offence to any in that Profession by imprudent Warmth. . . .

December 1758

18 MONDAY

I this Evening delivered to Mr. Field, a Declaration in Trespass for a Rescue. I was obliged to finish it, without sufficient examination. If it should escape an Abatement, it is quite indigested, and unclerklike. I

am ashamed of it, and concerned for it. If my first Writt should be abated, if I should throw a large Bill of Costs on my first Client, my Character and Business will suffer greatly. It will be said, I dont understand my Business. No one will trust his Interest in my hands. I never Saw a Writt, on that Law of the Province. I was perplexed, and am very anxious about. Now I feel the Dissadvantages of Putnams Insociability, and neglect of me. Had he given me now and then a few Hints concerning Practice, I should be able to judge better at this Hour than I can now. I have Reason to complain of him. But, it is my Destiny to dig Treasures with my own fingers. No Body will lend me or sell me a Pick axe. How this first Undertaking will terminate, I know not. I hope the Dispute will be settled between them, or submitted, and so my Writt never come to an Examination. But if it should I must take the Consequences. I must assume a Resolution, to bear without freting. . . .

December 18, 1760

Justice Dyer says there is more Occasion for Justices than for Lawyers. Lawyers live upon the sins of the People. If all Men were just, and honest, and pious, and Religious &c. there would be no need of Lawyers. But Justices are necessary to keep men just and honest and pious, and religious.—Oh sagacity!

But, it may be said with equal Truth, that all Magistrates, and all civil officers, and all civil Government, is founded and maintained by the sins of the People. All armies would be needless if Men were universally virtuous. Most manufacturers and Tradesmen would be needless. Nay, some of the natural Passions and sentiments of human Minds, would be needless upon that supposition. Resentment, e.g. which has for its object, Wrong and Injury. No man upon that supposition would ever give another, a just Provocation. And no just Resentment could take Place without a just Provocation. Thus, our natural Resentments are founded on the sins of the People, as much as the Profession of the Law, or that of Arms, or that of Divinity. In short Vice and folly are so interwoven in all human Affairs that they could not possibly be wholly separated from them without tearing and rending the whole system of human Nature, and state. Nothing would remain as it is. . . .

The Stamp Act[4]

December 1765

18 WEDNESDAY

How great is my Loss, in neglecting to keep a regular Journal, through the last Spring, Summer, and Fall. In the Course of my Business, as a Surveyor of High-Ways, as one of the Committee, for dividing, planning,

and selling the North-Commons, in the Course of my two great Journeys to Pounalborough and Marthas Vineyard, and in several smaller Journeys to Plymouth, Taunton and Boston, I had many fine Opportunities and Materials for Speculation.—The Year 1765 has been the most remarkable Year of my Life. That enormous Engine, fabricated by the British Parliament, for battering down all the Rights and Liberties of America, I mean the Stamp Act, has raised and spread, thro the whole Continent, a Spirit that will be recorded to our Honour, with all future Generations. In every Colony, from Georgia to New-Hampshire inclusively, the Stamp Distributors and Inspectors have been compelled, by the unconquerable Rage of the People, to renounce their offices. Such and so universal has been the Resentment of the People, that every Man who has dared to speak in favour of the Stamps, or to soften the detestation in which they are held, how great soever his Abilities and Virtues had been esteemed before, or whatever his fortune, Connections and Influence had been, has been seen to sink into universal Contempt and Ignominy.

The People, even to the lowest Ranks, have become more attentive to their Liberties, more inquisitive about them, and more determined to defend them, than they were ever before known or had occasion to be. Innumerable have been the Monuments of Wit, Humour, Sense, Learning, Spirit, Patriotism, and Heroism, erected in the several Colonies and Provinces, in the Course of this Year. Our Presses have groaned, our Pulpits have thundered, our Legislatures have resolved, our Towns have voted, The Crown Officers have every where trembled, and all their little Tools and Creatures, been afraid to Speak and ashamed to be seen.

This Spirit however has not yet been sufficient to banish, from Persons in Authority, that Timidity, which they have discovered from the Beginning. The executive Courts have not yet dared to adjudge the Stamp-Act void nor to proceed with Business as usual, tho it should seem that Necessity alone would be sufficient to justify Business, at present, tho the Act should be allowed to be obligatory. The Stamps are in the Castle. Mr. Oliver has no Commission. The Governor has no Authority to distribute, or even to unpack the Bales, the Act has never been proclaimed nor read in the Province; Yet the Probate office is shut, the Custom House is shut, the Courts of Justice are shut, and all Business seems at a Stand. Yesterday and the day before, the two last days of Service for January Term, only one Man asked me for a Writ, and he was soon determined to waive his Request. I have not drawn a Writ since 1st. Novr.

How long We are to remain in this languid Condition, this passive Obedience to the Stamp Act, is not certain. But such a Pause cannot be lasting. Debtors grow insolent. Creditors grow angry. And it is to be expected that the Public offices will very soon be forced open, unless such favourable Accounts should be received from England, as to draw away the Fears of the Great, or unless a greater Dread of the Multitude should drive away the Fear of Censure from G. Britain.

It is my Opinion that by this (*Timorous*) Inactivity we discover Cowardice, and too much Respect (*and Regard*) to the Act. This Rest appears to be by Implication at least an Acknowledgement of the Authority of Parliament to tax Us. And if this Authority is once acknowledged and established, the Ruin of America will become inevitable.

This long Interval of Indolence and Idleness will make a large Chasm in my affairs if it should not reduce me to Distress and incapacitate me to answer the Demands upon me. But I must endeavour in some degree to compensate the Disadvantage, by posting my Books, reducing my Accounts into better order, and by diminishing my Expences, but above all by improving the Leisure of this Winter, in a diligent Application to my Studies. I find that Idleness lies between Business and Study, i.e. The Transision from the Hurry of a multiplicity of Business, to the Tranquility that is necessary for intense Study, is not easy. There must be a Vacation, an Interval between them, for the Mind to recollect itself.

The Bar seem to me to behave like a Flock of shot Pidgeons. They seem to be stopped, the Net seems to be thrown over them, and they have scarcely Courage left to flounce and to flutter. So sudden an Interruption in my Career, is very unfortunate for me. I was but just getting into my Geers, just getting under Sail, and an Embargo is laid upon the Ship. Thirty Years of my Life are passed in Preparation for Business. I have had Poverty to struggle with—Envy and Jealousy and Malice of Enemies to encounter—no Friends, or but few to assist me, so that I have groped in dark Obscurity, till of late, and had but just become known, and gained a small degree of Reputation, when this execrable Project was set on foot for my Ruin as well as that of America in General, and of Great Britain.

To Be or not To Be a Politician[5]

May 1773

25 TUESDAY

Tomorrow is our General Election. The Plotts, Plans, Schemes, and Machinations of this Evening and Night, will be very numerous. By the Number of Ministerial, Governmental People returned, and by the Secrecy of the Friends of Liberty, relating to the grand discovery of the compleat Evidence of the whole Mystery of Iniquity, I much fear the Elections will go unhappily. For myself, I own I tremble at the Thought of an Election. What will be expected of me? What will be required of me? What Duties and Obligations will result to me, from an Election? What Duties to my God, my King, my Country, my Family, my Friends, myself? What Perplexities, and Intricacies, and Difficulties shall I be exposed to? What Snares and Temptations will be thrown in my Way? What Self denials and Mortifications shall I be obliged to bear?

If I should be called in the Course of Providence to take a Part in pub-

lic Life, I shall Act a fearless, intrepid, undaunted Part, at all Hazards—
tho it shall be my Endeavour likewise to act a prudent, cautious and considerate Part.

But if I should be excused, by a Non Election, or by the Exertions of
Prerogative from engaging in public Business, I shall enjoy a sweet Tran-
quility, in the Pursuit of my private Business, in the Education of my
Children and in a constant Attention to the Preservation of my Health.
This last is the most selfish and pleasant System—the first, the more
generous, tho arduous and disagreable.

But I was not sent into this World to spend my days in Sports, Diversions and Pleasures.

I was born for Business; for both Activity and Study. I have little Appetite, or Relish for any Thing else.

I must double and redouble my Diligence. I must be more constant to
my office and my Pen. Constancy accomplishes more than Rapidity. Continual Attention will do great Things. Frugality, of Time, is the greatest
Art as well as Virtue. This Economy will produce Knowledge as well as
Wealth. . . .

The Boston Tea Party[6]

December 17, 1773

Last Night 3 Cargoes of Bohea Tea were emptied into the Sea. This
Morning a Man of War sails.

This is the most magnificent Movement of all. There is a Dignity, a
Majesty, a Sublimity, in this last Effort of the Patriots, that I greatly
admire. The People should never rise, without doing something to be
remembered—something notable And striking. This Destruction of the
Tea is so bold, so daring, so firm, intrepid and inflexible, and it must have
so important Consequences, and so lasting, that I cant but consider it as
an Epocha in History.

This however is but an Attack upon Property. Another similar Exertion
of popular Power, may produce the destruction of Lives. Many Persons
wish, that as many dead Carcasses were floating in the Harbour, as there
are Chests of Tea:—a much less Number of Lives however would remove the Causes of all our Calamities.

The malicious Pleasure with which Hutchinson the Governor, the
Consignees of the Tea, and the officers of the Customs, have stood and
looked upon the distresses of the People, and their Struggles to get the
Tea back to London, and at last the destruction of it, is amazing. Tis
hard to believe Persons so hardened and abandoned.

What Measures will the Ministry take, in Consequence of this?—Will
they resent it? will they dare to resent it? will they punish Us? How? By

quartering Troops upon Us?—by annulling our Charter?—by laying on more duties? By restraining our Trade? By Sacrifice of Individuals, or how.

The Question is whether the Destruction of this Tea was necessary? I apprehend it was absolutely and indispensably so.—They could not send it back, the Governor, Admiral and Collector and Comptroller would not suffer it. It was in their Power to have saved it—but in no other. It could not get by the Castle, the Men of War &c. Then there was no other Alternative but to destroy it or let it be landed. To let it be landed, would be giving up the Principle of Taxation by Parliamentary Authority, against which the Continent have struggled for 10 years, it was loosing all our labour for 10 years and subjecting ourselves and our Posterity forever to Egyptian Taskmasters—to Burthens, Indignities, to Ignominy, Reproach and Contempt, to Desolation and Oppression, to Poverty and Servitude. . . .

Not the Famous Adams[7]

1779

11 FEBRUARY

When I arrived in France, the French Nation had a great many Questions to settle.

The first was—Whether I was the famous Adams, Le fameux Adams? —Ah, le fameux Adams?—In order to speculate a little upon this Subject, the Pamphlet entituled Common sense, had been printed in the Affaires de L'Angleterre et De L'Amerique, and expressly ascribed to M. Adams the celebrated Member of Congress, le celebre Membre du Congress. It must be further known, that altho the Pamphlet Common sense, was received in France and in all Europe with Rapture: yet there were certain Parts of it, that they did not choose to publish in France. The Reasons of this, any Man may guess. Common sense undertakes to prove, that Monarchy is unlawful by the old Testament. They therefore gave the Substance of it, as they said, and paying many Compliments to Mr. Adams, his sense and rich Imagination, they were obliged to ascribe some Parts to Republican Zeal. When I arrived at Bourdeaux, All that I could say or do, would not convince any Body, but that I was the fameux Adams.—Cette un homme celebre. Votre nom est bien connu ici.—My Answer was—it is another Gentleman, whose Name of Adams you have heard. It is Mr. Samuel Adams, who was excepted from Pardon by Gen. Gage's Proclamation.—Oh No Monsieur, cette votre Modestie.

But when I arrived at Paris, I found a very different Style. I found great Pains taken, much more than the Question was worth to settle the Point that I was not the famous Adams. There was a dread of a sensation —Sensations at Paris are important Things. I soon found too, that it was

effectually settled in the English News Papers that I was not the famous Adams. No body went so far in France or Ingland, as to say I was the infamous Adams. I make no scruple to say, that I believe, that both Parties for Parties there were, joined in declaring that I was not the famous Adams. I certainly joined both sides in this, in declaring that I was not the famous Adams, because this was the Truth.

It being settled that he was not the famous Adams, the Consequence was plain—he was some Man that nobody had ever heard of before—and therefore a Man of no Consequence—a Cypher. And I am inclined to think that all Parties both in France and England—Whiggs and Tories in England—the Friends of Franklin, Deane and Lee, differing in many other Things agreed in this—that I was not the fameux Adams.

Seeing all this, and saying nothing, for what could a Man say?—seeing also, that there were two Parties formed, among the Americans, as fixed in their Aversion to each other, as both were to G.B. if I had affected the Character of a Fool in order to find out the Truth and to do good by and by, I should have had the Example of a Brutus for my Justification. But I did not affect this Character. I behaved with as much Prudence, and Civility, and Industry as I could. But still it was a settled Point at Paris and in the English News Papers that I was not the famous Adams, and therefore the Consequence was settled absolutely and unalterably that I was a Man of whom Nobody had ever heard before, a perfect Cypher, a Man who did not understand a Word of French—awkward in his Figure —awkward in his Dress—No Abilities—a perfect Bigot—and fanatic. . . .

On Benjamin Franklin[8]

June 1779

23 WEDNESDAY

This Forenoon, fell strangely, yet very easily into Conversation with M.M.

I went up to him—M.M. said I, how many persons have you in your Train and that of the Chevalier who speak the German Language?— Only my Servant, said he, besides myself and the Chev[alier].—It will be a great Advantage to you said I in America, especially in Pensilvania, to be able to speak German. There is a great Body of Germans in P[enn-sylvania] and M[aryland]. There is a vast Proportion of the City of Philadelphia, of this Nation who have their Churches in it, two of which one Lutheran the other Calvinist, are the largest and most elegant Churches in the City, frequented by the most numerous Congregations, where the Worship is all in the German Language.

Is there not one Catholic, said M.M.?—Not a German Church said I. There is a Roman catholic Church in Philadelphia, a very decent Build-ing, frequented by a respectable Congregation, consisting partly of Ger-

mans, partly of French and partly of Irish.—All Religions are tolerated in America, said M.M., and the Ambassadors have in all Courts a Right to a Chappell in their own Way. But Mr. Franklin never had any.—No said I, laughing, because Mr. F. had no—I was going to say, what I did not say, and will not say here. I stopped short and laughed.—No, said Mr. M., Mr. F. adores only great Nature, which has interested a great many People of both Sexes in his favour.—Yes, said I, laughing, all the Atheists, Deists and Libertines, as well as the Philosophers and Ladies are in his Train—another Voltaire and Hume.—Yes said Mr. M., he is celebrated as the great Philosopher and the great Legislator of America. —He is said I a great Philosopher, but as a Legislator of America he has done very little. It is universally believed in France, England and all Europe, that his Electric Wand has accomplished all this Revolution but nothing is more groundless. He has [done] very little. It is believed that he made all the American Constitutions, and their Confederation. But he made neither. He did not even make the Constitution of Pennsylvania, bad as it is. The Bill of Rights is taken almost verbatim from that of Virginia, which was made and published two or three Months before that of Philadelphia was begun. It was made by Mr. Mason, as that of Pensilvania was by Timothy Matlack, James Cannon and Thomas Young and Thomas Paine. Mr. Sherman of Connecticutt and Dr. F. made an Essay towards a Confederation about the same Time. Mr. Shermans was best liked, but very little was finally adopted from either, and the real Confederation was not made untill a Year after Mr. F. left America, and but a few Days before I left Congress.

Who, said the Chevalier, made the Declaration of Independance?— Mr. Jefferson of Virginia, said I, was the Draughtsman. The Committee consisted of Mr. Jefferson, Mr. Franklin, Mr. Harrison, Mr. R. and myself, and We appointed [Mr.] Jefferson a subcommittee to draw it up.

I said that Mr. Franklin had great Merit as a Philosopher. His Discoveries in Electricity were very grand, and he certainly was a Great Genius, and had great Merit in our American Affairs. But he had no Title to the Legislator of America.

Mr. M. said he had Wit and Irony, but these were not the Faculties of Statesmen. His Essay upon the true Means of bring[ing] a great Empire to be a small one was very pretty.—I said he had wrote many Things, which had great Merit and infinite Wit and Ingenuity. His bonhomme Richard was a very ingenious Thing, which had been so much celebrated in France, gone through so many Editions, and been recommended by Curates and Bishops to so many Parishes and Diocesses.

Mr. M. asked, are natural Children admitted in America to all Priviledges like Children born in Wedlock.—I answered they are not Admitted to the Rights of Inheritance. But their fathers may give them Estates by Testament and they are not excluded from other Advantages.—In France, said M.M., they are not admitted into the Army nor any Office in Govern-

ment.—I said they were not excluded from Commissions in the Army, Navy, or State, but they were always attended with a Mark of Disgrace. —M.M. said this, No doubt, in Allusion to Mr. Fs. natural Son and natural Son of a natural Son. I let myself thus freely into this Conversation being led on naturally by the Chevalier and Mr. Marbois, on Purpose because I am sure it cannot be my Duty nor the Interest of my Country that I should conceal any of my sentiments of this Man, at the same Time that I due Justice to his Merits. It would be worse than Folly to conceal my Opinion of his great Faults. . . .

On British Policy Toward America[9]

December 1782

9 MONDAY

Visited C. Sarsfield who lent me his Notes upon America. Visited Mr. Jay, Mr. Oswald came in. We slided, from one Thing to another into a very lively Conversation upon Politicks.—He asked me what the Conduct of his Court and Nation ought to be, in Relation to America. I answered the Alpha and Omega of British Policy, towards America, was summed up in this one Maxim—See that American Independence is independent, independant of all the World, independent of yourselves as well as of France, and independent of both as well as of the rest of Europe. Depend upon it, you have no Chance for Salvation but by setting up America very high. Take care to remove from the American Mind all Cause of Fear of you. No other Motive but Fear of you, will ever produce in the Americans any unreasonable Attachment to the house of Bourbon.—Is it possible, says he that the People of America should be afraid of Us, or hate Us?—One would think Mr. Oswald says I, that you had been out of the World for these 20 Years past. Yes there are 3 millions of People in America who hate and dread you more than any Thing in the World.— What says he now We are come to our Senses?—Your Change of System, is not yet known in America, says I.—Well says he what shall We do to remove these Fears, and Jealousies?

In one Word says I, favour and promote the Interest, Reputation and Dignity of the United States in every Thing that is consistent with your own. If you pursue the Plan of cramping, clipping and weakening America, on the Supposition that She will be a Rival to you, you will make her really so, you will make her the natural and perpetual Ally of your natural and perpetual Ennemies.—But in what Instance says he have We discovered such a disposition?—In the 3 Leagues from your Shores and the 15 Leagues from Cape Breton, says I to which your Ministry insisted so earnestly to exclude our Fishermen. Here was a Point that would have done Us great harm and you no good, on the contrary harm. So that you would have hurt yourselves to hurt Us. This disposition must be guarded

against.—I am fully of your Mind about that, says he. But what else can
We do?—Send a Minister to Congress, says I, at the Peace, a clever Fel-
low, who Understands himself, and will neither set Us bad Examples, nor
intermeddle in our Parties. This will shew that you are consistent with
yourselves, that you are sincere in your Acknowledgment of American
Independence, and that you dont entertain hopes and designs of over-
turning it. Such a Minister will dissipate many fears, and will be of more
Service to the least obnoxious Refugees than any other Measure could be.
Let the King send a Minister to Congress and receive one from that
Body. This will be acting consistently and with Dignity, in the Face of
the Universe. . . .

John Yankee[10]

1785

AUTEUIL MAY 3

One of the foreign Ambassadors said to me, You have been often in
England.—Never but once in November and December 1783.—You have
Relations in England no doubt.—None at all.—None how can that be?
You are of English Extraction?—Neither my Father or Mother, Grandfather or Grandmother, Great Grandfather or Great Grandmother nor
any other Relation that I know of or care a farthing for have been in
England these 150 Years. So that you see, I have not one drop of Blood in
my Veins, but what is American. —Ay We have seen says he proofs
enough of that. —This flattered me no doubt, and I was vain enough to
be pleased with it. . . .

Letters

4. *"I Am Turned Politician"*

To Nathan Webb

Worcester, 12 October 1755

All that part of creation which lies within our observation, is liable to change. Even mighty states and kingdoms are not exempted.

If we look into history, we shall find some nations rising from contemptible beginnings, and spreading their influence till the whole globe is subjected to their sway. When they have reached the summit of grandeur, some minute and unsuspected cause commonly effects their ruin, and the empire of the world is transferred to some other place. Immortal Rome was at first but an insignificant village, inhabited only by a few abandoned ruffians; but by degrees it rose to a stupendous height, and excelled, in arts and arms, all the nations that preceded it. But the demolition of Carthage (what one should think would have established it in supreme dominion), by removing all danger, suffered it to sink into a debauchery, and made it at length an easy prey to barbarians.

England, immediately upon this, began to increase (the particular and minute causes of which I am not historian enough to trace) in power and magnificence, and is now the greatest nation upon the globe. Soon after the Reformation, a few people came over into this new world for conscience' sake. Perhaps this apparently trivial incident may transfer the great seat of empire into America. It looks likely to me: for if we can remove the turbulent Gallicks, our people, according to the exactest computations, will in another century become more numerous than England itself. Should this be the case, since we have, I may say, all the naval stores of the nation in our hands, it will be easy to obtain the mastery of the seas; and then the united force of all Europe will not be able to subdue us. The only way to keep us from setting up for ourselves is to disunite us. *Divide et impera.* Keep us in distinct colonies, and then, some great men in each colony desiring the monarchy of the whole, they will destroy each other's influence and keep the country *in equilibrio.*

178

Be not surprised that I am turned politician. This whole town is immersed in politics. The interests of nations, and all the *dira* of war, make the subject of every conversation. I sit and hear, and after having been led through a maze of sage observations, I sometimes retire, and by laying things together, form some reflections pleasing to myself.

5. *Miss Adorable*

Miss Adorable   *Octr. 4th. 1762*

By the same Token that the Bearer hereof *satt up* with you last night I hereby order you to give him, as many Kisses, and as many Hours of your Company after 9 O'Clock as he shall please to Demand and charge them to my Account: This Order, or Requisition call it which you will is in Consideration of a similar order Upon Aurelia for the like favour, and I presume I have good Right to draw upon you for the Kisses as I have given two or three Millions at least, when one has been received, and of Consequence the Account between us is immensely in favour of yours,   John Adams

6. *Lysander to His Diana*

To Abigail Smith

Boston May 7th. 1764

I promised you, Sometime agone, a Catalogue of your Faults, Imperfections, Defects, or whatever you please to call them. I feel at present, pretty much at Leisure, and in a very suitable Frame of Mind to perform my Promise. But I must caution you, before I proceed to recollect yourself, and instead of being vexed or fretted or thrown into a Passion, to resolve upon a Reformation—for this is my sincere Aim, in laying before you, this Picture of yourself.

In the first Place, then, give me leave to say, you have been extreamly negligent, in attending so little to Cards. You have very litle Inclination, to that noble and elegant Diversion, and whenever you have taken an Hand you have held it but aukwardly and played it, with a very uncourtly, and indifferent, Air. Now I have Confidence enough in your good sense, to rely upon it, you will for the future endeavour to make a better Figure in this elegant and necessary Accomplishment.

Another Thing, which ought to be mentioned, and by all means amended, is, the Effect of a Country Life and Education, I mean, a certain Modesty, sensibility, Bashfulness, call it by which of these Names you will, that enkindles Blushes forsooth at every Violation of Decency, in Company, and lays a most insupportable Constraint on the freedom of Behaviour. Thanks to the late Refinements of modern manners, Hypocrisy, superstition, and Formality have lost all Reputation in the World and the utmost sublimation of Politeness and Gentility lies, in Ease, and Freedom, or in other Words in a natural Air and Behaviour, and in expressing a satisfaction at whatever is suggested and prompted by Nature, which the aforesaid Violations of Decency, most certainly are.

In the Third Place, you could never yet be prevail'd on to learn to sing. This I take very soberly to be an Imperfection of the most moment of any. An Ear for Musick would be a source of much Pleasure, and a Voice and skill, would be a private solitary Amusement, of great Value when no other could be had. You must have remarked an Example of this in Mrs. Cranch, who must in all probability have been deafened to Death with the Cries of her Betcy if she had not drowned them in Musick of her own.

In the Fourth Place you very often hang your Head like a Bulrush. You do not sit, erected as you ought, by which Means, it happens that you appear too short for a Beauty, and the Company looses the sweet smiles of that Countenance and the bright sparkles of those Eyes.—This Fault is the Effect and Consequence of another, still more inexcusable in a Lady. I mean an Habit of Reading, Writing and Thinking. But both the Cause and the Effect ought to be repented and amended as soon as possible.

Another Fault, which seems to have been obstinately persisted in, after frequent Remonstrances, Advices and Admonitions of your Friends, is that of sitting with the Leggs across. This ruins the figure and the Air, this injures the Health. And springs I fear from the former source vizt. too much Thinking.—These Things ought not to be!

A sixth Imperfection is that of Walking, with the Toes bending inward. This Imperfection is commonly called Parrot-toed, I think, I know not for what Reason. But it gives an Idea, the reverse of a bold and noble Air, the Reverse of the stately strutt, and the sublime Deportment.

Thus have I given a faithful Portraiture of all the Spotts, I have hitherto discerned in this Luminary. Have not regarded Order, but have painted them as they arose in my Memory. Near Three Weeks have I conned and studied for more, but more are not to be discovered. All the rest is bright and luminous.

Having finished the Picture I finish my Letter, lest while I am recounting Faults, I should commit the greatest in a Letter, that of tedious and excessive Length. There's a prettily turned Conclusion for You! from yr.

Lysander

7. *Attachment to New England*

To Abigail Adams

Philadelphia, October 29, 1775

There is in the human breast a social affection which extends to our whole species, faintly indeed, but in some degree. The nation, kingdom, or community to which we belong is embraced by it more vigorously. It is stronger still towards the province to which we belong, and in which we had our birth. It is stronger and stronger as we descend to the county, town, parish, neighborhood and family, which we call our own. And here we find it often so powerful as to become partial, to blind our eyes, to darken our understandings and pervert our wills.

It is to this infirmity in my own heart that I must perhaps attribute that local attachment, that partial fondness, that overweening prejudice in favor of New England, which I feel very often, and which, I fear, sometimes leads me to expose myself to just ridicule.

New England has, in many respects, the advantage of every other colony in America, and, indeed, of every other part of the world that I know anything of.

1. The people are purer English blood; less mixed with Scotch, Irish, Dutch, French, Danish, Swedish, &c., than any other; and descended from Englishmen too, who left Europe in purer times than the present, and less tainted with corruption than those they left behind them.

2. The institutions in New England for the support of religion, morals, and decency exceed any other; obliging every parish to have a minister, and every person to go to meeting, &c.

3. The public institutions in New England for the education of youth, supporting colleges at the public expense, and obliging towns to maintain grammar schools, are not equalled, and never were, in any part of the world.

4. The division of our territory, that is, our counties, into townships; empowering towns to assemble, choose officers, make laws, mend roads and twenty other things, gives every man an opportunity of showing and improving that education which he received at college or at school, and makes knowledge and dexterity at public business common.

5. But in opposition to these we have labored under many disadvantages. The exorbitant prerogative of our Governors, &c., which would have overborne our liberties if it had not been opposed by the five preceding particulars.

8. *For an American Republic*

To Mercy Warren

Braintree, January 8, 1776

. . . Pray Madam, are you for an American monarchy or republic? Monarchy is the genteelest and most fashionable government, and I don't know why the ladies ought not to consult elegance and the fashion as well in government as gowns, bureaus or chariots.

For my own part I am so tasteless as to prefer a republic, if we must erect an independent government in America, which you know is utterly against my inclination. But a republic, although it will infallibly beggar me and my children, will produce strength, hardiness, activity, courage, fortitude, and enterprise, the manly, noble, and sublime qualities in human nature, in abundance. A monarchy would probably, somehow or other, make me rich, but it would produce so much taste and politeness, so much elegance in dress, furniture, equipage, so much music and dancing, so much fencing and skating, so much cards and backgammon; so much horse racing and cockfighting, so many balls and assemblies, so many plays and concerts that the very imagination of them makes me feel vain, light, frivolous, and insignificant.

It is the form of government which gives the decisive color to the manners of the people, more than any other thing. Under a well-regulated commonwealth, the people must be wise, virtuous, and cannot be otherwise. Under a monarchy they may be as vicious and foolish as they please, nay, they cannot but be vicious and foolish. As politics therefore is the science of human happiness, and human happiness is clearly best promoted by virtue, what thorough politician can hesitate who has a new government to build whether to prefer a commonwealth or a monarchy?

But, Madam, there is one difficulty which I know not how to get over.

Virtue and simplicity of manners are indispensably necessary in a republic among all orders and degrees of men. But there is so much rascality, so much venality and corruption, so much avarice and ambition, such a rage for profit and commerce among all ranks and degrees of men even in America, that I sometimes doubt whether there is public virtue enough to support a republic. There are two vices most detestably predominant in every part of America that I have yet seen which are as incompatible with the spirit of a commonwealth as light is with darkness; I mean servility and flattery. A genuine republican can no more fawn and cringe than he can domineer. Show me the American who cannot do all. I know two or three, I think, and very few more. However, it is the part of a great politician to make the character of his people, to extinguish among them

the follies and vices that he sees, and to create in them the virtues and abilities which he sees wanting. I wish I was sure that America has one such politician but I fear she has not. . . .

9. *Balance of Power*

To James Sullivan

Philadelphia, 26 May 1776

. . . Our worthy friend, Mr. Gerry, has put into my hands a letter from you, of the sixth of May, in which you consider the principles of representation and legislation, and give us hints of some alterations, which you seem to think necessary, in the qualification of voters.

I wish, Sir, I could possibly find time to accompany you, in your investigation of the principles upon which a representative assembly stands, and ought to stand, and in your examination whether the practice of our colony has been conformable to those principles. But, alas! Sir, my time is so incessantly engrossed by the business before me, that I cannot spare enough to go through so large a field; and as to books, it is not easy to obtain them here; nor could I find a moment to look into them, if I had them.

It is certain, in theory, that the only moral foundation of government is, the consent of the people. But to what an extent shall we carry this principle? Shall we say that every individual of the community, old and young, male and female, as well as rich and poor, must consent, expressly, to every act of legislation? No, you will say, this is impossible. How, then, does the right arise in the majority to govern the minority, against their will? Whence arises the right of the men to govern the women, without their consent? Whence the right of the old to bind the young, without theirs?

But let us first suppose that the whole community, of every age, rank, sex, and condition, has a right to vote. This community is assembled. A motion is made, and carried by a majority of one voice. The minority will not agree to this. Whence arises the right of the majority to govern, and the obligation of the minority to obey?

From necessity, you will say, because there can be no other rule.

But why exclude women?

You will say, because their delicacy renders them unfit for practice and experience in the great businesses of life, and the hardy enterprises of war, as well as the arduous cares of state. Besides, their attention is so much engaged with the necessary nurture of their children, that nature has made them fittest for domestic cares. And children have not judg-

ment or will of their own. True. But will not these reasons apply to others? Is it not equally true, that men in general, in every society, who are wholly destitute of property, are also too little acquainted with public affairs to form a right judgment, and too dependent upon other men to have a will of their own? If this is a fact, if you give to every man who has no property, a vote, will you not make a fine encouraging provision for corruption, by your fundamental law? Such is the frailty of the human heart, that very few men who have no property, have any judgment of their own. They talk and vote as they are directed by some man of property, who has attached their minds to his interest.

Upon my word, Sir, I have long thought an army a piece of clock-work, and to be governed only by principles and maxims, as fixed as any in mechanics; and, by all that I have read in the history of mankind, and in authors who have speculated upon society and government, I am much inclined to think a government must manage a society in the same manner; and that this is machinery too.

Harrington has shown that power always follows property. This I believe to be as infallible a maxim in politics, as that action and reaction are equal, is in mechanics. Nay, I believe we may advance one step farther, and affirm that the balance of power in a society, accompanies the balance of property in land. The only possible way, then, of preserving the balance of power on the side of equal liberty and public virtue, is to make the acquisition of land easy to every member of society; to make a division of the land into small quantities, so that the multitude may be possessed of landed estates. If the multitude is possessed of the balance of real estate, the multitude will have the balance of power, and in that case the multitude will take care of the liberty, virtue, and interest of the multitude, in all acts of government.

I believe these principles have been felt, if not understood, in the Massachusetts Bay, from the beginning; and therefore I should think that wisdom and policy would dictate in these times to be very cautious of making alterations. Our people have never been very rigid in scrutinizing into the qualifications of voters, and I presume they will not now begin to be so. But I would not advise them to make any alteration in the laws, at present, respecting the qualifications of voters.

Your idea that those laws which affect the lives and personal liberty of all, or which inflict corporal punishment, affect those who are not qualified to vote, as well as those who are, is just. But so they do women, as well as men; children, as well as adults. What reason should there be for excluding a man of twenty years eleven months and twenty-seven days old, from a vote, when you admit one who is twenty-one? The reason is, you must fix upon some period in life, when the understanding and will of men in general, is fit to be trusted by the public. Will not the same reason justify the state in fixing upon some certain quantity of property, as a qualification?

The same reasoning which will induce you to admit all men who have

no property, to vote, with those who have, for those laws which affect the person, will prove that you ought to admit women and children; for, generally speaking, women and children have as good judgments, and as independent minds, as those men who are wholly destitute of property; these last being to all intents and purposes as much dependent upon others, who will please to feed, clothe, and employ them, as women are upon their husbands, or children on their parents.

As to your idea of proportioning the votes of men, in money matters, to the property they hold, it is utterly impracticable. There is no possible way of ascertaining, at any one time, how much every man in a community is worth; and if there was, so fluctuating is trade and property, that this state of it would change in half an hour. The property of the whole community is shifting every hour, and no record can be kept of the changes.

Society can be governed only by general rules. Government cannot accommodate itself to every particular case as it happens, nor to the circumstances of particular persons. It must establish general comprehensive regulations for cases and persons. The only question is, which general rule will accommodate most cases and most persons.

Depend upon it, Sir, it is dangerous to open so fruitful a source of controversy and altercation as would be opened by attempting to alter the qualifications of voters; there will be no end of it. New claims will arise; women will demand a vote; lads from twelve to twenty-one will think their rights not enough attended to; and every man who has not a farthing, will demand an equal voice with any other, in all acts of state. It tends to confound and destroy all distinctions, and prostrate all ranks to one common level.

10. *The Declaration of Independence*

To Abigail Adams

July 3, 1776

... Yesterday the greatest question was decided which ever was debated in America, and a greater, perhaps, never was nor will be decided among men. A resolution was passed without one dissenting colony, "that these United Colonies are, and of right ought to be, free and independent States, and as such they have, and of right ought to have, full power to make war, conclude peace, establish commerce, and to do all other acts and things which other States may rightfully do." You will see in a few days a Declaration setting forth the causes which have impelled us to this mighty revolution, and the reasons which will justify it in the sight of God and man. A plan of confederation will be taken up in a few days.

When I look back to the year 1761, and recollect the argument con-

cerning writs of assistance in the superior court, which I have hitherto
considered as the commencement of this controversy between Great
Britain and America, and run through the whole period, from that time
to this, and recollect the series of political events, the chain of causes and
effects, I am surprised at the suddenness as well as greatness of this revolution. Britain has been filled with folly, and America with wisdom. At
least, this is my judgment. Time must determine. It is the will of Heaven
that the two countries should be sundered forever. It may be the will of
Heaven that America shall suffer calamities still more wasting, and distresses yet more dreadful. If this is to be the case, it will have this good
effect at least. It will inspire us with many virtues which we have not,
and correct many errors, follies, and vices which threaten to disturb, dis-
honor, and destroy us. The furnace of affliction produces refinement, in
states as well as individuals. And the new governments we are assuming
in every part will require a purification from our vices, and an augmentation of our virtues, or they will be no blessings. The people will have unbounded power, and the people are extremely addicted to corruption and
venality, as well as the great. But I must submit all my hopes and fears
to an overruling Providence, in which, unfashionable as the faith may
be, I firmly believe. . . .

The second day of July 1776 will be the most memorable epocha in the
history of America. I am apt to believe that it will be celebrated by succeeding generations as the great anniversary festival. It ought to be com-
memorated, as the day of deliverance, by solemn acts of devotion to God
Almighty. It ought to be solemnized with pomp and parade, with shows,
games, sports, guns, bells, bonfires, and illuminations, from one end of
this continent to the other, from this time forward, forevermore.

You will think me transported with enthusiasm, but I am not. I am
well aware of the toil, and blood, and treasure that it will cost us to
maintain this Declaration, and support and defend these States. Yet,
through all the gloom, I can see the rays of ravishing light and glory. I
can see that the end is more than worth all the means, and that posterity
will triumph in that day's transaction, even although we should rue it,
which I trust in God we shall not.

11. *For a Philosophical Society in Boston*

To Abigail Adams

August 4, 1776

I wonder extremely at the fondness of our people for scholars educated
at the southward, and for Southern preachers. Particular gentlemen here,
who have improved upon their education by travel, shine; but in general,

old Massachusetts outshines her younger sisters. Still in several particulars they have more wit than we. They have societies, the Philosophical Society particularly, which excites a scientific emulation, and propagates their fame. If ever I get through this scene of politics and war, I will spend the remainder of my days in endeavoring to instruct my countrymen in the art of making the most of their abilities and virtues; an art which they have hitherto too much neglected. A philosophical society shall be established at Boston, if I have wit and address enough to accomplish it, some time or other. Pray set brother Cranch's philosophical head to plodding upon this project. Many of his lucubrations would have been published and preserved, for the benefit of mankind and for his honor, if such a club had existed.

My countrymen want art and address. They want knowledge of the world. They want the exterior and superficial accomplishment of gentlemen, upon which the world has set so high a value. In solid abilities and real virtues they vastly excel, in general, any people upon this continent. Our New England people are awkward and bashful, yet they are pert, ostentatious, and vain, a mixture which excites ridicule and gives disgust. They have not the faculty of showing themselves to the best advantage, nor the art of concealing this faculty; an art and faculty which some people possess in the highest degree. Our deficiencies in these respects are owing wholly to the little intercourse we have with strangers, and to our inexperience in the world. These imperfections must be remedied, for New England must produce the heroes, the statesmen, the philosophers, or America will make no great figure for some time.

12. *"I Must Study Politics"*

To Abigail Adams

Without date, 1780

. . . Since my arrival this time, I have driven about Paris more than I did before. The rural scenes around this town are charming. The public walks, gardens, etc., are extremely beautiful. The gardens of the Palais Royal and the Gardens of the Tuileries are very fine. The Place de Louis XV, the Place Vendôme or Place de Louis XIV, the Place Victoire, the Place Royale, are fine squares, ornamented with very magnificent statues. I wish I had time to describe these objects to you in a manner that I should have done twenty-five years ago; but my head is too full of schemes, and my heart of anxiety, to use expressions borrowed from you know whom. To take a walk in the Gardens of the Palace of the Tuileries and describe the statues there, all in marble, in which the ancient divinities and heroes are represented with exquisite art, would be a very pleas-

ant amusement and instructive entertainment, improving in history, mythology, poetry, as well as in statuary. Another walk in the gardens of Versailles would be useful and agreeable. But to observe these objects with taste, and describe them so as to be understood, would require more time and thought than I can possibly spare. It is not indeed the fine arts which our country requires; the useful, the mechanic arts are those which we have occasion for in a young country as yet simple and not far advanced in luxury, although perhaps much too far for her age and character. I could fill volumes with descriptions of temples and palaces, paintings, sculptures, tapestry, porcelain, etc., etc., etc., if I could have time; but I could not do this without neglecting my duty. The science of government is my duty to study, more than all other sciences; the arts of legislation and administration and negotiation ought to take place of, indeed to exclude, in a manner, all other arts. I must study politics and war, that my sons may have liberty to study mathematics and philosophy. My sons ought to study mathematics and philosophy, geography, natural history and naval architecture, navigation, commerce, and agriculture, in order to give their children a right to study painting, poetry, music, architecture, statuary, tapestry, and porcelain. Adieu.

13. *The Divine Science of Politics*

To James Warren

The Hague, 17 June, 1782.

Broken to pieces and worn out with the diseases engendered by the tainted atmosphere of Amsterdam operating upon the effects of fatiguing journeys, dangerous voyages, a variety of climates, and eternal anxiety of mind, I have not been able to write you so often as I wished; but now I hope the fine season and the pure air of the Hague will restore me. Perhaps you will say that the air of a Court is as putrid as that of Amsterdam. In a moral and political sense, perhaps; but I am determined that the bad morals and false politics of other people shall no longer affect my repose of mind nor disturb my physical constitution. What is it to me, after having done all I can to set them right, whether other people go to heaven or to the devil? I may howl and weep, but this will have no effect. I may then just as well sing and laugh.

Pray, how do you like your new allies the Dutch? Does your imagination rove into futurity, and speculate and combine as it used to do? It is a pretty amusement to play a game with nations as if they were fox and geese, or coins upon a checker-board, or the personages at chess, is it not? It is, however, the real employment of a statesman to play such a

game sometimes; a sublime one, truly; enough to make a man serious, however addicted to sport. Politics are the divine science, after all. How is it possible that any man should ever think of making it subservient to his own little passions and mean private interests? Ye baseborn sons of fallen Adam, is the end of politics a fortune, a family, a gilded coach, a train of horses, and a troop of livery servants, balls at Court, splendid dinners and suppers? Yet the divine science of politics is at length in Europe reduced to a mechanical system composed of these materials. What says the muse, Mrs. Warren?

What is to become of an independent statesman, one who will bow the knee to no idol, who will worship nothing as a divinity but truth, virtue, and his country? I will tell you; he will be regarded more by posterity than those who worship hounds and horses; and although he will not make his own fortune, he will make the fortune of his country. The liberties of Corsica, Sweden, and Geneva may be overturned, but neither his character can be hurt, nor his exertions rendered ineffectual. Oh peace! when wilt thou permit me to visit Penns-hill, Milton-hill, and all the blue hills? I love every tree and every rock upon all those mountains. Roving among these, and the quails, partridges, squirrels, &c., that inhabit them, shall be the amusement of my declining years. God willing, I will not go to Vermont. I must be within the scent of the sea.

I hope to send along a treaty in two or three months. I love the Dutchmen with all their faults. There is a strong spirit of liberty among them, and many excellent qualities. Next year their navy will be so strong as to be able to do a great deal. They may do something this.

I am going to Court to sup with princes, princesses, and ambassadors. I had rather sup with you at one of our hills, though I have no objection to supping at Court. Adieu!

14. *Nobility*

To Count Sarsfield

Grosvenor Square, January 21, 1785

... How goes on your inquiry into fiefs? If you do not make haste, I may, perhaps, interfere with you. I have half a mind to devote the next ten years to the making of a book upon the subject of nobility. I wish to inquire into the practice of all nations, ancient and modern, civilized and savage, under all religions—Mahometan, Christian, and Pagan—to see how far the division of mankind into patricians and plebeians, nobles and simples, is necessary and inevitable, and how far it is not. *Nature has not made this discrimination. Art has done it. Art may then prevent it. Would*

*it do good or evil to prevent it? I believe good, think what you will of it.
How can it be prevented? In short, it is a splendid subject; and if I were
not too lazy, I would undertake it.*

I want to see nations in uniform. *No church canonicals, no lawyer's
robes, no distinctions in society, but such as sense and honesty make.*
What a fool! what an enthusiast! you will say. What then? Why should
not I have my hobby-horse to ride as well as my friend? I'll tell you
what. *I believe this many-headed beast, the people, will, some time or
other, have wit enough to throw their riders; and if they should, they will
put an end to an abundance of tricks with which they are now curbed
and bitted, whipped and spurred.*

15. *The Education of John Quincy Adams*

To Benjamin Waterhouse

Auteuil, April 24, 1785

This letter will be delivered you by your old acquaintance John Quincy
Adams, whom I beg leave to recommend to your attention and favor. He
is anxious to study some time at your university before he begins the
study of the law, which appears at present to be the profession of his
choice. He must undergo an examination, in which I suspect he will not
appear exactly what he is. In truth, there are few who take their degrees
at college who have so much knowledge. But his studies having been
pursued by himself, on his travels, without any steady tutor, he will be
found awkward in speaking Latin, in prosody, in parsing, and even, perhaps, in that accuracy of pronunciation in reading orations or poems in
that language which is often chiefly attended to in such examinations. It
seems to be necessary, therefore, that I make this apology for him to you,
and request you to communicate it in confidence to the gentlemen who
are to examine him, and such others as you think prudent. If you were to
examine him in English and French poetry, I know not where you would
find anybody his superior; in Roman and English history, few persons of
his age. It is rare to find a youth possessed of so much knowledge. He
has translated Virgil's Æneid, Suetonius, the whole of Sallust, and Tacitus's Agricola, his Germany, and several books of his Annals, a great part
of Horace, some of Ovid, and some of Cæsar's commentaries, in writing,
besides a number of Tully's orations. These he may show you; and although you will find the translations in many places inaccurate in point
of style, as must be expected at his age, you will see abundant proof that
it is impossible to make those translations without understanding his
authors and their language very well.

In Greek his progress has not been equal; yet he has studied morsels in Aristotle's Poetics, in Plutarch's Lives, and Lucian's Dialogues, the choice of Hercules, in Xenophon, and lately he has gone through several books in Homer's Iliad.

In mathematics I hope he will pass muster. In the course of the last year, instead of playing cards like the fashionable world, I have spent my evenings with him. We went with some accuracy through the geometry in the Preceptor, the eight books of Simpson's Euclid in Latin, and compared it, problem by problem and theorem by theorem, with le père de Chales in French; we went through plane trigonometry and plain sailing, Fleming's Algebra, and the decimal fractions, arithmetical and geometrical proportions, and the conic sections, in Ward's mathematics. I then attempted a sublime flight, and endeavored to give him some idea of the differential method of calculation of the Marquis de L'Hôpital, and the method of fluxions and infinite series of Sir Isaac Newton; but alas! it is thirty years since I thought of mathematics, and I found I had lost the little I once knew, especially of these higher branches of geometry, so that he is as yet but a smatterer, like his father. However, he has a foundation laid, which will enable him, with a year's attendance on the mathematical professor, to make the necessary proficiency for a degree. He is studious enough, and emulous enough, and when he comes to mix with his new friends and young companions, he will make his way well enough. I hope he will be upon his guard against those airs of superiority among the scholars, which his larger acquaintance with the world, and his manifest superiority in the knowledge of some things, may but too naturally inspire into a young mind, and I beg of you, Sir, to be his friendly monitor in this respect and in all others.

16. *"An Empire of Liberty"*

To Count Sarsfield

London, February 3, 1786

... It has ever been my hobby-horse to see rising in America an empire of liberty, and a prospect of two or three hundred millions of freemen, without one noble or one king among them. You say it is impossible. If I should agree with you in this, I would still say, let us try the experiment, and preserve our equality as long as we can. A better system of education for the common people might preserve them long from such artificial inequalities as are prejudicial to society, by confounding the natural distinctions of right and wrong, virtue and vice.

17. *"Confession of Political Faith"*

To James Warren

Grosvenor Square, January 9, 1787

. . . The appearance of county conventions and their resolutions set me upon throwing together some disquisitions concerning our governments, which are now printed. I will send you a copy of it. Popularity was never my mistress, nor was I ever or shall I ever be a popular man. This book will make me unpopular. But one thing I know, a man must be sensible of the errors of the people, and upon his guard against them, and must run the risk of their displeasure sometimes, or he will never do them any good in the long run. I deliver the book up, to the mercy of a world, that will never show me much mercy, as my confession of political faith. Unpopular as it may be at present, the time will come, after I am dead, when the system of it in general must be adopted, with bitter repentance that it was not heeded sooner. It is much easier to pull down a government in such a conjuncture of affairs as we have seen, than to build up, at such a season as the present. If the Massachusetts can be governed without a total separation of the executive power from the senate, the house, and the people, I am altogether ignorant of the character of that people, and have not made one sound observation upon the history of nations. . . .

18. *"Mobs Will Never Do"*

To Benjamin Hichborn

London, 27 January 1787

. . . I see, by some newspapers received to-day, that you have distinguished yourself in support of the laws, in a manner that does you great honor, and will not soon be forgotten. I begin to suspect that some gentlemen who had more zeal than knowledge in the year 1770, will soon discover that I had good policy, as well as sound law, on my side, when I ventured to lay open before our people the laws against riots, routs, and unlawful assemblies. Mobs will never do to govern States or command armies. I was as sensible of it in 1770 as I am in 1787. To talk of liberty in such a state of things! Is not a Shattuck or a Shays as great a tyrant, when he would pluck up law and justice by the roots, as a Bernard or a Hutchinson, when he would overturn them partially? . . .

19. *On the New U.S. Constitution*

To Thomas Jefferson

London, December 6, 1787

. . . You are afraid of the one, I, of the few. We agree perfectly that the many should have a full, fair, and perfect representation. You are apprehensive of monarchy, I, of aristocracy. I would, therefore, have given more power to the president, and less to the senate. The nomination and appointment to all offices, I would have given to the president, assisted only by a privy council of his own creation; but not a vote or voice would I have given to the senate or any senator unless he were of the privy council. Faction and distraction are the sure and certain consequences of giving to a senate a vote in the distribution of offices. You are apprehensive that the president, when once chosen, will be chosen again and again as long as he lives. So much the better, as it appears to me. You are apprehensive of foreign interference, intrigue, and influence. So am I. But as often as elections happen, the danger of foreign influence renews. The less frequently they happen, the less danger; and if the same man may be chosen again, it is possible he will be, and the danger of foreign influence will be less. Foreigners, seeing little prospect, will have less courage for enterprise. Elections, my dear sir, to offices which are a great object of ambition, I look at with terror. Experiments of this kind have been so often tried, and so universally found productive of horrors, that there is great reason to dread them. . . .

20. *"No Liberty without Balance"*

To Thomas Brand-Hollis

Fountain Inn, Portsmouth, April 5, 1788.

My dear sir,

If ever there was any philosophic solitude, your two friends have found it in this place, where we have been wind bound, a whole week, without a creature to speak to. Our whole business, pleasure and amusement has been reading Necker's Religious opinions, Halley's Old Maids, and Cumberland's fourth Observer. Our whole stock is now exhausted, and if the ship should not arrive with a fresh supply of books, we shall be obliged to write romances to preserve us from melancholy.

I know not whether atheism has made much progress in England: and perhaps it would do more hurt than good to publish any thing upon

the subject, otherwise Necker's book appears to me to deserve the best translation and edition that can be made of it. Mr. Mortimer perhaps might find his account in it. Necker's subject is so much more interesting to human nature, that I am almost disgusted with my own. Yet my countrymen have so much more need of arguments against errors in government, than in religion, that I am again comforted and encouraged. At this moment there is a greater fermentation throughout all Europe upon the subject of government, than was perhaps ever known, at any former period. France, Holland, and Flanders are alive to it. Is government a science or not? Are there any principles on which it is founded? What are its ends? If indeed there is no rule; no standard; all must be accident and change. If there is a standard, what is it?—It is easier to make a people discontented with a bad government, than to teach them how to establish and maintain a good one. Liberty can never be created and preserved without a people; and by a people, I mean a common people, in contradistinction from the gentlemen; and a people can never be created and preserved without an executive authority in one hand, separated entirely from the body of the gentlemen. The two ladies Aristocratia and Democratia will eternally pull caps, till one or other is mistress. If the first is the conqueress she never fails to depress and debase her rival into the most deplorable servitude. If the last conquers, she eternally surrenders herself into the arms of a ravisher. Kings, therefore, are the natural allies of the common people, and the prejudices against them are by no means favorable to liberty. Kings and the common people have both a common enemy in the gentlemen, and they must unite in some degree or other against them, or both will be destroyed; the one dethroned and the other enslaved. The common people too are unable to defend themselves against their own ally, the king, without another ally in the gentlemen. It is, therefore, indispensably necessary, that the gentlemen in a body, or by representatives, should be an independent and essential branch of the constitution. By a king, I mean a single person possessed of the whole executive power. You have often said to me, that it is difficult to preserve the balance. This is true. It is difficult to preserve liberty. But there can be no liberty without some balance: and it is certainly easier to preserve a balance of three branches than of two.—If the people cannot preserve a balance of three branches, how is it possible for them to preserve one of two only? If the people of England find it difficult to preserve their balance at present, how would they do, if they had the election of a king, and an house of lords to make, once a year, or once in seven years, as well as of an house of commons? It seems evident at first blush, that periodical elections of the king and peers in England, in addition to the commons, would produce agitations that must destroy all order and safety as well as liberty. The gentlemen too, can never defend themselves against a brace and united common people, but by an alliance with a king; nor against a king, without an alliance with the

common people. It is the insatiability of human passions, that is the foundation of all government. Men are not only ambitious, but their ambition is unbounded: they are not only avaricious, but their avarice is insatiable. The desires of kings, gentlemen and common people,—all increase, instead of being satisfied by indulgence. This fact being allowed, it will follow that it is necessary to place checks upon them all. —Pray write me upon these subjects when I arrive in America.

21. *Republican Systems*

To Benjamin Rush

New York June 19, 1789

Dear Sir,—Your single Principle in your Letter of the 15th must fail you. You say "that Republican Systems have never had a fair Tryal." What do you mean by a "fair Tryal"? and what by Republican systems? Every Government that has more than one Man in its sovereignty is a republican system. Tryals innumerable have been made—as many as there have existed Nations. There is not and never was, I believe, on earth, a Nation, which has not been, at some Period of its duration, under a Republican Government: *i.e.* under a Government of more than one. All the various combinations and modifications which the subtle Brains of Men could invent have been attempted, to no other purpose but to shew that Discord, Anarchy and Uncertainty of Life, Liberty and Property, can be avoided only by a perfect equilibrium in the Constitution. You seem determined not to allow a limited monarchy to be a republican system, which it certainly is, and the best that has ever been tryed.

There is no Proposition, of the Truth of which I am more clearly convinced than this, that the "Influence of general Science," instead of curing any defects in an unballanced Republick, would only increase and inflame them and make them more intollerable: for this obvious and unanswerable Reason, that Parties would have in them, a greater number of able and ambitious Men, who would only understand the better, how to worry one another with greater Art and dexterity. Religion itself by no means cures this inveterate evil, for parties are always founded on some Principle, and the more conscientious Men are, the more determined they will be in pursuit of their Principle, System and Party.

I should as soon think of closing all my window shutters, to enable me to see, as of banishing the Classicks, to improve Republican Ideas. How can you say that Factions have been few in America? Have they not rendered Property insecure? have they not trampled Justice under foot?

have not Majorities voted property out of the pocketts of others into their own, with the most decided Tyranny?

Have not our Parties behaved like all Republican Parties? is not the History of Hancock and Bowdoin, the History of the Medici and Albizi —that of Clinton and Yates, the same with that of the Cancellieri and the Panchiatichi? and so on through the Continent. And we shall find that without a Ballance the Progress will soon be, from Libels to Riots, from Riots to Seditions and from Seditions to Civil Wars.

Every Project to enlighten our Fellow Citizens has my most hearty good wishes: because it tends to bring them into a right way of thinking respecting the means of their Happiness, civil, political, social and religious.

I wish with all my heart, that the Constitution had expressed as much Homage to the Supreme Ruler of the Universe as the President has done in his first speech. The *Petit Maitres* who call themselves Legislators and attempt to found a Government on any other than an eternal Basis of Morals and Religion, have as much of my Pitty as can consist with Contempt.

22. *The Constitution and Limited Monarchy*

To Roger Sherman

Richmond Hill, July 18, 1789

. . . Let us . . . consider what our constitution is, and see whether any other name can with propriety be given it than that of a monarchical republic, or, if you will, a limited monarchy. The duration of our president is neither perpetual nor for life; it is only for four years; but his power during those four years is much greater than that of an avoyer, a consul, a podestà, a doge, a stadtholder; nay, than a king of Poland; nay, than a king of Sparta. I know of no first magistrate in any republican government, excepting England and Neuchâtel, who possesses a constitutional dignity, authority, and power comparable to his. The power of sending and receiving ambassadors, of raising and commanding armies and navies, of nominating and appointing and commissioning all officers, of managing the treasurers, the internal and external affairs of the nation; nay, the whole executive power, coextensive with the legislative power, is vested in him, and he has the right, and his is the duty, to take care that the laws be faithfully executed. These rights and duties, these prerogatives and dignities, are so transcendent that they must naturally and necessarily excite in the nation all the jealousy, envy, fears, apprehen-

sions, and opposition, that are so constantly observed in England against the crown.

That these powers are necessary, I readily admit. That the laws cannot be executed without them; that the lives, liberties, properties, and characters of the citizens cannot be secure without their protection, is most clear. But it is equally certain, I think, that they ought to have been still greater, or much less. The limitations upon them in the cases of war, treaties, and appointments to office, and especially the limitation on the president's independence as a branch of the legislative, will be the destruction of this constitution, and involve us in anarchy, if not amended. I shall pass over all particulars for the present, except the last; because that is now the point in dispute between you and me. Longitude, and the philosopher's stone, have not been sought with more earnestness by philosophers than a guardian of the laws has been studied by legislators from Plato to Montesquieu; but every project has been found to be no better than committing the lamb to the custody of the wolf, except that one which is called a *balance of power*. A simple sovereignty in one, a few, or many, has no balance, and therefore no laws. A divided sovereignty without a balance, or, in other words, where the division is unequal, is always at war, and consequently has no laws. In our constitution the sovereignty—that is, the legislative power—is divided into three branches. The house and senate are equal, but the third branch, though essential, is not equal. The president must pass judgment upon every law; but in some cases his judgment may be overruled. These cases will be such as attack his constitutional power; it is, therefore, certain he has not equal power to defend himself, or the constitution, or the judicial power, as the senate and house have.

Power naturally grows. Why? Because human passions are insatiable. But that power alone can grow which already is too great; that which is unchecked; that which has no equal power to control it. *The legislative power, in our constitution, is greater than the executive; it will, therefore, encroach, because both aristocratical and democratical passions are insatiable. The legislative power will increase, the executive will diminish. In the legislature, the monarchical power is not equal either to the aristocratical or democratical; it will, therefore, decrease, while the other will increase. Indeed, I think the aristocratical power is greater than either the monarchical or democratical. That will, therefore, swallow up the other two. . . .*

23. *Corruption in Elections*

To Benjamin Rush

New York, April 18, 1790

. . . How many follies and indiscreet speeches do your minutes in your note-book bring to my recollection, which I had forgotten forever! Alas! I fear I am not yet much more prudent. Your character of Mr. Paine is very well and very just. To the accusation against me which you have recorded in your note-book of the 17th of March last, I plead not guilty. I deny an attachment to monarchy, and I deny that I have changed my principles since 1776. No letter of mine to Mr. Hooper was ever printed that I know of. Indeed, I have but a very confused recollection of having ever written him any letter. If any letter has been printed in my name, I desire to see it. You know that a letter of mine to Mr Wythe was printed by Dunlap, in January 1776, under the title of "Thoughts on Government, in a letter from a gentlemen to his friend." In that pamphlet I recommended a leg- islature in three independent branches, and to such a legislature I am still attached. But I own that at that time I understood very little of the sub- ject, and if I had changed my opinions, should have no scruple to avow it. I own that awful experience has concurred with reading and reflection to convince me that Americans are more rapidly disposed to corruption in elections than I thought they were fourteen years ago.

My friend Dr. Rush will excuse me if I caution him against a fraudu- lent use of the words *monarchy* and *republic*. I am a mortal and irrecon- cilable enemy to monarchy. I am no friend to *hereditary limited* monarchy in America. This I know can never be admitted without an hereditary Senate to control it, and a hereditary nobility or Senate in America I know to be unattainable and impracticable. I should scarcely be for it if it were. Do not, therefore, my friend, misunderstand me and mis- represent me to posterity. I am for a balance between the legislative and executive powers, and I am for enabling the executive to be at all times capable of maintaining the balance between the Senate and House, or, in other words, between the aristocratical and democratical interests. Yet I am for having all three branches elected at stated periods, and these elections, I hope, will continue until the people shall be convinced that fortune, providence, or chance, call it which you will, is better than elec- tion. If the time should come when corruption shall be added to intrigue and manœuvre in elections, and produce civil war, then, in my opinion, chance will be better than choice for all but the House of Representa- tives.

Accept my thanks for your polite and obliging invitation to Philadel-

phia. Nothing would give me more pleasure than such a visit; but I must deny myself that satisfaction. I know I have friends in Pennsylvania, and such as I esteem very much as friends of virtue, liberty, and good government. What you mean by "more than British degrees of corruption" at New York, and by "sophisticated government," I know not. The continent is a kind of whispering gallery, and acts and speeches are reverberated round from New York in all directions. The report is very loud at a distance, when the whisper is very gentle in the centre. But if you see such corruption in your countrymen, on what do you found your hopes? I lament the deplorable condition of my country, which seems to be under such a fatality that the people can agree upon nothing. When they seem to agree, they are so unsteady that it is but for a moment. That changes may be made for the better, is probable. I know of no change that would occasion much danger, but that of President. I wish very heartily that a change of Vice-President could be made to-morrow. I have been too ill-used in the office to be fond of it—if I had not been introduced into it in a manner that made it a disgrace. I will never serve in it again upon such terms. Though I have acted in public with immense multitudes, I have had few friends, and those certainly not interested ones. These I shall love in public or private. Adieu.

24. *American and French Revolutions*

To Richard Price

New York, 19 April, 1790

My dear Friend,—Accept of my best thanks for your favor of February 1st, and the excellent discourse[1] that came with it. I love the zeal and the spirit which dictated this discourse, and admire the general sentiments of it. From the year 1760 to this hour, the whole scope of my life has been to support such principles and propagate such sentiments. No sacrifices of myself or my family, no dangers, no labors, have been too much for me in this great cause. The revolution in France could not therefore be indifferent to me; but I have learned by awful experience to rejoice with trembling. I know that encyclopedists and economists, Diderot and D'Alembert, Voltaire and Rousseau, have contributed to this great event more than Sidney, Locke, or Hoadley, perhaps more than the American revolution; and I own to you, I know not what to make of a republic of thirty million atheists. The Constitution is but an experiment, and must and will be altered. I know it to be impossible that France should be long

[1] On the Love of Country. This sermon was the occasion of Burke's *Reflections on the French Revolution.*

governed by it. If the sovereignty is to reside in one assembly, the king, princes of the blood, and principal quality, will govern it at their pleasure as long as they can agree; when they differ, they will go to war, and act over again all the tragedies of Valois, Bourbons, Lorraines, Guises, and Colignis, two hundred years ago. The Greeks sung the praises of Harmodius and Aristogiton for restoring equal laws. Too many Frenchmen, after the example of too many Americans, pant for equality of persons and property. The impracticability of this, God Almighty has decreed, and the advocates for liberty, who attempt it, will surely suffer for it.

I thank you, Sir, for your kind compliment. As it has been the great aim of my life to be useful, if I had any reason to think I was so, as you seem to suppose, it would make me happy. For "eminence" I care nothing; for though I pretend not to be exempt from ambition, or any other human passion, I have been convinced from my infancy and have been confirmed every year and day of my life, that the mechanic and peasant are happier than any nobleman, or magistrate, or king, and that the higher a man rises, if he has any sense of duty, the more anxious he must be. Our new government is an attempt to divide a sovereignty; a fresh essay at *imperium in imperio*. It cannot, therefore, be expected to be very stable or very firm. It will prevent us for a time from drawing our swords upon each other, and when it will do that no longer, we must call a new Convention to reform it. The difficulty of bringing millions to agree in any measures, to act by any rule, can never be conceived by him who has not tried it. It is incredible how small is the number, in any nation, of those who comprehend any system of constitution or administration, and those few it is wholly impossible to unite. I am a sincere inquirer after truth, but I find very few who discover the same truths. The king of Prussia has found one which has also fallen in my way. "That it is the peculiar quality of the human understanding, that example should correct no man. The blunders of the father are lost to his children, and every generation must commit its own." I have never sacrificed my judgment to kings, ministers, nor people, and I never will. When either shall see as I do, I shall rejoice in their protection, aid, and honor; but I see no prospect that either will ever think as I do, and therefore I shall never be a favorite with either. I do not desire to be; but I sincerely wish and devoutly pray, that a hundred years of civil wars may not be the portion of all Europe for want of a little attention to the true elements of the science of government. With sentiments, moral sentiments, which are and must be eternal, I am your friend, &c.

25. *Political Architecture*

To Samuel Adams

New York, October 18, 1790

. . . You agree that there are undoubtedly principles of political architecture. But, instead of particularizing any of them, you seem to place all your hopes in the universal, or at least more general, prevalence of knowledge and benevolence. I think with you that knowledge and benevolence ought to be promoted as much as possible; but, despairing of ever seeing them sufficiently general for the security of society, I am for seeking institutions which may supply in some degree the defect. If there were no ignorance, error, or vice, there would be neither principles nor systems of civil or political government.

I am not often satisfied with the opinions of Hume; but in this he seems well founded, that all projects of government founded in the supposition or expectation of extraordinary degrees of virtue are evidently chimerical. Nor do I believe it possible, humanly speaking, that men should ever be greatly improved in knowledge or benevolence, without assistance from the principles and system of government.

I am very willing to agree with you in fancying that in the greatest improvements of society, government will be in the republican form. It is a fixed principle with me that all good government is and must be republican. But, at the same time, your candor will agree with me that there is not in lexicography a more fraudulent word. Whenever I use the word *republic* with approbation, I mean a government in which the people have collectively, or by representation, an essential share in the sovereignty. The republican forms of Poland and Venice are much worse, and those of Holland and Bern very little better, than the monarchical form in France before the late revolution. By the republican form, I know you do not mean the plan of Milton, Nedham, or Turgot. For, after a fair trial of its miseries, the simple monarchical form will ever be, as it has ever been, preferred to it by mankind. Are we not, my friend, in danger of rendering the word *republican* unpopular in this country by an indiscreet, indeterminate, and equivocal use of it? The people of England have been obliged to wean themselves from the use of it, by making it unpopular and unfashionable, because they found it was artfully used by some, and simply understood by others, to mean the government of their interregnum parliament. They found they could not wean themselves from that destructive form of government so entirely as that a mischievous party would not still remain in favor of it, by any other means than by making the words *republic* and *republican* unpopular. They have succeeded to such a degree that, with a vast majority of that nation, a

republican is as unamiable as a witch, a blasphemer, a rebel, or a tyrant. If, in this country, the word *republic* should be generally understood, as it is by some, to mean a form of government inconsistent with a mixture of three powers, forming a mutual balance, we may depend upon it that such mischievous effects will be produced by the use of it as will compel the people of America to renounce, detest, and execrate it as the English do. With these explanations, restrictions, and limitations, I agree with you in your love of republican governments, but in no other sense.

With you, I have also the honor most perfectly to harmonize in your sentiments of the humanity and wisdom of promoting education in knowledge, virtue, and benevolence. But I think that these will confirm mankind in the opinion of the necessity of preserving and strengthening the dikes against the ocean, its tides and storms. Human appetites, passions, prejudices, and self-love will never be conquered by benevolence and knowledge alone, introduced by human means. The millennium itself neither supposes nor implies it. All civil government is then to cease, and the Messiah is to reign. That happy and holy state is therefore wholly out of this question. You and I agree in the utility of universal education; but will nations agree in it as fully and extensively as we do, and be at the expense of it? We know, with as much certainty as attends any human knowledge, that they will not. We cannot, therefore, advise the people to depend for their safety, liberty, and security upon hopes and blessings which we know will not fall to their lot. If we do our duty then to the people, we shall not deceive them, but advise them to depend upon what is in their power and will relieve them.

Philosophers, ancient and modern, do not appear to me to have studied nature, the whole of nature, and nothing but nature. Lycurgus's principle was war and family pride; Solon's was what the people would bear, &c. The best writings of antiquity upon government, those, I mean, of Aristotle, Zeno, and Cicero, are lost. We have human nature, society, and universal history to observe and study, and from these we may draw all the real principles which ought to be regarded. Disciples will follow their masters, and interested partisans their chieftains; let us like it or not, we cannot help it. But if the true principles can be discovered, and fairly, fully, and impartially laid before the people, the more light increases, the more the reason of them will be seen, and the more disciples they will have. Prejudice, passion, and private interest, which will always mingle inhuman inquiries, one would think might be enlisted on the side of truth, at least in the greatest number; for certainly the majority are interested in the truth, if they could see to the end of all its consequences. "Kings have been deposed by aspiring nobles." True, and never by any other. "These" (the nobles, I suppose) "have waged everlasting war against the common rights of men." True, when they have been possessed of the *summa imperii* in one body, without a check. So have the plebeians; so have the people; so have kings; so has human

nature, in every shape and combination, and so it ever will. But, on the other hand, the nobles have been essential parties in the preservation of liberty, whenever and wherever it has existed. In Europe, they alone have preserved it against kings and people, wherever it has been preserved; or, at least, with very little assistance from the people. One hideous despotism, as horrid as that of Turkey, would have been the lot of every nation of Europe if the nobles had not made stands. By nobles, I mean not peculiarly an hereditary nobility, or any particular modification, but the natural and actual aristocracy among mankind. The existence of this you will not deny. You and I have seen four noble families rise up in Boston—the CRAFTS, GORES, DAWES, and AUSTINS. These are as really a nobility in our town as the Howards, Somersets, Berties, &c., in England. Blind, undistinguishing reproaches against the aristocratical part of mankind, a division which nature has made, and we cannot abolish, are neither pious nor benevolent. They are as pernicious as they are false. They serve only to foment prejudice, jealousy, envy, animosity, and malevolence. They serve no ends but those of sophistry, fraud, and the spirit of party. It would not be true, but it would not be more egregiously false, to say that the people have waged everlasting war against the rights of men.

"The love of liberty," you say, "is interwoven in the soul of man." So it is, according to La Fontaine, in that of a wolf; and I doubt whether it be much more rational, generous, or social in one than in the other, until in man it is enlightened by experience, reflection, education, and civil and political institutions, which are at first produced and constantly supported and improved by a few; that is, by the nobility. The wolf, in the fable, who preferred running in the forest, lean and hungry, to the sleek, plump, and round sides of the dog, because he found the latter was sometimes restrained, had more love of liberty than most men. The numbers of men in all ages have preferred ease, slumber, and good cheer to liberty, when they have been in competition. We must not, then, depend alone upon the love of liberty in the soul of man for its preservation. Some political institutions must be prepared, to assist this love against its enemies. Without these, the struggle will ever end only in a change of impostors. When the people who have no property feel the power in their own hands to determine all questions by a majority, they ever attack those who have property, till the injured men of property lose all patience, and recur to finesse, trick, and stratagem to outwit those who have too much strength, because they have too many hands to be resisted any other way. Let us be impartial, then, and speak the whole truth. Till we do, we shall never discover all the true principles that are necessary. The multitude, therefore, as well as the nobles, must have a check. This is one principle.

"Were the people of England free after they had obliged King John to concede to them their ancient rights?" The people never did this.

There was no people who pretended to anything. It was the nobles
alone. The people pretended to nothing but to be villains, vassals, and
retainers to the king or the nobles. The nobles, I agree, were not free, because all was determined by a majority of their votes, or by arms, not by
law. Their feuds deposed their "Henrys, Edwards, and Richards" to
gratify lordly ambition, patrician rivalry, and "family pride." But if
they had not been deposed, those kings would have become despots,
because the people would not and could not join the nobles in any
regular and constitutional opposition to them. They would have become despots, I repeat it, and that by means of the villains, vassals, and
retainers aforesaid. It is not family pride, my friend, but family popularity that does the great mischief, as well as the great good. Pride, in
the heart of man, is an evil fruit and concomitant of every advantage; of
riches, of knowledge, of genius, of talents, of beauty, of strength, of
virtue, and even of piety. It is sometimes ridiculous, and often pernicious.
But it is even sometimes, and in some degree, useful. But the pride
of families would be always and only ridiculous if it had not family
popularity to work with. The attachment and devotion of the people to
some families inspires them with pride. As long as gratitude or interest,
ambition or avarice, love, hope, or fear, shall be human motives of
action, so long will numbers attach themselves to particular families.
When the people will, in spite of all that can be said or done, cry a
man or a family up to the skies, exaggerate all his talents and virtues,
not hear a word of his weakness or faults, follow implicitly his advice,
detest every man he hates, adore every man he loves, and knock down all
who will not swim down the stream with them, where is your remedy?
When a man or family are thus popular, how can you prevent them
from being proud? You and I know of instances in which popularity has
been a wind, a tide, a whirlwind. The history of all ages and nations is full
of such examples.

Popularity, that has great fortune to dazzle; splendid largesses, to excite
warm gratitude; sublime, beautiful, and uncommon genius or talents, to
produce deep admiration; or anything to support high hopes and strong
fears, will be proud; and its power will be employed to mortify enemies,
gratify friends, procure votes, emoluments, and power. Such family
popularity ever did and ever will govern in every nation, in every climate,
hot and cold, wet and dry, among civilized and savage people, Christians
and Mahometans, Jews and heathens. Declamation against family pride
is a pretty, juvenile exercise, but unworthy of statesmen. They know
the evil and danger is too serious to be sported with. The only way, God
knows, is to put these families into a hole by themselves, and set two
watches upon them; a superior to them all on one side, and the people
on the other.

There are a few popular men in the Massachusetts, my friend, who
have, I fear, less honor, sincerity, and virtue than they ought to have.

These, if they are not guarded against, may do another mischief. They may excite a party spirit and a mobbish spirit, instead of the spirit of liberty, and produce another Wat Tyler's rebellion. They can do no more. But I really think their party language ought not to be countenanced, nor their shibboleths pronounced. The miserable stuff that they utter about the *well-born* is as despicable as themselves. The εὐγενεῖς of the Greeks, the *bien nées* of the French, the *welgebohren* of the Germans and Dutch, the *beloved families* of the Creeks, are but a few samples of national expressions of the same thing, for which every nation on earth has a similar expression. One would think that our scribblers were all the sons of redemptioners or transported convicts. They think with Tarquin, *"In novo populo, ubi omnis repentina atque ex virtute nobilitas fit, futurum locum forti ac strenuo viro."*

Let us be impartial. There is not more of family pride on one side than of vulgar malignity and popular envy on the other. Popularity in one family raises envy in others. But the popularity of the least deserving will triumph over envy and malignity; while that which is acquired by real merit will very often be overborne and oppressed by it.

Let us do justice to the people and to the nobles; for nobles there are, as I have before proved, in Boston as well as in Madrid. But to do justice to both, you must establish an arbitrator between them. This is another principle.

It is time that you and I should have some sweet communion together. I do not believe that we, who have preserved for more than thirty years an uninterrupted friendship, and have so long thought and acted harmoniously together in the worst of times, are now so far asunder in sentiment as some people pretend; in full confidence of which, I have used this freedom, being ever your warm friend.

26. *On His Inauguration*

To Abigail Adams

Philadelphia, March 17, 1797

. . . It would have given me great pleasure to have had some of my family present at my inauguration, which was the most affecting and overpowering scene I ever acted in. I was very unwell, had no sleep the night before, and really did not know but I should have fainted in presence of all the world. I was in great doubt whether to say anything or not besides repeating the oath. And now the world is as silent as the grave. All the Federalists seem to be afraid to approve anybody but

Washington. The Jacobin papers damn with faint praise, and undermine with misrepresentation and insinuation. If the Federalists go to playing pranks, I will resign the office, and let Jefferson lead them to peace, wealth, and power if he will.

From the situation where I now am, I see a scene of ambition beyond all my former suspicions or imaginations; an emulation which will turn our government topsy-turvy. Jealousies and rivalries have been my theme, and checks and balances as their antidotes till I am ashamed to repeat the words; but they never stared me in the face in such horrid forms as at present. I see how the thing is going. At the next election England will set up Jay or Hamilton, and France, Jefferson, and all the corruption of Poland will be introduced; unless the American spirit should rise and say, we will have neither John Bull nor Louis Baboon.

Silence.

27. *The Encouragement of Learning*

To Benjamin Waterhouse

Quincy, August 7, 1805

. . . In 1774 on my journey to Congress, I was invited at Norwalk in Connecticut to see a collection made by a Mr. Arnold, an Englishman, of birds, insects, especially butterflies, made wholly in that neighborhood, and beautifully preserved. . . . I saw it again, ten or a dozen years afterwards in London. In 1778 I went to France, where I saw many cabinets, and some of more curiosity and magnificence than use; but they all served to impress upon my mind the utility of some establishment in America for collecting specimens of the works of nature peculiar to us. In 1779 in composing the frame of government for the State of Massachusetts I thought it the best opportunity which might ever occur to promote a design of this kind and impress upon the minds of the people a sense of the importance of it. . . . [Adams quotes section from Massachusetts Constitution, "The Encouragement of Literature." See No. 61]

As the words flowed from my pen, from the heart in reality rather than the head, in composing this paragraph, I could not help laughing, to myself alone in my closet, at the oddity of it. I expected it would be attacked in the convention from all quarters, on the score of affectation, pedantry, hypocrisy, and above all economy. Many ideas in it implied expense: and I knew then as well as I have known since that too large a portion of the people and their representatives had rather starve their souls than draw upon their purses to pay for nourishment of them; and

therefore no mercy was to be expected for a paragraph that I would not now exchange for a sceptre, and wish may be engraved on my tombstone.

But to my great surprise, instead of objections, it was received with applause and adopted I believe with unanimity, and without any amendment. Even the natural history of the country received no opposition. . . .

28. *"I Do Not Curse the Day When I Engaged in Public Affairs"*

To Benjamin Rush

Quincy, 1 May, 1807.

. . . You ask me, if I do not sometimes imprecate evils on the day on which I became a politician. I have endeavored to recollect that day. It is a remote one. . . . An odd accident has within a month brought to light the inclosed letter, which has lain fifty-one years and a half in darkness and silence, in dust and oblivion.[1] Pray tell me your reflections on the sight of this droll phenomenon. I fancy they will be, first, what would our tories and quakers and proprietors have said of this letter, had it been published in 1774, 5, or 6? But I will not guess at any more of your observations. You shall make them yourself and relate them to me. But I will make my own remarks first, and submit them to you.

1. Paine, in "Common Sense," says, that nobody in America ever thought, till he revealed to them the mighty truth, that America would ever be independent. I remember not the words, but this is the sense as I remember it. This I have always, at all times and in all places, contradicted, and have affirmed that the idea of American independence, sooner or later, and of the necessity of it some time or other, was always familiar to gentlemen of reflection in all parts of America, and I spoke of my own knowledge in this province.

2. I very distinctly remember, that in the war of 1755, a union of the colonies, to defend themselves against the encroachments of the French, was the general wish of the gentlemen with whom I conversed, and it was the opinion of some that we could defend ourselves, and even conquer Canada, better without England than with her, if she would but allow us to unite and exert our strength, courage, and skill, diffident as we were of the last.

3. It was the fear of this union of the colonies, which was indeed commenced in a Congress at Albany, which induced the English to take the war into their own hands.

---

[1] The letter to Nathan Webb, written in 1755.

4. The war was so ill conducted by Shirley, Lord Loudon, Braddock, and all other British commanders, till Wolfe and Amherst came forward, that the utmost anxiety prevailed, and a thousand panics were spread lest the French should overrun us all. All this time I was not alone in wishing that we were unshackled by Britain, and left to defend ourselves.

5. The treatment of the provincial officers and soldiers by the British officers during that war made the blood boil in my veins.

6. Notwithstanding all this, I had no desire of independence as long as Britain would do us justice. I knew it must be an obstinate struggle, and saw no advantage in it as long as Britain should leave our liberties inviolate.

7. Jefferson has acquired such glory by his declaration of independence in 1776, that I think I may boast of my declaration of independence in 1755, twenty-one years older than his.

8. Our governor elect, in his biographical sketch of Samuel Adams, ascribes to him the honor of the first idea and project of independence. In 1755, when my letter to Dr. Webb was written, I had never seen the face of Samuel Adams.

9. The English, the Scotch, the tories, and hyperfederalists will rebellow their execrations against me as a rebel from my infancy, and a plotter of independence more than half a hundred years ago.

10. The present ruling party in the United States will repeat, renew, and redouble their curses and sarcasms against me for having meditated the ruin of this country from a boy, from a mere chicken in the eggshell, by building a navy under pretence of protecting our commerce and seaports, but in reality only as a hobby-horse for myself to ride and to increase my patronage. For there can be no doubt but the boy, though not yet twenty years old, and though pinched and starved in a stingy country school, fully expected to be King of North America, and to marry his daughter to the Prince of Wales, and his son, John Quincy, to the princess royal of England.

11. There can be no doubt but this letter, puerile and childish as it is, will make a distinguished figure in the memoirs of my life. . . .

12. You may depend upon its authenticity, for I have copied it from the original, to every word and almost every letter of which I can attest, and so might any one else, who should compare it with this, from the similarity of hand and composition.

13. *Vive la bagatelle!*

Now, Sir, to be serious, I do not curse the day when I engaged in public affairs. I do not say when I became a politician, for that I never was. I cannot repent of any thing I ever did conscientiously and from a sense of duty. I never engaged in public affairs for my own interest, pleasure, envy, jealousy, avarice, or ambition, or even the desire of fame. If any of these had been my motive, my conduct would have been very different. In every considerable transaction of my public life, I have in-

variably acted according to my best judgment, and I can look up to God for the sincerity of my intentions. How, then, is it possible I can repent? Notwithstanding this, I have an immense load of errors, weaknesses, follies, and sins to mourn over and repent of, and these are the only afflictions of my present life.

But, notwithstanding all, St. Paul and Dr. Barrow have taught me to rejoice evermore, and be content. This phrase, "rejoice evermore," shall never be out of my heart, memory, or mouth again, as long as I live, if I can help it. This is my perfectibility of man.

Your "palace of ice" is a most admirable image. I agree that you and I have been employed in building a palace of ice. However, if we did not believe it to be marble, or silver, or gold, or ivory, or alabaster, or stone, or brick, we both thought it good, sound white oak, which would shelter its inhabitants from the inclemency of the weather, and last a long time. But the heat of the climate in summer has proved it to have been ice. It is all melted to water.

P. S. I forgot a principal point I had in view when I sat down; that is, to congratulate you that the Queen of Etruria has fallen in love with you. Tell Mrs. Rush that I congratulate her that the Queen of Sheba is not likely to visit Solomon at Philadelphia.

29. *The Defence of the Constitutions:* *"An American Boudoir"*

To William Cunningham

Quincy, January 3, 1809

I have sent to the Indian Queen the 2d and 3d vols. of a work which the English editor of the 2d edition calls an History of Republicks. It may be called *The American Boudoir.* What is a Boudoir? It is a *Pouting room.* And what is a Pouting room? In many gentlemen's houses in France, there is an apartment, of an octagonal form, twelve or fifteen feet across, or thirty six or forty-five feet round, and all the eight sides, as well as the ceiling over head, are all of the most polished glass Mirrors: so that, when a man stands in the centre of the room he sees himself in every direction, multiplied into a row of selfs, as far as the eye can reach.

The humour of it is, that when the lady of the house is out of temper, when she is angry, or when she weeps without a cause, she may be locked up in this chamber to pout, and to see in every direction how beautiful she is. There are settees and chairs round the sides and com-

monly a bath in the centre, which may be made hot or cold. So that persons may see themselves naked in every posture. Such a Boudoir is the Defence. Our States may see themselves in it, in every possible light, attitude and movement. They may see all their beauties and all their deformities. Happy they who are made cautious by others' dangers!

30. *On the Louisiana Purchase*

To Josiah Quincy

Quincy, February 9, 1811

Should I let loose my imagination into futurity, I could imagine that I foresee changes and revolutions such as eye hath not seen nor ear heard; changes in forms of government, changes in religion, changes in ecclesiastical establishments, changes in armies and navies, changes in alliances and foreign relations, changes in commerce, &c., &c., &c., without end. I cannot see any better principle at present than to make as little innovation as possible; keep things going as well as we can in the present train.

The Union appears to me to be the rock of our salvation, and every reasonable measure for its preservation is expedient. Upon this principle, I own, I was pleased with the purchase of Louisiana, because, without it, we could never have secured and commanded the navigation of the Mississippi. The western country would infallibly have revolted from the Union. Those States would have united with England, or Spain, or France, or set up an independence, or done anything else to obtain the free use of that river. I wish the Constitution had been more explicit, or that the States had been consulted; but it seems Congress have not entertained any doubts of their authority, and I cannot say that they are destitute of plausible arguments to support their opinion. . . .

Prophecies of division have been familiar in my ears for six-and-thirty years. They have been incessant, but have had no other effect than to increase the attachment of the people to the Union. However lightly we may think of the voice of the people sometimes, they not unfrequently see farther than you or I, in many great fundamental questions; and you may depend upon it, they see in a partition of the Union more danger to American liberty than poor Ames's distempered imagination conceived, and a total loss of independence for both fragments, or all the fragments, of the Union. . . .

31. *"After I Am Dead"*

To Benjamin Rush

Quincy, August 28, 1811

Your letter of the 20th, my dear friend, has filled my eyes with tears, and, indurated stoic as I am, my heart with sensations unutterable by my tongue or pen; not the feelings of vanity, but the overwhelming sense of my own unworthiness of such a panegyric from such a friend. Like Louis the sixteenth, I said to myself, *"Qu'est ce que j'ai fait pour le mériter?"*

Have I not been employed in mischief all my days? Did not the American Revolution produce the French Revolution? And did not the French Revolution produce all the calamities and desolations to the human race and the whole globe ever since? I meant well, however. My conscience was clear as a crystal glass, without a scruple or a doubt. I was borne along by an irresistible sense of duty. God prospered our labors; and, awful, dreadful, and deplorable as the consequences have been, I cannot but hope that the ultimate good of the world, of the human race, and of our beloved country, is intended and will be accomplished by it. While I was in this reverie, I handed your letter to my brother Cranch, the postmaster, of eight-five years of age, an Israelite indeed, who read it with great attention, and at length started up and exclaimed, "I have known you sixty years, and I can bear testimony as a witness to every word your friend has said in this letter in your favor." This completed my humiliation and confusion.

Your letter is the most serious and solemn one I ever received in my life. It has aroused and harrowed up my soul. I know not what to say in answer to it, or to do in consequence of it.

It is most certain that the end of my life cannot be remote. My eyes are constantly fixed upon it, according to the precept or advice of the ancient philosopher; and, if I am not in a total delusion, I daily behold and contemplate it without dismay.

If by dedicating all the rest of my days to the composition of such an address as you propose, I could have any rational assurance of doing any real good to my fellow-citizens of United America, I would cheerfully lay aside all other occupations and amusements and devote myself to it. But there are difficulties and embarrassments in the way, which to me, at present, appear insuperable.

The "sensibility of the public mind," which you anticipate at my decease, will not be so favorable to my memory as you seem to foresee. By the treatment I have received, and continue to receive, I should expect that a large majority of all parties would cordially rejoice to hear that my head was laid low.

I am surprised to read your opinion that "my integrity has never been called in question, and that friends and enemies agree in believing me to be an honest man." If I am to judge by the newspapers and pamphlets that have been printed in America for twenty years past, I should think that both parties believed me the meanest villain in the world.

If they should not suspect me of sinning in the grave, they will charge me with selfishness and hypocrisy before my death, in preparing an address to move the passions of the people, and excite them to promote my children, and perhaps to make my son a king. Washington and Franklin could never do anything but what was imputed to pure, disinterested patriotism; I never could do any thing but what was ascribed to sinister motives.

I agree with you in sentiment, that religion and virtue are the only foundations, not only of republicanism and of all free government, but of social felicity under all governments and in all the combinations of human society. But if I should inculcate this doctrine in my will, I should be charged with hypocrisy and a desire to conciliate the good will of the clergy towards my family, as I was charged by Dr. Priestley and his friend Cooper, and by Quakers, Baptists, and I know not how many other sects, for instituting a national fast, for even common civility to the clergy, and for being a church-going animal.

If I should inculcate those "national, social, domestic, and religious virtues" you recommend, I should be suspected and charged with an hypocritical, machiavelian, jesuitical, pharisaical attempt to promote a national establishment of Presbyterianism in America; whereas I would as soon establish the Episcopal Church, and almost as soon the Catholic Church.

If I should inculcate "fidelity to the marriage bed," it would be said that it proceeded from resentment to General Hamilton, and a malicious desire to hold up to posterity his libertinism. Others would say that it is only a vainglorious ostentation of my own continence. . . .

If I should recommend the sanctification of the sabbath, like a divine, or even only a regular attendance on public worship, as a means of moral instruction and social improvement, like a philosopher or statesman, I should be charged with vain ostentation again, and a selfish desire to revive the remembrance of my own punctuality in this respect; for it is notorious enough that I have been a church-going animal for seventy-six years, from the cradle. And this has been alleged as one proof of my hypocrisy.

Fifty-three years ago I was fired with a zeal, amounting to enthusiasm, against ardent spirits, the multiplication of taverns, retailers, and dram-shops, and tippling houses. . . . Sermons, moral discourses, philosophical dissertations, medical advice, are all lost upon this subject. Nothing but making the commodity scarce and dear will have any effect; and your Republican friend, and, I had almost said, mine, Jefferson, would not permit rum or whiskey to be taxed.

If I should then in my will, my dying legacy, my posthumous exhortation, call it what you will, recommend heavy, prohibitory taxes upon spirituous liquors, which I believe to be the only remedy against their deleterious qualities in society, every one of your brother Republicans and nine-tenths of the Federalists would say that I was a canting Puritan, a profound hypocrite, setting up standards of morality, frugality, economy, temperance, simplicity, and sobriety, that I knew the age was incapable of.

Funds and banks I never approved, or was satisfied with our funding system; it was founded in no consistent principle; it was contrived to enrich particular individuals at the public expense. Our whole banking system I ever abhorred, I continue to abhor, and shall die abhorring.

But I am not an enemy to funding systems. They are absolutely and indispensably necessary in the present state of the world. An attempt to annihilate or prevent them would be as romantic an adventure as any in Don Quixote or in Oberon. A national bank of deposit I believe to be wise, just, prudent, economical, and necessary. But every bank of discount, every bank by which interest is to be paid or profit of any kind made by the deponent, is downright corruption. It is taxing the public for the benefit and profit of individuals; it is worse than old tenor, continental currency, or any other paper money.

Now, Sir, if I should talk in this strain, after I am dead, you know the people of America would pronounce that I had died mad.

My opinion is, that a circulating medium of gold and silver only ought to be introduced and established; that a national bank of deposit only, with a branch in each State, should be allowed; that every bank in the Union ought to be annihilated, and every bank of discount prohibited to all eternity. Not one farthing of profit should ever be allowed on any money deposited in the bank. Now, my friend, if, in my posthumous sermon, exhortation, advice, address, or whatever you may call it, I should gravely deliver such a doctrine, nine-tenths of Republicans as well as Federalists will think that I ought to have been consigned to your tranquillizing chair rather than permitted to write such extravagances. Franklin, Washington, Hamilton, and all our disinterested patriots and heroes, it will be said, have sanctioned paper money and banks, and who is this pedant and bigot of a John Adams, who, from the ground, sounds the tocsin against all our best men, when every body knows he never had anything in view but his private interest from his birth to his death?

Free schools, and all schools, colleges, academies, and seminaries of learning, I can recommend from my heart; but I dare not say that a suffrage should never be permitted to a man who cannot read and write. What would become of the republic of France, if the lives, fortunes, character, of twenty-four millions and a half of men who can neither read nor write should be at the absolute disposal of five hundred thousand who can read?

I am not qualified to write such an address. The style should be pure,

elegant, eloquent, and pathetic in the highest degree. It should be revised, corrected, obliterated, interpolated, amended, transcribed twenty times, polished, refined, varnished, burnished. To all these employments and exercises I am a total stranger. To my sorrow, I have never copied, nor corrected, nor embellished. I understand it not. I never could write declamations, orations, or popular addresses.

If I could persuade my friend Rush, or my friend Jay, my friend Trumbull, or my friend Humphreys, or perhaps my friend Jefferson, to write such a thing for me, I know not why I might not transcribe it, as Washington did so often. Borrowed eloquence, if it contains as good stuff, is as good as one's own eloquence.

The example you recollect of Cæsar's will, is an awful warning. Posthumous addresses may be left by Cæsar as well as Cato, Brutus, or Cicero, and will oftener, perhaps, be applauded, and make deeper impressions; establish empires easier than restore republics; promote tyranny sooner than liberty. . . .

32. *On Renewing Friendship with Jefferson*

To Benjamin Rush

Quincy, December 25, 1811

. . . I perceive plainly enough, Rush, that you have been teasing Jefferson to write to me, as you did me some time ago to write to him. You gravely advise me "to receive the olive branch," as if there had been war; but there has never been any hostility on my part, nor that I know, on his. When there has been no war, there can be no room for negotiations of peace.

Mr. Jefferson speaks of my political opinions; but I know of no difference between him and myself relative to the Constitution, or to forms of government in general. In measures of administration, we have differed in opinion. I have never approved the repeal of the judicial law, the repeal of the taxes, the neglect of the navy; and I have always believed that his system of gunboats for a national defence was defective. To make it complete, he ought to have taken a hint from Molière's "*Femmes précieuses*," or his learned ladies, and appointed three or four brigades of horse, with a Major-General, and three or four brigadiers, to serve on board his galleys of Malta. I have never approved his non-embargo, or any non-intercourse, or non-importation laws.

But I have raised no clamors nor made any opposition to any of these measures. The nation approved them; and what is my judgment against

that of the nation? On the contrary, he disapproved of the alien law and sedition law, which I believed to have been constitutional and salutary, if not necessary.

He disapproved of the eight per cent loan, and with good reason. For I hated it as much as any man, and the army, too, which occasioned it. He disapproved, perhaps, of the partial war with France, which I believed, as far as it proceeded, to be a holy war. He disapproved of taxes, and perhaps the whole scheme of my administration, &c., and so perhaps did the nation. But his administration and mine are passed away into the dark backwards, and are now of no more importance than the administration of the old Congress in 1774 and 1775.

We differed in opinion about the French Revolution. He thought it wise and good, and that it would end in the establishment of a free republic. I saw through it, to the end of it, before it broke out, and was sure it could end only in a restoration of the Bourbons, or a military despotism, after deluging France and Europe in blood. In this opinion I differed from you as much as from Jefferson; but all this made me no more of an enemy to you than to him, nor to him than to you. I believe you both to mean well to mankind and your country. I might suspect you both to sacrifice a little to the infernal Gods, and perhaps unconsciously to suffer your judgments to be a little swayed by a love of popularity, and possibly by a little spice of ambition.

In point of republicanism, all the difference I ever knew or could discover between you and me, or between Jefferson and me, consisted,

1. In the difference between speeches and messages. I was a monarchist because I thought a speech more manly, more respectful to Congress and the nation. Jefferson and Rush preferred messages.

2. I held levees once a week, that all my time might not be wasted by idle visits. Jefferson's whole eight years was a levee.

3. I dined a large company once or twice a week. Jefferson dined a dozen every day.

4. Jefferson and Rush were for liberty and straight hair. I thought curled hair was as republican as straight.

In these, and a few other points of equal importance, all miserable frivolities, that Jefferson and Rush ought to blush that they ever laid any stress upon them, I might differ; but I never knew any points of more consequence on which there was any variation between us.

You exhort me to "forgiveness and love of enemies," as if I considered, or had ever considered, Jefferson as my enemy. This is not so; I have always loved him as a friend. If I ever received or suspected any injury from him, I have forgiven it long and long ago, and have no more resentment against him than against you. . . .

But why do you make so much ado about nothing? Of what use can it be for Jefferson and me to exchange letters? I have nothing to say to him, but to wish him an easy journey to heaven, when he goes, which I wish

may be delayed as long as life shall be agreeable to him. And he can have nothing to say to me, but to bid me make haste and be ready. Time and chance, however, or possibly design, may produce ere long a letter between us.

33. *Against Parties and Factions*

To Thomas Jefferson

Quincy, 9 July, 1813

. . . "The same political parties, which now agitate the United States, have existed through all time." Precisely; and this is precisely the complaint in the preface to the first volume of my Defence. While all other sciences have advanced, that of government is at a stand; little better understood, little better practised now than three or four thousand years ago. What is the reason? I say, parties and factions will not suffer improvements to be made. As soon as one man hints at an improvement, his rival opposes it. No sooner has one party discovered or invented any amelioration of the condition of man, or the order of society than the opposite party belies it, misconstrues it, misrepresents it, ridicules it, insults it, and persecutes it. Records are destroyed. Histories are annihilated or interpolated or prohibited; sometimes by Popes, sometimes by Emperors, sometimes by aristocratical, and sometimes by democratical assemblies, and sometimes by mobs. . . .

I recollect, near thirty years ago, to have said carelessly to you, that I wished I could find time and means to write something upon aristocracy. You seized upon the idea, and encouraged me to do it with all that friendly warmth that is natural and habitual to you. I soon began, and have been writing upon that subject ever since. I have been so unfortunate as never to be able to make myself understood. Your ἄριστοι are the most difficult animals to manage of any thing in the whole theory and practice of government. . . .

34. *Differences on French Revolution*

To Thomas Jefferson

Quincy, 13 July, 1813

... The first time that you and I differed in opinion on any material question was after your arrival from Europe; and that point was the French
revolution. You was well persuaded in your own mind that the nation
would succeed in establishing a free republican government. I was well
persuaded in mine, that a project of such a government, over five-and-
twenty millions of people, when four-and-twenty millions and five
hundred thousand of them could neither read nor write, was as unnatural,
irrational, and impracticable as it would be over the elephants, lions,
tigers, panthers, wolves, and bears, in the royal menagerie at Versailles.
Napoleon has lately invented a word, which perfectly expressed my opinion at that time and ever since. He calls the project *ideology;* and John
Randolph, though he was, fourteen years ago, as wild an enthusiast for
equality and fraternity as any of them, appears to be now a regenerated
proselyte to Napoleon's opinion and mine, that it was all madness.

The Greeks, in their allegorical style, said that the two ladies, ἀριστοκρατία
and δημοκρατία, always in a quarrel, disturbed every body in the neighborhood with their brawls. It is a fine observation of yours that whig and
tory belong to natural history. Inequalities of mind and body are so established by God Almighty in his constitution of human nature, that no art
or policy can ever plane them down to a level. I have never read reasoning more absurd, sophistry more gross, in proof of the Athanasian creed,
or transubstantiation, than the subtle labors of Helvetius and Rousseau to
demonstrate the natural equality of mankind. *Jus cuique*, the golden rule,
do as you would be done by, is all the equality that can be supported or
defended by reason or common sense.

It is very true, as you justly observe, I can say nothing new on this or
any other subject of government. But when Lafayette harangued you, and
me, and John Quincy Adams, through a whole evening, in your hotel in
the *Cul de Sac*, at Paris, and developed the plans now in operation to reform France, though I was silent as you was, I then thought I could say
something new to him. In plain truth, I was astonished at the grossness of
his ignorance of government and history, as I had been for years before,
at that of Turgot, Rochefoucauld, Condorcet, and Franklin. This gross
ideology of them all first suggested to me the thought and the inclination,
which I afterwards executed in London, of writing something upon
aristocracy. I was restrained for years by many fearful considerations.
Who and what was I? Why, a man of no name or consideration in Eu-

rope. The manual exercise of writing was painful and distressing to me, almost like a blow on the elbow or the knee; my style was habitually negligent, unstudied, unpolished; I should make enemies of all the French patriots, the Dutch patriots, the English republicans, dissenters, reformers, call them what you will; and, what came nearer home to my bosom than all the rest, I knew I should give offence to many, if not all, of my best friends in America, and, very probably, destroy all the little popularity I ever had in a country where popularity had more omnipotence than the British parliament assumed. Where should I get the necessary books? What printer or bookseller would undertake to print such hazardous writings? But, when the French assembly of notables met, and I saw that Turgot's "government in one centre, and that centre the nation," a sentence as mysterious or as contradictory as the Athanasian creed, was about to take place; and when I saw that Shays's rebellion was breaking out in Massachusetts; and when I saw that even my obscure name was often quoted in France as an advocate for simple democracy; when I saw that the sympathies in America had caught the French flame, I was determined to wash my own hands as clear as I could of all this foulness. I had then strong forebodings that I was sacrificing all the emoluments of this life; and so it has happened, but not in so great a degree as I apprehended.

In truth, my "Defence of the Constitutions" and "Discourses on Davila," were the cause of that immense unpopularity which fell like the tower of Siloam upon me. Your steady defence of democratical principles, and your invariable favorable opinion of the French revolution, laid the foundation of your unbounded popularity. *Sic transit gloria mundi.*

Now, I will forfeit my life, if you can find one sentiment in my Defence of the Constitutions, or the Discourses on Davila, which, by a fair construction, can favor the introduction of hereditary monarchy or aristocracy into America. They were all written to support and strengthen the Constitution of the United States.

The wood-cutter on Mount Ida, though he was puzzled to find a tree to drop at first, I presume knew how to leave off when he was weary. But I never know when to cease when I begin to write to you.

35. *On Natural Aristocracy*

To Thomas Jefferson

November 15, 1813

... though we are agreed in one point, in words, it is not yet certain that we are perfectly agreed in sense. Fashion has introduced an indeterminate use of the word talents. Education, wealth, strength, beauty, stature,

birth, marriage, graceful attitudes and motions, gait, air, complexion, physiognomy, are talents, as well as genius, science, and learning. Any one of these talents that in fact commands or influences two votes in society gives to the man who possesses it the character of an aristocrat, in my sense of the word. Pick up the first hundred men you meet, and make a republic. Every man will have an equal vote; but when deliberations and discussions are opened, it will be found that twenty-five, by their talents, virtues being equal, will be able to carry fifty votes. Every one of these twenty-five is an aristocrat in my sense of the word; whether he obtains one vote in addition to his own, by his birth, fortune, figure, eloquence, science, learning, craft, cunning, or even his character for good fellow-ship, and a *bon vivant*.

What gave Sir William Wallace his amazing aristocratical superiority? His strength. What gave Mrs. Clarke her aristocratical influence—to create generals, admirals and bishops? Her beauty. What gave Pompa-dour and Du Barry the power of making cardinals and popes? And I have lived for years in the Hotel de Valentinois, with Franklin, who had as many virtues as any of them. In the investigation of the meaning of the word "talents," I could write 630 pages as pertinent as John Taylor's, of Hazlewood; but I will select a single example; for female aristocrats are nearly as formidable as males. A daughter of a greengrocer walks the streets in London daily, with a basket of cabbage sprouts, dandelions, and spinach, on her head. She is observed by the painters to have a beautiful face, an elegant figure, a graceful step, and a *debonair*. They hire her to sit. She complies, and is painted by forty artists in a circle around her. The scientific Dr. William Hamilton outbids the painters, sends her to school for a genteel education, and marries her. This lady not only causes the triumphs of the Nile, Copenhagen, and Trafalgar, but separates Naples from France, and finally banishes the king and queen from Sicily. Such is the aristocracy of the natural talent of beauty. Millions of examples might be quoted from history, sacred and profane, from Eve, Hannah, Deborah, Susanna, Abigail, Judith, Ruth, down to Helen, Mrs. de Mainbenor, and Mrs. Fitzherbert. For mercy's sake do not compel me to look to our chaste States and territories to find women, one of whom let go would in the words of Holophernes's guards, deceive the whole earth. . . .

. . . Your distinction between natural and artificial aristocracy, does not appear to me founded. Birth and wealth are conferred upon some men as imperiously by nature as genius, strength, or beauty. The heir to honors, and riches, and power, has often no more merit in procuring these advan-tages than he has in obtaining a handsome face, or an elegant figure. When aristocracies are established by human laws, and honor, wealth and power are made hereditary by municipal laws and political institu-tions, then I acknowledge artificial aristocracy to commence; but this never commences till corruption in elections become dominant and un-

controllable. But this artificial aristocracy can never last. The everlasting envies, jealousies, rivalries, and quarrels among them; their cruel rapacity among the poor ignorant people, their followers, compel them to set up Cæsar, a demagogue, to be a monarch, a master; *pour mettre chacun à sa place.* Here you have the origin of all artificial aristocracy, which is the origin of all monarchies. And both artificial aristocracy and monarchy, and civil, military, political, and hierarchical despotism, have all grown out of the natural aristocracy of virtues and talents. . . .

36. *Improvement in Human Affairs*

To Thomas Jefferson

Quincy, July 16, 1814

. . . I am sometimes afraid that my machine will not surcease motions soon enough; for I dread nothing so much as "dying at top," and expiring like Dean Swift, a "driveller and a show," or like Sam. Adams, a grief and distress to his family, a weeping, helpless object of compassion for years.

I am bold to say that neither you nor I will live to see the course which the "wonders of the times" will take. Many years and perhaps centuries must pass before the current will acquire a settled direction. If the Christian religion, as I understand it, or as you understand it, should maintain its ground, as I believe it will, yet Platonic, Pythagoric, Hindoo, and cabilistical Christianity, which is Catholic Christianity, and which has prevailed for fifteen hundred years, has received a mortal wound, of which the monster must finally die. Yet so strong is his constitution that he may endure for centuries before he expires. Government has never been much studied by mankind; but their attention has been drawn to it in the latter part of the last century and the beginning of this, more than at any former period, and the vast variety of experiments which have been made of constitutions in America, in France, in Holland, in Geneva, in Switzerland, and even in Spain and South America, can never be forgotten. They will be studied, and their immediate and remote effects and final catastrophes noted. The result in time will be improvements; and I have no doubt that the horrors we have experienced for the last forty years will ultimately terminate in the advancement of civil and religious liberty, and amelioration in the condition of mankind. For I am a believer in the probable improvability and improvement, the ameliorability and amelioration in human affairs; though I never could understand the doctrine of the perfectibility of the human mind. . . .

37. *Equality v. Equal Rights*

To John Taylor

1814

I believe that none but Helvetius will affirm that all children are born with equal genius.

None will pretend that all are born of dispositions exactly alike,—of equal weight; equal strength; equal length; equal delicacy of nerves; equal elasticity of muscles; equal complexions; equal figure, grace, or beauty.

I have seen, in the Hospital of Foundlings, the *"Enfans Trouvés,"* at Paris, fifty babes in one room;—all under four days old; all in cradles alike; all nursed and attended alike; all dressed alike; all equally neat. I went from one end to the other of the whole row, and attentively observed all their countenances. And I never saw a greater variety, or more striking inequalities, in the streets of Paris or London. Some had every sign of grief, sorrow, and despair; others had joy and gayety in their faces. Some were sinking in the arms of death; others looked as if they might live to fourscore. Some were as ugly and others as beautiful as children or adults ever are; these were stupid; those sensible. These were all born to equal rights, but to very different fortunes; to very different success and influence in life.

The world would not contain the books, if one should produce all the examples that reading and experience would furnish. One or two permit me to hint.

Will any man say, would Helvetius say, that all men are born equal in strength? Was Hercules no stronger than his neighbors? How many nations, for how many ages, have been governed by his strength, and by the reputation and renown of it by his posterity? If you have lately read Hume, Robertson or the Scottish Chiefs, let me ask you if Sir William Wallace was no more than equal in strength to the average of Scotchmen? and whether Wallace could have done what he did without that extraordinary strength?

Will Helvetius or Rousseau say that all men and women are born equal in beauty? Will any philosopher say that beauty has no influence in human society? If he does, let him read the histories of Eve, Judith, Helen, the fair Gabrielle, Diana of Poitiers, Pompadour, Du Barry, Susanna, Abigail, Lady Hamilton, Mrs. Clark, and a million others. Are not despots, monarchs, aristocrats, and democrats, equally liable to be seduced by beauty to confer favors and influence suffrages?

Socrates calls beauty a short-lived tyranny; Plato, *the privilege of na-*

ture; Theophrastus, a mute eloquence; Diogenes, the best letter of recommendation; Carneades, a queen without soldiers; Theocritus, a serpent covered with flowers; Bion, a good that does not belong to the possessor, because it is impossible to give ourselves beauty, or to preserve it. Madame du Barry expressed the philosophy of Carneades in more laconic language, when she said, *"la véritable royauté, c'est la beauté,"*—the genuine royalty is beauty. And she might have said with equal truth that it is genuine aristocracy; for it has as much influence in one form of government as in any other; and produces aristocracy in the deepest democracy that ever was known or imagined, as infallibly as in any other form of government. What shall we say to all these philosophers, male and female? Is not beauty a privilege granted by nature, according to Plato and to truth, often more influential in society, and even upon laws and government, than stars, garters, crosses, eagles, golden fleeces, or any hereditary titles or other distinctions? The grave elders were not proof against the charms of Susanna. The Grecian sages wondered not at the Trojan war when they saw Helen. Holofernes's guards, when they saw Judith, said, "one such woman let go would deceive the whole earth." . . .

That all men are born to equal rights is true. Every being has a right to his own, as clear, as moral, as sacred, as any other being has. This is as indubitable as a moral government in the universe. But to teach that all men are born with equal powers and faculties, to equal influence in society, to equal property and advantages through life, is as gross a fraud, as glaring an imposition on the credulity of the people, as ever was practiced by monks, by Druids, by Brahmins, by priests of the immortal Lama, or by the self-styled philosophers of the French Revolution. For honor's sake, Mr. Taylor, for truth and virtue's sake, let American philosophers and politicians despise it.

Mr. Adams leaves to Homer and Virgil, to Tacitus and Quintilian, to Mahomet and Calvin, to Edwards and Priestley, or, if you will, to Milton's angels reasoning high in pandemonium, all their acute speculations about fate, destiny, foreknowledge absolute, necessity, and predestination. He thinks it problematical whether there is, or ever will be, more than one Being capable of understanding this vast subject. In his principles of legislation, he has nothing to do with these interminable controversies. He considers men as free, moral, and accountable agents; and he takes men as God has made them. And will Mr. Taylor deny that God has made some men deaf and some blind, or will he affirm that these will infallibly have as much influence in society, and be able to procure as many votes as any who can see and hear?

Honor the day, and believe me no enemy.

38. *The Age of Revolutions and Constitutions*

To James Lloyd

Quincy, 29 March 1815

. . . Did Mr. Pitt and Mr. Miranda believe me to be a lover of revolutions, deeply smitten with their charms, ready and eager to seize upon any and every opportunity to involve myself and my country in any revolutionary enterprise? I had been plunged head and ears in the American revolution from 1761 to 1798 (for it had been all revolution during the whole period). Did Mr. Pitt and Mr. Miranda think that I had trod upon feathers, and slept upon beds of roses, during those thirty-seven years? I had been an eye-witness of two revolutions in Holland; one from aristocracy to a mongrel mixture of half aristocracy and half democracy, the other back again to aristocracy and the splendid restoration of the Stadtholder. Did Mr. Pitt and Mr. Miranda think that I was so delighted with these electric shocks, these eruptions of volcanoes, these *tremblemens de terre,* as to be ambitious of the character of a chemist, who could produce artificial ones in South America? I had been an ear-witness of some of the first whispers of a revolution in France in 1783, 1784, and 1785, and had given all possible attention to its rise and progress, and I can truly say, that it had given me as much anxiety as our American revolution had ever done. Could Mr. Pitt and Mr. Miranda believe me so fascinated, charmed, enchanted, with what had happened in France, as to be desirous of engaging myself and my country in most hazardous and expensive and bloody experiments to excite similar horrors in South America?

The last twenty-five years of the last century, and the first fifteen years of this, may be called the age of revolutions and constitutions. We began the dance, and have produced eighteen or twenty models of constitutions, the excellences and defects of which you probably know better than I do. They are, no doubt, the best for us that we could contrive and agree to adopt.

39. *On His Administration*

To James Lloyd

Quincy, March 31, 1815

. . . I cannot repent of my "strong character." Whether I have one or not, I know not. I am not conscious of any character stronger than common. If I have such a nature, it was given me. I shall neither be rewarded nor punished for it. For all my foibles, strong or weak, I hold myself responsible to God and man. I hope to be forgiven for what I humbly acknowledge I cannot justify, and not be too severely censured for what, in my circumstances, *"humana parum cavet natura."* I did not humble France, nor have the combined efforts of emperors and kings humbled her, and, I hope, she never will be humbled below Austria, Russia, or England. But I humbled the French Directory as much as all Europe has humbled Bonaparte. I purchased navy yards, which would now sell for double their cost with compound interest. I built frigates, manned a navy, and selected officers with great anxiety and care, who perfectly protected our commerce, and gained virgin victories against the French, and who afterwards acquired such laurels in the Mediterranean, and who have lately emblazoned themselves and their country with a naval glory, which I tremble to think of. God forbid that American naval power should ever be such a scourge to the human race as that of Great Britain has been! I was engaged in the most earnest, sedulous, and, I must own, expensive exertions to preserve peace with the Indians, and prepare them for agriculture and civilization, through the whole of my administration. I had the inexpressible satisfaction of complete success. Not a hatchet was lifted in my time; and the single battle of Tippecanoe has since cost the United States a hundred times more money than it cost me to maintain universal and perpetual peace. I finished the demarcation of limits, and settled all controversies with Spain. I made the composition with England, for all the old Virginia debts, and all the other American debts, the most snarling, angry, thorny, *scabreux* negotiation that ever mortal ambassador, king, prince, emperor, or president was ever plagued with. I say I made it, and so I did, though the treaty was not ratified till Jefferson came in. My labors were indefatigable to compose all difficulties and settle all controversies with all nations, civilized and savage. And I had complete and perfect success, and left my country at peace with all the world, upon terms consistent with the honor and interest of the United States, and with all our relations with other nations, and all our obligations by the law of nations or by treaties. This is so true that no nation or individual ever

uttered a complaint of injury, insult, or offence. I had suppressed an insurrection in Pennsylvania, and effectually humbled and punished the insurgents; not by assembling an army of militia from three or four States, and marching in all the pride, pomp, and circumstance of war, at an expense of millions, but silently, without noise, and at a trifling expense. . . .

As I am not now writing a history of my administration, I will sum up all I have to say in a few words. I left my country in peace and harmony with all the world, and after all my "extravagant expenses" and "wanton waste of public money," I left navy yards, fortifications, frigates, timber, naval stores, manufactories of cannon and arms, and a treasury full of five millions of dollars. This was all done step by step, against perpetual oppositions, clamors and reproaches, such as no other President ever had to encounter, and with a more feeble, divided, and incapable support than has ever fallen to the lot of any administration before or since. For this I was turned out of office, degraded and disgraced by my country; and I was glad of it. I felt no disgrace, because I felt no remorse. It has given me fourteen of the happiest years of my life; and I am certain I could not have lasted one year more in that station, shackled in the chains of that arbitrary faction.

40. *"Eighteenth Century . . . Most Honorable to Human Nature"*

To Thomas Jefferson

Quincy, November 13, 1815

The fundamental article of my political creed is that despotism, or unlimited sovereignty, or absolute power, is the same in a majority of a popular assembly, an aristocratical council, an oligarchical junto, and a single emperor. Equally arbitrary, cruel, bloody, and in every respect diabolical. Accordingly, arbitrary power, wherever it has resided, has never failed to destroy all the records, memorials, and histories of former times, which it did not like, and to corrupt and interpolate such as it was cunning enough to preserve or to tolerate. We cannot therefore say with much confidence what knowledge or what *virtues* may have prevailed in some former ages in some quarters of the world.

Nevertheless, according to the few lights that remain to us, we may say that the eighteenth century, notwithstanding all its errors and vices, has been, of all that are past, the most honorable to human nature. Knowledge and virtue were increased and diffused; arts, sciences, useful

to men, ameliorating their condition, were improved more than in any former equal period.

But what are we to say now? Is the nineteenth century to be a contrast to the eighteenth? Is it to extinguish all the lights of its predecessor? Are the Sorbonne, the Inquisition, the Index expurgatorius, and the Knights-errant of St. Ignatius Loyola to be revived and restored to all their salutary powers of supporting and propagating the mild spirit of Christianity? The proceedings of the allies and their Congress at Vienna, the accounts from Spain and France, and the Chateaubriands, and the Genlis, indicate which way the wind blows. The priests are at their old work again; the Protestants are denounced, and another St. Bartholomew's day threatened. . . .

41. *Homo Sum*

To James Madison

Quincy, June 17, 1817

. . . There is nothing within the narrow compass of human knowledge more interesting than the subject of your letter. If the idea of a government in one centre seems to be everywhere "exploded," perhaps something remains undefined, as dangerous, as plausible, and pernicious as that idea. Half a million of people in England have petitioned Parliament for annual parliaments and universal suffrage. Parliament is unanimous against them. What is this state of things short of a declaration of war between the government and people? And is not this the picture of all Europe? Sovereigns, who modestly call themselves legitimate, are conspiring, in holy and unhallowed leagues, against the progress of human knowledge and human liberty.

War seems on the point of breaking out between government and people. Were the latter united, the question would be soon decided; but they are everywhere divided into innumerable sects, whereas the former are united, and have all the artillery and bayonets in their hands; and what is most melancholy of all, an appeal to arms almost always results in an exchange of one military tyranny for another.

The questions concerning universal suffrage, and those concerning the necessary limitations of the power of suffrage, are among the most difficult. It is hard to say that every man has not an equal right; but admit this equal right and equal power, and an immediate revolution would ensue. In all the nations of Europe, the number of persons who have not a penny is double those who have a groat; admit all these to an

equality of power, and you would soon see how the groats would be divided. Yet, in a few days, the party of the pennies and the party of the groats would be found to exist again, and a new revolution and a new division must ensue.

If there is anywhere an exception from this reasoning, it is in America; nevertheless, there is in these United States a majority of persons who have no property, over those who have any. I know of nothing more desirable in society than the abolition of all hereditary distinctions. But is not distinction among voters as arbitrary and aristocratical as hereditary distinctions? You will remember that, between thirty and forty years ago, the Irish patriots asked advice of the Duke of Richmond, Dr. Price, Dr. Jebb, &c. These three great statesmen, divines, and philosophers solemnly advised a universal suffrage. Tracy, in his review of Montesquieu, adopts this principle in its largest extent. A party among mankind countenanced, at this day, by such numbers and such names is not to be despised, neglected, nor easily overborne.

There is nothing more irrational, absurd, or ridiculous in the sight of philosophy than the idea of hereditary kings and nobles; yet all the nations of the earth, civilized, savage, and brutal, have adopted them. Whence this universal and irresistible propensity? How shall it be controlled, restrained, corrected, modified, or managed? A government, a mixed government, may be so organized, I hope, as to preserve the liberty, equality, and fraternity of the people without any hereditary ingredient in its composition. Our nation has attempted it, and, if any people can accomplish it, it must be this; and may God Almighty prosper and bless them!

I have seen the efforts of the people in France, Holland, and England. You have read them in all Europe. We both know the result. What is to come, we know not.

My personal interest in such disquisitions can last but a few hours; but, still, *homo sum*, and *homo* I shall be.

May you live to a greater age than mine, and be able to die with brighter prospects for your species than can fall to the lot of your friend.

42. *The American Revolution*

To H. Niles

Quincy, February 13, 1818

The American Revolution was not a common event. Its effects and consequences have already been awful over a great part of the globe. And when and where are they to cease?

But what do we mean by the American Revolution? Do we mean the American war? The Revolution was effected before the war commenced. The Revolution was in the minds and hearts of the people; a change in their religious sentiments of their duties and obligations. While the king, and all in authority under him, were believed to govern in justice and mercy, according to the laws and constitution derived to them from the God of nature and transmitted to them by their ancestors, they thought themselves bound to pray for the king and queen and all the royal family, and all in authority under them, as ministers ordained of God for their good; but when they saw those powers renouncing all the principles of authority, and bent upon the destruction of all the securities of their lives, liberties, and properties, they thought it their duty to pray for the Continental Congress and all the thirteen State congresses, &c.

There might be and there were others who thought less about religion and conscience, but had certain habitual sentiments of allegiance and loyalty derived from their education; but believing allegiance and protection to be reciprocal, when protection was withdrawn, they thought allegiance was dissolved.

Another alteration was common to all. The people of America had been educated in an habitual affection for England, as their mother country; and while they thought her a kind and tender parent (erroneously enough, however, for she never was such a mother), no affection could be more sincere. But when they found her a cruel beldam, willing like Lady Macbeth to "dash their brains out," it is no wonder if their filial affections ceased, and were changed into indignation and horror.

This radical change in the principles, opinions, sentiments, and affections of the people was the real American Revolution.

By what means this great and important alteration in the religious, moral, political, and social character of the people of thirteen colonies, all distinct, unconnected, and independent of each other, was begun, pursued, and accomplished, it is surely interesting to humanity to investigate, and perpetuate to posterity.

To this end, it is greatly to be desired that young men of letters in all the States, especially in the thirteen original States, would undertake the laborious, but certainly interesting and amusing task of searching and collecting all the records, pamphlets, newspapers, and even handbills, which in any way contributed to change the temper and views of the people and compose them into an independent nation.

The colonies had grown up under constitutions of government so different, there was so great a variety of religions, they were composed of so many different nations, their customs, manners, and habits had so little resemblance, and their intercourse had been so rare, and their knowledge of each other so imperfect, that to unite them in the same principles in theory and the same system of action was certainly a very difficult enterprise. The complete accomplishment of it, in so short a time and by

such simple means, was perhaps a singular example in the history of mankind. Thirteen clocks were made to strike together—a perfection of mechanism which no artist had ever before effected.

In this research, the gloriole of individual gentlemen, and of separate States, is of little consequence. The *means and the measures* are the proper objects of investigation. These may be of use to posterity, not only in this nation, but in South America and all other countries. They may teach mankind that revolutions are no trifles; that they ought never to be undertaken rashly; nor without deliberate consideration and sober reflection; nor without a solid, immutable, eternal foundation of justice and humanity; nor without a people possessed of intelligence, fortitude, and integrity sufficient to carry them with steadiness, patience, and perseverance, through all the vicissitudes of fortune, the fiery trials and melancholy disasters they may have to encounter. . . .

43. *"Man a Rational Creature!"*

To Thomas Jefferson

Quincy, May 29, 1818

I think, with you, that it is difficult to say at what moment the Revolution began. In my opinion, it began as early as the first plantation of the country. Independence of Church and Parliament was a fixed principle of our predecessors in 1620, as it was of Samuel Adams and Christopher Gadsden in 1776; and independence of Church and Parliament was always kept in view in this part of the country, and, I believe, in most others. The hierarchy and parliamentary authority ever were dreaded and detested even by a majority of professed Episcopalians. I congratulate you upon your "canine appetite" for reading. I have been equally voracious for several years, and it has kept me alive. It is policy in me to despise and abhor the writing-table, for it is a bunch of grapes out of reach. Had I your eyes and fingers, I should scribble forever such poor stuff as I have been writing by fits and by starts for fifty or sixty years, without ever correcting or revising any thing.

. . . When we come to be cool in the future world, I think we cannot choose but smile at the gambols of ambition, avarice, pleasure, sport, and caprices here below. Perhaps we may laugh as the angels do in the French fable. At a convivial repast of a club of choice spirits, of whom Gabriel and Michael were the most illustrious, after nectar and ambrosia had set their hearts at ease, they began to converse upon the *mécanique céleste*. After discussing the Zodiac, and the constellations of the solar system, they condescended to this speck of dirt, the earth, and remarked

some of its inhabitants, the lion, the elephant, the eagle, and even the fidelity, gratitude, and adroitness of the dog. At last, one of them recollected man. What a fine countenance! What an elegant figure! What subtilty, ingenuity, versatility, agility, and, above all, a rational creature! At this, the whole board broke out into a broad ha! ha! ha! that resounded through the vault of heaven, exclaiming, "Man a rational creature! How could any rational being ever dream that man was a rational creature?"

After all, I hope to meet my wife, and friends, ancestors and posterity, sages, ancient and modern. I believe I could get over all my objections to meeting Alexander Hamilton and Tim Pick, if I could see a symptom of penitence in either. . . .

44. *The Infamy of Slavery*

To Robert J. Evans

Quincy, June 8, 1819

. . . The turpitude, the inhumanity, the cruelty, and the infamy of the African commerce in slaves have been so impressively represented to the public by the highest powers of eloquence that nothing that I can say would increase the just odium in which it is and ought to be held. Every measure of prudence, therefore, ought to be assumed for the eventual total extirpation of slavery from the United States. If, however, humanity dictates the duty of adopting the most prudent measures for accomplishing so excellent a purpose, the same humanity requires that we should not inflict severer calamities on the objects of our commiseration than those which they at present endure, by reducing them to despair, or the necessity of robbery, plunder, assassination, and massacre, to preserve their lives, some provision for furnishing them employment, or some means of supplying them with the necessary comforts of life. The same humanity requires that we should not by any rash or violent measures expose the lives and property of those of our fellow-citizens who are so unfortunate as to be surrounded with these fellow-creatures by hereditary descent, or by any other means without their own fault. I have, through my whole life, held the practice of slavery in such abhorrence that I have never owned a Negro or any other slave, though I have lived for many years in times when the practice was not disgraceful, when the best men in my vicinity thought it not inconsistent with their character, and when it has cost me thousands of dollars for the labor and subsistence of free men, which I might have saved by the purchase of Negroes at times when they were very cheap. . . .

45. *On Making Constitutions*

To Richard Rush

Quincy, May 14, 1821

I have been tenderly affected by the kind expressions of your friendship, in your letter of the 9th of February.

In the course of forty years I have been called twice to assist in the formation of a constitution for this State. This kind of architecture, I find, is an art or mystery very difficult to learn, and still harder to practise. The attention of mankind at large seems now to be drawn to this interesting subject. It gives me more solicitude than, at my age, it ought to do; for nothing remains for me but submission and resignation. Nevertheless, I cannot wholly divest myself of anxiety for my children, my country, and my species. The probability is that the fabrication of constitutions will be the occupation or the sport, the tragedy, comedy, or farce, for the entertainment of the world for a century to come. There is little appearance of the prevalence of correct notions of the indispensable machinery of a free government, in any part of Europe or America. Neither Spain, Portugal, or Naples can long preserve their fundamental laws under their present constitutions. But I must recollect that I am not reading a lecture.

But, hazardous as it may be, I will venture one remark upon our national and state institutions.

The legislative and executive authorities are too much blended together. While the Senate of the United States have a negative on all appointments to office, we can never have a national President. In spite of his own judgment, he must be the President, not to say the tool, of a party. In Massachusetts, the legislature annually elect an executive council, which renders the Governor a mere Doge of Venice, a mere *"testa di legno,"* a mere head of wood.

Strait is the gate and narrow is the way that leads to liberty, and few nations, if any, have found it.

46. *Genius and Education*

To Benjamin Waterhouse

Montezillo, May 21, 1821

I am glad I forgot to return your son's beautiful morsel on *Industry* with my last letter; because it furnishes an apology for writing another. In answering a letter I commonly forget to notice two-thirds of it, till my answer is sent away.

Helvetius and Rousseau preached to the French nation *liberty*, till they made them the most mechanical slaves; *equality* till they destroyed all equity; *humanity* till they became weasels, and African panthers; and *fraternity* till they cut one another's throats like Roman gladiators.

Helvetius carried his enthusiasm for equality so far that he fills many pages with learned and ingenious arguments to prove that men are born equal in capacity, intellect, and genius. This doctrine, if I have correctly measured your inimitable wooden leg, is at antipodes with yours. You seem to imply that natural genius is all, and education nothing but artificial show.

Now, if I rightly ken you both, I cannot perfectly agree with Waterhouse or Helvetius: for

1. Barrow and Waterhouse have both proved the ancient maxim that the Gods *sell all things to industry.*

2. I have never known a studious youth who did not come to something; a student at the bar who did not make a lawyer; a student in medicine who did not become a physician; a student in theology who did not turn out a divine. No, nor a studious carpenter who did not appear an excellent architect; nor a diligent shoemaker who was not a good workman.

3. Genius is often produced by accident. Mrs. Morton says genius is sorrow's child. Extreme poverty, deep distress, severe affliction, sudden danger, cruel, inextricable embarrassments, often produce astonishing efforts of genius. Revolutions, they say, produce self-taught heroes, statesmen, philosophers, genius in abundance, out of multitudes of lumpish animals. Anger, hatred, revenge, jealousy, envy, and above all *love* are often productive of sublime and beautiful genius. Disappointment, too, often creates it.

4. Genius is often created by artificial and physical means. West India and even New England rum and Virginia whisky, mild English porter, and even good old cider, much more Burgundy champagne, old Madeira, cherry, and old hock are great inspirers. But, they say, for I never tried an atom or a drop, that opium and liquid laudanum are the very divini-

ties that stir within us, and will produce genius out of the coarsest clay. Arrack, and cognac brandy have plenty of genius in them.

5. To descend to examples. Tom. Paine could never write without several bottles of porter, or an equal quantity of alcohol, rum, or brandy, in his stomach. Churchill could not compose a verse without a bottle of Madeira wine before him. Abraham B[isho]p of Connecticut could not write upon the alliance of Church and State till he had a reasonable quantity of rum and water in him. And I have been told by Parson Montague of Dedham, though I will not vouch for the truth of it, that General Hamilton never wrote or spoke at the bar, or elsewhere in public, without a bit of opium in his mouth. But none of these causes can produce Helvetius's equality of genius. *Education,* after all, is a better leg, if it is wooden, than all the rest.

So much for octogenarian or nonagenarian badinage!

47. *The Art of Law Giving*

To Thomas Jefferson

Quincy, 19 May, 1821

Must we, before we take our departure from this grand and beautiful world, surrender all our pleasing hopes of the progress of society, of the improvement of the intellect and moral condition of the world, of the reformation of mankind?

The Piedmontese revolution scarcely assumed a form, and the Neapolitan bubble is burst. And what should hinder the Spanish and Portuguese constitutions from running to the same ruin? The Cortes is in one assembly vested with the legislative power. The king and his priests, armies, navies, and all other officers, are vested with the executive authority of government. Are not here two authorities up, neither supreme? Are they not necessarily rivals, constantly contending, like law, physic, and divinity, for superiority? Just ready for civil war?

Can a free government possibly exist with the Roman Catholic religion? The art of lawgiving is not so easy as that of architecture or painting. New York and Rhode Island are struggling for conventions to reform their constitutions, and I am told there is danger of making them worse. Massachusetts has had her convention; but our sovereign lords, the people, think themselves wiser than their representatives, and in several articles I agree with their lordships. Yet there never was a cooler, a more patient, candid, or a wiser deliberative body than that convention.

I may refine too much, I may be an enthusiast, but I think a free

government is a complicated piece of machinery, the nice and exact adjustment of whose springs, wheels, and weights, is not yet well comprehended by the artists of the age, and still less by the people. . . .

48. *Free Inquiry*

To Thomas Jefferson

Quincy, January 23, 1825

We think ourselves possessed, or, at least, we boast that we are so, of liberty of conscience on all subjects, and of the right of free inquiry and private judgment in all cases, and yet how far are we from these exalted privileges in fact! There exists, I believe, throughout the whole Christian world, a law which makes it blasphemy to deny or to doubt the divine inspiration of all the books of the Old and New Testaments, from Genesis to Revelations. In most countries of Europe it is punished by fire at the stake, or the rack, or the wheel. In England itself it is punished by boring through the tongue with a red-hot poker. In America it is not much better; even in our own Massachusetts, which I believe, upon the whole, is as temperate and moderate in religious zeal as most of the States, a law was made in the latter end of the last century, repealing the cruel punishments of the former laws, but substituting fine and imprisonment upon all those blasphemers upon any book of the Old Testament or New. Now, what free inquiry, when a writer must surely encounter the risk of fine or imprisonment for adducing any argument for investigation into the divine authority of those books? Who would run the risk of translating Dupuis? But I cannot enlarge upon this subject, though I have it much at heart. I think such laws a great embarrassment, great obstructions to the improvement of the human mind. Books that cannot bear examination, certainly ought not to be established as divine inspiration by penal laws. It is true, few persons appear desirous to put such laws in execution, and it is also true that some few persons are hardy enough to venture to depart from them. But as long as they continue in force as laws, the human mind must make an awkward and clumsy progress in its investigations. I wish they were repealed. The substance and essence of Christianity, as I understand it, is eternal and unchangeable, and will bear examination forever, but it has been mixed with extraneous ingredients, which I think will not bear examination, and they ought to be separated. Adieu.

49. *On the News that John Quincy Adams Is Elected President*

To John Quincy Adams

Quincy, February 18, 1825

My dear Son,—I have received your letter of the 9th. Never did I feel so much solemnity as upon this occasion. The multitude of my thoughts, and the intensity of my feelings are too much for a mind like mine, in its ninetieth year. May the blessing of God Almighty continue to protect you to the end of your life, as it has heretofore protected you in so remarkable a manner from your cradle! I offer the same prayer for your lady and your family, and am your affectionate father.

Other Writings

50. *Dissertation on the Canon and the Feudal Law*

February 1765

"Ignorance and inconsideration are the two great causes of the ruin of mankind." This is an observation of Dr. Tillotson, with relation to the interest of his fellow men in a future and immortal state. But it is of equal truth and importance if applied to the happiness of men in society, on this side the grave. In the earliest ages of the world, absolute monarchy seems to have been the universal form of government. Kings, and a few of their great counsellors and captains, exercised a cruel tyranny over the people, who held a rank in the scale of intelligence, in those days, but little higher than the camels and elephants that carried them and their engines to war.

By what causes it was brought to pass that the people in the Middle Ages became more intelligent in general would not, perhaps, be possible in these days to discover. But the fact is certain; and wherever a general knowledge and sensibility have prevailed among the people, arbitrary government and every kind of oppression have lessened and disappeared in proportion. Man has certainly an exalted soul; and the same principle in human nature—that aspiring, noble principle founded in benevolence, and cherished by knowledge; I mean the love of power, which has been so often the cause of slavery—has, whenever freedom has existed, been the cause of freedom. If it is this principle that has always prompted the princes and nobles of the earth, by every species of fraud and violence to shake off all the limitations of their power, it is the same that has always stimulated the common people to aspire at independency, and to endeavor at confining the power of the great within the limits of equity and reason.

The poor people, it is true, have been much less successful than the great. They have seldom found either leisure or opportunity to form a union and exert their strength; ignorant as they were of arts and letters, they have seldom been able to frame and support a regular opposition.

This, however, has been known by the great to be the temper of mankind; and they have accordingly labored, in all ages, to wrest from the populace, as they are contemptuously called, the knowledge of their rights and wrongs, and the power to assert the former or redress the latter. I say rights, for such they have, undoubtedly, antecedent to all earthly government—*Rights,* that cannot be repealed or restrained by human laws—*Rights,* derived from the great Legislator of the universe.

Since the promulgation of Christianity, the two greatest systems of tyranny that have sprung from this original are the canon and the feudal law. . . .

By the former of these, the most refined, sublime, extensive, and astonishing constitution of policy that ever was conceived by the mind of man was framed by the Romish clergy for the aggrandizement of their own order. . . .

In the latter we find another system, similar in many respects to the former; which, although it was originally formed, perhaps, for the necessary defence of a barbarous people against the inroads and invasions of her neighboring nations, yet for the same purposes of tyranny, cruelty, and lust which had dictated the canon law, it was soon adopted by almost all the princes of Europe, and wrought into the constitutions of their government. It was originally a code of laws for a vast army in a perpetual encampment. . . .

But another event still more calamitous to human liberty was a wicked confederacy between the two systems of tyranny above described. It seems to have been even stipulated between them that the temporal grandees should contribute everything in their power to maintain the ascendency of the priesthood, and that the spiritual grandees in their turn should employ their ascendency over the consciences of the people, in impressing on their minds a blind, implicit obedience to civil magistracy.

Thus, as long as this confederacy lasted, and the people were held in ignorance, liberty, and with her, knowledge and virtue too, seem to have deserted the earth, and one age of darkness succeeded another, till God in his benign providence raised up the champions who began and conducted the Reformation. From the time of the Reformation to the first settlement of America, knowledge gradually spread in Europe, but especially in England; and in proportion as that increased and spread among the people, ecclesiastical and civil tyranny, which I use as synonymous expressions for the canon and feudal laws, seem to have lost their strength and weight. The people grew more and more sensible of the wrong that was done them by these systems, more and more impatient under it, and determined at all hazards to rid themselves of it; till at last, under the execrable race of the Stuarts, the struggle between the people and the confederacy aforesaid of temporal and spiritual tyranny became formidable, violent, and bloody.

It was this great struggle that peopled America. It was not religion alone, as is commonly supposed; but it was a love of universal liberty, and a hatred, a dread, a horror, of the infernal confederacy before described, that projected, conducted, and accomplished the settlement of America.

It was a resolution formed by a sensible people—I mean the Puritans— almost in despair. They had become intelligent in general, and many of them learned. . . .

After their arrival here, they began their settlement, and formed their plan, both of ecclesiastical and civil government, in direct opposition to the canon and the feudal systems. . . . Tyranny in every form, shape, and appearance was their disdain and abhorrence; no fear of punishment, nor even of death itself in exquisite tortures, had been sufficient to conquer that steady, manly, pertinacious spirit with which they had opposed the tyrants of those days in church and state. They were very far from being enemies to monarchy; and they knew as well as any men the just regard and honor that is due to the character of a dispenser of the mysteries of the gospel of grace. But they saw clearly that popular powers must be placed as a guard, a control, a balance, to the powers of the monarch and the priest, in every government, or else it would soon become the man of sin, the whore of Babylon, the mystery of iniquity, a great and detestable system of fraud, violence, and usurpation. Their greatest concern seems to have been to establish a government of the church more consistent with the Scriptures, and a government of the state more agreeable to the dignity of human nature, than any they had seen in Europe, and to transmit such a government down to their posterity, with the means of securing and preserving it forever. To render the popular power in their new government as great and wise as their principles of theory, that is, as human nature and the Christian religion require it should be, they endeavored to remove from it as many of the feudal inequalities and dependencies as could be spared, consistently with the preservation of a mild limited monarchy. And in this they discovered the depth of their wisdom and the warmth of their friendship to human nature. But the first place is due to religion. They saw clearly that of all the nonsense and delusion which had ever passed through the mind of man, none had ever been more extravagant than the notions of absolutions, indelible characters, uninterrupted successions, and the rest of those fantastical ideas, derived from the canon law, which had thrown such a glare of mystery, sanctity, reverence, and right reverend eminence and holiness around the idea of a priest, as no mortal could deserve, and as always must, from the constitution of human nature, be dangerous in society. . . .

They knew that government was a plain, simple, intelligible thing, founded in nature and reason, and quite comprehensible by common sense. They detested all the base services and servile dependencies of the feudal system. They knew that no such unworthy dependencies took

place in the ancient seats of liberty, the republics of Greece and Rome; and they thought all such slavish subordinations were equally inconsistent with the constitution of human nature and that religious liberty with which Jesus had made them free. . . .

They were convinced, by their knowledge of human nature, derived from history and their own experience, that nothing could preserve their posterity from the encroachments of the two systems of tyranny, in opposition to which, as has been observed already, they erected their government in church and state, but knowledge diffused generally through the whole body of the people. Their civil and religious principles, therefore, conspired to prompt them to use every measure and take every precaution in their power to propagate and perpetuate knowledge. For this purpose they laid very early the foundations of colleges, and invested them with ample privileges and emoluments; and it is remarkable that they have left among their posterity so universal an affection and veneration for those seminaries, and for liberal education, that the meanest of the people contribute cheerfully to the support and maintenance of them every year, and that nothing is more generally popular than projections for the honor, reputation, and advantage of those seats of learning. But the wisdom and benevolence of our fathers rested not here. They made an early provision by law that every town consisting of so many families should be always furnished with a grammar school. They made it a crime for such a town to be destitute of a grammar schoolmaster for a few months, and subjected it to a heavy penalty. So that the education of all ranks of people was made the care and expense of the public, in a manner that I believe has been unknown to any other people ancient or modern.

The consequences of these establishments we see and feel every day. A native of America who cannot read and write is as rare an appearance as a Jacobite or a Roman Catholic, that is, as rare as a comet or an earthquake. It has been observed that we are all of us lawyers, divines, politicians, and philosophers. And I have good authorities to say that all candid foreigners who have passed through this country and conversed freely with all sorts of people here will allow that they have never seen so much knowledge and civility among the common people in any part of the world. . . . And liberty cannot be preserved without a general knowledge among the people, who have a right, from the frame of their nature, to knowledge, as their great Creator, who does nothing in vain, has given them understandings, and a desire to know; but besides this, they have a right, an indisputable, unalienable, indefeasible, divine right to that most dreaded and envied kind of knowledge—I mean, of the characters and conduct of their rulers. Rulers are no more than attorneys, agents, and trustees, for the people; and if the cause, the interest and trust, is insidiously betrayed, or wantonly trifled away, the people have a right to revoke the authority that they themselves have deputed, and to constitute

abler and better agents, attorneys, and trustees. And the preservation of the means of knowledge among the lowest ranks is of more importance to the public than all the property of all the rich men in the country. It is even of more consequence to the rich themselves, and to their posterity. The only question is, whether it is a public emolument; and if it is, the rich ought undoubtedly to contribute, in the same proportion as to all other public burdens—that is, in proportion to their wealth, which is secured by public expenses. But none of the means of information are more sacred, or have been cherished with more tenderness and care by the settlers of America, than the press. Care has been taken that the art of printing should be encouraged, and that it should be easy and cheap and safe for any person to communicate his thoughts to the public. . . . Let us tenderly and kindly cherish, therefore, the means of knowledge. Let us dare to read, think, speak, and write. Let every order and degree among the people rouse their attention and animate their resolution. Let them all become attentive to the grounds and principles of government, ecclesiastical and civil. Let us study the law of nature; search into the spirit of the British constitution; read the histories of ancient ages; contemplate the great examples of Greece and Rome; set before us the conduct of our own British ancestors, who have defended for us the inherent rights of mankind against foreign and domestic tyrants and usurpers, against arbitrary kings and cruel priests, in short, against the gates of earth and hell. Let us read and recollect and impress upon our souls the views and ends of our own more immediate forefathers, in exchanging their native country for a dreary, inhospitable wilderness. Let us examine into the nature of that power, and the cruelty of that oppression, which drove them from their homes. Recollect their amazing fortitude, their bitter sufferings—the hunger, the nakedness, the cold, which they patiently endured—the severe labors of clearing their grounds, building their houses, raising their provisions, amidst dangers from wild beasts and savage men, before they had time or money or materials for commerce. Recollect the civil and religious principles and hopes and expectations which constantly supported and carried them through all hardships with patience and resignation. Let us recollect it was liberty, the hope of liberty for themselves and us and ours, which conquered all discouragements, dangers, and trials. In such researches as these, let us all in our several departments cheerfully engage—but especially the proper patrons and supporters of law, learning, and religion!

Let the pulpit resound with the doctrines and sentiments of religious liberty. Let us hear the danger of thraldom to our consciences from ignorance, extreme poverty, and dependence, in short, from civil and political slavery. Let us see delineated before us the true map of man. Let us hear the dignity of his nature, and the noble rank he holds among the works of God—that consenting to slavery is a sacrilegious breach of trust, as offensive in the sight of God as it is derogatory from our own honor or

interest or happiness—and that God Almighty has promulgated from heaven liberty, peace, and good-will to man!

Let the bar proclaim "the laws, the rights, the generous plan of power" delivered down from remote antiquity—inform the world of the mighty struggles and numberless sacrifices made by our ancestors in defence of freedom. Let it be known that British liberties are not the grants of princes or parliaments, but original rights, conditions of original contracts, coequal with prerogative, and coeval with government; that many of our rights are inherent and essential, agreed on as maxims, and established as preliminaries, even before a parliament existed. Let them search for the foundations of British laws and government in the frame of human nature, in the constitution of the intellectual and moral world. There let us see that truth, liberty, justice, and benevolence are its everlasting basis; and if these could be removed, the superstructure is overthrown of course.

Let the colleges join their harmony in the same delightful concert. Let every declamation turn upon the beauty of liberty and virtue, and the deformity, turpitude, and malignity of slavery and vice. Let the public disputations become researches into the grounds and nature and ends of government, and the means of preserving the good and demolishing the evil. Let the dialogues, and all the exercises, become the instruments of impressing on the tender mind, and of spreading and distributing far and wide, the ideas of right and the sensations of freedom.

In a word, let every sluice of knowledge be opened and set a-flowing. The encroachments upon liberty in the reigns of the first James and the first Charles, by turning the general attention of learned men to government, are said to have produced the greatest number of consummate statesmen which has ever been seen in any age or nation. The Brookses, Hampdens, Vanes, Seldens, Miltons, Nedhams, Harringtons, Nevilles, Sidneys, Lockes, are all said to have owed their eminence in political knowledge to the tyrannies of those reigns. The prospect now before us in America ought in the same manner to engage the attention of every man of learning, to matters of power and of right, that we may be neither led nor driven blindfolded to irretrievable destruction. Nothing less than this seems to have been meditated for us, by somebody or other in Great Britain. There seems to be a direct and formal design on foot to enslave all America. This, however, must be done by degrees. The first step that is intended seems to be an entire subversion of the whole system of our fathers, by the introduction of the canon and feudal law into America. The canon and feudal systems, though greatly mutilated in England, are not yet destroyed. Like the temples and palaces in which the great contrivers of them once worshipped and inhabited, they exist in ruins; and much of the domineering spirit of them still remains. . . . But it seems very manifest from the Stamp Act itself that a design is formed to strip us in a great measure of the means of knowledge, by loading the press,

the colleges, and even an almanac and a newspaper, with restraints and duties; and to introduce the inequalities and dependencies of the feudal system, by taking from the poorer sort of people all their little subsistence, and conferring it on a set of stamp officers, distributors, and their deputies. . . . These are not the vapors of a melancholy mind, nor the effusions of envy, disappointed ambition, nor of a spirit of opposition to government, but the emanations of a heart that burns for its country's welfare. No one of any feeling, born and educated in this once happy country, can consider the numerous distresses, the gross indignities, the barbarous ignorance, the haughty usurpations, that we have reason to fear are meditating for ourselves, our children, our neighbors, in short, for all our countrymen and all their posterity, without the utmost agonies of heart and many tears.

51. *Instructions of the Town of Braintree to Their Representative*

September 1765

. . . In all the calamities which have ever befallen this country, we have never felt so great a concern, or such alarming apprehensions, as on this occasion. Such is our loyalty to the King, our veneration for both houses of Parliament, and our affection for all our fellow-subjects in Britain, that measures which discover any unkindness in that country towards us are the more sensibly and intimately felt. And we can no longer forbear complaining that many of the measures of the late ministry, and some of the late acts of Parliament, have a tendency, in our apprehension, to divest us of our most essential rights and liberties. We shall confine ourselves, however, chiefly to the act of Parliament, commonly called the Stamp Act, by which a very burthensome and, in our opinion, unconstitutional tax is to be laid upon us all; and we subjected to numerous and enormous penalties, to be prosecuted, sued for, and recovered at the option of an informer, in a court of admiralty, without a jury.

We have called this a burthensome tax because the duties are so numerous and so high, and the embarrassments to business in this infant, sparsely settled country so great, that it would be totally impossible for the people to subsist under it, if we had no controversy at all about the right and authority of imposing it. Considering the present scarcity of money, we have reason to think, the execution of that act for a short space of time would drain the country of its cash, strip multitudes of all their property, and reduce them to absolute beggary. And what the consequence would be to the peace of the province from so sudden a shock and such a convulsive change in the whole course of our business and

subsistence, we tremble to consider. We further apprehend this tax to be unconstitutional. We have always understood it to be a grand and fundamental principle of the constitution that no freeman should be subject to any tax to which he has not given his own consent, in person or by proxy. And the maxims of the law, as we have constantly received them, are to the same effect, that no freeman can be separated from his property but by his own act or fault. We take it clearly, therefore, to be inconsistent with the spirit of the common law, and of the essential fundamental principles of the British constitution, that we should be subject to any tax imposed by the British Parliament; because we are not represented in that assembly in any sense, unless it be by a fiction of law, as insensible in theory as it would be injurious in practice if such a taxation should be grounded on it.

But the most grievous innovation of all is the alarming extension of the power of courts of admiralty. In these courts, one judge presides alone! No juries have any concern there! The law and the fact are both to be decided by the same single judge, whose commission is only during pleasure, and with whom, as we are told, the most mischievous of all customs has become established, that of taking commissions on all condemnations; so that he is under a pecuniary temptation always against the subject. Now, if the wisdom of the mother country has thought the independency of the judges so essential to an impartial administration of justice as to render them independent of every power on earth—independent of the King, the Lords, the Commons, the people, nay, independent in hope and expectation of the heir-apparent, by continuing their commissions after a demise of the crown—what justice and impartiality are we, at three thousand miles' distance from the fountain, to expect from such a judge of admiralty? We have all along thought the acts of trade in this respect a grievance; but the Stamp Act has opened a vast number of sources of new crimes, which may be committed by any man, and cannot but be committed by multitudes, and prodigious penalties are annexed, and all these are to be tried by such a judge of such a court! What can be wanting, after this, but a weak or wicked man for a judge, to render us the most sordid and forlorn of slaves?—we mean the slaves of a slave of the servants of a minister of state. We cannot help asserting, therefore, that this part of the act will make an essential change in the constitution of juries, and it is directly repugnant to the Great Charter itself; for, by that charter, "no amerciament shall be assessed, but by the oath of honest and lawful men of the vicinage"; and "no freeman shall be taken, or imprisoned, or disseized of his freehold, or liberties of free customs, nor passed upon, nor condemned, but by lawful judgment of his peers, or by the law of the land." So that this act will "make such a distinction, and create such a difference between" the subjects in Great Britain and those in America as we could not have expected from the guardians of liberty in "both."

As these, sir, are our sentiments of this act, we, the freeholders and other inhabitants, legally assembled for this purpose, must enjoin it upon you to comply with no measures or proposals for countenancing the same, or assisting in the execution of it, but by all lawful means consistent with our allegiance to the King, and relation to Great Britain, to oppose the execution of it, till we can hear the success of the cries and petitions of America for relief.

We further recommend the most clear and explicit assertion and vindication of our rights and liberties to be entered on the public records, that the world may know, in the present and all future generations, that we have a clear knowledge and a just sense of them, and, with submission to Divine Providence, that we never can be slaves. . . .

52. *"Novanglus"*

Such events as the resistance to the Stamp Act, and to the Tea Act, particularly the destruction of that which was sent by the ministry, in the name of the East India Company, have ever been cautiously spoken of by the whigs, because they knew the delicacy of the subject, and they lived in continual hopes of a speedy restoration of liberty and peace. But we are now thrown into a situation, which would render any further delicacy upon this point criminal.

Be it remembered, then, that there are tumults, seditions, popular commotions, insurrections, and civil wars, upon just occasions as well as unjust.

Grotius B. 1, c. 3, § 1, observes, "that some sort of private war may be lawfully waged. It is not repugnant to the law of nature, for any one to repel injuries by force" . . . . [Adams here cites at length from Grotius, Sidney and Locke to develop the theme that "the general insurrection of a whole nation does not deserve the name of a rebellion."]

If there is any thing in these quotations, which is applicable to the destruction of the tea, or any other branch of our subject, it is not my fault; I did not make it. Surely Grotius, Pufendorf, Barbeyrac, Locke, Sidney, and Le Clerc, are writers of sufficient weight to put in the scale against the mercenary scribblers in New York and Boston, who have the unexampled impudence and folly, to call these, which are revolution principles, in question, and to ground their arguments upon passive obedience as a corner stone . . . we must go to the bottom of this great controversy. If parliament has a right to tax us, and legislate for us in all cases, the destruction of the tea was unjustifiable; but if the people of America are right in their principle, that parliament has no such right, that the act of parliament is null and void, and it is lawful to oppose and

resist it, the question then is, whether the destruction was necessary; for every principle of reason, justice, and prudence, in such cases, demands that the least mischief shall be done, the least evil, among a number, shall always be preferred. . . . All men will agree that such steps ought not to be taken but in cases of absolute necessity, and that such necessity must be very clear. But most people in America now think the destruction of the Boston tea was absolutely necessary, and therefore right and just. . . .

That "the colonies owe no allegiance to any imperial crown," provided such a crown involves in it a house of lords and a house of commons, is certain. Indeed, we owe no allegiance to any crown at all. We owe allegiance to the person of his majesty, King George III., whom God preserve. But allegiance is due universally, both from Britons and Americans to the person of the king, not to his crown; to his natural, not his politic capacity. . . .

Thus, we see, that in every instance which can be found, the observation proves to be true, that, by the common law, the laws of England, the authority of parliament, and the limits of the realm, were confined within seas. That the kings of England had frequently foreign dominions, some by conquest, some by marriage, and some by descent. But, in all those cases, the kings were either absolute in those dominions, or bound to govern them according to their own respective laws, and by their own legislative and executive councils. That the laws of England did not extend there, and the English parliament pretended no jurisdiction there, nor claimed any right to control the king in his government of those dominions. And, from this extensive survey of all the foregoing cases, there results a confirmation of what has been so often said, that there is no provision in the common law, in English precedents, in the English government or constitution, made for the case of the colonies. It is not a conquered, but a discovered country. It came not by marriage to the king, but was purchased by the settlers of the savages. It was not granted by the king of his grace, but was dearly, very dearly earned by the planters, in the labor, blood, and treasure which they expended to subdue it to cultivation. It stands upon no grounds, then, of law or policy, but what are found in the law of nature, and their express contracts in their charters, and their implied contracts in the commissions to governors and terms of settlement.

53. *Thoughts on Government*

January 1776

If I was equal to the task of forming a plan for the government of a colony, I should be flattered with your request, and very happy to comply with it; because, as the divine science of politics is the science of social happiness, and the blessings of society depend entirely on the constitutions of government, which are generally institutions that last for many generations, there can be no employment more agreeable to a benevolent mind than a research after the best.

Pope flattered tyrants too much when he said,

> *"For forms of government let fools contest,*
> *That which is best administered is best."*

Nothing can be more fallacious than this. But poets read history to collect flowers, not fruits; they attend to fanciful images, not the effects of social institutions. Nothing is more certain, from the history of nations and nature of man, than that some forms of government are better fitted for being well administered than others.

We ought to consider what is the end of government, before we determine which is the best form. Upon this point all speculative politicians will agree that the happiness of society is the end of government, as all divines and moral philosophers will agree that the happiness of the individual is the end of man. From this principle it will follow that the form of government which communicates ease, comfort, security, or, in one word, happiness, to the greatest number of persons, and in the greatest degree, is the best.

All sober inquirers after truth, ancient and modern, pagan and Christian, have declared that the happiness of man, as well as his dignity, consists in virtue. Confucius, Zoroaster, Socrates, Mahomet, not to mention authorities really sacred, have agreed in this.

If there is a form of government, then, whose principle and foundation is virtue, will not every sober man acknowledge it better calculated to promote the general happiness than any other form?

Fear is the foundation of most governments; but it is so sordid and brutal a passion, and renders men in whose breasts it predominates so stupid and miserable, that Americans will not be likely to approve of any political institution which is founded on it.

Honor is truly sacred, but holds a lower rank in the scale of moral excellence than virtue. Indeed, the former is but a part of the latter, and consequently has not equal pretensions to support a frame of government productive of human happiness.

The foundation of every government is some principle or passion in the minds of the people. The noblest principles and most generous affections in our nature, then, have the fairest chance to support the noblest and most generous models of government.

A man must be indifferent to the sneers of modern Englishmen to mention in their company the names of Sidney, Harrington, Locke, Milton, Nedham, Neville, Burnet, and Hoadly. No small fortitude is necessary to confess that one has read them. The wretched condition of this country, however, for ten or fifteen years past, has frequently reminded me of their principles and reasonings. They will convince any candid mind that there is no good government but what is republican. That the only valuable part of the British constitution is so; because the very definition of a republic is "an empire of laws, and not of men." That, as a republic is the best of governments, so that particular arrangement of the powers of society, or, in other words, that form of government which is best contrived to secure an impartial and exact execution of the laws, is the best of republics.

Of republics there is an inexhaustible variety, because the possible combinations of the powers of society are capable of innumerable variations.

As good government is an empire of laws, how shall your laws be made? In a large society, inhabiting an extensive country, it is impossible that the whole should assemble to make laws. The first necessary step, then, is to depute power from the many to a few of the most wise and good. But by what rules shall you choose your representatives? Agree upon the number and qualifications of persons who shall have the benefit of choosing, or annex this privilege to the inhabitants of a certain extent of ground.

The principal difficulty lies, and the greatest care should be employed, in constituting this representative assembly. It should be in miniature an exact portrait of the people at large. It should think, feel, reason, and act like them. That it may be the interest of this assembly to do strict justice at all times, it should be an equal representation, or, in other words, equal interests among the people should have equal interests in it. Great care should be taken to effect this, and to prevent unfair, partial, and corrupt elections. Such regulations, however, may be better made in times of greater tranquillity than the present; and they will spring up themselves naturally when all the powers of government come to be in the hands of the people's friends. At present, it will be safest to proceed in all established modes to which the people have been familiarized by habit.

A representation of the people in one assembly being obtained, a question arises whether all the powers of government, legislative, executive, and judicial, shall be left in this body? I think a people cannot be long free, nor ever happy, whose government is in one assembly. My reasons for this opinion are as follow:—

1. A single assembly is liable to all the vices, follies, and frailties of an individual; subject to fits of humor, starts of passion, flights of enthusiasm, partialities, or prejudice, and consequently productive of hasty results and absurd judgments. And all these errors ought to be corrected and defects supplied by some controlling power.

2. A single assembly is apt to be avaricious, and in time will not scruple to exempt itself from burdens, which it will lay, without compunction, on its constituents.

3. A single assembly is apt to grow ambitious, and after a time will not hesitate to vote itself perpetual. This was one fault of the Long Parliament; but more remarkably of Holland, whose assembly first voted themselves from annual to septennial, then for life, and after a course of years, that all vacancies happening by death or otherwise should be filled by themselves, without any application to constituents at all.

4. A representative assembly, although extremely well qualified, and absolutely necessary, as a branch of the legislative, is unfit to exercise the executive power, for want of two essential properties, secrecy and despatch.

5. A representative assembly is still less qualified for the judicial power, because it is too numerous, too slow, and too little skilled in the laws.

6. Because a single assembly, possessed of all the powers of government, would make arbitrary laws for their own interest, execute all laws arbitrarily for their own interest, and adjudge all controversies in their own favor.

But shall the whole power of legislation rest in one assembly? Most of the foregoing reasons apply equally to prove that the legislative power ought to be more complex; to which we may add that if the legislative power is wholly in one assembly, and the executive in another, or in a single person, these two powers will oppose and encroach upon each other, until the contest shall end in war, and the whole power, legislative and executive, be usurped by the strongest.

The judicial power, in such case, could not mediate, or hold the balance between the two contending powers, because the legislative would undermine it. And this shows the necessity, too, of giving the executive power a negative upon the legislative, otherwise this will be continually encroaching upon that.

To avoid these dangers, let a distinct assembly be constituted as a mediator between the two extreme branches of the legislature, that which represents the people, and that which is vested with the executive power.

Let the representative assembly then elect by ballot, from among themselves or their constituents, or both, a distinct assembly, which, for the sake of perspicuity, we will call a council. It may consist of any number you please, say twenty or thirty, and should have a free and independent exercise of its judgment, and consequently a negative voice in the legislature.

These two bodies, thus constituted, and made integral parts of the legislature, let them unite, and by joint ballot choose a governor, who, after being stripped of most of those badges of domination called prerogatives, should have a free and independent exercise of his judgment, and be made also an integral part of the legislature. This, I know, is liable to objections; and, if you please, you may make him only president of the council, as in Connecticut. But as the governor is to be invested with the executive power, with consent of council, I think he ought to have a negative upon the legislative. If he is annually elective, as he ought to be, he will always have so much reverence and affection for the people, their representatives and counsellors, that, although you give him an independent exercise of his judgment, he will seldom use it in opposition to the two houses, except in cases the public utility of which would be conspicuous; and some such cases would happen. . . .

The dignity and stability of government in all its branches, the morals of the people, and every blessing of society depends so much upon an upright and skilful administration of justice that the judicial power ought to be distinct from both the legislative and executive, and independent upon both, that so it may be a check upon both, as both should be checks upon that. The judges, therefore, should be always men of learning and experience in the laws, of exemplary morals, great patience, calmness, coolness, and attention. Their minds should not be distracted with jarring interest; they should not be dependent upon any man, or body of men. To these ends, they should hold estates for life in their offices; or, in other words, their commissions should be during good behavior, and their salaries ascertained and established by law. For misbehavior, the grand inquest of the colony, the house of representatives, should impeach them before the governor and council, where they should have time and opportunity to make their defence; but, if convicted, should be removed from their offices, and subjected to such other punishment as shall be thought proper. . . .

Laws for the liberal education of youth, especially of the lower class of people, are so extremely wise and useful, that, to a humane and generous mind, no expense for this purpose would be thought extravagant. . . .

A constitution founded on these principles introduces knowledge among the people, and inspires them with a conscious dignity becoming freemen; a general emulation takes place, which causes good humor, sociability, good manners, and good morals to be general. That elevation of sentiment inspired by such a government makes the common people brave and enterprising. That ambition which is inspired by it makes them sober, industrious, and frugal. You will find among them some elegance, perhaps, but more solidity; a little pleasure, but a great deal of business; some politeness, but more civility. If you compare such a country with the regions of domination, whether monarchical or aristocratical, you will fancy yourself in Arcadia or Elysium.

If the colonies should assume governments separately, they should be

left entirely to their own choice of the forms; and if a continental constitution should be formed, it should be a congress containing a fair and
adequate representation of the colonies, and its authority should sacredly
be confined to these cases, namely, war, trade, disputes between colony
and colony, the post-office, and the unappropriated lands of the crown, as
they used to be called.

These colonies, under such forms of government, and in such a union,
would be unconquerable by all the monarchies of Europe.

You and I, my dear friend, have been sent into life at a time when the
greatest lawgivers of antiquity would have wished to live. How few of
the human race have ever enjoyed an opportunity of making an election
of government, more than of air, soil, or climate, for themselves or their
children! When, before the present epocha, had three millions of people
full power and a fair opportunity to form and establish the wisest and
happiest government that human wisdom can contrive? I hope you will
avail yourself and your country of that extensive learning and indefatigable industry which you possess, to assist her in the formation of the happiest governments and the best character of a great people. . . .

54. *The Constitution of Massachusetts*

Preamble

The end of the institution, maintenance, and administration of government is to secure the existence of the body politic, to protect it and to
furnish the individuals who compose it with the power of enjoying, in
safety and tranquility, their natural rights and the blessings of life; and
whenever these great objects are not obtained, the people have a right to
alter the government and to take measures necessary for their safety,
happiness, and prosperity.

The body politic is formed by a voluntary association of individuals.
It is a social compact by which the whole people covenants with each
citizen and each citizen with the whole people, that all shall be governed
by certain laws for the common good. It is the duty of the people, therefore, in framing a Constitution of Government, to provide for an equitable mode of making laws, as well as for an impartial interpretation and
a faithful execution of them, that every man may, at all times, find his
security in them.

We, therefore, [the delegates of] the people of Massachusetts, [in
general convention assembled for the express and sole purpose of framing
a constitution or form of government to be laid before our constituents
according to their instructions] acknowledging with grateful hearts the
goodness of the great Legislator of the universe in affording *to this people*

in the course of His providence an opportunity *of entering into an original, explicit, and solemn compact with each other, deliberately and
peaceably, without fraud, violence, or surprise;* and of forming a new
constitution of civil government for *themselves* and [their] posterity; and
devoutly imploring His direction in *a design so interesting* [to them and
their posterity,] do, [by virtue of the authority vested in us by our con-
stituents] agree upon the following *Declaration of Rights and Frame of
Government* as the CONSTITUTION OF THE COMMONWEALTH OF MASSACHU-
SETTS.

Chapter I

A DECLARATION OF THE RIGHTS OF THE INHABITANTS OF THE COMMON-
WEALTH OF MASSACHUSETTS

ART. I. All men are born [equally] free and *independent,* and have
certain natural, essential, and unalienable rights, among which may be
reckoned the right of enjoying and defending their lives and liberties;
that of acquiring, possessing, and protecting [their] property; in fine, that
of seeking and obtaining their safety and happiness.

II. It is the —— duty of all men in society, publicly, and at stated seasons, to worship the SUPREME BEING, the great Creator and Preserver of
the universe. And no subject shall be hurt, molested, or restrained, in his
person, liberty, or estate, for worshipping GOD in the manner —— most
agreeable to the dictates of his own conscience; or, for his religious profession or sentiments, provided he does not disturb the public peace or
obstruct others in their religious worship. . . .

IV. The people of this commonwealth have the sole and exclusive right
of governing themselves as a free, sovereign, and independent state; and
do, and forever hereafter shall, exercise and enjoy every power, jurisdiction, and right, which *are* not, or may not hereafter be, by them expressly
delegated to the United States of America, in congress assembled.

V. All power residing originally in the people and being derived from
them, the several magistrates and officers of government vested with
authority, whether legislative, executive, or judicial, are their substitutes
and agents and are at all times accountable to them.

VI. No man, nor corporation or association of men, have any other title
to obtain advantages or particular and exclusive privileges distinct from
those of the community than what arises from the consideration of services rendered to the public; and this title, being in nature neither hereditary nor transmissible to children, or descendants, or relations by blood,
the idea of a man born a magistrate, lawgiver, or judge, is absurd and
unnatural.

VII. Government is instituted for the common good, for the protection,

safety, prosperity, and happiness of the people and not for the profit, honor, or private interest of any one man, family, or class of men. Therefore, the people alone have an incontestable, unalienable, and indefeasible right to institute government and to reform, alter, or totally change the same, when their protection, safety, prosperity, and happiness require it.

VIII. In order to prevent those who are vested with authority from becoming oppressors, the people have a right, at such periods and in such manner as *may be delineated in* their frame of government, to cause their public officers to return to private life, and to fill up vacant places by certain and regular elections.——

IX. All elections ought to be free, and all the [male] inhabitants of this commonwealth, having *sufficient qualifications,* have an equal right to elect officers and to be elected for public employments.

X. Each individual of the society has a right to be protected by it in the enjoyment of his life, liberty, and property, according to standing laws. He is obliged, consequently, to contribute his share to the expense of this protection, and to give his personal service, or an equivalent, when necessary. But no part of the property of any individual can, with justice, be taken from him or applied to public uses without his own consent or that of the representative body of the people. In fine, the people of this commonwealth are not controllable by any other laws than those to which their constitutional representative body have given their consent.

XI. Every subject of the commonwealth ought to find a certain remedy, by having recourse to the laws, for all injuries or wrongs which he may receive in his person, property, or character. He ought to obtain right and justice freely and without being obliged to purchase it, completely, and without any denial, promptly, and without delay, conformably to the laws. . . .

. . . XXX. [XXXI.] *The judicial department of the state ought to be separate from, and independent of, the legislative and executive powers.*

Chapter II

THE FRAME OF GOVERNMENT

The people inhabiting the territory *heretofore* called the Province of Massachusetts Bay do hereby solemnly and mutually agree with each other to form themselves into a free, sovereign, and independent body politic, or State, by the name of THE COMMONWEALTH OF MASSACHUSETTS.

In the government of the Commonwealth of Massachusetts the legislative, executive, and judicial power shall be placed in separate departments, to the end that it might be a government of laws and not of men. . . .

Chapter V

The Encouragement of Literature, etc.

Wisdom and knowledge, as well as virtue, diffused generally among the body of the people, being necessary for the preservation of their rights and liberties, and as these depend on spreading the opportunities and advantages of education in the various parts of the country and among the different orders of the people, it shall be the duty of legislators and magistrates in all future periods of this commonwealth to cherish the interests of literature and sciences and all seminaries of them—especially the university at Cambridge, public schools and grammar schools in the towns—to encourage private societies and public institutions, rewards and immunities for the promotion of agriculture, arts, sciences, commerce, trades, manufactures, and a natural history of the country; to countenance and inculcate the principles of humanity and general benevolence, public and private charity, industry and frugality, honesty and punctuality in their dealings, sincerity, good humor, and all social affections and generous sentiments among the people. . . .

55. *State Paper on Foreign Policy*

To Secretary Jay

Grosvenor Square, Westminster, August 10, 1785

The *arrêt* of the King of France, in his council of the 10th of July, has a preamble which deserves to be well considered in America. The increasing liberality of sentiment among philosophers and men of letters, in various nations, has for some time given reason to hope for a *reformation*, a kind of *protestantism*, in the commercial system of the world; but I believe that this *arrêt* is the first act of any sovereign which has openly avowed commercial principles so generous and noble. "Nothing could appear to the King more desirable, or suitable to his own principles, than a general liberty which, freeing from all kinds of fetters the circulation of all productions and goods of different countries, would make of all nations, as it were, but one, in point of trade; but, as long as that liberty cannot be universally admitted, and everywhere reciprocally, the interest of the kingdom requires of his Majesty's wisdom that he should exclude

from it, or suffer to be imported by the nation only, those foreign goods the free importation of which would be hurtful to his kingdom and manufactories, and might make the balance of trade to be against him."

The United States of America have done more than all the economists in France towards propagating in the world this magnanimous sentiment. But they have more cause than the court of France to complain that liberty is not universally and reciprocally admitted. They have cause to complain against France herself, in some degree, but more against Great Britain; for France, in some degree, calculates all her policy towards us, upon a principle which England pursues more steadily; a principle not so properly of enriching and strengthening herself at our expense as of impoverishing and weakening us even at her own expense. Simple selfishness, which is only the absence of benevolence, is much less unamiable than positive malevolence. As the French court has condescended to adopt our principle in theory, I am very much afraid we shall be obliged to imitate their wisdom in practice, and exclude from the United States, or suffer to be imported by our nation only, and in their own ships, those foreign goods which would be hurtful to the United States and their manufactories, make the balance of trade to be against them, or annihilate or diminish their shipping or mariners.

We have hitherto been the bubbles of our own philosophical and equitable liberality; and, instead of meeting correspondent sentiments, both France and England have shown a constant disposition to take a selfish and partial advantage of us because of them, nay, to turn them to the diminution or destruction of our own means of trade and strength. I hope we shall be the dupes no longer than we must. I would venture upon monopolies and exclusions, if they were found to be the only arms of defence against monopolies and exclusions, without fear of offending Dean Tucker or the ghost of Doctor Quesnay.

I observe further, with pleasure, in the preamble, that the King "is particularly occupied with the means of encouraging the industry of his subjects, and of propagating the extent of their trade, and reviving their manufactures." Great things may be done in this way, for the benefit of America as well as of France, if the measures are calculated upon the honest old principle of "live and let live." But, if another maxim is adopted, "I will live upon your means of living," or another still worse, "I will half starve that you may quite starve," instead of rejoicing at it, we must look out for means of preserving ourselves. These means can never be secured entirely, until Congress shall be made supreme in foreign commerce, and shall have digested a plan for all the States. But, if any of the States continue to refuse their assent, I hope that individual States will take it separately upon themselves, and confine their exports and imports wholly to ships and mariners of the United States, or even to their own ships and mariners, or, which is best of all, to the ships and mariners of those States which will adopt the same regulations.

I should be extremely sorry, however, that there ever should be a necessity of making any distinction between the ships and mariners of different States. It would be infinitely better to have all American ships and seamen entitled to equal privileges in all the thirteen States; but their privileges should be made much greater than those of foreign ships and seamen.

56. *A Defence of the Constitutions of Government of the United States of America—(1787-1788)*

Preface

The arts and sciences, in general, during the three or four last centuries, have had a regular course of progressive improvement. The inventions in mechanic arts, the discoveries in natural philosophy, navigation, and commerce, and the advancement of civilization and humanity, have occasioned changes in the condition of the world and the human character which would have astonished the most refined nations of antiquity. A continuation of similar exertions is every day rendering Europe more and more like one community, or single family. Even in the theory and practice of government, in all the simple monarchies, considerable improvements have been made. The checks and balances of republican governments have been in some degree adopted at the courts of princes. By the erection of various tribunals to register the laws and exercise the judicial power—by indulging the petitions and remonstrances of subjects, until by habit they are regarded as rights—a control has been established over ministers of state, and the royal councils, which, in some degree, approaches the spirit of republics. Property is generally secure, and personal liberty seldom invaded. The press has great influence, even where it is not expressly tolerated; and the public opinion must be respected by a minister, or his place becomes insecure. Commerce begins to thrive; and if religious toleration were established, personal liberty a little more protected, by giving an absolute right to demand a public trial in a certain reasonable time, and the states were invested with a few more privileges, or rather restored to some that have been taken away, these governments would be brought to as great a degree of perfection, they would approach as near to the character of governments of laws and not of men, as their nature will probably admit of. In so general a refinement, or more properly a reformation of manners and improvement in science, is it not unaccountable that the knowledge of the principles and construction of free governments, in which the happiness of life, and even the further progress of im-

provement in education and society, in knowledge and virtue, are so deeply interested, should have remained at a full stand for two or three thousand years?

According to a story in Herodotus, the nature of monarchy, aristocracy, and democracy, and the advantages and inconveniences of each, were as well understood at the time of the neighing of the horse of Darius as they are at this hour. A variety of mixtures of these simple species were conceived and attempted, with various success, by the Greeks and Romans. Representations, instead of collections, of the people; a total separation of the executive from the legislative power, and of the judicial from both; and a balance in the legislature, by three independent, equal branches, are perhaps the only three discoveries in the constitution of a free government since the institution of Lycurgus. Even these have been so unfortunate, that they have never spread: the first has been given up by all the nations, excepting one, which had once adopted it; and the other two, reduced to practice, if not invented, by the English nation, have never been imitated by any other, except their own descendants in America.

While it would be rash to say that nothing further can be done to bring a free government, in all its parts, still nearer to perfection, the representations of the people are most obviously susceptible of improvement. The end to be aimed at in the formation of a representative assembly seems to be the sense of the people, the public voice. The perfection of the portrait consists in its likeness. Numbers, or property, or both, should be the rule; and the proportions of electors and members an affair of calculation. The duration should not be so long that the deputy should have time to forget the opinions of his constituents. Corruption in elections is the great enemy of freedom. Among the provisions to prevent it, more frequent elections, and a more general privilege of voting, are not all that might be devised. Dividing the districts, diminishing the distance of travel, and confining the choice to residents, would be great advances towards the annihilation of corruption. The modern aristocracies of Holland, Venice, Bern, &c., have tempered themselves with innumerable checks, by which they have given a great degree of stability to that form of government; and though liberty and life can never be there enjoyed so well as in a free republic, none is perhaps more capable of profound sagacity. We shall learn to prize the checks and balances of a free government, and even those of the modern aristocracies, if we recollect the miseries of Greece, which arose from its ignorance of them. The only balance attempted against the ancient kings was a body of nobles; and the consequences were perpetual alternations of rebellion and tyranny, and the butchery of thousands upon every revolution from one to the other. When kings were abolished, aristocracies tyrannized; and then no balance was attempted but between aristocracy and democracy. This, in the nature of things,

could be no balance at all, and therefore the pendulum was forever on the swing. . . .

There can be no free government without a democratical branch in the constitution. Monarchies and aristocracies are in possession of the voice and influence of every university and academy in Europe. Democracy, simple democracy, never had a patron among men of letters. Democratical mixtures in government have lost almost all the advocates they ever had out of England and America. Men of letters must have a great deal of praise, and some of the necessaries, conveniences, and ornaments of life. Monarchies and aristocracies pay well and applaud liberally. The people have almost always expected to be served gratis, and to be paid for the honor of serving them; and their applauses and adorations are bestowed too often on artifices and tricks, on hypocrisy and superstition, on flattery, bribes, and largesses. It is no wonder then that democracies and democratical mixtures are annihilated all over Europe, except on a barren rock, a paltry fen, an inaccessible mountain, or an impenetrable forest. The people of England, to their immortal honor, are hitherto an exception; but, to the humiliation of human nature, they show very often that they are like other men. The people in America have now the best opportunity and the greatest trust in their hands that Providence ever committed to so small a number since the trangression of the first pair; if they betray their trust, their guilt will merit even greater punishment than other nations have suffered, and the indignation of Heaven. If there is one certain truth to be collected from the history of all ages, it is this: that the people's rights and liberties, and the democratical mixture in a constitution, can never be preserved without a strong executive, or, in other words, without separating the executive from the legislative power. If the executive power, or any considerable part of it, is left in the hands either of an aristocratical or a democratical assembly, it will corrupt the legislature as necessarily as rust corrupts iron, or as arsenic poisons the human body; and when the legislature is corrupted, the people are undone.

The rich, the well-born, and the able, acquire an influence among the people that will soon be too much for simple honesty and plain sense, in a house of representatives. The most illustrious of them must, therefore, be separated from the mass, and placed by themselves in a senate; this is, to all honest and useful intents, an ostracism. A member of a senate, of immense wealth, the most respected birth, and transcendent abilities, has no influence in the nation in comparison of what he would have in a single representative assembly. When a senate exists, the most powerful man in the state may be safely admitted into the house of representatives, because the people have it in their power to remove him into the senate as soon as his influence becomes dangerous. The senate becomes the great object of ambition; and the richest and the most sagacious wish to merit an advancement to it by services to the public

in the house. When he has obtained the object of his wishes, you may still hope for the benefits of his exertions, without dreading his passions; for the executive power being in other hands, he has lost much of his influence with the people, and can govern very few votes more than his own among the senators. . . .

The United States of America have exhibited, perhaps, the first example of governments erected on the simple principles of nature; and if men are now sufficiently enlightened to disabuse themselves of artifice, imposture, hypocrisy, and superstition, they will consider this event as an era in their history. Although the detail of the formation of the American governments is at present little known or regarded either in Europe or in America, it may hereafter become an object of curiosity. It will never be pretended that any persons employed in that service had interviews with the gods, or were in any degree under the inspiration of Heaven, more than those at work upon ships or houses, or laboring in merchandise or agriculture; it will forever be acknowledged that these governments were contrived merely by the use of reason and the senses. . . .

Unembarrassed by attachments to noble families, hereditary lines and successions, or any considerations of royal blood, even the pious mystery of holy oil had no more influence than that other one of holy water. The people were universally too enlightened to be imposed on by artifice; and their leaders, or more properly followers, were men of too much honor to attempt it. Thirteen governments thus founded on the natural authority of the people alone, without a pretence of miracle or mystery, and which are destined to spread over the northern part of that whole quarter of the globe, are a great point gained in favor of the rights of mankind. The experiment is made, and has completely succeeded; it can no longer be called in question whether authority in magistrates and obedience of citizens can be grounded on reason, morality, and the Christian religion, without the monkery of priests, or the knavery of politicians. As the writer was personally acquainted with most of the gentlemen in each of the states, who had the principal share in the first draughts, the following work was really written to lay before the public a specimen of that kind of reading and reasoning which produced the American constitutions. . . .

Against Government in a Single Assembly[1]

. . . Three writers in Europe of great abilities, reputation, and learning, M. Turgot, the Abbé de Mably, and Dr. Price, have turned their attention to the constitutions of government in the United States of America, and have written and published their criticisms and advice. They all had the most amiable characters, and unquestionably the purest inten-

tions. They all had experience in public affairs, and ample information respecting the nature of man, the necessities of society, and the science of government.

There are in the productions of all of them, among many excellent things, some sentiments, however, that it will be difficult to reconcile to reason, experience, the constitution of human nature, or to the uniform testimony of the greatest statesmen, legislators, and philosophers of all enlightened nations, ancient and modern.

M. Turgot, in his letter to Dr. Price, confesses, "that he is not satisfied with the constitutions which have hitherto been formed for the different states of America." He observes, "that by most of them the customs of England are imitated, without any particular motive. Instead of collecting all authority into one centre, that of the nation, they have established different bodies, a body of representatives, a council, and a governor because there is in England a house of commons, a house of lords, and a king. They endeavor to balance these different powers, as if this equilibrium, which in England may be a necessary check to the enormous influence of royalty, could be of any use in republics founded upon the equality of all the citizens, and as if establishing different orders of men was not a source of divisions and disputes."

There has been, from the beginning of the revolution in America, a party in every state who have entertained sentiments similar to these of M. Turgot. Two or three of them have established governments upon his principle; and, by advices from Boston, certain committees of counties have been held, and other conventions proposed in the Massachusetts, with the express purpose of deposing the governor and senate as useless and expensive branches of the constitution; and as it is probable that the publication of M. Turgot's opinion has contributed to excite such discontents among the people, it becomes necessary to examine it, and, if it can be shown to be an error, whatever veneration the Americans very justly entertain for his memory, it is to be hoped they will not be misled by his authority. . . .

M. Turgot . . . is for "collecting all authority into one centre, the nation." It is easily understood how all authority may be collected into "one centre" in a despot or monarch; but how it can be done when the centre is to be the nation is more difficult to comprehend. Before we attempt to discuss the notions of an author, we should be careful to ascertain his meaning. It will not be easy, after the most anxious research, to discover the true sense of this extraordinary passage. If, after the pains of "collecting all authority into one centre," that centre is to be the nation, we shall remain exactly where we began, and no collection of authority at all will be made. The nation will be the authority, and the authority the nation. The centre will be the circle, and the circle the centre. When a number of men, women, and children are simply congregated together, there is no political authority among them; nor any natural authority but that of

parents over their children. To leave the women and children out of the
question for the present, the men will all be equal, free, and independent
of each other. Not one will have any authority over any other. The
first "collection" of authority must be an unanimous agreement to form
themselves into a *nation, people, community,* or *body politic,* and to be
governed by the majority of suffrages or voices. But even in this case,
although the authority is collected into one centre, that centre is no
longer the nation, but the majority of the nation. Did M. Turgot mean
that the people of Virginia, for example, half a million of souls scattered
over a territory of two hundred leagues square, should stop here, and
have no other authority by which to make or execute a law, or judge a
cause, but by a vote of the whole people, and the decision of a majority!
Where is the plain large enough to hold them; and what are the means,
and how long would be the time, necessary to assemble them together?

A simple and perfect democracy never yet existed among men. If a
village of half a mile square, and one hundred families, is capable of
exercising all the legislative, executive, and judicial powers, in public
assemblies of the whole, by unanimous votes, or by majorities, it is more
than has ever yet been proved in theory or experience. In such a
democracy, for the most part, the moderator would be king, the town-
clerk legislator and judge, and the constable sheriff; and, upon more
important occasions, committees would be only the counsellors of both
the former, and commanders of the latter.

Shall we suppose, then, that M. Turgot intended that an assembly of
representatives should be chosen by the nation, and vested with all the
powers of government; and that this assembly should be the centre in
which all the authority was to be collected, and should be virtually
deemed the nation? After long reflection, I have not been able to discover any other sense in his words, and this was probably his real meaning. To examine this system in detail may be thought as trifling an occupation as the labored reasonings of Sidney and Locke to show the
absurdity of Filmer's superstitious notions appeared to Mr. Hume to be in
his enlightened day. Yet the mistakes of great men, and even the absurdities of fools, when they countenance the prejudices of numbers of
people, especially in a young country and under new governments, cannot be too fully confuted. I shall not then esteem my time misspent in
placing this idea of M. Turgot in all its lights; in considering the consequences of it; and in collecting a variety of authorities against it.

Equality and Natural Aristocracy[2]

... Let us now return to M. Turgot's idea of a government consisting in
a single assembly. He tells us our republics are "founded on the equality
of all the citizens, and therefore, 'orders' and 'equilibriums' are unneces-

sary, and occasion disputes." But what are we to understand here by equality? Are the citizens to be all of the same age, sex, size, strength, stature, activity, courage, hardiness, industry, patience, ingenuity, wealth, knowledge, fame, wit, temperance, constancy, and wisdom? Was there, or will there ever be, a nation whose individuals were all equal, in natural and acquired qualities, in virtues, talents, and riches? The answer of all mankind must be in the negative. It must then be acknowledged, that in every state, in the Massachusetts, for example, there are inequalities which God and nature have planted there, and which no human legislator ever can eradicate. I should have chosen to have mentioned Virginia, as the most ancient state, or indeed any other in the Union, rather than the one that gave me birth, if I were not afraid of putting suppositions which may give offence, a liberty which my neighbors will pardon. Yet I shall say nothing that is not applicable to all the other twelve.

In this society of Massachusettensians then, there is, it is true, a moral and political equality of rights and duties among all the individuals, and as yet no appearance of artificial inequalities of condition, such as hereditary dignities, titles, magistracies, or legal distinctions; and no established marks, as stars, garters, crosses, or ribbons; there are, nevertheless, inequalities of great moment in the consideration of a legislator, because they have a natural and inevitable influence in society. Let us enumerate some of them:—1. There is an inequality of *wealth;* some individuals, whether by descent from their ancestors, or from greater skill, industry, and success in business, have estates both in lands and goods of great value; others have no property at all; and of all the rest of society, much the greater number are possessed of wealth in all the variety of degrees between these extremes; it will easily be conceived that all the rich men will have many of the poor, in the various trades, manufactures, and other occupations in life, dependent upon them for their daily bread; many of smaller fortunes will be in their debt, and in many ways under obligations to them; others, in better circumstances, neither dependent nor in debt, men of letters, men of the learned professions, and others, from acquaintance, conversation, and civilities, will be connected with them and attached to them. Nay, farther, it will not be denied that among the wisest people that live, there is a degree of admiration, abstracted from all dependence, obligation, expectation, or even acquaintance, which accompanies splendid wealth, insures some respect, and bestows some influence. 2. *Birth.* Let no man be surprised that this species of inequality is introduced here. Let the page in history be quoted where any nation, ancient or modern, civilized or savage, is mentioned, among whom no difference was made between the citizens on account of their extraction. The truth is that more influence is allowed to this advantage in free republics than in despotic governments, or than would be allowed to it in simple monarchies, if severe laws had not been made from age to age to secure it. The children of illustrious families

have generally greater advantages of education, and earlier opportunities to be acquainted with public characters, and informed of public affairs, than those of meaner ones, or even than those in middle life; and what is more than all, an habitual national veneration for their names, and the characters of their ancestors described in history, or coming down by tradition, removes them farther from vulgar jealousy and popular envy, and secures them in some degree the favor, the affection, and respect of the public. . . .

. . . If there is, then, in society such a natural aristocracy as these great writers pretend, and as all history and experience demonstrate, formed partly by genius, partly by birth, and partly by riches, how shall the legislator avail himself of their influence for the equal benefit of the public? and how, on the other hand, shall he prevent them from disturbing the public happiness? I answer, by arranging them all, or at least the most conspicuous of them, together in one assembly, by the name of a senate; by separating them from all pretensions to the executive power, and by controlling in the legislative their ambition and avarice, by an assembly of representatives on one side, and by the executive authority on the other. Thus you will have the benefit of their wisdom, without fear of their passions. If among them there are some of Lord Bolingbroke's guardian angels, there will be some of his instruments of Divine vengeance too. The latter will be here restrained by a threefold tie,—by the executive power, by the representative assembly, and by their peers in the senate. But if these were all admitted into a single popular assembly, the worst of them might in time obtain the ascendency of all the rest. In such a single assembly, as has been observed before, almost the whole of this aristocracy will make its appearance, being returned members of it by the election of the people. These will be one class. There will be another set of members, of middling rank and circumstances, who will justly value themselves upon their independence, their integrity, and unbiased affection to their country, and will pique themselves upon being under no obligation. But there will be a third class, every one of whom will have his leader among the members of the first class, whose character he will celebrate, and whose voice he will follow; and this party, after a course of time, will be the most numerous. The question then will be, whether this aristocracy in the house will unite or divide? and it is too obvious, that destruction to freedom must be the consequence equally of their union or of their division. If they unite generally in all things, as much as they certainly will in respecting each other's wealth, birth, and parts, and conduct themselves with prudence, they will strengthen themselves by insensible degrees, by playing into each other's hands more wealth and popularity, until they become able to govern elections as they please, and rule the people at discretion. An independent member will be their aversion; all their artifices will be employed to destroy his popularity among his constituents, and bring in a disciple of their own in his place.

But if they divide, each party will, in a course of time, have the whole house, and consequently the whole state, divided into two factions, which will struggle in words, in writing, and at last in arms, until Cæsar or Pompey must be emperor, and entail an endless line of tyrants on the nation. But long before this catastrophe, and indeed through every scene of the drama, the laws, instead of being permanent, and affording constant protection to the lives, liberties, and properties of the citizens, will be alternately the sport of contending factions, and the mere vibrations of a pendulum. From the beginning to the end it will be a government of men, now of one set, and then of another; but never a government of laws. . . .

. . . It is from the natural aristocracy in a single assembly that the first danger is to be apprehended in the present state of manners in America; and with a balance of landed property in the hands of the people, so decided in their favor, the progress to degeneracy, corruption, rage, and violence might not be very rapid; nevertheless it would begin with the first elections, and grow faster or slower every year.

Rage and violence would soon appear in the assembly, and from thence be communicated among the people at large.

The only remedy is to throw the rich and the proud into one group, in a separate assembly, and there tie their hands; if you give them scope with the people at large or their representatives, they will destroy *all equality and liberty, with the consent and acclamations of the people themselves.* They will have much more power mixed with the representatives than separated from them. In the first case, if they unite, they will give the law and govern all; if they differ, they will divide the state, and go to a decision by force. But placing them alone by themselves, the society avails itself of all their abilities and virtues; they become a solid check to the representatives themselves, as well as to the executive power, and you disarm them entirely of the power to do mischief. . . .

Definition of Republic[3]

The elements and definitions in most of the arts and sciences are understood alike, by men of education, in all the nations of Europe; but in the science of legislation, which is not one of the least importance to be understood, there is a confusion of languages, as if men were but lately come from Babel. Scarcely any two writers, much less nations, agree in using words in the same sense. Such a latitude, it is true, allows a scope for politicians to speculate, like merchants with false weights, artificial credit, or base money, and to deceive the people, by making the same word adored by one party, and execrated by another. The union of the people, in any principle, rule, or system, is thus rendered impossible; because superstition, prejudice, habit, and passions, are so differently attached to words, that you can scarcely make any nation understand

itself. The words monarchy, aristocracy, democracy, king, prince, lords, commons, nobles, patricians, plebeians, if carefully attended to, will be found to be used in different senses, perpetually, by different nations, by different writers in the same nation, and even by the same writers in different pages.

The word *king*, for example. Ask a Frenchman, What is a king? His answer will be, A man with a crown and sceptre, throne and footstool, anointed at Rheims, who has the making, executing, and interpreting of all laws. Ask an Englishman. His idea will comprehend the throne, footstool, crown, sceptre, and anointing, with one third of the legislative power and the whole of the executive, with an estate in his office to him and his heirs. Ask a Pole; and he tells you, It is a magistrate chosen for life, with scarcely any power at all. Ask an inhabitant of Liege; and he tells you, It is a bishop, and his office is only for life. The word *prince* is another remarkable instance. In Venice, it means the senate, and some-times, by courtesy, the doge, whom some of the Italian writers call a mere *testa di legno*. In France, the eldest sons of dukes are princes, as well as the decendants of the blood royal; in Germany, even the rhingraves are princes; and in Russia, several families, not descended from nor allied to royal blood, anciently obtained, by grant of the sover-eign, the title of prince, descendible to all their posterity; the con-sequence of which has been, that the number of princes in that country is at this day prodigious; and the philosopher of Geneva, in imitation of the Venetians, professedly calls the executive power, wherever lodged, the Prince. How is it possible that whole nations should be made to comprehend the principles and rules of government, until they shall learn to understand one another's meaning by words?

But of all the words in all languages, perhaps there has been none so much abused in this way as the words *republic, commonwealth,* and *popular state.* In the *Rerum-Publicarum Collectio,* of which there are fifty and odd volumes, and many of them very incorrect, France, Spain, and Portugal, the four great empires, the Babylonian, Persian, Greek, and Roman, and even the Ottoman, are all denominated republics. If, indeed, a republic signifies nothing but public affairs, it is equally applicable to all nations; and every kind of government, despotisms, monarchies, aristocracies, democracies, and every possible or imaginable composi-tion of them are all republics. There is, no doubt, a public good and evil, a commonwealth and a common impoverishment in all of them. Others define a republic to be a government of more than one. This will exclude only the despotisms; for a monarchy administered by laws, requires at least magistrates to register them, and consequently more than one person in the government. Some comprehend under the term only aristocracies and democracies, and mixtures of these, without any distinct executive power. Others, again, more rationally, define a republic to signify only a government, in which all men, rich and poor, magistrates

and subjects, officers and people, masters and servants, the first citizen and the last, are equally subject to the laws. This, indeed, appears to be the true and only true definition of a republic. The word *res*, every one knows, signified in the Roman language wealth, riches, property; the word *publicus*, quasi populicus, and per syncope pôplicus, signified public, common, belonging to the people; *res publica*, therefore, was publica res, the wealth, riches, or property of the people. *Res populi*, and the original meaning of the word *republic* could be no other than a government in which the property of the people predominated and governed; and it had more relation to property than liberty. It signified a government, in which the property of the public, or people, and of every one of them, was secured and protected by law. This idea, indeed, implies liberty; because property cannot be secure unless the man be at liberty to acquire, use, or part with it, at his discretion, and unless he have his personal liberty of life and limb, motion and rest, for that purpose. It implies, moreover, that the property and liberty of all men, not merely of a majority, should be safe; for the people, or public, comprehends more than a majority, it comprehends all and every individual; and the property of every citizen is a part of the public property, as each citizen is a part of the public, people, or community. The property, therefore, of every man has a share in government, and is more powerful than any citizen, or party of citizens; it is governed only by the law. There is, however, a peculiar sense in which the words *republic, commonwealth, popular state*, are used by English and French writers; who mean by them a democracy, or rather a representative democracy; a "government in one centre, and that centre the nation;" that is to say, that centre a single assembly, chosen at stated periods by the people, and invested with the whole sovereignty; the whole legislative, executive, and judicial power, to be exercised in a body, or by committees, as they shall think proper. . . .

Elections[4]

It is agreed that the "people know where the shoe wrings, what grievances are most heavy," and, therefore, they should always hold an independent and essential part in the legislature, and be always able to prevent the shoe from wringing more, and the grievances from being made more heavy; they should have a full hearing of all their arguments, and a full share of all consultations, for easing the foot where it is in pain, and for lessening the weight of grievances or annihilating them. But it is denied that they have right, or that they should have power to take from one man his property to make another easy, and that they *only* know "what fences they stand in need of to shelter them from the injurious assaults of those powers that are above them;" meaning, by the powers

above them, senators and magistrates, though, properly speaking, there
are no powers above them but the law, which is above all men, governors
and senators, kings, and nobles, as well as commons.

The Americans have agreed . . . in the sentiment, that "it is but reason
that the people should see that none be interested in the supreme
authority but persons of their own election, and such as must, in a short
time, return again into the same condition with themselves." This
hazardous experiment they have tried, and, if elections are soberly made,
it may answer very well; but if parties, factions, drunkenness, bribes,
armies, and delirium come in, as they always have done sooner or later,
to embroil and decide every thing, the people must again have recourse
to conventions and find a remedy. Neither philosophy nor policy has yet
discovered any other cure, than by prolonging the duration of the first
magistrate and senators. The evil may be lessened and postponed, by
elections for longer periods of years, till they become for life; and if this is
not found an adequate remedy, there will remain no other but to make
them hereditary. The delicacy or the dread of unpopularity that should
induce any man to conceal this important truth from the full view and
contemplation of the people, would be a weakness, if not a vice. As to
"reaping the same benefit or burden, by the laws enacted, that befalls the
rest of the people," this will be secured, whether the first magistrate and
senate be elective or hereditary, so long as the people are an integral
branch of the legislature, can be bound by no laws to which they have
not consented, and can be subjected to no tax which they have not agreed
to lay. . . .

The Prospect in America[5]

. . . All nations, from the beginning, have been agitated by the same
passions. The principles developed here will go a great way in explaining
every phenomenon that occurs in the history of government. The vegetable and animal kingdoms, and those heavenly bodies whose existence
and movements we are as yet only permitted faintly to perceive, do not
appear to be governed by laws more uniform or certain that those which
regulate the moral and political world. Nations move by unalterable
rules; and education, discipline, and laws, make the greatest difference
in their accomplishments, happiness, and perfection. It is the master
artist alone who finishes his building, his picture, or his clock. The
present actors on the stage have been too little prepared by their early
views, and too much occupied with turbulent scenes, to do more than
they have done. Impartial justice will confess that it is astonishing they
have been able to do so much. It is for the young to make themselves
masters of what their predecessors have been able to comprehend and
accomplish but imperfectly.

A prospect into futurity in America is like contemplating the heavens through the telescopes of Herschell. Objects stupendous in their magnitudes and motions strike us from all quarters, and fill us with amazement! When we recollect that the wisdom or the folly, the virtue or the vice, the liberty or servitude, of those millions now beheld by us, only as Columbus saw these times in vision [Barlow's *Vision of Columbus*], are certainly to be influenced, perhaps decided, by the manners, examples, principles, and political institutions of the present generation, that mind must be hardened into stone that is not melted into the reverence and awe. With such affecting scenes before his eyes, is there, can there be, a young American indolent and incurious; surrendered up to dissipation and frivolity; vain of imitating the loosest manners of countries, which can never be made much better or much worse? A profligate American youth must be profligate indeed, and richly merits the scorn of all mankind.

The world has been too long abused with notions that climate and soil decide the characters and political institutions of nations. The laws of Solon and the despotism of Mahomet have, at different times, prevailed at Athens; consuls, emperors, and pontiffs have ruled at Rome. Can there be desired a stronger proof that policy and education are able to triumph over every disadvantage of climate? Mankind have been still more injured by insinuations that a certain celestial virtue, more than human, has been necessary to preserve liberty. Happiness, whether in despotism or democracy, whether in slavery or liberty, can never be found without virtue. The best republics will be virtuous, and have been so; but we may hazard a conjecture that the virtues have been the effect of the well-ordered constitution, rather than the cause. And, perhaps, it would be impossible to prove that a republic cannot exist even among highwaymen, by setting one rogue to watch another; and the knaves themselves may in time be made honest men by the struggle.

It is now in our power to bring this work to a conclusion with unexpected dignity. In the course of the last summer, two authorities have appeared, greater than any that have been before quoted, in which the principles we have attempted to defend have been acknowledged.

The first is an ORDINANCE of Congress, of the thirteenth of July 1787, for the Government of the Territory of the United States, Northwest of the River Ohio.

The second is the REPORT of the Convention at Philadelphia, of the seventeenth of September 1787.

The former confederation of the United States was formed upon the model and example of all the confederacies, ancient and modern, in which the federal council was only a diplomatic body. Even the Lycian, which is thought to have been the best, was no more. The magnitude of territory, the population, the wealth and commerce, and especially the rapid growth of the United States, have shown such a government to be

inadequate to their wants; and the new system, which seems admirably calculated to unite their interests and affections, and bring them to an uniformity of principles and sentiments, is equally well combined to unite their wills and forces as a single nation. A result of accommodation cannot be supposed to reach the ideas of perfection of anyone; but the conception of such an idea, and the deliberate union of so great and various a people in such a plan, is, without all partiality or prejudice, if not the greatest exertion of human understanding, the greatest single effort of national deliberation that the world has ever seen. That it may be improved is not to be doubted, and provision is made for that purpose in the report itself. A people who could conceive and can adopt it, we need not fear will be able to amend it, when, by experience, its inconveniences and imperfections shall be seen and felt.

57. *The Passion for Distinction*

Men, in their primitive conditions, however savage, were undoubtedly gregarious; and they continue to be social, not only in every stage of civilization, but in every possible situation in which they can be placed. As nature intended them for society, she has furnished them with passions, appetites, and propensities, as well as a variety of faculties, calculated both for their individual enjoyment, and to render them useful to each other in their social connections. There is none among them more essential or remarkable, than the *passion for distinction.* A desire to be observed, considered, esteemed, praised, beloved, and admired by his fellows, is one of the earliest, as well as keenest dispositions discovered in the heart of man. If any one should doubt the existence of this propensity, let him go and attentively observe the journeymen and apprentices in the first workshop, or the oarsmen in a cockboat, a family or a neighborhood, the inhabitants of a house or the crew of a ship, a school or a college, a city or a village, a savage or civilized people, a hospital or a church, the bar or the exchange, a camp or a court. Wherever men, women, or children, are to be found, whether they be old or young, rich or poor, high or low, wise or foolish, ignorant or learned, every individual is seen to be strongly actuated by a desire to be seen, heard, talked of, approved and respected, by the people about him, and within his knowledge. . . .

A regard to the sentiments of mankind concerning him, and to their dispositions towards him, every man feels within himself; and if he has reflected, and tried experiments, he has found, that no exertion of his reason, no effort of his will, can wholly divest him of it. In proportion to our affection for the notice of others is our aversion to their neglect; the

stronger the desire of the esteem of the public, the more powerful the aversion to their disapprobation; the more exalted the wish for admiration, the more invincible the abhorrence of contempt. Every man not only desires the consideration of others, but he frequently compares himself with others, his friends or his enemies; and in proportion as he exults when he perceives that he has more of it than they, he feels a keener affliction when he sees that one or more of them, are more respected than himself.

This passion, while it is simply a desire to excel another, by fair industry in the search of truth, and the practice of virtue, is properly called *Emulation*. When it aims at power, as a means of distinction, it is *Ambition*. When it is in a situation to suggest the sentiments of fear and apprehension, that another, who is now inferior, will become superior, it is denominated *Jealousy*. When it is in a state of mortification, at the superiority of another, and desires to bring him down to our level, or to depress him below us, it is properly called *Envy*. When it deceives a man into a belief of false professions of esteem or admiration, or into a false opinion of his importance in the judgment of the world, it is *Vanity*. These observations alone would be sufficient to show, that this propensity, in all its branches, is a principal source of the virtues and vices, the happiness and misery of human life; and that the history of mankind is little more than a simple narration of its operation and effects.

There is in human nature, it is true, simple *Benevolence*, or an affection for the good of others; but alone it is not a balance for the selfish affections. Nature then has kindly added to benevolence, the desire of reputation, in order to make us good members of society. *Spectemur agendo* expresses the great principle of activity for the good of others. Nature has sanctioned the law of self-preservation by rewards and punishments. The rewards of selfish activity are life and health; the punishments of negligence and indolence are want, disease, and death. Each individual, it is true, should consider, that nature has enjoined the same law on his neighbor, and therefore a respect for the authority of nature would oblige him to respect the rights of others as much as his own. But reasoning as abstruse, though as simple as this, would not occur to all men. The same nature therefore has imposed another law, that of promoting the good, as well as respecting the rights of mankind, and has sanctioned it by other rewards and punishments. The rewards in this case, in this life, are *esteem* and *admiration* of others; the punishments are *neglect* and *contempt;* nor may any one imagine that these are not as real as the others. The desire of the esteem of others is as real a want of nature as hunger; and the neglect and contempt of the world as severe a pain as the gout or stone. It sooner and oftener produces despair, and a detestation of existence; of equal importance to individuals, to families, and to nations. It is a principal end of government to regulate this passion, which in its turn becomes a principal means of

government. It is the only adequate instrument of order and subordination in society, and alone commands effectual obedience to laws, since without it neither human reason, nor standing armies, would ever produce that great effect. . . .

58. *Inaugural Address*

March 4, 1797

When it was first perceived, in early times, that no middle course for America remained between unlimited submission to a foreign legislature and a total independence of its claims, men of reflection were less apprehensive of danger from the formidable power of fleets and armies they must determine to resist than from those contests and dissensions which would certainly arise concerning the forms of government to be instituted over the whole and over the parts of this extensive country. Relying, however, on the purity of their intentions, the justice of their cause, and the integrity and intelligence of the people, under an overruling Providence, which had so signally protected this country from the first, the representatives of this nation, then consisting of little more than half its present numbers, not only broke to pieces the chains which were forging, and the rod of iron that was lifted up, but frankly cut asunder the ties which had bound them, and launched into an ocean of uncertainty.

The zeal and ardor of the people during the Revolutionary War, supplying the place of government, commanded a degree of order sufficient at least for the temporary preservation of society. The confederation which was early felt to be necessary was prepared from the models of the Batavian and Helvetic confederacies, the only examples which remain, with any detail and precision, in history, and certainly the only ones which the people at large had ever considered. But, reflecting on the striking difference in so many particulars between this country and those where a courier may go from the seat of government to the frontier in a single day, it was then certainly foreseen by some who assisted in Congress at the formation of it that it could not be durable.

Negligence of its regulations, inattention to its recommendations, if not disobedience to its authority, not only in individuals but in States, soon appeared, with their melancholy consequences; universal languor, jealousies, rivalries of States; decline of navigation and commerce; discouragement of necessary manufactures; universal fall in the value of lands and their produce; contempt of public and private faith; loss of consideration and credit with foreign nations; and, at length, in discontents, animosities, combinations, partial conventions, and insurrection; threatening some great national calamity.

In this dangerous crisis the people of America were not abandoned by their usual good sense, presence of mind, resolution, or integrity. Measures were pursued to concert a plan to form a more perfect union, establish justice, ensure domestic tranquillity, provide for the common defence, promote the general welfare, and secure the blessings of liberty. The public disquisitions, discussions, and deliberations issued in the present happy constitution of government.

Employed in the service of my country abroad, during the whole course of these transactions, I first saw the Constitution of the United States in a foreign country. Irritated by no literary altercation, animated by no public debate, heated by no party animosity, I read it with great satisfaction, as a result of good heads, prompted by good hearts; as an experiment better adapted to the genius, character, situation, and relations of this nation and country than any which had ever been proposed or suggested. In its general principles and great outlines, it was conformable to such a system of government as I had ever most esteemed, and in some States, my own native State in particular, had contributed to establish. Claiming a right of suffrage in common with my fellow-citizens, in the adoption or rejection of a constitution, which was to rule me and my posterity as well as them and theirs, I did not hesitate to express my approbation of it on all occasions, in public and in private. It was not then nor has been since any objection to it, in my mind, that the Executive and Senate were not more permanent. Nor have I entertained a thought of promoting any alteration in it, but such as the people themselves, in the course of their experience, should see and feel to be necessary or expedient, and by their representatives in Congress and the State legislatures, according to the Constitution itself, adopt and ordain.

Returning to the bosom of my country, after a painful separation from it for ten years, I had the honor to be elected to a station under the new order of things, and I have repeatedly laid myself under the most serious obligations to support the Constitution. The operation of it has equalled the most sanguine expectations of its friends; and, from an habitual attention to it, satisfaction in its administration, and delight in its effect upon the peace, order, prosperity, and happiness of the nation, I have acquired an habitual attachment to it, and veneration for it.

What other form of government, indeed, can so well deserve our esteem and love?

There may be little solidity in an ancient idea that congregations of men into cities and nations are the most pleasing objects in the sight of superior intelligences; but this is very certain, that, to a benevolent human mind, there can be no spectacle presented by any nation more pleasing, more noble, majestic, or august than an assembly like that which has so often been seen in this and the other chamber of Congress; of a government in which the executive authority, as well as that of all the branches of the legislature, are exercised by citizens selected at regular

periods by their neighbors, to make and execute laws for the general good. Can anything essential, anything more than mere ornament and decoration, be added to this by robes or diamonds? Can authority be more amiable or respectable when it descends from accidents or institutions established in remote antiquity than when it springs fresh from the hearts and judgments of an honest and enlightened people? For it is the people only that are represented; it is their power and majesty that is reflected, and only for their good, in every legitimate government, under whatever form it may appear. The existence of such a government as ours, for any length of time, is a full proof of a general dissemination of knowledge and virtue throughout the whole body of the people. And what object of consideration more pleasing than this can be presented to the human mind? If national pride is ever justifiable or excusable, it is when it springs, not from power or riches, grandeur or glory, but from conviction of national innocence, information, and benevolence.

In the midst of these pleasing ideas, we should be unfaithful to ourselves if we should ever lose sight of the danger to our liberties, if anything partial or extraneous should infect the purity of our free, fair, virtuous, and independent elections. If an election is to be determined by a majority of a single vote, and that can be procured by a party, through artifice or corruption, the government may be the choice of a party, for its own ends, not of the nation, for the national good. If that solitary suffrage can be obtained by foreign nations, by flattery or menaces, by fraud or violence, by terror, intrigue, or venality, the government may not be the choice of the American people, but of foreign nations. It may be foreign nations who govern us, and not we, the people, who govern ourselves. And candid men will acknowledge that, in such cases, choice would have little advantage to boast of over lot or chance.

Such is the amiable and interesting system of government (and such are some of the abuses to which it may be exposed) which the people of America have exhibited, to the admiration and anxiety of the wise and virtuous of all nations, for eight years; under the administration of a citizen who, by a long course of great actions regulated by prudence, justice, temperance, and fortitude, conducting a people inspired with the same virtues, and animated with the same ardent patriotism and love of liberty, to independence and peace, to increasing wealth and unexampled prosperity, has merited the gratitude of his fellow-citizens, commanded the highest praises of foreign nations, and secured immortal glory with posterity.

In that retirement which is his voluntary choice, may he long live to enjoy the delicious recollection of his services, the gratitude of mankind, the happy fruits of them to himself and the world, which are daily increasing, and that splendid prospect of the future fortunes of his country which is opening from year to year! His name may be still a rampart, and the knowledge that he lives, a bulwark against all open or secret enemies of his country's peace.

This example has been recommended to the imitation of his successors, by both Houses of Congress, and by the voice of the legislatures and the people throughout the nation.

On this subject it might become me better to be silent, or to speak with diffidence; but, as something may be expected, the occasion, I hope, will be admitted as an apology if I venture to say that, if a preference upon principle of a free republican government, formed upon long and serious reflection, after a diligent and impartial inquiry after truth; if an attachment to the Constitution of the United States, and a conscientious determination to support it, until it shall be altered by the judgments and the wishes of the people, expressed in the mode prescribed in it; if a respectful attention to the constitutions of the individual States, and a constant caution and delicacy towards the State governments; if an equal and impartial regard to the rights, interests, honor, and happiness of all the States in the Union, without preference or regard to a northern or southern, eastern or western position, their various political opinions on essential points, or their personal attachments; if a love of virtuous men of all parties and denominations; if a love of science and letters, and a wish to patronize every rational effort to encourage schools, colleges, universities, academies, and every institution for propagating knowledge, virtue, and religion among all classes of people, not only for their benign influence on the happiness of life in all its stages and classes and of society in all its forms, but as the only means of preserving our constitution from its natural enemies, the spirit of sophistry, the spirit of party, the spirit of intrigue, profligacy, and corruption, and the pestilence of foreign influence, which is the angel of destruction to elective governments; if a love of equal laws, of justice and humanity, in the interior administration; if an inclination to improve agriculture, commerce, and manufactures for necessity, convenience, and defence; if a spirit of equity and humanity towards the aboriginal nations of America, and a disposition to meliorate their condition by inclining them to be more friendly to us, and our citizens to be more friendly to them; if an inflexible determination to maintain peace and inviolable faith with all nations, and that system of neutrality and impartiality among the belligerent powers of Europe which has been adopted by the government, and so solemnly sanctioned by both Houses of Congress, and applauded by the legislatures of the States and the public opinion, until it shall be otherwise ordained by Congress; if a personal esteem for the French nation, formed in a residence of seven years chiefly among them, and a sincere desire to preserve the friendship which has been so much for the honor and interest of both nations; if, while the conscious honor and integrity of the people of America, and the internal sentiment of their own power and energies must be preserved, an earnest endeavor to investigate every just cause, and remove every colorable pretence of complaint; if an intention to pursue, by amicable negotiation, a reparation for the injuries that have been com-

mitted on the commerce of our fellow-citizens by whatever nation, and (if success cannot be obtained) to lay the facts before the legislature, that they may consider what further measures the honor and interest of the government and its constituents demand; if a resolution to do justice, as far as may depend upon me, at all times, and to all nations, and maintain peace, friendship, and benevolence with all the world; if an unshaken confidence in the honor, spirit, and resources of the American people, on which I have so often hazarded my all, and never been deceived; if elevated ideas of the high destinies of this country, and of my own duties towards it, founded on a knowledge of the moral principles and intellectual improvements of the people, deeply engraven on my mind in early life, and not obscured, but exalted by experience and age; and with humble reverence I feel it my duty to add, if a veneration for the religion of a people, who profess and call themselves Christians, and a fixed resolution to consider a decent respect for Christianity among the best recommendations for the public service—can enable me in any degree to comply with your wishes, it shall be my strenuous endeavor that this sagacious injunction of the two Houses shall not be without effect.

With this great example before me, with the sense and spirit, the faith and honor, the duty and interest of the same American people, pledged to support the Constitution of the United States, I entertain no doubt of its continuance in all its energy; and my mind is prepared without hesitation to lay myself under the most solemn obligations to support it to the utmost of my power.

And may that Being who is supreme over all, the patron of order, the fountain of justice, and the protector, in all ages of the world, of virtuous liberty, continue his blessing upon this nation and its government, and give it all possible success and duration, consistent with the ends of his providence!

PART III

THOMAS JEFFERSON

(1743-1826)

In April of 1962, President John F. Kennedy was entertaining the Nobel Laureates at the White House with a dinner in their honor. In a genial moment he turned to the impressive assemblage of men and women—America's prize-winning scientists, writers, artists—and said with a grin that he saw before him "probably the greatest concentration of talent and genius in this house except for perhaps those times when Thomas Jefferson ate alone."

Few men have been foolish enough to deny in their hearts what they may have denied with their lips: that Jefferson, in the brilliant reach of his mind and the limitless play of his interests, was one of the most gifted men ever to assume the tasks of democratic statesmanship. The historian, Henry Steele Commager, attempting to assess Jefferson's mighty influence over his countrymen, from the opening act of Independence to our present point in history, wrote: "Jefferson is the central figure in American history and—if freedom and democracy survive in our generation—he may yet prove to be the central figure of modern history." The philosopher, John Dewey, hailed Jefferson as "the first modern to state in human terms the principles of democracy." The great French sociologist, Alexis de Tocqueville, in his classic work, Democracy in America, stated without qualification: "I consider him the most powerful advocate democracy has ever had."

The young Virginian who became the symbol of America's most compelling ideals—so conclusively that both sides in every heated substantive policy from Jefferson's days to ours have claimed the sanction of his principles—was himself of the belief that politics per se was an inferior form of human life. His democratic faith, so properly coupled with the ideals he wrote into the Declaration of Independence, the human rights of equality, of life, liberty and the pursuit of happiness, was the faith of a humanist who had put himself to school in the method of the experimental sciences. Thus his comprehensive program was to establish a new social-political experiment, a democratic modern republic. Its base would be free men using their intelligence and information to play a responsible part, directly or indirectly, in the significant decisions of government. But the fruits and results of a democratic republic were

what he valued, not political power or political form in themselves. The chance to learn, to engage in enlightened discourse and debate, to work with some pride in a suitable task, to cultivate friendships, and enter the many-mansioned realm of art and culture as more than passive recipients, to quest endlessly, creatively, for the meanings of life, to win ever more of the inexhaustible truth—these were the moral goods for which free men would gratefully endure the burdens of self-government. So often is Jefferson cited as an "apostle of liberty"—as though liberty could be spoken for without questions for how, by what means, at what cost, *and* through what work, courage *and* sacrifice—*that it is essential to remember that he had no illusions that liberty was absolute and undivided! Not a cheap and easy liberty to which men are "transported in a featherbed," but the liberty which is the obverse side of responsibility, of intelligent concern and planning, and which at best ascends to a general rule, never to a universal dogma.*

Since Jefferson was the child of the European Enlightenment and in himself the superb fulfillment of the American Enlightenment, one must consider the underlying assumptions of his liberal social views. Long before Marx formulated the slogan that the role of philosophers was not merely to understand the world but to change it, Jefferson had come, through his own process of growth and through the selective affiliation with philosophers he would regard as his ideals, to link theory and action, ideals and reality, principles and practice. As a youth in Western Virginia, he was under the tutelage of his father, Peter Jefferson, a self-made man, a surveyor, cartographer, and skilled craftsman who had himself built the house at Shadwell on the farm where Jefferson was born. Jefferson's memories of his boyhood included less about his mother who came of good aristocratic Randolph stock, than of his father who taught him how to ride, manage a canoe, do carpentry and building, manage a farm, shoot, plant, judge livestock. His father died when Jefferson was fourteen years old, leaving a legacy of some 1400 acres to his son; and yet the fact that his father had arranged that the boy be given a complete training in the classics was mentioned in in Jefferson's Autobiography *in this way:* "I thank on my knees him who directed my early education, for having put into my possession this rich source of delight; and I would not exchange it for anything which I could then have acquired."

To this classical training, he soon added intensive exploration of the new world of natural science and mathematics, under the instruction of Dr. William Small at William and Mary College. Praised by Jefferson as "the most excellent Small," revered ever after as his beloved teacher, this professor of moral philosophy had been responsible for purchasing scientific apparatus for the college which has been described as "at least comparable to what Harvard then possessed." He also built up a library on scientific experiments and inventions for the college. Before this enlightened Scotsman returned to England, he had made a daily companion

of young Jefferson, and was responsible for introducing him to George Wythe, with whom Jefferson studied law for five years after college. Small and Wythe were also the men who conducted Jefferson into the intimate circle of friends who visited with Governor Fauquier at the Palace in Williamsburg. To their common interest in the advance of science, and the principles of law and government, these men joined the amateur's passion for impromptu musicales. Jefferson, who is said to have practiced three hours daily on the cello in these student days, was assigned performing parts.

Thus early the seamless web of knowledge, the Baconian challenge to take all knowledge for his empire became Jefferson's delight. He himself reflected in later years that he had been "a hard student" and his orderly, analytical notes on Montesquieu, Shaftesbury, Locke among others—as well as his careful annotation of the history of law and his more personal selections and comments in his literary commonplace book—bear him out. But important too were the occasions for good conversation, with affable and courteous manners, and the city pleasures of theatre-going, attendance at concerts, games and convivial meetings at the Williamsburg cafe. When Jefferson came to the ultimate test of defining his basic moral values, the use of the phrase "the pursuit of happiness" encompassed all these substantial, intellectual, artistic, and friendly human associations.

Tall, red-haired, soft-spoken and without a trace of arrogance, Jefferson travelled the path from law to public life that was even more compelling in Virginia than in Massachusetts. Henry Adams in characteristic exaggeration once propounded that "Law and politics were the only objects of Virginian thought; but within these bounds the Virginians achieved triumphs." Wythe, Jefferson, Madison, Marshall—these four alone, and at close distance dozens of others—attest to what is correct in the Adams judgment. By the time Jefferson appeared in Philadelphia, aged thirty-three, to represent Virginia at the second Continental Congress, he had practised law, served as a member of the House of Burgesses for Albemarle County from 1769 on, and had appeared in print as the author of a distinguished essay on the oppressive course of British rule in America, and the rationale of American rights, A Summary View of the Rights of British America, *which had placed him in the vanguard of the revolutionary leadership in his state. In the spring of 1776, when he was assigned to write the Declaration of Independence for Congress, he stepped across the threshold of "The Old Dominion" to enter the world stage as an American founder. We have John Adams' testimony that he, like the other members of the Committee on the Declaration, deferred to the younger man for this coveted role because Jefferson possessed the reputation of having written a most handsome public paper ("A Summary View") and was known to the delegates for the felicity of his pen.*

Wasting no time to preen his feathers, Jefferson wrote urgently to political associates in Virginia asking to be recalled so that he might

help to draft a new state constitution. Like John Adams, he sensed that Americans, who had solicited the attention of a candid world in their quest for freedom and self-government, had best create the framework of orderly republican institutions. "It is the whole object of the present controversy," he affirmed; "for should a bad government be instituted for us in future, it had been as well to have accepted at first the bad one offered to us from beyond the water without the risk of expense of contest." Through a series of accidental circumstances, Jefferson's draft of a constitution for Virginia arrived late in the proceedings of the Virginia Convention but nonetheless his preamble and several other features were incorporated into the Virginia constitution of 1776. Very shortly after, Jefferson was pressed into one of the most demanding assignments that could be dealt to a legal reformer. He was put on a committee charged with the revision of Virginia's laws, and since he was Jefferson, he alone drafted 126 bills before this Herculean task was over. His aim was to bring the laws of Virginia into conformity with republican principles, creating a system which he described in his Autobiography "by which every fibre would be eradicated of ancient or future aristocracy; and a foundation laid for a government truly republican." Justly famous among these important bills in the revisal of 1770 was the Bill for establishing religious freedom, a bill called by Julian Boyd "Jefferson's declaration of intellectual and spiritual independence." Unlike some of his other great bills, this one was at long last enacted into law in 1786, the first piece of legislation ever to provide expressly for full religious freedom. In this contribution alone, Jefferson advanced far beyond his revered John Locke whose philosophy of toleration "stopped short," as Jefferson said, of the full freedom required by the independent intelligence and conscience of man.

Other significant bills which contributed to the fame of "the philosophical legislation of Virginia" in France and throughout Europe in the decade of the 1780's were "A Bill on the more General Diffusion of Knowledge" and the bills abolishing primogeniture and entail. The object of the diffusion of knowledge bill was to "qualify citizens to understand their rights, to maintain them, and to exercise with intelligence their parts in self-government." As means to this end, Jefferson proposed a comprehensive new plan of education for the commonwealth of Virginia, providing for free elementary schools for all future citizens, and various higher levels of free education for students of proven ability or talent. This bill must be viewed as part of the revolutionary transformation of society that Jefferson considered to be the practical outcome of the ideals professed in the Declaration. It suffered the fate shared by many later wise educational proposals in America; it could not pass the legislature on grounds of "too much expence."

It is worth notice that Jefferson was also consciously trying to effect reform in the language of the law, as well as in its content. Eager to open

*the laws to the hard-headed intelligence of citizens who might neverthe-
less be perfectly innocent of legal scholarship, he tried to get rid of the
barbarisms of legal jargon, ornate, indirect and repetitive phrasing beneath which the logic of the law was often buried. Beyond any man of
his time, Jefferson had grasped the central principles that a free society
flourished with the freely flowing intelligence of its citizens; and that
communication, on the most extensive basis possible, was indispensable
to governments based upon the consent of the people. Both as means and
as ends, the morality of intelligence would conduct men to freedom and
renew their faith.*

*He was in no sense a provincial Virginia planter, consequently, when
he embarked for Europe in 1784 on a mission to join John Adams and
Benjamin Franklin in negotiating treaties of commerce for the needy
new United States. His success in Paris was second only to Franklin's,
whose affectionate introduction of Jefferson to his European network of
friends smoothed his path. Never did an American enter upon "the
vaunted scene of Europe" with more ardor and more determination to
study the best of European society, art, architecture, technology, invention, agriculture—even cuisine, in order to raise the level of life and
culture at home. Thus, observant travel notes were the product of one
phase of Jefferson's personal conquest of the old world. But his official
duties were pressing and important, especially after Franklin's return to
America when Jefferson was appointed American Minister in France.
Moreover, as a good friend of Lafayette and his circle, Jefferson was
consulted unofficially for political advice by this group who were the
leaders of the liberal "Patriot Party" in the early days of the French
Revolution. In sum, the crowded years of 1784-1789 challenged Jefferson
to compare his values and philosophy, his own country's qualities and
aspirations with those of France and indeed Europe as a civilization. On
the whole, they confirmed his earlier beliefs about free, republican government. With all the animated discussions he partook of in the most
brilliant salons, and the profuse opportunities he seized for opera and
theatre, he gained cosmopolitan sophistication—but nothing profoundly
new in the way of ideas. Matters of emphasis changed, of course. He
rethought his position on natural rights, and henceforth stressed, as he
had not before, the fundamental importance of economic rights. In connection with his powerful phrase, "the earth belongs to the living," he
developed his ideas of the primary claims men had upon society for the
opportunity to work and find satisfaction for their economic needs. He
was sensitive to human suffering and could not be indifferent to the
crushing poverty of the masses of men in the cities and the peasantry
in the countryside. These miseries, this inhuman indigence and accompanying ignorance he attributed to the "oppression" of stupid or
self-indulgent government policy. Monarchy, which he had always condemned on grounds of self-respect and freedom of action, he now de-*

tested as a visible system of evil that ground the faces of the poor. A new depth of moral passion awoke in him in Europe. This fact goes a long way in explaining the character of his feelings about the French Revolution. The opening events of this fateful upheaval he hailed as "the first chapter of the history of European liberty."

Even these few remarks about Jefferson in Paris would be inexcusable without at least a gesture towards the more personal side of his life there. He managed to surround himself with his adored and adoring daughters, Martha and Maria; and having placed them in a fine convent school, directed their studies and reading, even the details of their dress on important occasions, in a manner sufficiently attentive to violate the canons of so-called "permissiveness" which modern society has come to tolerate. He became an intimate friend of John Adams in these years and of his splendid lady and her young ones. Across the water, Madison was Jefferson's most valued correspondent, informing him of the course and climate of political changes at home; but across the Channel, when Adams became the American Ambassador at the Court of St. James's, Jefferson had an acute countryman nearby with whom he could review problems and share information and impressions. For example, as each of these diplomats received news of the new Federal Constitution, they exchanged appraising criticisms. Most affecting of all the events of these years, however, was the attractive middle-aged widower's infatuation with the ravishingly beautiful Mrs. Maria Cosway, portrait painter, musician, childlike lady of fashion—an exquisitely flirtatious creature of sensibility, gayety and melancholy. Jefferson's interest in Maria kept within bounds, as the elaborate love letter, the "Dialog between my Head and my Heart" unmistakably shows. But she remained a bright and glowing image in his emotional life while he lived. Their correspondence, once he had resumed his high but sober tasks in the United States, dwindled through the years; yet Jefferson's last letter to her from Monticello was dated 1822, when, as he described himself to her, he had become "octogenary."

In 1789 Jefferson returned to the United States for a "visit," to find himself under pressure as soon as he put his foot on American soil to remain at home and accept the post of Secretary of State in the new government under the Constitution. After strong misgivings and considerable delay, Jefferson joined the small Cabinet family of President Washington and soon found himself at close range with Hamilton, the Secretary of the Treasury. The classic enmity between these two brilliant men began very early: in 1790, it is already apparent in the clashing opinions sent to Washington on the question of arrearages in soldiers' pay in Virginia. As the enmity developed, and led to Jefferson's resignation as Secretary of State in December of 1793 (he expressed relief at quitting "the hated occupation of politics") the dynamics of a cleavage into two major parties had been set in motion. Jefferson and Madison, as joint leaders of the opposition party, soon captured for themselves the

appealing name of "Republicans"—an appeal far more extensive throughout the country than that of "Federalists." The entire decade of the 1790's, whether Jefferson was in retirement in Virginia, or at the capitol in Philadelphia, was intensely political for him in the hated sense. Fighting was rough on both sides, partly because big issues were at stake concerning the survival of democratic principles and institutions, and partly because of the dangerous inroads on the independence and growth of the infant United States by both England and France. To Jefferson and Madison as leaders of the emerging Republican Party must go the credit for creating and preserving a two-party system as a viable instrument of real political choice, and thus the sine qua non of free government.

In the plainer terms of political success and failure, Jefferson's Presidency commands attention. The results of a poll of the opinions of professional historians made by Arthur M. Schlesinger places Jefferson as one of the six "great" Presidents, the "Olympians" among all American statesmen. The grounds for this estimate of Jefferson were various: his successful negotiation of a turning point in the nation's history, by extending the national boundaries from the Mississippi to the Rockies; he "advanced the cause of human rights through precept and example"; he strengthened the powers of the Presidency, by his adroit management of the Congress and other means. Franklin Delano Roosevelt, himself a "great," suggested an entirely different basis for evaluating Jefferson's worth as President. He valued Jefferson as the deepest student of the cross-currents of our folk life, the hopes and fears of the common people. He praised Jefferson's "consecration" to social justice and to the freedom of the human mind. Interestingly enough, another "great," Woodrow Wilson, shifted the focus to a broader horizon still when he said "The immortality of Thomas Jefferson does not lie in any one of his achievements, but in his attitude toward mankind."

Thus, when the battles over the Kentucky and Virginia Resolutions, the constitutionality of the Bank of the United States, the Embargo policy, even Jefferson's "Agrarianism" or balanced budget fiscal policy are over, the campaign to deepen and extend Jefferson's "attitude toward mankind" is still being waged. The curious fact is that Jefferson's philosophy of human nature, and his profound understanding of the process of significant social order and social reform, made him insist that he had realized something substantial of the high ideals of "'76" and yet know that he had clearly failed to realize all he would have desired; and that successive generations of Americans would find themselves struggling with the agonizing ambiguities and tragic limitations similar to those for which he had expended a nonetheless fulfilling life! As he spoke across the barriers of time and space to men who would be born after he had died, he prepared instructions to his daughter that he wished only these three things inscribed on his tombstone—"because by these, as testimonials that I have lived, I wish most to be remembered:

Author of the Declaration of Independence;
of the Statute of Virginia for Religious Freedom
and Father of the University of Virginia."

The galaxy of his nation's highest office which he had held he passed over silently to choose the meaning of his life—his deepest and most abiding values. These were: political freedom, so that man may live with the dignity of a human person; equality, so that moral concern for every man, woman and child may strengthen his chance to live a fulfilling life and lessen his chance of being distorted into a creature of irrational violence and hatred; religious freedom, so that man's ultimate reading of his being and of nature may be free of coercive or persuasive intrusion by the state or organized pressure groups of his fellows; and intellectual freedom or freedom of the mind, the underlying pervasive value entering into the creation and safeguarding of the other freedoms. For this "freedom of the mind" education must be available, ideally from the cradle to the grave, for all.

The University of Virginia, the "darling" project of Jefferson's old age at Monticello after his retirement from politics, represented to him the culmination of his early love of the classics, his later induction into the enlightened and liberating sciences that could be put to use to improve the human estate, his long pilgrimage of test and trial in the hard decisions and bitter conflicts of creating and serving a powerful government based on faith in the people and functioning by the mandate of their consent. The University was more than that—it was a final embodiment of his distinctive ideal of "the pursuit of happiness." What greater happiness was there than learning, the love of books, of writing, of ideas, of learning, teaching, communicating? His last years were spent fussing over library catalogs for the University, planning the curriculum, the administration. Even the buildings were grouped as an "academical village" graced with serpentine walls and well-proportioned buildings —that art might enhance the students' lives.

On July 4, 1826, fifty years to the day since his Declaration of Independence had gone forth on its immortal journey, Jefferson died. He died a poor man, in debt, his extensive land holdings reduced in value through impersonal factors beyond his control, his capital savings nonexistent because of his long absences from Monticello for the three decades of active public service. The irony of this "planter aristocrat," who freed some of his slaves in his last will but could not afford to free them all, was that he poured his soul into the vision of human rights that he bequeathed to all his countrymen.

Lest this image be tarnished today, it is important to recall, if only briefly, Jefferson's efforts toward the abolition of slavery. Despite the fact that he was a man of his time and culture, from his first entry into politics in 1769 he made an effort in the Virginia legislature "for permission of the emancipation of the slaves, which was rejected." Again, in his draft of the Declaration of Independence, he declared that the

King "*waged cruel war against human nature itself, violating its most sacred rights of life and liberty in the persons of a distant people who never offended him, captivating and carrying them into slavery in another hemisphere. . . . Determined to keep open a market where men should be bought and sold, he has prostituted his negative for suppressing every legislative attempt to prohibit or to restrain this execrable commerce.*" This clause was stricken out on the floor of Congress. Even more important was Jefferson's proposal in 1784, in his "Report of Government for the Western Territories," "*that after the year 1800 of the Christian era, there should be no slavery nor involuntary servitude in any of the said states.*" Richard Morris, the historian, recently stated that had Congress adopted Jefferson's proposal, "*slavery would have been forbidden in all the Western territory after 1800, not only in the Northwest as it was by the Ordinance of 1787, and the grounds for the Civil War could have been removed.*" Finally, Jefferson's sentiments for equality reappear in 1814 in his letter to Edward Coles, President Madison's private secretary, who later removed with his freed slaves to Illinois, and became Governor of that state, a man heroically committed to the cause of abolition. Jefferson wrote, "*The love of justice and the love of country plead equally the cause of this people and it is a moral reproach to us that they should have pleaded it so long in vain, and should have produced not a single effort, nay, I fear not much serious willingness to relieve them and ourselves from our present condition of moral and political reprobation. . . . Yet the hour of emancipation is advancing, in the march of time.*"

It is against this setting of the American Experiment as a continuing revolution that we may view Jefferson's last extant letter, written less than two weeks before his death, regretfully declining the invitation to be present in Washington at the celebration of the fiftieth anniversary of American Independence. "*All eyes are opened, or opening, to the rights of man. The general spread of the light of science has already laid open to every view the palpable truth, that the mass of mankind has not been born with saddles on their backs, nor a favored few booted and spurred, ready to ride them legitimately, by the grace of God. These are grounds of hope for others. For ourselves, let the annual return of this day forever refresh our recollections of these rights, and an undiminished devotion to them.*"

Perhaps the last word should be the poet's—Robert Frost musing on "the pursuit of happiness":

> That's a hard mystery of Jefferson's.
> What did he mean? Of course the easy way
> Is to decide it simply isn't true.
> It may not be. I heard a fellow say so.
> But never mind, the Welshman got it planted
> Where it will trouble us a thousand years.
> Each age will have to reconsider it.

Autobiography

1. *Education and Marriage*

At the age of 77, I begin to make some memoranda, and state some recollections of dates and facts concerning myself, for my own ready reference, and for the information of my family.

The tradition in my family was, that their ancestor came to this country from Wales, and from near the mountain of Snowden, the highest in Great Britain. . . .

My father's education had been quite neglected; but being of a strong mind, sound judgment, and eager after information, he read much and improved himself, insomuch that he was chosen, with Joshua Fry, Professor of Mathematics in William and Mary College, to continue the boundary line between Virginia and North Carolina, which had been begun by Colonel Byrd; and was afterwards employed with the same Mr. Fry to make the first map of Virginia which had ever been made. . . . He died, August 17th, 1757, leaving my mother a widow, who lived till 1776, with six daughters and two sons, myself the elder. To my younger brother he left his estate on James River, called Snowdon, after the supposed birth-place of the family: to myself, the lands on which I was born and live.

He placed me at the English school at five years of age; and at the Latin at nine, where I continued until his death. My teacher, Mr. Douglas, a clergyman from Scotland, with the rudiments of the Latin and Greek languages, taught me the French; and on the death of my father, I went to the Reverend Mr. Maury, a correct classical scholar, with whom I continued two years; and then, to wit, in the spring of 1760, went to William and Mary college, where I continued two years. It was my great good fortune, and what probably fixed the destinies of my life, that Dr. William Small of Scotland, was then Professor of Mathematics, a man profound in most of the useful branches of science, with a happy talent of communication, correct and gentlemanly manners, and an enlarged and liberal mind. He, most happily for me, became soon attached to me, and made me his daily companion when not engaged in the school; and from his conversation I got my first views of the

expansion of science, and of the system of things in which we are placed. Fortunately, the philosophical chair became vacant soon after my arrival at college, and he was appointed to fill it *per interim:* and he was the first who ever gave, in that college, regular lectures in Ethics, Rhetoric and Belles Lettres. He returned to Europe in 1762, having previously filled up the measure of his goodness to me, by procuring for me, from his most intimate friend, George Wythe, a reception as a student of law, under his direction, and introduced me to the acquaintance and familiar table of Governor Fauquier, the ablest man who had ever filled that office. With him, and at his table, Dr. Small and Mr. Wythe, his *amici omnium horarum,* and myself, formed a *partie quarée,* and to the habitual conversations on these occasions I owed much instruction. Mr. Wythe continued to be my faithful and beloved mentor in youth, and my most affectionate friend through life. In 1767, he led me into the practice of the law at the bar of the General court, at which I continued until the Revolution shut up the courts of justice.

In 1769, I became a member of the legislature by the choice of the county in which I live, and so continued until it was closed by the Revolution. I made one effort in that body for the permission of the emancipation of slaves, which was rejected: and indeed, during the regal government, nothing liberal could expect success. . . .

On the 1st of January, 1772, I was married to Martha Skelton, widow of Bathurst Skelton, and daughter of John Wayles, then twenty-three years old. Mr. Wayles was a lawyer of much practice. . . . He acquired a handsome fortune, and died in May, 1773, leaving three daughters: the portion which came on that event to Mrs. Jefferson, after the debts should be paid, which were very considerable, was about equal to my own patrimony, and consequently doubled the ease of our circumstances. . . .

2. *Intellectual Leadership for Independence*

In May, 1769, a meeting of the General Assembly was called by the Governor, Lord Botetourt. I had then become a member; and to that meeting became known the joint resolutions and address of the Lords and Commons, of 1768–9, on the proceedings in Massachusetts. Counter-resolutions, and an address to the King by the House of Burgesses, were agreed to with little opposition, and a spirit manifestly displayed itself of considering the cause of Massachusetts as a common one. The Governor dissolved us: but we met the next day in the Apollo [public room] of the Raleigh tavern, formed ourselves into a voluntary convention, drew up articles of association against the use of any

merchandise imported from Great Britain, signed and recommended them to the people, repaired to our several counties, and were re-elected without any other exception than of the very few who had declined assent to our proceedings.

Nothing of particular excitement occurring for a considerable time, our countrymen seemed to fall into a state of insensibility to our situation; . . . But a court of inquiry held in Rhode Island in 1762, with a power to send persons to England to be tried for offences committed here, was considered, at our session of the spring of 1773, as demanding attention. Not thinking our old and leading members up to the point of forwardness and zeal which the times required, Mr. Henry, Richard Henry Lee, Francis L. Lee, Mr. Carr and myself agreed to meet in the evening, in a private room of the Raleigh, to consult on the state of things. . . . We were all sensible that the most urgent of all measures was that of coming to an understanding with all the other colonies, to consider the British claims as a common cause to all, and to produce a unity of action: and, for this purpose, that a committee of correspondence in each colony would be the best instrument of intercommunication: and that their first measure would probably be, to propose a meeting of deputies from every colony, at some central place, who should be charged with the direction of the measures which should be taken by all. . . .

The next event which excited our sympathies for Massachusetts, was the Boston port bill, by which that port was to be shut up on the 1st of June, 1774. This arrived while we were in session in the spring of that year. The lead in the House, on these subjects, being no longer left to the old members, Mr. Henry, R. H. Lee, Fr. L. Lee, three or four other members, whom I do not recollect, and myself, agreeing that we must boldly take an unequivocal stand in the line with Massachusetts, determined to meet and consult on the proper measures, in the council-chamber, for the benefit of the library in that room. We were under conviction of the necessity of arousing our people from the lethargy into which they had fallen, as to passing events; and thought that the appointment of a day of general fasting and prayer would be most likely to call up and alarm their attention. No example of such a solemnity had existed since the days of our distresses in the war of '55, since which a new generation had grown up. . . . The Governor dissolved us, as usual. We retired to the Apollo, as before, agreed to an association, and instructed the committee of correspondence to propose to the corresponding committees of the other colonies, to appoint deputies to meet in Congress at such place, *annually*, as should be convenient, to direct, from time to time, the measures required by the general interest: and we declared that an attack on any one colony, should be considered as an attack on the whole. This was in May. We further recommended to the several counties to elect deputies to meet at Williamsburg,

the 1st of August ensuing, to consider the state of the colony, and particularly to appoint delegates to a general Congress, should that measure be acceded to by the committees of correspondence generally. It was acceded to; Philadelphia was appointed for the place, and the 5th of September for the time of meeting. We returned home, and in our several counties invited the clergy to meet assemblies of the people on the 1st of June, to perform the ceremonies of the day, and to address to them discourses suited to the occasion. The people met generally, with anxiety and alarm in their countenances, and the effect of the day, through the whole colony, was like a shock of electricity, arousing every man, and placing him erect and solidly on his centre. They chose, universally, delegates for the convention. Being elected one for my own county, I prepared a draught of instructions to be given to the delegates whom we should send to the Congress, which I meant to propose at our meeting. In this I took the ground that, from the beginning, I had thought the only one orthodox or tenable, which was, that the relation between Great Britain and these colonies was exactly the same as that of England and Scotland, after the accession of James, and until the union, and the same as her present relations with Hanover, having the same executive chief, but no other necessary political connection; and that our emigration from England to this country gave her no more rights over us, than the emigrations of the Danes and Saxons gave to the present authorities of the mother country, over England. In this doctrine, however, I had never been able to get any one to agree with me but Mr. Wythe. He concurred in it from the first dawn of the question, What was the political relation between us and England? Our other patriots, Randolph, the Lees, Nicholas, Pendleton, stopped at the half-way house of John Dickinson, who admitted that England has a right to regulate our commerce, and to lay duties on it for the purposes of regulation, but not of raising revenue. But for this ground there was no foundation in compact, in any acknowledged principles of colonization, nor in reason: expatriation being a natural right, and acted on as such, by all nations, in all ages. I set out for Williamsburg some days before that appointed for our meeting, but was taken ill of a dysentery on the road, and was unable to proceed. I sent on, therefore, to Williamsburg, two copies of my draught. . . . Peyton Randolph informed the convention he had received such a paper from a member, prevented by sickness from offering it in his place, and he laid it on the table for perusal. It was read generally by the members, approved by many, though thought too bold for the present state of things; but they printed it in pamphlet form, under the title of "A Summary View of the Rights of British America." It found its way to England, was taken up by the opposition, interpolated a little by Mr. Burke so as to make it answer opposition purposes, and in that form ran rapidly through several editions. . . .

The convention met on the 1st of August, renewed their association, appointed delegates to the Congress, gave them instructions very temperately and properly expressed, both as to style and matter; and they repaired to Philadelphia at the time appointed. The splendid proceedings of that Congress, at their first session, belong to general history, are known to every one, and need not therefore be noted here. . . . The convention, at their ensuing session of March, '75, approved of the proceedings of Congress, thanked their delegates, and reappointed the same persons to represent the colony at the meeting to be held in May. . . .

3. *The Debates on Independence*

On the 15th of May, 1776, the convention of Virginia instructed their delegates in Congress, to propose to that body to declare the colonies independent of Great Britain, and appoint a committee to prepare a declaration of rights and plan of government. . . .

In Congress, Friday, June 7, 1776.

The delegates from Virginia moved, in obedience to instructions from their constituents, that the Congress should declare that these United colonies are, and of right ought to be, free and independent states, that they are absolved from all allegiance to the British crown, and that all political connection between them and the state of Great Britain is, and ought to be, totally dissolved; that measures should be immediately taken for procuring the assistance of foreign powers, and a Confederation be formed to bind the colonies more closely together.

The House being obliged to attend at that time to some other business, the proposition was referred to the next day, when the members were ordered to attend punctually at ten o'clock.

Saturday, June 8. They proceeded to take it into consideration, and referred it to a committee of the whole, into which they immediately resolved themselves, and passed that day and Monday, the 10th, in debating on the subject.

It was argued by Wilson, Robert R. Livingston, E. Rutledge, Dickinson, and others—

That, though they were friends to the measures themselves, and saw the impossibility that we should ever again be united with Great Britain, yet they were against adopting them at this time:

That the conduct we had formerly observed was wise and proper now, of deferring to take any capital step till the voice of the people drove us into it:

That they were our power, and without them our declarations could not be carried into effect:

That the people of the middle colonies (Maryland, Delaware, Pennsylvania, the Jerseys and New York) were not yet ripe for bidding adieu to British connection, but that they were fast ripening, and, in a short time, would join in the general voice of America: . . .

That some of them had expressly forbidden their delegates to consent to such a declaration, and others had given no instructions, and consequently no powers to give such consent. . . .

That if such a declaration should now be agreed to, these delegates must retire, and possibly their colonies might secede from the Union. . . .

That we had little reason to expect an alliance with those to whom alone, as yet, we had cast our eyes:

That France and Spain had reason to be jealous of that rising power, which would one day certainly strip them of all their American Possessions. . . .

On the other side, it was urged by J. Adams, Lee, Wythe, and others, that no gentleman had argued against the policy or the right of separation from Britain, nor had supposed it possible we should ever renew our connection; that they had only opposed its being now declared:

That the question was not whether, by a Declaration of Independence, we should make ourselves what we are not; but whether we should declare a fact which already exists:

That, as to the people or parliament of England, we had always been independent of them, their restraints on our trade deriving efficacy from our acquiescence only, and not from any rights they possessed of imposing them, and that so far, our connection had been federal only, and was now dissolved by the commencement of hostilities:

That, as to the King, we had been bound to him by allegiance, but that this bond was now dissolved by his assent to the last act of Parliament, by which he declares us out of his protection, and by his levying war on us, a fact which had long ago proved us out of his protection; it being a certain position in law, that allegiance and protection are reciprocal, the one ceasing when the other is withdrawn: . . .

That the people wait for us to lead the way:

That *they* are in favor of the measure, though the instructions given by some of their *representatives* are not:

That the voice of the representatives is not always consonant with the voice of the people, and that this is remarkably the case in these middle colonies: . . .

That it would be vain to wait either weeks or months for perfect

unanimity, since it was impossible that all men should ever become of one sentiment on any question: . . .

That though France and Spain may be jealous of our rising power, they must think it will be much more formidable with the addition of Great Britain; and will therefore see it their interest to prevent a coalition; but should they refuse, we shall be but where we are; whereas without trying, we shall never know whether they will aid us or not: . . .

4. *The Declaration of Independence*

It appearing in the course of these debates, that the colonies of New York, New Jersey, Pennsylvania, Delaware, Maryland, and South Carolina were not yet matured for falling from the parent stem, but that they were fast advancing to that state, it was thought most prudent to wait a while for them, and to postpone the final decision to July 1st; but, that this might occasion as little delay as possible, a committee was appointed to prepare a Declaration of Independence. The committee were John Adams, Dr. Franklin, Roger Sherman, Robert R. Livingston, and myself. Committees were also appointed, at the same time, to prepare a plan of confederation for the colonies, and to state the terms proper to be proposed for foreign alliance. The committee for drawing the Declaration of Independence, desired me to do it. It was accordingly done, and being approved by them, I reported it to the House on Friday, the 28th of June, when it was read, and ordered to lie on the table. On Monday, the 1st of July, the House resolved itself into a committee of the whole, and resumed the consideration of the original motion made by the delegates of Virginia, which, being again debated through the day, was carried in the affirmative by the votes of New Hampshire, Connecticut, Massachusetts, Rhode Island, New Jersey, Maryland, Virginia, North Carolina and Georgia. South Carolina and Pennsylvania voted against it. . . . The committee rose and reported their resolution to the House. Mr. Edward Rutledge, of South Carolina, then requested the determination might be put off to the next day, as he believed his colleagues, though they disapproved of the resolution, would then join in it for the sake of unanimity. The ultimate question, whether the House would agree to the resolution of the committee, was accordingly postponed to the next day, when it was again moved. . . . The whole twelve colonies who were authorized to vote at all gave their voices for it; and within a few days, the convention of New York approved of it. . . .

Congress proceeded the same day to consider the Declaration of Independence. . . .

The pusillanimous idea that we had friends in England worth keeping terms with, still haunted the minds of many. For this reason, those passages which conveyed censures on the people of England were struck out, lest they should give them offence. The clause too, reprobating the enslaving the inhabitants of Africa, was struck out in complaisance to South Carolina and Georgia, who had never attempted to restrain the importation of slaves, and who, on the contrary, still wished to continue it. Our northern brethren also, I believe, felt a little tender under those censures; for though their people had very few slaves themselves, yet they had been pretty considerable carriers of them to others. The debates, having taken up the greater parts of the 2d, 3d, and 4th days of July, were, on the evening of the last, closed; the Declaration was reported by the committee, agreed to by the House, and signed by every member present, except Mr. Dickinson. . . .

5. *"The General Pulse of Reformation"*

I knew that our legislation, under the regal government, had many very vicious points which urgently required reformation, and I thought I could be of more use in forwarding that work. I therefore retired from my seat in Congress on the 2d of September, resigned it, and took my place in the legislature of my State, on the 7th of October.

On the 11th, I moved for leave to bring in a bill for the establishment of courts of justice, the organization of which was of importance. I drew the bill; it was approved by the committee, reported and passed, after going through its due course.

On the 12th, I obtained leave to bring in a bill declaring tenants in tail to hold their lands in fee simple. In the earlier times of the colony, when lands were to be obtained for little or nothing, some provident individuals procured large grants; and, desirous of founding great families for themselves, settled them on their descendants in fee tail. The transmission of this property from generation to generation, in the same name, raised up a distinct set of families, who, being privileged by law in the perpetuation of their wealth, were thus formed into a Patrician order, distinguished by the splendor and luxury of their establishments. From this order, too, the king habitually selected his counsellors of State; the hope of which distinction devoted the whole corps to the interests and will of the crown. To annul this privilege, and instead of an aristocracy of wealth, of more harm and danger, than benefits, to society, to make an opening for the aristocracy of virtue and talent, which nature has wisely provided for the direction of the interests of society, and scattered with equal hand through all its conditions, was deemed

essential to a well-ordered republic.—To effect it, no violence was necessary, no deprivation of natural right, but rather an enlargement of it
by a repeal of the law. For this would authorize the present holder
to divide the property among his children equally, as his affections were
divided; and would place them, by natural generation, on the level of
their fellow citizens. But this repeal was strongly opposed by Mr.
Pendleton, who was zealously attached to ancient establishments; and
who, taken all in all, was the ablest man in debate I have ever met
with. . . . But the bill passed finally for entire abolition.

In that one of the bills organizing our judiciary system, which proposed
a court of Chancery, I had provided for a trial by jury of all matters of
fact, in that as well as in the courts of law. He defeated it by the introduction of four words only, *"if either party choose."* The consequence
has been, that as no suitor will say to his judge, "Sir, I distrust you,
give me a jury," juries are rarely, I might say, perhaps, never, seen in
that court, but when called for by the Chancellor of his own accord.

The first establishment in Virginia which became permanent, was
made in 1607. I have found no mention of negroes in the colony until
about 1650. The first brought here as slaves were by a Dutch ship;
after which the English commenced the trade, and continued it until
the revolutionary war. That suspended, *ipso facto,* their further importation for the present, and the business of the war pressing constantly
on the legislature, this subject was not acted on finally until the year
'78, when I brought in a bill to prevent their further importation. This
passed without opposition, and stopped the increase of the evil by
importation, leaving to future efforts its final eradication.

The first settlers of this colony were Englishmen, loyal subjects to their
king and church, and the grant to Sir Walter Raleigh contained an
express proviso that their laws "should not be against the true Christian
faith, now professed in the church of England." As soon as the state
of the colony admitted, it was divided into parishes, in each of which
was established a minister of the Anglican church, endowed with a fixed
salary, in tobacco, a glebe house and land with the other necessary
appendages. To meet these expenses, all the inhabitants of the parishes
were assessed, whether they were or not, members of the established
church. . . .

By the time of the revolution, a majority of the inhabitants had become dissenters from the established church, but were still obliged to
pay contributions to support the pastors of the minority. This unrighteous
compulsion, to maintain teachers of what they deemed religious errors,
was grievously felt during the regal government, and without a hope
of relief. But the first republican legislature, which met in '76, was
crowded with petitions to abolish this spiritual tyranny. These brought
on the severest contests in which I have ever been engaged. Our great
opponents were Mr. Pendleton and Robert Carter Nicholas; honest men,

but zealous churchmen. The petitions were referred to the committee of the whole house on the state of the country; and, after desperate contests in that committee, almost daily from the 11th of October to the 5th of December, we prevailed so far only, as to repeal the laws which rendered criminal the maintenance of any religious opinions, the forebearance of repairing to church, or the exercise of any mode of worship; and further, to exempt dissenters from contributions to the support of the established church; and to suspend, only until the next session, levies on the members of that church for the salaries of their own incumbents. . . .

This question, debated at every session, from '76 to '79, (some of our dissenting allies, having now secured their particular objects, going over to the advocates of a general assessment,) we could only obtain a suspension from session to session until '79, when the question against a general assessment was finally carried, and the establishment of the Anglican church entirely put down. . . .

In giving this account of the laws of which I was myself the mover and draughtsman, I, by no means, mean to claim to myself the merit of obtaining their passage. I had many occasional and strenuous coadjutors in debate, and one, most steadfast, able and zealous; who was himself a host. This was George Mason. . . .

Mr. Madison came into the House in 1776, a new member and young; which circumstances, concurring with his extreme modesty, prevented his venturing himself in debate before his removal to the Council of State, in November, '77. From thence he went to Congress, then consisting of few members. Trained in these successive schools, he acquired a habit of self-possession, which placed at ready command the rich resources of his luminous and discriminating mind, and of his extensive information, and rendered him the first of every assembly afterwards, of which he became a member. Never wandering from his subject into vain declamation, but pursuing it closely, in language pure, classical and copious, soothing always the feelings of his adversaries by civilities and softness of expression, he rose to the eminent station which he held in the great National Convention of 1787; and in that of Virginia which followed, he sustained the new constitution in all its parts, bearing off the palm against the logic of George Mason, and the fervid declamation of Mr. Henry. With these consummate powers, were united a pure and spotless virtue, which no calumny has ever attempted to sully. Of the powers and polish of his pen, and of the wisdom of his administration in the highest office of the nation, I need say nothing. They have spoken, and will forever speak for themselves.

6. *The Revisal of the Laws of Virginia*

So far we were proceeding in the details of reformation only; selecting points of legislation, prominent in character and principle, urgent, and indicative of the strength of the general pulse of reformation. When I left Congress, in '76, it was in the persuasion that our whole code must be reviewed, adapted to our republican form of government; and now that we had no negatives of Councils, Governors, and Kings to restrain us from doing right, it should be corrected, in all its parts, with a single eye to reason, and the good of those for whose government it was framed. Early, therefore, in the session of '76, to which I returned, I moved and presented a bill for the revision of the laws, which was passed. . . . Mr. Pendleton, Mr. Wythe, George Mason, Thomas L. Lee, and myself, were appointed a committee to execute the work. . . . The first question was, whether we should propose to abolish the whole existing system of laws, and prepare a new and complete Institute, or preserve the general system, and only modify it to the present state of things. Mr. Pendleton, contrary to his usual disposition in favor of ancient things, was for the former proposition, in which he was joined by Mr. Lee. To this it was objected, that to abrogate our whole system would be a bold measure, and probably far beyond the views of the legislature; that they had been in the practice of revising, from time to time, the laws of the colony, omitting the expired, the repealed, and the obsolete, amending only those retained, and probably meant we should now do the same, only including the British statutes as well as our own: that to compose a new Institute, like those of Justinian and Bracton, or that of Blackstone, which was the model proposed by Mr. Pendleton, would be an arduous undertaking, of vast research, of great consideration and judgment; and when reduced to a text, every word of that text, from the imperfection of human language, and its incompetence to express distinctly every shade of idea, would become a subject of question and chicanery, until settled by repeated adjudications; and this would involve us for ages in litigation, and render property uncertain, until, like the statutes of old, every word had been tried and settled by numerous decisions, and by new volumes of reports and commentaries; and that no one of us, probably, would undertake such a work, which to be systematical, must be the work of one hand. This last was the opinion of Mr. Wythe, Mr. Mason, and myself. When we proceeded to the distribution of the work, Mr. Mason excused himself, as, being no lawyer, he felt himself unqualified for the work, and he resigned soon after. Mr. Lee excused himself on the same ground, and died, indeed, in a short time. The other two gentlemen, therefore, and myself divided the work among us. The common law and statutes to the 4 James I. (when

our separate legislature was established) were assigned to me; the British statutes, from that period to the present day, to Mr. Wythe; and the Virginia laws to Mr. Pendleton. As the law of Descents, and the criminal law fell of course within my portion, I wished the committee to settle the leading principles of these, as a guide for me in framing them; and, with respect to the first, I proposed to abolish the law of primogeniture, and to make real estate descendible in parcenary to the next of kin, as personal property is, by the statute of distribution. Mr. Pendleton wished to preserve the right of primogeniture, but seeing at once that that could not prevail, he proposed we should adopt the Hebrew principle, and give a double portion to the elder son. I observed, that if the eldest son could eat twice as much, or do double work, it might be a natural evidence of his right to a double portion; but being on a par in his powers and wants, with his brothers and sisters, he should be on a par also in the partition of the patrimony; and such was the decision of the other members.

On the subject of the Criminal law, all were agreed, that the punishment of death should be abolished, except for treason and murder; and that, for other felonies, should be substituted hard labor in the public works, and in some cases, the *Lex talionis*. . . . How this last revolting principle came to obtain our approbation, I do not remember. There remained, indeed, in our laws, a vestige of it in a single case of a slave; it was the English law, in the time of the Anglo-Saxons, copied probably from the Hebrew law of "an eye for an eye, a tooth for a tooth," and it was the law of several ancient people; but the modern mind had left it far in the rear of its advances. These points, however, being settled, we repaired to our respective homes for the preparation of the work.

In the execution of my part, I thought it material not to vary the diction of the ancient statutes by modernizing it, nor to give rise to new questions by new expressions. The text of these statutes had been so fully explained and defined, by numerous adjudications, as scarcely ever now to produce a question in our courts. I thought it would be useful, also, in all new draughts, to reform the style of the later British statutes, and of our own acts of Assembly; which, from their verbosity, their endless tautologies, their involutions of case within case, and parenthesis within parenthesis, and their multiplied efforts at certainty, by *saids* and *aforesaids*, by *ors* and by *ands*, to make them more plain, are really rendered more perplexed and incomprehensible, not only to common readers, but to the lawyers themselves. We were employed in this work from that time to February, 1779, when we met at Williamsburg, . . . and meeting day by day, we examined critically our several parts, sentence by sentence, scrutinizing and amending, until we had agreed on the whole. We then returned home, had fair copies made of our several parts, which were reported to the General Assembly, June 18, 1779. . . .

We had, in this work, brought so much of the Common law as it was

thought necessary to alter, all the British statutes from *Magna Charta* to the present day, and all the laws of Virginia, from the establishment of our legislature, in the 4th Jac. I. to the present time, which we thought should be retained, within the compass of one hundred and twenty-six bills, making a printed folio of ninety pages only. Some bills were taken out, occasionally, from time to time, and passed; but the main body of the work was not entered on by the legislature until after the general peace, in 1785, when, by the unwearied exertions of Mr. Madison, in opposition to the endless quibbles, chicaneries, perversions, vexations and delays of lawyers and demi-lawyers, most of the bills were passed by the legislature, with little alteration.

The bill for establishing religious freedom, the principles of which had, to a certain degree, been enacted before, I had drawn in all the latitude of reason and right. It still met with opposition; but, with some mutilations in the preamble, it was finally passed; and . . . its protection of opinion was meant to be universal . . . to comprehend within the mantle of its protection, the Jew and the Gentile, the Christian and Mahometan, the Hindoo, and Infidel of every denomination.

Beccaria, and other writers on crimes and punishments, had satisfied the reasonable world of the unrightfulness and inefficacy of the punishment of crimes by death; and hard labor on roads, canals and other public works, had been suggested as a proper substitute. The Revisors had adopted these opinions; but the general idea of our country had not yet advanced to that point. The bill, therefore, for proportioning crimes and punishments, was lost in the House of Delegates by a majority of a single vote. . . .

7. *Systematic Plan of General Education*

The acts of Assembly concerning the College of William and Mary, were properly within Mr. Pendleton's portion of our work; but these related chiefly to its revenue, while its constitution, organization and scope of science, were derived from its charter. We thought that on this subject, a systematical plan of general education should be proposed, and I was requested to undertake it. I accordingly prepared three bills for the Revisal, proposing three distinct grades of education, reaching all classes. 1st. Elementary schools, for all children generally, rich and poor. 2d. Colleges, for a middle degree of instruction, calculated for the common purposes of life, and such as would be desirable for all who were in easy circumstances. And, 3d, an ultimate grade for teaching the sciences generally, and in their highest degree. The first bill proposed to lay off every county into Hundreds, or Wards, of a proper size and population for a school, in

which reading, writing, and common arithmetic should be taught; and that the whole State should be divided into twenty-four districts, in each of which should be a school for classical learning, grammar, geography, and the higher branches of numerical arithmetic. The second bill proposed to amend the constitution of William and Mary college, to enlarge its sphere of science, and to make it in fact a University. The third was for the establishment of a library. These bills were not acted on until the same year, '96, and then only so much of the first as provided for elementary schools. The College of William and Mary was an establishment purely of the Church of England; the Visitors were required to be all of that Church; the Professors to subscribe its thirty-nine Articles; its Students to learn its Catechism; and one of its fundamental objects was declared to be, to raise up Ministers for that church. The religious jealousies, therefore, of all the dissenters, took alarm lest this might give an ascendancy to the Anglican sect, and refused acting on that bill. Its local eccentricity, too, and unhealthy autumnal climate, lessened the general inclination towards it. And in the Elementary bill, they inserted a provision which completely defeated it; for they left it to the court of each county to determine for itself, when this act should be carried into execution, within their county. One provision of the bill was, that the expenses of these schools should be borne by the inhabitants of the county, every one in proportion to his general tax rate. This would throw on wealth the education of the poor; and the justices, being generally of the more wealthy class, were unwilling to incur that burden, and I believe it was not suffered to commence in a single county. . . .

8. *"These People are to be Free"*

The bill on the subject of slaves, was a mere digest of the existing laws respecting them, without any intimation of a plan for a future and general emancipation. It was thought better that this should be kept back, and attempted only by way of amendment, whenever the bill should be brought on. The principles of the amendment, however, were agreed on, that is to say, the freedom of all born after a certain day, and deportation at a proper age. But it was found that the public mind would not yet bear the proposition, nor will it bear it even at this day. Yet the day is not distant when it must bear and adopt it, or worse will follow. Nothing is more certainly written in the book of fate, than that these people are to be free; nor is it less certain that the two races, equally free, cannot live in the same government. Nature, habit, opinion have drawn indelible lines of distinction between them. It is still in our power to direct the process of emancipation and deportation, peaceably, and in such slow

degree, as that the evil will wear off insensibly, and their place be, *pari passu,* filled up by free white laborers. If, on the contrary, it is left to force itself on, human nature must shudder at the prospect held up. . . .

9. *"Foundation . . . for a Government Truly Republican"*

I consider four of these bills, passed or reported, as forming a system by which every fibre would be eradicated of ancient or future aristocracy; and a foundation laid for a government truly republican. The repeal of the laws of entail would prevent the accumulation and perpetuation of wealth, in select families, and preserve the soil of the country from being daily more and more absorbed in mortmain. The abolition of primogeniture, and equal partition of inheritances, removed the feudal and unnatural distinctions which made one member of every family rich, and all the rest poor, substituting equal partition, the best of all Agrarian laws. The restoration of the rights of conscience relieved the people from taxation for the support of a religion not theirs; for the establishment was truly of the religion of the rich, the dissenting sects being entirely composed of the less wealthy people; and these, by the bill for a general education, would be qualified to understand their rights, to maintain them, and to exercise with intelligence their parts in self-government; and all this would be effected, without the violation of a single natural right of any one individual citizen. To these, too, might be added, as a further security, the introduction of the trial by jury, into the Chancery courts, which have already ingulfed, and continue to ingulf, so great a proportion of the jurisdiction over our property. . . .

Letters

10. *The Advantages of Going to College*

To John Harvie

Shadwell, Jan. 14, 1760

I was at Colo. Peter Randolph's about a Fortnight ago, and my Schooling falling into Discourse, he said he thought it would be to my Advantage to go to the College, and was desirous I should go, as indeed I am myself for several Reasons. In the first place as long as I stay at the Mountains the Loss of one fourth of my Time is inevitable, by Company's coming here and detaining me from School. And likewise my Absence will in a great Measure put a Stop to so much Company, and by that Means lessen the Expences of the Estate in House-Keeping. And on the other Hand by going to the College I shall get a more universal Acquaintance, which may hereafter be serviceable to me; and I suppose I can pursue my Studies in the Greek and Latin as well there as here, and likewise learn something of the Mathematics. I shall be glad of your opinion.

11. *Renunciation of Public Service*

To James Monroe

Monticello, May 20, 1782

. . . If we are made in some degree for others, yet in a greater are we made for ourselves. It were contrary to feeling and indeed ridiculous to suppose a man had less right in himself than one of his neighbors or all of them put together. This would be slavery and not that liberty which the bill of rights has made inviolable and for the preservation of which our government has been changed. Nothing could so completely divest us of that liberty as the establishment of the opinion that the state has a

perpetual right to the services of all it's members. This to men of certain ways of thinking would be to annihilate the blessing of existence; to contradict the giver of life who gave it for happiness and not for wretchedness, and certainly to such it were better that they had never been born. However with these I may think public service and private misery inseparably linked together, I have not the vanity to count myself among those whom the state would think worth oppressing with perpetual service. I have received a sufficient memento to the contrary. I am persuaded that having hitherto dedicated to them the whole of the active and useful part of my life I shall be permitted to pass the rest in mental quiet. . . .

12. *The Death of His Wife*

To Francois Jean, Chevalier de Chastellux

Ampthill Nov. 26, 1782

I received your friendly letter of . . . June 30. . . . It found me a little emerging from that stupor of mind which had rendered me as dead to the world as she was whose loss occasioned it. Your letter recalled to my memory, that there were persons still living of much value to me. If you should have thought me remiss in not testifying to you sooner how deeply I had been impressed with your worth in the little time I had the happiness of being with you you will I am sure ascribe it to it's true cause the state of dreadful suspence in which I had been kept all the summer and the catastrophe which closed it. Before that event my scheme of life had been determined. I had folded myself in the arms of retirement, and rested all prospects of future happiness on domestic and literary objects. A single event wiped away all my plans and left me a blank which I had not the spirits to fill up. In this state of mind an appointment from Congress found me requiring me to cross the Atlantic.

13. *Low State of the Confederacy*

To Edmund Randolph

Baltimore Feb. 15, 1783

. . . I find . . . the pride of independance taking deep and dangerous hold on the hearts of individual states. I know no danger so dreadful and so probable as that of internal contests. And I know no remedy so likely to

prevent it as the strengthening the band which connects us. We have substituted a Congress of deputies from every state to perform this task: but we have done nothing which would enable them to enforce their decisions. What will be the case? They will not be enforced. The states will go to war with each other in defiance of Congress; one will call in France to her assistance; another Gr. Britain, and so we shall have all the wars of Europe brought to our own doors. Can any man be so puffed up with his little portion of sovereignty as to prefer this calamitous accompaniment to the parting with a little of his sovereign right and placing it in a council from all the states, who being chosen by himself annually, removeable at will, subject in a private capacity to every act of power he does in a public one, cannot possibly do him an injury, or if he does will be subject to be overhauled for it? It is very important to unlearn the lessons we have learnt under our former government, to discard the maxims which were the bulwark of that, but would be the ruin of the one we have erected. I feel great comfort on the prospect of getting yourself and two or three others into the legislature. My 'humble and earnest prayer to Almighty God' will be that you may bring into fashion principles suited to the form of government we have adopted, and not of that we have rejected, that you will first lay your shoulders to the strengthening the band of our confederacy and averting those cruel evils to which it's present weakness will expose us, and that you will see the necessity of doing this instantly before we forget the advantages of union, or acquire a degree of ill-temper against each other which will daily increase the obstacles to that good work. . . .

14. *The Ethics of Public Trust*

To Abner Nash

Philadelphia Mar. 11, 1783

Dear Sir

Since I had the pleasure of seeing you at Baltimore I have further reflected on the proposition you were so kind as to make me there of entering into a partnership for the purpose of purchasing some of the escheated territory in your state. I consider it as one of those fair opportunities of bettering my situation which in private prudence I ought to adopt, and which were I to consider myself merely as a private man I should adopt without condition or hesitation. But I find it is the opinion of some gentlemen that the interests of land companies may by possibility be brought on the carpet of negotiation in Europe. Whether I may or may

not participate in those negotiations remains still as incertain as it was in the moment of our conversation on this subject. However I having hitherto while concerned in the direction of public affairs made it a rule to avoid engaging in any of those enterprizes which on becoming the subjects of public deliberation might lay my judgment under bias or oblige me for fear of that to withdraw from the decision altogether, I would wish still to pursue that line of conduct. Indeed I feel the obligation to do it the stronger in proportion to the magnitude of the trust at present confided to me. If my mission to Europe be still pursued I would chuse for my own satisfaction as well as for that of Congress to have not a single interest which in any point of the negotiation might separate me from the great bulk of my countrymen, or expose me to a suspicion of having any object to pursue which might lead me astray from the general. You will therefore be sensible that my situation does not leave me an equal liberty with the other gentlemen of availing myself of this opportunity of repairing some of my losses; on the contrary that it calls for this in addition to the sacrifices I have already made. . . .

15. *Congress—"A House Incompetent to Business"*

To Edmund Pendleton

Annapolis Jan. 18, 1784

Dear Sir

Your letter of the 12th. inst. came to hand yesterday. I have the happiness of informing you that on the 14th. inst. we had nine states on the floor and ratified the definitive treaty. Two copies were immediately dispatched by different officers who were to embark in the first vessels they could find going to France. They had 48 days left for it's timely delivery. The important business now before Congress is as follows.

Foreign civil arrangement, and foreign treaties.

Domestic civil arrangement.

Domestic peace establishment of arsenals and posts.

Western territory.

Indian affairs.

Money.

None of these subjects can be transacted but with the concurrence of 9. states. Of the 9. now present 7 are represented by two members each. There are 14. gentlemen then, any one of whom differing from the rest, can stop any vote. The questions are important and difficult, and such as

the best and wisest men would divide on. I am satisfied therefore that we cannot get 9. states to concur in a single one of the above subjects. We shall begin tomorrow to bring them on. A few experiments will I expect evince the truth of my conjecture, and the necessity of our adjourning till the spring, informing the states that we adjourn because their business cannot be done in so thin a house, and urging them to instruct and to *enable* their delegates to come punctually to the day of adjournment, and never to be represented by less than three members. The true reason that the delegates do not attend is that their states do not furnish them with money, and if they advance them some to get them here they are then left in the lurch and obliged either to make mean shifts or to go home. Spirited members prefer the latter and thus we are kept with a house incompetent to business. I think if we had a full house, that is, 13 states with three members from each so that no votes might be lost by division we might clear our docket in two or three months, and that an annual session of two months will hereafter suffice. A committee of the states must be left to transact ordinary business. . . .

16. *"Rational Society"*

To James Madison

Annapolis, Feb. 20, 1784

. . . I hope you have found access to my library. I beg you to make free use of it. Key, the steward is living there now and of course will be always in the way. Monroe is buying land almost adjoining me. Short will do the same. What would I not give you could fall into the circle. With such a society I could once more venture home and lay myself up for the residue of life, quitting all it's contentions which grow daily more and more insupportable. Think of it. To render it practicable only requires you to think it so. Life is of no value but as it brings us gratifications. Among the most valuable of these is rational society. It informs the mind, sweetens the temper, chears our spirits, and promotes health. There is a little farm of 140 as. adjoining me, and within two miles, all of good land, tho' old, with a small indifferent house on it, the whole worth not more than £250. Such a one might be a farm of experiment and support a little table and houshold. It is on the road to Orange and so much nearer than I am. It is convenient enough for supplementary supplies from thence. Once more think of it, and Adieu.

17. *For a Constitutional Convention*

To Edmund Pendleton

Philadelphia May 25, 1784

Dear Sir

Your favor of the 17th. found me at this place from which I set out the day after tomorrow. I mean to go thro' the Eastern states in hopes of deriving some knolege of them from actual inspection and enquiry which may enable me to discharge my duty to them somewhat the better. I expect to embark at Boston about the 20th. of June.

If you will recur to the Confederation you will find the Committee of the states have no powers but what shall be given them by the votes of 9 states in Congress. The innovations in our constitution which you mention are so wild that I hope they are not the object of any rational man. To make the Executive and Judiciary branches independent of the Legislative; to give them some controul over the laws by forming them into a Council of revision as in New-York; to modify the election of the Senate so as to ensure a choice of the wisest men and thus rendering that branch of legislature more useful, the making our constitution paramount the powers of the ordinary legislature so that all acts contradictory to it may be adjudged null; these are objects which to me appear rational and necessary. For these purposes I have long wished to see a convention called. —But I now leave it among you, hoping that will be done which is best.

18. *Evils of Confederation*

To Richard Price

Paris, Feb. 1, 1785

Sir

The copy of your Observations on the American Revolution which you were so kind as to direct to me came duly to hand, and I should sooner have acknowledged the receipt of it but that I awaited a private conveiance for my letter, having experienced much delay and uncertainty in the posts between this place and London. I have read it with very great pleasure, as have done many others to whom I have communicated it. The spirit which it breathes is as affectionate as the observations themselves are wise and just. I have no doubt it will be reprinted in America and

produce much good there. The want of power in the federal head was early perceived, and foreseen to be the flaw in our constitution which might endanger its destruction. I have the pleasure to inform you that when I left America in July the people were becoming universally sensible of this, and a spirit to enlarge the powers of Congress was becoming general. Letters and other information recently received shew that this has continued to increase, and that they are likely to remedy this evil effectually. The happiness of governments like ours, wherein the people are truly the mainspring, is that they are never to be despaired of. When an evil becomes so glaring as to strike them generally, they arrouse themselves, and it is redressed. He only is then the popular man and can get into office who shews the best dispositions to reform the evil. This truth was obvious on several occasions during the late war, and this character in our governments saved us. Calamity was our best physician. Since the peace it was observed that some nations of Europe, counting on the weakness of Congress and the little probability of a union in measure among the States, were proposing to grasp at unequal advantages in our commerce. The people are become sensible of this, and you may be assured that this evil will be immediately redressed, and redressed radically. I doubt still whether in this moment they will enlarge those powers in Congress which are necessary to keep the peace among the States. I think it possible that this may be suffered to lie till some two States commit hostilities on each other, but in that moment the hand of the union will be lifted up and interposed, and the people will themselves demand a general concession to Congress of means to prevent similar mischiefs. Our motto is truly "nil desperandum." The apprehensions you express of danger from the want of powers in Congress, led me to note to you this character in our governments, which, since the retreat behind the Delaware, and the capture of Charlestown, has kept my mind in perfect quiet as to the ultimate fate of our union; and I am sure, from the spirit which breathes thro your book, that whatever promises permanence to that will be a comfort to your mind. . . .

19. *"An Honest Heart . . . A Knowing Head"*

To Peter Carr

Paris Aug. 19, 1785

Dear Peter

I received by Mr. Mazzei your letter of April 20. I am much mortified to hear that you have lost so much time, and that when you arrived in Williamsburgh you were not at all advanced from what you were when

you left Monticello. Time now begins to be precious to you. Every day you lose, will retard a day your entrance on that public stage whereon you may begin to be useful to yourself. However the way to repair the loss is to improve the future time. I trust that with your dispositions even the acquisition of science is a pleasing employment. I can assure you that the possession of it is what (next to an honest heart) will above all things render you dear to your friends, and give you fame and promotion in your own country. When your mind shall be well improved with science, nothing will be necessary to place you in the highest points of view but to pursue the interests of your country, the interests of your friends, and your own interests also with the purest integrity, the most chaste honour. The defect of these virtues can never be made up by all the other acquirements of body and mind. Make these then your first object. Give up money, give up fame, give up science, give the earth itself and all it contains rather than do an immoral act. And never suppose that in any possible situation or under any circumstances that it is best for you to do a dishonourable thing however slightly so it may appear to you. Whenever you are to do a thing tho' it can never be known but to yourself, ask yourself how you would act were all the world looking at you, and act accordingly. Encourage all your virtuous dispositions, and exercise them whenever an opportunity arises, being assured that they will gain strength by exercise as a limb of the body does, and that exercise will make them habitual. From the practice of the purest virtue you may be assured you will derive the most sublime comforts in every moment of life and in the moment of death. If ever you find yourself environed with difficulties and perplexing circumstances, out of which you are at a loss how to extricate yourself, do what is right, and be assured that that will extricate you the best out of the worst situations. Tho' you cannot see when you fetch one step, what will be the next, yet follow truth, justice, and plain-dealing, and never fear their leading you out of the labyrinth in the easiest manner possible. The knot which you thought a Gordian one will untie itself before you. Nothing is so mistaken as the supposition that a person is to extricate himself from a difficulty, by intrigue, by chicanery, by dissimulation, by trimming, by an untruth, by an injustice. This increases the difficulties tenfold, and those who pursue these methods, get themselves so involved at length that they can turn no way but their infamy becomes more exposed. It is of great importance to set a resolution, not to be shaken, never to tell an untruth. There is no vice so mean, so pitiful, so contemptible and he who permits himself to tell a lie once, finds it much easier to do it a second and third time, till at length it becomes habitual, he tells lies without attending to it, and truths without the world's believing him. This falshood of the tongue leads to that of the heart, and in time depraves all it's good dispositions.

An honest heart being the first blessing, a knowing head is the second. It is time for you now to begin to be choice in your reading, to begin to

pursue a regular course in it and not to suffer yourself to be turned to the right or left by reading any thing out of that course. I have long ago digested a plan for you, suited to the circumstances in which you will be placed. This I will detail to you from time to time as you advance. For the present I advise you to begin a course of antient history, reading every thing in the original and not in translations. First read Goldsmith's history of Greece. This will give you a digested view of that field. Then take up antient history in the detail, reading the following books in the following order. Herodotus. Thucydides. Xenophontis hellenica. Xenophontis Anabasis. Quintus Curtius. Justin. This shall form the first stage of your historical reading, and is all I need mention to you now. The next will be of Roman history. From that we will come down to Modern history. In Greek and Latin poetry, you have read or will read at school Virgil, Terence, Horace, Anacreon, Theocritus, Homer. Read also Milton's paradise lost, Ossian, Pope's works, Swift's works in order to form your style in your own language. In morality read Epictetus, Xenophontis memorabilia, Plato's Socratic dialogues, Cicero's philosophies. In order to assure a certain progress in this reading, consider what hours you have free from the school and the exercises of the school. Give about two of them every day to exercise; for health must not be sacrificed to learning. A strong body makes the mind strong. As to the species of exercise, I advise the gun. While this gives a moderate exercise to the body, it gives boldness, enterprize, and independance to the mind. Games played with the ball and others of that nature, are too violent for the body and stamp no character on the mind. Let your gun therefore be the constant companion of your walks. Never think of taking a book with you. The object of walking is to relax the mind. You should therefore not permit yourself even to think while you walk. But divert your attention by the objects surrounding you. Walking is the best possible exercise. Habituate yourself to walk very far. The Europeans value themselves on having subdued the horse to the uses of man. But I doubt whether we have not lost more than we have gained by the use of this animal. No one has occasioned so much the degeneracy of the human body. An Indian goes on foot nearly as far in a day, for a long journey, as an enfeebled white does on his horse, and he will tire the best horses. There is no habit you will value so much as that of walking far without fatigue. I would advise you to take your exercise in the afternoon. Not because it is the best time for exercise for certainly it is not; but because it is the best time to spare from your studies; and habit will soon reconcile it to health, and render it nearly as useful as if you gave to that the more precious hours of the day. A little walk of half an hour in the morning when you first rise is adviseable also. It shakes off sleep, and produces other good effects in the animal œconomy. Rise at a fixed and an early hour, and go to bed at a fixed and early hour also. Sitting up late at night is injurious to the health, and not useful to the mind.—Having ascribed proper hours to exercise, divide what remain (I

mean of your vacant hours) into three portions. Give the principal to history, the other two, which should be shorter, to Philosophy and Poetry. Write me once every month or two and let me know the progress you make. Tell me in what manner you employ every hour in the day. The plan I have proposed for you is adapted to your present situation only. When that is changed, I shall propose a corresponding change of plan. I have ordered the following books to be sent to you from London to the care of Mr. Madison. Herodotus. Thucydides. Xenophon's Hellenics, Anabasis, and Memorabilia. Cicero's works. Barretti's Spanish and English dictionary. Martin's philosophical grammar and Martin's philosophia Britannica. I will send you the following from hence. Bezout's mathematics. De la Lande's astronomy. Muschenbroek's physics. Quintus Curtius. Justin, a Spanish grammar, and some Spanish books. You will observe that Martin, Bezout, De la Lande and Muschenbroek are not in the preceding plan. They are not to be opened till you go to the University. You are now I expect learning French. You must push this: because the books which will be put into your hands when you advance into Mathematics, Natural philosophy, Natural history, &c. will be mostly French, these sciences being better treated by the French than the English writers. Our future connection with Spain renders that the most necessary of the modern languages, after the French. When you become a public man you may have occasion for it, and the circumstance of your possessing that language may give you a preference over other candidates. I have nothing further to add for the present, than to husband well your time, cherish your instructors, strive to make every body your friend, & be assured that nothing will be so pleasing, as your success. . . .

20. *"One Nation Only"*

To James Madison

Paris Feb. 8, 1786

. . . I have heard with great pleasure that our assembly have come to the resolution of giving the regulation of their commerce to the federal head. I will venture to assert that there is not one of it's opposers who, placed on this ground, would not see the wisdom of this measure. The politics of Europe render it indispensably necessary that with respect to every thing external we be one nation only, firmly hooped together. Interior government is what each state should keep to itself. If it could be seen in Europe that all our states could be brought to concur in what the Virginia assembly has done, it would produce a total revolution in their opinion

of us, and respect for us. And it should ever be held in mind that insult and war are the consequences of a want of respectability in the national character. As long as the states exercise separately those acts of power which respect foreign nations, so long will there continue to be irregularities committing by some one or other of them which will constantly keep us on an ill footing with foreign nations. . . .

21. *"A Crusade Against Ignorance"*

To George Wythe

Paris Aug 13, 1786

The European papers have announced that the assembly of Virginia were occupied on the revisal of their Code of laws. This, with some other similar intelligence, has contributed much to convince the people of Europe, that what the English papers are constantly publishing of our anarchy, is false; as they are sensible that such a work is that of a people only who are in perfect tranquillity. Our act for freedom of religion is extremely applauded. The Ambassadors and ministers of the several nations of Europe resident at this court have asked of me copies of it to send to their sovereigns, and it is inserted at full length in several books now in the press; among others, in the new Encyclopedie. I think it will produce considerable good even in these countries where ignorance, superstition, poverty and oppression of body and mind in every form, are so firmly settled on the mass of the people, that their redemption from them can never be hoped. If the almighty had begotten a thousand sons, instead of one, they would not have sufficed for this task. If all the sovereigns of Europe were to set themselves to work to emancipate the minds of their subjects from their present ignorance and prejudices, and that as zealously as they now endeavor the contrary, a thousand years would not place them on that high ground on which our common people are now setting out. Ours could not have been so fairly put into the hands of their own common sense, had they not been separated from their parent stock and been kept from contamination, either from them, or the other people of the old world, by the intervention of so wide an ocean. To know the worth of this, one must see the want of it here. I think by far the most important bill in our whole code is that for the diffusion of knowledge among the people. No other sure foundation can be devised for the preservation of freedom, and happiness. If any body thinks that kings, nobles, or priests are good conservators of the public happiness, send them here.

It is the best school in the universe to cure them of that folly. They will see here with their own eyes that these descriptions of men are an abandoned confederacy against the happiness of the mass of people. The omnipotence of their effect cannot be better proved than in this country particularly, where notwithstanding the finest soil upon earth, the finest climate under heaven, and a people of the most benevolent, the most gay, and amiable character of which the human form is susceptible, where such a people I say, surrounded by so many blessings from nature, are yet loaded with misery by kings, nobles and priests, and by them alone. Preach, my dear Sir, a crusade against ignorance; establish and improve the law for educating the common people. Let our Countrymen know that the people alone can protect us against these evils, and that the tax which will be paid for this purpose is not more than the thousandth part of what will be paid to kings, priests and nobles who will rise up among us if we leave the people in ignorance. . . .

22. *On the Society of the Cincinnati*

To George Washington

Paris Nov. 14, 1786

. . . What has heretofore passed between us on this institution makes it my duty to mention to you that I have never heard a person in Europe, learned or unlearned, express his thoughts on this institution, who did not consider it as dishonourable and destructive to our governments, and that every writing which has come out since my arrival here, in which it is mentioned, considers it, even as now reformed, as the germ whose developement is one day to destroy the fabric we have reared. I did not apprehend this while I had American ideas only. But I confess that what I have seen in Europe has brought me over to that opinion: and that tho' the day may be at some distance, beyond the reach of our lives perhaps, yet it will certainly come, when, a single fibre left of this institution, will produce an hereditary aristocracy which will change the form of our governments from the best to the worst in the world. To know the mass of evil which flows from this fatal source, a person must be in France, he must see the finest soil, the finest climate, the most compact state, the most benevolent character of people, and every earthly advantage combined, insufficient to prevent this scourge from rendering existence a curse to 24 out of 25 parts of the inhabitants of this country. With us the branches of this institution cover all the states. The Southern ones at this time are aristocratical in their disposition:

and that that spirit should grow and extend itself is within the natural order of things. I do not flatter myself with the immortality of our governments: but I shall think little also of their longevity unless this germ of destruction be taken out. When the society themselves shall weigh the possibility of evil against the impossibility of any good to proceed from this institution, I cannot help hoping they will eradicate it. I know they wish the permanence of our governments as much as any individuals composing them. . . .

23. *Amabile Amica!*

To Maria Cosway

Paris Dec. 24, 1786

Yes, my dear Madam, I have received your three letters, and I am sure you must have thought hardly of me, when at the date of the last, you had not yet received one from me. But I had written two. . . .

I wish they had formed us like the birds of the air, able to fly where we please. I would have exchanged for this many of the boasted pre-eminencies of man. I was so unlucky when very young, as to read the history of Fortunatus. He had a cap of such virtues that when he put it on his head, and wished himself anywhere, he was there. I have been all my life sighing for this cap. Yet if I had it, I question if I should use it but once. I should wish myself with you, and not wish myself away again. En attendant the cap, I am always thinking of you. If I cannot be with you in reality, I will in imagination. But you say not a word of coming to Paris. Yet you were to come in the spring, and here is winter. It is time therefore you should be making your arrangements, packing your baggage &c. unless you really mean to disappoint us. If you do, I am determined not to suppose I am never to see you again. I will believe you intend to go to America, to draw the Natural bridge, the Peaks of Otter &c., that I shall meet you there, and visit with you all those grand scenes. I had rather be deceived, than live without hope. It is so sweet! It makes us ride so smoothly over the roughnesses of life. When clambering a mountain, we always hope the hill we are on is the last. But it is the next, and the next, and still the next. Think of me much, and warmly. Place me in your breast with those who you love most: and comfort me with your letters. Addio la mia cara ed amabile amica!

After finishing my letter, the gentleman who brought yours sent me a roll he had overlooked, which contained songs of your composition. I am sure they are charming, and I thank you for them. The first words which met my eye on opening them, are I fear, ominous. "Qua l'attendo, e mai non vieni."

24. *"A Little Rebellion Now and Then"*

To James Madison

Paris Jan. 30, 1787

. . . I am impatient to learn your sentiments on the late troubles in the Eastern states. So far as I have yet seen, they do not appear to threaten serious consequences. Those states have suffered by the stoppage of the channels of their commerce, which have not yet found other issues. This must render money scarce, and make the people uneasy. This uneasiness has produced acts absolutely unjustifiable: but I hope they will provoke no severities from their governments. A consciousness of those in power that their administration of the public affairs has been honest, may perhaps produce too great a degree of indignation: and those characters wherein fear predominates over hope may apprehend too much from these instances of irregularity. They may conclude too hastily that nature has formed man insusceptible of any other government but that of force, a conclusion not founded in truth, nor experience. Societies exist under three forms sufficiently distinguishable. 1. Without government, as among our Indians. 2. Under governments wherein the will of every one has a just influence, as is the case in England in a slight degree, and in our states in a great one. 3. Under governments of force: as is the case in all other monarchies and in most of the other republics. To have an idea of the curse of existence under these last, they must be seen. It is a government of wolves over sheep. It is a problem, not clear in my mind, that the 1st. condition is not the best. But I believe it to be inconsistent with any great degree of population. The second state has a great deal of good in it. The mass of mankind under that enjoys a precious degree of liberty and happiness. It has it's evils too: the principal of which is the turbulence to which it is subject. But weigh this against the oppressions of monarchy, and it becomes nothing. Malo periculosam, libertatem quam quietam servitutem. Even this evil is productive of good. It prevents the degeneracy of government, and nourishes a general attention to the public affairs. I hold it that a little rebellion now and then is a good thing, and as necessary in the political world as

storms in the physical. Unsuccessful rebellions indeed generally establish the incroachments on the rights of the people which have produced them. An observation of this truth should render honest republican governors so mild in their punishment of rebellions, as not to discourage them too much. It is a medecine necessary for the sound health of government. . . .

As you are now returned into Congress it will become of importance that you should form a just estimate of certain public characters; on which therefore I will give you such notes as my knowledge of them has furnished me with. You will compare them with the materials you are otherwise possessed of, and decide on a view of the whole. You know the opinion I *formerly* entertained of *my friend Mr. Adams.* Yourself and the governor were the first who *shook* that opinion. I afterwards saw proofs which *convicted* him of a degree of *vanity,* and of a *blindness* to it, of which no germ *had appeared* in Congress. A *7-months'* intimacy with him *here* and *as* many *weeks* in *London* have given me opportunities of studying him closely. *He is vain, irritable and a bad calculator of* the force and probable effect of the motives which govern men. This is *all* the *ill* which can possibly be *said of him.* He is as disinterested as the being which made him: he is profound in his views: and accurate in his judgment *except where knowledge of the world* is necessary to form a judgment. He is so amiable, that I pronounce you will love him if ever you become acquainted with him. He would be, as he was, a great man in *Congress.* . . .

25. *Love of Two Houses*

To Madame la Comtesse de Tessé

Nismes, March 20, 1787

Here I am, Madam, gazing whole hours at the Maison Quarrée, like a lover at his mistress. The stocking weavers and silk spinners around it consider me a hypochondriac Englishman, about to write with a pistol the last chapter of his history. This is the second time I have been in love since I left Paris. The first was with a Diana at the Chateau de Laye-Epinaye in Beaujolois, a delicious morsel of sculpture, by M. A. Slodtz. This, you will say, was in rule, to fall in love with a female beauty; but with a house! it is out of all precedent. No, Madam, it is not without a precedent in my own history. While in Paris, I was violently smitten with the Hotel de Salm, and used to go to the Tuileries almost daily, to look at it. . . .

A *propos* of Paris. I have now been three weeks from there, without knowing anything of what has passed. I suppose I shall meet it all at Aix, where I have directed my letters to be lodged, *poste restante.* My journey has given me leisure to reflect on this Assemblée des Notables. Under a good and a young King, as the present, I think good may be made of it. I would have the deputies then, by all means, so conduct themselves as to encourage him to repeat the calls of this Assembly. Their first steps should be, to get themselves divided into two chambers instead of seven; the Noblesse and the Commons separately. The second, to persuade the King, instead of choosing the deputies of the Commons himself, to summon those chosen by the people for the Provincial administrations. The third, as the Noblesse is too numerous to be all of the Assemblée, to obtain permission for that body to choose its own deputies. Two Houses, so elected, would contain a mass of wisdom which would make the people happy, and the King great; would place him in history where no other act can possibly place him. They would thus put themselves in the track of the best guide they can follow; they would soon overtake it, become its guide in turn, and lead to the wholesome modifications wanting in that model, and necessary to constitute a rational government. Should they attempt more than the established habits of the people are ripe for, they may lose all, and retard indefinitely the ultimate object of their aim. These, Madam, are my opinions; but I wish to know yours, which, I am sure, will be better. . . .

26. *"We are Obliged to Invent and to Execute"*

To Martha Jefferson

Aix en Provence March. 28, 1787

I was happy, my dear Patsy, to receive, on my arrival here, your letter informing me of your health and occupations. I have not written to you sooner because I have been almost constantly on the road. My journey hitherto has been a very pleasing one. It was undertaken with the hope that the mineral waters of this place might restore strength to my wrist. Other considerations also concurred. Instruction, amusement, and abstraction from business, of which I had too much at Paris. I am glad to learn that you are employed in things new and good in your music and drawing. You know what have been my fears for some time past; that you do not employ yourself so closely as I could wish. You have promised me a more assiduous attention, and I have great confidence in what you promise. It is your future happiness which interests me, and nothing

can contribute more to it (moral rectitude always excepted) than the contracting a habit of industry and activity. Of all the cankers of human happiness, none corrodes it with so silent, yet so baneful a tooth, as indolence. Body and mind both unemployed, our being becomes a burthen, and every object about us loathsome, even the dearest. Idleness begets ennui, ennui the hypochrondria, and that a diseased body. No laborious person was ever yet hysterical. Exercise and application produce order in our affairs, health of body, chearfulness of mind, and these make us precious to our friends. It is while we are young that the habit of industry is formed. If not then, it never is afterwards. The fortune of our lives therefore depends on employing well the short period of youth. If at any moment, my dear, you catch yourself in idleness, start from it as you would from the precipice of a gulph. You are not however to consider yourself as unemployed while taking exercise. That is necessary for your health, and health is the first of all objects. For this reason if you leave your dancing master for the summer, you must increase your other exercise. I do not like your saying that you are unable to read the antient print of your Livy, but with the aid of your master. We are always equal to what we undertake with resolution. A little degree of this will enable you to decypher your Livy. If you always lean on your master, you will never be able to proceed without him. It is a part of the American character to consider nothing as desperate; to surmount every difficulty by resolution and contrivance. In Europe there are shops for every want. It's inhabitants therefore have no idea that their wants can be furnished otherwise. Remote from all other aid, we are obliged to invent and to execute; to find means within ourselves, and not to lean on others. Consider therefore the conquering your Livy as an exercise in the habit of surmounting difficulties, a habit which will be necessary to you in the country where you are to live, and without which you will be thought a very helpless animal, and less esteemed. Music, drawing, books, invention and exercise will be so many resources to you against ennui. But there are others which to this object add that of utility. These are the needle, and domestic economy. The latter you cannot learn here, but the former you may. In the country life of America there are many moments when a woman can have recourse to nothing but her needle for employment. In a dull company and in dull weather for instance. It is ill manners to read; it is ill manners to leave them; no card-playing there among genteel people; that is abandoned to blackguards. The needle is then a valuable resource. Besides without knowing to use it herself, how can the mistress of a family direct the works of her servants? You ask me to write you long letters. I will do it my dear, on condition you will read them from time to time, and practice what they will inculcate. Their precepts will be dictated by experience, by a perfect knowledge of the situation in which you will be placed, and by the fondest love for you. This it is which makes me wish to see

you more qualified than common. My expectations from you are high: yet not higher than you may attain. Industry and resolution are all that are wanting. No body in this world can make me so happy, or so miserable as you. Retirement from public life will ere long become necessary for me. To your sister and yourself I look to render the evening of my life serene and contented. It's morning has been clouded by loss after loss till I have nothing left but you. I do not doubt either your affection or dispositions. But great exertions are necessary, and you have little time left to make them. Be industrious then, my dear child. Think nothing unsurmountable by resolution and application, and you will be all that I wish you to be. . . .

27. "*You must Ferret the People Out*"

To the Marquis de LaFayette

Nice, April 11, 1787

Your head, my dear friend, is full of notable things; and being better employed, therefore, I do not expect letters from you. I am constantly roving about, to see what I have never seen before, and shall never see again. In the great cities, I go to see what travellers think alone worthy of being seen; but I make a job of it, and generally gulp it all down in a day. On the other hand, I am never satiated with rambling through the fields and farms, examining the culture and cultivators, with a degree of curiosity which makes some take me to be a fool, and others to be much wiser than I am. I have been pleased to find among the people a less degree of physical misery than I had expected. They are generally well clothed, and have a plenty of food, not animal indeed, but vegetable, which is as wholesome. Perhaps they are overworked, the excess of the rent required by the landlord obliging them to too many hours of labor in order to produce that, and wherewith to feed and clothe themselves. The soil of Champagne and Burgundy I have found more universally good than I had expected, and as I could not help making a comparison with England, I found that comparison more unfavorable to the latter than is generally admitted. The soil, the climate, and the productions are superior to those of England, and the husbandry as good, except in one point; that of manure. In England, long leases for twenty-one years, or three lives, to wit, that of the farmer, his wife, and son, renewed by the son as soon as he comes to the possession, for his own life, his wife's and eldest child's, and so on, render the farms there almost hereditary, make it worth the farmer's while to manure the lands highly, and

give the landlord an opportunity of occasionally making his rent keep pace with the improved state of the lands. Here the leases are either during pleasure, or for three, six, or nine years, which does not give the farmer time to repay himself for the expensive operation of well manuring, and, therefore, he manures ill, or not at all. I suppose, that could the practice of leasing for three lives be introduced in the whole kingdom, it would, within the term of your life, increase agriculture productions fifty per cent.; or were any one proprietor to do it with his own lands, it would increase his rents fifty per cent., in the course of twenty-five years. But I am told the laws do not permit it. The laws then, in this particular, are unwise and unjust, and ought to give that permission. . . .

I have often wished for you. I think you have not made this journey. It is a pleasure you have to come, and an improvement to be added to the many you have already made. It will be a great comfort to you, to know, from your own inspection, the condition of all the provinces of your own country, and it will be interesting to them at some future day, to be known to you. This is, perhaps, the only moment of your life in which you can acquire that knowledge. And to do it most effectually, you must be absolutely incognito, you must ferret the people out of their hovels as I have done, look into their kettles, eat their bread, loll on their beds under pretence of resting yourself, but in fact, to find if they are soft. You will feel a sublime pleasure in the course of this investigation, and a sublimer one hereafter, when you shall be able to apply your knowledge to the softening of their beds, or the throwing a morsel of meat into their kettle of vegetables. . . .

28. *The Pursuit of Knowledge*

To Peter Carr

Paris Aug. 10, 1787

Dear Peter

I have received your two letters of Decemb. 30. and April 18. and am very happy to find by them, as well as by letters from Mr. Wythe, that you have been so fortunate as to attract his notice and good will: I am sure you will find this to have been one of the most fortunate events of your life, as I have ever been sensible it was of mine. I inclose you a sketch of the sciences to which I would wish you to apply in such order as Mr. Wythe shall advise. . . . To this sketch I will add a few particular observations.

1. Italian. I fear the learning this language will confound your French and Spanish. . . .

2. Spanish. Bestow great attention on this, and endeavor to acquire an accurate knowledge of it. Our future connections with Spain and Spanish America will render that language a valuable acquisition. . . .

3. Moral philosophy. I think it lost time to attend lectures in this branch. He who made us would have been a pitiful bungler if he had made the rules of our moral conduct a matter of science. For one man of science, there are thousands who are not. What would have become of them? Man was destined for society. His morality therefore was to be formed to this object. He was endowed with a sense of right and wrong merely relative to this. This sense is as much a part of his nature as the sense of hearing, seeing, feeling; it is the true foundation of morality, and not the γοχαγου truth, &c., as fanciful writers have imagined. The moral sense, or conscience, is as much a part of man as his leg or arm. It is given to all human beings in a stronger or weaker degree, as force of members is given them in a greater or less degree. It may be strengthened by exercise, as may any particular limb of the body. This sense is submitted indeed in some degree to the guidance of reason; but it is a small stock which is required for this: even a less one than what we call Common sense. State a moral case to a ploughman and a professor. The former will decide it as well, and often better than the latter, because he has not been led astray by artificial rules. In this branch therefore read good books because they will encourage as well as direct your feelings. . . . and above all things lose no occasion of exercising your dispositions to be grateful, to be generous, to be charitable, to be humane, to be true, just, firm, orderly, couragious &c. Consider every act of this kind as an exercise which will strengthen your moral faculties, and increase your worth.

4. Religion. Your reason is now mature enough to receive this object. In the first place divest yourself of all bias in favour of novelty and singularity of opinion. Indulge them in any other subject rather than that of religion. It is too important, and the consequences of error may be too serious. On the other hand shake off all the fears and servile prejudices under which weak minds are servilely crouched. Fix reason firmly in her seat, and call to her tribunal every fact, every opinion. Question with boldness even the existence of a god; because, if there be one, he must more approve the homage of reason, than that of blindfolded fear. You will naturally examine first the religion of your own country. Read the bible then, as you would read Livy or Tacitus. The facts which are within the ordinary course of nature you will believe on the authority of the writer, as you do those of the same kind in Livy and Tacitus. The testimony of the writer weighs in their favor in one scale, and their not being against the laws of nature does not weigh against them. But those facts in the bible which contradict the laws of nature, must be examined with more care, and under a variety of faces. Here you must recur to the pretensions of the writer to inspiration from god. Examine upon

what evidence his pretensions are founded, and whether that evidence is so strong as that it's falshood would be more improbable than a change of the laws of nature in the case he relates. . . . Do not be frightened from this enquiry by any fear of it's consequences. If it ends in a belief that there is no god, you will find incitements to virtue in the comfort and pleasantness you feel in it's exercise, and the love of others which it will procure you. If you find reason to believe there is a god, a consciousness that you are acting under his eye, and that he approves you, will be a vast additional incitement. If that there be a future state, the hope of a happy existence in that increases the appetite to deserve it; if that Jesus was also a god, you will be comforted by a belief of his aid and love. In fine, I repeat that you must lay aside all prejudice on both sides, and neither believe nor reject any thing because any other person, or description of persons have rejected or believed it. Your own reason is the only oracle given you by heaven, and you are answerable not for the rightness but uprightness of the decision. . . .

5. Travelling. This makes men wiser, but less happy. When men of sober age travel, they gather knowledge which they may apply usefully for their country, but they are subject ever after to recollections mixed with regret, their affections are weakened by being extended over more objects, and they learn new habits which cannot be gratified when they return home. Young men who travel are exposed to all these inconveniences in a higher degree, to others still more serious, and do not acquire that wisdom for which a previous foundation is requisite by repeated and just observations at home. The glare of pomp and pleasure is analogous to the motion of their blood, it absorbs all their affection and attention, they are torn from it as from the only good in this world, and return to their home as to a place of exile and condemnation. Their eyes are for ever turned back to the object they have lost, and it's recollection poisons the residue of their lives. Their first and most delicate passions are hackneyed on unworthy objects here, and they carry home only the dregs, insufficient to make themselves or any body else happy. Add to this that a habit of idleness, an inability to apply themselves to business is acquired and renders them useless to themselves and their country. These observations are founded in experience. There is no place where your pursuit of knowledge will be so little obstructed by foreign objects as in your own country, nor any wherein the virtues of the heart will be less exposed to be weakened. Be good, be learned, and be industrious, and you will not want the aid of travelling to render you precious to your country, dear to your friends, happy within yourself. I repeat my advice to take a great deal of exercise, and on foot. Health is the first requisite after morality. Write to me often and be assured of the interest I take in your success. . . .

29. On "The Defence of the Constitutions"

To John Adams

Paris Sep. 28, 1787

Dear Sir

I received your favors by Mr. Cutting, and thank you sincerely for the copy of your book. The departure of a packet-boat, which always gives me full emploiment for some time before, has only permitted me to look into it a little. I judge of it from the first volume which I thought formed to do a great deal of good. The first principle of a good government is certainly a distribution of it's powers into executive, judiciary, and legislative, and a subdivision of the latter into two or three branches. It is a good step gained, when it is proved that the English constitution, acknowledged to be better than all which have proceeded it, is only better in proportion as it has approached nearer to this distribution of powers. From this the last step is easy, to shew by a comparison of our constitutions with that of England, how much more perfect they are. The article of Confederations is surely worthy of your pen. It would form a most interesting addition to shew what have been the nature of the Confederations which have existed hitherto, what were their excellencies and what their defects. A comparison of ours with them would be to the advantage of ours, and would increase the veneration of our countrymen for it. It is a misfortune that they do not sufficiently know the value of their constitutions and how much happier they are rendered by them than any other people on earth by the governments under which they live. . . .

30. On the New Constitution

To James Madison

Paris Dec. 20, 1787

The season admitting only of operations in the Cabinet, and these being in a great measure secret, I have little to fill a letter. I will therefore make up the deficiency by adding a few words on the Constitution proposed by our Convention. I like much the general idea of framing a government which should go on of itself peaceably, without needing continual recurrence to the state legislatures. I like the organization of the govern-

ment into Legislative, Judiciary and Executive. I like the power given the Legislature to levy taxes; and for that reason solely approve of the greater house being chosen by the people directly. For tho' I think a house chosen by them will be very illy qualified to legislate for the Union, for foreign nations &c. yet this evil does not weigh against the good of preserving inviolate the fundamental principle that the people are not to be taxed but by representatives chosen immediately by themselves. I am captivated by the compromise of the opposite claims of the great and little states, of the latter to equal, and the former to proportional influence. I am much pleased too with the substitution of the method of voting by persons, instead of that of voting by states: and I like the negative given to the Executive with a third of either house, though I should have liked it better had the Judiciary been associated for that purpose, or invested with a similar and separate power. There are other good things of less moment. I will now add what I do not like. First the omission of a bill of rights providing clearly and without the aid of sophisms for freedom of religion, freedom of the press, protection against standing armies, restriction against monopolies, the eternal and unremitting force of the habeas corpus laws, and trials by jury in all matters of fact triable by the laws of the land and not by the law of Nations. To say, as Mr. Wilson does that a bill of rights was not necessary because all is reserved in the case of the general government which is not given, while in the particular ones all is given which is not reserved might do for the Audience to whom it was addressed, but is surely gratis dictum, opposed by strong inferences from the body of the instrument, as well as from the omission of the clause of our present confederation which had declared that in express terms. It was a hard conclusion to say because there has been no uniformity among the states as to the cases triable by jury, because some have been so incautious as to abandon this mode of trial, therefore the more prudent states shall be reduced to the same level of calamity. It would have been much more just and wise to have concluded the other way that as most of the states had judiciously preserved this palladium, those who had wandered should be brought back to it, and to have established general right instead of general wrong. Let me add that a bill of rights is what the people are entitled to against every government on earth, general or particular, and what no just government should refuse, or rest on inference. The second feature I dislike, and greatly dislike, is the abandonment in every instance of the necessity of rotation in office, and most particularly in the case of the President. Experience concurs with reason in concluding that the first magistrate will always be re-elected if the constitution permits it. He is then an officer for life. . . .

An incapacity to be elected a second time would have been the only effectual preventative. The power of removing him every fourth year by the vote of the people is a power which will not be exercised. The king

of Poland is removeable every day by the Diet, yet he is never removed. —Smaller objections are the Appeal in fact as well as law, and the binding all persons Legislative, Executive and Judiciary by oath to maintain that constitution. I do not pretend to decide what would be the best method of procuring the establishment of the manifold good things in this constitution, and of getting rid of the bad. Whether by adopting it in hopes of future amendment, or, after it has been duly weighed and canvassed by the people, after seeing the parts they generally dislike, and those they generally approve, to say to them 'We see now what you wish. Send together your deputies again, let them frame a constitution for you omitting what you have condemned, and establishing the powers you approve. Even these will be a great addition to the energy of your government.'—At all events I hope you will not be discouraged from other trials, if the present one should fail of it's full effect.—I have thus told you freely what I like and dislike: merely as a matter of curiosity for I know your own judgment has been formed on all these points after having heard every thing which could be urged on them. I own I am not a friend to a very energetic government. It is always oppressive. The late rebellion in Massachusets has given more alarm than I think it should have done. Calculate that one rebellion in 13 states in the course of 11 years, is but one for each state in a century and a half. No country should be so long without one. Nor will any degree of power in the hands of government prevent insurrections. France with all it's despotism, and two or three hundred thousand men always in arms has had three insurrections in the three years I have been here in every one of which greater numbers were engaged than in Massachusets and a great deal more blood was spilt. In Turkey, which Montesquieu supposes more despotic, insurrections are the events of every day. In England, where the hand of power is lighter than here, but heavier than with us they happen every half dozen years. Compare again the ferocious depredations of their insurgents with the order, the moderation and the almost self extinguishment of ours.—After all, it is my principle that the will of the Majority should always prevail. If they approve the proposed Convention in all it's parts, I shall concur in it chearfully, in hopes that they will amend it whenever they shall find it work wrong. I think our governments will remain virtuous for many centuries; as long as they are chiefly agricultural; and this will be as long as there shall be vacant lands in any part of America. When they get piled upon one another in large cities, as in Europe, they will become corrupt as in Europe. Above all things I hope the education of the common people will be attended to; convinced that on their good sense we may rely with the most security for the preservation of a due degree of liberty. I have tired you by this time with my disquisitions and will therefore only add assurances of the sincerity of those sentiments of esteem and attachment with which I am Dear Sir your affectionate friend & servant,

TH: JEFFERSON

P.S. The instability of our laws is really an immense evil. I think it would be well to provide in our constitutions that there shall always be a twelvemonth between the ingrossing a bill and passing it: that it should then be offered to it's passage without changing a word: and that if circumstances should be thought to require a speedier passage, it should take two thirds of both houses instead of a bare majority.

31. *"An Enemy to Monarchy"*

To George Washington

Paris May 2, 1788

... I am anxious about every thing which may affect our credit. My wish would be to possess it in the highest degree, but to use it little. Were we without credit we might be crushed by a nation of much inferior resources but possessing higher credit. The present system of war renders it necessary to make exertions far beyond the annual resources of the state, and to consume in one year the efforts of many. And this system we cannot change. It remains then that we cultivate our credit with the utmost attention.—I had intended to have written a word to your Excellency on the subject of the new constitution, but I have already spun out my letter to an immoderate length. I will just observe therefore that according to my ideas there is a great deal of good in it. There are two things however which I dislike strongly. 1. The want of a declaration of rights. I am in hopes the opposition of Virginia will remedy this, and produce such a declaration. 2. The perpetual re-eligibility of the President. This I fear will make that an office for life first, and then hereditary. I was much an enemy to monarchy before I came to Europe. I am ten thousand times more so since I have seen what they are. There is scarcely an evil known in these countries which may not be traced to their king as it's source, nor a good which is not derived from the small fibres of republicanism existing among them. I can further say with safety there is not a crowned head in Europe whose talents or merit would entitle him to be elected a vestryman by the people of any parish in America. However I shall hope that before there is danger of this change taking place in the office of President, the good sense and free spirit of our countrymen will make the changes necessary to prevent it. Under this hope I look forward to the general adoption of the new constitution with anxiety, as necessary for us under our present circumstances. ...

32. *"Liberty or Despotism"*

To E. Rutledge

Paris, July 18, 1788

. . . We can surely boast of having set the world a beautiful example of a government reformed by reason alone, without bloodshed. But the world is too far oppressed, to profit by the example. On this side of the Atlantic, the blood of the people is become an inheritance, and those who fatten on it, will not relinquish it easily. The struggle in this country is, as yet, of doubtful issue. It is, in fact, between the monarchy and the parliaments. The nation is no otherwise concerned, but as both parties may be induced to let go some of its abuses, to court the public favor. The danger, is that the people, deceived by a false cry of liberty, may be led to take side with one party, and thus give the other a pretext for crushing them still more. If they can avoid the appeal to arms, the nation will be sure to gain much by this controversy. But if that appeal is made, it will depend entirely on the disposition of the army, whether it issue in liberty or despotism. Those dispositions are not as yet known. In the meantime, there is great probability that the war kindled in the east, will spread from nation to nation, and in the long run, become general. . . .

33. *"Taxation Will Be Necessary"*

To George Washington

Paris Nov. 4, 1788

Sir

Your favor of Aug. 31. came to hand yesterday; and a confidential conveiance offering, by the way of London, I avail myself of it to acknolege the receipt. I have seen, with infinite pleasure, our new constitution accepted by 11. states, not rejected by the 12th. and that the 13th. happens to be a state of the least importance. It is true that the minorities in most of the accepting states have been very respectable, so much so as to render it prudent, were it not otherwise reasonable, to make some sacrifices to them. I am in hopes that the annexation of a bill of rights to the constitution will alone draw over so great a propor-

tion of the minorities, as to leave little danger in the opposition of the residue; and that this annexation may be made by Congress and the assemblies, without calling a convention which might endanger the most valuable parts of the system. Calculation has convinced me that circumstances may arise, and probably will arise, wherein all the resources of taxation will be necessary for the safety of the state. For tho I am decidedly of opinion we should take no part in European quarrels, but cultivate peace and commerce with all, yet who can avoid seeing the source of war in the tyranny of those nations who deprive us of the natural right of trading with our neighbors? The produce of the U.S. will soon exceed the European demand. What is to be done with the surplus, when there shall be one? It will be employed, without question, to open by force a market for itself with those placed on the same continent with us, and who wish nothing better. Other causes too are obvious which may involve us in war; and war requires every resource of taxation and credit. The power of making war often prevents it, and in our case would give efficacy to our desire of peace. If the new government wears the front which I hope it will I see no impossibility in the availing ourselves of the wars of others to open the other parts of America to our commerce, as the price of our neutrality. . . .

34. *You Cannot "Array Yourself Against the People"*

To Lafayette

Paris May 6, 1789

My Dear Friend

As it becomes more and more possible that the Noblesse will go wrong, I become uneasy for you. Your principles are decidedly with the tiers état, and your instructions against them. A complaisance to the latter on some occasions and an adherence to the former on others, may give an appearance of trimming between the two parties which may lose you both. You will in the end go over wholly to the tiers etat, because it will be impossible for you to live in a constant sacrifice of your own sentiments to the prejudices of the Noblesse. But you would be received by the tiers état at any future day, coldly and without confidence. It appears to me the moment to take at once that honest and manly stand with them which your own principles dictate. This will win their hearts for ever, be approved by the world which marks and honours you as the man of the people, and will be an eternal consolation to yourself. The

Noblesse, and especially the Noblesse of Auvergne will always prefer men who will do their dirty work for them. You are not made for that. They will therefore soon drop you, and the people in that case will perhaps not take you up. Suppose a scission should take place. The priests and nobles will secede, the nation will remain in place and, with the king, will do it's own business. If violence should be attempted, where will you be? You cannot then take side with the people in opposition to your own vote, that very vote which will have helped to produce the scission. Still less can you array yourself against the people. That is impossible. Your instructions are indeed a difficulty. But to state this at it's worst, it is only a single difficulty, which a single effort surmounts. Your instructions can never embarrass you a second time, whereas an acquiescence under them will reproduce greater difficulties every day and without end. Besides, a thousand circumstances offer as many justifications of your departure from your instructions. Will it be impossible to persuade all parties that (as for good legislation two houses are necessary) the placing the privileged classes together in one house and the unprivileged in another, would be better for both than a scission. I own I think it would. People can never agree without some sacrifices; and it appears but a moderate sacrifice in each party to meet on this middle ground. The attempt to bring this about might satisfy your instructions, and a failure in it would justify your siding with the people even to those who think instructions are laws of conduct.—Forgive me, my dear friend, if my anxiety for you makes me talk of things I know nothing about. You must not consider this as advice. I know you and myself too well to presume to offer advice. Receive it merely as the expression of my uneasiness and the effusion of that sincere friendship with which I am, my dear sir, Your's affectionately. . . .

35. *The French Revolution*

To Richard Price

Paris July 12, 1789

Dear Sir

The delay of my Congé permits me still the pleasure of continuing to communicate the principal things which pass here. I have already informed you that the proceedings of the states general were tied up by the difficulty which arose as to the manner of voting, whether it should be by persons or orders. The Tiers at length gave an ultimate invitation to the other two orders to come and join them, informing them at the same time that if they did not they would proceed without them. The ma-

jority of the clergy joined them. The king then interposed by the seance royale of which you have heard. The decision he undertook to pronounce was declared null by the assembly and they proceeded in business. Tumults in Paris and Versailles and still more the declared defection of the Souldiery to the popular cause produced from the king an invitation to the Nobles and the minority of the clergy to go and join the common assembly. They did so, and since that time the three orders are in one room, voting by persons, and without any sensible dissension. Still the body of the nobles are rankling at the heart; but I see no reason to apprehend any great evil from it. Another appearance indeed, the approach of a great number of troops, principally foreigners, have given uneasiness. The Assembly addressed the king in an eloquent and masculine stile. His answer, tho' dry, disavows every object but that of keeping the two capitals quiet. The States then are in quiet possession of the powers of the nation, and have begun the great work of building up a constitution. They appointed a committee to arrange the order in which they should proceed, and I will give you the arrangement, because it will shew you they mean to begin the building at the bottom, and know how to do it. They entitle it 'Ordre du travail.' . . .

The Declaration of the rights of man, which constitutes the 1st. chapter of this work, was brought in the day before yesterday, and referred to the bureaus. You will observe that these are the outlines of a great work, and be assured that the body engaged in it are equal to a masterly execution of it. They may meet with some difficulties from within their body and some from without. There may be small and temporary checks. But I think they will persevere to it's accomplishment. The mass of the people is with them: the effective part of the clergy is with them: so I believe is the souldiery and a respectable proportion of the officers. They have against them the high officers, the high clergy, the noblesse and the parliaments. This you see is an army of officers without souldiers. Should this revolution succeed, it is the beginning of the reformation of the governments of Europe. . . .

36. *"The Earth Belongs to the Living"*

To James Madison

Paris September 6, 1789

I sit down to write to you without knowing by what occasion I shall send my letter. I do it because a subject comes into my head which I would wish to develope a little more than is practicable in the hurry of the moment of making up general dispatches.

The question Whether one generation of men has a right to bind another, seems never to have been started either on this or our side of the water. Yet it is a question of such consequences as not only to merit decision, but place also, among the fundamental principles of every government. The course of reflection in which we are immersed here on the elementary principles of society has presented this question to my mind; and that no such obligation can be so transmitted I think very capable of proof.—I set out on this ground, which I suppose to be self evident, 'that the earth belongs in usufruct to the living': that the dead have neither powers nor rights over it. The portion occupied by any individual ceases to be his when himself ceases to be, and reverts to the society. If the society has formed no rules for the appropriation of it's lands in severalty, it will be taken by the first occupants. These will generally be the wife and children of the decedent. If they have formed rules of appropriation, those rules may give it to the wife and children, or to some one of them, or to the legatee of the deceased. So they may give it to his creditor. But the child, the legatee, or creditor takes it, not by any natural right, but by a law of the society of which they are members, and to which they are subject. Then no man can, by *natural right*, oblige the lands he occupied, or the persons who succeed him in that occupation, to the paiment of debts contracted by him. For if he could, he might, during his own life, eat up the usufruct of the lands for several generations to come, and then the lands would belong to the dead, and not to the living, which would be the reverse of our principle.

What is true of every member of the society individually, is true of them all collectively, since the rights of the whole can be no more than the sum of the rights of the individuals.—To keep our ideas clear when applying them to a multitude, let us suppose a whole generation of men to be born on the same day, to attain mature age on the same day, and to die on the same day, leaving a succeeding generation in the moment of attaining their mature age all together. Let the ripe age be supposed of 21. years, and their period of life 34. years more, that being the average term given by the bills of mortality to persons who have already attained 21. years of age. Each successive generation would, in this way, come on, and go off the stage at a fixed moment, as individuals do now. Then I say the earth belongs to each of these generations, during it's course, fully, and in their own right. The 2d. generation receives it clear of the debts and incumberances of the 1st. the 3d. of the 2d. and so on. For if the 1st. could charge it with a debt, then the earth would belong to the dead and not the living generation. Then no generation can contract debts greater than may be paid during the course of it's own existence. At 21. years of age they may bind themselves and their lands for 34. years to come: at 22. for 33: at 23. for 32. and at 54. for one year only; because these are the terms of life which remain to them at those respective epochs.—But a material difference must be noted between the succession

of an individual, and that of a whole generation. Individuals are parts only of a society, subject to the laws of the whole. These laws may appropriate the portion of land occupied by a decedent to his creditor rather than to any other, or to his child on condition he satisfies the creditor. But when a whole generation, that is, the whole society dies, as in the case we have supposed, and another generation or society succeeds, this forms a whole, and there is no superior who can give their territory to a third society, who may have lent money to their predecessors beyond their faculties of paying.

What is true of a generation all arriving to self-government on the same day, and dying all on the same day, is true of those in a constant course of decay and renewal, with this only difference. A generation coming in and going out entire, as in the first case, would have a right in the 1st. year of their self-dominion to contract a debt for 33. years, in the 10th. for 24. in the 20th. for 14. in the 30th. for 4. whereas generations, changing daily by daily deaths and births, have one constant term, beginning at the date of their contract, and ending when a majority of those of full age at that date shall be dead. The length of that term may be estimated from the tables of mortality, corrected by the circumstances of climate, occupation &c. peculiar to the country of the contractors. Take, for instance, the table of M. de Buffon wherein he states 23,994 deaths, and the ages at which they happened. Suppose a society in which 23,994 persons are born every year, and live to the ages stated in this table. The conditions of that society will be as follows. 1st. It will consist constantly of 617,703. persons of all ages. 2ly. Of those living at any one instant of time, one half will be dead in 24. years 8. months. 3dly. 10,675 will arrive every year at the age of 21. years complete. 4ly. It will constantly have 348,417 persons of all ages above 21. years. 5ly. And the half of those of 21. years and upwards living at any one instant of time will be dead in 18. years 8. months, or say 19. years as the nearest integral number. Then 19. years is the term beyond which neither the representatives of a nation, nor even the whole nation itself assembled, can validly extend a debt. . . .

I suppose that the recieved opinion, that the public debts of one generation devolve on the next, has been suggested by our seeing habitually in private life that he who succeeds to lands is required to pay the debts of his ancestor or testator: without considering that this requisition is municipal only, not moral; flowing from the will of the society, which has found it convenient to appropriate lands, become vacant by the death of their occupant, on the condition of a paiment of his debts: but that between society and society, or generation and generation, there is no municipal obligation, no umpire but the law of nature. We seem not to have percieved that, by the law of nature, one generation is to another as one independant nation to another. . . .

On similar grounds it may be proved that no society can make a perpetual constitution, or even a perpetual law. The earth belongs always to

the living generation. They may manage it then, and what proceeds from it, as they please, during their usufruct. They are masters too of their own persons, and consequently may govern them as they please. But persons and property make the sum of the objects of government. The constitution and the laws of their predecessors extinguished then in their natural course with those who gave them being. This could preserve that being till it ceased to be itself, and no longer. Every constitution then, and every law, naturally expires at the end of 19 years. If it be enforced longer, it is an act of force, and not of right.—It may be said that the succeeding generation exercising in fact the power of repeal, this leaves them as free as if the constitution or law had been expressly limited to 19 years only. In the first place, this objection admits the right, in proposing an equivalent. But the power of repeal is not an equivalent. It might be indeed if every form of government were so perfectly contrived that the will of the majority could always be obtained fairly and without impediment. But this is true of no form. The people cannot assemble themselves. Their representation is unequal and vicious. Various checks are opposed to every legislative proposition. Factions get possession of the public councils. Bribery corrupts them. Personal interests lead them astray from the general interests of their constituents: and other impediments arise so as to prove to every practical man that a law of limited duration is much more manageable than one which needs a repeal.

This principle that the earth belongs to the living, and not to the dead, is of very extensive application and consequences, in every country, and most especially in France. . . .

Turn this subject in your mind, my dear Sir, and particularly as to the power of contracting debts; and develope it with that perspicuity and cogent logic so peculiarly yours. Your station in the councils of our country gives you an opportunity of producing it to public consideration, of forcing it into discussion. At first blush it may be rallied, as a theoretical speculation: but examination will prove it to be solid and salutary. It would furnish matter for a fine preamble to our first law for appropriating the public revenue; and it will exclude at the threshold of our new government the contagious and ruinous errors of this quarter of the globe, which have armed despots with means, not sanctioned by nature, for binding in chains their fellow men. We have already given in example one effectual check to the Dog of war by transferring the power of letting him loose from the Executive to the Legislative body, from those who are to spend to those who are to pay. I should be pleased to see this second obstacle held out by us also in the first instance. No nation can make a declaration against the validity of long-contracted debts so disinterestedly as we, since we do not owe a shilling which may not be paid with ease, principal and interest, within the time of our own lives.—Establish the principle also in the new law to be passed for protecting copyrights and new inventions, by securing the exclusive right for 19. instead of 14. years.

Besides familiarising us to this term, it will be an instance the more of our taking reason for our guide, instead of English precedent, the habit of which fetters us with all the political heresies of a nation equally remarkeable for it's early excitement from some errors, and long slumbering under others. . . .

37. *Why Washington Must Remain*

To the President of the United States

Philadelphia, May 23, 1792

Dear Sir,—I have determined to make the subject of a letter what for some time past has been a subject of inquietude to my mind, without having found a good occasion of disburthening itself to you in conversation, during the busy scenes which occupied you here. Perhaps, too, you may be able in your present situation, or on the road, to give it more time and reflection than you could do here at any moment.

When you first mentioned to me your purpose of retiring from the government, though I felt all the magnitude of the event, I was in a considerable degree silent. I knew that, to such a mind as yours, persuasion was idle and impertinent; that before forming your decision you had weighed all the reasons for and against the measure, had made up your mind on full view of them, and that there could be little hope of changing the result. Pursuing my reflections, too, I knew we were some day to try to walk alone, and if the essay should be made while you should be alive and looking on, we should derive confidence from that circumstance, and resource, if it failed. The public mind, too, was calm and confident, and therefore in a favorable state for making the experiment. Had no change of circumstances intervened, I should not, with any hopes of success, have now ventured to propose to you a change of purpose. But the public mind is no longer confident and serene; and that from causes in which you are no ways personally mixed. Though these causes have been hackneyed in the public papers in detail, it may not be amiss, in order to calculate the effect they are capable of producing, to take a view of them in the mass, giving to each the form, real or imaginary, under which they have been presented.

It has been urged, then, that a public debt, greater than we can possibly pay, before other causes of adding new debt to it will occur, has been artificially created by adding together the whole amount of the debtor and creditor sides of accounts, instead of only taking their balances, which could have been paid off in a short time: that this accumulation of debt

has taken forever out of our power those easy sources of revenue which, applied to the ordinary necessities and exigencies of government, would have answered them habitually, and covered us from habitual murmurings against taxes and tax-gatherers, reserving extraordinary calls for those extraordinary occasions which would animate the people to meet them: that though the calls for money have been no greater than we must expect generally, for the same or equivalent exigencies, yet we are already obliged to strain the impost till it produces clamor, and will produce evasion and war on our own citizens to collect it, and even to resort to an *excise* law of odious character with the people, partial in its operation, unproductive unless enforced by arbitrary and vexatious means, and committing the authority of the government in parts where resistance is most probable and coercion least practicable. They cite propositions in Congress, and suspect other projects on foot still to increase the mass of debt. . . .

They think . . . that it has furnished effectual means of corrupting such a portion of the legislature as turns the balance between the honest voters, whichever way it is directed: that this corrupt squadron, deciding the voice of the legislature, have manifested their dispositions to get rid of the limitations imposed by the Constitution on the general legislature, limitations, on the faith of which, the States acceded to that instrument: that the ultimate object of all this is to prepare the way for a change from the present republican form of government to that of a monarchy, of which the English Constitution is to be the model: that this was contemplated by the convention is no secret, because its partisans have made more of it. To effect it then was impracticable, but they are still eager after their object, and are predisposing everything for its ultimate attainment. . . .

Of all the mischiefs objected to the system of measures before mentioned, none is so afflicting and fatal to every honest hope, as the corruption of the Legislature. As it was the earliest of these measures, it became the instrument for producing the risk, and will be the instrument for producing in future a king, lords and commons, or whatever else those who direct it may choose. Withdrawn such a distance from the eye of their constituents, and these so dispersed as to be inaccessible to public information, and particularly to that of the conduct of their own representatives, they will form the most corrupt government on earth, if the means of their corruption be not prevented. The only hope of safety hangs now on the numerous representation which is to come forward the ensuing year. Some of the new members will be, probably, either in principle or interest, with the present majority; but it is expected that the great mass will form an accession to the republican party. . . .

. . . The division of sentiment and interest happens unfortunately to be so geographical, that no mortal can say that what is most wise and temperate would prevail against what is most easy and obvious? I can

scarcely contemplate a more incalculable evil than the breaking of the
Union into two or more parts. Yet when we consider the mass which opposed the original coalescence; when we consider that it lay chiefly in the
Southern quarter; that the Legislature have availed themselves of no occasion of allaying it, but on the contrary, whenever Northern and Southern prejudices have come into conflict, the latter have been sacrificed and
the former soothed; that the owners of the debt are in the Southern, and
the holders of it in the Northern division; that the anti-federal champions
are now strengthened in argument by the fulfillment of their predictions;
that this has been brought about by the monarchical federalists themselves, who, having been for the new government merely as a stepping
stone to monarchy, have themselves adopted the very constructions of the
Constitution, of which, when advocating its acceptance before the tribunal of the people, they declared it unsusceptible; that the republican federalists who espoused the same government for its intrinsic merits, are
disarmed of their weapons; that which they denied as prophecy, having
now become true history, who can be sure that these things may not
proselyte the small number which was wanting to place the majority on
the other side? And this is the event at which I tremble, and to prevent
which I consider your continuing at the head of affairs as of the last importance. The confidence of the whole Union is centred in you. Your being at the helm will be more than an answer to every argument which
can be used to alarm and lead the people in any quarter, into violence and
secession. North and South will hang together if they have you to hang
on; and if the first correction of a numerous representation should fail in
its effect, your presence will give time for trying others, not inconsistent
with the union and peace of the States. . . .

38. *"Lessons in Republicanism"*

To Thomas Paine

Philadelphia, June 19, 1792

Dear Sir,—I received with great pleasure the present of your pamphlets,
as well as for the thing itself as that it was a testimony of your recollection. Would you believe it possible that in this country there should be
high & important characters who need your lessons in republicanism, &
who do not heed them? It is but too true that we have a sect preaching
up & pouting after an English constitution of king, lords, & commons, &
whose heads are itching for crowns, coronets & mitres. But our people,
my good friend, are firm and unanimous in their principles of republican-

ism & there is no better proof of it than that they love what you write and read it with delight. The printers season every newspaper with extracts from your last, as they did before from your first part of the *Rights of Man*. They have both served here to separate the wheat from the chaff, and to prove that tho' the latter appears on the surface, it is on the surface only. The bulk below is sound & pure. Go on then in doing with your pen what in other times was done with the sword: shew that reformation is more practicable by operating on the mind than on the body of man, and be assured that it has not a more sincere votary nor you a more ardent well-wisher than Yrs. &c.

39. *On the Hamiltonian Program*

To the President of the United States

Monticello, September 9, 1792

. . . . I now take the liberty of proceeding to that part of your letter wherein you notice the internal dissensions which have taken place within our government, and their disagreeable effect on its movements. That such dissensions have taken place is certain, and even among those who are nearest to you in the administration. To no one have they given deeper concern than myself; to no one equal mortification at being myself a part of them. Though I take to myself no more than my share of the general observations of your letter, yet I am so desirous ever that you should know the whole truth, and believe no more than the truth, that I am glad to seize every occasion of developing to you whatever I do or think relative to the government; and shall, therefore, ask permission to be more lengthy now than the occasion particularly calls for, or could otherwise perhaps justify.

When I embarked in the government, it was with a determination to intermeddle not at all with the Legislature, and as little as possible with my co-departments. The first and only instance of variance from the former part of my resolution, I was duped into by the Secretary of the Treasury, and made a tool for forwarding his schemes, not then sufficiently understood by me; and of all the errors of my political life, this has occasioned me the deepest regret. It has ever been my purpose to explain this to you, when, from being actors on the scene, we shall have become uninterested spectators only. The second part of my resolution has been religiously observed with the War Department; and as to that of the Treasury, has never been further swerved from than by the mere enunciation of my sentiments in conversation, and chiefly among those

who, expressing the same sentiments, drew mine from me. If it has been supposed that I have ever intrigued among the members of the Legislature to defeat the plans of the Secretary of the Treasury, it is contrary to all truth. As I never had the desire to influence the members, so neither had I any other means than my friendships, which I valued too highly to risk by usurpation on their freedom of judgment, and the conscientious pursuit of their own sense of duty. That I have utterly, in my private conversations, disapproved of the system of the Secretary of the Treasury, I acknowledge and avow; and this was not merely a speculative difference. His system flowed from principles adverse to liberty, and was calculated to undermine and demolish the Republic, by creating an influence of his department over the members of the Legislature. I saw this influence actually produced, and its first fruits to be the establishment of the great outlines of his project by the votes of the very persons who, having swallowed his bait, were laying themselves out to profit by his plans; and that had these persons withdrawn, as those interested in a question ever should, the vote of the disinterested majority was clearly the reverse of what they made it. These were no longer the votes then of the representatives of the people, but of deserters from the rights and interests of the people; and it was impossible to consider their decisions, which had nothing in view but to enrich themselves, as the measures of the fair majority, which ought always to be respected. If, what was actually doing, begat uneasiness in those who wished for virtuous government, what was further proposed was not less threatening to the friends of the Constitution. For, in a report on the subject of manufactures, (still to be acted on), it was expressly assumed that the General Government has a right to exercise all powers which may be for the *general welfare,* that is to say, all the legitimate powers of government; since no government has a legitimate right to do what is not for the welfare of the governed. There was, indeed, a sham limitation of the universality of this power *to cases where money is to be employed.* But about what is it that money cannot be employed? Thus the object of these plans, taken together, is to draw all the powers of government into the hands of the general Legislature, to establish means for corrupting a sufficient corps in that Legislature to divide the honest votes, and preponderate, by their own, the scale which suited, and to have the corps under the command of the Secretary of the Treasury, for the purpose of subverting, step by step, the principles of the Constitution which he has so often declared to be a thing of nothing, which must be changed. Such views might have justified something more than mere expressions of dissent, beyond which, nevertheless, I never went. Has abstinence from the department, committed to me, been equally observed by him? To say nothing of other interferences equally known, in the case of the two nations, with which we have the most intimate connections, France and England, my system was to give some satisfactory distinctions to the former, of little cost to us, in return for the

solid advantages yielded us by them; and to have met the English with some restrictions which might induce them to abate their severities against our commerce. I have always supposed this coincided with your sentiments. Yet the Secretary of the Treasury, by his cabals with members of the Legislature, and by high-toned declamations on other occasions, has forced down his own system, which was exactly the reverse. He undertook, of his own authority, the conferences with the ministers of those two nations, and was, on every consultation, provided with some report of a conversation with the one or the other of them, adapted to his views. These views, thus made to prevail, their execution fell, of course, to me; and I can safely appeal to you, who have seen all my letters and proceedings, whether I have not carried them into execution as sincerely as if they had been my own, though I ever considered them as inconsistent with the honor and interest of our country. That they have been inconsistent with our interest is but too fatally proved by the stab to our navigation given by the French. So that if the question be by whose fault is it that Colonel Hamilton and myself have not drawn together? the answer will depend on that to two other questions, whose principles of administration best justify, by their purity, conscientious adherence? and which of us has, notwithstanding, stepped farthest into the control of the department of the other? . . .

40. *Republican Heresies*

To Phillip Mazzei

Monticello, April 24, 1796

. . . . The aspect of our politics has wonderfully changed since you left us. In place of that noble love of liberty and republican government which carried us triumphantly through the war, an Anglican monarchical aristocratical party has sprung up, whose avowed object is to draw over us the substance, as they have already done the forms, of the British government. The main body of our citizens, however, remain true to their republican principles; the whole landed interest is republican, and so is a great mass of talents. Against us are the Executive, the Judiciary, two out of three branches of the Legislature, all the officers of the government, all who want to be officers, all timid men who prefer the calm of despotism to the boisterous sea of liberty, British merchants and Americans trading on British capital, speculators and holders in the banks and public funds, a contrivance invented for the purposes of corruption, and for assimilating us in all things to the rotten as well as the sound parts of

the British model. It would give you a fever were I to name to you the apostates who have gone over to these heresies, men who were Samsons in the field and Solomons in the council, but who have had their heads shorn by the harlot England. In short, we are likely to preserve the liberty we have obtained only by unremitting labors and perils. But we shall preserve it; and our mass of weight and wealth on the good side is so great, as to leave no danger that force will ever be attempted against us. We have only to awake and snap the Lilliputian cords with which they have been entangling us during the first sleep which succeeded our labors. . . .

41. *"The Freedom of the Human Mind"*

To William Green Mumford

Monticello June 18, 1799

Dear Sir,

I have to acknolege the reciept of your favor of May 14. in which you mention that you have finished the 6. first books of Euclid, plane trigonometry, surveying and algebra and ask whether I think a further pursuit of that branch of science would be useful to you. There are some propositions in the latter books of Euclid, and some of Archimedes, which are useful, and I have no doubt you have been made acquainted with them. Trigonometry, so far as this, is most valuable to every man, there is scarcely a day in which he will not resort to it for some of the purposes of common life. The science of calculation also is indispensible as far as the extraction of the square and cube roots; Algebra as far as the quadratic equation and the use of logarithms are often of value in ordinary cases: but all beyond these is but a luxury; a delicious luxury indeed; but not to be indulged in by one who is to have a profession to follow for his subsistence. In this light I view the conic sections, curves of the higher orders, perhaps even spherical trigonometry, Algebraical operations beyond the 2d dimension, and fluxions. There are other branches of science however worth the attention of every man: astronomy, botany, chemistry, natural philosophy, natural history, anatomy. Not indeed to be a proficient in them; but to possess their general principles and outlines, so as that we may be able to amuse and inform ourselves further in any of them as we proceed through life and have occasion for them. Some knowledge of them is necessary for our character as well as comfort. The general elements of astronomy and of natural philosophy are best acquired at an academy where we can have the benefit of the instruments and apparatus usually provided there: but the others may well be ac-

quired from books alone as far as our purposes require. I have indulged myself in these observations to you, because the evidence cannot be unuseful to you of a person who has often had occasion to consider which of his acquisitions in science have been really useful to him in life, and which of them have been merely a matter of luxury.

I am among those who think well of the human character generally. I consider man as formed for society, and endowed by nature with those dispositions which fit him for society. I believe also, with Condorcet, as mentioned in your letter, that his mind is perfectible to a degree of which we cannot as yet form any conception. It is impossible for a man who takes a survey of what is already known, not to see what an immensity in every branch of science yet remains to be discovered, and that too of articles to which our faculties seem adequate. In geometry and calculation we know a great deal. Yet there are some desiderata. In anatomy great progress has been made; but much is still to be acquired. In natural history we possess knowledge; but we want a great deal. In chemistry we are not yet sure of the first elements. Our natural philosophy is in a very infantine state; perhaps for great advances in it, a further progress in chemistry is necessary. Surgery is well advanced; but prodigiously short of what may be. The state of medicine is worse than that of total ignorance. Could we divest ourselves of every thing we suppose we know in it, we should start from a higher ground and with fairer prospects. From Hippocrates to Brown we have had nothing but a succession of hypothetical systems each having it's day of vogue, like the fashions and fancies of caps and gowns, and yielding in turn to the next caprice. Yet the human frame, which is to be the subject of suffering and torture under these learned modes, does not change. We have a few medecines, as the bark, opium, mercury, which in a few well defined diseases are of unquestionable virtue: but the residuary list of the materia medica, long as it is, contains but the charlataneries of the art; and of the diseases of doubtful form, physicians have ever had a false knowledge, worse than ignorance. Yet surely the list of unequivocal diseases and remedies is capable of enlargement; and it is still more certain that in the other branches of science, great fields are yet to be explored to which our faculties are equal, and that to an extent of which we cannot fix the limits. I join you therefore in branding as cowardly the idea that the human mind is incapable of further advances. This is precisely the doctrine which the present despots of the earth are inculcating, and their friends here re-echoing; and applying especially to religion and politics; 'that it is not probable that any thing better will be discovered than what was known to our fathers.' We are to look backwards then and not forwards for the improvement of science, and to find it amidst feudal barbarians and the fires of Spital-fields. But thank heaven the American mind is already too much opened, to listen to these impostures; and while the art of printing is left to us, science can never be retrograde; what is once acquired of

real knowlege can never be lost. To preserve the freedom of the human mind then and freedom of the press, every spirit should be ready to devote itself to martyrdom; for as long as we may think as we will, and speak as we think, the condition of man will proceed in improvement. The generation which is going off the stage has deserved well of mankind for the struggles it has made, and for having arrested that course of despotism which had overwhelmed the world for thousands and thousands of years. If there seems to be danger that the ground they have gained will be lost again, that danger comes from the generation your contemporary. But that the enthusiasm which characterises youth should lift its parricide hands against freedom and science, would be such a monstrous phænomenon as I cannot place among possible things in this age and this country. Your college at least has shewn itself incapable of it; and if the youth of any other place have seemed to rally under other banners it has been from delusions which they will soon dissipate. I shall be happy to hear from you from time to time, and of your progress in study, and to be useful to you in whatever is in my power. . . .

42. *"This Whole Chapter in the History of Man Is New"*

To Dr. Joseph Priestley

Washington, March 21, 1801

Dear Sir,—I learned some time ago that you were in Philadelphia, but that it was only for a fortnight; and I supposed you were gone. It was not till yesterday I received information that you were still there, had been very ill, but were on the recovery. I sincerely rejoice that you are so. Yours is one of the few lives precious to mankind, and for the continuance of which every thinking man is solicitous. Bigots may be an exception. What an effort, my dear Sir, of bigotry in politics and religion have we gone through! The barbarians really flattered themselves they should be able to bring back the times of Vandalism, when ignorance put everything into the hands of power and priestcraft. All advances in science were proscribed as innovations. They pretended to praise and encourage education, but it was to be the education of our ancestors. We were to look backwards, not forwards, for improvement; the President himself declaring, in one of his answers to addresses, that we were never to expect to go beyond them in real science. This was the real ground of all attacks on you. Those who live by mystery and *charlatanerie*, fearing you would render them useless by simplifying the Christian philosophy,—the most sublime and benevolent, but most perverted system that ever shone

on man,—endeavored to crush your well-earned and well-deserved fame. But it was the Lilliputians upon Gulliver. Our countrymen have recovered from the alarm into which art and industry had thrown them; science and honesty are replaced on their high ground; and you, my dear Sir, as their great apostle, are on its pinnacle. It is with heartfelt satisfaction that, in the first moments of my public action, I can hail you with welcome to our land, tender to you the homage of its respect and esteem, cover you under the protection of those laws which were made for the wise and good like you, and disdain the legitimacy of that libel on legislation, which, under the form of a law, was for some time placed among them.

As the storm is now subsiding, and the horizon becoming serene, it is pleasant to consider the phenomenon with attention. We can no longer say there is nothing new under the sun. For this whole chapter in the history of man is new. The great extent of our republic is new. Its sparse habitation is new. The mighty wave of public opinion which has rolled over it is new. But the most pleasing novelty is, its so quietly subsiding over such an extent of surface to its true level again. The order and good sense displayed in this recovery from delusion, and in the momentous crisis which lately arose, really bespeaks a strength of character in our nation which augurs well for the duration of our republic; and I am much better satisfied now of its stability than I was before it was tried. I have been, above all things, solaced by the prospect which opened on us, in the event of a non-election of a President; in which case, the federal government would have been in the situation of a clock or watch run down. There was no idea of force, nor of any occasion for it. A convention, invited by the republican members of Congress, with the virtual President and Vice-President, would have been on the ground in eight weeks, would have repaired the Constitution where it was defective, and wound it up again. This peaceable and legitimate resource, to which we are in the habit of implicit obedience, superseding all appeal to force, and being always within our reach, shows a precious principle of self-preservation in our composition, till a change of circumstances shall take place, which is not within prospect at any definite period. . . .

43. *System of Finance*

To the Secretary of the Treasury. (Albert Gallatin.)

Washington, April 1, 1802

Dear Sir,—I have read and considered your report on the operations of the sinking fund, and entirely approve of it, as the best plan on which we can set out. I think it an object of great importance, to be kept in view and to be undertaken at a fit season, to simplify our system of finance, and

bring it within the comprehension of every member of Congress. Hamilton set out on a different plan. In order that he might have the entire government of his machine, he determined so to complicate it as that neither the President nor Congress should be able to understand it, or to control him. He succeeded in doing this, not only beyond their reach, but so that he at length could not unravel it himself. He gave to the debt, in the first instance, in funding it, the most artificial and mysterious form he could devise. He then moulded up his appropriations of a number of scraps and remnants, many of which were nothing at all, and applied them to different objects in reversion and remainder, until the whole system was involved in impenetrable fog; and while he was giving himself the airs of providing for the payment of the debt, he left himself free to add to it continually, as he did in fact, instead of paying it. I like your idea of kneading all his little scraps and fragments into one batch, and adding to it a complementary sum, which, while it forms it into a single mass from which everything is to be paid, will enable us, should a breach of appropriation ever be charged on us, to prove that the sum appropriated, and more, has been applied to its specific object.

But there is a point beyond this on which I should wish to keep my eye, and to which I should aim to approach by every tack which previous arrangements force on us. That is, to form into one consolidated mass all the moneys received into the treasury, and to the several expenditures, giving them a preference of payment according to the order in which they should be arranged. As for example. 1. The interest of the public debt. 2. Such portions of principal as are exigible. 3. The expenses of government. 4. Such other portions of principal as, though not exigible, we are still free to pay when we please. The last object might be made to take up the residuum of money remaining in the treasury at the end of every year, after the three first objects were complied with, and would be the barometer whereby to test the economy of the administration. It would furnish a simple measure by which every one could mete their merit, and by which every one could decide when taxes were deficient or superabundant. If to this can be added a simplification of the form of accounts in the treasury department, and in the organization of its officers, so as to bring everything to a single centre, we might hope to see the finances of the Union as clear and intelligible as a merchant's books, so that every member of Congress, and every man of any mind in the Union, should be able to comprehend them to investigate abuses, and consequently to control them. Our predecessors have endeavored by intricacies of system, and shuffling the investigator over from one officer to another, to cover everything from detection. I hope we shall go in the contrary direction, and that by our honest and judicious reformations, we may be able, within the limits of our time, to bring things back to that simple and intelligible system on which they should have been organized at first. . . .

44. *The Morals of Jesus*

To Doctor Benjamin Rush

Washington, April 21, 1803

Dear Sir,—In some of the delightful conversations with you, in the evenings of 1798–99, and which served as an anodyne to the afflictions of the crisis through which our country was then laboring, the Christian religion was sometimes our topic; and I then promised you, that one day or other, I would give you my views of it. They are the result of a life of inquiry and reflection, and very different from that anti-Christian system imputed to me by those who know nothing of my opinions. To the corruptions of Christianity I am, indeed, opposed; but not to the genuine precepts of Jesus himself. I am a Christian, in the only sense in which he wished any one to be; sincerely attached to his doctrines, in preference to all others; ascribing to himself every *human* excellence; and believing he never claimed any other. At the short interval since these conversations, when I could justifiably abstract my mind from public affairs, the subject has been under my contemplation. But the more I considered it, the more it expanded beyond the measure of either my time or information. In the moment of my late departure from Monticello, I received from Dr. Priestley, his little treatise of "Socrates and Jesus Compared." This being a section of the general view I had taken of the field, it became a subject of reflection while on the road, and unoccupied otherwise. The result was, to arrange in my mind a syllabus, or outline of such an estimate of the comparative merits of Christianity, as I wished to see executed by some one of more leisure and information for the task, than myself. This I now send you, as the only discharge of my promise I can probably ever execute. And in confiding it to you, I know it will not be exposed to the malignant perversions of those who make every word from me a text for new misrepresentations and calumnies. I am moreover averse to the communication of my religious tenets to the public; because it would countenance the presumption of those who have endeavored to draw them before that tribunal, and to seduce public opinion to erect itself into that inquisition over the rights of conscience, which the laws have so justly proscribed. It behooves every man who values liberty of conscience for himself, to resist invasions of it in the case of others; or their case may, by change of circumstances, become his own. It behooves him, too, in his own case, to give no example of concession, betraying the common right of independent opinion, by answering questions of faith, which the laws have left between God and himself. Accept my affectionate salutations.

*Syllabus of an Estimate of the Merit of the Doctrines of Jesus, compared
with those of others*

In a comparative view of the Ethics of the enlightened nations of
antiquity, of the Jews and of Jesus, no notice should be taken of the
corruptions of reason among the ancients, to wit, the idolatry and superstition of the vulgar, nor of the corruptions of Christianity by the learned
among its professors.

Let a just view be taken of the moral principles inculcated by the
most esteemed of the sects of ancient philosophy, or of their individuals;
particularly Pythagoras, Socrates, Epicurus, Cicero, Epictetus, Seneca,
Antoninus.

I. Philosophers. 1. Their precepts related chiefly to ourselves, and the
government of those passions which, unrestrained, would disturb our
tranquillity of mind.[1] In this branch of philosophy they were really great.

2. In developing our duties to others, they were short and defective.
They embraced, indeed, the circle of kindred and friends, and inculcated
patriotism, or the love of our country in the aggregate, as a primary
obligation: towards our neighbors and countrymen they taught justice,
but scarcely viewed them as within the circle of benevolence. Still
less have they inculcated peace, charity and love to our fellow men, or
embraced with benevolence the whole family of mankind.

II. Jews. 1. Their system was Deism; that is, the belief in one only God.
But their ideas of him and of his attributes were degrading and injurious.

2. Their Ethics were not only imperfect, but often irreconcilable with
the sound dictates of reason and morality, as they respect intercourse
with those around us; and repulsive and anti-social, as respecting other
nations. They needed reformation, therefore, in an eminent degree.

III. Jesus. In this state of things among the Jews, Jesus appeared. His
parentage was obscure; his condition poor; his education null; his natural
endowments great; his life correct and innocent: he was meek, benevolent, patient, firm, disinterested, and of the sublimest eloquence.

The disadvantages under which his doctrines appear are remarkable.

1. Like Socrates and Epictetus, he wrote nothing himself.

2. But he had not, like them, a Xenophon or an Arrian to write for
him. I name not Plato, who only used the name of Socrates to cover the
whimsies of his own brain. On the contrary, all the learned of his country,
entrenched in its power and riches, were opposed to him, lest his labors

---

[1] To explain, I will exhibit the heads of Seneca's and Cicero's philosophical works,
the most extensive of any we have received from the ancients. Of ten heads in
Seneca, seven relate to ourselves, viz. *de ira, consolatio, de tranquilitate, de constantia
sapientis, de otio sapientis, de vita beata, de brevitate vitae;* two relate to others,
de clementia, de beneficiis; and one relates to the government of the world, *de
providentia.* Of eleven tracts of Cicero, five respect ourselves, viz. *de finibus, Tus-
culana, academica, paradoxa, de Senectute;* one, *de officiis,* relates partly to ourselves, partly to others; one, *de amicitia,* relates to others; and four are on different
subjects, to wit, *de natura deorum, de divinatione, de fato,* and *somnium Scipionis.*
[Jefferson's footnote.]

should undermine their advantages; and the committing to writing his life and doctrines fell on unlettered and ignorant men; who wrote, too, from memory, and not till long after the transactions had passed.

3. According to the ordinary fate of those who attempt to enlighten and reform mankind, he fell an early victim to the jealousy and combination of the altar and the throne, at about thirty-three years of age, his reason having not yet attained the *maximum* of its energy, nor the course of his preaching, which was but of three years at most, presented occasions for developing a complete system of morals.

4. Hence the doctrines which he really delivered were defective as a whole, and fragments only of what he did deliver have come to us mutilated, misstated, and often unintelligible.

5. They have been still more disfigured by the corruptions of schismatizing followers, who have found an interest in sophisticating and perverting the simple doctrines he taught, by engrafting on them the mysticisms of a Grecian sophist, frittering them into subtleties, and obscuring them with jargon, until they have caused good men to reject the whole in disgust, and to view Jesus himself as an impostor.

IV. Notwithstanding these disadvantages, a system of morals is presented to us, which, if filled up in the style and spirit of the rich fragments he left us, would be the most perfect and sublime that has ever been taught by man.

The question of his being a member of the Godhead, or in direct communication with it, claimed for him by some of his followers, and denied by others, is foreign to the present view, which is merely an estimate of the intrinsic merits of his doctrines.

1. He corrected the Deism of the Jews, confirming them in their belief of one only God, and giving them juster notions of his attributes and government.

2. His moral doctrines, relating to kindred and friends, were more pure and perfect than those of the most correct of the philosophers, and greatly more so than those of the Jews; and they went far beyond both in inculcating universal philanthropy, not only to kindred and friends, to neighbors and countrymen, but to all mankind, gathering all into one family, under the bonds of love, charity, peace, common wants and common aids. A development of this head will evince the peculiar superiority of the system of Jesus over all others.

3. The precepts of philosophy, and of the Hebrew code, laid hold of actions only. He pushed his scrutinies into the heart of man; erected his tribunal in the region of his thoughts, and purified the waters at the fountain head.

4. He taught, emphatically, the doctrines of a future state, which was either doubted, or disbelieved by the Jews; and wielded it with efficacy, as an important incentive, supplementary to the other motives to moral conduct.

45. *Political Economy*

To Jean Baptiste Say

Washington, February 1, 1804

Dear Sir,—I have to acknowledge the receipt of your obliging letter, and with it, of two very interesting volumes on Political Economy. These found me engaged in giving the leisure moments I rarely find, to the perusal of Malthus' work on population, a work of sound logic, in which some of the opinions of Adam Smith, as well as of the economists, are ably examined. I was pleased, on turning to some chapters where you treat the same questions, to find his opinions corroborated by yours. I shall proceed to the reading of your work with great pleasure. In the meantime, the present conveyance, by a gentleman of my family going to Paris, is too safe to hazard a delay in making my acknowledgments for this mark of attention, and for having afforded to me a satisfaction, which the ordinary course of literary communications could not have given me for a considerable time.

The differences of circumstance between this and the old countries of Europe, furnish differences of fact whereon to reason, in questions of political economy, and will consequently produce sometimes a difference of result. There, for instance, the quantity of food is fixed, or increasing in a slow and only arithmetical ratio, and the proportion is limited by the same ratio. Supernumerary births consequently add only to your mortality. Here the immense extent of uncultivated and fertile lands enables every one who will labor, to marry young, and to raise a family of any size. Our food, then, may increase geometrically with our laborers, and our births, however multiplied, become effective. Again, there the best distribution of labor is supposed to be that which places the manufacturing hands alongside the agricultural; so that the one part shall feed both, and the other part furnish both with clothes and other comforts. Would that be best here? Egoism and first appearances say yes. Or would it be better that all our laborers should be employed in agriculture? In this case a double or treble portion of fertile lands would be brought into culture; a double or treble creation of food be produced, and its surplus go to nourish the now perishing births of Europe, who in return would manufacture and send us in exchange our clothes and other comforts. Morality listens to this, and so invariably do the laws of nature create our duties and interests, that when they seem to be at variance, we ought to suspect some fallacy in our reasonings. In solving this question, too, we should allow its just weight to the moral and physical preference of the agricultural, over the manufacturing, man. My occupations permit me

only to ask questions. They deny me the time, if I had the information, to answer them. Perhaps, as worthy the attention of the author of the *Traité d' Economie Politique,* I shall find them answered in that work. If they are not, the reason will have been that you wrote for Europe; while I shall have asked them because I think for America. Accept, Sir, my respectful salutations, and assurances of great consideration.

46. *Prudential Rules*

To Thomas Jefferson Randolph

Washington, November 24, 1808

My Dear Jefferson, ... Your situation, thrown at such a distance from us, and alone, cannot but give us all great anxieties for you. As much has been secured for you, by your particular position and the acquaintance to which you have been recommended, as could be done towards shielding you from the dangers which surround you. But thrown on a wide world, among entire strangers, without a friend or guardian to advise, so young too, and with so little experience of mankind, your dangers are great, and still your safety must rest on yourself. A determination never to do what is wrong, prudence and good humor, will go far towards securing to you the estimation of the world. When I recollect that at fourteen years of age, the whole care and direction of myself was thrown on myself entirely, without a relation or friend qualified to advise or guide me, and recollect the various sorts of bad company with which I associated from time to time, I am astonished I did not turn off with some of them, and become as worthless to society as they were. I had the good fortune to become acquainted very early with some characters of very high standing, and to feel the incessant wish that I could ever become what they were. Under temptations and difficulties, I would ask myself what would Dr. Small, Mr. Wythe, Peyton Randolph do in this situation? What course in it will insure me their approbation? I am certain that this mode of deciding on my conduct, tended more to correctness than any reasoning powers I possessed. Knowing the even and dignified line they pursued, I could never doubt for a moment which of two courses would be in character for them. Whereas, seeking the same object through a process of moral reasoning, and with the jaundiced eye of youth, I should often have erred. From the circumstances of my position, I was often thrown into the society of horse racers, card players, fox hunters, scientific and professional men, and of dignified men; and many a time have I asked myself, in the enthusiastic moment of the death of a

fox, the victory of a favorite horse, the issue of a question eloquently argued at the bar, or in the great council of the nation, well, which of these kinds of reputation should I prefer? That of a horse jockey? a fox hunter? an orator? or the honest advocate of my country's rights? Be assured, my dear Jefferson, that these little returns into ourselves, this self-catechising habit, is not trifling nor useless, but leads to the prudent selection and steady pursuit of what is right.

I have mentioned good humor as one of the preservatives of our peace and tranquillity. It is among the most effectual, and its effect is so well imitated and aided, artificially, by politeness, that this also becomes an acquisition of first rate value. In truth, politeness is artificial good humor, it covers the natural want of it, and ends by rendering habitual a substitute nearly equivalent to the real virtue. It is the practice of sacrificing to those whom we meet in society, all the little conveniences and preferences which will gratify them, and deprive us of nothing worth a moment's consideration; it is the giving a pleasing and flattering turn to our expressions, which will conciliate others, and make them pleased with us as well as themselves. How cheap a price for the good will of another! When this is in return for a rude thing said by another, it brings him to his senses, it mortifies and corrects him in the most salutary way, and places him at the feet of your good nature, in the eyes of the company. But in stating prudential rules for our government in society, I must not omit the important one of never entering into dispute or argument with another. I never saw an instance of one of two disputants convincing the other by argument. I have seen many, on their getting warm, becoming rude, and shooting one another. Conviction is the effect of our own dispassionate reasoning, either in solitude, or weighing within ourselves, dispassionately, what we hear from others, standing uncommitted in argument ourselves. It was one of the rules which, above all others, made Doctor Franklin the most amiable of men in society, "never to contradict anybody." If he was urged to announce an opinion, he did it rather by asking questions, as if for information, or by suggesting doubts. When I hear another express an opinion which is not mine, I say to myself, he has a right to his opinion, as I to mine; why should I question it? His error does me no injury, and shall I become a Don Quixote, to bring all men by force of argument to one opinion? If a fact be misstated, it is probable he is gratified by a belief of it, and I have no right to deprive him of the gratification. If he wants information, he will ask it, and then I will give it in measured terms; but if he still believes his own story, and shows a desire to dispute the fact with me, I hear him and say nothing. It is his affair, not mine, if he prefers error. There are two classes of disputants most frequently to be met with among us. The first is of young students, just entered the threshold of science, with a first view of its outlines, not yet filled up with the details and modifications which a further progress would bring to their knowledge. The other consists of the ill-

tempered and rude men in society, who have taken up a passion for politics. . . . From both of these classes of disputants, my dear Jefferson, keep aloof, as you would from the infected subjects of yellow fever or pestilence. Consider yourself, when with them, as among the patients of Bedlam, needing medical more than moral counsel. Be a listener only, keep within yourself, and endeavor to establish with yourself the habit of silence, especially on politics. . . .

47. *On Adams*

To Dr. Benjamin Rush

Monticello, January 16, 1811

. . . I receive with sensibility your observations on the discontinuance of friendly correspondence between Mr. Adams and myself, and the concern you take in its restoration. This discontinuance has not proceeded from me, nor from the want of sincere desire and of effort on my part, to renew our intercourse. You know the perfect coincidence of principle and of action, in the early part of the Revolution, which produced a high degree of mutual respect and esteem between Mr. Adams and myself. Certainly no man was ever truer than he was, in that day, to those principles of rational republicanism which, after the necessity of throwing off our monarchy, dictated all our efforts in the establishment of a new government. And although he swerved, afterwards, towards the principles of the English constitution, our friendship did not abate on that account. While he was Vice-President, and I Secretary of State, I received a letter from President Washington, then at Mount Vernon, desiring me to call together the Heads of departments, and to invite Mr. Adams to join us (which, by-the-bye, was the only instance of that being done) in order to determine on some measure which required despatch; and he desired me to act on it, as decided, without again recurring to him. I invited them to dine with me, and after dinner, sitting at our wine, having settled our question, other conversation came on, in which a collision of opinion arose between Mr. Adams and Colonel Hamilton, on the merits of the British constitution, Mr. Adams giving it as his opinion, that, if some of its defects and abuses were corrected, it would be the most perfect constitution of government ever devised by man. Hamilton, on the contrary, asserted, that with its existing vices, it was the most perfect model of government that could be formed; and that the correction of its vices would render it an impracticable government. And this you may be assured was the real line of difference between the

political principles of these two gentlemen. Another incident took place on the same occasion, which will further delineate Mr. Hamilton's political principles. The room being hung around with a collection of the portraits of remarkable men, among them were those of Bacon, Newton and Locke, Hamilton asked me who they were. I told him they were my trinity of the three greatest men the world had ever produced, naming them. He paused for some time: "the greatest man," said he, "that ever lived, was Julius Cæsar." Mr. Adams was honest as a politician, as well as a man; Hamilton honest as a man, but, as a politician, believing in the necessity of either force or corruption to govern men.

You remember the machinery which the federalists played off, about that time, to beat down the friends to the real principles of our Constitution, to silence by terror every expression in their favor, to bring us into war with France and alliance with England, and finally to homologize our Constitution with that of England. Mr. Adams, you know, was overwhelmed with feverish addresses, dictated by the fear, and often by the pen, of the *bloody buoy,* and was seduced by them into some open indications of his new principles of government, and in fact, was so elated as to mix with his kindness a little superciliousness towards me. Even Mrs. Adams, with all her good sense and prudence, was sensibly flushed. And you recollect the short suspension of our intercourse, and the circumstance which gave rise to it, which you were so good as to bring to an early explanation, and have set to rights, to the cordial satisfaction of us all. The nation at length passed condemnation on the political principles of the federalists, by refusing to continue Mr. Adams in the Presidency. On the day on which we learned in Philadelphia the vote of the city of New York, which it was well known would decide the vote of the State, and that, again, the vote of the Union, I called on Mr. Adams on some official business. He was very sensibly affected, and accosted me with these words: "Well, I understand that you are to beat me in this contest, and I will only say that I will be as faithful a subject as any you will have." "Mr. Adams," said I, "this is no personal contest between you and me. Two systems of principles on the subject of government divide our fellow citizens into two parties. With one of these you concur, and I with the other. As we have been longer on the public stage than most of those now living, our names happen to be more generally known. One of these parties, therefore, has put your name at its head, the other mine. Were we both to die to-day, to-morrow two other names would be in the place of ours, without any change in the motion of the machinery. Its motion is from its principle, not from you or myself." "I believe you are right," said he, "that we are but passive instruments, and should not suffer this matter to affect our personal dispositions." But he did not long retain this just view of the subject. I have always believed that the thousand calumnies which the federalists, in bitterness of heart, and mortification at their ejection, daily invented against me, were carried to

him by their busy intriguers, and made some impression. When the election between Burr and myself was kept in suspense by the federalists, and they were meditating to place the President of the Senate at the head of the government, I called on Mr. Adams with a view to have this desperate measure prevented by his negative. He grew warm in an instant, and said with a vehemence he had not used towards me before, "Sir, the event of the election is within your own power. You have only to say you will do justice to the public creditors, maintain the navy, and not disturb those holding offices, and the government will instantly be put into your hands. We know it is the wish of the people it should be so." "Mr. Adams," said I, "I know not what part of my conduct, in either public or private life, can have authorized a doubt of my fidelity to the public engagements. I say, however, I will not come into the government by capitulation. I will not enter on it, but in perfect freedom to follow the dictates of my own judgment." I had before given the same answer to the same intimation from Gouverneur Morris. "Then," said he, "things must take their course." I turned the conversation to something else, and soon took my leave. It was the first time in our lives we had ever parted with anything like dissatisfaction. And then followed those scenes of midnight appointment, which have been condemned by all men. The last day of his political power, the last hours, and even beyond the midnight, were employed in filling all offices, and especially permanent ones, with the bitterest federalists, and providing for me the alternative, either to execute the government by my enemies, whose study it would be to thwart and defeat all my measures, or to incur the odium of such numerous removals from office, as might bear me down. A little time and reflection effaced in my mind this temporary dissatisfaction with Mr. Adams, and restored me to that just estimate of his virtues and passions, which a long acquaintance had enabled me to fix. And my first wish became that of making his retirement easy by any means in my power; for it was understood he was not rich. I suggested to some republican members of the delegation from his State, the giving him, either directly or indirectly, an office, the most lucrative in that State, and then offered to be resigned, if they thought he would not deem it affrontive. They were of opinion he would take great offence at the offer; and moreover, that the body of republicans would consider such a step in the outset as auguring very ill of the course I meant to pursue. I dropped the idea, therefore, but did not cease to wish for some opportunity of renewing our friendly understanding. . . .

I have the same good opinion of Mr. Adams which I ever had. I know him to be an honest man, an able one with his pen, and he was a powerful advocate on the floor of Congress. He has been alienated from me, by belief in the lying suggestions contrived for electioneering purposes, that I perhaps mixed in the activity and intrigues of the occasion. My most intimate friends can testify that I was perfectly passive. They

would sometimes, indeed, tell me what was going on; but no man ever heard me take part in such conversations; and none ever misrepresented Mr. Adams in my presence, without my asserting his just character. With very confidential persons I have doubtless disapproved of the principles and practices of his administration. This was unavoidable. But never with those with whom it could do him any injury. Decency would have required this conduct from me, if disposition had not; and I am satisfied Mr. Adams' conduct was equally honorable towards me. But I think it part of his character to suspect foul play in those of whom he is jealous, and not easily to relinquish his suspicions. . . .

48. *"Fellow Laborers in the Same Cause"*

To John Adams

Monticello, January 21, 1812

. . . A letter from you calls up recollections very dear to my mind. It carries me back to the times when, beset with difficulties and dangers, we were fellow laborers in the same cause, struggling for what is most valuable to man, his right of self-government. Laboring always at the same oar, with some wave ever ahead, threatening to overwhelm us, and yet passing harmless under our bark, we knew not how we rode through the storm with heart and hand, and made a happy port. Still we did not expect to be without rubs and difficulties; and we have had them. First, the detention of the western posts, then the coalition of Pilnitz, outlawing our commerce with France, and the British enforcement of the outlawry. In your day, French depredations; in mine, English, and the Berlin and Milan decrees; now, the English orders of council, and the piracies they authorize. When these shall be over, it will be the impressment of our seamen or something else; and so we have gone on, and so we shall go on, puzzled and prospering beyond example in the history of man. And I do believe we shall continue to grow, to multiply and prosper until we exhibit an association, powerful, wise and happy, beyond what has yet been seen by men. As for France and England, with all their preëminence in science, the one is a den of robbers, and the other of pirates. And if science produces no better fruits than tyranny, murder, rapine and destitution of national morality, I would rather wish our country to be ignorant, honest and estimable, as our neighboring savages are. But whither is senile garrulity leading me? Into politics, of which I have taken final leave. I think little of them and say less. I have given up newspapers in exchange for Tacitus and Thucydides, for Newton and Euclid,

and I find myself much the happier. Sometimes, indeed, I look back to former occurrences, in remembrance of our old friends and fellow laborers, who have fallen before us. Of the signers of the Declaration of Independence, I see now living not more than half a dozen on your side of the Potomac, and on this side, myself alone. You and I have been wonderfully spared, and myself with remarkable health, and a considerable activity of body and mind. I am on horseback three or four hours of every day; visit three or four times a year a possession I have ninety miles distant, performing the winter journey on horseback. I walk little, however, a single mile being too much for me, and I live in the midst of my grandchildren, one of whom has lately promoted me to be a great-grandfather. I have heard with pleasure that you also retain good health, and a greater power of exercise in walking than I do. But I would rather have heard this from yourself, and that, writing a letter like mine, full of egotisms, and of details of your health, your habits, occupations and enjoyments, I should have the pleasure of knowing that in the race of life, you do not keep, in its physical decline, the same distance ahead of me which you have done in political honors and achievements. No circumstances have lessened the interest I feel in these particulars respecting yourself; none have suspended for one moment my sincere esteem for you, and I now salute you with unchanged affection and respect.

49. *On Parties*

To John Adams

Monticello, June 27, 1813

. . . Men have differed in opinion, and been divided into parties by these opinions, from the first origin of societies, and in all governments where they have been permitted freely to think and to speak. The same political parties which now agitate the United States, have existed through all time. Whether the power of the people or that of the aristoi should prevail, were questions which kept the States of Greece and Rome in eternal convulsions, as they now schismatize every people whose minds and mouths are not shut up by the gag of a despot. And in fact, the terms of whig and tory belong to natural as well as to civil history. They denote the temper and constitution of mind of different individuals. To come to our own country, and to the times when you and I became first acquainted, we well remember the violent parties which agitated the old Congress, and their bitter contests. There you and I were together, and the Jays, and the Dickinsons, and other anti-independents, were arrayed

against us. They cherished the monarchy of England, and we the rights of our countrymen. When our present government was in the mew, passing from Confederation to Union, how bitter was the schism between the Feds and Antis! Here you and I were together again. For although, for a moment, separated by the Atlantic from the scene of action, I favored the opinion that nine States should confirm the constitution, in order to secure it, and the others hold off until certain amendments, deemed favorable to freedom, should be made. I rallied in the first instant to the wiser proposition of Massachusetts, that all should confirm, and then all instruct their delegates to urge those amendments. The amendments were made, and all were reconciled to the government. But as soon as it was put into motion, the line of division was again drawn. We broke into two parties, each wishing to give the government a different direction; the one to strengthen the most popular branch, the other the more permanent branches, and to extend their permanence. Here you and I separated for the first time, and as we had been longer than most others on the public theatre, and our names therefore were more familiar to our countrymen, the party which considered you as thinking with them, placed your name at their head; the other, for the same reason, selected mine. But neither decency nor inclination permitted us to become the advocates of ourselves, or to take part personally in the violent contests which followed. We suffered ourselves, as you so well expressed it, to be passive subjects of public discussion. . . .

50. *Inventions and Property*

To Isaac McPherson

Monticello, August 13, 1813

. . . . It has been pretended by some, (and in England especially,) that inventors have a natural and exclusive right to their inventions, and not merely for their own lives, but inheritable to their heirs. But while it is a moot question whether the origin of any kind of property is derived from nature at all, it would be singular to admit a natural and even an hereditary right to inventors. It is agreed by those who have seriously considered the subject, that no individual has, of natural right, a separate property in an acre of land, for instance. By an universal law, indeed, whatever, whether fixed or movable, belongs to all men equally and in common, is the property for the moment of him who occupies it, but when he relinquishes the occupation, the property goes with it. Stable ownership is the gift of social law, and is given late in the progress of society. It would

be curious then, if an idea, the fugitive fermentation of an individual brain, could, of natural right, be claimed in exclusive and stable property. If nature has made any one thing less susceptible than all others of exclusive property, it is the action of the thinking power called an idea, which an individual may exclusively possess as long as he keeps it to himself; but the moment it is divulged, it forces itself into the possession of every one, and the receiver cannot dispossess himself of it. Its peculiar character, too, is that no one possesses the less, because every other possesses the whole of it. He who receives an idea from me, receives instruction himself without lessening mine; as he who lights his taper at mine, receives light without darkening me. That ideas should freely spread from one to another over the globe, for the moral and mutual instruction of man, and improvement of his condition, seems to have been peculiarly and benevolently designed by nature, when she made them, like fire, expansible over all space, without lessening their density in any point, and like the air in which we breathe, move, and have our physical being, incapable of confinement or exclusive appropriation. Inventions then cannot, in nature, be a subject of property. Society may give an exclusive right to the profits arising from them, as an encouragement to men to pursue ideas which may produce utility, but this may or may not be done, according to the will and convenience of the society, without claim or complaint from anybody. . . . .

51. *Natural Aristocracy*

To John Adams

Monticello, October 28, 1813

. . . I agree with you that there is a natural aristocracy among men. The grounds of this are virtue and talents. Formerly, bodily powers gave place among the aristoi. But since the invention of gunpowder has armed the weak as well as the strong with missile death, bodily strength, like beauty, good humor, politeness and other accomplishments, has become but an auxiliary ground of distinction. There is also an artificial aristocracy, founded on wealth and birth, without either virtue or talents; for with these it would belong to the first class. The natural aristocracy I consider as the most precious gift of nature, for the instruction, the trusts, and government of society. And indeed, it would have been inconsistent in creation to have formed man for the social state, and not to have provided virtue and wisdom enough to manage the concerns of the society. May we not even say, that that form of government is the best, which provides

the most effectually for a pure selection of these natural aristoi into the offices of government? The artificial aristocracy is a mischievous ingredient in government, and provision should be made to prevent its ascendency. . . . .

With respect to aristocracy, we should further consider, that before the establishment of the American States, nothing was known to history but the man of the old world, crowded within limits either small or overcharged, and steeped in the vices which that situation generates. A government adapted to such men would be one thing; but a very different one, that for the man of these States. Here every one may have land to labor for himself, if he chooses; or, preferring the exercise of any other industry, may exact for it such compensation as not only to afford a comfortable subsistence, but wherewith to provide for a cessation from labor in old age. Every one, by his property, or by his satisfactory situation, is interested in the support of law and order. And such men may safely and advantageously reserve to themselves a wholesome control over their public affairs, and a degree of freedom, which, in the hands of the *canaille* of the cities of Europe, would be instantly perverted to the demolition and destruction of everything public and private. The history of the last twenty-five years of France, and of the last forty years in America, nay of its last two hundred years, proves the truth of both parts of this observation.

But even in Europe a change has sensibly taken place in the mind of man. Science had liberated the ideas of those who read and reflect, and the American example had kindled feelings of right in the people. An insurrection has consequently begun, of science, talents, and courage, against rank and birth, which have fallen into contempt. It has failed in its first effort, because the mobs of the cities, the instrument used for its accomplishment, debased by ignorance, poverty, and vice, could not be restrained to rational action. But the world will recover from the panic of this first catastrophe. Science is progressive, and talents and enterprise on the alert. Resort may be had to the people of the country, a more governable power from their principles and subordination; and rank, and birth, and tinsel-aristocracy will finally shrink into insignificance, even there. This, however, we have no right to meddle with. It suffices for us, if the moral and physical condition of our own citizens qualifies them to select the able and good for the direction of their government, with a recurrence of elections at such short periods as will enable them to displace an unfaithful servant, before the mischief he meditates may be irremediable. . . .

52. *The Foundation of Morality*

To Thomas Law, Esq.

Poplar Forest, June 13, 1814

Dear Sir,—The copy of your Second Thoughts on Instinctive Impulses, with the letter accompanying it, was received just as I was setting out on a journey to this place, two or three days distant from Monticello. I brought it with me and read it with great satisfaction, and with the more as it contained exactly my own creed on the foundation of morality in man. It is really curious that on a question so fundamental, such a variety of opinions should have prevailed among men, and those, too, of the most exemplary virtue and first order of understanding. It shows how necessary was the care of the Creator in making the moral principle so much a part of our constitution as that no errors of reasoning or of speculation might lead us astray from its observation in practice. Of all the theories on this question, the most whimsical seems to have been that of Wollaston, who considers *truth* as the foundation of morality. The thief who steals your guinea does wrong only inasmuch as he acts a lie in using your guinea as if it were his own. Truth is certainly a branch of morality, and a very important one to society. But presented as its foundation, it is as if a tree taken up by the roots, had its stem reversed in the air, and one of its branches planted in the ground. Some have made the love of God the foundation of morality. This, too, is but a branch of our moral duties, which are generally divided into duties to God and duties to man. If we did a good act merely from the love of God and a belief that it is pleasing to Him, whence arises the morality of the Atheist? It is idle to say, as some do, that no such being exists. We have the same evidence of the fact as of most of those we act on, to wit: their own affirmations, and their reasonings in support of them. I have observed, indeed, generally, that while in Protestant countries the defections from the Platonic Christianity of the priests is to Deism, in Catholic countries they are to Atheism. Diderot, D'Alembert, D'Holbach, Condorcet, are known to have been among the most virtuous of men. Their virtue, then, must have had some other foundation than the love of God.

The το καλον of others is founded in a different faculty, that of taste, which is not even a branch of morality. We have indeed an innate sense of what we call beautiful, but that is exercised chiefly on subjects addressed to the fancy, whether through the eye in visible forms, as landscape, animal figure, dress, drapery, architecture, the composition of colors, etc., or to the imagination directly, as imagery, style, or measure in prose or poetry, or whatever else constitutes the domain of criticism or taste, a faculty entirely distinct from the moral one. Self-interest, or rather

self-love, or *egoism,* has been more plausibly substituted as the basis of morality. But I consider our relations with others as constituting the boundaries of morality. With ourselves we stand on the ground of identity, not of relation, which last, requiring two subjects, excludes self-love confined to a single one. To ourselves, in strict language, we can owe no duties, obligation requiring also two parties. Self-love, therefore, is no part of morality. Indeed it is exactly its counterpart. It is the sole antagonist of virtue, leading us constantly by our propensities to self-gratification in violation of our moral duties to others. Accordingly, it is against this enemy that are erected the batteries of moralists and religionists, as the only obstacle to the practice of morality. Take from man his selfish propensities, and he can have nothing to seduce him from the practice of virtue. Or subdue those propensities by education, instruction or restraint, and virtue remains without a competitor. Egoism, in a broader sense, has been thus presented as the source of moral action. It has been said that we feed the hungry, clothe the naked, bind up the wounds of the man beaten by thieves, pour oil and wine into them, set him on our own beast and bring him to the inn, because we receive ourselves pleasure from these acts. So Helvetius, one of the best men on earth, and the most ingenious advocate of this principle, after defining "interest" to mean not merely that which is pecuniary, but whatever may procure us pleasure or withdraw us from pain, [*de l'esprit,* 2, 1,] says, [ib. 2, 2,] "the humane man is he to whom the sight of misfortune is insupportable, and who to rescue himself from this spectacle, is forced to succor the unfortunate object." This indeed is true. But it is one step short of the ultimate question. These good acts give us pleasure, but how happens it that they give us pleasure? Because nature hath implanted in our breasts a love of others, a sense of duty to them, a moral instinct, in short, which prompts us irresistibly to feel and to succor their distresses, and protests against the language of Helvetius, [ib. 2, 5,] "what other motive than self-interest could determine a man to generous actions? It is as impossible for him to love what is good for the sake of good, as to love evil for the sake of evil." The Creator would indeed have been a bungling artist, had he intended man for a social animal, without planting in him social dispositions. It is true they are not planted in every man, because there is no rule without exceptions; but it is false reasoning which converts exceptions into the general rule. Some men are born without the organs of sight, or of hearing, or without hands. Yet it would be wrong to say that man is born without these faculties, and sight, hearing, and hands may with truth enter into the general definition of man.

The want or imperfection of the moral sense in some men, like the want or imperfection of the senses of sight and hearing in others, is no proof that it is a general characteristic of the species. When it is wanting, we endeavor to supply the defect by education, by appeals to reason and calculation, by presenting to the being so unhappily conformed, other motives to do good and to eschew evil, such as the love, or the hatred, or

rejection of those among whom he lives, and whose society is necessary to his happiness and even existence; demonstrations by sound calculation that honesty promotes interest in the long run; the rewards and penalties established by the laws; and ultimately the prospects of a future state of retribution for the evil as well as the good done while here. These are the correctives which are supplied by education, and which exercise the functions of the moralist, the preacher, and legislator; and they lead into a course of correct action all those whose disparity is not too profound to be eradicated. Some have argued against the existence of a moral sense, by saying that if nature had given us such a sense, impelling us to virtuous actions, and warning us against those which are vicious, then nature would also have designated, by some particular ear-marks, the two sets of actions which are, in themselves, the one virtuous and the other vicious. Whereas, we find, in fact, that the same actions are deemed virtuous in one country and vicious in another. The answer is, that nature has constituted *utility* to man, the standard and test of virtue. Men living in different countries, under different circumstances, different habits and regimens, may have different utilities; the same act, therefore, may be useful, and consequently virtuous in one country which is injurious and vicious in another differently circumstanced. I sincerely, then, believe with you in the general existence of a moral instinct. I think it the brightest gem with which the human character is studded, and the want of it as more degrading than the most hideous of the bodily deformities. I am happy in reviewing the roll of associates in this principle which you present in your second letter, some of which I had not before met with. To these might be added Lord Kaims, one of the ablest of our advocates, who goes so far as to say, in his Principles of Natural Religion, that a man owes no duty to which he is not urged by some impulsive feeling. This is correct, if referred to the standard of general feeling in the given case, and not to the feeling of a single individual. Perhaps I may misquote him, it being fifty years since I read his book.

The leisure and solitude of my situation here has led me to the indiscretion of taxing you with a long letter on a subject whereon nothing new can be offered you. I will indulge myself no farther than to repeat the assurances of my continued esteem and respect.

53. *"The Hour of Emancipation is Advancing"*

To Edward Coles

Monticello, August 25th, '14

Dear Sir,—Your favour of July 31, was duly received, and was read with peculiar pleasure. The sentiments breathed through the whole do honor to both the head and heart of the writer. Mine on the subject of slavery

of negroes have long since been in possession of the public, and time has only served to give them stronger root. The love of justice and the love of country plead equally the cause of these people, and it is a moral reproach to us that they should have pleaded it so long in vain, and should have produced not a single effort, nay I fear not much serious willingness to relieve them & ourselves from our present condition of moral & political reprobation. From those of the former generation who were in the fulness of age when I came into public life, which was while our controversy with England was on paper only, I soon saw that nothing was to be hoped. Nursed and educated in the daily habit of seeing the degraded condition, both bodily and mental, of those unfortunate beings, not reflecting that that degradation was very much the work of themselves & their fathers, few minds have yet doubted but that they were as legitimate subjects of property as their horses and cattle. The quiet and monotonous course of colonial life has been disturbed by no alarm, and little reflection on the value of liberty. And when alarm was taken at an enterprize on their own, it was not easy to carry them to the whole length of the principles which they invoked for themselves. In the first or second session of the Legislature after I became a member, I drew to this subject the attention of Col. Bland, one of the oldest, ablest, & most respected members, and he undertook to move for certain moderate extensions of the protection of the laws to these people. I seconded his motion, and, as a younger member, was more spared in the debate; but he was denounced as an enemy of his country, & was treated with the grossest indecorum. From an early stage of our revolution other & more distant duties were assigned to me, so that from that time till my return from Europe in 1789, and I may say till I returned to reside at home in 1809, I had little opportunity of knowing the progress of public sentiment here on this subject. I had always hoped that the younger generation receiving their early impressions after the flame of liberty had been kindled in every breast, & had become as it were the vital spirit of every American, that the generous temperament of youth, analogous to the motion of their blood, and above the suggestions of avarice, would have sympathized with oppression wherever found, and proved their love of liberty beyond their own share of it. But my intercourse with them, since my return has not been sufficient to ascertain that they had made towards this point the progress I had hoped. Your solitary but welcome voice is the first which has brought this sound to my ear; and I have considered the general silence which prevails on this subject as indicating an apathy unfavorable to every hope. Yet the hour of emancipation is advancing, in the march of time. . . .

54. *Jefferson's Library*

To Samuel H. Smith, Esq.

Monticello, September 21, 1814

Dear Sir,—I learn from the newspapers that the vandalism of our enemy has triumphed at Washington over science as well as the arts, by the destruction of the public library with the noble edifice in which it was deposited. Of this transaction, as of that of Copenhagen, the world will entertain but one sentiment. They will see a nation suddenly withdrawn from a great war, full armed and full handed, taking advantage of another whom they had recently forced into it, unarmed, and unprepared, to indulge themselves in acts of barbarism which do not belong to a civilized age. When Van Ghent destroyed their shipping at Chatham, and De Ruyter rode triumphantly up the Thames, he might in like manner, by the acknowledgment of their own historians, have forced all their ships up to London bridge, and there have burnt them, the Tower, and city, had these examples been then set. London, when thus menaced, was near a thousand years old; Washington is but in its teens.

I presume it will be among the early objects of Congress to re-commence their collection. This will be difficult while the war continues, and intercourse with Europe is attended with so much risk. You know my collection, its condition and extent. I have been fifty years making it, and have spared no pains, opportunity or expense, to make it what it is. While residing in Paris, I devoted every afternoon I was disengaged, for a summer or two, in examining all the principal bookstores, turning over every book with my own hand, and putting by everything which related to America, and indeed whatever was rare and valuable in every science. Besides this, I had standing orders during the whole time I was in Europe, on its principal book-marts, particularly Amsterdam, Frankfort, Madrid and London, for such works relating to America as could not be found in Paris. So that in that department particularly, such a collection was made as probably can never again be effected, because it is hardly probable that the same opportunities, the same time, industry, perseverance and expense, with some knowledge of the bibliography of the subject, would again happen to be in concurrence. During the same period, and after my return to America, I was led to procure, also, whatever related to the duties of those in the high concerns of the nation. So that the collection, which I suppose is of between nine and ten thousand volumes, while it includes what is chiefly valuable in science and literature generally, extends more particularly to whatever belongs to the American statesman. In the diplomatic and parliamentary branches, it is particu-

larly full. It is long since I have been sensible it ought not to continue private property, and had provided that at my death, Congress should have the refusal of it at their own price. But the loss they have now incurred, makes the present the proper moment for their accommodation, without regard to the small remnant of time and the barren use of my enjoying it. I ask of your friendship, therefore, to make for me the tender of it to the library committee of Congress, not knowing myself of whom the committee consists. I enclose you the catalogue, which will enable them to judge of its contents. . . .

55. On "Republic"

To John Taylor

Monticello, May 28, 1816

. . . It must be acknowledged, that the term *republic* is of very vague application in every language. Witness the self-styled republics of Holland, Switzerland, Genoa, Venice, Poland. Were I to assign to this term a precise and definite idea, I would say, purely and simply, it means a government by its citizens in mass, acting directly and personally, according to rules established by the majority; and that every other government is more or less republican, in proportion as it has in its composition more or less of this ingredient of the direct action of the citizens. Such a government is evidently restrained to very narrow limits of space and population. I doubt if it would be practicable beyond the extent of a New England township. The first shade from this pure element, which, like that of pure vital air, cannot sustain life of itself, would be where the powers of the government, being divided, should be exercised each by representatives chosen either *pro hac vice,* or for such short terms as should render secure the duty of expressing the will of their constituents. This I should consider as the nearest approach to a pure republic, which is practicable on a large scale of country or population. And we have examples of it in some of our State Constitutions, which, if not poisoned by priest-craft, would prove its excellence over all mixtures with other elements; and, with only equal doses of poison, would still be the best. Other shades of republicanism may be found in other forms of government, where the executive, judiciary and legislative functions, and the different branches of the latter, are chosen by the people more or less directly, for longer terms of years, or for life, or made hereditary; or where there are mixtures of authorities, some dependent on, and others independent of the people. The further the departure from direct and constant control by the citizens, the less has the government of the ingredient of repub-

licanism; evidently none where the authorities are hereditary, as in France, Venice, etc., or self-chosen, as in Holland; and little, where for life, in proportion as the life continues in being after the act of election.

The purest republican feature in the government of our own State, is the House of Representatives. The Senate is equally so the first year, less the second, and so on. The Executive still less, because not chosen by the people directly. The Judiciary seriously anti-republican, because for life; and the national arm wielded, as you observe, by military leaders, irresponsible but to themselves. . . .

If, then, the control of the people over the organs of their government be the measure of its republicanism, and I confess I know no other measure, it must be agreed that our governments have much less of republicanism than ought to have been expected; in other words, that the people have less regular control over their agents, than their rights and their interests require. And this I ascribe, not to any want of republican dispositions in those who formed these Constitutions, but to a submission of true principle to European authorities, to speculators on government, whose fears of the people have been inspired by the populace of their own great cities, and were unjustly entertained against the independent, the happy, and therefore orderly citizens of the United States. Much I apprehend that the golden moment is past for reforming these heresies. The functionaries of public power rarely strengthen in their dispositions to abridge it, and an unorganized call for timely amendment is not likely to prevail against an organized opposition to it. We are always told that things are going on well; why change them? *"Chista bene, non si muove,"* said the Italian, "let him who stands well, stand still." This is true; and I verily believe they would go on well with us under an absolute monarch, while our present character remains, of order, industry and love of peace, and restrained, as he would be, by the proper spirit of the people. But it is while it remains such, we should provide against the consequences of its deterioration. And let us rest in the hope that it will yet be done, and spare ourselves the pain of evils which may never happen.

On this view of the import of the term *republic,* instead of saying, as has been said, "that it may mean anything or nothing," we may say with truth and meaning, that governments are more or less republican, as they have more or less of the element of popular election and control in their composition; and believing, as I do, that the mass of the citizens is the safest depository of their own rights and especially, that the evils flowing from the duperies of the people, are less injurious than those from the egoism of their agents, I am a friend to that composition of government which has in it the most of this ingredient. And I sincerely believe, with you, that banking establishments are more dangerous than standing armies; and that the principle of spending money to be paid by posterity, under the name of funding, is but swindling futurity on a large scale.

I salute you with constant friendship and respect.

56. *"I Too Am An Epicurian"*

To William Short

Monticello, October 31, 1819

. . . As you say of yourself, I too am an Epicurian. I consider the genuine (not the imputed) doctrines of Epicurus as containing everything rational in moral philosophy which Greece and Rome have left us. Epictetus indeed, has given us what was good of the Stoics; all beyond, of their dogmas, being hypocrisy and grimace. Their great crime was in their calumnies of Epicurus and misrepresentations of his doctrines; in which we lament to see the candid character of Cicero engaging as an accomplice. Diffuse, vapid, rhetorical, but enchanting. His prototype Plato, eloquent as himself, dealing out mysticisms incomprehensible to the human mind, has been deified by certain sects usurping the name of Christians; because, in his foggy conceptions, they found a basis of impenetrable darkness whereon to rear fabrications as delirious, of their own invention. These they fathered blasphemously on Him whom they claimed as their Founder, but who would disclaim them with the indignation which their caricatures of His religion so justly excite. Of Socrates we have nothing genuine but in the Memorabilia of Xenophon; for Plato makes him one of his Collocutors merely to cover his own whimsies under the mantle of his name; a liberty of which we are told Socrates himself complained. Seneca is indeed a fine moralist, disfiguring his work at times with some Stoicisms, and affecting too much of antithesis and point, yet giving us on the whole a great deal of sound and practical morality. But the greatest of all the reformers of the depraved religion of His own country, was Jesus of Nazareth. Abstracting what is really His from the rubbish in which it is buried, easily distinguished by its lustre from the dross of His biographers, and as separable from that as the diamond from the dunghill, we have the outlines of a system of the most sublime morality which has ever fallen from the lips of man; outlines which it is lamentable He did not live to fill up. Epictetus and Epicurus give laws for governing ourselves, Jesus a supplement of the duties and charities we owe to others. The establishment of the innocent and genuine character of this benevolent Moralist, and the rescuing it from the imputation of imposture, which has resulted from artificial systems,[1] invented by ultra-Christian sects, unauthorized by a single word

[1] *E.g.* The immaculate conception of Jesus, His deification, the creation of the world by Him, His miraculous powers, His resurrection and visible ascension, His corporeal presence in the Eucharist, the Trinity, original sin, atonement, regeneration, election, orders of Hierarchy, etc. [Jefferson's note.]

ever uttered by Him, is a most desirable object, and one to which Priestley has successfully devoted his labors and learning. It would in time, it is to be hoped, effect a quiet euthanasia of the heresies of bigotry and fanaticism which have so long triumphed over human reason, and so generally and deeply afflicted mankind; but this work is to be begun by winnowing the grain from the chaff of the historians of His life. I have sometimes thought of translating Epictetus (for he has never been tolerably translated into English) by adding the genuine doctrines of Epicurus from the Syntagma of Gassendi, and an abstract from the Evangelists of whatever has the stamp of the eloquence and fine imagination of Jesus. The last I attempted too hastily some twelve or fifteen years ago. It was the work of two or three nights only, at Washington, after getting through the evening task of reading the letters and papers of the day. But with one foot in the grave, these are now idle projects for me. My business is to beguile the wearisomeness of declining life, as I endeavor to do, by the delights of classical reading and of mathematical truths, and by the consolations of a sound philosophy, equally indifferent to hope and fear. . . .

57. *The Missouri Question*

To John Holmes

Monticello, April 22, 1820

I thank you, dear Sir, for the copy you have been so kind as to send me of the letter to your constituents on the Missouri question. It is a perfect justification to them. I had for a long time ceased to read newspapers, or pay any attention to public affairs, confident they were in good hands, and content to be a passenger in our bark to the shore from which I am not distant. But this momentous question, like a fire-bell in the night, awakened and filled me with terror. I considered it at once as the knell of the Union. It is hushed, indeed, for the moment. But this is a reprieve only, not a final sentence. A geographical line, coinciding with a marked principle, moral and political, once conceived and held up to the angry passions of men, will never be obliterated; and every new irritation will mark it deeper and deeper. I can say, with conscious truth, that there is not a man on earth who would sacrifice more than I would to relieve us from this heavy reproach, in any *practicable* way. The cession of that kind of property, for so it is misnamed, is a bagatelle which would not cost me a second thought, if, in that way, a general emancipation and *expatriation* could be effected; and, gradually, and with due sacrifices, I think it might be. But as it is, we have the wolf by the ears, and we can

neither hold him, nor safely let him go. Justice is in one scale, and self-preservation in the other. Of one thing I am certain, that as the passage of slaves from one State to another, would not make a slave of a single human being who would not be so without it, so their diffusion over a greater surface would make them individually happier, and proportionally facilitate the accomplishment of their emancipation, by dividing the burden on a greater number of coadjutors. An abstinence too, from this act of power, would remove the jealousy excited by the undertaking of Congress to regulate the condition of the different descriptions of men composing a State. This certainly is the exclusive right of every State, which nothing in the Constitution has taken from them and given to the General Government. Could Congress, for example, say, that the non-freemen of Connecticut shall be freemen, or that they shall not emigrate into any other State?

I regret that I am now to die in the belief, that the useless sacrifice of themselves by the generation of 1776, to acquire self-government and happiness to their country, is to be thrown away by the unwise and unworthy passions of their sons, and that my only consolation is to be, that I live not to weep over it. If they would but dispassionately weigh the blessings they will throw away, against an abstract principle more likely to be effected by union than by scission, they would pause before they would perpetrate this act of suicide on themselves, and of treason against the hopes of the world. To yourself, as the faithful advocate of the Union, I tender the offering of my high esteem and respect.

58. *A Doctrine for Independence*

To the President of the United States (James Monroe)

Monticello, October 24, 1823

Dear Sir,—The question presented by the letters you have sent me, is the most momentous which has ever been offered to my contemplation since that of Independence. That made us a nation, this sets our compass and points the course which we are to steer through the ocean of time opening on us. And never could we embark on it under circumstances more auspicious. Our first and fundamental maxim should be, never to entangle ourselves in the broils of Europe. Our second, never to suffer Europe to intermeddle with cis-Atlantic affairs. America, North and South, has a set of interests distinct from those of Europe, and peculiarly her own. She should therefore have a system of her own, separate and apart from that of Europe. While the last is laboring to become the domi-

cile of despotism, our endeavors should surely be, to make our hemisphere that of freedom. One nation, most of all, could disturb us in this pursuit; she now offers to lead, aid, and accompany us in it. By acceding to her proposition, we detach her from the bands, bring her mighty weight into the scale of free government, and emancipate a continent at one stroke, which might otherwise linger long in doubt and difficulty. Great Britain is the nation which can do us the most harm of any one, or all on earth; and with her on our side we need not fear the whole world. With her then, we should most sedulously cherish a cordial friendship; and nothing would tend more to knit our affections than to be fighting once more, side by side, in the same cause. Not that I would purchase even her amity at the price of taking part in her wars. But the war in which the present proposition might engage us, should that be its consequence, is not her war, but ours. Its object is to introduce and establish the American system, of keeping out of our land all foreign powers, of never permitting those of Europe to intermeddle with the affairs of our nations. It is to maintain our own principle, not to depart from it. And if, to facilitate this, we can effect a division in the body of the European powers, and draw over to our side its most powerful member, surely we should do it. But I am clearly of Mr. Canning's opinion, that it will prevent instead of provoking war. With Great Britain withdrawn from their scale and shifted into that of our two continents, all Europe combined would not undertake such a war. For how would they propose to get at either enemy without superior fleets? Nor is the occasion to be slighted which this proposition offers, of declaring our protest against the atrocious violations of the rights of nations, by the interference of any one in the internal affairs of another, so flagitiously begun by Bonaparte, and now continued by the equally lawless Alliance, calling itself Holy.

But we have first to ask ourselves a question. Do we wish to acquire to our own confederacy any one or more of the Spanish provinces? I candidly confess, that I have ever looked on Cuba as the most interesting addition which could ever be made to our system of States. The control which, with Florida Point, this island would give us over the Gulf of Mexico, and the countries and isthmus bordering on it, as well as all those whose waters flow into it, would fill up the measure of our political well-being. Yet, as I am sensible that this can never be obtained, even with her own consent, but by war; and its independence, which is our second interest, (and especially its independence of England,) can be secured without it, I have no hesitation in abandoning my first wish to future chances, and accepting its independence, with peace and the friendship of England, rather than its association, at the expense of war and her enmity.

I could honestly, therefore, join in the declaration proposed, that we aim not at the acquisition of any of those possessions, that we will not

stand in the way of any amicable arrangement between them and the Mother country; but that we will oppose, with all our means, the forcible interposition of any other power, as auxiliary, stipendiary, or under any other form or pretext, and most especially, their transfer to any power by conquest, cession, or acquisition in any other way. . . .

59. *"The Parties . . . Are Those of Nature"*

To the Marquis de Lafayette

Monticello, November 4, 1823

. . . For in truth, the parties of Whig and Tory, are those of nature. They exist in all countries, whether called by these names, or by those of Aristocrats and Democrats, Coté Droite and Coté Gauche, Ultras and Radicals, Serviles and Liberals. The sickly, weakly, timid man, fears the people, and is a Tory by nature. The healthy, strong and bold, cherishes them, and is formed a Whig by nature. On the eclipse of federalism with us, although not its extinction, its leaders got up the Missouri question, under the false front of lessening the measure of slavery, but with the real view of producing a geographical division of parties, which might insure them the next President. The people of the North went blindfold into the snare, followed their leaders for awhile with a zeal truly moral and laudable, until they became sensible that they were injuring instead of aiding the real interests of the slaves, that they had been used merely as tools for electioneering purposes; and that trick of hypocrisy then fell as quickly as it had been got up. To that is now succeeding a distinction, which, like that of Republican and Federal, or Whig and Tory, being equally intermixed through every State, threatens none of those geographical schisms which go immediately to a separation. The line of division now, is the preservation of State rights, as reserved in the Constitution, or by strained constructions of that instrument, to merge all into a consolidated government. The Tories are for strengthening the Executive and General Government; the Whigs cherish the representative branch, and the rights reserved by the States, as the bulwark against consolidation, which must immediately generate monarchy. And although this division excites, as yet, no warmth, yet it exists, is well understood, and will be a principle of voting at the ensuing election, with the reflecting men of both parties. . . .

60. *"Take Care of Me When Dead"*

To James Madison

Monticello, February 17, 1826

. . . In the selection of our Law Professor, we must be rigorously attentive to his political principles. You will recollect that before the Revolution, Coke Littleton was the universal elementary book of law students, and a sounder Whig never wrote, nor of profounder learning in the orthodox doctrines of the British constitution, or in what were called English liberties. You remember also that our lawyers were then all Whigs. But when his black-letter text, and uncouth but cunning learning got out of fashion, and the honeyed Mansfieldism of Blackstone became the students' hornbook, from that moment, that profession (the nursery of our Congress) began to slide into toryism, and nearly all the young brood of lawyers now are of that hue. They suppose themselves, indeed, to be Whigs, because they no longer know what Whigism or republicanism means. It is in our seminary that that vestal flame is to be kept alive; it is thence it is to spread anew over our own and the sister States. If we are true and vigilant in our trust, within a dozen or twenty years a majority of our own legislature will be from one school, and many disciples will have carried its doctrines home with them to their several States, and will have leavened thus the whole mass. . . .

You will have seen in the newspapers some proceedings in the legislature, which have cost me much mortification. My own debts had become considerable, but not beyond the effect of some lopping of property, which would have been little felt, when our friend Nicholas gave me the *coup de grace*. Ever since that I have been paying twelve hundred dollars a year interest on his debt, which, with my own, was absorbing so much of my annual income, as that the maintenance of my family was making deep and rapid inroads on my capital, and had already done it. Still, sales at a fair price would leave me completely provided. Had crops and prices for several years been such as to maintain a steady competition of substantial bidders at market, all would have been safe. But the long succession of years of stunted crops, of reduced prices, the general prostration of the farming business, under levies for the support of manufacturers, etc., with the calamitous fluctuations of value in our paper medium, have kept agriculture in a state of abject depression. . . .

Reflecting on these things, the practice occurred to me, of selling, on fair valuation, and by way of lottery, often resorted to before the Revolution to effect large sales, and still in constant usage in every State for individual as well as corporation purposes. If it is permitted in my case,

my lands here alone, with the mills, etc., will pay everything, and leave me Monticello and a farm free. If refused, I must sell everything here, perhaps considerably in Bedford, move thither with my family, where I have not even a log hut to put my head into, and whether ground for burial, will depend on the depredations which, under the form of sales, shall have been committed on my property. The question then with me was *ultrum horum?* But why afflict you with these details? Indeed, I cannot tell, unless pains are lessened by communication with a friend. The friendship which has subsisted between us, now half a century, and the harmony of our political principles and pursuits, have been sources of constant happiness to me through that long period. And if I remove beyond the reach of attentions to the University, or beyond the bourne of life itself, as I soon must, it is a comfort to leave that institution under your care, and an assurance that it will not be wanting. It has also been a great solace to me, to believe that you are engaged in vindicating to posterity the course we have pursued for preserving to them, in all their purity, the blessings of self-government, which we had assisted too in acquiring for them. If ever the earth has beheld a system of administration conducted with a single and steadfast eye to the general interest and happiness of those committed to it, one which, protected by truth, can never know reproach, it is that to which our lives have been devoted. To myself you have been a pillar of support through life. Take care of me when dead, and be assured that I shall leave with you my last affections.

61. *The Rights of Man*

To Roger C. Weightman

Monticello, June 24, 1826

Respected Sir,—The kind invitation I receive from you, on the part of the citizens of the city of Washington, to be present with them at their celebration on the fiftieth anniversary of American Independence, as one of the surviving signers of an instrument pregnant with our own, and the fate of the world, is most flattering to myself, and heightened by the honorable accompaniment proposed for the comfort of such a journey. It adds sensibly to the sufferings of sickness, to be deprived by it of a personal participation in the rejoicings of that day. But acquiescence is a duty, under circumstances not placed among those we are permitted to control. I should, indeed, with peculiar delight, have met and exchanged there congratulations personally with the small band, the remnant of that host of worthies, who joined with us on that day, in the bold and doubtful

election we were to make for our country, between submission or the sword; and to have enjoyed with them the consolatory fact, that our fellow citizens, after half a century of experience and prosperity, continue to approve the choice we made. May it be to the world, what I believe it will be (to some parts sooner, to others later, but finally to all), the signal of arousing men to burst the chains under which monkish ignorance and superstition had persuaded them to bind themselves, and to assume the blessings and security of self-government. That form which we have substituted, restores the free right to the unbounded exercise of reason and freedom of opinion. All eyes are opened, or opening, to the rights of man. The general spread of the light of science has already laid open to every view the palpable truth, that the mass of mankind has not been born with saddles on their backs, nor a favored few booted and spurred, ready to ride them legitimately, by the grace of God. These are grounds of hope for others. For ourselves, let the annual return of this day forever refresh our recollections of these rights, and an undiminished devotion to them. . . .

Other Writings

62. *A Summary View of the Rights of British America (1774)*

RESOLVED, that it be an instruction to the said deputies, when assembled in General Congress, with the deputies from the other states of British America, to propose to the said Congress, that an humble and dutiful address be presented to his Majesty, begging leave to lay before him, as Chief Magistrate of the British empire, the united complaints of his Majesty's subjects in America; complaints which are excited by many unwarrantable encroachments and usurpations, attempted to be made by the legislature of one part of the empire, upon the rights which God, and the laws, have given equally and independentally to all. . . .

To remind him that our ancestors, before their emigration to America, were the free inhabitants of the British dominions in Europe, and possessed a right, which nature has given to all men, of departing from the country in which chance, not choice, has placed them, of going in quest of new habitations, and of there establishing new societies, under such laws and regulations as, to them, shall seem most likely to promote public happiness. That their Saxon ancestors had, under this universal law, in like manner, left their native wilds and woods in the North of Europe, had possessed themselves of the Island of Britain, then less charged with inhabitants, and had established there that system of laws which has so long been the glory and protection of that country. Nor was ever any claim of superiority or dependence asserted over them, by that mother country from which they had migrated: and were such a claim made, it is believed his Majesty's subjects in Great Britain have too firm a feeling of the rights derived to them from their ancestors, to bow down the sovereignty of their state before such visionary pretensions. And it is thought that no circumstance has occurred to distinguish, materially, the British from the Saxon emigration. America was conquered, and her settlements made and firmly established, at the expense of individuals, and not of the British public. Their own blood was spilt in acquiring lands for their settlement, their own fortunes expended in making that settlement effectual. For themselves they fought, for themselves they conquered, and for themselves alone they have right to hold. . . .

That the exercise of a free trade with all parts of the world, possessed by the American colonists, as of natural right, and which no law of their own had taken away or abridged, was next the object of unjust encroachment. . . . History has informed us, that bodies of men as well as of individuals, are susceptible of the spirit of tyranny. A view of these acts of Parliament for regulation, as it has been affectedly called, of the American trade, if all other evidences were removed out of the case, would undeniably evince the truth of this observation. . . . But, that we do not point out to his Majesty the injustice of these acts, with intent to rest on that principle the cause of their nullity; but to show that experience confirms the propriety of those political principles, which exempt us from the jurisdiction of the British Parliament. The true ground on which we declare these acts void, is, that the British Parliament has no right to exercise authority over us. . . .

Not only the principles of common sense, but the common feelings of human nature must be surrendered up, before his Majesty's subjects here, can be persuaded to believe, that they hold their political existence at the will of a British Parliament. Shall these governments be dissolved, their property annihilated, and their people reduced to a state of nature, at the imperious breath of a body of men whom they never saw, in whom they never confided, and over whom they have no powers of punishment or removal, let their crimes against the American public be ever so great? Can any one reason be assigned, why one hundred and sixty thousand electors in the island of Great Britain, should give law to four millions in the States of America, every individual of whom is equal to every individual of them in virtue, in understanding, and in bodily strength? Were this to be admitted, instead of being a free people, as we have hitherto supposed, and mean to continue ourselves, we should suddenly be found the slaves, not of one, but of one hundred and sixty thousand tyrants; distinguished, too, from all others, by this singular circumstance, that they are removed from the reach of fear, the only restraining motive which may hold the hand of a tyrant. . . .

That we next proceed to consider the conduct of his Majesty, as holding the Executive powers of the laws of these States, and mark out his deviations from the line of duty. By the Constitution of Great Britain, as well as of the several American States, his Majesty possesses the power of refusing to pass into a law, any bill which has already passed the other two branches of the legislature. . . . Yet this will not excuse the wanton exercise of this power, which we have seen his Majesty practice on the laws of the American legislature. For the most trifling reasons, and sometimes for no conceivable reason at all, his Majesty has rejected laws of the most salutary tendency. The abolition of domestic slavery is the great object of desire in those colonies, where it was, unhappily, introduced in their infant state. But previous to the enfranchisement of the slaves we have, it is necessary to exclude all further importations from

Africa. Yet our repeated attempts to effect this, by prohibitions, and by imposing duties which might amount to a prohibition, having been hitherto defeated by his Majesty's negative: thus preferring the immediate advantages of a few British corsairs, to the lasting interests of the American States, and to the rights of human nature, deeply wounded by this infamous practice. Nay, the single interposition of an interested individual against a law was scarcely ever known to fail of success, though, in the opposite scale, were placed the interests of a whole country. That this is so shameful an abuse of a power, trusted with his Majesty for other purposes, as if, not reformed, would call for some legal restrictions. . . .

That these are our grievances, which we have thus laid before his Majesty, with that freedom of language and sentiment which becomes a free people claiming their rights as derived from the laws of nature, and not as the gift of their Chief Magistrate. Let those flatter, who fear: it is not an American art. To give praise where it is not due might be well from the venal, but would ill beseem those who are asserting the rights of human nature. They know, and will, therefore, say, that Kings are the servants, not the proprietors of the people. . . . This, Sire, is the advice of your great American council, on the observance of which may perhaps depend your felicity and future fame, and the preservation of that harmony which alone can continue, both to Great Britain and America, the reciprocal advantages of their connection. It is neither our wish nor our interest to separate from her. We are willing, on our part, to sacrifice everything which reason can ask, to the restoration of that tranquillity for which all must wish. On their part, let them be ready to establish union on a generous plan. Let them name their terms, but let them be just. Accept of every commercial preference it is in our power to give, for such things as we can raise for their use, or they make for ours. But let them not think to exclude us from going to other markets to dispose of those commodities which they cannot use, nor to supply those wants which they cannot supply. Still less, let it be proposed, that our properties, within our own territories, shall be taxed or regulated by any power on earth, but our own. The God who gave us life, gave us liberty at the same time: the hand of force may destroy, but cannot disjoin them. This, Sire, is our last, our determined resolution. And that you will be pleased to interpose, with that efficacy which your earnest endeavors may insure, to procure redress of these our great grievances, to quiet the minds of your subjects in British America against any apprehensions of future encroachment, to establish fraternal love and harmony through the whole empire, and that that may continue to the latest ages of time, is the fervent prayer of all British America.

63. *Jefferson's Draft Constitution for Virginia (Third Draft, before 13 June 1776)*

A bill for new-modeling the form of Government and for establishing the fundamental principles thereof in future.

Whereas George Guelf, king of Great Britain and Ireland and Elector of Hanover, heretofore entrusted with the exercise of the kingly office in this government, has endeavored to pervert the same into a detestable and insupportable tyranny by putting his negative on laws the most wholesome and necessary for ye public good. . . .

[Here follows a list of a long "train of abuses," like those in *A Summary View* and later in the *Declaration*.]

Be it therefore enacted by the authority of the people that the said George Guelf be, and he hereby is, deposed from the kingly office within this government and absolutely divested of all its rights, powers and prerogatives . . . . and that the said office shall henceforth cease and never more either in name or substance be re-established within this colony.

And be it further enacted by the authority aforesaid that the following fundamental laws and principles of government shall henceforth be established:

The Legislative, Executive, and Judiciary offices shall be kept forever separate and no person exercising the one shall be capable of appointment to the others, or to either of them.

1. Legislative

Legislation shall be exercised by two separate houses, to wit, a house of Representatives and a house of Senators, which shall be called the General Assembly of Virginia.

The said house of Representatives shall be composed of persons chosen by the people annually. . . .

All male persons of full age and sane mind having a freehold estate in one fourth of an acre of land in any town or in 25 acres of land in the country, and all persons resident in the colony who shall have paid scot and lot to government the last two years shall have right to give their vote in the election of their respective representatives. . . .

II. Executive

The executive powers shall be exercised in manner following:

One person to be called the Administrator shall be annually appointed by the house of Representatives on the second day of their first session, who after having acted one year shall be incapable of being again appointed to that office until he shall have been out of the same three years. . . .

The Administrator shall possess the powers formerly held by the king, save only that:

he shall be bound by acts of legislature though not expressly named;

he shall have no negative on the bills of the legislature. . . .

III. Judiciary

[There follows a description of the judicial system, providing among other things for trial by jury and establishing a system of county courts.]

IV. Rights Private and Public

Every person of full age neither owning nor having owned fifty acres of land shall be entitled to an appropriation of fifty acres or to so much as shall make up what he owns or has owned fifty acres in full and absolute dominion, and no other person shall be capable of taking an appropriation. . . .

No person hereafter coming into this country shall be held within the same in slavery under any pretext whatever. . . .

All persons shall have full and free liberty of religious opinion; nor shall any be compelled to frequent or maintain any religious institution. . . .

Printing presses shall be free, except so far as by commission of private injury cause may be given of private action. . . .

None of these fundamental laws and principles of government shall be repealed or altered, but by the personal consent of the people on summons to meet in their respective counties on one and the same day by an act of Legislature to be passed for every special occasion; and if in such county meetings the people of two thirds of the counties shall give their suffrage for any particular alteration or repeal referred to them by the said act, the same shall be accordingly repealed or altered, and such repeal or alteration shall take its place among these fundamentals and stand on the same footing with them, in lieu of the article repealed or altered. . . .

64. *A Declaration By The Representatives Of The United States Of America, in* General *Congress Assembled**

When, in the course of human events, it becomes necessary for one people to dissolve the political bands which have connected them with another, and to assume among the powers of the earth the separate and equal station to which the laws of nature and of nature's God entitle them, a decent respect to the opinions of mankind requires that they should declare the causes which impel them to the separation.

We hold these truths to be self evident: that all men are created equal; that they are endowed by their Creator with CERTAIN [*inherent and*] inalienable rights; that among these are life, liberty, and the pursuit of happiness; that to secure these rights, governments are instituted among men, deriving their just powers from the consent of the governed; that whenever any form of government becomes destructive of these ends, it is the right of the people to alter or to abolish it, and to institute new government, laying its foundation on such principles, and organizing its powers in such form, as to them shall seem most likely to effect their safety and happiness. Prudence, indeed, will dictate that governments long established should not be changed for light and transient causes; and accordingly all experience hath shown that mankind are more disposed to suffer while evils are sufferable, than to right themselves by abolishing the forms to which they are accustomed. But when a long train of abuses and usurpations, [*begun at a distinguished period and*] pursuing invariably the same object, evinces a design to reduce them under absolute despotism, it is their right, it is their duty to throw off such government, and to provide new guards for their future security. Such has been the patient sufferance of these colonies; and such is now the necessity which constrains them to ALTER [*expunge*] their former systems of government. The history of the present king of Great Britain is a history of REPEATED [*unremitting*] injuries and usurpations, ALL HAVING [*among which appears no solitary fact to contradict the uniform tenor of the rest, but all have*] in direct object the establishment of an absolute tyranny over these states. To prove this, let facts be submitted to a candid world [*for the truth of which we pledge a faith yet unsullied by falsehood*].

* Jefferson wrote, in introducing this full version of the Declaration in his Autobiography, that "As the sentiments of men are known not only by what they receive, but what they reject also, I will state the form of the Declaration as originally reported. The parts struck out by Congress shall be distinguished by a black line drawn under them; and those inserted by them shall be placed in the margin, or in a concurrent column." In the text printed above, the editor has substituted the device of italicizing and enclosing in brackets the parts struck out by Congress.

He has refused his assent to laws the most wholesome and necessary for the public good.

He has forbidden his governors to pass laws of immediate and pressing importance, unless suspended in their operation till his assent should be obtained; and, when so suspended, he has utterly neglected to attend to them.

He has refused to pass other laws for the accommodation of large districts of people, unless those people would relinquish the right of representation in the legislature, a right inestimable to them, and formidable to tyrants only.

He has called together legislative bodies at places unusual, uncomfortable, and distant from the depository of their public records, for the sole purpose of fatiguing them into compliance with his measures.

He has dissolved representative houses repeatedly [and continually] for opposing with manly firmness his invasions on the rights of the people.

He has refused for a long time after such dissolutions to cause others to be elected, whereby the legislative powers, incapable of annihilation, have returned to the people at large for their exercise, the state remaining, in the meantime, exposed to all the dangers of invasion from without and convulsions within.

He has endeavored to prevent the population of these states; for that purpose obstructing the laws for naturalization of foreigners, refusing to pass others to encourage their migrations hither, and raising the conditions of new appropriations of lands.

He has OBSTRUCTED [suffered] the administration of justice BY [totally to cease in some of these states] refusing his assent to laws for establishing judiciary powers.

He has made [our] judges dependent on his will alone for the tenure of their offices, and the amount and payment of their salaries.

He has erected a multitude of new offices, [by a self-assumed power] and sent hither swarms of new officers to harass our people and eat out their substance.

He has kept among us in times of peace standing armies [and ships of war] without the consent of our legislatures.

He has affected to render the military independent of, and superior to, the civil power.

He has combined with others to subject us to a jurisdiction foreign to our constitutions and unacknowledged by our laws, giving his assent to their acts of pretended legislation for quartering large bodies of armed troops among us; for protecting them by a mock trial from punishment for any murders which they should commit on the inhabitants of these states; for cutting off our trade with all parts of the world; for imposing taxes on us without our consent; for depriving us IN MANY CASES of the benefits of trial by jury; for transporting us beyond seas

to be tried for pretended offences; for abolishing the free system of English laws in a neighboring province, establishing therein an arbitrary government, and enlarging its boundaries, so as to render it at once an example and fit instrument for introducing the same absolute rule into these COLONIES [states]; for taking away our charters, abolishing our most valuable laws, and altering fundamentally the forms of our governments; for suspending our own legislatures, and declaring themselves invested with power to legislate for us in all cases whatsoever.

He has abdicated government here BY DECLARING US OUT OF HIS PROTECTION, AND WAGING WAR AGAINST US [*withdrawing his governors, and declaring us out of his allegiance and protection*].

He has plundered our seas, ravaged our coasts, burnt our towns, and destroyed the lives of our people.

He is at this time transporting large armies of foreign mercenaries to complete the works of death, desolation and tyranny already begun with circumstances of cruelty and perfidy SCARCELY PARALLELED IN THE MOST BARBAROUS AGES, AND TOTALLY unworthy the head of a civilized nation.

He has constrained our fellow citizens taken captive on the high seas, to bear arms against their country, to become the executioners of their friends and brethren, or to fall themselves by their hands.

He has EXCITED DOMESTIC INSURRECTION AMONG US, AND HAS endeavored to bring on the inhabitants of our frontiers, the merciless Indian savages, whose known rule of warfare is an undistinguished destruction of all ages, sexes and conditions [*of existence*].

[*He has incited treasonable insurrections of our fellow citizens, with the allurements of forfeiture and confiscation of our property.*

He has waged cruel war against human nature itself, violating its most sacred rights of life and liberty in the persons of a distant people who never offended him, captivating and carrying them into slavery in another hemisphere, or to incur miserable death in their transportation hither. This piratical warfare, the opprobrium of INFIDEL powers, is the warfare of the CHRISTIAN king of Great Britain. Determined to keep open a market where MEN should be bought and sold, he has prostituted his negative for suppressing every legislative attempt to prohibit or to restrain this execrable commerce. And that this assemblage of horrors might want no fact of distinguished die, he is now exciting those very people to rise in arms among us, and to purchase that liberty of which he has deprived them, by murdering the people on whom he also obtruded them: thus paying off former crimes committed against the LIBERTIES of one people, with crimes which he urges them to commit against the LIVES of another.]

In every stage of these oppressions we have petitioned for redress in the most humble terms: our repeated petitions have been answered only by repeated injuries.

A prince whose character is thus marked by every act which may define a tyrant is unfit to be the ruler of a FREE people [*who mean to be free. Future ages will scarcely believe that the hardiness of one man adventured, within the short compass of twelve years only, to lay a foundation so broad and so undisguised for tyranny over a people fostered and fixed in principles of freedom.*]

Nor have we been wanting in attentions to our British brethren. We have warned them from time to time of attempts by their legislature to extend AN UNWARRANTABLE [*a*] jurisdiction over US [*these our states*]. We have reminded them of the circumstances of our emigration and settlement here, [*no one of which could warrant so strange a pretension: that these were effected at the expense of our own blood and treasure, unassisted by the wealth or the strength of Great Britain: that in constituting indeed our several forms of government, we had adopted one common king, thereby laying a foundation for perpetual league and amity with them: but that submission to their parliament was no part of our constitution, nor ever in idea, if history may be credited: and,*] we HAVE appealed to their native justice and magnanimity AND WE HAVE CONJURED THEM BY [*as well as to*] the ties of our common kindred to disavow these usurpations which WOULD INEVITABLY [*were likely to*] interrupt our connection and correspondence. They too have been deaf to the voice of justice and of consanguinity. WE MUST THEREFORE [*and when occasions have been given them, by the regular course of their laws, of removing from their councils the disturbers of our harmony, they have, by their free election, re-established them in power. At this very time too, they are permitting their chief magistrate to send over not only soldiers of our common blood, but Scotch and foreign mercenaries to invade and destroy us. These facts have given the last stab to agonizing affection, and manly spirit bids us to renounce forever these unfeeling brethren. We must endeavor to forget our former love for them, and hold them as we hold the rest of mankind, enemies in war, in peace friends. We might have a free and a great people together; but a communication of grandeur and of freedom, it seems, is below their dignity. Be it so, since they will have it. The road to happiness and to glory is open to us, too. We will tread it apart from them, and*] acquiesce in the necessity which denounces our [*eternal*] separation AND HOLD THEM AS WE HOLD THE REST OF MANKIND, ENEMIES IN WAR, IN PEACE FRIENDS!

[1] We therefore the representatives of the United States of America in General Congress assembled, do in the name, and by the authority of the good people of these [*states reject and renounce all allegiance and subjection to the*]

We, therefore, the representatives of the United States of America in General Congress assembled, appealing to the supreme judge of the world for the rectitude of our intentions, do in the name, and by the authority of the good people

kings of Great Britain and all others who may hereafter claim by, through or under them; we utterly dissolve all political connection which may heretofore have subsisted between us and the people or parliament of Great Britain: and finally we do assert and declare these colonies to be free and independent states,] and that as free and independent states, they have full power to levy war, conclude peace, contract alliances, establish commerce, and to do all other acts and things which independent states may of right do.

And for the support of this declaration, we mutually pledge to each other our lives, our fortunes, and our sacred honor.

of these colonies, solemnly publish and declare, that these united colonies are, and of right ought to be free and independent states; that they are absolved from all allegiance to the British crown, and that all political connection between them and the state of Great Britain is, and ought to be, totally dissolved; and that as free and independent states, they have full power to levy war, conclude peace, contract alliances, establish commerce, and to do all other acts and things which independent states may of right do.

And for the support of this declaration, with a firm reliance on the protection of divine providence, we mutually pledge to each other our lives, our fortunes, and our sacred honor.

The Declaration thus signed on the 4th, on paper, was engrossed on parchment, and signed again on the 2d of August.

65. *An Act for Establishing Religious Freedom (1779), Passed in the Assembly of Virginia in the Beginning of the Year 1786.*

Well aware that Almighty God hath created the mind free; that all attempts to influence it by temporal punishments or burdens, or by civil incapacitations, tend only to beget habits of hypocrisy and meanness, and are a departure from the plan of the Holy Author of our religion, who being Lord both of body and mind, yet chose not to propagate it by coercions on either, as was in his Almighty power to do; that the impious presumption of legislators and rulers, civil as well as ecclesiastical, who, being themselves but fallible and uninspired men have assumed dominion over the faith of others, setting up their own opinions and modes of thinking as the only true and infallible, and as such en-

---

[1] In this closing section, where additions and deletions have been lengthy, the editor follows Jefferson's device of printing his version in the left column, and the final adopted text in the right column.

deavoring to impose them on others, hath established and maintained false religions over the greatest part of the world, and through all time; that to compel a man to furnish contributions of money for the propagation of opinions which he disbelieves, is sinful and tyrannical; that even the forcing him to support this or that teacher of his own religious persuasion, is depriving him of the comfortable liberty of giving his contributions to the particular pastor whose morals he would make his pattern, and whose powers he feels most persuasive to righteousness, and is withdrawing from the ministry those temporal rewards, which proceeding from an approbation of their personal conduct, are an additional incitement to earnest and unremitting labors for the instruction of mankind; that our civil rights have no dependence on our religious opinions, more than our opinions in physics or geometry; that, therefore, the proscribing any citizen as unworthy the public confidence by laying upon him an incapacity of being called to the offices of trust and emolument, unless he profess or renounce this or that religious opinion, is depriving him injuriously of those privileges and advantages to which in common with his fellow citizens he has a natural right; that it tends also to corrupt the principles of that very religion it is meant to encourage, by bribing, with a monopoly of worldly honors and emoluments, those who will externally profess and conform to it; that though indeed these are criminal who do not withstand such temptation, yet neither are those innocent who lay the bait in their way; that to suffer the civil magistrate to intrude his powers into the field of opinion and to restrain the profession or propagation of principles, on the supposition of their ill tendency, is a dangerous fallacy, which at once destroys all religious liberty, because he being of course judge of that tendency, will make his opinions the rule of judgment, and approve or condemn the sentiments of others only as they shall square with or differ from his own; that it is time enough for the rightful purposes of civil government, for its offices to interfere when principles break out into overt acts against peace and good order; and finally, that truth is great and will prevail if left to herself, that she is the proper and sufficient antagonist to error, and has nothing to fear from the conflict, unless by human interposition disarmed of her natural weapons, free argument and debate, errors ceasing to be dangerous when it is permitted freely to contradict them.

Be it therefore enacted by the General Assembly, That no man shall be compelled to frequent or support any religious worship, place or ministry whatsoever, nor shall be enforced, restrained, molested, or burthened in his body or goods, nor shall otherwise suffer on account of his religious opinions or belief; but that all men shall be free to profess, and by argument to maintain, their opinions in matters of religion, and that the same shall in nowise diminish, enlarge, or affect their civil capacities.

And though we well know this Assembly, elected by the people for the ordinary purposes of legislation only, have no power to restrain the acts

of succeeding assemblies, constituted with the powers equal to our own, and that therefore to declare this act irrevocable, would be of no effect in law, yet we are free to declare, and do declare, that the rights hereby asserted are of the natural rights of mankind, and that if any act shall be hereafter passed to repeal the present or to narrow its operation, such act will be an infringement of natural right.

66. *Notes on the State of Virginia*

The Following Notes were written in Virginia in the year 1781, and somewhat corrected and enlarged in the winter of 1782, in answer to Queries proposed to the Author, by a Foreigner of Distinction, then residing among us . . . The subjects are all treated imperfectly; some scarcely touched on. To apologize for this by developing the circumstances of the time and place of their composition, would be to open wounds which have already bled enough. To these circumstances some of their imperfections may with truth be ascribed; the great mass to the want of information and want of talents in the writer. He had a few copies printed, which he gave among his friends: and a translation of them has been lately published in France, but with such alterations as the laws of the press in that country rendered necessary. They are now offered to the public in their original form and language.

Feb. 27, 1787.

Query XIII: The Constitution of the State?[1]

. . . This constitution was formed when we were new and unexperienced in the science of government. It was the first too which was formed in the whole United States. No wonder then that time and trial have discovered very capital defects in it.

1. The majority of the men in the state, who pay and fight for its support, are unrepresented in the legislature, the roll of freeholders intitled to vote, not including generally the half of those on the roll of the militia, or of the tax gatherers.

2. Among those who share the representation, the shares are very unequal. Thus the county of Warwick, with only one hundred fighting men, has an equal representation with the county of Loudon, which has 1746. So that every man in Warwick has as much influence in the government as 17 men in Loudon. . . .

3. The senate is, by its constitution, too homogeneous with the house of delegates. Being chosen by the same electors, at the same time, and out

of the same subjects, the choice falls of course on men of the same description. The purpose of establishing different houses of legislation is to introduce the influence of different interests or different principles. Thus in Great-Britain it is said their constitution relies on the house of commons for honesty, and the lords for wisdom; which would be a rational reliance if honesty were to be bought with money, and if wisdom were hereditary. In some of the American states the delegates and senators are so chosen, as that the first represent the persons, and the second the property of the state. But with us, wealth and wisdom have equal chance for admission into both houses. We do not therefore derive from the separation of our legislature into two houses, those benefits which a proper complication of principles is capable of producing, and those which alone can compensate the evils which may be produced by their dissensions.

4. All the powers of government, legislative, executive, and judiciary, result to the legislative body. The concentrating these in the same hands is precisely the definition of despotic government. It will be no alleviation that these powers will be exercised by a plurality of hands, and not by a single one. 173 despots would surely be as oppressive as one. Let those who doubt it turn their eyes on the republic of Venice. As little will it avail us that they are chosen by ourselves. An *elective despotism* was not the government we fought for; but one which should not only be founded on free principles, but in which the powers of government should be so divided and balanced among several bodies of magistracy, as that no one could transcend their legal limits, without being effectually checked and restrained by the others. For this reason that convention, which passed the ordinance of government, laid its foundation on this basis, that the legislative, executive and judiciary department should be separate and distinct, so that no person should exercise the powers of more than one of them at the same time. But no barrier was provided between these several powers. The judiciary and executive members were left dependant on the legislative, for their subsistence in office, and some of them for their continuance in it. If therefore the legislature assumes executive and judiciary powers, no opposition is likely to be made; nor, if made, can it be effectual; because in that case they may put their proceedings into the form of an act of assembly, which will render them obligatory on the other branches. They have accordingly, in many instances, decided rights which should have been left to judiciary controversy: and the direction of the executive, during the whole time of their session, is becoming habitual and familiar. And this is done with no ill intention. The views of the present members are perfectly upright. When they are led out of their regular province, it is by art in others, and inadvertence in themselves. And this will probably be the case for some time to come. But it will not be a very long time. Mankind soon learn to make interested uses of every right and power which they possess, or

may assume. The public money and public liberty, intended to have been deposited with three branches of magistracy, but found inadvertently to be in the hands of one only, will soon be discovered to be sources of wealth and dominion to those who hold them; distinguished too by this tempting circumstance, that they are the instrument, as well as the object of acquisition. With money we will get men, said Cæsar, and with men we will get money. Nor should our assembly be deluded by the integrity of their own purposes, and conclude that these unlimited powers will never be abused, because themselves are not disposed to abuse them. They should look forward to a time, and that not a distant one, when corruption in this, as in the country from which we derive our origin, will have seized the heads of government, and be spread by them through the body of the people; when they will purchase the voices of the people, and make them pay the price. Human nature is the same on every side of the Atlantic, and will be alike influenced by the same causes. The time to guard against corruption and tyranny, is before they shall have gotten hold on us. It is better to keep the wolf out of the fold, than to trust to drawing his teeth and talons afer he shall have entered. To render these considerations the more cogent, we must observe in addition,

5. That the ordinary legislature may alter the constitution itself. . . . Though this opinion seems founded on the first elements of common sense, yet is the contrary maintained by some persons. 1. Because say they, the conventions were vested with every power necessary to make effectual opposition to Great Britain. But to complete this argument, they must go on, and say further, that effectual opposition could not be made to Great Britain, without establishing a form of government perpetual and unalterable by the legislature; which is not true. . . . 2. They urge, that if the convention had meant that this instrument should be alterable, as their other ordinances were, they would have called it an ordinance: but they have called it a *constitution*, which *by force of the term* means "an act above the power of the ordinary legislature." I answer, that *constitutio, constitutum, statutum, lex,* are convertible terms. . . . Thus in the statute 25. Hen. 8. c. 19. sec. I. *"Constitutions and ordinances"* are used as synonimous. . . . No inference then of a different meaning can be drawn from the adoption of this title: on the contrary, we might conclude, that, by their affixing to it a term synonimous with ordinance, or statute, they meant it to be an ordinance or statute. But of what consequence is their meaning, where their power is denied? If they meant to do more than they had power to do, did this give them power? It is not the name, but the authority which renders an act obligatory. . . .

To get rid of the magic supposed to be in the word *constitution*, let us translate it into its definition as given by those who think it above the power of the law; and let us suppose the convention instead of say-

ing, "We, the ordinary legislature, establish a *constitution*," had said, "We, the ordinary legislature, establish an act *above the power of the ordinary legislature*." Does not this expose the absurdity of the attempt? 3. But, say they, the people have acquiesced, and this has given it an authority superior to the laws. It is true, that the people did not rebel against it: and was that a time for the people to rise in rebellion? Should a prudent acquiescence, at a critical time, be construed into a confirmation of every illegal thing done during that period? Besides, why should they rebel? At an annual election, they had chosen delegates for the year, to exercise the ordinary powers of legislation, and to manage the great contest in which they were engaged. These delegates thought the contest would be best managed by an organized government. They therefore, among others, passed an ordinance of government. They did not presume to call it perpetual and unalterable. They well knew they had no power to make it so; that our choice of them had been for no such purpose, and at a time when we could have no such purpose in contemplation. Had an unalterable form of government been meditated, perhaps we should have chosen a different set of people. There was no cause then for the people to rise in rebellion. But to what dangerous lengths will this argument lead? . . .

On every unauthoritative exercise of power by the legislature, must the people rise in rebellion, or their silence be construed into a surrender of that power to them? If so, how many rebellions should we have had already? One certainly for every session of assembly. The other states in the Union have been of opinion, that to render a form of government unalterable by ordinary acts of assembly, the people must delegate persons with special powers. They have accordingly chosen special conventions to form and fix their governments. The individuals then who maintain the contrary opinion in this country, should have the modesty to suppose it possible that they may be wrong and the rest of America right. But if there be only a possibility of their being wrong, if only a plausible doubt remains of the validity of the ordinance of government, is it not better to remove that doubt, by placing it on a bottom which none will dispute? If they be right, we shall only have the unnecessary trouble of meeting once in convention. If they be wrong, they expose us to the hazard of having no fundamental rights at all. True it is, this is no time for deliberating on forms of government. While an enemy is within our bowels, the first object is to expel him. But when this shall be done, when peace shall be established, and leisure given us for intrenching within good forms, the rights for which we have bled, let no man be found indolent enough to decline a little more trouble for placing them beyond the reach of question. . . .

Our situation is indeed perilous, and I hope my countrymen will be sensible of it, and will apply, at a proper season, the proper remedy; which is a convention to fix the constitution, to amend its defects, to

bind up the several branches of government by certain laws, which when they transgress their acts shall become nullities; to render unnecessary an appeal to the people, or in other words a rebellion, on every infraction of their rights, on the peril that their acquiescence shall be construed into an intention to surrender those rights.

Query XIV: A Description of the Laws? On the Law "To Diffuse Knowledge More Generally Through the Mass of the People²

. . . The general objects of this law are to provide an education adapted to the years, to the capacity, and the condition of every one, and directed to their freedom and happiness. Specific details were not proper for the law. These must be the business of the visitors entrusted with its execution. The first stage of this education being the schools of the hundreds, wherein the great mass of the people will receive their instruction, the principal foundations of future order will be laid here. Instead therefore of putting the Bible and Testament into the hands of the children, at an age when their judgments are not sufficiently matured for religious enquiries, their memories may here be stored with the most useful facts from Grecian, Roman, European and American history. The first elements of morality too may be instilled into their minds; such as, when further developed as their judgments advance in strength, may teach them how to work out their own greatest happiness, by shewing them that it does not depend on the condition of life in which chance has placed them, but is always the result of a good conscience, good health, occupation, and freedom in all just pursuits.—Those whom either the wealth of their parents or the adoption of the state shall destine to higher degrees of learning, will go on to the grammar schools, which constitute the next stage, there to be instructed in the languages. The learning Greek and Latin, I am told, is going into disuse in Europe. I know not what their manners and occupations may call for: but it would be very ill-judged in us to follow their example in this instance. There is a certain period of life, say from eight to fifteen or sixteen years of age, when the mind, like the body, is not yet firm enough for laborious and close operations. If applied to such, it falls an early victim to premature exertion; exhibiting indeed at first, in these young and tender subjects, the flattering appearance of their being men while they are yet children, but ending in reducing them to be children when they should be men. The memory is then most susceptible and tenacious of impressions; and the learning of languages being chiefly a work of memory, it seems precisely fitted to the powers of this period, which is long enough too for acquiring the most useful languages antient and modern. I do not pretend that language is science. It is only an instrument for the attainment of sci-

ence. But that time is not lost which is employed in providing tools for future operation: more especially as in this case the books put into the hands of the youth for this purpose may be such as will at the same time impress their minds with useful facts and good principles. If this period be suffered to pass in idleness, the mind becomes lethargic and impotent, as would the body it inhabits if unexercised during the same time. The sympathy between body and mind during their rise, progress and decline, is too strict and obvious to endanger our being misled while we reason from the one to the other.—As soon as they are of sufficient age, it is supposed they will be sent on from the grammar schools to the university, which constitutes our third and last stage, there to study those sciences which may be adapted to their views.—By that part of our plan which prescribes the selection of the youths of genius from among the classes of the poor, we hope to avail the state of those talents which nature has sown as liberally among the poor as the rich, but which perish without use, if not sought for and cultivated. But of all the views of this law none is more important, none more legitimate, than that of rendering the people the safe, as they are the ultimate, guardians of their own liberty. For this purpose the reading in the first stage, where *they* will receive their whole education, is proposed, as has been said, to be chiefly historical. History by apprising them of the past will enable them to judge of the future; it will avail them of the experience of other times and other nations; it will qualify them as judges of the actions and designs of men; it will enable them to know ambition under every disguise it may assume; and knowing it, to defeat its views. In every government on earth is some trace of human weakness, some germ of corruption and degeneracy, which cunning will discover, and wickedness insensibly open, cultivate, and improve. Every government degenerates when trusted to the rulers of the people alone. The people themselves therefore are its only safe depositories. And to render even them safe their minds must be improved to a certain degree. This indeed is not all that is necessary, though it be essentially necessary. An amendment of our constitution must here come in aid of the public education. The influence over government must be shared among all the people. If every individual which composes their mass participates of the ultimate authority, the government will be safe; because the corrupting the whole mass will exceed any private resources of wealth: and public ones cannot be provided but by levies on the people. In this case every man would have to pay his own price. The government of Great-Britain has been corrupted, because but one man in ten has a right to vote for members of parliament. The sellers of the government therefore get nine-tenths of their price clear. It has been thought that corruption is restrained by confining the right of suffrage to a few of the wealthier of the people: but it would be more effectually restrained by an extension of that right to such numbers as would bid defiance to the means of corruption.

Lastly, it is proposed, by a bill in this revisal, to begin a public library and gallery, by laying out a certain sum annually in books, paintings, and statues.

Query XVII: The Different Religions Received into That State?[3]

. . . The error seems not sufficiently eradicated, that the operations of the mind, as well as the acts of the body, are subject to the coercion of the laws. But our rulers can have authority over such natural rights only as we have submitted to them The rights of conscience we never submitted, we could not submit. We are answerable for them to our God. The legitimate powers of government extend to such acts only as are injurious to others. But it does me no injury for my neighbour to say there are twenty gods, or no god. It neither picks my pocket nor breaks my leg. If it be said, his testimony in a court of justice cannot be relied on, reject it then, and be the stigma on him. Constraint may make him worse by making him a hypocrite, but it will never make him a truer man. It may fix him obstinately in his errors, but will not cure them. Reason and free enquiry are the only effectual agents against error. Give a loose to them, they will support the true religion, by bringing every false one to their tribunal, to the test of their investigation. They are the natural enemies of error, and of error only. Had not the Roman government permitted free enquiry, Christianity could never have been introduced. Had not free enquiry been indulged, at the æra of the reformation, the corruptions of Christianity could not have been purged away. If it be restrained now, the present corruptions will be protected, and new ones encouraged. Was the government to prescribe to us our medicine and diet, our bodies would be in such keeping as our souls are now. Thus in France the emetic was once forbidden as a medicine, and the potatoe as an article of food. Government is just as infallible too when it fixes systems in physics. Galileo was sent to the inquisition for affirming that the earth was a sphere: the government had declared it to be as flat as a trencher, and Galileo was obliged to abjure his error. This error however at length prevailed, the earth became a globe, and Descartes declared it was whirled round its axis by a vortex. The government in which he lived was wise enough to see that this was no question of civil jurisdiction, or we should all have been involved by authority in vortices. In fact, the vortices have been exploded, and the Newtonian principle of gravitation is now more firmly established, on the basis of reason, than it would be were the government to step in, and to make it an article of necessary faith. Reason and experiment have been indulged, and error has fled before them. It is error alone which needs the support of government. Truth can stand by itself. Subject opinion to coercion: whom

will you make your inquisitors? Fallible men; men governed by bad passions, by private as well as public reasons. And why subject it to coercion? To produce uniformity. But is uniformity of opinion desireable? No more than of face and stature. Introduce the bed of Procrustes then, and as there is danger that the large men may beat the small, make us all of a size, by lopping the former and stretching the latter. Difference of opinion is advantageous in religion. The several sects perform the office of a Censor morum over each other. Is uniformity attainable? Millions of innocent men, women, and children, since the introduction of Christianity, have been burnt, tortured, fined, imprisoned; yet we have not advanced one inch towards uniformity. What has been the effect of coercion? To make one half the world fools, and the other half hypocrites. To support roguery and error all over the earth. Let us reflect that it is inhabited by a thousand millions of people. That these profess probably a thousand different systems of religion. That ours is but one of that thousand. That if there be but one right, and ours that one, we should wish to see the 999 wandering sects gathered into the fold of truth. But against such a majority we cannot effect this by force. Reason and persuasion are the only practicable instruments. To make way for these, free enquiry must be indulged; and how can we wish others to indulge it while we refuse it ourselves. . . .

Query XVIII: The Particular Customs and Manners . . . in That State?[4]

. . . There must doubtless be an unhappy influence on the manners of our people produced by the existence of slavery among us. The whole commerce between master and slave is a perpetual exercise of the most boisterous passions, the most unremitting despotism on the one part, and degrading submissions on the other. Our children see this, and learn to imitate it; for man is an imitative animal. This quality is the germ of all education in him. From his cradle to his grave he is learning to do what he sees others do. If a parent could find no motive either in his philanthropy or his self-love, for restraining the intemperance of passion towards his slave, it should always be a sufficient one that his child is present. But generally it is not sufficient. The parent storms, the child looks on, catches the lineaments of wrath, puts on the same airs in the circle of smaller slaves, gives a loose to his worst of passions, and thus nursed, educated, and daily exercised in tyranny, cannot but be stamped by it with odious peculiarities. The man must be a prodigy who can retain his manners and morals undepraved by such circumstances. And with what execration should the statesman be loaded, who permitting one half the citizens thus to trample on the rights of the other, transforms those into despots, and these into enemies, destroys the morals of

the one part, and the amor patriæ of the other. For if a slave can have a country in this world, it must be any other in preference to that in which he is born to live and labour for another: in which he must lock up the faculties of his nature, contribute as far as depends on his individual endeavours to the evanishment of the human race, or entail his own miserable condition on the endless generations proceeding from him. With the morals of the people, their industry also is destroyed. For in a warm climate, no man will labour for himself who can make another labour for him. This is so true, that of the proprietors of slaves a very small proportion indeed are ever seen to labour. And can the liberties of a nation be thought secure when we have removed their only firm basis, a conviction in the minds of the people that these liberties are of the gift of God? That they are not to be violated but with his wrath? Indeed I tremble for my country when I reflect that God is just: that his justice cannot sleep for ever: that considering numbers, nature and natural means only, a revolution of the wheel of fortune, an exchange of situation, is among possible events: that it may become probable by supernatural interference! The Almighty has no attribute which can take side with us in such a contest.—But it is impossible to be temperate and to pursue this subject through the various considerations of policy, of morals, of history natural and civil. We must be contented to hope they will force their way into every one's mind. I think a change already perceptible, since the origin of the present revolution. The spirit of the master is abating, that of the slave rising from the dust, his condition mollifying, the way I hope preparing, under the auspices of heaven, for a total emancipation, and that this is disposed, in the order of events, to be with the consent of the masters, rather than by their extirpation.

Query XIX: The Present State of Manufactures, Commerce, Interior and Exterior Trade?[5]

We never had an interior trade of any importance. Our exterior commerce has suffered very much from the beginning of the present contest. During this time we have manufactured within our families the most necessary articles of cloathing. Those of cotton will bear some comparison with the same kinds of manufacture in Europe; but those of wool, flax and hemp are very coarse, unsightly, and unpleasant: and such is our attachment to agriculture, and such our preference for foreign manufactures, that be it wise or unwise, our people will certainly return as soon as they can, to the raising raw materials, and exchanging them for finer manufactures than they are able to execute themselves.

The political œconomists of Europe have established it as a principle that every state should endeavour to manufacture for itself: and this principle, like many others, we transfer to America, without calculating the difference of circumstance which should often produce a difference

of result. In Europe the lands are either cultivated, or locked up against the cultivator. Manufacture must therefore be resorted to of necessity not of choice, to support the surplus of their people. But we have an immensity of land courting the industry of the husbandman. Is it best then that all our citizens should be employed in its improvement, or that one half should be called off from that to exercise manufactures and handicraft arts for the other? Those who labour in the earth are the chosen people of God, if ever he had a chosen people, whose breasts he has made his peculiar deposit for substantial and genuine virtue. It is the focus in which he keeps alive that sacred fire, which otherwise might escape from the face of the earth. Corruption of morals in the mass of cultivators is a phænomenon of which no age nor nation has furnished an example. It is the mark set on those, who not looking up to heaven, to their own soil and industry, as does the husbandman, for their subsistance, depend for it on the casualties and caprice of customers. Dependance begets subservience and venality, suffocates the germ of virtue, and prepares fit tools for the designs of ambition. This, the natural progress and consequence of the arts, has sometimes perhaps been retarded by accidental circumstances: but, generally speaking, the proportion which the aggregate of the other classes of citizens bears in any state to that of its husbandmen, is the proportion of its unsound to its healthy parts, and is a good-enough barometer whereby to measure its degree of corruption. While we have land to labour then, let us never wish to see our citizens occupied at a work-bench, or twirling a distaff. Carpenters, masons, smiths, are wanting in husbandry: but, for the general operations of manufacture, let our work-shops remain in Europe. It is better to carry provisions and materials to workmen there, than bring them to the provisions and materials, and with them their manners and principles. The loss by the transportation of commodities across the Atlantic will be made up in happiness and permanence of government. The mobs of great cities add just so much to the support of pure government, as sores do to the strength of the human body. It is the manners and spirit of a people which perserve a republic in vigour. A degeneracy in these is a canker which soon eats to the heart of its laws and constitution.

67. A Plan of Government for the Western Territory Report of the Committee, 1 March, 1784

The Committee appointed to prepare a plan for the temporary government of the Western territory have agreed to the following resolutions.

Resolved, that the territory ceded or to be ceded by Individual states to the United states shall be formed into distinct states, bounded in the

following manner as nearly as such cessions will admit, that is to say;
Northwardly and Southwardly by parallels of latitude so that each
state shall comprehend from South to North two degrees of latitude
beginning to count from the completion of thirty one degrees North of
the Equator: but any territory Northwardly of the 47th. degree shall
make part of the state next below. And Eastwardly and Westwardly they
shall be bounded, those on the Missisipi by that river on one side and
the meridian of the lowest point of the rapids of Ohio on the other; and
those adjoining on the East by the same meridian on their Western side,
and on their Eastern by the meridian of the Western cape of the mouth
of the Great Kanhaway. And the territory Eastward of this last meridian
between the Ohio, Lake Erie, and Pennsylvania shall be one state.

That the settlers within any of the said states shall, either on their own
petition, or on the order of Congress, receive authority from them, with
appointments of time and place for their free males of full age to meet
together for the purpose of establishing a temporary government, to
adopt the constitution and laws of any one of these states, so that such
laws nevertheless shall be subject to alteration by their ordinary legislature, and to erect, subject to a like alteration, counties or townships for
the election of members for their legislature.

That such temporary government shall only continue in force in any
state until it shall have acquired 20,000. free inhabitants; when giving
due proof thereof to Congress, they shall receive from them authority
with appointments of time and place to call a Convention of representatives to establish a permanent constitution and government for themselves.

Provided that both the temporary and permanent governments be established on these principles as their basis. 1. That they shall for ever
remain a part of the United states of America. 2. That in their persons,
property and territory they shall be subject to the government of the
United states in Congress assembled, and to the Articles of confederation
in all those cases in which the original states shall be so subject. 3. That
they shall be subject to pay a part of the federal debts contracted or to
be contracted to be apportioned on them by Congress according to the
same common rule and measure by which apportionments thereof shall
be made on the other states. 4. That their respective governments shall
be in republican forms, and shall admit no person to be a citizen who
holds any hereditary title. 5. That after the year 1800 of the Christian
æra, there shall be neither slavery nor involuntary servitude in any of the
said states, otherwise than in punishment of crimes, whereof the party
shall have been duly convicted to have been personally guilty.

That whensoever any of the said states shall have, of free inhabitants, as
many as shall then be in any one the least numerous of the thirteen original states, such state shall be admitted by it's delegates into the Congress
of the United states, on an equal footing with the said original states:
after which the assent of two thirds of the United states in Congress as-

sembled shall be requisite in all those cases, wherein by the Confederation, the assent of nine states is now required. Provided the consent of
nine states to such admission may be obtained according to the eleventh
of the articles of Confederation. Until such admission by their delegates
into Congress, any of the said states, after the establishment of their
temporary government, shall have authority to keep a sitting member in
Congress, with a right of debating, but not of voting. . . .

68. *Observations on the Whale-Fishery, 1788*

Whale oil enters, as a raw material, into several branches of manufacture, as of wool, leather, soap: it is used also in painting, architecture and
navigation. But its great consumption is in lighting houses and cities. For
this last purpose however it has a powerful competitor in the vegetable
oils. These do well in warm, still weather, but they fix with cold, they
extinguish easily with the wind, their crop is precarious, depending on
the seasons, and, to yield the same light, a larger wick must be used, and
greater quantity of oil consumed. Estimating all these articles of difference together, those employed in lighting cities find their account in
giving about 25 per cent. more for whale than for vegetable oils. But
higher than this the whale oil, in its present form, cannot rise; because it
then becomes more advantageous to the city-lighters to use others. This
competition then limits its price, higher than which no encouragement
can raise it, and becomes, as it were, a law of its nature but, at this low
price, the whale fishery is the poorest business into which a merchant or
sailor can enter. If the sailor, instead of wages, has a part of what is
taken, he finds that this, one year with another, yields him less than he
could have got as wages in any other business. It is attended too with
great risk, singular hardships, and long absences from his family. If the
voyage is made solely at the expence of the merchant, he finds that, one
year with another, it does not reimburse him his expences. As, for example, an English ship of 300 ton, and 42. hands brings home, communibus
annis, after a four months voyage, 25. ton of oil, worth 437 l. 10s. sterl.
but the wages of the officers and seamen will be 400 l. The Outfit then
and the merchant's profit must be paid by the government. And it is
accordingly on this idea that the British bounty is calculated. From the
poverty of this business then it has happened that the nations, who have
taken it up, have successively abandoned it. . . .

In the mean time too the inhabitants of the barren island of Nantucket
had taken up this fishery, invited to it by the whales presenting themselves on their own shore. To them therefore the English relinquished it,
continuing to them, as British subjects, the importation of their oils into
England duty free, while foreigners were subject to a duty of 18 l. 5s.
sterl. a ton. . . .

The Nantuckois then were the only people who exercised this fishery to any extent at the commencement of the late war. Their country, from it's barrenness, yielding no subsistence, they were obliged to seek it in the sea which surrounded them. Their economy was more rigorous than that of the Dutch. Their seamen, instead of wages, had a share in what was taken. This induced them to fish with fewer hands, so that each had a greater dividend in the profit. It made them more vigilant in seeking game, bolder in pursuing it, and parsimonious in all their expences. London was their only market. When therefore, by the late revolution, they became aliens in Great Britain, they became subject to the alien duty of 18 l. 5s. the ton of oil, which being more than equal to the price of the common whale oil, they were obliged to abandon that fishery. So that this people, who before the war had employed upwards of 300 vessels a year in the whale fishery, (while Great Britain had herself never employed one hundred) have now almost ceased to exercise it. But they still had the seamen, the most important material for this fishery; and they still retained the spirit of fishing: so that at the re-establishment of peace they were capable in a very short time of reviving their fishery in all its splendor. The British government saw that the moment was critical. They knew that their own share in that fishery was as nothing. That the great mass of fishermen was left with a nation now separated from them: that these fishermen however had lost their ancient market, had no other resource within their country to which they could turn, and they hoped therefore they might, in the present moment of distress, be decoyed over to their establishments, and be added to the mass of their seamen. To effect this they offered extravagant advantages to all persons who should exercise the whale fishery from British establishments. . . .

A vessel was already arrived from Halifax to Nantucket to take off some of those who proposed to remove; two families had gone on board and others were going, when a letter was received there, which had been written by Monsieur le Marquis de la Fayette to a gentleman in Boston, and transmitted by him to Nantucket. The purport of the letter was to dissuade their accepting the British proposals, and to assure them that their friends in France would endeavour to do something for them. This instantly suspended their design: not another went on board, and the vessel returned to Halifax with only the two families.

In fact the French government had not been inattentive to the views of the British, nor insensible of the crisis. They saw the danger of permitting five or six thousand of the best seamen existing to be transferred by a single stroke to the marine strength of their enemy, and to carry over with them an art which they possessed almost exclusively. The counterplan which they set on foot was to tempt the Nantuckois by high offers to come and settle in France. This was in the year 1785. The British however had in their favor a sameness of language, religion, laws, habits and kindred. 9 families only, of 33 persons in the whole came to Dun-

kirk; so that this project was not likely to prevent their emigration to the English establishments, if nothing else had happened.

France had effectually aided in detaching the U.S. of America from the *force* of Great Britain. But as yet they seemed to have indulged only a silent wish to detach them from her *commerce*. They had done nothing to induce that event. In the same year 1785, while M. de Calonne was in treaty with the Nantuckois, an estimate of the commerce of the U.S. was submitted to the Count de Vergennes, and it was shewn that, of 3. millions of pounds sterling to which their exports amounted, one third might be brought to France and exchanged against her productions and manufactures advantageously for both nations, provided the obstacles of prohibition, monopoly, and duty were either done away or moderated as far as circumstances would admit. . . .

The article of Whale oil was accordingly distinguished, in the letter of M. de Calonne, by an immediate abatement of duty, and promise of further abatement after the year 1790. This letter was instantly sent to America, and bid fair to produce there the effect intended, by determining the fishermen to carry on their trade from their own homes, with the advantage only of a free market in France, rather than remove to Great Britain where a free market and great bounty were offered them. . . .

The English had now begun to deluge the markets of France with their whale oils: and they were enabled by the great premiums given by their Government to undersell the French fisherman, aided by feebler premiums, and the American aided by his poverty alone. Nor is it certain that these speculations were not made at the risk of the British government, to suppress the French and American fishermen in their only market. Some remedy seemed necessary. . . . The remedy adopted was to prohibit all oils without exception.

To know how this remedy will operate we must consider the quantity of whale oil which France consumes annually, the quantity she obtains from her own fishery; and if she obtains less than she consumes, we are to consider what will follow this prohibition.

The annual consumption of France, as stated by a person who has good opportunities of knowing it, is as follows.

	pesant.	quintaux.	tons.
Paris according to the registers of 1786	2,800,000	28,000	1750
27. other cities lighted by M. Sangrain	800,000	8,000	500
Rouen	500,000	5,000	312½
Bordeaux	600,000	6,000	375
Lyon	300,000	3,000	187½
Other cities, leather and light	3,000,000	30,000	1875
	8,000,000	80,000	5,000

Other calculations, reduce the consumption to about half this. It is treating these with sufficient respect to place them on an equal footing with the estimate of the person before alluded to, and to suppose the truth half way between them. We will call then the present consumption of France only 60,000 quintals, or 3750 ton a year. This consumption is increasing fast as the practice of lighting cities is becoming more general, and the superior advantages of lighting them with whale oil are but now beginning to be known.

What do the fisheries of France furnish? She has employed this year 15. vessels in the Southern, and 2 in the Northern fishery, carrying 4500 tons in the whole or 265 each on an average. The English ships, led by Nantuckois as well as the French, have as I am told never averaged, in the Southern fishery, more than one fifth of their burthen, in the best year. The 15 ships of France, according to this ground of calculation, and supposing the present to have been one of the best years, should have brought, one with another, one fifth of 265 tons, or 53 tons each. But we are told they have brought near the double of that, to wit 100 tons each and 1500 tons in the whole. Supposing the 2. Northern vessels to have brought home the cargo which is common from the Northern fishery, to wit, 25 tons each, the whole produce this year will then be 1550 tons. This is 5½ months provision or two fifths of the annual consumption. To furnish for the whole year would require 40 ships of the same size, in years as fortunate as the present, and 85 communibus annis, 44 tons, or one sixth of the burthen, being as high an average as should be counted on, one year with another: and the number must be increased with the increasing consumption. France then is evidently not yet in a condition to supply her own wants. It is said indeed she has a large stock on hand unsold occasioned by the English competition. 33,000 quintals, including this year's produce, are spoken of. This is between 6. and 7. months provision: and supposing, by the time this is exhausted, that the next year's supply comes in, that will enable her to go on 5. or 6. months longer; say a twelvemonth in the whole. But, at the end of the twelvemonth, what is to be done? The Manufactures depending on this article cannot maintain their competition against those of other countries, if deprived of their equal means. When the alternative then shall be presented of letting them drop, or opening the ports to foreign whale oil, it is presumable the latter will be adopted, as the lesser evil. But it will be too late for America: her fishery annihilated during the late war, only began to raise its head on the prospect of market held out by this country. Crushed by the Arret of Sep. 28. in its first feeble effort to revive, it will rise no more. Expeditions, which require the expence of the outfit of vessels, and from 9. to 12. months navigation, as the Southern fishery does, most frequented by the Americans, cannot be undertaken in sole reliance on a market which is opened and shut from one day to another, with little or no warning. The English alone then will remain to furnish these supplies, and they must

be received even from them. We must accept bread from our enemies, if our friends cannot furnish it. This comes exactly to the point to which that government has been looking. She fears no rival in the whale fishery but America. Or rather, it is the whale fishery of America of which she is endeavoring to possess herself. It is for this object she is making the present extraordinary efforts by bounties and other encouragements: and her success so far is very flattering. Before the war she had not 100 vessels in the whale trade, while America employed 309. In 1786. Great Britain employed 151 vessels, in 1787. 286. in 1788. 314. nearly the ancient American number; while the latter is fallen to about 80. They have just changed places then, England having gained exactly what America has lost. France by her ports and markets holds the balance between the two contending parties, and gives the victory, by opening and shutting them, to which she pleases. We have still precious remains of seamen educated in this fishery, and capable by their poverty, their boldness and address, of recovering it from the English, in spite of their bounties. But this Arret endangers the transferring to Great Britain every man of them who is not invincibly attached to his native soil. There is no other nation in present condition to maintain a competition with Great Britain in the whale fishery. The expence at which it is supported on her part seems enormous. 255 vessels, of 75436 tons, employed by her this year in the Northern fishery, at 42 men each; and 59. in the Southern at 18 men each makes 11,772 men. These are known to have cost the government 15 l. each, or 176,580 l. in the whole, and that to employ the principal part of them from 3. to 4. months only. The Northern ships have brought home 20. and the Southern 60. tons of oil on an average, making 8640 tons. Every ton of oil then has cost the government 20 l. in bounty. Still, if they can beat us out of the field and have it to themselves, they will think their money well employed. If France undertakes solely the competition against them, she must do it at equal expence. The trade is too poor to support itself. The 85 ships necessary to supply even her present consumption, bountied as the English are, will require a sacrifice of 1,285,200 livres a year, to maintain 3570 seamen, and that a part of the year only. And if she will push it to 12,000 men in competition with England, she must sacrifice, as they do, 4. or 5. millions a year. The same number of men might, with the same bounty, be kept in as constant employ carrying stone from Bayonne to Cherburg, or coal from Newcastle to Havre, in which navigations they would be always at hand, and become as good seamen. The English consider among their best sailors those employed in carrying coal from Newcastle to London. France cannot expect to raise her fishery, even to the supply of her own consumption, in one year or in several years. Is it not better then, by keeping her ports open to the U.S. to enable them to aid in maintaining the field against the common adversary, till she shall be in condition to take it herself, and to supply her own wants? Otherwise her supplies must aliment that very force which is

keeping her under. On our part, we can never be dangerous competitors to France. The extent to which we can exercise this fishery is limited to that of the barren island of Nantucket, and a few similar barren spots; its duration to the pleasure of this government, as we have no other market. . . .

After this review of the whale fishery as a Political institution, a few considerations shall be added on its produce as a basis of Commercial exchange between France and the United States. The discussions it has undergone on former occasions, in this point of view, leaves little new to be now urged.

The United-States not possessing mines of the precious metals, they can purchase necessaries from other nations so far only as their produce is received in exchange. Without enumerating our smaller articles, we have three of principal importance, proper for the French market, to wit, Tobacco, whale oil, and rice. The first and most important is Tobacco. This might furnish an exchange for 8. millions of the productions of this country: but it is under a monopoly, and that not of a mercantile, but a financiering company, whose interest is to pay in money, and not in merchandize; and who are so much governed by the spirit of simplifying their purchases and proceedings, that they find means to elude every endeavor on the part of government to make them diffuse their purchases among the merchants in general. Little profit is derived from this then as an article of exchange for the produce and manufactures of France. Whale oil might be next in importance; but that is now prohibited. American Rice is not yet of great, but it is of growing consumption in France, and being the only article of the three which is free, it may become a principal basis of exchange. . . .

But of the three articles before mentioned, proved by experience to be suitable for the French market, one is prohibited, one under monopoly, and one alone free, and that the smallest and of very limited consumption. The way to encourage purchasers is to multiply their means of payment. Whale oil might be an important one. In one scale is the interest of the millions who are lighted, shod or clothed with the help of it, and the thousands of labourers and manufacturers who would be employed in producing the articles which might be given in exchange for it, if received from America. In the other scale are the interests of the adventurers in the whale fishery; each of whom indeed, politically considered may be of more importance to the state than a simple labourer or manufacturer: but to make the estimate with the accuracy it merits, we should multiply the numbers in each scale into their individual importance, and see which preponderates.

Both governments have seen with concern that their commercial intercourse does not grow as rapidly as they would wish. The system of the United States is to use neither prohibitions nor premiums. Commerce there regulates itself freely, and asks nothing better. Where a government

finds itself under the necessity of undertaking that regulation, it would seem that it should conduct it as an intelligent merchant would: that is to say, invite customers to purchase, by facilitating their means of payment, and by adapting goods to their taste. If this idea be just, government here has two operations to attend to, with respect to the commerce of the United States. 1. To do away, or to moderate, as much as possible, the prohibitions and monopolies of their materials for payment. 2. To encourage the institution of the principal manufactures which the necessities, or the habits of their new customers call for. . . .

69. Jefferson's Response to the Address of Welcome by the Citizens of Albemarle on His Return from Europe

February 12, 1790

Gentlemen

The testimony of esteem with which you are pleased to honour my return to my native county fills me with gratitude and pleasure. While it shews that my absence has not lost me your friendly recollection, it holds out the comfortable hope that when the hour of retirement shall come, I shall again find myself amidst those with whom I have long lived, with whom I wish to live, and whose affection is the source of my purest happiness. Their favor was the door thro' which I was ushered on the stage of public life; and while I have been led on thro' it's varying scenes, I could not be unmindful of those who assigned me my first part.

My feeble and obscure exertions in their service, and in the holy cause of freedom, have had no other merit than that they were my best. We have all the same. We have been fellow-labourers and fellow-sufferers, and heaven has rewarded us with a happy issue from our struggles. It rests now with ourselves alone to enjoy in peace and concord the blessings of self-government, so long denied to mankind: to shew by example the sufficiency of human reason for the care of human affairs and that the will of the majority, the Natural law of every society, is the only sure guardian of the rights of man. Perhaps even this may sometimes err. But it's errors are honest, solitary and short-lived.—Let us then, my dear friends, for ever bow down to the general reason of the society. We are safe with that, even in it's deviations, for it soon returns again to the right way. These are lessons we have learnt together. We have prospered in their practice, and the liberality with which you are pleased to approve my attachment to the general rights of mankind assures me we are still together in these it's kindred sentiments.

Wherever I may be stationed, by the will of my country, it will be my delight to see, in the general tide of happiness, that yours too flows on in just place and measure. That it may flow thro' all times, gathering strength as it goes, and spreading the happy influence of reason and liberty over the face of the earth, is my fervent prayer to heaven.

70. *Arrears in Soldiers' Pay*

June 3, 1790

The accounts of the souldiers of Virginia and North Carolina having been examined by the proper officer of government, the balances due to each individual ascertained, and a list of these balances made out, this list became known to certain persons before the souldiers themselves had information of it, and those persons, by unfair means, as is said, and for very inadequate considerations obtained assignments from many of the souldiers of whatever sum should be due to them from the public without specifying the amount. The legislature, to defeat this fraud, passed resolutions on the 21st. of May 1790. directing that, where paiment had not been made to the original claimant in person, or his representatives, it shall be made to him or them personally, or to their attorney producing a power for that purpose, attested by two justices of the county where he resides, and specifying the certain sum he is to recieve.

It has been objected to these resolutions that they annul transfers of property which were good by the laws under which they were made; that they take from the assignees their lawful property; are contrary to the principles of the constitution, which condemn retrospective laws; and are therefore not worthy of the President's approbation.

I agree in an almost unlimited condemnation of retrospective laws. The few instances of wrong which they redress are so overweighed by the insecurity they draw over all property, and even over life itself, and by the atrocious violations of both to which they lead, that it is better to live under the evil than the remedy. The only question I shall make is Whether these resolutions annul acts which were valid when they were done?

This question respects the laws of Virginia and North Carolina only. On the latter I am not qualified to decide, and therefore beg leave to confine myself to the former.

By the Common law of England (adopted in Virginia) the conveyance of a right to a debt or other thing, whereof the party is not in possession, is not only void, but severely punisheable under the names of Maintenance and champerty. The Law-merchant however, which is permitted

to have course between merchants, allows the assignment of a *bill of exchange,* for the convenience of commerce. This therefore forms one exception to the general rule that a mere right, or thing in action, is not assigneable. A 2d. exception has been formed by an English statute (copied into the laws of Virginia) permitting *Promisory notes* to be assigned. The laws of Virginia have gone yet further than the statute, and have allowed, as a 3d. exception, that a *bond* should be assigned, which cannot be done even at this day in England. So that in Virginia, when a debt has been settled between the parties, and put into the form of a bill of exchange, promisory note, or bond, the law admits it to be transferred by assignment. In all other cases, the assignment of a debt is void. The debts from the U.S. to the souldiers of Virginia not having been put into either of these forms, the assignments of them were void in law.

A creditor may give an order on his debtor in favor of another. But if the debtor does not accept it, he must be sued in the creditor's name: which shews that the *order* does not transfer the property of the debt.— So the creditor may appoint another to be his attorney to recieve and recover his debt; and he may covenant that when recieved, the attorney may apply it to his own use. But he must sue as attorney to the original proprietor, and not in his own right. This proves that a *power of attorney,* with such a *covenant,* does not transfer the property of the debt. A further proof in both cases is that the original creditor may, at any time before paiment, or acceptance, revoke either his order, or his power of attorney. In that event, the person in whose favor they were given has recourse to a court of equity. When there, asking equity, the judge examines whether he has done equity. If he finds his transaction has been a fair one, he gives him aid: if he finds it has been otherwise, not permitting his court to be made a handmaid to fraud, he leaves him without remedy in equity, as he was in law. The assignments in the present case therefore, if unfairly obtained, as seems to be admitted, are as void in equity as they are in law. And they derive their nullity from the laws under which they were made, not from the new resolutions of Congress. These are not retrospective: they only direct their treasurer not to give validity to an assignment which had it not before, by paiment to the assignee, until he in whom the legal property still is, shall order it in such a form as to shew he is apprised of the sum he is to part with, and it's readiness to be paid into his or any other hands and that he chuses notwithstanding to acquiesce under the fraud which has been practised on him. In that case he has only to execute, before two justices, a power of attorney to the same person, expressing the specific sum of his demand, and it is to be complied with. Actual paiment, in this case, is an important act. If made to the assignee, it would put the burthen of proof and process on the original owner. If made to that owner, it puts it on the assignee, who must then come forward and shew that his transaction has been that of an honest man. Government seems to be doing in this what

every individual, I think, would feel himself bound to do in the case of his own debt. For being free in law to pay to the one or the other, he would certainly give the advantage to the party, who has suffered wrong, rather than to him who had committed it. It is not honorable to take a mere legal advantage when it happens to be contrary to justice. But it is honorable to enforce a salutary principle of law, when a relinquishment of it is sollicited only to support a fraud.

I think the resolutions therefore merit approbation.

I have before professed my incompetence to say what are the laws of North Carolina on this subject. They, like Virginia, adopted the English laws in the gross. These laws forbid in general the buying and selling of debts, and their policy in this is so wise, that I should presume they had not changed it, till the contrary be shewn.

71. *First Inaugural Address, March 4, 1801*

Friends and Fellow Citizens:—

Called upon to undertake the duties of the first executive office of our country, I avail myself of the presence of that portion of my fellow citizens which is here assembled, to express my grateful thanks for the favor with which they have been pleased to look toward me, to declare a sincere consciousness that the task is above my talents, and that I approach it with those anxious and awful presentiments which the greatness of the charge and the weakness of my powers so justly inspire. A rising nation, spread over a wise and fruitful land, traversing all the seas with the rich productions of their industry, engaged in commerce with nations who feel power and forget right, advancing rapidly to destinies beyond the reach of mortal eye—when I contemplate these transcendent objects, and see the honor, the happiness, and the hopes of this beloved country committed to the issue and the auspices of this day, I shrink from the contemplation, and humble myself before the magnitude of the undertaking. Utterly indeed, should I despair, did not the presence of many whom I here see remind me, that in the other high authorities provided by our constitution, I shall find resources of wisdom, of virtue, and of zeal, on which to rely under all difficulties. To you, then, gentlemen, who are charged with the sovereign functions of legislation, and to those associated with you, I look with encouragement for that guidance and support which may enable us to steer with safety the vessel in which we are all embarked amid the conflicting elements of a troubled world.

During the contest of opinion through which we have passed, the animation of discussion and of exertions has sometimes worn an aspect which might impose on strangers unused to think freely and to speak and

to write what they think; but this being now decided by the voice of the nation, announced according to the rules of the constitution, all will, of course, arrange themselves under the will of the law, and unite in common efforts for the common good. All, too, will bear in mind this sacred principle, that though the will of the majority is in all cases to prevail, that will, to be rightful, must be reasonable; that the minority possess their equal rights, which equal laws must protect, and to violate which would be oppression. Let us, then, fellow citizens, unite with one heart and one mind. Let us restore to social intercourse that harmony and affection without which liberty and even life itself are but dreary things. And let us reflect that having banished from our land that religious intolerance under which mankind so long bled and suffered, we have yet gained little if we countenance a political intolerance as despotic, as wicked, and capable of as bitter and bloody persecutions. During the throes and convulsions of the ancient world, during the agonizing spasms of infuriated man, seeking through blood and slaughter his long-lost liberty, it was not wonderful that the agitations of the billows should reach even this distant and peaceful shore; that this should be more felt and feared by some and less by others; that this should divide opinions as to measures of safety. But every difference of opinion is not a difference of principle. We have called by different names brethren of the same principle. We are all republicans—we are federalists. If there be any among us who would wish to dissolve this Union or to change its republican form, let them stand undisturbed as monuments of the safety with which error of opinion may be tolerated where reason is left free to combat it. I know, indeed, that some honest men fear that a republican government cannot be strong; that this government is not strong enough. But would the honest patriot, in the full tide of successful experiment, abandon a government which has so far kept us free and firm, on the theoretic and visionary fear that this government, the world's best hope, may by possibility want energy to preserve itself? I trust not. I believe this, on the contrary, the strongest government on earth. I believe it is the only one where every man, at the call of the laws, would fly to the standard of the law, and would meet invasions of the public order as his own personal concern. Sometimes it is said that man cannot be trusted with the government of himself. Can he, then, be trusted with the government of others? Or have we found angels in the forms of kings to govern him? Let history answer this question.

Let us, then, with courage and confidence pursue our own federal and republican principles, our attachment to our union and representative government. Kindly separated by nature and a wide ocean from the exterminating havoc of one quarter of the globe; too high-minded to endure the degradations of the others; possessing a chosen country, with room enough for our descendants to the hundredth and thousandth generation; entertaining a due sense of our equal right to the use of our

own faculties, to the acquisitions of our industry, to honor and confidence from our fellow citizens, resulting not from birth but from our actions and their sense of them; enlightened by a benign religion, professed, indeed, and practiced in various forms, yet all of them including honesty, truth, temperance, gratitude, and the love of man; acknowledging and adoring an overruling Providence, which by all its dispensations proves that it delights in the happiness of man here and his greater happiness hereafter; with all these blessings, what more is necessary to make us a happy and prosperous people? Still one thing more, fellow citizens—a wise and frugal government, which shall restrain men from injuring one another, which shall leave them otherwise free to regulate their own pursuits of industry and improvement, and shall not take from the mouth of labor the bread it has earned. This is the sum of good government, and this is necessary to close the circle of our felicities.

About to enter, fellow citizens, on the exercise of duties which comprehend everything dear and valuable to you, it is proper that you should understand what I deem the essential principles of our government, and consequently those which ought to shape its administration. I will compress them within the narrowest compass they will bear, stating the general principle, but not all its limitations. Equal and exact justice to all men, of whatever state or persuasion, religious or political; peace, commerce, and honest friendship, with all nations—entangling alliances with none; the support of the state governments in all their rights, as the most competent administrations for our domestic concerns and the surest bulwarks against anti-republican tendencies; the preservation of the general government in its whole constitutional vigor, as the sheet anchor of our peace at home and safety abroad; a jealous care of the right of election by the people—a mild and safe corrective of abuses which are lopped by the sword of the revolution where peaceable remedies are unprovided; absolute acquiescence in the decisions of the majority—the vital principle of republics, from which there is no appeal but to force, the vital principle and immediate parent of despotism; a well-disciplined militia—our best reliance in peace and for the first moments of war, till regulars may relieve them; the supremacy of the civil over the military authority; economy in the public expense, that labor may be lightly burdened; the honest payment of our debts and sacred preservation of the public faith; encouragement of agriculture, and of commerce as its handmaid; the diffusion of information and the arraignment of all abuses at the bar of public reason; freedom of religion; freedom of the press; freedom of person under the protection of the habeas corpus; and trial by juries impartially selected—these principles form the bright constellation which has gone before us, and guided our steps through an age of revolution and reformation. The wisdom of our sages and the blood of our heroes have been devoted to their attainment. They should be the creed of our political faith—the text of civil instruction—the touchstone by

which to try the services of those we trust; and should we wander from them in moments of error or alarm, let us hasten to retrace our steps and to regain the road which alone leads to peace, liberty, and safety.

I repair, then, fellow citizens, to the post you have assigned me. With experience enough in subordinate offices to have seen the difficulties of this, the greatest of all, I have learned to expect that it will rarely fall to the lot of imperfect man to retire from this station with the reputation and the favor which bring him into it. Without pretensions to that high confidence reposed in our first and great revolutionary character, whose pre-eminent services had entitled him to the first place in his country's love, and destined for him the fairest page in the volume of faithful history, I ask so much confidence only as may give firmness and effect to the legal administration of your affairs. I shall often go wrong through defect of judgment. When right, I shall often be thought wrong by those whose positions will not command a view of the whole ground. I ask your indulgence for my own errors, which will never be intentional; and your support against the errors of others, who may condemn what they would not if seen in all its parts. The approbation implied by your suffrage is a consolation to me for the past; and my future solicitude will be to retain the good opinion of those who have bestowed it in advance, to conciliate that of others by doing them all the good in my power, and to be instrumental to the happiness and freedom of all.

Relying, then, on the patronage of your good will, I advance with obedience to the work, ready to retire from it whenever you become sensible how much better choice it is in your power to make. And may that Infinite Power which rules the destinies of the universe, lead our councils to what is best, and give them a favorable issue for your peace and prosperity.

72. *To the Inhabitants of Albemarle County, in Virginia*

Monticello, April 3, 1809

Returning to the scenes of my birth and early life, to the society of those with whom I was raised, and who have been ever dear to me, I receive, fellow citizens and neighbors, with inexpressible pleasure, the cordial welcome you are so good as to give me. Long absent on duties which the history of a wonderful era made incumbent on those called to them, the pomp, the turmoil, the bustle and splendor of office, have drawn but deeper sighs for the tranquil and irresponsible occupations of private life, for the enjoyment of an affectionate intercourse with you, my neighbors

and friends, and the endearments of family love, which nature has given us all, as the sweetener of every hour. For these I gladly lay down the distressing burden of power, and seek, with my fellow citizens, repose and safety under the watchful cares, the labors and perplexities of younger and abler minds. The anxieties you express to administer to my happiness, do, of themselves, confer that happiness; and the measure will be complete, if my endeavors to fulfil my duties in the several public stations to which I have been called, have obtained for me the approbation of my country. The part which I have acted on the theatre of public life, has been before them; and to their sentence I submit it; but the testimony of my native county, of the individuals who have known me in private life, to my conduct in its various duties and relations, is the more grateful, as proceeding from eye witnesses and observers, from triers of the vicinage. Of you, then, my neighbors, I may ask, in the face of the world, "whose ox have I taken, or whom have I defrauded? Whom have I oppressed, or of whose hand have I received a bribe to blind mine eyes therewith?" On your verdict I rest with conscious security. Your wishes for my happiness are received with just sensibility, and I offer sincere prayers for your own welfare and prosperity.

73. *Thoughts on Lotteries*

February, 1826

It is a common idea that games of chance are immoral. But what is chance? Nothing happens in this world without a cause. If we know the cause, we do not call it chance; but if we do not know it, we say it was produced by chance. If we see a loaded die turn its lightest side up, we know the cause, and that it is not an effect of chance; but whatever side an unloaded die turns up, not knowing the cause, we say it is the effect of chance. Yet the morality of a thing cannot depend on our knowledge or ignorance of its cause. Not knowing why a particular side of an unloaded die turns up, cannot make the act of throwing it, or of betting on it, immoral. If we consider games of chance immoral, then every pursuit of human industry is immoral; for there is not a single one that is not subject to chance, not one wherein you do not risk a loss for the chance of some gain. The navigator, for example, risks his ship in the hope (if she is not lost in the voyage) of gaining an advantageous freight. The merchant risks his cargo to gain a better price for it. A landholder builds a house on the risk of indemnifying himself by a rent. The hunter hazards his time and trouble in the hope of killing game. In all these pursuits, you stake some one thing against another which you hope to win. But the greatest of all gamblers is the farmer. He risks the seed he puts into

the ground, the rent he pays for the ground itself, the year's labor on it, and the wear and tear of his cattle and gear, to win a crop, which the chances of too much or too little rain, and general uncertainties of weather, insects, waste, &c., often make a total or partial loss. These, then, are games of chance. Yet so far from being immoral, they are indispensable to the existence of man, and every one has a natural right to choose for his pursuit such one of them as he thinks most likely to furnish him subsistence. Almost all these pursuits of chance produce something useful to society. But there are some which produce nothing, and endanger the well-being of the individuals engaged in them, or of others depending on them. Such are games with cards, dice, billiards, &c. And although the pursuit of them is a matter of natural right, yet society, perceiving the irresistible bent of some of its members to pursue them, and the ruin produced by them to the families depending on these individuals, consider it as a case of insanity, *quoad hoc,* step in to protect the family and the party himself, as in other cases of insanity, infancy, imbecility, &c., and suppress the pursuit altogether, and the natural right of following it. There are some other games of chance, useful on certain occasions, and injurious only when carried beyond their useful bounds. Such are insurances, lotteries, raffles &c. These they do not suppress, but take their regulation under their own discretion. The insurance of ships on voyages is a vocation of chance, yet useful, and the right to exercise it therefore is left free. So of houses against fire, doubtful debts, the continuance of a particular life, and similar cases. Money is wanting for a useful undertaking, as a school, &c., for which a direct tax would be disapproved. It is raised therefore by a lottery, wherein the tax is laid on the willing only, that is to say, on those who can risk the price of a ticket without sensible injury for the possibility of a higher prize. An article of property, insusceptible of division at all, or not without great diminution of its worth, is sometimes of so large value as that no purchaser can be found while the owner owes debts, has no other means of payment, and his creditors no other chance of obtaining it but by its sale at a full and fair price. The lottery is here a salutary instrument for disposing of it, where many run small risks for the chance of obtaining a high prize. . . . This method of selling was formerly very much resorted to, until it was thought to nourish too much a spirit of hazard. The legislature were therefore induced not to suppress it altogether, but to take it under their own special regulation. This they did for the first time by their act of 1769, c. 17, before which time every person exercised the right freely; and since which time, it is made unlawful but when approved and authorized by a special act of the legislature. . . .

We have seen, then, that every vocation in life is subject to the influence of chance; that so far from being rendered immoral by the admixture of that ingredient, were they abandoned on that account, man could no longer subsist; that, among them, every one has a natural right to choose

that which he thinks most likely to give him comfortable subsistence; but that while the greater number of these pursuits are productive of something which adds to the necessaries and comforts of life, others again, such as cards, dice, &c., are entirely unproductive, doing good to none, injury to many, yet so easy, and so seducing in practice to men of a certain constitution of mind, that they cannot resist the temptation, be the consequences what they may; that in this case, as in those of insanity, idiocy, infancy, &c., it is the duty of society to take them under its protection, even against their own acts, and to restrain their right of choice of these pursuits, by suppressing them entirely; that there are others, as lotteries particularly, which, although liable to chance also, are useful for many purposes, and are therefore retained and placed under the discretion of the Legislature, to be permitted or refused according to the circumstances of every special case, of which they are to judge; that between the years 1782 and 1820, a space of thirty-eight years only, we have observed seventy cases, where the permission of them has been found useful by the Legislature, some of which are in progress at this time. These cases relate to the emolument of the whole State, to local benefits of education, of navigation, of roads, of counties, towns, religious assemblies, private societies, and of individuals under particular circumstances which may claim indulgence or favor. The latter is the case now submitted to the Legislature, and the question is, whether the individual soliciting their attention, or his situation, may merit that degree of consideration which will justify the Legislature in permitting him to avail himself of the mode of selling by lottery, for the purpose of paying his debts.

That a fair price cannot be obtained by sale in the ordinary way, and in the present depressed state of agricultural industry, is well known. Lands in this State will not now sell for more than a third or fourth of what they would have brought a few years ago, perhaps at the very time of the contraction of the debts for which they are now to be sold. The low price in foreign markets, for a series of years past, of agricultural produce, of wheat generally, of tobacco most commonly, and the accumulation of duties on the articles of consumption not produced within our State, not only disables the farmer or planter from adding to his farm by purchase, but reduces him to sell his own, and remove to the western country, glutting the market he leaves, while he lessens the number of bidders. To be protected against this sacrifice is the object of the present application, and whether the applicant has any particular claim to this protection, is the present question.

Here the answer must be left to others. It is not for me to give it. I may, however, more readily than others, suggest the offices in which I have served. I came of age in 1764, and was soon put into the nomination of justice of the county in which I live, and at the first election following I became one of its representatives in the Legislature.

I was thence sent to the old Congress.

Then employed two years with Mr. Pendleton and Mr. Wythe on the revisal and reduction to a single code of the whole body of the British statutes, the acts of our Assembly, and certain parts of the common law.

Then elected Governor.

Next to the Legislature, and to Congress again.

Sent to Europe as Minister Plenipotentiary.

Appointed Secretary of State to the new government.

Elected Vice-President, and

President.

And lastly, a Visitor and Rector of the University.

In these different offices, with scarcely any interval between them, I have been in the public service now sixty-one years; and during the far greater part of the time, in foreign countries or in other States. Every one knows how inevitably a Virginia estate goes to ruin, when the owner is so far distant as to be unable to pay attention to it himself; and the more especially, when the line of his employment is of a character to abstract and alienate his mind entirely from the knowledge necessary to good, and even to saving management.

If it were thought worth while to specify any particular services rendered, I would refer to the specification of them made by the Legislature itself in their Farewell Address, on my retiring from the Presidency, February, 1809. There is one, however, not therein specified, the most important in its consequences, of any transaction in any portion of my life; to wit, the head I personally made against the federal principles and proceedings, during the administration of Mr. Adams. Their usurpations and violations of the constitution at that period, and their majority in both Houses of Congress, were so great, so decided, and so daring, that after combating their aggressions, inch by inch, without being able in the least to check their career, the republican leaders thought it would be best for them to give up their useless efforts there, go home, get into their respective Legislatures, embody whatever of resistance they could be formed into, and if ineffectual, to perish there as in the last ditch. All, therefore, retired. leaving Mr. Gallatin alone in the House of Representatives, and myself in the Senate, where I then presided as Vice-President. Remaining at our posts, and bidding defiance to the brow beatings and insults by which they endeavored to drive us off also, we kept the mass of republicans in phalanx together, until the Legislatures could be brought up to the charge; and nothing on earth is more certain, than that if myself particularly, placed by my office of Vice-President at the head of the republicans, had given way and withdrawn from my post, the republicans throughout the Union would have given up in despair, and the cause would have been lost forever. By holding on, we obtained time for the Legislatures to come up with their

weight; and those of Virginia and Kentucky particularly, but more especially the former, by their celebrated resolutions, saved the constitution at its last gasp. No person who was not a witness of the scenes of that gloomy period, can form any idea of the afflicting persecutions and personal indignities we had to brook. They saved our country however. The spirits of the people were so much subdued and reduced to despair by the X Y Z imposture, and other stratagems and machinations, that they would have sunk into apathy and monarchy, as the only form of government which could maintain itself.

If Legislative services are worth mentioning, and the stamp of liberality and equality, which was necessary to be imposed on our laws in the first crisis of our birth as a nation, was of any value, they will find that the leading and most important laws of that day were prepared by myself, and carried chiefly by my efforts; supported, indeed, by able and faithful coadjutors from the ranks of the House, very effective as seconds, but who would not have taken the field as leaders.

The prohibition of the further importation of slaves was the first of these measures in time.

This was followed by the abolition of entails, which broke up the hereditary and high-handed aristocracy, which, by accumulating immense masses of property in single lines of families, had divided our country into two distinct orders, of nobles and plebeians.

But further to complete the equality among our citizens so essential to the maintenance of republican government, it was necessary to abolish the principle of primogeniture. I drew the law of descents, giving equal inheritance to sons and daughters, which made a part of the revised code.

The attack on the establishment of a dominant religion, was first made by myself. It could be carried at first only by a suspension of salaries for one year, by battling it again at the next session for another year, and so from year to year, until the public mind was ripened for the bill for establishing religious freedom, which I had prepared for the revised code also. This was at length established permanently, and by the efforts chiefly of Mr. Madison, being myself in Europe at the time that work was brought forward.

To these particular services, I think I might add the establishment of our University, as principally my work, acknowledging at the same time, as I do, the great assistance received from my able colleagues of the Visitation. But my residence in the vicinity threw, of course, on me the chief burthen of the enterprise, as well of the buildings as of the general organization and care of the whole. The effect of this institution on the future fame, fortune and prosperity of our country, can as yet be seen but at a distance. But an hundred well-educated youths, which it will turn out annually, and ere long, will fill all its offices with men of superior qualifications, and raise it from its humble state to an eminence among its associates which it has never yet known; no, not in its brightest

days. That institution is now qualified to raise its youth to an order of science unequalled in any other State; and this superiority will be the greater from the free range of mind encouraged there, and the restraint imposed at other seminaries by the shackles of a domineering hierarchy, and a bigoted adhesion to ancient habits. Those now on the theatre of affairs will enjoy the ineffable happiness of seeing themselves succeeded by sons of a grade of science beyond their own ken. Our sister States will also be repairing to the same fountains of instruction, will bring hither their genius to be kindled at our fire, and will carry back the fraternal affections which, nourished by the same *alma mater*, will knit us to them by the indissoluble bonds of early personal friendships. The good Old Dominion, the blessed mother of us all, will then raise her head with pride among the nations, will present to them that splendor of genius which she has ever possessed, but has too long suffered to rest uncultivated and unknown, and will become a centre of ralliance to the States whose youth she has instructed, and, as it were, adopted.

I claim some share in the merits of this great work of regeneration. My whole labors, now for many years, have been devoted to it, and I stand pledged to follow it up through the remnant of life remaining to me. And what remuneration do I ask? Money from the treasury? Not a cent. I ask nothing from the earnings or labors of my fellow citizens. I wish no man's comforts to be abridged for the enlargement of mine. For the services rendered on all occasions, I have been always paid to my full satisfaction. I never wished a dollar more than what the law had fixed on. My request is, only to be permitted to sell my own property freely to pay my own debts. To *sell* it, I say, and not to *sacrifice* it, not to have it gobbled up by speculators to make fortunes for themselves, leaving unpaid those who have trusted to my good faith, and myself without resource in the last and most helpless stage of life. If permitted to sell it in a way which will bring me a fair price, all will be honestly and honorably paid, and a competence left for myself, and for those who look to me for subsistence. To sell it in a way which will offend no moral principle, and expose none to risk but the willing, and those wishing to be permitted to take the chance of gain. To give me, in short, that permission which you often allow to others for purposes not more moral.

Will it be objected, that although not evil in itself, it may as a precedent, lead to evil? But let those who shall quote the precedent, bring their case within the same measure. Have they, as in this case, devoted three-score years and one of their lives, uninterruptedly, to the service of their country? Have the times of those services been as trying as those which have embraced our Revolution, our transition from a colonial to a free structure of government? Have the stations of their trial been of equal importance? Has the share they have borne in holding their new government to its genuine principles, been equally marked? And has the cause of the distress, against which they seek a remedy, proceeded,

not merely from themselves, but from errors of the public authorities, disordering the circulating medium, over which they had no control, and which have, in fact, doubled and trebled debts, by reducing, in that proportion, the value of the property which was to pay them? If all these circumstances, which characterize the present case, have taken place in theirs also, then follow the precedent. Be assured, the cases will be so rare as to produce no embarrassment, as never to settle into an injurious habit. The single feature of a sixty years' service, as no other instance of it has yet occurred in our country, so it probably never may again. And should it occur, even once and again, it will not impoverish your treasury, as it takes nothing from that, and asks but a simple permission, by an act of natural right, to do one of moral justice.

74. *Epitaph*

Could the dead feel any interest in Monuments or other remembrances of them. . .
the following would be to my Manes the most
gratifying.
On the grave
    a plain die or cube of 3 f. without any
mouldings, surmounted by an Obelisk of
6 f. height, each of a single stone:
on the faces of the Obelisk the following
inscription, & not a word more
        'Here was buried
        Thomas Jefferson
Author of the Declaration of American Independence
        of the Statute of Virginia for religious freedom
    & Father of the University of Virginia.'
because by these, as testimonials that I have lived, I
wish most to be remembered.

PART IV

JAMES MADISON

(*1751-1836*)

Diderot once wrote to David Hume: "The reason I love you is because you would not demand of a poor wretch his baptismal certificate!" It was America's incalculable good fortune that one of its master builders, James Madison, was a man of this stripe. Modest, sagacious, and temperate, this great little Virginian devoted himself with such genuine fidelity to public service, that he has recently been described in Congress as "the most unhonored and unsung of the Founding Fathers." Even men who write and teach American history and government tend to give him conventional notice as the "father of the Constitution" but quickly pass from the human father to the paper child. Unlike John Adams, with whom Madison may be said to have shared an undeserved neglect from the American people, Madison never fought for a personal place in the artificial sunshine of history, never even availed himself of the opportunities tendered him by eager would-be biographers. Always cooperative when he was solicited for information and anecdotes on the other brilliant leaders of his time, he consistently refused to make himself the center of celebration or acclaim. As his brief autobiographical note conclusively indicates, he was a different man who shrank from self-display and directed inquirers to his papers on public subjects, letters, official transactions, finding this appropriate for "one whose whole life has in a manner been a public life." There is then a pleasing sense of the first faint stirrings of long-overdue justice in the campaign waged successfully by Irving Brant, Madison's first competent professional biographer, to have a monument built in his honor in Washington. In Brant's chiding words, "We should erect a memorial to Madison not because he needs it but because we do."

More than two generations younger than Benjamin Franklin, Madison, devoted to the same Enlightenment philosophy long before he met the aged statesman in person, had been impressed by his wisdom and genius. For the last four years of Franklin's life, while he attended the Constitutional Convention and served as President of the Council of Pennsylvania, Franklin and Madison became friends. The extent of the younger

*statesman's appreciation of the aged doctor is indicated by the notes
he took of the lively anecdotes the latter told in his hearing, and which
Madison re-told fondly in later years. Madison was also a close and
valued younger associate of George Washington; and for some time
before they became arch-enemies, a cordial associate of Alexander Hamilton; but, above all, he was for half a century the intimate and perfect
friend of Thomas Jefferson, whom he once called his "Tutelary Genius."
Thus, when Madison died in 1836, he brought to a close the most fruitful
era in American political thought and history. Madison himself was the
last great luminary of the American Enlightenment, who had had friendly
ties to all the men in that remarkable company of creative statesmen
who forged Independence, created a representative republic, developed
the American national party system, and definitively established the real
independence and character of America.*

*Although a century and a quarter has passed since Madison died,
only a tiny handful of scholars seem to understand the depth and solidity
of Madison's contribution to our system of representative government.
To be sure his role as the foremost architect of the Constitution is conceded by all, and this achievement did represent a high point in his
career. But it was by no means an isolated, nor his first, nor final contribution! Had Madison's work in Philadelphia not been prepared for by
his previous years of bold leadership in the movement for continental
unification; had it not been marked by his telling campaigns for religious
freedom and other legislative reforms in Virginia that brought him a
deserved reputation for devotion to liberty and justice; and had his
constitutional role not been followed by his constructive labors to organize the Republican party under the first administrations of the new
federal government—Madison's would have been an enigmatic performance, open to widely different speculations on its worth and significance. Moreover, although Madison himself clearly did not set supreme
value on the holding of public office, his Secretaryship of State and also
the two terms of his Presidency (that "splendid misery" in Jefferson's
phrase) were far from barren of distinctive results. Thus, it is not too
much to say that Madison's significant work, over time, is at last emerging from the shadows in the second half of the twentieth century, whence,
it is hoped, it will develop its own course in the future.*

*Since Madison was not Lincolnesque in person, nor gifted with the
magic of Jefferson's bright phrases and memorable prose, nor whirled
about with the turbulent passions of discovery and self-scrutiny of John
Adams, nor driven by the fierce flame of glory and masterful national
policy of Hamilton—one asks: wherein lay his power, and what was the
creative vision at the center of his being?*

*The answer is to be found somewhere in the following cluster of moti-
vations and character traits. From his early youth on, Madison was
apparently deeply concerned about religion and yet critical of orthodoxy*

and its presumptions to final truth, as well as to its intolerable practice of forcing men's conscience. He was thus both religiously oriented and rationally enlightened, and these strong interests were reinforced by the education he received at Dr. Witherspoon's hands when he attended Princeton College. We should note that in addition to the moral philosophy of the English and of the Scottish Enlightenment—his close reading of the works of Locke, Hume, Adam Ferguson, Adam Smith, Francis Hutcheson, Thomas Reid, and Lord Kames developed his "very early and strong impressions in favor of Liberty both Civil and Religious." An honest and earnest spirit, seeking more than fancy work and shunning the mere employment for gain (he would not be a Virginia planter on principle, since he was resolved "to depend as little as possible on the labour of slaves") naturally found an ideal vocation in the study of the principles and varieties of government; but that same conscience would not let him rest with theoretical or scholarly study only, driving him on to practice the politics of his reflective choice.

To this taste for social and political inquiry in their ethical bearings, he brought another distinctive mental talent—that of acute and penetrating logical analysis. Madison's Tenth Federalist Paper, unquestionably the most famous of the 85 essays that comprise this classic of American political literature, is only the most familiar of innumerable writings of Madison's that achieve admirable philosophical tidiness and clarity without sacrifice of observational content. Other land-marks are: Madison's cogent "Notes of Ancient and Modern Confederacies;" his speeches in the Constitutional Convention and in the Virginia Ratifying Convention; a goodly group of substantive letters expounding ideas or issues (such as his critique of Jefferson's proposed principle that "The earth belongs always to the living generation"); and his letters on union and nullification in the last years of his life; more than a few superb essays and public papers—notably his bold arguments for religious freedom and the separation of church and state in the "Memorial and Remonstrance Against Religious Assessments" (1785); his defense of intellectual freedom and limited but popular government in the Report of 1800 which he submitted to the Virginia legislature in 1799; and his Treatise, written while Secretary of State in Jefferson's second administration, on neutral trade in which he developed the doctrine of freedom of the seas and neutral rights (1806)—a report estimated by John Quincy Adams to be "a standard treatise in the Law of Nations, not inferior to the works of any writer upon those subjects since the day of Grotius."

Unifying the workings of his keen mind and his strong feelings about a serious vocation of public service was the alchemy of his temperament, his personal approach to men and values. His was the priceless gift of creative compromise, born of his deep-felt courtesy to others, and the schooled and "cool" judgment that permitted him to see and to understand points of view and desires widely different from his own. In his

mid-thirties, William Pierce of Georgia, a fellow delegate at the Constitutional Convention, described him in this fashion: "Mr. Madison . . . blends together the profound politician with the scholar. In the management of every great question he evidently took the lead in the convention, and though he cannot be called an orator, he is a most agreeable, eloquent and convincing speaker. From a spirit of industry and application which he possesses in a most eminent degree, he always comes forward the best informed man of any point in debate. The affairs of the United States, he perhaps has the most correct knowledge of, of any man in the Union. . . . Mr. Madison is about thirty-seven years of age, a gentleman of great modesty—with a remarkable sweet temper. He is easy and unreserved among his acquaintances, and has a most agreeable style of conversation." That "remarkable sweet temper" goes a long way to explain the quality and radiance of Madison's many friendships and his many triumphs as legislative leader and political organizer.

One should not imagine, however, that Madison's sweet temper clouded his judgment, or reduced his realistic estimate and flexible handling of men. On the contrary, though the sweet temper was there, to conciliate, to effect creative compromises and modifications, to persevere, it was fortified in hard and momentous cases, with steely courage and decisiveness. Thus Madison, who had opened the Constitutional Convention with the position of the nationalistic Virginia Plan, worked tirelessly to achieve a genuine federated union, and not, as he said, a mere treaty among sovereign states. He had balanced, throughout the deliberations, the often opposite claims of libertarian, democratic human rights with imperative needs for a stronger union. Although he was "conservative" if that label means that he was concerned to provide security for property, he was also "liberal" in his determination to advance the personal liberty and happiness of the people and to avert conditions that would "blast the glory of the Revolution." The constitution, with its inflexible provisions against absolute power—whether the absolutism of a monarchy, an aristocracy, an oligarchy, or a reckless and despotic majority—in effect established a unique new form, a modern large-scale republic of limited powers. In a revealing one-sentence gloss on the Constitution as a political experiment, Madison said: "Every step was a contest between power and liberty." His patient committee work and indefatigable contributions to the debate on the Constitution all bore fruit because he was not Utopian in his thought, nor fanatical in spirit. As he once commented, with seasoned insight, "That government is best which is the least imperfect."

Then, after having struggled unrelentingly for the far-from-ideal Constitution, Madison swiftly estimated that the big battle still lay ahead, and he lost no time in preparing the public opinion that alone could float it to victory. The Federalist Papers, with their full exploration of the need for and meaning of federation, and their equally persuasive

instruction on the nature of the American democratic republic, was an- other heroic task of daily and unremitting labor in the months following the close of the Convention in Philadelphia. They were offered to readers under the pseudonym "Publius," and Madison and Hamilton achieved a sensational teamwork, feeding the intricate essays to the press almost before the ink had dried. Although Madison's and Hamilton's views were far from identical, they stood together solidly in showing why the Articles of Confederation had failed to exercise adequate governmental control and why a strong but limited republican government, based on popular consent, would be a benefit to the various states and various interests of the people in the states rather than a Leviathan to fear. The last and crucial arena for constitutional struggle, however, was in the state con- ventions themselves as they went for ratification. Madison, whose sup- posedly "frail" constitution has been too much noticed by historians and critics (following his own youthful declaration that ill health after his graduate study made him doubt that he would live long) hastened to Virginia to take up the staggering burden of principal advocate for ratification against what appeared to be an invincible opposition, led by the peerless orator, Patrick Henry. But Madison's weaker voice, since it conveyed pertinent information, greater truth, and a more generous hope for the future of the United States, achieved a resonance that ultimately drowned Henry's.

Instructive, too, in revealing Madison's stature as a philosopher-states- man is the generalship he provided in the critical years that followed after he had engineered ratification of the Constitution by Virginia—then the largest, most populous and most powerful state on the North Ameri- can continent. As the first administration of President Washington opened, Madison quickly seized leadership in what was then the small and very select House of Representatives. Recent scholarship has shown that Madi- son was unquestionably the organizer of the Republican Party from early in the decade of the 1790's. In this period, Madison found himself in serious political disagreement with the political objectives and financial policies of Hamilton, his former collaborator in The Federalist Papers, *and Madison joined wholeheartedly with Jefferson in formulating the ideology of the Republican Party. Differences that had always existed between Madison's and Hamilton's outlook were now hardened. Madison believed that the Hamiltonian program was attempting to "administer" the government into something fundamentally different from what the Constitution had provided. In his view, Hamilton's program played to a moneyed elite and thus threatened to erode the faith of the majority of the people (who were predominantly farmers and workers) in the new federal system. In a dramatic piece of political journalism, Madison phrased the issue this way: men had "rights to property" but also "prop- erty in rights." The second kind of property was the "larger and juster" sense of the concept, including everything to which men attach values*

—religious opinions, the liberty and safety of their persons, the free use of their minds. Just governments will not confine their respect for property to the narrow concerns of money, possessions, external things—but will respect the property in rights of all the people. Not content with arguments based on the achievement of power alone, Madison interpreted the historic role of the Constitution and the government under it to be that of making power the means to the great human objective of liberty. In his philosophical reflections on the principles of government, when he was an old man, he summed up these thoughts in a phrase about America as "the workshop of liberty."

Greater challenge and days of stress lay ahead for Madison, but from the early 1790's on his political philosophy tallied in essential points with the increasingly democratic version of republican government that we normally associate with Jefferson's name alone. Although Jefferson would always be more emphatic in his formulations about civil liberties and the moral and political ideal of equality, Madison gave him essential and effective support. They stood together against the Alien and Sedition Acts, even though Madison, as the expert philosopher of the Constitution, cautioned and moderated Jefferson's position. The Kentucky Resolutions that Jefferson drafted and the Virginia Resolutions that Madison wrote brought to a focus the repeated charges they had made that the Federalists were bent upon destroying the residual powers of the states, that they were "unconstitutional" because prepared to stretch the express federal powers in the Constitution to the point where they made the provisions of the Constitution a meaningless exercise in the limbo of legal paperwork. Since both sets of resolutions, after protesting the tyranny over opinion and free political criticism inherent in the Alien and Sedition Acts, called upon their "sister states" to express their opinions, Madison always pointed out that there was no warranted connection between the South Carolina doctrine of nullification and secession and the Resolutions of '98 and '99.

Even more valuable, perhaps, was the solidarity of outlook, program and daily political decision that existed between Jefferson as President and Madison as his Secretary of State. In perfect accord with Jefferson's radical peace policy of Embargo, Madison himself as the next President had to contend with the war that policy had tried to avert. Although Madison's Presidency has never been given the highest marks by the standard-setting historians, Brant's study of his administration has corrected the general picture in several significant aspects. For one thing, Madison can no longer be considered a hapless instrument of the young "Warhawks" in Congress; for another, the effects of the War of 1812 are now considered along with the battle-by-battle setbacks that Henry Adams concentrated on with such deliberate irony, and once the effects—of a new confidence in the enterprise, integrity and spirit of America as an independent nation—are so re-introduced, the opera bouffe interpretation of the war becomes somewhat less persuasive. Meanwhile,

Madison emerged from the grinding agonies of the Presidency not reduced but raised in the estimation of his countrymen. Numerous congratulatory addresses and newspaper tributes were paid to Madison at the close of his administration, but a letter from Albert Gallatin, from Paris, must have brought balm to his soul because of the known worth of the writer. "Few indeed have the good fortune," Gallatin wrote, "after such career as yours, to carry in their retirement the entire approbation of their fellow citizens with that of their own conscience. Never was a country left in a more flourishing situation than the United States at the end of your administration; and they are more united at home and respected abroad than at any period since the war of the independence."

If we try to penetrate the veil that Madison self-effacingly drew over his private life, likes, and loves (and what American is chaste enough to be free of that temptation?), we are taken back to the scholarly young Virginian who described his family lineage as that of "respectable, though not the most opulent Class" of Virginia planters. Madison's father, a justice of the peace and a vestryman in the Anglican church, willingly undertook the expense of his son's education; but even when Madison was active in public life he continued to depend on economic support from his father, plus loans from time to time from friends. The revolutionary war created serious financial problems for the Madisons at home, and the depreciation of war and post-war, when Virginia was unable to pay the salaries of her delegates to the Congress, put the young legislator in acute embarrassment for funds. A credit line is due to Haym Solomon, the patriotic money-lender in Philadelphia, who bailed Madison out on repeated occasions (as he did other Congressmen), refusing to take any interest. On this score, one should recall that Madison had set for himself the most rigid standards of honesty, resolving "never to deal in public property, land, debts, or money whilst a member of a [political] body whose proceedings might influence these transactions."

From innumerable converging bits of evidence, it is clear that Madison was quite a different personality in his relaxed and friendly relationships from what he was in public. Gay and effusive letters to college friends are on record in his early years, even when his bantering leads up to an earnest moral point. He remained a methodical and constant reader all through his life and, as is usually true of bookish persons, knew how to maintain a necessary solitude. On the other hand, from his college days on Madison had a streak of broad humor in him and those who knew him well apparently found some of his off-color stories strong affairs. At Princeton, he had been a member of the brilliant group of young men who were the leaders of the American Whig Society on the campus, and Madison joined happily in their rompish exploits and "Diversions." He also wrote his share of supposedly witty poems and satires, although they were more ribald and less witty than one might ideally have wished.

In his forty-fifth year, Madison fell in love with an attractive young

*widow, Dolley Todd, whom he determined, practically on sight, would
be his wife. New York Senator Aaron Burr was asked to arrange a meeting. On learning this, Dolley hastily wrote to one of her confidantes,
"Aaron Burr says that the great little Madison has asked to be brought
to see me this evening." The meeting could not have been dull, for with
time out for Dolley's hesitations, they were married a few months later,
in September, 1794. Dolley Madison, although a Quaker, possessed infinite zest for society, for all its "do's," furbelows, and feathers. But she
did not cut corners on the culinary and managerial responsibilities of
her wifely role. A neighborly letter to the Monroes, for example, in 1798,
mentions that Mrs. Madison was sending "a few pickles and preserves,
with half a dozen bottles of gooseberries and a bag of dried cherries." In
short order, Dolley Madison charmed all of Madison's friends and her
reign in the White House was double that of any other woman in American history, since she gladly assumed the role of hostess when widower
Jefferson requested it. There is little doubt that this marriage, like that
of John and Abigail Adams, was a transformingly happy marriage for
both partners.*

*When Madison had withdrawn from public life, the Madisons at
Montpelier were visited by "everybody who was anybody or who thought
he was somebody." Every foreign visitor was certain to secure introductions to Jefferson at Monticello and Madison at Montpelier. The
diaries of a few of these observant visitors almost repay the inroads they
must have caused on the family budgets by their well-meant, but long-
staying visits. In the pages of Margaret Bayard Smith's diary, or Jared
Sparks' notes, or Harriet Martineau's sketches of life at the Madisons,
we find the most unmistakable impression of what Madison was like, face
to face. A fragment from a chapter devoted to the Madisons by the intelligent, liberal, and well-travelled English visitor, Miss Martineau,
comments on Madison in his eighty-third year:*

*"His voice was clear and strong, and his manner of speaking particu-
larly lively, often playful. . . . He seemed not to have lost any teeth,
and the form of the face was therefore preserved, without any striking
marks of age. It was an uncommonly pleasant countenance.*

*"His relish for conversation could never have been keener . . . There
is no need to add another to the many eulogies of Madison; I will only
mention that the finest of his characteristics appeared to me to be his
inexhaustible faith; faith that a well-founded commonwealth may . . .
be immortal; not only because the people, its constituency, never die, but
because the principles of justice in which such a commonwealth originates
never die out of the people's heart and mind. This faith shone brightly
through the whole of Mr. Madison's conversation. . . ."*

*Actually, this faith in the American Experiment, which Miss Martineau
truly read in Madison's words, was more troubled than she knew—
pre-occupied as he was with the unmistakable signs of sectional struggle
that threatened to undo all that his generation of creative statesmen*

had been able to construct. He had himself been the prophet of a society that must ever be turbulent to some extent, filled with factional stresses and strains, achieving equilibrium out of multiplicity of interests and give-and-take techniques of adjustment. At the very outset of that "Experiment" he had asked in The Federalist: *"What is government itself but the greatest of all reflections on human nature? If men were angels, no government would be necessary. If angels were to govern men, neither external nor internal controls on government would be necessary." But from 1820 on, with the harsh geographical line dividing sections of the country in the Missouri Compromise, Madison had worried about the carefully devised "controls" on the proud and extensive republic. Having argued always that liberty demands diversity, requires elbow room for arguments, opposing parties, mobility, growth and progress, he had subdued the forces that swept away all past ventures in free governments: he had designed a unique "extensive republic," a federative system that would not hobble opposing interests by depriving them of the chance to speak out—but would help them to live with their differences, to examine them, negotiate them, educate them. Self-government was, he believed, a "free system . . . so congenial with reason, with common sense, and with a universal feeling" that it would surely create friends, generation after generation. Men would grasp at this supreme opportunity to provide for their own happiness—if only the violent ones would not have their way, if only men would take care of the painstaking, endless, "great and advancing cause of representative government."*

A final testimonial to Madison may be read in the letter Jefferson wrote a few months before he died, to his dearest friend. "If ever the earth has beheld a system of administration conducted with a single and steadfast eye to the general interest and happiness of those committed to it, one which, protected by the truth, can never know reproach, it is that to which our lives have been devoted. To myself you have been a pillar of support through life. Take care of me when dead, and be assured that I shall leave with you my last affections." To his illustrious friend, Madison, normally a man of marked reserve, replied: "You cannot look back to the long period of our private friendship and political harmony, with more affecting recollections than I do. If they are a source of pleasure to you, what ought they not to be to me? We cannot be deprived of the happy consciousness of the pure devotion to the public good with which we discharged the trusts committed to us. And I indulge a confidence that sufficient evidence will find its way to another generation, to ensure, after we are gone, whatever of justice may be withheld whilst we are here. The political horizon is already yielding in your case at least, the surest auguries of it. Wishing and hoping that you may yet live to increase the debt which Our Country owes you, and to witness the increasing gratitude, which alone can pay it, I offer you the fullest return of affectionate assurances."

Madison's last message to his countrymen bespoke the vision of his

life: "the advice nearest to my heart and deepest in my convictions is that the Union of the States be cherished and perpetuated. Let the open enemy to it be regarded as a Pandora with her box opened; and the disguised one, as the Serpent creeping with his deadly wiles into Paradise." The very last day before Madison died, he dictated a letter of thanks to George Tucker who had dedicated his biography of Thomas Jefferson to the great little Madison. Madison concluded his thanks by tracing a barely legible signature, the last time he would ever sign his name.

A little couplet that Madison had often used to console Dolley Madison over the dreadful vexations brought to her by the spendthrift son of her first husband went:

"Errors like straws upon the surface flow;
Those who would seek for pearls must dive below."

Would his countrymen remember, and learn?

Autobiography

1. *My "Whole Life has ... been a Public Life"*

James Madison was born on the 5th of March, (O.S.) 1751. His parents James Madison & N. Conway Madison resided in the County of Orange in Virginia. At the time of his birth they were on a visit to her mother, who resided on the Rappahannoc, at Port Conway in the County of King George.

At the age of about 12 years, he was placed by his father under the tuition of Donald Robertson, from Scotland, a man of extensive learning, and a distinguished Teacher, in the County of King & Queen. With him he studied the Latin and Greek languages, was taught to read but not to speak French, and besides Arithmetic & Geography, made some progress in Algebra & Geometry. Miscellaneous literature was also embraced by the plan of the school.

Having remained 3 or 4 years with Mr. Robertson, he prosecuted his studies for a year or two under the Revd. Thos. Martin the Parish Minister of the Established Church, (of England as then called) who lived with his father as a private Tutor.

One of the earliest books which engaged his attention was the "Spectator," which from his own experience, he inferred to be peculiarly adapted to inculcate in youthful minds, just sentiments, an appetite for knowledge, and a taste for the improvement of the mind and manners. . . .

In the year 1769, by the advice of Mr. Martin, and his brother Alexander, both of whom had been educated at Nassau Hall, N. J.—he was sent to that college, of which Doct. Witherspoon was then President, in preference to William & Mary, the climate of which was unhealthy for persons going from a mountainous region. He there went thro' the ordinary course of studies, and in the autumn of 1771, received a Diploma of B. of Arts. His health being at the time too infirm for a journey home, he passed the ensuing winter in Princeton, employing his time in miscellaneous studies; but not without a reference to the profession of the Law; He availed himself of this opportunity of acquiring a slight knowledge of the Hebrew, which was not among the College Studies.

His very infirm health, had been occasioned not a little by a doubled

labour, in which he was joined by a fellow student Jos. Ross, in accomplishing the studies of two years within one, having obtained from the faculty a promise that in case their preparation for the usual degree, should be found unexceptionable, the honor should be conferred. The effect on his health was increased also by an indiscreet experiment of the minimum of sleep & the maximum of application, which the constitution would bear. The former was reduced for some weeks to less than five hours in the twenty four. He became satisfied that no real progress was gained by such a disproportionate extension of the hours of study, nor did he consider their success in performing the task of two years in one as any extraordinary achievement. It could have been effected by others with little more than ordinary exertion. The effect on his health proceeded from the extraordinary exertion made to justify the indulgence granted by the Faculty and to insure the attainment of his object. Hence it is probable they were better qualified in one year than they would have been in two by the ordinary application. . . .

On his return to Virginia he continued for several years in very feeble health, but without neglecting a course of reading, which mingled miscellaneous subjects with the studies intended to qualify him for the Bar, for a practice at which however he never formed any absolute determination.

On the commencement of the dispute with Great Britain, he entered with the prevailing zeal into the American Cause; being under very early and strong impressions in favour of Liberty both Civil & Religious. His devotion to the latter found a particular occasion for its exercise in the persecution instituted in his County as elsewhere against the preachers belonging to the sect of Baptists then beginning to spread thro' the Country. Notwithstanding the enthusiasm which contributed to render them obnoxious to sober opinion as well as to the laws then in force, against Preachers dissenting from the Established Religion, he spared no exertion to save them from imprisonment & to promote their release from it. This interposition tho' a mere duty prescribed by his conscience, obtained for him a lasting place in the favour of that particular sect. Happily it was not long before the fruits of Independence and of the spirit & principles which led to it, included a complete establishment of the Rights of Conscience, without any distinction of sects or individuals.

In 1775, he was elected a member of the Comee for the County, living at the time with his father (who was chairman of it) and had a part in the County proceedings belonging to the period. The spirit of the epoch may be seen in the address to P. H. on his expedition having for its object the military stores in Williamsburg, rifled by Gov. Dunmore.

He was restrained from entering into the military service by the unsettled state of his health and the discourageing feebleness of his constitution of which he was fully admonished by his experience during the exercises and movements of a minute Company which he had joined.

In the spring of 1776 he was initiated into the political career by a County election to the convention, which formed the original Constitution of the State with the Declaration of Rights prefixed to it; and which on the 16th day of May unanimously instructed her deputies in Congress to propose the final separation from G. Britain, as declared by that Body on the 4th of July following. Being young & in the midst of distinguished and experienced members of the Convention he did not enter into its debates; tho' he occasionally suggested amendments; the most material of which was a change of the terms in which the freedom of Conscience was expressed in the proposed Declaration of Rights. This important and meritorious instrument was drawn by Geo. Mason, who had inadvertently adopted the word *toleration* in the article on that subject. The change suggested and accepted, substituted a phraseology which— declared the freedom of conscience to be a *natural and absolute* right.

In the election of Delegates to the Legislature for the ensuing year (1777), he was an unsuccessful candidate. Previous to the Revolution the election of the County Representatives, was as in England, septennial, and it was as there the usage for the candidates to recommend themselves to the voters, not only by personal solicitation, but by the corrupting influence of spirituous liquors, and other treats, having a like tendency. Regarding these as equally inconsistent with the purity of moral and of republican principles; and anxious to promote, by his example, the proper reform, he trusted to the new views of the subject which he hoped would prevail with the people; whilst his competitors adhered to the old practice. The consequence was that the election went against him; his abstinence being represented as the effect of pride or parsimony.

In the course of the ensuing Session of the Legislature he was appointed by it a member of the Council of State, Patrick Henry being then Governor. Of that body he continued a member till late in the year 1779, Thos. Jefferson being then Governor, when he was appointed a Delegate to the Revolutionary Congress.

To prepare himself for this service, he employed an unavoidable detention from it, in making himself acquainted with the state of the Continental affairs, and particularly that of the finances which, owing to the depreciation of the paper currency, was truly deplorable. The view he was led to take of the evil and its causes, was put on a paper, now to be found in several periodical publications, particularly in Freneaus National Gazette.

He took his seat in Congress in March 1780, and was continued a member by annual re-elections till the expiration of the allowed term of three years, computed from the definitive ratification of the Articles of Confederation in 1781. On his arrival at Phila. he found that Congress had, after prolonged discussions, just adopted the new scheme of a Currency, by which forty of the paper dollars in circulation, were to be replaced by a single one. . . .

On his return to private life he resumed his law studies to which the forenoon was chiefly dedicated. In the afternoon he indulged in miscellaneous reading, which embraced among other works of philosophical cast, those of Buffon whose views of nature, however fanciful and even absurd in some instances were highly attractive in others, and especially by the fascinating eloquence which distinguishes them. Whilst engaged on the Zoological volumes, he availed himself of the means occasionally falling into his hands, of making minute comparisons of sundry of our quadrupeds, with those bearing the name, or having the resemblance of them in Europe. Among his papers are notes of the details, which might save in a small degree the labour of more scientific and systematic observers.

He was soon however called from this disposal of his time, by the wish of his country-men, that he should be one of their Representatives in the Legislature of the State; a service to which he yielded with the less reluctance, as it would give him an opportunity of pleading in a favorable position, the cause of reform in our federal system, then in the paroxism of its infirmities, and filling every well informed patriot with the most acute anxieties.

He was accordingly elected in the spring of 1784 & re-elected for the two successive years. For the Legislative proceedings of Virginia during that interesting period, embracing the Convention at Annapolis— the proposed grant of power to Congress and its recommendation of that at Philadelphia—the project of a Religious Establishment— the separation of Kentucky from Virginia—the effort for paper money— the revised code of laws . . . the case of British debts— the offered and declined donation to Genl. Washington— the attempted one to Thos. Paine &c— see his correspondence with Genl. W.— Edd R. and particularly the copious one with Mr. Jefferson during that period. See also the memorial & Remonstrance against the Religious Establishment, and an explanatory letter to Geo. Mason of Green Spring—notes of the proceedings at Annapolis, and an explanatory correspondence with Noah Webster as to the origin of the Convention there. . . .

The convention at Annapolis having recommended another with enlarged powers to be held at Phila. the year following, he brought forward the act of compliance on the part of the Virginia Assembly which availing itself of the early period of its acting set the first example of *deciding* on the measure, tho' it is believed that the Legislature of N. Jersey was the first in *taking* the measure *into consideration*. . . .

After his appointment as a deputy to that Convention, he turned his attention and researches to the sources ancient & modern of information and guidance as to its object. Of the result of these he had the use both in the Convention and afterwards in the "Federalist." . . .

During this period and until the expiration of the Old Congress he continued a member of that Body. . . . His main object in returning to

a service in that body, was to bring about, if possible, the cancelling of the project of Mr. Jay for shutting the Mississippi which threatened an alienation of Kentucky, then a part of Virginia, from any increase of federal power, with such an evidence in view of a disposition in those possessing it to make that sacrifice.

It was in this interval between the close of the Federal Convention and the meeting of the State Conventions that the "Federalist" was written. . . . The papers were first meant for the important and doubtful state of New York and signed a "Citizen of New York"— afterwards meant for all the States under "Publius". In the early stage the papers were shown by the writers to each other before going to the press. This was inconvenient four nos. being required for a week and committing . . . that was dropped. The numbers subsequent to the last written by him were first seen by him in print after his return to Virginia which was hastened by the approaching election.

In the month of April 1788, he was elected by the County of Orange a delegate to the State convention which was to decide on the Constitution proposed by the Federal Convention apart of the Session absent from confinement with bilious fever. . . .

In Feby. 1789 he was elected a Representative from the District in which he lived, to the first Congress under the new Constitution, and was continued a member by re-elections till March 1797, when he declined being longer a candidate. He had become wearied with public life, and longed for a return to a state in which he could indulge his relish for the intellectual pleasures of the closet, and the pursuits of rural life, the only resource of his future support. He had also in the year 1794 entered the married state, with a partner who favoured these views, and added every happiness to his life which female merit could impart. In retiring from the public service at that juncture, he had the example of Geo. Washington and his testimony of the prosperous condition of the Country. . . .

Whilst a member of the H. of Reps. he forbore to follow the example, to which he believes he was the sole exception, of receiving at the public expense the articles of stationary [sic] provided for the members, to which he thought he was no more entitled, than to the supply of other wants incident to his station. To this resolution he adhered throughout, tho' without attracting any notice to it that might lead to a reflection on others. On his first entering public life, he had laid down strict rules for himself in pecuniary matters— one invariably observed was, never to deal in public property, lands, debts or money, whilst a member of the body whose proceedings might influence these transactions. He highly disapproved of public bodies raising the wages of themselves, and declined receiving the addition made by the Legislature of Virginia to the wages of members whilst he was one. In this he was not singular. He was much surprized and disappointed at the incompleting of the

Ratification of the prohibitory Article proposed to the Constitution of the
U. S. in 1790, which he had eluded [sic] in the proposed amendments
in 1790, and had much at heart.

He disapproved also of Chaplains to Congress paid out of the public
Treasury—as a violation of principle. He thought the only legitimate
and becoming mode would be that of voluntary contribution from the
members. . . .

For his course whilst a member of the House of Reps. in relation to
amendments to the Constitution— to the trade with G. Britain and
particularly her West India Colonies— to the tariff— to the power of
Removal— to the funding system*— to the Bank— to the carriage tax—
to the Resolutions, called the Virginia Resolutions— for an alternative
impost on imports from nations not in Treaty with the U. S.—to Giles's
Resolutions against Secretary of Treasury— to Jay's treaty &c see
Debates in Congress. . . .

In 1799, being not disinclined, as urged by his friends particularly
Col. J. Taylor & W. C. Nicholas to be a candidate for the legislature
which would have before it the alien & sedition laws—he was elected
a delegate from the County for that year. He was the more bound to
co-operate on the occasion as he had drawn the Resolutions of the preceding Session, a vindication of which was called for by the animadversions on them, by other states. . . .

In 1800 he was appointed one of the Virginia Electors who voted for
Thos. Jefferson & Aaron Burr to be President & Vice President of the
U. S. It was with much difficulty that a unanimous vote could be obtained
in the Virginia College of Electors for both, lest an equality might throw
the choice into the House of Reps. or otherwise endanger the known
object of the people. J. Madison had received assurances from a confidential friend of Burr that in a certain quarter votes would be thrown
from B. with a view to secure a majority for Jefferson. This authority
alone with the persuasive language of the other electors overcame the
anxiety of Mr. Wythe, whose devoted regard for Mr. Jefferson made him

* His opinion in favour of dividing the payment of the public debt between
the original holders, and the purchasers, grew out of the enormous gain of the latter,
particularly out of Soldiers certificates and the sacrifice of these, to whom the public
faith had not been fulfilled. Whilst the case of this class of Creditors was less in view
he had opposed any discrimination; as in the Congress of 1782. Prior to the final
settlement with the Army in the address drawn by him recommending the plan providing for the debt, until indeed the subject came close into view & the sacrifice of the
soldiers was brought home to reflection, he had not sufficiently scanned and felt the
magnitude of the evil. Hence in a hasty answer to a letter from the Secretary of
the Treasury which followed him after the adjournment, he did not suggest the idea
of discrimination as one of the ingredients in a funding system. It grew rapidly on him
on his return to Congress as the subject unfolded itself; and the outrageous speculations on the floating paper pressed on the attention. Such was the spirit which was
stimulated by the prospect of converting the depreciated paper into par value, that
it seized members of Congress who did not shrink from the practice of purchasing
thro' Brokers the certificates at little price, and contributing by these at the same
moment to transmute them into the value of the precious metals. . . .

nearly inflexible. The event proved that he did not overrate the danger; the votes in the pledged quarter, being all given to Burr as well as to Jefferson, which produced the scene at the first choice by Congress. . . . Virginia was at that time extremely averse to the substitution of General Tickets for District Elections, and yielded only to the necessity of being on an equal footing with other states, by following their examples, and securing a unanimity in the voice of the State.

In 1801 he was appointed Secretary of State and remained such till 1809, when he was elected to the Presidency. In 1812 he was re-elected for another term ending in 1817. . . .

After the close of his public life under the U. S. he devoted himself to his farm & his books; with much avocation however from both by an extensive and often laborious correspondence (as his files shew) which seems to be entailed on Ex-Presidents, especially when they have passed a like prolonged & diversified career in the public service. . . .

A small part of his time had also been given to the Agricultural Body of Albemarle, of which he was appointed President and of course obliged to make an address . . . also a paper drawn up with a view to a professorship of Agriculture.

A larger portion of his time given as first a Visitor— then the Rector of the University. . . .

In 1829 he was prevailed on, notwithstanding his age & very feeble health, being but convalescent from a spell of sickness, to serve as a member of the Convention which revised the constitution of the State. . . . His main object was to promote a compromise of ideas between parties fixed in their hot opinion by their local interests, and threatening an abortive result to an experiment closely connected with the tranquillity of the State, and the capacity of man for self-government. His personal opinion on the rule of suffrage and apportionment of Reps. on the mode of choosing the Governor & the functions to be assigned him, were either controuled by the known will and *meditated* instructions of his Constituents or by the necessity of securing an effective & tranquil result by indulging the party, whose defeat would have been most pregnant with danger to it. His preference would have been the white basis for one branch, and the mixed or federal basis for the other: and in the appointment of Govr. he would have preferred the people to the Legislature; allowing the Govr. a qualified veto on the laws, and a nominating power to the Senate, as in the Government of U. S. and some of the individual States. Tho' aware of the danger of universal suffrage in a future state of Society such as the present state in Europe: he would have extended it so far as to secure in every event and change in the state of Society a majority of people on the side of power. A Government resting on a minority, is an aristocracy not a Republic, and could not be safe with a numerical & physical force against it, without a standing Army, and enslaved press, and a disarmed populace. He thought also the rates of

apportionment, as well as the right of suffrage, both being fundamental principles in free Governments ought to be prescribed by the Constitution and unalterable by the Legislature; which otherwise might so narrow the latter and new-model the former, as to transform the Republic into an Aristocracy. When it had been found impossible to obtain a fixed ratio of apportioning the Representatives, and it being obvius [sic], that inequalities would occur that would make a re-appt necessary, he proposed that the legislature should make an abuse of such a power being guarded against by requiring for the purpose 2/3 of each House. It was found that those most likely to suffer by the omission of some remedial provision, preferred that omission to the proposed supply of it. The explanation is that they wished for an impossibility of redress without a new Convention, as the ground of a struggle for a new Convention. . . .

It has been remarked that the biography of an author must be a history of his writings. So must that of one whose whole life has in a manner been a public life, be gathered from his official transactions, and his manuscript papers on public subjects including letters to as well as from him. This last fund of materials in the case of J. Madison is so voluminous, as doubtless in many other cases, as to make it a forbidding task to consult the whole and not a little & difficult to abridge the task by select & special references, separating the relevant from the redundant or irrelative. This with the little time that could be devoted to attempt, will account for the imperfect manner, in which the references to his files has been executed. A proper execution would have required not only a review of every thing penned by himself, but a great mass of letters from his correspondents; a labour irreconcileable, at his age, with other indispensable demands on his time.

Letters

2. *Liberty of Conscience*

To William Bradford

January 24, 1774

I congratulate you on your heroic proceedings in Philada. with regard to the Tea. I wish Boston may conduct matters with as much discretion as they seem to do with boldness: They seem to have great Tryals and difficulties by reason of the obduracy and *ministerialism* of their Governour. However Political Contests are necessary sometimes as well as military to afford excercise and practise and to instruct in the Art of defending Liberty and property. I verily believe the frequent Assaults that have been made on America[,] Boston especially [,] will in the end prove of real advantage. If the Church of England had been the established and general Religion in all the Northern Colonies as it has been among us here and uninterrupted tranquility had prevailed throughout the Continent, It is clear to me that slavery and Subjection might and would have been gradually insinuated among us. Union of Religious Sentiments begets a surprizing confidence and Ecclesiastical Establishments tend to great ignorance and Corruption all of which facilitate the Execution of mischievous Projects. But away with Politicks! Let me address you as a Student and Philosopher & not as a Patriot now. I am pleased that you are going to converse with the Edwards and Henry's & Charles &c&c who have swayed the British Sceptre though I believe you will find some of them dirty and unprofitable Companions unless you will glean Instruction from their follies and fall more in love with Liberty by beholding such detestable pictures of Tyranny and Cruelty. I was afraid you would not easily have loosened your Affections from the Belles Lettres. A Delicate Taste and warm imagination like yours must find it hard to give up such refined & exquisite enjoyments for the coarse and dry study of the Law: It is like leaving a pleasant flourishing field for a barren desert; perhaps I should not say barren either because the Law does bear fruit but it is sour fruit that must be gathered and pressed and distilled before it can bring pleasure or profit. I perceive I have made a very awkward Comparison but I got the thought by the end and

had gone to[o] far to quit it before I perceived that it was too much entangled in my brain to run it through. And so you must forgive it. I myself used to have too great a hankering after those amusing Studies. Poetry wit and Criticism Romances Plays &c captivated me much: but I begin [to] discover that they deserve but a moderate portion of a *mortal's* Time and that something more substantial more durable more profitable befits a riper Age. It would be exceeding improper for a labouring man to have nothing but flowers in his Garden or to determine to eat nothing but sweet-meats and Confections. Equally absurd would it be for a Scholar and man of Business to make up his whole Library with Books of Fancy and feed his Mind with nothing but such Luscious performances.

When you have an Opportunity and write to Mr. Brackinridge pray tell him I often think of him and long to see him and am resolved to do so in the Spring. George Luckey was with me at Christmas and we talked so much about old Affairs & Old Friends that I have a most insatiable desire to see you all. Luckey will accompany me and we are to set off on the 10th. of April if no disa[s]ter befalls either of us. I want again to breathe your free Air. I expect it will mend my Constitution & confirm my principles. I have indeed as good an Atmosphere at home as the Climate will allow: but have nothing to brag of as to the State and Liberty of my Country. Poverty and Luxury prevail among all sorts: Pride ignorance and Knavery among the Priesthood and Vice and Wickedness among the Laity. This is bad enough But It is not the worst I have to tell you. That diabolical Hell conceived principle of persecution rages among some and to their eternal Infamy the Clergy can furnish their Quota of Imps for such business. This vexes me the most of any thing whatever. There are at this [time?] in the adjacent County not less than 5 or 6 well meaning men in close Goal for publishing their religious Sentiments which in the main are very orthodox. I have neither patience to hear talk or think of any thing relative to this matter, for I have squabbled and scolded abused and ridiculed so long about it, [to so lit]tle purpose that I am without common patience. So I [leave you] to pity me and pray for Liberty of Conscience [to revive among us.] . . .

NB Our Correspondence is too far advanced to req[uire a]pologies for bad writing & [b]lots.

3. *The Critical Situation*

To Thomas Jefferson

Philadelphia, March 27, 1780

. . . Among the various conjunctures of alarm and distress which have arisen in the course of the revolution, it is with pain I affirm to you Sir, that no one can be singled out more truly critical than the present. Our army threatened with an immediate alternative of disbanding or living on free quarter; the public treasury empty; public credit exhausted, nay the private credit of purchasing Agents employed, I am told, as far as it will bear, Congress complaining of the extortion of the people; the people of the improvidence of Congress, and the army of both; our affairs requiring the most mature & systematic measures, and the urgency of occasions admitting only of temporizing expedients, and those expedients generating new difficulties. Congress from a defect of adequate Statesmen more likely to fall into wrong measures and of less weight to enforce right ones, recommending plans to the several states for execution and the states separately rejudging the expediency of such plans, whereby the same distrust of concurrent exertions that has damped the ardor of patriotic individuals, must produce the same effect among the States themselves. An old system of finance discarded as incompetent to our necessities, an untried & precarious one substituted, and a total stagnation in prospect between the end of the former & the operation of the latter: These are the outlines of the true picture of our public situation. I leave it to your own imagination to fill them up. Believe me Sir as things now stand, if the States do not vigorously proceed in collecting the old money and establishing funds for the credit of the new, that we are undone; and let them be ever so expeditious in doing this[,] still the intermediate distress to our army and hindrance to public affairs are a subject of melancholy reflection. Gen Washington writes that a failure of bread has already commenced in the army, and that for any thing he sees, it must unavoidably increase. Meat they have only for a short season and as the whole dependance is on provisions now to be procured, without a shilling for the purpose, and without credit for a shilling, I look forward with the most pungent apprehensions. . . .

4. *"The Rights of Sovereignty"*

To John Jay

October 17, 1780

Sir

Congress having in their instructions of the 4th. inst: directed you to adhere strictly to their former instructions relating to the boundaries of the United States, to insist on the navigation of the Mississippi for the Citizens of the United States in common with the subjects of his Catholic Majesty, as also on a free port or ports below the Northern limit of W. Florida & accessible to Merchant ships, for the use of the former; and being sensible of the influence which these claims on the part of the United States may have on your negociations with the Court of Madrid, have thought it expedient to explain the reasons and principles on which the same are founded, that you may be enabled to satisfy that Court of the equity and justice of their intentions.

With respect to the first of these articles by which the river Miss. is fixed as the boundary between the Spanish settlements and the United States, it is unnecessary to take notice of any pretensions founded on a priority of discovery, of occupancy or on conquest. It is sufficient that by the definitive treaty of Paris 1763 Art. 7 all the territory now claimed by the United States was expressly and irrevocably ceded to the King of G. Britain—and that the United States are in consequence of the revolution in their Government entitled to the benefits of that cession.

The first of these positions is proved by the treaty itself. To prove the last, it must be observed that it is a fundamental principle in all lawful Governments and particularly in the constitution of the British Empire, that all the rights of sovereignty are intended for the benefit of those from whom they are derived and over whom they are exercised. It is known also to have been held for an inviolable principle by the United States whilst they remained a part of the British Empire, that the Sovereignty of the King of England with all the rights & powers included in it, did not extend to them in virtue of his being acknowledged and obeyed as King by the people of England or of any other part of the Empire, but in virtue of his being acknowledged and obeyed as King by the people of America themselves; and that this principle was the basis, first of their opposition to, and finally of their abolition of, his authority over them. From these principles it results that all the territory lying within the limits of the States as fixed by the Sovereign himself, was held by him for their particular benefit, and must equally with his other rights and claims in quality of their sovereign be considered as having devolved on them in consequence of their resumption of the Sovereignty to themselves.

In support of this position it may be further observed that all the territorial rights of the King of G. Britain within the limits of the United States accrued to him from the enterprizes, the risks, the sacrifices, the expence in blood and treasure, of the present inhabitants and their progenitors. If in latter times expences and exertions have been borne by any other part of the Empire in their immediate defence it need only be recollected that the ultimate object of them was the general security and advantage of the empire, that a proportional share was borne by the States themselves, and that if this had not been the case, the benefits resulting from an exclusive enjoyment of their trade have been an abundant compensation. Equity and justice therefore perfectly coincide in the present instance with political and constitutional principles. . . .

5. *Observations on the Convention and the Constitution*

To Thomas Jefferson

New York, October 24, 1787

. . . You will herewith receive the result of the Convention, which continued its session till the 17th of September. I take the liberty of making some observations on the subject which will help to make up a letter, if they should answer no other purpose.

It appeared to be the sincere and unanimous wish of the Convention to cherish and preserve the Union of the States. No proposition was made, no suggestion was thrown out in favor of a partition of the Empire into two or more Confederacies.

It was generally agreed that the objects of the Union could not be secured by any system founded on the principle of a confederation of sovereign States. A voluntary observance of the federal law by all the members could never be hoped for. A compulsive one could evidently never be reduced to practice, and if it could, involved equal calamities to the innocent and the guilty, the necessity of a military force both obnoxious and dangerous, and in general, a scene resembling much more a civil war, than the administration of a regular Government.

Hence was embraced the alternative of a government which instead of operating, on the States, should operate without their intervention on the individuals composing them: and hence the change in the principle and proportion of representation.

This ground-work being laid, the great objects which presented themselves were 1. to unite a proper energy in the Executive and a proper sta-

bility in the Legislative departments, with the essential characters of Republican Government. 2. To draw a line of demarkation which would give
to the General Government every power requisite for general purposes,
and leave to the States every power which might be most beneficially administered by them. 3. To provide for the different interests of different
parts of the Union. 4. To adjust the clashing pretensions of the large and
small States. Each of these objects was pregnant with difficulties. The
whole of them together formed a task more difficult than can be well conceived by those who were not concerned in the execution of it. Adding to
these considerations the natural diversity of human opinions on all new
and complicated subjects, it is impossible to consider the degree of concord which ultimately prevailed as less than a miracle.

The first of these objects as it respects the Executive, was peculiarly
embarrassing. On the question whether it should consist of a single person,
or a plurality of co-ordinate members, on the mode of appointment, on
the duration in office, on the degree of power, on the re-eligibility, tedious
and reiterated discussions took place. The plurality of co-ordinate members had finally but few advocates. Governour Randolph was at the head
of them. The modes of appointment proposed were various, as by the people at large—by electors chosen by the people—by the Executives of the
States—by the Congress, some preferring a joint ballot of the two
Houses—some a separate concurrent ballot allowing to each a negative
on the other house—some a nomination of several candidates by one
House, out of whom a choice should be made by the other. Several other
modifications were started. The expedient at length adopted seemed to
give pretty general satisfaction to the members. As to the duration in
office, a few would have preferred a tenure during good behaviour—a
considerable number would have done so in case an easy and effectual
removal by impeachment could be settled. It was much agitated whether
a long term, seven years for example, with a subsequent and perpetual
ineligibility, or a short term with a capacity to be re-elected, should be
fixed. In favor of the first opinion were urged the danger of a gradual degeneracy of re-elections from time to time, into first a life and then a
hereditary tenure, and the favorable effect of an incapacity to be reappointed, on the independent exercise of the Executive authority. On the
other side it was contended that the prospect of necessary degradation
would discourage the most dignified characters from aspiring to the office,
would take away the principal motive to the faithful discharge of its
duties. The hope of being rewarded with a reappointment, would stimulate ambition to violent efforts for holding over the constitutional term,
and instead of producing an independent administration, and a firmer
defence of the constitutional rights of the department, would render the
officer more indifferent to the importance of a place which he would soon
be obliged to quit for ever, and more ready to yield to the incroachments
of the Legislature of which he might again be a member.—The questions

concerning the degree of power turned chiefly on the appointment to offices, and the control on the Legislature. An *absolute* appointment to all offices—to some offices—to no offices, formed the scale of opinions on the first point. On the second, some contended for an absolute negative, as the only possible mean of reducing to practice, the theory of a free government which forbids a mixture of the Legislative and Executive powers. Others would be content with a revisionary power to be overruled by three fourths of both Houses. It was warmly urged that the judiciary department should be associated in the revision. The idea of some was that a separate revision should be given to the two departments—that if either objected two thirds; if both three fourths, should be necessary to overrule.

In forming the Senate, the great anchor of the Government, the questions as they came within the first object turned mostly on the mode of appointment, and the duration of it. The different modes proposed were, 1. by the House of Representatives, 2. by the Executive, 3. by electors chosen by the people for the purpose, 4. by the State Legislatures. On the point of duration, the propositions descended from good behavior to four years, through the intermediate terms of nine, seven, six and five years. The election of the other branch was first determined to be triennial, and afterwards reduced to biennial.

The second object, the due partition of power, between the General and local Governments, was perhaps of all, the most nice and difficult. A few contended for an entire abolition of the States; Some for indefinite power of Legislation in the Congress, with a negative on the laws of the States, some for such a power without a negative, some for a limited power of legislation, with such a negative: the majority finally for a limited power without the negative. The question with regard to the Negative underwent repeated discussions, and was finally rejected by a bare majority. As I formerly intimated to you my opinion in favor of this ingredient, I will take this occasion of explaining myself on the subject. [Such a check on the States appears to me necessary 1. to prevent encroachments on the General authority, 2. to prevent instability and injustice in the legislation of the States.

1. Without such a check in the whole over the parts, our system involves the evil of imperia in imperio. If a compleat supremacy some where is not necessary in every Society, a controuling power at least is so, by which the general authority may be defended against encroachments of the subordinate authorities, and by which the latter may be restrained from encroachments on each other. If the supremacy of the British Parliament is not necessary as has been contended, for the harmony of that Empire, it is evident I think that without the royal negative or some equivalent controul, the unity of the system would be destroyed. The want of some such provision seems to have been mortal to the antient Confederacies, and to be the disease of the modern. Of the Lycian Con-

federacy little is known. That of the Amphyctions is well known to have
been rendered of little use whilst it lasted, and in the end to have been
destroyed by the predominance of the local over the federal authority.
The same observation may be made, on the authority of Polybius, with
regard to the Achæan League. The Helvetic System scarcely amounts to
a confederacy and is distinguished by too many peculiarities to be a
ground of comparison. The case of the United Netherlands is in point.
The authority of a Statholder, the influence of a standing army, the common interest in the conquered possessions, the pressure of surrounding
danger, the guarantee of foreign powers, are not sufficient to secure the
authority and interests of the generality, against the antifederal tendency
of the provincial sovereignties. The German Empire is another example.
A Hereditary chief with vast independent resources of wealth and power,
a federal Diet, with ample parchment authority, a regular Judiciary establishment, the influence of the neighbourhood of great and formidable
Nations, have been found unable either to maintain the subordination of
the members, or to prevent their mutual contests and encroachments.
Still more to the purpose is our own experience both during the war and
since the peace. Encroachments of the States on the general authority,
sacrifices of national to local interests, interferences of the measures of
different States, form a great part of the history of our political system.
It may be said that the new Constitution is founded on different principles, and will have a different operation. I admit the difference to be
material. It presents the aspect rather of a feudal system of republics, if
such a phrase may be used, than of a Confederacy of independent States.
And what has been the progress and event of the feudal Constitutions? In
all of them a continual struggle between the head and the inferior members, until a final victory has been gained in some instances by one, in
others, by the other of them. In one respect indeed there is a remarkable
variance between the two cases. In the feudal system the sovereign,
though limited, was independent; and having no particular sympathy of
interests with the great Barons, his ambition had as full play as theirs in
the mutual projects of usurpation. In the American Constitution the general authority will be derived entirely from the subordinate authorities.
The Senate will represent the States in their political capacity, the other
House will represent the people of the States in their individual capacity.
The former will be accountable to their constituents at moderate, the
latter at short periods. The President also derives his appointment from
the States, and is periodically accountable to them. This dependence of
the General, on the local authorities seems effectually to guard the latter
against any dangerous encroachments of the former: Whilst the latter
within their respective limits, will be continually sensible of the abridg-
ment of their power, and be stimulated by ambition to resume the surrendered portion of it. We find the representatives of counties and corporations in the Legislatures of the States, much more disposed to sacrifice the

aggregate interest, and even authority, to the local views of their Constituents, than the latter to the former. I mean not by these remarks to insinuate that an esprit de corps will not exist in the national Government, that opportunities may not occur of extending its jurisdiction in some points. I mean only that the danger of encroachments is much greater from the other side, and that the impossibility of dividing powers of legislation, in such a manner, as to be free from different constructions by different interests, or even from ambiguity in the judgment of the impartial, requires some such expedient as I contend for. Many illustrations might be given of this impossibility. How long has it taken to fix, and how imperfectly is yet fixed the legislative power of corporations, though that power is subordinate in the most compleat manner? The line of distinction between the power of regulating trade and that of drawing revenue from it, which was once considered as the barrier of our liberties, was found on fair discussion, to be absolutely undefinable. No distinction seems to be more obvious than that between spiritual and temporal matters. Yet wherever they have been made objects of Legislation, they have clashed and contended with each other, till one or the other has gained the supremacy. Even the boundaries between the Executive, Legislative and Judiciary powers, though in general so strongly marked in themselves, consist in many instances of mere shades of difference. It may be said that the Judicial authority under our new system will keep the States within their proper limits, and supply the place of a negative on their laws. The answer is that it is more convenient to prevent the passage of a law, than to declare it void after it is passed; that this will be particularly the case where the law aggrieves individuals, who may be unable to support an appeal against a State to the supreme Judiciary, that a State which would violate the Legislative rights of the Union, would not be very ready to obey a Judicial decree in support of them, and that a recurrence to force, which in the event of disobedience would be necessary, is an evil which the new Constitution meant to exclude as far as possible.

2. A Constitutional negative on the laws of the States seems equally necessary to secure individuals against encroachments on their rights. The mutability of the laws of the States is found to be a serious evil. The injustice of them has been so frequent and so flagrant as to alarm the most stedfast friends of Republicanism. I am persuaded I do not err in saying that the evils issuing from these sources contributed more to that uneasiness which produced the Convention, and prepared the public mind for a general reform, than those which accrued to our national character and interest from the inadequacy of the Confederation to its immediate objects. A reform therefore which does not make provision for private rights, must be materially defective. The restraints against paper emissions, and violations of contracts are not sufficient. Supposing them to be effectual as far as they go, they are short of the mark. Injustice may be effected by such an infinitude of legislative expedients, that where the dis-

position exists it can only be controuled by some provision which reaches all cases whatsoever. The partial provision made, supposes the disposition which will evade it. It may be asked how private rights will be more secure under the Guardianship of the General Government than under the State Governments, since they are both founded on the republican principle which refers the ultimate decision to the will of the majority, and are distinguished rather by the extent within which they will operate, than by any material difference in their structure. A full discussion of this question would, if I mistake not, unfold the true principles of Republican Government, and prove in contradiction to the concurrent opinions of theoretical writers, that this form of Government, in order to effect its purposes must operate not within a small but an extensive sphere. I will state some of the ideas which have occurred to me on this subject. Those who contend for a simple Democracy, or a pure republic, actuated by the sense of the majority, and operating within narrow limits, assume or suppose a case which is altogether fictitious. They found their reasoning on the idea, that the people composing the Society enjoy not only an equality of political rights; but that they have all precisely the same interests and the same feelings in every respect. Were this in reality the case, their reasoning would be conclusive. The interest of the majority would be that of the minority also; the decisions could only turn on mere opinion concerning the good of the whole of which the major voice would be the safest criterion; and within a small sphere, this voice could be most easily collected and the public affairs most accurately managed. We know however that no Society ever did or can consist of so homogeneous a mass of Citizens. In the savage State indeed, an approach is made towards it; but in that state little or no Government is necessary. In all civilized Societies, distinctions are various and unavoidable. A distinction of property results from that very protection which a free Government gives to unequal faculties of acquiring it. There will be rich and poor; creditors and debtors; a landed interest, a monied interest, a mercantile interest, a manufacturing interest. These classes may again be subdivided according to the different productions of different situations and soils, and according to different branches of commerce and of manufactures. In addition to these natural distinctions, artificial ones will be founded on accidental differences in political, religious and other opinions, or an attachment to the persons of leading individuals. However erroneous or ridiculous these grounds of dissention and faction may appear to the enlightened Statesman, or the benevolent philosopher, the bulk of mankind who are neither Statesmen nor Philosophers, will continue to view them in a different light. It remains then to be enquired whether a majority having any common interest, or feeling any common passion, will find sufficient motives to restrain them from oppressing the minority. An individual is never allowed to be a judge or even a witness in his own cause. If two individuals are under the biass of interest or enmity against a third, the rights of the

latter could never be safely referred to the majority of the three. Will two thousand individuals be less apt to oppress one thousand, or two hundred thousand, one hundred thousand? Three motives only can restrain in such cases. 1. A prudent regard to private or partial good, as essentially involved in the general and permanent good of the whole. This ought no doubt to be sufficient of itself. Experience however shews that it has little effect on individuals, and perhaps still less on a collection of individuals, and least of all on a majority with the public authority in their hands. If the former are ready to forget that honesty is the best policy; the last do more. They often proceed on the converse of the maxim: that whatever is politic is honest. 2. Respect for character. This motive is not found sufficient to restrain individuals from injustice, and loses its efficacy in proportion to the number which is to divide the praise or the blame. Besides as it has reference to public opinion, which is that of the majority, the standard is fixed by those whose conduct is to be measured by it. 3. Religion. The inefficacy of this restraint on individuals is well known. The conduct of every popular assembly, acting on oath, the strongest of religious ties, shews that individuals join without remorse in acts against which their consciences would revolt, if proposed to them separately in their closets. When Indeed Religion is kindled into enthusiasm, its force like that of other passions is increased by the sympathy of a multitude. But enthusiasm is only a temporary state of Religion, and whilst it lasts will hardly be seen with pleasure at the helm. Even in its coolest state, it has been much oftener a motive to oppression than a restraint from it. If then there must be different interests and parties in Society; and a majority when united by a common interest or passion can not be restrained from oppressing the minority, what remedy can be found in a republican Government, where the majority must ultimately decide, but that of giving such an extent to its sphere, that no common interest or passion will be likely to unite a majority of the whole number in an unjust pursuit. In a large Society, the people are broken into so many interests and parties, that a common sentiment is less likely to be felt, and the requisite concert less likely to be formed, by a majority of the whole. The same security seems requisite for the civil as for the religious rights of individuals. If the same sect form a majority and have the power, other sects will be sure to be depressed. Divide et impera, the reprobated axiom of tyranny, is under certain qualifications, the only policy, by which a republic can be administered on just principles. It must be observed however that this doctrine can only hold within a sphere of a mean extent. As in too small a sphere oppressive combinations may be too easily formed against the weaker party; so in too extensive a one a defensive concert may be rendered too difficult against the oppression of those entrusted with the administration. The great desideratum in Government is, so to modify the sovereignty as that it may be sufficiently neutral between different parts of the Society to controul one part from invading the rights of another,

and at the same time sufficiently controuled itself, from setting up an interest adverse to that of the entire Society. In absolute monarchies, the Prince may be tolerably neutral towards different classes of his subjects, but may sacrifice the happiness of all to his personal ambition or avarice. In small republics, the sovereign will is controuled from such a sacrifice of the entire Society, but it is not sufficiently neutral towards the parts composing it. In the extended Republic of the United States, the General Government would hold a pretty even balance between the parties of particular States, and be at the same time sufficiently restrained by its dependence on the community, from betraying its general interests.

Begging pardon for this immoderate digression, I return to the third object abovementioned, the adjustment of the different interests of different parts of the Continent. Some contended for an unlimited power over trade including exports as well as imports, and over slaves as well as other imports; some for such a power, provided the concurrence of two thirds of both Houses were required; some for such a qualification of the power, with an exemption of exports and slaves, others for an exemption of exports only. The result is seen in the Constitution. S. Carolina and Georgia were inflexible on the point of the slaves.

The remaining object, created more embarrassment, and a greater alarm for the issue of the Convention than all the rest put together. The little States insisted on retaining their equality in both branches, unless a compleat abolition of the State Governments should take place; and made an equality in the Senate a sine qua non. The large States on the other hand urged that as the new Government was to be drawn principally from the people immediately and was to operate directly on them, not on the States; and consequently as the States would lose that importance which is now proportioned to the importance of their voluntary compliances with the requisitions of Congress, it was necessary that the representation in both Houses should be in proportion to their size. It ended in the compromise which you will see, but very much to the dissatisfaction of several members from the large States. . . .

6. On Jefferson's "Earth Belongs to the Living"

To Thomas Jefferson

New York, February 4, 1790

Your favor of the 9th. of Jany. inclosing one of Sepr. last did not get to hand till a few days ago. The idea which the latter evolves is a great one, and suggests many interesting reflections to legislators; particularly when

contracting and providing for public debts. Whether it can be received in the extent your reasonings give it, is a question which I ought to turn more in my thoughts than I have yet been able to do, before I should be justified in making up a full opinion on it. My first thoughts though coinciding with many of yours, lead me to view the doctrine as not in *all* respects compatible with the course of human affairs. I will endeavor to sketch the grounds of my skepticism.

"As the earth belongs to the living, not to the dead, a living generation can bind itself only: In every society the will of the majority binds the whole: According to the laws of mortality, a majority of those ripe at any moment for the exercise of their will do not live beyond nineteen years: To that term then is limited the validity of *every* act of the Society; Nor within that limitation, can any declaration of the public will be valid which is not *express*." This I understand to be the outline of the argument.

The acts of a political Society may be divided into three classes.
1. The fundamental Constitution of the Government.
2. Laws involving stipulations which render them irrevocable at the will of the Legislature.
3. Laws involving no such irrevocable quality.
However applicable in Theory the doctrine may be to a Constitution, it seems liable in practice to some very powerful objections. Would not a Government so often revised become too mutable to retain those prejudices in its favor which antiquity inspires, and which are perhaps a salutary aid to the most rational Government in the most enlightened age? Would not such a periodical revision engender pernicious factions that might not otherwise come into existence? Would not, in fine, a Government depending for its existence beyond a fixed date, on some positive and authentic intervention of the Society itself, be too subject to the casualty and consequences of an actual interregnum?

In the 2d. class, exceptions at least to the doctrine seem to be *requisite* both in Theory and practice:

If the earth be the gift of nature to the living their title can extend to the earth in its natural State only. The *improvements* made by the dead form a charge against the living who take the benefit of them. This charge can no otherwise be satisfyed than by executing the will of the dead accompanying the improvements.

Debts may be incurred for purposes which interest the unborn, as well as the living: such are debts for repelling a conquest, the evils of which descend through many generations. Debts may even be incurred principally for the benefit of posterity; such perhaps is the present debt of the U. States, which far exceeds any burdens which the present generation could well apprehend for itself. The term of 19 years might not be sufficient for discharging the debts in either of these cases.

There seems then to be a foundation in the nature of things, in the relation which one generation bears to another, for the *descent* of obligations from one to another. Equity requires it. Mutual good is promoted by it. All that is indispensable in adjusting the account between the dead and the living is to see that the debits against the latter do not exceed the advances made by the former. Few of the incumbrances entailed on nations would bear a liquidation even on this principle.

The objections to the doctrine as applied to the 3d. class of acts may perhaps be merely practical. But in that view they appear to be of great force.

Unless such laws should be kept in force by new acts regularly anticipating the end of the term, all the rights depending on positive laws, that is, most of the rights of property would become absolutely defunct; and the most violent struggles be generated between those interested in reviving and those interested in new-modelling the former state of property. Nor would events of this kind be improbable. The obstacles to the passage of laws which render a power to repeal inferior to an opportunity of rejecting, as a security against oppression, would here render an opportunity of rejecting an insecure provision against anarchy. Add, that the possibility of an event so hazardous to the rights of property could not fail to depreciate its value; that the approach of the crisis would increase this effect; that the frequent return of periods superseding all the obligations depending on antecedent laws and usages, must by weak[en]ing the reverence for those obligations, co-operate with motives to licentiousness already too powerful; and that the uncertainty incident to such a state of things would on one side discourage the steady exertions of industry produced by permanent laws, and on the other, give a disproportionate advantage to the more, over the less, sagacious and interprizing part of the Society.

I find no relief from these consequences, but in the received doctrine that a tacit assent may be given to established Constitutions and laws, and that this assent may be inferred, where no positive dissent appears. It seems less impracticable to remedy, by wise plans of Government, the dangerous operation of this doctrine, than to find a remedy for the difficulties inseparable from the other.

May it not be questioned whether it be possible to exclude wholly the idea of tacit assent, without subverting the foundation of civil Society?— On what principle does the voice of the majority bind the minority? It does not result I conceive from the law of nature, but from compact founded on conveniency. A greater proportion might be required by the fundamental constitution of a Society if it were judged eligible. Prior then to the establishment of this principle, *unanimity* was necessary; and strict Theory at all times presupposes the assent of every member to the establishment of the rule itself. If this assent can not be given tacitly, or be not implied where no positive evidence forbids, persons born in Society

would not on attaining ripe age be bound by acts of the Majority; and either a *unanimous* repetition of every law would be necessary on the accession of new members, or an express assent must be obtained from these to the rule by which the voice of the Majority is made the voice of the whole.

If the observations I have hazarded be not misapplied, it follows that a limitation of the validity of national acts to the computed life of a nation, is in some instances not required by Theory, and in others cannot be accomodated to practice. The observations are not meant however to impeach either the utility of the principle in some particular cases; or the general importance of it in the eye of the philosophical Legislator. On the contrary it would give me singular pleasure to see it first announced in the proceedings of the U. States, and always kept in their view, as a salutary curb on the living generation from imposing unjust or unnecessary burdens on their successors. But this is a pleasure which I have little hope of enjoying. The spirit of philosophical legislation has never reached some parts of the Union, and is by no means the fashion here, either within or without Congress. The evils suffered and feared from weakness in Government, and licentiousness in the people, have turned the attention more towards the means of strengthening the former than of narrowing its extent in the minds of the latter. Besides this, it is so much easier to espy the little difficulties immediately incident to every great plan, than to comprehend its general and remote benefits, that our hemisphere must be still more enlightened before many of the sublime truths which are seen thro' the medium of Philosophy, become visible to the naked eye of the ordinary Politician. . . .

7. *The Whiskey Rebellion*

To James Monroe

Philadelphia, December 4, 1794

. . . You will learn from the Newspapers and official communications the unfortunate scene in the Western parts of Penn which unfolded itself during the recess. The history of its remote & immediate causes, the measures produced by it, and the manner in which it has been closed, does not fall within the compass of a letter. It is probable also that many explanatory circumstances are yet but imperfectly known. I can only refer to the printed accounts which you will receive from the Department of State, and the comments which your memory will assist you in making on them. The event was in several respects a critical one for the cause of liberty,

and the real authors of it, if not in the service, were in the most effectual manner, doing the business of Despotism. You well know the general tendency of insurrections to increase the momentum of power. You will recollect the particular effect of what happened some years ago in Massach. Precisely the same calamity was to be dreaded on a larger scale in this Case. There were eno' as you may well suppose, ready to give the same turn to the crisis, and to propagate the same impressions from it. It happened most auspiciously however that with a spirit truly Republican, the people every where and of every description condemned the resistance of the will of the Majority, and obeyed with alacrity the call to vindicate the authority of the laws. You will see, in the answer of the House of Rep[s] to the P's speech, that the most was made of this circumstance, as an antidote to the poisonous influence to which Republicanism was exposed. If the insurrection had not been crushed in the manner it was I have no doubt that a formidable attempt would have been made to establish the principle that a standing army was necessary for *enforcing the laws*. When I first came to this City about the middle of October, this was the fashionable language. Nor am I sure that the attempt would not have been made if the P. could have been embarked in it, and particularly if the temper of N. England had not been dreaded on this point. I hope we are over that danger for the present. You will readily understand the business detailed in the Newspapers, relating to the denunciation of the "self-created Societies." The introduction of it by the President was perhaps the greatest error of his political life. For his sake, as well as for a variety of obvious reasons, I wished it might be passed over in silence by the H. of Rep[s]. The answer was penned with that view and so reported. This moderate course would not satisfy those who hoped to draw a party advantage out of the P's popularity. The game was, to connect the democratic Societies with the odium of the insurrection—to connect the Republicans in Cong[s] with those Societies—to put the P. ostensibly at the head of the other party, in opposition to both, and by these means prolong the illusions in the North, & try a new experiment on the South. To favor the project, the answer of the Senate was accelerated & so framed as to draw the P. into the most pointed reply on the subject of the Societies. At the same time the answer of the H. of R. was procrastinated till the example of the Senate, & the commitment of the P. could have their full operation. You will see how nicely the House was divided, and how the matter went off. As yet, the discussion has not been revived by the newspaper combatants. If it should and equal talents be opposed, the result cannot fail to wound the P's popularity more than anything that has yet happened. It must be seen that no two principles can be either more indefensible in reason, or more dangerous in practice—than that—1. arbitrary denunciations may punish what the law permits, & what the Legislature has no right by law, to prohibit—and that 2. the Gov[t]. may stifle all censure whatever on its misdoings, for if it be itself the Judge it will

never allow any censures to be just, and if it can suppress censures flowing from one lawful source it may those flowing from any other—from the press and from individuals, as well as from Societies, &c. . . .

8. *Washington and Adams Compared*

To Thomas Jefferson

February, 1798

. . . I am glad to find the public opinion to be taking the turn you describe on the subject of arming. For the public opinion alone can now save us from the rash measures of our hotheaded Executive: it being evident from some late votes of the House of Rep[s], particularly in the choice of Managers for the Impeachment, that a majority there as well as in the Senate are ready to go as far as the controul of their constituents will permit. There never was perhaps a greater contrast between two characters than between those of the present President & his predecessor, altho' it is the boast & prop of the present that he treads in the steps of his predecessor. The one cool considerate & cautious, the other headlong & kindled into flame by every spark that lights on his passions: the one ever scrutinizing into the public opinion, and ready to follow where he could not lead it; the other insulting it by the most adverse sentiments & pursuits. W. a hero in the field, yet overweighing every danger in the Cabinet—A. without a single pretension to the character of a soldier, a perfect Quixote as a statesman: the former chief magistrate pursuing peace every where with sincerity, tho' mistaking the means; the latter taking as much pains to get into war, as the former took to keep out of it. The contrast might be pursued into a variety of other particulars—the policy of the one in shunning connections with the arrangements of Europe, of the other in holding out the U. S. as a makeweight in the Balances of power; the avowed exultation of W. in the progress of liberty every where, & his eulogy on the Revolution & people of France posterior even to the bloody reign & fate of Robespierre—the open denunciations by Adams of the smallest disturbance of the ancient discipline order & tranquillity of despotism, &c &c &c. . . .

9. *The Origins of the Federal Government*

To Noah Webster

Washington, October 12, 1804

I had observed, as you have done, that a great number of loose assertions have at different times been made with respect to the origin of the reform in our system of federal government, and that this has particularly happened on the late occasion which so strongly excited the effusions of party and personal zeal for the fame of Gen. Hamilton.

The change in our government like most other important improvements ought to be ascribed rather to a series of causes than to any particular and sudden one, and to the participation of many, rather than to the efforts of a single agent. It is certain that the general idea of revising and enlarging the scope of the federal authority, so as to answer the necessary purposes of the Union, grew up in many minds, and by natural degrees, during the experienced inefficacy of the old confederation. The discernment of Gen. Hamilton must have rendered him an early patron of the idea. That the public attention was called to it by yourself at an early period is well known.

In common with others, I derived from my service in the old Congress during the latter stages of the Revolutionary war, a deep impression of the necessity of invigorating the federal authority. I carried this impression with me into the legislature of Virginia; where, in the year 1784, if my recollection does not fail me, Mr. Henry co-operated with me and others in certain resolutions calculated to strengthen the hands of Congress.

In 1785, I made a proposition with success in the legislature of the same state, for the appointment of commissioners to meet at Annapolis such commissioners as might be appointed by other states, in order to form some plan for investing Congress with the regulation and taxation of commerce. This I presume to be the proceeding which gave you the impression that the first proposal of the present constitution was then made. It is possible that something more might have been the subject of conversation, or may have been suggested in debate, but I am induced to believe that the meeting at Annapolis was all that was regularly proposed at that session. I would have consulted the journals of it, but they were either lost or mislaid.

Although the step taken by Virginia was followed by the greater number of the states, the attendance at Annapolis was both so tardy and so deficient, that nothing was done on the subject immediately committed to the meeting. The consultations took another turn. The expediency of a

more radical reform than the commissioners had been authorized to undertake being felt by almost all of them, and each being fortified in his sentiments and expectations by those of others, and by the information gained as to the general preparation of the public mind, it was concluded to recommend to the states a meeting at Philadelphia, the ensuing year, of commissioners with authority to digest and propose a new and effectual system of government for the Union. The manner in which this idea rose into effect, makes it impossible to say with whom it more particularly originated. I do not even recollect the member who first proposed it to the body. I have an indistinct impression that it received its first formal suggestion from Mr. Abraham Clark of New Jersey. Mr. Hamilton was certainly the member who drafted the address.

The legislature of Virginia was the first I believe, that had an opportunity of taking up the recommendation, and the first that concurred in it. It was thought proper to express its concurrence in terms that would give the example as much weight and effect as possible; and with the same view to include in the deputation, the highest characters in the state, such as the governor and chancellor. The same policy led to the appointment of Gen. Washington, who was put at the head of it. It was not known at the time how far he would lend himself to the occasion. When the appointment was made known to him, he manifested a readiness to yield to the wishes of the legislature, but felt a scruple from his having signified to the Cincinnati, that he could not meet them at Philadelphia, near about the same time, for reasons equally applicable to the other occasion. Being in correspondence with him at the time and on the occasion, I pressed him to step over the difficulty. It is very probable that he might consult with others, particularly with Mr. Hamilton, and that their or his exhortations and arguments may have contributed more than mine to his final determination.

When the convention as recommended at Annapolis took place at Philadelphia, the deputies from Virginia supposed, that as that state had been first in the successive steps leading to a revision of the federal system, some introductory propositions might be expected from them. They accordingly entered into consultation on the subject, immediately on their arrival in Philadelphia, and having agreed among themselves on the outline of a plan, it was laid before the convention by Mr. Randolph, at that time governor of the state, as well as member of the convention. This project was the basis of its deliberations; and after passing through a variety of changes in its important as well as its lesser features, was developed and amended into the form finally agreed to.

I am afraid that this sketch will fall much short of the object of your letter. Under more favorable circumstances, I might have made it more particular. I have often had it in idea to make out from the materials in my hands, and within my reach, as minute a chronicle as I could, of the origin and progress of the last revolution in our government. I went

through such a task with respect to the declaration of independence, and the old confederation, whilst a member of Congress in 1783; availing myself of all the circumstances to be gleaned from the public archives, and from some auxilliary sources. To trace in like manner a chronicle or rather a history of our present constitution, would in several points of view be still more curious and interesting; and fortunately the materials for it are far more extensive. Whether I shall ever be able to make such a contribution to the annals of our country, is rendered every day more and more uncertain.

I will only add that on the slight view which I have taken of the subject to which you have been pleased to invite my recollections, it is to be understood, that in confining myself so much to the proceedings of Virginia, and to the agency of a few individuals, no exclusion of other states or persons is to be implied, whose share in the transactions of the period may be unknown to me.

10. *Gossip and News*

To Mrs. Madison

1809

Yours of the 1st instant my dearest gives me much happiness but it cannot be complete till I have you again with me. Let me know the moment you can of the time you will set out that I may make arrangements for paying the Dr. &c. My tob has been sold in Ricd but unfortunately the bills are not yet come on & are on N. York at 60 days so that some recognition will be necessary. I did not expect you would receive much from your Tenants. Dont forget to do something as to insuring the buildings. Your question as to Spain & England is puzzling, as one gets into ill humor it is possible the other may change her countenance. If a general war takes place in Europe Spain will probably be less disposed to insult us & England less sparing of her insults whether a war will be forced by either is more than can be foreseen. It certainly will not if they consult their interest. The power of deciding questions of war & providing measures that will make or meet it is with Congress & that is always our answer to Newspapers. Madam T[urreau] is here the General not. Your friends are all well except Capt T[ingey] who has been in extreme danger but is mending. Mrs. T also has been unwell. I enclose a letter from Payne & one from Mrs R. Miss P. postscript makes my mouth water. Cousin Isaac's would too, if he had ever had the taste which I have had. . . .

11. *Second War for Independence*

To ———

Sir,—I have rec^d. the address from "The Convention of Republican Delegates from the several Counties of the State of New Jersey," explaining the sentiments entertained, at this crisis, by that portion of my Constituents. The sentiments are worthy the character of Citizens, who know the value of the National rights at stake in the present contest; and who are willing to do justice to the sincere & persevering efforts which have been employed to obtain respect to them without a resort to arms.

The conduct of the nation agst. whom this resort has been proclaimed left no choice but between that & the greater evil of a surrender of our Sovereignty on the Element, on which all nations have equal rights, and in the free use of which, the U. S. as a nation whose agriculture & commerce are so closely allied, have an essential interest.

The appeal to force in opposition to the force so long continued against us, had become the more urgent, as every endeavor short of it, had not only been fruitless; but had been followed by fresh usurpations & oppressions. The intolerable outrages committed agst. the crews of our vessels which at one time were the result of alledged searches for deserters from British Ships of War, had grown into a like pretension, first as to all British Seamen, and next, as to all British subjects; with the invariable practice of seizing on all neutral seamen of every Nation, and on all such of our own seamen as British officers interested in the abuse might please to demand.

The blockading orders in Council, commencing on the plea of retaliating injuries indirectly done to G. Britain, through the direct operation of French Decrees agst. the trade of the U. S. with her, and on a professed disposition to proceed step by step with France in revoking them, have been since bottomed on pretensions more & more extended and arbitrary; till at length it is openly avowed, as indispensable to a repeal of the Orders as they affect the U. States, that the French Decrees, be repealed as they affect G. Britain directly, and all other neutrals, as well as the U. States. To this extraordinary avowal is superadded abundant evidence that the real object of the orders is, not to restore freedom to the American Commerce with G. B. which could indeed be little interrupted by the decrees of France, but to destroy our lawful commerce, as interfering with her own unlawful commerce with her enemies. The only foundation of this attempt to banish the American flag from the highway of Nations, or to render it wholly subservient to the commercial views of the B. Gov^t.

is the absurd and exploded doctrine that the ocean not less than the land is susceptible of occupancy & dominion; that this dominion is in the hands of G. Britain; and that her laws, not the law of nations, which is ours as well as hers, are to regulate our maritime intercourse with the rest of the world.

When the U. S. assumed & established their rank among the Nations of the Earth, they assumed & established a common Sovereignty on the high seas, as well as an exclusive sovereignty within their territorial limits. The one is as essential as the other to their Character as an Independent Nation. However conceding they may have been on controvertible points, or forbearing under casual and limited injuries, they can never submit to wrongs irreparable in their kind, enormous in their amount, and indefinite in their duration; and which are avowed and justified on principles degrading the U. States from the rank of a sovereign & independent Power. In attaining this high rank, and the inestimable blessings attached to it, no part of the American people, had a more meritorious share than the people of N. Jersey. From none therefore may more reasonably be expected a patriotic zeal in maintaining by the sword the unquestionable & unalienable rights acquired by it; and which it is found can no otherwise be maintained.

12. *The Political Experiment of Checks and Balances*

To John Adams

May 22d, 1817

Dear Sir,—I have received your favor of April 22d, with the two volumes bearing the name of Condorcet. If the length of time they remained in your hands had been in the least inconvenient to me, which was not the case, the debt would have been overpaid by the interesting observations into which you were led by your return of them.

The idea of a Government "in one centre," as expressed and espoused by this Philosopher and his theoretic associates, seems now to be every where exploded. And the views which you have given of its fallacy will be a powerful obstacle to its revival anywhere. It is remarkable that in each of our States which approached nearest to the theory changes were soon made, assimilating their constitutions to the examples of the other States, which had placed the powers of Government in different depositories, as means of controlling the impulse and sympathy of the passions, and affording to reason better opportunities of asserting its prerogatives.

The great question now to be decided, and it is one in which humanity is more deeply interested than in any political experiment yet made, is, whether checks and balances sufficient for the purposes of order, justice, and the general good, may not be created by a proper division and distribution of power among different bodies, differently constituted, but all deriving their existence from the elective principle, and bound by a responsible tenure of their trusts. The experiment is favored by the extent of our Country, which prevents the contagion of evil passions; and by the combination of the federal with the local systems of Government, which multiplies the divisions of power, and the mutual checks by which it is to be kept within its proper limits and direction. In aid of these considerations much is to be hoped from the force of opinion and habit, as these ally themselves with our political institutions. I am running, however, into reflections, without recollecting that all such must have fallen within the comprehensive reviews which your mind has taken of the principles of our Government, and the prospects of our Country.

I have always been much gratified by the favorable opinion you have been pleased occasionally to express of the public course pursued while the Executive trust was in my hands, and I am very thankful for the kind wishes you have added to a repetition of it. I pray you to be assured of the sincerity with which I offer mine, that a life may be prolonged which continues to afford proofs of your capacity to enjoy and make it valuable.

13. *"The Germ of Independence"*

To John Adams

Montpellier, Aug. 7, 1818

. . . Your remark is very just on the subject of Independence. It was not the offspring of a particular man or a particular moment. If Mr. Wirt be otherwise understood in his life of Mr. Henry, I cannot but suppose that his intention has been not clearly expressed, or not sufficiently scrutinized. Our forefathers brought with them the germ of Independence, in the principle of self-taxation. Circumstances unfolded & perfected it.

The first occasion which aroused this principle, was, if I can trust my recollection, the projected Union at Albany in 1754, when the proposal of the British Gov^t. to reimburse its advances for the Colonies by a Parliamentary tax on them was met by the letter from D^r. Franklin to Governor Shirley, pointing out the unconstitutionality, the injustice, and the impolicy of such a tax.

The opposition & discussions produced by the Stamp & subsequent Acts

of Parliament, make another stage in the growth of Independence. The attempts to distinguish between legislation on the subject of taxes, and on other subjects, terminated in the disclosure that no such distinction existed.

And these combats against the arrogated Authority of the British Legislature paved the way for burying in the same grave with it, the forfeited Authority of the British King.

If the merit of Independence as declared in 1776 is to be traced to Individuals, it belongs to those who first meditated the glorious measure, who were the ablest in contending for it, & who were the most decided in supporting it. Future times will be disposed to apportion this merit justly, and the present times ought to bequeath the means for doing it, unstained with the unworthy feelings which you so properly deprecate. . . .

14. *Emancipation of the Slaves*

To Robert J. Evans

Montpellier, June 15, 1819

. . . On the subject of an eventual extinguishment of slavery in the U. S. . . .

A general emancipation of slaves ought to be 1. gradual. 2. equitable & satisfactory to the individuals immediately concerned. 3. consistent with the existing & durable prejudices of the nation.

That it ought, like remedies for other deeprooted and wide-spread evils, to be gradual, is so obvious that there seems to be no difference of opinion on that point.

To be equitable & satisfactory, the consent of both the Master & the slave should be obtained. That of the Master will require a provision in the plan for compensating a loss of what he held as property guarantied by the laws, and recognised by the Constitution. That of the slave, requires that his condition in a state of freedom, be preferable in his own estimation, to his actual one in a state of bondage.

To be consistent with existing and probably unalterable prejudices in the U. S. the freed blacks ought to be permanently removed beyond the region occupied by or allotted to a White population. The objections to a thorough incorporation of the two people are, with most of the Whites insuperable; and are admitted by all of them to be very powerful. If the blacks, strongly marked as they are by Physical & lasting peculiarities, be retained amid the Whites, under the degrading privation of equal rights political or social, they must be always dissatisfied with their condition as

a change only from one to another species of oppression; always secretly confederated ag^st. the ruling & privileged class; and always uncontroulled by some of the most cogent motives to moral and respectable conduct. The character of the free blacks, even where their legal condition is least affected by their colour, seems to put these truths beyond question. It is material also that the removal of the blacks be to a distance precluding the jealousies & hostilities to be apprehended from a neighboring people stimulated by the contempt known to be entertained for their peculiar features; to say nothing of their vindictive recollections, or the predatory propensities which their State of Society might foster. Nor is it fair, in estimating the danger of Collisions with the Whites, to charge it wholly on the side of the Blacks. There would be reciprocal antipathies doubling the danger.

The colonizing plan on foot, has as far as it extends, a due regard to these requisites; with the additional object of bestowing new blessings civil & religious on the quarter of the Globe most in need of them. The Society proposes to transport to the African Coast all free & freed blacks who may be willing to remove thither; to provide by fair means, &, it is understood with a prospect of success, a suitable territory for their reception; and to initiate them into such an establishment as may gradually and indefinitely expand itself.

The experiment, under this view of it, merits encouragement from all who regard slavery as an evil, who wish to see it diminished and abolished by peaceable & just means; and who have themselves no better mode to propose. Those who have most doubted the success of the experiment must at least have wished to find themselves in an error.

But the views of the Society are limited to the case of blacks already free, or who may be *gratuitously* emancipated. To provide a commensurate remedy for the evil, the plan must be extended to the great Mass of blacks, and must embrace a fund sufficient to induce the Master as well as the slave to concur in it. Without the concurrence of the Master, the benefit will be very limited as it relates to the Negroes; and essentially defective, as it relates to the U. States; and the concurrence of Masters, must, for the most part, be obtained by purchase.

Can it be hoped that voluntary contributions, however adequate to an auspicious commencement, will supply the sums necessary to such an enlargement of the remedy? May not another question be asked? Would it be reasonable to throw so great a burden on the individuals distinguished by their philanthropy and patriotism?

The object to be obtained, as an object of humanity, appeals alike to all; as a National object, it claims the interposition of the nation. It is the nation which is to reap the benefit. The nation therefore ought to bear the burden.

Must then the enormous sums required to pay for, to transport, and to establish in a foreign land all the slaves in the U. S. as their Masters may

be will^g. to part with them, be taxed on the good people of the U. S. or be obtained by loans swelling the public debt to a size pregnant with evils next in degree to those of slavery itself?

Happily it is not necessary to answer this question by remarking that if slavery as a national evil is to be abolished, and it be just that it be done at the national expence, the amount of the expence is not a paramount consideration. It is the peculiar fortune, or, rather a providential blessing of the U. S. to possess a resource commensurate to this great object, without taxes on the people, or even an increase of the public debt.

I allude to the vacant territory the extent of which is so vast, and the vendible value of which is so well ascertained. . . .

And to what object so good so great & so glorious, could that peculiar fund of wealth be appropriated? Whilst the sale of territory would, on one hand be planting one desert with a free & civilized people, it would on the other, be giving freedom to another people, and filling with them another desert. And if in any instances, wrong has been done by our forefathers to people of one colour, by dispossessing them of their soil, what better atonement is now in our power than that of making what is rightfully acquired a source of justice & of blessings to a people of another colour? . . .

15. *"The Original Sin of the African Trade"*

To Marquis de la Fayette

Montpellier, November 25, 1820

. . . We feel here all the pleasure you express at the progress of reformation on your Continent. Despotism can only exist in darkness, and there are too many lights now in the political firmament, to permit it to reign any where, as it has heretofore done, almost every where. To the events in Spain & Naples has succeeded already, an auspicious epoch in Portugal. Free States seem indeed to be propagated in Europe, as rapidly as new States are on this side of the Atlantic: Nor will it be easy for their births or their growths if safe from dangers within to be strangled by external foes, who are not now sufficiently united among themselves, are controuled by the aspiring sentiments of their people, are without money of their own, and are no longer able to draw on the foreign fund which has hitherto supplied their belligerent necessities.

Here, we are, on the whole, doing well, and giving an example of a free system, which I trust will be more of a Pilot to a good Port, than a Beacon warning from a bad one. We have, it is true, occasional fevers, but they are of the transient kind flying off thro' the surface, without

preying on the vitals. A Gov^t. like ours has so many safety-valves giving vent to overheated passions, that it carries within itself a relief ag^st. the infirmities from which the best of human Institutions cannot be exempt. The subject which ruffles the surface of public affairs most at present, is furnished by the transmission of the "Territory" of Missouri from a state of nonage to a maturity for self-Gov^t. and for a membership in the Union. Among the questions involved in it, the one most immediately interesting to humanity is the question whether a toleration or prohibition of slavery Westward of the Mississippi, would most extend its evils. The humane part of the argument against the prohibition, turns on the position, that whilst the importation of slaves from abroad is precluded, a diffusion of those in the Country, tends at once to meliorate their actual condition, and to facilitate their eventual emancipation. Unfortunately, the subject which was settled at the last session of Congress, by a mutual concession of the parties, is reproduced on the Arena, by a clause in the Constitution of Missouri, distinguishing between free persons of Colour, and white persons; and providing that the Legislature of the new State shall exclude from it the former. What will be the issue of the revived discussion is yet to be seen. The case opens the wider field as the Constitutions & laws of the different States are much at variance in the civic character given to free people of colour; those of most of the States, not excepting such as have abolished slavery, imposing various disqualifications which degrade them from the rank & rights of white persons. All these perplexities develope more & more the dreadful fruitfulness of the original sin of the African trade.

16. *"The Gordian Knot of the Constitution"*

To Spencer Roane

Montpellier, June 29, 1821

... The Gordian Knot of the Constitution seems to lie in the problem of collision between the federal & State powers, especially as eventually exercised by their respective Tribunals. If the knot cannot be untied by the text of the Constitution it ought not, certainly, to be cut by any Political Alexander.

I have always thought that a construction of the instrument ought to be favoured, as far as the text would warrant, which would obviate the dilemma of a Judicial rencounter or a mutual paralysis; and that on the abstract question whether the federal or the State decisions ought to prevail, the sounder policy would yield to the claims of the former.

Our Governmental System is established by a compact, not between

the Government of the U. States, and the State Governments; but between the States, as sovereign communities, stipulating each with the others, a surrender of certain portions, of their respective authorities, to be exercised by a Common Gov^t. and a reservation, for their own exercise, of all their other Authorities. The possibility of disagreements concerning the line of division between these portions could not escape attention; and the existence of some Provision for terminating regularly & authoritatively such disagreements, not but be regarded as a material desideratum.

Were this trust to be vested in the States in their individual characters, the Constitution of the U. S. might become different in every State, and would be pretty sure to do so in some; the State Gov^{ts}. would not stand all in the same relation to the General Gov^t., some retaining more, others less of sovereignty; and the vital principle of equality, which cements their Union thus gradually be deprived of its virtue. Such a trust vested in the Gov^t. representing the whole and exercised by its tribunals, would not be exposed to these consequences; whilst the trust itself would be controulable by the States who directly or indirectly appoint the Trustees: whereas in the hands of the States no federal controul direct or indirect would exist the functionaries holding their appointments by tenures altogether independent of the General Gov^t.

Is it not a reasonable calculation also that the room for jarring opinions between the National & State tribunals will be narrowed by successive decisions sanctioned by the Public concurrence; and that the weight of the State tribunals will be increased by improved organizations, by selections of abler Judges, and consequently by more enlightened proceedings? Much of the distrust of these departments in the States, which prevailed when the National Constitution was formed has already been removed. Were they filled everywhere, as they are in some of the States, one of which I need not name, their decisions at once indicating & influencing the sense of their Constituents, and founded on united interpretations of constitutional points, could scarcely fail to frustrate an assumption of unconstitutional powers by the federal tribunals.

Is it too much to anticipate even that the federal & State Judges, as they become more & more coordinate in talents, with equal integrity, and feeling alike the impartiality enjoined by their oaths, will vary less & less also in their reasonings & opinions on all Judicial subjects; and thereby mutually contribute to the clearer & firmer establishment of the true boundaries of power, on which must depend the success & permanency of the federal republic, the best Guardian, as we believe, of the liberty, the safety, and the happiness of men. In these hypothetical views I may permit my wishes to sway too much my hopes. I submit the whole nevertheless to your perusal, well assured that you will approve the former, if you cannot join fully in the latter.

17. *The Constitutional Convention*

To John G. Jackson

Montpellier, December 27, 1821

That most of us carried into the Convention a profound impression produced by the experienced inadequacy of the old Confederation, and by
the monitory examples of all similar ones ancient & modern, as to the
necessity of binding the States together by a strong Constitution, is certain. The necessity of such a Constitution was enforced by the gross and
disreputable inequalities which had been prominent in the internal administrations of most of the States. Nor was the recent & alarming insurrection headed by Shays, in Massachusetts without a very sensible effect
on the pub. mind. Such indeed was the aspect of things that in the eyes
of all the best friends of liberty a crisis had arrived which was to decide
whether the Am^n. Experiment was to be a blessing to the world, or to
blast forever the hopes which the republican cause had inspired; and
what is not to be overlooked the disposition to give to a new system all
the vigour consistent with Republican principles, was not a little stimulated by a backwardness in some quarters towards a Convention for the
purpose, which was ascribed to a secret dislike to popular Gov^t. and a
hope that delay would bring it more into disgrace, and pave the way for
a form of Gov^t. more congenial with Monarchical or Aristocratical Pre-
dilections.

This view of the crisis made it natural for many in the Convention to
lean more than was perhaps in strictness warranted by a proper distinction between causes temporary as some of them doubtless were, and
causes permanently inherent in popular frames of Gov^t. It is true also, as
has been sometimes suggested that in the course of discussions in the
Convention, where so much depended on compromise, the patrons of
different opinions often set out on negotiating grounds more remote
from each other, than the real opinions of either were from the point at
which they finally met.

For myself, having from the first moment of maturing a political
opinion down to the present one, never ceased to be a votary of the principle of self Gov^t., I was among those most anxious to rescue it from the
danger which seemed to threaten it; and with that view was willing to
give to a Gov^t. resting on that foundation, as much energy as would insure the requisite stability and efficacy. It is possible that in some instances this consideration may have been allowed a weight greater than
subsequent reflection within the Convention, or the actual operation of
the Gov^t. would sanction. It may be remarked also that it sometimes happened that opinions as to a particular modification or a particular power

of the Gov^t. had a conditional reference to others which combined therewith would vary the character of the whole.

But whatever might have been the opinions entertained in forming the Constitution, it was the duty of all to support it in its true meaning as understood *by the nation* at the time of its ratification. No one felt this obligation more than I have done; and there are few perhaps whose ultimate & deliberate opinions on the merits of the Constitution accord in a greater degree with that Obligation.

The departures from the true & fair construction of the instrument have always given me pain, and always experienced my opposition when called for. The attempts in the outset of the Gov^t. to defeat those safe, if not necessary, & those politic if not obligatory amendments introduced in conformity to the known desires of the Body of the people, & to the pledges of many, particularly myself when vindicating & recommending the Constitution, was an occurrence not a little ominous. And it was soon followed by indications of political tenets, and by rules, or rather the abandonment of all rules of expounding it, wch. were capable of transforming it into something very different from its legitimate character as the offspring of the National Will. I wish I could say that constructive innovations had altogether ceased.

Whether the Constitution, as it has divided the powers of Gov^t. between the States in their separate & in their united Capacities, tends to an oppressive aggrandizement of the Genl. Gov^t. or to an Anarchical Independence of the State Gov^{ts}. is a problem which time alone can absolutely determine. It is much to be wished that the division as it exists, or may be made with the regular sanction of the people, may effectually guard agst. both extremes; for it cannot be doubted that an accumulation of all Power in the Genl. Gov^t. w^d. as naturally lead to a dangerous accumulation in the Executive hands, as that the resumption of all power by the several States w^d. end in the calamities incident to contiguous & rival Sovereigns; to say nothing of its effect in lessening the security for sound principles of administration within each of them.

There have been epochs when the Genl. Gov^t. was evidently drawing a disproportion of power into its vortex. There have been others when States threatened to do the same. At the present moment it w^d. seem that both are aiming at encroachments, each on the other. One thing however is certain, that in the present condition and temper of the Community, the Genl. Gov^t. cannot long succeed in encroachments contravening the will of a Majority of the States, and of the people. Its responsibility to these w^d., as was proved on a conspicuous occasion, quickly arrest its career. If, at this time, the powers of the Genl. Gov^t. be carried to unconstitutional lengths, it will be the result of a majority of the States & of the people, actuated by some impetuous feeling, or some real or supposed interest, overruling the minority, and not of successful attempts by the Genl. Gov^t. to overpower both.

In estimating the greater tendency in the political System of the Union to a subversion, or to a separation of the States composing it, there are some considerations to be taken into the account which have been little Adverted to by the most oracular Authors on the Science of Gov^t. and which are but imperfectly developed as yet by our own experience. Such are the size of the States, the number of them, the territorial extent of the whole, and the degree of external danger. Each of these, I am persuaded, will be found to contribute its impulse to the practical direction which our great Political Machine is to take.

18. *Separation Between Church and State*

To Edward Livingston

Montpellier, July 10, 1822

. . . I observe with particular pleasure the view you have taken of the immunity of Religion from civil jurisdiction, in every case where it does not trespass on private rights or the public peace. This has always been a favorite principle with me; and it was not with my approbation, that the deviation from it took place in Congress, when they appointed Chaplains, to be paid from the National Treasury. It would have been a much better proof to their Constituents of their pious feeling if the members had contributed for the purpose, a pittance from their own pockets. . . .

There has been another deviation from the strict principle in the Executive Proclamations of fasts & festivals, so far, at least, as they have spoken the language of *injunction,* or have lost sight of the equality of *all* religious sects in the eye of the Constitution. Whilst I was honored with the Executive Trust I found it necessary on more than one occasion to follow the example of predecessors. But I was always careful to make the Proclamations absolutely indiscriminate, and merely recommendatory; or rather mere *designations* of a day, on which all who thought proper might *unite* in consecrating it to religious purposes, according to their own faith & forms. . . . Notwithstanding the general progress made within the two last centuries in favour of this branch of liberty, & the full establishment of it, in some parts of our Country, there remains in others a strong bias towards the old error, that without some sort of alliance or coalition between Government & Religion neither can be duly supported. Such indeed is the tendency to such a coalition, and such its corrupting influence on both the parties, that the danger cannot be too carefully guarded against. And in a Government of opinion, like

ours, the only effectual guard must be found in the soundness and stability of the general opinion on the subject. Every new & successful example therefore of a perfect separation between ecclesiastical and civil matters, is of importance. And I have no doubt that every new example, will succeed, as every past one has done, in shewing that religion & Gov^t. will both exist in greater purity, the less they are mixed together. It was the belief of all sects at one time that the establishment of Religion by law, was right & necessary; that the true religion ought to be established in exclusion of every other; And that the only question to be decided was which was the true religion. The example of Holland proved that a toleration of sects, dissenting from the established sect, was safe & even useful. The example of the Colonies, now States, which rejected religious establishments altogether, proved that all Sects might be safely & advantageously put on a footing of equal & entire freedom; and a continuance of their example since the declaration of Independence, has shewn that its success in Colonies was not to be ascribed to their connection with the parent Country. If a further confirmation of the truth could be wanted, it is to be found in the examples furnished by the States, which have abolished their religious establishments. I cannot speak particularly of any of the cases excepting that of Virg^a. where it is impossible to deny that Religion prevails with more zeal, and a more exemplary priesthood than it ever did when established and patronised by Public authority. We are teaching the world the great truth that Gov^{ts}. do better without Kings & Nobles than with them. The merit will be doubled by the other lesson that Religion flourishes in greater purity, without than with the aid of Gov^t.

19. *Liberty and Learning*

To W. T. Barry

August 4, 1822

. . . The liberal appropriations made by the Legislature of Kentucky for a general system of Education cannot be too much applauded. A popular Government, without popular information, or the means of acquiring it, is but a Prologue to a Farce or a Tragedy; or, perhaps both. Knowledge will forever govern ignorance: And a people who mean to be their own Governors, must arm themselves with the power which knowledge gives.

I have always felt a more than ordinary interest in the destinies of Kentucky. Among her earliest settlers were some of my particular friends

and Neighbors. And I was myself among the foremost advocates for submitting to the Will of the "District" the question and the time of its becoming a separate member of the American family. Its rapid growth & signal prosperity in this character have afforded me much pleasure; which is not a little enhanced by the enlightened patriotism which is now providing for the State a Plan of Education embracing every class of Citizens, and every grade & department of Knowledge. No error is more certain than the one proceeding from a hasty & superficial view of the subject: that the people at large have no interest in the establishment of Academies, Colleges, and Universities, where a few only, and those not of the poorer classes can obtain for their sons the advantages of superior education. It is thought to be unjust that all should be taxed for the benefit of a part, and that too the part least needing it.

If provision were not made at the same time for every part, the objection would be a natural one. But, besides the consideration when the higher Seminaries belong to a plan of general education, that it is better for the poorer classes to have the aid of the richer by a general tax on property, than that every parent should provide at his own expence for the education of his children, it is certain that every Class is interested in establishments which give to the human mind its highest improvements, and to every Country its truest and most durable celebrity.

Learned Institutions ought to be favorite objects with every free people. They throw that light over the public mind which is the best security against crafty & dangerous encroachments on the public liberty. They are the nurseries of skilful Teachers for the schools distributed throughout the Community. They are themselves schools for the particular talents required for some of the Public Trusts, on the able execution of which the welfare of the people depends. They multiply the educated individuals from among whom the people may elect a due portion of their public Agents of every description; more especially of those who are to frame the laws; by the perspicuity, the consistency, and the stability, as well as by the just & equal spirit of which the great social purposes are to be answered.

Without such Institutions, the more costly of which can scarcely be provided by individual means, none but the few whose wealth enables them to support their sons abroad can give them the fullest education; and in proportion as this is done, the influence is monopolized which superior information every where possesses. At cheaper & nearer seats of Learning parents with slender incomes may place their sons in a course of education putting them on a level with the sons of the Richest. Whilst those who are without property, or with but little, must be peculiarly interested in a System which unites with the more Learned Institutions, a provision for diffusing through the entire Society the education needed for the common purposes of life. A system comprizing the Learned Institutions may be still further recommended to the more indigent

class of Citizens by such an arrangement as was reported to the General Assembly of Virginia, in the year 1779, by a Committee appointed to revise laws in order to adapt them to the genius of Republican Government. It made part of a "Bill for the more general diffusion of knowledge" that wherever a youth was ascertained to possess talents meriting an education which his parents could not afford, he should be carried forward at the public expence, from seminary to seminary, to the completion of his studies at the highest.

But why should it be necessary in this case, to distinguish the Society into classes according to their property? When it is considered that the establishment and endowment of Academies, Colleges, and Universities are a provision, not merely for the existing generation, but for succeeding ones also; that in Governments like ours a constant rotation of property results from the free scope to industry, and from the laws of inheritance, and when it is considered moreover, how much of the exertions and privations of all are meant not for themselves, but for their posterity, there can be little ground for objections from any class, to plans of which every class must have its turn of benefits. The rich man, when contributing to a permanent plan for the education of the poor, ought to reflect that he is providing for that of his own descendants; and the poor man who concurs in a provision for those who are not poor that at no distant day it may be enjoyed by descendants from himself. It does not require a long life to witness these vicissitudes of fortune.

It is among the happy peculiarities of our Union, that the States composing it derive from their relation to each other and to the whole, a salutary emulation, without the enmity involved in competitions among States alien to each other. This emulation, we may perceive, is not without its influence in several important respects; and in none ought it to be more felt than in the merit of diffusing the light and the advantages of Public Instruction. In the example therefore which Kentucky is presenting, she not only consults her own welfare, but is giving an impulse to any of her sisters who may be behind her in the noble career.

Throughout the Civilized World, nations are courting the praise of fostering Science and the useful Arts, and are opening their eyes to the principles and the blessings of Representative Government. The American people owe it to themselves, and to the cause of free Government, to prove by their establishments for the advancement and diffusion of Knowledge, that their political Institutions, which are attracting observation from every quarter, and are respected as Models, by the new-born States in our own Hemisphere, are as favorable to the intellectual and moral improvement of Man as they are conformable to his individual & social Rights. What spectacle can be more edifying or more seasonable, than that of Liberty & Learning, each leaning on the other for their mutual & surest support? . . .

20. *"The Republican Ascendency"*

To William Eustis

Montpellier, May 22, 1823

. . . . The people are now able every where to compare the principles & policy of those who have borne the name of Republicans or Democrats, with the career of the adverse party; and to see & feel that the former are as much in harmony with the spirit of the nation & the genius of the Government as the latter was at variance with both.

A great effort has been made by the fallen party to proclaim and eulogize an amalgamation of political sentiments & views. Who could be duped by it, when unmasked by the electioneering violence of the party where strong, and intrigues where weak?

The effort has been carried even further. It has been asserted that the Republicans have abandoned their Cause, and gone over to the policy of their opponents. Here the effort equally fails. It is true that under a great change of foreign circumstances, and with a doubled population, & more than doubled resources, the Republican party has been reconciled to certain measures & arrangements which may be as proper now as they were premature and suspicious when urged by the Champions of federalism. But they overlook, the overbearing & vindictive spirit, the apocryphal doctrines, & rash projects, which stamped on federalism its distinctive character; and which are so much in contrast with the unassuming & unavenging spirit which has marked the Republican Ascendency.

There has been in fact a deep distinction between the two parties or rather, between the mass of the Nation, and the part of it which for a time got possession of the Government. The distinction has its origin in the confidence of the former, in the capacity of mankind for self Government and in a distrust of it by the other or by its leaders; and it is the key to many of the phenomena presented by our political History. In all free Countries somewhat of this distinction must be looked for; but it can never be dangerous in a well informed Community and a well constructed Government both of which I trust will be found to be the happy lot of the U.S. The wrong paths into which the fathers may stray will warn the sons into the right one. . . .

21. *Necessity for Two Legislative Branches*

To John Cartwright

1824

. . . . I received your volume on the English Constitution. . . .

I am now able to say that I have found in your pages not a little to admire, very much to approve, but some things in which I cannot concur. Were I to name instances of the last, I should not omit your preference of a single to a double Legislature.

The infirmities most besetting Popular Governments, even in the Representative Form, are found to be defective laws which do mischief before they can be mended, and laws passed under transient impulses, of which time & reflection call for a change. These causes, render the Statute Book complex and voluminous, multiply disputed cases between individuals, increase the expence of Legislation, and impair that certainty & stability which are among the greatest beauties, as well as most solid advantages of a well digested Code.

A second Branch of the Legislature, consisting of fewer and riper members, deliberating separately & independently of the other, may be expected to correct many errors and inaccuracies in the proceedings of the other, and to controul whatever of passion or precipitancy may be found in them; and being in like manner with the other, elective & responsible, the probability is strengthened that the Will & interest of their Common Constituents will be duly pursued.

In support of this view of the subject, it may be remarked that there is no instance among us of a change of a double for a single Legislature, whilst there is more than one of a contrary change; and it is believed, that if all the States were now to form their Gov^{ts}. over again, with lights derived from experience, they would be unanimous in preferring two Legislative Chambers to a single one.

22. *Parties*

To Henry Lee   MAD. MSS.

Montpellier, June 25, 1824.

I have received, Sir, your letter of the 18th, inclosing the proposal of a new publication, under the title of "American Gazette & Literary Journal." Of the prospectus I cannot say less than that it is an interesting specimen of cultivated talents.

I must say at the same time that I think it concedes too much to a remedial power in the press over the spirit of party.

Besides the occasional and transient subjects on which parties are formed, they seem to have a permanent foundation in the variance of political opinions in free States, and of occupations and interests in all cilivized States. The Constitution itself, whether written or prescriptive, influenced as its exposition and administration will be, by those causes, must be an unfailing source of party distinctions. And the very peculiarity which gives pre-eminent value to that of the United States, the partition of power between different governments, opens a new door for controversies and parties. There is nevertheless sufficient scope for combating the spirit of party, as far as it may not be necessary to fan the flame of liberty, in efforts to divert it from the more noxious channels; to moderate its violence, especially in the ascendant party; to elucidate the policy which harmonizes jealous interests; and particularly to give to the Constitution that just construction, which, with the aid of time and habit, may put an end to the more dangerous schisms otherwise growing out of it.

With a view to this last object, I entirely concur in the propriety of resorting to the sense in which the Constitution was accepted and ratified by the nation. In that sense alone it is the legitimate Constitution. And if that be not the guide in expounding it, there can be no security for a consistent and stable, more than for a faithful exercise of its powers. If the meaning of the text be sought in the changeable meaning of the words composing it, it is evident that the shape and attributes of the Government must partake of the changes to which the words and phrases of all living languages are constantly subject. What a metamorphosis would be produced in the code of law if all its ancient phraseology were to be taken in its modern sense. And that the language of our Constitution is already undergoing interpretations unknown to its founders, will I believe appear to all unbiased Enquirers into the history of its origin and adoption. Not to look farther for an example, take the word "consolidate" in the Address of the Convention prefixed to the Constitution.

It there and then meant to give strength and solidity to the Union of the States. In its current & controversial application it means a destruction of the States, by transfusing their powers into the government of the Union.

23. *"Private Friendship and Political Harmony"*

To Thomas Jefferson

Montpellier, February 24, 1826

. . . . The awkward state of the Law Professorship is truly distressing, but seems to be without immediate remedy. Considering the hopeless condition of Mr. Gilmour, a temporary appointment, if an acceptable successor were at hand, whilst not indelicate towards the worthy moribund incumbent, might be regarded as equivalent to a permanent one. And if the hesitation of our Colleagues at Richmond has no reference to Mr. Terril, but is merely tenderness towards Mr. Gilmour, I see no objection to a communication to Mr. T. that would bring him to Virginia at once, and thus abridge the loss of time. The hardheartedness of the Legislature towards what ought to be the favorite offspring of the State, is as reproachful as deplorable. Let us hope that the reflections of another year, will produce a more parental sensibility. . . .

You do not overrate the interest I feel in the University, as the Temple thro which alone lies the road to that of Liberty. But you entirely do my aptitude to be your successor in watching over its prosperity. It would be the pretension of a mere worshipper "remplacer" the Tutelary Genius of the Sanctuary. The best hope is, in the continuance of your cares, till they can be replaced by the stability and selfgrowth of the Institution. Little reliance can be put even on the fellowship of my services. The past year has given me sufficient intimation of the infirmities in wait for me. In calculating the probabilities of survivorship, the inferiority of my constitution forms an equation at least with the seniority of yours. . . .

You cannot look back to the long period of our private friendship & political harmony, with more affecting recollections than I do. If they are a source of pleasure to you, what ought they not to be to me? We cannot be deprived of the happy consciousness of the pure devotion to the public good with which we discharged the trusts committed to us. And I indulge a confidence that sufficient evidence will find its way to another generation, to ensure, after we are gone, whatever of justice may be withheld whilst we are here. The political horizon is already yielding in your case

at least, the surest auguries of it. Wishing & hoping that you may yet live to increase the debt which our Country owes you, and to witness the increasing gratitude, which alone can pay it, I offer you the fullest return of affectionate assurances.

24. *Jefferson's Death*

To Nicholas P. Trist

Montpellier, July 6, 1826

I have just received yours of the 4th. A few lines from Dr. Dunglison had prepared me for such a communication; and I never doubted that the last Scene of our illustrious friend would be worthy of the life which it closed. Long as this has been spared to his Country & to those who loved him, a few years more were to have been desired for the sake of both. But we are more than consoled for the loss, by the gain to him; and by the assurance that he lives and will live in the memory and gratitude of the wise & good, as a luminary of Science, as a votary of liberty, as a model of patriotism, and as a benefactor of human kind. In these characters, I have known him, and not less in the virtues & charms of social life, for a period of fifty years, during which there has not been an interruption or diminution of mutual confidence and cordial friendship, for a single moment in a single instance. What I feel therefore now, need not, I should say, cannot, be expressed. If there be any possible way, in which I can *usefully* give evidence of it, do not fail to afford me an opportunity. I indulge a hope that the unforeseen event will not be permitted to impair *any* of the beneficial measures which were in progress or in project. It cannot be unknown that the anxieties of the deceased were for others, not for himself. . . .

25. *Washington*

To Henry Coleman

Montpellier, August 25, 1826

. . . In doing justice to the virtue and valour of the revolutionary army, you add as a signal proof of the former, their readiness in laying down their arms at the triumphant close of the war, "when they had the liberties of their Country within their grasp."

Is it a fact that they had the liberties of their country within their grasp; that the troops then in command, even if led on by their illustrious chief, and backed by the apostates from the revolutionary cause, could have brought under the Yoke the great body of their fellow Citizens, most of them with arms in their hands, no inconsiderable part fresh from the use of them, all inspired with rage at the patricidal attempt, and not only guided by the federal head, but organized & animated by their local Governments possessing the means of appealing to their interests, as well as other motives, should such an appeal be required?

I have always believed that if General Washington had yielded to a usurping ambition, he would have found an insuperable obstacle in the incorruptibility of a sufficient portion of those under his command, and that the exalted praise due to him & them, was derived not from a forbearance to effect a revolution within their power, but from a love of liberty and of country which there was abundant reason to believe, no facility of success could have seduced. I am not less sure that General Washington would have spurned a sceptre if within his grasp, than I am that it was out of his reach, if he had secretly sighed for it. It must be recollected also that the practicability of a successful usurpation by the army cannot well be admitted, without implying a folly or pusillanimity reproachful to the American character, and without casting some shade on the vital principle of popular Government itself. . . .

26. *Internal Improvements*

To Martin Van Buren

Montpellier, September 20, 1826

. . . I should certainly feel both gratification and obligation in giving any aid in my power towards making the Constitution more appropriate to its objects, & more satisfactory to the nation. But I feel also the arduousness of such a task, arising as well from the difficulty of partitioning and defining Legislative powers, as from the existing diversity of opinions concerning the proper arrangement of the power in question over internal improvements.

Give the power to the General Government as possessing the means most adequate, and the objections are, 1. the danger of abuses in the application of the means to objects so distant from the eye of a Government, itself so distant from the eye of the people, 2. the danger, from an increase of the patronage and pecuniary transactions of the General Government, that the equilibrium between that and the State Governments may not be preserved.

Leave the power exclusively with the States, and the objections are: 1. that being deprived by the Constitution, and even by their local relations (as was generally experienced before the present Constitution was established) of the most convenient source of revenue, the impost on commerce, improvements might not be made even in cases wholly within their own limits. 2. that in cases where roads, & canals ought to pass through contiguous States, the necessary co-operation might fail from a difficulty in adjusting conditions and details, from a want of interest in one of them, or possibly from some jealousy or rivalship in one towards the other. 3. that where roads and canals ought to pass thro' a number of States, particular views of a single State might prevent improvements deeply interesting to the whole nation.

This embarrassing alternative has suggested the expedient which you seem to have contemplated, of dividing the power between the General & State Governm^{ts}., by allotting the appropriating branch to the former, & reserving the jurisdiction to the latter. The expedient has doubtless a captivating aspect. But to say nothing of the difficulty of defining such a division, and maintaining it in practice will the nation be at the expence of constructing roads & canals, without such a jurisdiction over them as will ensure their constant subservience to national purposes? Will not the utility and popularity of these improvements lead to a constructive assumption of the jurisdiction by Congress, with the same sanction of their constituents, as we see given to the exercise of the appropriating power, already stretching itself beyond the appropriating limit.

It seems indeed to be understood, that the policy & advantage of roads & canals have taken such extensive & permanent hold of the public will, that the constructive authority of Congress to make them, will not be relinquished, either by that, or the Constituent Body. It becomes a serious question therefore, whether the better course be not to obviate the unconstitutional precedent, by an amendatory article expressly granting the power. Should it be found as is very possible, that no effective system can be agreed on by Congress, the amendment will be a recorded precedent against constructive enlargements of power; and in the contrary event, the exercise of the power will no longer be a precedent in favour of them.

In all these cases, it need not be remarked I am sure, that it is necessary to keep in mind, the distinction between a usurpation of power by Congress against the will, and an assumption of power with the approbation, of their constituents. When the former occurs, as in the enactment of the alien & sedition laws, the appeal to their Constituents sets everything to rights. In the latter case, the appeal can only be made to argument and conciliation, with an acquiescence, when not an extreme case, in an unsuccessful result.

If the sole object be to obtain the aid of the federal treasury for internal improvements by roads & canals, without interfering with the jurisdiction of the States, an amendment need only say, "Congress may make ap-

propriations of moneys for roads and canals, to be applied to such purposes by the Legislatures of the States within their respective limits, the jurisdiction of the States remaining unimpaired."

If it be thought best to make a constitutional grant of the entire Power, either as proper in itself, or made so by the moral certainty, that it will be constructively assumed, with the sanction of the national will, and operate as an injurious precedent, the amendment cannot say less, than that "Congress may make roads & canals, with such jurisdiction as the cases may require."

But whilst the terms "common defence & general welfare," remain in the Constitution unguarded agst. the construction which has been contended for, a fund of power, inexhaustible & wholly subversive of the equilibrium between the General and the State Gov^{ts}. is within the reach of the former. Why then, not precede all other amendments by one, expunging the phrase which is not required for any harmless meaning; or making it harmless by annexing to it the terms, "in the cases required by this Constitution." . . .

27. *Information on Mr. Jefferson*

To Samuel Harrison Smith

Montpellier, November 4, 1826

I have received your letter . . . requesting from me any information which would assist you in preparing a memoir of Mr. Jefferson. . . . Few things would give me more pleasure than to contribute to such a task. . . .

The period between his leaving Congress in 1776, and his mission to France, was filled chiefly by his labours on the Revised Code,—the preparation of his "Notes on Virginia" (an obiter performance):—his Governorship of that State:—and by his services as a member of Congress, and of the Committee of the States at Annapolis.

The Revised code in which he had a masterly share, exacted perhaps the most severe of his public labours. It consisted of 126 Bills, comprizing and recasting the whole statutory code, British & Colonial, then admitted to be in force, or proper to be adopted, and some of the most important articles of the unwritten law, with original laws on particular subjects; the whole adapted to the Independent & Republican form of Government. The work tho' not enacted in the mass, as was contemplated, has been a mine of Legislative wealth, and a model of statutory composition, containing not a single *superfluous* word, and preferring always words & phrases of a meaning fixed as much as possible by oracular treatises, or solemn adjudications. . . .

The University of Virginia, as a temple dedicated to science & Liberty, was after his retirement from the political sphere, the object nearest his heart, and so continued to the close of his life. His devotion to it was intense, and his exertions unceasing. It bears the stamp of his genius, and will be a noble monument of his fame. His general view was to make it a nursery of Republican patriots as well as genuine scholars. . . .

Your request includes "his general habits of study." With the exception of an intercourse in a session of the Virginia Legislature in 1776, rendered slight by the disparity between us, I did not become acquainted with M^r. Jefferson till 1779, when being a member of the Executive Council, and he the Governor, an intimacy took place. From that date we were for the most part separated by different walks in public & private life, till the present Govr. brought us together, first when he was Secretary of State and I a member of the House of Rep^s.; and next, after an interval of some years, when we entered, in another relation, the service of the U. S. in 1801. Of his earlier habits of study therefore I can not particularly speak. It is understood that whilst at College [Wm. & Mary] he distinguished himself in all the branches of knowledge taught there; and it is known that he never after ceased to cultivate them. The French language he had learned when very young, and became very familiar with it, as he did with the literary treasures which it contains. He read, and at one time spoke the Italian also; with a competent knowledge of Spanish; adding to both the Anglo-Saxon, as a root of the English, and an element in legal philosophy. The Law itself he studied to the bottom, and in its greatest breadth, of which proofs were given at the Bar which he attended for a number of years, and occasionally throughout his career. For all the fine arts, he had a more than common taste; and in that of architecture; which he studied in both its useful, and its ornamental characters, he made himself an adept; as the variety of orders and stiles, executed according to his plan founded on the Grecian & Roman models and under his superintendance, in the Buildings of the University fully exemplify. Over & above these acquirements, his miscellaneous reading was truly remarkable, for which he derived leisure from a methodical and indefatigable application of the time required for indispensable objects, and particularly from his rule of never letting the sun rise before him. His relish for Books never forsook him, not even in his infirm years and in his devoted attention to the rearing of the University, which led him often to express his regret that he was so much deprived of that luxury, by the epistolary tasks, which fell upon him, and which consumed his health as well as his time. He was certainly one of the most learned men of the age. It may be said of him as has been said of others that he was a "walking Library," and what can be said of but few such prodegies, that the Genius of Philosophy ever walked hand in hand with him.

28. *The Anti-Republican Heretic*

To Margaret B. Smith

Montpellier, September, 1830

. . . I recollect an incident . . . which . . . is characteristic of Mr. Jefferson. . . .

The new Constitution of the U. States having just been put into operation, forms of Government were the uppermost topics every where, more especially at a convivial board, and the question being started as to the best mode of providing the Executive chief, it was among other opinions, boldly advanced that a hereditary designation was preferable to any elective process that could be devised. At the close of an eloquent effusion against the agitations and animosities of a popular choice and in behalf of birth, as on the whole, affording even a better chance for a suitable head of the Government, M^r. Jefferson, with a smile remarked that he had heard of a university somewhere in which the Professorship of Mathematics was hereditary. The reply, received with acclamation, was a coup de grace to the Anti-Republican Heretic.

29. *The General and Particular Governments—Supplement to a letter on the phrase, "Common Defence and General Welfare"*

To A. Stevenson

Montpellier, Nov. 27, 1830

. . . As the people of the United States enjoy the great merit of having established a system of Government on the basis of human rights, and of giving to it a form without example, which, as they believe, unites the greatest national strength with the best security for public order and individual liberty, they owe to themselves, to their posterity, and to the world, a preservation of the system in its purity, its symmetry, and its authenticity. This can only be done by a steady attention and sacred regard to the chartered boundaries between the portion of power vested in the Government over the whole, and the position undivested from the several Governments over the parts composing the whole; and by a like attention and regard to the boundaries between the several departments,

Legislative, Executive, and Judiciary, into which the aggregate power is divided. Without a steady eye to the landmarks between these departments, the danger is always to be apprehended, either of mutual encroachments, and alternate ascendencies incompatible with the tranquil enjoyment of private rights, or of a concentration of all the departments of power into a single one, universally acknowledged to be fatal to public liberty.

And without an equal watchfulness over the great landmarks between the General Government and the particular Governments, the danger is certainly not less, of either a gradual relaxation of the band which holds the latter together, leading to an entire separation, or of a gradual assumption of their powers by the former, leading to a consolidation of all the Governments into a single one.

The two vital characteristics of the political system of the United States are, first, that the Government holds its powers by a charter granted to it by the people; second, that the powers of Government are formed into two grand divisions—one vested in a Government over the whole community, the other in a number of independent Governments over its component parts. Hitherto charters have been written grants of privileges by Governments to the people. Here they are written grants of power by the people to their Governments.

Hitherto, again, all the powers of Government have been, in effect, consolidated into one Government, tending to faction and a foreign yoke among a people within narrow limits, and to arbitrary rule among a people spread over an extensive region. Here the established system aspires to such a division and organization of power as will provide at once for its harmonious exercise on the true principles of liberty over the parts and over the whole, notwithstanding the great extent of the whole; the system forming an innovation and an epoch in the science of Government no less honorable to the people to whom it owed its birth, than auspicious to the political welfare of all others who may imitate or adopt it.

As the most arduous and delicate task in this great work lay in the untried demarkation of the line which divides the general and the particular Governments by an enumeration and definition of the powers of the former, more especially the legislative powers; and as the success of this new scheme of polity essentially depends on the faithful observance of this partition of powers, the friends of the scheme, or rather the friends of liberty and of man, cannot be too often earnestly exhorted to be watchful in marking and controlling encroachments by either of the Governments on the domain of the other.

30. *Franklin, Jefferson, Adams and Hamilton*

To James K. Paulding

Montpellier, April 1831

I have recd. your letter . . . and feel myself very safe in joining your
other friends in their advice on the Biographical undertaking you
meditate. The plan you adopt is a valuable improvement on the prevailing examples; which have too much usurped the functions of the
Historian; and by omitting the private features of character, and anecdotes which as condiments always add flavour and sometimes nutrition
to the repast, forfeit much of the due attraction. The more historical
mode has been recommended probably by the more ready command of
materials, such as abound in the contributions of the press, and the public
Archives. In a task properly biographical, the difficulty lies in the
evanescent or inaccessible information which it particularly requires.
Autographic Memorials are rare, and usually deficient on essential points,
if not otherwise faulty; and at the late periods of life, the most knowing
witnesses may have descended to the tomb, or their memories become no
longer faithful depositories. Where oral tradition is the resort, all know
the uncertainties and inaccuracies which beset it.

I ought certainly to be flattered by finding my name on the list of
subjects you have selected. . . . Yet I feel the awkwardness of attempting
"a sketch of the principal incidents of my life," such as the partiality of
your friendship has prompted you to request. . . . My life has been so
much a public one, that any review of it must mainly consist of the
agency which was my lot in public transactions. . . .

For portraits of the several characters you allude to, I know not that
I could furnish your canvas with any important materials. . . .

Of Doctor Franklin I had no personal knowledge till we served together in the Convention of 1787: and the part he took there has found
its way to the public; with the exception of a few anecdotes which
belong to the unveiled proceedings of that assembly. He has written
his own life: and no man had a finer one to write, or a better title to
be himself the writer. There is eno' of blank left however for a succeeding
pen.

With Mr. Jefferson I was not acquainted till we met as members of
the first Revolutionary Legislature of Virginia. I had of course no personal
knowledge of his early life. Of his public career, the records of his
Country give ample information. And of the general features of his
character, with much of his private habits, and of his peculiar opinions,
his writings before the world, to which additions are not improbable,

are equally explanatory. The Obituary Eulogiums, multiplied by the Epoch and other coincidences of his death, are a field where some things not unworthy of notice may perhaps be gleaned. It may on the whole be truly said of him, that he was greatly eminent for the comprehensiveness and fertility of his Genius; the vast extent and rich variety of his acquirements; and particularly distinguished by the philosophic impress left on every subject which he touched. Nor was he less distinguished for an early and uniform devotion to the cause of liberty, and for a systematic preference of a Form of Government squared in the strictest degree, to the equal rights of Man. In the social and domestic spheres he was a model of the virtues and manners which most adorn them.

In relation to Mr. John Adams I had no personal knowledge till he became Vice President of the U.S.; and then saw no side of his private character which was not visible to all; whilst my chief knowledge of his public character and career was acquired by means now accessible or becoming so to all. His private papers are said to be voluminous; and when opened to public view will doubtless be of much avail to a biographer. His official correspondence during the Revolutionary period just published, will be found interesting, both in a historical and a biographical view. That he had a mind rich in ideas of its own, as well as in its learned store; with an ardent love of Country, and the merit of being a Colossal Champion of its Independence, must be allowed by those most offended by the alloy in his Republicanism, and the fervors and flights originating in his moral temperament.

Of Mr. Hamilton I ought perhaps to speak with some restraint, tho' my feelings assure me that no recollection of political collisions could controul the justice due to his memory. That he possessed intellectual powers of the first order, and the moral qualities of integrity and honor in a captivating degree, has been decreed to him by a suffrage now universal. If his Theory of Govt. deviated from the Republican standard, he had the candor to avow it, and the greater merit of co-operating faithfully in maturing and supporting a System which was not his choice. The criticism to which his share in the administration of it, was most liable was that it had the aspect of an effort to give to the Instrument a constructive and practical bearing not warranted by its true and intended character. . . .

31. *Against Nullification and Secession*

To William Cabell Rives

Montpellier, March 12, 1833

I have received . . . a copy of your late Speech in the Senate. . . . I have found as I expected, that it takes a very able and enlightening view of its subject. I wish it may have the effect of reclaiming to the doctrine & language held by all from the birth of the Constitution, & till very lately by themselves, those who now Contend that the States have never parted with an Atom of their sovereignty; and consequently that the Constitutional band which holds them together, is a mere league or partnership, without any of the characteristics of sovereignty or nationality.

It seems strange that it should be necessary to disprove this novel and nullifying doctrine; and stranger still that those who deny it should be denounced as Innovators, heretics & Apostates. Our political system is admitted to be a new Creation—a real nondescript. Its character therefore must be sought within itself; not in precedents, because there are none; not in writers whose comments are guided by precedents. Who can tell at present how Vattel and others of that class, would have qualified (in the Gallic sense of the term) a Compound & peculiar system with such an example of it as ours before them.

What can be more preposterous than to say that the States as united, are in no respect or degree, a Nation, which implies sovereignty; altho' acknowledged to be such by all other Nations & Sovereigns, and maintaining with them, all the international relations, of war & peace, treaties, commerce, &c, and, on the other hand and at the same time, to say that the States separately are compleatly nations & sovereigns; although they can separately neither speak nor harken to any other nation, nor maintain with it any of the international relations whatever and would be disowned as Nations if presenting themselves in that character.

The nullifiers it appears, endeavor to shelter themselves under a distinction between a delegation and a surrender of powers. But if the powers be attributes of sovereignty & nationality & the grant of them be perpetual, as is necessarily implied, where not otherwise expressed, sovereignty & nationality according to the extent of the grant are effectually transferred by it, and a dispute about the name, is but a battle of words. The practical result is not indeed left to argument or inference. The words of the Constitution are explicit that the Constitution & laws of the U. S. shall be supreme over the Constitution & laws of the several States; supreme in their exposition and execution as well as in their authority. Without a supremacy in those respects it would be like a scabbard in

the hand of a soldier without a sword in it. The imagination itself is startled at the idea of twenty four independent expounders of a rule that cannot exist, but in a meaning and operation, the same for all.

The conduct of S. Carolina has called forth not only the question of nullification; but the more formidable one of secession. It is asked whether a State by resuming the sovereign form in which it entered the Union, may not of right withdraw from it at will. As this is a simple question whether a State, more than an individual, has a right to violate its engagements, it would seem that it might be safely left to answer itself. But the countenance given to the claim shows that it cannot be so lightly dismissed. The natural feelings which laudably attach the people composing a State, to its authority and importance, are at present too much excited by the unnatural feelings, with which they have been inspired agst. their brethren of other States, not to expose them, to the danger of being misled into erroneous views of the nature of the Union and the interest they have in it. One thing at least seems to be too clear to be questioned; that whilst a State remains within the Union it cannot withdraw its citizens from the operation of the Constitution & laws of the Union. In the event of an actual secession without the Consent of the Co-States, the course to be pursued by these involves questions painful in the discussion of them. God grant that the menacing appearances, which obtruded it may not be followed by positive occurrences requiring the more painful task of deciding them!

32. *The Great Political Experiment*

To ————

March, 1836

. . . The precise obligation imposed on a representative, by the instructions of his constituents, still divides the opinions, of distinguished statesmen. . . .

It being agreed by all, that whether an instruction be obeyed or disobeyed, the act of the Representative is equally valid & operative, the question is a moral one, between the Representative, and his Constituents. With him, if satisfied, that the instruction expresses the will of his constituents, it must be to decide whether he will conform to an instruction opposed to his judgment or will incur their displeasure by disobeying it and with them to decide in what mode they will manifest their displeasure. In a case necessarily appealing to the conscience of the Representative its paramount dictates must of course be his guide.

It is well known that the equality of the States in the Federal Senate was a compromise between the larger, & the smaller states, the former claiming a proportional representation in both branches of the Legislature, as due to their superior population; the latter, an equality in both, as a safeguard to the reserved sovereignty of the States, an object which obtained the concurrence of members from the larger States. But it is equally true tho' but little adverted to as an instance of miscalculating speculation that, as soon as the smaller States, had secured more than a proportional share in the proposed Government, they became favorable to augmentations of its powers; & that under the administration of the Gov^t., they have generally, in contests between it, & the State governments, leaned to the former. Whether the direct effect of instructions which could make the senators dependent on the pleasure of their Constituents . . . would be most favourable, to the General Government, or the state Governments, is a question which not being tested by practice, is left to individual opinions. . . .

Nothing is more certain than that the tenure of the Senate, was meant as an obstacle to the instability, which not only history, but the experience of our Country, had shewn to be the besetting infirmity of popular Gov^{ts}. Innovations therefore impairing the stability afforded by that tenure, without some compensating remodification of the powers of the Government, must affect the balance, contemplated by the Constitution.

My prolonged life has made me a witness of the alternate popularity, & unpopularity of each of the great branches of the Federal Government. I have witnessed, also, the vicissitudes, in the apparent tendencies in the Federal & State Governments to encroach each on the authorities of the other, without being able to infer with certainty, what would be the final operation of the causes as heretofore existing; whilst it is far more difficult, to calculate, the mingled & checkered influences, on the future from an expanding territorial Domain; from the multiplication of the parties to the Union, from the great & growing power of not a few of them, from the absence of external danger; from combinations of States in some quarters, and collisions in others, and from questions, incident to a refusal of unsuccessful parties to abide by the issue of controversies judicially decided. To these uncertainties, may be added, the effects of a dense population, & the multiplication, and the varying relations of the classes composing it. I am far however from desponding of the great political experiment in the hands of the American people. Much has already been gained in its favour, by the continued prosperity accompanying it through a period of so many years. Much may be expected from the progress and diffusion of political science in dissipating errors, opposed to the sound principles which harmonize different interests; from the Geographical, commercial, & social ligaments, strengthened as they are by mechanical improvements, giving so much advantage to time over space; & above all, by the obvious & inevitable consequences of the wreck of an ark, bearing

as we have flattered ourselves the happiness of our country & the hope of the world. Nor is it unworthy of consideration, that the 4 great religious Sects, running through all the States, will oppose an event placing parts of each under separate Governments.

It cannot be denied that there are in the aspect our country presents, Phenomena of an ill omen, but it w^d. seem that they proceed from a coincidence of causes, some transitory, others fortuitous, rarely if ever likely to recur, that of the causes more durable some can be greatly mitigated if not removed by the Legislative authority, and such as may require and be worthy the "intersit" of a higher power, can be provided for whenever, if ever, the public mind may be calm and cool enough for that resort.

Other Writings

33. *Address to the States*

April 18, 1783

. . . Let it be remembered . . . that it has ever been the pride and boast of America, that the rights for which she contended were the rights of human nature. By the blessing of the Author of these rights on the means exerted for their defence they have prevailed against all opposition and form the basis of thirteen independent States. No instance has heretofore occurred, nor can any instance be expected hereafter to occur, in which the unadulterated forms of Republican government can pretend to so fail an opportunity of justifying themselves by their fruits. In this view the citizens of the United States are responsible for the greatest trust ever confided to a political society. If justice, good faith, honor, gratitude and all the other qualities which enoble the character of a nation & fulfil the ends of government, be the fruits of our establishments, the cause of liberty will acquire a dignity and lustre, which it has never yet enjoyed, and an example will be set, which cannot but have the most favourable influence on the rights of Mankind. If on the other side, our governments should be unfortunately blotted with the reverse of these cardinal and essential virtues, the great cause which we have engaged to vindicate, will be dishonored and betrayed; the last and fairest experiment in favor of the rights of human nature will be turned against them; and their patrons and friends exposed to be insulted and silenced by the votaries of tyranny and usurpation.

34. *Proceedings in the Constitutional Convention, 1787:*

Republican Liberty and Majority Rule[1]

Wednesday June 6

. . . M^r. Madison considered an election of one branch at least of the Legislature by the people immediately, as a clear principle of free Gov^t. and that this mode under proper regulations had the additional advantage of securing better representatives, as well as of avoiding too great an agency of the State Governments in the General one. He differed from the member from Connecticut (Mr. Sherman) in thinking the objects mentioned to be all the principal ones that required a National Gov^t. Those were certainly important and necessary objects; but he combined with them the necessity of providing more effectually for the security of private rights, and the steady dispensation of Justice. Interferences with these were evils which had more perhaps than anything else, produced this convention. Was it to be supposed that republican liberty could long exist under the abuses of it practised in some of the States. The gentleman (M^r. Sherman) had admitted that in a very small State, faction & oppression w^d. prevail. It was to be inferred then that wherever these prevailed the State was too small. Had they not prevailed in the largest as well as the smallest tho' less than in the smallest; and were we not thence admonished to enlarge the sphere as far as the nature of the Gov^t. would Admit. This was the only defence ag^st. the inconveniences of democracy consistent with the democratic form of Gov^t. All civilized Societies would be divided into different Sects, Factions, & interests, as they happened to consist of rich & poor, debtors & creditors, the landed the manufacturing, the commercial interests, the inhabitants of this district or that district, the followers of this political leader or that political leader—the disciples of this religious Sect or that religious Sect. In all cases where a majority are united by a common interest or passion, the rights of the minority are in danger. What motives are to restrain them? A prudent regard to the maxim that honesty is the best policy is found by experience to be as little regarded by bodies of men as by individuals. Respect for character is always diminished in proportion to the number among whom the blame or praise is to be divided. Conscience, the only remaining tie is known to be inadequate in individuals: In large numbers, little is to be expected from it. Besides, Religion itself may become a motive to persecution & oppression. These observations are verified by the Histories of every country antient & modern. In Greece & Rome the rich & poor, the Creditors & debtors, as well as the patricians & plebeians alternately oppressed

each other with equal unmercifulness. What a source of oppression was the relation between the parent cities of Rome, Athens & Carthage, & their respective provinces; the former possessing the power, & the latter being sufficiently distinguished to be separate objects of it? Why was America so justly apprehensive of Parliamentary injustice? Because G. Britain had a separate interest real or supposed, & if her authority had been admitted, could have pursued that interest at our expence. We have seen the mere distinction of colour made in the most enlightened period of time, a ground of the most oppressive dominion ever exercised by man over man. What has been the source of those unjust laws complained of among ourselves? Has it not been the real or supposed interest of the major number? Debtors have defrauded their creditors. The landed interest has borne hard on the mercantile interest. The Holders of one species of property have thrown a disproportion of taxes on the holders of another species. The lesson we are to draw from the whole is that where a majority are united by a common sentiment, and have an opportunity, the rights of the minor party become insecure. In a Republican Gov^t. the majority if united have always an opportunity. The only remedy is to enlarge the sphere, & thereby divide the community into so great a number of interests & parties, that in the 1st. place a majority will not be likely at the same moment to have a common interest separate from that of the whole or of the minority; and in the 2^d place that in case they sh^d have such an interest, they may not be apt to unite in the pursuit of it. It was incumbent on us then to try this remedy, and with that view to frame a republican system on such a scale & in such a form as will controul all the evils wch. have been experienced. . . .

The Senate[2]

Tuesday, June 26

M^r. Madison. In order to judge of the form to be given to this institution, it will be proper to take a view of the ends to be served by it. These were first to protect the people agst. their rulers; secondly to protect the people agst. the transient impressions into which they themselves might be led. A people deliberating in a temperate moment, and with the experience of other nations before them, on the plan of Gov^t. most likely to secure their happiness, would first be aware, that those charg^d. with the public happiness might betray their trust. An obvious precaution agst. this danger w^d. be to divide the trust between different bodies of men, who might watch & check each other. In this they w^d. be governed by the same prudence which has prevailed in organizing the subordinate departments of Gov^t., where all business liable to abuses is made to pass thro' separate hands, the one being a check on the other. It w^d. next occur to such

people, that they themselves were liable to temporary errors, thro' want of information as to their true interest, and that men chosen for a short term, & employed but a small portion of that in public affairs, might err from the same cause. This reflection w^d. naturally suggest that the Gov^t. be so constituted as that one of its branches might have an opp^y. of acquiring a competent knowledge of the public interests. Another reflection equally becoming a people on such an occasion, w^d. be that they themselves, as well as a numerous body of Representatives, were liable to err also, from fickleness and passion. A necessary fence agst. this danger would be to select a portion of enlightened citizens, whose limited number, and firmness might seasonably interpose agst. impetuous councils. It ought finally to occur to a people deliberating on a Gov^t. for themselves, that as different interests necessarily result from the liberty meant to be secured, the major interest might under sudden impulses be tempted to commit injustice on the minority. In all civilized Countries the people fall into different classes hav^g. a real or supposed difference of interests. There will be creditors & debtors; farmers, merch^{ts}. & manufacturers. There will be particularly the distinction of rich & poor. It was true as had been observ^d. (by M^r. Pinkney) we had not among us those hereditary distinctions, of rank which were a great source of the contests in the ancient Gov^{ts}. as well as the modern States of Europe, nor those extremes of wealth or poverty which characterize the latter. We cannot however be regarded even at this time, as one homogeneous mass, in which every thing that affects a part will affect in the same manner the whole. In framing a system which we wish to last for ages, we sh^d. not lose sight of the changes which ages will produce. An increase of population will of necessity increase the proportion of those who will labour under all the hardships of life, & secretly sigh for a more equal distribution of its blessings. These may in time outnumber those who are placed above the feelings of indigence. According to the equal laws of suffrage, the power will slide into the hands of the former. No agrarian attempts have yet been made in this Country, but symptoms, of a levelling spirit, as we have understood, have sufficiently appeared in certain quarters, to give notice of the future danger. How is this danger to be guarded agst. on the republican principles? How is the danger in all cases of interested coalitions to oppress the minority to be guarded agst.? Among other means by the establishment of a body in the Gov^t. sufficiently respectable for its wisdom & virtue, to aid on such emergencies, the preponderance of justice by throwing its weight into that scale. Such being the objects of the second branch in the proposed Gov^t. he thought a considerable duration ought to be given to it. He did not conceive that the term of nine years could threaten any real danger; but in pursuing his particular ideas on the subject, he should require that the long term allowed to the 2^d. branch should not commence till such a period of life, as would render a perpetual disqualification to be re-elected little inconvenient either in a public or private view. He

observed that as it was more than probable we were now digesting a plan which in its operation w^d. decide for ever the fate of Republican Gov^t. we ought not only to provide every guard to liberty that its preservation c^d. require, but be equally careful to supply the defects which our own experience had particularly pointed out. . . .

Union and Liberty[3]

Friday, June 29

Mr. Madison . . .

He entreated the gentlemen representing the small States to renounce a principle wch. was confessedly unjust, which c^d. never be admitted, & if admitted must infuse mortality into a Constitution which we wished to last forever. He prayed them to ponder well the consequences of suffering the Confederacy to go to pieces. It had been s^d. that the want of energy in the large states w^d. be a security to the small. It was forgotten that this want of energy proceeded from the supposed security of the States agst. all external danger. Let each state depend on itself for its security, & let apprehensions arise of danger, from distant powers or from neighbouring States, & the languishing condition of all the States, large as well as small, w^d. soon be transformed into vigorous & high toned Gov^{ts}. His great fear was that their Gov^{ts}. w^d. then have too much energy, that these might not only be formidable in the large to the small States, but fatal to the internal liberty of all. The same causes which have rendered the old world the Theatre of incessant wars, & have banished liberty from the face of it, w^d. soon produce the same effects here. The weakness & jealousy of the small States w^d. quickly introduce some regular military force agst. sudden danger from their powerful neighbours. The example w^d. be followed by others, and w^d. soon become universal. In time of actual war, great discretionary powers are constantly given to the Executive Magistrate. Constant apprehension of war, has the same tendency to render the head too large for the body. A standing military force, with an overgrown Executive will not long be safe companions to liberty. The means of defence agst. foreign danger, have been always the instruments of tyranny at home. Among the Romans it was a standing maxim to excite a war, whenever a revolt was apprehended. Throughout all Europe, the armies kept up under the pretext of defending, have enslaved the people. It is perhaps questionable, whether the best concerted system of absolute power in Europe c^d. maintain itself, in a situation, where no alarms of external danger c^d. tame the people to the domestic yoke. The insular situation of G. Britain was the principal cause of her being an exception to the general fate of Europe. It has rendered less defence necessary, and admitted a kind of defence wch. c^d. not be used for the purpose of oppression.—These consequences he conceived ought to be apprehended

whether the States should run into a total separation from each other, or sh^d. enter into partial confederacies. Either event w^d. be truly deplorable; & those who might be accessary to either, could never be forgiven by their Country, nor by themselves. . . .

Judicial Review[4]

Saturday July 21

. . . M^r. Madison considered the object of the motion as of great importance to the meditated Constitution. It would be useful to the Judiciary departm^t. by giving it an additional opportunity of defending itself agst. Legislative encroachments: It would be useful to the Executive, by inspiring additional confidence & firmness in exerting the revisionary power: It would be useful to the Legislature by the valuable assistance it would give in preserving a consistency, conciseness, perspicuity & technical propriety in the laws, qualities peculiarly necessary; & yet shamefully wanting in our republican Codes. It would moreover be useful to the Community at large as an additional check agst. a pursuit of those unwise & unjust measures which constituted so great a portion of our calamities. If any solid objection could be urged agst. the motion, it must be on the supposition that it tended to give too much strength either to the Executive or Judiciary. He did not think there was the least ground for this apprehension. It was much more to be apprehended that notwithstanding this co-operation of the two departments, the Legislature would still be an overmatch for them. Experience in all the States had evinced a powerful tendency in the Legislature to absorb all power into its vortex. This was the real source of danger to the American Constitutions; & suggested the necessity of giving every defensive authority to the other departments that was consistent with Republican principles. . . .

M^r. Madison could not discover in the proposed association of the Judges with the Executive in the Revisionary check on the Legislature any violation of the maxim which requires the great departments of power to be kept separate & distinct. On the contrary he thought it an auxiliary precaution in favor of the maxim. If a Constitutional discrimination of the departments on paper were a sufficient security to each agst. encroachments of the others, all further provisions would indeed be superfluous. But experience had taught us a distrust of that security; and that it is necessary to introduce such a balance of powers and interests as will guarantee the provisions on paper. Instead therefore of contenting ourselves with laying down the Theory in the Constitution that each department ought to be separate & distinct, it was proposed to add a defensive power to each which should maintain the Theory in practice. In so doing we did not blend the departments together. We erected effectual

barriers for keeping them separate. The most regular example of this theory was in the British Constitution. Yet it was not only the practice there to admit the Judges to a seat in the legislature, and in the Executive Councils, and to submit to their previous examination all laws of a certain description, but it was a part of their Constitution that the Executive might negative any law whatever; a part of *their* Constitution which had been universally regarded as calculated for the preservation of the whole. The objection agst. a union of the Judiciary & Executive branches in the revision of the laws, had either no foundation or was not carried far enough. If such a Union was an improper mixture of powers, or such a Judiciary check on the laws, was inconsistent with the Theory of a free Constitution, it was equally so to admit the Executive to any participation in the making of laws; and the revisionary plan ought to be discarded altogether. . . .

35. *Factions and the Extensive Republic: The Federalist No. 10*

Among the numerous advantages promised by a well-constructed Union, none deserves to be more accurately developed than its tendency to break and control the violence of faction. The friend of popular governments never finds himself so much alarmed for their character and fate, as when he contemplates their propensity to this dangerous vice. He will not fail, therefore, to set a due value on any plan which, without violating the principles to which he is attached, provides a proper cure for it. The instability, injustice, and confusion introduced into the public councils, have, in truth, been the mortal diseases under which popular governments have everywhere perished; as they continue to be the favorite and fruitful topics from which the adversaries to liberty derive their most specious declamations. The valuable improvements made by the American constitutions on the popular models, both ancient and modern, cannot certainly be too much admired; but it would be an unwarrantable partiality, to contend that they have as effectually obviated the danger on this side, as was wished and expected. Complaints are everywhere heard from our most considerate and virtuous citizens, equally the friends of public and private faith, and of public and personal liberty, that our governments are too unstable, that the public good is disregarded in the conflicts of rival parties, and that measures are too often decided, not according to the rules of justice and the rights of the minor party, but by the superior force of an interested and overbearing majority. However anxiously we may wish that these complaints had no foundation, the evidence of known facts will not permit us to deny that they are in some degree true. It will be found, indeed, on a candid review of our situation, that some of the

distresses under which we labor have been erroneously charged on the operation of our governments; but it will be found, at the same time, that other causes will not alone account for many of our heaviest misfortunes; and, particularly, for that prevailing and increasing distrust of public engagements, and alarm for private rights, which are echoed from one end of the continent to the other. These must be chiefly, if not wholly, effects of the unsteadiness and injustice with which a factious spirit has tainted our public administrations.

By a faction, I understand a number of citizens, whether amounting to a majority or minority of the whole, who are united and actuated by some common impulse of passion, or of interest, adverse to the rights of other citizens, or to the permanent and aggregate interests of the community.

There are two methods of curing the mischiefs of faction: the one, by removing its causes; the other, by controlling its effects.

There are again two methods of removing the causes of faction: the one, by destroying the liberty which is essential to its existence; the other, by giving to every citizen the same opinions, the same passions, and the same interests.

It could never be more truly said than of the first remedy, that it was worse than the disease. Liberty is to faction what air is to fire, an aliment without which it instantly expires. But it could not be less folly to abolish liberty, which is essential to political life, because it nourishes faction, than it would be to wish the annihilation of air, which is essential to animal life, because it imparts to fire its destructive agency.

The second expedient is as impracticable as the first would be unwise. As long as the reason of man continues fallible, and he is at liberty to exercise it, different opinions will be formed. As long as the connection subsists between his reason and his self-love, his opinions and his passions will have a reciprocal influence on each other: and the former will be objects to which the latter will attach themselves. The diversity in the faculties of men, from which the rights of property originate, is not less an insuperable obstacle to a uniformity of interests. The protection of these faculties is the first object of government. From the protection of different and unequal faculties of acquiring property, the possession of different degrees and kinds of property immediately results; and from the influence of these on the sentiments and views of the respective proprietors, ensues a division of the society into different interests and parties.

The latent causes of faction are thus sown in the nature of man; and we see them everywhere brought into different degrees of activity, according to the different circumstances of civil society. A zeal for different opinions concerning religion, concerning government, and many other points, as well of speculation as of practice; an attachment to different leaders ambitiously contending for pre-eminence and power; or to persons of other descriptions whose fortunes have been interesting to the human passions, have, in turn, divided mankind into parties, inflamed

them with mutual animosity, and rendered them much more disposed to vex and oppress each other than to co-operate for their common good. So strong is this propensity of mankind to fall into mutual animosities, that where no substantial occasion presents itself, the most frivolous and fanciful distinctions have been sufficient to kindle their unfriendly passions and excite their most violent conflicts. But the most common and durable source of factions has been the various and unequal distribution of property. Those who hold and those who are without property have ever formed distinct interests in society. Those who are creditors, and those who are debtors, fall under a like discrimination. A landed interest, a manufacturing interest, a mercantile interest, a moneyed interest, with many lesser interests, grow up of necessity in civilized nations, and divide them into different classes, actuated by different sentiments and views. The regulation of these various and interfering interests forms the principal task of modern legislation, and involves the spirit of party and faction in the necessary and ordinary operations of the government.

No man is allowed to be a judge in his own cause, because his interest would certainly bias his judgment, and, not improbably, corrupt his integrity. With equal, nay with greater reason, a body of men are unfit to be both judges and parties at the same time; yet what are many of the most important acts of legislation, but so many judicial determinations, not indeed concerning the rights of single persons, but concerning the rights of large bodies of citizens? And what are the different classes of legislators but advocates and parties to the causes which they determine? Is a law proposed concerning private debts? It is a question to which the creditors are parties on one side and the debtors on the other. Justice ought to hold the balance between them. Yet the parties are, and must be, themselves the judges; and the most numerous party, or, in other words, the most powerful faction must be expected to prevail. Shall domestic manufactures be encouraged, and in what degree, by restrictions on foreign manufactures? are questions which would be differently decided by the landed and the manufacturing classes, and probably by neither with a sole regard to justice and the public good. The apportionment of taxes on the various descriptions of property is an act which seems to require the most exact impartiality; yet there is, perhaps, no legislative act in which greater opportunity and temptation are given to a predominant party to trample on the rules of justice. Every shilling with which they overburden the inferior number, is a shilling saved to their own pockets.

It is in vain to say that enlightened statesmen will be able to adjust these clashing interests, and render them all subservient to the public good. Enlightened statesmen will not always be at the helm. Nor, in many cases, can such an adjustment be made at all without taking into view indirect and remote considerations, which will rarely prevail over the immediate interest which one party may find in disregarding the rights of another or the good of the whole.

The inference to which we are brought is, that the *causes* of faction cannot be removed, and that relief is only to be sought in the means of controlling its *effects*.

If a faction consists of less than a majority, relief is supplied by the republican principle, which enables the majority to defeat its sinister views by regular vote. It may clog the administration, it may convulse the society; but it will be unable to execute and mask its violence under the forms of the Constitution. When a majority is included in a faction, the form of popular government, on the other hand, enables it to sacrifice to its ruling passion or interest both the public good and the rights of other citizens. To secure the public good and private rights against the danger of such a faction, and at the same time to preserve the spirit and the form of popular government, is then the great object to which our inquiries are directed. Let me add that it is the great desideratum by which this form of government can be rescued from the opprobrium under which it has so long labored, and be recommended to the esteem and adoption of mankind.

By what means is this object attainable? Evidently by one of two only. Either the existence of the same passion or interest in a majority at the same time must be prevented, or the majority, having such coexistent passion or interest, must be rendered, by their number and local situation, unable to concert and carry into effect schemes of oppression. If the impulse and the opportunity be suffered to coincide, we well know that neither moral nor religious motives can be relied on as an adequate control. They are not found to be such on the injustice and violence of individuals, and lose their efficacy in proportion to the number combined together, that is, in proportion as their efficacy becomes needful.

From this view of the subject it may be concluded that a pure democracy, by which I mean a society consisting of a small number of citizens, who assemble and administer the government in person, can admit of no cure for the mischiefs of faction. A common passion or interest will, in almost every case, be felt by a majority of the whole; a communication and concert result from the form of government itself; and there is nothing to check the inducements to sacrifice the weaker party or an obnoxious individual. Hence it is that such democracies have ever been spectacles of turbulence and contention; have ever been found incompatible with personal security or the rights of property; and have in general been as short in their lives as they have been violent in their deaths. Theoretic politicians, who have patronized this species of government, have erroneously supposed that by reducing mankind to a perfect equality in their political rights, they would, at the same time, be perfectly equalized and assimilated in their possessions, their opinions, and their passions.

A republic, by which I mean a government in which the scheme of representation takes place, opens a different prospect, and promises the cure for which we are seeking. Let us examine the points in which it

varies from pure democracy, and we shall comprehend both the nature of the cure and the efficacy which it must derive from the Union.

The two great points of difference between a democracy and a republic are: first, the delegation of the government, in the latter, to a small number of citizens elected by the rest; secondly, the greater number of citizens, and greater sphere of country, over which the latter may be extended.

The effect of the first difference is, on the one hand, to refine and enlarge the public views, by passing them through the medium of a chosen body of citizens, whose wisdom may best discern the true interest of their country, and whose patriotism and love of justice will be least likely to sacrifice it to temporary or partial considerations. Under such a regulation, it may well happen that the public voice, pronounced by the representatives of the people, will be more consonant to the public good than if pronounced by the people themselves, convened for the purpose. On the other hand, the effect may be inverted. Men of factious tempers, of local prejudices, or of sinister designs, may, by intrigue, by corruption, or by other means, first obtain the suffrages, and then betray the interests, of the people. The question resulting is, whether small or extensive republics are more favorable to the election of proper guardians of the public weal; and it is clearly decided in favor of the latter by two obvious considerations:

In the first place, it is to be remarked that, however small the republic may be, the representatives must be raised to a certain number, in order to guard against the cabals of a few; and that, however large it may be, they must be limited to a certain number, in order to guard against the confusion of a multitude. Hence, the number of representatives in the two cases not being in proportion to that of the two constituents, and being proportionally greater in the small republic, it follows that, if the proportion of fit characters be not less in the large than in the small republic, the former will present a greater option, and consequently a greater probability of a fit choice.

In the next place, as each representative will be chosen by a greater number of citizens in the large than in the small republic, it will be more difficult for unworthy candidates to practise with success the vicious arts by which elections are too often carried; and the suffrages of the people being more free, will be more likely to centre in men who possess the most attractive merit and the most diffusive and established characters.

It must be confessed that in this, as in most other cases, there is a mean, on both sides of which inconveniences will be found to lie. By enlarging too much the number of electors, you render the representative too little acquainted with all their local circumstances and lesser interests; as by reducing it too much, you render him unduly attached to these, and too little fit to comprehend and pursue great and national objects. The federal Constitution forms a happy combination in this respect; the great and ag-

gregate interests being referred to the national, the local and particular to the State legislatures.

The other point of difference is, the greater number of citizens and extent of territory which may be brought within the compass of republican than of democratic government; and it is this circumstance principally which renders factious combinations less to be dreaded in the former than in the latter. The smaller the society, the fewer probably will be the distinct parties and interests composing it; the fewer the distinct parties and interests, the more frequently will a majority be found of the same party; and the smaller the number of individuals composing a majority, and the smaller the compass within which they are placed, the most easily will they concert and execute their plans of oppression. Extend the sphere, and you take in a greater variety of parties and interests; you make it less probable that a majority of the whole will have a common motive to invade the rights of other citizens; or if such a common motive exists, it will be more difficult for all who feel it to discover their own strength, and to act in unison with each other. Besides other impediments, it may be remarked that, where there is a consciousness of unjust or dishonorable purposes, communication is always checked by distrust in proportion to the number whose concurrence is necessary.

Hence, it clearly appears, that the same advantage which a republic has over a democracy, in controlling the effects of faction, is enjoyed by a large over a small republic,—is enjoyed by the Union over the States composing it. Does the advantage consist in the substitution of representatives whose enlightened views and virtuous sentiments render them superior to local prejudices and to schemes of injustice? It will not be denied that the representation of the Union will be most likely to possess these requisite endowments. Does it consist in the greater security afforded by a greater variety of parties, against the event of any one party being able to outnumber and oppress the rest? In an equal degree does the increased variety of parties comprised within the Union, increase this security. Does it, in fine, consist in the greater obstacles opposed to the concert and accomplishment of the secret wishes of an unjust and interested majority? Here, again, the extent of the Union gives it the most palpable advantage.

The influence of factious leaders may kindle a flame within their particular States, but will be unable to spread a general conflagration through the other States. A religious sect may degenerate into a political faction in a part of the Confederacy; but the variety of sects dispersed over the entire face of it must secure the national councils against any danger from that source. A rage for paper money, for an abolition of debts, for an equal division of property, or for any other improper or wicked project, will be less apt to pervade the whole body of the Union than a particular member of it; in the same proportion as such a malady is more likely to taint a particular county or district, than an entire State.

In the extent and proper structure of the Union, therefore, we behold a

republican remedy for the diseases most incident to republican government. And according to the degree of pleasure and pride we feel in being republicans, ought to be our zeal in cherishing the spirit and supporting the character of Federalists.

36. *Republicanism: The Federalist No. 39*

. . . The first question that offers itself is, whether the general form and aspect of the government be strictly republican? It is evident that no other form would be reconcilable with the genius of the people of America; with the fundamental principles of the Revolution; or with that honorable determination which animates every votary of freedom, to rest all our political experiments on the capacity of mankind for self-government. If the plan of the convention, therefore, be found to depart from the republican character, its advocates must abandon it as no longer defensible.

What, then, are the distinctive characters of the republican form? Were an answer to this question to be sought, not by recurring to principles, but in the application of the term by political writers, to the constitutions of different States, no satisfactory one would ever be found. Holland, in which no particle of the supreme authority is derived from the people, has passed almost universally under the denomination of a republic. The same title has been bestowed on Venice, where absolute power over the great body of the people is exercised, in the most absolute manner, by a small body of hereditary nobles. Poland, which is a mixture of aristocracy and of monarchy in their worst forms, has been dignified with the same appellation. The government of England, which has one republican branch only, combined with an hereditary aristocracy and monarchy, has, with equal impropriety, been frequently placed on the list of republics. These examples, which are nearly as dissimilar to each other as to a genuine republic, show the extreme inaccuracy with which the term has been used in political disquisitions.

If we resort for a criterion to the different principles on which different forms of government are established, we may define a republic to be, or at least may bestow that name on, a government which derives all its powers directly or indirectly from the great body of the people, and is administered by persons holding their offices during pleasure, for a limited period, or during good behavior. It is *essential* to such a government that it be derived from the great body of the society, not from an inconsiderable proportion, or a favored class of it; otherwise a handful of tyrannical nobles, exercising their oppressions by a delegation of their powers, might aspire to the rank of republicans, and claim for their government the honorable title of republic. It is *sufficient* for such a govern-

ment that the persons administering it be appointed, either directly or indirectly, by the people; and that they hold their appointments by either of the tenures just specified; otherwise every government in the United States, as well as every other popular government that has been or can be well organized or well executed, would be degraded from the republican character. According to the constitution of every State in the Union, some or other of the officers of government are appointed indirectly only by the people. According to most of them, the chief magistrate himself is so appointed. And according to one, this mode of appointment is extended to one of the coördinate branches of the legislature. According to all the constitutions, also, the tenure of the highest offices is extended to a definite period, and in many instances, both within the legislative and executive departments, to a period of years. According to the provisions of most of the constitutions, again, as well as according to the most respectable and received opinions on the subject, the members of the judiciary department are to retain their offices by the firm tenure of good behavior.

On comparing the Constitution planned by the convention with the standard here fixed, we perceive at once that it is, in the most rigid sense, conformable to it. The House of Representatives, like that of one branch at least of all the State legislatures, is elected immediately by the great body of the people. The Senate, like the present Congress, and the Senate of Maryland, derives its appointment indirectly from the people. The President is indirectly derived from the choice of the people, according to the example in most of the States. Even the judges with all other officers of the Union, will, as in the several States, be the choice, though a remote choice, of the people themselves. The duration of the appointments is equally conformable to the republican standard, and to the model of State constitutions. The House of Representatives is periodically elective, as in all the States; and for the period of two years, as in the State of South Carolina. The Senate is elective, for the period of six years; which is but one year more than the period of the Senate of Maryland, and but two more than that of the Senates of New York and Virginia. The President is to continue in office for the period of four years; as in New York and Delaware the chief magistrate is elected for three years, and in South Carolina for two years. In the other States the election is annual. In several of the States, however, no constitutional provision is made for the impeachment of the chief magistrate. And in Delaware and Virginia he is not impeachable till out of office. The President of the United States is impeachable at any time during his continuance in office. The tenure by which the judges are to hold their places, is, as it unquestionably ought to be, that of good behavior. The tenure of the ministerial offices generally, will be a subject of legal regulation, conformably to the reason of the case and the example of the State constitutions.

Could any further proof be required of the republican complexion of

this system, the most decisive one might be found in its absolute prohibition of titles of nobility, both under the federal and the State governments; and in its express guaranty of the republican form to each of the latter. . . .

37. Checks and Balances: The Federalist No. 51

To what expedient, then, shall we finally resort, for maintaining in practice the necessary partition of power among the several departments, as laid down in the Constitution? The only answer that can be given is, that as all these exterior provisions are found to be inadequate, the defect must be supplied, by so contriving the interior structure of the government as that its several constituent parts may, by their mutual relations, be the means of keeping each other in their proper places. Without presuming to undertake a full development of this important idea, I will hazard a few general observations, which may perhaps place it in a clearer light, and enable us to form a more correct judgment of the principles and structure of the government planned by the convention.

In order to lay a due foundation for that separate and distinct exercise of the different powers of government, which to a certain extent is admitted on all hands to be essential to the preservation of liberty, it is evident that each department should have a will of its own; and consequently should be so constituted that the members of each should have as little agency as possible in the appointment of the members of the others. Were this principle rigorously adhered to, it would require that all the appointments for the supreme executive, legislative, and judiciary magistracies should be drawn from the same fountain of authority, the people, through channels having no communication whatever with one another. Perhaps such a plan of constructing the several departments would be less difficult in practice than it may in contemplation appear. Some difficulties, however, and some additional expense would attend the execution of it. Some deviations, therefore, from the principle must be admitted. In the constitution of the judiciary department in particular, it might be inexpedient to insist rigorously on the principle: first, because peculiar qualifications being essential in the members, the primary consideration ought to be to select that mode of choice which best secures these qualifications; secondly, because the permanent tenure by which the appointments are held in that department, must soon destroy all sense of dependence on the authority conferring them.

It is equally evident, that the members of each department should be as little dependent as possible on those of the others, for the emoluments annexed to their offices. Were the executive magistrate, or the judges,

not independent of the legislature in this particular, their independence in every other would be merely nominal.

But the great security against a gradual concentration of the several powers in the same department, consists in giving to those who administer each department the necessary constitutional means and personal motives to resist encroachments of the others. The provision for defence must in this, as in all other cases, be made commensurate to the danger of attack. Ambition must be made to counteract ambition. The interest of the man must be connected with the constitutional rights of the place. It may be a reflection on human nature, that such devices should be necessary to control the abuses of government. But what is government itself, but the greatest of all reflections on human nature? If men were angels, no government would be necessary. If angels were to govern men, neither external nor internal controls on government would be necessary. In framing a government which is to be administered by men over men, the great difficulty lies in this: you must first enable the government to control the governed; and in the next place oblige it to control itself. A dependence on the people is, no doubt, the primary control on the government; but experience has taught mankind the necessity of auxiliary precautions.

This policy of supplying, by opposite and rival interests, the defect of better motives, might be traced through the whole system of human affairs, private as well as public. We see it particularly displayed in all the subordinate distributions of power, where the constant aim is to divide and arrange the several offices in such a manner as that each may be a check on the other—that the private interest of every individual may be a sentinel over the public rights. These inventions of prudence cannot be less requisite in the distribution of the supreme powers of the State.

But it is not possible to give to each department an equal power of self-defence. In republican government, the legislative authority necessarily predominates. The remedy for this inconveniency is to divide the legislature into different branches; and to render them, by different modes of election and different principles of action, as little connected with each other as the nature of their common functions and their common dependence on the society will admit. It may even be necessary to guard against dangerous encroachments by still further precautions. As the weight of the legislative authority requires that it should be thus divided, the weakness of the executive may require, on the other hand, that it should be fortified. An absolute negative on the legislature appears, at first view, to be the natural defence with which the executive magistrate should be armed. But perhaps it would be neither altogether safe nor alone sufficient. On ordinary occasions it might not be exerted with the requisite firmness, and on extraordinary occasions it might be perfidiously abused. May not this defect of an absolute negative be supplied by

some qualified connection between this weaker department and the weaker branch of the stronger department, by which the latter may be led to support the constitutional rights of the former, without being too much detached from the rights of its own department?

If the principles on which these observations are founded be just, as I persuade myself they are, and they be applied as a criterion to the several State constitutions, and to the federal Constitution, it will be found that if the latter does not perfectly correspond with them, the former are infinitely less able to bear such a test.

There are, moreover, two considerations particularly applicable to the federal system of America, which place that system in a very interesting point of view.

First. In a single republic, all the power surrendered by the people is submitted to the administration of a single government; and the usurpations are guarded against by a division of the government into distinct and separate departments. In the compound republic of America, the power surrendered by the people is first divided between two distinct governments, and then the portion allotted to each subdivided among distinct and separate departments. Hence a double security arises to the rights of the people. The different governments will control each other, at the same time that each will be controlled by itself.

Second. It is of great importance in a republic not only to guard the society against the oppression of its rulers, but to guard one part of the society against the injustice of the other part. Different interests necessarily exist in different classes of citizens. If a majority be united by a common interest, the rights of the minority will be insecure. There are but two methods of providing against this evil: the one by creating a will in the community independent of the majority—that is, of the society itself; the other, by comprehending in the society so many separate descriptions of citizens as will render an unjust combination of a majority of the whole very improbable, if not impracticable. The first method prevails in all governments possessing an hereditary or self-appointed authority. This, at best, is but a precarious security; because a power independent of the society may as well espouse the unjust views of the major, as the rightful interests of the minor party, and may possibly be turned against both parties. The second method will be exemplified in the federal republic of the United States. Whilst all authority in it will be derived from and dependent on the society, the society itself will be broken into so many parts, interests and classes of citizens, that the rights of individuals, or of the minority, will be in little danger from interested combinations of the majority. In a free government the security for civil rights must be the same as that for religious rights. It consists in the one case in the multiplicity of interests, and in the other in the multiplicity of sects. The degree of security in both cases will depend on the number of interests and sects; and this may be presumed to depend on the extent

of country and number of people comprehended under the same government. This view of the subject must particularly recommend a proper federal system to all the sincere and considerate friends of republican government, since it shows that in exact proportion as the territory of the Union may be formed into more circumscribed Confederacies, or States, oppressive combinations of a majority will be facilitated; the best security, under the republican forms, for the rights of every class of citizens, will be diminished; and consequently the stability and independence of some member of the government, the only other security, must be proportionally increased. Justice is the end of government. It is the end of civil society. It ever has been and ever will be pursued until it be obtained, or until liberty be lost in the pursuit. In a society under the forms of which the stronger faction can readily unite and oppress the weaker, anarchy may as truly be said to reign as in a state of nature, where the weaker individual is not secured against the violence of the stronger; and as, in the latter state, even the stronger individuals are prompted, by the uncertainty of their condition, to submit to a government which may protect the weak as well as themselves; so, in the former state, will the more powerful factions or parties be gradually induced, by a like motive, to wish for a government which will protect all parties, the weaker as well as the more powerful. It can be little doubted that if the State of Rhode Island was separated from the Confederacy and left to itself, the insecurity of rights under the popular form of government within such narrow limits would be displayed by such reiterated oppressions of factious majorities that some power altogether independent of the people would soon be called for by the voice of the very factions whose misrule had proved the necessity of it. In the extended republic of the United States, and among the great variety of interests, parties, and sects which it embraces, a coalition of a majority of the whole society could seldom take place on any other principles than those of justice and the general good; whilst there being thus less danger to a minor from the will of a major party, there must be less pretext, also, to provide for the security of the former, by introducing into the government a will not dependent on the latter, or, in other words, a will independent of the society itself. It is no less certain than it is important, notwithstanding the contrary opinions which have been entertained, that the larger the society, provided it lie within a practical sphere, the more duly capable it will be of self-government. And happily for the *republican cause,* the practicable sphere may be carried to a very great extent, by a judicious modification and mixture of the *federal principle.*

38. *Remarks in the Virginia Ratifying Convention, 1788:*

Power[1]

MR. MADISON. Mr. Chairman, the honorable gentleman has laid much stress on the maxim, that the purse and sword ought not to be put in the same hands, with a view of pointing out the impropriety of vesting this power in the general government. But it is totally inapplicable to this question. What is the meaning of this maxim? Does it mean that the sword and purse ought not to be trusted in the hands of the same government? This cannot be the meaning; for there never was, and I can say there never will be, an efficient government, in which both are not vested. The only rational meaning is, that the sword and purse are not to be given to the same member. Apply it to the British government, which has been mentioned. The sword is in the hands of the British king; the purse in the hands of the Parliament. It is so in America, as far as any analogy can exist. Would the honorable member say that the sword ought to be put in the hands of the representatives of the people, or in other hands independent of the government altogether? If he says so, it will violate the meaning of that maxim. This would be a novelty hitherto unprecedented. The purse is in the hands of the representatives of the people. They have the appropriation of all moneys. They have the direction and regulation of land and naval forces. They are to provide for calling forth the militia; and the President is to have the command, and, in conjunction with the Senate, to appoint the officers. The means ought to be commensurate to the end. The end is general protection. This cannot be effected without a general power to use the strength of the Union.

We are told that both sides are distinguished by these great traits, confidence and distrust. Perhaps there may be a less or greater tincture of suspicion on one side than the other. But give me leave to say that, where power can be safely lodged, if it be necessary, reason commands its cession. In such case, it is imprudent and unsafe to withhold it. It is universally admitted that it must be lodged in some hands or other. The question, then, is, in what part of the government it ought to be placed; and not whether any other political body, independent of the government, should have it or not. I profess myself to have had a uniform zeal for a republican government. If the honorable member, or any other person, conceives that my attachment to this system arises from a different source, he is greatly mistaken. From the first moment that my mind was capable of contemplating political subjects, I never, till this moment, ceased wishing success to a well-regulated republican government. The establishment of such in America was my most ardent desire. I have considered atten-

tively (and my consideration has been aided by experience) the tendency of a relaxation of laws and a licentiousness of manners.

If we review the history of all republics, we are justified in the supposition that, if the bands of the government be relaxed, confusion will ensue. Anarchy ever has produced, and I fear ever will produce, despotism. What was the state of things that preceded the wars and revolutions in Germany? Faction and confusion. What produced the disorders and commotions of Holland? The like causes. In this commonwealth, and every state in the Union, the relaxed operation of the government has been sufficient to alarm the friends of their country. The rapid increase of population in every state is an additional reason to check dissipation and licentiousness. Does it not strongly call for the friends of republican government to endeavor to establish a republican organization? A change is absolutely necessary. I can see no danger in submitting to practice an experiment which seems to be founded on the best theoretic principles.

Ratification: "One of the Most Fortunate Events ... for Human Nature"[2]

MR. MADISON. Mr. Chairman, nothing has excited more admiration in the world than the manner in which free governments have been established in America; for it was the first instance, from the creation of the world to the American revolution, that free inhabitants have been seen deliberating on a form of government, and selecting such of their citizens as possessed their confidence, to determine upon and give effect to it. But why has this excited so much wonder and applause? Because it is of so much magnitude, and because it is liable to be frustrated by so many accidents. If it has excited so much wonder that the United States have, in the middle of war and confusion, formed free systems of government, how much more astonishment and admiration will be excited, should they be able peaceably, freely, and satisfactorily, to establish one general government, when there is such a diversity of opinions and interests—when not cemented or stimulated by any common danger! How vast must be the difficulty of concentrating, in one government, the interests, and conciliating the opinions, of so many different, heterogeneous bodies!

How have the confederacies of ancient and modern times been formed? As far as ancient history describes the former to us, they were brought about by the wisdom of some eminent sage. How was the imperfect union of the Swiss cantons formed? By danger. How was the confederacy of the United Netherlands formed? By the same. They are surrounded by dangers. By these, and one influential character, they were stimulated to unite. How was the Germanic system formed? By danger, in some degree, but principally by the overruling influence of individuals.

When we consider this government, we ought to make great allow-

ances. We must calculate the impossibility that every state should be gratified in its wishes, and much less that every individual should receive this gratification. It has never been denied, by the friends of the paper on the table, that it has defects; but they do not think that it contains any real danger. They conceive that they will, in all probability, be removed, when experience will show it to be necessary. I beg that gentlemen, in deliberating on this subject, would consider the alternative. Either nine states shall have ratified it, or they will not. If nine states will adopt it, can it be reasonably presumed, or required, that nine states, having freely and fully considered the subject, and come to an affirmative decision, will, upon the demand of a single state, agree that they acted wrong, and could not see its defects—tread back the steps which they have taken, and come forward, and reduce it to uncertainty whether a general system shall be adopted or not? Virginia has always heretofore spoken the language of respect to the other states, and she has always been attended to. Will it be that language to call on a great majority of the states to acknowledge that they have done wrong? Is it the language of confidence to say that we do not believe that amendments for the preservation of the common liberty, and general interests, of the states, will be consented to by them? This is the language neither of confidence nor respect. Virginia, when she speaks respectfully, will be as much attended to as she has hitherto been when speaking this language.

It is a most awful thing that depends on our decision—no less than whether the thirteen states shall unite freely, peaceably, and unanimously, for security of their common happiness and liberty, or whether every thing is to be put in confusion and disorder. . . .

I have revolved this question in my mind with as much serious attention, and called to my aid as much information, as I could, yet I can see no reason for the apprehensions of gentlemen; but I think that the most happy effects for this country would result from adoption, and if Virginia will agree to ratify this system, I shall look upon it as one of the most fortunate events that ever happened for human nature. . . .

39. *On Titles*

Congress, May 11, 1789

. . . I am not afraid of titles, because I fear the danger of any power they could confer, but I am against them because they are not very reconcilable with the nature of our Government or the genius of the people. Even if they were proper in themselves, they are not so at this juncture of time. But my strongest objection is founded in principle; instead of increasing,

they diminish the true dignity and importance of a Republic, and would in particular, on this occasion, diminish the true dignity of the first magistrate himself. If we give titles, we must either borrow or invent them. If we have recourse to the fertile fields of luxuriant fancy, and deck out an airy being of our own creation, it is a great chance but its fantastic properties would render the empty phantom ridiculous and absurd. If we borrow, the servile imitation will be odious, not to say ridiculous also; we must copy from the pompous sovereigns of the East, or follow the inferior potentates of Europe; in either case, the splendid tinsel or gorgeous robe would disgrace the manly shoulders of our chief. The more truly honorable shall we be, by showing a total neglect and disregard to things of this nature; the more simple, the more Republican we are in our manners, the more rational dignity we shall acquire. . . .

40. *Public Opinion*

National Gazette, *December 19, 1791*

Public opinion sets bounds to every government, and is the real sovereign in every free one.

As there are cases where the public opinion must be obeyed by the government; so there are cases, where not being fixed, it may be influenced by the government. This distinction, if kept in view, would prevent or decide many debates on the respect due from the government to the sentiments of the people.

In proportion as government is influenced by opinion, it must be so, by whatever influences opinion. This decides the question concerning a *Constitutional Declaration of Rights,* which requires an influence on government, by becoming a part of public opinion.

The larger a country, the less easy for its real opinion to be ascertained, and the less difficult to be counterfeited; when ascertained or presumed, the more respectable it is in the eyes of individuals.—This is favorable to the authority of government. For the same reason, the more extensive a country, the more insignificant is each individual in his own eyes.—This may be unfavorable to liberty.

Whatever facilitates a general intercourse of sentiments, as good roads, domestic commerce, a free press, and particularly a *circulation of newspapers through the entire body of the people,* and *Representatives going from, and returning among every part of them,* is equivalent to a contraction of territorial limits, and is favorable to liberty, where these may be too extensive.

41. *Charters: Power and Liberty*

National Gazette, *January 19, 1792*

In Europe, charters of liberty have been granted by power. America has set the example and France has followed it, of charters of power granted by liberty. This revolution in the practice of the world, may, with an honest praise, be pronounced the most triumphant epoch of its history, and the most consoling presage of its happiness. We look back, already, with astonishment, at the daring outrages committed by despotism, on the reason and rights of man; we look forward with joy, to the period, when it shall be despoiled of all its usurpations, and bound forever in the chains, with which it had loaded its miserable victims.

In proportion to the value of this revolution; in proportion to the importance of instruments, every word of which decides a question between power and liberty; in proportion to the solemnity of acts, proclaiming the will authenticated by the seal of the people, the only earthly source of authority, ought to be the vigilance with which they are guarded by every citizen in private life, and the circumspection with which they are executed by every citizen in public trust.

As compacts, charters of government are superior in obligation to all others, because they give effect to all others. As truths, none can be more sacred, because they are bound, on the conscience by the religious sanctions of an oath. As metes and bounds of government, they transcend all other land-marks, because every public usurpation is an encroachment on the private right, not of one, but of all.

The citizens of the United States have peculiar motives to support the energy of their constitutional charters.

Having originated the experiment, their merit will be estimated by its success.

The complicated form of their political system arising from the partition of government between the states and the union, and from the separations and subdivisions of the several departments in each, requires a more than common reverence for authority which is to preserve order thro' the whole.

Being republicans, they must be anxious to establish the efficacy of popular charters, in defending liberty against power, and power against licentiousness; and in keeping every portion of power within its proper limits; by this means discomforting the partizans of anti-republican contrivances for the purpose.

All power has been traced up to opinion. The stability of all governments and security of all rights may be traced to the same source. The most arbitrary government is controuled where the public opinion is

fixed. The despot of Constantinople dares not lay a new tax, because every slave thinks he ought not. The most systematic governments are turned by the slightest impulse from their regular path, where public opinion no longer holds them in it. We see at this moment the *executive* magistrate of Great-Britain, exercising under the authority of the representatives of the *people,* a *legislative* power over the West-India commerce.

How devoutly is it to be wished, then, that the public opinion of the United States should be enlightened; that it should attach itself to their governments as delineated in *great charters,* derived not from the usurped power of kings, but from the legitimate authority of the people; and that it should guarantee, with a holy zeal, these political scriptures from every attempt to add to or diminish from them. Liberty and order will never be *perfectly* safe, until a trespass on the constitutional provisions for either, shall be felt with the same keenness that resents an invasion of the dearest rights, until every citizen shall be an Argus to espy, and an Ægeon to avenge, the unhallowed deed.

42. *Parties*

National Gazette, *January 23, 1792*

In every political society, parties are unavoidable. A difference of interests, real or supposed, is the most natural and fruitful source of them. The great objects should be to combat the evil: 1. By establishing political equality among all. 2. By withholding *unnecessary* opportunities from a few, to increase the inequality of property, by an immoderate, and especially unmerited, accumulation of riches. 3. By the silent operation of laws, which, without violating the rights of property, reduce extreme wealth towards a state of mediocrity, and raise extreme indigence towards a state of comfort. 4. By abstaining from measures which operate differently on different interests, and particularly such as favor one interest, at the expence of another. 5. By making one party a check on the other, so far as the existence of parties cannot be prevented, nor their views accommodated. If this is not the language of reason, it is that of republicanism.

In all political societies, different interests and parties arise out of the nature of things, and the great art of politicians lies in making them checks and balances to each other. Let us then increase these *natural distinctions* by favoring an inequality of property; and let us add to them artificial distinctions, by establishing *kings* and *nobles,* and *plebeians.* We shall then have the more checks to oppose to each other; we

shall then have the more scales and the more weights to protect and maintain the equilibrium. This is as little the voice of reason, as it is of republicanism.

From the expediency, in politics, of making natural parties, mutual checks on each other, to infer the propriety of creating artificial parties, in order to form them into mutual checks, is not less absurd than it would be in ethics, to say, that new vices ought to be promoted, where they would counteract each other, because this use may be made of existing vices.

43. *Fashion*

National Gazette, *March 22, 1792*

An humble address has been lately presented to the Prince of Wales by the Buckle Manufacturers of Birmingham, Wassal, Wolverhampton, and their environs, stating that the Buckle Trade gives employment to more than Twenty Thousand persons, numbers of whom, in consequence of the prevailing fashion of Shoestrings & Slippers, are at present without employ, almost destitute of bread, and exposed to the horrors of want at the most inclement season; that to the manufactures of Buckles and Buttons, Birmingham owes its important figure on the map of England; that it is to no purpose to address Fashion herself, she being void of feeling and deaf to argument, but fortunately accustomed to listen to his voice, and to obey his commands: and finally *imploring* his Royal Highness to consider the deplorable condition of their trade, which is in danger of being ruined by the *mutability of fashion,* and to give that direction to the *public taste,* which will insure the lasting gratitude of the petitioners.

Several important reflections are suggested by this address.

I. The most precarious of all occupations which give bread to the industrious, are those depending on mere fashion, which generally changes so suddenly, and often so considerably, as to throw whole bodies of people out of employment.

II. Of all occupations those are the least desirable in a free state, which produce the most servile dependence of one class of citizens on another class. This dependence must increase as the *mutuality* of wants is diminished. Where the wants on one side are the absolute necessaries; and on the other are neither absolute necessaries, nor result from the habitual œconomy of life, but are the mere caprices of fancy, the evil is in its extreme; or if not,

III. The extremity of the evil must be in the case before us, where the absolute necessaries depend on the caprices of fancy, and the caprice of a

single fancy directs the fashion of the community. Here the dependence sinks to the lowest point of servility. We see a proof of it in the *spirit* of the address. Twenty thousand persons are to get or go without their bread, as a wanton youth, may fancy to wear his shoes with or without straps, or to fasten his straps with strings or with buckles. Can any despotism be more cruel than a situation, in which the existence of thousands depends on one will, and that will on the most slight and fickle of all motives, a mere whim of the imagination.

IV. What a contrast is here to the independent situation and manly sentiments of American citizens, who live on their own soil, or whose labour is necessary to its cultivation, or who are occupied in supplying wants, which being founded in solid utility, in comfortable accommodation, or in settled habits, produce a reciprocity of dependence, at once ensuring subsistence, and inspiring a dignified sense of social rights.

V. The condition of those who receive employment and bread from the precarious source of fashion and superfluity, is a lesson to nations, as well as to individuals. In proportion as a nation consists of that description of citizens, and depends on external commerce, it is dependent on the consumption and caprice of other nations. If the laws of propriety did not forbid, the manufacturers of Birmingham, Wassal, and Wolverhampton, had as real an interest in supplying the arbiters of fashion in America, as the patron they have addressed. The dependence in the case of nations is even greater than among individuals of the same nation: for besides the *mutability of fashion* which is the same in both, the *mutability of policy* is another source of danger in the former.

44. *Who Are the Best Keepers of the People's Liberties?*

National Gazette, *December 20, 1792*

Republican.—The people themselves.—The sacred trust can be no where so safe as in the hands most interested in preserving it.

Anti-republican.—The people are stupid, suspicious, licentious. They cannot safely trust themselves. When they have established government they should think of nothing but obedience, leaving the care of their liberties to their wiser rulers.

Republican.—Although all men are born free, and all nations might be so, yet too true it is, that slavery has been the general lot of the human race. Ignorant—they have been cheated; asleep—they have been surprized; divided—the yoke has been forced upon them. But what is the lesson? that because the people *may* betray themselves, they ought to

give themselves up, blindfold, to those who have an interest in betraying them? Rather conclude that the people ought to be enlightened, to be awakened, to be united, that after establishing a government they should watch over it, as well as obey it.

Anti-republican.—You look at the surface only, where errors float, instead of fathoming the depths where truth lies hid. It is not the government that is disposed to fly off from the people; but the people that are ever ready to fly off from the government. Rather say then, enlighten the government, warn it to be vigilant, enrich it with influence, arm it with force, and to the people never pronounce but two words—*Submission* and *Confidence.*

Republican.—The centrifugal tendency then is in the people, not in the government, and the secret art lies in restraining the tendency, by augmenting the attractive principle of the government with all the weight that can be added to it. What a perversion of the natural order of things! to make *power* the primary and central object of the social system, and *Liberty* but its satellite.

Anti-republican.—The science of the stars can never instruct you in the mysteries of government. Wonderful as it may seem, the more you increase the attractive force of power, the more you enlarge the sphere of liberty; the more you make government independent and hostile towards the people, the better security you provide for their rights and interests. Hence the wisdom of the theory, which, after limiting the share of the people to a third of the government, and lessening the influence of that share by the mode and term of delegating it, establishes two grand hereditary orders, with feelings, habits, interests, and prerogatives all inveterately hostile to the rights and interests of the people, yet by a *mysterious* operation all combining to fortify the people in both.

Republican.—Mysterious indeed!—But mysteries belong to religion, not to government; to the ways of the Almighty, not to the works of man. And in religion itself there is nothing mysterious to its author; the mystery lies in the dimness of the human sight. So in the institutions of man let there be no mystery, unless for those inferior beings endowed with a ray perhaps of the twilight vouchsafed to the first order of terrestrial creation.

Anti-republican.—You are destitute, I perceive, of every quality of a good citizen, or rather of a good *subject*. You have neither the light of faith nor the spirit of obedience. I denounce you to the government as an accomplice of atheism and anarchy.

Republican.—And I forbear to denounce you to the people, though a blasphemer of their rights and an idolater of tyranny.—Liberty disdains to persecute.

45. *The Alien and Sedition Acts: Address of the General Assembly to the People of the Commonwealth of Virginia*

January 23, 1799

Fellow-Citizens,—Unwilling to shrink from our representative responsibility, conscious of the purity of our motives, but acknowledging your right to supervise our conduct, we invite your serious attention to the emergency which dictated the subjoined resolutions. Whilst we disdain to alarm you by ill-founded jealousies, we recommend an investigation, guided by the coolness of wisdom, and a decision bottomed on firmness but tempered with moderation.

It would be perfidious in those entrusted with the guardianship of the State sovereignty, and acting under the solemn obligation of the following oath, "I do swear that I will support the Constitution of the United States," not to warn you of encroachments which, though clothed with the pretext of necessity, or disguised by arguments of expediency, may yet establish precedents which may ultimately devote a generous and unsuspicious people to all the consequences of usurped power.

Encroachments springing from a government whose organization can not be maintained without the co-operation of the States, furnish the strongest excitements upon the State Legislatures to watchfulness, and impose upon them the strongest obligation to preserve unimpaired the line of partition.

The acquiescence of the States under infractions of the federal compact, would either beget a speedy consolidation, by precipitating the State governments into impotency and contempt; or prepare the way for a revolution, by a repetition of these infractions, until the people are roused to appear in the majesty of their strength. It is to avoid these calamities that we exhibit to the people the momentous question, whether the Constitution of the United States shall yield to a construction which defies every restraint and overwhelms the best hopes of republicanism.

Exhortations to disregard domestic usurpation, until foreign danger shall have passed, is an artifice which may be forever used; because the possessors of power, who are the advocates for its extension, can ever create national embarrassments, to be successively employed to soothe the people into sleep, whilst that power is swelling, silently, secretly, and fatally. Of the same character are insinuations of a foreign influence, which seize upon a laudable enthusiasm against danger from abroad, and distort it by an unnatural application, so as to blind your eyes against danger at home.

The sedition act presents a scene which was never expected by the early friends of the Constitution. It was then admitted that the State sovereignties were only diminished by powers specifically enumerated, or necessary to carry the specified powers into effect. Now, Federal authority is deduced from implication; and from the existence of State law, it is inferred that Congress possess a similar power of legislation; whence Congress will be endowed with a power of legislation in all cases whatsoever, and the States will be stripped of every right reserved, by the concurrent claims of a paramount Legislature.

The sedition act is the offspring of these tremendous pretensions, which inflict a death-wound on the sovereignty of the States.

For the honor of American understanding, we will not believe that the people have been allured into the adoption of the Constitution by an affectation of defining powers, whilst the *preamble* would admit a construction which would erect the will of Congress into a power paramount in all cases, and therefore limited in none. On the contrary, it is evident that the objects for which the Constitution was formed were deemed attainable only by a particular enumeration and specification of each power granted to the Federal Government; reserving all others to the people, or to the States. And yet it is in vain we search for any specified power embracing the right of legislation against the freedom of the press.

Had the States been despoiled of their sovereignty by the generality of the preamble, and had the Federal Government been endowed with whatever they should judge to be instrumental towards union, justice, tranquillity, common defence, general welfare, and the preservation of liberty, nothing could have been more frivolous than an enumeration of powers.

It is vicious in the extreme to calumniate meritorious public servants; but it is both artful and vicious to arouse the public indignation against calumny in order to conceal usurpation. Calumny is forbidden by the laws, usurpation by the Constitution. Calumny injures individuals, usurpation, States. Calumny may be redressed by the common judicatures; usurpation can only be controlled by the act of society. Ought *usurpation,* which is most mischievous, to be rendered less hateful by *calumny,* which, though injurious, is in a degree less pernicious? But the laws for the correction of calumny were not defective. Every libellous writing or expression might receive its punishment in the State courts, from juries summoned by an officer, who does not receive his appointment from the President, and is under no influence to court the pleasure of Government, whether it injured public officers or private citizens. Nor is there any distinction in the Constitution empowering Congress exclusively to punish calumny directed against an officer of the General Government; so that a construction assuming the power of protecting the reputation of a citizen officer will extend to the case of any other citizen, and open to

Congress a right of legislation in every conceivable case which can arise between individuals.

In answer to this, it is urged that every Government possesses an inherent power of self-preservation, entitling it to do whatever it shall judge necessary for that purpose.

This is a repetition of the doctrine of implication and expediency in different language, and admits of a similar and decisive answer, namely, that as the powers of Congress are defined, powers inherent, implied, or expedient, are obviously the creatures of ambition; because the care expended in defining powers would otherwise have been superfluous. Powers extracted from such sources will be indefinitely multipled by the aid of armies and patronage, which, with the impossibility of controlling them by any demarcation, would presently terminate reasoning, and ultimately swallow up the State sovereignties.

So insatiable is a love of power that it has resorted to a distinction between the freedom and licentiousness of the press for the purpose of converting the third amendment of the Constitution, which was dictated by the most lively anxiety to preserve that freedom, into an instrument for abridging it. Thus usurpation even justifies itself by a precaution against usurpation; and thus an amendment universally designed to quiet every fear is adduced as the source of an act which has produced general terror and alarm.

The distinction between liberty and licentiousness is still a repetition of the Protean doctrine of implication, which is ever ready to work its ends by varying its shape. By its help, the judge as to what is licentious may escape through any constitutional restriction. Under it men of a particular religious opinion might be excluded from office, because such exclusion would not amount to an establishment of religion, and because it might be said that their opinions are licentious. And under it Congress might denominate a religion to be heretical and licentious, and proceed to its suppression. Remember that precedents once established are so much positive power; and that the nation which reposes on the pillow of political confidence, will sooner or later end its political existence in a deadly lethargy. Remember, also, that it is to the press mankind are indebted for having dispelled the clouds which long encompassed religion, for disclosing her genuine lustre, and disseminating her salutary doctrines. . . .

As if we were bound to look for security from the personal probity of Congress amidst the frailties of man, and not from the barriers of the Constitution, it has been urged that the accused under the sedition act is allowed to prove the truth of the charge. This argument will not for a moment disguise the unconstitutionality of the act, if it be recollected that opinions as well as facts are made punishable, and that the truth of an opinion is not susceptible of proof. By subjecting the truth of opinion to the regulation, fine, and imprisonment, to be inflicted by those who are

of a different opinion, the free range of the human mind is injuriously restrained. The sacred obligations of religion flow from the due exercise of opinion, in the solemn discharge of which man is accountable to his God alone; yet, under this precedent the truth of religion itself may be ascertained, and its pretended licentiousness punished by a jury of a different creed from that held by the person accused. This law, then, commits the double sacrilege of arresting reason in her progress towards perfection, and of placing in a state of danger the free exercise of religious opinions. But where does the Constitution allow Congress to create crimes and inflict punishment, provided they allow the accused to exhibit evidence in his defense? This doctrine, united with the assertion, that sedition is a common law offence, and therefore within the correcting power of Congress, opens at once the hideous volumes of penal law, and turns loose upon us the utmost invention of insatiable malice and ambition, which, in all ages, have debauched morals, depressed liberty, shackled religion, supported despotism, and deluged the scaffold with blood.

All the preceding arguments, arising from a deficiency of constitutional power in Congress, apply to the alien act; and this act is liable to other objections peculiar to itself. If a suspicion that aliens are dangerous constitute the justification of that power exercised over them by Congress, then a similar suspicion will justify the exercise of a similar power over natives; because there is nothing in the Constitution distinguishing between the power of a State to permit the residence of natives and of aliens. It is, therefore, a right originally possessed, and never surrendered, by the respective States, and which is rendered dear and valuable to Virginia, because it is assailed through the bosom of the Constitution, and because her peculiar situation renders the easy admission of artisans and laborers an interest of vast importance.

But this bill contains other features, still more alarming and dangerous. It dispenses with the trial by jury; it violates the judicial system; it confounds legislative, executive, and judicial powers; it punishes without trial; and it bestows upon the President despotic power over a numerous class of men. Are such measures consistent with our constitutional principles? And will an accumulation of power so extensive in the hands of the Executive, over aliens, secure to natives the blessings of republican liberty?

If measures can mould governments, and if an uncontrolled power of construction is surrendered to those who administer them, their progress may be easily foreseen, and their end easily foretold. A lover of monarchy, who opens the treasures of corruption by distributing emolument among devoted partisans, may at the same time be approaching his object and deluding the people with professions of republicanism. He may confound monarchy and republicanism, by the art of definition. He may varnish over the dexterity which ambition never fails to display, with

the pliancy of language, the seduction of expediency, or the prejudices of the times; and he may come at length to avow that so extensive a territory as that of the United States can only be governed by the energies of monarchy; that it cannot be defended, except by standing armies; and that it cannot be united except by consolidation. . . .

Let history be consulted; let the man of experience reflect: nay, let the artificers of monarchy be asked what further materials they can need for building up their favorite system.

These are solemn but painful truths; and yet we recommend it to you not to forget the possibility of danger from without, although danger threatens us from within. Usurpation is indeed dreadful; but against foreign invasion, if that should happen, let us rise with hearts and hands united, and repel the attack with the zeal of freemen who will strengthen their title to examine and correct domestic measures, by having defended their country against foreign aggression.

Pledged as we are, fellow-citizens, to these sacred engagements, we yet humbly and fervently implore the Almighty Disposer of events to avert from our land war and usurpation, the scourges of mankind; to permit our fields to be cultivated in peace; to instil into nations the love of friendly intercourse; to suffer our youth to be educated in virtue, and to preserve our morality from the pollution invariably incident to habits of war; to prevent the laborer and husbandman from being harassed by taxes and imposts; to remove from ambition the means of disturbing the commonwealth; to annihilate all pretexts for power afforded by war; to maintain the Constitution; and to bless our nation with tranquillity, under whose benign influence we may reach the summit of happiness and glory, to which we are destined by *nature* and *nature's God*.

46. *The Sedition Act—"A Precedent Fatal to the Liberty of Conscience"*

1799–1800

. . . Here is an express and solemn declaration by the Convention of the State, that they ratified the Constitution in the sense that no right of any denomination can be cancelled, abridged, restrained, or modified, by the Government of the United States, or any part of it, except in those instances in which power is given by the Constitution; and in the sense, particularly, "that among other essential rights, the liberty of conscience and freedom of the press cannot be cancelled, abridged, restrained, or modified, by any authority of the United States."

Words could not well express in a fuller or more forcible manner the

understanding of the Convention, that the liberty of conscience and the freedom of the press were *equally* and *completely* exempted from all authority whatever of the United States.

Under an anxiety to guard more effectually these rights against every possible danger, the Convention, after ratifying the Constitution, proceeded to prefix to certain amendments proposed by them a declaration of rights, in which are two articles providing, the one for the liberty of conscience, the other for the freedom of speech and of the press.

Similar recommendations having proceeded from a number of other States, and Congress, as has been seen, having, in consequence thereof, and with a view to extend the ground of public confidence, proposed, among other declaratory and restrictive clauses, a clause expressly securing the liberty of conscience and of the press, and Virginia having concurred in the ratifications which made them a part of the Constitution, it will remain with a candid public to decide whether it would not mark an inconsistency and degeneracy, if an indifference were now shown to a palpable violation of one of those rights—the freedom of the press; and to a precedent, therein, which may be fatal to the other—the free exercise of religion.

That the precedent established by the violation of the former of these rights may, as is affirmed by the resolution, be fatal to the latter, appears to be demonstrable by a comparison of the grounds on which they respectively rest, and from the scope of reasoning by which the power over the former has been vindicated.

First. Both of these rights, the liberty of conscience and of the press, rest equally on the original ground of not being delegated by the Constitution, and, consequently, withheld from the Government. Any construction, therefore, that would attack this original security for the one must have the like effect on the other.

Secondly. They are both equally secured by the supplement to the Constitution, being both included in the same amendment, made at the same time, and by the same authority. Any construction or argument, then, which would turn the amendment into a grant or acknowledgment of power with respect to the press, might be equally applied to the freedom of religion.

Thirdly. If it be admitted that the extent of the freedom of the press secured by the amendment is to be measured by the common law on this subject, the same authority may be resorted to for the standard which is to fix the extent of the "free exercise of religion." It cannot be necessary to say what this standard would be; whether the common law be taken solely as the unwritten, or as varied by the written law of England.

Fourthly. If the words and phrases in the amendment are to be considered as chosen with a studied discrimination, which yields an argument for a power over the press under the limitation that its freedom be not abridged, the same argument results from the same consideration for

a power over the exercise of religion, under the limitation that its freedom be not prohibited.

For if Congress may regulate the freedom of the press, provided they do not abridge it, because it is said only "they shall not abridge it," and is not said "they shall make no law respecting it," the analogy of reasoning is conclusive that Congress may *regulate* and even *abridge* the free exercise of religion, provided they do not *prohibit* it; because it is said only "they shall not prohibit it," and is *not* said "they shall make no law *respecting*, or no law *abridging* it."

The General Assembly were governed by the clearest reason, then, in considering the Sedition Act, which legislates on the freedom of the press, as establishing a precedent that may be fatal to the liberty of conscience; and it will be the duty of all, in proportion as they value the security of the latter, to take the alarm at every encroachment on the former. . . .

47. *First Inaugural Address*

March 4, 1809

Unwilling to depart from examples of the most revered authority, I avail myself of the occasion now presented to express the profound impression made on me by the call of my country to the station to the duties of which I am about to pledge myself by the most solemn of sanctions. So distinguished a mark of confidence, proceeding from the deliberate and tranquil suffrage of a free and virtuous nation, would under any circumstances have commanded my gratitude and devotion, as well as filled me with an awful sense of the trust to be assumed. Under the various circumstances which give peculiar solemnity to the existing period, I feel that both the honor and the responsibility allotted to me are inexpressibly enhanced.

The present situation of the world is indeed without a parallel, and that of our own country full of difficulties. The pressure of these, too, is the more severely felt because they have fallen upon us at a moment when the national prosperity being at a height not before attained, the contrast resulting from the change has been rendered the more striking. Under the benign influence of our republican institutions, and the maintenance of peace with all nations whilst so many of them were engaged in bloody and wasteful wars, the fruits of a just policy were enjoyed in an unrivaled growth of our faculties and resources. Proofs of this were seen in the improvements of agriculture, in the successful enterprises of commerce, in the progress of manufactures and useful arts, in the increase of the public

revenue and the use made of it in reducing the public debt, and in the valuable works and establishments everywhere multiplying over the face of our land.

It is a precious reflection that the transition from this prosperous condition of our country to the scene which has for some time been distressing us is not chargeable on any unwarrantable views, nor, as I trust, on any involuntary errors in the public councils. Indulging no passions which trespass on the rights or the repose of other nations, it has been the true glory of the United States to cultivate peace by observing justice, and to entitle themselves to the respect of the nations at war by fulfilling their neutral obligations with the most scrupulous impartiality. If there be candor in the world, the truth of these assertions will not be questioned; posterity at least will do justice to them.

This unexceptionable course could not avail against the injustice and violence of the belligerent powers. In their rage against each other, or impelled by more direct motives, principles of retaliation have been introduced equally contrary to universal reason and acknowledged law. How long their arbitrary edicts will be continued in spite of the demonstrations that not even a pretext for them has been given by the United States, and of the fair and liberal attempt to induce a revocation of them, can not be anticipated. Assuring myself that under every vicissitude the determined spirit and united councils of the nation will be safeguards to its honor and its essential interests, I repair to the post assigned me with no other discouragement than what springs from my own inadequacy to its high duties. If I do not sink under the weight of this deep conviction it is because I find some support in a consciousness of the purposes and a confidence in the principles which I bring with me into this arduous service.

To cherish peace and friendly intercourse with all nations having correspondent dispositions; to maintain sincere neutrality toward belligerent nations; to prefer in all cases amicable discussion and reasonable accommodation of differences to a decision of them by an appeal to arms; to exclude foreign intrigues and foreign partialities, so degrading to all countries and so baneful to free ones; to foster a spirit of independence too just to invade the rights of others, too proud to surrender our own, too liberal to indulge unworthy prejudices ourselves and too elevated not to look down upon them in others; to hold the union of the States as the basis of their peace and happiness; to support the Constitution, which is the cement of the Union, as well in its limitations as in its authorities; to respect the rights and authorities reserved to the States and to the people as equally incorporated with an essential to the success of the general system; to avoid the slightest interference with the rights of conscience or the functions of religion, so wisely exempted from civil jurisdiction; to preserve in their full energy the other salutary provisions in behalf of private and personal rights, and of the freedom of the press; to observe

economy in public expenditures; to liberate the public resources by an honorable discharge of the public debts; to keep within the requisite limits a standing military force, always remembering that an armed and trained militia is the firmest bulwark of republics—that without standing armies their liberty can never be in danger, nor with large ones safe; to promote by authorized means improvements friendly to agriculture, to manufactures, and to external as well as internal commerce; to favor in like manner the advancement of science and the diffusion of information as the best aliment to true liberty; to carry on the benevolent plans which have been so meritoriously applied to the conversion of our aboriginal neighbors from the degradation and wretchedness of savage life to a participation of the improvements of which the human mind and manners are susceptible in a civilized state;—as far as sentiments and intentions such as these can aid the fulfillment of my duty, they will be a resource which can not fail me.

It is my good fortune, moreover, to have the path in which I am to tread lighted by examples of illustrious services successfully rendered in the most trying difficulties by those who have marched before me. Of those of my immediate predecessor it might least become me here to speak. I may, however, be pardoned for not suppressing the sympathy with which my heart is full in the rich reward he enjoys in the benedictions of a beloved country, gratefully bestowed for exalted talents zealously devoted through a long career to the advancement of its highest interest and happiness.

But the source to which I look for the aids which alone can supply my deficiencies is in the well-tried intelligence and virtue of my fellow-citizens, and in the counsels of those representing them in the other departments associated in the care of the national interests. In these my confidence will under every difficulty be best placed, next to that which we have all been encouraged to feel in the guardianship and guidance of that Almighty Being whose power regulates the destiny of nations, whose blessings have been so conspicuously dispensed to this rising Republic, and to whom we are bound to address our devout gratitude for the past, as well as our fervent supplications and best hopes for the future.

48. *Second Annual Message*

December 5, 1810

. . . Whilst it is universally admitted that a well-instructed people alone can be permanently a free people, and whilst it is evident that the means of diffusing and improving useful knowledge form so small a proportion

of the expenditures for national purposes, I can not presume it to be unreasonable to invite your attention to the advantages of superadding to the means of education provided by the several States a seminary of learning instituted by the National Legislature within the limits of their exclusive jurisdiction, the expense of which might be defrayed or reimbursed out of the vacant grounds which have accrued to the nation within those limits.

Such an institution, though local in its legal character, would be universal in its beneficial effects. By enlightening the opinions, by expanding the patriotism, and by assimilating the principles, the sentiments, and the manners of those who might resort to this temple of science, to be redistributed in due time through every part of the community, sources of jealousy and prejudice would be diminished, the features of national character would be multiplied, and greater extent given to social harmony. But, above all, a well-constituted seminary in the center of the nation is recommended by the consideration that the additional instruction emanating from it would contribute not less to strengthen the foundations than to adorn the structure of our free and happy system of government. . . .

49. *Eighth Annual Message*

December 3, 1816

. . . The period of my retiring from the public service being at little distance, I shall find no occasion more proper than the present for expressing to my fellow-citizens my deep sense of the continued confidence and kind support which I have received from them. My grateful recollection of these distinguished marks of their favorable regard can never cease, and with the consciousness that, if I have not served my country with greater ability, I have served it with a sincere devotion will accompany me as a source of unfailing gratification.

Happily, I shall carry with me from the public theater other sources, which those who love their country most will best appreciate. I shall behold it blessed with tranquillity and prosperity at home and with peace and respect abroad. I can indulge the proud reflection that the American people have reached in safety and success their fortieth year as an independent nation; that for nearly an entire generation they have had experience of their present Constitution, the offspring of their undisturbed deliberations and of their free choice; that they have found it to bear the trials of adverse as well as prosperous circumstances; to contain in its combination of the federate and elective principles a reconcilement of public strength with individual liberty, of national power for the defense

of national rights with a security against wars of injustice, of ambition, and of vainglory in the fundamental provision which subjects all questions of war to the will of the nation itself, which is to pay its costs and feel its calamities. Nor is it less a peculiar felicity of this Constitution, so dear to us all, that it is found to be capable, without losing its vital energies, of expanding itself over a spacious territory with the increase and expansion of the community for whose benefit it was established.

And may I not be allowed to add to this gratifying spectacle that I shall read in the character of the American people, in their devotion to true liberty and to the Constitution which is its palladium, sure presages that the destined career of my country will exhibit a Government pursuing the public good as its sole object, and regulating its means by the great principles consecrated in its charter, and by those moral principles to which they are so well allied; a Government which watches over the purity of elections, the freedom of speech and of the press, the trial by jury, and the equal interdict against encroachments and compacts between religion and the state; which maintains inviolably the maxims of public faith, the security of persons and property, and encourages in every authorized mode that general diffusion of knowledge which guarantees to public liberty its permanency and to those who possess the blessing the true enjoyment of it; a Government which avoids intrusions on the internal repose of other nations, and repels them from its own; which does justice to all nations with a readiness equal to the firmness with which it requires justice from them; and which, whilst it refines its domestic code from every ingredient not congenial with the precepts of an enlightened age and the sentiments of a virtuous people, seeks by appeals to reason and by its liberal examples to infuse into the law which governs the civilized world a spirit which may diminish the frequency or circumscribe the calamities of war, and meliorate the social and beneficent relations of peace; a Government, in a word, whose conduct within and without may bespeak the most noble of all ambitions—that of promoting peace on earth and good will to man. . . .

50. *Speech in the Virginia Constitutional Convention.*

December 2, 1829

Although the actual posture of the subject before the Committee might admit a full survey of it, it is not my purpose, in rising, to enter into the wide field of discussion, which has called forth a display of intellectual resources and varied powers of eloquence, that any country might be

proud of, and which I have witnessed with the highest gratification. Having been, for a very long period, withdrawn from any participation in proceedings of deliberative bodies, and under other disqualifications now of which I am deeply sensible, though perhaps less sensible than others may perceive that I ought to be, I shall not attempt more than a few observations, which may suggest the views I have taken of the subject, and which will consume but little of the time of the Committee, become precious. It is sufficiently obvious, that persons now and property are the two great subjects on which Governments are to act; and that the rights of persons, and the rights of property, are the objects, for the protection of which Government was instituted. These rights cannot well be separated. The personal right to acquire property, which is a natural right, gives to property, when acquired, a right to protection, as a social right. The essence of Government is power; and power, lodged as it must be in human hands, will ever be liable to abuse. In monarchies, the interests and happiness of all may be sacrificed to the caprice and passions of a despot. In aristocracies, the rights and welfare of the many may be sacrificed to the pride and cupidity of the few. In republics, the great danger is, that the majority may not sufficiently respect the rights of the minority. Some gentlemen, consulting the purity and generosity of their own minds, without adverting to the lessons of experience, would find a security against that danger, in our social feelings; in a respect for character; in the dictates of the monitor within; in the interests of individuals; in the aggregate interests of the community. But man is known to be a selfish, as well as a social being. Respect for character, though often a salutary restraint, is but too often overruled by other motives. When numbers of men act in a body, respect for character is often lost, just in proportion as it is necessary to control what is not right. We all know that conscience is not a sufficient safe-guard; and besides, that conscience itself may be deluded; may be misled, by an unconscious bias, into acts which an enlightened conscience would forbid. As to the permanent interest of individuals in the aggregate interests of the community, and in the proverbial maxim, that honesty is the best policy, present temptation is often found to be an over-match for those considerations. These favourable attributes of the human character are all valuable, as auxiliaries; but they will not serve as a substitute for the coercive provision belonging to Government and Law. They will always, in proportion as they prevail, be favourable to a mild administration of both: but they can never be relied on as a guaranty of the rights of the minority against a majority disposed to take unjust advantage of its power. The only effectual safeguard to the rights of the minority, must be laid in such a basis and structure of the Government itself, as may afford, in a certain degree, directly or indirectly, a defensive authority in behalf of a minority having right on its side.

To come more nearly to the subject before the Committee, viz.: that

peculiar feature in our community, which calls for a peculiar division in the basis of our government, I mean the coloured part of our population. It is apprehended, if the power of the Commonwealth shall be in the hands of a majority, who have no interest in this species of property, that, from the facility with which it may be oppressed by excessive taxation, injustice may be done to its owners. It would seem, therefore, if we can incorporate that interest into the basis of our system, it will be the most apposite and effectual security that can be devised. Such an arrangement is recommended to me by many very important considerations. It is due to justice; due to humanity; due to truth; to the sympathies of our nature; in fine, to our character as a people, both abroad and at home, that they should be considered, as much as possible, in the light of human beings, and not as mere property. As such, they are acted upon by our laws, and have an interest in our laws. They may be considered as making a part, though a degraded part, of the families to which they belong.

If they had the complexion of the Serfs in the North of Europe, or of the Villeins formerly in England; in other terms, if they were of our own complexion, much of the difficulty would be removed. But the mere circumstance of complexion cannot deprive them of the character of men. The Federal number, as it is called, is particularly recommended to attention in forming a basis of Representation, by its simplicity, its certainty, its stability, and its permanency. Other expedients for securing justice in the case of taxation, while they amount in pecuniary effect, to the same thing, have been found liable to great objections: and I do not believe that a majority of this Convention is disposed to adopt them, if they can find a substitute they can approve. Nor is it a small recommendation of the Federal number, in my view, that it is in conformity to the ratio recognized in the Federal Constitution. The cases, it is true, are not precisely the same, but there is more of analogy than might at first be supposed. If the coloured population were equally diffused through the State, the analogy would fail; but existing as it does, in large masses, in particular parts of it, the distinction between the different parts of the State, resembles that between the slave-holding and non-slave-holding States: and, if we reject a doctrine in our own State, whilst we claim the benefit of it in our relations to other States, other disagreeable consequences may be added to the charge of inconsistency, which will be brought against us. If the example of our sister States is to have weight, we find that in Georgia, the Federal number is made the basis of Representation in both branches of their Legislature; and I do not learn, that any dissatisfaction or inconvenience has flowed from its adoption. I wish we could know more of the manner in which particular organizations of Government operate in other parts of the United States. There would be less danger of being misled into error, and we should have the advantage of their experience, as well as our own. In the case I mention, there can, I believe, be no error.

Whether, therefore, we be fixing a basis of Representation, for the one branch or the other of our Legislature, or for both, in a combination with other principles, the Federal ratio is a favourite resource with me. It entered into my earliest views of the subject, before this Convention was assembled: and though I have kept my mind open, have listened to every proposition which has been advanced, and given to them all a candid consideration, I must say, that in my judgment, we shall act wisely in preferring it to others, which have been brought before us. Should the Federal number be made to enter into the basis in one branch of the Legislature, and not into the other, such an arrangement might prove favourable to the slaves themselves. It may be, and I think it has been suggested, that those who have themselves no interest in this species of property, are apt to sympathise with the slaves, more than may be the case with their masters; and would, therefore, be disposed, when they had the ascendancy, to protect them from laws of an oppressive character, whilst the masters, who have a common interest with the slaves, against undue taxation, which must be paid out of their labour, will be their protectors when they have the ascendancy.

The Convention is now arrived at a point, where we must agree on some common ground, all sides relaxing in their opinions, not changing, but mutually surrendering a part of them. In framing a Constitution, great difficulties are necessarily to be overcome; and nothing can ever overcome them, but a spirit of compromise. Other nations are surprised at nothing so much as our having been able to form Constitutions in the manner which has been exemplified in this country. Even the union of so many States, is, in the eyes of the world, a wonder; the harmonious establishment of a common Government over them all, a miracle. I cannot but flatter myself, that without a miracle, we shall be able to arrange all difficulties. I never have despaired, notwithstanding all the threatening appearances we have passed through. I have now more than a hope—a consoling confidence, that we shall at last find, that our labours have not been in vain.

51. *Note During the Convention for Amending the Constitution of Virginia*

1829

The right of suffrage being of vital importance, and approving an extension of it to House keepers & heads of families, I will suggest a few considerations which govern my judgment on the subject.

Were the Constitution on hand to be adapted to the present circumstances of our Country, without taking into view the changes which time

is rapidly producing, an unlimited extension of the right wd probably vary little the character of our public councils or measures. But as we are to prepare a system of Gov^t. for a period which it is hoped will be a long one, we must look to the prospective changes in the condition and composition of the society on which it is to act.

It is a law of nature, now well understood, that the earth under a civilized cultivation is capable of yielding subsistence for a large surplus of consumers, beyond those having an immediate interest in the soil; a surplus which must increase with the increasing improvements in agriculture, and the labor-saving arts applied to it. And it is a lot of humanity that of this surplus a large proportion is necessarily reduced by a competition for employment to wages which afford them the bare necessaries of life. That proportion being without property, or the hope of acquiring it, can not be expected to sympathize sufficiently with its rights, to be safe depositories of power over them.

What is to be done with this unfavored class of the community? If it be, on one hand, unsafe to admit them to a full share of political power, it must be recollected, on the other, that it cannot be expedient to rest a Republican Gov^t. on a portion of the society having a numerical & physical force excluded from, and liable to be turned against it; and which would lead to a standing military force, dangerous to all parties & to liberty itself.

This view of the subject makes it proper to embrace in the partnership of power, every description of citizens having a sufficient stake in the public order, and the stable administration of the laws; and particularly the House keepers & Heads of families; most of whom "having given hostages to fortune," will have given them to their Country also.

This portion of the community, added to those, who although not possessed of a share of the soil, are deeply interested in other species of property, and both of them added to the territorial proprietors, who in a certain sense may be regarded as the owners of the Country itself, form the safest basis of free Government. To the security for such a Gov^t. afforded by these combined numbers, may be further added, the political & moral influence emanating from the actual possession of authority and a just & beneficial exercise of it.

It would be happy if a State of Society could be found or framed, in which an equal voice in making the laws might be allowed to every individual bound to obey them. But this is a Theory, which like most Theories, confessedly requires limitations & modifications, and the only question to be decided in this as in other cases, turns on the particular degree of departure, in practice, required by the essence & object of the Theory itself.

It must not be supposed that a crowded state of population, of which we have no example here, and which we know only by the image reflected from examples elsewhere, is too remote to claim attention.

The ratio of increase in the U. S. shows that the present

12 Millions will in	25 years be	24 Mils.
24 " " "	50 " "	48 "
48 " " "	75 " "	96 "
96 " " "	100 " "	192 "

There may be a gradual decrease of the rate of increase: but it will be small as long as agriculture shall yield its abundance. G. Britain has doubled her population in the last 50 years; notwithstanding its amount in proportion to its territory at the commencement of that period, and Ireland is a much stronger proof of the effect of an increasing product of food, in multiplying the consumers.

How far this view of the subject will be affected by the Republican laws of descent and distribution, in equalizing the property of the citizens and in reducing to the minimum mutual surplusses for mutual supplies, cannot be inferred from any direct and adequate experiment. One result would seem to be a deficiency of the capital for the expensive establishments which facilitate labour and cheapen its products on one hand, and, on the other, of the capacity to purchase the costly and ornamental articles consumed by the wealthy alone, who must cease to be idlers and become labourers. Another the increased mass of labourers added to the production of necessaries by the withdrawal for this object, of a part of those now employed in producing luxuries, and the addition to the labourers from the class of present consumers of luxuries. To the effect of these changes, intellectual, moral, and social, the institutions and laws of the Country must be adapted, and it will require for the task all the wisdom of the wisest patriots.

Supposing the estimate of the growing population of the U. S. to be nearly correct, and the extent of their territory to be 8 or 9 hundred Mils of acres, and one fourth of it to consist of inarable surface, there will in a century or a little more, be nearly as crowded a population in the U. S. as in G. Britain or France, and if the present Constitution (of Virginia) with all its flaws, lasted more than half a century, it is not an unreasonable hope that an amended one will last more than a century.

If these observations be just, every mind will be able to develop & apply them.—

52. *Sovereignty*

1835

It has hitherto been understood, that the supreme power, that is, the sovereignty of the people of the States, was in its nature divisible, and was in fact divided, according to the Constitution of the U. States, be-

tween the States in their united and the States in their individual capacities that as the States, in their highest sov. char., were competent to surrender the whole sovereignty and form themselves into a consolidated State, so they might surrender a part & retain, as they have done, the other part, forming a mixed Gov^t. with a division of its attributes as marked out in the Constitution.

Of late, another doctrine has occurred, which supposes that sovereignty is in its nature indivisible; that the societies denominated States, in forming the constitutional compact of the U. States, acted as indivisible sovereignties, and consequently, that the sovereignty of each remains as absolute and entire as it was then, or could be at any time.

This discord of opinions arises from a propensity in many to prefer the use of theoretical guides and technical language to the division and depositories of pol. power, as laid down in the const^l. charter, which expressly assigns certain powers of Gov^t. which are the attributes of sovereig^ty of the U. S., and even declares a practical supremacy of them over the powers reserved to the States; a supremacy essentially involving that of exposition as well as of execution; for a law could not be supreme in one depository of power if the final exposition of it belonged to another.

In settling the question between these rival claims of power, it is proper to keep in mind that all power in just & free Gov^ts. is derived from compact, that when the parties to the compact are competent to make it, and when the compact creates a Gov^t., and arms it not only with a moral power, but the physical means of executing it, it is immaterial by what name it is called. Its real character is to be decided by the compact itself; by the nature and extent of the powers it specifies, and the obligations imposed on the parties to it.

As a ground of compromise let then, the advocates of State rights acknowledge this rule of measuring the Federal share of sovereign power under the const. compact; and let it be conceded, on the other hand, that the States are not deprived by it of that corporate existence and political unity which w^d. in the event of a dissolution, voluntary or violent, of the Const^n. replace them in the condition of separate communities, that being the condition in which they entered into the compact.

At the period of our Revol^n. it was supposed by some that it dissolved the social compact within the Colonies, and produced a state of nature which required a naturalization of those who had not participated in the revol^n. The question was brought before Cong. at its first session by D^r. Ramsay, who contested the election of W^m. Smith; who, though born in S. C., had been absent at the date of Independence. The decision was, that his birth in the Colony made him a member of the society in its new as well as its original state.

To go to the bottom of the subject, let us consult the Theory which contemplates a certain number of individuals as meeting and agreeing to form one political society, in order that the rights the safety & the interest of each may be under the safeguard of the whole.

The first supposition is, that each individual being previously independent of the others, the compact which is to make them one society must result from the free consent of *every* individual.

But as the objects in view could not be attained, if every measure conducive to them required the consent of every member of the society, the theory further supposes, either that it was a part of the original compact, that the will of the majority was to be deemed the will of the whole, or that this was a law of nature, resulting from the nature of political society itself, the offspring of the natural wants of man.

Whatever be the hypothesis of the origin of the *lex majoris partis*, it is evident that it operates as a plenary substitute of the will of the majority of the society for the will of the whole society; and that the sovereignty of the society as vested in & exercisable by the majority, may do anything that could be *rightfully* done by the unanimous concurrence of the members; the reserved rights of individuals (of conscience for example) in becoming parties to the original compact being beyond the legitimate reach of sovereignty, wherever vested or however viewed.

The question then presents itself, how far the will of a majority of the society, by virtue of its identity with the will of the society, can divide, modify, or dispose of the sovereignty of the society; and quitting the theoretic guide, a more satisfactory one will perhaps be found—1, In what a majority of a society has done, and been universally regarded as having had a right to do; 2, What it is universally admitted that a majority by virtue of its sovereignty might do, if it chose to do.

1. The majority has not only naturalized, admitted into social compact again, but has divided the sovereignty of the society by actually dividing the society itself into distinct societies equally sovereign. Of this operation we have before us examples in the separation of Kentucky from Virginia and of Maine from Massachusetts; events wch. were never supposed to require a unanimous consent of the individuals concerned.

In the case of naturalization a new member is added to the social compact, not only without a unanimous consent of the members, but by a majority of the governing body, deriving its powers from a majority of the individual parties to the social compact.

2. As, in those cases just mentioned, one sovereignty was divided into two by dividing one State into two States; so it will not be denied that two States equally sovereign might be incorporated into one by the voluntary & joint act of majorities only in each. The Constitution of the U. S. has itself provided for such a contingency. And if two States, could thus incorporate themselves into one by a mutual surrender of the entire sovereignty of each; why might not a partial incorporation, by a partial surrender of sovereignty, be equally practicable if equally eligible. And if this could be done by two States, why not by twenty or more.

A division of sovereignty is in fact illustrated by the exchange of sovereign rights often involved in Treaties between Independent Nations,

and still more in the several confederacies which have existed, and particularly in that which preceded the present Constitution of the United States.

Certain it is that the constitutional compact of the U. S. has allotted the supreme power of Gov^t. partly to the United States by special grants, partly to the individual States by general reservations; and if sovereignty be in its nature divisible, the true question to be decided is, whether the allotment has been made by the competent authority, and this question is answered by the fact that it was an act of the *majority* of the people in each State in their highest sovereign capacity, equipollent to a *unanimous* act of the people composing the State in that capacity.

It is so difficult to argue intelligibly concerning the compound system of Gov^t. in the U. S. without admitting the divisibility of sovereignty, that the idea of sovereignty, as divided between the Union and the members composing the Union, forces itself into the view, and even into the language of those most strenuously contending for the unity & indivisibility of the *moral being* created by the social compact. "For security agst. oppression from abroad we look to the *sovereign power* of the U. S. to be exerted according to the compact of union; for security agst. oppression from within, or domestic oppression, we look to the sovereign power of the State. Now all sovereigns are equal; the sovereignty of the State is equal to that of the Union, for the sovereignty of each is but a *moral person*. That of the State and that of the Union are each a moral person, and in that respect precisely equal." These are the words in a speech which, more than any other, has analyzed & elaborated this particular subject, and they express the view of it finally taken by the speaker, notwithstanding the previous one in which he says, "the States, whilst the Constitution of the U. S. was forming, were not even shorn of *any* of their sovereign power by that process."

That a sovereignty would be lost & converted into a vassalage, if subjected to a foreign sovereignty over which it had no controul, and in which it had no participation, is clear & certain, but far otherwise is a surrender of portions of sovereignty by compacts among sovereign communities making the surrenders equal & reciprocal & of course giving to each as much as is taken from it.

Of all free Gov^{ts} compact is the basis & the essence, and it is fortunate that the powers of Gov^t. supreme as well as subordinate can be so moulded & distributed, so compounded and divided by those on whom they are to operate as will be most suitable to their conditions, will best guard their freedom, and best provide for their safety.

53. *Against Nullification*

1835-36

Altho' the Legislature of Virginia declared at a late session almost unanimously, that S. Carolina was not supported in her doctrine of nullification by the Resolutions of 1798, it appears that those resolutions are still appealed to as expressly or constructively favoring the doctrine.

That the doctrine of nullification may be clearly understood it must be taken as laid down in the Report of a special committee of the House of Representatives of S. C. in 1828. In that document it is asserted, that a single State has a constitutional right to arrest the execution of a law of the U. S. within its limits; that the arrest is to be presumed right and valid, and is to remain in force unless ¾ of the States, in a Convention, shall otherwise decide.

The forbidding aspect of a naked creed, according to which a process instituted by a single State is to terminate in the ascendancy of a minority of 7, over a majority of 17, has led its partizans to disguise its deformity under the position that a single State may rightfully resist an unconstitutional and tyrannical law of the U. S., keeping out of view the essential distinction between a constitutional right and the natural and universal right of resisting intolerable oppression. But the true question is whether a single state has a constitutional right to annul or suspend the operation of a law of the U. S. within its limits, the State remaining a member of the Union, and admitting the Constitution to be in force.

With a like policy, the nullifiers pass over the state of things at the date of the proceedings of Vir^a. and the particular doctrines and arguments to which they were opposed; without an attention to which the proceedings in this as in other cases may be insecure ag^st. a perverted construction. . . .

Recurring to the epoch of the proceedings, the facts of the case are that Cong^s. had passed certain acts, bearing the name of the alien and sedition laws, which Virg & some of the other States, regarded as not only dangerous in their tendency, but unconstitutional in their text; and as calling for a remedial interposition of the States. It was found also that not only was the constitutionality of the acts vindicated by a predominant party, but that the principle was asserted at the same time, that a sanction to the acts given by the supreme Judicial authority of the U. S. was a bar to any interposition whatever on the part of the States, even in the form of a legislative declaration that the acts in question were unconstitutional.

Under these circumstances, the subject was taken up by Virg^a. in her resolutions, and pursued at the ensuing session of the Legislature in a

comment explaining and justifying them; her main and immediate object, evidently being, to produce a conviction everywhere, that the Constitution had been violated by the obnoxious acts and to procure a concurrence and co-operation of the other States in effectuating a repeal of the acts. She accordingly asserted and offered her proofs at great length, that the acts were unconstitutional. She asserted moreover & offered her proofs that the States had a right in such cases, to interpose, first in their constituent character to which the gov^t. of the U. S. was responsible, and otherwise as specially provided by the Constitution; and further, that the States, in their capacity of parties to and creators of the Constitution, had an ulterior right to interpose, notwithstanding any decision of a constituted authority; which, however it might be the *last resort* under the forms of the Constitution in cases falling within the scope of its functions, could not preclude an interposition of the States as the parties which made the Constitution and, as such, possessed an authority paramount to it.

In this view of the subject there is nothing which excludes a natural right in the States individually, more than in any portion of an individual State, suffering under palpable and insupportable wrongs, from seeking relief by resistance and revolution.

But it follows, from no view of the subject, that a nullification of a law of the U. S. can as is now contended, belong rightfully to a single State, as one of the parties to the Constitution; the State not ceasing to avow its adherence to the Constitution. A plainer contradiction in terms, or a more fatal inlet to anarchy, cannot be imagined. . . .

These startling consequences from the nullifying doctrine have driven its partizans to the extravagant presumption that no State would ever be so unreasonable, unjust & impolitic as to avail itself of its right in any case not so palpably just and fair as to ensure a concurrence of the others, or at least the requisite proportion of them.

Omitting the obvious remark that in such a case the law would never have been passed or immediately repealed; and the surprize that such a defence of the nullifying right should come from S. C. in the teeth & at the time of her own example, the presumption of such a forbearance in each of the States, or such a pliability in all, among 20 or 30 independent sovereignties, must be regarded as a mockery by those who reflect for a moment on the human character, or consult the lessons of experience, not the experience of other countries & times, but that among ourselves; and not only under the former defective Confederation, but since the improved system took place of it. Examples of differences, persevering differences among the States on the constitutionality of Federal acts, will readily occur to every one; and which would, e'er this, have defaced and demolished the Union, had the nullifying claim of S. Carolina been indiscriminately exercisable. In some of the States, the carriage-tax would have been collected, in others unpaid. In some, the tariff on imports would

be collected; in others, openly resisted. In some, lighthouses w^d. be established; in others denounced. In some States there might be war with a foreign power; in others, peace and commerce. Finally, the appellate authority of the Supreme Court of the U. S. would give effect to the Federal laws in some States, whilst in others they would be rendered nullities by the State Judiciaries. In a word, the nullifying claims if reduced to practice, instead of being the conservative principle of the Constitution, would necessarily, and it may be said obviously, be a deadly poison. . . .

The true question therefore is whether there be a *constitutional* right in a single state to nullify a law of the U. S. We have seen the absurdity of such a claim in its naked and suicidal form. Let us turn to it as modified by S. C., into a right in every State to resist within itself, the execution of a Federal law deemed by it to be unconstitutional; and to demand a Convention of the States to decide the question of constitutionality, the annulment of the law to continue in the mean time, and to be permanent, unless ¾ of the states concur in over-ruling the annulment.

Thus, during the temporary nullification of the law, the results would be the same from those proceeding from an unqualified nullification, and the result of a convention might be, that 7 out of the 24 states, might make the temporary results permanent. It follows, that any State which could obtain the concurrence of six others, might abrogate any law of the U. S. constructively whatever, and give to the Constitution any shape they please, in opposition to the construction and will of the other seventeen, each of the 17 having an equal right & authority with each of the 7. Every feature in the Constitution, might thus be successively changed; and after a scene of unexampled confusion & distraction, what had been unanimously agreed to as a whole, would not as a whole be agreed to by a single party. The amount of this modified right of nullification is, that a single State may arrest the operation of a law of the United States, and institute a process which is to terminate in the ascendency of a minority over a large majority, in a Republican System, the characteristic rule of which is that the major will is the ruling will. And this newfangled theory is attempted to be fathered on Mr. Jefferson the apostle of republicanism, and whose own words declare that "acquiescence in the decision of the majority is the vital principle of it." [See his Inaugural Address.]

Well might Virginia declare, as her Legislature did by a resolution of 1833 "that the resolutions of 98-99, gave no support to the nullifying doctrine of South Carolina. And well may the friends of Mr. J. disclaim any sanction to it or to any *constitutional* right of nullification from his opinions. His memory is fortunately rescued from such imputations, by the very Document procured from his files and so triumphantly appealed to by the nullifying partisans of every description. In this Document, the remedial right of nullification is expressly called a *natural* right, and,

consequently, not a right derived from the Constitution, but from abuses or usurpations, releasing the parties to it from their obligation. . . .

It has been asked whether every right has not its remedy, and what other remedy exists under the Gov^t. of the U. S. agst. usurpations of power, but a right in the States individually to annul and resist them.

The plain answer is, that the remedy is the same under the government of the United States as under all other Gov^{ts}. established & organized on free principles. The first remedy is in the checks provided among the constituted authorities; that failing the next is in the influence of the Ballot-boxes & Hustings; that again failing, the appeal lies to the power that made the Constitution, and can explain, amend, or remake it. Should this resort also fail, and the power usurped be sustained in its oppressive exercise on a minority by a majority, the final course to be pursued by the minority, must be a subject of calculation, in which the degree of oppression, the means of resistance, the consequences of its failure, and consequences of its success must be the elements.

Does not this view of the case, equally belong to every one of the States, Virginia for example.

Should the constituted authorities of the State unite in usurping oppressive powers; should the constituent Body fail to arrest the progress of the evil thro' the elective process according to the forms of the Constitution; and should the authority which is above that of the Constitution, the majority of the people, inflexibly support the oppression inflicted on the minority, nothing would remain for the minority, but to rally to its reserved rights (for every citizen has his reserved rights, as exemplified in Declarations prefixed to most of the State constitutions), and to decide between acquiescence & resistance, according to the calculation above stated. . . .

Yes, it may be safely admitted that every right has its remedy; as it must be admitted that the remedy under the Constitution lies where it has been marked out by the Constitution; and that no appeal can be consistently made from that remedy by those who were and still profess to be parties to it, but the appeal to the parties themselves having an authority above the Constitution or to the law of nature & of nature's God. . . .

54. *"Advice to My Country"*

As this advice, if it ever see the light will not do it till I am no more, it may be considered as coming from the tomb where the truth alone can be respected, and the happiness of man alone consulted. It will be entitled therefore to whatever weight can be derived from good intentions,

and from the experience of one, who has served his Country in various stations through a period of forty years, who espoused in his youth and adhered through his life to the cause of its liberty and who has borne a part in most of the transactions which will constitute epochs of its destiny.

The advice nearest to my heart and deepest in my convictions is that the Union of the States be cherished and perpetuated. Let the open enemy to it be regarded as a Pandora with her box opened; and the disguised one, as the Serpent creeping with his deadly wiles into Paradise.

PART V

ALEXANDER
HAMILTON
(1755-1804)

PART V

ALEXANDER HAMILTON

(1755-1804)

The price of greatness, especially in statecraft, comes high. All the master-builders in the American Enlightenment were tormented by political enemies, wounded by lying or malicious critics, forced to breathe for years on end the withering fumes of political skull-duggery. All of them lived with some awareness that they would be reviewed and most likely re-crucified as future events would inspire fresh controversy. To say of that rare being, a philosopher-statesman, that he is "controversial" is therefore hardly a statement: it is more like a tautology.

Yet the brilliant and troubled life and career of Alexander Hamilton is controversial in a special sense. To him controversy was a way of life, a high adventure. He created it, often, without much regard to later results; he met it with bold and high-handed rebuttals and counter-attacks; and apart from days necessarily consumed by the professional tasks before him, or spent in the adoring society of his family, or among his political lieutenants to whom he imparted the directives of the day, Hamilton came to consciousness as a youth and died on the "field of honor" intensely and peculiarly a combatant. "The Little Lion" found life and politics tame without glory, without the stiff breezes of danger —fancied or real. To live dangerously, to outwit and out-maneuver others, to achieve something grand—no other life was worth playing out. The insatiable passion was pride—not Virgil's "greed of gold," but rather what the eighteenth century knew as "the craving for distinction." Many times Alexander Hamilton laid his life on the line, and won. But even before his unnecessary death at the age of 49, the wheel of fortune had played him out and in the debacle of those last years he doubted even what he had truly achieved.

In his own time, estimates of his character were profoundly tinctured with partisan politics. John Adams, who had been the victim of repeated covert vendettas on Hamilton's part, lashed out at Hamilton as "the most restless, impatient, artful, indefatigable and unprincipled intriguer in the United States, if not in the world." Others saw him as "a little Alex-

ander . . . who would be Great," a "Bonaparte," "chief of a corrupt squadron," "ambitious Cataline," "the greatest Machiavel in America."

However, the best of his political opponents admitted the marked talents Hamilton possessed. Although he was the classic enemy of Jefferson, the latter did not deny the stature of his antagonist. In the glaring heat of the fight over Jay's Treaty, for example, Jefferson wrote almost despairingly to Madison, "Without numbers, he is an host within himself." Without weakening a shred towards his opponent, Jefferson nevertheless exhibited his portrait at Monticello along with those of other great men of the time. In the 1830's Madison, answering a request for information, wrote of Hamilton: "He possessed intellectual powers of the first order, and the moral qualifications of integrity and honor in a captivating degree . . . If his Theory of Government deviated from the Republican Standard, he had the candor to avow it, and the greater merit of cooperating faithfully in maturing and supporting a system which was not his choice. The criticism to which his share in the administration of it was most liable was that it had the aspect of an effort to give to the instrument a constructive and practical bearing not warranted by its true and intended character."

As for his political friends, there is no doubt that Hamilton enjoyed intense hero-worship from numbers of them. Federalists in the highest offices under President Adams wrote unashamedly asking his advice. Timothy Pickering, the Secretary of State, lamented: "I wish you were in a situation not only 'to see all the cards', but to play them. With all my soul I would give you my hand." On more than one occasion, he was addressed as "Father Confessor." Most important was the esteem Washington held him in, listening willingly to Hamilton's proposals, vesting particular credence in his financial and constitutional views, although not unaware of Hamilton's impetuousness and high-handed style in politics. His last written estimate of Hamilton's character deserves attention. "By some he is considered as an ambitious man, and therefore a dangerous one. That he is ambitious I shall readily grant, but it is of that laudable kind which prompts a man to excell in whatever he takes in hand. He is enterprising, quick in his perceptions, and his judgment intuitively great; qualities essential to a Military character. . . ." After Hamilton's untimely death, no less a man than John Marshall confided his view to Timothy Pickering that Hamilton was "certainly one of the greatest men that ever lived."

Perhaps the true balance suggested by the views above is that Hamilton's "ambition" was in fact composed of two elements—personal ambition, for his own fame, acknowledged headship over all others in the field, glory (even of the obvious military kind), power (even to do favors, pay scores, punish whomever had offended or obstructed him); and national ambition, for his adopted country. For both, he was on the make, and often the two interests could be advanced together. He was de-

termined to make himself and his country emblematic images of superiority and power.

An illegitimate child, born in the West Indies, Alexander Hamilton had been thrown on his own resources in his early teens and vowed to win identity and achieve distinction for himself. Even when he was a lonely, castoff youngster, working for his own keep in a shipping firm on the island of St. Croix, Hamilton symbolically prepared "for futurity." One of his earliest letters is suffused with longing for a life grander, less "contemptible," than that of a mere clerk. The urgency with which he dreamed of the turns of fortune, the ardor with which he came round, at the end of the letter, to the theme of heroic escape by means of war ("I wish there was a war") are startlingly prophetic of the stormy drama ahead.

Through his own enterprise and brains, Hamilton had arranged to borrow sufficient passage money for the migration to the American colonies. Shortly after his arrival, he appeared in New Jersey to study at an academy; soon he tried to arrange a speed-up course for himself, one year shorter than the regular period, at Princeton College. He made his request in person, in an interview with President Witherspoon, who firmly said no. A little later, he studied for a short time at King's College in New York. These meager details provide the short foreground of his preparation for the role of "Alexander, Hero."

In the spring of 1775, he was a member of one of the militias of the gathering revolutionary struggle. At that early time, too, Hamilton demonstrated his command in the field of argument and debate. Important men noticed the clever and cogent youth as he talked up in political meetings. At the precocious age of a college sophomore, he displayed his literary powers by contributing two forceful pamphlets to the literature of colonial protest against the encroachments of Parliament. In these he rehearsed arguments that had achieved intercolonial currency by that time, but he made them arresting, and he evoked a grand vision of future economic power for North America. Some division of feeling may nevertheless have existed in him, to put the brake of law and orderly process on a movement that he found rife with mob violence, the flaunting of property rights, and disrespect for authority. These conservative impulses became greatly accentuated after the Revolution, when Hamilton became prominent as legal counsel for British and Loyalist litigants, and incidentally created the basis of his later political support on the part of conservative and well-to-do citizens in the New York area.

The Reverend Dr. Myles Cooper, Anglican President of King's College and a Tory propagandist, knew a different young scholar, a volatile blue-eyed, auburn-haired lad, to whom he was grateful for a warning that he believed had saved his life. Hamilton, who always responded to position, rank, and authority (and thus knew from the start that he would not settle for less than the highest), loathed the rash actions of crowds of

incensed men. Learning that a band of New Yorkers were planning to attack the President's house, he dashed ahead to warn the scholar, and accompanied him in his flight from the college grounds to the banks of the Hudson where a thoroughly terrified Reverend Doctor managed to board a British vessel. Hamilton, who was so intensely partisan in his political conduct when he was a great man of power in national affairs, could not abide "Tory-baiting."

Just as Hamilton had intimated in his prescient letter peeping into "futurity," he found his war. Soon after the Cooper episode, he became a captain of artillery and held off British troops at White Plains long enough for Washington's ragged troops to withdraw to New Jersey. Hamilton quickly rose to the position of lieutenant colonel in the Revolutionary Army via importunate requests to General Washington, whom he had served ably as an aide-de-camp at headquarters. There, in an inexcusable peeve, Hamilton manufactured the occasion for a quarrel with the beleaguered Washington in order to force his way clear to an active command. His early yearning for military glory was under no circumstances to be ignored for the mundane tasks of a military scribe.

From the early days when Hamilton, a youth in his twenties, joined General Washington's intimate family in the Revolutionary War, he discovered within himself the dynamism of personal influence. Without benefit of a "How to" manual, he influenced people and made friends—wealthy young men, powerful older men, foreigners of rank and importance who had come to assist in the military management of the American try for independence—Layfayette, for one, Baron Steuben for another. From his youthful taste of success, Hamilton developed the habit—for it did become automatic and reflexive—of drawing other ambitious men to his side as aids, abettors, confidants, and associates, many of them grateful to come within the radius of a talented personality who knew how to command.

During the war, Hamilton married, according to a plan he had playfully but with serious undertones recommended to a friend, a lovely and very rich wife of the highest social standing—Betsy Schuyler, one of the daughters of the aristocratic New Yorker, Philip Schuyler. This marriage was blessed by eight children and was marred by the sordid affair that Hamilton had with the illiterate and vulgar Mrs. Reynolds, acting as decoy for her extortionist husband—an affair that rivalled the sensationalism of the Profumo scandal in our own day, though the love nest was located on Philadelphia's Market Street. Hamilton's curious psychology, as he chose to publish a detailed confession of this episode rather than tolerate baseless accusations against his public conduct as Secretary of the Treasury, remains an enigma.

In the 1780's Hamilton was greatly concerned with the economic problems of the Confederation, and with the attendant problems of insufficient energy, authority, and control over the states. His powers as a draftsman

had sharpened and his mind, though neither learned nor nourished by broad humanistic study, was incisive, realistic and constructive. He had a twofold drive: to argue for a stronger continental government, and to develop his views of the economic supports that might oil and power the machinery of more effective government. In these years, he and Madison were without doubt the two foremost men—both young—directing the moves that led to the Constitutional Convention. Yet in that assembly of talented men from every state in the Confederation, Hamilton's political position represented the extreme right of the spectrum of belief. The majority of delegates, and the people whose approval they knew they would have to seek, were committed to the ideal of a new form of republicanism. Hamilton's frank admiration of the British monarchy, his wholesale distrust of self-government, his unqualified belief that "the goodness of a government consists in a vigorous execution," led him to recommend sweeping national powers and central authority "toned . . . as high as possible." This undemocratic political philosophy prevented him from making any significant contribution to the formation of the Constitution in 1787, although he decided to return to the Convention to sign the document and to work for its ratification. "No man's ideals were more remote from the plan" than his own, he said: "but is it possible to deliberate between anarchy and convulsion on one side, and the change of good to be expected from the plan on the other?"

In this spirit, Hamilton made an immeasurable contribution to the ratification of the Constitution, leading the fight in the hostile New York Convention and writing masterly expositions of the meaning and implications of the proposed constitutional system for The Federalist. The latter contribution, authorship of fifty of the 85 essays and probably joint authorship with Madison of three more, is in itself a major and lasting contribution to American political thought.

Shortly afterwards, Hamilton accepted the Secretaryship of the Treasury in the new government under George Washington. From that position of broad power, he developed his greatest service to his country. The heart of his contribution can be identified with faith in and formulation of the vast potentialities for economic development in the United States. Three fundamental propositions unified his series of financial reports and measures. First, Hamilton himself appreciated the role of private capital in winning economic gain for the nation, and therefore urged the development of private capital. Second, he caught up with the technological implications of the Industrial Revolution then in its infancy in England, and was trying to provide a theoretical defense of it appropriate to the national development of the United States. He understood the need to create the positive conditions for economic growth, and clearly explained the responsibility of the government in this regard. Many of his appeals to a supposedly preferred economic class—the moneyed men—are the result of his understanding that the interest of

the state and private property must be linked in order to assure increasing productivity. Third, Hamilton made an unprecedented contribution by working out a detailed and systematic program for the Federal Government to promote national economic growth and private capital. His measures included a tariff on imports; an excise tax on domestic products; a funding system to assume the outstanding debts, and issue interest-paying bonds in their place; the establishment of a Bank of the United States to create a free flow of currency, stimulate business and provide a pool from which the Government could borrow when necessary; the encouragement of manufactures by bounties; a protective tariff, and subsidiary government activities. All these measures were successfully put into operation under Hamilton's guidance, with the exception of his forward-looking proposals in the brilliant Report on Manufactures.

Men who disagreed with his political goals and with the methods he employed to reach them, found it hard to distinguish between the man and his national ideals. They fought him as a "Caesar" who would ride roughshod over the people. They found him callous about the liberties, interests and pride of the many—the farmers and the workers; and correspondingly persuaded of the special prerogatives and superior value of the moneyed interests, whose alliance with the government he had judged indispensable and worth courting above all. It was this betrayal of the democratic ethic that Jefferson and Madison and their followers opposed, and it was doubtless a compound of the man and his thorough program. For Hamilton's program was certainly not confined to fiscal and monetary affairs. Hamilton wished to ensure an energetic national government centered in the Federal administration; a strong growing economy was naturally required, but so was an army, and some of the symbols of authority similar to those of the English monarchy, a ruling class of the "wealthy, well-born and wise." His favorite word for this vision of a powerful United States that would not be subservient to European powers but would in time out-distance their power, was Empire. For an empire, vigorous action was the lifeline. Consequently clear, unswerving opposition had to be forth-coming against those who would oppose the dictates of government. Thus he seized upon the Whiskey Rebellion in Pennsylvania (in 1794) as an opportunity for the government to vindicate its strength. He himself thought it essential to play the chief role in the suppression of the opposition by the farmers to the whiskey tax. Similarly, when Virginia and Kentucky issued the Resolution of 1798 against the government's Alien and Sedition Acts, he found reinforcement for his conviction that the large states could not safely be permitted to co-exist with the central government, and advocated their subdivision into smaller, more manageable units. As a first response, he had moved, characteristically, to threaten Virginia and other "refractory" Southern states with the United States Army.

If to men like Jefferson and Madison the thrust of Hamilton's political

economy was "adverse to the principles of liberty," making the consolidation of all powers into the Federal structure a death-warrant for the powers of the states and indeed for any popular center of loyal opposition to central government, there were others who were less plagued by his "principles" and more by his conduct and character as a man. John Adams, an honored potentate in the same party that Hamilton sought to rule as "King of the Feds," saw in the man with his power plays and intrigues, the embodiment of evil—even though he shared some of his political philosophy and was in accord with some of his program. There is no doubt that John Adams had been singled out for rough handling. Hamilton never wanted Adams elevated by the Federalists to the second in public position after Washington. Among other hostile moves, he schemed to defeat Adams of an honest share of electoral votes in the Presidential contest of 1796; and he went to extremes of implacable and irrational egotism in strafing Adams' character to destroy his chances of re-election in 1800.

It must be said that in political contests which he regarded as tests of his power, Hamilton was sometimes unbelievably reckless and on one occasion at least flagrantly lawless. The occasion was the move that climaxed his last-ditch maneuvers in New York to circumvent a Republican victory at the polls in 1800. Infuriated that Burr had brought off a Republican victory in the New York City elections, he penned a hurried letter to John Jay, Governor of New York, urging that the Assembly reverse the election laws and undo the results of the legal election. It was a conscious proposal of a coup d'etat, argued for on the ground that "in times like these in which we live, it will not do to be over-scrupulous." John Jay would have no part of this deed—he merely endorsed the back of Hamilton's letter with the honorable words: "Proposing a measure for party purposes, which I think it would not become me to adopt."

On the other hand, Hamilton had far-seeing vision and grasp of the subsidiary details to construct a viable program out of his dream for a populous, thriving and powerful nation. In short, his capacity to provide energetic direction and clear-minded definition for his program persuaded men like Washington, John Marshall, Rufus King, John Jay, to rank him as super-statesman among his contemporaries. Tribute would be rendered him for one or another of his many significant contributions: Washington could rely on him for economic "intelligence" and for the quick, intuitive political judgments that so often proved to be penetrating and adroit. Marshall, whose own course as Chief Justice borrowed the Hamiltonian portion on judicial review, valued the strong unionist who paved the way for implied powers and judicial supremacy. And of course some of his admirers were simply attached to the man who could be very tolerant of his friends, loyal to them even when they were foolish or flagrant in business speculations. Men could not help responding to his confident and brilliant conversation, his social conviviality and

charm. The ladies saw all this, of course, in heightened terms and fancied in addition his easy chit-chat, the courtly compliments he paid, and a certain insouciance.

Hamilton's retirement from public office in January, 1795 was never expected to be permanent. Wishing to repair his financial position which had suffered by the $3,500 salary that his Cabinet position then carried, Hamilton resumed the practice of law in New York, engaged in land speculation, had a hand in various commercial ventures, and continued to be active as a Federalist party boss. However, his dire move against John Adams in 1800 lost him ground with his own Federalist circle and no sooner had he measured his declining influence, than he opened a new round of warfare with Aaron Burr. Hamilton was becoming more violent in his enmities and less skillful in his political plans and intrigues with each passing year. The loss of self-control all seemed to stem from the fateful turn of the century, when his illustrious protector, George Washington, died; and when President Adams took surprisingly stubborn command of his own Cabinet and frustrated Hamilton's last chance for a career of military glory on a continental scale.

In these various depredations on his reputation, his political prospects, and his self-confidence Hamilton had been injured in his most cherished aspirations. He had no deep fund of internal resources that could carry him over these hurts to his amour propre. A gloomy Cassandra-note sounds in many of the private letters of this period. Democracy is a "poison," the American world "is not made for me," his unrecognized supreme services for the strengthening of the Constitution oppressed him and alienated him further. From his childhood he had sought a way to win identity and cure the pangs of alienation; for these ends he had struggled to the top of the cliff and reached the sunlight. Now he felt his fall to be precipitous.

Disenchantment already had him in its grip when the crushing affliction of his eldest son's death in a duel, fought to protect his father's name from slander, fell upon him. The son, Philip, died in his early twenties of a gunshot wound inflicted by a young Republican lawyer on "the field of honor" at Weehawken. An intimate friend of Alexander Hamilton, Robert Troup, wrote: "Never did I see a man so completely overwhelmed with grief as Hamilton has been." This deadly encounter took place on July 4, 1801. Three years later, in the same month, on the same heights of Weehawken, the father took Aaron Burr's fire and on July 12, 1804 he died.

In the first half of the nineteenth century, Hamilton's reputation was in temporary eclipse, partly because of the disintegration of the Federalist Party and the transition from Jeffersonian to Jacksonian democracy. Post Civil War America was another matter; for with the transformation of America into an industrial society and with currents of aggressive nationalism running strong, historians and statesmen turned enthusi-

astically to Hamilton as a symbol. From that time to our own, the symbol has been repeatedly revised and re-shaped at the hands of conservatives, financiers, businessmen, romantic and not-so-romantic nationalists, and all admirers—native and foreign—of a dashing, energetic "doer," and administrative genius who could keep a governing finger on the remotest customs clerk at the same time that he could control Congress, advise the President and act as the chief of the Federalist Party.

Today Hamilton's reputation is at a higher peak than it has been for over a century. Leaders of the rising new nations who desire accelerated economic growth and national power read and quote Hamilton. Meanwhile, at home, biographies, administrative studies, and monographs on his contribution to the "living Constitution," or on "the founder of the American nation," or on his realistic understanding of the American "national interest" add their share to the burgeoning revival of the past decade.

Woodrow Wilson tried once to sum Hamilton up by saying he was "a great man, but not a great American." Senator Arthur Vandenburg, as though to reply, subtitled his book on Hamilton, "The Greatest American." The controversy continues. For men of different temperaments can hardly be expected to see the multiform content of the American Experiment in identical ways, nor will they be drawn with equal attachment to the principles and life styles of Hamilton and Jefferson. But as we learn more about these two great men we realize that their complementary play and very different views and abilities had much to do with the durability of the American Experiment. For these reasons there can be no serious disagreement with Walter Lippmann's assertion that "to be partisan, as between Jefferson and Hamilton, is like arguing whether men or women are more necessary to the procreation of the race."

This insight is caught in Rosemary and Stephen Vincent Benet's verse:

Jefferson said "the Many!"
Hamilton said "the Few!"
Like opposite sides of a penny
Were these exalted two.
If Jefferson said "It's black, Sir!"
Hamilton cried "It's white!"
But 'twixt the two, our Constitution started working right.

Autobiography

1. *The Way for Futurity*

To Edward Stevens

St. Croix, Novemr. 11th, 1769

Dear Edward

This just serves to acknowledge receipt of yours per Cap Lowndes which was delivered me Yesterday. The truth of Cap Lightbourn & Lowndes information is now verifyd by the Presence of your Father and Sister for whose safe arrival I Pray, and that they may convey that Satisfaction to your Soul that must naturally flow from the sight of Absent Friends in health, and shall for news this way refer you to them. As to what you say respecting your having soon the happiness of seeing us all, I wish, for an accomplishment of your hopes provided they are Concomitant with your welfare, otherwise not, tho doubt whether I shall be Present or not for to confess my weakness, Ned, my Ambition is prevalent that I contemn the grov'ling and condition of a Clerk or the like, to which my Fortune &c. condemns me and would willingly risk my life tho' not my Character to exalt my Station. Im confident, Ned that my Youth excludes me from any hopes of immediate Preferment nor do I desire it, but I mean to prepare the way for futurity. Im no Philosopher you see and may be jusly said to Build Castles in the Air. My Folly makes me ashamd and beg youll Conceal it, yet Neddy we have seen such Schemes successfull when the Projector is Constant I shall Conclude saying I wish there was a War.

2. *Feelings for Military Reputation*

To George Washington

[*Passaic Falls, New Jersey, November 22, 1780*]

Dear Sir,

Sometime last fall when I spoke to your Excellency about going to the Southward, I explained to you candidly my feelings with respect to military reputation, and how much it was my object to act a conspicuous part in some enterprise that might perhaps raise my character as a soldier above mediocrity. You were so good as to say you would be glad to furnish me with an occasion. When the expedition to Staten Island was on foot a favourable one seemed to offer. There was a batalion without a field officer, the command of which I thought, as it was accidental, might be given to me without inconvenience. I made an application for it through the Marquis, who informed me of your refusal on two principles —one that giving me a whole batalion might be a subject of dissatisfaction, the other that if an accident should happen to me, in the present state of your family, you would be embarrassed for the necessary assistance.

The project you now have in contemplation affords another opportunity. I have a variety of reasons that press me to desire ardently to have it in my power to improve it. I take the liberty to observe, that the command may be proportionned to my rank, and that the second objection ceases to operate, as during the period of establishing our winter quarters there will be a suspension of material business; besides which, my peculiar situation will in any case call me away from the army in a few days and Mr. Harrison may be expected back early next month. . . .

I suggest this mode to avoid the complaints that might arise from composing my party wholly of the light infantry, which might give umbrage to the officers of that corps, who on this plan can have no just subject for it.

The primary idea may be, if circumstances permit to attempt with my detachment Byards Hill. Should we arrive early enough to undertake it, I should prefer it to any thing else, both for the brilliancy of the attempt in itself and the decisive consequences of which its success would be productive. If we arrive too late to make this eligible (as there is reason to apprehend) my corps may form the van of one of the other attacks; and Byards Hill will be a pretext for my being employed in the affair, on a supposition of my knowing the ground, which is partly true.

I flatter myself also that my military character stands so well in the army as to reconcile the officers in general to the measure. All circumstances considered, I venture to say any exceptions which might be taken would be unreasonable.

I take this method of making the request to avoid the embarrassment of a personal explanation; I shall only add that however much I have the matter at heart, I wish your Excellency intirely to consult your own inclination; and not from a disposition to oblige me, to do any thing, that may be disagreeable to you. (It will, nevertheless, make me singularly) happy if your wishes correspond with mine. . . .

3. *Parting from Washington*

To Philip Schuyler

Headquarters, New Windsor, February 18, 1781

My Dear Sir:

Since I had the pleasure of writing you last, an unexpected change has taken place in my situation. I am no longer a member of the General's family. This information will surprise you, and the manner of the change will surprise you more. Two days ago, the General and I passed each other on the stairs. He told me he wanted to speak to me. I answered that I would wait upon him immediately. I went below, and delivered Mr. Tilghman a letter to be sent to the commissary, containing an order of a pressing and interesting nature.

Returning to the General, I was stopped on the way by the Marquis de La Fayette, and we conversed together about a minute on a matter of business. He can testify how impatient I was to get back, and that I left him in a manner which, but for our intimacy, would have been more than abrupt. Instead of finding the General, as is usual, in his room, I met him at the head of the stairs, where, accosting me in an angry tone, "Colonel Hamilton," said he, "you have kept me waiting at the head of the stairs these ten minutes. I must tell you, sir, you treat me with disrespect." I replied, without petulancy, but with decision: "I am not conscious of it, sir; but since you have thought it necessary to tell me so, we part." "Very well, sir," said he, "if it be your choice," or something to this effect, and we separated. I sincerely believe my absence, which gave so much umbrage, did not last two minutes.

In less than an hour after, Tilghman came to me in the General's name, assuring me of his great confidence in my abilities, integrity, usefulness, etc., and of his desire, in a candid conversation, to heal a difference which could not have happened but in a moment of passion. I requested Mr. Tilghman to tell him—1st. That I had taken my resolution in a manner not to be revoked. 2d. That, as a conversation could serve no other purpose than to produce explanations, mutually disagreeable, though I certainly would not refuse an interview if he desired it, yet I would be happy

if he would permit me to decline it. 3d. That, though determined to leave the family, the same principles which had kept me so long in it would continue to direct my conduct towards him when out of it. 4th. That, however, I did not wish to distress him, or the public business, by quitting him before he could derive other assistance by the return of some of the gentlemen who were absent. 5th. And that, in the mean time, it depended on him to let our behavior to each other be the same as if nothing had happened. He consented to decline the conversation, and thanked me for my offer of continuing my aid in the manner I had mentioned. . . .

I have given you so particular a detail of our difference from the desire I have to justify myself in your opinion. Perhaps you may think I was precipitate in rejecting the overture made by the General to an accommodation. I assure you, my dear sir, it was not the effect of resentment; it was the deliberate result of maxims I had long formed for the government of my own conduct.

I always disliked the office of an aide-de-camp as having in it a kind of personal dependence. I refused to serve in this capacity with two major-generals at an early period of the war. Infected, however, with the enthusiasm of the times, an idea of the General's character [which experience taught me to be unfounded] overcame my scruples, and induced me to *accept his invitation* to enter into his family. [It was not long before I discovered he was neither remarkable for delicacy nor good temper, which revived my former aversion to the station in which I was acting, and it has been increasing ever since.] It has been often with great difficulty that I have prevailed upon myself not to renounce it; but while, from motives of public utility, I was doing violence to my feelings, I was always determined, if there should ever happen a breach between us, never to consent to an accommodation. I was persuaded that when once that nice barrier, which marked the boundaries of what we owed to each other, should be thrown down, it might be propped again, but could never be restored.

[I resolved, whenever it should happen, not to be in the wrong. I was convinced the concessions the General might make would be dictated by his interest, and that his self-love would never forgive me for what it would regard as a humiliation.

I believe you know the place I held in the General's confidence and counsels, which will make it the more extraordinary to you to learn that for three years past I have felt no friendship for him and have professed none. The truth is, our dispositions are the opposites of each other, and the pride of my temper would not suffer me to profess what I did not feel. Indeed, when advances of this kind have been made to me on his part, they were received in a manner that showed at least that I had no desire to court them, and that I desired to stand rather upon a footing of military confidence than of private attachment.

You are too good a judge of human nature not to be sensible how this

conduct in me must have operated on a man to whom all the world is offering incense. With this key you will easily unlock the present mystery.

At the end of the war I may say many things to you concerning which I shall impose upon myself till then an inviolable silence.]

The General is a very honest man. His competitors have slender abilities, and less integrity. His popularity has often been essential to the safety of America, and is still of great importance to it. These considerations have influenced my past conduct respecting him, and will influence my future. I think it is necessary he should be supported.

4. *Vain Pursuit of Power and Glory*

To Mrs. Hamilton

Head of Elk, Sept. 6, 1781

Yesterday, my lovely wife, I wrote to you, inclosing you a letter in one to your father, to the care of Mr. Morris. To-morrow the post sets out, and to-morrow we embark for Yorktown. I cannot refuse myself the pleasure of writing you a few lines. Constantly uppermost in my thoughts and affections, I am happy only when my moments are devoted to some office that respects you. I would give the world to be able to tell you all I feel and all I wish, but consult your own heart and you will know mine. What a world will soon be between us! To support the idea, all my fortitude is insufficient. What must be the case with you, who have the most female of female hearts? I sink at the perspective of your distress, and I look to heaven to be your guardian and supporter. Circumstances that have just come to my knowledge assure me that our operations will be expeditious, as well as our success certain. Early in November, as I promised you, we shall certainly meet. Cheer yourself with this idea, and with the assurance of never more being separated. Every day confirms me in the intention of renouncing public life and devoting myself wholly to you. Let others waste their time and their tranquillity in a vain pursuit of power and glory; be it my object to be happy in a quiet retreat with my better angel.

5. *The Reynolds Affair*

. . . The charge against me is a connection with one James Reynolds for purposes of improper pecuniary speculation. My real crime is an amorous connection with his wife for a considerable time, with his privity and connivance, if not originally brought on by a combination between the husband and wife with the design to extort money from me.

This confession is not made without a blush. I cannot be the apologist of any vice because the ardor of passion may have made it mine. I can never cease to condemn myself for the pang which it may inflict in a bosom eminently entitled to all my gratitude, fidelity, and love. But that bosom will approve, that, even at so great an expense, I should effectually wipe away a more serious stain from a name which it cherishes, with no less elevation than tenderness. The public, too, will, I trust, excuse the confession. The necessity of it to my defence against a more heinous charge could alone have extorted from me so painful an indecorum. . . .

6. *A Short Account of His Life*

To Alexander Hamilton, the Laird of Cambuskeith

Albany, State of New York, May 2, 1797

My Dear Sir:

Some days since I received with great pleasure your letter of the 10th of March. The mark it affords of your kind attention, and the particular account it gives me of so many relations in Scotland are extremely gratifying to me. You, no doubt, have understood that my father's affairs at a very early day went to wreck, so as to have rendered his situation during the greatest part of his life far from eligible. This state of things occasioned a separation between him and me, when I was very young, and threw me upon the bounty of my mother's relatives, some of whom were then wealthy, though by vicissitudes to which human affairs are so liable, they have been since much reduced and broken up. Myself, at about sixteen, came to this country. Having always had a strong propensity to literary pursuits, by a course of study and laborious exertion, I was able, by the age of nineteen, to qualify myself for the degree of Bachelor of Arts in the College of New York, and to lay the foundation by preparatory study for the future profession of the law.

The American Revolution supervened. My principles led me to take part in it; at nineteen, I entered into the American army as captain of artillery. Shortly after I became, by his invitation, aide-de-camp to General Washington, in which station I served till the commencement of that campaign which ended with the siege of York in Virginia, and the capture of Cornwallis' army. The campaign I made at the head of a corps of light infantry, with which I was present at the siege of York, and engaged in some interesting operations.

At the period of the peace with Great Britain I found myself a member of Congress, by appointment of the legislature of this State.

After the peace, I settled in the city of New York, in the practice of the law, and was in a very lucrative course of practice, when the derange-

ment of our public affairs, by the feebleness of the general confederation, drew me again reluctantly into public life. I became a member of the Convention which framed the present Constitution of the United States; and having taken part in this measure, I conceived myself to be under an obligation to lend my aid towards putting the machine in some regular motion. Hence, I did not hesitate to accept the offer of President Washington to undertake the office of Secretary of the Treasury.

In that office I met with many intrinsic difficulties, and many artificial ones, proceeding from passions, not very worthy, common to human nature, and which act with peculiar force in republics. The object, however, was effected of establishing public credit and introducing order in the finances.

Public office in this country has few attractions. The pecuniary emolument is so inconsiderable as to amount to a sacrifice to any man who can employ his time with advantage in any liberal profession. The opportunity of doing good, from the jealousy of power and the spirit of faction, is too small in any station to warrant a long continuance of private sacrifices. The enterprises of party had so far succeeded as materially to weaken the necessary influence and energy of the executive authority, and so far diminish the power of doing good in that department, as greatly to take away the motives which a virtuous man might have for making sacrifices. The prospect was even bad for gratifying in future the love of fame, if that passion was to be the spring of action.

The union of these motives, with the reflections of prudence in relation to a growing family, determined me as soon as my plan had attained a certain maturity, to withdraw from office. This I did by a resignation about two years since, when I resumed the profession of the law in the city of New York under every advantage I could desire.

It is a pleasant reflection to me, that since the commencement of my connection with General Washington to the present time, I have possessed a flattering share of his confidence and friendship.

Having given you a brief sketch of my political career, I proceed to some further family details.

In the year 1780, I married the second daughter of General Schuyler, a gentleman of one of the best families of this country, of large fortune, and no less personal and political consequence. It is impossible to be happier than I am in a wife; and I have five children, four sons and a daughter, the eldest a son somewhat past fifteen, who all promise as well as their years permit, and yield me much satisfaction. Though I have been too much in public life to be wealthy, my situation is extremely comfortable, and leaves me nothing to wish for but a continuance of health. With this blessing, the profits of my profession and other prospects authorize an expectation of such addition to my resources, as will render the eve of life easy and agreeable; so far as may depend on this consideration.

It is now several months since I have heard from my father, who con-

tinued at the island of St. Vincent. My anxiety at this silence would be greater than it is, were it not for the considerable interruption and precariousness of intercourse which is produced by the war.

I have strongly pressed the old gentleman to come and reside with me, which would afford him every enjoyment of which his advanced age is capable; but he has declined it on the ground that the advice of his physicians leads him to fear that the change of climate would be fatal to him. The next thing for me is, in proportion to my means, to endeavor to increase his comforts where he is.

It will give me the greatest pleasure to receive your son Robert at my house in New York, and still more to be of use to him; to which end, my recommendation and interest will not be wanting, and I hope not unavailing. It is my intention to embrace the opening which your letter affords me to extend my intercourse with my relations in your country, which will be a new source of satisfaction to me.

7. Military Pretensions

To George Washington

June 2, 1798

. . . It is a great satisfaction to me to ascertain what I had anticipated in hope, that you are not determined in an *adequate emergency* against affording once more your military services. There is no one but yourself that would unite the public confidence in such an emergency, independent of other considerations, and it is of the last importance that this confidence should be *full and complete.* As to the wish of the country, it is certain that it will be *ardent and universal.* You intimate a desire to be informed what would be my part in such an event as to entering into military service. I have no scruple about opening myself to you on this point. If I am invited to *a station in which the service I may render may be proportionate to the sacrifice I am to make, I* shall be willing to go into the army. If you command, the place in which I should hope to be most useful is that of Inspector-General, with a command in the line. This I would accept. The public must judge for itself as to whom it will employ, but every individual must judge for himself as to the terms on which he will serve, and consequently must estimate his own pretensions. . . .

8. *Rules for His Son, Phillip*

(1798-1800)

From the first of April to the first of October he is to rise not later than six o'clock; the rest of the year not later than seven. If earlier, he will deserve commendation. Ten will be his hour of going to bed throughout the year.

From the time he is dressed in the morning till nine o'clock (the time for breakfast excepted), he is to read law. At nine he goes to the office, and continues there till dinner time. He will be occupied partly in writing and partly in reading law.

After dinner he reads law at home till five o'clock. From this time till seven he disposes of his time as he pleases. From seven to ten he reads and studies whatever he pleases.

From twelve on Saturday he is at liberty to amuse himself.

On Sunday he will attend the morning church. The rest of the day may be applied to innocent recreations.

He must not depart from any of these rules without my permission.

9. *On News of Washington's Death*

To Tobias Lear

January 2, 1800

. . . The very painful event which it announces had, previous to the receipt of it, filled my heart with bitterness. Perhaps no man in this community has equal cause with myself to deplore the loss. I have been much indebted to the kindness of the General, and he was an *Ægis very essential to me*. But regrets are unavailing. For great misfortunes it is the business of reason to seek consolation. The friends of General Washington have very noble ones. If virtue can secure happiness in another world, he is happy. In this the seal is now put upon *his* glory. It is no longer in jeopardy from the fickleness of fortune.

P. S.—In whose hands are his papers gone? Our very confidential situation will not permit this to be a point of indifference to me.

10. *On His Financial Situation*

(*1804*)

Herewith is a general statement of my pecuniary affairs, in which there can be no material error.

The result is that calculating my property at what it stands me in, I am now worth about £10,000, and that estimating according to what my lands are now selling for and are likely to fetch, the surplus beyond my debts may fairly be stated at nearly double that sum; yet I am pained to be obliged to entertain doubts, whether, if an accident should happen to me, by which the sales of my property should come to be forced, it would even be sufficient to pay my debts. In a situation like this, it is perhaps due to my reputation to explain why I have made so considerable an establishment in the country. This explanation shall be submitted.

To men who have been so much harassed in the base world as myself, it is natural to look forward to a comfortable retirement, in the sequel of life, as a principal desideratum. This desire I have felt in the strongest manner, and to prepare for it has latterly been a favorite object. I thought I might not only expect to accomplish the object, but might reasonably aim at it and pursue the preparatory measures, from the following considerations:

It has been for some time past pretty well ascertained to my mind, that the emoluments of my profession would prove equal to the maintenance of my family and the gradual discharge of my debts, within a period to the end of which my faculties for business might be expected to extend in full energy. I think myself warranted to estimate the annual product of those emoluments at twelve thousand dollars at the least. My expenses while the first improvements of my country establishment were going on have been great, but they would this summer and fall reach the point at which, it is my intention they should stop, at least till I should be better able than at present to add to them; and after a fair examination founded upon an actual account of my expenditures, I am persuaded that a plan I have contemplated for the next and succeeding years would bring my expenses of every kind within the compass of four thousand dollars yearly, exclusive of the interest of my country establishment. To this limit I have been resolved to reduce them, even though it should be necessary to lease that establishment for a few years. In the meantime, my lands now in a course of sale and settlement would accelerate the extinguishment of my debts, and in the end leave me a handsome clear property. It was also allowable for me to take into view collaterally the expectations of my wife: which have been of late partly realized. She is now entitled to a property of between 2,000 and 3,000 pounds (as I compute), by descent

from her mother, and her father is understood to possess a large estate. I feel all the delicacy of this allusion, but the occasion, I trust, will plead my excuses, and that venerable father, I am sure, will pardon. He knows well all the nicety of my past conduct.

Viewing the matter in these different aspects, I trust the opinion of candid men will be that there has been no impropriety in my conduct, especially when it is taken into the calculation, that my country establishment, though costly, promises, by the progressive rise of property on this island and the felicity of its situation, to become more and more valuable. My chief apology is to those friends who have from mere kindness endorsed my paper discounted at the banks. On mature reflection I have thought it justifiable to secure them in preference to other creditors, lest perchance there should be a deficit. Yet, while this may save them from eventual loss, it will not exempt them from present inconvenience. As to this I can only throw myself upon their kindness and entreat the indulgence of the banks for them. Perhaps the request may be supposed entitled to some regard. In the event which would bring this paper to the public eye, one thing at least would be put beyond doubt. This is that my public labors have amounted to an absolute sacrifice of the interests of my family, and that in all pecuniary concerns the delicacy no less than the probity of conduct in public stations has been such as to defy even the shadow of a question.

Indeed, I have not enjoyed the ordinary advantages incident to my military services. Being a member of Congress while the question of the commutation of the half pay of the army for a sum in gross was in debate, delicacy and a desire to be useful to the army by removing the idea of my having an interest in the question, induced me to write to the Secretary of War and relinquish my claim to half pay, which or the equivalent I have never received. Neither have I even applied for the lands allowed by the United States to officers of my rank. Nor did I ever obtain from this State the allowance of lands made to officers of similar rank. It is true that having served through the latter periods of the war on the general staff of the United States and not on the line of this State, I could not claim the allowance as a matter of course; but having before the war resided in this State, and having entered the military career at the head of a company of artillery raised for the particular defence of this State, I had better pretensions to the allowance than others to whom it was actually made, yet it has not been extended to me.

11. *His Motives in Meeting Burr*

(*1804*)

On my expected interview with Col. Burr, I think it proper to make some remarks explanatory of my conduct, motives, and views. I was certainly desirous of avoiding this interview for the most cogent reasons:

(1) My religious and moral principles are strongly opposed to the practice of duelling, and it would ever give me pain to be obliged to shed the blood of a fellow-creature in a private combat forbidden by the laws.

(2) My wife and children are extremely dear to me, and my life is of the utmost importance to them in various views.

(3) I feel a sense of obligation towards my creditors; who, in case of accident to me by the forced sale of my property, may be in some degree sufferers. I did not think myself at liberty as a man of probity lightly to expose them to this hazard.

(4) I am conscious of no ill-will to Col. Burr, distinct from political opposition, which, as I trust, has proceeded from pure and upright motives.

Lastly, I shall hazard much and can possibly gain nothing by the issue of the interview.

But it was, as I conceive, impossible for me to avoid it. There were intrinsic difficulties in the thing and artificial embarrassments, from the manner of proceeding on the part of Col. Burr.

Intrinsic, because it is not to be denied that my animadversions on the political principles, character, and views of Col. Burr have been extremely severe; and on different occasions I, in common with many others, have made very unfavorable criticisms on particular instances of the private conduct of this gentleman. In proportion as these impressions were entertained with sincerity and uttered with motives and for purposes which might appear to me commendable, would be the difficulty (until they could be removed by evidence of their being erroneous) of explanation or apology. . . .

As well, because it is possible that I may have injured Col. Burr, however convinced myself that my opinions and declarations have been well-founded, as from my general principles and temper in relation to similar affairs, I have resolved, if our interview is conducted in the usual manner, and it pleases God to give me the opportunity, to reserve and throw away my first fire, and I have thoughts even of reserving my second fire, and thus giving a double opportunity to Col. Burr to pause and reflect. It is not, however, my intention to enter into any explanations on the

ground. Apology from principle, I hope, rather than pride, is out of the question. To those who, with me, abhorring the practice of duelling, may think that I ought on no account to have added to the number of bad examples, I answer that my relative situation, as well in public as private, enforcing all the considerations which constitute what men of the world denominate honor, imposed on me (as I thought) a peculiar necessity not to decline the call. The ability to be in future useful, whether in resisting mischief or in effecting good, in those crises of our public affairs which seem likely to happen, would probably be inseparable from a conformity with public prejudice in this particular.

12. *Last Will and Testament*

In the name of God, Amen!

I, Alexander Hamilton, of the State of New York, counsellor at law, do make this my last will and testament, as follows: First, I appoint John B. Church, Nicholas Fish, and Nathaniel Pendleton, of the city aforesaid, esquires, to be executors and trustees of this my will, and I devise to them, their heirs and assigns, as joint tenants, and not as tenants in common, all my estate, real and personal, whatsoever and wheresoever upon trust, at their discretion to sell and dispose of the same at such time and times, in such manner, and upon such terms as they the survivors and survivor shall think fit, and out of the proceeds to pay all the debts which I shall owe at the time of my decease, in whole, if the fund shall be sufficient, proportionally, if it shall be insufficient, and the residue, if any there shall be, to pay and deliver to my excellent and dear wife, Elizabeth Hamilton.

Though, if it please God to spare my life, I may look for a considerable surplus out of my present property; yet if he should speedily call me to the eternal world, a forced sale, as is usual, may possibly render it insufficient to satisfy my debts. I pray God that something may remain for the maintenance and education of my dear wife and children. But should it on the contrary happen that there is not enough for the payment of my debts, I entreat my dear children, if they or any of them shall ever be able, to make up the deficiency. I without hesitation commit to their delicacy a wish which is dictated by my own. Though conscious that I have too far sacrificed the interests of my family to public avocations, and on this account have the less claim to burthen my children, yet I trust in their magnanimity to appreciate, as they ought, this my request. In so unfavorable an event of things, the support of their dear mother, with the most respectful and tender attention, is a duty all

the sacredness of which they will feel. Probably her own patrimonial resources will preserve her from indigence. But in all situations they are charged to bear in mind that she has been to them the most devoted and best of mothers. In testimony whereof, I have hereunto subscribed my hand, the ninth day of July, in the year of our Lord one thousand eight hundred and four.

Letters

13. *A Great Danger of Fatal Extremes*

To John Jay

New York, Novem 26, 1775

Dear Sir

I take the liberty to trouble you with some remarks on a matter which to me appears of not a little importance; doubting not that you will use your influence in Congress to procure a remedy for the evil I shall mention, if you think the considerations I shall urge are of that weight they seem in my judgment to possess.

You will probably ere this reaches you have heard of the late incursion made into this city by a number of horsemen from New England under the command of Capt Sears, who took away Mr. Rivington's types, and a Couteau or two. Though I am fully sensible how dangerous and pernicious Rivington's press has been, and how detestable the character of the man is in every respect, yet I cannot help disapproving and condemning this step.

In times of such commotion as the present, while the passions of men are worked up to an uncommon pitch there is great danger of fatal extremes. The same state of the passions which fits the multitude, who have not a sufficient stock of reason and knowlege to guide them, for opposition to tyranny and oppression, very naturally leads them to a contempt and disregard of all authority. The due medium is hardly to be found among the more intelligent, it is almost impossible among the unthinking populace. When the minds of these are loosened from their attachment to ancient establishments and courses, they seem to grow giddy and are apt more or less to run into anarchy. These principles, too true in themselves, and confirmed to me both by reading and my own experience, deserve extremely the attention of those, who have the direction of public affairs. In such tempestuous times, it requires the greatest skill in the political pilots to keep men steady and within proper bounds, on which account I am always more or less alarmed at every thing which is done of mere will and pleasure, without any proper authority. Irregu-

larities I know are to be expected, but they are nevertheless dangerous and ought to be checked, by every prudent and moderate mean. From these general maxims, I disapprove of the irruption in question, as serving to cherish a spirit of disorder at a season when men are too prone to it of themselves.

Moreover, New England is very populous and powerful. It is not safe to trust to the virtue of any people. Such proceedings will serve to produce and encourage a spirit of encroachment and arrogance in them. I like not to see potent neighbours indulged in the practice of making inroads at pleasure into this or any other province.

You well know too, sir, that antipathies and prejudices have long subsisted between this province and New England. To this may be attributed a principal part of the disaffection now prevalent among us. Measures of the present nature, however they may serve to intimidate, will secretly revive and increase those ancient animosities, which though smothered for a while will break out when there is a favorable opportunity.

Besides this, men coming from a neighbouring province to chastise the notorious friends of the ministry here, will hold up an idea to our enemies not very advantageous to our affairs. They will imagine that the New Yorkers are totally, or a majority of them, disaffected to the American cause, which makes the interposal of their neighbours necessary: or that such violences will breed differences and effect that which they have been so eagerly wishing, a division and quarrelling among ourselves. Every thing of such an aspect must encourage their hopes.

Upon the whole the measure is condemned, by all the cautious and prudent among the whigs, and will evidently be productive of secret jealousy and ill blood if a stop is not put to things of the kind for the future. . . .

14. *On A Representative Democracy*

To Gouverneur Morris

Head Quarters, Morris Town [New Jersey]
May 19th, 1777

. . . I partly agree and partly disagree with you respecting the deficiencies of your constitution. That there is a want of vigor in the executive, I believe will be found true. To determine the qualifications proper for the chief executive Magistrate requires the deliberate wisdom of a select assembly, and cannot be safely lodged with the people

at large. That instability is inherent in the nature of popular governments, I think very disputable; unstable democracy, is an epithet frequently in the mouths of politicians; but I believe that from a strict examination of the matter, from the records of history, it will be found that the fluctuation of governments in which the popular principle has borne a considerable sway, has proceeded from its being compounded with other principles and from its being made to operate in an improper channel. Compound governments, though they may be harmonious in the beginning, will introduce distinct interests; and these interests will clash, throw the state into convulsions & produce a change or dissolution. When the deliberative or judicial powers are vested wholly or partly in the collective body of the people, you must expect error, confusion and instability. But a representative democracy, where the right of election is well secured and regulated & the exercise of the legislative, executive and judiciary authorities, is vested in select persons, chosen *really* and not *nominally* by the people, will in my opinion be most likely to be happy, regular and durable. That the complexity of your legislative will occasion delay and dilatoriness is evident and I fear may be attended with much greater, evil; as expedition is not very material *in making* laws, especially when the government is well digested and matured by time. The evil I mean is, that in time, your senate, from the very name and from the mere circumstance of its being a separate member of the legislature, will be liable to degenerate into a body purely aristocratical. And I think the danger of an abuse of power from a simple legislative would not be very great, in a government where the equality and fulness of popular representation is so wisely provided for as in yours. On the whole, though I think there are the defects intimated, I think your Government far the best that we have yet seen, and capable of giving long and substantial happiness to the people. Objections to it should be suggested with great caution and reserve. . . .

15. *"There Should Be a Change"*

To George Clinton

Head Quarters [Valley Forge] Feb'y 13, 1778.

Dear Sir,

. . . There is a matter, which often obtrudes itself upon my mind, and which requires the attention of every person of sense and influence, among us. I mean a degeneracy of representation in the great council of America. It is a melancholy truth Sir, and the effects of which we dayly see and feel, that there is not so much wisdom in a certain body, as there

ought to be, and as the success of our affairs absolutely demands. Many members of it are no doubt men in every respect, fit for the trust, but this cannot be said of it as a body. Folly, caprice, a want of foresight, comprehension and dignity, characterise the general tenor of their actions. Of this I dare say, you are sensible, though you have not perhaps so many opportunities of knowing it as I have. Their conduct with respect to the army especially is feeble, indecisive and improvident—insomuch, that we are reduced to a more terrible situation than you can conceive. False and contracted views of economy have prevented them, though repeatedly urged to it, from making that provision for officers which was requisite to interest them in the service; which has produced such carelessness and indifference to the service, as is subversive of every officer-like quality. They have disgusted the army by repeated instances of the most whimsical favouritism in their promotions; and by an absurd prodigality of rank to foreigners and to the meanest staff of the army. They have not been able to summon resolution enough to withstand the impudent importunity and vain boasting of foreign pretenders; but have manifested such a ductility and inconstancy in their proceedings, as will warrant the charge of suffering themselves to be bullied, by every petty rascal, who comes armed with ostentatious pretensions of military merit and experience. Would you believe it Sir, it is become almost proverbial in the mouths of the French officers and other foreigners, that they have nothing more to do, to obtain whatever they please, than to assume a high tone and assert their own merit with confidence and perseverance? These things wound my feelings as a republican more than I can express; and in some degree make me contemptible in my own eyes.

By injudicious changes and arrangements in the Commissary's department, in the middle of a campaign, they have exposed the army frequently to temporary want, and to the danger of a dissolution, from absolute famine. At this very day there are complaints from the whole line, of having been three or four days without provisions; desertions have been immense, and strong features of mutiny begin to show themselves. It is indeed to be wondered at, that the soldiery have manifested so unparallelled a degree of patience, as they have. If effectual measures are not speedily adopted, I know not how we shall keep the army together or make another campaign.

I omit saying any thing of the want of Cloathing for the army. It may be disputed whether more could have been done than has been done.

If you look into their conduct in the civil line, you will equally discover a deficiency of energy, dignity and extensiveness of views; but of this you can better judge than myself, and it is unnecessary to particularise.

America once had a representation, that would do honor to any age or nation. The present falling off is very alarming and dangerous. What is the cause? or how is it to be remedied? are questions that the welfare of

these states requires should be well attended to. The great men who composed our first council; are they dead, have they deserted the cause, or what has become of them? Very few are dead and still fewer have deserted the cause;—they are all except the few who still remain in Congress either in the field, or in the civil offices of their respective states; far the greater part are engaged in the latter. The only remedy then is to take them out of these employments and return them to the place, where their presence is infinitely more important.

Each State in order to promote its own internal government and prosperity, has selected its best members to fill the offices within itself, and conduct its own affairs. Men have been fonder of the emoluments and conveniences, of being employed at home, and local attachment, falsely operating, has made them more provident for the particular interests of the states to which they belonged, than for the common interests of the confederacy. This is a most pernicious mistake, and must be corrected. However important it is to give form and efficiency to your interior constitutions and police; it is infinitely more important to have a wise general council; otherwise a failure of the measures of the union will overturn all your labours for the advancement of your particular good and ruin the common cause. You should not beggar the councils of the United States to enrich the administration of the several members. Realize to yourself the consequences of having a Congress despised at home and abroad. How can the common force be exerted, if the power of collecting it be put in weak foolish and unsteady hands? How can we hope for success in our European negociations, if the nations of Europe have no confidence in the wisdom and vigor, of the great Continental Government? This is the object on which their eyes are fixed, hence it is America will d[e]rive its importance or insignificance, in their estimation.

Arguments to you Sir, need not be multiplied to enforce the necessity of having a good general council, neither do I think we shall very widely differ as to the fact that the present is very far from being such.

The sentiments I have advanced are not fit for the vulgar ear; and circumstanced as I am, I should with caution utter them except to those in whom I may place an entire confidence. But it is time that men of weight and understanding should take the alarm, and excite each other to a proper remedy. For my part, my insignificance, allows me to do nothing more, than to hint my apprehensions to those of that description who are pleased to favour me with their confidence. In this view, I write to you.

As far, as I can judge, the remarks I have made do not apply to your state nearly so much as to the other twelve. You have a Duane, a Morris and may I not add a Duer? But why do you not send your Jay and your R. R. Livingston? I wish General Schuyler was either explicitly in the army or in the Congress. For yourself Sir, though I mean no compliments you must not be spared from where you are.

But the design of this letter is not so much that you may use your in-

fluence, in improving or enlarging your own representation, as in, discreetly, giving the alarm to other states, through the medium of your confidential friends. Indeed Sir it is necessary there should be a change. America will shake to its center, if there is not. . . .

16. "Give Them Their Freedom with Their Muskets"

To John Jay

[*Middlebrook, New Jersey, March 14, 1779*]

Dear Sir,

Col Laurens, who will have the honor of delivering you this letter, is on his way to South Carolina, on a project, which I think, in the present situation of affairs there, is a very good one and deserves every kind of support and encouragement. This is to raise two, three or four batalions of negroes; with the assistance of the government of that state, by contributions from the owners in proportion to the number they possess. If you should think proper to enter upon the subject with him, he will give you a detail of his plan. He wishes to have it recommended by Congress to the state; and, as an inducement, that they would engage to take those batalions into Continental pay.

It appears to me, that an expedient of this kind, in the present state of Southern affairs, is the most rational, that can be adopted, and promises very important advantages. Indeed, I hardly see how a sufficient force can be collected in that quarter without it; and the enemy's operations there are growing infinitely serious and formidable. I have not the least doubt, that the negroes will make very excellent soldiers, with proper management; and I will venture to pronounce, that they cannot be put in better hands than those of Mr. Laurens. He has all the zeal, intelligence, enterprise, and every other qualification requisite to succeed in such an undertaking. It is a maxim with some great military judges, that with sensible officers soldiers can hardly be too stupid; and on this principle it is thought that the Russians would make the best troops in the world, if they were under other officers than their own. The King of Prussia is among the number who maintain this doctrine and has a very emphatical saying on the occasion, which I do not exactly recollect. I mention this, because I frequently hear it objected to the scheme of embodying negroes that they are too stupid to make soldiers. This is so far from appearing to me a valid objection that I think their want of cultivation (for their natural faculties are probably as good as ours) joined to that habit of subordination which they acquire from a life of servitude,

will make them sooner become soldiers than our White inhabitants. Let officers be men of sense and sentiment, and the nearer the soldiers approach to machines perhaps the better.

I foresee that this project will have to combat much opposition from prejudice and self-interest. The contempt we have been taught to entertain for the blacks, makes us fancy many things that are founded neither in reason nor experience; and an unwillingness to part with property of so valuable a kind will furnish a thousand arguments to show the impracticability or pernicious tendency of a scheme which requires such a sacrifice. But it should be considered, that if we do not make use of them in this way, the enemy probably will; and that the best way to counteract the temptations they will hold out will be to offer them ourselves. An essential part of the plan is to give them their freedom with their muskets. This will secure their fidelity, animate their courage, and I believe will have a good influence upon those who remain, by opening a door to their emancipation. This circumstance, I confess, has no small weight in inducing me to wish the success of the project; for the dictates of humanity and true policy equally interest me in favour of this unfortunate class of men. . . .

17. *The Sober Views of A Politician*

To James Duane

[*Liberty Pole, New Jersey, September 3, 1780*]

Dr. Sir

Agreeably to your request and my promise I sit down to give you my ideas of the defects of our present system, and the changes necessary to save us from ruin. They may perhaps be the reveries of a projector rather than the sober views of a politician. You will judge of them, and make what use you please of them.

The fundamental defect is a want of power in Congress. It is hardly worth while to show in what this consists, as it seems to be universally acknowleged, or to point out how it has happened, as the only question is how to remedy it. It may however be said that it has originated from three causes—an excess of the spirit of liberty which has made the particular states show a jealousy of all power not in their own hands; and this jealousy has led them to exercise a right of judging in the last resort of the measures recommended by Congress, and of acting according to their own opinions of their propriety or necessity, a diffidence in Congress of their own powers, by which they have been timid and indecisive in their resolutions, constantly making concessions to the states, till they have

scarcely left themselves the shadow of power; a want of sufficient means at their disposal to answer the public exigencies and of vigor to draw forth those means; which have occasioned them to depend on the states individually to fulfil their engagements with the army, and the consequence of which has been to ruin their influence and credit with the army, to establish its dependence on each state separately rather than *on them,* that is rather than on the whole collectively.

It may be pleaded, that Congress had never any definitive powers granted them and of course could exercise none—could do nothing more than recommend. The manner in which Congress was appointed would warrant, and the public good required, that they should have considered themselves as vested with full power *to preserve the republic from harm.* They have done many of the highest acts of sovereignty, which were always chearfully submitted to—the declaration of independence, the declaration of war, the levying an army, creating a navy, emitting money, making alliances with foreign powers, appointing a dictator &c. &c.—all these implications of a complete sovereignty were never disputed, and ought to have been a standard for the whole conduct of Administration. Undefined powers are discretionary powers, limited only by the object for which they were given—in the present case, the independence and freedom of America. The confederation made no difference; for as it has not been generally adopted, it had no operation. But from what I recollect of it, Congress have even descended from the authority which the spirit of that act gives them, while the particular states have no further attended to it than as it suited their pretensions and convenience. It would take too much time to enter into particular instances, each of which separately might appear inconsiderable, but united are of serious import. I only mean to remark, not to censure.

But the confederation itself is defective and requires to be altered; it is neither fit for war, nor peace. The idea of an uncontrolable sovereignty in each state, over its internal police, will defeat the other powers given to Congress, and make our union feeble and precarious. . . .

The confederation gives the states individually too much influence in the affairs of the army; they should have nothing to do with it. The entire formation and disposal of our military forces ought to belong to Congress. It is an essential cement of the union; and it ought to be the policy of Congress to destroy all ideas of state attachments in the army and make it look up wholly to them. . . .

I shall now propose the remedies, which appear to me applicable to our circumstances, and necessary to extricate our affairs from their present deplorable situation.

The first step must be to give Congress powers competent to the public exigencies. This may happen in two ways, one by resuming and exercising the discretionary powers I suppose to have been originally vested in them for the safety of the states and resting their conduct on the

candor of their country men and the necessity of the conjuncture: the other by calling immediately a convention of all the states with full authority to conclude finally upon a general confederation, stating to them beforehand explicitly the evils arising from a want of power in Congress, and the impossibility of supporting the contest on its present footing, that the delegates may come possessed of proper sentiments as well as proper authority to give to the meeting. Their commission should include a right of vesting Congress with the whole or a proportion of the unoccupied lands, to be employed for the purpose of raising a revenue, reserving the jurisdiction to the states by whom they are granted.

The first plan, I expect will be thought too bold an expedient by the generality of Congress; and indeed their practice hitherto has so rivetted the opinion of their want of power, that the success of this experiment may very well be doubted.

I see no objection to the other mode, that has any weight in competition with the reasons for it. The Convention should assemble the 1st of November next, the sooner, the better; our disorders are too violent to admit of a common or lingering remedy. The reasons for which I require them to be vested with plenipotentiary authority are that the business may suffer no delay in the execution, and may in reality come to effect. A convention may agree upon a confederation; the states individually hardly ever will. We must have one at all events, and a vigorous one if we mean to succeed in the contest and be happy hereafter. As I said before, to engage the states to comply with this mode, Congress ought to confess to them plainly and unanimously the impracticability of supporting our affairs on the present footing and without a solid coercive union. I ask that the Convention should have a power of vesting the whole or a part of the unoccupied land in Congress, because it is necessary that body should have some property as a fund for the arrangements of finance; and I know of no other kind that can be given them.

The confederation in my opinion should give Congress complete sovereignty; except as to that part of internal police, which relates to the rights of property and life among individuals and to raising money by internal taxes. It is necessary, that every thing, belonging to this, should be regulated by the state legislatures. Congress should have complete sovereignty in all that relates to war, peace, trade, finance, and to the management of foreign affairs, the right of declaring war, of raising armies, officering, paying them, directing their motions in every respect, of equipping fleets and doing the same with them, of building fortifications, arsenals, magazines &c. &c., of making peace on such conditions as they think proper, of regulating trade, determining with what countries it shall be carried on, granting indulgencies laying prohibitions on all the articles of export or import, imposing duties granting bounties & premiums for raising, exporting, importing and applying to their own use the product of these duties, only giving credit to the states on whom they are

raised in the general account of revenues and expences, instituting Admiralty courts &c., of coining money, establishing banks on such terms, and with such privileges as they think proper, appropriating funds and doing whatever else relates to the operations of finance, transacting every thing with foreign nations, making alliances offensive and defensive, treaties of commerce, &c. &c. . . .

And why can we not have an American bank? Are our monied men less enlightened to their own interest or less enterprising in the persuit? I believe the fault is in our government which does not exert itself to engage them in such a scheme. It is true, the individuals in America are not very rich, but this would not prevent their instituting a bank; it would only prevent its being done with such ample funds as in other countries. Have they not sufficient confidence in the government and in the issue of the cause? Let the Government endeavour to inspire that confidence, by adopting the measures I have recommended or others equivalent to them. Let it exert itself to procure a solid confederation, to establish a good plan of executive administration, to form a permanent military force, to obtain at all events a foreign loan. If these things were in a train of vigorous execution, it would give a new spring to our affairs; government would recover its respectability and individuals would renounce their diffidence. . . .

The first step to establishing the bank will be to engage a number of monied men of influence to relish the project and make it a business. . . .

If a Convention is called the minds of all the states and the people ought to be prepared to receive its determinations by sensible and popular writings, which should conform to the views of Congress. There are epochs in human affairs, when *novelty* even is useful. If a general opinion prevails that the old way is bad, whether true or false, and this obstructs or relaxes the operation of the public service, a change is necessary if it be but for the sake of change. This is exactly the case now. 'Tis an universal sentiment that our present system is a bad one, and that things do not go right on this account. The measure of a Convention would revive the hopes of the people and give a new direction to their passions, which may be improved in carrying points of substantial utility. The Eastern states have already pointed out this mode to Congress; they ought to take the hint and anticipate the others.

And, in future, My Dear Sir, two things let me recommend, as fundamental rules for the conduct of Congress—to attach the army to them by every motive, to maintain an air of authority (not domineering) in all their measures with the states. The manner in which a thing is done has more influence than is commonly imagined. Men are governed by opinion; this opinion is as much influenced by appearances as by realities; if a Government appears to be confident of its own powers, it is the surest way to inspire the same confidence in others; if it is diffident, it may be

certain, there will be a still greater diffidence in others, and that its authority will not only be distrusted, controverted, but contemned.

I wish too Congress would always consider that a kindness consists as much in the manner as in the thing: the best things done hesitatingly and with an ill grace lose their effect, and produce disgust rather than satisfaction or gratitude. . . .

18. *A Plan for a National Bank*

To Robert Morris

[*De Peyster's Point, New York, April 30, 1781*]

Sir,

I was among the first who were convinced, that an administration by single men was essential to the proper management of the affairs of this country. I am persuaded now it is the only resource we have to extricate ourselves from the distresses, which threaten the subversion of our cause. It is palpable that the people have lost all confidence in our public councils, and it is a fact of which I dare say you are as well apprised as myself, that our friends in Europe are in the same disposition. I have been in a situation that has enabled me to obtain a better idea of this than most others; and I venture to assert, that the Court of France will never give half the succours to this Country while Congress holds the reins of administration in their own hands, which they would grant, if these were intrusted to individuals of established reputation and con(spicuous) for probity, abilities and fortune.

With respect to ourselves, there is so universal and rooted a diffidence of the government, that if we could be assured the future measures of Congress would be dictated by the most perfect wisdom and public spirit there would be still a necessity for a change in the forms of our administration to give a new spring and current to the passions and hopes of the people.

To me it appears evident that an executive ministry composed of men with the qualifications I have described would speedily restore the credit of government abroad and at home, would induce our allies to greater exertions in our behalf, would inspire confidence in monied men in Europe as well as in America to lend us (those) sums of which it may be demonstrated we (stand) in need from the disproportion of our national wealth to the expences of the War. . . . Tis by introducing order into our finances —by restoring public credit—not by gaining battles, that we are finally to gain our object. Tis by putting ourselves in a condition to continue the war not by temporary, violent and unnatural efforts to bring it to a deci-

sive issue, that we shall in reality bring it to a speedy and successful one. In the frankness of truth I believe, Sir, you are the Man best capable of performing this great work.

In expectation that all difficulties will be removed, and that you will ultimately act, on terms you approve, I take the liberty to submit to you some ideas, relative to the object of your department. I pretend not to be an able financier; it is a part of administration, which has been least in my way and of course has least occupied my inquiries and reflections. Neither have I had leisure or materials to make accurate calculations. I have been obliged to depend on memory for important facts for want of the authorities from which they are drawn. With all these disadvantages, my plan must necessarily be crude and defective; but if it may be a basis for something more perfect, or if it contains any hints that may be of use to you, the trouble I have taken myself, or may give you, will not be misapplied. At any rate the confidence I have in your judgment assures me that you will receive with pleasure Communications of this sort; if they contain any thing useful, they will promote your views and the public benefit; if not the only evil is the trouble of reading them and the best informed will frequently derive light even from the reveries of projectors and quacks. There is scarcely any plan so bad as not to have something good in it. I trust mine to your candor without further apology. You will at least do justice to my Intention.

The first step towards determining what ought to be done in the finances of this country is to estimate in the best manner we can its capacity for revenue and the proportion between what it is able to afford and what it stands in need of for the expences of its civil and military establishments. There occur to me two ways of doing this: 1st by examining what proportion the revenues of other countries have borne to their stock of wealth, and applying the rule to ourselves with proper allowance for the difference of circumstances. 2dly by comparing the result of this rule with the product of taxes in those states which have been the most in earnest in taxation. The reason for having recourse to the first Method is, that our own experience of our faculties in this respect has not been sufficiently clear or uniform to admit of a certain conclusion; so that it will be more satisfactory to judge of them by a general principle drawn from the example of other nations compared with what we have effected ourselves, than to rely intirely upon the latter.

The nations with whose wealth and revenues (we) are best acquainted are France, Great Britain, and the United provinces. The real wealth of a nation consisting in its labour and commodities, is to be estimated by the sign of that wealth, its circulating cash. There may be times, when from particular accidents, the quantity of (this) may exceed or fall short of a just representative, but (it) will return again to a proper level, and in the general course of things maintain itself in that state. . . .

To . . . give individuals ability and inclination to lend, in any proportion

to the wants of government, a plan must be devised, which by incorporating their means together and uniting them with those of the public, will on the foundation of that incorporation and Union, erect a mass of credit that will supply the defect of monied capitals and answer all the purposes of cash, a plan which will offer adventurers immediate advantages analagous to those they receive by employing their money in trade, and eventually greater advantages, a plan which will give them the greatest security the nature of the case will admit for what they lend, and which will not only advance their own interest and secure the independence of their country, but in its progress have the most beneficial influence upon its future commerce and be a source of national strength and wealth.

I mean the institution of a National Bank. This I regard, in some shape or other as an expedient essential to our safety and success, unless by a happy turn of European affairs the war should speedily terminate in a manner upon which it would be unwise to reckon. There is no other that can give to government that extensive and systematic credit, which the defect of our revenues makes indispensably necessary to its operations. The longer it is delayed, the more difficult it becomes; our affairs grow every day more relaxed and more involved; public credit hastens to a more irretrievable catastrophe; the means for executing the plan are exhausted in partial and temporary efforts. . . .

In the present system of things the health of a state particularly a commercial one depends on a due quantity and regular circulation of Cash, as much as the health of an animal body depends upon the due quantity and regular circulation of the blood. There are indisputable indications that we have not a sufficient medium and what we have is in continual fluctuation. The only cure to our public disorders is to fix the value of the currency we now have and increase it to a proper standard in a species that will have the requisite stability.

The error of those who would explode paper money altogether originates in not making proper distinctions. Our paper was in its nature liable to depreciations, because it had no funds for its support and was not upheld by private credit. The emissions under the resolution of March, 80 have partly the former advantage but are destitute of the latter which is equally essential. No paper credit can be substantial or durable which has not funds and which does not unite immediately the interest and influence of the monied men in its establishment and preservation. A credit begun on this basis will in process of time greatly exceed its funds but this requires time and a well settled opinion in its favour. 'Tis in a National Bank alone that we can find the ingredients to constitute a wholesome, solid and beneficial paper credit. . . .

A national debt if it is not excessive will be to us a national blessing; it will be powerfull cement of our union. It will also create a necessity for keeping up taxation to a degree which without being oppressive, will be a spur to industry; remote as we are from Europe and shall be from danger,

it were otherwise to be feard our popular maxims would incline us to too great parsimony and indulgence. We labour less now than any civilized nation of Europe, and a habit of labour in the people is as essential to the health and vigor of their minds and bodies as it is conducive to the welfare of the State. We ought not to Suffer our self-love to deceive us in a comparrison, upon these points. . . .

19. For "A Strong, Well-Mounted Government"

To Washington

New York, July 3, 1787.

Dear Sir:

In my passage through the Jerseys, and since my arrival here, I have taken particular pains to discover the public sentiment, and I am more and more convinced that this is the critical opportunity for establishing the prosperity of this country on a solid foundation. I have conversed with men of information, not only in this city, but from different parts of the State, and they agree that there has been an astonishing revolution for the better in the minds of the people.

The prevailing apprehension among thinking men is, that the Convention, from the fear of shocking the popular opinion, will not go far enough. They seem to be convinced that a strong, well-mounted government will better suit the popular palate than one of a different complexion. Men in office are indeed taking all possible pains to give an unfavorable impression of the Convention, but the current seems to be moving strongly the other way.

A plain but sensible man, in a conversation I had with him yesterday, expressed himself nearly in this manner: The people begin to be convinced that "their excellent form of government," as they have been used to call it, will not answer their purpose, and that they must substitute something not very remote from that which they have lately quitted.

These appearances, though they will not warrant a conclusion that the people are yet ripe for such a plan as I advocate, yet serve to prove that there is no reason to despair of their adopting one equally energetic, if the Convention should think proper to propose it. They serve to prove that we ought not to allow too much weight to objections drawn from the supposed repugnance of the people to an efficient constitution. I confess I am more and more inclined to believe that former habits of thinking are regaining their influence with more rapidity than is generally imagined. . . .

I own to you, sir, that I am seriously and deeply distressed at the aspect

of the counsels which prevailed when I left Philadelphia. I fear that we shall let slip the golden opportunity of rescuing the American empire from disunion, anarchy, and misery.

No motly or feeble measure can answer the end, or will finally receive the public support. Decision is true wisdom, and will be not less reputable to the Convention than salutary to the community. . . .

20. *Washington Is Indispensable*

To George Washington

New York, August 13, 1788

. . . . I take it for granted, sir, you have concluded to comply with what will no doubt be the general call of your country in relation to the new government. You will permit me to say that it is indispensable you should lend yourself to its first operations. It is of little purpose to have *introduced* a system, if the weightiest influence is not given to its firm *establishment* in the outset.

21. *On Madison and Jefferson*

To Colonel Edward Carrington

Philadelphia, May 26, 1792.

My Dear Sir:

Believing that I possess a share of your personal friendship and confidence, and yielding to that which I feel towards you; persuaded also, that our political creed is the same on two essential points—first, the necessity of Union to the respectability and happiness of this country, and second, the necessity of an efficient general government to maintain the Union, I have concluded to unbosom myself to you, on the present state of political parties and views. . . .

When I accepted the office I now hold, it was under full persuasion, that from similarity of thinking, conspiring with personal good-will, I should have the firm support of Mr. Madison, in the general course of my administration. Aware of the intrinsic difficulties of the situation, and of the powers of Mr. Madison, I do not believe I should have accepted under a different supposition. I have mentioned the similarity of thinking

between that gentleman and myself. This was relative, not merely to the general principles of national policy and government, but to the leading points, which were likely to constitute questions in the administration of the finances. I mean, first, the expediency of funding the debt; second, the inexpediency of discrimination between original and present holders; third, the expediency of assuming the State debts.

As to the first point, the evidence of Mr. Madison's sentiments, at one period, is to be found in the address of Congress, of April twenty-sixth, seventeen hundred and eighty-three, which was planned by him, in conformity to his own ideas, and without any previous suggestions from the committee, and with his hearty co-operation in every part of the business. His conversations upon various occasions since have been expressive of a continuance in the same sentiment; nor, indeed, has he yet contradicted it, by any part of his official conduct. How far there is reason to apprehend a change in this particular, will be stated hereafter. As to the second part, the same address is an evidence of Mr. Madison's sentiments at the same period. And I had been informed that at a later period he had been, in the Legislature of Virginia, a strenuous and successful opponent of the principle of discrimination. Add to this, that a variety of conversations had taken place between him and myself, respecting the public debt, down to the commencement of the new government, in none of which had he glanced at the idea of a change of opinion. I wrote him a letter after my appointment, in the recess of Congress, to obtain his sentiments on the subject of the finances. In his answer, there is not a lisp of his new system.

As to the third point, the question of an assumption of the State debts by the United States was in discussion when the convention that framed the present government was sitting at Philadelphia, and in a long conversation which I had with Mr. Madison in an afternoon's walk, I well remember that we were perfectly agreed in the expediency and propriety of such a measure; though we were both of opinion that it would be more advisable to make it a measure of administration than an article of Constitution, from the impolicy of multiplying obstacles to its reception on collateral details.

Under these circumstances you will naturally imagine that it must have been matter of surprise to me when I was apprised that it was Mr. Madison's intention to oppose my plan on both the last-mentioned points. Before the debate commenced, I had a conversation with him on my report; in the course of which I alluded to the calculation I had made of his sentiments, and the grounds of that calculation. He did not deny them; but alleged in his justification that the very considerable alienation of the debt, subsequent to the periods at which he had opposed a discrimination, had essentially changed the state of the question; and that as to the assumption, he had contemplated it to take place as matters stood at the peace. . . .

At this time and afterwards repeated intimations were given to me that

Mr. Madison, from a spirit of rivalship, or some other cause, had become personally unfriendly to me. . . .

Still I suspended my opinion on the subject. I knew the malevolent officiousness of mankind too well to yield a very ready acquiescence to the suggestions which were made, and resolved to wait till time and more experience should afford a solution. It was not till the last session that I became unequivocally convinced of the following truth: "that Mr. Madison, co-operating with Mr. Jefferson, is at the head of a faction decidedly hostile to me and my administration; and actuated by views, in my judgment, subversive of the principles of good government and dangerous to the Union, peace, and happiness of the country." . . .

I cannot persuade myself that Mr. Madison and I, whose politics had formerly so much the same point of departure, should now diverge so widely in our opinions of the measures which are proper to be pursued. The opinion I once entertained of the candor and simplicity and fairness of Mr. Madison's character, has, I acknowledge, given way to a decided opinion that it is one of a peculiarly artificial and complicated kind. . . .

When the Department of the Treasury was established, Mr. Madison was an unequivocal advocate of the principles which prevailed in it, and of the powers and duties which were assigned by it to the head of the department. This appeared, both from his private and public discourse, and I will add, that I have personal evidence that Mr. Madison is as well convinced as any man in the United States of the necessity of the arrangement which characterizes that establishment, to the orderly conducting of the business of the finances. Mr. Madison nevertheless opposed a reference to me to report ways and means for the Western expedition, and combated, on principle, the propriety of such references.

He well knew that if he had prevailed a certain consequence was my resignation; that I would not be fool enough to make pecuniary sacrifices and endure a life of extreme drudgery without opportunity either to do material good or to acquire reputation. . . .

Mr. Jefferson, it is known, did not in the first instance cordially acquiesce in the new Constitution for the United States; he had many doubts and reserves. He left this country before we had experienced the imbecilities of the former.

In France, he saw government only on the side of its abuses. He drank freely of the French philosophy, in religion, in science, in politics. He came from France in the moment of a fermentation, which he had a share in exciting, and in the passions and feelings of which he shared both from temperament and situation. He came here probably with a too partial idea of his own powers; and with the expectation of a greater share in the direction of our councils than he has in reality enjoyed. I am not sure that he had not peculiarly marked out for himself the department of the finances.

He came, electrified with attachment to France, and with the project of knitting together the two countries in the closest political bands.

Mr. Madison had always entertained an exalted opinion of the talents, knowledge, and virtues of Mr. Jefferson. The sentiment was probably reciprocal. A close correspondence subsisted between them during the time of Mr. Jefferson's absence from the country. A close intimacy arose upon his return. . . .

Another circumstance has contributed to widening the breach. 'Tis evident, beyond a question, from every movement, that Mr. Jefferson aims with ardent desire at the Presidential chair. This, too, is an important object of the party-politics. It is supposed, from the nature of my former personal and political connections, that I may favor some other candidate more than Mr. Jefferson, when the question shall occur by the retreat of the present gentleman. My influence, therefore, with the community becomes a thing, on ambitious and personal grounds, to be resisted and destroyed. . . .

A word on another point. I am told that serious apprehensions are disseminated in your State as to the existence of a monarchical party meditating the destruction of State and republican government. If it is possible that so absurd an idea can gain ground, it is necessary that it should be combated. I assure you, on my private faith and honor as a man, that there is not, in my judgment, a shadow of foundation for it. A very small number of men indeed may entertain theories less republican than Mr. Jefferson and Mr. Madison, but I am persuaded there is not a man among them who would not regard as both criminal and visionary any attempt to subvert the republican system of the country. Most of these men rather fear that it may not justify itself by its fruits, than feel a predilection for a different form; and their fears are not diminished by the factious and fanatical politics which they find prevailing among a certain set of gentlemen and threatening to disturb the tranquillity and order of the government.

As to the destruction of State governments, the great and real anxiety is to be able to preserve the national from the too potent and counteracting influence of those governments. As to my own political creed, I give it to you with the utmost sincerity. I am affectionately attached to the republican theory. I desire above all things to see the equality of political rights, exclusive of all hereditary distinction, firmly established by a practical demonstration of its being consistent with the order and happiness of society. As to State governments, the prevailing bias of my judgment is that if they can be circumscribed within bounds, consistent with the preservation of the national government, they will prove useful and salutary. . . .

I said that I was affectionately attached to the republican theory. This is the real language of my heart, which I open to you in the sincerity of friendship; and I add that I have strong hopes of the success of that

theory; but, in candor, I ought also to add that I am far from being without doubts. I consider its success as yet a problem. It is yet to be determined by experience whether it be consistent with that stability and order in government which are essential to public strength and private security and happiness.

On the whole, the only enemy which Republicanism has to fear in this country is in the spirit of faction and anarchy. If this will not permit the ends of government to be attained under it, if it engenders disorders in the community, all regular and orderly minds will wish for a change, and the demagogues who have produced the disorder will make it for their own aggrandizement. This is the old story. If I were disposed to promote monarchy and overthrow State governments, I would mount the hobby-horse of popularity; I would cry out "usurpation," "danger to liberty," etc., etc.; I would endeavor to prostrate the national government, raise a ferment, and then "ride in the whirlwind, and direct the storm." That there are men acting with Jefferson and Madison who have this in view, I verily believe; I could lay my finger on some of them. That Madison does not mean it, I also verily believe; and I rather believe the same of Jefferson, but I read him upon the whole thus: "A man of profound ambition and violent passions." . . .

22. *For Washington's Second Term*

To Washington

Philadelphia, July 30, 1792

Sir:

I received the most sincere pleasure at finding in our late conversation, that there was some relaxation in the disposition you had before discovered to decline a re-election. Since your departure, I have left no opportunity of sounding the opinions of persons, whose opinions were worth knowing on these two points. 1st. The effect of your declining, upon the public affairs, and upon your own reputation. 2dly. The effect of your continuing, in reference to the declarations you have made of your disinclination to public life; and I can truly say that I have not found the least difference of sentiment on either point. The impression is uniform, that your declining would be to be deplored as the greatest evil that could befall the country at the present juncture, and as critically hazardous to your own reputation; that your continuance will be justified in the mind of every friend to his country, by the evident necessity for it. 'T is clear, says every one with whom I have conversed, that the affairs of the national government are not yet firmly established—that its enemies, gen-

erally speaking, are as inveterate as ever—that their enmity has been sharpened by its success, and by all the resentments which flow from disappointed predictions and mortified vanity—that a general and strenuous effort is making in every State to place the administration of it in the hands of its enemies, as if they were its safest guardians—that the period of the next House of Representatives is likely to prove the crisis of its permanent character—that if you continue in office nothing materially mischievous is to be apprehended, if you quit, much is to be dreaded—that the same motives which induced you to accept or originally ought to decide you to continue till matters have assumed a more determined aspect—that indeed it would have been better, as it regards your own character, that you had never consented to come forward, than now to leave the business unfinished and in danger of being undone—that in the event of storms arising, there would be an imputation either of want of foresight or want of firmness—and, in fine, that on public and personal accounts, on patriotic and prudential considerations, the clear path to be pursued by you will be, again to obey the voice of your country, which, it is not doubted, will be as earnest and as unanimous as ever. . . .

I trust, sir, and I pray God, that you will determine to make a further sacrifice of your tranquillity and happiness to the public good. I trust that it need not continue above a year or two more; and I think that it will be more eligible to retire from office before the expiration of a term of election, than to decline a re-election. . . .

23. *On the Internal Situation, 1799: "Signs of a Gangrene Begun and Progressive"*

To Jonathan Dayton

1799

An accurate view of the internal situation of the United States presents many discouraging reflections to the enlightened friends of our government and country. Notwithstanding the unexampled success of our public measures at home and abroad—notwithstanding the instructive comments afforded by the disastrous and disgusting scenes of the French Revolution—public opinion has not been ameliorated; sentiments dangerous to social happiness have not been diminished; on the contrary, there are symptoms which warrant the apprehension that among the most numerous class of citizens, errors of a very pernicious tendency have not only preserved but have extended their empire. Though some thing may have been gained on the side of men of information and property, more has

probably been lost on that of persons of a different description. An extraordinary exertion of the friends of government, aided by circumstances of momentary impression, gave, in the last election for members of Congress, a more favorable countenance to some States than they had before worn; yet it is the belief of well-informed men that no real or desirable change has been wrought in those States. On the other hand, it is admitted by close observers that some of the parts of the Union which, in times past, have been the soundest, have of late exhibited signs of a gangrene begun and progressive.

It is likewise apparent that opposition to the government has acquired more system than formerly, is bolder in the avowal of its designs, less solicitous than it was to discriminate between the Constitution and the administration, and more open and more enterprising in its projects. The late attempt of Virginia and Kentucky to unite the State Legislatures in a direct resistance to certain laws of the Union can be considered in no other light than as an attempt to change the government.

It is stated in addition that the opposition party in Virginia, the headquarters of the faction, have followed up the hostile declarations which are to be found in the resolutions of their General Assembly by an actual preparation of the means of supporting them by force, that they have taken measures to put their militia on a more efficient footing—are preparing considerable arsenals and magazines, and (which is an unequivocal proof how much they are in earnest) have gone so far as to lay new taxes on their citizens. Amidst such serious indications of hostility, the safety and the duty of the supporters of the government call upon them to adopt vigorous measures of counteraction. It will be wise in them to act upon the hypothesis that the opposers of the government are resolved, if it shall be practicable, to make its existence a question of force. Possessing, as they now do, all the constitutional powers, it will be an unpardonable mistake on their part if they do not exert them to surround the Constitution with more ramparts and to disconcert the schemes of its enemies.

The measures proper to be adopted may be classed under heads.

FIRST.—Establishments which will extend the influence and promote the popularity of the government. Under this head three important expedients occur. *First.* The extension of the judiciary system. *Second.* The improvement of the great communications, as well interiorly as coastwise, by turnpike roads. *Third.* The institution of a society with funds to be employed in premiums for new inventions, discoveries, and improvements in agriculture and in the arts.

The extension of the judiciary system ought to embrace two objects: one, the subdivision of each State into small districts (suppose Connecticut into four, and so on in proportion), assigning to each a judge with a moderate salary; the other, the appointment in each county of conservators or justices of the peace, with only ministerial functions, and with no other compensation than fees for the services they shall perform. This

measure is necessary to give efficacy to the laws, the execution of which is obstructed by the want of similar organs and by the indisposition of the local magistrates in some States. The Constitution requires that *judges* shall have fixed salaries; but this does not apply to mere justices of the peace without judicial powers. Both those descriptions of persons are essential, as well to the energetic execution of the laws as to the purposes of salutary patronage.

The thing, no doubt, would be a subject of clamor, but it would carry with it its own antidote, and when once established, would bring a very powerful support to the government.

The improvement of the roads would be a measure universally popular. None can be more so. For this purpose a regular plan should be adopted, co-extensive with the Union, to be successively executed, and a fund should be appropriated sufficient for the basis of a loan of a million of dollars. The revenue of the post-office naturally offers itself. The future revenue from tolls would more than reimburse the expense, and public utility would be promoted in every direction. The institution of a society, with the aid of proper funds, to encourage agriculture and the arts, besides being productive of general advantage, will speak powerfully to the feelings and interests of those classes of men to whom the benefits derived from the government have been heretofore the least manifest.

SECOND.—Provision for augmenting the means and consolidating the strength of the government. A million of dollars may without difficulty be added to the revenue, by increasing the rates of some existing indirect taxes, and by the addition of some new items of a similar character.

The direct taxes ought neither to be increased nor diminished. Our naval force ought to be completed to six ships of the line, twelve frigates, and twenty-four sloops of war. More at this juncture would be disproportioned to our resources, less would be inadequate to the ends to be accomplished. Our military force should, for the present, be kept upon its actual footing; making provision for a re-enlistment of the men for five years in the event of a settlement of differences with France,—with this condition, that in case of peace between Great Britain, France, and Spain, the United States being then also at peace, all the privates of the twelve additional regiments of infantry, and of the regiment of dragoons, not exceeding twenty to a company, shall be disbanded. The corps of artillerists may be left to retain the numbers which it shall happen to have, but without being recruited until the number of officers and privates shall fall below the standard of the infantry and dragoons. A power ought to be given to the President to augment the four old regiments to their war establishment.

The laws respecting volunteer companies, and the *eventual army*, should be rendered permanent, and the Executive should proceed without delay to organize the latter. Some modifications of the discretion of the President will, however, be proper in a permanent law. And it will be

a great improvement of the plan, if it shall be thought expedient to allow the enlistment, for the purpose of instruction, of a corps of sergeants equal to the number requisite for the eventual army. The institution of a military academy will be an auxiliary of great importance. Manufactories of every article, the woollen parts of clothing included, which are essential to the supply of the army, ought to be established.

THIRD.—Arrangements for confirming and enlarging the legal powers of the government. There are several temporary laws which, in this view, ought to be rendered permanent, particularly that which authorizes the calling out of the militia to suppress unlawful combinations and insurrections.

An article ought to be proposed, to be added to the Constitution, for empowering Congress to open canals in all cases in which it may be necessary to conduct them through the territory of two or more States, or through the territory of a State and that of the United States. The power is very desirable for the purpose of improving the prodigious facilities for inland navigation with which nature has favored this country. It will also assist commerce and agriculture, by rendering the transportation of commodities more cheap and expeditious. It will tend to secure the connection, by facilitating the communication between distant portions of the Union, and it will be a useful source of influence to the government. Happy would it be if a clause could be added to the Constitution, enabling Congress, on the application of any considerable portion of a State, containing not less than a hundred thousand persons, to erect it into a separate State, on the condition of fixing the quota of contributions which it shall make toward antecedent debts, if any there shall be, reserving to Congress the authority to levy within such States, the taxes necessary to the payment of such quota, in case of neglect on the part of the State. *The subdivision of the great States is indispensable to the security of the general government, and with it of the Union.*

Great States will always feel a rivalship with the common head; will often be supposed to machinate against it, and in certain situations will be able to do it with decisive effect. The subdivision of such States ought to be a cardinal point in the federal policy, and small States are doubtless best adapted to the purposes of local regulation and to the preservation of the republican spirit. This suggestion, however, is merely thrown out for consideration. It is feared that it would be inexpedient and even dangerous to propose, *at this time,* an amendment of the kind.

FOURTH.—Laws for restraining and punishing incendiary and seditious practices. It will be useful to declare that all such writings, etc., which at common law are libels, if levelled against any officer whatsoever of the United States, shall be cognizable in the courts of the United States. To preserve confidence in the officers of the general government, by preserving their reputations from malicious and unfounded slanders, is essential to enable them to fulfil the ends of their appointment. It is, therefore, both

constitutional and politic to place their reputations under the guardianship of the courts of the United States. They ought not to be left to the cold and reluctant protection of State courts, always temporizing, and sometimes disaffected. But what avail laws which are not executed? Renegade aliens conduct more than one of the most incendiary presses in the United States—and yet, in open contempt and defiance of the laws, they are permitted to continue their destructive labors. Why are they not sent away? Are laws of this kind passed merely to excite odium and remain a dead letter? Vigor in the executive is at least as necessary as in the legislative branch. If the President requires to be stimulated, those who can approach him ought to do it.

24. "The Government ... Ought to Appear Like a Hercules"

To James McHenry

(*Private*)

New York, March 18, 1799.

Beware, my dear sir, of magnifying a riot into an insurrection, by employing, in the first instance, an inadequate force. 'T is better far to err on the other side.

Whenever the government appears in arms, it ought to appear like a *Hercules,* and inspire respect by the display of strength. The consideration of expense is of no moment compared with the advantages of energy. 'T is true this is always a relative question, but 't is always important to make no mistake. I only offer a *principle* and a *caution.*

25. On Adams and the Federal Party

To Theodore Sedgwick

New York, May 10, 1800

... He is, I am persuaded, much mistaken as to the opinion entertained of Mr. Adams by the federal party. Were I to determine from my own observation, I should say *most* of the most *influential men* of that party consider him as a very *unfit* and *incapable* character.

For my individual part my mind is made up. I will never more be responsible for him by my direct support, even though the consequence should be the election of *Jefferson*.

If we must have an *enemy* at the head of the government, let it be one whom we can oppose, and for whom we are not responsible, who will not involve our party in the disgrace of his foolish and bad measures. Under *Adams,* as under *Jefferson,* the government will sink. The party in the hands of whose chief it shall sink will sink with it, and the advantage will all be on the side of his adversaries.

'T is a notable expedient for keeping the federal party together, to have at the head of it a man who hates and is despised by those men of it who, in time past, have been its most efficient supporters. If the cause is to be sacrificed to a weak and perverse man, I withdraw from the party and act upon my own ground—never certainly against my principles, but in pursuance of them in my own way. I am mistaken if others do not do the same. . . .

26. *On Jefferson and Burr*

To James A. Bayard

New York, January 16, 1801

. . . I admit that his [Jefferson's] politics are tinctured with fanaticism; that he is too much in earnest in his democracy; that he has been a mischievous enemy to the principal measures of our past administration; that he is crafty and persevering in his objects; that he is not scrupulous about the means of success, nor very mindful of truth, and that he is a contemptible hypocrite. But it is not true, as is alleged, that he is an enemy to the power of the Executive, or that he is for confounding all the powers in the House of Representatives. It is a fact which I have frequently mentioned, that, while we were in the administration together, he was generally for a large construction of the Executive authority and not backward to act upon it in cases which coincided with his views. Let it be added that in his theoretic ideas he has considered as improper the participations of the Senate in the Executive authority. I have more than once made the reflection that, viewing himself as the reversioner, he was solicitous to come into the possession of a good estate. Nor is it true that Jefferson is zealot enough to do any thing in pursuance of his principles which will contravene his popularity or his interest. He is as likely as any man I know to temporize—to calculate what will be likely to promote his own reputation and advantage; and the probable result of such a temper

is the preservation of systems, though originally opposed, which, being once established, could not be overturned without danger to the person who did it. To my mind a true estimate of Mr. Jefferson's character warrants the expectation of a temporizing rather than a violent system. That Jefferson has manifested a culpable predilection for France is certainly true; but I think it a question whether it did not proceed quite as much from her *popularity* among us as from sentiment, and, in proportion as that popularity is diminished, his zeal will cool. Add to this that there is no fair reason to suppose him capable of being corrupted, which is a security that he will not go beyond certain limits. It is not at all improbable that under the change of circumstances Jefferson's Gallicism has considerably abated.

As to Burr these things are admitted, and indeed cannot be denied, that he is a man of *extreme* and *irregular* ambition; that he is *selfish* to a degree which excludes all social affections, and that he is decidedly *profligate*. . . .

The truth is, that Burr is a man of a very subtle imagination, and a mind of this make is rarely free from ingenious whimsies. Yet I admit that he has no fixed theory, and that his peculiar notions will easily give way to his interest. But is it a recommendation to have *no theory?* Can that man be a systematic or able statesman who has none? I believe not. *No general principles* will hardly work much better than erroneous ones. . . .

27. *"Mine Is an Odd Destiny"*

To Gouveneur Morris

New York, February 27, 1802

. . . Mine is an odd destiny. Perhaps no man in the United States has sacrificed or done more for the present Constitution than myself; and contrary to all my anticipations of its fate, as you know from the very beginning, I am still laboring to prop the frail and worthless fabric. Yet I have the murmurs of its friends no less than the curses of its foes for my reward. What can I do better than withdraw from the scene? Every day proves to me more and more, that this American world was not made for me. . . .

You, friend Morris, are by *birth* a native of this country, but by *genius* an exotic. You mistake, if you fancy that you are more of a favorite than myself, or that you are in any sort upon a theatre suited to you.

28. *For the "Christian Constitutional Society"*

To James A. Bayard

New York, April 1802

... Nothing is more fallacious than to expect to produce any valuable or permanent results in political projects by relying merely on the reason of men. Men are rather reasoning than reasonable animals, for the most part governed by the impulse of passion. This is a truth well understood by our adversaries, who have practised upon it with no small benefit to their cause; for at the very moment they are eulogizing the reason of men, and professing to appeal only to that faculty, they are courting the strongest and most active passion of the human heart, *vanity!* It is no less true, that the Federalists seem not to have attended to the fact sufficiently; and that they erred in relying so much on the rectitude and utility of their measures as to have neglected the cultivation of popular favor, by fair and justifiable expedients. The observation has been repeatedly made by me to individuals with whom I particularly conversed, and expedients suggested for gaining good will, which were never adopted. Unluckily, however, for us, in the competition for the passions of the people, our opponents have great advantages over us; for the plain reason that the vicious are far more active than the good passions; and that, to win the former to our side, we must renounce our principles and our objects, and unite in corrupting public opinion till it becomes fit for nothing but mischief. Yet, unless we can contrive to take hold of, and carry along with us some strong feelings of the mind, we shall in vain calculate upon any substantial or durable results. Whatever plan we may adopt, to be successful, must be founded on the truth of this proposition. And perhaps it is not very easy for us to give it full effects; especially not without some deviations from what, on other occasions, we have maintained to be right. But in determining upon the propriety of the deviations, we must consider whether it be possible for us to succeed, without, in some degree, employing the weapons which have been employed against us, and whether the actual state and future prospect of things be not such as to justify the reciprocal use of them. I need not tell you that I do not mean to countenance the imitation of things intrinsically unworthy, but only of such as may be denominated irregular; such as, in a sound and stable order of things, ought not to exist. Neither are you to infer that any revolutionary result is contemplated. In my opinion, the present Constitution is the standard to which we are to cling. Under its banners, *bona fide*, must we combat our political foes, rejecting all changes but through the channel itself provides for amendments. By these general views of the subject

have my reflections been guided. I now offer you the outline of the plan which they have suggested. Let an association be formed to be denominated "The Christian Constitutional Society." Its objects to be:

1st. The support of the Christian religion.

2d. The support of the Constitution of the United States. . . .

29. *A Disappointed Politician*

To General Charles Cotesworth Pinckney

Grange (New York), Dec. 29, 1802.

My Dear Sir:

A garden, you know, is a very useful refuge of a disappointed politician. Accordingly, I have purchased a few acres about nine miles from town, have built a house, and am cultivating a garden. The *melons* in your country are very fine. Will you have the goodness to send me some seed, both of the water and musk melons? My daughter adds another request, which is for three or four of your paroquets. She is very fond of birds. If there be any thing in this quarter the sending of which can give you pleasure, you have only to name them. As *farmers,* a new source of sympathy has arisen between us, and I am pleased with every thing in which our likings and tastes can be approximated. Amidst the triumphant reign of democracy, do you retain sufficient interest in public affairs to feel any curiosity about what is going on? In my opinion, the follies and vices of the administration have as yet made no material impression to their disadvantage. On the contrary, I think the malady is rather progressive than upon the decline in our Northern quarter. The last *lullaby* message, instead of inspiring contempt, attracts praise. Mankind are forever destined to be the dupes of bold and cunning imposture. But a difficult knot has been twisted by the incidents of the cession of Louisiana, and the interruption of the deposit of New Orleans. You have seen the soft turn given to this in the message. Yet we are told that the President, in conversation is very stout. The great embarrassment must be how to carry on the war without taxes. The pretty scheme of substituting economy to taxation will not do here. And a war would be a terrible comment upon the abandonment of the internal revenue. Yet how is popularity to be preserved with the Western partisans if their interests are tamely sacrificed? Will the artifice be for the chief to hold a bold language, and the subalterns to act a feeble part? Time must explain. You know my general theory as to our Western affairs. I have always held that the *unity of our empire* and the best interests of our nation require that we shall annex to the United States all the territory east of the Mississippi, New Orleans included. Of course I infer that, in an emergency like the present, energy is wisdom.

30. *"There Is Some Fault in Ourselves"*

New York, April 12, 1804

. . . 'T is by practice and perseverance that we can expect to vanquish difficulties, and better an unpleasant condition.

Arraign not the dispensations of Providence, they must be founded in wisdom and goodness; and when they do not suit us, it must be because there is some fault in ourselves which deserves chastisement; or because there is a kind intent, to correct in us some vice or failing, of which, perhaps, we may not be conscious; or because the general plan requires that we should suffer partial ill.

In this situation it is our duty to cultivate resignation, and even humility, bearing in mind, in the language of the poet, "that it was pride which lost the blest abodes."

31. *"Our Real Disease . . . Is Democracy"*

To Theodore Sedgwick

New York, July 10, 1804

. . . I will here express but one sentiment, which is, that dismemberment of our empire will be a clear sacrifice of great positive advantages without any counterbalancing good, administering no relief to our real disease, which is *democracy*, the poison of which, by a subdivision, will only be the more concentrated in each part, and consequently the more virulent. . . .

Other Writings

32. *A Full Vindication of the Measures of the Congress*

New-York [December 15] 1774

Friends and Countrymen,

It was hardly to be expected that any man could be so presumptuous, as openly to controvert the equity, wisdom, and authority of the measures, adopted by the congress: an assembly truly respectable on every account! Whether we consider the characters of the men, who composed it; the number, and dignity of their constituents, or the important ends for which they were appointed. But, however improbable such a degree of presumption might have seemed, we find there are some, in whom it exists. Attempts are daily making to diminish the influence of their decisions, and prevent the salutary effects, intended by them. The impotence of such insidious efforts is evident from the general indignation they are treated with; so that no material ill-consequences can be dreaded from them. But lest they should have a tendency to mislead, and prejudice the minds of a few; it cannot be deemed altogether useless to bestow some notice upon them.

And first, let me ask these restless spirits, whence arises that violent antipathy they seem to entertain, not only to the natural rights of mankind; but to common sense and common modesty. That they are enemies to the natural rights of mankind is manifest, because they wish to see one part of their species enslaved by another. That they have an invincible aversion to common sense is apparent in many respects: They endeavour to persuade us, that the absolute sovereignty of parliament does not imply our absolute slavery; that it is a Christian duty to submit to be plundered of all we have, merely because some of our fellow-subjects are wicked enough to require it of us, that slavery, so far from being a great evil, is a great blessing; and even, that our contest with Britain is founded entirely upon the petty duty of 3 pence per pound on East India tea; whereas the whole world knows, it is built upon this interesting question, whether the inhabitants of Great-Britain have a right to dispose of the lives and properties of the inhabitants of America, or not? And lastly, that

these men have discarded all pretension to common modesty, is clear from hence, first, because they, in the plainest terms, call an august body of men, famed for their patriotism and abilities, fools or knaves, and of course the people whom they represented cannot be exempt from the same opprobrious appellations; and secondly, because they set themselves up as standards of wisdom and probity, by contradicting and censuring the public voice in favour of those men. . . .

The only distinction between freedom and slavery consists in this: In the former state, a man is governed by the laws to which he has given his consent, either in person, or by his representative: In the latter, he is governed by the will of another. In the one case his life and property are his own, in the other, they depend upon the pleasure of a master. It is easy to discern which of these two states is preferable. No man in his senses can hesitate in choosing to be free, rather than a slave.

That Americans are intitled to freedom, is incontestible upon every rational principle. All men have one common original: they participate in one common nature, and consequently have one common right. No reason can be assigned why one man should exercise any power, or pre-eminence over his fellow creatures more than another; unless they have voluntarily vested him with it. Since then, Americans have not by any act of their's impowered the British Parliament to make laws for them, it follows they can have no just authority to do it.

Besides the clear voice of natural justice in this respect, the fundamental principles of the English constitution are in our favour. It has been repeatedly demonstrated, that the idea of legislation, or taxation, when the subject is not represented, is inconsistent with *that*. Nor is this all, our charters, the express conditions on which our progenitors relinquished their native countries, and came to settle in this, preclude every claim of ruling and taxing us without our assent.

Every subterfuge that sophistry has been able to invent, to evade or obscure this truth, has been refuted by the most conclusive reasonings; so that we may pronounce it a matter of undeniable certainty, that the pretensions of Parliament are contradictory to the law of nature, subversive of the British constitution, and destructive of the faith of the most solemn compacts.

What then is the subject of our controversy with the mother country? It is this, whether we shall preserve that security to our lives and properties, which the law of nature, the genius of the British constitution, and our charters afford us; or whether we shall resign them into the hands of the British House of Commons, which is no more privileged to dispose of them than the Grand Mogul? . . .

Are you willing then to be slaves without a single struggle? Will you give up your freedom, or, which is the same thing, will you resign all security for your life and property, rather than endure some small present inconveniences? Will you not take a little trouble to transmit the advan-

tages you now possess to those, who are to come after you? I cannot doubt it. I would not suspect you of so much baseness and stupidity, as to suppose the contrary.

Pray who can tell me why a farmer in America, is not as honest and good a man, as a farmer in England? or why has not the one as good a right to what he has earned by his labour, as the other? I can't, for my life, see any distinction between them. And yet it seems the English farmers are to be governed and taxed by their own Assembly, or Parliament; and the American farmers are not. The former are to choose their own Representatives from among themselves, whose interest is connected with theirs, and over whom they have proper controul. The latter are to be loaded with taxes by men three thousand miles off; by men, who have no interest, or connexions among them; but whose interest it will be to burden them as much as possible; and over whom they cannot have the least restraint. How do you like this doctrine my friends? Are you ready to own the English farmers for your masters? Are you willing to acknowledge their right to take your property from you, and when they please? I know you scorn the thought. You had rather die, than submit to it. . . .

33. *The Farmer Refuted*

New York, February 5, 1775

. . . I shall, henceforth, begin to make some allowance for that enmity, you have discovered to the *natural rights* of mankind. For, though ignorance of them in this enlightened age cannot be admitted, as a sufficient excuse for you; yet, it ought, in some measure, to extenuate your guilt. If you will follow my advice, there still may be hopes of your reformation. Apply yourself, without delay, to the study of the law of nature. I would recommend to your perusal, Grotius Puffendorf, Locke, Montesquieu, and Burlemaqui. I might mention other excellent writers on this subject; but if you attend, diligently, to these, you will not require any others.

There is so strong a similitude between your political principles and those maintained by Mr. Hobbs, that, in judging from them, a person might very easily *mistake* you for a disciple of his. His opinion was, exactly, coincident with yours, relative to man in a state of nature. He held, as you do, that he was then, perfectly free from all restraint of *law* and *government*. Moral obligation, according to him, is derived from the introduction of civil society; and there is no virtue, but what is purely artificial, the mere contrivance of politicians, for the maintenance of social intercourse. But the reason he ran into this absurd and impious doctrine, was, that he disbelieved the existence of an intelligent superin-

tending principle, who is the governor, and will be the final judge of the universe.

As you, sometimes, swear *by him that made you,* I conclude, your sentiment does not correspond with his, in that which is the basis of the doctrine, you both agree in; and this makes it impossible to imagine whence this congruity between you arises. To grant, that there is a supreme intelligence, who rules the world, and has established laws to regulate the actions of his creatures; and, still, to assert, that man, in a state of nature, may be considered as perfectly free from all restraints of *law* and *government,* appear to a common understanding, altogether irreconcileable.

Good and wise men, in all ages, have embraced a very dissimilar theory. They have supposed, that the deity, from the relations, we stand in, to himself and to each other, has constituted an eternal and immutable law, which is, indispensibly, obligatory upon all mankind, prior to any human institution whatever. . . .

Upon this law, depend the natural rights of mankind, the supreme being gave existence to man, together with the means of preserving and beatifying that existence. He endowed him with rational faculties, by the help of which, to discern and pursue such things, as were consistent with his duty and interest, and invested him with an inviolable right to personal liberty, and personal safety.

Hence, in a state of nature, no man had any *moral* power to deprive another of his life, limbs, property or liberty; nor the least authority to command, or exact obedience from him; except that which arose from the ties of consanguinity.

Hence also, the origin of all civil government, justly established, must be a voluntary compact, between the rulers and the ruled; and must be liable to such limitations, as are necessary for the security of the *absolute rights* of the latter; for what original title can any man or set of men have, to govern others, except their own consent? To usurp dominion over a people, in their own despite, or to grasp at a more extensive power than they are willing to entrust, is to violate that law of nature, which gives every man a right to his personal liberty; and can, therefore, confer no obligation to obedience. . . .

. . . If we examine the pretensions of parliament . . . we shall, presently detect their injustice. First, they are subversive of our natural liberty, because an authority is assumed over us, which we by no means assent to. And secondly, they divest us of that moral security, for our lives and properties, which we are intitled to, and which it is the primary end of society to bestow. For such security can never exist, while we have no part in making the laws, that are to bind us; and while it may be the interest of our uncontroled legislators to oppress us as much as possible. . . .

It is the unalienable birth-right of every Englishman, who can be con-

sidered as *a free agent* to participate in framing the laws which are to bind him, either as to his life or property. But, as many inconveniences would result from the exercise of this right, in person, it is appointed by the constitution, that he shall delegate it to another. Hence he is to give his vote in the election of some person he chuses to confide in as his representative. This right no power on earth can divest him of. It was enjoyed by his ancestors time immemorial; recognized and established by Magna Charta, and is essential to the existence of the constitution. Abolish this privilege, and the house of commons is annihilated.

But what was the use and design of this privilege? To secure his life and property from the attacks of exorbitant power. And in what manner is this done? By giving him the election of those, who are to have the disposal and regulation of them, and whose interest is in every respect connected with his.

The representative in this case is bound by every possible tie to consult the advantage of his constituent. Gratitude for the high and honourable trust reposed in him demands a return of attention and regard to the advancement of his happiness. Self-interest, that most powerful incentive of human actions, points and attracts towards the same object.

The duration of his trust is not perpetual; but must expire in a few years, and if he is desirous of the future favour of his constituents, he must not abuse the present instance of it; but must pursue the end, for which he enjoys it; otherwise he forfeits it, and defeats his own purpose. Besides, if he consent to any laws hurtful to his constituent, he is bound by the same, and must partake in the disadvantage of them. His friends, relations, children, all whose ease and comfort are dear to him, will be in a like predicament. And should he concur in any flagrant acts of injustice or oppression, he will be within the reach of popular vengeance, and this will restrain him within due bounds.

To crown the whole, at the expiration of a few years, if their representatives have abused their trust, the people have it in their power to change them, and to elect others, who may be more faithful and more attached to their interest.

But what merits still more serious atention is this. There seems to be, already, a jealousy of our dawning splendour. It is looked upon as portentous of aproaching independence. This we have reason to believe is one of the principal incitements to the present rigorous and unconstitutional proceedings against us. And though it may have chiefly originated in the calumnies of designing men, yet it does not entirely depend upon adventitious or partial causes; but is also founded in the circumstances of our country and situation. The boundless extent of territory we possess, the wholesome temperament of our climate, the luxuriance and fertility of our soil, the variety of our products, the rapidity of our population, the industry of our country men and the commodiousness of our ports, naturally lead to a suspicion of independence, and would always have an

influence pernicious to us. Jealousy is a predominant passion of human nature, and is a source of the greatest evils. Whenever it takes place between rulers and their subjects, it proves the bane of civil society.

The experience of past ages may inform us, that when the circumstances of a people render them distressed, their rulers generally recur to severe, cruel and oppressive measures. Instead of endeavouring to establish their authority in the *affection* of their subjects, they think they have no security but in their *fear*. They do not aim at gaining their fidelity and obedience, by making them flourishing, prosperous and happy; but by rendering them abject and dispirited. They think it necessary to intimidate and awe them, to make every accession to their own power, and to impair the people's as much as possible.

One great engine, to effect this in America, would be a large standing army, maintained out of our own pockets to be at the devotion of our oppressors. This would be introduced under pretence of defending us; but in fact to make our bondage and misery complete.

We might soon expect the martial law, universally prevalent to the abolition of trials by juries, the *Habeas Corpus* act, and every other bulwark of personal safety, in order to overawe the honest assertors of their country's cause. A numerous train of *court dependents* would be created and supported at our expence. The value of all our possessions, by a complication of extorsive methods, would be gradually depreciated, till it became a mere shadow.

This will be called too high-wrought a picture, a phantom of my own deluded imagination. The highest eulogies will be lavished on the wisdom and justice of the British nation. But deplorable is the condition of that people who have nothing else than the wisdom and justice of another to depend upon. . . .

Extraordinary emergencies, require extraordinary expedients. The best mode of opposition was that in which there might be an union of councils. This was necessary to ascertain the boundaries of our rights; and to give weight and dignity to our measures, both in Britain and America. A Congress was accordingly proposed, and universally agreed to.

You, Sir, triumph in the supposed *illegality* of this body; but, granting your supposition were true, it would be a matter of no real importance. When the first principles of civil society are violated, and the rights of a whole people are invaded, the common forms of municipal law are not to be regarded. Men may then betake themselves to the law of nature; and, if they but conform their actions, to that standard, all cavils against them, betray either ignorance or dishonesty. There are some events in society, to which human laws cannot extend; but when applied to them lose all their force and efficacy. In short, when human laws contradict or discountenance the means, which are necessary to preserve the essential rights of any society, they defeat the proper end of all laws, and so become null and void. . . .

34. *The Continentalist*

[*Fishkill, New York, April 18, 1782*]

The vesting Congress with the power of regulating trade ought to have been a principal object of the confederation for a variety of reasons. It is as necessary for the purposes of commerce as of revenue. There are some, who maintain, that trade will regulate itself, and is not to be bene- fitted by the encouragements, or restraints of government. Such persons will imagine, that there is no need of a common directing power. This is one of those wild speculative paradoxes, which have grown into credit among us, contrary to the uniform practice and sense of the most en- lightened nations. Contradicted by the numerous institutions and laws, that exist every where for the benefit of trade, by the pains taken to culti- vate particular branches and to discourage others, by the known advan- tages derived from those measures, and by the palpable evils that would attend their discontinuance—it must be rejected by every man ac- quainted with commercial history. Commerce, like other things, has its fixed principles, according to which it must be regulated; if these are understood and observed, it will be promoted by the attention of govern- ment, if unknown, or violated, it will be injured—but it is the same with every other part of administration.

To preserve the ballance of trade in favour of a nation ought to be a leading aim of its policy. The avarice of individuals may frequently find its account in pursuing channels of traffic prejudicial to that ballance, to which the government may be able to oppose effectual impediments. There may, on the other hand, be a possibility of opening new sources, which, though accompanied with great difficulties in the commencement, would in the event amply reward the trouble and expence of bringing them to perfection. The undertaking may often exceed the influence and capitals of individuals; and may require no small assistance, as well from the revenue, as from the authority of the state.

The contrary opinion, which has grown into a degree of vogue among us, has originated in the injudicious attempts made at different times to effect a REGULATION of PRICES. It became a cant phrase among the opposers of these attempts, that TRADE MUST REGULATE ITSELF; by which at first was only meant that it had its fundamental laws, agree- able to which its general operations must be directed; and that any violent attempts in opposition to these would commonly miscarry. In this sense the maxim was reasonable; but it has since been extended to mili- tate against all interference by the sovereign; an extreme as little recon- cileable with experience, or common sense, as the practice it was first framed to discredit. . . .

35. *Letter from Phocion in Defense of Loyalists' Rights*

New York, April, 1784

. . . . To place this matter in a still clearer light, let it be supposed, that instead of the mode of indictment and trial by jury, the legislature was to declare that every citizen who did not swear he had never adhered to the King of Great-Britain, should incur all the penalties which our treason laws prescribe. Would this not be a palpable evasion of the treaty, and a direct infringement of the constitution? The principle is the same in both cases, with only this difference in the consequences; that in the instance already acted upon, the citizen forfeits a part of his rights,—in the one supposed he would forfeit the whole. The degree of punishment is all that distinguishes the cases. In either justly considered, it is substituting a new and arbitrary mode of prosecution to that antient and highly esteemed one, recognized by the laws and the constitution of the state; I mean the trial by jury.

Let us not forget that the constitution declares that trial by jury in all cases in which it has been formerly used, should remain inviolate forever, and that the legislature should at no time, erect any new jurisdiction which should not proceed, according to the course of the common law. Nothing can be more repugnant to the true genius of the common law, than such an inquisition as has been mentioned into the consciences of men.

A share in the sovereignty of the state, which is exercised by the citizens at large, in voting at elections is one of the most important rights of the subject, and in a republic ought to stand foremost in the estimation of the law. It is that right, by which we exist a free people; and it certainly therefore will never be admitted, that less ceremony ought to be used in divesting any citizen of that right, than in depriving him of his property. Such a doctrine would ill suit the principles of the revolution, which taught the inhabitants of this country to risk their lives and fortunes in asserting their *liberty;* or in other words, their *right* to a *share* in the government. That portion of the sovereignty, to which each individual is entitled, can never be too highly prized. It is that for which we have fought and bled; and we should cautiously guard against any precedents, however they may be immediately directed against those we hate, which may in their consequences render our title to this great privilege, precarious. Here we may find the criterion to distinguish the genuine from the pretended whig. The man that would attack that right, in whatever shape, is an enemy to whiggism.

If any oath, with retrospect to past conduct, were to be made the con-

dition, on which individuals, who have resided within the British lines, should hold their estates; we should immediately see, that this proceeding would be tyrannical, and a violation of the treaty, and yet when the same mode is employed to divest that right, which ought to be deemed still more sacred, many of us are so infatuated as to overlook the mischief. . . .

It has been said too, that an oath to determine the qualifications of electors, is an usual precaution in free governments; but we may challenge those who make the assertion, to show that retrospective oaths have ever been administered, requiring electors to swear that they have not been guilty of past offences. In all the violence of party which has at different periods agitated Great Britain, nothing of this kind has ever been adopted; but even where religious fanaticism has given an edge to political opposition, and in an undecided contest for the crown, they have never gone further than to prescribe oaths for testing present dispositions towards the government on general principles, without retrospection to particular instances of past mal-conduct. The practical notions of legal liberty established in that country by a series of time would make such an experiment too odious to be attempted by the government. Wise men have thought that even there, they have carried the business of oaths to an exceptionable length; but we who pretend a purer zeal for liberty, in a decided contest, after a formal renunciation of claims by the adverse party, are for carrying the matter to a still more blameable extreme. . . .

It has been urged, in support of the doctrines under consideration, that every government has a right to take precautions for its own security, and to prescribe the terms on which its rights shall be enjoyed. . . .

In the first formation of a government the society may multiply its precautions as much, and annex as many conditions to the enjoyment of its rights, as it shall judge expedient; but when it has once adopted a constitution, that constitution must be the measure of its discretion, in providing for its own safety, and in prescribing the conditions upon which its privileges are to be enjoyed. If the constitution declares that persons possessing certain qualifications shall be entitled to certain rights, while that constitution remains in force, the government which is the mere creature of the constitution, can divest no citizen, who has the requisite qualifications, of his corresponding rights. . . .

Among the extravagancies with which these prolific times abound, we hear it often said that the constitution being the creature of the people, their sense with respect to any measure, if it even stand in opposition to the constitution, will sanctify and make it right.

Happily, for us, in this country, the position is not to be controverted; that the constitution is the creature of the people; but it does not follow that they are not bound by it, while they suffer it to continue in force; nor does it follow, that the legislature, which is, on the other hand, a

creature of the constitution, can depart from it, on any presumption of the contrary sense of the people.

The constitution is the compact made between the society at large and each individual. The society therefore, cannot without breach of faith and injustice, refuse to any individual, a single advantage which he derives under that compact, no more than one man can refuse to perform his agreement with another. If the community have good reasons for abrogating the old compact, and establishing a new one, it undoubtedly has a right to do it; but until the compact is dissolved with the same solemnity and certainty with which it was made, the society, as well as individuals, are bound by it. . . .

There is a bigotry in politics, as well as in religions, equally pernicious in both. The zealots, of either description, are ignorant of the advantage of a spirit of toleration: It was a long time before the kingdoms of Europe were convinced of the folly of persecution, with respect to those, who were schismatics from the established church. The cry was, these men will be equally the disturbers of the hierarchy and of the state. While some kingdoms were impoverishing and depopulating themselves, by their severities to the non-conformists, their wiser neighbours were reaping the fruits of their folly, and augmenting their own numbers, industry and wealth, by receiving with open arms the persecuted fugitives. Time and experience have taught a different lesson; and there is not an enlightened nation, which does not now acknowledge the force of this truth, that whatever speculative notions of religion may be entertained, men will not on that account, be enemies to a government, that affords them protection and security. The same spirit of toleration in politics, and for the same reasons, has made great progress among mankind, of which the history of most modern revolutions is a proof. Unhappily for this state, there are some among us, who possess too much influence, that have motives of personal ambition and interest to shut their minds against the entrance of that moderation, which the real welfare of the community teaches. . . .

Those, who are at present entrusted with power, in all these infant republics, hold the most sacred deposit that ever was confided to human hands. 'Tis with governments as with individuals, first impressions and early habits give a lasting bias to the temper and character. Our governments hitherto have no habits. How important to the happiness not of America alone, but of mankind, that they should acquire good ones.

If we set out with justice, moderation, liberality, and a scrupulous regard to the constitution, the government will acquire a spirit and tone, productive of permanent blessings to the community. If on the contrary, the public councils are guided by humour, passion and prejudice; if from resentment to individuals, or a dread of partial inconveniences, the constitution is slighted or explained away, upon every frivolous pretext, the future spirit of government will be feeble, distracted and arbitrary. The

rights of the subject will be the sport of every party vicissitude. There will be no settled rule of conduct, but every thing will fluctuate with the alternate prevalency of contending factions.

The world has its eye upon America. The noble struggle we have made in the cause of liberty, has occasioned a kind of revolution in human sentiment. The influence of our example has penetrated the gloomy regions of despotism, and has pointed the way to inquiries, which may shake it to its deepest foundations. Men begin to ask every where, who is this tyrant, that dares to build his greatness on our misery and degradation? What commission has he to sacrifice millions to the wanton appetites of himself and the few minions that surround his throne?

To ripen inquiry into action, it remains for us to justify the revolution by its fruits.

If the consequences prove, that we really have asserted the cause of human happiness, what may not be expected from so illustrious an example? In a greater or less degree, the world will bless and imitate!

But if experience, in this instance, verifies the lesson long taught by the enemies of liberty; that the bulk of mankind are not fit to govern themselves, that they must have a master, and were only made for the rein and the spur: We shall then see the final triumph of despotism over liberty. The advocates of the latter must acknowledge it to be an *ignis fatuus,* and abandon the pursuit. With the greatest advantages for promoting it, that ever a people had, we shall have betrayed the cause of human nature. . . .

36. *Report of a Committee of the New York State Society of the Society of the Cincinnati*

[New York, July 6, 1786]

. . . The alterations they have in view respect, principally, the duration or succession of the Society, and the distinction between Honorary and Regular Members. As to the first, the provision intended to be made appears to them to be expressed in terms not sufficiently explicit, and as far as it may intend an hereditary succession, by right of primogeniture, is liable to this objection, that it refers to birth what ought to belong to merit only, a principle inconsistent with the genius of a Society founded on friendship and patriotism. As to the second, the distinction holds up an odious difference between men who have served their country in one way and those who have served it in another, a difference ill-founded in itself, and improper in a Society where the character of Patriot ought to be an equal title to all its members. . . .

37. New York Assembly. Remarks on an Act for Regulating Elections

January 27, 1787

Mr. Hamilton observed they were going on dangerous ground. The best rule the committee could follow was that held out in the constitution; which it would be safest to adhere to without alteration or addition. If we once depart from this rule, there is no saying where it will end. To-day, a majority of the persons sitting here from a particular mode of thinking disqualify one description of men. A future legislature from a particular mode of thinking in another point, disqualify another set of men. One precedent is the pretext of another, 'till we narrow the ground of qualifications to a degree subversive of the spirit of the constitution. . . .

Let us on our part be cautious how we abridge the freedom of choice allowed them by the constitution or the right of being elected, which every citizen may claim under it.

I hold it to be a maxim which ought to be sacred in our form of government, that no man ought to be deprived of any right or privilege which he enjoys under the constitution; but for some offence proved in due course of law.

To declare qualifications or disqualifications by general descriptions, in legislative acts, would be to invade this important principle. It would be to deprive in the gross all those who had not the requisite qualifications, or who were objects of those disqualifications to that right to a share in the administration of the republic which the constitution gives them, and that without any offence to incur a forfeiture.

As to the objection that the electors might even choose a foreigner to represent them within the latitude of the constitution, the answer is that common sense would not tolerate such a construction. The constitution from the fundamental policy of a republican government must be understood to intend citizens. But the gentleman, (Mr. Jones) has not adverted that the same difficulty would attend the case of electors where he admits there is no power in the legislature to make alterations—the expression there is, every *male inhabitant* possessed of certain property shall vote; but there surely could never be a doubt that such male inhabitant must also be a citizen.

But let us pursue the subject a little further; commerce it will be admitted leads to an increase of individual property, property begets influence. Though a legislature composed as we are, will always take care of the rights of the middling and lower classes, suppose the majority of the legislature to consist at a future day, of wealthy men, what would

hinder them, if the right of innovating on the constitution be admitted, from declaring that no man not worth ten thousand pounds should be eligible to a seat in either house? and would not this introduce a principle of aristocracy fatal to the genius of our present constitution.

In making this observation I cannot be suspected of wishing to increase the jealousy already sufficiently high of property—my situation, prospects and connections forbid the supposition. But I mean to lay honestly before you the dangers to which we expose ourselves by letting in the principle which the clause under consideration rests upon.

I give no opinion on the expediency of the exclusion proposed. I only say, in my opinion, the constitution does not permit it, and I shall be against any qualification or disqualification either of electors or elected, not prescribed by the constitution.

To me it appears that the qualifications of both ought to be fundamental in a republican government; not liable to be varied or added to by the legislature, and that they should for ever remain where the constitution has left them. I see no other safe ground.

It is to be lamented that men to carry some favorite point in which their party or their prejudices are interested, will inconsiderately introduce principle and precedents, which lead to successive innovations destructive of the liberty of the subject and the safety of the government.

For my part, I shall uniformly oppose every innovation not known in the provisions of the constitution. . . .

38. *Speech on a Plan of Government in the Constitutional Convention*

James Madison's Version

June 18, 1787

Mr. Hamilton, had been hitherto silent on the business before the Convention, partly from respect to others whose superior abilities, age & experience rendered him unwilling to bring forward ideas dissimilar to theirs, and partly from his delicate situation with respect to his own State, to whose sentiments as expressed by his Colleagues, he could by no means accede. The crisis however which now marked our affairs, was too serious to permit any scruples whatever to prevail over the duty imposed on every man to contribute his efforts for the public safety & happiness. He was obliged therefore to declare himself unfriendly to both plans. He was particularly opposed to that from N. Jersey, being fully convinced, that no amendment of the Confederation,

leaving the States in possession of their Sovereignty could possibly answer the purpose. On the other hand he confessed he was much discouraged by the amazing extent of Country in expecting the desired blessings from any general sovereignty that could be substituted. As to the powers of the Convention, he thought the doubts started on that subject had arisen from distinctions & reasonings too subtle. A *federal* Govt. he conceived to mean an association of independent Communities into one. Different Confederacies have different powers, and exercise them in different ways. In some instances the powers are exercised over collective bodies; in others over individuals, as in the German Diet—& among ourselves in cases of piracy. Great latitude therefore must be given to the signification of the term. The plan last proposed[1] departs itself from the *federal* idea, as understood by some, since it is to operate eventually on individuals. He agreed moreover with the Honble gentleman from Va. (Mr. R.) that we owed it to our Country, to do on this emergency whatever we should deem essential to its happiness. The States sent us here to provide for the exigences of the Union. To rely on & propose any plan not adequate to these exigences, merely because it was not clearly within our powers, would be to sacrifice the means to the end. It may be said that the *States* can not *ratify* a plan not within the purview of the article of Confederation providing for alterations & amendments. But may not the States themselves in which no constitutional authority equal to this purpose exists in the Legislatures, have had in view a reference to the people at large. In the Senate of N. York, a proviso was moved, that no act of the Convention should be binding until it should be referred to the people & ratified; and the motion was lost by a single voice only, the reason assigned agst. it being, that it might possibly be found an inconvenient shackle.

The great question is what provision shall we make for the happiness of our Country? He would first make a comparative examination of the two plans—prove that there were essential defects in both—and point out such changes as might render a *national one*, efficacious. The great & essential principles necessary for the support of Government are 1. an active & constant interest in supporting it. This principle does not exist in the States in favor of the federal Govt. They have evidently in a high degree, the esprit de corps. They constantly pursue internal interests adverse to those of the whole. They have their particular debts—their particular plans of finance &c. All these when opposed to, invariably prevail over the requisitions & plans of Congress. 2. The love of power. Men love power. The same remarks are applicable to this principle. The States have constantly shewn a disposition rather to regain the powers delegated by them than to part with more, or to give effect to what they had parted with. The ambition of their demagogues is known to hate the controul of

---

[1] The New Jersey Plan.

the Genl. Government. It may be remarked too that the Citizens have not that anxiety to prevent a dissolution of the Genl. Govt. as of the particular Govts. A dissolution of the latter would be fatal; of the former would still leave the purposes of Govt. attainable to a considerable degree. Consider what such a State as Virga. will be in a few years, a few compared with the life of nations. How strongly will it feel its importance & self-sufficiency? 3. An habitual attachment of the people. The whole force of this tie is on the side of the State Govt. Its sovereignty is immediately before the eyes of the people: its protection is immediately enjoyed by them. From its hand distributive justice, and all those acts which familiarize & endear Govt. to a people, are dispensed to them. 4. *Force* by which may be understood a *coertion of laws* or *coertion of arms*. Congs. have not the former except in few cases. In particular States, this coertion is nearly sufficient; tho' he held it in most cases, not entirely so. A certain portion of military force is absolutely necessary in large communities. Mass. is now feeling this necessity & making provision for it. But how can this force be exerted on the States collectively. It is impossible. It amounts to a war between the parties. Foreign powers also will not be idle spectators. They will interpose, the confusion will increase, and a dissolution of the Union will ensue. 5. *influence*. he did not mean corruption, but a dispensation of those regular honors & emoluments, which produce an attachment to the Govt. Almost all the weight of these is on the side of the States; and must continue so as long as the States continue to exist. All the passions then we see, of avarice, ambition, interest, which govern most individuals, and all public bodies, fall into the current of the States, and do not flow in the stream of the Genl. Govt. The former therefore will generally be an overmatch for the Genl. Govt. and render any confederacy, in its very nature precarious. Theory is in this case fully confirmed by experience. The Amphyctionic Council had it would seem ample powers for general purposes. It had in particular the power of fining and using force agst. delinquent members. What was the consequence. Their decrees were mere signals of war. The Phocian war is a striking example of it. Philip at length taking advantage of their disunion, and insinuating himself into their Councils, made himself master of their fortunes. The German Confederacy affords another lesson. The authority of Charlemagne seemed to be as great as could be necessary. The great feudal chiefs however, exercising their local sovereignties, soon felt the spirit & found the means of, encroachments, which reduced the imperial authority to a nominal sovereignty. The Diet has succeeded, which tho' aided by a Prince at its head, of great authority independently of his imperial attributes, is a striking illustration of the weakness of Confederated Governments. Other examples instruct us in the same truth. The Swiss cantons have scarce any Union at all, and have been more than once at war with one another. How then are all these evils to be avoided? only by such a compleat sovereignty in the general

Governmt. as will turn all the strong principles & passions above mentioned on its side. Does the scheme of N. Jersey produce this effect? does it afford any substantial remedy whatever? On the contrary it labors under great defects, and the defect of some of its provisions will destroy the efficacy of others. It gives a direct revenue to Congs. but this will not be sufficient. The balance can only be supplied by requisitions: which experience proves can not be relied on. If States are to deliberate on the mode, they will also deliberate on the object of the supplies, and will grant or not grant as they approve or disapprove of it. The delinquency of one will invite and countenance it in others. Quotas too must in the nature of things be so unequal as to produce the same evil. To what standard will you resort? Land is a fallacious one. Compare Holland with Russia: France or Engd. with other countries of Europe. Pena. with N. Carola. will the relative pecuniary abilities in those instances, correspond with the relative value of land. Take numbers of inhabitants for the rule and make like comparison of different countries, and you will find it to be equally unjust. The different degrees of industry and improvement in different Countries render the first object a precarious measure of wealth. Much depends too on *situation*. Cont. N. Jersey & N. Carolina, not being commercial States & contributing to the wealth of the commercial ones, can never bear quotas assessed by the ordinary rules of proportion. They will & must fail in their duty, their example will be followed, and the Union itself be dissolved. Whence then is the national revenue to be drawn? from Commerce? even from exports which notwithstanding the common opinion are fit objects of moderate taxation, from excise, &c &c. These tho' not equal, are less unequal than quotas. Another destructive ingredient in the plan, is that equality of suffrage which is so much desired by the small States. It is not in human nature that Va. & the large States should consent to it, or if they did that they shd. long abide by it. It shocks too much the ideas of Justice, and every human feeling. Bad principles in a Govt. tho slow are sure in their operation, and will gradually destroy it. A doubt has been raised whether Congs. at present have a right to keep Ships or troops in time of peace. He leans to the negative. Mr. Ps. plan provides no remedy. If the powers proposed were adequate, the organization of Congs. is such that they could never be properly & effectually exercised. The members of Congs. being chosen by the States & subject to recall, represent all the local prejudices. Should the powers be found effectual, they will from time to time be heaped on them, till a tyrannic sway shall be established. The general power whatever be its form if it preserves itself, must swallow up the State powers. Otherwise it will be swallowed up by them. It is agst. all the principles of a good Government to vest the requisite powers in such a body as Congs. Two Sovereignties can not co-exist within the same limits. Giving powers to Congs. must eventuate in a bad Govt. or in no Govt. The plan of N. Jersey therefore will not do. What then is to

be done? Here he was embarrassed. The extent of the Country to be governed, discouraged him. The expence of a general Govt. was also formidable; unless there were such a diminution of expence on the side of the State Govts. as the case would admit. If they were extinguished, he was persuaded that great œconomy might be obtained by substituting a general Govt. He did not mean however to shock the public opinion by proposing such a measure. On the other hand he saw no *other* necessity for declining it. They are not necessary for any of the great purposes of commerce, revenue, or agriculture. Subordinate authorities he was aware would be necessary. There must be district tribunals: corporations for local purposes. But cui bono, the vast & expensive apparatus now appertaining to the States. The only difficulty of a serious nature which occurred to him, was that of drawing representatives from the extremes to the center of the Community. What inducements can be offered that will suffice? The moderate wages for the 1st. branch would only be a bait to little demagogues. Three dollars or thereabouts he supposed would be the utmost. The Senate he feared from a similar cause, would be filled by certain undertakers who wish for particular offices under the Govt. This view of the subject almost led him to despair that a Republican Govt. could be established over so great an extent. He was sensible at the same time that it would be unwise to propose one of any other form. In his private opinion he had no scruple in declaring, supported as he was by the opinions of so many of the wise & good, that the British Govt. was the best in the world: and that he doubted much whether any thing short of it would do in America. He hoped Gentlemen of different opinions would bear with him in this, and begged them to recollect the change of opinion on this subject which had taken place and was still going on. It was once thought that the power of Congs. was amply sufficient to secure the end of their institution. The error was now seen by every one. The members most tenacious of republicanism, he observed, were as loud as any in declaiming agst. the vices of democracy. This progress of the public mind led him to anticipate the time, when others as well as himself would join in the praise bestowed by Mr. Neckar on the British Constitution, namely, that it is the only Govt. in the world "which unites public strength with individual security." In every community where industry is encouraged, there will be a division of it into the few & the many. Hence separate interests will arise. There will be debtors & creditors &c. Give all power to the many, they will oppress the few. Give all power to the few, they will oppress the many. Both therefore ought to have power, that each may defend itself agst. the other. To the want of this check we owe our paper money, instalment laws &c. To the proper adjustment of it the British owe the excellence of their Constitution. Their house of Lords is a most noble institution. Having nothing to hope for by a change, and a sufficient interest by means of their property, in being faithful to the national interest, they form a permanent

barrier agst. every pernicious innovation, whether attempted on the part of the Crown or of the Commons. No temporary Senate will have the firmness eno' to answer the purpose. The Senate (of Maryland) which seems to be so much appealed to, has not yet been sufficiently tried. Had the people been unanimous & eager, in the late appeal to them on the subject of a paper emission they would have yielded to the torrent. Their acquiescing in such an appeal is a proof of it. Gentlemen differ in their opinions concerning the necessary checks, from the different estimates they form of the human passions. They suppose seven years a sufficient period to give the senate an adequate firmness, from not duly considering the amazing violence & turbulence of the democratic spirit. When a great object of Govt. is pursued, which seizes the popular passions, they spread like wild fire, and become irresistable. He appealed to the gentlemen from the N. England States whether experience had not there verified the remark. As to the Executive, it seemed to be admitted that no good one could be established on Republican principles. Was not this giving up the merits of the question: for can there be a good Govt. without a good Executive. The English model was the only good one on this subject. The Hereditary interest of the King was so interwoven with that of the Nation, and his personal emoluments so great, that he was placed above the danger of being corrupted from abroad—and at the same time was both sufficiently independent and sufficiently controuled, to answer the purpose of the institution at home. One of the weak sides of Republics was their being liable to foreign influence & corruption. Men of little character, acquiring great power become easily the tools of intermedling Neibours. Sweeden was a striking instance. The French & English had each their parties during the late Revolution which was effected by the predominant influence of the former. What is the inference from all these observations? That we ought to go as far in order to attain stability and permanency, as republican principles will admit. Let one branch of the Legislature hold their places for life or at least during good behaviour. Let the Executive also be for life. He appealed to the feelings of the members present whether a term of seven years, would induce the sacrifices of private affairs which an acceptance of public trust would require, so as to ensure the services of the best Citizens. On this plan we should have in the Senate a permanent will, a weighty interest, which would answer essential purposes. But is this a Republican Govt., it will be asked? Yes if all the Magistrates are appointed, and vacancies are filled, by the people, or a process of election originating with the people. He was sensible that an Executive constituted as he proposed would have in fact but little of the power and independence that might be necessary. On the other plan of appointing him for 7 years, he thought the Executive ought to have but little power. He would be ambitious, with the means of making creatures; and as the object of his ambition wd. be to *prolong* his power, it is probable that in case of a war, he would avail himself of the emergence,

to evade or refuse a degradation from his place. An Executive for life has not this motive for forgetting his fidelity, and will therefore be a safer depository of power. It will be objected probably, that such an Executive will be an *elective Monarch*, and will give birth to the tumults which characterize that form of Govt. He wd. reply that *Monarch* is an indefinite term. It marks not either the degree or duration of power. If this Executive Magistrate wd. be a monarch for life—the other propd. by the Report from the Comtte of the whole, wd. be a monarch for seven years. The circumstance of being elective was also applicable to both. It had been observed by judicious writers that elective monarchies wd. be the best if they could be guarded agst. the *tumults* excited by the ambition and intrigues of competitors. He was not sure that tumults were an inseparable evil. He rather thought this character of Elective Monarchies had been taken rather from particular cases than from general principles. The election of Roman Emperors was made by the *Army*. In *Poland* the election is made by great rival *princes* with independent power, and ample means, of raising commotions. In the German Empire, the appointment is made by the Electors & Princes, who have equal motives & means, for exciting cabals & parties. Might not such a mode of election be devised among ourselves as will defend the community agst. these effects in any dangerous degree? Having made these observations he would read to the Committee a sketch of a plan which he shd. prefer to either of those under consideration. He was aware that it went beyond the ideas of most members. But will such a plan be adopted out of doors? In return he would ask will the people adopt the other plan? At present they will adopt neither. But he sees the Union dissolving or already dissolved—he sees evils operating in the States which must soon cure the people of their fondness for democracies—he sees that a great progress has been already made & is still going on in the public mind. He thinks therefore that the people will in time be unshackled from their prejudices; and whenever that happens, they will themselves not be satisfied at stopping where the plan of Mr. R. wd. place them, but be ready to go as far at least as he proposes. He did not mean to offer the paper he had sketched as a proposition to the Committee. It was meant only to give a more correct view of his ideas, and to suggest the amendments which he should probably propose to the plan of Mr. R. in the proper stages of its future discussion. . . .

39. *Constitutional Convention. Remarks on Signing the Constitution*

[*Philadelphia, September 17, 1787*]

Mr. Hamilton expressed his anxiety that every member should sign. A few characters of consequence, by opposing or even refusing to sign the Constitution, might do infinite mischief by kindling the latent sparks which lurk under an enthusiasm in favor of the Convention which may soon subside. No man's ideas were more remote from the plan than his were known to be; but is it possible to deliberate between anarchy and Convulsion on one side, and the chance of good to be expected from the plan on the other.

40. *The Federalist No. 1: Introduction*

[*New York, October 27, 1787*]

To the People of the State of New York.

   After an unequivocal experience of the inefficacy of the subsisting Fœderal Government, you are called upon to deliberate on a new Constitution for the United States of America. The subject speaks its own importance; comprehending in its consequences, nothing less than the existence of the UNION, the safety and welfare of the parts of which it is composed, the fate of an empire, in many respects, the most interesting in the world. It has been frequently remarked, that it seems to have been reserved to the people of this country, by their conduct and example, to decide the important question, whether societies of men are really capable or not, of establishing good government from ref[l]ection and choice, or whether they are forever destined to depend, for their political constitutions, on accident and force. If there be any truth in the remark, the crisis, at which we are arrived, may with propriety be regarded as the æra in which that decision is to be made; and a wrong election of the part we shall act, may, in this view, deserve to be considered as the general misfortune of mankind.

   This idea will add the inducements of philanthropy to those of patriotism to heighten the sollicitude, which all considerate and good men must feel for the event. Happy will it be if our choice should be directed by a judicious estimate of our true interests, unperplexed and unbiassed by considerations not connected with the public good. But this is a thing

more ardently to be wished, than seriously to be expected. The plan offered to our deliberations, affects too many particular interests, innovates upon too many local institutions, not to involve in its discussion a variety of objects foreign to its merits, and of views, passions and prejudices little favourable to the discovery of truth.

Among the most formidable of the obstacles which the new Constitution will have to encounter, may readily be distinguished the obvious interest of a certain class of men in every State to resist all changes which may hazard a diminution of the power, emolument and consequence of the offices they hold under the State-establishments—and the perverted ambition of another class of men, who will either hope to aggrandise themselves by the confusions of their country, or will flatter themselves with fairer prospects of elevation from the subdivision of the empire into several partial confederacies, than from its union under one government.

It is not, however, my design to dwell upon observations of this nature. I am well aware that it would be disingenuous to resolve indiscriminately the opposition of any set of men (merely because their situations might subject them to suspicion) into interested or ambitious views: Candour will oblige us to admit, that even such men may be actuated by upright intentions; and it cannot be doubted, that much of the opposition which has made its appearance, or may hereafter make its appearance, will spring from sources, blameless at least, if not respectable, the honest errors of minds led astray by preconceived jealousies and fears. So numerous indeed and so powerful are the causes, which serve to give a false bias to the judgment, that we upon many occasions, see wise and good men on the wrong as well as on the right side of questions, of the first magnitude to society. This circumstance, if duly attended to, would furnish a lesson of moderation of those, who are ever so much persuaded of their being in the right, in any controversy. And a further reason for caution, in this respect, might be drawn from the reflection, that we are not always sure, that those who advocate the truth are influenced by purer principles than their antagonists. Ambition, avarice, personal animosity, party opposition, and many other motives, not more laudable than these, are apt to operate as well upon those who support as upon those who oppose the right side of a question. Were there not even these inducements to moderation, nothing could be more illjudged than that intolerant spirit, which has, at all times, characterised political parties. For, in politics as in religion, it is equally absurd to aim at making proselytes by fire and sword. Heresies in either can rarely be cured by persecution.

And yet however just these sentiments will be allowed to be, we have already sufficient indications, that it will happen in this as in all former cases of great national discussion. A torrent of angry and malignant passions will be let loose. To judge from the conduct of the opposite parties,

we shall be led to conclude, that they will mutually hope to evince the justness of their opinions, and to increase the number of their converts by the loudness of their declamations, and by the bitterness of their invectives. An enlightened zeal for the energy and efficiency of government will be stigmatised, as the off-spring of a temper fond of despotic power and hostile to the principles of liberty. An overscrupulous jealousy of danger to the rights of the people, which is more commonly the fault of the head than of the heart, will be represented as mere pretence and artifice; the bait for popularity at the expence of public good. It will be forgotten, on the one hand, that jealousy is the usual concomitant of violent love, and that the noble enthusiasm of liberty is too apt to be infected with a spirit of narrow and illiberal distrust. On the other hand, it will be equally forgotten, that the vigour of government is essential to the security of liberty; that, in the contemplation of a sound and well informed judgment, their interest can never be separated; and that a dangerous ambition more often lurks behind the specious mask of zeal for the rights of the people, than under the forbidding appearance of zeal for the firmness and efficiency of government. History will teach us, that the former has been found a much more certain road to the introduction of despotism, than the latter, and that of those men who have overturned the liberties of republics the greatest number have begun their career, by paying an obsequious court to the people, commencing Demagogues and ending Tyrants.

In the course of the preceeding observations I have had an eye, my Fellow Citizens, to putting you upon your guard against all attempts, from whatever quarter, to influence your decision in a matter of the utmost moment to your welfare by any impressions other than those which may result from the evidence of truth. You will, no doubt, at the same time, have collected from the general scope of them that they proceed from a source not unfriendly to the new Constitution. Yes, my Countrymen, I own to you, that, after having given it an attentive consideration, I am clearly of opinion, it is your interest to adopt it. I am convinced, that this is the safest course for your liberty, your dignity, and your happiness. I effect not reserves, which I do not feel. I will not amuse you with an appearance of deliberation, when I have decided. I frankly acknowledge to you my convictions, and I will freely lay before you the reasons on which they are founded. The consciousness of good intentions disdains ambiguity. I shall not however multiply professions on this head. My motives must remain in the depository of my own breast: My arguments will be open to all, and may be judged of by all. They shall at least be offered in a spirit, which will not disgrace the cause of truth.

I propose in a series of papers to discuss the following interesting particulars—*The utility of the UNION to your political prosperity*—*The insufficiency of the present Confederation to preserve that Union*—*The necessity of a government at least equally energetic with the one pro-*

posed to the attainment of this object—The conformity of the proposed constitution to the true principles of republican government—Its analogy to your own state constitution—and lastly, The additional security, which its adoption will afford to the preservation of that species of government, to liberty and to property.

In the progress of this discussion I shall endeavour to give a satisfactory answer to all the objections which shall have made their appearance that may seem to have any claim to your attention. . . .

41. *The Federalist No. 9: Union as a Barrier to Faction*

[New York, November 21, 1787]

To the People of the State of New-York.

A Firm Union will be of the utmost moment to the peace and liberty of the States as a barrier against domestic faction and insurrection. It is impossible to read the history of the petty Republics of Greece and Italy, without feeling sensations of horror and disgust at the distractions with which they were continually agitated, and at the rapid succession of revolutions, by which they were kept in a state of perpetual vibration, between the extremes of tyranny and anarchy. If they exhibit occasional calms, these only serve as short-lived contrasts to the furious storms that are to succeed. If now and then intervals of felicity open themselves to view, we behold them with a mixture of regret arising from the reflection that the pleasing scenes before us are soon to be overwhelmed by the tempestuous waves of sedition and party-rage. If momentary rays of glory break forth from the gloom, while they dazzle us with a transient and fleeting brilliancy, they at the same time admonish us to lament that the vices of government should pervert the direction and tarnish the lustre of those bright talents and exalted indowments, for which the favoured soils, that produced them, have been so justly celebrated.

From the disorders that disfigure the annals of those republics, the advocates of despotism have drawn arguments, not only against the forms of republican government, but against the very principles of civil liberty. They have decried all free government, as inconsistent with the order of society, and have indulged themselves in malicious exultation over its friends and partizans. Happily for mankind, stupendous fabrics reared on the basis of liberty, which have flourished for ages, have in a few glorious instances refuted their gloomy sophisms. And, I trust, America will be the broad and solid foundation of other edifices not less magnificent, which will be equally permanent monuments of their errors.

But it is not to be denied that the portraits, they have sketched of republican government, were too just copies of the originals from which they were taken. If it had been found impracticable, to have devised models of a more perfect structure, the enlightened friends to liberty would have been obliged to abandon the cause of that species of government as indefensible. The science of politics, however, like most other sciences has received great improvement. The efficacy of various principles is now well understood, which were either not known at all, or imperfectly known to the ancients. The regular distribution of power into distinct departments—the introduction of legislative ballances and checks—the institution of courts composed of judges, holding their offices during good behaviour—the representation of the people in the legislature by deputies of their own election—these are either wholly new discoveries or have made their principal progress towards perfection in modern times. They are means, and powerful means, by which the excellencies of republican government may be retained and its imperfections lessened or avoided. To this catalogue of circumstances, that tend to the amelioration of popular systems of civil government, I shall venture, however novel it may appear to some, to add one more on a principle, which has been made the foundation of an objection to the New Constitution, I mean the ENLARGEMENT of the ORBIT within which such systems are to revolve either in respect to the dimensions of a single State, or to the consolidation of several smaller States into one great confederacy. The latter is that which immediately concerns the object under consideration. It will however be of use to examine the principle in its application to a single State which shall be attended to in another place.

The utility of a confederacy, as well to suppress faction and to guard the internal tranquillity of States, as to increase their external force and security, is in reality not a new idea. It has been practiced upon in different countries and ages, and has received the sanction of the most applauded writers, on the subjects of politics. The opponents of the PLAN proposed have with great assiduity cited and circulated the observations of Montesquieu on the necessity of a contracted territory for a republican government. But they seem not to have been apprised of the sentiments of that great man expressed in another part of his work, nor to have adverted to the consequences of the principle to which they subscribe, with such ready acquiescence.

When Montesquieu recommends a small extent for republics, the standards he had in view were of dimensions, far short of the limits of almost every one of these States. Neither Virginia, Massachusetts, Pennsylvania, New-York, North-Carolina, nor Georgia, can by any means be compared with the models, from which he reasoned and to which the terms of his description apply. If we therefore take his ideas on this point, as the criterion of truth, we shall be driven to the alternative, either of taking refuge at once in the arms of monarchy, or of splitting ourselves into an

infinity of little jealous, clashing, tumultuous commonwealths, the wretched nurseries of unceasing discord and the miserable objects of universal pity or contempt. Some of the writers, who have come forward on the other side of the question, seem to have been aware of the dilemma; and have even been bold enough to hint at the division of the larger States, as a desirable thing. Such an infatuated policy, such a desperate expedient, might, by the multiplication of petty offices, answer the views of men, who possess not qualifications to extend their influence beyond the narrow circles of personal intrigue, but it could never promote the greatness or happiness of the people of America.

Referring the examination of the principle itself to another place, as has been already mentioned, it will be sufficient to remark here, that in the sense of the author who has been most emphatically quoted upon the occasion, it would only dictate a reduction of the SIZE of the more considerable MEMBERS of the Union; but would not militate against their being all comprehended in one Confederate Government. And this is the true question, in the discussion of which we are at present interested.

So far are the suggestions of Montesquieu from standing in opposition to a general Union of the States, that he explicitly treats of a CONFEDERATE REPUBLIC as the expedient for extending the sphere of popular government and reconciling the advantages of monarchy with those of republicanism.

"It is very probable (says he)* that mankind would have been obliged, at length, to live constantly under the government of a SINGLE PERSON, had they not contrived a kind of constitution, that has all the internal advantages of a republican, together with the external force of a monarchical government. I mean a CONFEDERATE REPUBLIC.

"This form of Government is a Convention, by which several smaller *States* agree to become members of a larger *one,* which they intend to form. It is a kind of assemblage of societies, that constitute a new one, capable of encreasing by means of new associations, till they arrive to such a degree of power as to be able to provide for the security of the united body.

"A republic of this kind, able to withstand an external force, may support itself without any internal corruption. The form of this society prevents all manner of inconveniencies.

"If a single member should attempt to usurp the supreme authority, he could not be supposed to have an equal authority and credit, in all the confederate states. Were he to have too great influence over one, this would alarm the rest. Were he to subdue a part, that which would still remain free might oppose him with forces, independent of those which he had usurped, and overpower him before he could be settled in his usurpation.

* *Spirit of Laws, Vol. I. Book IX. Chap. I.*

"Should a popular insurrection happen, in one of the confederate States, the others are able to quell it. Should abuses creep into one part, they are reformed by those that remain sound. The State may be destroyed on one side, and not on the other; the confederacy may be dissolved, and the confederates preserve their sovereignty.

"As this government is composed of small republics it enjoys the internal happiness of each, and with respect to its external situation it is possessed, by means of the association of all the advantages of large monarchies."

I have thought it proper to quote at length these interesting passages, because they contain a luminous abrigement of the principal arguments in favour of the Union, and must effectually remove the false impressions, which a misapplication of other parts of the work was calculated to produce. They have at the same time an intimate connection with the more immediate design of this Paper; which is to illustrate the tendency of the Union to repress domestic faction and insurrection.

A distinction, more subtle than accurate has been raised between *a confederacy* and a *consolidation* of the States. The essential characteristic of the first is said to be, the restriction of its authority to the members in their collective capacities, without reaching to the individuals of whom they are composed. It is contended that the national council ought to have no concern with any object of internal administration. An exact equality of suffrage between the members has also been insisted upon as a leading feature of a Confederate Government. These positions are in the main arbitrary; they are supported neither by principle nor precedent. It has indeed happened that governments of this kind have generally operated in the manner, which the distinction, taken notice of, supposes to be inherent in their nature—but there have been in most of them extensive exceptions to the practice, which serve to prove as far as example will go, that there is no absolute rule on the subject. And it will be clearly shewn, in the course of this investigation, that as far as the principle contended for has prevailed, it has been the cause of incurable disorder and imbecility in the government.

The definition of a *Confederate Republic* seems simply to be, an "assemblage of societies" or an association of two or more States into one State. The extent, modifications and objects of the Fœderal authority are mere matters of discretion. So long as the separate organisation of the members be not abolished, so long as it exists by a constitutional necessity for local purposes, though it should be in perfect subordination to the general authority of the Union, it would still be, in fact and in theory, an association of States, or a confederacy. The proposed Constitution, so far from implying an abolition of the State Governments, makes them constituent parts of the national sovereignty by allowing them a direct representation in the Senate, and leaves in their possession certain exclusive and very important portions of sovereign power. This fully cor-

responds, in every rational import of the terms, with the idea of a Fœderal Government.

In the Lycian confederacy, which consisted of twenty three CITIES, or republics, the largest were intitled to *three* votes in the COMMON COUNCIL, those of the middle class to *two* and the smallest to *one*. The COMMON COUNCIL had the appointment of all the judges and magistrates of the respective CITIES. This was certainly the most delicate species of interference in their internal administration; for if there be any thing, that seems exclusively appropriated to the local jurisdictions, it is the appointment of their own officers. Yet Montesquieu, speaking of this association, says "Were I to give a model of an excellent confederate republic, it would be that of Lycia." Thus we perceive that the distinctions insisted upon were not within the contemplation of this enlightened civilian, and we shall be led to conclude that they are the novel refinements of an erroneous theory.

42. *The Federalist No. 78: Judiciary*

[*New York, May 28, 1788*]

To the People of the State of New-York.

We proceed now to an examination of the judiciary department of the proposed government.

In unfolding the defects of the existing confederation, the utility and necessity of a federal judicature have been clearly pointed out. It is the less necessary to recapitulate the considerations there urged; as the propriety of the institution in the abstract is not disputed: The only questions which have been raised being relative to the manner of constituting it, and to its extent. To these points therefore our observations shall be confined.

The manner of constituting it seems to embrace these several objects— 1st. The mode of appointing the judges— 2d. The tenure by which they are to hold their places— 3d. The partition of the judiciary authority between different courts, and their relations to each other.

First. As to the mode of appointing the judges: This is the same with that of appointing the officers of the union in general, and has been so fully discussed in the two last numbers, that nothing can be said here which would not be useless repetition.

Second. As to the tenure by which the judges are to hold their places: This chiefly concerns their duration in office; the provisions for their support; and the precautions for their responsibility.

According to the plan of the convention, all the judges who may be ap-

pointed by the United States are to hold their offices *during good behaviour,* which is conformable to the most approved of the state constitutions; and among the rest, to that of this state. Its propriety having been drawn into question by the adversaries of that plan, is no light symptom of the rage for objection which disorders their imaginations and judgments. The standard of good behaviour for the continuance in office of the judicial magistracy is certainly one of the most valuable of the modern improvements in the practice of government. In a monarchy it is an excellent barrier to the despotism of the prince: In a republic it is a no less excellent barrier to the encroachments and oppressions of the representative body. And it is the best expedient which can be devised in any government, to secure a steady, upright and impartial administration of the laws.

Whoever attentively considers the different departments of power must perceive, that in a government in which they are separated from each other, the judiciary, from the nature of its functions, will always be the least dangerous to the political rights of the constitution; because it will be least in a capacity to annoy or injure them. The executive not only dispenses the honors, but holds the sword of the community. The legislature not only commands the purse, but prescribes the rules by which the duties and rights of every citizen are to be regulated. The judiciary on the contrary has no influence over either the sword or the purse, no direction either of the strength or of the wealth of the society, and can take no active resolution whatever. It may truly be said to have neither FORCE nor WILL, but merely judgment; and must ultimately depend upon the aid of the executive arm even for the efficacy of its judgments.

This simple view of the matter suggests several important consequences. It proves incontestibly that the judiciary is beyond comparison the weakest of the three departments of power;* that it can never attack with success either of the other two; and that all possible care is requisite to enable it to defend itself against their attacks. It equally proves, that though individual oppression may now and then proceed from the courts of justice, the general liberty of the people can never be endangered from that quarter; I mean, so long as the judiciary remains truly distinct from both the legislative and executive. For I agree that "there is no liberty, if the power of judging be not separated from the legislative and executive powers."† And it proves, in the last place, that as liberty can have nothing to fear from the judiciary alone, but would have every thing to fear from its union with either of the other departments; that as all the effects of such an union must ensue from a dependence of the former on the latter, notwithstanding a nominal and apparent separation; that as from the natural feebleness of the judiciary, it is in continual jeopardy of being overpowered, awed or influenced by its coordinate branches; and that as

* The celebrated Montesquieu speaking of them says, "of the three powers above mentioned, the JUDICIARY is next to nothing." Spirit of Laws, vol. I, page 186.

† Idem. page 181.

nothing can contribute so much to its firmness and independence, as permanency in office, this quality may therefore be justly regarded as an indispensable ingredient in its constitution; and in a great measure as the citadel of the public justice and the public security.

The complete independence of the courts of justice is peculiarly essential in a limited constitution. By a limited constitution I understand one which contains certain specified exceptions to the legislative authority; such for instance as that it shall pass no bills of attainder, no *ex post facto* laws, and the like. Limitations of this kind can be preserved in practice no other way than through the medium of the courts of justice; whose duty it must be to declare all acts contrary to the manifest tenor of the constitution void. Without this, all the reservations of particular rights or privileges would amount to nothing.

Some perplexity respecting the right of the courts to pronounce legislative acts void, because contrary to the constitution, has arisen from an imagination that the doctrine would imply a superiority of the judiciary to the legislative power. It is urged that the authority which can declare the acts of another void, must necessarily be superior to the one whose acts may be declared void. As this doctrine is of great importance in all the American constitutions, a brief discussion of the grounds on which it rests cannot be unacceptable.

There is no position which depends on clearer principles, than that every act of a delegated authority, contrary to the tenor of the commission under which it is exercised, is void. No legislative act therefore contrary to the constitution can be valid. To deny this would be to affirm that the deputy is greater than his principal; that the servant is above his master; that the representatives of the people are superior to the people themselves; that men acting by virtue of powers may do not only what their powers do not authorise, but what they forbid.

If it be said that the legislative body are themselves the constitutional judges of their own powers, and that the construction they put upon them is conclusive upon the other departments, it may be answered, that this cannot be the natural presumption, where it is not to be collected from any particular provision in the constitution. It is not otherwise to be supposed that the constitution could intend to enable the representatives of the people to substitute their *will* to that of their constituents. It is far more rational to suppose that the courts were designed to be an intermediate body between the people and the legislature, in order, among other things, to keep the latter within the limits assigned to their authority. The interpretation of the laws is the proper and peculiar province of the courts. A constitution is in fact, and must be, regarded by the judges as a fundamental law. It therefore belongs to them to ascertain its meaning as well as the meaning of any particular act proceeding from the legislative body. If there should happen to be an irreconcileable variance between the two, that which has the superior obligation and validity

ought of course to be preferred; or in other words, the constitution ought to be preferred to the statute, the intention of the people to the intention of their agents.

Nor does this conclusion by any means suppose a superiority of the judicial to the legislative power. It only supposes that the power of the people is superior to both; and that where the will of the legislature declared in its statutes, stands in opposition to that of the people declared in the constitution, the judges ought to be governed by the latter, rather than the former. They ought to regulate their decisions by the fundamental laws, rather than by those which are not fundamental.

This exercise of judicial discretion in determining between two contradictory laws, is exemplified in a familiar instance. It not uncommonly happens, that there are two statutes existing at one time, clashing in whole or in part with each other, and neither of them containing any repealing clause or expression. In such a case, it is the province of the courts to liquidate and fix their meaning and operation: So far as they can by any fair construction be reconciled to each other; reason and law conspire to dictate that this should be done: Where this is impracticable, it becomes a matter of necessity to give effect to one, in exclusion of the other. The rule which has obtained in the courts for determining their relative validity is that the last in order of time shall be preferred to the first. But this is mere rule of construction, not derived from any positive law, but from the nature and reason of the thing. It is a rule not enjoined upon the courts by legislative provision, but adopted by themselves, as consonant to truth and propriety, for the direction of their conduct as interpreters of the law. They thought it reasonable, that between the interfering acts of an *equal* authority, that which was the last indication of its will, should have the preference.

But in regard to the interfering acts of a superior and subordinate authority, of an original and derivative power, the nature and reason of the thing indicate the converse of that rule as proper to be followed. They teach us that the prior act of a superior ought to be prefered to the subsequent act of an inferior and subordinate authority; and that, accordingly, whenever a particular statute contravenes the constitution, it will be the duty of the judicial tribunals to adhere to the latter, and disregard the former.

It can be of no weight to say, that the courts on the pretence of a repugnancy, may substitute their own pleasure to the constitutional intentions of the legislature. This might as well happen in the case of two contradictory statutes; or it might as well happen in every adjudication upon any single statute. The courts must declare the sense of the law; and if they should be disposed to exercise *will* instead of *judgment*, the consequence would equally be the substitution of their pleasure to that of the legislative body. The observation, if it proved any thing, would prove that there ought to be no judges distinct from that body.

If then the courts of justice are to be considered as the bulwarks of a limited constitution against legislative encroachments, this consideration will afford a strong argument for the permanent tenure of judicial offices, since nothing will contribute so much as this to that independent spirit in the judges, which must be essential to the faithful performance of so arduous a duty.

This independence of the judges is equally requisite to guard the constitution and the rights of individuals from the effects of those ill humours which the arts of designing men, or the influence of particular conjunctures, sometimes disseminate among the people themselves, and which, though they speedily give place to better information and more deliberate reflection, have a tendency in the mean time to occasion dangerous innovations in the government, and serious oppressions of the minor party in the community. Though I trust the friends of the proposed constitution will never concur with its enemies* in questioning that fundamental principle of republican government, which admits the right of the people to alter or abolish the established constitution whenever they find it inconsistent with their happiness; yet it is not to be inferred from this principle, that the representatives of the people, whenever a momentary inclination happens to lay hold of a majority of their constituents incompatible with the provisions in the existing constitution, would on that account be justifiable in a violation of those provisions; or that the courts would be under a greater obligation to connive at infractions in this shape, than when they had proceeded wholly from the cabals of the representative body. Until the people have by some solemn and authoritative act annulled or changed the established form, it is binding upon themselves collectively, as well as individually; and no presumption, or even knowledge of their sentiments, can warrant their representatives in a departure from it, prior to such an act. But it is easy to see that it would require an uncommon portion of fortitude in the judges to do their duty as faithful guardians of the constitution, where legislative invasions of it had been instigated by the major voice of the community.

But it is not with a view to infractions of the constitution only that the independence of the judges may be an essential safeguard against the effects of occasional ill humours in the society. These sometimes extend no farther than to the injury of the private rights of particular classes of citizens, by unjust and partial laws. Here also the firmness of the judicial magistracy is of vast importance in mitigating the severity, and confining the operation of such laws. It not only serves to moderate the immediate mischiefs of those which may have been passed, but it operates as a check upon the legislative body in passing them; who, perceiving that obstacles to the success of an iniquitous intention are to be expected from the scruples of the courts, are in a manner compelled by the very motives of

* Vide Protest of the minority of the convention of Pennsylvania, Martin's speech, &c.

the injustice they meditate, to qualify their attempts. This is a circumstance calculated to have more influence upon the character of our governments, than but few may be aware of. The benefits of the integrity and
moderation of the judiciary have already been felt in more states than
one; and though they may have displeased those whose sinister expectations they may have disappointed, they must have commanded the esteem and applause of all the virtuous and disinterested. Considerate men
of every description ought to prize whatever will tend to beget or fortify
that temper in the courts; as no man can be sure that he may not be to-
morrow the victim of a spirit of injustice, by which he may be a gainer
to-day. And every man must now feel that the inevitable tendency
of such a spirit is to sap the foundations of public and private confidence,
and to introduce in its stead, universal distrust and distress.

That inflexible and uniform adherence to the rights of the constitution
and of individuals, which we perceive to be indispensable in the courts of
justice, can certainly not be expected from judges who hold their offices
by a temporary commission. Periodical appointments, however regulated,
or by whomsoever made, would in some way or other be fatal to their
necessary independence. If the power of making them was committed
either to the executive or legislature, there would be danger of an improper complaisance to the branch which possessed it; if to both, there
would be an unwillingness to hazard the displeasure of either; if to the
people, or to persons chosen by them for the special purpose, there would
be too great a disposition to consult popularity, to justify a reliance that
nothing would be consulted but the constitution and the laws.

There is yet a further and a weighty reason for the permanency of the
judicial offices; which is deducible from the nature of the qualifications
they require. It has been frequently remarked with great propriety, that
a voluminous code of laws is one of the inconveniences necessarily connected with the advantages of a free government. To avoid an arbitrary
discretion in the courts, it is indispensable that they should be bound
down by strict rules and precedents, which serve to define and point out
their duty in every particular case that comes before them; and it will
readily be conceived from the variety of controversies which grow out of
the folly and wickedness of mankind, that the records of those precedents
must unavoidably swell to a very considerable bulk, and must demand
long and laborious study to acquire a competent knowledge of them.
Hence it is that there can be but few men in the society, who will have
sufficient skill in the laws to qualify them for the stations of judges. And
making the proper deductions for the ordinary depravity of human nature,
the number must be still smaller of those who unite the requisite integrity
with the requisite knowledge. These considerations apprise us, that the
government can have no great option between fit characters; and that a
temporary duration in office, which would naturally discourage such
characters from quitting a lucrative line of practice to accept a seat on the

bench, would have a tendency to throw the administration of justice into hands less able, and less well qualified to conduct it with utility and dignity. In the present circumstances of this country, and in those in which it is likely to be for a long time to come, the disadvantages on this score would be greater than they may at first sight appear; but it must be confessed that they are far inferior to those which present themselves under the other aspects of the subject.

Upon the whole there can be no room to doubt that the convention acted wisely in copying from the models of those constitutions which have established *good behaviour* as the tenure of their judicial offices in point of duration; and that so far from being blameable on this account, their plan would have been inexcuseably defective if it had wanted this important feature of good government. The experience of Great Britain affords an illustrious comment on the excellence of the institution.

43. *Report on Public Credit*

January 9, 1790

. . . While the observance of that good faith, which is the basis of public credit, is recommended by the strongest inducements of political expediency, it is enforced by considerations of still greater authority. There are arguments for it which rest on the immutable principles of moral obligation. And in proportion as the mind is disposed to contemplate, in the order of Providence, an intimate connection between public virtue and public happiness, will be its repugnancy to a violation of those principles.

This reflection derives additional strength from the nature of the debt of the United States. It was the price of liberty. The faith of America has been repeatedly pledged for it, and with solemnities that give peculiar force to the obligation. There is, indeed, reason to regret that it has not hitherto been kept; that the necessities of the war, conspiring with inexperience in the subjects of finance, produced direct infractions; and that the subsequent period has been a continued scene of negative violation or non-compliance. But a diminution of this regret arises from the reflection, that the last seven years have exhibited an earnest and uniform effort, on the part of the Government of the Union, to retrieve the national credit, by doing justice to the creditors of the nation; and that the embarrassments of a defective Constitution, which defeated this laudable effort, have ceased.

From this evidence of a favorable disposition given by the former Government, the institution of a new one, clothed with powers com-

petent to calling forth the resources of the community, has excited correspondent expectations. A general belief accordingly prevails, that the
credit of the United States will quickly be established on the firm
foundation of an effectual provision for the existing debt. . . .

It cannot but merit particular attention, that, among ourselves, the
most enlightened friends of good government are those whose expectations are the highest.

To justify and preserve their confidence; to promote the increasing
respectability of the American name; to answer the calls of justice; to
restore landed property to its due value; to furnish new resources, both to
agriculture and commerce; to cement more closely the union of the
States; to add to their security against foreign attack; to establish public
order on the basis of an upright and liberal policy;—these are the great
and invaluable ends to be secured by a proper and adequate provision, at
the present period, for the support of public credit. . . .

The Secretary has too much deference for the opinions of every part of
the community not to have observed one, which has more than once
made its appearance in the public prints, and which is occasionally to be
met with in conversation. It involves this question: Whether a discrimination ought not to be made between original holders of the public
securities, and present possessors, by purchase? Those who advocate a
discrimination are for making a full provision for the securities of the
former at their nominal value, but contend that the latter ought to
receive no more than the cost to them, and the interest. And the idea
is sometimes suggested of making good the difference to the primitive
possessor.

In favor of this scheme it is alleged that it would be unreasonable to
pay twenty shillings in the pound to one who had not given more for it
than three or four. And it is added that it would be hard to aggravate the
misfortune of the first owner, who, probably through necessity, parted
with his property at so great a loss, by obliging him to contribute to the
profit of the person who had speculated on his distresses.

The Secretary, after the most mature reflection on the force of this
argument, is induced to reject the doctrine it contains, as equally unjust
and impolitic; as highly injurious, even to the original holders of public
securities; as ruinous to public credit.

It is inconsistent with justice, because, in the first place, it is a breach
of contract—a violation of the rights of a fair purchaser.

The nature of the contract, in its origin, is that the public will pay
the sum expressed in the security, to the first holder or his assignee. The
intent in making the security assignable is, that the proprietor may be
able to make use of his property, by selling it for as much as it may be
worth in the market, and that the buyer may be safe in the purchase.

Every buyer, therefore, stands exactly in the place of the seller; has the
same right with him to the identical sum expressed in the security; and,

having acquired that right by fair purchase and in conformity to the original agreement and intention of the Government, his claim cannot be disputed without manifest injustice.

That he is to be considered as a fair purchaser, results from this: whatever necessity the seller may have been under, was occasioned by the Government, in not making a proper provision for its debts. The buyer had no agency in it, and therefore ought not to suffer. He is not even chargeable with having taken an undue advantage. He paid what the commodity was worth in the market, and took the risks of reimbursement upon himself. He, of course, gave a fair equivalent, and ought to reap the benefit of his hazard—a hazard which was far from inconsiderable, and which, perhaps, turned on little less than a revolution in government.

That the case of those who parted with their securities from necessity is a hard one, cannot be denied. But, whatever complaint of injury, or claim of redress, they may have, respects the Government solely. They have not only nothing to object to the persons who relieved their necessities, by giving them the current price of their property, but they are even under an implied condition to contribute to the reimbursement of those persons. They knew that, by the terms of the contract with themselves, the public were bound to pay to those to whom they should convey their title the sums stipulated to be paid to them; and that, as citizens of the United States, they were to bear their proportion of the contribution for that purpose. This, by the act of assignment, they tacitly engaged to do; and, if they had an option, they could not, with integrity or good faith, refuse to do it, without the consent of those to whom they sold. . . .

The Secretary, after mature reflection on this point, entertains a full conviction that an assumption of the debts of the particular States by the Union, and a like provision for them as for those of the Union, will be a measure of sound policy and substantial justice.

It would, in the opinion of the Secretary, contribute, in an eminent degree, to an orderly, stable, and satisfactory arrangement of the national finances. Admitting, as ought to be the case, that a provision must be made, in some way or other, for the entire debt, it will follow that no greater revenues will be required whether that provision be made wholly by the United States, or partly by them and partly by the States separately.

The principal question, then, must be whether such a provision cannot be more conveniently and effectually made by one general plan, issuing from one authority, than by different plans, originating in different authorities? In the first case there can be no competition for resources; in the last there must be such a competition. The consequences of this, without the greatest caution on both sides, might be interfering regulations, and thence collision and confusion. Particular branches of industry

might also be oppressed by it. The most productive objects of revenue are not numerous. Either these must be wholly engrossed by one side, which might lessen the efficacy of the provisions by the other, or both must have recourse to the same objects, in different modes, which might occasion an accumulation upon them beyond what they could properly bear. If this should not happen, the caution requisite to avoiding it would prevent the revenue's deriving the full benefit of each object. The danger of interference and of excess would be apt to impose restraints very unfriendly to the complete command of those resources which are the most convenient, and to compel the having recourse to others, less eligible in themselves and less agreeable to the community. The difficulty of an effectual command of the public resources, in case of separate provisions for the debt, may be seen in another, and, perhaps, more striking light. It would naturally happen that different States, from local considerations, would, in some instances, have recourse to different objects, in others to the same objects, in different degrees, for procuring the funds of which they stood in need. It is easy to conceive how this diversity would affect the aggregate revenue of the country. By the supposition, articles which yielded a full supply in some States would yield nothing, or an insufficient product, in others. And hence, the public revenue would not derive the full benefit of those articles from State regulations; neither could the deficiencies be made good by those of the Union. It is a provision of the national Constitution that "all duties, imposts, and excises shall be uniform throughout the United States." And, as the General Government would be under a necessity, from motives of policy, of paying regard to the duty which may have been previously imposed upon any article, though but in a single State, it would be constrained either to refrain wholly from any further imposition upon such article, where it had been already rated as high as was proper, or to confine itself to the difference between the existing rate and what the article would reasonably bear. Thus the pre-occupancy of an article by a single State would tend to arrest or abridge the impositions of the Union on that article. And as it is supposable that a great variety of articles might be placed in this situation, by dissimilar arrangements of the particular States, it is evident that the aggregate revenue of the country would be likely to be very materially contracted by the plan of separate provisions.

If all the public creditors receive their dues from one source, distributed with an equal hand, their interest will be the same. And, having the same interests, they will unite in the support of the fiscal arrangements of the Government—as these, too, can be made with more convenience where there is no competition. . . .

Persuaded, as the Secretary is, that the proper funding of the present debt will render it a national blessing, yet he is so far from acceding to the position, in the latitude in which it is sometimes laid down, that "public debts are public benefits"—a position inviting to prodigality and

liable to dangerous abuse—that he ardently wishes to see it incorporated as a fundamental maxim in the system of public credit of the United States, that the creation of debt should always be accompanied with the means of extinguishment. This he regards as the true secret for rendering public credit immortal. And he presumes that it is difficult to conceive a situation in which there may not be an adherence to the maxim. At least, he feels an unfeigned solicitude that this may be attempted by the United States, and that they may commence their measures for the establishment of credit with the observance of it. . . .

44. *On Realism in Foreign Policy— Cabinet Paper to Washington*

September 15, 1790

. . . It is necessary, then, to reflect, however painful the reflection, that gratitude is a duty, a sentiment, which between nations can rarely have any solid foundation. Gratitude is only due to a kindness or service, the predominant object of which is the interest or benefit of the party to whom it is performed. Where the interest or benefit of the party performing is the predominant cause of it, however there may result a debt, in cases in which there is not an immediate adequate and reciprocal advantage, there can be no room for the sentiment of gratitude. Where there is such an advantage, there is then not even a debt. If the motive of the act, instead of being the benefit of the party to whom it was done, should be a compound of the interest of the party doing it and of detriment to some other, of whom he is the enemy and the rival, there is still less room for so noble and refined a sentiment. This analysis will serve as a test of our true situation in regard both to France and Spain.

It is not to be doubted, that the part which the courts of France and Spain took in our quarrel with Great Britain, is to be attributed, not to an attachment to our independence or liberty, but to a desire of diminishing the power of Great Britain by severing the British Empire. This they considered as an interest of very great magnitude to them. In this their calculations and their passions conspired. For this they united their arms with ours, and encountered the expenses and perils of war. This has been accomplished; the advantages of it are mutual; and so far the account is balanced. . . .

. . . It is possible, indeed, that the enthusiasm which the transition from slavery to liberty may inspire, may be a substitute for the energy of a good administration, and the spring of great exertions. But the ebullitions of enthusiasm must ever be a precarious reliance. And it is quite as possi-

ble that the greatness, and perhaps immaturity, of that transition, may prolong licentiousness and disorder. Calculations of what may happen in France must be unusually fallible, not merely from the yet unsettled state of things in that kingdom, but from the extreme violence of the change which has been wrought in the situation of the people. . . .

45. *Report on a National Bank*

December 13, 1790

. . . Considerations of public advantage suggest a further wish, which is—that the bank could be established upon principles that would cause the profits of it to redound to the immediate benefit of the State. This is contemplated by many who speak of a national bank, but the idea seems liable to insuperable objections. To attach full confidence to an institution of this nature, it appears to be an essential ingredient in its structure, that it shall be under a *private* not a *public* direction—under the guidance of *individual interest,* not of *public policy,* which would be supposed to be, and, in certain emergencies, under a feeble or too sanguine administration, would really be, liable to being too much influenced by *public necessity.* The suspicion of this would, most probably, be a canker that would continually corrode the vitals of the credit of the bank, and would be most likely to prove fatal in those situations in which the public good would require that they should be most sound and vigorous. It would, indeed, be little less than a miracle, should the credit of the bank be at the disposal of the government, if, in a long series of time, there was not experienced a calamitous abuse of it. It is true that it would be the real interest of the government not to abuse it; its genuine policy to husband and cherish it with the most guarded circumspection, as an inestimable treasure. But what government ever uniformly consulted its true interests in opposition to the temptations of momentary exigencies? What nation was ever blessed with a constant succession of upright and wise administrators?

The keen, steady, and, as it were, magnetic sense of their own interest as proprietors, in the directors of a bank, pointing invariably to its true pole—the prosperity of the institution,—is the only security that can always be relied upon for a careful and prudent administration. It is, therefore, the only basis on which an enlightened, unqualified, and permanent confidence can be expected to be erected and maintained. . . .

46. *Opinion as to the Constitutionality of the Bank of the United States*

February 23, 1791

. . . In entering upon the argument, it ought to be premised that the objections of the Secretary of State and the Attorney-General are founded on a general denial of the authority of the United States to erect corporations. The latter, indeed, expressly admits, that if there be anything in the bill which is not warranted by the Constitution, it is the clause of incorporation.

Now it appears to the Secretary of the Treasury that this *general principle* is *inherent* in the very *definition* of government, and *essential* to every step of the progress to be made by that of the United States, namely: That every power vested in a government is in its nature *sovereign*, and includes, by *force* of the *term*, a right to employ all the *means* requisite and fairly applicable to the attainment of the *ends* of such power, and which are not precluded by restrictions and exceptions specified in the Constitution, or not immoral, or not contrary to the *essential ends* of political society. . . .

This principle, in its application to government in general, would be admitted as an axiom; and it will be incumbent upon those who may incline to deny it, to prove a distinction, and to show that a rule which, in the general system of things, is essential to the preservation of the social order, is inapplicable to the United States.

The circumstance that the powers of sovereignty are in this country divided between the National and State governments, does not afford the distinction required. It does not follow from this, that each of the portion of *powers* delegated to the one or to the other, is not sovereign with *regard to its proper objects*. It will only *follow* from it, that each has sovereign power as to *certain things*, and not as to *other things*. To deny that the Government of the United States has sovereign power, as to its declared purposes and trusts, because its power does not extend to all cases, would be equally to deny that the State governments have sovereign power in any case, because their power does not extend to every case. The tenth section of the first article of the Constitution exhibits a long list of very important things which they may not do. And thus the United States would furnish the singular spectacle of a *political society* without *sovereignty*, or of a *people governed*, without *government*.

If it would be necessary to bring proof to a proposition so clear, as that which affirms that the powers of the Federal Government, as to *its objects*, were sovereign, there is a clause of its Constitution which would be decisive. It is that which declares that the Constitution, and the laws

of the United States made in pursuance of it, and all treaties made, or which shall be made, under their authority, shall be the *supreme law of the land*. The power which can create the *supreme law of the land* in *any case*, is doubtless *sovereign* as to such case.

This general and indisputable principle puts at once an end to the *abstract* question, whether the United States have power to erect a *corporation;* that is to say, to give a *legal* or *artificial capacity* to one or more persons, distinct from the *natural*. For it is unquestionably incident to *sovereign power* to erect corporations, and consequently to *that* of the United States, in *relation* to the *objects* intrusted to the management of the government. The difference is this: where the authority of the government is general, it can create corporations in *all cases;* where it is confined to certain branches of legislation, it can create corporations *only* in those cases.

Here, then, as far as concerns the reasonings of the Secretary of State and the Attorney-General, the affirmative of the constitutionality of the bill might be permitted to rest. It will occur to the President, that the principle here advanced has been untouched by either of them.

For a more complete elucidation of the point, nevertheless, the arguments which they had used against the power of the government to erect corporations, however foreign they are to the great and fundamental rule which has been stated, shall be particularly examined. And after showing that they do not tend to impair its force, it shall also be shown that the power of incorporation, incident to the government in certain cases, does fairly extend to the particular case which is the object of the bill.

The first of these arguments is, that the foundation of the Constitution is laid on this ground: "That all powers not delegated to the United States by the Constitution, nor prohibited by it to the States, are reserved to the States, or to the people." Whence it is meant to be inferred, that Congress can in no case exercise any power not included in those enumerated in the Constitution. And it is affirmed, that the power of erecting a corporation is not included in any of the enumerated powers.

The main proposition here laid down, in its true signification, is not to be questioned. It is nothing more than a consequence of this republican maxim, that all government is a delegation of power. But how much is delegated in each case is a question of fact, to be made out by fair reasoning and construction, upon the particular provisions of the Constitution, taking as guides the general principles and general ends of governments.

It is not denied that there are *implied*, as well as *express powers*, and that the *former* are as effectually delegated as the *latter*. And for the sake of accuracy it shall be mentioned that there is another class of powers, which may be properly denominated *resulting powers*. It will not be doubted that if the United States should make a conquest of any of the

territories of its neighbors, they would possess sovereign jurisdiction over the conquered territory. This would be rather a result from the whole mass of the powers of the government, and from the nature of political society, than a consequence of either of the powers specially enumerated.

But be this as it may, it furnishes a striking illustration of the general doctrine contended for; it shows an extensive case, in which a power of erecting corporations is either implied in, or would result from, some or all of the powers vested in the National Government. The jurisdiction acquired over such conquered country would certainly be competent to any species of legislation.

To return:—It is conceded that *implied powers* are to be considered as delegated equally with *express ones*. Then it follows, that as a power of erecting a corporation may as well be *implied* as any other thing, it may as well be employed as an *instrument* or *means* of carrying into execution any of the specified powers, as any other *instrument* or *means* whatever. The only question must be in this, as in every other case, whether the means to be employed, or, in this instance, the corporation to be erected, has a natural relation to any of the acknowledged objects or lawful ends of the government. Thus a corporation may not be erected by Congress for superintending the police of the city of Philadelphia, because they are not authorized to *regulate* the *police* of that city. But one may be erected in relation to the collection of taxes, or to the trade with foreign countries, or to the trade between the States, or with the Indian tribes; because it is the province of the Federal Government to *regulate* those objects, and because it is incident to a general *sovereign* or *legislative* power to *regulate* a thing, to employ all the means which relate to its regulation to the best and greatest advantage. . . .

47. *Report on Manufactures*

December 5, 1791

The Secretary of the Treasury, in obedience to the order of the House of Representatives, of the 15th day of January, 1790, has applied his attention, at as early a period as his other duties would permit, to the subject of Manufactures, and particularly to the means of promoting such as will tend to render the United States independent of foreign nations for military and other essential supplies; and he thereupon respectfully submits the following report:

The expediency of encouraging manufactures in the United States, which was not long since deemed very questionable, appears at this time

to be pretty generally admitted. The embarrassments which have obstructed the progress of our external trade, have led to serious reflections on the necessity of enlarging the sphere of our domestic commerce. The restrictive regulations, which, in foreign markets, abridge the vent of the increasing surplus of our agricultural produce, serve to beget an earnest desire that a more extensive demand for that surplus may be created at home; and the complete success which has rewarded manufacturing enterprise in some valuable branches, conspiring with the promising symptoms which attend some less mature essays in others, justify a hope that the obstacles to the growth of this species of industry are less formidable than they were apprehended to be, and that it is not difficult to find, in its further extension, a full indemnification for any external disadvantages, which are or may be experienced, as well as an accession of resources, favorable to national independence and safety. . . .

It ought readily be conceded that the cultivation of the earth, as the primary and most certain source of national supply, as the immediate and chief source of subsistence to a man, as the principal source of those materials which constitute the nutriment of other kinds of labor, as including a state most favorable to the freedom and independence of the human mind—one, perhaps, most conducive to the multiplication of the human species, has intrinsically a strong claim to pre-eminence over every other kind of industry.

But, that it has a title to any thing like an exclusive predilection, in any country, ought to be admitted with great caution; that it is even more productive than every other branch of industry, requires more evidence than has yet been given in support of the position. That its real interests, precious and important as, without the help of exaggeration, they truly are, will be advanced, rather than injured, by the due encouragement of manufactures, may, it is believed, be satisfactorily demonstrated. And it is also believed that the expediency of such encouragement, in a general view, may be shown to be recommended by the most cogent and persuasive motives of national policy. . . .

As to the division of labor

It has justly been observed, that there is scarcely any thing of greater moment in the economy of a nation than the proper division of labor. The separation of occupations causes each to be carried to a much greater perfection than it could possibly acquire if they were blended. This arises principally from three circumstances:

The greater skill and dexterity naturally resulting from a constant and undivided application to a single object. . . .

The economy of time, by avoiding the loss of it, incident to a frequent transition from one operation to another of a different nature.

An extension of the use of machinery. . . . on a single object will have it more in his power, and will be more naturally led to exert his imagina-

tion, in devising methods to facilitate and abridge labor, than if he were perplexed by a variety of independent and dissimilar operations. Besides this the fabrication of machines, in numerous instances, becoming itself a distinct trade, the artist who follows it has all the advantages which have been enumerated, for improvement in his particular art; and, in both ways, the invention and application of machinery are extended.

And from these causes united, the mere separation of the occupation of the cultivator from that of the artificer, has the effect of augmenting the productive powers of labor, and with them, the total mass of the produce or revenue of a country. In this single view of the subject, therefore, the utility of artificers or manufacturers, towards producing an increase of productive industry, is apparent.

As to an extension of the use of machinery, a point which, though partly anticipated, requires to be placed in one or two additional lights

The employment of machinery forms an item of great importance in the general mass of national industry. It is an artificial force brought in aid of the natural force of man; and, to all the purposes of labor, is an increase of hands, an accession of strength, unencumbered too by the expense of maintaining the laborer. May it not, therefore, be fairly inferred, that those occupations which give greatest scope to the use of this auxiliary, contribute most to the general stock of industrious effort, and, in consequence, to the general product of industry?

It shall be taken for granted, and the truth of the position referred to observation, that manufacturing pursuits are susceptible, in a greater degree, of the application of machinery, than those of agriculture. If so, all the difference is lost to a community which, instead of manufacturing for itself, procures the fabrics requisite to its supply from other countries. The substitution of foreign for domestic manufactures is a transfer to foreign nations of the advantages accruing from the employment of machinery, in the modes in which it is capable of being employed with most utility and to the greatest extent.

The cotton-mill, invented in England, within the last twenty years, is a signal illustration of the general proposition which has been just advanced. In consequence of it, all the different processes for spinning cotton are performed by means of machines, which are put in motion by water, and attended chiefly by women and children—and by a smaller number of persons, in the whole, than are requisite in the ordinary mode of spinning. And it is an advantage of great moment, that the operations of this mill continue with convenience during the night as well as through the day. The prodigious effect of such a machine is easily conceived. To this invention is to be attributed, essentially, the immense progress which has been so suddenly made in Great Britain, in the various fabrics of cotton.

As to the additional employment of classes of the community not originally engaged in the particular business

This is not among the least valuable of the means by which manufacturing institutions contribute to augment the general stock of industry and production. In places where those institutions prevail, besides the persons regularly engaged in them, they afford occasional and extra employment to industrious individuals and families, who are willing to devote the leisure resulting from the intermissions of their ordinary pursuits to collateral labors, as a resource for multiplying their acquisitions or their enjoyments. The husbandman himself experiences a new source of profit and support from the increased industry of his wife and daughters, invited and stimulated by the demands of the neighboring manufactories.

Besides this advantage of occasional employment to classes having different occupations, there is another, of a nature allied to it, and of a similar tendency. This is the employment of persons who would otherwise be idle, and in many cases a burthen on the community, either from the bias of temper, habit, infirmity of body, or some other cause, indisposing or disqualifying them for the toils of the country. It is worthy of particular remark that, in general, women and children are rendered more useful, and the latter more early useful, by manufacturing establishments, than they would otherwise be. Of the number of persons employed in the cotton manufactories of Great Britain, it is computed that four sevenths nearly are women and children, of whom the greatest proportion are children, and many of them of a tender age.

And thus it appears to be one of the attributes of manufactures, and one of no small consequence, to give occasion to the exertion of a greater quantity of industry, even by the same number of persons, where they happen to prevail, than would exist if there were no such establishments.

As to the promoting of emigration from foreign countries

Men reluctantly quit one course of occupation and livelihood for another, unless invited to it by very apparent and proximate advantages. Many who would go from one country to another, if they had a prospect of continuing with more benefit the callings to which they have been educated, will often not be tempted to change their situation by the hope of doing better in some other way. Manufacturers who, listening to the powerful invitations of a better price for their fabrics or their labor, of greater cheapness of provisions and raw materials, of an exemption from the chief part of the taxes, burthens, and restraints which they endure in the Old World, of greater personal independence and consequence, under the operation of a more equal government, and of what is far more precious than mere religious toleration, a perfect equality of religious privileges, would probably flock from Europe to the United States, to pursue their own trades or professions, if they were once made sensible

of the advantages they would enjoy, and were inspired with an assurance of encouragement and employment, will with difficulty, be induced to transplant themselves, with a view to becoming cultivators of land.

If it be true, then, that it is the interest of the United States to open every possible avenue to emigration from abroad, it affords a weighty argument for the encouragement of manufactures; which, for the reasons just assigned, will have the strongest tendency to multiply the inducements to it.

Here is perceived an important resource, not only for extending the population, and with it the useful and productive labor of the country, but likewise for the prosecution of manufactures, without deducting from the number of hands which might otherwise be drawn to tillage, and even for the indemnification of agriculture for such as might happen to be diverted from it. Many, whom manufacturing views would induce to emigrate, would, afterwards, yield to the temptations which the particular situation of this country holds out to agricultural pursuits. And while agriculture would, in other respects, derive many signal and unmingled advantages from the growth of manufactures, it is a problem whether it would gain or lose, as to the article of the number of persons employed in carrying it on.

As to the furnishing greater scope for the diversity of talents and dispositions, which discriminate men from each other

This is a much more powerful means of augmenting the fund of national industry, than may at first sight appear. It is a just observation, that minds of the strongest and most active powers for their proper objects, fall below mediocrity, and labor without effect, if confined to uncongenial pursuits. And it is thence to be inferred, that the results of human exertion may be immensely increased by diversifying its objects. When all the different kinds of industry obtain in a community, each individual can find his proper element, and can call into activity the whole vigor of his nature. And the community is benefited by the services of its respective members, in the manner in which each can serve it with most effect.

If there be any thing in a remark often to be met with, namely, that there is, in the genius of the people of this country, a peculiar aptitude for mechanic improvements, it would operate as a forcible reason for giving opportunities to the exercise of that species of talent, by the propagation of manufactures.

As to the affording a more ample and various field for enterprise

To cherish and stimulate the activity of the human mind, by multiplying the objects of enterprise, is not among the least considerable of the expedients by which the wealth of a nation may be promoted. Even things in themselves not positively advantageous sometimes become so, by their tendency to provoke exertion. Every new scene which is opened

to the busy nature of man to rouse and exert itself, is the addition of a new energy to the general stock of effort.

The spirit of enterprise, useful and prolific as it is, must necessarily be contracted or expanded, in proportion to the simplicity or variety of the occupations and productions which are to be found in a society. It must be less in a nation of mere cultivators, than in a nation of cultivators and merchants; less in a nation of cultivators and merchants, than in a nation of cultivators, artificers, and merchants.

As to the creating, in some instances, a new, and securing, in all, a more certain and steady demand for the surplus produce of the soil. . . .

It is evident that the exertions of the husbandman will be steady or fluctuating, vigorous or feeble, in proportion to the steadiness or fluctuation, adequateness or inadequateness, of the markets on which he must depend for the vent of the surplus which may be produced by his labor; and that such surplus, in the ordinary course of things, will be greater or less in the same proportion.

For the purpose of this vent, a domestic market is greatly to be preferred to a foreign one; because it is, in the nature of things, far more to be relied upon. . . .

To secure such a market there is no other expedient than to promote manufacturing establishments. Manufacturers, who constitute the most numerous class, after the cultivators of land, are for that reason the principal consumers of the surplus of their labor.

This idea of an extensive domestic market for the surplus produce of the soil, is of the first consequence. It is, of all things, that which most effectually conduces to a flourishing state of agriculture. If the effect of manufactories should be to detach a portion of the hands which would otherwise be engaged in tillage, it might possibly cause a smaller quantity of lands to be under cultivation; but, by their tendency to procure a more certain demand for the surplus produce of the soil, they would, at the same time, cause the lands which were in cultivation to be better improved and more productive. And while by their influence, the condition of each individual farmer would be meliorated, the total mass of agricultural production would probably be increased. For this must evidently depend as much upon the degree of improvement, if not more, than upon the number of acres under culture.

It merits particular observation, that the multiplication of manufactories not only furnishes a market for those articles which have been accustomed to be produced in abundance in a country, but it likewise creates a demand for such as were either unknown or produced in inconsiderable quantities. The bowels as well as the surface of the earth are ransacked for articles which were before neglected. Animals, plants, and minerals acquire a utility and a value which were before unexplored. . . .

Encouragement of Manufactures

. . . Industry, if left to itself, will naturally find its way to the most useful and profitable employment. Whence it is inferred that manufactures, without the aid of government, will grow up as soon and as fast as the natural state of things and the interest of the community may require. . . .

Experience teaches, that men are often so much governed by what they are accustomed to see and practise, that the simplest and most obvious improvements, in the most ordinary occupations, are adopted with hesitation, reluctance, and by slow gradations. The spontaneous transition to new pursuits, in a community long habituated to different ones, may be expected to be attended with proportionably greater difficulty. When former occupations ceased to yield a profit adequate to the subsistence of their followers, or when there was an absolute deficiency of employment in them, owing to the superabundance of hands, changes would ensue; but these changes would be likely to be more tardy than might consist with the interest either of individuals or of the society. In many cases they would not happen, while a bare support could be insured by an adherence to ancient courses, though a resort to a more profitable employment might be practicable. To produce the desirable changes as early as may be expedient may therefore require the incitement and patronage of government.

The apprehension of failing in new attempts is, perhaps, a more serious impediment. There are dispositions apt to be attracted by the mere novelty of an undertaking; but these are not always the best calculated to give it success. To this it is of importance that the confidence of cautious, sagacious capitalists, both citizens and foreigners, should be excited. And to inspire this description of persons with confidence, it is essential that they should be made to see in any project which is new—and for that reason alone, if for no other, precarious—the prospect of such a degree of countenance and support from governments, as may be capable of overcoming the obstacles inseparable from first experiments. . . .

There is, at the present juncture, a certain fermentation of mind, a certain activity of speculation and enterprise which, if properly directed, may be made subservient to useful purposes; but which, if left entirely to itself, may be attended with pernicious effects.

The disturbed state of Europe inclining its citizens to emigration, the requisite workmen will be more easily acquired than at another time; and the effect of multiplying the opportunities of employment to those who emigrate, may be an increase of the number and extent of valuable acquisitions to the population, arts, and industry of the country.

To find pleasure in the calamities of other nations would be criminal; but to benefit ourselves, by opening an asylum to those who suffer in consequence of them, is as justifiable as it is politic. . . .

Bounties

Except the simple and ordinary kinds of household manufacture or those for which there are very commanding local advantages, pecuniary bounties are, in most cases, indispensable to the introduction of a new branch. A stimulus and a support, not less powerful and direct, is, generally speaking, essential to the overcoming of the obstacles which arise from the competitions of superior skill and maturity elsewhere. Bounties are especially essential in regard to articles upon which those foreigners, who have been accustomed to supply a country, are in the practice of granting them.

The continuance of bounties on manufactures long established must almost always be of questionable policy; because a presumption would arise, in every such case, that there were natural and inherent impediments to success. But, in new undertakings, they are as justifiable as they are oftentimes necessary.

There is a degree of prejudice against bounties, from an appearance of giving away the public money without an immediate consideration, and from a supposition that they serve to enrich particular classes at the expense of the community.

But neither of these sources of dislike will bear a serious examination. There is no purpose to which public money can be more beneficially applied than to the acquisition of a new and useful branch of industry; no consideration more valuable than a permanent addition to the general stock of productive labor. . . .

A question has been made concerning the constitutional right of the Government of the United States to apply this species of encouragement, but there is certainly no good foundation for such a question. The National Legislature has express authority "to lay and collect taxes, duties, imposts, and excises, to pay the debts, and provide for the common defence and general welfare," with no other qualifications than that "all duties, imposts, and excises shall be uniform throughout the United States; and that no capitation or other direct tax shall be laid, unless in proportion to numbers ascertained by a census or enumeration, taken on the principles prescribed in the Constitution," and that "no tax or duty shall be laid on articles exported from any State."

These three qualifications excepted, the power to raise money is plenary and indefinite, and the objects to which it may be appropriated are no less comprehensive than the payment of the public debts, and the providing for the common defence and general welfare. The terms "general welfare" were doubtless intended to signify more than was expressed or imported in those which preceded; otherwise, numerous exigencies incident to the affairs of a nation would have been left without a provision. The phrase is as comprehensive as any that could have been used, because it was not fit that the constitutional authority of the Union to ap-

evenues should have been restricted within narrower limits
eneral welfare," and because this necessarily embraces a vast
f particulars, which are susceptible neither of specification nor
nition.

is, therefore, of necessity, left to the discretion of the National Legis-
ture to pronounce upon the objects which concern the general welfare,
and for which, under that description, an appropriation of money is
requisite and proper. And there seems to be no room for a doubt that
whatever concerns the general interests of learning, of agriculture, of
manufactures, and of commerce, are within the sphere of the national
councils, as far as regards an application of money.

The only qualification of the generality of the phrase in question,
which seems to be admissible, is this: That the object to which an appropriation of money is to be made be general, and not local: its operation
extending in fact or by possibility throughout the Union, and not being
confined to a particular spot.

48. *On the Motives of Treaties—Cabinet Paper on French Treaty to Washington*

April 1793

. . . This great and important question arises out of the facts which have
been stated:

Are the United States bound, by the principles of the laws of nations,
to consider the treaties heretofore made with France as in present force
and operation between them and the actual governing powers of the
French nation? or may they elect to consider their operation as suspended, reserving also a right to judge finally whether any such changes
have happened in the political affairs of France as may justify a renunciation of those treaties?

It is believed that they have an option to consider the operation of
those treaties as suspended, and will have eventually a right to renounce
them, if such changes shall take place as can *bona fide* be pronounced to
render a continuance of the connections which result from them disad-
vantageous or dangerous. . . .

If, then, a nation thinks fit to make changes in its government, which
render treaties that before subsisted between it and another nation useless, or dangerous, or hurtful to that other nation, it is a plain dictate of
reason, that the *latter* will have a right to renounce those treaties; because it also has a right to take care of its own happiness, and cannot be
obliged to suffer this to be impaired by the means which its neighbor or

ally may have adopted for its own advantage,
state of things. . . .

Nothing can be more evident than that the
ment of two nations may enter far into the mot
republics may contract an alliance, the princi
may be a similarity of constitutions, produci
defend their mutual rights and liberties. A chang
one of them into a monarchy or despotism may destroy the m
and the main link of common interest. . . .

A treaty pernicious to the state is of itself void, where no change in
the situation of either of the parties takes place. By a much stronger reason it must become *voidable* at the option of the other party, when the
voluntary act of one of the allies has made so material a change in the
condition of things as is always implied in a radical revolution of government.

Moreover, the maxim in question must, I presume, be understood with
this further limitation—that the revolution be *consummated*—that the
new government be *established,* and *recognized* among nations—that
there be an *undisputed* organ of the national will to obtain the performance of the stipulations made with the former government. . . .

The character of the United States may also be concerned in keeping
clear of any connection with the present government of France in other
views.

A struggle for liberty is in itself respectable and glorious; when conducted with magnanimity, justice, and humanity, it ought to command
the admiration of every friend to human nature; but if sullied by crimes
and extravagances, it loses its respectability. Though success may rescue
it from infamy, it cannot, in the opinion of the sober part of mankind,
attach to it much positive merit or praise. But in the event of a want of
success, a general execration must attend it.

It appears, thus far, but too probable, that the pending revolution of
France has sustained some serious blemishes. There is too much ground
to anticipate that a sentence uncommonly severe will be passed upon it
if it fails.

Will it be well for the United States to expose their reputation to the
issue, by implicating themselves as associates? Will their reputation be
promoted by a successful issue? What will it suffer by the reverse?

These questions suggest very serious considerations to a mind anxious
for the reputation of the country—anxious that it may emulate a character
of sobriety, moderation, justice, and love of order. . . .

...t of Revolution—
...ngton

May 2, 1793

...November, passed a decree in these

...declare, in the name of the French nation,
...RNITY and ASSISTANCE TO EVERY PEOPLE who
...erty; and they charge the executive power to
...ders to the generals to give assistance to such
...those citizens *who may have been or who may be*
...*of liberty.*" Which decree was ordered to be printed

The Convention
words:
"The National
that they will gr...
wish to recover th...
send the necessary
people, and to defen...
vexed for the cause
IN ALL LANGUAGES
This decree ou...
the government
...to assist a...

...ght justly to be regarded in an exceptionable light by
...of every country. For though it be lawful and meritorious... ...people in a virtuous and rational struggle for liberty, *when
the particular case happens,* yet it is not justifiable in any government
or nation to hold out to the world a *general invitation* and *encouragement* to *revolution* and insurrection, under a promise of *fraternity* and
assistance.

Such a step is of a nature to disturb the repose of mankind, to excite
fermentation in every country, to endanger government everywhere. Nor
can there be a doubt that wheresoever a spirit of this kind appears, it is
lawful to repress and repel it. . . .

The pretext of propagating liberty can make no difference. Every nation has a right to carve out its own happiness in its own way, and it is
the height of presumption in another to attempt to fashion its political
creed. . . .

50. *On Morality Between Nations—Pacificus, IV*

July 10, 1793

. . . Between individuals, occasion is not unfrequently given for the exercise of gratitude. Instances of conferring benefits from kind and benevolent dispositions or feelings toward the person benefited, without any
other interest on the part of the person who renders the service, than the
pleasure of doing a good action, occur every day among individuals. But
among nations they perhaps never occur. It may be affirmed as a gen-

eral principle,
tion to anothe
them.

Indeed, t
between na
fare the
upon the
of nationa
manency of the
millions, and for the mo
present measures of a governme
actions of an individual ordinarily ter
cumscribed within a narrow compass.

Whence it follows that an individual may, on
meritoriously indulge the emotions of generosity an
only without an eye to, but even at the expense of, his
a government can rarely, if at all, be justifiable in p
course; and, if it does so, ought to confine itself with
bounds. Good offices which are indifferent to the interest
forming them, or which are compensated by the existence or expectation of some reasonable equivalent, or which produce an essential good
to the nation to which they are rendered, without real detriment to the
affairs of the benefactors, prescribe perhaps the limits of national generosity or benevolence.

It is not here meant to recommend a policy absolutely selfish or interested in nations; but to show, that a policy regulated by their own interest, as far as justice and good faith permit, is, and ought to be, their
prevailing one; and that either to ascribe to them a different principle of
action, or to deduce, from the supposition of it, arguments for a self-
denying and self-sacrificing gratitude on the part of a nation which may
have received from another good offices, is to misrepresent or miscon-
ceive what usually are, and ought to be, the springs of national conduct. . . .

51. *On French Revolution—Americanus, I*

February 1, 1794

. . . There was a time when all men in this country entertained the same
favorable view of the French Revolution. At the present time, they all
still unite in the wish that the troubles of France may terminate in the
establishment of a free and good government; and dispassionate, well-
informed men must equally unite in the doubt whether this be likely to

take place under the auspices of those who now govern the affairs of that country. But, agreeing in these two points, there is a great and serious diversity of opinion as to the real merits and probable issue of the French Revolution.

None can deny that the cause of France has been stained by excesses and extravagances, for which it is not easy, if possible, to find a parallel in the history of human affairs, and from which reason and humanity recoil. Yet many find apologies and extenuations with which they satisfy themselves; they still see in the cause of France the cause of liberty; they are still sanguine in the hope that it will be crowned with success; that the French nation will establish for themselves not only a free but a republican government, capable of promoting solidly their happiness. Others, on the contrary, discern no adequate apology for the horrid and disgusting scenes which have been, and continue to be, acted. They conceive that the excesses which have been committed, transcend greatly the measure of those which, with every due allowance for circumstances, were reasonably to have been expected. They perceive in them proofs of atrocious depravity in the most influential leaders of the revolution. They observe that among these, a MARAT and a ROBESPIERRE, assassins still reeking with the blood of their fellow-citizens, monsters who outdo the fabled enormities of a *Busiris* and a *Procrustes,* are predominant in influence as well as iniquity. They find everywhere marks of an unexampled dissolution of all the social and moral ties. They see nowhere any thing but principles and opinions so wild, so extreme, passions so turbulent, so tempestuous, as almost to forbid the hope of agreement in any rational or well-organized system of government. They conclude that a state of things like this is calculated to extend disgust and disaffection throughout the nation, to nourish more and more a spirit of insurrection and mutiny, facilitating the progress of the invading armies, and exciting in the bowels of France commotions, of which it is impossible to compute the mischief, the duration, or the end; that if by the energy of the national character, and the intrinsic difficulty of the enterprise, the enemies of France shall be compelled to leave her to herself, this era may only prove the commencement of greater misfortunes; that after wading through seas of blood, in a furious and sanguinary civil war, France may find herself at length the slave of some victorious Sylla, or Marius, or Cæsar: and they draw this afflicting inference from the whole view of the subject, that there is more reason to fear that the CAUSE OF TRUE LIBERTY has received a deep wound in the mismanagements of it, by those who, unfortunately for the French nation, have for a considerable time past maintained an ascendant in its affairs, than to regard the revolution of France in the form it has lately worn, as entitled to the honors due to that sacred and all-important cause, or as a safe bark in which to freight the fortunes, the liberties, and the reputation of this now respectable and happy land. . . .

52. *Final Report on the Public Credit*

January 16, 1795

. . . There is no sentiment which can better deserve the serious attention of the legislators of a country than the one expressed in the speech of the President, which indicates the danger to every government from the progressive accumulation of debt. A tendency to it is, perhaps, the natural disease of all governments; and it is not easy to conceive any thing more likely than this to lead to great and convulsive revolutions of empire.

On the one hand, the exigencies of a nation, creating new causes of expenditure, as well from its own, as from the ambition, rapacity, injustice, intemperance, and folly of other nations, proceed in increasing and rapid succession. On the other, there is a general propensity in those who administer the affairs of a government, founded in the constitution of man, to shift off the burden from the present to a future day—a propensity which may be expected to be strong in proportion as the form of a state is popular.

To extinguish a debt which exists, and to avoid the contracting more, are ideas always favored by public feeling and opinion: but to pay taxes for the one or the other purpose, which are the only means of avoiding the evil, is always, more or less, unpopular. These contradictions are in human nature; and happy, indeed, would be the lot of a country that should ever want men ready to turn them to the account of their own popularity, or to some other sinister account.

Hence, it is no uncommon spectacle to see the same men clamoring for occasions of expense, when they happen to be in unison with the present humor of the community, whether well or ill directed, declaiming against a public debt, and for the reduction of it as an abstract thesis; yet vehement against every plan of taxation which is proposed to discharge old debts, or to avoid new, by the defraying expenses of exigencies as they emerge.

These unhandsome arts throw artificial embarrassment in the way of the administrators of a government, and, co-operating with the desire which they themselves are too apt to feel to conciliate public favor, by declining to lay even necessary burthens, or with the fear of losing it, by imposing them with firmness, serve to promote the accumulation of debt, by leaving that which exists without adequate provision for its reimbursement, and by preventing the levying, with energy, new taxes, when new occasions of expense occur. The consequence is, that the public debt swells till its magnitude becomes enormous, and the burthens of the people gradually increase, till their weight becomes intolerable. Of such

a state of things, great disorders in the whole political economy, convulsions and revolutions of government, are a natural offspring.

There can be no more sacred obligation, then, on the public agents of a nation, than to guard, with provident foresight and inflexible perseverance, against so mischievous a result. True patriotism and genuine policy cannot, it is respectfully presumed, be better demonstrated by those of the United States, at the present juncture, than by improving, efficaciously, the very favorable situation in which they stand, for extinguishing, with reasonable celerity, the actual debt of the country, and for laying the foundation of a system which may shield posterity from the consequences of the usual improvidence and selfishness of its ancestors, and which, if possible, may give IMMORTALITY TO PUBLIC CREDIT. . . .

53. *On War and Peace (Camillus Papers)*

1795

. . . It is only to know the vanity and vindictiveness of human nature, to be convinced, that while this generation lasts there will always exist among us men irreconcilable to our present national Constitution; embittered in their animosity in proportion to the success of its operations, and the disappointment of their inauspicious predictions. It is a material inference from this, that such men will watch, with lynx's eyes, for opportunities of discrediting the proceedings of the government, and will display a hostile and malignant zeal upon every occasion, where they think there are any prepossessions of the community to favor their enterprises. A treaty with Great Britain was too fruitful an occasion not to call forth all their activity.

It is only to consult the history of nations, to perceive, that every country, at all times, is cursed by the existence of men who, actuated by an irregular ambition, scruple nothing which they imagine will contribute to their own advancement and importance: in monarchies, supple courtiers; in republics, fawning or turbulent demagogues, worshipping still the idol—power—wherever placed, whether in the hands of a prince or of the people, and trafficking in the weaknesses, vices, frailties, or prejudices of the one or the other. It was to have been expected that such men, counting more on the passions than on the reason of their fellow-citizens, and anticipating that the treaty would have to struggle with prejudices, would be disposed to make an alliance with popular discontent, to nourish it and to press it into the service of their particular views. . . .

. . . National pride is generally a very untractable thing. In the councils of no country does it act with greater force than in those of Great

Britain. Whatever it might have been in her power to yield to negotiation, she could have yielded nothing to compulsion, without self-degradation, and without the sacrifice of that political consequence which, at all times very important to a nation, was peculiarly so to her at the juncture in question. It should be remembered, too, that from the relations in which the two countries have stood to each other, it must have cost more to the pride of Great Britain to have received the law from us than from any other power.

When one nation has cause of complaint against another, the course marked out by practice, the opinion of writers, and the principles of humanity, the object being to avoid war, is to precede reprisals of any kind by a demand of reparation. To begin with reprisals is to meet on the ground of war, and put the other party in a condition not to be able to recede without humiliation.

Had this course been pursued by us, it would not only have rendered war morally certain, but it would have united the British nation in a vigorous support of their government in the prosecution of it; while, on our part, we should have been quickly distracted and divided. The calamities of war would have brought the most ardent to their senses, and placed them among the first in reproaching the government with precipitation, rashness, and folly for not having taken every chance, by pacific means, to avoid so great an evil. . . .

Few nations can have stronger inducements than the United States to cultivate peace. Their infant state in general, their want of a marine in particular, to protect their commerce, would render war, in an extreme degree, a calamity. It would not only arrest our present rapid progress to strength and prosperity, but would probably throw us back into a state of debility and impoverishment, from which it would require years to emerge. . . .

To precipitate nothing, to gain time by negotiations, was to leave the country in a situation to profit by any events which might turn up, tending to restrain a spirit of hostility to Great Britain, and to dispose her to reasonable accommodation. . . .

By taking the ground of negotiation in the attitude of preparation for war, we at the same time carried the appeal to the prudence of the British Cabinet, without wounding its pride, and to the justice and interest of the British nation, without exciting feelings of resentment. . . .

A very powerful state may frequently hazard a high and haughty tone with good policy; but a weak state can scarcely ever do it without imprudence. The last is yet our character; though we are the embryo of a great empire. It is, therefore, better suited to our situation to measure each step with the utmost caution; to hazard as little as possible, in the cases in which we are injured; to blend moderation with firmness; and to brandish the weapons of hostility only when it is apparent that the use of them is unavoidable.

It is not to be inferred from this, that we are to crouch to any power on earth, or tamely to suffer our rights to be violated. A nation which is capable of this meanness will quickly have no rights to protect, or honor to defend.

But the true inference is, that we ought not lightly to seek or provoke a resort to arms; that, in the differences between us and other nations, we ought carefully to avoid measures which tend to widen the breach; and that we should scrupulously abstain from whatever may be construed into reprisals, till after the employment of all amicable means has reduced it to a certainty that there is no alternative.

If we can avoid a war for ten or twelve years more, we shall then have acquired a maturity, which will make it no more than a common calamity, and will authorize us, in our national discussions, to take a higher and more imposing tone.

This is a consideration of the greatest weight to determine us to exert all our prudence and address to keep out of war as long as it shall be possible; to defer, to a state of manhood, a struggle to which infancy is ill adapted. This is the most effectual way to disappoint the enemies of our welfare; to pursue a contrary conduct may be to play into their hands, and to gratify their wishes. If there be a foreign power which sees with envy or ill-will our growing prosperity, that power must discern that our infancy is the time for clipping our wings. We ought to be wise enough to see that this is not a time for trying our strength. . . .

. . . Nations, no more than individuals, ought to persist in error, especially at the sacrifice of their peace and prosperity; besides, nothing is more common, in disputes between nations, than each side to charge the other with being the aggressor or delinquent. This mutual crimination, either from the nature of circumstances, or from the illusions of the passions, is sometimes sincere; at other times it is dictated by pride or policy. But in all such cases, where one party is not powerful enough to dictate to the other, and where there is a mutual disposition to avoid war, the natural retreat for both is in compromise, which waives the question of first aggression or delinquency. This is the salvo for national pride; the escape for mutual error; the bridge by which nations, arrayed against each other, are enabled to retire with honor, and without bloodshed, from the field of contest. In cases of mutual delinquency, the question of the first default is frequently attended with real difficulty and doubt. One side has an equal right with the other to have and maintain its opinion. What is to be done when the pride of neither will yield to the arguments of the other? War, or a waiver of the point, is the alternative. What sensible man, what humane man, will deny that a compromise, which secures substantially the objects of interest, is almost always preferable to war on so punctilious and unmanageable a point?

Reject the principle of compromise, and the feuds of nations must become much more deadly than they have hitherto been. There would

scarcely ever be room for the adjustment of differences without an appeal to the sword; and, when drawn, it would seldom be sheathed but with the destruction of one or the other party. The earth, now too often stained, would then continually stream with human gore. . . .

54. *A Sacred Respect for Constitutional Law—Tully, III*

August 28, 1794

If it were to be asked, What is the most sacred duty, and the greatest source of security in a republic? the answer would be, An inviolable respect for the Constitution and laws—the first growing out of the last. It is by this, in a great degree, that the rich and the powerful are to be restrained from enterprises against the common liberty—operated upon by the influence of a general sentiment, by their interest in the principle, and by the obstacles which the habit it produces erects against innovation and encroachment. It is by this, in a still greater degree, that caballers, intriguers, and demagogues are prevented from climbing on the shoulders of faction to the tempting seats of usurpation and tyranny.

Were it not that it might require too long a discussion, it would not be difficult to demonstrate that a large and well-organized republic can scarcely lose its liberty from any other cause than that of anarchy, to which a contempt of the laws is the high-road.

But without entering into so wide a field, it is sufficient to present to your view a more simple and a more obvious truth, which is this: that a sacred respect for the constitutional law is the vital principle, the sustaining energy, of a free government.

Government is frequently and aptly classed under two descriptions—a government of FORCE, and a government of LAWS; the first is the definition of despotism—the last, of liberty. But how can a government of laws exist when the laws are disrespected and disobeyed? Government supposes control. It is that POWER by which individuals in society are kept from doing injury to each other, and are brought to co-operate to a common end. The instruments by which it must act are either the AUTHORITY of the laws or FORCE. If the first be destroyed, the last must be substituted; and where this becomes the ordinary instrument of government, there is an end to liberty!

Those, therefore, who preach doctrines, or set examples which undermine or subvert the authority of the laws, lead us from freedom to slavery; they incapacitate us for a GOVERNMENT of LAWS, and consequently prepare the way for one of FORCE, for mankind must have GOV-

ERNMENT OF ONE SORT OR ANOTHER. There are, indeed, great and urgent cases where the bounds of the Constitution are manifestly transgressed, or its constitutional authorities so exercised as to produce unequivocal oppression on the community, and to render resistance justifiable. But such cases can give no color to the resistance by a comparatively inconsiderable part of a community, of constitutional laws distinguished by no extraordinary features of rigor or oppression, and acquiesced in by the body of the community. . . .

55. *The Public Conduct and Character of John Adams*

1800

. . . Not denying to Mr. Adams patriotism and integrity, and even talents of a certain kind, I should be deficient in candor, were I to conceal the conviction that he does not possess the talents adapted to the *administration* of government, and that there are great and intrinsic defects in his character, which unfit him for the office of chief magistrate. . . .

I was one of that numerous class who had conceived a high veneration for Mr. Adams, on account of the part he acted in the first stages of our revolution. My imagination had exalted him to a high eminence, as a man of patriotic, bold, profound, and comprehensive mind. . . .

But this did not hinder me from making careful observations upon his several communications, and endeavoring to derive from them an accurate idea of his talents and character. This scrutiny enhanced my esteem in the main for his moral qualifications, but lessened my respect for his intellectual endowments. I then adopted an opinion, which all my subsequent experience has confirmed, that he is a man of an imagination sublimated and eccentric; propitious neither to the regular display of sound judgment, nor to steady perseverance in a systematic plan of conduct; and I began to perceive what has been since too manifest, that to this defect are added the unfortunate foibles of a vanity without bounds, and a jealousy capable of discoloring every object.

Strong evidence of some traits of this character is to be found in a journal of Mr. Adams, which was sent by the then Secretary of Foreign Affairs to Congress. The reading of this journal extremely embarrassed his friends, especially the delegates of Massachusetts, who, more than once, interrupted it, and at last, succeeded in putting a stop to it, on the suggestion that it bore the marks of a private and confidential paper, which, by some mistake, had gotten into its present situation, and never

could have been designed as a public document for the inspection of Congress. The good humor of that body yielded to the suggestion.

The particulars of this journal cannot be expected to have remained in my memory—but I recollect one which may serve as a sample. Being among the guests invited to dine with the Count de Vergennes, Minister for Foreign Affairs, Mr. Adams thought fit to give a specimen of American politeness, by conducting Madame de Vergennes to dinner; on the way, she was pleased to make retribution in the current coin of French politeness—by saying to him, "*Monsieur Adams, vous êtes le* Washington *de négociation.*" Stating the incident, he makes this comment upon it: "These people have a very pretty knack of paying compliments." He might have added, they have also a very dexterous knack of disguising a sarcasm.

The opinion, however, which I have avowed, did not prevent my entering cordially into the plan of supporting Mr. Adams for the office of Vice-President, under the New Constitution. I still thought that he had high claims upon the public gratitude, and possessed a substantial worth of character, which might atone for some great defects. In addition to this, it was well known that he was a favorite of New England, and it was obvious that his union with General Washington would tend to give the government, in its outset, all the strength which it could derive from the character of the two principal magistrates.

. . . It is time to conclude. This statement, which has been made, shows that Mr. Adams has committed some positive and serious errors of administration; that in addition to these, he has certain fixed points of character which tend naturally to the detriment of any cause of which he is the chief, of any administration of which he is the head; that by his ill humors and jealousies he has already divided and distracted the supporters of the government; that he has furnished deadly weapons to its enemies by unfounded accusations, and has weakened the force of its friends by decrying some of the most influential of them to the utmost of his power; and let it be added, as the necessary effect of such conduct, that he has made great progress in undermining the ground which was gained for the government by his predecessor, and that there is real cause to apprehend it might totter, if not fall, under his future auspices. A new government, constructed on free principles, is always weak, and must stand in need of the props of a firm and good administration, till time shall have rendered its authority venerable, and fortified it by habits of obedience.

Yet with this opinion of Mr. Adams, I have finally resolved not to advise the withholding from him a single vote. The body of Federalists, for want of sufficient knowledge of facts, are not convinced of the expediency of relinquishing him. It is even apparent, that a large proportion still retain the attachment which was once a common sentiment.

To refrain from a decided opposition to Mr. Adams' re-election has

been reluctantly sanctioned by my judgment; which has been not a little perplexed between the unqualified conviction of his unfitness for the station contemplated, and a sense of the great importance of cultivating harmony among the supporters of the government; on whose firm union hereafter will probably depend the preservation of order, tranquillity, liberty, property; the security of every social and domestic blessing.

56. *Louisiana: "A Question of Expediency"*

Pericles

(For the *Evening Post*.)

February 8, 1803

Since the question of independence, none has occurred more deeply interesting to the United States than the cession of Louisiana to France.

This event threatens the early dismemberment of a large portion of the country; more immediately, the safety of all the Southern States; and remotely, the independence of the whole Union. This is the portentous aspect which the affair presents to all men of sound and reflecting minds, of whatever party; and it is not to be concealed, that the only question which now offers itself, is how the evil is to be averted?

The strict right to resort at once to war, if it should be deemed expedient, cannot be doubted. A manifest and great danger to the nation; the nature of the cession to France, extending to ancient limits without respect to our rights by treaty; the direct infraction of an important article of the treaty itself, in withholding the deposit of New Orleans: either of these affords justifiable cause of war, and that they would authorize immediate hostilities, is not to be questioned by the most scrupulous mind.

The whole is then a question of expediency. Two courses only present: First, to negotiate, and endeavor to purchase; and if this fails, to go to war. Secondly, to seize at once on the Floridas and New Orleans, and then negotiate. A strong objection offers itself to the first. There is not the most distant probability that the ambitious and aggrandizing views of Buonaparte will commute the territory for money. Its acquisition is of immense importance to France, and has long been an object of her extreme solicitude. The attempt, therefore, to purchase, in the first instance, will certainly fail; and in the end, war must be resorted to, under all the accumulation of difficulties caused by a previous and strongly fortified possession of the country by our adversary.

The second plan is, therefore, evidently the best. First, because effectual; the acquisition easy; the preservation afterwards easy. The evils of a war with France at this time are certainly not very formidable: her fleet crippled and powerless; her treasury empty; her resources almost dried up; in short, gasping for breath after a tremendous conflict, which, though it left her victorious, left her nearly exhausted under her extraordinary exertions. On the other hand, we might count with certainty on the aid of Great Britain with her powerful navy.

Secondly, this plan is preferable, because it affords us the only chance of avoiding a long-continued war. When we have once taken possession the business will present itself to France in a new aspect. She will then have to weigh the immense difficulties, if not the utter impracticability, of wresting it from us. In this posture of affairs she will naturally conclude it is her interest to bargain. Now it may become expedient to terminate hostilities by a purchase, and a cheaper one may reasonably be expected. To secure the better prospect of final success, the following auxiliary measures ought to be adopted. The army should be increased to ten thousand men, for the purpose of insuring the preservation of the conquest. Preparations for increasing our naval force should be made. The militia should be classed, and effectual provision made for raising, on an emergency, forty thousand men. Negotiations should be pushed with Great Britain, to induce her to hold herself in readiness to co-operate fully with us, at a moment's warning. This plan should be adopted and proclaimed before the departure of our envoy. Such measures would astonish and disconcert Buonaparte himself; our envoy would be enabled to speak and treat with effect, and all Europe would be taught to respect us. These ideas have been long entertained by the writer, but he has never given himself the trouble to commit them to the public, because he despaired of their being adopted. They are now thrown out with very little hope of their producing any change in the conduct of the Administration, yet with the encouragement that there is a strong current of public feeling in favor of decisive measures. If the President would adopt this course, he might yet retrieve his character, induce the best part of the community to look favorably upon his political career, exalt himself in the eyes of Europe, save the country, and secure a permanent fame. But, for this, alas! Jefferson is not destined.

57. *On the Liberty of the Press: People vs. Croswell*

February 13, 1803

. . . The liberty of the press consists, in my idea, in publishing the truth, from good motives and for justifiable ends, though it reflect on the government, on magistrates, or individuals. If it be not allowed, it excludes the privilege of canvassing men, and our rulers. It is in vain to say, you may canvass measures. This is impossible without the right of looking to men. To say that measures can be discussed, and that there shall be no bearing on those who are the authors of those measures, cannot be done. The very end and reason of discussion would be destroyed. Of what consequence to show its object? Why is it to be thus demonstrated, if not to show, too, who is the author? It is essential to say, not only that the measure is bad and deleterious, but to hold up to the people who is the author, that, in this our free and elective government, he may be removed from the seat of power. If this be not to be done, then in vain will the voice of the people be raised against the inroads of tyranny. For, let a party but get into power, they may go on from step to step, and, in spite of canvassing their measures, fix themselves firmly in their seats, especially as they are never to be reproached for what they have done. This abstract mode, in practice, can never be carried into effect. But if, under the qualifications I have mentioned, the power be allowed, the liberty for which I contend will operate as a salutary check. In speaking thus for the freedom of the press, I do not say there ought to be an unbridled license; or that the characters of men who are good will naturally tend eternally to support themselves. I do not stand here to say that no shackles are to be laid on this license.

I consider this spirit of abuse and calumny as the pest of society. I know the best of men are not exempt from the attacks of slander. Though it pleased God to bless us with the first of characters, and though it has pleased God to take him from us and this band of calumniators, I say that falsehood eternally repeated would have affected even his name. Drops of water, in long and continued succession, will wear out adamant. This, therefore, cannot be endured. It would be to put the best and the worst on the same level.

I contend for the liberty of publishing truth, with good motives and for justifiable ends, even though it reflect on government, magistrates, or private persons. I contend for it under the restraint of our tribunals. When this is exceeded, let them interpose and punish. From this will follow none of those consequences so ably depicted. . . .

Chronologies

1. *Benjamin Franklin*

1706   Born January 17, in Boston, Massachusetts.

1718   Works as apprentice printer for brother James.

1722   The "Silence Dogood" letters published in *New England Courant.*

1723   Goes to Philadelphia and finds employment as a printer.

1724   Leaves for London. Works as printer, sets type for Wollaston's *Religion of Nature Delineated.*

1725   "A Dissertation on Liberty and Necessity, Pleasure and Pain."

1726   Returns to Philadelphia.

1730   Appointed Public Printer by the Assembly of Philadelphia.

1731   Founds the first subscription library in America, the Pennsylvania Library Company.

1733   Publishes first issue of *Poor Richard's Almanack* (published regularly until 1758).

1744   Founds American Philosophical Society.

1746   Begins experiments with Leyden jar and other electrical apparatus.

1749   Founds the academy later to become the University of Pennsylvania.

1751   Elected member of the Pennsylvania General Assembly.
       Publishes first book on electricity.

1752   Collinson's edition of Franklin's works published in French.

1753   Deputy postmaster of the Colonies.
       Awarded Copley Medal by the Royal Society of London and made a Fellow.
       Awarded the honorary degree of Master of Arts by Harvard and Yale.

1754   Goes as delegate from Pennsylvania to discuss plan for union of the Colonies at the Albany Congress.

1757   Goes to London as commissioner for the Colony of Pennsylvania.

1762   Honorary Degree of Doctor of Law at Oxford.
       Returns to America.

1764   Returns to London to petition Crown for change in Pennsylvania's status from Proprietary to Crown Colony.

1766   Wins temporary repeal of the Stamp Act.

1775   Returns to America.
       Elected member of the Second Continental Congress.

1776   Serves on committee to draft Declaration of Independence with Adams and Jefferson.
       Appointed one of three American agents in France, takes up residence there.

1778   Negotiates and signs treaty of alliance with the French.

1781   Member of peace commission.

1783	Signs Treaty of Paris with John Jay and Adams.
1785	Resigns as minister to France and returns to America.
1787	Delegate to Constitutional Convention.
	President of the Pennsylvania Society for the Abolition of Slavery until 1790.
	Founds Society for Political Enquiry, and elected first President.
1790	Dies, April 17, in Philadelphia.

2. *John Adams*

1735	Born October 30, Braintree, Massachusetts.
1751	Attends Harvard College until 1755.
1756	Reads law with James Putnam.
1758	Admitted to the Bar.
1765	"A Dissertation on the Canon and Feudal Law" and "Braintree Instructions."
1774	Attends First Continental Congress.
1775	Attends Second Continental Congress.
1776	Serves in Congress on Committee to draw up a Declaration of Independence.
	"Thoughts on Government."
1777	Attends Congress where he serves on many committees.
1778	Sails to Europe, as a joint commissioner to France.
1779	Returns to US to attend Massachusetts Constitutional Convention and drafts a "Constitution for the Commonwealth of Massachusetts," which is adopted, slightly amended, in 1780. Returns to Europe as minister to negotiate treaties of peace and commerce.
1780	Negotiates loans to the US in the Netherlands.
1782	Completes negotiations for first Dutch loan and joins the Peace Commission in Paris.
1784	Remains in Europe to negotiate treaties of amity and commerce.
1785	First Minister to the Court of St. James.
1787	Publishes first two volumes of "A Defence of the Constitutions of the United States," with the third volume in 1788.
1789	First Vice-President of the US under the new government.
1790	Begins publication of "Discourses on Davila" in Fenno's *Gazette*.
1791	Elected President of the American Academy of Arts and Sciences, and serves until 1813.
1793	Re-elected Vice-President.
1797	Second President of the US.
1798	Declares a state of quasi-war with France. Releases XYZ dispatches and signs the Alien and Sedition Acts.
1800	Peace agreement concluded with France.
1801	Appoints John Marshall as Chief Justice of Supreme Court.
1812	Resumes correspondence with Jefferson.
1826	Dies at Quincy, Massachusetts, on July 4th, the Jubilee celebration of the Declaration of Independence.

3. *Thomas Jefferson*

1743	Born April 13, Shadwell, Virginia.
1760	Attends William and Mary College until 1762.
1762	Reads law with George Wythe until 1767.
1767	Admitted to the Bar.
1769	Member, House of Burgesses until 1776.
1774	"A Summary View of the Rights of British America."
1775	Attends Continental Congress.
1776	Serves in Congress and writes the "Declaration of Independence."
	Attends Virginia General Assembly and serves on Committee to revise the laws of Virginia. Drafts a Constitution for Virginia—only its preamble adopted.
1777	Elected to House of Delegates and serves until 1779.
1779	Elected Governor of Virginia for two-year term. Reports on proposed "Revisal of the Laws of Virginia," including "Bills for the General Diffusion of Knowledge" and for "Establishment of Religious Freedom."
1780	Elected to American Philosophical Society.
1782	Drafts another constitution for Virginia.
1783	Elected to Congress—drafts report on the definitive treaty of peace which was eventually adopted.
1784	Presents plan for the government of the Western Territories.
	Appointed to join Franklin and Adams in negotiating treaties of commerce. Arrives in Paris, August 6.
1785	Succeeds Franklin as Minister to Versailles. Publishes "Notes on the State of Virginia."
1789	Arrives home, Monticello, December for "visit." Remains in US for the rest of his life.
1790	Secretary of State in new Cabinet under President Washington.
1791	Opinion of the Constitutionality of the Bank of the United States. Letter appears as Preface to Paine's "Rights of Man."
1793	Resigns as Secretary of State and retires to Monticello.
1797	Begins term as Vice-President of the US. Elected President of the American Philosophical Society, and serves until 1815.
1798	Organizes effort for Kentucky and Virginia Resolutions and drafts Kentucky Resolutions.
1801	Delivers first Inaugural and takes office as Third President of the US.
	Only American of his period to be elected as associé étranger of the Institute of France.
1809	Leaves office and retires to Monticello.
1812	Resumes correspondence with Adams.
1826	Dies at Monticello, Virginia, on July 4, a few hours before John Adams.

4. *James Madison*

1751	Born March 16, Port Conway, Virginia.
1769	Studied at College of New Jersey, receiving baccalaureate 1771.
1774	Elected to Orange County Committee of Safety, of which his father was chairman.
1776	Orange County delegate to Virginia Convention and General Assembly at Williamsburg, where he supports Jefferson's reform programs.
	Secures substitution of liberty of conscience provision for religious toleration provision in Virginia Declaration of Rights.
1777	Fails in his bid for re-election to General Assembly.
	Elected to Virginia's nine-member State Council for two years under Governors Patrick Henry and Thomas Jefferson.
1779	Elected to Continental Congress, serves until 1783. Realizes nation needs a stronger government.
1784	Member Virginia House of Delegates until 1787.
	Defeats public support of teachers of religion, secures passage of Jefferson's Statute of Religious Liberty.
	Puts much of Jefferson-Wythe-Pendleton revision of laws through legislature.
1786	Attends Annapolis Convention sponsored by himself a year earlier.
	Successfully sponsors convention to revise the Articles of Confederation.
1787	Constitutional Convention, leader of the Virginians, proponent of strong national government.
	Author of most extensive Journal of debates.
	The Federalist.
	Leads the fight for the Constitution at the Virginia Ratifying Convention.
1789	Elected to House of Representatives, serving until 1797.
	Speaker of the House.
	Defeats move for titles of nobility.
	Breaks with Hamilton on issue of National Bank charter.
1798	Retires to private life at Harewood.
	Drafts Virginia Resolutions in opposition to Alien and Sedition Acts.
	Attends House of Delegates in Virginia.
1801	Secretary of State until 1809, under President Jefferson.
1809	Fourth President of the United States.
1810	Proclamation taking possession of West Florida.
1812	Proclamation of War against Great Britain.
1815	Treaty of Peace with Great Britain.
1816	Signs bill establishing Second Bank of the US.
1817	Retires to Montpellier.
1826	Succeeds Thomas Jefferson as Rector of the University of Virginia.
1829	Participates in the Virginia Constitutional Convention.
1836	Dies, June 28, at Montpellier.

5. *Alexander Hamilton*

1755	Born, January 11, in Nevis, British West Indies.
1766	Serves as apprentice clerk in Nicholas Cruger's mercantile firm.
1772	Publication of "Hurricane Letter".
1773	Arrival in New York City.
	Enters King's College, now Columbia University.
1774	*A Full Vindication.*
1775	*The Farmer Refuted.*
	Member of militia company, "Corsicans".
1776	Appointed captain in command of the Provincial Company of Artillery.
1777	Appointed aide-de-camp to Washington with rank of lieutenant-colonel.
1778	*Publius* letters.
1781	Resigns as Washington's aide.
	Continentalist essays.
1782	Admitted to New York bar after three months' intensive study of law.
	Urges New York legislature to pass resolution for a general convention to amend the Articles of Confederation.
	Elected to Continental Congress, from New York.
1783	*Phocion Letters.*
1784	Founds and becomes director of the Bank of New York.
1785	Associated in founding of the New York Society for Promoting the Manumission of Slaves.
1786	Annapolis Convention; drafts resolution calling for new convention to enlarge powers of the Confederation.
1787	Delegate to New York State assembly.
	At Federal Convention in Philadelphia, spokesman for strong central government.
	The Federalist.
1788	Leads fight for ratification of US Constitution in New York Convention.
1789	First Secretary of the Treasury in the new government.
1790	First Report on the Public Credit.
	Report on a National Bank.
1791	Report on the US Mint.
	Report on Manufactures.
1794	*Americanus* papers.
	Takes field to suppress the Whiskey Rebellion.
1795	Second Report on Public Credit.
	Resigns as Secretary of the Treasury, January 31.
	Camillus letters.
1796	Prepares draft for Washington's Farewell Address.
1797	Discloses nature of liaison with Mrs. Reynolds.
1798	Appointed Inspector General of the Army with rank of major-general.
1800	"The Public Conduct and Character of John Adams," opposing the President's re-election.
1801	Founds the New York *Evening Post.*
	Criticizes Jefferson administration in series of articles.
1804	Counsel in *People v. Croswell*, argues in defense of freedom of the press.
	Mortally wounded in a duel with Aaron Burr, July 11, Alexander Hamilton dies July 12, in New York City.

Sources

1. *Benjamin Franklin*

The Smyth edition (Albert Henry Smyth, ed., *The Writings of Benjamin Franklin,* 10 vols., New York: Macmillan, 1905-1907), has been used as the basis of the text. Whenever the Smyth edition is not used as the source, the editor or author from which an item is taken is cited.

1. I, 238-247
2. I, 295-297; 324-332
3. I, 386-389
4. II, 214-16
5. Leonard Labaree, ed., *The Papers of Benjamin Franklin* (New Haven: Yale Univ. Press, 1959-), III, 30-31. Hereafter cited as Labaree.
6. II, 302-310
7. III, 40-42
8. III, 16-17
9. III, 100-101
10. III, 143-146
11^1. III, 231
11^2. III, 232-237
11^3. III, 238-241
12. IV, 12-14
13. V, 53-54
14. V, 155-156
15. V, 437-438
16. VII, 414-16
17. VIII, 9-10
18. VIII, 27-29
19. VIII, 153-154
20. VIII, 451-453
21. IX, 161-168
22. IX, 208-210
23. IX, 242-248
24. IX, 337-338
25. IX, 488-490
26. IX, 651
27. IX, 658-659
28. X, 72
29. X, 83-85
30. II, 88-90
31. II, 172-176; 178-179
32. Labaree, I, 28-33
33. II, 228-229

34. III, 407-410

35. V, 127-137

36. VI, 254-256

37. VI, 420-426

38. VII, 358-359

39. VIII, 603-612

40. X, 97-101

41. X, 120-121

42. X, 131-134; 135; 136-37

43. X, 607-609

44. X, 54-60

45. X, 66-68

46. Carl Van Doren, *Benjamin Franklin* (New York: Viking Press, 1938), 124.

2. *John Adams*

The C.F. Adams edition (Charles Francis Adams, ed., *The Works of John Adams,* 10 vols., Boston: Charles Little and James Brown, 1851) has been used as the basis of the text. Whenever the Adams edition is not used as the source, the editor or author from which an item is taken is cited.

1. Adams, IX, 610-613

2. Adams, IX, 616-618

3¹. Lyman H. Butterfield, *The Adams Papers: The Diary and Autobiography of John Adams,* 4 vols. (Cambridge, Mass.: Belknap Press of Harvard Univ. Press, 1961. Hereafter cited as Butterfield, *Diary.*)

3². Butterfield, *Diary,* I, 13-14

3³. Butterfield, *Diary,* I, 42-43; 62-63; 184

3⁴. Butterfield, *Diary,* I, 263-265

3⁵. Butterfield, *Diary,* II, 82

3⁶. Butterfield, *Diary,* II, 85-86

3⁷. Butterfield, *Diary,* II, 351-352

3⁸. Butterfield, *Diary,* II, 390-391

3⁹. Butterfield, *Diary,* III, 91-92

3¹⁰. Butterfield, *Diary,* III, 176

4. Adams, I, 23

5. Lyman H. Butterfield, *The Adams Papers: The Adams Family Correspondence,* 2 vols. to date (Cambridge, Mass.: Belknap Press, 1963), I, 2. (Hereafter cited as Butterfield, *Correspondence.*)

6. Butterfield, *Correspondence,* I, 44-46

7. C.F. Adams, ed., *Letters of John Adams to His Wife,* 2 vols. (Boston: 1841), I, 73-75 (Hereafter cited as *Letters to His Wife.*)

8. *Warren-Adams Letters,* 2 vols. (Boston: The Mass. Historical Society, 1917, 1925), I, 126-129. (Hereafter cited as *Warren Letters.*)

9. Adams, IX, 375-378

10. Adams, I, 230-231

11. *Familiar Letters of John Adams and His Wife Abigail Adams, during the Revolution* (New York: 1816), 206-207. (Hereafter cited as *Familiar Letters.*)

12. *Familiar Letters,* 381

13. Adams, IX, 511-513

14. Adams, III, 369-370
15. Adams, IX, 530-531
16. Adams, IX, 546
17. *Warren Letters*, II, 281-282
18. Adams, IX, 551
19. Adams, VIII, 464-465
20. John Disney, *Memoirs of Thomas Brand-Hollis* (London: 1808), 32-33
21. *Old Family Letters: Copied from the Originals for Alexander Biddle*, Series A (Philadelphia: 1892), 39-40
22. Adams, VI, 429-431
23. Adams, IX, 565-567
24. Adams, IX, 563-565
25. Adams, VI, 414-420
26. *Letters to His Wife*, II, 251-252
27. W.C. Ford, ed., *Statesman and Friend, Correspondence of John Adams with Benjamin Waterhouse, 1784-1822* (Boston: 1927), 23-26. (Hereafter cited as *Statesman and Friend*.)
28. Adams, IX, 591-593
29. *Correspondence of William Cunningham and John Adams, 73-74.*
30. Adams, IX, 630-631
31. Adams, IX, 635-640
32. Adams, X, 10-13
33. Adams, X, 50-51
34. Adams, X, 52-54
35. Paul Wilstach, ed., *Correspondence of John Adams and Thomas Jefferson, 1812-1826* (Indianapolis: 1925), 98-102.
36. Adams, X, 100-101
37. Adams, VI, 452-454
38. Adams, X, 148-149
39. Adams, X, 152-154
40. Adams, X, 174
41. Adams, X, 267-268
42. Adams, X, 282-284
43. Adams, X, 212-213
44. Adams, X, 379-380
45. Adams, X, 397
46. *Statesman and Friend*, 155-158
47. Adams, X, 398
48. Adams, X, 415
49. Adams, X, 416
50. Adams, III, 448-457; 462-464
51. Adams, III, 465-467
52. Adams, IV, 79; 84; 89-90; 114; 170
53. Adams, IV, 193-200
54. Adams, IV, 219-226; 230; 239
55. Adams, VIII, 298-300
56. Adams, IV, 283-285; 289-293
56[1]. Adams, IV, 299-302
56[2]. Adams, IV, 391-393; 414-415; 444-445
56[3]. Adams, V, 452-454
56[4]. Adams, VI, 66-67
56[5]. Adams, VI, 218-220
57. Adams, VI, 232-234
58. Adams, IX, 105-111

3. *Thomas Jefferson*

The Memorial Edition (Andrew A. Lipscomb and Albert Ellery Bergh, eds., *The Writings of Thomas Jefferson*, 20 vols., The Thomas Jefferson Memorial Association, Washington, D.C., 1905), and the Boyd edition (Julian Boyd, *The Papers of Thomas Jefferson*, 16 vols. to date, Princeton, N.J.: Princeton Univ. Press, 1950-) have been used as the basis of the text. Whenever the Memorial Edition or the Boyd edition have not been used as the source, the editor, author or manuscript collection from which an item is taken is cited.

1. Memorial Edition, I, 1-5
2. Memorial Edition, I, 6-14
3. Memorial Edition, I, 17-24
4. Memorial Edition, I, 25-28
5. Memorial Edition, I, 53-59; 60-62
6. Memorial Edition, I, 62-67
7. Memorial Edition, I, 70-72
8. Memorial Edition, I, 72-73
9. Memorial Edition, I, 73-74
10. Boyd, I, 3
11. Boyd, VI, 185-186
12. Boyd, VI, 203
13. Boyd, VI, 248-249
14. Boyd, VI, 255
15. Boyd, VI, 470-471
16. Boyd, VI, 550
17. Boyd, VII, 292-293
18. Boyd, VII, 630-631
19. Boyd, VIII, 405-408
20. Boyd, IX, 264
21. Boyd, X, 244-245
22. Boyd, X, 532-533
23. Boyd, X, 637-638
24. Boyd, XI, 92-93; 95-96
25. Memorial Edition, VI, 102, 104-105
26. Boyd, XI, 250-252
27. Memorial Edition, VI, 106-108, 109
28. Boyd, XII, 14-18
29. Boyd, XII, 189
30. Boyd, XII, 439-442
31. Boyd, XIII, 127-128
32. Memorial Edition, VII, 81-82
33. Boyd, XIV, 328
34. Boyd, XV, 97-98
35. Boyd, XV, 271-272
36. Boyd, XV, 392-397
37. Memorial Edition, VIII, 341-347
38. Paul L. Ford, ed., *The Writings of Thomas Jefferson*, 12 vols., The Federal Edition (New York: Knickerbocker Press, 1904), VII, 121-122.
39. Memorial Edition, VIII, 393-399
40. Memorial Edition, IX, 335-336
41. "A Tribute to Philip May Hamer on the Completion of Ten Years as Executive Director of the National Historical Publications Commission," New York, December 29, 1960.

42. Memorial Edition, X, 227-230
43. Memorial Edition, X, 306-308
44. Memorial Edition, X, 379-385
45. Memorial Edition, XI, 1-3
46. Memorial Edition, XII, 196-200
47. Memorial Edition, XIII, 2-9
48. Memorial Edition, XIII, 123-125
49. Memorial Edition, XIII, 279-281
50. Memorial Edition, XIII, 333-334
51. Memorial Edition, XIII, 396-402
52. Memorial Edition, XIV, 138-144
53. Paul L. Ford, ed., *The Writings of Thomas Jefferson,* 10 vols. (New York: Putnam, 1893), IX, 477-478 (Hereafter cited as Ford, *Writings.*)
54. Memorial Edition, XIV, 190-194
55. Memorial Edition, XV, 19-20, 22-23
56. Memorial Edition, XV, 219-221
57. Memorial Edition, XV, 248-250
58. Memorial Edition, XV, 477-479
59. Memorial Edition, XV, 492-493
60. Memorial Edition, XVI, 156-159
61. Memorial Edition, XVI, 181-182
62. Memorial Edition, I, 184-187; 189; 189-192; 194-195; 200-201; 209-211
63. Boyd, I, 356-359; 361-364
64. Memorial Edition, I, 28-38
65. Memorial Edition, II, 300-303
66. William Peden, ed., *Notes on the State of Virginia* (Chapel Hill: Univ. of North Carolina Press, 1955), 118-129 (Hereafter cited as *Notes.*)
66[1]. *Notes,* 118-129
66[2]. *Notes,* 147-149
66[3]. *Notes,* 159-160
66[4]. *Notes,* 162-163
66[5]. *Notes,* 164-165
67. Boyd, VI, 603-604
68. Boyd, XIV, 242-249; 250-253
69. Boyd, XVI, 178-179
70. Boyd, XVI, 468-470
71. Memorial Edition, III, 317-323
72. Memorial Edition, XII, 269-270
73. Ford, *Writings,* X, 362-364; 366-372
74. Memorial Edition, Facsimile facing I, 262

4. *James Madison*

The Hunt edition (Gaillard Hunt, *The Writings of James Madison,* 9 vols., New York: Putnam, 1900-1910) has been used as the basis of the text. Whenever the Hunt edition is not used as the source, the editor, author or manuscript collection from which an item is taken is cited.

1. Douglass Adair, ed., *Autobiography of James Madison* (*William and Mary Quarterly,* Third Series, no. II, April 1945.)

2. William T. Hutchinson, William M.E. Rachal, eds., *The Papers of James Madison* (Chicago: Univ. of Chicago Press, 1962-), I, 105-106. (Hereafter cited as Hutchinson.)
3. Hutchinson, II, 6
4. Hutchinson, II, 127-128
5. Julian Boyd, ed., *The Papers of Thomas Jefferson* (Princeton, N.J.: Princeton University Press, 1950-) XII, 271-280. (Hereafter cited as Boyd.)
6. Boyd, XVI, 147-150
7. Hunt, VI, 220-224
8. Hunt, VI, 309-310
9. Hunt, VII, 163-167
10. Hunt, VIII, 76-77
11. Hunt, VIII, 203-205
12. Hunt, VIII, 390-392
13. Hunt, VIII, 413-414
14. Hunt, VIII, 439-444
15. Hunt, IX, 35-37
16. Hunt, IX, 65-68
17. Hunt, IX, 71-76
18. Hunt, IX, 100-103
19. Hunt, IX, 103-108
20. Hunt, IX, 135-136
21. Hunt, IX, 181-182
22. Hunt, IX, 190-192
23. Hunt, IX, 243-246
24. Hunt, IX, 247-248
25. Hunt, IX, 250-251
26. Hunt, IX, 252-255
27. Hunt, IX, 256-261
28. Hunt, IX, 405-406
29. Hunt, IX, 429-431
30. Hunt, IX, 451-454
31. Hunt, IX, 511-513
32. Hunt, IX, 607-610
33. Hunt, I, 459-460
34[1]. Hunt, III, 102-105
34[2]. Hunt, III, 284-287
34[3]. Hunt, III, 316-318
34[4]. Hunt, IV, 22-23; 27-28
35. Benjamin F. Wright, ed., *The Federalist* (Cambridge, Mass.: Belknap Press of Harvard Univ. Press, 1961), 129-136. (Hereafter cited as Wright.)
36. Wright, 280-282
37. Wright, 355-359
38[1]. *Eliot's Debates,* Part I. v. III, 393-395
38[2]. *Eliot's Debates,* Part I, v. III, 616-619
39. Hunt, V, 356-357
40. Hunt, VI, 70
41. Hunt, VI, 83-85
42. Hunt, VI, 86
43. Hunt, VI, 99-101
44. Hunt, VI, 120-123
45. Hunt, VI, 332-340
46. Hunt, VI, 399-401
47. Hunt, VIII, 47-50
48. Hunt, VIII, 127

49. Hunt, VIII, 383-385
50. Hunt, IX, 358-364
51. Hunt, IX, 358n, 359n, 360n
52. Hunt, IX, 568-573
53. Hunt, IX, 573-575; 577-578; 588-589; 597-599
54. Hunt, IX, Facsimile facing 611

5. *Alexander Hamilton*

The Lodge edition (Henry Cabot Lodge, ed., *The Works of Alexander Hamilton,* 12 vols., New York: Putnam, 1904), and the Syrett edition (Harold C. Syrett, ed.. *The Papers of Alexander Hamilton,* 6 vols. to date, New York: Columbia University Press, 1961-), have been used as the basis of the text.

1. Syrett, I, 4
2. Syrett, II, 509-510
3. Lodge, IX, 232-236
4. Lodge, IX, 246
5. Lodge, VII, 378-379
6. Lodge, X, 257-261
7. Lodge, X, 286-287
8. Lodge, X, 480
9. Lodge, X, 357
10. Lodge, X, 476-480
11. Lodge, X, 471-472; 474
12. Lodge, X, 481-482
13. Syrett, I, 176-177
14. Syrett, I, 255
15. Syrett, I, 425-428
16. Syrett, II, 17-18
17. Syrett, II, 400-402; 406-408; 414-417
18. Syrett, II, 604-609; 617; 620; 635
19. Lodge, IX, 417-418
20. Lodge, IX, 441
21. Lodge, IX, 513-517; 520-521; 528-530; 532-535
22. Lodge, X, 7-8; 10
23. Lodge, X, 329-336
24. Lodge, X, 349
25. Lodge, X, 375-376
26. Lodge, X, 412-415
27. Lodge, X, 425-426
28. Lodge, X, 433-435
29. Lodge, X, 444-446
30. Lodge, X, 456
31. Lodge, X, 458
32. Syrett, I, 45-48; 66
33. Syrett, I, 86-88; 92-94; 136
34. Syrett, III, 75-77
35. Syrett, III, 544-546; 548; 550-551; 553-554; 556-557
36. Syrett, III, 676

37. Syrett, IV, 25-26; 28-29
38. Syrett, IV, 187-195
39. Syrett, IV, 253
40. Syrett, IV, 301-305
41. Syrett, IV, 333-339
42. Syrett, IV, 655-663
43. Lodge, II, 230-232; 236-239; 244-246; 283
44. Lodge, IV, 322-323; 333-334
45. Lodge, III, 427-428
46. Lodge, III, 446-450
47. Lodge, IV, 70-71; 73-74; 87-95; 97-98; 104-105; 142-143; 149-151
48. Lodge, IV, 374-377; 386-387
49. Lodge, IV, 401-402, 407
50. Lodge, IV, 464-465
51. Lodge, V, 75-78
52. Lodge, III, 261-263
53. Lodge, V, 190-191; 200-203; 206-207; 212-213
54. Lodge, VI, 418-419
55. Lodge, VII, 310-311; 314-316; 361-364
56. Lodge, VI, 333-336
57. Lodge, VIII, 389-391

For Further Reading

Benjamin Franklin

The best biography of Franklin is Carl Van Doren, *Benjamin Franklin* (New York: Viking, 1938). At present, Leonard W. Labaree is editing *The Papers of Benjamin Franklin* (6 vols. to date, New Haven: Yale Univ. Press, 1959-   ) which will make all of Franklin's letters and papers available. Although it does not live up to the high standards of accuracy and completeness of the Labaree edition, until that project has been completed, Albert Henry Smyth, ed., *The Writings of Benjamin Franklin*, 10 vols. (New York: Macmillan, 1905-1907) is the standard source for Franklin's writings. A good short anthology is Frank L. Mott and Chester E. Jorgenson, *Benjamin Franklin: Representative Selections* (New York: American Book Co., 1936), now available in paperback in the American Century Series (New York: Hill and Wang, 1962).

John Adams

The most recent biography of Adams is Page Smith, *John Adams*, 2 vols. (New York: Doubleday, 1962). Charles Francis Adams edited his grandfather's papers with a constant concern for accuracy and completeness, marred by an occasional concern for family reputation (*The Works of John Adams*, 10 vols. (Boston: Little, Brown, 1951). In progress at Harvard University is a project to publish the diaries, letters, and other writings of John, John Quincy and Charles Francis Adams. Under the general editor, Lyman H. Butterfield, six volumes of *The Adams Papers* have been published: *The Diary and Autobiography of John Adams*, 4 vols. (Cambridge, Mass.: Belknap Press of Harvard Univ. Press, 1961) and the first two volumes of *The Adams Family Correspondence* (1963). For a convenient one-volume selection of Adams' writings see Adrienne Koch and William Peden, *Selected Writings of John and John Quincy Adams* (New York: Knopf, 1946).

Thomas Jefferson

The best biography of Jefferson is Dumas Malone's multi-volume study, *Jefferson and His Time*. Three volumes have been completed: *Jefferson the Virginian* (Boston: Little, 1948); *Jefferson and the Rights of Man* (1951); *Jefferson and the Ordeal of Liberty* (1962). Two more volumes are in preparation to complete this set. When it has been completed, Julian Boyd, ed., *The Papers of Thomas Jefferson*, 16 vols. to date (Princeton, N.J.: Princeton Univ. Press, 1950-   ), will provide the most accurate and comprehensive record of the writings of Jefferson and the correspondence which he received. Of two other collections, P. L. Ford, ed., *The Writings of Thomas Jefferson*, 10 vols. (New York: Putnam, 1893) is the more accurate, but it does not have the quantity and variety of the Memorial Edition (Andrew A. Lipscomb and Albert Ellery Bergh, eds., *The Writings of Thomas Jefferson*, 20 vols., Washington, D.C.: The Thomas Jefferson Memorial Association, 1905). For a one-volume collection, see Adrienne Koch and William Peden, *The Life and Selected Writings of Thomas Jefferson* (New York: Random House, Inc., Modern Library, 1944).

The best source for the complete correspondence between Adams and Jefferson is Lester Cappon, ed., *The Adams-Jefferson Letters*, 2 vols. (Chapel Hill: Univ. of North Carolina Press, 1959).

James Madison

Irving Brant has written the most comprehensive biography, *James Madison*, 6 vols. (New York: Bobbs-Merrill, 1941-1961): 1. *The Virginia Revolutionist* 2. *The Nationalist* 3. *Father of the Constitution* 4. *Secretary of State* 5. *The President* 6. *Commander-in-Chief*. The standard edition of the papers, Gaillard Hunt, *The Writings of James Madison*, 9 vols. (New York: Putnam, 1900-1910), is being replaced by a new edition, William T. Hutchinson and William M. E. Rachal, eds., *The Papers of James Madison*, 2 vols. to date (Chicago: Univ. of Chicago Press, 1962). There is no satisfactory one-volume collection of Madison's writings.

Alexander Hamilton

The most recent biography of Hamilton is Broadus Mitchell, *Alexander Hamilton*, 2 vols. 1. *Youth to Maturity* 2. *The National Adventure* (New York: Macmillan, 1957, 1962). There is a project in progress to publish Hamilton's writings, and six volumes have appeared (Harold C. Syrett, ed., *The Papers of Alexander Hamilton*, New York: Columbia Univ. Press, 1961). Henry Cabot Lodge, ed., *The Works of Alexander Hamilton*, 12 vols. (New York: Putnam, 1904) has been the standard edition of Hamilton's writings and must serve until the project at Columbia has been completed. There is a good one-volume selection of Hamilton's writings, Richard B. Morris, ed., *Alexander Hamilton and the Founding of the Nation* (New York: Dial Press, 1957).

K O V E L S

ATT: ORDER DEPT. _____

NAME _____

ADDRESS _____

CITY & STATE _____ ZIP _____

PLEASE SEND ME THE FOLLOWING BOOKS:

ITEM NO.	QTY.	TITLE		PRICE	TOTAL
884623	_____	Kovels' Antiques & Collectibles Price List 28th Edition	PAPER	$14.95	_____
580128	_____	Kovels' American Art Pottery	HARDCOVER	$60.00	_____
54668X	_____	American Country Furniture 1780 –1875	PAPER	$14.95	_____
701375	_____	Kovels' Dictionary of Marks—Pottery & Porcelain	HARDCOVER	$16.00	_____
559145	_____	Kovels' New Dictionary of Marks	HARDCOVER	$19.00	_____
568829	_____	Kovels' American Silver Marks	HARDCOVER	$40.00	_____
589443	_____	Kovels' Bottles Price List, 9th Edition	PAPER	$14.00	_____
883821	_____	Kovels' Depression Glass & American Dinnerware Price List, 5th Edition	PAPER	$16.00	_____
578069	_____	Kovels' Know Your Antiques, Revised & Updated	PAPER	$16.00	_____
588404	_____	Kovels' Know Your Collectibles, Updated	PAPER	$16.00	_____
883139	_____	Kovels' Guide to Selling, Buying, and Fixing Your Antiques and Collectibles	PAPER	$18.00	_____
883813	_____	Kovels' Quick Tips: 799 Helpful Hints on How to Care for Your Collectibles	PAPER	$12.00	_____

_____ TOTAL ITEMS

TOTAL RETAIL VALUE _____

KOVELS' QUICK TIPS
799 Helpful Hints on How to
Care for Your Collectibles

Want to know how to clean your stuffed moosehead, remove the gum stain from a baseball card, dust a feather boa, repair a cracked porcelain figurine, hang a vintage dress, deodorize a matchcover, hide a scratch on your piano? KOVELS' QUICK TIPS offers these secrets and many more. Wearing their hats as the Heloise of the antiques world, the Kovels give you quick and handy tips on how to care for all the treasures in your home from your favorite jewelry, heirloom silver, and childhood toys to your Coca–Cola bottle collection, kitchen collectibles, books, and family photographs. Organized by subject matter and charmingly illustrated, this book includes 799 tips collected by the Kovels over the past twenty years.

883813 176 pages / $12.00 paperback

KOVELS' GUIDE TO SELLING, BUYING, AND FIXING YOUR ANTIQUES AND COLLECTIBLES

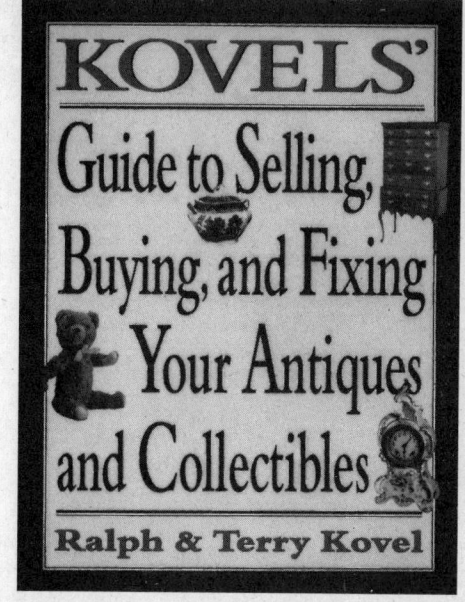

New!

Looking for parts and services needed to fix your antiques? Selling your antiques and collectibles? Thinking of having your treasures appraised? Renting space at a flea market? Having a house sale? These are some of the questions the Kovels address in this comprehensive book. Here in one place is almost everything the collector needs to know about repairing, buying, selling, and caring for antiques and collectibles. There is advice on how to sell more than one-hundred categories of collectibles—in all price ranges—from autographs, baseball cards, beer cans, carousel figures, decoys, furniture, and glass to movie memorabilia, musical instruments, paintings, toys, and Western art. Want a tail for your carousel horse or a belly button for your toy robot? The Kovels list names, addresses, and phone numbers of those who sell parts and know how to repair antiques and collectibles. The Kovels also list clubs, publications, auctions, appraisers, books, and much more. This is a book for easy, frequent reference. A must for dealers, dedicated collectors, and those who love their antiques.

883139 352 pages / $18.00 paperback

AMERICAN COUNTRY FURNITURE
1780–1875

More than 700 photographs identify styles, construction, woods, finishes, hardware, and other details. Here is all the information you need to be an expert on American country furniture. There are special sections on Pennsylvania, Shaker furniture, spool furniture, and furniture construction, plus an illustrated glossary of accessories and terms.

54668X 256 pages / $14.95 paperback

KOVELS' KNOW YOUR COLLECTIBLES
Updated Edition

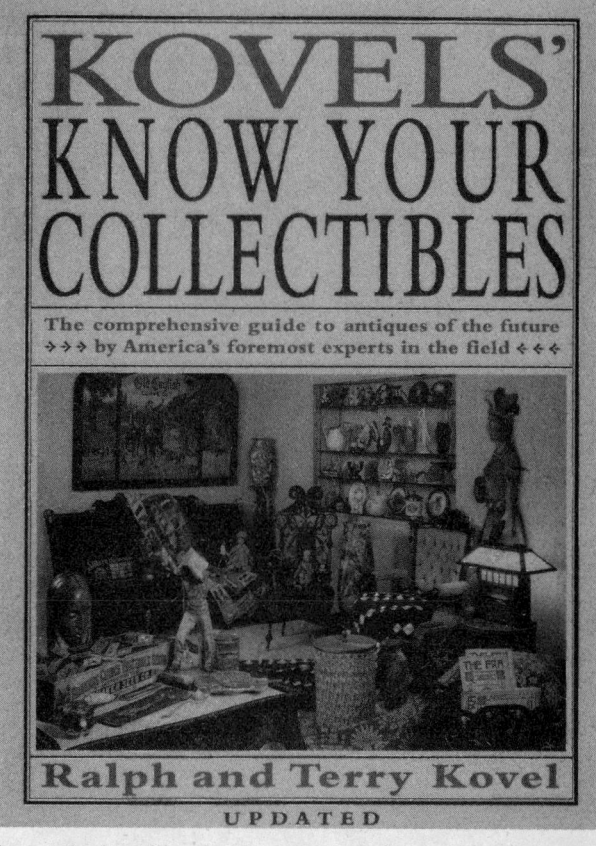

The guide to what's selling in shops and at shows today. The collectibles category covers items made since 1890, including the coveted Depression glass, Tiffany lamps, Mission furniture, and advertising items. Marks, catalog reprints, and photographs make every category clear. An in-depth study of jewelry, both American and foreign, includes names, dates, and artists information. Toys, art pottery, American dinnerware, and European pottery and porcelain all receive attention in this book, which is complete with bibliography, index, and terrific tips on care and collecting.

588404 416 pages / $16.00 paperback

KOVELS' KNOW YOUR ANTIQUES
Revised & Updated Edition

KOVELS'
KNOW YOUR
ANTIQUES

The best-selling guide to evaluating, buying, and caring
for antiques by America's foremost experts in the field

Ralph and Terry Kovel

REVISED & UPDATED

The best guide in print today for beginning collectors. Learn how to recognize, evaluate, and purchase virtually any type of antique—large or small—like an expert. There is detailed advice about caring for your antiques, identifying fakes, and finding bargains. This best-seller is used by collectors and college classes alike.

578069 368 pages / $16.00 paperback

KOVELS' BOTTLES PRICE LIST
Ninth Edition

Kovels' Bottles Price List is the complete guide to collecting bottles of all types. More than 10,000 current pieces are included in this, the most complete bottle book available. More than 200 illustrations in full color and black and white aid in identification of bottles. Included are old and new bottles, bitters, perfumes, figurals, flasks, Avons, Beams, and a host of others. Notes on styles of manufacturers, lists of bottles magazines and clubs, recommended reading, and a bibliography for the serious collector make *Kovels' Bottles Price List* the best listing of current bottle prices available.

589443 240 pages / $14.00 paperback

KOVELS' DEPRESSION GLASS & AMERICAN DINNERWARE PRICE LIST
Fifth Edition

The inexpensive pastel-colored glassware that became popular from 1925 on and the ceramic dinnerware produced during the same period are now attracting collectors in great numbers. Here are the latest and most accurate prices, based on a comprehensive survey of actual sales, shows, catalogs, auctions, and other reliable sources. The more than 6,000 pieces are listed by pattern, along with dates, descriptions, marks and illustrations. Also included are charts of factories with all the known patterns and their name variations, and a 16-page, full-color photographic glossary of Depression Glass and American Dinnerware terms.

883821 256 pages / $16.00 paperback

KOVELS' NEW DICTIONARY OF MARKS
Pottery & Porcelain (1850–Present)

Kovels' New Dictionary of Marks provides the quickest and easiest way to identify more than 3,500 American, European, and Oriental marks from 1850 to the present. The perfect companion to the Kovels' original best-seller *Dictionary of Marks—Pottery and Porcelain*, this is the most comprehensive reference manual for nineteenth- and twentieth-century marks. Together, the two volumes are an indispensable guide to the porcelain and pottery marks of the last four centuries.

559145 304 pages / $19.00 hardcover

KOVELS' DICTIONARY OF MARKS
Pottery & Porcelain
(1650–1850)

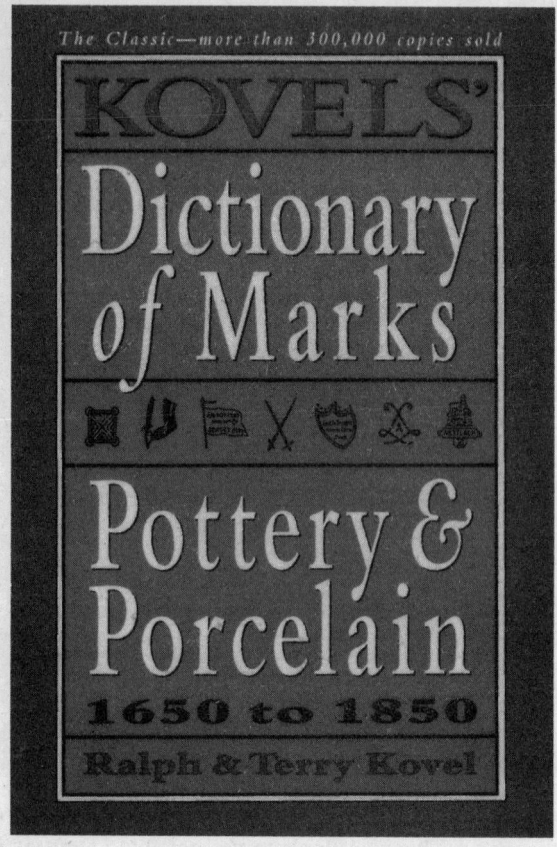

A classic in the field, *Kovels' Dictionary of Marks* is a comprehensive guide to more than 5,000 American and European pottery and porcelain marks. It shows at a glance the geographical location of the factory, family name or manufacturer's name, type of ware, color of mark, and the date the mark was used.

701375 288 pages / $16.00 hardcover

KOVELS' AMERICAN SILVER MARKS
(1650–Present)

Almost everyone owns an old piece of silver. Few know the complete history of that piece. This is a simple-to-use guide to identifying marks and monograms that appear on silver. Collectors and professional dealers can quickly determine the maker of a piece of silver. Each listing includes working dates, location, mark (if known), and bibliographic references to more than 200 books and articles. More than 10,000 silversmiths are listed in alphabetical order, with a cross-indexing system for monograms and pictorial marks.

568829 432 pages / $40.00 hardcover